HANDBOOK OF SOCIAL PSYCHOLOGY

Fifth Edition

HANDBOOK OF SOCIAL PSYCHOLOGY

Fifth Edition

Volume 2

Edited by

SUSAN T. FISKE

DANIEL T. GILBERT

GARDNER LINDZEY

John Wiley & Sons, Inc.

Published by John Wiley & Sons, Inc., Hoboken, New Jersey.
Published simultaneously in Canada.

For general information on our other products and services, please contact our Customer Care Department within the United States at (800) 762-2974, outside the United States at (317) 572-3993, or fax at (317) 572-4002.

Wiley also publishes its books in a variety of electronic formats. Some content that appears in print may not be available in electronic books. For more information about Wiley products, visit our website at www.wiley.com.

Library of Congress Cataloging-in-Publication Data:

Handbook of social psychology / edited by Susan T. Fiske, Daniel T. Gilbert, & Gardner Lindzey. —5th ed.
    p. cm.
Includes bibliographical references and index.
ISBN 978-0-470-13747-5 (set)—ISBN 978-0-470-13748-2 (v. 1 : cloth)—ISBN 978-0-470-13749-9 (v. 2 : cloth)   1. Social psychology.   I. Fiske, Susan T.
II. Gilbert, Daniel Todd.   III. Lindzey, Gardner.

    HM1011.H37 2010
    302--dc22

                                            2009023126

Printed in the United States of America

10 9 8 7 6 5 4 3 2 1

For Gardner Lindzey —
founding editor, scientist, and friend

Contents

VOLUME 2

Part III: The Social World

Fifth Edition Preface

You hold in your hands (or on your screens) an array of treasures. Since the first edition appeared in 1935, the *Handbook of Social Psychology* has been the standard reference work in the field, offering historical, integrative, and penetrating surveys of the topics that constitute the discipline. For this we have the authors to thank. Each chapter is written by the world's foremost authorities on the topic, and the list of contributors reads like an international who's who in social psychology. This fifth edition serves a new generation of students and researchers, reflecting the tremendous changes the field has experienced in the last decade. Most authors in this edition are new to the *Handbook,* as befits a vigorous, cutting-edge science. Many chapter topics remain from the previous edition (although in most cases their content has changed dramatically), and many others (social neuroscience, mind perception, experimental existential psychology, morality, and interpersonal stratification) are new to this edition.

This is the last edition of the *Handbook* that will bear the name of Gardner Lindzey, who passed away in 2008 at the age of 87. He helped organize this edition, but it is the first of the modern era to be completed without him. Carl Murchison brought out the first official edition of the *Handbook* in 1935, but empirical work in social psychology did not really explode until just after World War II, and it was then that Gardner founded the current *Handbook* series that every social psychologist knows so well. His first edition appeared in 1954; his second and third editions appeared in 1969 and 1985, respectively (with Elliot Aronson as his co-editor); and his fourth edition appeared in 1998 (with Daniel Gilbert and Susan Fiske as his co-editors).

From the start, Gardner determined his topics and chose his authors democratically—by soliciting opinions from leaders in the field—which at once gave his *Handbook* breadth, vision, and credibility. We have continued to use his method. Gardner's fingerprints are all over this fifth edition in many other ways as well—in our philosophy of representing the full field from neuron to nation, in our insistence that authors write for graduate students and not for one another, in our adherence to a prompt publication schedule, and we hope, in the continuing excellence of these volumes.

Gardner's impact extended beyond his half century as the editor of the *Handbook.* He also shaped the field of social psychology with his articles and books, although much of his influence occurred modestly, behind the scenes—advising, promoting, recommending, persuading. Neither of us will ever forget meeting with Gardner 15 years ago in a dark, smoke-filled restaurant in Boston, where he invited us to become part of this great tradition. We are proud to carry forward his legacy, and we trust that future editors will do the same—without the smoke, perhaps, but with the same respect for the institution that Gardner's *Handbook* has become and with the same enthusiasm it inspires in all of us for the hub discipline of social psychology.

STF, PRINCETON
DTG, CAMBRIDGE

Contributors to Volume 2

Eugene Borgida, Ph.D.
Department of Psychology
University of Minnesota
Minneapolis, Minnesota

Brad J. Bushman, Ph.D.
Institute for Social Research
University of Michigan
Ann Arbor, Michigan

Margaret S. Clark, Ph.D.
Department of Psychology
Yale University
New Haven, Connecticut

Carsten K. W. De Dreu, Ph.D.
Department of Psychology
University of Amsterdam
Amsterdam, The Netherlands

Stéphanie Demoulin, Ph.D.
Department of Psychology
Université catholique de Louvain
Louvain-la-neuve, Belgium

John F. Dovidio, Ph.D.
Department of Psychology
Yale University
New Haven, Connecticut

Susan T. Fiske, Ph.D.
Department of Psychology
Princeton University
Princeton, New Jersey

Samuel L. Gaertner, Ph.D.
Department of Psychology
University of Delaware
Newark, Delaware

Deborah H. Gruenfeld, Ph.D.
Graduate School of Business
Stanford University
Stanford, California

J. Richard Hackman, Ph.D.
Department of Psychology
Harvard University
Cambridge, Massachusetts

Jonathan Haidt, Ph.D.
Department of Psychology
University of Virginia
Charlottesville, Virginia

Joshua Harder
Boston Consulting Group
Washington D.C.

Steven J. Heine, Ph.D.
Department of Psychology
University of British Columbia
Vancouver, British Columbia, Canada

Michael A. Hogg, Ph.D.
School of Behavioral and Organizational Sciences
Claremont Graduate University
Claremont, California

Thomas Holtgraves, Ph.D.
Department of Psychological Science
Ball State University
Muncie, Indiana

L. Rowell Huesmann, Ph.D.
Department of Psychology
University of Michigan
Ann Arbor, Michigan

John T. Jost, Ph.D.
Department of Psychology
New York University
New York, New York

Nancy Katz, Ph.D.
Harvard Kennedy School
Harvard University
Cambridge, Massachusetts

Aaron C. Kay, Ph.D.
Department of Psychology
University of Waterloo
Waterloo, Ontario

Douglas T. Kenrick, Ph.D.
Department of Psychology
Arizona State University
Tempe, Arizona

Selin Kesebir, M. A.
Department of Psychology
University of Virginia
Charlottesville, Virginia

Margaret Bull Kovera, Ph.D.
John Jay College of Criminal Justice
City University of New York
New York, New York

Jon A. Krosnick, Ph.D.
Department of Communication
Stanford University
Stanford, California

Mark R. Leary, Ph.D.
Department of Psychology and Neuroscience
Duke University
Durham, North Carolina

Edward P. Lemay Jr
Department of Psychology
University of New Hampshire
Durham, New Hampshire

Steven L. Neuberg, Ph.D.
Department of Psychology
Arizona State University
Tempe, Arizona

Mark Schaller, Ph.D.
Department of Psychology
University of British Columbia
Vancouver, British Columbia, Canada

Larissa Z. Tiedens, Ph.D.
Graduate School of Business
Stanford University
Stanford, California

Penny S. Visser, Ph.D.
Department of Psychology
University of Chicago
Chicago, Illinois

Vincent Yzerbyt, Ph.D.
Department of Psychology
Université catholique de Louvain
Louvain-la-neuve, Belgium

PART III

The Social World

Chapter 21

Evolutionary Social Psychology

STEVEN L. NEUBERG, DOUGLAS T. KENRICK, AND MARK SCHALLER

Based merely on the scents of shirts worn recently by unknown men, women can, to a significant degree, assess the men's physical attractiveness—but only while ovulating. When worried about catching colds, people show greater prejudices against those who are disabled, obese, or foreign. When romantic inclinations are temporarily intensified, men—but not women—become more creative, confrontational, and nonconformist. Encountering a stranger with attitudes similar to one's own automatically activates thoughts of kinship. Pregnant women are more ethnocentric than their non-pregnant counterparts, but only during the first trimester. And upon viewing an opposite-sex face resembling one's own, people judge that person to be a desirable friend but undesirable sexual partner—to be trustworthy but not lustworthy.

These empirical findings, and many others like them, are difficult to explain—even post hoc—with most conventional social psychological theories. Yet, each was predicted from analyses of the psychological implications of human evolutionary biology (e.g., DeBruine, 2005; Gangestad & Thornhill, 1998; Griskevicius, Cialdini, & Kenrick, 2006; Navarrete, Fessler, & Eng, 2007; Park & Schaller, 2005; Park, Schaller, & Crandall, 2007). In addition to facilitating the discovery of diverse, sometimes counterintuitive, and often complex phenomena, an evolutionary perspective on social psychology also integrates these phenomena with one another and with a host of other findings, too. Evolutionarily informed empirical inquiries have produced deeper understandings of classic social psychological phenomena ranging from attraction to aggression, conflict to cooperation, person perception to prejudice, social cognition to social influence. The evolutionary approach has also served to open the field to phenomena long ignored, such as kin relations and child rearing—phenomena central to social life in the real world. The result is a comprehensive view of human social behavior

governed by a coherent set of rigorously logical general principles (Buss, 2005; Cosmides, Tooby, & Barkow, 1992; Crawford & Krebs, 2008; Gangestad & Simpson, 2007).

In this chapter, we review the current state of evolutionary social psychology. We begin with a brief primer on exactly what evolutionary social psychology is and is not, articulating its assumptions and the tools it provides for inquiry into social cognition and behavior. We then present an overview of what we call the *affordance management system*—a conceptual framework that articulates, in general terms, the manner in which many evolved psychological mechanisms influence cognition and behavior as individuals negotiate the many threats and opportunities inherent in social life. We proceed to review many different lines of evolutionarily informed research on a wide range of social psychological phenomena. This review highlights the many novel and nuanced hypotheses that have been deduced within an evolutionary framework, and illustrates the generative and integrative power of evolutionary logic when applied to the study of social psychology. We then address broader questions. We explore the relationships among evolved adaptations, development, learning, and culture. We discuss several epistemic and methodological issues that attend inquiries in evolutionary social psychology (and common misunderstandings that arise from these issues). We identify promising directions for future research. Finally, we reconsider the utility that an evolutionary perspective offers to scientific inquiry into social behavior.

WHAT IS EVOLUTIONARY SOCIAL PSYCHOLOGY?

Evolutionary psychology isn't a theory, model, or hypothesis. Rather, evolutionary psychology is a set of

The contributions of Steven L. Neuberg and Douglas T. Kenrick were supported by grants from the National Institute of Mental Health (MH064734) and National Science Foundation (#0642873); the contributions of Mark Schaller were supported by the Social Sciences and Humanities Research Council of Canada.

metatheoretical assumptions that govern how scientists approach conceptual and empirical inquiry into psychological phenomena (Buss, 1995; Ketelaar & Ellis, 2000). These assumptions (e.g., that cognition is the product of an underlying physiology, and that human physiology has been shaped by a long history of biological selection pressures) are scientifically noncontroversial, and are based on a vast empirical database within the biological sciences more broadly. When applied to the conceptual landscape of social psychology, these assumptions focus scientific inquiry on specific kinds of research questions and generate specific kinds of answers to those questions. These assumptions also provide a set of logical tools that, when applied rigorously, can be used to deduce specific theories, models, and hypotheses about social psychological phenomena. It is these theories, models, and hypotheses (not the metatheory of evolutionary social psychology) that offer specific predictions for social psychological phenomena, and that are directly tested by empirical evidence.

Thus, evolutionary social psychology is logically analogous to cognitive social psychology. Just as the cognitive sciences provide a metatheoretical context (and a set of conceptual tools) that can be used to derive hypotheses about social psychological phenomena, the evolutionary sciences provide a metatheoretical context (and a somewhat different set of conceptual tools) that can be used to derive hypotheses about social psychological phenomena. The analogy is apt in other ways, too: Just as the metatheory of cognitive science generates multiple, and sometimes competing, theories about social psychological phenomena, so too does the metatheory of evolutionary science. Just as the advent of the cognitive approach to social psychology was greeted with skepticism decades ago, so too has been the advent of evolutionary psychological inquiry. And, just as the cognitive revolution eventually reshaped the landscape of social psychology, the findings generated thus far by the evolutionary perspective suggest that it, too, has the potential to further revolutionize inquiry into social behavior (Kenrick, Schaller, & Simpson, 2006).

Because its metatheoretical assumptions are rooted in the biological sciences (rather than the traditional social sciences), evolutionary social psychology is sometimes viewed as exotic, and sometimes even as threatening to the basic assumptions of social psychology. In fact, an evolutionary approach is entirely consistent with the defining themes of social psychology. Evolutionary social psychology is emphatically focused on the *power of the situation*, assuming that the proximate impetus to action typically lies in the immediate social context. Evolutionary social psychology is also an *interactionist* perspective, recognizing that thoughts, feelings, and behavior emerge as an interactive function of variables pertaining to the person (e.g., specific motives, strategies, and capacities) and the situation (e.g., salient contextual cues connoting specific threats or opportunities within the immediate social context). It is explicitly interactionist in another way, too: An evolutionary perspective rejects any simplistic "nature *versus* nurture" approach to the causes of social behavior. Rather, it acknowledges, and seeks to unpack, the fascinating and complex relationships among evolved mechanisms, developmental processes, learning, and culture. Given these features, evolutionary analyses rarely generate hypotheses about inflexible, rigid forms of behavior. Instead, these hypotheses often explicitly articulate how evolved psychological adaptations imply predictably *flexible* responses to cues in the immediate environment. Finally, evolutionary social psychology generates hypotheses about mediating processes—about how particular cues in the social environment heuristically imply particular threats and opportunities, activate particular cognitive and affective mechanisms, and thereby incline individuals toward particular behaviors.

In other ways, however, evolutionary approaches move beyond traditional social psychological approaches. Evolutionarily informed deductions typically begin by identifying specific domains of fitness-relevant behavior (e.g., coalition formation, child-rearing, mate acquisition) and specific problems pertaining to each domain (e.g., how to avoid social exclusion, how to enhance parental commitment to offspring, how to identify a mate who maximizes one's own reproductive potential). The resulting deductions are *domain specific*: Psychological mechanisms that govern social inference and behavior in one social domain may be very different from those that govern inference and behavior in other, superficially similar, domains. The focus on recurrent fitness-relevant problems also encourages attention not only to specific underlying processes (e.g., the automatic activation of attitudes), but to the specific *contents* of those processes (e.g., the automatic activation of specific attitudes—rather than others—that are functionally relevant to particular fitness-relevant problems). The result is a set of hypotheses that are often more highly specific and nuanced than those deduced from other conceptual perspectives.

IMPORTANT ASSUMPTIONS AND CONCEPTUAL TOOLS

Some individual organisms have characteristics that enable them, compared to other individuals, to more successfully exploit the prospects and avoid the perils presented by their local ecologies. As a consequence, these organisms are more successful at transmitting their genes into future generations. Over many generations of differential reproductive success, this process—*natural selection*—produces populations possessing those characteristics that previously conferred relative reproductive fitness (Darwin, 1871). Natural selection applies to all living species, including humans, and has shaped the ways contemporary humans think about and interact within their social worlds. In this section, we highlight some key evolutionary concepts and their implications for understanding human social psychology.

Reproductive Fitness Is the Coin of the Realm

People are purpose-driven. They have goals, and their actions can be understood as attempts, conscious or not, to achieve these goals. Open nearly any contemporary social psychology journal and you will read about how people's thoughts, feelings, and behavior are driven by the goals to get along with others, conserve mental resources, maintain internal consistency, enhance self-esteem, or satisfy some other need or motive or goal.

Evolutionary approaches also begin with the tacit assumption that social behavior ultimately serves some function. The ultimate function of behavior is reproduction—the perpetuation of genes into subsequent generations. Evolutionary perspectives on psychological processes consider the implications that those processes—and the behaviors they produce—have for reproductive fitness.

This does not mean that reproductive fitness is a conscious goal. Reproductive fitness is not usually a psychological goal state at all (conscious or nonconscious). At an evolutionary level of analysis, behavior is functional not in the sense of being purpose-driven, but in the sense that these behaviors (and the psychological mechanisms that produce them) had positive implications for reproductive fitness in the past. This evolutionary understanding of "function" is entirely compatible with psychological approaches to function emphasizing motives, needs, and goals. Behaviors that are functional in an evolutionary sense (because they conferred reproductive fitness in ancestral environments) are typically driven—consciously or unconsciously—by more proximate goals (of the sort typically articulated by social psychological theories).

Reproduction may be the ultimate function of behavior, but this does not mean that each episode of behavior effectively promotes reproductive success. Evolutionary adaptations are not perfect (as we discuss more fully below), and behaviors inconsistent with reproductive fitness are inevitable. Such behaviors are often of considerable interest to evolutionary psychologists. Just as the study of cognitive errors and biases can provide insights into the proximate goals that underlie human cognition, the study of fitness-inconsistent behaviors may provide clues to the evolution of the psychological mechanisms that produce these puzzling

behaviors (e.g., Campero-Ciani, Corna, & Capiluppi, 2004; Kenrick, Keefe, Bryan, Barr, & Brown, 1995).

To assert that psychological mechanisms were designed by evolution to promote reproductive fitness is sometimes misunderstood to imply that all behavior is ultimately about sex. It's not. Successful reproduction typically requires solutions to a large number of problems (e.g., self-protection, acquisition of resources) and sub-problems that have nothing directly to do with copulation, per se. Any psychological process that bears on the solution to this broader set of problems may have enormous consequences for reproductive fitness.

Indeed, even individuals who never reproduce directly may nonetheless increase their reproductive fitness through a variety of indirect means. Reproductive fitness is defined not by the mere production of offspring but by the successful reproduction of genes. Actions that have implications for the survival and reproduction of close genetic relatives therefore have indirect implications for one's own reproductive fitness (the concept of *inclusive fitness*; Hamilton, 1964). Under predictable conditions, for instance, some birds actually fare better by helping their siblings raise a clutch than by mating on their own (Trivers, 1985). People may also enhance their own reproductive fitness by facilitating the survival and reproduction of close kin (Burnstein, Crandall, & Kitayama, 1994; Faulkner & Schaller, 2007; Hrdy, 1999). Consequently, evolutionary processes apply not only to the small set of behaviors bearing directly on sex and mating, but to all of human social cognition and behavior.

Adaptations Solved Problems

Adaptations are features of an organism that were naturally selected because they enhanced the reproductive fitness of its predecessors in ancestral environments. Adaptations solved recurring problems. Some solved problems related to movement (e.g., wings, legs); some solved problems related to the acquisition of nutrients (e.g., the giraffe's long neck, digestive enzymes in saliva). In this chapter, we focus on (a) adaptive problems defined by the recurring threats and opportunities presented by human *social* ecologies, and (b) the cognitive, emotional, and behavioral mechanisms that evolved to help ancestral humans solve them.

What kinds of recurring problems did early humans face? There is considerable overlap in the various answers that have been offered to that question (e.g., Bugental, 2000; Kenrick, Li, & Butner, 2003). Like most animals, humans must solve problems of self-protection (from non-human predators and human rivals), disease avoidance (including that posed by human–human pathogen transmission), and mate attraction. Like other animals that invest heavily in offspring, humans must also solve problems related to child rearing. Like the (relatively few) mammals that include long-term pair-bonding as a predominant mating strategy, humans must solve problems related to mate retention. And like other social animals, humans must solve the (sometimes competing) problems of coalitional cooperation, exchange of resources, and status-seeking.

These broad classes of problems can each be divided into hierarchically linked sub-problems. For instance, to solve the problem of successful social exchange, individuals must solve sub-problems that include identification of individuals with traits that facilitate or hinder successful exchange, detection of actual acts of non-reciprocation, and the discouragement of such acts (e.g., Cosmides & Tooby, 2005; Cottrell, Neuberg, & Li, 2007; Fehr, Fischbacher, & Gachter, 2002). To solve the problem of mate selection, individuals must also solve a myriad of sub-problems, including the ability to discriminate between individuals according to their fertility, parental potential, genetic quality, and degree of kinship (e.g., Gangestad & Simpson, 2000; Kenrick & Keefe, 1992; Lieberman, Tooby, & Cosmides, 2007). Most adaptations are designed to solve these kinds of specific sub-problems.

Adaptations Are Functionally Specialized and Domain-Specific

An assumption underlying most evolutionary approaches is that natural selection results in a large number of relatively specialized, problem-specific psychological mechanisms. For instance, rather than having a single all-purpose "survival system" that addresses the problems of extracting nutrients from food and moving those nutrients throughout the body, people possess functionally distinct (albeit linked) digestive, circulatory, and respiratory systems. These domain-specific systems are themselves made up of functionally distinct structures that perform necessary sub-tasks (e.g., the digestive system's salivary glands, stomach, and intestines). Similarly, rather than having a single "social survival system" that addresses all fitness-relevant problems presented by social ecologies (problems of status attainment, coalition formation, child-rearing, and the like), the human psyche is made up of functionally distinct (albeit linked) cognitive, emotional, and behavioral mechanisms—each adapted to a set of specific fitness-relevant challenges.

This view—that adaptations are functionally specialized—contrasts with explanatory perspectives invoking "domain-general" principles, such as some general desire to seek reward. Domain-general principles may appeal to parsimony, but an abundance of research on human cognition raises serious problems for these domain-general approaches. Just as there are multiple, functionally distinct visual systems, learning systems, and memory systems (e.g., Kanwisher,

McDermott, & Chun, 1997; Klein, Cosmides, Tooby, & Chance, 2002; Moore, 2004, Sherry & Schacter, 1987), it is becoming increasingly clear that there are also multiple, functionally-distinct systems for responding to the multiple, conceptually distinct prospects and perils of social life (Ackerman & Kenrick, 2008; Barrett & Kurzban, 2006; Kurzban & Aktipis, 2007; Pinker, 1997; Schaller, Park, & Kenrick, 2007; Tooby & Cosmides, 1992).

Many psychologists traditionally presumed that the mind emerges free of content and constraint—a "blank slate" to be written upon by experience and learning (Pinker, 2003). On the contrary, functionally specialized systems are domain-specific: They possess some amount of content that directs and constrains which information in the world "counts" as relevant input information and which outcomes potentially serve as solutions to the adaptive problem confronted. Research on associative learning illustrates this key point. Only certain stimuli get conditioned to nausea, and the particulars depend on the organism's evolutionary history and typical ecology. Rats, which have poor vision and rely on taste and smell to find food at night, condition nausea to novel tastes but not to novel visual stimuli (Garcia & Koelling, 1966). In contrast, quail, which have excellent vision and rely on visual cues in food choice, condition nausea easily to visual cues but not to taste (Wilcoxon, Dragoin, & Kral, 1971). The same principles apply to people. A fearful response is more easily conditioned to objects that posed a significant threat throughout humans' evolutionary past (e.g., snakes) than to objects that cause many more deaths in current-day environments (e.g., electrical outlets and automobiles) but that did not exist in ancestral ecologies (Öhman & Mineka, 2001). Similarly, people are faster and more accurate at detecting objects that posed threats in ancestral environments than at detecting objects that pose threats only in modern environments (New, Cosmides, & Tooby, 2007).

Evidence of evolved functional specificity has become increasingly common within the social psychological literature. We will review a wide range of such findings.

Adaptations Are Imperfect in Evolutionarily Sensible Ways

Biases, errors, and poor decisions are sometimes, naively, taken as evidence that the psychological processes underlying them could not have evolved, because evolution presumably would have created a better, smarter, less error-prone system. This is not so. Evolved psychological mechanisms are inevitably imperfect, for several reasons.

First, biological evolution is slow. Changes in gene frequencies within populations occur more slowly than changes in the environments inhabited by the organisms that house those genes. This is particularly the case for humans, who reproduce slowly but alter their environments rapidly and significantly. Recall that, to the extent than any psychological mechanism has evolved, it did so as an adaptation to selection pressures that existed over long periods of time in ancestral environments (sometimes known as the *environment of evolutionary adaptedness*, or *EEA* for short; Bowlby, 1969). Some of these historical environments had similar features to the ones humans currently reside in (e.g., families, neighbors, threats from outgroups). However, the EEA for other adaptations may differ substantially from contemporary human ecologies. For example, the small, kin-based coalitional groups that characterized much of human history are different in many respects from the large, urban, ethnically heterogeneous societies within which many humans live today. To the extent there are differences between ancestral and contemporary environments, psychological *adaptations* (to ancestral social ecologies) may not currently be *adaptive* (in contemporary social ecologies).

Second, given the way natural selection works, it is unlikely that any evolutionary adaptation will operate perfectly within any environment, even within the specific environment in which it was selected. Natural selection is not a creative process, per se; it does not generate new, ideal solutions to fitness-relevant problems. Instead, it is a winnowing process; it selectively eliminates from populations those genes (and their phenotypic expressions) that, compared to other genes (and their expressions), are less reproductively fit. What evolves within a population is rarely as perfect as what might have been created by a forward-thinking, omniscient intelligent designer. Existing adaptations are simply relatively less flawed than the biologically constrained set of alternatives from which blind processes of natural selection had to "choose."

Third, evolved psychological mechanisms were selected because, multiplied across instances and across individuals, they enhanced reproductive fitness more than did alternative mechanisms. One might usefully think of evolved psychological mechanisms as if-then *decision rules*, or *stimulus-response heuristics*, in which specific sets of psychological inputs (e.g., perceptions, inferences) trigger specific set of psychological outputs (e.g., cognitive, emotional, or behavioral responses). Consider, for instance, the tendency for the perception of an angry face to trigger an avoidant response. Averaged across many instances, this stimulus-response heuristic likely led to better fitness outcomes than did alternative stimulus-response associations. Of course, in some specific instances, this heuristic may be counterproductive (when, for example, the apparently angry person doesn't actually pose a threat).

The types of errors and biases generated by evolved, stimulus-response psychological mechanisms tend to be fitness-seeking (Gigerenzer, Todd, & the ABC Research Group, 1999; Haselton & Nettle, 2006). To respond to some stimulus in an adaptive fashion (e.g., to avoid a dangerous rival or approach a promising mate), one must first identify that stimulus (i.e., categorize a person as a dangerous rival or a promising mate). Such categorizations depend on imperfect, often superficial, cues, creating a classic *signal-detection problem*. At the simplest level of analysis, two distinct kinds of errors may occur: A false positive error (e.g., classifying a benign individual as dangerous) or a false negative error (e.g., classifying a truly dangerous person as benign). Because cues are imperfectly diagnostic, errors are inevitable, and any systematic attempt to minimize the likelihood of false positive errors inevitably increases the likelihood of false negative errors, and vice versa. How are these signal detection dilemmas resolved? The logic of reproductive fitness implies that psychological mechanisms will be biased in favor of whichever error (either false positive or false negative) leads, in the long run, to less deleterious outcomes for reproductive fitness.

This fundamental principle has a nickname: The *smoke detector principle* (Nesse, 2005). A smoke detector (the kind that homeowners install in their ceilings) may be calibrated to minimize (irritating) false positives, or to minimize (fatal) false negatives. Not surprisingly, they are deliberately (and wisely) calibrated to minimize the more costly false negative error, which inevitably results in the occasional irritating false positive. Analogously, natural selection has shaped perceptual, cognitive, and emotional systems to minimize the likelihood of making whichever form of error is most harmful to reproductive fitness. Consequently, these mechanisms have predictable biases, and regularly favor the alternative, less costly, form of error.

This fundamental logical insight underlies many evolutionary analyses of social psychological phenomena (e.g., Haselton & Nettle, 2006; Kurzban & Leary, 2001; Park, Schaller, & Van Vugt, 2008; Schaller & Duncan, 2007). One prominent example is *error management theory* (Haselton & Nettle, 2006). This theory helps explain why men misperceive women to be more sexually available than they actually are, and why women show a rather different bias in their perceptions of men (Haselton & Buss, 2000; Maner et al., 2005). Analyses of inference errors people regularly make (and do not make) can be an invaluable means of testing theories and hypotheses. We discuss many such biases below.

THE AFFORDANCE MANAGEMENT SYSTEM

The specialized adaptations making up the human psyche were designed by natural selection to manage the threats and opportunities afforded by the ecologies early humans and their ancestors inhabited. These threats and opportunities can collectively be called "affordances" (Gibson, 1979; McArthur & Baron, 1983; Zebrowitz & Montepare, 2006). This set of coordinated adaptations can therefore be considered an *affordance management system*. The simple template depicted in Figure 21.1 characterizes the basic contours of this system.

To illustrate, imagine walking alone down a dark, deserted street in an unfamiliar city. Suddenly you hear footsteps approaching rapidly from behind. Not knowing the source of the sounds, you may categorize it as a threat to your physical safety. This perception of threat rapidly initiates a suite of coordinated, self-protective responses—sensory vigilance toward the assumed threat, a rush of adrenaline, implicit activation of threat-relevant semantic concepts ("Danger!"), increased blood flow to large muscles in your legs and arms (and away from your digestive system), and a strong behavioral inclination to escape—all of which facilitate the likelihood that you flee. This example illustrates several key principles that characterize the affordance management system.

Cues Connote Affordances

Effective affordance management requires psychological mechanisms that translate perceptual stimuli (e.g., sounds, smells, morphological features) into fitness-relevant categorical inferences (e.g., threat to physical safety, mating opportunity, etc.). Many research programs in evolutionary psychology attempt to articulate specific cues likely to imply specific affordances. Specific characteristics of other people heuristically imply infectious disease, for instance (Schaller & Duncan, 2007). Other specific cues heuristically

Identification of Relevant Cues in the Environment

Perception of Cue-Relevant Threat or Opportunity

Activation of Affordance-Relevant
Cognitions, Emotions, and Behavioral Inclinations

Behavior

Figure 21.1 Affordance Management System.

connote kinship (Park et al., 2008). Still other cues heuristically connote fertility (Kenrick & Keefe, 1992). And so on. The implicit message, of course, is that in order to predict an individual's response to any social situation, one much attend not only to the superficial details of that situation but also to the fitness-relevant threats or opportunities that those details imply.

Thinking (and Feeling) Is for Doing

Perceptual, cognitive, and affective processes are integral to the affordance management system. But the eventual outcome is behavior—doing something. This emphasizes the fundamental axiom that thinking is for doing (S. T. Fiske, 1992). Feeling is for doing, too. These premises are particularly salient within the evolutionary approach, because cognitions and emotions cannot, by themselves, have any direct influence on reproductive fitness; natural selection can only operate on actual motor behavior (or the lack of it). Consequently, to understand why people think and feel different things in different situations, it is important to consider the implications of thought and feeling for the actual behavior likely to result.

The Focus Is on Function

The linkages between processes—cue perception, affordance categorization, response suites, and behavior—are *functional* linkages. They are coordinated to facilitate solving the problem implied by the initially perceived cue. For instance, although you *could* respond to the perception of approaching footsteps by contemplating a snack and licking your lips, you are unlikely to do so—because food fantasizing and lip licking were unlikely to have served fitness under analogous circumstances in ancestral worlds. Inherent to an evolutionary approach, and to the idea of an affordance management system, is the assumption that human social cognition and behavior is *motivated* social cognition and behavior.

Content Matters

In light of the functional nature of psychological mechanisms, an evolutionary approach implies that cognitive, affective, and behavioral systems must not only make gross distinctions between things that are good and bad (or requiring approach versus avoidance), but must also make much finer qualitative distinctions (Kenrick & Shiota, 2008). Many events may be evaluative unpleasant—a rapidly approaching stranger, the death of a child, a thief escaping with your bag of groceries—but they are unpleasant in fundamentally different ways, with different functional implications. Cognitive, affective, and behavioral responses must be calibrated to differentiate among them in textured ways so as to produce focused, functionally specific solutions. Thus, when evolutionary logic is applied to social psychological phenomena, it typically yields hypotheses not only about underlying processes but also, crucially, about *content*, too—and in ways that are often extraordinarily precise about the *particular* affective, cognitive, and behavioral responses one would expect in different social situations.

Context Matters, Too

For most psychological adaptations, there is no hardwired highway that necessarily links some specific set of perceptual cues to some specific threat or opportunity inference, or that necessarily links that threat or opportunity inference to some specific feeling, cognition, and/or behavioral response. These links are probabilistic, and their strength tends to be contingent upon additional information gleaned from the immediate environment. Sudden noises produce more exaggerated fear responses among people who are in the dark (Grillon, Pellowski, Merikangas, & Davis, 1997), and snakes are more readily detected by people who feel anxious (Öhman, Flykt, & Esteves, 2001). Similarly, inferences about, and adaptive reactions to, social stimuli are sensitive to inputs from both chronic and ephemeral elements of the perceptual context. As seen throughout this chapter, evolutionary approaches provide logical tools that allow one to derive novel predictions about how specific features of the immediate social situation and specific perceiver dispositions (e.g., current goals, traits, beliefs) facilitate or attenuate specific cognitive, affective, and behavioral phenomena. This appreciation for moderation effects, of course, is consistent with social psychology's traditional theme of person-situation interactionism.

This Applies to All of Social Psychology

The affordance management system provides a broad conceptual template that can be applied across all of social psychology. In the following sections, we summarize a variety of different ways in which evolutionary thinking has been applied productively to different social psychological topic areas. The vast majority of this work—both theoretical and empirical—fits the template of the affordance management system. Table 21.1 provides a complementary summary, highlighting specific examples that illustrate the functional linkages between specific adaptive problems, the cues that reveal them, the functional responses to them, and the contextual variables that moderate the extent to which these adaptive mechanisms are engaged.

EVOLUTIONARY PERSPECTIVES ON SOCIAL PSYCHOLOGICAL PHENOMENA

The landscape of social psychology is broad. Social psychological inquiry focuses on highly automatized perceptual and memory processes as well as on highly deliberative forms of actual interpersonal behavior. It includes the study of individuals, dyads, groups, and entire cultures. Evolutionary theorizing has been applied productively across this entire scholarly landscape. We cannot review it all here. Instead, in the following sections, we provide a selective review to illustrate both the breadth and depth of this research and to illustrate the generative utility that an evolutionary approach brings to the study of social psychology.

Ultrasociality, Belongingness, and Self-Esteem

In many species, including humans, reproductive fitness is enhanced by proximity to, and alliances with, conspecifics. Compared to those who pursued a solitary lifestyle, significant fitness benefits accrued to those who lived in cooperative, highly interdependent groups (e.g., Brewer & Caporael, 2006; Leakey & Lewin, 1977). Given these fitness benefits associated with *ultrasociality* (Campbell, 1982), one would expect humans to be highly motivated to be accepted by their fellow group members—to experience a profound *need to belong* (Baumeister & Leary, 1995; Leary, this volume).

When their bodies require nutrition, people experience hunger, which motivates them to find food and eat; when people encounter threatening footsteps on the dark city street, they feel fear, which motivates them to find a safe haven. Self-esteem may serve a similar signaling function for the belongingness motive, operating as a *sociometer* that informs people whether they are falling below the threshold for social inclusion (Leary & Baumeister, 2000). On this account, high self-esteem indicates successful social inclusion; lowered self-esteem signals actual or impending social exclusion. Indeed, variation in self-esteem is linked with the degree to which one feels included and/or accepted by others (Leary, Tambor, Terdal, & Downs, 1995; Leary, Haupt, Strausser, & Chokel, 1998; Murray, Griffin, Rose, & Bellavia, 2003). Moreover, neuroimaging (fMRI) results indicate that the psychological pain of social exclusion is produced by some of the same physiological mechanisms involved in the experience of physical pain (Eisenberger & Lieberman, 2004). This finding is consistent with speculation that neural mechanisms that once served simply to indicate the threat of physical injury may have undergone additional adaptation in response to the ultrasocial landscape of human (and pre-human) populations, and thus now function to signal the threat of social exclusion as well (MacDonald & Leary, 2005).

Table 21.1 Representative Illustrations of Functional Linkages Between Specific Fundamental Social Motives, Social Affordances (Opportunities and Threats) Germane to Them, Cues that Reveal These Affordances, Functional Psychological and Behavioral Responses to Them, and the Types of Contextual Variables that Moderate the Extent to Which These Adaptive Mechanisms are Engaged.

Motive	Relevant Affordances	Relevant Heuristic Cues	Functional Response "Syndromes"	Functionally Relevant Moderating Factors
To self-protect	*Opportunities*: Safety provided by others. *Threats*: Violence from outgroup members; violence from ingroup members.	Presence of familiar, similar others. Presence of unfamiliar, dissimilar, angry males.	Perceive such individuals as safe; feel friendly toward them; become braver; smile; approach; offer cooperation. Err on side of perceiving such individuals as dangerous; experience fear; attempt to escape or join similar, familiar others to defend.	Located in familiar surroundings; many similar, familiar others nearby; high dispositional trust in others. Located in unfamiliar surroundings; darkness; past experience of being physically harmed; being female or of small stature.
To attract mates	*Opportunities*: Availability of desirable, opposite-sex others. *Threats*: Presence of desirable, same-sex others.	Opposite-sex other's age, physical attractiveness, status, bodily symmetry, morphological abnormalities, scent, nonverbal (flirting or rejecting) behaviors. Same-sex other's age, status, symmetry, masculinity/femininity, flirting behaviors.	Subjective lust; increase in testosterone; over-interpretation of sexual interest by men; conservative bias in evaluating signs of men's commitment by women. Bias toward attending to and interpreting attractive and high status same-sex individuals as competitors; denigrating same-sex competitors; costly signaling to potential mates.	Relative mate value; age; restricted vs. unrestricted sexual strategies; current ovulatory status; histocompatibility. Relative mate value; male-female ratio of available mates; status-linked distribution of resources; unpredictability of resource availability.
To retain mates	*Opportunities*: Long-term parental alliances. *Threats*: Sexual infidelity, Mate-poaching.	Other's expressions of love, intimacy, commitment; other's and own age and apparent fertility. Partner's flirtation behaviors; presence of nearby, high mate-value, opposite-sex individuals.	Own expressions of love, intimacy, commitment; feelings of love; enhanced attention to other's needs; diminished concern with equity between mates; bias toward viewing mate favorably, other potential partners less favorably. Jealousy; mate-guarding; enhanced vigilance and memory for desirable members of other sex; aggression against mate or suspected mate-poacher.	Shared children; own mate value; own resources; availability of desirable alternative mates. Relative mate value; own resources; availability of desirable alternative mates; ovulatory status.

768

Social motive	Opportunities/Threats	Inputs/Cues	Affective, cognitive, and behavioral responses	Moderators
To care for offspring	*Opportunities*: Enhanced reproductive fitness. *Threats*: Especially high costs imposed by children.	Apparent relatedness of child; physical similarity of child. Apparent (un)relatedness of child; physical (dis)similarity of child; child's health; health, age, and other qualities of one's other children.	Vigilance to child and nearby unfamiliar others; feelings of parental love; resource provision without expectation of reciprocity. Enhanced attention to one's other children, or to alternative mate; withholding of resources; child abuse, infanticide.	Oxytocin levels; gender; number of other children of one's own, siblings, or nieces/nephews; age of child; availability of tangible resources. Degree of paternal uncertainty: step-parenthood; age of child; number of other children of one's own, siblings, or nieces/nephews.
To form and maintain cooperative alliances	*Opportunities*: Share resources, receive material support, enhanced self-protection, access to mates. *Threats*: Exposure to disease, cheating/free-riding, incompetence, excessive demands.	Familiarity; past acts of reciprocity, trustworthiness; other's adherence to group norms; facial characteristics signaling trustworthiness. Subjective "foreignness" of others; unfamiliarity of other; other's acts of cheating, norm violation.	Feelings of trust and respect; commitment to other; willingness to share, reciprocate; work with others to achieve group goals; adherence to group norms. Hypersensitivity to unfair exchanges, disease-linked cues, or rejection cues in others; sensitivity to existing social norms; feelings of moral disgust, fear, and anger; stigmatization and other forms of informal and formal social control; tit-for-tat interactional strategies.	Coalitional identity or investment; gender; "collectivistic" cultural context and proximity to kin networks; dispositional trust in others; need for belongingness, social approval. Own inclinations to cheat; personal vulnerability to disease; location (central vs. peripheral) within group network.
To seek status	*Opportunities*: Status-enhancing alliances, improved access to resources and (for males) mating opportunities. *Threats*: Loss of status, social regard, status-linked resources and mates.	Nonverbal status-conferring displays (e.g., eye-contact, bodily orientation, etc.) by others; shifts in exchange rules; others' willingness to invest in oneself. Nonverbal dominance displays by others; shifts in exchange rules; lack of apparent respect from others.	Public displays of resources, abilities (costly signaling), dominance, self-efficacy, inclinations toward leadership; sensitivity to cues implying one's own position in hierarchy and to presence of others with similar concerns. Embarrassment, shame; vigilance toward those higher in status hierarchy and toward those on their way up; join with related others of similar status to try to overthrow current high status; denigrate others.	Current status level; presence of potential familial coalitional partners; presence of desirable (female) mates. Current status level; public vs. private nature of interactional context; optimism, self-efficacy.

From the evolutionary perspective, thinking and feeling are for doing: It is not enough to feel the sting of rejection, but one must also do something to redress the deficit. One strategy is to actively avoid and punish those doing the rejecting, and the literature on social exclusion indicates that the aversive state of exclusion precipitates various kinds of antisocial behavior (e.g., Leary, Twenge, & Quinlivan, 2006; Twenge, Baumeister, DeWall, Ciarocco, & Bartels, 2007). Strategies for re-establishing social connections, however, are likely to solve the problem of exclusion more effectively than aggression, which can trigger increased rejection. Consistent with this reconnection hypothesis, when people are threatened with social exclusion, they tend to express greater interest in making new friends, increase their desire to work cooperatively with others, and form more positive first impressions of new potential interaction partners (Maner, DeWall, Baumeister, & Schaller, 2007).

Although the above research is consistent with certain evolutionary analyses, the kinds of nuanced hypotheses we highlighted in our opening paragraph haven't yet emerged within this arena. For instance, it seems likely that the need to belong may currently be conceptualized too broadly; other evolutionary views would suggest, instead, greater modularity—that there are distinct sets of problems and opportunities linked to relationships with kin, friends, and one's broader coalition (e.g., Ackerman, Kenrick, & Schaller, 2007), and that these distinct needs would be attuned to different social cues, elicit different cognitive and behavioral responses, lead to different behavioral strategies, and be modulated by different person variables and ecological circumstances. Similarly, recent evidence suggests that self-esteem may be sensitive not only to social acceptance and rejection, but also to other cues as well, depending on sex and prominent current goals (e.g., appearance, status, others' assessments of one's mate value, etc.; Anthony, Holmes, & Wood, 2007; Johnson, Burk, & Kirkpatrick, 2007; Penke & Denissen, 2008).

Social Attention, Perception, and Person Memory

From an evolutionary perspective, it makes little sense to cognitively process just any information, but to selectively process information that was highly relevant to ancestral reproductive fitness (Kenrick, 1994). Individuals quick to attend to and process rapidly approaching angry men, for example, would have likely outreproduced their inattentive and slower-witted neighbors.

Simply put, cognitive processing should be selective, and selective in particular ways. The mind should, as a default, expend its energy processing the kinds of information that implied threats and opportunities in ancestral social environments—for instance, angry male faces,

physically attractive members of the opposite sex, and crying children. Moreover, the informational grist selected by the cognitive mill should be sensitive to whatever evolutionarily relevant goal states are especially salient.

Consider the benefits of being beautiful, and its implications for visual attention. Physically attractive people are liked more, paid more, and are assumed to possess many desirable characteristics (Feingold, 1992). Evolutionary analyses suggest, however, that—depending on the context—attractive individuals may afford either opportunities *or* threats to reproductive fitness; this, in turn, has implications for the prediction of visual attention to (or away from) physically attractive individuals. Some of these implications are demonstrated in a set of highly nuanced findings from a series of studies by Maner, Gailliot, Rouby, and Miller (2007). Attractive opposite-sex targets were especially likely to hold attention of perceivers for whom the fitness-relevant problem of acquiring a mate was highly salient and who were also inclined toward an "unrestricted" (e.g., relatively promiscuous) mating style. No such attentional advantage was directed at opposite-sex targets in general, nor did attractive opposite-sex targets hold the attention of individuals with a more "restricted" approach to mate-seeking. What about attention to attractive *same-sex* targets? They were especially likely to hold the attention of perceivers for whom the fitness-relevant goal of retaining current mates was highly salient and who were also dispositionally inclined to employ a zealously protective and vigilant strategy of guarding mates from same-sex rivals. No such attentional advantage was directed at either same-sex or attractive targets in general, nor did attractive same-sex targets hold the attention of individuals less inclined toward mate-guarding. This pattern of textured findings illustrate that social attentional processes are attuned to the affordances implied by the perceptual environment, and that these affordances are defined jointly by the fitness-relevant goals of perceivers and the fitness-relevant features of the persons perceived.

This is just one example. There is a burgeoning body of evolutionarily informed empirical research documenting similar forms of process specificity in individuals' attention to their social environment (e.g., Becker, Kenrick, Guerin, & Maner, 2005; Duncan, Park, Faulkner, Schaller, Neuberg, & Kenrick, 2007; Fox, Russo, Bowles, & Dutton, 1991; Maner, DeWall, & Gailliot, 2008; Öhman & Mineka, 2001).

Similarly nuanced findings emerge in research that focuses not on social attention, per se, but on the detection of specific features in others' faces. Recall that an adaptive behavioral response to social exclusion is behavioral reconnection with potentially rewarding others (Maner et al., 2007). It follows that the experience of social exclusion should enhance individuals' ability to detect facial expressions that signal affiliative potential and to accurately discriminate these expressions from other facial expressions. This is indeed the case (Pickett & Gardner, 2005). For example, socially excluded individuals show a substantial increase in the ability to discriminate between real smiles and fake smiles (Bernstein, Young, Brown, Sacco, & Claypool, 2008). Another example reflects the fact that adult males and females have historically differed in their capacity to do physical harm, and in their tendencies toward aggression versus succorance. One implication of this sex difference—that men are more likely to afford aggression, women more likely to afford helpfulness—is that there may be an adaptive bias to detect anger in the faces of men and more affiliative expressions in the faces of women. Indeed, perceivers more quickly and accurately identify male faces as *angry*, but female faces as *happy*; conversely, angry expressions facilitate the identification of faces as male, whereas happy expressions facilitate identification of faces as female. Additional results reveal that this phenomenon cannot be readily attributed to learned stereotypes about men and women: When androgynous computer-generated faces are dressed in male versus female clothing, for example, they are perceived as stereotypically masculine or feminine, but not as correspondingly angry or happy (Becker, Kenrick, Neuberg, Blackwell, & Smith, 2007).

Content specificity of this sort emerges not only in perceivers' perception of actual information on others' faces, but also in the *mis*perception of information that isn't actually there. White perceivers for whom self-protection goals (but not other goals) are highly salient erroneously "see" anger (but not other negative emotions) in the neutrally expressive faces of Black men, but not in the neutrally expressive faces of White men or women, or in the faces of Black women (Maner et al., 2005). These results fit with speculation—common to many evolutionary analyses of intergroup relations (e.g., Navarrete, Olsson, Ho, Mendes, Thomsen, & Sidanius, in press; Schaller & Neuberg, 2008)—that unexpected interactions with outgroup males afforded a particularly potent threat to reproductive fitness.

The evolutionary importance of faces heuristically connoting threat also has implications for recognition memory. Consider the robust "outgroup homogeneity bias" in recognition memory: White perceivers, for example, are much more accurate at recognizing previously encountered White faces than Black faces (e.g., Anthony, Copper, & Mullen, 1992; Chance & Goldstein, 1996). An evolutionary analysis of this phenomenon suggests that the effect occurs because limited processing resources are selectively allocated to the faces of individuals who have clear fitness implications for perceivers. Since most fitness-relevant interactions have historically occurred within coalitional groups, this implies

a processing advantage for ingroup faces. However, when a facial expression implies imminent threat—as is implied by an angry facial expression—it is likely to attract processing resources regardless of ingroup/outgroup status. In fact, given the historically greater danger associated with intergroup (rather than intragroup) interactions, angry outgroup faces may be especially likely to attract the kind of processing resources that allow accurate identification later on. This implies that when White perceivers encounter angry faces (both White and Black), the usual outgroup homogeneity effect in recognition memory should be eliminated—and even reversed. It is (Ackerman et al., 2006).

Social Inference and Impression Formation

To effectively avoid a social threat or avail oneself of a reproductive opportunity, it is advantageous—and sometimes essential—to identify that threat or opportunity quickly. Just as there are evolutionary advantages associated with fast and frugal decision-making heuristics more broadly (e.g., Gigerenzer et al., 1999), there is also a need for speed in social inference. Indeed, people form trait impressions quickly, spontaneously, and with minimal cognitive effort (Carlston & Skowronski, 2005; Gilbert & Malone, 1995; Newman & Uleman, 1989).

Speedy and spontaneous impressions of others can be adaptive even if they are imperfect, as long as they are generally diagnostic of actual behavior. In fact, first impressions are often remarkably accurate given the impoverished information they are based upon (Ambady, Bernieri, & Richeson, 2000; Vanneste, Verplaetse, Van Hiel, & Braeckman, 2007; Yamagishi, Tanida, Mashima, Shimoma, & Kanazawa, 2003). For example, people are able to accurately estimate the upper-body strength of men based solely on facial photographs (Sell et al., 2009), and just 50 milliseconds are sufficient for perceivers to infer, at levels exceeding chance, a man's sexual orientation (Rule & Ambady, 2008). Such findings are consistent with speculation regarding an evolved *personality judgment instinct* (Haselton & Funder, 2006).

Not all trait impressions are equally relevant to reproductive fitness, however. Trait that best convey whether someone represents a threat or an opportunity should be most central to impression formation. The embodiment of a threat or opportunity depends upon an individual's intentions (e.g., whether someone intends harm or intends to share reproductively useful resources) and on that individual's skill at carrying out those intentions (greater skill implies greater threat and greater opportunity, depending on whether the person's intentions are nasty or nice.) Consistent with this functional analysis (Fiske, Cuddy, & Glick, 2007; Schaller, 2008), impressions of individuals (and of the social groups to which they belong) are consistently located within a two-dimensional space anchored by the broad evaluative dimensions of interpersonal warmth and competence (Fiske et al., 2007; Judd, James-Hawkins, Yzerbyt, & Kashima, 2005; Rosenberg, Nelson, & Vivekananthan, 1968). The warmth dimension—particularly as represented by traits that emphasize trustworthiness—is especially central to impression formation (Cottrell et al., 2007; Kelley, 1950; Oosterhof & Todorov, 2008; Peeters & Czapinski, 1990).

Many initial trait impressions are inspired by superficial characteristics, and recent evolutionarily analyses have yielded empirical findings linking specific superficial cues to specific impressions and identifying the specific conditions under which these linkages are especially strong. One such line of research focuses on psychological defenses against disease transmission and their implications for impression formation. Because pathogenic diseases pose powerful fitness costs, perceivers should be sensitive to cues signaling the possibility that another person carries an infectious disease. Many of these cues are morphological anomalies. In line with the smoke detector principle, perceivers often make overinclusive inference errors, responding inferentially to many truly healthy, but superficially anomalous-looking, individuals as though they were sick. For instance, even specific physical anomalies not diagnostic of pathogen transmission—including accident-caused facial disfigurement, physical disability, and obesity—spontaneously trigger disease-connoting implicit impressions, especially among perceivers who feel specifically vulnerable to disease transmission (Park, Faulkner, & Schaller, 2003; Park, Schaller, & Crandall, 2007; Schaller & Duncan, 2007). In fact, it has been suggested that physical unattractiveness of any kind may serve as a crude heuristic cue for ill-health, and thus lead to aversive trait inferences (Zebrowitz, Fellous, Mignault, & Andreoletti, 2003).

A second illustrative line of research examines heuristic cues to kinship and the impressions these cues inspire (Park et al., 2008). Many animal species employ superficial heuristic cues such as phenotypic similarity to distinguish kin from non-kin (Hepper, 1991; Rendall, 2004). Although humans have more recently evolved additional mechanisms that improve identification of close kin (based on capacities for language and symbolic thought), human inferences also appear to be implicitly influenced by evolutionarily ancient heuristic cue-based mechanisms. One consequence is that people respond to phenotypically similar individuals in a more kin-like way, even when those individuals are total strangers. For instance, perceived facial similarity leads to impressions connoting greater liking and trustworthiness, and also—in contrast to alternative explanations suggesting that similarity implies positive evaluations of all kinds—to *reduced* sexual attractiveness (DeBruine, 2002, 2005; see

also Ackerman, Kenrick, & Schaller, 2007). Moreover, perceived attitude similarity implicitly activates semantic cognitions connoting kinship (Park & Schaller, 2005). This latter finding suggests that evolved kin-detection mechanisms may help account for the classic similarity-liking effect (Byrne et al., 1971)—an interpretation bolstered by evidence that the similarity-liking effect emerges more strongly when the similar attitudes are those that are highly heritable (Tesser, 1993), and thus more diagnostic of actual kinship.

Prosocial Behavior

Why do people act in ways that benefit others? From an evolutionary perspective, there are many answers to this question; we explore a few of them here.

Kinship

Kinship provides one foundation for understanding the evolution of prosocial behavior, and for predicting variability in prosocial behavior across different circumstances. The logic of inclusive fitness (Hamilton, 1964) implies that, to the extent another individual is a close genetic relative, any action that directly enhances that individual's reproductive fitness indirectly enhances one's own fitness as well. This forms the basis of a process through which a particular form of altruism—nepotism—may have evolved. Evidence of nepotistic altruism is found widely across the animal kingdom (Greenberg, 1979; Holmes & Sherman, 1983; Suomi, 1982), including humans. Compared with dizygotic twins, for instance, monozygotic (identical) twins are more cooperative in mixed-motive games (Segal & Hershberger, 1999). In other contexts, too, people are more inclined to help genetically closer kin, and this tendency is exaggerated under conditions that have more direct implications for the kin member's actual reproductive fitness (Burnstein, Crandall, & Kitayama, 1994; Neyer & Lang, 2003; Stewart-Williams, 2008).

The evolved psychology of kinship also has important implications for prosocial behavior among total strangers. As with many other animals, ancestral humans were often unable to directly identify kin—one cannot "see" genes—but instead inferred kinship implicitly on the basis of superficial cues such as familiarity and similarity (Lieberman et al., 2007; Park et al., 2008). One implication of readily employing such cues is that persons may heuristically respond prosocially to individuals who appear either familiar or highly similar in some way—even when they know, rationally, that the individuals are total strangers. For instance, just as facial similarity promotes trust (DeBruine, 2002), it also promotes cooperative behavior in a public goods game (Krupp, DeBruine, & Barclay, 2008).

A variety of other cues may also heuristically imply kinship. Several different lines of evolutionary theorizing converge in suggesting that friendship may be a cue connoting kinship, and that this may especially be the case among women. Consistent with this analysis, women—but not men—behave just as benevolently toward friends as they do toward actual kin (Ackerman et al., 2007). Emotions may also serve as heuristic cues. Empathy likely evolved as part of a functional system for aiding kin in distress, and thus kinship may be implicitly connoted by the emotional experience of empathy—even when the empathy is elicited by non-kin (Hoffman, 1981; Krebs, 1987; Park et al., 2008). This suggests that the well-known relation between empathy and helping behavior among strangers may be rooted, in part, in the evolved psychology of kinship and kin-recognition.

Reciprocal Exchange

In exchange for the benefits people receive from fellow group members, they are obligated to provide benefits to them. Although some of the specific rules of social exchange vary across societies, the norm of reciprocal exchange is universal (Brown, 1991; A. Fiske, 1992). Fitness benefits for sharing emerge at both group and individual levels of analysis: By sharing resources, the individual helps other members of the group survive, and accrues credit for the future when his or her own luck may be down (Hill & Hurtado, 1989). Moreover, generous sharing enhances an individual's status within the group, and such status portends significant benefits of its own, including access to future group resources and enhanced mate value (Griskevicius et al., 2007).

From a purely economic perspective, one might expect prosocial behavior toward an unrelated individual only when a person was confident that others would, in fact, reciprocate. In fact, however, people often share resources with total strangers with whom they have no reciprocal alliances and will never interact again. Trying to explain such seemingly irrational behavior is an active domain of interdisciplinary inquiry (e.g., Henrich et al., 2005). An evolutionary perspective on social cognition helps resolve this issue. When making behavioral decisions, individuals respond not merely to rational assessments but also to heuristic cues (e.g., a sense of familiarity) that connote, imperfectly, potential reciprocity. In addition, the vast majority of interactions in ancestral environments involved coalitional group members who would, in fact, reciprocate. Therefore, following the smoke detector principle, psychological mechanisms that govern prosocial behavior between unrelated individuals may well have evolved in such a way to err on the side of assuming reciprocity (an assumption that helped maintain and promote social bonds) rather than non-reciprocity (an assumption that would have

undermined social bonds, thereby generating a broader set of costs). If so, mechanisms that evolved to promote reciprocal exchange and cooperation will be overinclusive, leading to many acts of prosocial behavior that, in reality, are unlikely to ever to be reciprocated (Burnham & Johnson, 2005; Johnson, Price, & Takezawa, 2008).

An evolutionary perspective has also recently been applied to better understand an aspect of exchange that appears puzzling from a simple economic perspective—the fact that people sometimes reject offers of help from others. Such behavior is less puzzling, however, when one realizes that offers of benefits from others often come—explicitly or implicitly—with associated costs and obligations. How the trade-offs between the benefits of receiving help versus the costs of accepting it depend importantly on the recipient's current goals and the salient aspects of the social context relevant to those goals (Ackerman & Kenrick, 2008).

Stigmatization

Any implicit trust in coalitional ingroup members (the assumption that they will reciprocate and share) has a flip side: Groups are vulnerable to the invasion of "cheaters" and "free-riders"—individuals who strategically avail themselves of others' benevolence while failing to reciprocate or otherwise hold up their end of the implied exchange relationship. There is an enormous interdisciplinary literature on this problem, and on the evolved cognitive and behavioral strategies that might help solve the problem. One line of work has direct implications for the psychology of stigmatization, indicating that there may be evolved psychological mechanisms (and complementary cultural norms) that promote *altruistic punishment*—the willingness to punish (and potentially socially exclude) free-riders, even if doing so requires the expenditure of valuable resources oneself (e.g., Fehr & Gächter, 2002; Henrich et al., 2006).

A large body of research supports the hypothesis that there are specialized cognitive adaptations that function to identify others who intentionally violate norms of social exchange (Cosmides & Tooby, 2005)—the necessary first step in the stigmatization of these individuals. More broadly, evolutionary theorizing has identified a number of different threats that individuals may pose to the successful operation of cooperative groups (e.g., inability to reciprocate, carrying of contagious disease, counter-socialization of children, challenge to accepted authority structures), and that form the basis of different forms of social stigmatization (Kurzban & Neuberg, 2005; Neuberg, Smith, & Asher, 2000). From this perspective, many acts of stigmatization and social exclusion may be viewed as altruistic acts of prosocial policing and punishment.

Aggression

Like altruistic behaviors, aggressive behaviors should be viewed as possible manifestations of conditional strategies that evolved to facilitate survival and reproduction (Campbell, 2005; Duntley, 2005). Across many animal species, aggression serves a number of fitness-relevant goals, including control over territorial boundaries, division of limited resources, and defense of offspring against predators (Scott, 1992). Evolutionary analyses of human aggression take a similar conceptual approach (Buss & Duntley, 2006; Kirkpatrick, Waugh, Valencia, & Webster, 2002). Further, because of the substantial fitness costs that often attend aggressive acts (e.g., risk of injury and retaliation), most evolutionary analyses presume people are likely to behave aggressively only when other strategies for reaching goals have failed (Dabbs & Morris, 1990; Wilson & Daly, 1985). Thus, rather than treating aggression as a single psychological construct, it is helpful to consider different fitness-relevant problems that might be solved via aggressive behavior, and to identify the multiple, domain-specific mechanisms and variables that may precipitate different forms of aggressive behavior within different social contexts.

This evolutionarily informed approach to aggression has led to a number of productive lines of research on various specific forms of aggression, such as violence against stepchildren, spousal homicide, rape, and infanticide (e.g., Daly & Wilson, 1984, 1996, 2005; Wilson & Daly, 1992; Thornhill & Thornhill, 1992). It has also led to nuanced predictions and novel empirical discoveries bearing on the specific contexts within which specific psychological variables, such as self-esteem, predict aggression (e.g., Kirkpatrick et al., 2002).

One line of inquiry has focused on male aggression as a strategy for acquiring mating opportunities. The evolutionary principle of differential parental investment implies that females, compared to males (who are required to invest relatively less in offspring), maximize fitness outcomes by exercising considerable discrimination in choosing mates. Consequently, men find themselves in the position of competing with each other for the opportunity to mate with highly selective women. Two strategies could accomplish this end. One is to display characteristics highly prized by women (e.g., traits connoting good genes, resources, status, etc.; Miller, 2000). The other strategy is to beat out the competition directly (e.g., fighting one's way to the top of the local dominance hierarchy). In both cases, the capacity for physical aggression confers reproductive fitness to men (Alcock, 1993). Indeed, there is a dramatic sex difference in physically violent behavior, and this holds across human societies and across historical time periods (Archer, 2000;

Campbell, 2005; Daly & Wilson, 1988; see Bushman & Huesmann, this volume).

If aggression provides a means of meeting this very specific reproduction-relevant goal (mating), then aggression should be facilitated or inhibited depending on the extent to which that mating goal is salient. Cross-species comparisons reveal that as species become more polygynous (with some males likely to attract no mates while others attract many), males become more violent (Buss & Duntley, 2006). Within many different species, male aggressiveness increases just before the mating season, when territories and females are being contested (Gould & Gould, 1989). Developmental analyses of human aggression reveal conceptually similar findings. Boys increase dominance displays at puberty, which is also when evidence of successful competitiveness (such as being a sports star) results in greater popularity with girls (Weisfeld, 1994). And men are most violent in their late teens and twenties, the developmental phase during which they are most vigorously competing for mates (Daly & Wilson, 1988). Once a male has attracted a long-term mate, aggression decreases (Palmer, 1993). Much of this behavioral variation is the consequence of variation in testosterone, which not only regulates male sexual activity but is also implicated in the development of muscle mass, competitiveness, status-striving, and violence (Dabbs & Dabbs, 2000; Mazur & Booth, 1998; McIntyre et al., 2006).

The link between mating motives and status concerns varies not only developmentally, but also moment to moment, depending on the immediate context. This, too, has consequences for aggressive behavior: Under specific conditions in which either status or mating motives are temporarily activated, men—but not women—show an exaggerated tendency to engage in direct physical aggression (Griskevicius, Tybur, Gangestad et al., 2009). This same research indicated that women typically responded to status or mating motives with indirect aggression, rather than having an immediate public interchange with their opponent. Furthermore, women's aggression can be triggered by resource threats, especially when these have implications for their offspring (Campbell, 1999, 2005; Griskevicius, Tybur, Gangestad et al., 2009).

Sexual Attraction and Mate Selection

Differential reproduction is at the heart of natural selection, and much research in the biological sciences focuses on the evolution of features that attract members of the opposite sex. The resulting insights have informed many studies of human sexual attraction and mate selection, and many empirical findings in this literature are difficult to explain without the logical tools provided by an evolutionary perspective.

One body of evolutionary research has revealed the importance of bilateral symmetry to the subjective perception of physical attractiveness. In many animal species, symmetry is associated with developmental stability and reproductive success, implying that symmetry may be a useful heuristic cue connoting "good genes" (Moller & Thornhill, 1998). Individuals' own reproductive fitness is enhanced by choosing mates with good genes (increasing the likelihood of producing healthy and reproductively fit offspring). Symmetry is subjectively attractive to humans, too: People perceive symmetrical faces to be healthier and more attractive than asymmetrical faces (Jones, Little, Penton-Voak, Tiddeman, Burt, & Perrett, 2001; Mealey, Bridgstock, & Townsend, 1999; Rhodes, Zebrowitz, Clark, Kalick, Hightower, & McKay, 2001; Thornhill & Gangestad, 1999a).

The attraction to symmetry is not limited to face perception. Bodily symmetry is also a likely indicator of good genes, and women appear to be especially attuned to selectively favor more symmetrical men as sexual partners (Gangestad & Thornhill, 1997). Women are sensitive to a variety of cues that correlate with bodily symmetry, including a man's skill at rhythmic dancing (Brown et al., 2005), and even olfactory cues (perceived simply from the scent of a man's unwashed t-shirt; Thornhill & Gangestad, 1999b). Further, women appear especially attracted to men with "good genes" under conditions in which these genes have the greatest functional implications for female reproductive fitness—when women are especially liable to become pregnant (Gangestad, Thornhill, & Garver-Apgar, 2005). For instance, when presented with men's unwashed t-shirts, women in the most fertile phase of their ovulatory cycles are especially likely to prefer the scent of symmetrical men (Thornhill & Gangestad, 1999b).

Prior to the application of evolutionary theorizing to the social psychology of attraction, it was largely unknown that female social cognition and behavior varies predictably across the ovulatory cycle. Other evidence indicates that women in the most fertile phase of their cycle show an increased interest in men who possess genes that would enhance the immune system competence of potential offspring (Garver-Apgar, Gangestad, Thornhill, Miller, & Olp, 2006). Ovulating women also show an increased preference for men with masculine sex-typed features (such as a deep voice or taller stature), which also are hypothesized to serve as signals of underlying genetic quality (e.g., Johnston, Hagel, Franklin, Fink, & Grammer, 2001; Pawlowski & Jasienska, 2005; Penton-Voak, Little, Jones, Burt, Tiddeman, & Perrett, 2003; Puts, 2005). Another such finding revealed that ovulating women are relatively more interested in extramarital affairs with masculine men,

especially if their current partners are relatively unattractive (Pillsworth & Haselton, 2006).

Whereas that line of research has necessarily focused on female preferences, other lines of evolutionarily informed research have compared the mating behaviors and mate preferences of men and women. Much of this work is informed by the evolutionary implications of *differential parental investment* (Trivers, 1972). Throughout evolutionary history, female mammals have been obligated by physiology to make a large investment in offspring, both prior to birth (during gestation) and afterwards (during nursing). Male mammals have not. The maximum number of offspring a female can potentially produce is, therefore, relatively small compared to the maximum number that a male might produce. The implication is that female reproductive fitness has historically been facilitated by a relatively choosy approach to sexual relations. In addition, for species with helpless offspring such as humans, female reproductive fitness has been enhanced when mating with a male who commits resources to the care of a child after it is born. This further implies a female priority on monogamous relationships, and a preference for mates who have the capacity and willingness to expend resources on offspring care. In contrast, and in keeping with their relatively minimal obligate parental investment, male reproductive fitness has historically been facilitated by a somewhat more unrestricted approach to sexual relations, and by a preference for mates whose physical features heuristically connote fertility.

An enormous body of empirical evidence has tested, and supported, these predicted sex differences. Men generally show a greater interest than women in casual sexual relationships (Buss & Schmitt, 1993; Clark & Hatfield, 1989; Li & Kenrick, 2006). Compared to men, women hold higher standards for potential romantic partners, especially for sexual relationships (Kenrick, Groth, Trost, & Sadalla, 1993; Kenrick, Sadalla, Groth, & Trost, 1990). Women generally place a higher priority on variables that connote a mate's ability to commit resources to offspring (e.g., wealth, status), whereas men generally place a higher priority on variables that connote a mate's fertility (e.g., youth, facial attractiveness; Badahdah & Tiemann, 2005; Buss & Schmitt, 1993; Hanko, Master, & Sabini, 2004; Li & Kenrick, 2006; Wiederman, 1993). These effects emerge across many different cultures (Buss, 1989; Kenrick & Keefe, 1992; Schmitt, 2005; Schmidt et al., 2003). It is worth noting that these sex differences emerge most strongly under conditions in which individuals must prioritize. Without constraints on their choices, both men and women prefer mates who are both attractive and resource-rich; when forced to compromise, however, women prioritize a mate's status over his physical appearance, whereas men prioritize a mate's attractiveness over her wealth (Li, Bailey, Kenrick, & Linsenmeier, 2002).

These consequences of differential parental investment emerge not only on straightforward assessments of sexual behavior and mate preferences; they also have more subtle effects. Research on counterfactual thinking reveals that when asked about their regrets in life, men are more likely to wish they had slept with more partners, whereas women wish they had tried harder to avoid getting involved with losers (Roese, Pennington, Coleman, Janicki, Li, & Kenrick, 2006). Predictable biases in person perception emerge as well. Women tend to be skeptical about a man's commitment even when it may be sincere, whereas men are biased to perceive sexual desire in a woman even when it may not be there (Haselton & Buss, 2000). And, of course, context matters: Men's tendency to project sexual interest onto women emerges especially when romantic goals are highly salient to the men and the women are physically attractive (Maner et al., 2005).

By drawing on the evolutionary logic of reproductive fitness, it is also possible to make many nuanced predictions about mate preferences that are difficult to deduce from alternative perspectives. For instance, the male preference for relatively youthful mates might be predicted by stipulating the existence of a social norm encouraging men to date younger women (Eagly & Wood, 1999). Although such an alternative might account for the finding that 45-year-old men are attracted to women in their 20s, it cannot account for the fact that men in their 20s are attracted to women their own age, nor for the fact that teenage boys are actually attracted to somewhat *older* women (Buunk, Dijstra, Kenrick, & Warntjes, 2001; Kenrick, Gabrielidis, Keefe, & Cornelius, 1996; Otta, Queiroz, Campos, daSilva, & Silveira, 1998). Nor can it account for the fact that those differences are found across cultures and historical time periods, actually becoming more pronounced in societies not subject to Euro-American sex-role norms (Kenrick & Keefe, 1992; Kenrick, Nieuweboer, & Buunk, 2010). The entire set of findings, however, was explicitly predicted by the hypothesis that men have an evolved preference for mates whose features connote fertility and fits with a broader nomological network of evolution-based findings (Kenrick, 2006b; Kenrick & Li, 2000).

Of course, there is also considerable variability within the sexes, both in mate preferences and in sexual strategies more generally (Simpson & Gangestad, 1991). An evolutionary metatheoretical perspective suggests that within-sex variability may be attributable, in part, to the same underlying physiological mechanisms that account for differences between sexes. At a proximal level of analysis, many evolved sex differences are likely to result from different levels of androgens—such as testosterone, which masculinizes the body (and therefore the brain). Individual differences in testosterone, in both men and women, would

therefore be expected to influence mating behavior and mate preferences. This is the case (Regan & Berscheid, 1999).

Mating strategies and mate preferences also vary cross-culturally (Buss, 1989; Kenrick, Nieuweboer et al., 2010; Schmitt, 2005). Although such cross-cultural variation is sometimes offered as evidence against an evolutionary explanation (e.g., Eagly & Wood, 1999; Wood & Eagly, 2002), the logical tools offered by an evolutionary approach actually provide the basis for multiple (and sometimes competing) hypotheses about specific ecological variables that have specific implications for fitness-relevant costs and benefits associated with different mating preferences, and thus have clear implications for cross-cultural differences. There is now abundant evidence supporting evolutionarily informed predictions about cross-cultural differences in mating behavior, including evidence casting doubt on alternative explanations based on sociocultural variables alone (e.g., Gangestad, Haselton, & Buss, 2006; Schaller & Murray, 2008; Schmitt, 2005). Employed rigorously, the logical tools of evolutionary psychology not only predict universal tendencies, but can also predict deviations from these tendencies that occur under unique ecological circumstances.

Evolutionary inquiry into these cultural differences reflects a broader body of work that has arisen in the literature on human evolution and sexual behavior. This body of research has emerged from the recognition that, in terms of implications for reproductive fitness, there are *trade-offs* that arise when choosing to employ a mating strategy that emphasizes relatively unrestricted casual sexual liaisons versus a strategy that emphasizes relatively monogamous committed relationships (Buss & Schmidt, 1993; Gangestad & Simpson, 2000; Kenrick et al., 2003). The particular nature of these trade-offs (i.e., the ratio of reproductive costs and benefits) may vary considerably according to the specific contexts that individuals find themselves in. These contexts may be relatively enduring, with implications for chronic individual differences in mating preferences and mating strategies. Consequently, there has arisen an important line of research examining *sociosexual orientation* and its implications for social cognition and interpersonal behavior (e.g., Bleske-Rechek & Buss, 2001; Duncan et al., 2007; Simpson & Gangestad, 1991, 1992). These contexts may also be temporary, with the implication that individuals may be adaptively equipped to flexibly employ different strategies, and to prioritize different features of potential mates, under different mating contexts. There has therefore arisen another important line of research examining the ways in which social cognition and behavior varies depending on whether individuals—both men and women—find themselves in a *short-term* or *long-term* mating context, and on other variables that influence the reproductive trade-off between short-term and long-term mating (Buss & Schmidt, 1993; DeBruine, 2005; Fletcher, Tither, O'Loughlin, Friesen, & Overall, 2004; Gangestad & Simpson, 2000; Kenrick, Sundie, Nicastle, & Stone, 2002; Li & Kenrick, 2006; Puts, 2005; Regan, Medina, & Joshi, 2001; Shackelford, Goetz, LaMunyon, Quintus, & Weekes-Shackelford, 2004).

Long-Term Romantic Relationships

For the vast majority of mammals, the adult male contributes little more than sperm to his offspring. Humans are different. Long-term relationships (with both parents often contributing substantially to offspring care) are common in human populations, and these committed dual-parent relationships have beneficial consequences for the reproductive fitness of offspring (Geary, 2000). Given these fitness benefits, it's not surprising that an evolutionary perspective has been brought to bear on many different social psychological phenomena pertaining to long-term romantic relationships.

One body of research focuses on psychological adaptations that promote commitment to existing romantic relationships. These adaptive mechanisms include positive biases favoring existing partners over potential alternatives (Johnson & Rusbult, 1989; Miller, 1997). For instance, compared with individuals who are not in committed relationships, those who are in long-term relationships often perceive alternative mates as less physically and sexually desirable (Simpson, Gangestad, & Lerma, 1990). Moreover, when feelings of romantic love are psychologically salient, people selectively reduce their visual attention to attractive members of the opposite sex (Maner, Rouby, & Gonzaga, 2008).

These cognitive and attentional biases may be rooted, at a physiological level of analysis, in hormonal changes that accompany commitment to long-term romantic relationships. For instance, compared to men in short-term sexual relationships, those in long-term relationships have relatively lower levels of testosterone (Gray, Chapman, Burnham, McIntyre, Lipson, & Ellison, 2004). In addition, oxytocin appears to play an important role in the experience of companionate love, and in the formation and maintenance of long-term romantic attachments (Brown & Brown, 2006; Carter, 1998; Diamond, 2004). Oxytocin is also secreted when mothers nurse infant children and appears to play an important role in the forging of mother-child attachments. Given this neuroendocrinological similarity, it has been suggested that long-term romantic attachments may be facilitated by some of the same cognitive, affective, and neurophysiological systems that evolved to facilitate adaptive attachments between mammalian mothers and their infants (Bowlby, 1969; Hazan & Shaver, 1994; Zeifman & Hazan, 1997). This does not mean, of course, that these two forms of attachment are equivalent. Because parent–child bonds and adult romantic bonds solve different adaptive problems, there are important differences in the decision biases governing attachments to children and lovers (Kenrick, 2006a).

Another body of research has focused on psychological responses to a partner's real or imagined infidelities. Individuals typically express strong negative reactions to the thought that their partner might flirt or have sex with another. Jealousy is found across a wide variety of cultures and is commonly implicated in spousal assault and homicide (Buss, 1994; Buunk & Hupka, 1987; Daly, Wilson, & Weghorst, 1982). The logic of differential parental investment implies predictable sex differences in the experience of jealousy. Consistent with this analysis, jealous women pay more attention to a potential rival's beauty, whereas jealous men attend more to a rival's social dominance (Dijkstra & Buunk, 1998). A sex difference is also predicted in the extent to which jealousy is aroused by sexual infidelity versus emotional infidelity (i.e., the formation of a close emotional attachment to a mating rival). A female mate's sexual infidelity is expected to be especially upsetting to men, because it raises the possibility that they might unwittingly invest resources in a biologically unrelated child. In contrast, a male mate's emotional infidelity is expected to be especially upsetting to women, as it raises the possibility that her mate might redirect his resources to children who aren't her own. Some have argued that, because the survival of human infants ancestrally required a close bond between both parents, both sexes should be similarly upset by sexual and emotional infidelity (DeSteno, Bartlett, Braverman, & Salovey, 2002; Harris, 2003). Consistent with the logic of differential parental investment, however, the predicted sex differences emerge across studies done in multiple countries and with multiple methods (Buss, Larsen, Westen, & Semmelroth, 1992; Buunk, Angleitner, Oubaid, & Buss, 1996; Pietrzak, Laird, Stevens, & Thompson, 2002; Sagarin, Becker, Guadagno, Nicastle, & Millevoi, 2003; Shackelford, LeBlanc, & Drass, 2000; Wiederman & Allgeier, 1993). Although there is continuing debate about the exact nature of sex differences in jealousy, a number of findings using different methods converge to support an evolutionary model (Sagarin, 2005).

Offspring Care

From an evolutionary perspective, the formation and maintenance of romantic relationships serves the ultimate function of producing offspring and sustaining those offspring until they are successful reproducers themselves. The investment of resources in children involves trade-offs, however. According to *life-history theory*, all animals (including humans) divide their resources between (1) their own survival and somatic development, (2) mating effort, and (3) parenting effort (Kaplan & Gangestad, 2007; Kenrick & Luce, 2000; Stearns, Allal, & Mace, 2008). Decision rules about how to allocate those resources are predicted to have evolved in such a way as to be sensitive to cues and circumstances connoting the relative fitness benefits and costs associated with specific allocation priorities. Therefore, the extent that a parent will invest resources in caring for a child (rather than in attempts to produce additional children, for instance) is expected to depend upon many additional variables, including the availability of resources, the child's needs, the child's apparent reproductive potential, the existence of other offspring, and—for men especially—the extent one is confident the child is one's own.

There is now a large body of research supporting specific predictions based on this analysis. For instance, mothers give more to offspring who are healthy and withhold from those with a lower probability of reproductive success (Hrdy, 2000). Children with greater reproductive potential are more likely to receive help under life-and-death circumstances (Burnstein et al., 1994). The actual or apparent genetic relatedness of offspring also influences the extent to which parents invest in them. Parents provide more nurturant care to actual biological offspring than to stepchildren (Daly & Wilson, 1998; Tooley, Karakis, Stokes, Ozanne-Smith, 2006). And men provide better care to children to whom they bear a physically resemblance, a superficial cue that heuristically implies confidence in their paternity (Apicella & Marlowe, 2004; Burch & Gallup, 2000; Platek et al., 2004).

The effects of parental uncertainty extend to the investment of resources in grandchildren and other relatives, too. For instance, a maternal grandmother knows with a high degree of certainty that her daughter is hers and that her daughter's children are truly her daughter's. In contrast, a paternal grandfather is considerably more uncertain; he cannot be sure that his ostensible son is truly his, nor that his son's ostensible children are truly his son's. These variations in parental uncertainty are reflected in the extent that individuals invest resources (e.g., money, emotional support) in their grandchildren and other relatives: Higher degrees of parental uncertainty result in lower investment (Laham, Gonsalkorale, & von Hippel, 2005; Michalski & Shackelford, 2005; Pollet, Nettle, & Nelissen, 2007; Webster, 2003). These effects are further moderated by additional variables bearing on reproductive fitness (e.g., Laham et al., 2005; Webster, 2003).

Social Influence

Research on social influence covers a wide range of topics, including the study of conformity, obedience to authority, compliance, and persuasion (see Hogg, this volume). Textbooks often treat these different topics (and the phenomena identified with each) as conceptually independent, united merely by the superficial fact they are examples of social influence. In contrast, an evolutionary approach reveals deep conceptual commonalities underlying these ostensibly distinct phenomena. In so doing, it provides a unique explanatory perspective (and generates novel hypotheses) that answer fundamental research questions about social influence processes.

Classic studies of social influence—for example, those by Sherif, Asch, and Milgram—are often viewed as surprising evidence that individuals are not as independent and free-thinking as they might wish to believe. From an evolutionary perspective, however, people's obedient and conformist tendencies are not so surprising (Campbell, 1975). Historically, hierarchical status structures appear to have offered many competitive advantages to groups (Sidanius & Pratto, 1999). It seems reasonable to presume that deference to authority figures has historically conferred fitness advantages, providing an evolutionary basis not only for obedience, but for authoritarian attitudes more broadly (Kessler & Cohrs, 2008).

Conformity, too, has multiple evolutionary roots. Conforming to the actions of others reduces the likelihood of social exclusion, which is likely to benefit reproductive fitness. Moreover, in most stable ancestral ecological contexts, behaving like others was likely to have led to fitness-enhancing decisions, thereby selecting for mimicry, imitation, and other manifestations of conformity (Coultas, 2004; Henrich & Boyd, 1998; Kessler & Cohrs, 2008). These two lines of fitness-relevant logic indicate evolutionary foundations for "normative" and "informational" influence, respectively. These evolutionary analyses also suggest a conceptual linkage between classic social influence phenomena with other kinds of phenomena entirely, such as the tendencies toward highly automatic behavioral mimicry (Lakin, Jefferis, Cheng, & Chartrand, 2003) and implicitly accepting others' assertions to be true (Gilbert, 1991).

People are more susceptible to social influence under some situations than others, and an evolutionary approach is useful for understanding this cross-situational variability. Our analysis of belongingness needs suggests that conformity will especially pronounced under conditions in which the risk of social exclusion is exaggerated, such as when one's own attitudes and actions deviate from group norms; this is the case (Snyder & Fromkin, 1980). Moreover, if conformity has a positive impact on fitness, then the natural tendency toward conformity will be amplified under circumstances that represent immediate threats to one's fitness. Indeed, conformity to salient norms is enhanced when death or fear-inducing physical threats are made salient (Gailliot, Stillman, Schmeichel, Maner, & Plant, 2008; Griskevicius, Goldstein, Mortensen, Cialdini, & Kenrick, 2006). Cross-cultural evidence is consistent with this analysis as well: In geographical regions historically characterized by a higher prevalence of pathogenic diseases, there have emerged cultural value systems that most strongly encourage conformity to behavioral norms (Fincher, Thornhill, Murray, & Schaller, 2008).

The evolutionary perspective also provides conceptual leverage for predicting the characteristics of those individuals that people are most likely to imitate, obey, conform to, or otherwise be influenced by. Conformity may be an evolutionarily adaptive behavioral strategy, in general, but it is especially adaptive to selectively imitate the actions of prestigious individuals (Henrich & Gil-White, 2001). Prestige is a fluid concept; the specific features that confer prestige may vary across different cultural contexts. It is clear, however, that people endowed with higher levels of prestige-connoting traits—for example, expertise, attractiveness, or fame—exert greater influence in a variety of ways (Heath, McCarthy, & Mothersbaugh, 1994; Henrich & Gil-White, 2001; Kamins, 1989; Milgram, 1974; Wilson & Sherrell, 1993).

Finally, although the fitness benefits of conformity may generally outweigh the benefits associated with deviance, deviance may nonetheless have specific kinds of fitness benefits that, under specific and predictable circumstances, may trump those associated with conformity. In ancestral populations, only a minority of males had access to female reproductive resources, and males' reproductive fitness was substantially influenced by their ability to distinguish themselves from other males competing for access to the same females. In such a competitive mating context, blending in with the crowd may have been disadvantageous, and presenting oneself as distinctive and different is likely to have led to greater reproductive fitness. This implies that, whereas conformity may be the default behavioral strategy among both men and women, men (but not women) will show anti-conformity tendencies under specific circumstances in which mating motives are salient. Recent experimental findings support this logic (Griskevicius et al., 2006).

Group Dynamics

Most evolutionary analyses focus specifically on reproductive fitness at the level of the gene or the individual organism, and there is rarely much logical need to consider groups as an additional level of analysis. It can be argued, however, that in highly interdependent ultrasocial species such as *Homo sapiens*, individuals' outcomes have manifold consequences for all other individuals in their social groups and, reciprocally, the group's outcomes have substantial implications for fitness at the levels of individuals and the genes making them up. Consequently, evolutionary frameworks that consider the logical relations between outcomes at the levels of genes, individuals, and groups might provide useful tools for understanding intra-group dynamics. *Multilevel selection theory* (Sober & Wilson, 1998) provides one such conceptual framework, emphasizing the impact that group-level outcomes have on the reproductive fitness of individuals (and genes) within the group. This framework has been used to generate hypotheses and empirical discoveries bearing on brainstorming, distributed cognition, cooperative behavior, and social dilemmas (O'Gorman, Sheldon, & Wilson, 2008; Sheldon & McGregor, 2000; Wilson, Van Vugt, & O'Gorman, 2008).

There is also a wide-ranging body of literature stimulated by the observation that group living affords specific kinds of coordination problems to solve (Kameda & Tindale, 2006). One illustrative example is provided by recent evolutionary analyses of leadership (Van Vugt, 2006; Van Vugt, Hogan, & Kaiser, 2008). The psychology of leadership can best be understood within a context that considers the evolved psychology of followership, too. Evolutionary analyses have also yielded hypotheses about the particular characteristics of leaders that are appealing under different kinds of circumstances. For instance, masculine facial morphologies (connoting higher levels of testosterone, competitiveness, and aggression) are more highly desired in political leaders during times of war versus peace (Little, Burriss, Jones, & Roberts, 2007). In addition, whereas there is a preference for male leaders to manage potential intergroup competition, there is a preference for female leaders to manage potential *intragroup* competition (Van Vugt & Spisak, 2008)—perhaps because females tend to be more concerned with preserving within-group unity (Eagly & Johnson, 1990; Geary, 1998).

A third line of research has applied evolutionary insights to the complex dynamical processes through which norms emerge within groups (e.g., Kameda, Takezawa, & Hastie, 2003; 2005; Kenrick et al., 2003). This work not only contributes to an understanding of group processes and group outcomes, but also to an understanding of the origins of culture—a topic we discuss in somewhat more detail below.

These applications of evolutionary theorizing to group dynamics are all relatively recent, and they offer hope for a revival of social psychological interest in the study of group dynamics. Despite its centrality to social psychology, interest in group dynamics has not been in the mainstream for some time (Moreland, Hogg, & Hains, 1994; Sanna & Parks, 1997; Steiner, 1974). The application of evolutionarily informed theorizing in this domain may help reverse that trend. Just as the study of sex-differences (which, after an initial flurry of popularity, had became somewhat marginalized in the absence of rigorous theorizing) was re-energized by the introduction of evolutionary theorizing (e.g., Buss, 1995; Kenrick, 1994), so too an evolutionary approach has the potential to bring the study of group dynamics back into vogue.

Intergroup Prejudices and Intergroup Conflicts

Although traditional social psychology often speaks simply of "prejudice" as though it were a single, unitary thing, an evolutionary approach—emphasizing particularized domain-specific adaptations—suggests that it may be more appropriate to speak of *prejudices*, plural. For instance, prejudices predicated on gender or on sexual orientation may be psychologically distinct from one another and from prejudices based on facial disfigurement. Even within the more specific context of intergroup relations, there appear to be multiple, evolutionarily distinct mechanisms that produce discrimination between ingroup and outgroup, and in doing so, produce psychologically distinct intergroup prejudices (Cottrell & Neuberg, 2005; Neuberg & Cottrell, 2006). From this perspective, the nature of prejudices is predictable from a functional analysis of emotions and the threats they are designed to address. For instance, people prejudiced against gay men tend to perceive them as posing threats to health and values; consequently, their prejudices are characterized by physical and moral disgust, and their discriminatory inclinations heuristically focus on avoiding close physical contact and keeping gay men out of positions of social policy and socialization influence. In contrast, people prejudiced against African Americans (especially African American men) tend to perceive them as posing threats to physical safety; consequently, their prejudices contain a stronger component of fear, and their discriminatory inclinations focus of strategies of self-protection.

Several lines of research proceed from the premise that small coalitional groups provided early humans with access to many fitness-relevant opportunities and also with protection from many kinds of fitness-relevant perils. This provides an evolutionary foundation for the psychology of social identity and its implications for ingroup favoritism (Brewer & Caporael, 2006). By emphasizing the point that coalitional social structure (rather than mere group categorization) lies at the heart of intergroup cognition, this approach implies that contemporary categorical distinctions (e.g., perceptual discrimination according to racial or ethnic categories) can be psychologically eliminated by cross-cutting categorizations that are more immediately coalitional in nature (Kurzban, Tooby, & Cosmides, 2001); people respond to coalitions and the threats and opportunities they pose, not to race *per se*. Another implication is that any perceived threat to one's coalitional ingroup—even if the threat does not originate in a coalitional outgroup—may lead to exaggerated ingroup favoritism (e.g., Navarrete, Kurzban, Fessler, & Kirkpatrick, 2004).

Another line of research begins with the recognition that hierarchical group structures may confer relatively positive fitness outcomes to group members. The evolutionary implication—articulated by *social dominance theory* (Sidanius & Pratto, 1999)—is that humans may be characterized by psychological adaptations that favor the establishment and maintenance of dominance hierarchies. These adaptations may produce effects at the cognitive and behavioral level of analysis, and also at a societal level, in the creation of institutions that legitimize and reify existing dominance hierarchies (e.g., Mitchell & Sidanius, 1995). Different kinds of prejudices (e.g., sexism, racism) may be viewed, in part, as manifestations of these cognitive mechanisms and social institutions. People who are dispositionally favorable to social dominance hierarchies are likely to show these prejudices at especially high levels (Pratto, Sidanius, Stallworth, & Malle, 1994), and these prejudices may be especially likely to emerge under circumstances within which dominance considerations are temporarily paramount (Guimond, Dambrun, Michinov, & Duarte, 2003; Pratto, Sidanius, & Levin, 2006).

Additional evolutionary research programs focus less on the nature of ingroups and more on outgroups and the specific fitness costs associated with intergroup contact. One line of inquiry draws on evidence that, historically, intergroup contact was likely to be associated with an increased chance of interpersonal aggression and physical injury. One might thus expect the evolution of adaptations that dispose individuals to associate outgroup members with traits connoting aggression, violence, and danger, and to do so especially under conditions in which perceivers feel especially vulnerable to danger. For instance, when people (especially those who chronically perceive the world to be a dangerous place) are in the dark, they are more prone to the implicit activation of danger-connoting stereotypes of ethnic outgroups (Schaller, Park, & Faulkner, 2003; Schaller, Park, & Mueller, 2003). Evolutionary analyses often generate very specific predictions, and that is the case here: The darkness-stereotyping finding was specific to stereotypes relevant to physical safety threat (e.g., aggressive); no such effect is observed on equally negative stereotypes irrelevant to physical safety (e.g., ignorant). In fact, in real-life intergroup conflict situations, an increased sense of vulnerability may actually lead to more positive outgroup stereotypes along trait dimensions connoting competence, while simultaneously leading to more negative stereotypes along trait dimensions connoting warmth and trustworthiness—a constellation of stereotypic traits that most clearly implies an actual fitness-relevant threat (Schaller & Abeysinghe, 2006).

The threat of interpersonal violence is not the only fitness-relevant cost associated with intergroup contact. Historically, intergroup contact was associated with increased exposure to pathogenic diseases (Schaller & Duncan, 2007). It follows that a functionally specific form of intergroup prejudice is likely to be exaggerated when people perceive themselves to be especially vulnerable to infection. This is indeed the case. People who perceive themselves to be more vulnerable to disease show stronger implicit cognitive associations linking outgroups to danger, but not to negativity in general (Faulkner, Schaller, Park, & Duncan, 2004). Xenophobia and ethnocentrism are also predicted by disease-relevant individual difference variables (Faulkner et al., 2004; Navarrete & Fessler, 2006), and by naturally occurring circumstances (such as the first trimester of pregnancy) in which individuals' immune functioning is temporary suppressed (Navarrete, Fessler, & Eng, 2007). Empirical results such as these are impossible to explain with traditional theories of prejudice that focus primarily on processes pertaining to social categorization, social identity, and realistic conflict. They follow directly from hypotheses deduced within an evolutionary framework, however.

Several of these evolutionary perspectives imply sex differences in prejudice and intergroup conflict (e.g., Van Vugt, De Cremer, & Janssen, 2007; Yuki & Yokota, 2009). For instance, dominance hierarchies have historically been especially pertinent to male reproductive fitness. Social dominance theory thus implies that, compared to women, men are more chronically concerned with the maintenance of social dominance hierarchies, and should exhibit especially strong prejudices toward others who threaten one's own status in an existing dominance hierarchy (e.g., Sidanius, Pratto, & Brief, 1995). Also, historically, intergroup contact occurred primarily between males. This implies that men are especially likely to perceive outgroup members as a threat and that, among men, these prejudicial perceptions are especially likely to be triggered by contextual cues connoting vulnerability to harm. Evidence from several studies supports this implication (Schaller & Neuberg, 2008). Finally, outgroup men (compared to outgroup women) were especially likely to inflict mortal wounds ancestrally—a phenomenon true in modern societies, as well—thereby suggesting that male (compared to female) outgroup members will be especially likely to trigger danger-connoting cognitive associations. This also

appears to be the case (Maner et al., 2005; Navarrete et al., 2009).

The Affordance Management System Revisited

This body of research, of which we have only glossed the surface, illustrates the value of thinking about psychological mechanisms in terms of the specific kinds of adaptive problems they solve—problems related to, for instance, self-protection, coalition maintenance, mate selection, child rearing, and other challenges to reproductive fitness. The adaptive, problem-solving nature of psychological mechanisms is revealed by the functionally specialized, domain-specific manner in which they are engaged. Interpersonal attraction, for instance, is not a single construct. There are very different forms of attraction, and they are governed by very different psychological principles in very different adaptive contexts. In contexts that emphasize the adaptive value of coalitions and cooperative behavior, individuals are especially attracted to people who seem familiar or physically similar; in sexual contexts, however, familiarity and physical similarity are repellant instead (Ackerman et al., 2007; DeBruine, 2005; Lieberman et al., 2007).

This brief review has illustrated, in a variety of ways, how evolved psychological mechanisms are sensitive to predictable categories of cues in the perceptual environment—cues that heuristically connote very specific opportunities or threats. These cues are often very subtle (the scent of symmetry, for instance; Thornhill & Gangestad, 1999b), and their discovery as important social psychological variables emerged only after psychologists equipped themselves with the logical tools of evolutionary inquiry. These fitness-relevant cues—even very subtle ones—trigger predictable, functionally specific cascades of affect, cognition, and behavior. For instance, superficial cues connoting female fertility trigger (among male perceivers, but not female perceivers) very specific consequences on attention and memory, as well as on more overt judgments and behavior (Becker et al., 2005; Duncan et al., 2007; Kenrick & Keefe, 1992).

Psychological adaptations are imperfect, but in evolutionarily sensible ways, and thus help to explain many of the inferential biases and prejudices that are of central interest to social psychologists. The evolutionary consequences of differential parental investment, for instance, manifest not only in sex differences in mate preferences, but also in the fact that men (but not women) often misperceive sexual interest in the faces of attractive opposite-sex others, whereas women (but not men) often erroneously assume that their suitors are cads (Haselton & Buss, 2000; Maner et al., 2005). The substantial fitness costs associated with infectious diseases lead perceivers not only to respond aversely to individuals who actually are diseased, but also to predictable prejudices against a variety of objectively healthy individuals who just happen to appear morphologically, behaviorally, or culturally anomalous (Faulkner et al., 2004; Park et al., 2003; 2007).

Content matters. Psychological adaptations respond to specific cues, and these cues trigger the activation of highly specific affective states and associative knowledge structures with highly specific contents. In the realm of prejudice, for instance, particular categories of fitness-relevant threat are associated with very particular prejudices—defined by particular emotional responses and by very particular kinds of negative stereotypes but not by other, equally negative, stereotypes (Cottrell & Neuberg, 2005; Schaller, Park, & Faulkner, 2003).

Context matters too. Evolved stimulus-response associations are highly sensitive to the intrapersonal context created by perceivers' own preexisting dispositions and goals, and by immediate ecological circumstances within which perceivers finds themselves. The scent of a symmetrical man is sexually attractive to women, but primarily under circumstances in which those women are most prone to become pregnant (Thornhill & Gangestad, 1999b). Facial cues connoting female fertility are especially likely to draw and hold men's' attention, but primarily among men with a dispositional tendency toward unrestricted mating (Duncan et al., 2007). White people misperceive anger in the faces of African American men, especially under conditions in which self-protective motives have been made temporarily salient (Maner et al., 2005). Morphological, behavioral, and cultural anomalies trigger disease-connoting prejudices especially among perceivers who are, or merely perceive themselves to be, especially vulnerable to infection (Faulkner et al., 2004; Navarrete et al., 2007; Park et al., 2007). These psychological phenomena are malleable—not despite being the products of evolution, but *because* they are the products of evolution.

Finally, the implications of underlying evolutionary principles apply across the entire landscape of social psychology. Adaptations that facilitate kin-recognition have implications not only for person perception, but also for altruism, aggression, mate selection, and offspring care (Apicella & Marlowe, 2004; DeBruine, 2005; Lieberman et al., 2007; Park et al., 2008). Adaptations that facilitate avoidance of physical harm have implications for phenomena as superficially distinct as person memory, intergroup prejudice, and conformity (Ackerman et al., 2006; Griskevicius, Goldstein, et al., 2006; Schaller, Park, & Faulkner, 2003). Adaptations that serve the ultimate function of sexual selection have implications for topics as ostensibly irrelevant to mating as altruism, aggression, conformity, and creativity (Griskevicius, Cialdini, & Kenrick, 2006, Griskevicius et al., 2006, 2007, 2009).

LINKAGES TO DEVELOPMENT, LEARNING, AND CULTURE

Many people assume that evolutionary theories of social behavior imply a hardwired genetic determinism, a diminished role of developmental and learning processes, and an absence of cultural differences. None of these assumptions are correct.

Development

The human genotype is not a blueprint depicting the phenotypic features of people; rather, it is more like a recipe book, providing instructions for the assembly and generation of those phenotypic characteristics. This assembly process is more commonly referred to as development. Developmental processes are fundamental to any evolutionary approach to human behavior (Bjorklund & Pellegrini, 2002; Geary, 2006; Marcus, 2004).

There is no simple inflexible relation between a gene and its role in the assembly of phenotypic features (Carroll, 2005; Ridley, 2003). Genes may or may not be expressed. Even if they are expressed, the exact location and timing of their expression may vary considerably. Gene expression may vary depending on the presence of other pieces of genetic code. Gene expression may vary depending on the gene's immediate physiological environment (e.g., hormone levels within the developing organism). And gene expression may vary depending on features of the physical and social environment within which the organism itself is located. For instance, genetically identical butterflies may take on entirely different appearances depending on local climatic conditions during development (Beldade & Brakefield, 2002) and, among some species of fish, ecological variables such as social density and local sex ratio influence the expression of genes that govern whether the developing organism ultimately becomes male or female (Godwin, Luckenbach, & Borski, 2003). Among humans, qualities of the family environment influence the expression of genes that precipitate sexual maturation (Ellis, 2004). Phenotypic plasticity of this sort is itself adaptive, given that a particular phenotypic trait may or may not confer relative fitness advantages, depending on the local ecological circumstances.

This principle of adaptive phenotypic plasticity applies not only to the development of physiological features, but also to the development of behavioral tendencies as well. This evolutionary logic has been applied toward the understanding of individual differences in attachment style (Bowlby, 1969), mating strategies (Bjorklund & Shackelford, 1999; Gangestad & Simpson, 2000), kin recognition (Lieberman et al., 2007), and many other phenomena central to social cognition and social behavior.

Learning

Learning mechanisms provide means through which information about chronic developmental environments are acquired. Learning mechanisms also provide means through which organisms acquire information about temporary contexts, thus allowing them to flexibly (and functionally) adjust behavioral responses. Because the fitness benefits of learning are enormous, it is no surprise that so many different learning mechanisms have evolved (Moore, 2004).

Particularly relevant to many social psychological phenomena is the concept of prepared associative learning—the evolved tendency to acquire specific fitness-relevant associations more quickly and efficiently than other (less fitness-relevant) associations. As noted earlier, there is extensive evidence that people are biologically prepared to acquire a fear response to stimuli (such as snakes) that represented significant sources of threat in ancestral environments (Öhman & Mineka, 2001). Analogously, there is evidence that people are especially efficient at learning, and especially slow to unlearn, fearful responses to coalitional outgroups (Olsson, Ebert, Banaji, & Phelps, 2005). This effect is specific to perceptions of male (but not female) outgroup members, a finding that is consistent with speculation that male outgroup members historically posed an especially substantial fitness threat (Navarrete et al., 2009).

Prepared learning of this sort can operate through nonsocial associative mechanisms, but social learning is implicated too. Rhesus monkeys, for instance, learn to fear snakes simply from observing other monkeys' fearful reactions to them (Cook & Mineka, 1990). It is likely that social learning mechanisms contribute to the extraordinarily efficient learning of fitness-relevant interpersonal impressions and prejudices as well (Schaller, 2006).

Cross-Cultural Variability

Humans inhabit many different cultural environments. These different cultural contexts create different developmental circumstances and different learning environments. Evolved mechanisms would thus be expected to manifest differently across different human cultures. Evidence of cross-cultural differences is therefore entirely compatible with an evolutionary perspective on human social behavior (Buss, 2001; Kenrick et al., 2003; Norenzayan & Heine, 2005; Norenzayan, Schaller, & Heine, 2006; Schaller, 2007).

In fact, evolutionary theorizing can be extraordinarily useful as a means of predicting the origins of cross-cultural differences in the first place. Here the concept of *evoked culture* is important: Cultural differences may themselves reflect differences in the extent to which evolved psychological mechanisms are expressed differently under different ecological circumstances (Gangestad, Haselton, & Buss, 2006; Schmitt, 2005; Schmitt et al., 2003; Tooby & Cosmides, 1992). One sustained program of research has focused on regional differences in pathogen prevalence and its implications for the origins of many cultural differences, including in food preparation (Sherman & Billing, 1999), parenting practices (Quinlan, 2007), marriage systems (Low, 1990), and mate preferences (Gangestad & Buss, 1993; Gangestad et al., 2006). Research employing an evolutionary cost/benefit analysis has also provided evidence that regional variability in pathogen prevalence may have contributed to the emergence of worldwide differences in extraversion and other basic dispositional tendencies (Schaller & Murray, 2008) and to cultural differences in individualism, collectivism, and other fundamental value systems (Fincher et al., 2008; Thornhill, Fincher, & Aran, 2009).

It's worth making one last point here. Researchers and others often posit a role for socialized norms and culture as "alternatives" to evolutionary explanations. This will rarely be correct. Particular norms and culture sometimes collaborate in creating behavior (e.g., by potentially altering the expression of evolved inclinations) and are sometimes phenomena themselves to be explained by evolutionary processes. Moreover, positing a particular norm or cultural process as an alternative to an evolution-inspired hypothesis (e.g., that males are socialized to prefer younger women as mates) begs the question of why that particular norm exists as opposed to its opposite. The nature *versus* nurture debate has been roundly rejected in the biological sciences as assuming a false dichotomy; it makes no more sense to pursue that dichotomy in the psychological sciences.

THINKING STRAIGHT ABOUT THEORY AND RESEARCH IN EVOLUTIONARY SOCIAL PSYCHOLOGY

The general principles underlying evolutionary hypotheses have been tested extensively across many different animal species and are well established (Alcock, 1993; Daly & Wilson, 1983; Trivers, 1985; Wilson, 1975). Evolutionary approaches have resulted in the rigorous deduction of many novel hypotheses about social cognition and behavior. Some of these have generated compelling empirical support, some have been refuted, and others have yet to be fully tested. Evolutionarily informed hypotheses in psychology are subjected to the same high standards of empirical evidence as any other hypotheses. Despite their heuristic and integrative successes, evolutionary inquiries about social psychological phenomena have elicited especially high levels of skepticism and controversy. Some of this controversy is driven by misconception, misinterpretation, and ideology;

some is driven by the fact that evolutionary hypotheses can involve extra layers of inference compared to more proximate hypotheses (Alcock & Crawford, 2008; Conway & Schaller, 2002; Cosmides, Tooby, Fiddick, & Bryant, 2005; Daly & Wilson, 2005; Kurzban, 2002). We briefly discuss the most common issues and questions raised about evolutionary inquiry in the psychological sciences.

The Epistemic Status of Evolutionary Psychological Hypotheses

The paleontologist Stephen Jay Gould argued that many evolved characteristics have no adaptive function whatsoever, and so—despite the enormous success of the adaptationist research program in evolutionary biology (Alcock, 2001; Williams, 1966)—criticized evolutionists for adopting an adaptationist perspective on animal behavior. As part of this critique, he famously characterized adaptationist explanations as "just-so stories"—fanciful speculations that "do not prove anything" (Gould, 1977, p. 26). The "just-so story" accusation has been regularly trotted out by critics of evolutionary approaches to human psychology as well, typically as a shorthand means of asserting that evolutionary analyses are untestable, or are merely post-hoc explanations for common knowledge, or both.

Both critiques are logically unfounded. We noted at the outset that the evolutionary approach to social psychology isn't a specific theory or a hypothesis, but is instead a metatheoretical framework within which specific theories and hypotheses can be deduced. That important epistemic distinction is blurred by critics who suggest that evolutionary explanations are untestable (Ketelaar & Ellis, 2000). As we have reviewed above, the metatheoretical assumptions and logical tools of evolutionary inquiry have led to numerous highly specific hypotheses about social psychological phenomena, and these hypotheses are exactly as testable—exactly as falsifiable—as other hypotheses in the psychological sciences. Similarly, it is abundantly clear that evolutionary analyses do far more than simply provide post-hoc accounts for common knowledge. We have reviewed a large number of empirical discoveries that have emerged as a result of evolutionary inquiry. Some of these findings (just like other social psychological findings) may be consistent with intuition and lay observation. But many more are so nuanced, complex, or counterintuitive that they are unlikely to be part of any common knowledge (such as the links between ovulation and social behavior). Nor were they found within the scientific literature until they were revealed as the result of empirical inquiry guided by evolutionary theorizing.

This is not to say that there aren't additional epistemic and methodological complexities that attend evolutionary social psychology. There are. Compared to traditional social psychological theories (which merely specify sets of psychological processes), theories that draw on evolutionary theorizing (and thus also specify the evolutionary origins of those psychological processes) introduce an additional level of logical inference at which additional kinds of alternative explanations must be entertained (Conway & Schaller, 2002). There are many empirical strategies for dealing with these additional inferential complexities (Simpson & Campbell, 2005). The use of multiple methods is especially important. The most compelling support for any alleged social psychological adaptation is likely to draw on results from standard psychological experiments in conjunction with results from cross-species analyses, cross-cultural surveys, brain imaging, genetic analyses, and other diverse methods of inquiry (Schmitt & Pilcher, 2004). In addition, simple findings rarely yield fully compelling conclusions. Whereas alternative explanations may be readily found for main effects (e.g., a sex difference in mate preferences), alternative explanations can often be ruled out by more complex findings (e.g., a sex difference that appears and disappears under very specific conditions predicted by the logic of inclusive fitness). Deliberate attempts to deduce and test more complex interactions can therefore lead to especially compelling empirical findings.

A somewhat different epistemic issue is rooted in scientists' inability to directly observe ancestral environments and to measure the constraints they posed on reproductive fitness. Skeptics sometimes wonder whether one can deduce plausible theories and hypotheses in the absence of such observations and measurements. The answer is yes. Considerable bodies of archeological, anthropological, and biological evidence have yielded many confident conclusions about the ecologies of ancestral humans; these inferences (about group sizes, infectious diseases, homicide rates, etc.) form the basis for the deduction of many hypotheses bearing on social psychological phenomena. In addition, many evolutionary hypotheses can be informed by information that actually is measurable in contemporary environments, including evidence obtained from contemporary small-scale societies and comparative evidence from many other mammalian species. For instance, comparative evidence has been instrumental in guiding theory and research on attachment processes (Fraley, Brumbaugh, & Marks, 2005). Also, contemporary cross-cultural and comparative evidence indicates with a high degree of certainty that ancestral females played a much more substantial role than ancestral males in bearing and nurturing children. From that inference alone, the principles of differential parental investment can be presumed to apply to the evolution of human beings (Geary, 2000). As the chapter has illustrated, this has further implications for the deduction of an enormous number of specific hypotheses bearing on social cognition and behavior.

The Logical Implications of Evolved Psychological Mechanisms

People sometimes think that, if human behavior is influenced by evolved adaptations, then people would never act against their own interests. This is wrong. As discussed above, evolved mechanisms are not foolproof and, like financial investments, operate on expected average payoffs. Psychological tendencies that are adaptive in the long term may still sometimes produce instances of costly and even maladaptive behavior. Such actions may also reflect environmental influences against which there are no evolutionary safeguards, because the environmental feature was rare or nonexistent in ancestral environments (e.g., birth control, easily available potent psychotropic drugs). Finally, of course, it is important keep in mind that evolutionary processes operate in the service of genetic replication, not in the service of the organisms that house those genes (Dawkins, 1976). Ostensibly maladaptive behaviors may produce hidden benefits for one's genes. Aggression, for example, occasionally leads to the aggressor's death, but aggressive tendencies may historically have resulted in net reproductive benefits (especially among men). And, as the enormous literature on the evolution of altruism reveals, selfish genes need not result in selfish people.

Another common misunderstanding is that if a psychological phenomenon is the result of evolved mechanisms, then the phenomenon itself must be evident at birth. This is actually rarely the case. Although the presence of a psychological phenomenon in infants may, in some cases, contribute compelling evidence of an innate predisposition, this is by no means necessary evidence. As we have discussed, developmental processes (including learning processes) are essential to the emergence of many evolved psychological phenomena, and much of this development occurs postpartum. Sexual maturation provides one obvious example: The onset of human puberty is a genetically programmed event, but does not occur until after a developing person has reached a particular size and physical condition. More broadly, many evolved adaptations require environmental input before they are expressed phenotypically. Even if a psychological phenomenon is absent at birth, it may still reflect the operation of adaptations.

It is also sometimes assumed that, because many evolved psychological mechanisms manifest in highly automatized stimulus-response associations, evidence of automaticity is necessary to support an evolutionary interpretation. As a corollary, it is sometimes assumed that if a phenomenon is moderated by manipulations of cognitive load, then the phenomenon cannot reflect an evolved adaptation (DeSteno, Bartlett, Braverman, & Salovey, 2002). These assumptions are wrong, and fail to consider the different ways in which different adaptations may manifest at a psychological level of analysis (Barrett, Frederick, Haselton, & Kurzban, 2006). Both automatic as well as more effortful cognitive responses may be produced as a result of evolved mechanisms.

Finally, there is the gross misconception that evolutionary influences on human behavior imply genetic determinism—that individuals' thoughts, feelings, and actions are inflexibly governed by their genes. This misconception may emerge from the fact that genes are associated with some relatively inflexible physical features (eye color, for example). But genes also encode for the development of many highly flexible traits as well. Even overt physical characteristics can change dependent on ecological variations (e.g., Godwin et al., 2003). Genetically endowed cognitive and behavioral flexibility is a central feature of the adapted mind. As our review of the social psychological literature reveals, evolved mechanisms play an important role in directing individuals' attention to fitness-relevant information in their immediate ecological context and thus enable these individuals to respond adaptively, and flexibly, to those circumstances.

So, are evolution-inspired hypotheses untestable? No. Are such hypotheses merely post hoc accounts of common sense knowledge? No. Does the inability to directly observe ancestral environments preclude the generation of well-grounded evolution-inspired hypotheses? No. Does an evolutionary perspective presume that people never act against their apparent best interest? No. Must a mechanism be observable at birth to be considered an evolved adaptation? No. Is evidence of automaticity necessary to claim that a psychological mechanism has evolved? No. And does the evolutionary approach imply that human thought and behavior are biologically determined, inflexibly controlled by genes? Emphatically, no.

FUTURE DIRECTIONS

Underlying Mechanisms

Like most social psychological inquiries, evolutionary social psychological research focuses on social cognition and social behavior. It is assumed that these cognitive and behavioral outcomes are the product of adaptations that have a physical manifestation—in the anatomy of the nervous system, the neurotransmission of neurotransmitters, the release of androgens into the bloodstream, and so forth.

Recent advances in brain imaging techniques (e.g., fMRI) reveal that specific anatomical structures are implicated in sexual attraction, social exclusion, self-esteem, intergroup prejudice, and many other fitness-relevant social psychological responses (e.g., Eisenberger & Lieberman, 2004; Fisher, Aron, Mashek, Li, & Brown, 2002; Harris & Fiske, 2006; Heatherton, Macrae, & Kelley, 2004; Phelps et al., 2000). Research in neuroendocrinology reveals relations between endocrine activity and specific kinds of cognitive and behavioral responses. Sex hormones, for instance, influence not only sexual behavior but many other forms of social behavior as well. Variation in testosterone levels has been associated with aggression, expressive behavior, empathic mimicry, and intellectual performance under conditions of stereotype threat, among many other social psychological outcomes (Archer, 1991; Dabbs, Bernieri, Strong, Campo, & Milun, 2001; Hermans, Putman, & van Hong, 2006; Josephs, Newman, Brown, & Beer, 2003). Other hormones matter, too. For instance, women's estradiol levels predict their preference for facial cues of men's testosterone (Roney & Simmons, 2008), women's progesterone levels predict sensitivity to fearful and disgusted facial expressions that suggest the presence of nearby threats (C. Conway et al., 2007), and oxytocin is implicated in feelings of interpersonal trust and attachment in close relationships (Insel & Young, 2001; Kosfeld et al., 2005). And the study of neurotransmitter systems is also obviously relevant. Dopamine and serotonin transporter systems have each been implicated in a wide range of social behaviors with consequences for reproductive fitness (e.g., Knutson, Wolkowitz, & Cole, 1998; Melis & Argiolas, 1995).

A fruitful avenue for future research in evolutionary social psychology is to more explicitly explore the role of evolution in designing anatomical structures and neurochemical processes that give rise to social cognition and behavior. The benefits will be reciprocal: Evolutionary explanations for social psychological phenomena will benefit from a more rigorous anchoring in the "meat" of the mind; the study of social neuroscience will benefit from the rigorously functional perspective that is provided by the evolutionary sciences (Duchaine, Cosmides, & Tooby, 2001).

Evolutionary explanations imply events that operate at multiple levels of analysis, including a genetic level. Although it is not necessary to articulate genetic mechanisms to conduct rigorous research in evolutionary social psychology, it can potentially be useful to do so—especially as advances in behavior genetics and functional genomics begin to reveal specific genes (and their context-contingent expressions) implicated in fitness-relevant behaviors. Ample evidence now links specific alleles expressed in the dopamine and serotonin transporter systems (e.g., different variants of the DRD4 allele, and of the 5-HTTLPR allele) to a variety of traits bearing on social cognition and social behavior (e.g., Ebstein, 2006; Munafo, Yalcin, Willis-Owen, & Flint, 2008; Schinka, Busch, & Robinchaux-Keene, 2004), and

the expression of these genes is moderated by specific elements of an individual's social environment (e.g., Taylor et al., 2006). As discoveries in behavioral genetics and functional genomics yield new information about specific genes and their relation to social psychological phenomena—and about the specific environmental circumstances that lead these genes to be expressed—there will emerge fruitful opportunities to employ genetic mechanisms as means of articulating the important connection between human evolutionary origins and social psychological outcomes.

Broader Applications

An emerging subdiscipline of psychology (with links to other biological, social, and cognitive sciences) addresses questions at the intersection of evolutionary and cultural psychology and, in so doing, identifies evolved psychological mechanisms that may have contributed to the origins of culture (Norenzayan, Schaller, & Heine, 2006). Specific lines of inquiry have focused, for instance, on the evolved psychology underlying moral norms and religious practices (e.g., Atran & Norenzayan, 2005; Krebs & Janicki, 2004; Weeden, Cohen, & Kenrick, 2008). Evolutionary analyses—particularly those that consider how different cognitive and behavioral tendencies are likely to have different implications for reproductive fitness under different ecological circumstances—are also proving useful for explaining the origins of cross-cultural differences (e.g., Fincher et al., 2008; Gangestad et al., 2006; Kenrick, Nieuweboer et al., 2010; Schaller & Murray, 2008; Schmitt, 2005; Schmitt et al., 2003). These lines of inquiry are still young, and additional work must address other cultural differences and other ecological pressures that may influence the manner in which universal human capacities are expressed. Additional work must also address the exact mechanisms through which ecological variability produces cultural variability. Different ecologies may promote differential selection of genes, differential expression of common genes, differential activation of common neural structures, differential constraints on social learning, and so forth. Elucidation of these mechanisms will constitute an important part of future research in evolutionary cultural psychology.

There are also exciting developments in the integration of evolutionary social psychology and economics. Evolutionary analyses within the fields of biology and anthropology often rely on economic models (e.g., Henrich et al., 2006), and this work overlaps considerably with social psychological research on mixed-motive games and decision making (e.g., Kahneman & Tversky, 1991; Van Vugt & Van Lange, 2006). Social psychologists and economists alike have typically applied domain-general decision models to these problems, overlooking the important implications likely to result from the fact that very different decision rules often apply when interacting with strangers, relatives, romantic partners, children, and other functionally distinct categories of people (e.g., Clark & Mills, 1993; Fiske & Haslam, 1996). The application of evolutionary analyses—based on domain-specific consequences for reproductive fitness—potentially yields novel implications for the computation of expected utility and novel predictions about the decisions people are likely to make when presented with economic decisions and mixed-motive dilemmas (Kenrick, Griskevicius et al., 2009; Kenrick, Sundie, & Kurzban, 2008).

Emerging literatures also highlight additional applications of evolutionary social psychology—applications to study of crime and punishment, for instance, and to politics and public policy (Crawford & Salmon, 2004; Duntley & Shackelford, 2008). Social psychology has always had powerful implications for the study of—and potential solutions to—social issues. These implications may be made even more powerful through a rigorous application of an evolutionary approach to social psychology.

FINAL COMMENTS

The most useful theories (and those that are least likely to be wrong) are those that are logically coherent and deductively rigorous. Evolutionary approaches bring with them many sophisticated tools that ensure deductive rigor (e.g., the strict computational logic of evolutionary game theory, inclusive fitness theory, and means of mathematically modeling the relative fitness outcomes associated with different behavioral strategies).

Useful theories must also be generative, producing novel, testable hypotheses (Lakatos, 1970; Ketelaar & Ellis, 2000). Darwin's theory of evolution by natural selection is arguably the most generative scientific theory of all time. And when these basic evolutionary principles are applied to human behavior, they can be used to deduce psychological theories that have proven to be extraordinarily generative as well, including theories pertaining to reasoning processes (Cosmides & Tooby, 2005), person perception (Zebrowitz & Montepare, 2006), interpersonal relationships (Buss & Schmitt, 1993; Gangestad & Simpson, 2001), and more. Evolutionarily informed theories in social psychology have yielded many novel—and often very subtle and non-obvious—hypotheses bearing on a wide range of topics, including not only those that are straightforwardly linked to human evolution, but also many that are not. Many of these novel hypotheses involve predictive constructs (e.g., likelihood of conception, ambient darkness) that are straightforwardly derived from

evolutionary analyses but lie well outside the conceptual architecture of traditional psychological theories. Further demonstrating the value of the approach, other novel evolutionary hypotheses focus on finer-level outcomes well beyond the specifications of traditional conceptualizations (e.g., specific emotional reactions rather than general prejudice; short-term versus long-term mate value rather than general level of attraction).

Another important criterion for evaluating scientific theories is explanatory coherence (Thagard, 2000). An evolutionarily perspective reveals deep conceptual connections between many different, and superficially unrelated, forms of social behavior. For example, evolved kin recognition mechanisms provide conceptual links between phenomena as superficially different as altruistic behavior, the similarity-liking effect, and incest avoidance, and the theory of differential parental investment has implications for domains as diverse as altruism, aggression, conformity, and creativity. An evolutionary approach can conceptually integrate many of social psychology's "mini-theories," forging a less piecemeal, more conceptually coherent understanding of social behavior.

An evolutionary approach also integrates findings across different levels of analysis and description, connecting phenomena at the individual level of analysis (e.g., attentional processes) with phenomena at the population level (the evolution of the mechanisms that produce those attentional processes). Evolutionary explanations connect empirical observations of ongoing cognitive processes with very different kinds of facts and speculations about pre-human ancestors, primate relatives, and life on Earth more broadly. Therefore, an evolutionary approach to social psychology provides a unique means of integrating social psychological findings with a much broader set of scientific findings within the biological, historical, cognitive, and social sciences (e.g., behavioral ecology, paleontology, linguistics, anthropology). In contrast to some of psychology's subdisciplines (such as sensation and perception), social psychology has traditionally fallen closer to the social sciences than the biological sciences, with its findings being of greater interest to sociologists and political scientists than to colleagues in the natural sciences. But that is changing, following the emergence of evolutionary social psychology and parallel developments in social neuroscience. This bodes well for the long-term vitality of social psychology.

ENVOI

Humans are animals. As such, human brains, like the brains of all animals, evolved via natural selection to solve the types of recurring fitness-relevant problems that our ancestors faced long ago. Perhaps more important, people are *social* animals. The problems faced by our ancestors thus included not only those faced by all animals (e.g., resource acquisition, self-protection, mating), but also those specific to social life (e.g., affiliation and coalition maintenance, status-seeking, intergroup conflict). These assertions should be uncontroversial. Yet the discipline of social psychology, which has dedicated itself to the exploration of human social life, traditionally disregarded the fact of this evolved nature in its attempts to uncover the principles and facts of social behavior. This was a mistake. Three decades ago, one of us encountered more than one senior social psychologist who vehemently denigrated "grand theories" and advocated instead for the value of "mid-level" theories—as if seeking the former would be akin to Icarus's folly. In light of impressive conceptual and empirical advances in recent years, it is our sense that any folly lies instead in ignoring the demonstrably most powerful, integrated set of ideas in the natural sciences—evolutionary theory—in social psychology's efforts to truly understand the fascinating complexities of human behavior.

REFERENCES

Ackerman, J. M., & Kenrick, D. T. (2008). The costs of benefits: Help-refusals highlight key trade-offs of social life. *Personality & Social Psychology Review, 12*, 118–140.

Ackerman, J. M., Kenrick, D. T., & Schaller, M. (2007). Is friendship akin to kinship? *Evolution and Human Behavior, 28*, 365–374.

Ackerman, J. M., Shapiro, J. R., Neuberg, S. L., Kenrick, D. T., Becker, D. V., Griskevicius, V., et al. (2006). They all look the same to me (unless they're angry): From out-group homogeneity to out-group heterogeneity. *Psychological Science, 17*, 836–840.

Alcock, J. (1993). *Animal behavior* (5th ed.). Sunderland, MA: Sinauer.

Alcock, J. (2001). *The triumph of sociobiology*. New York: Oxford University Press.

Alcock, J., & Crawford, C. (2008). Evolutionary questions for evolutionary psychologists. In C. Crawford & D. L. Krebs (Eds.), *Foundations of evolutionary psychology* (pp. 25–45). Mahwah, NJ: Erlbaum.

Ambady, N., Bernieri, F. J., & Richeson, J. A. (2000). Toward a histology of social behavior: Judgmental accuracy from thin slices of the behavioral stream. *Advances in Experimental Social Psychology, 32*, 201–271.

Anthony, D. B., Holmes, J. G., & Wood, J. V. (2007). Social acceptance and self-esteem: Tuning the sociometer to interpersonal value. *Journal of Personality and Social Psychology, 92*, 1024–1039.

Anthony, T., Copper, C., & Mullen, B. (1992). Cross-racial facial identification: A social cognitive integration. *Personality and Social Psychology Bulletin, 18*, 296–301.

Apicella, C. L., & Marlowe, F. W. (2004). Perceived mate fidelity and paternal resemblance predict men's investment in children. *Evolution and Human Behavior, 25*, 371–378.

Archer, J. (1991). The influence of testosterone on human aggression. *British Journal of Psychology, 82*, 1–28.

Archer, J. (2000) Sex differences in aggression between heterosexual partners: A meta-analytic review. *Psychological Bulletin, 126*, 651–680.

Atran, S., & Norenzayan, A. (2004). Religion's evolutionary landscape: Counterintuition, commitment, compassion, communion. *Behavioral and Brain Sciences, 27*, 713–770.

Badahdah, A. M., & Tiemann, K. A. (2005). Mate selection criteria among Muslims living in America. *Evolution & Human Behavior, 26*, 432–440.

Barrett, H. C., & Kurzban, R. (2006). Modularity in cognition: Framing the debate. *Psychological Review, 113*, 628–647.

Barrett, H. C., Frederick, D. A., Haselton, M. G., & Kurzban, R. (2006). Can manipulations of cognitive load be used to test evolutionary hypotheses? *Journal of Personality and Social Psychology, 91*, 513–518.

Baumeister, R. F., & Leary, M. R. (1995). The need to belong: Desire for interpersonal attachments as a fundamental human motivation. *Psychological Bulletin, 117*, 497–529.

Becker, D. V., Kenrick, D. T., Guerin, S., & Maner, J. K. (2005). Concentrating on beauty: Sexual selection and sociospatial memory. *Personality & Social Psychology Bulletin, 31*, 1643–1652.

Becker, D. V., Kenrick, D. T., Neuberg, S. L., Blackwell, K. C., & Smith, D. M. (2007). The confounded nature of angry men and happy women. *Journal of Personality & Social Psychology, 92*, 179–190.

Beldade, P., & Brakefield, P. M. (2002). The genetics and evo-devo of butterfly wing pattern. *Nature Reviews Genetics, 3*, 442–452.

Bernstein, M. J., Young, S. G., Brown, C. M., Sacco, D. F., & Claypool, H. M. (2008). Adaptive responses to social exclusion: Social rejection improves detection of real and fake smiles. *Psychological Science, 19*, 981–983.

Bjorklund, D. F., & Pellegrini, A. D. (2002). *The origins of human nature: Evolutionary developmental psychology*. Washington DC: APA.

Bjorklund, D. F., & Shackelford, T. K. (1999). Differences in parental investment contribute to important differences between men and women. *Current Directions in Psychological Science, 8*, 86–89.

Bleske-Rechek, A. L., & Buss, D. M. (2001). Opposite-sex friendship: Sex differences and similarities in initiation, selection, and dissolution. *Personality and Social Psychology Bulletin, 27*, 1310–1323.

Bowlby, J. (1969). *Attachment and loss: Vol. 1, Attachment*. New York: Basic Books.

Brewer, M. B., & Caporael, L. (2006). An evolutionary perspective on social identity: Revisiting groups. In M. Schaller, J. A. Simpson, & D. T. Kenrick (Eds.), *Evolution and social psychology* (pp. 143–161). New York: Psychology Press.

Brown, D. E. (1991). *Human universals*. New York: McGraw-Hill.

Brown, S. L., & Brown, R. M. (2006). Selective Investment Theory: Recasting the functional significance of close relationships. *Psychological Inquiry, 17*, 1–29.

Brown, W. M., Cronk, L., Grochow, K., Jacobson, A. Liu, C. K., Popovic, Z., et al. (2005). Dance reveals symmetry especially in young men. *Nature, 438*, 1148–1150.

Bugental, D. B. (2000). Acquisition of the algorithms of social life: a domain-based approach. *Psychological Bulletin, 126*, 187–219.

Burch, R. L., & Gallup, G. G., Jr. (2000). Perceptions of paternal resemblance predict family violence. *Evolution and Human Behavior 21*, 429–435.

Burnham, T., & Johnson, D. D. P. (2005). The evolutionary and biological logic of human cooperation. *Analyse Kritik, 27*, 113–135.

Burnstein, E., Crandall, C., & Kitayama, S. (1994). Some neo-Darwinian rules for altruism: Weighing cues for inclusive fitness as a function of the biological importance of the decision. *Journal of Personality & Social Psychology, 67*, 773–789.

Buss, D. M. (1989). Conflict between the sexes: Strategic interference and the evocation of anger and upset. *Journal of Personality & Social Psychology, 56*, 735–747.

Buss, D. M. (1994). The strategies of human mating. *American Scientist, 82*, 238–249.

Buss, D. M. (1995). Psychological sex differences: Origins through sexual selection. *American Psychologist, 50*, 164–168.

Buss, D. M. (2001). Human nature and culture: An evolutionary psychological perspective. *Journal of Personality, 69*, 955–978.

Buss, D. M. (2005). *The handbook of evolutionary psychology*. Hoboken, NJ: Wiley.

Buss, D. M., & Duntley, J. D. (2006). The evolution of aggression. In M. Schaller, J. A. Simpson, & D. T. Kenrick (Eds.), *Evolution and social psychology*. New York: Psychology Press.

Buss, D. M., Larsen, R. J., Westen, D., & Semmelroth, J. (1992). Sex differences in jealousy: Evolution, physiology, and psychology. *Psychological Science, 3*, 251–255.

Buss, D. M., & Schmitt, D. P. (1993). Sexual strategies theory: A contextual evolutionary analysis of human mating. *Psychological Review, 100*, 204–232.

Buunk, B. P., Angleitner, A., Oubaid, V., & Buss, D. M. (1996). Sex differences in jealousy in evolutionary and cultural perspective: Tests from the Netherlands, Germany, and the United States. *Psychological Science, 7*(6), 359–363.

Buunk, B. P., Dijstra, P., Kenrick, D. T., & Warntjes, A. (2001). Age differences in preferences for mates are related to gender, own age, and involvement level. *Evolution and Human Behavior, 22*, 241–250.

Buunk, B., & Hupka, R. B. (1987). Cross-cultural differences in the elicitation of sexual jealousy. *Journal of Sex Research, 23*, 12–22.

Byrne, D., Gouaux, C., Griffitt, W., Lamberth, J., Murakawa, N., Prasad, M. B., et al. (1971). The ubiquitous relationship: Attitude similarity and attraction: A cross-cultural study. *Human Relations, 24*, 201–207.

Campbell, A. (1999). Staying alive: Evolution, culture, and women's intrasexual aggression. *Behavioral and Brain Sciences, 22*, 203–252.

Campbell, A. (2005). Aggression. In D.M. Buss (Ed.), *Handbook of evolutionary psychology* (pp. 628–652). Hoboken, NJ: John Wiley & Sons.

Campbell, D. T. (1975). On the conflicts between biological and social evolution and between psychology and moral tradition. *American Psychologist, 30*, 1103–1126.

Campbell, D. T. (1982). Legal and primary-group social controls. *Journal of Social and Biological Structures, 5*, 431–438.

Campero-Ciani, A., Corna, F., & Capiluppi, C. (2004). Evidence for maternally inherited factors favouring male homosexuality and promoting female fecundity. *Proceedings of the Royal Society B, 271*, 2217–2221.

Carlston, D. E., & Skowronski, J. J. (2005). Linking versus thinking: Evidence for the different associative and attributional bases of spontaneous trait transference and spontaneous trait inference. *Journal of Personality and Social Psychology, 89*, 884–898.

Carroll, S. B. (2005). *Endless forms most beautiful*. New York: Norton.

Carter, C. S. (1998). Neuroendocrine perspectives on social attachment and love. *Psychoneuroendocrinology, 23*, 779–818.

Chance, J. E., & Goldstein, A. G. (1996). The other-race effect and eyewitness identification. In S. L. Sporer & R. S. Malpass (Eds.), *Psychological issues in eyewitness identification* (pp. 153–176). Hillsdale, NJ: Erlbaum.

Clark, M. S., & Mills, J. (1993). The difference between communal and exchange relationships: What it is and is not. *Personality and Social Psychology Bulletin, 19*, 684–691.

Clark, R. D., & Hatfield, E. (1989). Gender differences in receptivity to sexual offers. *Journal of Psychology and Human Sexuality, 2*, 39–55.

Conway, C. A., Jones, B. C., DeBruine, L. M., Welling, L. L. M., Law Smith, M. J., Perrett, D. I., et al. (2007). Salience of emotional displays of danger and contagion in faces is enhanced when progesterone levels are raised. *Hormones and Behavior, 51*, 202–206.

Conway, L. G., III, & Schaller, M. (2002). On the verifiability of evolutionary psychological theories: An analysis of the psychology of scientific persuasion. *Personality and Social Psychology Review, 6*, 152–166.

Cook, M., & Mineka, S. (1990). Selective associations in the observational conditioning of fear in rhesus monkeys. *Journal of Experimental Psychology: Animal Behavior Processes, 16*, 372–389.

Cosmides, L., & Tooby, J. (2005). Neurocognitive adaptations designed for social exchange. In D. M. Buss (Ed.), *The handbook of evolutionary psychology*. New York: Wiley.

Cosmides, L., Tooby, J. & Barkow, J. (1992). Evolutionary psychology and conceptual integration. In J. Barkow, L. Cosmides, & J. Tooby (Eds.), *The adapted mind: Evolutionary psychology and the generation of culture*. New York: Oxford University Press.

Cosmides, L., Tooby, J., Fiddick, L, & Bryant, G. A. (2005). Detecting cheaters. *Trends in Cognitive Sciences, 9*, 505–506.

Cottrell, C. A., & Neuberg, S. L. (2005). Different emotional reactions to different groups: A sociofunctional threat-based approach to 'prejudice.' *Journal of Personality and Social Psychology, 88*, 770–789.

Cottrell, C. A., Neuberg, S. L., & Li, N. P. (2007). What do people desire in others? A sociofunctional perspective on the importance of different valued characteristics. *Journal of Personality and Social Psychology, 92*, 208–231.

Coultas, J. C. (2004). When in Rome… An evolutionary perspective on conformity. *Group Processes and Intergroup Relations, 7*, 317–331.

Crawford, C., & Krebs, D. (2008). *Foundations of evolutionary psychology*. Mahwah, NJ: Erlbaum.

Crawford, C. B., & Salmon, C. (2004). *Evolutionary psychology, public policy, and personal decisions*. Mahwah, NJ: Erlbaum.

Dabbs, J. M. Jr., & Dabbs, M. G. (2000). *Heroes, rogues, and lovers: Testosterone and behavior*. New York: McGraw-Hill.

Dabbs, J. M., Jr., & Morris, R. (1990). Testosterone, social class, and antisocial behavior in a sample of 4,462 men. *Psychological Science, 1*, 209–211.

Dabbs, J. M., Bernieri, F. J., Strong, R. K., Campo, R., & Milun, R. (2001). Going on stage: Testosterone in greetings and meetings. *Journal of Research in Personality, 35*, 27–40.

Daly, M., & Wilson, M. I. (1983). *Sex, evolution and behavior: Adaptations for reproduction* (2nd ed.). Boston, MA: Willard Grant Press.

Daly, M., & Wilson, M. I. (1984). A sociobiological analysis of human infanticide. In G. Hausfater & S. B. Hrdy (Eds.), *Infanticide: Comparative and evolutionary perspectives* (pp. 487–502). New York: Aldine Press.

Daly, M., & Wilson, M. I. (1988). *Homicide*. Hawthorne, NY: Aldine de Gruyter.

Daly, M., & Wilson, M. I. (1996). Violence against stepchildren. *Current Directions in Psychological Science, 5*, 77–81.

Daly, M., & Wilson, M. (1998). *The truth about Cinderella*. London: Weidenfeld & Nicolson.

Daly, M., & Wilson, M. (2005). Parenting and kinship. In D. M. Buss (Ed.), *Handbook of evolutionary psychology* (pp. 443–446). Hoboken, NJ: Wiley.

Daly, M., Wilson, M. I., & Weghorst, S. J. (1982). Male sexual jealousy. *Ethology & Sociobiology, 3*, 11–27.

Darwin, C. (1871). *The descent of man and selection in relation to sex*. New York: D. Appleton and Company.

Dawkins, R. (1976). *The selfish gene*. Oxford, UK: Oxford University Press.

DeBruine, L. M. (2002). Facial resemblance enhances trust. *Proceedings of the Royal Society of London B, 269*, 1307–1312.

DeBruine L. M. (2005). Trustworthy but not lust-worthy: Context-specific effects of facial resemblance. *Proceedings of the Royal Society of London, B, 272*, 919–922.

DeSteno, D., Bartlett, M. Y., Braverman, J., & Salovey, P. (2002). Sex differences in jealousy: Evolutionary mechanism or artifact of measurement? *Journal of Personality and Social Psychology, 87,* 876–893.

Diamond, L. M. (2004). Emerging perspectives on distinctions between romantic love and sexual desire. *Current Directions in Psychological Science, 13,* 116–119.

Dijkstra, P., & Buunk, B. P. (1998). Jealousy as a function of rival characteristics: An evolutionary perspective. *Personality & Social Psychology Bulletin, 24,* 1158–1166.

Duchaine, B., Cosmides, L., & Tooby, J. (2001). Evolutionary psychology and the brain. *Current Opinion in Neurobiology, 11,* 225–230.

Duncan, L. A., Park, J. H., Faulkner, J., Schaller, M., Neuberg, S. L., & Kenrick, D. T. (2007). Adaptive allocation of attention: Effects of sex and sociosexuality on visual attention to attractive opposite-sex faces. *Evolution and Human Behavior, 28,* 359–364.

Duntley, J. D. (2005). Adaptations to dangers from humans. In D.M. Buss (Ed.), *Handbook of evolutionary psychology* (pp. 224–254). New York: John Wiley & Sons.

Duntley, J. D., & Shackelford, T. K. (2008). *Evolutionary forensic psychology.* New York: Oxford University Press.

Eagly, A., & Johnson, B. T. (1990). Gender and leadership style: A meta-analysis. *Psychological Bulletin, 108,* 233–256.

Eagly, A. H., & Wood, W. (1999). The origins of sex differences in human behavior: Evolved dispositions versus social roles. *American Psychologist, 54,* 408–423.

Ebstein, R. P. (2006). The molecular genetic architecture of human personality: Beyond self-report questionnaires. *Molecular Psychiatry, 11,* 427–445.

Eisenberger, N. I., & Lieberman, M. D. (2004). Why rejection hurts: A common neural alarm system for physical and social pain. *Trends in Cognitive Sciences, 8,* 294–300.

Ellis, B. J. (2004). Timing of pubertal maturation in girls: An integrated life history approach. *Psychological Bulletin, 130,* 920–958.

Faulkner, J., & Schaller, M. (2007). Nepotistic nosiness: Inclusive fitness and vigilance of kin members' romantic relationships. *Evolution and Human Behavior, 28,* 430–438.

Faulkner, J., Schaller, M., Park, J. H., & Duncan, L. A. (2004). Evolved disease-avoidance mechanisms and contemporary xenophobic attitudes. *Group Processes and Intergroup Relations, 7,* 333–353.

Fehr, E., Fischbacher, U., & Gächter, S. (2002). Strong reciprocity, human cooperation and the enforcement of social norms. *Human Nature, 13,* 1–25.

Fehr, E. & Gächter, S. (2002). Altruistic punishment in humans. *Nature, 415,* 137–140.

Feingold, A. (1992). Good-looking people are not what we think. *Psychological Bulletin, 111,* 304–341.

Fincher, C. L., Thornhill, R., Murray, D. R., & Schaller, M. (2008). Pathogen prevalence predicts human cross-cultural variability in individualism / collectivism. *Proceedings of the Royal Society B: Biological Sciences, 275,* 1279–1285.

Fisher, H. E., Aron, A., Mashek, D., Li, H., & Brown. L. L. (2002). Defining the brain systems of lust, romantic attraction, and attachment. *Archives of Sexual Behavior, 31,* 413–419.

Fiske, A. P. (1992). The four elementary forms of sociality: Framework for a unified theory of social relations. *Psychological Review, 99,* 689–723.

Fiske, A. P., & Haslam, N. (1996). Social cognition is thinking about relationships. *Current Directions in Psychological Science, 5,* 143–148.

Fiske, S. T. (1992). Thinking is for doing: Portraits of social cognition from daguerreotype to laser photo. *Journal of Personality and Social Psychology, 63,* 877–889.

Fiske, S. T., Cuddy, A. J. C., & Glick, P (2007). Universal dimensions of social cognition: Warmth and competence. *Trends in Cognitive Sciences, 11,* 77–83.

Fletcher, G. J. O., Tither, J. M., O'Loughlin, C., Friesen, M., & Overall, N. (2004). Warm and homely or cold and beautiful? Sex differences in trading off traits in mate selection. *Personality & Social Psychology Bulletin, 30,* 659–672.

Fox, E., Russo, R., Bowles, R., & Dutton, K. (2001). Do threatening stimuli draw or hold visual attention in subclinical anxiety? *Journal of Experimental Psychology: General, 130,* 681–700.

Fraley, R. C., Brumbaugh, C. C., & Marks, M. J. (2005). The evolution and function of adult attachment: A comparative and phylogenetic analysis. *Journal of Personality and Social Psychology, 89,* 731–746.

Gailliot, M. T., Stillman, T. F., Schmeichel, B. J., Maner, J. K., & Plant, E. A. (2008). Mortality salience increases adherence to salient norms and values. *Personality and Social Psychology Bulletin, 34,* 993–1003.

Gangestad, S. W. & Buss, D. M. (1993). Pathogen prevalence and human mate preferences. *Ethology and Sociobiology, 14,* 89–96.

Gangestad, S. W., Haselton, M. G., & Buss, D. M. (2006). Evolutionary foundations of cultural variation: Evoked culture and mate preferences. *Psychological Inquiry, 17,* 75–95.

Gangestad, S. W., & Simpson, J. A. (2000). The evolution of human mating: Trade-offs and strategic pluralism. *Behavioral & Brain Sciences,* 573–587.

Gangestad, S. W., & Simpson, J. A. (2007). *The evolution of mind: Fundamental questions and controversies.* New York: Guilford.

Gangestad, S. W., & Thornhill, R. (1997). The evolutionary psychology of extra-pair sex: The role of fluctuating asymmetry. *Evolution and Human Behavior, 18,* 69–88.

Gangestad, S. W., & Thornhill, R. (1998). Menstrual cycle variation in women's preferences for the scent of symmetrical men. *Proceedings of the Royal Society of London B, 265,* 727–733.

Gangestad, S. W., Thornhill, R., & Garver-Apgar (2005). Adaptations to ovulation. In D. M. Buss (Ed.), *The handbook of evolutionary psychology* (pp. 344–371). Hoboken, NJ: Wiley.

Garcia, J., & Koelling, R. A. (1966). Relation of cue to consequence in avoidance learning. *Psychonomic Science, 4,* 123–124.

Garver-Apgar, C. E., Gangestad, S. W., Thornhill, R., Miller, R. D., & Olp, J. J. (2006). Major histocompatibility complex alleles, sexual responsivity, and unfaithfulness in romantic couples. *Psychological Science, 17,* 830–835.

Geary, D. C. (1998). *Male, female: The evolution of human sex differences.* New York: American Psychological Association.

Geary, D. C. (2000). Evolution and proximate expression of human paternal investment. *Psychological Bulletin, 126,* 55–77.

Geary, D. C. (2006). Evolutionary developmental psychology: Current status and future directions. *Developmental Review, 26,* 113–119.

Gibson, J. J. (1979). *The ecological approach to visual perception.* Boston: Houghton Mifflin.

Gigerenzer, G., Todd, P. M. & the ABC Research Group. (1999). *Simple heuristics that make us smart.* New York: Oxford University Press.

Gilbert, D. T. (1991). How mental systems believe. *American Psychologist, 46,* 107–119.

Gilbert, D. T., & Malone, P. S. (1995). The correspondence bias. *Psychological Bulletin, 117,* 21–38.

Godwin, J., Luckenbach, J. A., & Borski, R. J. (2003). Ecology meets endocrinology: Environmental sex determination in fishes. *Evolution and Development, 5,* 40–49.

Gould, J. L., & Gould, C. L. (1989). *Sexual selection.* New York: Scientific American Library.

Gould, S. J. (1977). The return of hopeful monsters. *Natural History, 86,* 22–30.

Gray, P. B., Chapman, J. F., Burnham, T. C., McIntyre, M. H., Lipson, S. F., & Ellison, P. T. (2004). Human male pair bonding and testosterone. *Human Nature, 15,* 119–131.

Greenberg, L. (1979) Genetic component of bee odor in kin recognition. *Science, 206,* 1095–1097.

Grillon, C., Pellowski, M., Merikangas, K. R., & Davis, M. (1997). Darkness facilitates acoustic startle reflex in humans. *Biological Psychiatry, 42,* 453–460.

Griskevicius, V., Cialdini, R. B., & Kenrick, D. T. (2006). Peacocks, Picasso, and parental investment: The effects of romantic motives on creativity. *Journal of Personality and Social Psychology, 91,* 63–76.

Griskevicius, V., Goldstein, N. J., Mortensen C. R., Cialdini, R. B., & Kenrick, D. T. (2006). Going along versus going alone: When fundamental motives facilitate strategic (non)conformity. *Journal of Personality and Social Psychology, 91,* 281–294.

Griskevicius, V., Tybur, J. M., Gangestad, S. W., Perea, E. F., Shapiro, J. R., & Kenrick, D. T. (2009). Aggress to impress: Hostility as an evolved context-dependent strategy. *Journal of Personality & Social Psychology, 96,* 980–994.

Griskevicius, V, Tybur, J. M., Sundie, J. M., Cialdini, R. B., Miller, G. F., & Kenrick, D. T. (2007). Blatant benevolence and conspicuous consumption: When romantic motives elicit strategic costly signals. *Journal of Personality and Social Psychology, 93,* 85–102.

Guimond, S., Dambrun, M., Michinov, N., & Duarte, S. (2003). Does social dominance generate prejudice? Integrating individual and contextual determinants of intergroup cognitions. *Journal of Personality and Social Psychology, 84,* 697–721.

Hamilton, W. D. (1964). The genetical evolution of social behavior: I & II. *Journal of Theoretical Biology, 7,* 1–32.

Hanko, K., Master, S., & Sabini, J. (2004). Some evidence about character and mate selection. *Personality & Social Psychology Bulletin, 30,* 732–742.

Harris, C. R. (2003). A review of sex differences in sexual jealousy, including self-report data, psychophysiological responses, interpersonal violence, and morbid jealousy. *Personality and Social Psychology Review, 7,* 102–128.

Harris, L. T., & Fiske, S. T. (2006). Dehumanizing the lowest of the low: Neuroimaging responses to extreme out-groups. *Psychological Science, 17,* 847–853.

Haselton, M. G., & Buss, D. M. (2000). Error management theory: A new perspective on biases in cross-sex mind reading. *Journal of Personality and Social Psychology, 78,* 81–91.

Haselton, M. G., & Funder, D. (2006). The evolution of accuracy and bias in social judgment. In M. Schaller, J. A. Simpson, & D. T. Kenrick (Eds.), *Evolution and social psychology* (pp. 15–37). New York: Psychology Press.

Haselton, M. G., & Nettle, D. (2006). The paranoid optimist: An integrative evolutionary model of cognitive biases. *Personality and Social Psychology Review, 10,* 47–66.

Hazan, C. & Shaver, P. R. (1994). Attachment as an organizational framework for research on close relationships. *Psychological Inquiry, 5,* 1–22.

Heath, T. B., McCarthy, M. S., & Mothersbaugh, D. L. (1994). Spokesperson fame and vividness effects in the context of issue-relevant thinking: The moderating role of competitive setting. *Journal of Consumer Research, 20,* 520–534.

Heatherton, T. F., Macrae, C. N., & Kelley, W. M. (2004). What the social brain sciences can tell us about the self. *Current Directions in Psychological Science, 13,* 190–193.

Henrich, J., & Boyd, R. (1998). The evolution of conformist transmission and between-group differences. *Evolution and Human Behavior, 19,* 215–242.

Henrich, J., Boyd, R., Bowles, S., Gintis, H., Fehr, E., Camerer, C., et al. (2005). 'Economic Man' in cross-cultural perspective: Ethnography and experiments from 15 small-scale societies. *Behavioral and Brain Sciences, 28,* 795–855.

Henrich, J., & Gil-White, F. J. (2001). The evolution of prestige: Freely conferred deference as a mechanism for enhancing the benefits of cultural transmission. *Evolution and Human Behavior, 22,* 165–196.

Henrich, J., McElreath, R., Barr, A., Ensimger, J., Barrett, C., Bolyanatz, A., et al. (2006). Costly punishment across human societies, *Science, 312,* 1767–1770.

Hepper, P. G. (1991). *Kin recognition.* New York: Cambridge University Press.

Hermans, E. J., Putman, P., & van Hong, J. (2006). Testosterone administration reduces empathetic behavior: A facial mimicry study. *Psychoneuroendocrinology, 31,* 859–866.

Hill, K. R., & Hurtado, A. M. (1989). Hunter-gatherers of lowland South America. *American Scientist, September-October,* 437–443.

Hoffman, M. (1981). Is altruism part of human nature? *Journal of Personality and Social Psychology, 40,* 121–137.

Holmes, W. G., & Sherman, P. W. (1983). Kin recognition in animals. *American Scientist, 71,* 46–55.

Hrdy, S. H. (1999). *Mother Nature: A history of mothers, infants, and natural selection.* New York: Pantheon.

Insel, T. R., & Young, L. J. (2001). The neurobiology of attachment. *Nature Reviews Neuroscience, 2,* 129–136.

Johnson, D. D. P., Price, M. E., & Takezawa, M. (2008). Renaissance of the individual: Reciprocity, positive assortment, and the puzzle of human cooperation. In C. Crawford & D. Krebs (Eds.), *Foundations of evolutionary psychology.* Mahwah, NJ: Erlbaum.

Johnson, D. J., & Rusbult, C. E. (1989). Resisting temptation: Devaluation of alternative partners as a means of maintaining commitment in close relationships. *Journal of Personality and Social Psychology, 57,* 967–980.

Johnson, R. T., Burk, J. A., Kirkpatrick, L. A. (2007). Dominance and prestige as differential predictors of aggression and testosterone levels in men. *Evolution and Human Behavior, 28,* 345–351.

Johnston, V. S., Hagel, R., Franklin, M., Fink, B., & Grammer, K. (2001). Male facial attractiveness: Evidence for hormone mediated adaptive design. *Evolution and Human Behavior, 22,* 251–267.

Jones, B. C., Little, A. C., Penton-Voak, I. S., Tiddeman, B. P., Burt, D. M., & Perrett, D. I. (2001). Facial symmetry and judgments of apparent health: Support for a 'good genes' explanation of the attractiveness-symmetry relationship. *Evolution and Human Behavior, 22,* 417–429.

Josephs, R. A., Newman, M. L., Brown, R. P., & Beer, J. M. (2003). Status, testosterone, and human intellectual performance: Stereotype threat as status concern. *Psychological Science, 14,* 158–163.

Judd, C. M., James-Hawkins, L., Yzerbyt, V., & Kashima, Y. (2005). Fundamental dimensions of social judgment: Understanding the relations between judgments of competence and warmth. *Journal of Personality and Social Psychology, 89,* 899–913.

Kahneman, D., & Tversky, A., (1991). Loss aversion in riskless choice: a reference dependent model. In D. Kahneman & A. Tversky (Eds.), *Choices, values and frames* (pp. 143–158). Cambridge, UK: Cambridge University Press.

Kameda, T., Takezawa, M., & Hastie, R. (2003). The logic of social sharing: An evolutionary game analysis of adaptive norm development. *Personality and Social Psychology Review, 7,* 2–19.

Kameda, T., Takezawa, M., & Hastie, R. (2005). Where do social norms come from?: The example of communal sharing. *Current Directions in Psychological Science, 14*, 331–334.

Kameda, T., & Tindale, R. S. (2006). Groups as adaptive devices: Human docility and group aggregation mechanisms in evolutionary context. In M. Schaller, J. A. Simpson, & D. T. Kenrick (Eds.), *Evolution and social psychology* (pp. 317–341). New York: Psychology Press.

Kamins, M. A. (1989). Celebrity and noncelebrity advertising in a two-sided context. *Journal of Advertising Research, 29*, 34–42.

Kanwisher, N. McDermott, J., & Chun, M. M. (1997). The fusiform face area: A module in human extrastriate cortex specialized for face perception. *Journal of Neuroscience, 17*, 4302–4311.

Kaplan, H. S., & Gangestad, S. W. (2007). Optimality approaches and evolutionary psychology: A call for synthesis. In S. W. Gangestad & J. A. Simpson (Eds.), *The evolution of mind: Fundamental questions and controversies* (pp. 121–129). New York: Guilford.

Kelley, H. H. (1950). The warm-cold variable in first impressions of persons. *Journal of Personality, 18*, 431–439.

Kenrick, D. T. (1994). Evolutionary social psychology: From sexual selection to social cognition. In M.P. Zanna (Ed.), *Advances in experimental social psychology, 26* (pp. 75–121). San Diego, CA: Academic Press.

Kenrick, D. T. (2006a). A dynamical evolutionary view of love. In R. J. Sternberg & K. Weis (Eds.), *Psychology of love* (2nd ed., pp. 15–34). New Haven, CT: Yale University Press.

Kenrick, D. T. (2006b). Evolutionary psychology: Resistance is futile. *Psychological Inquiry, 17*, 102–108.

Kenrick, D. T., Gabrielidis, C., Keefe, R. C., & Cornelius, J. (1996). Adolescents' age preferences for dating partners: Support for an evolutionary model of life-history strategies. *Child Development, 67*, 1499–1511.

Kenrick, D. T., Griskevicius, V., Sundie, J. M., Li, N. P., Li, Y. J. & Neuberg, S. L. (2009). Deep rationality: The evolutionary economics of decision-making. *Social Cognition, 27*, 763–784.

Kenrick, D. T., Groth, G. R., Trost, M. R., & Sadalla, E. K. (1993). Integrating evolutionary and social exchange perspectives on relationships: Effects of gender, self-appraisal, and involvement level on mate selection criteria. *Journal of Personality and Social Psychology, 64*, 951–969.

Kenrick, D. T., & Keefe, R. C. (1992). Age preferences in mates reflect sex differences in mating strategies. *Behavioral & Brain Sciences, 15*, 75–91.

Kenrick, D. T., Keefe, R. C., Bryan, A., Barr, A., & Brown, S. (1995). Age preferences and mate choice among homosexuals and heterosexuals: A case for modular psychological mechanisms. *Journal of Personality and Social Psychology, 69*, 1166–1172.

Kenrick, D. T., & Li, N. (2000). The Darwin is in the details. *American Psychologist, 55*, 1060–1061.

Kenrick, D. T., Li, N. P., & Butner, J. (2003). Dynamical evolutionary psychology: Individual decision-rules and emergent social norms. *Psychological Review, 110*, 3–28.

Kenrick, D. T., & Luce, C. L. (2000). An evolutionary life-history model of gender differences and similarities. In T. Eckes & H. M. Trautner (Eds.), *The developmental social psychology of gender* (pp. 35–64). Hillsdale, NJ: Erlbaum.

Kenrick, D. T., Nieuweboer, S., & Buunk, A. P. (2010). Universal mechanisms and cultural diversity: Replacing the blank slate with a coloring book. In M. Schaller, A. Norenzayan, S. Heine, T. Yamagishi, & T. Kameda (Eds.), *Evolution, culture, and the human mind* (pp. 257–271). New York: Psychology Press.

Kenrick, D. T., Sadalla, E. K., Groth, G., & Trost, M. R. (1990). Evolution, traits, and the stages of human courtship: Qualifying the parental investment model. *Journal of Personality, 58*, 97–116.

Kenrick, D. T., Schaller, M., & Simpson, J. A. (2006). Evolution is the new cognition. In M. Schaller, J. A. Simpson, & D. T. Kenrick (Eds.), *Evolution and social psychology* (pp. 1–13). New York: Psychology Press.

Kenrick, D. T., & Shiota, M. N. (2008). Approach and avoidance motivation(s): An evolutionary perspective. In A. J. Elliot (Ed.), *Handbook of approach and avoidance motivation* (pp. 271–285). Mahwah, NJ: Erlbaum.

Kenrick, D. T., Sundie, J. M., & Kurzban, R. (2008). Cooperation and conflict between kith, kin, and strangers: Game theory by domains. In C. Crawford & D. Krebs (Eds.), *Foundations of evolutionary psychology* (pp. 353–370). New York: Erlbaum.

Kenrick, D. T., Sundie, J. M., Nicastle, L. D., & Stone, G. O. (2001). Can one ever be too wealthy or too chaste? Searching for nonlinearities in mate judgment. *Journal of Personality and Social Psychology, 80*, 462–471.

Kessler, T., & Cohrs, C. J. (2008). The evolution of authoritarian processes: Fostering cooperation in large-scale groups. *Group Dynamics: Theory, Research, and Practice, 12*, 17–26.

Ketelaar, T., & Ellis, B. J. (2000). Are evolutionary explanations unfalsifiable? Evolutionary psychology and the Lakatosian philosophy of science. *Psychological Inquiry, 11*, 1–21.

Kirkpatrick, L. A., Waugh, C. E., Valencia, A., & Webster, G. D. (2002). The functional domain-specificity of self-esteem and the differential prediction of aggression. *Journal of Personality and Social Psychology, 82*, 756–767.

Klein, S. B., Cosmides, L., Tooby, J., & Chance, S. (2002). Decisions and the evolution of memory: Multiple systems, multiple functions. *Psychological Review, 109*, 306–329.

Knutson, B., Wolkowitz, O. M., & Cole, S. W. (1998). Selective alteration of personality and social behavior by serotonergic intervention. *American Journal of Psychiatry, 155*, 373–379.

Kosfeld, M., Heinrichs, M., Zak, P.J., & Fischbacher, U., & Fehr, E. (2005). Oxytocin increases trust in humans. *Nature, 435*, 673–676.

Krebs, D. (1987). The challenge of altruism in biology and psychology. In C. Crawford, M. Smith, & D. Krebs (Eds.), *Sociobiology and psychology: Ideas, issues, and applications* (pp. 81–118). Hillsdale, NJ: Erlbaum.

Krebs, D., & Janicki, M. (2004). Biological foundations of moral norms. In M. Schaller & C. S. Crandall (Eds.), *The psychological foundations of culture* (pp. 125–148). Mahwah NJ: Erlbaum.

Krupp, D. B., DeBruine, L. M., & Barclay, P. (2008). A cue of kinship promotes cooperation for the public good. *Evolution and Human Behavior, 29*, 49–55.

Kurzban, R. (2002). Alas poor evolutionary psychology: Unjustly accused, unjustly condemned. *The Human Nature Review, 2*, 99–109.

Kurzban, R., & Aktipis, C. A. (2007). Modularity and the social mind: Are psychologists too selfish? *Personality and Social Psychology Review, 11*(2), 131–149.

Kurzban, R., & Leary, M. R. (2001). Evolutionary origins of stigmatization: The functions of social exclusion. *Psychological Bulletin, 127*, 187–208.

Kurzban, R., & Neuberg, S. L. (2005). Managing ingroup and outgroup relationships. In D. Buss (Ed.), *Handbook of evolutionary psychology* (pp. 653–675). New York: John Wiley & Sons.

Kurzban, R., Tooby, J., & Cosmides, L. (2001). Can race be erased? Coalitional computation and social categorization. *Proceedings of the National Academy of Sciences, 98*, 15387–15392.

Laham, S. M., Gonsalkorale, K., & von Hippel, W. (2005). Darwinian grandparenting: Preferential investment in more certain kin. *Personality & Social Psychology Bulletin, 31*, 63–72.

Lakatos, I. (1970). Falsification and the methodology of scientific research programmes. In I. Lakatos & A. Musgrave (Eds.), *Criticism and the growth of knowledge* (pp. 91–196). Cambridge, UK: Cambridge University Press.

Lakin, J. L., Jefferis, V. E., Cheng, C. M., & Chartrand, T. L. (2003). The chameleon effect as social glue: Evidence for the evolutionary significance of nonconscious mimicry. *Journal of Nonverbal Behavior, 27*, 145–162.

Leakey, R. E., & Lewin, R. (1977). *Origins: What new discoveries reveal about the emergence of our species and its possible future.* New York: Dutton.

Leary, M. R., & Baumeister, R. F. (2000). The nature and function of self-esteem: Sociometer theory. *Advances in Experimental Social Psychology, 32*, 1–62.

Leary, M. R., Haupt, A. L., Strausser, K. S., & Chokel, J. T. (1998). Calibrating the sociometer: The relationship between interpersonal appraisals and state self-esteem. *Journal of Personality and Social Psychology, 74*, 1290–1299.

Leary, M. R., Tambor, E. S., Terdal, S. K., & Downs, D. L. (1995). Self-esteem as an interpersonal monitor: The sociometer hypothesis. *Journal of Personality and Social Psychology, 68*, 518–530.

Leary, M. R., Twenge, J. M., & Quinlivan, E. (2006). Interpersonal rejection as a determinant of anger and aggression. *Personality and Social Psychology Review, 10*, 111–132.

Li, N. P., Bailey, J. M., Kenrick, D. T., & Linsenmeier, J. A. (2002). The necessities and luxuries of mate preferences: Testing the trade-offs. *Journal of Personality and Social Psychology, 82*, 947–955.

Li, N. P., & Kenrick, D. T. (2006). Sex similarities and differences in preferences for short-term mates: What, whether, and why. *Journal of Personality and Social Psychology, 90*, 468–489.

Lieberman, D., Tooby, J., & Cosmides, L. (2007). The architecture of human kin detection. *Nature, 445*, 727–731.

Little, A. C., Burriss R. P., Jones, B. C., & Roberts, S. C. (2007). Facial appearance affects voting decisions. *Evolution and Human Behavior, 28*, 18–27.

Low, B. S. (1990). Marriage systems and pathogen stress in human societies. *American Zoologist, 30*, 325–339.

MacDonald, G., & Leary, M. R. (2005). Why does social exclusion hurt? The relationship between social and physical pain. *Psychological Bulletin, 131*, 202–223.

Maner, J. K., DeWall, C. N., Baumeister, R. F., & Schaller, M. (2007). Does social exclusion motivate interpersonal reconnection? Resolving the 'porcupine problem.' *Journal of Personality and Social Psychology, 92*, 42–55.

Maner, J. K., DeWall, C. N., & Gailliot, M. T. (2008). Selective attention to signs of success: Social dominance and early stage interpersonal perception. *Personality and Social Psychology Bulletin, 34*, 488–501.

Maner, J. K., Gailliot, M. T., Rouby, D. A., & Miller, S. L. (2007). Can't take my eyes off you: Attentional adhesion to mates and rivals. *Journal of Personality and Social Psychology, 93*, 389–401.

Maner, J. K., Kenrick, D. T., Becker, D. V., Robertson, T. E., Hofer, B., Neuberg, S. L., et al. (2005). Functional projection: How fundamental social motives can bias interpersonal perception. *Journal of Personality & Social Psychology, 88*, 63–78.

Maner, J. K., Rouby, D.A., & Gonzaga, G. C. (2008). Automatic inattention to attractive alternatives: The evolved psychology of relationship maintenance. *Evolution & Human Behavior, 29*, 343–349.

Marcus, G. (2004). *The birth of the mind.* New York: Basic Books.

Mazur, A., & Booth, A. (1998). Testosterone and dominance in men. *Behavioral and Brain Sciences, 21*, 353–397.

McArthur, L. Z., & Baron, R. M. (1983). Toward an ecological theory of social perception. *Psychological Review, 90*, 215–238.

McIntyre, M., Gangestad, S. W., Gray, P. B., Chapman, J. F., Burnham, T. C., O'Rourke, M. T., et al. (2006). Romantic involvement often reduces men's testosterone levels—but not always: The moderating role of extrapair sexual interest. *Journal of Personality & Social Psychology, 91*, 642–651.

Mealey, L., Bridgstock, R., & Townsend, G. C. (1999). Symmetry and perceived facial attractiveness: A monozygotic co-twin comparison. *Journal of Personality & Social Psychology, 76*, 151–158.

Melis, M. R., & Argiolas, A. (1995). Dopamine and sexual behavior. *Neuroscience and Biobehavioral Reviews, 19*, 19–38.

Michalski, R. L., & Shackelford, T. K. (2005). Grandparental investment as a function of relational uncertainty and emotional closeness with parents. *Human Nature, 16*, 292–304.

Milgram, S. (1974). *Obedience to authority.* New York: Harper Colophon.

Miller, G. F. (2000). *The mating mind: How sexual choice shaped the evolution of human nature.* New York: Doubleday.

Miller, R. S. (1997). Inattentive and contented: Relationship commitment and attention to alternatives. *Journal of Personality and Social Psychology, 73*, 758–766.

Mitchell, M., & Sidanius, J. (1995). Social hierarchy and executions in the United States: A social dominance perspective. The death penalty: A social dominance perspective. *Political Psychology, 16*, 591–619.

Moller, A. P., & Thornhill, R. (1998). Bilateral symmetry and sexual selection: A meta-analysis. *American Naturalist, 151*, 174–192.

Moore, B. R. (2004). The evolution of learning. *Biological Review, 79*, 301–335.

Moreland, R. L., Hogg, M. A., & Hains, S. C. (1994). Back to the future: Social psychological research on groups. *Journal of Experimental Social Psychology, 30*, 527–555.

Munafo, M. R., Yalcin, B., Willis-Owen, S. A., & Flint, J. (2008). Association of the dopamine D4 receptor (DRD4) gene and approach-related personality traits: Meta-analysis and new data. *Biological Psychiatry, 63*, 197–206.

Murray, S. L., Griffin, D. W., Rose, P., & Bellavia, G. M. (2003). Calibrating the sociometer: The relational contingencies of self-esteem. *Journal of Personality and Social Psychology, 85*, 63–84.

Navarrete, C. D., & Fessler, D. M. T. (2006). Disease avoidance and ethnocentrism: The effects of disease vulnerability and disgust sensitivity on intergroup attitudes. *Evolution and Human Behavior, 27*, 270–282.

Navarrete, C. D., Fessler, D. M. T., & Eng, S. J. (2007). Elevated ethnocentrism in the first trimester of pregnancy. *Evolution and Human Behavior, 28*, 60–65.

Navarrete, C. D., Kurzban, R., Fessler, D. M. T., & Kirkpatrick, L. A. (2004). Anxiety and intergroup bias: Terror management or coalitional psychology. *Group Processes and Intergroup Relations, 7*, 370–377.

Navarrete, C. D., Olsson, A., Ho, A. K., Mendes, W. B., Thomsen, L., & Sidanius, J. (2009). Prepared learning and the gendered nature of outgroup fear. *Psychological Science, 20*, 155–158.

Nesse, R. M. (2005). Natural selection and the regulation of defenses: A signal detection analysis of the smoke detector principle. *Evolution and Human Behavior, 26*, 88–105.

Neuberg, S. L., & Cottrell, C. A. (2006). Evolutionary bases of prejudices. In M. Schaller, J.A. Simpson, & D.T. Kenrick (Eds.), *Evolution and social psychology* (pp. 163–187). New York: Psychology Press.

Neuberg, S. L., Smith, D. M., & Asher, T. (2000). Why people stigmatize: Toward a biocultural framework. In T. Heatherton, R. Kleck, J. G. Hull, & M. Hebl (Eds.), *The social psychology of stigma* (pp. 31–61). New York: Guilford.

New, J., Cosmides, L. & Tooby, J. (2007). Category-specific attention for animals reflects ancestral priorities, not expertise. *Proceedings of the National Academy of Sciences, 104*, 16593–16603.

Newman, L. S., & Uleman, J. S. (1989). Spontaneous trait inference. In J. S. Uleman & J. A. Bargh (Eds.), *Unintended thought* (pp. 155–188). New York: Guilford.

Neyer, F. J., & Lang, F. R. (2003). Blood is thicker than water: Kinship orientation across adulthood. *Journal of Personality and Social Psychology, 84*, 310–321.

Norenzayan, A., & Heine, S. J. (2005). Psychological universals across cultures: What are they and how do we know? *Psychological Bulletin, 131*, 763–784.

Norenzayan, A., Schaller, M., & Heine, S. J. (2006). Evolution and culture. In M. Schaller, J. A. Simpson, & D. T. Kenrick (Eds.), *Evolution and social psychology* (pp. 343–366). New York: Psychology Press.

O'Gorman, R., Sheldon, K. M., & Wilson, D. S. (2008). For the good of the group? Exploring group-level evolutionary adaptations using multilevel selection theory. *Group Dynamics: Theory, Research, and Practice, 12,* 17–26.

Öhman, A., Flykt, A., & Esteves, F. (2001). Emotion drives attention: Detecting the snake in the grass. *Journal of Experimental Psychology: General, 130,* 466–478.

Öhman, A, & Mineka, S. (2001). Fears, phobias, and preparedness: Toward an evolved module of fear and fear learning. *Psychological Review, 108,* 483–522.

Olsson, A., Ebert, J. P., Banaji, M. R., & Phelps, E. A. (2005). The role of social groups in the persistence of learned fear. *Science, 309,* 785–787.

Oosterhof, N. N., & Todorov, A. (2008). The functional basis of face evaluation. *Proceedings of the National Academy of Sciences, 105,* 11087–11092.

Otta, E., Queiroz, R. D. S., Campos, L. D. S., da Silva, M. W. D., & Silveira, M. T. (1998). Age differences between spouses in a Brazilian marriage sample. *Evolution and Human Behavior, 20,* 99–103.

Palmer, C. T. (1993). Anger, aggression, and humor in Newfoundland floor hockey: An evolutionary analysis. *Aggressive Behavior, 19,* 167–173.

Park, J. H., Faulkner, J., & Schaller, M. (2003). Evolved disease-avoidance processes and contemporary anti-social behavior: Prejudicial attitudes and avoidance of people with physical disabilities. *Journal of Nonverbal Behavior, 27,* 65–87.

Park, J. H., & Schaller, M. (2005). Does attitude similarity serve as a heuristic cue for kinship? Evidence of an implicit cognitive association. *Evolution and Human Behavior, 26,* 158–170.

Park, J. H., Schaller, M., & Crandall, C. S. (2007). Pathogen-avoidance mechanisms and the stigmatization of obese people. *Evolution and Human Behavior, 28,* 410–414.

Park, J., Schaller, M., & Van Vugt, M. (2008). The psychology of human kin recognition: Heuristic cues, erroneous inferences, and their implications. *Review of General Psychology, 12,* 215–235.

Pawlowski, B., & Jasienska, G. (2005). Women's preferences for sexual dimorphism in height depend on menstrual cycle phase and expected duration of relationship. *Biological Psychology, 70,* 38–43.

Peeters, G., & Czapinski, J. (1990). Positive-negative asymmetry in evaluations: The distinction between affective and informational negativity effects. *European Review of Social Psychology, 1,* 33–60.

Penke, L., & Denissen, J. J. A. (2008). Sex differences and lifestyle-dependent shifts in the attunement of self-esteem to self-perceived mate value: Hints to an adaptive mechanism? *Journal of Research in Personality, 42,* 1123–1129.

Penton-Voak, I. S., Little, A. C., Jones, B. C., Burt, D. M., Tiddeman, B. P., & Perrett, D. J. (2003). Female condition influences preferences for sexual dimorphism in faces of male humans (*Homo sapiens*). *Journal of Comparative Psychology, 117,* 264–271.

Phelps, E. A., O'Conner, K. J., Cunningham, W. A., Funayama, E. S., Gatenby, J. C., Gore, J. C., et al. (2000). Performance on indirect measures of race evaluation predicts amygdala activation. *Journal of Cognitive Neuroscience, 12,* 729–738.

Pickett, C. L., & Gardner, W. L. (2005). The social monitoring system: Enhanced sensitivity to social cues and information as an adaptive response to social exclusion and belonging need. In K. D. Williams, J. P. Forgas, & W. von Hippel (Eds.), *The social outcast: Ostracism, social exclusion, rejection, and bullying* (pp. 213–226). New York: Psychology Press.

Pietrzak, R. H., Laird, J. D., Stevens, D. A., Thompson, N. S. (2002, March). Sex differences in human jealousy: A coordinated study of forced-choice, continuous rating-scale, and physiological responses on the same subjects. *Evolution and Human Behavior, 23*(2), 83–94.

Pillsworth, E. G. & Haselton, M. G. (2006). Male sexual attractiveness predicts differential ovulatory shifts in female extra-pair attraction and male mate retention. *Evolution and Human Behavior, 27,* 247–258.

Pinker, S. (1997). *How the mind works.* New York: W. W. Norton.

Pinker, S. (2003). *The blank slate.* New York: Penguin.

Platek, S. M., Raines, D. M., Gallup G. G. Jr., Mohamed, F. B., Thomson, J. W., Myers, T. E., et al. (2004). Reactions to children's faces: Males are more affected by resemblance than females are, and so are their brains. *Evolution and Human Behavior, 25,* 394–405.

Pollet, T. V., Nettle, D., & Nelissen, M. (2007). Maternal grandmothers do go the extra mile: Factoring distance and lineage into differential contact with grandchildren. *Evolutionary Psychology, 5,* 832–843.

Pratto, F., Sidanius, J., & Levin, S. (2006). Social dominance theory and the dynamics of intergroup relations: Taking stock and looking forward. In W. Stroebe & M. Hewstone (Eds.), *European Review of Social Psychology, 17,* 271–320.

Pratto, F. Sidanius, J., Stallworth, L. M., & Malle, B. F. (1994). Social dominance orientation: A personality variable relevant to social roles and intergroup relations. *Journal of Personality and Social Psychology, 67,* 741–763.

Puts, D. A. (2005). Mating context and menstrual phase affect women's preferences for male voice pitch. *Evolution & Human Behavior, 26,* 388–397.

Quinlan, R. J. (2007). Human parental effort and environmental risk. *Proceedings of the Royal Society B, 274,* 121–125.

Regan, P. C., & Berscheid, E. (1999). *Lust: What we know about sexual desire.* Thousand Oaks, CA: Sage.

Regan, P. C., Medina, R., & Joshi, A. (2001). Partner preferences among homosexual men and women: What is desirable in a sex partner is not necessarily desirable in a romantic partner. *Social Behavior & Personality, 29,* 625–634.

Rendall, D. (2004). "Recognizing" kin: Mechanisms, media, minds, modules, and muddles. In B. Chapais & C. M. Berman (Eds.), *Kinship and behavior in primates* (pp. 295–316). Oxford, UK: Oxford University Press.

Rhodes, G., Zebrowitz, L. A., Clark, A., Kalick, S. M., Hightower, A., & McKay, R. (2001). Do facial averageness and symmetry signal health? *Evolution and Human Behavior, 22,* 31–46.

Ridley, M. (2003). *The agile gene.* New York: HarperCollins.

Roese, N., Pennington, G. L., Coleman, J., Janicki, M., Li, N. P., & Kenrick, D. T. (2006). Sex differences in regret: All for love or some for lust? *Personality & Social Psychology Bulletin, 32,* 770–780.

Roney, J. R., & Simmons, Z. L. (2008). Women's estradiol predicts preference for facial cues of men's testosterone. *Hormones and Behavior, 53,* 14–19.

Rosenberg, S., Nelson, C., & Vivekananthan, P. S. (1968). A multidimensional approach to the structure of personality impressions. *Journal of Personality and Social Psychology, 9,* 283–294.

Rule, N. O., & Ambady, N. (2008). Brief exposures: Male sexual orientation is accurately perceived at 50 ms. *Journal of Experimental Social Psychology, 44,* 1100–1105.

Sagarin, B. J. (2005). Reconsidering evolved sex differences in jealousy: Comment on Harris (2003). *Personality & Social Psychology Review, 9,* 62–75.

Sagarin, B. J., Becker, D. V. Guadagno, R. E., Nicastle, L. D., Millevoi, A. (2003). Sex differences (and similarities) in jealousy: The moderating influence of infidelity experience and sexual orientation of the infidelity. *Evolution & Human Behavior, 24,* 17–23.

Sanna, L. J., & Parks, C. D. (1997). Group research trends in social and organizational psychology: Whatever happened to intragroup research? *Psychological Science, 8,* 261–267.

Schaller, M. (2006). Parasites, behavioral defenses, and the social psychological mechanisms through which cultures are evoked. *Psychological Inquiry, 17*, 96–101.

Schaller, M. (2007). Turning garbage into gold: Evolutionary universals and cross-cultural differences. In S. W. Gangestad & J. A. Simpson (Eds.), *The evolution of mind* (pp. 363–371). New York: Guilford.

Schaller, M. (2008). Evolutionary bases of first impressions. In N. Ambady & J. J. Skowronski (Eds.), *First impressions* (pp. 15–34). New York: Guilford.

Schaller, M., & Abeysinghe, A. M. N. D. (2006). Geographical frame of reference and dangerous intergroup attitudes: A double-minority study in Sri Lanka. *Political Psychology, 27*, 615–631.

Schaller, M., & Duncan, L. A. (2007). The behavioral immune system: Its evolution and social psychological implications. In J. P. Forgas, M. G. Haselton, & W. von Hippel (Eds.), *Evolution and the social mind: Evolutionary psychology and social cognition* (pp. 293–307). New York: Psychology Press.

Schaller, M., & Murray, D. R. (2008). Pathogens, personality and culture: Disease prevalence predicts worldwide variability in sociosexuality, extraversion, and openness to experience. *Journal of Personality and Social Psychology, 95*, 212–221.

Schaller, M., & Neuberg, S. L. (2008). Intergroup prejudices and intergroup conflicts. In C. Crawford & D. L. Krebs (Eds.), *Foundations of evolutionary psychology* (pp. 399–412). Mahwah, NJ: Erlbaum.

Schaller, M., Park, J. H., & Faulkner, J. (2003). Prehistoric dangers and contemporary prejudices. *European Review of Social Psychology, 14*, 105–137.

Schaller, M., Park, J. H., & Kenrick, D. T. (2007). Human evolution and social cognition. In R. I. M. Dunbar & L. Barrett (Eds.), *Oxford handbook of evolutionary psychology* (pp. 491–504). Oxford, UK: Oxford University Press.

Schaller, M., Park, J. H., & Mueller, A. (2003). Fear of the dark: Interactive effects of beliefs about danger and ambient darkness on ethnic stereotypes. *Personality and Social Psychology Bulletin, 29*, 637–649.

Schinka, J. A., Busch, R. M., & Robinchaux-Keene, N. (2004). A meta-analysis of the association between the serotonin transporter gene polymorphism (5-HTTLPR) and trait anxiety. *Molecular Psychiatry, 9*, 197–202.

Schmitt, D. P. (2005). Sociosexuality from Argentina to Zimbabwe: A 48-nation study of sex, culture, and strategies of human mating. *Behavioral and Brain Sciences, 28*, 247–311.

Schmitt, D. P., and 118 members of International Sexuality Description Project. (2003). Universal sex differences in the desire for sexual variety: Tests from 52 nations, 6 continents, and 13 islands. *Journal of Personality & Social Psychology, 85*, 85–104.

Schmitt, D. P., & Pilcher, J. J. (2004). Evaluating evidence of psychological adaptation: How do we know one when we see one? *Psychological Science, 15*, 643–649.

Scott, J. P. (1992). Aggression: Functions and control in social systems. *Aggressive Behavior, 18*, 1–20.

Segal, N. L., & Hershberger, S. L. (1999). Cooperation and competition in adolescent twins: Findings from a prisoner's dilemma game. *Evolution and Human Behavior, 20*, 29–51.

Sell, A., Cosmides, L., Tooby, J., Sznycer, D., von Rueden, C., & Gurven, M. (2009). Human adaptations for the visual assessment of strength and fighting ability from the body and face. *Proceedings of the Royal Society, 276*(1656), 575–584.

Shackelford, T. K., Goetz, A. T., LaMunyon, C. W., Quintus, B. J., & Weekes-Shackelford, V. A. (2004). Sex differences in sexual psychology produce sex similar preferences for a short-term mate. *Archives of Sexual Behavior, 33*, 405–412.

Shackelford, T. K., LeBlanc, G. J., & Drass, E. (2000). Emotional reactions to infidelity. *Cognition and Emotion, 14*, 643–659.

Sheldon, K. M., & McGregor, H. (2000). Extrinsic Value Orientation and the "tragedy of the commons." *Journal of Personality, 68*, 383–411.

Sherman, P. W., & Billing, J. (1999). Darwinian gastronomy: Why we use spices. *BioScience, 49*, 453–463.

Sherry, D. F., & Schacter, D. L. (1987). The evolution of multiple memory systems. *Psychological Review, 94*, 439–454.

Sidanius, J., & Pratto, F. (1999). *Social dominance: An intergroup theory of social hierarchy and oppression.* New York: Cambridge University Press.

Sidanius, J., Pratto, F., & Brief, D. (1995). Group dominance and the political psychology of gender: A cross-cultural comparison. *Political Psychology, 16*, 381–396.

Simpson, J. A., & Campbell, L. (2005). Methods of evolutionary sciences. In D. M. Buss (Ed.), *The handbook of evolutionary psychology* (pp. 119–144). Hoboken, NJ: John Wiley & Sons.

Simpson, J. A., & Gangestad, S. W. (1991). Individual differences in sociosexuality: Evidence for convergent and discriminant validity. *Journal of Personality and Social Psychology, 67*, 870–883.

Simpson, J. A., & Gangestad, S. W. (1992). Sociosexuality and romantic partner choice. *Journal of Personality, 60*, 31–51.

Simpson, J. A., Gangestad, S. W., & Lerma, M. (1990). Perception of physical attractiveness: Mechanisms involved in the maintenance of romantic relationships. *Journal of Personality and Social Psychology, 59*, 1192–1201.

Snyder, C. R., & Fromkin, H. L (1980). *Uniqueness: The human pursuit of difference.* New York: Plenum Press.

Sober, E., & Wilson, D. S. (1998). *Unto others: The evolution and psychology of unselfish behavior.* Cambridge, MA: Harvard University Press.

Stearns, S. C., Allal, N. & Mace, R. (2008). Life history theory and human development. In C. Crawford & D. L. Krebs (Eds.), *Foundations of evolutionary psychology* (pp. 47–69). Mahwah, NJ: Erlbaum.

Steiner, I. D. (1974). Whatever happened to the group in social psychology? *Journal of Experimental Social Psychology, 10*, 94–108.

Stewart-Williams, S. (2008). Human beings as evolved nepotists: Exceptions to the rue and effects of cost of help. *Human Nature, 19*, 414–425.

Suomi, S. J. (1982). Sibling relationships in nonhuman primates. In M. E. Lamb & B. Sutton-Smith (Eds.), *Sibling relationships.* Mahwah, NJ: Erlbaum.

Taylor, S., Way, B., Welch, W., Hilmert, C., Lehman, B., & Eisenberger, N. (2006). Early family environment, current adversity, the serotonin transporter promoter polymorphism, and depressive symptomatology. *Biological Psychiatry, 60*, 671–676.

Tesser, A. (1993). The importance of heritability in psychological research: The case of attitudes. *Psychological Review, 100*, 129–142.

Thagard, P. (2000). *Coherence in thought and action.* Cambridge, MA: MIT Press.

Thornhill, R., Fincher, C. L., & Aran, D. (2009). Parasites, democratization, and the liberalization of values across contemporary countries. *Biological Reviews, 84,* 113–131.

Thornhill, R., & Gangestad, S. W. (1999a). Facial attractiveness. *Trends in Cognitive Sciences, 3*, 452–460.

Thornhill, R., & Gangestad, S. W. (1999b). The scent of symmetry: A human sex pheromone that signals fitness? *Evolution and Human Behavior, 20*, 175–201.

Thornhill, R., & Thornhill, N. W. (1992). The evolutionary psychology of men's sexual coercion. *Behavioral and Brain Sciences, 15*, 363–375.

Tooby, J., & Cosmides, L. (1992). The psychological foundations of culture. In J. H. Barkow, L. Cosmides, & J. Tooby (Eds.), *The adapted mind* (pp. 19–136). New York: Oxford University Press.

Tooley, G. A., Karakis, M., Stokes, M., Ozanne-Smith, J. (2006). Generalising the Cinderella effect to unintentional childhood fatalities. *Evolution and Human Behavior, 27,* 224–230.

Trivers, R. L. (1972). Parental investment and sexual selection. In B. Campbell (Ed.), *Sexual selection and the descent of man* (pp. 136–179). Chicago: Aldine-Atherton.

Trivers, R. L. (1985). *Social evolution*. Menlo Park, NJ: Benjamin/Cummings.

Twenge, J. M., Baumeister, R. F., DeWall, C. N., Ciarocco, N. J., & Bartels, J. M. (2007). Social exclusion decreases prosocial behavior. *Journal of Personality and Social Psychology, 92*, 56–66.

Van Vugt, M. (2006). Evolutionary origins of leadership and followership. *Personality and Social Psychology Review, 10*, 354–371.

Van Vugt, M., De Cremer, D. & Janssen, D. (2007). Gender differences in cooperation and competition: The male warrior hypothesis. *Psychological Science, 18*, 19–23.

Van Vugt, M., Hogan, R., & Kaiser, R. (2008). Leadership, followership, and evolution: Some lessons from the past. *American Psychologist*, 63, 182–196.

Van Vugt, M., & Spisak, B. R. (2008). Sex differences in the emergence of leadership during competitions within and between groups. *Psychological Science, 19*, 854–858.

Van Vugt, M., & Van Lange, P. A. M. (2006). The altruism puzzle: Psychological adaptations for prosocial behavior. In M. Schaller, J. A. Simpson, & D. T. Kenrick (Eds.), *Evolution and social psychology* (pp. 237–261). New York: Psychology Press.

Vanneste, S., Verplaetse, J., Van Hiel, A., & Braeckman, J. (2007). Attention bias toward noncooperative people. A dot probe classification study in cheating detection. *Evolution and Human Behavior, 28*, 272–276.

Webster, G. D. (2003). Prosocial behavior in families: Moderators of resource sharing. *Journal of Experimental Social Psychology, 39*, 644–652.

Weeden, J., Cohen, A. B., & Kenrick, D. T. (2008). Religious attendance as reproductive support. *Evolution & Human Behavior, 29*, 327–334.

Weisfeld, G. (1994). Aggression and dominance in the social world of boys. In J. Archer (Ed.), *Male violence* (pp. 43–69). New York: Routledge.

Wiederman, M. W. (1993). Evolved gender differences in mate preferences: Evidence from personal advertisements. *Ethology and Sociobiology, 14*, 331–352.

Wiederman, M. W., & Allgeier, E. R. (1992). Gender differences in mate selection criteria: Sociobiological or socioeconomic explanation? *Ethology and Sociobiology, 13*, 115–124.

Wilcoxon, H. C., Dragoin, W. B., & Kral, P. A. (1971). Illness-induced aversions in rat and quail: Relative salience of visual and gustatory cues. *Science, 171*, 826–828.

Williams, G. C. (1966). *Adaptation and natural selection*. Princeton, NJ: Princeton University Press.

Wilson, D. S., Van Vugt, M., & O'Gorman, R. (2008). Multilevel selection theory and major evolutionary transitions: Implications for psychological science. *Current Directions in Psychological Science, 17*, 6–9.

Wilson, E. J., & Sherrell, D. L. (1993). Source effects in communication and persuasion research: A meta-analysis of effect size. *Journal of the Academy of Marketing Science, 21*, 101–112.

Wilson, E. O. (1975). *Sociobiology: The new synthesis*. Cambridge, MA: Harvard University Press.

Wilson, M. I., & Daly, M. (1985). Competitiveness, risk-taking and violence: The young male syndrome. *Ethology and Sociobiology, 6*, 59–73.

Wilson, M. I., & Daly, M. (1992). Who kills whom in spouse killings? On the exceptional sex ratio of spousal homicides in the United States. *Criminology, 30*, 189–215.

Wood, W., & Eagly, A. H. (2002). A cross-cultural analysis of the behavior of women and men: Implications for the origins of sex differences. *Psychological Bulletin, 128*, 699–727.

Yamagishi, T., Tanida, S., Mashima, R., Shimoma, E., & Kanazawa, S. (2003). You can judge a book by its cover: Evidence that cheaters may look different from cooperators. *Evolution and Human Behavior, 24*, 290–301.

Yuki, M., & Yokota, K. (2009). The primal warrior: Outgroup threat priming enhances intergroup discrimination in men but not women. *Journal of Experimental Social Psychology, 45*, 271–274.

Zebrowitz, L. A., Fellous, J. M., Mignault, A., & Andreoletti, C. (2003). Trait impressions as overgeneralized responses to adaptively significant facial qualities: Evidence from connectionist modeling. *Personality and Social Psychology Review, 7*, 194–215.

Zebrowitz, L. A., & Montepare, J. (2006). The ecological approach to person perception: Evolutionary roots and contemporary offshoots. In M. Schaller, J. A. Simpson, & D. T. Kenrick (Eds.), *Evolution and social psychology* (pp. 81–113). New York: Psychology Press.

Zeifman, D., & Hazan, C. (1997). Attachment: The bond in pair-bonds. In J. A. Simpson & D. T. Kenrick (Eds.), *Evolutionary social psychology*. Mahwah, NJ: Erlbaum.

Chapter 22

Morality

JONATHAN HAIDT AND SELIN KESEBIR

In one of the earliest textbooks of social psychology, William McDougall wrote that "The fundamental problem of social psychology is the moralization of the individual by the society into which he is born as a creature in which the non-moral and purely egoistic tendencies are so much stronger than any altruistic tendencies" (McDougall, 1908/1998, p. 18). McDougall dreamed of a social psychology that would span the study of individuals and societies, and he believed morality would be the main bridge. He hoped that social psychology would one day document the full set of "instincts" and other endowments present in individual minds, and then demonstrate how these were activated and combined to create large and cooperative groups of individuals. If McDougall could come back today and see how his beloved field has fared, what would he think of its progress?

A brief survey of five of the top current textbooks (Aronson, Wilson, & Akert, 2007; Baumeister & Bushman, 2008; Gilovich, Keltner, & Nisbett, 2006; Kassin, Fein, & Markus, 2008; Myers, 2008) shows that social psychology has made uneven progress on the study of morality in the last century. On one hand, the words "moral" and "morality" are minor entries in the indices of these books, referring to an average of 6.8 pages combined. The field known as "moral psychology" was, until recently, a part of developmental psychology, focused on the cognitive-developmental approach of Lawrence Kohlberg (1969). On the other hand, the terms "altruism" and "prosocial behavior" are very prominent in these textbooks, given a full chapter in four of the books and a half-chapter in the fifth. Furthermore, social psychologists have long studied topics related to morality—such as aggression, empathy, obedience, fairness, norms, and prejudice—without calling it morality. So just as Molière's Monsieur Jourdain discovers that he had been speaking in prose his whole life, social

psychology can, perhaps, claim to have been speaking about morality its whole life.

But if so, then what does it have to say? Is the social psychology of morality the claim that situational factors predominate (e.g., Milgram, 1963), but that they often interact with personality traits such as self-esteem (Bushman & Baumeister, 1998)? Is it the sum of research on nice behaviors (primarily altruism) and nasty behaviors (such as conformity, aggression, and racial discrimination)? Is there any theoretical or explanatory framework that links these phenomena and approaches together?

This chapter assesses the state of the art in moral psychology from a social-psychological perspective. Moral psychology is undergoing a multidisciplinary renaissance, and social psychology is one of the central fields in this "new synthesis" (Haidt, 2007). Even if no grand unified theory of morality is ever supported—morality may simply be too heterogeneous and multifaceted—progress is so rapid, and the bridges between disciplines are now so numerous that the days of unconnected mini-theories are over. Whatever happens over the next ten years, the trend will likely be toward greater integration and "consilience"—a term revived by E. O. Wilson (1998) that refers to the "jumping together" or unification of knowledge across fields.

The chapter begins with the story of the "great narrowing"—the historical process in which morality got reduced from virtue-based conceptions of the good person down to quandaries about what people should do. In social psychology this narrowing led to a focus on issues related to harm (including antisocial and prosocial behavior) and fairness (including justice and equity). The chapter argues for a return to a broader conception of the moral domain that better accommodates the diverse and often group-focused moralities found around the world. The chapter then tells

We thank David DeSteno, Peter Ditto, Susan Fiske, Dan Gilbert, Jesse Graham, Craig Joseph, Robert Kurzban, Ara Norenzayan, and David Pizarro for helpful comments and criticisms of earlier drafts. Contact information: e-mail: Haidt@virginia.edu.

the story of the "new synthesis" in moral psychology that has shifted attention away from reasoning (and its development) and onto emotions, intuitions, and social factors (which are more at home in social psychology than in developmental psychology).

The chapter's review of empirical research is organized under three principles that have emerged as unifying ideas in this new synthesis: (1) Intuitive primacy (but not dictatorship); (2) moral thinking is for social doing; and (3) morality binds and builds. The chapter is entirely descriptive; it is about how moral psychology works. It does not address normative questions about what is really right or wrong, nor does it address prescriptive questions about how moral judgment or behavior could be improved. The goal of this chapter is to explain what morality really is and why McDougall was right to urge social psychologists to make morality one of their fundamental concerns.

WHAT IS MORALITY ABOUT?

Soon after human beings figured out how to write, they began writing about morality, law, and religion, which were often the same thing. Kings and priests were fond of telling people what to do. As the axial age progressed (800 BCE to 200 BCE), many societies East and West began to supplement these lists of rules with a sophisticated psychology of virtue (Aristotle, 1941; Leys, 1997). An important feature of virtue-based approaches is that they aim to educate children not just by teaching rules, but by shaping perceptions, emotions, and intuitions. This is done in part through providing exemplars of particular virtues, often in the form of narratives (MacIntyre, 1981; Vitz, 1990). In epic poems (e.g., Homer's *Iliad*, the *Mahabharata* in India, the *Shahnameh* in Persia), and in stories of the lives of saints and other moral exemplars (e.g., the Gospels or the *Sunna* of Muhammad), protagonists exemplify virtuous conduct and illustrate the terrible consequences of moral failings.

A second important feature of virtue ethics is that virtues are usually thought to be multiple (rather than being reducible to a single "master virtue" or principle[1]), local (saturated with cultural meaning), and often context- or role-specific. The virtues prized by a nomadic culture differ from those of settled agriculturalists, and from those of city-dwellers (Ibn-Khaldun, 2004; MacIntyre, 1981; Nisbett & Cohen, 1996). A third feature of virtue-based approaches is that they emphasize practice and habit, rather than propositional

knowledge and deliberative reasoning. Virtues are skills of social perception and action (Churchland, 1998; Dewey, 1922; McDowell, 1979) that must be acquired and refined over a lifetime. Morality is not a body of knowledge that can be learned by rote or codified in general ethical codes or decision procedures.

Virtue-based approaches to morality remained dominant in the West up through the Middle Ages (Christian and Islamic philosophers relied directly on Aristotle). They are still in evidence in the "character education" approaches favored by many conservative and religious organizations (Bennett, 1993; Hunter, 2000), and they are undergoing a renaissance in philosophy today (Chappell, 2006; Crisp, 1996).

The Great Narrowing

European philosophers, however, began developing alternate approaches to morality in the eighteenth century. As God retreated from the (perceived) management of daily life, and as traditions lost their authority, Enlightenment philosophers tried to reconstruct ethics (and society) from secular first principles (MacIntyre, 1981; Pincoffs, 1986). Two approaches emerged as the leading contenders: *deontology* and *consequentialism*. Deontologists focused on duties—on the rightness or wrongness of actions considered independently of their consequences. Immanuel Kant produced the most important deontological theory by grounding morality in the logic of non-contradiction: He argued that actions were right only if a person could consistently and rationally will that the rule governing her action be a universal rule governing the actions of others. In contrast, consequentialists (such as Jeremy Bentham and John Stuart Mill) proposed that actions be judged by their consequences alone. Their rule was even simpler than Kant's: Act always in the way that will bring about the greatest total good.

These two approaches have been among the main combatants in moral philosophy for 200 years. But despite their many differences, they have much in common, including an emphasis on parsimony (ethics can be derived from a single rule), an insistence that moral decisions must be reasoned (by logic or calculation) rather than felt or intuited, and a focus on the abstract and universal, rather than the concrete and particular. Most important, deontologists and consequentialists have both shrunk the scope of ethical inquiry from the virtue ethicist's question of "whom should I *become*?" down to the narrower question of "what is the right thing to *do*?" The philosopher Edmund Pincoffs (1986) documents and laments this turn to what he calls "quandary ethics." He says that modern textbooks present ethics as a set of tools for resolving dilemmas, which encourages explicit rule-based thinking.

---

[1]But see McDowell (1979) for the view that each virtue is a special case of a single general perceptual capacity.

Ethics has been narrowed to quandary ethics in psychology too. Freud (1923/1962) and Durkheim (1925/1973) both had thick conceptions of morality; both men asked how it happened that individuals became willing participants in complex and constraining social orders. (This was the very question that McDougall said was fundamental for social psychology.) Yet by the 1970s, moral psychology had largely become a subfield of developmental psychology that examined how children and young adults solved quandaries. The most generative quandaries were "Should Heinz steal a drug to save his wife's life?" (Kohlberg, 1969) and "Should I have an abortion?" (Gilligan, 1982). Social psychology had also dropped the question of moralization, focusing instead on situational factors that influenced the resolution of quandaries, for example, about obedience (Milgram, 1963), bystander intervention (Latane & Darley, 1970), and other forms of prosocial behavior (Batson, O'Quinn, Fulty, Vanderplass, & Isen, 1983; Isen & Levin, 1972). One of the most active areas of current research in moral psychology uses quandaries in which one choice is deontologically correct (don't throw a switch that will divert a trolley and kill one person) and the other is consequentially correct (do kill the one person if it will save five others [Greene, 2008; Hauser, 2006]).

Moral psychology, then, has become the study of how individuals resolve quandaries, pulled not just by self-interest, but also by two distinctively moral sets of moral concerns. The first set might be labeled *harm/care* (including concerns about suffering, nurturance, and the welfare of people and sometimes animals); the second set can be called *fairness/reciprocity* (including justice and related notions of rights, which specify who owes what to whom). The greatest debate in the recent history of moral psychology was between proponents of these two sets of concerns. Kohlberg (1969; Kohlberg, Levine, & Hewer, 1983) argued that moral development *was* the development of reasoning about justice, whereas Gilligan (1982) argued that the "ethic of care" was an independent part of moral psychology, with its own developmental trajectory. Gilligan's claims that the ethic of care was more important for women than men has received at best mixed support (Walker, 1984), but the field of moral development ultimately came to general agreement that both sets of concerns are the proper domain of moral psychology (Gibbs, 2003). In fact, the *Handbook of Moral Development* (Killen & Smetana, 2006) summarizes the field symbolically on its cover with two images: the scales of justice and a sculpture of a parent and child. It is not surprising, therefore, that when psychologists have offered definitions of morality, they have followed philosophers in proposing definitions tailored for quandary ethics. Here is the most influential definition in moral psychology, from Turiel (1983, p. 3), who defined the moral domain as "prescriptive judgments of justice, rights, and welfare pertaining to how people ought to relate to each other." Turiel specifically excludes rules and practices that don't directly prevent harmful or unfair consequences to other people. Such rules and practices are mere social conventions, useful for efficient social regulation, but not part of morality itself. This way of thinking (morality = not harming or cheating others) has become a kind of academic common sense, an assumption shared widely by educated secular people. For example, in *Letter to a Christian Nation*, Harris (2006, p. 8) gives us this definition of morality: "Questions of morality are questions about happiness and suffering . . . To the degree that our actions can affect the experience of other creatures positively or negatively, questions of morality apply." He then shows that the Bible and the Koran are immoral books because they are not primarily about happiness and suffering, and in many places they advocate harming people.

But can it really be true that the two books most widely revered as moral guides in the history of humanity are not really about morality? Or is it possible that Turiel and Harris have defined morality in a parochial way, one that works well for educated, secular Westerners, but that excludes much that other people value?

Redefining Morality: Beyond Harm and Fairness

A good way to escape from parochialism is to travel, or, at least, to read reports from those who have gone abroad. Anthropologists and cultural psychologists have offered several ways of describing variations in the world's cultures, and the most frequent element is the idea that construals of the self vary on a dimension from collectivism/interdependence to individualism/independence (Hogg, 2010; Markus & Kitayama, 1991; Shweder & Bourne, 1984; Triandis, 1995). The anthropologist Mary Douglas (1982, p. 206) called this dimension "group," which refers to the degree to which "the individual's life is absorbed in and sustained by group membership."

One of the earliest and still richest treatments of this idea is Tönnies's (1887/2001) classic dimension running from *Gemeinschaft* (community) to *Gesellschaft* (civil society). *Gemeinschaft* refers to the traditional and (until recently) most widespread form of human social organization: relatively small and enduring communities of people bound together by the three pillars (whether real or imagined) of shared blood, shared place, and shared mind or belief. People keep close track of what everyone else is doing, and every aspect of behavior (including clothing, food, and sexual choices) can be regulated, limited, and judged by others. But as technology, capitalism, mobility, and new ideas about individualism transformed European ways of life in the nineteenth century, social organization moved increasingly toward *Gesellschaft*—the kind of civil society in which individuals are free to move about, make choices for themselves, and design whatever lives they choose so long as they don't harm or cheat others. (For more recent accounts of how modernity created a thinner and less binding morality, see Hunter, 2000; Nisbet, 1933/1966; Shweder, Mahapatra, & Miller, 1987; see A. P. Fiske, 1991, on the decreasing reliance on "communal sharing" and increasing use of "market pricing" in social relationships.)

Moral psychology to date has been largely the psychology of *Gesellschaft*. In part to gain experimental control, researchers usually examine people harming, helping, or cooperating with strangers in the lab (e.g., Batson et al., 1983; Sanfey et al., 2003) or judging hypothetical strangers who hurt or cheat other strangers (e.g., Greene, Sommerville, Nystrom, Darley, & Cohen, 2001; Kohlberg, 1969). Morality as defined by psychologists is mostly about what we owe to each other in order to make *Gesellschaft* possible: Don't hurt others, don't infringe on their rights, and if some people are having particularly serious problems, then it is good (but not always obligatory) to help them. If the entire world was one big *Gesellschaft*, then this moral psychology would be adequate. But it is as clear today as it was in Tönnies's time that real towns and real nations are mixtures of the two types. The wealthiest districts of New York and London may approximate the *Gesellschaft* ideal, but just a few miles from each are ethnic enclaves with honor codes, arranged marriages, and patriarchal families, all of which are markers of *Gemeinschaft*.

A comprehensive moral psychology must therefore look beyond the psychology of *Gesellschaft*. It should study the full array of psychological mechanisms that are active in the moral lives of people in diverse cultures. It should go beyond what's "in the head" to show how psychological mechanisms and social structures mutually influence each other (A. P. Fiske, 1991; Shweder, 1990). To encourage such a broadening, Haidt (2008) proposed an alternative to Turiel's (1983) definition. Rather than specifying the *content* of moral issues (e.g., "justice, rights, and welfare"), this definition specifies the *function* of moral systems:

> Moral systems are interlocking sets of values, virtues, norms, practices, identities, institutions, technologies, and evolved psychological mechanisms that work together to suppress or regulate selfishness and make cooperative social life possible.[2]

This functionalist approach allows psychology to move from moral parochialism (i.e., the belief that there is one universal moral domain that happens to include the values most prized by the secular academics who defined the domain) to moral pluralism (i.e., the belief that there are multiple incompatible but morally defensible ways of organizing a society [Shweder, Much, Mahapatra, & Park, 1997]). In this functionalist approach, there are multiple defensible moralities because societies have found multiple ways to suppress selfishness. The free and open social order of a big Western city is a moral system (requiring rights and justice to protect the welfare of others) just as is the more binding and constricting social order of a small Indian village. The suppression of selfishness in a big city may rely more upon padlocks, police, and norms of noninterference than on caste, gossip, and norms of respect, but in either case, selfish behavior is controlled not just by individual conscience and direct concerns about harm, but by an interlocking combination of physical, psychological, cultural, and institutional mechanisms.

The study of such complex combinations clearly requires collaboration among many disciplines. Social psychology is well suited to be the central field in this study—as McDougall had hoped—because social psychologists are adept at research on values, norms, identities, and psychological mechanisms that suppress selfishness (such as empathy and reciprocity). But social-psychological work must be integrated "up" a level of analysis and made consilient with "outside-the-head" elements studied by anthropologists and sociologists (such as institutions and social practices). Social psychological work must also be integrated "down" a level of analysis and made consilient with brain-based explanations of those mechanisms and with evolutionary accounts of how those mechanisms evolved (Hogg, 2010; Neuberg, Shaller, & Kenrick, 2010). The next section of this chapter describes how multiple disciplines are indeed coming together to study morality at multiple levels of analysis.

THE NEW SYNTHESIS IN MORAL PSYCHOLOGY

In 1975, E. O. Wilson predicted that ethics would soon become part of the "new synthesis" of sociobiology, in which distal mechanisms (such as evolution), proximal mechanisms (such as neural processes), and the socially constructed web of meanings and institutions (as studied by the humanities and social sciences) would all be integrated into a full explanation of human morality. The key to this integration, Wilson argued, was to begin with the moral intuitions given to us by our evolved emotions.

---

[2]This definition is an expansion of the one originally offered in Haidt (2008).

Wilson suggested that moral philosophers had in fact been following their intuitions all along:

> ethical philosophers intuit the deontological canons of morality by consulting the emotive centers of their own hypothalamic-limbic system. This is also true of the developmentalists [such as Kohlberg], even when they are being their most severely objective. Only by interpreting the activity of the emotive centers as a biological adaptation can the meaning of the canons be deciphered (p. 563).

Philosophers did not take kindly to this debunking of their craft. Neither did moral psychologists, who at that time were deeply invested in the study of reasoning. Even social psychologists, who were studying moral-emotional responses such as empathy (Batson et al., 1983) and anger (Berkowitz, 1965) were slow to embrace sociobiology, kept away in part by the perception that it had some morally and politically unpalatable implications (Pinker, 2002). In the 1980s, Wilson's prediction seemed far from prophetic, and the various fields that studied ethics remained resolutely unsynthesized.

But two trends in the 1980s laid the groundwork for E. O. Wilson's synthesis to begin in the 1990s. The first was the affective revolution—the multidisciplinary upsurge of research on emotion that followed the cognitive revolution of prior decades (Fischer & Tangney, 1995; see Frank, 1988; Gibbard, 1990; and Kagan, 1984 for important early works on emotion and morality). The second was the rebirth of sociobiology as evolutionary psychology (Barkow, Cosmides, & Tooby, 1992). These two trends had an enormous influence on social psychology, which had a long history of questioning the importance of conscious reasoning (e.g., Nisbett & Wilson, 1977; Zajonc, 1980), and which became a key player in the new interdisciplinary science of emotion that emerged in the 1990s (see the first edition of the *Handbook of Emotions*, Lewis & Haviland-Jones, 1993). Emotion and evolution were quickly assimilated into dual-process models of behavior in which the "automatic" processes were the ancient, fast emotions and intuitions that E. O. Wilson had described, and the "controlled" process was the evolutionarily newer and motivationally weaker language-based reasoning studied by Kohlberg and relied upon (too heavily) by moral philosophers. (See Chaiken & Trope, 1999, but this idea goes back to Zajonc, 1980, and before him to Freud, 1900/1976, and Wundt, 1907).

In telling this story of the shift from moral reasoning to moral emotion and intuition, two books published in the 1990s deserve special mention. Damasio's (1994) *Descartes' Error* showed that areas of the prefrontal cortex that integrate emotion into decision making were crucial for moral judgment and behavior, and de Waal's (1996) *Good Natured* showed that most of the "building blocks" of human morality could be found in the emotional reactions of chimpanzees and other primates. A well-written trade book can reach across disciplinary lines more effectively than can any journal article. In the late 1990s, as these and other trade books (e.g., Ridley, 1996; Wright, 1994) were read widely by researchers in every field that studied ethics, E. O. Wilson's prediction began to come true. The move to emotion and affectively laden intuition as the new anchors of the field accelerated in 2001 when the research of Greene and colleagues (2001) on the neural basis of moral judgment was published in *Science*. The next month, Haidt's (2001) cross-disciplinary review of the evidence for an intuitionist approach to morality was published in *Psychological Review*.

In the years since 2001, morality has become one of the major interdisciplinary topics of research in the academy. Three of the fields most active in this integration are social psychology, social-cognitive neuroscience, and evolutionary science, but many other scholars are joining in, including anthropologists (Boehm, in press; A. P. Fiske, 2004; Henrich & Henrich, 2007), cognitive scientists (Casebeer, 2003; Lakoff, 2008), developmental psychologists (Bloom, 2004), economists (Clark, 2007; Gintis, Bowles, Boyd, & Fehr, 2005a; Fehr & Gächter, 2002), historians (McNeill 1995; Smail, 2008); legal theorists (Kahan, 2005; Robinson, Kurzban, & Jones, 2007; Sunstein, 2005), and philosophers (Appiah, 2008; Caruthers, Laurence, & Stich, 2006; Joyce, 2006; Prinz, 2008).

Haidt (2007) described three principles that have characterized this new synthesis, and these principles organize the literature review presented in the next three sections of this chapter: (1) Intuitive primacy (but not dictatorship); (2) moral thinking is for social doing, and (3) morality binds and builds. It should be noted that the chapter focuses on moral judgment and moral thinking rather than on moral behavior. Behavior will be mentioned when relevant, but because of the great narrowing, the term "moral behavior" has until now largely been synonymous for social psychologists with the terms "altruism," "helping," and "prosocial behavior" (and sometimes fairness and honesty as well). Many excellent reviews of this work are available (Batson, 1998; Dovidio, Piliavin, Schroeder, & Penner, 2006). If this chapter is successful in arguing for a broadened conception of moral psychology and the moral domain, then perhaps in the future there will be a great deal more work to review beyond these well-studied topics.

INTUITIVE PRIMACY (BUT NOT DICTATORSHIP)

According to a prominent moral philosopher, "There has been a controversy started of late . . . concerning the general foundation of morals; whether they be derived from reason, or from sentiment; whether we attain the knowledge of them by a chain of argument and induction, or by an immediate feeling and finer internal sense." These words were published in 1777 by David Hume (1777/1960, p. 2), who, like E. O. Wilson, argued for sentiment as the foundation and "finer internal sense" (i.e., intuition) as the mechanism by which we attain knowledge of right and wrong. The controversy is now in its third century, but recent evidence points to a potential resolution: Hume was mostly right, although moral reasoning still matters, even if it is not the original source from which morals are "derived." A central challenge for modern moral psychology is to specify when, where, and how reason and sentiment interact.

But first, it is crucial that terminology be clarified. There is a long history in social psychology of contrasting "cognition" with "emotion" (or with "affect" more broadly). Partisans of either side can show that their favored term is the more important one just by making it more inclusive and the other term less so. Do you think "affect" rules? If so, then you can show, as Zajonc (1980) did, that people often have quick reactions of liking or disliking before they have done enough "cognitive" processing to know, *consciously*, what the object is. But if you favor "cognitive" approaches, you need only expand your definition so that "cognition" includes all information processing done anywhere in the brain, at which point it's easy to show that "affect" can't happen until some neural activity has processed some kind of perceptual information. (This is the basis of Lazarus's 1984 response to Zajonc and of Hauser's 2006 critique of "Humean" moral judgment; see also Huebner, Dwyer, & Hauser, 2009).

Moral psychology has long been hampered by debates about the relative importance of "cognition" versus "emotion" and "affect." Some clarity may be achieved by noting that moral judgment, like nearly all mental activity, is a kind of cognition. The question is: what kind? Two important kinds of cognition in current moral psychology are moral intuition and moral reasoning; or, as Margolis (1987) put it, "seeing-that" and "reasoning-why."

Moral intuition has been defined as "the sudden appearance in consciousness, or at the fringe of consciousness, of an evaluative feeling (like-dislike, good-bad) about the character or actions of a person, without any conscious awareness of having gone through steps of search, weighing evidence, or inferring a conclusion" (Haidt & Bjorklund, 2008, p. 188). Moral intuition is an example of the automatic processes that Bargh and Chartrand (1999) say comprise most of human mental life. But whereas many automatic processes involve no affect, moral intuitions (as defined here) are a subclass of automatic

processes that always involve at least a trace of "evaluative feeling." Moral intuitions are about good and bad. Sometimes these affective reactions are so strong and differentiated that they can be called moral emotions, such as disgust or gratitude, but usually they are more like the subtle flashes of affect that drive evaluative priming effects (Fazio, Sanbonmatsu, Powell, & Kardes, 1986; Greenwald, Nosek, & Banaji, 2003). Moral intuitions include the moral heuristics described by Sunstein (2005) and Gigerenzer (2007), such as "people should clean up their own messes," which sometimes oppose utilitarian public policies (such as letting companies trade pollution credits).

In contrast to moral intuition, moral reasoning has been defined as "conscious mental activity that consists of transforming given information about people (and situations) in order to reach a moral judgment" (Haidt, 2001, p. 818). To say that moral reasoning is a conscious process means that the process is intentional, effortful, and controllable and that the reasoner is aware that it is going on (Bargh, 1994). Kohlberg himself stated that he was studying such processes: "moral reasoning is the conscious process of using ordinary moral language" (Kohlberg et al., 1983, p. 69).

The contrast of intuition and reasoning, it must be repeated, is a contrast between two *cognitive* processes, one of which almost always has an affective component (see Shweder & Haidt, 1993). This contrast is similar to the one made in Chaiken's (1980) Heuristic-Systematic Model, as well as the one widely used by behavioral economists between "system 1" and "system 2" (Sloman, 1996). "Emotion" and "cognition" cannot fruitfully be contrasted because emotions include so much cognition (Lazarus, 1991). But when intuition and reasoning are contrasted as relatively distinct cognitive processes, the empirical questions become clear: How do the two interact, and what is their relative importance? Existing dual process models allow for many ways of putting the two processes together (Gilbert, 1999). Commonly, the two processes are thought to run with some independence, and reasoning (or "systematic processing," or "system 2") plays the crucial role of correcting the occasional errors of faster and cognitively cheaper intuition (or "heuristic processing," or "system 1"). In moral thinking, however, reasoning appears to have less power and independence; a variety of motives bias it toward finding support for the conclusions already reached by intuitive processes (see Chen & Chaiken, 1999, on the effects of defensive and impression motives; see Ditto, Pizarro, & Tannenbaum, 2009, on motivated moral reasoning). Here are ten brief summaries of work supporting this idea of "intuitive primacy" in moral cognition and a closing section summarizing challenges to the view.

1. People Make Rapid Evaluative Judgments of Others

Zajonc (1980) argued that brains are always and automatically evaluating everything they perceive, even irregular polygons and Chinese ideographs (Monahan, Murphy, & Zajonc, 2000), so when the thing perceived is another person, rapid evaluation is inevitable. Subsequent research has supported his contention. From early work on spontaneous trait inferences (Winter & Uleman, 1984) and evaluative priming (Fazio et al., 1986) through later research using the implicit association test (Greenwald, McGhee, & Schwartz, 1998), thin slices of behavior (Ambady & Rosenthal, 1992), judgments of trustworthiness (Todorov, Mandisodza, Goren, & Hall, 2005), and photographs of moral violations viewed inside an fMRI scanner (Luo et al., 2006), the story has been consistent: People form an initial evaluation of social objects almost instantly, and these evaluations are hard to inhibit or change by conscious will-power. Even when people engage in moral reasoning, they do so in a mental space that has already been prestructured by intuitive processes, including affective reactions that prepare the brain to approach or avoid the person or proposition being considered.

2. Moral Judgments Involve Brain Areas Related to Emotion

People who have damage to the ventro-medial prefrontal cortex (VMPFC) lose the ability to integrate emotions into their judgments and decisions (Damasio, 1994). They still perform well on tests of moral reasoning—they know the moral norms of their society. But when "freed" from the input of feelings, they do not become hyper-ethical Kantians or Millians, able to apply principles objectively. Rather, they lose the ability to know, instantly and intuitively, that ethically suspect actions should not be undertaken. Deprived of intuitive feelings of rightness, they can't decide which way to go, and they end up making poor choices or no choices at all. Like the famous case of Phineas Gage, they often show a decline of moral character (Damasio, 1994). When the damage occurs in early childhood, depriving the person of a lifetime of emotional learning, the outcome goes beyond moral cluelessness to moral callousness, with behavior similar to that of a psychopath (Anderson, Bechara, Damasio, Tranel, & Damasio, 1999).

Complementary work on healthy people has used trolley-type dilemmas pitting consequentialist and deontological outcomes against each other (Greene, Nystrom, Engell, Darley, & Cohen, 2004). This work shows that the choices people make can be predicted (when aggregated across many judgments) by the intensity and time course of activation in emotion areas (such as the VMPFC and the amygdala), relative to areas associated with cool deliberation (including the dorsolateral prefrontal cortex and the anterior cingulate cortex). When emotion areas are most strongly activated, people tend to choose the deontological outcome (don't push the person off of a footbridge, even to stop a train and save five others). But in scenarios that trigger little emotional response, people tend to choose the utilitarian response (go ahead and throw a switch to divert a train that will end up killing one instead of five [Greene et al., 2004; Greene et al., 2001]).

Utilitarian responding is not by itself evidence of reasoning: It is immediately and intuitively obvious that saving five people is better than saving one. More compelling evidence of reasoning is found in the frequency of internal conflicts in these studies. People don't always just go with their first instincts, and in these cases of apparent overriding, there is (on average) a longer response time and increased activity in the anterior cingulate cortex, an area linked to the resolution of response conflicts (Botvinick, Braver, Barch, Carter, & Cohen, 2001). Controlled processing, which might well involve conscious reasoning, seems to be occurring in these cases. Furthermore, patients who have damage to the VMPFC tend to judge all of these dilemmas in a utilitarian way (Koenigs et al., 2007); they seem to have lost the normal flash of horror that most people feel at the thought of pushing people to their (consequentially justifiable) deaths.

3. Morally Charged Economic Behaviors Involve Brain Areas Related to Emotion

Many of the landmark studies in the new field of "neuroeconomics" are demonstrations that people's frequent departures from selfish rationality are well correlated with activity in emotion-related areas, which seem to index judgments of moral condemnation, just as the economist Robert Frank had predicted back in 1988. For example, in the "ultimatum game" (Thaler, 1988), the first player chooses how to divide a sum of money; if the second player rejects that division, then both players get nothing. When the first player proposes a division that departs too far from the fair 50% mark, the second player usually rejects it, and the decision to reject is preceded by increased activity in the anterior insula (Sanfey et al., 2003). That area is often implicated in emotional responding; it receives autonomic feedback from the body, and it links forward to multiple areas of prefrontal cortex involved in decision making (Damasio, 2003). Activity in the insula has been found to correlate directly with degree of concern about equity (Hsu, Anen, & Quartz, 2008). When people cooperate in trust games, they show greater activity in brain areas related to emotion and feelings of reward, including VMPFC, orbitofrontal cortex, nucleus accumbens, and caudate nucleus (Rilling et al., 2007). Similarly, when people choose to make costly charitable donations, they show increased activation in emotion and reward areas (Moll et al., 2006).

4. Psychopaths Have Emotional Deficits

Roughly 1% of men (and many fewer women) are psychopaths, yet this small subset of the population commits as much as 50% of some of the most serious crimes, including serial murder and the killing of police officers (Hare, 1993). Much research on psychopathy points to a specific deficit in the moral emotions. Cleckley (1955) and Hare (1993) give us chilling portraits of psychopaths gliding through life with relatively full knowledge of social and moral norms, but without the emotional reactions that make them *care* about those norms or about the people they hurt along the way. Psychopaths have some emotions; when Hare (p. 53) asked one if he ever felt his heart pound or stomach churn, the man responded: "Of course! I'm not a robot. I really get pumped up when I have sex or when I get into a fight." Furthermore, psychopaths show normal electrodermal responses to images of direct threat (e.g., a picture of a shark's open jaw). But when shown pictures of children in distress, of mutilated bodies, or of piles of corpses, their skin conductance does not change, and they seem to feel nothing (Blair, 1999).

Recent research on psychopaths points to reduced activity (compared to controls) in many areas of the brain, but among the most widely reported are those related to emotionality, including the VMPFC, amygdala, and insula (Blair, 2007; Kiehl, 2006). Those who study psychopaths behaviorally and those who study their brains have converged on the conclusion that the central deficit from which most of the other symptoms may be derived is the inability to feel sympathy, shame, guilt, or other emotions that make the rest of us *care* about the fates of others and the things we do to hurt or help them.

5. Moral-Perceptual Abilities Emerge in Infancy

Before infants can talk, they can recognize and evaluate helping and hurting. Hamlin, Wynn, and Bloom (2007) showed infants (ages 6 or 10 months) puppet-like performances in which a "climber" (a wooden shape with eyes glued to it) struggles to climb up a hill. In some trials the climber is helped by another figure, who gently pushes from below. In other trials the climber is hindered by a third figure, who appears at the top of the hill and repeatedly bashes the climber down the slope. After habituating to these displays, infants were presented with the helper

and the hinderer on a tray in front of them. Infants of both ages showed a strong preference in their reaching behavior: They reached out to touch or pick up the helper. In a subsequent phase of the study, the 10-month-old infants (but not the younger group) looked longer at a display of the climber seeming to cozy up to the hinderer, rather than the helper. The authors conclude that their findings "indicate that humans engage in social evaluation far earlier in development than previously thought, and support the view that the capacity to evaluate individuals on the basis of their social interactions is universal and unlearned" (p. 559).

Just as Baillargeon (1987) showed that infants arrive in the world with an understanding of intuitive physics, these studies suggest that infants are also born with at least the rudiments of an intuitive ethics. They recognize the difference between kind and unkind actors, and prefer puppets who act kindly. If so, then Hume was right that the "general foundation of morals" cannot have been "derived from reason." A more promising candidate is an innate and early-emerging moral-perceptual system that creates negative affect toward harmdoers and positive affect toward helpers. There may be other innate moral-perceptual systems as well, including the ability by 5 months of age to detect and prefer members of one's ingroup based on their accent (Kinzler, Dupoux, & Spelke, 2007), and the ability by 18 months of age to detect when another person needs help and then to offer appropriate help (Warneken & Tomasello, 2006).

6. Manipulating Emotions Changes Judgments

If you change the facts of a case (e.g., say that Heinz stole a drug to save his dog, rather than his wife), people's judgments change too (Kohlberg, 1969), as would be predicted either by a rationalist or an intuitionist. But if you leave the facts alone and manipulate people's feelings instead, you find evidence that emotions play a causal role in moral judgment. Valdesolo and DeSteno (2006), for example, used a dose of positive affect to counteract the normal flash of negative affect caused by the "footbridge" dilemma. Participants who watched a comedy video immediately before completing a questionnaire on which they judged the appropriateness of pushing a man to his (useful) death were more likely to judge in the utilitarian way, whereas an emotionally neutral video had no such effect. The positive affect from the comedy video reduced or counteracted the flash of negative affect that most people get and many follow when responding to the footbridge dilemma.

Conversely, Wheatley, and Haidt (2005) used posthypnotic suggestion to implant an extra flash of disgust whenever participants read a particular word ("take" for half of the participants; "often" for the other half). Participants later made harsher judgments of characters in vignettes that contained the hypnotically enhanced word, compared to vignettes with the non-enhanced word. Some participants even found themselves condemning a character in a story who had done no wrong—a student council representative who "tries to take" or "often picks" discussion topics that would have wide appeal.

Schnall, Haidt, Clore, and Jordan (2008) extended these findings with three additional disgust manipulations: seating participants at a dirty desk (versus a clean one), showing a disgusting video clip (versus a sad or neutral one), and asking participants to make moral judgments in the presence of a bad smelling "fart spray" (or no spray). A notable finding in these studies was that moral judgments grew more severe primarily for those who scored above average on a measure of "private body consciousness" (Miller, Murphy, & Buss, 1981), which is the degree to which people attend to their own bodily sensations. This finding raises the importance of individual differences in the study of morality: Even if the ten literatures reviewed here converge on a general picture of intuitive primacy, there is variation in the degree to which people have gut feelings, follow them, or override them (see Bartels, 2008; Epstein, Pacini, Denes-Raj, & Heier, 1996). For example, individual differences on a measure of disgust sensitivity (Haidt, McCauley, & Rozin, 1994) have been found to predict participants' condemnation of abortion and gay marriage, but not their stances on non-disgust-related issues such as gun control and affirmative action (Inbar, Pizarro, & Bloom, in press). Disgust sensitivity also predicts the degree to which people condemn homosexuals, even among a liberal college sample, and even when bypassing self-report by measuring anti-gay bias using two different implicit measures (Inbar, Pizarro, Knobe, & Bloom, in press).

7. People Sometimes Can't Explain Their Moral Judgments

In the course of several studies on harmless taboo violations (e.g., a family that eats its dead pet dog; a woman who masturbates in unusual ways), Haidt found frequent instances in which participants said that they knew something was morally wrong, even though they could not explain why (Haidt & Hersh, 2001; Haidt, Koller, & Dias, 1993). Cushman, Young, and Hauser (2006), using trolley-type dilemmas, found that participants had conscious access to some of the principles that correlated with their judgments (e.g., harmful actions are worse than harmful omissions), but not others (e.g., harm intended as the means to a goal is worse than harm foreseen as a side effect). These findings are consistent with the notion that the judgment process and the justification process are somewhat independent

(Margolis, 1987; Nisbett & Wilson, 1977; Wilson, 2002). They also illustrate the idea that moral judgment draws on a great variety of intuitive principles—not just emotions. Hauser (2006) and Mikhail (2007) have analogized moral knowledge to rules of grammar that are known intuitively by native speakers who were never taught them explicitly and who cannot articulate them. In this analogy, "a chain of argument and induction" is not the way people learn morals any more than it is the way they learned the grammar of their native language.

8. Reasoning Is Often Guided by Desires

Reasoning involves multiple steps, and any one of them could be biased by intuitive processes. Yet research on everyday reasoning (Kuhn, 1991) and on motivated reasoning (Kunda, 1990) converge on the importance of one particular step: the search for relevant evidence. People do not seem to work very hard to evaluate the quality of evidence that supports statements, medical diagnoses, or personality evaluations that are consistent with their own preferences (Ditto & Lopez, 1992; Ditto, Scepansky, Munro, Apanovitch, & Lockhart, 1998). However, when faced with statements that contradict what they want to believe, people scrutinize the evidence presented to them more closely.

When forced to reason (either by an experimental task or by an unwanted conclusion), people are generally found to be biased hypothesis testers (Pyszczynski & Greenberg, 1987; Snyder & Swann, 1978; Wason, 1969). People choose one side as their starting point and then show a strong confirmation bias (Nickerson, 1998); they set out to find *any* evidence to support their initial idea. If they succeed, they usually stop searching (Perkins, Farady, & Bushey, 1991). If not, they may then consider the other side and look for evidence to support it. But studies of everyday reasoning usually involve questions that are not freighted with emotional commitments (e.g., what are the causes of unemployment? Kuhn, 1991). In such cases, a slight initial preference may be undone or even reversed by the failure to find good supporting evidence.

When making moral judgments, however, the initial preference is likely to be stronger, sometimes even qualifying as a "moral mandate"—a commitment to a conclusion, which makes people judge procedures that lead to the "right" conclusion as fair procedures, even though they reject those same procedures when they lead to the "wrong" conclusion (Mullen & Skitka, 2006; Skitka, Bauman, & Sargis, 2005). If a moral issue is tied to one's political identity (e.g., pro-choice vs. pro-life) so that defensive motivations are at work (Chaiken, Giner-Sorolla, & Chen, 1996), the initial preference may not be reversible by any possible evidence or failure to find evidence. Try, for example, to make the case for the position you oppose on abortion, eugenics, or the use of torture against your nation's enemies. In each case there are utilitarian reasons available on both sides, but many people find it difficult or even painful to search for reasons on the other side. Motivated reasoning is ubiquitous in the moral domain (for a review, see Ditto, Pizarro, & Tannenbaum, 2009).

9. Research in Political Psychology Points to Intuitions, Not Reasoning

There is a long tradition in political science of studying voters using rational choice models (reviewed in Kinder, 1998). But psychologists who study political behavior have generally found that intuition, framing, and emotion are better predictors of political preferences than are self-interest, reasoning about policies, or even assessments of the personality traits of a candidate (Abelson, Kinder, Peters, & Fiske, 1982; Kinder, 1998). Lakoff (1996, 2004) argued that policy issues become intuitively appealing to voters to the extent that they fit within one of two underlying cognitive frames about family life that get applied, unconsciously, to national life: the "strict father" frame (for conservatives) and the "nurturant parent" frame (for liberals).

Westen (2007), based on a broader review of empirical research, argued that "successful campaigns compete in the marketplace of emotions and not primarily in the marketplace of ideas" (p. 305). He describes his own research on four controversial political issues in which he and his colleagues collected measures of people's knowledge of each case and their overall feelings toward the political parties and the main figures involved. In each case, overall feelings of liking (e.g., for Bill Clinton and the Democratic Party) predicted people's judgments about specific issues very well (e.g., "Does the President's behavior meet the standard set forth in the Constitution for an impeachable offense?"). Variables related to factual knowledge, in contrast, contributed almost nothing. Even when relevant evidence was manipulated experimentally (by providing a fake news story that supported or failed to support a soldier accused of torture at Abu Ghraib), emotional variables explained nearly all of the variance in moral judgment. Westen summarizes his findings as follows: "The results are unequivocal that when the outcomes of a political decision have strong emotional implications and the data leave even the slightest room for artistic license, reason plays virtually no role in the decision making of the average citizen" (pp. 112–113). Westen and Lakoff both agree that liberals in the United States have made a grave error in adopting a rationalist or "Enlightenment" model of the human mind and therefore assuming that good arguments about good

policies will convince voters to vote for the Democratic Party. Republicans, they show, have better mastered intuitionist approaches to political persuasion such as framing (for Lakoff) and emotional appeals (for Westen), at least in the three decades before Barack Obama became president.

10. Research on Prosocial Behavior Points to Intuitions, Not Reasoning

From donating a dollar to standing up against genocide, most of the research on prosocial behavior indicates that rapid intuitive processes are where the action is (Loewenstein & Small, 2007; Slovic, 2007). Batson's classic work on the "empathy-altruism hypothesis" demonstrated that people are sometimes motivated to help—even willing to take electric shocks in place of a stranger—by feelings of empathy for another person who is suffering (Batson et al., 1983). Cialdini challenged the interpretation that such behavior reflected true altruism by proposing a "negative state relief hypothesis." He demonstrated that helping is less likely when people think they can escape from their own negative feelings of distress without helping the victim (Cialdini et al., 1987). Subsequent rounds of experiments established that empathic and selfish motives are both at work under some circumstances, but that empathic feelings of concern, including the goal of helping the victim, really do exist, and sometimes do motivate people to help strangers at some cost to themselves (Batson et al., 1988). Even when participants were given a good justification for not helping, or when others couldn't know whether the participant helped, those who felt empathy still helped (Fultz, Batson, Fortenbach, McCarthy, & Varney, 1986). (For reviews of the debate, see Batson, 1991; Dovidio et al. 2006, Chapter 4). There is also evidence that feelings of gratitude can motivate helping behavior, above and beyond considerations of reciprocity (Bartlett & DeSteno, 2006).

Moral intuitions related to suffering and empathy sometimes lead to undesirable consequences such as a radically inefficient distribution of charity. In one study, participants who were encouraged to feel more sympathy toward a fictitious child with a fatal illness were more likely to assign the child to receive immediate help, at the expense of other children who had been waiting for a longer time, were more needy, or had more to gain from the help (Batson, Klein, Highberger, & Shaw, 1995). On a larger scale, charitable giving follows sympathy, not the number of people in need. One child who falls down a well or who needs an unusual surgery triggers an outpouring of donations if the case is covered on the national news (see Loewenstein and Small, 2007 for a review). Lab studies confirm the relative power of sympathy over numbers: Small, Loewenstein, and Slovic (2007) found that a charitable appeal with a single identifiable victim became *less* powerful when statistical information was added to the appeal. Even more surprising, Vastfjall, Peters, and Slovic (in prep) found that a charitable appeal with one identifiable victim became less effective when a second identifiable victim was added. Anything that interferes with one's ability to empathize appears to reduce the charitable response (see also Schelling, 1968; and Kogut & Ritov, 2005).

In addition to feelings of sympathy for the victim, irrelevant external factors often push people toward helpful action, further suggesting the primacy of intuitive reactions. Good weather (Cunningham, 1979), hearing uplifting or soothing music (Fried & Berkowitz, 1979; North, Tarrant, & Hargreaves, 2004), remembering happy memories (Rosenhan, Underwood, & Moore, 1974), eating cookies (Isen & Levin, 1972), and smelling a pleasant aroma such as roasted coffee (Baron, 1997) all led participants to offer more help.

Even if intuitions have "primacy," there is still room for conscious reasoning to exert some direction; manipulations of basic facts, such as the cost-benefit ratio of the helpful action, do alter behavior (Dovidio, Piliavin, Gaertner, Schroeder, Clark, 1991; Latane & Darley, 1970; Midlarsky & Midlarsky, 1973; Piliavin, Piliavin, & Rodin, 1975). It is not clear, however, whether participants evaluated costs and benefits consciously and deliberatively, or whether they did it intuitively and automatically.

Counter-Evidence: When Deliberation Matters

The review so far indicates that most of the action in moral psychology is in automatic processes—particularly but not exclusively emotional reactions. It is crucial to note that no major contributors to the empirical literature say that moral reasoning doesn't happen or doesn't matter. In the social intuitionist model, for example (Haidt, 2001), four of the six links are reasoning links, and reasoning is said to be a frequent contributor to moral judgment in discussions *between people* (who can challenge each others' confirmation bias), and within individuals *when intuitions conflict* (as they often do in lab studies of quandary ethics). The two most critical reviews of the SIM (Huebner et al., 2009; Saltzstein & Kasachkoff, 2004) reduce it erroneously to the claims that emotions (not intuitions) are necessary for all judgments and that reasoning never has causal efficacy, not even between people.

The modal view in moral psychology nowadays is that reasoning and intuition both matter, but that intuition matters more. This is not a normative claim (for even a little bit of good reasoning can save the world from disaster); it is a descriptive one. It is the claim that automatic, intuitive processes happen more quickly and frequently than moral reasoning, and when moral intuitions occur, they alter and guide the ways in which people subsequently (and only sometimes) deliberate. Those deliberations can—but rarely do—overturn one's initial intuitive response. This is what is meant by the principle "intuitive primacy—but not dictatorship."

There are, however, important researchers who do not endorse this principle. First and foremost, there is a large and important group of moral psychologists based mostly in developmental psychology that is strongly critical of the shift to intuitionism (see Killen & Smetana, 2006). Turiel (2006) points out that people make judgments that are intentional, deliberative, and reflective in many realms of knowledge such as mathematics, classification, causality, and intentionality. Children may acquire concepts in these domains slowly, laboriously, and consciously, but once mastered, these concepts can get applied rapidly and effortlessly. Therefore, even when moral judgments are made intuitively by adults, moral knowledge might still have been acquired by deliberative processes in childhood. (Pizarro and Bloom, 2003, make a similar point about the acquisition of moral expertise in adulthood).

Even among moral psychologists who endorse the principle of intuitive primacy, there are active debates about the relationships between intuition and reasoning. How are they to be put together into a dual-process model? The social intuitionist model proposes a dual process model in which reasoning is usually the servant of intuitive processes, sent out to find confirming evidence, but occasionally returning with a finding so important that it triggers new intuitions, and perhaps even a change of mind. In contrast to the SIM, Greene and colleagues (2004) have proposed a more traditional dual process model in which the two processes work independently and often reach different conclusions (for a review of such models in social psychology, see Chaiken & Trope, 1999). Greene (2008) describes these two modes of processing as "controlled cognitive processing," which generally leads to consequentialist conclusions that promote the greater good, and "intuitive emotional processing," which generally leads to deontological conclusions about the inviolability of rights, duties, and obligations. Hauser (2006) argues for yet another arrangement in which moral "cognition" comes first in the form of rapid, intuitive applications of an innate "grammar of action," which leads to moral judgments, which give rise to moral emotions.

The precise roles played by intuition and reasoning in moral judgment cannot yet be established based on the existing empirical evidence. Greene, Morelli, Lowenberg, Nystrom, and Cohen (2008) used cognitive load to try to resolve this question, but their results are equivocal. Cognitive load did slow down consequentialist responses to difficult dilemmas, suggesting that reasoning played some role in judgment, but cognitive load did not alter the judgments made, which is inconsistent with the view of two independent processes pushing against each other to reach the final judgment.

A further difficulty is that most research has used stories about dying wives, runaway trolleys, lascivious siblings, or other highly contrived situations. In these situations, usually designed to pit nonutilitarian intuitions (about rights or disgust) against extremely bad outcomes (often involving death), people do sometimes override their initial gut feelings and make the utilitarian choice. But do these occasional overrides show us that moral reasoning is best characterized—contra Hume—as an independent process that can easily veto the conclusions of moral intuition (Greene, 2008)? Or might it be the case that moral reasoning is rather like a lawyer (Baumeister & Newman, 1994) employed by moral intuition, which largely does its client's bidding, but will occasionally resist when the client goes too far and asks it to make an argument it knows to be absurd? It is useful to study judgments of extreme cases, but much more work is needed on everyday moral judgment—the evaluations that people make of each other many times each day (rare examples include Nucci & Turiel, 1978; Sabini & Silver, 1982). How rapidly are such judgments made? How often are initial judgments revised? When first reactions are revised, is the revision driven by competing intuitions, by questions raised by a discussion partner, or by the person's own private and unbiased search for alternative conclusions? What are the relevant personality traits or ecological contexts that lead to more deliberative judgments? When is deliberative judgment superior to judgment that relies on intuitions and heuristics? Progress will be made on these questions in coming years. In the meantime, we can prepare for the study of everyday moral judgment by examining what it is good for. Why do people judge each other so frequently in the first place? The second principle of the New Synthesis offers an answer.

MORAL THINKING IS FOR SOCIAL DOING

Functionalist explanations have long been essential in many sciences. Broadly speaking, functionalist explanations involve "interpreting data by establishing their consequences for larger structures in which they are implicated" (Merton, 1968, p. 101). The heart contracts in the complex ways that it does *in order to* propel blood at variable rates within a larger circulatory system, which is itself a functional component of a larger structure, the body. Psychology has long been a functionalist science, not just about behavior (which produces consequences for the organism; Skinner, 1938), but also about thought (Katz, 1960; Tetlock, 2002). William James (1890/1950, p. 333) insisted

on this approach: "My thinking is first and last and always for the sake of my doing." Our goal in this section is to apply James's dictum by exploring the different kinds of "doing" that moral thinking (including intuition and reasoning) might be for. (See S. T. Fiske, 1993, for a previous application of James's dictum to social cognition.)

A crucial first step in any functionalist analysis is to specify the larger structure within which a component and its effects are implicated. For moral thinking, there are three larger structures that have been discussed in the literature, which give us three kinds of functionalism.[3] In *intrapsychic functionalism*,[4] the larger structure is the psyche, and moral thinking is done in order to provide intrapsychic benefits such as minimizing intrapsychic conflict (Freud, 1923/1962), or maintaining positive moods or self-esteem (Cialdini et al., 1987; Jost & Hunyady, 2002). In *epistemic functionalism* the larger structure is a person's representation of the world, and moral thinking is done in order to improve the accuracy and completeness of that knowledge structure (e.g., Kohlberg, 1971). In *social functionalism*, the larger structure is the social agent embedded in a still larger social order, and moral thinking is done in order to help the social agent succeed in the social order (e.g., Dunbar, 1996). This section of the chapter examines various literatures in moral psychology from a social-functional perspective. Many of the puzzles of human morality turn out to be puzzles only for epistemic functionalists, who believe that moral thinking is performed *in order to* find moral truth.

The Puzzle of Cooperation

The mere existence of morality is a puzzle, one that is deeply intertwined with humanity's search for its origins and its uniqueness (Gazzaniga, 2008). Two of the most dramatic and plot-changing moments in the Hebrew Bible involve the receipt of moral knowledge—in the Garden of Eden and on Mt. Sinai. Both stories give Jews and Christians a narrative structure in which they can understand their obligations (especially obedience to authority), the divine justification of those obligations, and the causes and consequences of failures to live up to those obligations.

Morality plays a starring role in evolutionary thinking about human origins as well. Darwin was keenly aware

---

[3]These three functionalisms are similar to Katz's (1960) list of the four functions of attitudes: knowledge, ego-defense, utilitarian, and value-expressive. We merge the last two together as social functions.

[4]It should be noted that intrapsychic functionalism can often be subsumed within social functionalism because evolution often uses feelings of pleasure and displeasure as the proximal mechanisms that motivate organisms to engage in adaptive behaviors.

that altruism, in humans and other animals, seemed on its face to be incompatible with his claims about competition and the survival of the fittest. He offered a variety of explanations for how altruism might have evolved, including group-level selection—groups with many virtuous members outcompete groups with fewer. But as the new sciences of genetics and population genetics developed in the twentieth century, a new mathematical rigor led theorists to dismiss group selection (Williams, 1966) and to focus instead on two other ideas—kin selection and reciprocal altruism.

Kin selection refers to the process in which genes spread to the extent that they cause organisms to confer benefits on others who share the same gene because of descent from a recent common ancestor (Hamilton, 1964). Evidence for the extraordinary degree to which resources and cooperation are channeled toward kin can be found throughout the animal kingdom (Williams, 1966) and the ethnographic record (Fiske, 1991; Henrich & Henrich, 2007). Trivers (1971, p. 35) sought to move beyond kin selection when he defined altruism as "behavior that benefits another organism, not closely related, while being apparently detrimental to the organism performing the behavior." He proposed *reciprocal altruism* as a mechanism that could promote the spread of genes for altruism, if those genes led their bearers to restrict cooperation to individuals likely to return the favor. Evidence for the extraordinary power of reciprocity is found throughout the ethnographic (A. P. Fiske, 1991) and the experimental literature (Axelrod, 1984) with humans, but, contrary to Trivers's expectations, reciprocal altruism among animals is extremely rare (Hammerstein, 2003). There is some ambiguous experimental evidence for inequity aversion among chimpanzees and capuchin monkeys (Brosnan & De Waal, 2003; Wynne, 2004), and there is some compelling anecdotal evidence for several kinds of fairness among other primates (Brosnan, 2006), but the difficulty of documenting clear cases of reciprocal altruism among non-kin suggests that it may be limited to creatures with very advanced cognitive capacities.

Kin selection and reciprocal altruism are presented as the evolutionary foundations of morality in many social psychology textbooks and in most trade books on morality (e.g., Dawkins, 1976; Hauser, 2006; Ridley, 1996; Wright, 1994). Rather than dwell any further on these two overemphasized processes, this chapter now skips ahead to what they cannot explain: cooperation in large groups. The power of both processes falls off rapidly with increasing group size. For example, people share 50% of their variable genes with full siblings, 12.5% with first cousins, and just 3% with second cousins. Kin selection therefore cannot explain the intense cooperation found among extended families and clans in many cultures. Reciprocal altruism has a slightly greater reach: People can know perhaps a few hundred others well

enough to have had direct interactions with them and remember how those interactions went. Yet even if reciprocal altruism can create hundreds of cooperative *dyads*, it is powerless to create small cooperative *groups*. Commons dilemmas, in which the group does best when all cooperate but each person does best free-riding on the contributions of others (Hardin, 1968), cannot be solved if each player's only options are to cooperate or defect. When there is no mechanism by which defectors can be singled out for punishment, the benefits of free-riding outweigh the benefits of cooperating and, as evolutionary and economic theories both predict, cooperation is rare (Fehr & Gächter, 2002). Even in collectivist cultures such as Japan, when participants are placed in lab situations that lack the constant informal monitoring and sanctioning systems of real life, cooperation rates in small groups are low, even lower than those of Americans (Yamagishi, 2003). Collectivism is not just an "inside-the-head" trait that expresses itself in cooperative behavior; it requires "outside-the-head" environmental constraints and triggers to work properly.

Yet somehow, hunter-gatherers cooperate with groups of non-kin on difficult joint projects such as hunting buffalo, weaving large fishnets, and defending territory. And once humans domesticated plants and animals and began living in larger and denser groups, they began to engage in large-scale cooperative projects such as building city walls, changing the course of rivers, and conquering their neighbors. How did this happen, and happen so suddenly in several places over the course of just a few thousand years?

We can think of large-scale cooperation as the Rubicon that our ancestors crossed, founding a way of life on the other side that created a quantum leap in "non-zero-sumness" (Wright, 2000). The enormous and accelerating gains from cooperation in agriculture, trade, infrastructure, and governance are an example of what has been called a "major transition" in evolution (Maynard Smith & Szathmary, 1997), during which human beings went from being a social species like chimpanzees to being an "ultrasocial" species (Campbell, 1983; Richerson & Boyd, 1998), like bees and ants, able to live in groups of thousands with substantial division of labor. What "inside the head" mechanisms were already in place in preagricultural minds such that when early agriculturalists created the right "outside the head" products—such as virtues, institutions, social practices, and punitive gods—ultra-large-scale cooperation (i.e., civilization) materialized so rapidly? Many explanations have been offered, but two of the most widely discussed are reputation and moralistic rule enforcement.

Reputation, Rules, and the Origin of Conscience

Scholars have long wondered why people restrain themselves and follow rules that contradict their self-interest.

Plato opened *The Republic* with the question of why anyone would behave justly if he possessed the mythical "ring of Gyges," which made the wearer invisible at will. One of the first speakers, Glaucon, is a social-functionalist: He proposes that it is only concern for one's reputation that makes people behave well. Socrates, however, eventually steers the group to an epistemically functional answer: Goodness is a kind of truth, and those who know the truth will eventually embrace it. Freud (1900/1976), in contrast, was an intrapsychic-functionalist; he proposed that children internalize the rules, norms, and values of their opposite-sex parent *in order to* escape from the fear and shame of the Oedipus complex.

Darwin sided with Glaucon. He wrote extensively about the internal conflicts people feel between the "instincts of preservation" such as hunger and lust, and the "social instincts" such as sympathy and the desire for others to think well of us (Darwin, 1871/1998, Part I Ch. IV). He thought that these social instincts were acquired by natural selection—individuals that lacked them would be shunned and would therefore be less likely to prosper. Alexander (1987) developed this idea further; he proposed that "indirect reciprocity" occurs when people help others in order to develop a good reputation, which elicits future cooperation from others.

Game-theoretic approaches have elucidated the conditions under which indirect reciprocity can produce high rates of cooperation in one-shot interactions among large groups of strangers. The most important requirement is that good information is available about reputations—i.e., an overall measure of the degree to which each person has been a "good" player in the past (Nowak & Sigmund, 1998). But "good" does not mean "always cooperative," because a buildup of undiscriminating altruists in a population invites invasion by selfish exploiters. The second requirement for indirect reciprocity to stabilize cooperation is that individuals punish those with a bad reputation, at least by withholding cooperation from them (Panchanathan & Boyd, 2004). A "good" indirect reciprocator is therefore a person who carefully monitors the reputations of others and then limits cooperation to those with good reputations. When people have the capacity to do more than shun—when they have the ability to punish defectors at some cost to themselves—cooperation rates rise particularly quickly (Fehr & Gächter, 2002). Such punishment has been called "altruistic punishment" because it is a public good: It costs the punisher more than it earns the punisher, although the entire group benefits from the increased levels of cooperation that result from the punisher's actions (Fehr & Gächter, 2002).

Gossip, then, has emerged as a crucial catalyst of cooperation (Nowak, 2006; Wiessner, 2005). In a gossipy social world, reputations matter for survival, and natural selection favors those who are good at tracking the reputations of others while simultaneously restraining or concealing their own selfish behavior. Dunbar (1996) has even suggested that language and the large human frontal cortex evolved in part for the selective advantages they conferred on those who could most effectively share and manipulate information about reputations.

Norms and rules provide cultural standards that make it easy for people to identify possible violators and then share their concerns with friends. Other primates have norms—shared expectations about each others' behavior—such as when and how to show deference, or who is "allowed" to mate with whom (de Waal, 1996). However, there is no evidence that any non-human animal feels shame or guilt about violating such norms—only fear of punishment (Boehm, in press). Humans, in contrast, live in a far denser web of norms, mores, and folkways (Sumner, 1907) and have an expanded suite of emotions related to violations, whether committed by others (e.g., anger, contempt, and disgust) or by the self (e.g., shame, embarrassment, and guilt, although the differentiation of these emotions varies across cultures; see Haidt, 2003, for a review). Furthermore, humans devote an enormous portion of their gossip to discussions of norm violators within the immediate social group, particularly free-riders, cheaters, and liars (Dunbar, 1996). Given that gossip is often a precursor to collective judgment and some degree of social exclusion, it can be quite costly to become the object of gossip. In a gossipy world where norms are clear and are carefully and collectively monitored, the possession of a conscience is a prerequisite for survival. As the humorist H. L. Mencken once quipped: "Conscience is the inner voice that warns us somebody may be looking." Glaucon and Darwin would agree.

Turning now to the social psychological literature, what is the evidence for a social-functionalist approach to morality? The literature can be divided into research on people as actors, and research on people as judges or prosecutors who investigate the actions of others.

The Intuitive Politician

Tetlock (Lerner & Tetlock, 2003; Tetlock, Skitka, & Boettger, 1989) has argued that accountability is a universal feature of social life. It is a pre-requisite for any non-kin-based cooperative enterprise, from a hunting party to a multi-national corporation. Tetlock points out that the metaphor of people as intuitive scientists searching for truth with imperfect tools is not generally applicable in a world of accountability pressures. In place of such epistemic functionalism, Tetlock (2002) has proposed a social-functionalist framework for the study of judgment and choice. He suggests the metaphor that people often become "intuitive politicians" who strive to maintain positive identities with multiple constituencies; at other times they become "intuitive prosecutors" who try to catch cheaters and free-riders.

The condition that activates the mindset of an intuitive politician is the knowledge that one is "under the evaluative scrutiny of important constituencies in one's life who control valuable resources and who have some legitimate right to inquire into the reasons behind one's opinions or decisions" (Tetlock, 2002, p. 454). Because people are so often under such scrutiny, many phenomena in moral psychology reveal the intuitive politician in action.

1. *Impression management*. Rationalists are usually epistemic functionalists; they believe that moral thinking is like thinking about science and math (Turiel, 2006), and it is done *in order to* find a closer approximation of the truth. For a rationalist, the presence or absence of an audience should not affect moral thinking any more than it should affect scientific thinking. But intuitive politicians are not scientists; they are intuitive (good politicians have sensitive instincts and respond rapidly and fluently, not necessarily logically), and they are politicians (who are hypersensitive to the desires of each audience). Tetlock's research on decision making shows that complex, open-minded "exploratory" thinking is most common when people learn prior to forming any opinions that they will be accountable to a legitimate audience whose views are unknown, who is interested in accuracy, and who is reasonably well informed (Lerner & Tetlock, 2003). Because this confluence of circumstances rarely occurs, real decision makers usually engage in thought that is more simple-minded, more likely to conform to the audience's desires, and more "confirmatory"—that is, designed to find evidence to support the decision makers' first instinct. A great deal of research in classic (e.g., Newcomb, 1943) and recent (e.g., Pennington & Schlenker, 1999; Sinclair, Lowery, Hardin, & Colangelo, 2005) social psychology shows that people have a tendency to "tune" their attitudes to those of the people and groups with whom they interact, or expect to interact. The tuning process is so automatic and ubiquitous that it even results in behavioral mimicry, which improves the impression one makes on the person mimicked (Chartrand & Bargh, 1999).

Audiences alter moral behavior in several ways. In general, people are more likely to behave prosocially in the presence of others (Baumeister, 1982). For example, in one study, people donated several times more money to a research fund when the donation was made publicly rather than privately (Satow, 1975). The audience need not even be present: Security cameras increase helping (van Rompay, Vonk, & Fransen, 2009). The audience need not even be

real: People are more generous in a dictator game when they play the game on a computer that has stylized eyespots on the desktop background, subliminally activating the idea of being watched (Haley & Fessler, 2005).

When politicians have mollified their audiences, they can lower their guard a bit. Monin and Miller (2001) found that participants who established their "moral credentials" as being non-prejudiced by disagreeing with blatantly sexist statements were subsequently more likely to behave in a sexist manner than participants who first responded to more ambiguous statements about women, and who were therefore more concerned about impressing their audience. And finally, when the politician's constituents prefer antisocial behavior, there is a strong pressure to please. Vandalism and other crimes committed by teenagers in groups are, in Tetlock's terms, politically motivated.

2. *Moral confabulation*. People readily construct stories about why they did things, even though they do not have access to the unconscious processes that guided their actions (Nisbett & Wilson, 1977; T. D. Wilson, 2002). Gazzaniga (1985) proposed that the mind contains an "interpreter module" that is always on, always working to generate plausible rather than veridical explanations of one's actions. In a dramatic recent example, participants chose which of two female faces they found most attractive. On some trials, the experimenter used sleight-of-hand to swap the picture of the chosen face with the rejected face and then asked participants why they had chosen that picture. Participants did not notice the switch 74% of the time; in these cases they readily generated reasons to "explain" their preference, such as saying they liked the woman's earrings when their original choice had not been wearing earrings (Johansson, Hall, Sikstrom, & Olsson, 2005).

For an epistemic functionalist, the interpreter module is a puzzle. Why devote brain space and conscious processing capacity to an activity that does more to hide truth than to find it? But for an intuitive politician, the interpreter module is a necessity. It is like the press secretary for a secretive president, working to put the best possible spin on the administration's recent actions. The press secretary has no access to the truth (he or she was not present during the deliberations that led to the recent actions) and no particular interest in knowing what really happened. (See Kurzban & Aktipis, 2007, on modularity and the social mind.) The secretary's job is to make the administration look good. From this perspective, it is not surprising that—like politicians—people believe that they will act more ethically than the average person, whereas their predictions for others are usually more accurate (Epley & Dunning, 2000). People think that they are less likely than their peers to deliver electric shocks in the Milgram paradigm, and more likely to donate blood, cooperate in the prisoner's dilemma, distribute collective funds fairly, or give up their seat on a crowded bus to a pregnant woman (Allison, Messick & Goethals, 1989; Bierbrauer, 1976; Goethals, Messick, & Allison, 1991; Van Lange, 1991; Van Lange & Sedikides, 1998).

3. *Moral hypocrisy.* The ease with which people can justify or "spin" their own bad behavior means that, like politicians, people are almost certain to practice some degree of hypocrisy. When people behave selfishly, they judge their own behavior to be more virtuous than when they watch the same behavior performed by another person (Valdesolo & DeSteno, 2007). When the same experimental procedure is carried out with participants under cognitive load, the self-ratings of virtue decline to match those of the other groups, indicating that people employ conscious, controlled processes to find excuses for their own selfishness, but they do not use these processes when judging others, at least in this situation (Valdesolo & DeSteno, 2008). People also engage in a variety of psychosocial maneuvers—often aided by the institutions that organize and direct their actions (Darley, 1992)—which absolve them from moral responsibility for harmful acts. These include reframing the immoral behavior into a harmless or even worthy one; the use of euphemisms; diffusion or displacement of responsibility; disregarding or minimizing the negative consequences of one's action; attribution of blame to victims; and dehumanizing victims (Bandura, 1999; Glover, 2000; Zimbardo, 2007).

People are especially likely to behave in morally suspect ways if a morally acceptable alibi is available. Batson and colleagues (Batson, Kobrynowicz, Dinnerstein, Kampf, & Wilson, 1997; Batson, Thompson, Seuferling, Whitney, & Strongman, 1999) asked participants to decide how to assign two tasks to themselves and another participant. One of the tasks was much more desirable than the other, and participants were given a coin to flip, in a sealed plastic bag, as an optional decision aid. Those who did not open the bag assigned themselves the more desirable task 80 to 90% of the time. But the same was true of participants who opened the bag and (presumably) flipped the coin. Those who flipped may well have believed, before the coin landed, that they were honest people who would honor the coin's decision: A self-report measure of moral responsibility, filled out weeks earlier, correlated with the decision to open the bag, yet it did not correlate with the decision about task assignment. As with politicians, the ardor of one's declarations of righteousness does not predict the rightness of choices made in private, with no witnesses, and with an airtight alibi available. The coin functioned, in effect, as the Ring of Gyges. (See also Dana, Weber, & Kuang, 2007, on

the ways that "moral wiggle room" and plausible deniability reduce fairness in economic games.)

In another study, participants were more likely to avoid a person with a disability if their decision could be passed off as a preference for one movie over another (Snyder, Kleck, Strenta, & Mentzer, 1979). Bersoff (1999) created even more unethical behavior in the lab by handing participants an overpayment for their time, apparently as an experimenter error, which only 20% of participants corrected. But when deniability was reduced by the experimenter specifically asking, "Is that correct?" 60% did the right thing. Politicians are much more concerned about getting caught in a direct lie than they are about preventing improper campaign contributions.

4. *Charitable giving.* Conscience, for an epistemic functionalist, is what motivates people to do the right thing when faced with a quandary. The philosopher Peter Singer (1979) has argued that we are all in a quandary at every moment, in that we could all easily save lives tomorrow by increasing our charitable giving today. Singer has further argued that letting a child die in a faraway land is not morally different from letting a child drown in a pond a few feet away. Whether one is a utilitarian or a deontologist, it is hard to escape the unsettling conclusion that most citizens of wealthy nations could and should make greater efforts to save other people's lives. But because the conclusion is unsettling, people are strongly motivated to find counterarguments and rationalizations (Ditto & Lopez, 1992; Ditto et al., 1998), such as the fallacious "drop in the bucket" argument.

Because charitable giving has such enormous reputational consequences, the intuitive politician is often in charge of the checkbook. Charitable gifts are sometimes made anonymously, and they are sometimes calculated to provide the maximum help per dollar. But in general, charitable fundraisers gear their appeals to intuitive politicians by selling opportunities for reputation enhancement. They appoint well-connected people to boards and then exploit those people's social connections; they throw black-tie fundraisers and auctions; and they offer to engrave the top donors' names in stone on new buildings. An analysis of the 50 largest philanthropic gifts made in 2007 (all over $40 million) shows that 28 went to universities and cultural or arts organizations (http://philanthropy.com/topdonors/, retrieved October 14, 2008). The remainder went to causes that can be construed as humanitarian, particularly hospitals, but even these cases support the general conclusion that megagifts are usually made by a very rich man, through a foundation that bears his name, to an institution that will build a building or program that bears his name. These patterns of charitable giving are more consistent with a social-functionalist perspective that stresses reputational enhancement than with an epistemic functionalist perspective that stresses a concern for the objectively right or most helpful thing to do. The intuitive politician cares first and foremost about impressing his constituents. Starving children in other countries don't vote.

The Intuitive Prosecutor

In order to thrive socially, people must protect themselves from exploitation by those who are trying to advance through manipulation, dishonesty, and backstabbing. Intuitive politicians are therefore up against intuitive prosecutors who carefully track reputations, are hypervigilant for signs of wrong-doing, and are skillful in building a case against the accused. Many documented features and oddities of moral judgment make more sense if one adopts a social-functionalist view in which there is an eternal arms race between intuitive politicians and intuitive prosecutors, both of whom reside in everyone's mind. The adaptive challenge that activates the intuitive prosecutor is "the perception that norm violation is both common and commonly goes unpunished" (Tetlock, 2002, p. 454).

1. *Negativity bias in moral thinking.* Across many psychological domains, bad is stronger than good (Baumeister, Bratlavsky, Finenauer, & Vohs, 2001; Rozin & Royzman, 2001; Taylor, 1991). Given the importance of reputation for social success, the same is true for morality. Reputation and liking are more strongly affected by negative information than by equivalent positive information (Fiske, 1980; Riskey & Birnbaum, 1974; Skowronski & Carlston, 1987). One scandal can outweigh a lifetime of public service, as many ex-politicians can attest. The intuitive prosecutor's goal is to catch cheaters, not to hand out medals for good citizenship, and so from a signal detection or "error management" perspective (Haselton & Buss, 2000), it makes sense that people are hypervigilant and hyperreactive to moral violations, even if that blinds them to some cases of virtuous action.

A recent illustration of negativity bias is the Knobe effect (Knobe, 2003), in which people are more likely to say that a person intentionally caused an outcome if the outcome was unintended, foreseeable, and negative (e.g., harming the environment) than if the outcome was unintended, foreseeable, and positive (e.g., improving the environment). From an epistemic functionalist perspective, this makes no sense: Appraisals of intentionality are assumed to precede moral judgments and should therefore be independent of them. But from a social functionalist perspective, the Knobe effect makes good sense: The person who caused the negative outcome is a bad person who should be punished, and in order to convince a jury, the prosecutor must show that the defendant intended to cause the harm. Therefore, the prosecutor interprets the question about "intention" in whatever way will yield the highest possible value of intentionality, within the range permitted by the facts at hand. Similarly, Alicke (1992) showed that judgments about the degree to which a young man had control over his car just before an accident depended on why the man was speeding home. If he was driving fast to hide cocaine from his parents, then he was judged to have had more control (and therefore to be more culpable for the accident) than if he was driving fast to hide an anniversary gift for his parents. As with appraisals of intentionality, appraisals of control are commissioned by the prosecutor, or, at least, they are revised by the prosecutor's office when needed for a case.

2. *A cheater detection module?* Much of evolutionary psychology is a sustained argument against the idea that people solve social problems using their general intelligence and reasoning powers. Instead, evolutionary psychologists argue for a high degree of modularity in the mind (Barrett & Kurzban, 2006; Tooby, Cosmides, & Barrett, 2005). Specialized circuits or modules that gave individuals an advantage in the arms race between intuitive prosecutors and intuitive politicians (to use Tetlock's terms) have become part of the "factory-installed" equipment of human morality. Cosmides (1989; Cosmides & Tooby, 2005) argued that one such module is specialized for social exchange, with a subroutine or sub-module for the detection of cheaters and norm violators. Using variants of the Wason four-card problem (which cards do you have to turn over to verify a particular rule?), she has shown that people perform better when the problem involves rules and cheaters (e.g., the rule is "if you are drinking in the bar, you must be 18 or older") than when the problem does not involve any cheating (e.g., the rule is "if there is an A on one side, there must be a 2 on the other"). More specifically, when the task involves a potential cheater, people show an increase in their likelihood of correctly picking the "cheater" card (the card that describes a person who is drinking in a bar, who may or may not be 18); this is the one people often miss when the task is described abstractly. (For a critique of this work, see Buller, 2005; for a response, see Cosmides, Tooby, Fiddick, & Bryant, 2005.) Regardless of whether there is an innate module, there is other evidence to support Cosmides' contention that people have a particular facility for cheater detection. People are more likely to recognize faces of individuals who were previously labeled as cheaters than those labeled non-cheaters (Mealy, Daood, & Krage, 1996). People are also above chance in guessing who defected in a Prisoner's dilemma game, suggesting that they can detect

subtle cues given off by cheaters (Yamagishi, Tanida, Mashima, Shimoma, & Kanazawa, 2003).

3. *Prosecutorial confabulations.* Intuitive prosecutors are not impartial judges. They reach a verdict quickly and then engage in a biased search for evidence that can be presented to a judge (Kunda, 1990; Pyszczynski & Greenberg, 1987). When evidence is not forthcoming, intuitive prosecutors, like some overzealous real prosecutors, sometimes make it up. In the study by Wheatley and Haidt (2005) described earlier, some participants made up transparently post-hoc fabrications to justify their hypnotically influenced judgments that "Dan" had done something wrong by choosing discussion topics that would appeal to professors as well as students. Having just leveled a charge against Dan in their ratings, these participants wrote out supporting justifications such as "Dan is a popularity-seeking snob" and "It just seems like he's up to something." The motto of the intuitive prosecutor is "make the evidence fit the crime."

Pizarro, Laney, Morris, and Loftus (2006) caught the prosecutor tampering with evidence in a different way. Participants read a story about "Frank," who walked out of a restaurant without paying the bill. One-third of participants were given extra information indicating that Frank was a dishonest person; one-third were given extra information indicating that Frank was an honest person and the action had been unintentional; and one-third were given no extra information. When asked a week later to recall what they could about the story, participants who had been told that Frank was a bad person remembered the restaurant bill to have been larger than it actually was, and the degree of distortion was proportional to the degree of blame in participants' original ratings.

All Cognition Is for Doing

Epistemic functionalism was popular during the cognitive revolution, when theorists assumed that the mind must first create accurate maps of the world before it can decide upon a course of action. This assumption underlies Kohlberg's (1969) argument that children move up through his six stages of cognitive development because each level is more "adequate" than the one before.[5] But

it is now becoming increasingly clear that cognition is embodied and adapted for biological regulation (Smith & Semin, 2004). Animal brains cannot and do not strive to create full and accurate mental maps of their environments (Clark, 1999). Even cockroaches can solve a variety of complex problems, and they do so by using a grab-bag of environment-specific tricks and heuristics that require no central representations. As Clark (1999, p. 33) states in his review of animal, human, and robotic cognition: "The rational deliberator turns out to be a well camouflaged Adaptive Responder. Brain, body, world, and artifact are discovered locked together in the most complex of conspiracies."

Even perceiving is for doing. When people are asked to estimate the steepness of a hill, their estimates are influenced by the degree of effort they would have to make to climb the hill. Wearing a heavy backpack makes estimates higher; standing beside a friend makes them lower (see review in Proffitt, 2006). These distortions are not evidence of bad thinking or motivated inaccuracy, but they do suggest that visual perceptions, like memories and many judgments, are constructed on the fly and influenced by the task at hand (Loftus, 1975) and by the feelings one has as one contemplates the task (Clore, Schwarz, & Conway, 1994). When we move from the physical world to the social world, however, we find many more cases where distorted perceptions may be more useful than accurate ones. Chen and Chaiken (1999) describe three motives that drive systematic processing, including an "accuracy motive," which is sometimes overridden by a "defense motive" (to preserve one's self-concept and important social identities, including moral identities) and by an "impression motive" (to advance one's reputation and other social goals).

The many biases, hypocrisies, and outrageous conclusions of (other) people's moral thinking are hard to explain from an epistemic functionalist perspective, as is the frequent failure of intelligent and well-meaning people to converge on a shared moral judgment. But from a social-functionalist perspective, these oddities of moral cognition appear to be design features, not bugs.

MORALITY BINDS AND BUILDS

The previous section adopted a social functionalist perspective and examined moral psychology as a means by which individuals compete for advantage within groups. The section focused on gossip and punishment as long-standing and ubiquitous features of human society that made natural selection favor individuals who were skilled as intuitive politicians and prosecutors. This section takes the social functionalist approach a step further, exploring

---

[5]The claim that children move up along the same path in all cultures, coupled with the claim that higher levels are more adequate, was the warrant for one of Kohlberg's most audacious claims: that one could in fact derive an "ought" (a normative claim about justice) from an "is" (about how children develop toward a justice-based morality; see Kohlberg, 1971).

the possibility that humanity's moral nature was shaped not just by the competition of individuals *within* groups, but also by the competition of groups *with other groups* (Brewer & Caporael, 2006; Henrich, 2004; Richerson & Boyd, 2005; Turchin, 2006; D. S. Wilson, 2002). Humanity's ancestors have been living in groups with at least occasional violent intergroup hostility for most or all of the last seven million years (Boehm, in press). Human beings therefore can be expected to have many ancient "inside the head" mechanisms (such as for coalitions, tribalism, and territoriality [Kurzban, Tooby, & Cosmides, 2001]) that co-evolved in more recent times with "outside the head" cultural creations (such as law, religion, and political institutions), to serve the function of suppressing selfishness and increasing group cohesion, trust, and coordinated action.

The idea that natural selection works on multiple levels simultaneously was stated clearly by Darwin, but it was rejected forcefully by evolutionary theorists beginning in the 1960s (Dawkins, 1976; Williams, 1966). This section of the chapter shows that the main objection to group-level selection—the free-rider problem—has been answered. It also shows how the multilevel perspective has the potential to broaden and improve thinking about morality. Morality is not just about issues of harm and fairness, as many came to believe during the "great narrowing." From a descriptive point of view, morality is also about binding groups together in ways that build cooperative moral communities, able to achieve goals that individuals cannot achieve on their own. The next major section of the chapter will suggest that this broadening of the moral domain is a crucial analytical move that must be made in order to understand the moralities of traditional societies and of political conservatives within Western societies.

Multilevel Selection

Natural selection does not require genes or organisms. It is a process that occurs whenever there is competition among variations that are in some way heritable. When a fast-food restaurant chain modifies its menu and its sales rise (at the expense of its competitors), more outlets will be opened, each with the modified menu, and this is an example of natural selection. In *The Descent of Man*, Darwin (1998/1871) focused on competition among individual organisms, but he recognized the generality of his theory and he believed that human tribes are higher-level entities subject to natural selection:

A tribe including many members who, from possessing in a high degree the spirit of patriotism, fidelity, obedience, courage, and sympathy, were always ready to aid one another,

and to sacrifice themselves for the common good, would be victorious over most other tribes; and this would be natural selection. At all times throughout the world tribes have supplanted other tribes; and . . . morality is one important element in their success. (p. 137)

Darwin was well aware that the free-rider problem worked against group-level selection:

It is extremely doubtful whether the offspring of the more sympathetic and benevolent parents, or of those who were the most faithful to their comrades, would be reared in greater numbers than the children of selfish and treacherous parents belonging to the same tribe. (p. 135)

Darwin believed, however, that there were a variety of forces at work among human groups that solved the free-rider problem and made selfishness unprofitable; foremost among these was the need for a good reputation. Darwin also believed that religion helped bind groups together and suppress selfishness.

But in the 1960s, as claims proliferated about evolution working for the "good of the group" or even the "good of the species," Williams (1966) wrote a devastating critique that largely blocked discussion of group-level selection for three decades. Williams acknowledged that multilevel selection was possible in principle, and he reviewed purported instances of it among many animals, such as restraints on fertility and consumption when food supplies are limited. He concluded that these behaviors were all better explained by the natural selection of alternative alleles as individuals competed with other individuals. A fleet herd of deer is really just a herd of fleet deer, he said; nothing is gained by talking about groups as emergent entities. Given prevailing (and erroneous) assumptions about the slowness of genetic change, the porousness of groups, and the difficulty of suppressing free-riding, Williams argued that the math just does not work out to enable group-level selection to have any appreciable effect on genes. Williams disagreed with Darwin that morality was an adaptation; rather, he believed that morality was "an accidental capability produced, in its boundless stupidity, by a biological process that is normally opposed to the expression of such a capability" (Williams, 1988, p. 438). Dawkins (1976) cemented this idea in the popular and scientific imaginations with his metaphor of the "selfish gene," and his demonstrations that apparently altruistic acts in animals (including humans) can always be explained as benefiting the individual or other people likely to share the individual's genes. For the rest of the twentieth century, most books and essays on the evolution of morality focused on kin selection and reciprocal altruism (including indirect reciprocity).

In the last 20 years, however, three breakthroughs have enabled theorists to escape from the de facto ban imposed by Williams and Dawkins. The first was the formulation of "major transitions" theory (Maynard Smith & Szathmary, 1997). At several points in the history of life, mechanisms emerged that solved the free-rider problem and created larger emergent entities. Replicating molecules joined together to form chromosomes; prokaryotes merged together to become the cooperative organelles of eukaryotic cells; single-cell eukaryotes stayed together after division to form multi-cellular organisms; and some multi-cellular organisms stayed together after birth to form hives, colonies, and societies. In each of these cases, the evolution of a mechanism for suppressing free-riding at one level led to cooperation by entities at that level, which produced enormous gains for the emergent group, largely through division of labor.

Major transitions are rare in nature, but their effects are transformative. The super-organisms produced spread rapidly, outcompeting and marginalizing less cooperative groups (Wilson, 1990). Maynard Smith and Szathmary (1997) note that the transition from small primate societies to large human societies meets all the requirements for being a major transition. The explosion of human biomass, the rapid human domination of so many varied ecosystems, and the frequency of intergroup competition all exemplify the patterns seen after previous major transitions. Group-level analyses are no longer heretical in biology; in a sense, all life forms are now understood to be groups, or even groups of groups. (For reviews see Wilson, Van Vugt, & O'Gorman, 2008; Wilson & Wilson, 2007).

For all previous major transitions, the resolution of the free-rider problem involved suppression of individual opportunities for replication, for example by concentrating all breeding in a single queen. Human groups obviously do not reproduce in this way. The second major theoretical breakthrough was to recognize that culture was a biological adaptation that made it possible for humans to find many new solutions to the free-rider problem. Boyd and Richerson (1985) proposed "dual inheritance theory," which posited that the gene pool of a population and the cultural pool of a population are two separate pools of information that undergo natural selection across many generations. The evolutionary processes are different—cultural mutations can spread rapidly and laterally when they are copied by other group members, whereas genetic change is slower and spreads only by descent—but the two pools of information interact and mutually shape each other over the course of dozens or hundreds of generations. This co-evolutionary process has been occurring in humans for several hundred thousand years, with an upsurge in its speed and intensity in the last forty or fifty thousand years—the period of massively cumulative cultural learning (Richerson & Boyd, 2005).

Natural selection can shape genes only by acting on the expressed phenotype (Mayr, 1963), but human phenotypes, at least for traits related to morality, are usually jointly shaped by genes and culture (Richerson & Boyd, 2005). When cultural groups promote uniformity in dress, food choice, ritual practice, and other behaviors used as markers of group membership, they are reducing the phenotypic variation of members within their group, increasing the phenotypic differences between the group and other groups, and setting up the kind of clustering that can allow pockets of cooperation to form within larger populations (Kurzban, DeScioli, & O'Brien, 2007; D.S. Wilson, 2002). These effects of culture make human groups more like single entities or organisms—at least, when compared to herds or flocks of other animals—and therefore better candidates for group-level selection. Williams' (1966) debunking of group-level selection in other species may not be relevant to the special case of humans, who went through a major transition only after becoming cultural creatures. Most important, a great deal of cultural innovation involves practices and institutions that detect and punish cheaters and that reward and promote group-beneficial behaviors. Williams was surely right that a fleet herd of deer is just a herd of (individually) fleet deer, but it is obviously not true that a cohesive group of humans is just a group of (individually) cohesive humans. Darwin appears to have been correct: Human groups are good candidates for being the sorts of entities that natural selection can work upon. Tribes have long supplanted other tribes, and morality has indeed been a crucial element in their success.

The third breakthrough has only occurred in the last few years, and is not yet well known by psychologists. It is the discovery that genetic evolution can happen rapidly, and that it sped up greatly in the last 10,000 years. The prevailing assumption among psychologists, even evolutionary psychologists, has long been that biological adaptation occurs at a glacial pace, requiring tens of thousands of years of sustained selection pressure to leave any lasting mark on the genome. A corollary of this view is that there has been little genetically based behavioral change since human beings spread beyond Africa 50,000 years ago. The period of greatest interest has therefore been the Pleistocene (from 1.8 million years ago until 10,000 years ago). Reconstructions based on interpolation from primate behavior, archeological evidence, and extant isolated societies suggests that our Pleistocene ancestors lived as hunter-gatherers in small mobile groups of a few dozen or less, with egalitarian relationships among the adult males (Boehm, in press). When Cosmides and Tooby say that "our modern skulls house a Stone Age mind" (1997,

p. 85), they mean that the set of genetically encoded modules and subroutines that make up the human mind were shaped largely by the adaptive pressures of Pleistocene life.

But only in the last few years have human genomes from around the world been available, and when genomes from multiple populations are compared using techniques that can distinguish genetic variations due to selection pressure from those due to random drift, the results show something astonishing: Hundreds and perhaps thousands of genes have changed in response to selection pressures within local populations during the Holocene era—the last 10,000 years (Voight, Kudaravalli, Wen, & Pritchard, 2006; Williamson et al., 2007). The human genome has not been changing at a glacial pace; in fact, the rate of change accelerated rapidly throughout the last 50,000 years (Hawks, Wang, Cochran, Harpending, & Moyzis, 2007), particularly after the agricultural revolution. Human beings developed new food sources, increased their population density, exposed themselves to new pathogens from livestock and from each other, and in dozens of other ways subjected their cultures and genomes to new selection pressures as they set up camp on the far bank of the Rubicon.

One of the best studied examples of Boyd and Richerson's dual inheritance model in action is the co-evolution of genes for adult lactose tolerance with the cultural innovation of dairy farming (Richerson & Boyd, 2005). This co-evolutionary process occurred independently in several populations, leading to different genetic changes in each case, all within the last 7,000 years (Tishkoff et al., 2007). If cow-herding can lead to rapid genetic changes in localized populations, then social changes such as the adoption of hierarchical societies, caste systems, monotheistic religions, monogamy, and dozens of other innovations during the Holocene era can be expected to have altered patterns of cooperation, competition, and reproduction, leading to the co-evolution of civilization with brains that were better adapted for living in those civilizations. Ten thousand years is surely not enough time to create a new cognitive module from scratch, and one should be careful generalizing from the case of a single-gene mutation such as the one involved in lactose tolerance. Nevertheless, this new work, combined with other research on the rapidity with which new behavioral traits can emerge (such as in foxes domesticated in just 30 years [Trut, 1999]), justifies an equally strong caution: No longer can psychologists make genetic stasis in the last 50,000 years the null hypothesis, placing the entire burden of proof (at p < .05) on the shoulders of those who would argue for recent gene-culture co-evolution.

Co-evolution does not imply group-level selection. Co-evolution is discussed here to help readers escape from the old and deep prejudice that genes change too slowly, groups are too porous and similar to each other, and free-riding is too profitable to have permitted group-level selection to influence human genes. A corollary of the new and more dynamic view of evolution is that the last 10,000 years is an important and underappreciated period for the evolution of human morality. Our modern skulls do not house stone-age minds; they house modern minds that still bear strong traces of many earlier eras. An implication of this corollary is that intergroup conflict may have played a larger role in human evolution than is generally thought, based on analyses of Pleistocene life with its very low population densities. The last 10,000 years has been a long era of struggle, conquest, coalition-building, and sometimes genocide among hierarchically organized and symbolically marked tribes and empires (Bowles, 2006; Turchin, 2006). The Holocene is part of our cultural *and* genetic heritage; it is likely to have left some mark on our modern moral psychology.

Group Selection in Action

Long before Darwin, the fourteenth-century Arab philosopher Ibn Khaldun explained how tribes supplant other tribes. The process is driven, he said, by *asabiya*, the Arabic word for solidarity (Turchin, 2006). Ibn Khaldun noted that kingdoms and empires along the northern coast of Africa went through cycles in which a tribe with high *asabiya* came out of the desert to conquer an existing state, but then, after three or four generations of urban life, solidarity declined and a new tribe came out of the desert to repeat the cycle. Ibn Khaldun hit upon Darwin's essential insight that natural selection operates on tribes and selects for virtues that increase group solidarity, cohesion, and trust. The desert was a particularly fertile ground for the creation of solidarity because, as Ibn Khaldun noted, only tribes that had found ways to cooperate intensively could survive in such a harsh and lawless place. Turchin (2006) has recently expanded Ibn Khaldun's thesis to demonstrate that new empires almost always arise on the fault lines or "meta-ethnic frontiers" between religious or racial groups because the protracted wars in those regions spur cultural innovations that increase the solidarity of each group. Ultimately one group prevails and uses its amplified cohesiveness to conquer other opponents as well.

Just as Darwin said, "tribes have supplanted other tribes; and . . . morality is one important element in their success." But this morality is not Turiel's (1983) morality of harm, rights, and justice, which protects the autonomy of individuals; this is a more traditional morality of patriotism, fidelity, obedience, and solidarity. This is a morality that binds individuals together, suppresses selfishness, and directs people's strongest moral passions toward the heroes and martyrs who die for the group and toward the traitors and apostates who must be put to death in the name of the group. This is morality as it is defined it in this chapter—as a moral system in which inside-the-head psychological mechanisms and outside-the-head cultural products interlock and work together to suppress selfishness and make social life possible.

It should be noted that Ibn Khaldun's work demonstrates *cultural* group selection, not necessarily genetic group selection. Cultural group selection is the process by which cultural innovations that lead groups to prosper and grow (e.g., a new religion or technology) become more widespread as groups with the innovation replace or assimilate less successful groups (Richerson & Boyd, 2005). There is now a widespread consensus that cultural group selection occurs, and there has never been any serious objection to the idea that "outside-the-head" stuff spreads in this way. The controversy over group selection is limited to the issue of whether the *genes* that contribute to the "inside-the-head" stuff were selected in part by the process of "tribes supplanting other tribes." Some leading theorists say yes (e.g., Wilson & Wilson, 2007). Others say no (e.g., Dawkins, 2006), or are uncertain (Richerson & Boyd, 2005).

One way to pick sides in this controversy is to look at the empirical facts about morality. Do any social-psychological phenomena make more sense when viewed as adaptations that helped groups cohere, coordinate, and compete with other groups, rather than as adaptations that helped individuals outcompete their neighbors? As Brewer and Caporael (2006) state, "the result of selection in groups would be the evolution of perceptual, affective, and cognitive processes that support the development and maintenance of membership in groups" (p. 145).

Seeing and Being Groups

Campbell (1958) addressed the question of when aggregations of people can be called entities. He drew on principles of gestalt psychology that govern the perception of entities in the physical world, and he concluded that the most important cause of social "entitativity" was common fate, followed by similarity, proximity, and "pregnanz" or good continuation with clear borders. Groups that move together, share the ups and downs of fortune together, come together periodically, mark and patrol their borders (physical or social), and mark their group membership with clothing, hairstyles, bodily alterations, or other badges are more likely to be perceived as entities. Such groups also meet Campbell's requirement for *being* entities—for being proper objects of scientific study. The fact that ethnic groups, sports teams, military units, and college fraternities go to great lengths to exploit all four of these gestalt principles suggests that groups—particularly those in competition with other groups—are trying to enhance their entitativity, and by extension, their solidarity.

The fact that people easily see faces in the clouds, but never see clouds in faces, is due to the presence of specialized circuits in the visual system for facial detection (Guthrie, 1993). Similarly, if people have a hyperactive tendency to see social groups where groups don't exist, it suggests the presence of specialized social-cognitive structures designed for intergroup relations (see Yzerbyt & Demoulin, this volume, for a review). Tajfel's work on "minimal groups" suggests that we do indeed have such a tendency. People readily identify with and discriminate in favor of groups to which they have been assigned based on arbitrary criteria such underestimating versus overestimating the number of dots on a screen (Tajfel, Billig, Bundy, & Flament, 1971). Even a random lottery assignment is sufficient to make people identify with groups and treat ingroup members better (Locksley, Ortiz, & Hepburn, 1980). Sherif's famous "Robbers Cave" study examined what happened when two groups of boys who had previously not known of each other's presence suddenly came into competition (Sherif et al., 1961). Illustrating Turchin's (2006) thesis, the discovery of a "frontier" made both groups rapidly develop practices that increased their solidarity, including creating new customs, folkways, and moral identities for themselves (e.g., Rattlers cursed, but Eagles used clean language), using disgust to express shared revulsion for the other side (e.g., holding their noses in the vicinity of outgroup members), becoming more hierarchical, and suppressing divisions that had existed within groups before the intergroup conflict.

According to Social Identity Theory, one's identity and self-esteem are intimately tied to the standing of the groups to which one belongs (Tajfel & Turner, 1979). People sometimes adopt the interests of their groups as their own, even when doing so compromises their self-interest. A well-documented example of this effect is found in research on voting and public opinion. Many people cynically assume that people vote for the politician who panders to them by promising them money and other benefits, but in fact "self interest is surprisingly unimportant when it comes to predicting American public opinion" (Kinder, 1998, p. 801). Rather, public opinions function as badges of social membership; one's views on abortion, war, and gay marriage are in part declarations of social identities (Smith, Bruner, & White 1956). Kinder (1998, p. 808) summarizes decades of research in this way:

> Interests, it is now clear, do have a part to play in public opinions—that is, interests that are collective rather than personal,

group-centered rather than self-centered. In matters of public opinion, citizens seem to be asking themselves not "What's in it for me?" but rather "What's in it for my group?" (as well as "What's in it for other groups?"). (p. 808)

Prosociality Within Groups

Most Western philosophical approaches to morality call for impartiality and universalism as normative ideals (Hare, 1981; Kant, 1785/1959; Singer, 1979). But if multi-level selection shaped human beings, then we can expect that parochialism is, descriptively, the normal, default, evolutionarily prepared (Seligman, 1971) form of human sociality. A basic requirement for group-level selection to occur is that group members preferentially channel their altruism and cooperation to other group members, rather than helping or cooperating with all individuals equally and indiscriminately. The empirical evidence shows that people are indeed more likely to care for ingroup members than for outgroup members across various types of helping behavior (e.g., Dovidio, 1984, Levine & Thomson, 2004). For example, a bystander is more likely to offer help in an emergency situation if she perceives the victim as a member of the same social group as herself (Levine, Cassidy, Brazier, & Reicher; 2002), and ingroup favoritism becomes even more common when group membership is made salient (Levine, Prosser, Evans, & Reicher, 2005). Pointing to shared identity and creating psychological fusion with others such as feelings of "one-ness," "we-ness," or common fate leads to the same effect (Cialdini, Brown, Lewis, Luce, & Neuberg, 1997; Dovidio, Gaertner, Validzic, & Matoka, 1997; Flippen, Hornstein, Siegal, & Weitzman, 1996; Gaertner et al., 1999). We-ness helps to solve cooperative problems too; higher identification with the group leads to higher investment in a public goods dilemma and higher self-restraint in consuming the group's resources (Barreto & Ellemers, 2002; De Cremer & Van Vugt, 1999; Kramer & Brewer, 1984).

It's as though human beings have a slider switch in their heads that runs from "me" to "we." Brewer and Caporael (2006, p. 148) posit that selfish and group-oriented motivations are "two separate, semiautonomous regulatory systems that hold each other in check . . . which is to be expected from selection at both individual and group levels." People are well equipped to survive in social situations governed by "every man for himself," but they take just as readily, and a lot more joyfully, to situations in which it is "one-for-all, all-for-one."

Maintaining Groups

The joy of we-ness may draw people together into groups, but to keep them there, to keep groups stable over time and to

prevent the dissipation of solidarity requires psychological and institutional mechanisms for group maintenance in the face of external threats and internal divisions. Chimpanzee groups—which compete in sometimes lethal combat with neighboring groups—have a variety of such mechanisms, including the ability of high-ranking individuals to broker reconciliation among feuding members (de Waal, 1982; Goodall, 1986).

People have a larger suite of tools for maintaining intragroup harmony and cohesion. Foremost among these is the human propensity to generate norms for behavior, adhere to them, and work together to sanction those who do not (Fehr & Fischbacher, 2004). Many classic studies show that people tend to follow norms generated by those around them (Asch, 1956; Deutsch & Gerard, 1955; Sherif, 1936; for a review see Hogg, this volume). Yet norms do not exist in a free-floating Kantian space shared by all rational creatures; they are group-bound and they achieve their full power to regulate behavior in real groups. For example, people are much more likely to follow norms set by ingroup members. In one Asch-type study, participants who were psychology students conformed 58% of the time to other psychology students, whereas they conformed only 8% of the time to ancient history students (Abrams, Wetherell, Cochrane, & Hogg, 1990). The more people identify with a group, the more they like others who follow the group's norms, and this effect is larger for moral norms than for non-moral norms (Christensen, Rothgerber, Wood, & Matz, 2004). People also exert more pressure on ingroup members to adhere to norms: According to the "black sheep effect," people are generally less tolerant toward an ingroup member who transgresses social norms than they are toward an equally transgressive outgroup member (Abrams, Marques, Bown, & Henson, 2000; Marques, Yzerbyt, & Leyens, 1988).

Ethnicity appears to be a major factor in the generation of cooperation within multiethnic societies (Henrich & Henrich, 2007). Groups of strangers playing an anonymous coordination game in which they can use arbitrary pseudo-ethnic markers to improve coordination learn to use those markers and increase their payoffs (Efferson, Lalive, & Fehr, 2008). Ethnic enclaves within diverse cities have long created moral systems saturated with parochial trust, which sometimes enables them to gain an economic edge over less groupish competitors and thereby dominate certain trades and professions (Henrich & Henrich, 2007). A widely cited example is the dominance in the diamond trade of ultra-orthodox Jews, whose ability to trust each other greatly reduces the transaction costs that non-ethnic merchants would incur as they tried to monitor and guard each diamond sent out for examination, trade, or sale (Coleman, 1988). On the other hand, it should be noted that

Putnam (2007) has found that ethnic diversity within towns and cities in the United States correlates with reduced trust, cooperation, and social capital, not just across groups (which he calls "bridging capital") but within groups as well ("bonding capital"). A possible resolution of this paradox may come from Ibn-Khaldun (Turchin, 2006): If we take "bonding capital" to be a synonym of *asabiya* or collective solidarity, then it stands to reason that some ethnic groups respond to diversity by increasing their separateness and solidarity, thereby creating a more binding moral system; others move gradually toward assimilation with the dominant culture, thereby becoming more individualistic and creating a less binding and less consensually shared moral system.

A willingness to punish norm-violators, cheaters, and free-riders is a crucial component of group maintenance. In economic games, people often punish defectors even if they have to pay for it themselves (Fehr & Gächter, 2002). Moreover, when people punish free-riders, brain areas related to the processing of rewards are activated, suggesting that such punishment feels good (de Quervain et al., 2004). Such "altruistic punishment"[6] in turn has been shown to uphold cooperation levels in public goods games, in the absence of which cooperation quickly dissipates (Fehr & Gächter, 2002). When subjects in a lab experiment are given the choice of playing a cooperative game in a group that allows punishment versus one that does not, many people initially choose to take part in the group that seems "nicer." They quickly discover, however, that in the absence of punishment there is little cooperation, and the majority of participants soon elect to move to the group that allows punishment (Gürerk, Irlenbusch, & Rockenbach, 2006). Those who move cooperate fully on the next round; they need no trial-and-error experience to understand that cooperative behavior is now required and rewarded.

The discussion of group maintenance so far has focused on norms and the punishment of norm violators, for that is where the lab-based empirical research has been concentrated. But if one takes a more ethnographic approach and simply lists a few additional group-maintenance mechanisms, the list would include harsh initiation rites with shaming for those who refuse to take part or who later fail to live up to the group's standards (Herdt, 1981); the use of monuments, holidays, and other techniques for memorializing and sacralizing heroes and martyrs (Eliade, 1957/1959;

Lowenthal, 1986); the widespread practice of punishing treason and apostasy with death (Ben-Yehuda, 2001); the reflex to rally around the flag and the leader when the group is under assault (Duckitt, 1989; Stenner, 2005); and the use of synchronized group movement to build *esprit de corps*, a practice that stretches back long before recorded history (McNeill, 1995) and that has recently been shown to increase cooperation and trust in the lab (Wiltermuth & Heath, 2008).

Religion and Morality

Across cultures and eras, people have often thought that religion was the foundation of morality. That claim was challenged in the Enlightenment; philosophers tried to offer secular justifications for doing good when it is not in one's self-interest to do so. But even Enlightenment icons such as John Locke (1689/1983) argued that religious toleration should not be extended to atheists: "Promises, covenants, and oaths, which are the bonds of human society, can have no hold upon an atheist" (p. 51).

A new chapter opened recently in the debate over atheism and morality when several books appeared in quick succession merging scientific evidence and philosophical argument to claim that God is not just a "delusion" (Dawkins, 2006); deities and religions are in fact *obstacles* to ethical behavior because they blind people to scientific and moral truths and then lead to socially destructive behavior (Dennett, 2006; Harris, 2006). A feature common to these books (see also Atran, 2002) is that they raise the possibility that religion evolved because it is adaptive for groups, but then they dismiss group selection by citing Williams (1966) and the free-rider problem. They then go on to search for ways that religiosity might have helped individuals outcompete their less-religious neighbors. Finding no such advantages and many disadvantages, they conclude that human minds were not shaped by natural selection to be religious. Rather, they argue that religion is a byproduct, a cultural parasite that exploits mental structures that evolved for other purposes, such as a "hyperactive agency detection device" (Barrett, 2000) that is so prone to detecting agency that it misfires and detects agency when no real agent is present. On this view, religion is like a parasite that infects ants' brains and makes them climb to their death at the top of blades of grass, where grazing animals can consume the ant and continue the life cycle of the parasite (Dennett, 2006).

But from a multilevel selection perspective, religions are generally well suited for solving the free-rider problem within groups, increasing their levels of cohesion, cooperation, and coordination, and improving their chances of outcompeting less religious groups. The idea that religions

---

[6]See Kurzban, DeScioli, and O'Brien (2007) for a critique of altruistic punishment, including evidence that people engage in little such punishment when the action is fully anonymous. This pattern suggests that it is done for reputational enhancement and is not truly altruistic.

are really about creating group cohesion was stated clearly by Durkheim (1915/1965, p. 47):

> A religion is a unified system of beliefs and practices relative to sacred things, that is to say, things set apart and forbidden—beliefs and practices which unite into one single moral community called a church, all those who adhere to them.

David Sloan Wilson (2002) has developed Durkheim's perspective into an evolutionary theory in which religion played a key role in pulling human beings through the last major transition in evolutionary history (Maynard Smith & Szathmary, 1997). Religions differ enormously around the world, but despite their diversity, supernatural agents are inordinately concerned about the promises people make to each other and the degree to which they help or harm ingroup members (Boyer, 2001). Furthermore, the world's major religions generally include a well-developed set of practices and beliefs for suppressing not just selfishness but also the discomfort of self-consciousness (Leary, 2004). Religion might even be described as a co-evolved set of psychological mechanisms, social practices, and factual beliefs that use gods in the service of shifting the balance between the two regulatory systems described by Brewer and Caporael (2006): down with the self-oriented system, up with the group-oriented system.

Even if the byproduct theorists are right that the initial tendency to perceive supernatural agency was a byproduct, not an adaptation, this byproduct could easily have been drawn into co-evolutionary processes with enormous consequences for the survival and spread of groups. Consistent with this view, a review of the historical and cross-cultural evidence indicates that gods seem to become more powerful, moralistic, and punitive as group size grows (Shariff, Norenzayan, & Henrich, in press). "Meaner" gods can better serve the social function of suppressing free-riding and cheating, thereby making larger groups possible. In fact, a recent lab study found that cheating on a math test was positively correlated with the niceness of participants' god-concepts. People who believed in an angry, punishing god cheated less; people who believed in a loving, forgiving god cheated the most (Shariff & Norenzayan, 2009).

A great deal of research has examined whether religious people are more prosocial than others. There is evidence on both sides: Religious people report giving much more to charities, even to non-religious charities, than do secular people (Brooks, 2006). But in experimental studies, people's self-reported religiosity rarely predicts actual helping or cooperative behavior (Norenzayan & Shariff, 2008); situational factors are usually much more powerful (e.g., Darley & Batson, 1973). From a multilevel selection perspective, however, there is no reason to expect that religion would turn people into unconditional altruists.

Religious prosociality should be targeted primarily toward co-religionists, and it should be most vigorous when one believes that others, particularly God or ingroup members, will know of one's actions. A recent review (Norenzayan & Shariff, 2008) concludes that these two conditions are indeed important moderators of the relationship between religion and prosociality. When religious people can interact with fellow group members, they do indeed achieve higher rates of cooperation than do members of a matched secular group (Sosis & Ruffle, 2003). An examination of the longevity of communes in nineteenth-century America shows the same thing: During each year after the founding of the commune, religious communes were four times as likely to survive as were communes based on secular principles such as socialism (Sosis & Bressler, 2003). Religions do indeed function to increase trust, cooperation, generosity, and solidarity within the moral community. Religions bind and build, and the psychology of religion should be integrated with the psychology of morality.

THE MANY FOUNDATIONS OF A BROADER MORALITY

An earlier section of this chapter asserted that moral psychology to date has been largely the psychology of *Gesellschaft*—a search for the psychological mechanisms that make it possible for individuals to interact with strangers in a large modern secular society. The two centers of gravity in such a psychology are harmdoing vs. helping (involving a large literature on altruism toward strangers, linked explicitly or implicitly to the philosophical tradition of consequentialism) and fairness/justice/rights (involving a large literature on justice and social justice, linked explicitly or implicitly to the philosophical tradition of deontology).

What's missing? What else could morality be? Haidt and Joseph (2004) reviewed four works that offered lists or taxonomies of moral values or social practices across cultures (Brown, 1991; Fiske, 1991; Schwartz, 1992; Shweder et al., 1997). They also included de Waal's (1996) description of the "building blocks" of morality that are found in other primates. Haidt and Joseph did not aim to identify virtues that appeared in all cultures, nor did they try to create a comprehensive taxonomy that would capture every human virtue. Rather, they tried to identify the best candidates for being the psychological foundations (the "inside-the-head" mechanisms) upon which cultures create an enormous variety of moral systems.

Haidt and Joseph found five groups of virtues or issues discussed by most or all of the five theorists. For each one, a plausible evolutionary story had long been told, and for four of them (all but Purity), there was some evidence of continuity with the social psychology of other primates. The five hypothesized foundations are:

1. Harm/care: Concerns for the suffering of others, including virtues of caring and compassion.
2. Fairness/reciprocity: Concerns about unfair treatment, cheating, and more abstract notions of justice and rights.
3. Ingroup/loyalty: Concerns related to obligations of group membership, such as loyalty, self-sacrifice, and vigilance against betrayal.
4. Authority/respect: Concerns related to social order and the obligations of hierarchical relationships, such as obedience, respect, and the fulfillment of role-based duties.
5. Purity/sanctity: Concerns about physical and spiritual contagion, including virtues of chastity, wholesomeness, and control of desires.

The five best candidates ended up being most closely related to Shweder's "three ethics" of moral discourse (Shweder et al., 1997): the ethics of *autonomy*, in which the self is conceived of as an autonomous agent with preferences and rights (and therefore moral virtues related to harm/care and fairness/reciprocity are highly developed); the ethics of *community*, in which the self is conceived of as an office holder in a larger interdependent group or social system (and therefore virtues related to ingroup/loyalty and authority/respect are highly developed); and the ethics of *divinity*, in which the self is conceived of as a creation of God, housing a divine soul within (and therefore virtues related to purity, self-control, and resistance to carnal pleasures become highly developed). Moral Foundations Theory (Haidt & Joseph, 2004; Haidt & Graham, 2009) can therefore be seen as an extension of Shweder's three ethics, bringing it into the "new synthesis" by describing psychological mechanisms and their (speculative) evolutionary origins. Shweder's theory of the three ethics has long proven useful for describing variations in moral judgments across and within nations (Haidt et al., 1993; Jensen, 1997; Shweder et al., 1997).

Graham, Haidt, and Nosek (2009) investigated whether moral foundations theory could be used to understand the "culture war" (Hunter, 1991) between political liberals and conservatives in the United States. They devised three very different self-report measures for assessing the degree to which a person's morality is based on each of the five foundations. These questionnaires were completed by three large Internet samples, and all three methods produced the same conclusion: Political liberals greatly value the first two foundations (Harm and Fairness) and place much less value on the remaining three, whereas political conservatives construct their moral systems on all five foundations. This pattern was also found across nations, and it was found in two studies using more naturalistic methods. One study examined the frequency of words related to each foundation that were used in religious sermons given in liberal and conservative Christian churches (Graham, Haidt, & Nosek, 2009, study 4). The second study used qualitative methods to code the narrative statements offered by religious Americans who were asked to narrate important events in their lives (McAdams et al., 2008). McAdams et al. summarized their findings as follows:

> When asked to describe in detail the most important episodes in their self-defining life narratives, conservatives told stories in which authorities enforce strict rules and protagonists learn the value of self-discipline and personal responsibility, whereas liberals recalled autobiographical scenes in which main characters develop empathy and learn to open themselves up to new people and foreign perspectives. When asked to account for the development of their own religious faith and moral beliefs, conservatives underscored deep feelings about respect for authority, allegiance to one's group, and purity of the self, whereas liberals emphasized their deep feelings regarding human suffering and social fairness. (p. 987)

This quote, and other writing on political ideology (Sowell, 2002), suggest that liberals and conservatives are trying to build different kinds of moral systems using different but overlapping sets of moral intuitions. Liberals are trying to build the ideal *Gesellschaft*, an open, diverse, and cosmopolitan place in which the moral domain is limited to the issues described by Turiel (1983): justice, rights, and welfare. Moral regulation that does not further those goals (e.g., restraints on sexuality or gender roles) is immoral. The harm/care and fairness/reciprocity foundations may be sufficient for generating such a secular, contractual society, as John Rawls (1971) did with his "veil of ignorance" thought experiment.[7] In such a society the other three foundations are less important, and perhaps even morally suspect: Ingroup/loyalty is associated with racism, ethnocentrism, and nationalism; authority/respect is associated

---

[7]In which he asked what kind of society and government people would choose to create if they did so while not knowing what role or position they would occupy in that society. Rawls asserted that people would prioritize individual rights and liberties, and would have a special concern for the welfare of those at the bottom.

with oppression, authoritarianism, and system justification (Jost & Hunyady, 2002); and purity/sanctity is associated with homophobia and other disgust-based restrictions on the rights of women and some minority or immigrant groups (Nussbaum, 1999).

Conservatives—at least, social conservatives of the sort exemplified by the Religious Right in the United States—are trying to build a very different kind of moral system. That system is much more like the *Gemeinschaft* described by Tönnies. It uses all five moral foundations to create tighter local communities and congregations within which free-rider problems are solved effectively and therefore trust, cooperation, and mutual aid can flourish (Ault, 2005). It uses God as a coordination and commitment device (Graham & Haidt, in press; Shariff, Norenzayan, & Henrich, in press; D. S. Wilson, 2002), which increases similarity, conformity, and solidarity among community members.

This social-functional approach, which interprets liberalism and conservatism as two families of approaches to creating two very different kinds of moral systems, may be a useful corrective to the tendency in social psychology to explain conservatism (but not liberalism) using an intrapsychic functionalist perspective. Conservatives have often been equated with authoritarians, and their moral and political values have long been explained away as means for channeling hostility, raising self-esteem, or justifying either a high or a low position in a social hierarchy (Adorno, Frenkel-Brunswik, Levinson, & Sanford, 1950; Jost, Glaser, Kruglanski, & Sulloway, 2003). From a social-functional perspective, conservatism is no puzzle; it is a way—the most common way, historically—of creating moral systems, although not ones that liberals approve of.

CONCLUSION AND FUTURE DIRECTIONS

The goal of this chapter was to offer an account of what morality really is, where it came from, how it works, and why McDougall was right to urge social psychologists to make morality one of their fundamental concerns. The chapter used a simple narrative device to make its literature review more intuitively compelling: It told the history of moral psychology as a fall followed by redemption. (This is one of several narrative forms that people spontaneously use when telling the stories of their lives [McAdams, 2006]). To create the sense of a fall, the chapter began by praising the ancients and their virtue-based ethics; it praised some early sociologists and psychologists (e.g., McDougall, Freud, and Durkheim) who had "thick" emotional and sociological conceptions of morality; and it praised Darwin for his belief that intergroup competition

contributed to the evolution of morality. The chapter then suggested that moral psychology lost these perspectives in the twentieth century as many psychologists followed philosophers and other social scientists in embracing rationalism and methodological individualism. Morality came to be studied primarily as a set of beliefs and cognitive abilities, located in the heads of individuals, which helped individuals to solve quandaries about helping and hurting other individuals. In this narrative, evolutionary theory also lost something important (while gaining much else) when it focused on morality as a set of strategies, coded into the genes of individuals, that helped individuals optimize their decisions about cooperation and defection when interacting with strangers. Both of these losses or "narrowings" led many theorists to think that altruistic acts performed toward strangers are the quintessence of morality.

The chapter tried to create a sense of redemption, or at least of hopeful new directions, in each of the three principles that structured the literature review. The long debate over the relative roles of "emotion" and "cognition" seems to have given way to an emerging consensus on the first principle: "intuitive primacy but not dictatorship." New discoveries about emotion, intuition, and the ways that brains respond to stories about moral violations have led to a pronounced shift away from information processing models and toward dual process models. In these models, most (but not all) of the action is in the automatic processes, which are cognitive processes that are usually affectively valenced. The second principle, "moral thinking is for social doing," reflects the growing recognition that much of human cognition was shaped by natural selection for life in intensely social groups. Human cognition is socially situated and socially functional, and a great deal of that functionality can be captured by viewing people as intuitive politicians and prosecutors, not as intuitive scientists. The third principle, "morality binds and builds," reflects the emergence of multilevel selection theory and of gene-culture co-evolutionary theory. Groups may not be significant units of selection for the great majority of other species, but once human beings developed the capacity for cumulative cultural learning, they invented many ways to solve the free-rider problem, increase the entitativity of their groups, and increase the importance of group-level selection pressures relative to individual-level pressures (which are always present and powerful).

Many other narratives could be told about the last century of moral psychology, and any narrative leaves out inconvenient exceptions in order to create a coherent and readable story. The particular narrative told in this chapter will probably be rejected by psychologists who were already united by a competing narrative. For example, many cognitive developmentalists believe the redemption occurred forty years ago when Lawrence Kohlberg (1969) vanquished the twin demons of behaviorism and psychoanalysis. Moral psychology, like any human endeavor, is influenced by moral psychology, which means that there is often a tribal or team aspect to it. It remains to be seen whether the intuitionist team replaces the rationalist team and gets to write the history of moral psychology that graduate students will learn in 20 years.

For today's young researchers, however, this chapter closes with three suggestions, each meant to be analogous to the nineteenth-century American journalist Horace Greeley's advice to "go west young man!"

1. *Go beyond harm and fairness!* The psychology of harm/care and fairness/reciprocity has been studied so extensively that it will be difficult for young researchers to make big contributions in these areas. But if you re-examine the psychology of ingroups, authority, and purity from a social-functionalist perspective—one that takes them seriously as part of our moral nature, rather than dismissing them with intrapsychic-functionalist explanations—you will find it much easier to say or discover something new.

2. *Transcend your own politics!* One reason that nearly all moral psychology has focused on harm/care and fairness/reciprocity may be that nearly everyone doing the research is politically liberal. A recent study of professors in the humanities and social sciences at elite American schools found that 95% voted for John Kerry in 2004, and 0% voted for George Bush (Gross & Simmons, 2007). An analysis that focused on academic psychology (Redding, 2001) reached a similar conclusion about the politics of the profession and warned that the lack of sociopolitical diversity creates a hostile climate for the few young conservatives who try to enter the field. When almost everyone in an academic field is playing on the same team, there is a high risk that motivated reasoning and conformity pressures will create political correctness, herd-like behavior, and collective blindness to important phenomena. As in most investment situations, when the herd goes one way, you should go the other. If you want to do or discover something big, look for credible scientific ideas that are politically unpopular (e.g., group-level selection and fast genetic evolution) and apply them to moral psychology. Expose yourself to people and cultures whose moral values differ from your own, and do it in a way that will trigger empathy in you, rather than hostility. Good places to start include Ault (2005) for religious conservatism, Sowell (2002) for conservatism more broadly, and Shweder, Much, Mahapatra, and Park (1997) for a Hindu perspective on morality.

3. *Read widely!* The new synthesis in moral psychology really is a synthesis. No longer can a graduate student in one field read only work from that field. Basic literacy in moral psychology now requires some knowledge of neuroscience (Damasio, 2003; Greene, in press), primatology (de Waal, 2008), and the related fields of game theory and evolutionary theory (Gintis, Bowles, Boyd, & Fehr, 2005b; Richerson & Boyd, 2005).

If major transitions in evolution happen when disparate elements begin to work together for the common good, then one can almost say that moral psychology is in the middle of a major transition. The enormous benefits of division of labor are beginning to be felt, and a few large-scale multidisciplinary projects are bearing fruit (e.g., Henrich et al., 2005). The analogy is imperfect—there was no suppression of free-riding or competition with other academic superorganisms—but something has changed in moral psychology in recent years as the questions asked, tools used, and perspectives taken have expanded. Social psychology has been a major contributor to, and beneficiary of, these changes. If McDougall were to come back in a few years to examine social psychology's progress on its "fundamental problem," he'd likely be quite pleased.

REFERENCES

Abelson, R. P., Kinder, D. R., Peters, M. D., & Fiske, S. T. (1982). Affective and semantic components in political person perception. *Journal of Personality and Social Psychology, 42,* 619–630.

Abrams, D., Marques, J. M., Bown, N., & Henson, M. (2000). Pro-norm and anti-norm deviance within and between groups. *Journal of Personality and Social Psychology, 78,* 906–912.

Abrams, D., Wetherell, M., Cochrane, S., & Hogg, M. A. (1990). Knowing what to think by knowing who you are: Self-categorization and the nature of norm formation, conformity and group polarization. *British Journal of Social Psychology, 29,* 97–119.

Adorno, T. W., Frenkel-Brunswik, E., Levinson, D. J., & Sanford, R. N. (1950). *The authoritarian personality* (1st ed.). New York: Harper & Row.

Alexander, R. (1987). *The biology of moral systems.* New York: Aldine De Gruyter.

Alicke, M. D. (1992). Culpable causation. *Journal of Personality and Social Psychology, 63,* 368–378.

Allison, S. T., Messick, D. M., & Goethals, G. R. (1989). On being better but not smarter than others: The Muhammad Ali effect. *Social Cognition, 7,* 275.

Ambady, N., & Rosenthal, R. (1992). Thin slices of expressive behavior as predictors of interpersonal consequences: A meta-analysis. *Psychological Bulletin, 111,* 256–274.

Anderson, S. W., Bechara, A., Damasio, H., Tranel, D., & Damasio, A. R. (1999). Impairment of social and moral behavior related to early damage in human prefrontal cortex. *Nature Neuroscience, 2,* 1032–1037.

Appiah, K. A. (2008). *Experiments in ethics.* Cambridge, MA: Harvard.

Aristotle. (1941). *Nichomachean ethics* (W. D. Ross, Trans.). New York: Random House.

Aronson, E., Wilson, T. D., & Akert, R. M. (2007). *Social psychology* (6th ed.). Upper Saddle River, NJ: Pearson Prentice Hall.

Asch, S. (1956). Studies of independence and conformity: A minority of one against a unanimous majority. *Psychological Monographs, 70*, (Whole No. 416).

Atran, S. (2002). *In gods we trust*. New York: Oxford.

Ault, J. M. J. (2005). *Spirit and flesh: Life in a fundamentalist Baptist church*. New York: Knopf.

Axelrod, R. (1984). *The evolution of cooperation*. New York: Basic Books.

Baillargeon, R. (1987). Object permanence in 3 1/2- and 4 1/2-month-old infants. *Developmental Psychology, 23*, 655–664.

Bandura, A. (1999). Moral disengagement in the perpetration of inhumanities. *Personality and Social Psychology Review, 3*, 193–209.

Bargh, J. A. (1994). The four horsemen of automaticity: Awareness, efficiency, intention, and control in social cognition. In J. R. S. Wyer & T. K. Srull (Eds.), *Handbook of social cognition* (2nd ed., pp. 1–40). Hillsdale, NJ: Erlbaum.

Bargh, J. A., & Chartrand, T. L. (1999). The unbearable automaticity of being. *American Psychologist, 54*, 462–479.

Barkow, J. H., Cosmides, L., & Tooby, J. (Eds.). (1992). *The adapted mind : Evolutionary psychology and the generation of culture*. New York: Oxford.

Baron, R. A. (1997). The sweet smell of . . . helping: Effects of pleasant ambient fragrance on prosocial behavior in shopping malls. *Personality and Social Psychology Bulletin, 23*, 498–503.

Barreto, M., & Ellemers, N. (2002). The impact of anonymity and group identification on progroup behavior in computer-mediated groups. *Small Group Research, 33*, 590.

Barrett, H. C., & Kurzban, R. (2006). Modularity in cognition: Framing the debate. *Psychological Review, 113*, 628–647.

Barrett, J. L. (2000). Exploring the natural foundations of religion. *Trends in Cognitive Sciences, 4*, 29.

Bartels, D. M. (2008). Principled moral sentiment and the flexibility of moral judgment and decision making. *Cognition, 108*, 381–417.

Bartlett, M. Y., & DeSteno, D. (2006). Gratitude and prosocial behavior: Helping when it costs you. *Psychological Science, 17*, 319–325.

Batson, C. D. (1991). *The altruism question: Toward a social-psychological answer*. Hillsdale, NJ: Erlbaum.

Batson, C. D. (1998). Altruism and prosocial behavior. In D. T. Gilbert & S. T. Fiske (Eds.), *The handbook of social psychology* (4th ed., Vol. 2, pp. 262–316). Boston: McGraw-Hill.

Batson, C. D., Dyck, J. L., Brandt, J. R., Batson, J. G., Powell, A. L., McMaster, M. R., et al. (1988). Five studies testing two new egoistic alternatives to the empathy-altruism hypothesis. *Journal of Personality and Social Psychology, 55*, 52–77.

Batson, C. D., Klein, T. R., Highberger, L., & Shaw, L. L. (1995). Immorality from empathy-induced altruism: When compassion and justice conflict. *Journal of Personality and Social Psychology, 68*, 1042–1054.

Batson, C. D., Kobrynowicz, D., Dinnerstein, J. L., Kampf, H. C., & Wilson, A. D. (1997). In a very different voice: Unmasking moral hypocrisy. *Journal of Personality and Social Psychology, 72*, 1335–1348.

Batson, C. D., O'Quinn, K., Fulty, J., Vanderplass, M., & Isen, A. M. (1983). Influence of self-reported distress and empathy on egoistic versus altruistic motivation to help. *Journal of Personality and Social Psychology, 45*, 706–718.

Batson, C. D., Thompson, E. R., Seuferling, G., Whitney, H., & Strongman, J. A. (1999). Moral hypocrisy: Appearing moral to oneself without being so. *Journal of Personality and Social Psychology, 77*, 525–537.

Baumeister, R. F. (1982). A self-presentational view of social phenomena. *Psychological Bulletin, 91*, 3–26.

Baumeister, R. F., Bratlavsky, E., Finenauer, C., & Vohs, K. D. (2001). Bad is stronger than good. *Review of General Psychology, 5*, 323–370.

Baumeister, R. F., & Bushman, B. J. (2008). *Social psychology and human nature*. Belmont, CA: Thomson/Wadsworth.

Baumeister, R. F., & Newman, L. S. (1994). Self-regulation of cognitive inference and decision processes. *Personality and Social Psychology Bulletin, 20*, 3–19.

Ben-Yehuda, N. (2001). *Betrayals and treason: Violations of trust and loyalty*. Boulder, CO: Westview Press.

Bennett, W. J. (1993). *The book of virtues: A treasury of great moral stories*. New York: Simon & Schuster.

Berkowitz, L. (1965). Some aspects of observed aggression. *Journal of Personality and Social Psychology, 2*, 359–369.

Bersoff, D. (1999). Why good people sometimes do bad things: Motivated reasoning and unethical behavior. *Personality and Social Psychology Bulletin, 25*, 28–39.

Bierbrauer, G. (1979). Why did he do it? Attribution of obedience and the phenomenon of dispositional bias. *European Journal of Social Psychology, 9*, 67.

Blair, R. J. R. (1999). Responsiveness to distress cues in the child with psychopathic tendencies. *Personality and Individual Differences, 27*, 135–145.

Blair, R. J. R. (2007). The amygdala and ventromedial prefrontal cortex in morality and psychopathy. *Trends in Cognitive Sciences, 11*, 387–392.

Bloom, P. (2004). *Descartes' baby: How the science of child development explains what makes us human*. New York: Basic.

Boehm, C. (in press). Conscience origins, sanctioning selection, and the evolution of altruism in homo sapiens. *Brain and Behavioral Sciences*.

Botvinick, M. M., Braver, T. S., Barch, D. M., Carter, C. S., & Cohen, J. D. (2001). Conflict monitoring and cognitive control. *Psychological Review, 108*, 624–652.

Bowles, S. (2006). Group competition, reproductive leveling, and the evolution of human altruism. *Science, 314*, 1569–1572.

Boyd, R., & Richerson, P. J. (1985). *Culture and the evolutionary process*. Chicago: University of Chicago Press.

Boyer, P. (2001). *Religion explained: The evolutionary origins of religious thought*. New York: Basic.

Brewer, M. B., & Caporael, L. R. (2006). An evolutionary perspective on social identity: Revisiting groups. In M. Schaller, J. Simpson, & D. Kenrick (Eds.), *Evolution and social psychology* (pp. 143–161). New York: Psychology Press.

Brooks, A. C. (2006). *Who really cares: The surprising truth about compassionate conservatism*. New York: Basic Books.

Brosnan, S. F. (2006). Nonhuman species' reactions to inequity and their implications for fairness. *Social Justice Research, 19*, 153–185.

Brosnan, S. F., & De Waal, F. (2003). Monkeys reject unequal pay. *Nature, 425*, 297–299.

Brown, D. E. (1991). *Human universals*. Philadelphia: Temple University Press.

Buller, D. J. (2005). Evolutionary psychology: The emperor's new paradigm. *Trends in Cognitive Science, 9*, 277–283.

Bushman, B. J., & Baumeister, R. F. (1998). Threatened egotism, narcissism, self-esteem, and direct and displaced aggression: Does self-love or self-hate lead to violence? *Journal of Personality and Social Psychology, 75*, 219–229.

Campbell, D. T. (1958). Common fate, similarity, and other indices of the status of aggregates of persons as social entities. *Behavioral Science, 3*, 14–25.

Campbell, D. T. (1983). The two distinct routes beyond kin selection to ultrasociality: Implications for the humanities and social sciences. In D. Bridgeman (Ed.), *The nature of prosocial development: Theories and strategies* (pp. 11–39). New York: Academic Press.

Carruthers, P., Laurence, S., & Stich, S. (2006). *The innate mind Volume 2: Culture and cognition*. New York: Oxford University Press.

Casebeer, W. D. (2003). *Natural ethical facts*. Cambridge, MA: MIT Press.

Chaiken, S. (1980). Heuristic versus systematic information processing and the use of source versus message cues in persuasion. *Journal of Personality and Social Psychology, 39*, 752–766.

Chaiken, S., Giner-Sorolla, R., & Chen, S. (1996). Beyond accuracy: Defense and impression motives in heuristic and systematic information processing. In P. M. Gollwitzer & J. A. Bargh (Eds.), *The psychology of action: Linking cognition and motivation to behavior* (pp. 553–578). New York: Guilford.

Chaiken, S., & Trope, Y. (Eds.). (1999). *Dual process theories in social psychology*. New York: Guilford.

Chappell, T. D. J. (2006). *Values and virtues: Aristotelianism in contemporary ethics*. Oxford, UK: Oxford University Press.

Chartrand, T. L., & Bargh, J. A. (1999). The chameleon effect: The perception-behavior link and social interaction. *Journal of Personality and Social Psychology, 76*, 893–910.

Chen, S., & Chaiken, S. (1999). The heuristic-systematic model in its broader context. In S. Chaiken & Y. Trope (Eds.), *Dual process theories in social psychology* (pp. 73–96). New York: Guilford.

Christensen, P. N., Rothgerber, H., Wood, W., & Matz, D. C. (2004). Social norms and identity relevance: A motivational approach to normative behavior. *Personality and Social Psychology Bulletin, 30*, 1295–1309.

Churchland, P. M. (1998). Toward a cognitive neuriobiology of the moral virtues. *Topoi, 17*, 83–96.

Cialdini, R., Schaller, M., Houlihan, D., Arps, K., Fultz, J., & Beaman, A. (1987). Empathy based helping: Is it selflessly or selfishly motivated? *Journal of Personality and Social Psychology, 52*, 749–758.

Cialdini, R. B., Brown, S. L., Lewis, B. P., Luce, C., & Neuberg, S. L. (1997). Reinterpreting the empathy-altruism relationship: When one into one equals oneness. *Journal of Personality and Social Psychology, 73*, 481.

Clark, A. (1999). *Being there: Putting brain, body, and world together again*. Cambridge, MA: MIT Press.

Clark, G. (2007). *A farewell to alms: A brief economic history of the world*. Princeton, NJ: Princeton University Press.

Cleckley, H. (1955). *The mask of sanity*. St. Louis, MO: Mosby.

Clore, G. L., Schwarz, N., & Conway, M. (1994). Affective causes and consequences of social information processing. In R. S. Wyer & T. K. Srull (Eds.), *Handbook of social cognition* (Vol. 1, pp. 323–417). Hillsdale, NJ: Erlbaum.

Coleman, J. S. (1988). Social capital in the creation of human capital. *American Journal of Sociology, 94*, S95–S120.

Cosmides, L. (1989). The logic of social-exchange—Has natural selection shaped how humans reason—Studies with the Wason Selection Task. *Cognition, 31*, 187–276.

Cosmides, L., & Tooby, J. (1997). The modular nature of human intelligence. In A. B. Scheibel & J. W. Schopf (Eds.), *The origin and evolution of intelligence* (pp. 71–101). Boston: Jones and Bartlett.

Cosmides, L., & Tooby, J. (2005). Neurocognitive adaptations designed for social exchange. In D. M. Buss (Ed.), *The handbook of evolutionary psychology*. (pp. 584–627). Hoboken, NJ: John Wiley & Sons.

Cosmides, L., Tooby, J., Fiddick, L., & Bryant, G. A. (2005). Detecting cheaters: Comment. *Trends in Cognitive Sciences, 9*, 505–506.

Crisp, R. (Ed.). (1996). *How should one live?: Essays on the virtues*. Oxford, UK: Oxford University Press.

Cunningham, M. R. (1979). Weather, mood, and helping behavior: Quasi experiments with the sunshine samaritan. *Journal of Personality and Social Psychology, 37*, 1947–1956.

Cushman, F., Young, L., & Hauser, M. (2006). The role of conscious reasoning and intuition in moral judgment: Testing three principles of harm. *Psychological Science, 17*, 1082–1089.

Damasio, A. (1994). *Descartes' error: Emotion, reason, and the human brain*. New York: Putnam.

Damasio, A. (2003). *Looking for Spinoza*. Orlando, FL: Harcourt.

Dana, J., Weber, R. A., & Kuang, J. X. (2007). Exploiting moral wiggle room: Experiments demonstrating an illusory preference for fairness. *Economic Theory, 33*, 67–80.

Darley, J. M. (1992). Social organization for the production of evil. *Psychological Inquiry, 3*, 199–218.

Darley, J. M., & Batson, C. D. (1973). From Jerusalem to Jericho: A study of situational and dispositional variables in helping behavior. *Journal of Personality & Social Psychology, 27*, 100–108.

Darwin, C. (1998/1871). *The descent of man and selection in relation to sex*. Amherst, NY: Prometheus Books.

Dawkins, R. (1976). *The selfish gene*. London: Oxford University Press.

Dawkins, R. (2006). *The God delusion*. Boston: Houghton Mifflin.

de-Quervain, D. J. F., Fischbacher, U., Treyer, V., Schellhammer, M., Schnyder, U., Buck, A., et al. (2004). The neural basis of altruistic punishment. *Science, 305*, 1254–1258.

De Cremer, D., & Van Vugt, M. (1999). Social identification effects in social dilemmas: A transformation of motives. *European Journal of Social Psychology, 29*, 871.

de Waal, F. B. M. (1982). *Chimpanzee politics*. New York: Harper & Row.

de Waal, F. B. M. (1996). *Good natured: The origins of right and wrong in humans and other animals*. Cambridge, MA: Harvard University Press.

de Waal, F. B. M. (2008). Putting the altruism back into altruism: The evolution of empathy. *Annual Review of Psychology, 59*, 279–300.

Dennett, D. C. (2006). *Breaking the spell*: Religion as a natural phenomenon. New York: Penguin.

Deutsch, M., & Gerard, H. B. (1955). A study of normative and informational social influences upon individual judgment. *The Journal of Abnormal and Social Psychology, 51*, 629–636.

Dewey, J. (1922). *Human nature and conduct: An introduction to social psychology*. New York: Holt.

Ditto, P. H., & Lopez, D. F. (1992). Motivated skepticism: Use of differential decision criteria for preferred and nonpreferred conclusions. *Journal of Personality and Social Psychology, 63*, 568–584.

Ditto, P. H., Pizarro, D. A., & Tannenbaum, D. (2009). Motivated moral reasoning. In D. M. Bartels, C. W. Bauman, L. J. Skitka & D. L. Medin (Eds.), *The Psychology of Learning and Motivation, Vol. 50* (Vol. 50, pp. 307–338). Burlington, VT: Academic Press.

Ditto, P. H., Scepansky, J. A., Munro, G. D., Apanovitch, A. M., & Lockhart, L. K. (1998). Motivated sensitivity to preference-inconsistent information. *Journal of Personality and Social Psychology, 75*, 53–69.

Douglas, M. (1982). *In the active voice*. London: Routledge.

Dovidio, J. F. (1984). Helping behavior and altruism: An empirical and conceptual overview. In *Advances in experimental social psychology* (Vol. 17, pp. 361–427). New York: Academic Press.

Dovidio, J. F., Gaertner, S. L., Validzic, A., & Matoka, K. (1997). Extending the benefits of recategorization: Evaluations, self-disclosure, and helping. *Journal of Experimental Social Psychology, 33*, 401.

Dovidio, J. F., Piliavin, J. A., Gaertner, S. L., Schroeder, D. A., & Clark, R. D., III. (1991). The arousal: Cost-reward model and the process of intervention: A review of the evidence. In M. S. Clark (Ed.), *Prosocial behavior* (pp. 86–118). Newbury Park, CA: Sage Publications.

Dovidio, J. F., Piliavin, J. A., Schroeder, D. A., & Penner, L. (2006). *The social psychology of prosocial behavior*. Mahwah, NJ: Erlbaum.

Duckitt, J. (1989). Authoritarianism and group identification: A new view of an old construct. *Political Psychology, 10*, 63–84.

Dunbar, R. (1996). *Grooming, gossip, and the evolution of language.* Cambridge, MA: Harvard University Press.

Durkheim, E. (1965). *The elementary forms of religious life* (J. W. Swain, Trans.). New York: The Free Press. (Original work published in 1915.)

Durkheim, E. (1973). *Moral education* (E. Wilson & H. Schnurer, Trans.). New York: The Free Press. (Original work published in 1925.)

Efferson, C., Lalive, R., & Fehr, E. (2008). The coevolution of cultural groups and ingroup favoritism. *Science, 321,* 1844–1849.

Eliade, M. (1957/1959). *The sacred and the profane: The nature of religion.* W. R. Task (trans.). San Diego: Harcourt Brace.

Epley, N., & Dunning, D. (2000). Feeling "holier than thou": Are self-serving assessments produced by errors in self- or social prediction? *Journal of Personality & Social Psychology, 79,* 861–875.

Epstein, S., Pacini, R., Denes-Raj, V., & Heier, H. (1996). Individual differences in intuitive-experiential and analytical-rational thinking styles. *Journal of Personality and Social Psychology, 71,* 390–405.

Fazio, R. H., Sanbonmatsu, D. M., Powell, M. C., & Kardes, F. R. (1986). On the automatic evaluation of attitudes. *Journal of Personality and Social Psychology, 50,* 229–238.

Fehr, E., & Fischbacher, U. (2004). Social norms and human cooperation. *Trends in Cognitive Science, 8,* 185–190.

Fehr, E., & Gächter, S. (2002). Altruistic punishment in humans. *Nature, 415,* 137–140.

Fischer, K. W., & Tangney, J. P. (1995). Self-conscious emotions and the affect revolution: Framework and overview. In J. P. Tangney & K. W. Fischer (Eds.), *Self-conscious emotions: The psychology of shame, guilt, embarrassment, and pride.* New York: Guilford.

Fiske, A. P. (1991). *Structures of social life.* New York: Free Press.

Fiske, A. P. (2004). Relational Models Theory 2.0. In N. Haslam (Ed.), *Relational models theory: A contemporary overview* (pp. 3–25). Mahwah, NJ: Erlbaum.

Fiske, S. T. (1980). Attention and weight in person perception: The impact of negative and extreme behavior. *Journal of Personality and Social Psychology, 38,* 889–906.

Fiske, S. T. (1993). Social cognition and social perception. *Annual Review of Psychology, 44,* 155–194.

Flippen, A. R., Hornstein, H. A., Siegal, W. E., & Weitzman, E. A. (1996). A comparison of similarity and interdependence as triggers for in-group formation. *Personality and Social Psychology Bulletin, 22,* 882.

Frank, R. (1988). *Passions within reason: The strategic role of the emotions.* New York: Norton.

Freud, S. (1962). *The ego and the id* (J. Riviere, Trans.). New York: Norton. (Original work published in 1923.)

Freud, S. (1976). *The interpretation of dreams* (J. Strachey, Trans.). New York: Norton. (Original work published in 1900.)

Fried, R., & Berkowitz, L. (1979). Music hath charms . . . and can influence helpfulness. *Journal of Applied Social Psychology, 9,* 199.

Fultz, J., Batson, C. D., Fortenbach, V. A., McCarthy, P. M., & Varney, L. L. (1986). Social evaluation and the empathy-altruism hypothesis. *Journal of Personality and Social Psychology, 50,* 761–769.

Gaertner, S. L., Dovidio, J. F., Rust, M. C., Nier, J. A., Banker, B. S., Ward, C. M. et al. (1999). Reducing intergroup bias: Elements of intergroup cooperation. *Journal of Personality and Social Psychology, 76,* 388.

Gazzaniga, M. S. (1985). *The social brain.* New York: Basic Books.

Gazzaniga, M. S. (2008). *Human: The science behind what makes us unique.* New York: Ecco.

Gibbard, A. (1990). *Wise choices, apt feelings.* Cambridge, Mass: Harvard University Press.

Gibbs, J. C. (2003). *Moral development and reality: Beyond the theories of Kohlberg and Gibbs.* Thousand Oaks, CA: Sage.

Gigerenzer, G. (2007). *Gut feelings: The intelligence of the unconscious.* New York: Penguin.

Gilbert, D. (1999). What the mind's not. In S. Chaiken & Y. Trope (Eds.), *Dual process theories in social psychology* (pp. 3–11). New York: Guilford.

Gilligan, C. (1982). *In a different voice: Psychological theory and women's development.* Cambridge, MA: Harvard University Press.

Gilovich, T., Keltner, D., & Nisbett, R. E. (2006). *Social psychology.* New York: Norton.

Gintis, H., Bowles, S., Boyd, R., & Fehr, E. (2005a). Moral sentiments and material interests: Origins, evidence, and consequences. In H. Gintis, S. Bowles, R. Boyd & E. Fehr (Eds.), *Moral sentiments and material interests: The foundations of cooperation in economic life.* (pp. 3–39). Cambridge, MA: MIT Press.

Gintis, H., Bowles, S., Boyd, R., & Fehr, E. (Eds.). (2005b). *Moral sentiments and material interests: The foundations of cooperation in economic life.* Cambridge, MA: MIT Press.

Glover, J. (2000). *Humanity: A moral history of the twentieth century.* New Haven, CT: Yale University Press.

Goethals, G. R., Messick, D. M., & Allison, S. T. (1991). The uniqueness bias: Studies of constructive social comparison. In J. Suls & T. A. Wills (Eds.), *Social comparison: Contemporary theory and research* (pp. 149–176). Hillsdale, NJ: Erlbaum.

Goodall, J. (1986). *The chimpanzees of Gombe: Patterns of behavior.* Cambridge, MA: Belknap Press.

Graham, J., & Haidt, J. (in press). Beyond beliefs: Religion binds individuals into moral communities. *Personality and Social Psychology Review.*

Graham, J., Haidt, J., & Nosek, B. (2009). Liberals and conservatives rely on different sets of moral foundations. *Journal of Personality and Social Psychology, 96,* 1029–1046.

Greene, J. D. (2008). The secret joke of Kant's soul. In W. Sinnott-Armstrong (Ed.), *Moral psychology: Vol. 2. The cognitive science of morality (pp.* 35-79). Cambridge, MA: MIT Press.

Greene, J. D. (in press). The cognitive neuroscience of moral judgment. In M. Gazzaniga (Ed.), *The cognitive neurosciences IV.* Cambridge, MA: MIT Press.

Greene, J. D., Morelli, S. A., Lowenberg, K., Nystrom, L. E., & Cohen, J. D. (2008). Cognitive load selectively interferes with utilitarian moral judgment. *Cognition, 107,* 1144–1154.

Greene, J. D., Nystrom, L. E., Engell, A. D., Darley, J. M., & Cohen, J. D. (2004). The neural bases of cognitive conflict and control in moral judgment. *Neuron, 44,* 389–400.

Greene, J. D., Sommerville, R. B., Nystrom, L. E., Darley, J. M., & Cohen, J. D. (2001). An fMRI study of emotional engagement in moral judgment. *Science, 293,* 2105–2108.

Greenwald, A. G., McGhee, D. E., & Schwartz, J. L. (1998). Measuring individual differences in implicit cognition: The implicit association test. *Journal of Personality and Social Psychology, 74,* 1464–1480.

Greenwald, A. G., Nosek, B. A., & Banaji, M. R. (2003). Understanding and using the Implicit Association Test. *Journal of Personality and Social Psychology, 85,* 197–216.

Gross, N., & Simmons, S. (2007). *The social and political views of American professors.* Unpublished manuscript, Harvard University.

Gurerk, O., Irlenbusch, B., & Rockenbach, B. (2006). The competitive advantage of sanctioning institutions. *Science, 312,* 108–111.

Guthrie, S. E. (1993). *Faces in the clouds.* New York: Oxford.

Haidt, J. (2001). The emotional dog and its rational tail: A social intuitionist approach to moral judgment. *Psychological Review, 108,* 814–834.

Haidt, J. (2003). The moral emotions. In R. J. Davidson, K. R. Scherer & H. H. Goldsmith (Eds.), *Handbook of affective sciences* (pp. 852–870). Oxford, UK: Oxford University Press.

Haidt, J. (2007). The new synthesis in moral psychology. *Science, 316,* 998–1002.

Haidt, J. (2008). Morality. *Perspectives on Psychological Science, 3,* 65–72.

Haidt, J., & Bjorklund, F. (2008). Social intuitionists answer six questions about morality. In W. Sinnott-Armstrong (Ed.), *Moral psychology: Vol. 2. The cognitive science of morality* (pp. 181–217). Cambridge, MA: MIT Press.

Haidt, J., & Graham, J. (2009). Planet of the Durkheimians, where community, authority, and sacredness are foundations of morality. In J. Jost, A. C. Kay & H. Thorisdottir (Eds.), *Social and psychological bases of ideology and system justification* (pp. 371–401). New York: Oxford.

Haidt, J., & Hersh, M. A. (2001). Sexual morality: The cultures and reasons of liberals and conservatives. *Journal of Applied Social Psychology, 31,* 191–221.

Haidt, J., & Joseph, C. (2004, Fall). Intuitive ethics: How innately prepared intuitions generate culturally variable virtues. *Daedalus,* 55–66.

Haidt, J., Koller, S., & Dias, M. (1993). Affect, culture, and morality, or is it wrong to eat your dog? *Journal of Personality and Social Psychology, 65,* 613–628.

Haidt, J., McCauley, C., & Rozin, P. (1994). Individual differences in sensitivity to disgust: A scale sampling seven domains of disgust elicitors. *Personality and Individual Differences, 16,* 701–713.

Haley, K. J., & Fessler, D. M. T. (2005). Nobody's watching? Subtle cues affect generosity in an anonymous economic game. *Evolution and Human Behavior, 26,* 245–256.

Hamilton, W. D. (1964). The genetical evolution of social behavior, parts 1 and 2. *Journal of Theoretical Biology, 7,* 1–52.

Hamlin, J. K., Wynn, K., & Bloom, P. (2007). Social evaluation by preverbal infants. *Nature, 450,* 557–560.

Hammerstein, P. (2003). Why is reciprocity so rare in social animals? In P. Hammerstein (Ed.), *Genetic and cultural evolution of cooperation* (pp. 55–82). Cambridge, MA: MIT Press.

Hardin, G. (1968). Tragedy of the commons. *Science, 162,* 1243–1248.

Hare, R. D. (1993). *Without conscience.* New York: Pocket Books.

Hare, R. M. (1981). *Moral thinking: Its levels, method, and point.* Oxford, UK: Oxford University Press.

Harris, S. (2006). *Letter to a Christian nation.* New York: Knopf.

Haselton, M. G., & Buss, D. M. (2000). Error management theory: A new perspective on biases in cross-sex mind reading. *Journal of Personality and Social Psychology, 78,* 81–91.

Hauser, M. (2006). *Moral minds: How nature designed our universal sense of right and wrong.* New York: HarperCollins.

Hawks, J., Wang, E. T., Cochran, G. M., Harpending, H. C., & Moyzis, R. K. (2007). Recent acceleration of human adaptive evolution. *Proceedings of the National Academy of Sciences of the United States of America, 104,* 20753–20758.

Henrich, J. (2004). Cultural group selection, coevolutionary processes and large-scale cooperation. *Journal of Economic Behavior & Organization, 53,* 3–35.

Henrich, J., Boyd, R., Bowles, S., Camerer, C., Fehr, E., Gintis, H., et al. (2005). 'Economic man' in cross-cultural perspective: Behavioral experiments in 15 small-scale societies. *Behavioral and Brain Sciences, 28,* 795–855.

Henrich, N., & Henrich, J. (2007). *Why humans cooperate: A cultural and evolutionary explanation.* Oxford: Oxford University Press.

Herdt, G. (1981). *The Sambia: Ritual and gender in New Guinea.* New York: Holt, Rinehart and Winston.

Hogg, M. A. (2010). Influence and leadership. In S. Fiske & D. Gilbert (Eds.), *The handbook of social psychology* (5th ed.). Hoboken, NJ: Wiley & Sons.

Hsu, M., Anen, C., & Quartz, S. R. (2008). The right and the good: Distributive justice and neural encoding of equity and efficiency. *Science, 320,* 1092–1095.

Huebner, B., Dwyer, S., & Hauser, M. (2009). The role of emotion in moral psychology. *Trends in Cognitive Sciences, 13,* 1–6.

Hume, D. (1960). *An enquiry concerning the principles of morals.* La Salle, IL: Open Court. (Original work published in 1777.)

Hunter, J. D. (1991). *Culture wars: The struggle to define America.* New York: Basic Books.

Hunter, J. D. (2000). *The death of character: Moral education in an age without good and evil.* New York: Basic.

Ibn-Khaldun. (2004). *The Muqaddimah* (F. Rosenthal, Trans. Abridged and edited by N. J. Dawood ed.). Princeton, NJ: Princeton University Press.

Inbar, Y., Pizarro, D. A., & Bloom, P. (in press). Conservatives are more easily disgusted than liberals. *Emotion.*

Inbar, Y., Pizarro, D. A., Knobe, J., & Bloom, P. (in press). Disgust sensitivity predicts intuitive disapproval of gays. *Emotion.*

Isen, A. M., & Levin, P. F. (1972). Effect of feeling good on helping: Cookies and kindness. *Journal of Personality and Social Psychology, 21,* 384–388.

James, W. (1950). *The principles of psychology* (Vol. 2). New York: Dover. (Original work published in 1890.)

Jensen, L. A. (1997). Different worldviews, different morals: America's culture war divide. *Human Development, 40,* 325–344.

Johansson, P., Hall, L., Sikstrom, S., & Olsson, A. (2005). Failure to detect mismatches between intention and outcome in a simple decision task. *Science, 310,* 116–119.

Jost, J. T., Glaser, J., Kruglanski, A. W., & Sulloway, F. J. (2003). Political conservatism as motivated social cognition. *Psychological Bulletin, 129,* 339–375.

Jost, J. T., & Hunyady, O. (2002). The psychology of system justification and the palliative function of ideology. *European Review of Social Psychology, 13,* 111–153.

Joyce, R. (2006). *The evolution of morality.* Cambridge, MA: MIT.

Kagan, J. (1984). *The nature of the child.* New York: Basic Books.

Kahan, D. M. (2005). The logic of reciprocity: Trust, collective action, and law. In H. Gintis, S. Bowles, R. Boyd, & E. Fehr (Eds.), *Moral sentiments and material interests* (pp. 339–378). Cambridge, MA: MIT Press.

Kant, I. (1959). *Foundation of the metaphysics of morals* (L. W. Beck, Trans.). Indianapolis: Bobbs-Merrill. (Original work published in 1785.)

Kassin, S. M., Fein, S., & Markus, H. R. (2008). *Social psychology* (7th ed.). Boston: Houghton Mifflin.

Katz, D. (1960). The functional approach to the study of attitudes. *The Public Opinion Quarterly, 24,* 163–204.

Kiehl, K. A. (2006). A cognitive neuroscience perspective on psychopathy: Evidence for paralimbic system dysfunction. *Psychiatry Research, 142,* 107–128.

Killen, M., & Smetana, J. G. (2006). *Handbook of moral development.* Mahwah, NJ: Erlbaum.

Kinder, D. E. (1998). Opinion and action in the realm of politics. In D. Gilbert, S. Fiske, & G. Lindzey (Eds.), *Handbook of social psychology* (pp. 778-867). New York: McGraw-Hill.

Kinzler, K. D., Dupoux, E., & Spelke, E. S. (2007). The native language of social cognition. *Proceedings of the National Academy of Sciences of the United States of America, 104,* 12577–12580.

Knobe, J. (2003). Intentional action in folk psychology: An experimental investigation. *Philosophical Psychology, 16,* 309–324.

Koenigs, M., Young, L., Adolphs, R., Tranel, D., Cushman, F., Hauser, M., et al. (2007). Damage to the prefrontal cortex increases utilitarian moral judgements. *Nature, 446*, 908–911.

Kogut, T., & Ritov, I. (2005). The 'identified victim' effect: An identified group, or just a single individual? *Journal of Behavioral Decision Making, 18*, 157–167.

Kohlberg, L. (1969). Stage and sequence: The cognitive-developmental approach to socialization. In D. A. Goslin (Ed.), *Handbook of socialization theory and research* (pp. 347–480). Chicago: Rand McNally.

Kohlberg, L. (1971). From is to ought: How to commit the naturalistic fallacy and get away with it in the study of moral development. In T. Mischel (Ed.), *Psychology and genetic epistemology* (pp. 151–235). New York: Academic Press.

Kohlberg, L., Levine, C., & Hewer, A. (1983). *Moral stages: A current formulation and a response to critics.* Basel, Switzerland: Karger.

Kramer, R. M., & Brewer, M. B. (1984). Effects of group identity on resource use in a simulated commons dilemma. *Journal of Personality and Social Psychology, 46*, 1044.

Kuhn, D. (1991). *The skills of argument.* Cambridge: Cambridge University Press.

Kunda, Z. (1990). The case for motivated reasoning. *Psychological Bulletin, 108*, 480–498.

Kurzban, R., & Aktipis, C. A. (2007). Modularity and the social mind: Are psychologists too self-ish?. *Personality and Social Psychology Review, 11*, 131–149.

Kurzban, R., DeScioli, P., & O'Brien, E. (2007). Audience effects on moralistic punishment. *Evolution and Human Behavior, 28*, 75–84.

Kurzban, R., Tooby, J., & Cosmides, L. (2001). Can race be erased? Coalitional computation and social categorization. *Proceedings of the National Academy of Sciences of the United States of America, 98*, 15387–15392.

Lakoff, G. (1996). *Moral politics: What conservatives know that liberals don't.* Chicago: University of Chicago Press.

Lakoff, G. (2004). *Don't think of an elephant: Know your values and frame the debate.* White River Junction, VT: Chelsea Green.

Lakoff, G. (2008). *The political mind.* New York: Viking.

Latane, B., & Darley, J. M. (1970). *The unresponsive bystander.* Englewood Cliffs: Prentice Hall.

Lazarus, R. S. (1991). Cognition and motivation in emotion. *American Psychologist, 46*, 352–367.

Lazarus, R. S. (1984). On the primacy of cognition. *American Psychologist, 39*, 124–129.

Leary, M. (2004). *The curse of the self: Self-awareness, egotism, and the quality of human life.* Oxford, UK: Oxford.

Lerner, J. S., & Tetlock, P. E. (2003). Bridging individual, interpersonal, and institutional approaches to judgment and decision making: The impact of accountability on cognitive bias. In S. L. Schneider & J. Shanteau (Eds.), *Emerging perspectives on judgment and decision research* (pp. 431–457). New York: Cambridge.

Levine, M., Cassidy, C., Brazier, G., & Reicher, S. (2002). Self-categorization and bystander non-intervention: Two experimental studies. *Journal of Applied Social Psychology, 32*, 1452.

Levine, M., Prosser, A., Evans, D., & Reicher, S. (2005). Identity and emergency intervention: how social group membership and inclusiveness of group boundaries shape helping behavior. *Personality and Social Psychology Bulletin, 31*, 443.

Levine, M., & Thompson, K. (2004). Identity, place, and bystander intervention: Social categories and helping after natural disasters. *Journal of Social Psychology, 144*, 229.

Lewis, M., & Haviland-Jones J. M. (Eds.). (1993). *Handbook of emotions.* New York: Guilford Press.

Leys, S. (1997). *The analects of Confucius* (S. Leys, Trans.). New York: Norton.

Locke, J. (1983/1689). *A letter concerning toleration* (J. Tully, Trans.). Indianapolis: Hackett Publishing.

Locksley, A., Ortiz, V., & Hepburn, C. (1980). Social categorization and discriminatory behavior: Extinguishing the minimal intergroup discrimination effect. *Journal of Personality and Social Psychology, 39*, 773–783.

Loewenstein, G., & Small, D. A. (2007). The Scarecrow and the Tin Man: The vicissitudes of human sympathy and caring. *Review of General Psychology, 11*, 112–126.

Loftus, E. F. (1975). Leading questions and eyewitness report. *Cognitive Psychology, 7*, 560–572.

Lowenthal, D. (1986). *The past is a foreign country.* New York: Cambridge University Press.

Luo, Q., Nakic, M., Wheatley, T., Richell, R., Martin, A., & Blair, R. J. R. (2006). The neural basis of implicit moral attitude—An IAT study using event-related fMRI. *Neuroimage, 30*, 1449–1457.

MacIntyre, A. (1981). *After virtue.* South Bend, IN: University of Notre Dame Press.

Margolis, H. (1987). *Patterns, thinking, and cognition.* Chicago: University of Chicago Press.

Markus, H. R., & Kitayama, S. (1991). Culture and the self: Implications for cognition, emotion, and motivation. *Psychological Review, 98*, 224–253.

Marques, J. M., Yzerbyt, V. Y., & Leyens, J.-P. (1988). The 'Black Sheep Effect': Extremity of judgments towards ingroup members as a function of group identification. *European Journal of Social Psychology, 18*, 1–16.

Maynard Smith, J., & Szathmary, E. (1997). *The major transitions in evolution.* Oxford, UK: Oxford University Press.

Mayr, E. (1963). *Animal species and evolution.* Cambridge, MA: Harvard.

McAdams, D. P. (2006). *The redemptive self: stories Americans live by.* New York: Oxford University Press.

McAdams, D. P., Albaugh, M., Farber, E., Daniels, J., Logan, R. L., & Olson, B. (2008). Family metaphors and moral intuitions: How conservatives and liberals narrate their lives. *Journal of Personality and Social Psychology, 95*, 978–990.

McDougall, W. (1998). *An introduction to social psychology.* Boston: John W. Luce. (Original work published in 1908.)

McDowell, J. (1979). Virtue and reason. *Monist, 62*, 331–350.

McNeill, W. H. (1995). *Keeping together in time: Dance and drill in human history.* Cambridge, MA: Harvard University Press.

Mealy, L., Daood, C., & Krage, M. (1996). Enhanced memory for faces of cheaters. *Ethology and Sociobiology, 17*, 119–128.

Merton, R. K. (1968). *Social theory and social structure.* New York: Free Press.

Midlarsky, E., & Midlarsky, M. (1973). Some determinants of aiding under experimentally-induced stress. *Journal of Personality, 41*, 305–327.

Mikhail, J. (2007). Universal moral grammar: Theory, evidence and the future. *Trends in Cognitive Sciences, 11*, 143–152.

Milgram, S. (1963). Behavioral study of obedience. *Journal of Abnormal and Social Psychology, 67*, 371–378.

Miller, L. C., Murphy, R., & Buss, A. H. (1981). Consciousness of body: Private and public. *Journal of Personality and Social Psychology, 41*, 397–406.

Moll, J., Krueger, F., Zahn, R., Pardini, M., de Oliveira-Souza, R., & Grafman, J. (2006). Human fronto-mesolimbic networks guide decisions about charitable donation. *Proceedings of the National Academy of Sciences of the United States of America, 103*, 15623–15628.

Monahan, J. L., Murphy, S. T., & Zajonc, R. B. (2000). Subliminal mere exposure: Specific, general, and diffuse effects. *Psychological Science, 11*, 462–466.

Monin, B., & Miller, D. T. (2001). Moral credentials and the expression of prejudice. *Journal of Personality and Social Psychology, 81*, 33–43.

Mullen, E., & Skitka, L. J. (2006). Exploring the psychological underpinnings of the moral mandate effect: Motivated reasoning, group differentiation, or anger? *Journal of Personality and Social Psychology, 90*, 629–643.

Myers, D. (2008). *Social psychology* (9th ed.). New York: McGraw-Hill.

Neuberg, S., Shaller, M., & Kenrick, D. (2010). Evolution. In S. Fiske & D. Gilbert (Eds.), *The handbook of social psychology* (5th ed.). Hoboken, NJ: John Wiley & Sons.

Newcomb, T. M. (1943). *Personality and social change: Attitude formation in a student community*. New York: Dryden.

Nickerson, R. S. (1998). Confirmation bias: A ubiquitous phenomenon in many guises. *Review of General Psychology, 2*, 175–220.

Nisbet, R. A. (1966/1993). *The sociological tradition* (2nd ed.). New Brunswick, NJ: Transaction. (Original work published 1966).

Nisbett, R. E., & Cohen, D. (1996). *Culture of honor: The psychology of violence in the South*. Boulder, CO: Westview Press.

Nisbett, R. E., & Wilson, T. D. (1977). Telling more than we can know: Verbal reports on mental processes. *Psychological Review, 84*, 231–259.

Norenzayan, A., & Shariff, A. F. (2008). The origin and evolution of religious prosociality. *Science, 322*, 58–62.

North, A. C., Tarrant, M., & Hargreaves, D. J. (2004). The effects of music on helping behavior: A field study. *Environment and Behavior, 36*, 266.

Nowak, M. A. (2006). Five rules for the evolution of cooperation. *Science, 314*, 1560–1563.

Nowak, M. A., & Sigmund, K. (1998). The dynamics of indirect reciprocity. *Journal of Theoretical Biology, 194*, 561–574.

Nucci, L., & Turiel, E. (1978). Social interactions and the development of social concepts in preschool children. *Child Development, 49*, 400–407.

Nussbaum, M. C. (1999). "Secret sewers of vice": Disgust, bodies, and the law. In S. A. Bandes (Ed.), *The passions of law* (pp. 19–62). New York: New York University Press.

Panchanathan, K., & Boyd, R. (2004). Indirect reciprocity can stabilize cooperation without the second-order free rider problem. *Nature, 432*, 499–502.

Pennington, J., & Schlenker, B. R. (1999). Accountability for consequential decisions: Justifying ethical judgments to audiences. *Personality and Social Psychology Bulletin, 25*, 1067–1081.

Perkins, D. N., Farady, M., & Bushey, B. (1991). Everyday reasoning and the roots of intelligence. In J. F. Voss, D. N. Perkins & J. W. Segal (Eds.), *Informal reasoning and education* (pp. 83–105). Hillsdale, NJ: Erlbaum.

Piliavin, I. M., Piliavin, J. A., & Rodin, J. (1975). Costs, diffusion, and the stigmatized victim. *Journal of Personality and Social Psychology, 32*, 429–438.

Pincoffs, E. L. (1986). *Quandaries and virtues: Against reductivism in ethics*. Lawrence: University of Kansas.

Pinker, S. (2002). *The blank slate: The modern denial of human nature*. New York: Viking.

Pizarro, D. A., & Bloom, P. (2003). The intelligence of the moral intuitions: Comment on Haidt (2001). *Psychological Review, 110*, 193–196.

Pizarro, D. A., Laney, C., Morris, E. K., & Loftus, E. F. (2006). Ripple effects in memory: Judgments of moral blame can distort memory for events. *Memory & Cognition, 34*, 550–555.

Prinz, J. J. (2008). *The emotional construction of morals*. New York: Oxford.

Proffitt, D. R. (2006). Embodied perception and the economy of action. *Perspectives on Psychological Science, 1*, 110–122.

Putnam, R. D. (2007). E Pluribus Unum: Diversity and community in the twenty-first century. *Scandinavian Political Studies, 30*, 137–174.

Pyszczynski, T., & Greenberg, J. (1987). Toward an integration of cognitive and motivational perspectives on social inference: A biased hypothesis-testing model. *Advances in Experimental Social Psychology, 20*, 297–340.

Rawls, J. (1971). *A theory of justice*. Cambridge, MA: Harvard University Press.

Redding, R. E. (2001). Sociopolitical diversity in psychology: The case for pluralism. *American Psychologist, 56*, 205–215.

Richerson, P. J., & Boyd, R. (1998). The evolution of human ultra-sociality. In I. Eibl-Eibesfeldt & F. K. Salter (Eds.), *Indoctrinability, ideology, and warfare: Evolutionary perspectives* (pp. 71–95). New York: Berghahn.

Richerson, P. J., & Boyd, R. (2005). *Not by genes alone: How culture transformed human evolution*. Chicago: University of Chicago Press.

Ridley, M. (1996). *The origins of virtue*. Harmondsworth, UK: Penguin.

Rilling, J. K., Glenn, A. L., Jairam, M. R., Pagnoni, G., Goldsmith, D. R., Elfenbein, H. A., et al. (2007). Neural correlates of social cooperation and non-cooperation as a function of psychopathy. *Biological Psychiatry, 61*, 1260–1271.

Riskey, D. R., & Birnbaum, M. H. (1974). Compensatory effects in moral judgment: Two rights don't make up for a wrong. *Journal of Experimental Psychology, 103*, 171–173.

Robinson, P. H., Kurzban, R., & Jones, O. D. (2007). The origins of shared intuitions of justice. *Vanderbilt Law Review, 60*, 1633–1688.

Rosenhan, D. L., Underwood, B., & Moore, B. (1974). Affect moderates self-gratification and altruism. *Journal of Personality and Social Psychology, 30*, 546–552.

Rozin, P., & Royzman, E. B. (2001). Negativity bias, negativity dominance, and contagion. *Personality and Social Psychology Review, 5*, 296–320.

Sabini, J., & Silver, M. (1982). *Moralities of everyday life*. Oxford: Oxford University Press.

Saltzstein, H. D., & Kasachkoff, T. (2004). Haidt's moral intuitionist theory. *Review of General Psychology, 8*, 273–282.

Sanfey, A. G., Rilling, J. K., Aronson, J. A., Nystrom, L. E., & Cohen, J. D. (2003). The neural basis of economic decision-making in the ultimatum game. *Science, 300*, 1755–1758.

Satow, K. L. (1975). Social approval and helping. *Journal of Experimental Social Psychology, 11*, 501–509.

Schelling, T. C. (Ed.). (1968). *The life you save may be your own*. Washington DC: The Brookings Institute.

Schnall, S., Haidt, J., Clore, G. L., & Jordan, A. H. (2008). Disgust as embodied moral judgment. *Personality and Social Psychology Bulletin, 34*, 1096–1109.

Schwartz, S. H. (1992). Universals in the content and structure of values. In M. P. Zanna (Ed.), *Advances in experimental social psychology* (Vol. 25, pp. 1–65). New York: Academic Press.

Seligman, M. E. P. (1971). Phobias and preparedness. *Behavior Therapy, 2*, 307–320.

Shariff, A. F., & Norenzayan, A. (2009). *Mean gods make good people: Different views of god predict cheating behavior*. Unpublished manuscript, University of British Columbia.

Shariff, A. F., Norenzayan, A., & Henrich, J. (in press). The birth of high gods: How the cultural evolution of supernatural policing influenced the emergence of complex, cooperative human societies, paving the way for civilization. In M. Schaller, A. Norenzayan, S. Heine, T. Yamagishi & T. Kameda (Eds.), *Evolution, culture and the human mind*. Mahwah, NJ: Erlbaum.

Sherif, M. (1936). *The psychology of social norms*. New York: Harper.

Sherif, M., Harvey, O. J., White, B. J., Hood, W., & Sherif, C. (1961). *Intergroup conflict and cooperation: The Robbers Cave experiment*. Norman: University of Oklahoma Institute of Group Relations.

Shweder, R. A. (1990). Cultural psychology: What is it? In J. W. Stigler, R. A. Shweder & G. Herdt (Eds.), *Cultural psychology: Essays on comparative human development* (pp. 1–43). New York: Cambridge University Press.

Shweder, R. A., & Bourne, E. (1984). Does the concept of the person vary cross-culturally? In R. Shweder & R. LeVine (Eds.), *Culture theory* (pp. 158–199). Cambridge, UK: Cambridge University Press.

Shweder, R. A., & Haidt, J. (1993). The future of moral psychology: Truth, intuition, and the pluralist way. *Psychological Science, 4*, 360–365.

Shweder, R. A., Mahapatra, M., & Miller, J. (1987). Culture and moral development. In J. Kagan & S. Lamb (Eds.), *The emergence of morality in young children* (pp. 1–83). Chicago: University of Chicago Press.

Shweder, R. A., Much, N. C., Mahapatra, M., & Park, L. (1997). The "big three" of morality (autonomy, community, and divinity), and the "big three" explanations of suffering. In A. Brandt & P. Rozin (Eds.), *Morality and health* (pp. 119–169). New York: Routledge.

Sinclair, S., Lowery, B. S., Hardin, C. D., & Colangelo, A. (2005). Social tuning of automatic racial attitudes: The role of affiliative motivation. *Journal of Personality and Social Psychology, 89*, 583–592.

Singer, P. (1979). *Practical ethics*. Cambridge, UK: Cambridge University Press.

Skinner, B. F. (1938). *The behavior of organisms*. New York: Appleton-Century-Crofts.

Skitka, L. J., Bauman, C. W., & Sargis, E. G. (2005). Moral conviction: Another contributor to attitude strength or something more? *Journal of Personality and Social Psychology, 88*, 895–917.

Skowronski, J. J., & Carlston, D. E. (1987). Social judgment and social memory—the role of cue diagnosticity in negativity, positivity, and extremity biases. *Journal of Personality and Social Psychology, 52*, 689–699.

Sloman, S. A. (1996). The empirical case for two systems of reasoning. *Psychological Bulletin, 119*, 3–22.

Slovic, P. (2007). 'If I look at the mass I will never act': Psychic numbing and genocide. *Judgment and Decision Making, 2*, 79–95.

Smail, D. L. (2008). *On deep history and the brain*. Berkeley, CA: University of California.

Small, D. A., Loewenstein, G., & Slovic, P. (2007). Sympathy and callousness: The impact of deliberative thought on donations to identifiable and statistical victims. *Organizational Behavior and Human Decision Processes, 102*, 143–153.

Smith, E. R., & Semin, G. R. (2004). Socially situated cognition: Cognition in its social context. In M. P. Zanna (Ed.), *Advances in experimental social psychology* (Vol. 36, pp. 53–117). San Diego, CA: Elsevier Academic Press.

Smith, M. B., Bruner, J., & White, R. W. (1956). *Opinions and personality*. New York: Wiley.

Snyder, M., & Swann, W. B. (1978). Hypothesis-testing processes in social interaction. *Journal of Personality and Social Psychology, 36*, 1202–1212.

Snyder, M. L., Kleck, R. E., Strenta, A., & Mentzer, S. J. (1979). Avoidance of the handicapped: An attributional ambiguity analysis. *Journal of Personality and Social Psychology, 37*, 2297.

Sosis, R., & Bressler, E. R. (2003). Cooperation and commune longevity: A test of the costly signaling theory of religion. *Cross-Cultural Research: The Journal of Comparative Social Science, 37*, 211–239.

Sosis, R., & Ruffle, B. J. (2003). Religious ritual and cooperation: Testing for a relationship on Israeli religious and secular kibbutzim. *Current Anthropology, 44*, 713–722.

Sowell, T. (2002). *A conflict of visions: The ideological origins of political struggles*. New York: Basic.

Stenner, K. (2005). *The authoritarian dynamic*. New York: Cambridge University Press.

Sumner, W. G. (1907). *Folkways: A study of the sociological importance of usages, manners, customs, and morals*. Boston: Ginn & Co.

Sunstein, C. R. (2005). Moral heuristics. *Brain and Behavioral Sciences, 28*, 531–573.

Tajfel, H., Billig, M. G., Bundy, R. P., & Flament, C. (1971). Social categorization and intergroup behaviour. *European Journal of Social Psychology, 1*(2), 149–178.

Tajfel, H., & Turner, J. C. (1979). An integrative theory of intergroup conflict. In W. G. Austin & S. Worchel (Eds.), *The social psychology of intergroup relations* (pp. 33–47). Monterey, CA.: Brooks-Cole.

Taylor, S. E. (1991). Asymmetrical effects of positive and negative events: The mobilization-minimization hypothesis. *Psychological Bulletin, 110*, 67–85.

Tetlock, P. E. (2002). Social functionalist frameworks for judgment and choice: Intuitive politicians, theologians, and prosecutors. *Psychological Review, 109*, 451–457.

Tetlock, P. E., Skitka, L., & Boettger, R. (1989). Social and cognitive strategies for coping with accountability: Conformity, complexity, and bolstering. *Journal of Personality and Social Psychology, 57*, 632–640.

Thaler, R. (1988). The ultimatum game. *Journal of Economic Perspectives, 2*, 195–206.

Tishkoff, S. A., Reed, F. A., Ranciaro, A., Voight, B. F., Babbitt, C. C., Silverman, J. S., et al. (2007). Convergent adaptation of human lactase persistence in Africa and Europe. *Nature Genetics, 39*, 31–40.

Todorov, A., Mandisodza, A. N., Goren, A., & Hall, C. C. (2005). Inferences of competence from faces predict election outcomes. *Science, 308*, 1623–1626.

Tönnies, F. (2001). *Community and civil society* (J. Harris & M. Hollis, Trans.). Cambridge, UK: Cambridge University Press. (Original work published in 1887.)

Tooby, J., Cosmides, L., & Barrett, H. C. (2005). Resolving the debate on innate ideas: Learnability constraints and the evolved interpenetration of motivational and conceptual functions. In P. Carruthers, S. Laurence, & S. Stich (Eds.), *The innate mind: Structure and contents* (pp. 305–337). New York: Oxford University Press.

Triandis, H. C. (1995). *Individualism and collectivism*. Boulder, CO: Westview.

Trivers, R. L. (1971). The evolution of reciprocal altruism. *Quarterly Review of Biology, 46*, 35–57.

Trut, L. N. (1999). Early canid domestication: The farm fox experiment. *American Scientist, 87*, 160–169.

Turchin, P. (2006). *War and peace and war*. New York: Pi Press.

Turiel, E. (1983). *The development of social knowledge: Morality and convention*. Cambridge, UK: Cambridge University Press.

Turiel, E. (2006). Thought, emotions, and social interactional processes in moral development. In M. Killen & J. G. Smetana (Eds.), *Handbook of moral development* (pp. 7–35). Mahwah, NJ: Erlbaum.

Valdesolo, P., & DeSteno, D. (2006). Manipulations of emotional context shape moral judgment. *Psychological Science, 17*, 476.

Valdesolo, P., & DeSteno, D. (2007). Moral hypocrisy: Social groups and the flexibility of virtue. *Psychological Science, 18*, 689–690.

Valdesolo, P., & DeSteno, D. (2008). The duality of virtue: Deconstructing the moral hypocrite. *Journal of Experimental Social Psychology, 44*, 1334–1338.

Van Lange, P. A. (1991). Being better but not smarter than others: The Muhammad Ali effect at work in interpersonal situations. *Personality and Social Psychology Bulletin, 17,* 689–693.

Van Lange, P. A. M., & Sedikides, C. (1998). Being more honest but not necessarily more intelligent than others: Generality and explanations for the Muhammad Ali effect. *European Journal of Social Psychology, 28,* 675–680.

van Rompay, T. J. L., Vonk, D. J., & Fransen, M. L. (2009). The eye of the camera: Effects of security cameras on prosocial behavior. *Environment and Behavior, 41,* 60–74.

Vastfjall, D., Peters, E., & Slovic, P. (in prep). *Representation, affect, and willingness to donate to children in need.* Unpublished manuscript.

Vitz, P. C. (1990). The use of stories in moral development: New psychological reasons for an old educational method. *American Psychologist, 45,* 709–720.

Voight, B. F., Kudaravalli, S., Wen, X., & Pritchard, J. K. (2006). A map of recent positive selection in the human genome. *Plos Biology, 4,* e72.

Walker, L. J. (1984). Sex differences in the development of moral reasoning: A critical review. *Child Development, 55,* 677–691.

Warneken, F., & Tomasello, M. (2006). Altruistic helping in human infants and young chimpanzees. *Science, 311,* 1301–1303.

Wason, P. C. (1969). Regression in reasoning? *British Journal of Psychology, 60,* 471–480.

Westen, D. (2007). *The political brain.* New York: Public Affairs.

Wheatley, T., & Haidt, J. (2005). Hypnotic disgust makes moral judgments more severe. *Psychological Science, 16,* 780–784.

Wiessner, P. (2005). Norm enforcement among the Ju/'hoansi Bushmen. *Human Nature, 16,* 115–145.

Williams, G. C. (1966). *Adaptation and natural selection: A critique of some current evolutionary thought.* Princeton, NJ: Princeton University Press.

Williams, G. C. (1988). Reply to comments on "Huxley's evolution and ethics in sociobiological perspective." *Zygon, 23,* 437–438.

Williamson, S. H., Hubisz, M. J., Clark, A. G., Payseur, B. A., Bustamante, C. D., & Nielsen, R. (2007). Localizing recent adaptive evolution in the human genome. *Plos Genetics, 3,* e90.

Wilson, D. S. (2002). *Darwin's cathedral: Evolution, religion, and the nature of society.* Chicago: University of Chicago Press.

Wilson, D. S., Van Vugt, M., & O'Gorman, R. (2008). Multilevel selection theory and major evolutionary transitions: Implications for psychological science. *Current Directions in Psychological Science, 17,* 6–9.

Wilson, D. S., & Wilson, E. O. (2007). Rethinking the theoretical foundation of sociobiology. *Quarterly Review of Biology, 82,* 327–348.

Wilson, E. O. (1975). *Sociobiology.* Cambridge, MA: Harvard University Press.

Wilson, E. O. (1990). *Success and dominance in ecosystems: The case of the social insects.* Oldendorf, Germany: Ecology Institute.

Wilson, E. O. (1998). *Consilience: The unity of knowledge.* New York: Alfred A. Knopf.

Wilson, T. D. (2002). *Strangers to ourselves: Discovering the adaptive unconscious.* Cambridge, MA: Belknap Press.

Wiltermuth, S., & Heath, C. (2008). Synchrony and cooperation. *Psychological Science, 20,* 1–5.

Winter, L., & Uleman, J. S. (1984). When are social judgments made? Evidence for the spontaneousness of trait inferences. *Journal of Personality and Social Psychology, 47,* 237–252.

Wright, R. (1994). *The moral animal.* New York: Pantheon.

Wright, R. (2000). *Non-zero: The logic of human destiny.* New York: Vintage.

Wundt, W. (1907). *Outlines of psychology.* Leipzig, Germany: Wilhelm Englemann.

Wynne, C. D. L. (2004). Animal behaviour: Fair refusal by capuchin monkeys. *Nature, 428,* 140.

Yamagishi, T. (2003). Cross-societal experimentation on trust: A comparison of the United States and Japan. In E. Ostrom & J. Walker (Eds.), *Trust and reciprocity: Interdisciplinary lessons from experimental research* (pp. 352–370). New York: Russell Sage Foundation.

Yamagishi, T., Tanida, S., Mashima, R., Shimoma, E., & Kanazawa, S. (2003). You can judge a book by its cover—Evidence that cheaters may look different from cooperators. *Evolution and Human Behavior, 24,* 290–301.

Yzerbyt, V. Y., & Demoulin. (2010). Intergroup relations. In S. Fiske & D. Gilbert (Eds.), *The handbook of social psychology* (5th ed.). Hoboken, NJ: John Wiley & Sons.

Zajonc, R. B. (1980). Feeling and thinking: Preferences need no inferences. *American Psychologist, 35,* 151–175.

Zimbardo, P. G. (2007). *The Lucifer effect: Understanding how good people turn evil.* New York: Random House.

Chapter 23

Aggression

BRAD J. BUSHMAN AND L. ROWELL HUESMANN

WHAT IS AGGRESSION?

> Man must evolve for all human conflict a method which rejects revenge, aggression and retaliation. The foundation of such a method is love.
>
> —Martin Luther King Jr. (1929–1968)

There is little doubt that aggression was an adaptive behavior for many of our ancient ancestors who lived in small groups. Males used aggression to gain access to females, food, shelter, and other resources. Females used aggression to defend their offspring and gain resources for them. Thus, the most aggressive individuals in our evolutionary past were at one time the ones who were most likely to pass on their genes to subsequent generations. As humans became more social, however, aggression toward others in the social group on which one's survival depended became less adaptive and prosocial genes became common. Aggression today, in fact, seems maladaptive and destructive. Aggression breeds aggression, and seems to cause more problems than it solves. Even if it works in the short run, it fails in the long run. Most social psychologists today are interested in understanding why people become aggressive, what factors influence aggression, and how to reduce it.

In this chapter we begin by defining the terms aggression and violence. We also discuss different forms and functions of aggression. The forms and functions of aggression change from childhood to adulthood and differ for males and females (perhaps as a result of their evolutionary past). We discuss whether the amount of aggression and violence is changing over time, and whether the amount differs across cultures. Next, we describe different theoretical explanations for aggression, some based on nature, some based on nurture, and some based on both nature and nurture. We describe situational, personal, and environmental factors that influence aggression. Finally, we discuss different approaches for reducing aggression.

Aggression and Violence Defined

The scientific study of aggressive behavior was hampered for years because of different understandings of the word "aggression." Aggressive toddlers are generally considered bad. However, in sports and in business, the term "aggressive" is frequently given a positive connotation as a trait to be admired. Consequently, one of the first steps scientists had to undertake was to define aggressive behavior clearly as a negative social behavior.

In social psychology, the term *aggression* is generally defined as any behavior that is intended to harm another person who does not want to be harmed (e.g., Baron & Richardson, 1994). Aggression is an external behavior that you can see. For example, you can see a person shoot, stab, hit, slap, or curse someone. Aggression is not an emotion that occurs inside a person, such as an angry feeling. Aggression is not a thought inside someone's brain, such as mentally rehearsing a murder. Note also that aggression is a social behavior—it involves at least two people. In addition, aggression is intended to hurt. Aggression is not accidental, such as when a drunk driver accidentally runs over a child on a tricycle. In addition, not all intentional behaviors that hurt others are aggressive behaviors. For example, a dentist might intentionally give a patient a shot of Novocain (and the shot hurts!), but the goal is to help rather than hurt the patient.

Social psychologists and laypeople also differ in their use of the term *violence*. A meteorologist might call a storm "violent" if it has intense winds, rain, thunder, and lightning. In social psychology, *violence* is aggression that has extreme physical harm as its goal, such as injury or death. One child intentionally pushing another child down is an act of aggression but is not an act of violence. One person intentionally hitting, kicking, shooting, or stabbing another person is an act of violence. Thus, violence is a subset of aggression. All violent acts are aggressive,

Correspondence should be addressed to: Brad J. Bushman, Institute for Social Research, University of Michigan, 426 Thompson Street, Ann Arbor, MI, 48106, U.S.A., Telephone: (734) 615-6631, Fax: (734) 763-1202, E-mail: bbushman@umich.edu. We thank Roy Baumeister for his assistance on this chapter.

but not all aggressive acts are violent (only the ones that are intended to cause extreme physical damage are called violent). The U.S. Federal Bureau of Investigation (FBI) classifies four crimes as violent: murder, assault, rape, and robbery. Social psychologists would also classify other physically aggressive acts as violent even if they do not meet the FBI definition of a violent crime, such as slapping someone really hard across the face. But a husband who calls his wife every name in the book would not be committing an act of violence by this definition.

Forms and Functions of Aggression

Different Forms of Aggression

It is useful to distinguish between forms and functions of aggression. By *forms* we mean how the aggressive act is expressed, such as physical versus verbal, direct versus indirect, and active versus passive (Buss, 1961). *Physical aggression* involves harming others physically (e.g., hitting, kicking, stabbing, or shooting them). *Verbal aggression* involves harming others with words (e.g., yelling, screaming, swearing, name calling). *Relational aggression* (also called *social aggression*) is defined as intentionally harming another person's social relationships, feelings of acceptance, or inclusion within a group (e.g., Crick & Grotpeter, 1995). Some examples of relational aggression include saying bad things about people behind their backs, withdrawing affection to get what you want, excluding others from your circle of friends, and giving someone the "silent treatment." "Recent research shows that social pain may even linger longer than physical pain (Chen, Williams, Fitness, & Newton, 2008). Participants in these studies recalled an event that caused social pain (e.g., betrayal by a person very close to them) and an event that caused physical pain. They rated how intense the initial pain had been and how intense it was as they relived it. The initial levels of social and physical pain did not differ, but relived pain was more intense for social pain than for physical pain. Social pain also impaired cognitive performance more than physical pain did.

The different forms of aggression can be expressed directly or indirectly (Lagerspetz, Bjorkqvist, & Peltonen, 1988). With *direct aggression*, the victim is physically present. With *indirect aggression*, the victim is absent. For example, physical aggression can be direct (e.g., hitting a person in the face) or indirect (e.g., destroying another person's property when he or she isn't looking). Likewise, verbal aggression can be direct (e.g., screaming in a person's face) or indirect (e.g., spreading rumors behind a person's back).

In *displaced aggression*, a substitute aggression target is used (e.g., Marcus-Newhall, Pedersen, Carlson, & Miller, 2000). The substitute target is innocent of any wrongdoing and just happens to be in wrong place at the wrong time. For example, a man is berated by his boss at work but does not retaliate. When he gets home, he yells at his daughter instead. Sometimes the substitute target is not entirely innocent, but has committed a minor or trivial offense, called *triggered displaced aggression* (Pedersen, Gonzales, & Miller, 2000). For example, the man berated by his boss might yell at his daughter because she forgot to clean her room. Triggered displaced aggression is especially likely to occur when the aggressor ruminates about the initial offense (Bushman, Bonacci, Pedersen, Vasquez, & Miller, 2005) and when the aggressor does not like the substitute target, such as when the target is an outgroup member or has a personality flaw (e.g., Pederson, Bushman, Vasquez, & Miller, 2008). People displace aggression for two main reasons. First, directly aggressing against the source of provocation may be unfeasible because the source is unavailable (e.g., the provoker has left the area), or because the source is an intangible entity (e.g., hot temperature). Second, fear of retaliation or punishment from the provoker may inhibit direct aggression. For example, the employee who was reprimanded by his boss may be reluctant to retaliate because he does not want to lose his job.

The form of aggression may be active or passive. With *active aggression*, the aggressor responds in a hurtful manner (e.g., hitting, swearing). With *passive aggression*, the aggressor fails to respond in a helpful manner. For example, the aggressor might "forget" to deliver an important message to the person.

Direct and active forms of aggression can be quite risky, leading to injury or even death. Thus, most people prefer to use indirect and passive forms of aggression instead.

Different Functions of Aggression

Aggressive acts may also differ in their function. Consider two examples. In the first, a husband finds his wife and her lover together in bed. He takes his rifle from the closet, and shoots and kills both individuals. In the second, a "hitman" uses a rifle to kill another person for money. The form of aggression is the same in both examples (i.e., physical aggression caused by shooting and killing victims with a rifle). However, the motives appear quite different. In the first example, the husband appears to be motivated by anger. He is enraged when he finds his wife making love to another man, so he shoots them both. In the second example, the "hitman" appears to be motivated by money. The "hitman" probably does not hate his victim. He might not even know his victim, but he kills the person anyway for the money. To capture different functions or motives for aggression, psychologists make a distinction between *reactive aggression* (also called hostile, affective, angry, impulsive, or retaliatory aggression) and *proactive aggression* (also called instrumental aggression; e.g., Buss, 1961; Dodge & Coie, 1987; Feshbach, 1964). Reactive aggression is "hot," impulsive, angry behavior that is motivated by a desire to harm someone. Proactive aggression is "cold," premeditated, calculated behavior that is motivated by some other goal (obtaining money, restoring one's image, restoring justice). Some social psychologists have argued that it is difficult (if not impossible) to distinguish between reactive and proactive aggression because they are highly correlated and because motives are often mixed (Bushman & Anderson, 2001). For example, what if the husband who finds his wife making love to another man hires a "hitman" to kill his wife and her illicit lover? Would this be reactive or proactive aggression?

FREQUENCY OF VIOLENT AND AGGRESSIVE BEHAVIOR

Is the World Less Violent Now Than in the Past?

World War I was called "the war to end all wars," but that title went out of fashion after World War II. The colossal slaughter and destruction of World War II might have taught humanity some lessons about the importance of peace, yet wars continued. In the 40 years after the end of World War II there were approximately 150 wars and only 26 days of world peace (out of 14,610 days), defined as the absence of international wars (Sluka, 1992). (Civil wars didn't count; if you count civil wars, there was probably no peace at all.) In the early twenty-first century, international wars continue to be waged. The world seems more violent today than ever before. Yet quantitative studies of body counts, such as the proportion of prehistoric skeletons with axe and arrowhead wounds, suggest that prehistoric societies were far more violent than our own (Pinker, 2007). Although one can kill a lot more people with a bomb than with an axe, the death rates per battle were much higher in the past. Estimates show that if the wars of the twentieth century killed the same proportion of the population as ancient tribal wars, then the death toll would have been 20 times higher—2 billion rather than 100 million (Pinker, 2007).

More recent data also show that violence is decreasing over time. European murder rates have decreased dramatically since the Middle Ages (e.g., Eisner, 2001; Gurr, 1981). For example, estimated murders in England dropped from 24 per 100,000 in the fourteenth century to 0.6 per 100,000 by the early 1960s. The major decline in violence seems to have occurred in the seventeenth century during the "Age of Reason," beginning in the Netherlands and England and then spreading to other European countries (Pinker, 2007). Global violence has also been steadily falling since the middle of the twentieth century (*Human Security Brief,* 2007). For example, the number of battle deaths in interstate wars has declined from more than 65,000 per year in the 1950s to less than 2,000 per year in the 2000s. There also are global declines in the number of armed conflicts and combat deaths, the number of military coups, and the number of deadly violence campaigns waged against civilians.

A number of other observations are consistent with the idea that human society is becoming less violent over time. Pinker (2007, p. 18) notes:

> Cruelty as entertainment, human sacrifice to indulge superstition, slavery as a labor-saving device, conquest as the mission statement of government, genocide as a means of acquiring real estate, torture and mutilation as routine punishment . . . all were unexceptionable features of life for most of human history. But, today, they are rare to nonexistent in the West, far less common elsewhere than they used to be, concealed when they do occur, and widely condemned when they are brought to light.

In today's digital age we certainly are more informed about wars and other acts of violence than in past ages. In the media, if it bleeds it leads. Because violent images are more available to us now than ever before, we might assume that violence levels are also higher. However, while terrible violence still kills thousands or even millions in places like Cambodia, Croatia, Chechnya, and Rwanda, it seems that over time this planet is actually becoming a less violent place to live.

Cross-National Comparisons of Murder Rates

Murder rates vary widely across the world. The 10 countries with the highest murder rates per 100,000 population are Colombia (61.7), South Africa (49.6), Jamaica (32.4), Venezuela (31.6), Russia (20.2), Mexico (13.0), Estonia (10.7), Latvia (10.4), Lithuania (10.3), and Belarus (9.8) (United Nations Survey of Crime, 1998- 2000). The USA at 4.3 per 100,000 in this survey had the highest rate of Western democracies. The heterogeneity in murder rates reflects, in part, the role of culture and social learning on violence. However, a word of caution is in order. Murder rates can be distorted by political reasons and reflect the availability of weapons. Thus, they do not necessarily reflect overall violence rates. For example, national victimization surveys (which are the most accurate assessments of violence) show that the United States is less violent than Britain today even though the United States has a higher murder rate (U.S. Department of Justice, 2008).

Recent Murder Trends in the United States

Even though violence has gone down over the centuries, an examination of murder rates of the past 100 years in the

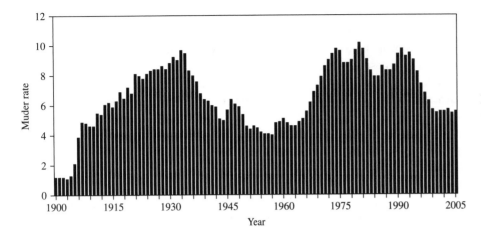

Figure 23.1 USA murder rates (per 100,000 population) from 1900–2006 (US Department of Justice, 2008).

United States looks somewhat like the stock market—murder rates go up and down (see Figure 23.1, U.S. Department of Justice, 2008). In recent years murder rates have been going down. The simplest explanation for the recent downturn in murders is that the U.S. population is getting older, and very few elderly people are murderers. About 30% of the current U.S. population was born in the post–World War II baby boom between 1946 and the early 1960s (U.S. Census Bureau, 2008). The large aging baby boomer population may be driving down the murder statistics. However, other explanations ranging from increased imprisonment rates and increased abortion rates to increased surveillance of the population have been offered. There is no way to know for certain what the cause is.

DEVELOPMENTAL TRENDS AND GENDER DIFFERENCES IN AGGRESSION

Emergence of Aggression in Early Childhood

In all cultures, aggressive behavior appears very early in children's lives. Angry facial expressions are apparent in most infants 4 to 7 months old (Stenberg, Campos, & Emde, 1983). Interpersonal behaviors that can be called aggressive (although it is difficult to be certain about "intent" to harm) appear shortly afterwards. For example, protest and aggressive retaliation in response to provocations (e.g., grabbing toys) is frequent in infants (Caplan, Vespo, Pedersen, & Hay, 1991), and physical aggression to obtain instrumental goals is frequent in 1- to 3-year-olds (Tremblay et al., 1996).

As empirical data from multiple longitudinal studies have accumulated, it has become clear that most people are more physically aggressive when they are 1 to 3 years old than at any other time in their lives (e.g., Broidy et al., 2003; Cote, Vaillancourt, LeBlanc, Nagin, & Tremblay, 2006;

Miner & Clarke-Steward, 2008; Tremblay et al., 2004). In daycare settings, about 25% of interactions among toddlers involve some kind of physical aggression (e.g., one child pushes another child out of the way and takes her toy [Tremblay, 2000]). No other group, not even violent youth gangs or hardened criminals, resorts to physical aggression 25% of the time. Fortunately, most toddler aggression isn't severe enough to qualify as violence. Children can't do much damage at that age, being smaller and weaker and subject to external control.

Toddlers may resort to physical aggression 25% of the time, but as they grow up, they learn to inhibit aggression. In the later preschool and early elementary years physical aggression generally decreases, whereas verbal aggression and indirect aggression increases (Loeber & Hay, 1997; Tremblay, 2000; Tremblay & Nagin, 2005).

There are important implications of this early emergence of anger and aggression for the understanding of aggressive behavior. Certainly, these findings cast doubt on any "pure learning theory" explanation of aggressive behavior in young children. Anger in response to frustration and pushing, hitting, and shoving obstacles to obtain goals appears too early in almost all toddlers' lives to be explained solely in terms of learning. It is more plausible to explain these behaviors as part of inborn proclivities. The key role for early learning processes is to socialize children "out of aggression" and into socially acceptable behaviors for obtaining goals.

Age Trends in Aggression and Violence

Although most people become less aggressive over time, a subset of people become *more* aggressive over time. The most dangerous years for this subset of individuals (and for society) are late adolescence and early adulthood. This is because aggressive acts become more extreme, and the consequences are more severe (e.g., weapons are used more frequently [Cairns & Cairns, 1994]). Official records show that violent criminal offending is highest for both males and females between ages 15 and 30, and declines significantly after that. For example, the average age of murderers is about 27 years old (U.S. Department of Justice, 2008).

Although these generalizations summarize the empirical data accurately, exact developmental trends in general aggression are difficult to measure because aggressiveness manifests itself in different ways at different ages—for example, in taking things at age 4, fighting at age 8, telling lies about others at age 12, vandalism at age 16, and murder at age 27. In addition, boys and girls show different trajectories for different types of aggression. Girls not only show greater use of indirect aggression than boys, but their use of indirect aggression increases with age (Vaillancourt, Miller, Fagbemi, Cote, & Tremblay, 2007). Different environments may also influence the growth of aggression quite differently. For example, in high-risk inner city schools, average aggression by children increases dramatically during the first year of school (Guerra, Huesmann, Tolan, Van Acker, & Eron, 1995). Similarly, the prevalence of a gang culture radically increases the growth curve of aggression in adolescence (Goldstein, 1994).

Continuity of Aggression From Childhood to Adulthood

Shortly after aggressive behavior emerges in children, individual differences in aggressiveness become detectable—by the late preschool and early elementary school years (Eron, Walder, & Lefkowitz, 1971; Huesmann, Eron, Lefkowitz, & Walder, 1984). Such early differences are highly predictive of aggression later in life (Farrington, 1982, 1989, 1995; Huesmann et al., 1984; Huesmann, Dubow, & Boxer, 2009; Huesmann, Eron, & Dubow, 2002; Huesmann & Moise, 1998; Juon, Doherty, & Ensminger, 2006; Kokko, Pulkkinen, Huesmann, Dubow, & Boxer, 2009; Loeber & Dishion, 1983; Magnusson, Duner, & Zetterblom, 1975; Moffitt, Caspi, Rutter, & Silva, 2001; Olweus, 1979; Tremblay, 2000; Zumkley, 1992). The "stability" for aggression indicated by these data refers to "continuity of position" within the population: The more aggressive child grows up to be the more aggressive adult (Huesmann et al., 1984; Olweus, 1979). Continuity correlations range from .76 for one year to .60 for 10 years for both males and females (Olweus, 1979). Indeed, aggressiveness is almost as stable over time as intelligence. One study reported 22-year continuity correlations of .50 for males and .35 for females (Huesmann et al., 1984).

Some researchers have suggested that the continuity in aggression is due only to a few highly aggressive people

remaining aggressive over time (e.g., Loeber, 1982). However, the continuity occurs all along the entire range of aggression. The statistical continuity of aggression over time is as much due to non-aggressive individuals remaining non-aggressive as it is due to aggressive individuals remaining aggressive (Hartup, 2005). For example, 18% of children who are classified as very low in aggressiveness at age 8 remain very low for the next 40 years, whereas 22% of those who are classified as very high in aggressiveness at age 8 remain very high for the next 40 years (Huesmann et al., 2009; Huesmann & Moise, 1998). It is rare for adolescents to suddenly become very aggressive and continue to remain aggressive through adulthood (Brame, Nagin, & Tremblay, 2001; Huesmann et al., 2009).

According to Moffitt's (1993) developmental taxonomy, there are two types of aggressive people: (1) those for whom aggression is stable and persistent (*life-course-persistent*) and (2) those for whom aggression is temporary and situational (*adolescent-limited*). A significant number of individuals who fit the pattern of adolescent-limited aggression have now been identified in several longitudinal studies (Broidy et al., 2003; Moffitt, 2007; Huesmann et al., 2009), and their aggressive behaviors are much less severe than the aggressive behaviors for life-course-persistent individuals.

Emergence of Gender Differences

Gender differences in aggression are very noticeable by the preschool years, with boys showing higher levels of physical aggression than girls (Loeber & Hay, 1997). However, many preschool girls are physically aggressive, and they show levels of verbal and indirect aggression similar to or greater than boys (Crick & Grotpeter, 1995; Rys & Bear, 1997). In later elementary grades and in adolescence, gender differences in indirect and physical aggression increase. Indirect aggression becomes much greater for girls than boys; physical aggression becomes much greater for boys than girls; and verbal aggression is about the same for girls and boys (Crick & Grotpeter, 1995; Lagerspetz et al., 1988; Vaillancourt, 2005). These gender differences culminate in dramatic differences in violent behavior in young adulthood, reflected by large gender differences in murder rates. Nevertheless, this should not lead one to believe that females are never physically aggressive. Females do display physical aggression in social interactions, particularly when they are provoked by other females (Collins, Quigley, & Leonard, 2007). When it comes to heterosexual domestic partners, women are slightly *more* likely than men to use physical aggression against their partners (e.g., Archer, 2000; Straus, 1997)! However men are more likely than women to inflict serious injuries and death on their partners.

Laboratory studies with college students often yield higher aggression by men, but provocation apparently has a greater effect on aggression than does biological sex. Sex differences in aggression practically disappear under high provocation (Bettencourt & Miller, 1996).

Developmental research suggests that many gender differences in aggression result both from nature and nurture. Innate factors (discussed in more detail later) have led to substantial evolutionary theorizing about the reasons for gender differences in aggression (Archer & Conte, 2005; Buss & Shackelford, 1997b; Campbell, 1999; Geary, 1998). These are described below in the section on evolutionary theorizing.

THEORETICAL ORIENTATIONS FOR THE STUDY OF AGGRESSION

As long as there has been violence in the world, people have tried to determine why it occurs. For example, is it due to biological abnormalities or poor upbringing? More generally, why is it that most people can be aggressive at least some of the time?

Instinctive and Psychoanalytic Theories of Aggression

One early theory that gained popularity in intellectual circles in the nineteenth century was that violence was instinctive in humans just as it was in many other animals. First given scientific prominence by Darwin (1871), the instinct theory of aggression viewed aggressive behavior as motivated neither by the seeking of pleasure nor the avoidance of pain, but rather as an evolutionary adaptation that had enabled humans to survive better. Empirical evidence supporting the existence of innate, relatively automatic, aggressive responses has been demonstrated for many species (e.g., Lorenz, 1966). For example, for the male Stickleback fish, a red object triggers attack 100% of the time (Timbergen, 1952). However, for humans no exactly parallel innate aggressive response has been demonstrated (Hinde, 1970).

However, it does appear that most humans innately derive "pleasure" from hurting people who have provoked, angered, or attacked them. This has been demonstrated in a variety of clever experiments. In one experiment (Baron, 1979), half the participants were first strongly angered by a confederate who insulted them, whereas the other half had a neutral interaction with the confederate. All participants then "shocked" the confederate every time he made an error on a task. They could select the intensity of the shock, from mild to severe. Half of the people giving the shocks could see a "pain meter" that supposedly told them how much pain the confederate was experiencing from the shocks, whereas the other half got no pain information. The pain meter always showed that the confederate was experiencing "high pain." Of course, the angered people gave stronger shocks than nonangered people, but the interesting result was the effect of the pain meter. The somewhat depressing results showed that angry people gave more intense shocks when the pain meter indicated that the confederate was suffering. In contrast, non-angry people gave less intense shocks when the pain meter indicated that the confederate was suffering. Apparently, humans enjoy hurting those who have provoked them. However, that does not mean that aggression is an automatic instinctive response to provocation.

A more complex and plausible view of human aggression as a product of instincts was offered by Freud (1933/1950). Depressed by the horrors of World War I, Freud became interested in explaining aggressive behavior. He advanced the theory that humans have both an instinct to live and an instinct to die. The life instinct supposedly counteracts the death instinct and preserves life by diverting destructive urges outward toward others in aggressive acts (Freud, 1917/1961). Freud's views undoubtedly influenced Lorenz (1966) whose instinct theory of aggression posited a more specific buildup of aggressive urges (like hydraulic pressure inside a closed environment) that, if not released through some other activity, would inevitably lead to aggression. Although little empirical evidence has ever been found to support the "hydraulic" model of aggression, the theory that aggression is due to the buildup of an internal drive or tension that must be released still has a profound influence on clinical psychology. It motivates popular venting and cathartic therapies even though numerous studies have shown that the hydraulic model is false (for reviews see Berkowitz, 1993; Geen & Quanty, 1977; Scott, 1958).

Frustration-Aggression Theory

In 1939, psychologists from Yale University published an important book titled *Frustration and Aggression* (Dollard, Doob, Miller, Mowrer, & Sears, 1939). In this book, partially as a reaction to the spreading influence of the Freud's theory, the authors proposed that aggression was due to frustration. They defined frustration an unpleasant emotion that arises when a person is blocked from achieving a goal. Their theory was summarized in two bold statements on the first page of their book: (1) "The occurrence of aggressive behavior always presupposes the existence of frustration," and (2) "the existence of frustration always leads to some form of aggression." In their view, frustration depended on an "expected" or "hoped for" goal being denied and was not simply absence of achieving a goal.

This theory seemed to explain a large amount of everyday occurrences of aggression, but it readily became apparent to the authors that not every frustration led to observable aggression. Miller (1941), one of the original authors, was the first to revise the theory. He explained that frustrations actually stimulate a number of different inclinations besides an inclination to aggress, such as an inclination to escape or to find a way around the obstacle to the goal. The inclination that eventually dominates, he theorized, is the one that is most successful in reducing frustration. In other words, people learn through experience to respond to frustrations with aggressive or non-aggressive responses. This idea opened the door for learning theory explanations of aggression.

Learning Theory Formulations

The earliest learning theory explanations for individual differences in human aggressiveness focused on operant and, to a lesser extent, classical conditioning processes. *Operant conditioning theory*, developed by behaviorists such as Edward Thorndike and B. F. Skinner, proposes that people are more likely to repeat behaviors that have been rewarded and are less likely to repeat behaviors that have been punished. *Classical conditioning theory*, developed by Ivan Pavlov, proposes that through repeated pairing of an unconditioned stimulus with a conditioned stimulus, the unconditioned stimulus eventually elicits a response similar to that elicited by the conditioned stimulus. For example, dogs that hear a bell every time they receive meat powder will eventually salivate when they hear the bell alone. The bell becomes a conditioned stimulus by being paired with the meat powder, which is the unconditioned stimulus. Research showed that children could be taught to behave aggressively through *positive reinforcement*—adding pleasure (Cowan & Walters, 1963; Lovaas, 1961) or *negative reinforcement*—subtracting pain (Patterson, Littman, & Bricker, 1967). Children not only learn to behave aggressively, they also learn to discriminate between situations when aggression pays and when it does not. Through stimulus generalization they apply what they have learned to new situations (Sears, Whiting, Nowlis, & Sears, 1953). Taken together these processes explained how aggressive behavior could be learned (Eron, 1987; Eron et al., 1971).

By the early 1960s, however, it became clear that conditioning by itself could not explain individual differences in aggression. Bandura theorized that the more powerful learning processes in understanding social behavior (including aggression) were *observational learning* or *imitation* (also called *social learning*) (e.g., Bandura, 1977;

Bandura, Ross, & Ross 1961; 1963) in which people learn how to behave aggressively by observing and imitating others. In several classic experiments, he showed that young children imitated specific aggressive acts they observed in aggressive models (e.g., hitting a "bobo" doll that they had seen an actor hit). Furthermore, he developed the concept of *vicarious learning* of aggression by showing that children were especially likely to imitate models that had been rewarded for behaving aggressively (Bandura, 1965; Bandura et al., 1963). Bandura argued that the imitation was the key to social learning. The idea is that one does not just imitate the specific social behaviors one sees, but one makes cognitive inferences based on the observations, and these inferences lead to generalizations in behavior. What is important is how the child interprets social events and how competent the child feels in performing the behaviors he or she observes (Bandura, 1986). These cognitions provide a basis for stability of behavior tendencies across a variety of situations. Watching one parent hit the other parent may not only increase a child's likelihood of hitting, but may also increase the child's belief that hitting is OK when someone provokes you.

Aversive Stimulation Theory

Building on ideas from frustration-aggression theory, learning theory, and cognitive psychology, Berkowitz (1974, 1989, 1990) proposed a theory of "aversively stimulated aggression" that subsumes frustration-aggression theory. The idea is that aversive stimuli (including frustrations) automatically produce primitive reaction tendencies (e.g., flight or fight). When people experience an unpleasant event, they want to stop it (fight) or get away from it (flight). This fight-or-flight response is an adaptive stress-reducing response that occurs in humans and other animals (Cannon, 1915). The theory suggests that "anything that makes us feel bad" is an aversive instigation to aggression. Whether aggression occurs depends on the cognitive interpretation of the aversive event and the presence of aggressive cues (Berkowitz, 1993). For example, a person who experiences an aversive event (e.g., frustration) and sees an aggressive cue (e.g., a weapon) is likely to behave aggressively.

Social-Cognitive, Information-Processing Models of Aggression

The introduction of ideas from cognitive psychology into theorizing about aggression was given another boost in the early 1980s with the formulation of two cognitive information-processing models. One model, developed by Huesmann and his colleagues (Huesmann, 1982, 1988,

1998; Huesmann & Eron, 1984), focused particularly on scripts, beliefs, and observational learning. In a play or movie, scripts tell actors what to say and do. In memory, *scripts* define situations and guide behavior: The person first selects a script to represent the situation and then assumes a role in the script. One example is a restaurant script (i.e., enter restaurant, go to table, look at menu, order food, eat food, pay for food, leave tip, exit restaurant [see Abelson, 1981]). Scripts can be learned by direct experience or by observing others (e.g., parents, siblings, peers, mass media characters). The second model, developed by Dodge and his colleagues (Dodge, 1980, 1986, 1993; Dodge & Frame, 1982; Fite, Goodnight, Bates, Dodge, & Pettit, 2008), focused particularly on perceptions and attributions. *Attributions* are the explanations people make about why others behave the way they do. For example, if a person bumps into you, a hostile attribution would be that the person did it on purpose to hurt you. These two models were supplemented in the late 1990s and early 2000s by a third similar model, called the General Aggression Model, developed by Anderson and his colleagues (e.g., Anderson & Bushman, 2002a). Although these three models differ in their details, all view aggression as the outcome of a social problem-solving process in which situational factors are evaluated, social scripts are retrieved, and these scripts are evaluated until one is selected to guide behavior.

Huesmann and Kirwil (2007) have attempted to integrate these three models into one unified model. According to the unified model, information processing begins with evaluation of the social situation and ends with the decision to follow a particular script for behaving. People also evaluate the consequences of behaving that way. If the consequences are positive, the script is likely to be used again in the future. Four individual differences in social problem solving play a central role in the unified model: scripts (described above), world schemas, normative beliefs, and emotional predispositions. *World schemas* are beliefs about what the world is like. They are used to evaluate environmental cues and make attributions about others' intentions. These attributions, in turn, influence the search for a script for behaving. People who believe the world is a mean place are more likely to make hostile attributions about others' intentions and thus to retrieve an aggressive script. *Normative beliefs* are beliefs about what types of behavior are normal. They are used to judge the appropriateness of aggressive behavior and to filter out inappropriate scripts and behaviors. For example, a man who believes it is wrong to hit a woman is likely to reject retrieved scripts that involving hitting women. *Emotional predispositions* are individual differences in a variety of emotion-related tendencies (e.g., emotional reactivity, arousal level). These predispositions affect how people evaluate scripts. For

example, non-aggressive individuals may reject aggressive scripts because they think they might feel bad after behaving in an aggressive manner.

In any given social setting, the characteristics of the situation interact with these four individual-difference factors to determine behavior. Many of the cognitive processes happen in an automatic fashion (Berkowitz, 2008; Schneider & Shiffrin, 1977). Aversive events automatically arouses negative emotions, which makes aggressive scripts more accessible. If these aggressive scripts pass through a filter of normative and moral beliefs and seem to lead to a desirable goal, people use the script to guide their behavior. Individual differences in aggressiveness are therefore linked to individual differences in the four kinds of social cognitions involved in social problem solving—one's repertoire of scripts, world schemas, normative beliefs, and emotional reactivity. Once these cognitions are crystallized, they produce stable aggressive tendencies over the life span.

Recent Advances in Observational Learning Theory

Recent research helps us better understand imitation and observational learning processes. Human and primate young have an innate tendency to imitate what they observe (Meltzoff, 2005; Meltzoff & Moore, 1977). They imitate expressions in early infancy, and they imitate behaviors by the time they can walk. Aggressive behaviors are no different from other motor behaviors in this regard. Thus, the hitting, grabbing, pushing behaviors that young children see around them or in the mass media are generally immediately mimicked unless the child has been taught not to mimic them (Bandura, 1977; Bandura, Ross, & Ross, 1961, 1963). Furthermore, automatic imitation of expressions on others' faces can lead to the automatic activation of the emotion that the other was experiencing. For example, angry expressions stimulate angry emotions in observers (Prinz, 2005; Zajonc, Murphy, & Inglehart, 1989).

This empirical evidence for automatic imitation in humans has been given added import by an explosion of neurophysiological findings. The demonstration in the mid-1990s of the existence of "mirror neurons" that fire either when an action is observed or when it is executed provided a strong basis for understanding why children imitate others (Gallese, Fadiga, Fogassi, & Rizzolatti, 1996; Iacoboni, Woods, Brass, Bekkering, Mazziotta, & Rizzolatti, 1999; Rizzolatti, 2005). The immediate "mimicry" of aggressive behaviors does not require a complex cognitive representation of the observed act, but only a simple "mirror" representation of it. However, that does not mean that more delayed imitation is not a complex cognitive process. As Hurley and Chater (2005) wrote,

Imitation is often thought of as a low level, cognitively undemanding, even childish form of behavior. But recent work across a variety of sciences argues that imitation is a rare ability, fundamentally linked to characteristically human forms of intelligence, and in particular to language, culture, and the ability to understand other minds. (p. 1)

Within the cognitive information-processing theories of aggression described above, imitation is seen as a key learning process for the acquisition of scripts, schemas, and beliefs. Priming and simple imitation (mimicry) can explain why exposure to violence increases aggressive behavior in the short run, whereas complex delayed imitation, observational learning of cognitions, and emotional desensitization can explain why exposure to violence increases aggressive behavior in the long run (Bushman & Huesmann, 2006; Huesmann & Kirwil, 2007).

Ego Depletion Theory

Another theoretical approach with implications for aggression is "ego depletion theory" (Baumeister, Bratslavsky, Muraver, & Tice, 1998; DeWall, Baumeister, Stillman, & Gailliot, 2005). Self-regulating internal standards and normative beliefs are important elements for inhibiting aggression. Inhibiting behavior to satisfy such standards requires cognitive effort, which is limited. *Self-control* is a general capacity for bringing one's behavior into line with rules and standards. Self-control can be depleted by demanding tasks, which makes aggression more likely. For example, people who have to exercise self-control (e.g., by restraining themselves from eating chocolate or by performing demanding cognitive tasks) behave more aggressively than those who do not have to exercise self-control.

CAUSES OF AGGRESSION

Aggression is complex and multiply determined. We conceptualize aggression as the product of precipitating situational factors and predisposing personological factors. In this section we describe both types of factors.

Situational Factors That Precipitate Aggression

Unpleasant Events

According to Berkowitz's (1989) aversive stimulation theory (described earlier), all unpleasant events—instead of only frustration—deserve to be recognized as important causes of aggression. Some unpleasant events are nonsocial, such as hot temperatures. The evidence from laboratory experiments, field studies, correlational studies, and archival studies of violent crimes indicates that hotter temperatures are associated with higher levels of aggression and violence (for a review see Anderson, Anderson, Dorr, DeNeve, & Flanagan, 2000). Hotter regions generally have higher violent crime rates than cooler regions. Time period studies generally show higher violent crime rates in hot years, hot seasons, hot months, and hot days. Field and archival studies have found similar results. For example, in baseball games, the hotter the temperature, the more common it is for the pitcher to hit the batter with a pitched ball, which really hurts because the (hard!) ball is often thrown about 90 miles (145 kilometers) per hour (Reifman, Larrick, & Fein, 1991).

Scientists now agree that the average global air temperature near the Earth's surface is increasing, and it is projected to continue to increase (IPCC, 2007). When people think about the harmful effects of global warming, they mainly consider the effects on crops and flooding. People rarely consider the effects of global warming on violent crime rates. Projections indicate that by the middle of the twenty-first century, global warming could cause an increase of about 100,000 serious and deadly assaults each year in the United States alone (Anderson, Bushman, & Groom, 1997).

Other unpleasant environmental events can also increase aggression. Numerous studies have shown that loud noises can increase aggression, including traffic noise (Gaur, 1988). Noise is especially likely to increase aggression in when it is uncontrollable (Geen, 1978; Geen & McCown, 1984) and when it is paired with other aggression-eliciting factors, such as provocation (Donnerstein & Wilson, 1976) or violent media (Geen & O'Neal, 1969). Irritants in the air that we breathe can make us more aggressive, such as foul odors (Rotton, 1979), secondhand smoke (Jones & Bogat, 1978), and air pollution (Rotton & Frey, 1985).

Social stress may be even more unpleasant than nonsocial stress. There is an important difference between *density* (the number of people in a given area) and *crowding* (the subjective and unpleasant feeling that there are too many people in a given area). Crowding is a better predictor of aggression than density per se. In fact, high population density can produce positive emotions and behaviors in desirable environments, such as in football stadiums or concert halls. Crowding, on the other hand, can increase aggression in undesirable environments, such as in psychiatric wards (e.g., Nijman & Rector, 1999) and prisons (e.g., Lawrence & Andrews, 2004).

Social rejection is another aversive social stimulus. Common observation suggests that people who have been rejected by others often become angry and aggressive. Consider, for example, the reactions of some contestants who try out for the TV show *American Idol*, but do not pass the initial screening. The words they say about the judges often must be bleeped out. The term "going postal" is used to describe the behavior of some disgruntled postal workers who shot and killed managers, fellow workers, police officers, and even ordinary citizens after being rejected at work (Barling, Dupré, & Kelloway, 2009). An analysis of 15 school shooters found that social rejection (e.g., from a romantic partner) was present in all but two of the cases (Leary, Kowalski, Smith, & Phillips, 2003).

In experimental studies, social psychologists have used a number of different procedures to make research participants feel rejected. For example, participants are tested in groups and are told that they have been voted out of the group (as in the reality TV show *Survivor*), they are left out of a ball-tossing game, or they are given false test feedback stating they will be alone and isolated most of their lives. Aggression is measured by allowing participants to give confederates loud blasts of noise through headphones or very spicy hot sauce to eat (they are told the confederate hates spicy food). In these experiments, rejected individuals are more aggressive than non-rejected individuals (for a review see Leary, Twenge, & Quinlivan, 2006). If a rejecter's group membership is salient, the rejected person is also more likely to retaliate against the entire group, even though the other group members had nothing to do with the rejection (Gaertner, Iuzzini, & O'Mara, 2008). The effects of social rejection on aggression are especially pronounced for individuals who are sensitive to rejection (Ayduk, Gyurak, & Luerssen, 2008).

One extreme form of social rejection is ostracism. *Ostracism* refers to being excluded, rejected, and ignored by others (e.g., giving someone the "silent treatment"). For example, the close-knit Amish community will sometimes ostracize someone who violates the community's rules, such as by cheating someone, breaking religious rules, or misbehaving sexually. The silent treatment is sometimes also used in military groups, such as if someone is believed to have cheated or broken the military code of honor. In such cases, no one speaks to the person or even acknowledges the soldier's existence. William James (1890) wrote, "If no one turned around when we entered, answered when we spoke, or minded what we did, but if every person we met 'cut us dead,' and acted as if we were nonexistent things, a kind of rage and impotent despair would ere long well up in us, from which the cruelest bodily torture would be a relief" (p. 281). Ostracism is very painful and does increase aggression (e.g., Warburton, Williams, & Cairns, 2006).

All unpleasant events have one thing in common—they put people in a bad mood. But why do unpleasant moods increase aggression? One possible explanation is that angry people aggress in the hope that doing so will enable them to feel better. Research has consistently shown that people who feel bad often try to remedy or repair their moods (Morris & Reilly, 1987). Because many people believe that venting is a healthy way to reduce anger and aggression, they might vent by lashing out at others to improve their mood. A series of studies (Bushman, Baumeister, & Phillips, 2001) replicated the standard finding that provocation increases aggression—but also found a revealing exception. When participants believed that their angry moods would not change for the next hour no matter what they did (ostensibly because of "mood freezing" side effects of a pill they had taken), anger did not lead to aggression. The implication is that anger does not directly or inevitably cause aggression. Rather, angry people attack others because they believe that lashing out will help get rid of their anger and enable them to feel better.

The fact that aversive emotional states lead to aggression has been supported by many research findings (for a review see Berkowitz, 1983). However, being in a bad mood is neither a necessary nor a sufficient condition for aggression. All people in a bad mood do not behave aggressively, and all aggressive people are not in a bad mood.

Presence of Weapons

> Guns not only permit violence, they can stimulate it as well. The finger pulls the trigger, but the trigger may also be pulling the finger.
>
> — Len Berkowitz (1968, p. 22)

Research has shown that the mere presence of weapons, even if they are not used, can increase aggression. In the first study on this topic (Berkowitz & LePage, 1967), participants were seated at a table that had a shotgun and revolver on it—or, in the control condition, badminton racquets and some shuttlecocks. The items on the table were described as part of another experiment, and the other researcher had supposedly forgotten to put them away. Participants decided how many shocks to deliver to a confederate who had previously angered or not angered them. Angered participants who saw the guns were more aggressive than were angered participants who saw the sports items. Several other studies have replicated this effect (dubbed the *weapons effect*). In a field study (Turner, Layton, & Simons, 1975), for example, a confederate driving a pickup truck purposely remained stalled at a traffic light to see whether the motorists trapped behind him would honk their horns (the measure of aggression). The truck contained either a military rifle in a gun rack and a bumper sticker that said VENGEANCE (two aggressive cues), a military rifle and a bumper sticker that said FRIEND (one aggressive cue), or no gun and no bumper sticker (no aggressive cues). The more aggressive cues the trapped motorists saw, the more likely they were to honk their horns. Why would people honk their horn at a driver with a military rifle and a VENGEANCE bumper sticker? This seems very stupid and dangerous. It is certainly much safer to honk at someone who is not driving around with weapons and violent bumper stickers. But people probably were not thinking about what they were doing. Aggressive cues can automatically activate aggressive thoughts and impulses (Anderson, Benjamin, & Bartholow, 1998), influencing people to react more aggressively than they normally would. A meta-analysis of 56 published studies confirmed that the mere sight of weapons increases aggression in both angry and non-angry individuals (Carlson, Marcus-Newhall, & Miller, 1990).

Situational Stimuli That Arouse

Many stimuli, such as provocation, media violence, and heat, that increase aggression also increase arousal levels, suggesting that arousal may have a role in stimulating aggression. But why would arousal increase aggression? There are at least four possible reasons. First, high levels of arousal may be experienced as aversive (e.g., Mendelson, Thurston, & Kubzansky, 2008), and may therefore stimulate aggression in the same way as other aversive stimuli. Second, arousal narrows our span of attention (Easterbrook, 1959). If aggressive cues are salient in the situation, then people will focus most of their attention on the aggressive cues. Third, arousal increases the dominant response, which is defined as the most common response in that situation (Zajonc, 1965). Thus, whatever people are normally inclined to do (including behaving aggressively), they will be even more strongly inclined to do when they are physiologically aroused. Fourth, arousal may be mislabeled as anger in situations involving provocation, thus producing anger-motivated aggressive behavior. This mislabeling process has been demonstrated in several studies by Dolf Zillmann, who has named it *excitation transfer*. Excitation-transfer theory assumes that physiological arousal, however produced, dissipates slowly. If two arousing events are separated by a short amount of time, some of the arousal caused by the first event may transfer to the second event and add to the arousal caused by the second event. In other words, arousal from the first event may be misattributed to the second event. If the second event increases anger, then the additional arousal should make the person even angrier. In one study (Zillmann, Katcher, & Milavsky 1972), half the participants exercised by riding a stationary bike. In the second part of the study, participants were provoked or not provoked by a confederate. Participants were then given an opportunity to punish the confederate by shocking him. The results showed that unprovoked participants were not very aggressive, regardless of whether they rode the bike. Provoked participants,

however, were more aggressive if they rode the bike than if they did not. Excitation transfer theory also suggests that anger may be extended over long periods of time, if the person has attributed his or her heightened arousal to anger and ruminates about it. Thus, even after the arousal has dissipated, the person may remain ready to aggress for as long as the self-generated label of anger persists.

Some Situational Factors That Interfere with Aggression Inhibition

This discussion of aversive stimulation raises the question of why there isn't even more aggression and violence in the world. After all, who hasn't experienced frustration, anger, insult, or hot weather in the past year? Yet most people do not hurt or kill anyone. These factors may give rise to violent impulses, but mostly people restrain themselves. People don't have to learn how to behave aggressively; it comes naturally. What people have to learn is how to inhibit their aggressive impulses. However, even after the inhibition of aggression is learned, situational factors can interfere with inhibiting aggression. We discuss two of those factors in this section: alcohol and anonymity. Other factors, such as aggressive role models, are discussed in a later section.

Alcohol

Alcohol has long been associated with violent and aggressive behavior. Numerous studies have found that over 50% of people who commit violent crimes were intoxicated when the crimes occurred (e.g., Innes, 1988; Pernanen, 1991). There is ample evidence of a positive correlation between alcohol and aggression. For example, a meta-analytic review of 130 studies found that alcohol was correlated with both criminal and domestic violence (Lipsey, Wilson, Cohen, & Derzon, 1997). However, there are numerous difficulties with using correlational evidence to establish a causal link between alcohol and aggression (Brain, 1986). For example, the aggressor may misreport alcohol ingestion as an excuse or to avoid punishment. But meta-analytic reviews of experimental studies also show that alcohol increases aggression (e.g., Bushman & Cooper, 1990; Ito, Miller & Pollock, 1996; Lipsey et al., 1997). In fact, alcohol is sometimes deliberately used to promote aggression. It has been standard practice for many centuries to issue soldiers some alcohol before they went into battle, both to increase aggression and to reduce fear (Keegan, 1993).

Does all of this mean that alcohol is a direct cause of aggression? No. Alcohol mainly seems to increase aggression in combination with other factors. Factors that normally increase aggression (e.g., frustration, provocation) have a stronger effect on intoxicated people than on sober people (Bushman, 1997). If someone is insulted, his or her response will be more violent if he or she is drunk than sober. When there is no provocation, however, the effect of alcohol on aggression may be negligible.

There are several possible explanations for why alcohol increases aggression. One explanation is that alcohol reduces inhibitions. Normally people have strong inhibitions against behaving aggressively, and alcohol reduces these inhibitions. To use a car analogy, alcohol increases aggression by cutting the brake line rather than by stepping on the gas. One interesting theory, based on ego-depletion theory described previously, provides a plausible explanation of how alcohol might cut the brake line (Gailliot & Baumeister, 2007). The brain's activities rely almost exclusively on glucose for energy. Self-control takes a lot of energy, and acts of self-control deplete relatively large amounts of glucose. Alcohol reduces glucose throughout the brain and body and also impairs many forms of self-control, including the self-control needed to restrain aggressive impulses.

A second explanation is that alcohol creates a "myopic" or narrowing effect on attention (Steele & Josephs, 1990). This causes people to focus attention on the more salient provocative features of a situation and to pay less attention to more subtle inhibitory features. Several experiments have found support for this theory (e.g., Denson et al., 2008; Giancola & Corman, 2007).

A third explanation is that alcohol increases aggression by decreasing self-awareness (Hull, 1981). People become more aware of their internal standards when attention is focused on the self. Most people have internal standards against behaving aggressively, but alcohol reduces people's ability to focus on these internal standards.

A fourth explanation is that alcohol disrupts *executive functions*, which are cognitive abilities that help us plan, organize, reason, achieve goals, control emotions, and inhibit behavior tendencies (e.g., Giancola, 1995). It appears that executive functioning is both a mediator and moderator of alcohol-related aggression. It is a mediator because alcohol intoxication disrupts executive functioning, which, in turn, heightens the probability of aggression. It is a moderator because acute alcohol consumption is more likely to facilitate aggression in persons with low, rather than high, executive functioning abilities.

Alcohol is so closely linked to aggression that people don't even need to drink alcohol for it to have an effect. The mere sight of a bottle of alcohol or an alcohol advertisement increases aggressive thoughts and hostile attributions about others (Bartholow & Heinz, 2006). Moreover, the mere belief that one has consumed alcohol increases aggression (Bègue, Subra, Arvers, Muller, Bricout, & Zorman, 2009).

Anonymity

Another factor that might reduce aggressive inhibitions is being anonymous, probably because the perpetrators think they will be less likely to be caught and held responsible for their aggressive actions. When people become anonymous, they lose their sense of individuality, a state called *deindividuation*. Some ways people can achieve anonymity are by wearing a mask or disguise, by being part of a large group, or by performing behaviors in the dark. This might explain why bank robbers and members of the Ku Klux Klan wear masks when they commit violent crimes, why larger crowds are more likely to taunt a suicidal person to jump off a building, bridge, or tower (Mann, 1981), and why violent crimes are much more likely to occur during nighttime hours than during daytime hours (e.g., Bushman, Wang, & Anderson, 2005; Tamura, 1983).

Anonymity increases aggression both inside and outside the lab (Anderson & Bushman, 1997). In an analysis of 500 violent assaults in Northern Ireland, attackers who wore disguises inflicted more serious physical injuries, attacked more people at the scene, and were more likely to threaten victims after the attacks than were attackers who did not wear disguises (Silke, 2003). In a field study (Ellison, Govern, Petri, & Figler, 1995), a confederate driver remained stationary at an intersection when the light turned green. Participants were stalled motorists behind the confederate who were driving vehicles in which the tops could be put up or down (e.g., convertibles, Jeeps). (Drivers of other types of vehicles were not included in the study.) Drivers with tops up (and hence more anonymous) honked more and longer than drivers with tops down. Similar effects have been found in simulation tests of aggressive driving behavior (e.g., Ellison-Potter, Bell, & Deffenbacher, 2001). In an early laboratory experiment (Zimbardo, 1969), female college students were randomly assigned to one of two conditions. Half wore large lab coats, wore hoods over their heads, and were not referred to by name. The other half did not wear lab coats, wore large nametags, and were referred to by name. First, they listened to an interview between the researcher and a female confederate who was either obnoxious or nice. Participants were tested in groups of three. As a group, participants decided how long the female confederate should be shocked, presumably as part of a separate study on conditioning. The anonymous groups gave the confederate longer shocks than did the identified group, especially if she was obnoxious during the interview.

PREDISPOSING PERSONAL FACTORS

Aggression is the consequence of situational factors interacting with predisposing factors. We described the major situational factors above. In this section we describe the major predisposing personal factors that influence aggression. In the next section we focus on the major predisposing environmental factors.

Personality

Many predisposing factors, once established, are viewed as part of an individual's personality. However, their origins may stem from early interactions of the child with the environment, or they may be more innate. From a social-cognitive perspective, personality is the sum of a person's knowledge structures and emotional proclivities (Mischel & Shoda, 1995; Sedikides & Skowronski, 1990). *Knowledge structures* are organized packets of information that are stored in memory. These knowledge structures form when a set of related concepts is frequently brought to mind, or activated. How people construe and respond to their world depends in part on the knowledge structures they use. Situational realities impose constraints on how people construe their world, but individual differences in emotional reactivity and in the structure, accessibility, and use of underlying knowledge structures create a range of possible construals.

Psychopathy

One personality characteristic associated with aggression and violence is *psychopathy* (Hare, Harpur, Hakstian, Forth, Hart, & Newman, 1990), defined as a syndrome of callous and unemotional affective reactions and low empathy. Psychopaths are more likely to engage in proactive cold-blooded aggression than in reactive hot-blooded aggression (Nouvion, Cherek, Lane, Tcheremissine, & Lieving 2007). Because most murders are committed in a fit of rage, psychopaths are not frequently murderers (Hare & McPherson, 1984; Williamson, Hare, & Wong, 1987). Psychopaths mainly focus on obtaining their own goals, regardless of whether they hurt others in the process. Although psychopaths normally don't "feel" empathy toward others, if they are forced to adopt the victim's perspective, their aggression levels can be reduced (Van Baardewijk, Stegge, Bushman, & Vermeiren, 2009). Unfortunately, the origins of psychopathy remain unclear. It is also difficult (some say impossible) to treat psychopaths.

Narcissism

How are self-views related to aggression? For many years, the prevailing view held that aggressive people have low self-esteem. Despite this apparent consensus, no compelling theoretical rationale existed to explain why low self-esteem would cause aggression. Even more problematic, a persuasive body of empirical evidence was lacking. Research has contradicted the prevailing view (Baumeister, Smart, & Boden, 1996). Violent individuals typically have the trait of *narcissism*, which includes thinking oneself superior or special, feeling entitled to preferential treatment, being willing to exploit others, having low empathy for "lesser" human beings, and entertaining grandiose fantasies or other ideas about oneself as a great person (Morf & Rhodewalt, 2001). Several studies have shown that narcissistic individuals respond with high levels of aggression when they receive a blow to their ego (e.g., Bushman & Baumeister, 1998). Aggression often starts when someone questions or challenges those favorable self-views. Wounded pride seems to be the most apt descriptor of how self-views are linked to aggression.

Poor Self-Control

In their book titled *A General Theory of Crime*, Gottfredson and Hirschi (1990) propose that poor self-control is the major cause of crime. Research supports this proposition; poor self-control is one of the "strongest known correlates of crime" (Pratt & Cullen, 2000, p. 952), especially violent crime (Henry, Caspi, Moffitt, & Silva, 1996). Criminals seem to be impulsive individuals who don't show much respect for rules in general. In the movies, criminals often specialize in one specific kind of crime, almost like any other job. But in reality, most criminals are arrested multiple times for several different kinds of crimes. Another sign is that the lives of criminals show low self-control even in behaviors that are not illegal. For example, criminals are more likely than law-abiding citizens to smoke cigarettes, to be involved in traffic accidents, to be involved in unplanned pregnancies, to fail to show up for work regularly, and the like.

Predisposing Biological Factors

A number of different biological characteristics predispose individuals from birth to be more or less aggressive. Although the exact mechanisms are not entirely clear, most of them are triggered by environmental factors, and few (or none) of them determine aggression by themselves.

Low Arousal

Individuals with lower than average baseline levels of physiological arousal (e.g., heart rate, blood pressure) are inclined to behave aggressively. This finding has been replicated in several groups of individuals with aggressive tendencies, including conduct disordered children (Rogeness, Cepeda, Macedo, Fischer, & Harris, 1990), antisocial youth (Raine, 1993), and psychopaths (Hare, 1978). Men who show little negative emotion in response to scenes of violence in movies are also more aggressive inside and outside the laboratory (Moise-Titus, 1999). Longitudinal studies have shown that youth with low levels of arousal are more likely to engage in criminal activities 10 years later (Raine, Venables, & Williams, 1995; Wadsworth, 1976).

One social-cognitive interpretation of this effect is that low arousal individuals are less likely to experience negative affect during evaluation of aggressive scripts for behavior (Huesmann, 1997). An alternative interpretation presumes an optimal arousal level for everyone. Low arousal individuals may engage in more risky and sensation-producing behaviors (including antisocial and aggressive acts) to increase their arousal to a more optimal level.

Some individual differences in baseline arousal are innate, but learning also plays a role. Researchers have shown that people habituate to repeated exposures to scenes of violence, displaying less emotional reaction to real-life violence over time (Smith & Donnerstein, 1998; Lazarus, Speisman, Mordkoff, & Davison, 1962).

Low Serotonin

In our brains, information is communicated between neurons (nerve cells) by the movement of chemicals across a small gap called the synapse. The chemical messengers are called neurotransmitters. Serotonin is one of these neurotransmitters. Its chemical name is 5-hydroxytryptamine, or 5-HT. It has been called the "feel good" neurotransmitter. If people don't have enough of it, they feel bad and may therefore behave more aggressively. Studies of humans and animals (even invertebrates) have found low serotonin levels in individuals who engage in aggressive and violent behavior repeatedly (e.g., Linnolia et al., 1983; Miczek, Mirsky, Carey, DeBold, & Raine, 1994; Virkkunen, De Jong, Bartko, Goodwin, & Linnolia, 1989; Virkkunen, De Jong, Bartko, & Linnolia, 1989; Virkkunen & Narvanen, 1987). In experiments involving animals, decreasing serotonin levels increases aggression levels, which shows a causal link between serotonin and aggression (Kantak, Hegstrand, & Eichelman, 1981). This causal link has also been shown in experiments involving humans. In one experiment (Berman, McCloskey, Fanning, Schumacher, & Coccaro, 2009), participants with and without a past history of aggression were randomly assigned to receive either 40 mg of paroxetine (raises serotonin) or a placebo. Next, participants completed a competitive reaction time task with an ostensible opponent in which the winner got to punish the loser with electric shocks. Over the series of 28 trials, the "opponent" kept setting more and more intense shocks for participants. Participants who had a history of aggression were much more likely to retaliate by administering severe shocks to their opponent, especially if they had ingested the placebo. The paroxetine, however, significantly reduced aggression levels. Low serotonin appears to produce an inability to inhibit impulsive responses to unpleasant events such as provocation (Soubrie, 1986). For example criminals convicted of impulsive violent crimes have lower serotonin levels than criminals convicted of premeditated crimes (Linnolia et al., 1983).

High Testosterone

Testosterone is the male sex hormone. It is a simple chemical arrangement of carbon rings, a derivative of the molecule cholesterol. Both males and females have testosterone, but males have much more of it. During puberty, testosterone levels are at their lifetime peak, and they begin to decline around the age of 23. Testosterone has repeatedly been linked to aggression. Robert Sapolsky (1998), author of *The Trouble with Testosterone*, writes: "Remove the source of testosterone in species after species and levels of aggression typically plummet. Reinstate normal testosterone levels afterward with injections of synthetic testosterone, and aggression returns."

Testosterone seems to affect aggression through long-term and short-term effects (Archer, 1991). In the long run, testosterone seems to affect the development and organization of various collections of cells in the brain (functional modules) that are associated with sex typed behaviors (ranging from sex to hunting—see Cosmides & Tooby, 2006) as well as affecting bodily structures (e.g., muscles, height) that influence the likelihood and the success rate of aggression. In the short run, testosterone may also have an instigating effect on aggression by increasing feelings of dominance. Although both effects are well established in animals, only the long-term effects are well established in humans (Book, Starzyk, & Quinsey, 2002; Brain, 1994; Reinisch, 1981). In humans, the presence of an instigating effect is difficult to demonstrate. One problem is that various behavioral outcomes closely related to aggression also affect circulating testosterone levels (Archer, 1988). Meta-analytic reviews have found a weak but significant positive correlation (about $r = .14$) between current level of circulating testosterone and various measures of human aggression (Archer, 1991; Book et al., 2002). Studies investigating whether testosterone levels in humans are affected by certain outcomes (e.g., winning, losing) also tend to show weak positive effects, but with many exceptions. Laboratory studies of competitions have shown that male winners usually experience an increase in testosterone, and sometimes female winners do, too (Gladue, Boechler, & McCaul, 1989; Mazur, Susman, & Edelbrock, 1997; McCaul, Gladue, & Joppa, 1992). Similar results have occurred in naturalistic studies of judo martial artists (Salvador, Simon, Suay, Llorens, 1987), wrestlers and tennis players (Elias, 1981), and chess players (Mazur, Booth, & Dabbs, 1992). Even the fans of a winning team show greater increases in testosterone compared to fans of a losing team (Mazur & Booth, 1998). Taken together, this research strongly suggests a reciprocal influence process for the short-term relation between testosterone and aggression in humans. Higher levels of plasma testosterone probably increase aggression slightly, but the outcome of winning and dominating affects testosterone levels just as much.

Executive Functioning Deficits and IQ

As was mentioned previously, one explanation why alcohol increases aggression is that it disrupts executive functioning. A significant body of research has linked deficits in executive functioning to aggression (Giancola, 1995; Giancola, Mezzich, & Tarter, 1998; Seguin & Zelazo, 2005). Neurologically, executive functioning is thought to take place in the prefrontal cortex (the front of the brain, located just behind the forehead), and damage to the prefrontal cortex has also been linked to increased aggression. Deficits in executive functioning may also be linked to early Attention-Deficit/Hyperactivity Disorder (ADHD) and to low IQ. Low IQ in turn has been linked to aggression (Huesmann, Eron, Yarmel, 1987; Moffitt & Lynam, 1994; Wilson & Herrnstein, 1985). Some researchers have argued that a verbal IQ deficit makes it difficult for a child to develop appropriate social problem-solving skills that are useful in solving conflict (Moffitt & Lyman, 1994). It takes real skill and insight to negotiate and resolve a problem peacefully. It is much easier to resort to violence to get what you want.

Attention-Deficit/Hyperactivity Disorder (ADHD)

Early ADHD is strongly correlated with early aggression (Hinshaw, 1987). ADHD also predicts aggression in adolescence and young adulthood (Farrington, Loeber, & Van Kammen, 1990; Magnusson, 1987; Moffitt, 1990; Satterfield, Hoppe, & Schell, 1982). Pharmacological treatment of ADHD symptoms also lowers short-term aggression, though it has little effect on long-term aggression (Hinshaw, Heller, & McHale, 1992).

Genetic Predispositions to Aggress

Research has shown that a number of individual neurophysiological factors are related to aggression. The extent to which these factors are inherited is an important question. In animals, the hereditability of aggression is well established (see Lagerspetz & Lagerspetz, 1971). In humans, although aggression does not appear to be "inherited," genetic factors can predispose individuals to be more or less aggressive. The evidence for this conclusion comes both from behavior genetic studies and from recent examinations of specific genes and DNA sequences.

A substantial number of twin and adoption studies show some hereditability of aggressive or antisocial tendencies (Coie & Dodge, 1998, p. 35; Miles & Carey, 1997). For example, in a large sample of Danish twins born between 1880 and 1910, criminal behavior was correlated .74 for identical twins that have 100% of their genes in common and .46 for fraternal twins that have 50% of their genes in common (Christiansen, 1977; Cloninger & Gottesman, 1987). Similarly, a large sample of American same-sexed twins reared apart, aggression scores in adulthood were correlated .64 for identical twins and .34 for fraternal twins (Tellegen et al., 1988). However, the size of the estimated size of genetic effects decreases when measuring specific rather than general behaviors (DiLalla & Gottesman, 1991; Miles & Carey, 1997), so the behavior genetic effects of heritability may be overestimated.

The second line of evidence comes from the analysis of specific candidate genes and DNA sequences. For example, one important study demonstrated that individuals who possessed a certain variation of the gene that determined monoamine oxidase activity (MAOA) were more at risk to grow up to be antisocial and aggressive adults, but only when they were mistreated as children (Caspi et al., 2002). The MAOA gene is located on the X chromosome, and the enzyme it produces breaks down serotonin and other neurotransmitters. In this study it was demonstrated that if children with the gene for low MAOA activity were severely maltreated as children, they grew up to be more aggressive than either severely maltreated children who did not have the gene or than other children with the gene who were not maltreated. Another study found that a gene variation that lowers serotonin and dopamine activity seems to predispose individuals to be at risk for adolescent antisocial behavior (Burt & Mikolajewski, 2008). Although much more research is needed, it appears that aggressive behavior, like most other behaviors, is affected but not determined by genetic variations.

Evolutionary Underpinnings for Aggression

If genes affect individual differences in aggression, then, obviously, evolution should have influenced characteristic levels of aggression in male and female humans. In particular, to the extent that aggressive or non-aggressive behaviors are adaptive for survival, for the production of offspring, and for the survival of offspring, central nervous system (CNS) mechanisms should evolve that promote those behaviors. The mechanisms may not be "expressed" until certain stimuli occur, but they should evolve.

Evolutionary psychologists who have addressed aggressive behavior have suggested a number of different social problems where evolved neurophysiological mechanisms might play particularly strong roles (Buss & Shackelford, 1997b). These include driving away sexual competitors, mating by force, defending one's offspring, co-opting the resources of others to support one's offspring, and reducing the risk of investing in non-genetic offspring by enforcing sexual fidelity. For males and females, somewhat different social problems are most relevant, and these different adaptive problems could be one explanation for gender differences in forms and amounts of aggression (Archer & Conte, 2005; Vaillancourt, 2005). According to evolutionary theorists, males are more likely than females to use aggression to ensure sexual fidelity in their partners because such aggression makes it more likely that their partners' offspring have the male's genes. Females know that their offspring have their own genes and do not need to use aggression for this purpose. A female, on the other hand, is more prone to use aggression to ensure that her partner does not devote any of his resources to the offspring of other sexual partners but stays committed to her (e.g., Buss & Shackelford, 1997a; Geary, Rumsey, Bow-Thomas, & Hoard, 1995). Consequently, females are more likely to be aggressive toward their partners or toward rivals over issues of commitment than over issues of sexual fidelity. In support of these ideas, women are angered somewhat more by thinking their partners love someone else than by thinking they have had sex with someone else, whereas the opposite is true for men (Buss & Shackelford, 1997a).

Evolutionary theories have also been advanced for why females use more indirect aggression. On average, males are stronger and more easily able to dominate their partners with physical aggression, whereas females, of necessity, must resort to other aggressive tactics such as indirect aggression. Also, from an evolutionary standpoint, the most important type of aggression for females is that directed against other females who compete for access to the best mates (Vaillancourt, 2005). Evolutionary theorists argue that indirect aggression is particularly valuable for damaging female rivals because females' reproductive success depends on their reputation among males. Males want sexual partners with a reputation of monogamy because they want to be sure that all of their partner's offspring are genetically their own.

Evolutionary theories have also been used to explain other differences in aggression, such as aggression in honor cultures (Nisbett & Cohen, 1996) and aggression against outgroup members (Pyszczynski, Greenberg, & Solomon, 1999). However, a cautionary note is in order: Evolutionary theories are not readily "falsifiable" and alternative theories can often make similar predictions.

PREDISPOSING ENVIRONMENTAL FACTORS

Within the framework of the social-cognitive information-processing model, there can be a large number of environmental factors that can exert long-lasting effects on aggression by influencing what people learn, what they believe, and what emotions they feel. For example,

parenting practices, community environments, culture, peers, exposure to violence, and socioeconomic level are all environmental modifiers by this definition. For all of these factors, observational learning plays a major role in the development of various knowledge structures that support aggression.

Family Environment

Children closely observe those around them, so, not surprisingly, their aggressiveness is strongly influenced by how aggressive their parents are (Capaldi, Pears, Patterson, & Owen, 2003; Connell & Goodman, 2002; Huesmann et al., 1984). The influence is long lasting, too. When children grow up, their aggressive behaviors and beliefs as adults are correlated with the amount of inter-parental violence they witnessed in the home when they were children (Hill & Nathan, 2008).

Longitudinal studies have identified a number of family child-rearing variables have been linked to the development of life-long aggression, including inconsistent discipline, failure to monitor the child, rejection and coldness toward the child, and use of harsh physical punishment on the child (Eron, Huesmann, & Zelli, 1991; McCord, 1983; Olweus, 1980, 1995; Patterson, DeBaryshe, & Ramsey, 1989). For example, a study of parental acceptance and rejection in 60 different societies found that rejected children around the world are significantly more hostile and aggressive than are non-rejected children (Rohner, 1975).

Harsh physical punishment deserves special attention because of its close connection to abuse. Abused or neglected children are particularly likely to become abusing and neglecting parents themselves (e.g., Azar & Rohrbeck, 1986; Peterson, Gable, Doyle, & Ewugman, 1997). Furthermore, a number of prospective longitudinal studies have found that corporal punishment of children leads to later increases in aggression against parents, peers, and dating partners (Straus, 2000). There appears to be a reciprocal relation between aggressiveness in children and physical punishment, with each stimulating more of the other (Eron et al., 1991; Sheehan & Watson, 2008). However, the effects also seem to be moderated by cultural norms and identification with parents. Moderate (but not harsh) levels of punishment may actually reduce aggression in ethnic cultures (e.g., African American) that consider punishment normal and acceptable (Lansford et al., 2005) and in children who identify strongly with their parents (Eron et al., 1971).

Coercive Family Interactions

Serious aggressive and antisocial behavior in adolescence most often is the product of a confluence of a number of interacting child-rearing and child-behavior problems (Dishion & McMahon, 1998; Patterson, Dishion, & Bank, 1984). The parents fail to monitor the child well; the child misbehaves; the parents exert inconsistent and overly harsh discipline. At that point the child and parents begin to have "coercive family interactions" that "teach" the child to behave aggressively. The child refuses to behave as the parents want. The parents respond to the child's misbehavior with aggression in an attempt to coerce the child to do what they want. The angered child aggresses back. The parents retreat, which reinforces the child's aggression. The downward cycle continues with the child learning that aggressive behavior produces desirable outcomes.

Peer Environment

As children begin attending school, peer interactions become important (Boivin, Vitaro, & Poulin, 2005; Cairns, Cairns, Neckerman, Gest, & Gariepy, 1988). In general, aggressive children are not well liked by their peers, particularly in elementary school (Cairns et al., 1988; Coie & Dodge, 1983; Eron & Huesmann, 1984; Leary et al., 2006). One possible reason is that children do not like violence and will avoid bullies and others whom they regard as dangerous. Rejected aggressive children often seek out other rejected aggressive peers, or they withdraw from peers altogether and spend their time on isolated activities such as watching TV or playing video games. In either case, these children are likely to become even more aggressive, because they are surrounded by aggressive role models to imitate (Huesmann, 1986).

However, there are some cases where moderately aggressive children are viewed as popular, such as when they are viewed as attractive role models (Rodkin, Farmer, Pearl, & Van Acker, 2000; Vaillancourt & Hymel, 2006). In these studies, however, popularity seems to be defined more in terms of who has social power than in terms of who is liked.

Bullying

Bullying refers to persistent aggression by one individual against another for the purpose of establishing a power relationship over the person (Olweus, 1978). Bullying can occur almost anywhere: at school, at work, or even online (called *cyber bullying*). Being bullied can be a living hell for the victim. In extreme cases, the victim may even commit suicide. For example, one 14-year-old girl from Vancouver, Canada, hung herself with a dog leash after being repeatedly bullied by three girls at her school. She left a note that said: "If I try to get help it will get worse. They are always looking for a new person to beat up and they are the toughest girls. If I ratted they would get suspended and there would be no stopping them. I love you all so much."

Unfortunately, some use the term bullying to refer to any aggression by one peer against another. In fact, most so called "one-time bullying behavior" can be explained using the same theoretical models used for other aggressive behavior. But research suggests that real bullies (as defined above) have some characteristics that distinguish them from other aggressive individuals. Most notably, they have a reduced capacity to experience empathy for others (Gianluca Albiero, Benelli, Altoe, et al., 2007; Jolliffe & Farrington, 2006) a characteristic that bullies share with narcissists and psychopaths.

Cultural and Community Environment

"*Amok*" is one of the few Indonesian words used in the English language. The term dates back to 1665, and means "a murderous frenzy that has traditionally been regarded as occurring especially in Malaysian culture" (*Merriam-Webster Dictionary*, 2008). A young Malay man who had suffered some loss of face or other setback would "run amok," recklessly performing violent acts. The Malays believed it was impossible for young men to control their aggressive impulses under those circumstances. However, when the British colonial administration disapproved of the practice and began to hold the young men responsible for their actions, including punishing them for their violent acts, most Malays suddenly stopped running amok. The history of "running amok" thus reveals three important points about violence. First, it shows the influence of culture: The violence was accepted by one culture and prohibited another culture, and when the local culture changed, the practice of running amok died out. Second, it shows that cultures can promote violence without placing a positive value on it. There is no sign that the Malaysians ever approved of running amok (e.g., those who ran amok didn't receive trophies), but positive value wasn't necessary. All that was necessary was for the culture to believe that it was normal for people to lose control under some circumstances and act violently as a result. Third, it shows that when people believe their violence is beyond control, they are often mistaken—the supposedly "uncontrollable" pattern of running amok died out when the British government cracked down on it. The influence of culture was therefore mediated through self-control.

Cultures of violence can contribute to aggressive and violent behavior. For example, certain parts of the southern United States have long been associated with greater levels of violent attitudes and behaviors than the northern United States. These regional differences might be caused by a southern *culture of honor*, which calls for violent response to threats to one's honor (Nisbett & Cohen, 1996). Youth who grow up in the South even behave more aggressively when provoked in laboratory settings at northern universities. Nisbett and Cohen suggest that the culture of honor dates back to the Europeans who first came to the United States. Many of the settlers in the areas where the culture of honor can be found came from herder families where protecting the herd (with violence, if necessary) was particularly important. Research has shown that herding cultures around the world tend to be more violent than agricultural cultures (e.g., Campbell, 1965; Figueredo, Tal, McNeil, & Guillén, 2003; Peristiany, 1965).

Honor cultures exist throughout the world. One example is ethnic Albania. The Kanun describes the laws that govern customs and practices in Albania. The following quotation is from the Kanun:

> An offence to honor is never forgiven. The person dishonored has every right to avenge his honor; no pledge is given, no appeal is made to the Elders, no judgment is needed, no fine is taken. The strong man collects the fine himself. A man who has been dishonored is considered dead according to the Kanun.

In some societies women are killed if they bring "dishonor" to their family, such as by refusing to accept an arranged marriage, seeking a divorce (even from an abusive husband), committing adultery, or having sex before marriage (even if the man forced her). This practice, called honor killing, supposedly restores the family's honor from the disgrace caused by the woman. It is estimated that about 5,000 women are killed each year this way (United Nations Population Fund, 2007/2008). For example, one Egyptian father paraded his daughter's severed head through the streets shouting, "I avenged my honor."

Other kinds of cultural influences on aggression have also been demonstrated. In one study, the longer Lebanese immigrants were in the United States, the more they "accepted" violence in general, but they became less accepting of violence by men against women (Souweidane & Huesmann, 1999). Children who grow up in violent cultures or communities, observing or experiencing violence around them, have been shown to develop numerous problems (Osofsky, 1995). They behave more violently (Guerra et al., 1995) and are more likely to later physically aggress against their own children (Widom, 1989). Observations of violence seem to lead to the development of beliefs and scripts supporting aggression that stimulate aggressive behavior (Guerra, Huesmann, & Spindler, 2002; Schwartz & Proctor, 2000).

Community poverty has long been investigated as an instigator to aggression for its inhabitants. To the extent poverty is an aversive stimulus, one would expect it to increase aggression (Berkowitz, 1989). However, there are different views of how psychologically aversive poverty is. Certainly, poverty makes life more difficult, increases the risk of a child being exposed to violence, and reduces resources to help families. Consequently, there are generally significant negative correlations between socioeconomic status and violent and aggressive behavior (Farrington, 1995; Huesmann, Eron, & Dubow, 2002; Huesmann, Moise-Titus, Podolski, & Eron, 2003; Winslow & Shaw, 2007). However, impoverished neighborhoods do not need to be breeding grounds for aggression. Research has shown that neighborhood and community activism and social support can mitigate the effects of impoverished neighborhoods on the development of aggression (Gatti, Tremblay, & Schadee, 2007; Sampson, Raudenbush, & Earls, 1997; Scarpa & Haden, 2006).

Other community characteristics besides violence and poverty also increase the risk of children growing up to be aggressive. Growing up in a community of ethnic prejudice and hate may well be the most extreme version of an aggression-fostering environment. Observational learning in such environments may well account for generations of ethnic and religious hatreds and genocidal tendencies that occasionally erupt into genocidal wars (Keltner & Robinson, 1996; Staub, 1989, 1998). When normative beliefs become completely accepting of violence against another ethnic group, genocide can result. Normal aggression inhibitions are sometimes overridden when one grows up in such prejudiced environments (Bandura, Barbaranelli, Caprara, & Pastorelli, 1996; Keltner & Robinson, 1996; Staub, 1989, 1998).

Most people do not commit extreme acts of violence, even if they could do so with little chance of punishment, because of their own self-regulating normative beliefs and moral standards inhibit aggression. However, there appear to be at least two particularly important mechanisms that allow people to disengage their moral standards—dehumanizing the victim and finding overriding other "moral" beliefs. When the potential victims are placed in the ultimate outgroup—one that has no human qualities—typical moral beliefs need not apply (see also Diener, 1976; Prentice-Dunn & Rogers, 1983). Enemies are called "cockroaches," "rats," "vermin," "beasts," and so on. Alternatively, prejudiced societies often develop overriding beliefs about why it is good for the society to "cleanse" itself of the other "inferior" ethnic group.

Mass Media Environment

Children today are immersed in the media, like fish in water. By age 2, most children are frequently viewing television and movies and are playing some video games. By age 12, children spend more time consuming media than attending school. It should not be surprising, then, that decades of research have shown that observing violence in the mass media stimulates aggressive behavior. Regardless of how one studies the media violence/aggression link, the outcomes are the same. This is true for longitudinal studies, cross-sectional correlational studies, field studies, and laboratory experiments (Anderson, Berkowitz, et al., 2003; Anderson & Bushman, 2002b; Bushman & Huesmann, 2000; Paik & Comstock, 1994). The average correlations from meta-analytic reviews are as large as those for other risks that are considered public health threats (e.g., second-hand smoke, exposure to lead)—ranging between .2 and .4. Violent media stimulate aggression in the short run by priming aggressive scripts and by influencing children to mimic what they see. Violent media stimulate aggression in the long run by changing schemas, scripts, and beliefs about aggression, and by desensitizing viewers to violence (Bushman & Huesmann, 2006; Huesmann & Kirwil, 2007).

Experiments on Short-Term Effects of Media-Violence

Ever since Bandura's classical early studies on imitation of film violence (Bandura et al., 1961), laboratory experiments have played an important role in showing that exposure to violent media causes a short-term increase in aggressive behavior. There can no longer be any dispute about this conclusion, and more recent studies using more valid measures of aggression have shown similar results. In one field experiment (Josephson, 1987), for example, a group of 396 7- to 9-year-old boys were randomly assigned to watch either a violent or a nonviolent film before they played a game of floor hockey in school. Observers who did not know what movie any boy had seen recorded the number of times each boy physically attacked another boy during the game (e.g., hitting, elbowing, tripping, kneeing, hair pulling). For some of the games, the referees carried walkie-talkies that were similar to those carried by characters in the violent film. The most aggressive boys were those who saw the violent film and the walkie-talkies carried by the referees.

A number of recent experiments have shown similar effects for violent video games. In one study (Konijn, Nije Bijvank, & Bushman, 2007), Dutch boys about 14 years old were randomly assigned to play a violent or nonviolent video game for 20 minutes and rated how much they identified with the main character in the game. Next, they completed a competitive task in which the winner blasted the loser with a noise through a pair of headphones. The noise levels ranged from 60 decibels (*level 1*) to 105 decibels (*level 10*)—about the same level as a fire alarm. (A nonaggressive no noise option was also included, although none of the boys used it.) The boys were told that inflicting higher noise levels could cause "permanent hearing damage" to their partners. Of course, nobody actually got hearing damage. But the results showed that violent game players acted more aggressively than nonviolent game players, especially if they identified strongly with the game

character. These boys were even willing to give another boy noise levels loud enough to cause permanent hearing damage. One boy said, "I blasted him with level 10 noise because he deserved it. I know he can get hearing damage, but I don't care!" Another boy said he liked the violent game "because in this game you can kill people and shoot people, and I want to do that too."

An obvious question is whether playing violent video games has a larger effect in stimulating aggression than watching violent TV programs or movies. There are at least three reasons to believe that violent video games might stimulate more aggression. First, video game play is active, whereas watching TV is passive. People learn better when they are actively involved. Suppose you wanted to teach a person how to fly an airplane. What would be the best method to use: read a book, watch a TV program, or practice on a video game flight simulator? Second, players of violent video games are more likely to identify with violent characters. If the game is a first-person shooter, players have the same visual perspective as the killer. If the game is third person, the player controls the actions of the violent character from a more distant visual perspective. In either case, the player is linked to a violent character. In a violent TV program, viewers might or might not identify with a violent character. Third, violent games directly reward violent behavior by awarding points or allowing players to advance to the next game level. In some games, players are also rewarded through verbal praise, such as hearing the words "Nice shot!" or "Impressive!" after killing an enemy. It is well known that rewarding behavior increases its frequency. In TV programs, reward is not directly tied to the viewer's behavior. A recent study provided the first evidence that playing violent games produce stronger effects than simply observing violence (Polman, Orobio de Castro, & Van Aken, 2008). In this study, some participants played violent games while others watched the games being played, and the effects on aggression were stronger for the players than the watchers.

Some experiments have also provided support for more long-term processes. In particular several studies have shown how people who consume violent media become more tolerant of violence (*cognitive desensitization*) and experience less physiological arousal to violence (*emotional desensitization*) (Drabman & Thomas, 1974). Here again violent video games are of particular concern. Feeling empathy requires taking the perspective of the victim, whereas violent video games encourage players to take the perspective of the perpetrator. In one experiment, people who played a violent video game were less physiologically aroused (i.e., had lower heart rate and skin conductance levels) by real depictions of violence than were those who played a nonviolent game (e.g., Carnagey, Anderson, & Bushman, 2007).

In another experiment (Bushman & Anderson, 2009), people who had played a violent video game took 450% longer to help a violence victim in a staged emergency in comparison to those who played a nonviolent game. Violent game players also were less likely to notice the emergency and rated it as less serious if they did notice it.

Longitudinal Studies of Long-Term Effects of Media Violence

It is not so much the immediate effects of media violence on aggression that are of concern, but rather the aggregated long-term effects. A study initiated in 1960 on 856 8-year-old children in New York State found that boys' early childhood viewing of violence on TV was positively related to their aggressive and antisocial behavior 10 years later (after graduating from high school), even controlling for initial aggressiveness, social class, education, and other variables (Eron, Huesmann, Lefkowitz, & Walder, 1972; Lefkowitz, Eron, Walder, & Huesmann, 1977). A 22-year follow-up of these same boys revealed that early violence viewing was independently related to adult criminal behavior at age 30 (Huesmann, 1986; Huesmann & Miller, 1994).

The long-term effects of violent media exposure are not limited to American children. A three-year longitudinal study of children in five countries (Australia, Finland, Poland, Israel, USA) found that the television habits of children as young as 6 years old predicted subsequent childhood aggression, even controlling for initial level of aggression (Huesmann & Eron, 1986; Huesmann, Lagerspetz, & Eron, 1984). In contrast to earlier longitudinal studies, this effect was obtained for both boys and girls, even in countries without large amounts of violent programming. A 15-year follow-up of the U.S. children in this study revealed that both boys and girls who had been high violence viewers in childhood behaved significantly more aggressively in their mid-20s (Huesmann, Moise-Titus, Podolski, & Eron, 2003). For males, this included being convicted of more crimes. For females this included being both more physically aggressive and more indirectly aggressive. Importantly, this study also found that children's aggression did not significantly predict their later tendency to view or not view violent media as adults. Thus, it is unlikely that the results are simply due to more aggressive kids wanting to watch more violent programs.

Another large longitudinal study followed over 2,500 middle-school students over 2 years (Slater, Henry, Swaim, & Anderson, 2003). The results found a significant lagged effect of prior violence viewing on subsequent aggression, and a smaller and less significant effect of prior aggression on subsequent violence viewing. The authors concluded that the relation seemed to be a "downward spiral" of violence, viewing stimulating aggression and aggressive youth turning to more violence viewing.

Other longitudinal studies involving elementary school children in the United States and Japan found that playing violent video games predicted aggressive behaviors and thoughts several months later, even after controlling for initial level of aggression (Anderson, Gentile, & Buckley, 2007; Anderson, Sakamoto, Gentile, Ihori, & Shibuya, 2008; Ihori, Sakamoto, Kobayashi, & Kimura, 2003). In summary, the results from these longitudinal studies and others show that exposure to violent media has a cumulative effect and can increase aggression in the long run.

Sexually Explicit Violent Media

One type of media deserves special mention because it can lead to aggression against women—violent sexual media (e.g., rape depictions). The evidence is clearest for short-term effects. In one experiment (Donnerstein & Berkowitz, 1981), for example, college men watched one of four film clips: (1) a clip containing no violence or sex, (2) a nonviolent-sexually explicit clip of a couple enjoying making love, (3) a violent-sexual clip of a man raping a woman who resists the rape, or (4) a violent-sexual clip of a man raping a woman who initially resists the rape, but then seems to enjoy it. Afterwards, participants were provoked by either a male or female confederate and were then given the chance to punish the confederate using electric shocks. The results showed that men who viewed a rape scene were more aggressive than men who did not view a rape scene, especially when the aggression target was the female provoker. Men who saw the clip showing the woman enjoying being raped showed the highest levels of aggression. There was no evidence of an aggression-enhancing effect from viewing nonviolent sex. In fact, the men who viewed nonviolent sex were *less* aggressive toward the female provoker than toward the male provoker.

There are also long-term effects of viewing violent sexual media, such as desensitization. Research has shown that even several days after watching violent sex scenes (e.g., in "slasher" films), men still displayed an increased tolerance to aggression directed toward women (Malamuth & Check, 1981; Mullin & Linz, 1995). Additionally, field studies have shown a positive relation between pornography use and sexual aggression (e.g., Kingston, Fedoroff, Firestone, Curry & Bradford, 2008).

REDUCING AGGRESSION

Most people are greatly concerned about the amount of aggression and violence in society. Because aggression directly interferes with our basic needs of safety and security, it is urgent to find ways to reduce it. The fact that there is no single cause for aggression makes it difficult to design effective interventions. A treatment that works for one person may not work for another. Some people, such as psychopaths, are even considered untreatable. Indeed, many people have started to accept the fact that aggression and violence have become an inevitable, intrinsic part of our society.

This being said, there certainly are things that can be done to reduce aggression and violence. There are two important general points we would like to make. First, successful interventions target as many causes of aggression as possible and attempt to tackle them collectively. Most often, these interventions are aimed at reducing factors that promote aggression in the direct social environment (family, friends), general living conditions (housing and neighborhood, health, poverty), and occupation (school, work, spare time). Interventions that are narrowly focused at removing a single cause of aggression, however well conducted, are bound to fail.

Aggression is quite stable over time. Therefore, if young children display excessive levels of aggression (often in the form of hitting, biting, or kicking), it places them at high risk for becoming violent adolescents and even violent adults. It is much more difficult to alter aggressive behaviors when they are part of an adult personality than when they are still in development. Thus, as a second general rule, aggressive behavior problems are best treated in early development, when they are still malleable.

In this section we discuss some methods for reducing aggression. Before discussing the effective methods, we first debunk two ineffective methods: catharsis and punishment.

Catharsis

The word catharsis comes from the Greek word *katharsis*, which means to cleanse or purge. The term dates back to Aristotle, who taught that viewing tragic plays gave people emotional release from negative emotions. In Greek drama, the heroes didn't just grow old and retire—they often suffered a violent demise.

Sigmund Freud, who believed that repressed negative emotions could build up inside an individual and cause psychological symptoms, revived the ancient notion of catharsis. Freud's ideas form the basis of the hydraulic model of anger (described earlier), which suggests that frustrations lead to anger and that anger, in turn, builds up inside an individual like hydraulic pressure inside a closed environment until it is vented or released. If the anger is not vented, the build-up will presumably cause the individual to explode in an aggressive rage.

According to *catharsis theory*, acting aggressively or even viewing aggression purges angry feelings and aggressive impulses into harmless channels. Almost as soon as researchers started testing catharsis theory, it ran into trouble.

In one early experiment (Hornberger, 1959), participants who had been insulted by a confederate either pounded nails with a hammer for 10 minutes or did nothing. After this, all participants had a chance to criticize the confederate who had insulted them. If catharsis theory is true, the act of pounding nails should reduce anger and subsequent aggression. Unfortunately for catharsis theory, the results showed the opposite effect. Participants who pounded nails were *more* hostile toward the confederate afterward than were the ones who didn't get to hammer any nails.

In 1973, Albert Bandura issued a moratorium on catharsis theory and the use of venting in therapy, and research evidence supported Bandura's views (e.g., Geen & Quanty, 1977). Venting doesn't work even among people who believe in the value of venting, and even among people who report feeling better after venting (Bushman, Baumeister, & Stack, 1999). In fact, venting has the opposite effect—it increases aggression. The better people feel after venting, the more aggressive they are. Venting can even increase aggression against innocent bystanders.

One variation of venting is intense physical exercise, such as running. When angry, some people go running or try some other form of physical exercise. Although exercise is good for your heart, it is not good for reducing anger (Bushman, 2002). The reason exercise doesn't work very well is that it increases rather than decreases arousal levels. Angry people are highly aroused, and should try to calm down. Also, if someone provokes you after exercising, excitation transfer might occur (Zillmann, 1979). That is, the arousal from the exercise might transfer to the provocation, producing an exaggerated and possibly more violent response.

Punishment

Most cultures assume that punishment is an effective way to deter violence and aggression. *Punishment* is defined as inflicting pain (*positive punishment*) or removing pleasure (*negative punishment*) for a misdeed. Punishment can range in intensity from spanking a child to executing a convicted murderer. Parents use it, organizations use it, and governments use it. But does it work? Today, aggression researchers have their doubts about the effectiveness of punishment. Punishment is most effective when it is: (1) intense, (2) prompt (before the person can derive pleasure from the misdeed), (3) applied consistently and with certainty, (4) perceived as justified, and (5) replaced by a more desirable alternative behavior (Berkowitz, 1993). Even if punishment occurs under these ideal conditions, it may only suppress aggressive behavior temporarily, and it has several undesirable long-term consequences (Baron & Richardson, 1994; Berkowitz, 1993; Eron et al., 1971). Punishment models the behavior it seeks to prevent. For example, suppose a father sees an older brother beating up his younger sister. The father starts spanking boy while proclaiming, "I'll teach you not to hit your little sister." Yes, the father is teaching the son something; he is teaching the boy that it is okay to behave aggressively as long as you are an authority figure. Punishment is also unpleasant. Its application can classically condition children to avoid their parents, and in the short run can instigate retaliatory aggression. Longitudinal studies have shown that children who are physically punished by their parents at home are more aggressive outside the home, such as in school (e.g., Lefkowitz. Huesmann, & Eron, 1978).

The most extreme form of punishment is capital punishment. Obviously, one way to stop violent people from hurting others is to kill them so they can't do it again. Unfortunately, capital punishment doesn't seem to deter murders, perhaps because many murderers kill their victims in a fit of rage without considering the consequences of their actions. In the United States, FBI Unified Crime reports show that states with the death penalty have murder rates 48 to 101% higher than states without the death penalty. Similar findings have been reported in other countries. An international study of criminal violence analyzed data from 110 nations over a period of 74 years and found that the death penalty does not deter criminals (Archer & Gartner, 1987). Of course, another problem with capital punishment is that it is irreversible. An innocent person (rather than the actual murderer) might be executed. There have been more than 75 documented cases of wrongful conviction of murder, and the death sentence was carried out in 8 of these cases (Draper, 1985). As use of DNA evidence becomes more common, these numbers are likely to increase.

Developing Nonaggressive Ways of Behaving

Aggressive people need to develop nonaggressive ways of behaving. Most aggression treatment programs can be divided into one of two broader categories, depending upon whether aggression is viewed as proactive or reactive (see Berkowitz, 1993, pp. 358–370). Recall from an earlier section that proactive aggression is the cold-blooded, premeditated type of aggression that is a means to some other end, whereas reactive aggression is the hot-blooded, impulsive type of aggression that is an end in itself.

Approaches to Reducing Proactive Aggression

People may resort to aggression because it seems to be the easiest way for them to get what they want in the short run. Negotiating, inducing guilt, compromising, ingratiating, and other ways of influencing others all require considerable skills and self-control, whereas aggression may not. (Indeed, aggression may flourish best in the absence of

self-control and other social skills!) People may therefore turn to aggression as a seemingly rational and appealing way of pursuing their goals.

Psychologists who view aggression as proactive (instrumental) behavior concentrate on teaching aggressive people that they will be more effective in achieving their goals if they behave in a nonaggressive manner. This approach to reducing aggression uses *behavior modification* learning principles that focus on reinforcing nonaggressive behaviors.

One of the main problems with punishment is that does not teach the aggressor new, prosocial forms of behavior. One way to get rid of an undesirable behavior is to replace it with a desirable behavior (called *differential reinforcement of alternative behavior* in behavior modification terminology). The idea is that if one behavior increases as a result of reinforcement, then behaviors that are incompatible with the increased behavior must decrease. Thus, by reinforcing nonaggressive behavior, aggressive behavior should decrease.

The Oregon Social Learning Center uses behavior modification principles to reduce aggression in children and adolescents (e.g., Patterson, Reid, Jones, & Conger, 1975). According to this approach, parents play a key role in forming aggressive tendencies in their children by nagging them, failing to reward desirable behavior, and inconsistently punishing undesirable behavior. Thus, parents are involved in the treatment plan. The treatment is based on a contract the counselor makes with the aggressive child. The contract specifies the rewards the child will receive if he or she complies with the contract. For example, the child might gain 3 points for listening to parents, and lose 3 points for swearing at someone. The points can be exchanged for privileges (e.g., watching TV, favorite treats). If the first contract is successful, a second one is negotiated in which new behaviors are added. The counselor monitors and advises the family through the process. The program is effective in reducing aggression in about one of three children. Additional programs are sometimes required for the other children, such as school programs.

Other effective programs include social skills training, where people are taught about the verbal and nonverbal behaviors involved in social interactions (e.g., Pepler, King, Craig, Byrd, & Bream, 1995). For example, they are taught how to make "small talk" in social settings, how to maintain good eye contact during a conversation, and how to "read" the subtle cues contained in social interactions. By learning how to interact better with others, people don't have to resort to aggression to get what they want.

Having prosocial role models also helps. In one study (Spivey & Prentice-Dunn, 1990), participants played a computer game with a partner. During the game they could punish their partner by pressing shock buttons (1 = *low intensity*, 10 = *high intensity*), or reward their partner by pressing money-dispensing buttons (1 = $*0.25* to 10 = $*2.50*). Before the actual task, the experimenter asked a confederate to press several of the buttons to make sure they were "working." In the antisocial modeling condition, the confederate repeatedly pressed the two highest shock level buttons and said: "I'm going to give this guy 10s every time" (during the task). In the prosocial modeling condition, the confederate repeatedly pressed the two highest money dispensing buttons and said: "I'm going to give this guy $2.50 every time" (during the task). The results showed that participants exposed to the prosocial model gave their partner the most money and the least shock, whereas participants exposed to the antisocial model gave their partner the least money and the most shock. Just as exposure to violent models in the media can increase aggression in viewers, exposure to prosocial models in the media can decrease aggression and increase cooperation (for a meta-analytic review see Mares & Woodward, 2005). Prosocial video games, like prosocial TV programs, can increase helping and decrease aggression (e.g., Gentile et al., 2009).

Approaches to Reducing Reactive Aggression

Other approaches to reducing aggression focus on reducing anger and arousal levels using relaxation and cognitive-behavioral techniques (for a meta-analytic review see DiGuiseppe & Tafrate, 2003). Most relaxation-based techniques involve deep breathing, visualizing relaxing images (e.g., a peaceful meadow), or tightening and loosening muscle groups in succession. People practice relaxing after imaging or experiencing a provocative event. In this way, they learn to calm down after they have been provoked.

Cognitive-based treatments focus on how an event is appraised or interpreted. When provocative events occur, people talk to themselves (in their minds), a process called *self-instructional training* (e.g., Novaco, 1975). When preparing for a provocation, people rehearse statements such as: "If I find myself getting upset, I'll know what to do" and "I can manage this situation. I know how to regulate my anger." When confronting the provocation, people rehearse statements such as: "Stay calm. Just continue to relax" and "You don't need to prove yourself." To cope with arousal and agitation that arises following provocation, people rehearse statements such as: "My muscles are starting to feel tight. Time to relax and slow things down" and "I'm not going to get pushed around, but I'm not going to lose control either." If the conflict is resolved, people rehearse statements such as: "That wasn't as hard as I thought" and "It could have been a lot worse." If the conflict is not resolved, people rehearse statements such as: "These are difficult situations, and they take time to work out." Research shows that it is especially helpful to combine relaxation and cognitive techniques to reduce angry arousal (e.g., Novaco, 1975).

SUMMARY

In some ways, humans are far more aggressive than other animals on this planet. Most fighting between other animals stops far short of serious injury or death, whereas humans kill each other. Humans have even gone to great lengths to invent tools to make killing easier and more "efficient" (from spears to guns to nuclear weapons). The good news is that human society is becoming less violent over time. Hopefully, that trend will continue.

We know a lot more today than we did even a few decades ago about what makes people aggressive. Social psychological theory and research can play an important role in reducing the amount of aggression and violence in society. Social psychological research has shed light on many of the situational and personal factors that are related to aggression. Social psychological research has also helped dispel some myths that have contributed to the level of violence and aggression in society. One myth is that venting anger is an effective way to reduce anger and aggression. Another myth is that aggressive people suffer from low self-esteem.

We don't have a crystal ball, and predictions of the future are hazardous to say the least. We are, however, optimistic about some areas of future research on human aggression. The link between brain activity and human aggression is a promising area of current and future research. Another promising research direction is self-control. Aggression often starts when self-control stops. Another promising research direction is forgiveness (e.g., McCullough, 2008). Dr. Martin Luther King Jr. was correct. The best way to reduce aggression is to reject revenge and retaliation and to embrace love and forgiveness. Hopefully, social psychologists will be at the forefront conducting research on these and other important topics that will help make the world a more peaceful place.

REFERENCES

Abelson, R. P. (1981). Psychological status of the script concept. *American Psychologist, 36*, 715–729.

Anderson, C. A., Anderson, K. B., Dorr, N., DeNeve, K. M., & Flanagan, M. (2000). Temperature and aggression. In M. Zanna (Ed.), *Advances in experimental social psychology*, volume 32 (pp. 63–133). New York: Academic Press.

Anderson, C. A., Benjamin, A. J., & Bartholow, B. D. (1998). Does the gun pull the trigger? Automatic priming effects of weapon pictures and weapon names. *Psychological Science, 9*, 308–314.

Anderson, C. A., Berkowitz, L., Donnerstein, E., Huesmann, L. R., Johnson, J., Linz, D., et al. (2003). The influence of media violence on youth. *Psychological Science in the Public Interest, 4*(3), 81–110.

Anderson, C. A., & Bushman, B. J. (1997). External validity of "trivial" experiments: The case of laboratory aggression. *Review of General Psychology, 1*, 19–41.

Anderson, C. A., & Bushman, B. J. (2002a). Human aggression. *Annual Review of Psychology, 53*, 27–51.

Anderson, C. A., & Bushman, B. J. (2002b). The effects of media violence on society. *Science, 295*, 2377–2378.

Anderson, C. A., Bushman, B. J., & Groom, R. W. (1997). Hot years and serious and deadly assault: Empirical tests of the heat hypothesis. *Journal of Personality and Social Psychology, 16*, 1213–1223.

Anderson, C. A., Gentile, D. A., & Buckley, K. E. (2007). *Violent video game effects on children and adolescents.* New York: Oxford University Press.

Anderson, C. A., Sakamoto, A., Gentile, D. A., Ihori, N., & Shibuya, A. (2008). Longitudinal effects of violent video games on aggression in Japan and the United States. *Pediatrics, 122*(5), 1067–1072.

Archer, D., & Gartner, R. (1987). *Violence and crime in cross-national perspective.* New Haven, CT: Yale University Press.

Archer, J. (1988). *The behavioral biology of aggression.* Cambridge, UK: Cambridge University Press.

Archer, J. (1991). The influence of testosterone on human aggression. *British Journal of Psychology, 82*, 1–28.

Archer, J. (2000). Sex differences in aggression between heterosexual partners: A meta-analytic review. *Psychological Bulletin, 126*, 697–702.

Archer, J., & Conte, S. (2005). Sex differences in aggressive behavior: A developmental and evolutionary perspective. In R.E. Tremblay, W. W. Hartup, & J. Archer (Eds.), *Developmental origins of aggression* (pp. 425–443). New York: Guilford.

Ayduk, Ö, Gyurak, A., & Luerssen, A. (2008). Individual differences in the rejection-aggression link in the hot sauce paradigm: The case of rejection sensitivity. *Journal of Experimental Social Psychology, 44*(3), 775–782.

Azar, S. T., & Rohrbeck, C. A. (1986). Child abuse and unrealistic expectations: Further validation of the Parent Opinion Questionnaire. *Journal of Consulting and Clinical Psychology, 54*, 867–868.

Bandura, A. (1965). Influence of models' reinforcement contingencies on the acquisition of imitative responses. *Journal of Abnormal and Social Psychology, 66*, 575–582.

Bandura, A. (1973). *Aggression: A social learning theory analysis.* Englewood Cliffs, NJ: Prentice-Hall.

Bandura, A. (1977). *Social learning theory.* Englewood Cliffs, NJ: Prentice Hall.

Bandura, A. (1986). *Social foundations of thought and action: A social-cognitive theory.* Englewood Cliffs, NJ: Prentice-Hall.

Bandura, A., Barbaranelli, C., Caprara, G. V., & Pastorelli, C. (1996). Mechanisms of moral disengagement in the exercise of moral agency. *Journal of Personality and Social Psychology, 71*, 364–374.

Bandura, A., Ross, D., & Ross, S.A. (1961). Transmission of aggression through imitation of aggressive models. *Journal of Abnormal and Social Psychology, 63*, 575–582.

Bandura, A., Ross, D., & Ross, S.A. (1963). Vicarious reinforcement and imitative learning. *Journal of Abnormal and Social Psychology, 67*, 601–607.

Barling, J., Dupré, K. E., & Kelloway, E. K. (2009). Predicting workplace aggression and violence. *Annual Review of Psychology.*

Baron, R. A. (1979). Aggression, empathy, and race: Effects of victim's pain cures, victim's race, and level of instigation on physical aggression. *Journal of Applied Social Psychology, 9*, 103–114.

Baron, R. A., & Richardson, D. R. (1994). *Human aggression* (2nd ed.). New York: Plenum.

Bartholow, B. D., & Heinz, A. (2006). Alcohol and aggression without consumption: Alcohol cues, aggressive thoughts, and hostile perception bias. *Psychological Science, 17*, 30–37.

Baumeister, R. F., Bratslavsky, E., Muraver, M. & Tice, D. M. (1998). Ego depletion: Is the active self a limited resource? *Journal of Personality and Social Psychology*, 74, 1152–1165.

Baumeister, R. F., Smart, L., & Boden, J. M. (1996). Relation of threatened egotism to violence and aggression: The dark side of high self-esteem. *Psychological Review, 103*, 5–33.

Berkowitz, L. (1968). Impulse, aggression, and the gun. *Psychology Today, 2*(4), 18–22.

Berkowitz, L. (1974). Some determinants of impulsive aggression: The role of mediated associations with reinforcements for aggression. *Psychological Review, 81*, 165–176.

Berkowitz, L. (1983). Aversively stimulated aggression: Some parallels and differences in research with animals and humans. *American Psychologist, 38*, 1135–1144.

Berkowitz, L. (1989). Frustration-aggression hypothesis: Examination and reformulation. *Psychological Bulletin, 106*, 59–73.

Berkowitz, L. (1990). On the formation and regulation of anger and aggression: A cognitive-neoassociationistic analysis. *American Psychologist, 45*, 494–503.

Berkowitz, L. (1993). *Aggression: Its causes, consequences, and control.* New York: McGraw-Hill.

Berkowitz, L. (2008). On the consideration of automatic as well as controlled psychological processes in aggression. *Aggressive Behavior, 34*(2), 117–129.

Berkowitz, L., & LePage, A. (1967). Weapons as aggression-eliciting stimuli. *Journal of Personality and Social Psychology*, 7, 202–207.

Bettencourt, B. A., & Miller, N. (1996). Gender differences in aggression as a function of provocation: A meta-analysis. *Psychological Bulletin, 119*, 422–447.

Boivin, M., Vitaro, F., & Poulin, F. (2005). Peer relationships and the development of aggressive behavior in early childhood. In R.E. Tremblay, W.W. Hartup, & J. Archer (Eds.), *Developmental origins of aggression* (pp. 376–397). New York: Guilford.

Book, A. S., Starzyk, K. B., & Quinsey, V. L. (2002). The relationship between testosterone and aggression: A meta-analysis. *Aggression and Violent Behavior, 6*, 579–599.

Brain, P. F. (1986). Multidisciplinary examinations of the 'causes' of crime: The case of the link between alcohol and violence. *Alcohol and Alcoholism, 21*, 237–240.

Brain, P. F. (1994). Hormonal aspects of aggression and violence. In A. J. Reis, Jr. & J. A. Roth (Eds.), *Understanding and control of biobehavioral influences on violence* (Vol. 2., pp. 177–244). Washington, DC: National Academy Press.

Brame, B., Nagin, D. S., Tremblay, R. E. (2001). Developmental trajectories of physical aggression from school entry to late adolescence. *Journal of Child Psychology and Psychiatry, 42*(4), 503–512.

Broidy, L. M., Nagin, D. S., Tremblay, R. E., Bates, J. E., Brame, B., Dodge, K. A., et al. (2003). Developmental trajectories of childhood disruptive behaviors and adolescent delinquency: A six-site, cross-national study. *Developmental Psychology, 39*, 222–245.

Burt, S. A., & Mikolajewski, A. J. (2008). Preliminary evidence that specific candidate genes are associated with adolescent onset antisocial behavior. *Aggressive Behavior, 34*(4), 437–445.

Bushman, B. J. (1997). Effects of alcohol on human aggression: Validity of proposed explanations. In D. Fuller, R. Dietrich, & E. Gottheil (Eds.), *Recent developments in alcoholism: Alcohol and violence* (Vol. 13, pp. 227–243). New York: Plenum.

Bushman, B. J. (2002). Does venting anger feed or extinguish the flame? Catharsis, rumination, distraction, anger, and aggressive responding. *Personality and Social Psychology Bulletin, 28*, 724–731.

Bushman, B. J., & Anderson, C. A. (2001). Is it time to pull the plug on the hostile versus instrumental aggression dichotomy? *Psychological Review, 108*, 273–279.

Bushman, B. J., & Anderson, C. A. (2009). Comfortably numb: Desensitizing effects of violent media on helping others. *Psychological Science, 21*(3), 273–277.

Bushman, B. J., & Baumeister, R. F. (1998). Threatened egotism, narcissism, self-esteem, and direct and displaced aggression: Does self-love or self-hate lead to violence? *Journal of Personality and Social Psychology, 75*, 219–229.

Bushman, B. J., Baumeister, R. F., & Phillips, C. M. (2001). Do people aggress to improve their mood? Catharsis beliefs, affect regulation opportunity, and aggressive responding. *Journal of Personality and Social Psychology, 81*, 17–32.

Bushman, B. J., Baumeister, R. F., & Stack, A. D. (1999). Catharsis, aggression, and persuasive influence: Self-fulfilling or self-defeating prophecies? *Journal of Personality and Social Psychology, 76*, 367–376.

Bushman, B. J., Bonacci, A. M., Pedersen, W. C., Vasquez, E. A., & Miller, N. (2005). Chewing on it can chew you up: Effects of rumination on triggered displaced aggression. *Journal of Personality and Social Psychology, 88*, 969–983.

Bushman, B. J., & Cooper, H. M. (1990). Alcohol and human aggression: An integrative research review. *Psychological Bulletin, 107*, 341–354.

Bushman, B. J., & Huesmann, L. R. (2000). Effects of televised violence on aggression. In D. Singer & J. Singer (Eds.), *Handbook of children and the media* (pp. 223–254). Thousand Oaks, CA: Sage.

Bushman, B. J., & Huesmann, L. R. (2006). Short-term and long-term effects of violent media on aggression in children and adults. *Archives of Pediatrics & Adolescent Medicine, 160*, 348–352.

Bushman, B. J., Wang, M. C., & Anderson, C. A. (2005). Is the curve relating temperature to aggression linear or curvilinear? Assaults and temperature in Minneapolis reexamined. *Journal of Personality and Social Psychology, 89*, 62–66.

Buss, A. H. (1961). *The psychology of aggression*. New York: Wiley.

Buss, D. M., & Shackelford, T. K. (1997a). From vigilance to violence: Mate retention tactics in married couples. *Journal of Personality and Social Psychology, 72*, 346–361.

Buss, D. M., & Shackelford, T. K. (1997b). Human aggression in evolutionary psychological perspective. *Clinical Psychology Review, 17*, 605–619.

Cairns, R. B., & Cairns, B. D. (1994). *Lifelines and risks: Pathways of youth in our time*. New York: Cambridge University Press.

Cairns, R. B., & Cairns, B. D., Neckerman, H. J., Gest, S. D., & Gariepy, J. L. (1988). Social networks and aggressive behavior: Peer support of peer rejection? *Developmental Psychology*, 24, 815–823.

Campbell, A. (1999). Staying alive: Evolution, culture, and women's intrasexual aggression. *Behavioral and Brain Sciences, 22*, 203–252.

Campbell, J. K. (1965). Honour and the devil. In J. G. Peristiany (Ed.), *Honour and shame: The values of Mediterranean society* (pp. 112–175). London: Weidenfeld & Nicolson.

Cannon, W. B. (1915). *Bodily changes in pain, hunger, fear and rage: An account of recent researches into the function of emotional excitement*. New York: Appleton.

Capaldi, D. M., Pears, K. C., Patterson, G. R., & Owen, L. D. (2003). Continuity of parenting practices across generations in an at-risk sample: A prospective comparison of direct and mediated associations. *Journal of Abnormal Child Psychology, 31*, 127–142.

Caplan, M., Vespo, J., Pedersen, J., & Hay, D. F. (1991). Conflict over resources in small groups of one-and two-year-olds. *Child Development, 62*, 1513–1524.

Carlson, M., Marcus-Newhall, A., & Miller, N. (1990). Effects of situational aggression cues: A quantitative review. *Journal of Personality and Social Psychology, 58*, 622–633.

Carnagey, N. L., Anderson. C. A., & Bushman, B. J. (2007). The effect of video game violence on physiological desensitization to real life violence. *Journal of Experimental Social Psychology, 43*, 489–496.

Caspi, A., McClay, J., Moffitt, T. E., Mill, J., Martin, J., Craig, I. W., et al. (2002). Role of genotype in the cycle of violence in maltreated children. *Science, 297*, 851–854.

Chen, Z., Williams, K. D., Fitness, J., & Newton, N. C. (2008). When hurt won't heal: Exploring the capacity to relive social pain. *Psychological Science, 19*(8), 789–795.

Christiansen, K. (1977). A preliminary study of criminality among twins. In S. A. Mednick & K. O. Christiansen (Eds.), *Biosocial bases of criminal behavior* (pp. 89–108). New York: Gardner Press.

Cloninger, C. R., & Gottesman, I. I. (1987). Genetic and environmental factors in antisocial behavior disorders. In S. A. Mednick, T. E. Moffitt, & S. Stack (Eds.), *The causes of crime: New biological approaches*. Cambridge, UK: Cambridge University Press.

Coie, J. D., & Dodge, K. A. (1983). Continuities and changes in children's social status: A five-year longitudinal study. *Merrill-Palmer Quarterly, 29*, 261–282.

Coie, J. D., & Dodge, K. A. (1998). Aggression and anti-social behavior. In W. Damon & N. Eisenberg (Eds.), *Handbook of child psychology* (pp. 779–862). New York: Wiley.

Collins, R. L., Quigley, B., & Leonard, K. (2007). Women's physical aggression in bars: An event-based examination of precipitants and predictors of severity. *Aggressive Behavior, 33*(4), 304–313.

Connell, A. M., & Goodman, S. H. (2002). The association between psychopathology in fathers versus mothers and children's internalizing and externalizing behavior problems: A meta-analysis. *Psychological Bulletin, 128*, 746–773.

Cosmides, L. & Tooby, J. (2006). Origins of domain specificity: The evolution of functional organization. In J. L. Bermudez (Ed.), *Philosophy of psychology: Contemporary readings* (pp. 539–555). New York: Routledge.

Cote, S., Vaillancourt, T., LeBlanc, J., Nagin, D. W., & Tremblay, R. E. (2006). The development of physical aggression from toddlerhood to pre-adolescence: A nation wide longitudinal study of Canadian children. *Journal of Abnormal Child Psychology, 34*(1), 71–85.

Cowan, P. A., & Walters, R. A. (1963). Studies of reinforcement of aggression: I. Effects of scheduling. *Child Development*, 34, 543–551.

Crick, N. R., & Grotpeter, J. K. (1995). Relational aggression, gender, and social-psychological adjustment. *Child Development, 66*, 710–722.

Darwin, C. (1871/1948). *Origin of species*. New York: Modern Library.

Denson, T. F., Aviles, F. E., Pollock, V. E., Earleywine, M., Vasquez, E. A., & Miller, N. (2008). The effects of alcohol and the salience of aggressive cues on triggered displaced aggression. *Aggressive Behavior, 34*(1), 25–33.

DeWall, C. N., Baumeister, R. F., Stillman, R. G., & Gailliot, M. T. (2007). Violence restrained: Effects of self-regulation and its depletion on aggression. *Journal of Experimental Social Psychology*, 43, 62–76.

Diener, E. (1976). Effects of prior destructive behavior, anonymity, and group presence on deindividuation and aggression. *Journal of Personality and Social Psychology, 33*, 497–507.

DiGuiseppe, R., & Tafrate, R. C. (2003). Anger treatment for adults: A meta-analytic review. *Clinical Psychology: Science and Practice, 10*(1), 70–84.

DiLalla, L. F., & Gottesman, I. I. (1991). Biological and genetic contributors to violence: Widom's untold tale. *Psychological Bulletin, 109*, 125–129.

Dishion, T. J., & McMahon, R. J. (1998). Parental monitoring and the prevention of child and adolescent problem behaviour: A conceptual and empirical formulation. *Clinical Child and Family Psychology, 1*, 61–75.

Dodge, K. A. (1980). Social cognition and children's aggressive behavior. *Child Development, 51*, 620–635.

Dodge, K. A. (1986). A social information processing model of social competence in children. In M. Perlmutter (Ed.), *The Minnesota Symposium on Child Psychology* (Vol. 18, pp. 77–125). Hillsdale, NJ: Erlbaum.

Dodge, K. A. (1993). Social-cognitive mechanisms in the development of conduct disorder and depression. *Annual Review of Psychology, 44*, 559–584.

Dodge, K. A. & Coie, J. D. (1987). Social-information-processing factors in reactive and proactive aggression in children's peer groups. *Journal of Personality and Social Psychology*, 53, 1146–1158.

Dodge, K. A., & Frame, C. L. (1982). Social cognitive biases and deficits in aggressive boys. *Child Development*, 53, 620–635.

Dollard, J., Doob, L. W., Miller, N. E., Mower, O. H., & Sears, R. R. (1939). *Frustration and aggression*. New Haven: Yale University Press.

Donnerstein, E., & Berkowitz, L. (1981). Victim reactions in aggressive erotic films as a factor in violence against women. *Journal of Personality and Social Psychology, 41*, 710–724.

Donnerstein, E., & Wilson, D. W. (1976). Effects of noise and perceived control on ongoing and subsequent aggressive behavior. *Journal of Personality and Social Psychology, 34*, 774–781.

Drabman, R. S., & Thomas, M. H. (1974). Does media violence increase children's tolerance for real-life aggression? *Developmental Psychology, 10*, 418–421.

Draper, T. (1985). *Capital punishment*. New York: H. W. Wilson.

Easterbrook, J. A. (1959). The effect of emotion on the utilization and the organization of behavior. *Psychological Review, 66*, 183–201.

Eisner, M. (2001). Modernization, self-control and lethal violence: The long-term dynamics of European homicide rates in theoretical perspective. *The British Journal of Criminology, 41*, 618–638.

Elias, M. (1981). Serum cortisol, testosterone, and testosterone-binding globulin responses to competitive fighting in human males. *Aggressive Behavior, 7*, 215–224.

Ellison, P. A., Govern, J. M., Petri, H. L., & Figler, M. H. (1995). Anonymity and aggressive driving behavior: A field study. *Journal of Social Behavior & Personality, 10*(1), 265–272.

Ellison-Potter, P., Bell, P., & Deffenbacher, J. (2001). The effects of trait driving anger, anonymity, and aggressive stimuli on aggressive driving behavior. *Journal of Applied Social Psychology, 31*(2), 431–443.

Eron, L. D. (1987). The development of aggressive behavior from the perspective of a developing behaviorist. *American Psychologist, 42*, 435–442.

Eron, L. D., & Huesmann, L. R. (1984). The relation of prosocial behavior to the development of aggression and psychopathology. *Aggressive Behavior*, 10, 201–211.

Eron, L. D., Huesmann, L. R., Lefkowitz, M. M., & Walder, L. O. (1972). Does television violence cause aggression? *American Psychologist, 27*, 253–263.

Eron, L. D. Huesmann, L. R. & Zelli, A. (1991). The role of parental variables in the learning of aggression. In D. Pepler & K. Rubin (Eds.), *The development and treatment of childhood aggression* (pp. 169–188). Hillsdale, NJ: Erlbaum.

Eron, L. D., Walder, L. O., & Lefkowitz, M. M. (1971). *The learning of aggression in children*. Boston: Little Brown.

Farrington, D. P. (1982). Longitudinal analyses of criminal violence. In M. E. Wolfgang & N. A. Weiner (Eds.), *Criminal violence* (pp. 171–200). Beverly Hills, CA: Sage.

Farrington, D. P. (1989). Early predictors of adolescent aggression and adult violence. *Violence and Victims, 4*, 79–138.

Farrington, D. P. (1995). The development of offending and antisocial behavior from childhood: Key findings from the Cambridge study in delinquent development. *Journal of Child Psychiatry and Psychology, 360*, 929–964.

Farrington, D. P., Loeber, R., & Van Kammen, W. B. (1990). Long-term criminal outcomes of hyperactivity-impulsivity-attention deficit and conduct problems in childhood. In L. N. Robins & M. Rutter (Eds.), *Straight and devious pathways from childhood to adulthood* (pp. 62–81). Cambridge, UK: Cambridge University Press.

Feshbach, S. (1964). The function of aggression and the regulation of aggressive drive. *Psychological Review, 71*, 257–272.

Figueredo, A., Tal, I., McNeil, P., & Guillén, A. (2003). Farmers, herders, and fishers: The ecology of revenge. *Evolution and Human Behavior, 25*(5), 336–353.

Fite, J. E., Goodnight, J. A., Bates, J. E., Dodge, K. A., & Pettit, G. S. (2008). Adolescent aggression and social cognition in the context of personality: Impulsivity as a moderator of predictions from social information processing. *Aggressive Behavior, 34*(5), 511–520.

Freud, S. (1933/1950). Why war? In *Collected Works of Sigmund Freud* (Vol. 16). London: Imagio.

Freud, S. (1961). *Mourning and melancholia* (standard ed.). London: Norton. (Original work published 1917.)

Gaertner, L., Iuzzini, J., & O'Mara, E. M. (2008). When rejection by one fosters aggression against many: Multiple-victim aggression as a consequence of social rejection and perceived groupness. *Journal of Experimental Social Psychology, 44*(4), 958–970.

Gailliot, M. T., & Baumeister, R. F. (2007). The physiology of willpower: Linking blood glucose to self-control. *Personality and Social Psychology Review, 11*(4), 303–327.

Gallese, V., Fadiga, L., Fogassi, L., & Rizzolatti, G. (1996). Action recognition in the premotor cortex. *Brain, 119*, 593–609.

Gatti, U., Tremblay, R. E., & Schadee, H. (2007). Civic community and violent behavior in Italy. *Aggressive Behavior, 33*(1), 56–62.

Gaur, S. D. (1988). Noise: Does it make you angry? *Indian Psychologist, 5*, 51–56.

Geary, D. C. (1998). *Male, female: The evolution of human sex differences*. Washington, DC: American Psychological Association.

Geary, D. C., Rumsey, M., Bow-Thomas, C. C., & Hoard, M. K. (1995). Sexual jealousy as a facultative trait: Evidence from the pattern of sex differences in adults from China and the United States. *Ethology and Sociobiology, 16*, 355–383.

Geen, R. G. (1978). Effects of attack and uncontrollable noise on aggression. *Journal of Research in Personality, 12*(1), 15–29.

Geen, R. G., & McCown, E. J. (1984). Effects of noise and attack on aggression and physiological arousal. *Motivation and Emotion, 8*, 231–241.

Geen, R. G., & O'Neal, E. C. (1969). Activation of cue-elicited aggression by general arousal. *Journal of Personality and Social Psychology, 11*, 289–292.

Geen, R. G. & Quanty, M. B. (1977). The catharsis of aggression: An evaluation of a hypothesis. In L. Berkowitz (Ed.), *Advances in experimental social psychology* (Vol. 10, pp. 1–37) New York: Academic Press.

Gentile, D. A., Anderson, C. A., Yukawa, S., Ihori, N., Saleem, M., Ming, L. K., Liau, A. K., Khoo, A., Bushman, B. J., Huesmann, L. R., & Sakamoto, A. (2009). The effects of prosocial video games on prosocial behaviors: International evidence from correlational, longitudinal, and experimental studies. *Personality and Social Psychology Bulletin, 35*(6), 752–763.

Giancola, P. R. (1995). Evidence for dorsolateral and orbital prefrontal cortical involvement in the expression of aggressive behavior. *Aggressive Behavior, 21*, 431–450.

Giancola, P. R., & Corman, M. D. (2007). Alcohol and aggression: A test of the attention-allocation model. *Psychological Science, 18*(7), 649–655.

Giancola, P. R., Mezzich, A. C., & Tarter, R. E. (1998). Executive cognitive functioning, termperament, and antisocial behavior in conduct-disordered adolescent females. *Journal of Abnormal Psychology, 107*, 629–641.

Gianluca, G., Albiero, P., Benelli, B., Altoe, G., et al. (2007). Does empathy predict adolescents' bullying and defending behavior? *Aggressive Behavior, 33*(5), 467–476.

Gladue, B. A., Boechler, M., & McCaul, K. D. (1989). Hormonal responses to competition in human males. *Aggressive Behavior, 17*, 313–326.

Goldstein, A. P. (1994). Delinquent gangs. In L. R. Huesmann (Ed.), *Aggressive behavior: Current perspectives. Plenum series in social/clinical psychology* (pp. 255–273). New York: Plenum Press.

Gottfredson, M. R., & Hirschi, T. (1990). *A general theory of crime.* Stanford, CA: Stanford University Press.

Guerra, N. G., Huesmann, L. R., & Spindler, A. J. (2002). *Community violence exposure, social cognition, and aggression among urban elementary-school children.* Ann Arbor: Institute for Social Research, University of Michigan.

Guerra, N. G., Huesmann, L. R., Tolan, P., Van Acker, R., & Eron, L. D. (1995). Stressful events and individual beliefs as correlates of economic disadvantage and aggression among urban children. *Journal of Consulting and Clinical Psychology, 63*(4), 518–528.

Gurr, T. R. (1981). Historical trends in violent crime: A critical review of the evidence. *Crime and Justice, 3*, 295.

Hare, R. D. (1978). Electrodermal and cardiovascular correlates of psychopathy. In R. D. Hare & D. Schalling (Eds.), *Psychopathic behavior: Approaches to research* (pp. 107–144). New York: Wiley.

Hare, R. D., Harpur, T. J., Hakstian, A. R., Forth, A. E., Hart, S. D., & Newman, J. P. (1990). The Revised Psychopathy Checklist: Descriptive statistics, reliability, and factor structure. *Psychological Assessment: A Journal of Consulting and Clinical Psychology, 2*, 338–341.

Hare, R. D., & McPherson, L. M. (1984). Violent and aggressive behavior by criminal psychopaths. *International Journal of Law and Psychiatry, 7*, 35–50.

Hartup, W. W. (2005). The development of aggression: Where do we stand? In R. E. Tremblay, W. W. Hartup, & J. Archer (Eds.), *Developmental origins of aggression* (pp. 3–24). New York: Guilford.

Henry, B., Caspi, A., Moffitt, T. E., & Silva, P. A. (1996). Temperamental and familial predictors of violent and nonviolent criminal convictions: Age 3 to age 18. *Developmental Psychology, 32*, 614–623.

Hill, J. & Nathan, R. (2008). Childhood antecedents of serious violence in adult male offenders. *Aggressive Behavior, 34*(3), 329–338.

Hinde, R. A. (1970). *Animal behavior.* New York: McGraw-Hill.

Hinshaw, S. P. (1987). On the distinction between attentional deficits/hyperactivity and conduct problems/aggression in child psychopathology. *Psychological Bulletin, 101*, 443–463.

Hinshaw, S. P., Heller, T., & McHale, J. P. (1992). Covert antisocial behavior in boys with attention-deficit hyperactivity disorder: External validation and effects of methylphenidate. *Journal of Consulting and Clinical Psychology, 60*, 274–281.

Hornberger, R. H. (1959). The differential reduction of aggressive responses as a function of interpolated activities. *American Psychologist, 14*, 354.

Huesmann, L. R. (1982). Information processing models of behavior. In N. Hirschberg & L. Humphreys (Eds.), *Multivariate applications in the social sciences* (pp. 261–288). Hillsdale, NJ: Erlbaum.

Huesmann, L. R. (1986). Psychological processes promoting the relation between exposure to media violence and aggressive behavior by the viewer. *Journal of Social Issues, 42*, 3, 125–139.

Huesmann, L. R. (1988). An information processing model for the development of aggression. *Aggressive Behavior, 14*, 13–24.

Huesmann, L. R. (1997). Observational learning of violent behavior: Social and biosocial processes. In A. Raine, D. P. Farrington, P. O. Brennen, & S. A. Mednick (Eds.), *The biosocial basis of violence* (pp. 69–88). New York: Plenum Press.

Huesmann, L. R. (1998). The role of social information processing and cognitive schemas in the acquisition and maintenance of habitual aggressive behavior. In R. G. Geen & E. Donnerstein (Eds.),

Human aggression: Theories, research, and implications for policy (pp. 73–109). New York: Academic Press.

Huesmann, L. R., Dubow, E. F., & Boxer, P. (2009). Continuity of childhood, adolescent, and early adulthood aggression as predictors of adult criminality and life outcomes: Implications for the adolescent-limited and life-course-persistent models. *Aggressive Behavior, 35*(2), 136–149.

Huesmann, L. R., & Eron, L. D. (1984). Cognitive processes and the persistence of aggressive behavior. *Aggressive Behavior, 10*, 243–251.

Huesmann, L. R., & Eron, L. D. (Eds.). (1986). *Television and the aggressive child: A cross-national comparison.* Hillsdale, NJ: Erlbaum.

Huesmann, L. R., Eron, L. D., & Dubow, E. F. (2002). Childhood predictors of adult criminality: Are all risk factors reflected in childhood aggressiveness? *Criminal Behavior and Mental Health, 12*(3), 185–208.

Huesmann, L. R., Eron, L. D, Lefkowitz, M. M., & Walder, L. O. (1984). Stability of aggression over time and generations. *Developmental Psychology, 20*, 1120–1134.

Huesmann, L. R., Eron, L. D., & Yarmel, P. W. (1987). Intellectual functioning and aggression. *Journal of Personality and Social Psychology, 52*, 232–240.

Huesmann, L. R., & Kirwil, L. (2007). Why observing violence increases the risk of violent behavior in the observer. In D. J. Flannery, A. T. Vaxsonyi, & I. D. Waldman (Eds.), *The Cambridge handbook of violent behavior and aggression* (pp. 545–570). Cambridge, UK: Cambridge University Press.

Huesmann, L. R., Lagerspetz, K., & Eron, L. D. (1984). Intervening variables in the television violence–aggression relation: Evidence from two countries. *Developmental Psychology, 20*(5), 746–775.

Huesmann, L. R. & Miller, L. S. (1994). Long-term effects of repeated exposure to media violence in childhood. In L. R. Huesmann (Ed.), *Aggressive behavior: Current perspective* (pp. 153–186). New York: Plenum.

Huesmann, L. R., & Moise, J. (1998). The stability and continuity of aggression from early childhood to young adulthood. In D. J. Flannery, & C. R. Huff (Eds.), *Youth violence: Prevention, intervention, and social policy* (pp. 73–95). Washington, DC: American Psychiatric Press.

Huesmann, L. R., Moise-Titus, J., Podolski, C. L., & Eron, L. D. (2003). Longitudinal relations between children's exposure to TV violence and their aggressive and violent behavior in young adulthood: 1977–1992. *Developmental Psychology, 39*, 201–221.

Hull, J. G. (1981). A self-awareness model of the causes and effects of alcohol consumption. *Journal of Abnormal Psychology, 90*, 586–600.

Human Security Brief (2007). Retrieved July 29, 2009 from http://www.humansecuritybrief.info/.

Hurley, S., & Chater, N. (2005). *Perspectives on imitation: From neuroscience to social science.* (Vols. 1 & 2). Cambridge, MA: MIT Press.

Iacoboni, M., Woods, R., Brass, M., Bekkering, H., Mazziotta, J., & Rizzolatti, G. (1999). Cortical mechanisms of human imitation. *Science, 286*, 2526–2528.

Ihori, N., Sakamoto, A., Kobayashi, K., & Kimura, F. (2003). Does video game use grow children's aggressiveness? Results from a panel study. In K. Arai (Ed.), *Social contributions and responsibilities of simulation & gaming* (pp. 221–230). Tokyo: Japan Association of Simulation and Gaming.

Innes, C. A. (1988). *Drug use and crime.* Washington, DC: U.S. Department of Justice.

IPCC. (2007). Summary for policymakers. In S. Solomon, D. Qin, M. Manning, Z. Chen, M. Marquis, K. B. Averyt, M. Tignor, & H. L. Miller (Eds.). *Climate change 2007: The physical science basis. Contribution of Working Group I to the Fourth Assessment Report of the Intergovernmental Panel on Climate Change.* Cambridge, UK & New York: Cambridge University Press.

Ito, T. A., Miller, N., & Pollock, V. E. (1996). Alcohol and aggression: A meta-analysis on the moderating effects of inhibitory cues, triggering events, and self-focused attention. *Psychological Bulletin, 120*, 60–82.

James, W. (1890). *The principles of psychology.* Chicago: Encyclopedia Britannica.

Jolliffe, D., & Farrington, D. P. (2006). Development and validation of the Basic Empathy Scale. *Journal of Adolescence, 29*(4), 589–611.

Jones, J. W., & Bogat, G. (1978). Air pollution and human aggression. *Psychological Reports, 43*(3, Pt 1), 721–722.

Josephson, W. L. (1987). Television violence and children's aggression: Testing the priming, social script, and disinhibition predictions. *Journal of Personality and Social Psychology, 53*, 882–890.

Juon, H. S., Doherty, E. E., & Ensminger, M. E. (2006). Childhood behavior and adult criminality: Cluster analysis in prospective study of African Americans. *Journal of Quantitative Criminology, 38*(5), 553–563.

Kantak, K. M., Hegstrand, L. R., Eichelman, B. (1981). Facilitation of shock-induced fighting following intraventricular 5, 7-dihydroxytryptamine and 6-hydroxydopa. *Psychopharmacology*, 157–160.

Keegan, J. (1993). *A history of warfare.* New York: Knopf.

Keltner, D., & Robinson, R. J. (1996). Extremism, power, and the imagined basis of social conflict. *Current Directions in Psychological Science, 5*, 101–105.

Kingston, D. A., Fedoroff, P., Firestone, P., Curry, S., & Bradford, J. M. (2008). Pornography use and sexual aggression: The impact of frequency and type of pornography use on recidivism among sexual offenders. *Aggressive Behavior*, 34, 341–351.

Kokko, K., Pulkkinen, L., Huesmann, L. R., Dubow, E. F., & Boxer, P. (in press). Intensity of aggression in childhood as a predictor of different forms of adult aggression: A two-country (Finland and United States) analysis. *Journal of Research in Adolescence.*

Konijn, E. A., Nije Bijvank, M., & Bushman, B. J. (2007). I wish I were a warrior: The role of wishful identification in effects of violent video games on aggression in adolescent boys. *Developmental Psychology, 43*, 1038–1044.

Lagerspetz, K. M., Bjorkqvist, K., & Peltonen, T. (1988). Is indirect aggression typical of females? Gender differences in aggressiveness in 11- to 12-year-old children. *Aggressive Behavior, 14*, 403–414.

Lagerspetz, K., & Lagerspetz, K. M. J. (1971). Changes in aggressiveness of mice resulting from selective breeding, learning and social isolation. *Scandinavian Journal of Psychology, 12*, 241–278.

Lansford, J. E, Chang, L., Dodge, K. A., Malone, P. S., Oburu, P., Palmérus, K., et al. (2005). Cultural normativeness as a moderator of the link between physical discipline and children's adjustment: A comparison of China, India, Italy, Kenya, Philippines, and Thailand. *Child Development, 76*, 1234–1246.

Lawrence, C., & Andrews, K. (2004). The influence of perceived prison crowding on male inmates' perception of aggressive events. *Aggressive Behavior, 30*(4), 273–283.

Lazarus, R. S., Speisman, M., Mordkoff, A. M., & Davison, L. A. (1962). A laboratory study of psychological stress produced by a motion picture film. *Psychological Monographs: General and Applied, 76*(34), Whole No. 553.

Leary, M. R., Kowalski, R. M., Smith, L., & Phillips, S. (2003). Teasing, rejection, and violence: Case studies of the school shootings. *Aggressive Behavior, 29*(3), 202–214.

Leary, M. R., Twenge, J. M., & Quinlivan, E. (2006). Interpersonal rejection as a determinant of anger and aggression. *Personality and Social Psychology Review, 10*(2), 111–132.

Lefkowitz, M. M., Eron, L. D., Walder, L. O., & Huesmann, L. R. (1977). *Growing up to be violent: A longitudinal study of the development of aggression.* New York: Pergamon.

Lefkowitz, M. M., Huesmann, L. R., & Eron, L. D. (1978). Parental punishment: A longitudinal analysis of effects. *Archives of General Psychiatry, 35*(2), 186–191.

Linnolia, M., Virkkunnen, M., Scheinin, M., Nuttila, A., Rimon, R., & Goodwin, F. K. (1983). Low cerebrospinal fluid 5-Hydroxyindoleacetic acid concentration differentiates impulsive from non-impulsive violent behavior. *Life Sciences, 33*, 2609–2614.

Lipsey, M. W., Wilson, D. B., Cohen M. A., & Derzon, J. H. (1997). Is there a causal relationship between alcohol use and violence? A synthesis of the evidence. In M. Galanter (Ed.), *Recent developments in alcoholism: Vol. 13. Alcohol and violence: Epidemiology, neurobiology, psychology, and family issues* (pp. 245–282). New York: Plenum.

Loeber, R. (1982). The stability of antisocial and delinquent child behavior: A review. *Child Development, 53*, 1431–1446.

Loeber, R., & Dishion, T. J. (1983). Early predictors of male delinquency: A review. *Psychological Bulletin, 94*, 68–94.

Loeber, R., & Hay, D. (1997). Key issues in the development of aggression from childhood to early adulthood. *Annual Review of Psychology, 48*, 371–410.

Lorenz, K. (1966). *On aggression.* (M. K. Wilson, trans.) New York: Harcourt, Brace.

Lovaas, O. I. (1961). Interaction between verbal and non-verbal behavior. *Child Development, 32*, 329–336.

Magnusson, D. (1987). Adult delinquency and early conduct and physiology. In D. Magnusson & A. Ohman (Eds.), *Psychopathology: An international perspective* (pp. 221–234). New York: Academic Press.

Magnusson, D., Duner, A. & Zetterblom, G. (1975). *Adjustment: A longitudinal study.* Stockholm: Almqvist & Wiksell.

Malamuth, N. M., & Check, J. V. P. (1981). The effects of mass media exposure on acceptance of violence against women: A field experiment. *Journal of Research in Personality, 15*, 436–446.

Mann, L. (1981). The baiting crowd in episodes of threatened suicide. *Journal of Personality and Social Psychology, 41*, 703–709.

Marcus-Newhall, A., Pedersen, W. C., Carlson, M., & Miller, N. (2000). Displaced aggression is alive and well: A meta-analytic review. *Journal of Personality and Social Psychology, 78*, 670–689.

Mares, M. L., & Woodard, E. (2005). Positive effects of television on children's social. interactions: A meta-analysis. *Media Psychology, 7*, 301–322.

Mazur, A., & Booth, A. (1998). Testosterone and dominance in men. *Behavioral and Brain Sciences, 21*, 353–397.

Mazur, A., Booth, A., & Dabbs, J. M., Jr. (1992). Testosterone and chess competition. *Social Psychology Quarterly 55*(1), 70–77.

Mazur, A., Susman, E. J., & Edelbrock, S. (1997). Sex differences in testosterone response to a video game contest. *Evolution and Human Behavior, 18*, 317–326.

McCaul, K. D., Gladue, B. A., & Joppa, M. (1992). Winning, losing, mood, and testosterone. *Hormones and Behavior, 26*, 486–504.

McCord, J. (1983). A longitudinal study of aggression and antisocial behavior. In K. T. Van Dusen & S. A. Mednick (Eds.), *Prospective studies of crime and delinquency* (pp. 269–275). Boston: Kluwer-Nijhoff.

McCullough, M. (2008). *Beyond revenge: The evolution of the forgiveness instinct.* New York: Wiley.

Meltzoff, A. N. (2005). Imitation and other minds: The "Like Me" hypothesis. In S. Hurley & N. Chater (Eds.), *Perspectives on imitation: From mirror neurons to memes* (Vol. 2, pp. 55–78). Cambridge, MA: MIT Press.

Meltzoff, A.N., & Moore, K.M. (1977). Imitation of facial and manual gestures by human neonates. *Science, 109*, 77–78.

Mendelson, T., Thurston, R. C., & Kubzansky, L. D. (2008). Arousal and stress: Affective and cardiovascular effects of experimentally-induced social status. *Health Psychology, 27*(4), 482–489.

Miczek, K. A., Mirsky, A. F., Carey, G., DeBold, J., & Raine, A. (1994). An overview of biological influences on violent behavior. In National

Research Council, *Understanding and preventing violence* (Vol. 2, pp. 1–20). Washington, DC: National Academy Press.

Miles, D. R., & Carey, G. (1997). Genetic and environmental architecture of aggression. *Journal of Personality and Social Psychology, 72*, 207–217.

Miller, N. E. (1941). The frustration-aggression hypothesis. *Psychological Review, 48*, 337–342.

Miner, J. L. & Clarke-Steward, K. A. (2008). Trajectories of externalizing behavior from age 2 to age 9: Relations with gender, temperament, ethnicity, parenting, and rater. *Developmental Psychology, 44*(3), 771–786.

Mischel, W., & Shoda, Y. (1995). A cognitive-affective system theory of personality: Reconceptualizing situations, dispositions, dynamics, and invariance in personality structure. *Psychological Review, 102*, 246–268.

Moffitt, T. E. (1990). Juvenile delinquency and attention-deficit disorder: Boys' developmental trajectories from age 3 to 15. *Child Development, 61*, 893–910.

Moffitt, T. E. (1993). Adolescence-limited and life-course-persistent antisocial behavior: A developmental taxonomy. *Psychological Review, 100 (4)*, 674–701.

Moffitt, T. E. (2007). A review of research on the taxonomy of life-course-persistent versus adolescence-limited antisocial behaviour. In D. J. Flannery, A. T. Vaxsonyi, & I. D. Waldman (Eds.), *The Cambridge handbook of violent behavior and aggression* (pp. 545–570). Cambridge, UK: Cambridge University Press.

Moffitt, T. E., Caspi, A., Rutter, M., & Silva, P. A. (2001). *Sex differences in antisocial behaviour*. Cambridge, UK: Cambridge University Press.

Moffitt, T. E., & Lynam, D. R. (1994). The neuropsychology of conduct disorder and delinquency: Implications for understanding antisocial behavior. In D. C. Fowles, P. Sutker, & S. H. Goodman (Eds.), *Progress in experimental personality & psychopathology research* (pp. 233–262). New York: Springer-Verlag.

Moise-Titus, J. (1999). *The role of negative emotions in the media violence-aggression relation*. Unpublished doctoral dissertation, University of Michigan, Ann Arbor.

Morf, C. C., & Rhodewalt, F. (2001). Unraveling the paradoxes of narcissism: A dynamic self-regulatory processing model. *Psychological Inquiry, 12*, 177–196.

Morris, W. N., & Reilly, N. P. (1987). Toward the self-regulation of mood: Theory and research. *Motivation and Emotion, 11*, 215–249.

Mullin, C. R., & Linz, D. (1995). Desensitization and resensitization to violence against women: Effects of exposure to sexually violent films on judgments of domestic violence victims. *Journal of Personality and Social Psychology, 69*, 449–459.

Nijman, H. L. I., & Rector, G. (1999). Crowding and aggression on inpatient psychiatric wards. *Psychiatric Services, 50*(6), 830–831.

Nisbett, R. E., & Cohen, D. (1996). *Culture of honor: The psychology of violence in the South*. Boulder, CO: Westview Press.

Nouvion, S. O., Cherek, D. R., Lane, S. D., Tcheremissine, O. V., & Lieving, L. F. (2007). Human proactive aggression: Association with personality disorders and psychopathy. *Aggressive Behavior, 33*(6), 552–562.

Novaco, R. W. (1975). *Anger control: The development and evaluation of an experimental treatment*. Lexington, MA: Lexington Books.

Olweus, D. (1978). *Aggression in the schools: Bullies and whipping boys*. Washington, DC: Hemisphere (Wiley).

Olweus, D. (1979). The stability of aggressive reaction patterns in males: A review. *Psychological Bulletin, 86*, 852–875.

Olweus, D. (1980). Familial and temperamental determinants of aggressive behavior in adolescent boys: A causal analysis. *Developmental Psychology, 16*, 644–660.

Olweus, D. (1995). Bullying or peer abuse at school: Facts and intervention. *Current Directions in Psychological Science, 4*, 196–200.

Osofsky, J. D. (1995). The effects of exposure to violence on young children. *American Psychologist, 50*, 782–788.

Paik, H., & Comstock, G. (1994). The effects of television violence on antisocial behavior: A meta-analysis. *Communication Research, 21*, 516–546.

Patsy, R. (1999). *Homicide statistics, research paper 99/56*. House of Commons Library, Social and General Statistics Section. United Kingdom.

Patterson, G. R., DeBaryshe, B. D., & Ramsey, E. (1989). A developmental perspective on antisocial behavior. *American Psychologist, 44*, 329–335.

Patterson, G. R., Dishion, T. J., & Bank, L. (1984). Family interaction: A process model of deviancy training. *Aggressive Behavior, 10*, 253–267.

Patterson, G. R., Littman, R. A., & Bricker, W. (1967). Assertive behavior in children: A step toward a theory of aggression. *Monographs of the Society for Research in Child Development. 32*, 1–43.

Patterson, G. R., Reid, J. B., Jones, R. R., & Conger, R. E. (1975). *A social learning approach to family intervention: Vol. 1. Families with aggressive children*. Eugene, OR: Castalia.

Pedersen, W. C., Bushman, B. J., Vasquez, E. A., & Miller, N. (2008). Kicking the (barking) dog effect: The moderating role of target attributes on triggered displaced aggression. *Personality and Social Psychology Bulletin, 34*(10), 1382–1395.

Pedersen, W. C., Gonzales, C., & Miller, N. (2000). The moderating effect of trivial triggering provocation on displaced aggression. *Journal of Personality and Social Psychology, 78*, 913–927.

Pepler, D., King, G., Craig, W., Byrd, B., & Bream, L. (1995). The development and evaluation of a multisystem social skills group training program for aggressive children. *Child & Youth Care Forum, 24*(5), 297–313.

Peristiany, J. G. (1965). (Ed.), *Honour and shame: The values of Mediterranean society*. London: Weidenfeld & Nicolson.

Pernanen, K. (1991). *Alcohol in human violence*. New York: Guilford.

Peterson, L., Gable, S., Doyle, C. & Ewugman, B (1997). Beyond parenting skills: Battling barriers and building bonds to prevent child abuse and neglect. *Cognitive and Behavioral Practice, 4*, 53–74.

Pinker, S. (2007, March 19). A history of violence. *The New Republic, 236*(12), 18.

Polman, J., Orobio de Castro, B., & Van Aken, M. (2008). Experimental study of the differential effects of playing versus watching violent video games on children's aggressive behavior. *Aggressive Behavior, 34*(3), 256–264.

Pratt, T. C., & & Cullen, F. T. (2000). The empirical status of Gottfredson and Hirschi's general theory of crime: A meta-analysis. *Criminology, 38*, 931–964.

Prentice-Dunn, S., & Rogers, R. (1983). Deindividuation in aggression. In R.G. Geen & E. Donnerstein (Eds.), *Aggression: Theoretical and empirical reviews* (Vol. 2, pp. 155–171). New York: Academic Press.

Prinz, J. J. (2005). Imitation and moral development. In S. Hurley & N. Chater (Eds.), *Perspectives on imitation: From mirror neurons to memes* (Vol. 2, pp. 267–282). Cambridge, MA: MIT Press.

Pyszczynski, T., Greenberg, J., & Solomon, S. (1999). A dual process model of defense against conscious and unconscious death-related thought: An extension of terror management theory. *Psychological Review, 106*, 835–845.

Raine, A. (1993). *The psychopathology of crime: Criminal behavior as a clinical disorder*. San Diego: Academic Press.

Raine, A., Venables, P. H., & Williams, M. (1995). High autonomic arousal and electrodermal orienting at age 15 years as protective factors against criminal behavior at age 29 years. *American Journal of Psychiatry, 152*, 1595–1600.

Reifman, A. S., Larrick, R. P., & Fein, S. (1991). Temper and temperature on the diamond: The heat-aggression relationship in major league baseball. *Personality and Social Psychology Bulletin, 17*, 580–585.

Reinisch, J. M. (1981). Prenatal exposure to synthetic progestins increases potential for aggression in humans. *Science, 211*, 1171–1173.

Rizzolatti, G. (2005). The mirror neuron system and imitation. In S. Hurley & N. Chater (Eds.), *Perspectives on imitation: From mirror neurons to memes* (Vol. 1, pp. 55–76). Cambridge, MA: MIT Press.

Rodkin, P. C., Farmer, T. W., Pearl, R., & Van Acker, R. (2000). Heterogeneity of popular boys: Antisocial and prosocial configurations. *Developmental Psychology, 36*, 14–24.

Rogeness, G. A., Cepeda, C., Macedo, C. A., Fischer, C., Harris, W. R. (1990). Differences in heart rate and blood pressure in children with conduct disorder, major depression, and separation anxiety. *Psychiatry Research, 33*, 199–206.

Rohner, R. P. (1975). *They love me, they love me not: A worldwide study of the effects of parental acceptance and rejection*. New Haven, CT: Human Relations Area Files Press.

Rotton, J. (1979). The air pollution experience and physical aggression. *Journal of Applied Social Psychology, 9*, 397–412.

Rotton, J., & Frey, J. (1985). Air pollution, weather, and violent crime: Concomitant time-series analysis of archival data. *Journal of Personality and Social Psychology, 49*, 1207–1220.

Rys, G. S., & Bear, G. G. (1997). Relational aggression and peer relations: Gender and developmental issues. *Merrill-Palmer Quarterly, 43*, 87–106.

Salvador, A., Simon, V., Suay, F., & Llorens, L. (1987). Testosterone and cortisol responses to competitive fighting in human males: A pilot study. *Aggressive Behavior, 13*, 9–13.

Sampson, R. J., Raudenbush, S. W., & Earls, F. (1997). Neighborhoods and violent crime: A multilevel study of collective efficacy. *Science, 277*, 918–924.

Sapolsky, R. M. (1998). *The trouble with testosterone: And other essays on the biology of the human predicament*. New York: Scribner.

Satterfield, J. H., Hoppe, C. M., & Schell, A. M. (1982). A prospective study of delinquency in 110 adolescent boys with attention deficit disorder and 88 normal adolescent boys. *American Journal of Psychiatry, 139*, 795–798.

Scarpa, A., & Haden, S. C. (2006). Community violence victimization and aggressive behavior: The moderating effects of coping and social support. *Aggressive Behavior, 32*(5), 502–515.

Schneider, W., & Shiffrin, R. M. (1977). Controlled and automatic human information processing: I. Detection, search, and attention. *Psychological Review, 84*, 1–66.

Schwartz, D., & Proctor, L. J. (2000). Community violence exposure and children's social adjustment in the school peer group: The mediating roles of emotion regulation and social cognition. *Journal of Consulting and Clinical Psychology, 68*(4), 670–683.

Scott, J. P. (1958). *Aggression*. Chicago: University of Chicago Press.

Sears, R. R., Whiting, J. W., Nowlis, V., & Sears, P. S. (1953). Some child-rearing antecedents of aggression and dependency in young children. *Genetic Psychology Monographs, 47*, 135–236.

Sedikides, C., & Skowronski, J. J. (1990). Towards reconciling personality and social psychology: A construct accessibility approach. *Journal of Social Behavior and Personality, 5*, 531–546.

Seguin, J. R., & Zelazo, P.D. (2005). Executive function in early physical aggression. In R. E. Tremblay, W. W. Hartup, & J. Archer (Eds.), *Developmental origins of aggression* (pp. 307–329). New York: Guilford.

Sheehan, M. J., & Watson, M. (2008). Reciprocal influences between maternal discipline techniques and aggression in children and adolescents. *Aggressive Behavior, 34*, 245–255.

Silke, A. (2003). Deindividuation, anonymity, and violence: Findings from Northern Ireland. *Journal of Social Psychology, 143*(4), 493–499.

Slater, M. D., Henry, K. L., Swaim, R. C., & Anderson, L. L. (2003). Violent media content and aggressiveness in adolescents: A downward spiral model. *Communication Research, 30*, 713–736.

Sluka, J. (1992). The anthropology of conflict (pp. 18–36). In C. Nordstrom & J. Martin (Eds.), *The paths to domination, resistance, and terror*. Berkeley: University of California Press.

Smith, S. L., & Donnerstein, E. (1998). Harmful effects of exposure to media violence: Learning of aggression emotional desensitization, and fear. In R. G. Geen & E. Donnerstein (Eds.), *Human aggression: Theories, research, and implications for social policy* (pp. 167–202). New York: Academic Press.

Soubrie, P. (1986). Reconciling the role of central serotonin neurons in humans and animal behavior. *The Behavioral and Brain Sciences, 9*, 319–364.

Souweidane, V., & Huesmann, L. R. (1999). The influence of American urban culture on the development of normative beliefs about aggression in Middle-Eastern immigrants. *American Journal of Community Psychology, 27*(2), 239–254.

Spivey, C. B., & Prentice-Dunn S. (1990). Assessing the directionality of deindividuated behavior: Effects of deindividuation, modeling, and private self-consciousness on aggressive and prosocial responses. *Basic and Applied Social Psychology, 11*(4), 387–403.

Staub, E. (1989). *The roots of evil: The origins of genocide and other group violence*. New York: Cambridge University Press.

Staub, E. (1998). Breaking the cycle of genocidal violence: Healing and reconciliation. In J. Harvey (Ed.), *Perspectives on loss: A sourcebook*. Philadelphia: Taylor & Francis.

Steele, C. M., & Josephs, R. A., (1990). Alcohol myopia: Its prized and dangerous effects. *American Psychologist, 45*, 921–933.

Stenberg, C., Campos, J., & Emde, R. (1983). The facial expression of anger in seven-month-old infants. *Child Development, 54*, 178–184.

Straus, M. A. (1997). Physical assaults by women partners: A major social problem. In M. R. Walsh (Ed.), *Women, men and gender: Ongoing debates* (pp. 210–221). New Haven, CT: Yale University Press.

Straus, M. A. (2000). *Beating the devil out of them: Corporal punishment by American families and its effects on children* (2nd ed.). Somerset, NJ: Transaction Publishers.

Tamura, M. (1983). Changes in the patterns of criminal homicide for recent three decades. *Reports of National Research Institute of Police Science, 24*, 149–161.

Tellegen, A., Lykken, D. T., Bouchard, Jr., T. J., Wilcox, K. J., Segal, N. L., & Rich, S. (1988). Personality similarity in twins reared apart and together. *Journal of Personality and Social Psychology, 54*, 1031–1039.

Timbergen, N. (1952). The curious behavior of the Stickleback. *Scientific American, 187*, 22–26.

Tremblay, R. E. (2000). The development of aggressive behavior during childhood: What have we learned in the past century? *International Journal of Behavioral Development, 24*, 129–141.

Tremblay, R. E., Boulerice, B., Harden, P. W., McDuff, P., Perusse, D., Pihl, R. O., et al. (1996). Do children in Canada become more aggressive as they approach adolescence? In Human Resources Development Canada (Ed.), *Growing up in Canada: National Longitudinal Survey of Children and Youth* (pp. 127–137). Ottawa: Statistics Canada.

Tremblay, R. E., & Nagin, D. S. (2005). The developmental origins of physical aggression in humans. In R. E. Tremblay, W. W. Hartup, & J. Archer (Eds.), *Developmental origins of aggression* (pp. 83–106). New York: Guilford Press.

Tremblay, R. E., Nagin, D. S., Seguin, J. R., Zoccolillo, M., Zelazo, P., Boivin, M., Perusse, et al. (2004). Physical aggression during early childhood: Trajectories and predictors. *Pediatrics, 114*(1), e43–e50.

Turner, C. W., Layton, J. F., & Simons, L. S. (1975). Naturalistic studies of aggressive behavior: Aggressive stimuli, victim visibility, and horn honking. *Journal of Personality and Social Psychology, 31*, 1098–1107.

United Nations Population Fund. (2007/2008). A human rights and health priority. Retrieved October 17, 2008, from http://www.unfpa.org/swp/2000/english/ch03.html.

United Nations Survey of Crime Trends and Operations of Criminal Justice Systems. (1998-2000): Retrieved August 12 2009, from http://www.nationmaster.com/red/graph/ cri_mur_percap-crime-murders-per-capita&int=-1.

U.S. Census Bureau (2008). Retrieved July 29, 2009 from: http://www.census.gov/.

U.S. Department of Justice, Bureau of Justice Statistics. (2008). *Homicide trends in the United States*. Retrieved July 30, 2009 from http/www.ojp.usdoj.gov/bjs/homicide/homtrnd.htm.

Vaillancourt, R. (2005). Indirect aggression among humans: Social construct or evolutionary adaption? In R. E. Tremblay, W. W. Hartup, & J. Archer (Eds.), *Developmental origins of aggression* (pp. 158–177). New York: Guilford.

Vaillancourt, T., & Hymel, S. (2006). Aggression and social status: The moderating roles of sex and peer-valued characteristics. *Aggressive Behavior, 32*(4), 396–408.

Vaillancourt, T., Miller, J. L., Fagbemi, J., Cote, S., & Tremblay, R. E. (2007). Trajectories and predictors of indirect aggression: Results from a nationally representative longitudinal study of Canadian children aged 2–10. *Aggressive Behavior, 33*(4), 314–326.

Van Baardewijk, Y., Stegge, H., Bushman, B. J., & Vermeiren, R. (2009). Psychopathic traits, victim distress and aggression in children. *Journal of Child Psychology and Psychiatry, 50*(6), 718–725.

Virkkunen, M., De Jong, J., Bartko, J., Goodwin, F. K., & Linnola, M. (1989). Relationship of psychobiological variables to recidivism in violent offenders and impulsive fire setters. *Archives of General Psychiatry, 46*, 600–603.

Virkkunen, M., De Jong, J., Bartko, J., & Linnolia, M. (1989). Psychobiological concomitants of history of suicide attempts among violent offenders and impulsive fire setters. *Archives of General Psychiatry, 46*, 604–606.

Virkkunen, M., & Narvanen, S. (1987). Plasma insulin, tryptophan and serotonin levels during the glucose tolerance test among habitually violent and impulsive offenders. *Neuropsychobiology, 17*, 19–23.

Wadsworth, M. E. J. (1976). Delinquency, pulse rate and early emotional deprivation. *British Journal of Criminology, 16*, 245–256.

Warburton, W. A., Williams, K. D., & Cairns, D. R. (2006). When ostracism leads to aggression: The moderating effects of control deprivation. *Journal of Experimental Social Psychology, 42*(2), 213–220.

Widom, C. S. (1989). Does violence beget violence? A critical examination of the literature. *Psychological Bulletin, 106*(1), 3–28.

Williamson, S., Hare, R. D., & Wong, S. (1987). Violence: Criminal psychopaths and their victims. *Canadian Journal of Behavioral Science, 19*, 454–462.

Wilson, J. Q., & Herrnstein, R. J. (1985). *Crime and human nature*. New York: Simon & Schuster.

Winslow, E. B., & Shaw, D. S. (2007). Impact of neighborhood disadvantage on overt behavior problems during early childhood. *Aggressive Behavior, 33*(3), 207–219.

Zajonc, R. B. (1965). Social facilitation. *Science, 149*, 269–274.

Zajonc, R. B., Murphy, S. T., & Inglehart, M. (1989). Feeling and facial efference: Implications of vascular theory of emotions. *Psychological Review, 96*, 395–416.

Zillmann, D. (1979). *Hostility and aggression*. Hillsdale, NJ: Erlbaum.

Zillmann, D., Katcher, A.H., & Milavsky, B. (1972). Excitation transfer from physical exercise to subsequent aggressive behavior. *Journal of Experimental Social Psychology, 8*, 247–259.

Zimbardo, P. G. (1969). The human choice: Individuation, reason, and order, versus deindividuation, impulse, and chaos. In W. Arnold & D. Levine (Eds.), *Nebraska Symposium on Motivation, 1969*. Lincoln: University of Nebraska Press.

Zumkley, H. (1992). Stability of individual differences in aggression. In A. Fraczek & H. Zumkley (Eds.), *Socialization and aggression* (pp. 45–57). New York: Springer-Verlag.

Chapter 24

Affiliation, Acceptance, and Belonging

The Pursuit of Interpersonal Connection

MARK R. LEARY

The science of social psychology is predicated on the simple fact that human thought, emotion, and behavior are powerfully affected by the real, implied, and imagined presence of other people (Allport, 1954). Sometimes, people's thoughts, feelings, and actions are affected when they merely think about other people, wonder about their intentions, imagine their reactions, or even fantasize about them, and a great deal of attention has been paid to how people respond when they think about other people. Yet, much of social psychology is fundamentally concerned with how people are influenced by those with whom they actually interact. Even when researchers conduct studies in nonsocial contexts (such as when they ask participants to respond to hypothetical situations or react to computer-administered stimuli), they are usually interested in understanding psychological and interpersonal processes that they believe play out during actual social encounters in everyday life. Indeed, most social psychological phenomena—even those that occur when people are by themselves—make sense only with respect to the fact that people interact with one another, form relationships, and join groups. A social psychology of the solitary individual who thought about, but never associated with, other people would be an impoverished one indeed.

Given the centrality of social interaction in human behavior, understanding how and why people seek contact with others is of central concern to social psychology. People are highly motivated to spend time with certain other people and make choices on an ongoing basis regarding with whom they will interact. However, affiliation is a two-way street. People can sustain both single interactions and ongoing relationships with other people only to the extent that they can entice others to want to relate to them as well. As a result, people are interested not only in being with and developing connections with other individuals but also in showing other people that they have something to offer as social interactants, relational partners, and group members.

As a result, interpersonal behavior is rooted in two complementary processes by which people simultaneously seek to relate with other people and try to get others to want to relate with them as well. This chapter focuses on these two fundamental interpersonal processes.

The chapter is organized as follows. The first section examines factors that motivate people to affiliate and spend time with others. Most work in this area has focused on the effects of stressful situations on affiliation, but people obviously desire to interact with others under nonstressful conditions as well, and we examine an array of reasons that people affiliate with one another. As noted, people who are interested in interacting with others must also induce the others to interact with them, so we also touch on the ways in which people promote counteraffiliation. As discussed in this chapter, much of this research was conducted in the 1950s and 1960s; although social psychologists once devoted a good deal of attention to understanding the bases of affiliation, interest has nearly disappeared since then.

Because merely affiliating with other people is of limited usefulness in providing many desired outcomes, people are motivated not only to get others to affiliate with them, but also for others to value and accept them as well. The chapter discusses ways in which people foster and maintain their relational value by showing other people that they possess attributes that make them a good relational partner (friend, romantic partner, group member, or whatever) and monitoring their relational value in others' eyes for signs that their value to other people is low or declining. Of course, people are often not successful in being accepted as a relational partner or group member, so the chapter also examines the causes and consequences of interpersonal rejection, with sections devoted to the effects of rejection on emotion, self-esteem, and interpersonal behavior. The chapter concludes with an examination of the effects of interpersonal rejection on physical and psychological well-being.

AFFILIATION

Affiliation is the act of associating or interacting with one or more other people. The concept of affiliation carries no indication of the quality, affective tone, or length of the social encounter or the nature of the relationship between the people. When people want to affiliate, they merely seek to be in the company of and to interact with others. Many theorists have suggested that being with or interacting with other people is a fundamental social behavior (Bakan, 1966; Hogan & Roberts, 2000; Murray, 1938; Saucier & Goldberg, 1996).

At one level, the motive to affiliate appears to emerge without any special evocative circumstances. All well-adjusted people desire to interact with others to some degree even when doing so provides no tangible benefits other than the experience of interacting itself. Often, people who find themselves in close proximity, such as waiting in line or seated together on an airplane, will interact with one another even though there is no instrumental reason for doing so. Presumably, the strong and pervasive urge to affiliate has evolutionary underpinnings. In tracing the origins of human sociality, theorists have proposed that affiliation and group living enhanced our prehistoric ancestors' chances of survival and reproduction, as well as the survival of their offspring (Ainsworth, 1989; Kameda & Tindale, 2006). Not only are solitary human beings a poor match for most predators, but they are not likely to thrive when they must single-handedly obtain food, defend themselves against threats of various kinds, care for their children, and successfully survive occasions on which they are too ill or injured to fend for themselves. As a result, natural selection may have forged a strong motive for affiliation as part of the human psyche. Group living is characteristic of our closest primate relatives—the chimpanzees, bonobos, and gorillas—suggesting that it might have evolved before the human lineage split from that leading to other modern great apes (De Waal, 2005). (In contrast, orangutans, whose family tree diverged earlier, are notably solitary and nonaffiliative.) Thus, the urge to affiliate with other people probably springs from evolutionary pressures to remain in proximity to other people for purposes of protection and to form groups that allow people to solve recurrent adaptive problems more effectively (Kameda & Tindale, 2006).

Situational Determinants of Affiliation

Although people are motivated to affiliate with others, their desire for social contact fluctuates across situations and time. As Altman (1975, p. 22) observed, "There are times when people want to be alone and out of contact with others and there are times when others are sought out, to be heard and to hear, to talk and to listen." Theorists and researchers have examined some of the factors that determine the degree to which people wish to affiliate in a particular situation, although, as noted, recent research on this topic is surprisingly sparse.

One perspective on why and when people will want to affiliate is offered by the social affiliation model, which proposes that people seek to maintain an optimal level of social contact (O'Connor & Rosenblood, 1996). As with all homeostatic models, the social affiliation model suggests that deviations from a preferred level of interpersonal contact motivates people to adjust their behavior so that an optimal degree of contact is restored. Thus, after an episode of solitude, people will be motivated to seek out additional opportunities for affiliation, whereas after having a high amount of contact with others, people will draw back and affiliate less for a time. Of course, people differ in their optimal or preferred level of interaction overall, which accounts for individual differences in affiliation tendencies (Cheek & Buss, 1981).

Research has generally supported the hypothesis that the affiliation motive responds in a homeostatic fashion in human beings (Gerwitz & Baer, 1958; O'Connor & Rosenblood, 1996; Peay & Peay, 1983; Zeedyk-Ryan & Smith, 1983) and in rats (Latané & Werner, 1978). In fact, people who merely expect to experience a nonoptimal level of affiliation in the near future (either lower or higher than they prefer) may adjust their behavior beforehand (Baum & Greenberg, 1975). Although research supports the idea that people adjust their affiliative behavior in a homeostatic fashion, one shortcoming of the social affiliation model is that it does not attempt to explain why external circumstances other than prior (or expected) interaction motivate people to seek or avoid affiliation.

According to the multidimensional model of affiliation (Hill, 1987), people affiliate with others for four primary reasons: to obtain positive stimulation, for emotional support, to gain social comparison information, and to get attention from other people (see also Murray, 1938). First, people may affiliate because contact and interaction with others are often enjoyable (i.e., positive stimulation; Hill, 1987). People are biased to rate other people positively and to expect that other people will be rewarding (Sears, 1983), and brain imaging studies show that similar regions of the brain are activated by other people as by social rewards (Harris, McClure, van den Bos, Cohen, & Fiske, 2007; van den Bos, McClure, Harris, Fiske, & Cohen, 2007). Because social interaction and harmonious relationships are inherently pleasant (probably because evolution rendered them so as a means of inducing people to seek social connections), people may desire to interact even when the encounter has no purpose other than to associate with others. Of course, specific features of the interaction partner and interaction may add to the pleasure and to the desire to affiliate with particular people, as when people engage in particularly interesting, enjoyable, or humorous encounters. Second, people sometimes affiliate to obtain relief from stressful or fearful situations (Hill, 1987). People who face a distressing situation not only receive support, sympathy, compassion, and nurturance from others, but often the mere presence of other people can reduce fear or stress (Schachter, 1959).

The third reason that people affiliate is to obtain information about other people's behaviors, attitudes, and reactions that may reduce uncertainty, ambiguity, and confusion, and provide guidance for how they should respond to the situation (Hill, 1987; Schachter, 1959; Veroff & Veroff, 1980). Because people compare themselves with others to assess their opinions and reactions (Festinger, 1954), they may seek opportunities to interact when their uncertainty is high (Buunk, van Yperen, Taylor, & Collins, 1991; Gerard, 1963). Finally, people sometimes affiliate out of the desire to receive attention and to be held in high regard (Derber, 2000; Hill, 1987). Although people undoubtedly affiliate when they desire attention and approval, the question arises whether attention and praise are actually the focal goals that motivate affiliation or whether people seek approval and praise because they ultimately desire to be valued and accepted, as is discussed later.

Of the many reasons that people may affiliate, two have received the bulk of research attention—emotional support and social comparison. Indeed, the earliest programmatic research on affiliation focused on these two motives.

Affiliation Under Conditions of Anxiety and Stress

The earliest systematic investigations of affiliation were conducted by Schachter (1959), who published his findings in an influential book, *The Psychology of Affiliation*. Schachter's starting point was to note that people find it necessary to associate with one another in everyday life to satisfy a variety of goals. Some of these goals are nonsocial in nature (such as interacting with a store clerk to buy groceries), whereas some are inherently social in that they are satisfied only by other people (such as the desire for approval, friendship, or social support). Schachter's initial interest was in people's use of affiliation to evaluate their own reactions and to attain a state of "cognitive clarity" regarding the situation in which they found themselves. Just as people cannot easily evaluate their own opinions and abilities without comparing themselves with other people (Festinger, 1954), they sometimes are unable to assess whether they are responding appropriately to an ambiguous situation without seeing how other people are reacting.

As a result, Schachter proposed that people who are uncertain about the nature of a situation and how they should react desire to affiliate with other people to find out.

Schachter (1959) studied this process in the context of ambiguous threatening events. In his first study, female participants were given the choice to wait alone or to wait with other people for 10 minutes for a study in which they believed they would receive electric shocks that were or were not described as painful. His results showed that the women who were waiting to receive painful shocks preferred to wait with other people significantly more than the women waiting for benign shocks. In a second study, women who were waiting for painful shocks were given the opportunity to wait alone, to wait with women who were ostensibly waiting for the same shock experiment, or to wait with women who were waiting to talk to their academic advisors. Whereas 60% of the women who could wait with other women in the same experiment chose to do so, all of those who had the opportunity to wait with women who were seeing their advisors chose to wait alone instead. The fact that participants preferred to wait only with other women who were also waiting to be shocked led Schachter to conclude that participants' primary goal was to obtain social comparison information that they needed to assess their own reactions to the impending shocks. Because waiting with women who were not in the experiment would provide no information about the threatening and ambiguous situation, women who were given the option of being with students who were waiting for their advisors opted to wait alone.

The results of this study led Schachter to quip that "misery does not love just any kind of company, it loves miserable company" (1959, p. 24), but this conclusion is certainly an overgeneralization. Not only do people who are distressed often desire to affiliate with people who are not facing the same stressor, but "miserable" people sometimes appear not to want company of any kind. In addition, contrary to Schachter's conclusion that this preference is fueled by a desire for social comparison information, people who are distressed gain much more from being with similar others than merely an opportunity for social comparison. In fact, in a subsequent study designed to understand why women chose to wait with others who were in the same threatening situation more than those in another situation, Schachter told women in one condition that they should not talk about anything relating to the experiment and told those in another condition that they should not talk to one another at all. Results suggested that anxious women preferred waiting with others regardless of whether they could talk about their common plight, which seems to cast doubt on the social comparison explanation.

Schachter (1959) also conducted studies on the relationship between birth order and affiliation under stress.

He hypothesized that adults who were first-born children would prefer to wait with other people when afraid more than those who were later-born children, because first-born children experience faster and more consistent parental support when they are distressed than do later-borns. Because parents become less concerned about minor episodes of distress as they have more experience raising children and because the presence of other children in the house interferes with parental responsiveness to any particular child, later-born children receive less rapid and consistent parental support when upset, and thus learn to manage their distress on their own. His results supported this hypothesis: Participants who were first-born or only children were almost twice as likely to want to wait with other people when they were worried about the upcoming shocks than were later-born participants. Furthermore, Schachter found a linear relationship between birth order and preferring to wait with others when anxious; the proportion of participants who wanted to wait with other people decreased steadily with birth order. Interestingly, in the absence of anxiety, Schachter found a tendency for later-borns to prefer to wait with others more than first-borns and only-borns, a finding borne out by other research suggesting that later-born children are generally more sociable (e.g., Beck, Burnet, & Vosper, 2006). He also found that, although first-born and only children reported greater anxiety about the impending shocks than later-born children, differences in preferences for waiting alone versus with others were obtained even when self-reported anxiety was statistically controlled.

Schachter (1959) extended his thinking about birth order and affiliation to real-world instances in which people affiliate with other people to relieve their distress. Later research showed that people who were first-born and only children were more likely to use psychotherapy (a means of coping that requires affiliation with a counselor or psychotherapist), whereas later-borns were more likely to abuse alcohol (a nonsocial means of coping with anxiety). He integrated all of this work on birth order by suggesting that ordinal position is related to dependency, which is reflected in higher affiliation when people are anxious or otherwise distressed. In later studies, Schachter began to wonder whether any drive that is satisfied during childhood by parental responsiveness would yield the same findings. In an experiment involving the effects of hunger on affiliation, participants were deprived of food for 0, 6, or 20 hours, then given the option of participating alone or with another subject. Participants who had not eaten for 20 hours were about twice as likely to want to participate with another subject as those who had eaten within the last 6 hours.

Schachter (1959) explained the patterns that he observed across these experiments with respect to two processes.

First, as noted earlier, he suggested that people affiliate when anxious for social comparison reasons—to compare the appropriateness of their emotional reactions with the reactions of other people. Uncertain about whether their reactions to a threatening situation are "correct," people seek information about their emotions just as they do their attitudes and beliefs. Second, Schachter suggested that people seek others' company in an effort to reduce their anxiety by talking about the situation, obtaining support, and engaging in distracting conversation.

Soon afterward, another article claimed to refute the conclusion that anxiety increases affiliation by showing that a "fear" manipulation increased affiliation, whereas an "anxiety" manipulation reduced it (Sarnoff & Zimbardo, 1961). However, the induction of fear versus anxiety used in this research was based on a Freudian notion of these constructs: fear was induced by threatening participants with shock, whereas anxiety was induced by leading participants to believe that they would suck on infantile objects. Later research showed that this so-called anxiety induction actually caused a concern with embarrassment (Teichman, 1973), which reliably causes people to disassociate from others (Miller, 1996).

Even so, later research revealed numerous exceptions to the general finding that people prefer to affiliate when anxious. For example, pregnant women in one study preferred to be alone immediately before delivery (when anxiety is presumably high) but to be with other people afterward (Rofé, Lewin, & Padeh, 1977). Similarly, people who were most upset by the assassination of President Kennedy preferred to be alone more than those who were less distressed (Sheatsley & Feldman, 1964).

In an effort to reconcile these contradictory patterns regarding the relationship between stress and affiliation, Rofé (1984) proposed utility affiliation theory. Utility affiliation theory suggests that the strength of people's preference to affiliate in a stressful situation is a function of the perceived benefits and costs of being with other people. Being with other people when under stress can result in both positive outcomes (such as clarifying the situation, providing emotional support, or increasing safety) and negative outcomes (such as embarrassment or an escalation of panic). Specific features of the stressful event and the characteristics of the others who are present, as well as personality characteristics of the person himself or herself, influence the relative benefits and costs of affiliating when one is distressed (Rofé & Lewin, 1988). So, for example, whether misery actually loves miserable company as Schachter (1959) suggested should depend on whether people think that miserable versus nonmiserable company can best help them deal with a particular situation. Also, whether emotional upset increases affiliation may depend on whether the upset is exacerbated by the presence of other people, as may be the case when one has been or expects to be embarrassed (as in Sarnoff & Zimbardo, 1961). When the presence of other people raises concerns with social evaluation or increases the possibility of embarrassment, people prefer not to affiliate.

Opportunities for Relationship Formation

Although theorists acknowledge that people affiliate for many reasons, research on affiliation tended to follow Schachter's (1959) lead in focusing primarily on affiliation under conditions of anxiety or stress as if people want to interact with others only when they are upset. This focus has been unfortunate in terms of understanding everyday affiliation because the majority of instances in which people seek to interact with others do not involve stressful or distressing circumstances.

Relationships with other people—friendships, romantic relationships, group memberships, and so on—typically emerge from interactions among people. Although exceptions exist (such as arranged marriages in some cultures), people usually view affiliation as necessary for the development of interpersonal relationships of all kinds. As a result, people may be particularly prone to affiliate when they desire relationships. Also, they are particularly likely to affiliate with those with whom relationships are both more desirable and more likely.

The effects of physical proximity on interpersonal attraction and the development of relationships have been well documented (Back, Schmukle, & Egloff, 2008; Festinger, Schachter, & Back, 1950; Johnson, 1989). Typically, such findings are interpreted to show that proximity is a strong determinant of interpersonal attraction. Although true, this framing may miss the important role that affiliation plays in this process. That is, people are most likely to like and form relationships with people who are proximal because those are the people with whom they are most likely to affiliate.

However, ongoing social contact can have both positive and negative effects on interpersonal attraction and the desire for continued affiliation. On one hand, research on the mere exposure effect (Bornstein, 1989; Zajonc, 1968) suggests that people who have regular contact, even if they merely see one another from afar, should come to like one another more, and this pattern has been shown in laboratory and field experiments (Moreland & Beach, 1992; Moreland & Zajonc, 1982). However, proximity and familiarity can also undermine attraction and the desire to affiliate when the other individual is socially unpleasant (Ebbesen, Kjos, & Konecni, 1976), when excessive contact elicits boredom (Bornstein, 1989), or when repeated exposure reveals that one shares less in common with another

person than was first imagined (Norton, Frost, & Ariely, 2007). The positive effects of mere exposure on liking may be confined to situations in which additional exposures to the other person do not provide new information about him or her (as in Moreland & Beach, 1992). Even so, because frequent contact is typically a precondition to affiliation and relationship formation, people who wish to continue to affiliate must risk the hazards of overexposure and the possibility that familiarity might breed contempt rather than liking (Norton et al., 2007).

Behaviors That Promote Affiliation in Others

Affiliation is a two-way street. When people wish to affiliate, they must behave in ways that lead people to want to affiliate with them. Thus, people who desire to affiliate tend to display so-called immediacy behaviors that indicate an open, friendly, interested, and pleasant interpersonal stance (Mehrabian, 1969). These "nonverbal immediacy behaviors" include smiling, an appropriate interpersonal distance (close enough to imply approachability but not so close as to be seen as imposing or threatening), eye contact, an open body position, and a body orientation toward the other person (McAndrew, Gold, Lenney, & Ryckman, 1984; Patterson, 1976).

Given the role that immediacy plays in promoting affiliation and closeness (Mehrabian, 1969), people who are highly motivated to seek enjoyable, close interactions with others should display more immediacy behaviors. In support of this hypothesis, people who report that they talk with other people either for the pleasure of interacting or to express caring and appreciation use immediacy behaviors at a higher level than those who report talking to others primarily to fill time or to control other people (Myers & Ferry, 2001).

One means of inducing other people to affiliate involves prompting them to talk about themselves. Thus, people who are good at getting other people to talk about themselves, so-called openers (Miller, Berg, & Archer, 1983), more easily induce others to affiliate with them (Pegalis, Shaffer, Bazzini, & Greenier, 1994; Shaffer, Ruammake, & Pegalis, 1990). Research shows that high openers display a more attentive facial expression, appear more comfortable during interactions, are more agreeable, and give the sense of enjoying interactions with other people more (Colvin & Longueuil, 2001; Purvis, Dabbs, & Hopper, 1984), all of which should prompt affiliative behaviors from other people. Furthermore, high opener men (but not women) use more back-channel responses—that is, vocal utterances that convey attentiveness and receipt of information (such as "uh-huh" and "hmm"; Purvis et al., 1984). These immediacy behaviors appear to pay off. People who score high on the Opener Scale (Miller et al., 1983) are better liked than those who score low, presumably because they appear more attentive and affirming.

Research on nonverbal immediacy was once popular in social psychology but has waned considerably in recent years. Current interest in the topic can be seen primarily in education, where the effects of teachers' immediacy behaviors on students' motivation and learning have been studied (e.g., Christensen & Menzel, 1998). In addition, research has investigated the impact of immediacy behaviors on doctor-patient interactions (Harrigan, Oxman, & Rosenthal, 1985) and marital relationships (Hinkle, 1999).

In part, social psychologists' declining interest in immediacy may be because of the failure of early theories to explain both when people will use particular immediacy behaviors and the separate interpersonal effects of particular behaviors (smiling, eye contact, stance, etc.). In retrospect, the problem may have been that the theories did not account adequately for the fact that the most effective behaviors for sustaining a particular level of conversational interest, depth, and closeness depend on the social context, the nature of the relationship between the people, the roles in which people find themselves, and their goals for the interaction (McAndrew et al., 1984). Not only do these factors influence the type and intensity of particular immediacy behaviors (such as eye contact, physical closeness, and facial expressiveness), but a particular behavior can have quite different effects on other people's reactions and the course of an interaction depending on these factors. Even though it may be difficult to model the degree to which a particular pattern of nonverbal behaviors influences the likelihood that others will affiliate with another person in a given context, certain levels of immediacy are more likely to promote affiliation than others.

SEEKING ACCEPTANCE AND BELONGING

Although affiliating, interacting, and "hanging out" with other people can provide many positive outcomes, mere affiliation goes only so far toward helping people meet their physical, material, and social needs, and satisfying an array of other goals that depend on other people. To capitalize fully on their social connections, people must not only affiliate with others, but they also must establish interpersonal relationships of various kinds. In all cultures, people develop and maintain a variety of interpersonal relationships such as kin relationships, friendships, mating relationships, instrumental coalitions, and so on. Because people are necessarily selective in the number and kinds of relationships that they develop (Tooby & Cosmedes, 1996), individuals must take steps to show other people that they

are good prospects for various kinds of relationships and group memberships. Furthermore, once they develop a relationship or become a member of a group, people must protect themselves against the possibility that they will be rejected from that relationship or group.

Because pre-human individuals who sought to be accepted and to belong were most likely to survive, reproduce, and help their offspring reach maturity, a motivational disposition likely evolved that orients people toward seeking acceptance and avoiding rejection (Baumeister & Leary, 1995). Because rejection would have compromised the likelihood of survival and reproduction, mechanisms probably evolved for monitoring and responding to indications that one was, or was likely to be, rejected by other people (Ainsworth, 1989; Gardner, Pickett, Jefferis, & Knowles, 2005; Leary & Downs, 1995).

Although many theorists have acknowledged that people seek to develop and maintain social bonds with other people (e.g., Bowlby, 1969; Horney, 1945; James, 1890; Maslow, 1968), Baumeister and Leary (1995) suggested that social psychologists had overlooked the centrality of this motive in human behavior, cognition, and emotion. They observed that people in every culture belong to small, primary groups and form a variety of relationships with family members, friends, mates, and others (Coon, 1946; Fiske, 1992; Mann, 1980), and that people who lack the desire for any social connections are at risk for psychological problems (Chapman, Chapman, Kwapil, Eckblad, & Zinser, 1994; Kwapil, 1998). People typically form social bonds with individuals and groups very easily, often without any special eliciting circumstances (Festinger et al., 1950; Tajfel, Flament, Billig, & Bundy, 1971). Once they develop relationships with others, people are reluctant to allow those relationships to end, even when they no longer have any instrumental value and may even exact costs on them. Based on evidence such as this, Baumeister and Leary concluded that people possess an evolved need to "form and maintain at least a minimum quantity of lasting, positive, and significant interpersonal relationships" (p. 497), and that this desire for acceptance and belonging underlies a great deal of human behavior.

Importantly, not all efforts to seek acceptance and belonging necessarily arise from this evolved need for social acceptance. Being accepted into relationships and groups offers a wide array of benefits, and people sometimes seek acceptance because they believe that it will lead to specific rewards or opportunities, not because they are driven to do so by an evolved need for belonging. For example, a man who applies for membership in a country club may do so to spend his weekends on its golf course and not because he is seeking new interpersonal relationships. But whether people desire acceptance and belonging in a particular instance because of an evolved motivational impetus or because of the perceived benefits of acceptance in a specific case, they must take care to behave in ways that will lead others to accept them (Baumeister & Leary, 1995; Leary & Baumeister, 2000).

Relational Value as the Basis of Acceptance and Rejection

Although the terms "acceptance" and "rejection" are often treated as dichotomous (i.e., one is either accepted or rejected), shades of acceptance/rejection actually fall along a continuum (Leary, 2001). At the extreme pole of acceptance, a person may be actively sought after as a relational partner or group member, whereas moderate levels of acceptance may involve welcoming the person (but not seeking him or her out), and minimal acceptance may involve merely tolerating the person's presence (Leary, 1990). Similarly, the term "belonging"—acceptance by a group of individuals who include the individual as a member—is also problematic, because it too is treated as a dichotomy (i.e., one either does or does not belong) and because people may "belong" to a group that wishes that they were not a member. In such cases, people may not feel that they belong or are accepted even though they are technically a group member and included in the group's activities.

Likewise, rejection can range from merely ignoring people to avoiding or not including them to explicitly excluding or banishing them from encounters or groups in which they are already a participant (Leary, 1990). The term "ostracism," defined as "any act or acts of ignoring and excluding of an individual or groups by an individual or group" (Williams, 2001, p. ix), is sometimes used as synonymous with rejection but is perhaps best regarded as a subtype of rejection because people can be psychologically rejected by others without being ignored or excluded. For example, people may find themselves working or interacting with others who dislike, devalue, and despise them. Such individuals could not be said to be ostracized (i.e., they are not excluded or ignored), but they certainly might feel that they are being "rejected" despite the fact that the group fully includes them. As can be seen, the terms that are used to refer to the experiences of acceptance and rejection (including belonging and ostracism) are often insufficiently precise, and people experience degrees of acceptance and rejection that are difficult to describe using these terms (Leary, 2001). Furthermore, people sometimes *feel* rejected even though they technically belong to a group or are included in other people's activities (Bourgeois & Leary, 2001).

The subjective experiences of acceptance (and belonging) and rejection may be conceptualized as areas along a continuum of *perceived relational value* to provide greater

conceptual clarity and precision. Relational value refers to the degree to which one person regards his or her relationship with another individual as valuable or important (Leary, 2001). People value their relationships with other people to varying degrees, regarding relationships with certain individuals as very valuable and important, and viewing certain other relationships as less valuable and important or as having no value at all. When people perceive that their relational value to a particular individual or group of individuals is acceptably high, they perceive that they are accepted. In contrast, feelings of rejection arise when people perceive that their relational value to a particular person or group is unacceptably low—that is, when they believe that others do not value having a relationship with them as much as they desire the others to value it (Leary, 2001, 2005).

The degree to which people desire to be relationally valued and the indicators that they use to assess their relational value are relationship specific. For example, talking to an acquaintance at a party, a person may desire that the acquaintance value their transient "relationship" only to the point that he or she remains engaged in the conversation for a few minutes. As long as the acquaintance seems reasonably interested and engaged, perceived relational value will be sufficiently high (relative to the individual's desire), and the person will feel accepted. If, however, the acquaintance seems disengaged while scanning the party for a more interesting conversational partner, the person may experience a sense of having low relational value, and thus feel rejected.

Furthermore, because the psychological experience of being accepted and rejected depends on whether relational value is as high as one desires, subjective experiences of acceptance and rejection are only loosely linked to how accepted or rejected people are in an absolute sense. Indeed, people sometimes *feel* rejected by people who they know like and accept them because they perceive that their relational value is not as high as they would like it to be (Leary, 2001). For example, when a long-time romantic partner whose love and commitment are assured declines an invitation to do something that one wants to do (such as go out to dinner, take a trip, or have sex), people may nonetheless feel rejected and hurt because, at that moment, they perceive that their relational value in the partner's mind is not as high as they desire it to be.

Promoting Relational Value

Being relationally valued by other people increases the likelihood of acceptance and access to desired social and material outcomes, such as companionship, friendship, group memberships, romantic relationships, social support, logistical help, financial and material resources, social influence, and a broad range of social, occupational, financial, recreational, and sexual opportunities (Baumeister & Leary, 1995; Williams, Forgas, von Hippel, & Zadro, 2005). Put simply, people who have higher relational value accrue greater benefits in life. Not surprisingly, then, people are highly motivated to maintain high relational value in the minds of those with whom they desire to interact and have relationships.

People increase their chances of forming relationships and being accepted into groups when they are perceived as possessing characteristics that make them a desirable group member, friend, romantic partner, colleague, companion, teammate, or whatever. As a result, a great deal of human behavior appears centered on efforts to promote and maintain one's relational value (Baumeister & Leary, 1995; Leary, 1995; Williams, 2001). Some interpersonal behaviors are motivated primarily by the desire to promote relational value and acceptance, but even when social acceptance is not their primary objective in a particular context, people typically pursue their goals in ways that do not jeopardize their relational value in others' eyes. In this sense, the desire for acceptance and belonging constrains much of what people do, leading them to behave in ways that do not lead other people to devalue or reject them.

An important first step in facilitating acceptance and belonging involves self-disclosure, the voluntary presentation of personal or intimate information about oneself to another person (Miller, 2002). Theories of relationship development suggest that relationships develop and deepen as the people involved disclose increasingly intimate information about themselves to one another over time (Altman & Taylor, 1973; Reis & Shaver, 1988). Unless people disclose too quickly or their disclosures reveal negative information about them (Berger, Gardner, Parks, Shulman, & Miller, 1976), self-disclosure both increases others' attraction to the individual and elicits more disclosure in return (Berg & Wright-Buckley, 1988; Worthy, Gary, & Kahn, 1969). In fact, self-disclosure by a member of an outgroup can also improve others' evaluations of the person's group in general (Turner, Hewstone, & Voci, 2007).

Of course, the content of people's disclosures is critical in promoting acceptance, and people try to establish and maintain their relational value by behaving in ways that will convey particular desired impressions of themselves to others. People engage in self-presentation (or impression management) to achieve a variety of goals (Baumeister, 1982; Leary & Kowalski, 1990; Schlenker, 1980), but a great deal of impression management appears to involve direct or indirect efforts to promote relational value and acceptance. Jones and Pittman (1982) identified five primary self-presentational tactics (although there are undoubtedly more), involving efforts to be perceived as friendly and likeable (ingratiation), intelligent and competent (self-promotion), responsible and morally exemplary (exemplification), helpless (supplication), and threatening (intimidation). People may use each of these self-presentational tactics to foster their relational value. First, because people who are perceived as likeable, competent, and exemplary are virtually always valued and accepted more than those who are viewed as unlikable, incompetent, and reprehensible, people who desire to be accepted try to portray themselves in one or more of these socially desirable ways. Of course, being viewed as likable, competent, or moral can have other consequences in addition to social acceptance (such as earning a higher salary), but many of the payoffs of conveying desirable impressions come in the form of interpersonal consequences such as attention, friendship, group memberships, romantic relationships, and so on.

Paradoxically, conveying socially undesirable images of oneself can also increase one's relational value. For example, people who show others that they are the sort who respond with anger and aggression to signs of disinterest or rejection may lead others to value their relationship as a means of avoiding social costs. Intimidating self-presentations may enhance relational value at the price of liking and goodwill, but nonetheless promote value via the threat of punishment. Likewise, people may convey impressions of neediness or helplessness (supplication) to enhance their relational value to those who wish to be helpful.

Seeking Approval and Liking

Theorists have traced a wide variety of behaviors to people's desire for social approval. Behaviors as diverse as working hard in school, earning a good deal of money, performing well in sports, taking drugs, practicing safe sex, cheating on tests, and having an eating disorder have been attributed to people's efforts to obtain approval (Baumeister, 1990; Matell & Smith, 1970; Moulton, Moulton, & Roach, 1998; St. Lawrence, Eldridge, Reitman, Little, Shelby, & Brasfield, 1998; Stein, Newcomb, & Bentler, 1987). That people behave in these ways to garner approval from other people is beyond doubt. Yet, focusing on social approval may overlook the deeper interpersonal motive that underlies people's desire to seek approval from others. Learning, or even imagining, that one is evaluated positively or regarded approvingly is certainly satisfying, but mere approval is functionally unimportant unless it is associated with positive outcomes. Thus, people may not be generally motivated to seek approval per se but rather seek approval because people with high relational value receive a variety of benefits.

Perhaps the primary way in which people seek approval, thereby increasing their relational value and social acceptance, is by trying to lead others to like them. Although disliked individuals may be tolerated and even valued if they have something special to offer a relationship or group (such as being particularly competent at an important task), the emotional costs that they exact on other people generally lower their relational value. As a result, people typically prefer to be seen as possessing characteristics that lead others to like rather than dislike them. For this reason, people indicate that the images that they generally want others to form of them include being perceived as friendly, sincere, caring, fun, and easy to talk to (Leary, 1995). At the same time, people usually do not want others to regard them as boring, conceited, obnoxious, superficial, self-centered, and mean (Leary, 1995), traits that reliably lead others to dislike and reject them.

Research also shows that people are more likely to like, interact with, befriend, and fall in love with people whom they perceive as similar to themselves (for reviews, see AhYun, 2002; Montoya, Horton, & Kirchner, 2008). In the terms we are using here, a person's relational value increases with the degree to which others perceive him or her as similar to them. Not surprisingly, people identify and capitalize on areas of similarity when they interact and foster impressions of similarity by conforming to others' opinions and behavior (Jellison & Gentry, 1978; Jones, Gergen, Gumpert, & Thibaut, 1965; Kacmar, Carlson, & Bratton, 2004). Furthermore, people who score high in the need to belong are more likely to cooperate in group settings than those who score low (DeCremer & Leonardelli, 2003), presumably because others are more likely to accept those who are seen as cooperative. A great deal of conformity is probably enacted in the service of social acceptance.

Research suggests that people may even promote their similarity to others nonconsciously. For example, participants in one study automatically mimicked the nonverbal behaviors of an experimental confederate, shaking their feet and rubbing their faces more when the confederate shook and rubbed his (Chartrand & Bargh, 1999). Furthermore, this effect was strongest among people who scored high in the need for affiliation (Lakin & Chartrand, 2003), suggesting that behavioral mimicry is at least partly designed to promote social interactions. Furthermore, people like others who behaviorally mimic them more than those who do not (Chartrand & Bargh). The fact that behavioral mimicry operates automatically and nonconsciously suggests that people may be hardwired to behave in ways that stimulate liking and acceptance.

People also increase their chances of acceptance and belonging through behaviors that convey that they like other people, such as flattery, praise, and expressing interest in the other person (Deluga & Perry, 1991; Gordon, 1996; Jones, 1964; Jones & Wortman, 1973; Stevens & Kristof, 1995; Wayne & Kacmar, 1991). Engaging in these kinds of other-directed behaviors increases liking not only by the target of these actions but by uninvolved observers as well (Folkes & Sears, 1977). Of course, insincere flattery may backfire, but research suggests that targets tend to accept ingratiators' behavior at face value (whereas observers tend to be more skeptical) and may appreciate others' efforts to ingratiate them even if they do not believe that the person is being genuine (Vonk, 2002).

Achievement and Competence

Most theoretical discussions of achievement assume that people strive for competence and mastery either for their own sake or because being competent and successful allows them to achieve other important outcomes. Yet, people appear to enact a great deal of achievement-oriented behavior in the service of interpersonal goals, including acceptance and belonging. People often seek to be competent or successful not because they intrinsically value competence or success, or for the tangible outcomes that achievement produces, but rather because excellence and achievement lead to recognition, approval, and acceptance by other people (Baumeister, 1990). This is not to say that all striving for competence, achievement, and success is motivated by interpersonal rewards, but there is little doubt that people who are seen as competent and successful have higher relational value than those who are regarded as incompetent and unsuccessful. Successful people are more likely to be sought for groups and relationships, either because their skills benefit other people, the rewards of their achievements (such as a high salary) are desired by others, they are regarded as more interesting interactants and relational partners, or others wish, for their own reasons, to be associated with successful people. Theory and research on achievement-related goals show that interpersonal concerns with appearing competent to others, obtaining approval, and pleasing other people constitute one source of the motivation to perform well and to achieve (see Miller, Greene, Montalvo, Ravindran, & Nichols, 1996; Urdan & Mestas, 2006). However, the deeper goal may be to enhance relational value, acceptance, and belonging.

Although people generally try to project images of themselves as intelligent and competent, they sometimes "play dumb" instead. When they think that they can increase their chances of social acceptance by appearing less competent than they really are, people may pretend to know less than they really do (Dean, Braito, Powers, & Britton, 1975; Thornton, Audesse, Ryckman, & Burckle, 2006). People play dumb for a variety of reasons, but perhaps the most common is to increase their desirability and relational value to someone who might be put off or threatened by their knowledge or competence. The classic, stereotypic case of playing dumb involves women who underplay their intelligence to avoid threatening men (Gove, Hughes, & Geerken, 1980; Thornton et al.), but men also play dumb to play up the intelligence and ability of their bosses (Dean et al.; Gove et al.). Interestingly, people who tend to play dumb also tend, in other contexts, to claim more knowledge than they actually have, suggesting that both self-enhancing and self-effacing tactics are motivated by concerns with other people's evaluations and acceptance (Thornton et al.).

Being a Good Relational Partner or Group Member

A third set of images that promote relational value involves being viewed as a responsible, trustworthy, loyal, cooperative, and dedicated individual who supports the goals and norms of the relationship or group. Often, the issue is only whether the person demonstrates these characteristics in the context of a particular group or relationship. We are often willing to form relationships with those who are less than fully honest and dependable in their dealings with others as long as we believe that they are truthful and responsible with us.

Given that people devalue, dislike, and reject those who do not conform to their judgments, decisions, and behaviors (Schachter, 1951), people understandably conform to others' views (see Cialdini, Kallgren, & Reno, 1991; Insko, Smith, Alicke, Wade, & Taylor, 1985). They are particularly likely to conform when they see others being ridiculed for nonconformity (Janes & Olson, 2000) and less likely to conform when other nonconformists are present (Asch, 1956; Insko et al., 1985). Furthermore, people who score high in the need to belong are more likely to cooperate in group settings than those who score low (DeCremer & Leonardelli, 2003). All of these findings reflect people's efforts to show others that they should be regarded as trustworthy members-in-good-standing to minimize the likelihood of losing relational value and being rejected from the group.

Many social psychological phenomena can be explained in terms of people going along with others to avoid jeopardizing their position in the group. For example, because many people desire to avoid conflict and do not wish to rock the boat, they may censor their objections to options being discussed by the group, withhold information that might undermine group harmony or make them appear oppositional, and conform to emerging group decisions. Thus, many of the factors that undermine effective group deliberations (and promote groupthink) reflect people's concerns with their acceptance by other members of the group (McCauley, 1989).

Even reciprocity, which many theorists consider to be the foundation of any mutually satisfying interpersonal encounter, is enforced chiefly through the implied threat of rejection for those who fail to reciprocate (Cotterell, Eisenberger, & Speicher, 1992). A great deal of interpersonal reciprocity, as well as modes of social influence that are based on reciprocity, such as the reciprocal concessions technique (in which people in a dispute are more likely to offer concessions when their opponent does; Cialdini, Vincent, Lewis, Catalan, Wheeler, & Darby, 1975; Hale & Laliker, 1999), are undergirded by people's concerns with being accepted by others.

Physical Appearance

Although a few exceptions exist, physically attractive people are typically better liked and more highly sought as companions, friends, group members, and romantic partners than people who are less attractive. Meta-analyses show that attractive children and adults are judged and treated more positively than unattractive people, even by those who know them well (Feingold, 1990; Langlois, Kalakanis, Rubenstein, Larson, Hallam, & Smoot, 2000). Some physical features, such as facial symmetry and unblemished skin, appear to be universally regarded as attractive, and thus associated with greater social acceptance, possibly because of their role in signaling genetic fitness and an absence of pathogens and illness (Jones et al., 2001; Rhodes, 2006). However, other criteria for attractiveness differ across groups and social contexts so that people who wish to be accepted by a particular individual must abide by the prevailing norms regarding appearance.

Viewed in this way, virtually anything that people do to enhance their physical appeal is done primarily to promote relational value and acceptance. Many people in Western cultures try to maintain their weight within an acceptable range (with varying degrees of success) and exercise to appear slim and fit. Not only do those who exercise regularly develop a physique that others view as more attractive, but also the mere fact that someone exercises can lead others to draw more positive inferences about the person's personal and social qualities (Martin Ginis, Lindwall, & Prapavessis, 2007). Likewise, people with light skin may strive to maintain a tan despite knowing of the health risks of excessive sun exposure because they believe (correctly, as it turns out) that being tan will enhance their attractiveness to others (Leary & Jones, 1993). The multibillion-dollar cosmetics, personal grooming, and cosmetic surgery industries are based on the notion that enhancing one's appearance (and one's scent) leads to greater social acceptance and the attendant social outcomes (Davis & Vernon, 2002).

One of the most conscious and deliberate ways in which people try to enhance their appearance involves the clothes that they choose to wear. People desire to wear clothing that they believe, correctly or incorrectly, enhances their appearance and that conforms to the accepted wardrobe of their primary social groups (Peluchette, Karl, & Rust, 2006). Although people's clothing preferences are also influenced by an array of nonsocial factors, including comfort and price, concerns with social image and, ultimately, social acceptance are undoubtedly involved (Frith & Gleeson, 2004; Simpson & Littrell, 1984).

Self-presentation and Relational Value

As we have seen, people pursue relational value and acceptance primarily through the images that they convey of themselves to other people. Fostering images of being likable, competent, an exemplary partner or group member, or physically attractive increases people's relational value compared with being regarded as unlikable, incompetent, an undesirable partner or group member, and unattractive. Although people sometimes misrepresent themselves to others to increase their relational value (Feldman, Forrest, & Happ, 2002; Tyler & Feldman, 2004; Weiss & Feldman, 2006), their self-presentations are more-or-less accurate representations of their characteristics when overly positive self-presentations are held in check by the possibility of detection (Schlenker, 1975). Being caught misrepresenting one's characteristics, abilities, or personal history invariably reduces people's relational value and the likelihood of acceptance.

The lure of relational value is so strong that people sometimes do things that are dangerous to themselves or to others to make the kinds of impressions that they believe will lead others to value and accept them. For example, teenagers and young adults may ingest large quantities of alcohol, take drugs, engage in excessive suntanning, drive recklessly, show-off by performing dangerous stunts, and fail to practice safe sex to gain others' approval and acceptance (Hingson & Howland, 1993; Leary, Tchividjian, & Kraxberger, 1994; Martin & Leary, 1999, 2000). Even older adults may engage in risky behaviors, such as refusing to use aids to help them walk safely, because they are concerned with making undesired impressions on other people (Martin, Leary, & Rejeski, 2000).

MONITORING RELATIONAL VALUE AND SOCIAL CONNECTIONS

Given the importance of cooperative group living to human survival and reproduction, natural selection favored individuals who sought the company of others and behaved in ways that led others to value and accept them. Because social acceptance was literally vital, a psychological system likely evolved to monitor and respond to cues relevant to interpersonal acceptance and rejection. Although researchers have devoted little attention to precisely how people

monitor their relational value, two perspectives—sociometer theory and social monitoring theory—have described the features that this monitoring system might have.

The Sociometer

Sociometer theory proposes that people possess a psychological system—a sociometer—that monitors the social environment for cues relevant to relational value (i.e., acceptance and rejection), alerts the individual via negative affect and lowered self-esteem when signs of low or declining relational value are detected, and motivates behaviors that attempt to maintain or, if necessary, increase relational value (Leary, 2006; Leary & Baumeister, 2000; Leary & Downs, 1995). This system appears to operate nonconsciously in background mode until indications of low or declining relational value are detected. Then the system prompts the individual to consider the situation consciously.

Evidence suggests that people are highly sensitive to information that might be relevant to their relational value, processing such information quickly, automatically, and often nonconsciously. In a classic article on dichotic listening, Cherry (1953) described what has become known as the cocktail party phenomenon. Even when people are consciously attending closely to certain stimuli (such as a conversation that they are having at a lively party) and seemingly oblivious to everything else in their environment (such as the myriad other conversations around them), they nonetheless can detect and respond to extraneous stimuli that are self-relevant (such as the mention of their name in another conversation) (Moray, 1959; Wood & Cowan, 1995). At the time this work was published, the central conclusion was that the brain processes the content of information outside of conscious awareness even while people consciously attend to other things (Cherry, 1953). For our purposes, it is noteworthy that people are particularly attuned to self-relevant information, such as their name, but no one addressed the broader question of why people are peculiarly sensitive to such cues aside from the broad conclusion that they are "self-relevant."

From a social psychological standpoint, the answer would seem to be not just that such stimuli are self-relevant but rather that they are relevant to one's image and standing in the minds of other people. When people experience the cocktail party effect while engaged in conversation at an actual party, they not only hear and orient toward whoever mentioned their name, but they often wonder, if not inquire, what was being said about them. Given the importance of others' impressions and evaluations of them, people must be attuned to any information that might provide information about their relational value and particularly to indications that their relational value might be low.

Thus, the brain processes such information below the level of conscious awareness and alerts the person when information that might be relevant to their public image and relational value is detected.

More recent evidence shows more clearly that people process information regarding others' judgments of them vis-à-vis acceptance and rejection automatically and nonconsciously. A variety of priming manipulations, including guided visualizations (Baldwin & Sinclair, 1996) and subliminal presentations of a significant other's face (Baldwin, Carrell, & Lopez, 1990) or name (Baldwin, 1994), have produced effects on people's self-judgments and emotions that resemble the effects of explicit rejection. This research has shown that minimal cues can activate relational knowledge in memory in ways that lead people to feel and act as if they are devalued or rejected (Baldwin & Main, 2001).

According to sociometer theory, one output of the sociometer system is state self-esteem, people's feelings about themselves at a particular moment in time, which rises and falls with changes in perceived relational value (Leary & Baumeister, 2000). Changes in state self-esteem alert people to real and potential rejection, and motivate actions that maintain relational value and social acceptance. A good deal of research shows that state self-esteem fluctuates like a gauge of acceptance and rejection in response to social feedback (for a meta-analysis, see Blackhart, Knowles, & Bieda, 2009). Not only does explicit rejection decrease state self-esteem, but people's feelings about themselves when they perform certain behaviors mirror the degree to which they think their actions will lead others to accept or reject them. In one study (Leary, Tambor, Terdal, & Downs, 1995), participants rated how they would feel about themselves if they performed each of several behaviors that varied in social desirability (e.g., I saved a drowning child; I cheated on a final exam), as well as the degree to which other people would accept or reject them if they knew about each behavior. Results showed a strong concordance between participants' feelings about themselves (i.e., state self-esteem) and the degree to which they thought other people would accept or reject them.

Furthermore, people's self-evaluations on particular dimensions predict their self-esteem primarily to the degree to which they believe that those dimensions are relevant to their social acceptance and rejection by other people (MacDonald, Saltzman, & Leary, 2003). For example, people who think that they are physically unattractive have lower self-esteem if they believe that their relational value to others depends on their physical appearance than if they think that appearance is less important for social acceptance.

Sociometer theory also offers a novel conceptualization on the nature of the self-esteem motive, which has traditionally been regarded as a mechanism that helps people maintain high self-esteem (e.g., Taylor & Brown, 1988). In contrast, sociometer theory proposes that, when people do things that appear intended to maintain or raise their self-esteem, their goal is usually to protect and enhance their relational value to increase their likelihood of interpersonal acceptance. Thus, many behaviors that have been attributed to a motive to maintain self-esteem, such as self-serving attributions, self-handicapping behaviors, biased social judgments, prejudices, and ego-defensive reactions, may reflect efforts to promote acceptance rather than to raise self-esteem per se (Leary & Baumeister, 2000). The theory acknowledges that people sometimes try to feel good about themselves in their own minds but maintains that the fundamental function of the self-esteem system is to monitor and respond to threats to relational value and social acceptance.

Presumably, people monitor cues relevant to relational value in all types of interpersonal encounters, including interactions with friends, romantic partners, fellow group members, acquaintances, family members, and even strangers. The question has been raised, however, of whether people have a single sociometer that monitors cues that are relevant to acceptance and rejection across all relationships or a set of sociometers, each of which deals specifically with acceptance/rejection in a particular kind of relationship. An evolutionary analysis suggests that people might possess different sociometer systems to monitor their acceptance in fundamentally different types of social relationships (Kirkpatrick & Ellis, 2001). First, people form into macrolevel groups, such as tribes, villages, communities, or nations. They may or may not have direct contact with all other members, but these collectives offer benefits such as access to resources and defense against other groups. Second, people form instrumental coalitions, that is, groups of people who work together toward mutually desired goals. The earliest instrumental coalitions may have been hunting parties, but people today join committees, teams, gangs, work groups, civic organizations, neighborhood associations, and other task-oriented groups. Third, people seek mating relationships that range from one-time liaisons to permanent monogamous pairings. Fourth, people have many kin relationships that are based on genetic relatedness. A fifth type of relationship involves supportive friendships that provide ongoing companionship and support that span time, roles, and tasks, and provide an interpersonal insurance policy for occasions when one is in dire need and has nowhere else to turn (Tooby & Cosmedes, 1996).

People are accepted into, and rejected from, these various kinds of relationships for different reasons (Kirkpatrick & Ellis, 2001). Community memberships are typically based on shared heritage or attitudes, instrumental coalitions on one's ability to contribute to the group, mating relationships on mate value, kin relationships on genetic relatedness, and friendships on the basis of being a reliable source of companionship and support. Given that different adaptive problems require different solutions and that a separate mechanism is needed for each qualitatively different problem (see Symons, 1992), it seems unlikely that a single mechanism could have evolved to monitor one's value in all types of relationships (Kirkpatrick & Ellis, 2001, 2006), although some bases of acceptance and rejection seem to apply across all types of relationships. For example, a person who behaves in a selfish, untrustworthy, or duplicitous manner is not valued as a relational partner no matter what type of relationship we might imagine. Thus, people might have a general sociometer and specific systems that monitor particular kinds of relationships.

Social Monitoring System

Gardner, Pickett, and Brewer (2000; see also Pickett & Gardner, 2005) extended the concept of the sociometer to suggest that people possess a social monitoring system that responds specifically in instances in which people become particularly concerned with their acceptance or belonging. They proposed that an increase in belonging need increases people's sensitivity to social information in ways that help them navigate their social worlds more successfully. The social monitoring system is hypothesized to be activated whenever people become concerned about rejection. For example, a recently rejected person may become more attuned to cues regarding his or her relational value, show greater sensitivity to other people's thoughts and feelings about him or her, and devote more cognitive resources to thinking about social situations. (Although the theory suggests that sensitivity to social information increases when belonging needs are heightened, it is probably more accurate to say that sensitivity increases in response to perceived threats to acceptance and belonging even if the person's need for belonging remains constant.)

Concerns with acceptance and rejection may become salient because people have detected cues that their relational value is low in a particular situation, they are dispositionally high in traits that are associated with wanting to be accepted (e.g., they are high in the need to belong or desire for approval), or they chronically feel that their social relationships are deficient (as in the case of loneliness) (Gardner et al., 2000). Whatever their source, high concerns about social acceptance and belonging lead people to become particularly sensitive to cues regarding how others feel about them, as well as information that might help them maintain or restore their social connections. Experimental manipulations that lead people to feel socially excluded cause them to selectively remember

socially relevant information about another person but not nonsocial information (Gardner et al., 2000), supporting the hypotheses that the system increases the degree to which people are attuned to the social matrix when social acceptance is at risk. Similarly, people who are experiencing a chronic deficiency in perceived belonging by virtue of being lonely show greater selective memory for social information (Gardner, Pickett, Jefferis, & Knowles, 2005). Likewise, people who scored high on a measure of the dispositional need to belong were more accurate in identifying facial expressions and vocal tone, and displayed greater empathic accuracy than people who scored lower on the need to belong (Pickett, Gardner, & Knowles, 2004). Similarly, participants who were primed with rejection by writing about a time that they were rejected were more accurate at distinguishing Duchenne (true) smiles from feigned smiles than participants who wrote about acceptance or a control topic (Bernstein, Young, Brown, Sacco, & Claypool, in press).

Together, sociometer theory and social monitoring theory suggest that people possess systems that monitor and respond to indications that their relational value is low or declining. These systems monitor cues that are relevant to acceptance and rejection on an ongoing basis, alert the individual when potential threats to relational value are detected, motivate behaviors that protect or restore relational value, and increase people's sensitivity to social information that will enhance the probability that they will be accepted.

VARIETIES OF REJECTION-RELATED EVENTS

People's efforts to affiliate, to be accepted, and to belong are not always successful. Other people are not always interested in interacting or maintaining relationships with us, and even when they are, our relational value in their eyes is sometimes not as high as we desire it to be. Interestingly, social psychologists have long been interested in situations and events that lead people to feel rejected, although they have not always recognized the common role that low relational value and rejection play in them. This section focuses on interpersonal phenomena that involve low relational value, and the subsequent section examines the psychological reactions to rejection-related phenomena.

Explicit Rejection and Ostracism

When people think of rejection, they typically envision receiving explicit indications that others do not wish to associate with a person—deliberate actions in which one or more people ignore, exclude, or reject the individual. Being purposefully excluded from a social gathering, fired from a job, rejected by a romantic partner, or not chosen for a team each involve explicit indications that others do not wish to associate with or have a relationship with the individual. A number of experimental paradigms have been used to cause participants to experience explicit rejection (also called "active disassociation") by leading them to believe that other participants had voted not to include them in a laboratory group (Maner, DeWall, Baumeister, & Schaller, 2007), they were chosen last for a laboratory team (Bourgeois & Leary, 2001), another person was disinterested in what they were saying about themselves (Snapp & Leary, 2001), others had excluded them from a real or computerized ball-tossing game (Eisenberger, Lieberman, & Williams, 2003; Williams & Sommer, 1997), other participants indicated that they preferred to work alone rather than with the participant (Buckley, Winkel, & Leary, 2004, Study 1), or that others had little interest in getting to know the participant better (Buckley et al., 2004, Study 2).

Stigmatization

Traditionally, stigmatization has been conceptualized in terms of the possession of a negative attribute or "mark" that taints, spoils, or discredits a person's social identity (Crocker & Major, 1989; Fiske, this volume; Goffman, 1963; Swann & Bosson, volume 1). However, the central feature of stigmatization may involve not merely a tainted identity but also low relational value and, possibly, outright rejection. One conceptualization suggests that stigmatization occurs "when a shared characteristic of a category of people becomes consensually regarded as a basis for disassociating from (that is, avoiding, excluding, ostracizing, or otherwise minimizing interaction with) individuals who are perceived to be members of that category" (Leary & Schreindorfer, 1998, p. 15). According to this conceptualization, people are not stigmatized simply because they have a spoiled identity or are evaluated negatively, but rather because others view them as possessing a characteristic for which they should be avoided or excluded.

When one examines the reasons that people are typically stigmatized, they mostly involve reasons that, in the eye of the stigmatizer, qualify the target for devaluation, avoidance, and possibly rejection. In fact, many instances of stigmatization may involve evolved dispositions to distance oneself from others who are perceived to pose a threat to one's well-being (Kurzban & Leary, 2001; Neuberg et al., this volume; Neuberg & Cottrell, 2008). Specifically, people tend to stigmatize and exclude those who are perceived as poor social exchange partners (e.g., homeless people, convicted felons, known cheaters),

members of outgroups that are perceived to be in competition for resources with one's own group, and those whose appearance or manner suggest that they might be infected with contagious parasites (e.g., people with skin lesions, behavioral abnormalities, or obvious psychological problems). In each instance, stigmatization may serve to protect people from costs associated with contact with the stigmatized person (Kurzban & Leary, 2001; Neuberg & Cottrell, 2008). Of course, people are sometimes stigmatized for reasons that have nothing to do with actual costs or risks, but even then the rejector typically believes that the stigmatized person poses some sort of threat, should be devalued, and is not a viable relational partner.

Stigma-by-association is particularly interesting in this regard. People are sometimes stigmatized merely because of their association with a stigmatized individual—for example, when a heterosexual is stigmatized for having a homosexual friend (Neuberg, Smith, Hoffman, & Russell, 1994). Thus, people's relational value can be influenced by the relational value of those with whom they associate.

Prejudice and Discrimination

Although prejudice and discrimination are usually conceptualized in terms of negative attitudes and behavior, respectively, they also typically involve low relational value. When people are prejudiced against members of a particular group, they not only evaluate those individuals negatively, but often place a low value on interacting and developing relationships with them (unless the individual provides some desired commodity such as sex or cheap labor). Similarly, the targets of discrimination are people whose relational value is perceived to be low. (People do not discriminate against those whose relationships they value.) In some cases, the prejudiced person may even acknowledge that the target possesses what most people view as socially desirable attributes but nonetheless harbors negative feelings toward the target, devalues him or her as a viable relational partner or group member, and acts in discriminatory ways.

In many ways, the psychological impact of prejudice and discrimination on their targets may come more from relational devaluation and rejection than from negative evaluations or prejudicial attitudes. Although people may be frustrated or angered when others perceive them negatively, being avoided, excluded, and ostracized may take a larger toll on people's well-being (Richman & Leary, 2009; Williams, 2007). Given that people possess a strong and pervasive motive to be accepted, chronic deprivation of acceptance and belonging produces a number of negative effects that go beyond negative emotion. For example, studies of people who are targets of ongoing prejudice and discrimination find strong support for an association between self-reports of discrimination and lower psychological well-being (Dion & Earn, 1995; Kessler, Mickelson, & Williams, 1999; Landrine & Klonoff, 1996; Sellers & Shelton, 2003; Thompson, 1996). For example, among immigrants, perceived discrimination in the new country was the strongest single predictor of stress and homesickness (Tartakovsky, 2007).

Laboratory analogues of ethnic discrimination and mistreatment are also associated with cardiovascular reactions that mirror the effects of explicit rejection (Armstead, 1989; Harrell, Hall, & Taliaferro, 2003; Merritt, Bennett, Williams, Edwards, & Sollers, 2006). Chronic experiences of mistreatment and discrimination may also increase the degree to which people react to subsequent stressors. Research shows, for example, that past experiences of subtle mistreatment (e.g., being ignored or treated with less courtesy and respect than other people) were related to higher diastolic blood pressure reactivity among African Americans, but not European Americans, during a speech task (Guyll, Matthews, & Bromberger, 2001). Such findings suggest that pervasive and chronic rejection may have long-term effects on physiological responses to socially stressful events.

Implicit Devaluation and Rejection

Relational devaluation is often subtle, and people sometimes feel rejected when other people treat them in ways that, although not explicitly rejecting, convey that they have low relational value.

Criticism

Although criticism is not necessarily explicitly rejecting, it can hurt people's feelings and make them feel rejected because it connotes low relational value in two ways (Feeney, 2004; Leary, Springer, et al., 1998). First, criticism inherently conveys that another person believes that the target possesses some undesirable characteristic, and as discussed in this chapter, possessing undesirable attributes undermines one's relational value. Therefore, although a criticism may contain no explicit suggestion of relational devaluation or rejection, the fact that another person regards something about the target negatively may connote that the target's relational value is lower than he or she desires it to be.

Second, the fact that another person voiced a criticism might be interpreted as an indication of low relational value. Even among close friends, critical comments can lead people to reason that "If you really valued our relationship, you wouldn't say such a thing." People may view the expression of a criticism as reflecting lower-than-desired

relational value even if they recognize that the criticism is accurate and justified.

Bullying

Bullying and malicious teasing also connote that the target has low relational value in the eyes of the bully. As in the case of criticism, people who are bullied may conclude, quite reasonably, that people do not bully and harass those whose relationships they value, and thus bullying is prima facie evidence of low relational value. Thus, whatever other effects bullying may have—humiliation, fear of physical harm, and lowered status, for example—being bullied has many of the same effects as "purer" forms of rejection, such as depression, social withdrawal, avoidant behaviors, anger, and lowered self-esteem (Vernberg, Abwender, Ewell, & Beery, 1992; Schwartz, Dodge, & Coie, 1993). Interestingly, children who are bullied suffer less severe psychological consequences if they witness other children being bullied as well (Nishina & Juvonen, 2005), possibly because widespread bullying does not connote that one has uniquely low relational value.

Betrayal

Betrayal undermines relationships in a number of ways, but one source of its potency involves the fact that being betrayed connotes that one has low relational value to the betrayer. Based on her review of the literature on betrayal, Fitness (2001) concluded that "every betrayal implies interpersonal rejection and/or a devaluation of the relationship between two parties" (p. 77). Put simply, people typically do not engage in acts of betrayal with respect to people whose relationships they value greatly. Thus, when a spouse has an affair, the betrayed partner cannot help but to conclude that the partner did not sufficiently value the marital relationship.

Interpersonal Favoritism

People also experience lower-than-desired relational value when they perceive that another person favors some other person, whom they regard as an equal or even inferior, over them. For example, an employee who perceives that the boss unjustly favors another worker or a child who believes that a parent favors a sibling over him or her will likely feel rejected.

In a study of perceived favoritism within families (Fitness, 2005), nearly 69% of college students perceived that there had been a favorite in their family, and about half of those indicated that the family favorite was a sibling rather than them. Given that the average family size is larger than two, this pattern suggests a bias to assume that the family favorite was oneself more than is probably the case, but overall, about a third of all respondents thought that their parents had favored a brother or sister over them. In addition, about 80% of the respondents indicated that their family also had a "black sheep"—someone who was not approved of, liked, or included as much as other family members—and 21% indicated that they were the black sheep of their family. According to respondents, other family members reacted toward black sheep with responses that included chilly politeness (7%), coldness (9%), and total exclusion (51%). The consequences of being a family nonfavorite, or worse, the black sheep, have not been widely studied in adults (see, however, Brody, Copeland, Sutton, Richardson, & Guyer, 1998; Fitness, 2005), but they presumably resemble the consequences of other types of rejection.

The Common Link

As can be seen, interpersonal rejection can take many forms that include not only explicit indications that one is not accepted but also phenomena such as stigmatization, discrimination, bullying, betrayal, favoritism, and so on. These various manifestations of rejection differ in important ways, but they share low relational value as a common feature. Whatever other implications these events may have, they convey to people that others do not regard their relationships to be as valuable or important as the person desires them to be. Unfortunately, researchers who study each of these phenomena have rarely considered ways in which each one resembles and differs from the others. More integration across social psychological phenomena in which low relational value is involved would be useful.

REACTIONS TO REJECTION

Perceiving that one is rejected by other people is a potent experience, with widespread effects on emotions, self-perceptions, social judgments, and interpersonal behavior. In attempting to understand the ways in which real and imagined rejections affect people, theorists have stressed that rejection episodes are typically complex and multifaceted events that have important implications for the person beyond the fact that he or she merely has low relational value or suffered the loss of a social relationship. Williams's (2001) model of ostracism directly addresses this point, noting that rejection poses a threat not only to belonging but also to self-esteem, perceived control, and one's sense of having a meaningful existence. A number of studies have confirmed this notion, showing that people who have been rejected, even in relatively trivial ways (such as not being included in an online ball-tossing game), consistently report lowered belonging, self-esteem, control, and sense of having a meaningful life (for reviews,

see Williams, 2001, 2007). In addition to constituting a threat to these important predictors of psychological well-being, being rejected often has other implications for other aspects of people's lives, such as their safety (as when a young adult is kicked out of the house by his or her parents and has nowhere else to go), financial security (as when a person's well-paid spouse ends the marriage or a person is fired from a job), and reputation (as when public breakups bring information to light that damages one's social image). Because rejections often threaten more than a person's relational value, acceptance, and belonging, researchers must be careful to distinguish the effects of rejection per se from the effects of other factors that may accompany or result from rejection.

Emotional Responses

A clear example of the importance of determining whether certain effects are caused by rejection or by other factors, involves the array of strong emotions that people experience when they are rejected. Rejection experiences typically evoke negative emotions such as hurt feelings, sadness, anger, and loneliness. However, the question arises whether each of these emotions arises from rejection per se or whether some arise from other factors that may accompany episodes of rejection.

Hurt Feelings

The emotion that is most closely associated with perceiving that one's relational value is lower than desired is hurt feelings. Cognitive appraisals of low or declining relational value reliably cause people's feelings to be hurt (Buckley, Winkel, & Leary, 2004; Snapp & Leary, 2001). Thus, the situations that cause hurt feelings invariably involve events that lead people to infer that others do not value their relationship as much as they would like them to.

A content analysis of people's descriptions of instances in which their feelings had been hurt identified six categories of hurtful events, all of which connoted low relational evaluation: active disassociation (i.e., explicit rejection), passive dissociation (i.e., being ignored or avoided), criticism, betrayal, teasing, and feeling unappreciated or taken for granted (Leary, Springer, Negel, Ansell, & Evans, 1998). Similarly, a study of hurt feelings in romantic relationships identified five categories of hurtful events that occur specifically in close relationships: active disassociation, passive disassociation, criticism, infidelity, and deception (e.g., lying and breaking promises) (Feeney, 2004). In each instance, interpreting such events as indications that their partner does not adequately value their relationship leads people to experience hurt feelings. Along the same lines, most of the categories of hurtful events identified in another study of hurt feelings connoted that another person does not adequately value one's relationship, as when one is explicitly rejected, betrayed, or personally attacked (Vangelisti, Young, Carpenter-Theune, & Alexander, 2005). In other cases, low relational evaluation is implicit but nonetheless present, as when others damage one's self-concept, shatter one's hopes, say insulting things, or use inappropriate or spiteful humor (Vangelisti et al.). In a study of hurt feelings in parent-child relationships, most of the events that children and mothers considered hurtful involved relational devaluation, such as being disparaged or disregarded (Mills, Nazar, & Farrell, 2002).

Experimental investigations also show that inducing a sense of low relational value—for example by leading the participant to believe that others do not wish to interact with or get to know them—elicits hurt feelings. When research participants have been led to believe that they were selected last for a team (Bourgeois & Leary, 2001), that another person was disinterested in what they were saying (Snapp & Leary, 2001), that others excluded them from a ball-tossing game (Eisenberger et al., 2003), or that others did not want to work with them (Buckley et al., 2004), participants reported feeling hurt (compared with participants who received feedback indicating that others valued and accepted them). Furthermore, participants' ratings of how accepted or valued they felt, whether in laboratory experiments or when reporting on real-life rejection episodes, correlated strongly with how hurt they reported feeling (e.g., Buckley et al., 2004; Leary, Springer, et al., 1998). Also, the greater the discrepancy between people's ratings of desired and perceived relational value, the more hurt they felt (Leary & Leder, 2009).

An intriguing question that has garnered considerable interest is why hurt feelings "hurt" in ways that other aversive emotions, such as sadness or anxiety, do not (see Eisenberger & Lieberman, 2005; MacDonald, in press). Theorists have speculated that, during the course of mammalian evolution, the neurological system that responds to threats to social connections was built on top of more primitive systems that are involved the experience of physical pain (MacDonald, in press; MacDonald & Leary, 2005a; MacDonald, Kinsbury, & Shaw, 2005; Panksepp, 1998). The experience of physical pain involves activity in two distinct neurological systems (Craig & Dostrovsky, 1999; Price, 2000). The pain sensation system transfers sensory information from the site of a physical injury to the brain. At the same time, the pain affect system mediates the emotional and motivational features of pain—creating emotional distress and a desire to terminate the painful sensations. The "hurt feelings" that result from rejection may be painful because the sting of social rejection is processed via the pain affect system that imbues physical injury with its emotionally aversive qualities (MacDonald & Leary, 2005a, b).

Growing evidence supports this hypothesis. An experiment in which participants' brains were imaged using functional magnetic resonance imaging while they were ostracized showed that social exclusion activated the anterior cingulate cortex and right ventral pre-frontal cortex (Eisenberger et al., 2003), areas that are also involved in the pain affect system (Rainville, 2002). Furthermore, certain personality characteristics, such as extraversion, trait anxiety, aggressiveness, and depression, moderate reactions to physical and social sources of pain in similar ways (see MacDonald & Leary, 2005a). Additional evidence from animal models implicates similar areas of the neuroendocrine system and brain in reactions to both physical injury and social separation (Panksepp, 1998). Furthermore, being rejected lowers people's tolerance for physical pain (DeWall & Baumeister, 2006), and analgesics that are typically taken for physical pain may attenuate hurt feelings that are caused by rejection (DeWall, MacDonald, Webster, Tice, & Baumeister, 2007). Together, these findings suggest that the hurt feelings that people experience when they feel relationally devalued and rejected may arise from some of the same neurological mechanisms as those involved in processing physical pain. The evolutionary reason for this link seems clear: just as physical pain warns people of threats to their physical well-being and motivates actions that minimize further injury to their bodies, social pain (i.e., hurt feelings) warns people of threats to their social connections, which during evolutionary history would have had negative consequences for their physical survival as well.

Although feeling devalued reliably elicits hurt feelings, rejection can also evoke other emotions such as sadness and anger. However, whereas hurt feelings result from perceived low relational value per se, the other emotions that often accompany hurt appear to be caused by other features of the situation. Rejection episodes typically involve multiple outcomes in addition to relational devaluation, and these other features may evoke other emotions. For example, if a rejection event frustrates the person's efforts to obtain certain outcomes, particularly in an unjustified manner, the person might feel angry because appraisals of unjustified harm elicit anger (Smith & Lazarus, 1993). Similarly, because appraisals of loss elicit sadness, interpersonal rejections that involve the loss of an existing or potential relationship should cause people to feel sad. Likewise, a rejection episode that puts the person in danger of harm might cause anxiety. Research shows that, although rejection consistently causes hurt feelings, whether other emotions also occur depends on how people appraise the causes and implications of the rejection episode (Leary & Leder, 2009).

Loneliness and Homesickness

Two additional emotional experiences that are closely linked to perceived deficiencies in one's social connections are loneliness and homesickness. Loneliness and homesickness are not always caused by rejection, but they sometimes are, as when a person is abandoned by his or her romantic partner soon after the couple moves to a new city. Both loneliness and homesickness are tied to the perception that one's social network is inadequate, and there may be good reasons for considering homesickness a special case of loneliness with the added feature that the lonely person longs for home.

People feel lonely when their social relationships are less satisfying than they desire (Peplau & Perlman, 1982). Loneliness is not the same as being alone, and it is not necessarily attenuated by being with other people. Even so, people tend to feel lonelier when their social networks are small, and when they have fewer interactions with friends and family members (Dykstra, van Tilburg, & de Jong Gierveld, 2005; Pinquart & Sörensen, 2003). Thus, factors that reduce the opportunity for social interactions with close others increase loneliness (Shaver, Furman, & Buhrmester, 1985), and the quality of people's social relationships is more important in predicting loneliness than the frequency or length of social interactions (Pinquart & Sörensen, 2003). For example, close marriages that satisfy the partners' needs for a confidant reduce loneliness more than marriages that are less close even if the amount of interaction between the partners is the same in both cases (Olson & Wong, 2001).

Once people feel lonely, they react more strongly to negative social events and experience fewer benefits from positive interpersonal experiences (Hawkley, Preacher, & Cacioppo, 2007). As a result, lonely people tend to perceive social exchanges, even supportive ones, as less fulfilling (Hawkley, Burleson, Berntson, & Cacioppo, 2003) and believe that they do not have control over their ability to fulfill their needs for acceptance and social contact (Solano, 1987). Furthermore, people who feel lonely often act in ways that are seen by others as anxious and negative in tone, which can lead other people to view them less positively (Lau & Gruen, 1992). For example, studies showed that lonely people are less accepting of other people than are the nonlonely (Rotenberg & Kmill, 1992; Wittenberg & Reis, 1986), and that lonely students were less responsive to their classmates during class discussions and provided less appropriate and less effective feedback than nonlonely students (Anderson & Martin, 1995). Paradoxically, then, the behaviors of lonely people often lead others to distance themselves, further lowering perceived acceptance, diminishing interpersonal contact, and increasing loneliness (Cacioppo & Hawkley, 2005).

When the possibility of rejection is salient, people who already feel lonely become particularly attuned to signs of social acceptance and rejection (Gardner et al., 2005; Pickett et al., 2004). However, their greater attentiveness to social cues does not necessarily lead lonely people to perceive other people's reactions more accurately. In fact, people who feel lonely are less accurate at decoding facial and postural expressions of emotion than less lonely people (Pickett & Gardner, 2005; Pitterman & Nowicki, 2004). Whether this effect is due to the fact that being lonely biases people's perceptions of other people or reflects pre-existing differences in emotional intelligence among people who are predisposed versus are not predisposed to be lonely is unclear. Given that this finding contradicts other research showing that people who feel rejected are more accurate in their perceptions of others (Bernstein et al., in press; Gardner et al., 2005; Pickett et al., 2004), more research is needed on this question.

In contrast with loneliness, which has been studied extensively, research on homesickness is in its infancy. People who are homesick feel sad and lonely, are apathetic and listless, ruminate about their relationships back home, and long to return to a more familiar environment (Fisher & Hood, 1987; Van Tilberg, 2005). Much of the distress of homesickness arises from the loss of regular contact with family and friends in one's previous environment, but some of the feelings associated with homesickness may also come from being in an unfamiliar, unpredictable environment in which one has less control than one had in the "home" environment, and experiencing changes in one's roles and self-concept. People who feel homesick also may experience a conflict between the desire to acclimate to and take advantage of the new situation, and the desire to flee the new situation and return home (Fisher, 1989). The intensity of homesickness is further increased when the person genuinely dislikes his or her new social environment (Archer, Ireland, Amos, Broad, & Currid, 1998).

Emotional Numbing

As we have seen, most studies show that rejection episodes cause an array of negative emotions, some of which are due to perceiving that one has low relational value and some of which are due to the perceived causes and consequences of being rejected. (For a meta-analysis of findings involving the effects of laboratory-manipulated rejection on negative affect, see Blackhart et al., 2009). However, some experiments have found evidence that rejection may cause "emotional numbing" instead (Baumeister & DeWall, 2005; Twenge, Catanese, & Baumeister, 2003).

Most (although not all) of the studies that have failed to find emotional effects of rejection have used a paradigm in which participants are told, on the basis of a measure that they completed earlier, that they are the type of person "who will end up alone later in life" and that "when you're past the age where people are constantly forming new relationships, you'll end up being alone more and more" (Twenge et al., 2003, p. 416). Unlike paradigms that lead participants to feel rejected by people in the current situation, the you-will-be-alone-later-in-life manipulation presumably does not make participants feel rejected at the present time, but rather raises the specter of future social isolation at some unspecified time in the future. Thus, this method of inducing rejection should not be expected to evoke precisely the same emotional reactions as when people feel devalued or rejected in their current situation. Furthermore, the unexpected, vague, and distal nature of the feedback may cause people to be puzzled or consternated rather than to feel relationally devalued.

A few other studies that have induced rejection more directly have also found no effects of acceptance versus rejection on emotion, but null effects are always difficult to interpret. Clearly, rejection sometimes fails to evoke negative emotions, but the dominant finding is that it usually does (Blackhart et al., 2009). In fact, even when efforts are made to counterbalance the negative emotions that arise from rejection, by offering financial gain for being ostracized for example, participants still report negative feelings (Van Beest & Williams, 2006).

State Self-esteem

Perceiving that one is devalued or rejected reliably causes changes in state self-esteem—how people feel about and evaluate themselves at the present time. In laboratory experiments, manipulations that convey low relational value through rejection, disapproval, disinterest, or ostracism consistently reduce participants' state self-esteem (Leary, Cottrell, & Phillips, 2001; Leary, Haupt, Strausser, & Chokel, 1998; Leary et al., 1995; Nezlek, Kowalski, Leary, Blevins, & Holgate, 1997; Williams, Govan, Croker, Tynan, Cruickshank, & Lam, 2002; Zadro, Williams, & Richardson, 2005). Similarly, rejecting events in everyday life, such as unrequited love and being bullied, are associated with negative self-feelings (Baumeister, Wotman, & Stillman, 1993; Nishina & Juvonen, 2005), and longitudinal research shows that perceived relational value prospectively predicts changes in self-esteem over time (Murray, Griffin, Rose, & Bellavia, 2003; Srivastava & Beer, 2005). Even imagining being rejected can lower state self-esteem (Vandevelde & Miyahara, 2005). Although some people claim that their feelings about themselves are not affected by whether others value and accept them, research shows that even people who claim to be wholly unconcerned with other people's approval and acceptance show changes in

state self-esteem when they receive devaluing feedback from other people (Leary, Gallagher, et al., 2003). (See Blackhart et al., 2009, for a meta-analysis of the effects of rejection on self-esteem.)

Many researchers have been surprised to find that rejection can evoke negative emotions and lower self-esteem regardless of the identity of the rejector and whether the rejection has any meaningful consequences for the rejected person. People are distressed and deflated when rejected by people whose acceptance is inconsequential and even by people whom they dislike (Gonsalkorale & Williams, 2007). Most laboratory-based experiments that have shown effects of rejection on emotions and state self-esteem have not only involved rejections by strangers, but often participants never actually meet the person who ostensibly rejected them (the feedback was conveyed via written rating or by computer). Furthermore, rejection causes changes in emotion and state self-esteem even when others have little or no basis for judging the target as an individual and, thus, the devaluing feedback does not reflect in any way on the target's personal qualities. For example, effects of rejection of emotion and self-esteem have been obtained when participants are left out of an online ball-tossing computer game with anonymous people located in other parts of the world (Williams, Cheung, & Choi, 2000) and when the rejector has only superficial information about the rejectee, such as his or her name, hometown, and favorite class (Snapp & Leary, 2001). Even rejection by a computer can reduce self-esteem and elicit negative emotions (Zadro, Williams, & Richardson, 2004).

Perhaps more surprisingly, people can be as affected by rejections by members of outgroups as by members of their own group (Williams et al., 2000) and are even hurt when rejected by members of outgroups that they despise (such as the Ku Klux Klan; Gonsalkorale & Williams, 2007). Also, when inconsequential ostracism (being ignored during a computer ball-tossing game) was paired with financial rewards and inclusion led to financial loss, participants still experienced threats to belonging and self-esteem, and reported negative affect (van Beest & Williams, 2006).

The fact that people are affected by inconsequential rejections by strangers who the person will not meet and who have no information about him or her as an individual suggests that people are predisposed to react to cues indicating low relational value regardless of their source, at least initially. Williams and Zadro (2005) suggested that the early warning system that alerts people to possible threats to belonging is indiscriminate with respect to the identity of the rejector. Although people may be able to override their initial response by telling themselves that the other person's acceptance of them is irrelevant and inconsequential, their first response is to experience negative affect and lowered self-esteem. This feature of the sociometer may reflect the fact that, in the ancestral environment in which human evolution occurred, virtually all of a person's interactions were with members of one's own clan, individuals whose acceptance and good will always mattered. Thus, psychological mechanisms did not evolve to distinguish important from unimportant rejections; any indication that one had low relational value had to be taken seriously. In contrast, people living in modern industrialized societies interact regularly with scores of people whose acceptance does not matter in any way, but the early warning system that Williams and Zadro described was designed to respond to any and all signs of possible rejection.

Ancillary Effects of Rejection

Fundamentally, rejection threatens people's desire to be relationally valued and accepted, and yet, as noted earlier, rejection episodes can have other consequences as well. Williams (2001) suggested that rejection threatens four fundamental needs: for belonging (acceptance), self-esteem, control, and meaningful existence. We have already dealt in depth with the impact of rejection on acceptance and belonging, and as we have seen, rejection invariably lowers state self-esteem (although proponents of sociometer theory would suggest that this is because self-esteem is an aspect of the system that monitors acceptance and belonging, and not because people have a "need" for self-esteem; Leary, 2006).

In addition, being rejected undermines people's sense of control over important outcomes (Williams, 2001). Rejection usually reflects a unilateral decision by one or more people to distance themselves from the target individual, and the target typically has no recourse or control. Furthermore, people's sense of control may be lowered further when the cause of the rejection is unclear, as if often the case because rejectors do not always provide full and true reasons for the rejection. Consistent with the suggestion that lack of interpretative control makes it more difficult for people to cope with stressful events, rejections that are causally unclear are more distressing (Sommer, Williams, Ciarocco, & Baumeister, 2001).

Williams's (2001) model also suggests that rejection undermines people's sense of having a meaningful existence because social connections are essential for the sense that one's life has meaning (James, 1890). The effects of rejection on meaningfulness are obvious in extreme cases in which people are shunned by everyone in their community or chronically ostracized by significant others. Case studies of people who have been given the silent treatment, banished, or ostracized by a large number of people suggest that wholesale ostracism leads people to feel that they do not exist and that their life has no meaning (Williams, 2001). However, research evidence shows that even minor

rejection episodes can also lead to a decrease in meaning (Zadro et al., 2004).

The fact that rejection episodes threaten more than one's relational value, acceptance, and belonging suggests that some of the emotional and behavioral consequences of rejection are not due to relational devaluation per se but rather to the effects of rejection on other psychological processes. For example, the depression that may arise in the aftermath of an important rejection might not be merely because one is not relationally valued but also because of the learned helplessness that arises from a perceived lack of control over the situation (Abramson, Seligman, & Teasdale, 1978). Similarly, some of the ways in which people react after being rejected may arise from their sense that life has lost some (or all) of its meaning rather than from low relational value per se (Williams, 2007; Zadro et al., 2004).

DEALING WITH THREATS TO AFFILIATION, ACCEPTANCE, AND BELONGING

People's behavioral reactions when they perceive that they are insufficiently accepted are quite complex. When rejected, people often seek ways to strengthen their social connections with those who have rejected them or with other people who were not involved in the rejection episode, or both, but they may also withdraw socially or behave in antisocial fashion, reactions that undermine rather than restore their social connections. Overall, people's reactions to rejection seem to reflect a mixture of three goals: to increase relational value and acceptance, to protect themselves from further rejection and hurt, and to exact revenge on those who have devalued or rejected them. How people respond in any particular moment after a rejection episode reflects which of these goals is dominant at the time (Richman & Leary, 2009; Williams, 2007).

Restoring Social Connections

Interpersonal rejection appears to stimulate a desire to affiliate and connect with other people. People who are rejected cooperate more with others (Ouwerkerk, Kerr, Galluci, & Van Lange, 2005), conform more to other people's opinions (Williams et al., 2000), work harder in group settings (Williams & Sommer, 1997), and allocate higher cash awards to other people (Maner et al., 2007), all of which may reflect efforts to increase relational value and social acceptance. Furthermore, priming participants to think about a time that they had been excluded increased their desire to meet new people and to make new friends (Maner et al., 2007, Study 1). In another study, participants who were given feedback, ostensibly based on a personality inventory they had completed earlier, that they were likely to end up alone later in life showed an increased preference to work with others rather than alone on a subsequent task (Maner et al., 2007, Study 2). However, as noted earlier, this experimental manipulation may not induce a sense of being currently rejected as opposed to opening the prospect of being rejected many years in the future.

Being rejected may also increase the degree to which people perceive that others who were not involved in the rejection are nicer, friendlier, and more desirable (Maner et al., 2007, Study 3). Similarly, people who are high in the need to belong appear to downplay the degree to which they have personally experienced discrimination (Carvallo & Pelham, 2006). Such biases in perceptions of other people may make it easier for people who feel inadequately accepted to seek out alternative sources of acceptance. However, under certain circumstances, being rejected by one person or group may lead people to regard other people as potentially more threatening and rejecting as well. For example, people who are high in fear of negative evaluation do not perceive other people as nicer and friendlier after being rejected (Maner et al., Study 4). Research is needed to identify the conditions under which people who are rejected perceive others as more versus less friendly and approachable.

Some of the behaviors that rejected people enact to strengthen social connections may be automatic and nonconscious. As noted earlier, behavioral mimicry—the tendency to imitate the behavior of others without awareness—increases after rejection. Participants who were excluded from an online ball-tossing game nonverbally mimicked a confederate more than those who were included (Lakin & Chartrand, 2003). Given that nonconscious mimicry enhances the target's liking for the mimicker and ratings of the positivity of the interaction (Chartrand & Bargh, 1999), this effect may reflect a nonconscious tactic for increasing acceptance after being rejected. Indeed, the experimental confederate in a behavioral mimicry study rated interactions with excluded participants who mimicked him more positively than interactions with participants who had been included (Lakin & Chartrand).

Presumably, people who perceive that they have been rejected would prefer to restore their acceptance and belonging by building social connections with real people. However, in instances in which people who feel rejected are unable to increase their relational value and acceptance by other people, they may use cognitive means to restore a subjective sense of belonging. For example, people who feel inadequately connected with others sometimes "snack" on symbolic reminders of their social connections, just as people who cannot eat a meal may snack to hold off their hunger (Gardner, Pickett, Jefferis, & Knowles, 2005).

People may engage in social snacking by rereading e-mail messages or letters from friends and loved ones, recalling pleasant social connections, daydreaming about significant others, or looking at photographs that remind them of their social relationships. Research shows that people who score high in the need to belong engage in social snacking more often than those who score low in the need to belong, presumably as a means of maintaining a subjective sense of acceptance. Furthermore, participants who imagined being alone all day showed a higher tendency to engage in social snacking (Gardner, Jefferis, & Knowles, 2009).

Social snacking and other reminders of one's interpersonal connections appear to ameliorate some of the negative effects of being rejected. For example, thinking and writing about one's friends lowered people's reactions to being rejected (Twenge, Baumeister, DeWall, Ciarocco, & Bartels, 2007). Likewise, parasocial relationships—attachments to movie stars, television personalities, musicians, sports figures, and other favorite celebrities—may provide comfort and a sense of social connection even though the "relationship" is distal and nonreciprocated (Gardner et al., 2005; Koenig & Lessan, 1985). Parasocial relationships may provide these emotional benefits because evolution had no reason to design the human brain to distinguish real people from televised images.

Companion animals can also provide social connections and a sense of acceptance. Relationships with pets give many people an ongoing source of social contact that reduces loneliness, provides emotional support, and promotes well-being (Collis & McNicholas, 1998; Krause-Parello, 2008; Serpell, 2002). Research also shows that human-pet relationships promote physical health among individuals, such as the elderly, who lack sufficient social contacts with other people (Staats, Pierfelice, Kim, & Crandell, 1999).

When people lose relational value because they have behaved in a way that has damaged their image as a desirable interpersonal partner or group member, they may engage in an array of remedial behaviors that attempt to repair their social image and restore their relational value. Often, people's first remedial step involves apologizing. Apologies have historically been conceptualized as tactics that repair one's social image (Schlenker & Weigold, 1992), but they may be viewed more broadly as ways of reestablishing one's relational value in the aftermath of an undesired behavior or outcome that has lowered the person's relational value to other people. A sincere apology conveys that people recognize that their behavior has violated foundational conditions of social acceptance, and are concerned enough about its impact and others' judgments to acknowledge and correct it. In contrast, the person who does not apologize after misbehaving conveys either that he or she is unaware that the action might undermine social acceptance or, worse, simply does not care. This functional understanding of apologies appears at a young age, presumably because most parents are adamant about ingraining in their children the importance of saying "I'm sorry" when they do something wrong. Children as young as 3 years old evaluate those who apologize for a wrongdoing more favorably than those who do not apologize (Darby & Schlenker, 1982).

When the infraction is minor, a casual and brief apology is usually sufficient to repair the damage to one's image and to restore relational value. However, when transgressions are more serious, people must apologize more strongly and accompany their apologies with expressions of distress and remorse. The more severe the incident, the more effortful apology the perpetrator is expected to express before the apology is accepted by other people (Schlenker & Darby, 1981). Of course, in extreme cases of antisocial behavior, even strong, sincere apologies cannot repair the person's image sufficiently to restore relational value to its pre-infraction level.

Most research has focused on apologies that are made after one has behaved in a way that damaged one's image and undermined relational value. However, people sometimes apologize before or at the same time that the undesired behavior occurs (*ex ante* apologies). For example, people may apologize in advance for negative outcomes that they will create in the future (e.g., "I'm sorry, but I will be late for our meeting tomorrow.") or apologize concurrently with performance of an action that may lead others to devalue them (e.g., "I'm sorry that I have to do this, but you're fired."). Research suggests that apologies offered beforehand may have different effects than those offered afterward on perceptions of the apologizer, judgments of fairness, and motives for revenge (Skarlicki, Folger, & Gee, 2004), but more research on *ex ante* apologies is needed.

People also reduce the impact of undesirable behaviors on interpersonal acceptance through accounts, which are explanations for why one engaged in an unacceptable behavior (Gonzales, Pederson, Manning, & Wetter, 1990; Schlenker, 1980; Scott & Lyman, 1968). Theorists have distinguished among three primary types of accounts: refusals, excuses, and justifications (Austin, 1956; Schlenker, 1980; Turnbull, 1992). (Other, less frequently used types of accounts include concessions, requests, and disclaimers.) The refusal account, also known as a defense of innocence, involves a denial that the person was responsible for a wrongdoing or, often, that a wrongdoing even occurred. When successful, a refusal account immediately restores the person's relational value to its pre-incident level.

When people cannot plausibly maintain their innocence, they often offer excuses. Excuses admit that a negative behavior or outcome occurred but try to reduce one's perceived responsibility for it (Snyder & Higgins, 1988). If others accept them, excuses reduce the person's perceived responsibility for the behavior in question, and thus reduce somewhat the degree to which people draw negative inferences about the person from his or her actions. Put differently, successful excuses help to mitigate damage to the person's relational value.

Whereas excuses minimize one's responsibility for negative outcome, justifications reduce the perceived negativity of the event itself (Schlenker, 1980; Scott & Lyman, 1968). A justification accepts personal responsibility for the outcome but offers reasons why the outcome was not as bad as others believe it to be. For example, people can claim that the misbehavior was really not serious (direct minimization), that the negative event was the result of an otherwise positive action (claimed beneficence), that the behavior was not as bad as what other people do (comparative justification), or that behaving appropriately took a back seat to some superordinate goal (principled justification) (Schlenker, 1980). When successful, these various forms of justification help to protect the person's public image and relational value by decreasing the perceived negativity of his or her behavior.

In addition to repairing one's relational value verbally through apologies, excuses, and justifications, people may engage in nonverbal behaviors that convey that they recognize that they performed an action that may result in undesired impressions and relational devaluation (Castelfranchi & Poggi, 1990). These nonverbal appeasement behaviors include facial blushing, gaze aversion, and nervous smiling. People who enact such behaviors after a transgression, whether intentionally or automatically, elicit more favorable reactions from observers. For example, parents are less likely to punish children for a wrongdoing if the children appear embarrassed than if they do not (Semin & Papadopoulou, 1990), and people who appear embarrassed after behaving clumsily are liked more than people who do not seem to be embarrassed (Semin & Manstead, 1982). Thus, although people's first inclination may be to hide their embarrassment, they may benefit by conveying to others that they recognize their misbehavior and feel badly about it. At some level, people seem to realize that nonverbal signs of embarrassment help to repair their social images and protect belonging because believing that others know that one is embarrassed reduces people's distress and reduces their efforts to repair their public image in other ways (Leary, Landel, & Patton, 1996; Miller, 1996).

The nonverbal behaviors that accompany embarrassment, guilt, and shame may reflect human analogues of the appeasement displays that are observed in certain nonhuman primates. When threatened socially, many nonhuman primates perform a set of stereotypic actions that diffuse the threat, and features of these actions can be seen in the nonverbal behaviors of people who have behaved in an undesired fashion that potentially damaged their relational value. For example, the lowered gaze and appeasement grins of chimpanzees resemble the averted eyes and nervous smiling that human beings display after a public blunder (Leary, Britt, Cutlip, & Templeton, 1992). Although primatologists have stressed that the function of appeasement is to reduce conflict and aggression (which it does), appeasement also reduces the likelihood that the offending individual will be ostracized or ignored (De Waal, 2000; Kutsukake & Castles, 2004).

In some instances, a stronger means of demonstrating one's remorse and goodwill is needed, and the transgressor may be required to provide compensation or penance for the wrongdoing (Bottom, Gibson, Daniels, & Murnighan, 2002). Rituals of apology often require some form of repayment or the presentation of a gift (Arno, 1976), and today, people often pay a penance when they have behaved in an inappropriate manner (in terms of buying the offended party a gift, doing favors, or paying fines, among other examples). Offers of penance convey that the transgressor is willing to sacrifice something to be accepted back into the relationship (Bottom, Gibson, Daniels, & Murnighan, 2002). Other people are more likely to forgive others' misdeeds when the perpetrator admits that he or she caused harm and offers to compensate for it (Schmitt, Gollwitzer, Förster, & Montada, 2004). Offers of compensation may be particularly beneficial when they involve a clear sacrifice on the part of the individual (Van Lange, Rusbult, Drigotas, Arriaga, Witcher, & Cox, 1997; Wieselquist, Rusbult, Foster, & Agnew, 1999).

Social Withdrawal

Although people who perceive that their relational value is low often wish to restore their social connections with the rejector or others, they sometimes behave in ways that undermine rather than increase the probability of future acceptance (Richman & Leary, 2009). As Maner and colleagues (2007) observed, people who have been recently rejected can be characterized as "vulnerable but needy" (p. 52). Although they feel a strong need to foster their bonds with other people, their feelings of vulnerability may lead them to distance themselves from others to avoid being hurt further (Vangelisti, 2001; Vangelisti et al., 2005). Not only does continued interaction with the rejector raise the specter of further rejection and hurt, but once they are rejected by one person, people may lose confidence in their acceptability to other people as well. Furthermore, even if they are not worried about being hurt again, people often see little value in interacting with those who do not adequately accept them,

so their motivation to affiliate with those individuals is low. People who are low in self-esteem are particularly likely to engage in defensive withdrawal when they believe that they are not as accepted as they would like to be (Murray, Holmes, MacDonald, & Ellsworth, 1998; Sommer et al., 2001).

Although little research has examined the effects of rejection on social withdrawal and avoidance, shreds of evidence support the idea that people who are concerned about acceptance sometimes distance themselves from others by physically leaving the situation in which they feel rejected or withdrawing socially and psychologically even while remaining physically present (Maner et al., 2007, Study 4). One experiment that explicitly examined behavioral reactions to rejection found that participants who interacted with a person who had previously been disinterested in them dreaded interacting with the person, reported a lower desire to communicate, sat farther away from the person, and oriented their bodies more away from him or her (Waldrip & Jensen-Campbell, 2007). People who are rejected may also display a "sour grapes" reaction (as in the fable of the fox and the grapes) in which they downplay the degree to which they wish to be accepted (Bourgeois & Leary, 2001), a tactic that may both reduce the sting of rejection and make it easier for them to withdraw from further efforts to be accepted.

Similar effects can be seen in social encounters in which the possibility of devaluation and rejection is salient, as when one person in the interaction is stigmatized or belongs to a marginalized social group (Shelton & Richeson, 2006; Shelton, Richeson, & Salvatore, 2005). In a study in which Latino and Asian American participants believed that an interaction partner held prejudiced beliefs about their group, participants not only reported feeling more anxious and hostile about an upcoming interaction with that person, but were also less positive about interacting with outgroup members in general compared with participants who expected to interact with someone who held race-neutral beliefs (Tropp & Wright, 2003).

Of course, members of majority groups are also often concerned about rejection by minorities and, thus, feel anxious about real or impending intergroup interactions (Hyers & Swim, 1998; Swim, Cohen, & Hyers, 1997), particularly when they are concerned about appearing prejudiced (Shelton, 2003). However, unlike members of minority groups, who can often not avoid having to interact with majority group members, members of majority groups sometimes try to avoid intergroup interactions altogether (Fiske & Ruscher, 1993; Swim et al., 1997).

Antisocial Responses

A great deal of research has shown that children and adults who feel rejected often react in antisocial, if not blatantly aggressive ways (e.g., Asher & Coie, 1990; Asher, Rose, & Gabriel, 2001; Buckley et al., 2004; Kupersmidt, Burchinal, & Patterson, 1995; McDougall, Hymel, Vaillancourt, & Mercer, 2001; Twenge, Baumeister, Tice, & Stucke, 2001; Warburton, Williams, & Cairns, 2006). Likewise, certain instances of real-world violence appear to be precipitated by rejection, such as when estranged husbands kill their wives (Barnard, Vera, Vera, & Newman, 1982; Crawford & Gartner, 1992), ostracized students shoot their classmates (Leary, Kowalski, Smith, & Phillips, 2003), and people attack those who have treated them disrespectfully (Cohen, Nisbett, & Bowdle, 1996). People who score high in rejection sensitivity are particularly prone to respond antisocially when they feel rejected (Ayduk, Downey, Testa, Yen, & Shoda, 1999).

These patterns are intriguing because anger, aggression, and other antisocial actions usually fracture rather than repair people's interpersonal relationships. Why, then, are people prone to aggress when rejected? After reviewing the literature on the relationship between rejection and aggression, Leary, Twenge, and Quinlivan (2006) offered several plausible hypotheses that might explain why people sometimes sacrifice acceptance to hurt others. Some such explanations involve processes that are not specific to rejection, such as the possibility that the pain or frustration that results from rejection may lead people to aggress. Other explanations are more directly social-psychological, involving the possibility that people use aggression in an effort to influence others not to abandon them or to control other people (some domestic violence appears to fall into this category; Johnson & Ferraro, 2000), or merely to punish those who have hurt them or treated them unfairly. Another possibility is that rejection lowers the normal restraints against antisocial reactions. People ordinarily hesitate to aggress against those with whom they have relationships because aggression would damage those social bonds. But once people are rejected, the potential costs of aggression are reduced and people are more likely to behave antisocially when they feel inclined to do so.

Research also suggests that rejection may interfere with self-regulation so that rejected people more easily lose control when provoked (Baumeister, DeWall, Ciarocco, & Twenge, 2005; Twenge, Catanese, & Baumeister, 2002). Not only do experimental rejection inductions reduce intelligent thought (Baumeister, Twenge, & Nuss, 2002), but merely making people's stigmatized status salient, even without explicitly rejecting them, can undermine cognitive performance in ways that might impair self-control (Inzlicht, McKay, & Aronson, 2006; Schmader & Johns, 2003). An experiment that used magnetoencephalography to image participants' brains showed that social exclusion compromises executive control of attention in ways

that undermine cognitive performance on a self-control task (Campbell et al., 2006). Interestingly, ostracizing another person can similarly deplete self-control resources (Ciarocco, Sommer, & Baumeister, 2001).

As noted earlier, angry and aggressive reactions to signs of rejection are more common among people who are high rather than low in rejection sensitivity. Downey and her colleagues (Downey & Feldman, 1996; Downey, Freitas, Michaelis, & Khouri, 1998) conceptualized rejection sensitivity as a cognitive-affective processing disposition whereby people anxiously expect, readily perceive, and intensely react to cues of rejection in the behavior of other people. Highly rejection-sensitive people are hypervigilant for cues of rejection when entering interpersonal situations where rejection is possible (Downey, Mougios, Ayduk, London, & Shoda, 2004). When signs of rejection are detected, rejection-sensitive people feel rejected, judge others negatively (Ayduk et al., 1999), and react with hostility, avoidance, depression, or socially inappropriate efforts to avoid rejection (Ayduk, Mendoza-Denton, Mischel, Downey, Peake, & Rodriguez, 2000; Downey & Feldman, 1996; Downey, Feldman, & Ayduk, 2000; Downey et al., 1998). Paradoxically, these reactions tend to elicit rejecting responses from other people, making the feared outcome a reality.

In diary studies of romantic couples, rejection-sensitive women were more likely to become embroiled in conflicts with their partners on days that followed a day on which they felt more rejected (Ayduk et al., 1999; Downey et al., 1998). Similarly, rejection sensitivity predicted greater relationship violence by male college students who were highly invested in their relationships (Downey et al., 2000). Highly rejection-sensitive people are also more likely to aggress against strangers who reject them (Ayduk, Gyurak, & Luerssen, 2007). Similarly, in a study of singers in auditions, rejection sensitivity predicted contestants' aggression and derogation of judges after rejection, as well as indirect efforts to sabotage other singers' success in the audition (DiBenigno, Romero-Canyas, & Downey, 2007). The rejection-hostility link is also evident in rejection-sensitive people's reactions to distant, powerful others who they believe have treated them unfairly. Rejection sensitivity predicts people's withdrawal of support from politicians who they feel betrayed them (Romero-Canyas & Downey, 2003), and hostility toward and distancing from God among religious people who are facing personal difficulties (Anderson, Romero-Canyas, & Downey, 2008).

People who are high in rejection sensitivity have a stronger cognitive association between rejection and hostile thoughts. In sequential priming-pronunciation paradigms, rejection-related words facilitate pronunciation of hostility-related words among people who are high in rejection sensitivity but not among people who are low in rejection sensitivity (Ayduk et al., 1999; Romero-Canyas, Downey, Berenson, Ayduk, & Kang, in press), suggesting an automatic link between rejection and hostile cognitions. These hostile thoughts presumably translate to a higher incidence of anger and aggression among highly rejection-sensitive people.

As noted earlier, antisocial reactions to rejection are paradoxical in that they often undermine one's relational value and cause others to withdraw. This self-fulfilling cycle can be seen in the context of conflicts in dating relationships (Downey et al., 1998). When embroiled in a conflict with their dating partner, high (compared with low) rejection-sensitive women engaged in more negative behaviors such as using a negative tone of voice, criticizing or mocking their partner, and using nonverbal gestures that convey disapproval or disgust. Not surprisingly, such responses tended to lead their partners to distance themselves, which fueled further overreactions from the women. Importantly, women high in rejection sensitivity reacted with greater hostility than women low in rejection sensitivity only when the situation involved feeling rejected, demonstrating that the effect is specific to rejection and not to negative events in general (Ayduk et al., 1999).

Although Downey and colleagues (1998) did not find this pattern in men, they did find that men who were both high in rejection sensitivity and very invested in their romantic relationships were more likely to behave violently toward their dating partners than men who were low in rejection sensitivity or men who were high in rejection sensitivity but less invested in their relationships. Thus, the degree of commitment and investment in a relationship may moderate rejection-sensitive men's reactions to perceived rejection (Downey et al., 1998; Levy, Ayduk, & Downey, 2001). It is unclear why people who are most worried about rejection and invested in their relationships are most likely to behave in ways that damage those relationships when they feel relationally devalued, and this self-defeating pattern deserves further attention.

LONG-TERM CONSEQUENCES OF REJECTION

As discussed in this chapter, transient episodes in which people perceive that others do not adequately value having a relationship with them are highly distressing. Although negative reactions to permanent rejections from close relationships can linger for some time (Leary, Springer, et al., 1998; Vangelisti & Maguire, 2002; Williams, 2001), as long as people eventually restore the damaged relationship or find others to replace it, the hurt is temporary and people show few, if any, long-term effects. However, some people live for long periods with a chronic deficit in acceptance and belonging. For example, people who are stigmatized, who lack the social skills or personal characteristics needed to attract relational partners, or who have little to offer as group members may perceive that others do not value having relationships with them, or worse, that others actively avoid having anything to do with them at all.

Such chronic perceptions of low relational value can have detrimental effects on both psychological well-being and physical health. Most notably, a chronic sense that one is not valued and accepted by other people predicts depression. For example, although the symptoms of loneliness and depression are conceptually and empirically distinct, being lonely strongly predicts depression (Nolen-Hoeksema & Ahrens, 2002). Furthermore, loneliness predicts depression longitudinally in prospective studies (Heikkinen & Kauppinen, 2004) even when certain risk factors that are common to both loneliness and depression are controlled (Cacioppo, Hughes, Waite, Hawkley, & Thisted, 2006). Not surprisingly, people who are high in rejection sensitivity are particularly prone to becoming depressed when they feel rejected (Ayduk, Downey, & Kim, 2001). Unfortunately, once people are depressed, they react more strongly to indications that they are not being accepted (Nezlek et al., 1997), which may compromise their relationships further and fuel further loneliness and dysphoria.

Similarly, children who feel rejected by their peers tend to be depressed, and changes in their status—to more or less rejected—prospectively predict corresponding changes in depression (Boivin, Hymel, & Bukowski, 1995; Boivin, Poulin, & Vitaro, 1994). In fact, some evidence suggests that perceived rejection is the primary predictor of childhood depression (Kupersmidt & Patterson, 1991). This relationship between chronic rejection and depression in children is mediated by awareness of their own rejection. That is, children who were objectively rejected by their peers but who did not recognize (or refused to admit) that they were rejected did not show signs of depression (Panak & Gerber, 1992).

People who feel chronically disconnected from other people experience physical health problems as well. For example, indices of social isolation—such as living alone, reporting low social support, feeling lonely, and experiencing chronic ostracism—are associated with negative health outcomes such as high blood pressure (Uchino, Cacioppo, & Kiecolt-Glaser, 1996), increased likelihood of heart attack (Case, Moss, Case, McDermott, & Eberly, 1992), and increased levels of stress-related hormones that are related to immunological function.

What is unclear is whether these effects are due to having a chronically low sense of relational value, belonging, and social support or to the effects of explicit rejection. Rejection elicits a stresslike response that involves increased systolic and diastolic blood pressure (Stroud, Tanofsky-Kraff, Wilfley, & Salovey, 2000), and the release of cortisol (Blackhart, Echel, & Tice, 2007). Even situations that involve the potential for negative evaluations by other people, such as giving a speech or performing a difficult task in front of an evaluative audience, elicit cortisol release (Dickerson, Gruenewald, & Kemeny, 2004; Dickerson & Kemeny, 2004; Dickerson, Mycek, & Zaldivar, in press). Similarly, feelings of loneliness (which, as noted, arise from perceived deficits in people's social relationships) are associated with greater levels of cortisol on the following day (Adam, Hawkley, Kudielka, & Cacioppo, 2006). Cortisol is beneficial in helping people deal with immediate threats, but ongoing threats to social acceptance may lead to excessive cortisol activity that puts the person at risk for cardiovascular damage, compromised immune function, and other health problems over the long run (Miller, Chen, & Zhou, 2007). Even events that connote relational devaluation more subtly, such as being treated unfairly, are related to elevated blood pressure readings (Matthews, Salomon, Kenyon, & Zhou, 2005). Laboratory analogues of ethnic discrimination and mistreatment are also associated with immediate physiological arousal (see Harrell et al., 2003 for review; see also Armstead, 1989; Guyll et al., 2001; Merritt et al., 2006).

The persistence or chronicity of stressors over time contributes to more negative cardiovascular outcomes than the experience of an acute event or series of discrete events (Williams, Spencer, & Jackson, 1999). Even so, repeated activation of these physiological pathways increases the risk for cardiovascular outcomes such as hypertension (Krieger, 2000). Thus, people who perceive themselves to be regularly devalued or rejected because of ongoing discrimination, rejection, or ostracism are presumably at greater risk. In support of this hypothesis, research on loneliness and chronically low levels of acceptance or belonging finds increased morbidity and premature mortality (Cacioppo & Hawkley, 2005).

To make matters worse, chronic experiences of relational devaluation and discrimination may heighten reactivity to subsequent stressors so that pervasive and chronic rejection may have long-term effects on physiological responses to socially stressful events, possibly paving the way for pathogenic processes associated with heightened physiological reactivity. For example, past experiences of subtle mistreatment (e.g., being ignored or being treated with less courtesy and respect than other people) were related to higher diastolic blood pressure reactivity among African American women during a speech task, whereas this effect was not observed among European Americans (Guyll et al., 2001).

SUMMARY

Human life is predicted on social interaction and the maintenance of a variety of interpersonal relationships. People's efforts to affiliate and to be accepted underlie a great deal of their behavior, and failures to be relationally valued and to foster desired relationships have a strong impact on people's emotions, self-views, social behavior, psychological well-being, and physical health. Although processes that involve affiliation, acceptance, and belonging were understudied for most of the 20th century, we have seen a marked increase in interest in these topics more recently, not only by social and personality psychologists but by developmental and clinical psychologists as well. Even so, research on these fundamental interpersonal processes is in its infancy, and the far-reaching impact of people's efforts to develop and maintain social connections remains a ripe topic for future theorizing and research.

REFERENCES

Abramson, L. Y., Seligman, M. E. P., & Teasdale, J. D. (1978). Learned helplessness in humans: Critique and reformulation. *Journal of Abnormal Psychology, 87*, 49–74.

Adam, E. K., Hawkley, L., Kudielka, M. M., & Cacioppo, J. T. (2006). Day-to-day dynamics of experience-cortisol associations in a population-based sample of older adults. *Proceedings of the National Academy of Sciences, 103*, 17058–17063.

AhYun, K. (2002). Similarity and attraction. In M. Allen, R. W. Preiss, B. M. Gayle, & N. A. Burrell (Eds.), *Interpersonal communication research* (pp. 145–167). Mahwah, NJ: Erlbaum.

Ainsworth, M. S. (1989). Attachments beyond infancy. *American Psychologist, 44*, 709–716.

Allport, G. W. (1954). The historical background of modern social psychology. In G. Lindzey (Ed.), *Handbook of social psychology* (Vol. 1, pp. 3–56). Reading, MA: Addison-Wesley.

Altman, I. (1975). *The environment and social behavior*. Monterey, CA: Brooks/Cole.

Altman, I., & Taylor, D. A. (1973). *Social penetration: The development of interpersonal relationships*. New York: Holt, Rinehart, & Winston.

Anderson, C. M., & Martin, M. M. (1995). The effects of communication motives, interaction involvement, and loneliness on satisfaction. *Small Group Research, 26*, 118–137.

Anderson, V. T., Romero-Canyas, R., & Downey, G. (2008). *Rejection sensitivity predicts attributing distressing events to powerful others. It's all in God's hands and he doesn't love me*. Unpublished manuscript, Columbia University, New York.

Archer, J., Ireland, J., Amos, S. L., Broad, H., & Currid, L. (1998). Derivation of a homesickness scale. *British Journal of Psychology, 89*, 205–221.

Armstead, C. (1989). Relationship of racial stressors to blood pressure responses and anger expression in Black college students. *Health Psychology, 8*, 541–556.

Arno, A. (1976). Ritual reconciliation and conflict management in Fiji. *Oceania, 47*, 49–65.

Asch, S. E. (1956). Studies of independence and submission to group pressure: I. A minority of one against a unanimous majority. *Psychological Monographs, 70*(9, Whole No. 417).

Asher, S. R., & Coie, J. D. (1990). *Peer rejection in childhood*. New York: Cambridge University Press.

Asher, S. R., Rose, A. J., & Gabriel, S. W. (2001). Peer rejection in everyday life. In M. R. Leary (Ed.), *Interpersonal rejection* (pp. 105–142). New York: Oxford University Press.

Austin, J. L. (1970). *Philosophical papers* (2nd ed.). New York: Oxford University Press.

Ayduk, Ö., Downey, G., & Kim, M. (2001). Rejection sensitivity and depressive symptoms in women. *Personality & Social Psychology Bulletin, 27*, 868–877.

Ayduk, Ö., Downey, G., Testa, A., Yen, Y., & Shoda, Y. (1999). Does rejection elicit hostility in rejection sensitive women? *Social Cognition, 17*, 245–271.

Ayduk, Ö., Gyurak, A., & Luerssen, A. (2007). Individual differences in the rejection-aggression link in the hot sauce paradigm: The case of rejection sensitivity. *Journal of Experimental Social Psychology, 44*, 775–782.

Ayduk, Ö., Mendoza-Denton, R., Mischel, W., Downey, G., Peake, P. K., & Rodriguez, M. (2000). Regulating the interpersonal self: Strategic self-regulation for coping with rejection sensitivity. *Journal of Personality & Social Psychology, 79*, 776–792.

Back, M. D., Schmukle, S. C., & Egloff, B. (2008). Becoming friends by chance. *Psychological Science, 19*, 439–440.

Bakan, D. (1966). *The duality of human existence*. Boston: Beacon.

Baldwin, M. W. (1994). Primed relational schemas as a source of self-evaluative reaction. *Journal of Social and Clinical Psychology, 13*, 380–403.

Baldwin, M. W., Carrell, S. E., & Lopez, D. F. (1990). Priming relationship schemas: My advisor and the pope are watching me from the back of my mind. *Journal of Experimental Social Psychology, 26*, 435–454.

Baldwin, M. W., & Main, K. J. (2001). Social anxiety and the cued activation of relational knowledge. *Personality and Social Psychology Bulletin, 27*, 1637–1647.

Baldwin, M. W., & Sinclair, L. (1996). Self-esteem and "if . . . then" contingencies of interpersonal acceptance. *Journal of Personality and Social Psychology, 71*, 1130–1141.

Barnard, G. W., Vera, H., Vera, M. I., & Newman, G. (1982). Till death do us part: A study of spouse murder. *Bulletin of the American Academy of Psychiatry and the Law, 10*, 271–280.

Baum, A., & Greenberg, C. I. (1975). Waiting for a crowd: The behavioral and perceptual effects of anticipated crowding. *Journal of Personality and Social Psychology, 32*, 671–679.

Baumeister, R. F. (1982). A self-presentational view of social phenomena. *Psychological Bulletin, 91*, 3–26.

Baumeister, R. F. (1990). Motives and costs of self-presentation in organizations. In R. A. Giacalone & P. Rosenfeld (Eds.), *Impression management in the organization* (pp. 57–71). Hillsdale, NJ: Erlbaum.

Baumeister, R. F., & DeWall, C. N. (2005). Inner disruption following social exclusion: Reduced intelligent thought and self-regulation failure. In K. D. Williams & W. von Hippel (Eds.), *The social outcast: Ostracism, social exclusion, rejection, and bullying* (pp. 53–73). New York: Psychology Press.

Baumeister, R. F., Dewall, C. N., Ciarocco, N. J., & Twenge, J. M. (2005). Social exclusion impairs self-regulation. *Journal of Personality and Social Psychology, 88*, 589–604.

Baumeister, R. F., & Leary, M. R. (1995). The need to belong: Desire for interpersonal attachments as a fundamental human motivation. *Psychological Bulletin, 117*, 497–529.

Baumeister, R. F., Twenge, J. M., & Nuss, C. K. (2002). Effects of social exclusion on cognitive processes: Anticipated aloneness reduces intelligent thought. *Journal of Personality and Social Psychology, 83*, 817–827.

Baumeister, R. F., Wotman, S. R., & Stillwell, A. M. (1993). Unrequited love: On heartbreak, anger, guilt, scriptlessness, and humiliation. *Journal of Personality and Social Psychology, 64*, 377–394.

Beck, E., Burnet, K. L., & Vosper, J. (2006). Birth-order effects on facets of extraversion. *Personality and Individual Differences, 40*, 953–959.

Berg, J. H., & Wright-Buckley, C. (1988). Effects of racial similarity and interviewer intimacy in a peer counseling analogue. *Journal of Counseling Psychology, 35*, 377–384.

Berger, C. R., Gardner, R. B., Parks, M. R., Schulman, L., & Miller, G. R. (1976). Interpersonal epistemology and interpersonal communication. In G. R. Miller (Ed.), *Explorations in interpersonal communication* (pp. 149–171). Beverly Hills, CA: Sage Publications.

Bernstein, M., Young, S., Brown, C., Sacco, D., & Claypool, H. (2008). Adaptive responses to social exclusion: Social rejection improves detection of real and fake smiles. *Psychological Science, 19*, 981–983.

Blackhart, G. C., Echel, L. A., & Tice, D. M. (2007). Salivary cortisol in response to acute social rejection and acceptance by peers. *Biological Psychology, 75*, 267–276.

Blackhart, G. C., Knowles, M. L., & Bieda, K. (2009). *A meta-analytic review of affective reactions and self-esteem in response to social rejection: Support for the belongingness and sociometer theories.* Manuscript submitted for publication.

Boivin, M., Hymel, S., & Bukowski, W. M. (1995). The roles of social withdrawal, peer rejection, and victimization by peers in predicting loneliness and depressed mood in childhood. *Development and Psychopathology, 7*, 765–785.

Boivin, M., Poulin, F., & Vitaro, F. (1994). Depressed mood and peer rejection in childhood. *Development and Psychopathology, 6*, 483–498.

Bornstein, R. F. (1989). Exposure and affect: Overview and meta-analysis of research, 1968–1987. *Psychological Bulletin, 106*, 265–289.

Bottom, W., Gibson, K. S., Daniels, S., & Murnighan, J. K. (2002). When talk is not cheap: Substantive penance and expressions of intent in rebuilding cooperation. *Organization Science, 13*, 497–513.

Bourgeois, K. S., & Leary, M. R. (2001). Coping with rejection: Derogating those who choose us last. *Motivation and Emotion, 25*, 101–111.

Bowlby, J. (1969). *Attachment and loss, Vol. 1: Attachment*. New York: Basic Books.

Brody, L., Copeland, A., Sutton, L., Richardson, D., & Guyer, M. (1998). Mommy and daddy like you best: Perceived family favoritism in relation to affect, adjustment, and family process. *Journal of Family Therapy, 20*, 269–291.

Buckley, K. E., Winkel, R. E., & Leary, M. R. (2004). Reactions to acceptance and rejection: Effects of level and sequence of relational evaluation. *Journal of Experimental Social Psychology, 40*, 14–28.

Buunk, B. P., van Yperen, N. W., Taylor, S. E., & Collins, R. L. (1991). Social comparison and the drive upward revisited: Affiliation as a response to marital stress. *European Journal of Social Psychology, 21*, 529–546.

Cacioppo, J. T., & Hawkley, L. C. (2005). Social isolation and health, with an emphasis on underlying mechanisms. *Perspectives in Biology and Medicine, 46*, 839–852.

Cacioppo, J. T., Hughes, M. E., Waite, L. J., Hawkley, L. C., & Thisted, R. (2006). Loneliness as a specific risk factor for depressive symptoms in older adults: Cross-sectional and longitudinal analyses. *Psychology and Aging, 21*, 140–151.

Campbell, W. K., Krusemark, E. A., Dyckman, K. A., Brunell, A. B., McDowell, J. E., Twenge, J. M., et al. (2006). A magnetoencephalography investigation of neural correlates for social exclusion and self-control. *Social Neuroscience, 1*, 124–134.

Carvallo, M., & Pelham, B. W. (2006). When fiends become friends: The need to belong and perceptions of personal and group discrimination. *Journal of Personality and Social Psychology, 90*, 94–108.

Case, R. B., Moss, A. J., Case, N., McDermott, M., & Eberly, S. (1992). Living alone after myocardial infarction impact on prognosis. *Journal of the American Medical Association, 267,* 515–519.

Castelfranchi, C., & Poggi, I. (1990). Blushing as a discourse: Was Darwin wrong? In W. R. Crozier (Ed.), *Shyness and embarrassment: Perspectives from social psychology* (pp. 230–254). Cambridge: Cambridge University Press.

Chapman, L. J., Chapman, J. P., Kwapil, T. R., Eckblad, M., & Zinser, M. C. (1994). Putatively psychosis–prone subjects 10 years later. *Journal of Abnormal Psychology, 103,* 171–183.

Chartrand, T. L., & Bargh, J. A. (1999). The chameleon effect: The perception-behavior link and social interaction. *Journal of Personality and Social Psychology, 76,* 893–910.

Cheek, J. M., & Buss, A. H. (1981). Shyness and sociability. *Journal of Personality and Social Psychology, 41,* 330–339.

Cherry, E. C. (1953). Some experiments on the recognition of speech, with one and with two ears. *Journal of Acoustical Society of America, 25,* 975–979.

Christensen, L. J., & Menzel, K. E. (1998). The linear relationship between student reports of teacher immediacy behaviors and perceptions of state motivation and of cognitive, affective, and behavioral learning. *Communication Monographs, 55,* 58–79.

Cialdini, R. B., Kallgren, C. A., & Reno, R. R. (1991). A focus theory of normative conduct: A theoretical refinement and reevaluation of the role of norms in human behavior. In M. Zanna (Ed.), *Advances in experimental social psychology* (Vol. 24, pp. 201–234). New York: Academic Press.

Cialdini, R. B., Vincent, J. E., Lewis, S. K., Catalan, J., Wheeler, D., & Darby, B. L. (1975). Reciprocal concessions procedure for inducing compliance: The door-in-the-face technique. *Journal of Personality and Social Psychology, 31,* 206–215.

Ciarocco, N. J., Sommer, K. L., & Baumeister, R. F. (2001). Ostracism and ego depletion: The strains of silence. *Personality and Social Psychology Bulletin, 27,* 1156–1163.

Cohen, D., Nisbett, R. E., & Bowdle, B. F. (1996). Insult, aggression, and the southern culture of honor: An 'experimental ethnography.' *Journal of Personality and Social Psychology, 70,* 945–960.

Collis, G. M., & McNicholas, J. (1998). A theoretical basis for health benefits of pet ownership: Attachment versus psychological support. In C. C. Wilson & D. C. Turner (Eds.), *Companion animals in human health* (pp. 105–122). Thousand Oaks, CA: Sage.

Colvin, C. R., & Longueuil, D. (2001). Eliciting self-disclosure: The personality and behavioral correlates of the Opener Scale. *Journal of Research in Personality, 35,* 238–246.

Coon, C. S. (1946). The universality of natural groupings in human societies. *Journal of Educational Sociology, 20,* 163–168.

Cotterell, N., Eisenberger, R., & Speicher, H. (1992). Inhibiting effects of reciprocation wariness on interpersonal relationships. *Journal of Personality and Social Psychology, 62,* 658–668.

Craig, A. D., & Dostrovsky, J. O. (1999) Medulla to thalamus. In P. Wall & R. Melzack (Eds.), *Textbook of pain* (pp. 183–214). New York: Churchill Livingstone.

Crawford, M., & Gartner, R. (1992). *Women killing: Intimate femicide in Ontario, 1974–1990.* Toronto: Women We Honour Action Committee.

Crocker, J., & Major, B. (1989). Social stigma and self-esteem: The self-protective properties of stigma. *Psychological Review, 96,* 608–630.

Darby, B. W., & Schlenker, B. R. (1982). Children's reactions to apologies. *Journal of Personality and Social Psychology, 43,* 742–753.

Davis, D., & Vernon, M. L. (2002). Sculpting the body beautiful: Attachment style, neuroticism, and use of cosmetic surgeries. *Sex Roles, 47,* 129–138.

Dean, D. G., Braito, R., Powers, E. A., & Britton, B. (1975). Cultural contradictions and sex roles revisited: A replication and reassessment. *The Sociological Quarterly, 16,* 201–215.

DeCremer, D., & Leonardelli, G. J. (2003). Cooperation in social dilemmas and the need to belong: The moderating effect of group size. *Group Dynamics: Theory, Research, and Practice, 7,* 168–174.

Deluga, R. J., & Perry, J. T. (1991). The relationship of subordinate upward influence behavior, satisfaction, and perceived superior effectiveness with leader-member exchanges. *Journal of Occupational Psychology, 64,* 239–252.

Derber, C. (2000). *The pursuit of attention.* New York: Oxford University Press.

De Waal, F. (2000). Primates: A natural heritage of conflict resolution. *Science, 289,* 586–590.

De Waal, F. (2005). *Our inner ape.* New York: Riverhead Books.

DeWall, C. N., & Baumeister, R. F. (2006). Alone but feeling no pain: Effects of social exclusion on physical pain tolerance and pain threshold, affective forecasting, and interpersonal empathy. *Journal of Personality and Social Psychology, 91,* 1–15.

DeWall, C. N., MacDonald, G., Webster, G. D., Tice, D. M., & Baumeister, R. F. (2007). *Acetaminophen reduces psychological hurt feelings over time.* Manuscript under review, Lexington, KY: University of Kentucky.

DiBenigno, J., Romero-Canyas, R., & Downey, G. (2007). *Do rejection sensitivity and performance predict extreme reactions to rejection for performing artists?* Paper presented at the meeting of the Society for Personality and Social Psychology, Memphis, TN.

Dickerson, S. S., Gruenewald, T. L., & Kemeny, M. E. (2004). When the social self is threatened: Shame, physiology, and health. *Journal of Personality, 72,* 1192–1216.

Dickerson, S. S., & Kemeny, M. E. (2004). Acute stressors and cortisol responses: A theoretical integration and synthesis of laboratory research. *Psychological Bulletin, 130,* 355–391.

Dickerson, S. S., Mycek, P. J., & Zaldivar, F. (2008). Negative social evaluation—but not mere social presence—elicits cortisol responses to a laboratory stressor task. *Health Psychology, 27,* 116–121.

Dion, K. L., & Earn, B. M. (1995). The phenomenology of being a target of prejudice. *Journal of Personality and Social Psychology, 32,* 944–950.

Downey, G., & Feldman, S. I. (1996). Implications of rejection sensitivity for intimate relationships. *Journal of Personality and Social Psychology, 70,* 1327–1343.

Downey, G., Feldman, S., & Ayduk, O. (2000). Rejection sensitivity and male violence in romantic relationships. *Personal Relationships, 7,* 45–61.

Downey, G., Freitas, A. L., Michaelis, B., & Khouri, H. (1998). The self-fulfilling prophecy in close relationships: Rejection sensitivity and rejection by romantic partners. *Journal of Personality and Social Psychology, 75,* 545–560.

Downey, G., Mougios, V., Ayduk, O., London, B. E., & Shoda, Y. (2004) Rejection sensitivity and the defensive motivational system: Insights from the startle response to rejection cues. *Psychological Science, 15,* 668–673.

Dykstra, P. A., van Tilburg, T. G., & de Jong Gierveld, J. (2005). Changes in older adult loneliness: Results from a seven-year longitudinal study. *Research on Aging, 27,* 725–747.

Ebbesen, E. B., Kjos, G. L., & Konecni, V. J. (1976). Spatial ecology: Its effects on the choice of friends and enemies. *Journal of Experimental Social Psychology, 12,* 505–518.

Eisenberger, N. I., & Lieberman, M. D. (2005). Why it hurts to be left out: The neurocognitive overlap between physical and social pain. In K. D. Williams, J. P. Forgas, & W. von Hippel (Eds.), *The social outcast: Ostracism, social exclusion, rejection, and bullying* (pp. 109–127). New York: Psychology Press. Eisenberger, N. I., Lieberman, M. D., & Williams, K. D. (2003). Does rejection hurt? An fMRI study of social exclusion. *Science, 302,* 290–292.

Feeney, J. A. (2004). Hurt feelings in couple relationships: Towards integrative models of the negative effects of hurtful events. *Journal of Social and Personal Relationships, 21,* 487–508.

Feeney, J. (2005). Hurt feelings in couple relationships: Exploring the role of attachment and perceptions of personal injury. *Personal Relationships, 12,* 253–272.

Feingold, A. (1990). Gender differences in effects of physical attractiveness on romantic attraction: A comparison across five research paradigms. *Journal of Personality and Social Psychology, 59,* 981–993.

Feldman, R. S., Forrest, J. A., & Happ, B. R. (2002). Self-presentation and verbal deception: Do self-presenters lie more? *Basic and Applied Social Psychology, 24,* 163–170.

Festinger, L. (1954). A theory of social comparison processes. *Human Relations, 7,* 117–140.

Festinger, L., Schachter, S., & Back, K. W. (1950) *Social pressures in informal groups: A study of human factors in housing.* New York: Harper.

Fisher, S. (1989). *Homesickness, cognition, and health.* London: Erlbaum.

Fisher, S., & Hood, B. (1987). The stress of the transition to university: A longitudinal study of psychological disturbance, absent-mindedness and vulnerability to homesickness. *British Journal of Psychology, 78,* 425–441.

Fiske, A. P. (1992). The four elementary forms of sociality: Framework for a unified theory of social relations. *Psychological Review, 99,* 689–723.

Fiske, S. T., & Ruscher, J. B. (1993). Negative interdependence and prejudice: Whence the affect? In D. M. Mackie & D. L. Hamilton (Eds.), *Affect, cognition, and stereotyping: Interactive processes in group perception* (pp. 239–268). San Diego, CA: Academic Press.

Fitness, J. (2001). Betrayal, rejection, revenge, and forgiveness. In M. R. Leary (Ed.), *Interpersonal rejection* (pp. 73–103). New York: Oxford University Press.

Fitness, J. (2005). Bye bye, black sheep: The causes and consequences of rejection in family relationships. In K. D. Williams, J. P. Forgas, & W. von Hippel (Eds.), *The social outcast: Ostracism, social exclusion, rejection, and bullying* (pp. 263–276). New York: Psychology Press.

Folkes, V. S., & Sears, D. O. (1977). Does everybody like a liker? *Journal of Experimental Social Psychology, 13,* 505–519.

Frith, H., & Gleeson, K. (2004). Clothing and embodiment: Men managing body image and appearance. *Psychology of Men and Masculinity, 5,* 40–48.

Gardner, W. L., Jefferis, V., & Knowles, M. L. (2009). *Social snacking: The use of social symbols in sustaining subjective social connection.* Unpublished manuscript, University of Georgia.

Gardner, W. L., Pickett, C. L., & Brewer, M. B. (2000). Social exclusion and selective memory: How the need to belong influences memory for social events. *Personality and Social Psychology Bulletin, 26,* 486–496.

Gardner, W. L., Pickett, C. L., Jefferis, V., & Knowles, M. (2005). On the outside looking in: Loneliness and social monitoring. *Personality and Social Psychology Bulletin, 31,* 1549–1560.

Gerard, H. B. (1963). Emotional uncertainty and social comparison. *Journal of Abnormal and Social Psychology, 66,* 568–573.

Gerwitz, J. S., & Baer, D. M. (1958). The effect of brief social deprivation on behavior for a social reinforcer. *Journal of Abnormal and Social Psychology, 56,* 49–56.

Goffman, E. (1963). *Stigma: Notes on the management of spoiled identity.* Englewood Cliffs, NJ: Prentice-Hall.

Gonsalkorale, K., & Williams, K. D. (2007). The KKK won't let me play: Ostracism even by a despised outgroup hurts. *European Journal of Social Psychology, 37,* 1176–1186.

Gonzales, M. H., Pederson, J. H., Manning, D. J., & Wetter, D. W. (1990). Pardon my gaffe: Effects of sex, status, and consequence severity on accounts. *Journal of Personality and Social Psychology, 58,* 610–621.

Gordon, R. A. (1996). Impact of ingratiation on judgments and evaluations: A meta-analytic investigation. *Journal of Personality and Social Psychology, 71,* 54–70.

Gove, W. R., Hughes, M., & Geerken, M. R. (1980). Playing dumb: A form of impression management with undesirable side effects. *Social Psychology Quarterly, 43,* 89–102.

Guyll, M., Matthews, K. A., & Bromberger, J. T. (2001). Discrimination and unfair treatment: Relationship to cardiovascular reactivity among African American and European American women. *Health Psychology, 20,* 315–325.

Hale, J. L., & Laliker, M. (1999). Explaining the door-in-the-face: Is it really time to abandon reciprocal concessions? *Communication Studies, 50,* 203–210.

Harrell, J. P., Hall, S., & Taliaferro, J. (2003). Physiological responses to racism and discrimination: An assessment of the evidence. *American Journal of Public Health, 93,* 243–248.

Harrigan, J., Oxman, T., & Rosenthal, R. (1985). Rapport expressed through nonverbal behavior. *Journal of Nonverbal Behavior, 9,* 95–110.

Harris, L. T., McClure, S. M., van den Bos, W., Cohen, J. D., & Fiske, S. T. (2007). Regions of MPFC differentially tuned to social and nonsocial affective evaluation. *Cognitive and Behavioral Neuroscience, 7,* 309–316.

Hawkley, L. C., Burleson, M. H., Berntson, G. G., & Cacioppo, J. T. (2003). Loneliness in everyday life: Cardiovascular activity, psychosocial context, and health behaviors. *Journal of Personality and Social Psychology, 85,* 105–120.

Hawkley, L. C., Preacher, K. J., & Cacioppo, J. T. (2007). Multilevel modeling of social interactions and mood in lonely and socially connected individuals: The MacArthur Social Neuroscience Studies. In A. D. Ong & M. H. M. van Dulmen (Eds.), *Oxford handbook of methods in positive psychology* (pp. 559–575). New York: Oxford University Press.

Heikkinen, R., & Kauppinen, M. (2004). Depressive symptoms in late life: A 10-year follow-up. *Archives of Gerontology and Geriatrics, 38,* 239–250.

Hill, C. A. (1987). Affiliation motivation: People who need people . . . but in different ways. *Journal of Personality and Social Psychology, 52,* 1008–1018.

Hingson, R., & Howland, J. (1993). Promoting safety in adolescents. In S. G. Milllstein, A. C. Petersen, & E. O. Nightingale (Eds.), Promoting the health of adolescents (pp. 305–327). New York: Oxford University Press.

Hinkle, L. L. (1999). Nonverbal immediacy communication behaviors and liking in marital relationships. *Communication Research Reports, 16,* 81–90.

Hogan, R., & Roberts, B. W. (2000). A socioanalytic perspective on person/environment interaction. In W. B. Walsh, K. H. Craik, & R. H. Price (Eds.), *New directions in person-environment psychology* (pp. 1–24). Hillsdale, NJ: Lawrence Erlbaum.

Horney, K. (1945). *Our inner conflicts.* New York: Norton.

Hyers, L. L., & Swim, J. K. (1998). A comparison of the experiences of dominant and minority group members during an intergroup encounter. *Group Processes & Intergroup Relations, 1,* 143–163.

Insko, C. A., Smith, R. H., Alicke, M. D., Wade, T. J., & Taylor, S. (1985). Conformity and group size: The concern with being liked and the concern with being right. *Personality and Social Psychology Bulletin, 11,* 41–50.

Inzlicht, M., McKay, L., & Aronson, J. (2006). Stigma as ego depletion: How being the target of prejudice affects self-control. *Psychological Science, 17,* 262–269.

James, W. (1890). *The principles of psychology* (2 vols.). New York: Henry Holt.

Janes, L., & Olson, J. M. (2000). Jeer pressure: The behavioral effects of observing ridicule of others. *Personality and Social Psychology Bulletin, 26,* 474–485.

Jellison, J. M., & Gentry, K. W. (1978). A self-presentational interpretation of the seeking of social approval. *Personality and Social Psychology Bulletin, 4,* 227–230.

Johnson, M. A. (1989). Variables associated with friendship in an adult population. *Journal of Social Psychology, 129,* 379–390.

Johnson, M. P., & Ferraro, K. (2000). Research on domestic violence in the 1990s: Making distinctions. *Journal of Marriage and the Family, 62,* 948–963.

Jones, B. C., Little, A. C., Penton-Voak, I. S., Tiddeman, B. P., Burt, D. M., Perrett, D. I. (2001). Facial symmetry and judgments of apparent health: Support for a 'good genes' explanation of the attractiveness-symmetry relationship. *Evolution and Human Behavior, 22,* 417–429.

Jones, E. E. (1964). *Ingratiation.* New York: Appleton-Century-Crofts.

Jones, E. E., Gergen, K. J., Gumpert, P., & Thibaut, J. (1965). Some conditions affecting the use of ingratiation to influence performance evaluation. *Journal of Personality and Social Psychology, 1,* 613–625.

Jones, E. E., & Pittman, T. S. (1982). Toward a general theory of strategic self-presentation. In J. Suls (Ed.), *Psychological perspectives on the self* (Vol. 1, pp. 231–262). Hillsdale, NJ: Erlbaum.

Jones, E. E., & Wortman, C. (1973). *Ingratiation: An attributional approach.* Morristown, NJ: General Learning Press.

Kacmar, K. M., Carlson, D. S., & Bratton, V. K. (2004). Situational versus dispositional factors as antecedents of ingratiatory behaviors in organizational settings. *Journal of Vocational Behavior, 65,* 309–331.

Kameda, T., & Tindale, R. S. (2006). Groups as adaptive devices: Human docility and group aggregation mechanisms in evolutionary context. In M. Schaller, J. A. Simpson, & D. T. Kenrick (Eds.), *Evolution and social psychology* (pp. 317–341). New York: Psychology Press.

Kessler, R. C., Mickelson, K. D., & Williams, D. R. (1999). The prevalence, distribution, and mental health correlates of perceived discrimination in the United States. *Journal of Health and Social Behavior, 40,* 208–230.

Kirkpatrick, L. A., & Ellis, B. J. (2001). An evolutionary-psychological approach to self-esteem: Multiple domains and multiple functions. In G. J. O. Fletcher & M. S. Clark (Eds.), *Blackwell handbook of social psychology: Interpersonal processes* (pp. 411–436). Oxford: Blackwell.

Kirkpatrick, L. A., & Ellis, B. J. (2006). The adaptive functions of self-evaluative psychological mechanisms. In M. H. Kernis (Ed.), *Self-esteem: Issues and answers* (pp. 334–339). New York: Psychology Press.

Koenig, F. & Lessan, G. (1985). Viewers' relationship to television personalities. *Psychological Reports, 57,* 263–266.

Krause-Parello, C. A. (2008). The mediating effect of pet attachment support between loneliness and general health in older females living in the community. *Journal of Community Health Nursing, 25,* 1–14.

Krieger, N. (2000). Discrimination and health. In L. F. Berkman & I. Kawachi (Eds.), *Social epidemiology* (pp. 36–75). New York: Oxford University Press.

Kupersmidt, J. B., Burchinal, M., & Patterson, C. J. (1995). Developmental patterns of childhood peer relation as predictors of externalizing behavior problems. *Development and Psychopathology, 7,* 825–843.

Kupersmidt, J. B., & Patterson, C. J. (1991). Childhood peer rejection, aggression, withdrawal, and perceived competence as predictors of self-reported behavior problems in preadolescence. *Journal of Abnormal Child Psychology, 19,* 437–449.

Kurzban, R., & Leary, M. R. (2001). Evolutionary origins of stigmatization: The functions of social exclusion. *Psychological Bulletin, 127,* 187–208.

Kutsukake, N., & Castles, D. L. (2004). Reconciliation and post-conflict third-party affiliation among wild chimpanzees in the Mahale Mountains, Tanzania. *Primates, 45,* 157–165.

Kwapil, T. R. (1998). Social anhedonia as a predictor of the development of schizophrenia–spectrum disorders. *Journal of Abnormal Psychology, 107,* 558–565.

Lakin, J., & Chartrand, T. L. (2003). Increasing nonconscious mimicry to achieve rapport. *Psychological Science, 27,* 145–162.

Landrine, H., & Klonoff, E. A. (1996). The schedule of racist events: A measure of racial discrimination and a study of its negative physical and mental health consequences. *Journal of Black Psychology, 22,* 144–168.

Langlois, J. H., Kalakanis, L., Rubenstein, A. J., Larson, A., Hallam, M., & Smoot, M. (2000). Maxims or myths of beauty? A meta-analytic and theoretical review. *Psychological Bulletin, 126,* 390–423.

Latané, B., & Werner, C. (1978). Regulation of social contact in laboratory rats: Time, not distance. *Journal of Personality and Social Psychology, 36,* 1128–1137.

Lau, S., & Gruen, G. E. (1992). The social stigma of loneliness: Effect of target person's and perceiver's sex. *Personality & Social Psychology Bulletin, 18,* 182–189.

Leary, M. R. (1990). Responses to social exclusion: Social anxiety, jealousy, loneliness, depression, and low self-esteem. *Journal of Social and Clinical Psychology, 9,* 221–229.

Leary, M. R. (1995). *Self-presentation: Impression management and interpersonal behavior.* Boulder, CO: Westview.

Leary, M. R. (2001). Toward a conceptualization of interpersonal rejection. In M. R. Leary (Ed.), *Interpersonal rejection* (pp. 3–20). New York: Oxford University Press.

Leary, M. R. (2005). Varieties of interpersonal rejection. In K. D. Williams, J. P. Forgas, & W. von Hippel (Eds.), *The social outcast* (pp. 35–51). New York: Psychology Press.

Leary, M. R. (2006). Sociometer theory and the pursuit of relational value: Getting to the root of self-esteem. *European Review of Social Psychology, 16,* 75–111.

Leary, M. R., & Baumeister, R. F. (2000). The nature and function of self-esteem: Sociometer theory. In M. P. Zanna (Ed.), *Advances in experimental social psychology* (Vol. 32, pp. 1–62). San Diego: Academic Press.

Leary, M. R., Britt, T. W., Cutlip, W. D., & Templeton, J. L. (1992). Social blushing. *Psychological Bulletin, 112,* 446–460.

Leary, M. R., Cottrell, C. A., & Phillips, M. (2001). Deconfounding the effects of dominance and social acceptance on self-esteem. *Journal of Personality and Social Psychology, 81,* 898–909.

Leary, M. R., & Downs, D. L. (1995). Interpersonal functions of the self-esteem motive: The self-esteem system as a sociometer. In M. Kernis (Ed.), *Efficacy, agency, and self-esteem* (pp. 123–144). New York: Plenum.

Leary, M. R., Gallagher, B., Fors, E. H., Buttermore, N., Baldwin, E., Lane, K. K., et al. (2003). The invalidity of personal claims about self-esteem. *Personality and Social Psychology Bulletin, 29,* 623–636.

Leary, M. R., Haupt, A. L., Strausser, K. S., & Chokel, J. T. (1998). Calibrating the sociometer: The relationship between interpersonal appraisals and state self-esteem. *Journal of Personality and Social Psychology, 74,* 1290–1299.

Leary, M. R., & Jones, J. L. (1993). The social psychology of tanning and sunscreen use: Self-presentational variables as a predictor of health risk. *Journal of Applied Social Psychology, 23,* 1390–1406.

Leary, M. R., & Kowalski, R. M. (1990). Impression management: A literature review and two-component model. *Psychological Bulletin, 107,* 34–47.

Leary, M. R., Kowalski, R. M., Smith, L., & Phillips, S. (2003). Teasing, rejection, and violence: Case studies of the school shootings. *Aggressive Behavior, 29,* 202–214.

Leary, M. R., Landel, J. L., & Patton, K. M. (1996). The motivated expression of embarrassment following a self-presentational predicament. *Journal of Personality, 64,* 619–636.

Leary, M. R., & Leder, S. (2009). The nature of hurt feelings: Emotional experience and cognitive appraisals. In A. Vangelisti (Ed.), *Feeling hurt in close relationships.* New York: Cambridge University Press.

Leary, M. R., & Schreindorfer, L. S. (1998). The stigmatization of HIV and AIDS: Rubbing salt in the wound. In V. Derlega & A. Barbee (Eds.), *HIV infection and social interaction* (pp. 12–29). Thousand Oaks, CA: Sage.

Leary, M. R., Springer, C., Negel, L., Ansell, E., & Evans, K. (1998). The causes, phenomenology, and consequences of hurt feelings. *Journal of Personality and Social Psychology, 74,* 1225–1237.

Leary, M. R., Tambor, E. S., Terdal, S. K., & Downs, D. L. (1995). Self-esteem as an interpersonal monitor: The sociometer hypothesis. *Journal of Personality and Social Psychology, 68,* 518–530.

Leary, M. R., Tchividjian, L. R., & Kraxberger, B. E. (1994). Self-presentation can be hazardous to your health: Impression management and health risk. *Psychological Bulletin, 13,* 461–470.

Leary, M. R., Twenge, J. M., & Quinlivan, E. (2006). Interpersonal rejection as a determinant of anger and aggression. *Personality and Social Psychology Review, 10,* 111–132.

Levy, S., Ayduk, O., & Downey, G. (2001). The role of rejection sensitivity in people's relationships with significant others and valued social groups. In M. R. Leary (Ed.), *Interpersonal rejection* (pp. 251–289). New York: Oxford University Press.

MacDonald, G. (in press). Social pain and hurt feelings. In P. J. Corr & G. Matthews (Eds.), *Cambridge handbook of personality psychology.* New York: Cambridge University Press.

MacDonald, G., Kingsbury, R., & Shaw, S. (2005). Adding insult to injury: Social pain theory and response to social exclusion. In K. D. Williams, J. P. Forgas, & W. von Hippel (Eds.), *The social outcast* (pp. 77–90). New York: Psychology Press.

MacDonald, G., & Leary, M. R. (2005a). Roles of social pain and defense mechanisms in response to social exclusion: Reply to Panksepp (2005) and Corr (2005). *Psychological Bulletin, 131,* 237–240.

MacDonald, G., & Leary, M. R. (2005b). Why does social exclusion hurt? The relationship between social and physical pain. *Psychological Bulletin, 131,* 202–223.

MacDonald, G., Saltzman, J. L., & Leary, M. R. (2003). Social approval and trait self-esteem. *Journal of Research in Personality, 37,* 23–40.

Maner, J. K., DeWall, C. N., Baumeister, R. F., & Schaller, M. (2007). Does social exclusion motivate interpersonal reconnection? Resolving the "porcupine problem." *Journal of Personality and Social Psychology, 92,* 42–55.

Mann, L. (1980). Cross-cultural studies of small groups. In H. Triandis & R. Brislin (Eds.), *Handbook of cross-cultural psychology: Social psychology* (Vol. 5, pp. 155–209). Boston: Allyn & Bacon.

Martin, K. A., & Leary, M. R. (1999). Would you drink after a stranger? The influence of self-presentational motives on willingness to take a health risk. *Personality and Social Psychology Bulletin, 25,* 1092–1100.

Martin, K. A., & Leary, M. R. (2000). Self-presentational determinants of health risk behavior among college freshmen. *Psychology and Health, 16,* 17–27.

Martin, K. A., Leary, M. R., & Rejeski, W. J. (2000). Self-presentational concerns in older adults: Implications for health and well-being. *Basic and Applied Social Psychology, 22,* 169–179.

Martin Ginis, K. A., Lindwall, M., & Prapavessis, H. (2007). Who cares what other people think? Self-presentation in sport and exercise. In G. Tenenbaum & R. Eklund (Eds.), *Handbook of sport psychology* (3rd ed., pp. 136–157). New York: Wiley.

Maslow, A. H. (1968). *Toward a psychology of being* (2nd ed.). New York: Van Nostrand Reinhold.

Matell, M. S., & Smith, R. E. (1970). Approval motive and academic behaviors: The self-reinforcement hypothesis. *Journal of Consulting and Clinical Psychology, 35,* 229–232.

Matthews, K. A., Salomon, K., Kenyon, K., & Zhou, F. (2005). Unfair treatment, discrimination, and ambulatory blood pressure in Black and White adolescents. *Health Psychology, 24,* 258–265.

McAndrew, F. T., Gold, J. A., Lenney, E., & Ryckman, R. M. (1984). Explorations in immediacy: The nonverbal system and its relationship to affective and situational factors. *Journal of Nonverbal Behavior, 8,* 210–228.

McCauley, C. (1989). The nature of social influence in *groupthink*: Compliance and internalization. *Journal of Personality and Social Psychology, 57,* 250–260.

McDougall, P., Hymel, S., Vaillancourt, T., & Mercer, L. (2001). The consequences of childhood peer rejection. In M. R. Leary (Ed.), *Interpersonal rejection* (pp. 213–247). New York: Oxford University Press.

Mehrabian, A. (1969). Significance of posture and position in the communication of attitude and status relationships. *Psychological Bulletin, 71,* 359–372.

Merritt, M. M., Bennett, G., Williams, R. B., Edwards, C. L., & Sollers, J. J. (2006). Perceived Racism and cardiovascular reactivity and recovery to personally relevant stress. *Health Psychology, 25,* 364–369.

Miller, G. E., Chen, E., & Zhou, E. S. (2007). If it goes up, must it come down? Chronic stress and the hypothalamic-pituitary-adrenocorticol axis in humans. *Psychological Bulletin, 133,* 25–45.

Miller, L. C., Berg, J. H., & Archer, R. L. (1983). Openers: Individuals who elicit intimate self-disclosure. *Journal of Personality & Social Psychology, 44,* 1234–1244.

Miller, N. (2002). Personalization and the promise of contact theory. *Journal of Social Issues, 58,* 387–410.

Miller, R. B., Greene, B. A., Montalvo, G., Ravindran, B. & Nichols, J. (1996). Engagement in academic work: The role of learning goals, future consequences, pleasing others and perceived ability. *Contemporary Educational Psychology, 21,* 388–422.

Miller, R. S. (1996). *Embarrassment: Poise and peril in everyday life.* New York: Guilford.

Mills, R. S. L., Nazar, J., & Farrell, H. M. (2002). Child and parent perceptions of hurtful messages. *Journal of Social and Personal Relationships, 19,* 731–754.

Montoya, R. M., Horton, R. S., & Kirchner, J. (2008). Is actual similarity necessary for attraction? A meta-analysis of actual and perceived similarity. *Journal of Social and Personal Relationships, 25,* 889–922.

Moray, N. (1959). Attention in dichotic listening: Affective cues and the influence of instructions. *Quarterly Journal of Experimental Psychology, 11,* 56–60.

Moreland, R. L., & Beach, S. R. (1992). Exposure effects in the classroom: The development of affinity among students. *Journal of Experimental Social Psychology, 28,* 255–276.

Moreland, R. L., & Zajonc, R. B. (1982). Exposure effects in person perception: Familiarity, similarity, and attraction. *Journal of Experimental Social Psychology, 18,* 395–415.

Moulton, P., Moulton, M., & Roach, S. (1998). Eating disorders: A means for seeking approval? *Eating Disorders: The Journal of Treatment & Prevention, 6,* 319–327.

Murray, H. A. (1938). *Explorations in personality.* New York: Oxford University Press.

Murray, S. L., Griffin, D. W., Rose, P., & Bellavia, G. (2003). Calibrating the sociometer: The relational contingencies of self-esteem. *Journal of Personality and Social Psychology, 85,* 63–84.

Murray, S. L., Holmes, J. G., MacDonald, G., & Ellsworth, P. (1998). Through the looking glass darkly? When self-doubts turn into relationship insecurities. *Journal of Personality and Social Psychology, 75,* 1459–1480.

Myers, S. A., & Ferry, M. F. (2001). Interpersonal communication motives and nonverbal immediacy behaviors. *Communication Research Reports, 18,* 182–191.

Neuberg, S. L., & Cottrell, C. A. (2008). Managing the threats and opportunities afforded by human sociality. *Group Dynamics: Theory, Research, and Practice, 12,* 63–72.

Neuberg, S. L., Smith, D. M., Hoffman, J. C., & Russell, F. J. (1994). When we observe stigmatized and 'normal' individuals interacting: Stigma by association. *Personality and Social Psychology Bulletin, 20,* 196–209.

Nezlek, J. B., Kowalski, R. M., Leary, M. R., Blevins, T., & Holgate, S. (1997). Personality moderators of reactions to interpersonal rejection: Depression and trait self-esteem. *Personality and Social Psychology Bulletin, 23,* 1235–1244.

Nishina, A., & Juvonen, J. (2005). Daily reports of witnessing and experiencing peer harassment in middle school. *Child Development, 76,* 435–450.

Nolen-Hoeksema, S., & Ahrens, C. (2002). Age differences and similarities in the correlates of depressive symptoms. *Psychology and Aging, 17,* 116–124.

Norton, M. I., Frost, J. H., & Ariely, D. (2007). Less is more: The lure of ambiguity, or why familiarity breeds contempt. *Journal of Personality and Social Psychology, 92,* 97–105.

O'Connor, S. C., & Rosenblood, L. K. (1996). Affiliation motivation in everyday experience: A theoretical comparison. *Journal of Personality and Social Psychology, 70,* 513–522.

Olson, K., & Wong, E. H. (2001). Loneliness in marriage. *Family Therapy, 28,* 105–111.

Ouwerkerk, J. W., Kerr, N. L., Gallucci, M., & Van Lange, P. (2005). Avoiding the social death penalty: Ostracism and cooperation in social dilemmas. In K. D. Williams & W. von Hippel (Eds.), *The social outcast: Ostracism, social exclusion, rejection, and bullying* (pp. 321–332). New York: Psychology Press.

Panak, W. F., & Gerber, J. (1992). Role of aggression, rejection, and attributions in the prediction of depression in children. *Development and Psychopathology, 7,* 145–165.

Panksepp, J. (1998). *Affective neuroscience.* New York. Oxford University Press.

Patterson, M. L. (1976). An arousal model of interpersonal intimacy. *Psychological Review, 83,* 235–245.

Peay, M. Y., & Peay, E. R. (1983). The effects of density, group size, and crowding on behavior in an unstructured situation. *British Journal of Social Psychology, 22,* 13–18.

Pegalis, L. J., Shaffer, D. R., Bazzini, D. G., & Greenier, K. (1994). On the ability to elicit self-disclosure: Are there gender-based and contextual limitations on the opener effect? *Personality and Social Psychology Bulletin, 20,* 412–420.

Peluchette, J., Karl, K., & Rust, K. (2006). Dressing to impress: Beliefs and attitudes regarding workplace attire. *Journal of Business and Psychology, 21,* 45–63.

Peplau, L. A., & Perlman, D. (1982). Perspectives on loneliness. In L. A. Peplau & D. Perlman (Eds.), *Loneliness: A sourcebook of current theory, research and therapy* (pp. 1–20). New York: John Wiley & Sons.

Pickett, C. L., & Gardner, W. L. (2005). The social monitoring system: Enhanced sensitivity to social cues as an adaptive response to social exclusion. In K. Williams, J. Forgas, and W. von Hippel (Eds.), *The social outcast: Ostracism, social exclusion, rejection, and bullying* (pp. 213–225). New York: Psychology Press.

Pickett, C. L., Gardner, W. L., & Knowles, M. (2004). Getting a cue: The need to belong and enhanced sensitivity to social cues. *Personality and Social Psychology Bulletin, 30,* 1095–1107.

Pinquart, M., & Sörensen, S. (2003). Risk factors for loneliness in adulthood and old age: A meta-analysis. *Advances in Psychology Research, 19,* 111–143.

Pitterman, H., & Nowicki, S., Jr. (2004). A test of the ability to identify emotion in human standing and sitting postures: The diagnostic analysis of nonverbal accuracy-2 posture test (DANVA-POS). *Genetic, Social, and General Psychology Monographs, 130,* 146–162.

Price, D. D. (2000). Psychological and neural mechanisms of the affective dimension of pain. *Science, 288,* 1769–1772.

Purvis, J. A., Dabbs, J. M., & Hopper, C. H. (1984). The 'opener': Skilled user of facial expression and speech pattern. *Personality and Social Psychology Bulletin, 10,* 61–66.

Rainville, P. (2002). Brain mechanisms of pain affect and pain modulation. *Current Opinion in Neurobiology, 12,* 195–204.

Reis, H. T., & Shaver, P. (1988). Intimacy as an interpersonal process. In S. Duck (Ed.), *Handbook of personal relationships* (pp. 367–389). Chichester, United Kingdom: Wiley.

Rhodes, G. (2006). The evolutionary psychology of facial beauty. *Annual Review of Psychology, 57,* 199–226.

Richman, L. S., & Leary, M. R. (2009). Reactions to discrimination, stigmatization, ostracism, and other forms of interpersonal rejection: A multi-motive model. *Psychological Review, 116,* 365–383.

Rofé, Y. (1984). Stress and affiliation: A utility theory. *Psychological Review, 91,* 235–250.

Rofé, Y., & Lewin, I. (1988). Social comparison or utility: An experimental examination. *Social Behavior and Personality, 16,* 5–10.

Rofé, Y., Lewin, I., & Padeh, B. (1977). Affiliation before and after child delivery as a function of repression-sensitization. *British Journal of Social and Clinical Psychology, 16,* 311–315.

Romero-Canyas, R., & Downey, G. (2003, February). *Sensitivity to rejection by groups (rejection sensitivity-G) as a predictor of political behavior.* Poster presented at the meeting of the Society for Personality and Social Psychology, Los Angeles.

Romero-Canyas, R., Downey, G., Berenson, K., Ayduk, O., & Kang, J. (in press). Rejection sensitivity and the rejection-hostility link in romantic relationships. *Journal of Personality.*

Rotenberg, K. J., & Kmill, J. (1992). Perception of lonely and non-lonely persons as a function of individual differences in loneliness. *Journal of Social and Personal Relationships, 9,* 325–330.

Sarnoff, I., & Zimbardo, P. (1961). Anxiety, fear and social affiliation. *Journal of Abnormal and Social Psychology, 62,* 356–363.

Saucier, G., & Goldberg, L. R. (1996). The language of personality: Lexical perspectives on the five-factor model. In J. S. Wiggins (Ed.), *The five-factor model of personality* (pp. 21–50). New York: Guilford.

Schachter, S. (1951). Deviance, rejection, and communication. *Journal of Abnormal and Social Psychology, 46,* 190–207.

Schachter, S. (1959). *The psychology of affiliation.* Stanford, CA: Stanford University Press.

Schlenker, B. R. (1975). Self-presentation: Managing the impression of consistency when reality interferes with self-enhancement. *Journal of Personality and Social Psychology, 32,* 1030–1037.

Schlenker, B. R. (1980). *Impression management: The self-concept, social identity, and interpersonal relations.* Monterey, CA: Brooks/Cole.

Schlenker, B. R., & Darby, B. (1981). The use of apologies in social predicaments. *Social Psychology Quarterly, 44,* 271–278.

Schlenker, B. R., & Weigold, M. F. (1992). Interpersonal processes involving impression regulation and management. *Annual Review of Psychology, 43,* 133–168.

Schmader, T., & Johns, M. (2003). Converging evidence that stereotype threat reduces working memory capacity, *Journal of Personality & Social Psychology, 85,* 440–452.

Schmitt, M., Gollwitzer, M., Förster, N., & Montada, L. (2004). Effects of objective and subjective account components on forgiving. *Journal of Social Psychology, 144,* 465–485.

Schwartz, D., Dodge, K. A., & Coie, J. D. (1993). The emergence of chronic peer victimization in boys' play groups. *Child Development, 64,* 1755–1772.

Scott, M. B., & Lyman, S. M. (1968). Accounts. *American Sociological Review, 33,* 46–62.

Sears, D. O. (1983). The person-positivity bias. *Journal of Personality and Social Psychology.* 44, 233–250.

Sellers, R. M., & Shelton, J. N. (2003). The role of racial identity in perceived racial discrimination. *Journal of Personality & Social Psychology, 84,* 1079–1092.

Semin, G. R., & Manstead, A. S. R. (1982). The social implications of embarrassment displays and restitution behaviour. *European Journal of Social Psychology, 12,* 367–377.

Semin, G. R., & Papadopoulou, K. (1990). The acquisition of reflexive social emotions: The transmission and reproduction of social control through joint action. In G. Duveen & B. Lloyd (Eds.), *Social representations and the development of knowledge* (pp. 107–125). New York: Cambridge University Press.

Serpell, J. A. (2002). Anthropomorphism and anthropomorphic selection— Beyond the "cute response." *Society and Animals, 10,* 437–453.

Shaffer, D. R., Ruammake, C., Pegalis, L. J. (1990). The "opener": Highly skilled as interviewer or interviewee. *Personality and Social Psychology Bulletin, 16,* 511–520.

Shaver, P., Furman, W., & Buhrmester, D. (1985). Transition to college: Network changes, social skills, and loneliness. In S. Duck & D. Perlman (Eds.), *Understanding personal relationships: An interdisciplinary approach* (pp. 193–219). Thousand Oaks, CA: Sage Publications.

Sheatsley, P. B., & Feldman, J. J. (1964). The assassination of President Kennedy: A preliminary report on public reactions and behavior. *Public Opinion Quarterly, 28,* 189–215.

Shelton, J. N. (2003). Interpersonal concerns in social encounters between majority and minority group members. *Group Processes & Intergroup Relations, 6,* 171–185.

Shelton, J. N., & Richeson, J. A. (2006). Interracial interactions: A relational approach. *Advances in Experimental Social Psychology, 38,* 121–181.

Shelton, J. N., Richeson, J. A., & Salvatore, J. (2005). Expecting to be the target of prejudice: Implications for interethnic interactions. *Personality and Social Psychology Bulletin, 31,* 1189–1202.

Simpson, M. M., & Littrell, M. A. (1984). Attitudes toward clothing of elderly men. *Journal of Applied Gerontology, 3,* 171–180.

Skarlicki, D. P., Folger, R., & Gee, J. (2004). When social accounts backfire: Effects of a polite message or an apology on reactions to an unfair outcome. *Journal of Applied Social Psychology, 34,* 322–341.

Smith, C. A., & Lazarus, R. S. (1993). Appraisal components, core relational themes and the emotions. *Cognition and Emotion, 7,* 233–269.

Snapp, C. M., & Leary, M. R. (2001). Hurt feelings among new acquaintances: Moderating effects of interpersonal familiarity. *Journal of Personal and Social Relationships, 18,* 315–326.

Snyder, C. R., & Higgins, R. L. (1988). Excuses: Their effective role in the negotiation of reality. *Psychological Bulletin, 104,* 23–35.

Solano, C. H. (1987). Loneliness and perceptions of control: General traits versus specific attributions. *Journal of Social Behavior and Personality, 2,* 201–214.

Sommer, K. L., Williams, K. D., Ciarocco, N. J., & Baumeister, R. F. (2001). When silence speaks louder than words: Explorations into the intrapsychic and interpersonal consequences of social ostracism. *Basic and Applied Social Psychology, 23,* 225–243.

Srivastava, S., & Beer, J. S. (2005). How self-evaluations relate to being liked by others: Integrating sociometer and attachment perspectives. *Journal of Personality and Social Psychology, 89,* 966–977.

St. Lawrence, J. S., Eldridge, G. D., Reitman, D., Little, C. E., Shelby, M. C., & Brasfield, T. L. (1998). Factors influencing condom use among African American women: Implications for risk reduction interventions. *American Journal of Community Psychology, 26,* 7–28.

Staats, S., Pierfelice, L., Kim, C., & Crandell, R. (1999). A theoretical model for human health and the pet connection. *Journal of American Veterinary Medical Association, 214,* 483–487.

Stein, J. A., Newcomb, M. D., & Bentler, P. M. (1987). An 8-year study of multiple influences on drug use and drug use consequences. *Journal of Personality and Social Psychology, 53,* 1094–1105.

Stevens, C. K., & Kristof, A. L. (1995). Making the right impression: A field study of applicant impression management during job interviews. *Journal of Applied Psychology, 80,* 587–606.

Stroud, L. R., Tanofsky-Kraff, M., Wilfley, D. E., & Salovey, P. (2000). The Yale Interpersonal Stressor (YIPS): Affective, physiological, and behavioral responses to a novel interpersonal rejection paradigm. *Annals of Behavioral Medicine, 22,* 204–213.

Swim, J. K., Cohen, L. L., & Hyers, L. L. (1997). Experiencing everyday prejudice and discrimination. In J. K. Swim & C. Stangor (Eds), *Prejudice: The target's perspective* (pp. 37–60). San Diego, CA: Academic Press.

Symons, D. (1992). On the use and misuse of Darwinism in the study of human behavior. In J. H. Barkow, L. Cosmides, & J. Tooby J (Eds.), *The adapted mind: evolutionary psychology and the generation of culture.* New York: Oxford University Press.

Tajfel, H., Flament, C., Billig, M. G., & Bundy, R. F. (1971). Social categorization and intergroup behaviour. *European Journal of Social Psychology, 1,* 149–177.

Tartakovsky, E. (2007). A longitudinal study of acculturative stress and homesickness: High-school adolescents immigrating from Russia and Ukraine to Israel without parents. *Social Psychiatry and Psychiatric Epidemiology, 42,* 485–494.

Taylor, S. E., & Brown, J. D. (1988). Illusion and well-being: A social psychological perspective on mental health. *Psychological Bulletin, 103,* 193–210.

Teichman, Y. (1973). Emotional arousal and affiliation. *Journal of Experimental Social Psychology, 9,* 591–605.

Thompson V. L. (1996). Perceived experiences of racism as stressful life events. *Community Mental Health, 32,* 223–233.

Thornton, B., Audesse, R. J., Ryckman, R. M., & Burckle, M. J. (2006). Playing dumb and knowing it all: Two sides of an impression management coin. *Individual Differences Research, 4,* 37–45.

Tooby, J., & Cosmedes, L. (1996). Friendship and the banker's paradox: Other pathways in the evolution of altruism. *Proceedings of the British Academy, 88,* 119–143.

Tropp, L. R., & Wright, S. C. (2003). Evaluations and perceptions of self, ingroup, and outgroup: Comparisons between Mexican-American and European-American children. *Self and Identity, 2,* 203–221.

Turnbull, W. (1992). A conversation approach to explanation, with emphasis on politeness and accounting. In M. L. McLaughlin, M. J. Cody, & S. J. Read (Eds.), *Explaining oneself to others: Reason-giving in a social context* (pp. 105–130). Hillsdale, NJ: Erlbaum.

Turner, R. N., Hewstone, M., & Voci, A. (2007). Reducing explicit and implicit outgroup prejudice via direct and extended contact: The mediating role of self-disclosure and intergroup anxiety. *Journal of Personality and Social Psychology, 93,* 369–388.

Twenge, J. M., Baumeister, R. F., DeWall, C. N., Ciarocco, N. J., & Bartels, J. M. (2007). Social exclusion decreases prosocial behavior. *Journal of Personality and Social Psychology, 92,* 56–66.

Twenge, J. M., Baumeister, R. F., Tice, D. M., & Stucke, T. S. (2001). If you can't join them, beat them: Effects of social exclusion on aggressive behavior. *Journal of Personality and Social Psychology, 81,* 1058–1069.

Twenge, J. M., Catanese, K. R., & Baumeister, R. F. (2003). Social exclusion and the deconstructed state: Time perception, meaninglessness, lethargy, lack of emotion, and self-awareness. *Journal of Personality and Social Psychology, 85,* 409–423.

Tyler, J. M., & Feldman, R. S. (2004). Truth, lies, and self-presentation: How gender and anticipated future interaction relate to deceptive behavior. *Journal of Applied Social Psychology, 34,* 2602–2615.

Uchino, B. N., Cacioppo, J. T., & Kiecolt-Glaser, J. K. (1996). The relationship between social support and physiological processes: A review with emphasis on underlying mechanisms and implications for health. *Psychological Bulletin, 119,* 488–531.

Urdan, T., & Mestas, M. (2006). The goals behind performance goals. *Journal of Educational Psychology, 98,* 354–365.

Van Beest, I., & Williams, K. D. (2006). When inclusion costs and ostracism pays, ostracism still hurts. *Journal of Personality and Social Psychology, 91,* 918–928.

van den Bos, W., McClure, S. M., Harris, L. T., Fiske, S. T., & Cohen, J. D. (2007). Dissociating affective evaluation and social cognitive processes in ventral medial prefrontal cortex. *Cognitive and Behavioral Neuroscience, 7,* 337–346.

Vandevelde, L., & Miyahara, M. (2005). Impact of group rejections from a physical activity on physical self-esteem among university students. *Social Psychology of Education, 8,* 65–81.

Vangelisti, A. L. (2001). Making sense of hurtful interactions in close relationships: When hurt feelings create distance. In V. Manusov & J. H. Harvey (Eds.), *Attribution, communication behavior, and close relationships: Advances in personal relations* (pp. 38–58). New York: Cambridge University Press.

Vangelisti, A. L., & Maguire, K. (2002). Hurtful messages in family relationships: When the pain lingers. In J. H. Harvey & A. Wenzel (Eds.), *A clinician's guide to maintaining and enhancing close relationships* (pp. 43–62). Mahwah, NJ: Lawrence Erlbaum Associates.

Vangelisti, A. L., Young, S. L., Carpenter-Theune, K., & Alexander, A. L. (2005). Why does it hurt? The perceived causes of hurt feelings. *Communication Research, 32,* 443–477.

Van Lange, P. A. M., Rusbult, C. E., Drigotas, S. M., Arriaga, X. B., Witcher, B. S., & Cox, C. L. (1997). Willingness to sacrifice in close relationships. *Journal of Personality and Social Psychology, 72,* 1373–1395.

Van Tilburg, M. A. L. (2005). The psychological context of homesickness. In M. A. L. Van Tilburg & A. J. J. M. Vingerhoets (Eds.), *Psychological aspects of geographical moves: Homesickness and acculturation stress* (pp. 35–48). Tilburg, The Netherlands: Tilburg University Press.

Vernberg, E. M., Abwender, D. A., Ewell, K. K., & Beery, S. H. (1992). Social anxiety and peer relationships in early adolescence: A prospective analysis. *Journal of Clinical Child Psychology, 21,* 189–196.

Veroff, J., & Veroff, J. B. (1980). *Social incentives: A life-span developmental approach.* New York: Academic Press.

Vonk, R. (2002). Self-serving interpretations of flattery: Why ingratiation works. *Journal of Personality and Social Psychology, 82,* 515–526.

Waldrip, A., & Jensen-Campbell, L. (2007). *Why do I feel so bad after being excluded? The mediational effects of threatened needs on social exclusion.* Manuscript under review.

Warburton, W. A., Williams, K. D., & Cairns, D. R. (2006). When ostracism leads to aggression: The moderating effects of control deprivation. *Journal of Experimental Social Psychology, 42,* 213–220.

Wayne, S. J., & Kacmar, K. M. (1991). The effects of impression management on the performance appraisal process. *Organizational and Human Decision Processes, 48,* 70–88.

Weiss, B., & Feldman, R. S. (2006). Looking good and lying to do it: Deception as an impression management strategy in job interviews. *Journal of Applied Social Psychology, 36,* 1070–1086.

Wieselquist, J., Rusbult, C. E., Foster, C. A., & Agnew, C. R. (1999). Commitment, pro-relationship behavior, and trust in close relationships. *Journal of Personality and Social Psychology, 77,* 942–966.

Williams, D. R., Spencer, M. S., & Jackson, J. S. (1999). Race, stress, and physical health: The role of group identity. In R. J. Contrada & R. D. Ashmore (Eds.), *Self, social identity, and physical health: Interdisciplinary explorations* (pp. 71–100). New York: Oxford University Press.

Williams, K. D. (2001). *Ostracism: The power of silence.* New York: Guilford Publications.

Williams, K. D. (2007). Ostracism. *Annual Review of Psychology, 58,* 425–452.

Williams, K. D., Cheung, C. K. T., & Choi, W. (2000). CyberOstracism: Effects of being ignored over the Internet. *Journal of Personality and Social Psychology, 79,* 748–762.

Williams, K. D., Forgas, J. P., von Hippel, W., & Zadro, L. (2005). The social outcast: An overview. In K. D. Williams, J. P. Forgas, & W. von Hippel (Eds.), *The social outcast* (pp. 1–16). New York: Psychology Press.

Williams, K. D., Govan, C. L., Croker, V., Tynan, D., Cruickshank, M., & Lam, A. (2002). Investigations into differences between social- and Cyberostracism. *Group Dynamics: Theory, Research, and Practice, 6,* 65–77.

Williams, K. D., & Sommer, K. L. (1997). Social ostracism by one's coworkers: Does rejection lead to loafing or compensation? *Personality and Social Psychology Bulletin, 23,* 693–706.

Williams, K. D., & Zadro, L. (2005). Ostracism: The indiscriminate early detection system. In K. D. Williams, J. P. Forgas, & W. von Hippel (Eds.), *The social outcast* (pp. 19–34). New York: Psychology Press.

Wittenberg, M. T., & Reis, H. T. (1986). Loneliness, social skills, and social perception. *Personality and Social Psychology Bulletin, 12,* 121–130.

Wood, N., & Cowan, N. (1995). The cocktail party phenomenon revisited: How frequent are attention shifts to one's name in an irrelevant auditory channel? *Journal of Experimental Psychology: Learning, Memory, and Cognition, 21,* 255–260.

Worthy, C. B., Gary, A. L., & Kahn, G. M. (1969). Self-disclosure as an exchange process. *Journal of Personality and Social Psychology, 13,* 59–63.

Zadro, L., Williams, K. D., & Richardson, R. (2004). How low can you go? Ostracism by a computer is sufficient to lower self-reported levels of belonging, control, self-esteem and meaningful existence. *Journal of Experimental Social Psychology, 40,* 560–567.

Zadro, L., Williams, K. D., & Richardson, R. (2005). Riding the 'O' train: Comparing the effects of ostracism and verbal dispute on targets and sources. *Group Processes and Intergroup Relations, 8,* 125–143.

Zajonc, R. B. (1968). Attitudinal effects of mere exposure. *Journal of Personality and Social Psychology Monographs, 9*(2 Pt 2), 1–27.

Zeedyk-Ryan, J., & Smith, G. F. (1983). The effects of crowding on hostility, anxiety, and desire for social interaction," *Journal of Social Psychology, 120,* 245–252.

Chapter 25

Close Relationships

MARGARET S. CLARK AND EDWARD P. LEMAY, JR.

The field of research on close relationships is burgeoning. In the not so distant past it was possible to summarize most social psychological research on friendships, romantic relationships, and marriages in a handbook chapter. This is no longer true. Thus, this chapter addresses some specific and important questions about close relationships without trying to cover all recent relationship research. The questions include: What do people mean when they say they have a "close" relationship with someone? What psychological processes are involved in becoming close to another person, and what processes interfere with attaining closeness? Why do people value close relationships? Finally, what is it about close relationships that may account for the now very large body of literature showing links between having close relationships and having good mental and physical health?

A great deal of research arising from many different laboratories is converging on the idea that answers to these questions center around each member of a relationship being successfully responsive to their partners' actual needs and desires, as well as on making it easy for their partners to do the same for them. Pulling this off provides each relationship member with a person other than the self willing to watch out for and support them, together with a sense of purpose and generativity as they watch out for their partner. As attachment theorists have taught us, these relationships provide a secure base from which individuals can confidently venture forth, explore the world, and attain success, as well as a safe haven to which to retreat when stressors arise. They also provide us with an important sense of identity.

This chapter starts with a conceptualization of the nature of closeness itself, as well as some commentary about the field itself. It then moves on to discussing factors that draw people into such relationships before discussing in detail a model of responsiveness dynamics within relationships. We conclude with some comments about what remains to be done. Processes that support the health of mutually responsive relationships (as well as some that are inimical to effective mutual responsiveness) are outlined.

The view that responsiveness is key to optimal relationship functioning and, indeed, the sine qua non of close relationships, is strongly advocated. Some may disagree, positing instead, perhaps, that sexuality, commitment, stability or satisfaction, a lack of conflict or some combination of these factors are the key determinants of a high quality close relationship. Certainly, such criteria have often been used as markers of relationship success or well-being by social psychologists, sociologists, and clinicians. Moreover, all these factors *relate* to responsiveness in important ways. Yet, each can be high (or low in the case of conflict) *without* relationship members being responsive to one another, and if that is the case, the relationship would not be considered a high-quality, close relationship from the present perspective.

The view that responsiveness is key to success in relationships has been suggested by others and is central to *many* current theories in the adult close relationship field including attachment theory (e.g., Cassidy & Shaver, 1999; Mikulincer & Shaver, 2007; Rholes & Simpson, 2004), risk-regulation theory (e.g., Murray, Holmes, & Griffin, 2000; Murray, Holmes, & Collins, 2006), theories of intimacy (Gable & Reis, 2006; Reis & Patrick, 1996; Reis & Shaver, 1988), communal relationships theory (e.g., Clark & Monin, 2006), efforts to understand people's drive to "belong" (Baumeister & Leary, 1995; Leary & Cox, 2008), as well as to research on interpersonal rejection (e.g., Leary, Twenge, & Quinlivan, 2006; Williams, Forgas, & von Hippel, 2005), empathic sharing, accuracy, and care (e.g., Zaki, Bolger, & Ochsner, 2009; Zaki, Bolger, & Ochsner, 2008), prosocial behavior (e.g., Bierhoff, 2002; Dovidio, Piliavin, Schroeder, & Penner, 2006), and social support (e.g., Cohen, 2004; Cohen & Janicki-Deverts, in press). So, too, is the importance of the concept of interpersonal responsiveness central to much work on individual differences such as rejection sensitivity (Ayduk, Zayas, Downey, Cole, Shoda, & Mischel, 2008; Downey & Feldman, 1996; London, Downey, Bonica, & Paltin, 2007) and self-esteem (Leary, 2005). Reis, Clark, and Holmes

(2004) presented a case that the concept of responsiveness is central and essential to understanding relationships, and the same premise underlies this chapter.

WHAT IS CLOSENESS?

The term "close relationship" is often used and rarely defined. Certainly people have an implicit feel for what a close relationship is and use the term often. When the term is used, no one asks, "Well, what exactly do you mean by closeness?" Instead, when asked to name types of close relationships, people readily point to friendships, romantic relationships, and family relationships. Yet, these are just labels. Moreover, the very same people who point to such relationships as prototypical "close relationships" often will not hesitate to add that they are not close with their own *particular* father or mother or sister.

Only a handful of researchers in the relationships field have offered explicit definitions of the term. Berscheid, Snyder, and Omoto (2004) were among the first. They equated closeness with the degree of interdependence between two people. The more frequent, diverse, and strong the impacts of each person's thoughts, feelings, and behavior on the other, and the longer the duration of the relationship, the closer the relationship. This definition proved useful in predicting such things as the degree of distress on relationship breakup (e.g., Simpson, 1987), and a more recent "atlas" of types of interdependence (Kelley, Holmes, Kerr, Reis, Rusbult, & Van Lange, 2002) might be utilized as a basis for investigating different forms of this type of closeness.

Other definitions, more akin to lay use of the term "close relationship," equate closeness with intimacy, which can be viewed as the outcomes of a set of interpersonal processes in which two people understand, validate, and care for one another (Reis & Patrick, 1996; Reis & Shaver, 1988). Compatible with this are definitions that equate closeness with the degree of motivation to respond supportively to the other's welfare. This degree of motivation refers to the extent to which the person is willing to act, non-contingently, in ways that promote the other's welfare, and is indexed by the costs in time, effort, money, and emotional investments the person is willing to incur to benefit the partner (Mills, Clark, Ford, & Johnson, 2004). Still others equate closeness with an incorporation of the other into one's self-concept (Aron, Aron, Tudor, & Nelson, 2004). Beyond this, some people might equate closeness with commitment to the relationship (intent to remain in the relationship) and with the various outcomes that have been linked to commitment including seeing the partner as a part of the self (Agnew, Van Lange, Rusbult, & Langston, 1998), and willingness to

accommodate, sacrifice, and forgive (Rusbult, Bissonnette, Arriaga, & Cox, 1998; Rusbult, Hannon, Stocker, & Finkel, 2005; Rusbult, Kumashiro, Finkel, & Wildschut, 2002; Van Lange, Rusbult, Drigotas, Arriaga, Witcher, & Cox, 1997; Whitton, Stanley, & Markman, 2002; Wieselquist, Rusbult, Foster, & Agnew, 1999).

There is, of course, no one correct conceptual definition of closeness. Yet, as this is a chapter on close relationships, it is important to define what closeness *means in this particular chapter*, for that defines the scope of the chapter. Here closeness refers to the degree to which a relationship serves two broad functions for its members: (1) providing both members a sense of security that their welfare has been, is, and will continue to be protected and enhanced by their partner's responsiveness; and (2) providing both members a sense that they, themselves, have been, are, and will continue to be responsive to their partners (Reis, Clark, & Holmes, 2004). These functions are best served, we assert, when both members of a relationship are non-contingently responsive to one another's welfare and allow themselves to be dependent on their partner's responsiveness, alerting partners to their needs and comfortably accepting support when it is needed. A quantitative dimension of responsiveness exists as well, for people can vary in terms of how responsive they are to one another in terms of the costs, time, and effort they are willing to devote to monitoring and supporting the other's welfare, as well as in terms of their willingness to depend on the other for support. The greater the degree of responsiveness felt and enacted by each member, the closer that relationship is.

Whereas in many, perhaps most, close relationships partners are both the providers and recipients of responsiveness, we do not believe a relationship must be mutual and symmetrical for a sense of closeness to exist. Because, at times, one person has greater ability, motivation, or both to provide responsiveness and the other is primarily a recipient of responsiveness (e.g., the prototypical example of this being relationship between a parent and a very young child), a sense of closeness can and often does exist even in relationships that might be described as fairly "one-sided." In these relationships, one person (e.g., the parent) provides most of the care, whereas the other (e.g., the young child) receives most of the care. For example, a mother may feel very close to her very young child as a result of feeling and enacting tremendous responsiveness toward that child, and the child may share the sense of closeness as a result of being the recipient of that care even though the levels of responsiveness given and received are clearly asymmetrical. Of course, in this example, the asymmetry is natural for the type of relationship in question. If a similar degree of asymmetry in communal responsiveness were to occur within a relationship normatively expected to be characterized by a symmetry in responsiveness (e.g., a friendship between two able-bodied [physically and mentally] persons), the same feelings of closeness would not exist.

Importantly, closeness, as defined for the purposes of this chapter, may be related to many of the other constructs just discussed. It overlaps conceptually with intimacy, as defined by Reis and colleagues (Reis & Patrick, 1996; Reis & Shaver, 1988), and with the concept of communal strength, as defined by Mills et al. (2004). It is also greatly facilitated by trust (Holmes, 1991; Holmes & Rempel, 1989; Simpson, 2007), because trust allows the fortitude to care for others unconditionally and is crucial for being willing to reveal one's vulnerabilities and allow others to care for the self (Murray, Holmes, & Collins, 2006). It is also facilitated in important ways by commitment, as defined by Rusbult and her colleagues (Rusbult, Olsen, Davis, & Hannon, 2001), because commitment keeps one in a relationship, allowing one to keep being responsive even in the face of a partner's poor behavior (Rusbult et al., 1998), and facilitates the difficult behaviors of forgiveness (Rusbult et al., 2002, 2005) and sacrifice (Van Lange, Resbult, Arriaga, Witcher, & Cox, et al., 1997; Whitton et al., 2002). Commitment seems to keep members of close relationships in an implemental frame of mind (cf. Gagne & Lydon, 2001a, 2001b; Gollwitzer, 1999) with regard to the relationship; that is, commitment seems to promote certainty regarding one's decision to maintain a relationship, as well as striving for responsiveness rather than continually strategically presenting oneself as a desirable partner, evaluating the other, and protecting oneself from risking dependence on the other (Clark & Beck, in press). In addition, because adopting a norm of being non-contingently responsive involves provision of support in response to a partner's needs if and when they arise in the future, and because cultivating responsive relationships likely involves sharing information about needs across time, adopting and applying a norm of non-contingent high responsiveness when with a relationship partner almost always requires some degree of intent to persist in the relationship.

Conceptually, closeness as we define it here is distinct from the constructs of the degree of interdependence and inclusion of other in the self. We can, for instance, imagine two highly interdependent enemies who have frequent, diverse, and strong impacts on one another over a long period, but the impacts are largely negative, aimed not at providing mutual support but rather at competing with and possibly harming the partner. Such a relationship is close in terms of interdependence, but not necessarily in terms of mutual responsiveness. (Of course, it is difficult to imagine a highly responsive relationship that is not also highly interdependent, so, empirically, the constructs will overlap). So,

too, is responsiveness a distinct construct from including the other in the self. People may include others in the self-concept without necessarily seeking or providing responsiveness, although, again, it is difficult to imagine that in highly responsive relationships there would not also be a good deal of including the other in the self.

THE MANY FORMS OF RESPONSIVENESS

Responsiveness takes many forms (Reis et al., 2004). Perhaps the first to come to mind is provision of help to partners when those partners have needs that cannot be met independently. Yet responsiveness takes many other forms as well. It includes endorsing a partner's goals and providing the partner with the time, space, and support necessary to pursue the goal or to explore (Feeney, 2004), spending time with a partner, including him or her in joint activities or groups (Aron, Norman, Aron, McKenna, & Heyman, 2000; Leary & Baumeister, 2000), and celebrating a partner's accomplishments (Gable, Reis, Impett, & Asher, 2004; Gable, Gonzaga, & Strachman, 2006). It can be largely symbolic as when one simply tells a partner than one likes or loves that partner. It may involve affirming a partner's self-concept (Drigotas, 2002; Drigotas, Rusbult, Wieselquist, & Whitton, 1999; Rusbult, Kumashiro, Kubacka, & Finkel, 2009; Swann, 1987). It can take the form of restraining oneself from taking actions, such as not telling a partner a new haircut looks bad or encouraging a partner to engage in activities independent of the self that promote the partner's well-being. Sacrifice, forgiveness, and sometimes even just being quiet while putting up with a partner's grumpy behavior are responsive behaviors as well (Rusbult et al., 2005; Whitton et al., 2002). Responsiveness may, at times, even appear a bit negative on the surface, as when one offers a partner constructive criticism or restrains oneself from helping a partner who ultimately will be better off working through a problem himself or herself as a parent might do when a toddler tries to tie his own shoes. What is key to a responsive action is that it supports and promotes the partner's welfare.

Notably, our definition of closeness is not linked to sexuality. We realize that a considerable body of recent work, much of it based on evolutionary theory, focuses on determinants of sexual interest or mating goals. Moreover, sexual interest is often an important determinant of desires and attempts to establish and maintain a romantic relationship. We do not review that literature here. Instead, we focus on the concept of mutual responsiveness as it is enacted in and serves as a basis not only for close romantic relationships but also for friendships and family relationships. In romantic relationships, a mating goal may motivate people to form a mutually responsive bond with another person, yet it may remain separate from such bonds. (See the chapter on evolution by Neuberg, Kenrick & Schaller, this volume, for coverage of much of the work on sexual determinants of forming romantic relationships and of behavior in those relationships.)

FOCUSING ON PROCESS

How are we to understand such closeness and the well-being it confers? A focus on identifying and understanding the multiple and interrelated intrapersonal and interpersonal processes that characterize and promote (and sometimes detract from) relationships being responsive seems essential. We believe high- versus low-quality, close relationships must be defined in terms of these processes if we are to truly understand them, together with understanding just how and why they promote individual well-being. We need to know what actually occurs in these relationships that contributes to people feeling good, enjoying the relationships, and experiencing the positive consequences of these relationships (as well as what may go wrong process-wise, and how negative processes hurt relationships and the individuals who make up the relationship).

In much "close relationship" work, this simply has not been done. Rather, it has been common in both sociology and psychology to measure static markers of some aspect of a relationship (e.g., the individuals within the relationship share or do not share a religion; the individuals in a marriage were very young at the time they married; an individual in the relationship has a particular personality trait) and to correlate such variables with one of a number of possible "markers" that the relationship is either good (e.g., high ratings of relationship satisfaction, the relationship has lasted a long time) or bad (e.g., divorce occurs, members say they are dissatisfied). However, as House, Landis, and Umberson (1988) noted some time ago, we already know the association between having relationships and well-being, but we need to know the mechanisms through which the association is mediated. Moreover, these mechanisms, as Cohen (2004) pointed out, will be varied. Some will buffer people in the face of acute stress. Others will promote positive feelings day to day. Yet others may be harmful and erase the health-promoting qualities of relationships for some individuals and perhaps even harm members' well-being (Cohen), and their absence should be considered markers of relationship well-being.

We believe that identifying high (low)-quality relationships by intrapersonal and interpersonal processes will provide the clearest picture of just what such relationships are and will provide the best basis for intervention in troubled relationships. Yet, this mapping out of processes that promote and inhibit noncontingent responsiveness and happiness in relationships is going to be complex. It is not going to simply involve producing a list of "good" processes and "bad" ones because research increasingly makes it evident that whether certain processes are good or bad often depends on relationship context. Consider forgiveness, for example. Forgiveness is often labeled a virtue, and consistent with that view, evidence exists that it promotes relationships (Fincham, Beach, & Davila, 2004), and among spouses married to partners who rarely behave negatively, being more forgiving in the face of negative partner behavior *is* linked to remaining more satisfied across time (McNulty, 2008). From our perspective, we would say that such forgiveness is responsive to the errant partner; it likely makes the partner feel accepted and cared for even in the face of having flaws. In addition, it should promote feelings of being caring in the forgiver, which also ought to benefit the relationship. Yet, among spouses married to partners whose typical behavior is destructive, being more forgiving has actually been shown to be associated with steeper declines in satisfaction across time (McNulty). In other words, it seems to be terrific to forgive a partner who likely has good overarching intentions and makes minor slipups, as we all do, but bad to forgive a partner who is truly abusive, as forgiveness in such a case does nothing to correct the bad habits and may even reinforce them. In this case, a seemingly responsive behavior may promote or even allow to accelerate nonresponsive behaviors on the part of the forgiven partner. Therefore, seemingly "good" relationship processes may not be "good" in all contexts.

Likewise, seemingly "bad" behaviors may not always be bad. Consider expressing anger to one's partner. Many studies have shown that people say they do not like others who express anger (cf. Sommers, 1984). Yet Yoo, Clark, Salovey, Lemay, and Monin (2009) have found that expressing anger results in declines in liking for partners when a communal (i.e., mutually responsive) relationship is not desired or when the communal strength of a relationship is weak. However, expressing anger can also convey needs and does not cause declines in liking when a communal relationship is strong (Yoo et al.). Indeed, in such a case expressions of anger actually have been shown to elicit enhanced levels of social support (Graham et al., 2008; Yoo et al.). So, too, has expressing anxiety to a securely attached partner been shown to elicit support, whereas expressing similar levels of anxiety to a partner who characteristically avoids intimacy appears to drive that partner away (Simpson, Rholes, & Nelligan, 1992).

Thus, it should be possible to paint good pictures of what high-quality, responsive, close relationships look like and what poor-quality relationships look like in terms of intrapersonal and interpersonal processes. Yet, pictures of what good and bad close relationships look like will not be perfect mirror images of one another. For just this reason it is also now clear that for purposes of intervention in troubled relationships, it will be insufficient and naïve to point to differences in how troubled versus happy partnerships operate, and simply to tell troubled couples to stop what they are doing and substitute with behaviors that characterize happy relationships. Context matters. A final point to be made in this regard is that we clearly need more work that integrates findings arising from samples of normally functioning dyads (typically done by social psychologists) with findings arising from samples of more troubled dyads (typically done by clinicians).

It also is important to consider the developmental trajectories of close relationships. We currently have bodies of literature on determinants of initial attraction and much on the functioning of established relationships, most typically focusing established romantic relationships among young adults. Yet, we have little data that track actual relationship formation, that is, little data on what happens between initial attraction and the establishment of close, ongoing relationships. We have some, but not much, developmental data on what unfolds over the course of ongoing romantic relationships, particularly in the early years and particularly across the transition to parenthood for married couples, but more is needed. We have little data on the actual unfolding and deterioration of relationships, particularly in the case of friendships. It is important to fill these gaps, for not only is it the case that the processes that characterize these stages may be distinct in nature and degree from those that characterize other stages, but processes that may be normative or beneficial to relationships in one stage may be non-normative or harmful to relationships in another stage. Consider, for instance, being anxious, cautious, and guarded in a relationship. This sort of anxiety may be healthy and adaptive early in relationships (Clark & Beck, in press; Eastwick & Finkel, 2008b) but a sign that all is not well in established relationships. Or consider having positive illusions about one's romantic partner. This appears to be a good sign and to facilitate a partner's positive growth in established relationships (Murray, Holmes, & Griffin, 1996a, 1996b, 2003; and see Murray & Derrick, 2005 for context), yet seeing one's partner clearly and without bias may be far more functional when forming a relationship (Gagne & Lydon, 2001a; 2004) lest one miss the potential partner's negative attributes and end up unwisely committed to a partner whose negative attributes subsequently erode satisfaction (Clements, Stanley, & Markman, 2004; Markman, 1979, 1981). To illustrate the importance of focusing on the development of interpersonal processes across time, we note the considerable attention received by Gottman's list of four attitudes that predict marital failure (Gottman, 1994): criticism (or attacking a partner's

character), contempt (attacking a partner's sense of self), defensiveness (seeing oneself as a victim and warding off perceived attacks), and stonewalling (or withdrawing from a relationship to avoid conflict). We applaud the focus on interpersonal process. Yet, importantly, noting a relationship is characterized by these four processes, and therefore bad, and predicting its demise is insufficient. Can one simply tell people to stop such behaviors and all will be well? Likely not. Something drove people to engage in these processes in the first place, and changing the "symptom" likely leaves its antecedent causes in place and does not give individuals a clue regarding what healthy processes ought to replace whatever poor relational processes led to the symptoms in the first place. We need to know how and why an initially desired, and perhaps well-functioning, relationship became characterized by criticism, contempt, defensiveness, and stonewalling, and therapists need to know what intrapersonal and interpersonal processes people need to learn and practice if there is to be any hope of eliminating such bad behaviors.

Fortunately, relationship researchers are rapidly informing us of the nature of many of the processes that likely form the constellation of specific, helpful and harmful, intrapersonal and interpersonal processes that promote (and sometimes detract) from relationship health, and thus individual mental and physical health. Moreover, individuals such as McNulty are keeping us from making the simple and tempting generalizations from our studies of relatively well-functioning dyads to all dyads. There is, unfortunately, still little work on relational trajectories and processes as they unfold across relationship initiation, commitment, maintenance, and deterioration, but there is some and we will mention some examples throughout this chapter.

Unfortunately, we cannot say much about developmental trajectories in this chapter because this is an area in which little extant work exists and much work remains to be done.

A BROAD, INTEGRATIVE PROCESS MODEL OF RESPONSIVENESS DYNAMICS

As noted earlier, we focus our review on the dynamics of responsiveness within close relationships that involve a system of integrated processes (see Reis, Collins, & Berscheid, 2000), including providing, perceiving, receiving, desiring, seeking, and benefiting from responsiveness within close relationships. Also, as noted earlier, we conceive of the construct of responsiveness broadly following Reis et al. (2004) so that we can highlight similarities across research areas. Hence, constructs and processes emphasized in diverse research areas, such as reactions to evaluative feedback, social support, attraction, attachment, caregiving, and social inclusion, are often related closely to responsiveness as we conceive it; research on these issues often seems more similar than different to us in terms of their implications for interpersonal responsiveness dynamics. As such, we treat them somewhat interchangeably. Of course, important differences exist across these constructs, but here, in the interest of theoretical parsimony, our goal is to highlight their commonalities.

Although the belief that a partner is motivated to respond supportively to one's needs is a critical component of perceived responsiveness, other forms of responsiveness have been studied and we address these other forms in our review. Another commonly studied form is the specific belief that a potential or existing partner has positive regard for the self. Perceiving that the partner has positive regard for the self may indirectly contribute to the more global belief that a partner will respond supportively to the self. Positive evaluation is widely believed to be a predictor and indicator of approach motivation—people approach objects (including other people) that they view positively. People desire to avoid negatively evaluated others. Hence, those who feel positively regarded may be confident that the partner wishes to approach the relationship to form a close bond characterized by mutual responsiveness. Moreover, people desire to be valuable relationship partners in others' eyes (Leary & Baumeister, 2000), and believing that others have positive regard helps fulfill this desire. Beyond feeling valued, however, people seem to desire to be understood by their relationship partners and to receive feedback that verifies importantly held identities (Reis & Shaver, 1988; Swann, 1987). Such feedback may be responsive for many reasons. First, and probably foremost, feeling understood by a partner likely contributes to the belief that the partner is motivated and able to be responsive to the self. After all, a partner who has not made the effort to understand one and who does not know one's unique perspectives, interests, desires, and needs cannot possibly be expected to respond supportively to these things. Indeed, understanding of needs is often included in measures of caregiving (Kunce & Shaver, 1994), and observed support provision has been related to wives' accurate views of their husbands' specific abilities and traits (Neff & Karney, 2005). People also reported greater intimacy in their marriages when their spouse's views of their abilities matched their own views of their abilities, whether positive or negative. In addition, people may desire feedback that confirms existing self-views because they rely on their self-views to navigate their social environments and predict future outcomes (Swann, 1987; Swann, Stein-Seroussi, & Giesler, 1992). They seem to rely on romantic partners to help them diffuse self-discrepant feedback (De La Ronde & Swann, 1998; see also Swann & Predmore, 1985). Of course, being positively regarded can

sometimes conflict with being understood, which can produce ambivalent reactions to either form of responsiveness (Shrauger, 1975; Swann, Griffin, Predmore, & Gaines, 1987). One compelling model of how both forms of responsiveness can occur and have benefits distinguishes among levels of abstraction. Most people seem to simultaneously enhance their spouses in regard to rather broad qualities (e.g., global worth) and perceive them rather accurately in regard to specific, circumscribed qualities (e.g., tidy) (Neff & Karney, 2002, 2005). This pattern of responsiveness likely causes partners to feel that they are both valued and understood.

RESPONSIVENESS AS A RELATIONSHIP-SPECIFIC CONSTRUCT

Consistent with a view of relationships as somewhat autonomously functioning systems (see Reis et al., 2000), we view responsiveness to a partner and perceptions of that responsiveness as largely relationship-specific phenomena. Although this point is not frequently made, we believe it is an important point because it is one that is often overshadowed by the prominence of individual difference work in the close relationships area, which may be taken, by some, to suggest that responsiveness and perceived responsiveness are qualities of individuals rather than of relationships.

Theoretically, responsiveness should be mainly relationship specific for a number of reasons. First, a mundane but powerful reason is that we simply do not have the capacity to have highly responsive relationships with too many people. We have the resources to carefully monitor and respond to the needs of only a limited number of individuals. Moreover, the more highly responsive relationships we do have, the fewer we need. Thus, people tend to have sets of hierarchically ordered responsive relationships that vary in communal strength from low (with, for instance, strangers and casual acquaintances) to moderate (with, for instance, friends) to very strong (perhaps with a child or spouse) (Clark & Monin, 2006; Mills & Clark, 1982; Reis et al., 2004). To whom we are responsive and from whom we expect responsiveness depend on who the partner is, where in our communal hierarchy our relationship with them sits and where, in their hierarchy, their relationship with us sits (see Monin, Clark, & Lemay, 2008). These relationships tend to be mutual. Indeed, as we discuss later, mutually responsive relationships may be created by detecting a partner's responsiveness and then feeling more motivated or able to be responsive in return. The very nature of such hierarchies dictates that responsiveness will vary most by relationship, not by the individual differences in tendencies to be responsive or to elicit responsiveness from others.

Second, just how attributes, skills, and needs mesh to facilitate (or impede) responsiveness is, logically, dependent on the combination of attributes two people bring to a relationship. A good example of this is provided by some recent research on empathic accuracy that demonstrates that empathic accuracy is not dependent just on the perceiver's skills. Instead, for a perceiver to be empathically accurate regarding a partner's emotional states, not only must that person be motivated and skilled enough to detect emotion accurately, but the partner also must be emotionally expressive (Zaki et al., 2008). Other examples include the likelihood that people who share intense interests in wine-tasting or tennis may be the only ones who can appropriately respond to one another's desire to discuss wine or engage in a skilled and high-level tennis game and that those who share sorrows such as a loss of a child may also be best able to be responsive to one another, perhaps in a support group. This is an important reason, we believe, for the powerful effects similarities have on relationship formation and satisfaction. Finally, shared histories, investments, and goals may motivate both partners' responsiveness in relationships, which may create mutually responsive relationships.

Empirical studies support the view that responsiveness is, to a large extent, relationship specific rather than individually based. For instance, although some people generally like others and feel liked by others, substantial relationship-specific variance components are also present; people like and feel liked by different people to different degrees (Kenny & DePaulo, 1993; Levesque, 1997). More closely related to our theoretical construct, care for others' needs and perceived care by others varies substantially from one relationship to the next (Lemay & Clark, 2008a), as does perceived social support (Barry, Lakey, & Orehek, 2007; Davis, Morris, & Kraus, 1998; Lakey, McCabe, Fisicaro, & Drew, 1996; Pierce, Sarason, & Sarason, 1991), desires for closeness (Baldwin, Keelan, Fehr, Enns, & Koh-Rangarajoo, 1996; Barry et al., 2007; Cook, 2000; Klohnen, Weller, Luo, & Choe, 2005; La Guardia, Ryan, Couchman, & Deci, 2000; Pierce & Lydon, 2001), fears of abandonment (Baldwin et al.; Barry et al.; Cook; La Guardia et al.; Pierce & Lydon), and felt intimacy (Pierce & Lydon). That is, people seem to differentially feel responsive and differentially perceive responsiveness across their multiple relationship partners.

Interestingly, recent research suggests that people (and cultures) vary in terms of the extent to which relationships are emphasized as aspects of self-concept (Cross, Gore, & Morris, 2003; Cross, Morris, & Gore, 2002; Gore & Cross, 2006). Viewing oneself as inconsistent across relationships seems to be more troubling and more detrimental for well-being among those who have independent self-construals than for those who emphasize interdependence

and relationships in their self-concepts. This is intriguing, as it suggests that those who are relationally interdependent are also likely to be the ones whose levels of responsiveness vary most according to the relationship in which they find themselves.

This is not to say that individual differences and features of the external relationship environment (see Berscheid, 1999) are irrelevant. To the contrary, such factors are extremely important for understanding relationship phenomena (as we review later). However, the existence of relationship-specific processes seems to us to be quite normative, and relationship-specific processes may frequently overwhelm other factors once relationships are established (e.g., Barry et al., 2007; Cook, 2000; Cozzarelli, Hoekstra, & Bylsma, 2000; Klohnen et al., 2005; Murray, Bellavia, Rose, & Griffin, 2003). We emphasize the importance of normative relationship-specific variation in responsiveness primarily because this has sometimes been obscured by an emphasis in the literature on the impact of work on individual differences, particularly individual differences in attachment styles. Yet, this point is not at all at odds with attachment theory because that theory itself emphasizes that the natural course of events is for individuals to become especially attached to particular other individuals and not to all others.

We would also note that the very fact that all people seem to have hierarchies of close relationships that vary in responsiveness raises intriguing new questions about these individual differences. Do people who are especially responsive have more "close" relationships altogether than others? If so, where in their hierarchies do these additional responsive relationships sit? Are they at the bottom with people being more responsive to acquaintances? At the top with people being more responsive to spouses? All along the hierarchy? Do people who are especially responsive have stronger communal relationships altogether than others? In other words, to say that some people are more responsive than other people (an individual difference focus) leaves open several possibilities regarding *how* this additional responsiveness is manifested in communal relationship hierarchies.

DO PEOPLE WANT RESPONSIVENESS?

To this point we have suggested that good, high quality, close relationships are characterized by responsiveness. This may seem obvious, but it is worth examining whether empirical evidence exists for this assumption. Although global measures of relationship satisfaction and general relationship quality are somewhat ambiguous, they do seem to index the extent to which one's relationship conforms to one's ideals and expectations (Hassebrauck & Aron, 2001). Hence links between measures of responsiveness and such global measures may be taken as evidence relevant to whether people want responsiveness. The fact that strong correlations are routinely observed between perceived relationship quality and perceptions of partner's care (Cross, Bacon, & Morris, 2000; Lemay, Clark, & Feeney, 2007), social support (Abbey, Andrews, & Halman, 1995; Campbell, Simpson, Boldry, & Kashy, 2005; Collins & Feeney, 2000; Deci, La Guardia, Moller, Scheiner, & Ryan, 2006; Gable et al., 2004; Kaul & Lakey, 2003; Srivastava, McGonigal, Richards, Butler, & Gross, 2006), love (Murray, Holmes, Griffin, Bellavia, & Rose, 2001), regard (Murray, Holmes, & Griffin, 2000; Overall, Fletcher, & Simpson, 2006), valuing (La Guardia et al., 2000), and willingness to sacrifice (Wieselquist, Rusbult, Foster, & Agnew, 1999) indicates people do desire responsiveness in their relationships. In addition, the fact that people value communal traits (e.g., empathy, friendliness, helpfulness) (Abele & Wojciszke, 2007) and trustworthiness (Cottrell, Neuberg, & Li, 2007) in relationship partners, and that they value them more than they value agentic traits (see also Fletcher, Simpson, Thomas, & Giles, 1999; Sprecher, 1998) and more than they say they value such attributes as a partner having resources and beauty (Buss, 1989; Buss & Barnes, 1986) provides further support for the value of responsiveness in relationships. The common belief that responsive self-disclosure and emotional support are critical for the development of closeness (Fehr, 2004), as well as the actual covariation between felt closeness and beliefs of being understood, accepted, and cared for (Laurenceau, Barrett, & Pietromonaco, 1998) provide additional support. Hence, people generally seem to desire close relationships to be characterized by mutual responsiveness.

It is, however, worth noting two caveats. First, attachment researchers have uncovered considerable evidence that a small but significant proportion of people, those classified as avoidant, deny vulnerability, do not seek support and intimacy, and emphasize their own self-sufficiency (Mikulincer & Shaver, 2003) while still associating and socializing with other people (Mikulincer & Shaver, 2007). On the surface, this might be taken to indicate that avoidantly attached persons care little about partner responsiveness and, indeed, have some disdain for it if it requires, as it often does, being vulnerable and intimate. Yet, considerable evidence has been reported that their avoidance of intimacy and dependence is a self-protective veneer, and that even they show signs of desire for intimacy. In particular, they react with distress and arousal when rejected, signs that, we would note, belie their seeming lack of interest in responsiveness (Beck & Clark, 2008; Diamond, Hicks & Otter-Henderson, 2006; Roisman, Tsai & Chiang, 2004).

A second caveat relates to the fact that individuals characterized by attachment-related anxiety—that is, those who claim to fear abandonment by relationship partners—have been observed to display some discomfort when partners do act in communally responsive ways (Bartz & Lydon, 2006, study 2; Beck & Clark, 2008). This, especially when taken together with findings regarding the existence of people characterized by unmitigated communion, who provide support to partners but seem very reluctant to seek or accept support (Helgeson & Fritz, 1998), might also be taken to indicate the existence of a subset of people who do not desire to be recipients of partners' responsiveness. We suggest, however, as have others, that reluctance to seek responsiveness may arise from fears that dependency will not be met with responsiveness, and that initial acceptance and responsiveness might not be followed by sustained responsiveness across time. Thus, we maintain our claim that people, in general, desire responsiveness but note that self-protective defensive processes, at times, mask that desire.

MODEL OF RESPONSIVENESS GIVEN AND RECEIVED

We present a broad, integrative model of responsiveness in Figure 25.1. In most of the remaining sections of this review, we describe empirical results that are broadly consistent with this model. The model posits that confidence in a partner's responsiveness and desire for a mutually responsive relationship are products of a variety of precipitating factors such as traits of the partner, traits of the perceiver, and the external environment. In addition, confidence in a partner's responsiveness and relationship desire mutually influence one another, and each cause both provision of responsiveness to a partner and seeking of responsiveness from a partner. Beyond confidence and desire, provision of responsiveness is thought to occur as a result of perceiving a partner's need for responsiveness, and one's own need is thought to drive seeking of responsiveness from the partner.

Figure 25.1 also illustrates coordination between partners (shown as dashed lines), such that one's partner's provision of responsiveness affects the other's confidence in responsiveness, relief of need, and promotion of well-being. Likewise, one partner's seeking of responsiveness affects the other partner's perceptions of that partner's need for responsiveness.

Figure 25.1 illustrates effects of "Partner B" on "Partner A." Of course, Partner A influences Partner B as well, but to minimize complexity, we omitted the analogous effects of "Partner A" on "Partner B." Figure 25.1 implies several feedback loops, which characterize a systems approach to close relationships (see Reis et al., 2000). For example, a

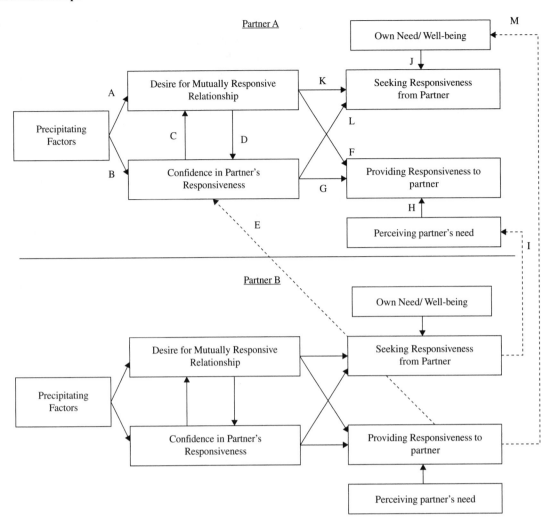

Figure 25.1   An Integrative Model of Responsiveness.

state of need is a cause and consequence of the illustrated processes, such that the presence of a need (ideally) predicts seeking responsiveness, which causes the partner (ideally) to detect the need and provide responsiveness, which (again, ideally) alleviates the need. In addition, convergence across partners may occur through a conjunction of the illustrated processes. For example, one's desire for a mutually responsive relationship may cause one to provide responsiveness, which increases the partner's confidence in that responsiveness, which may increase that partner's desire for a mutually responsive relationship.

What Figure 25.1 does not include are some of the hurtful behaviors that commonly occur in relationships that our culture dictates ought to be responsive and communal in nature but, in practice, may not be. Such behaviors exist and will be raised in connection to the model as exceptions to the links depicted in that model.

Our discussion of the model shown in Figure 25.1 starts with "precipitating factors" (Paths A and B) or, in

other words, factors that influence whether people desire responsive relationships with a particular other (Path A) and have confidence in the target's potential responsiveness toward them (Path B). Many precipitating factors influence both desire and confidence so they are discussed together here.

Path A: Precipitating Factors That Motivate Desire for a Close, Responsive Relationship

A number of "background factors," such as individual differences in both partners and qualities of the relationship environment may determine whether people desire to form and maintain a mutually responsive relationship with a particular partner.

Nepotism

In thinking about what drives people to be motivated to be responsive to one another, we commonly think of factors that drive physical attraction to others (such as beauty) or ones that influence liking for potential partners (e.g., they are kind). Yet, there are other, very important factors that seem to motive forming responsive bonds with others, particularly our kin. With the exception of romantic partners (who are rated the closest), people feel closer to kin than nonkin. Moreover, the degree of felt closeness varies with the degree of genetic relatedness. However, there are individual differences in these effects (Neyer & Lang, 2003). Among close relatives people tend to feel more responsiveness toward and to expect more responsiveness from those with the closest biological ties (e.g., more responsiveness is felt toward and expected from mothers than aunts), and among those with equally strong ties they tend to feel more responsiveness toward and to expect more responsiveness from female than male relatives (Monin, Clark, & Lemay, 2008).

Much evidence has been reported to suggest that we may be hardwired to form attachment bonds with our own infants and with other kin (Bowlby, 1969). Increasing evidence has also been reported suggesting that hormones such as oxytocin function to bind parents to offspring (see Pedersen, 2006 for a commentary on this and Feldman, Weller, Zagoory-Sharon, & Levine, 2007) and to bind sexual partners, who will be the basis of new kinship ties, to one another (Floyd, 2006). Levels of this hormone in the bloodstream are linked to levels of trust in humans (Kirsch et al., 2005; Kosfeld et al., 2005). There do seem to be individual differences in these effects. Feldman et al. [2007] and many others have suggested that both our natural tendencies to form attachment bonds and the natural functioning of systems involving oxytocin can be disrupted by negative experiences within relationships.

Of course cultural dictates also motivate a sense of duty to kin. Thus, duty and biological factors are factors that push us toward responsiveness to others, and these factors can operate even in the absence of liking for these people.

Pre-existing Bonds with Others

If maintaining mutually responsive bonds is a need that can be satiated, people should be especially eager to establish a relationship with any particular new potential partner to the extent to which they lack such bonds elsewhere (see Baumeister & Leary, 1995). People who have just lost a particularly strong communal bond through death or divorce, or perhaps most commonly, through moving to a new physical location may be especially interested in forming close relationships with new individuals. Consistent with the idea that people who lack close bonds ought to be especially attracted to others, reminding people about social rejection from a current partner increases their interest in meeting new people (Maner, DeWall, Baumeister, & Schaller, 2007, studies 1 and 2; see also Williams & Sommer, 1997).

In addition, a number of studies have now provided evidence that people who have established romantic relationships characterized by commitment are less prone to have their attention captured by attractive alternatives (Maner, Gailliot, & Miller, 2009; Maner, Rouby, & Gonzaga, 2008; Miller, 1997), and that when they do attend to attractive others, they judge them to be less attractive than do people who are available for new relationships (Johnson & Rusbult, 1989; Lydon, Fitzsimons, & Naidoo, 2003; -; Simpson, Gangestad, & Lerma, 1990). In addition, partners in committed, happy relationships appear biased to perceive their relationship to be better than the relationships others have (Buunk, 2001; Rusbult, Van Lange, Wildschut, Yovetich, & Verette, 2000), and thus ought to be less interested in alternative relationships than others will be. For all these reasons, and perhaps more yet to be discovered, existing relationships are important determinants of the likelihood of forming new close relationships with additional target persons.

The degree to which establishing a new relationship would disrupt pre-existing bonds also seems to influence attraction toward new partners. People report less commitment toward romantic partners when they believe that other partners disapprove of the relationship (Cox, Wexler, Rusbult, & Gaines, 1997; Lehmiller & Agnew, 2006). In contrast, approval of the relationship from one's broader social network predicts relationship persistence (Sprecher & Felmlee, 1992).

Qualities of the Target

Various partner assets in the interpersonal "marketplace" may enhance one's attraction to current or potential partners. Perhaps the most researched of these assets is physical attractiveness, which clearly does enhance attraction (Eastwick & Finkel, 2008a; Huston & Levinger, 1978; Walster, Aronson, Abrahams, & Rottman, 1966) and predicts desires to maintain bonds in ongoing relationships (Lemay, Clark, & Greenberg, in press). From an evolutionary perspective, people may desire attractive relationship partners because attractiveness signals (or at least signaled during our evolutionary history, if not today—see Kalick, Zebrowitz, Langlois, & Johnson, 1998) health, and hence low threat of contagion (Thornhill & Gangestad, 1999). So, too, does the cultural value people place on beauty likely account, in part, for our liking of the physically attractive.

Other interpersonal assets that enhance attraction include qualities such as intelligence, popularity, or assertiveness. People may desire such qualities in their relationship partners to the extent that outcome dependency is high and these qualities are anticipated to fulfill personal goals (Abele & Wojciszke, 2007; Cottrell et al., 2007). In addition, having partners with such desirable qualities sometimes boosts one's own feelings of self-worth or one's own sense of being interpersonally desirable through a process in which the partner is thought to reflect on the self (Cialdini, Borden, Thorne, Walker, Freeman, & Sloan, 1976; Tesser, 1988) and, indeed, may actually reflect (Sigall & Landy, 1973) on the self. The extent to which such reflection is a concern may vary across individuals. For instance, narcissists—those with low desires for intimacy and grandiose, volatile self-concepts—especially desire to have "perfect" relationship partners (e.g., popular, attractive, athletic, successful), in part because they anticipate feeling better about themselves and being more popular if they had such partners (Campbell, 1999). Similarly, some evidence suggests that individuals with low self-esteem may be especially concerned with reflection (Lemay & Clark, 2009; Tesser, 1988; Tesser & Cornell, 1991). This is a matter of degree, however, for even non-narcissists and individuals with high self-esteem tend to be attracted to partners with many of these interpersonal assets, and Tesser (1988) conceived of reflection as a largely normative process with which everyone is concerned at times.

A partner's positive qualities, however, can reduce attraction if individuals make upward social comparisons. The self-evaluation maintenance model posits that people are less attracted to individuals who outperform them in a domain that is highly relevant to self-definition, and some findings support this view (Tesser, 1988). Importantly, affective reactions to social comparison appear to be moderated by the established degree of closeness. In relationships that are already close, the threat of upward comparison seems mitigated by empathic, positive affective reactions to a close other's positive performance (Beach, Tesser, Fincham, Jones, Johnson, & Whitaker, 1998). In very close relationships, a cognitive inclusion of the other in the self (see Aron & Fraley, 1999) also seems to operate independently of empathic effects, such that positive outcomes for others are experienced as positive outcomes for the self (McFarland, Buchler, & MacKay, 2001). Priming of self as distinct causes contrast effects in social comparison, such that people feel better when exposed to unsuccessful relative to successful others, whereas priming of self as related causes assimilation effects, such that people feel more positively about themselves when exposed to a successful relative to unsuccessful comparison target (Stapel & Koomen, 2001; see also Gabriel, Carvallo, Dean, Tippin, & Renaud, 2005; Gardner, Gabriel, & Hochschild, 2002). When a close partner outperforms the self, people also may focus on their connection with the partner, and being connected to a desirable partner may be a means of indirect self-enhancement (Lockwood, Dolderman, Sadler, & Gerchak, 2004; see also Locke & Nekich, 2000). In contrast, upward comparisons seem threatening when closeness is not already established, although such comparisons seem rare

during interaction (Locke & Nekich). Also, upward comparisons even with currently distant others may not be threatening if people have expectancies that they can be similar to the other on the comparison dimension (Collins, 1996).

Similarity/Dissimilarity

Broadly speaking, whether a target person's dissimilarities and similarities cause people to become attracted to one another has remained an area of interest to relationship researchers and, as it has, it becomes clear that neither the claim that "opposites attract" nor that "birds of a feather flock together" is clearly true or false. Instead, a more nuanced approach that takes into account interpersonal and intrapersonal processes better serves our understanding of this issue.

Some evidence has been reported that people desire partners who are distinct from themselves. For instance, evidence exists that people prefer complementary interaction partners on the dominance-submissiveness dimension (Dryer & Horowitz, 1997; see also Tiedens & Jimenez, 2003) presumably because that combination allows both people to behave as preferred within a relationship. Of course, the literature on social comparison just mentioned also suggests that in performance domains, at least, another person's good performance may threaten one's own sense of competence in that same domain, leading one to experience negative emotion (e.g., DeSteno & Salovey, 1996; Tesser, Millar, & Moore, 1988) and to prefer or feel more comfortable with a person "opposite from the self" in performance skills. For instance, a person who excels in acting may be most comfortable with a person who would never consider acting but loves doing scientific research. If the scientist performs well, the actor will not suffer from painful comparisons and can bask in that person's glory. Indeed, some evidence exists that we seek complementarity with relationship partners in performance domains, are more comfortable around people who are distinct from us in performance domains, and are attracted to such people (Beach, Whitaker, Jones, & Tesser, 2001). Finally, it is also the case that Aron and his colleagues' work on including the other in the self (Aron, McLaughlin-Volpe, Mashek, Lewandowski, Wright, & Aron, 2004) suggests that a partner who is distinct from the self may facilitate the positive feelings that accompany such expansion, and this provides yet another reason why people with distinct attributes or those who are different in some ways (if not exactly opposite) may be attracted to one another (see Aron, Steele, Kashdan, & Perez, 2006 for male participants).

Yet it is simultaneously true (and not contradictory) that similarity draws people together. Researchers found this long ago (Byrne, 1971; Byrne & Griffitt, 1973; Newcomb, 1961), and recent research reaffirms that similarity in attitudes, demographic variables, and activity preferences do, in fact, draw people together (Klohnen & Luo, 2003; Singh, Ng, Ong, & Lin, 2008). It is also now clear that these effects cannot be attributed merely to discoveries of dissimilarity producing repulsion (Drigotas, 1993; Smeaton, Byrne, & Murnen, 1989) as had once been suggested, although dissimilarity clearly can lead to avoidance or distancing from people (Drigotas, 1993). At the same time, new research shows that different types of similarity may well be more or less important to different people (see Jamieson, Lydon, & Zanna, 1987), perceived similarity may be distinct from actual similarity (Dryer & Horowitz, 1997; Murray, Holmes, Bellavia, Griffin, & Dolderman, 2002), and similarity itself may be more or less important to different individuals (see Michinov & Michinov, 2001). Still, although our understanding of exactly how similarity influences attraction is certainly becoming more nuanced, the finding that similarity does attract people to one another remains one of social psychology's most replicated findings.

New research offers more support for established thinking about the processes through which similarity may lead to greater attraction, as well as new evidence about additional processes that are influential in this regard. As suggested early on, others' similarities may be affirming and make us feel good (Byrne & Clore, 1970; Singh, Yeo, Lin, & Tan, 2007), they enhance trust that the other will reciprocate liking and care (Condon & Crano, 1988; Singh et al., 2007) and they lead to more positive evaluations of potential partners (Montoya & Horton, 2004; Singh et al., 2007), which, we note, may facilitate positive reflection processes. Intriguingly, thinking about similarity (rather than uniqueness) also seems to push us to focus on partners as part of a unit, a "we," and to reduce feelings of defensiveness and that may also draw us toward other similar potential partners (Tesser, Beach, Mendolia, Crepaz, Davies, & Pennebaker, 1998).

Are these the only processes through which similarity has its potent effects? Probably not, for current research also suggests an intriguing new mediating process that seems decidedly less rational. In particular, Burger, Messian, Patel, del Prado, and Anderson (2004), and Miller, Downs, and Prentice (1998) all found evidence that similarities in such mundane things as people's birth dates, names, and even fingerprints (if pointed out) increase cooperation between people, and Jones, Pelham, Carvallo, and Mirenberg (2004) reported studies showing striking links between such similarities and liking. They argue for a sort of "implicit egoism" that occurs whereby when people note even mundane similarities between the self and a partner, they will automatically and without effort come to have positive reactions to that partner. Finally, it is important to keep in mind that, as mentioned

earlier, when it comes to similarity in generally desired attributes (e.g., physical attractiveness), similar people may end up together not because similarity leads to greater attraction, but rather because of everyone desiring partners with the best attributes but people either settling or being forced to settle for those they can "get." It is also important to keep in mind that similar people may end up together because they choose to enter similar situations. Thus they may simply be more likely to meet one another and become attracted.

Activated Thoughts Relevant to Other Relationships

Newer research also suggests that qualities of new targets may activate concepts of relationship (or past relationship) partners who share those qualities, with implications for whether people approach or avoid the new target (Andersen & Chen, 2002). For instance, it is now clear that if attributes of a new person remind us of attributes of someone with whom we have had a good or a bad relationship in the past, then judgments from the past and affective feelings from specific past relationships feed forward and influence whether we feel attracted to or repulsed from the new partner. This can occur even when the attributes of a new person that "prime" thoughts about existing or past relationships are quite trivial and seemingly relationship irrelevant. For instance, the hair color or voice of a new person may influence our desire for a relationship with that person not necessarily because we care about those attributes, but because they bring to mind feelings about another person who shared those attributes.

Moreover, this occurs without our having to be aware of that fact (Andersen & Chen, 2002; Andersen, Reznik, & Manzella, 1996). When a current partner reminds us of a past partner for any reason, it does seem to bring back not just that relevant memory of the partner but many others as well (Glassman & Andersen, 1999). Moreover, because past partners may have had both good and bad attributes, it even appears that if a negative attribute of a potential partner reminds us of something negative about a past partner about whom we *also* happen to have had some very positive feelings, the same negative trait in a new person ironically can, through priming, elicit positive feelings. For instance, Berenson and Anderson (2006) observed that when women who were abused by parents met a new person who reminded them of that parent, they experienced both enhanced dysphoria *and* enhanced positive feelings (presumably because even abused children likely have positive as well as negative memories of their parents). Sadly, this may be one reason people are sometimes attracted to others who are not "good for them."

Other likely nonconscious effects that target attributes or behavior have on attraction include a person mimicking our moves causing us to like them more (Chartrand & Bargh, 1999), primes of hostility somewhere in our environment causing us to like people less even though they did not cause the hostile prime (Bargh & Pietromonaco, 1982), primes of power causing us to approach people (Smith & Bargh, 2008), thinking of friends causing us to be helpful and responsive to entirely new individuals encountered soon after those thoughts have occurred (Fitzsimons & Bargh, 2003), being primed with thoughts (e.g., names) of existing partners with whom we feel secure, anxious, or avoidant, influencing the nature of interpersonal goals we pursue when with new people (Gillath, Mikulincer, Fitzsimons, Shaver, Schachner, & Bargh, 2006), and even feelings of physical warmth caused by something independent of a target person (such as holding a warm vs. iced drink) leading us to feel "warmly" toward another person, liking that person more and being more responsive to him or her (Williams & Bargh, 2008; Zhong & Leonardelli, 2008). Clearly, we do not always have control over or even conscious awareness of our momentary feelings of liking or urges to approach or help new people we meet. Yet, these feelings of liking and urges to approach or help are all linked to our concept of responsiveness, and thus may well influence the initiation of new relationships.

At the same time, some recent research suggests limits on the effects of nonconscious primes on our attraction toward others. Specifically, Kruglanski and Pierro's (2008) research suggests primes are most likely to have an impact on us when our cognitive resources are limited. (In their case, cognitive resources were low for "evening persons" tested in the morning and "morning persons" tested in the evening). The current bottom line to us seems to be that we now know such processes may be important "players" in relationship processes. Yet, much work remains to be done to nail down just when, for whom, how, and to what degree these unconscious processes influence relationship processes.

Attachment Dimensions

According to Bowlby (1969), early interactions with significant others generate expectations and beliefs that guide interpersonal perception and behavior in adulthood. Hazan and Shaver (1987) developed a framework of how such expectations and beliefs operate in adult romantic relationships. Many attachment theorists distinguish such perception, beliefs, and behavior into two primary dimensions, commonly termed "attachment-related anxiety" and "attachment-related avoidance" (see Bartholomew & Horowitz, 1991 for an early dimensional model; and Brennan, Clark, & Shaver, 1998; Collins & Read, 1990; Fraley & Waller, 1998; Fraley, Waller & Brennan, 2000; Simpson, Rholes, & Phillips, 1996). Secure individuals are thought to be low on both anxiety and avoidance.

People high on the anxiety dimension tend to worry and ruminate about abandonment by close others. Hence, such individuals chronically desire responsive relationships. For instance, relative to secure individuals, they report more distress over separating from their romantic partners (Fraley & Shaver, 1998), are over involved in others' problems (Fritz & Helgeson, 1998), show chronic activation of proximity-related concepts (Mikulincer, Birnbaum, Woddis, & Nachmias, 2000), hold strong goals to win others' approval (Pietromonaco & Barrett, 2006), exaggerate the extent to which they are similar to others (Mikulincer, Orbach, & Iavnieli, 1998), and report especially strong desires for closeness (Hazan & Shaver, 1987). Low self-esteem, a conceptually and empirically related construct, seems to be associated with a form of vicarious self-enhancement in which associations with others are used to regulate feelings of self-worth (Brown, Collins, & Schmidt, 1988; Schutz, 1998; Schutz & DePaulo, 1996; Schutz & Tice, 1997; Suls, Lemos, & Stewart, 2002).

The avoidance dimension refers to desires for minimal emotional and psychological investment in close others. Relative to secure individuals, individuals high on this dimension are uninterested in forming strong attachments. They avoid "socially diagnostic" situations in which they will find out whether another is interested in a responsive relationship with them (Beck & Clark, 2009a). They are not strongly committed to getting married, are less likely to be married, and are more likely to get divorced (Klohnen & Bera, 1998). They are less likely to fall in love (Feeney & Noller, 1990; Hazan & Shaver, 1987) and their limited interaction with opposite-sex partners may suggest an avoidance of romantic relationships (Tidwell, Reis, & Shaver, 1996). They seem relatively unattached to their existing partners, being especially adept at suppressing thoughts about a partner's abandonment (Fraley & Shaver, 1997), reporting less emotional distress when their relationships actually dissolve (Simpson, 1990), reporting weaker feelings of commitment to romantic partners (Simpson, 1990), and exhibiting less desire to maintain contact during separation (Fraley & Shaver, 1998). Their especially low feelings of similarity toward others suggest they do not feel a sense of connection with others (Mikulincer et al., 1998; see also Gabriel et al., 2005). Their emotional responses also suggest minimal attachment. They show reduced emotional expression (Bartholomew & Horowitz, 1991; Klohnen & Bera, 1998) and experience more negative affect in their interactions (Simpson, 1990; Tidwell et al., 1996). They seem rather uninterested in others' emotion as well, showing reduced encoding of others' emotions (Fraley, Garner, & Shaver, 2000) and relative lack of interest in learning about their romantic partner's thoughts and feelings (Rholes, Simpson, Tran, Martin, & Friedman, 2007).

These general proclivities to avoid closeness seem to be applied to new relationship partners, especially if those partners resemble prior partners (Brumbaugh & Fraley, 2006). In terms of social process, it seems fair to say that avoidant people are people who self-protect by literally avoiding closeness, as defined in this chapter, either by sidestepping relationship formation altogether or by resisting mutual responsiveness within dating relationships and friendships that, normatively, are close.

Other individual differences, such as differences in relational-interdependent self-construal (Cross et al., 2000) and unmitigated communion (Fritz & Helgeson, 1998) seem to similarly reflect chronic differences in desires to establish close, mutually responsive relationships.

Consistent with attachment theory, these individual differences in tendencies to feel anxious or avoidant in regard to close relationships seem to have roots in early interpersonal experiences. Secure individuals describe their parents as more consistently responsive relative to anxious and avoidant individuals (Brennan & Shaver, 1998; Collins & Read, 1990; Diehl, Elnick, Bourbeau, & Labouvie-Vief, 1998; Feeney & Noller, 1990; Hazan & Shaver, 1987; Levy, Blatt, & Shaver, 1998). Avoidant individuals are especially likely to have experienced conflict with parents or a death of a parent in childhood (Brennan & Shaver, 1998; Klohnen & Bera, 1998). In an impressive longitudinal study spanning several decades, relationship quality in young adulthood was predicted by feelings of attachment security in adolescence, which, in turn, was predicted by peer competence in childhood, which, in turn, was predicted by attachment security in infancy (Simpson, Collins, Tran, & Haydon, 2007; see also Collins, Cooper, Albino, & Allard, 2002). These individual differences in attachment anxiety and avoidance likely act as "external" causes of relationship desire or lack thereof.

Proximity

Closeness in physical space also seems to predict attraction. Students randomly assigned to sit next to each other during a classroom task were more likely to be friends a year later relative to students sitting in the same row, who were, in turn, more likely to be friends than students sitting in other rows (Back, Schmukle, & Egloff, 2008). These findings confirm the importance of a mundane determinant of relationship formation identified long ago (Bossard, 1932) and replicate the classic finding that proximity of living quarters predicts formation of friendships (Festinger, Schachter, & Back, 1950). From the perspective of our model, this is hardly surprising because it is difficult to be responsive to others without coming into contact with them. Of course people may come into close contact because they share similarities. However, even assuming suitable relationship partners are randomly distributed across physical space, people may be more likely to satisfy their needs to belong with proximal partners simply because those others come into contact with them first. Even so what is very striking about some of these studies, is that they reveal that being right next door, directly across the hall (Festinger et al., 1950; Segal, 1974), or in an adjacent seat (Back et al., 2008) as opposed to just being in the same building or the same classroom makes a difference. Surely, one might think, it is worthwhile to search one's immediate environment (those who live in one's building or share classes) a bit more thoroughly than simply turning to the person one sits next to or lives next to in order to find the best available person with whom to form a mutually responsive, close relationship. In this regard, recent research on how much rejection hurts (MacDonald & Leary, 2005), as well as recent theorizing and evidence that people follow a risk-regulation strategy in forming relationships in which they balance appearing interested in and investing in relationships with protecting themselves from rejection (Murray, Derrick, Leder, & Holmes, 2008; Murray, Holmes, & Collins, 2006) may provide some insight. It suggests to us that very close, immediate propinquity may be as powerful a determinant of attraction as it is because conversing with or offering minor sorts of support to people whom one literally just runs into need not reveal that one has sought the other person out, whereas intentionally making one's way down the hall or across the classroom to seek another out does communicate degree of interest. It may be people's self-protective desire not to too openly reveal interest in others that makes them reluctant to even cross a room or walk down a hall to meet and get to know others.

Path B: Precipitating Factors Especially Likely to Predict Interpersonal Confidence

"Background" factors about the self such as self-views, self-esteem, attachment anxiety, and match between self and partner may independently predict felt confidence regarding a partner's current or potential responsiveness.

Self-views and Self-esteem

People with positive self-views and people with high self-esteem are more likely than those with negative self-views and low self-esteem to have a sense of confidence in potential or existing relationship partners' responsiveness. Strong correlations exist between individuals' perceptions of themselves and their perceptions of how others see them, and this pertains to specific views (e.g., personality traits, domain-specific abilities) and to global evaluation of the self (Kenny & DePaulo, 1993; Leary & Baumeister, 2000; Murray et al., 2000, 2001; Shrauger & Schoeneman, 1979). Through a projection of self-evaluation on the evaluations made by others, it appears that people who have negative thoughts or feelings about themselves naively assume that their partners have similarly negative thoughts and feelings. Moreover, people with low self-esteem seem to have a conditional sense of approval, feeling loved and valued by their partners only when they meet certain perceived contingencies. Response-latency studies revealing activation of rejection-related constructs in response to failure and acceptance-related constructs in response to success suggest that this contingent sense of approval can automatically bias judgments of others' responsiveness (Baldwin & Sinclair, 1996). Such contingencies are also evident in studies in which participants with chronic low self-esteem, but not participants with chronic high self-esteem, react to intellectual failures (Murray, Holmes, MacDonald, & Ellsworth, 1998, study 4; see also Murray, Griffin, Rose, & Bellavia, 2006), their own perceived transgressions (Murray et al., 1998, studies 1 through 3), and indeed, their own personal self-disclosures of failures (Cameron, Holmes, & Vorauer, 2009) with reduced confidence about their romantic partner's acceptance. (Sadly, much of this same work reveals that the low confidence of these individuals in their partner's regard is not grounded in reality. Their partners often regard them highly.) Interestingly, people with high self-esteem not only do have confidence in their partner's view of them, they sometimes perceive partners to have more positive views of them than those partners' self-reports suggest is the case (e.g., Cameron et al., 2009; Murray, Rose, Bellavia, Holmes, & Kusche, 2002).

With regard to specific self-views, the stage of relationship is likely to determine which specific self-views are most relevant to inferring a partner's responsiveness. Having valuable social commodities, such as physical attractiveness or superb conversational abilities, likely most strongly affects confidence about relationship formation, whereas having valuable communal qualities, such as kindness and responsiveness, likely most strongly affects confidence about relationship maintenance. Indeed, those involved in romantic relationships show stronger correlations between their global self-esteem (thought to be an indicator of confidence in others' acceptance) and perceptions of their communal qualities relative to those not involved (Anthony, Holmes, & Wood, 2007, study 2), and others' physical attractiveness is judged to be more important during initial stages of attraction than during maintenance of ongoing relationships (Sprecher, 1998).

Match Between Self and Partner

Beyond level of self-esteem, people also appear to consider the match between their own and their partner's social desirability. According to the matching hypothesis discussed long ago by Walster and Murstein (see Murstein, 1972; Walster, Walters, & Berscheid, 1978), people expect to be rejected by those who are substantially more socially desirable than they are (e.g., physically attractive, personable, wealthy). Hence, they feel more confident in their ability to secure the romantic affections of those who are more or less similar to themselves in terms of general value on the social marketplace, despite the ideal of obtaining more desirable partners. In support of these ideas, research has consistently shown that romantic couples do tend to "match" in attractiveness. Murstein and Walster reported evidence for this effect early on on, and the effect has been repeatedly replicated (see Lee, Loewenstein, Ariely, Hong, & Young, 2008 for a recent example). In addition, research has shown that confidence about a potential dating partner's acceptance is reduced when participants considered themselves to be unattractive or when the partner was highly attractive (Huston, 1973), and attractive male individuals were lower in fear of negative evaluation by women relative to unattractive male individuals (Reis et al., 1982). Again, relationship stage may play a role in these links. It is possible that when people are forming relationships they heavily weigh such matches (and the equity of what each member brings to the relationship), and that this emphasis fades as they move from a more deliberative phase of the relationship to an implemental phase, marked by high commitment (see Gollwitzer, Heckhausen, & Steller, 1990).

Attachment-Related Anxiety

As described earlier, attachment anxiety refers to individual differences in fears of abandonment by close others. Although high anxiety reflects, in part, high desire for closeness, it also reflects lack of confidence in others' responsiveness. These individuals exhibit automatic links between stress-related concepts and worries about separation and rejection (Mikulincer et al., 2000). They worry about their partner's love and commitment (Pierce & Lydon, 2001), especially if new partners resemble prior partners (Brumbaugh & Fraley, 2006), which suggests a transference of global models onto specific partners. Relative to individuals low in anxiety, individuals high in attachment-related anxiety perceive the same ambiguous behaviors committed by their partners as more upsetting, inconsiderate, and disappointing (Collins & Feeney, 2004). They also perceive more conflict in their relationships than their partners perceive, feel more hurt by those conflicts, and have exaggerated perceptions of the detrimental effects of conflict on their partner's satisfaction and optimism for the future of the relationship (Campbell et al., 2005). They report less trust in their relationship partner's responsiveness (Collins, 1996; Collins & Read, 1990; Hazan & Shaver, 1987; Mikulincer, 1998c; Simpson,

1990). Similarly, those high in rejection sensitivity (i.e., anxious expectations about rejection) perceive intentional rejection in the insensitive behaviors of their romantic partners (Downey & Feldman, 1996). These individual difference factors likely act as "background" or external predictors of confidence in a particular partner's responsiveness.

Path C: Interpersonal Confidence Breeds Desire

People seek to form close relationships with potential partners whom they believe are likely to respond supportively to the self. In ongoing relationships, they desire to maintain the relationship and contribute to its well-being if they perceive that partners are responsive. Likewise, they reduce their desire for a mutually responsive relationship when they doubt a partner's responsiveness. This point has been made explicitly in Murray, Holmes, and Collins' risk-regulation model (Murray, Derrick, Leder, & Holmes, 2008; Murray, Holmes, & Collins, 2006).

Studies examining breakup as an outcome variable suggest effects on desire to remain in a relationship. In this respect, findings that unstable views of a partner's commitment (Arriaga, Reed, Goodfriend, & Agnew, 2006), anxious expectations of rejection (Downey, Freitas, Michaelis, & Khouri, 1998), perceived lack of partner support (Srivastava et al., 2006), and negative views of partner's communal qualities (Murray, Holmes, & Griffin, 1996b) predict relationship breakup suggest that confidence in a partner's responsiveness predicts relationship desire.

Other findings regarding evaluation and attraction to partners suggest a similar process in which desire is regulated in accord with confidence. Substantial correlations have been found between liking for a specific relationship partner and perceptions of that partner's liking for the self (Kenny & DePaulo, 1993). In romantic relationships, people seem to reciprocate evaluations, such that those who believe that they are evaluated positively by their partners evaluate their partners positively in return (Murray et al., 2000; Murray, Holmes, & Collins, 2006).

People also freely report others' liking as a reason for attraction (Sprecher, 1998). Such findings suggest that people view partners positively, which indicates approach motivation, to the extent to which they feel valued by those partners. Similar processes occur at the daily level as well; people with chronic doubts about their spouse's regard appear to respond to their spouse's daily negative behavior with reduced feelings of closeness (Murray, Bellavia, et al., 2003). Believing that spouses devalue the self (in comparison with self-evaluations) also predicts reduced feelings of commitment and greater thoughts of divorce (Katz, Beach, & Anderson, 1996).

A common source of information regarding another's liking for one, and hence a very common confidence builder

(or buster) in a partner's likely responsiveness, is that other person's emotional expressions. A person who smiles at one is likely to be seen as more attractive and judged more benevolently (cf. Reis et al., 1990) precisely because the person is seen as a responsive, warm individual. Likewise, a person with an angry expression may be disliked and avoided as a relationship partner precisely because that person appears not only nonresponsive but to exemplify the antithesis of responsiveness in that he or she may harm one's welfare. Even young children seem to know that others who do not know one well will dislike you if you express anger (Zeman & Garber, 1996).

Studies of social support similarly suggest that confidence leads to desire. People who perceive their partners to respond supportively to their positive events (e.g., responding with enthusiasm) and to refrain from negative responses (e.g., quashing the event) tend to report high commitment to their partners (Gable et al., 2004), as do people who perceive their partners as responding supportively to their needs for competence, relatedness, and autonomy (Patrick, Knee, Canevello, & Lonsbary, 2007). In addition to the emotional benefits of the support itself, people seem attracted to providers of help because of the underlying message that the provider has positive feelings toward the self and cares about one's needs (Ames, Flynn, & Weber, 2004). In addition, those who believe that their partners are willing to sacrifice self-interest for the benefit of the relationship claim a similar willingness for themselves (Van Lange, Agnew, Harinck, & Steemers, 1997). In the same manner, partners of women who respond to conflict with hostility and derogation (women high in rejection sensitivity) tend to report greater thoughts of ending the relationship after conflicts (Downey et al., 1998).

Of course, many of these correlational findings may be explained by a causal effect in the reverse direction or by third variables. Experimental studies provide clearer evidence for the direction of causality being discussed here. For instance, classic studies show that participants who were assigned randomly to receive negative feedback from an evaluator were subsequently less attracted to the evaluator relative to participants who were assigned to receive positive feedback (Deutsch & Solomon, 1959; Dittes, 1959; Jacobs, Berscheid, & Walster, 1971; Jones & Panitch, 1971; Shrauger & Lund, 1975). Such findings suggest a reduction in motivation to approach targets for relationship formation once people felt devalued. More recent experimental work suggests similar effects. People who believed they were chosen last for a team task derogated team captains, and this effect was explained by feelings of rejection (Bourgeois & Leary, 2001). This effect also extends to romantic relationships. Experimentally inducing doubts about a partner's acceptance, such as by reminding individuals with low self-esteem of their own prior transgressions, inconsiderateness, or failures (Murray et al., 1998), or by directly stirring their doubts about their partner's acceptance (Murray, Rose, Bellavia, Holmes, & Kusche, 2002), caused negative evaluations of partners, reduced felt dependence on partners, and/or reduced feelings of closeness to partners. Also, early studies on attraction suggest that beliefs about partners beings attracted to the self predict desires to interact with those partners (Huston & Levinger, 1978), just as beliefs about partners being receptive to forming mutually responsive relationships predicts desires to form them (Clark, 1986).

Doubts about a partner's regard for the self brought about in less direct ways also seem to reduce interpersonal desire. For instance, according to the matching hypothesis described earlier (see Walster et al., 1966 and Walster & Walster, 1969), people not only feel more confident of acceptance by those who are within one's league, but they also expect and attempt to date individuals of similar desirability, and are even thought to like them more. Although several studies have failed to support this prediction, many of them suffer methodological limitations (Stroebe, 1977). Some studies do suggest that one's own attractiveness constrains selection of dating partners (Berscheid, Dion, Walster, & Walster, 1971; Stroebe, Insko, Thompson, & Layton, 1971). Likewise, people with low self-esteem doubt their partners regard when their partners seem to have superior interpersonal qualities, which, somewhat ironically, caused them to evaluate their partners negatively (Murray et al., 2005). This same phenomenon might explain the pratfall effect—a generally desirable individual tends to be even more liked when he or she exhibits some minor blunder or imperfection (Aronson, Willerman, & Floyd, 1966). Perceived similarity in attitudes seems to be another indirect manipulation of felt confidence; those who were led to believe that a stranger shared their attitudes regarding a variety of issues inferred that the stranger would be attracted to them, which, in turn, predicted their attraction to the stranger (Huston & Levinger, 1978; Singh, Yeo, Lin, & Tan, 2007, study 2), and reassuring people that they will be liked by others reversed the typical similarity-attraction effect for men (Aron et al., 2006).

In addition to positive regard, there is evidence that feeling validated and understood increases interpersonal desire. People seem to feel attracted to those who have matching subjective perspectives on the world, as when they have a similar musical taste or similar senses of humor (Pinel, Long, Landau, Alexander, & Pyszczynski, 2006). Believing that partners are similar to the self may cause people to feel especially understood by those partners, which can enhance feelings of satisfaction independently of feeling positively regarded (Murray, Holmes, et al., 2002). Some findings

suggest that people are most attracted to potential romantic partners who provide both positive and self-consistent feedback, and are least attracted to those who provide neither (Katz & Beach, 2000). However, one important difference between positive regard and self-consistent regard is that the former has the capacity to threaten one's confidence in the partner's attraction and commitment. Indeed, with regard to feedback that is viewed as highly relevant to relationship functioning or the partner's attraction and commitment, desires for positive regard seem to outweigh desires to receive feedback that is consistent with self-views (Boyes & Fletcher, 2007; Murray et al., 2000; Swann, Bosson, & Pelham, 2002). In new relationships, in which commitment is especially uncertain, negative but self-verifying feedback may be especially threatening and cause reductions in felt closeness (Campbell, Lackenbauer, & Muise, 2006; Swann, de la Ronde, & Hixon, 1994).

Beyond relationship length and relevance to partners' commitment, individual differences in self-esteem and attachment security may predict the relative dominance of regard and understanding goals. People with low self-esteem seem more adversely affected by negative evaluation relative to people with high self-esteem (for a review of early literature, see Jones, 1973). Findings that individuals with low self-esteem are less likely than individuals with high self-esteem to seek feedback that confirms a negative specific self-view are consistent with this view (Bernichon, Cook, & Brown, 2003), as are findings that individuals with low self-esteem prefer to interact with globally accepting partners, regardless of whether they provide self-verifying feedback (Rudich & Vallacher, 1999). Murray and colleagues, in tests of their dependency-regulation model, tend to have found that individuals with low self-esteem, but not individuals with high self-esteem, evaluate their partners negatively and reduce feelings of closeness or dependence in response to manipulations about a partner's acceptance (Murray et al., 1998; Murray, Rose, et al., 2002). Anxiously attached individuals similarly exhibit especially strong links between their perceptions of others' positive regard and their evaluation of others (Pietromonaco & Barrett, 2006). Similarly, they exhibited stronger relationships between their relationship-specific feelings of rejection and their reports of interaction quality and intimacy (Pierce & Lydon, 2001).

Do these effects represent differences in reactions or differences in perception? Some studies suggest that individuals with low self-esteem and those with high self-esteem equally desire positive regard from their close partners (Murray et al., 2000). It may be the case that findings of self-esteem or attachment differences in reactions to others' approval reflect a tendency for individuals with low self-esteem or insecure individuals to more readily believe that they are truly rejected. Individuals with high self-esteem may more readily distinguish between negative evaluation of specific attributes and global rejection (see Baldwin & Sinclair, 1996). Indeed, in Murray and colleagues' research, these self-esteem differences are typically fully explained by measured perceptions of partners' acceptance (Murray et al., 1998; Murray, Rose, et al., 2002), and persuading individuals with low self-esteem to take their partner's positive feedback to heart renders them just as secure and satisfied as individuals with high self-esteem (Marigold, Holmes, & Ross, 2007). Such findings suggest differences in perceptions of rejection rather than differences in reactions to equivalently perceived rejection.

Some puzzling findings exist regarding effects of manipulations designed to increase perceived acceptance by romantic partners. Rather than causing individuals with low self-esteem to have especially positive evaluations of partners, such manipulations have sometimes been shown to have the unintended consequence of operating as a threat, causing individuals with low self-esteem to derogate partners and doubt partners' acceptance (Murray et al., 1998, studies 3 and 4). Similarly, as noted earlier, those with chronic attachment-related anxiety responded to knowledge about a potential relationship partner's use of communal norms with increased feelings of interpersonal anxiety (Bartz & Lydon, 2006, study 2). A similar effect has been reported by Beck and Clark (2008), who found that anxious people who experienced a mild acceptance manipulation (an attractive confederate in an experimental setting indicating that she would like to work jointly with the participant as opposed to working alone) responded with increased feelings of fear across time, as well as relative to changes in feelings of fear when receiving mild rejection feedback (the confederate indicating she wishes to work alone). Although surprising, such effects are striking and important findings. It may be the case that chronic distrust causes people to think of rejection in response to cues of acceptance perhaps because they especially fear rejection after beginning to think about acceptance. Fitting with this viewpoint are findings suggesting that people activate cognitions that are incongruent with a given message when they are primed to be distrustful (Schul, Mayo, & Burnstein, 2004).

This research does convincingly suggest a path between confidence in a partner's responsiveness and desire for a responsive relationship, with high confidence leading to high desire for a responsive relationship and a willingness to enter and maintain one, and low confidence preventing that, leading to doubt, and surprisingly even leading to partner derogation. However, the research does not reveal why this effect exists. Murray and colleagues (Murray et al., 1998, 2008; Murray, Holmes, & Collins, 2006; Murray, Holmes, Aloni, Pinkus, Derrick, & Leder, 2009), fortunately, present an elegant risk-regulation model suggesting that the key may be the presence or absence of a self-protection motive and they provide data to back their model. According to their model, people with low self-esteem tend to doubt their partner's responsiveness and perceive rejection risks to be high. This automatically activates a self-protection goal directing them away from situations that would lead to dependency on the partner and require trusting the partner. People who doubt a partner's acceptance therefore pre-emptively reduce the pain of rejection by devaluing their partners and their relationships. We find this perspective compelling.

Sadly, evidence has also been reported that the self-protection efforts of those low in self-esteem who doubt partner regard do not simply result in their devaluing partners and withdrawing from them. They may strike back at partners pre-emptively in hurtful ways that may cause the relationship to deteriorate (Murray, Bellavia, et al., 2003; Murray, Rose, et al., 2002). There is also evidence that when people who are chronically low in self-esteem feel threatened because social comparisons with their partner suggest they are inferior, an exchange script is automatically triggered together with the behavioral tendency to make heightened contributions to the relationship presumably to heighten the partner's dependence on them (Murray, Aloni, et al., 2009). The person with low self-esteem making the greater contributions is comforted by so doing, and the partner may well like the increased contributions to the relationship. However, the benefits of this "insurance policy" may be short-lived, for once an exchange script is adopted, the person making the greater contributions may come to feel inequitably treated in the longer run (cf. Walster, Walster, & Berscheid, 1978) and use of an exchange script has been linked with poorer relationship functioning in general (Buunk & Van Yperen, 1991; Murstein, Cerreto, & MacDonald, 1977). So, too, may feeling that a partner is sticking with one only because one has provided increased benefits undermine one's own sense that the partner truly cares for one.

It also could be the case that confidence in a partner's regard is a reward, which enhances relationship satisfaction and, in turn, commitment to the relationship (see Rusbult, 1983). In other words, the link may reflect approach in response to perceived responsiveness, in addition to avoidance in response to a lack thereof. Indeed, perceiving partners as responsive (i.e., willing to sacrifice for the relationship and accommodating) affects relationship commitment through its effect on satisfaction (and other indices of dependence) (Wieselquist et al., 1999). Approach motivation arising from perceiving partners as responsive also may be mediated through feelings of gratitude, which seem to increase in response to perceived responsiveness from partners, promote feelings of closeness and satisfaction, and motivate helping behavior (Algoe, Haidt, & Gable, 2008; Bartlett & DeSteno, 2006). Gratitude, when felt, may serve as a secondary signal to the help recipient that desired support has been received. When expressed, it may convey to the donor of support that it was welcomed and ought to be continued or repeated and has been shown to increase the expresser's perceptions of his or her felt communal strength toward the recipient (Lambert, Clark, Durtsch, Fincham & Graham, in press). It seems to us that gratitude likely serves its most important function in growing responsiveness in relationships when benefits slightly greater than what was expected by the recipient are both desired and received. It is possible, we suspect, for the magnitude of benefits to exceed what is desired, and thus to produce distress rather than gratitude. It also seems likely to us that receipt of benefits well within the range of what is expected will not elicit gratitude. The primary function of gratitude, we suspect, is to grow responsiveness in relationships.

In addition to self-protection in response to lack of partner responsiveness and relationship approach in response to presence of partner responsiveness, it also may be the case that perceiving partners as unresponsive undermines self-control or cognitive abilities (see Baumeister, DeWall, Ciarocco, & Twenge, 2005; Baumeister, Twenge, & Nuss, 2002), which are thought to be needed for maintaining a pro-relationship orientation during threat (Arriaga & Rusbult, 1998; Ayduk, Mendoza-Denton, Mischel, Downey, Peake, & Rodriguez, 2000; Ayduk, Mischel, & Downey, 2002; Finkel & Campbell, 2001; Vohs & Ciarocco, 2004; Warburton, Williams, & Cairns, 2006; Yovetich & Rusbult, 1994). Feeling that one is victimized by a hurtful or rejecting partner also may reduce feelings of power, which may undermine reconciliation (Shnabel & Nadler, 2008). As another potential process, some findings suggest that people may cope with rejection experiences by claiming to have chosen the rejection (Williams & Sommer, 1997), and such a process may involve claiming disinterest in perpetrators. This is subtly different from a self-protection mechanism, because it involves an attempt to explain prior events rather than preparing oneself for future events (i.e., mitigating future threat). Desire for revenge, perhaps to re-establish a belief in an orderly and just world, also may explain the effect of confidence on desire. Hence, additional studies that clarify the mechanisms underlying the confidence leading to the desire link seem necessary. Of course, multiple mechanisms ultimately may account for the link. It is our guess that they do.

Whereas a link between confidence and desire suggests that people desire partners' responsiveness, it may be the case that this effect is suppressed for people who do not generally claim to desire mutual, dependent relationships, or who have ambivalent feelings about having responsive relationships. For instance, as noted earlier in this chapter, people high in attachment avoidance claim to experience negative emotions and reduced attraction when their relationship

partners behave in a communal manner (Bartz & Lydon, 2006, 2008). Whether attachment avoidance truly reflects low desire for interpersonal bonds or whether it reflects defensive disavowal of dependence is a debated issue. Some evidence suggests the latter (for a review, see Shaver & Mikulincer, 2002); individuals high in attachment avoidance appear to actively suppress proximity-related worries when not "cognitively loaded" for other reasons, whereas they do show accessibility of such worries under cognitive load manipulations (Mikulincer et al., 2000; Mikulincer, Dolev, & Shaver, 2004) and elevated skin conductance while talking about separation from attachment figures (Dozier & Kobak, 1992). Moreover, their generally positive characterizations of self seem to be a response to distress and are more negative in situations that undermine defensive self-presentation (Mikulincer, 1998a). Some findings suggest that they have more negative views of self than secure individuals (Cooper, Shaver, & Collins, 1998). Trained judges perceive avoidant individuals as overly defensive and as repressing feelings of anxiety (Klohnen & Bera, 1998), and their high scores on social desirability scales and reduced accessibility of negative emotional events corroborate such views (Mikulincer & Orbach, 1995). In addition, some findings suggest that, contrary to their proclamations of independence, they feel positive emotion and boosts in self-esteem in response to interpersonal acceptance (Carvallo & Gabriel, 2006) and seem even more likely to feel calmed by their partner's support relative to secure individuals (Simpson, Rholes, & Nelligan, 1992). Hence it is not clear whether the confidence to desire link is consistently moderated by individual differences in attachment avoidance. The link, we postulate, is always there, but outward behavioral manifestations may vary.

Paths D and E: Relationship-Specific Predictors of Felt Confidence

As shown in Figure 25.1, beyond effects of the precipitating factors described earlier, confidence in a partner's responsiveness is both rooted in reality, predicted by the partner's actual responsiveness-relevant behavior (see Path E, the dashed cross-partner line in Figure 25.1), and somewhat biased by the perceiver's desires for a mutually responsive relationship with the partner (Path D). That accuracy of something as important as a partner's responsiveness is considerably less than perfect and that perceptions are somewhat biased may seem surprising. Many factors likely contribute to this state of affairs.

First, consider that, in natural social interaction, explicit feedback regarding others' evaluation or liking is rarely given (Blumberg, 1972; Felson, 1980; Tesser & Rosen, 1975; Yariv, 2006), and there is evidence that this can be especially true if the other is perceived to be highly "sensitive" to negative feedback (Lemay & Clark, 2008c), as well as some evidence that this can be especially true when dependence is high (Uysal & Oner-Ozkan, 2007, study 1), as it typically is in relationships. Instead, negative feedback is often expressed subtly, through nonverbal channels (Swann, Stein-Seroussi, & McNulty, 1992), if at all. In addition, when explicit feedback is given, it is often dishonestly positive (DePaulo & Kashy, 1998; DePaulo, Kashy, Kirkendol, Wyer, & Epstein, 1996). (All new babies are cute. All new haircuts look good.)

One may think that people should be able to detect a partner's sentiments. However, accurately detecting the sentiments underlying a partner's behavior is a complex process that is likely to be error-prone. Any particular observed behavior may be attributed to a handful of potential causes. Indeed, research examining accuracy of perceptions has produced rather weak correlations between one's beliefs regarding how one is viewed by others and others' actual views. This pertains to others' views regarding one's specific abilities and others' global evaluation of the self, although the latter seems somewhat more accurately detected than the former (Shrauger & Schoeneman, 1979). For instance, in Walster et al.'s study cited earlier (Walster et al., 1966), participants' perceptions of their dates' liking and the dates' actual liking was .23 for male and .36 for female individuals. In addition, round-robin studies have found moderate accuracy regarding how much one is generally liked by others, but virtually no accuracy regarding how one is differentially liked by different partners (Kenny & DePaulo, 1993). This pattern pertains to social support as well. For example, participants reported receiving social support on only 65% of the days that their partners claimed to provide support, suggesting they missed many instances of support provision. They also reported receiving support on 44% of the days on which their partners claimed to not have provided support, suggesting many "false" perceptions of support receipt (Bolger, Zuckerman, & Kessler, 2000). Similarly, on average, laboratory observations of social support are only moderately related to recipients' perceptions of support received (Collins & Feeney, 2000; Feeney, 2004). Such moderate levels of accuracy may be difficult for people to reconcile with their feelings of confidence regarding their partners' sentiments. Yet, such confidence is often based on only pseudo-relevant factors, such as informational complexity and richness (Gill, Swann, & Silvera, 1998). That is, although it may be the case that we have an abundance of detailed, vivid information about our relationships and partners, this does not necessarily mean we have very high levels of accuracy.

Often compounding the effect of communication barriers is the salience of one's own interpersonal desires.

Research on social projection and false consensus suggests that one's own salient attributes or goals tend to be attributed to others (e.g., Ames, 2004; Kawada, Oettingen, Gollwitzer, & Bargh, 2004; Krueger & Clement, 1994; Ross, Greene, & House, 1977; for reviews see Holmes, 1968; Marks & Miller, 1987; Robbins & Krueger, 2005). This projection occurs even in close relationships (e.g., Cobb, Davila, & Bradbury, 2001; Kenny & Acitelli, 2001; Lemay, Pruchno, & Feild, 2006; Murray, Holmes, et al., 2002; Ruvolo & Fabin, 1999; Schul & Vinokur, 2000; Thomas, Fletcher, & Lange, 1997). Similarly, research on related biases suggests that the conclusions people draw regarding others' judgments are often driven by an egocentric tendency to place undue weight on salient aspects of self (Savitsky, Epley, & Gilovich, 2001; Savitsky & Gilovich, 2003). When discerning a partner's responsiveness, it is likely that one's own desire for a responsive relationship is very salient and, hence, very biasing.

Beyond such cognitive factors is the likely powerful motivation to see one's desire reciprocated by partners. When people care for a partner's needs, when they are committed to a partner, or when they are otherwise approach oriented or invested, they strongly desire reciprocation of these sentiments (see Holmes & Rempel, 1989). Consistent with the idea that strong motivations are often subjectively fulfilled (Bruner & Goodman, 1947), these desires may cause perceivers to see responsiveness in partners, even when "reality" contradicts such perceptions. Findings that positively biased perceptions of partners are tied to the importance of the domain for relationship quality (with perceived warmth and trustworthiness ranking high in importance) suggest such interpersonally motivated construal processes (Boyes & Fletcher, 2007; see also Kenny & Acitelli, 2001). These findings are reminiscent of the classic finding that people positively misconstrue others' likability when they learn that they must interact with those others (Berscheid, Boye, & Darley, 1968; Tyler & Sears, 1977). Once a decision to invest in a relationship has been made (or made by somebody else), people seem to justify the investment by subjectively construing a responsive partner. To some extent, people in satisfying relationships even seem to be aware that their perceptions of their close relationship partners' warmth and trustworthiness are positively biased (Boyes & Fletcher, 2007). By the same token, when people do not desire a highly responsive relationship, seeing lack of responsiveness in the partner can alleviate guilt (see Baumeister, Stillwell, & Heatherton, 1994), stave off the temptation to invest in an undesired relationship, or orient self-protection mechanisms (see Murray, Holmes, & Collins, 2006).

This perspective provides a second interpretation of the observed correlations between perceived partner responsiveness and indices of relationship desire. Rather than it reflecting only a unidirectional process in which perceived partner responsiveness is accurately detected (or affected by the precipitating factors noted previously) and then affects desire, it also may be the case that desire affects perceptions of the partner's responsiveness. Studies that model both accuracy and projection bias (by examining the unique predictive effects of indices of a partner's responsiveness and indices of own responsiveness on perceptions of the partner's responsiveness) actually tend to produce stronger evidence of bias than accuracy. This is the case in regard to perceptions of partner's recent caring feelings (Kenny & Acitelli, 2001), feelings of closeness (Cross & Morris, 2003; Kenny & Acitelli), intimacy goals (Sanderson & Evans, 2001), relationship involvement and satisfaction (Schul & Vinokur, 2000), and perceptions of the partner's motivation to respond to one's needs (Lemay et al., 2007). In each case, one's own standing was a strong predictor of perceptions of the partner's standing even after controlling for the partner's reports. Research on positive relationship illusions also provides evidence for this effect. People who claimed to have many communal attributes (e.g., warm, responsive to needs, patient, accepting) reported seeing their romantic partners as having similar communal attributes, independently of the partner's self-reported attributes (Murray, Holmes, & Griffin, 1996a; Murray et al., 2000). Round-robin studies of liking suggest a similar process; whereas the actual reciprocity of liking between relationship partners has been observed to be moderate, the perception of reciprocity of liking has been observed to be substantial (Kenny & DePaulo, 1993; Levesque, 1997). Apparently, people who liked their relationship partners saw more reciprocation of liking than was warranted by those partners' reports. In a classic study of acceptance and rejection in small groups, group members perceived a substantial degree of congruence between their own sentiments and those of other group members, although the actual congruence of these sentiments did not exceed chance (Tagiuri, Blake, & Bruner, 1953). Likewise, comparisons of correlations suggest that perceptions that partners reciprocate one's commitment (Adams & Jones, 1997), one's provision of social support (Abbey et al., 1995; Brunstein, Dangelmayer, & Schultheiss, 1996; Deci et al., 2006; Trobst, 2000), one's self-disclosure (Brunell, Pilkington, & Webster, 2007), one's willingness to sacrifice for the relationship (Van Lange, Agnew, et al., 1997), and one's communal orientation (McCall, Reno, Jalbert, & West, 2000) are exaggerated in comparison with the partner's actual reciprocation. These findings suggest that people who desire a close relationship see the target of their desire as responsive, somewhat independently of the target partner's actual responsiveness as indexed by his or her self-reports. Related to these findings are findings that people attribute their own cooperative or competitive

choices in a Prisoner's Dilemma game to others, especially if the other is their game partner (Messe & Sivacek, 1979).

Individual differences in attachment-related avoidance, which reflect variability in explicitly claimed desire for mutually responsive relationships, have similar biasing effects. For instance, those who are high in avoidance perceive the same unsupportive messages written by their romantic partner as less supportive than individuals low in avoidance (Collins & Feeney, 2004), and they claim to trust their partners less (Mikulincer, 1998c). Reflecting a similar process, individuals who value relationships as aspects of their self-concepts seem to exaggerate their roommate's feelings of closeness (Cross & Morris, 2003). Of course, because these studies are correlational, these findings may reflect causal effects in the reverse direction or third variable effects.

Experimental studies provide clearer evidence for a desire to confidence effect. Although not focusing on responsiveness per se, some studies suggest goal-driven perceptions of others. Sexually aroused men perceived available women to be sexually receptive (Stephan, Berscheid, & Walster, 1971). Similarly, men who were primed with a mate-search goal perceived sexual arousal in attractive opposite-sex targets (Maner et al., 2005, study 1). These findings suggest that activating a desire for formation of a sexual relationship caused men to perceive women as responsive to their specific, salient need. This effect extends beyond the sexual domain. Manipulations designed to incite doubts about future social inclusion not only cause increases in desires for forming bonds with new individuals, but such desires seem to cause people to see new individuals as especially receptive to forming bonds (i.e., sociable) (Maner et al., 2007, studies 3 and 4). Desires to avoid the formation of trusting, responsive relationships seem to have opposite effects. For instance, priming self-protection goals caused people to see anger in the faces of members of outgroups that are stereotypically associated with physical threat (Maner et al., 2005, studies 1 and 2), and manipulating people to lie to others causes them to see others as similarly dishonest (Sagarin, Rhoads, & Cialdini, 1998).

This basic phenomenon has been extended to perceived care. When people were randomly assigned to experience difficulty recalling their own responsiveness to a partner's needs (Lemay et al., 2007, study 3), to recall a time in which they were not responsive to a partner's needs (Lemay & Clark, 2008a, study 1), or to behave in an unresponsive manner toward a new acquaintance (Lemay & Clark, 2008a, study 2), they perceived their partner as similarly unresponsive to the self. Therefore, causing people to feel that they do or do not care for a partner seems to cause analogous changes in confidence about the partner's responsiveness. Likewise, when participants felt close to a partner who outperformed them on an ostensible intelligence test (and when they were motivated to dispel the threat of a superior partner or to bond with a desirable partner), they were especially likely to construe the partner as interpersonally responsive (Lockwood et al., 2004). More recent research suggests that desires to bond with physically attractive individuals explain why those individuals are seen as especially interpersonally responsive (Lemay et al., in press). In other words, beautiful people are seen as "good" people because they are desired relationship partners. This research suggests that the desire to confidence effect may be relevant to explaining the classic "beautiful is good" effect.

Even some studies designed to provide evidence of a confidence in a partner's responsiveness to desire effect might be seen as providings evidence for the reciprocal desire to confidence effect. For instance, Murray and colleagues (1998, studies 1–3) found that priming individuals with low self-esteem to think about their own prior transgressions caused them to see their partners as less responsive (i.e., they perceived the partner to have less positive regard for the self). It is possible that the reminders of prior misdeeds convinced participants with low self-esteem that they are not responsive or do not desire a responsive relationship, which, in turn, affected their perceptions of the partner's responsiveness. Likewise, in correlational work by Murray and colleagues (1996a, 2000), in which self-esteem was modeled as a predictor of evaluation of partner, the predictor—self-esteem—was measured by averaging self-ratings on a variety of attributes that largely referred to interpersonal responsiveness (e.g., responsive to needs, warm, tolerant, patient). The outcome measure—evaluation of partner—was evaluation of the partner on these same attributes. The finding that "self-esteem" predicted evaluation of the partner is consistent with the idea that individuals with high self-esteem evaluate partners positively. It is also consistent with the idea that people who care for partners see partners as caring in return.

Of course, some of a partner's responsiveness is accurately detected. Many of the studies cited earlier suggest accuracy in perceiving partner's commitment (Wieselquist et al., 1999), caring feelings (Kenny & Acitelli, 2001), closeness (Kenny & Acitelli), social support (Brunstein et al., 1996), willingness to sacrifice (Van Lange, Rusbult, et al., 1997; Wieselquist et al.), constructive responses to conflict (Wieselquist et al.), motivation to respond to needs (Lemay & Clark, 2008a; Lemay et al., 2007), liking (Kenny & DePaulo, 1993; Levesque, 1997), intimacy goals (Sanderson & Evans, 2001), relationship involvement (Schul & Vinokur, 2000), regard (Murray et al., 2000; Overall et al., 2006), and daily expressions of support and affection (Gable, Reis, & Downey, 2003). In addition, people who are committed to their relationships have partners who trust them (Wieselquist et al.). Other findings are consistent with this notion. For

example, those who claimed to be caring and responsive to others have romantic partners who view them as caring and responsive (Murray et al., 2000). Laboratory studies have revealed positive correlations between a romantic partner's supportive behavior as indexed by objective observers and the recipient's perceptions of being supported, suggesting their perceptions of support were somewhat rooted in reality (Collins & Feeney, 2000; Feeney, 2004). Likewise, laboratory studies have revealed positive correlations between a romantic partner's observed hostile and derogating behavior and the partner's feelings of anger (Downey et al., 1998).

Of interest are factors likely to moderate the degree to which people are reading their partner's behavior for signs of responsiveness and the degree to which they use heuristics (i.e., their own desire) to infer a partner's behavior. Individuals high in attachment-related anxiety imbue relationship events with heightened interpersonal meaning, such that the partner's behavior is seen as especially diagnostic of the partner's desire for a close relationship (Bartz & Lydon, 2006, study 3). Such individuals may avoid the use of the desire-driven biases outlined earlier. Indeed, high-anxiety participants seemed more accurate than low-anxiety participants in inferring their partner's thoughts and feelings when such thoughts and feelings could threaten the relationship (Simpson, Ickes, & Grich, 1999). Similarly, people with chronic fears of negative evaluation do not readily perceive new individuals as socially receptive, even when a prior rejection experience might motivate a desire for forming new bonds (Maner et al., 2007, study 4). Of course, these insecure individuals are undoubtedly biased in other ways (i.e., underestimating partners' responsiveness). The stage of a relationship's development may also constrain the use of a goal-driven bias. People who are in the process of establishing a close relationship seem to read more into the partner's behavior relative to individuals who have already established closeness (Lydon, Jamieson, & Holmes, 1997), and people seem less likely to see partners in positively biased ways when they are deliberating about the future of the relationship, as opposed to when they have made a decision and are actively pursing the relationship (Gagne & Lydon, 2004).

Will such subjectively constructed feelings of security satisfy people's needs? In many cases, confidence in responsiveness should predict relationship outcomes largely irrespective of how that confidence was derived. Of course, there are limitations to the effect of self-generated confidence. For instance, it may cause people to overlook problems in their relationships that, if detected, could be remedied (see McNulty, O'Mara, & Karney, 2008) or could, perhaps quite wisely, serve as a cause for choosing to leave a relationship. Such possibilities are directions for future research. Yet, because doubts about a partner's responsiveness can undermine motivation to maintain responsive relationships, lack of a partner's responsiveness may not be the sort of problem that can be easily addressed once it is perceived and, ironically, may be better addressed by not perceiving it. Why? Perceiving partners to be more responsive than they are can create self-fulfilling prophecies in which partners become more responsive (Murray et al., 1996b), predict increased relationship satisfaction (Gable et al., 2003; Lemay et al., 2007; Murray et al., 1996a; Sanderson & Evans, 2001), and predict engaging in pro-relationship acts, such as self-disclosure, expressions of warmth, and support provision (Lemay & Clark, 2008a). Moreover, accurately inferring a romantic partner's thoughts and feelings predicts reduced closeness and increased probability of breakup (the latter for anxiously attached individuals) when such thoughts were threatening to the relationship (Simpson, Ickes, & Blackstone, 1995; Simpson et al., 1999; Simpson, Orina, & Ickes, 2003).

People are not so likely to exaggerate a partner's care that they miss truly serious problems in the relationship, because large gaps between self and partner, although rare, may be especially likely to be detected. Confidence in a partner's responsiveness seems to provide many people with a means to feel secure in relationships despite the difficulty of reading others' motivations, thoughts, and feelings. In other words, the bias to feel confident when such confidence is most desired may be more beneficial and less costly than refraining from biases and limiting oneself to "bottom up" perception (see Haselton & Buss, 2000), as it aids in relationship formation and maintenance, as we discuss in the following sections. Whether such biases are primarily due to the cognitive mechanisms or the motivational mechanisms we described are directions for future research, although we would anticipate that both accessibility and desire for reciprocation play a role in the desire to confidence effect.

Paths F, G, H, and I: Enactment of Responsivene Acts

A desire for a mutually responsive relationship should predict provision of responsive support to relationship partners, because such behavior is normative in such relationships (Clark & Mills, 1979), and because increased interdependence and intimacy cause people to develop concern for their partner's welfare.

Consistent with this idea, people claim greater willingness to provide help to partners and potential partners with whom they would like to be close relative to relationship partners with whom they do not feel close and would not like to be close (Lydon et al., 1997). A feeling of "oneness" or merged identity with relationship partners, which may be another index of desire to maintain a responsive relationship, predicts self-reported willingness to help partners in need (Cialdini, Brown, Lewis, Luce, & Neuberg, 1997). Such feelings of "oneness" also predict actual helping of strangers (Maner, Luce, Neuberg, Cialdini, Brown, & Sagarin, 2002). People who report intimacy goals in their close relationships provide more support to their partners (Sanderson & Evans, 2001). Experimental manipulations of closeness with new acquaintances eliminate the typical tendency to take credit for success and blame others for failure (Sedikides, Campbell, Reeder, & Elliot, 1998), and experimental manipulations that activate feelings of closeness cause more empathic reactions to others' distress and a reduced focus on one's own personal distress (Mikulincer, Gillath, Halevy, Avihou, Avidan, & Eshkoli, 2001). So, too, do experimental manipulations that produce desire for a close, responsive communal relationship result in more help being given (Clark, Ouellette, Powell, & Milberg, 1987), more responsiveness to partner's distressed affect (Clark et al., 1987), and more attention to a partner's needs (Clark, Mills, & Corcoran, 1989; Clark, Mills, & Powell, 1986).

These effects may emerge because those who desire mutually responsive relationships are genuinely concerned for their partner's welfare. Recent studies by Batson and colleagues (Batson, Eklund, Chermok, Hoyt, & Ortiz, 2007) support this idea. Those who were manipulated to value a stranger's welfare (by presenting the stranger as a compassionate and likable person) felt more empathic concern for the stranger, which, in turn, predicted increased helping behavior. Feelings of love also correlate with feelings of sympathy toward partners (Gonzaga, Keltner, Londahl, & Smith, 2001). To say this, importantly, is not the equivalent of saying that those who desire mutually responsive relationships do so for entirely altruistic reasons. Rather, we suspect, people often may desire mutually responsive relationships for selfish reasons. They may know, for instance, that the very existence of such relationships will make them feel accepted, secure, and perhaps generative as well, so they adopt communal norms of responsiveness for the relationship. Other times, as with relatives, social or evolutionary forces may drive use of that norm, and still other times true empathy may drive it. No matter. Once it is adopted, they may also adopt the attitude and habit of focusing on the partner when the partner can be supported (and focusing on the self when the self needs support, as we describe in the next section), resulting in desire for the relationship, true empathic concern, genuine care, and responsiveness.

Relationship commitment, which is typically conceptualized as involving feelings of psychological attachment to a partner and a long-term orientation toward the relationship (Rusbult, 1983), may be another index of desire to maintain a mutually responsive relationship. People who are strongly committed to their relationships report willingness to sacrifice some of their personal goals as a means of benefiting the relationship (Van Lange, Rusbult, et al., 1997; Wieselquist et al., 1999). Their willingness to exert themselves to benefit their partners also was experimentally observed (Van Lange, Rusbult, et al., 1997, study 4). Commitment also seems to promote pro-relationship responses to conflict, such as increased forgiveness (Finkel, Rusbult, Kumashiro, & Hannon, 2002; McCullough, Rachal, Sandage, Worthington, Brown, & Hight, 1998) and reduced negative reciprocity (i.e., reacting to negativity with negativity) (Rusbult et al., 1991; Wieselquist et al., 1999). The links between commitment and pro-relationship processes suggest to us that commitment is the point demarking individuals moving from a deliberative frame of mind regarding their relationships (i.e., carefully considering whether to establish or maintain a relationship) to an implemental frame of mind (i.e., deciding to establish or maintain a relationship) (see Gollwitzer et al., 1990).

Individual differences in desire for responsive relationships also predict provision of responsiveness. Relational-interdependent self-construal, a tendency to construe the self in terms of relationships with close others, is correlated with self-reported desires for mutually responsive relationships (communal orientation) (Cross et al., 2000, study 1), a tendency to take other's needs and wishes into account when making decisions (Cross et al., 2000, study 2), and greater accuracy in predicting new relationship partners' values (Cross & Morris, 2003).

To the extent that attachment avoidance reflects a defensive lack of desire for mutually responsive relationships, findings regarding avoidance also suggest a link between desire and provision of responsiveness. Individuals high in attachment avoidance provide less responsive support (e.g., less physical affection, less sensitivity to partner's needs, less emotional support, more neglect) to their romantic partners relative to individuals low in attachment avoidance, and they appear to do so, in part, because they feel less committed and close to their specific partners and, in part, because they are less empathic and communally oriented generally (Feeney & Collins, 2001). Indeed, attachment avoidance is associated with reduced empathic reactions to others' distress (Mikulincer et al., 2001) and reduced willingness to help others in distress (Mikulincer, Shaver, Gillath, & Nitzberg, 2005), and avoidant individuals and their partners report avoidant individuals to be critical and aggressive (Collins et al., 2002). Similarly, avoidant individuals were less likely to provide responsive caregiving to alleviate a partner's distress while parting with those partners at airports (Fraley & Shaver, 1998) and in laboratory observations (Simpson, Rholes, Orina, & Grich, 2002; see also Bartholomew & Horowitz, 1991). Moreover, laboratory observations of their behavior indicate they are less

warm and supportive toward their romantic partners than are low avoidance individuals when discussing a major relationship conflict (Simpson et al., 1996). When they do help their romantic partners, they report more self-focused motivations for providing the help (i.e., to reduce one's own costs or reap rewards) and fewer motivations related to care for the partner (Feeney & Collins, 2003). When they themselves are distressed, avoidant individuals seem to respond to a partner's lack of support or a partner's anger with reciprocated anger, frustration, and statements expressing unhappiness with their partner (Rholes, Simpson, & Orina, 1999; see also Mikulincer, 1998b). In contrast, individuals low in avoidance responded to the same situation with reductions of such negative responses. Hence, evidence strongly suggests that various indices of desire to form close, mutually responsive relationships are associated with provision of responsiveness to partners.

As shown in Figure 25.1, confidence in a partner's responsiveness may independently predict responsive behavior toward the partner (Path G). As people may be unwilling to invest in relationships in which partners are unresponsive, people who are insecure about a partner's responsiveness may feel compelled to be focused on their own needs rather than the partner's needs. In addition, providing responsiveness requires trust that partners desire such responsiveness from the self. Consistent with this overall idea (and the specific idea that confidence may influence people to be self-protective), people who doubt their particular spouse's regard respond to daily feelings of rejection with hurtful behaviors toward their spouse (Murray, Bellavia et al., 2003). In contrast, those who perceive their partners as supportive exhibit constructive behaviors (e.g., listening, trying to understand, refraining from criticism) during conflict situations (Srivastava et al., 2006, study 2) and report providing support in return (Deci et al., 2006). People who perceive their partner to be secure (i.e., trusting, comfortable with closeness) provide more support while their partners discuss personal goals relative to those who perceived insecure partners (Cobb et al., 2001). Studies testing circumplex models of interpersonal behavior not only find that agreeable and quarrelsome behavior is reciprocated, but also suggest a tendency for people to provide responsiveness only when they are certain of receiving responsiveness (Markey, Funder, & Ozer, 2003; Moskowitz, Ho, & Turcotte-Tremblay, 2007; Tiedens & Jimenez, 2003).

Experimental manipulations of confidence suggest a similar pattern. People who feel rejected by a target person (i.e., low confidence in responsiveness) allocated fewer rewards to that target relative to people who did not feel rejected (Maner et al., 2007, study 5). People who were led to feel noncontingently accepted (i.e., based on their true selves) showed less defensiveness, including reduced tendencies to engage in downward social comparisons and reduced distancing from an undesirable person relative to people who felt that their acceptance was contingent (based on performance) (Schimel, Arndt, Pyszczynski, & Greenberg, 2001). Activating concepts of attachment security similarly causes more empathic reactions to others' distress and a greater willingness to help others (Mikulincer et al., 2005), and activates communal goals such as kindness and warmth (Bartz & Lydon, 2004; Mikulincer et al., 2003).

A similar pattern is found using individual difference variables that tap confidence in responsiveness. Participants with partners high in attachment anxiety received less support from those partners after discussing a personal problem relative to participants with partners low in attachment anxiety. Instead, such anxious partners engaged in seemingly defensive negative behaviors, such as blaming, minimizing the importance of the problem, or ignoring emotional displays (Collins & Feeney, 2000). In part, anxious partners' intentions to punish partners and engage in conflict seem to be a result of their tendencies to doubt their partner's responsiveness (Collins, 1996; Collins, Ford, Guichard, & Allard, 2006). For anxiously attached women, increases in personal distress were related to subsequent increases in negative behaviors such as derogating the partner, and expressing anger and distrust toward the partner. In contrast, personal distress was inversely related to such reactions for women low in attachment anxiety (Rholes et al., 1999). Similarly, women high in rejection sensitivity—anxious expectations of being rejected by others—expressed hostility and derogated their romantic partners during an observed interaction (Downey et al., 1998). These various findings point not only to a link between confidence in a partner's responsiveness and provision of responsiveness, but also to a link between lack of confidence in a partner's responsiveness and behavior that is the antithesis of responsiveness.

In many ways, it is paradoxical that anxious individuals who are hypersensitive to issues of responsiveness and those especially wary of rejection act in ways that likely drive partners away from them. Their behavior has been explained as "pre-emptive" defense. That does make a certain amount of sense because rejecting the other before the other can reject you may hurt less than relying on another and then not receiving support or even being actively hurt by them. Moreover, pre-emptive attacks may result in one feeling "in control" of the situation. Yet, defensiveness is self-serving only in the moment. Attacking one's partner certainly does nothing to promote the relationship and likely does much to harm it. Thus, it is reasonable to ask *why* people who are hypersensitive to issues of responsiveness do not consider the almost immediate negative reaction

their actions are likely to draw from partners along with the longer-term, almost certainly negative, consequences of such actions.

An analysis of how goal striving relates to relational focus of attention suggests an answer (Clark, Graham, Williams, & Lemay, 2008). Anxious, rejection-sensitive individuals or those with low self-esteem (all overlapping constructs) may have chronic self-protective goals and a chronic relational self-focus (meaning that when with partners they focus on the self and the implications of the partner for the self). Given the goal of self-protection and where their attention is focused, they may simply be attentionally blind to signs of partner needs and opportunities to support the partner (cf. Most et al., 2005; Simmons & Chabris, 1999). It may not be until after they lash out, thereby reaching their goal of immediate self-protection, that they can "see" the negative consequences of their behavior.

The same analysis of how goal striving relates to relational focus of attention has broader implications for how confidence in a partner's responsiveness relates to providing responsiveness to partners as well. Clark et al. (2008) suggest that people who have confidence in a partner's responsiveness tend also to have flexibility in relational focus of attention (i.e., where they focus when with partners). When the partner has a need, they can focus on the partner and what they can do for their partner, which ought to lead to providing appropriate responsiveness. When they have a need, they switch to focusing on the self and what the partner can do for the self (which ought to lead to seeking appropriate responsiveness, as discussed in the next section), and when neither person has a pressing need, they can focus on joint activities (e.g., a conversational topic, dancing, sexual activity), which will often result in providing different sorts of responsiveness to the partner as well. In contrast, people with low confidence in a partner's responsiveness tend to be stuck in relational self-focus (i.e., thinking about the self and the implications of the partner for the self), which may not only mean being less apt to notice cues to partner needs, but also, when such cues are noted, being especially apt to think of the implications of the neediness for the self than for the partner and consequently less apt to help the partner even when needs are noted.

Unfortunately, the same insecurity that leads people to focus on self and that undermines providing responsiveness, if expressed, has been shown to further undermine the expresser's insecurity. Some recent research, for example, suggests that continued expressions of heightened insecurity may perpetuate feelings of insecurity through providing insecure people with an external attribution for the partner's expressions of positive regard and affection (Lemay & Clark, 2008b, 2008c; Lemay & Dudley, in press), and this lashing out may cause one to feel that one lacks the positive communal qualities that a partner desires, thereby perpetuating doubt about the partner's positive regard.

Even though, as just reviewed, much research suggests that a lack of confidence in a partner's responsiveness predicts not just low responsiveness toward a partner but also relationship-harming behavior, other findings also exist that instead suggest that lack of confidence in a partner's responsiveness predicts provision of responsiveness to the partner. For example, people with chronic attachment-related anxiety seem especially eager to follow communal norms with potential relationship partners (Bartz & Lydon, 2006, study 1). Moreover, relative to secure individuals, they wrote more emotionally supportive messages to their partners, and more instrumentally supportive messages when their partners were distressed (Feeney & Collins, 2001). In a daily diary study of support provision in romantic couples, people who claimed to be worried or fearful in their relationships provided more support to their partners relative to people who did not show this anxiety (Iida, Seidman, Shrout, Fujita, & Bolger, 2008; see also Bartholomew & Horowitz, 1991). These findings suggest a more complex picture than we have painted previously. Attachment-related anxiety reflects a *combination* of low confidence in a partner's responsiveness and high desire for the relationship. This combination may produce especially strong efforts to secure a responsive relationship, but the effect may be unstable because it likely depends on the degree of threat relative to the degree of desire. When desire is "greater than" threat, anxious people may seek to provide responsiveness to secure a close relationship. When threat is "greater than" desire, anxious people may defensively back away from the relationship. In addition and importantly, it is almost certainly the case that the help provided is motivated by qualitatively different factors. In particular, it is likely designed to alleviate the anxious person's own felt insecurity rather than to respond to a partner's needs. Fitting well with this idea is the fact that anxious attachment is correlated with feelings of personal distress and reduced feelings of empathy in response to others' needs (Mikulincer et al., 2001, 2005). Although they follow communal norms in close relationships, they are vigilant about others' reciprocation (Bartz & Lydon, 2008). Moreover, whereas all participants exhibited intimacy goals in trust-related contexts, anxiously attached individuals also exhibited goals to reduce their feelings of insecurity (Mikulincer, 1998c), and their motivations for helping more often include relationship concerns such as bolstering the partner's commitment, which, in turn, predicts compulsive, overinvolved forms of caregiving that, somewhat ironically, reduce partners' satisfaction (Feeney & Collins, 2003). They get overly involved with alleviating their romantic

partner's problems, and they appear to do so, in part, because they lack trust and they desire to reduce their own anxiety (Feeney & Collins, 2001; see also Fritz & Helgeson, 1998). They exhibit a manic, obsessive, overly dependent style of love (Collins & Read, 1990; Feeney & Noller, 1990). Thus, the support provided by anxiously attached individuals may be rather self-focused and ultimately often uncoordinated with partners' particular needs both in the sense that (nonresponsive) "help" will be given when it is neither needed nor desired and in the sense that situations requiring help are likely to be "missed." Of course, it is also possible that appropriate help will sometimes be given, but the overall pattern of responsiveness is likely to be far from ideal. Fitting well with this argument, researchers have noted that anxious peoples' own self-disclosures (which can be responsive) are relatively uncoordinated with others' self-disclosures (Mikulincer & Nachshon, 1991) and, therefore, likely unresponsive to their needs.

In addition to being predicted by felt desire for and confidence in a mutual responsiveness relationship, the provision of responsiveness, ideally, should be sensitive to the partner's needs (see Path H in Figure 25.1). In laboratory studies, observed seeking of support from one's romantic partner while discussing a personal problem predicted the partner's provision of responsive caregiving as indexed by objective observers (Collins & Feeney, 2000; Simpson et al., 2002). Likewise, manipulated beliefs about a partner's distress predicted more emotionally supportive written messages to the partner, as indexed by outside observers and by the partner (Feeney & Collins, 2001). In daily diary studies, support provision was coordinated with romantic partners' anxious mood, daily stressors, and support seeking (Iida et al., 2008), and individuals gave less support to their partners and received more support from their partners as an upcoming personal, major stressor approached (Gleason, Iida, Shrout, & Bolger, 2008). That is, people seem to focus more on support provision than on support receipt when their partners' needs outweigh their own.

Hence, detection of partner's needs seems to be a critical determinant of responsiveness above and beyond the effects of desire and confidence for a mutually responsive relationship. Indeed, people are more likely to monitor another person's needs when they believe the individual is available to establish a close relationship (Clark, Mills, & Powell, 1986) or when the individual is already a friend (Clark, Mills, & Corcoran, 1989). Studies suggest that missing signs of need is detrimental to recipients' well-being. For instance, pregnant women with partners who underestimated their stressful life events were more likely to become more depressed from their second to the third trimester relative to women with partners who did not underestimate their stressful life events (Chapman, Hobfoll, & Ritter, 1997). In another study, providing support to encourage a partner's goals predicted the partner's relationship satisfaction only if participants were well aware of their partner's most important goals (Brunstein et al., 1996). Such findings suggest the relevance of accurately detecting the nature of a partner's distress to efforts at promoting the partner's well-being.

Desire and detection of need also likely interact to predict responsiveness, such that detection of need promotes supportively responding to that need primarily when interpersonal desire is high. People who are high in attachment avoidance, who appear to have low desire for responsive relationships, responded to a partner's expressions of distress or support seeking with increased anger and less support. The opposite was the case for people low in attachment avoidance (Rholes et al., 1999; Simpson et al., 1992). Similarly, whereas low avoidance individuals provided more support to their romantic partners as their partner's distress increased, high avoidance individuals did not (Feeney & Collins, 2001). Individuals high in communal orientation, a proclivity to desire communal relationships with others, provided help that was commensurate with the recipient's sad mood, whereas individuals low in communal orientation did not increase helping in response to the other's sad mood (Clark, Ouellette, Powell, & Milberg, 1987).

Paths J, K, L: Seeking Responsive Acts

When people have a need, they ought to seek their partner's responsive acts (see Path J in Figure 25.1). Several findings suggest that, in general, people do seek responsiveness from their close relationship partners. In laboratory observations of participants discussing a personal problem with their romantic partners, the perceived stressfulness of the participant's problem predicted their seeking of emotional support from the partner, as measured by objective observers (Collins & Feeney, 2000). Reaction-time studies reveal automatic associations of stress-related concepts with proximity-related concepts, suggesting that people automatically bring close others to mind when confronted with stress (Mikulincer et al., 2000).

Desire for a responsive relationship ought to moderate such effects, because receiving responsiveness from partners is an important means by which people build intimate, close relationships (see Path K in Figure 25. 1). Such intimacy may be one motivator for seeking responsiveness (in addition to more tangible benefits). Indeed, feelings of intimacy and closeness do seem tied to one's own self-disclosure, especially disclosure of emotions (Laurenceau et al., 1998; Levesque, Steciuk, & Ledley, 2002). Self-disclosure is related to goals of creating intimacy in relationships (Sanderson & Evans, 2001), relationship satisfaction (Hendrick, 1981), and commitment (Sprecher & Hendrick, 2004). Self-disclosure of

vulnerabilities, such as anxiety and fear, to friends is more likely when people chronically desire for their relationships to be mutually responsive (Clark & Finkel, 2005), and expression of emotion is especially likely to occur when people believe others are available to establish a close, communal bond (Clark, Fitness, & Brissette, 2000) or when such a bond is already established (Clark & Taraban, 1991, study 2).

There is likely to be both a tendency for people to seek responsiveness from those with whom they feel close and a closeness-enhancing mechanism of seeking and then receiving responsiveness (see Reis & Shaver, 1988; for a review of bidirectional effects linking self-disclosure and liking, see Collins & Miller, 1994). Indeed, just as the prior research suggests that desire for closeness causes self-disclosure, experimentally manipulated self-disclosure also creates feelings of closeness (Aron et al., 1997). Some additional findings point to the relational benefits of seeking responsiveness. People who desire warmth and trustworthiness in their relationships seem to communicate such desires to their romantic partners, which seem to engender partners' self-regulatory efforts to become more warm and trustworthy (Overall et al., 2006), and perceiving partners to have positive communal qualities predicts temporal changes in partners' self-perceptions (Murray et al., 1996b). People who are willing to express negative emotions to others elicit help from those others, and have more intimate friendships and more intimacy in the strongest of their friendships (Graham, Huang, Clark, & Helgeson, 2008). Therefore, responsiveness seeking seems to derive from and further contribute to desires for mutually responsive relationships.

On the other side of this coin, individuals who prefer to avoid interpersonal dependence seem to refrain from support seeking. When people are uncomfortable with consciously admitting their dependence on others (but have unconscious dependency needs), they seem unlikely to seek support unless that seeking can be done indirectly or unless the support being sought is not obviously a form of support (Bornstein, 1998). Similarly, while discussing a personal problem with their romantic partners, people high in attachment avoidance, who generally avoid dependence on others, sought their partner's social support in rather subtle and indirect ways, including fidgeting, sulking, complaining, or hinting about a need for support (Collins & Feeney, 2000). Moreover, whereas a positive relationship was found between the stressfulness of one's problem and observed support-seeking behavior for low avoidance individuals, this effect was not found for high avoidance individuals. Indeed, some findings suggest that individuals high in avoidance seek less support when they are distressed (Simpson et al., 1992). Attachment avoidance is inversely related to self-reported reliance on partners during emotion-laden situations (La Guardia et al., 2000), self-reported willingness to express emotions (Gross & John, 2003), self-reported self-disclosure (Collins et al., 2002; Collins & Read, 1990; Gillath et al., 2006; Mikulincer & Nachshon, 1991), self-reported support seeking (Florian, Mikulincer, & Bucholtz, 1995; Gillath et al.; Mikulincer & Florian, 1995), and interviewer-assessed self-disclosure, emotional expressiveness, and reliance on others (Bartholomew & Horowitz, 1991). Other indices of desire for mutually responsive relationships also seem to predict responsiveness seeking. Individuals high in relational-interdependent self-construal not only have a communal orientation (as reviewed earlier), but they tend to engage in more intimate self-disclosures (Cross et al., 2000, studies 1 and 3), which is a form of responsiveness seeking.

As depicted in Figure 25.1, confidence in a partner's responsiveness also ought to predict support seeking (Path L). When people are confident that a partner is responsive, they are more likely to accept the risks of revealing needs and vulnerabilities and seeking support. Concerns about seeking responsive support from others, such as fearing criticism, a tarnished reputation, incurring costs to others, or disrupting harmony may reduce responsiveness seeking. Such factors explain cultural differences in seeking social support (Taylor, Sherman, Kim, Jarcho, Takagi, & Dunagan, 2004). People who believe they do not have others to turn to for emotional or instrumental support are less likely to express their emotions (Deci et al., 2006; Gross & John, 2003). Similarly, people who believe that closeness is risky because it offers the potential of hurt tend to refrain from self-disclosure (Brunell et al., 2007). Likewise, people who see their friends as providing support are more likely to seek emotional support (Deci et al., 2006; Ognibene & Collins, 1998), and those who believe that partners care for their needs are willing to express vulnerabilities such as sadness and hurt (Lemay & Clark, 2008a). Moreover, people are more willing to discuss and seek support regarding their personal goals with their relationship partners when those partners behave in a supportive and responsive manner (Feeney, 2004). Even subliminal primes related to interpersonal acceptance predicted increased self-reported willingness to seek emotional support to cope with a stressful situation (Pierce & Lydon, 1998; see also Gillath et al., 2006) and willingness to self-disclose (Gillath et al.). Classic findings that people are sometimes unwilling to ask for help from physically attractive strangers also may be explained by concerns about the other's rejection as a result of needing help (i.e., appearing inadequate) (Nadler, Shapira, & Ben-Itzhak, 1982).

Again, some findings regarding individual differences reveal a similar pattern. When secure individuals experience romantic jealousy, they claim to directly confront and express their anger to their partners, which may be a means of seeking responsiveness and reassurance. In contrast,

anxiously attached individuals claim to suppress their anger (Mikulincer, 1998b; Sharpsteen & Kirkpatrick, 1997), claim to be unwilling to rely on their partners to help them regulate their emotions (La Guardia et al., 2000), and report reduced support seeking (Florian et al., 1995). Similarly, couples characterized by low trust in the other's responsiveness seem unwilling to express to their partners the rather negative attributions they make for their partner's behavior, perhaps as a means of avoiding confrontation (Rempel, Ross, & Holmes, 2001). People also reported expressing their anger to their relationship partners to the extent that they believed that their partners would respond in a positive manner (Lundgren & Rudawsky, 2000).

However, some contrary findings exist. In another study, individuals high in attachment anxiety claimed more daily self-disclosure and greater intimacy in daily interaction than individuals low in attachment anxiety, especially after conflict (Pietromonaco & Barrett, 1997; see also Bartholomew & Horowitz, 1991). They reported greater reassurance seeking relative to individuals low in attachment anxiety (Shaver, Schachner, & Mikulincer, 2005), and greater emotional expressiveness and reliance on others (Bartholomew & Horowitz, 1991). They also seem to characterize themselves in negative ways to elicit compassion from others (Mikulincer, 1998a). Such unstable results are not surprising given that, as we discussed previously, high anxiety is related to a strong desire for close bonds (which would increase responsiveness seeking), as well as insecurity regarding others' responsiveness (which would decrease responsiveness seeking). Perhaps the combination of desiring close relationships but fearing that they do not have them causes them to withdraw from seeking responsiveness when social threat seems especially high, but to redouble their efforts to obtain others' support and reassurance in lower threat situations. In addition, because attachment anxiety is associated with both increased personal distress and doubts about others' responsiveness, a suppressor effect may occur; those who feel increased distress may be more likely to seek support to alleviate that distress, but those who doubt others' responsiveness may be less likely to seek support to alleviate their distress. This suggests a need for delineating under what conditions one versus the other effect predominates.

Path M: Responsiveness and Well-being

As shown in Figure 25.1, the receipt of responsiveness should reduce the partner's needs for responsiveness and increase the partner's well-being. Much evidence suggests that close, responsive relationships can contribute to one's physical and mental well-being (Reis et al., 2000). We review some recent findings.

In a laboratory study of caregiving processes that Collins and Feeney (2000) conducted, participants discussed a personal problem with their romantic partners. Their perceptions of their partner's supportiveness, the partner's supportiveness observed by objective observers, and the partner's reports of their own supportive behavior each predicted positive changes in mood relative to pre-interaction mood (see also Feeney, 2004). Research on capitalization suggests that partner's responsiveness to positive events also can have an impact on emotional well-being. For instance, those who believed that their close partners responded constructively (e.g., with enthusiasm) and refrained from destructive responses (e.g., quashing or ignoring the event) to their positive events reported greater positive affect and life satisfaction (Gable et al., 2004). The effect of perceived support on measures of psychological well-being has been replicated many times (e.g., Barry et al., 2007; Davila, Bradbury, Cohan, & Tochluk, 1997; Deci et al., 2006; McCaskill & Lakey, 2000). Receiving feedback that verifies existing aspects of self-definition also appears to have affective benefits. Not only does it predict feeling understood, but it predicts positive emotion (Campbell et al., 2006). More general indices of relatedness (i.e., a sense of connection with others) also predict variability in subjective well-being (Patrick et al., 2007; Sheldon & Niemiec, 2006), as do measures of attachment anxiety and avoidance, both as a generalized model of self with others (Cozzarelli et al., 2000; Klohnen et al., 2005; La Guardia et al., 2000; Roberts, Gotlib, & Kassel, 1996) and in terms of relationship-specific models (Barry et al., 2007).

Receiving responsiveness also facilitates coping. Women undergoing an abortion experienced more subsequent positive adjustment and less subsequent distress to the extent that they perceived their relationship partners as responding supportively to their decision to have an abortion (Major, Zubek, Cooper, Cozzarelli, & Richards, 1997). Women with rheumatoid arthritis experienced more psychological well-being when they had supportive spouses (Manne & Zautra, 1989). Similarly, secure attachment is related to more effective coping with stressors such as having an abortion (Cozzarelli, Sumer, & Major, 1998) and international conflict (Mikulincer, Florian, & Weller, 1993). Even subliminal presentations of concepts related to interpersonal acceptance orient people to cope with stress in a growth-oriented manner, whereas presentations of concepts related to rejection orient people to cope with stress in a self-denigrating manner (Pierce & Lydon, 1998). These effects also are evident in physiological studies. People with large social support networks exhibited faster cardiovascular recovery after a stressor relative to people with small social support networks (Roy, Steptoe, & Kirschbaum, 1998). Examination of salivary cortisol levels suggests that insecurely attached

individuals have greater physiological stress reactions relative to securely attached individuals (Powers, Pietromonaco, Gunlicks, & Sayer, 2006). Moreover, insecurely attached individuals show increased cardiovascular reactivity to stressors relative to securely attached individuals (Feeney & Kirkpatrick, 1996).

Even the individual differences we view as precipitating factors, such as attachment styles and self-esteem, may change as a result of having responsive partners. People who believed their romantic partner saw many virtues in them increased in their global self-esteem over time (Murray et al., 2000). Likewise, people who felt secure in regard to a specific partner's acceptance developed more secure global attachment models over time (Pierce & Lydon, 2001). Those who were viewed positively by their partners (i.e., possessing many positive communal attributes) decreased in their attachment anxiety over time (Murray et al., 1996b). Those who perceived the availability of social support developed more secure attachment orientations over time (Cozzarelli, Karafa, Collins, & Tagler, 2003). Some evidence even suggests intergenerational transmission of self-esteem via conditional regard. Mothers who perceived their own parents to have provided conditional regard had lower self-esteem and had daughters who perceived them to similarly provide conditional regard (Assor, Roth, & Deci, 2004).

The beneficial effects of partners' responsiveness extend to pursuit and achievement of goals. People with romantic partners who report being attentive and responsive to their needs report greater self-efficacy, greater pursuit of personal goals, and more confidence regarding achievement of those goals relative to those who had partners who claimed to be inattentive and unresponsive (Feeney, 2007, studies 1 and 2; see also Brunstein et al., 1996; Feeney, 2004). Laboratory components of this research corroborate these findings, suggesting that people with romantic partners who behave in a sensitive and responsive manner were more likely to openly discuss and plan goal pursuits relative to people with partners who did not behave in a sensitive and responsive manner (Feeney, 2007, studies 1 and 2). People with responsive partners also exhibit more independent functioning by paying less attention and being less accepting of their partner's ostensible efforts to intrusively provide unsolicited task assistance (Feeney, 2007, study 1). People also were more receptive to negative information after poor intellectual performance, information that could facilitate growth, when they visualized a close relationship partner (Kumashiro & Sedikides, 2005). Moreover, partner responsiveness predicts temporal increases in self-efficacy and goal pursuit, and even greater likelihood of achieving goals (Feeney, 2007, study 2). Perceiving partners as generally supportive (Ruvolo & Brennan, 1997) and as supportive of one's ideals (Drigotas,

Rusbult, Wieselquist, & Whitton, 1999) predicts achievement of ideals over time. Just reminding individuals of a significant other increases their confidence, goal pursuit, and performance if the significant other is believed to have high expectations for their performance (Shah, 2003). Similarly, activating thoughts of secure attachment increases interest in exploring new activities (Green & Campbell, 2000). Individual differences in tendencies to perceive and depend on close partners' responsiveness, as reflected in attachment security, predict appetitive achievement and mastery goals. That is, secure individuals appear to focus on potential gains in achievement situations, whereas insecure individuals appear to focus on potential threats (Elliot & Reis, 2003). This may explain why chronically insecure individuals report less interest in exploratory activities (Green & Campbell).

A number of findings suggest that receiving responsiveness has implications for physical health. For instance, loneliness is a risk factor for morbidity and mortality. Effects of greater cumulative stress on organs and regulatory systems, as well as reduced efficiency of restorative mechanisms (e.g., sleep) may be pathways that explain such effects (Cacioppo et al., 2002; Uchino, Cacioppo, & Kiecolt-Glaser, 1996). In addition, having diverse social networks seems to have a main effect on physical health, whereas perceiving social support seems to buffer effects of stress on health (Cohen, 2004; Cohen & Wills, 1985). Partners who care for one's welfare also may exert pressure to engage in health-promoting activities (Lewis & Butterfield, 2007; Tucker, 2002). Social bonds also may mediate effects of seemingly more intrapsychic variables. For instance, individuals with low self-esteem experienced poorer quality social bonds (e.g., low satisfaction, doubts about acceptance, discomfort with closeness, general interpersonal stress), which, in turn, explained their greater health problems (Stinson et al., 2008).

Not all findings, however, are consistent with the view that receiving responsiveness enhances well-being. For instance, in a daily diary study of law students preparing to take the bar exam (Bolger et al., 2000), perceiving that partners provided social support predicted increased depression the following day, whereas partners' reports of providing support predicted reduced depression. (The former finding, but not the latter finding, also was significant for anxiety.) These authors argued that receiving "invisible support"—support that is provided but not detected—is more supportive than receiving visible support because the knowledge that one has been supported threatens self-esteem and self-efficacy. These findings do not fit well with the findings of support provision described earlier. It is possible that the measure of support receipt—that is, whether the partner "listened to and comforted" one—was

confounded with severity or nature of stress subjectively experienced on that day. In addition, law students preparing to take the bar exam may be a group under extraordinary ego threat, such that they easily feel threatened by needing support. Recent experimental work suggests that visible support increases distress relative to no support only to the extent that it is seen as communicating doubts about one's efficacy, and that invisible support decreases distress relative to no support to the extent that it provides reassurance regarding one's efficacy (Bolger & Amarel, 2007). These results suggest that visible support that includes bolstering feelings of efficacy may not have a detrimental effect. The research described previously suggests that promotion of self-efficacy, rather than visibility, is the critical issue, because visible, nonintrusive support that included encouragement seemed to enhance recipients' emotional well-being (e.g., Feeney, 2004, 2007). Moreover, whether social support increases negative affect seems to vary across individuals (Gleason et al., 2008). Perhaps it occurs primarily for individuals whose egos are easily threatened, and primarily with the support is related to something central to one's identity. A law student may feel threatened when receiving visible support for something on which he or she is supposed to have expertise. In contrast, a friend, very visibly, helping one to carry boxes into one's apartment ought not be threatening. Fitting with this reasoning, some research suggests that securely attached individuals seem more emotionally calm when their partners provided emotional support relative to insecure individuals, and that avoidant individuals tend to prefer instrumental (i.e., task-focused) support (Simpson, Winterheld, Rholes, & Orina, 2007).

Providing responsiveness to partners also may enhance one's own well-being. For instance, daily provision of support to romantic partners not only predicted partners' relationship satisfaction, but it also predicted one's own relationship satisfaction (Iida et al., 2008). Both daily giving and daily receiving support combined to predict lowest levels of negative mood and highest levels of closeness (Gleason, Iida, Bolger, & Shrout, 2003; Gleason et al., 2008). Giving support to and receiving support from a friend independently predicted relationship satisfaction, closeness, positive emotion, and feelings of attachment security (Brunstein et al., 1996; Deci et al., 2006). Experimental manipulations corroborate these findings, suggesting that people experience more positive mood and self-evaluations after helping (Williamson & Clark, 1989). Effects occurred primarily when participants believed the other was open to forming a close relationship, suggesting that some of the effect of helping on mood and self-evaluation is mediated by beliefs about promoting close relationships (for a review, see Clark & Grote, 1998).

SUMMARY

This chapter defines close relationships as those that are characterized by the giving and receipt of responsiveness to a partner, with responsiveness itself defined as thoughts, feelings, and especially behaviors geared toward promoting the partner's welfare through understanding, validating, and caring for that partner (cf. Reis & Shaver, 1988). Responsiveness in its many forms, as it inheres in specific relationships, is the key to people feeling close and connected to other people and, in turn, to their mental and physical well-being.

Responsiveness itself takes many forms, and in most adult close relationships, responsiveness is mutual involving both the provision of support to partners and the receipt of support from partners. Ideally, both the giving and receiving of responsiveness is noncontingent, with the giving of responsiveness prompted by opportunities to promote partner welfare, and the seeking and acceptance of responsiveness prompted by opportunities for the partner to promote one's own welfare. When responsiveness is noncontingently given, partners can infer that they and their partners care for one another, and they can feel secure. It is also ideal for individuals in such relationships to be able to flexibly move their interpersonal goals and relational focus of attention to focus on partners when partners need support, to self when the self needs support, and to mutual activities when engaging in such activities that will benefit both relationship partners (cf. Clark et al., 2008).

Research abounds that people desire close, responsive relationships. Yet, "pulling off" a responsive, noncontingent, communal relationship is not easy. Recent research, especially that generated by attachment theory (cf. Mikulincer & Shaver, 2007) and that associated with a model of risk regulation in relationships (cf. Murray, Holmes, & Collins, 2006, and a forthcoming book by Murray & Holmes, 1999), but much other research as well suggests that worries about being dependent, vulnerable, and neglected or even abused by a partner or potential partner can interfere with the establishment of a close, responsive relationship by kicking self-protective motives into gear. This means, sadly, that a desire for such a relationship and the implicit knowledge of the value of such relationships is not sufficient to lead one to successful close relationships. If there is one lesson to be learned from recent research in this area, it is that trust in the likelihood that one's partner will care about one is absolutely crucial to being able to un-self-consciously pull off these relationships. Anything that threatens such trust, be it past experiences and the models of relationships that one brings to new relationships, poor partner behavior, or the interaction of these factors, often twists the process in relationships desired to be close, responsive relationships

in undesirable ways. Low trust and confidence in partner care can simply halt the giving and receiving of responsiveness. It can prompt self-defensive attacks on partners (cf. Murray, Bellavia, et al., 2003). It can lead to unrealistically positive or negative views of partners (cf. Graham & Clark, 2006), which, itself, can interfere with effective giving and receipt of support. It can lead individuals to abandon noncontingent care in favor of safer, more self-protective ways of interacting such as following or attempting to follow an exchange norm (cf. Grote & Clark, 2001; Murray et al., 2009), or it can lead to providing more responsiveness to one's partner than one expects for the self in the hopes of keeping the relationship (cf. Murray et al., 2009). Ironically, such reactions can perpetuate feelings of insecurity through projection processes (Lemay & Clark, 2008a) or through providing external attributions for partners' expressions of affection and positive regard (Lemay & Clark, 2008b).

On a happier note, high desire for responsive relationships combined with reasonably high trust in partners and, eventually, commitment to these relationships promotes these relationships and can buffer people from the normal ups and downs that our own imperfections and those of our partners present to us. For instance, high desire can lead us to perceive partners as more responsive than they might actually be (cf. Lemay et al., 2007; Lemay & Clark, 2008a), and high trust and commitment is associated with viewing partners as having more positive traits than they themselves or outsiders to the relationship consider them to have, which, in turn, can lead to self-fulfilling prophecies (cf. Murray et al., 1996a, 1996b) or sculpting partners into who they wish to be (Drigotas et al., 1999) and to processes such as seeing one's relationship as better than others' relationships (Rusbult, Van Lange, Wildschut, Yovetich, & Verette, 2000), derogating the attractiveness of alternative partners (Simpson, Gangestad, & Lerma, 1990), and even seeing positives in partners' faults (Murray & Holmes, 1999), together with other processes such as forgiveness, accommodation, and sacrifice, all of which may protect the present relationship by buffering it from the normal ups and downs of relationship life.

Not long ago, researchers spoke of the "greening" of the field of close relationship work (Berscheid, 1999). It is fair to say that the field has now blossomed. The field is well populated, current research programs are leading to new discoveries daily, and a nicely converging view of the intrapersonal and interpersonal processes that characterize optimal and sub-optimal relationships is emerging. At the same time, some topics and issues in this field have hardly been touched. Much of our research has focused on heterosexual romantic dating relationships and marriages among relatively young individuals. More work is needed on close relationships among family members, friendships, same-sex relationships, be they romantic or not, and relationships among quite young, middle-aged, and elderly people. Little is known about how people negotiate the initiation phase of relationships, that is, how they get from initial attraction to a committed, ongoing relationship, or about how they manage entire networks of responsive relationships balancing responsibilities in each against responsibilities in others and choosing whom to depend upon for what. Work also is needed on how people decide what partners need and deserve. Ties between the research social psychologists do on normative samples of relationships and that done by clinicians dealing with couples in distress ought to be better integrated. Importantly, explorations of the implications of variations in relationship context for understanding social phenomena long of interest to social psychologists have barely begun despite signs those implications will be profound (Reis & Collins, 2004). Yet, with the rate of progress in this field of research and the number of interesting issues yet to be explored but under discussion, little doubt remains that the next *Handbook* chapter on close relationships will look very different from this one.

REFERENCES

Abbey, A., Andrews, F. M., & Halman, L. J. (1995). Provision and receipt of social support and disregard: What is their impact on the marital life quality of infertile and fertile couples? *Journal of Personality and Social Psychology, 68,* 455–469.

Abele, A. E., & Wojciszke, B. (2007). Agency and communion from the perspective of self versus others. *Journal of Personality and Social Psychology, 93,* 751–763.

Adams, J. M., & Jones, W. H. (1997). The conceptualization of marital commitment: An integrative analysis. *Journal of Personality and Social Psychology, 72,* 1177–1196.

Agnew, C. R., Van Lange, P. A. M., Rusbult, C. E., & Langston, C. A. (1998). Cognitive interdependence: Commitment and the mental representation of close relationships. *Journal of Personality and Social Psychology, 74,* 939–954.

Algoe, S. B., Haidt, J., & Gable, S. L. (2008). Beyond reciprocity: Gratitude and relationships in everyday life. *Emotion, 8,* 425–429.

Ames, D. R. (2004). Inside the mind reader's tool kit: Projection and stereotyping in mental state inference. *Journal of Personality and Social Psychology, 87,* 340–353.

Ames, D. R., Flynn, F. J., & Weber, E. U. (2004). It's the thought that counts: On perceiving how helpers decide to lend a hand. *Personality and Social Psychology Bulletin, 30,* 461–474.

Andersen, S. M., & Chen, S. (2002). The relational self: An interpersonal social-cognitive theory. *Psychological Review, 109,* 619–645.

Andersen, S. M., Reznik, I., & Manzella, L. M. (1996). Eliciting facial affect, motivation, and expectancies in transference: Significant other presentations in social relationships. *Journal of Personality and Social Psychology, 71,* 1108–1129.

Anthony, D. B., Holmes, J. G., & Wood, J. V. (2007). Social acceptance and self-esteem: Tuning the sociometer to interpersonal value. *Journal of Personality and Social Psychology, 92,* 1024–1039.

Aron, A., Aron, E.N., Tudor, M. & Nelson, G. (1991). Close relationships as including other in the self. *Journal of Personality and Social Psychology, 60,* 241–253.

Aron, A., & Fraley, B. (1999). Relationship closeness as including other in the self: Cognitive underpinnings and measures. *Social Cognition, 17,* 140–160.

Aron, A., McLaughlin-Volpe, T., Mashek, D., Lewandowski, G., Wright, S. C., & Aron, E. N. (2004). Including others in the self. In W. Stroebe & M. Hewstone (Eds.), *European review of social psychology* (Vol. 15, pp. 101–132). Hove, United Kingdom: Psychology Press/Taylor & Francis.

Aron, A., Melinat, E., Aron, E. N., Vallone, R. D., et al. (1997). The experimental generation of interpersonal closeness: A procedure and some preliminary findings. *Personality and Social Psychology Bulletin, 23,* 363–377.

Aron, A., Norman, C. C., Aron, E. N., McKenna, C., & Heyman, R. E. (2000). Couples' shared participation in novel and arousing activities and experienced relationship quality. *Journal of Personality and Social Psychology, 78,* 273–284.

Aron, A., Steele, J. L., Kashdan, T. B., & Perez, M. (2006). When similars do not attract: Tests of a prediction from the self-expansion model. *Personal Relationships, 13,* 387–396.

Aronson, E., Willerman, B., & Floyd, J. (1966). The effect of a pratfall on increasing interpersonal attractiveness. *Psychonomic Science, 4,* 227–228.

Arriaga, X. B., Reed, J. T., Goodfriend, W., & Agnew, C. R. (2006). Relationship Perceptions and persistence: Do fluctuations in perceived partner commitment undermine dating relationships? *Journal of Personality and Social Psychology, 91,* 1045–1065.

Arriaga, X. B., & Rusbult, C. E. (1998). Standing in my partner's shoes: Partner perspective taking and reactions to accommodative dilemmas. *Personality and Social Psychology Bulletin, 24,* 927–948.

Assor, A., Roth, G., & Deci, E. L. (2004). The emotional costs of parents' conditional regard: A self-determination theory analysis. *Journal of Personality, 72,* 47–88.

Ayduk, O., Mendoza-Denton, R., Mischel, W., Downey, G., Peake, P. K., & Rodriguez, M. (2000). Regulating the interpersonal self: Strategic self-regulation for coping with rejection sensitivity. *Journal of Personality and Social Psychology, 79,* 776–792.

Ayduk, O., Mischel, W., & Downey, G. (2002). Attentional mechanisms linking rejection to hostile reactivity: The role of "hot" versus "cool" focus. *Psychological Science, 13,* 443–448.

Ayduk, O., Zayas, V., Downey, G., Cole, A. B., Shoda, Y., & Mischel, W. (2008). Rejection sensitivity and executive control: Joint predictors of borderline personality features. *Journal of Research in Personality, 42,* 151–168.

Back, M. D., Schmukle, S. C., & Egloff, B. (2008). Becoming friends by chance. *Psychological Science, 19,* 439–440.

Baldwin, M. W., Keelan, J. P. R., Fehr, B., Enns, V., & Koh-Rangarajoo, E. (1996). Social-cognitive conceptualization of attachment working models: Availability and accessibility effects. *Journal of Personality and Social Psychology, 71,* 94–109.

Baldwin, M. W., & Sinclair, L. (1996). Self-esteem and "if . . . then" contingencies of interpersonal acceptance. *Journal of Personality and Social Psychology, 71,* 1130–1141.

Bargh, J. A., & Pietromonaco, P. (1982). Automatic information processing and social perception: The influence of trait information presented outside of conscious awareness on impression formation. *Journal of Personality and Social Psychology, 43,* 437–449.

Barry, R. A., Lakey, B., & Orehek, E. (2007). Links among attachment dimensions, affect, the self, and perceived support for broadly generalized attachment styles and specific bonds. *Personality and Social Psychology Bulletin, 33,* 340–353.

Bartholomew, K., & Horowitz, L. M. (1991). Attachment styles among young adults: A test of a four-category model. *Journal of Personality and Social Psychology, 61*, 226–244.

Bartlett, M. Y., & DeSteno, D. (2006). Gratitude and prosocial Behavior: Helping when it costs you. *Psychological Science, 17*, 319–325.

Bartz, J. A., & Lydon, J. E. (2004). Close relationships and the working self-concept: Implicit and explicit effects of priming attachment on agency and communion. *Personality and Social Psychology Bulletin, 30*, 1389–1401.

Bartz, J. A., & Lydon, J. E. (2006). Navigating the interdependence dilemma: Attachment goals and the use of communal norms with potential close others. *Journal of Personality and Social Psychology, 91*, 77–96.

Bartz, J. A., & Lydon, J. E. (2008). Relationship-specific attachment, risk regulation, and communal norm adherence in close relationships. *Journal of Experimental Social Psychology, 44*, 655–663.

Batson, C. D., Eklund, J. H., Chermok, V. L., Hoyt, J. L., & Ortiz, B. G. (2007). An additional antecedent of empathic concern: Valuing the welfare of the person in need. *Journal of Personality and Social Psychology, 93*, 65–74.

Baumeister, R. F., DeWall, C. N., Ciarocco, N. J., & Twenge, J. M. (2005). Social exclusion impairs self-regulation. *Journal of Personality and Social Psychology, 88*, 589–604.

Baumeister, R. F., & Leary, M. R. (1995). The need to belong: Desire for interpersonal attachments as a fundamental human motivation. *Psychological Bulletin, 117*, 497–529.

Baumeister, R. F., Stillwell, A. M., & Heatherton, T. F. (1994). Guilt: An interpersonal approach. *Psychological Bulletin, 115*, 243–267.

Baumeister, R. F., Twenge, J. M., & Nuss, C. K. (2002). Effects of social exclusion on cognitive processes: Anticipated aloneness reduces intelligent thought. *Journal of Personality and Social Psychology, 83*, 817–827.

Beach, S. R., Whitaker, P. J., Jones, D. J., & Tesser, A. (2001). When does performance feedback prompt complentarity in romantic relationships. *Personal Relationships, 8*, 231–248.

Beach, S. R. H., Tesser, A., Fincham, F. D., Jones, D. J., Johnson, D., & Whitaker, D. J. (1998). Pleasure and pain in doing well, together: An investigation of performance-related affect in close relationships. *Journal of Personality and Social Psychology, 74*, 923–938.

Beck, L. A., & Clark, M. S. (2008). Emotional reactions to mild acceptance and rejection by potential relationship partners. Submitted manuscript, Yale University.

Beck, L. A., & Clark, M. S. (2009a). Choosing to enter or avoid diagnostic social situations. *Psychological Science, 20*, 1175–1181.

Beck, L. A., & Clark, M. S. (2009b). Offering more support than we seek. *Journal of Experimental Social Psychology, 45*, 267–270.

Berenson, K. R., & Andersen, S. M. (2006). Childhood physical and emotional abuse by a parent: Transference effects in adult interpersonal relationship. *Personality and Social Psychology Bulletin, 32*, 1509–1522.

Bernichon, T., Cook, K. E., & Brown, J. D. (2003). Seeking self-evaluative feedback: The interactive role of global self-esteem and specific self-views. *Journal of Personality and Social Psychology, 84*, 194–204.

Berscheid, E. (1999). The greening of relationship science. *American Psychologist, 54*, 260–266.

Berscheid, E., Boye, D., & Darley, J. M. (1968). Effect of forced association upon voluntary choice to associate. *Journal of Personality and Social Psychology, 8*(1), 13–19.

Berscheid, E., Dion, K., Walster, E., & Walster, G. W. (1971). Physical attractiveness and dating choice: A test of the matching hypothesis. *Journal of Experimental Social Psychology, 7*, 173–189.

Berscheid, E., Snyder, M., Omoto, A. M. (1989): The relationship closeness inventory: Assessing the closeness of interpersonal relationships. *Journal of Personality and Social Psychology, 57*, 792–807.

Bierhoff, H. (2002). *Prosocial behaviour*. New York: Psychology Press, Taylor & Francis Group.

Blumberg, H. H. (1972). Communication of interpersonal evaluations. *Journal of Personality and Social Psychology, 23*, 157–162.

Bolger, N., & Amarel, D. (2007). Effects of social support visibility on adjustment to stress: Experimental evidence. *Journal of Personality and Social Psychology, 92*, 458–475.

Bolger, N., Zuckerman, A., & Kessler, R. C. (2000). Invisible support and adjustment to stress. *Journal of Personality and Social Psychology, 79*, 953–961.

Bornstein, R. F. (1998). Implicit and self-attributed dependency strivings: Differential relationships to laboratory and field measures of help seeking. *Journal of Personality and Social Psychology, 75*, 778–787.

Bossard, J. H. S. (1932). Residential propinquity as a factor in marriage selection. *American Journal of Sociology, 38*, 218–224.

Bourgeois, K. S., & Leary, M. R. (2001). Coping with rejection: Derogating those who choose us last. *Motivation and Emotion, 25*, 101–111.

Bowlby, J. (1969). *Attachment and loss: Vol. 1. Attachment*. New York: Basic Books.

Boyes, A. D., & Fletcher, G. J. O. (2007). Meta-perceptions of bias in intimate relationships. *Journal of Personality and Social Psychology, 92*, 286–306.

Brennan, K. A., Clark, C. L., & Shaver, P. R. (1998). Self-report measurement of adult attachment: An integrative overview. In J. A. Simpson & W. S. Rholes (Eds.), *Attachment theory and close relationships* (pp. 46–76). New York: Guilford Press.

Brennan, K. A., & Shaver, P. R. (1998). Attachment styles and personality disorders: Their connections to each other and to parental divorce, parental death, and perceptions of parental caregiving. *Journal of Personality, 66*, 835–878.

Brown, J. D., Collins, R. L., & Schmidt, G. W. (1988). Self-esteem and direct versus indirect forms of self-enhancement. *Journal of Personality and Social Psychology, 55*, 445–453.

Brumbaugh, C. C., & Fraley, R. C. (2006). Transference and attachment: How do attachment patterns get carried forward from one relationship to the next? *Personality and Social Psychology Bulletin, 32*, 552–560.

Brunell, A. B., Pilkington, C. J., & Webster, G. D. (2007). Perceptions of risk in intimacy in dating couples: Conversation and relationship quality. *Journal of Social & Clinical Psychology, 26*, 92–119.

Bruner, J. S., & Goodman, C. C. (1947). Value and need as organizing factors in perception. *Journal of Abnormal and Social Psychology, 42*, 33–44.

Brunstein, J. C., Dangelmayer, G., & Schultheiss, O. C. (1996). Personal goals and social support in close relationships: Effects on relationship mood and marital satisfaction. *Journal of Personality and Social Psychology, 71*, 1006–1019.

Buunk, B. P. (2001). Perceived superiority of one's own relationship and perceived prevalence of happy and unhappy relationships. *British Journal of Social Psychology, 40*, 565–574.

Buunk, B. P., & Van Yperen, N. W. (1991). Referential comparisons, relational comparisons, and exchange orientation: Their relation to marital satisfaction. *Personality and Social Psychology Bulletin, 17*, 709–717.

Burger, J. M., Messian, N., Patel, S., del Prado, A., & Anderson, C. (2004). What a coincidence! The effects of incidental similarity on compliance. *Personality and Social Psychology Bulletin, 30*, 35–43.

Buss, D. M. (1989). Sex differences in human mate preferences: Evolutionary hypotheses tested in 37 cultures. *Behavioral and Brain Sciences, 12*, 1–49.

Buss, D. M., & Barnes, M. L. (1986). Preferences in human mate selection. *Journal of Personality & Social Psychology, 50*(3), 559–570.

Byrne, D. (1971). *The attraction paradigm*. New York: Academic Press.

Byrne, D., & Clore, G. L. (1970). A reinforcement model of evaluative responses. *Personality: An International Journal, 1*, 103–128.

Byrne, D., & Griffitt, W. (1973). Interpersonal attraction. *Annual Review of Psychology, 11*, 317–336.

Cacioppo, J. T., Hawkley, L. C., Crawford, E., Ernst, J. M., Burleson, M. H., Kowalewski, R. B., et al. (2002). Loneliness and health: Potential mechanisms. *Psychosomatic Medicine, 64*, 407–417.

Cameron, J. J., Holmes, J. G., & Vorauer, J. D. (2009). When self-disclosure goes awry: Negative consequences of revealing personal failure for lower self-esteem individuals. *Journal of Experimental Social Psychology, 45*, 217–222.

Campbell, L., Lackenbauer, S. D., & Muise, A. (2006). When is being known or adored by romantic partners most beneficial? Self-percep- tions, relationship length, and responses to partner's verifying and enhancing appraisals. *Personality and Social Psychology Bulletin, 32*, 1283–1294.

Campbell, L., Simpson, J. A., Boldry, J., & Kashy, D. A. (2005). Perceptions of conflict and support in romantic relationships: The role of attachment anxiety. *Journal of Personality and Social Psychology, 88*, 510–531.

Campbell, W. K. (1999). Narcissism and romantic attraction. *Journal of Personality and Social Psychology, 77*, 1254–1270.

Carvallo, M., & Gabriel, S. (2006). No man is an island: The need to belong and dismissing avoidant attachment style. *Personality and Social Psychology Bulletin, 32*, 697–709.

Cassidy, J., & Shaver, P. R. (Eds.). (1999). *Handbook of attachment: Theory, research, and clinical applications*. New York: Guilford Press.

Chapman, H. A., Hobfoll, S. E., & Ritter, C. (1997). Partners' stress under- estimations lead to women's distress: A study of pregnant inner-city women. *Journal of Personality and Social Psychology, 73*, 418–425.

Chartrand, T., L., & Bargh, J. A. (1999). The chameleon effect: The perception-behavior link and social interaction. *Journal of Personality and Social Psychology, 76*, 893–910.

Cialdini, R. B., Borden, R. J., Thorne, A., Walker, M. R., Freeman, S., & Sloan, L. R. (1976). Basking in reflected glory: Three (football) field studies. *Journal of Personality and Social Psychology, 34*, 366–375.

Cialdini, R. B., Brown, S. L., Lewis, B. P., Luce, C., & Neuberg, S. L. (1997). Reinterpreting the empathy-altruism relationship: When one into one equals oneness. *Journal of Personality and Social Psychology, 73*, 481–494.

Clark, M. S. (1986). Evidence for the effectiveness of manipulations of communal and exchange relationships. *Personality and Social Psychology Bulletin, 12*, 414–425.

Clark, M.S. & Beck, L.A. (in press). Initiating and evaluating close rela- tionships: A task central to emerging adults. In F. Fincham & M. Cui (Eds). *Romantic Relationships in Emerging Adulthood*. New York: Cambridge University Press.

Clark, M. S., & Finkel, E. J. (2005). Willingness to express emotion: The impact of relationship type, communal orientation, and their interac- tion. *Personal Relationships, 12*, 169–180.

Clark, M. S., Fitness, J., & Brissette, I. (2000). Understanding people's perceptions of relationships is crucial to understanding their emotional lives. In G. Fletcher & M. S. Clark (Eds.), *Blackwell Handbook of Social Psychology: Interpersonal Processes* (pp. 253–278). Oxford: Blackwell Publishers.

Clark, M. S., Graham, S. M., Williams, E., & Lemay, E. P. (2008) Understanding relational focus of attention may help us understand relational phenomena. In J. Forgas and J. Fitness (Eds.), *Social relation- ships: Cognitive, affective, and motivational processes* (pp. 131–146). New York: Psychology Press.

Clark, M. S., & Grote, N. K. (1998). Why aren't indices of relationship costs always negatively related to indices of relationship quality? *Personality and Social Psychology Review, 2*, 2–17.

Clark, M. S., & Mills, J. (1979). Interpersonal attraction in exchange and communal relationships. *Journal of Personality and Social Psychology, 37*, 12–24.

Clark, M. S., Mills, J., & Powell, M. C. (1986). Keeping track of needs in communal and exchange relationships. *Journal of Personality and Social Psychology, 51*, 333–338.

Clark, M. S., Mills, J. R., & Corcoran, D. M. (1989). Keeping track of needs and inputs of friends and strangers. *Personality and Social Psychology Bulletin, 15*, 533–542.

Clark, M. S., & Monin, J. (2006). Giving and receiving communal respon- siveness as love. In R. J. Sternberg & K. Weis (Eds.), *The new psychol- ogy of love* (pp. 200–221). New Haven, CT: Yale University Press.

Clark, M. S., Ouellette, R., Powell, M. C., & Milberg, S. (1987). Recipient's mood, relationship type, and helping. *Journal of Personality and Social Psychology, 53*, 94–103.

Clark, M. S., & Taraban, C. (1991). Reactions to and willingness to express emotion in communal and exchange relationships. *Journal of Experimental Social Psychology, 27*, 324–336.

Clements, M. I., Stanley, S. M., & Markman, H. J. (2004). Before they said "I do": Discriminating among marital outcomes over 13 years. *Journal of Marriage and Family, 66*, 613–626.

Cobb, R. J., Davila, J., & Bradbury, T. N. (2001). Attachment security and marital satisfaction: The role of positive perceptions and social support. *Personality and Social Psychology Bulletin, 27*, 1131–1143.

Cohen, S. (2004). Social relationships and health. *American Psychologist, 59*, 676–684.

Cohen, S., & Janicki-Deverts, D. (in press). Can we improve our physical health by altering our social networks? *Perspectives in Psychological Science, 4*, 375–378.

Cohen, S., & Wills, T. A. (1985). Stress, social support, and the buffering hypothesis. *Psychological Bulletin, 98*, 310–357.

Collins, N. L. (1996). Working models of attachment: Implications for explanation, emotion, and behavior. *Journal of Personality and Social Psychology, 71*, 810–832.

Collins, N. L., Cooper, M. L., Albino, A., & Allard, L. (2002). Psychosocial vulnerability from adolescence to adulthood: A prospective study of attachment style differences in relationship functioning and partner choice. *Journal of Personality, 70*, 965–1008.

Collins, N. L., & Feeney, B. C. (2000). A safe haven: An attachment theory perspective on support seeking and caregiving in intimate relationships. *Journal of Personality and Social Psychology, 78*, 1053–1073.

Collins, N. L., & Feeney, B. C. (2004). Working models of attachment shape perceptions of social support: Evidence from experimental and observational studies. *Journal of Personality and Social Psychology, 87*, 363–383.

Collins, N. L., Ford, M. B., Guichard, A. C., & Allard, L. M. (2006). Working models of attachment and attribution processes in intimate relationships. *Personality and Social Psychology Bulletin, 32*, 201–219.

Collins, N. L., & Miller, L. C. (1994). Self-disclosure and liking: A meta- analytic review. *Psychological Bulletin, 116*, 457–475.

Collins, N. L., & Read, S. J. (1990). Adult attachment, working models, and relationship quality in dating couples. *Journal of Personality and Social Psychology, 58*, 644–663.

Collins, R. L. (1996). For better or worse: The impact of upward social comparison on self-evaluations. *Psychological Bulletin, 119*, 51–69.

Condon, J. W., & Crano, W. D. (1988). Inferred evaluation and the rela- tion between attitude similarity and interpersonal attraction. *Journal of Personality and Social Psychology, 54*, 789–797.

Cook, W. L. (2000). Understanding attachment security in family context. *Journal of Personality and Social Psychology, 78*, 285–294.

Cooper, M. L., Shaver, P. R., & Collins, N. L. (1998). Attachment styles, emotion regulation, and adjustment in adolescence. *Journal of Personality and Social Psychology, 74*, 1380–1397.

Cottrell, C. A., Neuberg, S. L., & Li, N. P. (2007). What do people desire in others? A sociofunctional perspective on the importance of different valued characteristics. *Journal of Personality and Social Psychology, 92*, 208–231.

Cox, C. L., Wexler, M. O., Rusbult, C. E., & Gaines, S. O., Jr. (1997). Prescriptive support and commitment processes in close relationships. *Social Psychology Quarterly, 60*, 79–90.

Cozzarelli, C., Hoekstra, S. J., & Bylsma, W. H. (2000). General versus specific mental models of attachment: Are they associated with different outcomes? *Personality and Social Psychology Bulletin, 26*, 605–618.

Cozzarelli, C., Karafa, J. A., Collins, N. L., & Tagler, M. J. (2003). Stability and change in adult attachment styles: Associations with personal vulnerabilities, life events, and global construals of self and others. *Journal of Social & Clinical Psychology, 22*, 315–346.

Cozzarelli, C., Sumer, N., & Major, B. (1998). Mental models of attachment and coping with abortion. *Journal of Personality and Social Psychology, 74*, 453–467.

Cross, S. E., Bacon, P. L., & Morris, M. L. (2000). The relational-interdependent self-construal and relationships. *Journal of Personality and Social Psychology, 78*, 791–808.

Cross, S. E., Gore, J. S., & Morris, M. (2003). The relational self-construal, self-consistency, and well-being. *Journal of Personality and Social Psychology, 85*, 933–944.

Cross, S. E., Morris, M., & Gore, J. (2002). Thinking about oneself and others: The relational-interdependent self-construal and social cognition. *Journal of Personality and Social Psychology, 82*, 399–418.

Cross, S. E., & Morris, M. L. (2003). Getting to know you: The relational self-construal, relational cognition, and well-being. *Personality and Social Psychology Bulletin, 29*, 512–552.

Davila, J., Bradbury, T. N., Cohan, C. L., & Tochluk, S. (1997). Marital functioning and depressive symptoms: Evidence for a stress generation model. *Journal of Personality and Social Psychology, 73*, 849–861.

Davis, M. H., Morris, M. M., & Kraus, L. A. (1998). Relationship-specific and global perceptions of social support: Associations with well-being and attachment. *Journal of Personality and Social Psychology, 74*, 468–481.

De La Ronde, C., & Swann, W. B., Jr. (1998). Partner verification: Restoring shattered images of our intimates. *Journal of Personality and Social Psychology, 75*, 374–382.

Deci, E. L., La Guardia, J. G., Moller, A. C., Scheiner, M. J., & Ryan, R. M. (2006). On the benefits of giving as well as receiving autonomy support: Mutuality in close friendships. *Personality and Social Psychology Bulletin, 32*, 313–327.

DePaulo, B. M., & Kashy, D. A. (1998). Everyday lies in close and casual relationships. *Journal of Personality and Social Psychology, 74*, 63–79.

DePaulo, B. M., Kashy, D. A., Kirkendol, S. E., Wyer, M. M., & Epstein, J. A. (1996). Lying in everyday life. *Journal of Personality and Social Psychology, 70*, 979–995.

DeSteno, D., & Salovey, P. (1996). Jealousy and the characteristics of one's rival: A self-evaluation maintenance perspective. *Personality and Social Psychology Bulletin, 22*, 920–932.

Deutsch, M., & Solomon, L. (1959). Reactions to evaluations by others as influenced by self-evaluations. *Sociometry, 22*, 93–112.

Diamond, L. M., Hicks, A. M., & Otter-Henderson, K. (2006). Psysiological evidence for repressive coping among avoidantly attached adults. *Journal of Social and Personal Relationships, 23*, 205–229.

Diehl, M., Elnick, A. B., Bourbeau, L. S., & Labouvie-Vief, G. (1998). Adult attachment styles: Their relations to family context and personality. *Journal of Personality and Social Psychology, 74*, 1656–1669.

Dittes, J. E. (1959). Attractiveness of group as function of self-esteem and acceptance by group. *The Journal of Abnormal and Social Psychology, 59*, 77–82.

Dovidio, J. F., Piliavin, J. A., Schroeder, D. A., & Penner, L. A. (2006). *The social psychology of prosocial behavior.* Mahwah, NJ: Erlbaum.

Downey, G., & Feldman, S. I. (1996). Implications of rejection sensitivity for intimate relationships. *Journal of Personality and Social Psychology, 70*, 1327–1343.

Downey, G., Freitas, A. L., Michaelis, B., & Khouri, H. (1998). The self-fulfilling prophecy in close relationships: Rejection sensitivity and rejection by romantic partners. *Journal of Personality and Social Psychology, 75*, 545–560.

Dozier, M., & Kobak, R. R. (1992). Psychophysiology in attachment interviews: Converging evidence for deactivating strategies. *Child Development, 63*, 1473–1480.

Drigotas, S. M. (1993). Similarity revisited: A comparison of similarity-attraction versus dissimilarity-repulsion. *British Journal of Social Psychology, 32*, 365–377.

Drigotas, S. M. (2002). The Michelangelo phenomenon and personal well-being. *Journal of Personality, 70*, 59–70.

Drigotas, S. M., Rusbult, C. E., Wieselquist, J., & Whitton, S. W. (1999). Close partner as sculptor of the ideal self: Behavioral affirmation and the Michelangelo phenomenon. *Journal of Personality and Social Psychology, 77*, 293–323.

Dryer, D. C., & Horowitz, L. M. (1997). When do opposites attract? Interpersonal complementarity versus similarity. *Journal of Personality and Social Psychology, 72*, 592–603.

Eastwick, P. W., & Finkel, E. J. (2008a). Sex differences in mate preferences revisited: Do people know what they initially desire in a romantic partner? *Journal of Personality and Social Psychology, 94*, 245–264.

Eastwick, P. W., & Finkel, E. J. (2008b). The attachment system in fledgling relationships: An activating role for attachment anxiety. *Journal of Personality and Social Psychology, 95*, 628–647.

Elliot, A. J., & Reis, H. T. (2003). Attachment and exploration in adulthood. *Journal of Personality and Social Psychology, 85*, 317–331.

Feeney, B. C. (2004). A secure base: Responsive support of goal strivings and exploration in adult intimate relationships. *Journal of Personality and Social Psychology, 87*, 631–648.

Feeney, B. C. (2007). The dependency paradox in close relationships: Accepting dependence promotes independence. *Journal of Personality and Social Psychology, 92*, 268–285.

Feeney, B. C., & Collins, N. L. (2001). Predictors of caregiving in adult intimate relationships: An attachment theoretical perspective. *Journal of Personality and Social Psychology, 80*, 972–994.

Feeney, B. C., & Collins, N. L. (2003). Motivations for caregiving in adult intimate relationships: Influences on caregiving behavior and relationship functioning. *Personality and Social Psychology Bulletin, 29*, 950–968.

Feeney, B. C., & Kirkpatrick, L. A. (1996). Effects of adult attachment and presence of romantic partners on physiological responses to stress. *Journal of Personality and Social Psychology, 70*, 255–270.

Feeney, J. A., & Noller, P. (1990). Attachment style as a predictor of adult romantic relationships. *Journal of Personality and Social Psychology, 58*, 281–291.

Fehr, B. (2004). Intimacy expectations in same-sex friendships: A prototype interaction-pattern model. *Journal of Personality and Social Psychology, 86*, 265–284.

Feldman, R., Weller, A., Zagoory-Sharon, O., & Levine, A. (2007). Evidence for a neuroencocrinological foundation of human affiliation: Plasma osytocin levels across pregnancy and the postpartum period predict mother-infant bonding. *Psychological Science, 18*, 965-970.

Felson, R. B. (1980). Communication barriers and the reflected appraisal process. *Social Psychology Quarterly, 43*, 223–233.

Festinger, L., Schachter, S., & Back, K. (1950). *Social pressures in informal groups; a study of human factors in housing* (p. x). Oxford: Harper.

Fincham, F. D., Beach, S. R. H., & Davila, J. (2004). Forgiveness and conflict resolution in marriage. *Journal of Family Psychology, 18,* 72–81.

Finkel, E. J., & Campbell, W. K. (2001). Self-control and accommodation in close relationships: An interdependence analysis. *Journal of Personality and Social Psychology, 81,* 263–277.

Finkel, E. J., Rusbult, C. E., Kumashiro, M., & Hannon, P. A. (2002). Dealing with betrayal in close relationships: Does commitment promote forgiveness? *Journal of Personality and Social Psychology, 82,* 956–974.

Fitzsimons, G. M., & Bargh, J. A. (2003). Thinking of you: Nonconscious pursuit of interpersonal goals associated with relationship partners. *Journal of Personality and Social Psychology, 84,* 148–164.

Fletcher, G. J. O., Simpson, J. A., Thomas, G., & Giles, L. (1999). Ideals in intimate relationships. *Journal of Personality and Social Psychology, 76,* 72–89.

Florian, V., Mikulincer, M., & Bucholtz, I. (1995). Effects of adult attachment style on the perception and search for social support. *Journal of Psychology: Interdisciplinary and Applied, 129,* 665–676.

Floyd, K. (2006). *Communicating affection: Interpersonal behavior and social context.* New York: Cambridge University Press.

Fraley, R. C., Garner, J. P., & Shaver, P. R. (2000). Adult attachment and the defensive regulation of attention and memory: Examining the role of preemptive and postemptive defensive processes. *Journal of Personality and Social Psychology, 79,* 816–826.

Fraley, R. C., & Shaver, P. R. (1997). Adult attachment and the suppression of unwanted thoughts. *Journal of Personality and Social Psychology, 73,* 1080–1091.

Fraley, R. C., & Shaver, P. R. (1998). Airport separations: A naturalistic study of adult attachment dynamics in separating couples. *Journal of Personality and Social Psychology, 75,* 1198–1212.

Fraley, R. C., & Waller, N. G. (1998). Adult attachment patterns: A test of the typological model. In J. A. Simpson & W. S. Rholes (Eds.), *Attachment theory and close relationships* (pp. 77–114). New York: Guilford Press.

Fraley, R. C., Waller, N. G., & Brennan, K. A. (2000). An item-response theory analysis Of self-report measures of adult attachment. *Journal of Personality and Social Psychology, 78,* 350–365.

Fritz, H. L., & Helgeson, V. S. (1998). Distinctions of unmitigated communion from communion: Self-neglect and overinvolvement with others. *Journal of Personality and Social Psychology, 75,* 121–140.

Gable, S. L., Gonzaga, G., & Strachman, A. (2006). Will you be there for me when things go right? Social support for positive events. *Journal of Personality and Social Psychology, 91,* 904–917.

Gable, S. L., & Reis, H. T. (2006). Intimacy and the self: An iterative model of the self and close relationships. In P. Noller & J. A. Feeney (Eds.), *Close relationships: Functions, forms and processes.* (pp. 211–225). Hove, United Kingdom: Psychology Press/Taylor & Francis.

Gable, S. L., Reis, H. T., & Downey, G. (2003). He said, she said: A quasi-signal detection analysis of daily interactions between close relationship partners. *Psychological Science, 14,* 100–105.

Gable, S. L., Reis, H. T., Impett, E. A., & Asher, E. R. (2004). What do you do when things go right? The intrapersonal and interpersonal benefits of sharing positive events. *Journal of Personality and Social Psychology, 87,* 228–245.

Gabriel, S., Carvallo, M., Dean, K. K., Tippin, B., & Renaud, J. (2005). How I see me depends on how I see you: The role of attachment style in social comparison. *Personality and Social Psychology Bulletin, 31,* 1561–1572.

Gagne, F., & Lydon, J. (2001a). Mindset and relationship illusions: The moderating effects of domain specificity and relationship commitment. *Personality and Social Psychology Bulletin, 27,* 1144–1155.

Gagne, F. M., & Lydon, J. E. (2001b). Mind-set and close relationships: When bias leads to (in)accurate predictions. *Journal of Personality and Social Psychology, 81,* 85–96.

Gagne, F. M., & Lydon, J. E. (2004). Bias and accuracy in close relationships: An integrative review. *Personality and Social Psychology Review, 8,* 322–338.

Gardner, W. L., Gabriel, S., & Hochschild, L. (2002). When you and I are "we," you are not threatening: The role of self-expansion in social comparison. *Journal of Personality and Social Psychology, 82,* 239–251.

Gill, M. J., Swann, W. B., Jr., & Silvera, D. H. (1998). On the genesis of confidence. *Journal of Personality and Social Psychology, 75,* 1101–1114.

Gillath, O., Mikulincer, M., Fitzsimons, G. M., Shaver, P. R., Schachner, D. A., & Bargh, J. A. (2006). Automatic activation of attachment-related goals. *Personality and Social Psychology Bulletin, 32,* 1375–1388.

Glassman, N. S., & Andersen, S. M. (1999). Activating transference without consciousness: Using significant-other representations to go beyond what is subliminally given. *Journal of Personality and Social Psychology, 77,* 1146–1162.

Gleason, M. E. J., Iida, M., Bolger, N., & Shrout, P. E. (2003). Daily supportive equity in close relationships. *Personality and Social Psychology Bulletin, 29,* 1036–1045.

Gleason, M. E. J., Iida, M., Shrout, P. E., & Bolger, N. (2008). Receiving support as a mixed blessing: Evidence for dual effects of support on psychological outcomes. *Journal of Personality and Social Psychology, 94,* 824–838.

Gollwitzer, P. M. (1999). Implementation intentions: Strong effects of simple plans. *American Psychologist, 54,* 493–503.

Gollwitzer, P. M., Heckhausen, H., & Stellar, B. (1990). Deliberative versus implemental mind-sets: Cognitive tuning toward congruous thoughts and information. *Journal of Personality and Social Psychology, 59,* 1119–1127.

Gonzaga, G. C., Keltner, D., Londahl, E. A., & Smith, M. D. (2001). Love and the commitment problem in romantic relations and friendship. *Journal of Personality and Social Psychology, 81,* 247–262.

Gore, J. S., & Cross, S. E. (2006). Pursuing goals for us: Relationally-autonomous reasons in long-term goal pursuit. *Journal of Personality and Social Psychology, 90,* 858–861.

Gottman, J. M. (1994). *What predicts divorce?* Hillsdale, NJ: Lawrence Erlbaum Associates.

Graham, S. M., & Clark, M. S. (2006). Self-esteem and organization of valenced information about others: The "Jekyll and Hyde"-ing of relationship partners. *Journal of Personality and Social Psychology, 90,* 652–665.

Graham, S. M., Huang, J. Y., Clark, M. S., & Helgeson, V. S. (2008). The positives of negative emotions: Willingness to express negative emotions promotes relationships. *Personality and Social Psychology Bulletin, 34,* 394–406.

Green, J. D., & Campbell, W. K. (2000). Attachment and exploration in adults: Chronic and contextual accessibility. *Personality and Social Psychology Bulletin, 26,* 452–461.

Gross, J. J., & John, O. P. (2003). Individual differences in two emotion regulation processes: Implications for affect, relationships, and well-being. *Journal of Personality and Social Psychology, 85,* 348–362.

Grote, N. K., & Clark, M. S. (2001). Perceiving unfairness in the family: Cause or consequence of marital distress. *Journal of Personality and Social Psychology, 80,* 281–293.

Haselton, M. G., & Buss, D. M. (2000). Error management theory: A new perspective on biases in cross-sex mind reading. *Journal of Personality and Social Psychology, 78,* 81–91.

Hassebrauck, M., & Aron, A. (2001). Prototype matching in close relationships. *Personality and Social Psychology Bulletin, 27,* 1111–1122.

Hazan, C., & Shaver, P. (1987). Romantic love conceptualized as an attachment process. *Journal of Personality and Social Psychology, 52*, 511–524.

Helgeson, V. S. (1994). The relation of agency and communion to well-being: Evidence and potential explanations. *Psychological Bulletin, 116*, 412–428.

Helgeson, V. S., & Fritz, H. L. (1998). A theory of unmitigated communion. *Personality and Social Psychology Review, 2*, 173–183.

Hendrick, S. S. (1981). Self-disclosure and marital satisfaction. *Journal of Personality and Social Psychology, 40*, 1150–1159.

Holmes, D. S. (1968). Dimensions of projection. *Psychological Bulletin, 69*, 248–268.

Holmes, J. G. (1991). Trust and the appraisal process in close relationships. In W. H. Jones & D. Perlman (Eds.), *Advances in personal relationships* (Vol. 2, pp. 57–106). London: Jessica Kingsley.

Holmes, J. G., & Rempel, J. K. (1989). Trust in close relationships. In C. Hendrick (Ed.), *Close relationships* (pp. 187–220). Thousand Oaks, CA: Sage Publications, Inc.

House, J. S., Landis, K. R., & Umberson, B. (1988). Social relationships and health. *Science, 29*, 540–545.

Huston, T. L. (1973). Ambiguity of acceptance, social desirability, and dating choice. *Journal of Experimental Social Psychology, 9*, 32–42.

Huston, T. L., & Levinger, G. (1978). Interpersonal attraction and relationships. *Annual Review of Psychology, 29*, 115–156.

Iida, M., Seidman, G., Shrout, P. E., Fujita, K., & Bolger, N. (2008). Modeling support provision in intimate relationships. *Journal of Personality and Social Psychology, 94*, 460–478.

Jacobs, L., Berscheid, E., & Walster, E. (1971). Self-esteem and attraction. *Journal of Personality and Social Psychology, 17*, 84–91.

Jamieson, D. W., Lydon, J. E., & Zanna, M. P. (1987). Attitude and activity preference similarity: Differential bases of interpersonal attraction for low and high self-monitors. *Journal of Personality and Social Psychology, 53*, 1052–1060.

Johnson, D. J., & Rusbult, C. E. (1989). Resisting temptation: Devaluation of alternative partners as a means of maintaining commitment in close relationships. Journal of Personality and Social Psychology, *57*, 967–980.

Jones, J. T., Pelham, B. W., Carvallo, M., & Mirenberg, M. C. (2004). How do I love three? Let me count the Js: Implicit egotism and interpersonal attraction. *Journal of Personality and Social Psychology, 87*, 665–683.

Jones, S. C. (1973). Self- and interpersonal evaluations: Esteem theories versus consistency theories. *Psychological Bulletin, 79*, 185–199.

Jones, S. C., & Panitch, D. (1971). The self-fulfilling prophecy and interpersonal attraction. *Journal of Experimental Social Psychology, 7*, 356–366.

Kalick, S. M., Zebrowtiz, L. A., Langlois, J. H., & Johnson, R. M. (1998). Does human facial attractiveness honestly advertise health? *Psychological Science, 9*, 8–13.

Katz, J., & Beach, S. R. H. (2000). Looking for love? Self-verification and self-enhancement effects on initial romantic attraction. *Personality and Social Psychology Bulletin, 26*, 1526–1539.

Katz, J., Beach, S. R. H., & Anderson, P. (1996). Self-enhancement versus self-verification: Does spousal support always help? *Cognitive Therapy and Research, 20*, 345–360.

Kaul, M., & Lakey, B. (2003). Where is the support in perceived support? The role of generic relationship satisfaction and enacted support in perceived support's relation to low distress. *Journal of Social & Clinical Psychology, 22*, 59–78.

Kawada, C. L. K., Oettingen, G., Gollwitzer, P. M., & Bargh, J. A. (2004). The projection of implicit and explicit goals. *Journal of Personality and Social Psychology, 86*, 545–559.

Kelley, H. H., Holmes, J. G., Kerr, N., Reis, H. T., Rusbult, C. E., & Van Lange, P. A. M. (2003). *An atlas of interpersonal situations.* New York: Cambridge University Press.

Kenny, D. A., & Acitelli, L. K. (2001). Accuracy and bias in the perception of the partner in a close relationship. *Journal of Personality and Social Psychology, 80*, 439–448.

Kenny, D. A., & DePaulo, B. M. (1993). Do people know how others view them? An empirical and theoretical account. *Psychological Bulletin, 114*, 145–161.

Kirsch, P., Esslinger, C., Chen, Q., Mier, D., Lis, S., Siddhanti, S., et al. (2005). Oxytocin modulates neural circuitry for social cognition and fear in humans. *Journal of Neuroscience, 25*, 11489–11489.

Klohnen, E. C., & Bera, S. (1998). Behavioral and experiential patterns of avoidantly and securely attached women across adulthood: A 31-year longitudinal perspective. *Journal of Personality and Social Psychology, 74*, 211–223.

Klohnen, E. C., & Luo, S. (2003). Interpersonal attraction and personality: What is attractive—self similarity, ideal similarity, complementarity or attachment security. *Journal of Personality and Social Psychology, 85*, 709–722.

Klohnen, E. C., Weller, J. A., Luo, S., & Choe, M. (2005). Organization and predictive power of general and relationship-specific attachment models: One for all, and all for one? *Personality and Social Psychology Bulletin, 31*, 1665–1682.

Kosfeld, M., Heinriches, M., Zak, P. J., Fischbacker, U., & Fehr, E. (2005). Oxytocin increases trust in humans. *Nature, 435*, 673–676.

Krueger, J., & Clement, R. W. (1994). The truly false consensus effect: An ineradicable and egocentric bias in social perception. *Journal of Personality and Social Psychology, 67*, 596–610.

Kruglanski, A. W., & Pierro, A. (2008). Night and day, you are the one: On circadian mismatches and the transference effect. *Psychological Science, 19*, 296–301.

Kumashiro, M., & Sedikides, C. (2005). Taking on board liability-focused information: Close positive relationships as a self-bolstering resource. *Psychological Science, 16*, 732–739.

Kunce, L. J., & Shaver, P. R. (1994). An attachment-theoretical approach to caregiving in romantic relationships. In K. Bartholomew & D. Perlman (Eds.), *Attachment processes in adulthood* (pp. 205–237). Philadelphia: Jessica Kingsley Publishers.

La Guardia, J. G., Ryan, R. M., Couchman, C. E., & Deci, E. L. (2000). Within-person variation in security of attachment: A self-determination theory perspective on attachment, need fulfillment, and well-being. *Journal of Personality and Social Psychology, 79*, 367–384.

Lakey, B., McCabe, K. M., Fisicaro, S. A., & Drew, J. B. (1996). Environmental and personal determinants of support perceptions: Three generalizability studies. *Journal of Personality and Social Psychology, 70*, 1270–1280.

Lambert, W., Clark, M.S., Durtschi, J., Fincham, F. D., & Graham, S. (in press). Benefits of expressing gratitude: Does expressing gratitude to a partner change one's view of the relationship? *Psychological Science.*

Laurenceau, J.-P., Barrett, L. F., & Pietromonaco, P. R. (1998). Intimacy as an interpersonal process: The importance of self-disclosure, partner disclosure, and perceived partner responsiveness in interpersonal exchanges. *Journal of Personality and Social Psychology, 74*, 1238–1251.

Leary, M. R. (2005). Sociometer theory and the pursuit of relational value: Getting to the root of self-esteem. *European Review of Social Psychology, 16*, 75–111.

Leary, M. R., & Baumeister, R. F. (2000). The nature and function of self-esteem: Sociometer theory. In M. P. Zanna (Ed.), *Advances in experimental social psychology* (Vol. 32, pp. 1–62). San Diego, CA: Academic Press.

Leary, M. R., & Cox, C. B. (2008). Belongingness motivation: A mainspring of social action. In J. Y Shah & W. L. Gardern (Eds.), *Handbook of motivation science* (pp. 27–40). New York: Guilford Press.

Leary, M. R., Twenge, J., & Quinlivan, E. (2006). Interpersonal rejection as a determinant of anger and aggression. *Personality and Social Psychology Review, 10,* 111–132.

Lee, L., Loewenstein, G., Ariely, D., Hong, J., & Young, J. (2008). If I'm not hot, are you hot or not? Physical-attractiveness evaluations and dating preferences as a function of one's own attractiveness. *Psychological Science, 19,* 669–677.

Lehmiller, J. J., & Agnew, C. R. (2006). Marginalized relationships: The impact of social disapproval on romantic relationship commitment. *Personality and Social Psychology Bulletin, 32,* 40–51.

Lemay, E. P., Jr., & Clark, M. S. (2008a). How the head liberates the heart: Projection of communal responsiveness guides relationship promotion. *Journal of Personality and Social Psychology, 94,* 647–671.

Lemay, E. P., Jr., & Clark, M. S. (2008b). Walking on eggshells: How expressing relationship insecurities perpetuates them. *Journal of Personality and Social Psychology, 95,* 420–441.

Lemay, E. P., Jr., & Clark, M. S. (2008c). You're just saying that: Contingencies of self-worth, suspicion, and authenticity in the partner affirmation process. *Journal of Experimental Social Psychology, 44,* 1376–1382.

Lemay, E. P., Jr., & Clark, M. S. (2009). Self-esteem and communal responsiveness toward a flawed partner: The fair-weather care of low self-esteem individuals. *Personality and Social Psychology Bulletin, 35,* 698–712.

Lemay, E. P., Jr., Clark, M. S., & Feeney, B. C. (2007). Projection of responsiveness to needs and the construction of satisfying communal relationships. *Journal of Personality and Social Psychology, 92,* 834–853.

Lemay, E. P., Jr., Clark, M. S., & Greenberg, A. (in press). What is beautiful is good because what is beautiful is desired: Physical attractiveness stereotyping as projection of interpersonal goals. *Personality and Social Psychology Bulletin.*

Lemay, E. P., Jr., & Dudley, K. L. (in press). Implications of reflected appraisals of interpersonal insecurity for suspicion and power. *Personality and Social Psychology Bulletin.*

Lemay, E. P., Jr., Pruchno, R. A., & Feild, L. (2006). Accuracy and bias in perceptions of spouses' life-sustaining medical treatment preferences. *Journal of Applied Social Psychology, 36,* 2337–2361.

Levesque, M. J. (1997). Meta-accuracy among acquainted individuals: A social relations analysis of interpersonal perception and metaperception. *Journal of Personality and Social Psychology, 72,* 66–74.

Levesque, M. J., Steciuk, M., & Ledley, C. (2002). Self-disclosure patterns among well-acquainted individuals: Disclosers, confidants and unique relationships. *Social Behavior and Personality, 30,* 579–592.

Levy, K. N., Blatt, S. J., & Shaver, P. R. (1998). Attachment styles and parental representations. *Journal of Personality and Social Psychology, 74,* 407–419.

Lewis, M. A., & Butterfield, R. M. (2007). Social control in marital relationships: Effect of one's partner on health behaviors. *Journal of Applied Social Psychology, 37,* 298–319.

Locke, K. D., & Nekich, J. C. (2000). Agency and communion in naturalistic social comparison. *Personality and Social Psychology Bulletin, 26,* 864–874.

Lockwood, P., Dolderman, D., Sadler, P., & Gerchak, E. (2004). Feeling better about doing worse: Social comparisons within romantic relationships. *Journal of Personality and Social Psychology, 87,* 80–95.

London, B., Downey, G., Bonica, C. & Paltin, I. (2007). Social causes and consequences of rejection sensitivity in adolescents. *Journal of Research in Adolescence, 17,* 481–506.

Lundgren, D. C., & Rudawsky, D. J. (2000). Speaking one's mind or biting one's tongue: When do angered persons express or withhold feedback in transactions with male and female peers? *Social Psychology Quarterly, 63,* 253–263.

Lydon, J. E., Fitzsimons, G. M., & Naidoo, L. (2003). Devaluation versus enhancement of attractive alternatives: A critical test using the calibration paradigm. *Personality and Social Psychology Bulletin, 29,* 349–359.

Lydon, J. E., Jamieson, D. W., & Holmes, J. G. (1997). The meaning of social interactions in the transition from acquaintanceship to friendship. *Journal of Personality and Social Psychology, 73,* 536–548.

MacDonald, G., & Leary, M. R. (2005). Why does social exclusion hurt? The relationship between social and physical pain. *Psychological Bulletin, 131,* 202–223.

Major, B., Zubek, J. M., Cooper, M. L., Cozzarelli, C., & Richards, C. (1997). Mixed messages: Implications of social conflict and social support within close relationships for adjustment to a stressful life event. *Journal of Personality and Social Psychology, 72,* 1349–1363.

Maner, J. K., DeWall, C. N., Baumeister, R. F., & Schaller, M. (2007). Does social exclusion motivate interpersonal reconnection? Resolving the "porcupine problem." *Journal of Personality and Social Psychology, 92,* 42–55.

Maner, J. K., Gailliot, M. T., & Miller, S. L. (2009). The implicit cognition of relationship maintenance: Inattention to attractive alternatives. *Journal of Experimental Social Psychology,* 174–179.

Maner, J. K., Kenrick, D. T., Becker, D. V., Robertson, T. E., Hofer, B., Neuberg, S. L., et al. (2005). Functional projection: How fundamental social motives can bias interpersonal perception. *Journal of Personality and Social Psychology, 88,* 63–78.

Maner, J. K., Luce, C. L., Neuberg, S. L., Cialdini, R. B., Brown, S., & Sagarin, B. J. (2002). The effects of perspective taking on motivations for helping: Still no evidence for altruism. *Personality and Social Psychology Bulletin, 28,* 1601–1610.

Maner, J. K., Rouby, D. A., & Gonazaga, G. C. (2008). Automatic inattention to attractive alternatives: The evolved psychology of relationship maintenance, *Evolution and Human Behavior, 29,* 343–349.

Manne, S. L., & Zautra, A. J. (1989). Spouse criticism and support: Their association with coping and psychological adjustment among women with rheumatoid arthritis. *Journal of Personality and Social Psychology, 56,* 608–617.

Marigold, D. C., Holmes, J. G., & Ross, M. (2007). More than words: Reframing compliments from romantic partners fosters security in low self-esteem individuals. *Journal of Personality and Social Psychology, 92,* 232–248.

Markey, P. M., Funder, D. C., & Ozer, D. J. (2003). Complementarity of interpersonal behaviors in dyadic interactions. *Personality and Social Psychology Bulletin, 29,* 1082–1090.

Markman, H. J. (1979). Application of a behavioral model of marriage in predicting relationship satisfaction of couples planning marriage. *Journal of Consulting and Clinical Psychology, 47,* 743–749.

Markman, H. J. (1981). Prediction of marital distress: A 5-year follow-up. *Journal of Consulting and Clinical Psychology, 49,* 760–762.

Marks, G., & Miller, N. (1987). Ten years of research on the false-consensus effect: An empirical and theoretical review. *Psychological Bulletin, 102,* 72–90.

McCall, M., Reno, R. R., Jalbert, N., & West, S. G. (2000). Communal orientation and attributions between the self and other. *Basic and Applied Social Psychology, 22,* 301–308.

McCaskill, J. W., & Lakey, B. (2000). Perceived support, social undermining, and emotion: Idiosyncratic and shared perspectives of adolescents and their families. *Personality and Social Psychology Bulletin, 26,* 820–832.

McCullough, M. E., Rachal, K. C., Sandage, S. J., Worthington, E. L., Jr., Brown, S. W., & Hight, T. L. (1998). Interpersonal forgiving in close relationships: II. Theoretical elaboration and measurement. *Journal of Personality and Social Psychology, 75*, 1586–1603.

McFarland, C., Buchler, R., & MacKay, L. (2001). Affective responses to social comparisons with extremely close others. *Social Cognition, 19*, 547–586.

McNulty, J. K. (2008). Forgiveness in marriage: Putting the benefits into context. *Journal of Family Psychology, 22*, 171–175.

McNulty, J. K., O'Mara, E. M., & Karney, B. R. (2008). Benevolent cognitions as a strategy of relationship maintenance: "Don't sweat the small stuff"…But it is not all small stuff. *Journal of Personality and Social Psychology, 94*, 631–646.

Messe, L. A., & Sivacek, J. M. (1979). Predictions of others' responses in a mixed-motive game: Self-justification or false consensus? *Journal of Personality and Social Psychology, 37*, 602–607.

Michinov, E., & Michinov, N. (2001). The similarity hypothesis: A test of the moderating role of social comparison orientation. *European Journal of Social Psychology, 31*, 549–555.

Mikulincer, M. (1998a). Adult attachment style and affect regulation: Strategic variations in self-appraisals. *Journal of Personality and Social Psychology, 75*, 420–435.

Mikulincer, M. (1998b). Adult attachment style and individual differences in functional versus dysfunctional experiences of anger. *Journal of Personality and Social Psychology, 74*, 513–524.

Mikulincer, M. (1998c). Attachment working models and the sense of trust: An exploration of interaction goals and affect regulation. *Journal of Personality and Social Psychology, 74*, 1209–1224.

Mikulincer, M., Birnbaum, G., Woddis, D., & Nachmias, O. (2000). Stress and accessibility of proximity-related thoughts: Exploring the normative and intraindividual components of attachment theory. *Journal of Personality and Social Psychology, 78*, 509–523.

Mikulincer, M., Dolev, T., & Shaver, P. R. (2004). Attachment-related strategies during thought suppression: Ironic rebounds and vulnerable self-representations. *Journal of Personality and Social Psychology, 87*, 940–956.

Mikulincer, M., & Florian, V. (1995). Appraisal of and coping with a real-life stressful situation: The contribution of attachment styles. *Personality and Social Psychology Bulletin, 21*, 406–414.

Mikulincer, M., Florian, V., & Weller, A. (1993). Attachment styles, coping strategies, and posttraumatic psychological distress: The impact of the Gulf War in Israel. *Journal of Personality and Social Psychology, 64*, 817–826.

Mikulincer, M., Gillath, O., Halevy, V., Avihou, N., Avidan, S., & Eshkoli, N. (2001). Attachment theory and reactions to others' needs: Evidence that activation of the sense of attachment security promotes empathic responses. *Journal of Personality and Social Psychology, 81*, 1205–1224.

Mikulincer, M., Gillath, O., Sapir-Lavid, Y., Yaakobi, E., Arias, K., Tal-Aloni, L., et al. (2003). Attachment theory and concern for others' welfare: Evidence that activation of the sense of secure base promotes endorsement of self-transcendence values. *Basic and Applied Social Psychology, 25*, 299–312.

Mikulincer, M., & Nachshon, O. (1991). Attachment styles and patterns of self-disclosure. *Journal of Personality and Social Psychology, 61*, 321–331.

Mikulincer, M., & Orbach, I. (1995). Attachment styles and repressive defensiveness: The accessibility and architecture of affective memories. *Journal of Personality and Social Psychology, 68*, 917–925.

Mikulincer, M., Orbach, I., & Iavnieli, D. (1998). Adult attachment style and affect regulation: Strategic variations in subjective self-other similarity. *Journal of Personality and Social Psychology, 75*, 436–448.

Mikulincer, M., & Shaver, P. R. (2003). The attachment behavioral system in adulthood: Activation, psychodynamics and interpersonal processes. In M. P. Zanna (Ed.), *Advances in experimental social psychology* (Vol. 35). San Diego, CA: Academic Press.

Mikulincer, M., & Shaver, P. R. (2007). *Attachment in adulthood: Structure, dynamics, and change.* New York: Guilford Press.

Mikulincer, M., Shaver, P. R., Gillath, O., & Nitzberg, R. A. (2005). Attachment, caregiving, and altruism: Boosting attachment security increases compassion and helping. *Journal of Personality and Social Psychology, 89*, 817–839.

Miller, D. T., Downs, J. S., & Prentice, D. A. (1998). Minimal conditions for the creation of a unit relationship: The social bond between birthday mates. *European Journal of Social Psychology, 28*, 475–481.

Miller, R. J. (1997). Inattentive and contented: Relationship commitment and attention to alternatives. *Journal of Personality and Social Psychology, 73*, 758–766.

Mills, J., & Clark, M. S. (1982). Exchange and communal relationships. In L. Wheeler (Ed.), *Review of personality and social psychology* (pp. 121–144). Beverly Hills, CA: Sage.

Mills, J., Clark, M. S., Ford, T. E., & Johnson, M. (2004). Measurement of communal strength. *Personal Relationships, 11*, 213–230.

Monin, J., Clark, M. S., & Lemay, E. P. (2008). Expecting more responsiveness from and feeling more responsiveness to female than to male family members. *Sex Roles, 95*, 420–441.

Montoya, R. M., & Horton, R. S. (2004). On the important of cognitive evaluation as a determinant of interpersonal attraction. *Journal of Personality and Social Psychology, 86*, 696–712.

Moskowitz, D. S., Ho, M.-h. R., & Turcotte-Tremblay, A.-M. (2007). Contextual influences on interpersonal complementarity. *Personality and Social Psychology Bulletin, 33*, 1051–1063.

Most, S. A. B., Scholl, B. J., Clifford, E. R., & Simons, D. J. (2005) What you see is what you set: Sustained inattentional blindness and the capture of awareness. *Psychological Review, 112*, 217–242.

Murray, S. L., Aloni, M., Holmes, J. G., Derrick, J. L., Stinson, D. A., & Leder, S. (2009). Fostering partner dependence as trust insurance: The implicit contingencies of the exchange script in close relationships. *Journal of Personality and Social Psychology, 96*, 324–348.

Murray, S. L., Bellavia, G. M., Rose, P., & Griffin, D. W. (2003). Once hurt, twice hurtful: How perceived regard regulates daily marital interactions. *Journal of Personality and Social Psychology, 84*, 126–147.

Murray, S. L., & Derrick, J. (2005). A relationship-specific sense of felt security: How perceived regard regulates relationship enhancement processes. In M. W. Baldwin (Ed.), *Interpersonal cognition* (pp. 153–179). New York: Guilford Press.

Murray, S. L., Derrick, J. L., Leder, S., & Holmes, J. G. (2008). Balancing connectedness and self-protection goals in close relationships: A levels-of-processing perspective on risk regulation. *Journal of Personality and Social Psychology, 94*, 429–459.

Murray, S. L., Griffin, D. W., Rose, P., & Bellavia, G. (2006). For better or worse? Self-esteem and the contingencies of acceptance in marriage. *Personality and Social Psychology Bulletin, 32*, 866–880.

Murray, S. L., & Holmes, J. G. (1999). The (mental) ties that bind: Cognitive structures that predict relationship resilience. *Journal of Personality and Social Psychology, 77*, 1228–1244.

Murray, S. L., Holmes, J. G., Aloni, M., Pinkus, R. T., Derrick, J. L., & Leder, S. (2009). Commitment insurance: Compensating for the autonomy costs of interdependence in close relationships. *Journal of Personality and Social Psychology, 97*, 256–278.

Murray, S. L., Holmes, J. G., Bellavia, G., Griffin, D. W., & Dolderman, D. (2002). Kindred spirits? The benefits of egocentrism in close relationships. *Journal of Personality and Social Psychology, 82*, 563–581.

Murray, S. L., Holmes, J. G., & Collins, N. L. (2006). Optimizing assurance: The risk regulation system in relationships. *Psychological Bulletin, 132*, 641–666.

Murray, S. L., Holmes, J. G., & Griffin, D. W. (1996a). The benefits of positive illusions: Idealization and the construction of satisfaction in close relationships. *Journal of Personality and Social Psychology, 70,* 79–98.

Murray, S. L., Holmes, J. G., & Griffin, D. W. (1996b). The self-fulfilling nature of positive illusions in romantic relationships: Love is not blind, but prescient. *Journal of Personality and Social Psychology, 71,* 1155–1180.

Murray, S. L., Holmes, J. G., & Griffin, D. W. (2000). Self-esteem and the quest for felt security: How perceived regard regulates attachment processes. *Journal of Personality and Social Psychology, 78,* 478–498.

Murray, S. L., Holmes, J. G., & Griffin, D. W. (2003). Reflections on the self-fulfilling effects of positive illusions. *Psychological Inquiry, 14,* 289–295.

Murray, S. L., Holmes, J. G., Griffin, D. W., Bellavia, G., & Rose, P. (2001). The mismeasure of love: How self-doubt contaminates relationship beliefs. *Personality and Social Psychology Bulletin, 27,* 423–436.

Murray, S. L., Holmes, J. G., MacDonald, G., & Ellsworth, P. C. (1998). Through the looking glass darkly? When self-doubts turn into relationship insecurities. *Journal of Personality and Social Psychology, 75,* 1459–1480.

Murray, S. L., Rose, P., Bellavia, G. M., Holmes, J. G., & Kusche, A. G. (2002). When rejection stings: How self-esteem constrains relationship-enhancement processes. *Journal of Personality and Social Psychology, 83,* 556–573.

Murray, S. L., Rose, P., Holmes, J. G., Derrick, J., Podchaski, E. J., Bellavia, G., et al. (2005). Putting the partner within reach: A dyadic perspective on felt security in close relationships. *Journal of Personality and Social Psychology, 88,* 327–347.

Murstein, B. I. (1972). Physical attractiveness and martial choice. *Journal of Personality and Social Psychology, 22,* 8–12.

Murstein, B. I., Cerreto, M., & MacDonald, M. G. (1977). A theory and investigation of the effect of exchange-orientation on marriage and friendship. *Journal of Marriage and the Family, 39,* 543–548.

Nadler, A., Shapira, R., & Ben-Itzhak, S. (1982). Good looks may help: Effects of helper's physical attractiveness and sex of helper on males' and females' help-seeking behavior. *Journal of Personality and Social Psychology, 42,* 90–99.

Neff, L. A., & Karney, B. R. (2002). Judgments of a relationship partner: Specific accuracy but global enhancement. *Journal of Personality, 70,* 1079–1112.

Neff, L. A., & Karney, B. R. (2005). To know you is to love you: The implications of global adoration and specific accuracy for marital relationships. *Journal of Personality and Social Psychology, 88,* 480–497.

Newcomb, T. M. (1961). *The acquaintance process.* New York: Holt, Rinehart, & Winston.

Neyer, F. J., & Lang, F. R. (2003). Blood is thicker than water: Kinship orientation across adulthood. *Journal of Personality and Social Psychology, 84,* 310–321.

Ognibene, T. C., & Collins, N. L. (1998). Adult attachment styles, perceived social support and coping strategies. *Journal of Social and Personal Relationships, 15,* 323–345.

Overall, N. C., Fletcher, G. J. O., & Simpson, J. A. (2006). Regulation processes in intimate relationships: The role of ideal standards. *Journal of Personality and Social Psychology, 91,* 662–685.

Patrick, H., Knee, C. R., Canevello, A., & Lonsbary, C. (2007). The role of need fulfillment in relationship functioning and well-being: A self-determination theory perspective. *Journal of Personality and Social Psychology, 92,* 434–457.

Pedersen, C. A. (2006). Biological aspects of social bonding and the roots of human violence. *Annals of the New York Academy of Sciences, 1036,* 106–127.

Pierce, G. R., Sarason, I. G., & Sarason, B. R. (1991). General and relationship-based perceptions of social support: Are two constructs

better than one? *Journal of Personality and Social Psychology, 61,* 1028–1039.

Pierce, T., & Lydon, J. (1998). Priming relational schemas: Effects of contextually activated and chronically accessible interpersonal expectations on responses to a stressful event. *Journal of Personality and Social Psychology, 75,* 1441–1448.

Pierce, T., & Lydon, J. E. (2001). Global and specific relational models in the experience of social interactions. *Journal of Personality and Social Psychology, 80,* 613–631.

Pietromonaco, P. R., & Barrett, L. F. (1997). Working models of attachment and daily social interactions. *Journal of Personality and Social Psychology, 73,* 1409–1423.

Pietromonaco, P. R., & Barrett, L. F. (2006). What can you do for me? Attachment style and motives underlying esteem for partners. *Journal of Research in Personality, 40,* 313–338.

Pinel, E. C., Long, A. E., Landau, M. J., Alexander, K., & Pyszczynski, T. (2006). Seeing I to I: A pathway to interpersonal connectedness. *Journal of Personality and Social Psychology, 90,* 243–257.

Powers, S. I., Pietromonaco, P. R., Gunlicks, M., & Sayer, A. (2006). Dating couples' attachment styles and patterns of cortisol reactivity and recovery in response to a relationship conflict. *Journal of Personality and Social Psychology, 90,* 613–628.

Reis, H. T., Clark, M. S., & Holmes, J. G. (2004). Perceived partner responsiveness as an organizing construct in the study of intimacy and closeness. In D. J. Mashek & A. P. Aron (Eds.), *Handbook of closeness and intimacy* (pp. 201–225). Mahwah, NJ: Lawrence Erlbaum Associates.

Reis, H. T., & Collins, W. A. (2004). Relationships, human behavior and psychological science. *Current Directions in Psychological Science, 13,* 233–237.

Reis, H. T., Collins, W. A., & Berscheid, E. (2000). The relationship context of human behavior and development. *Psychological Bulletin, 126,* 844–872.

Reis, H. T., & Patrick, B. C. (1996). Attachment and intimacy: Component processes. In E. T. Higgins & A. W. Kruglanski (Eds.), *Social psychology: Handbook of basic principles* (pp. 523–563). New York: Guilford Press.

Reis, H. T., & Shaver, P. (1988). Intimacy as an interpersonal process. In S. Duck, D. F. Hay, S. E. Hobfoll, & W. Ickes (Eds.), *Handbook of personal relationships: Theory, research and interventions* (pp. 367–389). Oxford: John Wiley & Sons.

Reis, H. T., Wheeler, L., Spiegel, N., & Kernis, M. H. (1982). Physical attractiveness in social interaction: II. Why does appearance affect social experience? *Journal of Personality and Social Psychology, 43,* 979–996.

Reis, H. T., Wilson, I. M., Monestere, C., Bernstein, S., Clark, K., Seidl, E., Franco, M., Gioioso, E., Freeman, L., & Radoane, K. (1990). What is smiling is beautiful and good. *European Journal of Social Psychology, 20,* 259–267.

Rempel, J. K., Ross, M., & Holmes, J. G. (2001). Trust and communicated attributions in close relationships. *Journal of Personality and Social Psychology, 81,* 57–64.

Rholes, W. S., & Simpson, J. A. (Eds.). (2004). *Adult attachment: Theory, research and clinical implications.* New York: Guilford.

Rholes, W. S., Simpson, J. A., & Orina, M. M. (1999). Attachment and anger in an anxiety-provoking situation. *Journal of Personality and Social Psychology, 76,* 940–957.

Rholes, W. S., Simpson, J. A., Tran, S., Martin, A. M., III, & Friedman, M. (2007). Attachment and information seeking in romantic relationships. *Personality and Social Psychology Bulletin, 33,* 422–438.

Robbins, J. M., & Krueger, J. I. (2005). Social projection to ingroups and outgroups: A review and meta-analysis. *Personality and Social Psychology Review, 9,* 32–47.

Roberts, J. E., Gotlib, I. H., & Kassel, J. D. (1996). Adult attachment security and symptoms of depression: The mediating roles of dysfunctional attitudes and low self-esteem. *Journal of Personality and Social Psychology, 70*, 310–320.

Roisman, G. I., Tsai, J. L., & Chiang, K. H. S. (2004). The emotional integration of childhood Experience: Physiological, facial expressive, and self-reported emotional response during the adult attachment interview. *Developmental Psychology, 40*, 776–789.

Ross, L., Greene, D., & House, P. (1977). The false consensus effect: An egocentric bias in social perception and attribution processes. *Journal of Experimental Social Psychology, 13*, 279–301.

Roy, M. P., Steptoe, A., & Kirschbaum, C. (1998). Life events and social support as moderators of individual differences in cardiovascular and cortisol reactivity. *Journal of Personality and Social Psychology, 75*, 1273–1281.

Rudich, E. A., & Vallacher, R. R. (1999). To belong or to self-enhance? Motivational bases for choosing interaction partners. *Personality and Social Psychology Bulletin, 25*, 1387–1404.

Rusbult, C. E. (1983). A longitudinal test of the investment model: The development (and deterioration) of satisfaction and commitment in heterosexual involvements. *Journal of Personality and Social Psychology, 45*, 101–117.

Rusbult, C. E., Bissonnette, V. L., Arriaga, X. B., & Cox, C. L. (1998). Accommodation processes during the early years of marriage. In T. N. Bradbury (Eds.), *The developmental course of marital dysfunction* (pp. 74–113). New York: Cambridge University Press.

Rusbult, C. E., Hannon, P. A., Stocker, S. L., & Finkel, E. J. (2005). Forgiveness and relational repair. In E. L. Worthington, Jr. (Ed.), *Handbook for forgiveness* (pp. 185–206). New York: Brunner-Routledge.

Rusbult, C. E., Kumashiro, M., Finkel, E. J., & Wildschut, T. (2002). The war of the roses: An interdependence analysis of betrayal and forgiveness. In P. Noller & J. A. Feeney (Eds.), *Understanding marriage: Developments in the study of couple interaction* (pp. 251–281). New York: Cambridge University Press.

Rusbult, C. E., Kumashiro, M., Kubacka, K. E., & Finkel, E. J. (2009). "The part of me that you bring out": Ideal similarity and the Michelangelo Phenomenon. *Journal of Personality and Social Psychology, 96*(1), 61–82.

Rusbult, C. E., Olsen, N., Davis, J. L., & Hannon, M. A. (2001). Commitment and relationship maintenance mechanisms. In J. H. Harvey & A. E. Wenzel (Eds.), *Close romantic relationships: Maintenance and enhancement* (pp. 87–113). Mahwah, NJ: Erlbaum.

Rusbult, C. E., Van Lange, P. A. M., Wildschut, T., Yovetich, N. A., & Verette, J. (2000). Perceived superiority in close relationships: Why it exists and persists. *Journal of Personality and Social Psychology, 79*, 521–545.

Rusbult, C. E., Verette, J., Whitney, G. A., Slovik, L. F., Lipkus, I. (1991). Accommodation processes in close relationships: Theory and preliminary empirical evidence. *Journal of Personality and Social Psychology, 60*, 53–78.

Ruvolo, A. P., & Brennan, C. J. (1997). What's love got to do with it? Close relationships and perceived growth. *Personality and Social Psychology Bulletin, 23*, 814–823.

Ruvolo, A. P., & Fabin, L. A. (1999). Two of a kind: Perceptions of own and partner's attachment characteristics. *Personal Relationships, 6*, 57–79.

Sagarin, B. J., Rhoads, K. v. L., & Cialdini, R. B. (1998). Deceiver's distrust: Denigration as a consequence of undiscovered deception. *Personality and Social Psychology Bulletin, 24*, 1167–1176.

Sanderson, C. A., & Evans, S. M. (2001). Seeing one's partner through intimacy-colored glasses: An examination of the processes underlying the intimacy goals-relationship satisfaction link. *Personality and Social Psychology Bulletin, 27*, 463–473.

Savitsky, K., Epley, N., & Gilovich, T. (2001). Do others judge us as harshly as we think? Overestimating the impact of our failures, shortcomings, and mishaps. *Journal of Personality and Social Psychology, 81*, 44–56.

Savitsky, K., & Gilovich, T. (2003). The illusion of transparency and the alleviation of speech anxiety. *Journal of Experimental Social Psychology, 39*, 618–625.

Schimel, J., Arndt, J., Pyszczynski, T., & Greenberg, J. (2001). Being accepted for who we are: Evidence that social validation of the intrinsic self reduces general defensiveness. *Journal of Personality and Social Psychology, 80*, 35–52.

Schul, Y., Mayo, R., & Burnstein, E. (2004). Encoding under trust and distrust: The spontaneous activation of incongruent cognitions. *Journal of Personality and Social Psychology, 86*, 668–679.

Schul, Y., & Vinokur, A. D. (2000). Projection in person perception among spouses as a function of the similarity in their shared experiences. *Personality and Social Psychology Bulletin, 26*, 987–1001.

Schutz, A. (1998). Autobiographical narratives of good and bad deeds: Defensive and favorable self-description moderated by trait self-esteem. *Journal of Social & Clinical Psychology, 17*, 466–475.

Schutz, A., & DePaulo, B. M. (1996). Self-esteem and evaluative reactions: Letting people speak for themselves. *Journal of Research in Personality, 30*, 137–156.

Schutz, A., & Tice, D. M. (1997). Associative and competitive indirect self-enhancement in close relationships moderated by trait self-esteem. *European Journal of Social Psychology, 27*, 257–273.

Sedikides, C., Campbell, W. K., Reeder, G. D., & Elliot, A. J. (1998). The self-serving bias in relational context. *Journal of Personality and Social Psychology, 74*, 378–386.

Segal, M.W. (1974). Alphabet & attraction: An unobtrusive measure of the effect of propinquity in a field setting. *Journal of Personality and Social Psychology, 30*, 654–657.

Shah, J. (2003). The motivational looking glass: How significant others implicitly affect goal appraisals. *Journal of Personality and Social Psychology, 85*, 424–439.

Sharpsteen, D. J., & Kirkpatrick, L. A. (1997). Romantic jealousy and adult romantic attachment. *Journal of Personality and Social Psychology, 72*, 627–640.

Shaver, P. R., & Mikulincer, M. (2002). Attachment-related psychodynamics. *Attachment & Human Development, 4*, 133–161.

Shaver, P. R., Schachner, D. A., & Mikulincer, M. (2005). Attachment style, excessive reassurance seeking, relationship processes, and depression. *Personality and Social Psychology Bulletin, 31*, 343–359.

Sheldon, K. M., & Niemiec, C. P. (2006). It's not just the amount that counts: Balanced need satisfaction also affects well-being. *Journal of Personality and Social Psychology, 91*, 331–341.

Shnabel, N., & Nadler, A. (2008). A needs-based model of reconciliation: Satisfying the differential emotional needs of victim and perpetrator as a key to promoting reconciliation. *Journal of Personality and Social Psychology, 94*, 116–132.

Shrauger, J. S. (1975). Responses to evaluation as a function of initial self-perceptions. *Psychological Bulletin, 82*, 581–596.

Shrauger, J. S., & Lund, A. K. (1975). Self-evaluation and reactions to evaluations from others. *Journal of Personality, 43*, 94–108.

Shrauger, J. S., & Schoeneman, T. J. (1979). Symbolic interactionist view of self-concept: Through the looking glass darkly. *Psychological Bulletin, 86*, 549–573.

Sigall, H., & Landy, D. (1973). Radiating beauty: Effects of having a physically attractive partner on person perception. *Journal of Personality and Social Psychology, 28*, 218–224.

Simmons, D. J., & Chabris, S. E. (1999). Gorillas in our midst: Sustained inattentional blindness for dynamical events. *Perception, 28*, 1069–1074.

Simpson, J. A. (1987). The dissolution of romantic relationships: Factors involved in relationship stability and emotional distress. *Journal of Personality and Social Psychology, 53*, 683–692.

Simpson, J. A. (1990). Influence of attachment styles on romantic relationships. *Journal of Personality and Social Psychology, 59*, 971–980.

Simpson, J. A. (2007). Psychological foundations of trust. *Current Directions in Psychological Science, 16*, 264–268.

Simpson, J. A., Collins, W. A., Tran, S., & Haydon, K. C. (2007). Attachment and the experience and expression of emotions in romantic relationships: A developmental perspective. *Journal of Personality and Social Psychology, 92*, 355–367.

Simpson, J. A., Gangestad, W. W. & Lerma, M. (1990). Perception of physical attractiveness: Mechanisms involved in the maintenance of romantic relationships. *Journal of Personality and Social Psychology, 59*, 1192–1201.

Simpson, J. A., Ickes, W., & Blackstone, T. (1995). When the head protects the heart: Empathic accuracy in dating relationships. *Journal of Personality and Social Psychology, 69*, 629–641.

Simpson, J. A., Ickes, W., & Grich, J. (1999). When accuracy hurts: Reactions of anxious-ambivalent dating partners to a relationship-threatening situation. *Journal of Personality and Social Psychology, 76*, 754–769.

Simpson, J. A., Orina, M. M., & Ickes, W. (2003). When accuracy hurts, and when it helps: A test of the empathic accuracy model in marital interactions. *Journal of Personality and Social Psychology, 85*, 881–893.

Simpson, J. A., Rholes, W. S., & Nelligan, J. S. (1992). Support seeking and support giving within couples in an anxiety-provoking situation: The role of attachment styles. *Journal of Personality and Social Psychology, 62*, 434–446.

Simpson, J. A., Rholes, W. S., Orina, M. M., & Grich, J. (2002). Working models of attachment, support giving, and support seeking in a stressful situation. *Personality and Social Psychology Bulletin, 28*, 598–608.

Simpson, J. A., Rholes, W. S., & Phillips, D. (1996). Conflict in close relationships: An attachment perspective. *Journal of Personality and Social Psychology, 71*, 899–914.

Simpson, J. A., Winterheld, H. A., Rholes, W. S., & Orina, M. M. (2007). Working models of attachment and reactions to different forms of caregiving from romantic partners. *Journal of Personality and Social Psychology, 93*, 466–477.

Singh, R., Ng, R., Ong, E. L., & Lin, P. K. F (2008). Different mediators for the age, sex and attitude similarity effects in interpersonal attraction. *Basic and Applied Social Psychology, 30*, 1–17.

Singh, R., Yeo, S. E. L., Lin, P. K. F., & Tan, L. (2007). Multiple mediators of the attitude similarity-attraction relationship: Dominance of inferred attraction and substley of affect. *Basic and Applied Social Psychology, 29*, 61–74.

Smeaton, G., Byrne, D., & Murnen, S. K. (1989). The repulsion hypothesis revisited: Similarity irrelevance or dissimilarity bias? *Journal of Personality and Social Psychology, 56*, 54–59.

Smith, P., & Bargh, J. A. (2008). Nonconscious effects of power on basic approach and avoidance tendencies. *Social Cognition, 26*, 1–24.

Sommers, S. (1984). Reported emotions and conventions of emotionality among college students. *Journal of Personality and Social Psychology, 46*, 207–215.

Sprecher, S. (1998). Insiders' perspectives on reasons for attraction to a close other. *Social Psychology Quarterly, 61*, 287–300.

Sprecher, S., & Felmlee, D. (1992). The influence of parents and friends on the quality and stability of romantic relationships: A three-wave longitudinal investigation. *Journal of Marriage & the Family, 54*, 888–900.

Sprecher, S., & Hendrick, S. S. (2004). Self-disclosure in intimate relationships: Associations with individual and relationship characteristics over time. *Journal of Social & Clinical Psychology, 23*, 857–877.

Srivastava, S., McGonigal, K. M., Richards, J. M., Butler, E. A., & Gross, J. J. (2006). Optimism in close relationships: How seeing things in a positive light makes them so. *Journal of Personality and Social Psychology, 91*, 143–153.

Stapel, D. A., & Koomen, W. (2001). I, we, and the effects of others on me: How self-construal level moderates social comparison effects. *Journal of Personality and Social Psychology, 80*, 766–781.

Stephan, W., Berscheid, E., & Walster, E. (1971). Sexual arousal and heterosexual perception. *Journal of Personality and Social Psychology, 20*, 93–101.

Stinson, D. A., Logel, C., Zanna, M. P., Holmes, J. G., Cameron, J. J., Wood, J. V., et al. (2008). The cost of lower self-esteem: Testing a self- and social-bonds model of health. *Journal of Personality and Social Psychology, 94*, 412–428.

Stroebe, W. (1977). Self-esteem and interpersonal attraction. In S. W. Duck (Ed.), *Theory and practice in interpersonal attraction* (pp. 79–104). London: Academic Press.

Stroebe, W., Insko, C. A., Thompson, V. D., & Layton, B. D. (1971). Effects of physical attractiveness, attitude similarity, and sex on various aspects of interpersonal attraction. *Journal of Personality and Social Psychology, 18*, 79–91.

Suls, J., Lemos, K., & Stewart, H. L. (2002). Self-esteem, construal, and comparisons with the self, friends, and peers. *Journal of Personality and Social Psychology, 82*, 252–261.

Swann, W. B. (1987). Identity negotiation: Where two roads meet. *Journal of Personality and Social Psychology, 53*, 1038–1051.

Swann, W. B., Jr., Bosson, J. K., & Pelham, B. W. (2002). Different partners, different selves: Strategic verification of circumscribed identities. *Personality and Social Psychology Bulletin, 28*, 1215–1228.

Swann, W. B., de la Ronde, C., & Hixon, J. G. (1994). Authenticity and positivity strivings in marriage and courtship. *Journal of Personality and Social Psychology, 66*, 857–869.

Swann, W. B., Griffin, J. J., Predmore, S. C., & Gaines, B. (1987). The cognitive-affective crossfire: When self-consistency confronts self-enhancement. *Journal of Personality and Social Psychology, 52*, 881–889.

Swann, W. B., & Predmore, S. C. (1985). Intimates as agents of social support: Sources of consolation or despair? *Journal of Personality and Social Psychology, 49*, 1609–1617.

Swann, W. B., Stein-Seroussi, A., & Giesler, R. B. (1992). Why people self-verify. *Journal of Personality and Social Psychology, 62*, 392–401.

Swann, W. B., Stein-Seroussi, A., & McNulty, S. E. (1992). Outcasts in a white-lie society: The enigmatic worlds of people with negative self-conceptions. *Journal of Personality and Social Psychology, 62*, 618–624.

Tagiuri, R., Blake, R. R., & Bruner, J. S. (1953). Some determinants of the perception of positive and negative feelings in others. *Journal of Abnormal and Social Psychology, 48*, 585–592.

Taylor, S. E., Sherman, D. K., Kim, H. S., Jarcho, J., Takagi, K., & Dunagan, M. S. (2004). Culture and social support: Who seeks it and why? *Journal of Personality and Social Psychology, 87*, 354–362.

Tesser, A. (1988). Toward a self-evaluation maintenance model of social behavior. In L. Berkowitz (Ed.), *Advances in experimental social psychology, Vol. 21: Social psychological studies of the self: Perspectives and programs* (pp. 181–227).

Tesser, A. (1999). Toward a self-evaluation maintenance model of social behavior. In R. F. Baumeister (Ed.), *The self in social psychology* (pp. 446–460). New York: Psychology Press.

Tesser, A., Beach, S. R. H., Mendolia, M., Crepaz, N., Davies, B., & Pennebaker, J. (1998). Similarity and uniqueness focus: A paper tiger and a surprise. *Personality and Social Psychology Bulletin, 24*, 1190–1204.

Tesser, A., & Cornell, D. P. (1991). On the confluence of self processes. *Journal of Experimental Social Psychology, 27*, 501–526.

Tesser, A., Millar, M., & Moore, J. (1988). Some affective consequences of social comparison and reflection processes: The pain and pleasure of being close. *Journal of Personality and Social Psychology, 54*, 49–61.

Tesser, A., & Rosen, S. (1975). The reluctance to transmit bad news. In Berkowitz, L. (Ed.), *Advances in experimental social psychology, 8* (pp. 193–232). New York: Academic Press.

Thomas, G., Fletcher, G. J. O., & Lange, C. (1997). On-line empathic accuracy in marital interaction. *Journal of Personality and Social Psychology, 72*, 839–850.

Thornhill, R., & Gangestad, S. W. (1999). Facial attractiveness. *Trends in Cognitive Sciences, 3*, 452–460.

Tidwell, M.-C. O., Reis, H. T., & Shaver, P. R. (1996). Attachment, attractiveness, and social interaction: A diary study. *Journal of Personality and Social Psychology, 71*, 729–745.

Tiedens, L. Z., & Jimenez, M. C. (2003). Assimilation for affiliation and contrast for control: Complementary self-construals. *Journal of Personality and Social Psychology, 85*, 1049–1061.

Trobst, K. K. (2000). An interpersonal conceptualization and quantification of social support transactions. *Personality and Social Psychology Bulletin, 26*, 971–986.

Tucker, J. S. (2002). Health-related social control within older adults' relationships. *Journals of Gerontology: Series B: Psychological Sciences and Social Sciences, 5*, 387.

Tyler, T. R., & Sears, D. O. (1977). Coming to like obnoxious people when we must live with them. *Journal of Personality and Social Psychology, 35*, 200–211.

Uchino, B. N., Cacioppo, J. T., & Kiecolt-Glaser, J. K. (1996). The relationship between social support and physiological processes: A review with emphasis on underlying mechanisms and implications for health. *Psychological Bulletin, 119*, 488–531.

Uysal, A., & Oner-Ozkan, B. (2007). A self-presentational approach to transmission of good and bad news. *Social Behavior and Personality, 35*, 63–78.

Van Lange, P. A. M., Agnew, C. R., Harinck, F., & Steemers, G. E. M. (1997). From game theory to real life: How social value orientation affects willingness to sacrifice in ongoing close relationships. *Journal of Personality and Social Psychology, 73*, 1330–1344.

Van Lange, P. A. M., Rusbult, C. E., Drigotas, S. M., Arriaga, X. B., Witcher, B. S., & Cox, C. L. (1997). Willingness to sacrifice in close relationships. *Journal of Personality and Social Psychology, 72*, 1373–1395.

Vohs, K. D., & Ciarocco, N. J. (2004). Interpersonal functioning requires self-regulation. In R. Baumeister & K. Vohs (Eds.), *Handbook of self-regulation: Research, theory, and applications* (pp. 392–407).

Walster, E., Aronson, V., Abrahams, D., & Rottman, L. (1966). Importance of physical attractiveness in dating behavior. *Journal of Personality and Social Psychology, 4*, 508–516.

Walster, E., & Walster, G. W. (1969). The matching hypothesis. *Journal of Personality and Social Psychology, 6*, 248–253.

Walster, E., Walster, G.W., & Berscheid, E. (1978*). Equity: Theory and Research*. Boston: Allyn & Bacon.

Warburton, W. A., Williams, K. D., & Cairns, D. R. (2006). When ostracism leads to aggression: The moderating effects of control deprivation. *Journal of Experimental Social Psychology, 42*, 213–220.

Whitton, S., Stanley, S., & Markman, H. (2002). Sacrifice in romantic relationships: An exploration of relevant research and theory. In A. L. Vangelistic, H. T. Reis, & M. A. Fitzpatrick (Eds.), *Stability and change in relationships* (pp. 156–181). Cambridge: Cambridge University Press.

Wieselquist, J., Rusbult, C. E., Foster, C. A., & Agnew, C. R. (1999). Commitment, pro-relationship behavior, and trust in close relationships. *Journal of Personality and Social Psychology, 77*, 942–966.

Williams, K. D., Forgas, J. P., & von Hippel, W. (Eds.). (2005). *The social outcast: Ostracism, social exclusion, rejection, and bullying*. New York: Psychology Press.

Williams, K. D., & Sommer, K. L. (1997). Social ostracism by coworkers: Does rejection lead to loafing or compensation? *Personality and Social Psychology Bulletin, 23*, 693–706.

Williams, L. E., & Bargh, J. A. (2008). Experiencing physical warmth promotes interpersonal warmth. *Science, 322*, 606–607.

Williamson, G. M., & Clark, M. S. (1989). Providing help and desired relationship type as determinants of changes in moods and self-evaluations. *Journal of Personality and Social Psychology, 56*, 722–734.

Yariv, E. (2006). "Mum effect": Principals' reluctance to submit negative feedback. *Journal of Managerial Psychology, 21*, 533–546.

Yoo, S., Clark, M. S., Salovey, P., Lemay, E. P., & Monin, J. (2009). The impact of expressing anger depends upon the communal strength of a relationship. Yale University, unpublished manuscript.

Yovetich, N. A., & Rusbult, C. E. (1994). Accommodative behavior in close relationships: Exploring transformation of motivation. *Journal of Experimental Social Psychology, 30*, 138–164.

Zaki, J., Bolger, N., & Ochsner, D. (2009). Unpacking the informational bases of empathic accuracy. *Emotion, 9*, 478–487.

Zaki, J., Bolger, N., & Ochsner, K. (2008). It takes two: The interpersonal nature of empathic accuracy. *Psychological Science, 19*, 399–404.

Zeman, J., & Garber, J. (1996). Display rules for anger, sadness, and pain: It depends on who is watching. *Child Development, 67*, 957–953.

Zhong, C., & Leonardelli, G. (2008). Cold and lonely: Does social exclusion literally feel cold? *Psychological Science, 19*, 838–842.

Chapter 26

Interpersonal Stratification

Status, Power, and Subordination

SUSAN T. FISKE

Empires rise and fall. Majority groups shrink to mere plurality. Political generations succeed each other. Parents age, and children grow up. Even department chairs come and go. Each instance shifts global, national, demographic, familial, or professional hierarchies—with important differences, to be sure—but some enduring similarities describe the individuals inhabiting these shifting spheres. With the passing of the American Century, this waning superpower could learn from past superpowers, for example, Russia, Britain, Spain, Rome, Greece, and resurgent China, about the risks and rewards of empire. With immigration and changing birth rates, Whites in Western countries, especially the United States, will soon relinquish the majority moniker and could learn more about power sharing. The millennial Generation O replaces the Boomer generation in politics, who earlier replaced the Greatest Generation, each claiming not to repeat the mistakes of the past. Further, in countless workplaces and families, the younger always eventually supplant the older, who rarely see it coming. When hierarchies remain stable, no one heeds them much. When hierarchies change, people finally notice the stratification that subtly structures their every social interaction.

This chapter aims to illuminate the interpersonal dynamics of stratification, first defining it and related terms such as hierarchy, status, power, subordination, and oppression. Current research typically promotes either the advantages or disadvantages, respectively, of being at the top or the bottom of the social heap, revealing short- and long-term effects of hierarchy. Overall, however, the social psychology of stratification demonstrates both personal gains and losses to individuals, no matter what their hierarchical context. Analyzing hierarchy in this interpersonal way shows people's interplay with people, more personal than neighborhoods (Massey, 2007) and more holistic than hormones

(Sapolsky, 2005), although the chapter touches on both, at the boundaries.

DEFINITIONS

Social psychologists do not normally use the term "stratification" but might usefully import it from the social sciences because it encompasses several more common terms. *Stratification* ranks people vertically by their social categories, creating unequal access to scarce resources. Social psychologists often study social categories, intergroup relations, bias, inequality, group status, and conflict over resources (respectively, in this volume: Macrae & Quadflieg, volume 1; Yzerbyt & Demoulin, Dovidio & Gaertner, Hackman & Katz, De Dreu this volume). Stratification overlaps with these phenomena, as well as a collection of related terms also familiar to social psychologists: "hierarchy," "status," and "power."

Pure *hierarchy* occurs in groups that order parties along a valued dimension, sometimes distinguishing leaders from followers (Hogg, this volume; Magee & Galinsky, 2008) and sometimes ranking more continuously, for example, by seniority. Upper levels of the hierarchy carry more *status*, defined here as social respect, recognition, importance, and prestige. Workplaces supply people's most common daily experience of hierarchy outside the family. Bosses and managers have more status, but so do more senior, experienced, and prominent peers who may not hold that title. Regardless of whether they control resources, people designated as being at the top carry more status, gain respect, and enjoy recognition.

The features of power generally are more tangible than those of status. Granted, status often correlates with power. But *power* specifically controls valued resources, according

---

The author gratefully acknowledges the following colleagues for suffering through and improving an earlier version at a particularly busy time: Daniel L. Ames, Mina Cikara, Daniel T. Gilbert, and Stephen V. Shepherd.

to current definitions (e.g., Fiske, 1993; Keltner, Gruenfeld, & Anderson, 2003; Magee & Galinsky, 2008). Control over valued resources comprises outcomes that are physical (e.g., office), economic (e.g., salary), and social (e.g., inclusion). True, managers both have a title and distribute tangible resources, showing the correlation of status (rank) and power (resource control). However, power does not always correlate with status, as, for example, when a respected senior employee controls no tangible resources (e.g., does not set subordinates' salaries) but maybe offers intangible resources such as advice and networking. The power–status lines get fuzzy at the edges. Status of course can yield control over resources, but not always, as in a lame-duck administrator who still has a title but not power.

Status and power often but not always confer *influence* (Hogg, this volume), that is, the ability to change other people's beliefs and behavior. The older power definition most familiar to social psychologists, French and Raven's (1959) half-dozen *bases of power*, names various forms of *potential* for influence. Some bases of power confer status (i.e., recognition that someone is expert, informed, legitimate, or admired/referent), and some bases of power confer power as control (reward, coercion). In the current view, the older bases of power combine power (control) and status (recognition) variables.

How to decide among these concepts of power? For simplicity's sake, consider definitions of power as representing three traditions (Fiske & Berdahl, 2007). Some older definitions of power, for example, focus on outcome control (Emerson, 1962; Kipnis, 1976; Thibaut & Kelley, 1959), others indicate power's potential for influence (Cartwright, 1965; French & Raven, 1959; Weber, 1914/1978), and others demand evidence of actual influence (Dahl, 1957; B. Russell, 1938; Simon, 1957). The advantage of the current outcome–control definition includes, first, its concreteness (for ease of operationalization). Second, the outcome–control definition focuses on the situation of the powerful person, regardless of potential effects on less powerful people (Fiske & Dépret, 1996).

Besides—and this matters psychologically—power's control is a matter of degree. The powerholder's control operates in comparison to each party's control over own outcomes. *Interdependence* describes people's patterns of control within a dyadic relationship, that is, in what ways they need each other (or not) to attain valued goals. Power is not typically absolute. Each person may have *fate control* over the other party (P determines O's outcomes) and *reflexive control* over own outcomes (P determines P's own outcomes). Plus, together they can have *mutual control* over each other's outcomes (Thibaut & Kelley, 1959). Degree and symmetry of power both determine how interpersonal encounters proceed, as this chapter will show.

Finally, note that power and status mostly adhere to situations, not people. The boss at work may be a pussycat at home. If the boss consistently tries to control people across situations, that person is high *dominance*, a personality trait (e.g., Gough, 1990). The dominant person enters every situation expecting to be in charge or to compete for control. High-dominance people often end up situated in power because they seek it. This chapter describes how they do it.

If the boss perhaps believes in principle that group power organizes society and that group hierarchies are inevitable and good, the boss is high on *social dominance orientation*, most relevant in intergroup encounters (Sidanius & Pratto, 1999). For example, the boss might believe in the inevitability of patriarchy, generational authority, white racial dominance, and upper-class hegemony.

Throughout, this chapter mentions and explains such individual differences, but the point here is merely to emphasize the situational nature of power in most social psychological research and theory, as a complement to personality approaches less emphasized here. Altogether, the care that social psychologists have applied to defining power reflects its fascination for scholars as well as everyday folks.

Presumably motivated to help the downtrodden, social psychologists have ironically attended less to the oppressed, except as subordinates acted upon by the powerful. Lately, researchers have begun to study those at the bottom of the heap, examining their experience as more than passive victims (e.g., Crocker, Major, & Steele, 1998; S. Levin & van Laar, 2006; Shelton, 2003; Swim & Stangor, 1998). Being *oppressed* implies being exploited by someone powerful, who deliberately harms or controls the less powerful person. Social psychologists rarely use this politically loaded term. A more frequent term, *stigma*, accompanies someone's perceived possession of a socially devalued characteristic (Crocker et al., 1998; cf. Goffman, 1963; Edward E. Jones et al., 1984). Society marks the stigmatized person as inferior, based on an individual attribute (facial birthmark, disability) or group membership (sometimes called a tribal stigma). Stigma overlaps with being low status and low power. Being *subordinate* simply means being lower on a hierarchy, so the chapter employs this generic term.

OVERVIEW

Building on this shared vocabulary, the review begins with status, moves to power, and ends with subordinates. The status section reviews top-of-the-ladder, high-status groups, separating short- and long-term effects. That section shows the ubiquity of immediate status encounters across primates and humans in various aggregates and then focuses on common long-term arrangements that differentiate by gender, age, race, and class. The following section still inhabits the ladder's top rungs but looks at individuals with power, again separating the immediate and the durable interactions. The issues for power, although often paralleling status, differ psychologically because power varies across situations more than societal status does. The final section, subordination, focuses on the bottom of the heap, which social psychologists have studied most as stigma, that is, as a durable low status in society rather than as changeable power.

Besides elaborating these points, all three sections contrast immediate, short-term phenomena—what happens immediately when a person walks in the door—versus how status or power effects accumulate over time—the domain the person inhabits. The accretion of status and power influences health, well-being, and other important life outcomes, which is why stratification matters, but not always in the ways people think. Being at the top has obvious advantages but unrecognized disadvantages. Conversely, being at the bottom hinders people but can have hidden advantages, as this chapter shows.

GROUP-BASED STATUS: OPENING DOORS

Status opens doors. Group-based status confers competence, agency, access, and privilege, as this section explains. People toward the top of the ladder receive respect and recognition—but not necessarily control over others, according to the most precise understandings of status. The immediate advantages of status accrue across levels from orangutans to organizations. The longer-term pros and cons of status tell a more mixed story.

Immediate Effects

In the short-term, status coordinates interactions. In particular, high status commands attention, binds groups, creates social intelligence, regulates resources, demands verbal and nonverbal deference, and appears instantly, as this section shows. Most short-term effects favor the high status over the low, but not always.

Primates Attend Up and Make Way

Attention binds individuals together into social organizations (Chance & Jolly, 1970). In nonhuman primates, attention promotes prediction and potential control over an individual's own safety and resources. In this sense, then, primates' status (position) typically correlates with their power (resource control). Certainly, in primate dominance

hierarchies, high-status families gain privileged access to valued resources (e.g., safety, food). Lower-status families' outcomes depend on dealing with the higher-status animals. One important means of coordinating is attention. Primate status (often termed "dominance rank") reliably demands attention from lower-ranked animals.

Although nonspecialists often cite the privileged alpha-male, primate leadership does not always have its clear-cut privileges. Primate societies vary not only between species but even between research sites for the same species, and far more than most social psychologists might assume—a useful reminder that nature is not tidy. Primate species vary, first, in how aggressively they maintain hierarchies. That is, threat-oriented species contrast with display-oriented species. The *threat-oriented* ones (sometimes called "agonistic," as in antagonistic) engage in more open conflict, opposition, and aggression, with animals harming each other to attain or maintain rank. These threat-oriented groups tend to be unstable, with rank changing relatively rapidly. The *display-oriented* species (sometimes called "hedonic," as in hedonism) engage in more show-off behavior, demonstrating size, strength, and the potential for damage to foolhardy challengers, without needing to act much on aggressive potential, because subordinates take the hint. These display-oriented species can afford more symbolic exhibitions of aggression because their hierarchies tend to be more stable.

Either actual aggression or mere muscle-flexing can maintain a hierarchy. In both cases, subordinates' attention upward can be wise, either to avoid unprovoked high-rankers' aggression in threat-oriented species or to defer properly to high-ranked show-offs in display-oriented species (Chance, 1988; Chance & Larsen, 1976). Whether conflicts are more or less open, the attentional dynamic is similar.

Primate species differ in a second relevant way. The hierarchy can be variably dominance-based, to greater (*centric*) or lesser (*acentric*) degrees. That is, many primate bands protect the important individuals in the middle, with the expendable ones at the fringes, hence "centric." The more centric ones tend to be more *despotic*, compared with more egalitarian hierarchies (Sapolsky, 2005).

Species' dominance hierarchies thus differ on both degree of overt aggression and strictness of the hierarchy. For example, baboons seem more threat-oriented and centric—that is, among the more aggressively competitive and dominance-oriented. Orangutans seem more display-oriented and acentric—that is, among the less compulsively hierarchical. Chimpanzees combine centric (rank-sensitive) and display-oriented features, in both cooperation and competition (de Waal, 2005). That said, competition especially brings out the chimpanzees' social intelligence (Hare & Tomasello, 2004). Chimpanzees probably provide the better model for human hierarchy.

In general, like humans, male primates aggress more overtly than females do (see Bushman & Huesmann, this volume). Dominant male primates contend with competitors either mainly within-group (if from multimale groups) or between groups (if unimale groups; Strier, 2000). Female primates form weaker but more egalitarian relationships when competition is indirect. For example, females might compete over resources such as food, refuge, or mates, in a *scramble* (first-come, first served). More overt female competition (*contests*), when they do occur, tend to have the side effect of forging alliances for mutual defense against the female opponents.

Despite all these varieties, both human and primate perceivers rely on degrees of attention upward to understand hierarchies. For example, in male rhesus macaques, low-status monkeys automatically follow the gaze of familiar conspecifics, ever vigilant, whereas high-status monkeys can afford to be more selective, following the gaze of only other high-status monkeys (Shepherd, Deaner, & Platt, 2006). Humans and monkeys both generally orient where conspecifics do (Deaner & Platt, 2003), although men follow gaze less reliably than women do (Bayliss, di Pellegrino, & Tipper, 2005); perhaps men's gaze-following behavior would differ by status as well, although this apparently has not been tested. In any event, the human attentional processes resemble those of our evolutionary cousins, as a later section indicates.

Beyond direct resource acquisition and staying out of the big guy's way, recognizing hierarchy also reflects social or political intelligence (Boehm, 1997). Various primates understand not only their own place in their hierarchy (who is above and below them) but also other individuals' places relative to each other (Cheney & Seyfarth, 2007; Seyfarth, Cheney, & Bergman, 2005). In one Botswana game reserve, loudspeakers hidden in the bushes played rank-consistent and -inconsistent sequences of accepting grunts and fearful barks between known pairs of female baboons. These familiar voices elicited longer visual attention (staring in the direction of the loudspeakers) when the combinations were expectancy-inconsistent than -consistent. This indicates the baboons' knowledge of others' relative rank. *Social intelligence* encodes interindividual patterns that ease daily navigation. Social intelligence confers an ongoing adaptive advantage that goes beyond moment-by-moment acquisition of resources.

Ironically, those at the bottom must maintain more social intelligence, or at least more complex social representations. Keeping track of relationships often falls on the lower ranks more than the upper. In many species, the burden of social attention descends on the subordinates. That is, the subordinates often enact rank even more than the dominant animals do (Chance & Jolly, 1970). Subordinates must deploy attention, get out of the way, and suffer the consequences of mistakes, at least within highly

centric (rank-focused) hierarchies. Hence, despotism aptly characterizes the subordinates' situation.

Despotism can be better or worse for all concerned, depending on the degree of overt aggression involved. Despotism characterized by merely intimidating displays, termed *stable despotism*, requires subordinates to keep track, but dominants merely to strut. Not surprisingly, then, these underlings show more signs of physiological stress (Sapolsky, 2004a, 2005): They must track the powerful, but the powerful do not actually have to pay much attention or to fight. In conflictual, *unstable despotism*, the dominants are more chronically stressed because they actually have to battle frequently to maintain their position; in these physically contending, threat-oriented troops, the dominants show more stress-related glucocoicoids, such as cortisol.

Stress is useful for nimble reactions in the short term, but hypervigilance is pathogenic in the long term (e.g., Cheney & Seyfarth, 2007; Sapolsky, 2004b; Schneiderman, Ironson, & Siegel, 2005). In humans and other species, mild or short-term stress enhances cognition and memory, primarily through neuroendocrine effects on the brain's hippocampus. However, the same processes, when sustained, impair cognition and memory. Stress cuts both ways (Blascovich & Mendes, volume 1), depending on its severity and duration. Stress can foster vigilance and learning about hierarchies, among other adaptive knowledge.

No wonder primates attend up and make way for dominance. Examining humans' nearest neighbors provides some pertinent principles for social psychology. Nevertheless, the connection between social structure and cognition in human evolution remains an area of intensive investigation (Tomasello, Carpenter, Call, Behne, & Moll, 2005).

People Defer Nonverbally to Status

People also attend up and make way but usually go beyond friendly grunts and fearful barks. From preschool onward, even children know the relative social ranks of their peers (Peter K. Smith, 1988). People immediately acknowledge status hierarchies through nonverbal, verbal, and attitudinal routes.

Nonverbal cues reveal hierarchy, although less than most people think, according to meta-analyses of both perceived and actual nonverbal correlates of verticality (Hall, Coats, & LeBeau, 2005). High-status people generally do (a) express freely (more facial activity, posing skill), (b) relax more (open body, calm voice, vocal stability), and (c) intrude more (direct gaze, closer interpersonal distance, more interruptions, louder voices). People accurately expect some of these high-status cues, but they also import some unjustified stereotypes: People falsely predict status to convey both (a) more severity (unsmiling, direct gaze, lowered brows, no self-touching, lower voice, fluent speech, few "um, er" filled pauses) and simultaneously (b) more commotion (nodding, gesturing, body-shifting, touching others, less relaxed body, talking fast, laughing, more vocal variability). People apparently expect high-status others to channel a cold, manic villain with blatantly contradictory features. Of course, whatever the inaccuracies and contradictions, people respond to the status cues as they perceive them, and these perceptions demonstrably matter.

Despite inaccurately reporting how they do it, people can automatically detect the dominance–subordination between two people (Moors & De Houwer, 2005), although this may stem from the expressivity and clarity of high-status nonverbal behavior (Hall et al., 2006). Some apparent cues seem simple, such as relative vertical position (elevating "your highness" on a dais; Schubert, 2005). In interactions across status, the open body of dominants can expand posture, literally taking up more space by sitting upright, draping arms over adjacent chairs, and crossing one leg with its ankle on the other knee, relative to sitting with hands in lap, knees together, and slouching (Tiedens & Fragale, 2003).

In a face-to-face interaction, this nonverbal dominance evokes a predictable response, literally shrinking the partner's posture over time (Tiedens & Fragale, 2003). Nevertheless, conversation partners on both sides of the status divide feel most comfort and mutual liking when their nonverbal dominance and subordination complement each other (see also Stapel & van der Zee, 2006). Reciprocity occurs most in work rather than social settings (Moskowitz, Ho, & Turcotte-Tremblay, 2007), especially when people care about the task (Tiedens, Unzueta, & Young, 2007). People's motivation to reciprocate emerges in their propensity to change even their self-concepts, at least temporarily, to contrast self–other control in relationships (Tiedens & Jimenez, 2003).

Status often confers nonverbal influence. People defer to status cues with compliance. For example, direct gaze while speaking (vs. listening) reliably communicates dominance (e.g., Dovidio & Ellyson, 1982; for a review, see Hall et al., 2005). Dominant visual behavior works, in the sense that staring at people makes them flee, at least from elevators (Elman, Schulte, & Bukoff, 1977) and intersections (Ellsworth, Carlsmith, & Henson, 1972). Direct gaze also influences impressions: It captures attention (Baron-Cohen, 1995; Senju & Hasegawa, 2005; von Grünau & Anston, 1995), facilitates categorization (Mason & Macrae, 2004), engraves memory (Hood, Macrae, Cole-Davies, & Dias, 2003; Mason, Hood, & Macrae, 2004), conveys likability (Mason, Tatkow, & Macrae, 2005), and helps identify approach emotions such as joy and anger (Adams & Kleck, 2003, 2005).

Other nonverbal status cues, such as clothing, also inspire conformity, regardless of whether the status relates to the domain. Pedestrians will follow apparently high-status jaywalkers into traffic (Guéguen & Pichot, 2001; Lefkowitz, Blake, & Mouton, 1955), although one might wonder why a suit inspires confidence regarding crosswalks. Drivers inhibit horn honking to high-status vehicles that frustrate them (Doob & Gross, 1968). Overall, status can communicate itself nonverbally, eliciting deferential nonverbal behavior and sometimes exerting nonverbal influence.

People Heed and Respect Status

Status extracts influence verbally as well. A high-status authority's orders (Milgram, 1974) famously demand obedience (see Blass, 1999, for a review). Another well-known effect, *communicator status*—essentially credibility and apparent expertise—reliably affects persuasion (e.g., doctors vs. nurses: Hofling, Brotzman, Dalrymple, Graves, & Pierce, 1966; for a review, see Pornpitakpan, 2004). For example, communicator expertise facilitates HIV/AIDS interventions, according to meta-analysis, and low-status groups especially defer to expertise (Durantini, Albarracín, Mitchell, Earl, & Gillette, 2006).

Expertise operates through two routes (for a review, see Petty & Wegener, 1998). The more automatic, unconscious route is immediate believability and acceptance. Expertise can act as a peripheral cue that makes distracted, confused, indifferent, or ignorant recipients just go along with the communicator (e.g., Andreoli & Worchel, 1978; Kiesler & Mathog, 1968; Petty, Cacioppo, & Goldman, 1981; Wood & Kallgren, 1988). The more thoughtful, deliberate route is scrutiny. Expertise can trigger attention, elaboration, and consideration, for motivated recipients (e.g., Chaiken & Maheswaran, 1994; DeBono & Harnish, 1988; Heesacker, Petty, & Cacioppo, 1983; Moore, Hausknecht, & Thamodaran, 1986). Credible sources thus can predispose people's thinking to favor the arguments, but even after-the-fact attribution of a communication to a credible source instills confidence in one's own reactions to it (Tormala, Briñol, & Petty, 2007). Confidence in one's thoughts (pro or con) enhances their influence on persuasion (Petty, Briñol, & Tormala, 2002). Overall, communicator expertise generally persuades, through a variety of routes.

Although expert power may change attitudes, possessing a title often makes other people do what the titular leader says. Mere *legitimate power* (simply being named to leadership, without resources, expertise, or affection) elicits behavioral compliance (Rahim & Afza, 1993). All else being equal, people will generally follow the titular leader, although they may not change their minds or even much respect and like the merely-in-name leader.

Being adopted as a role model, *referent power* creates deeper changes, because it elicits both attitudinal and behavioral compliance. A leader who can combine both legitimate and referent power can create lasting change. For example, a legitimately elected president, who is also young and appealing enough to serve as a referent role model, can inspire the entire upcoming generation. For different generations, Franklin Roosevelt, John F. Kennedy, and Barack Obama come to mind. All three motivated community service (behavior) and crafted new hopes (attitudes).

Regardless of credentials, speaking style conveys status, as many self-appointed experts know, to their benefit. Sociolinguists have established some practical principles (Holtgraves, this volume).

Rule 1: *Sound confident.* Avoid hesitant, uncertain speech, which undermines the message. Taboo are *tag questions* ("right?"), *hedges* ("mostly"), *intensifiers* ("very much so"), and *hesitations* ("um"). Also avoid *deitic phrases*—namely, terms that gesture vaguely, depending on the momentary shared context. In "let's do it to it," each word's meaning depends entirely on idiosyncratic and transitory features of the communication (which "us"? "doing" what? "to" in what sense? which "it"?) (Areni & Sparks, 2005; Sparks & Areni, 2008). High-status speech requests no reassurance from the audience, conveying communicator assurance. For example, tag questions raise doubts about the communicator's own certainty, undermine attributions to the person's underlying attitude, and thereby sabotage a low-status communication (Blankenship & Craig, 2007). Buyers may decide merely from a salesperson's linguistic style (Sparks & Areni, 2002). Audio communications especially cue speaker-related linguistic heuristics that affect acceptance (Sparks, Areni, & Cox, 1998).

Rule 2: *Be direct.* A high-status style gets to the point without *excess politeness* ("if that's OK") or preamble ("excuse me, is this a good time, would you mind, please"). A strong style establishes credibility and competence (e.g., Bradac & Mulac, 1984; Erickson, Lind, Johnson, & O'Barr, 1978), and with them, persuasion (e.g., Blankenship & Holtgraves, 2005). The key variable is status (Crosby & Nyquist, 1977; Erickson et al., 1978), although gender interacts with these effects (Carli, 1990). Being direct does not mean being informal: Formality conveys competence (H. Levin, Giles, & Garrett, 1994; Nath, 2007).

Rule 3: *Talk fast, but not too fast.* As noted, hesitation undermines credibility, so a quick clip conveys competence (e.g., Brown, Giles, & Thackerar, 1985), but excessive speed can backfire (Street, Brady, & Putnam, 1983), revealing anxiety (Harrigan, Wilson, & Rosenthal, 2004). Speech rate predicts both credibility and persuasiveness (S. M. Smith & Schaffer, 1995). (Other, less controllable vocal qualities also matter: For example, listeners accurately judge self-rated dominance from mature vocal qualities; Berry, 1991.)

Rule 4: *Pronounce all consonants.* High-status speakers' pronunciation demands respect, conveying and inspiring confidence (see Holtgraves, this volume, for a review). For example, low-status speakers drop their "r"s (Labov, 1972) and their "g"s in gerunds' "ing" endings (Campbell-Kibler, 2007). Listeners know this (Labov, 2001).

Rule 5: *Use sophisticated speech.* Status emerges variously in using refined vocabulary (Bradac, Bowers, & Courtright, 1979; Bradac & Wisegarver, 1984), syntax (Callary, 1974), and intonation (Guy & Vonwiller, 1984). Listeners evaluate speakers accordingly (Cargile, Giles, Ryan, & Bradac, 1994; Ng & Bradac, 1993). For example, varied word choice conveys competence and confidence (Howeler, 1972).

Rule 6. *Use standard speech.* Nonstandard speech (slang, street talk, ethnic dialect) impugns competence to listeners' ears. Nonstandard speech undermines societal status, communicating lower social class (Ryan & Sebastian, 1980) and, with it, stereotypically less competence. Although nonstandard usages may increase solidarity and warmth (Holtgraves, this volume), they do not communicate status, which is orthogonal (Fiske, Cuddy, & Glick, 2007).

Rule 7. *Talk.* The length of any particular statement communicates dominance (Scherer, 1979), and talking time generally communicates leadership, according to meta-analysis (Mast, 2002; Mullen, Salas, & Driskell, 1989). Effects are stronger when observers (rather than members) nominate leaders, when the talker is a member of a large group, when the group is real outside the lab (Mullen et al., 1989), on inferences of dominance, and for male speakers (Mast, 2002). Although quality matters as well as quantity (Eric E. Jones & Kelly, 2007), and excess quantity can reveal anxiety (Harrigan et al., 2004), talking is a necessary condition for status.

Rule 8. *No need to mind manners.* If the goal is simple dominance, politeness can undermine perceived status (Holtgraves, this volume; Ng & Bradac, 1993). Dominance can entail being rude (perhaps even vulgar, but see Rules 6 and 7). Of course, politeness promotes likability, which as noted is orthogonal to respect (Fiske et al., 2007).

Altogether, field and experimental research converge on linguistic cues—namely, being confident, direct, rapid, articulate, sophisticated, standard, abundant, and even impolite—as communicating status, at least in Western contexts. Together with nonverbal cues of status and actual expertise, linguistic status immediately confers competence and often influence.

Groups Immediately Bestow Leadership

Other immediately accessible features of people confer immediate status. *Status characteristics theory* (Berger, Cohen, & Zelditch, 1972) observes that certain salient features of people convey societal status, most commonly being male, White, middle-aged, having educational credentials, or holding a high occupational position. Such status characteristics create expectations that influence behavior on both sides: The process familiar to social psychologists and sociologists as *self-fulfilling prophecy* or *behavioral confirmation* entails the expectancy-holder behaving such that the target responds as anticipated (e.g., Merton, 1948; Rosenthal, 1994; Snyder, 1992). In status characteristics theory, *diffuse* status characteristics generalize: If an individual has a status characteristic ranked by society in one arena (e.g., occupation: engineer vs. janitor), then—the crucial point—observers attribute the corresponding capacities, even in arenas irrelevant to the status (e.g., becoming jury foreperson). In other words, nominal societal status conveys dispositional ability because people expect it. The characteristic is diffuse because it then spills over to areas beyond its relevance.

People socially construct status (Ridgeway, 1991, 1997). Even an initially neutral characteristic, such as wearing a tie, acquires value when people observe correlations between a status characteristic and rewards. They then interpret task performance as justifying those rewards and over time value one status over another. To illustrate, in one study, four-person groups assembled in the lab, two men and two women, with one person the assigned coordinator (legitimated leader). They discussed four dilemmas (e.g., risk vs. rewards in choosing a job, how to decide about getting married), and afterward all rated each other's participation performance. For the male coordinators, other members overevaluated their performance, whereas for female nonleaders, other members undervalued their performance (e.g., the extent to which they guided the discussion, had ideas; Burke, Stets, & Cerven, 2007). As another example (Ridgeway & Erickson, 2000), students in small decision-making dyads worked with a confederate who allegedly differed according to a minimal criterion (valuing one modern artist over another), which they learned made them respectively an S or Q type. The pairs then made "insight associations," choosing an English word for an unfamiliar foreign word. When the confederate behaved in a deferential (e.g., hesitant) manner, participants

inferred that their own type was higher status and remained immune to influence. The reverse occurred when the confederate behaved in a dominant manner. In another study, third-party observers accurately inferred the status hierarchy. These studies illustrate how an initially neutral characteristic acquires status and influence.

A plausible psychological mechanism is attributing expertise to diffuse status cues, which results in influence within the group. This analysis fits self-managed production teams in a high-tech Fortune 100 company (Bunderson, 2003). A diffuse status characteristic can also acquire and spread value in the public domain (Berger & Fisek, 2006). Thus, status generalization links societal status to interpersonal influence, but the diffusion can depend on the fit of status to context: That is, an older person is influential in university administration but not in student clubs, and vice versa (Oldmeadow, 2007). Moreover, people know where they stand because accurate self-perception of status is adaptive in groups (Anderson, Srivastava, Beer, Spataro, & Chatman, 2006).

Having high status in a group, however obtained, allows more freedom from norms. High-status members have *idiosyncrasy credits*, that is, they can deviate more with less punishment. Traditionally, leadership research viewed this as resulting from an equity analysis; the leader accumulates more inputs on the way up, so followers accord the leader more credits to spend on innovation and non-normative outputs (Hollander, 1958, 1985).

In more recent views, status apparently comes from representing the group's ideal (Hogg, this volume; Hogg & van Knippenberg, 2003). Thus, leaders may represent even more extreme positions, in the valued direction, than the group average on salient norms. When leaders deviate from established norms (e.g., go to an extreme), group members trust the leader, so they assume the leader's counter-normative behavior promotes the group's good. Because leaders attract attention, followers are more likely to attribute their behavior to dispositional essences, rather than accidents of the situation (Hogg, this volume).

Overall, groups quickly assign and trust leaders, using readily apparent cues to status. The leader's freedom from strictly adhering to norms anticipates findings in the power literature, covered in a later section.

Organizations Grant Instant Advantage by Status

Organizations universally favor hierarchy for smoother, more unified functioning (Gruenfeld & Tiedens, this volume). Moreover, distribution of people into top roles is far from random. Societal status predicts occupying the upper organizational strata as well, partly because the high-status people already there prefer homogeneity and similar others (e.g., Byrne, 1997). Moreover, high-status groups actively discriminate in their own favor, especially on status-relevant traits, according to meta-analyses (Bettencourt, Charlton, Dorr, & Hume, 2001; Mullen, Brown, & Smith, 1992). Their bias cuts across real and experimental groups, dispelling actual merit differences as the main explanation.

According to *uncertainty reduction theory*, category-based ingroup favoritism reassures ingroup members by structuring ambiguous situations (Hogg, 2001). Reducing uncertainty plausibly explains preference for similar others: Ingroup bias is highest when group boundaries are unstable, illegitimate, and permeable, and the similarity dimensions are relevant (Bettencourt et al., 2001). Favoring one's high-status ingroup can bolster security and conveniently maintain one's place in the hierarchy.

Thus, high-status groups in an organization tend to replicate themselves (Gruenfeld & Tiedens, this volume). Left to their spontaneous reactions, organizational decision makers tend to network, attract, hire, socialize, and appreciate similar others, from job-hunting onward. Thus, organizations tend to segregate by external status characteristics (gender, race, class) within rank (consider female secretaries and lower-class janitors). Even with an influx of dissimilar others into the overall organization, stratification tends to maintain homogeneity within status strata. For example, from the get-go, employees make job referrals to friends, who resemble them on education and gender. Coming into the organization via personal recommendation then confers advantages, even though the referred individuals do not necessarily have better information or success on the job (Fernandez, Castilla, & Moore, 2000). All this promotes homogeniety within status levels.

How should organizations diversify, assuming this would be desirable? According to *intergroup contact theory*, high-status people would have to encounter lower-status people under the right conditions—and these implausibly include equalizing status in context. As this section would predict, authorities in the situation carry a lot of weight in the outcomes of intergroup contact (Pettigrew & Tropp, 2006). Arguably, authority sanction matters more than other constructive contact conditions, such as the well-established bundle including equal status, shared goals, and cooperation.

Nevertheless, given the right circumstances, higher-status groups do reduce bias by contact with lower-status outgroups, although not vice versa (Tropp & Pettigrew, 2005a). Contact effects are smaller for lower-status groups, who presumably have already been required to know the higher status. Moreover, higher- and lower-status groups may need different outcomes from intergroup contact: High-status groups seek social acceptance and moral validation, whereas low-status groups seek respect and empowerment (Fiske, Harris, Russell, & Shelton, 2009; Shelton, Richeson & Vorauer 2006;

Shnabel & Nadler, 2008; Shnabel, Nadler, Canetti-Nisim, & Ullrich, 2008).

Overall, a variety of benefits instantly accrue to status in organizations, just as it does in interpersonal encounters and in small groups. In organizations, the clearest effect of status is the ability to replicate oneself by supporting similar others.

Between Societal Groups, Status Awards Apparent Competence

Consider what status confers, in society more generally. Recall that for high-status individuals within organizations, status bestows expected competence, a status-relevant trait. Likewise, high-status ingroups especially favor themselves on competence (see Bettencourt et al., 2001, meta-analysis). So, too, for societies: For example, nations within the European Union (EU) favor the national ingroup, depending on the status-relevance of the dimension. When rating their own country and other EU member nations, higher-status nationals favor their ingroup on the status-relevant dimension (competence), whereas lower-status nationals favor their ingroup on the status-irrelevant dimension (warmth; Cuddy, Fiske, & Glick, 2008; Ellemers, van Rijswijk, Roefs, & Simons, 1997; Mummendey & Wenzel, 1999; Poppe, 2001; Spears & Manstead, 1989; van Knippenberg & van Oers, 1984).

The *stereotype content model* provides context for these findings: Two traits matter most to groups, which array along the two fundamental dimensions of warmth and competence (Fiske, Cuddy, Glick, & Xu, 2002). Warmth answers the question of the others' apparent intent for good or ill; cooperative versus competitive relationships, respectively, predict perceived warmth or its lack (Cuddy et al., 2008).

More relevant here, the second dimension, perceived competence, answers the question of whether the others can enact their benign or ill intent. Status relationships robustly predict perceived group competence, for several reasons: (a) Social perception serves interaction goals (Fiske, 1992), so inferring others' capacity to carry out their goals is central. Groups use status-equals-competence stereotypes as a shortcut perhaps because status is more immediately evident than its inferred implication—namely, capability. (b) Social perception can also enhance perceivers' sense of legitimacy. People are motivated to believe that people generally deserve what they get, according to *just world theory* (i.e., outcomes are fair; Lerner & Miller, 1978) and *social dominance theory* (i.e., hierarchies are inevitable; Sidanius & Pratto, 1999). (c) People prefer system stability, supposing that the system rewards and punishes the right people, even when the system disadvantages their own group (Jackman, 1994; Jost, Burgess, & Mosso, 2001). And (d) perceivers attribute a group's position to their inherent features (e.g., dispositions)—rather than to circumstances, connections, inheritance, or luck. In effect, people observing group status infer that corresponding group dispositions must be the cause (Pettigrew, 1979), paralleling how they make correspondent inferences from behavior to traits for individuals (Gilbert & Malone, 1995; Edward E. Jones, 1979; Ross, 1977).

Correlational evidence from five U.S. samples (convenience samples of students and adults, as well as a representative sample) assessed 25 groups' societal status by asking whether group members are generally viewed as having prestigious jobs and economic success (Cuddy, Fiske, & Glick, 2007; Fiske et al., 2002; Fiske, Xu, Cuddy, & Glick, 1999). Perceived competence included items assessing societal perceptions of the groups' traits: competence, efficacy, skill, creativity, confidence, and intelligence. The structural scale Societal Status correlated substantially with the trait scale Competence. Meritocracy is not just an American disease. In 20 international samples—including European, Middle Eastern, Asian, and South American participants—perceived status also correlated highly with competence ratings. This holds equally for individualist and collectivist societies. Although the size and consistency of this status = competence relationship might raise issues of divergent validity between the two scales, the status and competence items clearly do not measure the same construct: The status measure is wholly demographic, whereas the competence measure comprises traits. Apparently, people generally view their societies as meritocratic, inferring that high-status groups must also be high-competence groups.

Of course, correlations are only correlations. Experiments suggest that the causal direction goes from high status to perceived competence, more than the reverse. Intergroup experiments (Caprariello, Cuddy, & Fiske, 2009) varied status in vignettes describing an unfamiliar immigrant group (in their home country, "they typically have prestigious jobs and are well educated and economically successful" vs. "they have low-status jobs and are uneducated and economically unsuccessful"). Participants predicted how "people here" would view the immigrant group. As predicted, status affected expected competence but not warmth ratings, such that high-status groups were rated as more competent than low-status groups. (The effect is not a mere positivity halo: By contrast, the other manipulation, competitiveness, affected warmth but not competence ratings, such that competitive groups were rated as less warm than cooperative groups.) Further, people who endorse belief in a just world or a social dominance orientation exaggerate the link between experimentally manipulated status (images of high- and low-status houses) and the competence of the inhabitants (Oldmeadow & Fiske, 2007). Thus, evidence for high status (the relevant social

structural predictor) bestowing perceived competence (the trait) is not only correlational but also causal.

Some but not all of the prior evidence included education on both sides of the equation, so a pair of interpersonal experiments eliminated that possible confound (A. M. Russell & Fiske, 2009). Undergraduates played a computer game (prisoner's dilemma in one study, trivia challenge in another) with a peer described incidentally as high or low status (by social class background in one study, arbitrary boss–subordinate assignment in the other). Competition also varied but is not relevant here. In the first study, participants rated their partners both before and after a standardized interaction and, in the second, only after a spontaneous interaction. In all cases, status affected competence ratings, and participants reported that only the partner's dispositions, not the game circumstances, affected their ratings. Yoked observers also reported, wrongly, that the structural manipulations would not affect their trait judgments.

Status-to-competence effects appear for varied groups, including gay male subgroups (Clausell & Fiske, 2005), immigrants (Lee & Fiske, 2006), European nationalities (Cuddy et al., 2009; Linssen & Hagendoorn, 1994; Peeters, 1993; Phalet & Poppe, 1997; Poppe & Linssen, 1999), enemy outgroups (Alexander et al., 1999, 2005), linguistic groups (Ruscher, 2001; Yzerbyt et al., 2005), American stereotypes changing over 80 years (Bergsieker, Leslie, Constantine, & Fiske, 2009), and Fascist depictions of racial groups (Volpato et al., 2009) (for a review, see Cuddy et al., 2008). All fit the stereotype content model (SCM) predictions that perceived status predicts perceived competence.

Related social psychology models also imply a status/power correlation with agency/competence and related dimensions. For example, *enemy images theory* (EIT) in political psychology (Alexander et al., 1999, 2005) also presupposes that social structural factors determine stereotypes. Groups differ in perceived cultural status and relative power, as well as goal compatibility. The first two dimensions, status and power, appear as distinct elements in EIT, unlike the SCM. The four main EIT images (ally, barbarian, dependent, imperialist) capture important elements of intergroup reactions that indirectly imply differences in both hierarchical position and competence. Both theories describe how structural variables can predict stereotypes, and Alexander et al. provide further evidence to that effect.

Although focused on gender per se, *social role theory* (Eagly, 1987; Eagly, Wood, & Diekman, 2000; see Wood & Eagly, volume 1) posits that social structure commonly divides men and women into roles of higher (wage-earning) and lower (child-rearing) status. People observe these diagnostic distributions by gender, throughout society, and infer more agency (competence) for men and communality (warmth) for women. When people observe role-constrained behavior, they infer the corresponding traits, another example of the group-based correspondent inference noted earlier. For example, in a hypothetical society, the "city workers" acquired male stereotypes, whereas the "child raisers" acquired female stereotypes (Hoffman & Hurst, 1990). This approach focuses on roles as carriers of status, but the corresponding competence stereotypes fit the overall pattern that group status confers competence.

Social identity theory has long examined group status and its interplay with legitimacy (Spears, Greenwood, & de Lemus, 2010; see Yzerbyt & Demoulin, this volume). One way that group status differences can appear legitimate is by apparently corresponding to differences in competence or deservingness; in practice, these are dimensions relevant to the social identity of the high-status group. Ingroup bias often is higher for high-status groups (Sachdev & Bourhis, 1987; for meta-analysis, see Bettencourt et al., 2001; Mullen et al., 1992): They show more ingroup favoritism, evaluate themselves more positively, and evaluate the outgroup more negatively. This particularly holds for status-relevant dimensions that legitimate the status quo. For high-status groups, legitimacy ("we deserve our privileges") supports ingroup bias and cements the status hierarchy, having symbolic importance. The low-status groups often also recognize the high-status group's advantages on status-relevant dimensions. Perhaps low-status groups show intergroup biases for more practical reasons. Instrumental concerns especially matter to low-status group members, whereas high-status groups can afford to deal with more symbolic identity expression (Scheepers, Spears, Doosje, & Manstead, 2006).

However, even low-status groups evaluate themselves favorably on dimensions relevant to their own identity, although these are less valued dimensions (Bettencourt et al., 2001) and less likely to be competence related. This fits social identity theory's *social creativity hypothesis* about finding alternative dimensions for the positive distinctiveness of even a low-status social identity. Nevertheless, the high-status groups do not recognize the identity-relevant strengths of the low-status groups (Bettencourt et al., 2001).

The status = competence link is relentless unless people perceive the system to be illegitimate. Under unstable circumstances, low-status groups will invoke (il)legitimacy to resist the status quo and favor themselves (Spears, Jetten, & Doosje, 2001).

One key insight from social identity theory is the role of ingroup identification in perceiving status legitimacy (e.g., status = competence). High-status group members typically identify more strongly with their ingroups (Bettencourt et al., 2001). High-identifiers stick with the group, even when its status is under threat, but low-identifiers may opt out, for example engaging in individual mobility, if possible (Ellemers, Spears, & Doosje, 1997; Spears, Doosje, & Ellemers, 1997). If they succeed in rising above their group, then of course this affirms their individual competence. However, the general case, under stable circumstances, according to meta-analyses (Bettencourt et al., 2001), is that high-status groups show the most ingroup bias and outgroup derogation, especially when the status reliably results from subjectively fair intergroup competition (Jost & Burgess, 2000). Whether they are correct is another matter, but right or wrong, the status = competence perceptions of course determine people's responses to society's groups.

Elites Control Political Discourse

Societies allow elites to construct the overall framing of politics, which prominently concerns status and power relations at the institutional level. At a societal level, *top-down processes* import ideologies constructed by political elites (Jost, Federico, & Napier, 2009). That is, the current culture frames particular political bundles of attitudes in socially recognizable ways, a type of *social representation* or socially shared schema (Moscovici, 1988). High-status groups especially influence the framing of current issues, for example, whether immigrants are allegedly invaders or helpers. High-status groups then disproportionately influence political discourse because they have more access to media and a more focused message (Converse, 2000; Gerth & Mills, 1948; Zaller, 1992). In comparison, the larger public possesses a less articulated, more latent, emotionally attuned interpretation of political events, institutions, and values (e.g., Westen, 2007). Arguably, certain interpretations appeal to elites—namely, system-justifying perspectives—but lower-status groups may also justify the system (Jost et al., 2009), being motivated to maintain system stability. For example, under system threat, men and women alike endorse status quo gender inequality in sheer numbers of female political and business leaders (Kay et al., 2009).

Nevertheless, high-status, relatively advantaged people especially exhibit group-serving explanations (as just noted). More relevant to status and its political implications, manipulations of *relative gratification* (status advantage) specifically increase enthusiasm for a variety of status-serving beliefs: endorsement of social dominance hierarchies, restrictive immigration policies, as well as outgroup prejudice (Guimond & Dambrun, 2002; Guimond, Dambrun, Michinov, & Duarte, 2003). According to the *group socialization model*, a favorable social position encourages social dominance orientation, which in turn facilitates prejudice.

Summary of Short-Term Status Effects

Immediate effects of status appear from primates up through human dyads and groups, all the way to human organizations, society, and politics. Status has its privileges, garnering attention, access, credit, respect, and agenda-setting, certainly positive in the short-term.

Lifelong Effects: What's So Special About Certain Categories?

Surely, a lifetime of experiencing immediate high-status abundance must influence habitual social responses. Even absent system-justifying ideologies, affirming social identities, and privileged societal roles, the mere experience of being repeatedly accorded respect and its rewards must eventually affect people. Social psychologists do not typically study lifetime interventions, although in theory one could compare twins adopted into families of contrasting social classes. Alternatives, such as random assignment to lifelong low or high status, are not ethical research options. Instead, social psychologists have interpreted responses that differ by several ascribed social categories, most often in terms of their category's correlated social status. Clearly, comparing the status accorded to particular genders, ages, races, and even social classes is fraught with natural confounds. Nevertheless, social psychologists have produced some useful insights about commonalities based on ascribed statuses. One insight is that although lifelong status has advantages, all is not rosy at the top; each of the high-status positions entails considerable ambivalence, although in different forms, depending on distinct features of each status contrast.

Gender

Others overview the social psychology of gender (Rudman & Glick, 2008; Wood & Eagly, volume 1), so this section focuses narrowly on gender as a societal status characteristic that affects interpersonal experiences. An earlier section described the immediate impact of other status characteristics in general, but this section considers gender as a status characteristic correlated with longer-term social responses. Communication, belief systems, and prejudices will especially illustrate these phenomena that mix gender and status.

Men in general clearly possess higher social status than women in general. Children as young as 6 years old know this (Martin & Ruble, 2010). Every culture displays male status: in business and government positions and on development indices (education, health, literacy; United Nations Development Fund for Women, 2005). American men earn more than their female counterparts (U.S. Department of Labor, 2005) and in dual-career couples do less housework than their wives do (Business and Professional Women's Foundation, 2005; Crosby, 1991; Deutsch, 1999). Male single-adult households, with or without children, are less likely to be in poverty, contrary to female-headed households

(Holden & Smock, 1991). Male fetuses and infants are less likely to be destroyed, worldwide (Sen, 2003). All this attests to the simple societal fact of male hegemony.

Not surprisingly, male societal advantage has interpersonal consequences, for example, in everyday communication. Being male is the default assumption in most social communication. For example, maleness is the unmarked form in most languages, whereas femaleness is the more complex, marked form (Holtgraves, this volume). Masculine forms describe the generic human, and people think of men when they encounter masculine generics (Gastil, 1990). Feminine forms reduce status (think major–majorette, governor–governess), and carry gender-stereotypic associations (actor–actress). No wonder women reject "poetess" or "chairwoman," preferring to be poets and chairs.

Holding the default gender and having higher societal status, men more often figuratively or literally own most workplaces and signal their intentions regarding the role of women in male-dominated settings. Language can be the canary in the coalmine (Boggs & Giles, 1999) that presages more overt, conscious forms of hostility. According to *communication accommodation theory*, workplace communications can either accommodate or fail to accommodate the lower-status group. Accommodation failure reinforces group-based advantages. Existing group-based structures may be portrayed or experienced as morally or normatively correct: "This is how we've always done things." Consider single-sex communication networks that result from ad hoc, all-male golfing, fishing, or drinking groups. Communication may emphasize male-metaphor jargon (sports, military), patronizing speech ("girls"), or sexual innuendo and joking. All these communication patterns signal intent not to accommodate. So communication styles convey whether the work environment aims for inclusion and collegiality across genders.

Not just verbal behavior but also nonverbal behavior expresses gendered dominance. As noted, dominance appears in a high ratio of looking while talking (vs. listening), especially for stereotypically male expertise (Dovidio, Brown, Heltman, Ellyson, & Keating, 1988). Certain nonverbal behaviors in men communicate high status (e.g., taking up space, relaxed posture, unreciprocated touching); in bars, this attracts women (Renninger, Wade, & Grammer, 2004). Perhaps women respond to the high-status cues (as noted later). Being the higher-status gender, men's communication patterns can implicitly reinforce gender hierarchy.

As the higher-status, default gender, men could reasonably be motivated to maintain that arrangement but also could just be relatively less worried about equality. On average, men are indeed more likely to endorse social dominance orientation; this general group-hierarchy ideology accounts for gender differences in more specific attitudes toward social compassion, women's and gay/lesbian rights, and the military (Pratto, Stallworth, & Sidanius, 1997). However, men's average commitment to social dominance might be most relevant on specifically status-related issues, such as women's rights. Indeed, although men more often endorse conservatism and group-based dominance, their social dominance best predicts their underendorsement of women's rights (Eagly, Diekman, Johannesen-Schmidt, & Koenig, 2004). Among the relevant general ideologies (conservatism, group-based dominance, and equality), the biggest gender differences occur in men's lesser endorsement of equality in general. All this fits a status-motivated explanation of gender difference in social dominance orientation for men but a status-improvement motivation for women's greater endorsement of an equality ideology. Furthermore, men's endorsement of social dominance orientation itself is mediated by the intensity of their gender identification (Dambrun, Duarte, & Guimond, 2004). Apparently, the higher-status gender group takes its status for granted, prefers its position, and on average is not as motivated to undermine the hierarchy as is the lower-status gender.

The universality of male dominance lends itself to sociobiological explanations (Neuberg, Kenrick, & Schaller, this volume; Wood & Eagly, volume 1). In the most common evolutionary view as well as in the biosocial view, differential parental investment and role requirements dictated by biology mean that men need not necessarily devote as much time to their progeny as must pregnant and lactating women (Trivers, 1985). One account of the consequences of differential parental investment posits that men are predisposed to promiscuity and women to sexual selectivity, although this vastly oversimplifies the universal human investment in one's children. Nevertheless, evolutionists cite men's relative preference for younger and apparently fertile mates, facilitating their reproductive odds, along with women's relative preference for older and high-status mates with resources, increasing their child-rearing success (e.g., Buss & Kenrick, 1998). Meta-analyses indicate that women do weight social class and ambition more heavily than do men, who weight attractiveness more heavily than women do (Feingold, 1992).

Evolutionary explanations are not the only way to understand these status-related mate-preference patterns. A biosocial model observes that these common patterns vary by a culture's degree of gender inequality, so, for example, women's status and resource preference attenuates when women hold more resources of their own (Wood & Eagly, volume 1). A biosocial approach acknowledges gender differences in parental investment and physical strength but then goes on to argue that the result, differential gender distribution into social roles (breadwinner, child-raiser), does not go unnoticed. People observing these gender roles develop status-related expectations about men and women.

At the same time, status dynamics do not explain everything about gender. Both men and women make enormous joint contributions to child-rearing and breadwinning (Wood & Eagly, 2002). Gender preferences in mates are more similar than different: Across 37 cultures, everyone puts as their top criteria the kindness, intelligence, and social skills of a prospective mate (Buss, 1989). (As Hyde, 2005, notes, most other gender differences also are small.) What the ascribed-status analysis misses is men's and women's unique needs for each other.

Of all societal groups differing in status, women and men are arguably the most interdependent, relying on each other for a variety of humans' most crucial outcomes. Unlike other ingroup–outgroup interactions, men and women live and love together, in the most intimate, deeply invested relationships. The *social distance scale* (Bogardus, 1933)—in which people rate an outgroup on, for example, "could accept in my nation, . . . neighborhood, . . . home"—would hardly do to measure gender relations. Because the genders certainly cannot and do not want to ignore each other, interdependence tempers the status relationships in at least two demonstrated ways: prescriptions and ambivalence.

Prescriptive gender-role stereotypes aim to preserve the status quo, controlling the behavior of both genders (Ruble & Ruble, 1982). Men must conform to high-status male roles requiring *agency* (action, leadership, autonomy) and not especially *communion* (emotional sensitivity and expressivity, social harmony). Indeed, according to meta-analyses, male agency appears consistently: Boys are more active and intense, compared with girls, who are more inhibited and perceptually sensitive (Else-Quest, Hyde, Goldsmith, & van Hulle, 2006). Men resist another's incivility as a status challenge more readily than women do (Porath, Overbeck, & Pearson, 2008). Masculine negotiating styles produce more one-sided outcomes (Kray, Reb, Galinsky, & Thompson, 2004). Men aggress physically and overtly, whereas women aggress socially (Eagly & Steffen, 1986). Men help heroically, whereas women help by caretaking over the long haul (Eagly & Crowley, 1986). Small wonder that men and women embody power differently: Men associate physical force with power, whereas women associate physical force with loss of power (Schubert, 2004). Violating these gender rules invites ridicule and rejection (Carranza, Larsen, & Prentice, 2009). Similarly, women who behave agentically, by self-promoting, for example, risk rejection, sabotage, and backlash (Rudman, 1998; Rudman & Glick, 1999, 2001) and forfeit romantic appeal (Rudman & Heppen, 2003). For both men and women, gender-atypical success threatens peers (Rudman & Fairchild, 2004), so both genders tend to conform.

Gender and leadership style provides a case in point. People implicitly and explicitly associate men with authority and management (Heilman, Block, Martell, & Simon, 1989; Rudman & Kiliansky, 2000). Leadership fits the prescriptive male gender role, and men do more often emerge as leaders in unstructured groups, according to meta-analyses (Eagly & Karau, 1991). However, women more often emerge as social leaders, befitting female gender roles. Further, across studies, atypical women who do lead organizations run them in a more democratic and participatory way, rather than an autocratic or directive way (Eagly & Johnson, 1990). Such women leaders are rewarded for their less masculine leadership styles (Eagly, Makhijani, & Klonsky, 1992). Occupational stereotypes and realities more generally sort by gender; for example, consider who stereotypically as well as actually occupies jobs such as secretary, elementary school teacher, or nurse (Cejka & Eagly, 1999; Glick, Wilk, & Perreault, 1995). Overall, prescriptive gender roles simultaneously reinforce status differences and genuine interdependence (Rudman & Glick, 2008).

The result is ambivalence (Glick & Fiske, 1996), with sexist men both rewarding women who fit traditional roles and holding subjectively benevolent attitudes that idealize, cherish, and paternalize them. The flip side is sexist hostility toward women who violate traditional gender roles. Men's degree of ambivalent sexism predicts stereotyping of women, failing to hire female managers, tolerating sexual harassment, derogating promiscuous (but not chaste) women, lacking sympathy toward rape victims, endorsing feminine beauty ideals, and neurally objectifying bikini-clad women (Cikara, Eberhardt, & Fiske, 2009; Forbes, Collinsworth, Jobe, Braun, & Wise, 2007; Masser & Abrams, 2004; B. L. Russell & Trigg, 2004; Sakalli-Ugurlu, Sila Yalçin, & Glick, 2007; Sibley & Wilson, 2004). Patterns of ambivalence hold up across cultures (Glick et al. 2000, 2004), suggesting the plausibility of a biosocial model. Most relevant here, ambivalently sexist men favor hierarchies: Sexist hostility correlates with competitive social dominance, and sexist "benevolence" correlates with controlling authoritarianism (Sibley, Wilson, & Duckitt, 2007). Hostile sexist men value power but not universalism and compassion (Feather, 2004).

Overall, male status correlates with long-term responses that correspond to repeated experiences of privilege: assuming leadership, disproportionately accepting inequality, even endorsing group dominance, and displaying higher activity levels, consistent with agency (see the upcoming section on power and agency). Although the relationships are necessarily correlational, the pattern extends the immediate effects of status to lifelong responses from living with hierarchy.

Age

Another status characteristic with long-term consequences is age, although of course membership in particular categories is stage-long, not lifelong, as it is with gender. Most people begin life by hoping to increase their age status, then wind-down reluctantly to accept the lower status of old age for longevity if possible. Old age is uniquely a low-status outgroup that people seek eventually to join, health permitting. Generally, the age–status correlation is curvilinear, so middle age has its privileges, more than youth or old age. Thus, the ascribed status of age shifts, but nevertheless, most people have the middle-aged period of their lives when they benefit from age-related status. Scant research examines middle-aged status, although it follows from research targeting younger and older people as low status. For example, people talk down to both young and old people (e.g., respectively, Caporael, 1981; Giles & Williams, 1994). In effect, middle age forms the privileged control condition for ageism studies that compare middle age as the better-off default to old age as the stigmatized condition.

Middle-aged people do show dominance, more than younger and older people. At the prime of life, people are more dominant, agreeable, conscientious, and emotionally stable (Caspi, Roberts, & Shiner, 2005). In particular, extraversion-type traits related to dominance peak at ages 30 to 50, but then social vitality begins to decrease (Roberts, Walton, & Viechtbauer, 2006). Middle-aged adults most invest in actively social roles within family, work, and community. Middle-agers flexibly exploit opportunities in the environment rather than trying to change everything (as younger people do) or giving up (as older people do) (Wrosch, Heckhausen, & Lachman, 2006). As a later section indicates, this effective use of environmental affordances characterizes powerful people in general (Guinote, 2008).

As a status characteristic, age resembles gender in that people have older and younger people in their families. Further, like gender, people are interdependent across ages, so the status tensions mix with contingency, arguably resulting in three kinds of ambivalence that should inform middle-age high-status privilege, revolving around pity, identity, and succession (North & Fiske, 2009), as follows.

The most common old-age prejudice involves pity, and the associated stereotype assumes benign incompetence, correlated with low status (Cuddy, Norton, & Fiske, 2005; Fiske et al., 2002; Richeson & Shelton, 2006; for reviews, see Nelson, 2002; for a meta-analysis, see Kite & Johnson, 1988). Consigning oldsters to low status appears across cultures (Cuddy et al., 2009). Older adults appear incompetent socially, cognitively, and physically (e.g., Pasupathi, Carstensen, & Tsai, 1995). This low-agency image contrasts with images of people in their prime, who appear strong and agentic. Young people may be active but not accorded competence. In the attitude literature, for example, communicator research has used age to operationalize status, prestige, influence, or power. Low-impact sources in one study were jean-clad undergraduates, whereas high-impact sources were more professionally dressed 38-year-olds (Jackson & Latané, 1981).

Identity is another ambivalent status domain. Strong, vital, middle-aged adults acknowledge the advantage of their agentic position by resisting the approaching old-age boundary; middle-aged people are in no hurry to believe themselves old. Although adults acknowledge their chronological age, they see "old age" as a moving boundary that recedes as they approach it (Seccombe & Ishii-Kuntz, 1991). Older adults automatically associate self with young stereotypes faster than with old stereotypes (Hummert, Garstka, O'Brien, Greenwald, & Mellott, 2002). Older people may try to retain one of the more positive youngold (55–75 years old) subtypes, such as the golden-ager or wise elder (Brewer, Dull, & Lui, 1981; Hummert, Garstka, Shaner, & Strahm, 1994, 1995; Neugarten, 1974). Variations in valence, vitality, and maturity characterize the different images (Hummert et al., 1994; Knox, Gekoski, & Kelly, 1995), some of which maintain more of the respect accorded middle-aged people. It helps to look younger (Hummert, 1994). Maintaining a positive (middle-aged) identity has health benefits (Hummert et al., 2002; Levy, Slade, Kunkel, & Kasl, 2002; Tuckman & Lavell, 1957). Even subliminal exposure to old-age stereotypes increases older people's cardiovascular and skin conductance reactivity to the short-term stress of math and verbal challenges (Levy, Hausdorff, Hencke, & Wei, 2000).

Relevant to identity, reminders of one's own mortality inspire a variety of coping mechanisms, among them reaffirming one's enduring core values (for a review of *terror management theory*, see Pyszczynski, Greenberg, Koole, & Solomon, volume 1; Greenberg, Schimel, & Mertens, 2002). Negative stereotypes of older adults may help younger and middle-aged adults to distance and protect themselves (Snyder & Meine, 1994). Middle-aged adults try to duck all these torments by maintaining their identity as separate from old age.

So where is the ambivalence in enjoying a middle-aged identity? At the height of adults' middle-aged status, they can see younger people await their turn, raising issues of age-appropriate *succession*. Intergenerational allocations are governed by egotism, uncertainty, power, and stewardship. That is, older people may act in self-interested ways, especially when primed with power, but can make fairer decisions when uncertain about the future consequences for the succeeding generations (Wade-Benzoni, Hernandez,

Medvec, & Messick, 2008). To the extent that older people control resources, envy will result; middle-age, contrasting with much older people and much younger people, would be the default category that inspires pride (Fiske et al., 2002).

With gender and race, age is one of the top-three most rapidly used social categories (for review, see Fiske, 1998). Like gender, but unlike race, people include all age categories in their families. Unlike both gender and race, people mostly move (and hope to do so) across age categories, from lower-status youngsters, to high-status middle-agers, to low-status oldsters. Despite the possibility of cultures that revere their elders, social psychologists apparently have yet to document this phenomenon.

Race

Like being male or at the prime of life, being White might seem unambiguously positive. For example, being White is the automatic default association for Americans with being American (Devos & Banaji, 2005). "White" English, as the standard, has more status than does African American vernacular English (Labov, 1972). Countless prejudice studies show Whites and other ethnic groups favoring White targets over Black and Latino ones (Dovidio & Gaertner, this volume). Even "model-minority" Asian targets evoke a more complicated pattern, but on the whole, being White is more positive (e.g., Lin, Kwan, Cheung, & Fiske, 2005.)

To be sure, over the past century, Whites' reported attitudes toward Blacks have improved (Schuman, Steeh, Bobo, & Krysan, 1997). In one 70-year series of studies, Princeton undergraduates described 10 ethnic and national groups, using a trait-adjective checklist (chronologically: D. Katz & Braly, 1933; Gilbert, 1951; Karlins, Coffman, & Walters, 1969; Bergsiecker et al., 2009; for parallel samples elsewhere, see Devine & Elliot, 1995; Madon et al., 2001). Trends for Black Americans showed the most dramatic positive change, with stereotypes gradually omitting negative traits (all competence-related: *lazy, ignorant, superstitious*, and *stupid*) and substituting positive traits (all warmth-related: *gregarious, passionate*, and *talkative*). Nevertheless, note the aspersion cast on competence implied by its absence, a phenomenon dubbed *stereotyping by omission*. That is, Whites no longer report low-competence stereotypes, but instead of substituting high-competence stereotypes, they mention high-warmth stereotypes instead. As this example illustrates, White negativity lingers in subtle ways—automatic, ambiguous, and ambivalent (Dovidio & Gaertner, this volume; Fiske, 1998)—and in not-so-subtle ways (e.g., Devine & Elliot, 1995).

As the higher-status group, Whites generally endorse hierarchy-maintaining ideologies more than Blacks do, a reliable-enough finding to be termed the *ideological asymmetry effect* (Fang, Sidanius, & Pratto, 1998; Sidanius,

Levin, Federico, & Pratto, 2001). Whites generally are more conservative than Blacks; Whites persistently tend to tolerate inequality, disapprove government social spending, disfavor poverty programs, and favor the death penalty (Davis, 2005). Conservative ideology predicts specific beliefs about who deserves what, which in turn predicts opposition to compensatory polices such as affirmative action for Blacks (although not for women: Reyna, Henry, Korfmacher, & Tucker, 2006). Given that conservatism resists change, by definition and by motivation (Jost, Glaser, Kruglanski, & Sulloway, 2003), greater White conservatism functions to protect Whites' racial status. Moderately prejudiced Whites favor the ingroup with sympathy and admiration more than they derogate racial outgroups (Dovidio, Esses, Beach, & Gaertner, 2002). Similar subtle prejudices occur in Europe with regard to its new immigrants (Pettigrew & Meertens, 1995).

White ideologies about their privileged position rely on biological explanations, implying fixed, objective, and unassailable differences that the data do not necessarily support. Although gender and age do have biological correlates, creating ongoing debates about essentialism, racial essentialism is harder to support. Genetic differences between "races" are 10 times smaller than those within "races," by some estimates (Lewontin, 1972; Nei & Roychoudhury, 1993). Society's racial categories do not fit any consistent underlying genetic patterns (Graves, 2001; Hirschfeld, 1996; Marks, 1995); even skin color does not reliably indicate shared genetic heritage (Parra et al., 2003). Genetics fail to explain race differences on intelligence tests (Nisbett, 2009). As increasingly recognized through the use of "multiracial" identifiers, definitions of race change with time, place, and power structure (Banks & Eberhardt, 1998). Racial categories are not natural kinds, but instead "social kinds."

Nor is racial bias plausibly a hardwired, evolved boundary. Arguably, gender and age bias could have evolved precisely because social groups inevitably mix these categories. In contrast, in ancestral times, racially mixed encounters would be implausible, and modern experiments suggest rapid distinctions by race are more malleable than gender and age differentiation (Cosmides, Tooby, & Kurzban, 2003). To be sure, people have doubtless adapted other systems to apply to race, for example, recognizing natural kinds that do differ perceptually and essentially. People also attune to distinct social coalitions (Kurzban & Leary, 2001; Kurzban, Tooby, & Cosmides, 2001); such tribes with specific markers could adapt to phenotypic markers such as race (or hair color, build, height). People's current concepts of race more probably built on general orientations to social groups and their coalitions.

Certainly, evidence for social construction is strong (Maddox, 2004; Markus, 2008). Phenotype determines racial category, but it operates through a variety of substitutable features, such as skin tone or hair texture or feature shapes, no one of which is necessary or sufficient. To identify race, people use a flexible configuration of race-related features (Blair, Judd, Sadler, & Jenkins, 2002; Livingston & Brewer, 2002). Standards for categorizing race depend on context (e.g., Maddox & Gray, 2002, Maddox & Chase, 2004) and on individual ideology (e.g., holding fixed views of racial categories, Eberhardt, Dasgupta, & Banaszynski, 2003). Racial categorization depends on people's specific beliefs: Semantic associations to light and dark, lay theories, cultural beliefs, and personal experiences together configure the social context (Maddox, 2004). For example, racially prejudiced individuals care more about accurately categorizing racially ambiguous people (Blascovich, Wyer, Swart, & Kibler, 1997). Racial categorization uses individual features associated closely with stereotypes and prejudices (Blair et al., 2002; Livingston & Brewer, 2002), fueled by the media (e.g., Dixon & Maddox, 2005). Even a person typically viewed as White might have some Afrocentric facial features, which carry stereotypic and affective associations, independent of race (Blair et al., 2002). Consistent with the idea that specific features can have major consequences, even White defendants with Afrocentric features receive harsher sentences than other Whites (Blair, Judd, & Chapleau, 2004). Blacks with especial Afrocentric faces are more likely to land on death row for murdering a White person, relative to Blacks without such features (Eberhardt, Davies, Purdie-Vaughns, & Johnson, 2006). Social constructions, however biologically based or not, are real in their consequences. Typically, such life-and-death consequences privilege Whites over minorities, especially Black Americans. Other cultures have their own racial constructions as well.

Perhaps the best indicator of White privilege is continuing residential racial segregation, as severe in the United States as in apartheid-era South Africa (Massey, 2007). Unlike gender and age as intergroup experiences, in which most people have both groups in their families, race challenges Euro-Americans because few have interracial families. Racial segregation occurs at all income levels and dramatically targets Black Americans and dark-skinned Latinos (Massey & Denton, 1993). White Americans prefer and obtain more racially segregated neighborhoods than Black Americans do. Neighborhood choice ramifies to Whites having advantages in schooling, employment, safety, social networks, and health care. Generally, then, Whites are accorded status (default prototype, standard language, stereotypic respect, residential choice, life advantages). However, Whites' high status is not so simple: clear privilege, yes, but fraught for the high-status race because of a unique intergroup history involving slavery, political and civil turmoil, progress, and backlash (see, e.g., Fredrickson, 2002; J. M. Jones, 1997; Sears, 1998).

The population-level racial advantages come with limited interracial contact for Whites. Granted, both sides may avoid contact, thinking the other side is not interested (Shelton & Richeson, 2005) or potentially prejudiced (Vorauer, Hunter, Main, & Roy, 2000). Focusing here on the high-status group, Whites generally find interracial contact unpleasant, experiencing various negatives:

- Whites are bad at remembering cross-race faces, beginning with a failure to activate fully the brain's fusiform "face area" (Golby, Gabrieli, Chiao, & Eberhardt, 2001).
- Whites often worry that Blacks will be resentful, perhaps hostile (e.g., Devine & Elliot, 1995; Shelton, 2003).
- Whites may fret about revealing themselves as racist, to self as well as others (Dovidio & Gaertner, this volume).
- Whites often worry about how they are being evaluated by their Black counterparts (Shelton & Richeson, 2006; Vorauer et al., 2000; Vorauer & Kumhyr, 2001).
- Whether because of such worries or sheer inexperience, Whites often experience anxiety, discomfort, threat, and fear about interracial interactions (e.g., Blascovich, Mendes, Hunter, Lickel, & Kowai-Bell, 2001; Gaertner & Dovidio, 1986; Mendes, Blascovich, Lickel, & Hunter, 2002; Stephan et al., 2002; Stephan & Stephan, 2000; Towles-Schwen & Fazio, 2003).
- Whites' nonverbal behavior also telegraphs discomfort during interracial interactions (e.g., Dovidio, Kawakami, Johnson, Johnson, & Howard, 1997; Vanman, Paul, Ito, & Miller, 1997; Word, Zanna, & Cooper, 1974).
- Whites' discomfort occurs rapidly and automatically, so the initial reaction is out of control, according to behavioral and neural indicators (e.g., Cunningham et al., 2004; Devine, 1989; Hart et al., 2000; Lieberman, Hariri, Jarcho, Eisenberger, & Bookheimer, 2005; Phelps et al., 2000; see Eberhardt, 2005).
- Whites' efforts at control kick in immediately for most well-intentioned people (e.g., Amodio, Harmon-Jones, & Devine, 2003; Cunningham et al. 2004; Wheeler & Fiske, 2005).
- Finally, all these worries, concerns, anxieties, discomforts, failures, and cover-ups together consume cognitive capacity (Amodio et al., 2004; Cunningham et al., 2004; Lieberman et al., 2005; Richeson et al., 2003), leaving people depleted afterward (Richeson & Shelton, 2003).

Not surprisingly, this kind of affective–evaluative, relatively automatic component of White racial attitudes predicts their behavior, particularly voluntary interracial contact (Dovidio et al., 2002; Esses & Dovidio, 2002). In an ironic twist, the more White people worry about it, the more they distance themselves (Goff, Steele, & Davies, 2008), the more biased they appear (Frantz, Cuddy, Burnett, Ray, & Hart, 2004; Vorauer & Turpie, 2004), and worse they feel (Fazio & Hilden, 2001).

Because Whites are the high-status and the current majority group, if they dread intergroup contact, then they can resist such contact to a greater degree than minorities can. Indeed, Whites have few Black friends (Aboud, Mendelson, & Purdy, 2003; Hallinan & Williams, 1989; Kao & Joyner, 2004; Massey, Charles, Lundy, & Fischer, 2003). For all racial groups, intergroup anxiety and ingroup favoritism predict fewer outgroup friendships (S. Levin, van Laar, & Sidanius, 2003). However, when outgroup friendships do occur, subsequent anxiety and ingroup favoritism reliably decrease, in both longitudinal settings (S. Levin et al., 2003) and in experimentally induced friendships (Page-Gould, Mendoza-Denton, & Tropp, 2008). Both individual differences, based on childhood experiences and parental values (e.g., Towles-Schwen & Fazio, 2001), and local norms (Crandall, Eshleman, & O'Brien, 2002), shape reactions to interracial interaction dilemmas for Whites.

When the majority, higher-status Whites brave the perceived landmines, and when their Black counterparts choose to join them, interracial contact can have an especially salutary influence, under the right circumstances. Because of Whites' numerical and societal dominance, they have less interracial experience and more to learn from the right kind of contact (Tropp & Pettigrew, 2005b). According to meta-analysis, benefits accrue the more the contact is cooperative, sanctioned, to common purpose, and equal-status in the immediate situation (Pettigrew & Tropp, 2006). In keeping with the emotion-laden character of Whites' interracial experiences, contact mainly reduces affective prejudice, with cognitive adjustments catching up (Tropp & Pettigrew, 2005a). Majority groups, such as Whites, experience contact as more novel and consequently more of a shock to their affective and emotional systems.

Generally, then, Whites carry status (in the West at least), being the default citizen and linguistic standard. White prejudices toward non-Whites are abundantly documented, although improving. As with other high-status groups, Whites tend to maintain privilege through beliefs that on average more often favor ingroup dominance, tolerate inequality, conserve the status quo, and interpret racial differences as essential. Whites also maintain segregation and minimize contact with non-Whites. These reactions are not without ambivalence (I. Katz & Hass, 1988), but because fewer Whites have non-White people in their families and the interdependence is less intimate, the ambivalence is more tempered than for age and gender.

Social Class

Psychological social psychologists, as compared with their neighbors in sociology, rarely examine social class variables. Nonetheless, a growing literature uncovers some curiosities. Reaching back to our evolutionary cousins, social class perhaps resembles primate hierarchies (Sapolsky, 2004a), involving whole families across generations. Among long-term hierarchies, the most obviously social and not biological is class, which segregates people (as does race), allows mobility (as does age), and determines roles (as does gender). Although social class differs from other long-term status markers, its dynamics raise by-now familiar themes of benefits for the high status, qualified by some ambivalence, but less ambivalent than more intimate forms of interdependence. Class has its (interpersonal) privileges, as this section shows: flattering dispositional attributions for affluence, presumed competence, enhanced self-esteem, no obligation for nonverbal engagement, and an enjoyable status quo.

Dispositional attributions reward the upper classes. Unlike all three other long-term categories, which carry externally assigned or *ascribed* status, social class carries *achieved* status, allegedly earned by internal factors such as effort and talent. Unlike all three kinds of ascribed status (gender, age, and race), then, people are supposedly responsible for their social class standing: They get credit for high status and blame for low status. (Absent major medical intervention, most people are not credited and blamed for their gender, age, or race.) Although fewer studies examine how people explain wealth than how they explain poverty, some evidence favors perceived personal responsibility also for affluence. Conservatives in particular credit wealth to individual character (Furnham, 1983).

Most people have theories about how society operates, and they believe in meritocracy: Higher-status people get credit for competence, as noted earlier. Consistent with the robust phenomenon of equating status to competence, ambiguous performance gives the benefit of the doubt to upper-class students. In a classic study, undergraduates all watched the same videotaped oral exam of little Hannah, who performed variably, sometimes well and sometimes poorly, across items (Darley & Gross, 1983). Before the 12-minute videotape, they saw a six-minute tape revealing Hannah in her social-class background, either privileged (suburban, large homes, tree-lined streets, modern school, attractive playground) or not (rundown, two-family homes, asphalt schoolyard), with parents whose jobs reflected family social class as high (attorney, freelance writer) or not (meatpacker, seamstress). Participants rated Hannah's standard, mixed performance as better when she came from a higher-status background. More to the dispositional point, they credited her with better work habits in general. Even without the videotape but just given the social-class expectations, they saw her as more likely to be motivated, sociable, mature, and cognitively skilled.

As early as elementary school, children rate the academic competence of rich children as higher than poor children (Woods, Kurtz-Costes, & Rowley, 2005). Samples across cultures assign competence to both rich and middle-class people, whereas the poor appear incompetent (Cuddy et al., 2007, 2009). Although both obtain high status, rich people differ from the middle class in having both higher status and seeming less warm and trustworthy. Besides enjoying respect (if not liking), affluence acquires some flattering attributions. Implicit in the robust correlations between status and competence is the idea that the wealthy somehow deserve it. As noted earlier, experiments manipulating status confirm how competence presumptively follows from class (Caprariello et al., 2009; Oldmeadow & Fiske, 2007; A. M. Russell & Fiske, 2008). As in the case of little Hannah, higher-class people stereotypically have a good work ethic (A. M. Russell & Fiske, 2009).

Not only do other people respect the well-off, the wealthy also tend to think highly of themselves. Socioeconomic status grants high self-esteem, which increases from childhood through middle age, according to meta-analysis (Twenge & Campbell, 2002). Social class is a more salient aspect of self-concept for groups who view themselves having earned it. Hence, the correlation is higher for adults than children, for women of later birth cohorts given their greater workforce participation, for more recent immigrants with ambitions for mobility, and for occupational and educational measures of class, which reflect effort more than income does. All these patterns fit a *self-salience interpretation*, viewing class as a central part of the self, more than *reflected appraisals*, whereby others' opinions reinforce one's self-esteem.

To the extent one already enjoys respect and feels confident, one has less need to engage with others. Consistent with this interpretation (Kraus & Keltner, 2009), higher social class appears in more nonverbal cues to disengagement (doodling, self-grooming, fiddling) and fewer to engagement (gazing at one's partner, nodding, laughing, and raised eyebrows). People's social class (e.g., parent education and income) predicts their nonverbal expression of privilege, and other people know this, allowing them to detect social class from nonverbal behavior. Partly because it affords actual and experienced control over one's own outcomes, higher social class also lowers risk of depression, distress (Link, Lennon, & Dohrenwend, 1993), and illness (Adler et al., 1994), among other privileges (Lachman & Weaver, 1998). People with higher social status experience fewer negative life events and have more resources for coping with those that do occur (Adler et al., 1994). People enjoying the advantages of social status might well wish to maintain the status quo, and income does correlate with more conservative ideologies (Sidanius & Pratto, 1999).

If higher social status provides much of what people want, then they depend less on others. Certainly, the direct, daily, interpersonal interdependence of individuals from different classes is less than that of different genders or age groups, who more often inhabit the same family. Just as with race, then, ambivalence across social classes should be less evident than between genders and ages. Generally, as this section indicates, higher status buys privilege: dispositional attributions for affluence, presumed competence, self-esteem, nonverbal freedom from engagement, and enjoying the status quo.

Summary of Lifelong Status Effects

This section commenced with a question—namely, How do the long-term effects of status overlap and differ for some salient groups, including gender, age, race, and class? The correlational evidence for these effects necessarily differs from the experimental evidence for effects of short-term status. Nevertheless, much of the message is the same: On the whole, higher status carries undeniable privileges, as it does for short-term status. Short-term status, as noted previously, garners attention, access, credit, respect, and agenda setting. Long-term status works much the same way.

However, long-term status reveals a complexity less obvious in short-term encounters—namely, ambivalence. Over a lifetime, even high-status people become acutely aware of their dependence on those lower in status. The moderating effects of interdependence on status particularly appear in intimate interdependence within the family, as occurs with gender and age. Both men and middle-aged people have more respect, wealth, and influence than their counterparts, maintaining on average more system-sustaining ideologies but at the same time cherishing their less lucky intimates. For status relations that are less intimate, Whites and higher classes enjoy favorable outcomes but experience less ambivalence toward those of lower rank.

POWER: VIEWS FROM THE TOP

Power, defined earlier as controlling valued resources, often correlates with status, the respect accorded by society. Yet power and status do not always correlate, as in the earlier-cited lame-duck official who retains the title but no longer as many resources, once a successor appears. The opposite example would be a low-status underling who acts as a powerful gatekeeper. Power's effects overlap but remain distinct from status effects. Because virtually all the social psychology of power entails experimental data, this section focuses on short-term phenomena that dissect the interpersonal dynamics of power difference. Where relevant, the section notes parallel effects of dominant personalities, who over time presume power over others.

Power has excited sharply contrasting viewpoints that even so come together (Brauer & Bourhis, 2006; Fiske & Berdahl, 2007; Magee & Galinsky, 2008). Roughly, the major perspectives translate as follows: Power liberates, versus power corrupts, which finally unite as power focuses the mind.

Power Liberates

In this view, powerful people have a wonderful life: Their *behavioral approach system* runs in full gear, because the world affords control, rewards, and opportunities (Keltner et al., 2003). Many of the blissful reactions to controlling resources (or feeling personally dominant) are mediated by a subjective sense of personal power (Anderson & Berdahl, 2002). The variety of liberating effects is impressive, as this section reviews.

Powerful people feel and express positive affect (Keltner et al., 2003). In one experiment, three-person groups discussed an emotion-laden topic (explanations for poverty), with one person publicly assigned to lead the group and distribute prize money. Leadership appeared legitimate (based on participant background questionnaires), but in fact was random. High-power individuals reported and expressed more positive emotions and less anger than did the less powerful (Berdahl & Martorana, 2006). Similar effects occur for both personality dominance and situational manipulations of resource control (Anderson & Berdahl, 2002).

To the extent that power matters only if others perceive it, the good feelings should come from control ascribed by other people. In any dyad, each partner perceives the other's level of power. In a correlational study, romantic partners each rated their partner's general influence over them in the relationship, allowing researchers to separate each person's perception of the other person's power within each couple (Langner & Keltner, 2008). People's power, as perceived by their partner, indeed predicted their own experienced positive affect in conversations about the couple's relationship; that is, people rated as powerful in the relationship were the same ones who reported more positive affect in the conversation. However, the partner's perception of that other person's power predicted negative affect for the partner's own self; that is, feeling that one's partner has a lot of power predicts experiences of negative emotion during an interaction. Because these data are correlational, a follow-up experiment randomly assigned one dyad member (high power) to interview and evaluate the other (low power) and found the same effects: High sense of own power generated positive affect, whereas a high sense of partner power separately generated negative affect.

Why are powerholders so cheerful? They see rewards everywhere (Keltner et al., 2003) because they recognize that they have access to resources, both material and social. Personally dominant and situationally powerful people both perceive their partners as liking them more (Anderson & Berdahl, 2002), and they enjoy a partner who ingratiates, that is, seeks to be likable and aims to please (Operario & Fiske, 2001). The powerful should in general see opportunities everywhere.

The approach system activates to opportunities afforded the powerful. Power researchers have operationalized the approach system in a variety of ways. The most straightforward is action orientation. For example (Galinsky, Gruenfeld, & Magee, 2003), studies can either manipulate structural power (i.e., dyadic resource control) or prime past experiences of holding power. The powerful then take the extra card in blackjack, move the annoying fan that disrupts their current task, and take action in a social dilemma regardless of the pro- or anti-social consequences. The powerful also express their true attitudes more freely (Anderson & Berdahl, 2002; Berdahl & Martorana, 2006), initiate competition (Magee, Galinsky, & Gruenfeld, 2007), and take risks (Anderson & Galinsky, 2006). The risk-seeking behavior of powerholders has limits, notably for dominant personalities whose position of power may be in jeopardy (Maner, Gailliot, Butz, & Peruche, 2007), perhaps because their action orientation is tempered by a concern for holding onto power.

Other people also recognize powerholders by their action orientation, whether in personal or policy decisions, in small groups and in organizations, in decisions to act and actual actions (Magee, 2009). In the long term, extraversion (a personality oriented toward sheer social activity) relatedly predicts perceived status (Anderson, John, Keltner, & Kring, 2001). Ironically, the last people to understand the two-way action–power link may be the powerholders themselves. Despite the findings that other people recognize them by their activity, the link appears unconscious for the powerholder (Pamela K. Smith & Bargh, 2008), who more often responds automatically (Keltner et al., 2003).

Along with being cheerful and action-oriented, powerholders typically do wield influence (French & Raven, 1959), creating a self-reinforcing world. For example, powerholders can influence subordinates to confirm their expectancies about them (Copeland, 1994). Although powerholders may be motivated to get to know the other, this often entails checking out their expectations and confirming a stable impression, so powerholder motivations merely confirm expectations, both perceptually and behaviorally (Snyder & Haugen, 1994, 1995; Snyder & Kiviniemi, 2001).

Generally, powerholders are confident in their preexisting ideas or, when newly persuaded, they may become equally confident in their new ideas (Briñol, Petty, Valle, Rucker, & Becerra, 2007). Either way, they self-validate. Powerholders have confidence in their internal states (Anderson & Galinsky, 2006; Weick & Guinote, 2008). This self-sufficiency spills over to freedom from outside influence, under some circumstances (Galinsky, Magee, Gruenfeld, Whitson, & Liljenquist, 2008; Overbeck, Tiedens, & Brion, 2006).

Generally, powerholders display a variety of self-assured action orientations: They feel and express positive affect, see rewards, operate on approach, generate activity, feel confident, and are immune to influence. All this sounds well and good, but another interpretation is that the powerful are often clueless at best and narcissistic at worst.

Power Corrupts

Predating the rosy view of power, earlier perspectives had taken a grimmer viewpoint. In a *metamorphic theory of power*, Kipnis (1972, 1976; Kipnis, Castell, Gergen, & Mauch, 1976) studied participants given legitimate power in a number of experiments: All participants were titled "managers", paid more than subordinates, responsible for outcomes, and more prestigious than the "workers," but only some powerholders controlled subordinates' raises, penalties, job transfer, and firing. The more powerful managers worked harder to influence subordinates, derogated their motivation, devalued their work, kept their distance, and viewed them as easily manipulated objects. In any interpersonal interaction, people overestimate their own agency and underestimate the agency of those they influence (Gilbert, Jones, & Pelham, 1987). Powerholders especially view themselves as causal, even if their control is illusory (Fast, Gruenfeld, Sivanathan, & Galinsky, 2009). Moreover, illusory control in turn raises people's self-regard, optimism, and action orientation. As power levels increase, evaluations of others become increasingly negative, and evaluations of the self become increasingly positive, according to meta-analysis (Georgesen & Harris, 1998). Both perceiver and target awareness of the power relationship increase its effects (Georgesen & Harris, 2000), as does the powerholder feeling threatened (Georgesen & Harris, 2006).

Analyzing power as actual command of resources, Fiske (1993) proposed the *power-as-control theory*. Because powerholders by definition depend less on others, because they may be personally motivated to dominate others, and because their underlings outnumber them, they are vulnerable to a host of unpleasant biases. Most boil down to being undermotivated to pay attention to those below, whether by default (too busy) or by design (to maintain one's position). The *by-default process* fits being clueless, whereas the *by-design process* fits motivated cognition. Powerholders do tend to stereotype more than individuate their subordinates (Goodwin, Gubin, Fiske, & Yzerbyt, 2000). Moreover, when motivated to suppress their stereotypes, they experience suppression difficulty, which translates to exaggerated postsuppression rebound; perhaps concluding that they must want to use the stereotypes, they later express stereotypes more than do the less powerful (Guinote, 2007c). Powerholders' stereotyping holds especially for negative stereotypes and for illegitimate power positions, consistent with threatened powerholders being motivated to legitimate their positions through demeaning stereotypes to (Rodríguez Bailón, Moya, & Yzerbyt, 2000). Thus, besides being unconstrained from taking the easy default way out, powerholders may be actively motivated by the status quo to defend their position.

Indeed, powerful people appear relentlessly self-oriented, rather than other-oriented, focusing on their own perspective (Galinsky, Magee, Inesi, & Gruenfeld, 2006). Powerholders may treat others instrumentally (Gruenfeld, Inesi, Magee, & Galinsky, 2008) and not notice their relatively impotent anger (Anderson & Berdahl, 2002). Under some circumstances at least, powerful people are less accurate about their underlings than vice versa (Ebenbach & Keltner, 1998; Keltner & Robinson, 1997). They show less distress and compassion for others' suffering (van Kleef et al., 2008). This follows from simple inattention downward (Fiske, 1993).

At the individual level, a variety of power-related effects conspire toward power accumulating more power (Magee & Galinsky, 2008), stabilizing the hierarchy (Gruenfeld & Tiedens, this volume). So far, this grim litany has included controlling subordinates, derogating them, failing to individuate them, and undermining their agency, all the while being instrumental.

What is worse, powerholders are prone to exploiting others. As noted, powerholders treat others instrumentally, in that, for example, when primed with power and oriented toward rewards, people are more likely to approach an unappealing but competent partner than otherwise (Gruenfeld et al., 2008). More directly, although most partners in commons games orient toward equal division of resources, leaders self-appropriate more than followers do, and they do so from a reported sense of entitlement (De Cremer & van Dijk, 2005).

Even in more intimate encounters, high-power partners tease in more hostile ways (Keltner, Capps, Kring, Young, & Heerey, 2001). Teasing often arises out of norm violations and conflicts, so the higher-status teasing implicitly sanctions and controls the lower-status partner. More overt intimate exploitation emerges in sexual harassment. When subliminally primed with power, men already inclined to sexually harass (high on a scale of likelihood to sexually harass) find a female subordinate more sexually attractive (Bargh, Raymond, Pryor, & Strack, 1995). Men individually high in power motivation, with a strong power–sex association, report more sexual aggression against women (Zurbriggen, 2000). The most probable sexual harassers are men who are particularly motivated to maintain their status as men, that is, highly gender-identified but threatened (Maass, Cadinu, Guarnieri, & Grasselli, 2003), consistent with the power dynamics of sexual harassment. Of course, quid-pro-quo harassment, the most obvious form of sexual harassment, involves a powerholder making resources contingent on sexual favors.

Overt discrimination works better if one actually possesses the resource to bestow selectively. Hence, powerholders (who by definition control resources) can discriminate more effectively than the powerless. In the *minimal group paradigm* (groups defined by merely arbitrary categories; see Yzerbyt & Demoulin, this volume), powerful group members do allocate fewer resources to others, and they report feeling comfortable and satisfied (Sachdev & Bourhis, 1985). High-status minority powerholders discriminate the most (Sachdev & Bourhis, 1991). Moreover, people who prefer power also see others as power-motivated (Schmid-Mast, Hall, & Ickes, 2006), creating a competitive environment.

All these bleak tendencies of powerholders are nevertheless malleable, depending on both person and situation. Generally, all these antisocial effects mitigate when *social responsibility*—obligation to others—is salient. Shortly after the admittedly paranoid power-as-control theory hit the stands (Fiske, 1993), various studies discovered more optimistic exceptions. Various individual differences moderate power's effects: Powerholders who are individually relationship-oriented respond more favorably than those who are individually exchange-oriented (S. Chen, Lee-Chai, & Bargh, 2001). Leaders take more for themselves only if they have a pro-self orientation, not a pro-social one (van Dijk & De Cremer, 2006). Powerholders high on interdependence (either chronically or temporarily primed) are more generous in dyadic dispute negotiations (Howard, Gardner, & Thompson, 2007).

Contexts that emphasize powerholders' duty to others also mitigate abuses: Leaders take more joint resources for themselves if appointed, but not if elected, because then they have more felt social responsibility (De Cremer & van Dijk, 2008). Although appointed powerholders generally take more, this reverses when their partner has absolutely no power whatsoever, making temporary powerholders sensitive to the asymmetry (Handgraaf, van Dijk, Vermunt, Wilke, & De Dreu, 2008). In settings that focus on the people involved, rather than the organization, product, and outcome, powerholders accordingly attune to the other as an individual (Overbeck & Park, 2001). Parallel results occur in contexts that are caretaking (health care) versus more competitive (conflict) (Magee & Langner, 2008). Priming social responsibility (egalitarian values) motivates powerholders to individuate and thus to bring their behavior in line with internal standards (Goodwin et al., 2000). Overall, when power-holders are primed with responsibility or attuned to their internal values, they are more likely to individuate the less powerful—they are more accuracy motivated.

To be sure, then, powerholders may be governed by a sense of responsibility. Sometimes indeed this becomes a burden. Both observers and powerholders perceive power to afford more control over the powerholder's own behavior (Magee, 2009), so their choices can produce the discomfort of internal conflict (Galinsky et al., 2008). In particular, if they have no legitimate explanation for their position, powerholders feel guilt and unease (Pamela K. Smith, Jost, & Vijay, 2008). Similarly, powerful group members who see their group's position as illegitimate also feel guilt and shame (for a review, see Yzerbyt & Demoulin, this volume).

Sometimes, the powerholders have good reason to feel uneasy. As they freely act on their own interests, no one dares to criticize (see later section on subordination). Being in power results in a lack of feedback. Can this possibly be good?

Power Focuses

Does power liberate one to act freely or corrupt one to abuse others? Perhaps both. Power focuses people on whatever high-level goals they want to follow, for good or ill (Fiske & Berdahl, 2007). Powerful people, being in control, can be flexible, attend to the big picture, and not sweat the details. Powerholders are free to focus on their goals and not worry about much else.

Powerful people concentrate. They more flexibly focus their attention by goal relevance, avoiding distractions, which enables them to act effectively (Guinote, 2007a). Powerholders focus on their own ideas, rather than being influenced by others, showing innovative creativity, independence from conformity, relying on their own social values (regardless of others' reputations), and exercising greater choice in their behavior (Galinsky et al., 2008).

Executives execute. That is, powerholders exercise some effective *executive functions*, specifically, updating information (Pamela K. Smith, Jostmann, Galinsky, & van Dijk, 2008).

Powerholders also use the available. Power makes people more likely to judge based on their momentary subjective experience of what easily comes to mind (Weick & Guinote, 2008). Power also makes people more responsive to what the situation affords, in a series of studies (Guinote, 2008). Undergraduates assigned randomly (but apparently legitimately, based on a test) to high power were more likely to plan as the situation suggested: work for weekdays and leisure for weekends, and in another study to plan work for an imaginary internship and socializing for a friend's imaginary visit. Using the minimal group paradigm, people assigned to be the majority (typically powerful) also planned imaginary activities by situational affordances. Undergraduates imagining themselves to be managers (rather than subordinates) planned a summer day with more active, extraverted, cheerful, outdoor activities, compared with planning a winter's day. In another study, undergraduates, first primed to think of their powerful selves, then planned their first day of summer holiday, focusing on situationally relevant leisure activities, undistracted by the irrelevancies of academic duty. In a final study, power-primed undergraduates also attended more selectively to such situation-relevant information (tourism for a friend's imagined visit, work activities for an internship). Altogether, relative to the less powerful, powerholders took more advantage of what each situation afforded.

Consistent with powerholders' focus on the most salient goal, they also focus on the more abstract, higher levels of thought. Because power increases psychological distance, it elevates thinking to the more abstract: emphasizing gist, primary patterns, and higher-level categorizations, as well as activating the brain's right hemisphere (Pamela K. Smith & Trope, 2006). The power-abstraction link is so strong that the reverse also holds; priming abstract thinking increases feelings of power (Pamela K. Smith, Wigboldus, & Dijksterhuis, 2008).

Summary

Power concentrates the mind. All these patterns favor powerholders enacting their goals (e.g., Guinote, 2007b). An earlier section noted that powerholders orient toward action; this section has specified further: They tend to enact higher-level goals, being less distracted by irrelevancy. The focusing effects of power help to explain both the earlier views that power corrupts (powerholders neglect their irrelevant subordinates) and that power liberates (they follow their own salient goals). Because powerholders respond to situational affordances, they behave more variably than the less powerful (Guinote, Judd, & Brauer, 2002). This can drive their subordinates to distraction, as the next section indicates.

SUBORDINATION: LOOKING UP FROM THE BOTTOM

This final section combines low power and low status because most of the work on power reflects short-term manipulations (as just reviewed for powerholders), and most of the work on status reflects long-term lower status. Also, the perspective of the oppressed appears elsewhere in this volume (see treatment in chapters by Dovidio & Gaertner regarding minorities, Gruenfeld & Tiedens regarding role internalization; Jost & Kay on system justification, Swann & Bosson regarding stigma and attributional ambiguity, Yzerbyt & Demoulin regarding low status) and in other reviews (Crocker et al., 1998; S. Levin & van Laar, 2006; Major & O'Brien, 2005; Shelton, 2003; Swim & Stangor, 1998). The current review differs from the others cited: Beyond the well-documented short- and long-term disadvantages, subordinates may even create some unexpected advantages for themselves.

Short-Term Consequences of Being Subordinate

Defining power as resource control leads to a straightforward short-term prediction—namely, the powerless will attend to those who do control valued resources in an effort to increase their own prediction and potential influence over their own outcomes (Fiske & Dépret, 1996; Fiske & Neuberg, 1990; Guinote, Brown, & Fiske, 2006). Being low on power demonstrably changes one's sense of control (Fiske & Dépret, 1996), as does being a minority (Guinote, Brown, & Fiske, 2006). As this section indicates, the less powerful attend up, individuate, strive for accuracy, and feel anxious; they also accommodate the more powerful, experiencing hassles, harassment, and aggression. They may envy the powerful. However, the less powerful sometimes enjoy side benefits: being treasured or nurtured, becoming accurate or detail-oriented, and understanding how others view them.

Vigilance

Being *outcome dependent* captures people's attention. The decreased control over resources makes people compensate by seeking information about those who do control what matters, whether money, recognition, love, reassurance, or safety. In an early study (Erber & Fiske, 1984), participants expected to create educational games with wind-up

toys, collaborating with an education-student confederate who admitted to being probably either skilled or not. The participants and their partners could win cash creativity prizes either separately for their individual work or together for their joint work. Beforehand, they read a series of peer teaching evaluations that were mixed, that is, both positive and negative. When outcome-dependent, participants selectively attended to the most diagnostic information about their partner, that is, expectancy-inconsistent reports. Moreover, they individuated, drawing dispositional inferences about that unique individual, and their evaluations became more idiosyncratic to themselves as perceivers, showing that they used the information to draw their own conclusions. Outcome-dependency per se, not just being a team, is key: Negatively correlated outcomes (i.e., individual competitions, also interdependent) show similar effects (Ruscher & Fiske, 1990; Ruscher, Fiske, Miki, & Van Manen, 1991). These effects moderate according to perceivers' expected possibility of control (Dépret & Fiske, 1999; Ruscher & Fiske, 1990), underlining its functional motivation. Attention and individuation likewise function for people with asymmetrical outcome dependency, that is, when people only depend on their partners but not vice versa, so the effects do not result from responsibility for one's partner (Dépret & Fiske, 1999; Goodwin et al., 2000; Stevens & Fiske, 2000).

Accuracy motivation both mediates (Neuberg & Fiske, 1987) and moderates (Dépret & Fiske, 1999; Ruscher & Fiske, 1990) outcome dependency's effects on how low-power people form impressions of powerholders. That is, dependency apparently operates through accuracy motivation to affect attention and inferences. Consistent with this path, dependency under low accuracy motivation does not promote vigilance. People apparently control impression-formation processes, depending on goals (Fiske & Von Hendy, 1992). Low-power people generally try to be more accurate and gather information that would allow them to be more accurate, and sometimes they succeed (Neuberg & Fiske, 1987), although sometimes they fall prey to wishful thinking (Goodwin, Fiske, Rosen, & Rosenthal, 2002; Stevens & Fiske, 2000). Nonetheless, they try. Subordinates better recall some of their superiors' nonverbal behavior and rate their behavior more accurately than vice versa (e.g., Hall, Carter, & Horgan, 2001). Indeed, people chronically (by personality) low on dominance use more accurate cues to make hiring decisions (Operario & Fiske, 2001).

Consistent with the idea of dependency-driven accuracy motivation, less powerful negotiators ask more diagnostic questions of their partners, as a result of greater accuracy and impression motivation (De Dreu & van Kleef, 2004). Further, in a job interview, accuracy-motivated interviewers give their interviewee more opportunities to belie an expectancy (Neuberg, 1989), consistent with the idea that control-induced accuracy motives make people seek not only information (Pittman & D'Agostino, 1989; Pittman & Pittman, 1980) but also more diagnostic information (Swann, Stephenson, & Pittman, 1981). Granted, low-power perceivers sometimes perceive what is not there: Low-power's control-deprivation induces people to see patterns where none exist (Whitson & Galinsky, 2008). The brain appears oriented toward processing the intentions of those up the hierarchy (Zink, Tong, Chen, Bassett, Stein, & Meyer-Lindenberg, 2008), whether accurate or not. For the powerless, more generally, their dependence motivates them to observe the powerful, trying to understand the contingencies for receiving valued outcomes.

Both contingency and vigilance take their toll. Low-power group members report performance anxiety, according to meta-analysis (Mullen, 1985). Low power specifically impairs certain executive functions; low-power individuals do not as effectively update, inhibit irrelevancies, and plan (Pamela K. Smith et al., 2008). Further, low power theoretically may inhibit activity (Keltner et al., 2003), though experiments are scarce.

Moving to correlational inferences about subordination, a variety of low-power (or strictly, low-status) groups show apparent vigilance and its consequences. Strongly identified minorities especially experience interracial interactions aware of possibly encountering racism (Hyers & Swim, 1998; Operario & Fiske, 2001; Sellers & Shelton, 2003; Shelton, 2000). Although individuals and contexts differ, Blacks more commonly believe in the reality of discrimination compared with Whites (see Dovidio, Gaertner, Kawakami, & Hodson, 2002, for a review). Actual intergroup interaction brings concern about encountering racism, which requires active coping (Shelton, 2003) and exacts a toll on highly identified (ingroup-favoring) Blacks (Richeson, Trawalter, & Shelton, 2005). In such interactions, low-power victimized groups often seek status and power (Shnabel & Nadler, 2008; Shnabel et al., 2008), which entails respect (Fiske et al., 2009), so they are selectively contingent on their interaction partner in that sense.

Whites, even as the higher-status majority, can also feel contingent in interracial interactions, because they fear appearing racist (Frantz et al., 2004; Goff et al., 2008; Shelton et al., 2006). Most Whites do not want to appear prejudiced (Dunton & Fazio, 1997; Plant & Devine, 1998); prevention requires monitoring their behavior (Shelton, 2000). They become more inhibited, more distant, and show more implicit prejudice, under threat of appearing racist. The cost to executive function occurs for the most ingroup-favoring Whites (Richeson et al., 2003; Richeson & Shelton, 2003). No wonder one of the important intergroup emotions for Whites is anxiety (as noted earlier; Stephan & Stephan, 2000) because as the high-power

group, they seek public moral affirmation (Shnabel & Nadler, 2008; Shnabel et al., 2008). Whites may want Black people to like them because they associate a Black person's dislike with that person believing they are prejudiced (Winslow, 2004). Each side's expectation about the other's prejudice depends on salience and meaning of group membership, so it differs for minorities and majorities (Tropp & Bianchi, 2007).

Another relatively low-status group, in societal terms, shows arguably related contingency effects. Although girls and boys, women and men, interact too often to feel anxious each time, some gender differences in behavior fit the vigilance interpretation. For example, girls show more inhibition and perceptual sensitivity, according to meta-analyses (Else-Quest et al., 2006). Highly identified women may be indicated by high scores on ambivalence toward men (Glick & Fiske, 1999); they emphasize male dominance. Women's ambivalence toward men relates to not valuing their own self-direction (Feather, 2004), potentially relevant to vigilance, inhibition, and low perceived control. These interpretations await empirical test.

Accommodation

In experiments, lower-power people adjust to higher-power people. For example (Galinsky et al., 2003), in a commons dilemma, low-power people shared resources better than did powerholders. Subordinates are motivated to have an agreeable interaction (Copeland, 1994) and to get along with powerholders (Snyder & Kiviniemi, 2001). Low-power negotiators notice and consider their opponent's emotion more than do powerful negotiators (van Kleef, De Dreu, & Manstead, 2004; van Kleef, De Dreu, Pietroni, & Manstead, 2006). In close relationships, the lower-power partner adopts the emotions of the more powerful partner (Anderson, Keltner, & John, 2003). More generally, close-relationship dependence promotes strong commitment, which in turn promotes pro-relationship behavior (Wieselquist, Rusbult, Foster, & Agnew, 1999). Even outside intimacy, the less personally dominant and less situationally powerful decision makers accommodate the more dominant and powerful, going along with their preferences (Anderson & Berdahl, 2002), although personal-belief strength can limit accommodation (Berdahl & Martorana, 2006). Low status and female gender predict avoidant responses to incivility, arguably related to accommodation (Porath et al., 2008).

Indeed, low status demands verbal accommodation, otherwise known as polite address. As noted earlier, power affects language, with low-power speakers being more polite than high-power speakers (Holtgraves, this volume; Ng & Bradac, 1993). For example, low-status people make more polite requests, queries, reminders, complaints, critiques, explanations, and bad-news delivery (see Holtgraves, this volume). Low-power people request less directly and assert less forcefully, both of which accommodate the listener's comfort and decrease potential conflict. Because the low-power speaker has less chance of prevailing in a conflict anyway, perhaps this strategy is functional in a stable power structure.

Hassles, Harassment, Aggression

Subordinates experience various unpleasant interactions. According to the rules for communicating status, covered earlier, dominant, high-status, or high-power people can freely monopolize, offend, discount, and otherwise control subordinates in interactions (unless of course the power-holders' sense of social responsibility happens to be especially accessible, as noted earlier).

Everyday hassles plague women as one societally low-status group. College women reported one or two sexist incidents per week in a diary study (Swim, Hyers, Cohen, & Ferguson, 2001). These experiences of stereotyping, prejudice, degrading comments, and sexual objectification undermined their well-being. Although most women did not respond directly, they stewed privately (Swim & Hyers, 1999). Failures to confront such disrespect likely stemmed from diffused responsibility, normative pressures, politeness norms, and potential retaliation. Such low-grade but tiresome hassles torment many low-status groups.

Interpersonal disrespect and harassment reinforces gender hierarchy (Berdahl, 2007a). For example, harassment targets agentic ("masculine") women more than traditionally feminine women in university and workplace alike (Berdahl, 2007b). Ethnic minority women suffer both sex-based and race-based harassment (Berdahl & Moore, 2006). Although men can be targets of sexual harassment, they do not react as negatively, perhaps feeling less threatened, except for sexual coercion by either male or female perpetrators (Berdahl, Magley, & Waldo, 1996; Waldo, Berdahl, & Fitzgerald, 1998). One form of male–male harassment also enforces gender status systems, as when *not-man-enough harassment* imposes conventional gender roles (Berdahl et al., 1996). Overt sabotage of uppity women also reinforces gender hierarchy, as when agentic women elicit backlash, reviewed earlier (e.g., Rudman & Fairchild, 2004; Rudman & Glick, 2001). Even more direct evidence of harassment as protecting gender hierarchies comes from findings that the men most likely to harass are the highly identified ones whose male identity feels threatened as insufficiently legitimate, valued, or distinctive (Maass, Cadinu, Guarnieri, & Grasselli, 2003). Egalitarian women are particularly at risk (Dall'Ara & Maass, 1999).

Besides these *hard power* forms of aggression, *soft power* can patronize women, which selectively sabotages them in traditionally male domains (e.g., athletic competition, strategic planning). For example, praise without substantive rewards angers both men and women but undermines only women's performance (Vescio, Gervais, Snyder, & Hoover, 2005). As another example, excessive kindness can damage performance, if it comes in the form of paternalistic benevolent sexism, which then creates intrusive doubts that damage women's performance (Dardenne, Dumont, & Bollier, 2007). The power relevance of all this soft-power toxicity comes from evidence that power interacts with prejudice, such that female stereotypes include weakness and therefore fit subordination; thus powerful men (but not women) use stereotype-based influence strategies that stifle women in masculine domains (Vescio, Snyder, & Butz, 2003).

Related interpersonal hassles and racial harassment plague Blacks. In the specific case of interpersonal, power-related events, specifically low-power Black people get derogated by powerful, prejudiced Whites in stereotypic domains such as academic performance (Vescio, Heidenreich, & Snyder, 2005). Everyday racial hassles, as reported in Black students' daily diaries, include verbal insults, bad service, hostile glares, and disrupted interactions (that is, rude, awkward, or nervous: Swim, Hyers, Cohen, Fitzgerald, & Bylsma, 2003). These incidents evoke threat, discomfort, anger, and confrontation. More generally, such micro-aggressions reveal modern racism in interpersonal interactions (Pettigrew, 1989; see Dovidio & Gaertner, this volume).

Worse of course are immediate impulses to interpret all Black men as dangerous criminals, with potentially murderous consequences. Racial bias facilitates split-second decisions to shoot unarmed Black men (Correll, Park, Judd, & Wittenbrink, 2002; Correll, Urland, & Ito, 2006). Because people instantly associate Black men's faces with crime (Eberhardt, Goff, Purdie, & Davies, 2004), this infects the criminal justice system (Eberhardt et al., 2006). Even beyond police encounters, automatic racial associations contaminate civilian interracial encounters, heightening tension on both sides. No surprise, then, that Blacks incur cognitive costs after interracial interaction (especially if they are highly identified; Richeson et al., 2005).

People from lower social classes also suffer everyday hassles, harassment, and aggression. For example, nonpoor people distance themselves from poor people (for a review, see Lott, 2002). A variety of stereotypes haunt cross-class encounters, which reportedly include insults, exclusion, and humiliation. People who are not poor experience physiological threat reactions to people of lower social classes, comparable to their cross-race threat responses, even during cooperative interactions (Blascovich, Spencer, Quinn, & Steele, 2001). Class and race appear to operate additively.

Exposure to prejudice understandably makes people feel distressed, anxious, angry, and agitated (Branscombe, Schmitt, & Harvey, 1999; Dion & Earn, 1975; Sellers & Shelton, 2003; Swim et al., 2003; Tropp, 2003). No surprise that low power more generally predicts negative emotion, as noted (Langner & Keltner, 2008). Beyond interpersonal hassles, harassment, and aggression, of course, low-status groups suffer life-determining discrimination on an intergroup scale (see Wood & Eagly, volume 1; Dovidio & Gaertner and Yzerbyt & Demovlin this volume), as well as on a societal scale, measured in education, housing, wages, and health (e.g., Massey, 2007).

Envy

Subordinates are vulnerable to a particular negative emotion—namely, envy. Social competition generally can create envy, frustration, anger, and fear (Yzerbyt & Demoulin, this volume). Envy especially targets competitive upward comparison (R. H. Smith, 2008; R. H. Smith & Kim, 2007). In intergroup space, people report that the competitive, high-status groups elicit envy (e.g., Fiske et al., 2002), and photographs of individuals from those groups (e.g., a rich person) elicit self-reports of envy (Harris & Fiske, 2006). At least sometimes, people reveal unconscious preferences for high-status groups (Jost, Pelham, & Carvallo, 2002). However, subjective injustice about the relative positions is the key to envy (R. H. Smith, Parrott, Ozer, & Moniz, 1994), perhaps underlying its famously corrosive effects. Envy is "an unpleasant, often painful emotion characterized by feelings of inferiority, hostility, and resentment, caused by an awareness of a desired attribute enjoyed by another" (R. H. Smith & Kim, 2008, p. 46), so it may be an inherent risk of low status, which is arguably not good for mental health (R. H. Smith, Combs, & Thielke, 2008).

Envy does not necessarily entail resentment because people can aspire to resemble the envied other. *Benign envy* admittedly frustrates but also motivates. Benign envy, a distinction understood even by those whose language does not have separate words for the benign and malicious kinds, involves wanting the self to move up. *Malicious envy* involves wanting to move the other downward (van de Ven, Zeelenberg, & Rik, 2009). If social comparisons conclude that the superior other's position is self-relevant, then people will forfeit self-interest to bring down the other (Turner, Brown, & Tajfel, 1979). *Schadenfreude*—pleasure at the other's misfortune—entails resentment (Feather & Naim, 2005; Feather & Sherman, 2002) and targets envied outgroups (Cikara, Botvinik, & Fiske, 2009). Being dominated in a competition, especially in an apparently illegitimate outcome, produces ill feelings such as envy, as well as frustration, and anger (Mikula, Scherer, & Athenstaedt, 1998).

Protection

For symmetry, one might ask whether subordination has any benefits. If the hierarchy reflects stable, cooperative interdependence perceived as legitimate, then low status or low power might enable a kind of relaxation, allowing oneself to be cherished, protected, and tended (see Yzerbyt & Demoulin, this volume). Ambivalent sexism's *benevolent sexism* (BS) recognizes that even women can endorse BS (Glick & Fiske, 1996), although not typically as much as men do. In the most sexist settings, women may endorse BS more than men, because a pedestal still looks better than the gutter (Z. Chen, Fiske, & Lee, 2009; Glick et al., 2000). During courtship, even in more traditional settings, both genders may endorse BS over *hostile sexism* (HS), although traditional marriage norms may turn out to have more HS, with its dominative hierarchy (Z. Chen et al., 2009). Benevolence predicts people's romantic ideals (Lee, Fiske, & Glick, 2010).

Of course, being subordinate in the ideal and actual case may differ considerably. When resources are provided, lower-power groups may thrive. For example, women, minorities, and lower classes make better use of information to guide their preventive health behavior, if provided training; the training makes less difference to higher-status groups (see Albarracin & Vargas, volume 1; Durantini et al., 2006). Explicit remediation, however, has its costs, depending on the message of inferiority versus challenge (e.g., Cohen, Steele, & Ross, 1999).

Accuracy

Besides potential emotional benefits of receiving care, subordinates have more opportunity for accuracy, for example, in forming impressions. Work reviewed earlier notes their attention upward, focus on diagnostic information, and motivation to be accurate, to gain a sense of prediction and possible influence. A focus on details instead of abstractions provides the possibility of accuracy in impressions.

Moreover, less powerful people are better at taking the role of others and knowing how they themselves appear, according to the flip side of the work reviewed earlier regarding powerholders. Perspective-taking specifically allows the powerless to understand how others stereotype them, for instance (Lammers, Gordijn, & Otten, 2008). Understanding how one is seen has advantages and disadvantages because although one might be accurate, it punctures illusions.

Conclusions Regarding Short-Term Effects of Subordination

Although low power and low status might have some silver linings (potential accuracy, protection, and striving to improve), most of the short-term effects appear frankly unappealing: vigilance, accommodation, micro and macro aggressions, and corrosive envy. In the long-term, the sheer accumulation can be especially bad.

Long-Term Consequences of Being Subordinate

In the last decades of the 20th century, social psychologists expanded their focus from the prejudiced perpetrators to the stigmatized targets (Crocker et al., 1998; S. Levin & van Laar, 2006; Major & O'Brien, 2005; Shelton, 2003; Swim & Stangor, 1998). Consequently, the literature on long-term costs of subordinate status is clear-cut and reviewed elsewhere, fortunately, because space limits its full acknowledgment here (as noted earlier, see chapters by Dovidio & Gaertner regarding minorities; Gruenfeld & Tiedens regarding role internalization; Jost & Kay on system justification; Swann & Bosson regarding stigma and attributional ambiguity; Yzerbyt & Demoulin regarding low status). Nevertheless, some outlines here provide useful closure to this chapter's story of stratification.

Reputational Threat

Consensus regarding the stigma of marked status as inferior developed following Goffman's (1963) book and Edward E. Jones et al.'s (1984) book, both focused on the interpersonal phenomena of subordinate status. Group subordination goes by the earlier-noted term tribal stigma, whereas individual lack of power typifies all the stigmatized (Edward E. Jones et al., 1984). Reputational threat conceivably varies by a stigma's concealability, time course, disruptiveness, responsibility, and peril (Edward E. Jones et al., 1984). Although subsequent analyses did not mostly focus on these dimensions per se, this and contemporaneous work focused on *expectancy confirmation*, whereby targets inadvertently conform to stereotypes that the more powerful perceiver communicates nonverbally (Edward E. Jones, 1990; Major & O'Brien, 2005). Subsequently, new major streams of research did emerge, among them two noted here.

The first stream, *attributional ambiguity*, reflects uncertainty about whether one's outcomes reflect oneself as an individual or as a member of a stigmatized group (Crocker & Major, 1989). Blaming discrimination for an overtly negative event may buffer self-esteem in the moment, but it backfires for positive outcomes, does not work well for subtle prejudice, does not sit well with others, and does not provide veridical knowledge of feedback (for review, see Major & O'Brien, 2005).

The second research stream, *stereotype threat*, describes the effect of stereotypes in the air, which endanger people targeted by those ambient beliefs. Knowing one might confirm the cultural stereotype undermines performance through a variety of mechanisms distinct from expectancy confirmation. That is, stereotype threat likely interferes via added pressure, self-integrity protection, and stereotype priming (for reviews, see Spencer, Logel, & Davies, 2010; Steele, Spencer, & Aronson, 2002). Unlike expectancy confirmation, one does not have to encounter a prejudiced person to worry about confirming a cultural stereotype.

All kinds of reputational threats invoke immediate physiological responses (Major & O'Brien, 2005); the low-status groups' stress and coping endanger self-esteem and health, as the previous sections indicate. The link between reputational threat and physiological stress also appears in experiments. Stereotype threat links to cardiovascular reactivity, alike for Blacks (Blascovich et al., 2001) and for women (Vick, Seery, Blascovich, & Weisbuch, 2008). Attributional ambiguity similarly implicates physiological threat and vigilance responses by Blacks in response to Whites (Mendes, Major, McCoy, & Blascovich, 2008). Upward comparison appears intrinsically threatening, as cardiovascular reactivity indicates, even under cooperative conditions (Mendes, Blascovich, Major, & Seery, 2001). Correlational evidence linking reputational threat and perceived discrimination is more ambiguous because reverse causality and third variables raise alternative explanations (Major & O'Brien, 2005). Nevertheless, exposure to naturally occurring dominance (independent of hostility) evokes cardiovascular reactivity (Newton & Bane, 2001).

Besides the more commonly studied race and gender, social class presents reputational threat. Stereotype threat can undermine lower-class academic performance (Croizet & Claire, 1998; Spencer & Castano, 2007). Attributional processes also punish the poor. Others—especially middle class and conservative people—routinely attribute poverty to personal irresponsibility: Alleged lack of hard work is chief among the attributions (Bullock, 1999; Bullock & Limbert, 2003; Cozzarelli, Wilkinson, & Tagler, 2001; Henry, Reyna, & Weiner, 2004; Lott, 2002; Singh, 1989; Weiner, 1993; Zucker & Weiner, 1993), resulting in polarized evaluations (A. M. Russell & Fiske, 2009).

Coping with Self-Esteem Threats

Beyond threatening one's external image, subordination threatens one's internal image. Although stigma research at first assumed that targets must have lower self-esteem, two decades of research now indicate otherwise. Targets actively cope, and most do not internalize collective derogation (Crocker et al., 1998). Self-esteem effects of stigma are variable within and across subordinated groups (Major & O'Brien, 2005).

Under some circumstances, self-esteem does suffer under a loss of power (Wojciszke & Struzynska-Kujalowicz, 2007). However, these effects moderate according to the individual's particular interpretation of identity threat. Generally, highly identified individuals perceive more discrimination (e.g., Branscombe et al., 1999; Sellers & Shelton, 2003), detect subtle discrimination (Major, Quinton, & Schmader, 2003; Operario & Fiske, 2001), and perceive it as self-relevant

(McCoy & Major, 2003). So they react: High identification under threat predicts outgroup derogation (C. A. Wong, Eccles, & Sameroff, 2003) and discrimination (Jetten, Spears, & Manstead, 1997), perhaps perpetuating group conflict (Swann & Bosson, volume 1). At the same time, attributions to discrimination can protect personal self-esteem (Major, Kaiser, & McCoy, 2003; Major, Quinton, & Schmader, 2003) and elevate collective self-esteem (Branscombe & Wann, 1994; Jetten, Branscombe, Schmitt, & Spears, 2001). Group identification buffers self-esteem against experienced discrimination.

Low-status groups can also adopt a social creativity approach and value themselves on alternative dimensions (e.g., warmth instead of competence). According to a meta-analysis noted earlier, low-status groups favor their groups more on status-irrelevant dimensions (Mullen et al., 1992), perhaps to compensate for their disadvantage (van Knippenberg, 1978). This helps explain circumstances under which subordinated groups show outgroup favoritism (Sachdev & Bourhis, 1991), justify the unfair system (Jost & Kay, this volume), and endorse its justice (Major et al., 2002). Generally, meta-analyses suggest lower self-esteem among Asians, Latinos, and Native Americans, although higher self-esteem among Black Americans than White Americans (Twenge & Crocker, 2002). Between women and men, self-esteem is domain-specific, women scoring higher on behavioral–conduct and moral–ethical self-esteem, but lower on appearance, athletic, personal, and self-satisfaction self-esteem (Gentile et al., 2009). Overall, the cultural context, political ideology, individual identity, specific domain, and immediate context all contribute to self-esteem among subordinated group members.

Besides moderating self-esteem, identification has a life of its own for subordinated groups. At baseline, according to meta-analysis, low-status group members identify with their ingroups less than do high-status group members (Bettencourt et al., 2001). Contrary to common intuition, however, discrimination mostly increases identification (Major & O'Brien, 2005), except for the very least identified (McCoy & Major, 2003). When people are not identified, they respond to group threat by individual mobility, that is, abandoning the group, if they can. When strongly identified, they affirm their threatened group (for review, see Ellemers et al., 2002). They may also endorse their devalued identity because uncertainty and chaos are worse even than stable low status (Hogg, this volume; Jost & Kay, this volume). Low-status, typical group members also increase their identification under uncertainty (Reid & Hogg, 2005).

Health Risks

Subordinated groups are wise to cope with psychological threats because these accumulate, correlating over time with health risks. For example, as noted, stress-heightened cortisol facilitates immediate adaptation to stigma, but sustained stress-based cortisol elevation damages mental and physical health (McEwen, 2000; Schneiderman et al., 2005). Identity threats fit this physiological pattern when they entail motivated performance, characterized by social-evaluative threat (one could be negatively judged by others; Dickerson & Kemeny, 2004). One's performance being experienced as uncontrollable also exacerbates negative stress-related outcomes from identity threat.

Consistent with the importance of perceived control as a stressor, men's social class predicts their risk of coronary heart disease. The risk gradient dramatically depends on lack of perceived job control (Marmot, 2003; Marmot, Bosma, Hemingway, Brunner, & Stansfeld, 1997). Among status variables, wealth best predicts health disparities (M. D. Wong, Shapiro, Boscardin, & Ettner, 2002). Income correlates with race, gender, and age, so their effects easily overlap, but some independent effects of race and probable discrimination do endanger health (Mays, Cochran, & Barnes, 2007). Class generally relates to health (especially cardiovascular disease but also mortality in general), and the effect may be mediated by negative emotions and cognitions (Gallo & Matthews, 2003). Besides experiencing more depression, anxiety, anger, hostility, and hopelessness, lower social classes also express more worries and cynicism but have fewer reserves for coping. Eventually, these cognitive–emotional stressors take a toll.

Returning to the primates that opened this chapter's discussion of status, recall that low-status male primates experience the most stress in stable configurations, but that high-status males experience stress in unstable settings in which they must fight to keep their place. Consistent with those results, socially dominant male monkeys in unstable groups have more atherosclerosis, compared with nondominant males in the same group and with dominant males in stable groups (Manuck, Kaplan, & Clarkson, 1983). Dominant female monkeys, studied separately, show similar cardiovascular effects (Kaplan, Adams, Clarkson, & Manuck, 1996).

Benefits?

A variety of threats—to reputation, self-esteem and health—plague lower-status people over the long haul. What could possibly be beneficial about long-term subordination? Again, for symmetry, one might entertain long-term benefits involving deniability and moral credibility.

For example, as noted earlier, speakers communicate power by, for example, talking a lot, being direct, and so on. Because low-power people talk less and use more indirect forms, they risk less. Indirect speech provides deniability, should events turn sour or should others allege hostile or immoral intent (Pinker, Nowak, & Lee, 2008).

Lower-status groups enjoy morality credibility, at least generically. That is, people infer that if a group is competent, as they reliably do for high-status groups (see earlier review), they also reliably infer that the group is not warm (e.g., not trustworthy). Conversely, low-status groups by default are less competent but more warm (Judd, James-Hawkins, Yzerbyt, & Kashima, 2005; Kervyn, Yzerbyt, Demoulin, & Judd, 2008; Kervyn, Yzerbyt, Judd, & Nunes, 2009; Yzerbyt, Kervyn, & Judd, 2008). Real-world athletic and academic rivals show such compensation effects (Oldmeadow & Fiske, 2010). Warmth often confers benign intent and moral credibility.

Compensation (e.g., stereotyping the poor as happy or honest, both representing warmth) also justifies the system (Kay & Jost, 2003). Warmth may play a particularly important role in legitimizing social inequalities because this kind of compensation effect occurs in allegedly legitimate status systems (Oldmeadow & Fiske, under review). Consistent with emphasizing warmth, characteristics associated with lower-status groups garner less respect than those associated with high-status groups (Ellemers, van Rijswijk, Roefs, & Simons, 1997).

Generally, groups may mutually acknowledge each other's standing on particular characteristics—a phenomenon termed *social cooperation* (van Knippenberg & Ellemers, 1990)—but it differs by status. For example, a high-status group may favor itself on academics, and a low-status group on community service (Oldmeadow & Fiske, 2010). According to meta-analysis (Bettencourt et al., 2001), low-status groups generally attribute respective strengths to both high- and low-status groups, but high-status members are less even-handed. Although the low-status group's ingroup bias on its comparative advantage favors themselves but does not derogate the high-status outgroup, again the high-status group is less even-handed, rating themselves lower on that dimension relative to their strong point, but not as inferior to the low-status group, even on the dimension that favors the low status. For example, a prestigious school may see themselves as superior on academics relative to community service and superior on academics relative to a lower-status school. However, they will not see themselves as inferior on community service compared with a lower-status school, so they are not even-handed. Conversely, the lower-status school agrees that the prestigious school rates better on academics than they do but sees themselves as better than the prestigious school on community service and maybe better in that than on academics, so they are even-handed in allocating each group its own relative advantage.

Although these patterns imply that the low-status groups adjust to and endorse the system that disadvantages them, they need not do so (see Yzerbyt & Demoulin, this volume).

For example, lower social classes recognize and report more personal deprivation and ingroup deprivation in Eurobarometer studies (Pettigrew et al., 2008). Further, perceived ingroup deprivation drives intergroup resentments. The moral credibility of the lower-status group appears in their conviction that they are not to blame for their position.

In the *minority-influence* literature, opinion minorities influence the majority when they persist, partly because their low-status position means their motives do not appear self-serving: They have so little to gain from advocating their unpopular perspective. Hence, their motives must be pure, or at least driven by sincere conviction (see Wood, 2000, for a review). This also constitutes a kind of moral credibility. Minorities seldom succeed on the main issue, according to meta-analysis (Wood, Lundgren, Ouellette, Busceme, & Blackstone, 1994). Nonetheless, they more often succeed indirectly, on issues tangential to the appeal. On these indirect issues, the majority may converge without risking alignment with the low-status minority. Minorities can thus prevail in roundabout ways that do not threaten the majority's apparent integrity and self-concept.

Moral credibility for low-status groups also comes from mutual support. Under threat, devalued groups can thrive by differentiating themselves and respecting each other (Jetten, Schmitt, Branscombe, & McKimmie, 2005), strategies termed social creativity in social identity and self-categorization theory. Social identity protects group members under stress, when it facilitates mutual support (Haslam, O'Brien, Jetten, Vormedal, & Penna, 2005). Subordinates can have power, when they act collectively. Even primates know the value of solidarity in subordinate coalitions (Boehm, 1997).

SUMMARY

Stratification matters. Group-based status provides immediate prestige, granting attention, access, and respect, from primate bands to human societies, and all the intermediate interpersonal interactions. High status over the longer haul also benefits the fortunate, but is tempered by greater ambivalence, especially in interdependent, long-term status relations between gender and ages, although to a lesser degree between races and classes.

Interpersonal power liberates and corrupts because it focuses the powerful on salient goals. Powerholders forge ahead, not sweating the small stuff but neglecting the small people, unless nudged to be socially responsible.

Subordination requires stressful short-term vigilance, with long-term risks to health and well-being. Nevertheless, subordinates cope and reap some benefits not often considered.

Although hierarchies matter, they are not the only game going in social encounters. Indeed, interdependence matters more because people immediately detect others' intentions for good or ill and live in cooperative or competitive relationships over time. Relationships have horizontal, enmeshed dimensions of interdependence, as well as vertical power–status dimensions.

This review's focus on the second dimension of social cognition, status–power–competence, stems from the discomfort it evokes. Americans particularly find stratification an awkward topic. Despite national consensus on generally egalitarian values, shared by other developed countries, Americans especially resist acknowledging the vertical differences that divide us. So, at the risk of seeming paranoid, angry, or cynical, one would prefer to bring stratification's dynamics out into the open, where people so inclined can better tackle their effects on human well-being and potential.

REFERENCES

Aboud, F. E., Mendelson, M. J., & Purdy, K. T. (2003). Cross-race peer relations and friendship quality. *International Journal of Behavioral Development, 27*, 165–173.

Adams, R. B., Jr., & Kleck, R. E. (2003). Perceived gaze direction and the processing of facial displays of emotion. *Psychological Science, 14*, 644–647.

Adams, R. B., Jr., & Kleck, R. E. (2005). Effects of direct and averted gaze on the perception of facially communicated emotion. *Emotion, 5*, 3–11.

Adler, N. E., Boyce, T., Chesney, M. A., Cohen, S., Folkman, S., Kahn, R. L., & Syme, S. L. (1994). Socioeconomic status and health: The challenge of the gradient. *American Psychologist, 49*, 15–24.

Alexander, M. G., Brewer, M. B., & Hermann, R. K. (1999). Images and affect: A functional analysis of out-group stereotypes. *Journal of Personality and Social Psychology, 77*, 78–93.

Alexander, M. G., Brewer, M. B., & Livingston, R. W. (2005). Putting stereotype content in context: Image theory and interethnic stereotypes. *Personality and Social Psychology Bulletin, 31*, 781–794.

Amodio, D. M., Harmon-Jones, E., & Devine, P. G. (2003). Individual differences in the activation and control of affective race bias as assessed by startle eyeblink response and self-report. *Journal of Personality and Social Psychology, 84*, 738–753.

Amodio, D. M., Harmon-Jones, E., Devine, P. G., Curtin, J. J., Hartley, S. L., & Covert, A. E. (2004). Neural signals for the detection of unintentional race bias. *Psychological Science, 15*, 88–93.

Anderson, C., & Berdahl, J. L. (2002). The experience of power: Examining the effects of power on approach and inhibition tendencies. *Journal of Personality and Social Psychology, 83*, 1362–1377.

Anderson, C., & Galinsky, A. D. (2006). Power, optimism, and risk-taking. *European Journal of Social Psychology, 36*, 511–536.

Anderson, C., John, O. P., Keltner, D., & Kring, A. M. (2001). Who attains social status? Effects of personality and physical attractiveness in social groups. *Journal of Personality and Social Psychology, 81*, 116–132.

Anderson, C., Keltner, D., & John, O. P. (2003). Emotional convergence between people over time. *Journal of Personality and Social Psychology, 84*, 1054–1068.

Anderson, C., Srivastava, S., Beer, J. S., Spataro, S. E., & Chatman, J. A. (2006). Knowing your place: Self-perceptions of status in face-to-face groups. *Journal of Personality and Social Psychology, 91*, 1094–1110.

Andreoli, V., & Worchel, S. (1978). Effects of media, communicator, and message position on attitude change. *Public Opinion Quarterly, 42*, 59–70.

Areni, C. S., & Sparks, J. R. (2005). Language power and persuasion. *Psychology & Marketing, 22*, 507–525.

Banks, R. R., & Eberhardt, J. L. (1998). Social psychological processes and the legal bases of racial categorization. In J. L. Eberhardt & S. T. Fiske (Eds.), *Confronting racism: The problem and the response* (pp. 54–75). Thousand Oaks, CA: Sage.

Bargh, J. A., Raymond, P., Pryor, J. B., & Strack, F. (1995). Attractiveness of the underling: An automatic power ' sex association and its consequences for sexual harassment and aggression. *Journal of Personality and Social Psychology, 68*, 768–781.

Baron-Cohen, S. (1995). *Mindblindness*. Cambridge, MA: MIT Press/Bradford.

Bayliss, A. P., di Pellegrino, G., & Tipper, S. P. (2005). Sex differences in eye gaze and symbolic cuing of attention. *Quarterly Journal of Experimental Psychology, A 58*, 631–650.

Berdahl, J. L. (2007a). Harassment based on sex: Protecting social status in the context of gender hierarchy. *Academy of Management Review, 32*, 641–658.

Berdahl, J. L. (2007b). The sexual harassment of uppity women. *Journal of Applied Psychology, 92*, 425–437.

Berdahl, J. L., Magley, V. J., & Waldo, C. R. (1996). The sexual harassment of men? *Psychology of Women Quarterly, 20*, 527–547.

Berdahl, J. L., & Martorana, P. (2006). Effects of power on emotion and expression during a controversial group discussion. *European Journal of Social Psychology, 36*, 497–509.

Berdahl, J. L., & Moore, C. (2006). Workplace harassment: Double jeopardy for minority women. *Journal of Applied Psychology, 91*, 426–436.

Berger, J., Cohen, B. P., & Zelditch, M. (1972). Status characteristics and social interaction. *American Sociological Review, 37*, 241–255.

Berger, J., & Fisek, M. H. (2006). Diffuse status characteristics and the spread of status value: A formal theory. *American Journal of Sociology, 111*, 1038–1079.

Bergsieker, H., Leslie, L. M., Constantine, V. S., & Fiske, S. T. (2009). *Stereotyping by omission: "You've got to eliminate the negative, accentuate the positive."* Unpublished manuscript, Princeton University.

Berry, D. S. (1991). Accuracy in social perception: Contributions of facial and vocal information. *Journal of Personality and Social Psychology, 61*, 298–307.

Bettencourt, B. A., Charlton, K., Dorr, N., & Hume, D. L. (2001). Status differences and in-group bias: A meta-analytic examination of the effects of status stability, status legitimacy, and group permeability. *Psychological Bulletin, 127*, 520–542.

Blair, I. V., Judd, C. M., & Chapleau, K. M. (2004). The influence of Afrocentric facial features in criminal sentencing. *Psychological Science, 15*, 674–679.

Blair, I. V., Judd, C. M., Sadler, M. S., & Jenkins, C. (2002). The role of Afrocentric features in person perception: Judging by features and categories. *Journal of Personality and Social Psychology, 83*, 5–25.

Blankenship, K. L., & Craig, T. Y. (2007). Powerless language markers and the correspondence bias: Attitude confidence mediates the effects of tag questions on attitude attributions. *Journal of Language and Social Psychology, 26*, 28–47.

Blankenship, K., & Holtgraves, T. (2005). The role of different markers of linguistic powerlessness in persuasion. *Journal of Language and Social Psychology, 24*, 3–24.

Blascovich, J., Mendes, W. B., Hunter, S. B., Lickel, B., & Kowai-Bell, N. (2001). Perceiver threat in social interactions with stigmatized others. *Journal of Personality and Social Psychology, 80*, 253–267.

Blascovich, J., Spencer, S. J., Quinn, D., & Steele, C. (2001). African Americans and high blood pressure: The role of stereotype threat. *Psychological Science, 12*, 225–229.

Blascovich, J., Wyer, N. A., Swart, L. A., & Kibler, J. L. (1997). Racism and racial categorization. *Journal of Personality and Social Psychology, 72*, 1364–1372.

Blass, T. (1999). The Milgram Paradigm after 35 years: Some things we now know about obedience to authority. *Journal of Applied Social Psychology, 29*, 955–978.

Boehm, C. (1997). Egalitarian behavior and the evolution of political intelligence. In A. Whiten & R. W. Byrne (Eds.), *Machiavellian intelligence II: Extensions and evaluations* (pp. 341–365). New York: Cambridge University Press.

Bogardus, E. S. (1933). A social distance scale. *Sociology & Social Research, 17*, 265–271.

Boggs, C., & Giles, H. (1999). The canary in the coalmine: The nonaccommodation cycle in the gendered workplace. *International Journal of Applied Linguistics, 9*, 223–245.

Bradac, J. J., Bowers, J. W., & Courtright, J. A. (1979). Three language variables in communication research: Intensity, immediacy, and diversity. *Human Communication Research, 5*, 257–269.

Bradac, J. J., & Mulac, A. (1984). A molecular view of powerful and powerless speech styles: Attributional consequences of specific language features and communicator intentions. *Communication Monographs, 51*, 307–319.

Bradac, J. J., & Wisegarver, R. (1984). Ascribed status, lexical diversity, and accent: Determinants of perceived status, solidarity, and control of speech style. *Journal of Language and Social Psychology, 3*, 239–256.

Branscombe, N. R., Schmitt, M. T., & Harvey, R. D. (1999). Perceiving pervasive discrimination among African Americans: Implications for group identification and well-being. *Journal of Personality and Social Psychology, 77*, 135–149.

Branscombe, N. R., & Wann, D. L. (1994). Collective self-esteem consequences of outgroup derogation when a valued social identity is on trial. *European Journal of Social Psychology, 6*, 641–657.

Brauer, M., & Bourhis, R. Y. (2006). Social power. *European Journal of Social Psychology, 36*, 601–616.

Brewer, M. B., Dull, V., & Lui, L. (1981). Perceptions of the elderly: Stereotypes as prototypes. *Journal of Personality and Social Psychology, 41*, 656–670.

Briñol, P., Petty, R. E., Valle, C., Rucker, D. D., & Becerra, A. (2007). The effects of message recipients' power before and after persuasion: A self-validation analysis. *Journal of Personality and Social Psychology, 93*, 1040–1053.

Brown, B. L., Giles, H., & Thackerar, J. N. (1985). Speaker evaluations as a function of speech rate, accent and context. *Language and Communication, 5*, 107–220.

Bullock, H. E. (1999). Attributions for poverty: A comparison of middle-class and welfare recipient attitudes. *Journal of Applied Social Psychology, 29*, 2059–2082.

Bullock, H. E., & Limbert, W. M. (2003). Scaling the socioeconomic ladder: Low-income women's perceptions of class status and opportunity. *Journal of Social Issues, 59*, 693–709.

Bunderson, J. S. (2003). Recognizing and utilizing expertise in work groups: A status characteristics perspective. *Administrative Science Quarterly, 48*, 557–591.

Burke, P. J., Stets, J. E., & Cerven, C. (2007). Gender, legitimation, and identity verification in groups. *Social Psychology Quarterly, 70*, 27–42.

Business and Professional Women's Foundation. (2005, July). 101 facts on the status of working women. Retrieved July 31, 2006, from http://www.bpwusa.org

Buss, D. M. (1989). Sex differences in human mate preferences: Evolutionary hypothesis tested in 37 cultures. *Behavioral and Brain Sciences, 12*, 1–49.

Buss, D. M., & Kenrick, D. T. (1998). Evolutionary social psychology. In D. T. Gilbert, S. T. Fiske, & G. Lindzey (Eds.), *Handbook of social psychology* (4th ed., Vol. 2, pp. 982–1026). New York: McGraw-Hill.

Byrne, D. (1997). An overview (and underview) of research and theory within the attraction paradigm. *Journal of Social and Personal Relationships, 14*, 417–431.

Callary, R. E. (1974). Status perception through syntax. *Language and Speech, 17*, 187–192.

Campbell-Kibler, K. (2007). Accent, (ing), and the social logic of listener's perceptions. *American Speech, 82*, 32–64.

Caporael, L. R. (1981). The paralanguage of caregiving: Baby talk to the institutionalized aged. *Journal of Personality and Social Psychology, 40*, 876–884.

Caprariello, P. A., Cuddy, J. C., & Fiske, S. T. (2009). Social structure shapes cultural stereotypes and emotions: A causal test of the stereotype content model. *Group Processes and Intergroup Behavior, 12*, 147–155.

Cargile, A. C., Giles, H., Ryan, E. B., & Bradac, J. J. (1994). Language attitudes as a social process: A conceptual model and new directions. *Language and Communication, 14*, 211–236.

Carli, L. (1990). Gender, language, and influence. *Journal of Personality and Social Psychology, 59*, 941–951.

Carranza, E., Larsen, J., & Prentice, D. A. (2009). *Derogation of deviates as an ingroup process.* Unpublished manuscript, Princeton University.

Cartwright, D. (1965). Influence, leadership, control. In J. G. March (Ed.), *Handbook of organizations* (pp. 1–47). Chicago: Rand McNally & Company.

Caspi, A., Roberts, B. W., & Shiner, R. L. (2005). Personality development: stability and change. *Annual Review of Psychology, 56*, 453–484.

Cejka, M. A., & Eagly, A. H. (1999). Gender-stereotypic images of occupations correspond to the sex segregation of employment. *Personality and Social Psychology Bulletin, 25*, 413–423. Erratum. *Personality and Social Psychology Bulletin, 25*, 1059.

Chaiken, S., & Maheswaran, D. (1994). Heuristic processing can bias systematic processing: Effects of source credibility, argument ambiguity, and task importance on attitude judgment. *Journal of Personality and Social Psychology, 66*, 460–473.

Chance, M. R. A. (Ed.). (1988). *Social fabrics of the mind.* Hillsdale, NJ: Erlbaum.

Chance, M. R. A., & Jolly, C. J. (1970). *Social groups of monkeys, apes, and men.* New York: Dutton.

Chance, M. R. A., & Larsen, R. R. (Eds.). (1976). *The social structure of attention.* New York: Wiley.

Chen, S., Lee-Chai, A. Y., & Bargh, J. A. (2001). Relationship orientation as a moderator of the effects of social power. *Journal of Personality and Social Psychology, 80*, 173–187.

Chen, Z., Fiske, S. T., & Lee, T. L. (2009). Ambivalent sexism and power-related gender-role ideology in marriage. *Sex Roles, 60*, 765–778.

Cheney, D. L., & Seyfarth, R. M. (2007). *Baboon metaphysics: The evolution of a social mind.* Chicago: University of Chicago Press.

Cikara, M., Eberhardt, J. L., & Fiske, S. T. (2009). *From agents to objects: Sexist attitudes and neural responses to sexualized targets.* Unpublished manuscript, Princeton University.

Cikara, M., Botvinick, M., & Fiske, S. T. (2009). *Red Sox v. Yankees: Neural responses to rival group's pleasures and pains.* Unpublished manuscript, Princeton University.

Clausell, E., & Fiske, S. T. (2005). When do the parts add up to the whole? Ambivalent stereotype content for gay male subgroups. *Social Cognition, 23,* 157–176.

Cohen, G. L., Steele, C. M., & Ross, L. D. (1999). The mentor's dilemma: Providing critical feedback across the racial divide. *Personality and Social Psychology Bulletin, 25,* 1302–1318.

Converse P. E. (2000). Assessing the capacity of mass electorates. *Annual Review of Political Science, 3,* 331–353.

Copeland, J. T. (1994). Prophecies of power: Motivational implications of social power for behavioral confirmation. *Journal of Personality and Social Psychology, 67,* 264–277.

Correll, J., Park, B., Judd, C. M., & Wittenbrink, B. (2002). The police officer's dilemma: Using ethnicity to disambiguate potentially threatening individuals. *Journal of Personality and Social Psychology, 83,* 1314–1329.

Correll, J., Urland, G. R., & Ito, T. A. (2006). Event-related potentials and the decision to shoot: The role of threat perception and cognitive control. *Journal of Experimental Social Psychology, 42,* 120–128.

Cosmides, L., Tooby, J., & Kurzban, R. (2003). Perception of race. *Trends in Cognitive Sciences, 7,* 173–179.

Cozzarelli, C., Wilkinson, A. V., & Tagler, M. J. (2001). Attitudes toward the poor and attributions for poverty. *Journal of Social Issues, 57,* 207–227.

Crandall, C. S., Eshleman, A., & O'Brien, L. (2002). Social norms and the expression and suppression of prejudice: The struggle for internalization. *Journal of Personality and Social Psychology, 82,* 359–378.

Crocker, J., & Major, B. (1989). Social stigma and self-esteem: The self-protective properties of stigma. *Psychological Review, 96,* 608–630.

Crocker, J., Major, B., & Steele, C. (1998). Social stigma. In D. T. Gilbert, S. T. Fiske, & G. Lindzey (Eds.), *The handbook of social psychology* (4th ed., Vol. 2, pp. 504–553). New York: McGraw-Hill.

Croizet, J., & Claire, T. (1998). Extending the concept of stereotype and threat to social class: The intellectual underperformance of students from low socioeconomic backgrounds. *Personality and Social Psychology Bulletin, 24,* 588–594.

Crosby, F. J. (1991). *Juggling: The unexpected advantages of balancing career and home for women and their families.* New York: Free Press.

Crosby, F. J., & Nyquist, L. (1977). The female register: An empirical study of Lakoff's hypothesis. *Language in Society, 6,* 313–322.

Cuddy, A. J. C., Fiske, S. T., & Glick, P. (2007). The BIAS Map: Behaviors from intergroup affect and stereotypes. *Journal of Personality and Social Psychology, 92,* 631–648.

Cuddy, A. J. C., Fiske, S. T., & Glick, P. (2008). Competence and warmth as universal trait dimensions of interpersonal and intergroup perception: The Stereotype Content Model and the BIAS Map. In M. P. Zanna (Ed.), *Advances in Experimental Social Psychology* (Vol. 40, pp. 61–149). New York: Academic.

Cuddy, A. J. C., Fiske, S. T., Kwan, V. S. Y., Glick, P., Demoulin, S., Leyens, J.-Ph., Bond, M. H., Croizet, J.-C., Ellemers, N., Sleebos, E., Htun, T. T., Yamamoto, M., et al. (2009). Is the stereotype content model culture-bound? A cross-cultural comparison reveals systematic similarities and differences. *British Journal of Social Psychology, 48,* 1–33.

Cuddy, A. J. C., Norton, M. I., & Fiske, S. T. (2005) This old stereotype: The pervasiveness and persistence of the elderly stereotype. *Journal of Social Issues, 61,* 265–283.

Cunningham, W. A., Johnson, M. K., Raye, C. L., Gatenby, J. C., Gore, J. C., & Banaji, M. R. (2004). Separable neural components in the processing of Black and White faces. *Psychological Science, 15,* 806–813.

Dahl, R. A. (1957). The concept of power. *Behavioral Science, 2,* 201–218.

Dall'Ara, E., & Maass, A. (1999). Studying sexual harassment in the laboratory: Are egalitarian women at higher risk? *Sex Roles, 41,* 681–704.

Dambrun, M., Duarte, S., & Guimond, S. (2004). Why are men more likely to support group-based dominance than women? The mediating role of gender identification. British *Journal of Social Psychology, 43,* 287–297.

Dardenne, B., Dumont, M., & Bollier, T. (2007). Insidious dangers of benevolent sexism: Consequences for women's performance. *Journal of Personality and Social Psychology, 93,* 764–779.

Darley, J. M., & Gross, P. H. (1983). A hypothesis-confirming bias in labeling effects. *Journal of Personality and Social Psychology, 44,* 20–33.

Davis, T. J., Jr. (2005). The political orientation of Blacks and Whites: Converging, diverging, or remaining constant? *Social Science Journal, 42,* 487–498.

Deaner, R. O., & Platt, M. L. (2003). Reflexive social attention in monkeys and humans. *Current Biology, 13,* 1609–1613.

DeBono, K. G., & Harnish, R. J. (1988). Source expertise, source attractiveness, and the processing of persuasive information: A functional approach. *Journal of Personality and Social Psychology, 55,* 541–546.

De Cremer, D., & van Dijk, E. (2005). When and why leaders put themselves first: Leader behaviour in resource allocations as a function of feeling entitled. *European Journal of Social Psychology, 35,* 553–563.

De Cremer, D., & van Dijk, E. (2008). Leader-follower effects in resource dilemmas: The roles of leadership selection and social responsibility. *Group Processes and Intergroup Relations, 11,* 355–369.

De Dreu, C. K. W., & van Kleef, G. A. (2004). The influence of power on the information search, impression formation, and demands in negotiation. *Journal of Experimental Social Psychology, 40,* 303–319.

Dépret, E. F., & Fiske, S. T. (1999). Perceiving the powerful: Intriguing individuals versus threatening groups. *Journal of Experimental Social Psychology, 35,* 461–480.

Deutsch, F. M. (1999). *Halving it all: How equally shared parenting works.* Cambridge, MA: Harvard University Press.

Devine, P. G. (1989). Stereotypes and prejudice: Their automatic and controlled components. *Journal of Personality and Social Psychology, 56,* 5–18.

Devine, P. G., & Elliot, A. J. (1995). Are racial stereotypes really fading? The Princeton trilogy revisited. *Personality and Social Psychology Bulletin, 21,* 1139–1150.

Devos, T., & Banaji, M. R. (2005). American = White? *Journal of Personality and Social Psychology, 88,* 447–466.

de Waal, F. B. M. (2005). A century of getting to know the chimpanzee. *Nature, 437,* 56–59.

Dickerson, S., & Kemeny, M.E. (2004). Acute stressors and cortisol responses: A theoretical integration and synthesis of laboratory research. *Psychological Bulletin, 130,* 355–931.

Dion, K. L., & Earn, B. M. (1975). The phenomenology of being a target of prejudice. *Journal of Personality and Social Psychology, 32,* 944–950.

Dixon, T. L., & Maddox, K. B. (2005). Skin tone, crime news, and social reality judgments: Priming the stereotype of the dark and dangerous black criminal. *Journal of Applied Social Psychology, 35,* 1555–1570.

Doob, A. N., & Gross, A. E. (1968). Status of frustrator as an inhibitor of horn-honking responses. *The Journal of Social Psychology, 76,* 213–218.

Dovidio, J. F., Brown, C. E., Heltman, K., Ellyson, S. L., & Keating, C. F. (1988). Power displays between women and men in discussions of gender-linked tasks: A multichannel study. *Journal of Personality and Social Psychology, 55,* 580–587.

Dovidio, J. F., & Ellyson, S. L. (1982). Decoding visual dominance: Attributions of power based on relative percentages of looking while speaking and looking while listening. *Social Psychology Quarterly, 45,* 106–113.

Dovidio, J. F., Esses, V. M., Beach, K. R., & Gaertner, S. L. (2002). The role of affect in determining intergroup behavior: The case of willingness to engage in intergroup contact. In D. M. Mackie & E. R. Smith (Eds.),

From prejudice to intergroup emotions (pp. 153–172). New York: Psychology Press.

Dovidio, J. F., Gaertner, S. E., Kawakami, K., & Hodson, G. (2002). Why can't we just get along? Interpersonal biases and interracial distrust. *Cultural Diversity and Ethnic Minority Psychology, 8,* 88–102.

Dovidio, J. F., Kawakami, K., Johnson, C., Johnson, B., & Howard, A. (1997). On the nature of prejudice: Automatic and controlled processes. *Journal of Experimental Social Psychology, 33,* 510–540.

Dunton, B. C., & Fazio, R. H. (1997). An individual difference measure of motivation to control prejudiced reactions. *Personality and Social Psychology Bulletin, 23,* 316–326.

Durantini, M. R., Albarracín, D., Mitchell, A. L., Earl, A. N., & Gillette, J. C. (2006). Conceptualizing the influence of social agents of behavior change: A meta-analysis of the effectiveness of HIV-prevention interventionists for different groups. *Psychological Bulletin, 132,* 212–248.

Eagly, A. H. (1987). *Sex differences in social behavior: A social-role interpretation.* Hillsdale, NJ: Lawrence Erlbaum Associates.

Eagly, A. H., & Crowley, M. (1986). Gender and helping behavior: A meta-analytic review of the social psychological literature. *Psychological Bulletin, 100,* 283–308.

Eagly, A. H., Diekman, A. B., Johannesen-Schmidt, M. C., & Koenig, A. M. (2004). Gender gaps in sociopolitical attitudes: A social psychological analysis. *Journal of Personality and Social Psychology, 87,* 796–816.

Eagly, A. H., & Johnson, B. T. (1990). Gender and leadership style: A meta-analysis. *Psychological Bulletin, 108,* 233–256.

Eagly, A. H., & Karau, S. J. (1991). Gender and the emergence of leaders: A meta-analysis. *Journal of Personality and Social Psychology, 60,* 685–710.

Eagly, A. H., Makhijani, M. G., & Klonsky, B. G. (1992). Gender and the evaluation of leaders: A meta-analysis. *Psychological Bulletin, 111,* 3–22.

Eagly, A. H., & Steffen, V. J. (1986). Gender and aggressive behavior: A meta-analytic review of the social psychological literature. *Psychological Bulletin, 100,* 309–330.

Eagly, A. H., Wood, W., & Diekman, A. (2000). Social role theory of sex differences and similarities: A current appraisal. In T. Eckes & H. M. Trautner (Eds.), *The developmental social psychology of gender* (pp. 123–174). Mahwah, NJ: Lawrence Erlbaum.

Ebenbach, D. H., & Keltner, D. (1998). Power, emotion, and judgmental accuracy in social conflict: Motivating the cognitive miser. *Basic and Applied Social Psychology, 20,* 7–21.

Eberhardt, J. L. (2005). Imaging race. *American Psychologist, 60,* 181–190.

Eberhardt, J. L., Dasgupta, N., & Banaszynski, T. L. (2003). Believing is seeing: The effects of racial labels and implicit beliefs on face perception. *Personality and Social Psychology Bulletin, 29,* 360–370.

Eberhardt, J. L., Davies, P. G., Purdie-Vaughns, V. J., & Johnson, S. L. (2006). Looking deathworthy: Perceived stereotypically of black defendants predicts capital sentencing outcomes. *Psychological Science, 17,* 383–386.

Eberhardt, J. L., Goff, P. A., Purdie, V. J., & Davies, P. G. (2004). Seeing black: Race, crime, and visual processing. *Journal of Personality and Social Psychology, 87,* 876–893.

Ellemers, N., Spears, R., & Doosje, B. (1997). Sticking together of falling apart: In-group identification as a psychological determinant of group commitment versus individual mobility. *Journal of Personality and Social Psychology, 72,* 617–626.

Ellemers, N., van Rijswijk, W., Roefs, M., & Simons, C. (1997). Bias in intergroup perceptions: Balancing group identity with social reality. *Personality and Social Psychology Bulletin, 23,* 186–198.

Ellsworth, P. C., Carlsmith, J. M., & Henson, A. (1972). The stare as a stimulus to flight in human subjects: A series of field experiments. *Journal of Personality and Social Psychology, 21,* 302–311.

Elman, D., Schulte, D. C., & Bukoff, A. (1977). Effects of facial expression and stare duration on walking speed: Two field experiments. *Environmental Psychology & Nonverbal Behavior, 2,* 93–99.

Else-Quest, N. M., Hyde, J. S., Goldsmith, H. H., & van Hulle, C. A. (2006). Gender differences in temperament: A meta-analysis. *Psychological Bulletin, 132,* 33–72.

Emerson, R. M. (1962). Power-dependence relations. *American Sociological Review, 27,* 31–41.

Erber, R., & Fiske, S. T. (1984). Outcome dependency and attention to inconsistent information. *Journal of Personality and Social Psychology, 47,* 709–726.

Erickson, B., Lind, A. E., Johnson, B. C., & O'Barr, W. M. (1978). Speech style and impression formation in a court setting: The effects of "powerful" and "powerless" speech. *Journal of Experimental Social Psychology, 14,* 266–279.

Esses, V. M., & Dovidio, J. F. (2002). The role of emotions in determining willingness to engage in intergroup contact. *Personality and Social Psychology Bulletin, 28,* 1202–1214.

Fang, C. Y., Sidanius, J., & Pratto, F. (1998). Romance across the social status continuum: Interracial marriage and the ideological asymmetry effect. *Journal of Cross-Cultural Psychology, 29,* 290–305.

Fast, N. J., Gruenfeld, D. H., Sivanathan, N., & Galinsky, A. D. (2009). Illusory control: A generative force behind power's far-reaching effects. *Psychological Science,* in press.

Fazio, R. H., & Hilden, L. E. (2001). Emotional reactions to a seemingly prejudiced response: The role of automatically activated racial attitudes and motivation to control prejudiced reactions. *Personality and Social Psychology Bulletin, 27,* 538–549.

Feather, N. T. (2004). Value correlates of ambivalent attitudes toward gender relations. *Personality and Social Psychology Bulletin, 30,* 3–12.

Feather, N. T., & Naim, K. (2005). Resentment, envy, Schadenfreude, and sympathy: Effects of own and other's deserved or undeserved status. *Australian Journal of Psychology, 57,* 87–102.

Feather, N. T., & Sherman, R. (2002). Envy, resentment, Schadenfreude, and sympathy: Reactions to deserved and underserved achievement and subsequent failure. *Personality and Social Psychology Bulletin, 28,* 953–961.

Feingold, A. (1992). Gender differences in mate selection preferences: A test of the parental investment model. *Psychological Bulletin, 112,* 125–139.

Fernandez, R. M., Castilla, E. J., & Moore, P. (2000). Social capital at work: Networks and employment at a phone center. *American Journal of Sociology, 105,* 1288–1356.

Fiske, S. T. (1992). Thinking is for doing: Portraits of social cognition from daguerreotype to laserphoto. *Journal of Personality and Social Psychology, 63,* 877–889.

Fiske, S. T. (1993). Controlling other people: The impact of power on stereotyping. *American Psychologist, 48,* 621–628.

Fiske, S. T. (1998). Stereotyping, prejudice, and discrimination. In D. T. Gilbert, S. T. Fiske, & G. Lindzey (Eds.), *Handbook of social psychology* (4th ed., Vol. 2, pp. 357–411). New York: McGraw-Hill.

Fiske, S. T., & Berdahl, J. (2007). Social power. In A. Kruglanski & E. T. Higgins (Eds.), *Social psychology: Handbook of basic principles* (2nd ed., pp. 678–692). New York: Guilford.

Fiske, S. T., Cuddy, A. J. C., & Glick, P. (2007). Universal dimensions of social perception: Warmth and competence. *Trends in Cognitive Science, 11,* 77–83.

Fiske, S. T., Cuddy, A. J. C., Glick, P., & Xu, J. (2002). A model of (often mixed) stereotype content: Competence and warmth respectively follow from perceived status and competition. *Journal of Personality and Social Psychology, 82,* 878–902.

Fiske, S. T., & Dépret, E. (1996). Control, interdependence, and power: Understanding social cognition in its social context. In W. Stroebe & M. Hewstone (Eds.), *European Review of Social Psychology* (Vol. 7, pp. 31–61).

Fiske, S. T., Harris, L. T., Russell, A. M., & Shelton, J. N. (2009). Divergent social realities: Depending on where you sit: Perspectives from the stereotype content model. In S. Demoulin, J. P. Leyens, & J. F. Dovidio (Eds.), *Intergroup misunderstandings: Impact of divergent social realities* (pp 173–190). Philadelphia: Psychology Press.

Fiske, S. T., & Neuberg, S. L. (1990). A continuum model of impression formation, from category-based to individuating processes: Influence of information and motivation on attention and interpretation. In M. P. Zanna (Ed.), *Advances in experimental social psychology* (Vol. 23, pp. 1–74). New York: Academic Press.

Fiske, S. T., & Von Hendy, H. M. (1992). Personality feedback and situational norms can control stereotyping processes. *Journal of Personality and Social Psychology, 62,* 577–596.

Fiske, S. T., Xu, J., Cuddy, A. C., & Glick, P. (1999). (Dis)respecting versus (dis)liking: Status and interdependence predict ambivalent stereotypes of competence and warmth. *Journal of Social Issues, 55,* 473–491.

Forbes, G. B., Collinsworth, L. L., Jobe, R. L., Braun, K. D., & Wise, L. M. (2007). Sexism, hostility toward women, and endorsement of beauty ideals and practices: Are beauty ideals associated with oppressive beliefs? *Sex Roles, 56,* 265–273.

Frantz, C. M., Cuddy, A. J. C., Burnett, M., Ray, H., & Hart, A. (2004). A threat in the computer: The Race Implicit Association Test as a stereotype threat experience. *Personality and Social Psychology Bulletin, 30,* 1611–1624.

Fredrickson, G. M. (2002). *Racism: A short history.* Princeton, NJ: Princeton University Press.

French, J. R. P., Jr., & Raven, B. (1959). The bases of social power. In D. Cartwright (Ed.), *Studies in social power* (pp. 150–167). Ann Arbor: University of Michigan, Institute for Social Research.

Furnham, A. F. (1983). Attributions for affluence. *Personality and Individual Differences, 4,* 31–40.

Gaertner, S. L., & Dovidio, J. F. (1986). The aversive form of racism. In J. F. Dovidio & S. L. Gaertner (Eds.), *Prejudice, discrimination, and racism* (pp. 61–90). Orlando, FL: Academic Press.

Galinsky, A. D., Gruenfeld, D. H., & Magee, J. C. (2003). From power to action. *Journal of Personality and Social Psychology, 85,* 453–466.

Galinsky, A. D., Magee, J. C., Gruenfeld, D. H., Whitson, J. A., & Liljenquist, K. A. (2008). Power reduces the press of the situation: Implications for creativity, conformity, and dissonance. *Journal of Personality and Social Psychology, 95,* 1450–1466.

Galinsky, A. D., Magee, J. C., Inesi, M. E., & Gruenfeld, D. H. (2006). Power and perspectives not taken. *Psychological Science, 17,* 1068–1074.

Gallo, L. C., & Matthews, K. A. (2003). Understanding the association between socioeconomic status and physical health: Do negative emotions play a role? *Psychological Bulletin, 129,* 10–51.

Gastil, J. (1990). Generic pronouns and sexist language: The oxymoronic character of masculine generics. *Sex Roles, 23,* 629–643.

Gentile, B., Grabe, S., Dolan-Pascoe, B., Twenge, J. M., Wells, B. E., & Maitino, A. (2009). Gender differences in domain-specific self-esteem: A meta-analysis. *Review of General Psychology, 13,* 34–45.

Georgesen, J., & Harris, M. J. (2006). Holding onto power: Effects of powerholders' positional instability and expectancies on interactions with subordinates. *European Journal of Social Psychology, 36,* 451–468.

Georgesen, J. C., & Harris, M. J. (1998). Why's my boss always holding me down? A meta-analysis of power effects on performance evaluations. *Personality and Social Psychology Review, 2,* 184–195.

Georgesen, J. C., & Harris, M. J. (2000). The balance of power: Interpersonal consequences of differential power and expectations. *Personality and Social Psychology Bulletin, 26,* 1239–1257.

Gerth, H. H., & Mills, C. W. (1948). *Essays from Max Weber.* London: Routledge & Kegan Paul.

Gilbert, D. T., Jones, E. E., & Pelham, B. W. (1987). Influence and inference: What the active perceiver overlooks. *Journal of Personality and Social Psychology, 52,* 861–870.

Gilbert, D. T., & Malone, P. S. (1995). The correspondence bias. *Psychological Bulletin, 117,* 21–38.

Gilbert, G. M. (1951). Stereotype persistence and change among college students. *Journal of Abnormal and Social Psychology, 46,* 245–254.

Giles, H., & Williams, A. (1994). Patronizing the young: Forms and evaluations. *International Journal of Aging & Human Development, 39,* 33–53.

Glick, P., & Fiske, S. T. (1996). The Ambivalent Sexism Inventory: Differentiating hostile and benevolent sexism. *Journal of Personality and Social Psychology, 70,* 491–512.

Glick, P., & Fiske, S. T. (1999). The Ambivalence toward Men Inventory: Differentiating hostile and benevolent beliefs about men. *Psychology of Women Quarterly, 23,* 519–536.

Glick, P., Fiske, S. T., Mladinic, A., Saiz, J. L., Abrams, D., Masser, B., Adetoun, B., et al. (2000). Beyond prejudice as simple antipathy: Hostile and benevolent sexism across cultures. *Journal of Personality and Social Psychology, 79,* 763–775.

Glick, P., Lameriras, M., Fiske, S. T., Eckes, T., Masser, B., Volpato, C., et al. (2004). Bad but bold: Ambivalent attitudes toward men predict gender inequality in 16 nations. *Journal of Personality and Social Psychology, 86,* 713–728.

Glick, P., Wilk, K., & Perreault, M. (1995). Images of occupations: Components of gender and status in occupational stereotypes. *Sex Roles, 32,* 9–10.

Goff, P. A., Steele, C. M., & Davies, P. G. (2008). The space between us: Stereotype threat and distance in interracial contexts. *Journal of Personality and Social Psychology, 94,* 91–107.

Goffman, E. (1963). *Stigma: Notes on the management of spoiled identity.* New York: Prentice-Hall.

Golby, A. J., Gabrieli, J. D. E., Chiao, J. Y., & Eberhardt, J. L. (2001). Differential responses in the fusiform region to same-race and other-race faces. *Nature Neuroscience, 4,* 845–850.

Goodwin, S. A., Fiske, S. T., Rosen, L. D., & Rosenthal, A. M. (2002). The eye of the beholder: Romantic goals and impression biases. *Journal of Experimental Social Psychology, 38,* 232–241.

Goodwin, S. A., Gubin, A., Fiske, S. T., & Yzerbyt, V. Y. (2000). Power can bias impression processes: Stereotyping subordinates by default and by design. *Group Processes and Intergroup Relations, 3,* 227–256.

Gough, H. G. (1990). Testing for leadership with the California Psychological Inventory. In K. E. Clark & M. B. Clark (Eds.), *Measures of leadership* (pp. 355–379). West Orange, NJ: Leadership Library of America.

Graves, J. (2001). *The emperor's new clothes: Biological theories of race at the millennium,* New Brunswick, NJ: Rutgers University Press.

Greenberg, J., Schimel, J., & Mertens, A. (2002). Ageism: Denying the face of the future. In T. D. Nelson (Ed.), *Ageism: Stereotyping and prejudice against older persons* (pp. 27–48). Cambridge, MA: MIT Press.

Guéguen, N., & Pichot, N. (2001). The influence of status on pedestrians' failure to observe a road-safety rule. *Journal of Social Psychology, 141,* 413–415.

Gruenfeld, D. H., Inesi, M. E., Magee, J. C., & Galinsky, A. D. (2008). Power and the objectification of social targets. *Journal of Personality and Social Psychology, 95,* 111–127.

Guimond, S., & Dambrun, M. (2002). When prosperity breeds intergroup hostility: The effects of relative deprivation and relative gratification on prejudice. *Personality and Social Psychology Bulletin, 28,* 900–912.

Guimond, S., Dambrun, M., Michinov, N., & Duarte, S. (2003). Does social dominance generate prejudice? Integrating individual and contextual determinants of intergroup cognitions. *Journal of Personality and Social Psychology, 84*, 697–721.

Guinote, A. (2007a). Power affects basic cognition: Increased attentional inhibition and flexibility. *Journal of Experimental Social Psychology, 43*, 685–697.

Guinote, A. (2007b). Power and goal pursuit. *Personality and Social Psychology Bulletin, 33*, 1076–1087.

Guinote, A. (2007c). Power and the suppression of unwanted thoughts: Does control over others decrease control over the self? *Journal of Experimental Social Psychology, 43*, 433–440.

Guinote, A. (2008). Power and affordances: When the situation has more power over powerful than powerless individuals. *Journal of Personality and Social Psychology, 95*, 237–252.

Guinote, A., Brown, M., & Fiske, S. T. (2006). Minority status decreases sense of control and increases interpretive processing. *Social Cognition, 24*, 169–186.

Guinote, A., Judd, C. M., & Brauer, M. (2002). Effects of power on perceived and objective group variability: Evidence that more powerful groups are more variable. *Journal of Personality and Social Psychology, 82*, 708–721.

Guy, G. R., & Vonwiller, J. (1984). The meaning of intonation in Australian English. *Australian Journal of Linguistics, 4*, 1–17.

Hall, J. A., Carter, J. D., & Horgan, T. G. (2001). Status roles and recall of nonverbal cues. *Journal of Nonverbal Behavior, 25*, 79–100.

Hall, J. A., Coats, E. J., & LeBeau, L. S. (2005). Nonverbal behavior and the vertical dimension of social relations: A meta-analysis. *Psychological Bulletin, 131*, 898–924.

Hall, J. A., Rosip, J. C., Smith LeBeau, L., Horgan, T. G., & Carter, J. D. (2006). Attributing the sources of accuracy in unequal-power dyadic communication: Who is better and why? *Journal of Experimental Social Psychology, 42*, 18–27.

Hallinan, M. T., & Williams, R. A. (1989). Interracial friendship choices in secondary schools. *American Sociological Review, 54*, 67–78.

Handgraaf, M. J. J., Van Dijk, E., Vermunt, R. C., Wilke, H. A. M., & De Dreu, C. K. W. (2008). Less power or powerless? Egocentric empathy gaps and the irony of having little versus no power in social decision making. *Journal of Personality and Social Psychology, 95*, 1136–1149.

Hare, B., & Tomasello, M. (2004). Chimpanzees are more skilful in competitive than in cooperative cognitive tasks. *Animal Behavior 68*, 571–581.

Harrigan, J. A., Wilson, K., & Rosenthal, R. (2004). Detecting state and trait anxiety from auditory and visual cues: A meta-analysis. *Personality and Social Psychology Bulletin, 30*, 56–66.

Harris, L. T., & Fiske, S. T. (2006). Dehumanizing the lowest of the low: Neuro-imaging responses to extreme outgroups. *Psychological Science, 17*, 847–853.

Hart, A. J., Whalen, P. J., Shin, L. M., McInerney, S. C., Fischer, H., & Rauch, S. L. (2000). Differential response in the human amygdala to racial outgroup vs. ingroup face stimuli. *Neuroreport: For Rapid Communication of Neuroscience Research, 11*, 2351–2355.

Haslam, S. A., O'Brien, A., Jetten, J., Vormedal, K., & Penna, S. (2005). Taking the strain: Social identity, social support, and the experience of stress. *British Journal of Social Psychology, 44*, 355–370.

Heesacker, M., Petty, R. E., & Cacioppo, J. T. (1983). Field dependence and attitude change: Source credibility can alter persuasion by affecting message-relevant thinking. *Journal of Personality, 51*, 653–666.

Heilman, M. E., Block, C. J., Martell, R. F., & Simon, M. C. (1989). Has anything changed? Current characterizations of men, women, and managers. *Journal of Applied Psychology, 74*, 935–942.

Henry, P. J., Reyna, C., & Weiner, B. (2004). Hate welfare but help the poor: How the attributional content of stereotypes explains the paradox of reactions to the destitute in America. *Journal of Applied Social Psychology, 34*, 34–58.

Hirschfeld, L. (1996). *Race in the making*. Cambridge, MA: MIT Press.

Hoffman, C., & Hurst, N. (1990). Gender stereotypes: Perception or rationalization? *Journal of Personality and Social Psychology, 58*, 197–208.

Hofling, C. K., Brotzman, E., Dalrymple, S., Graves, N., & Pierce, C. M. (1966). An experimental study in nurse-physician relationships. *Journal of Nervous and Mental Disease, 143*, 171–180.

Hogg, M. A. (2001). A social identity theory of leadership. *Personality and Social Psychology Review, 5*, 184–200.

Hogg, M. A. (2007). Uncertainty-identity theory. In M. P. Zanna (Ed.), *Advances in experimental social psychology* (Vol. 39, pp. 69–126). San Diego: Elsevier Academic Press.

Hogg, M. A., & van Knippenberg, D. (2003). Social identity and leadership processes in groups. In M. P. Zanna (Ed.), *Advances in experimental social psychology* (Vol. 35, pp. 1–52). San Diego: Elsevier Academic Press.

Holden, K. C., & Smock, P. J. (1991). The economic costs of marital dissolution: Why do women bear a disproportionate cost? *Annual Review of Sociology, 17*, 51–78.

Hollander, E. P. (1958). Conformity, status, and idiosyncrasy credit. *Psychological Review, 65*, 117–127.

Hollander, E. P. (1985). Leadership and power. In G. Lindzey & E. Aronson (Eds.), *Handbook of social psychology* (3rd ed., Vol. 2, pp. 485–537). New York: Random House.

Hood, B. M., Macrae, C. N., Cole-Davies, V. & Dias, M. (2003). Eye remember you! The effects of gaze direction on face recognition in children and adults. *Developmental Science, 6*, 69–73.

Howard, E. S., Gardner, W. L., & Thompson, L. (2007). The role of the self-concept and the social context in determining the behavior of power holders: Self-construal in intergroup versus dyadic dispute resolution negotiations. *Journal of Personality and Social Psychology, 93*, 614–631.

Howeler, M. (1972). Diversity of word usage as a stress indicator in an interview situation. *Journal of Psycholinguistic Research, 1*, 243–248.

Hummert, M. L. (1994). Physiognomic cues to age and the activation of stereotypes of the elderly in interaction. *International Journal of Aging and Human Development, 39*, 5–19.

Hummert, M. L., Garstka, T. A., O'Brien, L. T., Greenwald, A. G., & Mellott, D. S. (2002). Using the implicit association test to measure age differences in implicit social cognitions. *Psychology and Aging, 17*, 482–495.

Hummert, M. L., Garstka, T. A., Shaner, J. L., & Strahm, S. (1994). Stereotypes of the elderly held by young, middle-aged, and elderly adults. *Journals of Gerontology, 49*, (pp. 240–249).

Hummert, M. L., Garstka, T. A., Shaner, J. L., & Strahm, S. (1995). Judgments about stereotypes of the elderly: Attitudes, age associations, and typicality ratings of young, middle-aged, and elderly adults. *Research on Aging, 17*, 168–189.

Hyde, J. S. (2005). The gender similarities hypothesis. *American Psychologist, 60*, 581–592.

Hyers, L. L., & Swim, J. K. (1998). A comparison of the experiences of dominant and minority group members during an intergroup encounter. *Group Processes & Intergroup Relations, 1*, 143–163.

Jackman, M. R. (1994). *The velvet glove: Paternalism and conflict in gender, class, and race relations*. University of California Press, Berkeley.

Jackson, J. M., & Latané, B. (1981). Strength and number of solicitors and the urge toward altruism. *Personality and Social Psychology Bulletin, 7*, 415–422.

Jaffee, C. L., & Lucas, R. L. (1969). Effects of rates of talking and correctness of decisions on leader choice in small groups. *Journal of Social Psychology, 79*, 247–254.

Jetten, J., Branscombe, N. R., Schmitt, M. T., & Spears, R. (2001). Rebels with a cause: Group identification as a response to perceived discrimination from the mainstream. *Personality and Social Psychology Bulletin, 27*, 1204–1213.

Jetten, J., Schmitt, M. T., Branscombe, N. R., & McKimmie, B. M. (2005). Suppressing the negative effect of devaluation on group identification: The role of intergroup differentiation and intragroup respect. *Journal of Experimental Social Psychology, 41*, 208–215.

Jetten, J., Spears, R., & Manstead, A. S. R. (1997). Distinctiveness threat and prototypicality: Combined effects on intergroup discrimination and collective self-esteem. *European Journal of Social Psychology, 27*, 635–657.

Jones, E. E. (1979). The rocky road from acts to dispositions. *American Psychologist, 34*, 107–117.

Jones, E. E. (1990). *Interpersonal perception*. New York: W H Freeman/ Times Books/ Henry Holt.

Jones, E. E., Farina, A., Hastorf, A. H., Markus, H., Miller, D. T., & Scott, R. A. (1984). *Social stigma: The psychology of marked relationships*. New York: Freeman.

Jones, E. E., & Kelly, J. R. (2007). Contributions to a group discussion and perceptions of leadership: Does quantity always count more than quality? *Group Dynamics: Theory, Research, and Practice, 11*, 15–30.

Jones, J. M. (1997). *Prejudice and racism* (2nd ed.). New York: McGraw-Hill.

Jost, J. T., & Burgess, D. (2000). Attitudinal ambivalence and the conflict between group and system justification motives in low status groups. *Personality and Social Psychology Bulletin, 26*, 293–305.

Jost, J. T., Burgess, D., & Mosso, C. O. (2001). Conflicts of legitimation among self, group, and system: The integrative potential of system justification theory. In J. Jost & B. Major (Eds.), *The Psychology of Legitimacy* (pp. 363–390). Cambridge, England: Cambridge University Press.

Jost, J. T., Federico, C. M., & Napier, J. L. (2009). Political ideology: Its structure, functions, and elective affinities. *Annual Review of Psychology, 60*, 307–337.

Jost, J. T., Glaser, J., Kruglanski, A. W., & Sulloway, F. J. (2003). Political conservatism as motivated social cognition. *Psychological Bulletin, 129*, 339–375.

Jost, J. T., Pelham, B. W., & Carvallo, M. R. (2002). Non-conscious forms of system justification: Implicit and behavioral preferences for higher status groups. *Journal of Experimental Social Psychology, 38*, 586–602.

Judd, C. M., James-Hawkins, L., Yzerbyt, V., & Kashima, Y. (2005). Fundamental dimensions of social judgment: Understanding the relations between judgments of competence and warmth. *Journal of Personality and Social Psychology, 89*, 899–913.

Kao, G., & Joyner, K. (2004). Do race and ethnicity matter among friends? Activities among interracial, interethnic, and intraethnic adolescent friends. *Sociological Quarterly, 45*, 557–573.

Kaplan, J. R., Adams, M. R., Clarkson, T. B., & Manuck, S. B. (1996). Psychosocial factors, sex differences, and atherosclerosis: Lessons from animal models. *Psychosomatic Medicine, 58*, 598–611.

Karlins, M., Coffman, T. L., & Walters, G. (1969). On the fading of social stereotypes: Studies in three generations of college students. *Journal of Personality and Social Psychology, 13*, 1–16.

Katz, D., & Braly, K. W. (1933). Racial stereotypes of one hundred college students. *Journal of Abnormal and Social Psychology, 28*, 280–290.

Katz, I., & Hass, R. G. (1988). Racial ambivalence and American value conflict: Correlational and priming studies of dual cognitive structures. *Journal of Personality and Social Psychology, 55*, 893–905.

Kay, A. C., Gaucher, D., Peach, J. M., Laurin, K., Friesen, J., Zanna, M. P., et al. (2009). Inequality, discrimination, and the popwer of the status quo: Direct evidence for a motivation to see the way things are as the way they should be. *Journal of Personality and Social Psychology, 97*, 421–434.

Kay, A. C., & Jost, J. T. (2003). Complementary justice: Effects of "poor but happy" and "poor but honest" stereotype exemplars on system justification and implicit activation of the justice motive. *Journal of Personality and Social Psychology, 85*(5), 823–837.

Keltner, D., Capps, L., Kring, A. M., Young, R. C., & Heerey, E. A. (2001). Just teasing: A conceptual analysis and empirical review. *Psychological Bulletin, 127*, 229–248.

Keltner, D., Gruenfeld, D. H., & Anderson, C. (2003). Power, approach, and inhibition. *Psychological Review, 110*, 265–284.

Keltner, D., & Robinson, R. J. (1997). Defending the status quo: Power and bias in social conflict. *Personality and Social Psychology Bulletin, 23*, 1066–1077.

Kervyn, N., Yzerbyt, V. Y., Demoulin, S., & Judd, C. M. (2008). Competence and warmth in context: The compensatory nature of stereotypic views of national groups. *European Journal of Social Psychology, 38*, 1175–1183. doi: 10.1002/ejsp.526

Kervyn, N., Yzerbyt, V. Y., Judd, C. M., & Nunes, A. (2009). A question of compensation: The social life of the fundamental dimensions of social perception. *Journal of Personality and Social Psychology, 96*, 828–842. doi: 10.1037/a0013320

Kiesler, S. B., & Mathog, R. B. (1968). Distraction hypothesis in attitude change: Effects of effectiveness. *Psychological Reports, 23*, 1123–1133.

Kipnis, D. (1972). Does power corrupt? *Journal of Personality and Social Psychology, 24*, 33–41.

Kipnis, D. (1976). *The powerholders*. Chicago: University of Chicago Press.

Kipnis, D., Castell, J., Gergen, M., & Mauch, D. (1976). Metamorphic effects of power. *Journal of Applied Psychology, 61*, 127–135.

Kite, M. E., & Johnson, B. T. (1988). Attitudes toward older and younger adults: A meta-analysis. *Psychology and Aging, 3*, 233–244.

Knox, V. J., Gekoski, W. L., & Kelly, L. E. (1995). The Age Group Evaluation and Description (AGED) Inventory: A new instrument for assessing stereotypes of and attitudes toward age groups. *International Journal of Aging and Human Development, 40*, 31–55.

Kraus, M. W., & Keltner, D. (2009). Signs of socioeconomic status: A thin-slicing approach. *Psychological Science, 20*, 99–106.

Kray, L. J., Reb, J., Galinsky, A. D., & Thompson, L. (2004). Stereotype reactance at the bargaining table: The effect of stereotype activation and power on claiming and creating value. *Personality and Social Psychology Bulletin, 30*, 399–411.

Kurzban, R., & Leary, M. R. (2001). Evolutionary origins of stigmatization: The functions of social exclusion. *Psychological Bulletin, 127*, 187–208.

Kurzban, R., Tooby, J., & Cosmides, L. (2001). Can race be erased? Coalitional computation and social categorization. *Proceedings of the National Academy of Sciences, 98*, 15387–15392.

Labov, W. (1972). *Sociolinguistic patterns*. Philadelphia: University of Pennsylvania Press.

Labov, W. (2001). *Principles of linguistic change: Social factors*. Oxford: Blackwell.

Lachman, M. E., & Weaver, S. L. (1998). The sense of control as a moderator of social class differences in health and well-being. *Journal of Personality and Social Psychology, 74*, 763–773.

Lammers, J., Gordijn, E. H., & Otten, S. (2008). Looking through the eyes of the powerful. *Journal of Experimental Social Psychology, 44*, 1229–1238.

Langner, C. A., & Keltner, D. (2008). Social power and emotional experience: Actor and partner effects within dyadic interactions. *Journal of Experimental Social Psychology, 44*, 848–856.

Lee, T. L., & Fiske, S. T. (2006). Not an outgroup, but not yet an ingroup: Immigrants in the stereotype content model. *International Journal of Intercultural Relations, 30*, 751–768.

Lee, T. L., Fiske, S. T., & Glick, P. (2010). Ambivalent sexism in close relationships: (Hostile) power and (benevolent) romance shape relationship ideals. *Sex Roles*.

Lefkowitz, M., Blake, R. R., & Mouton, J. S. (1955). Status factors in pedestrian violation of traffic signals. *Journal of Abnormal and Social Psychology, 51*, 704–706.

Lerner, M. J., & Miller, D. T. (1978). Just world research and the attribution process: Looking back and ahead. *Psychology Bulletin, 85*, 1030–1051.

Levin, H., Giles, H., & Garrett, P. (1994). The effects of lexical formality and accent on trait attributions. *Language and Communication, 14*, 265–274.

Levin, S., & van Laar, C. (Eds.). (2006). Stigma and group inequality: Social psychological perspectives. *The Claremont Symposium on Applied Social Psychology* (pp. 65–81). Mahwah, NJ: Erlbaum.

Levin, S., van Laar, C. Y., & Sidanius, J. H. (2003). The effects of ingroup and outgroup friendships on ethnic attitudes in college: A longitudinal study. *Group Processes and Intergroup Relations, 6*, 76–92.

Levy, B. R., Hausdorff, J. M., Hencke, R., & Wei, J. Y. (2000). Reducing cardiovascular stress with positive self-stereotypes of aging. *Journals of Gerontology: Series B: Psychological Sciences and Social Issues, 55B*, 205–213.

Levy, B. R., Slade, M. D., Kunkel, S. R., & Kasl, S. V. (2002). Longevity increased by positive self perceptions of aging. *Journal of Personality and Social Psychology, 83*, 261–270.

Lewontin, R. (1972). The apportionment of human diversity. *Evolutionary Biology, 6*, 381–398.

Lieberman, M. D., Hariri, A., Jarcho, J. M., Eisenberger, N. I., & Bookheimer, S. Y. (2005). An fMRI investigation of race-related amygdala activity in African-American and Caucasian-American individuals. *Nature Neuroscience, 8*, 720–722.

Lin, M. H., Kwan, V. S. Y., Cheung, A., & Fiske, S. T. (2005). Stereotype content model explains prejudice for an envied outgroup: Scale of Anti-Asian American Stereotypes. *Personality and Social Psychology Bulletin, 31*, 34–47.

Link, B. G., Lennon, M. C., & Dohrenwend, B. P. (1993). Socioeconomic status and depression: The role of occupations involving direction, control, and Planning. *American Journal of Sociology, 98*, 1351–1387.

Linssen, H., & Hagendoorn, L. (1994). Social and geographical factors in the explanation of the content of European nationality stereotypes. *British Journal of Social Psychology, 33*, 165–182.

Livingston, R. W., & Brewer, M. B. (2002). What are we really priming? Cue-based versus category-based processing of facial stimuli. *Journal of Personality and Social Psychology, 82*, 5–18.

Lott, B. (2002). Cognitive and behavioral distancing from the poor. *American Psychologist, 57*, 100–110.

Maass, A., Cadinu, M., Guarnieri, G., & Grasselli, A. (2003). Sexual harassment under social identity threat: The computer harassment paradigm. *Journal of Personality and Social Psychology, 85*, 853–870.

Maddox, K. B. (2004). Perspectives on racial phenotypicality bias. *Personality and Social Psychology Review, 8*, 383–401.

Maddox, K. B., & Chase, S. G. (2004). Manipulating subcategory salience: Exploring the link between skin tone and social perception of Blacks. *European Journal of Social Psychology, 34*, 533–546.

Maddox, K. B., & Gray, S. A. (2002). Cognitive representations of Black Americans: Re-exploring the role of skin tone. *Personality and Social Psychology Bulletin, 28*, 250–259.

Madon, S., Guyll, M., Aboufadel, K., Montiel, E., Smith, A., Palumbo, P., & Jussim, L. (2001). Ethnic and national stereotypes: The Princeton trilogy revisited and revised. *Personality and Social Psychology Bulletin, 27*, 996–1010.

Magee, J. C. (2009). Seeing power in action: The roles of deliberation, implementation, and action in inferences of power. *Journal of Experimental Social Psychology, 45*, 1–14.

Magee, J. C. & Galinsky, A. D. (2008). Social hierarchy: The self-reinforcing nature of power and status. *Academy of Management Annals, 2*, 351–398.

Magee, J. C., Galinsky, A. D., & Gruenfeld, D. H. (2007). Power, propensity to negotiate, and moving first in competitive interactions. *Personality and Social Psychology Bulletin, 33*, 200–212.

Magee, J. C., & Langner, C. A. (2008). How personalized and socialized power motivation facilitate antisocial and prosocial decision-making. *Journal of Research in Personality, 42*, 1547–1559.

Major, B., Gramzow, R. H., McCoy, S. K., Levin, S., Schmader, T., & Sidanius, J. (2002). Perceiving personal discrimination: The role of group status and legitimizing ideology. *Journal of Personality and Social Psychology, 82*, 269–282.

Major, B., Kaiser, C. R., & McCoy, S. K. (2003). It's not my fault: When and why attributions to prejudice protect self-esteem. *Personality and Social Psychology Bulletin, 29*, 772–781.

Major, B., & O'Brien, L. T. (2005). The social psychology of stigma. *Annual Review of Psychology, 56*, 393–421.

Major, B., Quinton, W. J., & Schmader, T. (2003). Attributions to discrimination and self-esteem: Impact of group identification and situational ambiguity. *Journal of Experimental Social Psychology, 39*, 220–231.

Maner, J. K., Gailliot, M. T., Butz, D. A., & Peruche, B. M. (2007). Power, risk, and the status quo: Does power promote riskier or more conservative decision making? *Personality and Social Psychology Bulletin, 33*, 451–462.

Manuck, S. B., Kaplan, J. R., & Clarkson, T. B. (1983). Behaviorally induced heart rate reactivity and atherosclerosis in cynomolgus monkeys. *Psychosomatic Medicine, 45*, 95–108.

Marks, J. (1995). *Human biodiversity: Genes, races, and history.* Aldine de Gruyter.

Markus, H. R. (2008). Pride, prejudice, and ambivalence: Toward a unified theory of race and ethnicity. *American Psychologist, 63*, 651–670.

Marmot, M. (2003). Social resources and health. In F. Kessel, P. L. Rosenfield, & N. B. Anderson (Eds.), *Expanding the Boundaries of Health and Social Science* (pp. 259–285). New York: Oxford University Press.

Marmot, M. G., Bosma, H., Hemingway, H., Brunner, E. J., & Stansfeld, S. (1997). Contribution of job control and other risk factors to social variations in coronary heart disease incidence. *Lancet, 350*, 235–239.

Martin, C. L., & Ruble, D. N. (2010). Patterns of gender development. *Annual Review of Psychology, 61*.

Mason, M. F., Hood, B. M., & Macrae, C. N. (2004). Look into my eyes: Gaze direction and person memory. *Memory, 12*, 637–643.

Mason, M. F., & Macrae, C. N. (2004). Categorizing and individuating others: The neural substrates of person perception. *Journal of Cognitive Neuroscience, 16*, 1785–1795.

Mason, M. F., Tatkow, E. P., & Macrae, C. N. (2005). The look of love: Gaze shifts and person perception. *Psychological Science, 16*, 236–239.

Masser, B. M., & Abrams, D. (2004). Reinforcing the glass ceiling: The consequences of hostile sexism for female managerial candidates. *Sex Roles, 51*, 609–615.

Massey, D. S. (2007). *Categorically unequal: The American stratification system.* New York: Russell Sage.

Massey, D. S., Charles, C. Z., Lundy, G. F., & Fischer, M. J. (2003). *The source of the river: The social origins of freshman at America's selective colleges and universities.* Princeton, NJ: Princeton University Press.

Massey, D. S., & Denton, N. A. (1993). *American apartheid: Segregation and the making of the underclass.* Cambridge MA: Harvard University Press.

Mast, M. (2002). Dominance as expressed and inferred through speaking time: A meta-analysis. *Human Communication Research, 28*, 420–450.

Mays, V. M., Cochran, S. D., & Barnes, N. W. (2007). Race, race-based discrimination, and health outcomes among African Americans. *Annual Review of Psychology, 58*, 201–225.

McCoy, S. K., & Major, B. (2003). Group identification moderates emotional responses to perceived prejudice. *Personality and Social Psychology Bulletin, 29*, 1005–1017.

McEwen, B. S. (2000). The neurobiology of stress: from serendipity to clinical relevance. *Brain Research, 886*, 172–189.

Mendes, W. B., Blascovich, J., Lickel, B., & Hunter, S. (2002). Challenge and threat during social interaction with White and Black men. *Personality and Social Psychology Bulletin, 28*, 939–952.

Mendes, W. B., Blascovich, J., Major, B., & Seery, M. (2001). Challenge and threat responses during downward and upward social comparisons. *European Journal of Social Psychology, 31*, 477–497.

Mendes, W. B., Major, B., McCoy, S., & Blascovich, J. (2008). How attributional ambiguity shapes physiological and emotional responses to social rejection and acceptance. *Journal of Personality and Social Psychology, 94*, 278–291.

Merton, R. K. (1948). The self-fulfilling prophecy. *Antioch Review, 8*, 193–210.

Mikula, G., Scherer, K. R., & Athenstaedt, U. (1998). The role of injustice in the elicitation of differential emotional reactions. *Personality and Social Psychology Bulletin, 24*, 769–783.

Milgram, S. (1974). *Obedience to authority*. New York: Harper and Row.

Moore, D. L., Hausknecht, D., & Thamodaran, K. (1986). Time compression, response opportunity, and persuasion. *Journal of Consumer Research, 13*, 85–99.

Moors, A., & De Houwer, J. (2005). Automatic processing of dominance and submissiveness. *Experimental Psychology, 52*, 296–302.

Moscovici S. (1988). Some notes on social representations. *European Journal of Social Psychology, 18*, 211–250.

Moskowitz, D. S., Ho, M. R., & Turcotte-Tremblay, A. (2007). Contextual influences on interpersonal complementarity. *Personality and Social Psychology Bulletin, 33*, 1051–1063.

Mullen, B. (1985). Strength and immediacy of sources: A meta-analytic evaluation of the forgotten elements of social impact theory. *Journal of Personality and Social Psychology, 48*, 1458–1466.

Mullen, B., Brown, R., & Smith, C. (1992). Ingroup bias as a function of salience, relevance, and status: An integration. *European Journal of Social Psychology, 22*, 103–122.

Mullen, B., Salas, E., & Driskell, J. E. (1989). Salience, motivation, and artifact as contributions to the relation between participation rate and leadership. *Journal of Experimental Social Psychology, 25*, 545–559.

Mummendey, A., & Wenzel, M. (1999). Social discrimination and tolerance in intergroup relations: Reactions to intergroup differences. *Personality and Social Psychology Review, 3*, 158–175.

Nath, L. E. (2007). Expectation states: Are formal words a status cue for competence? *Current Research in Social Psychology, 13*, 50–63.

Nei, M., & Roychoudhury, A. (1993). Evolutionary relationships of human populations on a global scale. *Molecular Biology Evolution, 10*, 927–943.

Nelson, T. D. (Ed.). (2002). *Ageism: Stereotyping and prejudice against older persons*. Cambridge, MA: MIT Press.

Neuberg, S. L. (1989). The goal of forming accurate impressions during social interactions: Attenuating the impact of negative expectancies. *Journal of Personality and Social Psychology, 56*, 374–386.

Neuberg, S. L., & Fiske, S. T. (1987). Motivational influences on impression formation: Outcome dependency, accuracy-driven attention, and individuating processes. *Journal of Personality and Social Psychology, 53*, 431–444.

Neugarten, B. (1974, September). Age groups in American society and the rise of the young old. *Annals of the American Academy of Political and Social Science*, 187–198.

Newton, T. L., & Bane, C. M. H. (2001). Cardiovascular correlates of behavioral dominance and hostility during dyadic interaction. *International Journal of Psychophysiology, 40*, 33–46.

Ng, S. H., & Bradac, J. J. (1993). *Power in language: Verbal communication and social influence*. Newbury Park, CA: Sage.

Nisbett, R. E. (2009). *Intelligence and how to get it: Why schools and cultures count*. New York: Norton.

North, M., & Fiske, S. T. (2009). Succession, Identity, and Consumption: Dimensions of control in ageism. Unpublished manuscript, Princeton University.

Oldmeadow, J. (2007). Status generalization in context: The moderating role of groups. *Journal of Experimental Social Psychology, 43*, 273–279.

Oldmeadow, J., & Fiske, S. T. (2007). System-justifying ideologies moderate status = competence stereotypes: Roles for belief in a just world and social dominance orientation. *European Journal of Social Psychology, 37*, 1135–1148.

Oldmeadow, J. A., & Fiske, S. T. (under review). *Contentment to corruption: A model of stereotype content across status systems*. Unpublished manuscript, University of York.

Oldmeadow, J. A., & Fiske, S. T. (2010). Social status and the pursuit of positive social identity: Systematic domains of intergroup differentiation and discrimination for high and low status groups. *Group Processes and Intergroup Relations*.

Operario, D., & Fiske, S. T. (2001). Effects of trait dominance on power-holders' judgments of subordinates. *Social Cognition, 19*, 161–180.

Overbeck, J. R., & Park, B. (2001). When power does not corrupt: Superior individuation processes among powerful perceivers. *Journal of Personality and Social Psychology, 81*, 549–565.

Overbeck, J. R., Tiedens, L. Z., & Brion, S. (2006). The powerful want to, the powerless have to: Perceived constraint moderates causal attributions. *European Journal of Social Psychology, 36*, 479–496.

Page-Gould, E., Mendoza-Denton, R., & Tropp, L. R. (2008). With a little help from my cross-group friend: Reducing anxiety in intergroup contexts through cross-group friendship. *Journal of Personality and Social Psychology, 95*, 1080–1094.

Parra, F. C., Amado, R. C., Lambertucci, J. R., Rocha, J., Antunes, C. M., & Pena, S. D. (2003). Color and genomic ancestry in Brazilians. *Proceedings of the National Academy of Sciences, 100*, 177–182.

Pasupathi, M., Carstensen, L. L., & Tsai, J. L. (1995). Ageism in interpersonal settings. In B. Lott & D. Maluso (Eds.), *The social psychology of interpersonal discrimination*. New York: Guilford Press.

Peeters, G. (1993). Self-other anchored evaluations of national stereotypes. Unpublished manuscript, Catholic University of Leuven, Leuven, Belgium.

Pettigrew, T. F. (1979). The ultimate attribution error: Extending Allport's cognitive analysis of prejudice. *Personality and Social Psychology Bulletin, 5*, 461–476.

Pettigrew, T. F. (1989). The nature of modern racism in the United States. *Revue Internationale de Psychologie Sociale, 2*, 291–303.

Pettigrew, T. F., Christ, O., Wagner, U., Meertens, R. W., van Dick, R., & Zick, A. (2008). Relative deprivation and intergroup prejudice. *Journal of Social Issues, 64*, 385–401.

Pettigrew, T. F., & Meertens, R. W. (1995). Subtle and blatant prejudice in Western Europe. *European Journal of Social Psychology, 25*, 57–75.

Pettigrew, T. F., & Tropp, L. R. (2006). A meta-analytic test of intergroup contact theory. *Journal of Personality and Social Psychology, 90*, 751–783.

Petty, R. E., Briñol, P., & Tormala, Z. L. (2002). Thought confidence as a determinant of persuasion: The self-validation hypothesis. *Journal of Personality and Social Psychology, 82*, 722–741.

Petty, R. E., Cacioppo, J. T., & Goldman, R. (1981). Personal involvement as a determinant of argument-based persuasion. *Journal of Personality and Social Psychology, 41*, 847–855.

Petty, R. E., & Wegener, D. T. (1998). Attitude change: Multiple roles for persuasion variables. In D. T. Gilbert, S. T. Fiske, & G. Lindzey (Eds.),

Handbook of Social Psychology (4th ed., Vol. 1, pp. 323–390). New York: McGraw-Hill.

Phalet, K., & Poppe, E. (1997). Competence and morality dimensions in national and ethnic stereotypes: A study in six eastern-European countries. *European Journal of Social Psychology, 27*, 703–723.

Phelps, E. A., O'Connor, K. J., Cunningham, W. A., Funayama, E. S., Gatenby, J. C., Gore, J. C., et al. (2000). Performance on indirect measures of race evaluation predicts amygdala activation. *Journal of Cognitive Neuroscience, 12*, 729–738.

Pinker, S., Nowak, M. A., & Lee, J. J. (2008) The logic of indirect speech. *Proceedings of the National Academy of Sciences, 105*, 833–838.

Pittman, T. S., & D'Agostino, P. R. (1989). Motivation and cognition: Control deprivation and the nature of subsequent information processing. *Journal of Experimental Social Psychology, 25*, 465–480.

Pittman, T. S., & Pittman, N. L. (1980). Deprivation of control and the attribution process. *Journal of Personality and Social Psychology, 39*, 377–389.

Plant, E. A., & Devine, P. G. (1998). Internal and external motivation to respond without prejudice. *Journal of Personality and Social Psychology, 75*, 811–832.

Poppe, E. (2001). Effects of changes in GNP and perceived group characteristics on national and ethnic stereotypes in Central and Eastern Europe. *Journal of Applied Social Psychology, 31*, 1689–1708.

Poppe, E., & Linssen, H. (1999). In-group favouritism and the reflection of realistic dimensions of difference between national states in Central and Eastern European nationality stereotypes. *British Journal of Social Psychology, 38*, 85–102.

Porath, C. L., Overbeck, J. R., & Pearson, C. M. (2008). Picking up the gauntlet: How individuals respond to status challenges. *Journal of Applied Social Psychology, 38*, 1945–1980.

Pornpitakpan, C. (2004). The persuasiveness of source credibility: A critical review of five decades' evidence. *Journal of Applied Social Psychology, 34*, 243–281.

Pratto, F., Stallworth, L. M., & Sidanius, J. (1997). The gender gap: Differences in political attitudes and social dominance orientation. *British Journal of Social Psychology, 36*, 49–68.

Rahim, M. A., & Afza, M. (1993). Leader power, commitment, satisfaction, compliance, and propensity to leave a job among U.S. accountants. *Journal of Social Psychology, 133*, 611–625.

Reid, S. A., & Hogg, M. A. (2005). Uncertainty reduction, self-enhancement, and ingroup identification. *Personality and Social Psychology Bulletin, 31*, 804–817.

Renninger, L. A., Wade, T. J., & Grammer, K. (2004). Getting that female glance: Patterns and consequences of male nonverbal behavior in courtship contexts. *Evolution and Human Behavior, 25*, 416–431.

Reyna, C., Henry, P. J., Korfmacher, W., & Tucker, A. (2006). Examining the principles in principled conservatism: The role of responsibility stereotypes as cues for deservingness in racial policy decisions. *Journal of Personality and Social Psychology, 90*, 109–128.

Richeson, J. A., Baird, A. A., Gordon, H. L., Heatherton, T. F., Wyland, C. L., Trawalter, S., et al. (2003). An fMRI investigation of the impact of interracial contact on executive function. *Nature Neuroscience, 6*, 1323–1328.

Richeson, J. A., & Shelton, J. N. (2003). When prejudice does not pay: Effects of interracial contact on executive function. *Psychological Science, 14*, 287–290.

Richeson, J. A., & Shelton, J. N. (2006). A social psychological perspective on the stigmatization of older adults. In L. L. Carstensen & C. R. Hartel (Eds.), *When I'm 64* (pp. 174–208). Washington, DC: National Research Council Committee on Aging Frontiers in Social Psychology, Personality, and Adult Developmental Psychology. The National Academies Press.

Richeson, J. A., Trawalter, S., & Shelton, J. N. (2005). African Americans' implicit racial attitudes and the depletion of executive function after interracial interactions. *Social Cognition, 23*, 336–352.

Ridgeway, C. L. (1991). The social construction of status value: Gender and other nominal characteristics. *Social Forces, 70*, 367–86.

Ridgeway, C. L. (1997). Interaction and the conservation of gender inequality: Considering employment. *American Sociological Review, 62*, 218–35.

Ridgeway, C. L., & Erickson, K. G. (2000). Creating and spreading status beliefs. *American Journal of Sociology, 106*, 579–615.

Roberts, B.W., Walton, K. E., & Viechtbauer, W. (2006). Patterns of mean-level change in personality traits across the life course: A meta-analysis of longitudinal studies. *Psychological Bulletin, 132*, 1–25.

Rodríguez-Bailón, R., Moya, M., & Yzerbyt, V. (2000). Why do superiors attend to negative stereotypic information about their subordinates? Effects of power legitimacy on social perception. *European Journal of Social Psychology, 30*, 651–671.

Rosenthal, R. (1994). Interpersonal expectancy effects: A 30-year perspective. *Current Directions in Psychological Science, 3*, 176–179.

Ross, L. (1977). The intuitive psychologist and his shortcomings: Distortions in the attribution process. In L. Berkowitz (Ed.), *Advances in experimental social psychology* (Vol. 10, pp. 174–221). New York: Academic Press.

Ruble, D. N., & Ruble, T. L. (1982). Sex stereotypes. In A. G. Miller (Ed.), *In the eye of the beholder: Contemporary issues in stereotyping* (pp. 188–252). New York: Praeger.

Rudman, L. A. (1998). Self-promotion as a risk factor for women: The costs and benefits of counterstereotypical impression management. *Journal of Personality and Social Psychology, 74*, 629–645.

Rudman, L. A., & Fairchild, K. (2004). Reactions to counterstereotypic behavior: The role of backlash in cultural stereotype maintenance. *Journal of Personality and Social Psychology, 87*, 157–176.

Rudman, L. A., & Glick, P. (1999). Feminized management and backlash toward agentic women: The hidden costs to women of a kinder, gentler image of middle managers. *Journal of Personality and Social Psychology, 77*, 1004–1010.

Rudman, L. A., & Glick, P. (2001). Prescriptive gender stereotypes and backlash toward agentic women. *Journal of Social Issues, 57*, 743–762.

Rudman, L. A., & Glick, P. (2008). *Social psychology of gender: How power and intimacy shape gender relations.* New York: Guilford Press.

Rudman, L. A., & Heppen, J. B. (2003). Implicit romantic fantasies and women's interest in personal power: A glass slipper effect? *Personality and Social Psychology Bulletin, 29*, 1357–1370.

Rudman, L. A., & Kilianski, S. E. (2000). Implicit and explicit attitudes toward female authority. *Personality and Social Psychology Bulletin, 26*, 1315–1328.

Ruscher, J. B. (2001). *The social psychology of prejudiced communication.* New York: Guilford.

Ruscher, J. B., & Fiske, S. T. (1990). Interpersonal competition can cause individuating processes. *Journal of Personality and Social Psychology, 58*, 832–843.

Ruscher, J. B., Fiske, S. T., Miki, H., & Van Manen, S. (1991). Individuating processes in competition: Interpersonal versus intergroup. *Personality and Social Psychology Bulletin, 17*, 595–605.

Russell, A. M., & Fiske, S. T. (2008). It's all relative: Social position and interpersonal perception. *European Journal of Social Psychology, 38*, 1193–1201.

Russell, A. M., & Fiske, S. T. (2009, February). Social class ambivalence: Polarized reactions to the poor. Paper presented to *Society for Personality and Social Psychology*, Tampa.

Russell, B. (1938). *Power: A new social analysis.* New York: Norton.

Russell, B. L., & Trigg, K. Y. (2004). Tolerance of sexual harassment: An examination of gender differences, ambivalent sexism, social dominance, and gender roles. *Sex Roles, 50,* 565–573.

Ryan, E. B., & Sebastian, R. (1980). The effects of speech style and social class background on social judgments of speakers. *British Journal of Social and Clinical Psychology, 19,* 229–233.

Sachdev, I., & Bourhis, R. Y. (1985). Social categorization and power differentials in group relations. *European Journal of Social Psychology, 15,* 415–434.

Sachdev, I., & Bourhis, R. Y. (1987). Status differentials and inter-group behavior. *European Journal of Social Psychology, 17,* 277–293.

Sachdev, I., & Bourhis, R. Y. (1991). Power and status differentials in minority and majority group relations. *European Journal of Social Psychology, 21,* 1–24.

Sakalli-Ugurlu, N., Sila Yalçin, Z., & Glick, P. (2007). Ambivalent sexism, belief in a just world, and empathy as predictors of Turkish students' attitudes toward rape victims. *Sex Roles, 57,* 889–895.

Sapolsky, R. M. (2004a). Social status and health in humans and other animals. *Annual Review of Anthropology, 33,* 393–418.

Sapolsky, R. M. (2004b). Stress and cognition. In M. S. Gazzaniga (Ed.), *The cognitive neurosciences* (3rd ed., pp. 1031–1042). Cambridge MA: MIT Press.

Sapolsky, R. M. (2005). The influence of social hierarchy on primate health. *Science, 308,* 648–652.

Scheepers, D., Spears, R., Doosje, B., & Manstead, A. S. R. (2006). Diversity in in-group bias: Structural factors, situational features, and social functions. *Journal of Personality and Social Psychology, 90,* 944–960.

Scherer, K. R. (1979). Personality markers in speech. In K. R. Scherer & H. Giles (Eds.), *Social markers in speech* (pp. 147–209). Cambridge: Cambridge University Press.

Schmid-Mast, M., Hall, J. A., & Ickes, W. (2006). Inferring power-relevant thoughts and feelings in others: A signal detection analysis. *European Journal of Social Psychology, 36,* 469–478.

Schneiderman, N., Ironson, G., & Siegel, S. D. (2005). Stress and health: Psychological, behavioral, and biological determinants. *Annual Review of Clinical Psychology, 1,* 607–28.

Schubert, T. W. (2004). The power in your hand: Gender differences in bodily feedback from making a fist. *Personality and Social Psychology Bulletin, 30,* 757–769.

Schubert, T. W. (2005). Your Highness: Vertical positions as perceptual symbols of power. *Journal of Personality and Social Psychology, 89,* 1–21.

Schuman, H., Steeh, C., Bobo, L., & Krysan, M. (1997). *Racial attitudes in America: Trends and interpretations* (rev. ed.). Cambridge, MA: Harvard University Press.

Sears, D. O. (1998). Racism and politics in the United States. In J. L. Eberhardt, & S. T. Fiske (Eds.), *Confronting racism: The problem and the response* (pp. 76–100). Thousand Oaks, CA: Sage.

Seccombe, K., & Ishii-Kuntz, M. (1991). Perceptions of problems associated with aging: Comparisons among four older age cohorts. *Gerontologist, 31,* 527–533.

Sellers, R. M., & Shelton, J. N. (2003). The role of racial identity in perceived racial discrimination. *Journal of Personality and Social Psychology, 84,* 1079–1092.

Sen, A. (2003). Missing women: Revisited. *BMJ, 327,* 1297–1298.

Senju, A., & Hasegawa, T. (2005). Direct gaze captures visuospatial attention. *Visual Cognition, 12,* 127–144.

Seyfarth, R. M., Cheney, D. L., & Bergman, T. J. (2005). Primate social cognition and the origins of language. *Trends in Cognitive Sciences, 9,* 264–266.

Shelton, J. N. (2000). A reconceptualization of how we study issues of racial prejudice. *Personality and Social Psychology Review, 4,* 374–390.

Shelton, J. N. (2003). Interpersonal concerns in social encounters between majority and minority group members. *Group Processes and Intergroup Relations, 6,* 171–185.

Shelton, J. N., & Richeson, J. A. (2005). Intergroup contact and pluralistic ignorance. *Journal of Personality and Social Psychology, 88,* 91–107.

Shelton, J. N., & Richeson, J. A. (2006). Interracial interactions: A relational approach. In M. P. Zanna (Ed.), *Advances in experimental social psychology* (pp. 121–181). New York: Academic Press.

Shelton, J. N., Richeson, J. A., & Vorauer, J. D. (2006). Threatened identities and interethnic interactions. In W. Stroebe & M. Hewstone (Eds.), *European review of social psychology* (Vol. 17, pp. 312–358). New York: Psychology Press.

Shepherd, S. V., Deaner, R. O., & Platt, M. L. (2006). Social status gates social attention in monkeys. *Current Biology, 16,* R119–R120.

Shnabel, N., & Nadler, A. (2008). A needs-based model of reconciliation: Satisfying the differential emotional needs of victim and perpetrator as a key to promoting reconciliation. *Journal of Personality and Social Psychology, 94,* 116–132.

Shnabel, N., Nadler, A., Canetti-Nisim, D., & Ullrich, J. (2008). The role of acceptance and empowerment in promoting reconciliation from the perspective of the Needs-Based Model. *Social Issues and Policy Review, 2,* 159–186.

Sibley, C. G., & Wilson, M. S. (2004). Differentiating hostile and benevolent sexist attitudes toward positive and negative sexual female subtypes. *Sex Roles, 51,* 687–696.

Sibley, C. G., Wilson, M. S., & Duckitt, J. (2007). Antecedents of men's Hostile and Benevolent Sexism: The dual roles of Social Dominance Orientation and Right-Wing Authoritarianism. *Personality and Social Psychology Bulletin, 33,* 160–172.

Sidanius, J., Levin, S., Federico, C. M., & Pratto, F. (2001). Legitimizing ideologies: The social dominance approach. In J. T. Jost & B. Major (Eds.), *The psychology of legitimacy: Emerging perspectives on ideology, justice, and intergroup relations* (pp. 307–331). New York: Cambridge University Press.

Sidanius, J., & Pratto, F. (1999). *Social dominance: An intergroup theory of social hierarchy and oppression.* New York: Cambridge University Press.

Simon, H. A. (1957). *Models of man.* New York: Wiley.

Singh, A. K. (1989). Attribution research on poverty: A review. *Psychologia: An International Journal of Psychology in the Orient, 32,* 143–148.

Smith, Pamela K., & Bargh, J. A. (2008). Nonconscious effects of power on basic approach and avoidance tendencies. *Social Cognition, 26,* 1–24.

Smith, Pamela K., Jost, J. T., & Vijay, R. (2008). Legitimacy crisis? Behavioral approach and inhibition when power differences are left unexplained. *Social Justice Research, 21,* 358–376.

Smith, Pamela K., Jostmann, N. B., Galinsky, A. D., & van Dijk, W. W. (2008). Lacking power impairs executive functions. *Psychological Science, 19,* 441–447.

Smith, Pamela K., & Trope, Y. (2006). You focus on the forest when you're in charge of the trees: Power priming and abstract information processing. *Journal of Personality and Social Psychology, 90,* 578–596.

Smith, Peter K. (1988). The cognitive demands of children's social interactions with peers. In R. W. Byrne & A. Whiten (Eds.), *Machiavellian Intelligence* (pp. 94–110). Oxford: Oxford University Press.

Smith, R. H. (Ed.). (2008). *Envy: Theory and research.* New York: Oxford University Press.

Smith, R. H., Combs, D. J. Y., & Thielke, S. M. (2008). Envy and the challenges to good health. In R. H. Smith (Ed.), *Envy: Theory and research* (pp. 290–314). New York: Oxford University Press.

Smith, R. H., & Kim, S. H. (2007). Comprehending envy. *Psychological Bulletin, 133*, 46–64.

Smith, R. H., Parrott, W. G., Ozer, D., & Moniz, A. (1994). Subjective injustice and inferiority as predictors of hostile and depressive feelings in envy. *Personality and Social Psychology Bulletin, 20*, 705–711.

Smith, S. M., & Schaffer, D. R. (1995). Speed of speech and persuasion: Evidence for multiple effects. *Personality and Social Psychology Bulletin, 21*, 1051–1060.

Snyder, M. (1992). Motivational foundations of behavioral confirmation. In M. P. Zanna (Ed.), *Advances in experimental social psychology* (Vol. 25, pp. 67–114). San Diego: Academic Press.

Snyder, M., & Haugen, J. A. (1994). Why does behavioral confirmation occur? A functional perspective on the role of the perceiver. *Journal of Experimental Social Psychology, 30*, 218–246.

Snyder, M., & Haugen, J. A. (1995). Why does behavioral confirmation occur? A functional perspective on the role of the target. *Personality and Social Psychology Bulletin, 21*, 963–974.

Snyder, M., & Kiviniemi, M. T. (2001). Getting what they came for: How power influences the dynamics and outcomes of interpersonal interaction. In A. Y. Lee-Chai & J. A. Bargh (Eds.), *The use and abuse of power: Multiple perspectives on the causes of corruption.* (pp. 133–155). New York: Psychology Press.

Snyder, M., & Miene, P. K. (1994). Stereotyping of the elderly: A functional approach. *British Journal of Social Psychology, 33*, 63–82.

Sparks, J. R., & Areni, C. S. (2002). The effects of sales presentation quality an initial perceptions on persuasion: A multiple role perspective. *Journal of Business Research, 55*, 517–528.

Sparks, J. R., & Areni, C. S. (2008). Style versus substance: Multiple roles of language power in persuasion. *Journal of Applied Social Psychology, 38*, 37–60.

Sparks, J. R., Areni, C. S., & Cox, K. C. (1998). An investigation of the effects of language style and communication modality on persuasion. *Communication Monographs, 65*, 108–125.

Spears, R., Doosje, B., & Ellemers, N. (1997). Self-stereotyping in the face of threats to group status and distinctiveness: The role of group identification. *Personality and Social Psychology Bulletin, 23*, 538–553.

Spears, R., Greenwood, R., & de Lemus, S. (2010). Legitimacy, social identity, and power. In A. P. Guinote & T. K. Vescio (Eds.), *The social psychology of power*. New York: Guilford.

Spears, R., Jetten, J., & Doosje, B. (2001). The (il)legitimacy of ingroup bias: From social reality to social resistance. In J. T. Jost & B. Major (Eds.), *The psychology of legitimacy: Emerging perspectives on ideology, justice, and intergroup relations* (pp. 332–362). New York: Cambridge University Press.

Spears, R., & Manstead, A. S. (1989). The social context of stereotyping and differentiation. *European Journal of Social Psychology, 19*, 101–121.

Spencer, B., & Castano, E. (2007). Social class is dead. Long live social class! Stereotype threat among low socioeconomic status individuals. *Social Justice Research, 20*, 418–432.

Spencer, S. J., Logel, C., & Davies, P. G. (2010). Stereotype threat. *Annual Review of Psychology, 61*.

Stapel, D. A., & van der Zee, K. I. (2006). The self salience model of other-to-self effects: Integrating principles of self-enhancement, complementarity, and imitation. *Journal of Personality and Social Psychology, 90*, 258–271.

Stephan, W. G., Boniecki, K. A., Ybarra, O., Bettencourt, A., Ervin, K. S., Jackson, L. A., McNatt, P. S., & Renfro, C. L. (2002). The role of threats in the racial attitudes of Blacks and White. *Personality and Social Psychology Bulletin, 28*, 1242–1254.

Stephan, W. G., & Stephan, C. W. (2000). An integrated threat theory of prejudice. In S. Oskamp (Ed.), *Reducing prejudice and discrimination* (pp. 23–45). Mahwah, NJ: Erlbaum.

Stevens, L. E., & Fiske, S. T. (2000). Motivated impressions of a powerholder: Accuracy under task dependency and misperception under evaluative dependency. *Personality and Social Psychology Bulletin, 26*, 907–922.

Steele, C. M., Spencer, S. J., & Aronson, J. (2002). Contending with group image: The psychology of stereotype and social identity threat. In M. P. Zanna (Ed.), *Advances in experimental social psychology* (Vol. 34, pp. 379–440). San Diego: Academic Press.

Street, R. L., Jr., Brady, R. M., & Putnam, W. B. (1983). The influence of speech rate stereotypes and rate similarity on listeners' evaluations of speakers. *Journal of Language and Social Psychology, 2*, 37–356.

Strier, K. B. (2000). *Primate behavioral ecology*. Boston: Pearson Allyn and Bacon.

Swann, W. B., Stephenson, B., & Pittman, T. S. (1981). Curiosity and control: On the determinants of the search for social knowledge. *Journal of Personality and Social Psychology, 40*, 635–642.

Swim, J. K., & Hyers, L. L. (1999). Excuse me—What did you just say?!: Women's public and private responses to sexist remarks. *Journal of Experimental Social Psychology, 35*, 68–88.

Swim, J. K., Hyers, L. L., Cohen, L. L., & Ferguson, M. J. (2001). Everyday sexism: Evidence for its incidence, nature, and psychological impact from three daily diary studies. *Journal of Social Issues, 57*, 31–53.

Swim, J. K., Hyers, L. L., Cohen, L. L., Fitzgerald, D. C., & Bylsma, W. H. (2003). African American college students' experiences with everyday racism: Characteristics of and responses to these incidents. *Journal of Black Psychology, 29*, 38–67.

Swim, J. K., & Stangor, C. (Eds.). (1998). *Prejudice: The target's perspective*. San Diego, Academic Press.

Thibaut, J. W., & Kelley, H. H. (1959). *The social psychology of groups*. New York: Wiley.

Tiedens, L. Z., & Fragale, A. R. (2003). Power moves: Complementarity in dominant and submissive nonverbal behavior. *Journal of Personality and Social Psychology, 84*, 558–568.

Tiedens, L. Z., & Jimenez, M. C. (2003). Assimilation for affiliation and contrast for control: complementary self-construals. *Journal of Personality and Social Psychology, 85*, 1049–1061.

Tiedens, L. Z., Unzueta, M. M., & Young, M. J. (2007). An unconscious desire for hierarchy? The motivated perception of dominance complementarity in task partners. *Journal of Personality and Social Psychology, 93*, 402–414.

Tomasello, M., Carpenter, M., Call, J., Behne, T., & Moll, H. (2005). Understanding and sharing intentions: The origins of cultural cognition. *Behavioral and Brain Sciences, 28*, 675–735.

Tormala, Z. L., Briñol, P., & Petty, R. E. (2007). Multiple roles for source credibility under high elaboration: It's all in the timing. *Social Cognition, 25*, 536–552.

Towles-Schwen, T., & Fazio, R. H. (2001). On the origins of racial attitudes: Correlates of childhood experiences. *Personality and Social Psychology Bulletin, 27*, 162–175.

Towles-Schwen, T., & Fazio, R. H. (2003). Choosing social situations: The relation between automatically activated racial attitudes and anticipated comfort interacting with African Americans. *Personality and Social Psychology Bulletin, 29*, 170–182.

Trivers, R. L. (1985). *Social evolution*. Menlo Park, CA: Benjamin/Cummings.

Tropp, L. R. (2003). The psychological impact of prejudice: Implications for intergroup contact. *Group Processes and Intergroup Relations, 6*, 131–149.

Tropp, L. R., & Bianchi, R. A. (2007). Interpreting references to group membership in context: Feelings about intergroup contact depending on who says what to whom. *European Journal of Social Psychology, 37*, 153–170.

Tropp, L. R., & Pettigrew, T. F. (2005a). Differential relationships between intergroup contact and affective and cognitive dimensions of prejudice. *Personality and Social Psychology Bulletin, 31*, 1145–1158. [Erratum: *31*, 1456.]

Tropp, L. R., & Pettigrew, T. F. (2005b). Relationships between intergroup contact and prejudice among minority and majority status groups. *Psychological Science, 16*, 951–957.

Tropp, L. R., Stout, A. M., Boatswain, C., Wright, S. C., & Pettigrew, T. F. (2006). Trust and acceptance in response to references to group membership: Minority and majority perspectives on cross-group interactions. *Journal of Applied Social Psychology, 36*, 769–794.

Tuckman, J., & Lavell, M. (1957). Self classification as old or not old. *Geriatrics, 12*, 666–671.

Turner, J. C., Brown, R. J., & Tajfel, H. (1979). Social comparison and group interest in ingroup favouritism. *European Journal of Social Psychology, 9*, 187–204.

Twenge, J. M., & Campbell, W. K. (2002). Self-esteem and socioeconomic status: A meta-analytic review. *Personality and Social Psychology Review, 6*, 59–71.

Twenge, J. M., & Crocker, J. (2002). Race and self-esteem: Meta-analyses comparing Whites, Blacks, Hispanics, Asians, and American Indians and comment on Gray-Little and Hafdahl (2000). *Psychological Bulletin, 128*, 371–408.

United Nations Development Fund for Women. (2005). Overview: Women, work, and poverty. *Progress of World's Women 2005*. Retrieved August 2, 2006, from http://www.unifem.org/attachments/products/PoWW2005_overview_eng.pdf.

United States Department of Labor. (2005, May). Women in the labor force, A databook. Retrieved July 28, 2006, from http://www.bls.gov/cps/wlf-databook2005.htm.

van de Ven, N., Zeelenberg, M., & Rik, P. (2009). Leveling up and down: The experiences of benign and malicious envy. *Emotion 9*, 419–429.

van Dijk, E., & De Cremer, D. (2006). Self-benefiting in the allocation of scarce resources: Leader-follower effects and the moderating effect of social value orientations. *Personality and Social Psychology Bulletin, 32*, 1352–1361.

van Kleef, G. A., De Dreu, C. K. W., & Manstead, A. S. R. (2004). The interpersonal effects of emotions in negotiations: A motivated information processing approach. *Journal of Personality and Social Psychology, 87*, 510–528.

van Kleef, G. A., De Dreu, C. K. W., Pietroni, D., & Manstead, A. S. R. (2006). Power and emotion in negotiation: Power moderates the interpersonal effects of anger and happiness on concession making. *European Journal of Social Psychology, 36*, 557–581.

van Kleef, G. A., Oveis, C., van der Löwe, I., LuoKogan, A., Goetz, J., & Keltner, D. (2008). Power, distress, and compassion: Turning a blind eye to the suffering of others. *Psychological Science, 19*, 1315–1322.

van Knippenberg, A. (1978). Status differences, comparative relevance, and intergroup differentiation. In H. Tajfel (Ed.), *Differentiation between social groups: Studies in the social psychology of intergroup relations* (pp. 171–199). London: Academic Press.

van Knippenberg, A., & Ellemers, N. (1990). Social identity and intergroup differentiation processes. *European Review of Social Psychology, 1*, 137–169.

van Knippenberg, A., & van Oers, H. (1984). Social identity and equity concerns in intergroup perceptions. *British Journal of Social Psychology, 23*, 351–361.

Vanman, E. J., Paul, B. Y., Ito, T. A., & Miller, N. (1997). The modern face of prejudice and structural features that moderate the effect of cooperation on affect. *Journal of Personality and Social Psychology, 73*, 941–959.

Vescio, T. K., Gervais, S. J., Heidenreich, S., & Snyder, M. (2006). The effects of prejudice level and social influence strategy on powerful people's responding to racial out-group members. *European Journal of Social Psychology, 36*, 435–450.

Vescio, T. K., Gervais, S. J., Snyder, M., & Hoover, A. (2005). Power and the creation of patronizing environments: The stereotype-based behaviors of the powerful and their effects on female performance in masculine domains. *Journal of Personality and Social Psychology, 88*, 658–672.

Vescio, T. K., Snyder, M., & Butz, D. A. (2003). Power in stereotypically masculine domains: A social influence strategy x stereotype match model. *Journal of Personality and Social Psychology, 85*, 1062–1078.

Vick, S. B., Seery, M. D., Blascovich, J., & Weisbuch, M. (2008). The effect of gender stereotype activation on challenge and threat motivational states. *Journal of Experimental Social Psychology, 44*, 624–630.

Volpato, C., Durante, F. & Fiske, S. T. (2009). Using the stereotype content model to examine the evils of Fascism: An archival approach. *European Journal of Social Psychology, 39*, 1–19.

von Grünau, M., & Anston, C. (1995). The detection of gaze direction: A stare-in-the-crowd effect. *Perception, 24*, 1297–1313.

Vorauer, J. D., Hunter, A. J., Main, K. J., & Roy, S. A. (2000). Meta-stereotype activation: Evidence from indirect measures for specific evaluative concerns experienced by members of dominant groups in intergroup interaction. *Journal of Personality and Social Psychology, 78*, 690–707.

Vorauer, J., & Kumhyr, S. M. (2001). Is this about you or me? Self- versus other-directed judgments and feelings in response to intergroup interaction. *Personality and Social Psychology Bulletin, 27*, 706–719.

Vorauer, J., & Turpie, C. A. (2004). Disruptive effects of vigilance on dominant group members' treatment of outgroup members choking versus shining under pressure. *Journal of Personality and Social Psychology, 87*, 384–399.

Wade-Benzoni, K. A., Hernandez, M., Medvec, V., & Messick, D. (2008). In fairness to future generations: The role of egocentrism, uncertainty, power, and stewardship in judgments of intergenerational allocations. *Journal of Experimental Social Psychology, 44*, 233–245.

Waldo, C. R., Berdahl, J. L., & Fitzgerald, L. F. (1998). Are men sexually harassed? If so, by whom? *Law and Human Behavior, 22*, 59–79.

Weber, M. (1978). *Economy and Society*. G. Roth & C. Wittich (trans.). Berkeley: University of California Press. (Original work published 1914)

Weick, M., & Guinote, A. (2008). When subjective experiences matter: Power increases reliance on the ease of retrieval. *Journal of Personality and Social Psychology, 94*, 956–970.

Weiner, B. (1993). On sin versus sickness: A theory of perceived responsibility and social motivation. *American Psychologist, 48*, 957–965.

Westen, D. (2007). *The political brain: The role of emotion in deciding the fate of the nation*. New York: Public Affairs Books.

Wheeler, M. E., & Fiske, S. T. (2005). Controlling racial prejudice: Social cognitive goals affect amygdala and stereotype activation. *Psychological Science, 16*, 56–63.

Whitson, J. A., & Galinsky, A. D. (2008). Lacking control increases illusory pattern perception. *Science, 322*, 115–117.

Wieselquist, J., Rusbult, C. E., Foster, C. A., & Agnew, C. R. (1999). Commitment, pro-relationship behavior, and trust in close relationships. *Journal of Personality and Social Psychology, 77*, 942–966.

Winslow, M. P. (2004). Reactions to the imputation of prejudice. *Basic and Applied Social Psychology, 26*, 289–297.

Wojciszke, B., & Struzynska-Kujalowicz, A. (2007). Power influences self-esteem. *Social Cognition, 25*, 472–494.

Wong, C. A. (2003). The influence of ethnic discrimination and ethnic identification on African American adolescents' school and socioemotional adjustment. *Journal of Personality, 71*, 1197–1232.

Wong, C. A. Eccles, J. S., & Sameroff, A. (2003). The influence of ethnic discrimination and ethnic identification on African American adolescents' school and socioemotional adjustment. *Journal of Personality, 71*, 1197–1232.

Wong, M. D., Shapiro, M. F., Boscardin, W. J., & Ettner, S. L. (2002). Contribution of major diseases to disparities in mortality. *New England Journal of Medicine, 347*, 1585–1592.

Wood, W. (2000). Attitude change: Persuasion and social influence. *Annual Review of Psychology, 51*, 539–570.

Wood, W., & Eagly, A. H. (2002). A cross-cultural analysis of the behavior of women and men: Implications for the origins of sex differences. *Psychological Bulletin, 128*, 699–727.

Wood, W., & Kallgren, C. A. (1988). Communicator attributes and persuasion: Recipients' access to attitude-relevant information in memory. *Personality and Social Psychology Bulletin, 14*, 172–182.

Wood, W., Lundgren, S., Ouellette, J., Busceme, S., & Blackstone, T. (1994). Minority influence: a meta-analytic review of social influence processes. *Psychological Bulletin, 115*, 323–345.

Woods, T. A., Kurtz-Costes, B., & Rowley, S. J. (2005). The development of stereotypes about the rich and poor: Age, race, and family income differences in beliefs. *Journal of Youth and Adolescence, 34*, 437–445.

Word, C. O., Zanna, M. P., & Cooper, J. (1974). The nonverbal mediation of self-fulfilling prophecies in interracial interaction. *Journal of Experimental Social Psychology, 10*, 109–120.

Wrosch, C., Heckhausen, J., & Lachman, M. E. (2006). Goal management across adulthood and old age: The adaptive value of primary and secondary control. In D. K. Mroczek & T. D. Little (Eds.), *Handbook of Personality Development* (pp. 399–421). Mahwah, NJ: Erlbaum.

Yzerbyt, V. Y., Kervyn, N., & Judd, C. M. (2008). Compensation versus halo: The unique relations between the fundamental dimensions of social judgment. *Personality and Social Psychology Bulletin, 34*, 1110–1123.

Yzerbyt, V., Provost, V., & Corneille, O. (2005). Not competent but warm . . . Really? Compensatory stereotypes in the French-speaking world. *Group Processes and Intergroup Relations, 8*, 291–308.

Zaller, J. (1992). *The nature and origins of mass opinion*. New York: Cambridge University Press.

Zink, C., Tong, Y., Chen, Q., Bassett, D., Stein, J., & Meyer-Lindenberg, A. (2008). Know your place: Neural processing of social hierarchy in humans. *Neuron, 58*, 273–283.

Zucker, G. S., & Weiner, B. (1993). Conservatism and perceptions of poverty: An attributional analysis. *Journal of Applied Social Psychology, 23*, 925–943.

Zurbriggen, E. L. (2000). Social motives and cognitive power–sex associations: Predictors of aggressive sexual behavior. *Journal of Personality and Social Psychology, 78*, 559–581.

Chapter 27

Social Conflict

The Emergence and Consequences of Struggle and Negotiation

CARSTEN K. W. DE DREU

In 2004, a patient nearly died at the operating table because his anesthetist and surgeon got into a heated debate. Their fistfight, which ended in a broken thumb and a bruised eye, led them to an adjacent room, leaving the patient in the middle of the operation. The patient only survived because of the swift intervention by a cool-headed assistant who took over the medical procedures. In 2006, an employee of the Santa Barbara Processing and Distribution Center who was forced out of her job shot five former colleagues. In 1994, the world was shocked when it learned of the 500,000 Tutsi massacred in Rwanda by members of the Hutu, a rivaling ethnic group. What had been a well-functioning African country was crippled in less than a few months.

Clearly, conflict can have devastating consequences for individuals, small groups such as organizational teams, or larger communities and nations. However, conflict does not always result in violence and death, and its consequences are rarely exclusively negative and detrimental. Conflict can also be a source of creativity and a catalyst of change and innovation. Scientific progress such as the discovery of DNA has been attributed to the intense hatred and rivalry among the leaders of world-famous laboratories (White, 2001); similarly, the discovery of nuclear energy and the development of the atomic bomb were primarily stimulated by World War II (Simonton, 2003). And the other way around, a lack of conflict and dissent among members of decision-making teams can substantially hurt decision quality, as was putatively the case during the months preceding the Bay of Pigs invasion in 1961 (Janis, 1972). In fact, conflict resolution often is needed to achieve the agreements underlying close relationships, group decision making, or other forms of collective action. Well-crafted agreements that meet conflict parties' needs and aspirations

create order and stability, foster social harmony, reduce the probability of future conflict, and may stimulate economic prosperity. In short, social conflict can both hamper or impede and facilitate or strengthen the functioning of individuals, groups, and larger social systems.

But what triggers these conflicts? Why do people get into conflict, and what motivates the manner in which they treat opposing parties? Why do people sometimes opt for competition and struggle and at other times engage in more constructive negotiation and joint problem solving? What are the psychological mechanisms responsible for conflict escalation? Is conflict escalation necessarily detrimental to the individuals or groups involved or to the larger social system within which they operate? What are, in other words, the possible consequences of social conflict, and when do these emerge? These and related questions are considered in the current chapter. It considers the emergence, management, and functions of social conflict at the interpersonal, small group, and intergroup level of analysis. The social-psychological literature forms the core of this discussion, but because the study of conflict is a multidisciplinary enterprise, the chapter ventures into related areas such as the organizational sciences and behavioral economics or neuroeconomics.

The chapter is designed to accomplish several goals. First, this chapter connects and integrates the currently disparate literatures on cooperation and competition in social dilemmas with work on the psychological and behavioral processes in conflict escalation, negotiation, and joint problem solving. Second, theoretical and empirical work on social conflict has typically focused on the interpersonal, the small group, or the intergroup level of analysis. Thus, this chapter provides a side-by-side

This chapter was written while the author was on sabbatical leave at Leiden University, The Netherlands. Financial support was provided by grants from the Dutch National Science Foundation (NWO 400.07.701). The author gratefully acknowledges the inputs from Lindy Greer, Fieke Harinck, Wolfgang Steinel, Ilja van Beest, Eric van Dijk, and Arjaan Wit.

discussion of theoretical principles and research findings at these levels of analysis, highlights similarities and dissimilarities, and further explores the cross-level influences on social conflict. Third, the study of cooperation and conflict is often narrowly focused on the negative, destructive, and aversive outcomes of conflict. However, the functions of social conflict are much broader, and its impact stretches beyond immediate gains and losses. Accordingly, the chapter reviews negative and positive effects of conflict on well-being, learning and creativity, group decision making and team performance, and formation and change of small groups and larger social systems.

To achieve these three goals, the chapter proceeds on the basis of several assumptions. The first assumption is that conflict requires interdependence: Individuals and groups need and depend on one another to achieve outcomes that are important to them. Conflict emerges to the extent that one party feels deprived of important outcomes and attributes this state of deprivation to the actions or inactions by the interdependent other or others. Thus, whereas interdependence structures inherently involve latent, or potential, conflict, only when current or anticipated deprivation is attributed to another party's behavior does such potential conflict become real and manifest conflict. The second assumption is that individuals or groups who feel (they will be) deprived by others engage in strategic action—they may withdraw from the situation and avoid further interaction, go to court, engage in warfare, initiate a negotiation or problem-solving session, or engage in some other form of strategic action. These strategic choices signal when latent conflict has become manifest.

Such choices may create (fear of) deprivation in the conflict counterpart, who in turn has strategic choices to make (engage a lawyer, mobilize an army, agree to negotiate, etc.). The emerging action–reaction cycles may intensify and escalate the conflict or may take the form of more constructive negotiation and joint problem solving. These action–reaction cycles may take a few minutes or several years. Along the way, they may have an enormous effect on individuals and groups, including affecting their sense of well-being, creativity, decision making, and performance.

Figure 27.1 provides a flowchart that summarizes this conflict process. The figure also highlights the structure of this chapter. The emerging phase in which interdependent parties may fail to cooperate and deprive others is discussed in first section. This section covers the large literatures on two-person and n-person social dilemmas, on intergroup competition, and on formal and informal mechanisms that operate at the system level to reduce noncooperation. The second section is about the procedural and strategic choices that individuals and groups have when facing conflict. Two related theories of strategic choice are considered: Deutsch's (1973) theory of cooperation and competition and Pruitt and Rubin's (1986) dual concern theory. The two subsequent sections discuss two broad classes of conflict management processes in further detail, namely, struggle and conflict escalation and, later, negotiation and joint problem solving. Another section examines the functions and consequences of social conflict at the individual, small group, and intergroup levels. The concluding section provides a summary of the main themes in this chapter and highlights some avenues for future research.

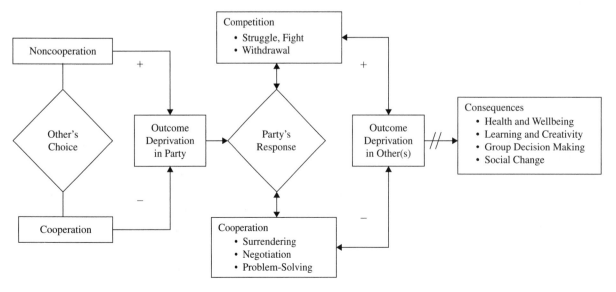

Figure 27.1   Flowchart of conflict process.

EMERGENCE OF SOCIAL CONFLICT

The efforts of men [sic] are utilized in two different ways: They are directed to the production or transformation of economic goods, or else to the appropriation of goods produced by others.

—Vittoro Pareto (1902)

Conflict has many definitions, and many of them are problematic. Dictionaries often define conflict in terms of a struggle or fight and thus focus on participants' behavior. Such a definition has no place for withdrawal or constructive negotiation and problem solving. Scholarly definitions tend to be more inclusive yet focus on parts of the conflict process. Some define conflict as the clashing of aspirations and thus focus on antecedent conditions (e.g., Pruitt & Rubin, 1986). Others focus on interaction processes and define conflict in terms of incompatible behaviors, with one party's goal pursuit blocking or impeding another party's goal striving (e.g., Deutsch, 1973).

An alternative approach that is adopted in this chapter is to avoid a single, encompassing definition of conflict. Instead, conflict is considered a process that has distinguishable phases—it emerges for some reason, triggering emotional experiences and motivational goals in one or both parties, which feed into behavioral strategies and patterns of exchange. These interaction processes produce various consequences at the intrapersonal, interpersonal, or group level. The current section considers the emerging phase—that is, what triggers social conflict. Subsequent sections cover subsequent phases, including interaction processes and proximal, as well as more distal, consequences.

Social conflict emerges when individuals and groups depend on one another for valuable outcomes and deprive one another of such valued outcomes through their independent or coordinated actions. Interpersonal conflicts emerge when an individual attributes *egoistic* deprivation—personal outcomes falling below the reasonable standard—to another individual's actions or inactions. Intergroup conflicts emerge when (the representative of) a group attributes *fraternalistic* deprivation—the outcomes to one's group, organization, or nation falling below a reasonable standard—to another group's actions or inactions (Pruitt, 1998). Both egoistic and fraternalistic deprivation can be relative to outcomes achieved by a counterpart, to some aspiration level or ideal standard, or to the (potential) outcomes from an alternative interdependent relationship (Kelley & Thibaut, 1978).

Outcomes derive from tangible goods such as money or territory and from intangible goods such as status, love, and respect. Deprivation thus relates to the access to and distribution of scarce resources but also to the way in which one is treated—when people are denied the respect to which they believe they are entitled, people feel as unjustly treated as when they are denied the material resources to which they believe they are entitled (Miller, 2001). Furthermore, deprivation may relate to attitudes, beliefs, and preferences that are ignored, contested, or otherwise derogated. The large literature on interpersonal and group decision making considers this form of outcome deprivation and its consequences for human thinking and decision making (Brehmer, 1976; Schulz-Hardt, Mojzisch, & Vogelgesang, 2008; see also the Functions of Social Conflict section).

To understand when and why individuals deprive others of valuable outcomes, and thus create social conflict, interdependence theory (Kelley & Thibaut, 1978) provides a useful starting point. The theory models the exchange relationship between individuals or groups, including power differences, and identifies core motives underlying people's decisions to cooperate or compete with one another. This section briefly introduces the theory (for more extensive treatments, see, e.g., Kelley et al., 2004, and Rusbult & Van Lange, 2003). Subsequently, the section reviews classic and contemporary research on cooperative decision making that highlights the conditions moderating the emergence of conflict among individuals, within small groups, and among social groups.

Interdependence Theory

Interdependence theory (Kelley & Thibaut, 1978) builds on and extends the theory of games (Colman, 2003; Luce & Raiffa, 1957) by considering the ways in which parties (individuals or groups) can influence one another's outcomes through their individual or coordinated actions. Outcome interdependence may take one of three basic forms (Schelling, 1960/1980). The first type of interdependence involves pure noncorrespondence, or competition. These are "zero-sum" situations likely to produce conflict because pursuing self-interest inevitably produces outcome deprivation in the other. An example is that of two companies both entering the same new market—the greater market share acquired by one company is at the expense of the other company's market share. Such competitive situations trigger conflict when the emerging deprivation is attributed by one company to the other's foul play, inappropriate power play, intentional misrepresentation of fact and figures, or some similar sort of strategic action with malicious intent.

The second type of interdependence identified by Schelling involves pure coordination situations that reflect a symbiotic relationship between parties. An example is that of Harry and Sally, who travel on different trains.

They are both rewarded when Harry meets Sally and gets off at the same station but not when they get off at different stations. Pure correspondence is unlikely to produce conflict because parties lack the motivation to deprive the other of valuable outcomes, and pursuing self-interest fosters the other's outcomes, and vice versa. In pure correspondence, conflict only emerges when parties attribute their failure to coordinate (e.g., Harry and Sally get off at different stations) to the other's clumsiness or have otherwise biased perceptions.

Pure coordination and pure competition capture a rather small portion of the possible interdependence structures individuals and groups encounter. Most situations, Schelling (1960/1980) notes, are *mixed motive* because joint cooperation creates better outcomes for each party than mutual competition yet each party is better off by competing when the other is cooperating: "These are the 'nonzero-sum' games involved in wars and threats of war, strikes, negotiations, criminal deterrence, race war, price war, and blackmail; maneuvering in a bureaucracy or in a traffic jam; the coercion of one's own children. . . . These are the 'games' in which, though an element of conflict provides the dramatic interest, mutual dependence is part of the logical structure and demands some kind of collaboration or mutual accommodation—tacit, if not explicit—even if only in the avoidance of mutual disaster" (Schelling, 1960/1980, p. 83).

A classic and widely studied form of mixed-motive interdependence is the prisoner's dilemma (PD). As can be seen in Figure 27.2, which shows an ordinal example of the PD, both parties are better off when both cooperate than when both defect, yet each party is best off when he or she defects and the other cooperates (Komorita & Parks, 1995). For example, a husband and wife each prefer doing nothing to cleaning the house, yet each party prefers a clean house to a dirty one. Mutual cooperation (both clean

the house) generates more value than mutual defection, but each party is best off when he or she defects and the other cooperates. Numerous studies, including several discussed in this section, used the PD game to study the conditions leading people to make cooperative or noncooperative choices.

Some interdependence situations, such as the ones modeled in the PD in Figure 27.2, are symmetrical in that both parties benefit equally from mutual cooperation and are equally hurt by the other's defection. In many cases, asymmetries exist. First, one party may affect the other's outcomes to a greater extent than that the other affects the party's outcomes. One party thus controls the other's fate to a greater extent than that the other controls the party's fate. Such "fate control" (Kelley & Thibaut, 1978) relates to punitive capability or threat capacity (Bacharach & Lawler, 1981) and represents an important source of power. Second, individuals may differ in the extent to which they depend on their counterpart. Employees can look for a job elsewhere, married couples may divorce, and customers may go to a different store. Sometimes, such exit options apply to only one of the two parties. For example, a seller may have another customer interested in buying a classic Volvo, but the customer cannot find this particular car elsewhere. Dependency on the other is another important source of power. Thus, power differences emerge when one party has more fate control, better or more exit options, or some combination of the two. However, it is conceivable that there is a power balance because one party has more fate control than the other but the other party has more or better exit options.

It should be noted that interdependent parties are not always fully aware of the consequences of their independent actions. Many analysts have argued that in most situations parties know at best half of the story—the way their decisions affect their own outcomes is known, but it is unclear how their decisions affect their partner's outcomes. To quote Schelling (1960/1980, p. 162), this is "particularly applicable whenever the facilities for communication are short of perfect, where there is inherent uncertainty about each other's value systems or choices of strategies, and especially when an outcome must be reached by a sequence of moves or maneuvers." Thus, parties may lack information of what is and is not valued by their counterpart. They may then infer their counterpart's value function by relying on imperfect assumptions such as "your gain is my loss" or "rational people like me see the world as I do" (Ross & Ward, 1995). This may lead to over- or underestimation of entitlements, and of power and influence, and this in itself may become a source of social conflict. Finally, parties may withhold or distort information about their preferences and priorities, especially when they fear their counterpart might

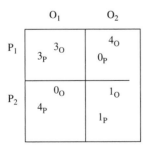

Figure 27.2   The prisoner's dilemma as an example of mixed-motive interdependence.

Note: P and O refer to "party" and "other," respectively; their choice options are denoted by subscripts 1 and 2. Option 1 is commonly referred to as "cooperation" and option 2 is commonly referred to as "noncooperation" or "defection."

abuse such information to its own advantage (Steinel & De Dreu, 2004).

Greed, Fear, and Fairness

As discussed earlier, conflict emerges when individuals or groups attribute current or future deprivation to an interdependent other's lack of cooperativeness. The critical question then becomes why individuals or groups fail to cooperate and thus deliberately or inadvertently deprive others of valuable outcomes. In a partial answer to this question, Coombs (1973) distinguished between two core motives underlying noncooperation. The first motive is *greed*—by making a noncooperative choice one accumulates more personal gain, or incurs fewer personal losses, than by making a cooperative choice. Greed as a motive captures various human goals and aspirations. Tangible aspirations such as making money or gaining access to scarce resources such as water, oil, or fertile land drive greed. But greed also manifests itself in the search for status and power or in the tendency to see oneself, or one's group, as superior to other individuals, or groups.

The second motive underlying failures to cooperate is *fear*—by making a noncooperative choice, one protects oneself against exploitation by a partner. Fear often results from expectations about the partner's behavior that are grounded in, for example, past behavior or beliefs about what the partner's most likely choice is going to be. Consider, for example, a study by De Dreu, Yzerbyt, and Leyens (1995). They engaged psychology students in a PD with another student they were told majored in business studies or, in another condition, in theology. At the time of the study, psychology students perceived business students as egoistic, noncooperative individuals and theology students as moral and essentially cooperative people. These stereotypic beliefs influenced expectations and initial choices toward the counterpart—participants expected more competition from a business major, and to preempt being exploited by the business student, participants made a noncooperative opening move. Such a noncooperative initiation by the participants triggered an equally noncooperative move by the (preprogrammed) counterpart, thus confirming the participant's initial belief that business students are indeed competitive and dangerous and that theology students are indeed cooperative and trustworthy. Interestingly, this also shows that whereas the initial interaction is driven by fear grounded in stereotypic beliefs, after a few exchanges noncooperation becomes grounded in the other's actual (noncooperative) behavior in the previous rounds of exchange. Participants thus created their own "proof" that the other party was to be feared for its noncooperative stance.

Fear as a motive is closely related to trust—the positive expectation that an interdependent partner will not abuse or otherwise take advantage of one's vulnerability (Ostrom, 1998). Trust is often seen as a necessary but not sufficient cause of cooperation. Specifically, Pruitt and Kimmel (1977) advanced their goal–expectation hypothesis, which states that people cooperate to the extent that they have cooperative goals (i.e., lack greed) and expect their interdependent other or others not to violate trust (i.e., lack of fear). Put differently, noncooperation and ensuing deprivation in others emerge because people experience greed, fear, or both.

Although most evidence for fear and greed as motives for noncooperation derives from studies on realistic conflicts over tangible resources, the analysis can be fruitfully applied to understand symbolic conflicts that emerge because of the human tendency toward developing, maintaining, and enhancing a positive self-view (Baumeister, Smart, & Boden, 1996). To some extent, ego enhancement and positive identity striving imply that people are seeing and positioning themselves as better, smarter, and more likable than others, and this is similar to the greed motive discussed earlier. Positive identity striving may also manifest itself in emphasizing others' negative features and attributes while deemphasizing others' positive features and attributes (other derogation). Fear of being derogated by others and being denied a positive self-view corresponds to the fear motive discussed earlier.

In addition to greed and fear, cooperation may be motivated by fairness considerations, and noncooperation may be the result of (expected) violations of fairness. The preference for fairness has been proposed to be a basic human impulse (Tyler & Blader, 2006), possibly rooted in a fundamental desire to be accepted by others (Baumeister & Leary, 1995). Indeed, unfairness triggers negative emotional responses, inferred from anterior insula activation, and fairness activates brain regions associated with reward, including the ventral striatum, the orbitofrontal cortex, and midbrain dopamine regions (Tabibnia, Satpuute, & Lieberman, 2008). Unfairness is associated with anger and contempt; fairness is associated with positive hedonic experiences. Violating fairness principles, including disrespectful acts and insults, represents an important source of deprivation and social conflict (Miller, 2001).

Fairness as a driving motive has been revealed in studies using the ultimatum bargaining game (UBG), in which an allocator divides a certain amount of money (e.g., 10) between oneself and a recipient. The recipient either accepts the proposed distribution, in which case the proposed distribution takes effect, or rejects the proposed distribution, in which case neither allocator nor recipient receives anything. From a "rational self-interest maximizing" perspective, one would expect recipients to accept any offer that provides them with an outcome greater than 0 and, as a corollary, allocators to offer as little as possible (e.g., out of 10, offering 1 and keeping 9). Interestingly, however, an exceedingly long list of studies shows that allocators tend to propose fair, or close to fair distributions and that recipients reject unfair distributions (Camerer & Thaler, 1995).

It should be noted that the tendency toward fairness revealed in the UBG only refers to fairness as *equality* in the distribution of outcomes. Fairness may derive from other distribution rules, such as *equity* (participants receive outcomes proportional to their respective inputs; Deutsch, 1975). Messick and Sentis (1985; Loewenstein, Thompson, & Bazerman, 1989) illustrated the equity rule. Participants rated their satisfaction with distributions of money to themselves and another worker. Satisfaction was highest when distributions were proportional to the investments made by oneself and the other worker. Thus, when the participant worked 10 hours and their partner worked 5 hours, participants were more satisfied with a 100–50 distribution than with a 100–100 (or 50–50) distribution. Getting less than the other was even more satisfactory than getting an equal amount when getting less (e.g., 50–100) best reflected the inputs of oneself and the partner (e.g., 5 vs. 10 hours).

Finally, fairness may derive from the decision procedures that were used—to the extent that one is allowed voice and invited to participate in the decision process, people tend to perceive greater *procedural fairness* (e.g., Schroeder, Steele, Woodell, & Bernbenek, 2003; Tyler & Blader, 2000). Violations of procedural fairness have been shown to trigger negative emotions, including anger, and to produce retaliation. For example, in a study of workers being laid off, Barclay, Skarlicki, and Pugh (2005) found that when the procedures used to lay off employees were perceived as fair, employees experienced less outward-focused negative emotions such as anger and hostility, and this in turn reduced their intentions to retaliate against the organization. In other words, procedural fairness may substantially dampen the conflict-triggering effects of outcome deprivation.

To sum up, good evidence shows that cooperation is largely driven by trust and fairness considerations—a desire to be fair, to do just, and to divide resources equally or proportionally. Noncooperation, in contrast, results from greed and fear, as well as from perceived or expected violations of fairness.

Noncooperation Within and Between Groups

Greed, fear, and fairness considerations mediate the effects of various chronic traits and temporary states on cooperation and noncooperation among individuals, within small groups, and among groups. This section reviews this work. Studies on larger groups and intergroup situations highlight some additional motives that will be reviewed as well.

Most of the studies reviewed as follows engage research participants in a (variant of the) PD game or UBG. In experiments using the PD game, participants are informed that they and some other participant should independently and simultaneously choose between option 1 (the cooperative choice) and option 2 (the noncooperative, or competitive choice; see also Figure 27.2). The combination of their own and the other's choice provides outcomes (e.g., money) to both oneself and the other participant. The payoff matrix, such as the one shown in Figure 27.2, is explained, and participants move on to make their choice. Sometimes, repeated choices with or without feedback about other's decisions are requested. Before decision making, specific traits are measured or more transient states are experimentally manipulated.

Participants in UBG experiments are assigned either to the role of allocator and asked to propose a division of some valuable amount or to the role of recipient and asked to accept or reject a proposed division by their (real or simulated) allocator. The allocator proposes a division of some goods (e.g., chips to be converted into money), and the responder subsequently decides whether to accept or reject the proposed division. Sometimes, only the proposals made are being studied, with more generous proposals being taken as reflecting a greater tendency toward cooperation. Likewise, greater willingness among responders to accept disadvantageous offers can be seen as reflecting greater cooperation.

Traits Influencing Greed, Fear, and Fairness

In their review of experiments on two-person games, Rubin and Brown (1975) concluded that personality and individual differences have little consistent influence on noncooperation. Since their review, however, researchers have uncovered several chronic individual differences that reliably predict cooperation in both two-person and *n*-person games. A prominent example is the individual's *social value orientation*—the chronic preference for a particular distribution of value between oneself and interdependent others (McClintock, 1977; Van Lange, 1999). Social value orientations are usually measured by having participants make a series of choices between outcome distributions between themselves and an unknown other person. Examples include a choice between $50 to oneself and $50 to the other, versus $60 to oneself and $30 to the other, versus $40 to oneself and $0 to the other. Those opting for the 50–50 distribution are considered "prosocial" because they prefer a fairly split collective gain over maximizing individual reward (the $60 in option 2) or maximizing relative gain (the 40–0 = $40 in option 3). Those opting for the 60–30 split are considered "individualistic," and those opting for the 40–0 split are considered "competitive" (Kuhlman & Marshello, 1975). Across a large amount of studies, it appears that in North America and northwest Europe approximately 40% to 50% of the individuals can be classified as prosocial, 40% as individualistic, and approximately 10% as competitive. Most studies on social value orientations collapse the individualists and competitors into one proself category (Van Lange, 1999).

Individuals with a prosocial value orientation seek harmony and fairness and value collective welfare. Those with a proself orientation seek good outcomes for themselves and ignore or derogate those of others. Individuals with a proself motivation experience both greed and fear, whereas prosocials seek fairness and lack greed but may experience fear. Proself individuals tend toward noncooperation, and prosocials tend toward cooperation, provided they do not fear being exploited by their counterpart (Kelley & Stahelski, 1970; Parks, Sanna, & Berel, 2001; Steinel & De Dreu, 2004; Van Lange, 1992). Likewise, in ultimatum bargaining, prosocial as well as proself individuals distribute resources rather evenly between themselves and their responder. However, proself individuals propose fair distributions for instrumental reasons—they fear that an overly self-serving and greedy distribution will be rejected by their responder. Prosocial individuals, in contrast, appear to propose fair distributions because of genuine fairness considerations (Van Dijk, De Cremer, & Handgraaf, 2004).

The goal–expectation hypothesis (Pruitt & Kimmel, 1977) mentioned earlier would predict prosocial individuals to withhold cooperation when they fear noncooperation by others, and there is solid evidence for this prediction (e.g., Kelley & Stahelski, 1970; Van Lange, 1992). Recent work indicates that fear tends to be moderated by the neuropeptide oxytocin (Kosfeld, Heinrichs, Zak, Fishbacher, & Fehr, 2006), which is released when the individual affiliates with a close other, such as when a mother nurtures her infant. Depue and Morrone-Strupinsky (2005) propose that differential exposure to these temporary increases in oxytocin over time develops into chronic differences in affiliation tendencies and trust. Dispositional tendencies to affiliate and trust enhance cooperation (Barry & Friedman, 1998; Graziano, Jenssen-Campbell, & Hair, 1996), most likely because they enhance fairness considerations and increase generalized trust (i.e., lack of fear; Parks & Hulbert, 1995).

Transient States Influencing Greed, Fear, and Fairness

Fear, greed, or fairness considerations can also be triggered by external cues. For example, Kahneman and Tversky (1979) argued that losses are more aversive than

gains of objectively equal size are attractive—losing $10 is more painful and unpleasant than gaining $10 is pleasant. Accordingly, people are motivated to reduce burdens and losses more than to approach and maximize benefits and gains. Put differently, greed becomes more important when decisions are about burdens and losses rather than about benefits and gains. Indeed, proself individuals (who experience greed) defect more when outcomes are loss- rather than gain-framed—they appear more motivated to avoid personal loss than to achieve personal gain. Prosocials, to whom fairness and concern for others play an important role, cooperate more when outcomes are loss framed—they appear more motivated to avoid collective losses and burdens to others than to achieve collective gain and benefits for others (De Dreu & McCusker, 1997; also see Leliveld, Van Dijk, Van Beest, & Tenbrunsel, 2009).

The importance of greed, fear, and fairness also depends on the labeling of the situation and the options. Thus, participants cooperated less when the PD game was introduced as the "Wall Street broker game," a label that primes greed, than when it was called the "community game," a label that primes fairness-related constructs (Ross & Ward, 1995). Other work showed that subliminal priming of money- or business-related materials (e.g., boardroom tables and business suits) increased noncooperative tendencies (Kay, Wheeler, Bargh, & Ross, 2004; Vohs, Meed, & Goode, 2006). Fear seems to be reduced, and people cooperate more when the counterpart is referred to as "partner" than as "opponent" (Burnham, McGabe, & Smith, 2000), when individuals are subliminally primed with cooperation- rather than competition-related words (Smeesters, Warlop, Van Avermaet, Corneille, & Yzerbyt, 2003), or when the interdependent ("we") rather than the independent ("I") self-concept is activated (Utz, 2004). Subtle cues, even when processed outside of conscious awareness, can shift the focus of attention from fairness and trust to greed and fear and thereby profoundly increase the rate of noncooperation among individuals.

An important source of greed is feelings of entitlement. In ultimatum bargaining, people make more self-serving offers when they feel the endowment is theirs, compared with when they feel the endowment is their partner's (Leliveld, Van Dijk, & Van Beest, 2008). Feelings of entitlement, or "ownership," may also explain why people in exchange situations ask a higher price for some goods they own and wish to sell than they are willing to pay for the exact same goods when they do not own them and seek acquisition (De Dreu & Van Knippenberg, 2005; Kahneman, Knetch, & Thaler, 1990). Finally, feelings of entitlement are higher among powerful rather than powerless individuals. For example, individuals randomly assigned to leader positions take more for themselves than those not assigned to a leader position. That these tendencies are indeed related to greed is supported by a study showing that leaders with a proself orientation (who experience greed) make more self-serving offers in ultimatum bargaining than do leaders with a prosocial orientation (who are mainly driven by fairness considerations; Van Dijk & De Cremer, 2006). Along similar lines, Handgraaf, Van Dijk, Vermunt, Wilke, and De Dreu (2008) found that allocators in a modified UBG offered less when their counterpart became less powerful. Remarkably, however, offers increased when recipients were powerless: When the recipient was without power, allocators experienced feelings of social responsibility and hence offered more to their powerless partner.

In recent years, cooperation and noncooperation have been studied as functions of emotions and emotion displays. This work shows, for example, that individuals with high levels of trait anger are less cooperative than participants with low levels of trait anger (Kassinove, Roth, Owens, & Fuller, 2002) or that those who feel guilty toward their partner cooperate more than those who do not feel guilty (Ketelaar & Au, 2003). These effects suggest that emotion states moderate greed, with anger augmenting and guilt reducing it. Reversely, it appears that fear and trust are moderated by a counterpart's emotional displays. For example, Krumhuber and colleagues engaged participants in a mixed-motive game before which the facial dynamics of the other player were manipulated using brief (less than 6 seconds), but highly realistic facial animations. Results showed that facial dynamics significantly influenced participants' cooperation, an effect mediated by inferences about the other player's trustworthiness (Krumhuber et al., 2007). Another indication that other's emotion displays influence fear comes from a study showing that allocators make less generous ultimatum offers to angry as opposed to happy recipients when the consequences of rejection and concomitant fear are low. But when the consequences of rejection and concomitant fear are high, participants made more generous offers to angry recipients (Van Dijk, Van Kleef, Steinel, & Van Beest, 2008).

Group Size, Self-Efficacy, Anonymity, and Identification

When group size increases from two to three or more participants, fairness, greed, and fear are complemented by self-efficacy concerns. In so-called *n*-person social dilemmas, for example, each individual is best off when he or she defects and the others cooperate, but all members are better off when all cooperate rather than not (Dawes, 1980; Weber, Kopelman, & Messick, 2004). A classic example of such a situation is given by Hardin (1968) in the article "The Tragedy of the Commons": Herdsmen overgraze a common

village pasture to the point of permanent destruction. Another example is writing reviews for academic journals. Each scholar is best off by not writing reviews and concentrating on his or her own writing. But if no one contributes by reviewing others' work, the peer-review system collapses and the academic community as a whole suffers. These examples highlight that individuals may feel their personal actions do not matter much. They may wonder how sending a few sheep to the common pasture causes permanent destruction or how refusing to write a review causes the entire system to collapse. Put differently, in *n*-person social dilemmas people may fail to cooperate not only because of greed and fear but also because of low self-efficacy—the feeling that their behavior cannot make a difference (Kerr, 1989).

Another effect of increased group size is that it becomes exceedingly difficult to trace who did or did not cooperate (e.g., academic journals sometimes list ad hoc reviewers but never those who consistently refused to write reviews). Noncooperation can thus be anonymous, and deprivation cannot always be unambiguously attributed to one or more fellow group members (Komorita, Parks, & Hulbert, 1992). As such, deprivation in small groups may be associated with suspicion, gossip, finger pointing, and accusatory remarks. Moreover, members of larger groups have less identification with the group as a whole (Brewer & Kramer, 1986) and a stronger tendency to identify with and contribute to subgroups within the overarching system (Wit & Kerr, 2002). The combination of reduced self-efficacy, increased anonymity, and lowered identification explains why noncooperation is more likely in larger groups.

Individual–Group Discontinuity and Intergroup Conflict

Within larger groups, individual members may be aligned into subgroups because of, for example, shared interests or distinguishable features and characteristics (Dovidio & Gaertner, this volume; Yzerbyt & Demoulin, this volume; Tajfel & Turner, 1979). Such categorization of self and others into ingroup and outgroups lays the foundation for intergroup conflict, which emerges when one group or subgroup attributes current or anticipated fraternalistic deprivation to another group's or subgroup's actions or inactions (e.g., Sherif & Sherif, 1953; Taylor & Moghaddam, 1987). As with egoistic deprivation, fraternalistic deprivation can be about tangible outcomes (e.g., money, territory, or access to scarce resources such as oil or water) or intangible outcomes (e.g., status or a positive identity).

Similar to the analysis at the interpersonal level, Insko, Schopler, and colleagues reasoned and demonstrated that noncooperation among groups is driven by greed (seeking to maximize the ingroup's interests), by fear of being exploited by the outgroup, or by some combination of greed and fear (Schopler & Insko, 1992). Their work also revealed that moving from the interpersonal level to the intergroup level of analysis introduces new issues. Across many studies, they uncovered an *individual–group discontinuity effect*—the rate of noncooperation is much lower in interpersonal rather than in intergroup mixed-motive interdependence (Wildschut, Pinter, Vevea, Insko, & Schopler, 2003). For example, Robert and Carnevale (1997) compared individuals making an offer in a UBG with groups making an offer. Their results showed that individuals were more generous toward another individual than groups were toward another group.

This steep increase in competitiveness largely appears to occur because individual group members feel that greedy, noncooperative behavior toward outgroups can be justified as being loyal to the ingroup (i.e., social support for shared self-interest, or patriotism; see Arrow, 2007). It thus is "easier" and more in line with dominant norms to be noncooperative toward another group in intergroup settings than toward another individual in interpersonal or small group settings. In addition, individuals appear to have greater fear of being exploited by an outgroup than by another individual. Patriotism and increased fear both mean that compared with egoistic deprivation, fraternalistic deprivation is more common and likely to emerge; social conflict is more likely and more intense among groups than among individuals.

The discovery of individual–group discontinuity highlights the mutual influence between intergroup processes on the one hand and within-group dynamics on the other. Dawes (1980) noted that "soldiers who fight in a large battle can reasonably conclude that no matter what their comrades do, they personally are better off taking no chances; yet if no one takes chances, the result will be rout and slaughter worse for all the soldiers than is taking chances" (p. 170). This tension between the collective interest of the group and the interests of its individual members is unavoidable because the outcomes of the intergroup competition (e.g., territory, status, and pride) are public goods that accrue to all group members regardless of the individual's contribution. Furthermore, the problem of public goods provision in intergroup competition is fundamentally different from that in the single-group case discussed in the previous section on interpersonal and group conflicts—in the case of a single group, the level of contribution needed to provide for the public good (e.g., collective prosperity) is determined by nature, which may be uncertain but never competes back. In contrast, the provision in intergroup competition needed to provide for the public good (e.g., victory) is determined by comparing the levels of contribution made by the competing groups (Bornstein, 2003).

The effect of intergroup competition on within-group cooperation was nicely illustrated in a field experiment reported by Erev, Bornstein, and Galili (1993). The authors took advantage of the orange harvesting season in Israel and created three conditions under which groups of four workers were rewarded. In the first condition, group members were rewarded for their individual performance—the more oranges they personally picked, the more money they earned. In the second condition, group members were rewarded for their group's performance—the more oranges their group harvested, the more money the group received. Consistent with the notion that noncooperation increases in larger groups, harvesting performance under group reward plummeted by about 30% compared with the individual reward condition. In the third condition, group members were rewarded for their group's relative performance—when their group harvested more oranges than a competing outgroup, they would be rewarded; but if there was a tie or when they harvested less than the competing outgroup, no reward would be earned. Results showed that the latter condition led to greatest harvesting behavior—intergroup competition stimulated individuals to work harder and to contribute to their ingroup.

The orange-picking study captures simultaneously between-group competition and within-group dynamics. Bornstein (2003; Bornstein & Rapoport, 1988) formalized these dynamics in *team games*. A team game involves a competition between two groups of players, with each player independently choosing how much to contribute toward the group effort. Contribution is costly in that the more one contributes, the less one's self-interest is served. Payoffs to an individual player increase as a function of the total contributions made by one's own group and decrease as a function of the total contributions made by the outgroup. As in an *n*-person social dilemma, within each group, each member is individually better off by not cooperating when all others cooperate. But because the group with the largest total contribution receives a higher payoff than the group with the lower total contribution, it is in each group's interest to mobilize cooperation. This increases the probability to win from the other group and provides an additional incentive for individual group members to cooperate (Bornstein & Ben-Yossef, 1994). Consistent with the findings from Erev et al. (1993), several studies show that the more individual group members cooperate with their ingroup, the more intense the intergroup competition becomes, and vice versa (for a review, see Bornstein, 2003). Such enhanced intragroup cooperation results in an escalatory spiral at the intergroup level with, at some point, one group being fraternalistically deprived by the other group. This is where intergroup competition turns into intergroup conflict.

One issue in the emergence of intergroup conflict is whether it is primarily driven by group members' desire to promote and favor their ingroup, to derogate and punish the outgroup, or some combination of both desires. Halevy, Bornstein, and Sagiv (2008) developed a team game in which individuals could, at a cost to themselves, contribute to a pool that benefited their ingroup and to a pool that punished the outgroup. Results showed strong support for ingroup favoritism and little support for outgroup derogation—individual group members donated personal resources to the pool benefiting their ingroup and much less to the pool that punished the outgroup. Moreover, preplay intragroup communication increased ingroup favoritism but did not affect outgroup derogation. These results are important because they suggest that intergroup conflicts arise out of a desire among group members not necessarily to hurt outgroups but, rather, to help their ingroup.

The analysis of team games does more than highlight the complex interdependencies at the intergroup level. In the present context, perhaps more importantly, the analysis of team games shows that in intergroup systems both cooperation and noncooperation can cause deprivation in others, thereby creating conflict among groups (Wit & Kerr, 2002). What is collectively beneficial at the intergroup level and individually beneficial at the personal level (e.g., not fighting) is disloyal at the within-group level and likely to deprive fellow ingroup members who take risks to defend the ingroup and to defeat the outgroup. Likewise, what is collectively beneficial at the within-group level (e.g., contributing to the fight) is likely to create fraternalistic deprivation in the outgroup.

Institutional Solutions to Noncooperation

The preceding review and analysis revealed that especially larger social systems are susceptible to high rates of noncooperation among its members. To avert such noncooperation and to reduce the emergence of social conflict, several formal and informal measures can be employed. Through legislation, individuals and groups are deterred from being overly exploitative and depriving others of valuable outcomes. Entitlements are regulated, and as long as rules and regulations are adhered to, the likelihood of deprivation due to another person's or group's actions is reduced and so is the emergence of social conflict. Along similar lines, management scientists have long argued that the bureaucratization of companies is mainly a response to recurrent social conflicts in the workplace. Through an increasingly large number of exceedingly detailed protocols, recurrent conflicts are either prevented or regulated as much as possible (Jaffee, 2008). Although discussing these institutionalized systems in greater detail is beyond the current scope of this chapter, this section discusses a few critical ingredients of these and related systems, namely, privatization, leadership, and sanctions. In addition, several more tacit, informal practices that prevent the adverse impact of relative deprivation and social conflict are reviewed.

Privatization, Leadership, and Sanctioning Systems

To prevent noncooperation in n-person social dilemmas (both as single-group and intergroup systems), three institutional interventions have been examined. The first is *privatization*, which means that the common resource is privatized and individuals depend less, or not at all, on others' decisions. This structural change reduces the interdependence among parties and thereby the likelihood of social conflict (Messick & McClelland, 1983). A related but less drastic intervention is the appointment of a leader who decides about the access to and allocation of resources. Again, appointing an authority reduces or eliminates outcome interdependence in the sense described thus far, although it may lead to outcome deprivation attributed to the leader and thus vertical conflicts between followers and their leader (e.g., Wit & Wilke, 1988). Indeed, parties prefer a leader more when a common resource is being overused and when managing a common resource is perceived to be a difficult task (Van Vugt & De Cremer, 1999). Put differently, privatization and the delegation of decision making to a higher authority are often triggered by (the anticipation of) others' noncooperation.

In addition to privatization and delegation to authority, noncooperation is deterred by implementing sanction systems. In general, sanctioning systems reduce noncooperation (McCusker & Carnevale, 1995; Yamagishi, 1986). This is most likely because the attractiveness of defection is decreased and, therefore, cooperation becomes a relatively more attractive course of action. However, sanction systems can have adverse effects. Tenbrunsel and Messick (1999) showed that a sanctioning system changes people's perception of the social dilemma from an ethical decision (to cooperate is ethically appropriate) to a business-related decision in which calculative instead of ethical motives prevail. Indeed, when there is a sanction on defection, trust in others being internally motivated to cooperate is reduced and the motivation to cooperate declines, especially among individuals with high propensity to trust (Mulder, Van Dijk, De Cremer, & Wilke, 2006).

Communication and Cooperative Norms

In addition to formal institutions, more informal tendencies exist in groups and larger social systems to prevent noncooperation. One is the establishment of cooperation norms that may be induced and enhanced through communication before decision making. Through communication, parties augment the importance of fairness by devising cooperative norms and putting pressure on those who do not (intend to) subscribe to these norms (e.g., Deutsch, 1973). Second, discussion allows individuals to commit themselves to cooperation, thereby reducing fear in their counterpart (Orbell, van der Kragt, & Dawes, 1988). Finally, participants develop a sense of collective identity through discussion that shifts the emphasis from individual self-interest and greed to fairness and collective benefits (Bouas & Komorita, 1996).

Numerous studies examined the impact of tacit communication, or repeated play, on tendencies to cooperate or compete. In these studies, participants play the game several times, mostly with the same partner, and thus can adapt to the partner's previous move (Axelrod, 1984; Messick & Liebrand, 1995). This work revealed, among other things, that noncooperation may deter the counterpart from continuing to make noncooperative moves, as much as the other's cooperation may be rewarded and reinforced by reciprocating with a cooperative move. Axelrod (1984) showed, for example, that tit for tat is a suitable strategy for arriving at sustainable cooperation and thus averting the emergence of social conflict. In tit for tat, players initiate interactions with a cooperative move and subsequently mimic their counterpart's previous move. That is, if the individual's cooperative opening move meets with a noncooperative opening move by a partner, the individual subsequently defects, only to return to cooperation when the partner cooperated on the previous trial. Such a tit-for-tat strategy is deemed effective because it is nice (the individual begins with cooperation) but not weak (the individual retaliates against the other's exploitative, noncooperative moves). It also is clear and predictable in that the partner learns that cooperation begets cooperation as much as noncooperation begets noncooperation.

Studies by Van Lange and colleagues revealed that tit for tat does not necessarily produce sustainable cooperation when there is environmental noise and the counterpart may misinterpret the other party's action. An apologetic letter may get lost, what was meant as a friendly joke is interpreted as a derogatory remark, and someone's late arrival was not a strategic ploy but entirely due to unexpected traffic. In such "noisy" situations, a cooperative move by one's partner may be mistaken for a noncooperative move, thus inducing noncooperative responses. Such a noncooperative response leads one's partner to reciprocate with defection, and this may be the beginning of an escalatory spiral of competitive exchanges. Indeed, in such noisy situations a more benevolent and forgiving strategy is more likely to produce sustainable cooperation—instead of mimicking the other's prior move, parties should forgive a single instance of noncooperative action and only change from cooperation to noncooperation when the partner fails to cooperate on two

consecutive trials (e.g., Tazelaar, Van Lange, & Ouwerkerk, 2004; Van Lange, Ouwerkerk, & Tazelaar, 2002).

Altruistic Punishment

Behavioral economists have uncovered another route by which cooperation is enforced—*altruistic punishment*. Altruistic punishment emerges when an individual punishes someone else for being noncooperative even though this noncooperation had no consequences for the individual and punishment comes at a cost to the individual (Fehr & Gächter, 2002; Folger & Skarlicki, 2001; also see Price, Cosmides, & Tooby, 2002). Examples of altruistic punishment include a "citizen arrest" and anonymous tips about a neighbor not paying taxes.

To examine altruistic punishment, economists have developed a so-called third-party punishment game, in which two players play a PD game and a third party is informed about the choices made by the two players. The third party then decides whether to punish the PD players. This is costly not only to the player being punished but also to the third party who punishes—it thus is individually rational for the third party not to punish. However, it is collectively rational to punish those players who defected, to deter them from defecting again on later occasions when the third party may be involved as well—the system functions better if each individual member not only cooperates but also engages in altruistic punishment when witnessing noncooperation toward others.

Research using this and similar games consistently reveals that a substantial portion of third parties incur costs by punishing a norm violator (i.e., someone making a defective move in the PD; e.g., Fehr & Fishbacher, 2004), and this appears especially when the norm violator is a member of the third parties' ingroup (Shinada, Yamagishi, & Ohmura, 2004). Shinada and Yamagishi (2007) further showed that such third-party altruistic punishment, or the mere threat of it, reduces noncooperation among principal parties. It thus appears that at the least two motives drive altruistic punishment. First, moral outrage and anger are felt at perceiving moral wrongdoing and noncooperative behavior exploiting otherwise well-intending individuals. Second, altruistic punishment is driven by deterrence motives—the desire to prevent or curb future crimes (Carlsmith, Darley, & Robinson, 2002).

Summary and Synthesis

Numerous chronic dispositions and transient states lead people to promote and seek fairness, to promote their personal self-interests (greed), or to protect their self-interests (fear). Fairness considerations drive toward cooperation. Greed and fear drive toward noncooperation and deliberately or inadvertently create deprivation in interdependent others. Social conflict thus is likely to emerge when individuals have or adopt proself value orientations, when they feel powerful and entitled to great outcomes, when materialistic desires have been primed, or when individuals feel anger. Social conflict is less likely to emerge with a cooperative or trustworthy counterpart or when fairness and community norms are being primed. Most of these processes operate at the interpersonal level and reproduce in larger groups. However, as group size increases, anonymity, reduced self-efficacy, and lowered identification alone and in combination drive toward exceedingly high levels of noncooperation. Social conflict is indeed more likely in larger rather than smaller groups.

Greed and fear also drive conflict among groups, and evidence indicates that individuals and groups are far less likely to cooperate with other groups than with other individuals. This individual–group discontinuity effect is partially explained by individual group members' tendency to show ingroup loyalty. It is partially explained by the greater fear and distrust of groups rather than individuals. Recent work suggests, however, that the desire to serve the ingroup is a stronger motive for noncooperation with outgroups than is the desire to derogate and hurt the outgroup.

Social systems use several formal and informal mechanisms to reduce noncooperation among members and to prevent the emergence of social conflict. Examples of formal systems include legislation and sanction systems and the appointment of leaders. At the informal level, communication and the establishment of cooperative norms reduce fear and emphasize the importance of fairness, and altruistic punishment caps overly greedy, noncooperative behavior. The formal and informal mechanisms moderate noncooperation at the system level but cannot eliminate localized noncooperation among subsets of individuals or groups. This begs the question of how individuals or groups respond to egoistic and fraternalistic deprivation: What strategies and tactics do they employ, what feelings are involved, and what cognitive processes emerge once an interdependent other derogates one's identity, claims one's territory or asks too high a price for a desirable product? These and related questions are considered in the next three sections on strategic choices, on struggle and conflict escalation, and on negotiation and joint problem solving.

STRATEGIC CHOICE IN SOCIAL CONFLICT

There is a time to be timid. There is a time to be conciliatory. There is a time, even, to fly and there is a time to fight. And I'm going to fight like hell.

—Richard M. Nixon (1913–1994)

In the face of deprivation and conflict, such as former U.S. President Richard Nixon was facing when Congress moved toward his impeachment in 1973, individuals or groups have the choice between competitive moves, including struggling and fighting, and cooperative moves, including surrendering, collaborative problem solving, and negotiation (Deutsch, 1973). Sometimes, they have a withdrawal or exit option and can leave the situation (Hayashi & Yamagishi, 1998; Miller & Holmes, 1975). Throughout the years, scholars have developed several taxonomies of conflict management strategies. Some take a systems perspective and explore how large systems, such as organizations, can create high-quality systems for grievance filing and conflict intervention (for reviews, see, Goldman, Cropanzano, Stein, & Benson, 2008; Olson-Buchanan & Boswell, 2008). This section considers the disputant's perspective to identify what conflict management procedures parties prefer and why. Subsequently, two broad theories are reviewed that consider the motivational basis of strategic choice—when and why parties opt for negotiation, struggle, surrendering, or withdrawal.

Taxonomies of Conflict Management Procedures

Many different procedures can be used to manage social conflict, some of which involve a third party in the role of autocratic decision-maker (e.g., an intervening manager or police officer), arbitrator (e.g., a judge), or mediator. Common procedures not involving a third party include debate and struggle, as well as negotiation and problem solving (e.g., Heuer & Penrod, 1986; Thibaut & Walker, 1975). In general, disputants prefer procedures that afford them two types of control. First, disputants seek *decision control*, which refers to the power to prescribe and enforce the resolution of the conflict—to the extent that the party's agreement is needed for a solution to take effect, the party is more likely to endorse that procedure. Second, disputants seek *process control*, which refers to the control over the conflict resolution process, including the arguments to be presented or the format and timing of exchanges—the more that a party controls the process, the more likely a procedure is to be endorsed (Thibaut & Walker, 1975). Both types of control are higher in procedures not involving a third party, such as struggle or negotiation and problem solving. Among those procedures involving a third party, both types of control tend to be higher when the third party acts as a mediator rather than as an arbitrator or autocratic decision-maker (Heuer & Penrod, 1986; Shestowsky, 2004).

The preference for decision and process control implies that people gravitate toward struggle and competition, or toward negotiation and joint problem solving, rather than toward some form of third-party intervention. Heuer and Penrod (1986) found that individuals with a prosocial, cooperative orientation, regardless of how strongly they felt their case, preferred negotiation and problem solving to mediation, which in turn was preferred to struggle, arbitration, and autocratic decision making. For individuals with a proself, competitive orientation, however, things changed when the felt strength of their case was taken into consideration. When proself disputants felt strongly about the issue at hand, they preferred autocratic decision making and arbitration more than struggle and negotiation. When they did not feel strongly about the issue, such third-party procedures were actually preferred less. This pattern of results may reflect a self-serving bias, in which procedures are selected to the extent that they best serve one's personal goals (among proself individuals) or some joint goal (among prosocial individuals).

The finding that procedural preferences differ as a function of social motivation is echoed in cross-cultural research. Leung (1987) compared procedural preferences among collectivistic Chinese and individualistic American participants. He found stronger preferences for negotiation and mediation among the collectivist group. One explanation, which was supported by his data, is that disputants with a collectivistic background perceive negotiation and mediation as better able to reduce animosity and to maintain or promote harmonious relations.

Motivational Approaches to Strategic Choice

Whereas work in law and human behavior tends to focus on the conditions under which disputants accept third-party intervention (e.g., Tyler, Lind, & Huo, 2000), the social-psychological analysis primarily focuses on the motivational antecedents of broader classes of strategic choice—struggle, inaction, and withdrawal, as well as negotiation and joint problem solving. Two general theories of strategic choice are discussed—Deutsch's theory of cooperation and competition and then Pruitt and Rubin's dual concern theory.

Theory of Cooperation and Competition

According to the theory of cooperation and competition (Deutsch, 1973), strategic choices depend on the way a party perceives the goal interdependence with another individual or group. When goals are seen as positively correlated (parties swim or sink together), parties are likely to opt for cooperation and joint problem solving. When, in contrast, parties perceive goals to be separate, or even to be negatively linked (one sinks when the other swims), struggle and withdrawal tend to prevail.

How goal interdependence is perceived depends on those factors discussed earlier under the rubric of social

value orientation and social motivation. Those with a prosocial value orientation are more likely to emphasize positive linkages between their own and other's goals. They are thus more likely to opt for negotiation and joint problem solving. Those with an individualistic or competitive orientation are more likely to emphasize negative linkages between their own and other's goals. They are thus more likely to opt for struggle and, if possible, withdrawal (De Dreu, Weingart, & Kwon, 2000; Deutsch, 1982; Rubin & Brown, 1975). Reversing the causal order, evidence also points to positively (negatively) linked goals being more likely to induce prosocial (proself) motivation, which then fosters cooperation (competition). This close interplay among goal interdependence, motivational orientation, and strategic choice in social conflict has been documented extensively in both laboratory experiments and survey research in organizational settings (for reviews, see Deutsch, 1973; Pruitt & Kimmel, 1977; Tjosvold, 1998).

Dual Concern Theory

An alternative to the theory of cooperation and competition is provided by dual concern theory (Carnevale & Pruitt, 1992; Pruitt, 1998; Pruitt & Rubin, 1986). In contrast to Deutsch's theory, dual concern theory distinguishes between two motives—concern for self and concern for other—that are independent of each other and range from weak to strong. Concern for self refers to the extent to which conflict parties are concerned with their own needs, interests, values, and beliefs; concern for other refers to the extent to which conflict parties are concerned with their counterpart's needs, interests, values, and beliefs. Although there may be situations in which these two concerns covary, dual concern theory views self-concern and other-concern as essentially orthogonal and independent. Thus, a conflict party can have high self-concern and low other-concern but can also combine high self-concern with high other-concern, low self-concern with low other-concern, or low self-concern with high concern for the other.

Self-concern and other-concern can be rooted in various traits and states, some of which have been discussed in the first section on cooperation in experimental games. Dual concern theory would, indeed, assume higher self-concern to emerge when the conflict involves losses and burdens rather than gains and benefits and when parties have high rather than low aspirations, more rather than less power, and good rather than poor alternatives (e.g., Pruitt, 1998). With regard to other-concern, it is noteworthy that other-concern can be instrumental and reflective of "enlightened self-interest." For example, other-concern may be high because one needs the other party on future occasions or because the other party is more powerful and may lash out when his or her interests or beliefs are not taken seriously.

But other-concern can be genuine as well, such as when one likes to other party or feels that party's claims are justified and legitimate. Some evidence that other-concern can be genuine and based on empathy derives from a study by Batson and Ahmad (2001). These authors placed female participants in a PD in which they knew the other had already defected. Before making their own choice between cooperation and defection, half of the participants received a message from their (noncooperative) partner stating, "I'm supposed to write about something interesting that's happened to me lately . . . the only thing that I can seem to think of is that two days ago I broke up with my boyfriend. We've been dating since our junior year in high school and have been really close. . . . I've been kind of upset. It's all I think about. My friends all tell me that I'll meet other guys and all I need is for something good to happen to cheer me up. I guess they're right, but so far that hasn't happened" (p. 30). This message, not shown to the other half of the participants, induced empathic feelings toward the partner. Results showed that among those not induced to feel empathy, most made a noncooperative move. However, among those induced to feel empathy for the other, almost half cooperated and thus incurred a cost to themselves at the benefit of their counterpart.

The combination of self- and other-concern is proposed to predict strategic behavior. When self-concern is high and other-concern is low, parties are expected to prefer forcing, contending, and struggle. When, in contrast, self-concern is low and other-concern is high, parties are expected to prefer yielding, concession making, and obliging. When both self- and other-concern are low, parties are expected to remain inactive and to withdraw from the situation, and when both self- and other-concern are high, parties are expected to prefer constructive negotiation and joint problem solving. Thus, in contrast to the theory of cooperation and competition, dual concern theory has a place for inaction and withdrawal and distinguishes between two forms of cooperation (yielding and problem solving) (e.g., Pruitt & Lewis, 1975; Weingart, Brett, Olekalns, & Smith, 2007). Empirical evidence is largely consistent with these core aspects of dual concern theory—the distinction between two basic motives jointly predicting four strategic tendencies (Carnevale & Pruitt, 1992; De Dreu, Weingart, et al., 2000). For example, scale development studies and psychometric analysis (e.g., De Dreu, Evers, Beersma, Kluwer, & Nauta, 2001; Van de Vliert, 1997) corroborated the distinction among these four strategies: withdrawal, struggle, problem solving, and yielding. Also consistent with dual concern theory, this work points to two underlying dimensions, or motives: concern for self and concern for other (see Figure 27.3).

Although dual concern theory has good support (Carnevale & Pruitt, 1992; De Dreu, Weingart, et al., 2000; Van de Vliert, 1997), recent work in cross-cultural psychology raises some important issues. In individualistic cultures such as those found in Europe and North America, individuals tend to prefer contending along with problem solving (Holt & DeVore, 2005; Tinsley, 2001). In contrast, individuals in collectivistic cultures found in Africa and eastern Asia tend to prefer contending along with avoiding and withdrawal (Holt & DeVore, 2005; Morris et al., 1998), especially in intense disputes and disputes with ingroup members and superiors (Brew & Cairns 2004; Derlega, Cukur, Kuang, & Forsyth, 2002). Furthermore, Gabrielidis and colleagues (Gabrielidis, Stephan, Ybarra, Pearson, & Villareal, 1997; Cai & Fink, 2002) showed that avoidance reflects a *concern for others*, rather than a lack thereof, as originally conceived in dual

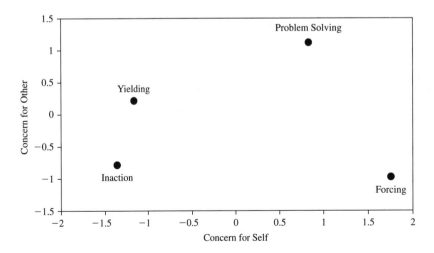

Figure 27. 3　Dual concern theory.

Adapted from De Dreu et al. (2001), reprinted with permission from Wiley.

Note: The spatial distances are based on multidimensional scaling of correlational data obtained from 2,500 professionals in various occupations and job functions.

concern theory. Similarly, while silence and avoidance are strategies viewed negatively in Western cultures, they are viewed quite positively in Eastern cultures (Brett & Gelfand, 2005; Tinsley & Brett, 2001). Future research on avoidance needs to capture this complexity.

Summary and Synthesis

Numerous procedures for dealing with conflict have been uncovered. Research shows that people tend toward those procedures that give both decision control and process control, namely, contending and struggle or negotiation and joint problem solving. When and why disputants choose a particular strategy is covered in both the theory of cooperation and competition (Deutsch, 1973) and dual concern theory (Pruitt & Rubin, 1986). Both predict struggle and competition when disputants see their own and other's goals as negatively linked and have low concern for their partner. Both predict negotiation and joint problem solving when disputants see their own and other's goals to be positively linked and to have high concern for their partner. The difference between the two theoretical perspectives is that, for negotiation and joint problem solving to happen, dual concern theory adds that parties should have a high (rather than low) concern for their own outcomes. As mentioned, there is good support for this additional prediction.

Theories of strategic choice do not address the dynamic process of action and reaction, the sequences of behavior conflict parties cycle through, and the factors that reinforce or inhibit the intensification and escalation of the conflict or a constructive exchange leading to mutually beneficial agreement. These processes are the focus of the next two sections.

STRUGGLE AND CONFLICT ESCALATION

> Karadzic . . . said that our draft proposal was unacceptable. Suddenly, Mladic erupted. Pushing to the center of the circle, he began a long, emotional diatribe. . . . This was the intimidating style he had used with the Dutch commander at Srebrenica, with Janvier, and with so many others. He gave off a scent of danger. . . . I did not know if his rage was real or feigned, but this was the genuine Mladic, the one who could unleash a murderous rampage.
>
> —Richard Holbrooke (*To End a War*, 1999, p. 150–151)

In 1995, the Muslim enclave Srebrenica in Bosnia-Herzegovina, declared by the United Nations as a "safe haven" and protected by approximately 400 armed Dutch peacekeepers, was invaded by the Serbian Republican Army. Under the command of General Ratko Mladic and with the putative consent of his political superior Radovan

Karadzic, more than 8,000 male Muslim refugees were separated from their women and children. As it later turned out, the men were transported and killed by a paramilitary unit known as the Scorpions in what became the biggest mass murder in Europe since World War II.

This case, and many others that may be less well publicized but no less appalling, begs the question as to what drives fathers, farmers, and factory workers to arm themselves and commit mass murder. How can conflicts within or between groups escalate to a point where civilians are uprooted and imprisoned without trial, unarmed men are shot at gunpoint, and former neighbors deny one another the right to live? Why do individuals and groups react with struggle and competition to current or anticipated deprivation, and what psychological processes drive conflict escalation? This section considers these questions.

Struggle Begets Struggle Begets More Struggle

As discussed in the first section, research on repeated play in PD games consistently shows that individuals tend to match their counterpart's noncooperative move by making a noncooperative move (e.g., Axelrod & Hamilton, 1981). This is especially likely when individuals or groups pair low other-concern with high self-concern, as explained in the section on dual concern theory. This basic human tendency toward reciprocity (Gouldner, 1960) is also reflected in the finding that receiving unfair offers in ultimatum bargaining triggers anger and spite (Pillutla & Murnighan, 1996). These outward-focused, negative emotions in turn trigger approach-motivated, competitive responses (Allred, Mallozzi, Matsui, & Raia, 1997; Forgas, 1998). Reversely, to accept an unfair offer that is experienced as disrespectful and insulting requires prefrontal down-regulation of negative emotional responses (Tabibnia et al., 2008; also see Knoch, Pascual, Meyer, Trever, & Fehr, 2006). In short, a competitive action by an interdependent other is likely to trigger competitive responses, and countering such competitive impulses requires cognitive resources and nonautomated action.

Competitive exchanges and struggle easily lead to conflict escalation—the intensification of conflict over time (Pruitt & Rubin, 1986). Escalation occurs when a party to a conflict first uses a contentious (aggressive) tactic or employs heavier contentious tactics than before. Table 27.1, based on Neuman and Baron (1997; Pruitt, 2008), gives examples of retaliatory behaviors. Grounded in a social-psychological analysis of aggression (e.g., Berkowitz, 1989), it shows that retaliation can be physical or verbal and can be direct or indirect. As can be inferred, some of these retaliatory tactics have immediate consequences for the target, while others have more delayed and, perhaps,

Table 27.1 Eight Types of Escalatory Responses in Conflict

	Direct	Indirect
Physical		
Active	Homicide, assault	Theft, sabotage
	Displaying anger	Defacing property
	Obscene gestures	Consuming, hiding needed resources
	Unfriendly, cold behavior	
Passive	Going on strike	Making target look bad
	Quitting	Failing to protect target's welfare
	Chronic lateness	
	Work slowdown	
	Failing to help	
Verbal		
Active	Threats	Filing a grievance or lawsuit
	Yelling	Attacking target's protégé
	Insults and sarcasm	Whistle blowing
	Hostile comments	Transmitting damaging information
	Criticism or blame	Talking behind target's back
Passive	Failing to return phone calls	Failing to transmit information
	Giving the silent treatment	Failing to warn of impending damage
	Refusing target's requests	Failing to defend target
	Damning with faint praise	Failing to refer clients to target

Based on Neuman and Baron (1997, p. 40) and Pruitt (2008, p. 246).

less traceable effects. Some are thus more likely to trigger counterretaliation and a sequence of escalatory exchanges than others. Note that such moves from low to high contentiousness may differ across contexts. In labor-management conflict, for example, labor may start out with placing high demands, threaten with work slowdowns, and then break off communication and call a strike. In close relationships, such escalatory cycles may begin with negotiations but then turn into psychological aggression, ultimately ending with physical abuse and sexual coercion (Straus, Hamby, Boney-McCoy, & Sugarman, 1996).

There are two types of escalation sequences: bilateral and unilateral. Bilateral escalation sequences usually develop through conflict spirals entailing repeated retaliation and counterretaliation, or defense and counterdefense. Thus, an employee might criticize a management policy, provoking disciplinary action such as failure to receive a raise. Annoyed by this treatment, the employee might then talk to the press and be fired as a result (Pruitt, 2008). In the

context of international conflict and security, Jervis (1976) discusses an escalation of defense and counterdefense, where one party increasingly expands its (military) power base to protect itself against the other, a putative enemy. The other interprets the party's tendency to increase its power base as a hostile act and, to preempt attack, sees no other option than to increase its own power base. In the second half of the last century, such escalatory tendencies resulted in the United States and the former Soviet Union having a nuclear arsenal capable of destroying each other more than 60 times.

In unilateral sequences, only one party escalates. Usually this is a party seeking change in its counterpart, which in turn has little or no incentive to change and instead wants to preserve the status quo (De Dreu, Kluwer, & Nauta, 2008). An example is that of a spouse demanding that an evasive, nonresponding partner become more involved in household duties. Research typically finds demand–withdrawal tendencies, with the demanding spouse becoming increasingly persistent and the evasive partner becoming increasingly nonresponsive (Kluwer, Heesink, & Van de Vliert, 1997). Mikolic, Parker, and Pruitt (1997) studied reactions to persistent annoyance by having confederates of the experimenter withhold supplies needed by the participants to complete a project. Participants worked, alone or in a group, on a creative project for which supplies such as scissors, pencils, glue, and paper were available in a central room. One could take these supplies and, after using them, return them to the central room for others to use in completing their own projects. Confederates acting as other participants would, however, take supplies but not return them, thereby depriving participants of valuable resources. Through an internal telephone system, participants could contact these confederates or the experimenter. A content analysis of these telephone messages to the confederates showed an orderly progression of tactics. Participants would begin with polite requests to have supplies being returned, but when this had no effect, they turned to more explicit demands, followed by angry statements and threats. Ultimately, phone messages showed harassment and abuse.

Psychological Processes in Conflict Escalation

The most common type of escalation involves retaliation aimed at punishing an annoying and offending other. The actor may be responding to self-annoyance or to another party with whom the actor identifies (as in altruistic punishment, as discussed in the first section). The motivation for retaliation may be rooted in the desire to express anger, to deter further annoyance from the offender, to establish a tough impression, or to prop up social norms. Also, there may be an element of evening up the score—the actor feels "one down" as a result of the offender's prior action and seeks to restore status, sense of power, or material well-being by responding aggressively (Pruitt, 2008; Skarlicki & Folger, 2004).

Entrapment and Escalated Commitment

An interesting feature of many escalating conflicts is that the disputants become increasingly committed to their competitive course of action (Teger, 1980). Commitments beget commitments, and investments beget investments, as the parties slide progressively into a morass from which there is little possibility of escape. This entrapment into a "too much invested to quit" tendency can be seen in former U.S. President Lyndon Johnson, who kept investing financial and military resources into Vietnam after he had determined that the cause was hopeless and the United States would not win the war (McMaster, 1998). More recent examples may include the U.S. "war on terrorism" and the contested rule over Tibet by the People's Republic of China.

Critical in escalated commitment is the "sunk cost fallacy," which holds that in making decisions people fail to ignore the costs that have been incurred and that cannot be recovered to any significant degree. Thus, when an initial competitive response is not creating the expected victory or change in the counterpart, it leads to escalated commitment to further struggle. Escalated commitment is partly due to the need to justify and rationalize prior moves and to recoup incurred losses (e.g., Brockner & Rubin, 1985; Staw & Ross, 1989; Teger, 1980). In social conflict, escalated commitment is complemented by "competitive arousal" (Ku, Malhotra, & Murnighan, 2004). A diverse set of factors such as rivalry, social facilitation, and time pressure fuel arousal that, in turn, impairs decision making and leads parties to "throw good money after bad."

Hostile Attributions

Retaliation is more likely and more extensive if the offender is seen as responsible for the annoyance, that is, as taking action that was "both controllable and intentional, without significant mitigating circumstances" (Martinko & Zellars, 1998, p. 25). Such attributions of responsibility are the rule rather than the exception, according to work on the hostile attribution error (Baron, 1997). It holds that relatively minor transgressions by another individual or group are overweighted—the actor takes precautions by attributing hostility and shrewd intentions to the offender, assuming that these hostile intentions reflect the other's dispositional trait more than some transient state (Dodge & Coie, 1987).

Hostile attribution leads the actor to see its offender as less moral and trustworthy and as more dangerous and unreasonable. In the extreme case, the offender is dehumanized and represented as a dangerous, inferior creature that does not deserve living (Yzerbyt & Demoulin, this volume). Because such deteriorated perceptions lower the threshold for retaliation and offensive behavior, hostile attributions ultimately increase the probability that the actor "strikes back" overly hard. Much like a self-fulfilling prophecy, this retaliatory act triggers hostile attributions and perceptual changes in the offender, and the conflict process continues its escalatory spiral.

Naïve Realism and Egocentric Misperceptions

To manage informational complexities and uncertainties, people act as *naïve realists*—they assume that they are rational and reasonable and that other rational and reasonable people thus perceive the world as they do. If others appear to see things differently, this must be due to others being less intelligent or less informed or to some hidden agenda (Ross & Ward, 1995). Such naïve realism may create the feeling that there is no point in cooperating with an adversary because the conflict is just too large—the two sides are simply too far apart from each other (Robinson, Keltner, Ward, & Ross, 1995)—and it may trigger a "biased-perception conflict spiral." Thus, Kennedy and Pronin (2008) showed that people perceive those who disagree with them as biased and that this perception of bias triggers conflict-escalating approaches toward those others. Finally, their study revealed that such conflict-escalating approaches prompts those others to see the actor as more biased and less worthy of cooperative gestures. Like the hostile attribution bias, naïve realism triggers conflict escalation through a self-fulfilling and self-sustaining spiral of perceptual distortions and conflict-ridden behaviors.

Complementing work on naïve realism, Chambers and colleagues describe how egocentric misperceptions fuel conflict escalation. Whereas partisans tend to exaggerate differences of opinion with their adversaries, these exaggerations are particularly tied to issues central to the partisan's own ideology, not to issues central to their adversaries' ideology. For example, Republicans assume greater conflict with Democrats on issues such as gun control and free markets than on social welfare, health care, and environmental policy. Vice versa, Democrats assume greater conflict on these latter issues, which are more central to their own ideology (Chambers, Baron, & Inman, 2006). In follow-up studies, Chambers and Melnyk (2006) uncovered that these assumed (rather than real) conflicts predict disliking and negative stereotyping of adversaries. Interestingly, this work also revealed that partisans suppose others' opposition is geared toward blocking the partisans' point of view rather than promoting the adversaries' own perspective. This is quite ironic when we realize that group members are motivated more to favor their ingroup than to derogate their outgroup (e.g., Halevy et al., 2008; see also the first section of this chapter). Put differently, whereas individuals are driven by self-serving motives, they perceive and expect their counterparts to be primarily driven by other-derogating motives.

Conditions Promoting Conflict Escalation

Although hostile attributions and egocentric misperceptions operate at a basic level, several factors, at both the individual and the group level of analysis, mitigate or amplify their effects. The remainder of this section considers these moderators of conflict escalation. Several important individual differences are reviewed, including need for power, level and stability of self-esteem, and lay-person beliefs about the malleability of personality. Subsequently, group-level moderators are discussed, including vicarious retribution. The latter section is relatively short, as much of the literature about intergroup conflict and hostility is reviewed elsewhere in this volume (e.g., the chapters by Dovidio & Gaertner and by Yzerbyt & Demoulin).

Individual Differences

People who score high on power motive are concerned about having an impact on other people and about having formal social power and prestige (Winter, 2007). High need for power is associated with greater systematic nervous system reactivity (Fodor, 1985), a confrontational and exploitative negotiation style (Terhune, 1968), and tendencies toward both verbal and physical aggression (Winter & Barenbaum, 1985). These tendencies suggest that high-power motivation is also associated with greater retaliation, and this is indeed what has been found. For example, Winter (2007) identified several national and international crises, some of which did, and some of which did not, escalate to war. He scored documents such as diplomatic messages, speeches, and official media commentary from each crisis for power, affiliation, and achievement motivation. His results showed that war crises had significantly higher levels of power and achievement motivation than peace crises. In a similar vein, studies found that type A people who are hard driven, competitive, and time urgent engage in more retaliation than type B individuals, who are easygoing (Baron, Neuman, & Geddes, 1999). Carver and Glass (1978) found, for example, that type A students who were insulted about their task progress and given a chance to shock the insulter employed more shock than did type B individuals.

In contrast to the need for power, the affiliation motive is usually associated with cooperative and friendly behavior, at least when the situation is perceived as being safe (Winter, 2007). Individuals with high affiliation needs may, however, also be relatively prone to retaliation, as is suggested in work on social value orientation. Somewhat counterintuitively perhaps, several studies revealed that prosocial individuals faced with a competitive other "overassimilate" and respond even more competitively than do individuals with a proself orientation (e.g., Kelley & Stahelski, 1970; Van Lange, 1992). Overassimilation may be based on punitive sentiment and the moralistic desire to "teach the other a lesson" (Price et al., 2002; Van Lange, 1992). Such overassimilation is not limited to direct retaliation; it also shows up in more covert tendencies to deceive and mislead the counterpart (Steinel & De Dreu, 2004).

Retaliation is stronger among individuals with high rather than low self-esteem, especially when such high self-esteem is unstable (Kernis, Grannemann, & Barclay, 1989), ill-defined (i.e., low self-concept clarity; Stucke & Sprore, 2002), or yielding an inflated and grandiose view of oneself (Bushman & Baumeister, 1998; Exline, Baumeister, Bushman, Campbell, & Finkel, 2004). For example, Bushman and Baumeister (1998) gave students strikingly unfavorable evaluations of essays they had written and then provided them with a chance to blast the evaluator with noise. Those who were higher in narcissism gave louder and hence more punitive blasts, an effect that was not found when positive evaluations of the essays were given. Likewise, people respond with more verbal aggression, and less attitude change toward their counterparts' position, after negative feedback or after failure when they have low rather than high self-concept clarity (De Dreu & Van Knippenberg, 2005; Stucke & Spore, 2002). The explanation for these and similar results is that people with unstable high self-esteem, or low self-concept clarity, suffer especially uncomfortable self-doubts when others assert superiority over them or put them down. Hence, they lash out to protect or regain their self-esteem.

Fitting the idea that hostile attributions contribute to the escalatory process, work by Kammrath and Dweck (2006) suggests that conflict escalation is more likely when individuals hold so-called entity beliefs about their partner than when they hold incremental beliefs. Entity theorists assume personality to be rather fixed and stable and that not much change in personality is to be expected. Incremental theorists, in contrast, assume personality is flexible and that people can change. Kammrath and Dweck (2006) applied these notions to understand how people respond to transgressions in interpersonal settings. In a study of dating relationships, and in a prospective study of daily conflict experiences, they found that incremental theorists were likely to voice their displeasure with others openly and constructively during conflicts. Entity theorists, on the other hand, were less likely to voice their dissatisfactions directly. Interestingly, this divergence between incremental and entity theorists was increasingly pronounced as conflicts increased in severity: the higher the stakes, the stronger the effects. As the authors note: "One likely explanation is that . . . incremental theorists are motivated to voice their greatest dissatisfactions because they see in these issues both an urgent need for improvement and a real possibility for its realization. Entity theorists may shy away from exactly these discussions because they see the potential benefits as low (little hope of change) and the potential costs as high (irredeemable and relationship-threatening personal flaws may be brought to light). For people who do not believe in personal change, . . . constructive voice may appear no more than useless shouting at the mountain" (p. 1505).

Group-Level Factors and Escalation of Intergroup Conflict

Work on individual–group discontinuity discussed in the first section of this chapter revealed that groups tend to be far more noncooperative than individuals and that intergroup conflict thus is more likely to emerge than interpersonal conflict (Wildschut et al., 2003). Furthermore, conflicts between groups escalate further than interpersonal conflicts (Mikolic et al., 1997)— whereas individuals tend to stop at issuing threats and making angry remarks, groups are more likely to move to actual harassment and abuse.

In addition to the ingroup loyalty and schema-based distrust explanations discussed in the first section, inter-group conflicts escalate because of vicarious retribution. Vicarious retribution emerges when some members of an outgroup provoke or otherwise hurt an ingroup member and other ingroup members who are not personally involved lash out and behave aggressively. This retaliatory behavior can be directed not only toward these perpetrating outgroup members but also toward outgroup members who did not actively participate in the initial provocation. As such, the act of aggression is vicarious in that neither the agent of retaliation nor the target of retribution was directly involved in the original event that precipitated the intergroup conflict (Lickel, Miller, Stenstrom, Denson, & Schmader, 2006).

Vicarious retribution causes a spread of the conflict within the ingroup, as well as the outgroup. Where initially only a handful of people are involved, through vicarious retribution and subsequent reactions to it, a relatively small-scale conflict "blows up" and escalates into large-scale intergroup conflicts. This is what happened in 2005, when a Danish newspaper, the *Jyllands-Posten,* published a series of 12 cartoons showing Muhammad. In one cartoon, he appeared to have a bomb in his turban. According to Muslim faith, it is forbidden to display images of Muhammad, and many people of Muslim faith considered the cartoons offending and blasphemous. Not only were the Danish newspaper and the artist severely attacked, but across the Muslim world protests emerged, some of which

escalated into violence with police firing on the crowds (resulting in more than 100 deaths in total). Fire was set to the Danish embassies in Syria, Lebanon, and Iran; European buildings were stormed; and Danish, Dutch, Norwegian, and German flags were desecrated. Some Muslim leaders issued death threats. In the Western world, various groups responded by endorsing the Danish policies, including "buy Danish" campaigns and other displays of support (*Der Spiegel*, 2006). What began as a provocative act by an individual escalated into a large-scale conflict, described by Danish Prime Minister Anders Fogh Rasmussen as Denmark's worst international crisis since World War II (*Times Online*, 2006).

In their analysis of vicarious retribution, Lickel and colleagues (2006) highlight several amplifying factors, including the extent to which ingroup members identify with their ingroup. Ingroup identification causes people to experience group pride, to feel empathy for fellow ingroup members, and to be susceptible to normative pressures to defend and promote the ingroup. The more one identifies with one's ingroup, the more likely one is to engage in vicarious retribution. Vicarious retribution is also amplified when ingroup members see the outgroup as high in *entitativity*—the perception of the outgroup as a unified and coherent whole in which the members are perceived to be bonded together in some way (Hamilton & Sherman, 1996; Yzerbyt & Demoulin, this volume). In highly entitative outgroups, members are seen as highly similar and interchangeable; therefore, retribution can be relatively indiscriminant (e.g., although one outgroup member committed the provoking act, the others are highly similar and thus equally to blame). Interestingly, Stenstrom, Lickel, Denson, and Miller (2008) found that ingroup identification and outgroup entitativity are closely connected. Across two studies they found evidence of motivated cognition— highly identified individuals perceived the outgroup as higher in entitativity than did individuals low in identification. Structural equation modeling demonstrated that part of the effect of identification on retribution against the outgroup was mediated through perceptions of entitativity.

Other conditions that cause the spread of conflict through vicarious retribution include the public–private context and power differences among groups. In public settings, vicarious retribution is more likely because publicity enhances the salience of social identities and magnifies the humiliation associated with affronts (Tedeschi & Felson, 1994). In addition, in public settings, normative pressures to retaliate become more prominent (Lickel et al., 2006). Ingroup power also promotes vicarious retribution: Low-power outgroups that provoke powerful ingroups induce anger and retaliatory tendencies in the ingroup, whereas high-power outgroups that provoke powerless ingroups induce fear and withdrawal tendencies in the ingroup (Mackie, Devos, & Smith, 2000; Yzerbyt & Demoulin, this volume). Likewise, status hierarchies between groups tend to be justified by its members (Jost, Banaji, & Nosek, 2004). Noncooperation by low-status outgroup members is seen as illegitimate by members of high-status ingroups more than the other way around. As a result, high-status ingroup members may feel more justified to retaliate than do low-status outgroup members.

Self-Sustaining Nature of Escalated Conflicts

Much of the work reviewed thus far shows, one way or the other, that conflict escalation is a rather self-sustaining phenomenon—perceptions and expectations feed into hostile behaviors that trigger perceptual change in one's counterpart, who thus engages in hostile tendencies as well, thereby both confirming initial perceptions and further fueling the escalatory spiral. This self-sustaining nature of conflict escalation can be seen in the numerous conflicts between ethnic, religious, or linguistic groups within and across states: The conflicts between Catholics and Protestants in Northern Ireland, between Muslims and Serbs in Bosnia, or between Hutu and Tutsi in Rwanda are just a few examples.

Although different in many respects, these conflicts are, without exception, intractable conflicts that last decades if not generations (Burton, 1990). They usually involve violent events, including limited military actions or terrorist attacks, leading to civilian and military casualties and causing property destruction and, sometimes, population displacement. The violence and its vividness and saliency generate intense animosity that becomes integrated into the socialization processes in each society and through which conflict-related emotions and cognitions are transmitted to new generations (Rouhana & Bar-Tal, 1998). This sustains stereotypic beliefs and prejudices, which feed and form collective memories. Thoughts related to the conflict are highly accessible, and memories of conflict-related events permeate public discussions and discourse (Bar-Tal, Raviv, & Freund, 1994). Over time, the conflicts "penetrate the societal fabric of both parties and force themselves on individuals and institutions. Leaders, publics, and institutions—such as educational and cultural systems—become involved in the conflicts. At some stages of the conflicts, even intellectual life and scholarly inquiry become politicized as interest in the other society originates in the motivation to 'know your enemy' and inquiries become guided by security needs and considerations" (Rouhana & Bar-Tal, 1998, pp. 761–762).

Summary and Synthesis

Social conflict intensifies and escalates when deprivation is responded to with competition and struggle which, in

turn, triggers in one's counterpart either withdrawal and avoidance or reciprocal competition and struggle. Others' withdrawal provides no solution to deprivation and thus requires renewed and more intense struggle—unilateral escalation sets in. Likewise, others' reciprocal competition amplifies rather than reduces deprivation and thus motivates renewed and more intense struggle—bilateral escalation sets in. These behavioral tendencies are fueled by several closely related psychological processes, including hostile attributions, naïve realism, and egocentric misperceptions. Although emphasizing different aspects of the biases in thought processes, all three psychological processes show that much of what happens in conflict escalation is, in fact, a self-fulfilling prophecy—people see their counterpart as biased and hostile and lash out to preempt another's competitive move, thereby enhancing the likelihood that the other indeed responds competitively and thus confirming the initial perception of the other as biased and hostile.

Several chronic and transient states were identified that fuel conflict escalation. Individuals with high need for power and with inflated, narcissistic self-views are more likely to see others as unworthy and biased and respond to ego threat with greater hostility. Intergroup conflicts also escalate more readily, and further, than interpersonal conflicts. Intergroup conflicts escalate partly because initially uninvolved group members "help out" their ingroup members by attacking outgroup members. Such vicarious retribution explains why relatively local conflicts among a few individuals spread out and reproduce at a broader, intergroup level. This process sets the stage for conflicts to become deep rooted, protracted, and self-sustaining—conflicts become part and parcel of public and private life, survey in individual and collective memories and narratives, and become exceedingly difficult to resolve.

NEGOTIATION AND JOINT PROBLEM SOLVING

Had we begun negotiations then, I think at least half of the casualties and injuries on both sides could have been avoided. . . . [After meeting recently] the Hanoi officials agreed that they also missed these opportunities. (58,000 U.S. soldiers perished, as did 3.8 million Vietnamese.)

—Robert McNamara (*The Brown Daily Herald*, April 27, 1999, p. 13)

In the second section, we saw that parties are likely to resort to cooperation when they have high other-concern and perceive cooperative goal interdependence. An additional motive for negotiation and joint problem solving is that disputants find themselves in a hurting stalemate—a point where disputants refuse to back down yet also lack the strength to push further (Pruitt & Rubin, 1986). Such a hurting stalemate most likely triggered the negotiations among the United States, North Vietnam, and South Vietnam, referred to at the start of this section by former U.S. State Secretary of Defense, Robert McNamara. Hurting stalemates may also have triggered the relaxation of other protracted conflicts, such as the one between Catholics and Protestants in Northern Ireland.

Pruitt (2007) specified that for a hurting stalemate to lead to negotiation and problem solving, two things are needed. First, parties need to have a motivational goal to end the conflict, which is grounded in a sense that victory is unrealistic either because it carries unacceptable costs or risks or because pressure comes from allies or some powerful third party. Second, parties need to have some optimism about the outcome of negotiation and problem solving. Such optimism may derive from lowered aspirations on one or both sides, from the belief that the other party also wants to escape the conflict, or from the perception that an acceptable agreement is shaping up and that one's adversary is ready to make important concessions.

Hurting stalemates are not the only reason for conflict parties to engage in negotiation and joint problem solving. Sometimes disputants start negotiations because they perceive mutually enticing opportunities or seek to avoid an impending catastrophe (Carnevale & De Dreu, 2006). These two motives refer to negotiation as "deal making," and not as a means of conflict management and dispute resolution—the focus of this chapter. Negotiation and joint problem solving that emerge following a hurting stalemate probably involve greater (initial) levels of distrust and higher need for reconciliation and willingness to forgive (Kelman, 2006). For example, negotiation and joint problem solving is more difficult and produces less mutually beneficial agreements when parties have a history of competition (e.g., Lindskold & Han, 1988) or have a competitive reputation (Tinsley, O'Connor, & Sullivan, 2002). However, whether negotiation and joint problem solving unfolds differently as a function of the reasons for initiating a negotiation is an empirical issue in need of new research.

Single-Issue and Multi-Issue Negotiation

Negotiation is usually defined as the communication between parties aimed at resolving their differences. Such negotiations can be informal, as in the case of a husband and wife negotiating the distribution of household chores, or it can be formal, as in the case of union and management representatives negotiating new labor contracts. Negotiations may thus take a few minutes or involve many rounds of exchanges over extended periods. For example, many labor contract negotiations between unions and employers easily stretch several months, and the negotiations in Strategic Arms Limitation Talks I and II about nuclear arms reductions between the United States and the former Soviet Union in the late seventies and early eighties of the last century continued for several years before agreements were reached.

Negotiation involves mixed-motive interdependence, in that each party is better off with rather than without an agreement (providing an incentive to cooperate) but at the same time is better off by taking all and giving nothing (thus providing a competitive incentive). Whereas mixed-motive "games" such as the PD discussed in the first section involve independent choices by interdependent actors, negotiation involves joint decision making, with parties making concessions and proposals for agreement that only take effect when accepted by all sides. Agreements often represent a change in the status quo, for example, terms of an exchange (a new joint venture or change in ownership) or a new common understanding, shared perception, belief, attitude, or feeling (Carnevale, 2007). Agreements can take many forms. They can be a straightforward compromise, in which parties accommodate and meet one another halfway, or they can involve logrolling, in which parties concede on unimportant issues and hold firm on important issues.

Negotiation scholars typically distinguish between single-issue and multi-issue negotiation. A single-issue negotiation (e.g., about salary increases in a labor–management negotiation) has a single dimension of value, and the main goal in the negotiation is to distribute value among participants. An example involves the UBG discussed in the first section, with only a single dimension of value at stake—the resource to be distributed.

Many single-issue negotiations involve multiple rounds of exchange, in that parties make demands and concessions until an agreement is reached. For example, in the game-of-nine developed by Kelley, Beckman, and Fischer (1967), two parties hold up cards depicting a number between 1 and 9 and reach an agreement only if the sum of their numbers does not exceed 9. Because one party benefits from lower numbers and the other from high numbers, they need to make concessions to reach an agreement. One important finding using a repeated-play variation of this game is that bargaining pairs who assessed themselves, before the experiment, as cooperative were more likely to reach agreements than bargaining pairs who assessed themselves as competitive and that this effect was stronger when bargaining involved high stakes (money) rather than low stakes (points; Kelley et al., 1970).

Behavioral Strategies in Single-Issue Negotiations

Work using single-issue negotiation tasks has revealed that negotiators tend to match their counterpart's concessions in terms of size, frequency, or both (Pruitt & Carnevale, 1993). However, negotiators may decide not to reciprocate their counterpart's behavior. For example, reciprocating the other's competitive and tough strategy may lead to an impasse, providing neither party with positive outcomes. Reversely, reciprocating the other's cooperative behavior may be unwise when one's goal is to maximize personal gain or when the other's cooperative behavior reflects a strategic ploy and reciprocating the other's cooperativeness leads to being exploited.

That reciprocity is indeed not always the best option is reflected in negotiators occasional engagement in mismatching—they place high demands when their counterpart appears soft, and low demands when their counterpart appears tough (e.g., Liebert, Smith, Hill, & Keiffer, 1968). This mismatching phenomenon was nicely illustrated by Diekmann, Tenbrunsel, and Galinsky (2003). Whereas participants anticipating a competitive counterpart forecasted that they themselves would be competitive, too, an analysis of actual behavior showed that negotiators who expected a competitive opponent actually became less competitive, as evidenced by setting lower, less aggressive reservation prices; making less demanding counteroffers; and ultimately agreeing to lower negotiated outcomes. Other work has shown that mismatching occurs especially when time pressure and deadlines are looming (Smith, Pruitt, & Carnevale, 1982). Interestingly, mismatching also occurs when negotiators lack information about the partner's outcomes and limits. This suggests that, from the counterpart's concessions, negotiators derive insights into the other's limit (Pruitt, 1981). Indeed, mismatching is more likely in the early phases of negotiation when parties seek information and in the last phase of negotiation when parties try to convince their counterpart to make a concession to avoid a mutually harmful impasse.

Structure of Multi-Issue Negotiations

A multi-issue negotiation involves several dimensions of value and often allows for the development of "integrative" or win–win agreements. Consider, for example, the negotiation between Harry and Sally who divorce and move to different apartments. They negotiate about five items that they bought together (the current market value is in parentheses)—a ping-pong table ($125), a set of tennis rackets ($50), two baseball bats ($25), a guitar ($125), and an MP3 docking station ($75). One possibility would be to seek a distribution of these goods so that Harry and Sally walk away with the same value (e.g., Harry gets the ping-pong table and the MP3 docking station [125 + 75 = 200], and Sally takes the tennis rackets, the baseball bats, and the guitar [50 + 25 + 125 = 200]). A more integrative solution would be to take into consideration that Harry loves music,

whereas Sally is a true sports fan. Harry thus values more music-related items (e.g., the guitar and the MP3 docking station), whereas Sally values more the sports-related items (the pin-pong table, the baseball bats, and the tennis rackets). Whereas the market value of their deal is the same (i.e., [125 + 75 = 200] to Harry; [125 + 25 + 50 = 200] to Sally), the subjective value of this deal is higher because underlying interests and preferences were taken into account to a greater extent.

To understand integrative negotiation, researchers typically used a task that captures the integrative aspects of many multi-issue negotiations. Consider, for example, the task used in a classic study by Pruitt and Lewis (1975). These researchers engaged participants in a simulated negotiation between a seller and a buyer of three commodities (iron, sulfur, and coal). Each negotiator received a chart listing for each commodity several possible agreement levels (A through I) with each agreement level providing some value. As can be seen in Table 27.2, the values for each issue were structured so that when the buyer received more value (e.g., $800), the seller got less (e.g., $0). However, Table 27.2 also shows that coal was not valuable to the buyer (level A = $800 to level I = $0) and iron was extremely valuable (A = $2,000 to I = $0). The exact opposite was true for the seller (i.e., coal being most and iron being least valuable). This provided a logrolling opportunity—when the buyer makes small concessions on iron but large concessions on coal and the seller holds firm on coal but concedes on iron, both parties achieve more than when they split the difference on each of these issues. Typically, participants only see their own chart and are not given their counterpart's chart. They can only uncover the differences in preferences and priorities through communication. As such, the task provides ample opportunity for researchers to describe what negotiators do and how this relates to the likelihood of them finding integrative agreements, as well as for the testing of explanatory principles—why negotiators engage in some behavioral strategies more than in others, thus leading toward or away from mutually beneficial, integrative agreements.

Behavioral Strategies in Multi-Issue Negotiation

Content coding of the negotiation process, focusing on what negotiators say to one another, and in what sequence, revealed a distinction between distributive and integrative strategies and tactics (e.g., Ben-Yoav & Pruitt, 1984; Carnevale & Lawler, 1986; De Dreu, Giebels, & Van de Vliert, 1998; Pruitt & Lewis, 1975; Weingart, Hyder & Prietula, 1996; Weingart et al., 2007). Distributive strategies concern the way outcomes within an agreement are distributed among the parties and can be subdivided into contending and conceding tactics (see also dual concern

Table 27.2   Buyer and Seller Profit Sheets in the Pruitt and Lewis (1975) Study of Integrative Negotiation

Buyer						Seller					
Iron		Sulfur		Coal		Iron		Sulfur		Coal	
Price	(Profit)	Price	(Profit)	Price	(Profit)	Price	(Profit)	Price	(Profit)	Price	(Profit)
A	$2,000	A	$1,200	A	$800	A	$ 0	A	$ 0	A	$ 0
B	$1,750	B	$1,050	B	$700	B	$100	B	$ 150	B	$ 250
C	$1,500	C	$ 900	C	$600	C	$200	C	$ 300	C	$ 500
D	$1,250	D	$ 750	D	$500	D	$300	D	$ 450	D	$ 750
E	$1,000	E	$ 600	E	$400	E	$400	E	$ 600	E	$1,000
F	$ 750	F	$ 450	F	$300	F	$500	F	$ 750	F	$1,250
G	$ 500	G	$ 300	G	$200	G	$600	G	$ 900	G	$1,500
H	$ 250	H	$ 200	H	$100	H	$700	H	$1,050	H	$1,750
I	$ 0	I	$ 0	I	$ 0	I	$800	I	$1,200	I	$2,000

Note: Prices are referred to by letter; the numbers under each commodity represent profits to be made on that commodity at the particular price. Buyer and seller are only shown their own profit chart.

theory in Figure 27.3). *Contending tactics* involve the use of threats and bluffs, persuasive arguments, and commitments to a particular position or course of action. They may also involve strategic withdrawal from the situation, stalling, and avoiding issues, if doing so is serving one's goals and interests. *Conceding tactics* involve unilateral concessions, unconditional promises, and offering help. Some scholars also distinguish *compromising tactics*, which involve matching other's concessions, making conditional promises and threats, and actively searching for a middle ground (e.g., Van de Vliert, 1997). Integrative strategies concern the way in which opposing parties' interests and positions can be reconciled into a mutually satisfying agreement. *Problem solving* is a prime example of integrative behavior. In negotiation, it involves a full and open exchange of information about priorities and preferences, the revelation and verification of insights, and logrolling. Sometimes problem solving is implicit, as in "heuristic trial-and-error." It means that negotiators make, over time, a series of offers each having the same overall value to oneself but, perhaps, different value to one's partner (Pruitt & Lewis, 1975).

In their work on multi-issue negotiation, Walton and McKersie (1965) detected a "differentiation-before-integration" pattern: Negotiations begin in quite a harsh and competitive manner, and, after a series of competitive exchanges, parties come to realize that this leads nowhere but to a costly impasse and accordingly change toward mutual problem solving as a more viable strategy for safeguarding and promoting their self-interest. Gottman (1979) uncovered a similar pattern in a study of conflict in marital couples—after an agenda-building phase in which issues and feelings are voiced, couples enter an argumentation phase in which they attempt to persuade the other. Happily married couples more than others then enter a negotiation phase geared toward solving their differences. In general, such shifts from contending to problem solving produce mutually beneficial, integrative agreements (Harinck & De Dreu, 2004; Olekalns, Brett, & Weingart, 2003). Negotiators perhaps fear that their counterpart will return to contending when the attempt at problem solving fails and thus cooperate without restraint (Brodt & Tuchinsky, 2000). Alternatively, the attempt at problem solving may loom as particularly constructive when it is embedded in, and contrasted with, a tough and contending strategy that preceded it (Hilty & Carnevale, 1992).

Motivational and Cognitive Processes in Integrative Negotiation

Research into the psychological mechanisms underlying integrative negotiation has been conducted within two distinct research traditions. The motivational tradition largely evolved around dual concern theory, testing whether and when social motivation and resistance to yielding interact to produce problem solving and integrative agreements. Social motivation is seen as similar to concern for the other, with prosocial motivation producing higher concern for the other than proself motivation. Resistance to yielding is seen as similar to concern for self, with higher resistance reflecting higher concern for self (Carnevale & Pruitt, 1992; Pruitt, 1998; Van de Vliert, 1997).

Social motivation is assumed to vary as a function of the parties' relationship (friends vs. strangers), whether they expect cooperative future interaction or not, whether they have prosocial or proself value orientation, whether they are rewarded for joint or for personal performance, and whether they are categorized as members of the same or different social groups. Resistance to yielding is assumed to vary as a function of the negotiator's level of aspiration and their limit, whether they have an exit option and outside alternative or not, whether outcomes are framed as losses rather than gains, whether there is low or high time pressure, and whether there is constituent surveillance or not (Pruitt, 1998). A meta-analysis of this work provided good support for the theory. Regardless of the way in which social motivation or resistance to yielding was induced or measured, negotiators who combined a prosocial motivation with high resistance to yielding engaged in more problem solving and achieved more integrative agreements than when such high resistance to yielding was missing or negotiators had a proself, noncooperative motivation (De Dreu, Weingart et al., 2000).

Core notions from dual concern theory can also be used to understand the role of affect and emotions in negotiation. For example, a pioneering study by Carnevale and Isen (1986) showed that negotiators induced to feel positively engaged in more problem solving and achieved more integrative agreements than did negotiators in a mood-neutral control condition (also see e.g., Forgas, 1998; Kramer, Pommerenke, & Newton, 1993). These findings may reflect that a positive mood enhances a prosocial, cooperative motivation and increases cognitive flexibility and creative problem solving. Reversely, negative moods such as sadness produce evasiveness (Forgas & Cromer, 2004), while anger produces toughness (Butt, Choi, & Jaeger, 2005). Angry negotiators report lower prosocial motivation, achieve lower joint gains, and have lower desire to work with the other in the future than negotiators with more positive emotional regard for their partner (Allred et al., 1997). Whereas anger raises proself motivation and resistance to yielding (thus producing contending behavior), sadness lowers proself motivation and resistance to yielding (thus producing inaction and withdrawal; see Figure 27.3).

The cognitive tradition largely evolved around the behavioral decision approach (Bazerman, Curhan, Moore, & Valley, 2000). Grounded in work on bounded rationality and heuristics and on biases in human judgment and decision making (e.g., Kahneman & Tversky, 1973), it describes various cognitive errors that prohibit negotiators from uncovering and achieving mutually beneficial, integrative agreements. For example, negotiators tend to make a *fixed-pie assumption*—they assume their own and their counterparts' interests are diametrically opposed (i.e., your gain is my loss). It brings a distributive mindset to the negotiation and crowds out tendencies toward problem solving and integrative negotiation. Indeed, a large majority of negotiators, both nonexperts and professionals,

make a fixed-pie assumption and, as a result, fail to reach integrative agreements (Thompson & Hrebec, 1996). Other biases and heuristics include gain-loss framing, anchoring and adjustment, overconfidence, and reliance on stereotypes (for reviews, see Bazerman et al., 2000; Carnevale & Pruitt, 1992; De Dreu, Beersma, Steinel, & Van Kleef, 2007).

Cognitive processes in negotiation have a motivational basis (De Dreu & Carnevale, 2003; O'Connor, 1997). For example, the motivated information processing perspective (De Dreu & Carnevale, 2003) proceeds on the basis of the assumption that negotiators engage in more or less automatic and shallow, versus deep and deliberate, information processing and exchange. Deep processing is more likely when negotiators have high rather than low epistemic motivation, which is defined as the desire to develop a rich and accurate understanding of the world, including the negotiation task. Epistemic motivation is higher when negotiators are process accountable (De Dreu, Koole, & Steinel, 2000), experience mild rather than severe time pressure (De Grada, Kruglanski, Mannetti, & Pierro, 1999), have low rather than high need for closure (De Dreu, Koole, & Oldersma, 1999), or high rather than low need for cognition (Schei, Rognes, & Mykland, 2007).

High epistemic motivation and concomitant systematic information processing reduce the impact of reasoning errors such as the fixed-pie assumption (e.g., De Dreu, Koole, et al., 2000) or cognitive biases in person perception (e.g., De Dreu et al., 1999). The motivated information processing perspective further assumes that more accurate understanding of the task, and one's counterpart, leads to more problem solving when negotiators also have a prosocial motivation. Under prosocial motivation, there is enough trust to exchange information in an open and truthful way, and deep processing is oriented toward finding solutions that serve both rather than one party. However, when there is proself motivation, deep processing is oriented toward finding solutions that serve oneself rather than one's partner. Under proself motivation, deep processing thus leads away from rather than toward integrative agreements. This is indeed what has been found: Negotiators with a prosocial motive achieved more integrative agreements than those with a proself motivation, especially when they had high rather than low epistemic motivation (De Dreu, Beersma, Stroebe, & Euwema, 2006; Halevy, 2008).

The motivated information processing perspective provides a framework for understanding the intimate interplay between motivational and cognitive processes underlying integrative negotiation. It also helps to understand why negotiators are influenced by their partner's emotion displays—how do the counterpart's emotions influence the focal negotiator's strategic choice? For example, in one study, Van Kleef, De Dreu, and Manstead (2004a) provided participants in a two-party negotiation with information about their (simulated) opponent's emotional state. Negotiators who learned that their opponent was angry estimated the other's limit to be high, and to avoid a costly impasse, they made relatively large concessions. Conversely, negotiators with a happy partner judged the other's limit to be low, felt no need to concede to avoid an impasse, and made relatively small concessions. Follow-up studies show that the other's emotional displays had effects in particular when the focal negotiator had high epistemic motivation and engaged in deep information processing (Van Kleef, De Dreu, & Manstead, 2004b; Van Kleef, De Dreu, & Manstead, 2006; also see Steinel, Van Kleef, & Harinck, 2008).

Negotiation and Problem Solving in Small Groups

Many processes uncovered in interpersonal negotiation also apply to negotiations involving three or more parties. However, a few critical aspects of small group negotiations are noteworthy. First, small group negotiations are cognitively taxing because parties need to consider multiple counterparts with whom more or less disagreement exists (Kramer, 1991). Second, small group negotiation involves coalition formation. Parties need to determine not only how to distribute outcomes but also whom to include in (or exclude from) the coalition that benefits from the reward (Komorita & Parks, 1995). Whereas it may be in each party's self-interest to become a member of a small coalition (i.e., the rewards are distributed among fewer people), agreements that exclude some members tend to be less stable and groups may face renewed conflict when excluded members seek to improve their position. In the long run, all-inclusive "grand coalitions" thus may be both individually and collectively more beneficial (Mannix, 1993). Indeed, one important reason underlying the formation of all-inclusive, grand coalitions is a concern among group members that excluded members would feel hurt and deprived. This "do-no-harm" principle is particularly influential when excluded members would incur a loss and less so when excluded others would forego a gain (Van Beest, Van Dijk, De Dreu, & Wilke, 2005). It is also more likely when group members have a prosocial rather than a proself motivation and value fairness more than their personal self-interests (Van Beest, Andeweg, Koning, & Van Lange, 2008; also see Van Beest & Van Dijk, 2008).

Fairness considerations aside, group members may be led away from grand coalitions when preferences align better with those of only some other group members (Weingart, Bennett, & Brett, 1993). Polzer, Mannix, and Neale (1998) studied such a situation in which two parties (the majority) had identical preferences while the remaining party (the minority) had opposite preferences. Their study showed that majority members join forces through coalition formation, thus excluding the minority. This produced relatively good outcomes for the majority parties compared with the minority party. Follow-up studies revealed that this effect emerges especially when the group employs a majority rather than unanimity rule. This is because, when unanimity is required, the minority uses its veto power to prohibit agreements that favor the majority at the minority's expense (Beersma & De Dreu, 2002). This effect emerges especially when the minority member has a proself rather than a prosocial motivation—even when unanimity rule applies and the minority can block disadvantageous agreements, it refrains from doing so when it has a prosocial motivation (Ten Velden, Beersma, & De Dreu, 2007).

Between-Group Negotiation and Problem Solving

Many conflicts, especially the escalated and more protracted ones discussed in the section on struggle and conflict escalation, involve groups rather than individuals. For intergroup conflicts, too, negotiation and joint problem solving constitute important strategies for conflict resolution. Akin to the analysis at the individual level, between-group negotiation and problem solving emerges when there is a hurting stalemate in the escalated and protracted intergroup conflict yet parties also experience "readiness" (Pruitt, 2007). This section considers negotiation and problem solving between groups. It considers negotiation teams—small groups of individuals negotiating with another small group of individuals—as well as representative negotiation, in which two or more individuals negotiate on behalf of their ingroups. Finally, this section considers how features and characteristics of the group individual negotiators affect these individuals' negotiation behavior. Particular attention is given to recent work on cross-cultural encounters.

Negotiation Teams: Are Two Heads Better Than One?

Several studies compared the performance of solo negotiators with that of unitary teams (Morgan & Tindale, 2002; O'Connor, 1997; Polzer, 1996; Thompson, Peterson, & Brodt, 1996). In this work, either two individuals negotiate with each other or a team of two or three individuals negotiates with another team. Teams are unitary in that all members within a team have identical information and preferences. Two possible predictions have been tested. First, the individual–group discontinuity effect discussed in the first section suggests that teams are tougher and less oriented toward problem solving than individuals. Alternatively, the idea that people are bounded in their rationality and that "two heads are better than one" suggests that teams are less susceptible to reasoning errors and have greater information processing capacity—teams should be more likely to uncover integrative potential and more easily reach win–win agreements than individuals.

The research evidence is inconclusive, with some studies finding team negotiations to be less integrative (e.g., Polzer, 1996) and others finding support for the two-heads-are-better-than-one idea (e.g., Thompson et al., 1996). In one study, Morgan and Tindale (2002) compared integrative negotiation between two individuals to such negotiation between two three-person groups. After reaching agreement, negotiators were given the opportunity either to stick with the agreement (a cooperative choice) or to defect from the agreement (a noncooperative choice yielding greater personal or ingroup gain). Results showed that groups reached more integrative agreements than individuals, supporting the two-heads-are-better-than-one prediction. However, groups were also more likely to defect from the agreement than were individuals, supporting an ingroup-loyalty explanation (also see Howard, Gardner, & Thompson, 2007).

Halevy (2008) argued that negotiating teams rarely operate as monolithic entities and, instead, are often divided—some team members have different priorities and preferences regarding the between-group negotiation than other team-members, and such preference diversity creates intrateam conflicts. In a large experiment involving integrative negotiation between two four-person groups, Halevy showed that between-group negotiations produced more integrative agreements when within-group conflict was absent rather than present. Other results revealed this occurs because within-group conflict stimulated deliberate information processing among team members geared toward bolstering individual rather than collective goals. Such motivated information processing, combined with a desire to benefit the ingroup, undermined the capability of teams to do well in the between-group negotiation.

Taken together, more work is needed on team negotiation. First, opposing predictions made by the two-heads-are-better-than-one perspective and the ingroup-loyalty argument both received support. We need to know why, and under what conditions, ingroup loyalty prevails and renders between-group negotiation more difficult. Second, most work in this area assumes teams to be unitary, monolithic entities. Oftentimes, teams are internally divided, and how this plays out in the between-group negotiation requires a more systematic analysis.

Representative Negotiation

Intergroup negotiations are often conducted by individuals representing their ingroups. Groups engage representatives for many reasons. The group may be divided and cannot settle on one particular and consensually agreed strategy, group members may feel a need to shift responsibility and accountability, or they may believe matters can be better handled by one individual than by the entire group (Pruitt & Carnevale, 1993). Furthermore, groups may delegate negotiations to a representative because the group lacks specific expertise and domain-relevant knowledge. Thus, groups may engage a lawyer to represent them because group members lack the necessary judicial expertise or because the lawyer has relevant professional contacts. Finally, groups may select a representative because of some desirable dispositional temperament or other features believed to make that individual particularly well suited to negotiation and representation of the group (Mnookin & Susskind, 1999). For example, a coalition of community members desiring a local synagogue to be closed may seek representation by a publicly known orthodox Jewish lawyer. Because of his faith, the lawyer can never be accused of having a vested interest himself, lending further credibility to his arguments (and the interests of the coalition).

Representative negotiation can be seen as a special case of interpersonal negotiation to which many principles and processes identified earlier can be applied. However, while representatives may have considerable discretion to negotiate, they are bound by implicit or explicit directions provided by their constituents and they face accountability pressures (De Dreu et al., 2007; Druckman, 1994; Pruitt & Carnevale, 1993). Representatives thus are in a quite different position than those negotiating on their own behalf—not only do they need to consider their counterpart's needs, desires, preferences, strategic intentions, and tactical maneuvers, they also need to take into account and manage the preferences, ideas, and suggestions of their constituency. Accordingly, representatives monitor their constituency and adapt their goals and behavior accordingly (Carnevale, Pruitt, & Seilheimer, 1981), partly also to impress their constituents (Wall, 1991). One sensible hypothesis thus is that representative negotiation is cognitively taxing, making representatives more vulnerable to cognitive biases and errors than individuals negotiating on their own behalf.

Compared with situations in which individuals negotiate on their own behalf, representative negotiation tends to be less cooperative and more competitive. Representatives are relatively tough, place high demands, and concede slowly (Pruitt & Carnevale, 1993). One explanation for this competitive shift is that representatives tend to believe that their constituents favor an aggressive approach (Druckman, 1994). Indeed, when representatives believe that their constituency favors a cooperative approach toward the outgroup, they become relatively cooperative and lenient in their negotiation behavior (e.g., Enzle, Harvey, & Wright, 1992; Gelfand & Realo, 1999).

Within-constituency dynamics can influence the between-representative negotiation. For example, during the Camp David negotiations between Israel and the Palestine Liberation Organization in 2000, Yasser Arafat "did nothing to control the fratricidal competition in his delegation, effectively giving license to those who were attacking other members who were trying to find ways to bridge the differences" (Carnevale, 2007, pp. 428–429). Research has indeed shown that it requires a few hawks within the constituency to "spoil" the atmosphere and render between-group negotiations relatively tough and competitive (Steinel, De Dreu, Ouwehand, & Ramirez, 2009). One explanation is that hawks have relatively more influence because they appeal to ingroup loyalty. Another explanation is that the negative competitiveness in a hawkish position is more vivid and salient and attracts more weight in the representative's judgment and decision making.

Cross-Cultural Differences

A case can be made that even interpersonal negotiations are influenced by the features and characteristics of the groups these individuals belong to, including possible intergroup relations and perceptions of the outgroup. In other words, the social identities people have, with their dominant norms and values, "spill over" in negotiations between individuals acting on their own behalf. This possibility is illustrated well in work on cross-cultural differences in negotiation.

Culture shapes and determines the norms people have for managing disputes and for resolving conflicts (Tinsley & Brett, 2001). Culture also drives the cognitive representations people have of conflict. In the landmark study on single-issue negotiation by Kelley and colleagues (1970), individuals tested in the laboratories of Columbia University and the University of North Carolina were found to define bargaining more in terms of active–passive than in terms of good–bad; the reverse pattern emerged among participants tested in the laboratories of the Katholieke Universiteit Leuven (Leuven, Belgium) and the École Pratique des Hautes Études (Paris, France). Work comparing American to East Asian students revealed that individuals with a collectivist background view conflict more as compromise focused, whereas individuals with an individualist background view these same conflicts more as win–lose focused (Gelfand et al., 2001). This suggests that individuals scoring high on collectivism may have a stronger prosocial motivation than individuals scoring high on individualism, who may have a stronger proself orientation (see also Chen, Mannix, & Okumura, 2003; Hulbert, Correa da Silva, & Adegboyega, 2001;

Probst, Carnevale, & Triandis, 1999). It also suggests that fairness principles—such as the equality rule—may be more prominent in collectivist than individualistic cultures (e.g., Leung, 1987). Indeed, collectivist individuals are more inclined to make concessions, to engage in problem solving, or to accept a 50–50 compromise. However, this holds when the counterpart is not seen as outgroup—when this is the case, individuals from collectivist backgrounds tend to become more hostile and competitive than those with an individualist background (Carnevale & Leung, 2001; Gelfand & Brett, 2004).

Related to individualism–collectivism is the distinction between low- and high-context cultures (Triandis, 1989). In high-context cultures, such as Japan and China, meaning is communicated not only by a person's words or acts but also by the context in which those words or acts are communicated. Many Western cultures (e.g., United States and Germany) are low-context cultures, in which meaning is carried by words or acts and communication is typically direct. Negotiators from the United States indeed relied on logic and reasoning to make their point, whereas negotiators from Taiwan (a high-context culture) relied more on normative statements, referrals to social roles, and relationships (Drake, 1995). Negotiators from low-context cultures engaged in more direct communication (e.g., saying "no") than did negotiators from high-context cultures (e.g., Adair, Okumura, & Brett, 2001).

Mediation

Because negotiation can be difficult and easily breaks down into more hostile exchanges, conflict parties sometimes invite a mediator to assist the negotiation process. In some collectivist cultures, mediation is preferred over direct negotiations. In these cultures, harmony and peaceful relations are highly valued and mediators provide a buffer between the parties, thus preventing overt hostility (Leung, 1987; Wall, Stark, & Standifer, 2001). In individualistic cultures, mediation is sought, for example, when negotiators have low self-efficacy regarding the negotiation process (Arnold & O'Connor, 2006).

How mediators behave—what they do to facilitate negotiation—is modeled in Carnevale's (1986) strategic choice model. This model presents mediator behavior as a function of, first, perceived common ground. Perceived common ground refers to the mediator's estimate of the probability that disputants can find a mutually satisfying agreement. When the mediator sees that the parties trust one another, or have a history of cooperative exchange, for example, the mediator perceives common ground to be high. But when the conflict involves deeply rooted yet clearly opposing values, as in the prolife–prochoice debate, for example, the mediator perceives common ground to be much lower. Second, mediator behavior is a function of the mediator's concern for parties' aspirations—the value placed by the mediator on parties achieving their aspirations. When a mediator knows the parties well and considers them to be friends, for example, concern for aspirations tends to be high. Or when the mediator perceives the claims made by the parties to be legitimate and justified, concern for aspirations tends to be high. Finally, concern for parties' aspirations tends to be higher when the mediator has a vested interest in seeing the parties being happy with a particular settlement.

Generally, when both factors are low, mediators are predicted to employ pressing tactics, to force parties into some kind of agreement; when both factors are high, mediators are predicted to employ problem-solving tactics to help parties find a mutually beneficial, integrative agreement. When perceived common ground is low but concern for aspirations is high, mediators are predicted to use compensation tactics—they try to entice parties into making concessions but also seek to compensate such concessions through other means. For example, the Camp David agreement in 1977 involved not only return of the Sinai Peninsula to Egypt by Israel but also United States–Israel trade treaties that were quite advantageous to Israel. Finally, when perceived common ground is high but concern for aspirations is low, mediators are predicted to remain inactive and to let the parties work it out themselves.

Several studies support the strategic choice model (Carnevale & Pruitt, 1992). For example, Ross and Wieland (1996) found that mediators under high time pressure, which is assumed to lower concern for aspirations, became less inactive and increased the use of pressing tactics. However, this was the case especially when high trust between negotiators increased the mediator's perception of common ground. In addition, mediators tend to steer toward integrative agreements more when negotiators act friendly toward each other and perceived common ground is high than when the relationship appears to be hostile and perceived common ground is lower (Thompson & Kim, 2000).

There has been some debate about the value of the strategic choice model. Despite the good empirical support, some have argued that mediators rarely value both disputants' aspirations equally—more often, mediators are biased and have a preference for one party or for one party's aspirations. Such bias may lead mediators to side with one party and to ignore the needs and interests of the other. In addition, mediators may be biased because their personal interests are served more when one of the disputants wins the conflict (Van de Vliert, 1992). More work is needed to understand the origins of mediator biases and, more importantly, their consequences for mediation behavior,

the way disputants see their mediator, and the quality of the agreement reached.

Summary and Synthesis

Negotiation and joint problem solving represent constructive alternatives to struggle and to withdrawal and avoiding. When multiple issues are at stake, trade-offs and mutually beneficial agreements are possible. Motivational and cognitive processes alone and in combination determine behavioral actions and reactions that ultimately feed into integrative agreements. Such agreements become more likely when negotiators pair a prosocial rather than a proself orientation to a high rather than a low resistance to concession making. To overcome information processing errors and biases, it further helps for negotiators to have high epistemic motivation and to engage in deep and deliberate rather than shallow and automatic information search, dissemination, and processing. These conclusions appear to apply to interpersonal negotiations, as well as to the cognitively more taxing small group negotiations.

Negotiations in intergroup conflict may be conducted by teams or by individuals who represent their ingroups. Research supports both the two-heads-are-better-than-one idea that teams are better able to achieve integrative agreements and the ingroup-loyalty idea that between-team negotiations become relatively hostile and inefficient. More work is needed, also because much work on team negotiations proceeded on the basis of the questionable assumption that teams are monolithic entities in which all members think and act alike. The same holds for work on representative negotiation, which suggests that representatives are quite heavily influenced by the (presumed) norms in their constituency because of accountability, a basic desire to please, or some combination. But work on representative negotiation essentially ignored that constituencies often are rather heterogeneous mixtures that do anything but speak with one voice.

This section touched on several critical issues that are hardly addressed and about which we know little. When considering intergroup negotiations, we know, for example, exceedingly little about the way representative negotiation influences the dynamics within the respective constituencies—is a more constructive negotiation mitigating or heating up conflicts and disagreements within constituencies? Are between-representative animosities welcomed by their constituencies, or are these met with worry and anxiety? Reversely, we know little about the ways in which intergroup relations influence the representative negotiations. Do representatives feel empowered when constituencies fight rather than coexist peacefully? Do they benefit, and how, from knowing their counterpart's constituency is divided and ridden by internal conflicts? These and similar questions are important in understanding when and why negotiations between groups, with their constructive potential, deteriorate into hostile exchanges and result in (renewed) escalation of intergroup conflicts.

FUNCTIONS OF SOCIAL CONFLICT

> And if you calculate cost, then even in case of victory, one's losses greatly exceed the gains.
> —Desiderius Erasmus (1466–1536)

> Truth springs from argument amongst friends.
> —David Hume (1711–1776)

The preceding sections predominantly considered the emergence of conflict, the psychological and behavioral processes underlying conflict escalation, and negotiation and joint problem solving. They showed that parties sometimes end up with lose–lose agreements and destroy value and sometimes develop integrative agreements and create value. Value destroyed or created occupied the thinking of the Dutch humanist Desiderius Erasmus. But as the quote from the Scottish philosopher David Hume suggests, conflict may have several other consequences for the functioning and development of individuals and small groups and for the ways in which intergroup relations change and evolve (Coser, 1956). This section reviews several of these other functions of social conflict, including individual health and well-being, learning and creativity, group decision making and team performance, and the ways in which group composition and group size change.

Individual-Level Consequences

Health and Well-Being

Social conflict involves anger and anxiety, threatens self-esteem, and taxes cognitive resources. Negative emotions, threatened self-esteem, and heightened cognitive effort affect the physiological system in a multitude of ways: Adrenaline levels go up, heartbeat accelerates, and muscle tension increases (Kamarck et al., 1998). When conflict persists and stretches over longer periods, it may lead to psychosomatic complaints and increase susceptibility to mental breakdown and burnout (e.g., Spector & Bruke-Lee, 2008). Evidence also shows that prolonged conflict and concomitant high arousal come together with increased release of cortisol, a corticosteroid that causes an atrophy of the lymphoid structures, thus injuring the functioning of the immune system and ultimately increasing the likelihood of "real" illnesses (Pennebaker, 1982).

The detrimental impact of conflict can be seen in the sometimes disastrous consequences of workplace bullying—a situation in which an individual frequently and for longer periods is harassed, bullied, or otherwise derogated by one or more peers or supervisors. Although bullying is an extreme case of escalated conflict, extrapolating from a large survey suggests that several million people in the European labor force alone are the victim of continuous and systematic bullying behavior, sexual harassment, or physical aggression (e.g., Zapf, Knorz, & Kulla, 1996). Evidence shows that exposure to systematic bullying gives rise to psychosomatic complaints and, in some cases, post-traumatic anxiety disorders (Einarsen, 1999). Interestingly, even passive bystanders of systematic bullying tend to report more health problems and lower job satisfaction than employees not witnessing systematic bullying at work (Steensma, Hubert, Furda, & Groot, 2004). In other words, both experiencing and witnessing systematic bullying at work creates health problems, lowers job satisfaction, and increases turnover and absenteeism (Zapf et al., 1996).

The adverse impact of witnessing conflict is not limited to workplace conflicts and systematic bullying. A large literature on parental conflict shows that "exposure to high levels of interparental conflict increases the child's risk for a wide array of psychological problems, including emotional (e.g., depressive symptoms, anxiety), behavioral (e.g., aggression, delinquency), social (e.g., poor peer relations), and academic difficulties" (Davies, 2002, p. 1). According to the *emotional security hypothesis*, interparental conflict threatens a child's sense of interparental and parent–child security, which in turn increases the child's vulnerability to these psychological and behavioral problems (e.g., Davies & Cummings, 1994). Davies (2002) provides an overview of the specific mediators and moderators of these relationships that may serve as entry points for further studying the effects of witnessing conflict on psychological functioning both inside and outside of the family context.

Learning and Creativity

Conflict may stimulate learning, creativity, and intellectual development (e.g., Levine, Resnick, & Higgins, 1993). A large literature on *minority dissent* shows that being confronted with a dissenting point of view stimulates divergent thinking and creative processing when the dissenter is a numerical minority (Nemeth, 1986). For example, in a classic study by Nemeth and Kwan (1987), participants were shown a series of slides displaying large squares of a greenish color. Participants overwhelmingly labeled the slides' color as green but were told that a majority (or in another condition, minority) of other participants saw the slides as blue. Then, participants were asked to freely associate on the word "blue." Analyses of these free associations revealed that participants confronted with a deviating minority generated more original thoughts and associations with "blue" (e.g., jeans, jazz) than did participants confronted with a deviating majority (e.g., sky, ocean).

Other work has replicated and extended these findings. Thus, individuals finding themselves in conflict with a minority tend to generate more original word-associations, diverge more in their task strategies (e.g., Nemeth & Kwan, 1985); display greater cognitive complexity (e.g., Gruenfeld, Thomas-Hunt, & Kim; 1998); generate more divergent, novel problem solutions (Van Dyne & Saavreda, 1996); and design better task strategies (Choi & Levine, 2004). One explanation for these findings is that a minority dissenter is somewhat surprising in that dissent violates the naïve realist assumption that "rational individuals like me think like me." Yet as long as the minority message is not too threatening, it can be processed in a relatively open-minded way (Crano & Chen, 1998). As a result, issues and problems are considered from several perspectives and people detect new solutions and find more correct answers (Nemeth, 1986).

The notion that dissent drives learning and creativity resonates with work on social judgment theory (Brehmer, 1976). It deals with conflicts that involve differences of opinions and beliefs. While the correct solution to a problem may not be known to either party, each party has relevant information in the form of multiple, mostly redundant cues, each with some true relationship to the correct or best solution. These are the conflicts that emerge over what is the best business strategy, what stocks to invest in, what the shortest route to a holiday destination may be, what the optimal job candidate is, and so on. For example, participants have to agree on which horse will win a race and are given cues such as the horses' median speed, their positions at the start, their jockeys, and their winning records of last year (Harmon & Rohrbauch, 1990). When disputants have different cues at their disposal (e.g., the horses' median speed and starting position vs. their jockeys and last year's records), different preferences for cue utilization (e.g., a preference for median speed data rather than for last year's records), or both, participants initially come up with a solution that contradicts the one advanced by their partner. Moreover, these initial and contradictory predictions are less than optimal because only part of the available cues is being used.

The task facing parties in such conflicts is to decide what cues to use, and what cues to ignore, in designing their joint decision. One important research finding is that the extent to which parties arrive at an agreement that approximates the optimal solution depends on their prosocial versus proself motivation. For example, Summers

(1968) showed that with naturally occurring differences in beliefs, participants compromised more often when they were given a cooperative rather than a competitive orientation. Reversely, disputants given a competitive goal were less accurate in their predictions than disputants given no goal (Cosier & Rose, 1977), and disputants learn less when they try to avoid doing worse than others than when they try to outperform others (Darnon, Harackiewicz, Butera, Mugny, & Quiamzade, 2007). Finally, a meta-analysis by Roseth, Johnson, and Johnson (2008) showed that adolescents develop more positive peer relations and attain higher scholastic achievement when they operate under cooperative rather than competitive goal interdependence. In other words, conflict can help people learn and create better insight into reality. Such learning is facilitated by a prosocial, cooperative motivation and hindered by a competitive motivation.

Consistent with the idea that social motivation moderates the extent to which conflicting parties learn and develop, Carnevale and Probst (1998) proposed that whether and how conflict influences creativity also depend on the individual's social motivation—or "conflict mental set," as they called it. In their experiments, some participants anticipated a cooperative and constructive negotiation (cooperation set, akin to prosocial motivation), while others anticipated a competitive and hostile negotiation (conflict set, akin to proself motivation). Before the actual negotiation, participants performed tasks that assessed cognitive flexibility and inclusiveness. Results showed that participants in a conflict set were less flexible in their thinking, and less inclusive, than participants in a cooperation set. Accordingly, Carnevale and Probst (1998) concluded that compared with a cooperation mental set, a conflict mental set appears to shut down the system. It reduces one's scope and results in narrow-minded, black-and-white thinking, reduced creativity, and increased cognitive rigidity (for similar conclusions, see Golec & Federico, 2004; Jervis, 1976; Judd, 1978; Peterson, Winter, & Doty, 1994; Whyte, 1984). De Dreu and Nijstad (2008) uncovered that this is because individuals with a conflict set focus their cognitive resources on the conflict, whereas those with a cooperation set maintain a broad and open-minded perspective on issues and topics not specifically tied to the conflict at hand.

Taken together, various lines of work indicate that social conflict facilitates learning and improves creative thinking when prosocial motivation and cooperative mental sets are activated. This seems to hold for conflicts involving opposing views and opinions, as well as for conflicts involving the distribution of scarce resources. When proself motivation and conflict mental sets are activated, however, social conflict appears to undermine learning and to reduce cognitive flexibility and creative performance at large (but not creative thinking about the conflict itself; De Dreu & Nijstad, 2008). These effects may be due to the more open and truthful exchange of information under cooperative rather than competitive conditions, along with more positive affect and a more general versus more conflict-specific focus of cognitive resources.

Consequences to Groups and Intergroup Relations

Group Decision Making and Team Performance

Building on the work on groupthink by Janis (1972), studies on group decision making have explored whether, and under what conditions, conflict and dissent affects decision quality. The idea is that lack of conflict leads groups to move into premature consensus and extremely high levels of conflict break down communication and information processing. At moderate levels of conflict, however, group members are aroused to process information, motor performance is facilitated, and group members become relatively creative and reach high-quality decisions (De Dreu, 2006; Schulz-Hardt et al., 2008).

This effect of moderate conflict was nicely demonstrated in a study by Schulz-Hardt, Brodbeck, Mojzisch, Kerschreiter, and Frey (2006). The authors constructed three-person groups that had to select the best of four possible job candidates. Although each group member was given information about each of the four candidates, not all group members received the same information a priori. In one condition, information was distributed so that all group members, before group discussion, preferred the same but suboptimal candidate. In this "no prediscussion preference diversity" condition, no conflict emerged, and groups overwhelmingly opted for their initially preferred but suboptimal candidate. In another condition, initial preferences were manipulated so that group members preferred different candidates but in no case was the optimal candidate preferred (i.e., group member 1 preferring candidate A, group member 2 preferring candidate B, and group member 3 preferring candidate C, candidate D being the optimal one). In these preference diversity groups, conflict emerged, and groups were more likely to uncover that their initial preferences were suboptimal, ultimately settling for the optimal solution. Thus, preference diversity and concomitant conflict helped groups to achieve high-quality decisions (for similar studies and findings, see Brodbeck, Kerschreiter, Mojzich, Frey, & Schulz-Hardt, 2002; Galinsky & Kray, 2004; Postmes, Spears, & Cihangir, 2001; Scholten, Van Knippenberg, Nijstad, & De Dreu, 2007; Stasser & Titus, 1985; Wittenbaum, 1998).

It should be noted that, almost without exception, the studies revealing such positive effects of conflict involved group members sharing the cooperative goal of reaching a joint decision without also having vested interests in particular decision alternatives (Wittenbaum, Hollingshead, & Botero, 2004). As such, it is reasonable to conclude that these positive effects of conflict on group decision making occur within a cooperative context, where group members perceive positive goal interdependence and have a prosocial orientation (De Dreu, Nijstad, & Van Knippenberg, 2008). Indeed, a recent study by Toma and Butera (2009) showed that groups were far less likely to arrive at the optimal solution when members had a proself rather than a prosocial orientation.

Another issue with this group decision–making research is that it is almost exclusively focused on situations in which the group has to make a decision. It has not systematically examined the possibility that groups may delay their decision making, or decide not to decide. An exception is a study by Nijstad and Kaps (2008), who manipulated preference diversity so that group members either mildly or strongly opposed one another's decision preference. Groups were instructed to reach a decision but, in contrast to other research in this area, were allowed to "decide to not make a decision." Results showed that groups experiencing strong preference opposition more often decided not to make a decision. In other words, when groups experience conflict over decision preferences, they may be tempted not to make a decision rather than to continue their debate until they reach a high-quality decision. Because outside the social psychology laboratory groups often have the possibility to procrastinate and postpone decision making, it cannot be excluded that diversity and conflict more readily lead to costly delay than to high-quality decisions.

Related to work on group decision making is research into the consequences of conflict for the functioning and performance of task groups, such as work teams in organizations. Pioneering work by Jehn and colleagues (Jehn, 1995; Jehn & Mannix, 2001) distinguished between two forms of conflict in task groups—task-related conflict concerned with the way in which tasks are formulated and executed and relationship conflict concerned with the social relations among group members. Initial work revealed that whereas relationship conflict negatively relates to group functioning and task performance, moderate levels of task-related conflict are associated with enhanced performance (e.g., Jehn, 1995). Subsequent studies indicated that task-related conflict may promote performance, first, when the group task is complex and nonroutine and, second, when the team is characterized by high levels of trust and psychological safety (e.g., Simons & Peterson, 2000). However, a meta-analysis of these and other studies showed that, across task complexity and levels of trust, task-related conflict associates as negatively with team performance as relationship conflict (De Dreu & Weingart, 2003). As with the effects of conflict on group decision making, it thus seems that conflict may have a positive effect on team performance but only under limited circumstances (De Dreu, 2008).

Group Formation and Social Change

Conflict affects the structure of social relations, both interpersonally and within and across groups. Karney and Bradbury (1997) suggest that conflict behavior in marital couples is related to the slope of deterioration in marital satisfaction, which in turn is related to divorce and separation. In work settings, conflicts among peers, or between supervisors and employees, predicts lowered job satisfaction and organizational commitment, which in turn predicts absenteeism and turnover (Spector & Bruke-Lee, 2008). Intergroup conflict may make manifest latent within-group tensions and disparities, sometimes resulting in the dissolution of the group (Gaertner & Dovidio, 1992). Finally, history provides ample examples of conflicts in which one party dominated the partner to the extent that distinguishing features of the subordinated party's identity (e.g., culture and language) ceased to exist or the subordinated party itself vanished.

An outcome of conflict, especially those involving ideology and beliefs, is that members of an opposing faction or group convert to the ingroup perspective and come to be seen as members of the ingroup (e.g., Prislin, Limbert, & Bauer, 2000). This explains why consensually shared views (e.g., abortion is immoral) over time become minority positions and why what began as a minority position (e.g., abortion is a personal choice) over time changes into a majority position (e.g., Moscovici, 1985). Through conflict and ensuing social influence, group size changes. A large literature on social influence and attitude change speaks to the processes that facilitate or inhibit such conflict-driven social change (for reviews, see Cialdini & Trost, 1998; Hogg, this volume).

Summary and Synthesis

Clearly, conflict has broader implications than value destroyed or created. Prolonged conflict can seriously affect health and well-being, even among passive bystanders not directly involved in the conflict itself. Conflicts also change the social landscape, affecting the composition and size of entire groups. When conflict parties have a proself orientation and manage their conflicts through struggle and contending, social conflict impedes learning and creativity, undermines group performance, and reduces the quality of

group decision making. When conflict parties have a prosocial orientation and engage in constructive negotiation and joint problem solving, creativity and learning may be facilitated and group performance and the quality of group decision making may benefit from the conflict.

The immediate outcomes a conflict may have, such as increased stress or increased learning, may not be aligned with the more distal effects in terms of, for example, innovation or changes in member composition (O'Connor, Gruenfeld, & McGrath, 1993). For example, Beersma and De Dreu (2005) showed that groups that constructively negotiated integrative agreements subsequently performed quite poorly on tasks requiring creativity and quite well on tasks requiring planning and coordination. In the short run, constructive conflict management and integrative negotiation yielded high joint value; in the longer run, this cooperative approach seemed to predispose the group toward being overly harmonious, reducing the tendency toward independent thinking needed to perform creatively.

The social-psychological literature is relatively mute about postconflict processes, including reconciliation and trust building. Reconciliation and forgiveness have been shown to be key to the restoration of interpersonal relationships (e.g., Karremans, Van Lange, Ouwerkerk, & Kluwer, 2003), and in many large-scale conflicts that span years, if not decades, conflict resolution entails more than a cease-fire or the signing of a peace treaty (Kelman, 2006; Pruitt, 2007; Rouhana & Bar-Tal, 1998). For example, following a formal settlement of the conflict in Northern Ireland, the two antagonists issued the following statement: "A key impediment to completing the evolution to [a stable society] in Northern Ireland is that both major traditions have lacked confidence and trust in each other. . . . The two Governments recognise that Northern Ireland remains a deeply divided society, with ingrained patterns of division that carry substantial human and financial costs. They recognise the importance of building trust and improving community relations, tackling sectarianism and addressing segregation, including initiatives to facilitate and encourage integrated education and mixed housing" (cited in Tam, Hewstone, Kenworthy, & Cairns, 2009, pp. 45–46). Tam and colleagues showed how intensified contacts between members of the formerly opposing groups builds trust, which in turn enhances positive and reduces negative behavioral tendencies toward the outgroup.

These are initial steps toward a better understanding of the psychological processes underlying postconflict settlement. However, more systematic research is much needed. For example, it seems conceivable that the rather fragile agreements negotiated by representatives are easily destroyed by otherwise localized and relative minor transgressions of the members of one group against some members of the outgroup. The process of vicarious retribution, which was discussed in the section on struggle and conflict escalation, constitutes an important force driving against, or at least potentially undermining, the fragile processes of trust building and reconciliation.

SUMMARY

This chapter took a process view to understand conflict and to connect relatively disparate literatures. Conflict emerges when outcome deprivation is attributed to an interdependent other's intentional actions or inactions. The large literature on two-person, n-person, and team games provides a thorough understanding of both the structural and the psychological factors that drive individuals and groups to act noncooperatively and to violate fairness principles, thereby creating deprivation and social conflict. Responses to deprivation can be understood from a strategic choice perspective, showing that people gravitate toward procedures that afford them decision, as well as process, control. From Deutsch's theory of cooperation and competition and Pruitt and Rubin's dual concern theory, we learned that negotiation and joint problem solving take precedence over struggle and competition when parties value not only their own needs and desires but those of their conflict counterparts' as well. Obviously, initiating negotiation and joint problem solving does not necessarily mean that conflict will be resolved and that integrative, win–win agreements will be achieved. Hostile attributions, naïve realism, egocentric misperceptions, and at the intergroup level, vicarious retribution conspire to a move away from constructive communication and toward intractable conflicts.

The fifth section of this chapter highlighted various functions and consequences of social conflict—it influences health and well-being, learning and creativity, the quality of group decision making, and at a higher level of analysis, group formation and social change. An implicit assumption underlying the study of the functions of conflict is that social systems exist over longer periods and cycle through multiple conflicts. This draws attention to social conflicts not only crossing levels of analysis—from the individual to the intergroup system and back—but also being embedded in different layers of time. De Dreu and Gelfand (2008) invoked the work of Braudel (1947), a historian, and distinguished among structure, conjuncture, and events. Structure refers to those aspects of the context that are fixed and hardly change, an example being the geographical context within which conflict emerges. Van de Vliert, Huang, and Parker (2004) discovered that thermodynamic features including ambient temperature have notable and quite stable influences on the emergence and management of conflicts, with more noncooperation and escalatory tendencies in areas either extremely hot or extremely cold than in areas with more moderate ambient temperature. Other examples of structures within which conflicts take place involve the national, cultural, and historical context that provides a relatively stable background. For example, for quite some time worker relations between U.S. citizens and Japanese managers or between Dutch employees and German managers were influenced by and interpreted in light of World War II. Many of the ethnopolitical conflicts we have witnessed in the past decades, such as the wars between Tutsi and Hutu in Rwanda or between Israelis and Palestinians have become such stable historical and cultural backgrounds within which new conflicts are experienced and interpreted (Rouhana & Bar-Tal, 1998).

Within the relatively fixed structural layer of time, conjunctures emerge. We may think about the rise and fall of economies that change the power relations among groups or the legislative changes within a society that provide rights and privileges to individuals and groups, raise or reduce feelings of entitlement, and change access to scarce resources. And within conjunctures, we have events that rapidly emerge and dissipate yet can profoundly influence the way in which conflict processes evolve. The attack on the World Trade Center in New York in 2001, the murdering of a highly controversial politician in the Netherlands in 2005, and the publication of blasphemous cartoons that same year in a Danish newspaper are just some examples of events that not only created conflicts but also dramatically influenced the way ongoing conflicts evolved. Another example is that the Israeli–Palestinian conflict is, to some extent, depending on the perceived support from the United States. Elections taking place in the United States influence the strategic choices made by conflict parties in the Middle East.

Although not an easy task, future research and theory development would benefit tremendously from explicitly incorporating these three layers of time into the analysis. This would produce cross-level theories linking more distal and relatively fixed aspects of the context (e.g., national culture and history) with institutional, legislative, and organizational practices, cultures, and systems (conjunctures), as well as with more dynamic and fluid events.

Stepping away from the specifics of certain research findings, theoretical positions, or avenues for future research, the present review and analysis suggests several conclusions about social conflict. First, social conflict is part of the interdependent relationship among individuals and within and between groups. Greed, fear, and violations of fairness, whether deliberate or inadvertent, deprive others of valuable outcomes and create social conflicts. Second, social conflict easily escalates into aggressive exchanges and hostile interaction, but it does not have to. Cooperative interdependence structures, along with pro-social motivation, enhance the likelihood that parties can manage their conflicts through negotiation and joint problem solving. Finally, conflict triggers various negative, adverse consequences, including impoverished health and well-being and broken relationships. But when managed properly through negotiation and joint problem solving, conflict can be a catalyst for change and may stimulate creativity, innovation, and high-quality decision making.

REFERENCES

Adair, W. L., Okumura, T., & Brett, J. M. (2001). Negotiation behavior when cultures collide: The United States and Japan. *Journal of Applied Psychology, 86*, 371–385.

Allred, K., Mallozzi, J., Matsui, F., & Raia, C. (1997). The influence of anger and compassion on negotiation performance. *Organizational Behavior and Human Decision Processes, 70*, 175–187.

Arnold, J. A., & O'Connor, K. M. (2006). How negotiator self-efficacy drives decisions to pursue mediation. *Journal of Applied Social Psychology, 36*, 2649–2669.

Arrow, H. (2007). The sharp end of altruism. *Science, 318*, 581–582.

Axelrod, R. (1984). *The evolution of cooperation.* New York: Basic Books.

Axelrod, R., & Hamilton, W.D. (1981). The evolution of cooperation. *Science, 211*, 1390–1396.

Bacharach, S. B., & Lawler, E. J. (1981). *Bargaining: Power, tactics and outcomes.* Greenwich, CT: JAI Press.

Barclay, L. J., Skarlicki, D., & Pugh, S. D. (2005). Exploring the role of emotions in injustice perceptions and retaliation. *Journal of Applied Psychology, 90*, 629–643.

Baron, R. A. (1997). Positive effects of conflict: Insights from social cognition. In C. K. W. De Dreu & E. Van de Vliert (Eds.), *Using conflict in organizations* (pp. 177–191). London: Sage.

Baron, R. A., Neuman, J. H., & Geddes, D. (1999). Social and personal determinants of workplace aggression: Evidence for the impact of perceived injustice and the type A behavior pattern. *Aggressive Behavior, 25*, 281–297.

Barry, B., & Friedman, R. A. (1998). Bargainer characteristics in distributive and integrative negotiation. *Journal of Personality and Social Psychology, 74*, 345–359.

Bar-Tal, D., Raviv, A., & Freund, T. (1994). An anatomy of political beliefs: A study of their centrality, contents, and epistemic authority. *Journal of Applied Social Psychology, 24*, 849–872.

Batson, C. D., & Ahmad, N. (2001). Empathy-induced altruism in a prisoner's dilemma II: What if the target of empathy has defected? *European Journal of Social Psychology, 31*, 25–36.

Baumeister, R. F., & Leary, M. R. (1995). The need to belong: Desire for interpersonal attachments as a fundamental human motivation. *Psychological Bulletin, 117*, 497–529.

Baumeister, R. F., Smart, L., & Boden, J. M. (1996). Relation of threatened egotism to violence and aggression: The dark side of high self-esteem. *Psychological Review, 103*, 5–33.

Bazerman, M. H., Curhan, J. R., Moore, D. A., & Valley, K. L. (2000). Negotiation. *Annual Review of Psychology, 51*, 279–314.

Beersma, B., & De Dreu, C. K. W. (2002). Integrative and distributive negotiation in small groups: Effects of task structure, decision rule, and social motive. *Organizational Behavior and Human Decision Processes, 87*, 227–252.

Beersma, B., & De Dreu, C. K. W. (2005). Conflict's consequences: Effects of social motives on post-negotiation creative and convergent group functioning and performance. *Journal of Personality and Social Psychology, 89*, 358–374.

Ben-Yoav, O., & Pruitt, D. (1984). Resistance to yielding and the expectation of cooperative future interaction in negotiation. *Journal of Experimental Social Psychology, 34*, 323–335.

Berkowitz, L. (1989). Frustration–aggression hypothesis: Examination and reformulation. *Psychological Bulletin, 106*, 59–73.

Bornstein, G. (2003). Intergroup conflict: Individual, group, and collective interests. *Personality and Social Psychology Review, 7*, 129–145.

Bornstein. G., & Ben-Yossef, M. (1994). Cooperation in intergroup and single-group social dilemmas. *Journal of Experimental Social Psychology, 30*, 52–67.

Bornstein, G., & Rapoport, A. (1988). Intergroup competition for the provision of step-level public goods: Effects of preplay communication. *European Journal of Social Psychology, 18*, 125–142.

Bouas, K. S., & Komorita, S. S. (1996). Group discussion and cooperation in social dilemmas. *Personality and Social Psychology Bulletin, 22*, 1144–1150.

Braudel, F. (1947). *Mémoires de la méditerranée.* Paris: Livres de Poches.

Brehmer, B. (1976). Social judgment theory and the analysis of interpersonal conflict. *Psychological Bulletin, 83*, 985–1003.

Brett, J. M., & Gelfand, M. J. (2005). A cultural analysis of the underlying assumptions of negotiation theory. In L. Thompson (Ed.), *Frontiers of social psychology: Negotiations* (pp. 173–201). New York: Psychology Press.

Brew, F. P., & Cairns, D. R. (2004). Do culture or situational constraints determine choice of direct or indirect styles in intercultural workplace conflicts? *International Journal of Intercultural Relations, 28*, 331–352.

Brewer, M. B., & Kramer, R. M. (1986). Choice behavior in social dilemmas: Effects of social identity, group size, and decision framing. *Journal of Personality and Social Psychology, 50*, 543–549.

Brockner, J., & Rubin, J. Z. (1985). *Entrapment in escalating conflicts: A social psychological analysis.* New York: Springer-Verlag.

Brodbeck, F. C., Kerschreiter, R., Mojzisch, A., Frey, D., & Schulz-Hardt, S. (2002). The dissemination of critical unshared information in decision-making groups: The effect of pre-discussion dissent. *European Journal of Social Psychology, 32*, 35–56.

Brodt, S. E., & Tuchinsky, M. (2000). Working together but in opposition: An examination of the "good cop/bad cop" negotiating team tactic. *Organizational Behavior and Human Decision Processes, 81*, 155–177.

Burnham, T., McGabe, K., & Smith, V. L. (2000). Friend-or-foe intentionality priming in an extensive form trust game. *Journal of Economic Behavior & Organization, 43*, 57–73.

Burton, J. W. (1990). *Conflict resolution and prevention.* Boston: St Martin's Press.

Bushman, B. J., & Baumeister, R. F. (1998). Threatened egotism, narcissism, self-esteem, and direct and displaced aggression: Does self-love or self-hate lead to violence? *Journal of Personality and Social Psychology, 75*, 219–229.

Butt, A. N., Choi, J. N., & Jaeger, A. M. (2005). The effects of self-emotion, counterpart emotion, and counterpart behavior on negotiator behavior: A comparison of individual-level and dyad-level dynamics. *Journal of Organizational Behavior, 26*, 681–704.

Cai, D. A., & Fink, E. L. (2002). Conflict style differences between individualists and collectivists. *Communication Monographs, 69*, 67–87.

Camerer, C. F., & Thaler, R. H. (1995). Ultimatums, dictators and manners. *Journal of Economic Perspectives, 9*, 209–219.

Carlsmith, K. M., Darley, J. M., & Robinson, P. H. (2002). Why do we punish? Deterrence and just deserts as motives for punishment. *Journal of Personality and Social Psychology, 83,* 284–299.

Carnevale, P. J. (1986). Strategic choice in mediation. *Negotiation Journal, 2,* 41–56.

Carnevale, P. J. (2007). Creativity in the outcomes of conflict. In E. C. Marcus, M. Deutsch, & P. T. Coleman (Eds.), *The handbook of conflict resolution: Theory and practice* (2nd ed., pp. 414–435). Hoboken, NJ: Wiley.

Carnevale, P. J., & De Dreu, C. K. W. (2006). Motive: The negotiator's raison d'être. In L. L. Thompson & J. M. Brett (Eds.), *The social psychology of negotiation* (pp. 55–76). New York: Psychology Press.

Carnevale, P. J., & Isen, A. M. (1986). The influence of positive affect and visual access on the discovery of integrative solutions in bilateral negotiation. *Organizational Behavior and Human Decision Processes, 37,* 1–13.

Carnevale, P. J., & Lawler, E. J. (1986). Time pressure and the development of integrative agreements in bilateral negotiation. *Journal of Conflict Resolution, 30,* 636–659.

Carnevale, P. J., & Leung, K. (2001). Cultural dimensions of negotiation. In M. A. Hogg & R. S. Tindale (Eds.), *Blackwell handbook of social psychology* (Vol. 3, pp. 482–496). Oxford: Blackwell.

Carnevale, P. J., & Probst, T. M. (1998). Social values and social conflict in creative problem solving and categorization. *Journal of Personality and Social Psychology, 74,* 1300–1309.

Carnevale, P. J., & Pruitt, D. G. (1992). Negotiation and mediation. *Annual Review of Psychology, 43,* 531–582.

Carnevale, P. J., Pruitt, D. G., & Seilheimer, S. (1981). Looking and competing: Accountability and visual access in integrative bargaining. *Journal of Personality and Social Psychology, 40,* 111–120.

Carver, C. S., & Glass, D. C. (1978). Coronary-prone behavior pattern and interpersonal aggression. *Journal of Personality and Social Psychology, 36,* 361–366.

Chambers, J. R., Baron, R. S., & Inman, M. L. (2006). Misperceptions in intergroup conflict. *Psychological Science, 17,* 38–45.

Chambers, J. R., & Melnyk, D. (2006). Why do I hate thee? Conflict misperceptions and intergroup trust. *Personality and Social Psychology Bulletin, 32,* 1295–1311.

Chen, Y. R., Mannix, E. A., & Okumura, T. (2003). The importance of who you meet: Effects of self- versus other-concerns among negotiators in the United States, the People's Republic of China, and Japan. *Journal of Experimental Social Psychology, 39,* 1–15.

Choi, H.-S., & Levine, J. M. (2004). Minority influence in work teams: The impact of newcomers. *Journal of Experimental Social Psychology, 40,* 273–280.

Cialdini, R. B., & Trost, M. R. (1998). Social influence: Social norms, conformity and compliance. In D. T. Gilbert, S. T. Fiske, & G. Lindzey (Eds.), *The handbook of social psychology* (4th ed., Vol. 2, pp. 151–192). Boston: McGraw-Hill.

Colman, A. M. (2003). Cooperation, psychological game theory, and limitations of rationality in social interaction. *Behavioral and Brain Sciences, 26,* 139–198.

Coombs, C. H. (1973). A reparameterization of the prisoner's dilemma game. *Behavioral Science, 18,* 424–428.

Coser, L. A. (1956). *The functions of social conflict.* New York: Free Press.

Cosier, R., & Rose, G. (1977). Cognitive conflict and goal conflict effects on task performance. *Organizational Behavior and Human Performance, 19,* 378–391.

Crano, W. D., & Chen, X. (1998). The leniency contract and persistence of majority and minority influence. *Journal of Personality and Social Psychology, 74,* 1437–1450.

Darnon, C., Harackiewicz, J. M., Butera, F., Mugny, G., & Quiamzade, A. (2007). Performance-approach and performance-avoidance goals: When uncertainty makes a difference. *Personality and Social Psychology Bulletin, 33,* 813–827.

Davies, P. T., (2002). *Child emotional security and interparental conflict.* Malden, MA: Blackwell.

Davies, P. T., & Cummings, E. M. (1994). Marital conflict and child adjustment: An emotional security hypothesis. *Psychological Bulletin, 116,* 387–411.

Dawes, R. M. (1980). Social dilemmas. *Annual Review of Psychology, 31,* 169–193.

De Dreu, C. K. W. (2006). When too much and too little hurts: Evidence for a curvilinear relationship between task conflict and innovation in teams. *Journal of Management, 32,* 83–107.

De Dreu, C. K. W. (2008). The vice and virtue of workplace conflict: Food for (pessimistic) thought. *Journal of Organizational Behavior, 29,* 5–18.

De Dreu, C. K. W., Beersma, B., Steinel, W., & Van Kleef, G. A. (2007). The psychology of negotiation: principles and basic processes. In A. W. Kruglanski & E. T. Higgins (Eds.), *Handbook of basic principles in social psychology* (2nd ed., pp. 608–629). New York: Guilford.

De Dreu, C. K. W., Beersma, B., Stroebe, K., & Euwema, M. C. (2006). Motivated information processing, strategic choice, and the quality of negotiated agreement. *Journal of Personality and Social Psychology, 90,* 927–943.

De Dreu, C. K. W., & Carnevale, P. J. (2003). Motivational bases of information processing and strategy in conflict and negotiation. In M. P. Zanna (Ed.), *Advances in experimental social psychology* (Vol. 35, pp. 235–291). New York: Academic Press.

De Dreu, C. K. W., Evers, A., Beersma, B., Kluwer, E. S., & Nauta, A. (2001). A theory-based measure of conflict management strategies in the work place. *Journal of Organizational Behavior, 22,* 645–668.

De Dreu, C. K. W., & Gelfand, M. J. (2008). Conflict in the workplace: Sources, dynamics, and functions across multiple levels of analysis. In C. K. W. De Dreu & M. J. Gelfand (Eds.), *The psychology of conflict and conflict management in organizations* (pp. 3–54). New York: Lawrence Erlbaum.

De Dreu, C. K. W., Giebels, E., & Van de Vliert, E. (1998). Social motives and trust in integrative negotiation: The disruptive effects of punitive capability. *Journal of Applied Psychology, 83,* 408–422.

De Dreu, C. K. W., Kluwer, E. S., & Nauta, A. (2008). The structure and management of conflict: Fighting or defending the status quo. *Group Processes and Intergroup Relations, 11,* 331–353.

De Dreu, C. K. W., Koole, S., & Oldersma, F. L. (1999). On the seizing and freezing of negotiator inferences: Need for cognitive closure moderates the use of heuristics in negotiation. *Personality and Social Psychology Bulletin, 25,* 348–362.

De Dreu, C. K. W., Koole, S., & Steinel, W. (2000). Unfixing the fixed-pie: A motivated information processing account of integrative negotiation. *Journal of Personality and Social Psychology, 79,* 975–987.

De Dreu, C. K. W., & McCusker, C. (1997). Gain-loss frames in two-person social dilemmas: A transformational analysis. *Journal of Personality and Social Psychology, 72,* 1093–1106.

De Dreu, C. K. W., & Nijstad, B. A. (2008). Conflict and creativity: Threat-rigidity or motivated focus? *Journal of Personality and Social Psychology, 95,* 648–661.

De Dreu, C. K. W., Nijstad, B. A., & Van Knippenberg, D. (2008). Motivated information processing in group judgment and decision making. *Personality and Social Psychology Review, 12,* 22–49.

De Dreu, C. K. W., & Van Knippenberg, D. (2005). The possessive self as a barrier to conflict resolution: Effects of mere ownership, process accountability, and self-concept clarity on competitive cognitions and behavior. *Journal of Personality and Social Psychology, 89,* 345–357.

De Dreu, C. K. W., & Weingart, L. R. (2003). Task versus relationship conflict, team performance and team member satisfaction: A meta-analysis. *Journal of Applied Psychology, 88,* 741–749.

De Dreu, C. K. W., Weingart, L. R., & Kwon, S. (2000). Influence of social motives on integrative negotiation: A meta-analytic review and test of two theories. *Journal of Personality and Social Psychology, 78,* 889–905.

De Dreu, C.K.W., Yzerbyt, V., & Leyens, J-Ph. (1995). Dilution of stereotype-based cooperation in mixed-motive interdependence. *Journal of Experimental Social Psychology, 31,* 575–593.

De Grada, E., Kruglanski, A. W., Mannetti, L., & Pierro, A. (1999). Motivated cognition and group interaction: Need for closure affects the contents and processes of collective negotiations. *Journal of Experimental Social Psychology, 35,* 346–365.

Depue, R. A., & Morrone-Strupinsky, J. V. (2005). A neurobehavioral model of affiliative bonding: Implications for conceptualizing a human trait of affiliation. *Behavior and Brain Sciences, 28,* 313–395.

Derlega, V. J., Cukur, C. S., Kuang, J. C., & Forsyth, D. R. (2002). Independent construal of self and the endorsement of conflict resolution strategies in interpersonal, intergroup and international disputes. *Journal of Cross-Cultural Psychology, 33,* 610–625.

Der Spiegel. (2006). Arson and death threats as Muhammad caricature controversy escalates. Retrieved on November 5, 2008, from http://www.spiegel.de/international/0,1518,399177,00.html.

Deutsch, M. (1973). *The resolution of conflict: Constructive and destructive processes.* New Haven, CT: Yale University Press.

Deutsch, M. (1975). Equity, equality, and need: What determines which value will be used as the basis of distributive justice? *Journal of Social Issues, 31,* 137–149.

Deutsch, M. (1982). Interdependence and psychological orientation. In V. Derlega & J. Gezelak (Eds.), *Cooperation and helping behavior* (pp. 15–42). Cambridge, England: Cambridge University Press.

Diekmann, K. A., Tenbrunsel, A. E., & Galinsky, A. D. (2003). From self-prediction to self-defeat: Behavioral forecasting, self-fulfilling prophecies, and the effect of competitive expectations. *Journal of Personality and Social Psychology, 85,* 672–683.

Dodge, K. A., & Coie, J. D. (1987). Social-information-processing factors in reactive and proactive aggression in children's peer groups. *Journal of Personality and Social Psychology, 53,* 1146–1158.

Drake, L. E. (1995). Negotiation styles in intercultural communication. *International Journal of Conflict Management, 6,* 72–90.

Druckman, D. (1994). Determinants of compromising behavior in negotiation: A meta-analysis. *Journal of Conflict Resolution, 38,* 507–556.

Einarsen, S. (1999). The nature and causes of bullying at work. *International Journal of Manpower, 20,* 16–27.

Enzle, M., Harvey, M., & Wright, E. (1992). Implicit role obligations versus social responsibility in constituency representation. *Journal of Personality and Social Psychology, 62,* 238–245.

Erev. I., Bornstein, G., & Galili, R. (1993). Constructive intergroup competition as a solution to the free-rider problem: A field experiment. *Journal of Experimental Social Psychology, 29,* 463–478.

Exline, J.J., Baumeister, R.F., Bushman, B.J., Campbell, W.K., & Finkel, E.J. (2004). To proud to let go: Narcissistic entitlement as a barrier to forgiveness. *Journal of Personality and Social Psychology, 87,* 894–912.

Fehr, E., & Fishbacher, U. (2004). Social norms and human cooperation. *Trends in Cognitive Sciences, 8,* 187–190.

Fehr, E., & Gächter, S. (2002). Altruistic punishment in humans. *Nature, 415,* 137–140.

Fodor, E. M. (1985). The power motive, group conflict, and physiological arousal. *Journal of Personality and Social Psychology, 49,* 1408–1415.

Folger, R., & Skarlicki, D. P. (2001). Fairness as a dependent variable: Why tough times can lead to bad management. In R. Cropanzano (Ed.), *Justice in the workplace: From theory to practice* (Vol. 2, pp. 97–118). Mahwah, NJ: Erlbaum.

Forgas, J. P. (1998). On feeling good and getting your way: Mood effects on negotiator cognition and behavior. *Journal of Personality and Social Psychology, 74,* 565–577.

Forgas, J. P., & Cromer, M. (2004). On being sad and evasive: Affective influences on verbal communication strategies in conflict situations. *Journal of Experimental Social Psychology, 40,* 511–518.

Gabrielidis, C., Stephan, W. G., Ybarra, O., Pearson, V. M., & Villareal, L. (1997). Preferred styles of conflict resolution: Mexico and the United States. *Journal of Cross-Cultural Psychology, 28,* 661–677.

Gaertner, S. L., & Dovidio, J. F. (1992). Toward the elimination of racism: The study of intergroup behavior. In R. M. Baird & S. E. Rosenbaum (Eds.), *Bigotry, prejudice and hatred: Definitions, causes and solutions* (pp. 203–207). Amherst, NY: Prometheus.

Galinsky, A. D., & Kray, L. J. (2004). From thinking about what might have been to sharing what we know: The effects of counterfactual mind-sets on information sharing in groups. *Journal of Experimental Social Psychology, 40,* 606–618.

Gelfand, M. J., & Brett, J. M. (Eds.). (2004). *The handbook of negotiation and culture.* Stanford, CA: Stanford University Press.

Gelfand, M. J., Higgins, M., Nishii, L., Raver, J., Dominguez, A., Yamaguchi, S., Murakami, F., & Toyama, M. (2001). Culture and egocentric biases of fairness in conflict and negotiation. *Journal of Applied Psychology, 86,* 1059–1074.

Gelfand, M. J., & Realo, A. (1999). Individualism-collectivism and accountability in intergroup negotiations. *Journal of Applied Psychology, 84,* 721–736.

Goldman, B. M., Cropanzano, R., Stein, J., & Benson, L. (2008). The role of third parties/mediation in managing conflict in organizations. In C. K. W. De Dreu & M. J. Gelfand (Eds.), *The psychology of conflict and conflict management in organizations* (pp. 291–320). New York: Lawrence Erlbaum.

Golec, A., & Federico, C. (2004). Understanding responses to political conflict: Interactive effects of need for cognitive closure and salient conflict schemas. *Journal of Personality and Social Psychology, 87,* 750–762.

Gottman, J. M. (1979). *Marital interaction: Experimental investigations.* San Diego: Academic Press.

Gouldner, A. W. (1960). The norm of reciprocity: A preliminary statement. *American Sociological Review, 25,* 161–178.

Graziano, W. G., Jensen-Campbell, L., & Hair, E. (1996). Perceiving interpersonal conflict and reacting to it: The case for agreeableness. *Journal of Personality and Social Psychology, 70,* 820–835.

Gruenfeld, D. H., Thomas-Hunt, M. C., & Kim, P. H. (1998). Cognitive flexibility, communication strategy, and integrative complexity in groups: Public versus private reactions to majority and minority status. *Journal of Experimental Social Psychology, 34,* 202–226.

Halevy, N. (2008). Team negotiation: Social, epistemic, economic, and psychological consequences of subgroup conflict. *Personality and Social Psychology Bulletin, 34,* 1687–1702.

Halevy, N., Bornstein, G., & Sagiv, L. (2008). "In-group love" and "out-group hate" as motives for individual participation in intergroup conflict. *Psychological Science, 19,* 405–411.

Hamilton, D. L., & Sherman, S. J. (1996). Perceiving persons and groups. *Psychological Review, 103,* 336–355.

Handgraaf, M. J. J., Van Dijk, E., Vermunt, R., Wilke, H. A. M., & De Dreu, C. K. W. (2008). Less power or powerless? Egocentric empathy gaps and the irony of having little versus no power in social decision making. *Journal of Personality and Social Psychology, 95,* 1136–1149.

Hardin, G. (1968). The tragedy of the commons. *Science, 162,* 1243–1244.

Harinck, F., & De Dreu, C. K. W. (2004). Negotiating interests or values and reaching integrative agreements: The importance of time pressure and temporary impasses. *European Journal of Social Psychology, 34,* 595–612.

Harmon, J., & Rohrbauch, J. (1990). Social judgment analysis and small group decision making: Cognitive feedback effects on individual and collective performance. *Organizational Behavior and Human Decision Processes, 46*, 34–54.

Hayashi, N., & Yamagishi, T. (1998). Selective play: Choosing partners in an uncertain world. *Personality and Social Psychology Review, 2*, 276–289.

Heuer, L. B., & Penrod, S. (1986). Procedural preferences as a function of conflict intensity. *Journal of Personality and Social Psychology, 51*, 700–710.

Hilty, J.A., & Carnevale, P. J. (1992). Black-hat White-hat strategy in bilateral negotiation. *Organizational Behavior and Human Decision Processes, 55*, 444–469.

Holt, J. L., & DeVore, C. J. (2005). Culture, gender, organizational role, and styles of conflict resolution: A meta-analysis. *International Journal of Intercultural Relations, 29*, 165–196.

Howard, E. S., Gardner, W. L., & Thompson, L. L. (2007). The role of the self-concept and the social context in determining the behavior of power holders: Self-construal in intergroup versus dyadic dispute resolution negotiations. *Journal of Personality and Social Psychology, 93*, 614–631.

Hulbert, L. G., Correa da Silva, M., & Adegboyega, G. (2001). Cooperation in social dilemmas and allocentrism: A social values approach. *European Journal of Social Psychology, 31*, 641–658.

Jaffee, D. (2008). Conflict at work throughout the history of organizations. In C. K. W. De Dreu & M. J. Gelfand (Eds.), *The psychology of conflict and conflict management in organizations*. New York: Lawrence Erlbaum.

Janis, I. L. (1972). *Victims of groupthink: A psychological study of foreign-policy decisions and fiascos*. Boston: Houghton Mifflin.

Jehn, K. (1995). A multimethod examination of the benefits and detriments of intragroup conflict. *Administrative Science Quarterly, 40*, 256–282.

Jehn, K., & Mannix, E. (2001). The dynamic nature of conflict: A longitudinal study of intragroup conflict and group performance. *Academy of Management Journal, 44*, 238–251.

Jervis, R. (1976). *Perception and misperception in international relations*. Princeton, NJ: Princeton University Press.

Jost, J. T., Banaji, M., & Nosek, B. (2004). A decade of system justification theory: Accumulated evidence of conscious and unconscious bolstering of the status quo. *Political Psychology, 25*, 881–920.

Judd, C. M. (1978). Cognitive effects of attitude conflict resolution. *Journal of Conflict Resolution, 22*, 483–498.

Kahneman, D., Knetch, J. L., & Thaler, R. H. (1990). Experimental tests of the endowment effect and the Coase-theorem. *Journal of Political Economy, 98*, 1325–1348.

Kahneman, D., & Tversky, A. (1973). On the psychology of prediction. *Psychological Review, 80*, 237–251.

Kahneman, D., & Tversky, A. (1979). Prospect theory: An analysis of decision under risk. *Econometrica, 47*, 263–291.

Kamarck, T. W., Shiffman, S. M., Smithline, L., Goodle, J. L., Paty, J. A., Gnys, M., & Jong, J. Y.-K. (1998). Effects of task strain, social conflict, and emotional activation on ambulatory cardiovascular activity: Daily life consequences of recurring stress in a multiethnic adult sample. *Health Psychology, 17*, 17–29.

Kammrath, L. K., & Dweck, C. (2006). Voicing conflict: Preferred conflict strategies among incremental and entity theorists. *Personality and Social Psychology Bulletin, 32*, 1497–1508.

Karney, B. R., & Bradbury, T. N. (1997). Neuroticism, marital interaction, and the trajectory of marital satisfaction. *Journal of Personality and Social Psychology, 72*, 1075–1092.

Karremans, J. C., Van Lange, P. A. M., Ouwerkerk, J. W., & Kluwer, E. S. (2003). When forgiving enhances psychological well-being: The role of interpersonal commitment. *Journal of Personality and Social Psychology, 84*, 1011–1026.

Kassinove, H., Roth, D., Owens, S. G., & Fuller, J. R. (2002). Effects of trait anger and anger expression style on competitive attack responses in a wartime prisoner's dilemma game. *Aggressive Behavior, 28*, 117–125.

Kay, A. C., Wheeler, S. C., Bargh, J. A., & Ross, L. (2004). Material priming: The influence of mundane physical objects on situational construal and competitive behavioral choice. *Organizational Behavior and Human Decision Processes, 95*, 83–96.

Kelley, H. H., Beckman, L. L., & Fischer, C. S. (1967). Negotiation the division of reward under incomplete information. *Journal of Experimental Social Psychology, 3*, 361–389.

Kelley, H. H., Holmes, J. G., Kerr, N. L., Reis, H. T., Rusbult, C. E., & Van Lange, P. A. M. (2004). *An atlas of interpersonal situations*. Cambridge, England: Cambridge University Press.

Kelley, H. H., Shure, G. H., Deutsch, M., Faucheux, C., Lanzetta, J. T., Moscovici, S., Nuttin, J. M., Jr., Rabbie, J. M., & Thibaut, J. W. (1970). A comparative experimental study of negotiation behaviour. *Journal of Personality and Social Psychology, 16*, 411–438.

Kelley, H. H., & Stahelski, A. J. (1970). Social interaction basis of cooperators' and competitors' beliefs about others. *Journal of Personality and Social Psychology, 16*, 66–91.

Kelley, H. H., & Thibaut, J. W. (1978). *Interpersonal relations: A theory of interdependence*. New York: Wiley.

Kelman, H. (2006). Interests, relationships, identities: Three central issues for individuals and groups in negotiating their social environment. *Annual Review of Psychology, 57*, 1–26.

Kennedy, K. A., & Pronin, E. (2008). When disagreement gets ugly: Perceptions of bias and the escalation of conflict. *Personality and Social Psychology Bulletin, 28*, 385–392.

Kernis, M. H., Grannemann, B. D., & Barclay, L. C. (1989). Stability and level of self-esteem as predictors of anger arousal and hostility. *Journal of Personality and Social Psychology, 56*, 1013–1022.

Kerr, N. L. (1989). Illusions of self-efficacy: The effects of group size on perceived efficacy in social dilemmas. *Journal of Experimental Social Psychology, 25*, 287–313.

Ketelaar, T., & Au, W. T. (2003). The effects of feelings of guilt on the behaviour of uncooperative individuals in repeated social bargaining games: An affect-as-information interpretation of the role of emotion in social interaction. *Cognition and Emotion, 17*, 429–453.

Kluwer, E. S., Heesink, J. A. M., & Van de Vliert, E. (1997). The marital dynamics of conflict over the division of labor. *Journal of Marriage and the Family, 59*, 635–653.

Knoch, D., Pascual, L. A., Meyer, K., Trever, V., & Fehr, E. (2006). Diminishing reciprocal fairness by disrupting the right prefrontal cortex. *Science, 314*, 829–832.

Komorita, S. S., & Parks, C. D. (1995). Interpersonal relations: Mixed-motive interaction. *Annual Review of Psychology, 46*, 183–207.

Komorita, S. S., Parks, C., & Hulbert, L. (1992). Reciprocity and the induction of cooperation in social dilemmas. *Journal of Personality and Social Psychology, 62*, 607–617.

Kosfeld, M., Heinrichs, M., Zak, P. J., Fishbacher, U., & Fehr, E. (2006). Oxytocin increases trust in humans, *Nature, 435*, 673–676.

Kramer, R. M. (1991). The more the merrier? Social psychological aspects of multiparty negotiations in organizations. In R. Lewicki, B. Sheppard, & M. Bazerman (Eds.), *Research on negotiation in organizations* (Vol. 3, pp. 307–332). Greenwich, CT: JAI Press.

Kramer, R. M., Pommerenke, P., & Newton, E. (1993). The social context of negotiation. *Journal of Conflict Resolution, 37*, 633–654.

Krumhuber, E., Manstead, A. S. R., Cosker, D., Marshall, D., Rosin, P. L., & Kappas, A. (2007). Facial dynamics as indicators of trustworthiness and cooperative behavior. *Emotion, 7*, 730–735.

Ku, G., Malhotra, D., & Murnighan, J. K. (2004). Towards a competitive arousal model of decision making: A study of auction fever in internet and real life auctions. *Organizational Behavior and Human Decision Processes, 96*, 86–103.

Kuhlman, M.D., & Marshello, A. (1975). Individual differences in game motivation as moderators of pre-programmed strategic effects in prisoner's dilemma. *Journal of Personality and Social Psychology, 32*, 922–931.

Leliveld, M. C., Van Dijk, E., & Van Beest, E. (2008). Initial ownership in bargaining: Introducing the giving, splitting, and taking ultimatum bargaining game. *Personality and Social Psychology Bulletin, 34*, 1214–1225.

Leliveld, M. C., Van Dijk, E., Van Beest, I., & Tenbrunsel, A.E. (2009). Understanding the influence of outcome valence in bargaining: A study of fairness accessibility, norms, and behavior. *Journal of Experimental Social Psychology, 45*, 505–514.

Leung, K. (1987). Some determinants of reactions to procedural models for conflict resolution: A cross-national study. *Journal of Personality and Social Psychology, 53*, 898–908.

Levine, J. M., Resnick, L. B., & Higgins, E. T. (1993). Social foundations of cognition. *Annual Review of Psychology, 44*, 586–612.

Lickel, B., Miller, N., Stenstrom, D. M., Denson, T. F., & Schmader, T. (2006). Vicarious retribution: The role of collective blame in intergroup aggression. *Personality and Social Psychology Review, 10*, 372–390.

Liebert, R. M., Smith, W. P., Hill, J. H., & Keiffer, M. (1968). The effects of information and magnitude of initial offer on interpersonal negotiation. *Journal of Experimental Social Psychology, 4*, 431–441.

Lindskold, S., & Han, G. (1988). GRIT as a foundation for integrative bargaining. *Personality and Social Psychology Bulletin, 14*, 335–345.

Loewenstein, G. F., Thompson, L. L., & Bazerman, M. H. (1989). Social utility and decision making in interpersonal contexts. *Journal of Personality and Social Psychology, 57*, 426–441.

Luce, D. R., & Raiffa, H. (1957). *Games and decisions: Introduction and critical survey.* Oxford: Wiley.

Mackie, D. M., Devos, T., & Smith, E. R. (2000). Intergroup emotions: Explaining offensive action tendencies in an intergroup context. *Journal of Personality and Social Psychology, 79*, 602–616.

Mannix, E. A. (1993). Organizational as resource dilemmas: The effects of power balance on coalition formation in small groups. *Organizational Behavior and Human Decision Processes, 55*, 1–22.

Martinko, M. J., & Zellars, K. L. (1998). Toward a theory of workplace violence and aggression: A cognitive appraisal perspective. In R. W. Griffin, A. O'Leary-Kelly, & J. M. Collins (Eds.), *Dysfunctional behavior in organizations: Violent and deviant behavior* (pp. 1–42). Stamford, CT: JAI Press.

McClintock, C. (1977). Social motives in settings of outcome interdependence. In D. Druckman (Ed.), *Negotiations: Social psychological perspective* (pp. 49–77). Beverly Hills, CA: Sage.

McCusker, C., & Carnevale, P. J. (1995). Framing in resource dilemmas: Loss aversion and the moderating effects of sanctions. *Organizational Behavior and Human Decision Processes, 61*, 190–201.

McMaster, H.R. (1998). *Dereliction of duty: Johnson, McNamara, the Joint Chiefs of Staff, and the lies that led to Vietnam.* Boston: HarperCollins.

Messick, D. M., & Liebrand, W. B. G. (1995). Individual heuristics and the dynamics of cooperation in large groups. *Psychological Review, 102*, 131–146.

Messick, D. M., & McClelland, C. L. (1983). Social traps and temporal traps. *Personality and Social Psychology Bulletin, 9*, 105–110.

Messick, D. M., & Sentis, K. P. (1985). Estimating social and nonsocial utility from ordinal data. *European Journal of Social Psychology, 15*, 389–399.

Mikolic, J. M., Parker, J. C., & Pruitt, D. G. (1997). Escalation in response to persistent annoyance: Groups vs. individuals and gender effects. *Journal of Personality and Social Psychology, 72*, 151–163.

Miller, D. T. (2001). Disrespect and the experience of injustice. *Annual Review of Psychology, 52*, 527–553.

Miller, D. T., & Holmes, J. G. (1975). The role of situational restrictiveness on self-fulfilling prophecies: A theoretical and empirical extension of Kelley and Stahelski's triangle hypothesis. *Journal of Personality and Social Psychology, 31*, 661–673.

Mnookin, R. H., & Susskind, L. E. (Eds.). (1999). *Negotiating on behalf of others: Advice to lawyers, business executives, sports agents, diplomats, politicians, and everyone else.* Thousand Oaks, CA: Sage.

Morgan, P. M., & Tindale, R. S. (2002). Group vs. individual performance in mixed-motive situations: Exploring an inconsistency. *Organizational Behavior and Human Decision Processes, 87*, 44–65.

Morris, M. W., Williams, K. Y., Leung, K., Larrick, R., & Mendoza, M. T. (1998). Conflict management style: Accounting for cross-national differences. *Journal of International Business Studies, 29*, 729–747.

Moscovici, S. (1985). Social influence and conformity. In G. Lindzey & E. Aronson (Eds.), *The handbook of social psychology* (3rd ed., pp. 347–412). New York: Random House.

Mulder, L. B., Van Dijk, E., De Cremer, D., & Wilke, H. A. M. (2006). Undermining trust and cooperation: The paradox of sanctioning systems in social dilemmas. *Journal of Experimental Social Psychology, 42*, 147–162.

Nemeth, C. (1986). Differential contributions of majority and minority influence processes. *Psychological Review, 93*, 10–20.

Nemeth, C., & Kwan, J. (1985). Originality of word associations as a function of majority vs. minority influence processes. *Social Psychology Quarterly, 48*, 277–282.

Nemeth, C., & Kwan, J. (1987). Minority influence, divergent thinking and the detection of correct solutions. *Journal of Applied Social Psychology, 9*, 788–799.

Neuman, J. H., & Baron, R. A. (1997). Aggression in the workplace. In R. A. Giacalone & J. Greenberg (Eds.), *Antisocial behavior in organizations* (pp. 37–67). Thousand Oaks, CA: Sage.

Nijstad, B. A., & Kaps, S. C. (2008). Taking the easy way out: Preference diversity, decision strategies, and decision refusal in groups. *Journal of Personality and Social Psychology, 94*, 860–870.

O'Connor, K. (1997). Motives and cognitions in negotiation: A theoretical integration and empirical test. *International Journal of Conflict Management, 8*, 114–131.

O'Connor, K. M., Gruenfeld, D. H., & McGrath, J. E. (1993). The experience and effects of conflict in continuing work groups. *Small Group Research, 24*, 362–382.

Olekalns, M., Brett, J. M., & Weingart, L. R. (2003). Phases, transitions, and interruptions. Modelling processes in multi-party negotiations. *International Journal of Conflict Management, 14*, 191–211.

Olson-Buchanan, J., & Boswell, W. R. (2008). Organizational dispute resolution systems. In C. K. W. De Dreu & M. J. Gelfand (Eds.), *The psychology of conflict and conflict management in organizations* (pp. 321–352). New York: Lawrence Erlbaum.

Orbell, J. M., Van der Kragt, A. J., & Dawes, R. M. (1988). Explaining discussion-induced cooperation. *Journal of Personality and Social Psychology, 54*, 811–819.

Ostrom, E. (1998). A behavioural approach to the rational choice theory in collective action. *American Political Science Review, 92*, 1–22.

Parks, C. D., & Hulbert, L. G. (1995). High and low trusters' responses to fear in a payoff matrix. *Journal of Conflict Resolution, 39*, 718–730.

Parks, C. D., Sanna, L. J., & Berel, S. R. (2001). Actions of similar others as inducements to cooperate in social dilemmas. *Personality and Social Psychology Bulletin, 27*, 345–354.

Pennebaker, J. W. (1982). *The psychology of physical symptoms.* New York: Springer-Verlag.

Peterson, B. E., Winter, D. G., & Doty, R. M. (1994). Laboratory tests of a motivational-perceptual model of conflict escalation. *Journal of Conflict Resolution, 38,* 719–748.

Pillutla, M. M., & Murnighan, J. K. (1996). Unfairness, anger, and spite: Emotional rejections of ultimatum offers. *Organizational Behavior and Human Decision Processes, 68,* 208–224.

Polzer, J. T. (1996). Intergroup negotiations: The effects of negotiating teams. *Journal of Conflict Resolution, 40,* 678–698.

Polzer, J. T., Mannix, E. A., & Neale, M. A. (1998). Interest alignment and coalitions in multiparty negotiation. *Academy of Management Journal, 41,* 42–54.

Postmes, T., Spears, R., & Cihangir, S. (2001). Quality of decision making and group norms. *Journal of Personality and Social Psychology, 80,* 918–930.

Price, M. E., Cosmides, L., & Tooby, J. (2002). Punitive sentiment as an anti-free rider psychological device. *Evolution and Human Behavior, 23,* 203–231.

Prislin, R., Limbert, W. M., & Bauer, E. (2000). From majority to minority and vice versa: The asymmetrical effects of losing and gaining majority position within a group. *Journal of Personality and Social Psychology, 79,* 385–397.

Probst, T., Carnevale, P. J., & Triandis, H. (1999). Cultural values in intergroup and single-group social dilemmas. *Organizational Behavior and Human Decision Processes, 77,* 171–191.

Pruitt, D. G. (1981). *Negotiation behavior.* New York: Academic Press.

Pruitt, D. G. (1998). Social conflict. In D. Gilbert, S. T. Fiske, & G. Lindzey (Eds.), *Handbook of social psychology* (4th ed., Vol. 2, pp. 89–150). New York: McGraw-Hill.

Pruitt, D. G. (2007). Readiness theory and the Northern Ireland conflict. *American Behavioral Scientist, 50,* 1520–1541.

Pruitt, D. G. (2008). Conflict escalation in organizations. In C. K. W. De Dreu & M. J. Gelfand (Eds.), *The psychology of conflict and conflict management in organizations* (pp. 245–266). New York: Lawrence Erlbaum.

Pruitt, D. G., & Carnevale, P. J. (1993). *Negotiation in social conflict.* Buckingham, England: Open University Press.

Pruitt, D. G., & Kimmel, M. J. (1977). Twenty years of experimental gaming: Critique, synthesis, and suggestions for the future. *Annual Review of Psychology, 28,* 363–392.

Pruitt, D. G., & Lewis, S. A. (1975). Development of integrative solutions in bilateral negotiation. *Journal of Personality and Social Psychology, 31,* 621–633.

Pruitt, D. G., & Rubin, J. Z. (1986). *Social conflict: escalation, stalemate, and settlement.* New York: McGraw-Hill.

Robert, C., & Carnevale, P. J. (1997). Group choice in ultimatum bargaining. *Organizational Behavior and Human Decision Processes. 72,* 256–279.

Robinson, R. J., Keltner, D., Ward, A., & Ross, L. (1995). Actual versus assumed differences in construal: "Naïve realism" in intergroup perception and conflict. *Journal of Personality and Social Psychology, 68,* 404–417.

Roseth, C. J., Johnson, D. W., & Johnson, R. T. (2008). Promoting early adolescents' achievement and peer relationships: The effects of cooperative, competitive, and individualistic goal structures. *Psychological Bulletin, 134,* 223–246.

Ross, L., & Ward, A. (1995). Psychological barriers to dispute resolution. In M. Zanna (Ed.), *Advances in experimental social psychology* (Vol. 27, pp. 255–304). San Diego: Academic Press.

Ross, W. H., & Wieland, C. (1996). Effects of interpersonal trust and time pressure on managerial mediation strategy in a simulated organizational dispute. *Journal of Applied Psychology, 81,* 228–248.

Rouhana, N. N., & Bar-Tal, D. (1998). Psychological dynamics of intractable ethnonational conflicts: The Israeli–Palestinian case. *American Psychologist, 53,* 761–770.

Rubin, J. Z., & Brown, R. (1975). *Social psychology of bargaining and negotiation.* New York: Academic Press.

Rusbult, C. E., & Van Lange, P. A. M. (2003). Interdependence, interaction and relationships. *Annual Review of Psychology, 54,* 351–375.

Schei, V., Rognes, J. K., & Mykland, S. (2007). Thinking deeply may sometimes help: Cognitive motivation and role effects in negotiation. *Applied Psychology: An International Review, 55,* 73–90.

Schelling, T. (1960/1980). *The strategy of conflict.* Cambridge, MA: Harvard University Press.

Scholten, L., Van Knippenberg, D., Nijstad, B. A., & De Dreu, C. K. W. (2007). Motivated information processing and group decision making: Effects of process accountability on information processing and decision quality. *Journal of Experimental Social Psychology, 43,* 539–552.

Schopler, J., & Insko, C. A. (1992). The discontinuity effect in interpersonal and intergroup relations: Generality and mediation. In W. Stroebe & M. Hewstone (Eds.), *European review of social psychology* (Vol. 3, pp. 121–151). Chichester, England: Wiley.

Schroeder, D. A, Steele, J. E., Woodell, A. J., & Bernbenek, A. F. (2003). Justice in social dilemmas. *Personality and Social Psychology Review, 7,* 374–387.

Schulz-Hardt, S., Brodbeck, F. C., Mojzisch, A., Kerschreiter, R., & Frey, D. (2006). Group decision making in hidden profile situations: Dissent as a facilitator for decision quality. *Journal of Personality and Social Psychology, 91,* 1080–1093.

Schulz-Hardt, S., Mojzisch, A., & Vogelgesang, F. (2008). Dissent as a facilitator: Individual and group-level effects on creativity and performance. In C. K. W. De Dreu & M. J. Gelfand (Eds.), *The psychology of conflict and conflict management in organizations.* New York: Lawrence Erlbaum.

Sherif, M., & Sherif, C. W. (1953). *Groups in harmony and tension: An integration of studies of intergroup relations.* New York: Harper and Brothers.

Shestowsky, D. (2004). Procedural preferences in alternative dispute resolution: A closer, modern look at an old idea. *Psychology, Public Policy, and Law, 10,* 211–249.

Shinada, M., & Yamagishi, T. (2007). Punishing free riders: Direct and indirect promotion of cooperation. *Evolution and Human Behavior, 28,* 330–339.

Shinada, M., Yamagishi, T., & Ohmura, Y. (2004). False friends are worse than bitter enemies: "Altruistic" punishment of in-group members. *Evolution and Human Behavior, 25,* 379–393.

Simons, T. L., & Peterson, R. S. (2000). Task conflict and relationship conflict in top management teams: The pivotal role of intragroup trust. *Journal of Applied Psychology, 85,* 102–111.

Simonton, D. K. (2003). Creative cultures, nations, and civilizations: Strategies and results. In P. Paulus & B. A. Nijstad (Eds.), *Group creativity: Innovation through collaboration* (pp. 304–325). Oxford: Oxford University Press.

Skarlicki, D. P., & Folger, R. (2004). Broadening our understanding of organizational retaliatory behavior. In R. W. Griffin & A. M. O'Leary-Kelly (Eds.), *The dark side of organizational behavior* (pp. 373–402). San Francisco, CA: Jossey-Bass.

Smeesters, D., Warlop, L., Van Avermaet, E., Corneille, O., & Yzerbyt, V. (2003). Do not prime hawks with doves: The interplay of construct activation and consistency of social value orientation on cooperative behavior. *Journal of Personality and Social Psychology, 84,* 972–987.

Smith, D. L., Pruitt, D. G., & Carnevale, P. J. (1982). Matching and mismatching: The effect of own limit, other's toughness, and time pressure on concession rate in negotiation. *Journal of Personality and Social Psychology, 42*, 876–883.

Spector, P. E., & Bruke-Lee, V. (2008). Conflict, health and well-being. In C. K. W. De Dreu & M. J. Gelfand (Eds.), *The psychology of conflict and conflict management in organizations*. New York: Lawrence Erlbaum.

Stasser, G., & Titus, W. (1985). Pooling of shared and unshared information in group decision making: Biased information sampling during discussion. *Journal of Personality and Social Psychology, 48*, 1467–1478.

Staw, B. M., & Ross, J. (1989). Understanding behavior in escalation situations. *Science, 246*, 216–220.

Steensma, H., Hubert, A., Furda, J., & Groot, F.D. (2004). Ripple effects of bullying in the workplace on bystanders and family members of the target of bullying. *International Journal of Psychology, 39*, 393.

Steinel, W., & De Dreu, C. K. W. (2004). Social motives and strategic misrepresentation in social decision making. *Journal of Personality and Social Psychology, 86*, 419–434.

Steinel, W., De Dreu, C. K. W., Ouwehand, E., & Ramirez-Marin, J. Y. (2009). When the constituency speaks in multiple tongues: The relative persuasiveness of hawkish minorities in representative negotiation. *Organizational Behavior and Human Decision Processes,109*, 67–78.

Steinel, W., Van Kleef, G. A., & Harinck, F. (2008). Are you talking to me?! Separating the people from the problem when expressing emotions in negotiation. *Journal of Experimental Social Psychology, 44*, 362–369.

Stenstrom, D. M., Lickel, B., Denson, T. F., & Miller, N. (2008). The roles of in-group identification and out-group entitativity in intergroup retribution. *Personality and Social Psychology Bulletin, 34*, 1570–1582.

Straus, M. A., Hamby, S. L., Boney-McCoy, S., & Sugarman, D. B. (1996). The revised conflict tactics scale (CST2): Development and preliminary psychometric data. *Journal of Family Issues, 17*, 283–316.

Stucke, T. S., & Spore, S. L. (2002). When a grandiose self-image is threatened: Narcissism and self-concept clarity as predictors of negative emotions and aggression following ego-threat. *Journal of Personality, 70*, 509–532.

Summers, D. A. (1968). Conflict, compromise, and belief change in a decision-making task. *Journal of Conflict Resolution, 12*, 215–221.

Tabibnia, G., Satpuute, A. B., & Lieberman, M. D. (2008). The sunny side of fairness. *Psychological Science, 19*, 339–347.

Tajfel, H., & Turner, J. (1979). The social identity of intergroup behavior. In W. A. S. Worchel (Ed.), *Psychology and intergroup relations*. Chicago: Nelson-Hall.

Tam, T., Hewstone, M., Kenworthy, J., & Cairns, E. (2009). Intergroup trust in Northern Ireland. *Personality and Social Psychology Bulletin, 35*, 45–59.

Taylor, D. M., & Moghaddam, F. M. (1987). *Theories of intergroup relations: International social psychological perspectives*. New York: Praeger.

Tazelaar, M. J. A., Van Lange, P. A. M., & Ouwerkerk, J. W. (2004). How to cope with "noise" in social dilemmas: The benefits of communication. *Journal of Personality and Social Psychology, 87*, 845–859.

Tedeschi, J. T., & Felson, R. B. (1994). *Violence, aggression, and coercive action*. Washington, DC: APA.

Teger, A. I. (1980). *Too much invested to quit*: New York: Elsevier.

Tenbrunsel, A. E., & Messick, D. M. (1999). Sanctioning systems, decision frames, and cooperation. *Administrative Science Quarterly, 44*, 694–707.

Ten Velden, F. S., Beersma, B., & De Dreu, C. K. W. (2007). Heterogeneous social motives in negotiating groups: The moderating effects of decision rule and interest position. *Journal of Applied Psychology, 92*, 259–268.

Terhune, K. W. (1968). Motives, situation, and interpersonal conflict within prisoner's dilemma. *Journal of Personality and Social Psychology, 8*, 1–24.

Thibaut, J., & Walker, L. (1975). *Procedural justice: A psychological analysis*. Hillsdale, NJ: Erlbaum.

Thompson, L. L., & Hrebec, D. (1996). Lose–lose agreements in interdependent decision making. *Psychological Bulletin, 120*, 396–409.

Thompson, L. L., & Kim, P. H. (2000). How the quality of third parties' settlement solutions is affected by the relationship between negotiators. *Journal of Experimental Psychology: Applied, 6*, 3–14.

Thompson, L. L., Peterson, E., & Brodt, S. E. (1996). Team negotiation: An examination of integrative and distributive bargaining. *Journal of Personality and Social Psychology, 70*, 66–78.

Times Online. (2006). 70,000 gather for violent Pakistan cartoons protest. Retrieved November 5, 2008, from www.timesonline.co.uk/tol/news/world/asia/article731005.ece.

Tinsley, C. H. (2001). How negotiators get to yes: Predicting the constellation of strategies used across cultures to negotiate conflict. *Journal of Applied Psychology, 86*, 583–593.

Tinsley, C. H., & Brett, J. M. (2001). Managing workplace conflict in the United States and Hong Kong. *Organizational Behavior and Human Decision Processes, 85*, 360–381.

Tinsley, C. H., O'Connor, K. M., & Sullivan, B. (2002). Tough guys finish last: The perils of a distributive reputation. *Organizational Behavior and Human Decision Processes, 88*, 621–642.

Tjosvold, D. (1998). Cooperative and competitive goal approach to conflict: Accomplishments and challenges. *Applied Psychology: An International Review, 47*, 285–342.

Toma, C., & Butera, F. (2009). Hidden profiles and concealed information: Strategic information sharing and use in group decision making. *Personality and Social Psychology Bulletin, 35*, 793–806.

Triandis, H. C. (1989). The self and social behavior in different cultural contexts. *Psychological Review, 96*, 506–520.

Tyler, T.R., & Blader, S. (2000). *Cooperation in groups: Procedural justice, social identity, and behavioral engagement*. New York: Psychology Press.

Tyler, T. R., Lind, E., & Huo, Y. (2000). Cultural values and authority relations: The psychology of conflict resolution across cultures. *Psychology, Public Policy, and Law, 6*, 1138–1163.

Utz, S. (2004). Self-activation is a two-edged sword: The effects of I primes on cooperation. *Journal of Experimental Social Psychology, 40*, 769–776.

Van Beest, I., Andeweg, R.B., Koning, L., & Van Lange, P.A.M. (2008). Do groups exclude others more readily than individuals in coalition formation? *Group Processes and Intergroup Relations, 11*, 55–67.

Van Beest, I., & Van Dijk, E. (2008). Self-interest and fairness in coalition formation: A social utility approach to understanding partner selection and payoff allocations in group. In W. Stroebe & M. Hewstone (Eds.), *European Review of Social Psychology* (pp. 132–174). New York: Psychology Press.

Van Beest, I., Van Dijk, E., De Dreu, C. K. W., & Wilke, H. A. M. (2005). Do-no-harm in coalition formation: Why losses inhibit exclusion and promote fairness cognitions. *Journal of Experimental Social Psychology, 41*, 609–617.

Van de Vliert, E. (1992). Questions about the strategic choice model of mediation. *Negotiation Journal, 8*, 379–386.

Van de Vliert, E. (1997). *Complex interpersonal conflict behavior*. New York: Psychology Press.

Van de Vliert, E., Huang, X., & Parker, P. M. (2004). Do colder and hotter climates make richer societies more, but poorer societies less happy and altruistic? *Journal of Environmental Psychology, 24*, 17–30.

Van Dijk, E., & De Cremer, D. (2006). Self-benefiting in the allocation of scarce resources: Leader–follower effects and the moderating effect of social value orientations. *Personality and Social Psychology Bulletin, 32*, 1352–1361.

Van Dijk, E., De Cremer, D., & Handgraaf, M. J. J. (2004). Social value orientations and the strategic use of fairness in ultimatum bargaining. *Journal of Experimental Social Psychology, 40*, 697–707.

Van Dijk, E., Van Kleef, G. A., Steinel, W., & Van Beest, I. (2008). A social functional approach to emotions in bargaining: When communicating anger pays and when it backfires. *Journal of Personality and Social Psychology, 94*, 600–614.

Van Dyne, L., & Saavedra, R. (1996). A naturalistic minority influence experiment: Effect son divergent thinking, conflict, and originality. *British Journal of Social Psychology, 35*, 151–167.

Van Kleef, G. A., De Dreu, C. K. W., & Manstead, A. (2004a). The interpersonal effects of anger and happiness in negotiations. *Journal of Personality and Social Psychology, 86*, 57–76.

Van Kleef, G. A., De Dreu, C. K. W., & Manstead, A. (2004b). The interpersonal effects of emotions in negotiations: A motivated information processing approach. *Journal of Personality and Social Psychology, 87*, 510–528.

Van Kleef, G. A., De Dreu, C. K. W., & Manstead, A. S. R. (2006). Supplication and appeasement in conflict and negotiation: The interpersonal effects of disappointment, worry, guilt and regret. *Journal of Personality and Social Psychology, 91*, 124–142.

Van Lange, P. A. M. (1992). Confidence in expectations: A test of the triangle hypothesis. *European Journal of Personality, 6*, 371–379.

Van Lange, P. A. M. (1999). The pursuit of joint outcomes and equality in outcomes: An integrative model of social value orientations. *Journal of Personality and Social Psychology, 77*, 337–349.

Van Lange, P. A. M., Ouwerkerk, J. W., & Tazelaar, M. J. A. (2002). How to overcome the detrimental effects of noise in social interaction: The benefits of generosity. *Journal of Personality and Social Psychology, 82*, 768–780.

Van Vugt, M., & De Cremer, D. (1999). Leadership in social dilemmas: The effects of group identification on collective actions to provide public goods. *Journal of Personality and Social Psychology, 76*, 587–599.

Vohs, K. D., Mead, N. L., & Goode, M. R. (2006). The psychological consequences of money. *Science, 314*, 1154–1156.

Wall, J. A. (1991). Impression management in negotiations. In R. A. Giacalone & P. Rosenfeld (Eds.), *Applied impression management: How image-making affects managerial decisions* (pp. 133–156). Thousand Oaks, CA: Sage.

Wall, J. A., Stark, J. B., & Standifer, R. L. (2001). Mediation: A current review and theory development. *Journal of Conflict Resolution, 45*, 370–391.

Walton, R. E., & McKersie, R. (1965). *A behavioral theory of labor negotiations: An analysis of a social interaction system.* New York: McGraw-Hill.

Weber, J. M., Kopelman, S., & Messick, D. M. (2004). A conceptual review of decision making in social dilemmas: Applying a logic of appropriateness. *Personality and Social Psychology Review, 8*, 281–307.

Weingart, L. R., Bennett, R. J., & Brett, J. M. (1993). The impact of consideration of issues and motivational orientation on group negotiation process and outcome. *Journal of Applied Psychology, 78*, 504–517.

Weingart, L. R., Brett, J. M., Olekalns, M., & Smith, P. L. (2007). Conflicting social motives in negotiating groups. *Journal of Personality and Social Psychology, 93*, 994–1010.

Weingart, L.R., Hyder, E.B., & Prietula, M.J. (1996). Knowledge matters: The effect of tactical descriptions on negotiation behavior and outcome. *Journal of Personality and Social Psychology, 70*, 1205–1217.

White, M. (2001). *Rivals: Conflict as the fuel of science.* London: Secker & Warburg.

Whyte, R. K. (1984). *Fearful warriors: A psychological profile of U. S.–Soviet relations.* New York: Free Press.

Wildschut, T., Pinter, B., Vevea, J. L., Insko, C. A., & Schopler, J. (2003). Beyond the group mind: A quantitative review of the interindividual–intergroup discontinuity effect. *Psychological Bulletin, 129*, 698–722.

Winter, D. G. (2007). The role of motivation, responsibility, and integrative complexity in crisis escalation: Comparative studies of war and peace crises. *Journal of Personality and Social Psychology, 92*, 920–937.

Winter, D. G., & Barenbaum, N. B. (1985). Responsibility and the power motive in women and men. *Journal of Personality, 53*, 335–365.

Wit, A., & Kerr, N. (2002). "Me versus just us versus us all" categorization and cooperation in nested social dilemmas. *Journal of Personality and Social Psychology, 83*, 616–637.

Wit, A., & Wilke, H. (1988). Public good provision under environmental social uncertainty. *European Journal of Social Psychology, 28*, 249–256.

Wittenbaum, G. M. (1998). Information sampling in decision-making groups: The impact of members' task relevant status. *Small Group Research, 29*, 57–84.

Wittenbaum, G. M., Hollingshead, A. B., & Botero, I. C. (2004). From cooperative to motivated information sharing groups: Moving beyond the hidden profile paradigm. *Communication Monographs, 71*, 286–310.

Yamagishi, T. (1986). The provision of a sanctioning system as a public good. *Journal of Personality and Social Psychology, 51*, 110–116.

Zapf, D., Knorz, C., & Kulla, M. (1996). On the relationship between mobbing factors and job content, social work environment, and health outcomes. *European Journal of Work and Organizational Psychology, 5*, 215–237.

Chapter 28

Intergroup Relations

VINCENT YZERBYT AND STÉPHANIE DEMOULIN

The primary elections that set the stage for the 2008 U.S. presidential elections constituted a *"première"* in American history. Traditionally, party delegates end up choosing among "mainstream" European American male candidates. This time, the votes from the members of the Democratic Party were split between a woman, Sen. Hillary Clinton, and an African American man, Sen. Barack Obama, both representatives of minority groups in North American society, whether in power, in numbers, or both. Some 40 years after the assassination of Dr. Martin Luther King, Jr. and a little more than a century after the demonstrations of the Suffragettes, relations between the dominant group of European American men and other groups that comprise U.S. society seem to have evolved, permitting events that were simply unimaginable a few decades earlier. As is well known, Sen. Obama eventually won the election over Sen. John McCain, becoming the first minority president in American history. This is but one example of a series of encouraging signs regarding the nature of the relations between groups in general, and minorities and majorities in particular. In addition to other prominent examples of minority members achieving stature and power, such as Kofi Annan as head of the United Nations (U.N.) or Angela Merkel as Chancellor of Germany, perhaps the most convincing piece of data concerns the steady improvement of indicators documenting sex and ethnic inequalities in United Nations statistics.

Not all relations between groups, however, follow this reassuring path. Around the world, examples abound of the difficult, at times ferocious, relations between human groups. The message here, however, should not be that some countries are bad, whereas others are on a decidedly good path. During the latest presidential elections in the United States, several states ended up passing anti-gay laws. Surveys reveal that some Obama voters also contributed to restricting the civil rights of homosexuals. Obviously, the picture is a complex one, and oftentimes good news hides less cheering realities.

The groups taken into consideration in intergroup relations research are quite diverse (Lickel et al., 2000; for a collection, see Brown & Gaertner, 2001). Whenever scholars examine social entities, be they small (e.g., classes, sports teams), large (neighborhoods, universities, companies), or even very large (women, African Americans, Christians), they speak of intergroup research. In addition, researchers tackle intergroup issues using a variety of approaches. For instance, although they devoted most of their good work to examine interactions between various social entities, they also paid attention to intragroup processes. But intergroup research does not only involve groups as the unit of observation. In fact, the bulk of contemporary work concerns individual responses (Fiske & Taylor, 2008). Every time individuals react in a way that is influenced by their own or their partner's group membership, it falls under the umbrella of research on intergroup relations. Interactions between groups and between members of various groups take many forms. Researchers' best efforts deal with troublemakers, disputes, clashes, and conflicts. But groups may also choose to ignore each other and live in what appear to be segregated and separate worlds. Finally, at the other end of the continuum, groups and their members also engage in peaceful and harmonious interactions or even cooperate with other groups. It is not unusual to see different groups join forces and work together to alter situations that are detrimental to one or several of them.

We thank our colleagues and graduate students of the Center for the Study of Social Behavior of the Université catholique de Louvain at Louvain-la-Neuve and, in particular, the members of the Social Psychology Laboratory. This chapter has greatly benefited from the expertise of Olivier Corneille, Jacques-Philippe Leyens, Brian Lickel, and Bernadette Park. We also express our deep gratitude to Susan Fiske and Daniel Gilbert for their comments and their support during the process of writing this chapter Vincent Yzerbyt dedicates this chapter to his wife, Isabelle, and their three children, Simon, Mathilde, and Lucas. Last but not least, we wish to dedicate this chapter to our mentor, Jacques-Philippe Leyens.

This chapter deals with the recent literature on the various factors that shape intergroup relations, as well as with their results and consequences. Beyond this review, several other contributions, such as the ones on social conflict (De Dreu, this volume), on intergroup bias (Dovidio & Gartner, this volume), on power structures (Fiske, this volume), and on implicit measures (Banaji & Heiphetz, volume 1), also deal, either directly or indirectly, with aspects of intergroup relations. After having been a subsidiary issue in early editions of this *Handbook*, intergroup relations has established itself as a major topic of research in the two most recent editions, one that can be approached from a variety of angles.

The importance of intergroup relations, as a topic on researchers' agendas, is hardly surprising. People live and act in a world of groups. The way individuals think about the world, how they feel, and how they behave—indeed, all behavior—is guided and sometimes constrained by the group(s) to which they belong. Social psychologists have come to agree that a limited number of distal structural factors characterize the relations between the various groups that compose a given social system (Fiske, Xu, Cuddy, & Glick, 1999). At the same time, a tenet of the discipline is that these factors influence behavior only insofar as they affect people's perception of the situation (Lewin, 1948). A first key determinant of the interactions between members of various groups and between groups themselves is the malevolent versus benevolent nature of their relations, resulting, in part, from the objective state of affairs in terms of available material and symbolic resources, and also, from the subjective interpretation of the situation by perceivers. Although this chapter focuses quite a bit on conflictual and otherwise competitive relations, it also looks at more complex relations in which the ascription of positive qualities to the group may sometimes lead to negative emotional or behavioral reactions.

A second structural factor that shapes intergroup relations and determines the phenomenology of group members is the relative standing of the groups in the social structure—that is, whether a specific group is in a dominant position or, in contrast, occupies a subordinate position. This is why, beyond a series of invariants that affect group members in most if not all situations, various issues also need to be examined in light of the specific vantage point (i.e., dominant vs. dominated) of the group. Each subsection of this chapter will initially stress a series of issues that are common to all groups and group members before turning to specific aspects resulting from the dominant versus subordinate position of the group.

This chapter comprises five major sections. The first section, Theories of Group Attachment, reviews theories that account for the special relationship between individuals and the group(s) to which they belong. This section focuses on

evolutionary and social psychological theories that build on basic needs, such as the need to belong and the need to control, or on other motivational or cognitive processes (such as social identity and self-categorization theories). Appraisals of Intergroup Relations, From Prejudice to Emotions, and Intergroup Behaviors assess the classic and more recent work on the three aspects that characterize people's reactions in intergroup contexts, namely, their beliefs and representations (i.e., stereotypes), their feelings and emotions (i.e., prejudice), and their behavioral intentions, as well as their behaviors (i.e., discrimination). Finally, Challenges and Promises deals with a number of challenges and new issues that emerged since the late 1990s and proposes a series of directions for future research.

This chapter focuses on the fabric of intergroup relations. The main ambition is to clarify the role played by representations, emotions, and behaviors insofar as they set the stage for fruitful or conflictual interactions between groups or their members. This chapter thus is not concerned with the abundant and fascinating research regarding the factors that may improve intergroup relations and reduce conflict. The task of examining the strategies that may reduce intergroup disagreements or clashes is left to the intergroup bias chapter (Dovidio & Gaertner, this volume). Both chapters should be seen as complementary and allow readers, when read in combination, to gain a fuller sense of what researchers accomplished in the domain of intergroup relations.

THEORIES OF GROUP ATTACHMENT

Broadly speaking, theories of group attachment address two questions: "why" people feel attached to their group and "how" this attachment unfolds (see also the chapter on belonging, attraction, and affiliation, Leary, this volume). The "why" question tackles the issue of group identification and speaks to the role that groups occupy in people's lives. In this perspective, groups are tools or instruments for the fulfillment of individual (or collective) needs and goals. The individual is a given, and the focus is on those cognitive and motivational processes that lead to the formation, existence, and persistence of social groups. Other theories of group attachment concentrate on the "how" question. They reverse the individual-to-group path and take membership in social groups as their point of departure to examine the consequences of such membership for individuals' behavior.

Group Attachment: From Individual and Collective Needs to Group Formation

In his five-stage hierarchy of human needs, Maslow (1943) placed the need for affiliation and belongingness in-between the primary physiological and safety needs (i.e., survival and reproduction), and linked the higher-level needs to self-development (i.e., self-esteem and self-actualization). In this conception of human motivations, people seek to overcome feelings of loneliness and alienation by providing and receiving love and affection to and from close others. Contemporary theories of group attachment depart from this proposition in substantial ways. Most, if not all, of today's dominant theories consider group affiliation and belongingness not as a motivation in itself, but rather as a means for the fulfillment of other significant individual and collective needs (Correll & Park, 2005). Put differently, groups are instrumental to individuals and mainly serve to overcome the deficiencies associated with solitary human existence. Among the functions that groups fulfill, some are more cognitive, whereas others are largely motivational.

Motivational Determinants of Attachment

Evolutionary perspectives on group attachment share the basic premise that human beings have adapted for group living (Neuberg, Kenrick, & Schaller, this volume). According to these perspectives, joining a collective has proved over the millennia to be more efficient than remaining alone to respond to humans' most basic needs, namely, survival and reproduction. Groups provide opportunities for mating and parental investment, and constitute important improvements for defense and protection against external threats. Evolutionary theorists postulate that individuals who were better adapted for group life benefited from a selection advantage that resulted in the "evolution of perceptual, affective, and cognitive processes that support the development and maintenance of membership in groups" (Caporael, 2005, p. 820). In other words, human beings face *obligatory interdependence*, and the group plays the role of a buffer between the individual and the physical environment. For these authors (Brewer, 2004; Caporael & Brewer, 1995), demands of social interdependence have shaped all aspects of human psychology.

Recent theories explaining the reasons for the surprisingly relative large size of the human brain as compared to other animals fit well with this perspective (Dunbar, 1998). Although conventional wisdom and early scientific explanations generally stressed the role of the brain in sensory or technical competence, Dunbar and Shultz (2007) suggest that it was the computational demands of living in complex societies that resulted in the adaptive selection of large brains. In other words, it is the cognitive requirements of the uniquely social life of primates, and in particular the demands of the more intense forms of pair bonding, that promoted this evolutionary development of the human brain. In a related vein, Tomasello, Carpenter, Call, Behne, and Moll (2005) argued that human cognition is fundamentally different from other primate species. Although great apes understand the basics of intentional action, a species-unique motivation exists in human beings to share emotions, experiences, and activities with other people. This *shared intentionality* might have developed out of a need to search for and dominate scarce resources in ancestral times, an activity that can more easily be dominated by small groups of individuals to the exclusion of others (Tomasello et al., 2005). Recently, Hermann, Call, Hernandez-Lloreda, Hare, and Tomasello (2007) proposed that human beings do not simply evidence more general intelligence than primate species, but that they possess greater and more sophisticated cognitive skills for dealing with the social world. They call this phenomenon the "cultural intelligence hypothesis," and it derives from humans' unique motivation to participate and exchange knowledge in cultural groups (Epley & Waytz, volume 1).

Being attuned to social life does not imply that attachment is undifferentiated. As Kurzban and Leary (2001) argued, human adaptation to sociality is specific and includes cognitive mechanisms that cause individuals to be selective both about their interaction partners and the types of interactions which they are willing to engage in with those partners. The same argument is put forward by the Need to Belong theory (Baumeister & Leary, 1995). According to this theoretical framework, individuals are innately prepared (for health, survival, and reproduction reasons) to form and to maintain at least a minimal number of interpersonal relationships involving frequent interactions and persistent caring. For social contact to be satisfactory, it should take place on a long term basis and involve intimate partners rather than strangers. Research confirms that people value intimacy groups (such as family and friendship groups), characterized by their small size and high levels of interpersonal interactions, more than task groups, social categories, or loose associations (Deaux, Reid, Mizrahi, & Ethier, 1995; Lickel et al., 2000). Such findings substantiate the fact that issues of trust and reciprocity are at stake.

A motivation for self-preservation is also at the heart of *terror management theory* (TMT; Greenberg, Solomon, & Pyszczynski, 1997; Pyszczynski, Greenberg, & Solomon, 1997; Solomon, Greenberg, & Pyszczynski, 1991, 2004). From the perspective of TMT, human beings are the only animal species that combines the natural and fundamental instinct for self-preservation with the cruel awareness of the inevitability of their own mortality. This combination creates the potential for the experience of paralyzing terror, which can undermine human functioning. To reduce the threat of the consequences of death, TMT suggests that individuals attempt to seek symbolic immortality through a dual-component death anxiety buffer. Cultural worldviews and the belief that one is living up to cultural standards (i.e., self-esteem) are the two mechanisms that are used as terror management strategies in daily life. Not surprisingly, people devote a great deal of energy to this existential maintenance and defense (Pyszczynski et al., 1997).

In this perspective, ingroups are of critical importance because they are considered as a primary source of support for people's cultural worldviews, and they provide individuals with a kind of vicarious immortality (Castano & Dechesne, 2005; Greenberg et al., 1997). Indeed, ingroup bias is increased in the evaluations of minimal ingroups and outgroups when mortality is made salient (Harmon-Jones, Greenberg, Solomon, & Simon, 1996). Moreover, mortality salience increases both ingroup identification and perceived ingroup entitativity, and both mechanisms act as mediators for the occurrence of ingroup bias (Castano, Yzerbyt, Paladino, & Sacchi, 2002). People also seem more willing to embrace stronger group leaders under mortality salience (Landau et al., 2004).

Thus, group membership clearly serves as an insurance policy of sorts. Because groups serve humans' survival and reproductive needs, people who were better able to manage living in a group and to keep track of their social relations have likely derived some evolutionary advantage. Of course, groups also ought to deliver specific rewards if they are to trigger any attachment and identification in their members. Research confirms that people prove sensitive to cues that are indicative of group efficiency (Castano, Yzerbyt, & Bourguignon, 2003; Yzerbyt, Castano, Leyens, & Paladino, 2000) and react strongly against questionable group members (Abrams, Marques, Bown, & Henson, 2000; Leyens & Yzerbyt, 1992; Marques & Páez, 1994; Marques, Yzerbyt & Leyens, 1988). As the next subsection details, often from these (symbolic) self-preservation and efficacy concerns, groups also fulfill people's need for control and certainty.

Cognitive Determinants of Attachment

One of the most celebrated human motives is the desire for control (Skinner, 1996; Haidt & Rodin, 1999). Control is essential to human functioning because it allows for predictions about and confidence in how to behave and what to expect from the physical and social environment. Research has provided ample evidence that human beings strive to render the world a predictable and controllable place (Pittman, 1998). The more control and autonomy people enjoy, the more comfortable they feel and the better they perform. In contrast, experiencing a lack of control is aversive (Fiske & Taylor, 1991, 2008). Many theories of group attachment can be related to this desire for control motivation.

As a recent illustration, the *uncertainty management model* suggests that people have a fundamental need to feel certain about their world and their place within it, that the world is largely uncertain, and that people strive to eliminate

or reduce threats to certainty (Lind & van den Bos, 2002; van den Bos & Lind, 2002). In fact, several authors have begun to question the explanation of TMT effects in terms of self-preservation motives, proposing instead that the impact of mortality salience reflects the influence of a diminished feeling of control and an increased sense of uncertainty (van den Bos, Poortvliet, Maas, Miedema, & van den Ham, 2005). In a series of experiments, Fritsche, Jonas, and Fankhänel (2008) disentangled mortality and lack of control by contrasting the mortality salience manipulation with a control anxiety treatment (i.e., dental pain) and, more importantly, with a condition in which salience of death was accompanied by controllability (suicide, i.e., a self-determined death). Suggesting the crucial role of control restoration motivations in explaining the traditional effects of mortality salience, increased worldview defense (i.e., ingroup bias, ingroup homogeneity, ingroup identification, and social consensus estimates) emerged only after traditional mortality salience manipulations but not when participants contemplated a self-determined death. Gailliot, Schmeichel, and Baumeister (2006) found similar evidence in that individuals high in self-control ability reported less death anxiety and less worldview defense strategies when mortality was made salient than did individuals who were low in self-control ability (Gailliot, Schmeichel, & Maner, 2007).

One of the early theoretical propositions that rested on the idea of control is *social comparison theory*. According to Festinger (1954), people who face an environment in which reality checks are unavailable or where there are no objective referents tend to compare their own vision of the world with that of others. Through this process of "social reality testing," people try to validate their opinions and beliefs by comparing them with social referents in their environment (Mussweiler, 2003; Stapel & Suls, 2007). Initially formulated as an interpersonal process, social comparison has also proved sensitive to social factors: only ingroup, but not outgroup, members have the ability to reduce subjective uncertainty (for a recent collection, see Guimond, 2006).

Although research has long suggested that affiliation can be a response to stress and uncertainty (Schachter, 1959), and can serve as a means for processes of self-evaluation, this proposition has only recently been linked to the issue of group attachment (Hogg & Abrams, 1993; Hogg & Mullin, 1999). Hogg's (2000) *uncertainty reduction theory* states that uncertainty motivates people to self-categorize and identify with a group to the extent that this group provides them with clear norms for structuring their beliefs and guiding their behaviors (Hogg & Mullin, 1999). Hogg and his colleagues (Hogg & Grieve, 1999; Grieve & Hogg, 1999) showed that identification with minimal groups is contingent on the existence of subjective uncertainty. However, the uncertainty reduction motivation is effective only when it touches on a domain that is subjectively important to the individual (Hogg & Mullin, 1999). Uncertain individuals also identify with self-inclusive categories that are relevant to the contextual self-definition but much less so with irrelevant ones (Hogg & Mullin, 1999). Finally, group identification is strongest when individuals feel uncertain and the ingroup is perceived as a coherent social entity (Hogg, Sherman, Dierselhuis, Maitner, & Moffitt, 2007).

Uncertainty reduction theory blends cognitive aspects of *self-categorization theory* (SCT; Turner, Hogg, Oakes, Reicher, & Wetherell, 1987), which is presented later, with motivational elements (Brown & Capozza, 2006). In a similar vein, *optimal distinctiveness theory* (ODT; Brewer, 1991, 1993) combines an evolutionary perspective on social identification (Caporael, Dawes, Orbell, & van de Kragt, 1989) with cognitive aspects laid out by SCT (Turner et al., 1987). Specifically, ODT holds that identification with social groups plays an important role in the satisfaction of two fundamental yet conflicting motivations (see also Codol, 1984, 1987). On the one hand, individuals strive for assimilation, that is, the need for ingroup inclusion; on the other hand, they face a need for differentiation from others. According to ODT, the importance that a person will attach to a particular social identity (i.e., his or her willingness to become or be considered as a member of a given social group) will depend on the strength of assimilation and differentiation needs, and the perceived level of inclusiveness of the contextually salient social group (Brewer & Pickett, 2002). In two studies, Pickett, Silver, and Brewer (2002) experimentally induced the need for assimilation, the need for differentiation, or no need, and found that participants primed with a need for differentiation perceived broad social categories as less important to them than those primed with a need for assimilation. In addition, the induction of a need for differentiation (vs. assimilation) led to a stronger (vs. weaker) perception of ingroup overinclusiveness and to an underestimation (vs. overestimation) of ingroup size. Future research should confirm that differentiation and assimilation needs impact a whole range of personal and group behaviors (Hornsey & Jetten, 2004).

Finally, Johnson and colleagues (2006) investigated the different social motivational functions of intimacy, task, and social category groups. They predicted and found that people perceive intimacy groups to be associated with affiliation needs and task groups to fulfill achievement needs. The predicted perceived association between social categories and identity needs was much weaker. Although these authors concentrated their work on cognitive representations of the functionality of different types of groups rather than on their actual properties, it remains that their work points to a more differentiated view of the reasons for group attachment (see also Lickel, Rutchick, Hamilton, & Sherman, 2006).

Summary

Human beings are intrinsically social. Recent theorizing suggests that evolution favored those individuals who proved more apt to living and organizing themselves in groups, presumably because doing so afforded clear rewards in terms of survival and reproduction. Several lines of work converge to stress the key role of the aptitude for sociality in the development of the human brain. The idea of preservation, albeit in a more symbolic sense, is also central to perspectives that stress the role of humans' painful awareness of their own finitude in triggering a variety of group-favoring reactions. Whereas motivational factors hang on the group's efficacy, i.e., its ability to secure desired advantages and to be up to the challenges of the physical and social environment, people affiliate with groups for more cognitive reasons as well. Subjective feelings of control and certainty are key motives that encourage people to join together and to select certain groups over others. People will strive for membership in social entities that propose clear lines of conduct, and offer an adequate balance between a sense of uniqueness and a sense of community. Finally, specific attachment to different types of groups seems to result from the specific needs (i.e., affiliation, achievement, and identity needs) these groups are perceived to fulfill.

Group Attachment: From Group Categorization to Individual Identification

Social perceivers lack the cognitive capacity to deal with an overly complex environment (Fiske & Taylor, 2008). Categorization is the process by which individuals simplify their environment, creating categories on the basis of attributes that objects appear to have (or to not have) in common. Categorization processes apply not only to physical but also to social targets. This so-called cognitive miser perspective has generated a massive amount of research and, as discussed later in this chapter, has exerted a lasting influence in the area of stereotypes. But what is the impact of these presumably unavoidable categorization processes on an individual's attachment to social groups? Moreover, what are the contextual variables that may drive people to define themselves at a given hierarchical level in the categorical structure? These questions are at the heart of two of the most prominent social psychological models of the last 50 years: social identity theory and SCT.

Social Identity Theory and Self-Categorization Theory

In 1971, Tajfel, Billig, Bundy, and Flament created what is known as the *minimal group paradigm*. In their experiments, these authors attempted to assess the impact of social categorization on intergroup behavior in a situation in which individual self-interest and prior attitudes were neither present nor relevant. To do so, they used an arbitrary criterion to randomly divide participants into two groups. Their results and many others afterward (for reviews, see Brown, 2000; Messick & Mackie, 1989; and Mullen, Brown, & Smith, 1992) demonstrated that, under most conditions, mere categorization is sufficient to produce discriminatory intergroup behaviors in the form of ingroup favoritism but not outgroup derogation (Brewer, 1979, 1993).

To explain these surprising results, Tajfel and Turner (1979; Tajfel, 1972; Turner, 1975) developed the *social identity theory* (SIT), according to which categorization of people into social groups grants them a social identity. Social identity is that aspect of a person's self-concept that derives from the person's membership in a group. Once people define and evaluate themselves in terms of their social identity, Tajfel (1979) argued, a social comparison process is triggered in which individuals start to compare their ingroup with relevant outgroups in the social environment. This social comparison process, combined with an intrinsic motivation to perceive one's social self in a positive light, causes positive intergroup differentiation and ingroup biases. Thus, an individual's behavior greatly depends on the extent to which that individual's self-concept is defined in terms of personal versus group characteristics. Tajfel (1974) relied on this so-called interpersonal-intergroup continuum to explain changes in behavioral patterns as a function of a person's self-definition.

Motivation for a positive social identity alone, however, does not determine intergroup behaviors. For Tajfel and Turner (1979), intergroup attitudes and behaviors depend on both the strength of social identification with the group and the social structure of intergroup relationships. According to SIT, three main characteristics of the social structure combine with social identity to determine the behavioral direction taken by the categorized individual: the perceived legitimacy of the structure, the stability of the structure, and the permeability of group boundaries (Ellemers, 1993; Ellemers, Spears, & Doosje, 1999, 2002; Ellemers, van Knippenberg, de Vries, & Wilke, 1988). Depending on whether group members perceive status relationships as secure or insecure and intergroup boundaries as permeable or impermeable, they will adopt different types of strategies to achieve a positive social identity. The section on Appraisals of Intergroup Relations examines the role of the intergroup structure in more detail. Last but not least, SIT postulates that, to the extent that people define their self-concept in terms of the group to which they belong, all value connotations and emotional experiences associated with the group become associated with the individuals themselves. The section From Prejudice to Emotions returns to this issue.

Reconceptualizing Tajfel's (1974) proposition of an interpersonal-intergroup continuum where personal and social identity are considered as the two poles of the spectrum, Turner and his colleagues (Turner, 1985, 1987; Turner et al., 1987; Turner & Oakes, 1989) proposed that personal and social identity represent the categorization of the self at different levels of inclusiveness. Building on Rosch's (1978) work on categorical inclusiveness and exemplar prototypicality, SCT postulates that the self can be categorized at different levels of abstraction. It is the context that determines which inclusive level is most salient at any particular moment. Contextual factors that influence the salience of a specific self-categorization are category accessibility, perceived match between the category and the current environment, and strength of a person's social identification with the category—that is, the extent to which category is central and valued by the individual (Doosje & Ellemers, 1997). The metacontrast principle, another idea found in Rosch's work, further suggests that social categorization will occur to the extent that perceived differences between members of one's own group and members of the other group are greater than the perception of differences within the ingroup.

SCT deviates from SIT in a number of ways. Regarding their specific focus, Otten and Epstude (2006) note, "Whereas SIT especially tries to understand the emergence of ingroup favoritism, SCT more generally addresses the conditions and consequences when people define themselves in terms of their group membership" (p. 957). Also, motivational processes are at the heart of SIT, whereas SCT centers its analysis on the cognitive elements of social categorization. According to SCT, the self-concept is a cognitive representation of the self that is contextually dependent and thus variant. Although this idea contrasts with early versions of *self-schema theory* (Markus, 1977; Markus & Sentis, 1982), which postulate that representations of the self are stable schemas that facilitate information processing (for a thorough discussion, see Onorato & Tuner, 2004), a great deal of overlap exists with later versions incorporating the idea of a working self-concept (Markus & Kunda, 1986; Markus & Nurius, 1986; Markus & Wurf, 1987).

For SCT, categorization of the self at the social level will lead to depersonalization and self-stereotyping. In addition, the definition of oneself at the social level accentuates intragroup similarities (i.e., assimilation) and intergroup differences (i.e., contrast), as is the case with all other systems of categorization. The self is perceived as an interchangeable representative of the shared social category. This leads individuals to attach less importance to their unique personal characteristics (depersonalization), and to experience themselves and behave according to their prototypical representation of the category (self-stereotyping).

As such, self-categorization is the "cognitive mechanism which makes group behavior possible" (Turner, 1984, p. 527).

Elaborations and Criticisms of Social Identity Theory and Self-Categorization Theory

SIT and SCT have generated hundreds of studies that show strong empirical support for their theoretical propositions (for reviews, see Brown, 2000; Ellemers, Spears, & Doosje, 2002). However, both theories have also received a fair amount of qualification and criticism. As mentioned earlier, intergroup differentiation in minimal intergroup situations is better understood as a bias toward ingroup favoritism rather than outgroup derogation (Brewer, 1979; Hewstone, Rubin, & Willis, 2002). Research by Mummendey and colleagues (Blanz, Mummendey, & Otten, 1995; Mummendey & Otten, 1998; Mummendey, Otten, Berger, & Kessler, 2000; Otten, Mummendey, & Blanz, 1996) demonstrated the importance of the judgment's valence in the existence of such biases. Specifically, mere categorization in minimal intergroup contexts seems insufficient to induce preferential treatment of one's own group and discrimination against an outgroup. That is, when group members have to evaluate their ingroup and an outgroup on a positive dimension or to allocate positive resources to these groups, people favor ingroup members over outgroup members. However, when judgments are made on negative dimensions, or when people are required to punish or inflict aversive treatment, differential behaviors toward ingroup and outgroup members are not observed (Amiot & Bourhis, 2005; Buhl, 1999). For Mummendey and colleagues (2000), the absence of discrimination under negative valence conditions is a consequence of a change in the level of salience of the categorization. That is, in the negative domain, people tend to elaborate more systematically the categorical information, and this process leads them to the conclusion that the minimal group distinction, in this case, is not a legitimate basis for differentiation. Seen this way, the positive-negative asymmetry supports, rather than undermines, the propositions made by SCT because the effect of valence on intergroup discrimination is mediated by perceived category salience.

Other authors are more critical. For instance, Rabbie and colleagues (Rabbie, 1991; Rabbie & Horwitz, 1988; Rabbie, Schot, & Visser, 1989; see also Gaertner & Insko, 2000) have argued that most of the results obtained in minimal group situations simply derive from self-interest. That is, people perceive that they depend on others to achieve personal profit and, as a consequence, they are motivated to associate with these others to serve their self-interest. Interdependence is thus what drives intergroup phenomena. Turner, Bourhis, and colleagues (Bourhis, Turner, &

Gagnon, 1997; Gagnon & Bourhis, 1996; Perreault & Bourhis, 1998) have extensively responded to this criticism at conceptual and empirical levels. As a matter of fact, Turner (1985) did consider that interdependence, together with many other contextual factors, can indeed be the cause of psychological group formation. However, interdependence can also be the result (rather than the cause) of shared group membership (Turner, 1999). The debate opposing the proponents of an SIT/SCT perspective versus those supporting the interdependence hypothesis is an ongoing one, and many advocate for a better assessment of the underlying assumptions of SIT/SCT. For instance, L. Gaertner and colleagues (Gaertner, Iuzzini, Guerrero Witt, & Oriña, 2006) have argued that intragroup (e.g., interaction and interdependence) rather than intergroup (e.g., intergroup comparison) processes might be at the heart of group formation and might trigger positive evaluations of the ingroup allowing for "us" to exist without "them."

Together with the idea that social groups are competing for scarce resources and that their members are guided by self-interest, the Lewinian view championed by Rabbie and others is often presented as antithetical to the Tajfelian approach in which people see themselves as category members who inherit the symbolic standing of their group. Scheepers and colleagues (Scheepers, Spears, Doosje, & Manstead, 2006) proposed to integrate rather than oppose what they call the instrumental and the identity concerns, arguing that both concerns may trigger bias in different people and different contexts (see also Correll & Park, 2005; Stroebe, Lodewijkx, & Spears, 2005). These authors appraise the identity function in terms of how ingroup bias can create, and thereafter express, a positive, distinct, and meaningful social identity. In contrast, how ingroup bias mobilizes ingroup members, raises solidarity, and motivates them to engage in competition with the outgroup all relate to the instrumental function. Clearly, the context of the minimal group paradigm favors the "creation" facet of the identity function. The "expression" facet of the identity function emerges when group relations are rather stable and members seek symbolic superiority. Not surprisingly, self-esteem constitutes the main dividend of the identity function. The situation changes when people belong to a low-status or otherwise threatened ingroup. Here, ingroup bias materializes the motivation to improve one's lot and to secure material benefits in the context of a realistic conflict. Scheepers and colleagues' work (Scheepers, Spears, Doosje, & Manstead, 2002, 2003, 2006) not only stresses the multifaceted nature of ingroup bias but also emphasizes the fact that group members act strategically in response to a complex array of contextual determinants.

Having said this, the exact role of self-esteem continues to remain under scrutiny, even among SIT supporters

(Aberson, Healy, & Romero, 2000; Hogg & Abrams, 1990; Rubin & Hewstone, 1998). Intergroup discrimination is often seen both as a consequence of low self-esteem and as a precursor of high self-esteem. Both empirical work and meta-analytic reviews suggest that, whereas discrimination is, indeed, conducive to higher levels of self-regard, high self-esteem is, perhaps paradoxically, more likely than low self-esteem to lead to differentiation. This issue is dealt with in more detail later in this chapter during the examination of the role of personality factors in the emergence of prejudice.

On a related note, Otten and colleagues (Otten & Moskowitz, 2000; Otten & Epstude, 2006; Otten & Wentura, 1999) have questioned the fundamental propositions of SIT and SCT in a line of research that is based on the *self-anchoring hypothesis* (Cadinu & Rothbart, 1996). First, these authors question the (i.e., "strive for positive social distinctiveness") motivational hypothesis as underlying ingroup favoritism in minimal group experiments. They argue that a novel ingroup directly acquires a positive value connotation because of a self-anchoring process (Gramzow & Gaertner, 2005; Otten & Wentura, 2001). Presumably, because the self is typically evaluated positively (Baumeister, 1998), novel ingroups to which the self has been assigned are evaluated positively by default. Thus, ingroup bias "might, at least partly, be based upon an automatically activated, implicit positive attitude towards the self-including social category" (Otten & Wentura, 1999, p. 1050).

Second, SCT predicts that, once individuals come to define themselves at the social level, they enter a process of depersonalization in which the self is assimilated into the social category, the ingroup. This phenomenon is called self-stereotyping and is presumed to account for the well-documented, overlapping descriptions of the self and the ingroup (Coats, Smith, Claypool, & Banner, 2000; Smith, Coats, & Walling, 1999; Smith & Henry, 1996). Otten and Epstude's research (2006), however, suggests that the overlap between the description of the self and the ingroup could also be explained as an assimilation of the ingroup to the individual self via a self-anchoring mechanism (Cadinu & Rothbart, 1996; see also Clement & Krueger's work [2000, 2002] on social projection and Gramzow, Gaertner, and Sedikides's work [2001] on the self-as-information-base model).

Summary

People grow up in the midst of a complex social world. They divide their social environment into discrete categories and find themselves in one of these groups. Distinguishing the social world into "us" and "them" entails major consequences in how individuals treat those who belong to

their own group or category and those who do not. Two major empirical and theoretical perspectives, SIT and SCT, directly address this issue and continue to be major references in the field. Over the past decade, researchers celebrated the explanatory power of these approaches while pursuing the critical evaluation of their core assumptions. Following up on the useful distinction between ingroup bias and outgroup derogation, recent work on the positive-negative asymmetry stresses the importance of taking into account the valence of the dimension of differentiation. In an attempt to overcome a heated debate about the motivational foundations of ingroup bias and opposing a more "interested and motivational" (i.e., Lewinian) view of people as group members to a more "symbolic and cognitive" (i.e., Tajfelian) conception of individuals as category members, some researchers now propose an integrated view in which both instrumental and identity concerns can be reconciled. As suggested, however, the dispute between these positions remains vivid, and the field needs further research for this question to be settled. Finally, research also assessed the exact status of self-esteem. The classic view holds that people like their group because its positive properties befall on them. Instead, recent work suggests that people view their group in a positive light because they like themselves and project their positive qualities onto their group.

APPRAISALS OF INTERGROUP RELATIONS

Ever since the Ancient Greeks, philosophers and intellectuals have celebrated three distinct facets of human functioning. Among psychologists, the all-time favorite tripartite conception refers to cognition, emotion, and behavior. Within intergroup relations and stereotyping research, this division translates into stereotypes, prejudice, and discrimination (Fiske, 1998). Partly because of Allport's (1954) influential contribution, researchers long took it for granted that prejudice assumes antecedence. Borrowing from theories in the area of attitudes and in the field of emotions, the dominant view is now that appraisals influence prejudice, which, in turn, orients behavior (Mackie & Smith, 1998; Talaska, Fiske, & Chaiken, 2008). Accordingly, this section and the two following sections examine these three aspects. This section starts by examining people's representations of groups and group members, dealing with questions of process and content, before examining in more detail the way perceivers see the various groups within the social environment, and more generally, the social structure and relations between groups. The next section focuses on the emotional reactions triggered in the context of intergroup relations. The third section in this trilogy surveys a wide range of intergroup behaviors.

Group Perception

Categorization, Stereotype Activation, and Stereotype Application

One message from early research on intergroup relations was that stereotypical features could be listed for any social group (Katz & Braly, 1933), even groups that do not exist (for reviews, see Leyens, Yzerbyt, & Schadron, 1994; Schneider, 2004). Nothing seemed to constrain the specific set of traits that may characterize a group except that these qualities join together to form a stereotypical image (Lippmann, 1922). This early work also promoted the view that stereotypes show a substantial level of inertia (Gilbert, 1951; Karlins, Coffman, & Walters, 1969; Sigall & Page, 1971; but see Devine & Elliot, 1995; Madon et al., 2001), even though the occasional occurrence of dramatic events could affect the perception of social groups (Sherif & Sherif, 1969).

These rather pessimistic interpretations encouraged a generation of researchers to devote most of their energy to process instead of content issues. Starting in the 1970s and up through the present day, the social cognition approach produced an enormous body of knowledge and shows no signs of waning (Fiske & Taylor, 2008; Hamilton, 1981; Kunda, 1999; Macrae & Bodenhausen, 2000; van Knippenberg & Dijksterhuis, 2000). Thanks to these efforts, one now has a much better understanding of the processes at work when people meet with members of social groups. Indeed, perceivers may well hold a rich system of stereotypical beliefs, but this does not mean that such knowledge will be used to judge a specific person (Kunda & Spencer, 2003). For a stereotype to exert an influence, the target person must be categorized as a member of the stereotyped group. Once categorization has taken place, the stereotype must be activated, that is, rendered accessible in the perceivers' mind. Only then can stereotypical knowledge be applied in judgment. The outcome of this process will be very much dependent on the nature of the target information in relation to preexisting stereotypical beliefs, as well as on the concerns and cognitive resources of the social perceiver (Fiske, Lin, & Neuberg, 1999; Yzerbyt & Corneille, 2005).

Turning to categorization first, research using category confusion techniques, such as the "who-said-what" paradigm (Taylor, Fiske, Etcoff, & Ruderman, 1978) has long suggested that category membership, especially race, sex, and age, are spontaneously used to classify people (Fiske, 1998; Klauer & Wegener, 1998; Maddox & Chase, 2004). Individuals identify sex or race of familiar people presented to them even before they can give the person's name (Macrae, Quinn, Mason, & Quadflieg, 2005). Recent neurophysiological evidence confirms that race, followed by sex, come into play both quickly and with little cognitive effort (Ito & Urland, 2003), although this does not mean that category activation always occurs, and that mere exposure would suffice to initiate categorization (Gilbert & Hixon, 1991; Macrae, Bodenhausen, Milne, Thorn, & Castelli, 1997; Macrae, Hood, Milne, Rowe, & Mason, 2002).

Assuming the presence of minimal processing objectives, several factors determine which category (of the three "primary" ones but also among a host of others) will eventually be selected, with the consequence that other categories will be neglected (Bodenhausen & Macrae, 1998). Obviously, features that directly concern the stimulus, such as its mere prototypicality (Blair, Judd, Sadler, & Jenkins, 2002; Livingston & Brewer, 2002; Maddox & Gray, 2002) or its accessibility (Castelli, Macrae, Zogmaister, & Arcuri, 2004), and contextual cues, such as the solo status of a particular category member, play an important role (Mitchell, Nosek, & Banaji, 2003). In one study emphasizing the role of target information in general and behavioral hints in particular (Macrae, Bodenhausen, & Milne, 1995), people categorized an Asian woman as a woman when they observed her putting on makeup but thought of her as an Asian when they witnessed her eating with chopsticks.

Beyond these reality constraints linked to the stimulus and its context, perceivers' specific goals (Pendry & Macrae, 1996) or their partisanship (Fazio & Dunton, 1997) also orient and facilitate the selection of a particular category. Illustrating the intrusion of motivational concerns, compared with people who are not strongly attached to their group, high identifiers more readily classify social targets as members of the outgroup (Castano, Yzerbyt, Bourguignon, & Seron, 2002), a phenomenon called "ingroup overexclusion" (Leyens & Yzerbyt, 1992). In general, stereotypical knowledge merges with prejudice to fuel categorization. When Hugenberg and Bodenhausen (2004) asked prejudiced and nonprejudiced participants to classify pictures that blended White and Black facial features, the former, but not the latter, relied on the faces' emotional expressions and more readily categorized an angry face as Black and a happy face as White.

Some researchers have challenged the idea that categorization is a prerequisite for stereotype activation, proposing instead that features of the stimulus may trigger stereotypical knowledge directly. For instance, Blair and her colleagues (2002) argued that people are conditioned through cultural experiences to associate prototypically African features (e.g., dark skin) with negative traits (e.g., lazy), allowing a person's characteristics to activate a stereotype independent of categorization. As a matter of fact, more prototypically African Black people are negatively stereotyped to a greater degree (Blair et al., 2002), arouse more negative emotions (Livingston & Brewer, 2002), and if presented as defendants considered for the death penalty, are more readily sentenced to death (Eberhardt, Davies, Purdie-Vaughns, & Johnson, 2006).

A wealth of evidence confirms that encountering a category label sets off stereotypical knowledge (Dovidio, Evans, & Tyler, 1986; Gaertner & McLaughlin, 1983; Perdue, Dovidio, Gurtman, & Tyler, 1990). However, a minimal amount of cognitive resources would seem necessary for this to occur (Gilbert & Hixon, 1991; Spencer, Fein, Wolfe, Fong, & Dunn, 1998). Building on this evidence, Wittenbrink, Judd, and Park (1997, 2001; see also Blair, 2001; Dovidio, Kawakami, Johnson, Johnson, & Howard, 1997) designed a stereotyping measure in which participants have to indicate whether a string of letters is a word or a nonword. Whereas some of the words are stereotypically associated with Blacks, others are associated with Whites. Before the presentation of the words and the nonwords, participants are subliminally presented with one of three primes: the label White, the label Black, or a string of Xs. As predicted, prejudiced participants respond faster (slower) to Black stereotypical words when primed with the Black (White) label and faster (slower) to White stereotypical words when presented with the White (Black) label. Other techniques, such as the *Implicit Association Test* (IAT; Greenwald, McGhee, & Schwartz, 1998), although primarily conceived as a measure of prejudice, have also been adapted to gauge stereotypical beliefs by assessing the association between a category label and selected stereotypical features (Amodio & Devine, 2006; Fazio & Olson, 2003; Rudman, Greenwald, & McGhee, 2001; Wittenbrink & Schwarz, 2007; see Banaji & Heiphetz, volume 1). Alternatively, a number of authors have looked at how the confrontation with a category label shapes people's perceptions of objects in ways that are indicative of their stereotypical views (Judd, Blair, & Chapleau, 2004; Payne, 2001; Payne, Lambert, & Jacoby, 2002). For instance, the mere presence of a Black face enhances perceivers' ability to detect degraded images of crime-relevant objects (Eberhardt, Dasgupta, & Banaszynski, 2003; Eberhardt, Goff, Purdie, & Davies, 2004).

The strength of people's stereotypical associations has also been gauged by asking people to take part in computer gamelike situations and make split-second reactions, as in the work on the shooter bias (Correll, Park, Judd, & Wittenbrink, 2002). In these studies, participants are shown pictures of a series of individual targets, some are African American and others are European American, who either hold harmless objects in their hands (e.g., a can of soda) or a weapon (e.g., a handgun) and are asked to make "shoot"/"don't shoot" decisions. The findings confirm that the stereotype linking African Americans to danger underlies participants' decisions (Correll, Park, Judd, & Wittenbrink, 2007). Importantly, the more police officers are trained, the less they fall prey to

the automatic evocation of the stereotype and the more they rely instead on the actual presence or absence of a weapon (Correll, Park, Judd, Wittenbrink, Sadler, et al., 2007). On a related note and building on the fact that group representations rest on deeply learned associations linking a category and stereotypical features, Kawakami and her colleagues (Kawakami, Dovidio, Moll, Hermsen, & Russin, 2000; Kawakami, Dovidio, & van Kamp, 2005) suggested that specific learning aimed at altering these associations should have a direct impact on the expression of, and possibly eliminate, prejudice and discrimination.

Several factors modulate the stereotype activation process. Again, cognitive load is a major player in the field. Processing consistent information frees cognitive resources (Macrae, Milne, & Bodenhausen, 1994). But when they have resources to do so, perceivers also allocate their attention to inconsistent information. They visibly do so to explain away conflicting evidence and keep their stereotypical impressions both coherent and unaltered (Yzerbyt, Coull, & Rocher, 1999), even when cognitive capacity is low and especially when they are prejudiced (Sherman, Conrey & Groom, 2004; Sherman, Lee, Bessenoff, & Frost, 1998; Sherman, Stroessner, Conrey, & Azam, 2005). Illustrating once more the role of reality constraints, contextual cues shape the specific stereotype content that is being activated. For instance, Wittenbrink, Judd, and Park (2001) found that photographs depicting Black men in positive contexts (e.g., in church) triggered more positive associations than photographs depicting Black men in negative contexts (e.g., in a ghetto-looking, graffiti-strewn background). Apparently, the different contexts led participants to categorize the targets according to different subtypes (e.g., churchgoer vs. gang member) within the larger category of African Americans (Devine & Baker, 1991; Stangor, Lynch, Duan, & Glass, 1992).

People's vested interests may also facilitate or inhibit stereotype activation (Blair, 2002; Kunda & Spencer, 2003; Yzerbyt & Corneille, 2005). For instance, the more perceivers aim at integrating information about the targets, understanding the targets, or even explaining why the targets behaved the way they did, the more stereotypical information is likely to be activated (Kunda, Davies, Adams, & Spencer, 2002). Next to this comprehension goal, stereotype activation may provide perceivers with a means to self-promote and self-protect (Fein, Hoshino-Browne, Davies, & Spencer, 2003; Fein & Spencer, 1997; Sinclair & Kunda, 1999), but also to adjust socially (Fein et al., 2003). In contrast, the motivation to avoid prejudice, typically found among people who hold chronic egalitarian goals, should decrease stereotype activation (Moskowitz, Gollwitzer, Wasel, & Schaal, 1999; Olson & Fazio, 2002, 2004; Towles-Schwen & Fazio, 2003).

Once a stereotype is activated, cognitive and motivational factors again determine whether this knowledge will be used to color judgments, shape emotions, and orient behaviors. Availability of cognitive resources has generally been associated with the inhibition of stereotype application (Bodenhausen, 1990; Gilbert & Hixon, 1991; Pendry & Macrae, 1994). Building on ego-depletion theory (Muraven & Baumeister, 2000), which holds that people's mental resources can be depleted through use, Govorun and Payne (2006) found that participants were more likely to use stereotypes when judging a Black person after having been confronted with a demanding Stroop task. Recent behavioral and neuropsychological evidence confirm that stereotype inhibition indeed comes at a cognitive cost (Richeson & Shelton, 2003, 2007; Richeson et al., 2003; Richeson & Trawalter, 2005; Richeson, Trawalter, & Shelton, 2005). Last but not least, incidental emotions—that is, those emotions not associated with a social target but that people bring with them to the situation—have also been found to moderate stereotype application as a function of the processing strategies that are used (Bodenhausen, Mussweiler, Gabriel, & Moreno, 2001). Regarding motivational factors, accuracy and accountability goals, for instance, encourage perceivers to neglect stereotypes and turn to individuating information instead (Lerner & Tetlock, 1999; Weary, Jacobson, Edwards, & Tobin, 2001). The same holds for interdependence concerns (Fiske, 1998). In contrast, self-enhancement goals, such as when self-esteem is under threat, facilitate the application of stereotypical knowledge (Sinclair & Kunda, 2000).

Content of Stereotypes

Most distinctive of the past decade is that, after a long intermission during which process issues occupied center stage, researchers returned to the question of the content of stereotypes. Echoing a viewpoint championed by the *realistic conflict theory* (RCT; LeVine & Campbell, 1972) and what continues to be its best-known empirical demonstration by Sherif (1966), contemporary theorizing about the appraisal step has confirmed that much of the way intergroup relations unfold can ultimately be traced back to the members' understanding of the nature of the relations between their group and other groups, as well as their understanding of the relative positions of the groups. These representations then shape group members' beliefs and opinions about themselves and about the members of the other group. Given the limited number of structural variables that constrain people's stereotypes, only a small number of stereotypical "themes" should emerge in people's characterization of social groups. Counter to the idea that social groups could, in principle, be associated with any sort of feature, the argument here is that stereotype content is, in fact, predictable.

Building on earlier work by Phalet and Poppe (1997) on national stereotypes, and echoing a great deal of work on person perception (Peeters, 1983; Wojciszke, 1997) and personality psychology (Bakan, 1966), the *stereotype content model* (SCM; Fiske, Cuddy, Glick, & Xu, 2002; Fiske, Xu, Cuddy, & Glick, 1999) defines two fundamental dimensions of social perception, warmth and competence, predicted, respectively, by perceived competition and status. Whereas allies are judged as warm and competitors are judged as not warm, high status confers competence and low status incompetence. Somewhat similarly, *image theory* (Alexander, Brewer, & Herrmann, 1999; Alexander, Brewer, & Livingston, 2005; Brewer & Alexander, 2002) holds that intergroup goal compatibility and relative status, but also power to attain goals, are three dimensions that trigger specific group images (ally, enemy, barbarian, dependent, and imperialist).

In several studies, Fiske, Cuddy, and Glick (Cuddy, Fiske, & Glick, 2008; Fiske, Cuddy, & Glick, 2007) asked participants to place a variety of social groups along the two dimensions of warmth and competence. The resulting locations were not only reliably predicted by the relative status and the cooperative nature of intergroup relations, but were also highly similar from one culture to another, suggesting the universal applicability of these dimensions (Cuddy et al., 2009). Whereas the correlation between status and competence is remarkably high, the link between cooperation and warmth is less impressive. One possible account for this pattern is that conflict may involve either actual resources or more symbolic aspects. Whereas the first type of conflict may connect more to issues of sociability, the second type may be more linked to issues of morality. Although both sociability and morality contribute to warmth, there is also room for discrepancy, thereby weakening the link between competition and warmth. In any event, more research is needed to uncover the impact of perceived threat on the ascription of warmth.

Research on the SCM shows that ingroups generally obtain high levels of warmth and competence. Also, all quadrants of the bidimensional space are populated. That is, several groups end up in the ambivalent quadrants that correspond to two kinds of mixed stereotypes, namely, one combining high competence but low warmth and in other encompassing high warmth but low competence. Compared with a simplistic view in which characterizations of social groups are either positive or negative, such a view of stereotypical content in terms of two dimensions allows one to understand the emergence of complex and seemingly conflicting perceptions of social groups. As will become clear later in this chapter, it also adds much power to the prediction of emotional and behavioral reactions.

Whereas early work on the relations between these two dimensions showed warmth and competence to be somewhat positively correlated (Rosenberg, Nelson, & Vivekananthan, 1968; for a review, see Abele, Cuddy, Judd, & Yzerbyt, 2008)—a phenomenon known as the halo effect—more recent efforts point to the existence of a moderately negative relation (Cuddy, Norton, & Fiske, 2005). For instance, Judd, Yzerbyt, and colleagues (Judd, James-Hawkins, Yzerbyt, & Kashima, 2005; Kervyn, Yzerbyt, Judd, & Nunes, 2009; Yzerbyt, Kervyn, & Judd, 2008) presented their participants with a series of behaviors allegedly performed by the members of two groups: one high and the other low on one of these two dimensions (e.g., competence), and both groups ambiguous on the second dimension (e.g., warmth). Impression ratings revealed the presence of a so-called *compensation effect* in that the group that was higher than the other on the first, manipulated dimension was now also seen as lower than the other on the second, unmanipulated dimension (see also, Yzerbyt, Provost, & Corneille, 2005). This compensatory relation emerges whenever observers compare social targets (Judd, James-Hawkins, et al., 2005), but only for these two dimensions (Yzerbyt et al., 2008), underscoring their fundamental nature.

Next to studying the beliefs and opinions of people with respect to the characteristics (i.e., physical features, personality traits, and behaviors) typically expected in members of certain social groups (i.e., stereotypes) (Devine & Elliot, 1995), research has also devoted growing attention to the role of metastereotypes—that is, people's beliefs regarding the stereotypes that members of other groups hold about them. In one of the first studies to provide evidence for the existence of such metastereotypes, Vorauer, Main, and O'Connell (1998; Vorauer, Hunter, Main, & Roy, 2000) asked White Canadian participants to estimate the beliefs that Aboriginal Canadians held about Aboriginal Canadians and White Canadians. As predicted, White Canadians thought that Aboriginal Canadians associated some traits more to the outgroup than to their ingroup. Vorauer et al. (1998) also showed that more prejudiced participants thought that Aboriginal Canadians held more positive views of White Canadians than less prejudiced participants. Judd, Park, Yzerbyt, Gordijn, and Muller (2005) further explored the nature of such attributed stereotypical beliefs and showed that people expect outgroup members to exhibit more intergroup evaluative bias and outgroup homogeneity than they themselves do.

As Vorauer (2006) has argued, individuals' sensitivity to metastereotypes will be a function of the evaluative concerns that they have as a result of the uncertainty of the situation and the importance attached to the outgroup's point of view in that setting. This work ties in to a number of other studies on intergroup pluralistic ignorance; that is, people may sometimes misconceive the views held by members of other groups and embrace a line of action that fuels segregatory reactions (Shelton, Dovidio, Hebl, & Richeson, 2009). For example, Shelton and Richeson (2005) found that Whites and Blacks give divergent explanations about their own and their potential outgroup partner's failure to initiate contact. Specifically, individuals explained their own inaction in terms of their fear of being rejected because of their race, but they attributed outgroup members' inaction to a lack of interest for the intergroup interaction. The work on metastereotypes is also related to recent efforts showing that skills such as perspective-taking can greatly improve the quality of intergroup relations. When people have some sense of how members of other groups appraise things, and themselves in particular, this may help to adjust behaviors and avoid misunderstandings (Galinsky, Ku, & Wang, 2005; Galinsky & Moskowitz, 2000).

Perhaps paradoxically, the emphasis on structural factors in orienting people's appraisals of social groups has the distinct advantage that it stresses the flexible nature of stereotypical depictions. Depending on the nature of the specific comparison being contemplated, groups can be characterized in various ways (Turner et al., 1987; van Rijswijk & Ellemers, 2002; van Rijswijk, Haslam, & Ellemers, 2006; Wyer, Sadler, & Judd, 2002). Research also suggests, however, that the two fundamental dimensions constrain social creativity. That is, inferiority on one of these two facets (e.g., competence) encourages people to affirm superiority on the other (e.g., warmth), with a compensatory relation emerging rather quickly (Demoulin, Geeraert, & Yzerbyt, 2007; Kervyn, Yzerbyt, Demoulin, & Judd, 2008).

Homogeneity, Entitativity, and Essentialism

Stereotyping others has, of course, much to do with the evaluative and semantic meaning of the features associated with a social category, but this is not the end of the story. People consider that traits are stereotypical of a given group when they think that these traits are more likely in this group than in another group or in the general population (McCauley & Stitt, 1978). Whereas stereotypicality corresponds to the percentage of group members believed to possess some attribute, dispersion concerns the perceived spread of the feature among group members (Park & Judd, 1990). In what comes close to a definitional issue, categorization reduces the perceived variability within groups and increases the perceived difference between groups. First noted by Tajfel and Wilkes (1963), this accentuation effect has since been replicated several times (McGarty & Penny, 1988; Queller, Schell, & Mason, 2006). Interestingly, this effect emerges more readily on dimensions that are likely to maximize discrimination (Corneille & Judd, 1999) and for uncertain judgments (Corneille, Klein, Lambert, & Judd, 2002). This categorical accentuation effect biases people's memory, as shown in the who-said-what paradigm studies (Taylor et al., 1978) and in more recent studies concerned with face perception and memory (e.g., Corneille, Huart, Becquart, & Brédart, 2004; Eberhardt et al., 2003; Levin & Banaji, 2006). Other research reexamined the classic cross-race bias (i.e., people's better memory for same-race than for cross-race faces) under a social categorization perspective (e.g., Hugenberg, Miller, & Claypool, 2007; Michel, Corneille, & Rossion, 2007). The important take-home message here is that differential levels of expertise with the ingroup versus the outgroup are not the sole factor at work. Instead, people tend to encode faces differently as a function of their ingroup versus outgroup status, with more individuation and holistic processes driving the encoding of ingroup compared with outgroup faces.

On a related note, one would anticipate that accentuation affects both categories equally, but a large body of evidence indicates that when perceivers belong to one of the two categories, outgroup rather members come across as more alike than ingroup members (Messick & Mackie, 1989; Mullen & Hu, 1989). Whereas some account for this so-called *outgroup homogeneity effect* in terms of greater amounts of interaction, and thus familiarity with ingroup members than with outgroup members (Linville, Fischer, & Salovey, 1989; Linville, Salovey, & Fisher, 1986), others favor a dual-storage model according to which people process information at a more abstract level when it concerns the outgroup rather than the ingroup (Park, Ryan, & Judd, 1992; van Bavel, Packer, & Cunningham, 2008). Still other authors argue that outgroup homogeneity emerges because people spontaneously appraise outgroups in the context of an intergroup comparison, whereas they examine ingroups more readily at the intragroup level (Haslam, Oakes, Turner, & McGarty, 1995). According to this reasoning, both groups should be seen as equally homogeneous when perceivers contemplate them at a comparable level of specificity. In addition to more cognitive and contextual factors, motivational concerns also seem to shape the perception of group homogeneity. Outgroups come across as more homogeneous when they are threatening (Corneille, Yzerbyt, Rogier, & Buidin, 2001). In contrast, the ingroup appears more homogeneous than the outgroup for members of numerical minorities (Kelley, 1989; Simon, 1992) and for people who identify with their ingroup (Castano & Yzerbyt, 1998), especially on ingroup-defining features and in a context where the value of the ingroup is questioned (Doosje, Ellemers, & Spears, 1995). In summary, whenever some sort of divergence or threat colors the relations between two groups, homogeneity emerges in social perception. Although accentuation is presented as faulty because it means going beyond the data, people may well

exaggerate the actual similarity between group members to respond to the demands of the situation, conferring validity to the perception of homogeneity.

Homogeneity is one aspect of *entitativity*, a concept initially coined by Campbell (1958) to refer to the "degree of having the nature of a real entity, of having real existence" (p. 17). It is fair to say that this concept gained much popularity since the late 1990s (Yzerbyt, Judd, & Corneille, 2004). Inspired by early efforts by Hamilton and Sherman (1996) and Brewer and Harasty (1996), Lickel and colleagues (2000) attempted to uncover how people perceive a variety of groups and how different group properties are associated with the degree to which a group is seen as an entity. Entitative groups are characterized by high levels of interaction and similarity, their importance, and the presence of common goals and outcomes. Perception of entitativity triggers what Hamilton, Sherman, and Maddox (1999) call "integrative processing," a mode of dealing with information that is more systematic and extensive, and resembles what perceivers do when confronted with an individual person (Hamilton, Sherman, & Castelli, 2002). Perhaps because people perceive entitative groups as more real and efficient, and therefore more likely to meet their members' needs, such groups stimulate ingroup members to identify with them (Castano et al., 2003; Yzerbyt et al., 2000) and incite potential new members to join (Hogg, 2004; Hogg et al., 2007).

Theoretical and empirical work also suggests that entitativity is related, though not identical, to *psychological essentialism* (Haslam, Rothschild, & Ernst, 2000; Keller, 2005; Miller & Prentice, 1999; Prentice & Miller, 2007; Yzerbyt, Rocher, & Schadron, 1997). Imported from cognitive (Medin, 1989) and developmental psychology (Gelman, 2003) into the social psychology of group perception by Rothbart and Taylor (1992), psychological essentialism refers to perceivers' tendency to ascribe an invisible shared essence (e.g., genes or social background) to all members of a particular group or social category. The evocation of an essence seemingly provides an explanation for visible similarities among members of a group and visible differences between them and members of another group. Importantly, essentialism does not only refer to biological determinism but also entails various other forms of determinism (e. g. social and historical, among others) that incriminate inherent and chronic features of the social targets as causes for what they are and what they do (Rangel & Keller, 2008; Yzerbyt et al., 1997). Even though observers cannot always define this "essence" and it retains a certain element of impenetrability and vagueness (Demoulin, Leyens, & Yzerbyt, 2006; Prentice & Miller, 2007; Yzerbyt, Rocher, & Schadron, 1997), psychological essentialism is now widely seen as a way of appraising human categories that have significant social-psychological consequences, mainly because it reliably associates with group differentiation (Martin & Parker, 1995; Yzerbyt, Corneille, & Estrada, 2001), with prejudice and stereotyping (Bastian & Haslam, 2006; Haslam, Rothschild, & Ernst, 2002; Keller, 2005; Levy, Stroessner, & Dweck, 1998; Williams & Eberhardt, 2008; but see Verkuyten, 2003), and with people's willingness to eliminate disparities between groups or across group boundaries (Williams & Eberhardt, 2008).

Several research efforts examined the exact nature of the relationship between entitativity and essentialism (for a review, see Hamilton, 2007). Essentialism is sometimes presented as a global construct encompassing both the underlying dimensions of entitativity on the one hand (uniformity, informativeness, inherence, and exclusivity) and natural kindness on the other (immutability, naturalness, stability, discreteness, and necessity) (Demoulin et al., 2006; Haslam et al., 2000), and indeed, these factors map rather well on what Rothbart and Taylor (1992) called "inductive potential and immutability." Other work more simply distinguishes entitativity and essentialism (Brewer, Hong, & Li, 2004; Yzerbyt et al., 1997), arguing that there is a dynamic relationship between the perception of entitativity (i.e., phenotypic or apparent resemblance among group members) and the ascription of essence (i.e., genotypic or deep-level similarity), each one reinforcing the other (Prentice & Miller, 2007; Yzerbyt et al., 2001). Such a reciprocal influence has been supported in studies that manipulate either essentialism (Brescoll & LaFrance, 2004) or entitativity (Yzerbyt, Rogier, & Fiske, 1998). In line with the idea that an essentialistic stance has more to do with beliefs about, rather than stable characterizations, of social targets, evidence is accumulating that essentialism is dynamic, motivated, and aptly serves strategic concerns in perceivers' specific intergroup context (Morton, Hornsey, & Postmes, 2009; Morton, Postmes, Haslam, & Hornsey, 2009; Plaks, Levy, Dweck, & Stroessner, 2004; Yzerbyt et al., 2004).

Summary

Intergroup relations orient but are also critically affected by people's appraisal of the people and the situations they encounter. Categorizing others as members of categories allows individuals to handle the enormous complexity of the social world. In turn, social categories, with their associated stereotypical beliefs, deliver a huge amount of information at a trivial cost. Research distinguishes three consecutive processes, namely, categorization, stereotype activation, and stereotype application that are shaped by reality constraints, such as cognitive load and target information, and motivational concerns. Recent research also improved our understanding of the factors that shape the content of stereotypes, in denotative and connotative terms.

Specifically, the level of cooperation of a group and its relative status orient perceptions of warmth and competence, the two fundamental underlying dimensions. In addition, earlier work on perceived homogeneity of groups not only led to a revival of interest in the concept of entitativity but also triggered efforts to examine the intrusion of so-called essentialist beliefs in people's representations of groups.

Intergroup Representations

Aside from the stereotypes that people associate with different types of groups, individuals also assess their social environment in terms of its structure and the threats that they face in that environment. It is now a well-established fact that people vary in the extent to which they appraise the intergroup structure in hierarchical terms. *Social dominance orientation* (SDO; Pratto, Sidanius, Stallworth, & Malle, 1994) is concerned with individuals' beliefs that some groups are superior (i.e., high status) to others (i.e., low status), and that such hierarchical organization of groups in a society is a normal and unavoidable situation. These ideologies have proved to be sensitive to contextual variables such as one's social status (Guimond, Dambrun, Michinov, & Duarte, 2003; see later in this chapter). In addition to hierarchy beliefs, other elements of the social environment also influence people's attitudes and behaviors in intergroup relations. By structural appraisals, one refers to the overall structure of intergroup relations encompassing not only specific groups and their relative positioning in the environment, but also other levels of self and group inclusiveness (e.g., individuals, superordinate categories), and the contextual variables that determine the potential for structural changes. The threat appraisals section discusses the different forms of threats (e.g., symbolic, realistic) that group members face when placed in an intergroup situation.

Appraisals of the Intergroup Structure

Ever since the early formulations of SIT, Tajfel and Turner (1979) defended the idea that intergroup behaviors and attitudes in real (rather than minimal) intergroup situations depend both on the strength of one's social identification and the social structural factors that shape the intergroup situation. SCT (Turner et al., 1987) also proposes that, depending on the context, individuals picture themselves at various levels of category inclusiveness. That is, they can categorize themselves as unique individuals (the less inclusive category), as human beings (the most inclusive), or as members of social groups at any intermediate level of inclusiveness. SCT postulates that higher-order, more inclusive social categories provide the background for comparisons among lower-order categories (see also Goethals & Darley, 1977). At the intergroup level, this means that the ingroup and the outgroup can be recategorized into a single common ingroup, and that the dimensions and norms defining the common ingroup serve as a reference standard against which people evaluate the groups. The more a group comes across as prototypical of the superordinate category, the more positive its evaluation. The *ingroup projection model* (IPM) developed by Mummendey and Wenzel (1999) builds on these notions.

IPM suggests that perceptions of the superordinate category (the frame of reference) are not fixed and stable. Rather, they are social constructions that depend on the vantage point of the perceivers. These social categories are often represented in ways that serve the objectives of the perceiver (Reicher & Hopkins, 2001). As a matter of fact, group members should tend to prefer representations of superordinate categories that favor the ingroup over outgroups. Because relative prototypicality is what influences evaluations of subcategories, groups should disagree on their relative prototypicality, with the ingroup claiming greater relative (but not necessarily absolute) prototypicality for the higher-order category than the outgroup (Wenzel, Mummendey, & Waldzus, 2007). Within the framework of IPM, the appraisal of a group's frame of reference is at stake, and this appraisal influences groups' evaluations. Because the superordinate category is usually appraised as a function of one's group membership, ingroup evaluations are, in most cases, more favorable than outgroup evaluations. The ingroup projection hypothesis has been tested in a variety of intergroup contexts, ranging from university majors (e.g., business vs. psychology in the student context) to national groups (e.g., Italian vs. German in the European context), and using explicit attribute rating method (i.e., calculating the relative profile dissimilarity between subgroup descriptions and the superordinate category; e.g., Wenzel, Mummendey, Weber, & Waldzus, 2003), as well as implicit measurement approaches (i.e., using implicit associations of the subgroups with a superordinate category; e.g., Bianchi, Mummendey, Steffens, & Yzerbyt, 2008; Devos & Banaji, 2005). These efforts suggest that subgroups disagree on each subgroup's relative ability to define the superordinate category that encompasses them.

In an intriguing extension of IPM, several authors argued that one could reduce ingroup's projection tendencies by modifying the inclusive category's representation (Waldzus, Mummendey, Wenzel, & Weber, 2003). Both vaguely defined prototypes and high superordinate complexity countered ingroup projection processes and, as a consequence, increased the outgroup's relative prototypicality of the superordinate category. In turn, the reduction of ingroup projection improved evaluations of the outgroup. Thus, one way to alleviate negative evaluations of outgroup members is by changing the inclusive category's representation. But there

is yet another possibility. If, as suggested by SCT, negative behaviors and attitudes toward a specific outgroup occur as a consequence of people's self-categorization at a certain level of inclusion, it is plausible to argue that by changing people's specific level of inclusion, one would be able to modify their reactions towards the specified outgroup. The change of inclusiveness can take place in both directions. On the one hand, decategorization would occur to the extent that people abandon their social identity to the benefit of their personal identity. On the other hand, recategorization would take place to the extent that people would categorize at a higher level of inclusion. Processes of categorization (recategorization, decategorization, dual categorization) are at the heart of much research that focuses on the implementation of positive intergroup relations (Brown & Hewstone, 2005; Brewer & Brown, 1998; Gaertner & Dovidio, 2000; Oskamp, 2000). These models share the idea that categorization processes affect groups' evaluations and intergroup relations, and that, by changing people's appraisal of social categories, one will also influence group perceptions in a way that benefits intergroup relations. On a similar note, a variety of efforts deal with the impact of people's simultaneous membership in multiple groups (Crisp, Ensari, Hewstone, & Miller, 2002; Crisp & Hewstone, 2007; Vanbeselaere, 1991; Urban & Miller, 1998; for a collection, see Crisp & Hewstone, 2006). Dovidio and Gaertner (this volume) develop and discuss these models in greater detail. It suffices say that changes in the appraisals of categories have a dramatic impact on people's attitudes and behaviors towards members of other groups.

At the most inclusive level of categorization (Turner et al., 1987), social perceivers envisage groups in terms of their human identity. Anthropologists have long recognized that members of human groups consider themselves to be prototypical human beings (Lévi-Strauss, 1952) and downgrade members of other groups to subhuman species levels of categorization. It is only recently, however, that social psychologists began to investigate this phenomenon, and they have considered two distinct, yet related, approaches: *infrahumanization* and *dehumanization*. Whereas the former explores people's perceptions of others as poorer representatives of the human category (*infra-*; Leyens et al., 2000), the latter examines situations in which others are categorized outside of the boundaries defined by the human species (*de-*; Opotow, 1990; Schwartz & Struch, 1989; Staub, 1989). Given that, by definition, all humans belong to the human species, infrahumanization and dehumanization can be considered as biased appraisals of outgroups.

Infrahumanization theory suggests that because people believe that social groups have essential differences (Leyens, Demoulin, Vaes, Gaunt, & Paladino, 2007; Rothbart & Taylor, 1992; Yzerbyt et al., 1997) and because they are ethnocentric (Sumner, 1906), ingroup members tend to reserve for themselves the human essence and concede to outgroups an infrahuman status (Demoulin et al., 2004; Leyens et al., 2003). The theory rests on three main findings. First, when asked to indicate what is uniquely human, people refer to complex emotions, called "uniquely human emotions" (e.g., love, contempt) as contrasted with nonuniquely human emotions that also characterize animals (e.g. joy, anger). Second, people attribute more uniquely human emotions to their ingroup than to (some) outgroups (Leyens et al., 2001; Paladino et al., 2002). Interestingly, people resent the fact that outgroup members express uniquely human emotions and transgress borders (Gaunt, Leyens, & Demoulin, 2002; Vaes, Paladino, Castelli, Leyens, & Giovanazzi, 2003). Finally, research also shows that the ingroup, but not the outgroup, is linked in memory with uniquely human emotions (Boccato, Cortes, Demoulin, & Leyens, 2007; Paladino et al., 2002). Recent efforts address the issue of moderators and behavioral consequences. For instance, Castano and Giner-Sorolla (2006) have shown that infrahumanization biases are intensified when people are made aware of atrocities perpetrated by their ingroup against outgroup members. It is also noteworthy that conflict is not necessary for infrahumanization to emerge, and low-status groups may also infrahumanize higher-status ones (Cortes, 2005). Infrahumanization constitutes a nice example of the simultaneous emergence of ingroup favoritism and outgroup derogation (Viki & Calitri, 2008).

According to Haslam (2006; see also Haslam, Bain, Douge, Lee, & Bastian, 2005), two different conceptions of humanity allow for two possible forms of dehumanization. When others are denied "uniquely human" features such as culture, logic, maturity, and refinement, one would talk about animalistic dehumanization, that is, the treatment of others as subhuman, animal species. In contrast, when others are deprived of "typical human" features, such as warmth, agency, and curiosity, they are being considered as automata and one would talk about mechanistic dehumanization. Research in the domain of dehumanization has also shown that depending on the stereotypes associated with specific social categories, perceivers activate different kinds of nonhuman stereotypes. For instance, whereas businesspeople (lacking emotionality and openness) are implicitly associated with automata, artists (lacking self-control and civility) are linked to subhuman, animal species (Loughnan & Haslam, 2007). In addition, outgroups that are viewed as lacking both warmth and competence (see the SCM discussed earlier, Fiske, Cuddy, Glick, & Xu, 2002) trigger dehumanizing responses as evidenced by neuroimaging research (Harris & Fiske, 2006) and perspective-taking data (Harris & Fiske, in press). Dehumanization

biases are not without dramatic consequences for their targets. For instance, Goff, Eberhardt, Williams, and Jackson (2008) have recently demonstrated that the stereotype of Blacks as apelike creatures in American society alters basic cognitive processes such as visual perception and attention. This stereotype has also been found to increase endorsement of violence against Black suspects.

Clearly, the way people appraise the structure of group relations at different hierarchical levels of inclusiveness has important consequences for intergroup relations and determines beliefs, attitudes, and behaviors. But the social world is also appraised for its potential to trigger threat for one group's resources, identity, or values.

Appraisals of Intergroup Threat

During the 1960s, Muzafer Sherif conducted a series of field studies that set the stage for the development of Realistic Conflict Theory (Sherif, 1966; see also Campbell, 1965; LeVine & Campbell, 1972, Sherif & Sherif, 1969) and, more broadly, for the foundation of the whole field of intergroup conflict (Fiske & Taylor, 2008). Participants in his studies were 11- and 12-year-old White, middle-class, Protestant boys who thought they were attending a summer camp. Boys were initially assigned to two groups and given time to get to know one another within each group. The existence of the other group was then revealed to them, and elements of competition were introduced by setting up a series of games in which goals could be attained by only one group at a time, (i.e., negative interdependence). These conditions were sufficient for the emergence of hostility, derogation, and aggressive behavior toward the other group. Sherif concluded that prejudice and discrimination arise as a result of competition between groups for resources (e.g., prestige, money, goods, land, status, or power) that both groups desire. To the extent that group members perceive that the other group represents a threat to their own resources, conflict will emerge and intergroup relations will deteriorate (for a review, see Jackson, 1993). Importantly, individual self-interest need not be involved for the perception of threat to be activated. Threatening the interest of one's own group is sufficient to produce outgroup derogation (Bobo, 1983). Finally, RCT emphasizes that hostility is directed toward the source of the threat. In contrast, classic scapegoat theories (Zawadzki, 1948), although recognizing that threat triggers hostility, propose that hostility is redirected to a weak and safe-to-target outgroup (for a critical argument, see Glick, 2002).

According to RCT, then, competition for scarce resources is a prerequisite for the emergence of conflict. As a matter of fact, Sherif and Sherif (1969) considered that, when goals are complementary rather than conflicting, (i.e., positive interdependence), relations between the groups should be positive. This view is questioned by recent work on *relative deprivation theory* (RDT; for a recent review, see Walker & Smith, 2002). RDT stipulates that when people compare their current situation with their past situation or with the current situation of others and this comparison turns out to be unfavorable, they feel deprived and experience dissatisfaction. That is, people need not be objectively deprived in absolute terms to experience deprivation. They need only to perceive that they fare poorly compared with others (Tyler & Smith, 1998).

A difference is made between personal, also called "egoistic," and group, also called "fraternal," relative deprivation (Runciman, 1966). Group relative deprivation refers to the perception that a group, with which one's identification is high is deprived relative to an outgroup. Only group, but not personal, relative deprivation is thought to be related to intergroup variables (e.g., prejudice; Vanneman & Pettigrew, 1972). Pettigrew, Christ, Wagner, Meertens, van Dick, and Zick (2008) tested this proposition using three large-scale European surveys. They found that both personal and group relative deprivation are stronger among low-status individuals and correlate with a sense of political inefficacy. Whereas the two measures tend to correlate highly, only group relative deprivation serves as a proximal correlate of prejudice, and it fully mediates any relationship observed between personal relative deprivation and prejudice (see also Tougas & Beaton, 2001). Such empirical evidence is far from trivial because it counters a mounting view that low-status groups are bound to legitimize the system (Jost & Banaji, 1994).

These studies largely demonstrated that when individuals perceive their group as deprived compared with other groups in their environment, they display greater levels of intergroup antagonism and prejudice. The subsequent question then is whether a favorable outcome in the comparison process would, in turn, attenuate or reverse detrimental effects of relative deprivation. Grofman and Muller (1973) were the first to contrast relative deprivation from relative gratification in a correlational study. Their conclusion was strikingly counterintuitive in that the obtained pattern of results revealed a V-curve relationship: Both relatively deprived and relatively gratified individuals manifested greater potential for political violence. Similarly, Guimond and Dambrun (2002) reasoned that the V-curve pattern should also characterize the relationship between both relative deprivation and gratification of a group and this group's propensity to express prejudice toward outgroups. They confirmed this hypothesis in two studies in which they manipulated and compared temporal relative deprivation and relative gratification (i.e., declining or improving job opportunities, respectively) with a control condition, and found that both deprivation and gratification increased

prejudiced tendencies (Dambrun, Taylor, McDonald, Crush, & Méot, 2006). This pattern is consistent with a large body of literature suggesting that prejudice and discrimination are not only exhibited by relatively deprived, low-status people, but that they also, and maybe even more intensely, characterize individuals and groups that occupy a relatively high, favorable position on the dimensions of comparison (Bettencourt, Dorr, Charlton, & Hume, 2001).

Concrete resources are not the only elements that can create threat for a given group and tensions between groups. As a case in point, symbolic threats refer to threats resulting from conflicting values and beliefs that can exist in the absence of conflict over material resources. For instance, Biernat, Vescio, and Theno (1996) found that, in the American society, Whites who believe that Blacks do not support White values evaluate Blacks more negatively than Whites who do not face such value threat. *Symbolic racism theory* (Kinder & Sears, 1981) proposes that contemporary prejudice against Blacks originates from the perception that Blacks violate traditional American values such as individualism (Sears, 1988; Sears & Henry, 2003, 2005; Zanna, 1994).

Stephan and Stephan (2000, 2001; Stephan & Renfro, 2002) have attempted to combine different types of threat into a single *integrated threat theory* (ITT). According to ITT, realistic and symbolic threats can simultaneously account for the prediction of intergroup attitudes (see also Neuberg & Cottrell, 2002, and their biocultural model of intergroup emotions and behavior presented later in this chapter). Realistic threats encompass intergroup conflict and competition over scarce resources, as well as relative group deprivation. Symbolic threats arise from perceived differences in values, attitudes, beliefs, and moral standards. Moreover, intergroup anxiety and negative stereotypes constitute additional threats that should be taken into account in the prediction of intergroup prejudice (these latter threats are extensively detailed in the next section). Strong support for ITT has been found across a number of different intergroup contexts such as ethnicity (Stephan et al., 2002), sex (Stephan, Stephan, Demitrakis, Yamada, & Clason, 2000), and immigration (Stephan, Ybarra, & Bachman, 1999).

Two additional intergroup threats, based in SIT (Tajfel & Turner, 1979), were not included in Stephan and Stephan's ITT. According to SIT, people seek membership in positively distinct social groups. Both the "positive" and the "distinct" facet of this assumption can be threatened in intergroup relations. Threats to positive evaluations of the ingroup, called "group esteem threat," occur when the image of the ingroup is threatened by an outgroup. As it turns out, group esteem threats impact attitudes and behaviors toward the source of threat (e.g., Branscombe, Spears, Ellemers, & Doosje, 2002) but also attitudes toward outgroups unrelated to the threat (Leach, Spears, Branscombe, & Doosje, 2003). Similarly, intergroup similarity, (i.e., *distinctiveness threat*), increases intergroup bias and influences intergroup behaviors, especially for high-identifying ingroup members (Jetten, Spears, & Manstead, 2001; Jetten, Spears, & Postmes, 2004).

In their 2006 meta-analytic review of intergroup threat, Riek, Mania, and Gaertner examined all six different types of threats (i.e., realistic threat, symbolic threat, intergroup anxiety, negative stereotypes, group esteem threat, and distinctiveness threat) simultaneously. They concluded that integrated models of threats are efficient in understanding how threats impact intergroup attitudes and behaviors. They proposed a model of intergroup threat in which ingroup identification, distinctiveness threat, and stereotypes all act as antecedents to realistic, symbolic, and group esteem threats. The relationship between the latter threats and outgroup attitudes as well as intergroup behaviors is mediated by intergroup anxiety and other types of emotions. To date, this integrative model still lacks empirical support, and other moderators, such as group status, probably need to be included to fully understand the impact of threat appraisals on intergroup relations, but it is clear that current research efforts take the direction of a greater integration of structural and threat appraisals.

Summary

The distinction between structural and threat appraisals is reminiscent of similar distinctions in the intergroup literature. Take, for instance, the SCM described earlier (Fiske, Cuddy, & Glick, 2002). Stereotype content varies along two fundamental dimensions, that is, warmth and competence, which depend on appraisals of intergroup competition and relative status, respectively. In all likelihood, intergroup competition and status differential are just two incarnations of the ubiquitous appraisals of threat and structure, respectively, of an intergroup setting. As explained earlier, the critical issues are to determine the intentions of the other groups (their threat) and their potential to enact these intentions (their status).

FROM PREJUDICE TO EMOTIONS

This section first presents classic theories of prejudice, then turns to more recent contributions that specifically examined people's emotional reactions to intergroup situations, while clearly disentangling the cognitive, emotional, and behavioral components of attitudes. Although these theories often also address the cognitive and behavioral components of intergroup relations in their formulations, evaluations, affect, and emotions are their main focus. The section ends by looking at theories that focus on specific emotions.

Prejudice

Prejudice (i.e., the negative evaluation, affect, or emotion that a person feels when thinking about or interacting with members of other groups) has occupied the center stage in research on intergroup relations (Jones, 1997; for a recent collection, see Dovidio, Glick, & Rudman, 2005). More often than not, researchers examining prejudice focus on the perspective of the members of the dominant group. However, members of dominated groups are also likely to be prejudiced against members of dominant groups and, indeed, this issue has become a major focus in recent investigations (Swim & Stangor, 1998). First, this section examines the work on personality factors such as empathy and self-esteem. Next, the attention is directed to authoritarianism and social dominance, and recent efforts that cast these individual differences in terms of ideological beliefs influenced by specific types of socialization, as well as by transient considerations of the dynamic relations between groups and group members. This subsection ends with a quick discussion of the role of conservatism and religion. The next subsection reviews contemporary conceptions of prejudice, examining, in turn, modern racism, aversive racism, and ambivalent sexism.

From Personality Factors to Ideologies

Over the years, several individual difference variables have been linked to prejudice. Two outstanding personality characteristics are empathy and self-esteem. Empathy—that is, the ability to feel the emotions experienced by others as a result of being able to see the world from their point of view (Batson, Early, & Salvarani, 1997; Batson, Chang, Orr, & Rowland, 2002)—has been found to comprise four components (Davies, 1994): perspective taking, empathic concern, personal distress, and fantasy. Research shows that empathy is negatively related to several measures of prejudice (Whitley & Wilkinson, 2002), and that empathic concern produces powerful prosocial and even altruistic motivations (Dovidio, Piliavin, Schroeder, & Penner, 2006). Presumably, people take others' perspective because they value their welfare, which then facilitates empathic concern (Batson, Eklund, Chermok, Hoyt, & Ortiz, 2007). To the extent that group membership is associated with the plight of the target, the positive attitude directed toward the target likely generalizes to the entire group (Batson et al., 2002). Interestingly, temporary factors alter the amount of empathy that people feel for another person. In one illustrative study, Batson and colleagues (2002) confronted participants with a heroin addict and drug dealer serving a prison sentence. Compared with participants in a so-called objective perspective condition, which required them not to get caught up in how the target felt, and instead remain objective and detached, participants in the perspective-taking condition, which had them imagine how the target felt and how this affected his life, felt more empathy and showed less prejudice for the groups to whom the target belonged (Galinsky & Ku, 2004; Galinsky & Moskowitz, 2000; Vescio, Sechrist, & Paolucci, 2003).

For more than half a century, self-esteem—that is, people's evaluations of their personal characteristics—ranked high as a potential cause for prejudice. Presumably, people with low self-esteem rely on prejudice as a means to bolster their own self-image by looking down on others (Leary, 2007). As mentioned earlier, the proposition that successful discrimination enhances self-esteem has received substantial empirical support (Verkuyten, 2007; for reviews, see Aberson et al., 2000; Rubin & Hewstone, 1998). In contrast, the impact of self-esteem on bias and prejudice is less clear. Apparently, individuals high in self-esteem are more likely to be biased, perhaps because they are less troubled by expressing prejudice in explicit ways, whereas individuals low in self-esteem are more sensitive to situational factors that constrain the expression of bias (Aberson et al., 2000). In line with the self-projection view of group identity (Gramzow & Gaertner, 2005; Krueger, 2007; Otten & Wentura, 2001), individuals high in self-esteem may also be expected to manifest bias for their ingroup more easily because they project their characteristics, and thus their sense of self-worth, on other ingroup members. In contrast with chronic low self-esteem, momentary threats to self-esteem may fuel prejudice in the hopes of restoring self-esteem to prethreat levels (Fein & Spencer, 1997; Fein et al., 2003; Spencer et al., 1998; but see Crocker & Luhtanen, 1990).

After the Second World War, the Holocaust and its unimaginable horror triggered an enormous amount of research on anti-Semitism. This work pointed to the role of a character structure, known as the "authoritarian personality syndrome" (Adorno, Frenkel-Brunswick, Levinson, & Sanford, 1950; Allport, 1954), in the emergence of prejudice. Authoritarianism is characterized by blind submission to authority, rigid thinking, conventionalism and conservatism, patriotism, and aggression toward those who do not conform to one's standards. In line with a hydraulic view, the hatred toward outgroups observed among adults emerges as the result of internal conflict experienced in childhood between people's love for and idealization of their parents, and their unacceptable impulses toward their parents in response to a strict, punitive, and dominant parenting style. Much of the interest in this syndrome waned over the years, mainly because of methodological and conceptual problems, and a growing focus on social and cultural variables.

The modern version of authoritarianism, known as "right-wing authoritarianism" (RWA; Altemeyer, 1981, 1988, 1996) resurrected some of the main ideas. RWA avoids lots of the Freudian baggage that was present in prior versions of authoritarianism. People high in RWA are characterized by high levels of submission to established and legitimate authorities, of aggressiveness toward persons who appear to be sanctioned by those authorities, and of adherence to social conventions. Research shows that people high in RWA tend to view things in black or white and divide the world into ingroups and outgroups. They are mentally inflexible and have little tolerance or interest for complex answers and new experiences. In contrast, they have a high need for closure. They also view the world as a dangerous and threatening place, which makes finding security one of their prime concerns. For this reason, they value the protection of their group and the guidance afforded by its authority figures. As a set, these characteristics predispose people high in RWA to be prejudiced against a wide variety of groups (Altemeyer, 1998; Altemeyer & Hunsberger, 1992).

Another individual difference that is currently seen as a set of beliefs is SDO and refers to "the extent to which one desires that one's ingroup dominate and be superior to outgroups" (Pratto et al., 1994, p. 742). SDO comprises a component of group dominance, reflecting the belief that the ingroup ought to be at the top of the social ladder, and a component of opposition to equality, corresponding to the belief that subordinate groups should remain where they are (Jost & Thompson, 2000). Sidanius and Pratto (1999) showed that people high in SDO prefer to see inequality among groups, with their group occupying the higher position. Conversely, higher levels of SDO characterize people who belong to powerful groups. As one would expect, people high in SDO are prejudiced against members of groups who question the legitimacy of a system that puts them in the superior position and who strive to force them to share resources. Tough-minded and lacking empathy, they also see their relationship with other groups as a win-lose situation. Legitimizing myths are a key notion in SDO theory and consist of beliefs that people high in SDO use to justify the disadvantaged position of subordinate groups, despite the wide disapproval of prejudice. Instances of such myths are meritocracy, the Protestant Work Ethic, and just world beliefs. Stereotypes, both positive and negative, provide individuals high in SDO with a rationale for their convictions (Whitley, 1999). Positive stereotypes are particularly pernicious when they allow individuals high in SDO to maintain subordinate groups in a low-status position while appearing to attribute desirable features.

Although both RWA and SDO impact prejudice, research demonstrates that these two constructs are only weakly correlated (Duckitt, 2001), even if they seem to interrelate more as people grow older (Duriez & van Hiel, 2002). The key difference between RWA and SDO is that RWA is mainly concerned with threats perceived to be associated with other groups and, as a consequence, with relations within groups characterized by conformity and even submission to authority figures to avoid these threats (Petersen & Dietz, 2000). In contrast, SDO refers to relations between groups in the context of a competition for resources, with the dominance of the ingroup over the outgroup being the center of attention (Wilson & Liu, 2003). In an attempt to address both the similarities and differences between RWA and SDO, Duckitt (2001, 2005, 2006) proposed and tested a model that distinguishes a number of psychological dimensions leading to prejudice and ethnocentrism. The initial version of the model predicts that two socialization practice dimensions, called "punitive" and "unaffectionate socialization," impact two personality dimensions, social conformity and tough-mindedness, respectively. These two personality dimensions then influence two worldviews: belief in a dangerous and competitive-jungle world, respectively. In turn, both personality and worldview impact RWA and SDO. These ideological attitudes have independent causal influences on ethnocentrism (pro-ingroup attitudes) and prejudice (anti-outgroup attitudes). Research confirms that RWA and SDO predict negative attitudes toward the same groups but also prejudice against different groups (threatening groups such as drug dealers or homosexuals in the case of RWA and subordinate groups such as immigrants or the physically disabled in the case of SDO), reflecting the fact that RWA pertains to social cohesion and security concerns, whereas SDO is rooted in the motivation to maintain or establish group dominance and superiority (Duckitt, 2003; Duckitt & Fisher, 2003; Esses, Dovidio, Jackson, & Armstrong, 2001).

Both RWA and SDO are now widely seen as ideologies, that is, sets of beliefs and attitudes that predispose people to view the world in certain ways and to respond accordingly. As a matter of fact, social factors or even transient situational factors (e.g., failure on a test, positions of power) exert a direct influence on these apparently deeply engrained "personality" variables and, as a result, on the experience and expression of prejudice. Duckitt (2005, 2006) also emphasized the role of threatening and competitive group contexts on RWA and SDO, respectively, via the specific worldviews that these social situations promote. Also stressing the power of social factors, Guimond and colleagues (2003) showed that the specific major that people select in college affects their SDO. Not only do law school students manifest higher levels of SDO than do psychology students at the outset of their university trajectory, confirming the idea that people high in SDO are attracted to powerful professions, but SDO scores of law students

increase, whereas those of psychology students decrease over the years of study. Even more striking, Guimond and colleagues showed that a simple manipulation that assigned participants to a high-power as opposed to low-power role could influence SDO levels. In both cases, SDO mediated the impact between power and prejudice. These and other efforts (Danso & Esses, 2001; Schmitt, Branscombe, & Kappen, 2003) need replications, but they suggest that SDO is better seen as a set of beliefs that proves sensitive to strategic concerns emerging in a dynamic context of intergroup relations (Turner & Reynolds, 2003).

To be sure, researchers have examined other ideological orientations, as well as personal values that are thought to generate prejudice. Conservatism has long been linked to prejudice (Adorno et al., 1950; Allport, 1954; see Jones, 2002), and recent work indicates that this relationship can best be accounted for by the endorsement of various beliefs, such as RWA and SDO (Federico & Sidanius, 2002; Whitley & Lee, 2000), that are then likely to favor the adoption of a conservative political stance and to feed prejudiced responses. Conservatism is also conducive to prejudice because it entails a strong faith in personal responsibility for one's negative outcomes, whereas the propensity to blame the victim appears less strongly engrained among more liberal people (Skitka, Mullen, Griffin, Hutchinson, & Chamberlin, 2002). Jost, Glaser, Kruglanski, and Sulloway (2003) recently argued that political conservatism is best seen as motivated social cognition, serving a range of ideological (e.g., group-based dominance), existential (e.g., terror management), and epistemic (e.g., intolerance of ambiguity) motives.

Contrary to a widely held conception, greater religiosity is linked to prejudice and intolerance. Reviewing some 38 studies conducted over a 50-year period, Batson, Schoenrade, and Ventis (1993) concluded that religion is not related to increased compassion and love for others, but rather to stronger stereotyping, prejudice, and discrimination. Interestingly, research also shows that exposition to religious primes increases submission to both prosocial (Pichon, Boccato, & Saroglou, 2007) and antisocial (Saroglou, Corneille, & Van Cappellen, 2009) requests. The link between religious orientation and prejudice is thus a complex one. Viewing religion as a quest and a search for answers to the meaning of life is associated with open-mindedness and tolerance for outgroups (Batson, Floyd, Meyer, & Winner, 1999; Hunsberger, 1995). In contrast, fundamentalism is related to prejudice (Spilka, Hood, Hunsberger, & Gorsuch, 2003).

Types of Prejudice

Prejudice comes as a major determinant of discriminatory behavior, and one goal that stands high on the agenda of researchers on intergroup relations is to measure people's level of prejudice. Fortunately, explicit prejudice—or what is sometimes referred to as "Jim Crow Racism" in the race domain (Sears, Hetts, Sidanius, & Bobo, 2000)—has become a rarity, and few people would assert the biological superiority of Whites and express stereotypes that Blacks are lazy and stupid. But although old-fashioned forms of blatant prejudice have become markedly less common than when Bogardus (1925) proposed the social distance scale (Devine & Elliot, 1995), prejudice is still alive and well, albeit in more subtle forms (Gaertner & Dovidio, 1986; Swim, Aiken, Hall, & Hunter, 1995). Many people have not yet fully accepted the norm of equality, but they are also reluctant at seeing themselves (or being seen) as prejudiced, at least with respect to the vast majority of stigmatized groups (but see Crandall & Eshleman, 2003). For the sake of clarity, three broad perspectives on contemporary prejudice can be distinguished, embodied in the constructs of modern racism, aversive racism, and ambivalent sexism (Dovidio & Gaertner, 2004; Gawronski, Peters, Brochu, & Strack, 2008; McConahay, 1986; Sears & Henry, 2003; Glick & Fiske, 1996).

Theories of modern racism and symbolic racism (McConahay, 1986; Sears & Henry, 2003, 2005; Sears & McConahay, 1973) hold that the conflict between people's egalitarian goals and their negative feelings about minorities is best resolved by claiming that discrimination no longer exists (McConahay, 1986; Swim et al., 1995). Although they endorse equality (of opportunity) as an abstract principle, modern racists also see their hostility to antidiscrimination policies (such as affirmative action) as being based on rational grounds (such as issues of fairness and justice). The rationalization process builds on a series of interrelated arguments, namely, that prejudice and discrimination are things of the past, that any subsisting inequality is a consequence of the character of its victims, that protest about contemporary disadvantage is unjustified, that victims seek special favors, and that a number of benefits are illegitimate. At the end of the day, modern racists have the impression that they are treated unfairly and they feel deprived. According to Sears and colleagues (Sears, 1988; Sears & Henry, 2003; Sears, Henry, & Kosterman, 2000; Sears, Sidanius, & Bobo, 2000), this process is rooted in negative feelings about minorities in general, and African Americans in particular, acquired through socialization and in a set of beliefs that includes incomplete knowledge of the minority group, traditionalism, and high group self-interest. Closely linked to modern-symbolic racism, subtle prejudice is a construct that Pettigrew and Meertens developed to study prejudice against ethnic groups in Europe (Meertens & Pettigrew, 1997; Pettigrew & Meertens, 1995). Compared with modern racism, one belief that is

also associated with subtle prejudice is the exaggeration of cultural differences. Both strands of research focused on individual differences and contributed to the development of specific scales (McConahay; Pettigrew & Meertens, 1986, 1995). Although modern and subtle racism scales correlate with old-fashioned and blatant racism scales respectively, these scales are not entirely redundant and do uncover useful variability among individuals. Differences between more modern and more traditional forms of racism materialize into different types of discrimination.

The work on aversive racism (Dovidio & Gaertner, 1998, 2004) suggests that this dissociation between supporting an egalitarian value system while at the same time experiencing negative feelings toward minorities as a result of socialization encourages people to deny the existence of any unflattering emotional reactions and pretend that members of minority groups evoke only positive feelings. As detailed in the next section, the motivation to appear unprejudiced, combined with the inescapable experience of discomfort, uneasiness, and fear, leads aversive racists to avoidance behavior and disengagement or, when contact cannot be prevented, to ambiguous behaviors or even overcompensation. In this perspective, negative feelings toward minorities can leak out in subtle and rationalizable ways. More often than not, rather than discriminating against minorities, aversive racists may choose to favor their own group. Because the assumption here is that all people likely fall prey to this emotional ambivalence (Dovidio & Gaertner, 1991, 2004), research on aversive racism demonstrates a much stronger focus on the way situational demands modulate the expression of prejudice. That is, rather than counting on any specific scale to gauge the specific degree of aversive racism, researchers count on the emergence of a gap between more traditional measures of prejudice, where it is expected that respondents will show no prejudice, and more recent, so-called implicit, measures, on which the expression of prejudice is generally difficult to control (Blair, 2001; Dovidio, Kawakami, & Beach, 2001; Hofmann, Gawronski, Gschwendner, Le, & Schmitt, 2005; McConnell & Leibold, 2001; Rudman, Greenwald, Mellott, & Schwartz, 1999).

A variety of these implicit measures of prejudice, some more technologically demanding than others, are now part of the researcher's toolkit (Wittenbrink & Schwarz, 2007; see Banaji & Heiphetz, volume 1). Two popular techniques, known as affective priming (Dovidio, Kawakami, Johnson, Johnson, & Howard, 1997; Fazio, 2001; Fazio, Jackson, Dunton, & Williams, 1995; Klauer, 1998) and the IAT (Greenwald et al., 1998), rest on the assumption that concepts are associated with one another in memory (Fazio & Olson, 2003). Presumably, these and other tools (Payne, Cheng, Govorun, & Stewart, 2005) allow researchers to assess individuals' levels of prejudice in a way that bypasses their attempts to exert control over their responses and are, therefore, quite distinct from their overt responses (but see Olson, Fazio, & Hermann, 2007). There is, however, a growing debate as to the exact meaning of IAT responses and whether they remain truly impervious to extraneous influences and respondents' strategic considerations (de Houwer, Beckers, & Moors, 2007; Fiedler, Messner, & Bluemke, 2006; Klauer, Voss, Schmitz, & Teige-Mocigemba, 2007; Steffens & Buchner, 2003). Similar concerns surface with respect to affective priming (Teige-Mocigemba & Klauer, 2008). Also, because most implicit measures rely on semantic associations, they may not necessarily reflect respondents' endorsement of such associations but rather deeply engrained cultural influences. Related to the contemporary search for indirect measures of prejudice, a consideration of social neuroscience theory (see Lieberman, volume 1), methods, and techniques to examine intergroup phenomena is clearly growing. A number of authors now rely on neural activity to trace critical aspects of group processes and relations (Eberhardt, 2005; for a critical assessment, see Dovidio, Pearson, & Orr, 2008).

Conceptualizing conflict yet differently, the work on *ambivalent sexism* (Glick & Fiske, 1996) suggests that prejudiced people, mainly men, may simultaneously cultivate hostility against nontraditional women (i.e., showing hostile sexism), while praising traditional ones (i.e., manifesting benevolent sexism). In this framework, hostile sexism sees women and men as opponents, with women either trying to control men by marriage, sexual deceit, and a constant demand for attention, or fighting them in a battle of the sexes where feminists threaten men's power and identity. In contrast, benevolent sexism puts women on a pedestal, because they are considered pure and good creatures that stand by their men and nurture their children, but confines them to their traditional role of homemaker because they are presumed to be weak and incompetent (Glick & Fiske, 1999, 2001a, 2001b, 2001c). For many, the construct of benevolent prejudice may come across as an oxymoron, but within contemporary theorizing about racism, sexism, and other "isms," Glick and Fiske (1996) were among the first to suggest that prejudice does not only come in the conventional form of derogatory views and hostile affective reactions but may also be expressed in terms of flattering beliefs and positive emotional responses. According to Glick and colleagues, both sexisms serve to justify relegating women to stereotyped roles in society (Glick & Fiske, 2001a). This line of work led to the construction of the Ambivalent Sexism Inventory, a measure with good psychometric properties that assesses both types of sexism.

Confirming the prediction that ambivalent sexists would entertain a rather Manichean view of women, they tend to classify women in more polar-opposite categories (whore vs. caretaker) than nonsexist men (Glick, Diebold, Bailey-Werner, & Zhu, 1997; see also Haddock & Zanna, 1994). Research confirms that benevolent sexism correlates with hostile sexism (Glick & Fiske, 1996) and with negative implicit attitudes about women (Rudman, Greenwald, & McGhee, 2001), although this coexistence among men is generally underestimated by women (Kilianski & Rudman, 1998; Rudman & Kilianski, 2000). Together with the disturbing finding that benevolent sexist items are often endorsed by women themselves, the ironic consequence of such ignorance is increased resistance to the elimination of sexism. To the extent that women may actually hold a favorable attitude toward benevolent sexist men, women overlook their traditional beliefs while implicitly authorizing men's beliefs about male superiority (Glick & Fiske, 2001c). The same problem arises among men who may refrain from questioning their negative views about women in light of the presence of other (seemingly) positive attitudes. Research on ambivalent sexism spurred new work on ambivalent forms of group perception, which was referenced earlier in the section on representation, and prejudice, which we return to later when examining emotional reactions.

Summary

Since the 1990s, evaluations, affect, and emotions have (re)gained a prominent status within research on intergroup relations. Whereas classic work on prejudice emphasized chronic individual differences, current wisdom has it that the majority of these factors (i.e., authoritarianism, social dominance) are better conceptualized as ideological beliefs than as enduring personality syndromes. It is also clear that prejudice, rather than disappearing, has changed its appearance. More traditional forms of racism have receded, and most people openly support equality of opportunity. Unfortunately, many continue to feel negative about minorities and stigmatized groups. This psychological clash between socially appropriate responses and personal desires among people who hold contemporary prejudices can be seen as a modern version of the conflict idea at the heart of the work on authoritarianism. The research on modern racism, aversive racism, and ambivalent sexism constitute various proposals that address in more detail the mechanisms underlying this discrepancy. One noteworthy outcome of these efforts is the emergence of a variety of sophisticated measurement tools designed to bypass people's attempts at hiding their prejudiced reactions. One difficult issue with many of the so-called implicit measures is whether they truly reflect people's untainted and genuine prejudice rather than long-term cultural influences or short-lived strategic concerns.

Group-Based Emotions

The 2000s witnessed an outbreak of research on the various emotional reactions associated with intergroup contexts. First, the more traditional approaches often tended to examine affective reactions of individuals "as an individual" both toward ingroups and toward outgroups. If the impact of group membership on the nature and intensity of feelings was sometimes assumed, it was rarely assessed. Second, researchers simply tended to take into consideration positive feelings toward the ingroup (ingroup love) and negative feelings toward the outgroup (outgroup hate), often seeing them as opposites of each other and failing to consider them as potentially distinct. Today, the message is that a proper understanding of people's emotional reactions in intergroup contexts is best achieved by also taking into consideration their representations and beliefs on the one hand, and their intentions and behaviors toward the various groups on the other. Because they are shaped by such structural factors as interdependence and status, and the way these aspects are subjectively experienced, emotional reactions are not only diverse, they are also complex and highly specific. In turn, these distinctive emotional responses translate into specific patterns of attitudinal and behavioral responses. Moreover, there is a growing realization that one needs to distinguish between emotions felt as members of a group and those felt as individuals. Finally, and importantly, people may experience emotional reactions about the ingroup, about the outgroup, about their relations, as well as about a host of other events.

When examining contemporary work on this front, an influential source of inspiration remains Stephan and Stephan's (1985) work on intergroup anxiety. According to these authors, people experience a feeling of discomfort and distress in real or anticipated interactions with outgroup members. Because of negative prior contact or because of prejudicial attitudes, negative thoughts and beliefs about outgroups, individuals come to expect negative outcomes during interactions with members of these groups. Negative expectations vary from fear of rejection (by the outgroup if the interaction goes badly or by the ingroup if the interaction succeeds), of exploitation, or of domination, to the perception that one's values or beliefs might be attacked (Lazarus, 1991), or that the situation involves little control for the person (Dijker, 1987).

More recently, Smith (1993, 1999) developed the *intergroup emotion theory* (IET). IET can be seen as an adaptation of appraisal theories of emotion (Arnold, 1960; Frijda, 1986; Frijda, Kuipers, & ter Schure, 1989) in the intergroup domain (for early research along this line, see Dijker, 1987). Building on RDT (Runciman, 1966), SIT (Tajfel & Turner, 1979), and SCT (Turner et al., 1987), Smith (1993) proposed

that people likely appraise situations, experience emotions, and express behaviors as members of social groups rather than as individuals. In other words, people conduct their cognitive evaluation of a situation from the perspective of the group member. Situations are appraised, not for their relevance to the individual, but for their relevance to the group to which the individual belongs. This depersonalization process is crucial to understand what the appropriate stakes are *vis-à-vis* the stimulus. Just as people turn to their ingroup to determine what their beliefs and behaviors should be, a phenomenon at the heart of *referent informational theory* (Turner, 1991), they rely on their group identity to work out the fundamental characteristics of the situation, to react emotionally on them, and to take appropriate action. As a matter of fact, adding to a host of indirect demonstrations that people can psychologically function as group members rather than as individuals (Oakes, Haslam, & Turner, 1994; Turner et al., 1987), Smith and others (Smith et al., 1999; Smith & Henry, 1996; Tropp & Wright, 2001) have provided evidence that the way people define their self and their ingroup may overlap in significant ways.

Taking into account the fact that IET rests both on appraisal theories of emotions and on SCT, researchers have used two strategies to reveal the group nature of people's emotional reactions. The first, embraced by Smith, Mackie, and colleagues (Mackie & Smith, 2002), addresses the appraisal portion of the model. If people function at the group level, they should prove sensitive to changes in appraisals regarding the relation between their group and some other group. This is most easily achieved by modifying structural aspects of the intergroup situation. For instance, Mackie, Devos, and Smith (2000) reasoned that the strength of the ingroup position on some opinion debate should influence group members' emotions and action tendencies. Participants made to believe that their ingroup was in a strong (weak) position felt more (less) angry and wanted to oppose the outgroup more (less). Moreover, anger proved to be a mediator of the impact of collective support on the tendency to confront the outgroup (Mackie, Silver, & Smith, 2004). Further research confirmed that responding in accordance with the emotionally induced action tendency dissipated the emotion and triggered satisfaction (Maitner, Mackie, & Smith, 2006).

The second strategy directly speaks to the self-categorization aspect of the phenomenon and was adopted by Yzerbyt and colleagues (for a review, see Yzerbyt, Dumont, Mathieu, Gordijn, & Wigboldus, 2006). The key idea is that when people meet with specific events, how they appraise the situation will be crucially influenced by their salient social identity, which provides the lenses through which the situation is seen (Ray, Mackie, Rydell, & Smith, 2008; Smith, Seger, & Mackie, 2007; Yzerbyt et al., 2003, 2006). In a study taking advantage of the linguistic divide in Belgium, Yzerbyt, Dumont, Wigboldus, and Gordijn (2003) gave their French-speaking Belgian students a newspaper article informing them about a decision from the board of a Flemish-speaking university to enforce English as the standard language for Flemish-speaking students in their master's degree program. Presumably, students at this Flemish-speaking university strongly disapproved of this new policy. As predicted, inducing participants to see themselves as students in general rather than as students of their French-speaking university, together with their attachment to the group of students in general, combined to produce higher levels of anger (but not of other emotions) and stronger offensive action tendencies (but not other action tendencies). Moreover, in line with cognitive appraisal theories of emotion, participants' emotional reactions mediated the interactive impact of the transient contextual salience of a shared social identity and participants' chronic group identification with the group on action tendencies (Gordijn, Wigboldus, & Yzerbyt, 2001; Yzerbyt et al., 2003, 2006). Follow-up research confirmed that subtle manipulations of identity not only orient the way people appraise events (Gordijn, Yzerbyt, Wigboldus, & Dumont, 2006) but also how group-based emotions materialize in actual behaviors (Dumont, Yzerbyt, Wigboldus, & Gordijn, 2003; for a related approach on helping behavior, see Levine, Prosser, Evans, & Reicher, 2005; Stuermer, Snyder, & Omoto, 2005; Stuermer, Snyder, Kropp, & Siem, 2006).

Next to its emphasis on the flexible nature of people's identity, recent research on group-based emotions allows breaking the unitary construct of prejudice into various components: Several specific emotional reactions may be examined in response to specific appraisal dimensions. It thus comes as less of a surprise that some cognitive evaluations (i.e., stereotypes) that could be understood as positive characterizations of a group (e.g., competent) are sometimes associated with negative feelings (e.g., envy). Capitalizing on the benefits of this new conceptualization, a number of models related to IET emerged, such as *image theory* (Alexander et al., 1999; Alexander, Brewer, & Livingston, 2005), Neuberg and Cottrell's (2002) *sociofunctional threat-based approach*, and Fiske, Cuddy, and Glick's *SCM* and *BIAS map* (Cuddy, Fiske, & Glick, 2007; Fiske, Cuddy, & Glick, 2002, 2007). Previous sections dealt with the cognitive component of the SCM and of image theory, whereas the focus here is placed on the emotional aspects.

According to Neuberg and Cottrell (2002; Cottrell & Neuberg, 2005), people's dependence on the group during evolutionary history made them sensitive to threats to group-level resources and to obstructions to efficient group functioning. Intergroup emotions are a response to these group-level threats because they help people to deal with them effectively by fostering adaptive behavioral intentions. In one illustrative study, Cottrell and Neuberg predicted and found that different groups that were believed to pose qualitatively distinct threats to ingroup resources or processes evoked qualitatively distinct and functionally relevant emotional reactions, despite the fact that all groups scored equally high on a general prejudice measure. For instance, participants thought that gay men threatened their values and personal freedoms and posed a threat to their health (via a perceived association with HIV/AIDS). As a consequence, and in line with predictions, participants reported high levels of disgust and pity. This unique association for gay men was clearly distinguishable from appraisal and feelings observed for other groups. Such findings confirm that the traditional conception of prejudice as a general attitude may often obscure the rich panoply of emotions that people feel toward different groups. In a similar vein, *image theory* (Alexander et al., 1999; Brewer & Alexander, 2002) holds that the specific images associated with different groups (ally, enemy, barbarian, dependent, and imperialist) likely trigger different emotional reactions. For instance, in the enemy situation, the dominant emotional experience is characterized primarily by anger toward the other. However, perceived equal power and cultural status would also trigger respect, envy, and jealousy. Combination of these characteristics with a perception of threat triggers frustration, fear, and distrust (Alexander, Levin, & Henry, 2005).

The SCM (Fiske, Cuddy, Glick, & Xu, 2002; Fiske, Xu, Cuddy, & Glick, 1999; Glick & Fiske, 2001c) and its recent heir, the BIAS map (Cuddy, Fiske, & Glick, 2007, 2008), deal with the way specific relations between groups and their associated appraisals of groups and group members translate into a complex texturing of emotional reactions, which, in turn, feed into a range of unique behavioral reactions. Research on a wide variety of groups, replicated in several cultures (Cuddy et al., 2009), shows that the four quadrants defined by groups' relative status and their degree of competition/cooperation foster the emergence of four ambivalent stereotypes. Two of these stereotypical appraisals are in line with the traditional perspective of an all-positive versus all-negative stereotypical view of groups that commands positive prejudice associated with pride, admiration, affection, and respect on the one hand, and hostile prejudice linked to disrespect, contempt, and hostility on the other hand. The two remaining stereotypes feed a particular type of prejudice that generates a blend of positive and negative emotions. Specifically, the high-competence/low-warmth stereotype, associated with such groups as Asians, feminists, rich people, and the like, generates what Fiske and colleagues (Fiske, Cuddy, Glick, & Xu, 2002; Glick & Fiske, 2001c) call the "envious" prejudice. This "envious" prejudice provokes a mix of negative (envy, fear, resentment, hostility) and positive (respect, admiration) feelings (Lin, Kwan, Cheung, & Fiske, 2005). In sharp contrast, the low-competence/high-warmth stereotype, attached to groups such as disabled people, the elderly, or housewives, triggers "paternalistic" prejudice with its blend of pity, patronizing affection, and liking on the positive end, and disrespect and condescension on the negative end (Cuddy et al., 2005; Cuddy & Fiske, 2002). This model also spurred intriguing research using functional magnetic resonance imaging techniques (Harris & Fiske, 2006). In line with the prediction that low-competence, low-warmth social targets, such as addicts and the homeless, should trigger the nonsocial emotion of disgust (as opposed to social emotions such as pride, envy, and pity) and be dehumanized, confrontation with pictures of such targets failed to spontaneously activate the medial prefrontal cortex (mPFC), a brain zone implicated in social cognitive processing. As it happens, inducing perceivers to individuate such targets, by having them judge the target's food preference, increased activation of the mPFC (Harris & Fiske, 2007).

Even though the underlying rationale for all these efforts is that the beliefs people hold about a target group and its members trigger an intricate array of emotional responses, these recent models remain largely silent as to whether the person appraising the situation and experiencing the emotion is doing so as an individual or as a group member. Operating at either one of these levels is, psychologically speaking, equally real. At the personal level, behavior is shaped by individual emotional reactions to an appraised event or situation. In contrast, when working at the group level, people's beliefs and actions are aligned with their understanding of those features that define their group as opposed to a salient outgroup. Illustrating this mechanism, Verkuyten and Hagendoorn (1997) found that authoritarianism, as an individual difference variable, influenced prejudice when their participants' personal identity was made salient. In sharp contrast, ingroup stereotypes were related to prejudice when national identity was activated. In line with the long-time distinction made by Runciman (1966) between individual relative deprivation and fraternal relative deprivation, a particular social identity can somehow be "selected" so as to influence people's appraisals, emotions, and as we discuss later in this chapter, behavioral reactions.

When scanning this line of research, readers will come across several labels, such as collective emotions (Doosje et al., 1998), intergroup emotions (Mackie et al., 2000), group-based emotions (Bizman, Yinon, & Krotman, 2001; Dumont et al., 2003; Yzerbyt et al., 2006), or vicarious emotions (Lickel, Schmader, Curtis, Scarnier, & Ames, 2005). Each term is associated with nuances regarding the particular theoretical perspective and the researchers' focus of interest, but the general message remains: People experience emotions as a result of their group membership (Iyer & Leach, 2008; Parkinson, Fischer, & Manstead, 2005; Yzerbyt et al., 2006).

Specific Emotions

Although the earlier efforts address the emotions encountered among members of all sorts of groups and group members, several lines of research focused on specific emotions. Interestingly, some emotions are more readily associated with dominant groups, whereas others are more common for members of dominated groups.

Emotional Reactions of Dominant Groups

Members of dominant groups do not only experience positive emotions. Research has accumulated showing that feelings such as guilt and shame can emerge among members of dominant groups (for recent illustrations, see Brown, Gonzalez, Zagefka, Manzi, & Cehajic, 2008; McGarty et al., 2005). Much of the current interest in these two emotions in the context of group relations can be traced back to a series of studies conducted by Doosje and colleagues (1998) on so-called collective guilt. In one experiment, Dutch participants who were either high or low in identification with their national group read a thoroughly positive, a thoroughly negative, or an ambiguous account of the Dutch colonial history in Indonesia. When the text described the Dutch colonial occupation in ambivalent terms, those participants admitting to having a lower commitment to the group also reported feeling more collective guilt and being more willing to repair relations with the former colony. Presumably, high identifiers felt less guilt because they could count on a number of strategies to deal with and avoid the distressing reaction. Because participants obviously had no involvement in the wrongdoing, the pattern that Doosje and colleagues (1998) reported goes a long way to emphasize the group-based nature of the emotional reaction.

Paralleling guilt at the personal level (Tangney, Stuewig, & Mashek, 2007), group-based guilt is an unpleasant feeling said to occur when people self-categorize as a member of a group, are aware that this group's behavior is (or has been) harmful and unjustified or that its advantageous position is illegitimate, accept the ingroup's responsibility as the perpetrator, and appraise the cost of correcting the wrongdoing to be moderate (Wohl, Branscombe, & Klar, 2006). High identifiers (compared with low identifiers) and presumably those that tend to glorify their ingroup (as opposed to those who adopt a more critical view of their group; Roccas, Klar, & Liviatan, 2004), would seem to feel less group-based guilt by increasing the perceived variability of the ingroup. For instance, they consider that the members who did the wrongdoing are not "real members" but rather "black sheep" (Marques, Yzerbyt, & Leyens, 1988), or that the ingroup changed over time. More so than low identifiers, high identifiers are also inclined to compare the ingroup favorably with actions of other wrongdoers (Branscombe & Miron, 2004) or to consider the costs of reparation too high (Schmitt, Branscombe, & Brehm, 2004). In contrast, group-based guilt is increased when people focus on the illegitimate behavior of the ingroup rather than on the victimized outgroup (Harth, Kessler, & Leach, 2008; Iyer, Leach, & Crosby, 2003; Powell, Branscombe, & Schmitt, 2005) or recategorize the victims as members of a common ingroup (Gordijn et al., 2006).

Reminders of historical victimization of the ingroup do not render people more sympathetic to the predicament of the outgroup, but instead promote identity protection reactions. Typically, members of the "perpetrator" or advantaged group reduce the responsibility of the ingroup, blame the outgroup, and legitimize the harm inflicted on it (Swim & Miller, 1999; Wohl & Branscombe, 2008). Such a set of responses, in which the rationalization of the ingroup's harmful behavior seems paramount, is reminiscent of the work on relative gratification, which shows that ingroup advantage is often legitimized (Grofman & Muller, 1973; Guimond & Dambrun, 2002). Research confirms that the combination of an ingroup focus and the perception that the ingroup legitimately dominates the outgroup triggers group-based pride (Harth, Kessler, & Leach, 2008; see also Cialdini et al., 1976). Although empirical support remains ambiguous, one would expect people to feel contempt or disdain toward members of what appears to be a rightfully disadvantaged outgroup (Cuddy et al., 2007).

Group-based guilt is an important emotion in the context of intergroup relations because, negative and distressing as this feeling may be, it fuels a series of "approach" reactions aimed at correcting the wrong committed by the ingroup, such as apologies and reparative actions, that ultimately may contribute to positive consequences for the harmed individuals (Brown et al., 2008; Kanyangara, Rimé, Philippot, & Yzerbyt, 2007; McGarty et al., 2005). In contrast, shame, another self-condemnation emotion, is conceptualized as promoting avoidance responses because it puts a more global accent on the dispositional qualities of the wrongdoer and is, therefore, associated with fear of rejection (Tangney, 1995). Shame originates mainly in threats to one's image and, as such, is also more likely to emerge in relation to "identity-related" groups (e.g., ethnic groups) than to interdependence groups (e.g., friends) (Lickel et al., 2005). In addition to guilt or shame, members of dominant groups have also been found to experience

anger toward their own group on considering the illegitimate advantage it may enjoy over outgroups (Gordijn et al., 2006; Iyer, Schmader, & Lickel, 2007; Leach, Iyer, & Pedersen, 2006, 2007). A focus on the outgroup also facilitates the emergence of sympathy (Montada & Schneider, 1989).

Emotional Reactions of Dominated Groups

Occupying a low status position is by no means a sure predictor of people's emotional reactions toward the dominant group. In the context of cooperative intergroup relations, members of dominated groups may experience feelings of trust, respect, and admiration toward the people who belong to the dominant group. In contrast, competitive relations often result in envy, jealousy, and resentment, and under certain circumstances, anger or fear. In this regard, the perceived (il)legitimacy of the social hierarchy constitutes a key factor shaping dominated group members' emotional reactions. A large body of literature even addresses the fact that injustice lays the ground for feelings of frustration and anger (Mikula, Scherer, & Athenstaedt, 1998). For instance, relative deprivation theorists, introduced earlier in this chapter (Crosby, 1976; Folger, 1986; Gurr, 1970), suggested that the subjective experience of unjust disadvantage, rather than objective deprivation, is the key triggering factor.

Although perceptions of fraternal relative deprivation would seem to feed directly into collective action, research indicates that the feelings of frustration and anger associated with group-based deprivation are the more powerful predictor (Smith & Ortiz, 2002). Thus, congruent with contemporary approaches of group-based emotions, the affective reactions that derive from the appraisal of injustice fuel a series of behavioral tendencies aimed at changing the allegedly detrimental situation (van Zomeren, Spears, Fischer, & Leach, 2004). One note of caution is in order at this point. Just as a number of rationalization strategies allow guilt and shame to be relatively rare emotional experiences among members of dominant groups, anger with respect to the unfair treatment of the outgroup is not felt as often as one would imagine and even if so, does not necessarily lead to collective action (Klandermans, 1997, 2004; van Zomeren, Postmes, & Spears, 2008). First, in accordance with SIT and SCT, people ought to see themselves as members of the deprived group to feel angry and engage in collective action (Gordijn et al., 2006; van Zomeren, Spears, & Leach, 2008). Identification with the disadvantaged group paves the way for the mobilization of people in favor of social change (Ellemers, 1993, 2002) and allows for the emergence of a politicized identity (Drury & Reicher, 1999, 2000, 2005; Reicher, 2001; Simon & Klandermans, 2001; Simon, Trötschel, & Dähne, 2008; see also Ellemers, Platow, van Knippenberg, & Haslam, 2003). Another key determinant is the perception of group efficacy (Drury & Reicher, 2005; Reicher, 1996a, 1996b, 2001). In line with the work on group-based emotions, the higher the sense of subjective efficacy the more will people engage in collective actions (Hornsey et al., 2006).

But even before this, theory and research suggest that inequalities in distribution are often perceived as fair and, therefore, unlikely to trigger movements of protest (Jost & Major, 2001). Early on, SIT evoked the possibility that members of low-status groups deal with their predicament by relying on the strategy of social creativity (Lemaine, 1974; Tajfel & Turner, 1979). Social creativity is concerned with the redefinition of the attractiveness of existing group attributes. That is, members of the disadvantaged group come to valorize typically devalued features associated with their groups such as when African Americans claim that "Black is beautiful." Related to the idea of social creativity is the suggestion by *system justification theory* that people often tend to use complementary stereotypes to describe groups in a given society to bolster the system and to maintain the status quo (Kay et al., 2007). To the extent that dominant groups are associated with status and thus with competence, the work on *the compensation effect* suggests that the specific dimensions retained for such creativity are likely to revolve around sociability. Clearly, creativity may well provide some psychological comfort, but it hardly contributes to questioning the social hierarchy.

Although group-based emotions encountered among members of dominated groups are likely to be negative, ranging from envy and anger to sadness, resignation, or even fear, more positive feelings may also emerge in some circumstances. An intriguing line of work focuses on what is known as *schadenfreude*, or the malicious pleasure that derives from seeing a privileged other meet with some misfortune. Building on earlier work in emotion literature (Smith et al., 1996; for a review, see Smith & Kim, 2007), researchers started to examine this rather delicate emotion in intergroup contexts (Leach et al., 2003; Leach & Spears, 2008). A distinction can be made according to whether the spotlight is on the other group or whether people are more preoccupied with the ingroup. In the former case, the emergence of this opportunistic emotion is a reaction to the illegitimate success of the dominant group and the deservingness of its fall. In the latter approach, the pain associated with the inferiority of the ingroup triggers a displacement-like opportunity to compensate for threats to their ingroup status. Not surprisingly, such imaginary revenge emerges more strongly among those who consider the comparative dimension as more relevant and in contexts where such malicious pleasure is seen as legitimate.

Although mainly concerned with individual emotions, research on the impact of ostracism and exclusion on anger, sadness, and fear, and their associated behavioral tendencies also proves highly relevant here (Williams, 2001; for a review, Williams, 2007). In some cases, social rejection triggers antisocial behavior, and this link is mediated by anger but not by sadness (Chow, Tiedens, & Govan, 2008; Leary, Twenge, & Quinlivan, 2006). In other situations, exclusion prompts withdrawal from social contact (Twenge, Catanese, & Baumeister, 2003). Finally, threats to belonging may increase social sensitivity, with people manifesting renewed efforts to connect with others (Gardner, Pickett, & Brewer, 2000; Knowles & Gardner, 2008; Maner, DeWall, Baumeister, & Schaller, 2007; Williams, Cheung, & Choi, 2000). In line with cognitive appraisal theories of emotion, such findings point to the complexity and variability of negative affect in general. Recent work (Molden, Lucas, Gardner, Dean, & Knowles, 2009) suggests that people react rather differently according to whether they are rejected or ignored. Whereas explicit, active, and direct exclusion triggers feelings of agitation and anxiety, and more generally, a concern for preventing further social losses, implicit, passive, and indirect exclusion activates feelings of dejection and sadness, and a motivational state of eagerness and promotion (Higgins, 1997). This work on social exclusion is reminiscent of efforts in the intragroup literature showing that people want to be respected by their fellow ingroup members and, indeed, go a long way to improve their standing in the group if such respect is absent (Ellemers, Doosje, & Spears, 2004). In the intergroup relations domain, a prolific strand of research examined people's reactions to being a victim of discrimination (Crocker, Major, & Steele, 1998; Major & O'Brien, 2005). We come back to this important body of literature in the next section.

Summary

The late 1990s and early 2000s witnessed a real explosion in the attention devoted to emotions in the intergroup context. Combining the lessons from social identity theories with the strengths of appraisal theories of emotions, contemporary researchers went beyond a simplistic view of prejudice in terms of a general and undifferentiated positive or, more commonly, negative feeling toward outgroups and outgroup members. For one thing, people immersed in intergroup situations are likely to respond affectively to appraisals that are shaped not so much by their individual concerns but more so by group interests. For another, the fine distinction afforded by appraisal theories of emotion better correspond to the variety of feelings experienced in intergroup settings. All-purpose labels such as prejudice, favoritism, and bias have been replaced by more specific constructs such as guilt, shame, anger, envy, and *schadenfreude*, among others. Be it from the perspective of the members of dominant groups or those of dominated groups, current conceptions stress the highly contextual nature of the affects emerging in intergroup settings. The dividend of this more complex but at the same time more nuanced conceptualization of people's intergroup experiences is a more powerful prediction of their intergroup behaviors.

INTERGROUP BEHAVIORS

This section examines the behavioral consequences of cognitive and emotional processes for members of dominant and dominated groups in intergroup relations. Behaviors can take many guises. In regard to explicitness about a person's intention or attitude, behaviors can be more (e.g., rewarding someone's performance) or less (e.g., not commenting on someone's performance) explicit. Importantly, verbal behaviors are often considered to be explicit and nonverbal behaviors implicit forms of behaviors (Crosby, Bromley, & Saxe, 1980; Dotsch & Wigboldus, 2008; Fazio et al., 1995), but this is not necessarily the case (Hebl et al., 2009). Verbal behaviors may also seem more controlled than nonverbal behaviors (e.g., eye blinking), but again this need not be the case because verbal behaviors are sometimes uncontrolled (e.g., verbal [Freudian] slips) and nonverbal behaviors are sometimes very controlled (e.g., adopting a very open, assertive posture during a job interview) (DePaulo, 1992; DePaulo & Friedman, 1998; see Ambady & Weisbuch volume 1).

First, this section reviews those behaviors that arise in individuals as a consequence of their membership in social groups, irrespective of the position that these groups occupy in society. Second, the structural relationships between groups will be taken into account by looking at the specific behaviors of dominant and dominated groups in the intergroup situation. Because the intergroup bias chapter by Dovidio and Gaertner (this volume) is devoted to changes in intergroup relations, this chapter focuses on those behaviors that tend to maintain or reinforce the status quo, rather than on behaviors aimed at changing the situation (e.g., self-regulation, collective action). Behaviors related to maintenance and reinforcement of the status quo may be better understood as actions (i.e., behaviors that actors display to achieve their personal or group goals) on the part of majorities and dominant groups, and reactions (behaviors that actors display in "reaction" to another person or another group's action, or in "reaction" to an existing, "imposed," situation) in the case of minorities and stigmatized groups. Indeed, actions of dominant groups and reactions of dominated groups have largely been studied in relation to status quo maintenance or reinforcement. Importantly, minorities should not be considered as only

reactive "participants" and majorities as active "participants" (Jones et al., 1984; Shelton, 2000). However, again, studies investigating social change rather than status quo emphasize reactions of dominant groups and actions of dominated groups.

This section also follows the historical development in research on behaviors in intergroup relations. After a lengthy emphasis on the dominant side of the relationship, and a briefer focus on the dominated side of the relationship, a new generation of researchers now increasingly understands the importance of simultaneously examining both parts of the interaction (for a collection, see Demoulin, Leyens, & Dovidio, 2009). The ambition is to understand the nature of the interpersonal dynamics of intergroup contact when majority and minority group members are brought together in some specific interpersonal situation (Devine & Vasquez, 1998). In line with this concern, this section ends with a discussion of the more recent research on intergroup interactions.

Group Membership as a Determinant of Intergroup Behavior

The impact of group membership on intergroup behaviors can be examined in two different ways. On the one hand, researchers can assess the extent to which interpersonal behaviors depart from intergroup ones; on the other hand, researchers can contrast people's behaviors toward ingroup and outgroup members. The *interindividual-intergroup discontinuity effect* is concerned with the former (for a review, see Wildschut, Pinter, Vevea, Insko, & Schopler, 2003). Specifically, a discontinuity is said to occur when people display the tendency to be more competitive, or less cooperative, in intergroup than in interindividual situations. Two broad perspectives encompass most of the explanations proposed to account for these effects: the fear-and-greed perspective and the group decision-making perspective (Wildschut & Insko, 2007). In essence, the first account suggests that the interindividual-intergroup discontinuity effect is the consequence of greater fear, as well as greater greed, in intergroup than in interindividual settings. Fear because the greater level of distrust in intergroup contexts triggers the anticipation that outgroup members will compete, thereby enhancing the expectation that one will receive the lowest possible outcome. Greed because a greater probability exists of displaying behaviors that favor the pursuit of the highest possible outcome in the case others are willing to cooperate. In contrast, the group decision-making perspective rests on the assumption that group discussion facilitates the rational comprehension of mixed-motive situations, which triggers competitive responses. Indeed, most of the research in this domain rests on experiments that involve mixed-motive matrix games such as the prisoner's dilemma game (see also De Dreu, this volume). Although a complete understanding of the discontinuity effect is yet to be achieved (Wildschut & Insko, 2007), a greater amount of empirical evidence seems to support the fear-and-greed explanation over the group decision-making explanation.

A second consequence of group membership relates to the contrasting behaviors that individuals display toward ingroup and outgroup members (Hewstone et al., 2002). In 1906, Sumner introduced the term "ethnocentrism" to refer to people's universal tendency to preferentially be attached to ingroups over outgroups. Researchers traditionally differentiate between behaviors that favor ingroup members (i.e., ingroup favoritism) and behaviors that hurt outgroup members (i.e., outgroup derogation). Allocating more resources to an ingroup, preferring ingroup members in a voting or a recruitment procedure, or complimenting the ingroup's performance are all instances of ingroup favoritism. In contrast, punishing, insulting, beating, torturing, or even killing outgroup members exemplify outgroup derogation. Returning to Tajfel and colleagues' classic minimal group experiments (1971) presented earlier, we already mentioned that intergroup differentiation in minimal intergroup situations is better understood as a bias in favor of the ingroup rather than against the outgroup (Brewer, 1979, 1999). When group members must allocate positive resources to their ingroup and an outgroup, they favor ingroup members over outgroup members. However, when people are required to give aversive treatment, differential behaviors toward ingroup and outgroup members do not emerge as readily (for a review, see Buhl, 1999).

An interesting line of work on contrastive intergroup behaviors concerns the so-called *linguistic intergroup bias* (LIB). Building on earlier work by Semin and Fiedler (1988) on the *linguistic category model* (LCM), Maass (1999) focused on the way people talk about groups in general and groups members' behaviors in particular. The work on the LCM examines the language that perceivers use to communicate about what they observe in their social environment and distinguishes four increasingly abstract categories of language, namely, descriptive action verbs, interpretative action verbs, state verbs, and adjectives. Research has shown that perceivers use the more abstract categories to convey the idea that the observed behavior reveals an inherent and permanent characteristic of the actor (Semin & Fiedler, 1988). In one illustrative study, Maass, Salvi, Arcuri, and Semin (1989) provided evidence that positive (vs. negative) behaviors performed by ingroup members were described in more abstract (vs. concrete) terms, whereas the reverse was true for behaviors performed by outgroup members. In line with earlier work on the so-called ultimate attribution error (Hewstone,

1990; Pettigrew, 1979), the LIB contributes to the maintenance of a positive view of the ingroup and a negative view of the outgroup because more abstract descriptions of behaviors imply that they are caused by enduring features of the actor. Thus, positive and negative behaviors are more revealing of ingroup and outgroup members, respectively. Wigboldus, Spears, and Semin (2005) extended this work, talking about the linguistic expectancy bias. These authors argue that it is not merely the valence of the behavior that prompts different linguistic descriptions, but rather observers' expectations. If the behavior corresponds to (vs. contradicts) what observers expect of the target group, then this behavior will be described in more abstract (vs. concrete) terms. Therefore, even though for Whites, athletic achievements of African Americans are positive behaviors performed by outgroup members, Whites tend to describe them in abstract terms because being good in sports is something that is expected of African Americans. As a whole, this line of research shows that language constitutes a powerful means, and by the same token a rich source of information (von Hippel, Sekaquaptewa, & Vargas, 1997), to convey more or less desirable views about ingroup and outgroup members (Sutton & Douglas, 2008; Wigboldus & Douglas, 2007).

Group members also have the general tendency to avoid members of other groups, and to approach members of the ingroup (Paladino & Castelli, 2008). Encounters with strangers may be more emotionally arousing in intergroup than intragroup contexts, as is suggested, for example, by the higher activation of the amygdala (a subcortical structure known to play a role in emotional learning and evaluation) in White male individuals presented with photographs of Black versus White individuals (Cunningham, Johnson, et al., 2004; Phelps, Cannistraci, & Cunningham, 2003; Phelps et al., 2001; see also Hart et al., 2000). This is also the argument advanced by the intergroup anxiety theory described earlier in this chapter (Stephan & Stephan, 1985). Indeed, the feeling of discomfort that people experience because they expect negative consequences from interactions with outgroup members prompts avoidance of outgroup members and, ironically, reduces the likelihood of having positive intergroup contact that could undermine these negative expectations.

The exact negative expectations that trigger avoidance behaviors in high-status group members may well slightly differ from those expectations that provoke the same reactions in low-status group members. As a matter of fact, high-status individuals are afraid to appear prejudiced (Vorauer, Main, & O'Connell, 1998), whereas low-status individuals are concerned that they might confirm negative stereotypes associated with their ingroup or be discriminated against (Branscombe, Schmitt, & Harvey, 1999). Interestingly,

Shelton and Richeson (2005) argued that the underlying motivation is the same; that is, people fear rejection by the other during intergroup encounters. Fear of rejection-based avoidance behaviors from both parts combined with pluralistic ignorance (the failure to recognize that the same behavior is to be attributed to the same causes) reinforce intergroup misunderstandings, conflict, and the tendency to further avoid outgroup contact.

Summary

A first consequence of group membership is for individuals to behave more competitively, and less cooperatively, than they do when placed in an interindividual situation. A second effect is that people conduct themselves differently toward their ingroup and an outgroup. Favoring the ingroup is group members' preferred line of action and hurting the outgroup is less common. Framed in political terms, the first is reminiscent of patriotism that cherishes the positive features of one's fellow group members, whereas the latter corresponds to a nationalistic stance in which the active derogation of foreigners and enemies of the state stands high on the agenda. Even if the first inclination may appear more benign, both have their drawbacks. Oftentimes, people prefer to avoid outgroup members altogether because of the negative expectations as to how the intergroup encounter may unfold and the assumed potential for unpleasant emotions associated with such situations. A key underlying theme, for members of dominant and dominated groups alike, is fear of rejection.

Actions of Dominant Groups

Bias shows up in a variety of ways. Although it would appear that blatant discrimination has become less common than in the past (Dovidio & Gaertner, 2000), this does not mean that biased treatment based on membership in a social group has disappeared entirely. Rather, discrimination is likely to take on more subtle forms, and several factors moderate the concrete expression of prejudice (Crandall & Eshleman, 2003). Bias may occur at the individual level (i.e., in concrete interactions between members of different groups), or at higher levels of organizations, institutions, or cultures.

Individual Discriminatory Behaviors

Hate crimes are the most extreme and dramatic type of discriminatory behaviors. They consist of criminal offenses against victims chosen solely or primarily on the basis of group membership (Boeckmann & Turpin-Petrosino, 2002; Green, Strolovitch, & Wong, 1998; see also Lickel, Miller, Stenstrom, Denson, & Schmader, 2006). Such behaviors are primarily motivated by beliefs that these criminal actions are exciting and fun, that the targets are unlikely to react, that the crime is justified (because it is a response to some earlier attack on the offender's group), or that it is simply expected and unlikely to be disapproved by the other members of one's group (McDevitt, Levin, & Bennett, 2002). Both archival studies relying on police reports (Strom, 2001) and survey data (Franklin, 2000) suggest that such offenses are primarily committed by young male individuals. As much as 10% of Franklin's (2000) community college sample indicated having assaulted a homosexual, and another 24% reported engaging in antigay or antilesbian verbal abuse, suggesting that a large number of malevolent acts take place even in social environments that are usually considered to be highly tolerant.

Less visible or evident discriminatory behaviors also contribute to unequal and harmful treatment of members of stigmatized groups. Often unintentional and unnoticed by prejudiced people, subtle discrimination ranges from negative to ambivalent or even to positive behaviors. Perhaps the most obviously negative version of subtle discrimination emerges when offenders have the undisputable feeling that the (discriminatory) behaviors are normal or routine. This situation is likely to materialize when social consensus is believed to be strong. In a study by Sechrist and Stangor (2001), highly prejudiced participants sat significantly farther away from a Black female student than their low-prejudice counterparts, but this distance was greater (smaller) when participants had been led to believe that a majority (minority) of students on campus shared their views (Sechrist & Milford, 2007). Clearly, because people strongly adhere to social prescription when evaluating discriminatory acts, some stigmatized groups are more likely to be the target of prejudiced attitudes and behaviors simply because the (assumed) social norms support such reactions (Crandall, Eshleman, & O'Brien, 2002). People who display discriminatory behaviors against outgroup members may even count on the support of their group members, at least at an implicit level (Castelli, Tomelleri, & Zogmaister, 2008).

At the opposite end of the spectrum, some subtle discriminatory behaviors come across as decidedly positive. These reactions are especially insidious because the targets themselves seldom recognize these behaviors as discriminatory or have a hard time making attributions of prejudice. A nice illustration of such positive behaviors is patronizing speech, whether it takes the form of baby talk (to people seen as cognitively weak) or controlling talk (to people seen as having a low status) (Ruscher, 2001). Benevolent sexism provides another demonstration that behaviors of dominant people can be widely judged as positive yet contribute to reinforcing social hierarchies (Glick & Fiske, 1996; Hebl, King, Glick, Singletary, & Kazama, 2007). Positive as they may appear, such behaviors cause targets to underachieve, potentially justifying later unequal treatment (Dardenne, Dumont, & Bollier, 2007).

For the most part, behaviors produced by members of dominant groups toward stigmatized targets end up sending an ambivalent message because a general tendency exists to avoid the interaction, because they are expressed in contexts where causes other than prejudice exist or could be invoked as explanations, or because they comprise a mix of negative and positive behaviors. It is possible to contrast two major patterns of behaviors on the part of dominant groups. On the one hand, people try to avoid intergroup interactions; on the other hand, when avoidance would seem problematic or simply impossible, dominant group members do their best to blur the influence of prejudice. The *avoidance* strategy is more likely encountered among aversive racists. Aversive racists want to think of themselves as nonprejudiced and supporting egalitarian values, but they harbor unconscious negative feelings and beliefs about Blacks (Dovidio & Gaertner, 2004). On top of concerns about how they are seen by members of the dominated group (Vorauer, 2006; Vorauer et al., 2000), the level of discomfort, anxiety, and even threat experienced in intergroup encounters (Blascovich, Mendes, Hunter, Lickel, & Kowai-Bell, 2001; Mendes, Blascovich, Lickel, & Hunter, 2002; Plant & Devine, 2003; Stephan & Stephan, 2000) is such that the general preference of bigots is to stay away from interactions or at least intimate or nonscripted contacts, a strategy that is equally conducive to ambivalence by inaction rather than by action (Towles-Schwen & Fazio, 2003).

The *camouflage* strategy often emerges when interaction seems inevitable. In those cases, the implicit negative experience toward stigmatized persons will be actualized in ways that tend to conceal the fact that prejudice is present, often in the eyes of both the perpetrator and the victim (Dovidio, Smith, Donnella, & Gaertner, 1997; Esses, Dietz, & Bhardwaj, 2006; Gaertner & Dovidio, 1977, 2000; Gaertner, Dovidio, & Johnson, 1982; Uhlmann & Cohen, 2005). Factors that allow the expression of prejudice include ideological and religious beliefs, values, and stereotypes, and various rationalization processes that obscure the presence of bigotry such as attribution of blame or the furnishing of acceptable behavioral accounts (Crandall & Eshleman, 2003). In many ambiguous situations, behavior will not be so much antiminority, but rather biased in favor of the dominant group (Hodson, Dovidio, & Gaertner, 2002). Ambiguity sometimes serves the purpose of avoidance. In a clever study illustrating the way people conceal discrimination when they are forced to take action, Snyder, Kleck, Strenta, and Mentzer (1979) asked their nondisabled participants to watch a movie playing in a room with a disabled individual or in a room with a nondisabled individual (both of them confederates). When told that the exact same movie was playing in the two rooms, participants chose to watch the movie slightly more often alongside the disabled individual. In contrast, when instructions mentioned that different movies were playing in the two rooms, providing an occasion to explain their avoidance of the stigmatized person in terms of their movie preference, participants chose to watch the movie with the other person. A similar strategy prevails among modern racists who, for instance, will oppose affirmative action because, in their eyes, it violates equal opportunity, not because they refuse to accept racial equality (Sears, Sidanius, & Bobo, 2000). In other words, modern racists combine their deep antipathy for Blacks with a genuine endorsement of egalitarian values by trying to act in ways that appear unprejudiced.

In general, the fact that people can rely on justifications that allow them to escape external or internal sanction facilitates the expression of prejudice (Crandall & Eshleman, 2003). In accordance with this idea, Monin and Miller (2001) found that when majority members' past behaviors have established their moral credentials as nonprejudiced people, they seem more willing to act in ways that could be seen as prejudiced. In contrast, the salience of earlier prejudicial behavior may decrease the ease with which people come to discriminate. For instance, Son Hing, Li, and Zanna (2002) capitalized on induced hypocrisy (Aronson, 1999) to create a situation that mirrors the logic of moral credentials. These authors first gave their participants a chance to advocate egalitarian values and then asked them to recall past episodes in which they had reacted negatively toward members of stigmatized groups. Aversive racists felt more guilty and uncomfortable than nonaversive racists. They also responded with a marked reduction in prejudicial behavior in a subsequent discrimination task.

In the absence of good reasons to discriminate, dominant people exercise scrupulous censorship over their discriminatory responses and try their best to suppress their derogatory beliefs (Monteith, Sherman, & Devine, 1998). Suppression may be practiced to such an extent among some low-prejudiced people (Devine, 1989; Lepore & Brown, 1997; Monteith, Spicer, & Tooman, 1998) or people with chronic egalitarian goals (Moskowitz et al., 1999) that it becomes efficient and even automatized. Still, for other people, attempts at suppression are not always successful (Bodenhausen & Macrae, 1998). This means that suppression may have paradoxical rebound effects and even increase prejudice (Gordijn, Hindriks, Koomen, Dijksterhuis, & van Knippenberg, 2004; Macrae, Bodenhausen, Milne, & Jetten, 1994).

A key preoccupation among majority members is thus the control and suppression of prejudice. To tap this motivation, researchers developed several individual difference measures. According to Plant and Devine (1998, 2001), the desire to respond without prejudice may come from two sources. When stemming from internal sources, prejudice is deemed wrong because it conflicts with a personal belief system. In contrast, prejudice may also be restricted as a result of social pressure. The role of such normative responses should not be downplayed because, in due time, individuals accommodate to social norms (Crandall et al., 2002). Provided the environment is tailored to minimize or even proscribe stigmatizing reactions, people will likely develop an internal motivation to control prejudice. The more an individual has come to internalize the egalitarian norm, the lower the expressed prejudice will be, even on implicit measures (Amodio, Harmon-Jones & Devine, 2003; Devine, Plant, Amodio, Harmon-Jones, & Vance, 2002). The added value of Plant and Devine's (2001) distinction resides in the fact that violations against internal motivation should result in feelings of guilt about one's conduct, whereas failure in the case of external motivation should bring about reactions of anger and threat regarding other people's reactions.

A somewhat different perspective, suggested by Dunton and Fazio (1997), combines internal and external motivation to control prejudice into a general concern with acting prejudiced. This concern finds its roots in a pro-egalitarian upbringing and positive experiences with stigmatized people. Dunton and Fazio also point to people's restraint to avoid disputes that stem from a prejudiced background and negative experiences with stigmatized members, which involves staying away from trouble and arguments with targets of the prejudice. They use Higgins's (1998) basic psychological distinction in regulatory focus between nurturance needs and ideals, on the one hand, and security needs and oughts, on the other hand, and postulate that the concern with acting prejudiced could, indeed, be reformulated in terms of a promotion focus, whereas the restraint to avoid dispute can best be reframed in terms of a prevention focus.

Finally, even though prejudiced people such as aversive racists would seem to be in control of their behavior and act in a nonprejudiced manner, a sizeable share of their responses to the situation are less controllable than they would want, allowing prejudice to "leak out." Dovidio and colleagues (Dovidio, Kawakami, & Gaertner, 2002; Dovidio, Kawakami, Johnson, Johnson, & Howard, 1997) found evidence for such dissociation, and thus a mix of cues disconfirming and confirming prejudice, when they asked their White participants to meet with Black confederates. Whereas participants' explicit prejudice was correlated with the friendliness of what they said (a controlled behavior), their implicit prejudice was linked to the friendliness of their

nonverbal actions (an automatic behavior). In general, situations in which behavioral control is more difficult, such as when norms remain unclear or when the measures are unobtrusive, may facilitate the materialization of prejudice. Recent research also confirms that the suppression of prejudice requires cognitive resources (Richeson & Shelton, 2003; Richeson & Trawalter, 2005), and factors that undermine people's mental energy allow prejudice to be expressed in behavior.

Organizational, Institutional, and Cultural Discriminatory Behaviors

Bias percolates throughout all layers of society. In particular, the way companies and institutions are organized may also result in unequal treatment even though it is difficult, if not impossible, to pinpoint the prejudice of a specific individual as the culprit. Illustrating the malicious nature of "established" discrimination, Topolski, Boyd-Bowman, and Ferguson (2003) had their participants blindly judge fruits that had been bought in low-, middle-, or upper-class neighborhoods. These authors found a significant relation between socioeconomic status (SES) and the taste and appearance of the fruits, suggesting that low SES people were likely to consume lower-quality food than people of higher SES. On a related note, Oldmeadow and Fiske's study (2007) found that people judged the occupants of cheap houses to be less competent than the occupants of expensive houses, an effect that was also exaggerated by SDO and beliefs in a just world. Findings such as these underscore the fact that members of stigmatized groups may be at a disadvantage in ways that go unacknowledged by most of the population.

Many groups continue to be overrepresented or underrepresented in various professions or at various hierarchical levels of the same profession. Beyond race and ethnicity, sex and age are two important categories that seem to play a role in the way societal forces channel people's fate. Recent years have witnessed increased consideration for discrimination based on additional characteristics such as disability, religion or belief, sexual orientation, among others. What is striking is that even small biases in practices, rules, and policies at each step of a person's path through life can accumulate and end up in dramatic inequalities in various societal spheres (Martell, Lane, & Emrich, 1996). Clearly, stereotypes and prejudice play a major role in raising, schooling, and orienting individuals, but also in hiring, promoting, and dismissing them in the workplace, and even in arresting, prosecuting, and sentencing them.

For instance, women comprise 59% of university graduates in the European Union (EU) but continue to be largely underrepresented in engineering and science or technology. As a result, only 29% of scientists and engineers in the EU are women. Figures from the workforce in 2002 in the United States (U.S. Equal Employment Opportunity Commission [EEOC], 2004) reveal that, taking into account the respective numbers of White men and Black women in the workforce, the former are almost four times more likely than the latter to occupy managerial jobs. In Europe, the pay gap between women and men observed in 2006 remains steady at 15% since 2003, narrowing only one percentage point since 2000 (Commission of the European Communities [COM 10], 2008). Even when strong measures are in place to minimize the impact of preconceptions, more subtle features may orient decisions in an unfair direction (Ko, Muller, Judd, & Stapel, 2008). Analyzing a random sample of records of Black and White inmates, Blair, Judd, and Chapleau (2004; Blair, Chapleau, & Judd, 2005; Eberhardt, Davies, Purdie-Vaughns, & Johnson, 2006) found that they had been given roughly equivalent sentencing given equivalent criminal history. Still, inmates with more (vs. less) Afrocentric features received harsher (vs. lighter) sentences, revealing that judges bias their decision by relying on facial features of the offender (see also Maddox, 2004; Pager, 2003; Pager & Quillian, 2005).

There is a growing realization that concrete and large-scale organizational and institutional steps must be taken to challenge the subtle intrusion of bias and discrimination in different spheres of life (Goldin & Rouse, 2000; see Dovidio & Gaertner, this volume). As a case in point, certain European countries have enforced parity in the lists of candidates during elections, permitting the proportion of women to increase significantly in city, regional, and national political bodies. As of September 2009, the average number of female members of national parliaments has now attained more than 35% in Belgium, Spain, and Denmark, and even more than 40% in the Netherlands, Finland, and Sweden (at the same time, the figure reached some 17% in the U.S.A.). In line with the perspective underlying social-psychological research since Lewin (1948), discrimination needs to be combated on a daily basis by capitalizing on both individual and structural factors.

Summary

Bias and partiality come in many guises, and members of dominant groups manifest a host of discriminatory behaviors that contribute to their advantaged status. Although blatant discriminatory acts continue to be perpetrated, the unequal and unfair treatment of members of stigmatized and dominated groups usually rests on more subtle behaviors. Such "hidden" unfairness generally comes about when people think that their behavior is normative or positive, at least in appearance. Members of privileged groups will lean toward discrimination when their behavior can be concealed behind a curtain of ambiguity or respectability,

or both. Even if most people are motivated to appear tolerant and unbiased, suppressing prejudiced reactions is resource demanding unless it is practiced to the point that it becomes integrated and automatized. As a result, members of dominant groups often send out signals of prejudice via aspects of their conduct that are more difficult to control. Beyond individual actions, discrimination is also constitutive of the explicit and implicit routines that govern people's everyday interactions, whether in the workplace or in public settings.

Reactions of Dominated Groups

People generally experience anxiety at the prospect of an intergroup interaction. According to the intergroup anxiety model presented earlier (Stephan & Stephan, 1985), this anxiety derives, in part, from the negative expectations people develop concerning the possible reactions of outgroup members in the intergroup situation (Shelton & Richeson, 2005; Vorauer, 2006). Quite simply, individuals who belong to disadvantaged groups fear the potential prejudice and discrimination that they might experience during intergroup interactions (Branscombe et al., 1999; Tropp, 2003). Because a confrontation with a negative identity associated with the self may end up damaging self-esteem, the reaction of members of dominated groups to the anticipation of intergroup interaction is generally one of avoidance. But intergroup interaction can simply not be avoided at all times and in all circumstances. Two types of reactions are worth examining. On the one hand, dominated and low-status group members develop reactions to the various forms of behaviors that dominant, high-status outgroups display or are expected to display toward them. On the other hand, members of disadvantaged groups also react to their low-status stigmatized position in society independently of the actions undertaken by outgroup members. The two subsections that follow examine both responses in turn while restricting the discussion to those reactions that maintain rather than challenge the status quo in society.

Reactions Toward Behaviors of Dominant Group Members

Given the large disparity in behaviors of members of dominant groups examined earlier, it is reasonable to assume that members of the dominated group may show an assortment of differentiated reactions to discriminatory behaviors depending on whether these behaviors are explicitly or more subtly derogatory. Starting off with the worst case, victims of hate crimes experience heightened levels of anxiety, distress, anger, distrust, and fear in comparison with victims of similar crimes that were not motivated by social discrimination. They also report more difficulties in coping with the effects of victimization and greater cognitive troubles such as intrusive thoughts, problems at work, and problems with concentration (Ehrlich, Larcom, & Purvis, 1995; McDevitt, Balboni, Garcia, & Gu, 2001). Research also shows that hate crimes impact not only the victims but also members of the victim's group (i.e., secondary victimization; McDevitt, et al., 2001).

Not all forms of prejudice are as blatant as hate crimes. More often than not, dominated group members actually face a problem of uncertainty concerning the behaviors displayed by members of a dominant group. This is especially the case for members of groups who suffer from visible rather than invisible stigma (e.g., in terms of race, sex, and so forth; Goffman, 1963; Jones et al., 1984). Indeed, empirical evidence confirms that targets of discrimination are especially sensitive to cues that indicate prejudice and are more likely than dominant group members to attribute ambiguously racist behaviors to the actor's prejudiced attitudes toward them. That is, they find it difficult to interpret a particular behavior and to assess the extent to which that behavior should be attributed to discrimination, or whether other situational or personal variables are at play. Crocker, Voelkl, Testa, and Major (1991) refer to this difficulty in terms of *attributional ambiguity*. Research in this domain investigates how stigmatized people (e.g., ethnic minorities, overweight women) react to positive or negative feedback given by outgroup members about their performance (Major & O'Brien, 2005). Apparently, members of stigmatized groups weigh both positive and negative feedback differently as a function of whether they attribute this information to prejudice against them. Indeed, stigmatized group members who suspect that the negative feedback they receive is based on factors other than their performance and ability tend to discount it (i.e., attribute it to prejudice). This discounting process has important self-protective implications for the psychological well-being of the targets of such discrimination. For instance, Crocker, and colleagues (1991) demonstrated that Blacks who could attribute feedback to prejudice were less depressed than those who could not make such attribution (Crocker & Major, 1989; Major & Crocker, 1993; see also Crocker, Major, & Steele, 1998). Similarly, when White and Black participants had to face an outgroup evaluator, social acceptance (i.e., positive feedback) produced cardiovascular reactivity consistent with challenge states and, indeed, better performance among White but not among Black people (Mendes, Major, McCoy, & Blascovich, 2008; see also Major, Kaiser, & McCoy, 2003). Conversely, stigmatized group members' propensity to discount positive feedback has undermining consequences for their self-esteem (Hoyt, Aguilar, Kaiser, Blascovich, & Lee, 2007). Despite the attractiveness of the discounting hypothesis, empirical support for its claims remains open to question, and the effects on well-being have been qualified by a series of specific factors (e.g., Crocker, Cornwell, & Major, 1993; McCoy & Major, 2003; Mendoza-Denton, Downey, Purdie, & Davis, 2002).

Calling into question the discounting hypothesis that Crocker and Major (1989) proposed, Branscombe, Schmitt, and colleagues (e.g., Branscombe et al., 1999) reasoned that, although attributions to discrimination might be self-protective when people face unstable instances of prejudice, widespread bias against one's social group will, in the long run, trigger negative consequences for the well-being of targets of such discrimination. According to these authors, attribution of failure to discrimination may be damaging for one's self-esteem for at least two reasons. First, the recognition of widespread discrimination is a constant reminder of one's inability to lead and control one's own life (Schmitt & Branscombe, 2002a). Second, attribution to discrimination may call into question unmistakable internal factors linked to one's social identity (Schmitt & Branscombe, 2002b). As a consequence, members of discriminated groups should tend to minimize rather than maximize the importance of discrimination in their lives. Branscombe, Schmitt, and Harvey (1999) developed the *rejection-identification model* to account for the fact that members of stigmatized groups do not seem to suffer from huge losses in self-esteem. They proposed that identification with one's social ingroup acts as a buffer between discrimination and self-esteem. That is, although perceiving discrimination negatively impacts self-esteem, discriminated people react against discrimination by increasing their feelings of identification with the ingroup, with beneficial consequences for their self-esteem (Ellemers, Wilke, & van Knippenberg, 1993). Support for the rejection-identification model is solid and emerges for very different social groups (e.g., African Americans: Branscombe et al., 1999; women: Redersdorff, Martinot, & Branscombe, 2004; the elderly: Garstka, Schmitt, Branscombe, & Hummert, 2004).

Encounters with discrimination do not necessarily translate into awareness of disadvantage. In fact, the literature on the personal-group discrimination discrepancy (Crosby, 1982; Taylor, Wright, & Porter, 1994) has shown that people usually perceive themselves to be less discriminated against than members of their ingroup. Similarly, discriminated people perceive the world to be more just for nondiscriminated people and for themselves than for members of their ingroup (Sutton, Douglas, Wilkin, Elder, Cole, & Stathi, 2008). Several explanations, both motivational (Crosby, Clayton, Alksnis, & Hemker, 1986; Kaiser & Miller, 2001; Taylor et al., 1994) and cognitive (Crosby et al., 1986; Fuegen & Biernat, 2000; Taylor et al., 1994) in tone, account for these findings. For instance, Dupont and Leyens (2003) suggested that individuals deny or minimize personal instances of discrimination to maintain positive illusions about themselves and a sense of control over events.

Because personal and group discrimination may differentially relate to self-esteem and group identification, Bourguignon, Seron, Yzerbyt, and Herman (2006) proposed refining the rejection-identification model, taking into account the difference between perceptions of personal and group discrimination. These authors replicated Branscombe and colleagues' model (1999) for personal discrimination, but they also found that group and personal discrimination showed opposite relations with self-esteem. The more participants experienced self-discrimination, the lower was their self-esteem. In sharp contrast, the more participants perceived their group to be discriminated against, the higher was their self-esteem. Bourguignon and colleagues proposed that perceiving group discrimination together with the perception that one occupies an acceptable (less discriminated) position would raise self-esteem through a positive contrast with other members of the ingroup (Mussweiler, 2003).

Patronizing behaviors (i.e., treating others in a condescending manner) constitute yet another form of discriminatory behavior that members of dominated groups have to face. In a series of studies, Vescio, Gervais, Snyder, and Hoover (2005) looked at the impact of patronizing behaviors of a powerful person on both dominant (i.e., male) and dominated (i.e., female) targets. In one experiment, patronizing was operationalized by having the powerful person praise the target while at the same time assigning the target to a devalued position. Results revealed that both male and female individuals experienced anger as a result of the unfair treatment, but only men's performance increased in a subsequent allegedly masculine task, whereas female performance did not differ from a control condition. Apparently, men considered subsequent performance as a way to fight against the injustice and to decrease their experienced anger. Presumably, female individuals had a different reaction because they did not perceive their performance in a masculine task as an action that could effectively alter the situation (Harmon-Jones, Sigelman, Bohlig, & Harmon-Jones, 2003).

Thus, complimenting a target is obviously not sufficient to counter the negative effects of simultaneous discrimination on subsequent performance. Perhaps complimenting, in the absence of explicit devaluation, could produce more favorable outcomes for dominated group members. Dardenne, Dumont, and Bollier (2007) tested the effects of hostile and benevolent sexism (Glick & Fiske, 1996, 2001c) on female performance. In four studies, they used a job selection context in which the position required typically female characteristics. Independently of whether expressions of benevolent sexism were accompanied by references to unsolicited help or the mention of a preferential selection of female over male individuals, benevolent sexism led to poorer performance by women than did expressions of hostile sexism. Dardenne and colleagues showed that, because benevolent sexism is less easily identified as sexism than hostile sexism (and is, therefore, more ambiguous), it leads to more mental intrusions and self-doubt, which, in turn, decrease capacity and worsen performance (Dumont, Sarlet, & Dardenne, 2008).

The detrimental effects of the expression of positive stereotypes on performance are also accompanied by the target's negative reactions to such compliments. Although majority group members often fail to recognize the inappropriateness of positive stereotypes (Czopp & Monteith, 2006; Devine & Elliot, 1995; Mae & Carlston, 2005) and consequently do not correct for their influence on social judgments (Lambert, Khan, Lickel, & Fricke, 1997), dominated group members often resent the expression of positive stereotypes and evaluate the commentator less positively than when no such comments are made (Czopp, 2008).

Reactions About Their Disadvantaged Position

Members of dominated groups face specific discriminating episodes or chronic discrimination, but they also have to cope with their real or alleged disadvantaged position in the social ladder. A first aspect has to do with the impact of negative stereotypical expectations. The concern here is not so much for the consequences of an interaction with any specific prejudiced person, but for what Steele (1997) called the "threat in the air"—that is, the unfavorable stereotypes that are widely available in society about one or another group. Members of minority groups are often keenly aware of their presumed limitations in competence-related domains. For instance, women are thought to be less apt at math (Shih, Pittinsky, & Ambady, 1999; Spencer, Steele, & Quinn, 1999) and the same holds for Latinos and particularly Latinas (Gonzales, Blanton, & Williams, 2002). Stereotypes also hold that African Americans perform worse than European Americans on standardized intelligence tests (Steele & Aronson, 1995), that older people suffer from memory deficits (Chasteen, Bhattacharyya, Horhota, Tam, & Hasher, 2005), that people with low incomes perform more poorly than people with high income on linguistic tasks (Croizet & Claire, 1998), and that psychology students are less competent than their science colleagues (Croizet, Després, Gauzins, Huguet, Leyens, & Méot, 2004). Even members of groups who typically enjoy advantaged social status may at times be confronted with a negative stereotype on a particular dimension. For example, men are believed to face limitations in emotional sensitivity (Koenig & Eagly, 2005; Leyens, Désert, Croizet, & Darcis, 2000), Whites are perceived as worse than Blacks in athletic ability (Stone, Lynch, Sjomeling, & Darley, 1999), and Whites are perceived as worse in math than Asians (Aronson, Lustina, Keough, Brown, & Steele, 1999). Notably, shortcomings in the social, as opposed to the competence, domain are more readily associated with members of the dominant group, whereas the reverse appears to be true for dominated group members. This particular combination is reminiscent of the work on the two fundamental dimensions of social judgment, warmth and competence (Fiske, Cuddy, Glick, & Xu, 2002), and more particularly on the compensation phenomenon that suggests that people often evaluate groups in a compensatory manner such that what one group gains in terms of competence, it loses in terms of sociability, and vice versa (Judd et al., 2005; Yzerbyt et al., 2005, 2008).

The consequences of negative social reputations have been the focus of intensive research since the late 1990s (Schmader, Johns, & Forbes, 2008; Shapiro & Neuberg, 2007; Steele, 1997; Steele & Aronson, 1995; Steele, Spencer, & Aronson, 2002). Whether the bad reputation of a group in a particular area is or is not justified, performance tests pose a serious threat for group members. Failure not only constitutes a humiliating personal experience, it also carries with it the embarrassment of having validated unflattering preconceptions about the group as a whole. Schmader and colleagues (2008) recently proposed that stereotype threat rests on the activation of three unit relations (Heider, 1958): a positive relation between the concept of a group (e.g., women) and the self-concept (i.e., implying that the group is perceived as an ingroup), a positive relation between the concept of a domain (e.g., math) and the self-concept, and a negative relation between the concept of a group and the concept of a domain (e.g., women are not good in math and this is a diagnostic math test). Any of these three relations can be more or less prevalent as a function of individual differences and contextual factors. For instance, group identification (Schmader, 2002) or solo status (Inzlicht & Ben-Zeev, 2000; Sekaquaptewa & Thompson, 2003) may influence the salience of an individual's group membership (Marx, Stapel, & Muller, 2005). Building on the flexibility of social identity, Shih, Pittinsky, and Ambady (1999) illustrated the role of contextual factors by priming Asian women either with their gender identity, leading to a decrement in performance, or with their racial identity, causing an increase in performance. Clearly, it is the imbalance of the links between the three concepts that constitutes a menace for self-integrity, that is, the sense that one is a valuable and coherent individual (Steele, 1988).

Targets of negative stereotypes are generally motivated to try to disconfirm the group's negative reputation and do their best to prevent failure, but provided the task is complex and demanding enough (Spencer et al., 1999), this creates a sort of extra burden that interferes with the successful completion of the task. As far as the mechanisms by which stereotype threat undermines performance, stereotype threat triggers a disheartening combination of motivational and cognitive phenomena, all contributing to a decrement in performance. According to Schmader and colleagues (2008), physiological stress responses (Blascovich, Spencer, Quinn, & Steele, 2001; Croizet et al., 2004; O'Brien & Crandall, 2003), together with the monitoring of the situational cues, likely generate a host of negative thoughts (Cadinu, Maass, Rosabianca, & Kiesner, 2005; Marx & Stapel, 2006; Stangor, Carr, & Kiang, 1998) and negative feelings (Keller & Dauenheimer, 2003) that people try to suppress, with limited success (Steele et al., 2002; but see McGlone & Aronson, 2007). As a set, these factors disrupt people's working memory, resulting in a performance deficit (Schmader & Johns, 2003).

Research suggests a number of remedies to counter the detrimental impact of negative stereotypes. In one way or another, they confirm the view of stereotype threat as involving three unit relations. For instance, one can stress the fairness of the test and its insensitivity to group differences. Sticking to the link between the domain and the group, it is also possible to emphasize other strengths of the ingroup (Marx, Stapel, & Muller, 2005). Alternatively, one can affirm a unique attribute of the self (Martens, Johns, Greenberg, & Schimel, 2006) or minimize the link between the self and the cultural stereotype of the ingroup, a strategy called "identity bifurcation" (Pronin, Steele, & Ross, 2004). These efforts are important because stereotype threat is not simply a laboratory curiosity. It has dramatic real-life consequences that can be reduced if appropriate action is taken (Cohen, Garcia, Apfel, & Master, 2006). Clearly, psychological disengagement, that is, the detachment of one's self-esteem from a specific domain, is not inevitable (Crocker et al., 1998; Major, Spencer, Schmader, Wolfe, & Crocker, 1998). Disengagement creates disidentification in that people devalue a particular domain and de-emphasize the importance of success in this area (Schmader, Major, & Gramzow, 2001). These processes bear strong resemblance to social creativity, a reaction to which we alluded earlier and which is frequently observed among members of low-status groups.

As it happens, responses of minority group members to their disadvantaged position highly depend on their level of identification, as well as their perception of the intergroup structure. According to SIT (Tajfel & Turner, 1979), to the extent that the structure is perceived as illegitimate and unstable, disadvantaged group members come to form alternatives to the existing intergroup structure and are willing to engage in collective action aimed at social change (see Dovidio & Gaertner, this volume). However, as stressed by Taylor and colleagues (Taylor & McKirnan, 1984; Wright, Taylor, & Moghaddam, 1990), individual upward mobility is usually the default. Even a small number of tokens that are allowed to gain access to the advantaged group may undermine collective action (Wright et al., 1990). Examining the pursuit of individual mobility strategies, Ellemers, Spears, and Doosje (1997) found that people who primarily perceive themselves as individuals instead of group members (i.e., low identifiers) try to minimize their association with their group and to gain access to the more advantaged outgroup.

People are often reluctant to acknowledge group-based discrimination (Schmitt & Branscombe, 2002a) and do not feel good when reminded that their membership in a particular group makes it more difficult for them to achieve favorable individual products (Branscombe, 1998). In other words, people do not like to think that their outcomes may be shaped by their group membership instead of reflecting their individual worth (Major et al., 2002; Major & Schmader, 2001). In contrast, they want to believe that they possess sufficient control to overcome difficulties and to improve their social standing through merit and adequate performance (Bobo & Hutchings, 1996; Kluegal & Smith, 1986). Beliefs in meritocracy tend to increase perceived legitimacy of the system as a whole and to reinforce the status quo between social groups (Ellemers, 1993, 2001; Wright, 2001).

Given the importance of meritocracy beliefs, it is most interesting to consider the reactions of minority members who managed to climb the social ladder (Ellemers & Barreto, 2009; Ellemers, van den Heuvel, de Gilder, Maass, & Bonvini, 2004). Usually, not all individuals of a disadvantaged group necessarily suffer from inequality and a limited number of token minority members have gained access to advantaged positions. The question then is how these upwardly mobile individuals perceived themselves as representative of their disadvantaged ingroup. In particular, do successful individuals want to help change the negative stereotypes usually associated with their ingroup? Do they facilitate social change and the advancement of other ingroup members? Research suggests that the answers to these questions might well be negative. As a matter of fact, to achieve success and individual mobility, members of disadvantaged groups must emphasize the extent to which they differ from, rather than resemble, members of their own group. This makes it unlikely, first, for their ability to achieve success to be generalized to other members of their ingroup and, second, for they themselves to identify with other members of their disadvantaged group. Research by Wright and colleagues (Wright, 2001; Wright & Taylor,

1999) supports the idea that successful token members of disadvantaged groups tend to quickly shift their identity from the disadvantaged to the advantaged group and, as a consequence, are reluctant to support actions that would challenge the unjustified status quo. They thus legitimize rather than oppose existing intergroup status differences. Similarly, empirical evidence supporting the same claim is advanced by Ellemers and colleagues' work on sex differences (Ellemers, 1993, 2001; Ellemers & Barreto, 2009; Ellemers, van den Heuvel, et al., 2004). These authors have shown that successful professional women perceive themselves as exceptional individuals, describe themselves in more masculine terms than their male colleagues, and portray other women in a sex-stereotypical fashion. This tendency for successful women to distance themselves from other women indirectly contributes to the persistence of sex discrimination in Western societies.

Summary

Reactions to discriminatory behaviors depend on the form of the discrimination. The more overt the discrimination, the more members of dominated groups will experience anxiety, distrust, fear, anger, and the like. However, discrimination behaviors are rarely blatant, which means that members of stigmatized groups face a problem of attributional ambiguity. If the interpretation is in terms of discrimination, negative consequences ensue, mostly on the target's self-esteem and well-being. Even seemingly positive behaviors can lead to ironic negative consequences for the performance of these individuals. Members of subordinate groups not only react to specific acts but more generally to their disadvantaged position in society. Their knowledge of a negative stereotype attached to their group produces a threat, and motivates them to try and disconfirm the expectation. Ironically, this increased motivation produces a decrement in performance and leads to psychological disengagement and disidentification with the domain. Whether stigmatized group members opt for individual or collective strategies to overcome their disadvantage depends on their identification and their perception of the structural constraints in society. In addition, those individuals who managed to climb up the social ladder may well reinforce rather than modify the status quo.

Intergroup Interactions

To truly get a sense of what intergroup relations signify, one needs to study, investigate, and scrutinize real interactions between members of different social groups (Demoulin et al., 2009). Why is the study of intergroup interactions so crucial for the understanding of intergroup processes? The first obvious answer is that actions do not occur in a vacuum.

Individuals are influenced by a series of situational factors that shape the course of the interaction. The topic of discussion between the interactants (Saguy, Pratto, Dovidio, & Nadler, 2009; Trawalter & Richeson, 2008) and the evaluative potential of the situation (e.g., public vs. private) are variables likely to greatly influence the nature of intergroup interactions. Pearson and colleagues' study (2008) revealed, for instance, that external temporal disruptions in the discussion between interacting partners increased (vs. reduced) reports of anxiety in intergroup (vs. intragroup) dyads.

Second, aside from these contextual factors, antecedents of intergroup interactions also play a role in determining the shape of intergroup processes. It is commonly accepted that people hold more negative expectations regarding intergroup than intragroup interactions (Stephan & Stephan, 1985), and that these intergroup negative expectations are not always accurate. That is, intergroup interactions are usually more positive than people expect them to be. Mallett, Wilson, and Gilbert (2008) argued that this intergroup forecasting error is, in part, due to people's tendencies to focus on their dissimilarities (rather than similarities) with outgroup members. In one illustrative experiment, two White participants were assigned to the same Black interaction partner. One of the White participants (the forecaster) was removed from the room and asked to imagine what it would be like to talk with the Black participant. Measures of partner liking and perceived similarity were recorded. The other White person (the experiencer) entered into an interaction with the Black partner before answering the same questionnaire about the positivity of the interaction and perceived similarity with the partner. Results revealed that forecasters imagined the interaction with the Black partner to be less positive than the actual experience of experiencers. In addition, forecasters evaluated themselves as less similar to the Black partner than experiencers did, and these similarity evaluations mediated the relation between the type of person (forecaster vs. experiencer) and the partner evaluations. In summary, forecasters erred in believing that they would not be similar to the Black partner, and it is precisely this perceived dissimilarity that drove them to assume that the intergroup interaction would turn out to be negative (Wilson & Gilbert, 2008).

Other elements that influence one's own as well as the other person's behavior are concerned with expectancies about the partner's beliefs, attitudes, and behaviors. For example, Johnson and Lecci (2003) found that targets of discrimination generally hold expectations that their interactions with majority group members will include prejudice. Importantly, the extent to which a Black person expected a White interaction partner to be prejudiced (whether because of chronic or induced prejudice expectations) influenced

the experience they had in an interethnic interaction, with more negative experiences in prejudice expectation contexts (Shelton, Richeson, & Salvatore, 2005). The large literature on the self-fulfilling prophecy also reveals the powerful impact of a person's expectancies on behavioral confirmation (Klein & Snyder, 2003). Negative expectancies also lead to perceptual bias during the interaction. In Kleck and Strenta's (1980) classic experiment, individuals were led to believe that they were physically deviant (i.e., in the form of a facial disfigurement) in the eyes of an interactant. Although the interactant, in fact, never perceived the negative attribute, participants perceived strong negative reactivity to the facial stigma in the behavior of the interactant. Kleck and Strenta suggest that a perceptual bias was responsible for these findings, in that only the persons who thought that one member of the dyad had a facial disfigurement were prone to interpret eye gaze behavior from the part of the interactant as reaction to the supposed physical defect. Similarly, Inzlicht, Kaiser, and Major (2008) found that prejudice expectations affected the interpretation of emotional display of male individuals by female participants. Obviously, perceptual biases, as well as behavioral and cognitive biases that are at the heart of intergroup interactions (see also, Mendes, Blascovich, Hunter, Lickel, & Jost, 2002), will cause potentially dramatic misunderstandings and miscomprehensions between members of different groups. We return to the intergroup misunderstanding issue later in this chapter.

A third reason for studying intergroup processes in real interactions relates to the consequences of such intergroup interactions. By concentrating research efforts on one side only, researchers might not account for the full spectrum of outcomes that each specific behavior entails. In short, it is crucial to examine intergroup encounters in their entire complexity to grasp the potential causes for misunderstanding (Demoulin, Leyens, & Dovidio, 2009).

On several occasions, this chapter called attention to the fact that intergroup interactions are emotionally arousing for members of both minority and majority groups because evaluative pressures in these contexts are typically greater than in interpersonal (intragroup) interactions (Crandall & Eshleman, 2003; Richeson & Shelton, 2007; Stephan & Stephan, 1985; Vorauer & Kumhyr, 2001). The stress provoked by intergroup contact has a number of consequences for individuals. For instance, Richeson and colleagues (2005) found that intergroup (vs. intragroup) encounters between Whites and Blacks undermined subsequent executive control on a race-irrelevant Stroop color-naming task, confirming that interracial interactions can be cognitively costly. This suggests that, to cope with stressful situations and successfully negotiate intergroup interactions, individuals of all groups usually rely on self-regulation strategies.

As for the members of majority and dominant groups, self-regulation strategies often turn around prejudice reduction and vigilance for or suppression of discriminatory behaviors. Building on Higgins's (1998) regulatory focus theory, Trawalter and Richeson (2006) proposed that the goal of not appearing prejudiced could be pursued with either a prevention or a promotion focus. Prevention focus was manipulated by encouraging individuals to "avoid prejudice" during the interracial interaction, whereas promotion focus was encouraged by motivating individuals to achieve a "positive intercultural exchange." Prevention-focused individuals were found to perform worse on the subsequent Stroop task than promotion-focused individuals. In addition, prevention led to similar levels of cognitive depletion than those found among control individuals. These results are consistent with findings reported by Leyens, Demoulin, Désert, Vaes, and Philippot (2002), who found that when participants are instructed to be color-blind (i.e., not to make reference to intergroup differences), they were more anxious and less capable of expressing emotions to an outgroup target than when instructed to act in a color-conscious fashion (i.e., to act as a function of intergroup differences). These findings also relate to the work on color blindness and multiculturalism that shows that, overall, multiculturalism generates less explicit and implicit racial bias than color blindness (Richeson & Nussbaum, 2004; Wolsko, Park, Judd, & Wittenbrink, 2000).

Because members of dominant or dominated groups do not face the exact same types of threats in intergroup situations, the strategies they use to regulate their behaviors may differ. As suggested earlier, White majority group members are particularly concerned with appearing prejudiced in the interaction, and deploy strategies of vigilance, suppression, and effortful self-presentation to avoid appearing to behave in prejudiced ways (Richeson & Trawalter, 2008; Shelton, Richeson, Salvatore, & Trawalter, 2005). In contrast, Black minority group members who especially fear being the target of prejudice self-regulate by engaging in compensatory strategies in the sense that they display enhanced engagement and self-disclosure in the interaction as compared with racial minorities who do not expect to be prejudiced against (Shelton, Richeson, & Salvatore, 2005).

A unilateral perspective on these results would then conclude for a negative effect of intergroup interactions in the case of White majorities with high interracial concerns and an opposite positive effect in the case of Black minorities. But if one looks somewhat deeper and simultaneously investigates interpersonal in addition to intrapersonal outcomes of self-regulatory processes, a different picture emerges. For instance, Shelton, Richeson, Salvatore, and Trawalter (2005) have shown that the efforts displayed by high-prejudice Whites to regulate their behaviors do not go unrecognized by their Black interaction partners who actually reward those behaviors by forming more favorable impressions of them compared with low-bias individuals (see Dovidio et al., 2002). Similarly, compensatory strategies utilized by ethnic minority group members to avoid being discriminated against, although positive at first sight, are accompanied by negative affective outcomes for them (Shelton, Richeson, & Salvatore, 2005).

The divergent impact of interracial contact on intrapersonal and interpersonal outcomes has been modeled by Richeson and Shelton (2007), who proposed that individual differences (e.g., racial attitudes, previous contact), as well as situational factors (e.g., goals, topic of discussion), moderate the activation of interracial affective reactions (e.g., intergroup anxiety) and concerns (e.g., appearing prejudiced, confirming stereotypes). Once activated, affective reactions and interracial concerns promote the use of self-regulatory strategies (e.g., vigilance, suppression, compensatory behaviors) that result in a host of both positive (e.g., partner liking) and negative (e.g., cognitive depletion, negative affect) intrapersonal and interpersonal outcomes. Although it still requires empirical validation, the model is useful in that it constitutes a roadmap for further investigation in the domain of intergroup interactions. However, it remains unclear whether what the model proposes for interracial interactions could be usefully transposed onto other types of intergroup interactions.

Summary

One cannot get a complete sense of intergroup relations simply by juxtaposing findings obtained from the behaviors of the dominated and dominant group members taken in isolation. This is because interactions are influenced by several additional factors, some having to do with features of the interaction itself, such as the goals underlying the interaction. Other important determinants concern the expectations that people bring with them to the interaction. More often than not, people rely on negative and caricatured views of their interaction partner. This may limit the opportunity for disconfirmation because people are reluctant to even enter the interaction. And when encounters take place, they have consequences that should be considered more closely. Oftentimes, people experience a series of misunderstandings.

CHALLENGES AND PROMISES

> Two trains passing in the night . . .
> —Jones, Engelman, Turner, & Campbell (2009, p. 131)

Intergroup relations research is not conducted the same way it used to in the 1980s. As a matter of fact, the field has recently gone through a series of major modifications. This last section first reviews the various domains in which the field has made significant progress. These domains concern aspects of methods and techniques, issues of theory and conceptualization, as well as shifts in focus of interest. This section then concentrates on a series of future challenges that need to be addressed by our discipline.

As was evidenced in the introductory example about the 2008 U.S. presidential election and is now largely acknowledged in the field, the manner in which group members envisage their relations with members of other groups and the way intergroup interactions unfold have changed dramatically over the last century. In so-called egalitarian societies, overt and blatant discriminations of stigmatized social groups and minorities are no longer deemed acceptable. Rather, people are encouraged to treat all individuals in a fair manner and independently of the groups to which these individuals belong. This rather optimistic change in how one is supposed to go about intergroup relations is, however, tempered by two important considerations. First, antidiscrimination norms appear to apply more to some social targets than to others. That is, historical and cultural variables combine to determine which types of outgroups may benefit from egalitarian concerns and which outgroups will continue to suffer from continued bigotry and intolerance. Second, current theoretical propositions suggest that racism, sexism, and other "isms" have not, in fact, been suppressed but rather have changed in their form of expression by becoming less visible or less attributable to negative attitudes toward outgroup members. This evolution has given rise to the first major change in intergroup relation research that characterizes the late 1990s, that is, a profound modification in the research tools. Scholars now increasingly rely on sophisticated techniques that allow, for instance, for the measurement of reaction times or neural activity. As such, this emergence of new technologies has permitted researchers to investigate and test ideas and hypotheses that were simply unthinkable before.

Second, and as suggested throughout this chapter, recent theories of intergroup relations more systematically and more strictly rely on a tripartite view of human attitudes. Early on, researchers in social psychology were turning their attention to one of the three components at the expense of the other two. Even more problematic, they sometimes even failed to distinguish appraisals from feelings and feelings from behaviors, be it in their theoretical argument or in their empirical work. More recent theories of intergroup relations have revived the traditional tripartite perspective and now attempt to deal with more than one component at a time. That is, scholars try to include all three components of attitudes in their models, as well as in their experiments.

The third change that deserves to be stressed concerns researchers' focus of interest with respect to each of the three components just mentioned. After some 20 years of research on the cognitive component of attitudes, the beginning of the 21st century has witnessed growing interest in the power of emotions for the prediction of intergroup behaviors. In the previous edition of the *Handbook,* Brewer and Brown (1998) devoted a little less than three pages to what they called the "*emotional* consequences of classifying others as 'outgroups' (emphasis in original)." Emotions did pop up in a number of places in the chapter other than in the section on outgroup hostility and prejudice, most notably when talking about the importance of anxiety in the reduction of prejudice, but it is fair to say that the role afforded to feelings remained rather modest. Similarly, in Fiske's (1998) chapter on stereotypes, prejudice, and discrimination, three pages were explicitly dedicated to prejudice even though, again, a short discussion of early theories of prejudice included at the outset of the chapter should be added to this number. In contrast, a consideration for the role of feelings in the unfolding of relations between groups and group members does come across as a hallmark of the research conducted during since the late 1990s.

Another change in focus has to do with the specific vantage point that is adopted in research. For long, intergroup relations could be equated with the social psychology of the members of dominant groups. Researchers then enlarged the picture and took into consideration the social psychology of the members of subordinate groups. More recent work has begun to combine these two "partial" perspectives and now pays more attention to the dynamic processes that take place during intergroup contact (e.g., Richeson & Shelton, 2007).

A series of challenges also await future research. First, in keeping with what has just been said, it is important to pay more attention to reciprocal influence of both parties of the interaction. That is, members of subordinate and dominant groups do not appraise, feel, and act in a vacuum. Along the same lines, more efforts should be devoted to temporal aspects, that is, the way intergroup interactions unfold over time. This increased attention paid to the dynamics of intergroup interactions should certainly, in the decade to come, prove most useful in revealing new challenges for the study of intergroup relations. One fascinating item on researchers' agenda will be to understand disagreements and misunderstandings that emerge from a confrontation of groups with different viewpoints. As a matter of fact, people who occupy different positions in society are not identical. Members of dominant and dominated groups often live in very different psychological worlds because of their divergent cultural and historical backgrounds, their different subjective experiences of the immediate social setting, as well as the specific goals they pursue and their unique coping strategies (Demoulin et al., 2009).

Second, there is little doubt that researchers in the domain of intergroup relations will be forced to extend their definition and conception of intergroup relations. With the advent of new technologies that allow people from all over the world to converse with one another on a daily basis and with the expansion of person mobility programs, intergroup interactions will no longer be restricted to forced physical encounters between the parties. That is, social psychology will have to explore the impact and antecedents of intergroup encounters that occur on a voluntary basis, and that encompass the sincere willingness to explore and appreciate intergroup and intercultural differences.

Finally, at the opposite end of the spectrum, more attention should be devoted to those intergroup encounters that involve intense levels of intergroup aggression and large-scale violent behaviors such as wars, genocides, and the like (Lickel, Miller, Stenstrom, Denson, & Schmader, 2006). What brings about extreme manifestations of intergroup hatred (Staub, 1989, 2006) and how to recover from such dramatic episodes as ethnic cleansing and attempts at physical eradication of entire groups are topics that attract the attention of a growing number of scholars (Brown & Cehajic, 2008; Gibson, 2004; Kanyangara et al., 2007). This kind of research is not only likely to enrich existing knowledge on intergroup contact (Dovidio & Gaertner, this volume), but it also holds the potential to suggest fascinating new questions (Nadler, Malloy, & Fisher, 2008).

The goal of this chapter was to present contemporary knowledge in intergroup relations research. The amount of research accumulated since the last edition of the *Handbook* is nothing short of enormous, demonstrating if it were needed the role and importance of intergroup relations in people's lives. This chapter starts by reviewing the literature investigating how individuals connect with groups. The second section examines the way people appraise groups, as well as the intergroup situation. The third section details the emotional reaction people experience as a function of their group membership and the various feelings that arise in intergroup situations. Finally, the fourth section examines the various behaviors that people engage in and by which they, willingly or not, maintain the existing intergroup situation. Clearly, the new challenges that present themselves for the field will no doubt allow social psychologists to conduct equally prolific research in the next decade. Growing attention for the cultural dimensions of intergroup relations, as well as their neuropsychological foundations, will attract new generations of researchers, delivering new dividends

in terms of knowledge. This promises to be a wonderful scientific journey.

REFERENCES

Abele, A. E., Cuddy, A. J. C., Judd, C. M., & Yzerbyt, V. Y. (2008). Fundamental dimensions of social judgment: A view from different perspectives. *European Journal of Social Psychology, 38*, 1063–1065.

Aberson, C. L., Healy, M., & Romero, V. (2000). Ingroup bias and self-esteem: A meta-analysis. *Personality and Social Psychology Review, 4*, 157–173.

Abrams, D., Marques, J. M., Bown, N., & Henson, M. (2000). Pronorm and anti-norm deviance within and between groups. *Journal of Personality and Social Psychology, 78*, 906–912.

Adorno, T. W., Frenkel-Brunswick, E., Levinson, D. J., & Sanford, R. N. (1950). *The authoritarian personality*. New York: Harper & Row.

Alexander, M. G., Brewer, M. B., & Herrmann, R. (1999). Images and affect: A functional analysis of out-group stereotypes. *Journal of Personality and Social Psychology, 77*, 78–93.

Alexander, M. G., Brewer, M. B., & Livingston, R. W. (2005). Putting stereotype content in context: Image theory and interethnic stereotypes. *Personality and Social Psychology Bulletin, 31*, 781–794.

Alexander, M. G., Levin, S., & Henry, P. J. (2005). Image theory, social identity, and social dominance: Structural characteristics and individual motives underlying international images. *Political Psychology, 26*, 27–45.

Allport, G. W. (1954). *The nature of prejudice*. Cambridge, MA: Addison-Wesley.

Altemeyer, B. (1981). *Right-wing authoritarianism*. Winnipeg, Manitoba, Canada: University of Manitoba Press.

Altemeyer, B. (1988). *Enemies of freedom: Understanding right-wing authoritarianism*. San Francisco: Jossey-Bass.

Altemeyer, B. (1996). *The authoritarian specter*. Cambridge, MA: Harvard University Press.

Altemeyer, B. (1998). The other "authoritarian personality." *Advances in Experimental Social Psychology, 30*, 47–92.

Altemeyer, B., & Hunsberger, B. (1992). Authoritarianism, religious fundamentalism, and prejudice. *International Journal for the Psychology of Religion, 2*, 113–133.

Amiot, C. E., & Bourhis, R. Y. (2005). Discrimination and the positive-negative asymmetry effect between dominant and subordinate groups. *British Journal of Social Psychology, 44*, 289–308.

Amodio, D. M., & Devine, P. G. (2006). Stereotyping and evaluation in implicit race bias: Evidence for independent constructs and unique effects on behavior. *Journal of Personality and Social Psychology, 91*, 652–661.

Amodio, D. M., Harmon-Jones, E., & Devine, P. G. (2003). Individual difference in the activation and control of affective race boas as assessed by startle eye blink response and self-report. *Journal of Personality and Social Psychology, 84*, 738–753.

Arnold, M. B. (1960). *Emotion and personality*. New York: Columbia University Press.

Aronson, E. (1999). Dissonance, hypocrisy, and the self-concept. In E. Harmon-Jones & J. Mills (Eds.), *Cognitive dissonance: Progress on a pivotal theory in social psychology* (pp. 103–206). Washington, DC: American Psychological Association.

Aronson, J., Lustina, M., Keough, K., Brown, J. L., & Steele, C. M. (1999). When white men can't do math: necessary and sufficient factors in stereotype threat. *Journal of Experimental Social Psychology, 35*, 29–46.

Bakan, D. (1966). *The duality of human existence: An essay on psychology and religion*. Chicago: Rand McNally.

Bastian, B., & Haslam, N. (2006). Psychological essentialism and stereotype endorsement. *Journal of Experimental Social Psychology, 42*, 228–235.

Batson, C. D., Chang, J., Orr, R., & Rowland, J. (2002). Empathy, attitudes, and action: Can feeling for a member of a stigmatized group motivate one to help the group? *Personality and Social Psychology Bulletin, 28*, 1656–1666.

Batson, C. D., Early, S., & Salvarani, G. (1997). Perspective-taking: Imagining how another feels versus imagining how you would feel. *Personality and Social Psychology Bulletin, 23*, 751–758.

Batson, C. D., Eklund, J. H., Chermok, V. L., Hoyt, J. L., & Ortiz, B. G. (2007). An additional antecedent of empathic concern: Valuing the welfare of the person in need. *Journal of Personality and Social Psychology, 93*, 65–74.

Batson, C. D., Floyd, R. B., Meyer, J. M., & Winner, A. L. (1999). "And who is my neighbor?": Intrinsic religion as a source of universal compassion. *Journal for the Scientific Study of Religion, 38*, 445–457.

Batson, C. D., Schoenrade, P., & Ventis, W. L. (1993). *Religion and the individual: A social-psychological perspective*. New York: Oxford University Press.

Baumeister, R. F. (1998). The self. In D. T. Gilbert, S. T. Fiske, & G. Lindzey (Eds.), *The handbook of social psychology* (Vol. 1, pp. 680–740). New York: McGraw-Hill.

Baumeister, R. F., & Leary, M. R. (1995). The need to belong: Desire for interpersonal attachments as fundamental human motivation. *Psychological Bulletin, 117*, 497–529.

Bettencourt, B. A., Dorr, N., Charlton, K., & Hume, D. L. (2001). Status differences and ingroup bias: A meta-analytic examination of the effects of status stability, status legitimacy, and group permeability. *Psychological Bulletin, 127*, 520–542.

Bianchi, M., Mummendey, A., Steffens, M., & Yzerbyt, V. (2008). *What do you mean by European? Evidence for spontaneous ingroup projection*. Manuscript submitted for publication.

Biernat, M., Vescio, T. K., & Theno, S. A. (1996). Violating American values: A "value congruence" approach to understanding outgroup attitudes. *Journal of Experimental Social Psychology, 32*, 387–410.

Bizman, A., Yinon, Y., & Krotman, S. (2001). Group-based emotional distress: An extension of self-discrepancy theory. *Personality and Social Psychology Bulletin, 27*, 1291–1300.

Blair, I. V. (2001). Implicit stereotypes and prejudice. In G. B. Moskowitz (Ed.), *Cognitive social psychology: The Princeton Symposium on the Legacy and Future of Social Cognition* (pp. 359–374). Mahwah, NJ: Erlbaum.

Blair, I. V. (2002). The malleability of automatic stereotypes and prejudice. *Personality and Social Psychology Review, 6*, 242–261.

Blair, I. V., Chapleau, K. M., & Judd, C. M. (2005). The use of afrocentric features as cues for judgment in the presence of diagnostic information. *European Journal of Social Psychology, 35*, 59–68.

Blair, I. V., Judd, C. M., & Chapleau, K. M. (2004). The influence of afrocentric features in criminal sentencing. *Psychological Science, 15*, 674–679.

Blair, I. V., Judd, C. M., Sadler, M. S., & Jenkins, C. (2002). The role of Afrocentric features in person perception: Judging by features and categories. *Journal of Personality and Social Psychology, 83*, 5–25.

Blanz, M., Mummendey, A., & Otten, S. (1995). Positive-negative asymmetry in social discrimination: The impact of stimulus-valence, size, and status-differentials in intergroup evaluations. *British Journal of Social Psychology, 34*, 409–419.

Blascovich, J., Mendes, W. B., Hunter, S. B., Lickel, B., & Kowai-Bell, N. (2001). Perceiver threat in social interactions with stigmatized individuals. *Journal of Personality and Social Psychology, 80*, 253–267.

Blascovich, J., Spencer, S. J., Quinn, D. M., & Steele, C. M. (2001). African Americans and high blood pressure: The role of stereotype threat. *Psychological Science, 12*, 225–229.

Bobo, L. (1983). Whites' opposition to busing: Symbolic racism or realistic group conflict. *Journal of Personality and Social Psychology, 45*, 1196–1210.

Bobo, L., & Hutchings, V. L. (1996). Perceptions of racial group competition: Extending Blumer's theory of group position to a multiracial social context. *American Sociological Review, 61*, 951–972.

Boccato, G., Cortes, B., Demoulin, S., & Leyens, J.-Ph. (2007). The automaticity of infrahumanization. *European Journal of Social Psychology, 37*, 987–999.

Bodenhausen, G. V. (1990). Stereotypes as judgmental heuristics: Evidence of circadian variations in discrimination. *Psychological Science, 1*, 319–322.

Bodenhausen, G. V., & Macrae, C. N. (1998). Stereotype activation and inhibition. In R. S. Wyer (Ed.), *Stereotype activation and inhibition: Advances in social cognition* (Vol. 11, pp. 1–52). Mahwah, NJ: Erlbaum.

Bodenhausen, G. V., Mussweiler, T., Gabriel, S., & Moreno, K. N. (2001). Affective influences on stereotyping and intergroup relations. In J. P. Forgas (Ed.), *Handbook of affect and social cognition* (pp. 319–343). Mahwah, NJ: Erlbaum.

Boeckmann, R. J., & Turpin-Petrosino, C. (2002). Understanding the harm of hate crime. *Journal of Social Issues, 58*, 207–225.

Bogardus, E. S. (1925). Measuring social distances. *Journal of Applied Sociology, 9*, 299–308.

Bourguignon, D., Seron, E., Yzerbyt, V. Y., & Herman, G. (2006). Perceived group and personal discrimination: Differential effects on self-esteem. *European Journal of Social Psychology, 36*, 1–24.

Bourhis, R. Y., Turner, J. C., & Gagnon, A. (1997). Interdependence, social identity and discrimination. In R. Spears, P. J. Oakes, N. Ellemers, & S. A. Haslam (Eds.), *The social psychology of stereotyping and group life* (pp. 273–295). Oxford: Blackwell.

Branscombe, N. R. (1998). Thinking about one's gender group's privileges or disadvantages: Consequences for well-being in women and men. *British Journal of Social Psychology, 37*, 167–184.

Branscombe, N. R., & Miron, A. M. (2004). Interpreting the ingroup's negative actions toward another group: Emotional reactions to appraised harm. In L. Z. Tiedens & C. W. Leach (Eds.), *The social life of emotions* (pp. 314–335). New York: Cambridge University Press.

Branscombe, N. R., Schmitt, M. T., & Harvey, R. D. (1999). Perceiving pervasive discrimination among African Americans: Implications for group identification and well-being. *Journal of Personality and Social Psychology, 77*, 135–149.

Branscombe, N. R., Spears, R., Ellemers, N., & Doosje, B. (2002). Intragroup and intergroup evaluation effects on group behaviour. *Personality and Social Psychology Bulletin, 28*, 744–753.

Brescoll, V., & LaFrance, M. (2004). The correlates and consequences of newspaper reports of research on sex differences. *Psychological Science, 15*, 515–520.

Brewer, M. B. (1979). Ingroup bias in the minimal intergroup situation: A cognitive-motivational analysis. *Psychological Bulletin, 86*, 307–324.

Brewer, M. B. (1991). The social self: On being the same and different at the same time. *Personality and Social Psychology Bulletin, 17*, 475–482.

Brewer, M. B. (1993). The role of distinctiveness in social identity and group behaviour. In M. A. Hogg & D. Abrams (Eds.), *Group motivation: Social psychological perspectives* (pp. 1–16). New York: Harverster Wheatsheaf.

Brewer, M. B. (1999). The psychology of prejudice: Ingroup love or outgroup hate? *Journal of Social Issues, 55*, 429–444.

Brewer, M. B. (2004). Taking the social origins of human nature seriously: Toward a more imperialist social psychology. *Personality and Social Psychology Review, 8*, 107–113.

Brewer, M. B., & Alexander, M. G. (2002). Intergroup emotions and images. In D. M. Mackie & E. R. Smith (Eds.), *From prejudice to intergroup emotions* (pp. 209–225). New York: Psychology Press.

Brewer, M. B., & Brown, R. J. (1998). Intergroup relations. In D. T. Gilbert, S. T. Fiske, & G. Lindzey (Eds.), *The handbook of social psychology* (4th ed., Vol. 2, pp. 554–594). Boston: McGraw-Hill.

Brewer, M. B., & Harasty, A. S. (1996). Seeing groups as entities: The role of perceiver motivation. In R. M. Sorrentino & E. T. Higgins (Eds.), *Handbook of motivation and cognition* (Vol. 3, pp. 347–370). New York: Guilford Press.

Brewer, M. B., Hong, Y., & Li, Q. (2004). Dynamic entitativity: Perceiving groups as actors. In V. Yzerbyt, C. Judd, & O. Corneille (Eds.), *The psychology of group perception: Contributions to the study of homogeneity, entititavity, and essentialism*. New York: Psychology Press.

Brewer, M. B., & Pickett, C. L. (2002). The social self and group identification: Inclusion and distinctiveness motives in interpersonal and collective identities. In J. Forgas & K. Williams (Eds.), *The social self: Cognitive, interpersonal, and intergroup perspectives* (pp. 255–271). Philadelphia: Psychology Press.

Brown, R. J. (2000). Social identity theory: Past achievements, current problems, and future challenges. *European Journal of Social Psychology, 30*, 745–778.

Brown, R. J., & Capozza, D. (2006). *Social identity: Motivational, emotional, and cultural influences*. New York: Psychology Press.

Brown, R. J., & Cehajic, S. (2008). Dealing with the past and facing the future: Mediators of the effects of collective guilt and shame in Bosnia Herzegovina. *European Journal of Social Psychology, 38*, 669–684.

Brown, R. J., & Gaertner, S. L. (2001). *Blackwell handbook of social psychology. Vol. 4: Intergroup relations*. Oxford: Blackwell.

Brown, R. J., Gonzalez, R., Zagefka, H., Manzi, J., & Cehajic, S. (2008). Nuestra Culpa: Collective guilt and shame as predictors of reparation for historical wrongdoing. *Journal of Personality and Social Psychology, 94*, 75–90.

Brown, R. J., & Hewstone, M. (2005). An integrative theory of intergroup contact. In M. P. Zanna (Ed.), *Advances in experimental social psychology* (Vol. 37, pp. 255–343). San Diego, CA: Academic Press.

Buhl, T. (1999). Positive-negative asymmetry in social discrimination: A meta-analytical evidence. *Group Processes and Intergroup Relations, 2*, 51–58.

Cadinu, M. R., Maass, A., Rosabianca, A., & Kiesner, J. (2005). Why do women underperform under stereotype threat? Evidence for the role of negative thinking. *Psychological Science, 16*, 572–578.

Cadinu, M. R., & Rothbart, M. (1996). Self-anchoring and differentiation processes in minimal group setting. *Journal of Personality and Social Psychology, 70*, 661–677.

Campbell, D. T. (1958). Common fate, similarity, and other indices of the status of aggregates of persons as social entities. *Behavioral Sciences, 3*, 14–25.

Campbell, D. T. (1965). Ethnocentric and other altruistic motives. In D. Levine (Ed.), *Nebraska symposium on motivation* (pp. 283–311). Lincoln, NE: University of Nebraska Press.

Caporael, L. R. (2005). Psychology and groups at the junction of genes and culture. *Behavioral and Brain Science, 28*, 819–821.

Caporael, L. R., & Brewer, M. B. (1995). Hierarchical evolutionary theory: There is an alternative, and it's not creationism. *Psychological Inquiry, 6*, 31–34.

Caporael, L., Dawes, R., Orbell, J., & van de Kragt, A. (1989). Selfishness examined: Cooperation in the absence of egoistic incentives. *Behavioural and Brain Sciences, 12*, 683–699.

Castano, E., & Dechesne, M. (2005). On defeating death: Group reification and social identification as immortality strategies. In W. Strobe & M. Hewstone (Eds.), *European review of social psychology* (Vol. 16). Hove, England: Psychology Press.

Castano, E., & Giner-Sorolla, R. (2006). Not quite human: Infra-humanization in response to collective responsibility for intergroup killing. *Journal of Personality and Social Psychology, 90*, 804–819.

Castano, E., & Yzerbyt, V. Y. (1998). The high and lows of group homogeneity. *Behavioural Processes, 42*, 219–238.

Castano, E., Yzerbyt, V. Y., & Bourguignon, D. (2003). We are one and I like it: The impact of group entitativity on group identification. *European Journal of Social Psychology, 33*, 735–754.

Castano, E., Yzerbyt, V. Y., Bourguignon, D., & Seron, E. (2002). Who may come in? The impact of ingroup identification on ingroup-outgroup categorization. *Journal of Experimental Social Psychology, 38*, 315–322.

Castano, E., Yzerbyt, Y., Paladino, M. P., & Sacchi, S. (2002). I belong, therefore, I exist: Ingroup identification, ingroup entitativity, and ingroup bias. *Personality and Social Psychology Bulletin, 28*, 135–143.

Castelli, L., Macrae, N., Zogmaister, C., Arcuri, L. (2004). A tale of two primes: Contextual limits on stereotype activation. *Social Cognition, 22*, 233–247.

Castelli, L., Tomelleri, S., & Zogmaister, C. (2008). Implicit ingroup meta-favoritism: Subtle preference for ingroup members displaying ingroup bias. *Personality and Social Psychology Bulletin, 34*, 807–818.

Chasteen, A. L., Bhattacharyya, S., Horhota, M., Tam, R., & Hasher, L. (2005). How feelings of stereotype threat influence older adults' memory performance. *Experimental Aging Research, 31*, 235–260.

Chow, R. M., Tiedens, L. Z., & Govan, C. L. (2008). Excluded emotions: The role of anger in antisocial responses to ostracism. *Journal of Experimental Social Psychology, 44*, 896–903.

Cialdini, R. B., Borden, R. J., Thorne, A., Walker, M. R., Freeman, S., & Sloan, R. L. (1976). 'Basking in reflected glory: Three (football) field studies.' *Journal of Personality and Social Psychology, 34*, 366–375.

Clement, R. W., & Krueger, J. (2000). The primacy of self-referent information in perceptions of social consensus. *British Journal of Social Psychology, 39*, 279–299.

Clement, R. W., & Krueger, J. (2002). Social categorization moderates social projection. *Journal of Experimental Social Psychology, 38*, 219–231.

Coats, S., Smith, E. R., Claypool, H. M., & Banner, M. J. (2000). Overlapping mental representation of self and in-group: Reaction time evidence and its relationship with explicit measures of group identification. *Journal of Experimental Social Psychology, 36*, 304–315.

Codol, J.-P. (1984). Social differentiation and non-differentiation. In H. Tajfel (Ed.), *The social dimension: European developments in social psychology* (Vol. 1, pp. 314–337). Cambridge, England: Cambridge University Press.

Codol, J.-P. (1987). Comparability and incomparability between oneself and others: Means of differentiation and comparison reference points. *Cahier de Psychologie Cognitive/European Bulletin of Cognitive Psychology, 7*, 87–105.

Cohen, G. L., Garcia, J., Apfel, N., & Master, A. (2006). Reducing the racial achievement gap: A social-psychological intervention. *Science, 313*, 1307–1310.

Commission of the European Communities (COM, 2008, 10 Final). Report from the commission to the Council, the European Parliament, The European Economic and Social Committee, and the Committee of the Regions. Retrieved September 18, 2009, from http://eur-lex.europa.eu/LexUriServ/LexUriServ.do?uri=COM:2008:0010:FIN:EN:PDF

Corneille, O., Huart, J., Becquart, E., & Brédart, S. (2004). When memory shifts towards more typical category exemplars: Accentuation effects in the recollection of ethnically ambiguous faces. *Journal of Personality and Social Psychology, 86*, 236–250.

Corneille, O., & Judd, C. M. (1999). Accentuation and sensitization effects in the categorization of multi-faceted stimuli. *Journal of Personality and Social Psychology, 77*, 927–941.

Corneille, O., Klein, O., Lambert, S., & Judd, C. M. (2002). On the role of familiarity with units of measurement in categorical accentuation: Tajfel and Wilkes (1963) revisited and replicated. *Psychological Science, 4,* 380–383.

Corneille, O., Yzerbyt, V. Y., Rogier, A., & Buidin, G. (2001). Threat and the Group Attribution Error: When threat elicits judgments of extremity and homogeneity. *Personality and Social Psychology Bulletin, 27,* 437–446.

Correll, J., & Park, B. (2005). A model of the ingroup as a social resource. *Personality and Social Psychology Bulletin, 9,* 341–359.

Correll, J., Park, B., Judd, C. M., & Wittenbrink, B. (2002). The police officer's dilemma: Using ethnicity to disambiguate potentially threatening individuals. *Journal of Personality & Social Psychology, 83,* 1314–1329.

Correll, J., Park, B., Judd, C. M., & Wittenbrink, B. (2007). The influence of stereotypes on decisions to shoot. *European Journal of Social Psychology, 32,* 1102–1117.

Correll, J., Park, B., Judd, C. M., Wittenbrink, B., Sadler, M. S., & Keesee, T. (2007). Across the thin blue line: Police officers and racial bias in the decision to shoot. *Journal of Personality & Social Psychology, 92,* 1006–1023.

Cortes, B. P. (2005). *Looking for conditions leading to infra-humanization.* Unpublished doctoral thesis. Université Catholique de Louvain, Louvain-la-Neuve, Belgium.

Cottrell, C. A., & Neuberg, S. L. (2005). Different emotional reactions to different groups: A sociofunctional threat-based approach to "prejudice." *Journal of Personality and Social Psychology, 88,* 770–789.

Crandall, C. S., & Eshleman, A. (2003). A justification-suppression model of the expression and experience of prejudice. *Psychological Bulletin, 129,* 414–446.

Crandall, C. S., Eshleman, A., & O'Brien, L. (2002). Social norms and suppression of prejudice: The struggle for internalization. *Journal of Personality and Social Psychology, 82,* 359–378.

Crisp, R. J., Ensari, N., Hewstone, M., & Miller, N. (2002). A dual-route model of crossed categorization effects. *European Review of Social Psychology, 13,* 35–74.

Crisp, R. J., & Hewstone, M. (2006). *Multiple social categorization: Processes, models and applications.* Hove, England: Psychology Press.

Crisp, R. J., & Hewstone, M. (2007). Multiple social categorization. In M. P. Zanna (Ed.), *Advances in experimental social psychology* (Vol. 39, pp. 163–254). Orlando, FL: Academic Press.

Crocker, J., Cornwell, B., & Major, B. (1993). The stigma of overweight: Affective consequences of attributional ambiguity. *Journal of Personality and Social Psychology, 64,* 60–70.

Crocker, J., & Luhtanen, R. (1990). Collective self-esteem and ingroup bias. *Journal of Personality and Social Psychology, 58,* 60–67.

Crocker, J., & Major, B. (1989). Social stigma and self-esteem: The self-protective properties of stigma. *Psychological Review, 96,* 608–630.

Crocker, J., Major, B., & Steele, C. (1998). Social stigma. In D. T. Gilbert, S. T. Fiske, & G. Lindzey (Eds.), *The handbook of social psychology* (4th ed., Vol. 2, pp. 504–553). New York: McGraw-Hill.

Crocker, J., Voelkl, K., Testa, M., & Major, B. (1991). Social stigma: The affective consequences of attributional ambiguity. *Journal of Personality and Social Psychology, 60,* 218–228.

Croizet, J., Després, G., Gauzins, M., Huguet, P., Leyens, J.-Ph, & Méot, A. (2004). Stereotype threat undermines intellectual performance by triggering a disruptive mental load. *Personality and Social Psychology Bulletin, 30,* 721–731.

Croizet, J.-C., & Claire, T. (1998). Extending the concept of stereotype threat to social class: The intellectual underperformance of students from low socioeconomic backgrounds. *Personality and Social Psychology Bulletin, 24*(5), 88–94.

Crosby, F. J. (1976). A model of egoistic relative deprivation. *Psychological Review, 83,* 85–113.

Crosby, F. J. (1982). *Relative deprivation and working women.* New York: Oxford University Press.

Crosby, F. J., Bromley, S., & Saxe, L. (1980). Recent unobtrusive studies of black and white discrimination and prejudice: A literature review. *Psychological Bulletin, 87,* 546–563.

Crosby, F. J., Clayton, S., Alksnis, O., & Hemker, K. (1986). Cognitive biases in the perception of discrimination: The importance of format. *Sex Roles, 14,* 637–646.

Cuddy, A. J. C., & Fiske, S. T. (2002). Doddering, but dear: Process, content, and function in stereotyping of older persons. In T. Nelson (Ed.), *Ageism: Stereotyping and prejudice against older persons* (pp. 3–26). Cambridge, MA: MIT Press.

Cuddy, A. J. C., Fiske, S. T., & Glick, P. (2007). The BIAS map: Behaviors from intergroup affect and stereotypes. *Journal of Personality and Social Psychology, 92,* 631–648.

Cuddy, A. J. C., Fiske, S. T., & Glick, P. (2008). Warmth and competence as universal dimensions of social perception: The Stereotype Content Model and the BIAS Map. In M. P. Zanna (Ed.), *Advances in Experimental Social Psychology* (vol. 40, pp. 61–149). New York, NY: Academic Press.

Cuddy, A. J. C., Fiske, S. T., Kwan, V. S. Y., Glick, P., Demoulin, S., Leyens, J.-Ph., et al. (2009). Stereotype Content Model across cultures: Universal similarities and some differences. *British Journal of Social Psychology, 48,* 1–33.

Cuddy, A. J. C., Norton, M. I., & Fiske, S. T. (2005). This old stereotype: The stubbornness and pervasiveness of the elderly stereotype. *Journal of Social Issues, 61,* 265–283.

Cunningham, W. A., Johnson, M. K., Raye, C. L., Gatenby, J. C., Gore, J. C., & Banaji, M. R. (2004). Separate neural component in the processing of Black and White faces. *Psychological Science, 15,* 806–813.

Czopp, A. M. (2008). When is a compliment not a compliment? Evaluating expressions of positive stereotypes. *Journal of Experimental Social Psychology, 44,* 413–442.

Czopp, A. M., & Monteith, M. J. (2006). Thinking well of African Americans: Measuring complimentary stereotypes and negative prejudice. *Basic & Applied Social Psychology, 28,* 233–250.

Dambrun, M., Taylor, D. M., McDonald, D. A., Crush, J., & Méot, A. (2006). The relative deprivation-gratification continuum and the attitudes of South African toward immigrants: A test of the V-curve hypothesis. *Journal of Personality and Social Psychology, 91,* 1032–1044.

Danso, H. A., & Esses, V. M. (2001). Black experimenters and the intellectual test performance of White participants: The tables are turned. *Journal of Experimental Social Psychology, 37,* 158–165.

Dardenne, B., Dumont, M., & Bollier, T. (2007). Insidious dangers of benevolent sexism: Consequences for women's performance. *Journal of Personality and Social Psychology, 93,* 764–779.

Davies, M. (1994). Correlated of negative attitudes toward gay men: Sexism, male role norms, and male sexuality. *Journal of Sex Research, 41,* 259–266.

Deaux, K., Reid, A., Mizrahi, K., & Ethier, K. A. (1995). Parameters of social identity. *Journal of Personality and Social Psychology, 68,* 280–291.

de Houwer, J., Beckers, T., & Moors, A. (2007). Novel attitudes can be faked on the Implicit Association Test. *Journal of Experimental Social Psychology, 43,* 972–978.

Demoulin, S., Geeraert, N., & Yzerbyt, V. Y. (2007, September 5–9). *The impact of cultural exchange on national stereotypes: Evidence for projection and compensation effects in judgments of warmth and competence.* Paper presented at the 9th ESCON conference; Brno, Czech Republic.

Demoulin, S., Leyens, J.-Ph., & Dovidio, J. F. (2009). *Intergroup misunderstandings: Impact of divergent social realities.* New York: Psychology Press.

Demoulin, S., Leyens, J.-Ph., Paladino, P. M., Rodriguez, A. P., Rodriguez, R. T., & Dovidio, J. (2004). Dimensions of "uniquely" and "non uniquely" human emotions. *Cognition and Emotion, 18,* 71–96.

Demoulin, S., Leyens, J.-Ph., & Yzerbyt, V. Y. (2006). Lay theories of essentialism. *Group Processes and Intergroup Relations, 9*, 25–42.

DePaulo, B. M. (1992). Nonverbal behavior and self-presentation. *Psychological Bulletin, 111*, 203–243.

DePaulo, B. M., & Friedman, H. S. (1998). Nonverbal communication. In D. T. Gilbert, S. T. Fiske, & G. Lindzey (Eds.), *The handbook of social psychology* (pp. 3–40). New York: McGraw-Hill.

Devine, P. G. (1989). Stereotypes and prejudice: Their automatic and controlled components. *Journal of Personality and Social Psychology, 56*, 5–18.

Devine, P. G., & Baker, S. M. (1991). Measurement of racial stereotyping subtyping. *Personality and Social Psychology Bulletin, 17*, 44–50.

Devine, P. G., & Elliot, A. J. (1995). Are racial stereotypes *really* fading? The Princeton trilogy revisited. *Personality and Social Psychology Bulletin, 11*, 1139–1150.

Devine, P. G., Plant, E. A., Amodio, D. M., Harmon-Jones, E., & Vance, S. L. (2002). The regulation of explicit and implicit race bias: The role of motivations to respond without prejudice. *Journal of Personality and Social Psychology, 82*, 835–848.

Devine, P. G., & Vasquez, K. A. (1998). The rocky road to positive intergroup relations. In J. L. Eberhardt & S. T. Fiske (Eds.), *Confronting racism: The problem and the response* (pp. 234–262). London: Sage.

Devos, T., & Banaji, M. R. (2005). American = White? *Journal of Personality and Social Psychology, 88*, 447–466.

Dijker, A. J. M. (1987). Emotional reactions to ethnic minorities. *European Journal of Social Psychology, 17*, 305–325.

Doosje, B., Branscombe, N. R., Spears, R., & Manstead, A. S. R. (1998). Guilty by association: When one's group has a negative history. *Journal of Personality and Social Psychology, 75*, 872–886.

Doosje, B., & Ellemers, N. (1997). Stereotyping under threat: The role of group identification. In R. Spears, P. J. Oakes, N. Ellemers, & S. A. Haslam (Eds.), *The social psychology of stereotyping and group life*. Oxford: Blackwell.

Doosje, B., Ellemers, N. R., & Spears, R. (1995). Perceived intragroup variability as a function of group status and identification. *Journal of Experimental Social Psychology, 31*, 410–436.

Dotsch, R., & Wigboldus, D. H. J. (2008). Virtual prejudice. *Journal of Experimental Social Psychology, 44*, 1194–1198.

Dovidio, J. F., Evans, N. E., & Tyler, R. B. (1986). Racial stereotypes: The contents of their cognitive representations. *Journal of Experimental Social Psychology, 22*, 22–37.

Dovidio, J. F., & Gaertner, S. L. (1991). Changes in the expression and assessment of racial prejudice. In H. J. Knopke, R. J. Norrell, & R. W. Rogers (Eds.), *Opening doors: Perspectives on race relations in contemporary America* (pp. 119–148). Tuscaloosa: University of Alabama Press.

Dovidio, J. F., & Gaertner, S. L. (1998). On the nature of contemporary prejudice: The causes, consequences, and challenges of aversive racism. In J. L. Eberhardt & S. T. Fiske (Eds.), *Confronting racism: The problem and the response* (pp. 3–32). London: Sage.

Dovidio, J. F., & Gaertner, S. L. (2000). Aversive racism and selection decisions: 1989 and 1999. *Psychological Science, 11*, 315–319.

Dovidio, J. F., & Gaertner, S. L. (2004). Aversive racism. In M. P. Zanna (Ed.), *Advances in experimental social psychology* (Vol. 36, pp. 1–52). Thousand Oaks, CA: Sage.

Dovidio, J. F., Glick, P., & Rudman, L. (2005). *On the nature of prejudice: Fifty years after Allport*. Oxford: Blackwell.

Dovidio, J. F., Kawakami, K., & Beach, K. (2001). Implicit and explicit attitudes: Examination of the relationship between measures of intergroup bias. In R. Brown & S. L. Gaertner (Eds.), *Blackwell handbook of social psychology. Vol. 4: Intergroup relations* (pp. 175–197). Oxford: Blackwell.

Dovidio, J. F., Kawakami, K., & Gaertner, S. L. (2002). Implicit and explicit prejudice and interracial interaction. *Journal of Personality and Social Psychology, 82*, 62–68.

Dovidio, J. F., Kawakami, K., Johnson, C., Johnson, B., & Howard, A. (1997). On the nature of prejudice: Automatic and controlled processes. *Journal of Experimental Social Psychology, 33*, 510–540.

Dovidio, J. F., Pearson, A. R., & Orr, P. (2008). Social psychology and neuroscience: Strange bedfellows or a healthy marriage? *Group Processes and Intergroup Relations, 11*, 247–263.

Dovidio, J. F., Piliavin, J. A., Schroeder, D. A., & Penner, L. A. (2006). *The social psychology of prosocial behavior*. Mahwah, NJ: Erlbaum.

Dovidio, J. F., Smith, J. K., Donnella, A. G., & Gaertner, S. L. (1997). Racial attitudes and the death penalty. *Journal of Applied Social Psychology, 27*, 1468–1487.

Drury, J., & Reicher, S. (1999). The intergroup dynamics of collective empowerment: Substantiating the social identity model. *Group Processes and Intergroup Relations, 2*, 381–402.

Drury, J., & Reicher, S. (2000). Collective action and psychological change: The emergence of new social identities. *British Journal of Social Psychology, 39*, 579–604.

Drury, J., & Reicher, S. (2005). Explaining enduring empowerment: A comparative study of collective action and psychological outcomes. *European Journal of Social Psychology, 35*, 35–58.

Duckitt, J. (2001). A dual-process cognitive-motivational theory of ideology and prejudice. In M. P. Zanna (Ed.), *Advances in experimental social psychology* (Vol. 33, pp. 41–112). San Diego, CA: Academic Press.

Duckitt, J. (2003). Prejudice and intergroup hostility. In D. Sears, L. Huddy, & R. Jervis (Eds.), *Oxford handbook of political psychology* (pp. 559–600). Oxford: Oxford University Press.

Duckitt, J. (2005). Personality and prejudice. In J. Dovidio, P. Glick, & L. Rudman (Eds.), *On the nature of prejudice: Fifty years after Allport* (pp. 395–412). Cambridge, MA: Blackwell.

Duckitt, J. (2006). Differential effects of Right Wing Authoritarianism and Social Dominance Orientation on outgroup attitudes and their mediation by threat from competitiveness to outgroups. *Personality and Social Psychology Bulletin, 32*, 684–696.

Duckitt, J., & Fisher, K. (2003). Social threat, worldview, and ideological attitudes. *Political Psychology, 24*, 199–222.

Dumont, M., Sarlet, M., & Dardenne, B. (2008). Be too kind to a woman, she'll feel incompetent: Benevolent sexism shifts self-construal and autobiographical memories Toward Incompetence. *Sex Roles*, DOI 10.1007/s11199-008-9582-4.

Dumont, M., Yzerbyt, V., Wigboldus, D., & Gordijn, E. H. (2003). Social categorization and fear reactions to the September 11th terrorist attacks. *Personality and Social Psychology Bulletin, 29*, 1509–1520.

Dunbar, R. I. M. (1998). The social brain hypothesis. *Evolutionary Anthropology, 6*, 178–190.

Dunbar, R. I. M., & Shultz, S. (2007). Evolution in the social brain. *Science, 317*, 1344.

Dunton, B. C., & Fazio, R. H. (1997). An individual difference measure of motivation to control prejudiced reactions. *Personality and Social Psychology Bulletin, 23*, 316–326.

Dupont, E., & Leyens, J. Ph. (2003). Perceptions différentes des discriminations individuelle et groupale. In J.-C. Croizet & J.-Ph Leyens (Eds.), *Mauvaise réputation* (pp. 61–92). Paris: Armand Colin.

Duriez, B., & van Hiel, A. (2002). The march of modern fascism: A comparison of social dominance orientation and authoritarianism. *Personality and Individual Differences, 32*, 1199–1213.

Eberhardt, J. L. (2005). Imaging race. *American Psychologist, 60*, 181–190.

Eberhardt, J. L., Dasgupta, N., & Banaszynski, T. L. (2003). Believing is seeing: The effects of racial labels and implicit beliefs on face perception. *Personality and Social Psychology Bulletin, 29*, 360–370.

Eberhardt, J. L., Davies, P. G., Purdie-Vaughns, V. J., & Johnson, S. L. (2006). Looking deathworthy—Perceived stereotypicality of black defendants predicts capital-sentencing outcomes. *Psychological Science, 17*, 383–386.

Eberhardt, J. L., Goff, P. A., Purdie, V. J., & Davies, P.G. (2004). Seeing black: Race, crime, and visual processing. *Journal of Personality and Social Psychology, 87*, 876–963.

Ehrlich, H. J., Larcom, B. E. K., & Purvis, R. D. (1995). The traumatic impact of ethnoviolence. In L. J. Lederer & R. Delgado (Eds.), *The price we pay* (pp. 62–79). New York: Farrar, Straus and Giroux.

Ellemers, N. (1993). The influence of social structure variables on identity management strategies. In W. Stroebe & M. Hewstone (Eds.), *European review of social psychology* (Vol. 4, pp. 27–57). Chichester, England: Wiley.

Ellemers, N. (2001). Individual upward mobility and the perceived legitimacy of intergroup relations. In J. T. Jost & B. Major (Eds.), *The psychology of legitimacy*. Cambridge, England: Cambridge University Press.

Ellemers, N. (2002). Social identity and relative deprivation. In I. Walker & H. J. Smith (Eds.), *Relative deprivation: Specification, development and integration* (pp. 239–264). Cambridge, England: Cambridge University Press.

Ellemers, N., & Barreto, M. (2009). Maintaining the illusion of meritocracy. In S. Demoulin, J.-Ph. Leyens, & J. F. Dovidio (Eds.), *Intergroup misunderstandings: Impact of divergent social realities* (pp. 191–208). New York: Psychology Press.

Ellemers, N., Doosje, B., & Spears, R. (2004). Sources of respect: The effects of being liked by ingroups and outgroups. *European Journal of Social Psychology, 34*, 155–172.

Ellemers, N., Platow, M., van Knippenberg, D., & Haslam, A. (2003). Social identity at work: Definitions, debates, and directions. In A. Haslam, D. van Knippenberg, M. Platow, & N. Ellemers (Eds.), *Social identity at work: Developing theory for organizational practice* (pp. 3–28). New York: Psychology Press.

Ellemers, N., Spears, R., & Doosje, B. (1997). Sticking together or falling apart: Ingroup identification as a psychological determinant of group commitment versus individual mobility. *Journal of Personality and Social Psychology, 72*, 617–626.

Ellemers, N., Spears, R., & Doosje, B. (Eds.). (1999). *Social identity: Context, commitment, content*. Oxford: Blackwell.

Ellemers, N., Spears, R., & Doosje, B. (2002). Self and social identity. *Annual Review of Psychology, 53*, 161–186.

Ellemers, N., van den Heuvel, H., de Gilder, D., Maass, A., & Bonvini, A. (2004). The underrepresentation of women in science: Differential commitment or the queen bee syndrome? *British Journal of Social Psychology, 43*, 315–338.

Ellemers, N., van Knippenberg, A., de Vries, N., & Wilke, H. (1988). Social identification and permeability of group boundaries. *European Journal of Social Psychology, 18*, 497–513.

Ellemers, N., Wilke, H., & van Knippenberg, A. (1993). Effects of the legitimacy of low group or individual status on individual and collective identity enhancement strategies. *Journal of Personality and Social Psychology, 64*, 766–778.

Esses, V. M., Dietz, J., & Bhardwaj, A. (2006). The role of prejudice in the discounting of immigrant skills. In R. Mahalingam (Ed.), *The cultural psychology of immigrants* (pp. 113–130). Mahwah, NJ: Erlbaum.

Esses, V. M., Dovidio, J. F., Jackson, L. M., & Armstrong, T. L. (2001). The immigration dilemma: The role of perceived group competition, ethnic prejudice, and national identity. *Journal of Social Issues, 57*, 389–412.

Fazio, R. H. (2001). On the automatic activation of associated evaluations: An overview. *Cognition and Emotion, 15*, 115–141.

Fazio, R. H., & Dunton, B. C. (1997). Categorization by race: The impact of automatic and controlled components of racial prejudice. *Journal of Experimental Social Psychology, 33*, 451–470.

Fazio, R. H., Jackson, J. R., Dunton, B. C., & Williams, C. J. (1995). Variability in automatic activation as an unobtrusive measure of racial attitudes: A bona fide pipeline? *Journal of Personality and Social Psychology, 69*, 1013–1027.

Fazio, R. H., & Olson, M. A. (2003). Implicit measures in social cognition research: Their meaning and uses. *Annual Review of Psychology, 54*, 297–327.

Federico, C. M., & Sidanius, J. (2002). Racism, ideology, and affirmative action, revisited: The antecedents and consequences of 'principled objections' to affirmative action. *Journal of Personality and Social Psychology, 82*, 488–502.

Fein, S., Hoshino-Browne, E., Davies, P. G., & Spencer, S. J. (2003). Self-image maintenance goals and sociocultural norms in motivated social perception. In S. J. Spencer, S. Fein, M. Zanna, & J. M. Olson (Eds.), *Motivated social perception: The Ontario symposium* (Vol. 9, pp. 21–44). Mahwah, NJ: Erlbaum.

Fein, S., & Spencer, J. S. (1997). Prejudice as self-image maintenance: Affirming the self through derogating others. *Journal of Personality and Social Psychology, 73*, 31–44.

Festinger, L. (1954). A theory of social comparison processes. *Human Relations, 7*, 117–140.

Fiedler, K., Messner, C., & Bluemke, M. (2006). Unresolved problems with the 'I', the 'A', and the 'T': A logical and psychometric critique of the Implicit Association Test (IAT). *European Review of Social Psychology, 17*, 74–147.

Fiske, S. T. (1998). Stereotyping, prejudice, and discrimination. In D. T. Gilbert, S. T. Fiske, & G. Lindzey (Eds.), *The handbook of social psychology* (4th ed., Vol. 2, pp. 357–411). New York: McGraw-Hill.

Fiske, S. T., Cuddy, A. J. C., & Glick, P. (2002). Emotions up and down: Intergroup emotions result from status and competition. In D. M. Mackie & E. R. Smith (Eds.), *From prejudice to intergroup emotions: Differentiated reactions to social groups* (pp. 247–264). New York: Psychology Press.

Fiske, S. T., Cuddy, A. J. C., & Glick, P. (2007). First judge warmth, then competence: Fundamental social dimensions. *Trends in Cognitive Sciences, 11*, 77–83.

Fiske, S. T., Cuddy A. J. C., Glick, P., & Xu, J. (2002). A model of (often mixed) stereotype content: Competence and warmth respectively follow from perceived status and competition. *Journal of Personality and Social Psychology, 82*, 878–902.

Fiske, S. T., Lin, M., & Neuberg, S. L. (1999). The continuum model: Ten years later. In S. Chaiken & Y. Trope (Eds.), *Dual process theories in social psychology* (pp. 231–254). New York: Guilford.

Fiske, S. T., & Taylor, S. E. (1991). *Social cognition* (2nd ed.). New York: McGraw Hill.

Fiske, S. T., & Taylor, S. E. (2008). *Social cognition: From brains to culture*. New York: McGraw-Hill.

Fiske, S. T., Xu, J., Cuddy, A. J. C., & Glick, P. (1999). (Dis)respecting versus (Dis)liking: Status and interdependence predict ambivalent stereotypes of competence and warmth. *Journal of Social Issues, 55*, 473–490.

Folger, R. (1986). A referent cognitions theory of relative deprivation. In J. M. Olson, C. P. Herman, & M. P. Zanna (Eds.), *Relative deprivation and social comparison: The Ontario symposium* (Vol. 4, pp. 217–242). Hillsdale, NJ: Erlbaum.

Franklin, K. (2000). Antigay behaviors among young adults: Prevalence, patterns, and motivators in a noncriminal population. *Journal of Interpersonal Violence, 15*, 339–362.

Frijda, N. H. (1986). *The Emotions*. Cambridge University Press.

Frijda, N. H., Kuipers, P., & ter Schure, E. (1989). Relations among emotion, appraisal, and emotional action readiness. *Journal of Personality and Social Psychology, 57*, 212–228.

Fritsche, I., Jonas, E., & Fankhänel, T. (2008). The role of control motivation in mortality salience effects on ingroup support and defense. *Journal of Personality and Social Psychology, 95*(3), 524–541.

Fuegen, K., & Biernat, M. (2000). Defining discrimination in the personal-group discrimination discrepancy. *Sex Roles, 43*, 285–310.

Gaertner, L., & Insko, C. A. (2000). Intergroup discrimination in the minimal group paradigm: Categorization, reciprocation, or fear? *Journal of Personality and Social Psychology, 79*, 77–94.

Gaertner, L., Iuzzini, J., Guerrero Witt, M., & Oriña, M. M. (2006). Us without them: Evidence for an intragroup origin of positive ingroup regard. *Journal of Personality and Social Psychology, 90*, 426–439.

Gaertner, S. L., & Dovidio, J. F. (1977). The subtlety of white racism, arousal and helping behavior. *Journal of Personality and Social Psychology, 35*, 691–707.

Gaertner, S. L., & Dovidio, J. F. (1986). The aversive form of racism. In J. F. Dovidio & S. L. Gaertner (Eds.), *Prejudice, discrimination, and racism* (pp. 61–89). San Diego, CA: Academic Press.

Gaertner, S. L., & Dovidio, J. F. (2000). *Reducing intergroup bias: The Common Ingroup Identity Model*. Philadelphia: Psychology Press.

Gaertner, S. L., Dovidio, J. F., & Johnson, G., (1982). Race of victim, non-responsive bystanders and helping. *Journal of Social Psychology, 117*, 69–71.

Gaertner, S. L., & McLaughlin, J. P. (1983). The aversive form of racism. In S. L. Gaertner & J. F. Dovidio (Eds.), *Prejudice, discrimination, and racism* (pp. 1–34). Orlando, FL: Academic Press.

Gagnon, A., & Bourhis, R. Y. (1996). Discrimination in the minimal group paradigm: Social identity or self-interest? *Personality and Social Psychology Bulletin, 22*, 1289–1301.

Gailliot, M. T., Schmeichel, B. J., & Baumeister, R. F. (2006). Self-regulation processes defend against the threat of death: Effects of self-control depletion and trait self-control on thoughts and fears of dying. *Journal of Personality and Social Psychology, 91*, 49–62.

Gailliot, M. T., Schmeichel, B. J., & Maner, J. K. (2007). Differentiating the effects of self-control and self-esteem on reactions to mortality salience. *Journal of Experimental Social Psychology, 43*, 894–901.

Galinsky, A. D., & Ku, G. (2004). The effects of perspective-taking on prejudice: The moderating role of self-evaluation. *Personality and Social Psychology Bulletin, 30*, 594–604.

Galinsky, A. D., Ku, G., & Wang, C. S. (2005). Perspective-taking: Fostering social bonds and facilitating social coordination. *Group Processes and Intergroup Relations, 8*, 109–125.

Galinsky, A. D., & Moskowitz, G. B. (2000). Perspective-taking: Decreasing stereotype expression, stereotype accessibility, and ingroup favouritism. *Journal of Personality and Social Psychology, 78*, 708–724.

Gardner, W. L., Pickett, C. L., & Brewer, M. B. (2000). Social exclusion and selective memory: How the need to belong affects memory for social information. *Personality and Social Psychology Bulletin, 26*, 486–496.

Garstka, T. A., Schmitt, M. T., Branscombe, N. R., & Hummert, M. L. (2004). How young and older adults differ in their responses to perceived age discrimination. *Psychology and Aging, 19*, 326–335.

Gaunt, R., Leyens, J-Ph., & Demoulin, S. (2002). Intergroup relations and the attribution of emotions: Controllability of memory for secondary emotions associated to ingroup versus outgroup. *Journal of Experimental Social Psychology, 38*, 508–514.

Gawronski, B., Peters, K. R., Brochu, P. M., & Strack, F. (2008). Understanding the relations between different forms of racial prejudice: A cognitive consistency perspective. *Personality and Social Psychology Bulletin, 34*, 648–665.

Gelman, S. A. (2003). *The essential child: Origins of essentialism in everyday thought*. New York: Oxford University Press.

Gibson, J. L. (2004). Does truth lead to reconciliation? Testing the causal assumptions of the South African Truth and Reconciliation process. *American Journal of Political Science, 48*, 201–217.

Gilbert, D. T., & Hixon, J. G. (1991). The trouble of thinking: Activation and application of stereotypic beliefs. *Journal of Personality and Social Psychology, 60*, 509–517.

Gilbert, G. M. (1951). Stereotype persistence and change among college students. *Journal of Abnormal and Social Psychology, 46*, 245–254.

Glick, P. (2002). Sacrificial lambs dressed in wolves' clothing: Envious prejudice, ideology, and the scapegoating of Jews. In L. S. Newman & R. Erber (Eds.), *Understanding genocide: The social psychology of the Holocaust* (pp. 113–142). New York: Oxford University Press.

Glick, P., Diebold, J., Bailey-Werner, B., & Zhu, L. (1997). The two faces of Adam: Ambivalent sexism and polarized attitudes toward women. *Personality and Social Psychology Bulletin, 23*, 1323–1334.

Glick, P., & Fiske, S. T. (1996). The Ambivalent Sexism Inventory: Differentiating hostile and benevolent sexism. *Journal of Personality and Social Psychology, 70*, 491–512.

Glick, P., & Fiske, S. T. (1999). Sexism and other "isms": Interdependence, status, and the ambivalent content of stereotypes. In W. B. Swann, Jr., J. H. Langlois, & L. A. Gilbert (Eds.), *Sexism and stereotypes in modern society: The gender science of Janet Taylor Spence* (pp. 193–221). Washington, DC: American Psychological Association.

Glick, P., & Fiske, S. T. (2001a). Ambivalent sexism. In M. P. Zanna (Ed.), *Advances in experimental social psychology* (Vol. 33, pp. 115–188). Thousand Oaks, CA: Academic Press.

Glick, P., & Fiske, S. T. (2001b). Ambivalent stereotypes as legitimizing ideologies: Differentiating paternalistic and envious prejudice. In J. Jost & B. Major (Eds.), *The psychology of legitimacy* (pp. 278–306). Cambridge, England: Cambridge University Press.

Glick, P., & Fiske, S. T. (2001c). An ambivalent alliance: Hostile and benevolent sexism as complementary justifications of gender inequality. *American Psychologist, 56*, 109–118.

Goethals, G. R., & Darley, J. M. (1977). Social comparison theory: An attributional approach. In J. M. Suls & R. M. Miller (Eds.), *Social comparison processes* (pp. 259–278). Washington, DC: Hemisphere.

Goff, P. A., Eberhardt, J. L., Williams, M. J., & Jackson, M. C. (2008). Not yet human: implicit knowledge, historical dehumanization, and contemporary consequences. *Journal of Personality and Social Psychology, 94*, 292–306.

Goffman, E. (1963). *Stigma: Notes on the management of spoiled identity*. Englewood Cliffs, NJ: Prentice-Hall.

Goldin, C., & Rouse, C. (2000). Orchestrating impartiality: The impact of "Blind" auditions on female musicians. *American Economic Review, 90*, 715–741.

Gonzales, P. M., Blanton, H., & Williams, K. J. (2002). The effects of stereotype threat and double-minority status on the test performance of Latino women. *Personality and Social Psychology Bulletin, 28*, 659–670.

Gordijn, E. H., Hindriks, I., Koomen, W., Dijksterhuis, A., & van Knippenberg, A. (2004). Consequences of stereotype suppression and internal suppression motivation: A self-regulation approach. *Personality and Social Psychology Bulletin, 30*, 212–224.

Gordijn, E. H., Wigboldus, D., & Yzerbyt, V. (2001). Emotional consequences of categorizing victims of negative outgroup behavior as ingroup or outgroup. *Group Processes and Intergroup Relations, 4*, 317–326.

Gordijn, E. H., Yzerbyt, V. Y., Wigboldus, D., & Dumont, M. (2006). Emotional reactions to harmful intergroup behavior: The impact of being associated with the victims or the perpetrators. *European Journal of Social Psychology, 36*, 15–30.

Govorun, O., & Payne, B. K. (2006). Ego depletion and prejudice: Separating automatic and controlled components. *Social Cognition, 24*, 111–136.

Gramzow, R. H., & Gaertner, L. (2005). Self-esteem and favoritism toward novel in-groups: The self as an evaluative base. *Journal of Personality and Social Psychology, 88*, 801–815.

Gramzow, R. H., Gaertner, L., & Sedikides, C. (2001). Memory for ingroup and outgroup information in a minimal group context: The self as an informational base. *Journal of Personality and Social Psychology, 80*, 188–205.

Green, D. P., Strolovitch, D. Z., & Wong, J. S. (1998). Defended neighborhood, integration, and racially motivated crimes. *American Journal of Sociology, 104*, 372–403.

Greenberg, J., Solomon, S., & Pyszczynski, T. (1997). Terror management theory of self-esteem and cultural worldviews: Empirical assessments and conceptual refinements. In M. P. Zanna (Ed.), *Advances in Experimental Social Psychology, 29*, 61–139.

Greenwald, A. G., McGhee, D. E., & Schwartz, J. K. L. (1998). Measuring individual differences in implicit cognition: The implicit association test. *Journal of Personality and Social Psychology, 74*, 1464–1480.

Grieve, P. G., & Hogg, M. A. (1999). Subjective uncertainty and intergroup discrimination in the minimal group situation. *Personality and Social Psychology Bulletin, 25*, 926–940.

Grofman, B. N., & Muller, E. N. (1973). The strange case of relative gratification and potential for political violence: The V-curve hypothesis. *American Political Science Review, 57*, 514–539.

Guimond, S. (2006). *Social comparison processes and levels of analysis: Understanding cognition, intergroup relations, and culture.* Cambridge, England: Cambridge University Press.

Guimond, S., & Dambrun, M. (2002). When prosperity breeds intergroup hostility: The effects of relative deprivation and relative gratification on prejudice. *Personality and Social Psychology Bulletin, 28*, 900–912.

Guimond, S., Dambrun, M., Michinov, N., & Duarte, S. (2003). Does social dominance generate prejudice? Integrating individual and contextual determinants of intergroup cognition. *Journal of Personality and Social Psychology, 84*, 697–721.

Gurr, T. R. (1970). *Why men rebel.* Princeton, NJ: Princeton University Press.

Haddock, G., & Zanna, M. P. (1994). Preferring 'housewives' to 'feminists': Categorization and the favorability of attitudes toward women. *Psychology of Women Quarterly, 18*, 25–52.

Haidt, J., & Rodin, J. (1999). Control and efficacy as interdisciplinary bridges. *Review of General Psychology, 3*, 317–337.

Hamilton, D. (2007). Understanding the complexities of group perception: Broadening the domain. *European Journal of Social Psychology, 37*, 1077.

Hamilton, D. L. (1981). *Cognitive processes in stereotyping and intergroup behavior.* Hillsdale, NJ: Lawrence Erlbaum Associates.

Hamilton, D. L., & Sherman, S. J. (1996). Perceiving persons and groups. *Psychological Review, 103*, 336–355.

Hamilton, D. L., Sherman, S. J., & Castelli, L. (2002). A group by any other name: The role of entitativity in group perception. In W. Stroebe & M. Hewstone (Eds.), *European review of social psychology* (Vol. 12, pp. 139–166). Chichester, England: Wiley.

Hamilton, D. L., Sherman, S. J., & Maddox, K. B. (1999). Dualities and continua: Implications for understanding perceptions of persons and groups. In S. Chaiken & Y. Trope (Eds.), *Dual process theories in social psychology* (pp. 606–626). New York: Guilford.

Harmon-Jones, E., Greenberg, J., Solomon, S., & Simon, L. (1996). The effects of mortality salience on intergroup bias between minimal groups. *European Journal of Social Psychology, 26*, 677–681.

Harmon-Jones, E., Sigelman, J. D., Bohlig, A., & Harmon-Jones, C. (2003). Anger, coping, and frontal cortical activity: The effect of coping potential on anger-induced left frontal activity. *Cognition and Emotion, 17*, 1–24.

Harris, L. T., & Fiske, S. T. (2006). Dehumanizing the lowest of the low: Neuro-imaging responses to extreme outgroups. *Psychological Science, 17*, 847–853.

Harris, L. T., & Fiske, S. T. (2007). Social groups that elicit disgust are differentially processed in mPFC. *Scan, 2*, 45–51.

Harris, L. T., & Fiske, S. T. (in press). Perceiving humanity: Dehumanized perception demonstrates social neuroscience approach. In A. Todorov, S. Fiske, & D. Prentice (Eds.), *Social neuroscience: Toward understanding the underpinnings of the social mind.* New York: Oxford University Press.

Hart, A. J., Whalen, P. J., Shin, L. M., McInerney, S. C., Fischer, H., & Rauch, S. L. (2000). Differential response in the human amygdala to racial outgroup vs ingroup face stimuli. *Neuroreport: For Rapid Communication of Neuroscience Research, 11*, 2351–2355.

Harth, N. S., Kessler, T., & Leach, C. W. (2008). Advantaged group's emotional reactions to inter-group inequality: The dynamics of pride, guilt, and sympathy. *Personality and Social Psychology Bulletin, 34*, 115–129.

Haslam, N. (2006). Dehumanization: An integrative review. *Personality and Social Psychology Review, 10*, 252–264.

Haslam, N., Bain, P., Douge, L., Lee, M., & Bastian, B. (2005). More human than you: Attributing humanness to self and others. *Journal of Personality and Social Psychology, 89*, 937–950.

Haslam, N., Rothschild, L., & Ernst, D. (2000). Essentialist beliefs about social categories. *British Journal of Social Psychology, 39*, 113–127.

Haslam, N., Rothschild, L., & Ernst, D. (2002). Are essentialist beliefs associated with prejudice? *British Journal of Social Psychology, 41*, 87–100.

Haslam, S. A., Oakes, P. J., Turner, J. C., & McGarty, C. (1995). Social categorization and group homogeneity: Changes in the perceived applicability of stereotype content as a function of comparative context and trait favourableness. *British Journal of Social Psychology, 34*, 139–160.

Hebl, M., Dovidio, J. F., Richeson, J. A., Shelton, J. N., Gaertner, S. L., & Kawakami, K. (2009). Interpretation of interaction: Responsiveness to verbal and nonverbal cues. In S. Demoulin, J.-Ph. Leyens, & J. F. Dovidio (Eds.), *Intergroup misunderstandings: Impact of divergent social realities.* New York: Psychology Press.

Hebl, M., King, E. B., Glick, P., Singletary, S. L., & Kazama, S. (2007). Hostile and benevolent reactions toward pregnant women: Complementary interpersonal punishments and rewards that maintain traditional roles. *Journal of Applied Psychology, 92*, 1499–1511.

Heider, F. (1958). *The psychology of interpersonal relations.* New York: Wiley.

Hermann, E., Call, J., Hernandez-Lloreda, M. V., Hare, B., & Tomasello, M. (2007). Humans have evolved specialized skills of social cognition: The cultural intelligence hypothesis. *Science, 317*, 1360–1366.

Hewstone, M. (1990). The "ultimate attribution error"? A review of the literature on intergroup causal attribution. *European Journal of Social Psychology, 20*, 311–335.

Hewstone, M., Rubin, M., & Willis, H. (2002). Intergroup bias. *Annual Review of Psychology, 53*, 575–604.

Higgins, E. T. (1997). Beyond pleasure and pain. *American Psychologist, 52*, 1280–1300.

Higgins, E. T. (1998). From expectancies to worldviews: Regulatory focus in socialization and cognition. In J. M. Darley & J. Cooper (Eds.), *Attribution and social interaction: The legacy of Edward E. Jones* (pp. 243–309). Washington, DC: American Psychological Association.

Hodson, G., Dovidio, J. F., & Gaertner, S. L. (2002). Processes in racial discrimination: Weighting of conflicting information. *Personality and Social Psychology Bulletin, 28*, 460–471.

Hofmann, W., Gawronski, B., Gschwendner, T., Le, H., & Schmitt, M. (2005). A meta-analysis on the correlation between the Implicit Association Test and explicit self-report measures. *Personality and Social Psychology Bulletin, 31*, 1369–1385.

Hogg, M. A. (2000). Subjective uncertainty reduction through self-categorization: A motivational theory of social identity processes. *European Review of Social Psychology, 11*, 223–255.

Hogg, M. A. (2004). Uncertainty and extremism: identification with high entitative groups under condition of uncertainty. In V. Yzerbyt, C. M. Judd, & O. Corneille (Eds.), *The psychology of group perception: Perceived variability, entitativity, and essentialism* (pp. 401–418). New York: Psychology Press.

Hogg, M. A., & Abrams, D. (1990). Social motivation, self-esteem and social identity. In D. Abrams & M. A. Hogg (Eds.), *Social identity theory: Constructive and critical advances* (pp. 28–47). London: Harvester Wheatsheaf, & New York: Springer-Verlag.

Hogg, M. A., & Abrams, D. (1993). Towards a single-process uncertainty—reduction model of social motivation in groups. In M. A. Hogg, & D. Abrams (Eds.), *Group motivation: Social psychological perspectives* (pp. 173–190). London: Harvester Wheatsheaf.

Hogg, M. A., & Grieve, P. G. (1999). Social identity theory and the crisis of confidence in social psychology: A commentary, and some research on uncertainty reduction. *Asian Journal of Social Psychology, 2*, 79–93.

Hogg, M. A., & Mullin, B.-A. (1999). Joining groups to reduce uncertainty: Subjective uncertainty reduction and group identification. In D. Abrams & M. A. Hogg (Eds.), *Social identity and social cognition* (pp. 249–279). Oxford: Blackwell.

Hogg, M. A., Sherman, D. K., Dierselhuis, J., Maitner, A. T., & Moffitt, G. (2007). Uncertainty, entitativity, and group identification. *Journal of Experimental Social Psychology, 43*, 135–142.

Hornsey, M. J., Blackwood, L. M., Louis, W., Fielding, K., Morton, T., O'Brien, A., et al. (2006). Why do people engage in collective action? Revisiting the role of effectiveness. *Journal of Applied Social Psychology, 36*, 1701–1722.

Hornsey, M. J., & Jetten, J. (2004). The individual within the group: Balancing the need to belong with the need to be different. *Personality and Social Psychology Review, 8*, 248–264.

Hoyt, C. L., Aguilar, L., Kaiser, C. R., Blascovich, J., & Lee, K. (2007). The self-protective and undermining effects of attributional ambiguity. *Journal of Experimental Social Psychology, 43*, 884–893.

Hugenberg, K., & Bodenhausen, G. V. (2004). Ambiguity in social categorization: The role of prejudice and facial affect in race categorization. *Psychological Science, 15*, 342–345.

Hugenberg, K., Miller, J., & Claypool, H. (2007). Categorization and individuation in the Cross Race Recognition Deficit: Toward a solution for an insidious problem. *Journal of Experimental Social Psychology, 43*, 334–340.

Hunsberger, B. (1995). Religion and prejudice: The role of religious fundamentalism, quest, and right-wing authoritarianism. *Journal of Social Issues, 51*, 113–129.

Inzlicht, M., & Ben-Zeev, T. (2000). A threatening intellectual environment: Why females are susceptible to experiencing problem-solving deficits in the presence of males. *Psychological Science, 11*, 365–371.

Inzlicht, M., Kaiser, C. R., & Major, B. (2008). The face of chauvinism: How prejudice expectations shape perceptions of facial affect. *Journal of Experimental Social Psychology, 44*, 758–766.

Ito, T. A., & Urland, G. R. (2003). Race and gender on the brain: Electrocortical measures of attention to race and gender of multiply categorizable individuals. *Journal of Personality and Social Psychology, 85*, 616–626.

Iyer, A., & Leach, C. W. (2008). Emotion in inter-group relations. In W. Stroebe & M. Hewstone (Eds.), *European review of social psychology* (Vol. 19, pp. 86–125). Hove, England: Psychology Press.

Iyer, A., Leach, C. W., & Crosby, F. J. (2003). White guilt and racial compensation: The benefits and limits of self-focus. *Personality and Social Psychology Bulletin, 29*, 117–129.

Iyer, A., Schmader, T., & Lickel, B. (2007). Why individuals protest the perceived transgressions of their country: The role of anger, shame, and guilt. *Personality and Social Psychology Bulletin, 33*, 572–587.

Jackson, J. (1993). Realistic group conflict theory: A review and evaluation of the theoretical and empirical literature. *Psychological Record, 43*, 395–414.

Jetten, J., Spears, R., & Manstead, A. (2001). Similarity as a source of differentiation: The role of group identification. *European Journal of Social Psychology, 31*, 621–640.

Jetten, J., Spears, R., & Postmes, T. (2004). Intergroup distinctiveness and differentiation: A meta-analytic integration. *Journal of Personality and Social Psychology, 86*, 862–879.

Johnson, A. L., Crawford, M. T., Sherman, S. J., Rutchick, A. M., Hamilton, D. L., Ferreira, M., et al. (2006). A functional perspective on group memberships: Differential need fulfillment in a group typology. *Journal of Experimental Social Psychology, 42*, 709–719.

Johnson, J., & Lecci, L. (2003). Assessing antiWhite attitudes among Blacks and predicting perceived racism: The Johnson-Lecci Scale. *Personality and Social Psychology Bulletin, 29*, 299–312.

Jones, E. E., Farina, A., Hastorf, A. H., Markus, H., Miller, D. T., & Scott, R. A. (1984). *Social stigma: The psychology of marked relationship*. New York: Freeman.

Jones, J. M. (1997). *Prejudice and racism* (2nd ed.). New York: McGraw-Hill.

Jones, J. M., Engelman, S., Turner, C. E., Jr., & Campbell, S. (2009). Worlds apart: The universality of racism leads to divergent social realities. In S. Demoulin, J.-Ph. Leyens, & J. F. Dovidio (Eds.), *Intergroup misunderstandings: Impact of divergent social realities* (pp. 117–134). New York: Psychology Press.

Jones, M. (2002). *Social psychology of prejudice*. Upper Saddle River, NJ: Prentice Hall.

Jost, J. T., & Banaji, M. R. (1994). The role of stereotyping in system justification and the production of false consciousness. *British Journal of Social Psychology, 33*, 1–27.

Jost, J. T., Glaser, J., Kruglanski, A. W., & Sulloway, F. J. (2003). Political conservatism as motivated social cognition. *Psychological Bulletin, 129*, 339–375.

Jost, J., & Major, B. (2001). *The psychology of legitimacy: Emerging perspectives on ideology, justice, and intergroup relations*. New York: Cambridge University Press.

Jost, J. T., & Thompson, E. P. (2000). Group-based dominance and opposition to equality as independent predictors of self-esteem, ethnocentrism, and social policy attitudes among African Americans and European Americans. *Journal of Experimental Social Psychology, 36*, 209–232.

Judd, C. M., Blair, I. V., & Chapleau, K. M. (2004). Automatic stereotypes versus automatic prejudice: Sorting out the possibilities in the Payne (2001) weapon paradigm. *Journal of Experimental Social Psychology, 40*, 75–81.

Judd, C. M., James-Hawkins, L., Yzerbyt, V. Y., & Kashima, Y. (2005). Fundamental dimensions of social judgment: Understanding the relations between judgments of competence and warmth. *Journal of Personality and Social Psychology, 89*, 899–913.

Judd, C. M., Park, B., Yzerbyt, V., Gordijn, E., & Muller, D. (2005). Attributions of intergroup bias and outgroup homogeneity to ingroup and outgroup others. *European Journal of Social Psychology, 35*, 677–704.

Kaiser, C. R., & Miller, C. T. (2001). Stop complaining! The social costs of making attributions to discrimination. *Personality and Social Psychology Bulletin, 27*, 254–263.

Kanyangara, P., Rimé, B., Philippot, P., & Yzerbyt, V. Y. (2007). Collective rituals, emotional climate and intergroup perception: Participation in "Gacaca" tribunals and assimilation of the Rwandan genocide. *Journal of Social Issues, 63*, 387–403.

Karlins, M., Coffman, T. L., & Walters, G. (1969). On the fading of social stereotypes: Studies in three generations of college students. *Journal of Personality and Social Psychology, 13*, 1–16.

Katz, D., & Braly, K. W. (1933). Racial stereotypes in one hundred college students. *Journal of Abnormal and Social Psychology, 28*, 280–290.

Kawakami, K., Dovidio, J. F., Moll, J., Hermsen, S., & Russin, A. (2000). Just say no (to stereotyping): Effects of training in the negation of stereotypic associations on stereotype activation. *Journal of Personality and Social Psychology, 78*, 871–888.

Kawakami, K., Dovidio, J. F., & van Kamp, S. (2005). Kicking the habit: Effects of non-stereotypic association training and correction processes on hiring decisions. *Journal of Experimental Social Psychology, 41*, 68–75.

Kay, A. C., Jost, J. T., Mandisodza, A. N., Sherman, S. J., Petrocelli, J. V., & Johnson, A. L. (2007). Panglossian ideology in the service of system justification: How complementary stereotypes help us to rationalize inequality. In M. P. Zanna (Ed.), *Advances in Experimental Social Psychology* (Vol. 38, pp. 305–358). San Diego, CA: Academic Press.

Keller, J. (2005). In genes we trust: The biological component of psychological essentialism and its relationship to mechanisms of motivated social cognition. *Journal of Personality and Social Psychology, 88*, 686–702.

Keller, J., & Dauenheimer, D. (2003). Stereotype threat in the classroom: Dejection mediates the disrupting threat effect on women's math performance. *Personality and Social Psychology Bulletin, 29*, 371–381.

Kelley, C. (1989). Political identity and perceived intragroup homogeneity. *British Journal of Social Psychology, 28*, 239–250.

Kervyn, N., Yzerbyt, V. Y., Demoulin, S., & Judd, C. M. (2008). Competence and warmth in context: The compensatory nature of stereotypic views of national groups. *European Journal of Social Psychology, 38*, 1175–1183.

Kervyn, N., Yzerbyt, V. Y., Judd, C. M., & Nunes, A. (2009). A question of compensation: The social life of the fundamental dimensions of social perception. *Journal of Personality and Social Psychology, 96*(4), 828–842.

Kilianski, S. E., & Rudman, L. A. (1998). Wanting it both ways: Do women approve of benevolent sexism? *Sex Roles, 39*, 333–352.

Kinder, D. R., & Sears, D. O. (1981). Prejudice and politics: Symbolic racism versus racial threats to the good life. *Journal of Personality and Social Psychology, 40*, 414–431.

Klandermans, B. (1997). *The social psychology of protest.* Oxford: Basil Blackwell.

Klandermans, B. (2004). The demand and supply of participation: Socialpsychological correlates of participation in social movements. In D. A. Snow, S. A. Saule, & H. Kriesi (Eds.), *The Blackwell companion to social movements* (pp. 360–379). Oxford: Blackwell.

Klauer, K. C. (1998). Affective priming. *European Review of Social Psychology, 8*, 67–103.

Klauer, K. C., & Wegener, I. (1998). Unraveling social categorization in the "who said what?" paradigm. *Journal of Personality and Social Psychology, 75*, 1155–1178.

Klauer, K. C., Voss, A., Schmitz, F., & Teige-Mocigemba, S. (2007). Process components of the Implicit Association Test: A diffusion-model analysis. *Journal of Personality and Social Psychology, 93*, 353–368.

Kleck, R. E., & Strenta, A. (1980). Perceptions of the impact of negatively valued physical characteristics on social interaction. *Journal of Personality and Social Psychology, 39*, 861–873.

Klein, O., & Snyder, M. (2003). Stereotypes and behavioral confirmation: From interpersonal to intergroup perspectives. *Advances in Experimental Social Psychology, 35*, 153–234.

Kluegel, J. R., & Smith, E. R. (1986). *Beliefs about inequality: Americans' view of what is and what ought to be.* Hawthorne, NJ: Aldine de Gruyer.

Knowles, M. L., & Gardner, W. L. (2008). Benefits of membership: The activation and amplification of group identities in response to social rejection. *Personality and Social Psychology Bulletin, 34*, 1200–1213.

Ko, S. J., Muller, D., Judd, C. M., & Stapel, D. A. (2008). Sneaking in through the back door. How category-based stereotype suppression leads to rebound in feature based effects. *Journal of Experimental Social Psychology, 44*, 833–839.

Koenig, A. M., & Eagly, A. H. (2005). Stereotype threat in men on a test of social sensitivity. *Sex Roles, 52*, 489–496.

Krueger, J. I. (2007). From social projection to social behaviour. *European Review of Social Psychology, 18*, 1–35.

Kunda, Z. (1999). *Social cognition: Making sense of people.* Cambridge, MA: MIT Press.

Kunda, Z., Davies, P. G., Adams, B. D., & Spencer, S. J. (2002). The dynamic time course of stereotype activation: Activation, dissipation, and resurrection. *Journal of Personality and Social Psychology, 82*, 283–299.

Kunda, Z., & Spencer, S. J. (2003). When do stereotypes come to mind and when do they color judgment? A goal-based theoretical framework for stereotype activation and application. *Psychological Bulletin, 129*, 522–544.

Kurzban, R., & Leary, M. R. (2001). Evolutionary origins of stigmatization: The functions of social exclusion. *Psychological Bulletin, 127*, 187–208.

Lambert, A. J., Khan, S., Lickel, B., & Fricke, K. (1997). Mood and the correction of positive versus negative stereotypes. *Journal of Personality and Social Psychology, 72*, 1002–1016.

Landau, M. J., Solomon, S., Greenberg, J., Cohen, F., Pyszczynski, T., Arndt, J., et al. (2004). Deliver us from evil: The effects of mortality salience and reminders of 9/11 on support for President George W. Bush. *Personality and Social Psychology Bulletin, 30*, 1136–1150.

Lazarus, R. S. (1991). Progression on a cognitive-motivational-relational theory of emotion. *American Psychologist, 46*, 819–834.

Leach, C. W., Iyer, A., & Pedersen, A. (2006). Guilt and anger about ingroup advantage as explanations of the willingness for political action. *Personality and Social Psychology Bulletin, 32*, 1232–1245.

Leach, C. W., Iyer, A., & Pedersen, A. (2007). Angry opposition to government redress: When the structurally advantaged perceive themselves as relatively deprived. *British Journal of Social Psychology, 46*, 191–204.

Leach, C. W., & Spears, R. (2008). "A vengeful of the impotent": The pain of in-group inferiority and schadenfreude toward successful outgroups. *Journal of Personality and Social Psychology, 95*, 1383–1396.

Leach, C. W., Spears, R., Branscombe, N. R., & Doosje, B. (2003). Malicious pleasure: Schadenfreude at the suffering of another group. *Journal of Personality and Social Psychology, 84*, 932–943.

Leary, M. (2007). Motivational and emotional aspects of the self. *Annual Review of Psychology, 58*, 317–344.

Leary, M. R., Twenge, J. M., & Quinlivan, E. (2006). Interpersonal rejection as a determinant of anger and aggression. *Personality and Social Psychology Review, 10*, 111–132.

Lemaine, G. (1974). Social differentiation and social originality. *European Journal of Social Psychology, 4*, 17–52.

Lepore, L., & Brown, R. (1997). Category and stereotype activation: Is prejudice inevitable? *Journal of Personality and Social Psychology, 72*, 275–287.

Lerner, J. L., & Tetlock, P. E. (1999). Accounting for the effects of accountability. *Journal of Personality and Social Psychology, 125*, 255–275.

Levin, D. T., & Banaji, M. R. (2006). Distortions in the perceived lightness of faces: The role of race categories. *Journal of Experimental Psychology: General, 4*, 501–512.

Levine, M., Prosser, A., Evans, D., & Reicher, S. (2005). Identity and emergency intervention: How social group membership and inclusiveness of group boundaries shape helping behavior. *Personality and Social Psychology Bulletin, 31*, 443–453.

LeVine, R. A., & Campbell, D. T. (1972). *Ethnocentrism: Theories of conflict, ethnic attitudes, and group behavior.* New York: Wiley.

Lévi-Strauss, C. (1952). *Race and history*. Chicago: Chicago University Press.

Levy, S. R., Stroessner, S. J., & Dweck, C. S. (1998). Stereotype formation and endorsement: The role of implicit theories. *Journal of Personality and Social Psychology, 74*, 1421–1436.

Lewin, K. (1948). *Resolving social conflicts*. New York: Harper & Ross.

Leyens, J.-Ph., Cortes, B. P., Demoulin, S., Dovidio, J., Fiske, S. T., Gaunt, R., et al. (2003). Emotional prejudice, essentialism, and nationalism. *European Journal of Social Psychology, 33*, 703–717.

Leyens, J.-Ph., Demoulin, S., Désert, M., Vaes, J., & Phillipot, P. (2002). Expressing emotions and decoding them: In-groups and out-groups do not share the same advantages. In D. Mackie & E. Smith (Eds.), *From prejudice to intergroup emotions: Differentiated reactions to social groups*. Philadelphia: Psychology Press.

Leyens, J.-Ph., Demoulin, S., Vaes, J., Gaunt, R., & Paladino, M. P. (2007). Infra-humanization: The wall of group differences. *Journal of Social Issues and Policy Review, 1*, 139–172.

Leyens, J.-Ph., Désert, M., Croizet, J.-C., & Darcis, C. (2000). Stereotype threat: Are lower status and history of stigmatization preconditions of stereotype threat? *Personality and Social Psychology Bulletin, 26*, 1189–1199.

Leyens, J.-Ph., Paladino, M.-P., Rodriguez, R. T., Vaes, J., Demoulin, S., Rodriguez, A. P., et al. (2000). The emotional side of prejudice: The role of secondary emotions. *Personality and Social Psychology Review, 4*, 186–197.

Leyens, J.-Ph., Rodriguez, A. P., Rodriguez, R. T., Gaunt, R., Paladino, P. M., Vaes, J., et al. (2001). Psychological essentialism and the differential attribution of uniquely human emotions to ingroups and outgroups. *European Journal of Social Psychology, 31*, 395–411.

Leyens, J.-Ph., & Yzerbyt, V. Y. (1992). The ingroup overexclusion effect. Impact of valence and confirmation on stereotypical information search. *European Journal of Social Psychology, 22*, 549–569.

Leyens, J.-Ph., Yzerbyt, V. Y., & Schadron, G. (1994). *Stereotypes and social cognition*. London: Sage.

Lickel, B., Hamilton, D. L., Uhles, A. N., Wieczorkowska, G., Lewis, A., & Sherman, S. J. (2000). Varieties of groups and the perception of group entitativity. *Journal of Personality and Social Psychology, 78*, 223–246.

Lickel, B., Miller, N., Stenstrom, D. M., Denson, T. F., & Schmader, T. (2006). Vicarious retribution: The role of collective blame in intergroup aggression. *Personality and Social Psychology Review, 10*, 372–390.

Lickel, B., Rutchick, A., Hamilton, D. L., & Sherman, S. J. (2006). Intuitive theories of group types and relational principles. *Journal of Experimental Social Psychology, 42*, 28–39.

Lickel, B., Schmader, T., Curtis, M., Scarnier, M., & Ames, D. R. (2005). Vicarious shame and guilt. *Group Processes and Intergroup Relations, 8*, 145–147.

Lin, M. H., Kwan, V. S. Y., Cheung, A., & Fiske, S. T. (2005). Stereotype content model explains prejudice for an envied outgroup: Scale of Anti-Asian American Stereotypes. *Personality and Social Psychology Bulletin, 31*, 34–47.

Lind, E. A., & van den Bos, K. (2002). When fairness works: Toward a general theory of uncertainty management. In B. M. Staw & R. M. Kramer (Eds.), *Research in organizational behavior* (Vol. 24, pp. 181–223). Greenwich, CT: JAI Press.

Linville, P. W., Fischer, G. W., & Salovey, P. (1989). Perceived distributions of the characteristics of ingroup and outgroup members: Empirical evidence and a computer simulation. *Journal of Personality and Social Psychology, 57*, 165–188.

Linville, P. W., Salovey, P., & Fisher, G. W. (1986). Stereotyping and perceived distributions of social characteristics: An application to ingroup-outgroup perception. In J. F. Dovidio & S. L. Gaertner (Eds.), *Prejudice, discrimination, and racism* (pp. 165–208). Orlando, FL: Academic Press.

Lippmann, W. (1922). *Public opinion*. Oxford: Harcourt & Brace.

Livingston, R. W., & Brewer, M. B. (2002). What are we really priming? Cue-based versus category-based processing of facial stimuli. *Journal of Personality & Social Psychology, 82*, 5–18.

Loughnan, S., & Haslam, N. (2007). Animals and androids: Implicit associations between social categories and nonhumans. *Psychological Science, 18*, 116–121.

Maass, A. (1999). Linguistic intergroup bias: Stereotype perpetuation through language. In M. P. Zanna (Ed.), *Advances in experimental social psychology* (Vol. 31, pp. 79–121). New York: Academic Press.

Maass, A., Salvi, D., Arcuri, L., & Semin, G. (1989). Language use in intergroup contexts: The linguistic intergroup bias. *Journal of Personality and Social Psychology, 57*, 981–993.

Mackie, D. M., Devos, T., & Smith, E. R. (2000). Intergroup emotions: Explaining offensive action tendencies in an intergroup context. *Journal of Personality and Social Psychology, 79*, 602–616.

Mackie, D. M., Silver, L. A., & Smith, E. R. (2004). Intergroup emotions: Emotion as an intergroup phenomenon. In L. Z. Tiedens & C. W. Leach (Eds.), *The social life of emotions* (pp. 227–245). New York: Cambridge University Press.

Mackie, D. M, & Smith, E. R. (1998). Intergroup relations: Insights from a theoretically integrative approach. *Psychological Review, 105*, 499–529.

Mackie, D. M., & Smith, E. R. (2002). *From prejudice to intergroup emotions: Differentiated reactions to social groups*. Philadelphia: Psychology Press.

Macrae, C. N., & Bodenhausen, G. V. (2000). Social cognition: Thinking categorically about others. *Annual Review of Psychology, 51*, 93–120.

Macrae, C. N., Bodenhausen, G. V., & Milne, A. B. (1995). The dissection of selection in person perception: Inhibitory processes in social stereotyping. *Journal of Personality and Social Psychology, 69*, 397–407.

Macrae, C. N., Bodenhausen, G. V., Milne, A. B., & Jetten, J. (1994). Out of mind but back in sight: Stereotypes on the rebound. *Journal of Personality and Social Psychology, 67*, 808–817.

Macrae, C. N., Bodenhausen, G. V., Milne, A. B., Thorn, T. M. J., & Castelli, L. (1997). On the activation of social stereotypes: The moderating role of processing objectives. *Journal of Experimental Social Psychology, 33*, 471–489.

Macrae, C. N., Hood, B. M., Milne, A. B., Rowe, A. C., & Mason, M. F. (2002). Are you looking at me? Eye gaze and person perception. *Psychological Science, 13*, 460–464.

Macrae, C. N., Milne, A. B., & Bodenhausen, G. V. (1994). Stereotypes as energy-saving devices: A peek inside the cognitive toolbox. *Journal of Personality and Social Psychology, 66*, 37–47.

Macrae, C. N., Quinn, K. A., Mason, M. F., & Quadflieg, S. (2005). Understanding others: The face and person construal. *Journal of Personality and Social Psychology, 89*, 686–695.

Maddox, K. B. (2004). Perspectives on racial phenotypicality bias. *Personality and Social Psychology Review, 8*, 383–401.

Maddox, K. B., & Chase, S. G. (2004). Manipulating subcategory salience: Exploring the link between skin tone and social perception of blacks. *European Journal of Social Psychology, 34*, 1–14.

Maddox, K. B., & Gray, S. A. (2002). Cognitive representations of Black Americans: Reexploring the role of skin tone. *Personality and Social Psychology Bulletin, 28*, 250–259.

Madon, S., Guyll, M., Aboufadel, K., Montiel, E., Smith, A., Palumbo, P., et al. (2001). Ethnic and national stereotypes: The Princeton Trilogy revisited and revised. *Personality and Social Psychology Bulletin, 27*, 996–1010.

Mae, L., & Carlston, D. E. (2005). Boomerang effects of bigoted speech. *Journal of Experimental Social Psychology, 41*, 240–255.

Maitner, A. T., Mackie, D. M., & Smith, E. R. (2006). Evidence for the regulatory function of intergroup emotion: Emotional consequences of implemented or impeded intergroup action tendencies. *Journal of Experimental Social Psychology, 42*, 720–728.

Major, B., & Crocker, J. (1993). Social stigma: The affective consequences of attributional ambiguity. In D. M. Mackie & D. L. Hamilton (Eds.), *Affect, cognition, and stereotyping: Interactive process in intergroup perception* (pp. 345–370). New York: Academic Press.

Major, B., Gramzow, R. H., McCoy, S., Levin, S., Schmader, T., & Sidanius, J. (2002). Ideology and attributions to discrimination among low and high status groups. *Journal of Personality and Social Psychology, 82,* 269–282.

Major, B., Kaiser, C. R., & McCoy, S. K. (2003). It's not my fault: When and why attributions to prejudice protect self-esteem. *Personality and Social Psychology Bulletin, 29,* 772–781.

Major, B., & O'Brien, L. T. (2005). The social psychology of stigma. *Annual Review of Psychology, 56,* 393–421.

Major, B., & Schmader, T. (2001). From social devaluation to self-esteem: The impact of legitimacy appraisals. In B. Major & J. Jost (Eds.), *Psychology of legitimacy: Emerging perspectives on ideology, justice, and intergroup relations.* Cambridge, England: Cambridge University Press.

Major, B., Spencer, S. J., Schmader, T., Wolfe, C., & Crocker, J. (1998). Coping with negative stereotypes about intellectual performance: The role of psychological disengagement. *Personality and Social Psychology Bulletin, 24,* 34–50.

Mallett, R. K., Wilson, T. D., & Gilbert, D. T. (2008). Expect the unexpected: Failure to anticipate similarities leads to an intergroup forecasting error. *Journal of Personality and Social Psychology, 94,* 265–277.

Maner, J. K., DeWall, C. N., Baumeister, R. F., & Schaller, M. (2007). Does social exclusion motivate interpersonal reconnection? Resolving the "porcupine problem." *Journal of Personality and Social Psychology, 92,* 42–55.

Markus, H. (1977). Self-schemata and processing information about the self. *Journal of Personality and Social Psychology, 35,* 63–78.

Markus, H. R., & Kunda, Z. (1986). Stability and malleability of the self-concept. *Journal of Personality and Social Psychology, 51,* 858–866.

Markus, H. R., & Nurius, P. (1986). Possible selves. *American Psychologist, 41,* 954–969.

Markus, H. R., & Sentis, K. (1982). The self in social information processing. In J. Suls (Ed.), *Psychological perspectives on the self* (Vol. 1, pp. 41–70). Hillsdale, NJ: Lawrence Erlbaum.

Markus, H. R., & Wurf, E. (1987). The dynamic self-concept: A social psychological perspective. *Annual Review of Psychology, 38,* 299–337.

Marques, J. M., & Páez, D. (1994). The "black sheep effect": Social categorization, rejection of ingroup deviates, and perception of group variability. In W. Stroebe & M. Hewstone (Eds.), *European review of social psychology* (Vol. 5, pp. 38–68). Chichester, England: Wiley.

Marques, J. M., Yzerbyt, V. Y., & Leyens, J. P. (1988). The 'black sheep effect': Extremity of judgments towards ingroup members as a function of group identification. *European Journal of Social Psychology, 18,* 1–16.

Martens, A., Johns, M., Greenberg, J., & Schimel, J. (2006). Combating stereotype threat: The effect of self-affirmation on women's intellectual performance. *Journal of Experimental Social Psychology, 42,* 236–243.

Martell, R. F., Lane, D. M., & Emrich, C. (1996). Male-female differences: A computer simulation. *American Psychologist, 51,* 157–158.

Martin, C. L., & Parker, S. (1995). Folk theories about sex and race differences. *Personality and Social Psychology Bulletin, 21,* 45–57.

Marx, D. M., & Stapel, D. A. (2006). Distinguishing stereotype threat from priming effects: On the role of the social self and threat-based concerns. *Journal of Personality and Social Psychology, 91,* 243–254.

Marx, D. M., Stapel, D. A., & Muller, D. (2005). We can do it: The interplay of construal orientation and social comparisons under threat. *Journal of Personality and Social Psychology, 88,* 432–446.

Maslow, A. H. (1943). A theory of human motivation. *Psychological Review, 50,* 370–396.

McCauley, C., & Stitt, C. L. (1978). An individual and quantitative measure of stereotypes. *Journal of Personality and Social Psychology, 39,* 929–940.

McConahay, J. B. (1986). Modern racism, ambivalence, and the modern racism scale. In J. D. Dovidio & S. L. Gaertner (Eds.), *Prejudice, discrimination, and racism* (pp. 91–125). San Diego, CA: Academic Press.

McConnell, A. R., & Leibold, J. M. (2001). Relations between the Implicit Association Test, explicit racial attitudes, and discriminatory behavior. *Journal of Experimental Social Psychology, 37,* 435–442.

McCoy, S. K., & Major, B. (2003). Group identification moderates emotional responses to perceived prejudice. *Personality and Social Psychology Bulletin, 29,* 1005–1017.

McDevitt, J., Balboni, J., Garcia, L., & Gu, J. (2001). Consequences for victims: A comparison of bias- and non-bias-motivated assaults. *American Behavioral Scientist, 45*(4), 697–713.

McDevitt, J., Levin, J., & Bennett, S. (2002). Hate crime offenders: An expanded typology. *Journal of Social Issues, 58,* 303–317.

McGarty, C., Pedersen, A., Leach, C. W., Mansell, T., Waller, J., & Bliuc, A.-M. (2005). Group-based guilt as a predictor of commitment to apology. *British Journal of Social Psychology, 44,* 659–680.

McGarty, C., & Penny, R. E. C. (1988). Categorization, accentuation, and social judgement. *British Journal of Social Psychology, 22,* 147–157.

McGlone, M. S., & Aronson, J. (2007). Forewarning and forearming stereotype-threatened students. *Communication Education, 56,* 119–133.

Medin, D. L. (1989). Concepts and conceptual structure. *American Psychologist, 44,* 1469–1481.

Meertens, R. W., & Pettigrew, T. F. (1997). Is subtle prejudice really prejudice? *Public Opinion Quarterly, 61,* 54–71.

Mendes, W. B., Blascovich, J., Hunter, S. B., Lickel, B., & Jost, J. T. (2002). Threatened by the unexpected: Physiological responses during social interactions with expectancy-violating partners. *Journal of Personality and Social Psychology, 92,* 698–716.

Mendes, W. B., Blascovich, J., Lickel, B., & Hunter, S. B. (2002). Challenge and threat during social interactions with White and Black men. *Personality and Social Psychology Bulletin, 28,* 939–952.

Mendes, W. B., Major, B., McCoy, S. K., & Blascovich, J. (2008). How attributional ambiguity shapes physiological and emotional responses to social rejection and acceptance. *Journal of Personality and Social Psychology, 94,* 278–91.

Mendoza-Denton, R., Downey, G., Purdie, V., & Davis, A. (2002). Sensitivity to status-based rejection: Implications for African-American students' college experience. *Journal of Personality and Social Psychology, 83,* 896–918.

Messick, D. M., & Mackie, D. M. (1989). Intergroup relations. *Annual Review of Psychology, 40,* 45–81.

Michel, C., Corneille, O., & Rossion, B. (2007). Race categorization modulates holistic face encoding. *Cognitive Science, 31,* 911–924.

Mikula, G., Scherer, K. R., & Athenstaedt, U. (1998). The role of injustice in the elicitation of differential emotional reactions. *Personality and Social Psychology Bulletin, 24,* 769–783.

Miller, D. T., & Prentice, D. A. (1999). Some consequences of a belief in group essence: The category divide hypothesis. In D. A. Miller & D. T. Miller (Eds.), *Cultural divides: Understanding and resolving group conflict* (pp. 213–238). New York: Russell Sage Foundation.

Mitchell, J. P., Nosek, B. A., & Banaji, M. R. (2003). Contextual variations in implicit evaluation. *Journal of Experimental Psychology: General, 132,* 455–469.

Molden, D. C., Lucas, G. M., Gardner, W. L., Dean, K., & Knowles, M. L. (2009). Motivations for prevention or promotion following social exclusion: Being rejected versus being ignored. *Journal of Personality and Social Psychology, 96,* 415–431.

Monin, B., & Miller, D. T. (2001). Moral credentials and the expression of prejudice. *Journal of Personality and Social Psychology, 81,* 33–43.

Montada, L., & Schneider, A. (1989). Justice and emotional reactions to the disadvantaged. *Social Justice Research, 3,* 313–344.

Monteith, M. J., Sherman, J. W., & Devine, P. G. (1998). Suppression as a stereotype control strategy. *Personality and Social Psychology Review, 2,* 63–82.

Monteith, M. J., Spicer, C. V., & Tooman, G. (1998). Consequences of stereotype suppression: Stereotypes on and not on the rebound. *Journal of Experimental Social Psychology, 34,* 355–377.

Morton, T. A., Hornsey, M. J., & Postmes, T. (2009). Shifting ground: The variable use of essentialism in contexts of inclusion and exclusion. *British Journal of Social Psychology, 48,* 35–59.

Morton, T. A., Postmes, T., Haslam, S. A., & Hornsey, M. J. (2009). Theorizing gender in the face of social change: Is there anything essential about essentialism? *Journal of Personality and Social Psychology, 96,* 653–664.

Moskowitz, G. B., Gollwitzer, P. M., Wasel, W., & Schaal, B. (1999). Preconscious control of stereotype activation through chronic egalitarian goals. *Journal of Personality and Social Psychology, 77,* 167–184.

Mullen, B., Brown, R., & Smith, C. (1992). Ingroup bias as a function of salience, relevance, and status: An integration. *European Journal of Social Psychology, 22,* 103–122.

Mullen, B., & Hu, L. (1989). Perceptions of ingroup and outgroup variability: A meta-analytic integration. *Basic and Applied Social Psychology, 10,* 233–252.

Mummendey, A., & Otten, S. (1998). Positive-negative asymmetry in social discrimination. In W. Stroebe & M. Hewstone (Eds.), *European Review of Social Psychology* (Vol. 9, pp. 107–143). New York: Wiley.

Mummendey, A., Otten, S., Berger, U., & Kessler, T. (2000). Positive-negative asymmetry in social discrimination: Valence of evaluation and salience of categorization. *Personality and Social Psychology Bulletin, 26,* 1258–1270.

Mummendey, A., & Wenzel, M. (1999). Social discrimination and tolerance in intergroup relations: Reactions to intergroup difference. *Personality and Social Psychology Review, 3,* 158–174.

Muraven, M., & Baumeister, R. (2000). Self-regulation and depletion of limited resources: Does self-control resemble a muscle? *Psychological Bulletin, 126,* 247–259.

Mussweiler, T. (2003). Comparison processes in social judgment: Mechanisms and consequences. *Psychological Review, 110,* 472–489.

Nadler, A., Malloy, T., & Fisher, J. (2008). *Social psychology of intergroup reconciliation: From violent conflict to peaceful co-existence—going beyond victimization, guilt, and distrust.* Oxford: Oxford University Press.

Neuberg, S. L., & Cottrell, C. A. (2002). Intergroup emotions: A sociofunctional approach. In D. M. Mackie & E. R. Smith (Eds.), *From prejudice to intergroup emotions: Differentiated reactions to social groups* (pp. 265–283). New York: Psychology Press.

Oakes, P. J., Haslam, S. A., & Turner, J. C. (1994). *Stereotyping and Social Reality.* Oxford: Blackwell.

O'Brien, L. T., & Crandall, C. S. (2003). Stereotype threat and arousal: Effects on women's math performance. *Personality and Social Psychology Bulletin, 29,* 782–789.

Oldmeadow, J., & Fiske, S. T. (2007). System-justifying ideologies moderate status = competence stereotypes: Roles of beliefs in a just world and social dominance orientation. *European Journal of Social Psychology, 37,* 1135–1148.

Olson, M. A., & Fazio, R. H. (2002). Implicit acquisition and manifestation of classically conditioned attitudes. *Social Cognition, 20,* 89–103.

Olson, M. A., & Fazio, R. H. (2004). Trait inferences as a function of automatically-activated racial attitudes and motivation to control prejudiced reactions. *Basic and Applied Social Psychology, 26,* 1–11.

Olson, M. A., Fazio, R. H., & Hermann, A. D. (2007). Reporting tendencies underlie discrepancies between implicit and explicit measures of self-esteem. *Psychological Science, 18,* 287–291.

Onorato, R. S., & Tuner, J. S. (2004). Fluidity in the self-concept: The shift from personal to social identity. *European Journal of Social Psychology, 34,* 257–278.

Opotow, S. (1990). Moral exclusion and injustice: An introduction. *Journal of Social Issues, 46,* 173–182.

Oskamp, S. (2000). *Reducing intergroup discrimination.* Hillsdale, NJ: Lawrence Erlbaum.

Otten, S., & Epstude, K. (2006). Overlapping mental representations of self, ingroup and outgroup: Unraveling self-stereotyping and self-anchoring. *Personality and Social Psychology Bulletin, 32,* 957–969.

Otten, S., & Moskowitz, G. B. (2000). Evidence for implicit evaluative ingroup bias: Affect-biased spontaneous trait inference in a minimal group paradigm. *Journal of Experimental Social Psychology, 36,* 77–89.

Otten, S., Mummendey, A., & Blanz, M. (1996). Intergroup discrimination in positive and negative outcome allocations: Impact of stimulus valence, relative group status, and relative group size. *Personality and Social Psychology Bulletin, 22,* 568–581.

Otten, S., & Wentura, D. (1999). About the impact of automaticity in the minimal group paradigm: Evidence from affective priming tasks. *European Journal of Social Psychology, 29,* 1049–1071.

Otten, S., & Wentura, D. (2001). Self-anchoring and in-group favouritism: An individual profiles analysis. *Journal of Experimental Social Psychology, 37,* 525–532.

Pager, D. (2003). The mark of a criminal record. *American Journal of Sociology, 108,* 937–975.

Pager, D., & Quillian, L. (2005). Walking the talk? What employers say versus what they do. *American Sociological Review, 70,* 355–380.

Paladino, M. P., & Castelli, L. (2008). On the immediate consequences of intergroup categorization: Activation of approach and avoidance motor behavior toward ingroup and outgroup members. *Personality and Social Psychology Bulletin, 34,* 755–768.

Paladino, M. P., Leyens, J. Ph., Rodriguez, R. T., Rodriguez, A. P., Gaunt, R., & Demoulin, S. (2002). Differential association of uniquely and non uniquely human emotions with the ingroup and the outgroup. *Group Processes and Intergroup Relations, 5,* 105–117.

Park, B., & Judd, C. M. (1990). Measures and model of perceived group variability. *Journal of Personality and Social Psychology, 59,* 173–191.

Park, B., Ryan, C. S., & Judd, C. M. (1992). Role of meaningful subgroups in explaining differences in perceived variability for in-groups and outgroups. *Journal of Personality and Social Psychology, 63,* 553–567.

Parkinson, B., Fischer, A. H., & Manstead, A. S. R. (2005). *Emotion in social relations: Cultural, group, and interpersonal processes.* New York: Psychology Press.

Payne, B. K. (2001). Prejudice and perception: The role of automatic and controlled processes in misperceiving a weapon. *Journal of Personality and Social Psychology, 81,* 181–192.

Payne, B. K., Cheng, C. M., Govorun, O., & Stewart, B. D. (2005). An inkblot for attitudes: Affect misattribution as implicit measurement. *Journal of Personality and Social Psychology, 89,* 277–293.

Payne, B. K., Lambert, A. J., & Jacoby, L. L. (2002). Best laid plans: Effects of goals on accessibility bias and cognitive control in race-based misperceptions of weapons. *Journal of Experimental Social Psychology, 38,* 384–396.

Pearson, A., West, T., Dovidio, J., Powers, S., Buck, R., & Henning, R. (2008). The fragility of intergroup relations: Divergent effects of delayed audiovisual feedback in intergroup and intragroup interaction. *Psychological Science, 19*(12), 1272–1279.

Peeters, G. (1983). Relational and informational patterns in social cognition. In W. Doise & S. Moscovici (Eds.), *Current issues in European*

Social Psychology (pp. 201–237). Cambridge, England: Cambridge University Press.

Pendry, L. F., & Macrae, C. N. (1994). Stereotypes and mental life: The case of the motivated but thwarted tactician. *Journal of Experimental Social Psychology, 30*, 303–325.

Pendry, L. F., & Macrae, C. N. (1996). What the disinterested perceiver overlooks: Processing goals and stereotype activation. *Personality and Social Psychology Bulletin, 22*, 250–257.

Perdue, C. W., Dovidio, J. F., Gurtman, M. B., & Tyler, R. B. (1990). Us and them: Social categorization and the process of intergroup bias. *Journal of Personality and Social Psychology, 59*, 475–486.

Perreault, S., & Bourhis, R. Y. (1998). Social identification, interdependence, and discrimination. *Group Processes and Intergroup Relations, 1*, 49–66.

Petersen, L. E., & Dietz, J. (2000). Social discrimination in a personnel selection context: The effects of an authority's instruction to discriminate and followers' authoritarianism. *Journal of Applied Social Psychology, 30*, 206–220.

Pettigrew, T. F. (1979). The ultimate attribution error: Extending Allport's cognitive analysis of prejudice. *Personality and Social Psychology Bulletin, 5*, 461–476.

Pettigrew, T. F., Christ, O., Wagner, U., Meertens, R. W., van Dick, R., & Zick, A. (2008). Relative deprivation and intergroup prejudice. *Journal of Social Issues, 64*, 385–401.

Pettigrew, T. F., & Meertens, R. (1995). Subtle and blatant prejudice in Western Europe. *European Journal of Social Psychology, 25*, 57–75.

Phalet, K., & Poppe, E. (1997). Competence and morality dimensions of national and ethnic stereotypes: A study in six eastern-European countries. *European Journal of Social Psychology, 27*(6), 703–723.

Phelps, E. A., Cannistraci, C. J., & Cunningham, W. A. (2003). Intact performance on an indirect measure of race bias following amygdala damage. *Neuropsychologia, 41*, 203–208.

Phelps, E. A., O'Connor, K. J., Cunningham, W. A., Funayama, E. S., Gatenby, J. C., Gore, J. C., et al. (2001). Performance on indirect measures of race evaluation predicts amygdala activation. *Journal of Cognitive Neuroscience, 12*, 729–738.

Pichon, I., Boccato, G., & Saroglou, V. (2007). Nonconscious influences of religion on prosociality: A priming study. *European Journal of Social Psychology, 37*, 1032–1045.

Pickett, C. L., Silver, M. D., & Brewer, M. B. (2002). The impact of assimilation and differentiation needs on perceived group importance and judgments of ingroup size. *Personality and Social Psychology Bulletin, 28*, 546–558.

Pittman, T. S. (1998). Motivation. In D. T. Gilbert, S. T. Fiske, & G. Lindzey (Eds.), *The handbook of social psychology* (Vol. 1, 4th ed., pp. 549–590). New York: McGraw-Hill.

Plaks, J. E., Levy, S. R., Dweck, C. S., & Stroessner, S. J. (2004). In the eye of the beholder: Implicit theories and the perception of group variability, entitativity, and essence. In V. Yzerbyt, O. Corneille, & C. Judd (Eds.), *The psychology of group perception: Contributions to the study of homogeneity, entititavity, and essentialism* (pp. 127–146). New York: Psychology Press.

Plant, E. A., & Devine, P. G. (1998). Internal and external motivation to respond without prejudice. *Journal of Personality and Social Psychology, 75*, 811–832.

Plant, E. A., & Devine, P. G. (2001). Responses to other-imposed pro-Black pressure: Acceptance or backlash? *Journal of Experimental Social Psychology, 37*, 486–501.

Plant, E. A., & Devine, P. G. (2003). The antecedents and implications of interracial anxiety. *Personality and Social Psychology Bulletin, 29*, 790–801.

Powell, A. A., Branscombe, N. R., & Schmitt, M. T. (2005). Inequality as ingroup privilege or outgroup disadvantage: The impact of group focus on collective guilt and interracial attitudes. *Personality and Social Psychology Bulletin, 31*, 508–521.

Pratto, F., Sidanius, J., Stallworth, L. M., & Malle, B. F. (1994). Social dominance orientation: A personality variable predicting social and political attitudes. *Journal of Personality and Social Psychology, 67*, 741–763.

Prentice, D. A., & Miller, D. T. (2007). Psychological essentialism of human categories. *Current Directions in Psychological Science, 16*, 202–206.

Pronin, E., Steele, C. M., & Ross, L. (2004). Identity bifurcation in response to stereotype threat: Women and mathematics. *Journal of Experimental Social Psychology, 40*, 152–168.

Pyszczynski, T., Greenberg, J., & Solomon, S. (1997). Why do we need what we need? A terror management perspective on the roots of human social motivation. *Psychological Inquiry, 8*, 1–20.

Queller, S., Schell, T., & Mason, W. (2006). A novel view of between-categories contrast and within-category assimilation. *Journal of Personality and Social Psychology, 91*, 406–422.

Rabbie, J. M. (1991). Determinants of instrumental intra-group cooperation. In R. A. Hinde & J. Groebel (Eds.), *Cooperation and prosocial behaviour*. Cambridge, England: Cambridge University Press.

Rabbie, J. M., & Horwitz, M. (1988). Categories versus groups as explanatory concepts in intergroup relations. *European Journal of Social Psychology, 18*, 117–123.

Rabbie, J. M., Schot, J. C., & Visser, L. (1989). Social identity theory: A conceptual and empirical critique from the perspective of behavioural interaction model. *European Journal of Social Psychology, 19*, 171–202.

Rangel, U., & Keller, J. (2008). *Essentialism goes social: Belief in social determinism as a component of psychological essentialism*. University of Mannheim. Manuscript submitted for publication.

Ray, D. G., Mackie, D. M., Rydell, R. J., & Smith, E. R. (2008). Changing categorization of self can change emotions about outgroups. *Journal of Experimental Social Psychology, 44*, 1210–1213.

Redersdorff, S., Martinot, D., & Branscombe, N. R. (2004). The impact of thinking about group-based disadvantages or advantages on women's well-being: An experimental test of the rejection-identification model. *Current Psychology of Cognition, 22*, 203–222.

Reicher, S. D. (1996a). 'The Battle of Westminster': Developing the social identity model of crowd behaviour in order to explain the initiation and development of collective conflict. *European Journal of Social Psychology, 26*, 115–134.

Reicher, S. D. (1996b). Social identity and social change: Rethinking the context of social psychology. In P. Robinson (Ed.), *Social groups and identities: Developing the legacy of Henri Tajfel* (pp. 317–336). Oxford: Butterworth-Heinemann.

Reicher, S. D. (2001). Studying psychology studying racism. In M. Augoustinos & K. J. Reynolds (Eds.), *Understanding prejudice, racism, and social conflict*. London: Sage.

Reicher, S. D., & Hopkins, N. (2001). Psychology and the end of history: A critic and a proposal for the psychology of social categorization. *Political Psychology, 22*, 383–407.

Richeson, J. A., Baird, A. A., Gordon, H. L., Heatherton, T. F., Wyland, C. L., Trawalter, S., et al. (2003). An fMRI investigation of the impact of interracial contact on executive function. *Nature Neuroscience, 6*, 1323–1328.

Richeson, J. A., & Nussbaum, R. J. (2004). The impact of multiculturalism versus color-blindness on racial bias. *Journal of Experimental Social Psychology, 40*, 417–423.

Richeson, J. A., & Shelton, J. N. (2003). When prejudice does not pay: Effects of interracial contact on executive function. *Psychological Science, 14*, 287–290.

Richeson, J. A., & Shelton, J. N. (2007). Negotiating interracial interactions: Costs, consequences, and possibilities. *Current Directions in Psychological Science, 16*, 316–320.

Richeson, J. A., & Trawalter, S. (2005). Why do interracial interactions impair executive function? A resource depletion account. *Journal of Personality and Social Psychology, 88*, 934–947.

Richeson, J. A., & Trawalter, S. (2008). The threat of appearing prejudiced and race-based attentional biases. *Psychological Science, 19*, 98–102.

Richeson, J. A., Trawalter, S., & Shelton, J. N. (2005). African Americans' implicit racial attitudes and the depletion of executive function after interracial interactions. *Social Cognition, 23*, 336–352.

Riek, B. M., Mania, E. W., & Gaertner, S. L. (2006). Intergroup threat and outgroup attitudes: A meta-analytic review. *Personality and Social Psychology Review, 10*, 336–353.

Roccas, S., Klar, Y., & Liviatan, I. (2004). Exonerating cognitions, group identifications, and personal values as predictors of collective guilt among Jewish-Israelis. In N. R. Brancombe & B. Doosje (Eds.), *Collective guilt: International perspectives* (pp. 130–147). New York: Cambridge University Press.

Rosch, E. (1978). Principles of categorization. In E. Rosch & B. Lloyd (Eds.), *Cognition and categorization* (pp. 28–49). Hillsdale, NJ: Erlbaum.

Rosenberg, S., Nelson, C., & Vivekananthan, P. S. (1968). A multidimensional approach to the structure of personality impressions. *Journal of Personality and Social Psychology, 9*, 283–294.

Rothbart, M., & Taylor, M. (1992). Category labels and social reality: Do we view social categories as natural kinds? In G. Semin & F. Fiedler (Eds.), *Language, interaction and social cognition* (pp. 11–36). London: Sage Ltd.

Rubin, M., & Hewstone, M. (1998). Social identity theory's self-esteem hypothesis: A review and some suggestions for clarification. *Personality and Social Psychology Review, 2*, 40–62.

Rudman, L. A., Greenwald, A. G., & McGhee, D. E. (2001). Implicit self-concept and evaluative implicit gender stereotypes: Self and ingroup share desirable traits. *Personality and Social Psychology Bulletin, 27*, 1164–1178.

Rudman, L. A., Greenwald, A. G., Mellott, D. S., & Schwartz, J. L. K. (1999). Measuring the automatic components of prejudice: Flexibility and generality of the Implicit Association Test. *Social Cognition, 17*, 437–465.

Rudman, L. A., & Kilianski, S. E. (2000). Implicit and explicit attitudes toward female authority. *Personality and Social Psychology Bulletin, 26*, 1315–1328.

Runciman, W. G. (1966). *Relative deprivation and social justice*. London: Routledge & Kegan Paul.

Ruscher, J. B. (2001). *Prejudiced communication: A social psychological perspective*. New York: The Guilford Press.

Saguy, T., Pratto, F., Dovidio, J. F., & Nadler, A. (2009). Talking about power: Group power and the desired content of intergroup interactions. In Demoulin, S., Leyens, J.-Ph., & Dovidio, J. F. (Eds.), *Intergroup misunderstandings: Impact of divergent social realities* (pp. 213–232). New York: Psychology Press.

Saroglou, V., Corneille, O., & Van Cappellen, P. (2009). "Speak, Lord, your servant is listening": Religious priming activates submissive thoughts and behaviors. *International Journal for the Psychology of Religion, 19*, 143–154.

Schachter, S. (1959). *The psychology of affiliation*. Palo Alto, CA: Stanford University Press.

Scheepers, D., Spears, R., Doosje, B., & Manstead, A. S. R. (2002). Integrating identity and instrumental approaches to intergroup discrimination: Different contexts, different motives. *Personality and Social Psychology Bulletin, 28*, 1455–1467.

Scheepers, D., Spears, R., Doosje, B., & Manstead, A. S. R. (2003). Two functions of verbal intergroup discrimination: Identity and instrumental motives as a result of group identification and threat. *Personality and Social Psychology Bulletin, 29*, 568–577.

Scheepers, D., Spears, R., Doosje, B., & Manstead, A. S. R. (2006). The social functions of in-group bias: Creating, confirming, or changing social reality. In W. Stroebe & M. Hewstone (Eds.), *European review of social psychology* (Vol. 18, pp. 359–396). Hove, England: Psychology Press.

Schmader, T. (2002). Gender identification moderates stereotype threat effects on women's math performance. *Journal of Experimental Social Psychology, 38*, 194–201.

Schmader, T., & Johns, M. (2003). Converging evidence that stereotype threat reduces working memory capacity. *Journal of Personality and Social Psychology, 85*, 440–452.

Schmader, T., Johns, M., & Forbes, C. (2008). An integrated process model of stereotype threat effects on performance. *Psychological Review, 115*, 336–356.

Schmader, T., Major, B., & Gramzow, R. (2001). Coping with ethnic stereotypes in the academic domain: Perceived injustice and psychological disengagement. *Journal of Social Issues, 57*, 93–112.

Schmitt, M. T., & Branscombe, N. R. (2002a). The meaning and consequences of perceived discrimination in disadvantaged and privileged social groups. In W. Stroebe & M. Hewstone (Eds.), *European review of social psychology* (Vol. 12, pp. 167–199). Chichester, England: Wiley.

Schmitt, M. T., & Branscombe, N. R. (2002b). The internal and external causal loci of attributions to prejudice. *Personality and Social Psychology Bulletin, 28*, 484–492.

Schmitt, M. T., Branscombe, N. R., & Brehm, J. W. (2004). Gender inequality and the intensity of men's collective guilt. In N. R. Branscombe & B. Doosje (Eds.), *Collective guilt: International perspectives* (pp. 75–92). New York: Cambridge University Press.

Schmitt, M. T., Branscombe, N. R., & Kappen, D. M. (2003). Attitudes toward group-based inequality: Social dominance or social identity? *British Journal of Social Psychology, 42*, 161–186.

Schneider, D. J. (2004). *The psychology of stereotyping*. New York: The Guilford Press.

Schwartz, S. H., & Struch, N. (1989). Values, stereotypes, and intergroup antagonism. In D. Bar-Tal, C. F. Grauman, A. Kruglanski, & W. Stroebe (Eds.), *Stereotyping and prejudice: changing conceptions* (pp. 151–167). New York: Springer-Verlag.

Sears, D. O. (1988). Symbolic racism. In P. A. Katz & D. A. Taylor (Eds.), *Eliminating racism: Profiles in controversy*. New York: Plenum Press.

Sears, D. O., & Henry, P. J. (2003). The origins of symbolic racism. *Journal of Personality and Social Psychology, 85*, 259–275.

Sears, D. O., & Henry, P. J. (2005). Over thirty years later: A contemporary look at symbolic racism. In M. Zanna (Ed.), *Advances in experimental social psychology* (Vol. 37, pp. 95–150). San Diego, CA: Academic Press.

Sears, D. O., Henry, P. J., & Kosterman, R. (2000). Egalitarian values and contemporary racial politics. In D. O. Sears, J. Sidanius, & L. Bobo (Eds.), *Racialized politics: The debate about racism in America* (pp. 75–117). Chicago: University of Chicago Press.

Sears, D. O., Hetts, J. J., Sidanius, J., & Bobo, L. (2000). Race in American politics: Framing the debates. In D. O. Sears, J. Sidanius, & L. Bobo (Eds.), *Racialized politics: The debate about racism in America* (pp. 1–43). Chicago: University of Chicago Press.

Sears, D. O., & McConahay, J. B. (1973). *The politics of violence*. Boston: Houghton Mifflin.

Sears, D. O., Sidanius, J., & Bobo, L. (Eds.). (2000). *Racialized politics: Values, ideology, and prejudice in American public opinion*. Chicago: University of Chicago Press.

Sechrist, G. B., & Milford, L. R. (2007). Perceived consensus influences intergroup behavior and stereotype accessibility. *Basic and Applied Social Psychology, 29*, 365–374.

Sechrist, G. B., & Stangor, C. (2001). Perceived consensus influences intergroup behavior and stereotype accessibility. *Journal of Personality and Social Psychology, 88,* 645–654.

Sekaquaptewa, D., & Thompson, M. (2003). Solo status, stereotypes, and performance expectancies: Their effects on women's public performance. *Journal of Experimental Social Psychology, 39,* 68–74.

Semin, G., & Fiedler, K. (1988). The cognitive functions of linguistic categories in describing persons: Social cognition and language. *Journal of Personality and Social Psychology, 54,* 558–568.

Shapiro, J. S., & Neuberg, S. L. (2007). From stereotype threat to stereotype threats: Implications of a multi-threat framework for causes, moderators, mediators, consequences, and interventions. *Personality and Social Psychology Review, 11,* 107–130.

Shelton, J. N. (2000). A re-conceptualization of how we study issues of racial prejudice. *Personality and Social Psychology Review, 4,* 374–390.

Shelton, J. N., Dovidio, J. F., Hebl, M., & Richeson, J. A. (2009). Prejudice and intergroup interactions. In Demoulin, S., Leyens, J.-Ph., & Dovidio, J. F. (Eds.), *Intergroup misunderstandings: Impact of divergent social realities.* New York: Psychology Press.

Shelton, J. N., & Richeson, J. A. (2005). Intergroup contact and pluralistic ignorance. *Journal of Personality and Social Psychology, 88,* 91–107.

Shelton, J. N., Richeson, J. A., & Salvatore, J. (2005). Expecting to be the target of prejudice. Implications for interethnic interactions. *Personality and Social Psychology Bulletin, 31,* 1189–1202.

Shelton, J. N., Richeson, J. A., Salvatore, J., & Trawalter, S. (2005). Ironic effects of racial bias during interracial interactions. *Psychological Science, 16,* 397–402.

Sherif, M. (1966). *In common predicament: Social psychology of intergroup conflict and cooperation.* Boston: Houghton Mifflin.

Sherif, M., & Sherif, C. W. (1969). Ingroup and intergroup relations: Experimental analysis. In M. Sherif & C. W. Sherif (Eds.), *Social psychology* (pp. 221–266). New York: Harper & Row.

Sherman, J. W., Conrey, F. R., & Groom, C. J. (2004). Encoding flexibility revisited: Evidence for enhanced encoding of stereotype-inconsistent information under cognitive load. *Social Cognition, 22,* 214–232.

Sherman, J. W., Lee, A. Y., Bessenoff, G. R., & Frost, L. A. (1998). Stereotype efficiency reconsidered: Encoding flexibility under cognitive load. *Journal of Personality and Social Psychology, 75,* 589–606.

Sherman, J. W., Stroessner, S. J., Conrey, F. R., & Azam, O. A. (2005). Prejudice and stereotype maintenance processes: Attention, attribution, and individuation. *Journal of Personality and Social Psychology, 89,* 607–622.

Shih, M., Pittinsky, T. L., & Ambady, N. (1999). Stereotype susceptibility: Identity salience and shifts in quantitative performance. *Psychological Science, 10,* 80–83.

Sidanius, J., & Pratto, F. (1999). *Social dominance: An intergroup theory of social hierarchy and oppression.* New York: Cambridge University Press.

Sigall, H. H., & Page, R. (1971). Current stereotypes: A little fading, a little faking. *Journal of Personality and Social Psychology, 18,* 247–255.

Simon, B. (1992). The perception of ingroup and outgroup homogeneity: Reintroducing the intergroup context. In W. Stroebe, & M. Hewstone (Eds.), *European review of social psychology* (Vol. 3). Chichester, England: Wiley.

Simon, B., & Klandermans, B. (2001). Politicized collective identity: A social psychological analysis. *American Psychologist, 56,* 319–331.

Simon, B., Trötschel, R., & Dähne, D. (2008). Identity affirmation and social movement support. *European Journal of Social Psychology, 38,* 935–946.

Sinclair, L., & Kunda, Z. (1999) Reactions to a Black professional: Motivated inhibition and activation of conflicting stereotypes. *Journal of Personality and Social Psychology, 77,* 885–904.

Sinclair, L., & Kunda, Z. (2000). Motivated stereotyping of women: She's fine if she praised me but incompetent if she criticized me. *Personality and Social Psychology Bulletin, 26,* 1329–1342.

Skinner, E. A. (1996). A guide to constructs of control. *Journal of Personality and Social Psychology, 71,* 549–570.

Skitka, L. J., Mullen, E., Griffin, T., Hutchinson, S., & Chamberlin, B. (2002). Dispositions, scripts, or motivated correction? Understanding ideological differences in explanations for social problems. *Journal of Personality and Social Psychology, 83,* 470–487.

Smith, E. R. (1993). Social identity and social emotions: Toward new conceptualizations of prejudice. In D. M. Mackie & D. L. Hamilton (Eds.), *Affect, cognition, and stereotyping: Interactive processes in group perception* (pp. 297–315). San Diego, CA: Academic Press.

Smith, E. R. (1999). Affective and cognitive implications of a group becoming part of the self: New models of prejudice and of the self-concept. In D. Abrams & M. A. Hogg (Eds.), *Social identity and social cognition* (pp. 183–196). Malden, MA: Blackwell.

Smith, E. R., Coats, S., & Walling, D. (1999). Overlapping mental representations of self, ingroup and partner: Further response time evidence and a connectionist model. *Personality and Social Psychology Bulletin, 25,* 873–882.

Smith, E. R., & Henry, S. (1996). An in-group becomes part of the self: Response time evidence. *Personality and Social Psychology Bulletin, 22,* 635–642.

Smith, E. R., Seger, C. R., & Mackie, D. M. (2007). Can emotions be truly group level? Evidence regarding four conceptual criteria. *Journal of Personality and Social Psychology, 93,* 431–446.

Smith, H. J., & Ortiz, D. J. (2002). Is it just me? The different consequences of personal and group relative deprivation. In I. Walker & H. Smith (Eds.), *Relative deprivation: Specification, development, and integration* (pp. 91–115). Cambridge, England: Cambridge University Press.

Smith, R. H., & Kim, S. H. (2007). Comprehending envy. *Psychological Bulletin, 113,* 46–64.

Smith, R. H., Turner, T. J., Garonzik, R., Leach, C. W., Urch, V., & Weston, C. (1996). Envy and schadenfreude. *Personality and Social Psychology Bulletin, 22,* 158–168.

Snyder, M., Kleck, R. E., Strenta, A., & Mentzer, S. J. (1979). Avoidance of the handicapped: An attributional ambiguity analysis. *Journal of Personality and Social Psychology, 37,* 2297–2306.

Solomon, S., Greenberg, J., & Pyszczynski, T. (1991). A terror management theory of social behavior: The psychological functions of self-esteem and cultural worldviews. In M. P. Zanna (Ed.), *Advances in experimental social psychology* (Vol. 24, pp. 93–159). San Diego, CA: Academic Press.

Solomon, S., Greenberg, J., & Pyszczynski, T. (2004). The cultural animal: Twenty years of terror management theory and research. In J. Greenberg, S. L. Koole, & T. Pyszczynski (Eds.), *Handbook of experimental existential psychology* (p. 13–34). New York: Guilford Press.

Son Hing, L. S., Li, W. & Zanna, M. P. (2002). Inducing hypocrisy to reduce prejudicial responses among aversive racists. *Journal of Experimental Social Psychology, 38,* 71–78.

Spencer, S. J., Fein, S., Wolfe, C. T., Fong, C., & Dunn, M. A. (1998). Automatic activation of stereotypes: The role of self-image threat. *Personality and Social Psychology Bulletin, 24,* 1139–1152.

Spencer, S. J., Steele, C. M., & Quinn, D. (1999). Under suspicion of inability: Stereotype threat and women's math performance. *Journal of Experimental Social Psychology, 35,* 4–28.

Spilka, B., Hood, R. W., Hunsberger, B., & Gorsuch, R. (2003). *The psychology of religion: An empirical approach* (3rd ed.). New York: Guilford.

Stangor, C., Carr, C., & Kiang, L. (1998). Activating stereotypes undermines task performance expectations. *Journal of Personality and Social Psychology, 75,* 1191–1197.

Stangor, C., Lynch, L., Duan, C., & Glass, B. (1992). Categorization of individuals on the basis of multiple social features. *Journal of Personality and Social Psychology, 62,* 207–218.

Stapel, D. A., & Suls, J. (2007). (Eds.). *Assimilation and contrast in social psychology.* New York: Psychology Press.

Staub, E. (1989). *The roots of evil: The origin of genocide and other group violence.* Cambridge, England: Cambridge University Press.

Staub, E. (2006). Reconciliation after genocide, mass killing, or intractable conflict: Understanding the roots of violence, psychological recovery, and steps toward a general theory. *Political Psychology, 27,* 867–894.

Steele, C. M. (1988). The psychology of self-affirmation: Sustaining the integrity of the self. *Advances in experimental social psychology* (Vol. 21, pp. 261–302). San Diego, CA: Academic Press.

Steele, C. M. (1997). A threat in the air: How stereotype shapes intellectual identity and performance? *American Psychologist, 52,* 613–629.

Steele, C. M., & Aronson, J. (1995). Stereotype threat and the intellectual test performance of African Americans. *Journal of Personality and Social Psychology, 69,* 797–811.

Steele, C. M., Spencer, S. J., & Aronson, J. (2002). Contending with bias: The psychology of stereotype and social identity threat. In M. P. Zanna (Ed.), *Advances in experimental social psychology* (Vol. 34, pp. 277–341). San Diego, CA: Academic Press.

Steffens, M. C., & Buchner, A. (2003). Implicit association test: Separating transsituationally stable and variable components of attitudes toward gay men. *Experimental Psychology, 50,* 33–48.

Stephan, C. W., Stephan, W. G., Demitrakis, K. M., Yamada, A. M., & Clason, D. L. (2000). Women's attitudes toward men: An integrated threat theory approach. *Psychology of Women Quarterly, 24,* 63–73.

Stephan, W. G., Boniecki, K. A., Ybarra, O., Bettencourt, A., Ervin, K. S., Jackson, L. A., et al. (2002). The role of threats in the racial attitudes of Blacks and Whites. *Personality and Social Psychology Bulletin, 28,* 1242–1254.

Stephan, W. G., & Renfro, C. L. (2002). The role of threats in intergroup relations (pp. 191–208). In D. Mackie & E. R. Smith (Eds.), *From prejudice to intergroup emotions.* New York: Psychology Press.

Stephan, W. G., & Stephan, C. W. (1985). Intergroup anxiety. *Journal of Social Issues, 41,* 157–175.

Stephan, W. G., & Stephan, C. W. (2000). An integrated threat theory of prejudice. In S. Oskamp (Ed.), *Reducing prejudice and discrimination: The Claremont Symposium on Applied Psychology* (pp. 23–45). Mahwah, NJ: Erlbaum.

Stephan, W. G., & Stephan, C. W. (2001). *Improving intergroup relations.* Thousand Oaks, CA: Sage.

Stephan, W. G., Ybarra, O., & Bachman, G. (1999). Prejudice toward immigrants. *Journal of Applied Social Psychology, 29,* 2221–2237.

Stone, J., Lynch, C., Sjomeling, M., & Darley, J. M. (1999). Stereotype threat effects on black and white athletic performance. *Journal of Personality and Social Psychology, 77,* 1213–1227.

Stroebe, K., Lodewijkx, H. F. M., & Spears, R. (2005). Do unto others as they do unto you: Reciprocity and social identification as determinants of ingroup favoritism. *Personality and Social Psychology Bulletin, 31,* 831–845.

Strom, K. J. (2001). Hate crimes reported in NIBRS, 1997–99 (U.S. Department of Justice, Bureau of Justice Statistics Report No. NCJ 186765). Retrieved June 6, 2004, from http://www.ojp.usdoj.gov/bjs/pdf/hnrc99.pdf.

Stuermer, S., Snyder, M., Kropp, A., & Siem, B. (2006). Empathy-motivated helping: The moderating role of group membership. *Personality and Social Psychology Bulletin, 32,* 943–956.

Stuermer, S., Snyder, M., & Omoto, A. M. (2005). Prosocial emotions: The moderating role of group membership. *Journal of Personality and Social Psychology, 88,* 532–546.

Sumner, W. G. (1906). *Folkways.* New York: Ginn.

Sutton, R. M., & Douglas, K. M. (2008). Two decades of linguistic bias research: Introduction. *Journal of Language and Social Psychology, 27,* 105–109.

Sutton, R. M., Douglas, K. M., Wilkin, K, Elder, T. J., Cole, J. M., & Stathi, S. (2008). Justice for whom, exactly? Beliefs in justice for the self and various others. *Personality and Social Psychology Bulletin, 34,* 528–541.

Swim, J. K., Aiken, K. J., Hall, W. S., & Hunter, B. A. (1995). Sexism and racism: Old-fashioned and modern prejudices. *Journal of Personality and Social Psychology, 68,* 199–214.

Swim, J. K., & Miller, D. L. (1999). White guilt: Its antecedents and consequences for attitudes toward affirmative action. *Personality and Social Psychology Bulletin, 25,* 500–514.

Swim, J. K., & Stangor, C. (Eds.). (1998). *Prejudice: The target's perspective.* San Diego, CA: Academic Press.

Tajfel, H. (1972). La catégorisation sociale. In S. Moscovici (Ed.), *Introduction à la psychologie sociale.* Paris: Larousse.

Tajfel, H. (1974). Social identity and intergroup behaviour. *Social Science Information, 13,* 65–93.

Tajfel, H. (1979). Individuals and groups in social psychology. *British Journal of Social and Clinical Psychology, 18,* 183–190.

Tajfel, H., Billig, M., Bundy, R., & Flament, C. (1971). Social categorization and intergroup behaviour. *European Journal of Social Psychology, 1,* 149–178.

Tajfel, H., & Turner, J. C. (1979). An integrative theory of intergroup conflict. In W. G. Austin & S. Worchel (Eds.), *The social psychology of intergroup relations.* Monterey, CA: Brooks/Cole.

Tajfel, H., & Wilkes, A. L. (1963). Classification and quantitative judgment. *British Journal of Psychology, 54,* 101–114.

Talaska, C. A., Fiske, S. T., & Chaiken, S. (2008). Legitimating racial discrimination: Emotions, not beliefs, best predict discrimination in a meta-analysis. *Social justice research, 21,* 263–296.

Tangney, J. P. (1995). Shame and guilt in interpersonal relationships. In J. Tangney & K. W. Fischer (Eds.), *Self-conscious emotions: The psychology of shame, guilt, embarrassment, and pride* (pp. 114–139). New York: Guilford Press.

Tangney, J. P., Stuewig, J., & Mashek, D. (2007). Moral emotions and moral behavior. *Annual Review of Psychology, 58,* 345–372.

Taylor, D. M., & McKirnan, D. J. (1984). A five stage model of intergroup relations. *British Journal of Social Psychology, 23,* 291–300.

Taylor, D. M., Wright, S. C., & Porter, L. E. (1994). Dimensions of perceived discrimination: The personal/group discrimination discrepancy. In M. P. Zanna & J. M. Olson (Eds.), *The psychology of prejudice: The Ontario symposium* (Vol. 7, pp. 289–314). Hillsdale, NJ: Erlbaum.

Taylor, S. E., Fiske, S. T., Etcoff, N. J., & Ruderman, A. J. (1978). Categorical and contextual bases of person memory and stereotyping. *Journal of Personality and Social Psychology, 36,* 778–793.

Teige-Mocigemba, S., & Klauer, K. C. (2008). 'Automatic' evaluation? Strategic effects on affective priming. *Journal of Experimental Social Psychology, 44,* 1414–1417.

Tomasello, M., Carpenter, M., Call, J., Behne, T., & Moll, H. (2005). Understanding and sharing intentions: The origins of cultural cognition. *Behavioral and Brain Science, 28,* 675–691.

Topolski, R., Boyd-Bowman, K. A., & Ferguson, H. (2003). Grapes of wrath: Discrimination in the produce aisle. *Analyses of Social Issues and Public Policy, 3,* 111–119.

Tougas, F., & Beaton, A. M. (2001). Personal and group relative deprivations: Connecting the "I" to the "we." In I. Walker & H. Smith (Eds.) *Relative deprivation: Specification, development, and integration* (pp. 119–135). New York: Cambridge University Press.

Towles-Schwen, T., & Fazio, R. H. (2003). Choosing social situations: The relation between automatically-activated racial attitudes and anticipated comfort interacting with African Americans. *Personality and Social Psychology Bulletin, 29*, 170–182.

Trawalter, S., & Richeson, J. A. (2006). Regulatory focus and executive function after interracial interactions. *Journal of Experimental Social Psychology, 42*, 406–412.

Trawalter, S., & Richeson, J. A. (2008). Let's talk about race, baby! When whites' and blacks' interracial contact experiences diverge. *Journal of Experimental Social Psychology, 44*, 1214–1217.

Tropp, L. R. (2003). The psychological impact of prejudice: Implications for intergroup contact. *Group Processes and Intergroup Relations, 6*, 131–149.

Tropp, L. R., & Wright, S. C. (2001). Ingroup identification as the inclusion of ingroup in the self. *Personality and Social Psychology Bulletin, 27*, 585–600.

Turner, J. C. (1975). Social comparison and social identity: Some prospects for intergroup behaviour. *European Journal of Social Psychology, 5*, 5–34.

Turner, J. C. (1984). Social identification and psychological group formation. In H. Tajfel (Ed.), *The social dimension: European developments in social psychology* (Vol. 2, pp. 518–538). Cambridge, England: Cambridge University Press.

Turner, J. C. (1985). Social categorization and the self concept: A social cognitive theory of group behaviour. In E. J. Lawler (Ed.), *Advances in group processes: Theory and research* (Vol. 2, pp. 77–271). Greenwich, CT: JAL Press.

Turner, J. C. (1987). A self-categorization theory. In J. C. Turner, M. A. Hogg, P. J. Oakes, S. D. Reicher, & M. S. Wetherell (Eds.), *Rediscovering the social group: A self-categorization theory.* Oxford: Basil Blackwell.

Turner, J. C. (1991). *Social influence.* Milton Keynes, England: Open University Press.

Turner, J. C. (1999). Some current issues in research on social identity and self-categorization theories. In N. Ellemers, R. Spears, & B. Doosje (Eds.), *Social identity.* Oxford: Blackwell.

Turner, J. C., Hogg, M. A., Oakes, P. J., Reicher, S. D., & Wetherell, M. S. (1987). *Rediscovering the social group: A self-categorization theory.* Oxford: Basil Blackwell.

Turner, J. C., & Oakes, P. J. (1989). Self-categorization theory and social influence. In P. B. Paulus (Ed.), *Psychology of group influence* (2nd ed., pp. 233–275). Hillsdale, NJ: Lawrence Erlbaum.

Turner, J. C., & Reynolds, K. J. (2003). Why social dominance theory has been falsified. *British Journal of Social Psychology, 42*, 199–206.

Twenge, J. M., Catanese, K. R., & Baumeister, R. F. (2003). Social exclusion and the deconstructed state: Time perception, meaninglessness, lethargy, lack of emotion, and self-awareness. *Journal of Personality and Social Psychology, 85*, 409–423.

Tyler, T. R., & Smith, H. J. (1998). Social justice and social movements. In D. T. Gilbert, S. T. Fiske, & G. Lindzey (Eds.), *Handbook of social psychology* (4th ed., Vol. 2, pp. 595–629). Boston: McGraw-Hill.

Uhlmann, E. L., & Cohen, G. L. (2005). Constructed criteria: Redefining merit to justify discrimination. *Psychological Science 16*, 474–480.

Urban, L. M., & Miller, N. (1998). A theoretical analysis of crossed categorization effects: A meta-analysis. *Journal of Personality and Social Psychology, 74*, 894–908.

U.S. Equal Employment Opportunity Commission (2004, March 17). *Occupational employment in private industry by race/ethnic group/sex, and by industry, United States, 2002.* Retrieved September 18, 2009, from http://www.eeoc.gov/stats/jobpat/2002/us.html

Vaes, J., Paladino, M. P., Castelli, L., Leyens, J.-Ph., & Giovanazzi, A. (2003). On the behavioral consequences of infra-humanization: The implicit role of uniquely human emotions in intergroup relations. *Journal of Personality and Social Psychology, 85*, 1016–1034.

van Bavel, J. J., Packer, D. J., & Cunningham, W. A. (2008). The neural substrates of in-group bias: A functional magnetic resonance imaging investigation. *Psychological Science, 11*, 1131–1139.

van den Bos, K., & Lind, E. A. (2002). Uncertainty management by means of fairness judgements. In M. P. Zanna (Ed.), *Advances in experimental social psychology* (Vol. 34, pp. 1–60). San Diego, CA: Academic Press.

van den Bos, K., Poortvliet, P. M., Maas, M., Miedema, J., & van den Ham, E.-J. (2005). An enquiry concerning the principles of cultural norms and values: The impact of uncertainty and mortality salience on reactions to violations and bolstering of cultural worldviews. *Journal of Experimental Social Psychology, 41*, 91–113.

van Knippenberg, A., & Dijksterhuis, A. (2000). Social categorization and stereotyping: A functional perspective. In W. Stroebe & M. Hewstone (Eds.), *European review of social psychology* (Vol. 11, pp. 105–144). Chichester, England: Wiley.

van Rijswijk, W., & Ellemers, N. (2002). Context effects on the application of stereotype content to multiple categorizable target. *Personality and Social Psychology Bulletin, 28*, 90–101.

van Rijswijk, W., Haslam, S. A., & Ellemers, N. (2006). Who do we think we are? The interactive effect of social identification and comparative context on ingroup stereotyping. *British Journal of Social Psychology, 45*, 161–174.

van Zomeren, M., Postmes, T., & Spears, R. (2008). Toward an integrative Social Identity Model of Collective Action: A quantitative research synthesis of three socio-psychological perspectives. *Psychological Bulletin, 134*, 504–535.

van Zomeren, M., Spears, R., Fischer, A., & Leach, C. (2004). Put your money where your mouth is! Explaining collective action tendencies through group-based anger and group efficacy. *Journal of Personality and Social Psychology, 87*, 649–664.

van Zomeren, M., Spears, R., & Leach, C. (2008). Exploring psychological mechanisms of collective action: Does relevance of group identity influence how people cope with collective disadvantage? *British Journal of Social Psychology, 47*, 353–372.

Vanbeselaere, N. (1991). The different effects of simple and crossed categorizations: A result of the category differentiation process or of differential category salience? In W. Stroebe & M. Hewstone (Eds.), *European review of social psychology* (Vol. 2, pp. 247–278). Chichester, England: Wiley.

Vanneman, R. D., & Pettigrew, T. F. (1972). Race and relative deprivation in the urban United States. *Race, 13*, 461–486.

Verkuyten, M. (2003). Discourses about ethnic groups (de-)essentialism: Oppressive and progressive aspects. *British Journal of Social Psychology, 42*, 371–391.

Verkuyten, M. (2007). Ethnic in-group favoritism among minority and majority groups: Testing the self-esteem hypothesis among preadolescents. *Journal of Applied Social Psychology, 37*, 486–500.

Verkuyten, M., & Hagendoorn, L. (1997) Prejudice and self-categorization: The variable role of personality and in-group stereotypes. *Personality and Social Psychology Bulletin, 24*, 99–110.

Vescio, T. K., Gervais, S. J., Snyder, M., & Hoover, A. (2005). Power and the creation of patronizing environments: The stereotype-based behaviors of the powerful and their effects on female performance in masculine domains. *Journal of Personality and Social Psychology, 88*, 658–572.

Vescio, T. K., Sechrist, G. B., & Paolucci, M. P. (2003). Perspective taking and prejudice reduction: The mediational role of empathy arousal and situational attributions. *European Journal of Social Psychology, 33*, 455–472.

Viki, G. T., & Calitri, R. (2008). Infrahuman outgroup or suprahuman ingroup: The role of nationalism and patriotism in the infrahumanization of outgroups. *European Journal of Social Psychology, 38*, 1054–1061.

von Hippel, W., Sekaquaptewa, D., & Vargas, P. (1997). The linguistic intergroup bias as an implicit indicator of prejudice. *Journal of Experimental Social Psychology, 33*, 490–509.

Vorauer, J. (2006). An information search model of evaluative concerns in intergroup interaction. *Psychological Review, 113*, 862–886.

Vorauer, J. D., Hunter, A. J., Main, K. J., & Roy, S. A. (2000). Meta-stereotype activation: Evidence from indirect measures for specific evaluative concerns experienced by members of dominant groups in intergroup interaction. *Journal of Personality and Social Psychology, 78*, 690–707.

Vorauer, J. D., & Kumhyr, S. M. (2001). Is this about you or me? Self-versus other-directed judgments and feelings in response to intergroup interaction. *Personality and Social Psychology Bulletin, 27*, 706–719.

Vorauer, J. D., Main, K. J., & O'Connell, G. B. (1998). How do individuals expect to be viewed by members of lower status groups? Content and implications of meta-stereotypes. *Journal of Personality and Social Psychology, 4*, 917–937.

Waldzus, S., Mummendey, A., Wenzel, M., & Weber, U. (2003). Toward tolerance: Representations of superordinate categories and perceived in-group prototypicality. *Journal of Experimental Social Psychology, 39*, 31–47.

Walker, I., & Smith, H. J. (2002). *Relative deprivation: Specification, development, and integration.* New York: Cambridge University Press.

Weary, G., Jacobson, J. A., Edwards, J. A., & Tobin, S. J. (2001). Chronic and temporarily activated causal uncertainty beliefs and stereotype usage. *Journal of Personality and Social Psychology, 81*, 206–219.

Wenzel, M., Mummendey, A., & Waldzus, S. (2007). Superordinate identities and intergroup conflict: The ingroup projection model. *European Review of Social Psychology, 18*, 331–372.

Wenzel, M., Mummendey, A., Weber, U., & Waldzus, S. (2003). The ingroup as pars pro toto: Projection of the ingroup onto the inclusive category as a precursor to social discrimination. *Personality and Social Psychology Bulletin, 29*, 461–473.

Whitley, B. E., Jr. (1999). Right-wing authoritarianism, social dominance orientation, and prejudice. *Journal of Personality and Social Psychology, 77*, 126–134.

Whitley, B. E., Jr., & Lee, S. E. (2000). The relationship of authoritarianism and related constructs to attitudes toward homosexuality. *Journal of Applied Social Psychology, 30*, 144–170.

Whitley, B. E., Jr., & Wilkinson, W. W. (2002). *Authoritarianism, social dominance orientation, empathy, and prejudice: A test of three models.* Poster presented at the meeting of the American Psychological Society, New Orleans.

Wigboldus, D. H. J., & Douglas, K. M. (2007). Language, expectancies and intergroup relations. In K. Fiedler (Ed.), *Social communication* (pp. 79–106). New York: Psychology Press.

Wigboldus, D. H. J., Spears, R., & Semin, G. R. (2005). When do we communicate stereotypes? Influence of the social context on the linguistic expectancy bias. *Group Processes and Intergroup Relations, 8*, 215–230.

Wildschut, T., & Insko, C. A. (2007). Explanation of interindividual-intergroup discontinuity: A review of the evidence. *European Review of Social Psychology, 18*, 175–211.

Wildschut, T., Pinter, B., Vevea, J. L., Insko, C. A., & Schopler, J. (2003). Beyond the group mind: A quantitative review of the interindividual-intergroup discontinuity effect. *Psychological Bulletin, 129*, 698–722.

Williams, K. D. (2001). *Ostracism: The power of silence.* New York: Guilford Publications.

Williams, K. D. (2007). Ostracism. *Annual Review of Psychology, 58*, 425–452.

Williams, K. D., Cheung, K. T., & Choi, W. (2000). Cyberostracism: Effects of being ignored over the Internet. *Journal of Personality and Social Psychology, 79*, 748–762.

Williams, M. J., & Eberhardt, J. L. (2008). Biological conceptions of race and the motivation to cross racial boundaries. *Journal of Personality and Social Psychology, 94*, 1033–1047.

Wilson, M. S., & Liu, J. H. (2003). Social dominance orientation and gender: The moderating role of gender identity. *British Journal of Social Psychology, 42*, 187–198.

Wilson, T. D., & Gilbert, D. T. (2008). Explaining away: A model of affective adaptation. *Perspectives on Psychological Science, 5*, 372–388.

Wittenbrink, B., Judd, C. M., & Park, B. (1997). Evidence for racial prejudice at the implicit level and its relationship to questionnaire measures. *Journal of Personality and Social Psychology, 72*, 262–274.

Wittenbrink, B., Judd, C. M., & Park, B. (2001). Spontaneous prejudice in context: Variability in automatically activated attitudes. *Journal of Personality and Social Psychology, 81*, 815–827.

Wittenbrink, B., & Schwarz, N. (Eds.). (2007). *Implicit measures of attitudes.* New York: Guilford Press.

Wohl, M. J. A., & Branscombe, N. R. (2008). Remembering historical victimization: Collective guilt for current ingroup transgressions. *Journal of Personality and Social Psychology, 94*, 988–1006.

Wohl, M. J. A., Branscombe, N. R., & Klar, Y. (2006). Collective guilt: Emotional reactions when one's group has done wrong or been wronged. *European Review of Social Psychology, 17*, 1–37.

Wojciszke, B. (1997). Parallels between competence- versus morality-related traits and individualistic versus collectivistic values. *European Journal of Social Psychology, 27*, 245–256.

Wolsko, C., Park, B., Judd, C. M., & Wittenbrink, B. (2000). Framing interethnic ideology: Effects of multicultural and color-blind perspectives on judgments of groups and individuals. *Journal of Personality and Social Psychology, 78*, 635–654.

Wright, S. C. (2001). Strategic collective action: Social psychology and social change. In R. Brown & S. Gaertner (Eds.), *Blackwell handbook of social psychology. Vol. 4: Intergroup processes.* Oxford: Blackwell Press.

Wright, S. C., & Taylor, D. M. (1999). Success under tokenism: Co-option of the newcomer and the prevention of collective protest. *British Journal of Social Psychology, 38*, 369–396.

Wright, S. C., Taylor, D. M., & Moghaddam, F. M. (1990). Responding to membership in a disadvantaged group: From acceptance to collective protest. *Journal of Personality and Social Psychology, 58*, 994–1003.

Wyer, N. A., Sadler, M. S., & Judd, C. M. (2002). Contrast effects in stereotype formation and change: The role of comparative context. *Journal of Experimental Social Psychology, 38*, 443–458.

Yzerbyt, V. Y., Castano, E., Leyens, J.-P., & Paladino, M.-P. (2000). The primacy of the ingroup: The interplay of identification and entitativity. In W. Stroebe & M. Hewstone (Eds.), *European review of social psychology* (Vol. 11, pp. 258–295). Chichester, England: Wiley.

Yzerbyt, V. Y., & Corneille, O. (2005). Cognitive process: Reality constraints and integrity concerns in social perception. In J. F. Dovidio, P. Glick, & L. Rudman (Eds.), *On the nature of prejudice: 50 years after Allport.* London: Blackwell.

Yzerbyt, V. Y., Corneille, O., & Estrada, C. (2001). The interplay of subjective essentialism and entitativity in the formation of stereotypes. *Personality and Social Psychology Review, 5*, 141–155.

Yzerbyt, V. Y., Coull, A., & Rocher, S. J. (1999). Fencing off the deviant: The role of cognitive resources in the maintenance of stereotypes. *Journal of Personality and Social Psychology, 77*, 449–462.

Yzerbyt, V. Y., Dumont, M., Mathieu, B., Gordijn, E., & Wigboldus, D. (2006). Social comparison and group-based emotions. In S. Guimond (Ed.), *Social comparison processes and levels of analysis: Understanding cognition, intergroup relations, and culture* (pp. 174–205). Cambridge, England: Cambridge University Press.

Yzerbyt, V. Y., Dumont, M., Wigboldus, D., & Gordijn, E. H. (2003). I feel for us: The impact of categorization and identification on emotions and action tendencies. *British Journal of Social Psychology, 42*, 533–549.

Yzerbyt, V. Y., Judd, C. M., & Corneille, O. (2004). *The psychology of group perception: Perceived variability, entitativity, and essentialism.* London: Psychology Press.

Yzerbyt, V. Y., Kervyn, N., & Judd, C. M. (2008). Compensation versus halo: The unique relations between the fundamental dimensions of social judgment. *Personality and Social Psychology Bulletin, 34,* 1110–1123.

Yzerbyt, V. Y., Provost, V., & Corneille, O. (2005). Not competent but warm. Really? Compensatory stereotypes in the French-speaking world. *Group Processes and Intergroup Relations, 8,* 291–308.

Yzerbyt, V. Y., Rocher, S. J., & Schadron, G. (1997). Stereotypes as explanations: A subjective essentialistic view of group perception. In R. Spears, P. Oakes, N. Ellemers, & A. Haslam (Eds.), *The psychology of stereotyping and group life* (pp. 20–50). Oxford: Basil Blackwell.

Yzerbyt, V. Y., Rogier, A., & Fiske, S. (1998). Group entitativity and social attribution: On translating situational constraints into stereotypes. *Personality and Social Psychology Bulletin, 24,* 1090–1104.

Zanna, M. P. (1994). On the nature of prejudice. *Canadian Psychology, 35,* 11–23.

Zawadzki, B. (1948). Limitations of the scapegoat theory of prejudice. *Journal of Abnormal and Social Psychology, 43,* 127–141.

Chapter 29

Intergroup Bias

JOHN F. DOVIDIO AND SAMUEL L. GAERTNER

Bias is a term that encompasses a range of intergroup orientations, including beliefs about the traits and characteristics of groups, or individuals by virtue of their group membership, as well as unfair evaluative, affective, or behavioral responses to groups and their members. These types of bias generally relate to *stereotypes* (overgeneralized beliefs), *prejudice* (biased attitudes), and *discrimination* (unfair treatment). Moreover, prejudice and stereotypes, which involve intraindividual processes, may be explicit (overt and intentional) or implicit (involving the spontaneous, frequently automatic, activation of evaluations or beliefs; see Banaji's chapter, volume 1). However, bias does not relate only to beliefs about other groups (i.e., outgroups); intergroup bias is also a comparative concept involving how one views one's own group *relative to* other groups. Thus, ingroup favoritism is an important component of bias together with outgroup derogation. In this chapter, bias is defined broadly as *an unfair evaluative, emotional, cognitive, or behavioral response toward another group in ways that devalue or disadvantage the other group and its members either directly or indirectly by valuing or privileging members of one's own group.*

The chapter by Yzerbyt and Demoulin (this volume) examines different personal, contextual, social, and target group–related factors that influence intergroup bias. This chapter, in contrast, focuses on different manifestations of intergroup bias, the central role of social categorization in these effects, and ways to reduce intergroup bias. Specifically, in the next section, we outline basic distinctions and definitions relevant to intergroup bias. After that, we consider the common mechanism, *social categorization*, that provides the foundation for bias to arise and be maintained. Social categorization is the subjective process of classifying people into groups based on the appearance of shared similarities. We then discuss different approaches to reducing intergroup bias, focusing on three category-based

strategies for ameliorating bias. We conclude by suggesting promising avenues for future inquiry, identifying important moderating factors and mediating processes.

DISTINCTIONS AND DEFINITIONS

As noted earlier, bias is a broad and encompassing term that has been used by different researchers to refer to different phenomena. In this section, we attempt to introduce a conceptual framework that identifies basic dimensions of bias and use this framework to locate the different, commonly studied manifestations of bias. The three dimensions that we consider are: (1) type of bias (stereotypes, prejudice, and discrimination), (2) expression of bias (explicit or implicit), and (3) focus of orientation (outgroup derogation and ingroup favoritism).

Stereotypes, Prejudice, and Discrimination

Stereotypes are generally considered to represent a set of shared beliefs about a group, prejudice is typically conceived as an attitude, and discrimination is a type of behavior. By most historical accounts, Lippmann (1922) introduced the term "stereotype" to refer to the typical picture that comes to mind when thinking about a particular social group. Current definitions are similar, describing stereotypes as "qualities perceived to be associated with particular groups or categories of people" (Schneider, 2004, p. 24). Stereotypes, which contain information about qualities such as social roles, as well as about traits, reflect beliefs about the qualities that distinguish a group from others, that characterize the typical member of a group, and that indicate the consistency with which members of a group share a quality.

Whereas early researchers generally conceived of stereotyping as a faulty thought process, researchers now more

---

Preparation of this chapter was supported by the National Science Foundation (grant BCS-0613218).

commonly consider stereotypes as a functional means for simplifying a complex environment. In general, stereotypes produce a readiness to perceive behaviors or characteristics associated with the stereotype; when stereotypes are activated, individual group members are judged in terms of group-based expectations or standards. Stereotypes include affective reactions by the perceiver (e.g., disgust), as well as cognitive representations of the other group (e.g., they are ambitious). That is, stereotypes activate a "range of preferences, evaluations, moods, and emotions" (Fiske & Taylor, 1991, p. 410).

Although unique characteristics of groups are related to the specific intergroup context (e.g., related to the history of slavery of Blacks in the United States), systematic principles shape the content of stereotypes cross-culturally (Cottrell & Neuberg, 2005). The *Stereotype Content Model* (Fiske, Cuddy, Glick, & Xu, 2002; see also Cuddy, Fiske, & Glick, 2007) proposes that stereotypes are a function of perceptions of a particular group's position on two dimensions: warmth and competence. The specific associations for groups within each of the four combinations of high and low levels of competence and warmth may differ, but the type of orientation to each group and the emotions aroused by the groups within a particular combination are similar. Groups high in warmth and high in competence (e.g., the ingroup, close allies) elicit pride and admiration; groups high in warmth but low in competence (e.g., disabled persons, the elderly) produce pity and sympathy; those low in warmth but high in competence (e.g., rich people, businesspeople; in the United States, Asians and Jews as well) elicit envy and jealousy; and groups low on both warmth and competence (e.g., welfare recipients and poor Blacks) are associated with feelings of disgust, anger, and resentment.

Prejudice is generally conceptualized as an attitude that, like other attitudes, has a *cognitive component* (e.g., irrationally based beliefs about a target group), an *affective component* (e.g., dislike), and a *conative component* (e.g., a behavioral predisposition to avoid the target group). Perhaps because of the traditional focus on intergroup biases of Whites toward Blacks in the United States, researchers have often emphasized negative affect as a defining feature of prejudice. For example, Allport (1954) defined prejudice as "an antipathy based on faulty and inflexible generalization. It may be felt or expressed. It may be directed toward a group as a whole, or toward an individual because he [sic] is a member of that group" (p. 9). Other researchers have attended more to the cognitive component. Jones (1986) defined prejudice as "a faulty generalization from a group characterization (stereotype) to an individual member of that group irrespective of either (1) the accuracy of the group stereotype, or (2) the applicability of the group

characterization to the individual in question" (p. 288). Current definitions further emphasize the contextual nature of prejudice, describing it as "a less favorable attitude-in-context toward persons who are stereotypically mismatched with the requirements of a role, compared with attitudes toward those who are matched" (Eagly & Diekman, 2005, p. 23). Thus, prejudice represents *a negative (or a less positive) evaluative or affective response, or both, to others in a given context based on their group membership.*

Several different standardized scales measure prejudice based on people's degree of endorsement of a range of statements about attributes of the group, feelings about the group, and support for policies that affect the group. Common measures of prejudice against Blacks include the *Modern Racism Scale* (McConahay, 1986), the *Symbolic Racism Scale* (Henry & Sears, 2002), and the *Attitudes toward Blacks Scale* (Brigham, 1993). Examples of measures of sexism are the *Modern Sexism Scale* (Swim, Aiken, Hall, & Hunter, 1995) and the *Ambivalent Sexism Inventory* (Glick & Fiske, 1996). Other scales distinguish blatant from subtle prejudice and have been used to measure attitudes toward a range of outgroups (e.g., immigrants) in Europe (Pettigrew & Meertens, 1995). In addition, some scales assess the bias of Blacks toward Whites (Johnson & Lecci, 2003).

In the context of intergroup relations, *discrimination* has a pejorative meaning. It refers to more than simply distinguishing among social objects; it also implies inappropriate treatment of individuals because of their group membership. Discrimination may involve unjustified negative behavior toward members of the target group or less positive responses to an outgroup member than would occur for an ingroup member in comparable circumstances. According to Allport (1954), discrimination involves denying "individuals or groups of people equality of treatment which they may wish" (p. 51). Racial discrimination involves direct harm, failure to help, nonverbal behaviors, and overt pejorative evaluations of outgroup members.

Explicit and Implicit Bias

Whereas discrimination involves a behavioral response of a person to a member of a group or to a group as a whole, stereotypes and prejudice are intrapsychic phenomena. That is, stereotypes and prejudice occur within an individual and may vary not only in how apparent they are to others but also in the level of awareness of the person who harbors the stereotypes and prejudice. Traditionally, stereotypes and prejudice have been conceived as explicit responses, as beliefs and attitudes of which people are aware and can control in their expression (often strategically) (Fazio, Jackson, Dunton, & Williams, 1995). In contrast with these explicit processes, which are conscious and deliberative, implicit processes involve a lack of awareness and are unintentionally activated. The mere presence of the attitude object is often sufficient to activate the associated stereotype and attitude automatically (Gaertner & McLaughlin, 1983). Although people can generally perceive cues relating to multiple, different social categories to which others belong, when their cognitive capacities are taxed, people tend to activate only the category that is most relevant and accessible in the current context (Quinn & Macrae, 2005).

Whereas explicit measures of prejudice typically utilize self-reports, implicit measures utilize a variety of techniques, including psychophysiological measures, brain activity, as indicated by functional magnetic resonance imaging (see chapters by Blascovich & Mendes and by Lieberman, volume 1), and a range of indirect self-report responses, such as word fragment completions, linguistic cues, attributions, and explanations (for a review, see Fazio & Olson, 2003). The most widely used strategies to assess implicit biases involve response latency measures of association using *subliminal* priming (below the level of consciousness; see Dovidio, Kawakami, Johnson, Johnson, & Howard, 1997; Wittenbrink, Judd, & Park, 1997) or supraliminal priming (with awareness of the priming stimulus; see Fazio et al., 1995), the *Implicit Association Test* (IAT; Greenwald, McGhee, & Schwartz, 1998), and the *Go/No-Go Association Task* (GNAT; Nosek & Banaji, 2001). The general assumption underlying these response latency tests, which are also often used to assess stereotypes, as well as prejudice, is that people respond more quickly to stimuli with compatible than incompatible associations (e.g., negative category and negative words vs. negative category and positive words).

In priming tasks, the initial stimulus for a given trial is the name of a group or a picture of a member of the group. Participants then see another stimulus (e.g., a word) and make a decision about the word (e.g., indicate whether it is a positive or a negative word) by pressing alternative keys. In the IAT, in the first phase, participants classify stimuli, for example, pictures of Blacks and Whites in terms of race, by pressing one of two keys (e.g., "e" for Blacks and "i" for Whites). In the second phase, participants classify two concepts (e.g., positive and negative words) in terms of their valence using the same two keys ("e" for negative and "i" for positive). Then, in the third and fourth phases, which are counterbalanced between incompatible and compatible pairings, participants respond to all four categories. In one of these phases, participants respond to two categories of stimuli with one key (e.g., Blacks or positive words with the "e" key, which for most Whites are considered incompatible trials) and the other two categories of stimuli with

the other key (e.g., Whites or negative words with the "i" key). In the other four-category phase of the IAT, the category pairings are compatible for most Whites (e.g., Blacks and negative words with the "e" key, and Whites and positive words with the "i" key). Faster responses to compatible pairings (e.g., Whites with positive words and Blacks with negative words) than incompatible pairings indicate an implicit negative bias toward Blacks relative to Whites.

Although researchers commonly use implicit measures of attitudes and stereotypes (Fazio & Olson, 2003; see Banaji's chapter in volume 1), debate exists about the psychological meaning of these measures. Some researchers contend that implicit measures of bias primarily represent overlearned and "habitual" cultural associations rather than attitudes in the classic sense (Karpinski & Hilton, 2001). Others have argued that they reflect essentially a single attitude measured at different points in the process of expression, with social desirability concerns more strongly shaping overt expressions (Fazio et al., 1995). Still others consider implicit and explicit measures to reflect different components of a system of dual attitudes, with implicit responses often representing "older" attitudes and stereotypes that have been "overwritten" by newer, explicit forms of bias (Wilson, Lindsey, & Schooler, 2000).

Each of these positions on the nature of implicit bias suggests the possibility that implicit measures and explicit measures may not be highly correlated, particularly for more socially sensitive areas in which social desirability concerns are high (Nosek, Banaji, & Greenwald, 2002). Indeed, one meta-analysis, which examined a range of different implicit measures (including the physiological measure of galvanic skin response, as well as response latency measures), found a positive but only modest relationship (mean $r = .24$) with explicit measures of Whites' prejudice toward Blacks (Dovidio, Kawakami, & Beach, 2001). Alternatively, a meta-analysis that focused on one specific technique for measuring implicit responses, the IAT (Greenwald et al., 1998), but examined responses in a range of different domains, found the same overall correlation (mean $r = .24$) between implicit and explicit measures (Hofmann, Gawronski, Gschwendner, Le, & Schmitt, 2005). A more recent meta-analysis of IAT research showed an even weaker relationship between implicit and explicit measures in the domain of Black-White ($r = .12$) and other intergroup ($r = .15$) orientations (Greenwald, Poehlman, Uhlmann, & Banaji, 2009).

This general dissociation between explicit and implicit measures of bias is consistent with a number of different perspectives on contemporary prejudice. Frameworks such as *modern racism* (McConahay, 1986), *symbolic racism* (Sears, Henry, & Kosterman, 2000), and *aversive racism* (Dovidio & Gaertner, 2004; Gaertner & Dovidio, 1986) propose that contemporary racism is less blatant than in the past. These theories share a common premise that increasingly egalitarian norms have facilitated the development of conscious, nonprejudiced self-images among large portions of Whites, but many Whites who appear nonbiased on explicit measures (and who may genuinely believe they are not biased) still harbor unconscious negative feelings and beliefs toward Blacks.

Consistent with these theories of contemporary racism, an analysis of the responses of more than 100,000 Whites who completed race IAT on the web (https://implicit .harvard.edu/) revealed a significant preference for Whites over Blacks on this implicit measure (Nosek et al., 2002). Moreover, Whites showed much greater implicit bias than explicit bias (on a rating scale) against Blacks. Although Black respondents showed a substantial preference for Blacks over Whites on the explicit measure, they also exhibited a significant preference for Whites over Blacks on the implicit measure. A similar pattern of stronger implicit than explicit bias emerged for other social groups, for example, the preference for young over the elderly (Nosek et al., 2002). Thus, conclusions of bias drawn from studies of implicit measures are likely to diverge from those based on explicit measures of bias.

Outgroup Derogation and Ingroup Favoritism

The distinction between bias represented by outgroup derogation or reflected in *relative* ingroup-outgroup appraisals applies to both explicit and implicit measures. Explicit measures may involve evaluative ratings of the ingroup and outgroup or resource allocations on *Tajfel matrices*, for which people allocate points to their group and other groups. Tajfel matrices reveal ingroup favoritism, outgroup bias, or both, as well as other more specific motivations (e.g., to maximize or minimize the difference in outcomes between the groups, or to maximize their joint profit; Bourhis, Sachdev, & Gagnon, 1994). Whereas the traditional IAT produces only a measure of relative bias, other related techniques, such as the GNAT, assess responses to different groups independently.

The distinction between ingroup favoritism and outgroup derogation has important theoretical and practical implications. Theoretically, Allport (1954) argued that ingroup favoritism plays a particularly fundamental role in intergroup relations. He noted that "in-groups are psychologically primary. We live in them, and sometimes, for them" (p. 42), and proposed that "there is good reason to believe that this love-prejudice is far more basic to human life than is . . . hate-prejudice. When a person is defending a categorical value of his own, he may do so at the expense of other people's interests or safety. Hate

prejudice springs from a reciprocal love prejudice underneath" (pp. 25–26). Twenty-five years later, an influential review of the literature by Brewer (1979) concluded that establishing ingroup-outgroup distinctions in the absence of functional group relations (i.e., in the minimal group paradigm) primarily elicits more positive evaluations of people who become identified as ingroup members rather than more negative evaluations of those who become viewed as outgroup members. There is a general *positive-negative asymmetry of social discrimination* (Otten & Mummendey, 2000), which is characterized by greater allocations of positive resources for ingroup than for outgroup members than assignment of more negative outcomes to outgroup than to ingroup members. However, even in the absence of intergroup comparisons, intragroup factors, such as interaction and interdependence among members within a group, that increase the sense of *entitativity* of the ingroup (the sense that the ingroup is a functional entity) are sufficient to produce more positive ingroup evaluations (Gaertner, Iuzzini, Witt, & Oriña, 2006).

Although simply increasing the salience of intergroup boundaries does not necessarily create greater levels of bias in evaluations or in stereotyping of the ingroup relative to the outgroup, both relative (ingroup-outgroup) bias and outgroup derogation are more likely to occur when intergroup comparisons are salient (Mummendey, Klink, & Brown, 2001). Similarly, relative ingroup bias (i.e., more positive evaluations of the ingroup than outgroup) and outgroup derogation are stronger when groups have consequential relations (Mullen, Brown, & Smith, 1992), particularly in terms of competition (Scheepers, Spears, Doosje, & Manstead, 2006) and threat (Riek, Mania, & Gaertner, 2006).

High- and low-status groups both show bias, but in characteristically different ways. Members of high-status groups tend to show more intergroup bias on traits relevant to the group status differences. By contrast, consistent with the "social creativity" proposition of social identity theory (Jetten, Schmitt, Branscombe, & McKimmie, 2005; Tajfel & Turner, 1979), low-status or stigmatized groups show more intergroup bias on qualities irrelevant to the status distinction (Mullen et al., 1992), particularly when they view the status differences as illegitimate (Bettencourt, Dorr, Charlton, & Hume, 2001). For instance, people with body piercings emphasize the value of "shocking others" and being differentiated from the mainstream, particularly when they believe they are the target of unfair discrimination based on their appearance (Jetten, Branscombe, Schmitt, & Spears, 2001). Furthermore, a meta-analysis of relative ingroup-outgroup bias demonstrated that people tend to be more biased in their evaluations and judgments against groups that are more different than the ingroup, but they are more likely to engage in behavioral discrimination against outgroups whose similarity threatens the distinct identity of the ingroup (Jetten, Spears, & Postmes, 2004).

Even though much of the traditional research on bias has not made the distinction between outgroup derogation and relative ingroup-outgroup bias a central focus, empirically, these two measures can lead to very different conclusions. For example, a variety of different theories suggest that prejudice toward outgroups would be particularly strong among people who experience failure because it represents a form of downward comparison that can restore feelings of esteem (see Fein & Spencer, 1997; Knowles & Gardner, 2008). In part to test this hypothesis, Crocker and Luhtanen (1990) varied whether participants received (false) feedback indicating they had succeeded or failed on a task and then had participants evaluate outgroup and ingroup members. An examination of responses only to evaluations of outgroup members (i.e., prejudice) revealed little support for the anticipated greater bias among participants who failed. Outgroup members were evaluated the same by participants who believed they failed the task ($M = 75$) and those who were informed they succeeded ($M = 76$). However, bias in terms of the *relation* between ingroup and outgroup ratings did differ in the hypothesized ways across conditions. Participants who succeeded evaluated other ingroup members more highly than outgroup members ($M = 86$ vs. 76), whereas those who failed evaluated ingroup and outgroup members comparably ($M = 72$ vs. 75). Overall, strong ingroup favoritism drove the relational bias effect, not outgroup derogation. Nevertheless, proingroup biases can perpetuate unfair discrimination that provides systematic advantages to the ingroup, often with less personal awareness and recognition by others, and can be as pernicious as discrimination based on antioutgroup orientations (Gaertner et al. 1997).

The remainder of this chapter is organized around the basic processes that can initiate and ameliorate intergroup bias generally, rather than amplify the distinctions among stereotypes, prejudice (outgroup derogation), ingroup favoritism, and discrimination. Nevertheless, where most relevant, we note the different types of bias studied in various lines of research, and we later consider the theoretical and practical value of considering the distinctions among different forms of intergroup bias. In particular, we propose that intergroup bias, whether it concerns outgroup derogation or ingroup favoritism, explicit or implicit responses, or stereotypes, prejudice, and discrimination, has a common foundation: social categorization. Yzerbyt and Demoulin, in their chapter (this volume), address this issue broadly by considering the processes that underlie attachment to groups and the influences of group identity. In the next section, we consider the foundational role of social categorization in the creation and maintenance of intergroup bias.

SOCIAL CATEGORIZATION, IDENTITY, AND BIAS

Humans are fundamentally social animals. Group living is not only of obvious contemporary importance, it also represents the fundamental survival strategy that has likely characterized the human species from the beginning (see also chapters by Leary and by Neuberg this volume). Human activity is rooted in interdependence. Group systems involving greater mutual cooperation have substantial survival advantages for individual group members over those systems without reciprocally positive social relations. However, the decision to cooperate with nonrelatives (i.e., to expend resources for another's benefit) is a dilemma of trust because the ultimate benefit for the provider depends on others' willingness to reciprocate. Indiscriminate trust and altruism that are not reciprocated are not effective survival strategies.

Social categorization and group boundaries provide the basis for achieving the benefits of cooperative interdependence without the risk for excessive costs. Ingroup membership is a form of contingent cooperation. Total costs and risks for nonreciprocation can be contained by limiting aid to mutually acknowledged ingroup members. Thus, ingroups can be defined as bounded communities of mutual trust and obligation that delimit mutual interdependence and cooperation. The ways in which people perceive social categories and understand their group membership thus play a critical role in both prejudice toward members of other groups and social harmony within one's group.

Whether they are defined by culture, race or ethnicity, or role, group boundaries distinguish who is "in" from who is "out." Moreover, interactions between groups involve greater greed, fear, and mistrust than interactions between individuals (Insko et al., 2001). For instance, studies have examined how people make decisions in a *prisoner's dilemma game* when they participate as an individual or as a representative of their group. In a prisoner's dilemma game, like the Tajfel matrices, participants make decisions about allocating points to themselves and another participant. The choices represent cooperative or competitive orientations, and the final outcome is determined by both people's responses. People are much more competitive when groups collectively play another group than when individuals play another individual, and interventions that encourage mutual cooperation are less effective with groups than with individuals (Insko et al., 2001). In part as a consequence of this *interindividual-intergroup discontinuity effect*, in which groups are more competitive and greedy than individuals, conflict between groups is a ubiquitous phenomenon. It characterizes all cultures and has been a central theme across all of human history (Sidanius & Pratto, 1999).

In the remainder of this section, we discuss the basic functions and consequences of social categorization for intergroup bias, as well as the roles of functional relations between groups and collective identity for shaping intergroup relations and bias.

Functions and Consequences of Social Categorization

Categorization forms an essential basis for human perception, cognition, and functioning. Because of the adaptive significance of intellect in human survival, people have a fundamental need to understand their environment. To cope with the enormous complexity of the world, people abstract meaning from their perceptions and develop heuristics and other simplifying principles for thinking about important elements in their environment. Categorization is one of the most basic processes in the way that people actively derive meaning from complex environments.

Because of the fundamental importance of categorization for psychological functioning, one universal facet of human thinking essential for efficient functioning is the ability to quickly and effectively sort the many different objects, events, and people encountered into meaningful categories (Hamilton & Sherman, 1994). People often automatically categorize others on the basis of physical similarity, proximity, or shared fate (Campbell, 1958). Categorization enables decisions about incoming information to be made quickly because the instant an object is categorized, it is assigned the properties shared by other category members. Thus, it eliminates time-consuming and inefficient consideration of the meaning of every experience, and it frees up cognitive resources to perform other tasks. For example, in one set of studies (Macrae, Milne, & Bodenhausen, 1994), participants were asked to perform two tasks simultaneously. One was to form impressions of people based on pictures and limited information; the other was to attend to information from an audiotaped prose passage they heard. Participants who were first primed with category-related cues (e.g., skinhead) when they saw the pictures were better able attend to and recall information from the prose passage that they heard. Thus, category-based responses to seeing pictures of others freed up cognitive resources to process other information in the participants' environment. In this respect, people compromise total accuracy for efficiency when confronted with the often overwhelming complexity of their social world (Fiske & Taylor, 1991).

The operation of group-level processes associated with social categorization is dynamically distinct from the influence of individual-level processes. Different modes of functioning are involved, and these modes critically influence how people perceive others and experience their own sense of identity. In terms of perceptions of others, the primary distinction in influential dual-process models of impression formation (Brewer, 1988; see also the continuum model: Fiske, Lin, & Neuberg, 1999) is between person-based and category-based processing. Person-based processing is *bottom-up*. It is data-driven, involving the piecemeal acquisition of information that begins "at the most concrete level and stops at the lowest level of abstraction required by the prevailing processing objectives" (Brewer, 1988, p. 6). Category-based processing, in contrast, proceeds from global to specific; it is *top-down*. In top-down processing, how the external reality is perceived and experienced is influenced by category-based expectations. Category-based processing is more likely to occur than person-based processing because social information is typically organized around social categories.

When people or objects are categorized into groups, real differences between members of the same category tend to be perceptually minimized in making decisions or forming impressions (Tajfel, 1969). Members of the same category are regarded as more similar than they actually are, and more similar than they were before they were categorized together. In addition, distinctions between members of different categories become exaggerated. Thus, categorization enhances perceptions of similarities within and differences between groups. Furthermore, as the salience of the categorization increases, the magnitude of these distortions also increases (Turner, 1985). For *social* categorization, this process is more ominous than for nonhuman objects because these within- and between-group distortions have a tendency to be perceived as inherent in the nature of the groups (see Yzerbyt & Demoulin's this volume) and generalize to additional dimensions (e.g., character traits) beyond those that differentiated the categories originally (Allport, 1954).

Models of category-based processing (Brewer, 1988; see also Fiske et al., 1999) assume that "the mere presentation of a stimulus person activates certain classification processes that occur automatically and without conscious intent . . . The process is one of 'placing' the individual social object along well-established stimulus dimensions such as age, gender, and skin color" (Brewer, 1988, pp. 5–6). Moreover, a fundamental aspect of this type of categorization is the classification of individuals as members or not members of one's ingroup (Dovidio & Gaertner, 1993). Because of the centrality of the self in social perception, social categorization involves most fundamentally a distinction between the group containing the self, the ingroup, and other groups, the outgroups—between the "we's" and the "they's." The perceptions produced and motivations aroused by regarding oneself a member of one group and not a member of another group represent the cornerstone principles of Tajfel and Turner's (1979) *social identity theory*, historically one of the most influential perspectives in this area.

Individuals not only obtain material support from the ingroup, but they also experience substantial psychological benefit in terms of a sense of belonging and security from the ingroup (Correll & Park, 2005). People derive positive esteem from the status and distinctiveness of their group (Tajfel & Turner, 1979), and construe themselves in fundamental ways in terms of this collective identity, seeing themselves as embodying group values and characteristics. In addition, the mere recognition that another person shares ingroup membership brings the person closer to the self psychologically (Brewer, 1979).

This distinction between the ingroup and the outgroup has a profound influence on people's perceptions and evaluations of others (Sumner, 1906). Upon social categorization of people as members of the ingroup or outgroups, people favor ingroup members, both explicitly and implicitly in evaluations (Otten & Moskowitz, 2000; Otten & Wentura, 1999), particularly those ingroup members who are most prototypical of their group (Hogg & Hains, 1996). They also believe that ingroup members are more capable of expressing uniquely human emotions than are outgroup members (Leyens, Demoulin, Vaes, Gaunt, & Paladino, 2007). Cognitively, people process information more deeply for ingroup than for outgroup members (van Bavel, Packer, & Cunningham, 2008), retain information in a more detailed fashion for ingroup than for outgroup members (Park & Rothbart, 1982), have better memory for information about ways ingroup members are similar and outgroup members are dissimilar to the self (Wilder, 1981), and remember less positive information about outgroup members (Howard & Rothbart, 1980).

Because of the greater connection (Aron et al., 2005) and self-other overlap (Smith & Henry, 1996) in representations for people defined as ingroup members, people both perceive themselves as possessing qualities of the ingroup and view the ingroup as representing the characteristics they see in themselves (Otten & Epstude, 2006). Individuals process information about and make attributions to ingroup members more on the basis of self-congruency than they do for outgroup members (Gramzow, Gaertner, & Sedikides, 2001). In addition, people expect ingroup members to share their attitudes and values more than they do outgroup members (Robbins & Krueger, 2005).

In part as a consequence, people are more generous and forgiving in their attributions about the behaviors of ingroup relative to outgroup members. Positive behaviors and successful outcomes are more likely to be attributed to internal, stable characteristics of ingroup than outgroup members, whereas negative outcomes are more likely to be ascribed to the personalities of outgroup than ingroup members (Hewstone, 1990; Pettigrew, 1979). Also, people anticipate outgroup members to display bias toward one's own group (Judd, Park, Yzerbyt, Gordijn, & Muller, 2005), and they show a preference for ingroup members who show bias against an outgroup (Castelli, Tomelleri, & Zogmaister, 2008).

In addition, people encode behaviors of ingroup and outgroup members in memory at different levels of abstraction (Maass, Salvi, Arcuri, & Semin, 1989). Specifically, they encode the undesirable actions of outgroup members at more abstract levels that presume intentionality and dispositional origin (e.g., "She is hostile.") than identical behaviors of ingroup members (e.g., "She slapped the girl."). By contrast, they encode desirable actions of outgroup members at more concrete levels (e.g., "She walked across the street holding the old man's hand.") relative to the same behaviors of ingroup members (e.g., "She is helpful."). The *linguistic intergroup bias* (Maass et al., 1989) represents the tendency to describe positive ingroup and negative outgroup behaviors in abstract terms, and describe negative ingroup and positive outgroup behaviors in concrete terms.

These cognitive and linguistic biases help to perpetuate social biases and stereotypes even in the face of countervailing evidence. For example, because positive behaviors of outgroup members are encoded at relatively concrete levels, counterstereotypical positive behaviors less readily generalize across situations or to other outgroup members (see also Karpinski & von Hippel, 1996). People do not remember that an outgroup member was "helpful"; they recall only the concrete descriptive actions. Thus, outgroup stereotypes tend to be generally resistant to change by simply observing counterstereotypical outgroup behaviors. Moreover, people who are motivated to protect the esteem and integrity of their group are more likely to engage this bias when their group is threatened. One study, for instance, manipulated perceived threat from an outgroup (Maass, Ceccarelli, & Rudin, 1996). Participants who were hunters or environmentalists received a note, ostensibly from a member of the other group, containing critical (high-threat) or friendly (low-threat) remarks. Across both groups, threat exacerbated the linguistic intergroup bias: Although participants generally used more abstract language to describe the positive actions of ingroup members and the negative behavior of outgroup members, this tendency was more pronounced under high threat.

Another factor that promotes stereotyping is the systematic bias in how people perceive similarity within groups. In particular, people see the members of the outgroup as generally similar to one another, whereas ingroup members are perceived in more distinctive, individualistic ways (the *outgroup homogeneity effect*; see Boldry, Gaertner, & Quinn, 2007; Mullen & Hu, 1989). As a consequence, people are more likely to generalize the behavior of one member of the outgroup to other members of the outgroup and to the group as a whole (Quattrone & Jones, 1980). This generalization to the outgroup is particularly likely to occur for negative, stereotypical behaviors (Henderson-King & Nisbett, 1996), which may be seen as inherent in the character of the outgroup (Jost & Hamilton, 2005), and personally and socially threatening.

Language plays another role in intergroup bias because collective pronouns such as "we" or "they" that are used to define people's ingroup or outgroup status frequently occur in association with stimuli that have strong affective connotations. Thus, these pronouns may acquire important evaluative properties of their own. These words ("we," "they") can potentially increase the availability of positive or negative associations, and thus influence beliefs about, evaluations of, and behaviors toward other people, often spontaneously and without awareness (Perdue, Dovidio, Gurtman, & Tyler, 1990).

Categorization has immediate and profound effects on behavioral orientations toward others. Upon social categorization, people exhibit a "physical readiness" to approach ingroup members and avoid outgroup members (Paladino & Castelli, 2008). In terms of social relations and behavioral outcomes, people are more cooperative and trustful of ingroup than outgroup members (see Gaertner & Dovidio, 2000; Voci, 2006), as well as influenced more by their actions (Platow et al., 2007). Moreover, individuals display more positive forms of social behavior toward ingroup members. They exercise more personal restraint when using endangered resources shared with ingroup members than with others (Kramer & Brewer, 1984) and are more generous in their reward allocations with ingroup than with outgroup members (Mullen et al., 1992; Tajfel, Billig, Bundy, & Flament, 1971). In addition, shared group membership facilitates the arousal of *promotive tension*, an uncomfortable state that motivates people to address another person's needs, and other forms of empathy (e.g., compassion, sympathy) toward ingroup members (Hornstein, 1976). Moreover, empathy for a person in need of assistance is more strongly predictive of helping behavior when that target is an ingroup member than an outgroup member (Sturmer, Snyder, & Omoto, 2005). Relatedly, people are more helpful toward ingroup than toward outgroup members (Dovidio, Gaertner, Validzic, Matoka, Johnson, & Frazier, 1997; Piliavin, Dovidio, Gaertner, & Clark, 1981).

People also work harder on tasks associated with the ingroup than on activities not linked to their group identity (Worchel, Rothgerber, Day, Hart, & Butemeyer, 1998), and they are more concerned about procedural fairness within the group than about personal benefits and outcomes (Tyler & Blader, 2003). Moreover, expressing biases toward members of another group can enhance the social connection among members of the ingroup (Clark & Kashima, 2007). In general, individuals derive material benefit, receive valuable information, and experience a sense of belonging and security from the ingroup.

Although social categorization generally leads to intergroup bias, social categorization is not solely responsible for initiating social biases (Oakes, 2001). Rather, categorization is a necessary but not sufficient cause of intergroup bias. The intensity and nature of that bias—whether it is based on ingroup favoritism or extends to derogation and negative treatment of the outgroup—depend on a number of factors, such as whether the structural relations between groups and associated social norms foster and justify hostility or contempt (Mummendey & Otten, 2001). However, different treatment of ingroup versus outgroup members, whether rooted in favoritism for one group or derogation of another, can lead to different expectations, perceptions, and behavior toward ingroup versus outgroup members that can ultimately create a self-fulfilling prophecy. Initial ingroup favoritism also provides a foundation for embracing more negative intergroup feelings and beliefs that result from intrapersonal, cultural, economic, and political factors. In general, research on intergroup bias has adopted one of two perspectives, one with an emphasis on the functional relations between groups and the other on the role of collective identities.

Functional Relations Between Groups

Theories of functional relations between groups, in sociology as well as psychology, often point to competition as a fundamental cause of intergroup prejudice and conflict. Functional relations also determine the nature of the emotions aroused by other groups (Cottrell & Neuberg, 2005; see also *intergroup emotion theory*: Smith & Mackie, 2005). *Realistic group conflict theory* (Bobo, 1999; Campbell, 1965; Sherif, 1966), for example, posits that perceived group competition for resources produces efforts to reduce the access of other groups to the resources. This process was illustrated in classic work by Muzafer Sherif and his colleagues (Sherif, Harvey, White, Hood, & Sherif, 1961). In 1954, Sherif and his colleagues conducted a field study on intergroup conflict in an area adjacent to Robbers Cave State Park in Oklahoma. In this study, 22 12-year-old boys attending summer camp were randomly assigned to two groups (who subsequently named themselves Eagles and Rattlers). When the groups engaged in a series of competitive activities (tug-of-war, baseball, and touch football games), intergroup bias and conflict quickly developed.

Group members regularly exchanged verbal insults (e.g., "sissies," "stinkers," "pigs," "bums," and "cheaters"), and each group conducted raids on the other's cabins that resulted in the destruction and theft of property. Later, Sherif and his colleagues arranged intergroup contact under neutral, noncompetitive conditions. These interventions did not calm the ferocity of the exchanges, however. Mere intergroup contact was not sufficient to change the nature of the relations between the groups. Only after the investigators altered the functional relations between the groups by introducing a series of superordinate goals—that is, ones that could not be achieved without the full cooperation of both groups and that were successfully achieved—did the relations between the two groups become more harmonious and intergroup bias become greatly reduced.

Sherif et al. (1961) proposed that functional relations between groups are critical in determining intergroup attitudes. When groups are competitively interdependent, the interplay between the actions of each group results in positive outcomes for one group and negative outcomes for the other. Thus, in the attempt to obtain favorable outcomes for themselves, the actions of the members of each group are also realistically perceived to be calculated to frustrate the goals of the other group. Therefore, a win-lose, zero-sum competitive relation between groups can initiate mutually negative feelings and stereotypes toward the members of the other group. By contrast, cooperatively interdependent relations between members of different groups that have positive outcomes can reduce bias (e.g., Blanchard, Adelman, & Cook, 1975).

Functional relations do not have to involve explicit competition with members of other groups to generate biases. In the absence of any direct evidence, people typically presume that members of other groups are competitive and will hinder the attainment of one's goals (Fiske & Ruscher, 1993). Moreover, feelings of interdependence on members of one's *own* group may be sufficient to produce bias. Rabbie's *behavioral interaction model* (see Rabbie & Lodewijkx, 1996), for example, argues that either intragroup cooperation or intergroup competition can stimulate intergroup bias. That is, greater dependence on ingroup members alone can generate more intergroup bias (Gaertner & Insko, 2000). Perhaps as a consequence of feelings of outcome dependence, allowing opportunities for greater interaction among ingroup members increases intergroup bias (Gaertner & Schopler, 1998), whereas increasing interaction between members of different groups (Gaertner et al., 1999) decreases intergroup bias.

The *instrumental model of group conflict* (Esses, Dovidio, Jackson, & Armstrong, 2001; Esses, Jackson, & Armstrong, 1998) integrates work on *realistic group conflict theory* and *social dominance theory* (Sidanius & Pratto,

1999). This model proposes that *resource stress*, which represents the threat aroused by the perception that access to a desired resource (such as wealth or political power) is limited, and awareness of a potentially competitive outgroup produce perceptions of group competition for resources. The combination of resource stress and the presence of a potentially competitive outgroup lead to perceived group competition in the form of *zero-sum beliefs*—that is, beliefs that the more the other group obtains, the less is available for one's own group. The response is a strategic attempt to remove the source of competition.

Efforts to remove the other group from competition may include outgroup derogation, discrimination, and avoidance of the other group. One may express negative attitudes and attributions about members of the other group in an attempt to convince both one's own group and other groups of the competitors' lack of worth. Attempts to eliminate the competition may also entail discrimination and opposition to policies and programs that may benefit the other group. Limiting access of the other group to the resources also reduces competition. Consistent with this model, individuals in Canada and the United States perceive greater threat, are more biased against, and are more motivated to exclude immigrant groups who are seen as involved in a zero-sum competition for resources with citizens of the host country (see Esses, Jackson, Dovidio, & Hodson, 2005).

Discrimination can serve less tangible collective functions, as well as concrete instrumental objectives. The processes for establishing group position may involve goals such as gaining economic advantage, but they may also be associated with the acquisition of intangible resources such as prestige (Blumer, 1958). In fact, symbolic, psychological factors are frequently more important in intergroup bias than are tangible resources (Taylor, 2000). Theoretical developments in social psychology, stimulated by *social identity theory* (Tajfel & Turner, 1979), further highlight the role of group categorization, independent of actual realistic group conflict, in motivations to achieve favorable group identities ("positive distinctiveness") and, consequently, on the arousal of intergroup bias and discrimination.

Collective Identity

Social identity theory (Tajfel & Turner, 1979) and, more recently, *self-categorization theory* (Turner, 1985; Turner, Hogg, Oakes, Reicher, & Wetherell, 1987) consider the role of collective identity for intergroup bias. Because these frameworks are considered in some detail in the chapter by Yzerbyt and Demoulin (this volume), our coverage will be relatively brief.

With respect to one's sense of identity, social identity theory (Tajfel & Turner, 1979) and self-categorization theory

(Turner, 1985; see also Onorato & Turner, 2001) view the distinction between personal identity and social identity as a critical one. When personal identity is salient, a person's individual needs, standards, beliefs, and motives primarily determine behavior. In contrast, when social identity is salient, "people come to perceive themselves as more interchangeable exemplars of a social category than as unique personalities defined by their individual differences from others" (Turner et al., 1987, p. 50). Under these conditions, collective needs, goals, and standards are primary.

This perspective also proposes that a person defines or categorizes the self along a continuum that ranges at one extreme from the self as a separate individual with personal motives, goals, and achievements to the self as the embodiment of a social collective or group. At the individual level, one's personal welfare and goals are most salient and important. At the group level, the goals and achievements of the group are merged with one's own (see Brown & Turner, 1981), and the group's welfare is paramount. At each extreme, self-interest is represented fully by the pronouns "I" and "we," respectively. Intergroup relations begin when people think about themselves as group members rather than solely as distinct individuals.

Making group membership salient fundamentally changes the ways people see and respond to others. To isolate the influence of collective identity on intergroup relations from the affects of specific functional relations (e.g., competition) between groups, research has often used the *minimal group paradigm*. In this paradigm, groups are stripped of naturalistic meaning, functional interrelationships, and face-to-face interaction with ingroup or outgroup members. For example, researchers in minimal group studies designate people, ostensibly based on their performance on a dot-estimation task but actually randomly, as "overestimators" or "underestimators." Another common manipulation involves preferences for artists, such as Klee or Kandinsky (e.g., Peterson & Blank, 2003).

Identity, however, is a dynamic process. People can readily shift from personal to social identity and back in different contexts. Illustrating the dynamics and consequences of this process, experimenters have primed participants' personal identity by asking them to describe how they differ from other individuals or participants' social (national) identity by having them report their country of birth, native language, and nationality on their passport (Verkuyten & Hagendoorn, 1998). When individual identity was primed, individual differences in a personality-related variable, authoritarianism, primarily predicted Dutch respondents' prejudice toward Turkish migrants. In contrast, when social identity (i.e., national identity) was made salient, ingroup stereotypes and standards mainly predicted prejudiced attitudes. Thus, whether personal or

collective identity is more salient critically shapes how a person perceives, interprets, evaluates, and responds to situations and to others.

Although the categorization process may place the person at either extreme end of the continuum from personal identity to social identity, people often seek an intermediate point to balance their need to be different from others, and their need to belong and share a sense of similarity to others. *Optimal distinctiveness theory* (Brewer, 1991) proposes that people have competing motives for assimilation and differentiation, which lead them to prefer membership in smaller groups that provide a balance between these motives. Singular inclusive identities may threaten members' fundamental need for distinctiveness, a need for feeling unique and differentiated from others. Achieving balance between the motives for assimilation and differentiation enhances one's feelings of connection to the group, reduces feelings of uncertainty, and increases group cohesiveness (Hogg, 1996).

Social Categorization, Functional Relations, and Collective Identity: An Integration

Although functional and social categorization theories of intergroup bias suggest different psychological mechanisms, these approaches may offer complementary rather than necessarily competing explanations. Both sociological and psychological approaches, for example, have converged to recognize the importance of understanding the impact of group functions and collective identities on intergroup relations (see Bobo, 1999). In terms of group functions, sociologically based approaches (e.g., Blumer, 1958) focus on the importance of defending group position: Group competition and threat are fundamental processes in the development and maintenance of social biases. With respect to race relations in the United States, Blumer wrote: "Race prejudice is a defensive reaction to such challenging of the sense of group position . . . As such, race prejudice is a protective device. It functions, however shortsightedly, to preserve the integrity and position of the dominant group" (p. 5). From a psychological orientation, Sherif et al. (1961) similarly proposed that the functional relations between groups are critical in determining intergroup attitudes. According to this position, competition between groups produces prejudice and discrimination, whereas positive non-zero-sum intergroup interdependence and cooperative interaction that result in successful outcomes reduce intergroup bias (Campbell, 1965; Sherif, 1966).

Additional work demonstrates the reciprocal and often joint operation of realistic threats and symbolic threats to group identity in intergroup bias. In terms of reciprocal relations, not only do psychological biases produce perceptions of competition and motivate actual competition between groups, competition between groups itself further increases bias and distrust. When people perceive outgroup members as a threat, they tend to derogate and discriminate against them more directly (Esses et al., 2001). Thus, psychological biases and actual competition often reinforce each other to escalate intergroup biases.

With respect to complementary influences, according to *integrated threat theory* (Stephan, Renfro, Esses, Stephan, & Martin, 2005; see Stephan & Stephan, 2000), negative stereotypes, realistic group threat, and symbolic group threat all predict discrimination against other groups (e.g., immigrants), and each accounts for a unique portion of the effect. In addition, personal-level biases and collective biases may also have separate and additive influences. That is, group threat and personal prejudice can contribute independently to discrimination against other groups (Bobo, 1999). The independence of these effects points to the importance of considering each of these perspectives for a comprehensive understanding of intergroup bias, while at the same time reinforcing the theoretical distinctions among the hypothesized underlying mechanisms.

Given the centrality and spontaneity of the social categorization of people into ingroups and outgroups, and the important role of functional relations between groups in a world of limited resources, how can bias be reduced? Because categorization is a basic process that is fundamental to intergroup bias, some contemporary work has targeted this process as a place to begin to reduce intergroup bias. This work also considers the functional relations among groups. The next section explores how the forces of categorization can be disarmed or redirected to promote more positive intergroup attitudes, and potentially to begin to penetrate the barriers to reconciliation among groups with a history of antagonistic relations. One of the most influential strategies involves creating and structuring intergroup contact.

REDUCING INTERGROUP BIAS: INTERGROUP CONTACT AND CATEGORY-BASED MODELS

For more than 50 years, *intergroup contact theory* (Allport 1954; Williams, 1947; see also Dovidio, Gaertner, & Kawakami, 2003; Pettigrew, 1998) has represented one of psychology's most effective strategies for reducing bias and improving intergroup relations. This framework proposes that simple contact between groups is not necessarily sufficient to improve intergroup relations, but that it is possible to structure intergroup contact in specifiable ways to ameliorate intergroup prejudice and conflict.

In his reformulation of the *contact hypothesis*, Allport (1954) integrated and refined a range of ideas and evidence from different disciplines to identify when intergroup contact can most effectively reduce intergroup bias. Allport's contact hypothesis included four prerequisite features for contact to be successful at reducing intergroup conflict and achieving intergroup harmony: (1) equal status within the contact situation; (2) intergroup cooperation; (3) common goals; and (4) support of authorities, law, or custom. Since then, two other aspects of contact, opportunities for personal acquaintance between the members (particularly involving nonstereotypical elements; Cook, 1985) and intergroup friendships (Pettigrew, 1997, 1998), have been identified as particularly important. For instance, a longitudinal study reported that college students who had more outgroup friends in their second and third years of college were less biased in favor of their ethnic group at the end of their fourth year (Levin, van Laar, & Sidanius, 2003; see also van Laar, Levin, Sinclair, & Sidanius, 2005).

Moreover, research on *extended contact* demonstrates that simply learning that other ingroup members have friends in the outgroup can improve attitudes toward other outgroup members and reduce intergroup bias (Wright, Aron, McLaughlin-Volpe, & Ropp, 1997). In a laboratory simulation of Sherif et al.'s (1961) Robbers Cave studies, in each session, two groups of seven participants engaged in a series of competitive tasks (Wright et al., 1997). As expected, competition created conflict and negative intergroup attitudes. Then, one person from each group participated in friendship-building exercises, and each returned to their group. The main finding was that the other participants who simply learned that a member of their group had become friends with a member of the other group was sufficient to reduce intergroup tension and improve intergroup attitudes.

Allport's (1954) formulation, *contact theory*, which is a conceptual and empirical elaboration and update of the contact hypothesis, has stimulated extensive empirical work. In fact, interest appears to be escalating (see Dovidio et al., 2003), probably, in part, from the recognition of the robustness of the benefits of intergroup contact on attitudes between groups. Both laboratory and field research have yielded substantial documentation of improvement in intergroup relations when these prerequisite criteria have been established. Pettigrew and Tropp (2006) have provided an extensive meta-analysis of 515 studies involving 713 independent samples, conducted in a variety of intergroup contexts, testing the effects of intergroup contact on attitudes. Their findings demonstrated that intergroup contact, indeed, reduces intergroup prejudice (mean $r = -.215$). Furthermore, Pettigrew and Tropp found that the beneficial effect of contact was greater when Allport's optimal conditions were present in the contact situation than when they were not (mean $r = -.29$ vs. $-.20$).

Recent research, however, has moved beyond specifying what conditions moderate the reduction of bias to understanding what underlying processes, such as those involving social categorization, may be involved (see Pettigrew, 1998). This central question from a social categorization perspective involves how intergroup contact can be structured to alter inclusive-exclusive collective representations of others.

The process of social categorization, although fundamental to human perception, cognition, and social functioning, is fluid. Although category-based responses may be the cognitive "default," people engage in more individuating processes when they are in interdependent relationships with members of other groups or are motivated to form accurate impressions (Fiske, 1998, 2000). Also, people belong to many groups, and these groups are often hierarchically organized, with higher-level categories (e.g., nations) more inclusive of lower-level ones (e.g., cities or towns). Modifying a perceiver's goals, motives, and expectations, as well as the functional relationship between the groups, can alter the level of category inclusiveness that will be dominant within a particular context (Brewer, 1988; Fiske et al., 1999). This flexibility of social categorization, and consequently social identity, is important because of its implications for altering the way people think about members of other groups and, accordingly, how positively they feel about them.

Researchers have proposed a number of different approaches to structuring group contact to reduce intergroup bias. Although various models share common theoretical assumptions about the importance of social categorization and identity in intergroup relations, they represent different strategies for reducing bias and conflict. Three prominent category-based approaches are *decategorization, mutual differentiation between groups*, and *recategorization*. *Decategorization* refers to influencing whether people identify themselves primarily as group members or as distinct individuals (Brewer & Miller, 1984; Miller, 2002; Wilder, 1986). *Group differentiation* involves maintaining distinct group identities, which limits threats to valued social identity (Jetten et al., 2004), but within the context of positive interdependence between groups (Brown & Hewstone, 2005). *Recategorization*, like decategorization, is designed to alter group boundaries, but by redefining rather than eliminating group categorization (Gaertner & Dovidio, 2000).

Decategorization/Personalization

Based on the assumption that the categorization of people into different groups (specifically the ingroup and an outgroup) forms the foundation for bias, the goal of *decategorization* (see Wilder, 1981, 1986) is to weaken the salience of group boundaries. Specifically, decategorization interventions encourage people from different groups to regard one another primarily as distinct individuals and interact in interpersonal (i.e., "me" and "you") rather than group-based (i.e., "we" vs. "they") modes of relating to one another. In addition, decategorization that occurs through *personalized interactions* involving the exchange of information about each other's unique qualities further reduces intergroup bias by undermining the validity of the outgroup stereotypes (Brewer & Miller, 1984; Miller, 2002; Miller, Brewer, & Edwards, 1985).

Although similarities exist between perceiving ingroup and outgroup members in a decategorized way (as "separate individuals") and having "personalized interactions" with outgroup members, *decategorization* and *personalization* are theoretically distinct concepts. Decategorization involves viewing either outgroup members (see Wilder, 1986) or members of both groups as "separate individuals" and can promote individuated responses even in the absence of interaction or information exchange. For example, receiving information demonstrating variability in the opinions of outgroup members or seeing outgroup members respond as individuals rather than as a group renders each member more distinctive, potentially blurring the prior categorization scheme (Wilder, 1986). Another decategorization strategy of criss-crossing category memberships by forming new subgroups, each composed of members from former subgroups, changes the pattern of who is "in" and who is "out." Crossed categorization strategies have proved to be effective at reducing biases toward members of other groups relative to the original simple group categorization (see reviews by Crisp, Ensari, Hewstone, & Miller, 2003; see also Crisp & Hewstone, 2006), in part by rendering the earlier categorization less salient (Brown & Turner, 1979). Decategorization reduces intergroup bias, in part, by improving attitudes toward others previously seen primarily in terms of their outgroup membership, but also by producing less favorable responses to people formerly perceived mainly in terms of their membership in the ingroup (S. Gaertner, Mann, Murrell, & Dovidio, 1989).

In contrast with Wilder's individuation/decategorization approach, *personalization* (Brewer & Miller, 1984) involves receiving self-relevant, more intimate information about members of the outgroup. Thus, personalization involves perceiving outgroup members in a more individuated and differentiated way but further focuses on the impact of personally relevant information about an outgroup member. With personalized interaction, an individual's characteristics rather than their group memberships become primarily salient. Personalized impressions can thereby undermine group stereotypes as a source of information about members of that group (Brewer & Miller, 1984; Miller, 2002), producing more positive attitudes toward their group as a whole. Consistent with this reasoning, greater self-disclosure in intergroup contact relates to more positive intergroup attitudes and greater perceptions of the outgroup as more heterogeneous (Turner, Hewstone, & Voci, 2007). Nevertheless, Miller also observed that "if personalized information processing means that information concerning social category membership lacks any salience during the interaction, whatever information and/or affect was acquired cannot generalize to other members of the category . . . A key point, however, is that in most contact situations . . . cues providing information about the category identity of the interacting persons are constantly present" (p. 399). Thus, for the generalization of the benefits of personalized contact to occur and group stereotypes to be weakened, outgroup members' group identities must be salient to some degree (although not primary) during the interaction (see Brewer & Miller, 1984; Miller, 2002).

Miller (2002; see also Miller & Brewer, 1984) distinguished personalization from category-based and differentiated models of contact in Figure 29.1. With categorization (see Figure 29.1A), the outgroup is seen as homogeneous, tightly bounded, and distinct from the ingroup. The self, represented by the solid dot near the center of the ingroup circle, is seen as relatively prototypical of the ingroup.

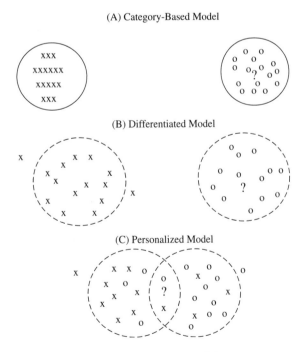

(A) Category-Based Model

(B) Differentiated Model

(C) Personalized Model

Figure 29.1 Miller's (2002) models of intergroup contact: (A) category based, (B) differentiated, and (C) personalized models.

Source: Adapted from Brewer, M. B., & Miller, N. (1984). Beyond the contact hypothesis: Theoretical perspectives on desegregation. In N. Miller & M. B. Brewer (Eds.), Groups in contact: The psychology of desegregation (pp. 281–302). Orlando, FL: Academic Press, by permission.

In the differentiated model (see Figure 29.1B), which reflects a degree of decategorization, differences among group members are recognized (as illustrated by the greater distances between members within a group), and group boundaries are more permeable. In personalized interaction (see Figure 29.1C), group membership is relatively unimportant, and others, both ingroup and outgroup members, are seen primarily in terms of similarity to the self.

A number of experimental studies provide evidence supporting the personalization perspective (Bettencourt, Brewer, Croak, & Miller, 1992; Miller et al., 1985; see also Miller, 2002). For instance, intergroup contact that permits more personalized interactions (e.g., when interactions are person focused rather than task focused) elicits more positive attitudes not only toward those outgroup members present but also toward other outgroup members (e.g., viewed on video; Miller et al., 1985). Thus, intergroup contact with personalized interaction can reduce bias in both an immediate and a generalizable fashion.

Whereas decategorization is designed to degrade group boundaries entirely and personalization attempts to make group membership secondary to personal connections between individuals, another approach allows group boundaries to be fully maintained. This alternative framework acknowledges the difficulty of eliminating perceptions of group identities; instead of attempting to degrade group boundaries, it focuses on changing perceptions of the *relationship* between the groups from competitive to cooperative, while emphasizing the positive distinctiveness of each group.

Mutual Intergroup Differentiation

One of the fundamental premises of social identity theory is that people are motivated to maintain the positive distinctiveness of their social identity. Interventions that threaten the integrity of collective identity, such as attempts to degrade group boundaries, can sometimes arouse resistance and exacerbate bias. Recognizing the potential of identity threat to arouse intergroup bias, Hewstone and Brown (1986) introduced a different categorization-based framework for reducing intergroup bias, the *mutual intergroup differentiation model*. This model posits that intergroup relations will be harmonious when group identities remain *mutually differentiated*, rather than threatened by extinction, but maintained in the context of cooperative intergroup interaction. Thus, relative to the decategorization strategies, this perspective proposes that maintaining group distinctiveness within a cooperative intergroup relationship would be associated with low levels of intergroup threat and, consequently, with lower levels of intergroup bias. In addition, the salience of intergroup boundaries provides an associative mechanism through which changes in outgroup attitudes that occur during intergroup contact can generalize to the outgroup as a whole. Because the most recent research has focused on the hypothesis that contact that makes the different category memberships salient is most effective for reducing bias, Brown and Hewstone (2005) no longer refer to their approach as the mutual intergroup differentiation model but prefer to label it simply as *intergroup contact theory*.

Figure 29.2 depicts this basic framework schematically. Opportunities for intergroup contact (quantity of contact) are important because they increase the possibility of forming close (high-quality) friendships with outgroup members. The *salience of the friend's outgroup membership* and the *perceived typicality of the friend as a member of that group* moderate the amount of *anxiety experienced* with other members of the group, and *perspective taking and empathy* for the group. Less intergroup anxiety and greater cognitive and affective empathy, in turn, mediate more positive attitudes toward the outgroup. In contrast with this set of paths for explicit intergroup attitudes, in recent work (e.g., Turner et al., 2007), the effects of contact on implicit attitudes (as assessed by the IAT) appear to be a function of attitude accessibility originating directly from the cross-group friendship.

Supportive of mutual intergroup differentiation/intergroup contact theory, several studies have demonstrated that positive contact produces more generalized reductions in bias toward the outgroup when people are aware of the *intergroup*, rather than the *interpersonal*, nature of the interaction (see Kenworthy, Turner, Hewstone, & Voci, 2005; Pettigrew, 1998). Evidence in support of this approach (see also Brown & Hewstone, 2005) comes from the results of an experiment by Brown and Wade (1987) in which work teams composed of students from two different faculties engaged in a cooperative effort to produce a two-page magazine article. When the representatives of the two groups were assigned separate roles in the team task (one group working on figures and layout, the other working on text), the contact experience had a more positive effect on intergroup attitudes than when the two groups were not provided with distinctive roles (see also Deschamps & Brown, 1983; Dovidio, Gaertner, & Validzic, 1998; Ensari & Miller, 2002; van Oudenhoven, Groenewoud, & Hewstone, 1996; Voci & Hewstone, 2003).

Mutual intergroup differentiation/intergroup contact theory further proposes that beyond the salience of social categories, the *perceived typicality* of outgroup members is a critical moderator of the extent to which positive intergroup contact can reduce bias toward the outgroup as a whole. Consistent with this proposition (see also Rothbart & John, 1985), the more representative (prototypical) of his or her group a person is perceived to be, the greater the likelihood that impressions about that person will generalize to change perceptions of the group (Rothbart & Lewis, 1988; Wilder, Simon, & Faith, 1996). Although people tend to make stronger generalizations from a member to the group for stereotype-consistent than stereotype-inconsistent impressions (Johnson, Ashburn-Nardo, Spicer, & Dovidio, 2008), typicality plays an important role in changing group stereotypes.

The relationship between exposure to counterstereotypical group members and amount of stereotype change toward the social group is influenced by the degree of perceived typicality of the group members. For instance, participants in a study read about eight different fraternity members, with descriptions that contained counterstereotypical information (Hewstone, Hassebrauck, Wirth, & Waenke, 2000). To manipulate perceived typicality of the group members, participants concentrated on the similarities or dissimilarities among the group members, or had no instructions in this regard. Compared with the other two conditions, participants rated the people they read about as most typical of fraternity

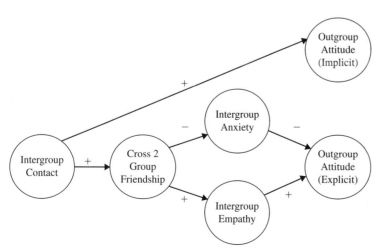

Figure 29.2 Depiction of Brown and Hewstone's (2005) mutual intergroup differentiation/intergroup contact theory framework.

members when they focused on similarities. Moreover, they stereotyped fraternity members the least in the similarities condition. Thus, with respect to group stereotypes, more change occurs when people learn about counterstereotypical information concerning others who are representative than nonrepresentative of the group (see also Weber & Crocker, 1983).

In addition, in terms of attitudes toward the outgroup, cooperation more effectively reduces prejudice when the partner is perceived as more typical of the group (Brown, Eller, Leeds, & Stace, 2007; Desforges et al., 1991). The moderating effect of typicality, however, occurs primarily when the outgroup is perceived as homogeneous rather than heterogeneous (Brown, Vivian, & Hewstone, 1999). Perceptions of typicality reduce the likelihood that group members who demonstrate counterstereotypical qualities will be seen as exceptions, which can be discounted, or as representing a subtype of the group, leaving the overall group stereotype intact and outgroup evaluation largely unaffected (Hewstone, 1994; Weber & Crocker, 1983).

Whereas decategorization focuses on degrading social categorization and mutual intergroup differentiation/intergroup contact theory emphasizes the importance of maintaining distinctive social identities, a third approach, the *common ingroup identity model* (Gaertner & Dovidio, 2000; Gaertner, Dovidio, Anastasio, Bachman, & Rust, 1993) posits the value of creating an overriding shared identity—*recategorization*—for members of different groups.

Common Ingroup Identity

The key idea of the *common ingroup identity model* is that factors that induce members of different groups to *recategorize* themselves as members of the same, more inclusive group can reduce intergroup bias through cognitive and motivational processes involving ingroup favoritism (Gaertner & Dovidio, 2000; Gaertner et al., 1993). Recategorization dynamically changes the conceptual representations of the

different groups from an "us" versus "them" orientation to a more inclusive, superordinate connection: "we." Thus, creating a common ingroup identity redirects the positive beliefs, feelings, and behaviors that are usually reserved for ingroup members and extends them to former outgroup members.

In a study that directly compared the effects of decategorization and recategorization (Gaertner et al., 1989), two three-person laboratory groups first separately performed a task in which they were instructed to imagine that their plane had crash-landed in the woods of northern Minnesota in mid-January and to rank-order 10 items salvaged from the plane (e.g., a gun, newspaper, can of shortening) in terms of their importance for survival. After that, the two groups came together to discuss the same task. The major focus of this study involved inducing the members of the three-person groups to recategorize the six participants as *one group*, to continue to categorize the participants as *two groups*, or to decategorize the participants and conceive of them as *separate individuals* (i.e., no groups) by systematically varying factors within the contact situation. Manipulated aspects included the spatial arrangement of the members (i.e. integrated, segregated, or separated seating pattern), the nature of the interdependence among the participants, and the assignment of names (i.e., assigning a group name to represent all six participants, maintaining the two earlier three-person group names, or using six different nicknames to represent the six participants).

In terms of intergroup bias, the one group's and the separate individuals' conditions each had lower levels of bias compared with the two groups' control condition, which maintained the salience of the intergroup boundary (see Table 29.1). However, recategorized (one group) and decategorized (separate individuals) conditions reduced bias in different ways. Specifically, the one group's condition reduced bias (compared with the two groups' control condition) primarily by increasing the attractiveness of former outgroup members, whereas the separate individuals' condition ameliorated bias primarily by decreasing the attractiveness of former ingroup members (see Table 29.1).

Table 29.1   Recategorization and Decategorization Reduce Bias, But in Different Ways

	Evaluations		
	Bias (Ingroup — Outgroup)	Ingroup	Outgroup
Control (two groups) condition	.49	5.80	5.39
Recategorization (one group) condition	.27	5.71	5.54
Decategorization (separate individuals) condition	.27	5.39	5.12

From Gaertner, S. L., Mann, J. A., Murrell, A. J., & Dovidio, J. F. (1989). Reduction of intergroup bias: The benefits of recategorization. *Journal of Personality and Social Psychology, 57*, 239–249, by permission.

Thus, consistent with self-categorization theory, "the attractiveness of an individual is not constant, but varies with the ingroup membership" (Turner, 1985, p. 60).

Figure 29.3 presents the general framework and specifies the causes and consequences of a common ingroup identity. According to the model, different types of intergroup interdependence and cognitive, perceptual, linguistic, affective, and environmental factors (listed on the left) can either independently or in concert alter individuals' cognitive representations of the aggregate (listed in the center). Included among the different factors that can increase the perception of a common ingroup identity are the features specified by Allport's (1954; see also Williams, 1947) contact hypothesis (i.e., cooperative intergroup interaction, equal status, egalitarian norms). In addition, common ingroup identity may be achieved by increasing the salience of existing common superordinate memberships (e.g., a school, a company, a nation) or categories (e.g., students; Gómez, Dovidio, Huici, Gaertner, & Cuardrado, 2008), or by introducing factors (e.g., common goals or fate; see Gaertner et al. 1999) that are perceived to be shared by the memberships.

These resulting cognitive representations (i.e., one group, two subgroups within one group [a dual identity], two groups, or separate individuals) then produce the specific cognitive, affective, and overt behavioral consequences (listed on the right in Figure 29.3). For instance, cooperative intergroup interaction improves outgroup attitudes and reduces bias between members of different groups through its effect on creating a more inclusive, common

identity. Once former outgroup members are regarded as ingroup members, they are accorded the benefits of ingroup status heuristically. They will be the recipients of more positive thoughts, feelings, and behaviors (listed on the right in Figure 29.3) by virtue of their inclusion now as ingroup members.

Consistent with this hypothesis, studies of a range of naturalistic groups report that stronger perceptions of a common ingroup identity mediate positive intergroup relations. These studies include students attending a multiethnic high school (Gaertner, Rust, Dovidio, Bachman & Anastasio, 1996), banking executives who had experienced a corporate merger (Gaertner et al., 1996), and college students from blended families whose households are composed of two formerly separate families trying to unite into one (Banker & Gaertner, 1998). Other field research demonstrates that more salient common identity relates to more favorable intergroup attitudes for members of majority (Smith & Tyler, 1996) and minority (Pfeifer et al., 2007) racial and ethnic groups and across national groups (Klandermans, Sabucedo, & Rodriguez, 2004). Experimental evidence of intergroup attitudes in support of the common ingroup identity model comes from research using both *ad hoc* and real groups, using children as well as adults, and in the United States (e.g., Houlette et al., 2004; Nier, Gaertner, Dovidio, Banker, & Ward, 2001; see Gaertner & Dovidio, 2000) and in other countries (e.g., Guerra, Rebelo, & Monteiro, 2004; Kessler & Mummendey, 2001; Montiero, Guerra, & Rebelo, 2009).

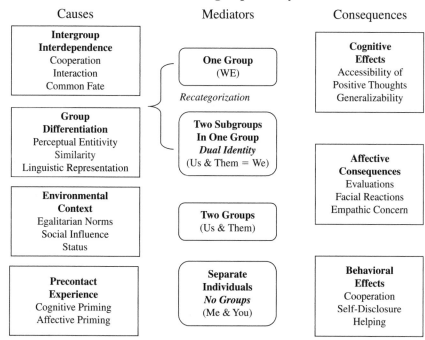

The Common Ingroup Identity Model

Figure 29.3 The common ingroup identity model.

A study conducted at the University of Delaware football stadium before a game between the University of Delaware and West Chester State University illustrates how a salient superordinate identity can increase compliance with a request for assistance from a person of a different race (Nier et al., 2001). In this experiment, Black and White, male and female interviewers approached fans of the same sex from both universities (indicated by their signature clothing) just before the fans entered the stadium. The interviewers, who wore University of Delaware or West Chester State University hats, asked fans to answer questions about their food preferences. White fans were significantly more compliant to a request from a Black who shared common university identity than from a Black interviewer ostensibly from the other university. When the interviewers were White, however, there was no significant difference in their levels of compliance as a function of university identity. These findings offer support for the idea that outgroup members will be treated more favorably in terms of prosocial behavior when they are perceived to also share a more inclusive, common ingroup affiliation.

Recategorization in terms of a common ingroup identity can also promote intergroup forgiveness and trust. For instance, increasing the salience of Jewish students' "human identity," in contrast with their "Jewish identity," increases their perceptions of similarity with Germans, willingness to forgive Germans for the Holocaust, and interest in associating with contemporary German students (Wohl & Branscombe, 2005). A shared superordinate identity also affects interest in and responsiveness to others. People are more accepting of a newcomer's innovation when the newcomer shares a superordinate identity with them than when the newcomer does not (Kane, Argote, & Levine, 2005). Also, people are more responsive to the needs of former outgroup members perceived within a common ingroup identity across a range of situations (Dovidio et al., 1997), including emergency situations (Levine, Prosser, Evans, & Reicher, 2005).

The successful induction of a common ingroup identity does not necessarily eliminate social biases entirely; instead, it may mainly redirect them. When recategorization occurs and a superordinate group identity is established, other outgroups at the same level of inclusiveness are likely to be recognized as relevant comparison groups. Because of the need to establish, maintain, or enhance the positive distinctiveness of the superordinate identity, biases toward these groups are likely to be aroused (Mummendey et al., 2001). For example, consistent with the common ingroup identity model, East Germans who recategorized West Germans and East Germans within the superordinate national identity of "Germans," relative to those who continued to use the East-West German categorization scheme,

displayed reduced bias toward West Germans. However, they also became more biased over time toward members of other countries (Kessler & Mummendey, 2001). Thus, "recategorization is a 2-edged process: Although it reduces conflict at the subgroup level, it may initiate conflict at the common ingroup level" (Kessler & Mummendey, p. 1099).

In addition, efforts to induce a common identity can sometimes be met with resistance that can increase bias between members of the original groups. Social identity theory (Tajfel & Turner, 1979) proposes that people are motivated to maintain the positive distinctiveness of their group relative to other groups. When the integrity of one's group identity is threatened, people are motivated to reestablish positive and distinctive group identities, and thereby maintain relatively high levels of intergroup bias (Brown & Wade, 1987) or show increased levels of bias (Deschamps & Brown, 1983; see Jetten et al., 2004, for a review). Consistent with this reasoning, introducing interventions such as emphasizing similarity or overlapping boundaries between the groups (Dovidio, Gaertner, Validzic, Matoka, Johnson, & Frazier, 1997; Jetten, Spears, & Manstead, 1997) or shared identity (Hornsey & Hogg, 2000) can exacerbate intergroup bias as a way of reaffirming positive distinctiveness. This effect is particularly likely to occur among people who value their original group highly, such as those more highly identified with their original group (Crisp, Walsh, & Hewstone, 2006), and when the initiative to form a superordinate identity is perceived to come from an outgroup rather than an ingroup member (Gómez et al., 2008).

However, within the context of the common ingroup identity model, the development of a common ingroup identity does not necessarily require each group to forsake its less inclusive group identity. Social identities are complex; every individual belongs to multiple groups simultaneously (Brewer, 2000). Thus, depending on their degree of identification with different categories and contextual factors that make particular identities more salient, individuals may activate one or more of these identities simultaneously (Roccas & Brewer, 2002), as well as sequentially (Turner, 1985). As depicted by the "subgroups within one group" (i.e., a dual identity) representation, people can conceive of two groups (e.g., science and art majors) as distinct units (thereby establishing "mutual group differentiation") within the context of a superordinate (i.e., University identity) social entity.

When group identities and their associated cultural values are adaptive or when identities are associated with high status or highly visible cues to group membership, it would be undesirable or impossible for people to relinquish these group identities completely or, as perceivers, to be "colorblind." Under these conditions, demands to forsake these group identities or to adopt a color-blind ideology often arouse strong reactance and exacerbate intergroup bias. However, people who regard themselves as members of different groups but all playing on the *same team* typically show positive attitudes toward the other "subgroups" relative to when they think only in terms of "separate groups." Although Allport (1954) observed that "concentric loyalties take time to develop, and often of course they fail completely to do so" (pp. 44–45), when subgroup identities are recognized, valued, and linked positively to the superordinate group identity, a dual identity may be effective for reducing intergroup bias and maintaining harmonious relations between groups.

Conceptually, whereas mutual intergroup differentiation/intergroup contact theory emphasizes the value of maintaining separate group identities within positive functional relations (i.e., cooperation) between groups, the common ingroup identity model posits that the superordinate identity component of a dual identity can be established in other ways as well, such as increasing the salience of overarching entities. From the perspective of the common ingroup identity model, it is the simultaneous salience of separate and superordinate group identities, not the particular mechanism that achieves this, that is important for intergroup bias. Consistent with this position, evidence has been reported that the intergroup benefits of a strong superordinate identity can be achieved for both majority and minority group members when the strength of the subordinate identity is also high (Gaertner et al., 1996; Huo & Molina, 2006; Huo, Smith, Tyler, & Lind, 1996; Smith & Tyler, 1996). These findings are also conceptually consistent with studies that reveal that interethnic attitudes are more favorable when participants are primed with a multicultural, pluralistic ideology for increasing interethnic harmony that emphasizes the value of a dual identity, relative to an assimilation ideology, which closely parallels a one-group representation (Richeson & Nussbaum, 2004). Moreover, with a dual identity relative to the pure one-group representation, the benefits of intergroup contact may more easily generalize to additional outgroup members because the associative link to their original group identity remains intact, as suggested by mutual intergroup differentiation/intergroup contact theory.

In contrast with the consistently positive relationship between the experience of a common identity (i.e., a one-group representation) and more favorable intergroup orientations, the strength of a dual identity can have divergent effects, associated with either positive or negative intergroup responses. For instance, in studies of banking executives involved in a merger and of members of blended families, a stronger sense of a dual identity was related to greater bias and conflict (see Gaertner, Bachman, Dovidio, & Banker, 2001).

The *ingroup projection model* (Mummendey & Wenzel, 1999) explains this latter effect as a consequence of projecting the standards of one's own group as the standards for the superordinate group. That is, when a common identity is salient for members of different groups, members of one group or both groups regard their subgroup's characteristics (such as norms, values, and goals) as more prototypical of the common, inclusive category compared with those of the other subgroup. When this occurs, the outgroup is judged as substandard, deviant, or inferior, leading to greater bias between the subgroups (e.g., Waldzus, Mummendey, Wenzel, & Boettcher, 2004). This type of group projection that exacerbates bias may be more likely to occur when the superordinate identity represents a dimension directly relevant to the subcategory identities (e.g., Germans for East Germans and West Germans); when the superordinate identity is irrelevant to the subgroup identities, the experience of a dual identity is likely to have more favorable intergroup consequences (Hall & Crisp, 2005; see also Dovidio, Gaertner, et al., 2008). Thus, further work is needed to understand the factors that can moderate the effectiveness of a dual identity for reducing bias and illuminate the mechanisms accounting for these effects.

Integration of Category-Based Models for Reducing Bias

Although decategorization, mutual group differentiation, and recategorization approaches suggest different ways of reducing bias, they all draw in some way on the fundamental role of social categorization in intergroup bias. Decategorization and recategorization focus directly on eliminating the original we-they distinction or replacing it with a new, superordinate identity to reduce intergroup bias in an immediate contact situation. However, both perspectives also note, consistent with the central premise of the mutual intergroup differentiation/intergroup contact theory approach, that some degree of salience of the original group boundaries is instrumental for promoting the immediate positive effects of intergroup contact to generalize beyond group members present to stereotypes and attitudes associated with the outgroup as a whole. Personalization is hypothesized to generalize primarily when group memberships are salient during the encounter and the other person is viewed as typical of the outgroup (Miller, 2002). The common ingroup identity model acknowledges a potential "trade-off" related to the salience of superordinate and subgroup identities within a dual identity: Attitudes toward outgroup members present may be more positive when only a superordinate identity is salient, but attitudes toward the outgroup will improve more when subgroup identity is simultaneously salient (Gaertner & Dovidio, 2000; see also Gaertner et al., 1989).

Each of the models has its own particular challenges. The basic need to categorize people and objects to simplify a world that is complex substantially undermines the ability to sustain decategorized representations over time. In addition, given the traditional and contemporary importance of certain social categories, which produces automatic activation of some categories such as age, race, and sex (Brewer, 1988; see Fiske, 1998, for a review), recategorized, as well as decategorized, representations may be highly unstable (Hewstone, 1996). Also with respect to recategorization, attempts to create new superordinate identities may arouse threats to valued subgroup identities, which can exacerbate intergroup bias (Crisp et al., 2006; Hornsey & Hogg, 2000). With respect to mutual intergroup differentiation/intergroup contact theory, exposure to an outgroup member who deviates from group-based expectations makes the person appear atypical of his or her group, which limits the generalization of the benefits of positive intergroup contact for changing group stereotypes and attitudes (Hewstone & Hamberger, 2000).

Rather than viewing decategorization, mutual intergroup differentiation, and recategorization approaches as competing perspectives, researchers in this area have recognized that the processes identified in these models may operate in a complementary fashion to reduce intergroup bias in a more general and sustained way (Gaertner & Dovidio, 2000; Hewstone, 1996; Pettigrew, 1998). For example, the more favorable impressions of and orientations toward outgroup members produced by recategorization within a common ingroup identity are not likely to be finely differentiated, at least initially (see Boldry et al., 2007). Rather, these more elaborated, personalized impressions can soon develop within the context of a common identity because the newly formed positivity bias is likely to encourage more open communication and greater self-disclosing interaction between former outgroup members (see Dovidio, Gaertner, Validzic, Matoka, Johnson, & Frazier, 1997). Thus, over time, a common identity can encourage personalization of outgroup members, which further reduces bias through decategorization (see Miller et al., 1985).

Other possible sequences may also be effective (see Gaertner & Dovidio, 2005). Success in cooperative activities in which groups maintain their separate identities (mutual intergroup differentiation) may facilitate the groups' subsequent acceptance of a common superordinate identity. The development of a common ingroup identity, in turn, may not only produce more positive attitudes toward people formerly perceived only as outgroup members but also may lead to more individuated perceptions

of them and encourage more self-disclosing interactions. Even though the salience of a common ingroup identity may be relatively unstable because of contextual pressures or historical relations between the original groups (Hewstone, 1996), these personalized interactions may then create more enduring positive attitudes, orientations, and social networks between members of the groups, as well as the recognition and development of cross-cutting group identities.

Alternatively, Pettigrew (1998) posited that intergroup interaction under the conditions proposed in contact theory might initially produce decategorized representations of the participating members, which results in a lessening of anxiety, reduced perceptions of threat, greater liking, and enhanced opportunities for personalized exchanges. Then, because of the greater resources involved in maintaining individuated rather than group representations (Brewer, 1988; Fiske et al., 1999), together with other immediate cues in the environment, salient categorization may be reinstated but now in the context of positive interdependence. With salient group representations, the benefits of contact are likely to generalize beyond those involved in the contact setting, because the outgroup members present are now directly associated with the outgroup as a whole (Brown & Hewstone, 2005). Furthermore, when members of one group recognize the heterogeneity of members of another group and develop more positive attitudes toward them, intergroup boundaries may become more permeable and flexible, thereby facilitating recategorization of both groups within a common superordinate identity.

The ongoing nature of the intergroup relationship likely influences how these different processes interrelate. When relations are highly antagonistic, attempts to form a common ingroup identity through recategorization are likely to be futile and may further increase bias because of identity threat. Under those conditions, decategorization may represent the most productive initial step (Pettigrew, 1998). Thus, future research may incorporate these basic principles and processes into a range of different contact situations and explore how the effectiveness of different *sequences* may be determined by the nature of the existing intergroup relations.

ADDITIONAL DIRECTIONS

The volume of research on intergroup bias reviewed in this chapter and in the chapter by Yzerbyt and Demoulin (this volume) demonstrates that a considerable amount is known about the processes that produce and ameliorate intergroup bias. Nevertheless, as the discussion of the potential sequential and complementary nature of decategorization, mutual intergroup differentiation, and recategorization frameworks reveals, there are also several other promising directions of research in this area. This final section of the chapter considers examples of three such areas, one related to moderating factors, another involving mediating processes, and a third about the relationships among different types of bias.

Moderation: Relationships Among Group Identities and Group Status

The relationships among group identities and relative group status (in terms of status, power, advantage, and size) are two potentially important moderators of processes relating to reduced bias. The former relates to symbolic relations between groups; the latter involves functional relations.

Relations Among Subgroup Identity, Superordinate Identity, and Functional Relations

Mutual intergroup differentiation/intergroup contact theory (Brown & Hewstone, 2005; Hewstone & Brown, 1986) proposes that maintaining distinctive group identities, which limits *identity threat*, within the context of positive functional relationship between groups is critical for reducing intergroup biases. The *dual identity* representation within the common ingroup identity model posits that the acceptance of a superordinate identity does not necessarily require members to forsake their subgroup identities (Gaertner & Dovidio, 2000; Gaertner et al., 1989). Establishing a common superordinate identity while simultaneously maintaining the salience of subgroup identities (i.e., developing a dual identity as two subgroups within one group) may be particularly effective because it permits the benefits of a common ingroup identity to operate without arousing countervailing motivations to achieve positive distinctiveness.

Nevertheless, appreciating the potential relations among subgroup identity, intergroup relations, and superordinate identity is critical for understanding the impact on intergroup bias. Different group identities may be complementary, independent, or competitive, and the consequences for bias may be quite different. When subgroup and superordinate identities involve different types of group identities (e.g., race and school identities; Gaertner et al., 1996), or complementary identities and expertise (Dovidio et al., 1998), appreciating group differences in a common endeavor or within a common superordinate identity is unlikely to produce identity threat or feelings of competition between groups. As a consequence, differentiated identities between groups and the simultaneous activation of common and subgroup identities should not arouse intergroup tension or bias. However, in many cases, the different group identities may be oppositional (e.g., reflecting mutually exclusive value systems)

or the subgroup and superordinate group identities may be incompatible. For example, because a second marriage can represent the formation of a new family composed of formerly separate families, the new stepfamily and its component families both serve the same primary function and are, therefore, within the same domain of group life—the family (Banker & Gaertner, 1998). Making these identities simultaneously salient can, therefore, exacerbate bias.

Previous research has explored the effects of assigning the same or different tasks to groups working together for a common purpose (Brown & Wade, 1987; Deschamps & Brown, 1983). Indeed, the mutual intergroup differentiation/intergroup contact theory perspective (Brown & Hewstone, 2005; Hewstone & Brown, 1986) posits that groups will experience greater identity threat and higher intergroup bias when they work toward a common goal and perform the same task as one another than when they perform different tasks. Whereas the work supporting the mutual intergroup differentiation/intergroup contact theory approach focuses on differences and similarities between the subgroups and the resulting threats to the group identities, it may also be enlightening to focus on the structural similarities and differences between the superordinate group and its component subgroups. Specifically, when subgroups and their superordinate group identities are in more highly related domains of group life or when subgroup identities relate more strongly to the activity or goals of the superordinate group, people are likely to perceive these identities more competitively.

Understanding the different potential relationships between subgroup and superordinate group identities represents one potential interpretation of the inconsistent relationship between a dual-identity and intergroup bias across settings. When subgroup and superordinate group identities are in different domains, stronger dual identity representations typically relate to less bias. For example, in a study of students attending a multiethnic high school (Gaertner et al., 1996), stronger endorsement of the belief that the student body felt like different groups playing on the same team was associated with lower bias toward students from other racial and ethnic groups at the school. Also, minority students at the school who described themselves using both a racial or ethnic group identity and as an American superordinate identity (e.g., Black American) had lower bias toward other groups in the school than those who described themselves only in terms of their racial or ethnic identity. Additional survey studies further reveal that a common identity has positive effects on intergroup relations when minority students' American and ethnic identities are seen as compatible (Huo, 2003); under these conditions, the benefits of a strong superordinate identity remain relatively stable even when the strength of the subordinate identity becomes equivalently high (Huo et al., 1996; Smith & Tyler, 1996). However, when subgroup and superordinate group identities are in comparable domains, and thus are potentially incompatible, the experience of a dual identity often relates to greater intergroup bias (e.g., Waldzus et al., 2004). For instance, in the context of bank mergers and blended families, the strength of dual identity was related to *less* favorable intergroup attitudes (see Gaertner & Dovidio, 2000).

Group Status

As noted earlier, high- and low-status groups differ generally in the amount of bias expressed toward each other and in the ways it is expressed. Overall, high-status groups show greater bias toward low-status groups, particularly on dimensions relevant to the group differentiation (Mullen et al.,1992). However, particularly when they perceive status relations as illegitimate, members of low-status groups often exhibit more bias than do members of high-status groups on irrelevant dimensions (Bettencourt et al., 2001). Nevertheless, perhaps because of the traditional emphasis of contact theory on equal status in the contact situation, group status has only recently received concerted attention in the literature on reducing intergroup bias. Even though contact may involve equal status in the context situation, the experiences, needs, and expectations of goals shaped by group status differences outside the context can have important implications for the impact of intergroup contact (Berger & Fisek, 2006; Demoulin, Leyens, & Dovidio, 2009).

A meta-analysis by Tropp and Pettigrew (2005), which involved the same database as the one used by Pettigrew and Tropp (2006), identified some important differences in the effectiveness of group contact as a function of group status. Overall, intergroup contact was significantly more effective at reducing intergroup bias for members of high-status groups (mean $r = -.23$) than it was for members of low-status groups (mean $r = -.18$). Moreover, status-related differences were present in the process of prejudice reduction. Whereas the optimal conditions specified by contact theory moderated the effect of contact for high-status group members, these conditions had no significant effect for low-status group members.

One fundamental difference between members of high- and low-status groups involves their motivations in the contact situation. Members of both high- and low-status groups often support the existing social structure (see *system justification theory* as detailed in Jost, Banaji, & Nosek, 2004). Nevertheless, several different theoretical perspectives, such as *social identity theory* (Tajfel & Turner, 1979), *social dominance theory* (Sidanius & Pratto, 1999), and the *group position* perspective (Bobo, 1999)

converge to posit that, whereas members of high-status groups are likely to desire the stability of the social system that benefits them, members of low-status groups are typically more motivated toward social change.

As a consequence, high- and low-status group members are likely to have different objectives for the nature and consequences of their contact (Dovidio, Gaertner, & Saguy, 2009). In particular, members of high-status groups tend to promote conditions that draw attention *away from* group differences and group-based inequality, preferring an emphasis on common identity in intergroup interactions. By contrast, members of low-status groups seek acknowledgment of differences (subgroup identities), as well as common identity, which can lead to recognition of unfair disparity between groups and motivate efforts to restore justice. Consistent with this hypothesis, members of high-status groups prefer to focus intergroup conversation on commonalities and away from differences, whereas members of low-status groups show a desire to talk about both types of topics (Saguy, Dovidio, & Pratto, 2008).

In addition, consistent with research showing that members of host countries typically endorse assimilation (one group) ideologies, whereas immigrants endorse integration (multicultural) ideologies (Berry, 1997; Verkuyten, 2006), Whites, the majority group in the United States, prefer common identity to a dual identity in intergroup contact situations (Dovidio, Gaertner, & Kafati, 2000); see also Ryan, Hunt, Weible, Peterson, & Casas, 2007). Moreover, for Whites, a stronger common identity but not dual identity mediates a lower level of bias. By contrast, racial and ethnic minority group members prefer a dual-identity representation, and the dual-identity representation is the most potent mediator of the effect of positive intergroup contact on reduced bias (Dovidio, Gaertner, & Kafati, 2000). Similarly, in an experiment using laboratory groups (González & Brown, 2006), participants who were members of a numerical minority group showed reduced bias toward the majority group as a whole only when the conditions of contact emphasized a dual identity (not when it emphasized common or separate group identities). Thus, to the extent to which general intergroup discourse (Ruscher, 2001) and the nature of intergroup contact fails to address intergroup differences and disparities (Jackman, 1994), intergroup contact will be less satisfying and effective for low-status group members than for high-status group members.

Future research might not only further investigate how group status differences moderate the extent and manner in which intergroup contact reduces bias, but also consider underlying factors. Differences in group prestige and privilege, power to control resources, and size can all contribute to these effects (Bettencourt et al., 2001; Goodwin, Gubin, Fiske, & Yzerbyt, 2000). Although these factors are typically confounded in naturalistic intergroup relations, theoretically they can be isolated experimentally to understand how each factor contributes to these effects (e.g., Gonzalez & Brown, 2006). In addition, other differences that can result from group position might also influence the nature and outcomes of intergroup contact. For example, the Needs-Based Model of Reconciliation (Shnabel, Nadler, Canetti-Nisim, & Ullrich, 2008) proposes that intergroup orientations will become more positive when contact satisfies the psychological needs of members of high-status and of low-status groups. However, members of high- and low-status groups have different basic needs: Members of low-status groups have a need for empowerment, whereas members of high-status groups seek acceptance and moral validation (Shnabel et al.; see also Fiske, Harris, Russell, & Shelton, 2009; Shelton, Richeson, & Vorauer, 2006). Thus, to fully understand intergroup relations, researchers need to consider more comprehensively the dynamics of group status differences and the nature of intergroup exchange. This leads us to the next general topic for further research: exploring proximal mediators of intergroup bias and its reduction.

Cognitive and Affective Mediators

Social categorization of people into ingroup and outgroups stimulates a range of cognitive and affective processes that produce intergroup biases. Much of the research on reducing bias has examined individual differences (see Yzerbyt & Demoulin's chapter, this volume) and social influences (e.g., intergroup contact) on bias. Moreover, as our earlier discussion indicated, attempts to reduce intergroup bias have focused on cognitive representations of the groups (e.g., through decategorization or recategorization). However, questions still remain about even more proximal cognitive and affective processes that may mediate the effects not only of social experiences on bias but also reflect "downstream" effects of new social representations. In this section, we review some of the potential cognitive and affective mediators of bias and bias reduction.

Cognitive Mediators

Based largely on popular beliefs that intergroup bias is rooted in ignorance, increased knowledge of other groups has long been hypothesized to be a potential mediator of reduced intergroup bias. Increased knowledge can have a range of possible benefits for reducing intergroup bias (Stephan & Stephan, 2001). Greater knowledge about a group may produce more positive attitudes through *mere exposure effects*, in which perceiving people or objects more frequently increases liking. Conversely, repeated exposure to the ingroup can produce more negative attitudes to outgroup members (Smith, Dijksterhuis, & Chaiken, 2008). Greater

knowledge can counteract negative expectancies and lead people to see more similarities with members of an outgroup than they anticipated (Mallett, Wilson, & Gilbert, 2008).

Negative expectancies are a key determinant of intergroup tension and negative intergroup interaction (Plant, 2004; Plant & Devine, 2003). Perceived similarities across group lines create more positive impressions of and orientations toward outgroups and their members (Stein, Hardyck, & Smith, 1965), reduce uncertainty in future interactions (Stephan & Stephan, 1985), and enhance trust (Poortinga & Pidgeon, 2006). Increased knowledge can help to create new cognitions that are inconsistent with previous biases, thereby arousing dissonance, which can be instrumental in reducing prejudice (Brewer & Miller, 1984; Leippe & Eisenstadt, 1994). In addition, enhanced knowledge may make people more aware of injustices against the outgroup (Dovidio et al., 2004), increase the accessibility of models for nonbiased relations, and alter perceptions of norms in a nonprejudiced direction (Crandall & Stangor, 2005).

Learning that other members of one's group are either more prejudiced or less prejudiced than one's group changes personal attitudes in a corresponding direction. In one study (Wittenbrink & Henly, 1996), for instance, participants read about how others responded to a questionnaire about racial issues. The questionnaire they saw was constructed to represent very high or very low levels of racial bias. For instance, in the high-prejudice condition, on one item, other respondents ostensibly indicated that they believed that 35% to 39% of Black men between the ages of 18 and 24 had served time in jail; in the low-prejudice condition, the others estimated 0% to 4%. Participants exposed to the high-prejudice consensus information reported greater personal prejudice and, in an ostensibly unrelated subsequent study, recommended harsher treatment for a Black defendant on trial than did those presented with low-prejudice consensus information. Participants already relatively high in prejudice were particularly susceptible to the high-prejudice consensus information. Knowledge concerning social norms is thus important for shaping attitudes and discrimination toward Blacks.

Recently, Pettigrew and Tropp (2008) conducted a new meta-analysis of the role of increased knowledge, using an updated database of studies published through 2005 testing mediators of the relationship between contact and reduced bias. Increased knowledge had a significant but weak mediating effect. The correlation between increased knowledge and prejudice was –.14. Pettigrew and Tropp concluded, "Thus, simply knowing more about the outgroup typically does not have a major effect on reducing prejudice" (p. 927).

Affective Mediators

In general, evidence for affective processes in bias and bias reduction is much more robust than that for the cognitive effects associated with increased knowledge. Two different meta-analyses, one by Pettigrew and Tropp (2008) examining the intergroup contact literature and the other by Talaska, Fiske, and Chaiken (2008) reviewing attitude-discrimination research, both found that measures of emotional bias (i.e., differential emotional reactions to ingroup and outgroup members beyond overall positive and negative reactions) were significantly better predictors of outcomes than were measures of cognitive bias. Talaska et al. concluded, "Emotional prejudices are twice as closely related to racial discrimination as stereotypes and beliefs are" (p. 263). The three affective mechanisms that have received the most empirical attention and support are anxiety, threat, and empathy.

Intergroup anxiety is a negative affective state that is aroused when people anticipate negative personal consequences during an immediate interaction or in anticipation of an upcoming interaction. Intergroup interactions are generally more anxiety-arousing than are intragroup interactions (Stephan & Stephan, 1985). This anxiety has a direct physiological basis in terms of physiological arousal and cortisol levels (Mendes, Major, McCoy, & Blascovich, 2008; see also the chapter by Blascovich & Mendes, volume 1).

Anxiety can have a range of effects that can influence intergroup bias. Anxiety produces a more narrow perceptual focus that can facilitate stereotype-confirming information searches (Wilder & Shapiro, 1989), and is associated with increased vigilance and sensitivity to negative cues from outgroup members in intergroup interactions (Vorauer, 2006). In addition, nonverbal cues of anxiety are similar to those for aversion; thus, anxiety can communicate bias toward others, which, in turn, can elicit reciprocal negative reactions and a mutual desire to avoid further relations (Pearson et al., 2008). Thus, high levels of anxiety, which are characteristic of intergroup interactions, can lead to disengagement from and the avoidance of future contact (Plant & Devine, 2003; Shelton & Richeson, 2006). Moreover, when contact does occur, it can contribute to awkward and uncomfortable experiences that can maintain or exacerbate bias (Shelton & Richeson, 2006). Riek et al.'s (2006) meta-analysis of 34 studies found that intergroup anxiety was related to less positive outgroup attitudes ($r = .46$).

Intergroup anxiety experienced by both non-Blacks and Blacks negatively impacts intergroup relations. One research report considered initial intergroup expectancies of non-Black and Black participants, and then assessed the consequences of interracial contact over the next 2 weeks (Plant, 2004). Non-Blacks (White, Asian, Latino, and biracial) who had more negative expectancies of interracial interactions, in part related to personal concerns about appearing biased, reported greater anxiety in their subsequent interracial interactions. Greater anxiety, in turn, related to a stronger

motivation to avoid intergroup contact. For Black participants, more negative expectancies of Whites' bias predicted their interracial anxiety, which was related to less positive experiences during intergroup contact over the following 2 weeks.

A considerable body of literature demonstrates that positive intergroup contact along the dimensions specified by contact theory reduces anxiety associated with intergroup interaction (Page-Gould, Mendoza-Denton, & Tropp, 2008; Pettigrew, 1998; Stephan et al., 2002; Turner, Hewstone, Voci, & Vonofakou, 2008; Voci & Hewstone, 2003). The Pettigrew and Tropp (2008) meta-analysis reported that anxiety is generally related to greater levels of prejudice, $r = .37$, but more intergroup contact predicts lower levels of anxiety, $r = -.29$. In addition, anxiety mediates the relationship between intergroup contact and reduced bias. Beyond personal contact, other research has found that knowing about intergroup friendships or imagining oneself successfully interacting with an outgroup member also reduces anxiety, which mediates the effects of extended contact (Turner et al., 2008) and imagined contact (Stathi & Crisp, 2008; Turner et al., 2007) on prejudice.

Closely related to anxiety are feelings of *intergroup threat*, which involve perceptions of imminent danger. Threats can be realistic, originating from actual or perceived conflicts over tangible resources, such as jobs, political power, or group position (Blumer, 1958; Sherif & Sherif, 1969), or symbolic, stemming from real or perceived cultural and value differences between groups (Riek et al., 2006; Stephan & Stephan, 2000). Riek et al. found in their meta-analysis that realistic and symbolic threats have similar, significant relationships to less positive outgroup attitudes ($r = .42$ and .45).

Moreover, ingroup identification can moderate people's responses to threat. People who identify more strongly with their ingroup are more sensitive to threats to the distinctiveness or value of their group's identity (Voci, 2006). In addition, in response to these threats to social identity, individuals who identify more strongly with their group self-stereotype (i.e., view themselves more in terms of the group prototype; Spears, Doosje, & Ellemers, 1997) and respond with greater bias toward other groups (Jetten et al., 2004).

However, positive intergroup contact reduces threat, in part by ameliorating personal feelings of anxiety that lead to intergroup bias and self-stereotyping (Abrams, Eller, & Bryant, 2006). With respect to the common ingroup identity model in particular, positive intergroup contact predicts more inclusive, one-group representations, which, in turn, predict lower levels of threat and more positive intergroup attitudes (Dovidio, Gaertner, John, Halabi, Saguy, Pearson, & Riek, 2008). In addition, experimentally increasing the salience of Democrats' and Republicans' shared identity as Americans increases positive outgroup attitudes by first reducing intergroup threat (Riek, Mania, Gaertner, Direso, & Lamoreaux, 2009).

Ingroup identification, though, also relates to the relationships among contact, threat, anxiety, and intergroup bias. In a study conducted in Northern Ireland (Tausch, Hewstone, Kenworthy, Cairns, & Christ, 2007; see also Tausch, Tam, Hewstone, Kenworthy, & Cairns, 2007), Catholic and Protestant respondents to a survey indicated how strongly they identified with their group, the quantity and quality of their intergroup contact, the anxiety and threat they experienced in these interactions, and their attitude toward the outgroup. Anxiety represents *personal discomfort*, whereas the threat measure reflected perceived realistic and symbolic *challenges to the group*. Although greater intergroup contact predicted lower levels of both anxiety and threat, the effects of these affective reactions depended on participants' levels of identification. Specifically, for low identifiers, for whom personal identity was presumably more salient in intergroup interactions, reductions in anxiety primarily mediated more positive attitudes toward the outgroup. By contrast, for high identifiers, who presumably viewed contact in intergroup terms, reductions in perceived group threats mainly mediated more positive attitudes toward the outgroup.

As explained earlier in this chapter, intergroup bias is not necessarily rooted in antipathy, but instead may reflect more positive feelings and orientations toward ingroup members. Thus, the absence of empathy accounts, at least in part, for many manifestations of intergroup bias. One form of empathy, cognitive empathy, involves taking the perspective of another person. In general, people, particularly those higher on ingroup identification, are less likely to adopt the perspective of an ingroup than an outgroup member (Galinsky, 2002; Mallett, Huntsinger, Sinclair, & Swim, 2008). In addition, perspective taking can evoke different emotional responses that can ultimately influence intergroup bias. Taking the perspective of a member of a stigmatized group who describes experiences of discrimination can increase the salience of perceived injustice and arouse feelings, such as anger, coordinated with those of the group member (Finlay & Stephan, 2000). Alternatively, people may feel guilt if they focus on their own group's role in this injustice (Mallet, Huntsinger, et al., 2008). As Stephan and Finlay (1999) explained, "Learning about suffering and discrimination while empathizing with the victims may lead people to . . . come to believe that the victims do not deserve the mistreatment. . . . If the victims do not deserve this unjust treatment, it may no longer be tenable to hold such negative attitudes toward them" (p. 735; see also Esses & Dovidio, 2002). Moreover, manipulations that create a stronger sense of common identity between ingroup and outgroup members can produce greater perspective taking for outgroup members, eliciting greater moral indignation for perceived injustice, and ultimately reduce intergroup biases (Dovidio et al., 2004).

One of the most common and studied responses to taking the perspective of a member of an outgroup is the experience of a form of affective empathy, empathic concern (e.g., feelings of sympathy and compassion for the other person). For example, asking participants to imagine how a person from another group is feeling, compared with attending primarily to the information presented, increases how positively people feel about that particular member of the target group and improves attitudes toward the larger group to which the person belongs (Batson et al., 1997). Perspective taking may increase the salience of the target as a prototype for his or her group; as a consequence, positive feelings toward that person generalize to the group as a whole. Consistent with this reasoning, other work (Batson, Chang, Orr, & Rowland, 2002) has shown that focusing on a particular group member's feelings, in this case, a drug addict's feelings as he described his misfortunes (how he became addicted, got arrested, and spent time in prison), elicited greater levels of empathic concern (e.g., feeling sympathetic) than did focusing on the facts of the person's situation. Stronger feelings of empathic concern, in turn, increased caring about the person's welfare, which then mediated improved attitudes toward the group as a whole. Arousing feelings of empathic concern through perspective taking similarly reduces Whites' prejudice toward Blacks (Vescio, Sechrist, & Paolucci, 2003).

Evidence is accumulating that one way intergroup contact can reduce intergroup bias is by increasing perspective taking and enhancing affective empathy for members of other groups. In a number of studies, the relationship between intergroup contact and reduced bias has been shown to be partially mediated by perspective taking and empathic concern (Aberson & Haag, 2007; Harwood, Hewstone, Paolini, & Voci, 2005; Tam, Hewstone, Harwood, Voci, & Kenworthy, 2005). Pettigrew and Tropp (2008) found in their meta-analysis of 14 studies that tested for mediation by cognitive and affective empathy that contact predicted greater empathy ($r = +.35$), and empathy, in turn, predicted lower levels of prejudice ($r = -.41$). Overall, empathy significantly mediated the relationship between contact and lower levels of prejudice.

Although studies on the mediators of bias and bias reduction have converged to identify a set of consistently influential processes (cognitive representations, anxiety, threat, and empathy), additional questions have arisen about how these processes relate to different forms of bias. For instance, affective factors may be more effective for changing attitudes, which can have a strong affective component, than stereotypes, for which semantic associations are more central (Esses & Dovidio, 2002). In addition, if explicit and implicit bias represent independent response systems (Wilson et al., 2000; see also Banaji's chapter in volume 1), they may have different fundamental bases and, thus, may be differentially responsive to interventions to reduce bias. We consider some of these issues in the next subsection.

Relationships Among Different Types of Bias

As discussed at the beginning of the chapter, bias comes in many forms, reflecting negative attitudes (prejudice), beliefs (stereotypes), and actions (discrimination). Prejudice and stereotyping may occur at a conscious (explicit) level or in unconscious (implicit) forms. Moreover, evaluative and action biases can involve ingroup favoritism, outgroup derogation, or both.

Conceptually, these different measures reflect some aspect of bias; thus, some substantial correlation among these measures might be anticipated. With respect to the relationships among prejudice, stereotypes, and discrimination, to the extent that prejudice is an attitude with both a belief component and a behavioral disposition component, prejudice might be expected to relate to both stereotyping and prejudice. Dovidio, Brigham, Johnson, and Gaertner (1996), who conducted a meta-analysis of the literature on Whites' stereotypes, prejudice, and discrimination against Blacks in the United States, wrote, "The traditional view of stereotypes, prejudice, and discrimination suggested a relatively straightforward relationship among these phenomena. . . . [T]o the extent that stereotypes represent the cognitive component of prejudice, a greater degree of stereotyping would be expected to be positively related to prejudice. . . . Prejudice, as a negative attitude, would then directly predict (negative) discrimination" (p. 283). Nevertheless, the relationships overall were quite modest. Prejudice related only moderately to discrimination ($r = .32$) and to stereotyping ($r = .25$). One reason for the moderate relationship between prejudice and stereotyping is that these phenomena may be rooted in different neural systems (Amodio & Devine, 2006). Also, stereotyping was only weakly related to discrimination ($r = .16$). The relationship remained similar even after controlling for a variety of methodological factors (e.g., different types of assessment instruments and implicit and explicit measures). A more recent meta-analysis (Talaska et al., 2008) similarly found that emotional prejudice was modestly related to discrimination ($r = .26$); cognitive measures of beliefs and stereotypes had an even weaker relationship with discrimination, with an r less than .15. As noted earlier, three different meta-analyses revealed only a modest relationship between explicit and implicit measures of prejudice (Dovidio et al., 2001; Greenwald et al., 2009; Hofmann et al., 2005). In addition,

greater levels of ingroup favoritism do not consistently relate to greater outgroup derogation (e.g., de Vries, 2003), nor does stronger ingroup identification consistently predict greater bias toward the outgroup (Brown & Zagefka, 2005).

The modest relationships among the various measures of bias suggest the need to refine different conceptions of the elements of bias and further delineate factors that might moderate the relations among these variables. In the next two subsections, we consider issues relating to implicit and explicit bias, and to understanding the relationship between intergroup attitudes and discrimination.

Implicit and Explicit Bias

Dovidio, Kawakami, Smoak, and Gaertner (2009) reviewed the literature on how people's motivation and resources for controlling bias can moderate the relation between implicit and explicit prejudice and discrimination. They hypothesized, guided by Fazio's (1990) MODE model (see also Strack & Deutsch, 2004), that implicit attitudes, which reflect habitual orientations toward another group that are activated without effort or intention, would be a better predictor of spontaneous behavioral responses, whereas explicit attitudes, which involve reflections on personal ideals and self-presentational concerns, would be a better predictor of more spontaneous behavior.

Supportive of these hypotheses, implicit prejudice generally predicts spontaneous nonverbal behaviors better than does explicit prejudice (see Dovidio et al., 2009), except when people are highly motivated and skilled at controlling these aspects of their behavior (Dasgupta & Rivera, 2006). In contrast, explicit prejudice is a better predictor of more controllable interpersonal behaviors, such as verbal behaviors and more blatant expressions of bias (Dovidio, Kawakami, Johnson, Johnson, Howard, 1997; Fazio et al., 1995; Rudman & Ashmore, 2007) than is implicit prejudice (see also Greenwald et al., 2009).

Because implicit prejudice "may be better than explicit measures in capturing the aspects of prejudiced attitudes that are most relevant in the parsing of nonverbal displays" (Hugenberg & Bodenhausen, 2004, p. 342), it may be a better predictor of stereotypical responses in situations in which the appropriateness of decisions are not clear-cut. Consistent with this hypothesis, an implicit measure of racial prejudice, but not an explicit measure, was related to the extent that Whites categorized a racially ambiguous person who displayed an angry expression as Black (Hugenberg & Bodenhausen, 2004). In addition, in other research, an implicit measure of prejudice, but not an explicit measure of prejudice, predicted the readiness of Whites to interpret a facial expression of a Black person as indicating anger (Hugenberg & Bodenhausen, 2003). Also, implicit prejudice toward Asians predicted discrimination in hiring an

Asian when the adequacy of the person's qualifications were unclear, but not when an Asian applicant was clearly qualified for the position (Son Hing, Chung-Yan, Hamilton, & Zanna, 2008).

The general dissociation between explicit and implicit measures of prejudice and their separate influences can help explain why people are poor at forecasting how they will actually respond in interracial situations. For instance, whereas most participants who read about or saw on videotape a White person make blatant remarks believed that they would confront or ostracize the racist, those who actually experienced the event were fundamentally unresponsive (Kawakami, Dunn, Karmali, & Dovidio, 2009).

In addition, the extent to which implicit attitudes and stereotypes represent overlearned, habitual cultural associations that are automatically activated, they may be less responsive to manipulations or less influenced over time by interventions designed to vary salient categorization than are explicit intergroup attitudes. Cognitive, social, and neuroscience evidence is increasing that explicit and implicit attitudes are learned and modified through different cognitive and neural processes (Amodio, Devine, & Harmon-Jones, 2007; Gawronski & Bodenhausen, 2006; Rydell & McConnell, 2006; Smith & DeCoster, 2000). In particular, explicit attitudes develop and operate in ways that permit more rapid change in social evaluations. Implicit attitudes, in contrast, are formed and modified through a relatively slow-learning cognitive system that relies on basic associative evaluations (Rydell, McConnell, Strain, Claypool, & Hugenberg, 2007).

Consistent with the proposition that explicit and implicit forms of bias reflect different cognitive processes and systems, the results of studies of the relation between intergroup contact and implicit bias are more mixed than those for measures of explicit bias. Henry and Hardin's (2006) study demonstrated that intergroup contact consistently related to lower levels of explicit bias among both majority and minority group members in the United States (Whites and Blacks) and in Lebanon (Muslims and Christians), but perhaps because of the greater mindfulness of people with lower power in their interactions, contact predicted lower levels of implicit prejudice only among minority group members in both countries. Research on the effects of contact with grandparents (Tam et al., 2005) found that the quantity (but not the quality) of contact was directly associated with less implicit bias toward the elderly. In contrast, both quantity and quality of contact predicted more positive explicit attitudes toward the elderly mediated by greater self-disclosure, less anxiety, and greater empathy with grandparents. Also, cross-group friendships and opportunity for contact directly predict White students' implicit attitudes toward Asians, independent of greater

self-disclosure or reduced anxiety, whereas the effects of cross-group friendship on explicit attitudes are mediated by greater self-disclosure and reduced anxiety with the group (Turner et al., 2007).

Given these dynamic differences, changing implicit attitudes may require more direct and focused interventions. Some of these may relate to interventions that have been demonstrated to influence explicit attitudes. For instance, a number of different techniques have attempted to capitalize on people's consciously endorsed egalitarian values to not only motivate inhibition of explicit bias but also to stimulate efforts to reduce their implicit biases once they become aware of them. Techniques that lead people to discover, apparently without much external pressure, inconsistencies among their self-images, values, and behaviors may arouse cognitive dissonance (Leippe & Eisenstadt, 1994) or other negative emotional states (Rokeach, 1973) that can produce more favorable attitudes toward outgroups and their members. These effects may be quite enduring and influence even subtle interracial behaviors (e.g., eye contact; Penner, 1971). Moreover, a "hypocrisy induction," in which people are made aware of how they may violate their personal nonprejudiced standards (Son Hing, Li, & Zanna, 2002), is particularly effective with aversive racists (Dovidio & Gaertner, 2004) who have nonprejudiced self-images (based on explicit measures) but who show high levels of implicit prejudice. Son Hing et al. (2002) concluded that "the hypocrisy induction procedure forced aversive racists to become aware of the negative aspects of their attitudes that they typically repress" (p. 77) and, presumably, to bring these biases under control.

These techniques aimed at self-regulatory processes can potentially also change implicit attitudes and stereotypes (Dasgupta, 2009). Considerable empirical evidence exists that, when appropriately motivated and with sufficient cognitive resources, people can avoid the influence of stereotypes in their conscious evaluations of others (Fiske, 1998). In addition, it is possible to moderate even the activation of unconscious negative attitudes and stereotypes, at least temporarily, for example, by priming subtypes (Wittenbrink, Judd, & Park, 2001), counterstereotypic or positive exemplars of an outgroup (Blair, Ma, & Lenton, 2001; Dasgupta & Greenwald, 2001), or the concept of equality (Zogmaister, Arcuri, Castelli, & Smith, 2008). Research in social neuroscience further reveals that, although implicit prejudice is associated with activation of the amygdala (a brain structure associated learning and emotional stimuli), activation of control mechanisms in the neocortex (associated with higher-order cognitive processing) can inhibit this amygdala activation (Cunningham et al., 2004; for reviews, see also Dovidio, Pearson, & Orr, 2008; Stanley, Phelps, & Banaji, 2008).

Because automaticity develops through repeated occurrence, practice, and ultimately overlearning, differences in the personal endorsement and application of negative attitudes and stereotypes can, over time, lead to systematic differences in their automatic activation. Higher prejudice people, for example, show greater activation of stereotypes on implicit measures when exposed to representatives of an outgroup, presumably because they rely on stereotypes more frequently (Kawakami, Dion, & Dovidio, 1998; Lepore & Brown, 1997). Conversely, people's repeated efforts to control activation of implicit biases can result in their ability to inhibit these biases. Although attempts to suppress stereotypes can initially produce a "rebound effect," reflecting an unintended hyperaccessibility of these thoughts (for a review, see Monteith, Sherman, & Devine, 1998), individuals can develop "auto-motive" control of their actions through frequent and persistent pursuit of a goal, such as one not to stereotype (Bargh, 2007). Monteith et al. noted, "Practice makes perfect. Like any other mental process, thought suppression processes may be proceduralized and become relatively automatic" (p. 71). When they become automatized, implicit motivations to control prejudice can inhibit activation of stereotypes and prejudice even when cognitive resources are depleted (Park, Glaser, & Knowles, 2008).

Consistent with this proposition, extensive practice in negating cultural stereotypical associations and affirming counterstereotypes can eliminate the automatic activation of cultural stereotypes (Kawakami, Dovidio, Moll, Hermsen, & Russin, 2000), and repeatedly associating approach responses with an outgroup reduces implicit prejudice toward the group, as well as subtle bias in nonverbal behavior in interactions with target group members (Kawakami, Phills, Steele, & Dovidio, 2007). Key elements in this process are the development of greater self-regulatory strength through practice (Gailliot, Plant, Butz, & Baumeister, 2007) and the creation of new strong associations that are incompatible with existing stereotypes or prejudice (Gawronski, Deutsch, Mbirkou, Seibt, & Strack, 2008). In addition, people who have strong internal motivations to control prejudice (Plant & Devine, 1998; Plant, Devine, & Brazy, 2003) and who develop chronic egalitarian values (Galinsky & Moskowitz, 2000) and stronger response control mechanisms (Amodio, Devine, & Harmon-Jones, 2008) appear to be able to, at least under some circumstances, inhibit the activation of implicit stereotypes and prejudice. In addition, individuals with the combination of high internal motivation and low external motivation to control prejudice, presumably because their motivations are both highly internalized and autonomous, exhibit generally low levels of implicit bias (Devine, Plant, Amodio, Harmon-Jones, & Vance, 2002).

According to the *self-regulation of prejudice model* (Monteith, Arthur, & Flynn, in press), the recognition by people that they have responded to a member of another group in a biased way that violates their personal egalitarian standards can stimulate basic self-regulatory processes. People experience feelings of guilt and attempt to inhibit further bias in their responses. For example, in one study (Monteith, 1993), an experimenter provided participants who scored high or low in a pretest of attitudes toward homosexuals with information that did or did not indicate that they were actually biased toward gays and lesbians. Because this information violated the personal standards of participants who were low in prejudice against homosexuals, they experienced particularly high levels of guilt. High-prejudiced participants, for whom this feedback was not discrepant from their standards, did not experience this same increased negative self-directed emotion. Moreover, to test for evidence of enhanced motivation to inhibit bias, the participants rated jokes in a subsequent, apparently unrelated study. Low-prejudiced participants who had received the feedback that violated their personal standards rated jokes about homosexuals as less humorous than did high-prejudiced participants, regardless of the feedback, and low-prejudiced participants whose self-image was not challenged by the feedback.

The self-regulation of prejudice model further posits that, when they recognize discrepancies from their nonprejudiced standards, individuals engage in *retrospective reflection*, in which they focus their attention on aspects of the situation that might have elicited the reaction, and subsequently attempt to develop cues for control in the future. As a result of this self-regulatory sequence, associations are created among stimuli that predict the occurrence of a discrepant response, the discrepant response itself, and the negative self-directed affect produced by awareness of one's discrepancy. With practice, this process results in the de-automatization of biased responses and their replacement with more positive implicit, as well as explicit, intergroup responses (see Dovidio, Kawakami, & Gaertner, 2000).

In addition to changing stereotypes and attitudes, both implicitly and explicitly, eliminating intergroup bias also requires reducing behavioral discrimination, removing structural barriers to equality, and improving intergroup relations generally. We consider the issues of intergroup interaction and social change in the next section.

Intergroup Attitude, Interaction, and Social Change

Understanding intergroup bias requires not only considering the intrapsychic dynamics of stereotyping and prejudice but also appreciating how prejudice and stereotypes affect intergroup interactions and social structures.

Intergroup interactions are typically more awkward and challenging than are interactions between members of the same group. Intergroup biases shape interactants' behaviors and attributions in intergroup exchanges, and the experiences in these interactions further influence, and often reinforce, intergroup biases and relations. Stereotypes affect the ways people perceive members of other groups in interactions, as well as beliefs about how others view them (i.e., *metastereotypes*; Vorauer, Hunter, Main, & Roy, 2000). These perceptions and metaperceptions, in turn, systematically shape behaviors in ways consistent with these views and often create confirming social realities through self-fulfilling prophecy effects (Snyder, Tanke, & Berscheid, 1977; Word, Zanna, & Cooper, 1974), in which members of the stereotyped group respond in stereotype-consistent ways.

Moreover, intentions, actions, and interpretations in intergroup interactions often relate in complex and paradoxical ways (Richeson & Shelton, in press; Shelton & Richeson, 2006; Shelton et al., 2006). Whites interacting with Blacks often become focused on not acting inappropriately (proposed as a major motive of aversive racists; Gaertner & Dovidio, 1986), and consequently attempt to adopt a color-blind orientation in the exchange (Norton, Sommers, Apfelbaum, Pura, & Ariely, 2006). They are often unaware that despite their conscious attempts to control their bias and often their beliefs that they did so successfully, their implicit biases are reflected in negative nonverbal behaviors. Preoccupation with suppressing recognition of group membership and behaving in a nonprejudiced manner can further contribute to inconsistencies between individuals' verbal and nonverbal behaviors in intergroup interactions (Hebl & Dovidio, 2005). Efforts to control the expression of bias during intergroup interactions are cognitively demanding and tax executive functioning (Richeson et al., 2003; Richeson & Shelton, 2003; Richeson & Trawalter, 2005; Richeson, Trawalter, & Shelton, 2005; Trawalter & Richeson, 2006), and as a consequence, can lead individuals to behave in ways that are directly opposite of their desired responses (Apfelbaum, Sommers, & Norton, 2008). In addition, when people are motivated to behave in unbiased ways because of external pressures (e.g., not to violate egalitarian norms), they are particularly likely to experience and exhibit anxiety both in anticipation of and during interracial interactions (Plant, 2004).

The obvious attempts to avoid acknowledgment of different group identities, the inconsistency between overt (e.g., verbal) and subtle (e.g., nonverbal) behaviors, and anxiety and more direct cues of bias that occur when cognitive resources are depleted are frequently interpreted and recognized by members of minority or stigmatized groups as indications of bias. Members of socially disadvantaged groups who have chronic or situational expectancies of bias are particularly vigilant for signs of bias (Inzlicht, Kaiser, & Major, 2008; Kaiser, Vick, & Major, 2006; Vorauer, 2006). Thus, concerns about appearing prejudiced among members of advantaged groups can, paradoxically, produce anxiety and other negative cues (Goff, Steele, & Davies, 2008) that can interfere with the intergroup exchange and the longer-term relationship between the interactants (West, Shelton, & Trail, 2009). The negative impressions and experiences in these interactions between members of different groups can, therefore, reinforce intergroup bias and tension more generally (Dovidio, Gaertner, Kawakami, & Hodson, 2002).

The relations between members of advantaged and disadvantaged groups involve other social motivations as well. Because groups in societies are characteristically hierarchically organized (Sidanius & Pratto, 1999), intergroup relations typically involve groups who differ in power or status. As we discussed in the section on group status as a moderator of the effects of intergroup contact on bias, high- and lower-power groups generally differ in their orientations toward the status quo (maintain vs. change the status quo), as well as in emotional needs (needs to be liked and morally validated vs. needs for respect and empowerment). Thus, although intergroup contact relates to lower levels of prejudice and more supportive policy attitudes, and prejudice generally relates to discrimination (Dovidio et al., 1996; Wagner, Christ, & Pettigrew, 2008), circumstances may occur in which the relation between attitudes and behavior is not direct.

Some researchers, for instance, have questioned the traditional focus of much of the work of traditional social psychology on intergroup attitudes as the ultimate measure of positive intergroup relations without adequate attention to the impact of attitudes on actual structural change toward equality (Dixon, Durrheim, & Tredoux, 2005, 2007). Dixon et al. "accept that contact may transform interpersonal attitudes and stereotypes, but caution that it may leave unaltered the ideological beliefs that sustain systems of racial discrimination" (Dixon et al., 2007, p. 868; see also Jackman & Crane, 1986). They further argue that "it is possible that the emotional benefits of contact may be offset by its tendency to promote acceptance of broader patterns of discrimination" (Dixon et al., 2005, p. 707). In support of this proposition, they document a general "principle-implementation gap" between high-status group members' widespread endorsement of equality in principle and weaker and less consistent support for policies for creating concrete social change between the groups in society (Dixon et al., 2005, 2007).

However, in both Dixon et al. (2007) and Jackman and Crane (1986), intergroup contact does relate to some degree to greater policy support among Whites to benefit Blacks, but not to the same extent that it relates to positive intergroup attitudes. Nevertheless, if positive intergroup contact satisfies majority group members' need to be liked, achieving this proximate goal may relax to some extent their motivation to actively support change toward social equality (Saguy, Tausch, Dovidio, & Pratto, 2009). In addition, even apparently positive forms of action, such as helping, can be executed strategically to maintain status differences between groups and promote the dependency of the disadvantaged group (Nadler, 2002; see also Nadler & Halabi, 2006). Thus, future research may benefit from a more complex view of the relationship among attitudes and behavior by including more direct consideration of the role of group motivations in this context.

SUMMARY

This chapter has considered the common and distinct aspects of psychological functioning that underlie different forms of bias, including stereotyping, prejudice, and discrimination; explicit and implicit responses; and ingroup favoritism and outgroup derogation. Social categorization provides the common base. Upon social categorization, people, often automatically without intent or control, experience more positive feelings toward others who are classified as part of the ingroup and are more responsive to their needs. Moreover, when people perceive psychological threat or material competition from the outgroup, they have more negative orientations toward the outgroup and its members. The biases originating in ingroup-outgroup categorization, which are magnified by perceptions of zero-sum outcomes and competitive intergroup relations, are robust and profound.

Because of the foundational role of social categorization in intergroup bias, a number of models have been developed that target group representations and functional relations between groups as central processes for reducing intergroup bias. The extensive literature on intergroup contact amply demonstrates that contact, particularly under the conditions specified by contact theory, has a robust impact in terms of reducing intergroup bias. The three category-based models we considered—decategorization, mutual intergroup differentiation, and recategorization—all focus on the psychological processes that account for the beneficial effects of contact. These models make different assumptions and differ substantially in how social categorization should be altered, but considerable experimental support is available for each. Rather than conceiving these as competing models, however, these different processes for reducing bias may be differentially effective under different circumstances

(e.g., mild vs. intense intergroup conflict) and may operate in a complementary fashion over time at different stages of intergroup relations.

A more comprehensive understanding of intergroup bias and its reduction, however, requires further consideration of the social and psychological forces that can moderate responses to contact and social categorization. Group status, distinctiveness, and ingroup identity are three such factors. In addition, the complexity of the effects of intergroup contact and group representations need to be appreciated. A variety of emotional (anxiety, threat, and empathy) and cognitive (perspective taking, inclusion of others in one's sense of identity) processes can mediate further "downstream" the effects of decategorization, recategorization, or introduction of cooperative functional relations. However, social experiences and interventions (e.g., intergroup contact) may affect different types of bias in fundamentally different ways. Thus, theoretically and practically, the distinct aspects of different forms of bias—their psychological components and bases, and relationship to personal and group-based motivations—merit further consideration to achieve a more accurate and comprehensive understanding of bias and its reduction.

REFERENCES

Aberson, C. L., & Haag, S. C. (2007). Contact, perspective taking, and anxiety as predictors of stereotype endorsement, explicit attitudes, and implicit attitudes. *Group Processes and Intergroup Relations, 10*, 179–201.

Abrams, D., Eller, A., & Bryant, J. (2006). An age apart: Intergenerational contact and stereotype threat on performance and intergroup bias. *Psychology and Aging, 21*, 691–702.

Allport, G. W. (1954). *The nature of prejudice.* Cambridge, MA: Addison-Wesley.

Amodio, D. M., & Devine, P. G. (2006). Stereotyping and evaluation in implicit race prejudice: Evidence for independent constructs and unique effects on behavior. *Journal of Personality and Social Psychology, 91*, 652–661.

Amodio, D. M., Devine, P. G., & Harmon-Jones, E. (2007). A dynamic model of guilt: Implications for motivation and self-regulation in the context of prejudice. *Psychological Science, 18*, 524–530.

Amodio, D. M., Devine, P. G., & Harmon-Jones, E. (2008). Individual differences in the regulation of intergroup bias: The role of conflict monitoring and neural signals for control. *Journal of Personality and Social Psychology, 94*, 60–74.

Apfelbaum, E. P., Sommers, S. R., & Norton, M. I. (2008). Seeing race and seeming racist? Evaluating strategic colorblindness in social interaction. *Journal of Personality and Social Psychology, 95*, 918–932.

Aron, A., McLaughlin-Volpe, T., Mashek, D., Lewandowski, G., Wright, S. C., & Aron, E. N. (2005). Including others in the self. In W. Stroebe & M. Hewstone (Eds.), *European review of social psychology* (Vol. 15, pp. 101–132). Hove, England: Psychology Press.

Banker, B. S., & Gaertner, S. L. (1998). Achieving stepfamily harmony: An intergroup relations approach. *Journal of Family Psychology, 12*, 310–325.

Bargh, J. A. (2007). *Social psychology and the unconscious: The automaticity of higher mental processes.* New York: Psychology Press.

Batson, C. D., Chang, J., Orr, R., & Rowland, J. (2002). Empathy, attitudes, and action: Can feeling for a member of a stigmatized group motivate one to help the group. *Personality and Social Psychology Bulletin, 28,* 1656–1666.

Batson, C. D., Polycarpou, M. P., Harmon-Jones, E., Imhoff, H. J., Mitchener, E. C., Bednar, L. L., et al. (1997). Empathy and attitudes: Can feeling for a member of a stigmatized group improve feelings toward the group? *Journal of Personality and Social Psychology, 72,* 105–118.

Berger, J., & Fisek, M. H. (2006). Diffuse status characteristics and the spread of status values: A formal theory. *American Journal of Sociology, 111,* 1038–1079.

Berry, J. W. (1997). Immigration, acculturation, and adaptation. *Applied Psychology: An International Review, 46,* 5–34.

Bettencourt, B. A., Brewer, M. B., Croak, M. R., & Miller, N. (1992). Cooperation and the reduction of intergroup bias: The roles of reward structure and social orientation. *Journal of Experimental Social Psychology, 28,* 301–319.

Bettencourt, B. A., Dorr, N., Charlton, K., & Hume, D. L. (2001). Status differences and in-group bias: A meta-analytic examination of the effects of status stability, status legitimacy, and group permeability. *Psychological Bulletin, 127,* 520–542.

Blair, I. V., Ma, J. E., & Lenton, A. P. (2001). Imagining stereotypes away: The moderation of implicit stereotypes through mental imagery. *Journal of Personality and Social Psychology, 81,* 824–841.

Blanchard, F. A., Adelman, L., & Cook, S. W. (1975). Effect of group success upon interpersonal attraction in cooperating interracial groups. *Journal of Personality and Social Psychology, 31,* 1021–1030.

Blumer, H. (1958). Race prejudice as a sense of group position. *Pacific Sociological Review, 1,* 3–7.

Bobo, L. D. (1999). Prejudice as group position: Microfoundations of a sociological approach to racism and race relations. *Journal of Social Issues, 55,* 445–472.

Boldry, J. G., Gaertner, L., & Quinn, J. (2007). Measuring the measures: A meta-analytic investigation of the measures of outgroup homogeneity. *Group Processes and Intergroup Relations, 10,* 147–178.

Bourhis, R. Y., Sachdev, I., & Gagnon, A. (1994). Intergroup research with Tajfel matrices: Methodological notes. In M. P. Zanna & J. M. Olson (Eds.), *The psychology of prejudice: The Ontario Symposium* (Vol. 7, pp. 209–232). Hillsdale, NJ: Erlbaum.

Brewer, M. B. (1979). Ingroup bias in the minimal intergroup situation: A cognitive-motivational analysis. *Psychological Bulletin, 86,* 307–324.

Brewer, M. B. (1988). A dual process model of impression formation. In T. S. Srull & R. S. Wyer (Eds.), *Advances in social cognition: Vol. I: A dual process model of impression formation* (pp. 1–36). Hillsdale, NJ: Erlbaum.

Brewer, M. B. (1991). On the social self: On being the same and different at the same time. *Personality and Social Psychology Bulletin, 17,* 475–482.

Brewer, M. B. (2000). Reducing prejudice through cross-categorization: Effects of multiple social identities. In S. Oskamp (Ed.), *Reducing prejudice and discrimination: The Claremont Symposium on Applied Social Psychology* (pp. 165–183). Mahwah, NJ: Erlbaum.

Brewer, M. B., & Miller, N. (1984). Beyond the contact hypothesis: Theoretical perspectives on desegregation. In N. Miller & M. B. Brewer (Eds.), *Groups in contact: The psychology of desegregation* (pp. 281–302). Orlando, FL: Academic Press.

Brigham, J. C. (1993). College students' racial attitudes. *Journal of Applied Social Psychology, 23,* 1933–1967.

Brown, R., Eller, A., Leeds, S., & Stace, K. (2007). Intergroup contact and intergroup attitudes: A longitudinal study. *European Journal of Social Psychology, 37,* 692–703.

Brown, R., & Hewstone, M. (2005). An integrative theory of intergroup contact. In M. P. Zanna (Ed.), *Advances in experimental social psychology* (Vol. 37, pp. 255–343). San Diego, CA: Academic Press.

Brown, R., & Zagefka, H. (2005). Ingroup affiliations and prejudice. In J. F. Dovidio, P. Glick, & L. A. Rudman (Eds.), *On the nature of prejudice: Fifty years after Allport* (pp. 54–70). Malden, MA: Blackwell.

Brown, R. J., & Turner, J. C. (1979). The criss-cross categorization effect in intergroup discrimination. *British Journal of Social and Clinical Psychology, 18,* 371–383.

Brown, R. J., & Turner, J. C. (1981). Interpersonal and intergroup behavior. In J. C. Turner & H. Giles (Eds.), *Intergroup behavior* (pp. 33–64). Chicago: University of Chicago Press.

Brown, R. J., Vivian, J., & Hewstone, M. (1999). Changing attitudes through intergroup contact: The effects of group membership salience. *European Journal of Social Psychology, 29,* 741–764.

Brown, R. J., & Wade, G. (1987). Superordinate goals and intergroup behavior: The effect of role ambiguity and status on intergroup attitudes and task performance. *European Journal of Social Psychology, 17,* 131–142.

Campbell, D. T. (1958). Common fate, similarity and other indices of the status of aggregates of persons as social entities. *Behavioral Science, 3,* 14–25.

Campbell, D. T. (1965). Ethnocentric and other altruistic motives. In D. Levine (Ed.), *Nebraska symposium on motivation* (Vol. 13, pp. 283–311). Lincoln, NE: University of Nebraska Press.

Castelli, L., Tomelleri, S., & Zogmaister, C. (2008). Implicit ingroup meta-favoritism: Subtle preference for ingroup members displaying ingroup bias. *Personality and Social Psychology Bulletin, 34,* 807–818.

Clark, A. E., & Kashima, Y. (2007). Stereotypes help people connect with others in the community. A situated functional analysis of the stereotype consistency bias in communication. *Journal of Personality and Social Psychology, 93,* 1028–1039.

Cook, S. W. (1985). Experimenting on social issues: The case of school desegregation. *American Psychologist, 40,* 452–460.

Correll, J., & Park, B. (2005). A model of the ingroup as a social resource. *Personality and Social Psychology Review, 9,* 341–359.

Cottrell, C. A., & Neuberg, S. L. (2005). Different emotional reactions to different groups: A sociofunctional threat-based approach to "prejudice." *Journal of Personality and Social Psychology, 88,* 770–789.

Crandall, C. S., & Stangor, C. (2005). Conformity and prejudice. In J. F. Dovidio, P. Glick, & L. A. Rudman (Eds.), *On the nature of prejudice: Fifty years after Allport* (pp. 295–309). Malden, MA: Blackwell.

Crisp, R. J., Ensari, N., Hewstone, M., & Miller, N. (2003). A dual-route model of crossed categorization effects. In W. Stroebe & M. Hewstone (Eds.), *European review of social psychology* (Vol. 13, pp. 35–73). Hove, England: Psychology Press.

Crisp, R. J., & Hewstone, M. (Eds.). (2006). *Multiple social categorization: Processes, models, and applications.* Philadelphia: Psychology Press.

Crisp, R. J., Walsh, J., & Hewstone, M. (2006). Crossed categorization in common ingroup contexts. *Personality and Social Psychology Bulletin, 32,* 1204–1218.

Crocker, J., & Luhtanen, R. (1990). Collective self-esteem and ingroup bias. *Journal of Personality and Social Psychology, 58,* 60–67.

Cuddy, A. J. C., Fiske, S. T., & Glick, P. (2007). The BIAS map: Behaviors from intergroup affect and stereotypes. *Journal of Personality and Social Psychology, 92,* 631–648.

Cunningham, W. A., Johnson, M. K., Raye, C. L., Getenby, J. C., Gore, J. J., & Banaji, M. R. (2004). Separable neural components in the processing of Black and White faces. *Psychological Science, 15,* 806–813.

Dasgupta, N. (2009). Mechanisms underlying the malleability of implicit prejudice and stereotypes; The role of automaticity and cognitive control. In T. Nelson (Ed.), *Handbook of prejudice, stereotyping, and discrimination* (pp. 267–284). New York: Psychology Press.

Dasgupta, N., & Greenwald, A. G. (2001). On the malleability of automatic attitudes: Combating automatic prejudice with images of admired and disliked individuals. *Journal of Personality and Social Psychology, 81,* 800–814.

Dasgupta, N., & Rivera, L. M. (2006). From automatic anti-gay prejudice to behavior: The moderating role of conscious beliefs about gender and behavioral control. *Journal of Personality and Social Psychology, 91,* 268–280.

Demoulin, S., Leyens, J. P., & Dovidio, J. F. (Eds.). (2009). *Intergroup misunderstandings: Impact of divergent social realities.* Philadelphia: Psychology Press.

Deschamps, J. C., & Brown, R. (1983). Superordinate goals and intergroup conflict. *British Journal of Social Psychology, 22,* 189–195.

Desforges, D. M., Lord, C. G., Ramsey, S. L., Mason, J. A., van Leeuwen, M. D., West, S. C., et al. (1991). Effects of structured cooperative contact on changing negative attitudes towards stigmatized social groups. *Journal of Personality and Social Psychology, 60,* 531–544.

Devine, P. G., Plant, E. A., Amodio, D. M., Harmon-Jones, E., & Vance, S. L. (2002). The regulation of explicit and implicit race bias: The role of motivations to respond without prejudice. *Journal of Personality and Social Psychology, 82,* 835–848.

de Vries, R. E. (2003). Self, in-group, and out-group evaluation: Bond or breach? *European Journal of Social Psychology, 33,* 609–621.

Dixon, J. A., Durrheim, K., & Tredoux, C. (2005). Beyond the optimal strategy: A "reality check" for the contact hypothesis. *American Psychologist, 60,* 697–711.

Dixon, J. A., Durrheim, K., & Tredoux, C. (2007). Intergroup contact and attitudes toward the principle and practice of racial equality. *Psychological Science, 18,* 867–872.

Dovidio, J. F., Brigham, J. C., Johnson, B. T., & Gaertner, S. L. (1996). Stereotyping, prejudice, and discrimination: Another look. In C. N. Macrae, M. Hewstone, & C. Stangor (Eds.), *Foundations of stereotypes and stereotyping* (pp. 276–319). New York: Guilford.

Dovidio, J. F., & Gaertner, S. L. (1993). Stereotypes and evaluative intergroup bias. In D. M. Mackie & D. L. Hamilton (Eds.), *Affect, cognition, and stereotyping: Interactive processes in intergroup perception* (pp. 167–193). Orlando, FL: Academic Press.

Dovidio, J. F., & Gaertner, S. L. (2004). Aversive racism. In M. P. Zanna (Ed.), *Advances in experimental social psychology* (Vol. 36, pp. 1–51). San Diego, CA: Academic Press.

Dovidio, J. F., Gaertner, S. L., John, M. S., Halabi, S., Saguy, T., Pearson, A. R., et al. (2008). Majority and minority perspectives in intergroup relations: The role of contact, group representation, threat, and trust in intergroup conflict and reconciliation. In A. Nadler, T. Malloy, & J. D. Fisher (Eds.), *Social psychology of intergroup reconciliation* (pp. 227–253). New York: Oxford University Press.

Dovidio, J. F., Gaertner, S. L., & Kafati, G. (2000). Group identity and intergroup relations: The Common In-Group Identity Model. In S. R. Thye, E. J. Lawler, M. W. Macy, & H. A. Walker (Eds.), *Advances in group processes* (Vol. 17, pp. 1–34). Stamford, CT: JAI Press.

Dovidio, J. F., Gaertner, S. L., & Kawakami, K. (2003). The Contact Hypothesis: The past, present, and the future. *Group Processes and Intergroup Relations, 6,* 5–21.

Dovidio, J. F., Gaertner, S. L., Kawakami, K., & Hodson, G. (2002). Why can't we just get along? Interpersonal biases and interracial distrust. *Cultural Diversity & Ethnic Minority Psychology, 8,* 88–102.

Dovidio, J. F., Gaertner, S. L., & Saguy, T. (2009). Commonality and the complexity of "we": Social attitudes and social change. *Personality and Social Psychology Review, 13,* 3–20.

Dovidio, J. F., Gaertner, S. L., & Validzic, A. (1998). Intergroup bias: Status, differentiation, and a common ingroup identity. *Journal of Personality and Social Psychology, 75,* 109–120.

Dovidio, J. F., Gaertner, S. L., Validzic, A., Matoka, K., Johnson, B., & Frazier, S. (1997). Extending the benefits of re-categorization: Evaluations, self-disclosure and helping. *Journal of Experimental Social Psychology, 33,* 401–420.

Dovidio, J., Kawakami, K., & Beach, K. (2001). Implicit and explicit attitudes: Examination of the relationship between measures of intergroup bias. In R. Brown & S. L. Gaertner (Eds.), *Blackwell handbook of social psychology* (Vol. 4, pp. 175–197). Oxford: Blackwell.

Dovidio, J., Kawakami, K., & Gaertner, S. L. (2000). Reducing contemporary prejudice: Combating explicit and implicit bias at the individual and intergroup level. In S. Oskamp (Ed.), *Reducing prejudice and discrimination* (pp. 137–163). Hillsdale, NJ: Erlbaum.

Dovidio, J., Kawakami, K., Johnson, C., Johnson, B., & Howard, A. (1997). The nature of prejudice: Automatic and controlled processes. *Journal of Experimental Social Psychology, 33,* 510–540.

Dovidio, J. F., Kawakami, K., Smoak, N., & Gaertner, S. L. (2009). The roles of implicit and explicit processes in contemporary prejudice. In R. E. Petty, R. H. Fazio, & P. Brinol (Eds.), *Attitudes: Insights from the new implicit measures* (pp. 165–192). New York: Psychology Press.

Dovidio, J. F., Pearson, A. R., & Orr, P. (2008). Social psychology and neuroscience: Strange bedfellows or happy marriage? *Group Processes and Intergroup Relations, 11,* 249–265.

Dovidio, J. F., ten Vergert, M., Stewart, T. L., Gaertner, S. L., Johnson, J. D., Esses, V. M., et al. (2004). Perspective and prejudice: Antecedents and mediating mechanisms. *Personality and Social Psychology Bulletin, 30,* 1537–1549.

Eagly, A. H., & Diekman, A. B. (2005). What is the problem? Prejudice as an attitude-in-context. In J. F. Dovidio, P. Glick, & L. A. Rudman (Eds.), *On the nature of prejudice: Fifty years after Allport* (pp. 71–19–35). Malden, MA: Blackwell.

Ensari, N., & Miller, N. (2002). The outgroup must not be so bad after all: The effects of disclosure, typicality, and salience on intergroup bias. *Journal of Personality and Social Psychology, 83,* 313–329.

Esses, V. M., & Dovidio, J. F. (2002). The role of emotions in determining willingness to engage in intergroup contact. *Personality and Social Psychology Bulletin, 28,* 1202–1214.

Esses, V. M., Dovidio, J. F., Jackson, L. M., & Armstrong, T. M. (2001). The immigration dilemma: The role of perceived group competition, ethnic prejudice, and national identity. *Journal of Social Issue, 57,* 389–412.

Esses, V. M., Jackson, L. M., & Armstrong, T. L. (1998). Intergroup competition and attitudes toward immigrants and immigration: An instrumental model of group conflict. *Journal of Social Issues, 54,* 699–724.

Esses, V. M., Jackson, L. M., Dovidio, J. F., & Hodson, G. (2005). Instrumental relations among groups: Group competition, conflict, and prejudice. In J. F. Dovidio, P. Glick, & L. A. Rudman (Eds.), *On the nature of prejudice: Fifty years after Allport* (pp. 227–243). Malden, MA: Blackwell.

Fazio, R. H. (1990). Multiple processes by which attitudes guide behavior: The MODE Model as an integrative framework. In M. P. Zanna (Ed.), *Advances in experimental social psychology* (Vol. 23, pp. 75–109). Orlando, FL: Academic Press.

Fazio, R. H., Jackson, J. R., Dunton, B. C., & Williams, C. J. (1995). Variability in automatic activation as an unobtrusive measure of racial attitudes: A *bona fide* pipeline? *Journal of Personality and Social Psychology, 69,* 1013–1027.

Fazio, R. H., & Olson, M. A., (2003). Implicit measures in social cognition research: Their meaning and uses. *Annual Review of Psychology, 54,* 297–327.

Fein, S., & Spencer, S. J. (1997). Prejudice as self-image maintenance: Affirming the self through derogating others. *Journal of Personality and Social Psychology, 73,* 31–44.

Finlay, K. A., & Stephan, W. G. (2000). Improving intergroup relations: The effects of empathy on racial attitudes. *Journal of Applied Social Psychology, 30*, 1720–1737.

Fiske, S. T. (1998). Stereotyping, prejudice, and discrimination. In D. T. Gilbert, S. T. Fiske, & G. Lindzey (Eds.), *The handbook of social psychology* (4th ed., Vol. 2, pp. 357–411). New York: McGraw-Hill.

Fiske, S. T. (2000). Interdependence and the reduction of prejudice. In S. Oskamp (Ed.), *Reducing prejudice and discrimination* (pp. 115–135). Hillsdale, NJ: Erlbaum.

Fiske, S. T., Cuddy, A. J. C., Glick, P., & Xu, J. (2002). A model of (often mixed) stereotype content: Competence and warmth respectively follow from perceived status and competition. *Journal of Personality and Social Psychology, 82*, 878–902.

Fiske, S. T., Harris, L. T., Russell, A. M., & Shelton, J. N. (2009). Divergent social realities: Depending on where you sit: Perspectives from the stereotype content model. In S. Demoulin, J. P. Leyens, & J. F. Dovidio (Eds.), *Intergroup misunderstandings: Impact of divergent social realities* (pp. 173–190). Philadelphia: Psychology Press.

Fiske, S. T., Lin, M., & Neuberg, S. L. (1999). The continuum model: Ten years later. In S. Chaiken & Y. Trope (Eds.), *Dual process theories in social psychology* (pp. 231–254). New York: Guilford.

Fiske, S. T., & Ruscher, J. B. (1993). Negative interdependence and prejudice: Whence the affect? In D. M. Mackie & D. L. Hamilton (Eds.), *Affect, cognition, and stereotyping: Interactive processes in group perception* (pp. 239–268). New York: Academic Press.

Fiske, S. T., & Taylor, S. E. (1991). *Social cognition* (2nd ed.). New York: McGraw-Hill.

Gaertner, L., & Insko, C. A. (2000). Intergroup discrimination in the minimal group paradigm: Categorization, reciprocation, or fear? *Journal of Personality and Social Psychology, 79*, 77–94.

Gaertner, L., Iuzzini, J., Witt, M. G., & Oriña, M. M. (2006). Us without them: Evidence for intragroup origin of positive in-group regard. *Journal of Personality and Social Psychology, 90*, 426–439.

Gaertner, L., & Schopler, J. (1998). Perceived ingroup entitativity and intergroup bias: An interconnection of self and others. *European Journal of Social Psychology, 28*, 963–980.

Gaertner, S. L., Bachman, B. A., Dovidio, J. D., & Banker, B. S. (2001). Corporate mergers and stepfamily marriages: Identity, harmony, and commitment. In M. A. Hogg & D. Terry (Eds.), *Social identity in organizations* (pp. 265–288). Oxford: Blackwell.

Gaertner, S. L., & Dovidio, J. F. (1986). The aversive form of racism. In J. F. Dovidio & S. L. Gaertner (Eds.), *Prejudice, discrimination, and racism* (pp. 61–89). Orlando, FL: Academic Press.

Gaertner, S. L., & Dovidio, J. F. (2000). *Reducing intergroup bias: The Common Ingroup Identity Model.* Philadelphia: Psychology Press.

Gaertner, S. L., & Dovidio, J. F. (2005). Categorization, recategorization, and intergroup bias. In J. F. Dovidio, P. Glick, & L. A. Rudman (Eds.), *On the nature of prejudice: Fifty years after Allport* (pp. 71–88). Malden, MA: Blackwell.

Gaertner, S. L., Dovidio, J. F., Anastasio, P. A., Bachman, B. A., & Rust, M. C. (1993). The common ingroup identity model: Recategorization and the reduction of intergroup bias. In W. Stroebe & M. Hewstone (Eds.), *European review of social psychology* (Vol. 4. pp. 1–26). New York: John Wiley & Sons.

Gaertner, S. L., Dovidio, J. F., Banker, B. S., Rust, M. C., & Nier, J. A., & Ward, C. M. (1997). Does pro-whiteness necessarily mean anti-blackness? In M. Fine, L. Powell, L. Weis, & M. Wong (Eds.), *Off White* (pp. 167–178). New York: Routledge.

Gaertner, S. L., Dovidio, J. F., Rust, M. C., Nier, J., Banker, B., Ward, C. M., et al. (1999). Reducing intergroup bias: Elements of intergroup cooperation. *Journal of Personality and Social Psychology, 76*, 388–402.

Gaertner, S. L., Mann, J. A., Murrell, A. J., & Dovidio, J. F. (1989). Reduction of intergroup bias: The benefits of recategorization. *Journal of Personality and Social Psychology, 57*, 239–249.

Gaertner, S. L., & McLaughlin, J. P. (1983). Racial stereotypes: Associations and ascriptions of positive and negative characteristics. *Social Psychology Quarterly, 46*, 23–30.

Gaertner, S. L., Rust, M. C., Dovidio, J. F., Bachman, B. A., & Anastasio, P. A. (1996). The Contact Hypothesis: The role of a common ingroup identity on reducing intergroup bias among majority and minority group members. In J. L. Nye & A. M. Brower (Eds.), *What's social about social cognition?* (pp. 230–360). Newbury Park, CA: Sage.

Gailliot, M. T., Plant, E. A., Butz, D. A., & Baumeister, R. F. (2007). Increasing self-regulatory strength can reduce the depleting effect of suppressing stereotypes. *Personality and Social Psychology Bulletin, 34*, 755–768.

Galinsky, A. D. (2002). Creating and reducing intergroup conflict: The role of perspective-taking in affecting out-group evaluations. In H. Sondak (Ed.), *Toward phenomenology of groups and group membership* (pp. 85–113). New York: Elsevier.

Galinsky, A. D., & Moskowitz, G. B. (2000). Perspective-taking: Decreasing stereotype expression, stereotype accessibility, and in-group favoritism. *Journal of Personality and Social Psychology, 78*, 708–724.

Gawronski, B., & Bodenhausen, G. V. (2006). Associative and propositional processes in evaluation: An integrative review of implicit and explicit attitude change. *Psychological Bulletin, 132*, 692–731.

Gawronski, B., Deutsch, R., Mbirkou, S., Seibt, B., & Strack, F. (2008). When "just say no" is not enough: Affirmation versus negation training and the reduction of automatic stereotype activation. *Journal of Experimental Social Psychology, 44*, 50–64.

Glick, P., & Fiske, S. T. (1996). The Ambivalent Sexism Inventory: Differentiating hostile and benevolent sexism. *Journal of Personality and Social Psychology, 70*, 491–512.

Goff, P. A., Steele, C. M., & Davies, P. G. (2008). The space between us: Stereotype threat and distance in interracial contexts. *Journal of Personality and Social Psychology, 94*, 91–107.

Gómez, A., Dovidio, J. F., Huici, C., Gaertner, S. L., & Cuardrado, I. (2008). The other side of We: When outgroup members express common identity. *Personality and Social Psychology Bulletin, 34*, 1613–1626.

González, R., & Brown, R. (2006). Dual identities and intergroup contact: Group status and size moderate the generalization of positive attitude change. *Journal of Experimental Social Psychology, 42*, 753–767.

Goodwin, S. A., Gubin, A., Fiske, S. T., & Yzerbyt, V. Y. (2000). Power can bias impression processes: Stereotyping subordinates by default and by design. *Group Processes and Intergroup Relations, 3*, 227–256.

Gramzow, R. H., Gaertner, L., & Sedikides, C. (2001). Memory for in-group and out-group information in a minimal group context: The self as an informational base. *Journal of Personality and Social Psychology, 80*, 188–205.

Greenwald, A., McGhee, D., & Schwartz, J. (1998). Measuring individual differences in implicit cognition: The Implicit Association Test. *Journal of Personality and Social Psychology, 74*, 1464–1480.

Greenwald, A. G., Poehlman, T. A., Uhlmann, E. L., & Banaji, M. R. (2009). Understanding and using the Implicit Association Test: III. Meta-analysis of predictive validity. *Journal of Personality and Social Psychology, 97*, 17–41.

Guerra, R., Rebelo, M., & Monteiro, M. B. (2004, June). *Changing intergroup relations: Effects of recategorization, decategorization and dual identity in the reduction of intergroup discrimination.* Paper presented at Change in Intergroup Relations: 7th Jena Workshop on Intergroup Processes, Friedrich Schiller University, Jena, Germany.

Hall, N. R., & Crisp, R. J. (2005). Considering multiple criteria for social categorization can reduce intergroup bias. *Personality and Social Psychology Bulletin, 31*, 1435–1444.

Hamilton, D. L., & Sherman, J. W. (1994). Stereotypes. In R. S. Wyer & T. K. Srull (Eds.), *Handbook of social cognition* (Vol. 2, pp. 1–68). Hillsdale, NJ: Erlbaum.

Harwood, J., Hewstone, M., Paolini, S., & Voci, A. (2005). Grandparent-grandchild contact and attitudes towards older adults: Moderator and mediator effects. *Personality and Social Psychology Bulletin, 31*, 393–406.

Hebl, M. R., & Dovidio, J. F. (2005). Promoting the "social" in the examination of social stigmas. *Personality and Social Psychology Review, 9*, 156–182.

Henderson-King, E. I., & Nisbett, R. E. (1996). Anti-Black prejudice as a function of exposure to the negative behavior of a single Black person. *Journal of Personality and Social Psychology, 71*, 654–664.

Henry, P. J., & Hardin, C. D. (2006). The Contact Hypothesis revisited: Status bias in the reduction of implicit prejudice in the United States and Lebanon. *Psychological Science, 17*, 862–868.

Henry, P. J., & Sears, D. O. (2002). The Symbolic Racism 2000 Scale. *Political Psychology, 23*, 253–283.

Hewstone, M. (1990). The "ultimate attribution error"? A review of the literature on intergroup attributions. *European Journal of Social Psychology, 20*, 311–335.

Hewstone, M. (1994). Revision and change of stereotypic beliefs: In search of the elusive subtyping model. *European Review of Social Psychology, 5*, 69–109.

Hewstone, M. (1996). Contact and categorization: Social psychological interventions to change intergroup relations. In C. N. Macrae, C. Stangor, & M. Hewstone (Eds.), *Stereotypes and stereotyping* (pp. 323–368). New York: Guilford.

Hewstone, M., & Brown, R. J. (1986). Contact is not enough: An intergroup perspective on the "Contact Hypothesis." In M. Hewstone & R. Brown (Eds.), *Contact and conflict in intergroup encounters* (pp. 1–44). Oxford: Basil Blackwell.

Hewstone, M., & Hamberger, J. (2000). Perceived variability and stereotype change. *Journal of Experimental Social Psychology, 36*, 103–124.

Hewstone, M., Hassebrauck, M., Wirth, A., & Waenke, M. (2000). Pattern of disconfirming information and processing instructions as determinants of stereotype change. *British Journal of Social Psychology, 39*, 399–411.

Hofmann, W., Gawronski, B., Gschwendner, T., Le H., & Schmitt, M. (2005). A meta-analysis on the correlation between the Implicit Association Test and explicit self-report measures. *Personality and Social Psychology Bulletin, 31*, 1369–1385.

Hogg, M. A. (1996). Social identity, self-categorization, and the small group. In E. H. Witte & J. H. Davis (Eds.), *Understanding group behavior. Vol. 2: Small group processes and interpersonal relations* (pp. 227–253). Hillsdale, NJ: Erlbaum.

Hogg, M. A., & Hains, S. C. (1996). Intergroup relations and group solidarity: Effects of group identification and social beliefs on depersonalized attraction. *Journal of Personality and Social Psychology, 70*, 295–309.

Hornsey, M. J., & Hogg, M. A. (2000). Subgroup relations: A comparison of mutual intergroup differentiation and common ungroup identity models of prejudice reduction. *Personality and Social Psychology Bulletin, 26*, 242–256.

Hornstein, H. A. (1976). *Cruelty and kindness: A new look at aggression and altruism*. Englewood Cliffs, NJ: Prentice Hall.

Houlette, M., Gaertner, S. L., Johnson, K. M., Banker, B. S., Riek, B. M., & Dovidio, J. F. (2004). Developing a more inclusive social identity: An elementary school intervention. *Journal of Social Issues, 60*, 35–56.

Howard, J. M., & Rothbart, M. (1980). Social categorization for in-group and out-group behavior. *Journal of Personality and Social Psychology, 38*, 301–310.

Hugenberg, K., & Bodenhausen, G. V. (2003). Facing prejudice: Implicit prejudice and the perception of facial threat. *Psychological Science, 14*, 640–643.

Hugenberg, K., & Bodenhausen, G. V. (2004). Ambiguity in social categorization: The role of prejudice and facial affect in race categorization. *Psychological Science, 15*, 342–345.

Huo, Y. J. (2003). Procedural justice and social regulation across group boundaries: Does subgroup identity undermine relationship-based governance. *Personality and Social Psychology Bulletin, 29*, 336–348.

Huo, Y. J., & Molina, L. E. (2006). Is pluralism a viable model of diversity? The benefits and limits of subgroup respect. *Group Processes and Intergroup Relations, 9*, 359–376.

Huo, Y. J., Smith, H. J., Tyler, T. R., & Lind, E. A. (1996). Superordinate identification, subgroup identification, and justice concerns: Is separatism the problem; is assimilation the answer? *Psychological Science, 7*, 40–45.

Insko, C. A., Schopler, J., Gaertner, L., Wildschut, T., Kozar, R., Pinter, B., et al. (2001). Interindividual-intergroup discontinuity reduction through the anticipation of future interaction. *Journal of Personality and Social Psychology, 80*, 95–111.

Inzlicht, M., Kaiser, C. R., & Major, B. (2008). The face of chauvinism: How prejudice expectations shape perceptions of facial affect. *Journal of Experimental Social Psychology, 44*, 758–766.

Jackman, M. R. (1994). *The velvet glove*. Berkeley, CA: University of California Press.

Jackman, M. R., & Crane, M. (1986). "Some of my best friends are black . . .": Interracial friendship and whites' racial attitudes. *Public Opinion Quarterly, 50*, 459–486.

Jetten, J., Branscombe, N. R., Schmitt, M. T., & Spears, R. (2001). Rebels with a cause: Group identification, as a response to perceived discrimination from the mainstream. *Personality and Social Psychology Bulletin, 27*, 1204–1213.

Jetten, J., Schmitt, M. T., Branscombe, N. R., & McKimmie, B. M. (2005). Suppressing the negative effect of devaluation on group identification: The role of intergroup differentiation and intragroup respect. *Journal of Experimental Social Psychology, 41*, 208–215.

Jetten, J., Spears, R., & Manstead, A. S. R. (1997). Strength of identification and intergroup differentiation: The influence of group norms. *European Journal of Social Psychology, 27*, 603–609.

Jetten, J., Spears, R., & Postmes, T. (2004). Intergroup distinctiveness and differentiation: A meta-analytic integration. *Journal of Personality and Social Psychology, 86*, 862–879.

Johnson, J. D., Ashburn-Nardo, L., Spicer, V., & Dovidio, J. F. (2008). The role of Blacks' discriminatory expectations in their prosocial orientations toward Whites. *Journal of Experimental Social Psychology, 44*, 1498–1505.

Johnson, J. D., & Lecci, L. (2003). Assessing anti-White attitudes and predicting perceived racism: The Johnson-Lecci scale. *Personality and Social Psychology Bulletin, 29*, 299–312.

Jones, J. M. (1986). Racism: A cultural analysis of the problem. In J. F. Dovidio & S. L. Gaertner (Eds.), *Prejudice, discrimination, and racism* (pp. 279–314). Orlando, FL: Academic Press.

Jost, J. T., Banaji, M., & Nosek, B. A. (2004). A decade of System Justification Theory: Accumulated evidence of conscious and unconscious bolstering of the *status quo*. *Political Psychology, 25*, 881–919.

Jost, J. T., & Hamilton, D. L. (2005). Stereotypes in our culture. In J. F. Dovidio, P. Glick, & L. A. Rudman (Eds.), *On the nature of prejudice: Fifty years after Allport* (pp. 208–224). Malden, MA: Blackwell.

Judd, C. M., Park, B., Yzerbyt, V., Gordijn, E. H., & Muller, D. (2005). Attributions of intergroup bias and outgroup homogeneity to ingroup and outgroup others. *European Journal of Social Psychology, 35*, 677–704.

Kaiser, C. R., Vick, S. B., & Major, B. (2006). Prejudice expectations moderate preconscious attention to cues that are threatening to social identity. *Psychological Science, 17*, 332–338.

Kane, A. A., Argote, L., & Levine, J. M. (2005). Knowledge transfer between groups via personnel rotation: Effects of social identity and knowledge quality. *Organizational Behavior and Human Decision Processes, 96*, 56–71.

Karpinski, A., & Hilton, J. L. (2001). Attitudes and the Implicit Association Test. *Journal of Personality and Social Psychology, 81*, 774–788.

Karpinski, A., & von Hippel, W. (1996). The role of the linguistic intergroup bias in expectancy maintenance. *Social Cognition, 14*, 141–163.

Kawakami, K., Dion, K., & Dovidio, J. F. (1998). Racial prejudice and stereotype activation. *Personality and Social Psychology Bulletin, 24*, 407–416.

Kawakami, K., Dovidio, J. F., Moll, J., Hermsen, S., & Russin, A. (2000). Just say no (to stereotyping): Effects of training in trait negation on stereotype activation. *Journal of Personality and Social Psychology, 78*, 871–888.

Kawakami, K., Dunn, E., Karmali, F., & Dovidio, J. F. (2009). Mispredicting affective and behavioral responses to racism. *Science, 323*, 276–279.

Kawakami, K., Phills, C., Steele, J., & Dovidio, J. F. (2007). (Close) Distance makes the heart grow fonder: Improving implicit racial attitudes and interracial interactions through approach behaviors. *Journal of Personality and Social Psychology, 92*, 957–971.

Kenworthy, J. B., Turner, R. N., Hewstone, M., & Voci, A. (2005). Intergroup contact: When does it work, and why? In J. F. Dovidio, P. Glick, & L. A. Rudman (Eds.), *On the nature of prejudice: Fifty years after Allport* (pp. 278–292). Malden, MA: Blackwell.

Kessler, T., & Mummendey, A. (2001). Is there any scapegoat around? Determinants of intergroup conflict at different categorization levels. *Journal of Personality and Social Psychology, 81*, 1090–1102.

Klandermans, B., Sabucedo, J. M., & Rodriguez, M. (2004). Inclusiveness of identification among farmers in the Netherlands and Galicia. *European Journal of Social Psychology, 34*, 279–295.

Knowles, M. L., & Gardner, W. L. (2008). Benefits of membership: The activation and amplification of group identities in response to social rejection. *Personality and Social Psychology Bulletin, 33*, 281–294.

Kramer, R. M., & Brewer, M. B. (1984). Effects of group identity on resource utilization in a simulated commons dilemma. *Journal of Personality and Social Psychology, 46*, 1044–1057.

Leippe, M. R., & Eisenstadt, D. (1994). Generalization of dissonance reduction: Decreasing prejudice through induced compliance. *Journal of Personality and Social Psychology, 67*, 395–413.

Lepore, L., & Brown, R. (1997). Category and stereotype activation: Is prejudice inevitable? *Journal of Personality and Social Psychology, 72*, 275–287.

Levin, S., van Laar, C., & Sidanius, J. (2003). The effects of ingroup and outgroup friendships on ethnic attitudes in college: A longitudinal study. *Group Processes and Intergroup Relations, 6*, 76–92.

Levine, M., Prosser, A., Evans, D., & Reicher, S. (2005). Identity and emergency intervention: How social group membership and inclusiveness of group boundaries shape helping behavior. *Personality and Social Psychology Bulletin, 31*, 443–453.

Leyens, J-P., Demoulin, S., Vaes, J., Gaunt, R., & Paladino, M. P. (2007). Infra-humanization: The wall of group differences. *Social Issues and Policy Review, 1*, 139–172.

Lippmann, W. (1922). *Public opinion*. New York: Harcourt, Brace.

Maass, A., Ceccarelli, R., & Rudin, S. (1996). Linguistic intergroup bias: Evidence for ingroup-protective motivation. *Journal of Personality and Social Psychology, 71*, 512–526.

Maass, A., Salvi, D., Arcuri, L., & Semin, G. R. (1989). Language use in intergroup contexts: The linguistic intergroup bias. *Journal of Personality and Social Psychology, 57*, 981–993.

Macrae, C. N., Milne, A. B., & Bodenhausen, G. V. (1994). Stereotypes as energy-saving devices: A peek inside the cognitive toolbox. *Journal of Personality and Social Psychology, 66*, 37–47.

Mallett, R. K., Huntsinger, J. R., Sinclair, S., & Swim, J. K. (2008). Seeing through their eyes: When majority group members take collective action on behalf of an outgroup. *Group Processes and Intergroup Relations, 11*, 451–470.

Mallett, R. K., Wilson, T. D., & Gilbert, D. T. (2008). Expect the unexpected: Failure to anticipate similarities when predicting the quality of an intergroup interaction. *Journal of Personality and Social Psychology, 94*, 265–277.

McConahay, J. B. (1986). Modern racism, ambivalence, and the modern racism scale. In J. F. Dovidio & S. L. Gaertner (Eds.), *Prejudice, discrimination, and racism* (pp. 91–125). Orlando, FL: Academic Press.

Mendes, W. B., Major, B., McCoy, S., & Blascovich, J. (2008). How attributional ambiguity shapes physiological and emotional responses to social rejection and acceptance. *Journal of Personality and Social Psychology, 94*, 278–291.

Miller, N. (2002). Personalization and the promise of Contact Theory. *Journal of Social Issues, 58*, 387–410.

Miller, N., Brewer, M. B., & Edwards, K. (1985). Cooperative interaction in desegregated settings: A laboratory analog. *Journal of Social Issues, 41*(3), 63–79.

Monteiro, M. B., Guerra, R., & Rebelo, M. (2009). Reducing prejudice: Common Ingroup and Dual Identity in unequal status intergroup encounters. In S. Demoulin, J. P. Leyens, & J. F. Dovidio (Eds.), *Intergroup misunderstandings: Impact of divergent social realities* (pp. 273–290). New York: Psychology Press.

Monteith, M. J. (1993). Self-regulation and prejudiced responses: Implications for progress in prejudice reduction efforts. *Journal of Personality and Social Psychology, 65*, 469–485.

Monteith, M. J., Arthur, S. A., & Flynn, S. M. (in press). Self-regulation and bias. In J. F. Dovidio, M. Hewstone, P. Glick, & V. M. Esses (Eds.), *Handbook of prejudice, stereotyping, and discrimination*. Thousand Oaks, CA: Sage.

Monteith, M. J., Sherman, J., & Devine, P. G. (1998). Suppression as a stereotype control strategy. *Personality and Social Psychology Review, 1*, 63–82.

Mullen, B., Brown, R. J., & Smith, C. (1992). Ingroup bias as a function of salience, relevance, and status: An integration. *European Journal of Social Psychology, 22*, 103–122.

Mullen, B., & Hu, L. T. (1989). Perceptions of ingroup and outgroup variability: A meta-analytic integration. *Basic and Applied Social Psychology, 10*, 233–252.

Mummendey, A., Klink, A., & Brown, R. (2001). Nationalism and patriotism: National identification and out-group rejection. *British Journal of Social Psychology, 40*, 159–172.

Mummendey, A., & Otten, S. (2001). Aversive discrimination. In R. Brown & S. L. Gaertner (Eds.), *Blackwell handbook of social psychology: Intergroup processes* (pp. 112–132). Malden, MA: Blackwell.

Mummendey, A., & Wenzel, M. (1999). Social discrimination and tolerance in intergroup relations: Reactions to intergroup difference. *Personality and Social Psychology Review, 3*, 158–174.

Nadler, A. (2002). Inter-group helping relations as power relations: Helping relations as affirming or challenging inter-group hierarchy. *Journal of Social Issues, 58*, 487–502.

Nadler, A., & Halabi, S. (2006). Intergroup helping as status relations: Effects of status stability in-group identification and type of help on receptivity to help from high status group. *Journal of Personality and Social Psychology, 91*, 97–110.

Nier, J. A., Gaertner, S. L., Dovidio, J. F., Banker, B. S., & Ward, C. M. (2001). Changing interracial evaluations and behavior: The effects of a common group identity. *Group Processes and Intergroup Relations, 4*, 299–316.

Norton, M. I., Sommers, S. R., Apfelbaum, E. P., Pura, N., & Ariely, D. (2006). Color blindness and interracial interaction: Playing the political correctness game. *Psychological Science, 17*, 949–953.

Nosek, B. A., & Banaji, M. R. (2001). The go/no go association task. *Social Cognition, 19*, 625–666.

Nosek, B. A., Banaji, M. R., & Greenwald, A. G. (2002). Harvesting implicit group attitudes and beliefs from a demonstration web site. *Group Dynamics: Theory, Research, and Practice, 6*, 101–115.

Oakes, P. (2001). The Root of all evil in intergroup relations? Unearthing the categorization process. In R. Brown & S. L. Gaertner (Eds.), *Blackwell handbook of social psychology: Intergroup processes* (pp. 3–21). Oxford: Blackwell.

Onorato, R. S., & Turner, J. C. (2001). The "I," "me," and the "us": The psychological group and self-concept maintenance and change. In C. Sedikides & M. B. Brewer (Eds.), *Individual self, relational self, collective self* (pp. 147–170). Philadelphia: Psychology Press.

Otten, S., & Epstude, K. (2006). Overlapping mental representations of self, ingroup, and outgroup: Unraveling self-stereotyping and self-anchoring. *Personality and Social Psychology Bulletin, 32*, 957–969.

Otten, S., & Moskowitz, G. B. (2000). Evidence for implicit evaluative ingroup bias: Affect-based spontaneous trait inference in a minimal group paradigm. *Journal of Experimental Social Psychology, 36*, 77–89.

Otten, S., & Mummendey, A. (2000). Valence-dependent probability of ingroup-favoritism between minimal groups: An integrative view on the positive-negative asymmetry in social discrimination. In D. Capozza & R. Brown (Eds.), *Social identity processes* (pp. 33–48). London: Sage.

Otten, S., & Wentura, D. (1999). About the impact of automaticity in the Minimal Group Paradigm: Evidence from affective priming tasks. *European Journal of Social Psychology, 29*, 1049–1071.

Page-Gould, E., Mendoza-Denton, R., & Tropp, L. R. (2008). With a little help from my cross-group friend: Reducing anxiety in intergroup contexts through cross-group friendship. *Journal of Personality and Social Psychology, 95*, 1080–1094.

Paladino, M-P., & Castelli, L. (2008). On the immediate consequences of ingroup categorization: Activation of approach and avoidance motor behavior toward ingroup and outgroup members. *Personality and Social Psychology Bulletin, 34*, 755–768.

Park, B., & Rothbart, M. (1982). Perception of out-group homogeneity and levels of social categorization: Memory for the subordinate attributes of in-group and out-group members. *Journal of Personality and Social Psychology, 42*, 1051–1068.

Park, S. H., Glaser, J., & Knowles, E. D. (2008). Implicit motivation to control prejudice moderates the effect of cognitive depletion on unintended discrimination. *Social Cognition, 26*, 401–419.

Pearson, A. R., West, T. V., Dovidio, J. F., Powers, S. R., Buck, R., & Henning, R. (2008). The fragility of intergroup relations. *Psychological Science, 19*, 1272–1279.

Penner, L. A. (1971). Interpersonal attraction to a black person as a function of value importance. *Personality: An International Journal, 2*, 175–187.

Perdue, C. W., Dovidio, J. F., Gurtman, M. B., & Tyler, R. B. (1990). "Us" and "them": Social categorization and the process of intergroup bias. *Journal of Personality and Social Psychology, 59*, 475–486.

Petersen, E., & Blank, H. (2003). Ingroup bias in the minimal group paradigm shown by three-person groups with high or low state self-esteem. *European Journal of Social Psychology, 33*, 149–162.

Pettigrew, T. F. (1979). The ultimate attribution error: Extending Allport's cognitive analysis of prejudice. *Personality and Social Psychology Bulletin, 5*, 461–476.

Pettigrew, T. F. (1997). Generalized intergroup contact effects on prejudice. *Personality and Social Psychology Bulletin, 23*, 173–185.

Pettigrew, T. F. (1998). Intergroup Contact Theory. *Annual Review of Psychology, 49*, 65–85.

Pettigrew, T. F., & Meertens, R. W. (1995). Subtle and blatant prejudice in Western Europe. *European Journal of Social Psychology, 25*, 57–76.

Pettigrew, T. F., & Tropp, L. (2006). A meta-analytic test of intergroup contact theory. *Journal of Personality and Social Psychology, 90*, 751–783.

Pettigrew, T. F., & Tropp, L. R. (2008). How does contact reduce prejudice? A meta analytic test of three mediators. *European Journal of Social Psychology, 38*, 922–934.

Pfeifer, J. H., Ruble, D. N., Bachman, M. A., Alvarez, J. M., Cameron, J. A., & Fuligni, A. J. (2007). Social identities and intergroup bias in immigrant and nonimmigrant children. *Developmental Psychology, 43*, 496–507.

Piliavin, J. A., Dovidio, J. F., Gaertner, S. L., & Clark, R. D., III. (1981). *Emergency intervention*. New York: Academic Press.

Plant, E. A. (2004). Responses to interracial interactions over time. *Personality and Social Psychology Bulletin, 30*, 1458–1471.

Plant, E. A., & Devine, P. G. (1998). Internal and external motivation to respond without prejudice. *Journal of Personality and Social Psychology, 75*, 811–832.

Plant, E. A., & Devine, P. G. (2003). The antecedents and implications of interracial anxiety. *Personality and Social Psychology Bulletin, 29*, 790–801.

Plant, E. A., Devine, P. G., & Brazy, P. C. (2003). The bogus pipeline and motivations to reduce prejudice: Revisiting the fading and faking of racial prejudice. *Group Processes and Intergroup Relations, 6*, 187–200.

Platow, M. J., Voudouris, N. J., Coulson, M., Gilford, N., Jamieson, R., Najdovski, L., et al. (2007). In-group reassurance in a pain setting produces lower levels of physiological arousal: Direct support for a self-categorization analysis of social influence. *European Journal of Social Psychology, 37*, 649–660.

Poortinga, W., & Pidgeon, N. F. (2006). Prior attitudes, salient value similarity, and dimensionality" toward an integrative model of trust in risk regulation. *Journal of Applied Social Psychology, 36*, 1674–1700.

Quattrone, G. A., & Jones, E. E. (1980). The perception of variability within in-groups and out-groups: Implications for the law of small numbers. *Journal of Personality and Social Psychology, 38*, 141–152.

Quinn, K. A., & Macrae, C. N. (2005). Categorizing others: The dynamics of person construal. *Journal of Personality and Social Psychology, 88*, 467–479.

Rabbie, J. M., & Lodewijkx, H. F. M. (1996). A behavioral interaction model: Toward an integrative theoretical framework for studying intra- and intergroup dynamics. In E. H. Witte & J. H. Davis (Eds.), *Understanding group behavior. Vol. 2: Small group processes and interpersonal relations. Understanding group behavior* (pp. 255–294). Hillsdale, NJ: Erlbaum.

Richeson, J. A., Baird, A. A., Gordon, H. L., Heatherton, T. F., Wyland, C. L., Trawalter, S., et al. (2003). An fMRI investigation of the impact of interracial contact on executive function. *Nature Neuroscience, 6*, 1323–1328.

Richeson, J. A., & Nussbaum, R. J. (2004). The impact of multiculturalism versus color-blindness on racial bias. *Journal of Experimental Social Psychology, 40*, 417–423.

Richeson, J., & Shelton, J. N. (2003). When prejudice does not pay: Effects of interracial contact on executive function. *Psychological Science, 14*, 287–290.

Richeson, J. A., & Shelton, J. N. (in press). Intergroup dyadic interactions. In J. F. Dovidio, M. Hewstone, P. Glick, & V. M. Esses (Eds.), *Handbook of prejudice, stereotyping, and discrimination*. Thousand Oaks, CA: Sage.

Richeson, J. A., & Trawalter, S. (2005). Why do interracial interactions impair executive function? A resource depletion account. *Journal of Personality and Social Psychology, 88*, 934–947.

Richeson, J. A., Trawalter, S., & Shelton, J. N. (2005). African American's implicit racial attitudes and the depletion of executive function after interracial interactions. *Social Cognition, 23*, 336–352.

Riek, B. M., Mania, E. W., & Gaertner, S. L. (2006). Intergroup threat and outgroup attitudes: A meta-analytic review. *Personality and Social Psychology Review, 10*, 336–353.

Riek, B. M., Mania, E. W., Gaertner, S. L., Direso, S. A., & Lamoreaux, M. (2009). *Does a common ingroup identity reduce intergroup threat?* Manuscript submitted for publication.

Robbins, J. M., & Krueger, J. I. (2005). Social projection to ingroups and outgroups: A review and meta-analysis. *Personality and Social Psychology Review, 9,* 32–47.

Roccas, S., & Brewer, M. (2002). Social identity complexity. *Personality and Social Psychology Review, 6,* 88–106.

Rokeach, M. (1973). *The nature of human values.* New York: Free Press.

Rothbart, M., & John, O. P. (1985). Social categorization and behavioral episodes: A cognitive analysis of the effects of intergroup contact. *Journal of Social Issues, 41*(3), 81–104.

Rothbart, M., & Lewis, S. (1988). Inferring category attributes from exemplar attributes: Geometric shapes and social categories. *Journal of Personality and Social Psychology, 55,* 861–872.

Rudman, L. A., & Ashmore, R. D. (2007). Discrimination and the Implicit Association Test. *Group Processes and Intergroup Relations, 10,* 359–372.

Ruscher, J. B. (2001). *Prejudiced communication: A social psychological perspective.* New York: Guilford Press.

Ryan, C. S., Hunt, J. S., Weible, J. A., Peterson, C. R., & Casas, J. F. (2007). Multicultural and colorblind ideology, stereotypes, and ethnocentrism among Black and White Americans. *Group Processes and Intergroup Relations, 10,* 617–637.

Rydell, R. J., & McConnell, A. R. (2006). Understanding implicit and explicit attitude change: A systems of reasoning analysis. *Journal of Personality and Social Psychology, 91,* 995–1008.

Rydell, R. J., McConnell, A. R., Strain, L. M., Claypool, H. M., & Hugenberg, K. (2007). Implicit and explicit attitudes respond differently to increasing amounts of counterattitudinal information. *European Journal of Social Psychology, 37,* 867–878.

Saguy, T., Dovidio, J. F., & Pratto, F. (2008). Beyond contact: Intergroup contact in the context of power relations. *Personality and Social Psychology Bulletin, 34,* 432–445.

Saguy, T., Tausch, N., Dovidio, J. F., & Pratto, F. (2009). The irony of harmony: Intergroup contact can produce false expectations for equality. *Psychological Science, 29,* 114–121.

Scheepers, D., Spears, R., Doosje, B., & Manstead, A. S. R. (2006). The social functions of ingroup bias: Creating, confirming, or changing social reality. In W. Stroebe & M. Hewstone (Eds.), *European review of social psychology* (pp. 359–396). New York: Psychology Press.

Schneider, D. J. (2004). *The psychology of stereotyping.* New York: Guilford.

Sears, D. O., Henry, P. J., & Kosterman, R. (2000). Egalitarian values and contemporary racial politics. In D. O. Sears, J. Sidanius, & L. Bobo (Eds.), *Racialized politics: The debate about racism in America* (pp. 75–117). Chicago: University of Chicago Press.

Shelton, J. N., & Richeson, J. A. (2006). Interracial interactions: A relational approach. In M. P. Zanna (Ed.), *Advances in experimental social psychology* (Vol. 38, pp. 121–181). New York: Academic Press.

Shelton, J. N., Richeson, J. A., & Vorauer, J. D. (2006). Threatened identities and interethnic interactions. In W. Stroebe & M. Hewstone (Eds.), *European review of social psychology* (Vol. 17, pp. 312–358). New York: Psychology Press.

Sherif, M. (1966). *Group conflict and cooperation: Their social psychology.* London: Routledge and Kegan Paul.

Sherif, M., Harvey, O. J., White, B. J., Hood, W. R., & Sherif, C. W. (1961). *Intergroup conflict and cooperation: The Robbers Cave experiment.* Norman, OK: University of Oklahoma Book Exchange.

Sherif, M., & Sherif, C. W. (1969). *Social psychology.* New York: Harper & Row.

Shnabel, N., Nadler, A., Canetti-Nisim, D., & Ullrich, J. (2008). The role of acceptance and empowerment in promoting reconciliation from the perspective of the Needs-Based Model. *Social Issues and Policy Review, 2,* 159–186.

Sidanius, J., & Pratto, F. (1999). *Social dominance: An intergroup theory of social hierarchy and oppression.* New York: Cambridge University Press.

Smith, E. R., & DeCoster, J. (2000). Dual-process models in social and cognitive psychology: Conceptual integration and links to underlying memory systems. *Personality and Social Psychology Review, 4,* 108–131.

Smith, E. R., & Henry, S. (1996). An ingroup becomes part of the self: Response time evidence. *Personality and Social Psychology Bulletin, 22,* 635–642.

Smith, E. R., & Mackie, D. M. (2005). Aggression, hatred, and other emotions. In J. F. Dovidio, P. Glick, & L. A. Rudman (Eds.), *On the nature of prejudice: Fifty years after Allport* (pp. 361–376). Malden, MA: Blackwell.

Smith, H. J., & Tyler, T. R. (1996). Justice and power: When will justice concerns encourage the advantaged to support policies which redistribute economic resources and the disadvantaged to willingly obey the law? *European Journal of Social Psychology, 26,* 171–200.

Smith, P. K., Dijksterhuis, A., & Chaiken, S. (2008). Subliminal exposure to faces and racial attitudes: Exposure to Whites makes Whites like Blacks less. *Journal of Experimental Social Psychology, 44,* 50–64.

Snyder, M., Tanke, E. D., & Berscheid, E. (1977). Social perception and interpersonal behavior: On the self-fulfilling nature of social stereotypes. *Journal of Personality and Social Psychology, 35,* 656–666.

Son Hing, L. S., Chung-Yan, G. A., Hamilton, L. K., & Zanna, M. P. (2008). A two-dimensional model that employs explicit and implicit attitudes to characterize prejudice. *Journal of Personality and Social Psychology, 94,* 771–987.

Son Hing, L. S., Li, W., & Zanna, M. P. (2002). Inducing hypocrisy to reduce prejudicial responses among aversive racists. *Journal of Experimental Social Psychology, 38,* 71–78.

Spears, R., Doosje, B., & Ellemers, N. (1997). Self-stereotyping in the face of threats to group status and distinctiveness: The role of group identification. *Personality and Social Psychology Bulletin, 23,* 538–553.

Stanley, D., Phelps, E., & Banaji, M. (2008). The neural basis of implicit attitudes. *Current Directions in Psychological Science, 17,* 164–170.

Stathi, S., & Crisp, R. J. (2008). Imagining intergroup contact promotes projection to outgroups. *Journal of Experimental Social Psychology, 44,* 943–957.

Stein, D. D., Hardyck, J. A., & Smith, M. B. (1965). Race and belief: An open and shut case. *Journal of Personality and Social Psychology, 1,* 281–289.

Stephan, W. G., Boniecki, K. A., Ybarra, O., Bettencourt, A., Ervin, K. S., Jackson, L. A., et al. (2002). The role of threats in the racial attitudes of blacks and whites. *Personality and Social Psychology Bulletin, 28*(9), 1242–1254.

Stephan, W. G., & Finlay, K. (1999). The role of empathy in improving intergroup relations. *Journal of Social Issues, 55,* 729–743.

Stephan, W. G., Renfro, C. L., Esses, V. M., Stephan, C. W., & Martin, T. (2005). The effects of feeling threatened on attitudes toward immigrants. *International Journal of Intercultural Relations, 29,* 1–19.

Stephan, W., & Stephan, C. W. (1985). Intergroup anxiety. *Journal of Social Issues, 41,* 157–175.

Stephan, W. G., & Stephan, C. W. (2000). An integrated threat theory of prejudice. In S. Oskamp (Ed.), *Reducing prejudice and discrimination* (pp. 23–45). Hillsdale, NJ: Erlbaum.

Stephan, W. G., & Stephan, C. W. (2001). *Improving intergroup relations.* Thousand Oaks, CA: Sage.

Strack, F., & Deutsch, R. (2004). Reflective and impulsive determinants of social behavior. *Personality and Social Psychology Review, 8,* 220–247.

Stürmer, S., Snyder, M., & Omoto, A. M. (2005). Prosocial emotions and helping: The moderating role of group membership. *Journal of Personality and Social Psychology, 88*, 532–546.

Sumner, W. G. (1906). *Folkways*. New York: Ginn.

Swim, J. K., Aiken, K. J., Hall, W. S., & Hunter, B. A. (1995). Sexism and racism: Old-fashioned and modern prejudices. *Journal of Personality and Social Psychology, 68*, 199–214.

Tajfel, H. (1969). Cognitive aspects of prejudice. *Journal of Social Issues, 25*(4), 79–97.

Tajfel, H., Billig, M. G., Bundy, R. F., & Flament, C. (1971). Social categorisation and intergroup behavior. *European Journal of Social Psychology, 1*, 149–177.

Tajfel, H., & Turner, J. C. (1979). An integrative theory of intergroup conflict. In W. G. Austin & S. Worchel (Eds.), *The social psychology of intergroup relations* (pp. 33–48). Monterey, CA: Brooks/Cole.

Talaska, C. A., Fiske, S. T., & Chaiken, S. (2008). Legitimating racial discrimination: Emotions, not beliefs, best predict discrimination in a meta-analysis. *Social Justice Research, 21*, 263–296.

Tam, T., Hewstone, M., Harwood, J., Voci, A., & Kenworthy, J. (2005). Intergroup contact and grandparent–grandchild communication: The effects of self-disclosure on implicit and explicit biases against older people. *Group Processes and Intergroup Relations, 9*, 413–429.

Tausch, N., Hewstone, M., Kenworthy, J., Cairns, E., & Christ, O. (2007). Cross-community contact, perceived status differences, and intergroup attitudes in Northern Ireland: The mediating roles of individual-level versus group-level threats and the moderating role of social identification. *Political Psychology, 28*, 53–68.

Tausch, N., Tam, T., Hewstone, M., Kenworthy, J. B., & Cairns, E. (2007). Individual-level and group-level mediators of contact effects in Northern Ireland: The moderating role of social identification. *British Journal of Social Psychology, 46*, 541–556.

Taylor, M. C. (2000). Social contextual strategies for reducing racial discrimination. In S. Oskamp (Ed.), *Reducing prejudice and discrimination* (pp. 71–89). Hillsdale, NJ: Erlbaum.

Trawalter, S., & Richeson, J. A. (2006). Regulatory focus and executive function after interracial interactions. *Journal of Experimental Social Psychology, 42*, 406–412.

Tropp, L. R., & Pettigrew, T. F. (2005). Relationship between intergroup contact and prejudice among minority and majority status groups. *Psychological Science, 16*, 951–957.

Turner, J. C. (1985). Social categorization and the self-concept: A social cognitive theory of group behavior. In E. J. Lawler (Ed.), *Advances in group processes* (Vol. 2, pp. 77–122). Greenwich, CT: JAI Press.

Turner, J. C., Hogg, M. A., Oakes, P. J., Reicher, S. D., & Wetherell, M. S. (1987). *Rediscovering the social group: A self-categorization theory.* Oxford: Basil Blackwell.

Turner, R. N., Hewstone, M., & Voci, A. (2007). Reducing explicit and implicit outgroup prejudice via direct and extended contact: The mediating role of self-disclosure and intergroup anxiety. *Journal of Personality and Social Psychology, 93*, 369–388.

Turner, R. N., Hewstone, M., Voci, A., & Vonofakou, C. (2008). A test of the extended intergroup contact hypothesis: The mediating role of perceived ingroup and outgroup norms, intergroup anxiety and inclusion of the outgroup in the self. *Journal of Personality and Social Psychology, 95*, 843–860.

Tyler, T., & Blader, S. L. (2003). The Group Engagement Model: Procedural justice, social identity, and cooperative behavior. *Personality and Social Psychology Review, 7*, 349–361.

van Bavel, J. J., Packer, D. J., & Cunningham, W. A. (2008). The neural substrates of in-group bias. *Psychological Science, 19*, 1131–1139.

van Laar, C., Levin, S., Sinclair, S., & Sidanius, J. (2005). The effect of university roommate contact on ethnic attitudes and behavior. *Journal of Experimental Social Psychology, 41*, 329–345.

van Oudenhoven, J. P., Groenewoud, J. T., & Hewstone, M. (1996). Cooperation, ethnic salience and generalization of inter ethnic attitudes. *European Journal of Social Psychology, 26*, 649–662.

Verkuyten, M. (2006). Multicultural recognition and ethnic minority rights: A social identity perspective. In W. Stroebe & M. Hewstone (Eds.), *European review of social psychology* (Vol. 17, pp. 148–184). Hove, England: Psychology Press.

Verkuyten, M., & Hagendoorn, L. (1998). Prejudice and self-categorization: The variable role of authoritarianism and in-group stereotypes. *Personality and Social Psychology Bulletin, 24*, 99–110.

Vescio, T. K., Sechrist, G. B., & Paolucci, M. P. (2003). Perspective taking and prejudice reduction: The mediational role of empathy arousal and situational attributions. *European Journal of Social Psychology, 33*, 455–472.

Voci, A. (2006). The link between identification and in-group favouritism: Effects of threat to social identity and trust-related emotions. *British Journal of Social Psychology, 45*, 265–284.

Voci, A., & Hewstone, M. (2003). Intergroup contact and prejudice toward immigrants in Italy: The mediational role of anxiety and the moderational role of group salience. *Group Processes and Intergroup Relations, 6*, 37–54.

Vorauer, J. D. (2006). An information search model of evaluative concerns in intergroup interaction. *Psychological Review, 113*, 862–886.

Vorauer, J. D., Hunter, A. J., Main, K. J., & Roy, S. A. (2000). Meta-stereotype activation: Evidence from indirect measures for specific evaluative concerns experienced by members of dominant groups in intergroup interaction. *Journal of Personality and Social Psychology, 78*, 690–707.

Wagner, U., Christ, O., & Pettigrew, T. F. (2008). Prejudice and group-related behavior in Germany. *Journal of Social Issues, 64*, 403–416.

Waldzus, S., Mummendey, A., Wenzel, M., & Boettcher, F. (2004). Of bikers, teachers, and Germans: Groups' diverging views about their prototypicality. *British Journal of Social Psychology, 43*, 385–400.

Weber, R., & Crocker, J. (1983). Cognitive processes in the revision of stereotypic beliefs. *Journal of Personality and Social Psychology, 45*, 961–977.

West, T. V., Shelton, J. N., & Trail, T. E. (2009). Relational anxiety in interracial interactions. *Psychological Science, 20*, 289–292.

Wilder, D. A. (1981). Perceiving persons as a group: Categorization and intergroup relations. In D. L. Hamilton (Ed.), *Cognitive processes in stereotyping and intergroup behavior* (pp. 213–257). Hillsdale, NJ: Erlbaum.

Wilder, D. A. (1986). Social categorization: Implications for creation and reduction of intergroup bias. In L. Berkowitz (Ed.), *Advances in experimental social psychology* (Vol. 19, pp. 291–355). Orlando, FL: Academic Press.

Wilder, D. A., & Shapiro, P. (1989). Effects of anxiety on impression formation in a group context: An anxiety-assimilation hypothesis. *Journal of Experimental Social Psychology, 25*, 481–499.

Wilder, D. A., Simon, A. F., & Faith, M. (1996). Enhancing the impact of counterstereotypic information. Dispositional attributions for deviance. *Journal of Personality and Social Psychology, 71*, 276–287.

Williams, R. M., Jr. (1947). *The reduction of intergroup tensions.* New York: Social Science Research Council.

Wilson, T. D., Lindsey, S., & Schooler, T. Y. (2000). A model of dual attitudes. *Psychological Review, 107*, 101–126.

Wittenbrink, B., & Henly, J. R. (1996). Creating social reality: Informational social influence and the content of stereotypic beliefs. *Personality and Social Psychology Bulletin, 22*, 598–610.

Wittenbrink, B., Judd, C., & Park, B. (1997). Evidence for racial prejudice at the implicit level and its relationship with questionnaire measures. *Journal of Personality and Social Psychology, 72*, 262–274.

Wittenbrink, B., Judd, C. M., & Park, B. (2001). Spontaneous prejudice in context: Variability in automatically activated attitudes. *Journal of Personality and Social Psychology, 81*, 815–827.

Wohl, M. J. A., & Branscombe, N. R. (2005). Forgiveness and collective guilt assignment to historical perpetrator groups depend on level of social category inclusiveness. *Journal of Personality and Social Psychology, 88*, 288–303.

Worchel, S., Rothgerber, H., Day, E. A., Hart, D., & Butemeyer, J. (1998). Social identity and individual productivity within groups. *British Journal of Social Psychology, 37*, 389–413.

Word, C. O., Zanna, M. P., & Cooper, J. (1974). The nonverbal mediation of self-fulfilling prophecies in interracial interaction. *Journal of Experimental Social Psychology, 10*, 109–120.

Wright, S. C., Aron, A., McLaughlin-Volpe, T., & Ropp, S. A. (1997). The extended contact effect: Knowledge of cross-group friendships and prejudice. *Journal of Personality and Social Psychology, 73*, 73–90.

Zogmaister, C., Arcuri, L., Castelli, L., & Smith, E. R. (2008). The impact of loyalty and equality on implicit ingroup favoritism. *Group Processes and Intergroup Relations, 11*, 493–512.

Chapter 30

Social Justice

History, Theory, and Research

JOHN T. JOST AND AARON C. KAY

> Justice is the first virtue of social institutions, as truth is of systems of thought. A theory however elegant and economical must be rejected or revised if it is untrue; likewise laws and institutions no matter how efficient and well-arranged must be reformed or abolished if they are unjust.
>
> —John Rawls (1971)

> The best safeguard against fascism is to establish social justice to the maximum possible extent.
>
> —Arnold Toynbee (1976)

Social justice is a concept that originates in philosophical discourse but is widely used in both ordinary language and social science, often without being clearly defined. By synthesizing the common elements of various philosophical treatments (e.g., Elster, 1992; Feinberg, 1973; Frankena, 1962; Miller, 1999; Walzer, 1983), it is possible to offer a general definition of social justice as a state of affairs (either actual or ideal) in which (a) benefits and burdens in society are dispersed in accordance with some allocation principle (or set of principles); (b) procedures, norms, and rules that govern political and other forms of decision making preserve the basic rights, liberties, and entitlements of individuals and groups; and (c) human beings (and perhaps other species) are treated with dignity and respect not only by authorities but also by other relevant social actors, including fellow citizens. The three aspects of our definition correspond, roughly, to *distributive*, *procedural*, and *interactional* justice, as we use the terms in this chapter. A theory of social justice need not address all three aspects, but it should address at least one of them. Conceived of in this way, social justice is a property of *social systems*—or perhaps a "predicate of societies" (Frankena, 1962)—as suggested also by Rawls (1971) and Toynbee (1976). A just social system is to be contrasted with those systems that foster arbitrary or unnecessary suffering, exploitation, abuse, tyranny, oppression, prejudice, and discrimination.

The foremost problem for scholars (or would-be practitioners) of social justice is that considerable disagreement persists,

This chapter is dedicated to the memory of George L. Jost (1916–2002), who worked for social justice in several different contexts: first as a communications specialist who received a Bronze Star in the U.S. military stationed in Italy during World War II; later as part of the Catholic Workers' anti-poverty movement led by Dorothy Day and Peter Maurin in New York City; and in the mid-1960s as a co-founder of the Friends of FIGHT civil rights organization in Rochester, NY, which worked with Saul Alinsky to challenge racial discrimination (see Horwitt, 1989, p. 486). The writing of this chapter was supported in part by research grants made available to John T. Jost by the New York University Center for Catastrophe Preparedness and Response and the National Science Foundation (BCS-0617558) and to Aaron C. Kay by the Canadian Social Sciences and Humanities Research Council. The authors wish to thank Mahzarin R. Banaji, Ramona Bobocel, Mitchell Callan, Irina Feygina, Susan T. Fiske, Danielle Gaucher, Daniel Gilbert, Erin Godfrey, Curtis D. Hardin, Erin Hennes, György Hunyady, Orsolya Hunyady, Lawrence J. Jost, Margarita Krochik, Ido Liviatan, Anesu Mandisodza, Gabe Mendlow, Jaime L. Napier, Tom R. Tyler, Kees Van den Bos, and Jojanneke Van der Toorn for extremely helpful advice and commentary on the material contained herein. We also acknowledge Tina Schweizer for her diligence in compiling the extensive bibliography. Finally, the authors would like to express their appreciation for all of the members of the International Society for Justice Research (ISJR) and wish that they could do "justice" to all of the many scientific and practical contributions made by the members of that society.

even after centuries of debate, concerning each of the elements incorporated in our definition (see Boucher & Kelly, 1998; Campbell, 2001; Miller, 1999; Solomon & Murphy, 2000). What is to be considered a truly fair principle for distributing benefits and burdens and why? Is it equity, equality, need, or some other principle of allocation? Similarly, what is a reasonable or appropriate set of rights, liberties, and entitlements? And what does it mean to treat others with dignity and respect? These are difficult questions, to be sure, but they are not in principle unanswerable. They have been addressed by some of the greatest minds in Western civilization, including Plato, Aristotle, Hobbes, Locke, Hume, Rousseau, Kant, Hegel, Marx, Mill, and Rawls. In this chapter, we summarize the major scientific contributions of social psychology to the understanding and practice of social justice.

LEWINIAN TRADITION IN SOCIAL PSYCHOLOGY

Social Justice as a Central Theoretical and Practical Concern of Social Psychology

It was not long ago that questions of social justice were at the forefront of theoretical and empirical inquiry in social psychology. The father of modern social psychology, Kurt Lewin, promoted the discipline as, among other things, a scientific means of fostering democratic, egalitarian norms and preventing tyranny and oppression from gaining the upper hand in society. Although he seldom (if ever) couched these goals in the explicit language of social justice, it is clear that his "applied" research programs on overcoming certain forms of prejudice, outgroup hostility, and self-hatred among Jews—to mention some of the most salient examples—reflected a commitment to social justice as well as a scathing critique of authoritarianism and the fascist ideology that had seized the hearts and minds of so many of his fellow citizens in 1930s Germany. Lewin self-consciously strove to integrate theoretical and applied goals, which he believed could be "accomplished in psychology, as it has been accomplished in physics, if the theorist does not look toward applied problems with high-brow aversion or with a fear of social problems" (Lewin, 1944/1951, p. 169). It is not surprising that one of Lewin's doctoral students, Morton Deutsch, went on to become one of the most illustrious contributors to the field of social justice research (see Deutsch, 1999).

Another prominent social psychologist of the postwar era, Gordon Allport, observed that, "Practical and humanitarian motives have always played an important part in the development of social psychology" (1962, p. 2). Specifically, he wrote that:

> Social psychology began to flourish soon after the First World War. This event, followed by the spread of communism, by the great depression of the '30s, by the rise of Hitler, the genocide of the Jews, race riots, the Second World War and its consequent anomie, stimulated all branches of social science. A special challenge fell to social psychology. The question was asked: how is it possible to preserve the values of freedom and individual rights under conditions of mounting social strain and regimentation? Can science help provide an answer? (p. 4)

Allport's own work on *The Nature of Prejudice* (1954) as well as a predecessor, *The Authoritarian Personality* by Adorno, Frenkel-Brunswik, Levinson, and Sanford (1950), sought to employ theories and methods in social psychology to diagnose and ultimately defeat prejudice, intolerance, and other apparent obstacles to social justice. It has been suggested darkly on more than one occasion that the individual who exerted the strongest influence over the development of social psychology in the 20th century was Adolf Hitler (e.g., Cartwright, 1979; Jones, 1985/1998).

World War II illustrated far too vividly both the devastating effects of social injustice and the human capacity to overcome it. In its aftermath, issues of social justice were central to social psychological theory and research. Textbooks routinely covered themes such as morality, conscience, crime and punishment, prejudice, authoritarianism, propaganda, war and peace, and the determinants of revolution (e.g., Brown, 1965; Doob, 1952; Klineberg, 1940; Krech & Crutchfield, 1948). However, as was the case with Lewin's writings, such themes were often approached in the absence of an explicit social justice framework, and terms such as "justice" and "fairness" were not necessarily used to illuminate them. As we shall see, it was not until decades later that social justice research became a subfield or area of specialization within social psychology. Before then, considerations of social justice seemed to permeate the field as a whole, albeit tacitly. None of the first three editions of *The Handbook of Social Psychology* contained a chapter devoted to studies of social justice *per se* (Miller, 2001, p. 528), but several chapters covered pertinent subjects, such as prejudice and ethnic relations, leadership, social structure, political behavior, international relations, collective action, and social movements.

Social psychological research on theories of justice (especially equity theory) began to flourish in the 1960s, but the demarcation of social justice research as a specific subfield came years later. For instance, *Social Justice Research* (a specialized interdisciplinary journal) was first published in 1987 under the editorship of Melvin Lerner, and the International Society for Justice Research (ISJR), whose members constitute the journal's core readership, was not officially created until a decade later. These professional developments have allowed researchers to delve more deeply into questions that are unique to justice-related theories and findings, but they also reflected (and may have even contributed to) some degree of separation (and, therefore, marginalization) of social justice research within the larger discipline of social psychology. By the mid-1960s, some social psychologists had already begun to have sober second thoughts about Lewin's vision of humanistic, action-oriented research aimed at human betterment and social justice (Ring, 1967). McGuire (1965), for instance, admonished his more "applied" colleagues for being "too preoccupied with the Berlin wall, the urban blight, the population bomb, and the plight of the Negro in the South" and quipped that students who wished to solve social problems should consider joining "the law or the ministry" (pp. 138–139).

In retrospect, social psychologists' commitment to social justice research in the middle of the 20th century may be attributable, at least in part, to the societal urgency that accompanied the need to defeat fascism in Europe and elsewhere (e.g., see Lewin, 1939/1948a). But, one might ask, do we not face urgent problems related to social justice even today? What, if anything, should be done about yawning economic inequality under capitalism; racial disparities in criminal sentencing, including the imposition of the death penalty; gender disparities in hiring, salary, and promotion at work; the persistence of prejudice; religious, ethnic, and other forms of violent conflict, including war, terrorism, and torture; and the problems posed by global climate change, environmental degradation, and species extinction? One need not be a doomsday prophet to suspect that the continued survival of the human race depends ultimately on its capacity to see past purely selfish, parochial sources of motivation and to embrace what social psychologists refer to as "the justice motive."

The Justice Motive in Human Behavior

Solomon Asch (1959) insisted that social psychologists study not only the perpetration of injustice but also "the vectors that make it possible for persons to think and care and work for others" (p. 372). More specifically, he wrote that: "It is of considerable consequence for any social psychology to establish the grounds of concern for the welfare of other persons or groups, and how these are related to the concern individuals feel for their own welfare" (p. 368). Such comments presage research programs on "altruism" (Krebs & Miller, 1985), prosocial behavior (Batson, 1998), and the

so-called "justice motive," that is, the extent to which people are motivated to promote fair treatment of others and not merely by considerations of self-interest (Lerner, 1977, 1980, 2003; Miller, 1977; Montada, 2002; Tyler, 1994; see also Tyler & Smith, 1998). The point is not that justice and self-interest are *always* opposed—plainly, they are not. In fact, the sense of justice may originate in humans and other primates in the self-protective desire to insure that they receive what they "deserve" (Brosnan, 2006; Brosnan & DeWaal, 2003). When members of disadvantaged groups band together to push for civil rights or other improvements in their quality of life, they are fighting on behalf of social justice *as well as* personal and collective self-interest (e.g., Piven & Cloward, 1978). Nevertheless, the purest evidence of a "justice motive" in human beings comes from cases in which people are willing to risk or sacrifice their own welfare to insure that *others* are treated fairly (e.g., Lerner, 2003; Monroe, 2004).

Rational Choice Theory and Its Discontents

Truly selfless behavior appears to violate both the normative and descriptive assumptions of rational choice theory, according to which individuals should (and at least sometimes do) act on the basis of self-interested preferences to maximize benefits and minimize costs (e.g., Becker, 1976; Kreps, 1990). It is generally assumed that in economic markets and other forms of social exchange, those preferences and behaviors that maximize individual welfare will predominate (e.g., Axelrod, 2006). As a result, rationally self-interested behavior should be more readily observable than other forms of behavior that do not, on average, offer equivalent benefits. Some rational choice theorists acknowledge that certain constraints (such as limits on the availability of information or material resources) can lead to nonrational behavior, but as a general rule this per-spective leaves relatively little room for any significant drivers of behavior other than self-interest. For this reason, rational choice theory has been widely criticized by psychologists and other social and behavioral scientists for being unrealistic—that is, descriptively inaccurate (e.g., see Green & Shapiro, 1994; Kahneman, Slovic, & Tversky, 1982; Nisbett & Ross, 1980).

One major line of attack emerged from work on "bounded rationality" (Simon, 1957) and shortcomings in human judgment and decision making (Kahneman et al., 1982). Both contributions suggested that the limited cognitive capacities of human beings insure major departures from normative standards of rationality. It has been less common to critique rational choice theory from a *motivational* perspective, but decades of research in social psychology have demonstrated that the motivational systems underlying human behavior are considerably more complex than is suggested by the rational choice model (see Fiske, 2004; Higgins & Kruglanski, 2000; Shah & Gardner, 2008). If Lerner (2003) is correct that humans—and perhaps other species as well (Brosnan, 2006; Brosnan & DeWaal, 2003)—possess a "justice motive," then it is sure to conflict with the unadulterated pursuit of rational self-interest on at least some occasions (e.g., Güth, Schmittberger, & Schwarze, 1982; Kahneman, Knetsch, & Thaler, 1986; Rabin, 1993). Or, to put the same point differently, the attainment of social justice is constrained by the extent to which individuals behave exclusively according to the principles of rational choice theory, insofar as social justice requires individuals to act on the basis of principles that sometimes conflict with the maximization of self-interest.

Similar questions concerning the relative importance of selfish versus prosocial motivations (including motivations for justice) have cropped up in evolutionary biology from time to time. Some, including Darwin (1871), suggest that evolutionary mechanisms are unlikely to privilege any traits that are not fundamentally selfish:

> It is extremely doubtful whether the offspring of the more sympathetic and benevolent parents, or those who were most faithful to their comrades, would be reared in greater number than the children of selfish and treacherous parents belonging to the same tribe. He who was ready to sacrifice his life . . . rather than betray his comrades, would often leave no offspring to inherit his noble nature. (Darwin, 1871, p. 475)

Several prominent evolutionary theorists have echoed the notion that evolution favors selfish over prosocial (or "altruistic") behaviors (e.g., Dawkins, 1989). The basic logic underlying such approaches is that any genes that fail to promote their own replication (at a significantly greater rate than they promote the replication of others' genes) will not survive for long.

Crucially, however, the alleged "selfishness" of genes does not necessarily translate into selfishness at the level of individual (or collective) behavior (e.g., Crespi, 2000; Krebs, 2008). It is possible that prosocial behaviors that evolved primarily to ensure the survival of genetic relatives facilitate the helping of other, nonkin individuals (Park, Schaller, & Van Vugt, 2008). Models of cultural evolution, according to which specific behavioral characteristics can be transmitted by social learning, can also explain the propagation of traits that are other- (rather than self-) regarding (Fehr & Fischbacher, 2003). For these reasons and others, there is no reason to assume that prosocial behavior is inconsistent with fitness or survival (especially in the span of a single lifetime), regardless of whether it is at odds with economic perspectives on human rationality. Although it is beyond the scope of this chapter, empirical research suggests that evolutionary processes did produce justice-oriented behavior in marmosets, Capuchin monkeys, and other nonhuman primates (see Brosnan, 2006; Brosnan & DeWaal, 2003; Burkart, Fehr, Efferson, & van Schaik, 2007).

The Altruism Debate

Quite apart from considerations of gene replication, social psychologists have debated the role of self-interest in supporting versus undermining prosocial behavior. The question, kicked around in many a dorm room over the years, is whether *bona fide* altruism really exists or whether helping behavior is always motivated by some form of egoism. Batson and Shaw (1991) characterize the dispute as follows:

> Advocates of universal egoism claim that everything we do, no matter how noble and beneficial to others, is really directed toward the ultimate goal of self-benefit. Advocates of altruism do not deny that the motivation for much of what we do, including much that we do for others, is egoistic. But they claim that there is more. They claim that at least some of us, to some degree, under some circumstances, are capable of a qualitatively different form of motivation, motivation with an ultimate goal of benefiting someone else. (p. 107)

In support of the latter conclusion, Batson and colleagues have offered into evidence a large number of studies addressing the "empathy–altruism hypothesis" (e.g., Batson, 1990; Batson et al., 1991; Batson & Shaw, 1991). They suggest that witnessing the distress of others instigates empathic emotions (such as compassion and tenderness) that facilitate perspective-taking and the setting of helping goals. Although helping behavior brings certain rewards—including the reduction of guilt and other negative emotions—one cannot conclude that the helper was *motivated* by those rewards. Thus, Batson (1990) sought to determine whether "the empathically aroused helper (a) benefits the other as an instrumental goal on the way to reaching some self-benefit as an ultimate goal (egoism) or (b) benefits the other as an ultimate goal, with any resulting self-benefits being unintended consequences (altruism)" (p. 340). Although it is not possible to review the specific details of individual studies here, Batson and colleagues (1991) have made a reasonably strong case for the existence of altruistic motivation.

This is not to say that their position is bereft of detractors. Most notably, Cialdini and his coauthors have argued that altruistic behavior, even when triggered by empathic emotions, is never truly selfless. Rather, they propose that the circumstances giving rise to empathic concern also elicit other feelings, such as sadness (Cialdini et al., 1987; Maner, Luce, Neuberg, Cialdini, Brown, & Sagarin, 2002; Schaller & Cialdini, 1988) and perceptions of "oneness" or "self-other overlap" (Cialdini, Brown, Lewis, Luce, & Neuberg, 1997; Maner et al., 2002; Neuberg et al., 1997), and that these are capable of generating seemingly selfless behaviors. From the standpoint of social justice, it may not matter greatly whether the motivation to help others (and to sustain sacrifices in doing so) stems from purely altruistic desires or from the so-called "moral emotions" or processes of social identification. The important point is that human beings do appear to be capable of setting aside narrow self-interest to make the world a "better" (i.e., putatively more just) place. The specific nature of these justice-related concerns is the subject of the next section.

A TYPOLOGY OF SOCIAL JUSTICE CONCERNS

The earliest theory-driven research in sociology and psychology on the topic of social justice tackled questions of *distributive* fairness, especially considerations of "equity" and relative deprivation in the allocation of resources (e.g., Adams, 1965; Crosby, 1976; Lerner, 1974; Walster, Walster, & Berscheid, 1978). Next came work on *procedural* justice, which addressed not only outcomes but the decision-making rules used to determine those outcomes (Folger, 1977; Leventhal, 1980; Lind & Tyler, 1988; Thibaut & Walker, 1975). Soon thereafter, a third type of justice was investigated—namely, *interpersonal* (or interactional) justice—to incorporate concerns about informal as well as formal treatment by others in everyday life (Bies & Moag, 1986; Colquitt, 2001; Greenberg, 1993). Finally, although Aristotle anticipated not only distributive but also *retributive* and *restorative* justice concerns nearly 24 centuries ago, empirical studies addressing these latter concerns have only recently become a cottage industry in social psychology and neighboring disciplines (Braithwaite, 1989; Carlsmith, Darley, & Robinson, 2002; Vidmar, 2002). We do our best to summarize theoretical and empirical progress on the social psychological understanding of each of these five types of social justice concerns, with an advance apology to our readers for the necessarily selective nature of our review.

Distributive Justice

Aristotle and the History of the Concept

One of the earliest influential accounts of distributive justice—that is, the issue of how to allocate scarce resources fairly and appropriately—was Aristotle's. In Book V of the *Nicomachean Ethics*, Aristotle (ca. 322 BCE) observes that "we call just the things that create and preserve happiness and its parts for the citizen community"

(2002, p. 159) and inquires about different types of justice and ways of being just (or unjust). According to one prominent interpretation, for Aristotle:

> The hallmark of a just apportionment is *equality*. In distribution, this consists in maintaining the same ratio of quantified goods or burdens to quantified merit for all recipients. In rectification, it consists in restoring the parties to the relative position (schematized as "equality") they were in before one harmed the other. (Broadie, 2002, p. 36)

Interpretational ambiguity arises from the fact that in Attic Greek the same word (*isotes*) is typically used to mean both *justice* and *equality*; the word is best translated as "geometrical equality" or "proportionality" (Vlastos, 1962/1997). Thus, Aristotle says that a just distribution is one that is impartial in the sense of "treating equals as equals" (see also Feinberg, 1973; Frankena, 1962; Mansbridge, 2005), but his conception of distributive justice emphasizes what social scientists today would call principles of equity, proportionality, or merit (Deutsch, 1975; Lerner, 1974; Walster, Walster, & Berscheid, 1978).

Aristotle appreciated one of the chief difficulties of justice theories based exclusively on equity or proportionality principles—namely, that decision makers disagree about which "inputs" (or merits) should be utilized in determining proportional outcomes (or rewards):

> The matter of distribution "according to merit" also makes this clear, since everybody agrees that what is just in distributions must accord with some kind of merit, but everybody is not talking about the same kind of merit: for democrats merit lies in being born a free person, for oligarchs in wealth or, for some of them, in noble descent, for aristocrats in excellence. (2002, p. 162, lines 1131a24–29)

Indeed, the notion that political or ideological factors influence one's conception of social justice is a central theme of this chapter, and we will return to it in our review of the research literature.

A few other aspects of Aristotle's theory of justice deserve mention, insofar as they, too, anticipate important social scientific contributions and controversies. For one thing, Aristotle addresses the relationship between what is *legal* and what is *just*, and he clearly sees a close relationship between them. He writes, for instance, that

> People regard as "unjust" both the person who breaks the law and the grasping (i.e., unequal-minded) one; hence, clearly, both the law-abiding person and the equal-minded one are just. In that case, the just is what is lawful and what is equal, while the unjust is what is unlawful and what is unequal. (p. 159)

Aristotle's discussion of the individual who is "grasping" or "unequal-minded" (*pleonexia:* the tendency to "get more for oneself"; Broadie, 2002, p. 36) presages research on dispositional or individual differences in selfishness (i.e., a "proself" orientation in the language of De Cremer & Van Vugt, 1999) and its consequences for justice-related outcomes. Aristotle also observes that, "The worst sort of person . . . is the one whose badness extends even to his treatment of himself and of those close to him, but the best sort is not the one whose excellence extends to his treatment of himself, but to his treatment of another; for it is this that is a difficult task" (2002, p. 160). This discussion foreshadows the social psychological distinction between "justice for oneself" and "justice for the other" (e.g., Gollwitzer, Schmitt, Schalke, Maes, & Baer, 2005; Sutton et al., 2008), as well as Lerner's (2003) more general thesis that, in its purest form, justice motivation opposes self-interest.

Although Aristotle equated justice with acting in an egalitarian (non-selfish), law-abiding manner, he recognized that the degree of impartiality (or perhaps universality) required by the law can lead to perverse outcomes if one ignores the particulars of a given case or situation. He argues that a *reasonable* person may (on occasion) depart from adhering to what is legal (and therefore what is just) to arrive at a superior outcome (or decree):

> It is clear, then, what the reasonable is; and that it is just, and better than just in one sense. From this it is also evident who the reasonable person is: the sort who decides on and does things of this kind, and who is not a stickler for justice in the bad sense but rather tends to take a less strict view of things, even though he has the law to back him up—this is the reasonable person. (2002, p. 175, lines 1137b33–1138a3)

Thus, justice may be the "mightiest of the excellences" (p. 160, lines 1129b27-8), but it is not the only excellence (see also Rawls, 1971). Courage, wisdom, and self-control were also cardinal virtues, along with justice (Adelson, 1995). John Stuart Mill (1869) likewise distinguished between justice and other moral principles, such as generosity and beneficence (see Frankena, 1962). Finally, it should be noted that Aristotle recognized the need for retributive (or rectificatory) justice, but by aligning his conception of justice with what is "law-abiding," he ruled out the possibility that certain acts of vengeance (or "vigilante justice") could be considered *just*, even if they are seemingly motivated by a desire for justice.

Marxian Tradition

The writings of Karl Marx have probably inspired more social justice movements than any other piece of literature, with the possible exceptions of religious texts (see Adelson, 1995; Solomon & Murphy, 2000). It is ironic, then, that Marx himself was notoriously suspicious about the meaning and use of the term "justice," which (having studied law) he equated with the concept of jurisprudence. Marx saw justice as an inherently bourgeois concern akin to *noblesse oblige*, and he expressed disdain for the "vulgar socialists" of his era who, in his view, championed empty slogans such as "a fair day's wages for a fair day's work." He was also skeptical about philosophical attempts to develop abstract or universal conceptions of justice that would transcend specific social and historical circumstances, such as those proffered by Kant or Hegel (see L. J. Jost & J. T. Jost, 2007). Thus, most scholars agree that Marx generally eschewed justice-based arguments in making the case for revolution and the overthrow of the capitalist system (see Tucker, 1969; Wood, 1972/1980). Instead, Marx appealed to collective self-interest, as in the famous line from *The Communist Manifesto*: "Workers of the world unite; you have nothing to lose but your chains!" That is, he saw it as obviously in the objective interests of the working class to overthrow the capitalist system, and he assumed that their material life circumstances would (eventually) lead them to this realization.

Even if Marx himself saw little revolutionary potential in appeals to social justice, many of his followers have discerned in his writings the seeds of a powerful justice-based critique of capitalism (e.g., Campbell, 2001; Husami, 1978/1980). For instance, Marx argued that capitalism depends for its very existence on "surplus value" being created through the labor process. The basic idea is that no worker is ever paid what his or her work is actually worth (to the employer; that is, the *value* of what is produced); otherwise, there would be no profit (or profit motive). But the worker who wants to survive and provide for his or her family has no real choice in a capitalist society but to produce wealth for those capitalists who happen to control the means of production. Marx clearly denounced this situation as a form of "exploitation," and it is one of the reasons that he predicted (and longed for) the transition from capitalism to socialism and communism, which he believed would finally put an end to class-based oppression. Thus, Marx objected to the stark economic inequality between social classes that characterizes the capitalist mode of production on grounds that are basically indistinguishable from considerations of social justice (see also Campbell, 2001; Husami, 1978/1980; Konow, 2003). At the same time, he worried that certain conceptions of justice would be used to provide ideological cover for the status quo.

There is also Marx's normative claim, in his *Critique of the Gotha Program*, that under socialism, the appropriate principle of distribution should be "from each according to their ability, to each according to their needs" (see Miller, 1999). As Lerner (1974) and Deutsch (1975) point out, taking into account the *needs* of individuals is a principle of distributive justice that is not necessarily incorporated in other theories of social justice, including Aristotle's. But "need considerations are more than a reaction to actual deficiencies of resources" (Schwinger, 1986, p. 223), and they function much like other distributive justice principles, especially in relationships built on trust. Similarly, value is often attached to the principle of *equality of outcomes* (as well as opportunities) across individuals and social classes, and many interpret Marx's demand for a "classless society" as a call for thoroughgoing egalitarianism with respect to distributive outcomes (e.g., see Campbell, 2001).

It is possible that as a practical matter Marx's condemnation of "utopian socialists" led him to underestimate the extent to which perceptions of social injustice based on principles of equality or need (and the accompanying sense of moral outrage that accompanies them) contain revolutionary potential. Research throughout the social and behavioral sciences reveals that *anger* in response to felt injustice—that is, *moral outrage*—is one of the most robust predictors of participation in collective action and motivation for social change (e.g., Gurr, 1970; Martin, Scully, & Levitt, 1990; Montada & Schneider, 1989; Moore, 1978; Tyler & Smith, 1998; Van Zomeren, Postmes, & Spears, 2008; Wakslak, Jost, Tyler, & Chen, 2007). Although Marx himself was deeply angered by the exploitation of workers in capitalist society, he sought to develop a dispassionate historical analysis and therefore said much less about social justice than he might otherwise have done.

Liberal-Progressive Tradition

Due in part to Marx's skepticism, the concept of "'social justice' was more readily embraced by liberals and progressives than by socialists proper," (Miller, 1999, p. 3). There are two major Western liberal traditions that are most responsible for scholarly and practical interest in questions of social justice. Sandel (1998) sums up these traditions succinctly in posing the following question: "Should justice be founded on utility, as Jeremy Bentham and John Stuart Mill argue, or does respect for individual rights require a basis for justice independent of utilitarian considerations, as Kant and Rawls maintain?" (p. 184). These two possibilities are generally referred to as the *utilitarian* and *deontological* perspectives, respectively, and each is considered in turn.

Utilitarianism   Utilitarianism is a *consequentialist* theory of justice, insofar as it assumes that the most just outcome or procedure is whatever results in the "greatest happiness of the greatest number." Of course, utilitarian philosophers disagree about how to gauge "happiness" and related constructs, such as "well-being," "public interest," and "general good" (see Bowie & Simon, 2007). Nevertheless,

support for the welfare state, which redistributes wealth and other valued resources in such a way as to reduce the misery of those who are worst off without extracting an equivalent amount of suffering from those who are better off, is justified or—in the language of Frankena (1962) and Feinberg (1973)—"justicized", that is, shown to be just, on largely *utilitarian* grounds (e.g., Campbell, 2001; Konow, 2003; Sen, 1979).

Although philosophical utilitarianism is quite clearly a normative theory about how people *ought* to behave, descriptive research in psychology suggests that in many situations people are indeed highly sensitive to the perceived *consequences* of an action (e.g., the degree of harm that results from it) when evaluating its moral soundness (e.g., Cushman, Young, & Hauser, 2006; Haidt & Graham, 2007; Kohlberg, 1978). In a series of experiments involving the well-known "trolley problem," which requires decision-makers to make hypothetical but morally troubling life-and-death decisions about appropriate and inappropriate ways of minimizing harm to innocent bystanders, research participants do make cost–benefit calculations and favor utilitarian solutions (e.g., taking action so that one bystander is killed while five others are spared)—as long as the emotional salience of the costs is relatively low for either situational or dispositional reasons (Greene, Sommerville, Nystrom, Darley, & Cohen, 2001; Koenigs, et al., 2007). Interestingly, cognitive load manipulations interfere with the type of moral reasoning that gives rise to utilitarian solutions (Greene, Morelli, Lowenberg, Nystrom, & Cohen, 2008). When emotional processing predominates, people look much more like "deontological" theorists adhering to moral absolutes than utilitarians making complex calculations (see also Baron, 1993).

Deontological Approaches   Deontologists hold that determinations of right and wrong depend not only on the consequences of human action but also on other considerations, including transcendent justice principles, such as the assumption that it is wrong to kill an innocent, healthy person under *any* circumstances. One of the most famous proponents of a deontological approach to justice, Immanuel Kant (1785/1993), proposed that a "categorical imperative" exists to "[a]ct only according to that maxim whereby you can at the same time will that it should become a universal law" (p. 30). In other words, justice requires us to do only those things that it would make rational sense to universalize. Lying to gain personal advantage, for instance, would violate the categorical imperative, because if everyone lied for personal gain it would be impossible to maintain trust and cooperation in society. Although some reject the notion that universal principles of justice could work in highly dissimilar cultures and societies, others find promise in the Kantian aspiration to develop an objective conception of justice—as embodied, for instance, in the work of John Rawls.

Rawls (1971) famously proposed that the most just social system is the one that would be chosen by rational decision makers under a "veil of ignorance," that is, in the absence of any specific knowledge of their own status or position within the adopted system. Drawing in part on psychological theory and research, including the work of Piaget (1932/1965) and Kohlberg (1969), Rawls concluded that under these circumstances rational individuals *ought* to (and in fact would) select a system that would, *ceteris paribus*: (a) minimize the degree of inequality in social and economic outcomes, and (b) maximize the outcomes of those who would occupy the worst position in the system. Taken together, these principles imply that *some degree of inequality in society is tolerable, but only to the extent that it benefits even those who are relatively disadvantaged*, for example, by creating enough wealth that everyone truly benefits. Rawls' work constitutes, among other things, a normative theory of justice that is meant to be "consistent with the laws of psychology," and, ultimately, a complex philosophical defense of political liberalism in the Kantian tradition of developing and enforcing a rational "social contract," that is, the consent of the individual to participate in society (see also Rawls, 1993).

Empirical studies cannot determine what Rawls' hypothetical decision makers would or should choose under the constraints he envisioned. This is because, as a practical matter, it is *impossible* to divorce actual decision makers from their own personal characteristics, experiences, beliefs, and opinions. Some philosophers have suggested that this impossibility represents a fatal flaw in Rawls' theory (rendering it, if not incoherent, useless for determining what justice principles *real* people would or should prefer). Nonetheless, the purpose of the "veil of ignorance" was to imagine the possibility of developing an objective conception of social justice by insuring decision-making *impartiality* and eliminating all potential sources of bias. Empirical studies can address the question of what distributive justice principles people generally prefer when personal sources of bias are at least muted (though not entirely removed).

The research literature provides mixed evidence for the notion that actual decision makers would favor Rawls' justice principles over attractive alternatives, such as sheer wealth maximization. In some studies, research participants who lack information that would enable them to act on the basis of self-interested motives do indeed evaluate the fairness of various distributional schemes in ways that are at least somewhat similar to how Rawls theorized they *should* behave (Bond & Park, 1991; Brickman, 1977;

Michelbach, Scott, Matland, & Bornstein, 2003; Schulz & May, 1989). For instance, Mitchell, Tetlock, Mellers, and Ordóñez (1993) found that most people sought to maximize the minimum standard of living in their society. However, there are studies showing clear departures from what Rawls would have expected (e.g., Curtis, 1979). Most damningly, a research program summarized by Frohlich and Oppenheimer (1992) revealed that most of the participants in their experiments, which were conducted in the United States, Canada, and Poland, opted for a "floor constraint" (some safety net) but without any "ceiling" (i.e., limitation on maximum income). Their preferences, in other words, included social systems that contained more inequality than Rawls' theory would allow. Although this evidence does not disconfirm Rawls' (1971) theory of what is objectively just, it does suggest that actual decision makers find it challenging to leave behind their own personal experiences and cultural baggage in placing themselves behind a "veil of ignorance." The fact that social group and ideological differences are frequently observed in experiments involving "hypothetical societies" suggests that people are anchored to a considerable extent by the economic realities and justice beliefs that operate in their own societies, even when they are explicitly instructed to ignore them (Bond & Park, 1991; Mitchell, Tetlock, Mellers, & Ordóñez, 1993; Mitchell, Tetlock, Newman, & Lerner, 2003; Scott, Matland, Michelbach, & Bornstein, 2001).

Conservative Critique of the Liberal–Socialist Tradition

It should be clear from the foregoing that most philosophical conceptions of social justice, especially those that emphasize egalitarian and welfare (i.e., need-based) principles, were developed by liberals or socialists who were critical of traditional social, economic, or political arrangements (e.g., see Barry, 2005). Miller (1999) notes, for example, that "social justice has always been, and must always be, a critical idea, one that challenges us to reform our institutions and practices in the name of greater fairness" (p. x). This explains why the concept of social justice is sometimes denounced by political conservatives and others on the political right who seek to vindicate existing institutions that they regard as—if not always perfectly just—at least necessary, efficient, or otherwise defensible (e.g., Hayek, 1976).

Historians often trace the origins of modern political conservatism to Edmund Burke, an Irish-born member of Parliament in England who famously opposed the French Revolution and encouraged his fellow citizens to "look backward to [the authority of] their ancestors" rather than turning to revolution (Burke, 1790/1987, p. 30; see also Viereck, 1956; White, 1950). Burke and his followers thus rejected liberal and socialist ideas as well as the broader intellectual context of the Scientific Enlightenment in which those ideas were developed (Jost, 2009), expressing "contempt for all forms of egalitarianism, which struck [Burke] as a doctrine that is profoundly at odds with all the evidence of nature and history" (Shapiro, 2003, p. 152). Burke also emphasized the importance of tradition and favored gradual, incremental reforms over more radical social change, because he believed that "conserving an imperfect inherited world from the worse imperfections that human beings are capable of contriving is the business of political leadership" (p. 152). To this day, political conservatism can be characterized in terms of two major principles, namely traditionalism (or resistance to change) and, relatedly, the justification of inequality or hierarchy (Jost, Glaser, Kruglanski, & Sulloway, 2003).

To the extent that conservatives (and libertarians) have offered new theories of social justice, they have tended not to dismiss principles of need and equality outright but rather to subordinate them (at least on occasion) to other principles, such as merit, prosperity, and personal freedom (e.g., Nozick, 1974; Smith, 1776; Solomon & Murphy, 2000). It has been suggested that conservatives possess unique "moral intuitions" and that they place a higher premium on loyalty to the ingroup, obedience to authority, and attaining purity (Haidt & Graham, 2007). However, the glorification of ingroup, authority, and purity concerns have (in a number of historical cases) been associated with authoritarianism and even genocide (e.g., Altemeyer, 1996; Kelman & Hamilton, 1989; Rummel, 1997; Staub, 1992). This makes them unlikely candidates (on normative grounds) to be considered general moral or justice principles. A stronger case can be made for moderate conservative principles such as desert, merit, prosperity, and personal freedom (e.g., Mitchell et al., 2003; Nozick, 1974; Smith, 1776; Solomon & Murphy, 2000). Some interpret the fact that political orientation is correlated with justice beliefs to mean that disagreements over what is just are ultimately ideological and therefore intractable; others aspire to elevate the terms of debate by bringing scientific evidence to bear on the selection and application of various justice principles in resource allocation.

Social Psychological Theories and Evidence

Equity Theory No theory has been more broadly influential to the empirical study of social justice than the one that arguably came first: equity theory. Aristotle (384–322 BCE) argued that justice requires proportionality, that is, "equality of ratios" (2002, p. 163; line 1131a31). This insight provides the starting point for equity theory, as developed by Homans (1961); Adams (1965); Blau (1968); Walster, Berscheid, & Walster (1973); and Walster, Walster, &

Berscheid (1978). The theory holds that in rendering judgments about distributive justice, people seek to determine whether there is a proportional relationship between their inputs (e.g., degree of effort, ability, time, training, etc.) and the outcomes they receive (e.g., payments and other rewards as well as costs or punishments). To make this determination in practice, people typically draw interpersonal comparisons involving similar or relevant others (e.g., Festinger, 1954) or intrapersonal comparisons based on their own prior experiences and expectations (Adams, 1965).

If an individual concludes that the ratio of inputs to outputs in a given case is disproportionate, psychological distress is theorized to ensue; such distress, in turn, is expected to motivate the individual to restore equity (Walster, Berscheid, & Walster, 1973; but see Greenberg, 1984). An important aspect of equity theory—an aspect that arguably is what makes it a theory of *justice* rather than simply a theory of attribution, social judgment, or preference—is that people are hypothesized to dislike being *over*benefited (i.e., rewarded in a disproportionately *favorable* manner) as well as being underbenefited. However, the latter is especially aversive because it violates both justice and self-interest (Walster, Walster, & Berscheid, 1978; see also Boll, Ferring, & Filipp, 2005; Loewenstein, Thompson, & Bazerman, 1989; Peters, Van den Bos, & Bobocel, 2004). In terms of emotional responses, those who are underbenefited are assumed to feel angry and resentful, whereas those who are overbenefited are assumed to feel guilty (e.g., Hegtvedt, 1990; Homans, 1961/1974; Jost, Wakslak, & Tyler, 2008; Schmitt, Behner, Montada, Müller, & Müller-Fohrbrodt, 2000). Anger, which is an approach-oriented, outward-directed emotion, is generally associated with protest, whereas guilt is not (e.g., Wakslak, Jost, Tyler, & Chen, 2007). According to equity theory, it is distressing to observe inequity in the relationships of others as well as in one's own relationships. There are two ways in which people can cope with aversive reactions engendered by the presence of inequity: (a) they can restore equity in actuality (i.e., objectively), by increasing or decreasing inputs (e.g., by working harder or withholding effort) or outputs (e.g., by giving or taking more or less in terms of benefits or burdens); or (b) they can restore equity *psychologically* (i.e., subjectively), by rationalizing or otherwise reconstruing the nature or relative evaluation of inputs and outputs so as to make the situation or relationship *seem* equitable (Hatfield & Sprecher, 1984).

The evidence has supported the basic tenets of equity theory to an impressive degree (Ambrose & Kulik, 1999; Greenberg, 1993; Mowday, 1991). Consequently, it has influenced several areas of social science, ranging from the study of close relationships (Utne, Hatfield,

Traupmann, & Greenberger, 1984; Van Yperen & Buunk, 1990) to organizational behavior (Ambrose & Kulik, 1999; Bolino & Turney, 2008). Inequity produces physiological arousal (Markowski, 1988), and the desire to establish (or restore) equity appears to be an important factor in children's resource allocations (Leventhal & Anderson, 1970; but see Lerner, 1974). Participants are especially likely to follow the equity norm when distributing rewards between themselves and a competitor in the presence of a mirror, presumably because the mirror increases adherence to salient social norms (Greenberg, 1980). Perceptions of equity are related to perceptions of stability and contentment in new marriages and other close relationships (Utne, Hatfield, Traupmann, & Greenberger, 1984; Van Yperen & Buunk, 1990; but see Montada, 2003; Sprecher & Schwartz, 1994), and perceptions of inequity (i.e., feeling overbenefited) can also help to explain negative reactions that are (ironically) caused by high levels of social support (Gleason, Iida, Bolger, & Shrout, 2003). Perceptions of inequity also explain seemingly anomalous behavior in workplace settings, including employee theft of property belonging to an organization that is seen as underrewarding its employees (Greenberg, 1993). A key contributor to "social loafing" (i.e., the tendency for people to exert less effort in the presence of others) is the assumption by some group members that their co-workers will do less than their share (Jackson & Harking, 1985); this assumption apparently causes people to diminish their own involvement to maintain the balance of equity. In one study, participants who were led to commit a transgression and then forgiven for it were more likely than others to comply with a subsequent request, presumably because "forgiveness . . . represent[s] a type of aid, or gift, that upsets the balance of a relationship" (Kelln & Ellard, 1999, p. 864) and creates a psychological need to reestablish balance (or equity).

Austin and Walster (1974) proposed that, when computing their equity ratios, people do not simply compare themselves with specific referents but also form perceptions of "transrelational" equity or *equity with the world* (EwW), which refers to the overall degree of equity (or inequity) that is present in the totality of a person's relationships. If a person is frequently manipulated or taken advantage of by others (e.g., the proverbial "sucker"), he or she falls well short of maintaining EwW. Similarly, if a person routinely exploits others (e.g., a racketeer, an unethical business person), he or she is generally aware of holding an inequitable position relative to "others in general." People also use stereotypes and social judgments to subjectively establish equity, balance, complementarity, and the "illusion of equality" with respect to the social system as a whole (Kay, Jost, & Young, 2005). Taken in conjunction, this work suggests that people not only monitor the degree of equity that characterizes their own dealings with others but also the degree of equity in society at large.

Criticisms and Limitations Despite the considerable evidence marshaled in support of equity theory, several limitations—both theoretical and empirical—have been noted. For one thing, cultural differences exist in the extent to which people prefer equity over other allocation principles, such as equality (Bolino & Turnley, 2008; Chen, 1995; Fischer & Smith, 2003). Furthermore, the original formulation of the theory does not specify whether people will respond to inequity by actively changing the circumstances to restore equity in objective terms or by engaging in subjective processes of reconstrual. Feelings of power or efficacy may play a large (and, on the basis of equity theory, unanticipated) role in determining which route will be pursued (Cook & Hegtvedt, 1986; Mowday, 1991; Weick, Bougan, & Maruyama, 1976). Those who are especially interested in preserving social harmony tend to restore equity through subjective, rather than objective, means (Bierhoff, Buck, & Klein, 1986).

Equity theory is noticeably silent about the specific social comparison standards (e.g., friends, siblings, coworkers, or bosses) that people invoke in determining whether their ratio of inputs to outputs is equitable. Although the referent may be obvious in the context of a dyadic relationship, it may not be so clear in many other real-world situations. It is assumed that people generally determine whether their rewards are equitable based on comparisons involving their own prior experiences, those of similar others (e.g., coworkers), and those based on system-specific expectations, such as organizational policies or promises (Goodman, 1977). The availability and relevance of specific referents likely dictate which ones are selected (Kulik & Ambrose, 1992; Levine & Moreland, 1987). Choices of referent type should also depend on individual differences in levels of "equity sensitivity" (e.g., Miles, Hatfield, & Huseman, 1994); people are expected to seek out those referents that best allow them to minimize psychological distress (O'Neill & Mone, 1998).

Another oft-cited limitation of equity theory is its apparent insensitivity to procedural justice concerns (e.g., Folger, 1986; Lind & Tyler, 1988; Thibaut & Walker, 1975). For instance, fairness judgments are not driven solely by input–output ratios but are also affected by procedural factors that interact with those ratios. Specifically, people react unfavorably to a state of inequity only if (a) it results from a decision that was made by another person (as opposed to oneself), and (b) they believe that a different decision could have reasonably been made (Cropanzano & Folger, 1989). If a situation of inequity is perceived as occurring because of one's own choices or because of unimpeachable decisions made by others (i.e., decisions made as a result of fair procedures), negative reactions do not generally ensue.

Principles of Equality and Need A number of authors have pointed out that equity is by no means the only appropriate principle of distributive justice (e.g., Clark & Mills, 1979; Deutsch, 1975; Elster, 1992; Feinberg, 1973; Konow, 2003; Jost & Azzi, 1996; Leventhal, 1980; Miller, 1999; Walzer, 1983). They take what is sometimes referred to as a pluralistic or "multidimensional" approach to justice norms (Cohen & Greenberg, 1982; Mikula, 1984; Reis, 1984). Along these lines, Lerner (1974) observed that people's conceptions of justice can take various forms, and that different situations call for different justice principles (see also Lerner & Whitehead, 1980; Törnblom & Foa, 1983). When recipients share a common "identity," as in the case of families, the Marxian principle of allocation based on *need* is much more likely to be adopted than when no such identity or affiliation exists (see also Deutsch, 1975; Lamm & Schwinger, 1980; Lerner, 1974). The idea of dishing out relative dinner portions to one's children on the basis of their report cards (e.g., merit)—regardless of their ages, sizes, or appetites—strikes one as inherently unjust if not downright absurd. Rather, a need-based allocation seems far more appropriate. Similarly, members of close-knit groups may prefer norms of *equality* (or parity) in dispersing benefits and burdens, presumably because of the value placed upon the maintenance of harmonious social relations (Deutsch, 1975; Konow, 2003; Wenzel, 2000).

Of all of the putative justice principles, *equality* has received far and away the most philosophical attention (e.g., Frankena, 1962; Miller, 1999; Nagel, 1991; Pojman & Westmoreland, 1997; Rawls, 1971; Solomon & Murphy, 2000; Vlastos, 1962/1997; Walzer, 1983). Demands for equal rights and equal treatment under the law have been fundamental causes of political revolution and constitution-building in Europe and the Americas since the time of the Enlightenment. Equality is central to the liberal–socialist tradition, and leftists today are distinguished largely by their advocacy for greater social, economic, and political equality (e.g., Nielsen, 1985). Although previous generations of conservatives, including Burke (1790/1987), objected to egalitarianism in various guises, most conservatives today endorse political equality (e.g., one person, one vote) and equality of *opportunity* in education and economic domains. But, as Parfit (1998) notes, to subscribe to egalitarianism as a justice principle also requires being "concerned with people's *being equally well off;*" that is, to believe that, "It is in itself bad if some

people are worse off than others" (p. 3; see also Williams, 1976/2000). Egalitarians assume, in other words, that the "demand for equality is built into the very concept of justice" (Frankena, 1962, p. 20), but they do not necessarily assume that justice always requires perfect equality or that equality is the only relevant principle of social justice. *Arbitrary* inequality, in which goods or access to goods are meted out capriciously, haphazardly, or in direct violation of notions of deservingness, is particularly objectionable to most people, including philosophers (Feinberg, 1973). In other cases, what really bothers egalitarians is not that some have less than others but that some simply do not have enough to meet their basic needs (Frankfurt, 1987). This may explain why principles of equality and need are frequently bundled together in liberal–socialist conceptions of social justice.

When individuals hold conflicting or competing goals, people tend to rely on formal rules—such as those codified by the legal system—to arrive at the fairest allocation of resources (Lerner, 1974). Equity is deemed most fair in situations in which people feel both dependent on and nonequivalent to other social actors, as in marketplace environments (Deutsch, 1975; Lerner, 1974). Thus, the importance of equity considerations (relative to other justice norms) depends upon perceptions of social relations; that is, the ways in which people see themselves as connected to others (or not) when it comes to sharing resources (Clayton & Opotow, 2003; Huo, 2002; Wenzel, 2001, 2002). Often what looks like the application of (or preference for) an equality principle is really the application of an equity principle under circumstances in which "the scrutineer perceived the relevant inputs to be equal" (Reis, 1984, p. 39). This returns us to the Aristotelian injunction to "treat equals as equals" (and to treat unequally those who are unalike in a relevant, that is, nonarbitrary way; Feinberg, 1973, pp. 100–101).

The most popular equity principle in common circulation is the principle of *merit;* that is, the rewarding of individuals on the basis of contributions or entitlements, such as ability, effort, motivation, and achievement (e.g., Frankena, 1962; Hayek, 1976; Nozick, 1974). Justifications for this principle are frequently utilitarian in nature, insofar as they suggest that a meritocratic system creates incentives for productivity that are beneficial to society as a whole. Miller (1999) has suggested that principles of equality and merit are compatible in certain ways and that social justice may require an integration of the two. For one thing, both equality and merit "stand opposed to a distribution of advantages on the basis of luck" (p. 201); this suggests that the extent to which the capitalist system may be considered just by egalitarians and meritarians alike depends upon the extent to which outcomes are *not* attributable to chance (or nepotism or simply being in the right place at the right time). Furthermore, Miller argues, on normative grounds, that the principle of merit should never be used to allocate "those goods and services that people regard as necessities, such as health care" (p. 200). On this point, there is general agreement between subjective and objective conceptions (see also Lupfer, Weeks, Doan, & Houston, 2000). Research participants do feel that different types of resources should be allocated on the basis of different justice principles (Fiske & Tetlock, 1997; Törnblom & Foa, 1983), and that burdens and necessities should be distributed with regard to considerations of need and equality rather than merit (e.g., Gamliel & Peer, 2006; Matania & Yaniv, 2007; but see Törnblom, Mühlhausen, & Jonsson, 1991).

Cooperative Versus Competitive Social Systems
Deutsch (1975) offered an analysis that was highly compatible with that of Lerner (1974) but differed in two significant ways. First, whereas Lerner focused on the forms of distribution that would be seen as most just in various social contexts, Deutsch (building on his earlier work in Lewin's Group Dynamics laboratory) addressed the related but distinct issue of which forms of distribution would be most effective at helping a group to reach a given goal. Second, Deutsch outlined three, rather than four, primary types of distributive justice, dropping the conception of justice as law-abidingness, possibly in recognition of the fact that the "laws of the state . . . may be themselves unjust" (Frankena, 1962, p. 3). Hence, Deutsch's taxonomy is a little less Aristotelian and a little more Marxian. The significance of overarching social systems is emphasized in Deutsch's (1985) "crude law of social relations," by which "the characteristic processes and effects elicited by a given type of social relationship also tend to elicit that type of social relationship" (p. 69); that is, competitively structured social systems beget competitive behavior, and cooperatively structured systems beget cooperation.

According to Deutsch (1975), the equity principle should be emphasized only in those situations in which "economic productivity is a primary goal" (p. 143), insofar as it breeds competition and even conflict as social by-products. By contrast, in the context of social systems that prioritize personal development, communal welfare, and cooperation, the most constructive method of distributing resources is on the basis of need and equality, consistent with Marxian social theory. Failing to consider the needs of its members, Deutsch argued, would "obviously be disruptive of any group that has a primary concern for the development and welfare of its members" (p. 147). Furthermore, if the goal is to maximize the harmoniousness of social relations, equality should be the distributive principle of choice.

According to Deutsch, distributing resources purely based on equity would disrupt the mutual respect required for fostering "enjoyable" social relationships. Deutsch (1985) reviewed several studies contradicting the commonly held notion that distributing rewards (and punishments) on the basis of the equality principle necessarily results in a loss of efficiency or productivity. He found that egalitarianism enhanced cooperation and, therefore, group performance.

Research has generally supported Deutsch's contention that the three principles of equity, equality, and need tend to vary in their applicability, and so are differentially valued as a function of situational and dispositional factors (e.g., Barrett-Howard & Tyler, 1986; Bolino & Turnley, 2008; Clark & Mills, 1979; Deutsch, 1985; Reis, 1984). However, it is not always clear whether this variability in allocation preferences is due to justice-related or instrumental concerns; that is, people might prefer one principle over another for reasons that have little to do with justice (Montada, 2003). People's allocations of resources appear to reflect a *blend* or combination of different justice principles along with considerations of self-interest (e.g., Jost & Azzi, 1996; Konow, 2003; Mikula, 1984), and they may engage in *post hoc* rationalizations of certain distributive principles and outcomes that they would not necessarily choose *ex ante* (Diekmann, Samuels, Ross, & Bazerman, 1997).

Do Liberals and Conservatives Prefer Different Justice Principles?   Given that one of the core ideological differences between political liberals and conservatives concerns the value that is placed on equality of outcomes (e.g., Jost, Glaser, Kruglanski, & Sulloway, 2003), it is not too surprising that justice preferences and judgments covary with political orientation (e.g., Bartels, 2008; Christiansen & Lavine, 1997; Emler, 2002; Furgeson, Babcock, & Shane, 2008; Rossi & Berk, 1997; Skitka & Tetlock, 1993). In so-called "hypothetical society" paradigms, for instance, liberals generally prefer more egalitarian distributions of wealth that also offer protections for those who are in greatest need, whereas conservatives are more likely to prioritize equity, efficiency, and individual merit (Mitchell, Tetlock, Mellers, Ordóñez, 1993; Mitchell, Tetlock, Newman, & Lerner, 2003). These differences in justice preferences are clearly consistent with philosophical differences among socialists, liberals, and conservatives that go back several centuries (Jost, 2009).

Mitchell and colleagues (1993) observed that ideological polarization was greatest for judgments of hypothetical societies containing moderate degrees of meritocracy. Presumably, this is because liberals see the justice glass as half-empty under such circumstances (emphasizing the role of chance), whereas conservatives see it as half-full (emphasizing ability and effort). Napier and Jost (2008a) found that economic inequality is differentially related to self-reported happiness levels for liberals and conservatives. Specifically, increasing economic inequality in U.S. society from 1974 to 2004 (measured in terms of various macro-economic indices) was associated with decreased subjective well-being in general, but liberals were more strongly affected than were conservatives, apparently because the conservative belief that inequality is often legitimate and meritorious provides a kind of "ideological buffer" against the negative hedonic effects of inequality.

Relative Deprivation and Social Comparison   Unlike the preceding accounts, relative deprivation theory does not specify which principles of distributive justice people will prefer under specific circumstances. Rather, it addresses a more general question about the social and psychological processes leading to the appraisal of a given situation as either just or unjust (Davies, 1962; Gurr, 1970). In essence, the theory holds that people will experience moral outrage and engage in collective action aimed at changing an unjust status quo if and only if they perceive themselves to be relatively deprived (Tyler & Smith, 1998). Theories that pivot on the concept of relative deprivation are not theories about how to recognize or implement social justice *per se*; rather they seek to understand when people will and will not perceive social injustice, and the question of whether such perceptions are accurate or inaccurate is largely unaddressed (e.g., see Walker & Smith, 2002). In other words, it is not specified and does not matter—from the perspective of relative deprivation approaches—whether people appeal to equity, equality, or need principles (or no justice principles at all) in formulating and acting upon perceptions of relative deprivation. What matters is simply whether or not they are aggrieved.

Origins of Relative Deprivation Theory   Relative deprivation theory began with a relatively simple empirical observation: when asked about their degree of satisfaction with the promotion system in the U.S. army, soldiers' judgments had little to do with current rank, promotion rates, or their actual likelihood of promotion. Instead, judgments were based largely on where the soldiers felt they stood in comparison with fellow soldiers of similar rank. If they were worse off than the other soldiers around them, they felt deprived (Stouffer, Suchman, DeVinney, Star, & Williams, 1949). Thus, soldiers' feelings of satisfaction (or dissatisfaction) were not due to a careful analysis of the characteristics of the system itself, but rather depended upon *social comparison* processes (Festinger, 1954; see also Brickman, Coates, & Janoff-Bulman, 1978; Olson & Hazlewood, 1986).

This initial observation inspired a slew of kindred theories addressing the phenomenon of relative deprivation

(e.g., Crosby, 1976; Davis, 1959; Gurr, 1970; Pettigrew, 1967; Runciman, 1966). The central insight for theories of social justice is that judgments of fairness and satisfaction (or, conversely, unfairness and dissatisfaction) are often derived not on the basis of some abstract or absolute standard. Rather, they are the result of an inherently comparative process in which one's own situation is contrasted with that of others—or, as with regard to equity comparisons, on the basis of intrapersonal comparisons involving one's own prior states and expectations (e.g., Albert, 1977; Davies, 1962; Guimond & Dambrun, 2002; Zagefka & Brown, 2005).

Davies (1962) proposed an influential theory of revolution in which he argued that social and political unrest is most likely to occur when a prolonged period of improvement in living conditions is followed by a brief but painful period of decline, such that the gap between people's subjectively rising expectations and their objectively worsening circumstances becomes intolerable. This argument sought to reconcile (a) Marx's claim that abject deprivation would lead members of underprivileged groups (such as the working class) to realize that they have "nothing to lose but their chains" and therefore rebel against the status quo, and (b) Tocqueville's historical observation that "the most overwhelming oppression often burst[s] into rebellion against the yoke the moment it begins to grow lighter." Several historical cases—including Dorr's Rebellion of 1842 and the Russian Revolution of 1917—seem to fit Davies' account, which is sometimes referred to as "progressive" relative deprivation theory. Building on this work, Gurr (1970) proposed that a significant gap between people's expectations and their capabilities creates "the necessary precondition for civil strife in any kind." In a series of cross-national studies, he found that both short-term economic deprivation and long-term strains (i.e., discrimination) tend to magnify frustration and the eventual likelihood of political rebellion.

The Distinction Between Individual and Group Deprivation   Runciman's (1966) well-known distinction between egoistic (individual) and fraternal (group) forms of relative deprivation has proven especially useful in social psychological research (e.g., Crosby, 1976; Walker & Smith, 2002). Studies show, for example, that relative deprivation at the group (but not individual) level of analysis is a powerful determinant of prejudice and outgroup hostility (e.g., Dubé & Guimond, 1986; Guimond & Dambrun, 2002; Fiske, 1998; Hafer & Olson, 1993; Pettigrew et al., 2008; Tyler & Smith, 1998; Walker & Pettigrew, 1984). Given the consistency of this result, it seems worthwhile to ask whether the converse—feeling that one's group is relatively *gratified* in comparison with another group—is associated with decreased hostility. Unfortunately, the answer is no; rather, group-based feelings of relative gratification (or perhaps *superiority*) are *also* associated with outgroup hostility (Dambrun, Taylor, McDonald, Crush, & Meot, 2006; Guimond & Dambrun, 2002). Perceptions of relative deprivation (and the anger elicited by such perceptions) may explain action taken by advantaged groups to stop government programs designed to help members of disadvantaged groups (Leach, Iyer, & Pederson, 2007; Pettigrew & Meertens, 1995). When those at the top claim injustice and discrimination from below (e.g., Major et al., 2002), it is difficult to know whether such claims are based sincerely on fairness concerns or are simply strategic ploys to maintain their own advantage, but the difference seems important.

Several studies have investigated the extent to which perceptions of relative deprivation motivate the disadvantaged to improve their own or their group's position—or to participate in collective action more generally (see Walker & Smith, 2002). Group deprivation contributes more strongly than individual deprivation to collective action, possibly because perceptions of group deprivation are more likely to elicit negative, outward-directed emotions, such as anger (Leach, Iyer, & Pedersen, 2007; Walker & Smith, 2002), whereas perceptions of individual deprivation may be associated with more inward-directed emotions, such as depression and anxiety (Hafer & Olson, 2003; Walker & Mann, 1987). Although most studies link group (rather than individual) relative deprivation to participation in collective action (Dion, 1986; Dubé & Guimond, 1986; Guimond & Dubé-Simard, 1983; Kessler & Mummendey, 2001; Walker & Mann, 1987), some evidence suggests that collective action is most likely to result when *both* forms of deprivation are experienced (Foster & Matheson, 1995).

Crosby (1976) originally proposed that five conditions must be met for feelings of individual (or egoistic) relative deprivation to ensue: (1) a person must notice that another possesses more than s/he does, (2) s/he must desire what the other person has, (3) s/he must feel entitled to it for some reason, (4) s/he must think that it can be realistically attained, and (5) s/he must not feel personally responsible for the state of deprivation. Reflecting on the results of survey research, Crosby, Muehrer, and Loewenstein (1986) trimmed the list of preconditions to two—*wanting* something and feeling that one *deserves* it. The other three factors, they concluded, were more distal causes of relative deprivation, and their effects were hypothesized to be mediated by the two more proximal states of wanting and deserving. The extent to which various preconditions are necessary and/or sufficient to engender feelings of relative deprivation is still largely unknown (but see Bernstein & Crosby, 1980; Olson & Hazlewood, 1986; Olson, Roese,

Meen, & Robertson, 1995). Nevertheless, feelings of personal deprivation have been linked to a number of consequential outcomes, including women's dissatisfaction with household divisions of labor (Freudenthaler & Mikula, 1998; but see Biernat & Wortman, 1991); career disengagement (Tougas, Rinfret, Beaton, & de la Sablonnière, 2005); and symptoms of stress among the unemployed (Walker & Mann, 1987).

Criticisms and Limitations   Relative deprivation theorists tend to assume, often tacitly, that members of disadvantaged groups are "revolutionaries-in-waiting," and that they will fight against the status quo as soon as the full and frustrating extent of their deprivation is made obvious through direct social comparison with others (or with what might have been). Members of advantaged groups, too, are hypothesized to feel relatively deprived when actual outcomes fall short of (even lofty, unrealistic) expectations. Thus, Gurr (1970) concluded that, "men are quick to aspire beyond their social means and quick to anger when those means prove inadequate, but slow to accept their limitations" (p. 58). The problem is that too many data sets fail to corroborate these strong claims (e.g., Gurney & Tierney, 1982; McPhail, 1971; Thompson, 1989; see also Kinder & Sears, 1985, pp. 701–702). The perception of relative deprivation *in and of itself* does not seem to be a sufficient cause of anger, protest behavior, or participation in collective action, as Crosby's (1976) original list of preconditions suggested (see also Klandermans, Van der Toorn, & Van Stekelenburg, 2008; Van Zomeren, Postmes, & Spears, 2008).

At the least, people must perceive the status quo as *illegitimate* to challenge it, but perceptions of illegitimacy are highly contingent on ideological and other factors (e.g., see Jost & Major, 2001; Tyler, 2006). As a result, rebellion is much rarer than relative deprivation and related theoretical perspectives would imply (Jost, Banaji, & Nosek, 2004). Contrary to Gurr's (1970) supposition that "men are quick to aspire" beyond their means, social psychological research reveals that "social comparison biases tend to prevent awareness of disadvantage, and attribution biases tend to legitimize disadvantage" (Major, 1994, p. 294; see also Crocker & Major, 1989; Jost, 1997). Thus, despite the fact that women are dramatically underpaid compared with men and suffer various other forms of discrimination, women generally show little discontent or resentment concerning their payment and employment status (Crosby, 1982) and no overall deficit in terms of satisfaction when compared with men (Diener, 1984; but see Fujita, Diener, & Sandvik, 1991).

It is telling that Pettigrew (2002) ultimately regarded the relative deprivation perspective "not [as] a fully developed theory itself," but rather "a key construct that can link different levels of analysis" (p. 353). Neither Stouffer and colleagues (1949) nor their many accomplished successors—including Davis (1959), Davies (1962), Runciman (1966), Pettigrew (1967), Gurr (1970), and Crosby (1976)—were able to specify the precise circumstances under which drawing upward social comparisons would consistently lead the disadvantaged to participate in collective action aimed at social change. As Kinder and Sears (1985) noted: "the deepest puzzle here is not occasional protest but pervasive tranquility—why, in Moore's (1978) words 'people so often put up with being the victims of their societies'" (p. 702). Collective action does not result simply from the perception that one's aspirations have been violated; rather, collective action most likely requires the dynamic interplay of a complicated set of social, psychological, and political variables.

Belief in a Just World   In seeking to establish a theoretical foundation in developmental psychology for his theory of the justice motive and belief in a just world, Lerner (1975) proposed that:

> "[T]he child (in order to gain better, more secure outcomes) develops a *personal contract* with the self. The terms of this contract are simply that he/she is willing to do certain things, give up certain things, on the assumption that a particular desired outcome will ensue. The child designs the child's goal-seeking, the adult patterns his/her life around this personal contract, mainly because it is to the person's benefit to develop the psychology of entitlement. People want to deserve their outcomes, get what they are entitled to receive. The concern with one's own deserving, or personal contract, gets linked to the commitment to justice—to an insistence that others get what *they* deserve—in various ways. . . . This psychology of entitlement provides the inevitable basis of the concern with justice for others." (p. 13)

On this view, human beings want adamantly to believe that their efforts and investments will be reciprocated; that is, that they will be rewarded for delaying personal gratification and participating in civilized society (Lerner, 1975, 1980). A natural extension of this "personal contract" is the motivated belief that people's outcomes (i.e., rewards or punishments) are caused by "who they are or what they have done" (Lerner, 1987, p. 108). According to Lerner (1980), people cling so strongly to this "fundamental delusion" that any information contradicting it—such as children suffering from terminal illness or innocent persons being victimized—causes psychological distress. To cope with distress, people convince themselves that the social world operates according to rules of *deservingness*, namely that people "get what they deserve and deserve what they get." The desire (or motive) to attain justice—both for oneself and for others—is thus

linked to the human need to commit to long-term goal pursuit (Hafer, Bègue, Choma, & Dempsey, 2005; Lerner, 1977, 1980; Lerner, Miller, & Holmes, 1976).

More than 40 years of empirical research has supported specific hypotheses derived from just world theorizing (Furnham, 2003; Hafer & Bègue, 2005; Lerner, 1980; Lerner & Miller, 1978). Much of this work has addressed psychological processes associated with victim derogation (see also Napier, Mandisodza, Andersen, & Jost, 2006; Ryan, 1971). For instance, research participants who learn about a woman's suffering and are denied the opportunity to help her directly are more likely to defame her character than are participants who are able to compensate her in some way (Lerner & Simmons, 1966). Studies of this type suggest that people are generally threatened by the presence of injustice and are therefore motivated to restore justice (i.e., through reparations); however, if they are prevented from doing so, they will engage in mental gymnastics (such as rationalization) to deny or minimize the unjust event (e.g., Reichle & Schmitt, 2002). Research reveals that (when opportunities to help are blocked) many people derogate those who are impoverished, unlucky, and unemployed; those who are sick with cancer, pneumonia, and HIV; and victims of sexual assault, spousal abuse, and electric shock (Hafer & Bègue, 2005). The desire to maintain the belief in a just world apparently even leads people to derogate themselves for their own misfortune (Olson & Hafer, 2001). It also encourages them to lionize those who are the beneficiaries of luck and good fortune, including those who are powerful and/or physically attractive (Callan, Powell, & Ellard, 2007; Dion & Dion, 1987; Ellard & Bates, 1990; Kay, Jost, & Young, 2005).

Experimental research on the belief in a just world has focused on victim-blaming as the most common behavioral outcome (Hafer & Bègue, 2005), possibly because it seems so paradoxical that the desire for *justice* would lead people to treat others so unjustly. Relatively little has been done to experimentally test other theoretical assumptions of the original theory, to pinpoint the psychological mechanisms involved, or to explore other possible means of satisfying the justice motive. But, there are exceptions to this generalization, including the demonstration that *denial*, *avoidance*, and *distancing* are effective means of coping with the threat posed by innocent victims (Drout & Gaertner, 1994; Hafer, 2000a, 2000b; Pancer, 1988). Exposure to *complementary* stereotypes in which an "illusion of equality" is created by ascribing positive, redeeming characteristics to members of disadvantaged groups and negative, offsetting characteristics to members of advantaged groups also helps to sustain the belief that societal arrangements are just (Jost & Kay, 2005; Kay & Jost, 2003; Kay, Jost, et al., 2007; see also Gaucher, Hafer, Kay, & Davidenko, in press).

To maintain the belief in a just world, people may reconstruct (or selectively recall) details of the past, such as misremembering that a smaller lottery prize was awarded to a "bad" person than was actually the case (Callan, Kay, Davidenko, & Ellard, in press; Haines & Jost, 2000). Reaction-time paradigms reveal that exposure to information that threatens (vs. satisfies) the belief in a just world (e.g., a criminal "getting away with it" vs. being apprehended) produces an automatic preoccupation with justice-related constructs (Hafer, 2000a; Kay & Jost, 2003). Knowledge of a victim's innocence (Correia, Vala, & Aguiar, 2007), prolonged suffering (Callan, Ellard, & Nicol, 2006), or status as an ingroup member (Aguiar, Vala, Correia, & Pereira, 2008) exacerbates justice concerns at an implicit as well as explicit level of awareness. Dalbert's (1998, 2001, 2002) work suggests that the belief in a just world serves an additional function that was not outlined in Lerner's original formulation of just world theory; specifically, it operates as a personal resource that helps people cope with unjust events that occur in their daily lives (see also Lipkus & Bissonnete, 1996; Lipkus, Dalbert, & Siegler, 1996; Schmitt & Dörfel, 1999; Tomaka & Blascovich, 1994; Vermunt, 2007). This may help to explain its prevalence and even its high degree of social desirability (Alves & Correia, 2008).

Research on dispositional measures of the belief in the just world, which was initiated by Rubin and Peplau (1975) and summarized first by Lerner and Miller (1978), has continued more or less unabated (Furnham, 2003). Some authors have questioned whether measuring the belief in a just world as a relatively stable personality variable (using explicit, self-report techniques) really captures the motivational construct as originally described in just world theorizing (Hafer & Bègue, 2005; Lerner, 1977, 1980), but there is little doubt that the individual differences approach has significantly shaped research agendas.[1] Studies show that those who score highly on the belief in a just world are more likely to engage in victim derogation (*inter alia*, Anderson, 1992; Braman & Lambert, 2001; Carr & MacLachlan, 1998; Crandall & Martinez, 1996; Dalbert, 2002; De Judicibus & McCabe, 2001; Furnham, 1995; Jost & Burgess, 2000; Kristiansen & Giuletti, 1990). Thus,

as with many other variables in social and personality psychology, there are both dispositional and situational sources of variability in the justice motive and the need to believe in a just world.

Deservingness and Entitlement   There may be no single theme more commonly enshrined in Western ideology than that of individual deservingness (Kluegel & Smith, 1986; Wegener & Liebig, 2000). It figures prominently in characterizations of the Protestant work ethic (Jones, 1997; Katz & Hass, 1988; Weber, 1958), culturally prevalent conceptions of personal control and causation (Nisbett & Ross, 1980), the belief in a just world (Lerner, 1980), and various system-justifying belief systems, including meritocratic ideology and faith in the American dream (Jost & Hunyady, 2005; McCoy & Major, 2007). The take-home message from empirical inquiry is that people are far more likely to feel that the existing social, economic, or political system is fair and just to the extent that they see recipients of various distributive outcomes (e.g., wealth and poverty) as personally *deserving* of those outcomes (e.g., Jost, Blount, Pfeffer, & Hunyady, 2003). People seem to feel more justified in discriminating against those who are stigmatized on the basis of characteristics that are seen as personally controllable, such as obesity (e.g., Crandall, & Martinez, 1996; Puhl & Brownell, 2003; Quinn & Crocker, 1999).

Social psychologists have devoted considerable research attention to understanding how notions of deservingness (and entitlement)[2] are related to processes of attribution, stereotyping and prejudice, perceptions of discrimination, political ideology, and appraisals of the legitimacy of social systems (e.g., Jost & Banaji, 1994; Jost & Major, 2001; Major, 1994). Studies show that perceptions of personal causation and

---

[1] There may be more than one type of belief in a just world (Furnham, 2003). Distinctions have been proposed, for example, between beliefs in a *just* vs. *unjust* world (Furnham, 1985), beliefs in a just world for the *self* vs. *others* (Bègue & Bastounis, 2003; Lipkus, Dalbert, & Siegler, 1996; Sutton et al., 2008), and beliefs in *immanent* vs. *ultimate* justice (Maes, 1998). Factor analyses confirm that a multidimensional factor structure exists, but the theoretical significance of such findings is not always entirely clear (Hafer & Bègue, 2005).

[2] Feather (1994) has distinguished crisply between concepts of deservingness and entitlement, noting that "whereas deservingness pertains more to the evaluative structure of actions and their outcomes . . . entitlement pertains more to an external, consensually based framework of laws, rights, and social norms that may be tacitly acknowledged or more formally prescribed" (p. 368; see also Feather, 1999). Major's (1994) account of entitlement, however, blurs the distinction: "If an individual fulfills certain preconditions, he or she will feel entitled to certain outcomes. These preconditions may be either ascribed (e.g., she is of a particular race or sex) or earned (e.g., he has made particular contributions)" (p. 299). Lerner's (1987) definition of entitlement-"a sense of requiredness between the actor's perceived outcomes and attributes or acts"-similarly amalgamates the two constructs. The important point is that symbolic and material resources are frequently allocated on the basis of *who* the recipient is and *what* he or she has done and that both of these are generally accepted as fair and legitimate (see Feather, 2008).

deservingness lead people to hold more and less favorable attitudes toward high and low status targets, respectively (e.g., Weiner, Perry, & Magnuson, 1988). Endorsement of just world beliefs and system-justifying ideologies that emphasize deservingness are associated with increased prejudice toward African Americans and obese people, among other stigmatized groups (Crandall & Martinez, 1996; Rim, 1988). Attributions of deservingness act not only as causes but also as *releasers* of prejudice (Crandall & Eshleman, 2003), insofar as they seem to justify the expression of preexisting negative attitudes toward certain social groups (Allport, 1954; Jost & Banaji, 1994). Espousing political conservatism, which often leans heavily on the assumption of personal deservingness (or individual responsibility), also predicts both implicit and explicit devaluation of those who are disadvantaged in society, including African Americans (e.g., Crandall, 1994; Jost, Banaji, & Nosek, 2004; Jost, Glaser, Kruglanski, & Sulloway, 2003; Nosek, Banaji, & Jost, 2009; Pratto, Sidanius, Stallworth, & Malle, 1994; Sears, van Laar, Carrillo, & Kosterman, 1997; Sidanius, Pratto, & Bobo, 1996).

The concept of deservingness is useful for understanding resentment directed at people who are extremely successful (i.e., "tall poppies"). According to Feather (1994), people first try to determine whether an individual is *personally responsible* for their outcome; that is, the extent to which "the outcome is assumed to be produced by the person and related to the person's intentions" (p. 13). Next, they consider the values of the behavior and the outcome. When a positively valued behavior is seen as leading to a positively valued outcome (e.g., training hard to win a competitive race) or a negatively valued behavior is seen as leading to a negatively valued outcome (e.g., cheating and losing the race), the perceiver will experience the outcome as deserved. By contrast, valence mismatches between the behavior and outcome (e.g., cheating and winning the race or training hard and losing it) lead to perceptions that the outcomes are undeserved. Thus, people tend to react negatively to success that is seen as undeserved and are eager to see "tall poppies" fall under such circumstances (Feather, 1994, 1999).

Much research, including studies of relative deprivation and social comparison processes mentioned previously, has explored the ways in which people's perceptions of entitlement relate to issues of social justice. One useful focus has been on the conditions that lead members of disadvantaged or low status groups (such as women) to develop a "depressed sense of entitlement" that leads them to be satisfied with less than others receive (Blanton, George, & Crocker, 2001; Callahan-Levy & Messé, 1979; Hogue & Yoder, 2003; Jost, 1997; Major, 1994; Pelham & Hetts, 2001). The endorsement of various ideological belief systems—especially those that reinforce notions of meritocracy and deservingness—have been associated with the tendency for members of low status groups to view their own state of disadvantage as relatively legitimate (Crandall, 1994; Jost, 1995; Jost, Banaji, & Nosek, 2004; Olson & Hafer, 2001; Quinn & Crocker, 1999). For example, women who score higher on the belief in a just world are less likely to report career-related discontentment (Hafer & Olson, 1993), and ethnic minorities who espouse the belief that it is possible to climb the status hierarchy are less likely to view negative outcomes as due to discrimination or unfairness (Major et al., 2002).

There is also experimental work showing that "depressed entitlement" (and tolerance of injustice more generally) can be produced or exacerbated under specific situational conditions. For instance, priming members of a low status group with meritocratic ideals makes them less likely to regard unfair treatment (by a higher status group member) as caused by sexism or discrimination (McCoy & Major, 2007; see also Biernat, Vescio, & Theno, 1996; Jost & Kay, 2005; Quinn & Crocker, 1999). Research on system justification theory similarly suggests that people may be motivated (for epistemic, existential, and relational reasons) to view inequalities among individuals and groups as fair, legitimate, and defensible rather than due to discrimination, unfairness, or historical accident (e.g., Jost, Banaji, & Nosek, 2004). As with regard to the belief in a just world and many other areas of social justice research, system justification tendencies vary as a function of both dispositional and situational variables (Jost, Glaser, Kruglanski, & Sulloway, 2003; Jost & Hunyady, 2005; Kay & Zanna, 2009; Kay, Gaucher, Peach, Laurin, Friesen, Zanna, & Spencer, 2009).

Social Dilemmas   Social dilemmas are situations that pit self-interest against collective interest. Although scholarly interest in these situations typically derives from an interest in how people with "mixed motives" make difficult decisions, there are clear implications for social justice—principally for the distribution of resources across individuals and even across generations of individuals. Experimentally created social dilemmas involve two essential characteristics: "(a) at any given decision point, individuals receive higher payoffs for making selfish choices than they do for making cooperative choices . . . and (b) everyone involved receives lower payoffs if everyone makes selfish choices than if everyone makes cooperative choices" (Weber, Kopelman, & Messick, 2004, p. 281). Defined in these terms, there are three major classes of social dilemmas (i.e., miniature social systems) studied by experimentalists (Komorita & Parks, 1995). These are the *prisoner's dilemma*, in which two individuals must choose between "cooperating" and "defecting," with the knowledge that, although defecting will offer an individual the highest possible payoff when his or her partner cooperates, if both defect, the outcome will be significantly worse than if both cooperate; the *public goods game*, in which people must decide how much to contribute to a common resource pool that others will benefit from, regardless of how much they actually contributed; and the *resource dilemma*, in which all group members are able to draw from a given resource pool, but with the awareness that overharvesting will deplete it entirely (because the resource is replenished only occasionally).

Although cooperative, prosocial behavior is by no means unheard of in these types of situations, it is less common overall than is competitive, self-interested behavior. People cooperate roughly 30%–40% of the time in laboratory studies, aggregating across different types of social dilemmas (Komorita & Parks, 1995). Because competitive strategies violate principles of equality and (assuming equivalent inputs) equity, understanding the factors that inhibit competition and promote cooperation is an important goal of social justice research (Schroeder, Steel, Woodell, & Bembenek, 2003). A comprehensive research literature (produced by social psychologists, economists, sociologists, political scientists, and others) highlights numerous factors associated with cooperative behavior in social dilemma situations, including shared social identification (Kramer & Brewer, 1984). Many excellent reviews of this literature exist, and theoretical integration has been achieved to a considerable extent (see Kollock, 1998; Komorita & Parks, 1995, 1996; Weber, Kopelman, & Messick, 2004). Thus, our summary will be confined to those empirical insights that speak most readily to the theme of social justice.

Individual Differences   A fruitful focus of research has addressed individual differences in *social value orientation*— that is, the extent to which people are concerned with *self* versus *other* regarding preferences and/or outcomes (Messick & McClintock, 1968; Van Lange, 2000). Individuals who hold prosocial orientations are more likely to cooperate in social dilemmas than are individuals with "proself"—or, as Aristotle would say, "grasping"—orientations (Bogaert, Boone, & Declerck, 2008; De Cremer & Van Lange, 2001; De Cremer & Van Vugt, 1999; Kollock, 1998; Kramer, McClintock, & Messick, 1986; Smeesters, Warlop, Van Avermaet, Corneille, & Yzerbyt, 2003; Weber, Kopelman, & Messick, 2004). Prosocial individuals are more likely than others to restrict their take of scarce resources (Roch & Samuelson, 1997), conserve environmental resources for the greater good (Van Vugt, Meertens, & Van Lange, 1995), and volunteer their time to help others (McClintock & Allison, 1989). They are also more likely to value *equality of outcomes* than are proselfs (Eek & Gärling, 2006). A similar distinction has been proposed between "altruistic cooperators," who seem to be more interested in positive

outcomes for others than for themselves, and "reciprocal cooperators," who engage in prosocial behavior only to the extent that they expect others to reciprocate (Kurzban & Houser, 2001; Perugini & Galluci, 2001).

But why, exactly, do prosocials cooperate more than proselfs? Two major explanations have been offered. First, it has been suggested that prosocials are more likely to construe the goal of social dilemma situations in terms of maximizing collective (as opposed to individual) rationality (Liebrand, Jansen, Rijken, & Suhre, 1986; Simpson, 2004; Utz, Ouwerkerk, & Van Lange, 2004). Second, it is possible that prosocials are more likely than proselfs to expect that others will cooperate rather than defect (e.g., Smeesters, Warlop, Van Avermaet, Corneille, & Yzerbyt, 2003). Interested readers are directed to more detailed reviews of how social value orientation (Bogaert, Boone, & Declerck, 2008) and other individual difference variables (Van Lange, De Cremer, Van Dijk, & Van Vugt, 2007) predict behavior in experimentally created social dilemmas. The general assumption is that justice-related behavior in these situations has fairly deep roots both in personality and socialization experiences (Au & Kwong, 2004; De Cremer & Van Lange, 2001; J. T. Jost & L. J. Jost, 2009; Kuhlman, Camac, & Cunha, 1986; Van Lange, 2000).

Structural Factors   Several studies have investigated the influence of dilemma *structure* on cooperative versus competitive behavior. For instance, cooperation increases whenever structural changes (such as direct social contact) foster the development of a common group identity (Gächter & Fehr, 1999; Kramer & Brewer, 1984; Orbell, Van de Kragt, & Dawes, 1988; Wit & Kerr, 2002). Although systems for monitoring and sanctioning the individual's behavior may be effective when they are firmly in place, they tend to undermine subsequent cooperation once they are removed because they reduce perceptions of others' cooperative intent (Yamagishi, 1988; see also Mulder, van Dijk, De Cremer, & Wilke, 2006; Tyler & Jost, 2007). When people are highly uncertain about the availability of a collective resource, they expect that others will engage in greater harvesting behavior and also harvest more resources themselves (Budescu, Rapoport, & Suleiman, 1990; Gustafsson, Biel, & Gärling, 1999; but see de Kwaadsteniet, van Dijk, Wit, De Cremer, & de Rooij, 2007; Van Dijk, Wilke, Wilke, & Metman, 1999; Wit & Wilke, 1998).

One common response to social dilemma situations is to appoint a leader who is expected to oversee the distribution of resources (Hardin, 1968). Studies show that group members are, indeed, more likely to appoint a leader when they are aware that a valued resource is being rapidly depleted (Messick et al., 1983) and when the use of resources is otherwise difficult to oversee (Samuelson, 1991). Group identification, as usual, plays an important role in determining the behavior of leaders and followers (Tajfel & Turner, 1986). Those who identify strongly (vs. weakly) with their group are more likely to support the democratic election of a leader (Van Vugt & De Cremer, 1999) and to be inspired by committed, fair leaders to increase their level of cooperation (De Cremer & Van Vugt, 2002). However, leaders may develop a sense of elevated entitlement, abandon norms of equality, and reserve an overabundance of resources for themselves—especially when they have been appointed rather than elected (De Cremer & Van Dijk, 2005). On the other hand, charismatic leaders can be effective at inducing even "proselfs" to cooperate (De Cremer, 2002), whereas autocratic leaders increase the likelihood that members will abandon the group when faced with a conflict between personal and group interests (Van Vugt, Jepson, Hart, & De Cremer, 2004). These and other findings attest to the enduring significance of Lewin's distinction between democratic versus autocratic leadership—and Deutsch's extrapolation to cooperative versus competitive social systems—for analyzing justice-related procedures and outcomes.

The choice of whether to cooperate or not when confronted with a social dilemma depends to a great extent on how the situation is "framed" (or construed). Does it call for cooperation and the privileging of collective (or communal) interests? Or does it offer a chance to maximize one's own outcomes? Subtle manipulations can influence the extent to which the same social dilemma situation is seen through one or the other of these frames. Specifically, the use of different labels (Batson & Moran, 1999; Liberman, Samuels, & Ross, 2004) or metaphors (Allison, Beggan, & Midgley, 1999) within the context of the same dilemma affects cooperation rates. Furthermore, the priming of specific mindsets (Elliott, Hayward, & Canon, 1998) and even incidental exposure to objects that symbolize competitiveness versus cooperativeness (Kay, Wheeler, Bargh, & Ross, 2004) can lead people to construe the same dilemma situation in drastically different terms and, therefore, to behave in more or less prosocial ways (Kay & Ross, 2003; Tenbrunsel & Messick, 1999; Weber, Kopelman, & Messick, 2004).

Procedural Justice

Although the terms "social justice" and "distributive justice" are often used interchangeably by philosophers and laypersons (e.g., Miller, 1999), social scientists in recent decades have come to recognize that justice considerations pertain not merely to the allocation of resources but also to the methods or procedures by which decisions are made at work, in political life, in the family, etc. A major thrust of contemporary social psychological research has demonstrated that justice

appraisals are determined at least as much, if not more, by the perceived fairness of procedural versus distributive factors (e.g., Tyler & Smith, 1998). The pioneers of this research tradition, Thibaut and Walker (1975), were primarily interested in third-party decision making, such as legal decisions made by judges or juries (see also Leventhal, 1980). This work demonstrated that the perceived fairness of the specific procedures used to render a verdict or decision influences people's evaluations of both the final outcome and the decision maker. Researchers have not looked back since; there has been far more research on aspects of procedural justice than on aspects of other types (including distributive justice) over the past quarter of a century.

"Voice" and Other Procedural Justice Criteria

According to Walker, Lind, and Thibaut (1979), "the belief that the techniques used to resolve a dispute are fair and satisfying in themselves" (p. 1402) follows from two major procedural features: "(a) process control, referring to how much people are allowed to present evidence on their behalf before the decision is made, and (b) decision control; that is, whether individuals have any say in the actual rendering of the decision" (Brockner & Wiesenfeld, 1996, p. 189; see also Ambrose & Arnaud, 2005). That is, people want to know that they will have input into (and are therefore able to exert at least some influence over) the decision-making process as well as the decision itself. Thibaut and Walker (1975) proposed that when people possess these two types of perceived control they are able to trust that procedures will be fair and that their short-term and especially long-term outcomes will be favorable in general (but see Azzi & Jost, 1997 for an application to majority–minority intergroup relations).

Research has been supportive of the notion that *process control* (i.e., the chance to present one's own "side" to a third-party decision maker) is a fundamental determinant of justice appraisals (e.g., Houlden, LaTour, Walker, & Thibaut, 1978; Thibaut & Walker, 1975; cf. Shapiro & Brett, 2005). Thibaut and Walker's pioneering work has influenced myriad research programs, including research on the so-called "voice effect;" that is, the demonstration that the opportunity to express one's views or feelings during the course of the decision-making process significantly increases perceptions of procedural fairness (Folger, 1977; Lind & Tyler, 1988; Van den Bos, 2005). Studies show that the presence of *voice* affects not only justice judgments but is also associated with increased positive affect, decreased negative affect, and greater trust in authorities (e.g., Brockner et al., 1998; Folger, Rosenfeld, Grove, & Corkran, 1979; Lind, Kanfer, & Earley, 1990; Lind & Tyler, 1988; Shapiro & Brett, 2005; Tyler & Blader, 2003; Tyler, Rasinki, & Spodick, 1985; Van den Bos, Wilke, & Lind,

1998; Van Prooijen, Karremans, & van Beest, 2006; Van Prooijen, Van den Bos, & Wilke, 2004).

At the same time, voice is by no means the only variable that influences perceptions of procedural justice. Leventhal, Karuza, and Fry (1980) identified six factors that can contribute to justice appraisals. To be considered fair, they argued, decisions must be made (a) *consistently* across instances and time periods; (b) *neutrally*, that is, without bias, preconceptions, or self-interest; (c) on the basis of *accurate* information; (d) with an opportunity to make *corrections* if necessary; (e) in consideration of the interests of *all* relevant parties; and (f) *ethically*. Leventhal (1980) pointed out that, depending upon the specific circumstances, some of these "rules" may be weighted more heavily than others. Consistent with this view, situational differences (e.g., variability in the formality of a given decision-making setting) affect the criteria that people use in making judgments of procedural fairness (Barrett-Howard & Tyler, 1986). Nevertheless, aggregating across a wide range of situations, people tend to prioritize three of these criteria—*consistency*, *accuracy*, and *ethicality*—in determining whether procedural justice requirements have been satisfied (Barrett-Howard & Tyler, 1986; Lind & Tyler, 1988).

Skitka (2002; Skitka & Houston, 2001; Skitka & Mullen, 2002) has argued that procedural justice concerns are suspended when people perceive "moral mandates"; that is, when they feel especially strongly about a specific issue or outcome, such as whether or not abortion is legally protected. Moral mandates, as defined by Skitka and her colleagues, are to be distinguished from strongly held attitudes (Skitka, Bauman, & Sargis, 2005) and are associated with anger directed at those who are seen as violating them (Mullen & Skitka, 2006). On the basis of her research, Skitka (2002) concluded that "when people have a moral mandate about an outcome, any means justifies the mandated end" and "fair procedures do not ameliorate the sense of injustice people experience when a morally mandated outcome is threatened or rejected" (p. 594). Napier and Tyler (2008) reviewed this evidence and arrived at a different conclusion, namely that even when people experience intense moral conviction about a given issue (e.g., immigration, abortion, or civil rights), they are still more likely to accept a decision made by authorities when they believe that procedural fairness norms have been observed than when they have not (see also Gibson, 2008; Tyler & Mitchell, 1994).

Why Do People Care About Procedures?

There is little question that procedural characteristics affect overall perceptions of fairness and satisfaction and also exert downstream effects on an extremely wide range of social and organizational variables (Van den Bos, 2005, pp.

274–277; see also Greenberg, 1993; Sweeney & McFarlin, 1993). At the same time, different theoretical models of procedural justice emphasize distinctive (and sometimes competing) underlying causes of procedural justice effects (e.g., Cropanzano & Folger, 1989; Lind & Tyler, 1988; Thibaut & Walker, 1975; Tyler & Lind, 1992; Van den Bos & Lind, 2002). The question is *why* people care as much as they do about the *procedures* that are used to determine their outcomes and not just about the favorability of the outcomes themselves.

Instrumental Models   Thibaut and Walker (1975) initially proposed that people seek control (or voice) over both the process and decision because they want to ensure that the ultimate outcome will be fair and favorable (see also Walker, Lind, & Thibaut, 1979).[3] The benefits of procedural fairness, in other words, were assumed to be tangible and instrumental. Given the fact that people often exhibit *naïve realism* by seeing their own "side" in a dispute as more correct and reasonable in comparison with that of their adversaries (Ross & Ward, 1996), it is possible to view the desire for fair procedures as a subtle expression of self-interest motivation (Folger et al., 1979; Shapiro & Brett, 2005; Tyler, 1994; Van Proojien et al., 2008). However, this interpretation was not the one favored by Thibaut and Walker. As Van den Bos (2005) noted, "An important aspect of the Thibaut and Walker (1975) model was the focus on whether people received *fair* outcomes and not so much on how *favorable* outcomes were to people . . . It is therefore more appropriate to label these authors' theory as the 'instrumental model,' and . . . it is wrong to call this the 'self-interest model'" (p. 284).

Relational Models   A clear alternative to instrumental explanations for why people care about procedural justice emerges from *relational* models of procedural justice (Tyler & Lind, 1992), such as the group-value model (Lind & Tyler, 1988). The basic idea is that people are concerned about the fairness of procedures largely because of the implications that these procedures hold for their feelings of *self-worth*, which are often derived from processes of social identification (Tajfel & Turner, 1986).

---

[3] Referent cognitions theory provides yet another account of procedural justice effects (Cropanzano & Folger, 1989; Folger, 1986). From this perspective, when a procedure is experienced as unfair, people begin to compare what actually happened to what "could" have happened. To the extent that other referents are available, that is, if people can easily imagine an alternative procedure, negative reactions (including perceptions of injustice) are more likely to ensue (see also Van den Bos, Lind, Vermunt, & Wilke, 1997).

As Tyler (1994) explains, "The basic assumption of the relational model is that people are predisposed to belong to social groups and that they are attentive to signs and symbols that communicate information about their position within groups" (p. 851). The quality of procedures, it is argued, reflects the extent to which people are *valued*, *respected*, and *understood* by decision-making authorities. The notion that individuals would be strongly motivated to obtain information about social standing is consistent not only with social identity theory but also with models of social belongingness, reputation, and shared reality (e.g., Baumeister & Leary, 1995; Hardin & Higgins, 1996).

Relational models of procedural justice can help to explain "voice" effects, insofar as the opportunity to express one's own point of view allows individuals to *express their values* to fellow group members and authorities (Lind, Kanfer, & Earley, 1990; Tyler, 1987). Such models also bring to the fore other benefits of procedural arrangements, including the communication and building up of trust, standing, and social status (Tyler, 1989; Van Prooijen, Van den Bos, & Wilke, 2002). People do infer from procedural treatment the extent to which authorities accord them with trust, standing, respect, and value, and consider them to be worthy group members (e.g., Heuer, Blumenthal, Douglas, & Weinblatt, 1999; Huo, 2002; Smith, Tyler, Huo, Ortiz, & Lind, 1998; Tyler, 1994; Tyler, Degoey, & Smith, 1996). To put the same point more negatively and, consequently, more dramatically, to treat someone unjustly is to deny them the benefits and trappings of social belongingness (see Baumeister & Leary, 1995).

Epistemic Models Social comparison processes are fundamental to prominent models of distributive justice, including theories of relative deprivation (Crosby, 1976), equity (Walster, Walster, & Berscheid, 1978), equality and need (Deutsch, 1975), and perceived entitlement (Major, 1994). That is, people often decide whether they have been treated fairly by comparing their own situation to that of relevant others (or, in the case of equity theory, comparing their own ratio of inputs to outputs to the ratios of others). In the real world, however, many people are largely ignorant about the sizes of their colleagues' salaries, their neighbors' inheritances, and their friends' tax breaks; thus, it is often difficult to make direct social comparisons, and many justice appraisals are made under conditions of uncertainty.

It has been suggested that people often rely on procedures as heuristic substitutes for social comparison information (Van den Bos & Lind, 2002; Van den Bos, Lind, Vermunt, & Wilke, 1997). In the absence of unambiguous information with which to draw conclusions about distributive justice, for example, people are compelled to rely on procedural

information (Skitka, 2002; Van den Bos, Wilke, Lind, & Vermunt, 1998).[4] Even abstract experimental manipulations of general self-uncertainty (having nothing to do with questions of fairness) are capable of increasing participants' attention to the procedural aspects of a given situation (see Van den Bos, 2001; Van den Bos, Wilke, & Lind, 1998; see also Diekmann, Barsness & Sondak, 2004, for an organizational field study).

Interactional (or Informal) Justice

The philosopher Frankena (1962) observed that "society does not consist merely of the law or the state: it has also a more informal aspect, comprised of its cultural institutions, conventions, moral rules, and moral sanctions." Thus, he argued, "In order for society to be fully just, it must be just in its informal as well as in its formal aspect" (p. 2). If this is correct, then it is possible to speak of social injustice as arising not merely as a consequence of unfair treatment proffered by institutionally sanctioned authority figures, such as politicians, judges, police officers, bosses, teachers, and so on, but also on the basis of how citizens tend to treat one another. It is in this sense that prejudice, discrimination, and authoritarianism on the part of ordinary citizens can contribute to a social climate that is undemocratic and fundamentally unjust, as Lewin (1939/1948a) noted with regard to fascist society. Several models of interpersonal justice have been put forth by social and organizational psychologists over the years; few of them deal explicitly with behavior or circumstances that are as extreme as those associated with fascism, but the models clearly do involve a broader conception of social justice than is suggested by more formal models of distributive or procedural justice.

Fairness of Interpersonal Treatment

Tyler and Lind (1992; Tyler, 1989) deserve credit for highlighting a number of ways in which aspects of social interaction affect perceptions of procedural justice (see also Leventhal, 1980; Thibaut & Walker, 1975). This idea was taken further by Bies and colleagues (Bies & Moag, 1986;

---

[4] Brockner & Wiesenfeld (1996) have also noted that perceptions of procedural and distributive justice frequently interact with one another, such that "when outcomes are unfair or have a negative valence, procedural justice is more likely to have a direct effect on individuals' reactions"; "when procedural justice is relatively low, outcome favorability is more apt to be positively correlated with individuals' reactions"; and "the combination of low procedural fairness and low outcome favorability engenders particularly negative reactions" (p. 191; regarding implications for self-evaluation, see also Brockner, Heuer, & Magner, 2003).

Folger & Bies, 1989; Tyler & Bies, 1990), who distinguished between "structural" and "interactional" components of decision-making procedures. In stressing the importance of the latter, Bies and Moag (1986) noted that people are sensitive not merely to the structure or content of a given procedure, but also to the "quality of interpersonal treatment they receive during the enactment of organizational procedures" (p. 44; see also Colquitt, Greenberg, & Zapata-Phelan, 2005). In other words, people do not just want fair procedures at work and elsewhere; they also want fair treatment in a much broader sense.

What constitutes fair interpersonal treatment? Bies and Moag (1986) initially focused on four aspects of social interaction: *respect*, *truthfulness*, *justification* (i.e., the provision of timely, adequate explanations for decisions), and *propriety* (i.e., sensitivity, appropriateness, and the avoidance of prejudicial treatment). The data speak favorably with respect to the predictive validity of each of these four facets of interactional justice (e.g., Colquitt, 2001; Colquitt, Conlon, Wesson, Porter, & Ng, 2001). This has only encouraged researchers to continue nominating additional candidates, such as *dignity*, the provision of *feedback*, and *consideration* of employees' (and other constituents') views (Folger & Bies, 1989; Greenberg, Bies, & Eskew, 1991; Tyler & Bies, 1990). Some authors have suggested that interactional justice is comprised of two separate constructs, namely *informational* justice, which emphasizes communicative aspects, such as truthfulness and justification, and *interpersonal* justice, which guarantees sensitive, respectful, and appropriate treatment. (See Bies, 2005; Colquitt, 2001; Greenberg, 1993).

Relationship Between Procedural and Interactional Justice

More than 20 years of research (most of which comes from the field of organizational behavior) confirms that perceptions of interactional justice help to explain how employees and others respond to decisions made by authority figures (Bies, 2005; Colquitt, Conlon, Wesson, Porter, & Ng., 2001; Colquitt, Greenberg, & Zapata-Phelan, 2005). Everyone agrees that—in addition to or in conjunction with formal mechanisms, such as rules and policies—informal aspects of social interaction matter a great deal when people are asked to evaluate the fairness of procedures and outcomes. Nevertheless, scholars disagree considerably about whether interactional justice concerns should fall under the rubric of procedural justice or be considered an entirely independent type of justice concern (see Bies, 2001, 2005; Bobocel & Holmvall, 2001; Colquitt, Greenberg, & Zapata-Phelan, 2005; Greenberg, 1993; Tyler & Blader, 2003). A fair amount of ink has been spilled in an effort to resolve this question, but from our point of view the study of social justice is too important to be mired in semantic or taxonomic disputes for long. There may well be circumstances in which it is useful to distinguish between cases involving procedural (or formal) and interactional (or informal) justice, but little is gained by exaggerating or reifying such divisions. It seems reasonable enough to assume that procedural justice and interactional justice constitute two important aspects of "fairness of treatment" (Van den Bos, 2005).

Probably the most compelling empirical case for separating the constructs comes from a series of studies suggesting that people spontaneously distinguish between structural and interactional aspects of procedures (see Bies, 2001). However, mapping this difference onto the concepts of procedural and interactional justice requires one to define procedural justice solely in terms of formal, structural aspects of procedures (Bobocel & Holmvall, 2001). In point of fact, the most influential research and theorizing on procedural justice does not treat procedural justice in such limited terms; rather, it views interpersonal treatment as a key determinant of perceptions of procedural justice (Folger & Bies, 1989; Lind & Tyler, 1988; Tyler & Bies, 1990; Tyler & Blader, 2000; Tyler & Lind, 1992). For example, relational models of procedural justice (e.g., group-value and group engagement models) stress that both formal structures and mechanisms and the manner in which these are implemented (i.e., fairness of treatment) are important for the same social psychological reasons: they signal one's degree of social acceptance, group inclusion, status, and worth (Tyler & Blader, 2003).

The notion that procedural and interactional justice are partially overlapping constructs also emerges from the research literature on themes of insult and disrespect, insofar as these refer to both qualities of treatment and social outcomes in themselves (see Miller, 2001, for a review). People tend to experience a wide range of violations, including structural forms of injustice, poor interpersonal treatment, and receipt of inequitable outcomes, as upsetting at least in part because they convey some measure of disrespect. Additional facts—such as the observation that people respond more harshly to perceived injustices when they are committed publicly rather than privately and that apologies can be quite effective at alleviating the sense of injustice—are supportive of the notion that feelings of *injustice* and *disrespect* are intertwined (Miller, 2001).

At the same time, there is some evidence indicating that people sometimes react differently to procedural versus interactional violations. Perceptions of procedural justice predict reactions to and evaluations of the system (e.g., one's organization), whereas perceptions of interactional justice predict reactions to and evaluations of representatives of the system (e.g., supervisors) who communicate the decisions (Ambrose, Seabright, & Schminke, 2002; Aryee, Budhwar, & Chen, 2002; Colquitt, 2001; Fuller & Hester, 2001). These results are easily interpretable from the standpoint of social exchange theories (e.g., Cropanzano, Prehar, & Chen, 2002; Masterson, Lewis, Goldman, & Taylor, 2000). To the extent that people view rules and procedures as under the control of the system, the perceived fairness of formal procedures should affect the "relationship" that people develop with the system. Likewise, to the extent that people view the quality of interpersonal treatment they receive as under the control of the person (or persons) with whom they are interacting, the perceived fairness of treatment should affect the relationships that people develop with those specific actors.

Finally, meta-analytic evidence reveals that procedural and interactional justice concerns are indeed correlated and partially overlapping, but they do predict somewhat different behavioral responses (Cohen-Charash & Spector, 2001; Colquitt, Conlon, Wesson, Porter, & Ng, 2001). Informational and interpersonal justice concerns also predict somewhat different behavioral outcomes (Colquitt, 2001; Greenberg, 1993; Kernan & Hanges, 2001). However, to justify conceptualizing procedural and interactional justice perceptions as fundamentally different phenomena, one would want to show that structural and interpersonal aspects of procedures exert their influence on justice-related judgments and behaviors through different psychological mechanisms (Bobocel & Holmvall, 2001; Miller, 2001). Apparently, this has yet to be demonstrated. But, rather than seeking to neatly compartmentalize different areas of social justice research, a better strategy for conveying the theoretical and practical significance of interactional justice might be to broaden the range of phenomena to be understood and explained. For example, experimental and other studies of hostility, aggression, stigmatization, harassment, social exclusion, and inappropriate humor are not necessarily considered part of the social justice canon, but this work should be incorporated, insofar as it speaks directly to the ways in which individuals are or are not treated with dignity and respect in their daily lives and why (e.g., Bargh, Raymond, Pryor, & Strack, 1995; Ford, Boxer, Armstrong, & Edel, 2008; Gelfand, Fitzgerald, & Drasgow, 1995; Kurzban & Leary, 2001; Link & Phelan, 2001; Maass, Cadinu, Guarnieri, & Grasselli, 2003; Rudman & Ashmore, 2007; Struch & Schwartz, 1989; Watson, Ottati, & Corrigan, 2003).

Retributive Justice

Following acts of clear injustice, individuals, groups, and societies often enact some form of punishment. When apprehended and found guilty, perpetrators are jailed, fined, or in some way reprimanded for their actions. Such punishment

schemes are typically seen as reasonable and legitimate by the public at large—indeed, they are seen as cornerstones of the "justice system." But how, specifically, are these systems of punishment justified or, more precisely, "justicized?" Questions such as these have been investigated most directly by scholars focused on the study of *retributive justice* concerns, namely the question of "how people who have intentionally committed known, morally wrong actions that either directly or indirectly harm others, should be punished for their misdeeds" (Carlsmith & Darley, 2008).

Is Vengeance Ours?

Two broad kinds of justifications for punishment have been offered, both of which originate in the seminal work of moral philosophers. Bentham (1962/1843) argued that punishment, to be justified, must serve some *utilitarian* purpose; that is, it must benefit society overall—making social life better or happier in some important way (cf. Greene & Cohen, 2004). How might punishment benefit society? It is certainly possible that the threat and/or execution of punishment serves to prevent or reduce the number of potential acts of injustice. Whether through *specific deterrence* (which aims to punish an offender sufficiently to deter him or her from committing similar offenses in the future), *incapacitation* (in which an offender is temporarily or even permanently prevented from committing additional offenses through incarceration or some other method), or *general deterrence* (in which certain individuals are punished so as to deter others from committing similar offenses), a utilitarian approach emphasizes the potential benefits punishment can have for society as a whole.

Kant (1790/1952) offered a different justification for punishment. He argued that punishment was fair insofar as people *deserve* to be punished for immoral behavior; punishment "balances the scales," so to speak. From a just-deserts perspective such as this, the worse the perpetrator's actions, the harsher the punishment that is required to restore justice. As Kant said, punishment "should be pronounced over all criminals in proportion to their wickedness" (as cited in Carlsmith, Darley, & Robinson, 2002, p. 397). Although there are clear parallels here to equity theory and other work on distributive justice, Carlsmith and Darley (2008) distinguish between concepts of distributive and retributive justice as follows:

> [D]istributive justice theories tend to assume positive outcomes and are concerned with whether those positive outcomes should be shared out equally, equitably . . . or on the basis of needs. In keeping with the standard conventions in this area, we will reserve the term "distributive justice" to discuss reward allocations, and use "retributive justice" to refer to punishments that people deserve for their wrongdoing. (p. 195)

Increasingly, researchers have sought to flesh out the social psychological underpinnings of support for policies that involve punishment. Generally, the aim is not to understand the best or most rational reasons to support policies of punishment (the normative question), but to discover *why* people support such policies, regardless of the objective quality of the reasons for their support (the descriptive question). For instance, researchers have pitted utilitarian, deterrence-related concerns against Kantian notions of just-deserts to determine which is the stronger motivation of support for strict punishment (Carlsmith, 2006; Carlsmith, Darley, & Robinson, 2002; Darley, Carlsmith, & Robinson, 2000). One firm conclusion emerges from these studies: People are far more attuned to the severity of a crime and its moral significance when assigning punishment than they are to information pertaining to the likelihood of either general or specific deterrence (Carlsmith & Darley, 2008; Darley & Pittman, 2003; Kahneman, Schkade, & Sunstein, 1998; McFatter, 1982).

More specifically, the desire for retribution is motivated by the perceived immorality of unjust behavior and the moral outrage that accompanies such perceptions. Studies show that people actively search for information related to morality when assigning punishment, that moral culpability and seriousness influence the harshness of recommended punishment, and that moral outrage mediates the relationship between the severity of an offense and recommended punishments (Carlsmith, 2006; Carlsmith, Darley, & Robinson, 2002; Darley, Carlsmith, & Robinson, 2000). Cultural and religious norms affect specific attitudes about retributive and other forms of justice (Cohen & Rozin, 2001; Henrich et al., 2001), but the desire to punish those who commit serious transgressions seems fairly universal.

A fascinating contrast exists between the objective determinants of punishment attitudes, which are largely Kantian, and the subjective reasons that people give in explaining their support for punishment, which lean toward utilitarianism (e.g., Ellsworth & Ross, 1983). Such a divergence has been observed, for example, in the dramatic context of debates over the use of torture in U.S. military prisons abroad. Although people who endorse torture generally say that their opinion is driven by their conviction that it successfully prevents future harm, experimental evidence reveals that support for harsh interrogation tactics is predicted by the perceived moral status of the target, and not by information concerning the likely effectiveness of the interrogation process (Carlsmith, 2008; Carlsmith & Sood, 2009; Janoff-Bulman, 2007). The motivation to justify the social system also plays a role in popular support for torture, insofar as citizens deem torture to be more acceptable and justifiable to the extent that it is seen as part of the societal status quo; that is, when they are told (falsely)

that the nation's military has been practicing torture for 40 years (Crandall, Eidelman, Skitka, & Morgan, 2009).

Studies such as these raise the important possibility that people may be *actually* motivated (consciously or unconsciously) to support highly aggressive forms of retribution (such as torture and capital punishment) by one set of justice-related reasons (e.g., intuitions about fairness and deservingness) or even *non*justice-related reasons, such as authoritarianism, social dominance, or racial prejudice (e.g., Dambrun, 2007; Ho, ForsterLee, ForsterLee, & Crofts, 2002; Johnson, Whitestone, Jackson, & Gatto, 1995; McKee & Feather, 2008; Rossi & Berk, 1997; Sidanius, Mitchell, Haley, & Navarrete, 2006) and yet offer a different set of justice-related reasons (e.g., utilitarianism, deterrence) as *post hoc* justifications or rationalizations for taking or supporting punitive action. Such a possibility is broadly consistent with the notion that moral judgment is often the result of automatic, intuitive judgments, rather than deliberative reasoning (Darley & Pittman, 2003; Haidt, 2001).

A far more optimistic image of retributive justice motives comes from theoretical models that emphasize the desire to affirm group or community values or standards (Tyler & Boeckman, 1997; Vidmar, 2002). The guiding idea is that unjust actions threaten the assumption that social consensus exists with regard to justice and morality and that meting out punishment can be an effective way of affirming shared values (Wenzel & Thielman, 2006). From this perspective, punishment serves to communicate the group's values and may therefore repair feelings of social identification—feelings that can be damaged when group members are confronted with an explicit challenge to their values (Vidmar, 2000). However, if one's primary goal in assigning punishment is to reaffirm social values and the consensus of group norms, *restorative justice*—which involves coming up with prosocial alternatives to traditional forms of punishment—is probably a better option.

Restorative Justice

The concept of restorative justice represents an alternative to traditional ways of thinking about crime and punishment (Bazemore, 1998; Braithwaite, 1989; Roberts & Stalans, 2004). More than any other approach discussed in this chapter (and perhaps even the entire *Handbook*), notions about restorative justice have developed out of professional practice rather than academic circles. As a result, restorative justice procedures have unfolded in realistic settings in fascinating ways, but there has been tremendous variety and, therefore, imprecision concerning the definition of restorative justice practices. Although the goals of most restorative justice programs appear to be similar, the methods for achieving them differ considerably. Roche (2006) offered the following description: "One way to think of restorative justice is simply as a particular method for dealing with crime that brings together an offender, his or her victims, and their respective families and friends to discuss the aftermath of an incident, and the steps that can be taken to repair the harm an offender has done" (p. 217). Thus, rather than relying on a third party to impose a unilateral punishment upon a particular offender, restorative justice programs give the justice process "back to their rightful owners: offenders, victims, and their respective communities" (Wenzel, Okimoto, Feather, & Platow, 2008, p. 376).

In restorative justice sentencing, the various parties are encouraged to express their feelings, come to an agreement about the harm that has occurred, and decide together what actions should be taken to reestablish a sense of justice. The aim of such programs is to promote healing and justice through open discussion, consensus, and forgiveness. Rather than simply meting out punishment—punishment can be part of restorative justice outcomes, but it is not usually considered to be necessary—the agreed upon actions often involve the offender participating in events or activities that are directly related to the restoration of justice (e.g., participation in community service, etc.). When applied appropriately, this procedure is thought to help the victim and the broader community feel that justice has been restored and to reintegrate the perpetrator into community life so that he or she will be more likely to respect its norms in the future. A well-known example concerns the "truth and reconciliation" commission established in South Africa, following the abolition of the apartheid system (Gibson, 2004).

Research provides modest support for the general effectiveness of restorative justice programs. It has been associated, for example, with decreased recidivism in groups of juveniles, bullies, and white-collar criminals (Ahmed & Braithwaite, 2006; Harris, 2006; Latimer, Dowden, & Muise, 2005; Murphy & Harris, 2007; Rodriguez, 2007). These data should be interpreted with caution, however, because self-selection biases and measurement problems limit the kinds of causal inferences that can be drawn. Furthermore, the effectiveness of restorative justice programs is likely to depend upon a number of contextual variables, including offense type (Braithwaite & Mugford, 1994). But, evidence from quasi-experimental paradigms in which a range of beneficial effects of restorative justice programs has been demonstrated across a range of contexts and offenses is especially impressive (Strang et al., 2006; Wallace, Exline, & Baumeister, 2008).

From a social psychological perspective, the crucial question is not simply whether such programs are effective but why. Although the earliest restorative justice programs originated in the late 1970s, serious intellectual attention was not devoted to the issue until roughly a decade later. Braithwaite (1989) was instrumental in drawing attention to the phenomenon of "reintegrative shaming"—a form of shaming behavior in which the community condemns the transgression but not the transgressor, seeks to treat all of the parties with dignity and respect, and attempts to broker a situation of forgiveness. Although it is not synonymous with restorative justice, reintegrative shaming theory (RST) was the first academic attempt to explain how and why restorative justice programs can succeed. Harris (2006) observed that "one of the most distinctive features of RST is its focus on the social process of shaming as the crucial mechanism in crime control" (p. 330). The generation of shame-related emotions is thought to discourage future offenses by introducing a powerful signal as to what is considered wrong and motivating the offender to preserve his or her (presumably valued) relationships with the "shamer" (Braithwaite, 1989; Braithwaite & Braithwaite, 2001). By focusing on the shameful act rather than the individual who committed it, reintegrative shaming is thought to foster reintegration rather than stigmatization, which frequently results from traditional legal proceedings. Research on specific social psychological mechanisms triggered by restorative justice sanctions is scarce, and the available data indicate considerable nuance and complexity concerning the emotion of shame and the important task of shame management. Nevertheless, there is empirical support for the notion that shame-based emotions are evoked by restorative justice procedures (Ahmed & Braithwaite, 2006; Harris, 2006; Murphy & Harris, 2007; for conflicting views on shame and guilt, see Leith & Baumeister, 1998; Tangney, 1995).

Other research programs emphasize different social psychological mechanisms. Wenzel and colleagues (2008), for example, stressed the role of social identification needs in driving the restorative justice process. When victims (and other observers) view themselves as sharing a common group identity with the offender, restorative justice is often preferred, presumably because it seeks to reestablish values and preserve a sense of community. When the offender is viewed as an outgroup member, however, more traditional forms of punishment are seen as appropriate, insofar as they restore the balance between the status of the offender and the victim or community (Wenzel & Thielmann, 2006). Drawing on the work of Kurt Lewin, Tyler (2007) observed that restorative justice, like procedural justice, has the potential to encourage individuals to rely upon intrinsic motivation rather than external pressures in regulating their behavior.

Following a transgression, both victims and perpetrators develop social psychological needs (pertaining to status and belongingness, respectively) that need to be addressed (Shnabel & Nadler, 2008). The opportunity for social exchange, in which victim and perpetrator can satisfy each other's needs, may be a particularly effective way to help both parties. Despite the potential benefits of restorative sentencing procedures, public opinion polls reveal that attitudinal support for restorative justice programs decreases significantly as the severity of the crime increases (Roberts & Stalans, 2004). For crimes that are particularly severe, experimental research suggests that combining retributive and restorative justice procedures may best satisfy the desire for justice (Gromet & Darley, 2006).

One final question can be raised about the overarching goals of restorative measures and whether they always serve the broader cause of social justice. Capehart and Milovanovic (2007) put it this way:

> The glaring question is "Restore to what?" If, for example, structures and a particular form of community organizations reduce or repress the search for self-development and actualization, then, the transformative theorists argue, *simply to restore relations to this previous state is by itself contributing to the sustaining of reductive or repressive practices* (p. 61; emphasis added).

The problem highlighted here is by no means limited to the study of restorative justice; it should serve as a reminder always to consider the "forest" as well as the "trees," that is, the overall extent to which the social system that is being created or reinforced by the implementation of specific principles or mechanisms (allegedly in the name of distributive, procedural, interactional, retributive, or restorative justice concerns) actually is worth reinforcing (see also Tyler & Jost, 2007).

OBSTACLES TO ATTAINING SOCIAL JUSTICE

There are numerous potential obstacles to the attainment of social justice, including both selfishness and laziness. There is also the tendency to dehumanize one's enemies or to otherwise exclude them from the "scope of justice," so that common standards of decency, fairness, and morality simply are not applied to certain groups or individuals (e.g., Clayton & Opotow, 2003; Deutsch, 1985; Hafer & Olson, 2003; Opotow, 1995). In this section we focus on the ways in which authoritarianism, social dominance, and system justification tendencies can threaten to undermine the cause of social justice.

Authoritarianism and Social Dominance

Adorno, Frenkel-Brunswik, Levinson, and Sanford (1950) identified a personality syndrome that they regarded as a threat not merely to social justice but to democracy itself (see also Reich, 1946/1970). Specifically, they proposed that economic frustration and harsh childrearing tactics, among other dynamics, lead certain individuals (including a majority of individuals in some circumstances, such as Nazi Germany) to develop fascist (or proto-fascist) tendencies. The result was a population containing a disproportionate share of citizens gravitating toward rigid, stereotypical ways of thinking and extreme forms of prejudice and intolerance toward others, especially those who are considered deviants or convenient scapegoats. Subsequent research has shown that highly threatening circumstances elicit increased authoritarianism, especially in individuals who are prone to such responses (e.g., Bonanno & Jost, 2006; Brown, 1965; Davis & Silver, 2004; Doty, Peterson, & Winter, 1991; Feldman, 2003; Jost, Glaser, Kruglanski, & Sulloway, 2003; Lavine, Lodge, & Freitas, 2005; Napier & Jost, 2008b; Stenner, 2005).

Altemeyer (1981) updated the "classic" theory of authoritarianism to emphasize three major characteristics of the disposition: (1) "a high degree of submission to the authorities who are perceived to be established and legitimate"; (2) "a general aggressiveness, directed against various persons, which is perceived to be sanctioned by established authorities"; and (3) "a high degree of adherence to the social conventions which are perceived to be endorsed by society" (1981, p. 148). Scores on the Right-Wing Authoritarianism (RWA) scale predict a wide range of attitudes and behaviors, including racial prejudice; sexism; homophobia; victim-blaming; punishment of deviants; severity of jury sentencing decisions; lack of support for civil liberties and freedoms; and approval of illegal governmental activities, such as wire-tapping, unconstitutional drug raids, and political harassment and intimidation (e.g., see Altemeyer, 1981, 1996, 1998).

Social Dominance Orientation (SDO) gauges individual differences in "general support for the domination of certain socially constructed groups over other socially constructed groups," whether on the basis of "race, sex, religion, social class, region, skin color, clan, caste, lineage, tribe, minimal groups, or any other group distinction that the human mind is capable of creating" (Sidanius & Pratto, 1999). Support for social dominance is comprised of two subfactors: the desire for ingroup superiority and generalized opposition to equality (e.g., Eagly, Diekman, Johannesen-Schmidt, & Koenig, 2004; Foels & Pappas, 2004; Freeman, Aquino, & McFerran, 2009; Jost & Thompson, 2000). Altemeyer (1998) estimated that, when combined in a statistical model, respondents' scores on RWA and SDO scales account for more than half of the observable variation in prejudice and ethnocentrism. Guimond, Dambrun, Michinov, and Duarte (2003) found that SDO mediates the effect of social position (i.e., belonging to a high status and/ or powerful group) on prejudice.

Perhaps the most succinct and compelling explanation for why social dominance poses an inherent threat to the attainment of social justice comes from Walzer (1983), who observed that:

> The critique of dominance and domination points toward an open-ended distributive principle. *No social good x should be distributed to men and women who possess some other good y merely because they possess y and without regard to the meaning of x.* This is a principle that has probably been reiterated, at one time or another, for every y that has ever been dominant. But it has not often been stated in general terms. (p. 20)

In other words, it is unjust for individuals to disproportionately receive benefits or burdens simply because of some other (arbitrary, irrelevant) characteristic that they possess, such as belonging to a dominant or subordinated group. This is because, among other things, it violates basic notions of deservingness, including the merit (or contribution) principle, as well as what Mansbridge (2005) referred to as the "logic of formal justice"—the prescription to "Treat everyone equally unless you can give *relevant* reasons for unequal treatment" (p. 337; emphasis added). As Sidanius and Pratto (1999) point out, it is a regrettable if not reprehensible fact about many social systems that—at least in part because of their social group memberships—some individuals possess a "disproportionately large share of *positive social value*," including "such things as political authority and power, good and plentiful food, splendid homes, the best available health care, wealth, and high social status," whereas others "possess a disproportionately large share of *negative social value*," including such things as low power and social status, high-risk and low-status occupations, relatively poor health care, poor food, modest or miserable homes, and severe negative sanctions (e.g., prison and death sentences)" (pp. 31–32).

System Justification: The Palliative Function of Ideology

It would be difficult to find a more astute justice theorist or a bigger authority on ethical behavior in the entire history of Western civilization than Aristotle. And yet, there are aspects of his belief system that strike contemporary audiences as anomalous and obviously wrong-headed, possibly even immoral. Probably the most obvious example is his spirited defense of the institution of slavery as practiced by so many of his fellow Athenian citizens (see Kraut, 2002; Miller, 1995).[5] It is not the case that no one in ancient

---

[5] Aristotle's views on women (and sex differences in general) are also easily subject to criticism on normative as well as descriptive grounds (e.g., Miller, 1995, pp. 239–246).

Greece had ever raised moral objections about slavery; several philosophers of Aristotle's era had criticized the practice, but Aristotle apparently rejected those criticisms (Kraut, 2002, pp. 277–8). How could such a brilliant ethical mind possibly find itself arguing that such a brutal, exploitative institution as slavery was not only necessary but also just? The answer, it seems, has to do with *system justification*, defined as the conscious or unconscious motivation to defend, bolster, and justify existing social, economic, and political institutions and arrangements (Jost, Banaji, & Nosek, 2004). Kraut (2002) writes:

> No doubt, Aristotle believed that slavery was justified in part because that was a convenient tenet for him to hold. Had he come to the opposite conclusion, he would have been forced to announce to the Greek world that its political institutions, which he greatly valued (however much he also criticized them), rested on resources that could not be justly acquired or used. The all too human tendency to avoid upheavals of thought and revolutions in social practice certainly played a role here. But . . . in order for Aristotle to have arrived at the sincere conviction that slavery was just, his social world had to present itself to him in a way that supported that thesis. (p. 279)

Thus, a combination of social, cognitive, and motivational factors apparently led Aristotle to the conclusion that some individuals are "natural slaves" (by virtue of their "child-like helplessness") and others are "natural masters" (by virtue of their "rational faculties"). Thus, he argued that both slaves and masters benefit from the institution of slavery. As a result of these beliefs, Aristotle and his fellow Athenians were able to feel better about their own society and to rationalize away any guilt, dissonance, or negative affect that they might have otherwise felt. To make matters worse, because of Aristotle's philosophical stature, his arguments were resurrected in 16th-century Spain to justify the enslavement of indigenous people in the New World (Kraut, 2002, p. 277).

Motivation to Justify the Societal Status Quo

If Aristotle himself was tempted to excuse the injustices inherent in the social system he knew and loved, what hope is there for the rest of us to avoid a similar fate, at least with respect to some subset of social issues? According to system justification theory, all of us are *motivated*—to varying degrees, as a function of both dispositional and situational factors (e.g., Jost & Hunyady, 2002, 2005; Kay & Zanna, 2009)—to rationalize away the moral and other failures of our social, economic, and political institutions and to derogate alternatives to the status quo (Jost, Liviatan, van der Toorn, Ledgerwood, Mandisodza, & Nosek, 2009; Kay, Gaucher, Peach, Laurin, Friesen, Zanna, & Spencer, 2009). Thus, despite the fact that most Americans espouse egalitarian ideals and acknowledge substantial income inequality in society, surveys show that a majority of U.S. respondents judge the economic system to be highly fair and legitimate (Bartels, 2008; Jost, Blount, Pfeffer, & Hunyady, 2003). In the context of a chapter on social justice, it is worth pointing out that in the United States today the combined net worth of the 400 wealthiest citizens exceeds $1 trillion (Mishel, Bernstein, & Allegretta, 2005) and that corporate chief executives earn more than 500 times the salary of their average employee (Stiglitz, 2004). It would be difficult to find *any* justice principle (i.e., equity, equality, need, etc.) that would "justicize" this degree of economic inequality, and in fact the inequality has arisen not because it was judged in advance to be fair but because of impersonal "market forces" that most citizens accept (consciously or unconsciously) as legitimate (see also Benabou & Tirole, 2006; Kluegel & Smith, 1986).

Stereotyping as System Justification One way in which people engage in system justification is through the use of stereotypes (such as Aristotle's stereotypes of slaves and masters) that ascribe to individuals and groups characteristics that render them especially well-suited to occupy the status or positions that they do in the current social order (e.g., Allport, 1954; Eagly & Steffen, 1984; Hoffman & Hurst, 1990; Jost & Banaji, 1994; Jost & Kay, 2005; Kay, Jost, et al., 2007; Kay et al., 2009; Sidanius & Pratto, 1999). It is important to point out that members of disadvantaged groups sometimes internalize system-justifying stereotypes and evaluations of themselves, and this almost surely has the consequence of decreasing their likelihood of rebelling against the status quo or participating in collective action aimed to change it (e.g., Ashburn-Nardo, Knowles, & Monteith, 2003; Jost, Banaji, & Nosek, 2004; Jost, Pelham, & Carvallo, 2002; Lewin, 1941/1948b; Rudman, Feinberg & Fairchild, 2002; Uhlmann, Dasgupta, Elgueta, Greenwald, & Swanson, 2002).

System-Justifying Aspects of Conservative Ideology Certain ideologies—such as political conservatism, which developed in part out of Edmund Burke's (1790/1987) critical resistance to the French Revolution and his efforts to "vindicate" the social order—satisfy the "goal" of system justification as well (see Jost, Glaser, Kruglanski, & Sulloway, 2003; Jost, 2009). More than two centuries after the French Revolution, political conservatives continue to show stronger implicit as well as explicit preferences for order, stability, conformity, and tradition (over chaos, flexibility, rebelliousness, and progress), in comparison with liberals and others (Jost, Nosek, & Gosling, 2008). The fact that political conservatives are motivated more strongly than liberals by system justification motivation helps to

explain why: (a) they strongly favor advantaged over disadvantaged groups on implicit as well as explicit measures (Jost, Banaji, & Nosek, 2004); (b) their Black–White racial attitudes lagged behind those of liberals by over thirty years in the United States (Nosek, Banaji, & Jost, 2009); (c) they are more likely to deny problems associated with global climate change and to resist efforts to change current environmental practices (Feygina, Goldsmith, & Jost, in press); and (d) they are relatively insulated against the negative hedonic effects of increasing inequality (Napier & Jost, 2008a). Thus, at least some of the attitudinal differences observed between liberals and conservatives can be understood in terms of variability in system justification tendencies.

Costs and Benefits of System Justification

System justification appears to satisfy a constellation of *epistemic* needs to attain certainty and create a stable, predictable worldview (Jost, Glaser, Kruglanski, & Sulloway, 2003); *existential* needs to manage threat and perceive a safe, reassuring environment (Kay, Gaucher, Napier, Callan, & Laurin, 2008); and *relational* needs to achieve shared reality with important others, including friends and family members who are also motivated by system justification concerns (Jost, Ledgerwood, & Hardin, 2008). Perhaps because it addresses these various needs, system justification conveys *palliative* psychological benefits, including increased positive affect and (especially) decreased negative affect (Janoff-Bulman, 1992; Jost & Hunyady, 2002; Kay, Gaucher, Napier, Callan, & Laurin, 2008; Kluegel & Smith, 1986; Lerner, 1980; Napier & Jost, 2008a; Wakslak, Jost, Tyler, & Chen, 2007). At the same time, however, system justification is associated with low self-esteem, depression, ambivalence, and outgroup favoritism among members of disadvantaged groups, who may be "caught" between competing desires to feel good about themselves and to feel good about the social system to which they belong (e.g., Ashburn-Nardo, Knowles, & Monteith, 2003; Jost & Burgess, 2000; Jost, Pelham, & Carvallo, 2002; Jost & Thompson, 2000; O'Brien & Major, 2005).

It has been suggested that system-justifying attitudes reflect a "moral motivation" to protect society and that "the benefits of justifying the system are not just palliative, they are meaning-providing and can often be important for human flourishing" (Haidt & Graham, 2009, p. 391). Without disputing that system justification contributes to social stability and carries with it a number of social and psychological advantages for the individual, group, and society, it seems important to point out that it is probably *neither* moral *nor* immoral in and of itself. System justification can indeed inspire people to celebrate and vindicate truly just institutions and practices. Nevertheless, the same motivation can lead us—as it may have led Aristotle—to venerate those features of the social system (e.g., customs, traditions, and practices) that should, on normative grounds, be changed. As Frankena (1962) pointed out, "All sorts of injustices may be enshrined in the rules of society, as those who settled this country knew and as many of those whose ancestors did not come willingly know even now" (pp. 8–9).

FROM THEORY TO PRACTICE: WHAT CAN SOCIAL PSYCHOLOGY CONTRIBUTE TO SOCIAL JUSTICE?

The topic of social justice brings into stark relief both the promise and challenges of social psychology in a way that perhaps no other subject matter covered in this *Handbook* does. Among other things, social justice is a theme that requires one to consider and integrate insights arising from individual, group, and system levels of analysis (Doise, 1986; Stangor & Jost, 1997). Students of social justice—like those who dare to confront questions of rationality or truth—must grapple with the uneasy relationship between the subjective and the objective or, what is nearly the same in this context, descriptive facts about how people actually think, feel, and act with respect to justice considerations and normative standards about how they *ought* to behave if their actions and institutions are to be considered just (see also Baron, 1993; Elster, 1992; Feinberg, 1973; Frankena, 1962; Konow, 2003; Lerner, 2003; Miller, 1999; Payne & Cameron, in press; Sandel, 1998; Tyler & Jost, 2007; Walzer, 1983).

Of course, reasonable (as well as unreasonable) parties can disagree about what justice entails, and many longstanding, seemingly intractable conflicts, such as the Arab-Israeli conflict, involve interpersonal or intergroup disputes over what is considered fair and legitimate (e.g., Deutsch, 2006; Gibson, 2008; Jost & Ross, 1999; Kelman, 2001; Leung & Stephan, 2000; Mikula & Wenzel, 2000). At the same time, it is not entirely satisfying to conclude simply that justice (like truth or beauty) is in the "eye of the beholder." As Miller (1999) observed, "Popular beliefs about social justice may turn out to be defective in various ways; for instance, they may prove to conceal deep contradictions, or involve serious factual errors" (p. x). If we accept this possibility, then we cannot merely assume that justice consists solely of what people *think* is just (see also Sampson, 1983), even though it may be a difficult task to determine what actually *is* just (or unjust) in any given situation.

Another reason why one cannot simply interpret the subjective acceptance of a given state of affairs as conclusive evidence of its objective fairness is that people sometimes tolerate circumstances, such as slavery, apartheid, or caste systems, that seem obviously unjust to outsiders, or in retrospect, or from the point of view of clearly established standards of just treatment (Crosby, 1982; Deutsch, 1985; Lerner, 1980; Martin, 1986; Moore, 1978). Some such cases are said to reflect "false consciousness," defined as false beliefs that serve to sustain injustice or oppression (Fox, 1999; Jost, 1995; Lind & Tyler, 1988). They may also suggest the presence of system justification motivation, that is, the desire to exonerate the existing social system and, in so doing, to minimize or overlook its injustices, whether petty or grand (see Jost, Banaji, & Nosek, 2004; Jost et al., 2009; Kay et al., 2009).

For all of these reasons, the scholar of social justice must at least bear in mind the possibility that there are objective standards of justice, even if specific candidates are bound to be controversial (e.g., see Feinberg, 1973; Hare, 1981; Miller, 1999; Rawls, 1971). Much as researchers use scientific means to identify the objective causes of subjective well-being (or happiness) of individuals (e.g., Kahneman, Diener, & Schwarz, 1999), it should be possible for social scientists to discover which characteristics of social systems are more and less likely to maximize equity, equality, need, liberty, respect, and other putative principles of social justice, and which characteristics lead disproportionately to unjust outcomes, such as suffering, exploitation, abuse, prejudice, and oppression. It seems like a daunting task to develop objective (as well as subjective) measures of well-being at the system or societal level, but there is no way of knowing whether scientific methods can gain traction on age-old problems of social justice unless and until it is attempted.

Work by Jasso (1999) suggests that it may be possible to draw meaningful comparisons among different societies with respect to their abilities to satisfy certain standards of distributive justice. By extending this general approach to incorporate objective, quantifiable indicators of well-being (e.g., health, wealth, education, work satisfaction, and quality of life) in drawing comparisons among nations that prioritize different justice principles, empirical research could leverage utilitarian and other insights concerning social justice. Likewise, it may be feasible to compare societies in terms of how well they adhere to specific deontological principles; indeed, some human rights organizations collect international data to draw precisely such comparisons. The most compelling normative theory (or metatheory) of social justice will probably combine elements of utilitarian and deontological approaches and reconcile multiple, potentially conflicting justice principles—such as equity, equality, need, merit, liberty, consistency, accuracy, and ethicality— in some hierarchical structure that weights such principles differentially as a function of contextual variables, local contingencies, and domains of application. As John Stuart

Mill (1910) observed, "Not only have different nations and individuals different notions of justice, but, in the mind of one and the same individual, justice is not some one rule, principle, or maxim, but many, which do not always coincide in their dictates" (p. 51).

Empirical research has a crucial role to play in clearing away common misconceptions—including erroneous assumptions, stereotypes, and misunderstandings about the causes of human behavior—and thereby updating and elevating public discourse about matters of social justice and morality (Greene, 2003; Payne & Cameron, in press). Over time, we have seen that scientific findings can change culturally prevalent representations of free will, consciousness, responsibility, and so on, and these changes slowly manifest themselves in legal and judicial transformations (e.g., Blasi & Jost, 2006; Greene & Cohen, 2004; Wegner, 2002).[6] Cognitive scientists have contributed mightily to refining normative theories of *rationality* (e.g., Kahneman et al., 1982; March & Simon, 1958; Thaler, 1991) as well as formerly philosophical (and even metaphysical) treatments of epistemological questions in general (Goldman, 1992; Kornblith, 1999; Quine, 1969; Stich, 1990). In recent years, philosophers have incorporated evidence from social and personality psychology in evaluating Aristotelian and other normative (as well as descriptive) theories of ethics, virtue, and moral character (Appiah, 2008; Doris, 2002; Flanagan, 1991; Harman, 1999; J. T. Jost & L. J. Jost, 2009). There is no *a priori* reason to assume that social psychological research will be less useful in forging the kinds of normative conceptions of justice and injustice that have traditionally been the bread and butter of moral philosophy and legal scholarship (see also Tyler & Jost, 2007).

Another basis for optimism concerning attempts to "naturalize" the study of social justice comes from explicit efforts to integrate legal studies with research in the social and behavioral sciences (e.g., Sunstein, 2000), including calls for "psychological jurisprudence" (Darley, Fulero, Haney, & Tyler, 2002; Haney, 1993; Tyler & Jost, 2007) and "behavioral realism" (Blasi & Jost, 2006; Hanson & Yosifon, 2004; Kang, 2005; Krieger & Fiske, 2006). Each of these represents a concerted attempt to bring the law and public policy into better alignment with conclusions

---

[6] Philosophers, including Rawls (1971), often strive to develop normative theories of justice that satisfy the principle of "minimal psychological realism," that is, theories that are at least consistent with what is known about the laws of human psychology. Legal authorities, too, have a vested interest in prescribing laws that are psychologically realistic in the sense that most citizens will be able to follow them.

drawn from the scientific study of human nature. It has been suggested, for instance, that current legal protections against racial discrimination (e.g., the Davis doctrine) are inadequate because they focus exclusively on conscious intention as an explanation for human behavior and the basis for assigning legal responsibility, whereas contemporary social and cognitive psychology has demonstrated that automatic, implicit (i.e., unintentional) processes are capable of producing discriminatory outcomes (Greenwald & Krieger, 2006; Kang & Banaji, 2006; Krieger, 1995; Lane, Kang, & Banaji, 2007; Lawrence, 2008; but see Mitchell & Tetlock, 2006 for a dissenting view).

All of this returns us to the grand Lewinian ambitions with which we began this chapter. The notion of solving social problems through rational, scientific means rather than ideological (or even coercive) means is particularly attractive (e.g., Allport, 1954, 1962; Deutsch, 1999; Lerner, 1980, 2003; Lewin, 1939/1948a; Mansbridge, 2005; McGuire, 1985; Walton & Dweck, 2009). Along these lines, Kurt Lewin (1939/1948a) argued that the objectives of science and social justice were in fact highly compatible:

> To believe in reason means to believe in democracy, because it grants to the reasoning partners a status of equality. It is therefore not an accident that not until the rise of democracy at the time of the American and French Revolutions was the goddess of "reason" enthroned in modern society. And again, it is not an accident that the first act of modern Fascism in every country has been officially and vigorously to dethrone this goddess and instead to make emotions and obedience the all-ruling principles in education and life from kindergarten to death.
>
> *I am persuaded that scientific sociology and social psychology based on an intimate combination of experiments and empirical theory can do as much, or more, for human betterment as the natural sciences have done.* However, the development of such a realistic, nonmystical social science and the possibility of its fruitful application presuppose the existence of a society which believes in reason. (p. 83; emphasis added)

Thus, Lewin was enthusiastic—even "heroic," according to some (e.g., Ring, 1967)—about the use of social science to serve the ends of social justice and, in so doing, to improve society. The evidence we have reviewed in this chapter suggests that considerable progress toward this most ambitious goal has been achieved (e.g., see Benabou & Tirole, 2006; Deutsch, 1985, 2006; Frohlich & Oppenheimer, 1992; Jasso, 1999; Konow, 2003; Lerner, 1987; Lind & Tyler, 1988; Major, 1994; Mikula & Wenzel, 2000; Miller, 2001; Payne & Cameron, in press; Pettigrew et al., 2008; Rossi & Berk, 1997; Skitka & Tetlock, 1993; Thibaut & Walker, 1986; Tyler, 2006, 2007; Tyler & Jost, 2007; Van den Bos, 2005; Van Lange, 2000; Wakslak et al., 2007). At the same time, the jury is still out on whether the theories and methods of social psychology can offer unique, indispensable insights that—when combined with those gathered from philosophy, law, history, anthropology, sociology, economics, political science, and other disciplines—will enable the human race to attain the highest degree of social justice in practice and to permanently overcome its most stubborn, pernicious obstacles. We follow Kurt Lewin in supposing, however optimistically, that they can.

REFERENCES

Adams, J. S. (1965). Inequality in social exchange. In L. Berkowitz (Ed.), *Advances in experimental social psychology*, (Vol. 2, pp. 267–299). New York: Academic Press.

Adelson, H. L. (1995). The origins of a concept of social justice. In K. D. Irani & M. Silver (Eds.), *Social justice in the ancient world* (pp. 25–38). Westport, CT: Greenwood Press.

Adorno, T. W., Frenkel-Brunswik, E., Levinson, D. J., & Sanford, R. N. (1950). *The authoritarian personality*. New York: Harper.

Aguiar, P., Vala, J., Correia, I., & Pereira, C. (2008). Justice in our world and in that of others: Belief in a just world and reactions to victims. *Social Justice Research, 21*, 50–68.

Ahmed, E., & Braithwaite, V. (2006). Forgiveness, reconciliation, and shame: Three key variables in reducing school bullying. *Journal of Social Issues, 62*, 347–370.

Albert, S. (1977). Temporal comparison theory. *Psychological Review, 84*, 485–503.

Allison, S. T., Beggan, J. K., & Midgley, E. H. (1996). The quest for "similar instances" and "simultaneous possibilities": Metaphors in social dilemma research. *Journal of Personality and Social Psychology, 71*, 479–497.

Allport, G. W. (1954). *The nature of prejudice*. Cambridge, MA: Addison-Wesley.

Allport, G. W. (1962). The historical background of modern social psychology. In G. Lindzey & E. Aronson (Eds.), *The handbook of social psychology* (2nd ed., Vol. 1, pp. 1–80). Reading, MA: Addison-Wesley. (Original work published in 1954)

Altemeyer, R. (1981). *Right wing authoritarianism*. Winnipeg, Manitoba, Canada: University of Manitoba Press.

Altemeyer, B. (1996). *The authoritarian specter*. Cambridge, MA: Harvard University Press.

Altemeyer, B. (1998). The other "authoritarian personality." In M. P. Zanna (Ed.), *Advances in experimental social psychology* (Vol. 30, pp. 47–92). New York: Academic Press.

Alves, H., & Correia, I. (2008). On the normativity of expressing the belief in a just world: Empirical evidence. *Social Justice Research, 21*, 106–118.

Ambrose, M. L., & Arnaud, A. (2005). Are procedural justice and distributive justice conceptually distinct? In J. Greenberg & J. A. Colquitt (Eds.), *Handbook of organizational justice* (pp. 59–84). Mahwah, NJ: Erlbaum.

Ambrose, M. L., & Kulik, C. T. (1999). Old friends, new faces: Motivation research in the 1990s. *Journal of Management, 25*, 231–292.

Ambrose, M. L., Seabright, M. A., & Schminke, M. (2002). Sabotage in the workplace: The role of organizational injustice. *Organizational Behavior and Human Decision Processes, 89*, 947–965.

Anderson, V. N. (1992). For whom is this world just? Sexual orientation and AIDS. *Journal of Applied Social Psychology, 22*, 248–259.

Appiah, K.A. (2008). *Experiments in ethics*. Cambridge, MA: Harvard University Press.

Aristotle (2002). *Nicomachean ethics* (S. Broadie & C. Rowe [Eds.], Trans.). New York: Oxford University Press. (Original work published 384-322 BCE).

Aryee, S., Budhwar, P. S., & Chen, Z. X. (2002). Trust as a mediator of the relationship between organizational justice and work outcomes: Test of a social exchange model. *Journal of Organizational Behavior, 23*, 267–286.

Asch, S. E. (1959). A perspective on social psychology. In S. Koch (Ed.), *Psychology: A study of a science* (Vol. 3, pp. 363–383). New York: McGraw-Hill.

Ashburn-Nardo, L., Knowles, M. L., & Monteith, M. J. (2003). Black Americans' implicit racial associations and their implications for intergroup judgment. *Social Cognition, 21*, 61–87.

Au, W. T., & Kwong, J. Y. Y. (2004). Measurements and effects of social-value orientation in social dilemmas: A review. In R. Suleiman, D. V. Budescu, I. Fischer, & D. M. Messick (Eds.), *Contemporary psychological research on social dilemmas*. (pp. 71–98). New York: Cambridge University Press.

Austin, W., & Walster, E. (1974). Participants' reactions to "equity with the world." *Journal of Experimental Social Psychology, 10*, 528–548.

Axelrod, R. (2006). *The evolution of cooperation* (Rev. ed.). New York: Perseus.

Azzi, A. E., & Jost, J. T. (1997). Votes without power: Procedural justice as mutual control in majority–minority relations. *Journal of Applied Social Psychology, 27*, 124–155.

Bargh, J. A., Raymond, P., Pryor, J. B., & Strack, F. (1995). Attractiveness of the underling: An automatic power-sex association and its consequences for sexual harassment and aggression. *Journal of Personality and Social Psychology, 68*, 768–781.

Baron, J. (1993). Heuristics and biases in equity judgments: A utilitarian approach. In B. A. Mellers & J. Baron (Eds.), *Psychological perspectives on justice* (pp. 109–137). New York: Cambridge University Press.

Barrett-Howard, E., & Tyler, T. R. (1986). Procedural justice as a criterion in allocation decisions. *Journal of Personality and Social Psychology, 50*, 296–304.

Barry, B. M. (2005). *A treatise on social justice*. Berkeley, CA: University of California Press.

Bartels, L. M. (2008). *Unequal democracy: The political economy of the new gilded age*. Princeton, NJ : Princeton University Press.

Batson, C. D. (1990). How social is an animal? The human capacity for caring. *American Psychologist, 45*, 336–346.

Batson, C. D. (1998). Altruism and prosocial behavior. In D. Gilbert, S. Fiske, & G. Lindzey (Eds.), *Handbook of social psychology* (pp. 282–316). New York: McGraw-Hill.

Batson, C. D., Batson, J. G., Singlsby, J. K., Harrell, K. L., Peekna, H. M., & Todd, R. M. (1991). Empathic joy and the empathy–altruism hypothesis. *Journal of Personality and Social Psychology, 61*, 413–426.

Batson, C. D., & Moran, T. (1999). Empathy-induced altruism in a prisoner's dilemma. *European Journal of Social Psychology, 29*, 909924.

Batson, C. D., & Shaw, L. L. (1991). Evidence for altruism: Toward a pluralism of prosocial motives. *Psychological Inquiry, 2*, 107–122.

Baumeister, R. F., & Leary, M. R. (1995). The need to belong: Desire for interpersonal attachments as a fundamental human motivation. *Psychological Bulletin, 117*, 497–529.

Bazemore, G. (1998). Restorative justice and earned redemption: Communities, victims, and offender reintegration. *American Behavioral Scientist, 41*, 768–813.

Becker, G. (1976). *The economic approach to human behavior*. Chicago: University of Chicago Press.

Bègue, L., & Bastounis, M. (2003). Two spheres of belief in justice: Extensive support for the bidimensional model of belief in a just world. *Journal of Personality, 71*, 435–463.

Benabou, R. & Tirole, J. (2006). Belief in a just world and redistributive politics. *Quarterly Journal of Economics, 121*, 1652–1678.

Bentham, J. (1962). Principles of penal law. In J. Bowring (Ed.), *The works of Jeremy Bentham* (pp. 396). Edinburgh: W. Tait. (Original work published 1843).

Bernstein, M., & Crosby, F. (1980). An empirical examination of relative deprivation theory. *Journal of Experimental Social Psychology, 16*, 442–456.

Bierhoff, H. W., Buck, E., & Klein, R. (1986). Social context and perceived injustice. In H. W. Bierhoff, R. L. Cohen, & J. Greenberg (Eds.), *Justice in social relations* (pp. 165–185). New York: Plenum.

Biernat, M., Vescio, T. K., & Theno, S. A. (1996). Violating American values: A "value congruence" approach to understanding outgroup attitudes. *Journal of Experimental Social Psychology, 32*, 387–410.

Biernat, M., & Wortman, C. B. (1991). Sharing of home responsibilities between professionally employed women and their husbands. *Journal of Personality and Social Psychology, 60*, 844–860.

Bies, R. J. (2001). Interactional (in)justice: The sacred and the profane. In J. Greenberg & R. Cropanzano (Eds.), *Advances in organizational justice* (pp. 89–118). Stanford, CA: Stanford University Press.

Bies, R. J. (2005). Are procedural justice and interactional justice conceptually distinct? In J. Greenberg & J. A. Colquitt (Eds.), *Handbook of organizational justice* (pp. 85–112). Mahwah, NJ: Erlbaum.

Bies, R. J., & Moag, J. S. (1986). Interactional justice: Communication criteria of fairness. In B. Sheppard (Ed.), *Research on negotiation in organizations* (pp. 43–55). Greenwich, CT: JAI Press.

Blanton, H., George, G., & Crocker, J. (2001). Contexts of system justification and system evaluation: Exploring the social comparison strategies of the (not yet) contented female worker. *Group Processes & Intergroup Relations, 4*, 126–137.

Blau, P. M. (1968). Social exchange. In D. L. Sills (Ed.), *International encyclopedia of the social sciences* (Vol. 7). New York: Macmillan.

Blasi, G., & Jost, J. T. (2006). System justification theory and research: Implications for law, legal advocacy, and social justice. *California Law Review, 94*, 1119–1168.

Bobocel, D. R., & Holmvall, C. M. (2001). Are interactional justice and procedural justice different? Framing the debate. In S. Gilliland, D. Steiner, & D. Skarlicki (Eds.), *Research in social research in social issues in management: Theoretical and cultural perspectives on organizational justice* (pp. 85–108). Greenwich, CT: Information Age.

Bogaert, S., Boone, C., & Declerck, C. (2008). Social value orientation and cooperation in social dilemmas: A review and conceptual model. *British Journal of Social Psychology, 47*, 453–480.

Bolino, M. C., & Turnley, W. H. (2008). Old faces, new places: Equity theory in cross-cultural contexts. *Journal of Organizational Behavior, 29*, 29–50.

Boll, T., Ferring, D., & Filipp, S. (2005). Effects of parental differential treatment on relationship quality with siblings and parents: Justice evaluations as mediators. *Social Justice Research, 18*, 155–182.

Bonanno, G. A., & Jost, J. T. (2006). Conservative shift among high-exposure survivors of the September 11 terrorist attacks. *Basic and Applied Social Psychology, 28*, 311–323.

Bond, D., & Park, J. (1991). An empirical test of Rawls's theory of justice: A second approach, in Korea and the United States. *Simulation & Gaming, 22*, 443–462.

Boucher, D., & Kelly, P. (Eds.). (1998). *Social justice from Hume to Walzer.* New York: Routledge.

Bowie, N. E., & Simon, R. L. (2007). *The individual and the political order: An introduction to social and political philosophy* (4th ed.). New York: Rowman & Littlefield.

Braithwaite, J. (1989). *Crime, shame, and reintegration.* New York: Cambridge University Press.

Braithwaite, J., & Braithwaite, V. (2001). Shame and shame management. In E. Ahmed, N. Harris, J. Braithwaite, & V. Braithwaite (Eds.), *Shame management and regulation* (pp. 3–69). Cambridge, England: Cambridge University Press.

Braithwaite, J., & Mugford, S. (1994). Conditions of successful reintegration ceremonies: Dealing with juvenile offenders. *British Journal of Criminology, 34*, 139–171.

Braman, A. C., & Lambert, A. J. (2001). Punishing individuals for their infirmities: Effects of personal responsibility, just-world beliefs, and in-group/out-group status. *Journal of Applied Social Psychology, 31*, 1096–1109.

Brickman, P. (1977). Preference for inequality. *Social Psychology Quarterly, 40*, 303–310.

Brickman, P., Coates, D., & Janoff-Bulman, R. (1978). Lottery winners and accident victims: Is happiness relative? *Journal of Personality and Social Psychology, 36*, 917–927.

Broadie, S. (2002). Philosophical introduction. In S. Broadie & C. Rowe (Eds.), *Aristotle, Nicomachean ethics: Translation, introduction, and commentary* (pp. 9–91). New York: Oxford University Press.

Brockner, J., Heuer, L., & Magner, N. (2003). High procedural fairness heightens the effect of outcome favorability on self-evaluations: An attributional analysis. *Organizational Behavior and Human Decision Processes, 91*, 51–68.

Brockner, J., Heuer, L., Siegel, P. A., Wiesenfeld, B., Martin, C., Grover, S., et al. (1998). The moderating effect of self-esteem in reaction to voice: Converging evidence from five studies. *Journal of Personality and Social Psychology, 75*, 394–407.

Brockner, J., & Wiesenfeld, B. (1996). An integrative framework for explaining reactions to decisions: Interactive effects of outcomes and procedures. *Psychological Bulletin, 120*, 189–208.

Brosnan, S. F. (2006). Nonhuman species' reactions to inequity and their implications for fairness. *Social Justice Research, 19*, 153–185.

Brosnan, S. F., & de Waal, F.B.M. (2003). Monkeys reject unequal pay. *Nature, 425*, 297–299.

Brown, R. (1965). *Social psychology.* New York: Free Press.

Budescu, D. V., Rapoport, A., & Suleiman, R. (1990). Resource dilemmas with environmental uncertainty and asymmetric players. *European Journal of Social Psychology, 20*, 475–487.

Burkart, J. M., Fehr, E., Efferson, C., & van Schaik, C. P. (2007). Other-regarding preferences in a non-human primate: Common marmosets provision food altruistically. *Proceedings of the National Academy of Sciences, 104*, 19762–19766.

Burke, E. (1987). Reflections on the revolution in France. In J.G.A. Pocock (Ed.), *Reflections on the revolution in France* (pp. 1–218). Indianapolis: Hackett. (Original work published 1790).

Callahan-Levy, C. M., & Messé, L. A. (1979). Sex differences in the allocation of pay. *Journal of Personality and Social Psychology, 37*, 433–446.

Callan, M. J., Ellard, J. H., & Nicol, J. E. (2006). The belief in a just world and immanent justice reasoning in adults. *Personality and Social Psychology Bulletin, 32*, 1646–1658.

Callan, M. J., Kay, A. C., Davidenko, N., & Ellard, J. H. (in press). The effects of justice motivation for memory for self- and other-relevant events. *Journal of Experimental Social Psychology.*

Callan, M. J., Powell, N. G., & Ellard, J. H. (2007). The consequences of victim physical attractiveness on reactions to injustice: The role of observers' belief in a just world. *Social Justice Research, 20*, 433–456.

Campbell, T. (2001). *Justice* (2nd ed.). New York: St. Martin's Press.

Capehart, L., & Milovanovic, D. (2007). *Social justice: Theories, issues, and movements.* New York: Rutgers University Press.

Carlsmith, K. M. (2006). The roles of retribution and utility in determining punishment. *Journal of Experimental Social Psychology, 42*, 437–451.

Carlsmith, K. M. (2008). On justifying punishment: The discrepancy between words and actions. *Social Justice Research, 21*, 119–137.

Carlsmith, K. M., & Darley, J. M. (2008). Psychological aspects of retributive justice. In M. P. Zanna (Ed.), *Advances in experimental social psychology* (pp. 193–236). San Diego, CA: Elsevier.

Carlsmith, K. M., Darley, J. M., & Robinson, P. H. (2002). Why do we punish? Deterrence and just deserts as motives for punishment. *Journal of Personality and Social Psychology, 83*, 284–299.

Carlsmith, K. M., & Sood, A. M. (2009). The fine line between interrogation and retribution. *Journal of Experimental Social Psychology, 45*, 191–196.

Carr, S. C., & MacLachlan, M. (1998). Actors, observers, and attributions for third world poverty: Contrasting perspectives from Malawi and Australia. *Journal of Social Psychology, 138*, 189–202.

Cartwright, D. (1979). Contemporary social psychology in historical perspective. *Social Psychology Quarterly, 42*, 82–93.

Chen, C. C. (1995). New trends in rewards allocation preferences: A Sino–U.S. comparison. *Academy of Management Journal, 38*, 408–428.

Christiansen, N. D., & Lavine, H. (1997). Need-efficiency trade-offs in the allocation of resources: Ideological and attributional differences in public aid decision making. *Social Justice Research, 10*, 289–310.

Cialdini, R. B., Brown, S. L., Lewis, B. P., Luce, C., & Neuberg, S. L. (1997). Reinterpreting the empathy–altruism relationship: When one into one equals oneness. *Journal of Personality and Social Psychology, 73*, 481–494.

Cialdini, R. B., Schaller, M., Houlihan, D., Arps, K., Fultz, J., & Beaman, A. L. (1987). Empathy-based helping: Is it selflessly or selfishly motivated? *Journal of Personality and Social Psychology, 52*, 749–758.

Clark, M. S., & Mills, J. (1979). Interpersonal attraction in exchange and communal relationships. *Journal of Personality and Social Psychology, 37*, 12–24.

Clayton, S., & Opotow, S. (2003). Justice and identity: Changing perspectives on what is fair. *Personality and Social Psychology Review, 7*, 298–310.

Cohen, A. B., & Rozin, P. (2001). Religion and the morality of mentality. *Journal of Personality and Social Psychology, 81*, 697–710.

Cohen, R. L., & Greenberg, J. (1982). The justice concept in social psychology. In J. Greenberg & R. L. Cohen (Eds.), *Equity and justice in social behavior* (pp. 1–41). New York: Academic Press.

Cohen-Charash, Y., & Spector, P. E. (2001). The role of justice in organizations: A meta-analysis. *Organizational Behavior and Human Decision Processes, 86*, 278–321.

Colquitt, J. A. (2001). On the dimensionality of organizational justice: A construct validation of a measure. *Journal of Applied Psychology, 86*, 386–400.

Colquitt, J. A., Conlon, D. E., Wesson, M. J., Porter, C. O. L. H., & Ng, K. Y. (2001). Justice at the millenium: A meta-analytic review of 25 years of organizational justice research. *Journal of Applied Psychology, 86*, 425–445.

Colquitt, J. A., Greenberg, J., & Zapata-Phelan, C. P. (2005). What is organizational justice? A historical overview. In J. Greenberg & J. A. Colquitt (Eds.), *Handbook of organizational justice* (pp. 3–56). Mahwah, NJ: Erlbaum.

Cook, K. S., & Hegtvedt, K. A. (1986). Justice and power: An exchange analysis. In H. W. Bierhoff, R. L. Cohen, & J. Greenberg (Eds.), *Justice in social relations* (pp. 19–41). New York: Plenum.

Correia, I., Vala, J., & Aguiar, P. (2007). Victim's innocence, social categorization, and the threat to the belief in a just world. *Journal of Experimental Social Psychology, 43*, 31–38.

Crandall, C. S. (1994). Prejudice against fat people: Ideology and self-interest. *Journal of Personality and Social Psychology, 66*, 882–894.

Crandall, C. S., Eidelman, S., Skitka, L. J., & Morgan, G. S. (2009). Status quo framing increases support for torture. *Social Influence, 4*, 1–10.

Crandall, C. S., & Eshleman, A. (2003). A justification–suppression of the expression and experience of prejudice. *Psychological Bulletin, 129*, 414–446.

Crandall, C. S., & Martinez, R. (1996). Culture, ideology, and antifat attitudes. *Personality and Social Psychology Bulletin, 22*, 1165–1176.

Crespi, B. J. (2000). The evolution of maladaptation. *Heredity, 84*, 623–629.

Crocker, J., & Major, B. (1989). Social stigma and self-esteem: The self-protective properties of stigma. *Psychological Review, 96*, 608–630.

Cropanzano, R., & Folger, R. (1989). Referent cognitions and task decision autonomy: Beyond equity theory. *Journal of Applied Psychology, 74*, 293–299.

Cropanzano, R., Prehar, C. A., & Chen, P. Y. (2002). Using social exchange theory to distinguish procedural from interactional justice. *Group & Organization Management, 27*, 324–351.

Crosby, F. (1976). A model of egoistical relative deprivation. *Psychological Review, 83*, 85–113.

Crosby, F. (1982). *Relative deprivation and the working woman.* New York: Oxford University Press.

Crosby, F., Muehrer, P., & Loewenstein, G. (1986). Relative deprivation and explanation: Models and concepts. In J. M. Olson, C. P. Herman, & M. P. Zanna (Eds.), *Relative deprivation and social comparison: The Ontario symposium* (Vol. 4, pp. 17–32). Hillsdale, NJ: Erlbaum.

Curtis, R. C. (1979). Effects of knowledge of self-interest and social relationship upon the use of equity, utilitarian, and Rawlsian principles of allocation. *European Journal of Social Psychology, 9*, 165–175.

Cushman, F., Young, L., & Hauser, M. (2006). The role of conscious reasoning and intuition in moral judgment: Testing three principles of harm. *Psychological Science, 17*, 1082–1089.

Dalbert, C. (1998). Belief in a just world, well-being, and coping with an unjust fate. In L. Montada & M. J. Lerner (Eds.), *Responses to victimizations and belief in a just world* (pp. 87–105). New York: Plenum.

Dalbert, C. (2001). *The justice motive as a personal resource: Dealing with challenges and critical life events.* New York: Plenum.

Dalbert, C. (2002). Beliefs in a just world as a buffer against anger. *Social Justice Research, 15*, 123–145.

Dambrun, M. (2007). Understanding the relationship between racial prejudice and support for the death penalty: The racist punitive bias hypothesis. *Social Justice Research, 20*, 228–249.

Dambrun, M., Taylor, D. M., McDonald, D. A., Crush, J., & Méot, A. (2006). The relative deprivation–gratification continuum and the attitudes of South Africans toward immigrants: A test of the V-curve hypothesis. *Journal of Personality and Social Psychology, 91*, 1032–1044.

Darley, J. M., Carlsmith, K. M., & Robinson, P. H. (2000). Incapacitation and just deserts as motives for punishment. *Law and Human Behavior, 24*, 659–683.

Darley, J. M., Fulero, S., Haney, C., & Tyler, T. (2002). Psychological jurisprudence: Taking psychology and law into the twenty-first century. In J. R. P. Ogloff (Ed.), *Taking psychology and law into the twenty-first century* (pp. 35–59). New York: Plenum.

Darley, J. M., & Pittman, T. S. (2003). The psychology of compensatory and retributive justice. *Personality and Social Psychology Review, 7*, 324–336.

Darwin, C. (1871). *The descent of man and selection in relation to sex.* London: John Murray.

Dawkins, R. (1989). *The selfish gene* (2nd ed.). Oxford: Oxford University Press.

Davies, J. C. (1962). Towards a theory of revolution. *American Sociological Review, 27*, 5–19.

Davis, J. A. (1959). A formal interpretation of the theory of relative deprivation. *Sociometry, 22*, 280–296.

Davis, D.W., & Silver, B. D. (2004). Civil liberties vs. security: Public opinion in the context of the terrorist attacks on America. *American Journal of Political Science, 48*, 28–46.

De Cremer, D. (2002). Charismatic leadership and cooperation in social dilemmas: A matter of transforming motives? *Journal of Applied Social Psychology, 32*, 997–1016.

De Cremer, D., & Van Dijk, E. (2005). When and why leaders put themselves first: Leader behaviour in resource allocations as a function of feeling entitled. *European Journal of Social Psychology, 35*, 553–563.

De Cremer, D., & Van Lange, P.A.M. (2001). Why prosocials exhibit greater cooperation than proselfs: The roles of social responsibility and reciprocity. *European Journal of Personality, 15*, 5–18.

De Cremer, D., & Van Vugt, M. (1999). Social identification effects in social dilemmas: A transformation of motives. *European Journal of Social Psychology, 29*, 871–893.

De Cremer, D., & Van Vugt, M. (2002). Intergroup and intragroup aspects of leadership in social dilemmas: A relational model of cooperation. *Journal of Experimental Social Psychology, 38*, 126–136.

De Judicibus, M., & McCabe, M. P. (2001). Blaming the target of sexual harassment: Impact of gender role, sexist attitudes, and work role. *Sex Roles, 44*, 401–417.

De Kwaadsteniet, E. W., van Dijk, E., Wit, A., De Cremer, D., & de Rooij, M. (2007). Justifying decisions in social dilemmas: Justification pressures and tacit coordination under environmental uncertainty. *Personality and Social Psychology Bulletin, 33*, 1648–1660.

Deutsch, M. (1973). *The resolution of conflict*. New Haven: Yale University Press.

Deutsch, M. (1975). Equity, equality, and need: What determines which value will be used as the basis of distributive justice? *Journal of Social Issues, 31*, 137–149.

Deutsch, M. (1985). *Distributive justice: A social–psychological perspective*. New Haven: Yale University Press.

Deutsch, M. (1999). A personal perspective on the development of social psychology in the twentieth century. In A. Rodrigues & R. Levine (Eds.), *Reflections on 100 years of experimental social psychology* (pp. 1–34). New York: Basic Books.

Deutsch, M. (2006). Justice and conflict. In M. Deutsch, P. T. Coleman, & E. C. Marcus (Eds.), *The handbook of conflict resolution: Theory and practice* (2nd ed., pp. 43–68). San Francisco: Jossey-Bass.

Diekmann, K.A., Barsness, Z. I., & Sondak, H. (2004). Uncertainty, fairness perceptions, and job satisfaction: A field study. *Social Justice Research, 17*, 237–255.

Diekmann, K. A., Samuels, S. M., Ross, L., & Bazerman, M. H. (1997). Self-interest and fairness in problems of resource allocation: Allocators versus recipients. *Journal of Personality and Social Psychology, 72*, 1061–1074.

Diener, E. (1984). Subjective well-being. *Psychological Bulletin, 95*, 542–575.

Dion, K. L., (1986). Responses to perceived discrimination and relative deprivation. In J. M. Olson, H. C. Peter, & M. P. Zanna (Eds.), *Relative deprivation and social comparison: The Ontario symposium* (Vol. 4, pp. 159–179). Hillsdale, NJ: Erlbaum.

Dion, K. L., & Dion, K. K. (1987). Belief in a just world and physical attractiveness stereotyping. *Journal of Personality and Social Psychology, 52*, 775–780.

Doise, W. (1986). *Levels of explanation in social psychology*. Cambridge, England: Cambridge University Press.

Doob, L. W. (1952). *Social psychology: An analysis of human behavior*. New York: Holt.

Doris, J. M. (2002). *Lack of character: Personality and moral behavior*. New York: Cambridge University Press.

Doty, R. M., Peterson, B. E., & Winter, D. G. (1991). Threat and authoritarianism in the United States, 1978–1987. *Journal of Personality and Social Psychology, 61*, 629–640.

Drout, C. E., & Gaertner, S. L. (1994). Gender differences in reactions to female victims. *Social Behavior and Personality, 22*, 267–277.

Dubé, L., & Guimond, S. (1986). Relative deprivation and social protest. In J. M. Olson, C. P. Herman, & M. P. Zanna (Eds.), *Relative deprivation and social comparison: The Ontario symposium* (Vol. 4, pp. 201–216). Hillsdale, NJ: Erlbaum.

Eagly, A. H., Diekman, A. B., Johannesen-Schmidt, M. C., & Koenig, A. M. (2004). Gender gaps in sociopolitical attitudes: A social psychological analysis. *Journal of Personality and Social Psychology, 87*, 796–816.

Eagly, A. H., & Steffen, V. J. (1984). Gender stereotypes stem from the distribution of women and men into social roles. *Journal of Personality and Social Psychology, 46*, 735–754.

Eek, D., & Gärling, T. (2006). Prosocials prefer equal outcomes to maximizing joint outcomes. *British Journal of Social Psychology, 45*, 321–337.

Ellard, J. H., & Bates, D. D. (1990). Evidence for the role of the justice motive in status generalization processes. *Social Justice Research, 4*, 115–134.

Elliott, C. S., Hayward, D. M., & Canon, S. (1998). Institutional framing: Some experimental evidence. *Journal of Economic Behavior and Organization, 35*, 455–464.

Ellsworth, P. C., & Ross, L. (1983). Public opinion and capital punishment: A close examination of the views of abolitionists and retentionists. *Crime & Delinquency, 29*, 116–169.

Elster, J. (1992). *Local justice: How institutions allocate scarce goods and necessary burdens*. New York: Russell Sage Foundation.

Emler, N. (2002). Morality and political orientations: An analysis of their relationship. *European Review of Social Psychology, 13*, 259–291.

Feather, N. T. (1994). Attitudes toward high achievers and reactions to their fall: Theory and research concerning tall poppies. In M. P. Zanna (Ed.), *Advances in experimental social psychology* (Vol. 26, pp. 1–73). San Diego, CA: Academic Press.

Feather, N. T. (1999). Judgments of deservingness: Studies in the psychology of justice and achievement. *Personality and Social Psychology Review, 3*, 86–107.

Feather, N. T. (2008). Perceived legitimacy of a promotion decision in relation to deservingness, entitlement, and resentment in the context of affirmative action and performance. *Journal of Applied Social Psychology, 38*, 1230–1254.

Fehr, E. & Fischbacher, U. (2003). The nature of human altruism. *Nature, 425*, 785–791.

Feinberg, J. (1973). *Social philosophy*. Englewood Cliffs, NJ: Prentice-Hall.

Feldman, S. (2003). Enforcing social conformity: A theory of authoritarianism. *Political Psychology, 24*, 41–74.

Festinger, L. (1954). A theory of social comparison processes. *Human Relations, 7*, 117–140.

Feygina, I., Goldsmith, R., & Jost, J. T. (in press). System justification and the disruption of environmental goal-setting: A self-regulatory perspective. In R. Hassin, K. Ochsner, & Y. Trope (Eds.), *Social cognitive and neuroscientific approaches to self-control*. New York: Oxford University Press.

Fischer, R., & Smith, P. B. (2003). Reward allocation and culture: A meta-analysis. *Journal of Cross-Cultural Psychology, 34*, 251–268.

Fiske, A. P., & Tetlock, P. E. (1997). Taboo trade-offs: Reactions to transactions that transgress the spheres of justice. *Political Psychology, 18*, 255–297.

Fiske, S. T. (1998). Stereotypes, prejudice, and discrimination. In D. Gilbert, S. T. Fiske, & G. Lindzey (Eds.), *Handbook of social psychology* (4th ed., pp. 357–414). Boston: McGraw-Hill.

Fiske, S. T. (2004). *Social beings: A core motives approach to social psychology*. New York: Wiley.

Flanagan, O. (1991). *Varieties of moral personality: Ethics and psychological realism*. Cambridge, MA: Harvard University Press.

Foels, R., & Pappas, C. J. (2004). Learning and unlearning the myths we are taught: Gender and social dominance orientation. *Sex Roles, 50*, 743–757.

Folger, R. (1977). Distributive and procedural justice: Combined impact of "voice" and improvement on experienced inequity. *Journal of Personality and Social Psychology, 35*, 108–119.

Folger, R. (1986). A referent cognitions theory of relative deprivation. In J. M. Olson, C. P. Herman, & M. P. Zanna (Eds.), *Social comparison and relative deprivation: The Ontario Symposium* (Vol. 4, pp. 33–55). Hillsdale, NJ: Erlbaum.

Folger, R., & Bies, R. J. (1989). Managerial responsibilities and procedural justice. *Employee Responsibilities and Rights Journal, 2*, 79–90.

Folger, R., Rosenfield, D., Grove, J., & Corkran, L. (1979). Effects of "voice" and peer opinions on responses to inequity. *Journal of Personality and Social Psychology, 37*, 2253–2261.

Ford, T. E., Boxer, C. F., Armstrong, J., & Edel, J. R. (2008). More than "just a joke": The prejudice-releasing function of sexist humor. *Personality and Social Psychology Bulletin, 34*, 159–170.

Foster, M. D., & Matheson, K. (1995). Double relative deprivation: Combining the personal and political. *Personality and Social Psychology Bulletin, 21*, 1167–1177.

Fox, D. R. (1999). Psycholegal scholarship's contribution to false consciousness about injustice. *Law and Human Behavior, 23*, 9–30.

Frankena, W. K. (1962). The concept of social justice. In R. B. Brandt (Ed.), *Social justice* (pp. 1–29). Englewood Cliffs, NJ: Prentice-Hall.

Frankfurt, H. (1987). Equality as a moral ideal. *Ethics, 98*, 21–42.

Freeman, D., Aquino, K., & McFerran, B. (2009). Overcoming beneficiary race as an impediment to charitable donations: Social dominance orientation, the experience of moral elevation, and donation behavior. *Personality and Social Psychology Bulletin, 35*, 72–84.

Freudenthaler, H. H., & Mikula, G. (1998). From unfulfilled wants to the experience of injustice: Women's sense of injustice regarding the lopsided division of household labor. *Social Justice Research, 11*, 289–312.

Frohlich, N., & Oppenheimer, J. A. (1992). *Choosing justice: An experimental approach to ethical theory*. Berkeley: University of California Press.

Fujita, F., Diener, E., & Sandvik, E. (1991). Gender differences in negative affect and well-being: The case for emotional intensity. *Journal of Personality and Social Psychology, 61*, 427–434.

Fuller, J. B., Jr., & Hester, K. (2001). A closer look at the relationship between justice perceptions and union participation. *Journal of Applied Psychology, 86*, 1096–1105.

Furgeson, J., Babcock, L., & Shane, P. (2008). Behind the mask of method: Political orientation and constitutional interpretive preferences. *Law & Human Behavior, 32*, 502–510.

Furnham, A. (1985). Just world beliefs in an unjust society: a cross-cultural comparison. *European Journal of Social Psychology, 15*, 363–366.

Furnham, A. (1995). The just world, charitable giving and attitudes to disability. *Personality and Individual Differences, 19*, 577–583.

Furnham, A. (2003). Belief in a just world: Research progress over the past decade. *Personality and Individual Differences, 34*, 795–817.

Gachter, S., & Fehr, E. (1999). Collective action as a social exchange. *Journal of Economic Behavior and Organization, 39*, 341–369.

Gamliel, E., & Peer, E. (2006). Positive versus negative framing affects justice judgments. *Social Justice Research, 19*, 307–322.

Gaucher, D., Hafer, C., Kay, A. C., & Davidenko, N. (in press). Compensatory rationalizations and the resolution of everyday underserved outcomes. *Personality and Social Psychology Bulletin*.

Gelfand, M. J., Fitzgerald, L. F., & Drasgow, F. (1995). The structure of sexual harassment: A confirmatory analysis across cultures and settings. *Journal of Vocational Behavior, 47*, 164–177.

Gibson, J. L. (2004). *Overcoming apartheid: Can truth reconcile a divided nation?* New York: Russell Sage Foundation.

Gibson, J. L. (2008). Group identities and theories of justice: An experimental investigation into the justice and injustice of land squatting in South Africa. *The Journal of Politics, 70*, 700–716.

Gleason, M. E. J., Iida, M., Bolger, N., & Shrout, P. E. (2003). Daily supportive equity in close relationships. *Personality and Social Psychology Bulletin, 29*, 1036–1045.

Goldman, A. (1992). *Liaisons: Philosophy meets the cognitive and social sciences*. Cambridge, MA: MIT Press.

Gollwitzer, M., Schmitt, M., Schalke, R., Maes, J., & Baer, A. (2005). Asymmetrical effects of justice sensitivity perspectives on prosocial and antisocial behavior. *Social Justice Research, 18*, 183–201.

Goodman, P. S. (1977). Social comparison processes in organizations. In B. Staw & G. Salancik (Eds.), *New directions in organizational behavior* (pp. 97–132). Chicago: St. Clair.

Green, D. P., & Shapiro, I. (1994). *Pathologies of rational choice theory: A critique of applications in political science*. New Haven, CT: Yale University Press.

Greenberg, J. (1980). Attentional focus and locus of performance causality as determinants of equity behavior. *Journal of Personality and Social Psychology, 38*, 579–585.

Greenberg, J. (1984). On the apocryphal nature of inequity distress. In R. Folger (Ed.), *The sense of injustice* (pp. 167–188). New York: Plenum.

Greenberg, J. (1993). Stealing in the name of justice: Informational and interpersonal moderators of theft reactions to underpayment inequity. *Organizational Behavior and Human Decision Processes, 54*, 81–103.

Greenberg, J., Bies, R. J., & Eskew, D. E. (1991). Establishing fairness in the eye of the beholder: Managing impressions of organizational justice. In R. A. Giacalone & P. Rosenfeld (Eds.), *Applied impression management: How image-making affects managerial decisions* (pp. 111–132). Thousand Oaks, CA: Sage.

Greenberger, E. (1984). Defining psychosocial maturity in adolescence. *Advances in Child Behavioral Analysis & Therapy, 3*, 1–37.

Greene, J. D. (2003). From neural "is" to moral "ought": What are the moral implications of neuroscientific moral psychology? *Nature Reviews Neuroscience, 4*, 846–849.

Greene, J. D., & Cohen, J. (2004). For the law, neuroscience changes nothing and everything. *Philosophical Transactions of the Royal Society of London B* (Special Issue on Law and the Brain), 359, 1775–17785.

Greene, J. D., Morelli, S. A., Lowenberg, K., Nystrom, L. E., & Cohen, J. D. (2008). Cognitive load selectively interferes with utilitarian moral judgment. *Cognition, 107*, 1144–1154.

Greene, J. D., Sommerville, R. B., Nystrom, L. E., Darley, J. M., & Cohen, J. D. (2001). An fMRI investigation of emotional engagement in moral Judgment. *Science, 293*, 2105–2108.

Greenwald, A. G., & Krieger, L. H. (2006). Implicit bias: Scientific foundations. *California Law Review, 94*, 945–967.

Gromet, D. M., & Darley, J. M. (2006). Restoration and retribution: How including retributive components affects the acceptability of restorative justice procedures. *Social Justice Research, 19*, 395–432.

Guimond, S., & Dambrun, M. (2002). When prosperity breeds intergroup hostility: The effects of relative deprivation and relative gratification on prejudice. *Personality and Social Psychology Bulletin, 28*, 900–912.

Guimond, S., Dambrun, M., Michinov, N., & Duarte, S. (2003). Does social dominance generate prejudice? Integrating individual and contextual determinants of intergroup cognitions. *Journal of Personality and Social Psychology, 84*, 697–721.

Guimond, S., & Dubé-Simard, L. (1983). Relative deprivation theory and the Quebec nationalist movement: The cognition–emotion distinction and the personal–group deprivation issue. *Journal of Personality and Social Psychology, 44*, 526–535.

Gurney, P., & Tierney, K. (1982). Relative deprivation and social movements: A critical look at twenty years of theory and research. *Sociological Quarterly, 23*, 33–47.

Gurr, T. (1970). *Why men rebel*. Princeton, NJ: Princeton University Press.

Gustafsson, M., Biel, A., & Gärling, T. (1999). Outcome-desirability bias in resource management problems. *Thinking & Reasoning, 5*, 327–337.

Güth, W., Schmittberger, R., & Schwarze, B. (1982). An experimental analysis of ultimatum bargaining. *Journal of Economic Behavior and Organization, 3*, 367–388.

Hafer, C. L. (2000a). Do innocent victims threaten the belief in a just world? Evidence from a modified Stroop task. *Journal of Personality and Social Psychology, 79*, 165–173.

Hafer, C. L. (2000b). Investment in long-term goals and commitment to just means drive the need to believe in a just world. *Personality and Social Psychology Bulletin, 26*, 1059–1073.

Hafer, C. L., & Bègue, L. (2005). Experimental research on just-world theory: Problems, developments, and future challenges. *Psychological Bulletin, 131*, 128–167.

Hafer, C. L., Bègue, L., Choma, B. L., & Dempsey, J. L. (2005). Belief in a just world and commitment to long-term deserved outcomes. *Social Justice Research, 18*, 429–444.

Hafer, C. L., & Olson, J. M. (1993). Beliefs in a just world, discontent, and assertive actions by working women. *Personality and Social Psychology Bulletin, 19*, 30–38.

Hafer, C. L., & Olson, J. M. (2003). An analysis of empirical research on the scope of justice. *Personality and Social Psychology Review, 7*, 311–323.

Haidt, J. (2001). The emotional dog and its rational tail: A social intuitionist approach to moral judgment. *Psychological Review, 108*, 814–834.

Haidt, J., & Graham, J. (2007). When morality opposes justice: Conservatives have moral intuitions that liberals may not recognize. *Social Justice Research, 20*, 98–116.

Haidt, J., & Graham, J. (2009). Planet of the Durkheimians, where community, authority, and sacredness are foundations of morality. In J. T. Jost, A. C. Kay, & H. Thorisdottir (Eds.), *Social and psychological bases of ideology and system justification* (pp. 371–401). New York: Oxford University Press.

Haines, E. L., & Jost, J. T. (2000). Placating the powerless: Effects of legitimate and illegitimate explanation on affect, memory, and stereotyping. *Social Justice Research, 13*, 219–236.

Haney, C. (1993). Psychology and legal change: The impact of a decade. *Law and Human Behavior, 17*, 371–398.

Hanson, J., & Yosifon, D. (2004). The situational character: A critical realist perspective on the human animal. *The Georgetown Law Journal, 93*, 1–179.

Hardin, C. D., & Higgins, E. T. (1996). Shared reality: How social verification makes the subjective objective. In R. M. Sorrentino & E. T. Higgins (Eds.), *Handbook of motivation and cognition*, (Vol. 3, pp. 28–84). New York: Guilford.

Hardin, G. (1968). The tragedy of the commons. *Science, 162*, 1243–1248.

Hare, R. M. (1981). *Moral thinking: Its levels, method, and point*. New York: Clarendon Press.

Harman, G. (1999). Moral philosophy meets social psychology: Virtue ethics and the fundamental attribution error. *Proceedings of the Aristotelian Society, 99*, 315–331.

Harris, N. (2006). Reintegrative shaming, shame, and criminal justice. *Journal of Social Issues, 62*, 327–346.

Hatfield, E., & Sprecher, S. (1984). Equity theory and behavior in organizations. *Research in the Sociology of Organizations, 3*, 95–124.

Hayek, F. A. (1976). *Law, legislation, and liberty: Volume 2—The mirage of social justice*. Chicago: University of Chicago Press.

Hegtvedt, K. A. (1990). The effects of relationship structure on emotional responses to inequity. *Social Psychology Quarterly, 53*, 214–228.

Henrich, J., Boyd, R., Bowles, S., Camerer, C., Fehr, E., Gintis, H., & McElreath, R. (2001). In search of homo economicus: Behavioral experiments in 15 small-scale societies. *The American Economic Review, 91*, 73–78.

Heuer, L., Blumenthal, E., Douglas, A., & Weinblatt, T. (1999). A deservingness approach to respect as a relationally based fairness judgment. *Personality and Social Psychology Bulletin, 25*, 1279–1292.

Higgins, E. T., & Kruglanski, A. W. (Eds.) (2000). *Motivational science: Social and personality perspectives*. New York: Psychology Press.

Ho, R., ForsterLee, L., ForsterLee, R., & Crofts, N. (2002). Justice versus vengeance: Motives underlying punitive judgements. *Personality and Individual Differences, 33*, 365–378.

Hoffman, C., & Hurst, N. (1990). Gender stereotypes: Perception or rationalization? *Journal of Personality and Social Psychology, 58*, 197–208.

Hogue, M., & Yoder, J. D. (2003). The role of status in producing depressed entitlement in women's and men's pay allocations. *Psychology of Women Quarterly, 27*, 330–337.

Homans, G. C. (1974). *Social behavior: Its elementary forms*. Oxford: Harcourt Brace Jovanovich. (Original work published 1961).

Horwitt, S. D. (1989). *Let them call me rebel: Saul Alinsky, his life and legacy*. New York: Knopf.

Houlden, P., LaTour, S., Walker, L., & Thibaut, J. (1978). Preference for modes of dispute resolution as a function of process and decision control. *Journal of Experimental Social Psychology, 14*, 13–30.

Huo, Y. J. (2002). Justice and the regulation of social relations: When and why do group members deny claims to social goods? *British Journal of Social Psychology, 41*, 535–562.

Husami, Z. (1980). Marx on distributive justice. In M. Cohen, T. Nagel, & T. Scanlon (Eds.), *Marx, justice, and history* (pp. 42–79). Princeton, NJ: Princeton University Press. (Original work published 1978).

Jackson, J. M., & Harkins, S. G. (1985). Equity in effort: An explanation of the social loafing effect. *Journal of Personality and Social Psychology, 49*, 1199–1206.

Janoff-Bulman, R. (1992). *Shattered assumptions: Towards a new psychology of trauma*. New York: Free Press.

Janoff-Bulman, R. (2007). Erroneous assumptions: Popular belief in the effectiveness of torture interrogation. *Peace and Conflict: Journal of Peace Psychology, 13*, 429–435.

Jasso, G. (1999). How much injustice is there in the world? Two new justice indexes. *American Sociological Review, 64*, 133–168.

Johnson, J. D., Whitestone, E., Jackson, L. A., & Gatto, L. (1995). Justice is still not colorblind: Differential racial effects of exposure to inadmissible evidence. *Personality and Social Psychology Bulletin, 21*, 893–898.

Jones, E. E. (1998). Major developments in five decades of social psychology. In D. T. Gilbert, S. T. Fiske, & G. Lindzey (Eds.), *Handbook of social psychology* (4th ed., Vol. 2, pp. 3–57). Boston: McGraw Hill. (Original work published 1985).

Jones, H. B., Jr. (1997). The Protestant ethic: Weber's model and the empirical literature. *Human Relations, 50*, 757–778.

Jost, J. T. (1995). Negative illusions: Conceptual clarification and psychological evidence concerning false consciousness. *Political Psychology, 16*, 397–424.

Jost, J. T. (1997). An experimental replication of the depressed–entitlement effect among women. *Psychology of Women Quarterly, 21*, 387–393.

Jost, J. T. (2009). "Elective affinities": On the psychological bases of left–right differences. *Psychological Inquiry, 20*, 129–141.

Jost, J. T., & Azzi, A. E. (1996). Microjustice and macrojustice in the allocation of resources between experimental groups. *Journal of Social Psychology, 136*, 349–365.

Jost, J. T., & Banaji, M. R. (1994). The role of stereotyping in system-justification and the production of false consciousness. *British Journal of Social Psychology, 33*, 1–27.

Jost, J. T., Banaji, M. R., & Nosek, B. A. (2004). A decade of system justification theory: Accumulated evidence of conscious and unconscious bolstering of the status quo. *Political Psychology, 25*, 881–920.

Jost, J. T., Blount, S., Pfeffer, J., & Hunyady, Gy. (2003). Fair market ideology: Its cognitive-motivational underpinnings. In R. M. Kramer & B. M. Staw (Eds.), *Research in organizational behavior* (Vol. 25, pp. 53–91). Oxford: Elsevier.

Jost, J. T., & Burgess, D. (2000). Attitudinal ambivalence and the conflict between group and system justification motives in low status groups. *Personality and Social Psychology Bulletin, 26*, 293–305.

Jost, J. T., Glaser, J., Kruglanski, A. W., & Sulloway, F. J. (2003). Political conservatism as motivated social cognition. *Psychological Bulletin, 129*, 339–375.

Jost, J. T., & Hunyady, O. (2002). The psychology of system justification and the palliative function of ideology. *European Review of Social Psychology, 13*, 111–153.

Jost, J. T., & Hunyady, O. (2005). Antecedents and consequences of system-justifying ideologies. *Current Directions in Psychological Science, 14*, 260–265.

Jost, J. T., & Jost, L. J. (2009). Virtue ethics and the social psychology of character: Philosophical lessons from the person-situation debate. *Journal of Research in Personality, 43*, 253–254.

Jost, J. T., & Kay, A. C. (2005). Exposure to benevolent sexism and complementary gender stereotypes: Consequences for specific and diffuse forms of system justification. *Journal of Personality and Social Psychology, 88*, 498–509.

Jost, J. T., Ledgerwood, A., & Hardin, C. D. (2008). Shared reality, system justification, and the relational basis of ideological beliefs. *Social and Personality Psychology Compass, 2*, 171–186.

Jost, J. T., Liviatan, I., van der Toorn, J., Ledgerwood, A., Mandisodza, A., & Nosek, B.A. (2009). System justification: How do we know it's motivated? In A.C. Kay et al. (Eds.), *The psychology of justice and legitimacy: The Ontario symposium* (Vol. 11). Hillsdale, NJ: Erlbaum.

Jost, J. T., & Major, B. (Eds.) (2001). *The psychology of legitimacy: Emerging perspectives on ideology, justice, and intergroup relations.* New York: Cambridge University Press.

Jost, J. T., Nosek, B. A., & Gosling, S. D. (2008). Ideology: Its resurgence in social, personality, and political psychology. *Perspectives on Psychological Science, 3*, 126–136.

Jost, J. T., Pelham, B. W., & Carvallo, M. R. (2002). Non-conscious forms of system justification: Implicit and behavioral preferences for higher status groups. *Journal of Experimental Social Psychology, 38*, 586–602.

Jost, J. T., & Ross, L. (1999). Fairness norms and the potential for mutual agreements involving majority and minority groups. In E. Mannix, M. Neale, & R. Wageman (Eds.), *Research on managing groups and teams/Volume 2: Context* (pp. 93–114). Greenwich, CT: JAI Press.

Jost, J. T., & Thompson, E. P. (2000). Group-based dominance and opposition to equality as independent predictors of self-esteem, ethnocentrism, and social policy attitudes among African Americans and European Americans. *Journal of Experimental Social Psychology, 36*, 209–232.

Jost, J. T., Wakslak, C., & Tyler, T.R. (2008). System justification theory and the alleviation of emotional distress: Palliative effects of ideology in an arbitrary social hierarchy and in society. In K. Hegtvedt & J. Clay-Warner (Eds.), *Justice: Advances in group processes* (Vol. 25, pp. 181–211). Bingley, England: JAI/Emerald.

Jost, L. J., & Jost, J. T. (2007). Why Marx left philosophy for social science. *Theory & Psychology, 17*, 297–322.

Kahneman, D., Diener, E., & Schwarz, N. (Eds.). (1999). *Well-being: The foundations of a hedonic psychology.* New York: Russell Sage Foundation.

Kahneman, D., Knetsch, J.L., & Thaler, R.H. (1986). Fairness as a constraint on profit seeking: Entitlement in the market. *American Economic Review, 76*, 728–741.

Kahneman, D., Schkade, D., & Sunstein, C. R. (1998). Shared outrage and erratic awards: The psychology of punitive damages. *Journal of Risk and Uncertainty, 16*, 49–86.

Kahneman, D., Slovic, P., & Tversky, A. (Eds.) (1982). *Judgment under uncertainty: Heuristics and biases.* New York: Cambridge University Press.

Kang, J. (2005). Trojan horses of race. *Harvard Law Review, 118*, 1489–1593.

Kang, J., & Banaji, M. R. (2006). Fair measures: A behavioral realist revision of "affirmative action." *California Law Review, 94*, 1063–1118.

Kant, I. (1952). The science of right. (W. Hastie, Trans.). In R. Hutchins (Ed.), *Great books of the Western world* (pp. 397–446). Edinburgh: T. & T. Clark. (Original work published 1790).

Kant, I. (1993). *Grounding for the metaphysics of morals* (3rd edition, J. W. Ellington, Trans.). Indianapolis, IN: Hackett. (Original work published 1785).

Katz, I., & Hass, R. G. (1988). Racial ambivalence and American value conflict: Correlational and priming studies of dual cognitive structures. *Journal of Personality and Social Psychology, 55*, 893–905.

Kay, A. C., Gaucher, D., Napier, J. L., Callan, M. J., & Laurin, K. (2008). God and the Government: Testing a compensatory control mechanism for the support of external systems. *Journal of Personality and Social Psychology, 95*, 18–35.

Kay, A. C., Gaucher, D., Peach, J. M., Laurin, K., Friesen, J., Zanna, M. P., & Spencer, S. J. (2009). Inequality, discrimination, and the power of the status quo: Direct evidence for a motivation to see is the way things are as the way they should be. *Journal of Personality and Social Psychology, 97*, 421–434.

Kay, A.C., & Jost, J.T. (2003). Complementary justice: Effects of "poor but happy" and "poor but honest" stereotype exemplars on system justification and implicit activation of the justice motive. *Journal of Personality and Social Psychology, 85*, 823–837.

Kay, A. C., Jost, J. T., Mandisodza, A. N., Sherman, S. J., Petrocelli, J. V., & Johnson, A. L. (2007). Panglossian ideology in the service of system justification: How complementary stereotypes help us to rationalize inequality. In M. Zanna (Ed.), *Advances in Experimental Social Psychology* (pp. 305–358). San Diego, CA: Academic Press/Elsevier.

Kay, A. C., Jost, J. T., & Young, S. (2005). Victim derogation and victim enhancement as alternate routes to system justification. *Psychological Science, 16*, 240–246.

Kay, A. C., & Ross, L. (2003). The perceptual push: The interplay of implicit cues and explicit situational construals on behavioral intentions in the prisoner's dilemma. *Journal of Experimental Social Psychology, 39*, 634–643.

Kay, A. C., Wheeler, S. C., Bargh, J. A., & Ross, L. (2004). Material priming: The influence of mundane physical objects on situational construal and competitive behavioral choice. *Organizational Behavior and Human Decision Processes, 95*, 83–96.

Kay, A. C., & Zanna, M. P. (2009). A contextual analysis of the social and psychological consequences of system justification. In J. T. Jost, A. C. Kay, & H. Thoristtodor (Eds.), *Social and psychological bases of ideology and system justification.* New York: Oxford University Press.

Kelln, B. R. C., & Ellard, J. H. (1999). An equity theory analysis of the impact of forgiveness and retribution on transgressor compliance. *Personality and Social Psychology Bulletin, 25*, 864–872.

Kelman, H. C. (2001). Reflections on the social and psychological processes of legitimization and delegitimization. In J. T. Jost & B. Major (Eds.), *The psychology of legitimacy: Emerging perspectives on ideology, justice, and intergroup relations* (pp. 54–73). Cambridge, England: Cambridge University Press.

Kelman, H. C., & Hamilton, V. L. (1989). *Crimes of obedience: Toward a social psychology of authority and responsibility*. New Haven, CT: Yale University Press.

Kernan, M. C., & Hanges, P. J. (2001). Survivor reactions to reorganization: Antecedents and consequences of procedural, interpersonal, and informational justice. *Journal of Applied Psychology, 87*, 916–928.

Kessler, T., & Mummendey, A. (2001). Is there any scapegoat around? Determinants of intergroup conflicts at different categorization levels. *Journal of Personality and Social Psychology, 81*, 1090–1102.

Kinder, D. R., & Sears, D. O. (1985). Public opinion and political action. In G. Lindzey & E. Aronson (Eds.), *Handbook of social psychology* (3rd ed., pp. 659–741). New York: Random House.

Klandermans, B., Van der Toorn, J., & Van Stekelenburg, J. (2008). Embeddedness and identity: How immigrants turn grievances into action. *American Sociological Review, 73*, 992–1012.

Klineberg, O. (1940). *Social psychology*. New York: Holt.

Kluegel, J. R., & Smith, E. R. (1986). *Beliefs about inequality: Americans' views of what is and what ought to be*. Hawthorne, NY: Aldine de Gruyter.

Koenigs, M., Young, L., Adolphs, R., Tranel, D., Cushman, F., & Hauser, M. et al. (2007). Damage to the prefrontal cortex increases utilitarian moral judgements, *Nature, 446*, 908–911.

Kohlberg, L. (1969). Stage and sequence: The cognitive-developmental approach to socialization. In D. Goslin (Ed.), *Handbook of socialization theory and research* (pp. 347–480). Chicago: Rand-McNally.

Kohlberg, L. (1978). Revisions in the theory and practice of moral development. In W. Damon (Ed.), *New directions for child development: Moral development* (Vol. 2, pp. 83–87). San Francisco: Jossey-Bass.

Kollock, P. (1998). Social dilemmas: The anatomy of cooperation. *Annual Review of Sociology, 24*, 183–214.

Komorita, S. S., & Parks, C. D. (1995). Interpersonal relations: Mixed-motive interaction. *Annual Review of Psychology, 46*, 183–207.

Komorita, S. S., & Parks, C. D. (1996). *Social dilemmas*. Boulder, CO: Westview.

Konow, J. (2003). Which is the fairest one of all? A positive analysis of justice theories. *Journal of Economic Literature, 41*, 1188–1239.

Kornblith, H. (Ed.) (1999). *Naturalizing epistemology*. Cambridge, MA: MIT Press.

Kramer, R. M., & Brewer, M. B. (1984). Effects of group identity on resource use in a simulated commons dilemma. *Journal of Personality and Social Psychology, 46*, 1044–1057.

Kramer, R. M., McClintock, C. G., & Messick, D. M. (1986). Social values and cooperative response to a simulated resource conservation crisis. *Journal of Personality, 54*, 576–592.

Kraut, R. (2002). *Aristotle: Political philosophy*. New York: Oxford University Press.

Krebs, D. L. (2008). How selfish by nature? In C. Crawford & D. L. Krebs (Eds), *Foundations of evolutionary psychology* (pp. 293–312). New York: Taylor & Francis.

Krebs, D., & Miller, D. T. (1985). Altruism and aggression. In G. Lindzey & E. Aronson (Eds.), *Handbook of social psychology* (3rd ed., pp. 1–71). New York: Random House.

Kreps, D. M. (1990). *A course in microeconomic theory*. Princeton, NJ: Princeton University Press.

Krieger, L. H. (1995). The content of our categories: A cognitive bias approach to discrimination and equal employment opportunity. *Stanford Law Review, 47*, 1161–1248.

Krieger, L. H., & Fiske, S. T. (2006). Behavioral realism in employment discrimination law: Implicit bias and disparate treatment. *California Law Review, 94*, 997–1062.

Krech, D., & Crutchfield, R. S. (1948). *Theory and problems of social psychology*. New York: McGraw-Hill.

Kristiansen, C. M., & Giulietti, R. (1990). Perceptions of wife abuse: Effects of gender, attitudes toward women, and just-world beliefs among college students. *Psychology of Women Quarterly, 14*, 177–189.

Kuhlman, D. M., Camac, C., & Cunha, D. A. (1986). Individual differences in social orientation. In H. Wilke, D. Messick, & C. Rutte (Eds.), *Experimental social dilemmas* (pp. 151–176). New York: Verlag Peter Lang.

Kulik, C. T., & Ambrose, M. L. (1992). Personal and situational determinants of referent choice. *Academy of Management Review, 17*, 212–237.

Kurzban, R., & Houser, D. (2001). Individual differences in cooperation in a circular public goods game. *European Journal of Personality, 15*, 37–52.

Kurzban, R., & Leary, M. R. (2001). Evolutionary origins of stigmatization: The functions of social exclusion. *Psychological Bulletin, 127*, 187–208.

Lamm, H., & Schwinger, T. (1980). Norms concerning distributive justice: Are needs taken into consideration in allocation decisions? *Social Psychology Quarterly, 4*, 425–429.

Lane, K. A., Kang, J. & Banaji, M. R. (2007). Implicit social cognition and the law. *Annual Review of Law and Social Science, 3*, 427–451.

Latimer, J., Dowden, C., & Muise, D. (2005). The effectiveness of restorative justice practices: A meta-analysis. *The Prison Journal, 85*, 127–144.

Lavine, H., Lodge, M., & Freitas, K. (2005). Threat, authoritarianism, and selective exposure to information. *Political Psychology, 26*, 219–244.

Lawrence, C.R. (2008). Unconscious racism revisited: Reflections on the impact and origins of "the id, the ego, and equal protection." *Connecticut Law Review, 40*, 931–978.

Leach, C. W., Iyer, A., & Pedersen, A. (2007). Angry opposition to government redress: When the structurally advantaged perceive themselves as relatively deprived. *British Journal of Social Psychology, 46*, 191–204.

Leith, K. P., & Baumeister, R. F. (1998). Empathy, shame, guilt, and narratives of interpersonal conflicts: Guilt-prone people are better at perspective taking. *Journal of Personality, 66*, 1–37.

Lerner, M. J. (1974). The justice motive: "Equity" and "parity" among children. *Journal of Personality and Social Psychology, 29*, 539–550.

Lerner, M. J. (1975). The justice motive of social behavior: Introduction. *Journal of Social Issues 31*, 1–19.

Lerner, M. J. (1977). The justice motive: Some hypotheses as to its origins and forms. *Journal of Personality, 45*, 1–52.

Lerner, M. J. (1980). *The belief in a just world: A fundamental delusion*. New York: Plenum Press.

Lerner, M. J. (1987). Integrating societal and psychological rules of entitlement: The basic task of each social actor and the fundamental problem for the social sciences. *Social Justice Research, 1*, 107–121.

Lerner, M. J. (2003). The justice motive: Where social psychologists found it, how they lost it, and why they may not find it again. *Personality and Social Psychology Review, 7*, 388–399.

Lerner, M. J., & Miller, D. T. (1978). Just world research and the attribution process: Looking back and ahead. *Psychological Bulletin, 85*, 1030–1051.

Lerner, M. J., Miller, D. T., & Holmes, J. G. (1976). Deserving and the emergence of forms of justice. In L. Berkowitz & E. Walster (Eds.), *Advances in experimental social psychology* (pp. 133–162). New York: Academic Press.

Lerner, M. J., & Simmons, C. H. (1966). Observer's reaction to the "innocent victim": Compassion or rejection? *Journal of Personality and Social Psychology, 4*, 203–210.

Lerner, M. J., & Whitehead, L. A. (1980). Procedural justice viewed in the context of justice motive theory. In G. Mikula (Ed.), *Justice and social interaction: Experimental and theoretical contributions from psychological research* (pp. 219–256). Bern, Austria: Huber.

Leung, K., & Stephan, W. G. (2000). Conflict and injustice in intercultural relations: Insights from the Arab-Israeli and Sino-British disputes. In S. Renshon & J. Duckitt (Eds.), *Political psychology: Cultural and cross-cultural perspectives* (pp. 128–145). New York: McMillan.

Leventhal, G. S. (1980). What should be done with equity theory? New approaches to the study of fairness in social relationships. In K. Gergen, M. Greenberg, & R. Willis (Eds.), *Social exchange* (pp. 27–55). New York: Plenum Press.

Leventhal, G. S., & Anderson, D. (1970). Self-interest and the maintenance of equity. *Journal of Personality and Social Psychology, 15*, 57–62.

Leventhal, G. S., Karuza, J., & Fry, W. R. (1980). Beyond fairness: A theory of allocation preferences. In G. Mikula (Ed.), *Justice and social interaction* (pp. 167–218). New York: Springer-Verlag.

Levine, J. M., & Moreland, R. L. (1987). Social comparison and outcome evaluation in group contexts. In J. C. Masters & W. P. Smith (Eds.), *Social comparison, social justice, and relative deprivation: Theoretical, empirical, and policy perspectives* (pp. 105–127). Hillsdale, NJ: Erlbaum.

Lewin, K. (1948a). Experiments in social space. In K. Lewin (Ed.), *Resolving social conflicts* (pp. 71–83). New York: Harper. (Original work published 1939).

Lewin, K. (1948b). Self-hatred among Jews. In K. Lewin (Ed.), *Resolving social conflicts* (pp. 186–200). New York: Harper. (Original work published 1941).

Lewin, K. (1951). Problems of research in social psychology. In K. Lewin (ed.), *Field theory in social science: Selected theoretical papers* (pp. 155–169). New York: Harper & Row. (Original work published 1944).

Liberman, V., Samuels, S. M., & Ross, L. (2004). The name of the game: Predictive power of reputations versus situational labels in determining prisoner's dilemma game moves. *Personality and Social Psychology Bulletin, 30*, 1175–1185.

Liebrand, W. B., Jansen, R. W., Rijken, V. M., & Suhre, C. J. (1986). Might over morality: Social values and the perception of other players in experimental games. *Journal of Experimental Social Psychology, 22*, 203–215.

Lind, E. A., Kanfer, R., & Earley, P. C. (1990). Voice, control, and procedural justice: Instrumental and noninstrumental concerns in fairness judgments. *Journal of Personality and Social Psychology, 59*, 952–959.

Lind, E. A., & Tyler, T. R. (1988). *The social psychology of procedural justice*. New York: Plenum.

Lind, E. A., & Van den Bos, K. (2002). When fairness works: Toward a general theory of uncertainty management. In B. M. Staw & R. M. Kramer (Eds.), *Research in organizational behavior* (pp. 181–223). Greenwich, CT: JAI Press.

Link, B. G., & Phelan, J. C. (2001). Conceptualizing stigma. *Annual Review of Sociology, 27*, 363–385.

Lipkus, I. M., & Bissonnette, V. L. (1996). Relationships among belief in a just world, willingness to accommodate, and marital well-being. *Personality and Social Psychology Bulletin, 22*, 1043–1056.

Lipkus, I. M., Dalbert, C., & Siegler, I. C. (1996). The importance of distinguishing the belief in a just world for self versus for others: Implications for psychological well-being. *Personality and Social Psychology Bulletin, 22*, 666–677.

Loewenstein, G. F., Thompson, L., & Bazerman, M. H. (1989). Social utility and decision making in interpersonal contexts. *Journal of Personality and Social Psychology, 57*, 426–441.

Lupfer, M. B., Weeks, K. P., Doan, K. A. & Houston, D. A. (2000). Folk conceptions of fairness and unfairness. *European Journal of Social Psychology, 30*, 405–428.

Maass, A., Cadinu, M., Guarnieri, G., & Grasselli, A. (2003). Sexual harassment under social identity threat: The computer harassment paradigm. *Journal of Personality and Social Psychology, 85*, 853–870.

Maes, J. (1998). Immanent justice and ultimate justice: Two ways of believing in justice. In L. Montada & M. J. Lerner (Eds.), *Responses to victimizations and belief in a just world* (pp. 9–40). New York: Plenum Press.

Major, B. (1994). From social inequality to personal entitlement: The role of social comparisons, legitimacy appraisals, and group membership. In M. P. Zanna (Ed.), *Advances in experimental social psychology* (Vol. 26, pp. 293–355). San Diego, CA: Academic Press.

Major, B., Gramzow, R. H., McCoy, S. K., Levin, S., Schmader, T., & Sidanius, J. (2002). Perceiving personal discrimination: The role of group status and legitimizing ideology. *Journal of Personality and Social Psychology, 82*, 269–282.

Major, B., Quinton, W. J., & McCoy, S. K. (2002). Antecedents and consequences of attributions to discrimination: Theoretical and empirical advances. In M. P. Zanna (Ed.), *Advances in experimental social psychology* (Vol. 34, pp. 251–330). San Diego, CA: Academic Press.

Maner, J. K., Luce, C. L., Neuberg, S. L., Cialdini, R. B., Brown, S., Sagarin, B. J. (2002). The effects of perspective taking on helping: Still no evidence for altruism. *Personality and Social Psychology Bulletin, 28*, 1601–1610.

Mansbridge, J. (2005). Cracking through hegemonic ideology: The logic of formal justice. *Social Justice Research, 18*, 335–347.

March, J. G., & Simon, H. A. (1958). *Organizations*. Oxford: Wiley.

Markowski, B. (1988). Injustice and arousal. *Social Justice Research, 2*, 223–233.

Martin, J. (1986). The tolerance of injustice. In J. M. Olson, C. P. Herman, & M. P. Zanna (Eds.), *Relative deprivation and social comparison: The Ontario Symposium* (pp. 217–242). Hillsdale, NJ: Erlbaum.

Martin, J., Scully, M., & Levitt, B. (1990). Injustice and the legitimation of revolution: Damning the past, excusing the present, and neglecting the future. *Journal of Personality and Social Psychology, 59*, 281–290.

Masterson, S. S., Lewis, K., Goldman, B. M., & Taylor, M. S. (2000). Integrating justice and social exchange: The differing effects of fair procedures and treatment on work relationships. *Academy of Management Journal, 43*, 738–748.

Matania, E. & Yaniv, I. (2007). Resource priority, fairness, and equality-efficiency compromises. *Social Justice Research, 20*, 497–510.

McClintock, C. G., & Allison, S. T. (1989). Social value orientation and helping behavior. *Journal of Applied Social Psychology, 19*, 353–362.

McCoy, S. K., & Major, B. (2007). Priming meritocracy and the psychological justification of inequality. *Journal of Experimental Social Psychology, 43*, 341–351.

McFatter, R. M. (1982). Purposes of punishment: Effects of utilities of criminal sanctions on perceived appropriateness. *Journal of Applied Psychology, 67*, 255–267.

McGuire, W. J. (1965). Discussion of William N. Schoenfeld's paper. In O. Klineberg & R. Christie (Eds.), *Perspectives in social psychology* (pp. 135–140). New York: Holt.

McGuire, W J. (1985). Attitudes and attitude change. In G. Lindzey & E. Aronson (Eds.), *Handbook of social psychology* (3rd ed., Vol. 2, pp. 233–346). New York: Random House.

McKee, I. R., & Feather, N. T. (2008). Revenge, retribution, and values: Social attitudes and punitive sentencing. *Social Justice Research, 21*, 138–163.

McPhail, C. (1971). Civil disorder participation: A critical examination of recent research. *American Sociological Review, 36*, 1058–1073.

Messick, D. M., & McClintock, C. G. (1968). Motivational bases of choice in experimental games. *Journal of Experimental Social Psychology, 4,* 1–25.

Messick, D. M., Wilke, H., Brewer, M. B., Kramer, R. M., Zemke, P. E., & Lui, L. (1983). Individual adaptations and structural change as solutions to social dilemmas. *Journal of Personality and Social Psychology, 44,* 294–309.

Michelbach, P. A., Scott, J. T., Mattland, R. E., & Bornstein, B. H. (2003). Doing Rawls justice: An experimental study of income distribution norms. *American Journal of Political Science, 47,* 523–539.

Mikula, G. (1984). Justice and fairness in interpersonal relations: Thoughts and suggestions. In H. Tajfel (Ed.), *The social dimension* (pp. 204–227). Cambridge, England: Cambridge University Press.

Mikula, G., & Wenzel, M. (2000). Justice and social conflict. *International Journal of Psychology, 35,* 126–135.

Miles, E. W., Hatfield, J. D., & Huseman, R. C. (1994). Equity sensitivity and outcome importance. *Journal of Organizational Behavior, 15,* 585–596.

Mill, J. S. (1869). *On liberty.* London: Longman, Roberts, & Green. (Original work published 1859.)

Mill, J. S. (1910). *Utilitarianism, liberty and representation.* New York: E.P. Dutton.

Miller, D. (1999). *Principles of social justice.* Cambridge, MA: Harvard University Press.

Miller, D. T. (1977). Personal deservingness versus justice for others: An exploration of the justice motive. *Journal of Experimental Social Psychology, 13,* 1–13.

Miller, D. T. (2001). Disrespect and the experience of injustice. *Annual Review of Psychology, 52,* 527–553.

Miller, F. D., Jr. (1995). *Nature, justice, and rights in Aristotle's politics.* New York: Oxford.

Mishel, L., Bernstein, J., & Allegretta, S. (2005). *The state of working America 2004/2005.* Ithaca, NY: Cornell University Press.

Mitchell, G., & Tetlock, P. E. (2006). Antidiscrimination law and the perils of mindreading. *Ohio State Law Journal, 67,* 1023–1121.

Mitchell, G., Tetlock, P. E., Mellers, B. A., & Ordóñez, L. D. (1993). Judgments of social justice: Compromises between equality and efficiency. *Journal of Personality and Social Psychology, 65,* 629–639.

Mitchell, G., Tetlock, P. E., Newman, D. G., & Lerner, J. S. (2003). Experiments behind the veil: Structural influences on judgments of social justice. *Political Psychology, 24,* 519–547.

Monroe, K. R. (2004). *The hand of compassion: Portraits of moral choice during the Holocaust.* Princeton, NJ: Princeton University Press.

Montada, L. (2002). Doing justice to the justice motive. In M. Ross & D. T. Miller (Eds.), *The justice motive in everyday life* (pp. 41–62). New York: Cambridge University Press.

Montada, L. (2003). Justice, equity, and fairness in human relations. In T. Millon & M. J. Lerner (Eds.), *Handbook of psychology: Personality and social psychology* (Vol. 5, pp. 532–568). Hoboken, NJ: John Wiley & Sons.

Montada, L., & Schneider, A. (1989). Justice and emotional reactions to the disadvantaged. *Social Justice Research, 3,* 313–344.

Moore, B. Jr. (1978). *Injustice: The social bases of obedience and revolt.* White Plains, NY: Sharpe.

Mowday, R. T. (1991). Equity theory predictions of behavior in organizations. In R. M. Steers & L. W. Porter (Eds.), *Motivation and work behavior* (3rd ed., pp. 91–112). New York: McGraw-Hill.

Mulder, L. B., van Dijk, E., De Cremer, D., & Wilke, H.A.M. (2006). Undermining trust and cooperation: The paradox of sanctioning systems in social dilemmas. *Journal of Experimental Social Psychology, 42,* 147–162.

Mullen, E., & Skitka, L. J. (2006). Exploring the psychological underpinnings of the moral mandate effect: Motivated reasoning, group differentiation, or anger? *Journal of Personality and Social Psychology, 90,* 629–643.

Murphy, K., & Harris, N. (2007). Shaming, shame and recidivism: A test of reintegrative shaming theory in the white-collar crime context. *British Journal of Criminology, 47,* 900–917.

Nagel, T. (1991). *Equality and partiality.* New York: Oxford University Press.

Napier, J. L., & Jost, J. T. (2008a). Why are conservatives happier than liberals? *Psychological Science, 19,* 565–572.

Napier, J. L., & Jost, J. T. (2008b). The "antidemocratic personality" revisited: A cross-national investigation of working-class authoritarianism. *Journal of Social Issues, 64,* 595–617.

Napier, J. L., Mandisodza, A. N., Andersen, S. M., & Jost, J. T. (2006). System justification in responding to the poor and displaced in the aftermath of Hurricane Katrina. *Analyses of Social Issues and Public Policy, 6,* 57–73.

Napier, J. L., & Tyler, T. R. (2008). Does moral conviction really override concerns about procedural justice? A reexamination of the value protection model. *Social Justice Research, 21,* 509–528.

Neuberg, S. L., Cialdini, R. B., Brown, S. L., Luce, C., Sagarin, B. J., & Lewis, B. P. (1997). Does empathy lead to anything other than superficial helping? Comment on Batson et al. (1997). *Journal of Personality and Social Psychology, 73,* 510–516.

Nielsen, K. (1985). *Equality and liberty: A defense of radical egalitarianism.* Totowa, NJ: Rowman & Allanheld.

Nisbett, R., & Ross, L. (1980). *Human inference: Strategies and shortcomings of social judgment.* Englewood Cliffs, NJ: Prentice Hall.

Nosek, B. A., Banaji, M. R., & Jost, J. T. (2009). The politics of intergroup attitudes. In J. T. Jost, A. C. Kay, & H. Thorisdottir (Eds.), *Social and psychological bases of ideology and system justification* (pp. 480–506). New York: Oxford University Press.

Nozick, R. (1974). *Anarchy, state, and utopia.* Oxford: Blackwell.

O'Neill, B. S., & Mone, M. A. (1998). Investigating equity sensitivity as a moderator of relations between self-efficacy and workplace attitudes. *Journal of Applied Psychology, 83,* 805–816.

O'Brien, L. T., & Major, B. (2005). System-justifying beliefs and psychological well-being: The roles of group status and identity. *Personality and Social Psychology Bulletin, 31,* 1718–1729.

Olson, J. M., & Hafer, C. L. (2001). Tolerance of personal deprivation. In J. T. Jost & B. Major (Eds.), *The psychology of legitimacy: Emerging perspectives on ideology, justice, and intergroup relations.* (pp. 157–175). New York: Cambridge University Press.

Olson, J. M., & Hazlewood, J. D. (1986). Relative deprivation and social comparison: An integrative perspective. In J. M. Olson, C. P. Herman, & M. P. Zanna (Eds.), *Relative deprivation and social comparison: The Ontario symposium* (Vol. 4, pp. 1–15). Hillsdale, NJ: Erlbaum.

Olson, J. M., Roese, N. J., Meen, J., & Robertson, D. J. (1995). The preconditions and consequences of relative deprivation: Two field studies. *Journal of Applied Social Psychology, 25,* 944–964.

Opotow, S. (1995). Drawing the line: Social categorization, moral exclusion, and the scope of justice. In B. Bunker & J. Z. Rubin (Eds.), *Conflict, cooperation, and justice: Essays inspired by the work of Morton Deutsch* (pp. 347–369). San Francisco: Jossey-Bass.

Orbell, J. M., van de Kragt, A. J. C., & Dawes, R. M. (1988). Explaining discussion-induced cooperation. *Journal of Personality and Social Psychology, 54,* 811–819.

Pancer, S. M. (1988). Salience of appeal and avoidance of helping situations. *Canadian Journal of Behavioural Science, 20,* 133–139.

Parfit, D. (1998). Equality and priority. In A. Mason (Ed.), *Ideals of equality* (pp. 1–20). Oxford: Blackwell.

Park, J. H., Schaller, M., & Van Vugt, M. (2008). Psychology of human kin recognition: Heuristic cues, erroneous inferences, and their implications. *Review of General Psychology, 12*, 215–235.

Payne, B. K., & Cameron, C. D. (in press). Divided minds, divided morals: How implicit social cognition underpins and undermines our sense of social justice. In B. Gawronski & B.K. Payne (Eds.), *Handbook of implicit social cognition: Measurement, theory, and applications*. New York: Guilford.

Pelham, B. W., & Hetts, J. J. (2001). Underworked and overpaid: Elevated entitlement in men's self-pay. *Journal of Experimental Social Psychology, 37*, 93–103.

Perugini, M., & Gallucci, M. (2001). Individual differences and social norms: The distinction between reciprocators and prosocials. *European Journal of Personality, 15*, 19–35.

Peters, S. L., Van den Bos, K., & Bobocel, D. R. (2004). The moral superiority effect: Self versus other differences in satisfaction with being overpaid. *Social Justice Research, 17*, 257–273.

Pettigrew, T. F. (1967). Social evaluation theory: Convergences and applications. *Nebraska Symposium on Motivation, 15*, 241–311.

Pettigrew, T. F. (2002). Summing up: Relative deprivation as a key social psychological concept. In I. Walker & H. J. Smith (Eds.), *Relative deprivation: Specification, development, and integration.* (pp. 351–373). New York: Cambridge University Press.

Pettigrew, T. F., Christ, O., Wagner, U., Meertens, R. W., van Dick, R., & Zick, A. (2008). Relative deprivation and intergroup prejudice. *Journal of Social Issues, 64*, 385–401.

Pettigrew, T. F., & Meertens, R. W. (1995). Subtle and blatant prejudice in Western Europe. *European Journal of Social Psychology, 25*, 57–75.

Piaget, J. (1965). *The moral judgment of the child.* New York: Free Press. (Original work published 1932).

Piven, F. F., & Cloward, R. A. (1978). *Poor people's movements: Why they succeed, how they fail.* New York: Vintage Books.

Pojman, L. P., & Westmoreland, R. (Eds.). (1997). *Equality: Selected readings.* New York: Oxford University Press.

Pratto, F., Sidanius, J., Stallworth, L. M., & Malle, B. F. (1994). Social dominance orientation: A personality variable predicting social and political attitudes. *Journal of Personality and Social Psychology, 67*, 741–763.

Puhl, R., & Brownell, K. D. (2003). Ways of coping with obesity stigma: Review and conceptual analysis. *Eating Behaviors, 4*, 53–78.

Quine, W. V. O. (1969). Epistemology naturalized. In *Ontological relativity and other essays.* New York: Columbia University Press.

Quinn, D. M., & Crocker, J. (1999). When ideology hurts: Effects of belief in the Protestant ethic and feeling overweight on the psychological well-being of women. *Journal of Personality and Social Psychology, 77*, 402–414.

Rabin, M. (1993). Incorporating fairness into game theory and economics. *American Economic Review, 83*, 1281–1302.

Rawls, J. (1971). *A theory of justice.* Oxford: Oxford University Press.

Rawls, J. (1993). *Political liberalism.* New York: Columbia University Press.

Reich, W. (1970). *The mass psychology of fascism* (V. R. Carfagno, Trans.). New York: Farrar, Straus, & Giroux. (Original work published 1946).

Reichle, B., & Schmitt, M. (2002). Helping and rationalization as alternative strategies for restoring the belief in a just world: Evidence from longitudinal change analyses. In M. Ross & D. T. Miller (Eds.), *The justice motive in everyday life* (pp. 127–148). New York: Cambridge University Press.

Reis, H. T. (1984). The multidimensionality of justice. In R. Folger (Ed.), *The sense of injustice: Social psychological perspectives* (pp. 25–61). New York: Plenum Press.

Rim, Y. (1988). Attitudes and the confluence model. *Small Group Behavior, 19*, 153–161.

Ring, K. (1967). Experimental social psychology: Some sober questions about some frivolous values. *Journal of Experimental Social Psychology, 3*, 113–123.

Roberts, J. V., & Stalans, L. J. (2004). Restorative sentencing: Exploring the views of the public. *Social Justice Research, 17*, 315–334.

Roch, S. G., & Samuelson, C. D. (1997). Effects of environmental uncertainty and social value orientation in resource dilemmas. *Organizational Behavior and Human Decision Processes, 70*, 221–235.

Roche, D. (2006). Dimensions of restorative justice. *Journal of Social Issues, 62*, 217–238.

Rodriguez, N. (2007). Restorative justice at work: Examining the impact of restorative justice resolutions on juvenile recidivism. *Crime & Delinquency, 53*, 355–379.

Ross, L., & Ward, A. (1996). Naïve realism in everyday life: Implications for social conflict and misunderstanding. In E. S. Reed, E. Turiel, & T. Brown (Eds.), *Values and knowledge* (pp. 103–135). Hillsdale, NJ: Erlbaum.

Rossi, P. H. & Berk, R. A. (1997). *Just punishments: Federal guidelines and public views.* New York: De Gruyter.

Rubin, Z., & Peplau, L. A. (1975). Who believes in a just world? *Journal of Social Issues, 31*, 65–89.

Rudman, L. A., & Ashmore, R. D. (2007). Discrimination and the Implicit Association Test. *Group Processes & Intergroup Relations, 10*, 359–372.

Rudman, L. A., Feinberg, J., & Fairchild, K. (2002). Minority members' implicit attitudes: Automatic ingroup bias as a function of group status. *Social Cognition, 20*, 294–320.

Rummel, R. J. (1997). *Death by government.* New Brunswick, NJ: Transactions.

Runciman, W. G. (1966). *Relative deprivation and social justice: A study of attitudes to social inequality in twentieth-century England.* Berkeley: University of California Press.

Ryan, W. (1971). *Blaming the victim.* New York: Pantheon Books.

Sampson, E. E. (1983). *Justice and the critique of pure psychology.* New York: Plenum.

Samuelson, C. D. (1991). Perceived task difficulty, causal attributions, and preferences for structural change in resource dilemmas. *Personality and Social Psychology Bulletin, 17*, 181–187.

Sandel, M. J. (1998). *Liberalism and the limits of justice* (2nd ed.). New York: Cambridge University Press.

Schaller, M., & Cialdini, R. B. (1988). The economics of empathic helping: Support for a mood-management motive. *Journal of Experimental Social Psychology, 24*, 163–181.

Schmitt, M., Behner, R., Montada, L., Müller, L., & Müller-Fohrbrodt, G. (2000). Gender, ethnicity, and education as privileges: Exploring the generalizability of the existential guilt reaction. *Social Justice Research, 13*, 313–337.

Schmitt, M., & Dorfel, M. (1999). Procedural injustice at work, justice sensitivity, job satisfaction and psychosomatic well-being. *European Journal of Social Psychology, 29*, 443–453.

Schroeder, D. A., Steel, J. E., Woodell, A. J., & Bembenek, A. F. (2003). Justice within social dilemmas. *Personality and Social Psychology Review, 7*, 374–387.

Schulz, U., & May, T. (1989). The recording of social orientations with ranking and pair comparison procedures. *European Journal of Social Psychology, 19*, 41–59.

Schwinger, T. (1986). The need principle of distributive justice. In H. W. Bierhoff, R. L. Cohen, & J. Greenberg (Eds.), *Justice in social relations* (pp. 211–226). New York: Plenum.

Scott, J. T., Matland, R. E., Michelbach, P. A., & Bornstein, B. H. (2001). Just deserts: An experimental study of distributive justice norms. *American Journal of Political Science, 45*, 749–767.

Sears, D. O., van Laar, C., Carrillo, M., & Kosterman, R. (1997). Is it really racism? The origins of White Americans' opposition to race-targeted policies. *Public Opinion Quarterly, 61,* 16–53.

Sen, A. (1979). The welfare basis of real income comparisons. *Journal of Economic Literature, 17,* 1–45.

Shah, J. Y., & Gardner, W. L. (Eds.). (2008). *Handbook of motivation science.* New York: Guilford Press.

Shapiro, D. L., & Brett, J. M. (2005). What is the role of control in organizational justice? In J. Greenberg & J. A. Colquitt (Eds.), *Handbook of organizational justice.* (pp. 155–177). Mahwah, NJ: Erlbaum.

Shapiro, I. (2003). *The moral foundations of politics.* New Haven, CT: Yale University Press.

Shnabel, N., & Nadler, A. (2008). A needs-based model of reconciliation: Satisfying the differential emotional needs of victim and perpetrator as a key to promoting reconciliation. *Journal of Personality and Social Psychology, 94,* 116–132.

Sidanius, J., Mitchell, M., Haley, H., & Navarrete, C. D. (2006). Support for harsh criminal sanctions and criminal justice beliefs: A social dominance perspective. *Social Justice Research, 19,* 433–449.

Sidanius, J., & Pratto, F. (1999). *Social dominance: An intergroup theory of social hierarchy and oppression.* New York: Cambridge University Press.

Sidanius, J., Pratto, F., & Bobo, L. (1996). Racism, conservatism, affirmative action, and intellectual sophistication: A matter of principled conservatism or group dominance? *Journal of Personality and Social Psychology, 70,* 476–490.

Simon, H. A. (1957). *Models of man.* New York: Wiley.

Simpson, B. (2004). Social values, subjective transformations, and cooperation in social dilemmas. *Social Psychology Quarterly, 67,* 385–395.

Skitka, L. J. (2002). Do the means always justify the ends, or do the ends sometimes justify the means? A value model of justice reasoning. *Personality and Social Psychology Bulletin, 28,* 588–597.

Skitka, L. J., Bauman, C. W., & Sargis, E. G. (2005). Moral conviction: Another contributor to attitude strength or something more? *Journal of Personality and Social Psychology, 88,* 895–917.

Skitka, L. J., & Houston, D. A. (2001). When due process is of no consequence: Moral mandates and presumed defendant guilt or innocence. *Social Justice Research, 14,* 305–326.

Skitka, L. J. & Mullen, E. (2002). Understanding judgments of fairness in a real-world political context: A test of the value protection model of justice reasoning. *Personality and Social Psychology Bulletin, 28,* 1419–1429.

Skitka, L. J., & Tetlock, P. E. (1993). Providing public assistance: Cognitive and motivational processes underlying liberal and conservative policy preferences. *Journal of Personality and Social Psychology, 65,* 1205–1223.

Smeesters, D., Warlop, L., Van Avermaet, E., Corneille, O., & Yzerbyt, V. (2003). Do not prime hawks with doves: The interplay of construct activation and consistency of social value orientation on cooperative behavior. *Journal of Personality and Social Psychology, 84,* 972–987.

Smith, A. (1776). *An inquiry into the nature and causes of the wealth of nations.* London: Dent.

Smith, H., Tyler, T., Huo, Y., Ortiz, D., & Lind, E. A. (1998). The self-relevant implications of the group-value model. *Journal of Experimental Social Psychology, 34,* 470–493.

Solomon, R. C., & Murphy, M. C. (Eds.). (2000). *What is justice? Classic and contemporary readings.* New York: Oxford University Press.

Sprecher, S., & Schwartz, P. (1994). Equity and balance in the exchange of contributions in close relationships. In M. J. Lerner & G. Mikula (Eds.), *Entitlement and the affectional bond: Justice in close relationships.* (pp. 11–41). New York: Plenum Press.

Stangor, C., & Jost, J. T. (1997). Individual, group and system levels of analysis and their relevance for stereotyping and intergroup relations.

In R. Spears, P. J. Oakes, N. Ellemers, & S. A. Haslam (Eds.), *The social psychology of stereotyping and group life* (pp. 336–358). Malden, MA: Blackwell Publishing.

Staub, E. (1992). *The roots of evil: The origins of genocide and other group violence.* New York: Cambridge University Press.

Stenner, K. (2005). *The authoritarian dynamic.* New York: Cambridge University Press.

Stich, S. (1990). *The fragmentation of reason.* Cambridge, MA: MIT Press.

Stiglitz, J. E. (2004). *The roaring nineties.* New York: Norton.

Stouffer, S. A., Suchman, E. A., Devinney, L. C., Star, S. A., & Williams, R. M., Jr. (1949). *The American soldier: Adjustment during army life (Studies in social psychology in World War II, vol. 1).* Princeton, NJ: Princeton University Press.

Strang, H., Sherman, L., Angel, C. M., Woods, D. J., Bennett, S., Newbury-Birch, D., et al. (2006). Victim evaluations of face-to-face restorative justice conferences: A quasi-experimental analysis. *Journal of Social Issues, 62,* 281–306.

Struch, N., & Schwartz, S. H. (1989). Intergroup aggression: Its predictors and distinctness from in-group bias. *Journal of Personality and Social Psychology, 56,* 364–373.

Sunstein, C. R. (Ed.) (2000). *Behavioral law and economics.* New York: Cambridge University Press.

Sutton, R. M., Douglas, K. M., Wilkin, K., Elder, T. J., Cole, J. M., & Stathi, S. (2008). Justice for whom, exactly? Beliefs in justice for the self and various others. *Personality and Social Psychology Bulletin, 34,* 528–541.

Sweeney, P. D., & McFarlin, D. B. (1993). Workers' evaluations of the "ends" and the "means": An examination of four models of distributive and procedural justice. *Organizational Behavior and Human Decision Processes, 55,* 23–40.

Tajfel, H., & Turner, J. C. (1986). The social identity theory of intergroup behavior. In S. Worchel & W. G. Austin (Eds.), *The psychology of intergroup relations* (pp. 7–24). Chicago: Nelson-Hall.

Tangney, J. P. (1995). Recent advances in the empirical study of shame and guilt. *American Behavioral Scientist, 38,* 1132–1145.

Tenbrunsel, A. E., & Messick, D. M. (1999). Sanctioning systems, decision frames, and cooperation. *Administrative Science Quarterly, 44,* 684–707.

Thaler, R. H. (1991). *Quasi rational economics.* New York: Russell Sage Foundation.

Thibaut, J., & Walker, L. (1975). *Procedural justice.* Hillsdale, NJ: Erlbaum.

Thibaut, J., & Walker, L. (1986). A theory of procedure. *California Law Review, 66,* 541–566.

Thompson, J. L. (1989). Deprivation and political violence in Northern Ireland, 1922–1985. *Journal of Conflict Resolution, 33,* 676–699.

Tomaka, J., & Blascovich, J. (1994). Effects of justice beliefs on cognitive appraisal of and subjective, physiological, and behavioral responses to potential stress. *Journal of Personality and Social Psychology, 67,* 732–740.

Törnblom, K. Y. & Foa, U. G. (1983). Choice of a distribution principle: Crosscultural evidence on the effects of resources. *Acta Sociologica, 26,* 161–173.

Törnblom, K. Y., Mühlhausen, S. M., & Jonsson, D. R. (1991). The allocation of positive and negative outcomes: When is the equality principle fair for both? In R. Vermunt & H. Steensma (Eds.), *Social justice in human relations* (Vol. 1, pp. 59–100). New York: Plenum.

Tougas, F., Rinfret, N., Beaton, A. M., & de la Sablonnière, R. (2005). Policewomen acting in self-defense: Can psychological disengagement protect self-esteem from the negative outcomes of relative deprivation? *Journal of Personality and Social Psychology, 88,* 790–800.

Toynbee, A. (1976). *The Toynbee-Ikeda dialogue: Man himself must choose* (Trans. R. L. Gage). Tokyo: Kodansha International.

Tucker, R. (1969). *The Marxian revolutionary idea*. New York: Norton.

Tyler, T. R. (1987). Conditions leading to value expressive effects in judgments of procedural justice: A test of four models. *Journal of Personality and Social Psychology, 52*, 333–344.

Tyler, T. R. (1989). The psychology of procedural justice: A test of the group-value model. *Journal of Personality and Social Psychology, 57*, 830–838.

Tyler, T. R. (1994). Psychological models of the justice motive: Antecedents of distributive and procedural justice. *Journal of Personality and Social Psychology, 67*, 850–863.

Tyler, T. R. (2006). Psychological perspectives on legitimacy and legitimation. *Annual Review of Psychology, 57*, 375–400.

Tyler, T. R. (2007). *Psychology and the design of legal institutions*. Netherlands: Wolf Legal.

Tyler, T. R., & Bies, R. (1990). Interpersonal aspects of procedural justice. In J. S. Carroll (Ed.), *Applied social psychology in business settings* (pp. 77–98). Hillsdale, NJ: Erlbaum.

Tyler, T. R., & Blader, S. L. (2000). *Cooperation in groups: Procedural justice, social identity, and behavioral engagement*. New York: Psychology Press.

Tyler, T. R., & Blader, S. L. (2003). The group engagement model: Procedural justice, social identity, and cooperative behavior. *Personality and Social Psychology Review, 7*, 349–361.

Tyler, T. R., & Boeckmann, R. J. (1997). Three strikes and you are out, but why? The psychology of public support for punishing rule breakers. *Law & Society Review, 31*, 237–265.

Tyler, T., Degoey, P., & Smith, H. (1996). Understanding why the justice of group procedures matters: A test of the psychological dynamics of the group-value model. *Journal of Personality and Social Psychology, 70*, 913–930.

Tyler, T. R., & Jost, J. T. (2007). Psychology and the law: Reconciling normative and descriptive accounts of social justice and system legitimacy. In A. W. Kruglanski & E. T. Higgins (Eds.), *Social psychology: Handbook of basic principles* (pp. 807–825). New York: Guilford.

Tyler, T. R., & Lind, E. A. (1992). A relational model of authority in groups. In M. P. Zanna (Ed.), *Advances in experimental social psychology* (Vol. 25, pp. 115–191). San Diego, CA: Academic Press.

Tyler, T. R., & Mitchell, G. (1994). Legitimacy and the empowerment of discretionary legal authority: The United States Supreme Court and abortion rights. *Duke Law Journal, 43*, 703–814.

Tyler, T. R., Rasinski, K. A., & Spodick, N. (1985). Influence of voice on satisfaction with leaders: Exploring the meaning of process control. *Journal of Personality and Social Psychology, 48*, 72–81.

Tyler, T. R., & Smith, H. J. (1998). Social justice and social movements. In D. T. Gilbert, S. T. Fiske, & G. Lindzey (Eds.), *The handbook of social psychology* (4th ed., pp. 595–629). Boston: McGraw-Hill.

Uhlmann, E., Dasgupta, N., Elgueta, A., Greenwald, A. G., & Swanson, J. (2002). Subgroup prejudice based on skin color among Hispanics in the United States and Latin America. *Social Cognition, 20*, 198–226.

Utne, M. K., Hatfield, E., Traupmann, J., & Greenberger, D. (1984). Equity, marital satisfaction, and stability. *Journal of Social and Personal Relationships, 1*, 323–332.

Utz, S., Ouwerkerk, J. W., & Van Lange, P. A. M. (2004). What is smart in a social dilemma? Differential effects of priming competence on cooperation. *European Journal of Social Psychology, 34*, 317–332.

Van den Bos, K. (2001). Uncertainty management: The influence of uncertainty salience on reactions to perceived procedural fairness. *Journal of Personality and Social Psychology, 80*, 931–941.

Van den Bos, K. (2005). What is responsible for the fair process effect? In J. Greenberg & J. A. Colquitt (Eds.), *Handbook of organizational justice*. (pp. 273–300). Mahwah, NJ: Erlbaum.

Van den Bos, K., & Lind, E. A. (2002). Uncertainty management by means of fairness judgments. In M. P. Zanna (Ed.), *Advances in experimental social psychology* (Vol. 34, pp. 1–60). San Diego, CA: Academic Press.

Van den Bos, K., Lind, E. A., Vermunt, R., & Wilke, H.A.M. (1997). How do I judge my outcome when I do not know the outcome of others? The psychology of the fair process effect. *Journal of Personality and Social Psychology, 72*, 1034–1046.

Van den Bos, K., Wilke, H. A. M., & Lind, E. A. (1998). When do we need procedural fairness? The role of trust in authority. *Journal of Personality and Social Psychology, 75*, 1449–1458.

Van den Bos, K., Wilke, H. A. M., Lind, E. A., & Vermunt, R. (1998). Evaluating outcomes by means of the fair process effect: Evidence for different processes in fairness and satisfaction judgments. *Journal of Personality and Social Psychology, 74*, 1493–1503.

Van Dijk, E., Wilke, H., Wilke, M., & Metman, L. (1999). What information do we use in social dilemmas? Environmental uncertainty and the employment of coordination rules. *Journal of Experimental Social Psychology, 35*, 109–135.

Van Lange, P. A. M. (2000). *Cooperation and competition*. New York: Oxford University Press.

Van Lange, P. A. M., De Cremer, D., Van Dijk, E., & Van Vugt, M. (2007). Self-interest and beyond: Basic principles of social interaction. In A. W. Kruglanski & E. T. Higgins (Eds.), *Social psychology: Handbook of basic principles* (2nd ed., pp. 540–561). New York: Guilford.

Van Prooijen, J., Karremans, J. C., & van Beest, I. (2006). Procedural justice and the hedonic principle: How approach versus avoidance motivation influences the psychology of voice. *Journal of Personality and Social Psychology, 91*, 686–697.

Van Prooijen, J., Van den Bos, K., & Wilke, H. A. M. (2002). Procedural justice and status: Status salience as antecedent of procedural fairness effects. *Journal of Personality and Social Psychology, 83*, 1353–1361.

Van Prooijen, J., Van den Bos, K., & Wilke, H. A. M. (2004). Group belongingness and procedural justice: Social inclusion and exclusion by peers affects the psychology of voice. *Journal of Personality and Social Psychology, 87*, 66–79.

Van Vugt, M., & De Cremer, D. (1999). Leadership in social dilemmas: The effects of group identification on collective actions to provide public goods. *Journal of Personality and Social Psychology, 76*, 587–599.

Van Vugt, M., Jepson, S. F., Hart, C. M., & De Cremer, D. (2004). Autocratic leadership in social dilemmas: A threat to group stability. *Journal of Experimental Social Psychology, 40*, 1–13.

Van Vugt, M., Meertens, R. M., & Van Lange, P. A. M. (1995). Car versus public transportation? The role of social value orientations in a real-life social dilemma. *Journal of Applied Social Psychology, 25*, 258–278.

Van Yperen, N. W., & Buunk, B. P. (1990). A longitudinal study of equity and satisfaction in intimate relationships. *European Journal of Social Psychology, 20*, 287–309.

Van Zomeren, M., Postmes, T., & Spears, R. (2008). Toward an integrative social identity model of collective action: A quantitative research synthesis of three socio-psychological perspectives. *Psychological Bulletin, 134*, 504–535.

Vermunt, R. (2007). *Social justice and the art of reducing stress*. Lecture delivered on September 28, 2007, at the University of Leiden, Holland.

Vidmar, N. (2000). Retribution and revenge. In J. Sanders & V. L. Hamilton (Eds.), *Handbook of justice research in law* (pp. 31–63). New York: Kluwer/Plenum.

Vidmar, N. (2002). Retributive justice: Its social context. In M. Ross & D. T. Miller (Eds.), *The justice motive in everyday life*. (pp. 291–313). New York: Cambridge University Press.

Viereck, P. (1956). *Conservatism*. Princeton, NJ: D. Van Nostrand.

Vlastos, G. (1997). Justice and equality. In L. P. Pojman & R. Westmoreland (Eds.), *Equality: Selected readings* (pp. 120–133). New York: Oxford University Press. (Original work published 1962).

Wakslak, C. J., Jost, J. T., Tyler, T. R., & Chen, E. S. (2007). Moral outrage mediates the dampening effect of system justification on support for redistributive social policies. *Psychological Science, 18*, 267–274.

Walker, I., & Mann, L. (1987). Unemployment, relative deprivation, and social protest. *Personality and Social Psychology Bulletin, 13*, 275–283.

Walker, I., & Pettigrew, T. F. (1984). Relative deprivation theory: An overview and conceptual critique. *British Journal of Social Psychology, 23*, 301–310.

Walker, I. & Smith, H. J. (Eds). (2002). *Relative deprivation: Specification, development, and integration.* New York: Cambridge University Press.

Walker, L., Lind, E. A., & Thibaut, J. (1979). The relation between procedural and distributive justice. *Virginia Law Review, 65*, 1401–1420.

Wallace, H. M., Exline, J. J., & Baumeister, R. F. (2008). Interpersonal consequences of forgiveness: Does forgiveness deter or encourage repeat offenses? *Journal of Experimental Social Psychology, 44*, 453–460.

Walster, E., Berscheid, E., & Walster, G. W. (1973). New directions in equity research. *Journal of Personality and Social Psychology, 25*, 151–176.

Walster, E., Walster, W., & Berscheid, E. (1978). *Equity: Theory and research.* Boston: Allyn & Bacon.

Walton, G., & Dweck, C. (2009). Solving social problems like a psychologist. *Perspectives on Psychological Science, 4*, 101–102.

Walzer, M. (1983). *Spheres of justice.* New York: Basic Books.

Watson, A. C., Ottati, V., & Corrigan, P. C. (2003). From whence comes mental illness stigma? *International Journal of Social Psychiatry, 49*, 142–157.

Weber, J. M., Kopelman, S., & Messick, D. M. (2004). A conceptual review of decision making in social dilemmas: Applying a logic of appropriateness. *Personality and Social Psychology Review, 8*, 281–307.

Weber, M. (1958). *The Protestant ethic and the spirit of capitalism* (T. Parsons, Trans.). New York: Scribner.

Wegener, B., & Liebig, S. (2000). Is the "inner wall" here to stay? Justice ideologies in unified Germany. *Social Justice Research, 13*, 177–197.

Wegner, D. M. (2002). *The illusion of conscious will.* Cambridge, MA: MIT Press.

Weick, K. E., Bougon, M. G., & Maruyama, G. (1976). The equity context. *Organizational Behavior and Human Performance, 15*, 32–65.

Weiner, B., Perry, R. P., & Magnusson, J. (1988). An attributional analysis of reactions to stigmas. *Journal of Personality and Social Psychology, 55*, 738–748.

Wenzel, M. (2000). Justice and identity: The significance of inclusion for perceptions of entitlement and the justice motive. *Personality and Social Psychology Bulletin, 26*, 157–176.

Wenzel, M. (2001). A social categorization approach to distributive justice: Social identity as the link between relevance of inputs and need for justice. *British Journal of Social Psychology, 40*, 315–335.

Wenzel, M. (2002). What is social about justice? Inclusive identity and group values as the basis of the justice motive. *Journal of Experimental Social Psychology, 38*, 205–218.

Wenzel, M., Okimoto, T. G., Feather, N. T., & Platow, M. J. (2008). Retributive and restorative justice. *Law and Human Behavior, 32*, 375–389.

Wenzel, M., & Thielmann, I. (2006). Why we punish in the name of justice: Just desert versus value restoration and the role of social identity. *Social Justice Research, 19*, 450–470.

White, R. J. (Ed.) (1950). *The conservative tradition.* New York: New York University Press.

Williams, B. (2000). Equality. In R. C. Solomon & M. C. Murphy (Eds.), *What is justice? Classic and contemporary readings* (pp. 188–194). New York: Oxford University Press. (Original work published 1976).

Wit, A., & Kerr, N. L. (2002). "Me versus just us versus us all" categorization and cooperation in nested social dilemmas. *Journal of Personality and Social Psychology, 83*, 616–637.

Wit, A., & Wilke, H. (1998). Public good provision under environmental social uncertainty. *European Journal of Social Psychology, 28*, 249–256.

Wood, A. (1980). The Marxian critique of justice. In M. Cohen, T. Nagel, & T. Scanlon (Eds.), *Marx, justice, and history* (pp. 3–41). Princeton, NJ: Princeton University Press. (Original work published 1972).

Yamagishi, T. (1988). Seriousness of social dilemmas and the provision of a sanctioning system. *Social Psychology Quarterly, 51*, 32–42.

Zagefka, H., & Brown, R. (2005). Comparisons and perceived deprivation in ethnic minority settings. *Personality and Social Psychology Bulletin, 31*, 467–482.

Chapter 31

Influence and Leadership

MICHAEL A. HOGG

Leaders are agents of influence. When people are influenced it is often because of effective leadership. Influence and leadership are thus tightly intertwined, phenomenologically and conceptually. Influence and leadership are also two of the most fundamental and thoroughly researched topics in social psychology. In one of the most widely cited definitions of social psychology, social psychology *is* the study of influence: "The scientific investigation of how the thoughts, feelings, and behaviors of individuals are influenced by the actual, imagined or implied presence of others" (Allport, 1954, p. 5). And the topic of leadership is so enormous and popular that Goethals, Sorenson, and Burns's (2004) *Encyclopedia of Leadership* ran to four volumes, 1,927 pages, 1.2 million words, and 373 substantive (1,000- to 6,000-word) entries written by 311 scholars.

Clearly, writing a handbook chapter that does justice to these two topics in isolation, let alone in conjunction, is a significant challenge. In taking on this challenge, it was immediately obvious that a comprehensive and in-depth coverage of over a century of research would be impossible. Instead, this chapter is organized around a particular perspective on influence and leadership. The most widespread and enduring forms of social influence rest on conformity to self-relevant group norms, in which norms are configured by normative conflict within and between groups and among majorities, minorities and factions. Furthermore, norms are often embodied by individuals who thus functionally occupy leadership positions in groups.

This perspective privileges the role of group and intergroup processes and representations in the explanation of influence (cf. Turner, 1991) and leadership (cf. Chemers, 1997). Other aspects of influence and leadership are dealt with elsewhere in this handbook. Albarracín and Vargas (volume 1) cover dynamics of interpersonal persuasion as attitude change; Gruenfeld and Tiedens discuss organizations and hierarchy; Yzerbyt and Demoulin cover intergroup relations; De Dreu discusses conflict, cooperation, and negotiation; Wood and Eagly (volume 1) discuss gender and leadership; and Fiske discusses status, power, and oppression.

This chapter opens with a brief discussion of processes of compliance, persuasion, and obedience, mainly to contrast the more group- and conformity-oriented focus of the body of the chapter. Next, the nature of group norms is discussed—what they look like, how they develop and change, and how people can determine the appropriate self-relevant norm of a group they feel they belong to. This is followed by a discussion of majority influence and conformity. Because the behavior of a majority of people in a particular context is often a powerful indication of what is normative, there are strong pressures to conform to the majority. However, some people remain independent and some contexts encourage independence. How can that happen? The fact of resistance to majority influence invites the more far-reaching question of how an individual or minority can sway the majority and produce a genuine normative change: the issue of minority influence and social change. This leads smoothly into the topic of leadership. A group that is mobilized to pursue social change or, less extremely, to forge new normative goals and practices usually coalesces around a leader who acts as the focus of influence for the group, defining its goals and motivating group members to internalize them and work together for their achievement.

INFLUENCE, LEADERSHIP, AND SOCIAL PSYCHOLOGY

A notable feature of influence and leadership research is that although leadership is clearly an influence phenomenon, social psychologists have tended to study the two phenomena relatively separately, with influence researchers and leadership researchers inhabiting relatively separate scientific universes. This has not always been the case. For example, the study of social influence processes and leadership were more closely interwoven during the heyday of small groups research in the 1940s, 1950s, and 1960s (e.g., Cartwright & Zander, 1953; Festinger, Schachter, & Back, 1950; Lewin, 1947; Stouffer, Suchman, DeVinney, Star, & Williams, 1949; see Shaw, 1976). Another example is Adorno, Frenkel-Brunswik, Levinson, and Sanford's (1950) classic study of the authoritarian personality that linked influence, albeit through psychodynamic processes, to reverence for and subservience to powerful leadership.

As social psychology matured and research activity exploded in the 1960s, the inevitable specialization focused researchers on influence *or* leadership rather than both. Then in the early 1970s, there was a well-publicized crisis of confidence in social psychology among some social psychologists (e.g., Elms, 1975; Strickland, Aboud & Gergen, 1976); among many concerns, one was that social psychological theories and methods were unsophisticated and fell far short of those developed in cognitive psychology. Although social psychology had always had a cognitive focus, one response to this critique was the rise of modern social cognition, which has had an enormous and some would say transformational impact on the discipline (e.g., Devine, Hamilton, & Ostrom, 1994; Fiske & Taylor, 2008). Another concern was that social psychology was no longer social enough, in the sense that it focused too much on individuals and interpersonal interaction and paid too little attention to large-scale social phenomena (e.g., Taylor & Brown, 1979). This concern underpinned the development of a European agenda for social psychology (Tajfel, 1984) that focused on intergroup relations, social representations, minority influence, and social identity processes.

Leadership

A correlate and consequence of all this was a dramatic shift of research interest and activity away from interactive small group processes including leadership (see Abrams & Hogg, 1998; Moreland, Hogg, & Hains, 1994; Wittenbaum & Moreland, 2008). Some scholars were led to the pessimistic conclusion that social psychology no longer studied small interactive groups (e.g., Steiner, 1974, 1986), and others to note that the study of group processes including leadership was alive and well but outside social psychology, in the organizational sciences (e.g., Sanna & Parks, 1997; Tindale & Anderson, 1998).

Regarding leadership, this is indeed true. Fiedler's (1964, 1967) contingency theory of leadership promoted substantial research in social psychology, but can in many ways be considered the high tide mark of significant social psychological interest in leadership. For example, although the first three editions of *The Handbook of Social Psychology* (in 1954, 1969, and 1985) had chapters on leadership, culminating in Hollander's (1985) chapter on leadership and power; the fourth edition (Gilbert, Fiske, & Lindzey, 1998)

did not. There are three other more recent social psychology handbooks, of which Hogg and Cooper's *The SAGE handbook of Social Psychology* (2003) also had no chapter on leadership. However, Kruglanski and Higgins's (2007) second edition of *Social Psychology: Handbook of Basic Principles* did have a chapter on leadership (Hogg, 2007a), and Hogg and Tindale's (2001) *Blackwell Handbook of Social Psychology: Group Processes* had two chapters on leadership (Chemers, 2001; Lord, Brown, & Harvey, 2001).

The study of leadership has a natural home in the organizational and management sciences. In the world of work, people's careers and prosperity hinge on securing leadership positions, becoming a member of the senior management team and perhaps ultimately the chief executive officer (CEO), and organizational success and societal prosperity rest heavily on effective organizational leadership. Although social psychology largely turned its back on leadership, leadership research has thrived and expanded exponentially in the organizational and management sciences. In recent years, however, social psychology has become notably more interested in leadership; as part of a revival in interest in small interactive group processes (Wittenbaum & Moreland, 2008) and a group perspective on leadership (e.g., Chemers, 1997, 2001), and as a development of research on power (e.g., Fiske & Dépret, 1996), gender (e.g., Eagly & Carli, 2007; Eagly & Karau, 2002; Eagly, Karau, & Makhijani, 1995), social cognition and social perception (e.g., Lord, Brown, & Harvey, 2001; Lord & Hall, 2003), and social identity and intergroup relations (e.g., Hogg, 2001; Hogg & Van Knippenberg, 2003).

Influence

What about social influence? Social psychology has continued to research social influence processes. Given the centrality of the phenomenon of influence to the definition of social psychology, this is not surprising. However, this research on influence takes many different forms and perspectives that are often somewhat isolated from one another. For example, one strand of research focuses on the social cognition of attitude change as a consequence of influence, rather than on influence itself (e.g., Chaiken, 1987; Eagly & Chaiken, 1984, 1993). The Yale attitude change program has provided another, classic line of research with a more practical and applied orientation—studying attitude change to understand theory and techniques of propaganda and mass transformation of attitudes (Hovland, Janis, & Kelley, 1953; Hovland, Lumsdaine, & Sheffield, 1949).

Another significant focus is on interpersonal persuasion—the psychology of getting someone to comply with requests (e.g., Burger, 1986; see Cialdini & Goldstein, 2004) or obey commands (e.g., Milgram, 1963, 1974; see Martin & Hewstone, 2003). Persuasion and attitude change have also been a focus of minority influence researchers who describe social cognitive processes and behavioral strategies and techniques that enable minorities to change the attitudes and practices of the majority (e.g., Moscovici, 1980; Mugny & Pérez, 1991; see Martin & Hewstone, 2008).

One of the best known approaches to influence focuses on how behavioral norms develop and change (e.g., Sherif, 1935, 1936) and on the processes whereby an individual is influenced by or remains independent of the normative behavior of a numerical majority (e.g., Asch, 1956; also see Allen, 1965, 1975). Other takes on the influence of behavioral regularities on people's behavior focus on how readily people conform to role prescriptions (e.g., Berger, Wagner, & Zelditch, 1985; Correll & Ridgeway, 2003; Haney, Banks, & Zimbardo, 1973; Hogg, Terry, & White, 1995) or are socialized by the group (e.g., Levine & Moreland, 1994; Moreland & Levine, 1982), and on how social-cognitive processes associated with identifying with a group generate group normative behavior and transform self-conception (e.g., Abrams & Hogg, 1990; Hogg & Turner, 1987; Turner, 1982; Turner & Oakes, 1989; see Turner, 1991).

Finally, what has sometimes been referred to as the Illinois school of small group research has focused on how the nature and distribution of opinions or positions in a small group influences the group's overall normative position that is accepted and endorsed by the group's members. The focus is mainly on group decision making, and rests on an analysis of social combination rules, unshared information, socially shared cognition, relative persuasive power, and the nature of the group task (e.g., Davis, 1973; Tindale, Davis, Vollrath, Nagao, & Hinsz, 1990; Tindale, Kameda, & Hinsz, 2003; Tindale, Meisenhelder, Dykema-Engblade, & Hogg, 2001).

MILESTONES IN THE SOCIAL PSYCHOLOGY OF INFLUENCE AND LEADERSHIP

Some of social psychology's most memorable and impactful research programs and studies have, explicitly or implicitly, been studies of influence and leadership. For example, in 1898, Triplett published what is often cited as the first social psychology experiment. Triplett, a keen cyclist, wanted to understand why cyclists sometime cycled faster when being paced by or in competition with other cyclists. In one experiment, he had children reeling in fishing lines alone or in competition with another child. Although Triplett did

not answer his question satisfactorily, his research was a platform for subsequent research on social facilitation that systematically investigated the influence of the mere presence of other people on people's performance of easy/well learned or difficult/poorly learned tasks (e.g., Allport, 1920; Bond & Titus, 1983; Guerin, 1993; Zajonc, 1965).

Still focusing on the influence of other people on task performance, Ringelmann (1913) reported a study in which he had groups of different sizes pulling on a rope and found that the amount of effort each person exerted became smaller as the group got larger. This influential study spawned an array of clever studies of social loafing to investigate the way that people's motivation to exert effort on a task is reduced if they know that others are also working on the task (e.g., Karau & Williams, 1993). An extreme case of loafing is free-riding (e.g., Kerr, 1983)—people exert no effort on a task when they believe that others will put in all the effort. Loafing and free-riding can be reduced if a person places a great deal of subjective importance on the task and the group and if they believe that their behavior is identifiable by the group.

Although social facilitation, social loafing, and free-riding all address situations where people's behavior is quite clearly *influenced* by the behavior of others, they are usually treated as social performance rather than social influence phenomena. In the same "performance" genre but more easily classified as influence is ostracism—a situation in which people believe an individual or group is intentionally ignoring them. The effects are quite dramatic and even disturbing, as has been demonstrated by studies in which someone is included for a while in a three-person ball-tossing game and then excluded by the other two people (see Williams, 2001, 2007).

More typically and centrally associated with the theme of social influence are studies of the development and persistence of group norms, and the enduring influence of norms and role prescriptions over individuals. These studies include Sherif's (1935, 1936) classic autokinetic experiments, showing how norms arise and persist in groups and influence members; Zimbardo's Stanford prison experiment (Haney, Banks, & Zimbardo, 1973), demonstrating the power of roles to influence behavior; Garfinkel's (1967) analysis of norms as the taken-for-granted background to everyday life that only become visible when they are violated; Newcomb's (1965) Bennington study, showing how students' conservative voting pattern became more liberal after two or three years' exposure to the college's liberal norms; and Kelley's (1952) research on reference groups and membership groups as sources of different forms of influence.

Other classic research has focused more on how individuals yield to majority influence. The classic studies here are Asch's (1956) studies of conformity to a face-to-face erroneous majority (also see Deutsch & Gerard, 1955). Turning this approach to influence on its head and focusing instead on how minorities can influence the majority are studies of minority influence. One ingenious paradigm discovered that when a minority called out blue slides as green, participants still called the slides blue but experienced a change in their afterimage that indicated that due to minority influence they had actually *seen* the slides as green (Moscovici, Lage, & Naffrechoux, 1969; also see Maass & Clark, 1984; Martin, 1998).

The role of social influence in changing people's attitudes and behavior has been the focus of a number of classic research programs and studies—for example, the Yale attitude change program that focused on persuasion and attitude change to understand propaganda and mass attitude transformation (Hovland, Janis, & Kelley, 1953; Hovland, Lumsdaine, & Sheffield, 1949). Drawing on cognitive dissonance theory (Festinger, 1957; see Cooper, 2007), Zimbardo, Weisenberg, Firestone, and Levy (1965) found that military cadets had more favorable attitudes toward eating, and actually ate, more fried grasshoppers after being "pressured" to do so by an unpleasant rather than pleasant senior officer. In another food-oriented study, Lewin (1943) discovered that group discussion was more effective than persuasion in changing American housewives' attitudes so that they were less negative toward eating beef hearts and other such foods.

The idea that group discussion is a powerful mechanism of influence is associated with a long tradition of research on group decision making. One classic piece of research is that on risky shift and group polarization—under some circumstances, group discussion can make a group adopt a more extreme position than the average of the members' prediscussion private opinions (Moscovici & Zavalloni, 1969; Wallach, Kogan, & Bem, 1962). Another classic is groupthink (Janis, 1972)—a situation in which a decision-making group comes to a group decision that is suboptimal and flawed because the group is too cohesive, the leader is too influential, and the members are consumed by pressure to seek concurrence and to avoid dissent.

The notion of concurrence with a powerful leader is most memorably explored by Milgram (1963) in his classic studies of obedience to authority, in which "ordinary" people administered deadly electric shocks to another participant simply because they were told to do so by an authority figure, and by Adorno, Frenkel-Brunswik, Levinson, and Sanford (1950) in their analysis of the authoritarian personality as a person who desperately needs to defer to powerful leadership.

Social psychological leadership research has largely separated power from leadership. For example, Lippitt and White (1943) conducted a classic early experiment in which groups of children exposed to different leadership styles operated most effectively when the leader was democratic rather than autocratic or *laissez-faire*. The huge Ohio State program of leadership studies (see Stogdill, 1974) identified two general leadership styles, one that focused on task activity and the other on social relationships, and argued that the most influential leaders are those who are both task and relationship oriented. Finally, Fiedler's (1964, 1967) heavily researched contingency theory of leadership was based on the idea that the effectiveness of particular leadership styles is contingent on the nature and context of the leadership task.

COMPLIANCE VERSUS CONFORMITY

Social influence is ultimately a process of change in which one's behaviors (what one does or says) or cognitions (attitudes, opinions and feelings), or both, are changed by the perceived cognitions and behaviors of others. A typical example of the result of influence would be a Conservative joining the Democratic Party and then voting for liberal politicians in elections. Influence can also be a process that *maintains* patterns of behavior or cognition. An example would be the way that cultural propaganda maintains cultural practices. However, this can probably also be considered a process of change, albeit less dramatic change that more resembles the light touch on the tiller that keeps a boat on course.

Given that influence involves change, a critical distinction pivots on the nature of the change. Is it a transitory change simply in what one publicly does and says (for example, saying one enjoys a particular piece of cacophonous music simply because one's friends say they like it), or is it an enduring and deep-seated cognitive change in one's private beliefs, attitudes, perceptions, and feelings (actually coming to like the cacophony and see it as genuinely melodious)? This is an important distinction—practically, because the consequences are different, and theoretically, because entirely different influence processes may be involved. But it is also a problematic distinction because it engages with the relationship between attitudes and behavior (e.g., Sheeran, 2002) and with the conceptualization and measurement of implicit attitudes and cognitions (e.g., Greenwald et al., 2002).

The distinction is captured in the attitude change literature by Kelman's (1958) differentiation among compliance, identification, and internalization; in the influence literature by a contrast between compliance or coercive compliance on the one hand and persuasive influence or genuine conformity on the other (e.g., Abrams & Hogg, 1990; Turner, 1991); and more generally in social psychology as a whole by a distinction between superficial, unelaborated and heuristic information processing, and deeper, more elaborated, and deliberative information processes (e.g., Bohner, Moskowitz, & Chaiken, 1995).

Moscovici (1976) puts the compliance–conformity distinction rather nicely. Public compliance is an outward change in behavior and expressed attitudes, often as a consequence of coercion. As compliance does not reflect internal change, it usually persists only while behavior is under surveillance and is based on the perception that the source of influence has coercive power over the target of influence. In contrast, persuasive influence or conformity is a "conversion" process that produces private acceptance and internalization—true internal change that persists in the absence of surveillance and is not based on coercive power. Rather, it is based on the subjective validity of social norms conveyed by the source's behavior (Festinger, 1950), that is, a feeling of confidence and certainty that the beliefs and actions described by the norm are correct, appropriate, valid, and socially desirable. Under these circumstances, the norm becomes an internalized standard for behavior.

The notion of perceived "power over" the target is a feature of this distinction between compliance and conformity (but note that power is a complicated construct with many different interpretations; for discussion see Fiske & Berdahl, 2007). Another feature is that compliance and conformity are associated with different relationships between the individual and the group. Kelley (1952) distinguishes between reference groups (groups that are psychologically significant for our attitudes and behavior—positively significant so that we behave in accordance with their norms or negatively significant so that we behave in opposition to their norms) and membership groups (groups to which we belong—are *in*—by some objective criterion, external designation, or social consensus). A positive reference group is a source of conformity (which is socially validated if that group also happens to be our membership group), whereas a negative reference group that is also our membership group has significant coercive power to produce compliance. From the perspective of social identity theory (Tajfel & Turner, 1979; Turner, Hogg, Oakes, Reicher, & Wetherell, 1987; also see Hogg, 2006; Hogg & Abrams, 1988), conformity is the influence process associated with groups that one identifies with as an important aspect of one's self-concept. However, compliance is a surface behavioral change in response to coercion and fear or aimed at pleasing (or irritating) others; it is not associated with group identification.

COMPLIANCE AND OBEDIENCE

Compliance and Persuasion

Research on compliance, which generally refers to a *behavioral* response to a *request by another individual*, has primarily focused on the conditions under which people acquiesce to a request, and on the strategies that are most effective in gaining compliance. Situations of compliance are extraordinarily common—for example, a salesperson trying to sell a car, a friend asking a favor, an employee asking for a raise, a charity asking for donations. Although compliance with small requests can rest on careful consideration of pros and cons, it can also be relatively "mindless" insofar as we comply without much thought. However, even if the request is small, we are more inclined to comply if some reason, any reason, even a spurious reason, is given for the request (Langer, Blank, & Chanowitz, 1978).

Strategic Self-Presentation

The tactics people use to gain compliance from others typically involve strategic self-presentation designed to elicit different emotions that will compel others to comply. Jones and Pittman (1982) describe five such strategies and emotions: *intimidation* is an attempt to elicit fear by getting others to think you are dangerous; *exemplification* is an attempt to elicit guilt by getting others to regard you as a morally respectable individual; *supplication* is an attempt to elicit pity by getting others to believe you are helpless and needy; *self-promotion* is an attempt to elicit respect and confidence by persuading others that you are competent; and *ingratiation* is simply an attempt to get others to like you to secure compliance with a subsequent request.

These last two, self-promotion and ingratiation, service two of the most common goals of social interaction: to get people to think you are competent and to get people to like you (Leary, 1995). Ingratiation, in particular, has been the focus of substantial research (Gordon, 1996; Jones, 1964). People can ingratiate themselves in a variety of ways; for example, by agreeing with someone to appear similar to them or make them feel good, making oneself look attractive, paying compliments, or name-dropping. Appropriately touching someone can also work. Smith, Pruitt, and Carnevale (1982) reported that shoppers who were approached to sample a new food product were more likely to sample and buy the item when they were touched in a socially acceptable way.

The psychology behind the effectiveness of ingratiation is the human tendency to be agreeable to those we like. It is much more difficult to decline a request from someone we feel we like than someone we feel we do not like. However, ingratiation can backfire. If it is too transparent that you are strategically trying to get someone to like you (you are pandering or engaging in deceptive flattery) to profit from their liking in some way, then the strategy is ineffective or worse: It can generate dislike that significantly reduces the probability of compliance.

Multiple Requests: Foot-in-the-Door, Door-in-the-Face, and Low-Balling

One of the most researched compliance tactics involves the use of multiple requests, in which softener or set-up requests prepare the ground for the focal request (see Cialdini & Goldstein, 2004, for a review). One strategy is to get one's foot-in-the-door by making a small request that no one could reasonably decline, and then following up with a more substantial request. This seems to work; we have all used it. For example, Freedman and Fraser (1966) contacted people in their homes to answer a few simple questions about the kind of soap they used, and then once they had agreed, they made the larger request to allow six people to make a thorough inventory of all household items. Only 22% complied when they received the larger request "cold," but 53% complied when they had been softened up by the initial questions about soap. Other studies have found that multiple small prior requests can make the foot-in-the-door even more effective—specifically, people who had agreed to two preliminary requests that were increasingly demanding, prior to the ultimate request, were more likely to agree to the ultimate request (e.g., Dolinski, 2000; Goldman, Creason, & McCall, 1981).

If properly used, gaining a foot-in-the-door can be effective; it may even, according to Saks (1978), induce people to act as organ and tissue donors. The tactic is, however, relatively ineffective if the link between the requests breaks down because the initial request is too small or the focal request too large (Foss & Dempsey, 1979; Zuckerman, Lazzaro, & Waldgeir, 1979). One reason why the foot-in-the-door may work is that complying with a small request changes a person's self-conception; people develop a picture of themselves in that situation as "giving" (DeJong, 1979.) Similarly, people seek self-consistency and find it inconsistent to comply on one occasion and refuse to comply on a second occasion in the same context; if we are charitable on one occasion then we should be charitable again on the second occasion (Cialdini & Trost, 1998). Others, however, are skeptical that something as dramatic as self-conceptual change is involved, instead proposing that the foot-in-the-door tactic simply changes people's attitudes toward compliance in the situation so that they favor compliance (e.g., Gorassini & Olson, 1995).

Another compliance-gaining tactic that can be quite effective is to first make a large request that no one will comply with, and then scale it down to make the smaller focal request—the door-in-the-face tactic. In the classic door-in-the-face study, Cialdini and his colleagues (Cialdini et al., 1975) approached students with a huge request: "Would you serve as a voluntary counselor at a youth offenders" center two hours a week for the next two years?" Virtually no one agreed. However, when they then made a considerably smaller request, "Would you chaperone a group of these offenders on a two-hour trip to the zoo?," 50% complied. When the second request was presented alone, less than 17% complied.

One reason why the door-in-the-face works may be that there is a contrast effect. The second request seems small and reasonable in contrast with the ludicrously large first request, much like lukewarm water feels cool when you have just had your hand in hot water. Another, more robust explanation is, according to Cialdini and his associates, that the second scaled-down request may be viewed as a concession that invites reciprocation. This is consistent with the fact that the tactic is most effective if both requests come from the same source, typically the same individual. Reciprocity is, in its own right, a powerful compliance tactic. It invokes the reciprocity principle: the general social expectation or norm that "we should treat others the way they treat us." If someone treats us well or does us a favor, we feel a strong urge to reciprocate, and we feel guilty if we are unable to reciprocate. From the point of view of compliance, people are more likely to comply with a request if the requester first does them a small favor (Regan, 1971). Guilt arousal has a similar effect. Guilt has been shown to increase compliance with requests to make a phone call to save native trees, to agree to donate blood, or to participate in an experiment (Carlsmith & Gross, 1969; Darlington & Macker, 1966; Freedman, Wallington, & Bless, 1967).

The final multiple requests tactic is called low-balling. Here the initial request is framed to conceal various drawbacks and hidden costs. Once people have agreed, the request is changed and they discover the drawbacks and costs. For example, Cialdini, Cacioppo, Bassett, and Miller (1978) asked half their participants to be in an experiment starting at 7:00 A.M. The other half were first asked simply to commit to participating in an experiment, and then they were informed that it would start at 7:00 A.M. The latter group had been low-balled. They complied more often (56%) than the control group (31%) and also tended to keep their appointments. Low-balling works because once people are committed to a decision or course of action, they are more likely to accept a slight increase in the cost of that action. Taken to an extreme, this reflects the notion of sunk costs (Fox & Hoffman, 2002), in which once a course of action is decided on, people will continue to invest in it even if the costs increase dramatically.

Obedience to Authority

One factor that can increase the probability of compliance is power. Under these circumstances, the request is no longer a request that we are free to accept or decline, but an order that we disobey at our peril. Rather than comply, we obey because the order comes from an authority we perceive to have coercive or legitimate power over us (e.g., Raven, 1993) or to have control over our outcomes (Fiske & Berdahl, 2007).

Stanley Milgram

The name most closely associated with the study of obedience to authority is Stanley Milgram. His obedience studies (Milgram, 1963, 1974) are some of the most influential pieces of research in social psychology (see Blass, 1992, 2004), not least due to the storm over research ethics that they stirred up (Baumrind, 1964, 1985; Miller, 1986). Milgram, like much of the rest of the world, was shocked at the "I was only following orders" justification given by many of the Nazis on trial for their involvement in the Holocaust—in particular the early 1960s trial of Adolf Eichmann, the Nazi official most directly responsible for the logistics of Hitler's "Final Solution," reported in Arendt's 1963 book *Eichmann in Jerusalem: A report on the banality of evil*. These "monsters" were often mild-mannered, softly spoken, courteous people who repeatedly and politely explained that they did what they did not because they hated Jews but because they were ordered to do it; they were simply obeying orders.

Milgram was also influenced by Solomon Asch's (1951; see later) conformity studies in which an individual conformed to the bizarrely erroneous judgments of a numerical majority. Like a number of others, Milgram was unimpressed with the Asch studies on the grounds that the task, judging line length, was trivial, and there were no significant consequences for conforming or resisting. So, he tried to replicate Asch's studies, but with a task that had important consequences attached to the decision to conform or remain independent, more like the Eichmann scenario.

Milgram had experimental confederates apparently administer electric shocks to another person to see whether true participants would conform to the confederates' behavior by doing the same. Before being able to start the study, Milgram needed to run a control group to obtain a base rate for people's willingness to shock someone *without* social pressure from confederates. For Milgram, this almost immediately became the crucial question in its own right. He never went ahead with his original conformity study, and the control group became the basis of one of social psychology's most dramatic research programs.

Milgram's obedience paradigm has been described in detail in many places (Milgram, 1963, 1974; also see Blass, 1992, 1999, 2004). Briefly, participants tested another participant (called the "learner," but actually a confederate) on a paired-associate learning task, and were told to give the learner an electric shock, moving systematically up

through a scale with labels indicating the severity of the shock, each time the learner got the associate wrong. The learner was incompetent, in some variants failing to respond at all, and so the participant was confronted by the prospect of moving up the scale past 375V, labeled "danger severe shock," into the 435–450V range, ominously labeled "XXX." Although the participant believed he was giving shocks, no shocks were actually given; the learner faked responses, which included crying out in pain, pleading with the participant to stop, and in some cases pounding on the wall. Throughout the experiment, the participant was agitated and tense, and often asked to break off. To such requests, the experimenter responded with an ordered sequence of replies proceeding from a mild "please continue" through "the experiment requires that you continue" and "it is absolutely essential that you continue," to the ultimate "you have no other choice, you must go on."

The remarkable finding was that obedience was extraordinarily high. In one of the 18 variants Milgram conducted, fully 65% of participants administered the maximum shock to a learner in another room who had ceased responding and who had previously reported having a heart complaint. Replications, some using slightly different paradigms, have been conducted all over the world (Blass, 1999; also see Smith, Bond, & Kağıtçıbaşı, 2006), with obedience rates ranging from a high of 90% in Spain and the Netherlands (Meeus & Raaijmakers, 1986) to a low of 16% among Australian women (Kilham & Mann, 1974).

Factors Influencing Obedience

Research has identified a number of factors that increase or diminish destructive obedience—that is, following orders that prescribe actions that harm others (victims). One of the most important is immediacy: the social proximity of the victim to the participant. For example, Milgram found 100% of participants administered the maximum shock when the victim was neither seen nor heard at all, but "only" 30% did so when they had to physically hold the victim's hand down on to the electrode to receive the shock. This is consistent with moral dilemmas research on what is called the "trolley problem" (e.g., Greene, Sommerville, Nystrom, Darley, & Cohen, 2001). Individuals who have to save the lives of five people lying on the tracks are less willing to do so by pushing someone onto the tracks to stop the train than by switching a switch that diverts the trolley onto another track on which only one person is lying. Immediacy is clearly involved here.

Immediacy may make it easier to view a victim as a living and breathing person like oneself and thus to empathize with their thoughts and feelings as a consequence of one's actions. Hence, pregnant women express greater commitment to their pregnancy after having seen an ultrasound that clearly reveals body parts (Lydon & Dunkel-Schetter, 1994), and it is easier to press a button to wipe out an entire village from 30,000 feet than it is to shoot an individual enemy from close range. There is substantial research on dehumanization that shows an association between believing a person not to be a human being at all and endorsement or commitment of atrocities against them (Haslam, 2006; Haslam, Loughnan, & Kashima, 2008; see Epley and Waytz, volume 1). Interestingly, if we return to Adolf Eichmann, it may not actually be the case that he, or his fellow Nazis, was blindly following orders, but rather that he was able to consider atrocities against Jews because he viewed Jews as less than human. Peter Malkin, the Israeli agent who captured Eichmann in 1960, interviewed him and reports that when confronted with irrefutable evidence of having murdered a Jewish child, Eichmann replied, "Yes, . . . but he was Jewish, wasn't he?" (Malkin & Stein, 1990, p. 110).

Another important factor that influences destructive obedience is the proximity or immediacy of the authority figure giving the orders. Milgram found that obedience was reduced to 20.5% when the experimenter was absent from the room and relayed directions by telephone. When the experimenter gave no orders at all and the participant was entirely free to choose when to stop, 2.5% still persisted to the end.

The most dramatic influence on obedience is group pressure. Milgram found that the presence of two disobedient peers (i.e., others who appeared to revolt and refused to continue after giving shocks in the 150–210V range) reduced complete obedience to 10%, while two obedient peers raised complete obedience to 92.5%. Group pressure, more accurately others' behavior, probably has its effects because the actions of relevant others establishes a prescriptive norm that confirms that it is either legitimate or illegitimate to continue administering the shocks.

Another critical factor is the legitimacy of the authority figure, which allows people to abdicate personal responsibility for their actions—to enter what Milgram called an agentic state in which people see themselves (followers) as agents for the authority figure (leader), carrying out orders but not being responsible for their consequences. Milgram's original experiments were conducted by laboratory-coated scientists at prestigious Yale University, and the purpose of the research was quite clearly the pursuit of scientific knowledge. What would happen if these trappings of legitimate authority were removed? Milgram ran one experiment in a run-down inner-city office building. The research was ostensibly sponsored by a private commercial research firm. Obedience dropped, but to a still remarkably high 48%.

A final factor that may be at play, particularly in the Milgram studies, is the psychology of sunk costs (Fox & Hoffman, 2002) that we discussed previously in the context of low-balling induced compliance; once committed, particularly publically, to a course of action, people will continue their commitment even if the costs increase dramatically. Milgram's experiments start innocuously with trivial shocks, but once people have committed themselves to giving these small shocks it may be difficult to know when or how to stop.

Taken together, research on obedience points to a recipe for destructive obedience: the victim should be remote and dehumanized, the authority figure issuing the orders should be close by and perceived as having legitimate authority, and relevant other "followers" should be seem to be uniformly obedient. To combat destructive obedience, the victim should be close by and be empathized with as a fellow human being, the authority figure should be remote and perceived as having little legitimate authority, and relevant other followers should be seen to be disobeying en masse.

Obedience is not entirely bad. It can sometimes be beneficial; for example, many organizations would grind to a halt or would be catastrophically dysfunctional if their members continually painstakingly negotiated orders (think about an emergency surgery team, a flight crew, a commando unit). However, the pitfalls of blind obedience are many and dramatic. For example, research has shown that medication errors in hospitals can be attributed to nurses overwhelmingly deferring to doctors' orders, even when metaphorical alarm bells are ringing (Krackow & Blass, 1995; Lesar, Briceland, & Stein, 1997), and that interviewers have obeyed bosses' orders to use interview tactics that they know will ruin interviewees' prospects of getting the job (Meeus & Raaijmakers, 1986, 1995). Blind obedience also plays a role in groupthink, in which members of cohesive decision-making groups that are under pressure and have a strong leader defer uncritically to the leader's will (Janis, 1972; also see Aldag & Fuller, 1993). For example, in an organizational study 77% of participants who were playing the role of board members of a pharmaceutical company advocated continued marketing of a hazardous drug merely because they felt that the chair of the board favored this decision (Brief, Dukerich, & Doran, 1991).

GROUP NORMS

If someone asks a favor and the target complies, then that is compliance. If the requester has authority and power over the target, the request is effectively an order and compliance is obedience. Conformity is a quite different form of influence. Above all, it is fundamentally a group, rather than interpersonal, process that rests on the power of group norms to influence people. The compliance and obedience literatures have little to say about norms, although there are exceptions; for example, we have just seen how obedience can be dramatically strengthened or weakened by normative support for obedience or for disobedience respectively. Norms are the focus of this section, largely as a transition to the discussion of conformity in the next section—a more extensive and broader discussion of norms is provided by Cialdini and Trost (1998).

Nature and Structure of Norms

Early on, Sumner (1906) talked about norms as "folkways": Habitual customs displayed by a group because they had originally been adaptive in meeting basic needs. Sherif (1936) described norms as "customs, traditions, standards, rules, values, fashions, and all other criteria of conduct which are standardized as a consequence of the contact of individuals" (p. 3). Garfinkel (1967) described norms as the taken-for-granted background to everyday life. People typically assume a practice is "natural" or "human nature" until the practice is disrupted by norm violation and people suddenly realize the practice is "merely" normative. Indeed, Piaget's theory of cognitive development describes how children only slowly begin to realize that norms are not objective facts and suggests that even adults find it difficult to come to this realization (Piaget, 1928, 1955). Finally, Cialdini and Trost (1998) define norms as "rules and standards that are understood by members of a group and that guide and/or constrain social behavior without the force of laws. These norms emerge out of interaction with others; they may or may not be stated explicitly, and any sanctions for deviating from them come from social networks, not the legal system" (p. 152).

Turner and other social identity theorists place a particular emphasis on the group-defining dimension of norms (e.g., Abrams & Hogg, 1990; Abrams, Wetherell, Cochrane, Hogg, & Turner, 1990; Turner, 1991; Hogg & Smith, 2007). Norms are attitudinal and behavioral regularities that map the contours of social groups (small groups or large social categories) such that normative discontinuities mark group boundaries. Norms capture attributes that describe one group and distinguish it from other groups, and because groups define who we are—our identity—group norms are also prescriptive, telling us how we should behave as group members. This perspective, to some extent, transcends (see Hogg & Reid, 2006) the traditional distinction drawn between descriptive norms ("is" norms) that describe behavioral regularities and injunctive norms ("ought" norms) that convey approval or disapproval of the behavior (e.g., Cialdini, Kallgren, & Reno, 1991).

Stereotypes and Roles

Norms and stereotypes are related constructs, but they are not identical and it can be difficult to disentangle them.

One key difference is that norms are studied from the perspective of social influence (how norms emerge and change and influence people), whereas stereotypes are studied from the perspective of social cognition (how the individual perceiver forms a generalized image of a group and how this generalized image influences individual perception and conduct; e.g., Hamilton & Sherman, 1996) and prejudice (derogatory stereotypes of outgroups lie at the psychological core of prejudice and discrimination; e.g., Fiske, 1998).

One immediate conceptual difference between norms and stereotypes is that the former tend to refer to behavioral regularities within a group, whereas the latter refer to people's shared perceptions of such regularities (e.g., Oakes, Haslam, & Turner, 1994). However, some consideration shows this distinction to be less clear-cut. If one were to believe that the French cycle around wearing berets and carrying baguettes, that would be one's perception or individual stereotype of a normative practice; this perception may be inaccurate, which reminds us that stereotypes and the normative practices they purport to capture are not objective facts but social constructs that people can disagree and negotiate over (see later). If one were to share this perception with fellow Americans, then to hold that attitude or have that perception would be a norm of one's own group; and it is often just such social agreement and consensual validation that makes a normative practice seem like an objective fact (cf. Festinger, 1954; Suls & Wheeler, 2000).

Also related to norms—but not identical—are roles. As with stereotypes, it can sometimes be difficult to distinguish the two. Like norms, roles describe and prescribe behaviors that distinguish one "group" of people from another, but here the relevant group is a subgroup of people within a larger group and there is an emphasis on how the subgroups relate to one another for the greater benefit of the larger group as a whole (e.g., cooks and waiters in a restaurant, or faculty and students in a university). Roles tend, within groups, to represent a division of labor, provide clear-cut social expectations, provide information about how members relate to one another, and furnish members with a self-definition and a place within the group. However, there can also be role conflict, and since roles within a group can often be based on wider social categories (e.g., race, socio-economic status, gender), intragroup role conflict can often be a manifestation of wider intergroup conflict in society.

Like norms, roles have a real influence on people's behavior and sense of who they are: their role identity (McCall & Simmons, 1978; Stryker & Statham, 1986; see Hogg, Terry, & White, 1995). The classic demonstration of the influence of roles is Zimbardo's simulated prison study (Zimbardo, 1971; also see Banuazizi & Movahedi, 1975) in which participants randomly assigned to prisoner or guard roles took on and enacted their role prescriptions with great gusto (cf. Haslam & Reicher, 2005).

Variation of Norms

Norms serve a function for the individual. They provide a frame of reference (Sherif, 1936) that regulates one's behavior and allows one to predict, with more or less accuracy, how others might behave. Because in this way norms reduce uncertainty (cf. Hogg, 2007b, in press), they are likely to persist and, like stereotypes, are resistant to change in response to disconfirmation.

However, norms are not monolithic; they are often situation specific, and they are subject to moderation in the face of changed circumstances. Norms often initially arise to deal with specific circumstances; they endure as long as those circumstances prevail but ultimately change with changing circumstances. Some norms can be quite generic, though typically these are normative practices attached to fundamental roles within a group. For example, leadership can be viewed as a role that has general normative properties or more specific normative properties catered closely to the leadership task (e.g., Lord & Brown, 2004). Another example comes from the group development and group socialization literatures that identify generic roles and associated normative expectations in groups. Tuckman (1965) famously described five stages, with associated normative practices, that all groups go through: forming, storming, norming, performing, and adjourning. Taking a slightly different approach, Moreland and Levine (e.g., Moreland & Levine, 1982; Levine & Moreland, 1994) describe a group socialization process in which normative expectations of members change quite dramatically as they move from prospective member, to newcomer, to full member, to marginal member, to ex-member.

Norms also vary in their latitude of acceptable behavior. Some norms are narrow and restrictive (e.g., military dress codes) and others wider and less restrictive (e.g., faculty dress codes). Generally, norms that relate to group loyalty and to central aspects of group life have a narrow latitude of acceptable behavior, whereas norms relating to more peripheral features of the group are less restrictive. But it is also the case that some group members are allowed greater latitude than others: higher-status members (e.g., leaders) can get away with more than lower-status members and followers (e.g., Hogg & Van Knippenberg, 2003; Hollander, 1958).

There is evidence for the patterning and structure of different types of norms from Sherif and Sherif's (1964) study of adolescent gangs in American cities. Participant observers infiltrated these gangs and studied them over several months. The gangs had given themselves names, had adopted various insignia, and had strict codes about how members should dress. Dress codes were important, as it was largely through dress that the gangs differentiated themselves from one another. The gangs also had strict norms concerning sexual mores and how to deal with outsiders (e.g., parents, police); however, leaders were allowed greater latitude in their adherence to these and other norms.

Emergence and Persistence of Norms

The classic studies of how norms develop are Sherif's (1935, 1936) autokinetic experiments. Sherif took advantage of the autokinetic effect: an optical illusion in which a fixed pinpoint of light in a completely dark room appears to move. People asked to estimate how much the light moves find the task difficult and generally feel uncertain about their estimates. Sherif presented the point of light a large number of times and had participants, who were on their own and were unaware that the movement was an illusion, estimate the amount of movement on each trial. People used their own estimates as a frame of reference. Over a series of 100 trials, they gradually focused on a narrow range of estimates, with different people adopting their own personal range, or norm. On subsequent days, Sherif had participants repeat the task but in groups of two or three in which they called out their estimates in random order. The well-known finding is that estimates converged quickly on a narrow range defined by the mean of the group's judgment, experimentally confirming Floyd Allport's (1924) earlier observation that people in groups gave less extreme and more conservative judgments of odors and weights than when they were alone. Allport speculated that it seemed as if, in the absence of direct pressure, the group could cause members to converge and thus become more similar to one another.

Sherif also discovered that once the group norm had been established, participants tested alone continued to make autokinetic estimates in line with the norm. Rohrer and colleagues (Rohrer, Baron, Hoffman, & Swander, 1954) found, quite remarkably, that people who were retested individually as much as a year later were still influenced by the group norm. Perhaps an even more powerful demonstration of the emergence and persistence of group norms comes from studies by Jacobs and Campbell (1961) and MacNeil and Sherif (1976) of arbitrarily extreme norms. In a group comprising three confederates (who gave extreme estimates of autokinetic movement) and one true participant, a relatively extreme norm emerged. The group went through a number of "generations," in which a confederate would leave and another true participant would join, until the membership of the group contained none of the original members. The original extreme norm still powerfully influenced participants' estimates. This is an elegant demonstration that a norm is a true group phenomenon: It can emerge only from a group, yet it can influence the behavior of the individual in the physical absence of the group (Turner, 1991). It is as if the group is carried in the head of the individual in the form of a norm.

A more naturalistic classic demonstration of normative persistence comes from Coch and French (1948), who studied factory production norms and described a group that set for itself a standard of 50 units per hour as the minimum level to secure job tenure. New members quickly adopted this norm; those who did not were strongly sanctioned by ostracism and in some cases had their work sabotaged. The norm persisted.

Although norms that emerge through face-to-face interaction can reflect an averaging process, as in Sherif's original studies and even the case in which an extreme norm is induced, this is not always the case. In most situations, some individuals have more influence than others over what the group perceives to be the relevant norm. Leadership is a case in point (see later). Leaders, almost by definition, disproportionately influence group norms. Indeed, the essence of transformational leadership (e.g., Avolio & Yammarino, 2003) is precisely that specific individuals—leaders—reconfigure or transform the group's norms for the group. In contrast, fringe members of the group tend to have less influence over what the group considers to be normative.

Also, group norms typically do not emerge or exist in isolation of the perceived normative practices of other groups that one does not belong to; there is a critical intergroup dimension of norms that is often underemphasized in discussions of norms (see Yzerbyt and Demoulin's discussion of intergroup behavior, this volume). This argument is most comprehensively made by social identity theory's perspective on norms and influence (e.g., Abrams & Hogg, 1990; Hogg & Smith, 2007; Hogg & Turner, 1987; Turner, 1991; Turner, Hogg, Oakes, Reicher, & Wetherell, 1987; Turner & Oakes, 1989). Norms are cognitively represented as group prototypes—fuzzy sets of attributes (e.g., attitudes and behaviors) that define ingroup membership. Prototypes are formed and configured according to the principle of meta-contrast; that is, they optimize the ratio of intergroup differences to intragroup differences, essentially striving to accentuate or maximize both intergroup differences and intragroup similarities (cf. Tajfel, 1959; 1969), and the perceived entitativity of groups (Campbell, 1958; Hamilton & Sherman, 1996). A clear consequence of this analysis is that prototypes/norms rarely embody the average of ingroup members' behavior; more often they are ideals that are displaced from the group mean in a direction away from the relevant comparison outgroup. Following from this, it can be seen that if the relevant outgroup changes

then the ingroup prototype/norm changes also. In this way, prototypes/norms are sensitive to context.

This analysis has been used to explain group polarization: the tendency for group discussion to produce a consensual group position that is more extreme than the mean of the prediscussion individual positions of the group's members in the direction favored by the mean (e.g., Isenberg, 1986; Moscovici & Zavalloni, 1969). The argument rests on the assumption that holding an "extreme" position means that most other people are moderate. So, if a collection of individuals with relatively extreme positions comes together as a psychologically real group (a group that they identify with), the prototype of the group will form not only to capture their similarities but to contrast the group with people who are not in the group, most of whom are "moderates." Hence the perceived prototype/norm is polarized to be even more extreme, and self-categorization as a group member produces prototype-consistent/normative behavior. A number of studies have supported this analysis (e.g., Abrams, Wetherell, Cochrane, Hogg, & Turner, 1990; Hogg, Turner, & Davidson, 1990; Mackie, 1986; Mackie & Cooper, 1984; Turner, Wetherell, & Hogg, 1989).

Detecting and Changing Norms

Given that group norms can have such a powerful influence over the way we behave and the way we perceive ourselves and the world we live in, people are continually in the business of determining what the appropriate norms are. This is no easy task. Although some groups have explicit guidelines, even regulations or laws, about normative conduct (e.g., the military, many organizations), many groups do not, and even groups with explicit guidelines almost always have a host of sometimes more important implicit norms that one needs to learn more informally.

How People Determine Norms

People generally learn normative information from the behavior of other people: what they do and what they say. In fact, a great deal of what groups do is talk directly or obliquely about normative practices and what it means to be a member of the group, about how things are done, and how one ought to behave. There is a great deal of "norm talk" in groups (Hogg & Reid, 2006). Although communication scholars focus on the role of communication in the development and learning of norms (e.g., Bendor & Swistak, 2001; Lapinski & Rimal, 2005), social psychologists focus more on information processing.

Because norms of subjectively important ingroups are, according to the social identity theory of norms and influence (e.g., Turner, 1991), cognitively internalized as self-defining prototypes, people are vigilant for reliable information about ingroup norms. They pay close attention to the relative prototypicality of group members including themselves (Haslam, Oakes, McGarty, Turner, & Onorato, 1995; Hogg, 2005), and are more likely to take a normative lead from highly prototypical ingroup members whose behavior is consistent with the group's identity than from prototypically marginal members or from noningroup members. For example, Reicher's (1984a; also see Reicher, 2001) analysis of an urban community riot showed how members of the crowd who were unsure of what behaviors they should engage in were guided by identity-consistent behavior of prototypical community members, rather than the behavior of nonprototypical members or identity-inconsistent behavior of prototypical members.

Because prototypical group members tend to occupy influential leadership positions in groups (Hogg, 2001; Hogg & Van Knippenberg, 2003), people tend to look to their leaders as a source of reliable information about norms. The effect is stronger to the extent that the group is subjectively important, and the leader is highly prototypical. Research shows that people can certainly pay close attention to their leaders and try to learn as much as they can about them (e.g., Fiske & Dépret, 1996). Less prototypical or marginal group members can also be informative about group norms but in a more indirect manner; they may provide information about what the group is not (Hogg, 2005). According to subjective group dynamics theory, one reason why marginal members are often derogated or rejected from the group is that such members threaten the integrity of group norms (e.g., Abrams, Marques, Bown, & Henson, 2000; Marques, Abrams, & Serôdio, 2001). However, marginal members can have a substantial impact on group norms if they unite and work together as an active minority (see discussion of minority influence later in the chapter).

One way to determine a group norm is to assess the degree of consensus existing within the group—if everyone else behaves in the same way then that is pretty reliable evidence for a norm (e.g., Asch, 1951). However, there is rarely consensus, so the question arises of how to combine information to arrive with relative confidence at a decision about what is normative. In some situations, groups—particularly decision-making groups—have explicit or implicit rules about how to combine information to determine the group norm. These social decision schemes (e.g., Davis, 1973; Miller, 1989) include rules such as "unanimity," "majority wins," "two thirds majority," and "truth wins." Other research focuses on how groups deal with shared or unshared information (e.g., Stasser & Titus, 1985). Overall, shared information is considered more valid and comes to the fore (Larson, Foster-Fishman, & Keys, 1994), people who communicate shared information are viewed more favorably (Wittenbaum, Hubbell, & Zuckerman, 1999),

and unshared information is strained out over time (e.g., Kashima, 2000). Overall, majority views are privileged over minority views or unshared information.

A notable aspect of how people detect norms is that people can get them wrong. One reason for this is that people often determine norms on the basis of the overt behavior of fellow group members. Yet, behavior can be a notoriously unreliable cue to what people really believe; in his classic 1969 paper, Wicker reported a correlation of only 0.30 between what people do or say and what they believe. Subsequent research by Ajzen and colleagues (e.g., Ajzen, 1991; Fishbein & Ajzen, 1974) built in parameters to improve the correspondence, but the improvement was not as great as one would expect. Most recently, social identity theory has been applied to attitude–behavior correspondence to show that people's attitudes are most in line with their behavior when people identify strongly with an important self-defining group for which the attitudes and behavior are normative (Hogg & Smith, 2007; Terry & Hogg, 1996, 2001). The implication of this is that it is unreliable to infer norms from behavior unless one is careful to only attend to the behavior of members who are themselves highly prototypical and highly identified with the group, which is the same point made previously.

Two well-documented distortions of how people understand group norms are pluralistic ignorance and ingroup projection. Pluralistic ignorance (Prentice & Miller, 1993, 1996) is a tendency for people to believe that everyone else in their group behaves in a certain way or shares a certain belief, whereas they themselves do not. The classic demonstration of this was a series of studies by Prentice and Miller (1993), in which they found that Princeton University students all reported that other Princeton students were significantly more comfortable with the alcohol drinking habits at Princeton than they were. Essentially they were reporting an erroneous norm: that all students were comfortable with the drinking habits when in fact very few were.

Ingroup projection (Mummendey & Wenzel, 1999; Wenzel, Mummendey, & Waldzus, 2007; Wenzel, Mummendey, Weber, & Waldzus, 2003) is a tendency for subgroups within a superordinate group to overestimate the extent to which their own characteristics are represented in (normative of) the superordinate group. The effect is, however, asymmetrical. Subgroups who consider themselves to be subordinate or have minority status within the larger group underestimate how normative their attributes are of the superordinate category and overestimate the normativeness of the higher status subgroup's attributes (see Sindic & Reicher, 2008).

Normative Disagreement and Normative Criticism

As noted previously, norms are not objective facts. They are social constructs that people can disagree over and that gain their sense of objectivity largely from consensual support within a group. In groups, people spend a substantial amount of time talking, directly or obliquely, about the group's norms. It is through this "norm talk" that groups fine-tune who they are and how they should behave (see Hogg & Reid, 2006; Hogg & Tindale, 2005).

Normative disagreement can be a constructive and adaptive process in which a group examines its identity and practices to adjust to a changing environment. In decision-making contexts normative disagreement and associated diversity of views can lead to better decisions (Stasser, Stewart, & Wittenbaum, 1995) and protect against groupthink (e.g., Postmes, Spears, & Cihangir, 2001). However, more often than not and in nondecision-making groups, normative disagreement is charged and conflictual. Because norms define the parameters of groups and therefore who we are, normative disagreement can be threatening; it raises self-conceptual uncertainty and may sponsor extreme reactions (Hogg, 2007b, in press), including marginalization and even rejection of those who express disagreement (cf. Marques, Abrams, & Serôdio, 2001).

Normative disagreement implies criticism of the group's practices and identity. According to the research on deviance and subjective group dynamics discussed previously (e.g., Abrams, Marques, Bown, & Henson, 2000; Marques, Abrams, & Serôdio, 2001), nonnormative (deviant) information and behavior is better tolerated within groups if it comes from an outgroup member. However, research by Hornsey (e.g., 2005) on the intergroup sensitivity effect reveals that people are more tolerant of criticism of group norms and practices if such criticism comes from an ingroup member. Internal criticism may even be encouraged as a basis for normative change. In contrast, outgroup criticism spawns defensiveness, and may enhance intergroup polarization and conflict.

The contradictory findings here probably rest on the difference between, on the one hand, being nonnormative and on the other engaging in criticism (Hogg & Reid, 2006; Hogg & Tindale, 2005). Violation of norms and criticism of normative practices may be quite different phenomena. The former conveys that one is not a group member or that one is marginal or does not wish to belong. The latter, if it comes from outside the group, conveys a deliberate attempt to discredit the group and all that it stands for. If it comes from inside the group, particularly from prototypical members (cf. discussion of leadership later), it may be viewed more positively as a constructive attempt to improve the group and promote its best interest.

Normative disagreement can take more of a collective form when, rather than an individual, it is a subgroup or faction that dissents. Later, we will see how a normative minority can sometimes dramatically change the normative practices of

a majority (minority influence—Moscovici, 1980; Mugny & Pérez, 1991; see Martin & Hewstone, 2008); here we discuss how schisms can unravel the normative fabric of groups. Schisms are usually associated with profound attitudinal and value differences within ideological groups such as religions, political parties, or artistic movements (e.g., Liebman, Sutton, & Wuthnow, 1988). According to Sani and Reicher (1998, 1999), identity threat, self-conceptual uncertainty, and a sense of self-conceptual impermanence and instability can arise in groups whose normative properties are suddenly changed by the actions of a subgroup or a leadership clique. Members feel that the group is no longer what it used to be; its normative attitudes, values, perceptions, and behaviors have uncompromisingly shifted, and thus the group's identity has changed. Taken off guard by this change, members feel acutely uncertain about how, and whether, they fit into the new group.

In response, members can try to reestablish the group's original identity through discussion, persuasion, and negotiation, or they can split into a separate subgroup that is in conflict with the rest of the group. A split, or schism, is most likely to occur if members feel the group is intolerant of dissent, unable to embrace diverse views, and inclined toward marginalization of dissenting individuals. A schism transforms one group, a single category, into two separate groups engaged in often highly charged intergroup conflict. The split rests on a profound social identity threat that engages a drive to reduce the acute self-conceptual uncertainty that has been aroused. Not surprisingly, schisms can sometimes be destructive of groups—for example, factional conflicts within political ideologies (e.g., Stalinists vs. Trotskyites within the Communist Party) and interpretational differences within religions (e.g., Sunnis vs. Shi'ites within Islam).

When a schism exists, the subgroup that holds the minority position may paradoxically stand a chance of winning over the rest of the group and reinstating a degree of normative consensus. This might happen if the minority's position was novel, the minority could lay some claim to being a bone fide part of the larger ingroup, and the minority adopted a consistent yet flexible style of social influence and persuasion (e.g., Mugny, 1982; Nemeth, 1986). Indeed, although schisms are often highly destructive, the fact that they may sponsor critical thinking, creativity and innovation may, if properly managed, enhance the larger group (e.g., Nemeth & Owens, 1996; Nemeth & Staw, 1989).

MAJORITY INFLUENCE AND CONFORMITY

Norms have an enormous influence on people. For example, Milgram, Bickman, and Berkowitz (1969) were able to make 84% of pedestrian passers-by gaze up into space at nothing at all by simply having a group of confederates set a norm by doing so. A classic early demonstration of the power of norms is Newcomb's (1965) study of 1930s norms at a small liberal arts college, Bennington College. The college had progressive and liberal norms but drew its students from conservative upper-middle-class families. The 1936 American presidential election allowed Newcomb to conduct a confidential ballot. First-year students strongly favored the conservative candidate, whereas third- and fourth-year students had shifted their voting preference toward the liberal and communist–socialist candidates. Presumably, prolonged exposure to liberal norms had produced the change in political preference. Siegel and Siegel (1957) conducted a better controlled study to rule out individual differences. New students at a private college were randomly assigned to different types of student accommodation: sororities and dormitories. At this college, sororities had a conservative ethos and dormitories had more progressive liberal norms. Siegel and Siegel measured the students' degree of conservatism at the beginning and end of the year. Exposure to liberal norms significantly reduced conservatism.

Why and how do people conform to norms? To answer these questions, social psychology has tended to downplay the norm concept, and instead reframe the question in terms of how and why people yield to group pressure or social pressure from a numerical majority.

Yielding to the Majority

The classic studies of conformity, as yielding to majority opinion, were conducted by Asch in the 1950s (Asch, 1956). Male students, participating in what they thought was a visual discrimination task, sat around a table in groups of seven to nine, and took turns in a fixed order to call out publicly which of three comparison lines was the same length as a standard line. There were 18 trials. In reality, only one person was a true naïve participant, and he answered second to last. The others were experimental confederates instructed to give erroneous responses on 12 focal trials; on six trials, they picked a line that was too long and on six trials, a line that was too short. There was a control condition in which participants performed the task privately with no group influence; as less than 1% of control participants' responses were errors, it can be assumed that the task was unambiguous.

The results were striking. There were large individual differences: 25% of participants remained steadfastly independent throughout; 50% conformed to the erroneous majority on six or more focal trials; and 5% conformed on all 12 focal trials. The average conformity rate was 33%, computed as the total number of instances of conformity across the experiment divided by the product of the number of participants in the experiment and the number of focal trials in the sequence.

When participants were asked about their experience in the experiment, they reported initially experiencing uncertainty and self-doubt, which gradually evolved into self-consciousness, fear of disapproval, and feelings of anxiety, even loneliness. They gave a variety of reasons for conforming: some said they felt their perceptions may have been inaccurate and that the group was actually correct; others that they knew the group was wrong but went along with the majority in order not to stand out; and a small minority claimed that they actually saw the lines as the group did. Independents (those who did not yield) were either entirely confident in the accuracy of their judgments or were emotionally affected by the group but guided by a belief in individualism or in doing the task as directed (i.e., being accurate and correct).

To pursue the idea that one reason why people conform, even when the stimulus is completely unambiguous, is to avoid censure, ridicule, and social disapproval, Asch (1951) conducted a variant of his experiment in which 16 naïve participants faced one confederate who gave incorrect answers. The participants found the confederate's behavior ludicrous and openly ridiculed him and laughed at him. Even the experimenter found the situation so bizarre that he could not contain his mirth and also ended up laughing at the poor confederate.

Perhaps if participants were not concerned about social disapproval, there would be no subjective pressure to conform? To investigate this, Asch conducted another variation of the experiment, in which the incorrect majority called out their judgments publicly but the single naïve participant wrote his down privately. Conformity dropped to 12.5%.

Deutsch and Gerard (1955) took this one step further. They believed that they could entirely eradicate pressure to conform if the task was unambiguous and the participant was anonymous, responded privately, and was not under any sort of surveillance by the group. Why should one conform to an erroneous majority when there is an obvious, unambiguous, and objectively correct answer, and the group has no way of knowing what one is doing?

To test this idea, Deutsch and Gerard confronted a naïve participant face-to-face with three confederates, who made unanimously incorrect judgments of lines, exactly as in Asch's original experiment. In another condition, the naïve participant was anonymous, isolated in a cubicle, and allowed to respond privately; no group pressure existed. There was a third condition in which participants responded face-to-face, but with an explicit group goal to be as accurate as possible; group pressure was maximized.

Deutsch and Gerard also manipulated subjective uncertainty by having half the participants respond while the stimuli were present (the procedure used by Asch) and half respond after the stimuli had been removed (there would be scope for feeling uncertain). As predicted, decreasing uncertainty and decreasing group pressure (i.e., the motivation and ability of the group to censure lack of conformity) reduced conformity. But, intriguingly, people still conformed at a rate of about 23% even when uncertainty was low (stimulus present) and responses were entirely private and anonymous.

Based on Deutsch and Gerard's (1955) discovery that participants still conformed when isolated in cubicles, Crutchfield (1955) devised an apparatus in which participants in cubicles believed they were communicating with one another by pressing buttons on a console that illuminated responses, when in reality the cubicles were not interconnected and the experimenter was the source of all communication. In this way, many participants could be run simultaneously and yet all would believe they were being exposed to a unanimous group. The time-consuming and costly practice of using confederates was no longer necessary, and data could now be collected much more quickly under more controlled and varied experimental conditions; there was an explosion of research into conformity (Allen, 1965, 1975).

Individual and Group Differences in Conformity

One obvious question to ask about conformity is whether some people conform more than others: Are there individual or group differences in conformity and are there personality attributes that predispose some people to conform more than others? Research has suggested that those who conform tend to have lower self-esteem, greater need for social support or social approval, a need for self-control, lower IQ, high anxiety, feelings of self-blame and insecurity in the group, feelings of inferiority, feelings of relatively low status in the group, and a generally authoritarian personality (e.g., Costanzo, 1970; Elms & Milgram, 1966; McGhee & Teevan, 1967; Stang, 1972; Strickland & Crowne, 1962).

However, other research suggests that people who conform in one situation may not conform in another situation: whether one conforms or not may be less influenced by predisposition than by situational and contextual factors (e.g., Barocas & Gorlow, 1967; Barron, 1953; McGuire, 1968; Vaughan, 1964). For example, research on gender and conformity initially confirmed the prevailing stereotype that women are more compliant and conformist than men. This has now been shown to overwhelmingly reflect the conformity tasks used in these early studies—tasks

with which women had less familiarity and expertise, and experienced greater subjective uncertainty, and thus were influenced more than men (Eagly & Carli, 1981; Eagly & Chrvala, 1986).

Sistrunk and McDavid (1971) illustrated this by having male and female participants identify various objects in group pressure situations. For some participants, the stimuli were traditional male items (e.g., a special type of wrench); for some, traditional female items (e.g., types of needlework); and for others, the stimuli were neutral (e.g., popular rock stars). As expected, women conformed more on male items, men more on female items, and both groups equally on neutral (nonsex-stereotypical) items. Women do, however, tend to conform a little more than men in public interactive settings like that involved in the Asch paradigm. One explanation is that it reflects women's greater concern with maintaining group harmony (Eagly, 1978). However, a later study put the emphasis on men's behavior; women conformed equally in public and private contexts whereas it was men who were particularly resistant to influence in public settings (Eagly, Wood, & Fishbaugh, 1981).

Cultural Norms

Conformity is universal, but the extent to which people conform is affected by cultural norms. Smith, Bond, and Kağitçibaşi (2006) surveyed conformity studies conducted in different nations using Asch's paradigm or a modified version of the Asch paradigm. They found that the level of conformity ranged from a low of 14% among Belgian students (Doms, 1983) to a high of 58% among Indian teachers in Fiji (Chandra, 1973), with an overall average of 31.2%. Conformity was lower among participants from individualist cultures in North America and northwestern Europe (25.3%) than among participants from collectivist or interdependent cultures in Africa, Asia, Oceania, and South America (37.1%).

A meta-analysis of 133 replications of the Asch paradigm in 17 countries (Bond & Smith, 1996) confirmed that people who score high on Hofstede's (1980) collectivism scale conform more than people who score low. For example, Norwegians, who have a reputation for social unity and responsibility, were more conformist than the French, who value critical judgment, diverse opinions, and dissent (Milgram, 1961), and the Bantu of Zimbabwe, who have strong sanctions against nonconformity, were highly conformist (Whittaker & Meade, 1967).

Cultural differences in level of conformity map onto not only Hofstede's (1980) societal-level distinction between collectivist and individualist societies, but also Markus and Kitayama's (1991) individual-level distinction between interdependent and independent self-construal. The interdependent self is relatively connected, fluid, and flexible and is tied to and guided by social relations that govern behavior, whereas the independent self is relatively bounded, stable, and autonomous, and in itself governs behavior (for further elaboration see Oyserman, Coon, & Kemmelmeier, 2002; Vignoles, Chryssochoou, & Breakwell, 2000; see Heine's discussion of culture, this volume).

From an individualistic perspective, interdependent self-construal and associated conformity can be pejoratively caricatured as slavish conformity that suppresses individual creativity and freedom and prevents social innovation; from a collectivist perspective, independent self-construal can also be pejoratively caricatured as brash disregard for and intolerance of others coupled with lack of sensitivity and immature lack of self-control. Both extremes are maladaptive in a social evolutionary sense (cf. Campbell, 1975) and because such caricatures have undesirable epistemological consequences (cf. Markus & Kitayama, 1994). In reality conformity—as yielding to the majority—is as essential to social cohesion and independence as resistance to majority views is vital for innovation and social change.

Situational Influences on Conformity

Privacy, Interdependence, and Attraction

A number of situational factors influence conformity. One important factor is privacy; people tend to conform less if their behavior is not under surveillance by the group. As we saw earlier, Deutsch and Gerard (1955) found that privacy reduced conformity in the Asch paradigm, but did not abolish it. Insko and colleagues found a similar effect using a different paradigm in which the judgment dimension was ambiguous (judging whether a blue–green slide was blue or green): Participants were less influenced in private than public by the majority judgment (Insko, Smith, Alicke, Wade, & Taylor, 1985).

Another factor that affects conformity is perceived interdependence. When individuals believe their fates are interdependent and that they must work together to achieve a common goal, conformity increases (Allen, 1965; Deutsch & Gerard, 1955). This is part of a wider psychological effect in which interdependence can enhance group serving motivation and cooperation (e.g., Sherif & Sherif, 1953) and increase effort exerted on behalf of the group (e.g., Karau & Williams, 1993).

Perhaps unsurprisingly, due to the similarity–attraction link (Byrne, 1971), people tend to conform more in settings in which they like fellow group members or the group as a whole. Conformity has been found to be greater when the group contains friends (e.g., Lott & Lott, 1961; Thibaut & Strickland, 1956), when the person values or feels valued by the group (Dittes & Kelley, 1956), when

people feel they are in the group because of shared characteristics (e.g., Gerard, 1954) or that others in the group are similar to them (e.g., Abrams, Wetherell, Cochrane, Hogg, & Turner, 1990), and when the group is more established (e.g., Williams & Sogon, 1984). However, attraction does not influence conformity when the group is faced with a perceptual task such as judgment of autokinetic movement (Downing, 1958) or judgment of line lengths (Harper, 1961); perhaps because the similarity–attraction link is less important here where perceptual validation is better grounded in triangulation from diverse perspectives (Gorenflo & Crano, 1989).

Group Size and Group Unanimity

Two situational factors in conformity that have been well researched are group size and group unanimity (Allen, 1965, 1975). Asch (1952) found that as the unanimous group increased from one person to two, to three, to four, to eight, to 10, and to 15, the conformity rate increased and then decreased slightly: 3, 13, 33, 35, 32, and 31%. Although some research reports a linear relationship between group size and conformity, the most robust finding is that conformity reaches its full strength with a three- to five-person majority, and additional members have little effect (e.g., Stang, 1976).

Campbell and Fairey (1989) suggest that group size affects conformity differently depending on the type of judgment being made and on the person's motivational goals. With matters of taste, in which there is no objectively correct answer (e.g., fashions), and in which people are concerned about "fitting in," group size has a relatively linear effect: The larger the majority, the more one is swayed. When there is a correct response and one is concerned about being correct, then the views of one or two others will usually be sufficient: The majority-consistent views of additional others will not increase confidence and will largely be redundant.

In addition, group size may not refer to the actual number of physically separate people in the group but to the number of seemingly *independent* sources of influence in the group (Wilder, 1977). For instance, a majority of three individuals who are perceived to be independent will be more influential than a majority of, say, five who are perceived to be in collusion and thus represent a single information source. People may actually find it difficult to represent more than four or five discriminable or independent pieces of information, and thus they assimilate additional group members into one or other of these initial sources of information—hence the relative lack of effect of group size above three to five members.

Unanimity plays a key role in conformity. Asch's original experiment in which there was a conformity rate of

33% used a unanimous erroneous majority. Subsequent experiments have shown that conformity is significantly reduced if the majority is not unanimous (Allen, 1975). Asch found that a correct supporter (i.e., a member of the majority who always gave the correct answer, and thus agreed with and supported the true participant) reduced conformity from 33 to 5.5%. The effectiveness of a supporter in reducing conformity is marginally greater if the supporter responds before rather than after the majority (Morris & Miller, 1975).

Support itself may not be the crucial factor in reducing conformity. Any lack of unanimity among the majority is effective. For example, Asch found that a dissenter who was even more wildly incorrect than the majority was equally effective, and Shaw, Rothschild, and Strickland (1957) found that a dithering and undecided deviate was also effective. Allen and Levine (1971) conducted a memorable experiment in which participants, who were making visual judgments, were provided with a "competent" supporter who had normal vision or an "incompetent" supporter who wore such thick glasses as to raise serious doubts about his ability to see anything at all, let alone judge lines accurately. In the absence of any support, participants conformed 97% of the time. The competent supporter reduced conformity to 36%, but most surprising was the fact that the incompetent supporter also reduced conformity to 64%.

Supporters, dissenters, and deviates are effective in reducing conformity because they shatter the unanimity of the majority, and this raises or legitimizes the possibility of alternative ways of responding or behaving. For example, Nemeth and Chiles (1988) confronted participants with four confederates who either all correctly identified blue slides as blue, or among whom one consistently called the blue slide "green." Participants were then exposed to another group that unanimously called red slides "orange." The participants who had previously been exposed to the consistent dissenter were more likely to correctly call the red slides "red."

Processes of Conformity

Research on conformity has led to the proposal of at least three main processes of influence (see Nail, 1986): informational influence, normative influence, and referent informational influence.

Informational and Normative Influence

The most enduring distinction concerning processes of conformity is between informational influence and normative influence (Deutsch & Gerard, 1955; Kelley, 1952). Informational influence is an influence to accept information from another as evidence about reality. Because people need to feel confident that their perceptions, beliefs, and feelings are correct, informational influence comes into play when people are uncertain, either because stimuli are intrinsically ambiguous or because there is social disagreement. Under these circumstances, people first make objective tests against reality, but if this is not possible they make social comparisons (Festinger, 1950, 1954; Suls & Wheeler, 2000). Effective informational influence causes true cognitive change: changes in people's underlying attitudes, beliefs and perceptions.

Informational influence was at least partially responsible for Sherif's (1935, 1936) autokinetic findings. Because reality was ambiguous, participants used other people's estimates as information to remove the ambiguity and resolve subjective uncertainty. When participants were told that the perceived movement was merely an illusion, they did not conform (Alexander, Zucker, & Brody, 1970). Presumably, since reality itself was uncertain, their own subjective uncertainty was interpreted as a correct and valid representation of reality, and thus informational influence did not operate. Although Asch's judgment task was designed to be unambiguous to exclude informational influence, Asch (1952) found that conformity increased when the comparison lines were made similar to one another and thus the task more ambiguous.

Normative influence is an influence to conform to the positive expectations of others. People have a need for social approval and acceptance, which causes them to go along with the group for instrumental reasons: to cultivate approval and acceptance, avoid censure or disapproval, or achieve specific goals. Thus, normative influence comes into play when the group is perceived to have the power and ability to mediate rewards and punishment contingent on our behavior. An important precondition is that one believes one is under surveillance by the group, and, therefore, that one's behavior is publicly observable. Effective normative influence creates situation-specific surface compliance in public settings rather than true enduring cognitive change. There is considerable evidence that people often conform to a majority in public but do not necessarily internalize this as it does not carry over to private settings or endure over time (Nail, 1986).

Normative influence was clearly the principal cause of conformity in the Asch paradigm. The stimuli were unambiguous (informational influence would not be operating), and participants' behavior was under direct surveillance by the group. We saw earlier how privacy, anonymity, and lack of surveillance reduced conformity in the Asch paradigm, presumably because normative influence was weakened. However, we also saw that Deutsch and Gerard (1955) tried to remove normative influence entirely, but were unsuccessful. Even under conditions in which neither informational nor normative influence would be expected to operate, they found residual conformity at a remarkably high rate of about 23%. Perhaps Deutsch and Gerard simply failed to completely remove the preconditions for informational and normative influence; for example, the participants did not feel the task was totally unambiguous or that their responses were entirely private. Another possibility is that there is either a third process of influence in groups, or that normative and informational influence need to be reconceptualized to fully capture the process of group influence.

Referent Informational Influence

This last possibility has been the focus of a critique of social influence research (e.g., Turner, 1981, 1982). It has been argued that normative and informational influence represents a dual-process model: a model that has drifted away from group norms and group belongingness and focused on *interpersonal* dependency that could just as well occur between individuals as among group members.

Grounded in social identity theory (Tajfel & Turner, 1979; Turner, Hogg, Oakes, Reicher, & Wetherell, 1987; also see Hogg, 2006; Hogg & Abrams, 1988), referent informational influence was developed to address this critique as a different way to explain social influence and conformity in groups (Abrams & Hogg 1990; Hogg & Turner, 1987; Turner, 1981, 1982; Turner & Oakes, 1989; also see Hogg & Smith, 2007; Turner, 1991). Its premise is that rather than being influenced by others because we are dependent on them for social approval and acceptance or for information that removes ambiguity and establishes subjective validity, we are influenced by others because we feel we belong, psychologically, to the group, and, therefore, the norms of the group are relevant standards for our behavior.

In situations in which we feel a sense of belonging and define ourselves in group terms (group membership is psychologically salient), we recruit information from memory and the immediate social context to determine the relevant normative attributes of our group. Although contextual information can be gleaned from the behavior of outgroup members or unrelated individuals, the most immediate and reliable source is the behavior of fellow ingroup members, particularly those who are generally group prototypical and behaving in a way that is broadly consistent with the essence of the group. As described earlier, the context-relevant ingroup norm that is constructed and cognitively represented as an ingroup prototype, obeys the metacontrast principle, capturing and accentuating intragroup similarities and intergroup differences.

The process of self-categorization associated with group identification, group belongingness, and group behavior (Turner, Hogg, Oakes, Reicher, & Wetherell, 1987) depersonalizes self-conception such that we define and see ourselves in group terms and assimilate our thoughts, feelings, and behavior to the prototype—thus we behave in group prototypical terms. To the extent that all members of the group construct a similar group prototype, self-categorization causes members to converge on the prototype; there is increased uniformity within the group—the characteristic conformity effect.

Referent informational influence differs from normative and informational influence in a number of ways. People conform because they are group members, not to validate physical reality or to avoid social disapproval. People conform not to other people but to a norm; other people act as a source of information about the appropriate ingroup norm. Because the norm is an internalized representation, people can conform to it in the absence of surveillance by group members or, for that matter, anybody else.

Support for referent informational influence comes from a wide range of studies of social identity and group influence (see Abrams & Hogg 1990; Hogg & Smith, 2007; Turner, 1991; Turner & Oakes, 1989). For example, across a series of four conformity experiments, Hogg and Turner (1987) found that under conditions of private responding (i.e., no normative influence), participants conformed to a nonunanimous majority containing a correct supporter (i.e., no informational influence) only if it was the participant's explicit or implicit ingroup. Turner, Wetherell, and Hogg (1989) found evidence for conformity to a polarized ingroup norm when there was a salient comparison outgroup and participants identified with the ingroup (cf. Mackie, 1986; Mackie & Cooper, 1984). Abrams, Wetherell, Cochrane, Hogg, and Turner (1990) found broad evidence for referent informational influence across an autokinetic study, an Asch paradigm study, and a group polarization study; and Reicher found similar evidence from an analysis of a riot (Reicher, 1984a) and an associated laboratory experiment analogue (Reicher, 1984b).

MINORITY INFLUENCE AND SOCIAL CHANGE

From the perspective of conformity research, social influence is a process whereby individuals yield to direct or indirect influence from a numerical majority; the majority prevails over the minority to maintain social stasis. There is, however, an entirely different type of social influence that we are all familiar with, in which lone individuals or small groups of individuals are able to change, often dramatically, the attitudes and behaviors of the larger majority; the minority prevails over the majority to promote social change. Minority influence and associated social change are the focus of this section.

Dissenters, Deviants, and Marginal Groups

For conformity research, individuals, alone or in small groups, who dissent or deviate from or are marginal within the majority, are treated as targets of influence that are resistant due to personality or situational factors. Typically, groups try to socialize and include dissenters and deviant members (e.g., Levine & Moreland, 1994; Schachter, 1959), particularly if the group is small or retaining members is important (e.g., Wicker, 1968), and only marginalize and reject members as a last resort (Darley, 2001).

Marginal members are not powerless. By the fact that they deviate from or are resistant to the group's normative practices, they can raise questions in members' minds about what the group stands for. As such, members can view them as posing a real threat to the group and its identity. Not surprisingly, normative deviates can be characterized as "black sheep" and rejected from the group, particularly if they are clearly ingroup members (Marques, Abrams, & Serôdio, 2001; Marques & Paez, 1994).

A different dynamic comes into play when a member is not merely normatively marginal, but is someone who actively criticizes the group's norms and, by implication, identity; here, it is outgroup critics who are censured and rejected more than ingroup critics (Hornsey, 2005). Ingroup critics who are constructively critical and viewed by the group to be highly prototypical members can sometimes be effective in transforming the group's norms and identity; these people may have a leadership function in groups (e.g., Hogg & Van Knippenberg, 2003; see discussion of leadership later).

Dissenters, "deviants," critics, and marginal members are not always lone individuals. In many cases, they are numerous, and more often than not, they represent a coherent and distinctive subgroup: a group that can acquiesce in its minority position, engineer a schism and split away from the majority group (e.g., Sani & Reicher, 1999; see previous), or actively promote its position in an attempt to influence and change the majority's position. These latter active minorities are a potent source of social influence oriented toward innovation and social change.

Minority Influence

Typically, minorities are at an influence disadvantage relative to majorities. Often, they are less numerous, and in the eyes of the majority, they have less legitimate power and are less worthy of serious consideration. Asch (1952) found, as we saw previously, that a lone deviate (a confederate giving erroneous line judgments) was ridiculed and laughed at by a majority comprising true participants giving correct line judgments. However, sometimes a minority can have some influence and be taken seriously by a majority. In a variant of the single deviate study, Asch (1952) found that a correct majority of 11 true participants confronted by a deviant/incorrect minority of nine confederates remained independent (i.e., continued responding correctly) but took the minority's responses far more seriously; no one laughed.

The minority had some influence over the majority, albeit not enough in this experiment to produce manifest conformity. In the real world, however, minorities can be enormously influential. Some of the key questions are whether minorities and majorities gain influence via different social practices and, more fundamentally, whether the underlying psychology is different. For recent conceptual and empirical overviews of minority influence research, see Martin and Hewstone (2003, 2008) and Martin, Hewstone, Martin, and Gardikiotis (2008), and for a meta-analysis of research findings, see Wood, Lundgren, Ouellette, Busceme, and Blackstone (1994).

Conformity Bias and the Genetic Model

The scientific study of minority influence really began with Moscovici and Faucheux's (1972; Moscovici, 1976) critique of social influence research. They argued that there had been a "conformity bias" and a functionalist assumption in the literature on social influence. Nearly all research focused on how individuals or minorities yield to majority influence and conform to the majority, and assumed that conformity is functional because people are dependent on majorities for normative and informational reasons. From this perspective social influence *is* conformity, and is a process that produces uniformity, perpetuates stability, and sustains the status quo—leaving no room for innovation and social change.

Moscovici and Faucheux (1972) also famously "turned Asch on his head," by cleverly suggesting that Asch's studies had actually been studies of minority influence, not majority influence. The Asch paradigm appears to pit a lone individual (true participant) against an erroneous majority (confederates) on an unambiguous physical perception task. However, in reality, virtually no judgment tasks are truly unambiguous; if we find we are in disagreement with others, even over the apparently most objective of perceptions, we feel uncertain and question our perceptions. This sense of uncertainty would be particularly acute when an obviously correct perception is challenged. Asch's lines were *not* "unambiguous": There was disagreement between confederates and participants over the length of the lines. In reality, Asch's lone participant was a member of a large majority (the rest of humanity who would call the lines "correctly") confronted by a small minority (the confederates who called the lines "incorrectly"). Asch's participants were influenced by a minority, and the participants who remained "independent" can be considered the conformists.

Building on this critique, Moscovici (1976) proposed a genetic model of social influence, calling it a "genetic" model because it focused on the way in which the dynamics of social conflict can generate (are genetic of) social change. The core premise was that all attempts at influence create disagreement-based conflict between the source and the target of influence. Because people generally do not like conflict, they try to resolve it. In the case of disagreement with a minority, an easy and common resolution is, as we saw earlier, to dismiss, discredit, or pathologize the minority (Papastamou, 1986).

However, it is more difficult to dismiss a minority if it "stands up to" the majority and adopts a behavioral style that conveys uncompromising certainty about and commitment to its position, and a genuine belief that the majority ought to change to adopt its position. Under these circumstances, the majority takes the minority seriously, reconsidering its own beliefs and considering the minority's position as a viable alternative. The most effective behavioral style a minority can adopt to prevail over the majority is one in which, among other things, the minority is diachronically and synchronically consistent, shows investment in its position by making significant personal and material sacrifices, and is seen to be acting out of principle rather than from ulterior motives.

Consistency is the most important minority behavioral style, as it speaks directly to the existence of an alternative norm and identity rather than merely an alternative opinion. When a number of people repeatedly agree on an alternative viewpoint, this draws attention to them as a distinct entity (e.g., Hamilton & Sherman, 1996) with a coherent and unshakable commitment to an alternative reality. From an attribution theory perspective (e.g., Kelley, 1967), this form of consistent and distinctive behavior cries out for explanation as it cannot be discounted. Furthermore, the behavior is likely to be internally attributed to invariant and perhaps essentialist (e.g., Haslam, Rothschild, & Ernst, 1998) properties of the minority rather than to transient situational factors, which makes the minority even more of a force to be reckoned with and a focus of cogitation by the majority.

The role of consistency has been demonstrated by Moscovici and his colleagues in a series of ingenious experiments, referred to as the "blue–green" studies (Maass & Clark, 1984). In a modified version of the Asch paradigm, Moscovici, Lage, and Naffrechoux (1969) had four participants confront two confederates for a color perception task involving blue slides that varied only in intensity. The confederates were either consistent, always calling the slides "green," or inconsistent, calling the slides "green" two-thirds of the time and "blue" one-third of the time. There was also

a control condition with no confederates, just six true participants. The consistent minority had significantly more influence (9% conformity) than the inconsistent minority (less than 2% conformity). Although the conformity rate is much lower than with a consistent majority (recall that Asch reported an average conformity rate of 33%), it is, nevertheless, remarkable that four people (a numerical majority) were influenced by two people (a minority).

Moscovici and Lage (1976) employed the same color perception task to compare consistent and inconsistent minorities with consistent and inconsistent majorities. There was also a control condition. As before, the only minority to produce conformity was the consistent minority (10% conformity). Although this does not compare well with the rate of conformity to the consistent majority (40%), it is comparable with the rate of conformity to the inconsistent majority (12%). Other studies have shown that the most important aspects of consistency are synchronic consistency (i.e., consensus) among members of the minority (Nemeth, Wachtler, & Endicott, 1977) and perceived consistency, not merely objective repetition (Nemeth, Swedlund, & Kanki, 1974).

Moscovici's (1976) focus on behavioral style was extended by Mugny (1982) who focused on the strategic use of behavioral styles by real, active minorities struggling to change societal practices. Mugny argued that because minorities are typically in powerless positions relative to majorities, they have to negotiate their influence with the majority rather than unilaterally adopt a behavioral style. Mugny distinguished between rigid and flexible negotiating styles, arguing that a rigid minority that refuses to compromise on any issues risks being rejected as dogmatic, and one that is too prepared to flexibly shift its ground and compromise risks being rejected as inconsistent (the classic case of "flip-flopping"). There is a fine line to tread, but a degree of flexibility is more effective than rigidity. A minority should be absolutely consistent with regard to its core position but should adopt a relatively open-minded and reasonable negotiating style on less core issues (e.g., Mugny & Papastamou, 1981).

Conversion Theory

Moscovici's (1980, 1985) conversion theory is still the dominant explanation of minority influence. While his genetic model focused largely on how a minority's behavioral style (in particular, attributions based on the minority's consistent behavior) could enhance its influence over a majority, conversion theory is a more cognitive account of how a member of the majority processes the minority's message.

Moscovici argued that majorities and minorities exert influence through different processes. Majority influence brings about direct public compliance for reasons of normative or informational dependence. People engage in a *comparison process* in which they concentrate attention on what others say to know how to fit in with them. Majority views are accepted passively without much thought. The outcome is public compliance with majority views with little or no private attitude change.

In contrast, minority influence brings about indirect, often latent, private change in opinion due to the cognitive conflict and restructuring that deviant ideas produce. People engage in a *validation process* in which they carefully examine and cogitate over the validity of their beliefs. The outcome is little or no overt public agreement with the minority, for fear of being viewed as a member of the minority, but a degree of private internal attitude change that may only surface later on. Minorities produce a conversion effect as a consequence of active consideration of the minority point of view.

It is worth noting that Moscovici's dual-process model of influence embodies a distinction that resembles, according to Turner (1991), the one discussed earlier between normative and informational influence. It also resembles Petty and Cacioppo's (1986) distinction between peripheral and central processing, and Chaiken's (e.g., Bohner, Moskowitz, & Chaiken, 1995) distinction between heuristic and systematic processing.

Martin and Hewstone's (2003) review of empirical evidence for conversion theory is organized around three testable hypotheses. The *direction-of-attention hypothesis* that majority influence causes people to focus on their relationship to the majority (interpersonal focus) whereas minority influence causes people to focus on the minority message itself (message focus) is supported (e.g., Campbell, Tesser, & Fairey, 1986). The *content-of-thinking* hypothesis that majority influence leads to superficial examination of arguments whereas minority influence leads to detailed evaluation of arguments has support from thought-listing studies of cognitive elaboration (e.g., Maass & Clark, 1983; Martin, 1996; Mucchi-Faina, Maass, & Volpato, 1991).

The *differential-influence* hypothesis that majority influence produces more public/direct influence than private/indirect influence whereas minority influence produces the opposite has received the most research attention and solid support (see meta-analysis by Wood, Lundgren, Ouellette, Busceme, and Blackstone, 1994). For example, the studies described previously by Moscovici, Lage, and Naffrechoux (1969) and Moscovici and Lage (1976) found, as would be expected from conversion theory, that conversion through minority influence took longer to manifest itself than compliance through majority influence; there was evidence for private change in color thresholds (i.e., conversion) among participants exposed to a consistent minority, although they did not behave (or had not yet behaved) publicly in accordance with this change.

Other support for the differential-influence hypothesis comes from an intriguing series of "blue–green" experiments by Moscovici and Personnaz (1980, 1986). Individual participants, judging the color of obviously blue slides, were exposed to a single confederate who always called the blue slides "green." They were told that most people (82%) would respond as the confederate did or that only few people (18%) would. In this way, the confederate was a source of majority or minority influence. Participants publicly called out the color of the slide and then (and this is the ingenious twist) the slide was removed and participants wrote down privately the color of the after-image. Unknown to most people, including the participants, the after-image is always the complementary color; for blue slides, the after-image would be yellow and for green slides, purple. There were three phases to the experiment: an influence phase in which participants were exposed to the confederate, preceded and followed by phases in which the confederate was absent and there was thus no influence. The remarkable finding was that majority influence hardly affected the after-image (it remained yellow, indicating that participants had seen a blue slide), but that minority influence shifted the after-image toward purple (indicating that participants had actually "seen" a green slide), and the effect persisted even when the minority confederate was absent. Because some other research teams have failed to replicate Moscovici and Personnaz's findings, Martin (1998) conducted a series of five careful replications to come to the relatively cautious conclusion that the finding may at least partially be an artifact of the amount of attention participants were paying to the slides: the greater the attention the greater the after-image shift.

Convergent-Divergent Theory

A slightly different account of majority/minority differences in influence has been proposed by Nemeth (1986, 1995). Because people expect to share attitudes with the majority, the discovery of disagreement associated with majority influence is surprising and stressful and leads to a self-protective narrowing of focus of attention. This produces convergent thinking that inhibits consideration of alternative views. In contrast, because people do not expect to share attitudes with a minority, the discovery of disagreement associated with minority influence is unsurprising and not stressful and does not narrow focus of attention. It allows divergent thinking that involves consideration of a range of alternative views, even ones not proposed by the minority. In this way, Nemeth believes that exposure to minority views can stimulate innovation and creativity, generate more and better ideas, and lead to superior decision making in groups. The key difference between Nemeth's (1986) convergent–divergent theory and Moscovici's (1980) conversion theory hinges on the relationship between "stress" and message processing: For Nemeth, majority-induced stress restricts message processing; for Moscovici, minority-induced stress elaborates message processing.

Convergent-divergent theory is supported by research using relatively straightforward cognitive tasks showing that minority influence improves performance relative to majority influence on tasks that benefit from divergent thinking (e.g., Martin & Hewstone, 1999; Nemeth & Wachtler, 1983), that majority influence improves performance relative to minority influence on tasks that benefit from convergent thinking (e.g., Peterson & Nemeth, 1996), and that minority influence leads to the generation of more creative and novel judgments than does majority influence (e.g., Mucchi-Faina, Maass, & Volpato, 1991; Nemeth & Wachtler, 1983). Research also shows that minority influence leads people to explore different strategies for problem solving whereas majority influence restricts people to the majority endorsed strategy (e.g., Butera, Mugny, Legrenzi, & Pérez, 1996; Peterson & Nemeth, 1996) and that minority influence encourages issue-relevant thinking whereas majority influence encourages message-relevant thinking (e.g., De Dreu, De Vries, Gordijn, & Schuurman, 1999).

Martin and Hewstone (2003) note in their review of minority influence that the role of stress has not been properly tested, and it is not clear whether convergent–divergent theory will hold up so well in studies using more complex cognitive tasks or in attitude domains (Kruglanski & Mackie, 1990).

Social Identity and Self-Categorization

We saw earlier that the social identity theory of influence in groups, referent informational influence theory (e.g., Abrams & Hogg, 1990; Hogg & Turner, 1987; Turner & Oakes, 1989), views prototypical ingroup members as the most reliable source of normative information and that through self-categorization and prototype-based depersonalization of self, members behave in line with the norm. From this perspective, minorities should be extremely ineffective sources of influence; they are low in prototypicality and, in many cases, are widely stigmatized by the majority group as social outgroups, or are "psychologized" as deviant individuals.

So, from a social identity perspective, how can a minority within one's group be influential? According to David and Turner (2001), the problem for ingroup minorities is that the majority makes intragroup social comparisons that highlight and accentuate the minority's otherness, essentially instantiating a majority–minority intergroup differentiation within the group. The key to effective minority influence is for the majority to shift its level of social comparison to focus on intergroup comparisons with a genuine shared outgroup; this automatically transcends perceived intragroup divisions and accentuates the minority's ingroup status. The minority is now viewed as part of the ingroup, and there is indirect attitude change that may not be manifested overtly. For example, a radical faction within Islam will have more influence within Islam if Muslims make intergroup comparisons between Islam and the West than if they dwell on intra-Islam comparisons between majority and minority factions.

Studies by David and Turner (1996, 1999) support this analysis; ingroup minorities produced more indirect attitude change (i.e., conversion) than did outgroup minorities, and majorities produced surface compliance. However, other research finds that an outgroup minority has just as much indirect influence as an ingroup minority (see review by Pérez & Mugny, 1998) and, according to Martin and Hewstone (2003), more research is needed to provide evidence that minority conversion is generated by a self-categorization process.

Vested Interest and the Leniency Contract

Overall, however, minorities are more influential if they can avoid being categorized by the majority as a despised outgroup and can be considered by the majority as part of the ingroup. The challenge for a minority is to be able to achieve this at the same time as promulgating an unwaveringly consistent alternative viewpoint that differs from the majority position.

Crano's context–comparison model of minority influence describes how this may happen (e.g., Crano & Alvaro, 1998; Crano & Chen, 1998; Crano & Seyranian, 2009). When a minority's message involves weak or unvested attitudes, an ingroup minority can be quite persuasive—the message is distinctive and attracts attention and elaboration, and, by virtue of the message being unvested and the minority a clear ingroup, there is little threat that might invite derogation or rejection of the minority. An outgroup minority is likely to be derogated and not influential.

When the message involves strong or vested attitudes, it is more difficult for the minority to prevail. The message is not only distinctive but speaks to core attributes; however, the fact that the minority is part of the ingroup makes members reluctant to derogate people who are, after all, ingroup members. One way out of this dilemma is to establish what Crano calls a leniency contract, which allows the target to elaborate on the ingroup minority's message without derogating the minority, open-mindedly with little defensiveness or hostility. This leniency toward an ingroup minority leads to indirect attitude change. An outgroup minority does not invite leniency and is therefore likely to be strongly derogated as a threat to core group attitudes.

Social Change

Minorities are a force for innovation and social change. Moscovici's (1976) original agenda in studying active minorities was to understand social change. As we saw earlier, his genetic model and subsequent research by Mugny (1982) outlined a number of behavioral styles and strategic behaviors that help an active minority prevail over a majority. However, subsequent research and theory has focused increasingly on information processing (e.g., Martin & Hewstone, 2008) and has been somewhat divorced from a separate literature that deals with social movements and collective mobilization in the service of social change.

Social Movements and Collective Mobilization

Active minorities often organize themselves into social movements that engage in collective mobilization and sustained social protest. Collective protest has often been characterized as crowd behavior and studied as if it were the primitive irrational behavior of a mob of uncoordinated and pathologically deviant individuals—people in the grip of a group mind and primitive emotions (cf. LeBon, 1896/1908; McDougall, 1920) or lacking a sense of responsibility due to deindividuation (cf. Zimbardo, 1970).

More recent social identity analyses of the crowd (e.g., Reicher, 2001) believe these approaches are metatheoretically predicated on an ideology that protects the establishment and perpetuates the status quo. Instead, social identity approaches see crowd behavior as collective protest in normatively unstructured contexts in which members of the crowd determine identity- and situation-appropriate behavioral norms through referent informational influence and then conform to these norms through self-categorization (e.g., Reicher, 1984a, 2001). From this perspective, deindividuation is not a loss of identity associated with regression to primitive instincts, but a change in identity associated with conformity to identity-defining group norms (Klein, Spears, & Reicher, 2007; Postmes & Spears, 1998; Reicher, Spears, & Postmes, 1995).

One key issue for social protest is what transforms individual discontents or grievances shared by a minority into collective action. How and why do sympathizers become mobilized as activists or participants? What triggers a minority to rise up and fight for social change? Klandermans (1997) provides a conceptual architecture showing how a number of social psychological processes may work together to mobilize collective action. According to Klandermans, mobilization involves translating individual attitudes into overt behavior. Sympathizers have sympathetic attitudes toward an issue, yet these attitudes do not automatically translate into behavior. Participation also resembles a social dilemma (e.g., Dawes & Messick,

2000). Protest is generally *for* a social good (e.g., equality) or *against* a social ill (e.g., pollution), and as success benefits everyone irrespective of participation but failure harms participants more, it is tempting to "free ride" (e.g., Kerr & Bruun, 1983): to remain a sympathizer rather than become a participant. Finally, Klandermans notes that protest can only be understood as intergroup behavior that occurs in what he calls "multiorganizational fields": That is, protest movements involve the clash of ideas and ideologies between groups and politicized and strategic articulation with other more or less sympathetic organizations.

Klandermans (1997; for overview see Stürmer & Simon, 2004) described four steps in social movement participation. The first step is to become part of the group's mobilization potential by being a sympathizer. This is determined by feeling that one's group has been collectively disadvantaged or deprived (cf. Walker & Pettigrew, 1984), by having an us-versus-them orientation that blames an outgroup for one's own group's plight, and by believing that social change through collective action is possible. The second step is to become a target of mobilization attempts. Being a sympathizer is not enough; one must also be informed, via media access and informal communication networks, about what forms of protest are occurring that one can engage in.

The third step is to become motivated to participate. Being a sympathizer and knowing what is going on is not sufficient; one must also be motivated to participate. Motivation arises from the value that people place on the outcome of protest and the extent to which they believe that the protest will deliver the goods. Motivation is strongest if the collective benefit of the outcome of protest is highly valued (collective motive), if important others value one's participation (normative motive), and if valued personal outcomes are anticipated (reward motive). The normative and reward motives are important to prevent sympathizers from free-riding on others' participation. This analysis of motivation is based on Ajzen and Fishbein's (1980) expectancy–value analysis and their theory of reasoned action account of attitude–behavior correspondence.

Finally, barriers to participation must be overcome. Even powerful motivation may not translate into action if there are insurmountable obstacles, such as no transport to the protest or ill health. However, these obstacles are more likely to be surmounted if motivation is high.

Empirical support for Klandermans's integrative model resides in empirical support for the various conceptual components that it rests on. Although they agree with most of Klandermans's analysis, Stürmer & Simon (2004) argue that the cost–benefit aspect places too much emphasis on individual decision making. Instead, they argue that when people identify strongly with a group, they have a powerfully shared perception of collective injustice, needs, and goals. They also share behavioral intentions, trust and like one another, and are collectively influenced by group norms and legitimate group leaders. Furthermore, group motivation eclipses personal motivation. Provided that members believe that protest is an effective way forward, these processes increase the probability of participation in collective protest.

LEADERSHIP

Social movements as agents of social change almost always coalesce behind and are motivated by leaders who focus and embody a vision of the group's distinctive goals and identity. Since leaders serve this function for almost all groups, big and small (leadership may serve an evolutionary function for the survival of our species; Van Vugt, Hogan, & Kaiser, 2008), no discussion of influence can be complete without a significant discussion of leadership. Leaders are the focus of influence, the individuals who give orders, make requests, define norms and identity, and motivate normative behavior. However, as explained at the start of this chapter, the study of influence now tends not to discuss leadership, and the study of leadership is largely conducted in the organization and management sciences with a focus on business leadership and the psychology of the CEO and with little linkage to the social psychology of influence. This section summarizes some of the key theories and research on leadership from social psychology and the organization sciences (Hogg, 2007a; also see Northhouse, 2007; Yukl, 2006). Research on gender and leadership is covered in full detail elsewhere in this book (see Wood and Eagly's chapter, volume 1), so it is not covered here.

Defining Leadership

It is difficult to find a single definition of leadership that embraces all the research done on leadership. There are numerous definitions that reflect and are closely tied to the variety of different theories of, approaches to, and perspectives on leadership. Leadership is a quintessentially social psychological phenomenon. Leaders influence other people, and *influence* is a core component of classic definitions of social psychology: "The scientific investigation of how the thoughts, feelings and behaviors of individuals are influenced by the actual, imagined or implied presence of others" (Allport, 1954, p. 5).

One useful definition is provided by Chemers, who defines leadership as "a process of social influence through which an individual enlists and mobilizes the aid of others in the attainment of a collective goal" (Chemers, 2001, p. 376). Leadership requires there to be an individual, or

clique, which influences the behavior of another individual or group of individuals; wherever there are leaders, there must be followers. Definitions of leadership are generally quite broad and inclusive, which begs the question of what is *not* leadership.

If I asked you to mow my lawn and you agreed because you liked me or were afraid of me, it would be influence and compliance (Cialdini & Trost, 1998), not leadership. Relatedly, the exercise of power is influence but is generally not considered to be leadership (Chemers, 2001; Lord, Brown, & Harvey, 2001; Moscovici, 1976; Raven, 1993). If you agreed because you knew that there was a neighborhood norm to mow neighbors' lawns, it would be conformity (e.g., Turner, 1991), not leadership. If, on the other hand, I had first convinced you that we should develop such a norm, and you subsequently adhered to that norm, then that most definitely would be leadership. Leaders play a critical role in defining collective goals, and, in this respect, leadership is more typically a group process than an interpersonal process; it is an influence process that plays out more noticeably in group than interpersonal contexts.

In defining leadership, an important distinction is between effective/ineffective leaders and good/bad leaders (e.g., Kellerman, 2004). Effective leaders are successful in setting new goals, whatever they might be, and influencing others to achieve them. Here, the evaluation of leadership is largely an objective matter of fact—how much influence did the leader have in setting new goals and were the goals achieved? Most leadership research is concerned with leadership effectiveness.

In contrast, evaluating whether a leader is good or bad is a subjective judgment based on one's preferences and perspective and one's goals and group memberships. We evaluate leaders in terms of their character (e.g., nice, nasty, charismatic), the ethics and morality of the means they use to influence others and achieve goals (e.g., persuasion, coercion, oppression, democratic decision making), and the nature of the goals that they lead their followers toward (e.g., saving the environment, reducing starvation and disease, producing a commodity, combating oppression, denying human rights, engaging in genocide). Good leaders are those who have attributes we applaud, use means we approve of, and set and achieve goals we value.

Individual Differences and Leadership Personalities

Leaders tend to stand out against the background of the group and are the focus of our attention. Not surprisingly, we tend to personify leadership, underemphasizing the context and process of leadership and explaining the leader's behavior in terms of invariant personality dispositions (cf. Gilbert & Malone, 1995; Haslam, Rothschild, & Ernst, 1998; Ross, 1977). There is evidence that we do indeed do this (e.g., Fiske & Dépret, 1996; Meindl, 1995; Meindl, Ehrlich, & Dukerich, 1985).

Social psychologists are little different from people in everyday life and have, therefore, tried to explain leadership in terms of personality constellations that make some people more effective leaders than others. The "great person" perspective on leadership has a long history, going as far back as Plato and ancient Greece. The view that leadership effectiveness is innate (e.g., Galton, 1892) is generally rejected by most "great person" scholars, who prefer the view that leadership ability is acquired early in life in the form of an enduring constellation of personality attributes that imbue people with charisma and a predisposition to lead (e.g., Carlyle, 1841; House, 1977).

Research has tried to identify these attributes. Early research identified a handful of weak correlates (among which intelligence and talkativeness are the most reliable), leading Stogdill to conclude that leadership is not "mere possession of some combination of traits" (Stogdill, 1948, p. 66), and others to proclaim that the search for a leadership personality is simplistic and futile (e.g., Conger & Kanungo, 1998). In general, correlations among traits and between traits and effective leadership are low (Stogdill, 1974, reports an average correlation of .30).

The belief that some people are better leaders than others because they have enduring traits that predispose them to effective leadership has reemerged, as we see later, in a different guise in modern theories of transformational leadership that place an emphasis on charisma (e.g., Avolio & Yammarino, 2003; Bass, 1985; Conger & Kanungo, 1998). Rather than focusing on specific traits, this tradition focuses on the wider Big Five personality dimensions of extraversion/surgency, agreeableness, conscientiousness, emotional stability, and intellect/openness to experience. A definitive meta-analysis by Judge, Bono, Ilies and Gerhardt (2002) reports a multiple correlation of .58 of these attributes with leadership, extraversion/surgency, intellect/openness to experience, and conscientiousness as the best predictors of effective leadership.

Situational Perspectives

In contrast to personality approaches is the view that anyone can lead effectively if the situation is right. However, this may be too extreme. For example, Simonton (1980) analyzed 300 military battles to find that situational factors did not account for all the outcomes; personal attributes of specific leaders were also significant correlates.

In reality, effective leadership is a function of a match between behavioral style or personality attributes and the particular requirements of a specific leadership situation. Different situations call for different leadership properties, and, therefore, the most effective leader in a given context is the group member who is best equipped to assist the group in achieving its objectives (Bales, 1950).

For example, Carter and Nixon (1949) had pairs of high school students perform three different tasks: an intellectual task, a clerical task, and a mechanical assembly task. Those who took the lead in the first two tasks rarely led in the mechanical assembly task. In another example, Sherif, Harvey, White, Hood, and Sherif (1961; Sherif, 1966) documented in one of their boys' camp studies a change of leader in one of the groups when the situation changed from intragroup norm formation to intergroup competition.

The Behavior of Leaders

Based on dissatisfaction with the validity and predictive reliability of the construct of personality, another perspective on leadership focused on what leaders do—their actual behavior. This perspective spawned some of social psychology's classic leadership research. For example, Lippitt and White (1943) manipulated leadership style (autocratic, democratic, and laissez-faire) and measured the effect on group atmosphere, morale, and effectiveness in after-school clubs for young boys. They found that a democratic leadership style was most effective; it produced a friendly, group-centered, task-oriented atmosphere that was associated with relatively high group productivity and was unaffected by whether the leader was physically present or not.

Another program of research identified two key leadership roles: *task specialist* and *socioemotional specialist* (Bales, 1950). No single person could occupy both roles simultaneously, and the task specialist was more likely to be the dominant leader. Task specialists tend to be centrally involved, often by offering opinions and giving directions, in the task-oriented aspects of group life, whereas socioemotional specialists tend to respond and pay attention to the feelings of other group members.

The Ohio State leadership studies constitute a third leadership program (e.g., Fleishman, 1973; Stogdill, 1974). A scale for measuring leadership behavior was devised—the *leader behavior description questionnaire* (LBDQ)—and a distinction was drawn between *initiating structure* and *consideration*. Leaders high on initiating structure define the group's objectives and organize members' work toward the attainment of these goals: they are task oriented. Leaders rating high on consideration are concerned with the welfare of subordinates and seek to promote harmonious relationships in the group; they are relationship oriented. Unlike Bales (1950), who believed that task-oriented and socioemotional attributes were inversely related, the Ohio State researchers believed their dimensions to be independent: A single person could be high on both initiating structure (task-oriented) and consideration (socioemotional), and such a person would be a particularly effective leader. Research supports this latter view (e.g., Sorrentino & Field, 1986; Stogdill, 1974).

The general distinction between a leadership style that pays attention to the group task and getting things done and one that pays attention to relationships among group members is pervasive in the literature. It appears in Fiedler's (1964) contingency theory of leadership and, in a slightly different guise, in leader–member exchange (LMX) theory's emphasis on the quality of the leader's relationship with his or her followers (e.g., Graen & Uhl-Bien, 1995). It is also a distinction that may hold across cultures, though what counts as task-oriented or socioemotional leadership behavior may vary from culture to culture (e.g., Smith, Misumi, Tayeb, Peterson, & Bond, 1989).

Contingency Theories

Contingency theories of leadership recognize that the leadership effectiveness of particular leadership behaviors or styles is contingent on the properties of the leadership situation. Some styles are better suited to some situations or tasks than are others.

Fiedler's Contingency Theory

Probably the best known contingency theory is that proposed by Fiedler (1964, 1967). Fiedler, like Bales (1950), distinguished between task-oriented and relationship-oriented leaders. He measured leadership style in a rather unusual way with his least preferred co-worker (LPC) scale, in which respondents rated their least preferred co-worker on semantic differentials. Respondents with high LPC scores were relationship oriented (because they were positive about a poor-performing co-worker); respondents with low LPC score were task oriented (because they were harsh on a poor performer).

Fiedler classified situations in terms of the quality of leader–member relations, the structural clarity of the task, and the power and authority the leader had by virtue of his or her position as leader. Good leader–member relations in conjunction with a clear task and substantial position-power furnished maximal "situational control" (making leadership easy), whereas poor leader–member relations, a fuzzy task, and low position-power furnished minimal "situational control" (making leadership difficult).

Fiedler predicted that task-oriented leaders would be most effective when situational control was low (the group needs a directive leader to focus on getting things done) *and* when it was high (the group is doing just fine so there is little need to worry about morale and relationships), and

relationship-oriented leaders would be more effective when situational control was between these extremes. Against a background of some controversy and criticism (e.g., Peters, Hartke, & Pohlmann, 1985) focused on the measurement of situational control and on the characterization of leadership style as an invariant personal quality, Fiedler's predictions have generally been supported—see meta-analyses by Strube and Garcia (1981) and Schriesheim, Tepper, and Tetrault (1994).

One troublesome finding, reported by Kennedy (1982), is that the 20% or so of leaders who have neither high nor low LPC scores are actually the most effective leaders of all, and their effectiveness is not influenced by situational control. Another limitation of Fiedler's theory is that it is somewhat static; it does not focus on the dynamic interactive processes that occur within a group between leaders and followers and among followers.

Normative Decision Theory

Normative decision theory (NDT) is a contingency model of leadership in group decision-making contexts (Vroom & Jago, 1988; Vroom & Yetton, 1973). NDT identifies three decision-making strategies among which leaders choose: autocratic (subordinate input is not sought), consultative (input is sought, but the leader retains authority to make the final decision), and group decision making (leader and subordinates are equal partners in a shared decision-making process). The efficacy of these strategies is contingent on the quality of leader–subordinate relationships (which influences how committed and supportive subordinates are) and on task clarity and structure (which influences the leader's need for subordinate input).

Autocratic leadership is fast and effective if subordinate commitment and support are high and the task is clear and well structured. When the task is less clear, subordinate involvement is needed and, therefore, consultative leadership is best. When subordinates are not committed or supportive, group decision making is required to increase participation and commitment. Predictions from NDT are reasonably well supported (e.g., Field & House, 1990); leaders and managers report better decisions and better subordinate ratings when they follow the prescriptions of the theory. However, there is a tendency for subordinates to prefer fully participative group decision making, even when it is not the most effective strategy.

Path-Goal Theory

Path-goal theory (PGT; House, 1971; House & Mitchell, 1974) is another well-known contingency theory, although it can also be classified as a transactional leadership theory (see later). For PGT, a leader's main function is to motivate followers by clarifying the paths (i.e., behaviors and actions) that will help them attain their goals. There are two types of behaviors available to leaders to do this: *structuring* behaviors whereby the leader directs task-related activities, and *consideration* behaviors whereby the leader addresses followers' personal and emotional needs (this distinction is that identified by the LBDQ described previously).

PGT predicts that structuring will be most effective when followers are unclear about their goals and how to reach them (e.g., when the task is new, difficult, or ambiguous). When tasks are well understood, structuring is less effective or can even backfire because it is viewed as meddling and micro-management. Consideration is most effective when the task is boring or uncomfortable but can backfire when followers are already engaged and motivated because it is considered distracting and unnecessary.

Empirical support for PGT is mixed, and most scholars agree that tests of the theory tend to suffer from flawed methodology and from being incomplete and simplistic (Schriesheim & Neider, 1996). For these reasons research on PGT tapered off in the early 1980s. Recently, House (1996) has reinvigorated the theory by addressing some of these concerns and by making it feel contemporary; for example, the interpersonal focus of the original formulation has been expanded to include ways in which a leader can motivate an entire work group rather than just individual followers.

Situational Leadership Theory

Situational leadership theory (Hersey & Blanchard, 1969) proposes that effective leaders need to be able to tailor their behavior to the situational demands of subordinates' level of task maturity (i.e., ability) and psychological maturity (i.e., willingness) to complete a task at hand. The distinction between task and relations behavior that surfaces repeatedly in leadership research is here relabeled *directing* and *supporting*. These dimensions are orthogonal, creating four leadership behaviors: *telling* (high directive, low supportive), *selling* (high directive, high supportive), *participating* (low directive, high supportive), and *delegating* (low directive, low supportive). So, for example, *telling* is best suited to low maturity/ability followers and *participating* to high maturity/willingness followers.

Intuitively this makes sense, but empirical support is sparse and the theory has a rather narrow conception of situational factors. However, it does underline the need for leaders to adapt their behavior to the situation, including the qualities of the followers. In leadership, followers matter (Shamir, Pillai, Bligh, & Uhl-Bien, 2006).

Transactional Leadership

One limitation of contingency theories is that they do not focus on the dynamic interaction between leaders and followers that allows leaders to lead and encourages followers to follow—an interaction in which leaders and followers provide support and gratification for one another (Messick, 2005).

Transactional theories view leadership as a process of exchange, similar to contractual relations in economic life that are based on good faith. Leaders transact with followers to get things done, setting expectations and goals, and providing recognition and rewards for task completion (Burns, 1978). Mutual benefits are exchanged (transacted) between leaders and followers against a background of contingent rewards and punishments that shape up cooperation and trust (Bass, 1985). The transactions may also have an equity dimension (Walster, Walster, & Berscheid, 1978). Because effective leaders play a greater role in steering groups to their goals than do followers, followers may reinstate equity by rewarding the leader with social approval, praise, prestige, status and power—the trappings of effective leadership.

Although path-goal theory (PGT) discussed previously (House, 1971) is a contingency theory because of its focus on the situation-contingent effectiveness of leadership behaviors, it can also be considered a transactional theory because it focuses on transactions between leaders and followers that enhance motivation and lead to goal attainment.

Idiosyncrasy Credit

An early transactional approach to leadership is Hollander's (1958; Hollander & Julian, 1970) analysis of idiosyncrasy credit. Hollander argued that effective leaders need to be allowed by the group to be innovative, to experiment with new ideas and new directions; to be idiosyncratic. Drawing on the equity argument above, Hollander argued that leaders who had behaved in a highly conformist manner as they climbed the organizational ladder accumulated credits, called "idiosyncrasy credits," from the group. When the leader arrived at the top of the organization, followers would effectively hand over these credits (as a resource) to the leader, who could then "spend" them by behaving idiosyncratically, innovatively, and creatively.

An early study by Merei (1949) is often cited as supporting this analysis. Merei introduced older children who had shown leadership potential into small groups of younger children in a Hungarian nursery and found that the most successful leaders were those who initially complied with existing group practices and who only gradually and later introduced minor variations.

Going beyond this strictly interpersonal approach, the idea that leaders who initially conform to group norms are ultimately allowed to be innovative and, paradoxically, nonnormative has recently been given a more group oriented treatment by social identity analyses of leadership (Hogg, 2001; Hogg & Van Knippenberg, 2003). As described later, the key idea is that normative leaders are assumed to identify strongly with the group and are considered "one of us," and if they behave nonnormatively and innovatively they are trusted to be doing so in the best interest of the group (cf. Abrams, Randsley de Moura, Marques, & Hutchison, 2008).

Vertical Dyad Linkage and Leader–Member Exchange Theories

Leader–member transactions are center stage in the vertical dyad linkage (VDL) model of leadership (Danserau, Graen, & Haga, 1975), which has evolved into leader–member exchange (LMX) theory (e.g., Graen & Uhl-Bien, 1995; Sparrowe & Liden, 1997). According to VDL, leaders develop dyadic exchange relationships with different specific subordinates. In these dyadic relationships, the subordinate can either be treated as a close and valued "ingroup" member with the leader or in a more remote manner as an "outgroup" member who is separate from the leader.

In LMX theory, this dichotomous, ingroup versus outgroup treatment of leader–member exchange relationships has been replaced by a continuum of quality of exchange relationships, ranging from ones that are based on mutual trust, respect, and obligation (high quality LMX relationships) to ones that are mechanically based on the terms of the formal employment contract between leader and subordinate (low quality LMX relationships). Effective leadership hinges on the development of high quality LMX relationships. High quality relationships motivate subordinates to internalize the group's and the leader's goals, whereas in low quality relationships, subordinates simply comply with the leader's goals without internalizing them as their own. However, from a leader's point of view, high quality relationships are labor intensive and so, over time, leaders tend to develop them with only a small subset of group members and develop low quality relationships with the rest of the group.

Research confirms that differentiated LMX relationships do exist in most organizations; that high quality LMX relationships are more likely to develop when the leader and the subordinate have similar attitudes, like one another, belong to the same sociodemographic groups, and both perform at a high level; and that high quality LMX relationships are associated with better performing and more satisfied workers who are more committed to the organization and less likely to leave (see Gerstner & Day, 1997; Graen & Uhl-Bien, 1995; Schriesheim, Castro, & Cogliser, 1999).

One limitation of LMX theory is its exclusive focus on dyadic leader–member relations. In reality, such relations are located in a wider context of shared group membership in which followers interact with one another as group members and are influenced by their perceptions of the leader's relations with other group members (Hogg, Martin & Weeden, 2004; Scandura, 1999). From a social identity perspective, one might expect that members who identify strongly with a group would find differentiated LMX relationships that favor some members over others to be uncomfortably personalized and fragmentary of the group and would not endorse such leaders. They might prefer a more depersonalized leadership style that treated all members relatively equally as group members, endorsing such leaders more strongly. Two field surveys of leadership perceptions in organizations in Wales and India have confirmed this hypothesis (Hogg et al., 2005).

Transformational Leadership

Transactional theories of leadership represent a focus on leadership, but transactional leadership is itself a leadership style that can be contrasted to other leadership styles. Transactional leaders appeal to followers' self-interest, whereas transformational leaders inspire followers to adopt a vision that involves more than individual self-interest (Burns, 1978; Judge & Bono, 2000). A third leadership style—laissez-faire (noninterfering) leadership, which involves not making choices or taking decisions and not rewarding others or shaping their behavior—has been added to transactional and transformational leadership to complete what Avolio (1999) calls the full-range leadership theory (see Antonakis & House, 2003).

The three main components of transformational leadership are: (a) individualized consideration (careful attention to followers' needs, abilities, and aspirations to raise aspirations, improve abilities, and satisfy needs); (b) intellectual stimulation (challenging of followers' basic thinking, assumptions, and practices to help them develop newer and better mind-sets and practices); and (c) charismatic/inspiring leadership which provides the energy, reasoning, and sense of urgency that transforms followers (Avolio & Bass, 1987; Bass, 1985). The components of transactional and transformational leadership are measured by the multifactor leadership questionnaire (MLQ), which (now in its fifth version) has been extraordinarily widely used and is the leadership questionnaire of choice of the organizational and management research communities, producing numerous large-scale meta-analyses of findings (e.g., Lowe, Kroeck, & Sivasubramaniam, 1996).

There is, however, some concern that the black box of transformation remains shut. What happens in the head of a follower to transform leader behavior into follower thought and behavior—what is the social psychology of transformation? In answer to this question, Shamir, House, and Arthur (1993) suggest that followers personally identify with the leader and, in this way, make the leader's vision their own;

Dvir, Eden, Avolio, and Shamir (2002) suggest that the behavior of transformational leaders causes followers to identify more strongly with the organization's core values. For the social identity theory of leadership (Hogg, 2001, see later), members look to and trust group prototypical leaders to define identity relevant group norms; members will follow and internalize leaders' innovative and transformational lead.

Charisma and Charismatic Leadership

Charisma is a key component of transformational leadership. Charisma facilitates effective leadership because charismatic people are emotionally expressive, enthusiastic, driven, eloquent, visionary, self-confident, and responsive to others (e.g., House, Spangler, & Woycke, 1991); all are attributes allowing a person to be influential and persuasive and, therefore, able to make others buy their vision for the group and sacrifice personal goals for collective goals. Meindl and Lerner (1983; Meindl, Ehrlich, & Dukerich, 1985) talk about visionary leaders heightening followers' sense of shared identity and how this shared identity produces a collective "heroic motive" that puts group goals ahead of personal goals.

The notion of charisma is so central to transformational leadership theory that a distinction was drawn between good and bad charisma (e.g., O'Connor, Mumford, Clifton, Gessner, & Connelly, 1995). Good charismatic leaders have socialized charisma that they use in a "morally uplifting" manner to improve society; they are transformational heroes (e.g., Gandhi). Bad charismatic leaders use personalized charisma to tear down groups and society; they are nontransformational villains (e.g., Hitler). The problem here is that one person's transformational leader can sometimes be another person's war criminal or vice versa (much like one person's freedom fighter is another's terrorist). For example, whether Osama Bin Laden is a transformational hero or nontransformational villain may rest more on one's ideological leanings than on transformational leadership theory's notion of good versus bad charisma.

There is another more general issue with the role of charisma in transformational leadership. Scholars talk of charismatic leadership as a product of the leader's personal charisma and followers' reactions to the leader's charisma; personal charisma alone may not guarantee charismatic leadership (e.g., Bryman, 1992). However, it is difficult to escape the inference that charisma is an enduring personality trait. For example, charismatic leadership has been linked to the Big Five personality traits of extraversion/surgency, agreeableness, and intellect/openness to experience (e.g., Judge, Bono, Ilies, & Gerhardt, 2002) and to the related construct of visionary leadership (e.g., Conger & Kanungo, 1998). Visionary leaders are special people who can identify attractive future goals and objectives for a group and mobilize followers to internalize these as their own. The worry is that this perspective recreates some of the problems of earlier personality theories of leadership (see Haslam & Platow, 2001).

An alternative perspective on the role of charisma in leadership is that a charismatic personality is constructed for the leader by followers; charisma is more a consequence or correlate, not a cause, of effective leadership. For example, Meindl's (1995; Meindl, Ehrlich, & Dukerich, 1985) *romance of leadership* argues that people have a strong tendency to attribute effective leadership to the leader's behavior and there is a halo effect in which the leader's shortcomings are overlooked. The social identity theory of leadership (e.g., Hogg, 2001; Hogg & Van Knippenberg, 2003; see later) provides a similar analysis. Social identity processes in salient groups that members identify strongly with render group prototypical leaders influential and attractive, imbue them with trust, and allow them to be innovative. Followers attribute these qualities internally to the leader's personality, thus constructing a charismatic leadership personality. Empirical studies provide some support for the attributional construction of charisma (e.g., Fiske & Dépret, 1996; Meindl, Ehrlich, & Dukerich, 1985) and for the social identity perspective on charisma and leadership (Haslam & Platow, 2001; Platow & Van Knippenberg, 2001).

Leader Perceptions and Leadership Schemas

Leader Categorization Theory

Leader categorization theory (LCT), also called implicit leadership theory, is a social cognitive theory of leadership that focuses on the content of people's leadership schemas and on the causes and consequences of categorization of someone as a leader (e.g., Lord, Brown, Harvey, & Hall, 2001; Lord, Foti, & DeVader, 1984; Lord, Foti, & Phillips, 1982; Lord & Hall, 2003; Lord & Maher, 1991). It assumes that leadership perceptions play a key role in leader selection decisions, leader endorsement, and in a leader's power base, and, thus, in how effectively a leader can lead and influence others.

In making leadership judgments, leadership schemas based on implicit leadership theories are activated, and characteristics of the leader are matched against the relevant schema. Earlier conceptions of LCT (e.g., Lord, Foti, & DeVader, 1984) viewed leader schemas as relatively general and fixed, whereas the contemporary version (e.g., Lord, Brown, Harvey, & Hall, 2001; Lord & Hall, 2003) views them as flexible cognitive structures that are regenerated in situ to meet contextual demands. In both cases, however, the better the match between the leader's characteristics and the perceiver's leadership schema, the more favorable are leadership perceptions.

LCT focuses on categories and associated schemas of leadership and leaders (e.g., military generals, CEOs, outward bound leaders), not on social groups as categories (e.g., a psychology department, a corporation, a sports team). LCT's leader categories are tied to tasks and functions and transcend groups; for example, a CEO schema applies similarly to companies such as Apple, Dell, GM, Toyota, Starbucks, Google, and so forth, whereas each company may have different group norms and prototypes.

Expectation States, Status Characteristics, and Role Congruity

Two other theories that also focus on leader categorization but do not go into social cognitive details quite so extensively are expectation states/status characteristics theory and role congruity theory. Both theories suggest that the match between an individual's characteristics and abstracted conceptions of status and leadership affect leadership perceptions.

Expectation states theory or status characteristics theory (e.g., Berger, Fisek, Norman, & Zelditch, 1977; Berger, Wagner, & Zelditch, 1985; Ridgeway, 2001) attributes influence (by implication leadership) within groups to possession of specific status characteristics (qualities that match what the group actually does) and diffuses status characteristics (stereotypical properties of high status groups in society). Influence is a function of the extent to which people possess characteristics that suit them to effective task performance (i.e., specific status characteristics) and possess characteristics that categorize them as members of high status sociodemographic categories (i.e., diffuse status characteristics). Influence, or leadership, is an additive function of perceived group task competence and perceived societal status (Ridgeway, 2003).

Role congruity theory focuses on gender and leadership (see Wood and Eagly's chapter on gender in this volume for detail). Briefly, because there is greater overlap between general leader schemas and male stereotypes than between leader schemas and female stereotypes, people tend to have more favorable perceptions of male leaders than of female leaders; this can make it generally easier for males than females to be effective leaders (e.g., Eagly & Karau, 2002; Heilman 1983).

Social Identity and Leadership

Leadership is a group process in which followers play a key role not only in the cognitive–perceptual sense described previously, but in the wider sense that leaders cannot lead unless followers follow. One way in which this idea has been explored is by research on "followership" that explores how followers can be empowered to create great and effective leaders (e.g., Kelley, 1992; Riggio, Chalefff, & Lipman-Blumen, 2008; Shamir, Pillai, Bligh, & Uhl-Bien, 2006).

Social Identity Theory of Leadership

Another perspective on leadership as a group process in which leader and follower roles are intertwined is provided by the social identity theory of leadership (Hogg, 2001, 2008; Hogg & Van Knippenberg, 2003; for empirical overviews, also see Ellemers, de Gilder, & Haslam, 2004; Van Knippenberg, Van Knippenberg, De Cremer, & Hogg, 2004); but here the key emphasis is on the identity function of leadership. Groups provide us with a social identity and our leaders are the most significant source of information about who we are as group members; we look to our leaders to express and epitomize our identity, to clarify and focus our identity, to forge and transform our identity, and to consolidate, stabilize, and anchor our identity.

A key tenet of the social identity theory of leadership is that as group membership becomes more important to self-definition and members identify more strongly with the group, leaders who are perceived to be more group prototypical are more effective than leaders who are perceived to be less prototypical of the group; and as prototypicality assumes greater importance, other determinants of effective leadership, such as leadership schemas, become less important (e.g., Hains, Hogg, & Duck, 1997; Hogg et al., 2006; Hogg, Hains, & Mason, 1998).

Prototypical leaders are effective because they are perceived by members to best embody the group's defining attributes and are, therefore, the source rather than target of conformity processes. Because members favorably evaluate the group prototype, tend to agree on the prototype, and consider prototypical members to be protecting and promoting the group, prototypical leaders are consensually liked as group members (Hogg, 1993). This facilitates influence (people comply more with requests from people they like; Berscheid & Reis, 1998), and accentuates the evaluative (status) differential between leader and followers.

Prototypical leaders find the group more central and important to self-definition and identify more strongly with it; they have greater investment in it and are more likely to behave in group-serving ways; they embody group norms more precisely and are more likely to favor the ingroup, treat ingroup members fairly, and act in ways that promote the ingroup. These behaviors confirm their prototypicality and membership credentials and communicate to the group that the leader is "one of us": A central member who identifies strongly and embodies the norms and aspirations of the group and is, therefore, unlikely to harm the group (e.g., Platow, Hoar, Reid, Harley, & Morrison, 1997; Platow & Van Knippenberg, 2001). Prototypical members are trusted to be acting in the best interest of the group even when it may not appear that they are (e.g., Brewer, 1981; Hogg, 2007c; Yamagishi & Kiyonari, 2000); they are furnished with legitimacy (Tyler, 1997; Tyler & Lind, 1992; see Platow, Reid, & Andrew, 1998). Together, this allows prototypical leaders to be innovative; they can, paradoxically, diverge from group norms and be less conformist than non- or less prototypical leaders.

This analysis of how prototypical leaders can be innovative describes the processes that may account for Hollander's (1958) idea, discussed earlier, that to be effective, a leader needs initially to conform to group norms to earn "idiosyncrasy credits," to be able later to diverge from such norms and be innovative. The social identity analysis is wider in that it is not tied to interpersonal transactions and conformity and the temporal dimension are not always necessary. The key factor is that the leader behaves in ways that build trust based on shared identity and the perception that the leader is centrally invested in the group (cf. Abrams, Randsley de Moura, Marques, & Hutchison, 2008).

Prototypical leaders are also often invested by the group with charisma, which further strengthens their authority and facilitates innovative and transformational leadership. However, as we saw earlier, this social identity perspective on charisma differs from the more personality oriented perspective of transformational leadership theories (cf. Conger & Kanungo, 1998). From a social identity perspective, similar to Meindl's (1995) *romance of leadership*, charisma is an attribution-based social construction (e.g., Haslam & Platow, 2001; Platow & Van Knippenberg, 2001). In salient groups, prototypical leaders are the focus of attention and members attribute their qualities (e.g., being influential and consensually attractive, having high status, being trusted, and being innovative and transformational) internally to stable and essentialist aspects of the leader's personality (c.f., Gilbert & Malone, 1995; Haslam, Rothschild, & Ernst, 1998; Ross, 1977).

Social identity based leadership processes confer on leaders considerable power to maintain their leadership position. Specifically, through talk, they can construct, reconstruct, or change the group prototype in ways that protect or promote their prototypically central position in the group—a process that can be referred to as norm talk (Hogg & Reid, 2006; Hogg & Tindale, 2005; also see Fiol, 2002; Reid & Ng, 2000). A key attribute of effective leadership is precisely this visionary and transformational activity in which a leader is an "entrepreneur of identity" who is adept at changing what the group sees itself as being (Reicher & Hopkins, 2003). Prototypical leaders can do this in different ways: talk-up prototypical aspects of their behavior and talk-down nonprototypical aspects; characterize as marginal those members who do not share their prototype of the group; vilify and cast as deviant those

who are contending for leadership; identify as relevant comparison outgroups those that are most favorable to their own prototypicality; and engage in a discourse that raises salience to favor a prototypical leader or lowers salience to favor a nonprototypical leader (e.g., Reicher & Hopkins, 1996, 2001, 2003). Nonprototypical leaders engage in group-oriented behaviors to strengthen their membership credentials (e.g., Platow & Van Knippenberg, 2001).

Trust and the Group Value Model

A key dimension of leadership is trust (e.g., Dirks & Ferrin, 2002). Can we trust our leaders? If we are to follow their lead, surely we should trust them (Kellerman, 2004)? Because shared group membership is a powerful basis of trust (e.g., Brewer, 1981; Hogg, 2007c; Yamagishi & Kiyonari, 2000), it follows that we are more likely to trust prototypical than nonprototypical leaders.

We are also more likely to trust and, thus, follow our leaders if they treat members fairly and with respect. According to Tyler's group value model (Lind & Tyler, 1988) and his relational model of authority in groups (Tyler, 1997; Tyler & Lind, 1992), fairness and justice perceptions are critical to group life. Because leaders make decisions that have important consequences for us (e.g., promotions, allocation of duties), we are concerned about how fair the leader is in making these decisions. In judging fairness, we focus on both distributive justice (how fair are the outcomes of the leader's decisions) and procedural justice (how fair are the procedures that the leader has used to make a decision). Justice and fairness judgments affect reactions to decisions and to the authorities making these decisions and, thus, influence leadership effectiveness (e.g., De Cremer, 2003).

Procedural justice is particularly important in building trust in leadership. One reason for this is that procedural justice serves a social identity function (Tyler, 2003). Because fair procedures convey a favorable social evaluation of followers as group members, the respect for group members conveyed by procedural fairness builds member identification and, thus, feeds into cooperative and compliant behavior. As members identify more strongly with the group, they care more that the leader is procedurally fair (e.g., Brockner, Chen, Mannix, Leung, & Skarlicki, 2000; Lipponen, Koivisto, & Olkkonen, 2005) and care less that the leader is distributively fair. This asymmetry arises because with increasing identification, instrumental outcome-oriented considerations (distributive justice) become less important relative to intragroup relational and membership considerations (procedural justice) (e.g., Vermunt, Van Knippenberg, Van Knippenberg, & Blaauw, 2001).

Another related line of research on trust and leadership focuses on the way that leadership can be an effective structural solution to social dilemmas. Social dilemmas are crises of trust that are notoriously difficult to resolve (Dawes & Messick, 2000; Kerr & Park, 2001). However, enhancing a sense of common social identity can build trust that resolves the dilemma (e.g., Brewer & Schneider, 1990; De Cremer & Van Vugt, 1999; also see Brewer, 1981; Hogg, 2007c; Yamagishi & Kiyonari, 2000). Leadership plays an often critical role in this process precisely because a leader can transform selfish individual goals into shared group goals by building a sense of common identity, shared fate, interindividual trust, and custodianship of the collective good (e.g., De Cremer & Van Knippenberg, 2003; De Cremer & Van Vugt, 2002; Van Vugt & De Cremer, 1999).

Intergroup Leadership

The social identity analysis of leadership has an intragroup focus: intragroup prototypicality, shared group membership, ingroup trust, and so forth. However, the great challenge of leadership is often not merely to transcend individual differences, but to bridge profound group divisions to build an integrative vision and identity. Leadership is often better characterized as intergroup leadership (Hogg, 2009; Pittinsky, 2009; Pittinsky & Simon, 2007).

Effective intergroup leadership confronts the wider challenge of building social harmony and a common purpose and identity out of conflict among groups. One problem is that intergroup leaders are often viewed as representing one group more than the other; they are outgroup leaders to one subgroup and, thus, suffer compromised effectiveness (Duck & Fielding, 1999, 2003). This problem has been well researched in the context of mergers and acquisitions. Mergers often fail precisely because the leader of the merged organization is viewed with suspicion as a member of the former outgroup organization (e.g., Terry, Carey, & Callan, 2001). These problems can be accentuated by ingroup projection. Subgroups overestimate the extent to which their characteristics are represented in the superordinate group (Wenzel, Mummendey, & Waldzus, 2007), in which case an outgroup leader will be viewed as particularly unprototypical.

One interesting wrinkle to this is that lower/minority status subgroups often do not engage in ingroup projection; both groups agree that the superordinate group reflects the dominant subgroup's attributes (Sindic & Reicher, 2008). The minority subgroup *will* view the outgroup leader as prototypical; but such a leader will not gain a prototypicality-based advantage because the minority group feels under-represented and, thus, is unlikely to identify sufficiently strongly with the superordinate group (Hohman, Hogg, & Bligh, in press).

Effective intergroup leaders need to build a common ingroup identity (Gaertner & Dovidio, 2000; Gaertner, Dovidio, Anastasio, Bachman, & Rust, 1993). But this can threaten the subgroup identity of subgroups, so another strategy is to balance the superordinate identity and associated vision with recognition of the integrity and valued contribution of subgroup identities (e.g., Hornsey & Hogg, 2000).

SUMMARY

Influence and leadership are core concerns of social psychology. Social psychology is often defined in terms of influence, and leadership is one of the most potent ways in which an individual can influence a large number of people. Research on influence has always been conducted within social psychology, though an early focus on norms has largely—with some important exceptions—been replaced by a focus on cognitive processing of potential persuasive information. Research on leadership was a major theme within social psychology, but some decades ago, the focus of research activity moved largely to the organizational and management sciences. However, leadership research is currently experiencing a revival within social psychology.

This chapter shows that, overall, we have a great deal of scientific knowledge about influence and leadership. However, there are loose ends and promising and important new directions. For example, mainstream social psychology is largely mute on the role of language and communication in influence and leadership—how else do people influence one another than by communication, largely through talk? The study of norms as social constructs would benefit from a more communication-oriented perspective such as this.

As a legacy of the transformational role of social cognition in social psychology, research on influence has tended over the past two decades to focus more on information processing than social interaction. We now know a great deal about this, and perhaps it is time to redress the balance. A good example is the study of minority influence; initially championed as a perspective on social change and societal transformation, it has become increasingly focused on the detail of cognitive change. Armed with what we now know, it would be timely and translational to revisit the role of active minorities in social change.

Finally, it is certainly gratifying to see that social psychology is once again paying attention to the quintessentially social psychological phenomenon of leadership. However, it is in its early days and much remains to be done to untether the study of leadership from a narrow focus on corporate leadership and the role of the CEO. A broader view of leadership needs to focus more on public and ideological leadership; the identity function of leadership; intergroup leadership; and leadership and social change.

REFERENCES

Abrams, D., & Hogg, M. A. (1990). Social identification, self-categorisation, and social influence. *European Review of Social Psychology, 1,* 195–228.

Abrams, D., & Hogg, M. A. (1998). Prospects for research in group processes and intergroup relations. *Group Processes and Intergroup Relations, 1,* 7–20.

Abrams, D., Marques, J. M., Bown, N. J., & Henson, M. (2000). Pro-norm and anti-norm deviance within ingroups and outgroups. *Journal of Personality and Social Psychology, 78,* 906–912.

Abrams, D., Randsley de Moura, G., Marques, J. M., & Hutchison, P. (2008). Innovation credit: When can leaders oppose their group's norms? *Journal of Personality and Social Psychology, 95,* 662–678.

Abrams, D., Wetherell, M. S., Cochrane, S., Hogg, M. A., & Turner, J. C. (1990). Knowing what to think by knowing who you are: Self-categorization and the nature of norm formation, conformity, and group polarization. *British Journal of Social Psychology, 29,* 97–119.

Adorno, T. W., Frenkel-Brunswik, E., Levinson, D. J., & Sanford, R. M. (1950). *The authoritarian personality.* New York: Harper.

Ajzen, I. (1991). The theory of planned behavior. *Organizational Behavior and Human Decision Processes, 50,* 179–211.

Ajzen, I., & Fishbein, M. (1980). *Understanding attitudes and predicting social behavior.* Englewood Cliffs, NJ: Prentice Hall.

Aldag, R. J., & Fuller, S. R. (1993). Beyond fiasco: A reappraisal of the groupthink phenomenon and a new model of group decision processes. *Psychological Bulletin, 113,* 533–552.

Alexander, C. N., Zucker, L. G., & Brody, C. L. (1970). Experimental expectations and autokinetic experiences: Consistency theories and judgmental convergence. *Sociometry, 33,* 108–122.

Allen, V. L. (1965). Situational factors in conformity. In L. Berkowitz (Ed.), *Advances in experimental social psychology* (Vol. 2, pp. 133–75). New York: Academic Press.

Allen, V. L. (1975). Social support for nonconformity. In L. Berkowitz (Ed.), *Advances in experimental social psychology* (Vol. 8, pp. 1–43). New York: Academic Press.

Allen, V. L., & Levine, J. M. (1971). Social support and conformity: The role of independent assessment of reality. *Journal of Experimental Social Psychology, 7,* 48–58.

Allport, F. H. (1920). The influence of the group upon association and thought. *Journal of Experimental Psychology, 3,* 159–182.

Allport, F. H. (1924). *Social psychology.* Boston, MA: Houghton-Mifflin.

Allport, G. W. (1954). The historical background of modern social psychology. In G. Lindzey (Ed.), *Handbook of social psychology* (Vol. 1, pp. 3–56). Reading, MA: Addison-Wesley.

Antonakis, J., & House, R. J. (2003). An analysis of the full-range leadership theory: The way forward. In B. J. Avolio & F. J. Yammarino (Eds.), *Transformational and charismatic leadership: The road ahead* (pp. 3–33). New York: Elsevier.

Arendt, H. (1963). *Eichmann in Jerusalem: A report on the banality of evil.* New York: Viking.

Asch, S. E. (1951). Effects of group pressure upon the modification and distortion of judgements. In H. Guetzkow (Ed.), *Groups, leadership and men* (pp. 177–190). Pittsburgh, PA: Carnegie Press.

Asch, S. E. (1952). *Social psychology.* Englewood Cliffs, NJ: Prentice Hall.

Asch, S. E. (1956). Studies of independence and conformity: A minority of one against a unanimous majority. *Psychological Monographs: General and Applied, 70,* 1–70.

Avolio, B. J. (1999). *Full leadership development: Building the vital forces in organizations.* Thousand Oaks, CA: Sage.

Avolio, B. J., & Bass, B. M. (1987). Transformational leadership, charisma and beyond. In J. G. Hunt, B. R. Balaga, H. P. Dachler, & C. A. Schriesheim (Eds.), *Emerging leadership vistas* (pp. 29–50). Elmsford, NY: Pergamon Press.

Avolio, B. J., & Yammarino, F. J. (Eds.). (2003). *Transformational and charismatic leadership: The road ahead.* New York: Elsevier.

Bales, R. F. (1950). *Interaction process analysis: A method for the study of small groups.* Reading, MA: Addison-Wesley.

Banuazizi, A., & Movahedi, S. (1975). Interpersonal dynamics in a simulated prison: A methodological analysis. *American Psychologist, 30,* 152–160.

Barocas, R., & Gorlow, L. (1967). Self-report personality measurement and conformity behaviour. *Journal of Social Psychology, 71,* 227–234.

Barron, F. (1953). Some personality correlates of independence of judgment. *Journal of Personality, 21,* 287–297.

Bass, B. M. (1985). *Leadership and performance beyond expectations.* New York: Free Press.

Baumrind, D. (1964). Some thoughts on ethics of research: After reading Milgram's "Behavioral study of obedience." *American Psychologist, 19,* 421–443.

Baumrind, D. (1985). Research using intentional deception: Ethical issues revisited. *American Psychologist, 40,* 165–174.

Bendor, J., & Swistak, P. (2001). The evolution of norms. *American Journal of Sociology, 106,* 1493–1545.

Berger, J., Fisek, M. H., Norman, R. Z., & Zelditch, M., Jr. (1977). *Status characteristics and social interaction.* New York: Elsevier.

Berger, J., Wagner, D., & Zelditch, M. Jr. (1985). Expectation states theory: Review and assessment. In J. Berger & M. Zelditch, Jr. (Eds.), *Status, rewards and influence* (pp. 1–72). San Francisco, CA: Jossey–Bass.

Berscheid, E., & Reis, H. T. (1998). Attraction and close relationships. In D. T. Gilbert, S. T. Fiske, & G. Lindzey (Eds.), *The handbook of social psychology* (4th ed., Vol. 2, pp. 193–281). New York: McGraw-Hill.

Blass, T. (1992). The social psychology of Stanley Milgram. In M. Zanna (Ed.), *Advances in experimental social psychology* (Vol. 25, pp. 227–329). San Diego, CA: Academic Press.

Blass, T. (1999). The Milgram paradigm after 35 years: Some things we now know about obedience to authority. *Journal of Applied Social Psychology, 29,* 955–978.

Blass, T. (2004). *The man who shocked the world: The life and legacy of Stanley Milgram.* New York: Basic Books.

Bohner, G., Moskowitz, G. B., & Chaiken, S. (1995). The interplay of heuristic and systematic processing of social information. *European Review of Social Psychology, 6,* 33–68.

Bond, C. F., Jr., & Titus, L. J. (1983). Social facilitation: A meta-analysis of 241 studies. *Psychological Bulletin, 94,* 265–292.

Bond, R., & Smith, P. B. (1996). Culture and conformity: A meta-analysis of the Asch line judgment task. *Psychological Bulletin, 119,* 111–137.

Brewer, M. B. (1981). Ethnocentrism and its role in interpersonal trust. In M. B. Brewer & B. Collins (Eds.), *Scientific inquiry and the social sciences* (pp. 345–360). San Francisco, CA: Jossey-Bass.

Brewer, M. B., & Schneider, S. (1990). Social identity and social dilemmas: A double-edged sword. In D. Abrams & M. A. Hogg (Eds.), *Social identity theory: Constructive and critical advances* (pp. 169–184). London: Harvester Wheatsheaf.

Brief, A. P., Dukerich, J. M., & Doran, L. I. (1991). Resolving ethical dilemmas in management: Experimental investigation of values, accountability, and choice. *Journal of Applied Social Psychology, 21,* 380–396.

Brockner, J., Chen, Y.R., Mannix, E. A., Leung, K., & Skarlicki, D. P. (2000). Culture and procedural fairness: When the effects of what you do depend on how you do it. *Administrative Science Quarterly, 45,* 1238–1259.

Bryman, A. (1992). *Charisma and leadership*. London: Sage.

Burger, J. M. (1986). Increasing compliance by improving the deal: The that's-not-all technique. *Journal of Personality and Social Psychology, 51*, 277–283.

Burns, J. M. (1978). *Leadership*. New York: Harper & Row.

Butera, F., Mugny, G., Legrenzi, P., & Pérez, J. A. (1996). Majority and minority influence, task representation and inductive reasoning. *British Journal of Social Psychology, 35*, 123–136.

Byrne, D. (1971). *The attraction paradigm*. New York: Academic Press.

Campbell, D. T. (1958). Common fate, similarity, and other indices of the status of aggregates of persons as social entities. *Behavioral Science, 3*, 14–25.

Campbell. D. T. (1975). On the conflicts between biological and social evolution and between psychology and moral tradition. *American Psychologist, 30*, 1103–1126.

Campbell, J. D., & Fairey, P. J. (1989). Informational and normative routes to conformity: The effect of faction size as a function of norm extremity and attention to the stimulus. *Journal of Personality and Social Psychology, 57*, 457–468.

Campbell, J. D., Tesser, A., & Fairey, P. J. (1986). Conformity and attention to the stimulus: Some temporal and contextual dynamics. *Journal of Personality and Social Psychology, 51*, 315–324.

Carlsmith, J. M., & Gross, A. E. (1969). Some effects of guilt on compliance. *Journal of Personality and Social Psychology, 11*, 232–239.

Carlyle, T. (1841). *On heroes, hero-worship, and the heroic*. London: Fraser.

Carter, L. F., & Nixon, M. (1949). An investigation of the relationship between four criteria of leadership ability for three different tasks. *The Journal of Psychology, 27*, 245–261.

Cartwright, D., & Zander, D. (Eds.). (1953). *Group dynamics: Research and theory*. New York: Harper & Row.

Chaiken, S. (1987). The heuristic model of persuasion. In M. P. Zanna, J. M. Olsen, & C. P. Herman (Eds.), *Social influence: The Ontario symposium* (Vol. 5, pp. 3–39). Hillsdale, NJ: Erlbaum.

Chandra, S. (1973). The effects of group pressure in perception: A cross-cultural conformity study. *International Journal of Psychology, 8*, 37–39.

Chemers, M. M. (1997). *An integrative theory of leadership*. Mahwah, NJ: Erlbaum.

Chemers, M. M. (2001). Leadership effectiveness: An integrative review. In M. A. Hogg & R. S. Tindale (Eds.), *Blackwell handbook of social psychology: Group processes* (pp. 376–399). Oxford: Blackwell.

Cialdini, R. B., Cacioppo, J. T., Bassett, R., & Miller, J. A. (1978). Low-balling procedure for producing compliance: Commitment then cost. *Journal of Personality and Social Psychology, 36*, 463–476.

Cialdini, R. B., & Goldstein, N. J. (2004). Social influence: Compliance and conformity. *Annual Review of Psychology, 55*, 591–621.

Cialdini, R. B., Kallgren, C. A., & Reno, R. R. (1991). A focus theory of normative conduct: Theoretical refinement and reevaluation of the role of norms in human behavior. In L. Berkowitz (Ed.), *Advances in experimental social psychology* (Vol. 21, pp. 201–234). New York: Academic Press.

Cialdini, R. B., & Trost, M. R. (1998). Social influence: Social norms, conformity, and compliance. In D. Gilbert, S. T. Fiske, & G. Lindzey (Eds.), *The handbook of social psychology* (4th ed., Vol. 2, pp. 151–192). New York: McGraw-Hill.

Cialdini, R. B., Vincent, J. E., Lewis, S. K., Catalan, J., Wheeler, D., & Darby, B. L. (1975). Reciprocal concessions procedure for inducing compliance: The door-in-the-face technique. *Journal of Personality and Social Psychology, 31*, 206–215.

Coch, L., & French, J. R. P., Jr (1948). Overcoming resistance to change. *Human Relations, 1*, 512–32.

Conger, J. A., & Kanungo, R. N. (1998). *Charismatic leadership in organizations*. Thousand Oaks, CA: Sage.

Cooper, J. (2007). *Cognitive dissonance: 50 years of a classic theory*. Los Angeles: Sage.

Correll, S. J., & Ridgeway, C. (2003). Expectation states theory. In J. Delamater (Ed.), *Handbook of social psychology* (pp. 29–52). New York: Kluwer Academic/Plenum.

Costanzo, P. R. (1970). Conformity development as a function of self-blame. *Journal of Personality and Social Psychology, 14*, 366–374.

Crano, W. D., & Alvaro, E. M. (1998). The context/comparison model of social influence: Mechanisms, structure, and linkages that underlie indirect attitude change. *European review of social psychology, 8*, 175–202.

Crano, W. D., & Chen, X. (1998). The leniency contract and persistence of majority and minority influence. *Journal of Personality and Social Psychology, 74*, 1437–1450.

Crano, W. D., & Seyranian, V. (2009). How minorities prevail: The context/comparison—leniency contract model. *Journal of Social Issues, 65*, 335–363.

Crutchfield, R. A. (1955). Conformity and character. *American Psychologist, 10*, 191–198.

Danserau, F., Jr, Graen, G., & Haga, W. J. (1975). A vertical dyad linkage approach to leadership within formal organizations: A longitudinal investigation of the role making process. *Organizational Behavior and Human Performance, 13*, 46–78.

Darley, J. (2001). Social comparison motives in ongoing groups. In M. A. Hogg & R. S. Tindale (Eds.), *Blackwell handbook of social psychology* (pp. 334–351). Oxford: Blackwell.

Darlington, R. B., & Macker, D. F. (1966). Displacement of guilt-produced altruistic behaviour. *Journal of Personality and Social Psychology, 4*, 442–443.

David, B., & Turner, J. C. (1996). Studies in self-categorization and minority conversion. Is being a member of the outgroup an advantage? *British Journal of Social Psychology, 35*, 179–199.

David, B., & Turner, J. C. (1999). Studies in self-categorization and minority conversion. The ingroup minority in intragroup and intergroup contexts. *British Journal of Social Psychology, 38*, 115–134.

David, B., & Turner, J. C. (2001). Majority and minority influence: A single process self-categorization analysis. In C. K. W. De Dreu & N. K. De Vries (Eds.), *Group consensus and innovation* (pp. 91–121). Oxford: Blackwell.

Davis, J. H. (1973). Group decision and social interaction: A theory of social decision schemes. *Psychological Review, 80*, 97–125.

Dawes, R. M., & Messick, D. M. (2000). Social dilemmas. *International Journal of Psychology, 35*, 111–116.

De Cremer, D. (2003). A relational perspective on leadership and cooperation: Why it matters to care and be fair. In D. van Knippenberg & M. A. Hogg (Eds.), *Leadership and power: Identity processes in groups and organizations* (pp. 109–122). London: Sage.

De Cremer, D., & Van Knippenberg, D. (2003). Cooperation with leaders in social dilemmas: On the effects of procedural fairness and outcome favorability in structural cooperation. *Organizational Behavior and Human Decision Processes, 91*, 1–11.

De Cremer, D., & Van Vugt, M. (1999). Social identification effects in social dilemmas: A transformation of motives. *European Journal of Social Psychology, 29*, 871–893.

De Cremer, D., & Van Vugt, M. (2002). Intergroup and intragroup aspects of leadership in social dilemmas: A relational model of cooperation. *Journal of Experimental Social Psychology, 38*, 126–136.

De Dreu, C.K.W., De Vries, N. K., Gordijn, E., & Schuurman, M. (1999). Convergent and divergent processing of majority and minority arguments: Effects on focal and related attitudes. *European Journal of Social Psychology, 29*, 329–348.

DeJong, W. (1979). An examination of self-perception mediation of the foot in the door effect. *Journal of Personality and Social Psychology, 37*, 2171–2180.

Deutsch, M., & Gerard, H. B. (1955). A study of normative and informational social influences upon individual judgment. *Journal of Abnormal and Social Psychology, 51*, 629–636.

Devine, P. G., Hamilton, D. L., & Ostrom, T. M. (Eds.). (1994). *Social cognition: Impact on social psychology.* San Diego, CA: Academic Press.

Dirks, K. T., & Ferrin, D. L. (2002). Trust in leadership: Meta-analytic findings and implications for research and practice. *Journal of Applied Psychology, 87*, 611–628.

Dittes, J. E., & Kelley, H. H. (1956). Effects of different conditions of acceptance upon conformity to group norms. *Journal of Abnormal and Social Psychology, 53*, 100–107.

Dolinski, D. (2000). On inferring one's beliefs from one's attempt and consequences for subsequent compliance. *Journal of Personality and Social Psychology, 78*, 260–272.

Doms, M. (1983). The minority influence effect: An alternative approach. In W. Doise & S. Moscovici (Eds.), *Current issues in European social psychology* (Vol. 1, pp. 1–32). Cambridge, England: Cambridge University Press.

Downing, J. (1958). Cohesiveness, perception, and values. *Human Relations, 11*, 157–166.

Duck, J. M., & Fielding, K. S. (1999). Leaders and subgroups: One of us or one of them? *Group Processes and Intergroup Relations, 2*, 203–230.

Duck, J. M., & Fielding, K. S. (2003). Leaders and their treatment of subgroups: Implications for evaluations of the leader and the superordinate group. *European Journal of Social Psychology, 33*, 387–401.

Dvir, T., Eden, D., Avolio, B. J., & Shamir, B. (2002). Impact of transformational leadership training on follower development and performance: A field experiment. *Academy of Management Journal, 45*, 735–744.

Eagly, A. H. (1978). Sex differences in influenceability. *Psychological Bulletin, 85*, 86–116.

Eagly, A. H., & Carli, L. L. (1981). Sex of researcher and sex-typed communications as determinants of sex differences in influenceability: A meta-analysis of social influence studies. *Psychological Bulletin, 90*, 1–20.

Eagly, A. H., & Carli, L. L. (2007). *Through the labyrinth: The truth about how women become leaders.* Boston: Harvard Business School Press.

Eagly, A. H., & Chaiken, S. (1984). Cognitive theories of persuasion. In L. Berkowitz (Ed.), *Advances in experimental social psychology* (Vol. 17, pp. 268–359). New York: Academic Press.

Eagly, A. H., & Chaiken, S. (1993). *The psychology of attitudes.* San Diego, CA: Harcourt Brace Jovanovich.

Eagly, A. H., & Chrvala, C. (1986). Sex differences in conformity: Status and gender role interpretations. *Psychology of Women Quarterly, 10*, 203–220.

Eagly, A. H., & Karau, S. J. (2002). Role congruity theory of prejudice toward female leaders. *Psychological Review, 109*, 573–598.

Eagly, A. H., Karau, S. J., & Makhijani, M. G. (1995). Gender and the effectiveness of leaders: A meta-analysis. *Psychological Bulletin, 117*, 125–145.

Eagly, A. H., Wood, W., & Fishbaugh, L. (1981). Sex differences in conformity: Surveillance by the group as a determinant of male nonconformity. *Journal of Personality and Social Psychology, 40*, 384–394.

Ellemers, N., de Gilder, D., & Haslam, S. A. (2004). Motivating individuals and groups at work: A social identity perspective on leadership and group performance. *Academy of Management Review, 29*, 459–478.

Elms, A. C. (1975). The crisis of confidence in social psychology. *American Psychologist, 30*, 967–976.

Elms, A. C., & Milgram, S. (1966). Personality characteristics associated with obedience and defiance toward authoritative command. *Journal of Experimental Research in Personality, 1*, 282–289.

Festinger, L. (1950). Informal social communication. *Psychological Review, 57*, 271–282.

Festinger, L. (1954). A theory of social comparison processes. *Human Relations, 7*, 117–140.

Festinger, L. (1957). *A theory of cognitive dissonance.* Stanford, CA: Stanford University Press.

Festinger, L., Schachter, S., & Back, K. (1950). *Social pressures in informal groups: A study of human factors in housing.* New York: Harper.

Fiedler, F. E. (1964). A contingency model of leadership effectiveness. In L. Berkowitz (Ed.), *Advances in experimental social psychology* (Vol. 1, pp. 149–190). New York: Academic Press.

Fiedler, F. E. (1967). *A theory of leadership effectiveness.* New York: McGraw-Hill.

Field, R. H. G., & House, R. J. (1990). A test of the Vroom-Yetton model using manager and subordinate reports. *Journal of Applied Psychology, 75*, 362–366.

Fiol, C. M. (2002). Capitalizing on paradox: The role of language in transforming organizational identities. *Organization Science, 13*, 653–666.

Fishbein, M., & Ajzen, I. (1974). Attitudes toward objects as predictors of single and multiple behavior criteria. *Psychological Review, 81*, 59–74.

Fiske, S. T. (1998). Stereotyping, prejudice, and discrimination. In D. T. Gilbert, S. T. Fiske, & G. Lindzey (Eds.), *The handbook of social psychology* (4th ed., Vol. 2, pp. 357–414). New York: McGraw-Hill.

Fiske, S. T., & Berdahl, J. (2007). Social power. In A. W. Kruglanski & E. T. Higgins (Eds.), *Social psychology: Handbook of basic principles* (2nd ed., pp. 678–692). New York: Guilford.

Fiske, S. T., & Dépret, E. (1996). Control, interdependence and power: Understanding social cognition in its social context. *European Review of Social Psychology, 7*, 31–61.

Fiske, S. T., & Taylor, S. E. (2008). *Social cognition: From brains to culture.* New York: McGraw-Hill.

Fleishman, E. A. (1973). Twenty years of consideration and structure. In E. A. Fleishman & J. F. Hunt (Eds.), *Current developments in the study of leadership.* Carbondale, IL: South Illinois University Press.

Foss, R. D., & Dempsey, C. B. (1979). Blood donation and the foot-in-the-door technique. *Journal of Personality and Social Psychology, 37*, 580–590.

Fox, S., & Hoffman, M. (2002). Escalation behavior as a specific case of goal-directed activity: A persistence paradigm. *Basic and Applied Social Psychology, 24*, 273–285.

Freedman, J. L., & Fraser, S. C. (1966). Compliance without pressure: The foot-in-the-door technique. *Journal of Personality and Social Psychology, 4*, 195–202.

Freedman, J. L., Wallington, S. A., & Bless, E. (1967). Compliance without pressure: The effect of guilt. *Journal of Personality and Social Psychology, 7*, 117–124.

Gaertner S. L., & Dovidio, J. F. (2000). *Reducing intergroup bias: The common ingroup identity model.* New York: Psychology Press.

Gaertner, S. L., Dovidio, J., Anastasio, P., Bachman, B., & Rust, M. (1993). The common ingroup identity model: Recategorization and the reduction of intergroup bias. *European Review of Social Psychology, 4*, 1–26.

Galton, F. (1892). *Heredity genius: An inquiry into its laws and consequences.* London: Macmillan.

Garfinkel, H. (1967). *Studies in ethnomethodology.* Englewood Cliffs, NJ: Prentice Hall.

Gerard, H. B. (1954). The anchorage of opinions in face-to-face groups. *Human Relations, 7*, 313–326.

Gerstner, C. R., & Day, D. V. (1997). Meta-analytic review of Leader-Member Exchange Theory: Correlates and construct issues. *Journal of Applied Psychology, 82*, 827–844.

Gilbert, D. T., Fiske, S. T., & Lindzey, G. (Eds.). (1998). *The handbook of social psychology* (4th ed.). New York: McGraw-Hill.

Gilbert, D. T., & Malone, P. S. (1995). The correspondence bias. *Psychological Bulletin, 117*, 21–38.

Goethals, G. R., Sorenson, G. J., & Burns, J. M. (Eds.). (2004). *Encyclopedia of leadership*. Thousand Oaks, CA: Sage.

Goldman, M., Creason, C. R., & McCall, C. G. (1981). Compliance employing a two-feet-in-the-door procedure. *Journal of Social Psychology, 114*, 259–265.

Gorassini, D. R., & Olson, J. M. (1995). Does self-perception change explain the foot-in-the-door effect? *Journal of Personality and Social Psychology, 69*, 91–105.

Gordon, R. A. (1996). Impact of ingratiation on judgments and evaluations: A meta-analytic investigation. *Journal of Personality and Social Psychology, 71*, 54–70.

Gorenflo, D. W., & Crano, W. D. (1989). Judgmental subjectivity/objectivity and locus of choice in social comparison. *Journal of Personality and Social Psychology, 57*, 605–614.

Graen, G. B., & Uhl-Bien, M. (1995). Relationship-based approach to leadership: Development of leader–member exchange (LMX) theory of leadership over 25 years: Applying a multi-level multi-domain approach. *The Leadership Quarterly, 6*, 219–247.

Greene, J. D., Sommerville, R. B., Nystrom, L. E., Darley, J. M., & Cohen, J. D. (2001). An fMRI investigation of emotional engagement in moral judgment. *Science, 293*, 2105–2108

Greenwald, A. G., Banaji, M. R., Rudman, L. A., Farnham, S. D., Nosek, B. A., & Mellott, D. S. (2002). A unified theory of implicit attitudes, stereotypes, self-esteem, and self-concept. *Psychological Review, 109*, 3–25.

Guerin, B. (1993). *Social facilitation*. Cambridge, England: Cambridge University Press.

Hains, S. C., Hogg, M. A., & Duck, J. M. (1997). Self-categorization and leadership: Effects of group prototypicality and leader stereotypicality. *Personality and Social Psychology Bulletin, 23*, 1087–1100.

Hamilton, D. L., & Sherman, S. J. (1996). Perceiving persons and groups. *Psychological Review, 103*, 336–335.

Haney, C., Banks, C., & Zimbardo, P. (1973). A study of prisoners and guards in a simulated prison. *Naval Research Review, 9*, 1–17 [Reprinted in E. Aronson (Ed.), *Readings about the social animal* (3rd ed., pp. 52–67). San Francisco, CA: W. H. Freeman.]

Harper, F.B.W. (1961). *The sociometric composition of the group as a determinant of yielding to a distorted norm*. Unpublished doctoral dissertation, University of California, Berkeley.

Haslam, N. (2006). Dehumanization: An integrative review. *Personality and Social Psychology Review, 10*, 252–264.

Haslam, N., Loughnan, S., & Kashima, Y. (2008). Attributing and denying humanness to others. *European Review of Social Psychology, 19*, 55–85.

Haslam, N., Rothschild, L., & Ernst, D. (1998). Essentialist beliefs about social categories. *British Journal of Social Psychology, 39*, 113–127.

Haslam, S. A., Oakes, P. J., McGarty, C., Turner, J. C., & Onorato, S. (1995). Contextual changes in the prototypicality of extreme and moderate outgroup members. *European Journal of Social Psychology, 25*, 509–530.

Haslam, S. A., & Platow, M. J. (2001). Your wish is our command: The role of shared social identity in translating a leader's vision into followers' action. In M. A. Hogg & D. J. Terry (Eds.), *Social identity processes in organizational contexts* (pp. 213–228). Philadelphia: Psychology Press.

Haslam, S. A., & Reicher, S. D. (2005). The psychology of tyranny. *Scientific American, 16*, 44–51.

Heilman, M. E. (1983). Sex bias in work settings: The lack of fit model. *Research in Organizational Behavior, 5*, 269–298.

Hersey, P., & Blanchard, K. H. (1969). An introduction to situational leadership. *Training and Development Journal, 23*, 26–34.

Hofstede, G. (1980). *Culture's consequences: International differences in work-related values*. Beverly Hills, CA: Sage.

Hogg, M. A. (1993). Group cohesiveness: A critical review and some new directions. *European Review of Social Psychology, 4*, 85–111.

Hogg, M. A. (2001). A social identity theory of leadership. *Personality and Social Psychology Review, 5*, 184–200.

Hogg, M. A. (2005). All animals are equal but some animals are more equal than others: Social identity and marginal membership. In K. D. Williams, J. P. Forgas, & W. von Hippel (Eds.), *The social outcast: Ostracism, social exclusion, rejection and bullying* (pp. 243–261). New York: Psychology Press.

Hogg, M. A. (2006). Social identity theory. In P. J. Burke (Ed.), *Contemporary social psychological theories* (pp. 111–136). Palo Alto, CA: Stanford University Press.

Hogg, M. A. (2007a). Social psychology of leadership. In A. W. Kruglanski & E. T. Higgins (Eds.), *Social psychology: Handbook of basic principles* (2nd ed., pp. 716–733). New York: Guilford.

Hogg, M. A. (2007b). Uncertainty-identity theory. In M. P. Zanna (Ed.), *Advances in experimental social psychology* (Vol. 39, pp. 69–126). San Diego, CA: Academic Press.

Hogg, M. A. (2007c). Social identity and the group context of trust: Managing risk and building trust through belonging. In M. Siegrist, T. C. Earle, & H. Gutscher (Eds.), *Trust in cooperative risk management: Uncertainty and scepticism in the public mind* (pp. 51–71). London: Earthscan.

Hogg, M. A. (2008). Social identity theory of leadership. In C. L. Hoyt, G. R. Goethals, & D. R. Forsyth (Eds.), *Leadership at the crossroads. Volume 1: Leadership and psychology* (pp. 62–77). Westport, CT: Praeger.

Hogg, M. A. (2009). From group conflict to social harmony: Leading across diverse and conflicting social identities. In T. Pittinsky (Ed.), *Crossing the divide: Intergroup leadership in a world of difference* (pp. 17–30). Cambridge, MA: Harvard Business Publishing.

Hogg, M. A. (in press). Uncertainty-identity theory. In P. A. M. van Lange, A. W. Kruglanski, & E. T. Higgins (Eds.), *Handbook of theories of social psychology*. Thousand Oaks, CA: SAGE.

Hogg, M. A., & Abrams, D. (1988). *Social identifications: A social psychology of intergroup relations and group processes*. London: Routledge.

Hogg, M. A., & Cooper, J. (Eds.). (2003). *The SAGE handbook of social psychology*. London: Sage.

Hogg, M. A., Fielding, K. S., Johnson, D., Masser, B., Russell, E., & Svensson, A. (2006). Demographic category membership and leadership in small groups: A social identity analysis. *The Leadership Quarterly, 17*, 335–350.

Hogg, M. A., Hains, S. C., & Mason, I. (1998). Identification and leadership in small groups: Salience, frame of reference, and leader stereotypicality effects on leader evaluations. *Journal of Personality and Social Psychology, 75*, 1248–1263.

Hogg, M. A., Martin, R., Epitropaki, O., Mankad, A., Svensson, A., & Weeden, K. (2005). Effective leadership in salient groups: Revisiting leader–member exchange theory from the perspective of the social identity theory of leadership. *Personality and Social Psychology Bulletin, 31*, 991–1004.

Hogg, M. A., Martin, R., & Weeden, K. (2004). Leader–member relations and social identity. In D. van Knippenberg & M. A. Hogg (Eds.), *Leadership and power: Identity processes in groups and organizations* (pp. 18–33). London: Sage.

Hogg, M. A., & Reid, S. A. (2006). Social identity, self-categorization, and the communication of group norms. *Communication Theory, 16*, 7–30.

Hogg, M. A., & Smith, J. R. (2007). Attitudes in social context: A social identity perspective. *European Review of Social Psychology, 18*, 89–131.

Hogg, M. A., Terry, D. J., & White, K. M. (1995). A tale of two theories: A critical comparison of identity theory with social identity theory. *Social Psychology Quarterly, 58*, 255–269.

Hogg, M. A., & Tindale, R. S. (Eds.). (2001). *Blackwell handbook of social psychology: Group processes.* Oxford: Blackwell.

Hogg, M.A., & Tindale, R. S. (2005). Social identity, influence, and communication in small groups. In J. Harwood & H. Giles (Eds.), *Intergroup communication: Multiple perspectives* (pp. 141–164). New York: Peter Lang.

Hogg, M. A., & Turner, J. C. (1987). Social identity and conformity: A theory of referent informational influence. In W. Doise & S. Moscovici (Eds.), *Current issues in European social psychology* (Vol. 2, pp. 139–182). Cambridge, England: Cambridge University Press.

Hogg, M. A., Turner, J. C., & Davidson, B. (1990). Polarized norms and social frames of reference: A test of the self-categorization theory of group polarization. *Basic and Applied Social Psychology, 11*, 77–100.

Hogg, M. A., & Van Knippenberg, D. (2003). Social identity and leadership processes in groups. In M. P. Zanna (Ed.), *Advances in experimental social psychology* (Vol. 35, pp. 1–52). San Diego, CA: Academic Press.

Hohman, Z. P., Hogg, M. A., & Bligh, M. C. (in press). Identity and intergroup leadership: Asymmetrical political and national identification in response to uncertainty. *Self and Identity.*

Hollander, E. P. (1958). Conformity, status, and idiosyncracy credit. *Psychological Review, 65*, 117–127.

Hollander, E. P. (1985). Leadership and power. In G. Lindzey & E. Aronson (Eds.), *Handbook of social psychology* (3rd ed., Vol. 2, pp. 485–537). New York: Random House.

Hollander, E. P., & Julian, J. W. (1970). Studies in leader legitimacy, influence, and innovation. In L. Berkowitz (Ed.), *Advances in experimental social psychology* (Vol. 5, pp. 34–69). New York: Academic Press.

Hornsey, M. J. (2005). Why being right is not enough: Predicting defensiveness in the face of group criticism. *European Review of Social Psychology, 16*, 301–334.

Hornsey, M. J., & Hogg, M. A. (2000). Assimilation and diversity: An integrative model of subgroup relations. *Personality and Social Psychology Review, 4*, 143–156.

House, R. J. (1971). A path–goal theory of leadership effectiveness. *Administrative Science Quarterly, 16*, 321–338.

House, R. J. (1977). A 1976 theory of charismatic leadership. In J. G. Hunt & L. Larson (Eds.), *Leadership: The cutting edge* (pp. 189–207). Carbondale, IL: Southern Illinois University Press.

House, R. J. (1996). Path–goal theory of leadership: Lessons, legacy, and a reformulated theory. *The Leadership Quarterly, 7*, 323–352.

House, R. J., & Mitchell, T. R. (1974). Path–goal theory of leadership. *Journal of Contemporary Business, 3*, 81–98.

House, R. J., Spangler, W. D., & Woycke, J. (1991). Personality and charisma in the U.S. presidency: A psychological theory of leader effectiveness. *Administrative Science Quarterly, 36*, 364–396.

Hovland, C. I., Janis, I. L., & Kelley, H. H. (1953). *Communication and persuasion.* New Haven, CT: Yale University Press.

Hovland, C. I., Lumsdaine, A. A., & Sheffield, F. D. (1949). *Experiments in mass communication.* Princeton, NJ: Princeton University Press.

Insko, C. A., Smith, R. H., Alicke, M. D., Wade, J., & Taylor, S. (1985). Conformity and group size: The concern with being right and the concern with being liked. *Personality and Social Psychology Bulletin, 11*, 41–50.

Isenberg, D. J. (1986). Group polarization: A critical review. *Journal of Personality and Social Psychology, 50*, 1141–1151.

Jacobs, R., & Campbell, D. T. (1961). The perpetuation of an arbitrary tradition through several generations of a laboratory microculture. *Journal of Abnormal and Social Psychology, 62*, 649–658.

Janis, I. L. (1972). *Victims of groupthink: A psychological study of foreign policy decisions and fiascoes.* Boston: Houghton Mifflin.

Jones, E. E. (1964). *Ingratiation: A social psychological analysis.* Des Moines, IA: Meredith Publishing Company.

Jones, E. E., & Pittman, T. S. (1982). Toward a general theory of strategic self-presentation. In J. Suls (Ed.), *Psychological perspectives on the self* (Vol. 1, pp. 231–262). Hillsdale, NJ: Erlbaum.

Judge, T. A., & Bono, J. E. (2000). Five-factor model of personality and transformational leadership. *Journal of Applied Psychology, 85*, 751–765.

Judge, T. A., Bono, J. E., Ilies, R., & Gerhardt, M. W. (2002). Personality and leadership: A qualitative and quantitative review. *Journal of Applied Psychology, 87*, 765–780.

Karau, S. J., & Williams, K. D. (1993). Social loafing: A meta-analytic review and theoretical integration. *Journal of Personality and Social Psychology, 65*, 681–706.

Kashima, Y. (2000). Maintaining cultural stereotypes in the serial reproduction of narratives. *Personality and Social Psychology Bulletin, 26*, 594–604.

Kellerman, B. (2004). *Bad leadership: What it is, how it happens, why it matters.* Cambridge, MA: Harvard Business School Press.

Kelley, H. H. (1952). Two functions of reference groups. In G. E. Swanson, T. M. Newcomb, & E. L. Hartley (Eds.), *Readings in social psychology* (2nd ed., pp. 410–414). New York: Holt, Rinehart & Winston.

Kelley, H. H. (1967). Attribution theory in social psychology. In D. Levine (Ed.), *Nebraska symposium on motivation* (pp. 192–238). Lincoln, NE: University of Nebraska Press.

Kelley, R. E. (1992). *The power of followership.* New York: Doubleday.

Kelman, H. C. (1958). Compliance, identification, and internalization: Three processes of attitude change. *Journal of Conflict Resolution, 2*, 51–60.

Kennedy, J. (1982). Middle LPC leaders and the contingency model of leader effectiveness. *Organizational Behavior and Human Performance, 30*, 1–14.

Kerr, N. L. (1983). Motivation losses in small groups: A social dilemma analysis. *Journal of Personality and Social Psychology, 45*, 819–828.

Kerr, N. L., & Bruun, S. (1983). The dispensability of member effort and group motivation losses: Free rider effects. *Journal of Personality and Social Psychology, 44*, 78–94.

Kerr, N. L., & Park, E. S. (2001). Group performance in collaborative and social dilemma tasks: Progress and prospects. In M. A. Hogg & R. S. Tindale (Eds.), *Blackwell handbook of social psychology: Group processes* (pp. 107–138). Oxford: Blackwell.

Kilham, W., & Mann, L. (1974). Level of destructive obedience as a function of transmitter and executant roles in the Milgram obedience paradigm. *Journal of Personality and Social Psychology, 29*, 696–702.

Klandermans, B. (1997). *The social psychology of protest.* Oxford: Blackwell.

Klein, O., Spears, R. & Reicher, S. D. (2007). Social identity performance: Extending the strategic side of SIDE. *Personality and Social Psychology Review, 11*, 28–45.

Krackow, A., & Blass, T. (1995). When nurses obey or defy inappropriate physician orders: Attributional differences. *Journal of Social Behavior and Personality, 10*, 585–594.

Kruglanski, A. W., & Higgins, E. T. (Eds.). (2007). *Social psychology: Handbook of basic principles* (2nd ed.). New York: Guilford.

Kruglanski, A. W., & Mackie, D. M. (1990). Majority and minority influence: A judgmental process analysis. *European Review of Social Psychology, 1*, 229–261.

Langer, E. J., Blank, A., & Chanowitz, B. (1978). The mindlessness of ostensibly thoughtful action. *Journal of Personality and Social Psychology, 36*, 635–642.

Lapinski, M. K., & Rimal, R. N. (2005). An explication of social norms. *Communication Theory, 15*, 127–147.

Larson, J. R., Jr., Foster-Fishman, P. G., & Keys, C. B. (1994). Discussion of shared and unshared information in decision-making groups. *Journal of Personality and Social Psychology, 67*, 446–461.

Leary, M. R. (1995). *Self-presentation: Impression management and interpersonal behavior.* Madison, WI: Brown & Benchmark.

LeBon, G. (1908). *The crowd: A study of the popular mind.* London: Unwin. (Original work published 1896.)

Lesar, T. S., Briceland, L., & Stein, D. S. (1997). Factors related to errors in medication prescribing. *Journal of the American Medical Association, 277*, 312–317.

Levine, J. M., & Moreland, R. L. (1994). Group socialization: Theory and research. *European Review of Social Psychology, 5*, 305–336.

Lewin, K. (1943). Forces behind food habits and methods of change. *Bulletin of National Research Council, 108*, 35–65.

Lewin, K. (1947). Frontiers in group dynamics. *Human Relations, 1*, 5–42.

Liebman, R. C., Sutton, J. R., & Wuthnow, R. (1988). Exploring the social sources of denominationalism: Schisms in American Protestant denominations, 1890–1980. *American Sociological Review, 53*, 343–52.

Lind, E. A., & Tyler, T. R. (1988). *The social psychology of procedural justice.* New York: Plenum Press.

Lippitt, R., & White, R. (1943). "The social climate" of children's groups. In R. G. Barker, J. Kounin, & H. Wright (Eds.), *Child behavior and development* (pp. 485–508). New York: McGraw-Hill.

Lipponen, J., Koivisto, S., & Olkkonen, M. E. (2005). Procedural justice and status judgements: The moderating role of leader ingroup prototypicality. *Leadership Quarterly, 16*, 517–528.

Lord, R. G., & Brown, D. J. (2004). *Leadership processes and follower identity.* Mahwah, NJ: Erlbaum.

Lord, R. G., Brown, D. J., & Harvey, J. L. (2001). System constraints on leadership perceptions, behavior and influence: An example of connectionist level processes. In M. A. Hogg & R. S. Tindale (Eds.), *Blackwell handbook of social psychology: Group processes* (pp. 283–310). Oxford: Blackwell.

Lord, R.G., Brown, D. J., Harvey, J. L., & Hall, R. J. (2001). Contextual constraints on prototype generation and their multilevel consequences for leadership perceptions. *Leadership Quarterly, 12*, 311–338.

Lord, R. G., Foti, R. J., & DeVader, C. L. (1984). A test of leadership categorization theory: Internal structure, information processing, and leadership perceptions. *Organizational Behavior and Human Performance, 34*, 343–378.

Lord, R. G., Foti, R. J., & Phillips, J. S. (1982). A theory of leadership categorization. In J. G. Hunt, U. Sekaran, & C. Schriesheim (Eds.), *Leadership: Beyond establishment views* (pp. 104–121). Carbondale, IL: Southern Illinois University Press.

Lord, R., & Hall, R. (2003). Identity, leadership categorization, and leadership schema. In D. van Knippenberg & M. A. Hogg (Eds.) *Leadership and power: Identity processes in groups and organizations* (pp. 48–64). London: Sage.

Lord, R. G., & Maher, K. J. (1991). *Leadership and information processing: Linking perceptions and performance.* Boston: Unwin Hyman.

Lott, A. J., & Lott, B. E. (1961). Group cohesiveness, communication level, and conformity. *Journal of Abnormal and Social Psychology, 62*, 408–412.

Lowe, K. B., Kroeck, K. G., & Sivasubramaniam, N. (1996). Effectiveness correlates of transformational and transactional leadership: A meta-analytic review. *The Leadership Quarterly, 7*, 385–425.

Lydon, J., & Dunkel-Schetter, C. (1994). Seeing is committing: A longitudinal study of bolstering commitment in amniocentesis patients. *Personality and Social Psychology Bulletin, 20*, 218–227.

Maass, A., & Clark, R. D., III. (1983). Internalisation versus compliance: Differential processes underlying minority influence and conformity. *European Journal of Social Psychology, 13*, 197–215.

Maass, A., & Clark, R. D., III. (1984). Hidden impact of minorities: Fifteen years of minority influence research. *Psychological Bulletin, 95*, 428–450.

Mackie, D. M. (1986). Social identification effects in group polarization. *Journal of Personality and Social Psychology, 50*, 720–728.

Mackie, D. M., & Cooper, J. (1984). Attitude polarization: The effects of group membership. *Journal of Personality and Social Psychology, 46*, 575–585.

MacNeil, M., & Sherif, M. (1976). Norm change over subject generations as a function of arbitrariness of prescribed norms. *Journal of Personality and Social Psychology, 34*, 762–773.

Malkin, P. Z., & Stein, H. (1990). *Eichmann in my hands.* New York: Warner Books.

Markus, H., & Kitayama, S. (1991). Culture and the self: Implications for cognition, emotion, and motivation. *Psychological Review, 98*, 224–253.

Markus, H., & Kitayama, S. (1994). A collective fear of the collective: Implications for selves and theories of selves. *Personality and Social Psychology Bulletin, 20*, 568–579.

Marques, J. M., Abrams, D., & Serôdio, R. (2001). Being better by being right: Subjective group dynamics and derogation of ingroup deviants when generic norms are undermined. *Journal of Personality and Social Psychology, 81*, 436–447.

Marques, J. M., & Paez, D. (1994). The "black sheep effect": Social categorization, rejection of ingroup deviates and perception of group variability. *European Review of Social Psychology, 5*, 37–68.

Martin, R. (1996). Minority influence and argument generation. *British Journal of Social Psychology, 35*, 91–103.

Martin, R. (1998). Majority and minority influence using the afterimage paradigm: A series of attempted replications. *Journal of Experimental Social Psychology, 34*, 1–26.

Martin, R., & Hewstone, M. (1999). Minority influence and optimal problem solving. *European Journal of Social Psychology, 29*, 825–832.

Martin, R., & Hewstone, M. (2003). Social influence processes of control and change: Conformity, obedience to authority, and innovation. In M. A. Hogg & J. Cooper (Eds.), *The SAGE handbook of social psychology* (pp. 347–366). London: Sage.

Martin, R., & Hewstone, M. (2008). Majority versus minority influence, message processing and attitude change: The source-context-elaboration model. In M. P. Zanna (Ed.), *Advances in experimental social psychology* (Vol. 40, pp. 237–326). San Diego, CA: Elsevier.

Martin, R., Hewstone, M., Martin, P. Y., & Gardikiotis, A. (2008). Persuasion from majority and minority groups. In W. Crano & R. Prislin (Eds.), *Attitudes and attitude change* (pp. 361–384). New York: Psychology Press.

McCall, G., & Simmons, R. (1978). *Identities and interactions* (2nd ed.). New York: Free Press.

McDougall, W. (1920). *The group mind.* London: Cambridge University Press.

McGhee, P. E., & Teevan, R. C. (1967). Conformity behavior and need for affiliation. *Journal of Social Psychology, 72*, 117–121.

McGuire, W. J. (1968). Personality and susceptibility to social influence. In E. F. Borgatta & W. W. Lambert (Eds.), *Handbook of personality: Theory and research* (pp. 1130–1187). Chicago: Rand McNally.

Meeus, W. H. J., & Raaijmakers, Q. A. W. (1986). Administrative obedience as a social phenomenon. In W. Doise & S. Moscovici (Eds.), *Current issues in European social psychology* (Vol. 2, pp. 183–230). Cambridge, England: Cambridge University Press.

Meeus, W. H. J., & Raaijmakers, Q. A. W. (1995). Obedience in modern society: The Utrecht studies. *Journal of Social Issues, 51*, 155–175.

Meindl, J. R. (1995). The romance of leadership as a follower-centric theory: A social constructionist approach. *The Leadership Quarterly, 6,* 329–341.

Meindl, J. R., Ehrlich, S. B., & Dukerich, J. M. (1985). The romance of leadership. *Administrative Science Quarterly, 30,* 78–102.

Meindl, J. R., & Lerner, M. (1983). The heroic motive: Some experimental demonstrations. *Journal of Experimental Social Psychology, 19,* 1–20.

Merei, F. (1949). Group leadership and institutionalization. *Human Relations, 2,* 23–39.

Messick, D. M. (2005). On the psychological exchange between leaders and followers. In D. M. Messick & R. M. Kramer (Eds.), *The psychology of leadership: New perspectives and research* (pp. 81–96). Mahwah, NJ: Erlbaum.

Milgram, S. (1961). Nationality and conformity. *Scientific American, 205(6),* 45–51.

Milgram, S. (1963). Behavioral study of obedience. *Journal of Abnormal and Social Psychology, 67,* 371–378.

Milgram, S. (1974). *Obedience to authority.* London: Tavistock.

Milgram, S., Bickman, L., & Berkowitz, L. (1969). Note on the drawing power of crowds of different size. *Journal of Personality and Social Psychology, 13,* 79–82.

Miller, A. G. (1986). *The obedience experiments: A case study of controversy in social science.* New York: Praeger.

Miller, C. E. (1989). The social psychological effects of group decision rules. In P. B. Paulus (Ed.), *Psychology of group influence* (2nd ed., pp. 327–55). Hillsdale, NJ: Erlbaum.

Moreland, R. L., Hogg, M. A., & Hains, S. C. (1994). Back to the future: Social psychological research on groups. *Journal of Experimental Social Psychology, 30,* 527–555.

Moreland, R. L., & Levine, J. M. (1982). Socialization in small groups: Temporal changes in individual–group relations. In L. Berkowitz (Ed.), *Advances in experimental social psychology* (Vol. 15, pp. 137–192). New York: Academic Press.

Morris, W. N., & Miller, R. S. (1975). The effects of consensus-breaking and consensus preempting partners on reduction of conformity. *Journal of Experimental Social Psychology, 11,* 215–223.

Moscovici, S. (1976). *Social influence and social change.* London: Academic Press.

Moscovici, S. (1980). Toward a theory of conversion behavior. In L. Berkowitz (Ed.), *Advances in experimental social psychology* (Vol. 13, pp. 202–239). New York: Academic Press.

Moscovici, S. (1985). Social influence and conformity. In G. Lindzey & E. Aronson (Eds.), *Handbook of social psychology* (3rd ed., Vol. 2, pp. 347–412). New York: Random House.

Moscovici, S., & Faucheux, C. (1972). Social influence, conforming bias, and the study of active minorities. In L. Berkowitz (Ed.), *Advances in experimental social psychology* (Vol. 6, pp. 149–202). New York: Academic Press.

Moscovici, S., & Lage, E. (1976). Studies in social influence: III. Majority vs. minority influence in a group. *European Journal of Social Psychology, 6,* 149–174.

Moscovici, S., Lage, E., & Naffrechoux, M. (1969). Influence of a consistent minority on the responses of a majority in a colour perception task. *Sociometry, 32,* 365–380.

Moscovici, S., & Personnaz, B. (1980). Studies in social influence: V. Minority influence and conversion behavior in a perceptual task. *Journal of Experimental Social Psychology, 16,* 270–282.

Moscovici, S., & Personnaz, B. (1986). Studies on latent influence by the spectrometer method: I. The impact of psychologization in the case of conversion by a minority or a majority. *European Journal of Social Psychology, 16,* 345–360.

Moscovici, S., & Zavalloni, M. (1969). The group as a polarizer of attitudes. *Journal of Personality and Social Psychology, 12,* 125–135.

Mucchi-Faina, A., Maass, A., & Volpato, C. (1991). Social influence: The role of originality. *European Journal of Social Psychology, 21,* 183–197.

Mugny, G. (1982). *The power of minorities.* London: Academic Press.

Mugny, G., & Papastamou, S. (1981). When rigidity does not fail: Individualization and psychologization as resistance to the diffusion of minority innovations. *European Journal of Social Psychology, 10,* 43–62.

Mugny, G., & Pérez, J. (1991). *The social psychology of minority influence.* Cambridge, England: Cambridge University Press.

Mummendey, A., & Wenzel, M. (1999). Social discrimination and tolerance in intergroup relations: Reactions to intergroup difference. *Personality and Social Psychology Review, 3,*158–174.

Nail, P. R. (1986). Toward an integration of some models and theories of social response. *Psychological Bulletin, 100,* 190–206.

Nemeth, C. (1986). Differential contributions of majority and minority influence. *Psychological Review, 93,* 23–32.

Nemeth, C. (1995). Dissent as driving cognition, attitudes and judgments. *Social Cognition, 13,* 273–291.

Nemeth, C., & Chiles, C. (1988). Modelling courage: The role of dissent in fostering independence. *European Journal of Social Psychology, 18,* 275–280.

Nemeth, C., & Owens, P. (1996). Making work groups more effective: The value of minority dissent. In M. A. West (Ed.), *The handbook of workgroup psychology* (pp. 125–141). Chichester, England: Wiley.

Nemeth, C., & Staw, B. M. (1989). The tradeoffs of social control and innovation in groups and organizations. In L. Berkowitz (Ed.), *Advances in experimental social psychology* (Vol. 22, pp. 175–210). San Diego, CA: Academic Press.

Nemeth, C., Swedlund, M., & Kanki, B. (1974). Patterning of the minority's response and their influence on the majority. *European Journal of Social Psychology, 4,* 53–64.

Nemeth, C., & Wachtler, J. (1983). Creative problem solving as a result of majority vs minority influence. *European Journal of Social Psychology, 13,* 45–55.

Nemeth, C., Wachtler, J., & Endicott, J. (1977). Increasing the size of the minority: Some gains and some losses. *European Journal of Social Psychology, 7,* 15–27.

Newcomb, T. M. (1965). Attitude development as a function of reference groups: The Bennington study. In H. Proshansky & B. Seidenberg (Eds.), *Basic studies in social psychology* (pp. 215–225). New York: Holt, Rinehart & Winston.

Northhouse, P. G. (2007). *Leadership: Theory and practice* (4th ed.). Thousand Oaks, CA: Sage.

Oakes, P. J., Haslam, S. A., & Turner, J. C. (1994). *Stereotyping and social reality.* Oxford, England: Blackwell.

O'Connor, J., Mumford, M. D., Clifton, T. C., Gessner, T. L., & Connelly, M. S. (1995). Charismatic leaders and destructiveness: A historiometric study. *The Leadership Quarterly, 6,* 529–558.

Oyserman, D., Coon, H. M., & Kemmelmeier, M. (2002). Rethinking individualism and collectivism: Evaluation of theoretical assumptions and meta-analyses. *Psychological Bulletin, 128,* 3–72.

Papastamou, S. (1986). Psychologization and processes of minority and majority influence. *European Journal of Social Psychology, 16,* 165–180.

Pérez, J. A., & Mugny, G. (1998). Categorization and social influence. In S. Worchel & J. M. Francisco (Eds.), *Social identity: International perspectives* (pp. 142–153). London: Sage.

Peters, L. H., Hartke, D. D., & Pohlmann, J. T. (1985). Fiedler's contingency theory of leadership: An application of the meta-analytic procedure of Schmidt and Hunter. *Psychological Bulletin, 97,* 274–285.

Peterson, R., & Nemeth, C. (1996). Focus versus flexibility: Majority and minority influence can both improve performance. *Personality and Social Psychology Bulletin, 22,* 14–23.

Petty, R. E., & Cacioppo, J. T. (1986). *Communication and persuasion: Central and peripheral routes to attitude change*. New York: Springer.

Pittinsky, T. (Ed.). (2009). *Crossing the divide: Intergroup leadership in a world of difference*. Cambridge, MA: Harvard Business Publishing.

Pittinsky, T. L., & Simon, S. (2007). Intergroup leadership. *The Leadership Quarterly, 18*, 586–605.

Piaget, J. (1928). *The child's conception of the world*. London: Routledge and Kegan Paul.

Piaget, J. (1955). *The child's construction of reality*. London: Routledge and Kegan Paul.

Platow, M. J., Hoar, S., Reid, S. A., Harley, K., & Morrison, D. (1997). Endorsement of distributively fair and unfair leaders in interpersonal and intergroup situations. *European Journal of Social Psychology, 27*, 465–94.

Platow, M. J., Reid, S. A., & Andrew, S. (1998). Leadership endorsement: The role of distributive and procedural behavior in interpersonal and intergroup contexts. *Group Processes and Intergroup Relations, 1*, 35–47.

Platow, M. J., & Van Knippenberg, D. (2001). A social identity analysis of leadership endorsement: The effects of leader ingroup prototypicality and distributive intergroup fairness. *Personality and Social Psychology Bulletin, 27*, 1508–1519.

Postmes, T., & Spears, R. (1998). Deindividuation and anti-normative behavior: A meta-analysis. *Psychological Bulletin, 123*, 238–259.

Postmes, T., Spears, R., & Cihangir, S. (2001). Quality of decision making and group norms. *Journal of Personality and Social Psychology, 80*, 918–930.

Prentice, D. A., & Miller, D. T. (1993). Pluralistic ignorance and alcohol use on campus: Some consequences of misperceiving the social norm. *Journal of Personality and Social Psychology, 64*, 243–256.

Prentice, D. A., & Miller, D. T. (1996). Pluralistic ignorance and the perpetuation of social norms by unwitting actors. In M. P. Zanna (Ed.), *Advances in experimental social psychology* (Vol. 28, pp. 161–209). New York: Academic Press.

Raven, B. H. (1993). The bases of power: Origins and recent developments. *Journal of Social Issues, 49*, 227–251.

Regan, J. (1971). Guilt, perceived injustice, and altruistic behaviour. *Journal of Personality and Social Psychology, 18*, 124–132.

Reicher, S. D. (1984a). The St. Pauls' riot: An explanation of the limits of crowd action in terms of a social identity model. *European Journal of Social Psychology, 14*, 1–21.

Reicher, S. D. (1984b). Social influence in the crowd: Attitudinal and behavioural effects of deindividuation in conditions of high and low group salience. *British Journal of Social Psychology, 23*, 341–350.

Reicher, S. D. (2001). The psychology of crowd dynamics. In M. A. Hogg & R. S. Tindale (Eds.), *Blackwell handbook of social psychology: Group processes* (pp. 182–208). Oxford: Blackwell.

Reicher, S. D., & Hopkins, N. (1996). Self-category constructions in political rhetoric: An analysis of Thatcher's and Kinnock's speeches concerning the British miners' strike (1984–5). *European Journal of Social Psychology, 26*, 353–371.

Reicher, S. D., & Hopkins, N. (2001). *Self and nation*. London: Sage.

Reicher, S., & Hopkins, N. (2003). On the science of the art of leadership. In D. van Knippenberg & M. A. Hogg (Eds.), *Leadership and power: Identity processes in groups and organizations* (pp. 197–209). London: Sage.

Reicher, S. D., Spears, R., & Postmes, T. (1995). A social identity model of deindividuation phenomena. *European Review of Social Psychology, 6*, 161–198.

Reid, S. A., & Ng, S. H. (2000). Conversation as a resource for influence: Evidence for prototypical arguments and social identification processes. *European Journal of Social Psychology, 30*, 83–100.

Ridgeway, C. L. (2001). Social status and group structure. In M. A. Hogg & R. S. Tindale (Eds.), *Blackwell handbook of social psychology: Group processes* (pp. 352–375). Oxford: Blackwell.

Ridgeway, C. L. (2003). Status characteristics and leadership. In D. van Knippenberg & M. A. Hogg (Eds.), *Leadership and power: Identity processes in groups and organizations* (pp. 65–78). London: Sage.

Riggio, R. E., Chaleff, I., & Lipman-Blumen, J. (Eds.). (2008). *The art of followership: How great followers create great leaders and organizations*. San Francisco: Jossey-Bass.

Ringelmann, M. (1913). Recherches sur les moteurs animés: Travail de l'homme. *Annales de l'Institut National Agronomique, 2*(12), 1–40.

Rohrer, J. H., Baron, S. H., Hoffman, E. L., & Swander, D. V. (1954). The stability of autokinetic judgments. *Journal of Abnormal and Social Psychology, 49*, 595–597.

Ross, L. (1977). The intuitive psychologist and his shortcomings. In L. Berkowitz (Ed.), *Advances in experimental social psychology* (Vol. 10, pp. 174–220). New York: Academic Press.

Saks, M. J. (1978). Social psychological contributions to a legislative committee on organ and tissue transplants. *American Psychologist, 33*, 680–690.

Sani, F., & Reicher, S. D. (1998). When consensus fails: An analysis of the schism within the Italian Communist Party (1991). *European Journal of Social Psychology, 28*, 623–45.

Sani, F., & Reicher, S. D. (1999). Identity, argument and schisms: Two longitudinal studies of the split in the Church of England over the ordination of women to the priesthood. *Group Processes and Intergroup Relations, 2*, 279–300.

Sanna, L. J., & Parks, C. D. (1997). Group research trends in social and organizational psychology: Whatever happened to intragroup research? *Psychological Science, 8*, 261–267.

Scandura, T. A. (1999). Rethinking leader-member exchange: An organizational justice perspective. *The Leadership Quarterly, 10*, 25–40.

Schachter, S. (1959). *The psychology of affiliation*. Stanford, CA: Stanford University Press.

Schriesheim, C. A., Castro, S. L., & Cogliser, C. C. (1999). Leader-member exchange (LMX) research: A comprehensive review of theory, measurement, and data-analytic practices. *The Leadership Quarterly, 10*, 63–113.

Schriesheim, C. A., & Neider, L. L. (1996). Path-goal leadership theory: The long and winding road. *The Leadership Quarterly, 7*, 317–321.

Schriesheim, C. A., Tepper, B. J., & Tetrault, L. A. (1994). Least preferred co-worker score, situational control, and leadership effectiveness: A meta-analysis of contingency model performance predictions. *Journal of Applied Psychology, 79*, 561–573.

Shamir, B., House, R., & Arthur, M. (1993). The motivational effects of charismatic leadership: A self-concept based theory. *Organization Science, 4*(3), 1–17.

Shamir, B., Pillai, R., Bligh, M. C., & Uhl-Bien, M. (Eds.). (2006). *Follower-centered perspectives on leadership: A tribute to the memory of James R. Meindl*. Greenwich, CT: Information Age Publishing.

Shaw, M. E. (1976). *Group dynamics* (2nd ed.). New York: McGraw-Hill.

Shaw, M. E., Rothschild, G., & Strickland, J. (1957). Decision process in communication networks. *Journal of Abnormal and Social Psychology, 54*, 323–330.

Sheeran, P. (2002). Intention-behavior relations: A conceptual and empirical review. *European Review of Social Psychology, 12*, 1–36.

Sherif, M. (1935). A study of some social factors in perception. *Archives of Psychology, 27*, 1–60.

Sherif, M. (1936). *The psychology of social norms*. New York: Harper.

Sherif, M. (1966). *In common predicament: Social psychology of intergroup conflict and cooperation*. Boston: Houghton-Mifflin.

Sherif, M., Harvey, O. J., White, B. J., Hood, W., & Sherif, C. (1961). *Intergroup conflict and cooperation: The robbers' cave experiment*. Norman, OK: University of Oklahoma Institute of Intergroup Relations.

Sherif, M., & Sherif, C. W. (1953). *Groups in harmony and tension: An integration of studies in intergroup behavior.* New York: Harper & Row.

Sherif, M., & Sherif, C. W. (1964). *Reference groups.* New York: Harper & Row.

Siegel, A. E., & Siegel, S. (1957). Reference groups, membership groups, and attitude change. *Journal of Abnormal and Social Psychology, 55,* 360–364.

Simonton, D. K. (1980). Land battles, generals and armies: Individual and situational determinants of victory and casualties. *Journal of Personality and Social Psychology, 38,* 110–119.

Sindic, D., & Reicher, S. D. (2008). The instrumental use of group prototypicality judgments. *Journal of Experimental Social Psychology, 44,* 1425–35.

Sistrunk, F., & McDavid, J. W. (1971). Sex variable in conforming behavior. *Journal of Personality and Social Psychology, 2,* 200–207.

Smith, D. L., Pruitt, D. G., & Carnevale, P. J. D. (1982). Matching and mismatching: The effect of own limit, other's toughness, and time pressure on concession rate in negotiation. *Journal of Personality and Social Psychology, 42,* 876–883.

Smith, P. B., Bond, M. H., & Kağıtçıbaşı, Ç. (2006). *Understanding social psychology across cultures: Living and working in a changing world.* London: Sage.

Smith, P. B., Misumi, J., Tayeb, M., Peterson, M., & Bond, M. (1989). On the generality of leadership style measures across cultures. *Journal of Occupational Psychology, 62,* 97–109.

Sorrentino, R. M., & Field, N. (1986). Emergent leadership over time: The functional value of positive motivation. *Journal of Personality and Social Psychology, 50,* 1091–1099.

Sparrowe, R. T., & Liden, R. C. (1997). Process and structure in leader–member exchange. *Academy of Management Review, 22,* 522–552.

Stang, D. J. (1972). Conformity, ability, and self-esteem. *Representative Research in Social Psychology, 3,* 97–103.

Stang, D. J. (1976). Group size effects on conformity. *Journal of Social Psychology, 98,* 175–181.

Stasser, G., Stewart, D. D., & Wittenbaum, G. M. (1995). Expert roles and information exchange during discussion: The importance of knowing who knows what. *Journal of Experimental Social Psychology, 31,* 244–265.

Stasser, G., & Titus, W. (1985). Pooling of unshared information in group decision making: Biased information sampling during discussion. *Journal of Personality and Social Psychology, 48,* 1467–1478.

Steiner, I. D. (1974). Whatever happened to the group in social psychology? *Journal of Experimental Social Psychology, 10,* 1467–1478.

Steiner, I. D. (1986). Paradigms and groups. *Advances in Experimental Social Psychology, 19,* 251–289.

Stogdill, R. M. (1948). Personal factors associated with leadership: A survey of the literature. *Journal of Psychology, 25,* 35–71.

Stogdill, R. (1974). *Handbook of leadership.* New York: Free Press.

Stouffer, S. A., Suchman, E. A., DeVinney, L. C., Star, S. A., & Williams, R. M., Jr. (1949). *The American soldier.* Princeton, NJ: Princeton University Press.

Strickland, B. R., & Crowne, D. P. (1962). Conformity under conditions of group pressure as a function of need for approval. *Journal of Social Psychology, 58,* 171–181.

Strickland, L. H., Aboud, F. E., & Gergen, K. J. (Eds.). (1976). *Social psychology in transition.* New York: Plenum.

Strube, M. J., & Garcia, J. E. (1981). A meta-analytic investigation of Fiedler's contingency model of leadership effectiveness. *Psychological Bulletin, 90,* 307–321.

Stryker, S., & Statham, A. (1986). Symbolic interaction and role theory. In G. Lindzey & E. Aronson (Eds), *The handbook of social psychology* (3rd ed., Vol. 1, pp. 311–378). New York: Random House.

Stürmer, S., & Simon, B. (2004). Collective action: Towards a dual-pathway model. *European Review of Social Psychology, 15,* 59–99.

Suls, J., & Wheeler, L. (Eds.). (2000). *Handbook of social comparison: Theory and research.* New York: Kluwer/ Plenum.

Sumner, W. G. (1906). *Folkways.* Boston: Ginn.

Tajfel, H. (1959). Quantitative judgement in social perception. *British Journal of Psychology, 50,* 16–29.

Tajfel, H. (1969). Social and cultural factors in perception. In G. Lindzey & E. Aronson (Eds.), *Handbook of social psychology* (Vol. 3, pp. 315–394). Reading, MA: Addison-Wesley.

Tajfel, H. (Ed.). (1984). *The social dimension: European developments in social psychology.* Cambridge, England: Cambridge University Press.

Tajfel, H., & Turner, J. C. (1979). An integrative theory of intergroup conflict. In W. G. Austin & S. Worchel (Eds.), *The social psychology of intergroup relations* (pp. 33–47). Monterey, CA: Brooks/Cole.

Taylor, D. M., & Brown, R. J. (1979). Towards a more social social psychology. *British Journal of Social and Clinical Psychology, 18,* 173–179.

Terry, D. J., Carey, C. J., & Callan, V. J. (2001). Employee adjustment to an organizational merger: An intergroup perspective. *Personality and Social Psychology Bulletin, 27,* 267–280.

Terry, D. J., & Hogg, M. A. (1996). Group norms and the attitude–behavior relationship: A role for group identification. *Personality and Social Psychology Bulletin, 22,* 776–793.

Terry, D. J., & Hogg, M. A. (2001). Attitudes, behaviour, and social context: The role of norms and group membership in social influence processes. In J. P. Forgas & K. D. Williams (Eds.), *Social influence: Direct and indirect processes* (pp. 253–270). New York: Psychology Press.

Thibaut, J. W., & Strickland, L. H. (1956). Psychological set and social conformity. *Journal of Personality, 25,* 115–129.

Tindale, R. S. & Anderson, E. M. (1998). Small group research and applied social psychology: An introduction. In R. S. Tindale, L. Heath, J. Edwards, E. J. Posavac, F. B. Bryant, Y. Suarez-Balcazar, et al. (Eds.), *Social psychological applications to social issues: Theory and research on small groups* (Vol. 4. pp 1–8). New York: Plenum.

Tindale, R. S., Davis, J. H., Vollrath, D. A., Nagao, D. H., & Hinsz, V. B. (1990). Asymmetrical social influence in freely interacting groups: A test of three models. *Journal of Personality and Social Psychology, 58,* 438–449.

Tindale, R. S., Kameda, T., & Hinsz, V. B. (2003). Group decision making. In M. A. Hogg & J. Cooper (Eds.), *The SAGE handbook of social psychology* (pp. 381–403). London: Sage.

Tindale, R. S., Meisenhelder, H. M., Dykema-Engblade, A. A., & Hogg, M. A. (2001). Shared cognition in small groups. In M. A. Hogg & R. S. Tindale (Eds.), *Blackwell handbook of social psychology: Group processes* (pp. 1–30). Oxford: Blackwell.

Triplett, N. (1898). The dynamogenic factors in pacemaking and competition. *American Journal of Psychology, 9,* 507–533.

Tuckman, B. W. (1965). Developmental sequence in small groups. *Psychological Bulletin, 63,* 384–399.

Turner, J. C. (1981). The experimental social psychology of intergroup behaviour. In J. C. Turner & H. Giles (Eds.), *Intergroup behaviour* (pp. 66–101). Oxford: Blackwell.

Turner, J. C. (1982). Towards a cognitive redefinition of the social group. In H. Tajfel (Ed.), *Social identity and intergroup relations* (pp. 15–40). Cambridge, England: Cambridge University Press.

Turner, J. C. (1991). *Social influence.* Buckingham, England: Open University Press.

Turner, J. C., Hogg, M. A., Oakes, P. J., Reicher, S. D., & Wetherell, M. S. (1987). *Rediscovering the social group: A self-categorization theory.* Oxford: Blackwell.

Turner, J. C., & Oakes, P. J. (1989). Self-categorization and social influence. In P. B. Paulus (Ed.), *The psychology of group influence* (2nd ed., pp. 233–275). Hillsdale, NJ: Erlbaum.

Turner, J. C., Wetherell, M. S., & Hogg, M. A. (1989). Referent informational influence and group polarization. *British Journal of Social Psychology, 28,* 135–147.

Tyler, T. R. (1997). The psychology of legitimacy: A relational perspective on voluntary deference to authorities. *Personality and Social Psychology Review, 1,* 323–345.

Tyler, T. R. (2003). Justice, identity, and leadership. In D. van Knippenberg & M. A. Hogg (Eds.), *Leadership and power: Identity processes in groups and organizations* (pp. 94–108). London: Sage.

Tyler, T. R., & Lind, E. A. (1992). A relational model of authority in groups. In M. P. Zanna (Ed.), *Advances in experimental social psychology* (Vol. 25, pp. 115–191). New York: Academic Press.

Van Knippenberg, D., Van Knippenberg, B., De Cremer, D., & Hogg, M. A. (2004). Leadership, self, and identity: A review and research agenda. *The Leadership Quarterly, 15,* 825–856.

Van Vugt, M., & De Cremer, D. (1999). Leadership in social dilemmas: The effects of group identification on collective actions to provide public goods. *Journal of Personality and Social Psychology, 76,* 587–599.

Van Vugt, M., Hogan, R., & Kaiser, R. (2008). Leadership, followership, and evolution: Some lessons from the past. *American Psychologist, 63,* 182–196.

Vaughan, G. M. (1964). The trans-situational aspect of conforming behavior. *Journal of Personality, 32,* 335–354.

Vermunt, R., Van Knippenberg, D., Van Knippenberg, B., & Blaauw, E. (2001). Self-esteem and outcome fairness: Differential importance of procedural and outcome considerations. *Journal of Applied Psychology, 86,* 621–628.

Vignoles, V. L., Chryssochoou, X., & Breakwell, G. M. (2000). The distinctiveness principle: Identity, meaning, and the bounds of cultural relativity. *Personality and Social Psychology Review, 4,* 337–354.

Vroom, V. H., & Jago, A. G. (1988). *The new leadership.* Englewood Cliffs, NJ: Prentice Hall.

Vroom, V. H., & Yetton, P. W. (1973). *Leadership and decision making.* Pittsburgh, PA: University of Pittsburgh Press.

Walker, I., & Pettigrew, T. F. (1984). Relative deprivation theory: An overview and conceptual critique. *British Journal of Social Psychology, 23,* 301–310.

Wallach, M. A., Kogan, N., & Bem, D. J. (1962). Group influence on individual risk taking. *Journal of Abnormal and Social Psychology, 65,* 75–86.

Walster, E., Walster, G. W., & Berscheid, E. (1978). *Equity theory and research.* Boston: Allyn & Bacon.

Wenzel, M., Mummendey, A., & Waldzus, S. (2007). Superordinate identities and intergroup conflict: The ingroup projection model. *European Review of Social Psychology, 18,* 331–372.

Wenzel, M., Mummendey, A., Weber, U., & Waldzus, S. (2003). The ingroup as pars pro toto: Projection from the ingroup onto the inclusive

category as a precursor to social discrimination. *Personality and Social Psychology Bulletin, 29,* 461–473.

Whittaker, J. O., & Meade, R. D. (1967). Social pressure in the modification and distortion of judgment: A cross-cultural study. *International Journal of Psychology, 2,* 109–113.

Wicker, A. W. (1968). Undermanning, performances, and students' subjective experiences in behavior settings of large and small high schools. *Journal of Personality and Social Psychology, 10,* 25–261.

Wicker, A. W. (1969). Attitudes versus actions: The relationship of verbal and overt behavioral responses to attitude objects. *Journal of Social Issues, 25,* 41–78.

Wilder, D. A. (1977). Perceptions of groups, size of opposition and social influence. *Journal of Experimental Social Psychology, 13,* 253–268.

Williams, K. D. (2001). *Ostracism: The power of silence.* New York: Guilford Press.

Williams, K. D. (2007). Ostracism. *Annual Review of Psychology, 58,* 425–452.

Williams, T. P., & Sogon, S. (1984). Group composition and conforming behavior in Japanese students. *Japanese Psychological Research, 26,* 231–234.

Wittenbaum, G. M., Hubbell, A., & Zuckerman, C. (1999). Mutual enhancement: Toward an understanding of the collective preference for shared information. *Journal of Personality and Social Psychology, 77,* 967–978.

Wittenbaum, G. M., & Moreland, R. L. (2008). Small group research in social psychology: Topics and trends over time. *Social and Personalitiy Psychology Compass, 2,* 187–205.

Wood, W., Lundgren, S., Ouellette, J. A., Busceme, S., & Blackstone, T. (1994). Minority influence: A meta-analytic review of social influence processes. *Psychological Bulletin, 115,* 323–345.

Yamagishi, T., & Kiyonari, T. (2000). The group as the container of generalized reciprocity. *Social Psychology Quarterly, 63,* 116–132.

Yukl, G. (2006). *Leadership in organizations* (6th ed.). Upper Saddle River, NJ: Prentice Hall.

Zajonc, R. B. (1965). Social facilitation. *Science, 149,* 269–274.

Zimbardo, P. G. (1970). The human choice: Individuation, reason, and order versus deindividuation, impulse, and chaos. In W. J. Arnold & D. Levine (Eds.), *Nebraska symposium on motivation 1969* (Vol. 17, pp. 237–307). Lincoln, NE: University of Nebraska Press.

Zimbardo, P. G. (1971). *The Stanford prison experiment.* Script of the slide show.

Zimbardo, P. G., Weisenberg, M., Firestone, I., & Levy, B. (1965). Communication effectiveness in producing public conformity and private attitude change. *Journal of Personality, 33,* 233–256.

Zuckerman, M., Lazzaro, M. M., & Waldgeir, D. (1979). Undermining effects of the foot-in-the-door technique with extrinsic rewards. *Journal of Applied Social Psychology, 9,* 292–296.

Chapter 32

Group Behavior and Performance

J. RICHARD HACKMAN AND NANCY KATZ

Although a scattering of influential empirical studies on group behavior and performance were conducted in the first half of the 20th century (e.g., Shaw, 1932), the psychological study of small groups did not begin to flourish until the war years of the 1940s. In the United States, nearly all available resources, including the nation's scientific talent, were brought to bear on winning World War II. Among the matters for which scientific knowledge was required were the dynamics and performance of small groups—for example, to identify the factors that shaped the performance of infantry squads in combat, or to properly design and lead groups that provided back-home support for the war effort.

The fruits of the research carried out in those years are summarized in the extensive compendia of empirical findings about group behavior and performance published by Hare (1976) and by McGrath and Altman (1966), and in the informative sampling of that research reprinted and discussed in Cartwright and Zander's influential *Group Dynamics* (1953; subsequent editions in 1960 and 1968). Despite often conflicting findings, gaps in knowledge, and a paucity of theory, it appeared that a reasonably solid platform of empirical knowledge about groups had been established. On that platform, surely, there would develop a steady stream of research that, in the Lewinian tradition, would simultaneously advance social psychological theory and provide evidence-based guidance about how best to structure, support, and lead groups of various kinds.

Those lofty aspirations were not fully realized. What had been a robust and fast-flowing stream of social psychological research on groups had by the 1970s gradually diminished to a trickle. Ivan Steiner, who himself had published a landmark text in the field (Steiner, 1972), was

eventually driven to publicly inquire of his scholarly colleagues, "Whatever happened to the group in social psychology?" (Steiner, 1974). The answer, Steiner suggested, was that the revival of interest in individual attitudes documented by McGuire (1969) in the second edition of the *Handbook of Social Psychology* had captured social psychologists' attention to such an extent that group research had entered a state of hibernation.

Research responds to the mood of the times, Steiner hypothesized, but with about a decade lag. The earlier flowering of group research had indeed been in response to the war years and the relatively tranquil period that followed. And, it was the pervasive individualism of the 1960s that prompted the subsequent focus in social psychology on intraindividual processes. The social unrest that characterized the late 1960s and early 1970s, he predicted, would soon reinvigorate small group research.

As John Levine and Richard Moreland documented in the previous edition of the *Handbook of Social Psychology*, it did not happen (Levine & Moreland, 1998; see also McGrath, Arrow, & Berdahl, 2000; Moreland, Hogg, & Hains, 1994; and Steiner, 1986). What happened is that small group research gradually but definitively changed its home address. Although group behavior and performance once again is a highly active field of study, it has moved out of its ancestral home in social psychology. As social psychologists increasingly have drawn upon cognitive neuroscience and evolutionary theories to explain social phenomena, small group research has migrated to the periphery of the field. And the discipline of sociology, now increasingly reliant on the models and methods of economics, has not taken up the slack. These days, it is mainly scholars in schools of communication,

Preparation of this chapter was supported in part by National Science Foundation Research Grant REC-0106070 to Harvard University, with support from Fred Ambrose and the Intelligence Technology Innovation Center. We gratefully acknowledge the research assistance of Sanden Averett and Susan Choi, and the helpful comments provided by Ruth Wageman and members of the Boston area Group workshop.

organizational behavior programs in business schools, and industrial–organizational psychology programs who are doing the bulk of the research on groups (see, for example, Frey, 1999, 2003; Hogg & Tindale, 2001; Ilgin, Hollenbeck, Johnson, & Jundt, 2005; Kozlowski & Bell, 2003; Kozlowski & Ilgen, 2006; Mathieu, Maynard, Rapp, & Gilson, 2008; Salas, Goodwin, & Burke, 2008; Salas, Stagl, & Burke, 2004).

Groups Are Changing

It is a time of transition not just in who is doing research on group behavior and performance but also in the very phenomena under study (Mortensen, 2009). Traditionally, groups tended to be intact, stable, and tightly bounded social systems. Now, the composition of many groups shifts so often that it can be nearly impossible to pin down who actually is a member (Wageman, Nunes, Burruss, & Hackman, 2008). Traditionally, group members tended to be co-located and to interact almost exclusively face to face. Now, many groups are so widely distributed across geographies and time zones that members may never even see one another, relying instead on an ever-expanding set of technological resources to coordinate their activities (O'Leary & Cummings, 2007). Traditionally, most task-performing groups generated some identifiable product, service, or decision. Now, groups handle a much wider variety of tasks that often have considerable complexity and uncertainty, such as providing organizational leadership (Berg, 2005), carrying out negotiations (Behfar, Friedman, & Brett, 2008), and managing organizational change initiatives (Hackman & Edmondson, 2008). Traditionally, work groups in organizations had a designated leader. Now, increasing numbers of groups are self-managing with members sharing leadership responsibilities (Manz & Sims, 1987). Traditionally, groups operated within a single organizational context. Now, groups often include members from two or more different organizations that may have different policies, practices, and cultures (Dess, Rasheed, McLaughlin, & Priem, 1995). And, finally, groups traditionally have been created top–down by an organizational manager or, in the laboratory, by the experimenter. Now, increasing numbers of groups are self-created, often using electronic technologies, to explore shared interests (Shirky, 2008) or to pursue activist social agendas (Andrews, Ganz, Baggetta, Han, & Lin, in press).

An iconic group from the past would be a coal mining team, a clearly bounded and highly stable group whose members are deeply dependent on one another for safely carrying out their collective work, and who commonly spend a considerable portion of their nonwork time together as well (Goodman & Leyden, 1991). An example

of the new kinds of groups that are seen these days is a research team consisting of both university researchers and pharmaceutical company scientists that is charged with investigating a new compound that may have therapeutic potential. These scientists work in laboratories in three different countries located in three different time zones, they communicate and coordinate using electronic technologies exclusively, and group composition gradually changes over time in response to the different expertise that is needed at different stages of the project. This team is emblematic of what Hackman and Wageman (2005b) call *sand dune* teams—dynamic social systems that have fluid rather than fixed composition and boundaries. Just as sand dunes change in number and shape as winds change, teams of various sizes and kinds form and reform within a larger social system in response to changing external demands and requirements.

Chapter Plan

The new group phenomena just described will require those of us who study them to reconsider our traditional conceptual paradigms and research methodologies. In particular, group scholars will need to move beyond reliance on laboratory experiments and survey-based field methods in studies of group dynamics and performance and give greater attention to structural, temporal, and contextual forces that powerfully shape group behavior. In the words of Moreland, Hogg, and Hains (1994), we may need to go "back to the future" if we are to generate conceptually interesting and practically useful theories and findings about new forms of group life. Several approaches to the study of group behavior reviewed in this chapter, although prominent in the early days of the field, have fallen from favor. As will be seen, these approaches offer some possibilities for research and theory that may be especially well suited to the emergent new realities of group life.

The first section of the chapter provides an analysis of just what is meant by the concept "group," exploration of what it means to say that a group is "effective," and identification of the major dimensions that distinguish various types of groups. The second section reviews and analyzes six approaches to the study of groups, each of which provides a distinctive "lens" through which groups can be observed and analyzed.

The third section explores a number of specific issues that lie at the frontier of scholarly work on group behavior and performance. Rather than provide a comprehensive review of all the work that has been carried out on groups since the excellent review by Levine and Moreland (1998) in the last edition of the *Handbook of Social Psychology*, the chapter emphasizes those issues that appear to lie on the present cutting edge of the field—some of which have received substantial attention by contemporary group researchers but others of which have not. Throughout, the focus is exclusively on the group *qua* group; other group-related phenomena, such as group influences on the beliefs, attitudes, and behaviors of individuals and the dynamics of intergroup relationships, are not addressed in detail (for an early review of group influences on individuals, see Hackman, 1992; for analyses of the dynamics of intergroup relations see the chapters by Dvoidio & Gaertner and by Yzerbyt & Demoulin in this volume).

GROUPS AND THEIR ATTRIBUTES

The term "group" is commonly and casually used to refer to an enormous variety of social forms, which is one reason why empirical findings about group and team behavior (we use the two terms interchangeably) have been less cumulative than one would hope and expect. This chapter deals only with the behavior and performance of *purposive groups*—that is, real groups that exist to accomplish something.

Numerous definitions of groups have been proposed in the scholarly literature (e.g., Baron, Kerr, & Miller, 1992; McGrath, 1984; Mohrman, Cohen, & Mohrman, 1995; Offermann & Spiros, 2001). Our use of the term, following Alderfer (1977), is relatively simple and inclusive: *A group is an intact social system, complete with boundaries, interdependence for some shared purpose, and differentiated member roles.* It is possible to distinguish members of groups from nonmembers even if they do not have regular face-to-face contact and even if membership changes frequently. Moreover, members depend on one another in pursuing their collective purposes, and they develop specialized roles within the group as they do so. Casual gatherings of people who have no shared purpose lie outside our domain, as do reference groups, identity groups, and statistical aggregations of the attributes, estimates, or preferences of people who do not actually interact with one another (e.g., the average SAT scores of a college's "group" of incoming students).

As social systems, groups are perceived as entities by both members and nonmembers (Hamilton, Sherman, & Rodgers, 2004), they create and redefine realities, and they generate outcomes that can be legitimately attributed to the group as a unit. The proper concepts for describing groups, therefore, are those that are situated at the group level of analysis, not those that describe the cognitive or affective processes of individual members (Larson & Christensen, 1993). To describe a collective entity such as a group as having thoughts and feelings is to significantly increase the difficulty of explicating how the states and processes of individual persons combine to shape group-level structures and interactions (Hutchins, 1995; James, Joyce, & Slocum, 1988).

Group Purposes and Performance

Because most groups have multiple purposes—some manifest and explicit but others latent and implicit—it is useful to partition them into three sets: those that have mainly to do with (1) accomplishing the work of the group, (2) strengthening the capabilities of the group itself, and (3) fostering the well-being of individual group members.

Accomplishing Work

Most groups, whether in laboratory experiments or field settings, have some piece of work to accomplish—some product, service, decision, or performance. Researchers commonly rely on relatively simple outcome measures to assess how well those groups have done, such as a group's score on an experimental task in the laboratory (e.g., the number of anagrams solved correctly) or organization-specified performance measures in field research (e.g., number of units produced, or an index of customer satisfaction).

In fact, it is conceptually and empirically challenging to develop measures of group performance that are both meaningful and psychometrically adequate. As Pritchard and Watson (1992) point out, the concept "group productivity" has been used in group research far too casually. A valid measure of productivity, they suggest, must consider both the efficiency of the group (i.e., its output relative to inputs) and its effectiveness (i.e., its output relative either to its own goals or to the expectations of others). The Pritchard–Watson approach, although attractive in theory, requires data that can be difficult or impossible to obtain in practice. An alternative that aspires to finesse that difficulty is to identify those who are served or affected by the group and rely on their assessments of the group's performance (Hackman, 2002). Although this approach accepts, for better or for worse, whatever criteria the assessors use, it does recognize the fact that consequences for a group are far more likely to derive from its clients' evaluations than from any researcher-constructed performance measure.

Strengthening Group Capabilities

Some groups have as an explicit purpose building the collective capability of the group *qua* group—for example, a research team or an educational seminar that seeks to enhance the learning capability of the group as a whole. Other examples include a crisis management team that rehearses its response strategy so the team will be ready when and if a real crisis occurs or a student string quartet that does not expect to perform publicly but whose members seek to continuously improve their ability to play together. Even the mere act of engaging in synchronous activities, such as marching, singing, or dancing, apparently can strengthen a group by fostering individual members' attachment to it (Wiltermuth & Heath, 2009). All of these activities can increase the "social capital" of the group, which, according to Oh, Labianca, and Chung (2006), is beneficial both to the group and to its members.

Even though a group can explicitly decide to build its social capital, purposes that have to do with strengthening the group itself often are latent and, therefore, not explicitly acknowledged or addressed by group members or their leaders. For this reason, group-focused purposes have, for the most part, been analyzed more by scholars in the psychodynamic tradition (e.g., Rioch, 1975) than by those who conduct empirical studies of group performance in laboratory or organizational settings.

Fostering Individual Well-Being

Groups also exist that have no specific task other than to foster the learning or well-being of their own members. Such groups are found mainly in schools (Aronson & Patnoe, 1997; Slavin, 1980; Thelen, 1981), in workshops intended to help individuals develop their interpersonal and group skills (Argyris, 1993; Jaques & Salmon (2007), in self-help groups (Alcoholics Anonymous, 2001; Zemore, Kaskutas, & Ammon, 2004), and in therapeutic settings that rely on group techniques to help individuals deal with emotional problems (Joyce, Piper, & Ogrodniczuk, 2007; Yalom & Leszcz, 2005). In all of these settings, the success of the group is a direct function of the degree to which individual members are helped.

Less well recognized and less frequently studied is the impact of group experiences on the members of groups whose manifest purpose is something else, such as accomplishing a piece of work or strengthening the group as a performing unit. In a study of a large number of professional symphony orchestras, Allmendinger, Hackman, and Lehman (1996) found that most orchestras accomplished their main work of performing concerts quite well—but at considerable cost to individual orchestra members. The mean job satisfaction of orchestra players ranked seventh of thirteen different kinds of groups that had been studied. And players ranked ninth of thirteen on satisfaction with opportunities for personal growth and development, just below a group of federal prison guards and just above an industrial production team. Group experiences clearly can contribute positively to member well-being, but they also

can have the opposite effect when the group is structured and led in ways that give collective accomplishment priority over individual well-being.

Group Effectiveness

The simplest way to assess the overall effectiveness of a given group would be to determine the degree to which it has achieved its purposes in each of the three domains just identified. Specifically, a robust assessment of group effectiveness might involve collecting data to generate answers to each of the following three questions (Hackman, 2002):

1. To what extent does the productive output of the group (i.e., its product, service, decision, or performance) meet the standards of the team's clients—the people who receive, review, or use the output?

2. To what extent do the group's social processes enhance members' collective capability to work together interdependently?

3. To what extent does the group experience contribute positively to the learning and personal well-being of individual members?

In practice, there are several nontrivial challenges and complications in using a multidimensional, cross-level criterion of effectiveness such as this. As the orchestra study mentioned previously illustrates, there commonly are tradeoffs among the three purposes. There, the work was accomplished at some cost to its members; one readily can imagine other circumstances in which the reverse would be true or in which building the capabilities of the group itself would be at the expense of the group's task performance. In an experimental study of group decision making by Kaplan (1979), for example, some groups received an intervention intended to improve the quality of members' interpersonal relationships. Compared with control groups that received an innocuous intervention, members became so entranced by their interpersonal explorations that they gave little attention to their work on subsequent tasks and group performance deteriorated significantly.

Moreover, some purposes may be irrelevant or latent for some groups in some circumstances. If a group were charged with a one-shot task of extraordinary importance such as defusing a bomb before it exploded, one would not worry much about the impact of the group experience on the group's capabilities or on members' learning. By contrast, those latter two criteria would be highly relevant for the long-term effectiveness of a police department bomb squad. Even though purposes having to do with group capability and individual learning might be latent rather than manifest, the squad's effectiveness over the long term clearly would be affected by the degree to which those latent purposes were accomplished.

Ultimately, the selection of the criteria to be used in assessing the effectiveness of a purposive group is a value choice. But that reality is often unrecognized or unacknowledged—for example, when a researcher constructs a task that has a simple performance measure such as the right solution to a problem or the number of puzzles solved in a given time, or when a practitioner finds something that can be readily counted, counts it, and then uses that as a measure of the group's effectiveness. Both research and practice would benefit from more thoughtful consideration of the criteria that are used to assess how well a group is performing. Indeed, the mere act of actively discussing with group members the criteria that are most appropriate for assessing their performance can make explicit that which may have been unacknowledged and implicit—and, thereby, increase the chances that the group's performance processes will be well aligned with the very criteria that are being discussed.

How Well Do Groups Perform?

That reasonable-sounding question has engendered a surprising level of partisan fervor. Some scholars, such as Harold Leavitt (1975), enthusiastically tout the benefits of using groups to accomplish work. In a classic essay titled, "Suppose we took groups seriously . . . ," Leavitt suggested that groups generate so many benefits that serious consideration should be given to using groups rather than individuals as the basic building blocks of organizations. Edwin Locke and his colleagues take the contrary position in a provocative article titled, "The importance of the individual in an age of groupism" (Locke et al., 2001). A "group frenzy" has so overtaken organizational life, these authors argue that the critical role of individuals, especially in providing critical thinking, is being lost. Other scholars concur that teams can be time-wasting social forms that coerce people and cap their human potential (Allen & Hecht, 2004; Barker, 1993).

Both sides can marshal ample support for their positions from essays and commentaries to hard empirical data. On one side are books with highly promising titles such as *Hot Groups* (Lipman-Blumen & Leavitt, 1999) and *The Wisdom of Teams* (Katzenbach & Smith, 1993) as well as a good number of empirical studies that document just how well groups can perform. A study by Groysberg, Healy, and Gui (2008), for example, assessed the performance of groups of financial analysts that selected stocks to be purchased. They found that the stocks recommended by a small selection committee (four to six members) performed significantly better than either stocks selected using traditional procedures or those selected by smaller or larger committees. On the other side is Irving Janis's classic work on "groupthink" (discussed later in this chapter) that documents just how wrong groups can be in making highly consequential decisions; the voluminous literature on free-riding (also known as "social loafing" or the "Ringlemann effect") in task-performing groups (Cornes & Sandler, 1996; Karau & Williams, 1993; Mas & Moretti, 2009); and the decidedly mixed research findings about the performance benefits of group brainstorming (Dugosh & Paulus, 2005; Litchfield, 2008; Nijstad & Stroebe, 2006; Parks & Sanna, 1999; Paulus, Dugosh, Dzindolet, Coskun, & Putman, 2002).

Perhaps the most succinct statement of skepticism about group performance is the simple equation that Steiner (1972) used to explore various models of group productivity: $AP = PP - PL$. The actual productivity (AP) of a group, he showed, can be estimated by first identifying its potential productivity (PP, what the group could achieve if all member resources were used optimally) and then subtracting from that the process losses (PL) it experiences—for example, motivation decrements such as free-riding, slippage in coordination, and inappropriate weighting of members' inputs to the group's deliberations. Neither Steiner nor subsequent researchers found it necessary to append a $+ PG$ (process gain) term to his equation. In the skeptical view, then, the question for researchers and theorists is how far below its potential a group will fall, not how much positive synergy members' interactions will generate.

The question of how well groups perform is sufficiently freighted with ideological considerations that it is unlikely ever to be empirically answered in a way that is satisfactory to all. Like many other matters that tap into ideological currents, this one will not be resolved either by meta-analysis or by the design of a "definitive" study whose findings will be convincing both to the group optimists and to the skeptics. In fact, it is the wrong question to ask. It is wrong because it confounds three separate and quite distinct issues:

1. When should groups be used, and when should they not?

2. How does group performance compare to that of individuals?

3. What differentiates groups that realize their full potential from those that do not?

When Groups, When Not In some circumstances there is no choice. Consider, for example, the generic task of flying an aircraft. Only individuals can fly single-seat planes, and only groups can operate planes that require synchronized input from multiple crew members. But technological imperatives such as these are a special case. Are there more general circumstances when groups are an inappropriate or ill-advised means to accomplish a piece of work? Although little systematic research has been done on this question, some evidence is available. Creative composition, for example, involves bringing to the surface, organizing, and expressing thoughts and ideas that are but partially formed or that reside in one's unconscious. As Miles Shore (2008) has found in his research on dyadic creativity, such work is inherently more suitable for individual than for collective performance. Even committee reports—mundane products compared with novels, poems, or musical scores—invariably are better done by one talented individual on behalf of a group than by the group as a whole writing in lockstep. The social system context within which a task is performed also can strongly mitigate against teamwork—for example, when organizational policies, practices, or culture make it impossible to properly design and support teams (Walton & Hackman, 1986).

Groups tend to be remarkably passive when given a task that is inappropriate for a collective work, or when the group is poorly structured or inadequately supported, or when the broader social context is unfriendly to collaboration. A case in point is the arrangement of the physical space in which the group does its work. As Steele (1973) has found, groups tend to view their spatial arrangements as fixed even when their work space could easily be reconfigured. Members are far more likely to unquestioningly soldier on in such circumstances than to rearrange the space to make it more amenable to teamwork. The same may be true for other structural or contextual features that impair group processes or performance: Although they potentially are open to group-initiated change, members take them as given. At present, little is known about the roots of this kind of passivity or what it would take to increase group proactivity about such matters. It would be good to know more.

Group Versus Individual Performance Among the first questions addressed in small group research was the relative performance of individuals and groups (Collins & Guetzkow, 1964) and the matter continues to engage group scholars (e.g., Kerr, MacCoun, & Kramer, 1996; Laughlin, VanderStoep, & Hollingshead, 1991; Stasser & Dietz-Uhler, 2001). In one of the first studies of individual versus group problem solving, Shaw (1932) asked 21 individuals and five four-person groups to solve an intellective problem. Three of the five groups (60%) solved the problem correctly, as did three of the 21 individuals (14%). Shaw concluded that groups were superior at problem solving, perhaps because group members corrected one another's errors as they worked through the problem.

Years later, Marquart (1955) corrected Shaw's logic by noting that any group would be successful in solving Shaw's problem if it included a member who was able to solve it alone. Perhaps, he suggested, the performance of a group was more a matter of its composition than the quality of members' interaction. In a replication of Shaw's study, Marquart created "nominal" groups by randomly assigning individuals who had worked on the problem alone to hypothetical groups that never actually met. The number of nominal groups that contained a member who had solved the problem closely approximated the number of real groups that solved it. The performance of groups on this problem, he demonstrated, reflected the performance of its most competent member. Subsequently, Steiner (1966) noted that the problem used by Shaw and Marquart was a special kind of task for which group performance tracks that of its best member. Steiner then went further and identified five distinct types of tasks for which different combinatorial rules apply:

1. *Disjunctive* tasks, for which the performance of the group as a whole is a direct function of the performance of its best-performing group member. For example: a track team whose score is that of its fastest runner, or a team of mathematicians that succeeds when any member comes up with a proof that works.

2. *Conjunctive* tasks, for which the group operates at the level of its least competent member. For example: a study group in a machine-paced language course, or a roped-together team of mountain climbers.

3. *Additive* tasks, for which group performance is the sum of members' contributions. For example: a production team in which members are working in parallel, or a tug-of-war in which the group's "pull" is the sum of the pulls of all its members.

4. *Compensatory* tasks, for which a group estimate is the simple average of individual members' independent estimates. The expectation is that individuals' errors will be compensated for by others' errors in the opposite direction. For example: estimating the number of beans in a jar or the number of people present at an outdoor event, or predicting next year's fossil fuel consumption.

5. *Complementary* tasks, which can be divided into subtasks that are assigned to different members. For example: a research task that requires different activities for which members may be differentially skilled; assembly of a complex device for which division of labor brings greater efficiency than otherwise would be the case.

By disaggregating the kinds of tasks that groups perform, Steiner laid the groundwork for much more informative comparisons of individual and group performance than previously had been possible. The present lack of consensus among scholars about the relative performance of groups and individuals, noted earlier, reflects in part the fact that groups and individuals are differentially advantaged for the various types of tasks that Steiner identified. It is regrettable that contemporary group scholars do not draw more extensively upon his simple, but powerful, conceptualization in framing and interpreting their research on group behavior and performance.

Achieving Groups' Full Potential   A large group performing a disjunctive task theoretically should do well, because its most competent member should be quite talented indeed. But there is no guarantee, since process problems—in this case, the risk that the best member's contribution will be ignored or lost in the shuffle in a large group—can derail even groups that have the resources needed to perform extraordinarily well (Straus, Parker, Bruce, & Dembrosky, 2009).

More generally, competent individuals, either working alone or in nominal groups, can outperform interacting groups that are poorly structured and supported. And a great group can generate synergistic outcomes that exceed what would be produced even by extraordinarily competent individuals (Laughlin, Bonner, & Miner, 2002) and do so in a way that simultaneously strengthens the group as a performing unit and contributes to the learning and development of individual members. It all depends on the degree to which the group has, and uses well, the full complement of resources that are required for exceptional performance.

An emerging theme in current research on group performance is identification of those aspects of the group's structure, its context, and the behavior of its leaders that, together, increase the likelihood that a group will evolve into an effective performing unit (Ancona & Bresman, 2007; Hackman, 2002; Wageman, Nunes, Burruss, & Hackman, 2008). In this way of thinking, groups are viewed more as social systems that chart their own development than as mechanistic entities in which specific causes are tightly linked to specific effects. Although integrated treatments such as these do draw on research findings about specific factors that affect performance outcomes, their emphasis is on identifying the general conditions that increase the chances that a group will be able to use well its full complement of resources in pursuing its purposes.

Attributes of Purposive Groups

As noted earlier, there has been a proliferation of new forms of groups in recent years, including many that bear only modest resemblance to those that historically have been most prominent in group research—the small groups created by researchers for laboratory experimental studies and the organizational work teams studied by field researchers. As a consequence, the development of cumulative knowledge about group behavior and performance has become more daunting than it was previously, since there is now greater risk that what is learned from research on one type of group may not generalize to groups of different kinds. It may be useful, therefore, to identify the attributes that can be used to partition the universe of purposive groups, thereby facilitating comparisons across types of groups as well as assessments of the external validity of empirical findings about groups of various kinds.

Four attributes that can be used to distinguish among different types of groups are: (1) the degree to which responsibility for achieving group purposes lies primarily with the group as a whole versus with individual members, (2) the degree to which members interact synchronously in real time versus asynchronously at their own discretion, (3) the level of authority groups have to manage their own processes, and (4) the substantive type of work the group is performing.

Responsibility and Synchrony

The first two attributes, taken together, identify four distinct types of purposive groups, shown in Table 32.1. As will be seen, some of these types are both more common and more commonly studied than are others.

Face-to-face groups, the upper right quadrant in the table, are what people usually have in mind when they talk about groups and teams, and most of the existing research literature on group behavior and performance is about them. Members of such groups are co-located and work together interdependently in real time to accomplish purposes for which they are collectively responsible. They most frequently are used when achieving the group's purposes requires coordinated contributions in real time from a diversity of members who have complementary expertise, experience, and perspectives (e.g., Mathieu, Heffner, Goodwin, Salas, & Cannon-Bowers, 2000; Stewart & Barrick, 2000).

Table 32.1 Four Types of Groups

	Responsibility for Achieving Group Purposes	
	Individual Members	Group as a Whole
Level of Synchronicity		
Real-Time Interaction	**"Surgical" Teams**	**Face-to-Face Groups**
Asynchronous Interaction	**Coacting Groups**	**Virtual Teams**

Adapted from Hackman & Wageman (2005).

In the lower right-hand quadrant of the matrix are virtual teams, which sometimes are called distributed or dispersed groups. Members of virtual teams also share responsibility and accountability for accomplishing collective purposes, but they are not co-located and they do not necessarily interact with one another in real time. With the rapid recent advances in information and communication technologies, members are able to interact mainly (and sometimes exclusively) using electronic means and on their own schedules. Virtual teams often are larger, more diverse, and collectively more knowledgeable than those whose members interact face to face. When they work well, they can bring widely dispersed information and expertise to bear on the team's work quickly and efficiently (Kirkman, Rosen, Tesluk, & Gibson, 2004; Townsend, DeMarie, & Hendrickson, 1998). Virtual teams are most frequently used when interdependent work is required but it would be difficult or impossible for team members to perform it face to face. As will be seen later in this chapter, researchers presently are working to identify the special conditions, beyond the mere availability of sophisticated communication capabilities, that are required for such teams to overcome their special challenges.

Groups in the upper-left quadrant are what Brooks (1995) has called surgical teams. Responsibility and accountability for outcomes lies primarily with one person, the surgeon, but accomplishing that work requires coordinated interaction among all members in real time to ensure that he or she has all the information and assistance that members can provide. Brooks noted that the best software development teams are of this type, with members working closely together but with one individual, the lead programmer, having primary responsibility for the quality of the team's product. This kind of team is most often seen when a group's purposes require an extremely high level of individual insight, expertise, or creativity—metaphorically, the writing of a play rather than its performance.

Responsibility for the performance of groups in the lower-left quadrant, which are known as coacting groups, also lies primarily with individual members. Each member's work does not depend upon what the others do, and the output of the group as a whole is simply the aggregation of individual members' contributions. Because there is no particular reason for members to coordinate their activities in real time, they may or may not work in close proximity to one another (when they do not, they are essentially the same as the nominal groups that sometimes are used in research to assess the relative performance of interacting groups). A great deal of organizational work is performed by sets of people that are called teams but that actually are coacting groups. Although coacting groups cannot generate synergistic collective products (because members are merely operating in parallel), they can benefit from social facilitation when members work in one another's presence and therefore can observe others performing the same well-learned task. And, of course, the presence of coactors also can impair performance when the work requires production of unfamiliar responses (Feinberg & Aiello, 2006; Zajonc, 1965) or when the group is so large that members are tempted to free-ride on others' contributions (Harkins & Szymanksi, 1989; Latane, Williams, & Harkins, 1979). Coacting groups are most often found in settings in which there is minimal need for interdependent work by relatively homogeneous sets of group members.

Level of Authority

Four generic functions must be fulfilled when a group pursues its particular purposes (Hackman, 1986). First, of course, is to execute the work. Second is to monitor and manage work processes, collecting and interpreting data about how the group is operating and then making corrections as needed. Third is designing the group itself and securing any outside resources or support that may be needed. Fourth is choosing or defining the purpose itself. Groups vary in the amount of authority they have to fulfill these four functions—the decision-making latitude of some groups is highly restricted, whereas others have control over all aspects of group life and work.

For the most restricted groups, most decision-making authority is held by an external agent. This agent will be referred to as the group's "manager," although in practice the agent may be an experimenter, a therapist, or even some other group, depending on the group's purpose and the setting in which it operates. In a *manager-led* group, members have authority only to actually execute the task; others monitor and manage performance processes, structure the group and its context, and specify overall purposes. This type of group was common in U.S. industry in the decades after the idea of "scientific management" took hold early in the 20th century—managers managed, workers worked, and the distinction between the two rarely was violated (Taylor, 1911). Manager-led groups continue to be seen today, not just in work organizations in which electronic technologies can facilitate continuous monitoring of team activities, but also for performing groups, such as a football team whose coach sends in every play or an orchestra whose players' only responsibility is to execute competently the conductor's instructions (Allmendinger, Hackman, & Lehman, 1996).

A *self-managing* group, in addition to its responsibility for executing the work, also has the authority to monitor and manage its own activities. This type of group has become prominent in organizations that seek to counter the dysfunctions of scientific management by fostering member commitment to collective purposes (Cummings, 1978; Kirkman & Shapiro, 1997; Wall, Kemp, Jackson, & Clegg, 1986; Walton, 1985). It also is commonplace in professional work—for example, a team of research assistants that has the authority to manage data collection processes within constraints set by, and for purposes chosen by, the principal investigator. Groups created in the laboratory for experimental purposes generally are either self-managing or, when instructions are tightly scripted, manager-led.

Members of *self-designing* groups have the authority to modify the structure of the group itself or aspects of its context that affect group behavior. Although others specify the purposes of such groups, members themselves have full authority to do whatever needs to be done to get group purposes accomplished. Many leadership teams in organizations are self-designing, as are task forces of various kinds. A faculty committee given a charge to review the college's curriculum, for example, would be self-designing if members had the authority to change its own composition, perhaps by adding student members, or to alter aspects of its context, perhaps by instructing the registrar to provide enrollment data in a nontraditional format.

Finally, *self-governing* groups have authority to deal with all four of the functions listed earlier: Members decide about the group's purposes, structure the group and aspects of its context, manage their own performance processes, and actually carry out the work. Professional string quartets exemplify self-governing groups (Butterworth, 1990; Murnighan & Conlon, 1991), as do some legislative bodies, corporate boards of directors, volunteer community service groups, and worker cooperatives.

The level of a group's authority powerfully shapes both its internal dynamics and its relationships with those who create, manage, support, or are served by the group (Smith & Berg, 1987). The less powerful group members are relative to their leader or manager, for example, the more they exhibit passivity and obedience in their interactions (Ancona & Nadler, 1989). Authority dynamics rarely are explicitly acknowledged or discussed by group members, in part because it is anxiety-arousing to do so but also because many of those dynamics operate below the level of conscious awareness (Argyris, 1969; Bion, 1961). It is challenging, therefore, to empirically study authority dynamics in laboratory experiments or field studies that rely on standard research methodologies. Even though such dynamics clearly are present in those settings (for example, in the role and behavior of the experimenter in laboratory studies, or the manager in organizational settings), standard research methods are likely to capture only the surface manifestations of deeper and less accessible forces.

Because of these limitations, little is known about the differences in authority dynamics that characterize group interaction in manager-led, self-managing, self-designing, self-governing groups. Research in the psychodynamic tradition, to be discussed later in this chapter, suggests that these dynamics may be quite powerful in shaping what happens in groups that have different levels of authority. But as of this writing, bridges between the psychodynamic tradition and what has been learned from normal science studies of group behavior and performance remain to be built.

Type of Work

There is no shortage of research on groups that perform different kinds of work. To illustrate, here is merely a sampling of the different kinds of groups that have been the subject of empirical research:

Groups that produce things, such as industrial work groups (Abramis, 1990), product development teams (Ancona & Caldwell, 1992b), and software development teams (Faraj & Sproull, 2000).

Groups that provide services to people, such as medical care (Denison & Sutton, 1990), social and community support (Cline, 1999; Howell, Brock, & Hauser, 2003), and psychotherapy (Forsyth, 2001).

Groups that decide things, such as juries (Hastie, Penrod, & Pennington, 1983; Kerr, Niedermeier, & Kaplan, 1999; Stasser & Davis, 1981; Tindale, Nadler, Krebel, & Davis, 2001), personnel selection teams (Tracy & Standerfer, 2003), and policy-making teams (Janis, 1982).

Groups that provide organizational and institutional leadership (Edmondson, Roberto, & Watkins, 2003; Wageman, Nunes, Burruss, & Hackman, 2008).

Groups that advocate and manage change, such as environmental advocacy groups (Ganz & Wageman, 2009), consulting groups (Sherblom, 2003), and organization development groups (Hackman & Edmondson, 2008).

Groups that conduct research, such as intelligence analysis teams (Hackman & Woolley, in press) and scientific collaborations (Cummings & Kiesler, 2005).

Groups that facilitate learning, such as classroom groups (Aronson & Patnoe, 1997; Johnson & Johnson, 1998) and student project teams (Druskat & Kayes, 2000; Gersick, 1990).

Groups that mount performances, such as sports teams (Wood, 1990) and musical ensembles (Murnighan & Conlon, 1991).

Groups that deal with adversarial or crisis situations, such as negotiating teams (Behfar, Friedman, & Brett, 2008), military teams (Salas, Bowers, & Cannon-Bowers, 1995), and crisis management teams (Klein, Ziegert, Knight, & Xiao, 2006).

We have learned a great deal about commonly-studied types of groups, such as juries, manufacturing and service teams, and temporary groups in the special context of the experimental laboratory. But much less is known about how the nature of a group's work affects either the character of group life or the emergent beliefs and attitudes of group members. It is one thing to do intellectual work with professionals, as leadership and consulting teams do, but quite another to put on a performance, to turn out an industrial product, or to engage an adversary in combat. The generalizability of findings from groups that do one kind of work to those that do different things remains mostly unexplored.

It is possible that comparisons across groups that perform different types of work would be at least as informative as comparisons involving the other attributes identified earlier—the degree of synchronicity in group interaction, the locus of responsibility for group outcomes, and the group's level of authority. It is unrealistic, however, to expect that many researchers will conduct research that explicitly compares groups that differ on these attributes. What *is* feasible is for researchers to include in their reports much more detail about the attributes of the groups they have studied than they typically do. That small innovation could greatly assist other scholars in assessing the generality of the findings obtained, and perhaps even prompt new insights about those attributes of groups that are of greatest consequence or conceptual interest.

A standard claim of cultural anthropologists is that any person is in some ways like all other people, like some other people, and like no other person (Kluckhohn & Murray, 1953). The same is true for groups: a particular group is in some ways like all others (which invites the development of general theory), like some others (which invites mid-range theory), and like no other (which invites case studies).

Case studies that focus on the "like no other" reality provide detailed accounts of specific groups but without reference to other groups of other kinds. They are valuable for teaching purposes, to be sure. But they also can provide deep understanding of particular groups that may be of special interest or importance and they can prompt ideas and hypotheses that would not have surfaced in the absence of detailed description.

The reality that all groups are like some other groups invites the development of mid-range theories that address the commonalities among all groups of a particular type, such as all juries or all industrial work teams. Because mid-range theories do not extend to groups of wholly different kinds, they can divert attention from generalities that actually *do* apply to all groups. That raises the third and most ambitious possibility: general theory that does purport to apply to all groups but that also includes

"translation rules" to guide the application of the general-level constructs to particular kinds of groups and contexts. The clarity of a group's goals, for example, is just as meaningful for an open-source programming group as it is for an athletic team or an industrial work group—but its salience, manifestations, and potency surely vary across these settings. Empirical and conceptual work that explicitly addresses the translation from what is known about groups in general to groups of particular kinds could contribute substantially to the eventual development of *demonstrably* general models of group behavior and performance.

APPROACHES TO THE STUDY OF GROUPS

As suggested at the beginning of this chapter, group research is in a transitional period—the phenomena are changing as new group forms emerge, and the scholars who study them now come from a wider range of disciplines than ever before. It also is likely that new conceptual approaches will be required to develop robust understanding of the emerging new forms. If that is so, then it might be instructive to reexamine the scholarly approaches that have guided group research over the decades. Buried in that history are ideas and perspectives that, if taken off the shelf and inspected, could help guide contemporary scholars in further advancing research and theory about group behavior and performance (McGrath, 1997).

This section examines six distinct approaches to the study of groups that have been, or are now becoming, influential in small group research. They are: psychodynamic, network, action, process-focused, decision-analytic, and complex systems approaches. These six approaches are complementary lenses for understanding and studying groups. Each lens brings certain phenomena into sharp focus, yet can obscure other phenomena. Drawing on multiple lenses in analyzing a group, therefore, can generate a substantially more robust understanding than otherwise would be the case.

Other scholars have divided the research into some of the same, but also some different categories (e.g., Poole & Hollingshead, 2005; Wheelan, 2005). This section does not delve into the nuances of these different categorization schemes. Rather, the goal of this section is for each approach to provide a vivid depiction of its origins, to highlight important recent contributions, and to identify its distinctive strengths and prospects.

The Psychodynamic Approach

The psychodynamic approach to the analysis of groups focuses on social and emotional forces that are hidden from view but that nonetheless can powerfully shape individual and group behavior. Although this approach draws heavily on psychoanalytic theories, it originated not with a Viennese analyst but with a French sociologist—Gustave Le Bon. In his book, *The Crowd: A Study of the Popular Mind* (1895/1995), Le Bon asserted that when individuals become part of a group, "the sentiments and ideas of all the persons in the gathering take one and the same direction, and their conscious personality vanishes" (p. 43). The mechanisms for this transformation, according to Le Bon, were heightened affectivity, suggestibility, and emotional contagion.

Le Bon viewed groups as more driven by instincts than individuals, and therefore less rational. He believed the capacity of a group to make wise decisions was always less than the capacity of its individual members. This was true for all groups—not just crowds but also elite groups vested with important decision-making authority. For example, even juries and parliamentary assemblies were, in Le Bon's view, incapable of exercising prudence and good judgment. Imposing democratic structures on such groups, he believed, would not tame their unruly instincts.

Le Bon's pessimistic views were reprised in the early 20th century by British psychologist William McDougall. In his book, *The Group Mind* (1920), written after his psychoanalysis with Carl Jung, McDougall described groups as:

> . . . excessively emotional, impulsive, violent, fickle, inconsistent, irresolute, and extreme in action, displaying only the coarser emotions and the less refined sentiments; extremely suggestible, careless in deliberation, hasty in judgment, incapable of any but the simpler and imperfect forms of reasoning; easily swayed and led, lacking in self-consciousness, devoid of self-respect and sense of responsibility, and apt to be carried away by the consciousness of its own force. (p. 64)

But McDougall did not share Le Bon's view that all groups were condemned to such a fate—only simple, unorganized groups were vulnerable. Organized groups, he asserted, could do better. He identified five conditions that could help in avoiding the worst aspects of group life: (1) a sense of continuity; (2) a sense of collective self consciousness; (3) specialization of functions among members; (4) interaction with other groups; and (5) group-generated traditions, customs, and habits.

Le Bon and McDougall greatly influenced Sigmund Freud's thinking about groups, who cited them approvingly in his essay, "Group Psychology and the Analysis of the Ego" (Freud, 1922/1959). In particular, he resonated with Le Bon's notion that unconscious motives can drive a group's behavior, but, following McDougall,

he also asserted that "organization" can check a group's primitive instincts and enable it to operate rationally. For Freud, organization is to the group what the ego is to the id; it restrains primitive instincts so that the group becomes capable of coordination and control.

The first psychoanalyst to apply Freud's techniques to a group as a whole was Wilfred Bion, whose thinking had been shaped by his mentor and analyst, Melanie Klein. As an officer in the British Army during World War II, Bion accumulated considerable experience working with groups—he led therapy groups in a military psychiatric hospital and also introduced the "leaderless group" as a device for identifying those soldiers who would make the best officers (Bion & Rickman, 1943). From these experiences, he concluded that all groups oscillate between rational and irrational states. When in the rational state, the group is ruled by what Bion called the "work group," focused on the stated task. When in the irrational state, the group is ruled by any one of three "basic assumptions." The basic assumptions operate outside of awareness, but profoundly shape the group's behavior (Bion, 1952, 1961).

According to Bion, the first basic assumption ("dependence") is that the group leader is omniscient and omnipotent, and the group members need his or her protection. The group might resent feeling dependent and helpless but is determined to remain so. The second basic assumption ("pairing") is that the group's purpose is reproduction; the group will, at some future time, bring forth a messianic figure. The group is suffused with optimism. The third basic assumption ("fight or flight") is that the group's life is at risk, and the group faces a choice between battling or running away. The dominant emotion is fear. Only one basic assumption is in evidence at any one moment, but, over time, the group can veer from one assumption to another. These basic assumptions interfere profoundly with the effective functioning of the work group.

If a group is to function well, Bion argued, it must explicitly acknowledge these basic assumptions. When a group brings the basic assumptions into consciousness and consistently interprets them, they lose their destructive power. An essential aspect of competent group functioning, therefore, is to identify and acknowledge the influence of the basic assumptions and the strong emotions they foster so the energy of the basic assumptions can serve the work group.

A more recent exemplar of the psychodynamic approach is the work of Smith and Berg (1987) on the paradoxes of group life. Smith and Berg observe that groups are pervaded by a wide range of tensions that defy members' attempts at resolution and often spawn circular processes that block forward movement. The tensions and contradictions that members experience, Smith and Berg argue, actually reflect true paradoxes—that is, both sides of the tension are simultaneously true. Among the paradoxes of group life they identify is the paradox of trust: "For trust to develop in a group, members must trust the group and the group must trust its members, for it is only through trusting that trust is built" (p. 641). The paradox of identity is "expressed in the struggle of individuals and the group to establish a unique and meaningful identity by attempting to indicate how each is separate from the other, while all the time turning out to actually be affirming the ways each is an integral part of the other" (p. 639). The paradox of authority is that "members must subordinate their autonomy to the group for it to become strong enough to represent members' collective interests; yet, in authorizing the group, members may diminish themselves and lessen the capacities of the group which derives its potency from the strength of its members" (p. 645). Not all group conflicts should be (or even can be) resolved, Smith and Berg argue, because when members think in terms of paradoxes rather than conflicts, it becomes clear that the tensions they are experiencing, although frustrating, are an integral aspect of group life.

Psychodynamic approaches continue to be seen in research on group dynamics, leadership, and intergroup relationships—although more as a trickle than a steady stream (e.g., Alderfer, 1987; Gillette & McCollom, 1990; Heifetz, 1998; Kets de Vries & Carlock, 2007). Psychodynamic constructs seem, on the whole, obsolete. Yet some of the assumptions that undergird the psychodynamic perspective are receiving new validation. Scholars increasingly recognize the power of emotional dynamics and implicit processes in shaping group behavior (Clark & Sline, 2003; McLeod & Kettner-Polley, 2005). Moreover, research on intergroup perceptions using the Implicit Association Test (Nosek, Greenwald, & Banaji, 2007) suggests that forces of which group members are wholly unaware can nonetheless profoundly affect what happens in groups (Dovidio, Kawakami, & Gaertner, 2002).

The Network Approach

The network approach to understanding group behavior, which charts and analyzes the relationships among group members, both complements and contrasts with the work of psychodynamic scholars. It is complementary in that it also focuses on emotions and the affective bonds among people. It departs from the psychodynamic tradition, however, by attending mainly to members' explicit, conscious feelings about one another. Jacob Levy Moreno, the founder of this approach, captures that difference in describing his first meeting, as a young man, with the much-older Sigmund Freud: "I said [to Freud], I start where you leave off. You

meet people in the artificial setting of your office. I meet them on the street and in their homes, in their natural surroundings. You analyze [people's] dreams. I give them the courage to dream again" (Marineau, 1989, p. 30).

Moreno invented the term, the concept, and the methodology of *sociometry*, which captures what he referred to as "the flow of feeling and sentiment" among group members. Moreno's methodology consisted of first surveying all the members of a group to determine their feelings about one another. This would show whether the affect between each member and every other member was positive or negative, and whether that sentiment was one-way or mutual. He then would create a diagram of the group. Each group member would be a node in the diagram, and the lines connecting nodes would represent the ties—positive or negative, uni- or bi-directional—between members. The resultant sociogram revealed what he called the group's depth structure as opposed to its formal structure.

The sociogram was a useful tool for operationalizing group-level constructs (Moreno, 1934, 1943). For example, when the sociogram revealed many mutual positive ties among group members, the group showed high "cohesion." When the network ties formed complex structures, such as chains, triangles, or squares, the group showed high "integration." When there were many mutual repulsions and one-way attractions, the group exhibited "disorganization and disharmony." Moreno applied this technique not only to relationships between individuals in a group, but to relationships between groups and to relationships between individuals and groups.

By tracking the changing pattern of network ties in a group or a society (which he called *sociodynamics*), Moreno believed he could predict many important phenomena, including the type of leadership that would emerge (democratic versus autocratic), the level of morale, the emergence of cliques, the alienation of minority groups, the spread of public opinion, and the distribution of wealth and power. Moreover, he asserted that the extent of the discrepancy between a group's formal social system and its sociogram determined the level of instability and conflict in the group (Moreno, 1934).

Moreno's writings convey an exuberant sense of possibility for what sociometry could contribute to understanding and improving group behavior. He dreamed of a future society in which every group's formal structure would mirror its depth structure, with all people free to join and leave groups as they wished. Under those conditions, every group would be a setting in which creativity and spontaneity were unleashed (Nehnevajsa, 1955). Sociometry thereby could provide "the cornerstone of a still undeveloped science of democracy" (Moreno, 1941, p. 35), which turned out to be a prescient aspiration given the increasing use of electronic technologies to create and deploy social networks in pursuit of democratic ideals (Noveck, 2009; Shirky, 2008).

The sociometric approach found a highly receptive audience in Kurt Lewin, and the journal Moreno founded, *Sociometry*, became the venue for a number of classic studies by Lewin and his colleagues on the social psychology of group behavior (e.g., Lewin & Lippitt, 1938; Lewin, Lippitt, & White, 1939). As early as 1935, Lewin had concluded that the study of groups had reached an impasse and would not realize its value if it continued to focus on purely descriptive analysis. Because Lewin viewed the rigorous, systematic nature of sociometry as a way to illuminate causal relationships through experimental methods, he adopted sociometric techniques for use in his own research.

In 1945, Lewin established the Research Center for Group Dynamics at MIT. The center was devoted to conducting controlled experiments in both laboratory and field settings (Lewin, 1945). The center became an intellectual incubator in which Lewin and his mentees designed imaginative studies of group communication (e.g., Bavelas, 1950; Guetzkow & Gyr, 1954; Guetzkow & Simon, 1955; Leavitt, 1951; Leavitt & Mueller, 1951) that generated hundreds of published articles (Monge & Contractor, 2003).

The early method for studying social networks at the Research Center for Group Dynamics was as follows: Study participants were randomly assigned to seats at adjoining cubicles. Participants could not see one another but could slip written messages to select others through slots in the walls. The researchers constrained who could pass notes to whom, thereby manipulating the pattern of ties and flow of information. Researchers compared the impact of various network configurations (e.g., circle, chain, y, wheel, and all-channel) on group functioning and performance.

After a flurry of early studies, the network approach to studying small groups became dormant from the 1960s through the 1980s. In the last fifteen years, however, this approach has resurfaced with renewed vigor, in part because of the availability of sophisticated software that quantifies key network features and creates visual displays of network patterns. Here is a sampling of findings that illustrate the kinds of things that can be learned from network studies. Groups with more internal ties outperform groups with fewer ties (Baldwin, Bedell, & Johnson, 1997; Reagans & Zuckerman, 2001). Teams with complex tasks perform better if their internal network is relatively decentralized (Sparrowe, Liden, Wayne, & Kraimer, 2001). The internal and external friendship ties of team leaders predict team performance (Mehra, Dixon, Brass, & Robertson, 2006).

Perhaps the greatest strength of the network approach is that it enables researchers to bridge the divide between a group's internal processes and its external context (Katz,

Lazer, Arrow, & Contractor 2004, 2005). With newly available technologies and analytic methods, the approach is now so powerful that network methods may soon become indispensable in social research. As Lazer and colleagues (2009) note, people now leave an enormous number of "digital traces" in their wake every day. By applying network methods to this vast aggregate of data, researchers now can study social processes, including the dynamics of widely distributed groups, at a level of detail never before possible.

The Action Approach

The action approach involves the development and use of group methods specifically to achieve positively valued outcomes. It seeks simultaneously to solve practical problems and to discover general laws of group life (Peters & Robinson, 1984). Typically, the approach involves a spiral process of data collection, feedback of results, and then more data collection—involving throughout, close collaboration with the people being studied.

Action research is most closely identified with Kurt Lewin who, in an early issue of the *Journal of Social Issues*, called on his colleagues to commit themselves to research in which "the diagnosis has to be complemented by comparative studies of the effectiveness of various techniques of change. Research that produces nothing but books will not suffice" (Lewin, 1946/1948, p. 203). Lewin's advocacy of action research was not merely an intellectual interest; it was driven by the profound anti-Semitism he witnessed and experienced while growing up Jewish in Europe. According to his social psychologist daughter, after learning that his mother, aunt, and cousins all had been killed in Nazi concentration camps he resolved to devote the rest of his career to conducting research that would directly combat bigotry and discrimination (Lewin, 1992).

Lewin not only coined the term *action research* but also was a pioneer in conducting it. In explaining why he relied on group methods in his action research projects, Lewin (1947a) wrote:

> Experience in leadership training, in changing of food habits, work production, criminality, alcoholism, prejudices, all seem to indicate that it is usually easier to change individuals formed into a group than to change any one separately. As long as group values are unchanged the individual will resist changes more strongly the farther he is to depart from group standards. If the group standard itself is changed, the resistance which is due to the relation between individual and group standard is eliminated. (p. 34)

One of Lewin's first action research projects was a two-week workshop, conducted in the summer of 1946 with his colleagues from the MIT Group Dynamics Research Laboratory, on behalf of the Advisory Committee on Race Relations of the State of Connecticut. The goal was to enhance the skills of teachers and social workers in dealing with interracial issues, and the primary methodology was small group discussion and role playing. Participants described problems in race relations that they were facing back home and then practiced alternative ways of understanding and dealing with those problems.

The experimental manipulation was based on Lewin's three-step model of change. Step 1 is "unfreezing": Confronted with a dilemma or a disconfirmation of existing beliefs, an individual or group becomes aware of a need for change. Step 2 is "changing": Participants experiment with new ways of behaving. Step 3 is "freezing": The new behavior is evaluated, and if positively reinforced, incorporated into the individual's or group's repertoire. Lewin predicted that those participants who came to the workshop in intact groups from their communities would show greater and more permanent attitudinal and behavioral change than those who came as individuals, thereby affirming the power of the group as a tool for social change.

At the end of the workshop's first day, the research team met to review members' notes and listen to audiotapes of the sessions. To the dismay of the rest of the research team, Lewin invited participants also to sit in on the debriefing. What transpired as participants discussed their behavior and its consequences galvanized everyone present. Here is how Benne (1964) subsequently described the process:

> A research observer might report [from his notes]: At 10:00 A.M. Mrs. X attacked the group leader. Mr. Y came to the defense of the leader, and he and Mrs. X became involved in a heated exchange. Some other members were drawn into taking sides. Other members seemed frightened and tried to make peace. But they were ignored by the combatants. At 10:10 A.M., the leader came in to redirect attention back to the problem, which had been forgotten in the exchange. Mrs. X and Mr. Y continued to contradict each other in the discussion that followed.

> Immediately, Mrs. X denied and Mr. Y defended the accuracy of the observation. Other members reinforced or qualified the data furnished by the observer. In brief, participants began to join observers and training leaders in trying to analyze and interpret behavioral events. . . . Participants reported that they were deriving important understandings of their own behavior and of the behavior of their groups. To the training staff it seemed that a potentially powerful medium and process of reeducation had been, somewhat inadvertently, hit upon. (p. 82)

This experiment—in particular what happened during the informal debriefing sessions—led to a follow-up series

of group workshops at the National Training Laboratory in Bethel, Maine. The Bethel groups were called "basic training groups" ("T-groups" for short). T-groups had multiple purposes: (1) to deepen participants' understanding of group dynamics and development; (2) to develop participants' skill in facilitating group effectiveness; (3) to increase participants' insight into themselves and their impact on others; (4) to provide an opportunity to experiment with new behaviors; (5) to enhance participants' ability to give and receive feedback; and (6) to make constructive use of conflict.

To achieve these aspirations, groups focused on members' thoughts, feelings, and behaviors as they occurred and were experienced in real time. Moreover, they were expected to learn how to engage fully in the group emotionally while simultaneously cultivating an analytic detachment that would allow them to learn from their feelings (Yalom, 1995). T-groups became extremely popular in the 1960s and 1970s as a form of management training and development and provided the foundation for the field of organization development. Offshoots of T-groups, such as sensitivity training and encounter groups, spread beyond industry to the wider culture.

As the years passed, interest in T-Groups began to wane, in part because the lessons participants learned on the "cultural island" that the groups provided tended not to persist in their back home environments. This development was especially troublesome to social psychologist Chris Argyris, who had been a leader in the T-Group movement and who, like Lewin, had great faith in the power of small groups as a crucible for individual change (Argyris, 1964).

Argyris eventually concluded that participants' default assumptions and values about social behavior were too strong to yield even to well-designed and well-led T-Group training. Specifically, he came to believe that behavior in groups is governed by the overriding goals of controlling the task, maximizing winning and minimizing losing, and avoiding embarrassment and threat. Rather than share valid data, Argyris concluded, people keep their true thoughts and feelings to themselves. Rather than test their assumptions and attributions, people discourage honest feedback from others. Disagreement is covered over, and a façade of pleasantness and politeness obscures what is really going on. Moreover, the cover-over is itself covered over. As a result, no one learns anything that is personally meaningful or useful in the wider world.

The only escape from this dead end, Argyris argued, was action research that departs radically from conventional social science. Whereas normal science strives to be objective and value-neutral, he concluded, action research *must* be normative and prescriptive (Argyris, Putnam, & Smith, 1985). The ultimate goal of action research, then, would be to develop a group's capacity for what Argyris calls *double loop learning*—that is, the capability not just to regulate behavior to achieve one's goals but to explore the validity of the goals themselves.

In recent years, scholars continue to explore how best to achieve ambitious objectives, such as those set forth by Lewin and Argyris, even as they draw on the methods and values of action research to pursue other scholarly objectives—from ways to use large groups to create systemic change in organizations or communities in real time (Bunker & Alban, 2006) to the development of group methods for carrying out planned organizational change programs (Hackman & Edmondson, 2008).

Perhaps the greatest overall strength of the action approach is the value it places on collaboration between those who conduct the research and those who participate in it. Researcher–participant collaboration helps keep action research focused on issues that have practical as well as scholarly significance. The risk, however, is that findings from such studies will be relegated to organization development journals rather than mainline academic journals—in which case the action research paradigm could become even more intellectually marginalized than it is now, lose its academic credibility, and fail to have the level of impact to which its founders aspired.

The Process-Focused Approach

> In the early days of "group dynamics," when therapists such as Wilfred Bion reported addressing their groups with interpretations that lumped all participants together, by saying "the group is" (doing or feeling so and so, such as "pairing" or "in flight"), the hair on the back of my neck always bristled in indignation as I read Bion's interpretation. In . . . groups I was always attuned to individual differences and interaction between different individuals and different value positions. I always made a point of looking for dissidents whenever a majority seemed to be forming. And I nearly always found them, even if there was only one of them, back in a corner or looking longingly toward the door. . . . (Bales, 1999, p. 115)

Thus wrote R. Freed Bales, whose system for analyzing group interaction launched the process-focused approach to understanding group behavior and performance. In his early work, Bales showed little interest in, or sympathy for, psychodynamic interpretations, or group members' self-reports about who they did and did not like, or action research that sought to alter how members thought, felt, or behaved. Instead, he set out to chart—concretely, reliably, and in detail—what actually transpires in group interaction (Bales, 1950). It is that insistent focus on group interaction

that is the essence of the process-focused approach to the study of groups.

Bales' particular methodology for assessing group interaction, Interaction Process Analysis (IPA), is a detailed coding system that breaks group interaction into its smallest constituent units, which he called "communication acts." For each act, trained observers record who performed the act, to whom it was directed, when it occurred, and the function it served. With those data in hand, researchers can then document how group members gradually develop distinctive roles, how alliances crystallize into subgroups, how the character of interaction changes over time, and more. Although labor intensive, IPA was so informative about group interaction that it became the standard method for coding group interaction throughout the last half of the 20th century (Forsyth & Burnette, 2005).

The IPA framework grew out of the work of Bales' mentor, sociologist Talcott Parsons. Parsons was perhaps best known for his theory of functionalism, which explains the evolution of societal structures such as economic, legal, and educational institutions in terms of the human needs they fulfill. Bales extended Parsons' theory of functionalism from the level of society to the level of the small group. Specifically, Bales posited that there are certain fundamental issues that every group must resolve. Some of those issues are in the task domain, and some are in the socioemotional domain. In the task domain are the challenges of orientation (developing a shared understanding of the task), evaluation (identifying which ideas to accept and which to reject), and control (keeping the group moving forward). In the socioemotional domain are challenges of decision (how members show agreement and disagreement), tension reduction (for example, by using humor), and reintegration (showing solidarity and support).

Bales found that the task and socioemotional needs of a group are in conflict. Because making progress on the task necessarily produces relational strain, a group needs to establish equilibrium through a cyclic pattern of interaction, with forward movement on the task followed by socioemotional communication that restores interpersonal harmony. He also documented the problems that arise when acts in one category are not balanced by acts in a complementary category. For example, conflict is likely to emerge when "giving opinions" is not balanced by "asking for opinions."

The list of substantive findings obtained using interaction process analysis is long. For example, two leaders typically emerge in a group, one who focuses on the task domain and the other on the socioemotional domain. The larger the group, the more likely one person will dominate.

Most acts in small groups are task-oriented rather than socioemotional. In order to successfully accomplish its task, a group needs more positive than negative communication acts. Newly formed groups progress through a predictable sequence of phases in problem solving: evaluation, orientation, and control (Bales & Strodtbeck, 1951; Seeger, 1983).

As informative as interaction process analysis has been about what actually happens in groups, it generated relatively few findings about what might be done to improve group functioning. Eventually, Bales developed a new model, based on the over five decades of work using IPA, that did have a more normative character. This model, known as SYMLOG ("systematic multiple level observation of groups") draws on multiple sources of data to generate a plot that situates each group member in three-dimensional space: dominant versus submissive, friendly versus unfriendly, and instrumentally controlled versus emotionally expressive (Bales & Cohen, 1979). That plot, which also depicts subgroups and their location in the three-dimensional space, provides an empirical basis for interventions intended to improve group interaction and performance.

In recent years, researchers in the process-focused tradition have been giving increasing attention to the ways patterns of interaction eventually generate stable group structures—a process known as *structuration* (Poole, Seibold, & McPhee, 1985). Structuration explains why groups that have an identical objective situation often carry out their work quite differently (Orlikowski, 2000; Perlow, Gittell, & Katz, 2004). To illustrate, consider the structure of a group's task. Members' work on that task is shaped not only by the objective task structure but also by their own preferences and values about working together. As Wageman and Gordon (2005) have shown, when members share egalitarian values, they are more likely to approach a task as a highly interdependent endeavor, but when they share meritocratic values, they are more likely to approach the same task as a low interdependence activity. Over time, these emergent behavioral patterns become normative and solidify into an aspect of the group's structure.

Overall, the major strength of the processed-focused approach is its capacity to capture nuance and meaning and to produce a rich and data-based understanding of how group members interact. Its major limitation is that generating process-focused descriptions of group interaction is an extremely labor-intensive undertaking. As hardware and software are developed to automate the coding of interaction processes, it is at least possible that the field of small group research will see a resurgence of interest in Bales-type process analyses.

The Decision-Analytic Approach

The decision-analytic approach to studying groups has two distinct research streams. The first stream has its origins in qualitative, case-based methods. The second stream is highly quantitative and largely laboratory-based. Despite these differences in methods, the streams share two key assumptions. One is that the purpose of using a group rather than individuals for decision making is primarily to enhance decision quality. The second is that variations in the quality of group decisions generally can be attributed to the quality of group interaction (Wittenbaum et al., 2004).

The qualitative stream of research originated with the work of Irving Janis with the publication in 1972 of his book, *Victims of Groupthink*. Though Janis was trained as a social psychologist, his method for studying groupthink, comparing case studies drawn from American history, was atypical of most of the social psychological research being conducted at that time. In the introduction to the second edition of the book, he explains how he found himself in that territory:

> The main theme of this book occurred to me while reading [historian] Arthur M. Schlesinger's chapters on the Bay of Pigs in *A Thousand Days*. At first, I was puzzled: How could bright, shrewd men like John F. Kennedy and his advisers be taken in by the CIA's stupid, patchwork plan? I began to wonder whether some kind of psychological contagion, similar to social conformity phenomena observed in studies of small groups, had interfered with their mental alertness. I kept thinking about the implications of this notion until one day I found myself talking about it, in a seminar of mine on group psychology at Yale University. (1982, p. vii)

Janis presented seven detailed case studies in his book, ranging from the decision in 1941 by Admiral Kimmel and his advisors to focus on training rather than on the defense of Pearl Harbor despite signs of an impending attack by Japan to the well-known decision in 1960 by President Kennedy and his advisers to invade Cuba at the Bay of Pigs. Especially well known is the contrast between the Kennedy group's Bay of Pigs fiasco and essentially the same group's successful management of the Cuban missile crisis two years later.

Janis constructed the case studies mainly from secondary sources: minutes of group meetings, diaries, memoirs, letters, prepared statements given to investigating committees, and published documents. These data provided the basis for his model of groupthink, which he specifically defined as "a mode of thinking that people engage in when they are deeply involved in a cohesive ingroup, when the members' strivings for unanimity override their motivation to realistically appraise alternative courses of action" (1982, p. 9).

Janis took pains to make clear that he believed in the potential of groups as effective decision-making units:

> I do not mean to imply that . . . group decisions are typically inefficient or harmful. On the contrary, a group whose members have properly defined roles, with traditions and standard operating procedures that facilitate critical inquiry, is probably capable of making better decisions than any individual in the group who works on the problem alone. And yet the advantages of having decisions made by groups are often lost because of psychological pressures that arise when the members work closely together, share the same values, and above all face a crisis situation in which everyone is subjected to stresses that generate a strong need for affiliation. (1982, p. 12)

The primary strengths of the groupthink model are its clarity, richness, and persuasiveness. Moreover, as Baron (2005) notes, the model offers a broad array of testable hypotheses since Janis carefully delineated the antecedents of groupthink, the symptoms exhibited by a team that is in its throes, and the consequences that follow. For these reasons, a great deal of empirical work has been carried out to test the model (e.g., Esser & Ahlfinger, 2001; Neck & Moorhead, 1992; Tetlock, Peterson, McGuire, Chang, & Feld, 1992) as well as to assess alternative models of groupthink-like phenomena (e.g., Baron, 2005; Kramer, 1998; McCauley, 1998; Raven, 1998; Turner & Pratkanis, 1998; Whyte, 1998). Baron (2005) offers this summary appraisal: "A review of the research and debate about Janis's model leads to the conclusion that after some 30 years of investigation, the evidence has largely failed to support the formulation's more ambitious and controversial predictions. . ." (p. 219).

Despite the decidedly mixed evidence about the validity of the model, it survives and, for the most part, prospers. Textbooks continue to discuss the groupthink model in detail, and it commonly is invoked to explain contemporary group decision-making fiascoes, ranging from the launch of the space shuttle *Challenger* to the Reagan administration's Iran–Contra scandal (Kramer, 1998, p. 238). What accounts for the resilience of groupthink? Clearly, the quality of Janis's writing and his skilled use of case studies play a role—in part because the cases invoke the *availability heuristic* (Aldag & Fuller, 1993). But perhaps most significant is the fact that his hypothesis is counterintuitive for most readers—that is, something people usually think of as good (group cohesiveness) can actually be quite dangerous. Together, these factors have rendered the groupthink hypothesis relatively immune to empirical correction, as badly needed as such corrections have turned out to be.

The second stream of research in the decision-analytic tradition is largely laboratory-based. In the 1960s and 1970s, this stream analyzed the ways group members combine their initial preferences to achieve a consensus position—for example, in jury decision making. More recently, this stream has emphasized the combination of members' information or expertise rather than their simple preferences (Kerr & Tindale, 2004).

Research on social combination models (e.g., Davis 1969, 1973; Kerr, 1981; Laughlin, 1980; Penrod & Hastie, 1981; Shiflett, 1979; Stasser & Davis, 1981) seeks to predict how group members will combine their diverse individual preferences into a single group response. The basic research paradigm requires a group to reach consensus regarding two or more prespecified alternatives (e.g., guilty versus not guilty). The inputs to the group decision are each group member's preference prior to group discussion, with group process simulated through alternative social combination models. Each way of resolving disagreement is represented probabilistically by a different decision rule for reaching consensus, such as voting, turn taking, demonstration, random selection, and the generation of a new alternative. According to Laughlin and Hollingshead (1995), voting can be represented as a majority wins model. Turn taking can be represented as a proportionality process. Demonstration can be represented as a truth wins or truth-supported wins model. Random assignment can be represented by a model that assigns equal probability to any alternative advocated by at least one group member. Researchers compare the actual proportion of groups selecting each decision rule with the proportion expected based on the initial distribution of individuals' preferences.

The type of model that best explains the data turns out to depend heavily on the type of group task being performed. For judgment tasks that have no demonstrably correct answer, majority models best predict the probability of the group choice, for example. For intellective tasks for which a demonstrably correct response exists, truth wins or truth-supported wins models best predict the probability that a group will select the correct answer. But, there is a twist: Unless at least one member advocates an alternative prior to the group discussion, that alternative is rarely even considered by the group and has almost no chance of being selected (Hollingshead, 1996; Laughlin, 1999).

Another line of research in the decision-analytic tradition focuses on how group members share information as they come to a decision or generate the solution to a problem. One benefit of group decision making is that the pooling of information held by different members can result in a more informed decision than otherwise would be the case. But, as demonstrated in a classic paper by Stasser and Titus (1985), groups actually tend to discuss only information that is shared by all members, rather than pieces of information that are uniquely held by single individuals. This phenomenon can compromise the group product both when the information most needed is held by a single individual and when many individuals have separate pieces of information that must be surfaced and integrated for the group to come up with the optimal course of action. As will be discussed later in this chapter, numerous scholars have explored the conditions that increase the likelihood that a group actually will elicit and use appropriately information that is uniquely held by individual members.

The quantitative, laboratory-based stream of research on group decision making is distinguished both by its formal elegance and its predictive power, especially for well-defined tasks such as jury decision making. Relative to qualitative research on group decision making, however, this line of research does not capture the substantive richness of what goes on in groups as members wrestle with difficult decisions—and, therefore, it can come across as relatively dry. Current developments in neuroscience offer new possibilities for exploring some intriguing parallels between groups and brains (Hinsz, Tindale, & Vollrath, 1997), as well as for the conduct of cross-level research on the ways that individual neural processes come to be assembled, through group interaction, into collective decisions.

The Complex Systems Approach

Many decades ago, Kurt Lewin conceptualized groups as holistic and dynamic systems, but at that time the tools needed to conceptually and empirically explore that view were not available. By the mid-1990s, complexity theory seemed to provide both a language and a methodology for bringing that approach to bear on group behavior (Wheelan, 1996).

Joseph McGrath and his colleagues at the University of Illinois took on the challenge of doing so. They had grown increasingly dissatisfied with established methods for studying and conceptualizing group process, for several reasons (McGrath, 1997; McGrath, Arrow, & Berdahl, 2000). First, groups typically were treated as simple systems, composed of chain-like, unidirectional cause–effect relationships. Second, the context in which groups were embedded often was ignored. Third, groups were studied as static entities, without a past or future. And fourth, groups were treated as generic entities, composed of generic people. The Illinois group sought an alternative approach, one that would be less mechanistic and more true to their own experience of group process as a sometimes baffling but always rich mix of routine and surprise, predictability and randomness, the obvious and the obscure. They turned to complex systems theory for that alternative approach.

Complex systems theory is an increasingly popular perspective emerging from work in biology, physics, mathematics, and computer science (Mathews, White, & Long, 1999). As McKelvey (1999) asserts, the study of complex adaptive systems "has become the ultimate in interdisciplinary science, focusing its modeling activities on how microstate events, whether particles, molecules, genes, neurons, human agents, or firms, self-organize into emergent aggregate structures" (p. 5). The basic premise of complexity theory, according to McClure (1998), is as follows: Even though the behaviors of natural systems are not predictable, there are patterns to their randomness or irregularity. Those patterns emerge over time. The aspiration is to track the patterns, both linear and nonlinear; to identify the contingencies that shape them; and to predict the exceptions or deviations from them.

Drawing on these few ideas, McGrath, Arrow, and Berdahl (2000) articulated a new approach to thinking about groups:

> We see groups as complex, adaptive, dynamic systems. Rather than simple, groups are complex entities embedded in a hierarchy of levels and characterized by multiple, bidirectional, and nonlinear causal relations. Rather than isolated, groups are intricately embedded within and have continual mutual adaptation with a number of embedding contexts. Rather than static, groups are inherently dynamic systems, operating via processes that unfold over time, with those processes dependent both on the group's past history and on its anticipated future. (p. 98)

A group is best understood, then, as a complex system made up of individuals who are themselves complex systems, each guided by goals and perceptions that change over time. Each individual belongs to multiple groups at the same time, and these groups are embedded in physical, temporal, sociocultural, and organizational contexts.

The distinctions among local, global, and contextual dynamics are central to the complex systems approach to understanding group behavior. Local dynamics involve the activity of group members and their links to tools and resources to accomplish tasks. Local elements interact with one another in a recursive, nonlinear way, and they cannot be meaningfully decomposed into standard independent and dependent variables (McGrath, Arrow, & Berdahl, 2000, p. 99). The pattern of interaction among local variables generates global variables—emergent aspects of the system, not mere aggregates of local variables—such as norms, cooperation, conflict, and leadership. Moreover, the higher level order that gradually emerges from the chaotic activity of lower level components cannot be fully specified from a detailed understanding of isolated system components. Thus, as Arrow (2005) notes, this approach requires "an appreciation for the paradox of coherent patterns arising out of group behavior that remains unpredictable in its particulars" (p. 202).

Contextual dynamics refer to the impact of system-level parameters whose values are determined in part by the group's embedding context, such as the level of organizational support, the supply of potential members, and the demand for group outputs. The interplay between micro and macro system levels operates in both directions: global variables emerge from local actions but then guide and constrain those same actions. Conventional methods of studying groups are not of much help in sorting this all out. When the elements of a system are strongly and complexly interconnected, for example, it is not useful to decompose that system into its basic elements and then attempt to vary them one at a time to assess their independent effects. In complex systems, the links are as important as the elements, and there are more of them. The focus of research, then, should be on identifying the rules that guide the interactions among variables rather than trying to predict the specific future values of particular variables (Arrow, McGrath, & Berdahl, 2000, p. 46).

A number of researchers have attempted to carry out empirical analyses of small groups as complex systems, including Arrow (1997), Arrow and Burns (2004), Arrow and Crosson (2003), Fuhriman and Burlingame (1994), Guastello (2007), Guastello and Guastello (1998), and Wheelan (1996), sometimes using computational modeling to analyze the dynamics of such systems (Berdahl, 1998). Yet research on group behavior using a complex systems approach has not yet become mainstream, perhaps because the approach poses difficult conceptual challenges and requires use of methodologies that are unfamiliar to most small group researchers. It also may be that the promise of the approach initially was oversold to some extent. As Cohen (1999) has pointed out:

> . . . we need to begin sharpening our appraisal of the promise and limitations of complex systems theories . . . To have real value, such new ideas cannot for very long be characterized as the potential answer to almost every question. A period of testing their applicability across a spectrum of issues is needed. This will help us to determine on which problems the ideas work best, and which are best attacked with other tools. (p. 373)

The period of testing is not yet over. But findings thus far suggest that the main contribution of the complex systems approach may lie in its potential for generating sophisticated answers to the question: What are the factors and conditions that influence group change and development over time? Other questions about small groups,

perhaps, will continue to be most appropriately addressed using other tools. In Arrow's (2005) words, "Work in this perspective is in an early stage of development. We are, in the terminology of the field, working far from equilibrium at the edge of chaos, a state in which creativity and disorganization are both readily available" (p. 202).

CURRENT FRONTIERS OF GROUP RESEARCH

The current flowering of research on purposive groups is generating a number of shoots that extend off into some new empirical and conceptual directions—some of which, as will be seen, have their roots in the intellectual history of the approaches just reviewed. This section explores several specific issues for which contemporary group research appears to be especially productive, promising, or problematic.

Assembly of Member Attributes

In an early review of research on group performance, Collins and Guetzkow (1964) coined the term "assembly effect" to refer to cases in which a group achieves collectively something beyond what could have been achieved by any of its members or by a simple combination of what members bring to the task. An example would be a group decision that is neither the average of individuals' preferences nor the adoption of the prior position of certain members. Although Collins and Guetzkow focused mainly on group performance, the idea of the assembly effect can be applied to any circumstance in which the attributes of individuals come together to create a genuinely *collective* reality. To illustrate, researchers have studied the assembly of members' emotions (Barsade, 2002), motivation (Chen & Kanfer, 2006), self-efficacy (Tasa, Taggar, & Seijtz, 2007), cognitions and concepts (Laughlin, 1999), skills and capabilities (Kozlowsiki, Gully, Nason, & Smith, 1999), social values (Wageman & Gordon, 2005), and personal dispositions and styles (Moynihan & Peterson, 2001).

Group polarization—that is, the tendency to settle on a riskier or more conservative position after group discussion—often is described as if it were an assembly effect (Brown, 1986, Isenberg, 1986). But the great majority of studies of polarization processes actually assess only changes in the level of risk that *individuals* are willing to accept after having discussed their choice with others. Research on group polarization has been more about the impact of group discussion on privately expressed individual preferences than about a genuinely group-level shift.

The attempt by numerous group researchers to generate and study the group-level manifestations of individual-level states, attributes, and processes raises two questions. One, how do assembly processes unfold and what do they generate? And two, which aspects of individuals can be assembled into group-level constructs, and which cannot or should not be?

A number of scholars have addressed these questions. Moreland, Levine, and Wingert (1996) provide a general model of group composition effects, with special attention to how "chemistry" develops in a group. Felps, Mitchell, and Byington (2006) present a model of how the ripples set in motion by troublesome individual members (i.e., "a bad apple") can alter the dynamic of the group as a whole. Kozlowski and his colleagues (Kozlowski, Gully, Nason, & Smith, 1999; Kozlowski, Watola, Nowakowski, Kim, & Botero, 2009) describe the way in which performance processes compile over time and the role of team leaders in facilitating that process. Goldstone, Roberts, and Guerckis (2008) draw a parallel between how neurons interconnect in the brain and how members' interactions result in emergent group processes such as bandwagon effects and population waves. Some researchers have gone even further, adopting the concept of a "group brain" quite literally, asserting that cognition happens not just at the individual level but also at the level of the group as a whole (Larson & Christensen, 1993).

Contemporary Models of Collective Cognition

Collective-level cognitive constructs have achieved considerable currency in contemporary group research and theory (Forbes & Miliken, 1999; Hinsz, Tindale, & Vollrath, 1997). The most prominent of these is the concept of *transactive memory*, developed by Daniel Wegner (Wegner, 1986, 1995; for a review of research on the construct, see Peltokorpi, 2008). Wegner posited that groups, like individuals, have memory systems that collect, encode, store, and retrieve information. Over time, different members of a group come to keep track of different matters, which results in the group as a whole having access to more information than any single individual—transactive memory.

Group members who spend time working together also can develop a *shared mental model*, a related concept that also brings what is known about individual cognition to the group level of analysis (Cannon-Bowers, Salas, & Converse, 1993; Klimoski & Mohammed, 1994; Mathieu, Heffner, Goodwin, Salas, & Cannon-Bowers, 2000). A mental model is a cognitive representation of how some system operates. When group members share the same mental model, coordination is enhanced and the likelihood of miscues is lessened (Ensley & Pearce, 2001; Waller, Gupta, & Giambatista, 2004).

A third collective construct is *collective mind*, which, as set forth by Weick and Roberts (1993), focuses more on cognitive activities than on the mind as an entity: "Our focus is at once on individuals and the collective, since only individuals can contribute to a collective mind, but a collective mind is distinct from an individual mind because it inheres in the pattern of interrelated activities among many people" (p. 360). Collective mind is explicitly social in character because it derives from what Weick and Roberts call "heedful interrelating" among members. The more attentively members interact, the more robust their collective mind will be.

Interpretive Cautions

Group-level cognitive constructs are not without interpretive risks, and the present day is not the first time they have been encountered. Early in the 20th century, William McDougall published *The Group Mind* (1920), which laid out the principles of what he called "collective psychology." The book prompted a blistering response from Floyd Allport (1924). Allport flatly rejected any notion of social cognition, emotion, or behavior, and asserted that McDougall had fallen victim to the group fallacy: "[T]he individual in the crowd behaves just as he would have alone, only more so. . . . There is no psychology of groups that is not essentially and entirely a psychology of individuals" (p. 4).

Although both McDougall and Allport may have stated their cases more vigorously than absolutely necessary, the study of assembly effects is in fact a risky and challenging undertaking. There is, of course, no problem with group-level properties that exist *only* at the collective level—for example, compositional features such as group size or the demographic diversity of members, and structural features such as group norms (whose conceptualization, following Jackson, 1966, centrally involves the variance among members, and variance is meaningful only at the collective level). Group properties that are obtained by aggregating the attributes or behaviors of individual members, however, require interpretive caution. To illustrate, the aggregated property of "group height," obtained by averaging the heights of all members, would seem to make no sense at the group level since only individuals can be tall or short. But, in the context of basketball, the concept becomes meaningful—some teams are indeed "taller" than others.

Aggregated properties often are established when a group is formed (e.g., the overall level of member skills), but they also emerge as a product of members' interactions (e.g., in the enhancement of collective talent as members learn from one another or in the development of a collective point of view about some matter). In either case, group scholars are obligated to establish that the aggregated property has both conceptual meaning and empirical integrity at the group level of analysis (Hackman, 2003; Walsh, 1995).

Concepts that describe group *processes* are more theoretically challenging than those that describe group properties. Descriptors of group decision making, task-performance activities, or learning processes pose no special problems because those processes generate outcomes that can be unambiguously attributed to the group as a collective—that is, a decision, a product, or alterations in how members work together. Difficulties arise, however, when collective processes are described using concepts whose actual referents are the biological, cognitive, or affective functioning of individual persons. It is hard to know exactly what is meant when a group is described as perceiving, thinking, or feeling. Because such invoked processes have no real collective referents, they may be more appropriately viewed as metaphors than as actual group-level realities.

Use of Member Information and Expertise

It is well established, both in research and in practice, that groups rarely draw on the full complement of members' information, knowledge, and expertise in pursuing collective purposes (Argote, Ingram, Levine, & Moreland, 2000; Dahlin, Weingart, & Hinds, 2005; Thomas-Hunt, Ogden, & Neale, 2003) and that group performance suffers as a consequence (Faraj & Sproull, 2000; Gruenfeld, Mannix, Williams, & Neale, 1996). A great deal of research has been conducted to document the reasons why groups underexploit the informational resources and expertise of their members and to identify interventions that might improve that state of affairs.

Vulnerabilities

Decision-making groups generally focus collective attention on information that is shared among all members, rather than on information that is uniquely held by different individuals. Studies of this phenomenon typically employ a *hidden profile* task, in which information that would identify the best alternative is distributed among members and, therefore, is not initially known to everyone in the group (Stasser & Titus, 1985, 2003). Groups performing hidden profile tasks (for example, making a decision about whom to hire or where to locate a business) rely so heavily on shared information that they rarely come up with the best answer unless individual members are somehow prompted to share with the group the information that they uniquely hold (Schulz-Hardt, Brodbeck, Mojzisch, Kerschreiter, & Frey, 2006; van Ginkel & van Knippenberg, 2009).

Not only do groups have difficulty finding ways to get all the relevant information onto the collective table, they also tend to *weight* the knowledge and expertise of their members suboptimally—for example, by misapprehending who actually knows what is needed for the group to make the right decision or turn in a good performance (Littlepage, Robison, & Reddington, 1997). The credence given to a member's contributions often depends much more on that person's demographic attributes (e.g., gender, age, or ethnicity), position (e.g., rank, role, or office), or behavioral style (e.g., talkativeness or verbal dominance) than on the person's actual expertise (Caruso & Woolley, 2008; Hackman & Morris, 1975).

Both overreliance on shared information and flawed weighting processes are generic problems for groups whose purposes require use of member knowledge and expertise. Some groups are considerably more vulnerable to these difficulties than others, however. The new group forms that are now emerging—larger groups with a greater diversity of membership, groups whose composition shifts continuously over time, and groups whose geographically dispersed members rely mainly on electronic technologies for communication—are likely to find managing member information and expertise to be especially challenging. It has been well established, for example, that the larger the group, the greater the chances that worthy individual ideas and insights will be overlooked (Steiner, 1972). The greater the diversity of group membership, the more likely that intergroup stereotypes and conflicts will compromise the full utilization of member resources (Caruso & Woolley, 2008). The more frequently group composition changes, the harder it is for members to keep track of which members have what task-relevant information or expertise (Gruenfeld, Martorana, & Fan, 2000; Lewis, Belliveau, Herndon, & Keller, 2007). And the more that a dispersed group relies on electronic technologies for communication, the more challenging it will be for members to get a good "take" on who knows what (Nemiro, M. M. Beyerlein, Bradley, & S. Beyerlein, 2008).

Overcoming the Vulnerabilities

To use member information and expertise fully and well requires overcoming three hurdles, each of which has been the subject of considerable research. One, the group must *recognize* that certain members do have special information or expertise relevant to the group's work (Bauman & Bonner, 2004; Bunderson, 2003; Littlepage, Robison, & Reddington, 1997). Two, the group must *value* what those individuals have to contribute (Caruso & Woolley, 2008; Scholten, van Knippenberg, Nijstad, & De Dreu, 2007). And three, the group must be sufficiently motivated and coordinated to actually *use* members' knowledge resources

(Faraj & Sproull, 2000; Quigley, Tesluk, Locke, & Bartol, 2007).

A number of conceptual models and empirical studies have sought to identify both the conditions and the leadership interventions that can increase the likelihood that a group actually will recognize, value, and use the information and expertise of its members. Among the structural and contextual factors that have been shown to facilitate use of the full complement of member resources on knowledge tasks are clear and challenging group goals coupled with incentives for achieving them (Quigley, Tesluk, Locke, & Bartol, 2007), a division of cognitive labor that publicly identifies members' areas of special expertise (Stasser, Stewart, & Wittenbaum, 1995), collective accountability for the process by which the team generates its output (Scholten, van Knippenberg, Nijstad, & De Dreu, 2007), an organizational culture that emphasizes shared collective interests rather than individual distinctiveness (Chatman, Polzer, Barsade, & Neale, 1998); and group norms that place a higher value on collaboration and critical thinking than on achieving consensus (Okhuysen & Eisenhardt, 2002; Postmes, Spears, & Cihangir, 2001).

Among the leader interventions that have been found to be helpful are those that elicit and legitimize dissenting views (Schulz-Hardt, Brodbeck, Mojzisch, Kerschreiter, & Frey, 2006); those that ask members to reflect on the group and its work, thereby prompting task representations that encourage them to draw upon one another's knowledge (van Ginkel & van Knippenberg, 2009); and those that invite members to explicitly plan the performance strategy the group will use in carrying out its work (Woolley, Gerbasi, Chabris, Kosslyn, & Hackman, 2008). Indeed, this last study suggests that merely having the right group composition (that is, having in the group people who have the expertise required for task success) can even *impair* group performance unless the group also is helped to use that expertise well. Successful performance of the intelligence analysis task used in the study by Woolley and colleagues required use of certain task-relevant cognitive capabilities. Teams either did or did not include members who had scored at the highest levels on a previously administered test of those capabilities and either did or did not receive an intervention that fostered collaborative planning about the use of those capabilities. Performance was enhanced only when groups were composed of members who had task-appropriate capabilities *and* when groups received the collaborative planning intervention. The presence of high expertise in the absence of the social intervention actually decreased team performance relative to teams that neither had the needed expertise nor received the intervention.

Research on the use of member information and expertise is one of the most vigorous and productive areas in the field of small group research. Additional evidence about the conditions and interventions that promote better utilization of the members' information and capabilities should yield not just advances in small group theory but also empirical findings that can constructively guide the practice of using groups to make decisions and perform work.

Group Learning

Groups are situated at the nexus of individuals and organizations. For that reason, they have considerable potential for fostering not just their own capabilities but also those of their members and of the organization as a whole (Edmondson, 2002; Senge, 1990).

The importance of group learning is widely recognized by scholars, and considerable research has been conducted on the topic (Argote, Gruenfeld, & Naquin, 2001; Kozlowski & Bell, 2008; Sessa & London, 2008). Yet, there remains considerable disagreement about exactly what group learning is. Ellis and his colleagues, for example, define it as a change in a group's level of knowledge and skill, produced by shared experiences (Ellis, Hollenbeck, Ilgen, Porter, & West, 2003). Zellmer-Bruhn and Gibson (2006) view learning as the creation of new collective routines. Gibson and Vermeulen (2003) define it as "a cycle of experimentation, reflective communication, and knowledge codification" (p. 206). Wilson, Goodman, and Cronin (2007) say that group learning is "a change in the group's repertoire of potential behavior . . . whether or not it is manifested in externally observable behavior" (p. 1044).

Despite these definitional disagreements, scholars generally concur with Wilson, Goodman, and Cronin (2007) that group learning involves three sequential processes: sharing, storage, and retrieval. According to these authors, the first process, *sharing*, begins when an individual member gains some new knowledge, learns a new routine, or invents a new behavior. Over time, as members become aware of what their fellow members know or know how to do, collective understanding of the group's overall store of knowledge and capabilities emerges. Eventually, what has been learned by various members becomes a property of the group as a whole—an emergent repertoire that exceeds what is known by any one of them.

Researchers have made considerable progress in identifying the conditions that increase the likelihood that learning-oriented sharing will occur in a group. A key condition for sharing is the level of required interdependence built into the team task, since that gives members both occasion and incentive to learn from one another (Wageman, 1995). Beyond the task itself, a broader array of structures, including specialization, formalization, and hierarchy, also can promote sharing and learning, especially in self-managing teams that may be more in need of structural supports than are manager-led teams (Bunderson & Boumgarden, in press).

Additional factors that have been shown to foster learning-oriented sharing include a climate of psychological safety (Edmondson, 1996, 1999b; Van den Bossche, Gijselaers, Segers, & Kirschner, 2006), a collective sense of group potency or efficacy (Van den Bossche et al., 2006), and strong identification with the group (Van der Vegt & Bunderson, 2005), all of which can be fostered by learning-oriented team leadership. In addition, research has identified a number of specific behaviors by group members that facilitate sharing and that are more likely to be exhibited when the conditions identified earlier are in place. These include speaking up about errors or lapses (Edmondson, 1996; 2003), active listening and communicating (Van den Bossche, Gijselaers, Segers, & Kirschner, 2006), and overt reflection on the group's objectives, strategies, and processes (Schippers, den Hartog, & Koopman, 2008).

Research on *storage*, the second of the three processes posited by Wilson, Goodman, and Cronin (2007), involves use of the group's transactive memory—that is, members' shared awareness of who in a group knows what. Transactive memory, discussed earlier in this chapter, has been shown to facilitate group learning as well as group performance (Austin, 2003; Faraj & Sproull, 2000; Lewis, 2004). Other kinds of repositories also can be useful in storing what is being collectively learned, including shared databases, bulletin boards, and expert systems, as well as standard roles, rules, and procedures developed by the group itself (Argote, 1999). Research is now exploring the differential appropriateness of various kinds of storage systems for different types of group knowledge (Goodman & Darr, 1996).

The third process involved in group learning is the *retrieval* of what has been learned. As Wilson, Goodman, and Cronin (2007) note, "It is not unusual for members of a group to think that they have stored new learning, only to discover that the group does not access it when the next opportunity to apply the learning presents itself" (p. 1050). Although some research has been done on the retrieval process (e.g., Cohen & Bacdayan, 1994; Hollingshead, 1998), much remains unknown about what is required for retrieval to occur smoothly and efficiently.

Group learning is a quite active field of research, but a good number of studies address its core concept only inferentially. That is, some manipulation or intervention is found to improve group performance—and then the inference is made that group learning must have occurred to have generated that improvement. Additional attention to measuring learning processes themselves would be helpful

in deepening knowledge about group learning, especially since learning and group performance are not isomorphic (Druskat & Kayes, 2000). That is, performance can improve in the absence of learning (perhaps merely because of increased effort for some kinds of tasks), and learning does not necessarily generate performance improvements (and, in some circumstances, can even result in performance decrements, as was found by Bunderson and Sutcliffe, 2003, and Wong, 2004). It would be good to know more about the circumstances under which group learning does and does not contribute positively to group performance as well as to the personal learning of individual members and to the collective capabilities of the broader organization in which the group operates.

Group Stability

Conventional wisdom about group stability is pessimistic about the viability and performance of groups whose members stay together for a long time. Although teams may become better at working together in the early phases of their lives, the argument goes, the improvements soon plateau and then, at some point, members become too comfortable with one another, too lax in enforcing standards of behavior, and too willing to forgive teammates' lapses. It is better, therefore, to have a continuous flow-through of members to keep teams fresh and sharp.

Conventional wisdom is wrong. Research findings, from both laboratory and field studies, overwhelmingly support the proposition that teams with stable membership have healthier dynamics and perform better than those that constantly have to deal with the arrival of new members and the departure of veterans. An analysis of National Transportation Safety Board (NTSB) records, for example, revealed that 73% of the incidents in the NTSB database occurred on a crew's first day of flying together, and 44% of those took place on a crew's first flight (National Transportation Safety Board, 1994). That there is a liability of newness in flight crew operations was confirmed in an experimental simulation by Foushee, Lauber, Baetge, and Acomb (1986), in which fatigued crews who had flown together for several days caught and corrected more errors than did well-rested crews who were just starting their work together. Similar findings have been obtained for teams as varied as coal miners (Goodman & Shah, 1992) and construction crews (Hapgood, 1994), and these field study findings documenting the benefits of team stability and longevity are affirmed by a number of laboratory experiments (Argote, Insko, Yovetich, & Romero, 1995; Gruenfeld & Hollingshead, 1993; Lewis, Bellieveau, Herndon, & Keller, 2007; Watson, Michaelsen, & Sharp, 1991).

There are, however, two exceptions to the main body of evidence summarized earlier, both of which have to do with the risk that a group whose members remain together for an extended period eventually will lose touch with critical aspects of the external environment. The first exception is research and development teams, for which there is some evidence in support of the conventional view that the relationship between time together and group performance is curvilinear. In a study of 50 research and development project teams, Katz (1982) found that team performance improved over the first two years that members worked together, remained high until around their fourth year, and then declined. Even if these teams had become increasingly competent in working together over a longer term, their *rate* of improvement would have decreased over time. And without the eventual addition of new members, the gains achieved by long-tenure groups surely would be reversed because of the absence of fresh input from external sources— a matter of some consequence for research teams.

The second exception is the risk that stable, long tenure groups may become increasingly insular and rely excessively on habitual routines for performing their standard tasks (Gersick & Hackman, 1990). When these routines are executed inattentively, which is not uncommon for long tenure groups, the accrued benefits of team longevity can be more than negated by unexpected and unnoticed contextual changes that render standard performance strategies irrelevant or inappropriate.

Mechanisms

Robust understanding of the main research findings about team stability and longevity (i.e., that more is better), as well as the two exceptions just discussed (i.e., research teams and the risk of overreliance on habitual routines), requires consideration of the *mechanisms* that generate these effects (Arrow & McGrath, 1995). Conventional wisdom is right that the longer group members work together, the more they are able to predict one another's behaviors, the more knowledgeable they are about other members' quirks, and the more mutual acceptance they are likely to develop. But, rather than posing problems for the group, these developments make it possible for group members to work together smoothly and, potentially, well.

How does this happen? Research and theory to date have focused mainly on the cognitive explanations previously described—specifically, the development of transactive memory (Wegner, 1986) and the creation of shared mental models. For example, Moreland and his colleagues have shown that groups whose members train together develop transactive memory systems that can significantly enhance group performance (Moreland, 1999; Moreland

& Myaskovsky, 2000). Moreover, they are likely to develop a robust shared mental model of their performance situation, which can both smooth group interaction and facilitate performance effectiveness (Moreland & Argote, 2003).

The benefits of team stability are not merely cognitive, however; affective and emotional processes also evolve as group members gain experience working together. Socialization processes, although generally viewed as applying exclusively to new members, actually continue to operate throughout members' time working together—and they shape the affective tone of a group as well as members' cognitive states (Levine, Moreland, & Choi, 2001). Specifically, affective socialization can reduce the degree to which members, both individually and collectively, experience ambiguity and anxiety and, thereby, can increase team learning capabilities (Goodman & Shah, 1992; also see the section on group learning in this chapter). Moreover, as group members spend more time together—especially if they come to feel that they are doing reasonably well in achieving the group's purposes—they are likely to develop a sense of collective efficacy (Bandura, 2000) and, perhaps, become a more cohesive social unit.

Group cohesiveness, although commonly invoked in distinguishing effective from failing groups, is something of a fraught concept (Beal, Cohen, Burke, & McLendon, 2003; Hogg, 1993; Mullen & Cooper, 1994). On the one hand, it has long been known that cohesive groups generate greater pressures for member conformity (Festinger, 1950) and, moreover, that members of such groups are disposed to accede to those pressures (Lott & Lott, 1965), which can inhibit both team learning and the correction of errors. On the other hand, cohesiveness often is viewed as a desirable state of affairs that helps groups succeed in achieving their purposes (Chang & Bordia, 2001). For lay persons, the latter view is not unreasonable. When one experiences the coincidence of high cohesiveness and group effectiveness, it can be hard to resist the logical error of assuming that the former is responsible for the latter. In fact, cohesiveness is neither as pernicious as the groupthink model posits nor as generally advantageous as lay persons and some scholars occasionally have suggested.

Knowledge about the antecedents and consequences of group cohesiveness has remained unsettled throughout more than 50 years of research on the topic, which may reflect problems with the construct validity of the concept itself, particularly regarding the *basis* of a group's cohesiveness. It has been suggested, for example, that cohesiveness based on a shared commitment to the work of the group is more functional for groups and their members than that based mainly on highly valued social relationships, since a focus on intragroup relationships can be at the expense of attention to changing external realities (Hackman, 1992; Chang & Bordia, 2001; Zaccarro & Lowe, 1988). Until such matters are resolved, any conclusion that the positive features of long tenure groups are due mainly to their greater cohesiveness should be drawn tentatively and with great caution.

Overcoming the Liabilities of Newness

The liabilities of newness discussed previously appear to be of a kind that could be remedied by leadership or consultative interventions that foster alertness to the risks of mindlessly executed habitual routines and that help groups develop strategies for staying closely in touch with developments in their external contexts. It is more challenging to identify ways of dealing with the uncertain and shifting membership of new group forms (e.g., groups with constantly changing composition whose members interact mainly using electronic technologies) as well as those whose primary purpose has to do with the development of the team or its members rather than execution of a specific, finite piece of work (e.g., academic seminars or research teams whose purposes include the development of junior members into autonomous scientists).

One managerial strategy for dealing with these problems would be to emphasize the training of individual members rather than the team as a whole, in hopes that people who have been well trained can be swapped in and out of teams much like parts of a standardized mechanical system. Such a strategy has the potential of minimizing both the inefficiencies involved in starting up a new team and the performance decrements that are encountered as members learn how to work together. This approach has been used with success with military aviators (Leedom & Simon, 1995), but the generality of its applicability remains to be assessed.

A second approach would be to establish team stability and continuity one level higher in the social system in which the team operates. That is, specific teams would form and reform in response to changing circumstances, but the social system from which members are drawn would remain relatively stable. Overall purposes, norms, and contextual supports are properties of the parent system, and would persist over time—only the composition of particular teams would change. Because members could import into those teams what they already know and are ready to execute, some of the normal costs and potential liabilities of team start up would be circumvented. These kinds of teams, which were characterized earlier in this chapter as "sand dune" teams, may be especially appropriate for the new, technology-intensive group and organizational forms that are emerging. It would be good

to have more empirical data about them, especially about the conditions that enable them to operate efficiently and productively.

Compositional Diversity

The study of diversity in groups is an extraordinarily active area of research on a topic of great scholarly and societal importance. Moreover, two superb reviews of the vast and rapidly expanding literature on diversity in groups recently have appeared: an *Annual Review of Psychology* chapter on "Work group diversity" by Daan van Knippenberg and Michaela Schippers (2007) and an analysis of "What differences make a difference?" in *Psychological Science in the Public Interest* by Elizabeth Mannix and Margaret Neale (2005). These reviews, along with an edited volume on diversity and groups in the *Research on Managing Groups and Teams* series (Phillips, 2008), provide comprehensive coverage of developments in research and theory on compositional diversity since the assessment of the state of the field published a decade ago by Williams and O'Reilly (1998).

Rather than undertake yet another review and analysis of the same material, therefore, this section raises some specific issues that appear to have special relevance for understanding diversity in purposive groups that operate within social systems, relying heavily on the insights and analyses provided in the reviews cited earlier.

What Is Compositional Diversity?

It would seem simple to assess how diverse a given group is—just see if the members are different from one another or if they are pretty much the same. But as the reviewers cited earlier have noted and explained in considerable detail, there actually are many different ways of conceptualizing the differences among members. The simplest definition of a "difference" is provided in the Williams and O'Reilly review: "[F]or our purposes, the effects of diversity can result from any attribute people use to tell themselves that another person is different" (1998, p. 81). But, for scholarly purposes, are some differences of greater interest or consequence than others? Which ones and how should they be conceptualized and measured? Although there are no straightforward answers to those questions, both Mannix and Neale (2005) and van Knippenberg and Schippers (2007) find the concept of "faultlines" to be a useful device for dealing with differences among members.

A faultline, as formulated by Lau and Murnighan (1998, 2005), is a constructed category used to divide a group into subgroups using multiple attributes simultaneously—for example, young Hispanic females versus older Asian males. The concept, which has much in common with Alderfer's

(1997) idea of "embedded intergroups," provides a way of partitioning a group that maximizes between-subgroup variation relative to within-subgroup variation. Faultlines have been shown to be an efficient and powerful concept for the analysis of compositional diversity and its effects (Homan, van Knippenberg, Van Kleef, & De Dreu, 2007; Polzer, Crisp, Jarvenpaa, & Kim, 2006).

What Are the Effects of Compositional Diversity?

Both the Mannix–Neale (2005) and van Kinppenberg–Schippers (2007) reviews conclude that there are no substantial main effects of diversity on group outcomes—it neither helps nor impairs groups reliably. Both reviewers then proceed to do what scholars almost always do when a presumably powerful factor does not generate strong, consistent main effects: They search for moderators and they find some good possibilities. That is the slippery slope that has tempted scholars in a wide variety of substantive areas, from the study of psychic phenomena to the search for the traits of effective leaders (to be discussed later in this chapter). As research progresses, so many contingencies are identified and documented that conceptual models become inelegant and practical advice impossible.

Moderators also invite conservatism in thought and action. If it should be, for example, that the effects of compositional diversity depend on certain enduring features of the social system context (Mannix & Neale, 2005, p. 43), what is to be done with that knowledge? Or how might one alter members' deeply seated diversity beliefs and perspectives if they turned out to moderate composition–outcome relationships (as they also do)? The implication would seem to be that homogeneous groups should be created in certain contexts, and diverse groups created in others. But that strategy implicitly overlooks an important reality about compositional diversity—namely, that diverse groups *always* have a greater pool of knowledge, skill, experience, and perspectives than do homogeneous groups. The question is how to capture and utilize those resources.

Beyond Mechanisms and Moderators

Both the Mannix–Neale (2005) and the van Knippenberg–Schippers (2007) reviews delve deeply and informatively into the mechanisms that are responsible for the dynamics of compositionally diverse groups. Multiple social and psychological processes operate simultaneously when group members deal with others who are distinctively different from themselves and their own groups. For one thing, members are more likely to like, affiliate with, and relate harmoniously to similar others. The other side of the same coin is the human tendency to categorize others based on their most salient or distinctive attributes, which can lay the groundwork for stereotyping other group members relative to members of one's own group. Together, these two mechanisms increase the likelihood that, at least initially, the dynamics of diverse groups will be more halting than harmonious.

Harmonious interaction is indeed pleasant, but it does not facilitate group performance or individual learning. Indeed, working through task-based conflicts and disagreements can be more helpful for performance and learning than either smoothing them over or basking in the pleasure of interacting with similar, like-minded colleagues. Once group members come to realize, if they do, that the knowledge, skills, perspectives, and experiences of their diverse teammates are valuable collective resources, group dynamics can become both more interesting and more productive than is typically the case for homogeneous groups.

Although research on the mechanisms that shape the dynamics of diverse groups generates interesting and informative findings, knowing why something happens is not the same thing as knowing how to create it or to repair it when it goes bad. As medical researchers know well, one does not really understand a malady until one can both create and cure it at will. The implications of this view for research on compositional diversity are clear. Rigorous scholarship on mechanisms and moderators should continue unabated. But it also may be of value to supplement those studies with research that is framed quite differently—specifically, to experiment with creating conditions that could increase the chances, although not guarantee, that diverse groups will become increasingly able to identify, value, and actually use the full complement of what their members bring.

Almost certainly such interventions would involve the simultaneous introduction of multiple conditions that are themselves intercorrelated and that may even be redundant in some ways. Introducing multiple, redundant, correlated interventions (independent variables) is of course taboo for scholars who aspire to tease out specific causes that are tightly linked to specific effects. But that is exactly what those who seek to make constructive differences in social systems do. And, interestingly, such interventions also would have a nice resonance with the concept of faultlines, itself a concept with multiple attributes that are intercorrelated within the ecologies of social systems.

Research on compositional diversity has come a long way in the decade since the Williams–O'Reilly (1998) review, as has been impressively demonstrated by Mannix and Neale (2005) and van Knippenberg and Schippers (2007). It may now be time to return to the Lewinian roots of group psychology and devise action research projects that have the potential to further advance knowledge even as they help groups find new ways to cultivate and use well their members' diverse resources.

The Context of Group Behavior and Performance

There are no truly freestanding groups. All groups operate within some broader social system whose properties and processes affect group behavior. Although contextual influences are more frequently discussed in reports of field research than of laboratory research, they also are present and powerful in the experimental laboratory. The difference is that, in the laboratory, they are established by the experimenter rather than by organizational authority figures. It is the experimenter who selects and arranges the physical space in which the research will be conducted, specifies group purposes, decides what rewards will be available and administers them, provides the resources that teams require for their work, and establishes the basic norms of conduct that guide behavior in the setting. In effect, the experimenter creates and manages a social system—albeit a small and temporary one—that serves as the context of the group. Precisely because contexts are so powerful, expert experimenters go to great lengths to ensure that contextual features are standardized for all groups in a given study.

Group contexts rarely are discussed in research reports, however. When context is mentioned at all, it usually is as a constraint on external validity: "Since the findings were obtained in a laboratory setting, generalizations to organizational life should be made with caution." Or: "Because the groups in this study all operated in a bureaucratic organization, the findings may not apply to network-type enterprises." Or: "These findings may not generalize to Asian cultures in which collective outcomes are more highly valued than they are in the United States." Although contextual features can indeed moderate the relationships among other variables, transactions between groups and their contexts also are an integral part of everyday group behavior (Ancona & Caldwell, 1992a; Haas, 2006). As group researchers are gradually coming to recognize, the context is part of the *phenomenon* of group dynamics, not merely a factor that constrains the generalizability of empirical findings about them (Frey, 2003; Ilgen, 1999; Lacey & Gruenfeld, 1999; Putnam & Stohl, 1990; Rousseau & Fried, 2001; Sundstrom, 1999; Wageman, 1999).

Contexts also shape both what is studied and what is found. Certain phenomena are highly constrained in some contexts. If one is interested in studying the effects of task design on group performance, for example, prospects for success are dim if the research is carried out in a setting in which a large number of groups perform essentially the same task, thereby limiting the variability of the very phenomenon under study. By contrast, Sutton and Hargadon (1996) chose to study group brainstorming in a product development firm, in which the phenomenon was both vivid and ubiquitous. The accessibility of certain contexts, moreover, can subtly shape researchers' choices about *what* to study. The ready availability to academically based researchers of laboratory experimental groups, student project teams, and classroom demonstrations such as "survival" and negotiation exercises, for example, can result in bodies of knowledge that may be more influenced than either scholars or research consumers realize by the special features of academic contexts. The following sections identify some specific contextual features that may deserve more attention by group researchers than they typically receive.

Cues and Contingencies

Groups in different contexts routinely deal with different kinds of content—the materials, ideas, or issues with which they work. Top management teams, for example, deal constantly with power and influence; task forces with ideas and plans; human service teams with emotions and relationships; production teams with technology; and so on. As is shown in collections of research studies on different types of teams, these differences in content strongly affect the character of group interaction (Frey, 2003; Hackman, 1990).

It has long been known that context-supplied cues activate the motivational and emotional states of individuals, and the mechanisms that drive these effects are well established (Atkinson, 1954; Schachter, 1964; Schultheiss & Brunstein, 1999). Since all members of any given group experience many of the same cues in the group's context, these states can diffuse across members and spawn a common emotional interpretation of an arousing situation or a heightened (or depressed) level of collective motivation (Brown, 1965; Edmondson, 1999a).

Contexts also differ in the contingencies that link group behaviors with outcomes. In some contexts, for example, achieving group purposes depends mainly on exerting sufficient collective effort; in others, it is more a matter of applying the right knowledge and skill; in still others, it depends heavily on how members approach and execute the work—the group's performance strategy (Hackman & Wageman, 2005a, b). A robust understanding of group behavior and performance, therefore, requires not just knowledge about the cues that are present in its context but also about the behavior–outcome contingences that characterize the social system within which the group operates. A great deal presently is understood about these matters at the individual level of analysis, but much remains to be learned about how they are assembled into processes and properties of the group as a whole.

Purposes, Places, and Resources

With the exception of self-governing groups, the purposes that groups pursue, as well as the places in which they operate and the resources and supports that are available for their work, are contextually supplied. Considerable empirical research has been conducted on certain aspects of the group context, such as reward contingencies (Beersma et al., 2003; Lawler, 2003; Wageman & Baker, 1997; Zenger & Marshall, 2000), the amount and kinds of information groups can obtain (Haas, 2006; Haas & Hansen, 2007; Hargadon, 1999), and the availability of educational resources to foster team learning (Salas, Nichols, & Driskell, 2007). Relatively little systematic evidence has accumulated about the appropriateness of groups' spatial arrangements or the munificence of the material resources that are available for carrying out group work.

Research on physical space would be especially welcome. Many years ago, Hall (1969) and Barker (1968) explored how settings shape social behavior. Hall used the terms "fixed feature space" and "semi-fixed" feature space to refer to the permanence versus moveability of the physical surround. Steele (1973) subsequently added the term "pseudo-fixed feature space" to designate physical features that are readily changeable but that are treated as if they were fixed—for example, when members of a small discussion group meet in a room in which all chairs are aligned in forward-facing rows but do not rearrange them before beginning their discussion. More recent commentators also have discussed how the properties of physical spaces shape and constrain group behavior (Burgoon, 1983; Gladwell, 2000), but the leads they have generated await systematic empirical investigation.

Authorities, Clients, and Other Groups

The contextual influences discussed previously are for the most part subtle, things one might not notice if one were not looking for them. By contrast, authority figures and other groups are among the most pervasive and salient features of a group's context. Few groups can accomplish their purposes without coordinating with external groups and authorities, obtaining information from them, receiving their feedback, or relying on them for assistance of some kind (Ancona & Caldwell, 1992a; Haas, 2006).

The relationship between groups and the authority figures in their contexts has long been of central concern in psychodynamic analyses of group behavior, discussed earlier in this chapter. These days, the field also is seeing substantially increased attention to groups' relationships with *other* groups—those a group serves, those with which it must coordinate to achieve its purposes, and those with which it is in competition (for details, see the chapters in this volume on intergroup relationships by De Dreu and by Yzerbyt & Demoulin). Indeed, the active stream of research in the communications literature on what are called "bona fide" groups gives extensive attention to the intergroup context of group behavior (Stohl & Walker, 2002), including transactions that extend even beyond groups' own organizational boundaries into the external environment (Lacey & Gruenfeld, 1999; Schopler, 1987). As interorganizational relationships become more extensive and more global in reach, it would not be surprising to see research on intergroup coordination become as extensive in future years as research on intragroup interaction has been heretofore.

Collective Values

Perhaps the most powerful contextual feature of all in shaping group behavior and performance is the *value* that the social system within which a group operates places on collaborative work. Some years ago, Walton (1985) identified two general constellations of organizational values, which he refers to as "control" versus "commitment" orientations. In the former, authorities impose control over all aspects of the work in the pursuit of efficiency; in the latter, they seek to generate and utilize member commitment to achieve collective purposes. As Walton subsequently demonstrated, group life was strikingly different under these two sets of values (Walton & Hackman, 1986). In control-type organizations, groups generally were spontaneously formed by organization members themselves to provide social satisfaction and some level of protection for members. Management, at best, ignored such groups and often attempted to kill them off. In commitment-type organizations, by contrast, management actively created and fostered work groups of various kinds and came to depend heavily upon them for accomplishing organizational objectives.

As Walton's research shows, group life is profoundly affected by the values that pervade the broader social system. Further research on the value context of groups, including those that differ across national cultures, could be highly informative in furthering understanding of the other features of organizational contexts discussed previously, as well as the dynamics of group-context relationships more generally.

Temporal Issues

Temporal issues have become an increasingly prominent theme in research on group behavior and performance.

Among the most influential early studies on time were Gersick's (1988, 1989) empirical studies of the temporal pacing of group development, research on the temporal entrainment of group activities by Kelly and McGrath (1985; McGrath & Kelly, 1986), and the analysis by Ancona and Chong (1996) of the ways pace, cycles, and rhythm shape group behavior. There followed numerous books and articles expanding on those topics and exploring other temporal phenomena (e.g., Ancona, Okhuysen, & Perlow, 2001; Blount, 2004; McGrath & Tschan (2004, 2007).

The flow of research on the temporal issues shows no sign of abating. As will be seen in the next section of this chapter, the impact of leader coaching strongly depends upon the time in the group life cycle when it is provided. But temporal dynamics also are consequential for groups in several additional ways described next.

Beginnings

Most frameworks that describe the process of group development specify a number of stages through which groups pass, with movement into each successive stage contingent on successful completion of the previous one. The "forming-storming-norming-performing" sequence described by Tuckman (1965) is perhaps the best known of the stage models. As plausible as the Tuckman model is, research on temporal dynamics in groups has raised questions about its generality and validity. In a field study of the entire life histories of a number of project teams, for example, Gersick (1988) found that each group she tracked developed a distinctive approach to its task immediately after commencing work, and stayed with that approach until almost exactly halfway between its first meeting and the project deadline. At that point, all teams experienced a "midpoint transition" that involved dropping previous patterns of behavior and adopting new roles and performance strategies. This new approach remained in place until near the project deadline, at which time the group focused on a new set of issues having to do with termination.

The most widely discussed of these findings, subsequently replicated in the experimental laboratory (Gersick, 1989), has been the midpoint transition, perhaps because it most clearly signaled that group development is shaped more by temporal factors than by progressing through a fixed series of stages (Okhuysen & Waller, 2002; Waller, Zellmer-Bruhn, & Giambatista, 2002). But equally as important in understanding group development is what happened at the beginning of the lives of the groups she studied—namely, that their initial pattern of interaction, which they typically fell into immediately and without deliberation, established the track on which they stayed for the entire first half of their life cycle. The same thing was found by Ginnett (1993) for an entirely different kind of group—aircraft flightdeck crews. Specifically, what happened during a crew's preflight briefing shaped members' behavior for a considerable time thereafter. Moreover, getting off to a good, fast start may be a prerequisite for success: In a study of high and low performing project teams, Ericksen and Dyer (2004) found that the high performing teams mobilized themselves more quickly and participatively than did low performing teams. The beginning of a group's life or task cycle, it appears, is highly consequential both for the life of the group and for its eventual performance.

Entrainment, Pacing, and Rhythm

The pace and rhythm that will characterize member interaction get established early in a group's life, as groups adjust their activities to synchronize with the phase, periodicity, or other temporal parameters of their work (Ancona & Chong, 1996, p. 36). A specific deadline, for example, can drive the group's pace and that pace will be maintained on subsequent tasks—even when the amount of time available for the subsequent work changes (Kelly & McGrath, 1985). When there is no deadline or it is ambiguous, groups do not establish a pace for their work and tend to flounder (Davis-Sacks, 1990).

Although a temporal anchor may be required for a group to be able to pace itself on a given type of task, entrainment apparently does not persist across different task types. In a study by Harrison, Mohammed, McGrath, Florey, and Vanderstoep (2003), groups that initially were entrained on a certain task changed their pace of work when, on a second trial, they were given a task of a different kind. But they returned to the original pacing when, on a third trial, they once again worked on a task of the first type.

Regular cycles, like time limits, can pace a group and generate a characteristic rhythm for work activities. Semesters in academia have this quality, as do quarters for sales teams in businesses (Gladstein, 1984). And even when there is no natural rhythm, as was the case for teams at a continuously operating semiconductor plant studied by Abramis (1990), arbitrary temporal markers almost always are put in place. At the semiconductor plant, these were six-week production periods. Although these periods had no external referent whatever, they served as the pivot around which all team planning and pacing took place. When natural temporal markers do not exist, we apparently are driven to create them—and then to use them to give rhythm to our work.

Constructions of Time

People differ in both their perspectives on time and their perceptions of temporal markers. Those differences can have profound effects, especially when groups are composed of members from different cultures (Ancona, Okhuysen, & Perlow, 2001; Gibson, Waller, Carpenter, & Conte, 2007). They affect matters of substantive interest, of course, such as how teams experience and deal with deadlines and the duration of time itself. But they also have implications for the methodologies used by group researchers. How, for example, should the temporal aspects of group behavior be studied when there is reason to believe that members may differ substantially in time perspectives or perceptions? What interpretive and external validity issues arise when research is done on groups whose members have a highly restricted time horizon—that is, when members know that they will meet only once for one hour to perform one task? To what extent do the temporal dynamics in such groups differ from those that have an extended or indefinite time horizon, such as the groups tracked by McGrath and his colleagues as their tasks and membership changed over time (McGrath, 1993)? As Ballard, Tschan, and Waller (2008) suggest, temporal issues such as these merit considerably more thought and attention by group researchers than they heretofore have received.

Team Leadership

The paradox about team leadership is this: On the one hand, observers so pervasively attribute to leaders responsibility for team successes and failures that the phenomenon has been characterized as the "leader attribution error" by Hackman and Wageman (2005b) and as part of the "romance of leadership" by Meindl (1990). On the other hand, researchers over the years have been unable to identify the particular traits or behavioral styles that reliably distinguish great from so-so team leaders. Many different attributes of individuals have been found to be modestly associated with rated leader effectiveness and (especially) with who is chosen to occupy leadership positions (for an early review on traits and group behavior, see Mann, 1959; for a contemporary and more trait-sympathetic review, see Zaccaro, 2007). But the usefulness of these findings for guiding either theory development or leadership practice is limited because the size of the empirical relationships typically has been so small.

Alternatives to Traits

If traits are not controlling, then perhaps *anyone* could be an effective group leader if he or she learned the right ways to behave. But no one leadership style has been found that works well across situations—a style that is effective in one situation may not work so well in another (for a review, see Bass, 1990). Research on leader styles, therefore, evolved from a search for the one best style to contingency models

that specify which leader behaviors work best in which circumstances (Fiedler & Garcia, 1987; Vroom & Jago, 1988; 2007). Such models identify those attributes of the situation and of the group being led that determine what leader behaviors are likely to be effective, thereby providing research-based guidance about how leaders ought to behave in various circumstances (for a review, see Yukl, 2002).

As research identifies more and more moderators of the leader behavior–group outcome relationship, contingency models necessarily become so complex that they can require of leaders a level of online cognitive processing that exceeds human capabilities (Gigerenzer, 1999; Simon, 1990). Moreover, direction of causality remains an open question. Although both scholars and lay persons generally view leader behavior as the cause of team behavior, it has long been known that in some circumstances the causal arrow points in the opposite direction (Farris & Lim, 1969; Lowin & Craig, 1968). For example, a team that exhibits cooperation and competence can elicit a considerate, participative leadership style, whereas one that is hostile and incompetent can prompt a more directive style.

These findings suggest that individual differences among leaders may be more usefully dealt with as *competencies* (McClelland, 1973), things the leader knows or knows how to do, rather than as either personality traits or behavioral styles (for a debate on this matter, see Hollenbeck, McCall, & Silzer, 2006). Identification of the competencies most needed for effective team leadership is still a work in progress (Gist & McDonald-Mann, 2000; Salas, Kosarzycki, Tannenbaum, & Carnegie, 2004). Whatever the specifics turn out to be, they clearly will include competencies both in diagnosing social systems (a cognitive capability that centrally involves inductive conceptualization) and in taking constructive action to address group or contextual problems and opportunities (Hackman & Walton, 1986).

Emergent Leadership

Although the main body of leadership research is about individuals who hold formal roles as leaders, scholars are giving increasing attention to the *emergence* of leaders within task-performing teams. This development can be at least partially attributed to the rise of interest in self-managing work teams, especially those that explicitly are designed without anyone designated as the formal team leader (Cohen, Ledford, & Spreitzer, 1996). Initially, research on leadership emergence focused mainly on the personal attributes of those individuals who were most likely to become group leaders. For example, general cognitive ability and certain personality traits, such as conscientiousness and extraversion, have been shown to enhance an individual's standing in the informal group structure (Neubert, 1999; Smith & Foti, 1998; Taggar, Hackett, & Saha, 1999).

More recently, scholars have begun to examine the impact of the behavior of emergent group leaders on group processes and performance. For example, emergent leaders who help a group set realistic goals have been shown to enhance group efficacy (De Souza & Klein, 1995; Pescosolido, 2001); and emergent leaders who help groups manage their emotional processes help foster group identity and solidarity (Pescosolido, 2002). These studies have laid the groundwork for recasting research on group leadership from its historical focus on individuals to an emphasis on the accomplishment of those leadership *functions* that are most critical to group effectiveness (Day, Gronn, & Salas, 2004; Hackman & Wageman, 2005b; Nye, 2008; Nohria & Khurana, 2010).

Leadership Functions

The functional approach to team leadership was first articulated by McGrath (1962), who suggested that a team leader's main job "is to do, or get done, whatever is not being adequately handled for group needs" (p. 5). Effective leaders, therefore, do, in their own idiosyncratic ways, whatever is necessary to ensure that those functions that are critical to the achievement of team purposes are accomplished.

Leadership functions can be partitioned into two general classes: designing the group and providing hands-on group leadership (Hackman & Walton, 1986). The latter class has received the major portion of research attention, from the classic study of autocratic, democratic, and laissez-faire leadership of boys' clubs by Lewin, Lippitt, and White (1939) to the present day. But as Wageman (2001) has shown, it is the former function—getting the group set up right—that turns out to make the most difference. Specifically, she found that leaders' design choices controlled more than four times as much variation in both team self-management and performance effectiveness as did their hands-on coaching activities. Moreover, well-designed teams benefitted greatly from competent leader coaching and were not much hurt by bad coaching. Poorly designed teams, by contrast, were not helped by competent coaching—and were devastated by bad coaching.

Timing

Group researchers are increasingly recognizing that *when* a leadership intervention is made can be as important as the content of that intervention or how skillfully it is delivered. Work by Kozlowski and his colleagues, for example, shows that the kind of leadership assistance teams need depends upon the stage of their development and, moreover, that

there are specific times in the group life cycle when teams are more and less open to receiving leadership interventions (Kozlowski, Gully, McHugh, Salas, & Cannon-Bowers, 1996; Kozlowski, Watola, Nowakowski, Kim, & Botero, 2009). Because the issues that are most salient for a group evolve as it develops, Kozlowski and his colleagues suggest that the proper focus of leader-facilitated "learning sessions" is quite different for newly formed versus mature groups. Similar conclusions are reached by Hackman and Wageman (2005a), who give special attention to the kinds of coaching interventions that are most impactful at the beginnings, midpoints, and ends of task performance cycles. They posit that even competently delivered coaching will not be helpful if it addresses issues that are not alive for a team at the time it is provided.

Overall, research has identified four times when leader actions can make a large and constructive difference in team behavior: (1) before the group even convenes, when the leader can structure the group and arrange for resources and contextual supports that facilitate competent teamwork (e.g., Hackman, 2002); (2) when the group begins work on its task, at which point the leader can bound the group, help members become oriented to one another and to their collective work, and foster collective motivation to perform that work well (e.g., Ginnett, 1993); (3) at the midpoint of the task cycle, when the group has logged some actual experience on the task and the leader can help members reflect on and improve the appropriateness of its performance strategy (e.g., Woolley, 1998); and (4) at the end of the task cycle, when the leader can help members learn from their collective experiences and thereby strengthen the group's overall complement of knowledge and skill (Smith-Jentsch, Cannon-Bowers, Tannenbaum, & Salas, 2008).

Shared Leadership

Shared leadership has been discussed, usually hopefully but not always favorably, since the earliest days of group research (Gibb, 1954). The phenomenon has become increasingly relevant recently as organizations experiment with co-leaders (Heenan & Bennis, 1999) and with widely distributed leadership in self-governing groups and organizations (Cheney, 1999). The research record on the efficacy of shared leadership is decidedly mixed (Pearce & Conger, 2003). On the one hand, when leadership is shared there are by definition more resources available to fulfill leadership functions; on the other, coordination difficulties, social loafing, and struggles for power or dominance can significantly erode the utilization of those resources.

The tension between the risks and benefits of shared leadership are perhaps most vividly seen in leadership teams—that is, teams composed of individual leaders whose collective task is to provide leadership to a broader organizational unit or to a whole enterprise (Berg, 2005; Edmondson, Roberto, & Watkins, 2003; Hambrick, 2007; Wageman, Nunes, Burruss, & Hackman, 2008). Such teams are composed of powerful, competent people who value being on the team and who, collectively, can command whatever resources as are needed to help the team succeed. Yet the teams themselves are underdesigned, underresourced, riddled with undiscussable authority dynamics, and so inefficient that members despair over the time they have to spend in them (Wageman & Hackman, 2010). Precisely because group processes in these teams are simultaneously vivid and fraught, the lessons learned from research on them may be especially useful in identifying what is required for the effective sharing of team leadership more generally.

Collaboration in Dispersed Groups

As organizations become more global in reach and as communications and information processing technologies become more powerful and pervasive, increasing numbers of groups are relying on these technologies for carrying out their work. Technology is evolving so quickly that social science research on virtual and distributed teams necessarily is lagging somewhat behind group and organizational practice. Nonetheless, a good deal has been learned about groups whose members communicate mainly electronically, and the pace of research on such groups is accelerating.

The earliest research on distributed team processes was carried out in the 1990s, and generally involved direct comparisons of face-to-face and "virtual" teams in laboratory settings. These studies treated virtuality as a dichotomous variable: Members interacted either face to face or using electronic technologies exclusively (e.g., Hollingshead, McGrath, & O'Conner, 1993; McLeod, Baron, Marti, & Yoon, 1997; Weisband, 1992). These days, even co-located teams employ one or more forms of computer-mediated interaction, whether email, instant messaging, desktop videoconferencing, file-and-application sharing, group decision support systems, electronic bulletin boards, or real-time calendar and scheduling systems. Thus, virtuality now is more appropriately understood as a matter of degree rather than as identifying a particular type of team (Bell & Kozlowski, 2002; Martins, Gilson, & Maynard, 2004).

Among the teams that rely most extensively on electronic technologies for communication and coordination are those whose members are geographically dispersed. Indeed, a recent analysis by O'Leary and Cummings (2007) suggests that the nature and extent of a team's dispersion, rather than the number or kind of electronic aids a group

uses, may provide the greatest leverage in understanding its dynamics. Specifically, O'Leary and Cummings distinguish among and provide indices for assessing three types of dispersion: spatial, temporal, and configural. Spatial dispersion, the average physical distance among team members, lessens the possibility of face-to-face communication. Temporal dispersion, the extent to which group members' work or awake hours overlap, lessens the possibility of synchronous problem solving. Configural dispersion, the number of different locations where members are located and the distribution of members across those locations, increases the complexity of coordination and subgroup relationships.

Dispersed groups can be just as "real" as face-to-face groups—that is, they can be as bounded, interdependent, and stable over time as those whose members do their work around a common table. The difference is their greater reliance on communication and information processing technologies for planning and executing the team's work. The body of research findings about what commonly are called virtual teams, therefore, can perhaps more appropriately be understood as providing insight into the dynamics of real-but-dispersed teams that necessarily use electronic technologies for communication and coordination.

What Is Known

It is reasonably well established that use of electronic technologies reduces both the overall amount of communication in a group and members' sense of a shared group identity (Bhappu, Griffith, & Northcraft, 1997; Hiltz, Johnson, & Turoff, 1986; Hollingshead, 1996; Straus, 1996), although to a lesser extent for groups whose members have experience working together (Alge, Wiethoff, & Klein, 2003; Bouas & Arrow, 1996). Use of electronic technologies does tend to equalize member participation (Kiesler, Siegel, & McGuire, 1984; Straus, 1996; Zigurs, Poole, & DeSanctis, 1988), as well as to increase the likelihood that minority members will express their views (McLeod, Baron, Marti, & Yoon, 1997), and to reduce members' attentiveness to ingroup–outgroup differences (Bhappu, Griffith, & Northcraft, 1997). These phenomena may occur because electronic technologies mask some social cues and, therefore, attenuate the impact of status differences and subgroup memberships on participation dynamics (Dubrovsky, Kiesler, & Sethna, 1991; Hollingshead, 1996; Sproull & Kiesler, 1986).

The *content* of group interaction can be problematic in groups that use electronic technologies, however. Members are more likely to exhibit uninhibited behavior such as insults, swearing, and name-calling (Siegel, Dubrovsky, Kiesler, & McGuire, 1986; Sproull & Kiesler, 1986). Moreover, they tend to make what Wageman (2003) calls "sinister" attributions about the commitment of teammates who do not respond quickly enough to team needs. When communications break down because of a technological failure, for example, the resulting silence may be wrongly assumed to reflect a member's poor work ethic (Cramton & Orvis, 2003).

Although teams that rely on electronic technologies do *not* apply less effort to their work than face-to-face teams, reliance on electronic technologies does impair group performance for tasks that require high levels of coordination in real time (Shepherd, Briggs, Reinig, Yen, & Nunamaker, 1996; Siegel, Dubrovsky, Kiesler, & McGuire, 1986; Straus & McGrath, 1994). Such groups generally take longer to get things done (Graetz, Boyle, Kimble, Thompson, & Garloch, 1998; Hollingshead, 1996; Straus, 1996; Weisband, 1992), and they tend to have problems staying on schedule and budget (McDonough, Kahn, & Barczak, 2001). Beyond the reality that typing is slower than talking, members of groups that communicate using computers also may be tempted to multitask while at the computer rather than to focus exclusively on the team's work (Lebie, Rhoades, & McGrath, 1996; Malhotra, Majchrzak, Carman, & Lott, 2001).

Research Frontiers

Advanced communication and computational technologies have become commonplace in collaborative work. Sometimes it is a matter of necessity, such as for groups whose members are globally dispersed. Or it may be for economic reasons—to lessen the costs in time and travel for group meetings. Or it may simply be because younger members have grown up with such technologies and would find it strange *not* to use them routinely. It may be time, therefore, for group scholars to move beyond studies that further document the risks and benefits of electronic technologies and to focus more on identifying the conditions that increase the likelihood that groups will use them well. Such a development would parallel what is happening in research on compositional diversity discussed earlier—movement from documentation of the main effect risks and benefits of diversity to identification of the conditions that enable groups to recognize, value, and fully utilize their members' differences.

Although it is not yet known what conditions will emerge as most critical in fostering the effective use of electronic tools by groups, one point of departure for research and theory could be what is already known about the conditions that foster team effectiveness (Gibson & Cohen, 2003). It is reasonably well established, for example, that performance is facilitated when teams are small and compositionally stable with clear, but permeable, boundaries and interdependence for some consequential

shared purpose (Hackman, 2002). What is *not* known is whether these same conditions are critical for teams whose members heavily use electronic means of communication and coordination. One could argue, for example, that electronic technologies render team structures less critical than otherwise would be the case, since these technologies make it possible for members to continuously and autonomously adjust in real time everything from their work strategies to the composition of the group itself. But, one also could argue that enabling structures are *more* important for technology-intensive dispersed groups because such groups run a greater risk of devolving into disorder and disorganization than those whose members work in the same place at the same time. Whatever the key conditions for effectiveness for dispersed teams turn out to be, it surely will be a significant team leadership challenge to create and maintain them when members are scattered across geographies and time zones—also a matter worthy of attention by group researchers (Cummings, 2007).

Another research challenge is to identify the proper mix of face-to-face and electronically mediated interaction. Research has shown that it is helpful to temper electronic collaboration in dispersed teams with periodic face-to-face interaction (Maznevski & Chudoba, 2001). The emerging question is to determine when in the team life cycle face-to-face contact is most useful. Studies of the temporal aspects of group leadership (discussed earlier) identified beginnings, midpoints, and ends as times when groups are most ready to accept and make use of leadership interventions. Might these three times also be ones when face-to-face interaction is most useful? The importance of face-to-face engagement at the beginning of a group's work has been empirically demonstrated (DeMeyer, 1991; Robey, Khoo, & Powers, 2000). Midpoints and ends of task cycles might also be times when it would be helpful for group members to come physically together to debrief and to reflect on how they might best utilize their electronic resources in carrying out their collective work.

The number of different technologies available for use by task-performing groups has increased dramatically in recent years, and the rate of growth shows no sign of abating. Indeed, a sufficient diversity of electronic resources has accumulated that it may now be possible to empirically identify those types of technologies that are, and are not, especially useful to groups that perform different types of tasks—for example, those that involve the generation of ideas versus the evaluation of issues versus the implementation of actions. As knowledge about such task by technology interactions accumulates, groups will become increasingly able to wisely select the kinds of electronic resources that are most appropriate for their particular circumstances. And, perhaps, they may become less inclined than some groups are at present either to resist using such technologies at all or, alternatively, to adopt relatively mindlessly whatever new technological resources as become available.

CONCLUSION

As noted at the outset of this chapter, groups evoke strong feelings—people tend either to love them or to despair of them. Scholars, through their research, pull in the tails of this distribution as they identify and document the structures, contexts, and leader behaviors that can help groups circumvent their nastiest dysfunctions—and, occasionally, capture the synergies of which the best groups actually are capable. The aspiration of this chapter has been to provide scholarly readers an enriched understanding of the intellectual history of group research as well as an overview of the current frontiers of the field.

The 1940s and 1950s were heady days for group research, a time when a variety of approaches were tried, found to not quite provide what was needed, and then were supplanted by fresh ideas about how to study group behavior and performance. The lessons learned in those years have much to teach contemporary group researchers. Specifically, the six approaches reviewed in this chapter—the psychodynamic, network, action, process-focused, decision-analytic, and complex systems approaches—offer some tantalizing leads for the future.

The psychodynamic approach reminds us that some of the most powerful influences on group dynamics are implicit and mostly hidden from view. The network approach invites us to apply today's powerful computational tools to generate new understanding of the evolution over time of relationships within and among groups. The action approach cautions us not to focus too much on the search for tight causal links between inputs, processes, and outputs and, instead, to explore ways to create conditions that foster the achievement of normatively valued outcomes. The process-focused approach also orients our attention to computational tools, this time to chart patterns of member interaction—who says what, to whom, when, with what effect—at a level of detail never before possible. The decision-analytic approach offers a way to go beyond the search for additional cognitive dysfunctions and to seek instead strategies that help groups draw on the full complement of members' information and expertise in making collective judgments and decisions. And the complex systems approach reminds us that groups, even if small and short-lived, really are dynamic social systems that create and redefine the very realities that shape their own behavior.

In 1974, Ivan Steiner ended his classic *Journal of Experimental Social Psychology* article on "Whatever Happened to the Group in Social Psychology?" with these words: "If the tea leaves tell me true, social psychology in the late 1970s is going to look a lot like social psychology in the late 1940s—better, of course, but groupy once more" (Steiner, p. 106). It did not happen back then, but if we combine the lessons from the history of small group research with the knowledge and research tools that now have become available, it very well could be that Steiner was absolutely right—if just a few decades early.

REFERENCES

Abramis, D. J. (1990). Semiconductor manufacturing team. In J. R. Hackman (Ed.), *Groups that work (and those that don't)* (pp. 449–470). San Francisco: Jossey Bass.

Alcoholics Anonymous. (2001). *Alcoholics anonymous.* New York: Alcoholics Anonymous World Services.

Aldag, R. J., & Fuller, S. R. (1993). Beyond fiasco: A reappraisal of the groupthink phenomenon and a new model of group decision processes. *Psychological Bulletin, 112,* 533–552.

Alderfer, C. P. (1977). Group and intergroup relations. In J. R. Hackman & J. L. Suttle (Eds.), *Improving life at work* (pp. 227–296). Santa Monica, CA: Goodyear.

Alderfer, C. P. (1987). An intergroup perspective on group dynamics. In J. Lorsch (Ed.), *Handbook of organizational behavior* (pp. 190–222). Englewood Cliffs, NJ: Prentice-Hall.

Alderfer, C. P. (1997). Embedded intergroup relations and racial identity theory. In C. E. Thompson & R. T. Carter (Eds.), *Applications of racial identity development theory: Individual, group, and organizational interventions* (pp. 237–263). Hillsdale, NJ: Erlbaum.

Alge, B. J., Wiethoff, C., & Klein, H. J. (2003). When does the medium matter? Knowledge-building experiences and opportunities in decision-making teams. *Organizational Behavior and Human Decision Processes, 91,* 26–37.

Allen, N. J., & Hecht, T. D. (2004). The "romance of teams": Toward an understanding of its psychological underpinnings and implications. *Journal of Occupational and Organizational Psychology, 77,* 439–461.

Allmendinger, J., Hackman, J. R., & Lehman, E. V. (1996). Life and work in symphony orchestras. *The Musical Quarterly, 80,* 194–219.

Allport, F. H. (1924). *Social psychology.* Boston: Houghton Mifflin.

Ancona, D., & Bresman, H. (2007). *X-teams: How to build teams that lead, innovate, and succeed.* Boston: Harvard Business School Press.

Ancona, D. G., & Caldwell, D. F. (1992a). Bridging the boundary: External activity and performance in organizational teams. *Administrative Science Quarterly, 37,* 634–665.

Ancona, D. G., & Caldwell, D. F. (1992b). Demography and design: Predictors of new product team performance. *Organization Science, 3,* 321–341.

Ancona, D. G., & Chong, C. (1996). Entrainment: Pace, cycle, and rhythm in organizational behavior. *Research in Organizational Behavior, 18,* 251–284.

Ancona, D. G., & Nadler, D. A. (1989, Fall). Top hats and executive tales: Designing the senior team. *Sloan Management Review,* 19–29.

Ancona, D. G., Okhuysen, G. A., & Perlow, L. A. (2001). Taking time to integrate temporal research. *Academy of Management Review, 26,* 512–529.

Andrews, K. T., Ganz, M., Baggetta, M., Han, H., & Lin, C. (in press). Leadership, membership, and voice: Civic associations that work. *American Journal of Sociology.*

Argote, L. (1999). *Organizational learning: Creating, retaining, and transferring knowledge.* Norwell, MA: Kluwer.

Argote, L., Gruenfeld, D., & Naquin, C. (2001). Group learning in organizations. In M. E. Turner (Ed.), *Groups at work: Theory and research* (pp. 369–411). Mahwah, NJ: Erlbaum.

Argote, L., Ingram, P., Levine, J. M., & Moreland, R. L. (2000). Knowledge transfer in organizations: Learning from the experience of others. *Organizational Behavior and Human Decision Processes, 82,* 1–8.

Argote, L., Insko, C. A., Yovetich, N., & Romero, A. A. (1995). Group learning curves: The effects of turnover and task complexity on group performance. *Journal of Applied Social Psychology, 25,* 512–529.

Argyris, C. (1964). T-Groups for organizational effectiveness. *Harvard Business Review, 42*(2), 60–74.

Argyris, C. (1969). The incompleteness of social psychological theory: Examples from small group, cognitive consistency, and attribution research. *American Psychologist, 24,* 893–908.

Argyris, C. (1993). Education for leading–learning. *Organizational Dynamics, 21*(3), 5–17.

Argyris, C., Putnam, R., & Smith, D. M. (1985). *Action science.* San Francisco: Jossey-Bass.

Aronson, E., & Patnoe, S. (1997). *The jigsaw method: Building cooperation in the classroom* (2nd ed.). New York: Longman.

Arrow, H. (1997). Stability, bistability, and instability in small group influence patterns. *Journal of Personality and Social Psychology, 72,* 75–85.

Arrow, H. (2005). Chaos, complexity, and catastrophe: The nonlinear dynamics perspective. In S. A. Wheelan (Ed.), *The handbook of group research and practice* (pp. 201–220). Thousand Oaks, CA: Sage.

Arrow, H., & Burns, K. L. (2004). Self-organizing culture: How norms emerge in small groups. In M. Schaller & C. S. Crandall (Eds.), *The psychological foundations of culture* (pp. 171–199). Mahwah, NJ: Erlbaum.

Arrow, H., & Crosson, S. B. (2003). Musical chairs: Membership dynamics in self-organized group formation. *Small Group Research, 5,* 523–556.

Arrow, H., & McGrath, J. E. (1995). Membership dynamics in groups at work: A theoretical framework. *Research in Organizational Behavior, 17,* 373–411.

Arrow, H., McGrath, J. E., & Berdahl, J. L. (2000). *Small groups as complex systems.* Thousand Oaks, CA: Sage.

Atkinson, J. W. (1954). Explorations using imaginative thought to assess the strength of human motives. In M. R. Jones (Ed.), *Nebraska symposium on motivation: 1954* (pp. 56–112). Lincoln: University of Nebraska Press.

Austin, J. R. (2003). Transactive memory in organizational groups: The effects of context, consensus, specialization, and accuracy on group performance. *Journal of Applied Psychology, 88,* 866–878.

Baldwin, T. T., Bedell, M. D., & Johnson, J. L. (1997). The social fabric of a team-based M.B.A. program: Network effects on student satisfaction and performance. *Academy of Management Journal, 40,* 1369–1397.

Bales, R. F. (1950). *Interaction process analysis: A method for the study of small groups.* Reading, MA: Addison-Wesley.

Bales, R. F. (1999). *Social interaction systems: Theory and measurement.* New Brunswick, NJ: Transaction Publishers.

Bales, R. F., & Cohen, S. P. (1979). *SYMLOG: A system for the multilevel observation of groups.* New York: Free Press.

Bales, R. F., & Strodtbeck, F. L. (1951). Phases in group problem solving. *Journal of Abnormal and Social Psychology, 46,* 485–495.

Ballard, D. I., Tschan, F., & Waller, M. J. (2008). All in the timing: Considering time at multiple stages of group research. *Small Group Research, 39,* 328–351.

Bandura, A. (2000). Exercise of human agency through collective efficacy. *Current Directions in Psychological Science, 9,* 75–78.

Barker, J. R. (1993). Tightening the iron cage: Concertive control in self-managing teams. *Administrative Science Quarterly, 38,* 408–437.

Barker, R. G. (1968). *Ecological psychology.* Palo Alto, CA: Stanford University Press.

Baron, R. S. (2005). So right it's wrong: Groupthink and the ubiquitous nature of polarized group decision making. In M. P. Zanna (Ed.), *Advances in experimental social psychology* (Vol. 37, pp. 219–253). San Diego, CA: Academic Press.

Baron, R. S., Kerr, N. L., & Miller, N. (1992). *Group process, group decision, group action.* Buckingham, England: Open University Press.

Barsade, S. G. (2002). The ripple effect: Emotional contagion and its influence on group behavior. *Administrative Science Quarterly, 47,* 644–675.

Bass, B. M. (Ed.). (1990). *Bass and Stogdill's handbook of leadership* (3rd ed.). New York: Free Press.

Baumann, M. R., & Bonner, B. L. (2004). The effects of variability and expectations on utilization of member expertise and group performance. *Organizational Behavior and Human Decision Processes, 93,* 89–101.

Bavelas, A. (1950). Communication patterns in task-oriented groups. *Journal of the Acoustical Society of America, 22,* 725–730.

Beal, D. J., Cohen, R. R., Burke, M. J., & McLendon, C. L. (2003). Cohesion and performance in groups: A meta-analytic clarification of construct relations. *Journal of Applied Psychology, 88,* 989–1004.

Beersma, B., Hollenbeck, J. R., Humphrey, S. E., Moon, H., Conlon, D. E., & Ilgen, D. R. (2003). Cooperation, competition, and team performance: Toward a contingency approach. *Academy of Management Journal, 46,* 572–590.

Behfar, K., Friedman, R. A., & Brett, J. M. (2008, November). The team negotiation challenge: Defining and managing the internal challenges of negotiating teams. Paper presented at the 21st Annual Conference of the International Association for Conflict Management, Chicago.

Bell, B. S., & Kozlowski, S. W. J. (2002). A typology of virtual teams. *Group and Organization Management, 27,* 14–49.

Benne, K. D. (1964). History of the T-Group in the laboratory setting. In L. P. Bradford, J. R. Gibb, & K. D. Benne (Eds.), *T-Group theory and laboratory method: Innovation in re-education* (pp. 136–167). New York: John Wiley & Sons.

Berdahl, J. L. (1998). The dynamics of composition and socialization in small groups: Insights gained from developing a computational model. In D. H. Gruenfeld (Ed.), *Research on managing groups and teams* (Vol. 1, pp. 209–227). Stamford, CT: JAI Press.

Berg, D. N. (2005). Senior executive teams: Not what you think. *Consulting Psychology Journal, 57,* 107–117.

Bhappu, A. D., Griffith, T. L., & Northcraft, G. B. (1997). Media effects and communication bias in diverse groups. *Organizational Behavior and Human Decision Processes, 70,* 19–205.

Bion, W. R. (1952). Group dynamics: A review. *International Journal of Psycho-analysis, 33,* 235–247.

Bion, W. R. (1961). *Experiences in groups.* London: Tavistock.

Bion, W. R., & Rickman, J. (1943, November). Intragroup tensions in therapy. *Lancet, 27,* 678–681.

Blount, S. (Ed.). (2004). *Time in groups*. Stamford, CT: JAI Press.

Bouas, K. S., & Arrow, H. (1996). The development of group identity in computer and face-to-face groups with membership change. *Computer Supported Cooperative Work*, *4*, 153–178.

Brooks, F. P., Jr. (1995). *The mythical man-month* (2nd ed.). Reading, MA: Addison-Wesley.

Brown, R. (1965). *Social psychology* (1st ed.). New York: Free Press.

Brown, R. (1965/1986). *Social psychology*. New York: Free Press. (Second edition, 1986).

Bunderson, J. S. (2003). Recognizing and utilizing expertise in work groups: A status characteristics approach. *Administrative Science Quarterly*, *48*, 557–591.

Bunderson, J. S., & Boumgarden, P. (in press). Structure and learning in self-managed teams: Why "bureaucratic" teams can be better learners. *Organization Science*.

Bunderson, J. S., & Sutcliffe, K. M. (2003). Management team learning orientation and business unit performance. *Journal of Applied Psychology*, *88*, 552–560.

Bunker, B. B., & Alban, B. T. (Eds.). (2006). *The handbook of large group methods: Creating systemic change in organizations and communities*. San Francisco: Jossey-Bass.

Burgoon, J. K. (1983). Spatial relationships in small groups. In R. S. Cathcart & L. A. Samovar (Eds.), *Small group communication* (pp. 276–292). Dubuque, IA: Brown.

Butterworth, T. (1990). Detroit String Quartet. In J. R. Hackman (Ed.), *Groups that work (and those that don't)* (pp. 207–224). San Francisco: Jossey-Bass.

Cannon-Bowers, J. A., Salas, E., & Converse, S. (1993). Shared mental models in expert team decision making. In N. J. Castellan (Ed.), *Individual and group decision making* (pp. 221–246). Hillsdale, NJ: Erlbaum.

Cartwright, D., & Zander, A. F. (1953). *Group dynamics: Research and theory*. New York: Harper (second edition: 1960; third edition: 1968).

Caruso, H. M., & Woolley, A. W. (2008). Harnessing the power of emergent interdependence to promote diverse team collaboration. In K. W. Phillips (Ed.), *Diversity and groups* (pp. 245–266). Stamford, CT: JAI Press.

Chang, A., & Bordia, P. (2001). A multidimensional approach to the group cohesion–group performance relationships. *Small Group Research*, *32*, 379–405.

Chatman, J. A., Polzer, J. T., Barsade, S. G., & Neale, M. A. (1998). Being different yet feeling similar: The influence of demographic composition and organizational culture on work processes and outcomes. *Administrative Science Quarterly*, *43*, 749–780.

Chen, G., & Kanfer, R. (2006). Toward a system theory of motivated behavior in work teams. *Research in Organizational Behavior*, *27*, 223–267.

Cheney, G. (1999). *Values at work*. Ithaca, NY: Cornell University Press.

Clark, C. C., & Sline, R. W. (2003). Teaming with emotion: The impact of emotionality on work-team collaboration. In R. Y. Hirokawa, R. S. Cathcart, L. A. Samovar, & L. D. Henman (Eds.), *Small group communication: Theory and practice* (8th ed., pp. 158–168). Los Angeles: Roxbury.

Cline, R. J. W. (1999). Communication in social support groups. In L. R. Frey (Ed.), *The handbook of group communication theory and research* (pp. 516–538). Thousand Oaks, CA: Sage.

Cohen, M. (1999). Commentary on the *Organization Science* special issue on complexity. *Organization Science*, *10*, 373–376.

Cohen, M., & Bacdayan, P. (1994). *Organizational routines* are stored as procedural memory: Evidence from a laboratory study. *Organization Science*, *5*, 554–568.

Cohen, S. G., Ledford, G. E., & Spreitzer, G. M. (1996). A predictive model of self-managing work team effectiveness. *Human Relations*, *49*, 643–676.

Collins, B. E., & Guetzkow, H. E. (1964). *The social psychology of group processes for decision making*. New York: Wiley.

Cornes, R., & Sandler, T. (1996). *The theory of externalities, public goods, and club goods* (2nd ed.). Cambridge, England: Cambridge University Press.

Cramton C. D., & Orvis, K. L. (2003). Overcoming barriers to information sharing in virtual teams. In C. B. Gibson & S. G. Cohen (Eds.), *Virtual teams that work: Creating conditions for virtual team effectiveness* (pp. 214–230). San Francisco: Jossey-Bass.

Cummings, J. N. (2007). Leading groups from a distance. In S. P. Weisband (Ed.), *Leadership at a distance: Research in technologically supported work* (pp. 33–50). Mahwah, NJ: Erlbaum.

Cummings, J. N., & Kiesler, S. (2005). Collaborative research across disciplinary boundaries. *Social Studies of Science*, *35*, 703–722.

Cummings, T. G. (1978). Self-regulating work groups: A socio-technical synthesis. *Academy of Management Review*, *3*, 625–634.

Dahlin, K. B., Weingart, L. R., & Hinds, P. J. (2005). Team diversity and information use. *Academy of Management Journal*, *48*, 1107–1123.

Davis, J. H. (1969). *Group performance*. Reading, MA: Addison-Wesley.

Davis, J. H. (1973). Group decision and social interaction: A theory of social decision schemes. *Psychological Review*, *80*, 97–125.

Davis-Sacks, M. L. (1990). Credit analysis team. In J. R. Hackman (Ed.), *Groups that work (and those that don't)* (pp. 126–145). San Francisco: Jossey-Bass.

Day, D. V., Gronn, P., & Salas, E. (2004). Leadership capacity in teams. *Leadership Quarterly*, *15*, 857–880.

DeMeyer, A. (1991, Spring). Tech talk: How managers are stimulating global R&D communication. *Sloan Management Review*, *32*, 49–59.

Denison, D. R., & Sutton, R. I. (1990). Operating room nurses. In J. R. Hackman (Ed.), *Groups that work (and those that don't)* (pp. 293–308). San Francisco: Jossey-Bass.

De Souza, G., & Klein, H. J. (1995). Emergent leadership in the group goal-setting process. *Small Group Research*, *26*, 475–496.

Dess, G. G., Rasheed, A.M.A., McLaughlin, K. J., & Priem, R. L. (1995, August). The new corporate architecture. *Academy of Management Executive*, 1–11.

Dovidio, J. F., Kawakami, K., & Gaertner, S. L. (2002). Implicit and explicit prejudice and interracial interaction. *Journal of Personality and Social Psychology*, *82*, 62–68.

Druskat, V. U., & Kayes, D. C. (2000). Learning versus performance in short-term project teams. *Small Group Research*, *31*, 328–353.

Dubrovsky, V. J., Kiesler, S., & Sethna, B. N. (1991). The equalization phenomenon: Status effects in computer-mediated and face-to-face decision making groups. *Human Computer Interaction*, *6*, 119–146.

Dugosh, K. L., & Paulus, P. B. (2005). Cognitive and social comparison processes in brainstorming. *Journal of Experimental Social Psychology*, *41*, 313–320.

Edmondson, A. C. (1996). Learning from mistakes is easier said than done: Group and organizational influences on the detection and correction of human error. *Journal of Applied Behavioral Sciences*, *32*, 5–32.

Edmondson, A. C. (1999a). A safe harbor: Social psychological conditions enabling boundary spanning in work teams. In R. Wageman (Ed.), *Groups in context* (pp. 179–199). Stamford, CT: JAI Press.

Edmondson, A. C. (1999b). Psychological safety and learning behavior in work teams. *Administrative Science Quarterly*, *44*, 350–383.

Edmondson, A. C. (2002). The local and variegated nature of learning in organizations: A group level perspective. *Organization Science*, *13*, 128–146.

Edmondson, A. C. (2003). Speaking up in the operating room: How team leaders promote learning in interdisciplinary action teams. *Journal of Management Studies, 40*, 1419–1452.

Edmondson, A. C., Roberto, M. A., & Watkins, M. D. (2003). A dynamic model of top management team effectiveness: Managing unstructured task streams. *Leadership Quarterly, 14*, 297–325.

Ellis, A. P., Hollenbeck, J. R., Ilgen, D. R., Porter, C. O., & West, B. (2003). Team learning: Collectively connecting the dots. *Journal of Applied Psychology, 88*, 821–832.

Ensley, M. D., & Pearce, C. L. (2001). Shared cognition in top management teams: Implications for new venture performance. *Journal of Organizational Behavior, 22*, 145–160.

Eriksen, J., & Dyer, L. (2004). Right from the start: Exploring the effects of early team events on subsequent project team development and performance. *Administrative Science Quarterly, 49*, 438–471.

Esser, J. K., & Ahlfinger, N. R. (2001). Testing the groupthink model: Effects of promotional leadership and conformity predisposition. *Social Behavior and Personality, 29*, 31–42.

Faraj, S., & Sproull, L. (2000). Coordinating expertise in software development teams. *Management Science, 46*, 1554–1568.

Farris, G. F., & Lim, F. G., Jr. (1969). Effects of performance on leadership, cohesiveness, influence, satisfaction, and subsequent performance. *Journal of Applied Psychology, 53*, 490–497.

Feinberg, J. M., & Aiello, J. R. (2006). Social facilitation: A test of competing theories. *Journal of Applied Social Psychology, 36*, 1087–1109.

Felps, W., Mitchell, T. R., & Byington, E. (2006). How, when, and why bad apples spoil the barrel: Negative group members and dysfunctional groups. *Research in Organizational Behavior, 27*, 175–222.

Festinger, L. (1950). Informal social communication. *Psychological Review, 57*, 157–166.

Fiedler, F. E., & Garcia, J. E. (1987). *New approaches to effective leadership: Cognitive resources and organizational performance.* New York: Wiley.

Forbes, D. P., & Milliken, F. J. (1999). Cognition and corporate governance: Understanding boards of directors as strategic decision-making groups. *Academy of Management Review, 24*, 489–505.

Forsyth, D. R. (2001). Therapeutic groups. In M. A. Hogg & R. S. Tindale (Eds.), *Blackwell handbook of social psychology: Group processes* (pp. 628–659). Oxford: Blackwell.

Forsyth, D. R., & Burnette, J. L. (2005). The history of group research. In S. A. Wheelan (Ed.), *The handbook of group research and practice* (pp. 3–18). Thousand Oaks, CA: Sage.

Foushee, H. C., Lauber, J. K., Baetge, M. M., & Acomb, D. B. (1986). *Crew factors in flight operations: III. The operational significance of exposure to short-haul air transport operations* (Technical Memorandum No. 88342). Moffett Field, CA: NASA Ames Research Center.

Freud, S. (1959). *Group psychology and the analysis of the ego.* New York: Norton. (Original work published 1922).

Frey, L. R. (Ed.). (1999). *The handbook of group communication theory and research.* Thousand Oaks, CA: Sage.

Frey, L. R. (Ed.). (2003). *Group communication in context: Studies of bona fide groups* (2nd ed.). Mahwah, NJ: Erlbaum.

Fuhriman, A., & Burlingame, G. M. (1994). Measuring small group process: A methodological application of chaos theory. *Small Group Research, 25*, 502–519.

Ganz, M., & Wageman, R. (2009). *Leadership development in a civic organization: Multi-level influences on effectiveness.* Manuscript submitted for publication.

Gersick, C. J. G. (1988). Time and transition in work teams: Toward a new model of group development. *Academy of Management Journal, 31*, 9–41.

Gersick, C. J. G. (1989). Marking time: Predictable transitions in task groups. *Academy of Management Journal, 31*, 9–41.

Gersick, C. J. G. (1990). The students. In J. R. Hackman (Ed.), *Groups that work (and those that don't)* (pp. 89–111). San Francisco: Jossey-Bass.

Gersick, C. J. G., & Hackman, J. R. (1990). Habitual routines in task-performing teams. *Organizational Behavior and Human Decision Processes, 47*, 65–97.

Gibb, C. A. (1954). Leadership. In G. Lindzey (Ed.), *Handbook of social psychology* (Vol. 2, pp. 877–917). Reading, MA: Addison-Wesley.

Gibson, C., & Vermeulen, F. (2003). A healthy divide: Subgroups as a stimulus for team learning behavior. *Administrative Science Quarterly, 48*, 202–224.

Gibson, C. B., & Cohen, S. G. (Eds.). (2003). *Virtual teams that work: Creating conditions for virtual team effectiveness.* San Francisco: Jossey-Bass.

Gibson, C. B., Waller, M. J., Carpenter, M. A., & Conte, J. M. (2007). Antecedents, consequences, and moderators of time perspective heterogeneity for knowledge management in MNO teams. *Journal of Organizational Behavior, 28*, 1005–1034.

Gigerenzer, G. (1999). Fast and frugal heuristics: The adaptive toolbox. In G. Gigerenzer & P. M. Todd (Eds.), *Simple heuristics that make us smart* (pp. 3–34). New York: Oxford University Press.

Gillette, J., & McCollom, M. (Eds.). (1990). *Groups in context: A new perspective on group dynamics.* Reading, MA: Addison-Wesley.

Ginnett, R. C. (1993). Crews as groups: Their formation and their leadership. In E. L. Wiener, B. G. Kanki, & R. L. Helmreich (Eds.), *Cockpit resource management* (pp. 71–98). Orlando, FL: Academic Press.

Gist, M. E., & McDonald-Mann, D. (2000). Advances in leadership training and development. In C. L. Cooper & E. A. Locke (Eds.), *Industrial and organizational psychology: Linking theory with practice* (pp. 52–71). Oxford: Blackwell.

Gladstein, D. L. (1984). Groups in context: A model of task group effectiveness. *Administrative Science Quarterly, 29*, 499–518.

Gladwell, M. (2000, Dec. 11). Designs for working. *The New Yorker*, 60–70.

Goldstone, R. L., Roberts, M. E., & Gureckis, T. M. (2008). Emergent processes in group behavior. *Current Directions in Psychological Science, 17*, 10–15.

Goodman, P. S., & Darr, E. D. (1996). Computer-aided systems for organizational learning. *Trends in Organizational Behavior, 3*, 81–97.

Goodman, P. S., & Leyden, D. P. (1991). Familiarity and group productivity. *Journal of Applied Psychology, 76*, 578–586.

Goodman, P. S., & Shah, S. (1992). Familiarity and work group outcomes. In S. Worchel, W. Wood, & J. Simpson (Eds.), *Group process and productivity* (pp. 276–298). London: Sage.

Graetz, K. A., Boyle, E. S., Kimble, C. E., Thompson, P., & Garloch, J. (1998). Information sharing in face-to-face, teleconferencing, and electronic chat groups. *Small Group Research, 29*, 714–743.

Groysberg, B., Healy, P., & Gui, Y. (2008). Can research committees add value for investors? *Journal of Financial Transformation, 24*, 123–130.

Gruenfeld, D. H., & Hollingshead, A. B. (1993). Sociocognition in work groups: The evolution of group integrative complexity and its relation to task performance. *Small Group Research, 24*, 383–405.

Gruenfeld, D. H., Mannix, E. A., Williams, K. Y., & Neale, M. A. (1996). Group composition and decision making: How member familiarity and information distribution affect process and performance. *Organizational Behavior and Human Decision Processes, 67*, 1–15.

Gruenfeld, D. H., Martorana, P. V., & Fan, E. T. (2000). What do groups learn from their worldliest members? Direct and indirect influence in dynamic teams. *Organizational Behavior and Human Decision Processes, 82*, 45–59.

Guastello, S. J. (2007). Nonlinear dynamics and leadership emergence. *Leadership Quarterly, 18*, 357–369.

Guastello, S. J., & Guastello, D. D. (1998). Origins of coordination and team effectiveness: A perspective from game theory and nonlinear dynamics. *Journal of Applied Psychology, 83*, 423–437.

Guetzkow, H., & Gyr, J. (1954). An analysis of conflict in decision-making groups. *Human Relations, 7*, 367–382.

Guetzkow, H., & Simon, H. A. (1955). The impact of certain communication nets upon organization and performance in task-oriented groups. *Management Science, 1*, 233–250.

Haas, M. R. (2006). Knowledge gathering, team capabilities, and project performance in challenging work environments. *Management Science, 52*, 1170–1184.

Haas, M. R., & Hansen, M. T. (2007). Different knowledge, different benefits: Toward a productivity perspective on knowledge sharing in organizations. *Strategic Management Journal, 28*, 1133–1153.

Hackman, J. R. (1986). The psychology of self-management in organizations. In M. S. Pallack & R. O. Perloff (Eds.), *Psychology and work: Productivity, change, and employment* (pp. 89–136). Washington, DC: American Psychological Association.

Hackman, J. R. (Ed.). (1990). *Groups that work (and those that don't).* San Francisco: Jossey-Bass.

Hackman, J. R. (1992). Group influences on individuals in organizations. In M. D. Dunnette & L. M. Hough (Eds.), *Handbook of industrial and organizational psychology* (Vol. 3, pp. 1455–1525). Palo Alto, CA: Consulting Psychologists Press.

Hackman, J. R. (2002). *Leading teams: Setting the stage for great performances.* Boston: Harvard Business School Press.

Hackman, J. R. (2003). Learning more from crossing levels: Evidence from airplanes, orchestras, and hospitals. *Journal of Organizational Behavior, 24*, 1–18.

Hackman, J. R., & Edmondson, A. C. (2008). Groups as agents of change. In T. Cummings (Ed.), *Handbook of organization development* (pp. 167–186). Thousand Oaks, CA: Sage.

Hackman, J. R., & Morris, C. G. (1975). Group tasks, group interaction process, and group performance effectiveness: A review and proposed integration. In L. Berkowitz (Ed.), *Advances in experimental social psychology* (Vol. 8, pp. 1–55). New York: Academic Press.

Hackman, J. R., & Wageman, R. (2005a). A theory of team coaching. *Academy of Management Review, 30*, 269–287.

Hackman, J. R., & Wageman, R. (2005b). When and how team leaders matter. *Research in Organizational Behavior, 26*, 37–74.

Hackman, J. R., & Walton, R. E. (1986). Leading groups in organizations. In P. S. Goodman (Ed.), *Designing effective work groups* (pp. 72–119). San Francisco: Jossey-Bass.

Hackman, J. R., & Woolley, A. W. (in press). Creating and leading analytic teams. In R. L. Rees & J. W. Harris (Eds.), *A handbook of the psychology of intelligence analysis: The human factor.* Burlington, MA: Centra.

Hall, E. T. (1969). *The hidden dimension* (2nd ed). Garden City, NY: Doubleday.

Hambrick, D. C. (2007). Upper echelons theory: An update. *Academy of Management Review, 32*, 334–343.

Hamilton, D. L., Sherman, S. J., & Rodgers, J. S. (2004). Perceiving the groupness of groups: Entitativity, homogeneity, essentialism, and stereotypes. In V. Yzerbyt, C. M. Judd, & O. Corneille (Eds.), *The psychology of group perception: Perceived variability, entitativity, and essentialism* (pp. 39–60). New York: Psychology Press.

Hapgood, F. (1994, August). Notes from the underground. *Atlantic Monthly*, 34–38.

Hare, A. P. (1976). Handbook of small group research (2nd ed.). New York: Free Press.

Hare, A. P. (1992). *Groups, teams, and social interaction: Theories and applications.* New York: Praeger.

Hargadon, A. B. (1999). Group cognition and creativity in organizations. In R. Wageman (Ed.), *Groups in context* (pp. 137–155). Stamford, CT: JAI Press.

Harkins, S. G., & Szymanski, K. (1989). Social loafing and group evaluation. *Journal of Personality and Social Psychology, 56*, 934–941.

Harrison, D. A., Mohammed, S., McGrath, J. E., Florey, A. T., & Vanderstoep, S. W. (2003). Time matters in team performance: Effects of member familiarity, entrainment, and task discontinuity on speed and quality. *Personnel Psychology, 56*, 633–669.

Hastie, R., Penrod, S. D., & Pennington, N. (1983). *Inside the jury.* Cambridge, MA: Harvard University Press.

Heenan, D. A., & Bennis, W. (1999). *Co-leaders: The power of great partnerships.* New York: Wiley.

Heifetz, R. A. (1998). *Leadership without easy answers.* Cambridge, MA: Harvard University Press.

Hiltz, S. R., Johnson, K., & Turoff, M. (1986). Experiments in group decision making: Communication process and outcome in face-to-face versus computerized conferences. *Human Communication Research, 13*, 225–252.

Hinsz, V. B., Tindale, R. S., & Vollrath, D. A. (1997). The emerging conceptualization of groups as information processors. *Psychological Bulletin, 121*, 43–64.

Hogg, M. A. (1993). Group cohesiveness: A critical review and some new directions. *European Review of Social Psychology, 4*, 85–111.

Hogg, M. A., & Tindale, R. S. (Eds.). (2001). *Blackwell handbook of social psychology: Group processes.* Oxford: Blackwell.

Hollenbeck, G. P., McCall, M. W., Jr., & Silzer, R. F. (2006). Leadership competency models. *Leadership Quarterly, 17*, 398–413.

Hollingshead, A. B. (1996). Information suppression and status persistence in group decision making. *Human Communication Research, 23*, 193–219.

Hollingshead, A. B. (1998). Communication, learning and retrieval in transactive memory systems. *Journal of Experimental Social Psychology, 34*, 423–442.

Hollingshead, A. B., McGrath, J. E., & O'Connor, K. M. (1993). Group task performance and communication technology: A longitudinal study of computer-mediated versus face-to-face work groups. *Small Group Research, 24*, 307–333.

Homan, A. C., van Knippenberg, D., Van Kleef, G. A., & De Dreu, K. W. (2007). Bridging faultlines by valuing diversity: Diversity beliefs, information elaboration, and performance in diverse work groups. *Journal of Applied Psychology, 92*, 1189–1199.

Howell, S., Brock, B., & Hauser, E. (2003). A multicultural, intergenerational youth program: Creating and sustaining a youth community group. In L. R. Frey (Ed.), *Group communication in context* (2nd ed., pp. 85–107). Mahwah, NJ: Erlbaum.

Hutchins, E. (1995). How a cockpit remembers its speeds. *Cognitive Science, 19*, 265–288.

Ilgen, D. (1999). Teams imbedded in organizations: Some implications. *American Psychologist, 54*, 129–139.

Ilgen, D. R., Hollenbeck, J. R., Johnson, M., & Jundt, D. (2005). Teams in organizations: From input–process–output models to IMOI models. *Annual Review of Psychology, 56*, 517–543.

Isenberg, D. J. (1986). Group polarization: A critical review and meta-analysis. *Journal of Personality and Social Psychology, 50*, 1141–1151.

Jackson, J. (1966). A conceptual and measurement model for norms and roles. *Pacific Sociological Review, 9*, 35–47.

James, L. R., Joyce, W. F., & Slocum, J. W. (1988). Organizations do not cognize. *Academy of Management Review, 13*, 129–132.

Janis, I. L. (1972). *Victims of groupthink.* Boston: Houghton Mifflin.

Janis, I. L. (1982). *Groupthink: Psychological studies of policy decisions and fiascoes* (2nd ed.). Boston: Houghton Mifflin.

Jaques, D., & Salmon, G. (2007). *Learning in groups: A handbook for face-to-face and online environments.* New York: Routledge.

Johnson, D. W., & Johnson, R. T. (1998). Cooperative learning and social interdependence theory. In R. S. Tindale (Ed.), *Theory and research on small groups* (pp. 9–35). New York: Plenum.

Joyce, A. S., Piper, W. E., & Ogrodniczuk, J. S. (2007). Therapeutic alliance and cohesion variables as predictors of outcome in short-term group psychotherapy. *International Journal of Group Psychotherapy, 57,* 269–297.

Kaplan, R. E. (1979). The utility of maintaining work relationships openly: An experimental study. *Journal of Applied Behavioral Science, 15,* 41–59.

Karau, S. J., & Williams, K. D. (1993). Social loafing: A meta-analytic review and theoretical integration. *Journal of Personality and Social Psychology, 65,* 681–706.

Katz, N., Lazer, D., Arrow, H., & Contractor, N. (2004). Network theory and small groups. *Small Group Research, 35,* 307–332.

Katz, N., Lazer, D., Arrow, H., & Contractor, N. (2005). The network perspective on small groups: Theory and research. In M. S. Poole & A. B. Hollingshead (Eds.), *Theories of small groups: Interdisciplinary perspectives* (pp. 277–312). Thousand Oaks, CA: Sage.

Katz, R. (1982). The effects of group longevity on project communication and performance. *Administrative Science Quarterly, 27,* 81–104.

Katzenbach, J. R., & Smith, D. K. (1993). *The wisdom of teams.* Boston: Harvard Business School Press.

Kelly, J. R., & McGrath, J. E. (1985). Effects of time limits and task types on task performance and interaction of four-person groups. *Journal of Personality and Social Psychology, 49,* 395–407.

Kerr, N. L. (1981). Social transition schemes: Charting the group's road to agreement. *Journal of Personality and Social Psychology, 41,* 684–702.

Kerr, N. L., MacCoun, R. J., & Kramer, G. P. (1996). Bias in judgment: Comparing individuals and groups. *Psychological Review, 103,* 687–719.

Kerr, N. L., Niedermeier, K. E., & Kaplan, M. F. (1999). Bias in jurors vs. bias in juries: New evidence from the SDS perspective. *Organizational Behavior and Human Decision Processes, 80,* 70–86.

Kerr, N. L., & Tindale, R. S. (2004). Group performance and decision making. *Annual Review of Psychology, 55,* 623–655.

Ketz de Vries, M. F. R., & Carlock, R. (2007). *The family business on the couch: A psychological perspective.* West Sussex, England: Wiley.

Kiesler, S., Siegel, J., & McGuire, T. W. (1984). Social psychological aspects of computer-mediated communication. *American Psychologist, 39,* 1123–1134.

Kirkman, B. L., Rosen, B., Tesluk, P. E., & Gibson, C. B. (2004). The impact of team empowerment on virtual team performance: The moderating role of face-to-face interaction. *Academy of Management Journal, 47,* 1–18.

Kirkman, B. L., & Shapiro, D. L. (1997). The impact of cultural values on employee resistance to teams: Toward a model of globalized self-managing work team effectiveness. *Academy of Management Review, 22,* 730–757.

Klein, K. J., Ziegert, J. C., Knight, A. P., & Xiao, Y. (2006). Dynamic delegation: Shared, hierarchical and deindividualized leadership in extreme action teams. *Administrative Science Quarterly, 51,* 590–621.

Klimoski, R., & Mohammed, S. (1994). Team mental model: Construct or metaphor? *Journal of Management, 20,* 403–437.

Kluckhohn, C., & Murray, H. A. (Eds.). (1953). *Personality in nature, society, and culture.* New York: Knopf.

Kozlowski, S. W. J., & Bell, B. S. (2003). Work groups and teams in organizations. In W. C. Borman, D. R. Ilgen, & R. J. Klimoski (Eds.), *Comprehensive handbook of psychology* (Vol. 12): *Industrial and organizational psychology* (pp. 333–375). New York: Wiley.

Kozlowski, S. W. J., & Bell, B. S. (2008). Team learning, development, and adaptation. In V. I. Sessa & M. London (Eds.), *Group learning* (pp. 15–44). Mahwah, NJ: Erlbaum.

Kozlowski, S. W. J., Gully, S. M., McHugh, P. P., Salas, E., & Cannon-Bowers, J. A. (1996). A dynamic theory of leadership and team effectiveness: Developmental and task contingent leader roles. In G. R. Ferris (Ed.), *Research in personnel and human resource management* (Vol. 14, pp. 253–305). Stamford, CT: JAI Press.

Kozlowski, S. W. J., Gully, S. M., Nason, E. R., & Smith, E. M. (1999). Developing adaptive teams: A theory of compilation and performance across levels and time. In D. R. Ilgen & E. D. Pulakos (Eds.), *The changing nature of work performance: Implications for staffing, personnel actions, and development* (pp. 240–292). San Francisco: Jossey-Bass.

Kozlowski, S. W. J., & Ilgen, D. R. (2006). Enhancing the effectiveness of work groups and teams. *Psychological Science in the Public Interest, 7,* 77–124.

Kozlowski, S. W. J., Watola, D. J., Nowakowski, J. M., Kim, B. H., & Botero, I. C. (2009). Developing adaptive teams: A theory of dynamic team leadership. In E. Salas, G. F. Goodwinh, & C. S. Burke (Eds.), *Team effectiveness in complex organizations: Cross-disciplinary perspectives* (pp. 113–156). New York: Psychology Press.

Kramer, R. M. (1998). Revisiting the Bay of Pigs and Vietnam decisions 25 years later: How well has the groupthink hypothesis stood the test of time? *Organizational Behavior and Human Decision Processes, 73,* 236–271.

Lacey, R., & Gruenfeld, D. (1999). Unwrapping the work group: How extra-organizational context affects group behavior. In R. Wageman (Ed.), *Groups in context* (pp. 157–177). Stamford, CT: JAI Press.

Larson, J. R., & Christensen, C. (1993). Groups as problem-solving units: Toward a new meaning of social cognition. *British Journal of Social Psychology, 32,* 5–30.

Latane, B., Williams, K. D., & Harkins, S. G. (1979). Many hands make light the work: The causes and consequences of social loafing. *Journal of Personality and Social Psychology, 37,* 823–832.

Lau, D., & Murnighan, J. K. (1998). Demographic diversity and faultlines: The compositional diversity of organizational groups. *Academy of Management Review, 23,* 325–340.

Lau, D., & Murnighan, J. K. (2005). Interactions within groups and subgroups: The effects of demographic faultlines. *Academy of Management Journal, 48,* 645–659.

Laughlin, P. R. (1980). Social combination processes of cooperative, problem-solving groups on verbal intellective tasks. In M. Fishbein (Ed.), *Progress in social psychology* (pp. 127–155). Hillsdale, NJ: Erlbaum.

Laughlin, P. R. (1999). Collective induction: Twelve postulates. *Organizational Behavior and Human Decision Processes, 80,* 50–69.

Laughlin, P. R., Bonner, B. L., & Miner, A. G. (2002). Groups perform better than the best individuals on Letters-to-Numbers problems. *Organizational Behavior and Human Decision Processes, 88,* 605–620.

Laughlin, P. R., & Hollingshead, A. B. (1995). A theory of collective induction. *Organizational Behavior and Human Decision Processes, 61,* 94–107.

Laughlin, P. R., VanderStoep, S. W., & Hollingshead, A. B. (1991). Collective versus individual induction: Recognition of truth, rejection of error, and collective information processing. *Journal of Personality and Social Psychology, 61,* 50–67.

Lawler, E. E. (2003). Pay systems for virtual teams. In C. B. Gibson & S. C. Cohen (Eds.), *Virtual teams that work: Creating conditions for virtual team effectiveness* (pp. 121–144). San Francisco: Jossey-Bass.

Lazer, D., Pentland, A., Adamic, L., Aral, S., Barabasi, A. L., Brewer, D., et al. (2009). Computational social science. *Science, 323*, 721–723.

Leavitt, H. J. (1951). Some effects of certain communication patterns on group performance. *Journal of Abnormal Psychology, 46*, 38–50.

Leavitt, H. J. (1975). Suppose we took groups seriously . . . In E. L. Cass & F. G. Zimmer (Eds.), *Man and work in society* (pp. 67–77). New York: Van Nostrand Reinhold.

Leavitt, H. J., & Mueller, R. A. (1951). Some effects of feedback on communication. *Human Relations, 4*, 401–410.

Lebie, L., Rhoades, J. A., & McGrath, J. E. (1996). Interaction process in computer-mediated and face-to-face groups. *Computer Supported Cooperative Work, 4*, 127–152.

Le Bon, G. (1995). *The crowd.* Piscataway, NJ: Transaction Publishers. (Original work published 1895).

Leedom, D. K., & Simon, R. (1995). Improving team coordination: A case for behavior-based training. *Military Psychology, 7*, 109–122.

Levine, J. M., & Moreland, R. L. (1998). Small groups. In D. T. Gilbert, S. T. Fiske, & G. Lindsey (Eds.), *The handbook of social psychology* (4th ed., Vol. 2, pp. 415–469). New York: McGraw-Hill.

Levine, J. M., Moreland, R. L., & Choi, H. S. (2001). Group socialization and newcomer innovation. In M. A. Hogg & R. S. Tindale (Eds.), *Blackwell handbook of social psychology: Group processes* (pp. 86–106). Oxford: Blackwell.

Lewin, K. (1945). The Research Center for Group Dynamics at Massachusetts Institute of Technology. *Sociometry, 8*, 126–136.

Lewin, K. (1947a). Frontiers in group dynamics, I. *Human Relations, 1*, 2–38.

Lewin, K. (1947b). Frontiers in group dynamics, II. *Human Relations, 1*, 143–153.

Lewin, K. (1948). Action research and minority problems. In G. W. Lewin (Ed.), *Resolving social conflicts: Selected papers on group dynamics* (pp. 201–216). New York: Harper & Row. (Original work published 1946).

Lewin, K., & Lippitt, R. (1938). An experimental approach to the study of autocracy and democracy: A preliminary note. *Sociometry, 1*, 292–300.

Lewin, K., Lippitt, R., & White, R. K. (1939). Patterns of aggressive behavior in experimentally created "social climates." *Journal of Social Psychology, 10*, 271–299.

Lewin, M. A. (1992). The impact of Kurt Lewin's life on the place of social issues in his work. *Journal of Social Issues, 48*, 15–30.

Lewis, K. (2004). Knowledge and performance in knowledge-worker teams: A longitudinal study of transactive memory systems. *Management Science, 50*, 1519–1533.

Lewis, K., Belliveau, M., Herndon, B., & Keller, J. (2007). Group cognition, membership change, and performance: Investigating the benefits and detriments of collective knowledge. *Organizational Behavior and Human Decision Processes, 103*, 159–178.

Lipman-Blumen, J., & Leavitt, H. J. (1999). *Hot groups: Seeding them, feeding them, and using them to ignite your organization.* New York: Oxford University Press.

Litchfield, R. C. (2008). Brainstorming reconsidered: A goal-based view. *Academy of Management Review, 33*, 649–668.

Littlepage, G., Robison, W., & Reddington, K. (1997). Effects of task experience and group experience on group performance, member ability, and recognition of expertise. *Organizational Behavior and Human Decision Processes, 69*, 133–147.

Locke, E. A., Tirnauer, D., Roberson, Q., Goldman, B., Latham, M. E., & Weldon, E. (2001). The importance of the individual in an age of groupism. In M. E. Turner (Ed.), *Groups at work: Theory and research* (pp. 501–528). Mahwah, NJ: Erlbaum.

Lott, A. J., & Lott, B. E. (1965). Group cohesiveness as interpersonal attraction: A review of relationships with antecedent and consequent variables. *Psychological Bulletin, 64*, 259–309.

Lowin, B., & Craig, J. R. (1968). The influence of level of performance on managerial style: An experimental object-lesson in the ambiguity of correlational data. *Organizational Behavior and Human Performance, 3*, 440–458.

Malhotra, A., Majchrzak, A., Carman, R., & Lott, V. (2001). Radical innovation without co-location: A case study at Boeing–Rocketdyne. *MIS Quarterly, 25*, 229–249.

Mann, R. D. (1959). A review of the relationships between personality and performance in small groups. *Psychological Bulletin, 56*, 241–270.

Mannix, E., & Neale, M. A. (2005). What difference does a difference make? The promise and reality of diverse teams in organizations. *Psychological Science in the Public Interest, 6*, 31–55.

Manz, C., & Sims, H. P., Jr. (1987). Leading workers to lead themselves: The external leadership of self-managing work teams. *Administrative Science Quarterly, 32*, 106–129.

Marineau, R. (1989). *Jacob Levy Moreno, 1889–1974: Father of psychodrama, sociometry, and group psychotherapy.* New York: Routledge.

Marquart, D. I. (1955). Group problem solving. *Journal of Social Psychology, 41*, 103–113.

Martins, L. L., Gilson, L. L., & Maynard, M. T. (2004). Virtual teams: What do we know and where do we go from here? *Journal of Management, 30*, 805–835.

Mas, A., & Moretti, E. (2009). Peers at work. *American Economic Review,* 112–145.

Mathews, K. M., White, M. C., & Long, R. G. (1999). Why study complexity in the social sciences? *Human Relations, 52*, 439–462.

Mathieu, J. E., Heffner, T. S., Goodwin, G. F., Salas, E., & Cannon-Bowers, J. A. (2000). The influence of shared mental models on team process and performance. *Journal of Applied Psychology, 85*, 273–283.

Mathieu, J. E., Maynard, M. T., Rapp, T., & Gilson, L. (2008). Team effectiveness 1997–2007: A review of recent advancements and a glimpse into the future. *Journal of Management, 34*, 410–476.

Maznevski, M. L., & Chudoba, K. M. (2001). Bridging space over time: Global virtual team dynamics and effectiveness. *Organization Science, 11*, 473–492.

McCauley, C. (1998). Group dynamics in Janis's theory of groupthink: Backward and forward. *Organizational Behavior and Human Decision Processes, 73*, 142–162.

McClelland, D. C. (1973). Testing for competence rather than intelligence. *American Psychologist, 28*, 1–14.

McClure, B. A. (1998). *Putting a new spin on groups: The science of chaos.* Mahwah, NJ: Erlbaum.

McDonough, E. F., Kahn, K. B., & Barczak, G. (2001). An investigation of the use of global, virtual, and co-located new product development teams. *Journal of Product Innovation Management, 18*, 110–120.

McDougall, W. (1920). *The group mind: A sketch of the principles of collective psychology with some attempt to apply them to the interpretation of national life and character.* New York: Putnam.

McGrath, J. E. (1962). *Leadership behavior: Some requirements for leadership training.* Washington, DC: U.S. Civil Service Commission.

McGrath, J. E. (1984). *Groups: Interaction and performance.* Englewood Cliffs, NJ: Prentice-Hall.

McGrath, J. E. (1993). The JEMCO Workshop: Description of a longitudinal study. *Small Group Research, 24*, 147–174.

McGrath, J. E. (1997). Small group research, that once and future field: An interpretation of the past with an eye to the future. *Group Dynamics, 1*, 7–27.

McGrath, J. E., & Altman, I. (1966). *Small group research.* New York: Holt.

McGrath, J. E., Arrow, H., & Berdahl, J. (2000). The study of groups: Past, present, and future. *Personality and Social Psychology Review, 4*, 95–105.

McGrath, J. E., & Kelly, J. R. (1986). *Time and social interaction.* New York: Guilford.

McGrath, J. E., & Tschan, F. (2004). *Temporal matters in social psychology: Examining the role of time in the lives of groups and individuals.* Washington, DC: American Psychological Association.

McGrath, J. E., & Tschan, F. (2007). Temporal matters in the study of work groups in organizations. *Psychologist-Manager Journal, 10,* 3–12.

McGuire, W. J. (1969). The nature of attitudes and attitude change. In G. Lindzey & E. Aronson (Eds.), *Handbook of social psychology* (2nd ed., Vol. 3, pp. 136–314). Reading, MA: Addison-Wesley.

McKelvey, B. (1999). Complexity theory in organization science: Seizing the promise or becoming a fad? *Emergence, 1,* 5–32.

McLeod, P. L., Baron, R. S., Marti, M. W., & Yoon, K. (1997). The eyes have it: Minority influence in face-to-face and computer-mediated groups. *Journal of Applied Psychology, 82,* 706–718.

McLeod, P. L., & Kettner-Polley, R. (2005). Psychodynamic perspectives on small groups. In M. S. Poole & A. B. Hollingshead (Eds.), *Theories of small groups: Interdisciplinary perspectives* (p. 99–138). Thousand Oaks, CA: Sage.

Mehra, A., Dixon, A. L., Brass, D. J., & Robertson, B. (2006). The social network ties of group leaders: Implications for group performance and leader reputation. *Organization Science, 17,* 64–79.

Meindl, J. R. (1990). On leadership: An alternative to conventional wisdom. *Research in Organizational Behavior, 12,* 159–203.

Mohrman, S. A., Cohen, S. G., & Mohrman, A. M. (1995). *Designing team-based organizations: New forms for knowledge work.* San Francisco: Jossey-Bass.

Monge, P. R., & Contractor, N. (2003). *Theories of communication networks.* New York: Oxford University Press.

Moreland, R. L. (1999). Transactive memory: Learning who knows what in work groups and organizations. In L. L. Thompson, J. M. Levine, & D. M. Messick (Eds.), *Shared cognition in organizations: The management of knowledge* (pp. 3–31). Mahwah, NJ: Erlbaum.

Moreland, R. L., & Argote, L. (2003). Transactive memory in dynamic organizations. In R. S. Peterson & E. A. Mannix (Eds.), *Leading and managing people in the dynamic organization* (pp. 135–162). Mahwah, NJ: Erlbaum.

Moreland, R. L., Hogg, M. A., & Hains, S. C. (1994). Back to the future: Social psychological research on groups. *Journal of Experimental Social Psychology, 30,* 527–555.

Moreland, R. L., Levine, J. M., & Wingert, M. L. (1996). Creating the ideal group: Composition effects at work. In E. H. Witte & J. H. Davis (Eds.), *Understanding group behavior* (Vol. 2, pp. 11–35). Hillsdale, NJ: Erlbaum.

Moreland, R. L., & Myaskovsky, L. (2000). Exploring the performance benefits of group training: Transactive memory or improved communication. *Organizational Behavior and Human Decision Processes, 82,* 117–133.

Moreno, J. L. (1934). *Who shall survive? A new approach to the problem of human interrelations.* Washington, DC: Nervous and Mental Disease Publishing Company.

Moreno, J. L. (1941). Foundations of sociometry: An introduction. *Sociometry, 4,* 15–35.

Moreno, J. L. (1943). Sociometry and the cultural order. *Sociometry, 6,* 299–344.

Mortensen, M. (2009). What is a team? The changing characteristics of teams and their effects on individual and team outcomes. Working Paper, Sloan School of Management, Massachusetts Institute of Technology.

Moynihan, L. M., & Peterson, R. S. (2001). A contingent configuration approach to the role of personality in organizational groups. *Research in Organizational Behavior, 23,* 327–378.

Mullen, B., & Copper, C. (1994). The relation between group cohesiveness and performance: An integration. *Psychological Bulletin, 115,* 210–227.

Murnighan, J. K., & Conlon, D. E. (1991). The dynamics of intense work groups: A study of British string quartets. *Administrative Science Quarterly, 36,* 165–186.

National Transportation Safety Board. (1994). *A review of flightcrew-involved major accidents of U.S. air carriers, 1978 through 1990.* Washington, DC: Author.

Neck, C. P., & Moorhead, G. (1992). Jury deliberations in the trial of *U.S. v. John DeLorean*: A case analysis of groupthink avoidance and an enhanced framework. *Human Relations, 45,* 1077–1091.

Nehnevajsa, J. (1955). Sociometry: Decades of growth. *Sociometry, 4,* 48–95.

Nemiro, J., Beyerlein, M. M., Bradley, L., & Beyerlein, S. (Eds.). (2008). *Handbook of high performance virtual teams: A toolkit for collaborating across boundaries.* San Francisco: Jossey-Bass.

Neubert, M. J. (1999). Too much of a good thing or the more the merrier? Exploring the dispersion and gender composition of informal leadership in manufacturing teams. *Small Group Research, 30,* 635–646.

Nijstad, B. A., & Stroebe, W. (2006). How the group affects the mind: A cognitive model of idea generation in groups. *Personality and Social Psychology Review, 10,* 186–213.

Nohria, N., & Khurana, R. (Eds.). (2010). *Advancing leadership.* Boston: Harvard Business School Press.

Nosek, B. A., Greenwald, A. G., & Banaji, M. R. (2007). The Implicit Association Test at age 7: A methodological and conceptual review. In J. A. Bargh (Ed.), *Automatic processes in social thinking and behavior* (pp. 265–292). New York: Psychology Press.

Noveck, B. S. (2009). *Wiki government: How technology can make government better, democracy stronger, and citizens more powerful.* Washington, DC: Brookings Institution.

Nye, J. S. (2008). *The powers to lead.* New York: Oxford University Press.

Offermann, L. R., & Spiros, R. K. (2001). The science and practice of team development. *Academy of Management Journal, 44,* 376–392.

Oh, H., Labianca, G., & Chung, M. H. (2006). A multilevel model of group social capital. *Academy of Management Review, 31,* 569–582.

Okhuysen, G. A., & Eisenhardt, K. M. (2002). Integrating knowledge in groups: How formal interventions enable flexibility. *Organization Science, 13,* 370–386.

Okhuysen, G. A., & Waller, M. J. (2002). Focusing on midpoint transitions: An analysis of boundary conditions. *Academy of Management Journal, 45,* 1056–1065.

O'Leary, M. B., & Cummings, J. N. (2007). The spatial, temporal, and configurational characteristics of geographic dispersion in teams. *MIS Quarterly, 31,* 433–452.

Orlikowski, W. J. (2000). Using technology and constituting structures: A practice lens for studying technology in organizations. *Organization Science, 11,* 404–428.

Parks, C. D., & Sanna, L. J. (1999). *Group performance and interaction.* Boulder, CO: Westview Press.

Paulus, P. B., Dugosh, K. L., Dzindolet, M. T., Coskun, H., & Putman, V. L. (2002). Social and cognitive influences in group brainstorming: Predicting production gains and losses. *European Review of Social Psychology, 12,* 299–325.

Pearce, C. A., & Conger, J. A. (Eds.). (2003). *Shared leadership: Reframing the hows and whys of leadership.* Thousand Oaks, CA: Sage.

Peltokorpi, V. (2008). Transactive memory systems. *Review of General Psychology, 12,* 378–394.

Penrod, S. D., & Hastie, R. (1981). A computer simulation of jury decision making. *Psychological Review, 87,* 133–159.

Perlow, L. A., Gittell, J. H., & Katz, N. (2004). Contextualizing patterns of work group interaction: Toward a nested theory of structuration. *Organization Science, 15*, 520–536.

Pescosolido, A. T. (2001). Informal leaders and the development of group efficacy. *Small Group Research, 32*, 74–93.

Pescosolido, A. T. (2002). Emergent leaders as managers of group emotion. *Leadership Quarterly, 18*, 1–18.

Peters, M., & Robinson, V. (1984). The origins and status of action research. *Journal of Applied Behavioral Sciences, 20*, 113–124.

Phillips, K. W. (Ed.). (2008). *Diversity and groups*. Stamford, CT: JAI Press.

Polzer, J. T., Crisp, C. B., Jarvenpaa, S. L., & Kim, J. W. (2006). Extending the faultline model to geographically dispersed teams: How collocated subgroups can impair group functioning. *Academy of Management Review, 49*, 679–692.

Poole, M. S., & Hollingshead, A. B. (2005). *Theories of small groups: Interdisciplinary perspectives*. Thousand Oaks, CA: Sage.

Poole, M. S., Seibold, D. R., & McPhee, R. D. (1985). Group decision making as a structuration process. *Quarterly Journal of Speech, 71*, 74–102.

Postmes, T., Spears, R., & Cihangir, S. (2001). Quality of decision making and group norms. *Journal of Personality and Social Psychology, 80*, 918–930.

Pritchard, R. D., & Watson, M. D. (1992). Understanding and measuring group productivity. In S. Worchel, W. Wood, & J. A. Simpson (Eds.), *Group process and productivity* (pp. 252–265). Newbury Park, CA: Sage.

Putnam, L. L., & Stohl, C. (1990). Bona fide groups: A reconceptualization of groups in context. *Communication Studies, 41*, 248–265.

Quigley, N. R., Tesluk, P. E., Locke, E. A., & Bartol, K. M. (2007). A multi-level investigation of the motivational mechanisms underlying knowledge sharing and performance. *Organization Science, 18*, 71–88.

Raven, B. H. (1998). Groupthink, Bay of Pigs, and Watergate reconsidered. *Organizational Behavior and Human Decision Processes, 73*, 352–361.

Reagans, R., & Zuckerman, E. W. (2001). Networks, diversity, and productivity: The social capital of corporate R&D teams. *Organization Science, 12*, 502–517.

Rioch, M. J. (1975). The work of Wilfred Bion on groups. In A. D. Colman & W. H. Bexton (Eds.), *Group relations reader* (pp. 21–33). Sausalito, CA: GREX.

Robey, D., Khoo, H. M., & Powers, C. (2000). Situated learning in cross-functional virtual teams. *IEEE Transactions on Professional Communications, 43*, 51–66.

Rosseau, D. M., & Fried, Y. (2001). Location, location, location: Contextualizing organizational research. *Journal of Organizational Behavior, 22*, 1–13.

Salas, E., Bowers, C. A., & Cannon-Bowers, J. A. (1995). Military team research: 10 years of progress. *Military Psychology, 7*, 55–75.

Salas, E., Goodwin, G. F., & Burke, C. S. (Eds.). (2008). *Team effectiveness in complex organizations: Cross-disciplinary perspectives and approaches*. Boca Raton, FL: CRC Press.

Salas, E., Kosarzycki, M. P., Tannenbaum, S. I., & Carnegie, D. (2004). Principles and advice for understanding and promoting effective teamwork in organizations. In R. J. Burke & C. L. Cooper (Eds.), *Leading in turbulent times: Managing in the new world of work* (pp. 95–120). Oxford: Blackwell.

Salas, E., Nichols, D. R., & Driskell, J. E. (2007). Testing three team training strategies in intact teams: A meta-analysis. *Small Group Research, 38*, 471–488.

Salas, E., Stagl, K. C., & Burke, C. S. (2004). 25 years of team effectiveness in organizations: Research themes and emerging needs. *Review of Industrial and Organizational Psychology, 19*, 47–91.

Schachter, S. (1964). The interaction of cognitive and physiological determinants of emotional state. In L. Berkowitz (Ed.), *Advances in experimental social psychology* (Vol. 1, pp. 49–80). New York: Academic Press.

Schippers, M. C., den Hartog, D. N., & Koopman, P. L. (2008). Reflexivity in teams: A measure and correlates. *Applied Psychology: An International Review, 56*, 189–211.

Scholten, L., van Knippenberg, D., Nijstad, B. A., & De Dreu, C. K. W. (2007). Motivated information processing and group decision making: Effects of process accountability on information processing and decision quality. *Journal of Experimental Social Psycyhology, 43*, 539–552.

Schopler, J. H. (1987). Interorganizational groups: Origins, structure, and outcomes. *Academy of Management Review, 12*, 702–713.

Schultheiss, O. C., & Brunstein, J. C. (1999). Goal imagery: Bridging the gap between implicit motives and explicit goals. *Journal of Personality, 67*, 1–34.

Schulz-Hardt, S., Brodbeck, F. C., Mojzisch, A., Kerschreiter, R., & Frey, D. (2006). Group decision making in hidden profile situations: Dissent as a facilitator for decision quality. *Journal of Personality and Social Psychology, 91*, 1080–1093.

Seeger, J. A. (1983). No innate phases in group problem solving. *Academy of Management Review, 8*, 683–689.

Senge, P. M. (1990). *The fifth discipline: The art and practice of the learning organization*. New York: Doubleday.

Sessa, V. I., & London, M. (Eds.). (2008). *Group learning*. Mahwah, NJ: Erlbaum.

Shaw, M. E. (1932). A comparison of individuals and small groups in the rational solution of complex problems. *American Journal of Psychology, 44*, 491–504.

Shepherd, M. M., Briggs, R. O., Reinig, B. A., Yen, J., & Nunamaker, J. F. (1996). Invoking social comparison to improve electronic brainstorming: Beyond anonymity. *Journal of Management Information Systems, 12*, 155–170.

Sherblom, J. C. (2003). Influences on the recommendations of international business consulting teams. In L. R. Frey (Ed.), *Group communication in context* (2nd ed., pp. 263–290). Mahwah, NJ: Erlbaum.

Shiflett, S. C. (1979). Toward a general model of small group productivity. *Psychological Bulletin, 86*, 67–79.

Shirky, C. (2008). *Here comes everybody: The power of organizing without organizations*. New York: Penguin.

Shore, M. (2008). Personal communication (manuscript in preparation).

Siegel, J., Dubrovsky, V., Kiesler, S., & McGuire, T. W. (1986). Group processes in computer-mediated communication. *Organizational Behavior and Human Decision Processes, 37*, 157–187.

Simon, H. A. (1990). Invariants of human behavior. *Annual Review of Psychology, 41*, 1–19.

Slavin, R. E. (1980). Cooperative learning in teams: State of the art. *Educational Psychologist, 15*, 93–111.

Smith, J. A., & Foti, R. J. (1998). A pattern approach to the study of leader emergence. *Leadership Quarterly, 9*, 147–160.

Smith, K. K., & Berg, D. N. (1987). *Paradoxes of group life*. San Francisco: Jossey-Bass.

Smith-Jentsch, K. A., Cannon-Bowers, J. A., Tannenbaum, S. I., & Salas, E. (2008). Guided team self-correction: Impacts on team mental models, processes, and effectiveness. *Small Group Research, 39*, 303–327.

Sparrowe, R. T., Liden, R. C., Wayne, S. J., & Kraimer, M. L. (2001). Social networks and the performance of individuals and groups. *Academy of Management Journal, 44*, 316–325.

Sproull, L., & Kiesler, S. (1986). Reducing social context cues: Electronic mail in organizational communication. *Management Science, 32*, 1492–1512.

Stasser, G., & Davis, J. H. (1981). Group decision making and social influence: A social interaction sequence model. *Psychological Review, 88,* 523–551.

Stasser, G., & Dietz-Uhler, B. (2001). Collective choice, judgment, and problem solving. In M. A. Hogg & R. S. Tindale (Eds.), *Blackwell handbook of social psychology: Group processes* (pp. 31–55). Oxford: Blackwell.

Stasser, G., Kerr, N. L., & Davis, J. H. (1989). Influence processes and consensus models in decision-making groups. In P. B. Paulus (Ed.), *Psychology of group influence* (pp. 431–477). Mahwah, NJ: Lawrence Erlbaum.

Stasser, G., Stewart, D. D., & Wittenbaum, G. M. (1995). Expert roles and information exchange during discussion: The importance of knowing who knows what. *Journal of Experimental Social Psychology, 31,* 244–265.

Stasser, G., & Titus, W. (1985). Pooling of unshared information in group decision-making: Biased information sampling during discussion. *Journal of Personality and Social Psychology, 48,* 1467–1478.

Stasser, G., & Titus, W. (2003). Hidden profiles: A brief history. *Psychological Inquiry, 14,* 304–313.

Steele, F. I. (1973). *Physical settings and organizational development.* Reading, MA: Addison-Wesley.

Steiner, I. D. (1966). Models for inferring relationships between group size and potential productivity. *Behavioral Science, 11,* 273–283.

Steiner, I. D. (1972). *Group process and productivity.* New York: Academic Press.

Steiner, I. D. (1974). Whatever happened to the group in social psychology? *Journal of Experimental Social Psychology, 10,* 94–108.

Steiner, I. D. (1986). Paradigms and groups. In L. Berkowitz (Ed.), *Advances in Experimental Social Psychology, 19,* 251–289.

Stewart, G. L., & Barrick, M. R. (2000). Team structure and performance: Assessing the mediating role of intrateam process and the moderating role of task type. *Academy of Management Journal, 43,* 135–148.

Stohl, C., & Walker, K. (2002). A bona fide perspective for the future of groups: Understanding collaborating groups. In L. R. Frey (Ed.), *New directions for group communication* (pp. 237–252). Thousand Oaks, CA: Sage.

Straus, S. G. (1996). Getting a clue: The effects of communication media and information distribution on participation and performance in computer-mediated and face-to-face groups. *Small Group Research, 27,* 115–142.

Straus, S. G., & McGrath, J. E. (1994). Does the medium matter? The interaction of task type and technology on group performance and member reactions. *Journal of Applied Psychology, 79,* 87–97.

Straus, S. G., Parker, A. M., Bruce, J. B., & Dembosky, J. W. (2009). *The group matters: A review of the effects of group interaction on processes and outcomes in analytic teams.* Arlington, VA: Rand Corporation (Report WR-580-USG).

Sundstrom, E. D. (Ed.). (1999). *Supporting work team effectiveness.* San Francisco: Jossey-Bass.

Sutton, R. I., & Hargadon. A. B. (1996). Brainstorming groups in context: Effectiveness in a product design firm. *Administrative Science Quarterly, 41,* 685–718.

Taggar, S., Hackett, R., & Saha, S. (1999). Leadership emergence in autonomous work teams: Antecedents and outcomes. *Personnel Psychology, 52,* 899–926.

Tasa, K., Taggar, S., & Seijts, G. H. (2007). The development of collective efficacy in teams: A multilevel longitudinal perspective. *Journal of Applied Psychology, 92,* 17–27.

Taylor, F. W. (1911). *The principles of scientific management.* New York: Harper.

Tetlock, P. E., Peterson, R. S., McGuire, C., Chang, S., & Feld, P. (1992). Assessing political group dynamics: A test of the groupthink model. *Journal of Personality and Social Psychology, 63,* 403–425.

Thelen, H. A. (1981). *The classroom society: The construction of educational experience.* New York: Wiley.

Thomas-Hunt, M. C., Ogden, T. Y., & Neale, M. A. (2003). Who's really sharing? Effects of social and expert status on knowledge exchange within groups. *Management Science, 49,* 464–477.

Tindale, R. S., Nadler, J., Krebel, A., & Davis, J. H. (2001). Procedural mechanisms and jury behavior. In M. A. Hogg & R. S. Tindale (Eds.), *Blackwell handbook of social psychology: Group processes* (pp. 574–602). Oxford: Blackwell.

Townsend, A. M., DeMarie, S. M., & Hendrickson, A. R. (1998). Virtual teams: Technology and the workplace of the future. *Academy of Management Executive, 12,* 17–29.

Tracy, K., & Standerfer, C. (2003). Selecting a school superintendent: Sensitivities in group deliberation. In L. R. Frey (Ed.), *Group communication in context* (2nd ed., pp. 109–134). Mahwah, NJ: Erlbaum.

Tuckman, B. W. (1965). Developmental sequence in small groups. *Psychological Bulletin, 63,* 384–399.

Turner, M. E., & Pratkanis, A. R. (1998). Twenty-five years of groupthink theory and research: Lessons from the evaluation of a theory. *Organizational Behavior and Human Decision Processes, 73,* 105–115.

Van den Bossche, P., Gijselaers, W. H., Segers, M., & Kirschner, P. A. (2006). Social and cognitive factors driving teamwork in collaborative learning environments: Team learning beliefs and behaviors. *Small Group Research, 37,* 490–521.

Van der Vegt, G. S., & Bunderson, J. S. (2005). Learning and performance in multidisciplinary teams: The importance of collective team identification. *Academy of Management Journal, 48,* 532–547.

van Ginkel, W. P., & van Knippenberg, D. (2009). Knowledge about the distribution of information and group decision making: When and why does it work? *Organizational Behavior and Human Decision Processes, 108,* 218–229.

van Knippenberg, D., & Schippers, M. C. (2007). Work group diversity. *Annual Review of Psychology, 58,* 515–541.

Vroom, V. H., & Jago, A. G. (1988). *The new leadership: Managing participation in organizations.* Englewood Cliffs, NJ: Prentice Hall.

Vroom, V. H., & Jago, A. G. (2007). The role of the situation in leadership. *American Psychologist, 62,* 17–24.

Wageman, R. (1995). Interdependence and group effectiveness. *Administrative Science Quarterly, 40,* 145–180.

Wageman, R. (Ed.). (1999). *Groups in context.* Stamford, CT: JAI Press.

Wageman, R. (2001). How leaders foster self-managing team effectiveness: Design choices versus hands-on coaching. *Organization Science, 12,* 559–577.

Wageman, R. (2003). Virtual process: Implications for coaching the virtual team. In E. A. Mannix & R. Peterson (Eds.), *Understanding the dynamic organization* (pp. 65–86). Mahwah, NJ: Erlbaum.

Wageman, R., & Baker, G. (1997). Incentives and cooperation: The joint effects of task and reward interdependence on group performance. *Journal of Organizational Behavior, 18,* 139–158.

Wageman, R., & Gordon, F. (2005). As the twig is bent: How group values shape emergent task interdependence in groups. *Organization Science, 16,* 687–700.

Wageman, R., & Hackman, J. R. (2010). What makes teams of leaders leadable? In N. Nohria & R. Khurana (Eds.), *Advancing leadership* (pp. 457–487). Boston: Harvard Business School Press.

Wageman, R., Nunes, D. A., Burruss, J. A., & Hackman, J. R. (2008). *Senior leadership teams: What it takes to make them great.* Boston: Harvard Business School Press.

Wall, T. D., Kemp, N. J., Jackson, P. R., & Clegg, C. W. (1986). Outcomes of autonomous work groups: A long-term field experiment. *Academy of Management Journal, 29,* 280–304.

Waller, M. J., Gupta, N., & Giambatista, R. C. (2004). Effects of adaptive behaviors and shared mental models on control crew performance. *Management Science, 50,* 1534–1544.

Waller, M. J., Zellmer-Bruhn, M. E., & Giambatista, R. C. (2002). Watching the clock: Group pacing behavior under dynamic deadlines. *Academy of Management Journal, 45,* 1046–1055.

Walsh, J. P. (1995). Managerial and organizational cognition: Notes from a trip down memory lane. *Organization Science, 6,* 280–321.

Walton, R. E. (1985). From control to commitment: Transforming workspace force management in the United States. In K. B. Clark, R. H. Hayes, & C. Lorenz (Eds.), *The uneasy alliance: Managing the productivity–technology dilemma* (pp. 237–265). Boston: Harvard Business School Press.

Walton, R. E., & Hackman, J. R. (1986). Groups under contrasting management strategies. In P. S. Goodman (Ed.), *Designing effective work groups* (pp. 168–201). San Francisco: Jossey-Bass.

Watson, W., Michaelsen, L. K., & Sharp, W. (1991). Member competence, group interaction, and group decision making: A longitudinal study. *Journal of Applied Psychology, 76,* 803–809.

Wegner, D. M. (1986). Transactive memory: A contemporary analysis of the group mind. In B. Mullen & G. R. Goethals (Eds.), *Theories of group behavior* (pp. 185–208). New York: Springer-Verlag.

Wegner, D. M. (1995). A computer network model of human transactive memory. *Social Cognition, 13,* 319–339.

Weick, K. E., & Roberts, K. H. (1993). Collective mind in organizations: Heedful interrelating on flight decks. *Administrative Science Quarterly, 38,* 357–381.

Weisband, S. P. (1992). Group discussion and first advocacy effects in computer-mediated and face-to-face decision making groups. *Organizational Behavior and Human Decision Processes, 53,* 352–380.

Wheelan, S. A. (1996). An initial exploration of the relevance of complexity theory to group research and practice. *Systems Practice, 9,* 47–70.

Wheelan, S. A. (Ed.). (2005). *The handbook of group research and practice.* Thousand Oaks, CA: Sage.

Whyte, G. (1998). Recasting Janis's groupthink model: The key role of collective efficacy in decision fiascoes. *Organizational Behavior and Human Decision Processes, 73,* 185–209.

Williams, K. Y., & O'Reilly, C. A., III. (1998). Demography and diversity in organizations: A review of 40 years of research. *Research in Organizational Behavior, 20,* 77–140.

Wilson, J. M., Goodman, P. S., & Cronin, M. A. (2007). Group learning. *Academy of Management Review, 32,* 1041–1059.

Wilson, J. M., O'Leary, M. B., Metiu, A., & Jett, Q. R. (2008). Perceived proximity in virtual, work: Explaining the paradox of far-but-close. *Organization Studies, 29,* 979–1002.

Wiltermuth, S. S., & Heath, C. (2009). Synchrony and cooperation. *Psychological Science, 20,* 1–5.

Wittenbaum, G. M., Hollingshead, A. B., Paulus, P. B., Hirokawa, R. Y., Ancona, D. G., Peterson, R. S., et al. (2004). The functional perspective as a lens for understanding groups. *Small Group Research, 35,* 17–43.

Wood, J. D. (1990). New Haven Nighthawks. In J. R. Hackman (Ed.), *Groups that work (and those that don't)* (pp. 265–279). San Francisco: Jossey-Bass.

Woolley, A. W. (1998). Effects of intervention content and timing on group task performance. *Journal of Applied Behavioral Science, 34,* 30–49.

Woolley, A. W., Gerbasi, M. E., Chabris, C. F., Kosslyn, S. M., & Hackman, J. R. (2008). Bringing in the experts: How team composition and collaborative planning jointly shape analytic effectiveness. *Small Group Research, 39,* 352–371.

Wong, S. S. (2004). Distal and local group learning: Performance trade-offs and tensions. *Organization Science, 15,* 645–656.

Yalom, I. D. (1995). *The theory and practice of group psychotherapy* (4th ed.). New York: Basic Books.

Yalom, I. D., & Leszcz, M. (2005). *Theory and practice of group psychotherapy* (5th ed.). New York: Basic Books.

Yukl, G. A. (2002). *Leadership in organizations* (5th ed.). Upper Saddle River, NJ: Prentice Hall.

Zaccaro, S. J. (2007). Trait-based perspectives of leadership. *American Psychologist, 62,* 6–16.

Zaccaro, S. J., & Lowe, C. A. (1988). Cohesiveness and performance on an additive task: Evidence for multidimensionality. *Journal of Social Psychology, i,* 547–558.

Zajonc, R. B. (1965). Social facilitation. *Science, 149,* 269–274.

Zellmer-Bruhn, M., & Gibson, C. (2006). Multinational organizational context: Implications for team learning and performance. *Academy of Management Journal, 49,* 501–518.

Zemore, S. E., Kaskutas, L. A., & Ammon, L. N. (2004). In 12-step groups, helping helps the helper. *Addiction, 99,* 1015–1023.

Zenger, T. R., & Marshall, C. R. (2000). Determinants of incentive intensity in group-based rewards. *Academy of Management Journal, 43,* 149–163.

Zigurs, I., Poole, M. S., & DeSanctis, G. L. (1988). A study of influence in computer-mediated group decision making. *MIS Quarterly, 12,* 625–644.

Chapter 33

Organizational Preferences and Their Consequences

DEBORAH H. GRUENFELD AND LARISSA Z. TIEDENS

As automatically as individuals feel, think, and behave, groups of individuals organize, and, like other species, humans organize for predictable reasons, in predictable patterns, and with predictable consequences. The study of human organizing behavior occurs across a variety of social science disciplines, including social psychology (Anderson, Srivastava, Beer, Spataro, & Chatman, 2006; Arrow, 1997), sociology (Blau, 1977; Merton, 1957; Homans, 1950), biology (Alexander, 1979), anthropology (Fiske, 1991; Malinowski, 1939; Radcliffe-Brown, 1952), and economics (Tirole, 1986), and is central to the interdisciplinary field of organizational behavior (March & Simon, 1958; Mayo, 1960; Pfeffer, 1998; Rousseau, 1997; Wilpert, 1995).

The purpose of this chapter is to make a series of novel claims, drawing on some of these literatures to provide evidence, about the social psychology of organizing (see also Homans, 1950; Scott, 1992; Weick, 1979). One claim is that among the ways people can organize themselves, certain structural forms tend to dominate organization life—for better or worse—because they serve basic human needs. A second claim is that these preferred social structures are intentionally and unintentionally created and re-created by organization members, independent of and often in opposition to the formal organization designs that are imposed for strategic purposes (see also Homans, 1950; Mulder, 1971; Roethlisberger & Dickson, 1939). To substantiate these claims about the social structure of organizations, this review draws on literatures that illustrate which types of structures dominate organization life and the social, psychological, and organizational processes that facilitate their construction and reconstruction.

The drive to organize stems from both evolutionary and existential logics. From an evolutionary stance, living and working in groups and organizations is more adaptive for survival than social isolation (see Neuberg et al., this volume). Existentially, human psychology has evolved to reinforce these adaptive arrangements. Human beings are plagued by a fundamental fear of death (Becker, 1973), which expresses itself in the fear of being alone and in the crisis of meaning (see Pyszczynski et al., volume 1). From these anxieties arise basic human strivings (Buck, 1976)—for affiliation and belonging on the one hand (see Leary, this volume) and for impact (i.e., status and power) on the other (McClelland, 1975; Swann, in press). People look to organizations to fulfill these strivings, some would say, naively (e.g., Pauchant, 2002; Whyte, 1956).

Indeed, it has been argued elsewhere that among the functions of work is to provide fulfillment of psychological needs (Cofer, 1959; Heath, 1999; Whyte, 1956), including the ability to establish and maintain social connections with others (Jahoda, 1982; Ouchi, 1981), to establish, develop, or change one's identity (Ashforth, 2001; Dutton, Duckerich, & Harquail, 1994), to acquire status and recognition (Homans, 1950; Mayo, 1960; Pfeffer, 1992; Roethlisberger & Dickson, 1939), and to derive meaning by having impact in the world (Herzberg, Mausner, Snyderman, 1959; McGregor & Cutcher-Gershenfeld, 2006).

It is our claim that certain types of organizations serve these purposes better than others and that these types of organizations should arise more frequently and with greater resiliency than other types of organizations. Specifically,

We wish to thank Lucia Guillory, Tamar Kreps, Jim Phills, and members of the Stanford Graduate School of Business behavioral faculty brown-bag for their helpful contributions to our work on this chapter.

we posit that *homogeneous* and *hierarchical* organizations are psychologically preferable to organizations that are more *heterogeneous* and *egalitarian*, because they provide a better context for achieving belongingness and impact goals. Organizations naturally gravitate toward social homogeneity and social hierarchy because members conspire, often without awareness, to homogenize and stratify the social environment, even despite—and sometimes in reaction to—moral, ideological, and strategic imperatives to do the opposite: that is, to embrace and promote more diversity and greater equality.

The homogenization of organizations is well documented from a variety of perspectives within sociology (for reviews see Fernandez, Castilla & Moore, 2000; McPherson, Smith-Lovin & Cook 2001; Reskin, McBrier & Kmec, 1999) and organizational behavior (O'Reilly & Chatman, 1996; Van Maanen & Schein, 1979; Westphal & Zajac, 1995), as well as social–organizational psychology (Asch, 1956; Janis, 1972; Newcomb, 1961). The stratification of organizations into hierarchically ordered groups and individuals is also documented, but not as evenly across disciplines. Within social–organizational psychology, for example, programmatic research on status, power, and social hierarchy is a relatively recent development, although studies of obedience to authority (Milgram, 1974) and of prisoner and guard roles in the Stanford Prison Experiment (Zimbardo, Maslach, & Haney, 2000), for example, are viewed as seminal in the field. In fact, much of the recent social psychological work on stratifying processes has been published within the past 10–15 years (for reviews see Fiske, this volume; Fiske & Berdahl, 2007; Keltner, Gruenfeld, & Anderson, 2003; Magee & Galinsky, 2008). Within sociology and organizational behavior, however, analysis of social and organizational stratification has a longer and more complex history (for a review see Saunders, 1990).

Our review is organized as follows. First, the evidence bearing on the preference for homogeneity is presented. This includes a discussion of definitional and measurement issues, a presentation of research bearing on the extent to which homogeneous organizing structures are preferable to and more prevalent than more heterogeneous structures, and a discussion of the major processes that create, reinforce and maintain organizational homogeneity. Next, we examine the evidence bearing on the preference for hierarchy (including definitional and measurement issues), a presentation of findings bearing on the extent to which hierarchical organizing structures are preferable to and more prevalent than more egalitarian structures, and a discussion of the major processes by which hierarchy is created, imposed and stabilized. These research summaries are followed by a discussion of the ways in which homogeneity and hierarchy are mutually reinforcing and the implications of these mutually reinforcing preferences for organizational performance.

WHAT IS AN ORGANIZATION?

One recent, accurate, and noncontroversial definition of an organization is: "a consciously coordinated social unit composed of two or more people that functions on a relatively continuous basis to achieve a common goal or set of goals" (Robbins & Judge, 2009, p. 6). Others, however, have recommended defining an organization further as a group of groups, noting that distinguishing an organization from a group illuminates some of the unique features of organization life (Simon, 1957; Weick, 1979). For example, acknowledging the multiple-group structure of an organization illuminates the distinctiveness of certain organizational roles, such as that of the manager, whose job is to link multiple groups. Defining an organization as a group of groups is also suggestive of a number of dynamics that are uniquely organizational, including the presence of multiple and competing objectives (Cyert & March, 1963), the competition for scarce resources (Pfeffer & Salancik, 1974), ingroup favoritism and outgroup discrimination (Levine & Campbell, 1972), the presence of faultlines along which coalitions emerge and change shape (Lau & Murnighan, 1998; 2005; Mannix, 1993), and the hierarchical stratification or ranking of groups along power and status dimensions (Pfeffer & Salancik, 1974).

In defining organizations, scholars emphasize different sets of assumptions about the main drivers of organization life (for a review see Scott, 2002). Some scholars emphasize a *rational* set of assumptions. This approach highlights the belief that organizations and their members act largely in pursuit of explicit goals via purposeful coordination and formalized rules. Alternatively, scholars can emphasize a *natural-systems* approach, which assumes that organizations and their members share a common interest in the survival of the system—independent of the achievement of other, more explicit purposes—and that they conspire informally to achieve this outcome. Finally, scholars using an *open-systems* approach assume that the actions of organizations and their members occur largely in response to changing conditions in the organization environment.

This chapter brings a natural-systems approach to bear on the question of how humans organize, for what purposes, and with what consequences. Specifically, it assumes that organizations, independent of their formal missions and business objectives and despite the strategic ideals of leaders, managers, and other organizational architects, reflect the ways in which all human groups serve social and psychological needs (Homans, 1950). Organization members develop patterns of interaction that reinforce social homogeneity and social hierarchy, often without awareness, because most people are more comfortable with these social arrangements than with the alternatives.

Organizing behavior, when it occurs in service of rational or performance outcomes, also affects natural or social outcomes, and organizing behavior driven by human needs affects performance outcomes as well. Thus, understanding the social process of organizing gives rise to basic, not just applied, psychological insights. Organizations are not just a context for understanding the effects of social psychology; they are a social psychological phenomenon in and of themselves. From this perspective, our task is to illuminate how understanding human organization can inform social psychology and vice versa.

ORGANIZATIONAL HOMOGENEITY

Definition of Homogeneity

In one sense, all organizations are heterogeneous, as no two individuals are exactly the same, and organizations are composed of multiple groups that differ from one another in terms of both functional and demographic characteristics. Conceptually, however, it is possible to distinguish between organizations that are characterized by a clear pattern of grouping members who belong to the same meaningful social, functional, or demographic category (i.e., organizations that are more homogeneous than heterogeneous) and those that exhibit more compositional diversity (i.e., organizations that are more heterogeneous than homogeneous).

There are, of course, many dimensions on which the homogeneity of an organization can be assessed (for a recent review see Mannix & Neale, 2005). Race, sex, age, class, educational background, personality, and nationality are all demographic attributes that people bring with them into the organization. Other dimensions of homogeneity are a function of organization membership, including tenure, rank, function, cohort membership (Pfeffer, 1983), and geographic location (Wiesenfeld, Raghuram, & Garud, 2001). Finally, there is homogeneity of underlying knowledge, beliefs, personality, and attitudes— the psychological attributes that are sometimes referred to as *deep* as opposed to *surface* characteristics (e.g., Harrison, Price, & Bell, 1998; Phillips & Loyd, 2006). And, there can be behavioral homogeneity, which is often a consequence of a strong organizational culture or subculture (Martin, 2002).

Some scholars treat all types of diversity as though they are equivalent, noting that diversity of any kind increases cognitive resources and, hence, performance (Wiersema & Bantel, 1992). Others have distinguished

among attributes that have high task-relevance and those that do not (e.g., Pelled, Eisenhardt, & Xin, 1999), noting that functional, educational, and industry background differences increase the knowledge, skills, and abilities necessary for the performance of specific organizational tasks, whereas differences that have no direct bearing on the performance of specific tasks are less likely to have positive effects (Simons, Pelled, & Smith, 1999).

There are also a number of ways to operationalize homogeneity (e.g., Bedeian & Mossholder, 2000; Lawrence, 1997). Some studies define homogeneity in terms of the extent to which certain demographic groups are either overrepresented or underrepresented relative to their proportions in the labor pool (e.g., Sorensen, 2004). Other studies define homogeneity as the extent to which demographic groups differ in their relative proportions within a firm (e.g., Baron, Hannan, Hsu, & Kocak, 2007; Mouw, 2002), and still others emphasize the extent to which different demographic groups are segregated across jobs and work sites within a firm (Baron & Bielby, 1980), a profession or industry (Bielby & Baron, 1986; Morales, 2008), or an economy (Baron & Bielby, 1984).

There is also a thriving literature on the demographic composition of work groups that measures homogeneity and examines its effects on performance (e.g., Blau, 1977; Jackson, Joshi, & Erhardt, 2003; Jehn, Northcraft, & Neale, 1999; Ruderman, Hughes-James, & Jackson, 1996), including in multidisciplinary or cross-functional teams (e.g, Dahlin, Weingart, & Hinds, 2005; Jackson, 1996), in sales teams (Jackson & Joshi 2004), in banking teams (Bantel & Jackson, 1989), and in top management teams (e.g., Barsade, Ward, Turner, & Sonnenfeld, 2000; Joshi, Liao, & Jackson, 2006; Kilduff, Angelmar, & Mehra, 2000). The findings on whether homogeneity is better or worse for organizational performance are inconsistent, perhaps, in part, due to the variation in contexts and forms of homogeneity.

The Preference for and Prevalence of Social Homogeneity

One of the most robust and widely documented organizing principles in human behavior is the preference for social homogeneity. Consistent with what has been called the homophily principle (e.g., Lazarsfeld & Merton, 1954; Blau, 1977), the similarity–attraction hypothesis (e.g., Byrne, 1971), and ingroup favoritism (Tajfel & Turner, 1986), the observation that people are drawn to similar others seems to apply to every type of human organization (for a review see McPherson, Smith-Lovin, & Cook, 2001). In studies of work organizations, it has been shown repeatedly that demographically similar co-workers like, are more attracted to, and prefer to work and communicate with one another more than with co-workers who are demographically different (Chatman & O'Reilly, 2004; but see Reagans, 2005).

Reasons for Social Homogeneity

There are also many theoretical traditions devoted to explaining why people prefer similar others (Schneider, 2004). Evolutionary theory predicts that we are drawn to those who are genetically similar (e.g., Rushton, 1989). Social comparison theory suggests that we are drawn to others who validate our own judgments about the world (Festinger, 1954; Goethals, 1986). Balance theory posits that we prefer cognitive symmetry to asymmetry and that liking others with whom we agree is more balanced and more consistent (Abelson et al., 1968) than liking others with whom we disagree (Heider, 1958; Newcomb, 1961). Other approaches posit that people are more drawn toward similar than dissimilar others because thinking that similar others are superior to dissimilar others is necessary for self-esteem. For example, terror management theory predicts greater attraction to those who uphold similar cultural values and greater disdain toward those who violate cultural values when mortality is salient (see Pyszczynski, volume 1). Social identity theory posits that people are more drawn to similar others because feeling good about one's social identity requires thinking that similar others are superior to dissimilar others on some important dimensions (Tajfel & Turner, 1986), and these identity dynamics have been applied to organizations (Ashforth & Mael, 1989; Pratt, 2001). The preference for similar others is also politically advantageous: The greater the proportion of organization members that are similar to oneself, the greater one's ability to form a dominant coalition (Mannix, 1993; Murnighan, 1978). It seems fair to conclude that the preference for social homogeneity is overdetermined and can be viewed as one of the most fundamental human phenomena (Schneider, 2004; West, 2002).

In sum, evidence about these psychological forces suggests that homogeneous structures, compared with heterogeneous structures, are preferred by the individuals who construct and inhabit them. This helps to explain why, despite contemporary legal, moral, and business imperatives calling for less discrimination, more equal opportunity, greater tolerance, and greater appreciation of diversity in the business world, most workplaces are still dominated by discernable homogeneity (Reskin, McBrier, & Kmec, 1999).

Homogeneity in Organizational Demography

As noted, one field of work that illustrates the homogeneity of social structures in organizations compares the demographic composition of work organizations with the demographic composition of the labor pools from which firm employees are drawn. Such analyses permit assessments of the extent to which certain types of employees are overrepresented or underrepresented within organizations. In the absence of a preference for homogeneity, one might expect that the demographic composition of firms should resemble a random draw from the pool of qualified workers who are available for hire. Yet the literature on organizational demography shows that organizations often do not resemble the proportion of qualified workers in relevant labor pools (e.g., Reskin, 2005; Reskin, McBrier, & Kmec, 1999). According to this literature, when data are aggregated across firms, at the national level for example, analyses of workplace discrimination underestimate the extent to which organizations are still characterized by homogeneity. Despite the increasing heterogeneity of qualified workers, demographic minorities are still significantly underrepresented in over half of U.S. establishments (Reskin, 2005). When analyses are computed at the workplace or job level, the persistent large-scale segregation of women and minorities becomes evident (e.g., Carrington & Troske, 1998a, b). One recent study found moderate to high levels of racial segregation in four major U.S. urban areas, noting that around half of the workers across firms would have to switch jobs in order to achieve an even distribution across workplaces (Sorensen, 2004). Segregation was worse in small than large firms (see also Moss & Tilly, 1996; Reskin & Roos, 1990; Szafran, 1982). As evidence for the potential pervasiveness of this pattern, firms with fewer than 20 employees account for 87% of U.S. workplaces (Reskin, McBrier, & Kmec, 1999).

National and ethnic groups tend to cluster in certain occupations and industries (e.g., Kaufman, 2002) and are segregated within firms (Hellerstein & Neumark, 2008; Queneau, 2005). For example, one recent study examined the labor market segmentation of members of 100 ethnic groups living in 216 metropolitan areas and found that indigenous minority and non-European groups tended to dominate in service and blue collar occupations, while European, Middle Eastern, and selected Asian groups tended to dominate in professional–managerial and technical occupations (Wilson & Hammer, 2003; see also Wright & Ellis, 2000).

Gender homogeneity is also evident. Reskin, McBrier, & Kmec (1999) reported that almost half of an average establishment's full-time employees were female, which corresponds roughly to the representation of women in the population. However, more than one of every 10 firms employed fewer than 10% full-time women, and one of every 14 firms employed more than 90% women. Moreover, the segregation of men and women into different jobs within the same organization is a pervasive feature of the organizational landscape (e.g, Baron, Hannan, Hsu, & Kocak, 2007; Peterson, Saporta, & Seidel, 2000; Tomaskovic-Devey & Skaggs, 2002).

A study of detailed job titles, for example, found 58% of the firms studied were totally sex segregated and 80% of the firms had 90% or more of the jobs held by one sex (Baron & Bielby, 1986). Furthermore, men and women doing the same work were assigned different job titles. More recently, sex segregation was observed in Silicon Valley high-tech startups (Baron, Hannan, Hsu, & Kocak, 2007). Specifically, averaging across all 167 firms sampled, women were vastly overrepresented in clerical (91%) and administrative positions (54%) and vastly underrepresented in technical roles (17%) and senior management (14%). Among female senior managers, a third were concentrated in human resources and administrative positions, with only 4% overseeing the core functions of engineering or R&D. Only 10% of the firms had had a woman CEO, president, or founder.

Thus, although demographic heterogeneity at the firm level seems to have increased at least somewhat with the heterogeneity of the labor pool, race-based homogeneity and sex-based homogeneity within organizations are both still evident, not so much because members of demographic minority groups are excluded from organizations altogether but, rather, because members of demographic groups tend to be segregated into relatively homogeneous social groupings (Weeden & Sorensen, 2003). The demographic heterogeneity of American society and the U.S. labor market has by all accounts increased steadily over time (Goldin, 1990). Yet organizations are still apparently more homogeneous and more segregated than the labor pool (Reskin, 1993).

If the skills and qualifications of different demographic groups explained their over- versus underrepresentation in various homogeneous workplaces, the findings showing such effects would not support the assertion that the homogeneity of organizations reflects a human preference. There is some evidence that skills and education play a role in workplace segregation (e.g., Browne, Hewitt, Tigges, & Green, 2001). Recent reviews of the literature on organizational demography indicate, however, that differential skills alone cannot account for these patterns (e.g., Moss & Tilly, 2001; Turner, 2008). One study tested this idea by looking at the proportion of African Americans hired by manufacturing plants in suburban versus urban areas (Holzer & Reaser, 2000). In this study, prospective African American workers were less skilled than comparable Whites, and the skill requirements of the suburban plants were lower than those in the urban plant. Yet, contrary to a differential skills explanation, the proportion of Blacks hired was lower in suburban than in urban firms.

Homogeneity in Social Networks

If the homogeneity of an organization's formal structure imposed constraints on employees that conflicted with their preferences, an examination of personal networks would presumably reveal that people go out of their way to create a more heterogeneous web of contacts than mere propinquity would allow. However, the literature on social networks indicates that, in fact, personal networks reinforce, and are in part responsible for, homogeneous formal structures. This is because the processes of identifying, selecting, recruiting, transferring, and promoting individuals occur largely through patterns of informal contact between co-network members, and social networks are also predominantly homogeneous. Moreover, when formal structures are not homogeneous enough, employees in the minority often go out of their way—reaching across formal work group and organization boundaries—to reach and establish contacts with similar others (Ibarra, 1993; Meyerson, 2001). Majority members in organizations that become too heterogeneous show signs of disengagement (Tsui, Egan, & O'Reilly, 1992) and, in studies of neighborhoods, they tend to exit altogether (Crowder, 2000; Granovetter, 1978; Schelling, 1971).

The study of social networks involves capturing the spatial representation of patterns of contact and relationship among social actors (for reviews, see Aldrich & Carter, 2004; McPherson, Smith-Lovin, & Cook, 2001). Among the strongest predictors of network co-membership are co-location and structural interdependence (Blau, 1977; Marsden, 1990). Thus, social networks correspond to the formal organizational structures within which work takes place: People are more likely to have contact with others in their department or functional area and with those they report to or manage. However, networks can also reveal an alternative reality to what appears in an organizational chart. Networks of personal relationships within an organization do not map perfectly onto what formal structures would predict, because although social networks reflect the co-location, or exposure, of actors to one another vis-a-vis their formal work relationships, they also reflect informal social groupings within and outside of the organization, which are driven by actor preferences (Laumann, 1966; Marsden, 1988).

The homogeneity of a social network is typically measured in terms of structural features such as *homophily* (the extent to which contacts with similar others are more frequent and stronger than contacts with dissimilar others), *range* (the extent to which a person's contacts span outside of his or her immediate work group), and *density* (the extent to which contacts within the network are all mutually connected with one another).

A recent review of the social networks literature concluded that the evidence for homogeneity in social networks is "voluminous" (McPherson, Smith-Lovin, & Cook, 2001, p. 416). Homogeneity in the form of homophily, in particular, characterizes social networks of every type, including friendship, work, advice, support, information transfer, exchange, and co-membership (but see Lawrence, 1997). Race and ethnicity are the strongest dividers, with age, religion, education, occupation, and gender following in roughly that order. The divide among races is so extreme that, one study found fewer than 10% of respondents to the General Social Survey reported discussing important matters with a person of another race (Marsden, 1987). Another study found evidence in five different workplaces of racial homogeneity in personal networks and greater racial homogeneity in friendship than in instrumental ties (Lincoln & Miller, 1979). More recently, despite the recent spread of network theory and management rhetoric about the performance benefits of diverse social networks (e.g., Reagans, Zuckerman, & McEvily, 2004; Seibert, Kraimer, & Liden, 2001), homogeneity in social networks persists (Seidel, Polzer, & Stewart, 2000).

To the extent that homogeneity in social networks is based purely on frequency of exposure, the networks of majority members should be more homogeneous than the networks of minority members (who are exposed to fewer similar contacts). Evidence for this *baseline homophily* pattern exists (e.g., Ridgeway & Smith-Lovin, 1999). However, a pure exposure explanation underestimates the homogeneity of minority members' networks, which tend to be more homogeneous than their immediate social environments (for a caveat, see Ibarra, 1997). When social networks are more homogeneous than their surrounding social setting, this is taken as evidence of *inbreeding homophily*. Inbreeding homophily provides evidence that network homogeneity reflects the preference for similar others, over and above propinquity or convenience (Byrne, 1971; Laumann, 1966, 1973; Marsden, 1988). Evidence of inbreeding homophily was obtained in a study showing that the social networks of high potential managers from minority groups (i.e., racial minorities and women), when compared with high potential White majority group managers, span more outside of the immediate work group to connect with similar others (Ibarra, 1995). Relatedly, network homogeneity is more pronounced among members of voluntary organizations, who choose to join, than among members of work organizations, who choose but are also chosen and assigned (McPherson & Smith-Lovin, 1987).

Further evidence of inbreeding homophily is the finding that ties among racial minority members also tend to be stronger—that is, closer and more resilient—than ties with majority members (Schneider, Dixon, & Udvari, 2007). When structural changes disrupt patterns of co-location, ties that are cross-sex or cross-race are more likely to be dropped than ties among demographically similar friends (Hallinan & Williams, 1989). Homogeneous relations help friendships survive other structural challenges. Homogeneity becomes more important to tie activation during times of crisis or trouble (Galaskiewicz & Shatin, 1981; Hurlbert, Haines, & Beggs, 2000). In sum, when similar others are scarce, people seek them out, and when patterns of exposure and co-location change, homogeneous ties outlast heterogeneous ties. These patterns all contribute to the homogeneity of individuals' personal networks.

Summary

The evidence from a number of literatures provides either direct or indirect support for the claim that homogeneous structures dominate organization life. Organizations, occupations, jobs, and social networks tend to be composed of homogeneous, segregated groups. This pattern is not merely a reflection of the pools from which employees are drawn, which are themselves segregated. Rather, homogeneous firms, jobs, and social networks are the product of choice on the part of organization members, who find their way into homogeneous social structures both when doing so is easy and when it is not, because it is preferable.

Homogenizing Processes

This section presents evidence that the preference for homogeneity drives a distinct set of structuring activities that lead to the establishment and reestablishment of homogeneous groupings within organizations. Organizations face opportunities to create more homogeneity or more diversity at multiple points in time, yet, homogeneity occurs throughout the organizational lifespan. First, homogeneity is often a founding principle at the time of an organization's creation and it continues to guide organizational recruitment efforts as members enter and exit the firm. The formal hiring practices through which new organization members are selected are homogeneity enhancing, and more informally, the widespread use of personal networks for job referrals homogenizes the outcomes of hiring, independent of the impact of formal hiring practices. Second, research on organizational culture shows that culture also homogenizes employees once they enter a firm via two routes: first, by attracting potential employees in search of a high degree of person–organization (P-O) fit; and second, by socializing and, thereby, purposefully increasing behavioral homogeneity among new recruits, effectively driving out whatever behavioral heterogeneity they bring with them. Research on the performance of organizational groups and teams shows, in addition, that diverse groups reliably reorganize themselves into homogeneous factions. Finally, the literatures on turnover (voluntary and involuntary) show how organizations rid themselves of employees who interfere with homogeneity goals.

Selection

It has been noted often that organizations engage in *homosocial reproduction*, which refers to the filling of organizational ranks with new employees who resemble the old employees (e.g., Kanter, 1977). For example, there are a number of types of homogenizing practices that occur at the time of recruiting (Reskin, 2005). One set of practices involves using application procedures that facilitate discrimination on the basis of observable qualities, such as in-person interviews or requiring a photograph with an application; another involves failing to keep records of the demography of new hires so that fairness in hiring cannot be tracked. Homogenizing job requirements have been documented as well, including forbidding the use of foreign languages at work and regulating hairstyles. Organizations can use subjective hiring procedures and vague criteria to create leeway for preferring candidates of one's own race or sex (Baron, 1984; Kanter, 1977). In experimental and field studies of hiring decisions, findings illustrate a positive relationship between applicant–rater similarity and the perceived quality of the applicant (Baskett, 1973; Wexley & Nemeroff, 1974). Organizations also offer more attractive jobs (e.g., Howell & Reese, 1986; Wallace & Chang, 1990) and more attractive terms of employment to certain types of employees, specifically, White men (e.g., Baron & Newman, 1990; England, 1992; Kilbourne, Farkas, Beron, Weir, & England, 1994).

It has also been noted that organization gatekeepers tend to evaluate prospective employees based on their demographic similarity to organizational elites (Baron, 1984). Consistent with this hypothesis, it has been shown that CEOs who had more power than their boards of directors appointed new directors who were demographically similar to themselves, yet when boards were more powerful than their CEOs, new directors resembled the existing board (Westphal & Zajac, 1995). Other studies have shown similar effects in other contexts; for example, educational administrators were typically the same sex and race as their predecessors, regardless of the composition of the recruitment pools (Konrad & Pfeffer, 1991), and the presence of a female CEO was associated with hiring significantly greater numbers of women in scientific and technical positions in Silicon Valley startups (Baron, Hannan, Hsu, & Kocak, 2007). Similarly, firms whose owners and supervisors are Black disproportionately hire Black workers (Carrington & Troske, 1998b).

Homogenization also comes from the supply side in hiring, as individuals search for employment in organizations in which they anticipate good person–organization (P–O) *fit*. P–O fit affects a broad range of outcomes that contribute to organizational homogeneity. For example, P–O fit affects organization choice and entry. Individuals seeking jobs tend to prefer organizations with personalities, goals, and values congruent with their own (Turban & Keon, 1993) and those with pay systems and internal structure that complement their needs (Cable & Judge, 1994). Similarly, individuals with a high need for achievement tend to select into organizations that reward competitive individual effort (Turban & Keon, 1993). High P–O fit (both in values and in goals) is also good for employees, who tend to show more motivation, satisfaction, commitment, work group cohesion, feelings of personal success, and less stress and turnover (e.g., Boxx, Odom, & Dunn, 1991; Chatman, 1991; B. Schneider, 1987). High P–O fit is also associated with fewer intentions to quit (Bretz & Judge, 1994), more positive attitudes about work (Dawis & Lofquist, 1984), and more prosocial and ethical behavior in the workplace (O'Reilly & Chatman, 1986).

Social Networks and Job Referrals

Independent of formal hiring practices, social networks play a critical role in the process of homosocial reproduction. Social networks are a key selection mechanism; more jobs are secured via social networks than any other matching process (Baker, 2000). Specifically, people regularly use personal contacts to find jobs (e.g., Bridges & Villemez, 1986; Granovetter, 1995; Montgomery, 1992) and to find prospective employees (Fernandez, Castilla, & Moore, 2000; Petersen, Saporta, & Seidel, 2000; Sorensen & Kelleberg, 1994). Since personal networks tend to be composed largely of homogeneous others, hiring based on personal referrals ensures greater homogeneity within rank and in the organization at large, as similar others are brought in (McPherson, Popielarz, & Drobnic, 1992). Informal networks reproduce firm composition because workers usually tell similar others about jobs (e.g., Kalleberg, Knoke, Marsden, & Spaeth, 1996; Waldinger & Bailey, 1991). Timing of application is also better with referrals, which increase the likelihood that similar others will submit applications at an opportune moment (Fernandez & Weinberg, 1997). One recent study of customer service phone center hiring found that (a) prospective hires referred to the firm by current employees were more similar (in their tenure at current employer, education, and gender) to referees than would be predicted by chance, but (b) hiring via personal referrals produced few of the other assumed benefits of hiring based on employee referrals, including the assumption that those referred have better information about the nature of the job, better timing of applications, a higher job acceptance rate, or better socialization post-hire (Fernandez, Castilla, & Moore, 2000). Thus, using social networks as a hiring mechanism does not appear to work in employers' interests, although it clearly serves workers' homosocial reproduction goals (Grieco, 1987; see also Granovetter, 1995).

It is also the case that most job openings are filled from within the firm, and within-firm networks play a key role in this process (Stewman, 1988). For example, it has been reliably shown that heterogeneous networks can be more advantageous than homogeneous networks for upward mobility within a firm (e.g., Burt, 1992). Individuals whose networks are characterized by many *structural holes*, which place the actor at the nexus between otherwise disconnected groups, are promoted faster than those whose networks are characterized by a preponderance of *clique networks*, which are homogeneous groups with strong boundaries (see also Seibert, Kraimer, & Liden, 2001). The advantage of structural holes is thought to come from the brokering activities they enable (Burt, 1992). The competitive advantage provided by brokering, however, depends on the absence of other equally effective brokers: that is, brokering provides unique recognition and promotion opportunities to the broker only if everyone else's networks are homogeneous. The fact that brokering reliably produces such benefits is an indication of how pervasive homogeneous networks are. Homogeneous networks are apparently still preferable to more heterogeneous networks, despite the demonstrable personal benefits that heterogeneity can provide (but see Podolny & Baron [1997] for an account of how homogeneous networks are also important for promotion and success).

Social networks are a source of not just demographic homogeneity, but behavioral homogeneity as well. People with regular contact adopt one another's attitudes, preferences, and behaviors (Burt, 1987; Coleman, Katz, & Menzel, 1966). Social networks affect how knowledge gets distributed, with members of discrete and bounded social structures developing unique pockets of common knowledge that are not shared across the boundary (Burt, 1992). Studies of personal networks within the nonprofit sector show that network co-membership predicts similar attitudes and preferences (Caldiera & Patterson, 1987; Galaskiewicz, 1985). These studies illustrate the power of social networks as an instrument of homogenization.

Organization Culture and Socialization

Socialization is another homogenizing process within organizations. Once members join a new organization, they are taught the ropes by more senior members (Van Maanen & Schein, 1979). Organization culture is a system of shared values, which define what is important, and norms, which dictate appropriate attitudes and behaviors (Chatman & Cha, 2003; Martin, 2002). Socialization is the process by which organization members learn the culture.

One way in which culture homogenizes organizations is through its impact on selection. Employees with ambitions and values that fit an organization's ambitions and values are more likely to be offered jobs, and to accept jobs, than employees who do not fit as well (Kristof, 1996). Culture is also a source of assimilation, however, such that individuals who join a particular firm will become more like one another as they attempt to fit and succeed. In fact, it has been argued that selection and socialization are somewhat substitutable as means of homogenizing employees (Chatman & Cha, 2003).

The literature on culture and socialization suggests that organization culture is an extremely powerful, perhaps the most powerful, mechanism of social control (Flynn & Chatman, 2001; Kunda, 1992; O'Reilly & Chatman, 1986). Organizations are ambiguous, complex and confusing, especially at first. This makes new organization members especially susceptible to social learning (Chatman, 1991; Morrison, 1993). Organizations can be characterized as strong situations (Davis-Blake & Pfeffer, 1988; O'Reilly & Chatman, 1996) that lead members to behave in normatively consistent ways. Then, because people seek to justify their own actions to themselves and others, they reconstruct their values to make them consistent with their actions (Chatman, Bell, & Staw, 1986). This motivated internalization of cultural values is what makes cultural norms such a powerful source of homogenization in organizations.

The mechanisms through which culture is transmitted and behavior homogenized are: (a) participation, which produces commitment; (b) use of language and symbols to emphasize what is important; (c) clear messages from co-workers about culturally valued behaviors; and (d) rewards for compliance with core norms and values (O'Reilly & Chatman, 1996).

The most powerful context for socialization is the work group (Roethlisberger & Dickson, 1939), especially when the groups are cohesive (Lipset, Trow, & Coleman, 1956; Seashore, 1964). Group members value conformity because it increases homogeneity, and they reward conformity by offering acceptance and belonging in return. *Groupthink* is the term most famously associated with the observation that groups making important decisions come to value conformity and consensus to such a degree that discordant viewpoints are effectively silenced, compromising decision quality (Janis, 1972). More recently it has been shown that heterogeneous groups prefer political correctness norms because these norms help downplay the differences among members (Goncalo, Chatman, Duguid, & Kennedy, 2009).

One reliable aspect of culture in work groups is the tendency to value consensus, which is useful for enhancing the sense of belongingness. Consistent with this observation, when belongingness goals are satisfied in work groups, there is some evidence that consensus seeking abates. For example, research on the *common knowledge problem* (Gigone & Hastie, 1993) shows that in typical laboratory groups, which tend to be composed of strangers, members spend the vast majority of their time discussing members' common knowledge, whereas the unique knowledge possessed by individuals is rarely mentioned and, when it is, is repeated less often (for a review, see Stasser & Titus, 2003). However, this problem is diffused when group members are familiar with one another (Gruenfeld, Mannix, Williams, & Neale, 1996), perhaps because belongingness within groups of familiar others is more secure than in groups of strangers. Work by Edmondson and colleagues on team cultures that are characterized by *psychological safety* explores the role of these kinds of belongingness dynamics in learning, and the detection and reporting of errors, in various work settings (Edmondson, 1999; Tucker, Nembhard, & Edmondson, 2007). The ability for groups and teams to learn and function effectively depends, they argue, on the extent to which team members believe they can speak up against the team without fear of being rejected (also see Baer & Frese, 2003).

Another important mechanism for homogenizing through socialization is the taking of roles (Van Maanen & Schein, 1979). A role is a set of behaviors that are expected of persons who occupy defined positions within a particular social system (e.g., Kahn, 1990; Van Mannen & Schein, 1979). If role expectations are met or exceeded, organizational rewards are passed on to the person performing the role (Podolny & Baron, 1997). If not, errant role occupants are punished. Thus, roles produce homogenization within segregated ranks.

Strong cultures put considerable pressure on employees to conform. They limit the range of values and behavioral styles that are acceptable. It has been pointed out that strong cultures do not necessarily stifle innovation, as cultural norms and values can induce conformity to behavioral norms of expressing unique ideas (Flynn & Chatman, 2001). Nonetheless, even a culture that values innovation and the expression of unique ideas produces a workforce in which heterogeneity in behavioral style is reduced, and thus, homogeneity in behavioral style is enhanced.

Segregation

As noted earlier, although the forces pushing organizations toward homogeneity are strong, it is also inevitable that there

will be sources of heterogeneity within organizations. One way that the reality of heterogeneity is reconciled with the preference for homogeneity is via segregation of those who differ from one another into different homogeneous jobs and work settings. Demographic segregation is a pervasive feature of organization life (Reskin, McBrier, & Kmec, 1999), and functional segregation has historically been a default structural feature of many organizations as well (e.g., Henke, Krachenberg, & Lyons, 1993). Organizations also typically have segregated subcultures (Martin, 2002). Segregation serves to maintain the individual psychological experience of homogeneity even in organizations that might appear diverse if viewed at a macro level. Thus, segregation is a process that supports homogeneity and, as such, we describe some of the literature about how segregation occurs.

Faultlines   An important construct in the organizations literature on how segregation occurs is the *faultline* (e.g., Lau & Murnighan, 1998; 2005), defined as the social boundary that emerges between homogeneous subgroups within a larger heterogeneous work group. Faultlines differentiate between coalitions that are internally homogeneous. The work on faultlines has primarily addressed how faultlines affect group performance, noting that strong faultlines typically hurt. Yet the negative impact of faultlines on performance does not seem to deter their emergence. In fact, a study of transnational teams found that cultural faultlines blocked team integration, yet they were exceedingly common, leading the authors to speculate that despite their negative effect on performance faultlines might satisfy some individual needs or preferences (Earley & Mosakowski, 2000).

Moreover, studies of congruence in heterogeneous work groups provide direct evidence that detectable faultlines are preferable to their absence. Members of heterogeneous work groups have been shown to prefer situations in which surface-level and deep-level differences (e.g., demographic and knowledge differences) are aligned, which would indicate the presence of strong faultlines, to situations in which surface-level and deep-level differences are not aligned, which would indicate weak or absent faultlines (K. W. Phillips, 2003; K. W. Phillips, Mannix, Neale, & Gruenfeld, 2004).

Job Titles and Roles   Whereas faultlines refer to informal and emergent separations within groups, organizations also produce formal separations between groups in order to segregate heterogeneous components of the organization. Several studies have demonstrated the use of job titles to segregate demographic groups. For example, the designers of the civil service used job title distinctions to segregate higher-status professional positions that employed mostly White men from lower-status clerical and manual jobs that employed women and people of color (DiPrete, 1989).

Similarly, within the California civil service, White males created more job titles as a way of continuing to differentiate themselves from and maintain superiority over women, who were being hired in increasing numbers (Strang & Baron, 1990).

Segregation practices are associated not just with the sorting of a diverse workforce into homogeneous categories, but also with pulling some employees (usually majority members) closer to the center of an organization, while pushing others (usually minority members) closer to its periphery (e.g., Klein, Lim, Saltz, & Mayer, 2004; Reskin & Roos, 1990).

Turnover

There are two potential mechanisms by which organization members at the margins become more likely to leave: They can be pushed out, as a consequence of negative performance evaluations, which ultimately lead to firing (i.e., involuntary turnover), or they can walk out, as a consequence of heightened exposure to attractive outside alternatives (voluntary turnover). Research suggests that both mechanisms operate and contribute to the higher attrition of organization members who interfere with homogeneity goals (e.g., Sorensen, 2004).

Negative Performance Evaluations and Involuntary Turnover Evaluators give lower ratings to dissimilar others (Tsui & O'Reilly, 1989). For example, a meta-analysis of 84 studies including nearly 20,000 respondents found that both Black and White raters gave significantly higher ratings to members of their own race (Kraiger & Ford, 1985). In this study and others, negative ratings for minority members were stronger in field settings when the proportion of minority members was smaller. For example, in one field study, women received lower performance ratings when the proportion of women in the group was small, even after controlling for education, job experience, and cognitive abilities (Sackett, DuBois, & Noe, 1991; also see Greenhaus & Parasuraman, 1993; for another view see Pulakos, White, Oppler, & Borman, 1989).

One implication of these findings is that organization members who are similar to their supervisors are more likely to be retained and less likely to be fired than those who are dissimilar. Consistent with this proposal, studies show that organization members who are most dissimilar are laid off first. For example, it has been shown that White employees in a White majority financial firm were less likely to be laid off than Blacks or Hispanics, controlling for business unit, occupation and job level, as well as tenure and performance ratings (Elvira & Zatzick, 2002). Whites were also more likely to be promoted, receive pay raises, and receive high performance ratings than Blacks

(see also Blau & Kahn, 1981; Kletzer, 1998). Another study found that controlling for seniority, layoffs of African Americans were justified based on a broader, more general set of outcomes than that for Whites, for whom layoffs tend to correspond to factors such as human capital credentials and job–labor market characteristics (Wilson & McBrier, 2005). Moreover, Blacks have a higher probability of being laid off overall, and their chances of layoff increase as their experience increases—which might affect their movement into more diverse ranks—while Whites encounter the opposite effect (Wolpin, 1992).

Job Satisfaction and Voluntary Turnover There are a number of studies showing that job satisfaction and intention to quit are also affected by the organization's demographic makeup (e.g., Pfeffer, 1981,1983). Demographic heterogeneity is associated with lower job satisfaction, lower work—group attachment, and greater turnover than homogeneity (Reskin, 2005; Williams & O'Reilly, 1998). These findings apply to studies of variables such as age and tenure (e.g., Pfeffer & O'Reilly, 1987), race (e.g., Sorensen, 2004), and sex (e.g., Tsui & O'Reilly, 1989). Some studies show that in heterogeneous organizations and work units, minority members are more likely to leave than majority members (e.g., Jackson et al., 1991; O'Reilly, Caldwell, & Burnett, 1989), while others show that it is majority members who are more disturbed by and eager to leave a heterogeneous workplace (Tsui, Egan, & O'Reilly, 1992; Wharton & Baron, 1987).

Using personnel data from a large number of bank branches, one recent study found that the turnover rate of a focal employee was increased if a person of the same race left the branch (Sorensen, 2004). Moreover, if a new co-worker of a different race joined the branch, turnover of the focal employee was also increased, but the addition of a same-race co-worker had no effect. This dynamic, in which organization members are compelled to leave whenever dissimilar others seem to be gaining representation, helps to explain how organizations homogenize themselves, and why racial integration is so difficult to achieve (also see Crowder, 2000; Granovetter, 1978; Schelling, 1971).

The relationship of demography to voluntary turnover has also been studied in the social networks literature. For example, it has been shown that people exit organizations in homogeneous clusters, because a similar co-worker exiting suggests that either the organization is hostile to similar others or that similar others can find better opportunities elsewhere (Krackhardt & Porter, 1986). Relatedly, groups remain homogeneous through greater attrition of the members at the edges of a social niche (Popielarz & McPherson 1995; also see Burt, 1997).

A recent meta-analysis found that women's turnover rates do not differ from men's, in contrast to stereotypes about women's instability on the job (Griffeth, Hom, & Gaertner, 2000). However, female quitting behavior does differ from male quitting behavior because better-educated women are more likely to quit their jobs, and this is not true for men (Viscusi, 1980). Presumably, this difference could be attributed in part to the relatively small number of women relative to men in higher job ranks and higher-status occupations.

Summary

The preference for homogeneity has profound organizational consequences. People are not only drawn to similar others within a work context, they are actively homogenized, growing more similar to existing members after joining organizations as well. When heterogeneity does increase, diverse workers are segregated into homogeneous work contexts. Similar workers are more likely to stay, whereas dissimilar workers are more likely to exit.

ORGANIZATIONAL HIERARCHY

Definition of Hierarchy

Hierarchy is most fundamentally about establishing, maintaining, and frequently formalizing differences among members of a group or organization. Hierarchical arrangements may be based on any difference, but hierarchy refers to the translation of that difference into a ranking of power, control, independence, resource allocation, value, and respect (Blau & Scott, 1962; Fiske, this volume). Some hierarchies are more concerned with rankings and distribution of power and control, whereas others are more concerned with status and respect; but in both cases, the notion is that members are ordered in terms of their value to the organization. Usually rankings of access to resources, control, and respect correlate highly with one another (e.g., Thye, 2000). Hierarchies are instantiated in terms of perceptions and beliefs about the value of group members (Berger, Rosenholtz, & Zelditch, 1980; Shils, 1968) and in terms of symbolic markers of positions (Eisenstadt, 1968; Nakao & Treas, 1990), as well as authority roles (Katz & Kahn, 1978), the ability to act in accordance with one's own desires (Cartwright, 1965; French & Raven, 1959), and in terms of behavior, with those at the highest levels engaging in more dominant behavior, and those at the lower levels tending to defer and submit (Hall, Coats, & LeBeau, 2005; Maclay & Knipe, 1972; Schmid Mast, 2002).

Hierarchies vary wildly in the degree to which they are formalized—that is, how easily observable and explicit the rankings are, and the extent to which a particular order is rigorously enforced (Mintzberg, 1983). For example, organizations sometimes downplay hierarchical differences, most frequently by removing signals and markers of positions. Yet, even in these circumstances, people are still aware of differences in the value and influence of different individuals or groups, they generally agree upon rank orderings of influence and value, and these perceptions of rank play out in social interactions (Berger, Cohen, & Zelditch, 1972; Ridgeway, 1987).

Organizations can be more or less hierarchical. The fewer the differences in perceived value, deference, and control between those at the top of these systems and those at the bottom, the more the organization could be considered egalitarian; the greater the differences between the top and the bottom, the more hierarchical the organization is. There are many examples of how investigators have measured the presence of hierarchy, including cultural measures, such as *power distance* (Hofstede, 1980), and organizational measures, such as the number and patterns of positions on organizational charts or official ranks and titles (Hambrick, 1981; Finkelstein, 1992), degree of upward mobility (Paulson, 1974), and salary dispersion (Bloom & Michel, 2002; Pfeffer & Langton, 1993; Shaw, Gupta, & Delery, 2002). More relational and individual measures capture subjective perceptions of one's own absolute or relative degree of power (Anderson & Berdahl, 2002; Maznevski, Gomez, Noorderhaven, & Wu, 1997), co-workers' perceptions of a target's level of power and influence (Anderson, Srivastava, Beer, Spataro, & Chatman, 2006; Hambrick, 1981), or implicit norms about how organization members relate to authority (Fiske, 1991; Kabanoff & Daly, 2002; van Oudenhoven, 2001). There is no consensus on which of these approaches is best, the extent to which they are correlated, or much investigation of whether they yield different results. Yet, perhaps most striking is the extent to which some degree of hierarchy appears to characterize relationships and organizations of all types (Leavitt, 2003; 2004; Lonner, 1980).

The Preference for and Prevalence of Hierarchy

Previous sections of this chapter reviewed evidence that people prefer homogeneity. That preference expresses itself both behaviorally (i.e., people enjoy it when they are exposed to it) and verbally (i.e., people say that they like being with similar others). There is, of course, some voiced ambivalence about the preference for homogeneity in a political climate that values diversity (e.g., Ely & Thomas, 2001; Thomas & Ely, 1996). However, a preference for hierarchy comes with even more ambivalence in a modern

American context in which hierarchy is seen as morally corrupt (Leavitt, 2004; de Tocqueville, 1836/1966). Thus, the preference for hierarchy is rarely acknowledged or articulated, and the assertion that hierarchy is preferable to more egalitarian structures is almost certainly controversial (Leavitt, 2003, 2004).

An explicit distaste for hierarchy and appreciation of equality can be found in nearly every study of values. In one, representative samples from 13 countries were asked to rate the extent to which 10 values represented important and guiding principles in their lives. Universalism, which includes a concern for equality and social justice (Schwartz & Boehnke, 2004), was the third highest across all settings, whereas tradition and power, the values most related to hierarchy, were eighth and tenth, respectively (Schwartz & Bardi, 2001). Similarly, managers from all over the world report that they desire less hierarchy in their workplaces than they currently have (House et al., 2004). And, when groups are given a choice about decision rules, members report a preference for complying with majority opinion over having an individual leader make the decision (Rutte & Wilke, 1985). Further, when a nonstudent sample of happily married couples was asked what produced their success, 51% of them gave a response that was coded as "equity" (Fletcher & Kininmonth, 1992). Other evidence comes from a study of founders of new technology firms. When asked about their preferences and ideals for their new organizations, many founders stated that they wanted equality and participation and sought out structures and practices that they believed would support those goals (Baron, Burton, & Hannan, 1996; Hannan, Burton, & Baron, 1996).

Certainly, there are contexts in which people are more welcoming of hierarchy. For example, some research suggests that people in Asia have more positive associations with hierarchy than do Americans (e.g., Brockner et al., 2001; Ying, Lee, Tsai, Lee, & Tsang, 2001). There are also individual differences in comfort with and preference for inequality. Some people, especially those at the top of hierarchies, desire hierarchies more than others (Pratto, Stallworth, Sidanius, & Siers, 1997). Groups performing poorly tend to seek greater hierarchy (De Cremer & Van Vugt, 1999; Samuelson, 1991, 1993) and the presence of experts and stars (Baron, Burton, & Hannan, 1996), task difficulty (Samuelson, 1991), and time pressure (Baron, Burton, & Hannan 1996) all increase the stated preference for hierarchical systems. Further, the extent to which hierarchy is avoided versus preferred depends on the rules by which hierarchies operate. Although Americans generally report that they oppose hierarchy, they typically embrace meritocracies in which people are rewarded in line with their efforts and contributions (Davey, Bobocel, Son Hing, & Zanna, 1999; Chow,

Lowery, & Knowles, 2008). Meritocracies are clearly hierarchical, yet the notion that differences in power and status are deserved makes them more palatable, even to some who think of themselves as hostile to inequality (Davey, Bobocel, Son Hing, & Zanna, 1999).

Despite the fact that people often do not acknowledge a preference for hierarchy, such a preference can be inferred from behavioral patterns, and from evolutionary and existential logics. The strongest piece of evidence is simply the regularity with which this form of organization is produced. As with homogeneity, people create hierarchies in all types of organizations. When scholars attempt to find an organization that is not characterized by hierarchy, they cannot (Lonner, 1980; Mannix & Sauer, 2006). When an organization touts itself as truly egalitarian, it garners much attention from the press, which itself is a signal of its rarity. So, some companies, such as IDEO and Gore Inc., promote their egalitarian ways as do other types of organizations, such as the chamber orchestra Orpheus, whose primary claim to fame is that it functions without a conductor (Seifter, Economy, & Hackman, 2001). However, closer investigations of these organizations show that, though they have ridded themselves of some of the usual trappings of hierarchy, many hierarchical patterns remain.

For example, the product design firm IDEO looks egalitarian from the perspective of formal positions. There are more than 150 employees, and almost everyone carries the formal title of "engineer." Yet, firsthand observations of brainstorming sessions there reveal that the engineers compete for respect and status at face-to-face meetings (Sutton & Hargadon, 1996). Engineers acquire status based on their respective abilities to come up with "cool" ideas at the brainstorming sessions. Status is doled out in the form of compliments ("neat" "wow" or "cool"), by pursuit of one person's idea by others, and by invitations to future brainstorming meetings. The brainstorming sessions are perceived as a chance for engineers to "strut their stuff" and when invitations to attend are not forthcoming, engineers often see this as a sign that they should leave the organization. Engineers who acquire these status markers also get paid more than those who do not. Thus, although it might look egalitarian at the surface, IDEO is hierarchical: "equal" members do not have equal influence, equal levels of respect from their colleagues, or equal access to resources.

Similarly, although the chamber orchestra Orpheus does not have a conductor and began with very few hierarchical levels for an orchestra, a different member is now appointed the "concert master" for each piece of music (Seifter, Economy, & Hackman, 2001). The founder and president has full control over the nature of the program, including what set of pieces are played and what the program looks like, and there is a "core group" comprised of the "principal" (i.e., highest ranked) string and woodwind players, which makes a number of key group decisions. Orpheus is not alone in the drift it has experienced in becoming more hierarchical over time. Newly formed Silicon Valley companies also tend to become more hierarchical over time (Baron & Hannan, 2002). Those that do not evolve toward hierarchy are less likely to survive.

A behavioral preference for hierarchy is also evident in studies that show a speedy emergence of hierarchical structures even when these structures are not necessary for task completion. In one classic study, discussion groups that were together for one hour, without directions to create a hierarchy or any task that required it, created hierarchies nonetheless (Bales & Slater, 1955; Slater, 1955). During the groups' one-hour life span, members came to conceptualize particular individuals as leaders, developed consensus about who these individuals were, and began deferring to them. Studies of dominant and submissive behaviors show the same pattern, with partners falling into a *complementary* dynamic in which one expresses dominance and the other submissiveness within minutes of social interaction (e.g., Sadler & Woody, 2003; Tiedens & Fragale, 2003).

Studies in more naturalistic settings also speak to the prevalence of hierarchy. When people casually gather on street corners, status rankings emerge even though there is no task that would appear to require them (Anderson, 1990; Whyte, 1981). Work partners who might value equality still tend to differentiate in terms of dominance and submission (Tracey & Hayes, 1989, Tracey, Sherry, & Albright, 1999).

Another illustration of the prevalence of hierarchy is evident in the literatures on empowerment and leadership. Empowerment theorists consider the empowerment of lower status workers an important goal all organizations should try to achieve (Conger & Kanungo, 1988; Drucker, 1988; Kanter, 1983). Importantly, the presence of low ranking workers is taken for granted, despite the motivational problems this entails. Another assumption is that organizations do not naturally empower those at the lowest levels. Instead, empowerment requires extra effort and even intervention into the structure that would naturally characterize work organizations (Bowen & Lawler, 1995; Thomas & Velthouse, 1990).

The literature on leadership is characterized by similar assumptions (see Hogg, this volume). This area, which has grown in popularity despite recent arguments about the benefits of flatter organizations, examines the attributes of individuals that predict whether they will become leaders (e.g., Bono & Judge, 2004), as well as what attributes

of people already in leadership positions result in good performance (Kaiser, Hogan, & Craig, 2008). Research in this area is also concerned with how to teach people better leadership skills (e.g., Thach, 2002; Yukl, 2002). The core assumptions here are that there will be leaders, hence hierarchy, in all organizations. It is also assumed that the people in leadership positions will have a greater impact on the development and effectiveness of the organization than other group members (Bass & Stogdill, 1990; Schein, 1992). Some even suggest that organizations as a whole are mere reflections of their upper echelons (Carpenter, Geletkanycz, & Sanders, 2004; Hambrick & Mason, 1984). In sum, an implicit assumption in all of these approaches is that hierarchy is not just prevalent, but inescapable.

Similarly, one reliable way of convincing the field that a particular variable is of interest and importance is to demonstrate that it predicts people's placement in the organizational hierarchy. In fact, a widely accepted way of thinking about success within an organizational context is in terms of one's hierarchical position (see Wrzesniewski, Dutton, & Debebe, 2003, for a different perspective). Thus, promotions, salaries, levels of influence, and status of title are all frequently used to measure success. An enormous number of variables have been found to be associated with these kinds of outcomes. As a taste, scholars have noted that aspects of individuals such as personality (e.g., Anderson, John, Keltner, & Kring, 2001; Judge, Bono, Ilies, & Gerhardt, 2002), demographic characteristics (e.g., Berger, Fisek, Zorman, & Zelditch, 1977; Bunderson, 2003), intelligence (Bass & Stogdill, 1990; Simonton, 1994), and physical features, most notably height (Judge & Cable, 2004; Wilson, 1968) and physical attractiveness (Anderson & Berdahl, 2002; Cherulnik, Turns, & Wilderman, 1990), predict hierarchical position. Research has also examined the impact of specific interpersonal behaviors on hierarchical position, such as the ability to give and receive feedback (Ashford, Blatt, & VandeWalle, 2003; Ashford & Tsui, 1991), to display trustworthiness and concern for others (Hogan, Curphy, & Hogan, 1994; Zaccaro, 2001), and to understand oneself (Walumbwa, Avolio, Gardner, Wernsing, & Peterson, 2008). Network position is associated with hierarchical position (Burt, 1992; Lin, 1999), as is the propensity to negotiate (Babcock & Laschever, 2003).

Although these literatures are full of interesting and important insights in their own right, the point here is simply to note that these kinds of variables are extremely popular in organizations research, and their popularity indicates how large hierarchies loom in organization life. The palpable concern with hierarchical placement is suggestive of how prevalent hierarchies are, and of how important they are to their members.

Evolutionary theorists have also pointed to consistencies in the ways in which hierarchies are enacted. Many have noted the parallels between the hierarchies created and maintained by animals and the similarity they bear to some of the basics of human organizing (Cheney & Seyfarth, 2007; De Waal, 1982; Sapolsky, 1998). Chimpanzees and some other nonhuman primates create hierarchies primarily through the expression of rather subtle nonverbal and verbal behavior signaling dominance and deference and occasionally through acts of violence in which one monkey physically dominates and subjugates another (De Waal, 1982). However, evolutionary theorists have generally argued that status ranks and their accompanying signals function to indicate to the group who would win a fight if it were to happen. In this way, hierarchy effectively bypasses violence. From this perspective, violence mainly occurs when status rankings are at issue (also see Gould, 2003). Once a particular group member is of higher rank he (and it usually is *he*) has access to more resources such as food, sex partners, and at times seems to direct the behavior of the group (De Waal, 1982) and to intimidate and control members of lower rank (Sapolsky, 1994). The basics of this process—subtle signaling to determine pecking order, more extreme acts either to overturn a preexisting hierarchy or when there are departures from established pecking orders, and the ultimate differentiation among members in terms of deference, control, and resources—bear a remarkable similarity to the processes humans use in the creation and maintenance of their organizational hierarchies.

There is also interest among evolutionary researchers about differences in the nature of hierarchy among species (Boehm, 1999), and this becomes particularly relevant to organizational scholars who seek to understand the particulars of human social hierarchies and the degree to which modern organizations either reflect our evolutionary origins or conflict with them (Nicholson, 2000; Van Vugt, 1996; Van Vugt, Hogan, & Kaiser, 2008). Although evolutionary approaches generally have a functionalist view that implies hierarchies exist because they are useful for meeting the ongoing challenges of organizational life, the evolutionary basis of the prevalence of hierarchy is sometimes seen as a remnant from our relatives that must be overcome in order to deal effectively with the organizational pressures and ideas of the modern world.

Existential Bases   As noted earlier, two of the most basic human strivings are for impact and belongingness (Buck, 1976). Both of these needs play a role in the creation and maintenance of social hierarchies. This section considers how these existential needs propel organizations toward hierarchical forms.

The need for impact is closely related to the desire for control. In social and organizational settings, in which individuals are interdependent, impact requires power and the ability to control the behavior of others (Fiske, 1993). The notion that people desire impact, power, control, and domination has a long history in both social and organizational psychology (e.g., Adler, 1966; Rotter, 1966; Sullivan, 1947). The existence of this psychological state is another reason why hierarchies are so common; if people want power, they will create structures that allow them to get it.

Most influential to the study of the social psychology of organizations has been the line of work on *power motive* and a set of related measures for assessing the degree to which people want power (McClelland, 1975). Power motive is not the only one of these constructs; for example, there is also a long standing interest in *trait dominance* (for a review, see Anderson & Kilduff, 2009) and a number of useful measures have emerged (Gough, McCloskey, & Meehl, 1951; Wiggins, Trapnell, & Phillips, 1988). *Social dominance orientation* (SDO) is another variable that reflects the preference for hierarchy (Sidanius & Pratto, 1999). These constructs have in common the idea that all people strive for impact, power, and control, but that individuals vary in the degree to which this outcome is important to them.

Because there is variation among individuals in the importance of having power over others, the extent to which people exhibit power-seeking behavior varies. Those who value power the most behave more in ways that lead to the acquisition of power. For example, those high in power motive are more likely to seek and accept jobs in which they can exercise power, and they stay in those jobs longer than individuals with lower power motive (Jenkins, 1994). They also share less information with others (Fodor & Smith, 1982) and like it when others are ingratiating toward them (Operario & Fiske, 2001). Once in high-power jobs, those high in power motive try to influence and direct other people, express their opinions forcefully, and try to assume leadership positions more than those low in power motive (McClelland, 1975). Those high in trait dominance engage in a range of *hierarchy enhancing* acts, such as speaking more and taking control of group processes, and as a result, they hold disproportionate sway over group decisions (Judge, Bono, Ilies, & Gerhardt, 2002), despite the fact that trait dominance is not associated with any important group-task-related competencies (e.g., Anderson & Kilduff, 2009).

Similarly, social dominance orientation is associated with hierarchy enhancing policy preferences, including support for racism, sexism, classism, the death penalty and painful executions, conquest-oriented military intervention in foreign countries, and opposition to humanitarian interventions (Sidanius, Liu, Shaw, & Pratto, 1994). Those high in SDO choose career paths on which hierarchical differences are enhanced (Pratto, Stallworth, Sidanius, & Siers, 1997; Sidanius, Pratto, Sinclair, &van Laar, 1996). Thus, the literatures on power motive, dominance, and social dominance orientation all suggest that hierarchies exist and are created to satisfy individuals' psycho-social needs for control. They also imply that who ends up in a particular position is at least in part a reflection of who puts the energy and effort into domination.

The need to belong is another central existential goal that underlies the prevalence of hierarchy. A feeling of belongingness may be more obviously associated with people's tendency to produce homogeneous organizations than with their tendency to produce hierarchical structures given how much similarity is associated with liking and affiliation. Yet some research suggests that interpersonal hierarchies can also increase a sense of affiliation and belongingness among interaction partners, especially when they share a task on which they must coordinate. This notion was expressed by scholars in the interpersonal circumplex tradition and their introduction of the notion of *interpersonal complementarity* (Carson, 1969; Kiesler, 1983; Leary, 1957; Wiggins, 1982). Interpersonal theorists have suggested that people tune their behavior in response to social partners as a way of producing smooth social interactions. Specifically, individuals match their interaction partners in terms of how much warmth they express, such that both parties end up behaving similarly in terms of warmth. Simultaneously, partners tune to one another in terms of how much dominance they express, but this kind of tuning requires engaging in behavior that is opposite to the partner's behavior. So, the prediction from interpersonal theory is that people engage in submissive behavior when interacting with a dominant other and dominant behavior when interacting with a submissive other.

Some authors have referred to this interpersonal dynamic more specifically as *dominance complementarity* since it refers distinctly to difference in terms of dominance and submission (Tiedens, Unzeuta, & Young, 2007), rather than to differences in general. Engaging in dominance complementarity produces informal hierarchies by differentiating relationship partners in terms of dominance and submission. Importantly, researchers from the interpersonal theory tradition have argued that dominance complementarity is an act of an affiliative and social nature (as opposed to a controlling one). In support of this notion, research shows that people feel greater relationship satisfaction when dominance is met with submission and submission

with dominance e.g., Glomb & Welsh, 2005; Horowitz et al., 2006; Tiedens & Fragale, 2003) and that people are more likely to create dominance complementarity when they care about and are invested in the relationship or the task the partners share (Tiedens, Fragale, & Young, 2007).

Another way in which hierarchies can promote affiliative goals is by reducing conflict. Hierarchies provide simple decision rules (i.e., individuals at the top have greater say than individuals lower down) and as such can reduce the time spent on discussions or disputes (Bass & Stogdill, 1990). In many instances, decisions are simply made by the highest ranked person, with little resistance from lower ranked others, whether right or wrong, fair or unfair. This kind of deference and conflict avoidance on the part of lower ranked organizational members is understandable in that frequently one role of higher ranked parties is to punish those who fail to fall in line (De Cremer & Van Vugt, 1999; Jung & Lake, 2008; Zimbardo, Maslach, & Haney, 2000). Thus, disagreeing or engaging in conflict can be dangerous for lower ranked members (Kabanoff, 1991) and therefore more hierarchical organizations can be less riddled by conflict than more egalitarian ones (Kabanoff, 1991; Strauss, 1982). Although hostility toward those in power can underlie this lack of conflict (Sampson, 1969), the organization may still be experienced as peaceful and harmonious as a consequence of the unwillingness of lower-ranked members to fight.

Members of groups in which there is no consensus about the status ordering like the group less and are less committed to the group than members of groups who agree on a ranking (Kilduff & Anderson, 2009). Low consensus groups are also less productive (Loch, Huberman, & Stout, 2000) and less effective (Groysberg, Polzer, & Elfenbein, 2007; Kilduff & Anderson, 2009; Overbeck, Correll, & Park, 2005) than groups with greater consensus about status ordering. When consensus is lacking, people engage in more politicking (Loch, Huberman, & Stout, 2000) and in more competitive status contests, which hinder coordination and cooperation on the task at hand (Kilduff & Anderson, 2009). Ambiguity over status ordering and the resulting contest to establish positions have even been cited as a major cause of world violence (Gould, 2003). Thus, even though people may generally dislike hierarchy, the structure does appear to provide some social glue.

People do, as noted earlier, have negative affective reactions to hierarchical structures. Researchers have found that people are less identified with and committed to more hierarchical organizations (Ashforth, 1989; Hornstein, 2002) and, as a consequence, are more passive (Kanter, 1983), less collaborative (Pfeffer & Langton, 1993; Siegel & Hambrick, 2005), less willing to go beyond the immediate confines of their jobs (Organ & Konovsky, 1989), less productive (Cowherd & Levine, 1992), and less satisfied (Pfeffer & Langton, 1993) than members of organizations that are more egalitarian. Others have argued that the low conflict observed in hierarchical structures may reflect the fear of expressing dissatisfaction rather than a true sense of belongingness (Kabanoff, 1991; Mulder, 1977; Strauss, 1982). This raises the possibility that it is only those at the top who prefer hierarchy over more egalitarian structures. However, some studies show that middle- and lower-ranking members are actually more invested in the hierarchy, despite their positions, than those at the top (Jost & Kay, this volume; Phillips & Zuckerman, 2001).

In sum, there is still much to learn about how hierarchy is experienced. Research programs on hierarchy differ from one another both in terms of how hierarchy is operationalized and in terms of how outcomes are assessed. For example, many of the studies demonstrating a negative impact of hierarchy examine pay differentials (e.g., Pfeffer & Langton, 1993), whereas many of those demonstrating the positive effects measure interpersonal behavior (e.g., Dryer & Horowitz, 1997). A systematic study of how and when hierarchy leads to greater satisfaction versus when it leaves people dissatisfied and despondent would constitute a major contribution to the study of the psychology of organizations (also see Fiske & Berdahl, 2007). The most common approach to this question has been to consider different ways in which power holders can enact their positions—that is, which *leadership styles* they adopt (Bass & Stogdill, 1990). A more traditional social psychological approach would be to locate variance in the nature of the system as whole, and this type of research would also make a valuable contribution. One observation toward this end is that in those cases where hierarchy promotes positive outcomes, it provides greater understanding of the roles and relationships within the organization and a sense of security about them. In the cases in which its results are negative, the hierarchy functions to deprive some people of information and understanding necessary for their jobs to be meaningful.

The literature on *Leader–Member Exchange* (LMX) illustrates the importance of what leaders and followers expect to give and take in their hierarchical relationship. This work has suggested that successful leadership requires that both leaders and members get what they expect from one another (for a review see Schriesheim, Castro, & Cogliser, 1999). Further, this literature suggests that affective reactions to hierarchical arrangements vary as a function of the nature of interpersonal interactions within the hierarchy, with quality exchange promoting innovation, productivity, trust, and organizational citizenship (e.g., Gomez & Rosen, 2001; Howell & Hall-Merenda, 1999).

Summary

These considerations suggest that, just as homogeneity dominates organizational life, so does hierarchy People form hierarchies to organize themselves, whether the task requires it or not. Like homogeneity, hierarchy is associated with both positive and negative outcomes, yet even in modern American business settings, in which hierarchical structures and cultures are not at all in favor, people consistently choose hierarchy over its less preferable alternatives.

Stratifying Processes

Just as the homogeneity of organizations is created and re-created as organizations grow and evolve, hierarchies are also established and reaffirmed at various stages in an organization's development. Sometimes hierarchy emerges through conscious and intentional decision making, with rational outcomes in mind, and other times the emergence of hierarchy reflects unintentional responses to bias and other dynamics in the social environment.

Creating Hierarchy

Multiple studies have shown that hierarchies spontaneously emerge. People interacting often produce hierarchies and negotiate their positions within them, quickly and spontaneously, without intending to do so or realizing that they have done so (e.g., Bales, 1950, 1999; Tiedens & Fragale, 2003). These unconscious negotiations also lead to consensus about members' respective hierarchical positions (Overbeck, Correll, & Park, 2005), resulting displays of dominance and deference (Tiedens & Fragale, 2003), greater influence for power holders than subordinates (Bales, 1950; Berger, Rosenholtz, & Zelditch, 1980), and differential access to resources (Bacharach & Lawler, 1980; Yukl, 2002). These hierarchies can be produced within minutes of the group members interacting and often go unnoticed until the group or organization is forced to contemplate members' respective roles.

Hierarchies are also explicitly discussed and chosen when organizations are being designed. In one study, conversations among the founders of new technology companies were observed at the time of organization founding. Company founders regularly grappled with how hierarchical to make their organizations (Baron, Burton, & Hannan, 1996). The degree to which the organization would have an authority structure, the bases of authority, and the power granted to authority figures were all components of these conversations. Those founders who opted for the greatest degree of hierarchy headed companies that relied on "stars" or people with unusual skills that were central to the company's mission and strategy. Hierarchical systems were used in these instances to reward the people (i.e., the stars) who were perceived as most valuable to the firm by giving them status symbols such as titles or other perks, high salaries, and the authority to control and coordinate the actions of other members of the organization.

In general, organizational scholars have argued that hierarchies can facilitate coordination across functions and business units and that the presence of authority roles is useful for motivating and regulating members' actions (Magee & Galinsky, 2008). Coordination and control are two of the most central problems organizations face (Daft, 2004; Galbraith, 1973; March & Simon, 1958). Thus, to the extent that hierarchies solve these problems, they become popular and purposefully chosen by organizations. Hierarchies facilitate coordination by assigning people managerial roles with responsibility for integrating across areas and domains. In theory, managerial roles could exist without providing extra status, authority, and power to the persons occupying them, yet some organizational scholars have argued that imbuing managerial roles with hierarchical elements such as power and authority makes these roles more effective (Etzioni, 1959; Urwick, 1943; Weber, 1947).

The use of hierarchy to reward, motivate, and control behavior has been discussed by numerous scholars and the literature suggests at least three ways in which hierarchies are used in this regard. First, gaining status is rewarding (Frank, 1985; Loch, Huberman, & Stout, 2000) and thus the presence of a status hierarchy allows organizations to offer the incentive of promotion. The existence of this form of rewards is often necessary to keep members active, committed, and engaged with the organization. Those organizations that do not offer opportunities for promotion risk high turnover as members seek the experience of being promoted by getting outside offers (Curry, Wakefield, Price, & Mueller, 1986; Lawler, 1973). Second, leaders are typically given the authority to dole out rewards and punishments, so they control incentive systems for others. Finally, a third way in which hierarchies are motivating is that leaders are considered high-status representatives of the group (Hogg, 2001). As such, their praise and attention become particularly meaningful for group members. Thus, people interpret their own value from how their leaders treat them and become motivated to act in a way that will gain them the simple approval of authority figures even when that approval is not directly linked to material gain. This idea is explored in the *Group Value Model* (Tyler & Lind, 1992) and is implied in the literatures on charismatic and transformational leadership (e.g., Kark, Shamir, & Chen, 2003: Shamir, House, & Arthur 1993).

Imposing Hierarchy

Even groups that start out more egalitarian sometimes impose hierarchy when they find that group goals are not being achieved. For example, researchers studying commons dilemmas have found that groups choose to move from leaderless structures to a system in which there is a leader when members' contributions cannot sustain the common good. These groups choose to have a leader who has the power to punish problematic individuals (e.g., Jung & Lake, 2008; Van Vugt & De Cremer, 1999). Similarly, research has found that people seek particularly authoritarian structures when they feel threatened, fearful, or unable to fend for themselves (Hamblin, 1958; McCann, 1991; Mulder & Stemerding, 1963), and organizations that face financial crises replace their top management teams and CEOs with outsiders who will institute greater control and change (Furtado & Karan, 1990). All of this suggests that organizations can become more hierarchical when they perceive themselves to be falling short of their goals or otherwise not functioning well.

Role Proliferation   A number of scholars have observed that over time the number of roles contained in an organization grows at a greater rate than the size of the organization itself (Baron & Bielby, 1986; Buss, 1984), and the establishment of new roles and job titles tends to increase hierarchical differentiation (Baron & Pfeffer, 1994). The division of labor and the creation of roles were traditionally seen as a rational and functional process engaged in by organizations for the sake of efficiency (Smith, 1937). More recently, role proliferation has come under scrutiny. Multiple roles within organizations have the potential to create coordination problems. It has been noted, for example, that occupants of different roles frequently pay attention only to their own tasks and lose track of the broader goals of the organization (Heath & Staudenmayer, 2000).

Although, in theory, roles could be defined solely in terms of task and need not imply differences in status and rank, organizational theorists have suggested that with a proliferation of roles also comes a differentiation in status for those roles (e.g., Baron & Bielby, 1986; Baron & Newman, 1990; Strang & Baron, 1990). For example, the more titles that exist in an organization, the greater the salary range, controlling for size of the organization (Pfeffer & Davis-Blake, 1990). In addition, the greater the number of roles within an organization, the more the workers feel that large pay differentials are acceptable, or even more desirable, than smaller pay differentials (Lansberg, 1989). If a greater salary range implies greater hierarchy or status difference, then this suggests that as organizations produce more roles, they also produce more hierarchy.

Some researchers have argued that the proliferation of roles may in fact occur in order to produce more stratification rather than to expedite the task (Baron & Bielby, 1986; Dreyfuss & Dreyfuss, 1986; Slater, 1955). Specifically, when industries or firms experience an influx of individuals from poorly represented demographic groups, more roles are created (Bielby & Baron, 1986; Strang & Baron, 1990). Further, these roles become stratified such that those at the top of the organizational hierarchy tend to be occupied by people from groups that have high status in society (i.e., White men), whereas those low in the organizational hierarchy are occupied by people with less status in society (i.e., women, people of color). Thus, the roles justify an organizational structure that provides more power to some people than others (Brass, 1984).

Seeking and Rewarding Competence Performance evaluations and promotions are another important means of imposing hierarchy. Most organizations engage in frequent formal and informal performance assessments (Bretz & Milkovich, 1989). Many organizations have formal evaluation programs on which raises and promotions are putatively based (Cleveland, Murphy, & Williams, 1989; Murphy & Cleveland, 1995), and group members also constantly engage in the informal evaluation of others, especially on those competencies that are most relevant to their shared tasks (Littlepage, Robinson, & Reddington, 1997). The literature is rife with examples of individual attributes that predict status-enhancing evaluations.

As noted earlier, some of these attributes are useful from a rational organizational performance standpoint (e.g., technical skill, interpersonal skills, networking and negotiation skills). There are also organization-specific skill sets that are associated with status achievement. Research taking this perspective on status achievement assumes that each organization faces a unique set of environmental challenges, and that those individuals and groups who are best at addressing those challenges acquire the greatest status and power (e.g., Hambrick, 1981; Salancik & Pfeffer, 1977). These kinds of findings illustrate instances in which organization's monitor individuals and groups for the likelihood that they will make positive contributions to the organization's goals and then reward these individuals with status and power.

There is also a large amount of literature on the non-rational biases that play a role in determining who ends up where in the organizational hierarchy. One particularly prominent perspective comes out of *status expectation states theory* and the related *status characteristics theory* (e.g., Berger, Rosenholtz, & Zelditch, 1980). This view

suggests that organization members want the most capable and competent people to occupy the highest positions in the hierarchy, but notes that it is often difficult to know who really is most competent. In the absence of clear evidence, people use cues to determine competence and these cues can be faulty indicators. Perhaps most representative of this line of research are the many findings showing that members of high status demographic categories attain positions of status in groups and organizations more easily than members of lower status demographic categories and that this pattern is mediated by expectations of competence (Berger, Cohen, & Zelditch, 1972; Berger, Fisek, Zorman, & Zelditch, 1977; Berger, Rosenholtz, & Zelditch, 1980; Bunderson, 2003).

Other nonrational bases of status attainment are nonverbal behaviors (for reviews see Hall, Coats, & LeBeau, 2005; Ridgeway, 1987), verbal attributes (e.g., Fragale, 2006; Gallois, Callan, & Palmer, 1992; Ng & Bradac, 1993), and physical characteristics (Anderson, John, Keltner, & Kring, 2001; Collins & Zebrowitz, 2006). These cues are not usually related to competence, yet they are reliably viewed as signals of capability. In work that highlights these biases, the preference for hierarchy is clearly evident; however, the inability to perceive and attribute status in ways that serve rational goals is highlighted.

Stabilizing Hierarchy

A long term concern for organizations is the stabilization of hierarchy. Since status contests and negotiations can hamper group productivity (Loch, Huberman, & Stout, 2000; Overbeck, Correll, & Park, 2005), it behooves organizations to achieve and maintain consensus about ranking. Many at the top of a hierarchy are overly vested in the existing order and engage in explicit attempts to retain their positions (Ashforth, 2003). There are also many other more subtle mechanisms that maintain hierarchies, often without participants' awareness or conscious cooperation, and these mechanisms have been of even greater interest to psychologists studying social ranking systems.

Role Internalization Hierarchies almost always appear in conjunction with roles. Roles are a public signal to the individual, to the organization, and to outsiders of the role-occupant's power, status, and rank in the organization (Allen & Van de Vliert, 1984). As such, roles are central to the existence of the hierarchy. One of the primary ways in which organizational hierarchies become stabilized is through the psychological internalization of these roles (Biddle, 1986). The notion that beliefs and behaviors are shaped by roles has a long history in psychology dating at least back to the observation that Nazi guards and prisoners in concentration camps seemed to merge their self-concept with the position they occupied (Bettelheim, 1943). This notion was further examined in Milgram's (1974) examination of obedience to authority and Zimbardo's prison study (Zimbardo, Maslach, & Haney, 2000). Each of these studies showed how psychological and behavioral responses become aligned with the roles that people enact, even when those roles call for extreme and distasteful behavior. Further, both the Milgram and Zimbardo studies emphasized the speed with which self and role are merged. Little time in role is needed for people to exhibit ownership.

These classic studies also illustrate the degree to which role internalization serves hierarchical systems. In these studies, the occupants of powerful roles saw themselves as justified in oppressing those in less powerful positions by mere dint of their role and those in less powerful roles felt compelled to go along with the wishes of the powerful. Even in cases of resistance to power holders, such as those observed in some of Zimbardo's prisoners and in a recent semi-replication (Haslam & Reicher, 2002), the powerless engage in a form of rebellion that takes the low power role to heart, acknowledging and accepting their lack of status in the system.

These kinds of ideas have also been studied in business organizations. One classic study found that union workers who shifted into managerial roles experienced attitude shifts in line with their roles (Lieberman, 1956). Similarly, variance in supervisory behavior among managers in a unit of a university was explained largely by variance in the way supervisory roles were defined (Pfeffer and Salancik, 1975), suggesting that supervisors' behaviors largely conformed to their roles. Conformity to roles is rewarded in organizations (Tsui, 1984), perhaps in part because it cements and stabilizes the hierarchy.

Positions of power and powerlessness do not just affect role-defined behavior, but instead seem to seep deeply into the very way in which role occupants describe their abilities, skills, and traits. For example, merely assigning individuals to roles that differ in terms of status and power can affect how competent and smart people think they are, with those in higher power roles attributing greater abilities to themselves than those in lower power roles (Humphrey, 1985; also see Fiske, Cuddy, Glick, & Xu, 2002; Kipnis, 1976).

Some have argued that it is especially the internalization of low status roles that maintains the hierarchy. The work on *system justification theory* suggests that although low status individuals and groups should be most invested in changing the system, they do not feel entitled to demand more for themselves, in part because

they internalize and adopt negative self-perceptions that are consistent with how their role is perceived by others (for a review, see Jost and Kay, this volume).

Hierarchical position can also affect the most basic psychological processes. In the last decade, there has been a heightened interest in the effect of having or not having power among social psychologists. There are a number of excellent reviews of this literature (Fiske, this volume; Fiske & Berdahl, 2007; Keltner, Gruenfeld, & Anderson, 2003; Magee & Galinsky, 2008; Vescio & Guinote, in press). Some in this area have suggested that a number of the cognitive consequences of possessing power function to maintain the hierarchy (Magee and Galinsky, 2008). These consequences include an action orientation (e.g., Galinsky, Gruenfeld, & Magee, 2003), risk-taking (Anderson & Galinsky, 2006; Fast & Gruenfeld, 2009; Maner, DeWall, Baumeister, & Schaller, 2007), seeing the big picture rather than the details (Guinote, 2007; Smith & Trope, 2006), social inattentiveness (Fiske, 1993; Galinsky, Magee, Inesi, & Gruenfeld, 2006), and instrumental attraction toward useful others (Galinsky, 2008, & Gruenfeld, Inesi, Magee).

These patterns of behavior can lead those with power to accumulate more power (Magee & Galinsky, 2008). The action orientation and appetite for risk lead power holders to demand more resources for themselves, and ultimately, to acquire even more power (Magee, Galinsky, & Gruenfeld, 2007). High levels of cognitive abstraction and egoism allow those in power to miss the details about how people at lower levels of the organization are faring, making it unlikely that they will give power away (Milliken, Magee, Lam, & Menezes, 2008). The heightened attraction of those in power to targets who are especially useful also facilitates exploiting others as means to an end (Gruenfeld, Inesi, Magee, & Galinsky, 2008). In short, the consequences of possessing power become the causes of acquiring more power, and this dynamic helps to stabilize the hierarchy.

Culture Earlier, we described how organizational culture contributes to homogeneity in organizations both through selection and socialization. Culture also contributes to hierarchy because cultures contain norms about power and status (Fiske, 1991). The extent to which an organization's culture promotes hierarchy versus equality is typically referred to as *power distance* (Hofstede, 1980). Much of the literature examining power distance uses national culture as a proxy for organization culture, but suggests that the more a culture accepts and promotes hierarchy—that is, the higher it is in power-distance—the more stable the hierarchy will be. For example, studies have shown that although individuals in low power distance contexts require voice and empowerment in their organizations in order to be satisfied, committed, and productive, the same is not true of people located in high power distance cultures (Brockner et al., 2001; Lam, Schaubroeck, & Aryee, 2002; Sue-Chan, & Ong, 2002). Members of high power distance cultures do not get satisfaction from having a say or being heard, suggesting they are less likely to request or value this kind of empowerment. Further, they are less aggrieved by maltreatment from their superiors (Bond, Wan, Leung, & Giacalone, 1985). Top management teams in companies with high power distance are more committed to the status quo than those with low power distance values (Geletkanycz, 1998).

In addition, the symbolism associated with authority varies across these cultural contexts. In high power distance settings, metaphors about the family are used in describing authority figures and their relationship with their subordinates, whereas in low power distance cultures, sports metaphors are more common (Gibson & Zellmer-Bruhn, 2001; see also Hofstede, Pedersen, & Hofstede, 2002). The family metaphor might help stabilize organizational hierarchy by contributing to the view that the hierarchy is a unit that cares for all individuals, whereas the sports metaphor is more likely to promote competition among individuals.

Another way in which power distance stabilizes hierarchy is that in high power distance contexts, higher status individuals have more influence (Earley, 1999). People in high power distance contexts also associate status and authority more closely than those in low power distance contexts (Chikudate, 1997). Similarly, in high power distance contexts, authorities can use their position to resolve conflicts and get their way in negotiations (Adair, Okumura & Brett, 2001; Tinsley, 2001; Tinsley & Brett, 2001). Further, people highest in the hierarchy are most likely to endorse and support cultural myths and practices that support hierarchical differentiation (Sidanius & Pratto, 1999). These findings suggest that people with status have more power when their culture supports and promotes hierarchy, which in turn likely allows them access to even greater power and status.

Summary

In sum, the production of hierarchy is a central and omnipresent component of organizing. Hierarchies meet evolutionary and existential demands. Organizations are characterized by hierarchy from the start, and they frequently become more hierarchical over time as they respond to crises, grow and produce more roles, and develop cultures and role systems that legitimate the status ordering. Hierarchies thus become unavoidable even when people seek greater equality.

HOMOGENEITY AND HIERARCHY ARE MUTUALLY REINFORCING

The respective preferences for homogeneity on the one hand and hierarchy on the other might, at first, seem incompatible. The former implies an interest in sameness, whereas the latter implies an interest in differentiation. However, we believe that these preferences work in concert and mutually persist, enabling the pursuit of belongingness and impact goals simultaneously.

This claim is consistent with findings in the cross-cultural literature showing that high power distance and collectivism tend to co-occur. In this literature, power distance is defined as a preference for hierarchy, and collectivism is defined as valuing expressions of sameness (e.g. Schermerhorn & Bond, 1991; Triandis & Gelfand, 1998). In an early psychological analysis of national cultures, more countries were characterized by the combination of collectivism and high power distance than by any of the other combinations of these variables (Hofstede, 1980). In fact, there were no countries in which collectivism was high and power distance was low. The two constructs were treated as independent despite their empirical association, but others have questioned this decision, asserting that collectivism and hierarchy are related. The term, *vertical collectivism* was introduced to capture the interdependence of these two constructs (Singelis, Triandis, Bhawuk, & Gelfand, 1995; Triandis & Gelfand, 1998). Vertical collectivism is evident in cultures in which "one perceives the self as part of a group while being accepting of power–status inequalities within the group" (Schermerhorn & Bond, 1991, p. 8). These studies provide empirical evidence that the preferences for homogeneity and hierarchy can and do co-occur (e.g., Bhagat, Kedia, Harveston, & Triandis, 2002; Earley & Gibson, 1998; Hofstede, 2005). The next sections of this chapter describe how within organizations, as within cultures, the preference for hierarchy operates in service of the preference for homogeneity, and the preference for homogeneity operates in service of the preference for hierarchy. We discuss each of these relationships in turn.

Hierarchy in Service of Homogeneity

When hierarchies are accepted and adhered to, belief in and reverence of the legitimacy of authority figures and their systems of control motivates conformity and within-group loyalty. Organization members internalize the vision, values, and behavior of strong (e.g., charismatic and transformational) leaders, and attempt to emulate them (see Hogg, this volume), thereby becoming more homogeneous. Deviance in such systems is considered disrespectful to superiors and is grounds for social rejection. When hierarchies are less rigid and less revered—for example, in the context of organization change efforts or in the early stages of an entrepreneurial venture—deviance and role innovation are sometimes rewarded (Aldrich & Ruef, 2006). Homogeneity and the sense of belonging that accompanies homogeneity are thus enhanced in organizations with a strong stable hierarchy.

Hierarchical organizations also foster homogeneity to the extent that they offer upward mobility. Sometimes the prospect of upward mobility is a measure of the degree to which an organization is hierarchical (Paulson, 1974). Since managers are most likely to hire and promote subordinates who are similar to themselves (Kanter, 1977), and workers tend to be preoccupied with status and prestige (Baron, 1984; Schwartz, 1995), the desire to move up in a hierarchy motivates conformity among workers. This dynamic is especially evident among middle-status managers, who exhibit greater conformity than both high-status and low-status managers: The former have less to gain by conforming, and the latter have less to lose by not conforming (Phillips & Zuckerman, 2001).

Hierarchical organizations can also facilitate homogeneity by providing a structure that has clear boundaries among stratified groups. Status boundaries provide a legitimate basis for restricting entry of dissimilar others (Baron & Pfeffer, 1994). As in the classic case of *old boys' networks*, members of elite ranks are often reluctant to change the demographic makeup of their membership as they feel protective of the status enjoyed by the group, and the sense of belongingness that accompanies homogeneous-group membership (Ellemers, 1993).

Hierarchical systems can also produce homogeneity within ranks because hierarchies are frequently formed through a tournament-like structure (Rosenbaum, 1979, 1984). Often, reaching the top of a hierarchy requires winning a series of preliminary contests (Lazear & Rosen, 1981). This narrowing process has the potential to homogenize because only a small number of people from the larger pool actually get to compete for the highest position. Winning competitions in early contests is not randomly distributed, but instead wins are disproportionately awarded to people from high status demographic groups (Rosenbaum, 1984), increasing the likelihood of homogeneity within ranks.

The notion of SDO also unites hierarchy and homogeneity. The finding that SDO is higher in men and Whites than women and non-Whites has been often replicated (Sidanius, 1993; Sidanius & Pratto, 1999), and the tendency for those high in SDO to support policies that segregate and separate their group from others has also received empirical support (e.g., Pratto, Stalworth, & Conway-Lanz, 1998). Thus, those most invested in creating hierarchies (high SDO individuals) use their power and status to maintain the boundary between themselves and the demographically different groups below. Membership in stigmatized,

low status ranks is also associated with enhanced feelings of belongingness, as the experience of common fate within rank, and differing fates across ranks reinforce a sense of shared within-rank identity and cohesion (Kanter, 1977; Mullen, Brown & Smith, 1992).

In sum, the preference for hierarchy, which drives the creation and maintenance of hierarchical social structures, serves the preference for homogeneity by inciting conformity among those who wish to emulate leaders and move into their ranks, and by creating segregated, stratified, homogeneous subgroups within which belongingness goals are satisfied.

Homogeneity in Service of Hierarchy

There are also ways that the preference for homogeneity operates in service of hierarchy. This idea is a central tenet of social identity and social categorization theories (for a review, see Yzerbyt, this volume). These theories posit that the social construction of ingroups and outgroups from a heterogeneous population bolsters self-esteem by providing a basis for downward social comparisons and, ultimately, judgments of ingroup superiority.

From an organizations perspective, a homogeneous work force is easier to control than a heterogeneous work force, and the ability to control lower ranking members reinforces existing hierarchy (Kandel & Lazear, 1992; O'Reilly, 1989). According to scholars in the Marxist tradition, a heterogeneous but unsegregated workforce is actually dangerous to hierarchical stability (e.g., Marglin, 1974; Stone, 1974). These qualitative historical analyses suggest that capitalist employers purposefully create divisions among demographic groups to prevent them from realizing their collective power and inciting a revolt (Wachtel, 1974).

Others have argued that the creation of homogeneous groups within organizations facilitates social comparisons necessary to determine which employees move up. For example, the ability to compare members of a cohort who are hired and socialized together with members of a single demographic category facilitates ranking them as well (Baron, 1984). Also, since it becomes more difficult to define and evaluate performance as jobs and workers move up the hierarchy, demographic categories are relied on more heavily in evaluations, appointments, and promotions within higher ranks (Dornbusch & Scott, 1975).

PERFORMANCE IMPLICATIONS OF ORGANIZING PREFERENCES

The fact that homogeneous, hierarchical structural forms dominate organization life creates tremendous challenges for those responsible for executing on performance goals and designing performance processes to meet changing strategic demands. Much attention has been devoted in the management literature to understanding how organizations should be designed to facilitate specific performance outcomes. A central tenet of this body of knowledge is that organizational structure should follow strategy (Amburgey & Dacin, 1994; Chandler, 1962). Other important ideas in this literature include the premise that organizations should be flexible and able to change in response to changing performance challenges (Galbraith, 1994; Hambrick, 2003; Miles & Snow, 2003), and that they should be designed to pursue several objectives at once (O'Reilly & Tushman, 2004; Tushman & O'Reilly, 1996). Homogeneity and hierarchy may be better suited for some strategic imperatives than others, and the fact that workers seem to prefer these structures over their alternatives poses performance challenges.

One framework for characterizing an organization's performance goals distinguishes between *exploration and exploitation* (Levinthal & March, 1993; March, 1991, 1994). Exploration refers to activities associated with learning and innovation for the sake of improving on current processes, whereas exploitation refers to activities associated with maximizing efficiency in execution of current processes.

In discussing the fit between strategy and structure, there are a number of ways that organizational design can be characterized. One framework distinguishes between what is called a *mechanistic model*, which supports exploitation and relies on hierarchy and homogeneity, and an *organic model*, which relies on the relative absence of hierarchy and on heterogeneity (Courtright, Fairhurst, & Rogers, 1989).

The mechanistic model is better suited for exploitation (e.g., Burns & Stalker, 1961; Katzenbach & Smith, 1993; Leavitt, 2003), because hierarchy facilitates the efficient and unquestioning fulfillment of established tasks and roles, whereas homogeneity facilitates communication and trust, and reduces conflict. The organic model is better suited for exploration, because heterogeneity facilitates clashes among differing perspectives, which stimulate learning and innovation, whereas the relative absence of hierarchy facilitates challenges to the status quo (Burns & Stalker, 1961; Katzenbach & Smith, 1993). One implication of the foregoing analysis is that mechanistic designs should be easier to construct and more sustainable than organic designs, and therefore, organizations should be better at executing exploitation than exploration strategies.

As some evidence of this, the management literature and management education both place much more emphasis on the challenges associated with exploration than exploitation, and on the challenges associated with the construction

and functioning of organic than mechanistic organizational forms. And, the preferences for hierarchy and homogeneity are seen as primary culprits in the problems that arise in organization management. For example, an American Psychologist Award address (Levinson, 1994) cited "difficulties with rigid corporate cultures and cumbersome hierarchies" (p. 428) as key factors in the demise of large, successful organizations such as IBM, Mercedes-Benz, and General Motors.

The final section of this chapter provides evidence that the insurmountable human attachments to homogeneity and hierarchy pose significant management challenges and that, in fact, the management literature has evolved in a way that reflects the overreliance on homogeneity and hierarchy and the challenges this overreliance creates (Leavitt, 2003; Levinson, 1994).

Management Challenges Related to Organizational Preferences

Management topics ebb and flow (Carson, Lanier, Carson, & Guidry, 2000; Sibbet, 1997), but there are a set of staples, many of which can be viewed as having secured their place in the literature because they address the intractable problems that arise from an overreliance on homogeneity and hierarchy. Some examples are discussed as follows.

Diversity

One challenge that has occupied management scholars for at least 40 years is how to create and utilize a diverse workforce (Kalev, Dobbin, & Kelly, 2006; Mannix & Neale, 2005; Williams & O'Reilly, 1998). The prominence of this topic within the fields of management and organizational behavior is a powerful testimony to the impact of human preferences on organizational structure.

Beginning in the 1960s, intolerance of the preference for homogeneity was legislated in the Civil Rights Act of 1964, the Equal Employment Opportunities Act of 1972, and various other executive orders. These policies reduced certain kinds of overt discrimination (Ely & Thomas, 2001; Kelly & Dobbin, 1998; Lorbiecki & Jack, 2000). However, the legal approach to reducing the preference for homogeneous work settings has not proven entirely effective. The EEOC prosecutes only a small fraction of the roughly 80,000 complaints it receives annually (Reskin, 2005), and the racial pay gap has widened (Cancio, Evans, & Maume, 1996). Many firms have focused on limiting their legal or financial liability, rather than actually reducing discriminatory practices (Bisom-Rapp, 2001).

Since true integration has not been forthcoming, scholars have shifted to an emphasis on "diversity management" (Ensari & Miller, 2006; Kelly & Dobbin, 1998), which attempts to motivate change via performance arguments, and to change behavior through education and training. Some have offered a "business case" for diversity (Richard, 2000; Robinson & Dechant, 1997; Ross & Schneider, 1992), arguing that differences are a source of competitive advantage (e.g., Jayne & Dipboye, 2004; Kochan et al., 2003; Thomas & Ely, 1996). These diversity management initiatives have emphasized attempts to counteract the tendency toward homogeneity in hiring and the tendency toward stratification that places members of certain demographic categories and functional backgrounds into different ranks. Yet, despite the persistent practical and moral imperatives to embrace greater diversity, homogeneous and stratified social groupings continue to dominate organizational life, and this pattern has proven to be surprisingly difficult to disrupt (Baron & Pfeffer, 1994). In short, sustained management interest in the topic of diversity belies a failure of organization design to conquer human preferences.

Teams

A related management initiative has advocated on behalf of functional diversity in teams, looking specifically at the potential benefits of using cross-functional teams, instead of functionally homogeneous departments (e.g., engineering, manufacturing, sales) that work sequentially on products rather than collaboratively (Katzenbach & Smith, 1993; Mohrman, Cohen, & Mohrman, 1995; Schuler, Jackson, & Luo, 2003). This literature also evolved in response to what was characterized in the 1990s as a dysfunctional reliance on homogeneous functional *silos* as a means of accomplishing work (Denison, Hart, & Kahn, 1996; Meyer & Gupta, 1994).

However, the teams movement in management was also a response to an overreliance on hierarchy, which made innovation difficult to achieve (e.g., Katzenbach & Smith, 1993; Leavitt, 1996; Mohrman, Cohen, & Mohrman, 1995). Consistent with this view, the positive impact of cross-functional teams on organization performance is achieved through increased idea generation and innovation (Guzzo & Dickson, 1996).

The notion of a flatter, networked organization, in which trust among equal actors replaces command and control as the primary driver of behavior, has also received much attention in recent years and, like the team-based organization, is also conceived as an antidote to too much hierarchy and insufficient diversity (Miles & Snow, 2003; Sheppard & Tuchinsky, 1996; Sproull & Kiesler, 1991). Here again, the sustained managerial interest in how to design and function within these alternative organizational forms has occurred against a backdrop of the preference for homogeneity on the one hand and for hierarchy on the other. In fact,

an important vein within these literatures has pursued the question of how to motivate teamwork among employees, who tend to focus on self-promotion within hierarchical systems (e.g., Coleman, 1988; Hamilton, Nickerson, & Owan, 2003).

Some have argued that the team-based and networked forms of organization are replacing more traditional hierarchical forms (e.g., Heckscher & Donnellon, 1994; Piore & Sabel, 1984; Sheppard & Tuchinsky, 1996). Others, like us, are less convinced (Ghittel, 2001). Leavitt (2003, 2004) argued recently that the intensity with which academics, consultants, and management gurus continue to struggle against hierarchies only serves to highlight their durability.

Innovation and Change

Another staple in the management literature are the topics of innovation and change. One of the most well-documented findings in organizations research is that organizations (Hannan & Freeman, 1988) and their members resist change (Dutton, Ashford, O'Neill & Lawrence, 2001; Fiss & Zajac, 2006; Huy, 2002). There have been many approaches to change management, ranging from action research (Eden & Huxham, 1996) and organizational development (e.g., Sinangil & Avallone, 2002) to sensitivity training (Highhouse, 2002) and process consultation (Schein, 1999).

Most recently the management literature has become enamored with the concept of innovation (e.g., Cohen & Levinthal, 1990; Kanter, 1988; Tushman & O'Reilly, 1996, 2002). Like change, innovation does not appear to come naturally; that is, there has been much research devoted to understanding its sources (for a review, see Damanpour, 1991). Given our analysis so far, it seems likely that change and innovation are so difficult because workers are loathe to (a) deal with organization outsiders and their heterogeneous viewpoints (Argyris, 1985; Beer & Eisenstat, 2000; Micklethwait & Wooldridge, 1996;), and (b) challenge the status quo, which inevitably involves weakening, if not destroying, the hierarchy (Ocasio, 1994; Pfeffer, 1992).

In sum, the abundant literatures on change and innovation reflect great management interest, which presumably reflects great management difficulty. Despite several decades of study, and plenty of knowledge dissemination via countless MBA programs and executive education courses, facility with change and innovation remain among the holy grails of management effectiveness.

Leadership and Empowerment

Among staples within the management literature, leadership effectiveness and worker empowerment also form a resilient partnership. Leadership is seen as the ultimate driver of organizational behavior and performance. However, the desire for knowledge about how to maximize one's power and influence as a leader (e.g., Pfeffer, 1992) is matched in the management literature only by the desire for knowledge about how to empower one's followers. The idea that effective leadership could be accomplished by giving power away was initially made explicit by Kanter (1983). The basic idea was that excessive bureaucracy (i.e., hierarchy) imposes constraints that make workers passive (Ashforth, 1989; Conger & Kanungo, 1988; Mondros & Wilson, 1994). Giving workers control over their work, in contrast, is motivating because of the increased sense of impact and self-determination they experience (Deci, Connell, & Ryan, 1989). Specifically, empowerment occurs when workers experience an intrinsic motivation toward work that is based on feelings of meaning, competence, self-determination, and impact (Thomas & Velthouse, 1990). Managers empower workers when they share information, resources, and power with subordinates, allowing them to have an impact on decision making (Spreitzer, 1996). Research suggests that when individuals experience these outcomes, they feel empowered. However, management scholars have also noted over the years that empowerment, for all the insight and inspiration it has provided, has not changed the face of corporate America. On this point, Argyris (1998) observed that instead of truly embracing the idea of letting employees make their own decisions, both managers and employees have tended to use the rhetoric of empowerment to justify yet another structure where employees are just following orders.

Empirical studies demonstrate additional ways that workers are committed to hierarchy, even when attempting to implement empowerment. For example, people attribute greater quality to work completed under supervision than to the same work completed with less supervision, and managers specifically feel better about work they have supervised than about the same work when they did not supervise it themselves (Pfeffer, Cialdini, Hanna, & Knopoff, 1998). Management scholars continue to observe that steep hierarchies and large bureaucracies engender not only worker disengagement, but corruption as well, and to call out for ways of reducing these structures to make it easier for workers to stop taking orders and start thinking and acting for themselves. Yet there is little evidence that such changes in behavior, or in the organizational structures necessary to support them, are becoming any more commonplace.

There are, of course, many other important management topics, but none we can identify provide evidence against our claims. Within the management literature, the challenges associated with creating more hierarchy, or more homogeneity, are simply dwarfed by the challenges associated with creating their opposites. Presumably, these former capabilities come more naturally. In contrast, the capabilities associated with making organizations diverse and flat require special training, management education, even intervention by consultants, and the industries devoted to providing this training are thriving. Yet, despite the proliferation of these abundant training resources, there is little evidence that the pendulum swings the other way. The preferences for homogeneity and hierarchy pervade organizational life, they constrain organizational structure, and they are at the root of many key management challenges.

SUMMARY

This chapter provides a framework for reviewing the organizations literature that emphasizes the social psychology of organizing—specifically, the human preference for certain organizational forms. Humans seem to prefer homogeneity and hierarchy over their opposites, and these preferences have profound consequences for organization life. The psychology that underlies organizing activity is at the heart of the intersection of social psychology and organizations.

This analysis is meant to help illuminate how understanding human organization can inform basic social psychology, as well as how understanding psychology helps to explain the forms organizations take. Although at one time this kind of perspective was central in social psychology (e.g., Lewin & Cartwright 1951; Milgram, 1974; Zimbardo, Maslach, & Haney, 2000), it has faded from view in the current discipline. The field of social psychology is built on the premise that situations are powerful, yet our social psychological understanding of situations is still relatively impoverished. An investigation of the psychology of organizing has the potential to provide a rich theoretical account of how situations are formed by, and transform, social behavior.

REFERENCES

Abelson, R. P., Aronson, E., McGuire, W. J., Newcomb, T. M., Rosenberg, M. J., & Tannenbaum, P. H. (1968). *Theories of cognitive consistency: A sourcebook*. Chicago: Rand-McNally.

Adair, W.L., Okumura, T., & Brett, J.M. (2001). Negotiation behavior when cultures collide: The United States and Japan. *Journal of Applied Psychology, 86*(3), 371–385.

Adler, A. (1966). *The individual psychology of Alfred Adler* (Ed. and annotated by H. L. Ansbacher & R. R. Ansbacher). New York: Harper & Row.

Aldrich, H.E., & Carter, N.M. (2004). Social networks. In W.B. Gartner, K.G. Shaver, N.M. Carter, & P.D. Reynolds (Eds.), *Handbook of entrepreneurial dynamics: The process of business creation* (pp. 324–335). Thousand Oaks, CA: Sage Publications.

Aldrich, H., & Ruef, M. (2006). *Organizations evolving*. Thousand Oaks, CA: Sage.

Alexander, C. (1979). *The timeless way of building*. New York: Oxford University Press.

Allen, V. L., & van de Vliert, E. (1984). A role theoretical perspective on transitional processes. In V. L. Allen & E. van de Vliert (Eds.), *Role transitions: Explorations and explanations* (pp. 3–18). New York: Plenum.

Amburgey, T. L., & Dacin, T. (1994). As the left foot follows the right? The dynamics of strategic and structural change. *Academy of Management Journal*, 1427–1452.

Anderson, C., & Berdahl, J. L. (2002). The experience of power: Examining the effects of power on approach and inhibition tendencies. *Journal of Personality and Social Psychology, 83*(6), 1362–1377.

Anderson, C., & Galinsky, A. D. (2006). Power, optimism, and risk-taking. *European Journal of Social Psychology, 36*(4), 511.

Anderson, C., John, O. P., Keltner, D., & Kring, A. (2001). Who attains social status? Effects of personality and physical attractiveness in social groups. *Journal of Personality and Social Psychology, 81*, 116–132.

Anderson, C., & Kilduff, G. (2009). Why do dominant personalities attain influence in groups? A competence-signaling account of personality dominance. *Journal of Personality and Social Psychology*, 296, *491*(13).

Anderson, C., Srivastava, S., Beer, J. S., Spataro, S. E., & Chatman, J. A. (2006). Knowing your place: Self-perceptions of status in face-to-face groups. *Journal of Personality and Social Psychology, 91*(6), 1094–1110.

Anderson, E. (1990). *Streetwise: Race, class, and change in an urban community*. Chicago: University of Chicago Press.

Argyris, C. (1985). *Strategy, change and defensive routines*. Marshfield, MA: Pitman Publishing Inc.

Argyris, C. (1998). Empowerment: The Emperor's New Clothes. *Harvard Business Review, 76*, 98–105.

Arrow, H. (1997). Stability, bistability, and instability in small group influence patterns. *Journal of Personality and Social Psychology, 72*(1), 75–85.

Asch, S. E. (1956). Studies of independence and conformity: A minority of one against a unanimous majority. *Psychological Monographs, 70*, 1–70.

Ashford, S. J., Blatt, R., & van de Walle, D. (2003). Reflections on the looking glass: A review of research on feedback-seeking behavior in organizations. *Journal of Management, 29*(6), 773.

Ashford, S. J., & Tsui, A. S. (1991). Self-regulation for managerial effectiveness: The role of active feedback seeking. *Academy of Management Journal, 34*, 251–280.

Ashforth, B. E. (1989). The experience of powerlessness in organizations. *Organizational Behavior and Human Decision Processes, 43*, 207–242.

Ashforth, B.E. (2001). *Role transitions in organizational life: An identity-based perspective*. Mahwah, NJ: Lawrence Erlbaum.

Ashforth, B. (2003). Petty tyranny in organizations. In L.W. Porter, H.L. Angle, & R.W. Allen (Eds.), *Organizational influence processes*. New York: Pearson Scott Foresman.

Ashforth, B. E., & Mael, F. (1989). Social identity theory and the organization. *Academy of Management Journal*, 14, 20–39.

Babcock, L., & Laschever, S. (2003). *Women don't ask: Negotiation and the gender divide*. Princeton, NJ: Princeton University Press.

Bacharach, S. B., & Lawler, E. J. (1980). *Power and politics in organizations*. London: Jossey-Bass.

Baer, M., & Frese, M. (2003). Innovation is not enough: Climates for initiative and psychological safety, process innovations, and firm performance. *Journal of Organizational Behavior, 24*(1), 45–68.

Baker, W. (2000). *Achieving success through social capital*. San Francisco: Jossey-Bass.

Bales, R. F. (1950). *Interaction process analysis: A method for the study of small groups*. Reading, MA: Addison-Wesley.

Bales, R.F. (1999). *Social interaction systems: Theory and measurement*. Edison: NJ: Transaction Publishers.

Bales, R. F., & Slater, P. E. (1955). Role differentiation in small decision-making groups. *Family, socialization and interaction process*, 259–306.

Bantel, K. A., & Jackson, S. E. (1989). Top management and innovations in banking: Does the composition of the top team make a difference? *Strategic Management Journal, 10*(1), 107–124.

Barchas, P. (1986). A sociophysiological orientation to small groups. In E. Lawler (Ed.), *Advances in group processes* (vol. 3, pp. 209–246). Greenwich, CT: JAI Press.

Baron, J. N. (1984). Organizational perspectives on stratification. *Annual Review in Sociology, 10*, 37–69.

Baron, J. N., & Bielby, W. T. (1980) Bringing the firms back in: Stratification, segmentation, and the organization of work. *American Sociological Review*, 45, 737–765.

Baron, J. N., & Bielby, W. T. (1984). The organization of work in a segmented economy. *American Sociological Review*, 49, 454–473.

Baron, J. N., & Bielby, W. T. (1986). The Proliferation of job titles in organizations. *Administrative Science Quarterly, 31*(4), 561–586.

Baron, J. N., Burton, M. D., & Hannan, M.T. (1996). The road taken: Origins and early evolution of employment systems in emerging companies. *Industrial and Corporate Change, 5*(2), 239–275.

Baron, J. N., & Hannan, M. T. (2002). Organizational blueprints for success in high-tech start-ups: Lessons from the Stanford project on emerging companies. *California Management Review, 44*(3), 8–36.

Baron, J. N., Hannan, M. T., Hsu, G., & Koçak, Ö. (2007). In the company of women: Gender inequality and the logic of bureaucracy in start-up firms. *Work and Occupations, 34*, 35–66.

Baron, J. N., & Newman A. E. (1990). For what it's worth: Organizations, occupations, and the value of work done by women and nonwhites. *American Sociological Review, 55*(2), 155–175.

Baron, J. N., & Pfeffer, J. (1994). The social psychology of organizations and inequality. *Social Psychology Quarterly, 57*(3), 190–209.

Barsade, S.G., Ward, A.J., Turner, J.D., & Sonnenfeld, J.A. (2000). To your heart's content: A model of affective diversity in top management teams. *Administrative Science Quarterly, 45*(4), 802–836.

Baskett, G. D. (1973). Interview decisions as determined by competency and attitude similarity. *Journal of Applied Psychology, 57*, 343–345.

Bass, B. M., & Stogdill, R. M. (1990). *Bass & Stogdill's handbook of leadership: Theory, research, and managerial applications*. New York: Free Press.

Becker, E. (1973). *The denial of death*. New York: Free Press.

Bedeian, A. G., & Mossholder, K. W. (2000). On the use of the coefficient of variation as a measure of diversity. *Organizational Research Methods, 3*, 285–297.

Beer, M., & Eisenstat, R. A. (2000). The silent killers of strategy implementation and learning. *Sloan Management Review, 41*, 29–40.

Berger, J., Cohen, B. P., & Zelditch, M., Jr. (1972). Status characteristics and social interaction. *American Sociological Review, 37*, 241–55.

Berger, J., M., Fisek, H., Zorman, R. Z., & Zelditch, M., Jr. (1977). *Status characteristics in social interaction: An expectations states approach*. New York: Elsevier-North Holland.

Berger, J., Rosenholtz, S. J., & Zelditch, M., Jr. (1980). Status Organizing Processes. *Annual Reviews in Sociology, 6*(1), 479–508.

Bettelheim, B. (1943). Individual and mass behavior in extreme situations. *Journal of Abnormal Social Psychology, 38*, 417–452.

Bhagat, R. S., Kedia, B. L., Harveston, P. D., & Triandis, H. C. (2002). Cultural variations in the cross-border transfer of organizational knowledge: An integrative framework. *Academy of Management Review, 27,* 204–221.

Biddle, B. J. (1986). Recent developments in role theory. *Annual Review of Sociology, 12,* 67–92.

Bielby, W. T., & Baron, J. N. (1986). Men and women at work: Sex segregation and statistical discrimination. *American Journal of Sociology, 91,* 759–99.

Bisom-Rapp, S. (2001). Ounce of prevention is a poor substitute for a pound of cure: Confronting the developing jurisprudence of education and prevention in employment discrimination law. *Berkeley Journal of Employment and Labor Law, 22*(1), 1–47.

Blau, P. M. (1977). *Inequality and heterogeneity: A primitive theory of social structure.* New York: The Free Press.

Blau, R. D., & Kahn, L. M. (1981). Race and sex differences in quits by young workers. *Industrial & Labor Relations Review, 34,* 563–577.

Blau, P. M., & Scott, W. R. (1962). *Formal Organizations: A Comparative Approach.* San Francisco: Chandler.

Bloom, M., & Michel, J. G. (2002). The relationships among organizational context, pay dispersion, and managerial turnover. *Academy of Management Journal, 45*(1), 33–44.

Boehm, C. (1999). *Hierarchy in the forest: The evolution of egalitarian behavior.* Cambridge, MA: Harvard University Press.

Bond, M. H., Wan, K. C., Leung, K., & Giacalone, R. A. (1985). How are responses to verbal insult related to cultural collectivism and power distance? *Journal of Cross-Cultural Psychology, 16*(1), 111–127.

Bono, J. E., & Judge, T. A. (2004). Personality and transformational and transactional leadership: A meta-analysis. *Journal of Applied Psychology, 89,* 901–910.

Bowen, D. E., & Lawler, E. E., III. (1995). Empowering service employees. *Sloan Management Review, 36*(4), 73.

Boxx, W. R., Odom, R.Y., & Dunn, M.G. (1991). Organizational values and value congruency and their impact on satisfaction, commitment, and cohesion. *Public Personnel Management, 20,* 195–205.

Brass, D. J. (1984). Being in the right place: A structural analysis of individual influence in an organization. *Administrative Science Quarterly, 29,* 518–539.

Bretz, R. D., & Judge, T.A. (1994). Person–organization fit and the theory of work adjustment: Implications for satisfaction, tenure, and career success. *Journal of Vocational Behavior, 44,* 32–54.

Bretz, R. D., & Milkovich, G. (1989). *Performance appraisal in large organizations: Practice and research implications.* Ithaca, NY: Cornell University.

Bridges, W. P., & Villemez, W. J. (1986). Informal hiring and income in the labor market. *American Sociological Review, 51,* 574–582.

Brockner, J., Ackerman, G., Greenberg, J., Gelfand, M. J., Francesco, A. M., Chen, Z. X., et al. (2001). Culture and procedural justice: The influence of power distance on reactions to voice. *Journal of Experimental Social Psychology, 37,* 300–315.

Browne, I., Hewitt, C., Tigges, L., & Green, G. (2001). Why does job segregation lead to wage inequality among African Americans? Person, place, sector, or skills? *Social Science Research, 30*(3), 473–495.

Buck, R. (1976). *Human Motivation and Emotion.* New York: John Wiley & Sons.

Bunderson, J. S. (2003). Recognizing and utilizing expertise in work groups: A status characteristics perspective. *Administrative Science Quarterly, 48,* 557–591.

Burns, T., & Stalker, G. M. (1961). *The management of innovation.* London: Tavistock.

Burt, R. S. (1987). Social contagion and innovation: Cohesion versus structural equivalence. *American Journal of Sociology, 92,* 1287–1335.

Burt, R. S. (1992). *Structural holes.* Cambridge, MA: Harvard University Press.

Burt, R.S. (1997). A note on social capital and network content. *Social Networks, 19,* 355–373.

Buss, D. M. (1984). Toward a psychology of person–environment (PE) correlation: The role of spouse selection. *Journal of Personality and Social Psychology, 47*(2), 361–377.

Byrne, D. (1971). *The attraction paradigm.* New York: Academic Press.

Cable, D. M., & Judge, T. A. (1994). Pay preferences and job search decisions: A person–organization fit perspective. *Personnel Psychology, 47,* 317–348.

Caldeira, G. A., & Patterson, S. C. (1987). Political friendship in the legislature. *The Journal of Politics,* 953–975.

Cancio, A. S., Evans, T. D., & Maume, D. J., Jr. (1996). Reconsidering the declining significance of race: Racial differences in early career wages. *American Sociological Review,* 541–556.

Carpenter, M. A., Geletkanycz, M. A., & Sanders, W. (2004). Upper echelons research revisited: Antecedents, elements, and consequences of top management team composition. *Journal of Management, 30*(6), 749.

Carrington W. J., & Troske, K. R. (1998a). Sex segregation in U.S. manufacturing. *Industrial and Labor Relations Review, 51,* 445–464.

Carrington W. J., & Troske, K. R. (1998b). Interfirm segregation and the Black–White wage gap. *Journal of Labor Economics, 16,* 231–260.

Carson, R. C. (1969). *Interaction concepts of personality.* Chicago: Aldine.

Carson, P. P., Lanier, P. A., Carson, K. D., & Guidry, B. N. (2000). Clearing a path through the management fashion jungle: Some preliminary trailblazing. *Academy of Management Journal, 43,* 1143–1158.

Cartwright, D. (1965). Influence, leadership, control. In J. G. March (Ed.), *Handbook of organizations* (pp. 1–47). Chicago: Rand McNally.

Chandler, A. (1962). *Strategy and structure.* Cambridge, MA: MIT Press.

Chatman, J. A. (1991). Matching people and organizations: Selection and socialization in public accounting firms. *Administrative Science Quarterly, 36,* 459–484.

Chatman, J. A., Bell, N. E., & Staw, B. M. (1986). The managed thought: The role of self-justification and impression management in organizational settings. In H. P. Sims & D. A. Gioia (Eds.), *The thinking organization: Dynamics of organizational social cognition* (pp. 191–214). San Francisco: Jossey-Bass.

Chatman, J. A., & Cha, S. E. (2003). Leading by leveraging culture. *California Management Review, 45*(4), 20–33.

Chatman, J., & O'Reilly, C. A. (2004). Asymmetric reactions to work group sex diversity among men and women. *Academy of Management Journal, 47,* 193–208.

Cheney, D. L., & Seyfarth, R. M. (2007). *Baboon metaphysics: The evolution of the social mind.* Chicago: University of Chicago Press.

Cherulnik, P. D., Turns, K. C., & Wilderman, S. K. (1990). Physical appearance and leadership: Exploring the role of appearance-based attribution in leader emergence. *Journal of Applied Social Psychology, 20,* 1530–1539.

Chikudate, N. (1997). Exploring the life–world of organizations by linguistic oriented phenomenology in sub-cultural analysis of organizations: A comparison between Japanese and U.S. banks. *Management International Review,* April, 1–17.

Chow, R. M., Lowery, B. S., & Knowles, E. D. (2007). The two faces of dominance: The differential effect of ingroup superiority and outgroup inferiority on dominant-group identity and group esteem. *Journal of Experimental Social Psychology, 44,* 1073–1081.

Cleveland, J. N., Murphy, K. R., & Williams, R. E. (1989). Multiple uses of performance appraisal: Prevalence and correlates. *Journal of Applied Psychology, 74,* 1, 130–135.

Cofer, C. N. (1959). Motivation. *Annual Review of Psychology, 10*, 173–202.

Cohen, W. M., & Levinthal, D. A. (1990). Absorptive capacity: A new perspective on learning and innovation. *Administrative science quarterly*, 128–152.

Coleman, J. S. (1988). Social capital in the creation of human capital. *American Journal of Sociology, 94*, 95–121.

Coleman. J S., Katz, E., & Menzel, H. (1966). *Medical innovation; A diffusion study* (2nd ed.). New York: Bobbs-Merrill.

Collins, M. A., & Zebrowitz, L. A. (2006). The contributions of appearance to occupational outcomes in civilian and military settings. *Journal of Applied Social Psychology, 25*, 129–163.

Conger, J. A., & Kanungo, R. N. (1988). The empowerment process: Integrating theory and practice. *Academy of Management Review, 13*, 471–482.

Courtright, J. A., Fairhurst, G. T., & Rogers, L. E. (1989). Interaction patterns in organic and mechanistic systems. *Academy of Management Journal, 32*, 773–802.

Cowherd, D. M., & Levine, D. I. (1992). Product Quality and Pay Equity Between Lower-level Employees and Top Management: An Investigation of Distributive Justice Theory. *Administrative Science Quarterly, 37*, 302–320.

Crowder, K. (2000). The racial context of white mobility: An individual-level assessment of the white flight hypothesis. *Social Science Research, 29*, 223–257.

Curry J. P., Wakefield, D. S., Price, J. L., & Mueller, C. W. (1986). On the causal ordering of job satisfaction and organizational commitment. *Academy of Management Journal, 29*, 847–858.

Cyert, R., & March, J.G. (1963). *A behavioral theory of the firm.* Englewood Cliffs, NJ: Prentice Hall.

Daft, R. L. (2004). *Organization theory and design.* Manson, OH: Thomson South-Western.

Dahlin, K. B., Weingart, L. R., & Hinds, P. J. (2005). Team diversity and information use. *Academy of Management Journal, 48*, 1107–1123.

Damanpour, F. (1991). Organizational innovation: A meta-analysis of effects of determinants and moderators. *Academy of Management Journal, 34*, 555–590.

Davey, L. M., Bobocel, D. R., Son Hing, L. S., & Zanna, M. P. (1999). Preference for the merit principle scale: An individual difference measure of distributive justice preferences. *Social Justice Research, 12*, 223–240.

Davis-Blake, A., & Pfeffer, J. (1988). Just a mirage: The search for dispositional effects in organizational research. *Academy of Management Review, 14*, 385–400.

Dawis, R. V., & Lofquist, L. H. (1984). *A psychological theory of work adjustment.* Minneapolis: University of Minnesota Press.

Deci, E. L., Connell, J. P., & Ryan, R. M. (1989). Self-determination in a work organization. *Journal of Applied Psychology, 74*, 580–590.

De Cremer, D., & Van Vugt, M. (1999). Social identification effects in social dilemmas: A transformation of motives. *European Journal of Social Psychology, 29*, 871–893.

de Tocqueville, A. (1966). *Democracy in America.* New York: Doubleday. (Original work published 1836).

De Waal, F. B. M. (1982). *Chimpanzee politics: Power and sex among the apes.* London: Jonathan Cape.

Denison, D. R., Hart, S. L., & Kahn, J. A. (1996). From chimneys to cross-functional teams: Developing and validating a diagnostic model. *Academy of Management Journal, 39*, 1005–1023.

DiPrete, T. A. (1989). *The bureaucratic labor market: The case of the federal civil service.* New York: Plenum Press.

Dornbusch, S. M., & Scott, W. R. (1975). *Evaluation and the exercise of authority.* San Francisco: Jossey-Bass.

Dreyfus, H., & Dreyfus, S. (1986). *Mind over machine.* New York: Free Press.

Drucker, P.F. (1988). The Coming of the New Organization. *Harvard Business Review, 66*, 45–53.

Dryer, D. C., & Horowitz, L. M. (1997). When do opposites attract? Interpersonal complementarity versus similarity. *Journal of Personality & Social Psychology, 72*, 592–603.

Dutton, J. E., Ashford, S. J., O'Neill, K. A., & Lawrence, K. A. (2001). Moves that matter: Issue selling and organizational change. *Academy of Management Journal*, 716–724.

Dutton, J. E., Dukerich, J. M., & Harquail, C. V. (1994). Organizational images and member identification. *Administrative Science Quarterly, 39*, 239–263.

Earley, P. C. (1999). Playing follow the leader: Status-determining traits in relation to collective efficacy across cultures. *Organizational Behavior and Human Decision Processes, 80*, 192–212.

Earley, P. C., & Gibson, C. B. (1998). Taking stock in our progress on individualism–collectivism: 100 years of solidarity and community. *Journal of Management, 24*, 265.

Earley, P. C., & Mosakowski, E. M. (2000). Creating hybrid team cultures: An empirical test of international team functioning. *Academy of Management Journal, 43*, 26–49.

Eden, C., & Huxham, C. (1996). Action research for management research. *British Journal of Management, 7*, 75–86.

Edmondson, A. (1999). Psychological safety and learning behavior in work teams. *Administrative Science Quarterly, 44*, 350–383.

Eisenstadt, S.N. (1968). *Social institutions: Comparative study. International Encyclopedia of the Social Sciences, 14*, 421–429.

Ellemers, N. (1993). The influence of socio-structural variables on identity management strategies. *European Review of Social Psychology, 1*, 27–57.

Elvira, M. M., & Zatzick, C. D. (2002). Who's displaced first? The role of race in layoff decisions. *Industrial Relations, 41*, 329–361.

Ely, R. J., & Thomas, D. A. (2001). Cultural diversity at work: The effects of diversity perspectives on work group processes and outcomes. *Administrative Science Quarterly, 46*, 229–273.

England, P. (1992). *Comparable worth: Theories and evidence.* New York: Aldine de Gruyter.

Ensari, N. K., & Miller, N. (2006). The application of the personalization model in diversity management. *Group Processes & Intergroup Relations, 9*, 589–607.

Etzioni, A. (1959). Authority structure and organizational effectiveness. *Administrative Science Quarterly, 4*, 43–67.

Fast, N. J., Gruenfeld, D. H., Sivanathan, N., & Galinsky, A. D. (2009). Illusory control: A generative force behind power's far-reaching effects. *Psychological Science, 420:4, 502*(7).

Fernandez, R. M., Castilla, E. J., & Moore, P. (2000). Social capital at work: Networks and employment at a phone center. *American Journal of Sociology, 105*, 1288–1356.

Fernandez, R. M., & Weinberg, N. (1997). Sifting and sorting: Personal contacts and hiring in a retail bank. *American Sociological Review, 62*, 883–903.

Festinger, L. (1954). A theory of social comparison processes. *Human Relations, 7*, 117–140.

Finkelstein, S. (1992). Power in top management teams: Dimensions, measurement, and validation. *The Academy of Management Journal, 35*, 505–538.

Fiske, A. P. (1991). *Structures of social life: The four elementary forms of human relations.* New York: Free Press.

Fiske, S. T. (1993). Controlling other people: The impact of power on stereotyping. *American Psychologist, 48*, 621–628.

Fiske, S. T., & Berdahl, J. L. (2007). Social power. In A. Kruglanski & E. T. Higgins (Eds.), *social psychology: A handbook of basic principles* (pp. 678–692). New York: Guilford Press.

Fiske, S. T., Cuddy, A. J. C., Glick, P., & Xu, J. (2002). A model of (often mixed) stereotype content: Competence and warmth respectively follow from perceived status and competition. *Journal of Personality and Social Psychology, 82*, 878–902.

Fiss, P. C., & Zajac, E. J. (2006). The symbolic management of strategic change: Sensegiving via framing and decoupling. *The Academy of Management Journal, 49*, 1173–1193.

Fletcher, G., & Kininmonth, L. (1992). Measuring relationship beliefs: An individual differences scale. *Journal of Research in Personality, 26*, 371–397.

Flynn, F. J., & Chatman. J. A. (2001). Strong cultures and innovation: Oxymoron and opportunity? In C. Cooper, S. Cartwright, & C. Earley (Eds.), *International handbook of organizational culture and climate* (pp. 263–287). Chichester, England: Wiley.

Fodor, E. M., & Smith, T. (1982). The power motive as an influence on group decision making. *Journal of Personality and Social Psychology, 42*, 178–185.

Fragale, A. R. (2006). The power of powerless speech: The effects of speech style and task interdependence on status conferral. *Organizational Behavior and Human Decision Processes, 101*, 243–261.

Frank, R. (1985). Choosing the right pond: Human behavior and quest for status. New York: Oxford.

French, J.R.P., & Raven, B. H. (1959). The bases of social power. In D. Cartwright (Ed.), *Studies in social power* (pp. 150–167). Ann Arbor: University of Michigan Press.

Furtado, E.P.H., & Karan, V. (1990). Causes, consequences, and shareholder wealth effects of management turnover: A review of the empirical evidence. *Financial Management, 19*, 60–75.

Galaskiewicz, J., (1985). Professional networks and the institutionalization of a single mind set. *American Sociological Review, 50*, 639–658.

Galaskiewicz, J., & Shatin, D. (1981). Leadership and networking among neighborhood human service organizations. *Administrative Science Quarterly, 26*, 434–448.

Galbraith, J. R. (1973). *Designing Complex Organizations*. Reading, MA: Addison-Wesley.

Galbraith, J. R. (1994). *Competing with flexible lateral organizations*. Reading, MA: Addison-Wesley.

Galinsky, A. D., Gruenfeld, D. H., & Magee, J. C. (2003). From power to action. *Journal of Personality and Social Psychology, 85*, 453–466.

Galinsky, A. D., Magee, J. C., Inesi, M. E., & Gruenfeld, D. H. (2006). Power and perspectives not taken. *Psychological Science, 17*, 1068–1074.

Gallois, C., Callan, V., & Palmer, J. M. (1992). The influence of applicant communication style and interviewer characteristics on hiring decisions. *Journal of Applied Social Psychology, 22*, 1041–1060.

Geletkanycz, M. A. (1998). The salience of "culture's consequences:" the effect of cultural values on top executive commitment to the status quo. *Strategic Management Journal 18*, 615–634.

Ghittell, J. H. (2001). Supervisory span, relational coordination and flight departure performance: A reassessment of postbureaucracy theory. *Organization Science, 12*, 468–483.

Gibson, C. B., & Zellmer-Bruhn, M. E. (2001). Metaphors and meaning: an intercultural analysis of the concept of teamwork. *Administrative Science Quarterly, 46*, 274–303.

Gigone, D., & Hastie, R. (1993). The common knowledge effect: Information sharing and group judgment. *Journal of Personality and Social Psychology, 65*, 959–974.

Glomb, T. M., & Welsh, E. T. (2005). Can opposites attract? Personality heterogeneity in supervisor–subordinate dyads as a predictor of subordinate osutcomes. *Journal of Applied Psychology, 90*, 749–757.

Goethals, G. R. (1986). Social comparison theory: Psychology from the lost and found. *Personality and Social Psychology Bulletin, 12*, 261–278.

Goldin, C. (1990). *Understanding the gender gap: An economic history of American women*. New York: Oxford University Press.

Gomez, C., & Rosen, B. (2001). The leader–member exchange as a link between managerial trust and employee empowerment. *Group & Organization Management, 26*, 53–69.

Goncalo, J., Chatman, J., Duguid, M., & Kennedy, J. (2009). Political correctness and creativity in mixed and same sex groups. Working paper, Department of Industrial and Labor Relations, Cornell University.

Gough, H. G., McCloskey, H., & Meehl, P. E. (1951). A personality scale for dominance. *Journal of Abnormal and Social Psychology, 46*, 360–366.

Gould, R. V. (2003). *Collision of wills: How ambiguity about social rank breeds conflict*. Chicago: University of Chicago Press.

Granovetter, M. S. (1978). Threshold models of collective behavior. *American Journal of Sociology 83*, 1420–1443.

Granovetter, M. S. (1995). *Getting a job: A study of contacts and careers* (2nd ed.). Chicago: University of Chicago Press.

Greenhaus, J. H., & Parasuraman, S. (1993). Job performance attributions and career advancement prospects: An examination of gender and race effects. *Organizational Behavior and Human Decision Processes, 55*, 273–297.

Grieco, M. (1987). *Keeping it in the family: Social networks and employment chance*. Cambridge, England: University Press.

Griffeth, R., Hom, P., & Gaertner, S. (2000). A meta-analysis of antecedents and correlates of employee turnover: Update, moderator tests, and research implications for the next millennium. *Journal of Management, 26*(3), 463–488.

Groysberg, B., Polzer, J. T., & Elfenbein, H. A. (2007). Too many cooks spoil the broth: How high status individuals decrease group effectiveness. Working Paper.

Gruenfeld, D. H., Mannix, E. A., Williams, K. Y., & Neale, M. A. (1996). Group composition and decision making: How member familiarity and information distribution affect process and performance. *Organizational Behavior and Human Decision Processes, 67*, 1–15.

Gruenfeld, D. H., Inesi, M. E., Magee, J. C., & Galinsky, A. D. (2008). Power and the objectification of social targets. *Journal of Personality and Social Psychology, 95*, 111–127.

Guinote, A. (2007). Power and goal pursuit. *Personality and Social Psychology Bulletin, 33*, 1076–1087.

Guzzo, R. A., & Dickson, M. W. (1996). Teams in organizations: Recent research on performance and effectiveness. *Annual Reviews in Psychology, 47*, 307–338.

Hall, J. A., Coats, E. J., & LeBeau, L. S. (2005). Nonverbal behavior and the vertical dimension of social relations: A meta-analysis. *Psychological Bulletin, 131*, 898.

Hallinan, M.T., & Williams, R. (1989). Interracial friendship choice in secondary schools. *American Sociological Review 54*, 67–78.

Hamblin, R. L. (1958). Group integration during a crisis. *Human Relations, 11*, 67–76.

Hambrick, D. C. (1981). Environment, strategy, and power within top management teams. *Administrative Science Quarterly, 26*, 253–275.

Hambrick, D. C. (2003). On the staying power of miles and snow's defenders, analyzers, and prospectors. *Academy of Management, 17*, 115–118.

Hambrick, D., & Mason, P. (1984). Upper echelons: The organization as a reflection of its top managers. *The Academy of Management Review, 9*, 193–206.

Hamilton, B. H., Nickerson, J. A., & Owan, H. (2003). Team incentives and worker heterogeneity: An empirical analysis of the impact of teams on productivity and participation. *Journal of Political Economy, 111,* 465–497.

Hannan, M. T., Burton, M. D., & Baron, J. N. (1996). Inertia and change in the early years: Employment relations in young, high-technology firms. *Industrial and Corporate Change, 5,* 503–36.

Hannan, M. T., & Freeman, J. (1988). The ecology of organizational mortality: American labor unions, 1836–1985. *The American Journal of Sociology, 94,* 25–52.

Harrison, D. A., Price, K. H., & Bell, M. P. (1998). Beyond relational demography: Time and the effects of surface and deep-level diversity on work group cohesion. *Academy of Management Journal, 41,* 96–107.

Haslam, S. A., & Reicher, S. D. (2002). A user's guide to "The Experiment": Exploring the psychology of groups and power. London: BBC Worldwide.

Heath, C. (1999). On the social psychology of agency relationships: Lay theories of motivation overemphasize extrinsic incentives. *Organizational Behavior and Human Decision Processes, 78,* 25–62.

Heath, C., & Staudenmayer, N. (2000). Coordination neglect: How lay theories of organizing complicate coordination in organizations. *Research in Organizational Behavior, 22,* 153–191.

Heckscher, C., & Donnellon, A. (1994). *The post-bureaucratic organization: New perspectives on organizational change.* London: Sage.

Heider, F. (1958). *The psychology of interpersonal relations.* New York: Wiley.

Hellerstein, J. K., & Neumark, D. (2008). Workplace segregation in the United States: Race, ethnicity, and skill. *The Review of Economics and Statistics, 90,* 459–477.

Henke, J. W., Krachenberg, A. R., & Lyons, T. F. (1993). Cross-functional Teams: Good concept, poor implementation! *Journal of Product Innovation Management, 10*(3), 216–229.

Herzberg, F., Mausner, B., & Snyderman, B.B. (1959). *The motivation to work.* New York: Wiley.

Highhouse, S. (2002). Assessing the candidate as a whole: A historical and critical analysis of individual psychological assessment for personnel decision making. *Personnel Psychology, 55*(2), 363–396.

Hofstede, G. (1980). *Culture's consequences: International differences in work-related values.* Beverly Hills, CA: Sage.

Hofstede, G. J. (2005). *Cultures and organizations: Software of the mind.* New York: McGraw-Hill Professional.

Hofstede, G. J., Pedersen, P. B., & Hofstede, G. (2002). *Exploring cultures: Exercises, stories and synthetic cultures.* Boston: Intercultural Press.

Hogan, R., Curphy, G. J., & Hogan, J. (1994). What we know about Leadership: effectiveness and personality. *American Psychologist, 49,* 493–493.

Hogg, M. A. (2001). A social identity theory of leadership. *Personality and Social Psychology Review, 5*(3), 184–200.

Holzer, H. J., & Reaser, J. (2000). Black applicants, black employees, and urban labor market policy. *Journal of Urban Economics, 48,* 365–387.

Homans, G. C. (1950). *The human group.* New York: Harcourt, Brace & Company.

Hornstein, H.A. (2002). *The haves and the have-nots: Abuse of power and privilege in the workplace and how to control it.* Upper Saddle River, NJ: Pearson Education.

Horowitz, L. M., Wilson, K. R., Turan, B., Zolotsev, P., Constantino, M. J., & Henderson, L. (2006). How interpersonal motives clarify the meaning of interpersonal behavior: A revised circumplex model. *Personality and Social Psychology Review, 10,* 67–86.

House, R. J., Hanges, P. J., Javidan, M., Dorfman, P., Gupta, V., & GLOBE Associates (Eds.). (2004). *Cultures, leadership, and organizations: GLOBE study of 62 societies.* Newbury Park, CA: Sage Publications.

Howell, J. M., & Hall-Merenda, K. E. (1999). The ties that bind: The impact of leader–member exchange, transformational and transactional leadership, and distance on predicting follower performance. *Journal of Applied Psychology, 84,* 680–694.

Howell, M. F., & Reese, W. A. (1986). Sex and mobility in the dual economy. *Work and Occupations, 13,* 77–96.

Humphrey, R. (1985). How work roles influence perception: Structural–cognitive processes and organizational behavior. *American Sociological Review, 50,* 242–252.

Hurlbert, J. S., Haines, V. A., & Beggs, J. J. (2000). Core networks and tie activation: What kinds of routine networks allocate resources in non-routine situations. *American Sociological Review, 65,* 598–618.

Huy, Q. N. (2002). Emotional balancing of organizational continuity and radical change: The contribution of middle managers. *Administrative Science Quarterly, 47,* 31–69.

Ibarra, H. (1993). Personal networks of women and minorities in management: A conceptual framework. *Academy of Management Review, 18,* 56–87.

Ibarra, H. (1995). Race, opportunity, and diversity of social circles in managerial managers' networks. *Academy of Management Journal, 38,* 673–703.

Ibarra, H. (1997). Paving an alternate route: Gender differences in network strategies for career development. *Social Psychology Quarterly, 60*(1), 91–102.

Jackson, S. E. (1996). The consequences of diversity in multidisciplinary work teams. In M. West (Ed.), *Handbook of work group psychology* (pp. 53–76). Chichester, England: Wiley.

Jackson, S. E., Brett, J. F., Sessa, V. I., Cooper, D. M., Julin, J. A., & Peyronnin, K. (1991). Some differences make a difference: Individual dissimilarity and group heterogeneity as correlates of recruitment, promotions, and turnover. *Journal of Applied Psychology, 76,* 675–689.

Jackson, S. E., & Joshi, A. (2004). Diversity in social context: A multi-attribute, multilevel analysis of team diversity and sales performance. *Journal of Organizational Behavior, 25,* 675–702.

Jackson, S., Joshi, A., & Erhardt, N. (2003). Recent research on team and organizational diversity: SWOT analysis and implications. *Journal of Management, 29,* 801–830.

Jahoda. M. (1982). *Employment and unemployment: A social-psychological analysis.* Cambridge, England: Cambridge University Press.

Janis, I. L. (1972). *Victims of groupthink.* Boston: Houghton Mifflin.

Jayne, M. E. A., & Dipboye, R. L. (2004). Leveraging diversity to improve business performance: Research findings and recommendations for organizations. *Human Resource Management, 43,* 409–424.

Jehn, K. A., Northcraft, G. B., & Neale, M. A. (1999). Why differences make a difference: A field study of diversity, conflict, and performance in work groups. *Administrative Science Quarterly, 44,* 741–763.

Jenkins, S. R. (1994). Need for power and women's careers over 14 years: Structural power, job satisfaction, and motive change. *Journal of Personality and Social Psychology, 66,* 155(11).

Joshi, A., Liao, H., & Jackson, S. E. (2006). Cross-level effects of workplace diversity on sales performance and pay. *Academy of Management Journal, 49*(3), 459.

Judge, T. A., Bono, J. E., Ilies, R., & Gerhardt, M. W. (2002). Personality and leadership: A qualitative and quantitative review. *Journal of Applied Psychology, 87,* 765–780.

Judge, T. A., & Cable, D. M. (2004). The effect of physical height on workplace success and income: Preliminary test of a theoretical model. *Journal of Applied Psychology, 89*(3), 428–441.

Judge, T. A., Heller, D., & Mount, M. K. (2002). Personality and job satisfaction: A meta-analysis. *Journal of Applied Psychology, 87,* 530–541.

Jung, D., & Lake, D. A. (2008). Markets, hierarchies, and networks: An agent-based organizational ecology. Paper presented at the Annual Meeting of the American Political Science Association, Boston.

Kabanoff, B. (1991). Equity, equality, power and conflict. *Academy of Management Review,* 16, 416–441.

Kabanoff, B., & Daly, J. P. (2002). Espoused values of organizations. *Australian Journal of Management, 27,* 89–104.

Kahn, W. A. (1990). Psychological conditions of personal engagement and disengagement at work. *Academy of Management Journal, 33,* 692–724.

Kaiser, R. B., Hogan, R., & Craig, S. B. (2008). Leadership and the fate of organizations. *American Psychologist, 63,* 96–110.

Kalev, A., Dobbin, F., & Kelly, E. (2006). Best practices or best guesses? Assessing the efficacy of corporate affirmative action and diversity Policies. *American Sociological Review, 71,* 589–617.

Kalleberg, A. L., Knoke, D., Marsden, P. V., & Spaeth, J. L. (1996). *Organizations in America: Analyzing their Structures and human resource practices.* Thousand Oaks, CA: Sage.

Kandel, E., & Lazear, E.P. (1992). Peer pressure and partnerships. *Journal of Political Economy, 100,* 801–817.

Kanter, R. M. (1977). *Men and women of the corporation.* New York: Basic Books.

Kanter, R. M. (1983). *The change masters: Innovation for productivity in the american corporation.* New York: Simon & Schuster.

Kanter, R. M. (1988). When a thousand flowers bloom: Structural, collective, and social conditions for innovation in organizations. *Research in organizational behavior, 10,* 169–211.

Kark, R., Shamir, B., & Chen, G. (2003). The two faces of transformational leadership: Empowerment and dependency. *Journal of Applied Psychology, 88,* 246–255.

Katz, D., & Kahn, R. (1978). *The social psychology of organizations.* New York: Wiley.

Katzenbach, J. R., & Smith, D. K. (1993). *The wisdom of teams: Creating the high performance organization.* Boston: Harvard Business School Press.

Kaufman, R. (2002). Assessing alternative perspectives on race and sex employment segregation. *American Sociological Review, 67,* 547–572.

Kelly, E., & Dobbin, F. (1998). How affirmative action became diversity management. *American Behavioral Scientist, 41,* 960–84.

Keltner, D., Gruenfeld, D. H., & Anderson, C. (2003). Power, approach, and inhibition. *Psychological Review, 110,* 265–284.

Kiesler, D. J. (1983). The 1982 interpersonal circle: A taxonomy for complementarity in human transactions. *Psychological Review, 90,* 185–214.

Kilbourne, B.S., Farkas, G., Beron, K., Weir, D., & England, P. (1994). Returns to skill, compensating differentials, and gender bias: Effects of occupational characteristics on the wages of white women and men. *The American Journal of Sociology, 100*(3), 689–719.

Kilduff, G. & Anderson, C. (2009). Status conflict: How disagreement over status ranking affects group performance and member behavior. Unpublished paper.

Kilduff, M., Angelmar, R., & Mehra, A. (2000). Top management team diversity and firm performance: Examining the role of cognitions. *Organization Science, 11,* 21–34.

King, R. G., & Levine, R. (1993). Finance and growth: Schumpeter might be right. *The Quarterly Journal of Economics,* 717–737.

Kipnis, D. (1976). *The powerholders.* Chicago: University of Chicago Press.

Klein, K. J., Lim, B. C., Saltz, J. L., & Mayer, D. M. (2004). How do they get there? An examination of the antecedents of centrality in team networks. *Academy of Management Journal, 47,* 952–963.

Kletzer, L. G. (1998). Job displacement. *The Journal of Economic Perspectives, 12*(1), 115–136.

Kochan, T., Bezrukova, K., Ely, R., Jackson, S., Joshi, A., Jehn, K., Leonard, J., Levine, D., & Thomas, D. (2003). The effects of diversity on business performance: Report of the diversity research network. *Human Resource Management, 42,* 3–21.

Konrad, A.M., and Pfeffer, J. (1991). Understanding the hiring of women and minorities in educational institutions. *Sociology of Education, 64*(3), 141–157.

Krackhardt, D., & Porter, L. W. (1986). The snowball effect: Turnover embedded in communication networks. *Applied Psychology, 71,* 50–55.

Kraiger, K., & Ford, J. (1985). A meta-analysis of ratee race effects in performance ratings. *Journal of Applied Psychology, 70,* 56–65.

Kristof, A. (1996). Person–organization fit: An integrative review of its conceptualizations, measurement, and implications. *Personnel Psychology, 49,* 1–49.

Kunda, G. (1992). *Engineering culture.* Philadelphia: Temple University Press.

Lam, S.S.K., Schaubroeck, J., & Aryee, S. (2002). Relationship between organizational justice and employee work outcomes: A cross-national study. *Journal of Organizational Behavior, 23,* 1–18.

Lansberg, I. (1989). Social categorization, entitlement, and justice in organizations: Contextual determinants and cognitive underpinnings. Human Relations *41,* 871–899.

Lau, D. C., & Murnighan, J. K. (1998). Demographic diversity and faultlines: The compositional dynamics of organizational groups. *The Academy of Management Review, 23,* 325–340.

Lau, D. C., & Murnighan, K. J. (2005). Interactions with groups and subgroups: The effects of demographic faultlines. *Academy of Management Journal, 48,* 645–659.

Laumann, E. O. (1966). *Prestige and association in an urban community.* Indianapolis, IN: Bobbs-Merrill.

Laumann, E. O. (1973). *Bonds of pluralism: The form and substance of urban social networks.* New York: Wiley.

Lawler, E. E., III. (1973). *Motivation in work organizations.* Monterey, CA: Brooks/Cole.

Lawrence, P. (Ed.). (1997). *Workflow handbook 1997: Workflow management coalition.* New York: John Wiley and Sons.

Lazarsfeld, P. F., & Merton, R. K. (1954). Friendship as a social process: A substantive and methodological analysis. In M. Berger (Ed.), *Freedom and control in modern society* (pp. 8–66). New York: Van Nostrand.

Lazear, E. P., & Rosen, S. (1981). Rank–order tournaments as optimum labor contracts. *Journal of Political Economy, 89,* 841–864.

Leary, T. (1957). *Interpersonal diagnosis of personality.* New York: Ronald Press.

Leavitt, H. J. (1996). The old days, hot groups, and managers' lib. *Administrative Science Quarterly, 41,* 288–300.

Leavitt, H. J. (2003). Why hierarchies thrive. *Harvard Business Review,* 81, 96–102.

Leavitt, H. (2004). *Top down: Why hierarchies are here to stay and how to manage them more effectively.* Cambridge, MA: Harvard Business School Press.

Levine, R. A., & Campbell, D. T. (1972). *Ethnocentrism: Theories of conflict, ethnic attitudes, and group behavior.* New York: Wiley.

Levinson, H. (1994). Why the behemoths fell: Psychological roots of corporate failure. *American Psychologist, 49,* 428–436.

Levinthal, D. A., & March, J. G. (1993). The myopia of learning. *Strategic Management Journal, 14,* 95–112.

Lewin, K., & Cartwright, D. (Eds.). (1951). *Field theory in social science: Selected theoretical papers*. New York: Harper.

Lieberman, S. (1956). The effects of changes in roles on the attitudes of role occupants. *Human Relations, 9*, 385.

Lin, N. (1999). Social networks and status attainment. *Annual Review of Sociology, 25*, 467–487.

Lincoln, J. R., & Miller, J. (1979). Work and friendship ties in organizations: A comparative analysis of relational networks. *Administrative Science Quarterly, 24*, 181–199.

Lipset, S. M., Trow, M., & Coleman, J. (1956). *Union democracy: The Inside politics of the international typographical union*. New York: Free Press.

Littlepage, G., Robinson, W., & Reddington, K. (1997). Effects of task experience and group experience on group performance, member ability, and recognition of expertise. *Organizational Behavior and Human Decision Processes, 69*, 133–147.

Loch, C. H., Huberman, B. A., & Stout, S. (2000). Status competition and performance in work groups. *Journal of Economic Behavior & Organization, 43*, 35–55.

Lonner, W. J. (1980). The search for psychological universals. In H. C. Triandis & W. W. Lambert (Eds.), *The Handbook of Cross Cultural Psychology* (vol. 1, pp. 143–204). Boston: Allyn & Bacon.

Lorbiecki, A., & Jack, G. (2000). Critical Turns in the evolution of diversity management. *British Journal of Management, 11*, 17–31.

Maclay, G., & Knipe, H. (1972). *The dominant man*. New York: Delacorte Press.

Magee, J. C., & Galinsky, A. D. (2008). Social hierarchy: The self-reinforcing nature of power and status. *Academy of Management Annals, 2*, 351–398.

Magee, J. C., Galinsky, A. D., & Gruenfeld, D. H (2007). Power, propensity to negotiate, and moving first in competitive interactions. *Personality and Social Psychology Bulletin, 33*, 200–212.

Malinowski, B. (1939). *A scientific theory of culture and other essays*. New York: Oxford University Press.

Maner, J. K., DeWall, C. N., Baumeister, R. F., & Schaller, M. (2007). Does social exclusion motivate interpersonal reconnection? Resolving the "Porcupine Problem." *Journal of Personaltiy and Social Psychology, 92*(1), 42–55.

Mannix, E. A., (1993). Organizations as resource dilemmas: The effects of power balance on coalition formation in small groups. *Organizational Behavior and Human Decision Processes, 55*, 1–22.

Mannix, E., & Neale, M. (2005). What differences make a difference? The promise and reality of diverse teams in organizations. *Psychological Science in the Public Interest, 6*, 31–55.

Mannix, E. A., & Sauer, S. J. (2006). Status and power in organizational group research: Acknowledging the pervasiveness of hierarchy. *Social Psychology of the Workplace: Advances in Group Processes, 26*, 149–182.

March, J. G. (1991). Exploration and exploitation in organizational learning. *Organization Science 2*, 71–87.

March, J. G. (1994). *A Primer on Decision Making. How Decisions Happen*. New York: Free Press.

March, J. G., & Simon, H. A. (1958). *Organizations*. New York: Wiley.

Marglin, S. A. (1974). What do bosses do? The origins and functions of hierarchy in capitalist production. *Review of Radical Political Economy, 6*, 60–112.

Marsden, P. V. (1987). Core discussion networks of America. *American Sociological Review, 52*, 122–131.

Marsden, P. V. (1988). Homogeneity in confiding relations. *Social Networks, 10*, 57–76.

Marsden, P. V. (1990). Network data and measurement. *Annual Review of Sociology, 16*, 435–463.

Martin, J. (2002). *Organizational culture: Mapping the terrain*. Thousand Oaks, CA: Sage Publications.

Mayo, E. (1960). *The human problems of an industrial civilization*. New York: Compass Books.

Maznevski, M. L., Gomez, C. B., Noorderhaven, N. G., & Wu, P. (1997). The cultural orientations framework and international management research. Presented at the Academy of International Business Annual Meeting, Monterrey, MX.

McCann, S. J. H. (1991). Threat, authoritarianism, and the power of U.S. presidents: New threat and power measures. *Journal of Psychology, 125*, 237–240.

McClelland, D. C. (1975). *Power: The inner experience*. New York: Irvington-Halsted-Wiley.

McGregor, D., & Cutcher-Gershenfeld, J. (2006). *The human side of enterprise*. New York: McGraw-Hill Professional.

McPherson, J. M., Popielarz, P., & Drobnic, S. (1992). Social networks and organizational dynamics. *American Sociology Review, 57*, 153–170.

McPherson, J. M., & Smith-Lovin, L. (1987). Homophily in voluntary organizations: Status distance and the composition of face-to-face groups. *American Sociology Review, 52*, 370–379.

McPherson, J. M., Smith-Lovin, L., & Cook, J. M. (2001). Birds of a feather: Homophily in social networks. *Annual Review of Sociology, 27*, 415–444.

Merton, R. (1957). The role-set: Problems in sociological theory. *The British Journal of Sociology, 8*, 106–120.

Meyer, M. W., & Gupta, V. (1994). The performance paradox. *Research in Organizational Behavior, 16*, 309–309.

Meyerson, D. (2001). *Tempered radicals: How people use difference to inspire change at work*. Boston: Harvard Business School Press.

Micklethwait, J., & Wooldridge, A. (1996). *The witch doctors: Making sense of management gurus*. New York: Time Books, Random House.

Miles, R. E., & Snow, C. C. (2003). Network organizations: New concepts for new forms. *California Management Review, 28*, 62–73.

Milgram, S. (1974). *Obedience to Authority*. New York: Harper & Row.

Milliken, F. J., Magee, J. C., Lam, N., & Menezes, D. (2008). The lens and language of power: Sense-making gaps in the aftermath of Hurricane Katrina. Manuscript submitted for publication.

Mintzberg, H. (1983). *Power in and around organizations*. Englewood Cliffs, NJ: Prentice Hall.

Mohrman, S. A. (1999). The contexts of geographically dispersed teams and networks. *Trends in organizational behavior, 6*, 63–80.

Mohrman, S. A., Cohen, S. G., & Morhman, A. M. (1995). *Designing team-based organizations: New forms for knowledge work*. San Francisco: Jossey-Bass.

Mondros, J. B., & Wilson, S. M. (1994). *Organizing for power and empowerment*. New York: Columbia University Press.

Montgomery, J. (1992). Job search and network composition: Implications of the strength-of-weak-ties hypothesis. *American Sociological Review, 57*, 586–596.

Morales, C. M. (2008). The ethnic niche as an economic pathway for the dark skinned. *Hispanic Journal of Behavioral Sciences, 30*, 280–298.

Morrison, E. W., (1993). Newcomer information seeking: Exploring types, modes, sources and outcomes. *Academy of Management Journal, 36*(3), 557–589.

Moss, P., & Tilly, C. (1996). "Soft" skills and race: An investigation of black men's employment problems. *Work and Occupations, 23*, 252.

Moss, P., & Tilly, C. (2001). *Stories employers tell: Race, skill, and hiring in America*. Thousand Oaks, CA: Russell Sage Publications.

Mouw, T. (2002). Are black workers missing the connection? The effect of spatial distance and employee referrals on interfirm racial segregation. *Demography 39*, 507–528.

Mulder, M. (1971). Power equalization through participation? *Administrative Science Quarterly, 16*, 31–38.

Mulder, M. (1977). *The daily power game.* Leiden, Neth.: Nijhoff.

Mulder, M., & Stemerding, A. (1963). Threat, attraction to group, and need for strong leadership. *Human Relations, 16*, 317–334.

Mullen, B., Brown, R., & Smith, C. (1992). Ingroup bias as a function of salience, relevance, and status: An integration. *European Journal of Social Psychology, 22*, 103–122.

Murnighan, K. J. (1978). Models of coalition behavior: Game theoretic, social-psychological, and political perspectives. *Psychological Bulletin, 85*, 1130–1153.

Murphy, K. R., & Cleveland, J. N. (1995). *Understanding performance appraisal: Social, organizational and goal-based perspectives.* Thousand Oaks, CA: Sage.

Nakao, K., & Treas, J. (1994). Updating occupational prestige and socioeconomic scores: How the new measures measure up. *Sociological methodology*, 1–72.

Newcomb, T. M. (1961). *The acquaintance process.* New York: Holt, Rinehart & Winston.

Ng, S. H., & Bradac, J. J. (1993). *Power in language.* Thousand Oaks, CA: Sage.

Nicholson, N. (2000). *Executive instinct.* New York: Crown Business Books.

Ocasio, W. (1994). Political dynamics and the circulation of power: CEO succession in U.S. industrial corporations, 1960–1990. *Administrative Science Quarterly, 39*, 285–312.

Operario, D., & Fiske, S. T. (2001). Effects of trait dominance on powerholders' judgments of subordinates. *Social Cognition, 19*, 161–180.

O'Reilly, C. A. (1989). Corporations, culture and commitment: Motivation and socialcontrol in organizations. *California Management Review, 31*, 9–25.

O'Reilly, C. A., Caldwell, D. F., & Barnett, W. P. (1989). Work group demography, social integration, and turnover. *Administrative Science Quarterly, 34*, 21–37.

O'Reilly, C., & Chatman, J. (1996). Cultures as social control: Corporations, cults, and commitment. *Research in Organizational Behavior, 18*, 157–200.

O'Reilly, C. A., III, & Chatman J. (1986). Organization commitment and psychological attachment: The effects of compliance, identification and internalization on prosocial behavior. *Journal of Applied Psychology, 71*, 492–499.

O'Reilly, C. A., & Tushman, M. L. (2004). The ambidextrous organization. *Harvard Business Review, 82*, 74–81.

Organ, D., & Konovsky, M. (1989). Cognitive versus affective determinants of organizational citizenship behavior. *Journal of Applied Psychology, 74*, 157–164.

Ouchi, W. (1981). *Theory Z: How American Business can meet the Japanese challenge.* Reading, MA: Addison-Wesley.

Overbeck, J. R., Correll, J., & Park, B. (2005). Internal status sorting in groups: The problem of too many stars. In M. A. Neale, E. A. Mannix, & M. Thomas-Hunt (Eds.), *Research on managing groups and teams* (vol. 7, pp. 169–199). Oxford: Elsevier.

Pauchant, T. C. (2002). *Ethics and spirituality at work: Hopes and pitfalls of the search for meaning in organizations.* Westport, CT: Quorum Books.

Paulson, S. K. (1974). Causal analysis of interorganizational relations: An axiomatic theory revised. *Administrative Science Quarterly, 19*, 319–337.

Pelled, L. H., Eisenhardt, K. M., & Xin, K. R. (1999). Exploring the black box: An analysis of work group diversity, conflict, and performance. *Administrative Science Quarterly, 44*(1), 1–28.

Petersen, T., Saporta, I., & Seidel, M.D.L. (2000). Offering a job: Meritocracy and social networks. *American Journal of Sociology, 106*(3), 763–816.

Pfeffer, J. (1981). *Power in organizations.* Marshfield, MA: Pitman.

Pfeffer, J. (1983). Organizational demography. *Research in Organizational Behavior, 5*, 299–357.

Pfeffer, J. (1992). *Managing with power: Politics and influence in organizations.* Boston: Harvard Business School Press.

Pfeffer, J. (1998). *The human equation: Building profits by putting people first.* Boston: Harvard Business School Press.

Pfeffer, J., & Davis-Blake, A. (1990). Unions and job satisfaction: An alternative view. *Work Occupations, 17*, 259–83.

Pfeffer, J., Cialdini, R. B., Hanna, B., & Knopoff, K. (1998). Faith in supervision and the self-enhancement bias: Two psychological reasons why managers don't empower workers. *Basic and Applied Psychology, 20*, 313–321.

Pfeffer, J., & Langton N. (1993). The effect of wage dispersion on satisfaction, *productivity*, and working collaboratively: Evidence from college and university faculty. *Administrative Science Quarterly, 38*, 382–408.

Pfeffer, J., & O'Reilly, C. A. (1987). Hospital demography and turnover among nurses. *Industrial Relations, 26*, 158–173.

Pfeffer, J., & Salancik, G. R. (1974). Organizational decision making as a political process: The case of a university budget. *Administrative Science Quarterly, 19*, 135–151.

Pfeffer, J., & Salancik, G. R. (1975). Determinants of supervisory behavior: A role set analysis. *Human Relations, 28*, 139–164.

Phillips, K. W. (2003). The effects of categorically based expectations on minority influence: The importance of congruence. *Personality and Social Psychology Bulletin, 29*, 3–13.

Phillips K. W., & Loyd, D. L. (2006). When surface and deep-level diversity collide: The effects on dissenting group members. *Organizational Behavior Human Decision Process, 99*, 143–160.

Phillips, K. W., Mannix, E. A., Neale, M. A., & Gruenfeld, D. H. (2004). Diverse groups and information sharing: The effects of congruent ties. *Journal of Experimental Social Psychology, 40*, 497–510.

Phillips, D. J., & Zuckerman, E. W. (2001). Middle-status conformity: Theoretical restatement and empirical demonstration in two markets. *American Journal of Sociology, 107*, 379–429.

Pinquart, M., & Sörensen, S. (2000). Influences of socioeconomic status, social network, and competence on subjective well-being in later life: A meta-analysis. *psychology and aging, 15*(2), 187.

Piore, M., & Sabel, C. (1984). *The second industrial divide: Possibilities for prosperity.* New York: Basic Books.

Podolny, J. M., & Baron, J. N. (1997). Resources and relationships: Social networks and mobility in the workplace. *American Sociological Review, 62*, 673–693.

Popielarz, P., & McPherson, J. M. (1995). On the edge or in between: Niche position, niche overlap, and the duration of voluntary memberships. *American Journal of Sociology, 101*, 698–720.

Pratt, M. G. (2001). Social identity dynamics in modern organizations: An organizational psychology–organizational behavior perspective. In M. Hogg & D. J. Terry (Eds.), *Social identity processes in organizational contexts* (pp. 13–30). Philadelphia: Psychology Press.

Pratto, F., Stallworth, L. M., & Conway-Lanz, S. (1998). Social dominance orientation and the ideological legitimization of social policy. *Journal of Applied Social Psychology, 28*(20), 1853–1875.

Pratto, F., Stallworth, L. M., Sidanius, J., & Siers B. (1997). The gender gap: Differences in political attitudes and social dominance orientation. *British Journal of Social Psychology, 36*, 49–68.

Pulakos, E. D., White, L. A., Oppler, S. H., & Borman, W. C. (1989). Examination of race and sex effects on performance ratings. *Journal of Applied Psychology, 74*, 770–780.

Queneau, H. (2005). Changes in occupational segregation by race and ethnicity in the USA. *Applied Economics Letters, 12*, 781–784.

Radcliffe-Brown, A. R. (1952). *Structure and function in primitive society: Essays and addresses*. Glencoe, IL: Free Press.

Reagans, R. (2005). Preferences, identity, and competition: Predicting tie strength from demographic data. *Management Science, 51*, 1374–1383.

Reagans, R., Zuckerman, E., & McEvily, B. (2004). How to make the team: Social networks vs. demography as criteria for designing effective teams. *Administrative Science Quarterly, 49*, 101–133.

Reskin, B. (1993). Sex Segregation in the Workplace. *Annual Reviews in Sociology, 19*, 241–270.

Reskin, B. F. (2005). Including mechanism in our models of ascriptive inequality. In L. B. Nielsen & R. L. Nelson (Eds.), *Handbook of Employment Discrimination Research* (pp. 75–99). Dordrecht, The Netherlands: Springer.

Reskin, B. F., McBrier, D. B., & Kmec, J. A. (1999). The determinants and consequences of workplace sex and race composition. *Annual Review of Sociology, 25*, 335–361.

Reskin, B.F., & Roos, P. (1990). *Job queues, gender queues: Explaining women's inroads into male occupations*. Philadelphia: Temple University Press.

Richard, O. C. (2000). Racial diversity, business strategy, and firm performance: A resource-based view. *Academy of Management Journal, 43*, 164–177.

Ridgeway, C. L. (1987). Nonverbal behavior, dominance, and the basis of status in task groups. *American Sociological Review, 52*, 683–694.

Ridgeway, C. L., & Smith-Lovin, L. (1999). The gender system and interaction. *Annual Review of Sociology, 25*, 191–216.

Robbins, S. P., & Judge, T. (2009). *Essentials of organizational behavior* (13th ed.). Englewood Cliffs, NJ: Prentice Hall.

Robinson, G., & Dechant, K. (1997). Building a business case for diversity. *Academy of Management Executive, 11*, 21–31.

Roethlisberger, F., & Dickson, W. (1939). *Management and the worker*. Cambridge, MA: Harvard University Press.

Rosenbaum, J. E. (1979). Tournament mobility: Career patterns in a corporation. *Administrative Science Quarterly*, 220–241.

Rosenbaum, J. E., (1984). *Career mobility in a corporate hierarchy*. Orlando, FL: Academic Press.

Ross, R., & Schneider, R. (1992). *From equality to diversity: A business case for equal opportunities*. London: Pitman.

Rotter, J. B. (1966). Generalized expectancies for internal versus external control of reinforcement. *Psychological Monographs, 80*, 1–28.

Rousseau, D. M. (1997). Organizational behavior in the new organizational era. *Annual Review of Psychology, 48*, 515–546.

Ruderman, M. N., Hughes-James, M. W., & Jackson, S. E. (Eds.). (1996). *Selected research on work team diversity*. Greensboro, NC: Center for Creative Leadership.

Rushton, J. P. (1989). Japanese inbreeding depression scores: Predictors of cognitive differences between Blacks and Whites. *Intelligence, 13*, 43–51.

Rutte, C., & Wilke, H. (1985). Preference for decision structures in a social dilemma situation. *European Journal of Social Psychology, 15*, 367–370.

Sackett P., DuBois C., & Noe A. (1991). Tokenism in performance evaluation: The effects of work group representation on male–female and white–black differences in performance ratings. *Journal of Applied Psychology, 76*, 263–267.

Sadler, P., & Woody, E. (2003). Is who you are who you're talking to? Interpersonal style and complementarity in mixed-sex interactions. *Journal of Personality and Social Psychology, 84*(1), 80–96.

Salancik, G. R., & Pfeffer, J. (1977). An examination of the need–satisfaction models of job attitudes. *Administrative Science Quarterly, 22*, 427–456.

Sampson, E. E. (1969). Studies of status congruence. In L. Berkowitz (Ed.), *Advances in experimental social psychology* (vol. 4, pp. 225–270). New York: Academic Press.

Samuelson, C. D. (1991). Perceived task difficulty, causal attributions, and preferences for structural change in resource dilemmas. *Personality and Social Psychology Bulletin, 17*, 181–187.

Samuelson, C. D. (1993). A multiattribute evaluation approach to structural change in resource dilemmas. *Organizational Behavior and Human Decision Processes, 55*, 283–324.

Sande, G., Ellard, J., & Ross, M. (1986). Effect of arbitrarily assigned status labels on self-perceptions and social perceptions: The mere position effect. *Journal of Personality and Social Psychology, 50*(4), 684–689.

Sapolsky, R. M. (1994). *Why zebras don't get ulcers*. New York: W. H. Freeman.

Sapolsky, R. M. (1998). *The trouble with testosterone*. New York: Simon & Schuster.

Saunders, P. (1990). *Social class and stratification*. London: Routledge.

Schein, E. H. (1992). *Organizational culture and leadership*. San Francisco: Jossey-Bass.

Schein, E.H. (1999). *Process consultation revisited: Building the helping relationship*. Reading, MA: Addison-Wesley.

Schelling, T. (1971). Dynamic models of segregation. *Journal of Mathematical Sociology, 1*, 143–186.

Schermerhorn, J. R., & Bond, M. H. (1991). Upward and downward influence tactics in managerial networks: A comparative study of Hong Kong Chinese and Americans. *Asia Pacific Journal of Management, 8*(2), 147–158.

Schmid Mast, M. (2002). Dominance as expressed and inferred through speaking time: A meta-analysis. *Human Communication Research, 28*, 420–450.

Schneider, B. (1987). The people make the place. *Personnel Psychology, 40*, 437–453.

Schneider, D. J. (2004). *The psychology of stereotyping*. New York: Guilford Press.

Schneider, B. H., Dixon, K., & Udvari, S. (2007). Closeness and competition in the inter-ethnic and co-ethnic friendships of early adolescents in Toronto and Montreal. *The Journal of Early Adolescence, 27*, 115.

Schriesheim, C. A., Castro, S. L., & Cogliser, C. C. (1999). Leader–member exchange (LMX) research: A comprehensive review of theory, measurement, and data-analytic practices. *The Leadership Quarterly, 10*(1), Spring, 63–113.

Schuler, R. S., Jackson, S. E., & Luo, Y. (2003). *Managing human resources in cross-border alliances*. London: Routledge.

Schwartz, H. S. (1995). Acknowledging the dark side of organizational life. In T. Pauchant (Ed.), *In search of meaning: Managing for the health of our organizations, our communities, and the natural world* (pp. 224–243). San Francisco: Jossey-Bass.

Schwartz, S. H., & Bardi, A. (2001). Value hierarchies across cultures: Taking a similarities perspective. *Journal of Cross-Cultural Psychology, 32*(3), 268.

Schwartz, S. H., & Boehnke, K. (2004). Evaluating the structure of human values with confirmatory factor analysis. *Journal of Research in Personality, 38*(3), 230–255.

Scott, J. (1992). *Social networking analysis: A handbook*. London: Sage.

Scott, J. (Ed.). (2002). *Social networks: Critical concepts in sociology.* London: Routledge.

Seashore, S. E. (1964). Field experiments with formal organizations. *Human Organizations, 23*, 164–170.

Seibert, S. E., Kraimer, M. L., & Liden, R. C. (2001). A social capital theory of career success. *Academy of Management Journal, 44*, 219–247.

Seidel, M.D.L., Polzer, J. T., & Stewart, K. J. (2000). Friends in high places: The effects of social networks on discrimination in salary negotiations. *Administrative Science Quarterly, 45*, 1–24.

Seifter, H., Economy, P., & Hackman, J. R. (2001). *Leadership ensemble: Lessons in collaborative management from world's only conductorless orchestra.* New York: Times Books.

Shamir, B., House, R. J., & Arthur, M. B. (1993). The motivational effects of charismatic leadership: A self-concept based theory. *Organization Science, 4*, 577–593.

Shaw, J. D., Gupta, N., & Delery, J. E. (2002). Pay dispersion and workforce performance: Moderating effects of incentives and interdependence. *Strategic Management Journal, 23*, 491–512.

Sheppard, B. H., & Tuchinsky, M. (1996). Micro-OB and the network organization. In R. M. Kramer & T. R. Tyler (Eds.), *Trust in organizations: Frontiers of theory and research* (pp. 140–165). Thousand Oaks, CA: Sage Publications.

Shils, E. A. (1968). Deference. In J. A. Jackson (Ed.), *Social Stratification* (pp. 104- 132). Cambridge, MA: Harvard University Press.

Sibbet, D. (1997). Years of Management Ideas and Practice: 1922–1997. *Harvard Business Review, 75*, 2–12.

Sidanius, J. (1993). The psychology of group conflict and the dynamics of oppression: A social dominance perspective. In S. Iyengar & W. McGuire (Eds.), *Explorations in political psychology* (pp. 183–219). Durham, NC: Duke University Press.

Sidanius, J., Liu, J., Shaw, J., & Pratto, F. (1994). Social dominance orientation, hierarchy-attenuators and hierarchy-enhancers: Social dominance theory and the criminal justice system. *Journal of Applied Social Psychology, 24*, 338–366.

Sidanius, J., & Pratto, F. (1999). *Social dominance: An intergroup theory of social hierarchy and oppression.* New York: Cambridge University Press.

Sidanius, J., Pratto, F., Sinclair, S., & van Laar, C. (1996). Mother Teresa meets Genghis Khan: The dialectics of hierarchy-enhancing and hierarchy-attenuating career choices. *Social Justice Research, 9*, 145–170.

Siegel, P. A., & Hambrick, D. C. (2005). Pay disparities within top management groups: Evidence of harmful effects on performance of high-technology firms. *Organization Science, 16*, 259–274.

Simon, H. A. (1957). *Models of man: Social and rational.* New York: John Wiley & Sons.

Simons, T., Pelled, L. H., & Smith, K. A. (1999). Making use of difference: Diversity, debate, and decision comprehensiveness in top management teams. *Academy of Management Journal, 42*(6), 662–674.

Simonton, D. K. (1994). *Greatness: Who makes history and why.* New York: Guilford Press.

Sinangil, H. K., & Avallone, F. (2002). Organizational development and change. *Handbook of industrial, work and organizational psychology, 2*, 332–345.

Singelis, T. M., Triandis, H. C., Bhawuk, D. P. S., & Gelfand, M. J. (1995). Horizontal and vertical dimensions of individualism and collectivism: A theoretical and measurement refinement. *Cross-Cultural Research, 29*(3), 240.

Slater, P. E. (1955). Roles differentiation in small groups. *American Sociological Review, 20*, 3, 300–310.

Smith, A. (1937). *An Inquiry into the Nature and the Causes of the Wealth of Nations.* New York: Modern Library.

Smith, P. K., & Trope, Y. (2006). You focus on the forest when you're in charge of the trees: Power priming and abstract information processing. *Journal of Personality and Social Psychology, 90*, 578–596.

Sørensen, J. B. (2004). The organizational demography of racial employment segregation. *American Journal of Sociology, 110*, 626–671.

Sørensen, A. B., & Kelleberg, A. L. (1994). An outline of a theory of the matching of persons to jobs. In D. B. Grusky (Ed.), *Social stratification in sociological perspective* (pp. 362–369). San Francisco: Westview Press.

Spreitzer, G. (1996). Social structural characteristics of psychological empowerment. *Academy of Management Journal, 39*, 483–504.

Sproull, L.S., & Kiesler S.B. (1991). *Connections: New ways of working in the networked organization.* Boston: MIT Press.

Stasser, G., & Titus, W. (2003). Hidden profiles: A brief history. *Psychological Inquiry, 14*, 302–311.

Stewman, S. (1988). Organizational demography. *Annual Review of Sociology, 14*, 173–202.

Stone, K. (1974). The origins of the labor process in the steel industry. *Review of Radical Political Economics, 6*, 61–97.

Strang, D., & Baron, J. N. (1990). Categorical imperatives: The structure of job titles in California state agencies. *American Sociology Review, 55*, 479–495.

Strauss, G. (1982). Workers participation in management: An international perspective. *Research in Organizational Behavior, 4*, 233–265.

Sue-Chan, C., & Ong, M. (2002). Goal assignment and performance: Assessing the mediating roles of goal commitment and self-efficacy and the moderating role of power distance. *Organizational Behavior and Human Decision Processes, 89*, 1140–1161.

Sullivan, H. S. (1947). *Conceptions of modern psychiatry.* Washington, DC: William Alanson White Foundation.

Sutton, R. I., & Hargadon, A. (1996). Brainstorming groups in context: Effectiveness in a product design firm. *Administrative Science Quarterly, 41*, 685–718.

Swann, W. B., Johnson, R. E., & Bosson, J. K. (in press). Identity negotiation at work. *Research in Organizational Behavior.*

Szafran, R. F. (1982). What kinds of firms hire and promote women and blacks? A review of the literature. *The Sociological Quarterly, 23*(2), 171–190.

Tajfel, H., & Turner, J. C. (1986). The social identity theory of intergroup behavior. In W. Austin & S. Worchel (Eds.), *The social psychology of intergroup relations* (pp. 7–24). Monterey, CA: Brooks/Cole.

Thach, E. C. (2002). The impact of executive coaching and 360 feedback on leadership effectiveness. *Leadership & Organization Development Journal, 23*, 205–214.

Thomas, D. A., & Ely, R. J. (1996). Making differences matter: A new paradigm for managing diversity. *Harvard Business Review, 74*, 79–91.

Thomas, K. W., & Velthouse, B. A. (1990). Cognitive elements of empowerment. *Academy of Management Review, 15*, 666–681.

Thye, S. R. (2000). Reliability in experimental sociology. *Social Forces, 74*, 1277–1309.

Tiedens, L. Z., & Fragale, A. R. (2003). Power moves: Complementarity in dominant and submissive nonverbal behavior. *Journal of Personality and Social Psychology, 84*, 558–568.

Tiedens, L. Z., Unzueta, M. M., & Young, M. J. (2007). An unconscious desire for hierarchy? The motivated perception of dominance complementarity in task partners. *Journal of Personality and Social Psychology, 93*(3), 402–414.

Tinsley, C. H. (2001). How negotiators get to yes: Predicting the constellation of strategies used across cultures to negotiate conflict. *Journal of Applied Psychology, 86*(4), 583–593.

Tinsley, C. H., & Brett, J. M. (2001). Managing workplace conflict in the United States and Hong Kong. *Organizational Behavior and Human Decision Processes, 85*(2), 360–381.

Tirole, J. (1986). Procurement and renegotiation. *Journal of Political Economy, 94*(2), 235–259.

Tomaskovic-Devey, D., & Skaggs, S. (2002). Sex segregation, labor process organization, and gender earnings inequality. *American Journal of Sociology, 108*(1), 102–128.

Tracey, T. J., & Hayes, K. (1989). Therapist complementarity as a function of experience and client stimuli. *Psychotherapy: Theory, Research, Practice, Training, 26*, 462–468.

Tracey, T. J., Sherry, P., & Albright, J. (1999). The interpersonal process of cognitive–behavioral therapy: An examination of complementarity over the course of treatment. *Journal of Counseling Psychology, 46*, 80–91.

Triandis, H. C., & Gelfand, M. J. (1998). Converging measurement of horizontal and vertical individualism and collectivism. *Journal of Personality and Social Psychology, 74*, 118–128.

Tsui, A. S. (1984). A multiple-constituency framework of managerial reputational effectiveness. In J. G. Hunt, D. Hosking, & C. Schriescheim (Eds.), *Leaders and managers: International perspectives on managerial behavior and leadership* (pp. 28–44). New York: Pergamon Press.

Tsui, A. S., Egan, T. D., & O Reilly, C. A. (1992). Being different: Relational demography and organizational attachment. *Administrative Science Quarterly, 37*, 549–579.

Tsui, A., & O'Reilly, C. (1989). Beyond simple demographic effects: The importance of relational demography in superior–subordinate dyads. *Academy of Management Journal, 32*, 402–423.

Tucker, A. L., Nembhard, I. M., & Edmondson, A. C. (2007). Implementing new practices: An empirical study of organizational learning in hospital intensive care units. *Management Science, 53*, 894–907.

Turban, D. B., & Keon, T. L. (1993). Organization attractiveness: An interactionist perspective. *Journal of Applied Psychology, 78*, 184–193.

Turner, M. A. (2008). Residential segregation and employment inequality. In J. H. Carr, S. L. Smith, & N. K. Kutty (Eds.), *Segregation* (pp. 151–196.) New York: Routledge.

Tushman, M. L., & O'Reilly, C. A. (1996). The ambidextrous organization: Managing evolutionary and revolutionary change. *California Management Review, 38*(4), 8–30.

Tushman, M., & O'Reilly, C. (2002). *Winning through innovation.* Boston: Harvard Business School Press.

Tyler, T. R., & Lind, E. A. (1992). A relational model of authority in groups. In M. Zanna (Ed.), *Advances in experimental social psychology* (Vol. 25, pp. 115–191). New York: Academic Press.

Urwick, L. (1943). *The elements of administration.* New York: Harper & Brothers.

Van Maanen, J., & Schein, E. H. (1979). Toward a theory of organizational socialization. *Research in Organizational Behavior, 1,* 204–264.

Van Oudenhoven, J. P. (2001). Do organizations reflect national cultures? A 10-nation study. *International Journal of Intercultural Relations, 25*(1), 89–107.

Van Vugt, M. (1996). Evolutionary origins of leadership and followership. *Personality and Social Psychology Review, 10,* 354–372.

Van Vugt, M,, & De Cremer, D. (1999). Leadership in social dilemmas: The effects of group identification on collective actions to provide public goods. *Journal of Personality and Social Psychology, 74*(4), 587–599.

Van Vugt, M., Hogan, R., & Kaiser, R. B. (2008). Leadership, followership, and evolution: Some lessons from the past. *The American Psychologist, 63*, 182–196.

Vescio, T., & Guinote, A. (Eds.). (in press). *The social psychology of power.*

Viscusi, W. K. (1980). Sex differences in worker quitting. *Review of Economics and Statistics, 62*, 388–398.

Wachtel, H. M. (1974). Class consciousness and stratification in the labor process. *Review of Radical Political Economy, 6,* 1–31.

Waldinger, R., & Bailey, T. (1991). The continuing significance of race: Racial conflict and racial discrimination in construction. *Politics and Society, 19,* 291–323.

Wallace, M., & Chang, C. F. (1990). Barriers to women's employment: Economic segmentation in American manufacturing. *Research in Social Stratification & Mobility, 9,* 337–361.

Walumbwa, F. O., Avolio, B. J., Gardner, W. L., Wernsing, T. S., & Peterson, S. J. (2008). Authentic leadership: Development and validation of a theory-based measure. *Journal of Management, 34*, 89.

Weber, M. (1947). *The theory of social and economic organization.* Detroit, MI: Free Press.

Weeden, K. A., & Sorensen, J. B. (2003). A framework for analyzing industrial and occupational sex segregation in the United States. In M. Charles & D. B. Grusky (Eds.), *Occupational Ghettos: The worldwide segregation of men and women* (pp. 245–294). Palo Alto, CA: Stanford University Press.

Weick, K. E. (1979). *The social psychology of organizing* (2nd ed.). Reading, MA: Addison-Wesley.

West, M. A. (2002). The human team: Basic motivations and innovations. In N. Anderson, D.S. Ones, H.K. Sinangil, & C. Viswesvaran (Eds.), *Handbook of industrial, work and organizational psychology* (vol. 2, pp. 270–288). London: Sage.

Westphal, J. D., & Zajac E. J. (1995). Who shall govern? CEO–board power, demographic similarity, and new director selection. *Administrative Science Quarterly 40,* 60–83.

Wexley, K. N., & Nemeroff, W. F. (1974). The effects of racial prejudice, race of applicant, and biographical similarity on interviewer evaluations of job applicants. *Journal of Social and Behavioral Sciences, 20*, 66–78.

Wharton, A. S., & Baron, J. N. (1987). So happy together? The impact of gender segregation on men at work. *American Sociological Review, 52*, 574–587.

Whyte, W. F. (1981). *Street corner society* (3rd ed.). Chicago: University of Chicago Press.

Whyte, W. H. (1956). *The organizational man.* New York: Anchor.

Wiersema, M. F., & Bantel, K. A. (1992). Top management team demography and corporate strategic change. *Academy of Management Journal, 35*(1), 91–121.

Wiesenfeld, B. M., Raghuram, S., & Garud, R. (2001). Organizational identification among virtual workers: The role of need for affiliation and perceived work-based social support. *Journal of Management, 27*, 213–229.

Wiggins, J. S. (1982). Circumplex models of interpersonal behavior in clinical psychology. In P. C. Kendall & J. N. Butcher (Eds.), *Handbook of research methods in clinical psychology* (pp. 183–221). New York: Wiley.

Wiggins, J., Trapnell, P., & Phillips, N. (1988). Psychometric and geometric characteristics of the revised Interpersonal Adjective Scales (IAS-R). *Multivariate Behavioral Research, 23*, 517–530.

Williams, K. Y., & O'Reilly, C. A. (1998). Demography and diversity in organizations: A review of 40 years of research. *Research in organizational behavior, 20*, 77–140.

Wilpert, B. (1995). Organizational Behavior. *Annual Review of Psychology, 46*, 59–90.

Wilson, F., & Hammer, R. (2003). Ethnic residential segregation and its consequences. In L. Bobo, et al. (Eds.), *Urban inequality in the United States: Evidence from four cities* (pp. 272–303). New York: Russell Sage Foundation.

Wilson, G., & McBrier, D. B. (2005). Race and Loss of Privilege: African American–White Differences in the Determinants of Job Layoffs From Upper-Tier Occupations. *Sociological Forum, 20*, 301–321.

Wilson, P. R. (1968). Perceptual distortion of height as a function of ascribed academic status. *Journal of Social Psychology, 74*, 97–102.

Wolpin, K.I. (1992). The determinants of Black–White differences in early employment careers: Search, layoffs, quits and endogenous wage growth. *The Journal of Political Economy*, 100, 3, 535–560.

Wright, R., & Ellis, M. (2000). The ethnic and gender division of labor compared among immigrants to Los Angeles. *International Journal of Urban and Regional Research*, 24, 583–600.

Wrzesniewski, A., Dutton, J.E., & Debebe, G. (2003). Interpersonal sensemaking and the meaning of work. *Research in Organizational Behavior*, 25, 93–135.

Ying, Y. W., Lee, P. A., Tsai, J. L., Lee, Y. J., & Tsang, M. (2001). Network composition, social integration, and sense of coherence in Chinese american young adults. *Journal of Human Behavior in the Social Environment, 3*(3/4), 83–98.

Yukl, G. (2002). *Leadership in organizations* (5th ed.). Englewood Cliffs, NJ: Prentice-Hall.

Zaccaro, S. J. (2001). *The nature of executive leadership: A conceptual and empirical analysis of success.* Washington, DC: American Psychological Association.

Zimbardo, P. G., Maslach, C., & Haney, C. (2000). Reflections on the Stanford Prison Experiment: Genesis, transformations, consequences. In T. Blass (Ed.), *Obedience to authority: Current perspectives on the Milgram paradigm* (pp. 193–237). Mahwah, NJ: Erlbaum.

Chapter 34

The Psychological Underpinnings of Political Behavior

JON A. KROSNICK, PENNY S. VISSER, AND JOSHUA HARDER

If social psychology's goal is to understand how people interact with and influence one another, the domain of politics offers a wonderful context in which to develop and test basic theory. In fact, a focus on politics has been central to social psychology since its birth. Kurt Lewin, Stanley Milgram, Solomon Asch, and many of our field's founders were motivated by the experience of Nazi Germany and sought to understand how authority figures and tendencies to conform to social norms could produce barbaric behavior (see Allport, 1985). Allport (1954) illuminated the nature of racial prejudice. Zimbardo's research clarified how assigning people to roles in a prison system could elicit shocking behaviors from them (Haney, Banks, & Zimbardo, 1973). Kelman (1982, 1983) and Ross (Hackley, Bazerman, Ross, & Shapiro, 2005) have shed light on international conflict. Countless studies of attitude change have used persuasive messages on political issues, illuminating the processes that induce variation in such attitudes over time. In these and other ways, the study of thinking about political matters and of the causes of political actions has been at the center of our discipline for decades.

Many scholars would argue that these studies of social relations were not studies about politics that were meant to illuminate the causes and consequences of political cognition and behavior. Instead, these observers would say, those studies *used* politics as a convenient device for basic research. Asch was not interested in politics, they would say; he was interested in conformity. Milgram was not interested in violence; he was interested in obedience. Zimbardo was not interested in prisons; he was interested in social roles.

In fact, however, the research of these pioneers illuminated important aspects of how political cognition and action unfold. This was probably a matter of great pride for Asch, Milgram, and Zimbardo. When asked why he chose a career in psychology, Robert Zajonc said it was to understand the human mind in ways that can help to prevent future wars (Thorpe, 2005). Indeed, research has

documented a great deal about the dynamics of political cognition and action, even if not yet providing tools to assure world peace.

This chapter tells the story of some of this research. Not addressed are topics of obvious relevance that chapters on politics in earlier editions of this Handbook have reviewed (Kinder, 1998; Kinder & Sears, 1985; Tetlock, 1998) and topics dealt with in other chapters in this edition of the Handbook (e.g., Jost & Kay, this volume; Yzerbyt & Demoulin, this volume). This chapter's focus is instead on the citizens of democratic nations, and this focus brushes off the table many fascinating political topics well worth the attention of social psychologists, including relations between governments, citizen life in nondemocratic nations, and more. In focusing on the domestic political affairs of Americans, the chapter seeks to illuminate the value of the study of politics for social psychology and to bring into focus many lessons learned about the basics of human nature and social relations as revealed through the careful study of this domain.

The next sections offer an overview of the field of political psychology and of the philosophical issue that guides this selective review of the literature: the requirements that citizens of a democracy may need to meet for the nation to thrive. The chapter then describes research findings on the determinants of people's decisions about whether to vote or not, people's decisions about which candidate to vote for, people's decisions about when to express their political preferences via other behaviors, and much more, always asking whether the empirical evidence suggests worry about the future of democracies or confidence in their longevity.

OVERVIEW OF POLITICAL PSYCHOLOGY

Political psychology is a thriving field of social scientific inquiry in its quest to understand the cognitive and social underpinnings and consequences of behaviors that entail the exercise of social power and the governance of collectives of people. Much political psychology explains political phenomena by taking a social-psychological perspective. Scholars could instead adopt an economic perspective, for example, attributing significant political events to economic forces that are typically easily observable (e.g., Alt & Chrystal, 1983). In contrast, political psychologists place emphasis on unobservable psychological processes unfolding in the minds of political actors and on the nature of social interaction among them.

In practice, two somewhat different forms of political psychology exist (see Krosnick, 2002). Some of this work attempts to understand political phenomena by applying theories that have already been developed through research done in psychological laboratories. Findings regarding mediation and moderation of real-world effects have often led to extensions and revisions of the inspiring psychological theories. Other political psychology research involves the development of completely new theory to provide psychological accounts of political phenomena, often without building on existing psychological research. The empirical testing and refinement of these new theories also contributes to basic understanding of how the mind works and how social interaction takes place.

A series of handbook publications document the vitality and longevity of the field. The first *Handbook of Political Psychology* was published in 1973 (edited by Jeanne Knutson), and new volumes have been published regularly since then (Borgida, Federico, & Sullivan, 2009; Hermann, 1986; Iyengar & McGuire, 1993; Monroe, 2002; Sears, Huddy, & Jervis, 2003). Two books of collected key readings in the field have been published (Jost & Sidanius, 2004; Kressel, 1993). The journal *Political Psychology* has been in print since 1979. Articles on political psychology often appear in the top journals of social psychology and political science. Courses on political psychology are routinely offered at colleges and universities around the world. Since 1978, the International Society of Political Psychology (ISPP) has been the field's professional association, sponsoring annual conferences and coordinating publication, outreach, and educational opportunities. Since 1991, the Summer Institute in Political Psychology has trained almost 1,000 young scholars and professionals in the field.

REQUIREMENTS OF DEMOCRACY

A guiding principal of much work in political psychology is the notion that for a democratic nation to survive and thrive, its government must be "by the people and for the people." Put simply, government should do what its citizens want done. One mechanism to encourage this outcome is for citizens to communicate their desires to government. If government knows what actions its population supports and what actions it opposes, policy can be designed accordingly, to be faithful to the public's will.

For such communication to occur and to be helpful, three conditions must be met: (1) citizens must have real attitudes toward government policy options; (2) those attitudes must be expressed behaviorally; and (3) those attitudes must be wise. Such behavioral expression can occur in many ways. One is voting in elections. However, voting for a particular candidate for president of the United States does not clearly and precisely indicate support or opposition for particular government actions. Voting is at best a blunt instrument with which to direct government policy making in a crude way. To the extent that candidates differ in their likely policy pursuits, voting for one over others can increase the likelihood that government will pursue particular policy directions. But a vote for one candidate does not, in itself, clearly communicate which policies a voter wishes to see enacted.

A second blunt mechanism of sending signals to government is the expression of approval or disapproval of political actors in national surveys. The news media routinely conduct surveys of representative samples of Americans and ask for performance appraisals of the president and of the U.S. Congress, as well as of governors, senators, and other legislators. If the public gives a thumbs up, this can be taken as endorsement of a politician's policy pursuits and thereby perpetuate them, and a thumbs down can similarly send a message requesting redirection.

One alternative approach that can be much more targeted and clear is participation in grassroots activism. A citizen can write a letter directly to the president or to a Congressional representative or can telephone the representative's office to express a preference. A citizen can write a letter to the editor of a newspaper or magazine, which may ultimately appear in print. Or a citizen can post a message on an Internet blog.

Another approach is to support the activities of lobbying organizations, who send such messages on behalf of many citizens. The National Rifle Association, Greenpeace, The American Civil Liberties Union, and numerous other such organizations exist importantly to pressure government to take particular actions on specific policy issues. Citizens who support these organizations by giving money to them and by participating in organized letter-writing campaigns, marches on the Capital steps, and get-out-the-vote efforts facilitate the expression of specific policy desires.

Lastly, citizens can send messages by answering policy-focused questions in national surveys that are widely publicized by the news media. These surveys offer opportunities to express positive or negative attitudes, and government officials are aware of such measurements of public opinion and often commission their own such measurements, so surveys constitute a pipeline for transferring public desires to government.

Much of the research done in political psychology informs an understanding of these processes. To what extent and under what circumstances do citizens have genuine attitudes toward government policy options? To what extent and under what circumstances are those attitudes well informed? To what extent and under what circumstances do citizens express their policy preferences behaviorally? This chapter reviews some of this evidence and considers its implications for the future of democratic governments.

Reconsidering Americans' Competence

Many analysts of the psychology of mass politics have made the observation that most Americans know little or nothing about national and international politics (e.g., Delli Carpini & Keeter, 1993, 1996; Kinder & Sears, 1985). Any such claim about the engagement and competence of democratic citizens has tremendously important implications for the health and longevity of a nation. If democratic government is to be by the people and for the people, the hands of a nation's citizens must be on the country's steering wheel. If this is true, and yet if most citizens are looking somewhere other than the road ahead most of the time while driving, the chances of disaster are far from minimal.

Are most Americans uninformed about most matters facing their government? Certainly, a great deal of empirical evidence has been put forth for decades to support this claim. Since the earliest scientific surveys of the American public, researchers asked quiz questions and have given respondents poor grades.

According to one review of many national surveys, almost all respondents were familiar with the president, and majorities recognized the names of some senators, but fewer than 50% of citizens recognized many other office holders and candidates (Kinder & Sears, 1985). Likewise, according to another review of survey results (Delli Carpini & Keeter, 1993), large majorities of respondents knew the name of the current vice president and their governor and of various well-publicized leaders of foreign countries, and majorities knew the party affiliation of the president, knew which party had the most seats in the House of Representatives, and knew whether the Republican party

was more conservative than the Democratic party. But minorities were familiar with various prominent U.S. senators and Congressional representatives or recognized the names of other foreign leaders.

In terms of the process of government, a large majority knew how many terms a person could be elected president of the United States, but minorities knew how long a senator's term in office lasts, who nominates federal judges, and the percent of Congressional votes that are needed to override a presidential veto (Delli Carpini & Keeter, 1993).

On specific policy issues, numerous surveys have documented rampant lack of knowledge. For example, although huge majorities of national survey respondents knew who would pay for the savings and loan bailout in 1990, knew that oil was in short supply in 1974, knew what happened at Three Mile Island in 1974, and knew in 1985 that the federal budget deficit had increased since 1981, small minorities could explain in 1986 what *Roe v. Wade* was about, knew the percent of poor people who were children, knew in 1980 what acid rain is, or knew in 1979 what thalidomide is (Delli Carpini & Keeter, 1996).

However, important new developments in political psychology raise questions about whether this sort of evidence convincingly documented a pervasive lack of essential knowledge among American citizens. To make claims about how knowledgeable Americans are about political matters, one would ideally first specify a universe of knowledge that people "should" possess to be competent at directing a nation. Then, one would randomly select a sample of pieces of information from that corpus and build questions to tap whether members of a representative sample of Americans possess each sampled bit.

This has never been done. Numerous surveys of representative samples of Americans have asked quiz questions to gauge possession of facts. However, no scholarly effort has begun by defining a universe of knowledge that those questions supposedly represent, and scholars have very rarely offered rationales for why they chose the question topics they did rather than others instead.

No doubt, it would be possible to design a test that most Americans would fail, asking about such obscure matters as the history of economic policy making in Peru. Likewise, it would be possible to design a test that most Americans would pass, asking who is currently serving as president of the United States, the name of the building in which the president usually sleeps when in Washington, D.C., and the month and day on which terrorists flew airplanes into the World Trade Center. Before claims are made about how knowledgeable Americans are about politics, this arbitrary quality of testing must be overcome. But to date, it has not. Any test of political knowledge can reveal how many people possess the specific facts sought by the test items, but generalizing from those items to the universe of knowledge seems tenuous.

Even if past survey questions assessing public knowledge are assumed to have addressed a representative sample of topics, the evidence thus produced cannot be trusted, because of the way the questions were constructed and administered. Two types of questions have been asked in surveys: closed-ended and open-ended. In closed-ended questions, respondents have usually been asked to choose from one of various offered response options, as in this example (see http://www.americancivicliteracy.org/resources/quiz.aspx):

Which of the following are the inalienable rights referred to in the Declaration of Independence?

A. life, liberty, and property
B. honor, liberty, and peace
C. liberty, health, and community
D. life, respect, and equal protection
E. life, liberty, and the pursuit of happiness

Educational testing research documents that performance on such items hinges not only on the respondent's familiarity with the question's subject matter but on how difficult the "distractor" response options are (e.g., Kline, 1986). For anyone who majored in American Politics in college, reading options A–D in this context might induce a smile. The distractors are all structurally similar to the right answer (naming three "rights"), and they are all plausible. But for people who have heard about the Declaration of Independence only very occasionally in school and have never read it, this might be a much tougher question.

What if the question were asked this way instead:

Which of the following are the inalienable rights referred to in the Declaration of Independence?

A. to own a boat, to laugh occasionally, and to have a good meal daily
B. to have a pet, to sleep in a bed every night, and to breathe air daily
C. to live, to learn, and to love
D. to vacation in a country away from home, to chop vegetables with a knife, and to get regular haircuts
E. life, liberty, and the pursuit of happiness

This question might bring smiles to the faces of all survey respondents, or worse, might lead respondents to wonder about the researchers' competence or seriousness

or both. Yet answers to such a question would also most likely indicate that the vast majority of Americans possess this piece of knowledge.

Pointing out such a basic element of test theory (that item difficulty hinges on the difficulty of the foils in a closed-ended question) might seem silly. But no empirical effort justifies the selection of distractors used in political knowledge quizzes. Most likely, no set of distractors is "optimal"—difficult distractors will yield poorer performance than easy distractors. Thus, closed-ended questions cannot be used to assess proportions of people who do or do not know a particular fact sufficiently well to receive credit for it.

One way to circumvent this challenge is to ask open-ended questions instead, thus avoiding the need to specify any answer choices. Numerous national surveys for decades have included such questions and have suggested that most Americans lack political knowledge. For example, the American National Election Studies (ANES) has asked questions like this:

Now we have a set of questions concerning various public figures. We want to see how much information about them gets out to the public from television, newspapers and the like . . . William Rehnquist—What job or political office does he NOW hold?

Recently, new revelations have cast doubt on findings produced using such questions. A new investigation revealed that using open-ended answers to decide whether a respondent has possession of a piece of information is tricky business—a subjective judgment call in many cases (Gibson & Caldeira, 2009). Some respondents clearly give what sounds like a correct answer (e.g., "He is Chief Justice of the U.S. Supreme Court"), and others clearly give an incorrect answer (e.g., "He is CEO of General Electric"), but many people give answers that are not exactly correct but would be considered by many observers to be close enough to count, such as:

- Supreme Court justice. The main one.
- He's the senior judge on the Supreme Court.
- He is the Supreme Court justice in charge.
- He's the head of the Supreme Court.

Yet, the ANES has coded these sorts of answers as incorrect. Furthermore, answers that are in the ballpark but were not right on the money (e.g., "He's a judge") were coded as incorrect (Krosnick & Lupia, 2008). This approach to coding has no doubt contributed to a misleading portrait of Americans as having less information about politics than they really possess.

That's not all. The measurement of political knowledge has been misleading because of its reliance on verbal questions. Almost all of the survey questions assessing knowledge of government officials have provided their names and asked respondents to indicate their job titles or have provided job titles and asked for names. However, people are sometimes significantly better able to identify a person when shown a photograph instead of the person's name, and sometimes, people are significantly better able to identify a person using a name rather than a photo (Prior, 2009a).

Furthermore, whereas performance on the verbal questions was better among more educated people—people more interested in politics, Whites, and males—performance on questions using photos was unrelated to education, gender, and race, and political interest was more weakly related to questions using photos than questions using names (Prior, 2009a). Also, people who prefer visual media (such as television) for learning political information performed better on quiz questions offering pictures and words than did people who prefer only verbal media (such as newspapers), whereas performance on verbal questions did not vary depending on medium preference (Prior, 2009b). Thus, how knowledge is measured affects conclusions about who possesses it, but no particular measurement method (e.g., verbal or visual or verbal plus visual) is obviously superior to others.

Another problem with knowledge measurement results from the use of interviewers, who have administered the most frequently studied knowledge questions in respondents' homes. In such situations, researchers hope that characteristics of the interviewer will not influence respondents' answers to questions. But unfortunately, this is not the case for attitude measurement (e.g., Anderson, Silver, & Abramson, 1988a, b; Davis, 1997), nor is it true for measurement of political knowledge. African American respondents perform significantly better on political knowledge quizzes when interviewed by an African American interviewer than when interviewed by a White interviewer, although race of interviewer seems not to influence the performance of White respondents (Davis & Silver, 2003). Davis and Silver (2003) attributed the effect of interviewer race on test performance by African Americans to stereotype threat (Spencer, Steele, & Quinn, 1999), though framing the quiz as a test or "not a test of any kind" did not alter the impact of interviewer race.

Yet another problem in measurement of knowledge involves handling "don't know" responses. Like most surveys, the ANES surveys have routinely instructed their interviewers to allow respondents to volunteer that they do not know the answer to a quiz question about political knowledge and to record that. Interviewers could instead have encouraged respondents to answer under those circumstances. When this is done, the number of respondents who answer accurately increases notably, more than would be expected by chance alone (Mondak & Davis, 2001; see also Barabas, 2002). Thus, some respondents who were in fact knowledgeable did not reveal it in most past surveys.

Another inherently psychological challenge to knowledge assessments is limited motivation during survey interviews. Some respondents who think and talk often about politics may find it easy to answer knowledge quiz questions correctly with little effort. But for other respondents, answering a quiz question correctly requires some cognitive work, to search their long-term memories and evaluate the diagnosticity of the information they retrieve. Furthermore, paying money to respondents for each correct answer they gave significantly increases the proportion of correct answers given—gigantically among people who expressed a moderate interest in politics and not at all among people who were highly interested in politics (for whom correct answering was presumably effortless) and among people with no interest in politics (who presumably could not offer a correct answer no matter how much effort they devoted to the task) (Prior & Lupia, 2008).

Another study illuminated people's capacity to become informed by giving some survey respondents 24 hours before they had to answer quiz questions, while a control group was asked to answer right away. Providing the extra time caused a substantial increase in the proportion of correct answers given by people with moderate political interest (Prior & Lupia, 2008). Thus, people can manifest higher levels of knowledge if given the opportunity to become better informed. When people need to become informed to make an important political decision, they can do so by gathering new information. So surveys should perhaps measure not what people know today but what they can know tomorrow.

The most fundamental criticism of research chastising Americans for their apparent lack of political knowledge asks whether it really matters that citizens lack knowledge. Some scholars have argued that a useful political knowledge test should tap a person's understanding of "what government is and does" (Delli Carpini & Keeter, 1993, p. 1182), as well as who political leaders are and what political parties stand for. But according to our account of the requirements of an effective democracy, focus should not be on knowing the name of the vice president or which political party controls the Congress or how many years a senator's term in office lasts or how a filibuster works. Rather, citizens simply need to know what they want government to do and to send signals to that effect.

Such signals are easy to send by attending a rally or making a contribution to a lobbying group, even without knowing anything about the people running government or the process by which they govern. Likewise, signals can be sent by answering survey questions asking for specific opinions on policy issues, regardless of broad knowledge about what government is and does. To send a signal via voting for president, people might simply need to know whether they are satisfied with current government policy (e.g., "Is abortion legal now, and is that the way I want the law to be?") and know the political party of the incumbent. Satisfaction would lead to voting for the incumbent's party's candidate, and dissatisfaction would lead to voting against that party's candidate.

Likewise, voting on a referendum can be done competently by knowing whether it is endorsed by political figures or groups that a citizen knows and trusts and does not require specific information about the technical details of the issue at stake (Lupia & McCubbins, 1998). This line of argument illustrates a broader point: Much of the knowledge sought by quiz questions asked in surveys is not needed by voters for them to perform their duties competently. So lack of knowledge does not indicate inability to perform adequately and responsibly (Lupia, 2006).

In sum, new insights in this literature and new lines of inquiry have cast new light on the old question of citizen competence. Clearly, some Americans lack some specific pieces of knowledge, but precisely how many people lack any given piece of knowledge is probably impossible to determine. Consequently, political psychologists should abandon making claims about absolute levels of knowledge in the electorate altogether and should assess public competence in other ways. Fortunately a great deal of research has done so, and that work is reviewed in the remainder of this chapter.

CAUSES OF BEHAVIOR

Why do People Vote?

One of the most fundamental questions challenging political psychologists is why citizens in a democratic country vote. Any discussion of turnout must begin with acknowledgment of an equation proposed by Downs (1957) that has powerfully shaped scholars' thinking in this arena:

$$R = (B)(P) - C + D$$

in which R is the total reward a citizen will gain from voting; B is the benefit a person thinks will accrue from having the citizen's preferred candidate win; P is the

person's perception of the probability the citizen's one vote will change the election outcome; C is the cost to the individual of voting in terms of time, money, and other resources; and D is the psychic satisfaction the person would gain from voting (Ferejohn & Fiorina, 1974; Riker & Ordeshook, 1968). If R is positive, the citizen is assumed to gain a reward from voting that outweighs the costs and will therefore participate in the election. The more positive R is, the more likely an individual is to vote. In any large election, the probability of casting the deciding vote is thought to be infinitesimally small and is likely to be perceived as such: much, much smaller than the costs of voting (e.g., Chamberlain & Rothschild, 1981). Therefore, the sense of satisfaction gained from voting (D) must make up any deficit caused by the cost and provide sufficient incentive for a citizen to participate.

This equation illustrates the "paradox of voting" (Ferejohn & Fiorina, 1974; Rosenstone & Hansen, 1993). Voting yields benefits only when supported by collective action, so most people should never pay the costs, because their effort will never assure the acquisition of benefits. The mystery, then, is why so many people vote. This surprising behavior is sometimes claimed to be evidence that voters are inherently irrational (though see Ferejohn & Fiorina, 1974).

Turnout can also be analyzed from a slightly different formal point of view, presuming that it is a function of people's motivation to vote, their ability to vote, and the difficulty of the act of voting for them:

Likelihood of voting = (Motivation to vote) × (Ability to vote) × (1 − Difficulty of voting)

in which all three predictors are coded to range from 0 (meaning no motivation, ability, or difficulty) to 1 (meaning maximum motivation, ability, or difficulty). The more motivation or ability people have, the more likely they are to turn out on Election Day, whereas the more difficult voting is for people, the less likely they are to vote. The multiplicative feature of this equation means that high motivation or high ability or low difficulty is not sufficient to assure turnout—a deficit in any area may be sufficient to undermine a person's turnout.

Motivation to vote can come from a strong preference for one candidate over that person's competitor(s). But motivation can also come from the belief that being a responsible citizen requires that a person vote, from pressure from one's friends or family to vote, or from other sources outlined later. The ability to vote refers to people's capacity to (1) make sense of information about political events and candidates to form a candidate preference; (2) understand and meet requirements for eligibility to vote legally; and (3) implement the required behavior to cast a ballot. Difficulty refers to conditions outside the voter's mind (e.g., the convenience of registration procedures, the physical closeness of a polling location to a person's home). Downs' (B) (P) term and (D) term are components of motivation, and his (C) term is a part of difficulty (1957). But motivation and difficulty have other components as well, as the research we have reviewed illustrates.

The existing literature addresses: (1) the factors that encourage or discourage registration, a necessary precursor to the act of voting; (2) the associations between turnout and various demographics, a person's social location, a person's psychological dispositions, and characteristics of a particular election contest; and (3) the impact of canvassing, polling, and election outcome projections on turnout. These literatures are reviewed next.

Registration

The costs of registering to vote are among the most significant reasons why many Americans fail to go to the polls on Election Day. To register, citizens must learn and follow a set of rules about how and when to register, and when a person moves from living in one residence to another, it is often necessary to take action to establish legitimate voting registration status at the new location. Turnout varies a great deal from state to state, and much of this variation appears to be attributable to variation in the difficulty of voter registration procedures (Kelley, Ayres, & Bowen, 1967; Kim, Petrocik, & Enokson, 1975). Indeed, registration requirements appear to impose such substantial barriers to turnout that if all such requirements were eliminated, turnout might rise by as much as 7% to 9% nationally (Mitchell & Wlezien, 1995; Wolfinger & Rosenstone, 1980; c.f., Nagler, 1991).

Barriers to Registration   People are less likely to register and to vote if they live in a place that imposes more, or more difficult, registration requirements. Such requirements have included annual reregistration, literacy tests, and early cutoff dates for registering before an election (e.g., Shinn, 1971; c.f., Katosh & Traugott, 1982). Other barriers include the accessibility of physical locations where citizens are permitted to register, the number of hours during which citizens can register, and whether citizens can register during evenings or on weekends (Caldeira, Patterson, & Markko, 1985; Wolfinger & Rosenstone, 1980). Interestingly, laws requiring employers to allow employees time off from work to vote do not appear to increase registration, suggesting that work requirements are not a serious impediment (Sterling, 1983).

Registration drives, wherein nonpartisan and partisan groups encourage people to register, attempt to reduce the difficulty of the registration process. Interestingly, people registered via registration drives usually vote at lower rates than do people who registered on their own (Cain & McCue, 1985; Hamilton, 1977; Vedlitz, 1985). Nonetheless, registration drives do appear to increase turnout rates.

The date when registration closes is often singled out as the most prominent contemporary requirement that impedes registration. An early closing date precludes voters from registering right at the time when they are most motivated to do so: during the height of a political campaign, in the very weeks just before Election Day. Thus, in states with early closing dates, registration is more likely among people who are chronically interested in politics and motivated to vote and less likely among people without that chronic interest but who are inspired to want to participate in an election by campaign events or by changes in local, regional, or national conditions close to Election Day. Election Day registration eliminates the closing date restriction and seems to have greatly increased turnout (Brians & Grofman, 2001; Knack & White, 2000).

Demographics

Education   Citizens with more formal education are more likely to vote; each additional year of education is associated with higher turnout (e.g., Gerber, Green, & Larimer, 2008; Shields & Goidel, 1997; Tenn, 2007; Verba, Schlozman, & Brady, 1995). Education may impart skills that enhance a person's ability to understand how the civic process operates and how to navigate the requirements of registration. Education may also motivate people to vote by instilling civic duty, interesting them in the political process, or placing them in social settings in which voting is normative.

Verbal SAT scores are positively associated with turnout, consistent with the notion that understanding language may facilitate understanding of politics. Math SAT scores are not related to turnout, suggesting that cognitive skills in general appear not to regulate turnout. College graduates who took more social science classes have more civic duty, and these people also vote more than other graduates (Hillygus, 2005; Nie & Hillygus, 2001).

The impact of education on a person's turnout depends partly on the educational attainment and political activity of other people in that individual's environment (Helliwell & Putman, 1999; Nie, Junn, & Stehlik-Barry, 1996). The more a person's educational attainment exceeds that of the people in that person's neighborhood, the more likely that person is to vote. Comparative educational attainment rates are much better predictors of a person's turnout than is the person's absolute educational attainment (Tenn, 2005).

Income   Wealthier people vote at higher rates (Gerber, Green, & Larimer, 2008; Leighley & Nagler, 1992b; Rosenstone & Hansen, 1993; Ulbig & Funk, 1999; c.f., Filer, Kenny, & Morton, 1993). And interestingly, when the health of the national economy declines, the citizens who are hurt most are the most likely to manifest reductions in turnout (Radcliff, 1992; Rosenstone, 1982). This relation could be due to differential motivation or ability or both. Perhaps less wealthy people have less time available to learn about elections and to cast votes than do wealthier people. Or perhaps more wealthy people perceive that they have a greater interest at stake in elections or have greater senses of political efficacy. People with higher incomes incur greater opportunity costs for spending time on politics and voting (Frey, 1971), but wealthier people may gain greater psychological or social rewards from voting (Rosenstone & Hansen, 1993).

Occupation   Workplace authority might be expected to create a greater feeling of social entitlement, which often translates into political participation (Sobel, 1993). However, managers and administrators have lower turnout than other professionals from the same economic class (Wolfinger & Rosenstone, 1980). Turnout does not seem to be influenced by the amount of decision making and power they are afforded at their workplaces, even if that power is given through democratic decisions (Elden, 1981; Greenberg, 1981). However, government employees turn out at especially high rates (Bennett & Orzechowski, 1983; Wolfinger & Rosenstone, 1980). This could be because government employees have a clear stake in the outcomes of elections: Whether they remain employed and what they work on may be influenced by which party occupies particular public offices (Bennett & Orzechowski, 1983; Wolfinger & Rosenstone, 1980).

Age   People appear to become increasingly likely to vote as they progress from early adulthood through middle adulthood; after about age 75, people become less likely to vote (Gerber, Green, & Larimer, 2008; Strate, Parrish, Elder, & Ford, 1989). In cross-sectional analyses, differences between age groups in turnout rates could be due to cohort effects: effects of historical events that occurred when a particular generation of people was a particular age and that shaped them for the rest of their lives. However, even after controlling for period and cohort effects, increasing age still appears to be associated with increased turnout until late in life.

Gender   The effect of gender on turnout has changed dramatically over the years. From the beginning of women's suffrage, women voted less than men (Arneson &

Eels, 1950; Glaser, 1959). And until the 1980s, women felt less efficacious and were less informed and politically interested and involved than men (Schlozman, Burns, & Verba, 1999; Verba, Burns, & Schlozman, 1997). Since the mid-1980s, though, women have voted at the same rate as men, and sometimes at even higher rates (e.g., Leighley & Nagler, 1992a; Schlozman, Burns, Verba, & Donahue, 1995; c.f., Gerber, Green, & Larimer, 2008).

Mobility   Residential mobility seems to depress turnout (Highton, 2000; Squire, Wolfinger, & Glass, 1987). Just after moving, people are less able to vote, because they must figure out how to reregister with a new address and must make time to do so amidst an inevitably busy postmove life. Longer moves do not seem to depress turnout more (Highton, 2000).

Residency   People who live in rural areas are more likely to vote than are people who live in urban areas (Wolfinger & Rosenstone, 1980). Farmers vote at substantially higher rates than would be expected based on their levels of education and income (Wolfinger & Rosenstone, 1980), perhaps because they see direct links of federal farming policies to their livelihoods. In contrast, farm laborers vote at very low rates that are unaccounted for solely by socioeconomic factors (Wolfinger & Rosenstone, 1980), perhaps because of their high residential mobility.

Race   Whites have voted at higher rates than some other racial groups (Uhlaner, Cain, & Kiewiet, 1989). For example, turnout among African Americans has been relatively low. During the 1950s and 1960s, African American turnout increased sharply because discriminatory voter registration laws were relaxed, feelings of efficacy increased due to the civil rights movement, and mobilization efforts by political parties were increased (Wolfinger & Rosenstone, 1993). As a result, African American turnout increased by 35 percentage points in only 15 years (Wolfinger & Rosenstone, 1993). As a result, African Americans have had similar, or often even higher, turnout than Whites after controlling for education and income (e.g., Bobo & Gilliam, 1990; Leighley & Vedlitz, 1999; Wolfinger & Rosenstone, 1980; c.f., Gerber, Green, & Larimer, 2008). But Latinos and Asians have manifested lower turnout rates than Whites, even after controlling for socioeconomic status (Aoki & Nakanishi, 2001; Barreto, 2005; Shaw, de la Garza, & Lee, 2000; Uhlaner, Cain, & Kiewiet, 1989).

Social and Psychological Factors

Neighborhood Characteristics   Living in a higher status neighborhood encourages political participation by people of higher socioeconomic status but decreases participation among less educated citizens (Huckfeldt, 1979). This may occur because people compare themselves with others around them and are motivated to participate in politics if they feel unusually qualified to have influence.

Turnout is also influenced by the match between one's political party affiliation and the affiliations of one's neighbors. Republicans vote at unusually low rates when they live in heavily Democratic areas, perhaps because perceived lack of local social support for one's views makes voting seem futile. Interestingly, turnout among Democrats is less affected by the party affiliations of their neighbors (Gimpel, Dyck, & Shaw, 2004). Living in politically diverse environments tends to depress turnout (Costa & Kahn, 2004; McClurg, 2006; Mutz, 2002a, b).

Marriage Married (and partnered) couples vote at higher rates than singles (Kingston & Finkel, 1987; c.f., Stoker & Jennings, 1995). The turnout of married citizens increases faster than the turnout of unmarried citizens as people grow older (Stoker & Jennings, 1995; Wolfinger & Rosenstone, 1980). Perhaps politically motivated people inspire less motivated spouses to vote, either through explicit persuasion efforts or simply by exposing the spouse to political information. Divorce greatly increases turnout among Whites (perhaps simply due to increased free time), though not among African Americans or Hispanics (Sandell & Plutzer, 2005).

Participation in Civic Organizations Voluntary involvement in social organizations can inspire turnout by motivating and enabling people through increasing civic skills (Verba, Schlozman, & Brady, 1995). The more a person is engaged in cooperative work with others, the more appealing casting a vote may appear to be.

Group Solidarity People who say that their lives are intrinsically tied to other members of their social group (especially if that group is disadvantaged) turn out at higher rates than do people lower in group solidarity (Miller, Gurin, Gurin, & Malanchuk, 1981). People with high solidarity could have higher motivation to vote because they are concerned with issues affecting their group, or their strong social connections to members of that group could give them skills that better enable them to vote.

Trust People who are especially trusting of others are more likely to vote (Cox, 2003; Timpone, 1998a). Perhaps distrustful people think of the political system as corrupt, which might sap their motivation to participate. During some recent decades, Americans' trust in people and in the federal government has declined significantly (Levi & Stoker, 2000; Miller, 1980), but these declines seem not to

be responsible for decreasing turnout (Hetherington, 1999; Wolfinger, Glass, & Squire, 1990).

Contagion Some people might choose to vote because they think that their decision to do so might inspire other like-minded people to vote as well (Quattrone & Tversky, 1984). Voters might also presume that their own behavior is diagnostic of the behavior of like-minded others, even if the former does not cause the latter. So voting may be perceived to provide an indication of a heightened chance of victory by one's preferred candidate (Acevedo & Krueger, 2004). Consistent with this reasoning, people are more confident that their preferred candidate will win an election in the moments just after they cast their own vote than during the moments just before casting their vote (Frenkel & Doob, 1976; Regan & Kilduff, 1988). And remarkably, a single person's decision to turn out can produce a "cascade" of turnout within that person's social network (Fowler, 2005; see also Coleman, 2004).

Strength of Party Identification People who identify more strongly with a political party are more likely to vote (Gerber, Green, & Larimer, 2008; Ulbig & Funk, 1999).

Political Efficacy Citizens who have a great sense of political efficacy turn out more (Acock, Clarke, & Stewart, 1985; Craig & Maggiotto, 1982; Ulbig & Funk, 1999). This is true for both internal efficacy—the belief in one's capability to understand and participate in politics—and external efficacy—the belief in the responsiveness of political institutions to citizen involvement (Rosenstone & Hansen, 1993).

Knowledge The more a citizen has to work to determine candidates' ideological positions, the higher the person's information costs and the less likely that person is to vote (Gant, 1983; Panning, 1982).

Personal Importance of Policy Issues If voting is a way to express policy preferences, then one might imagine that people who possess many strong preferences on policy issues may be especially motivated to turn out. And indeed, the more policy issues that citizens attach great personal important to, the more likely they are to intend to vote prior to an election, and the more likely they are to successfully carry out that intention on Election Day (Visser, Krosnick, & Simmons, 2003).

Civic Duty People who believe that all citizens have the obligation to vote go to the polls more than those who do not hold this belief (Knack, 1992; Rosenstone & Hansen, 1993). Presumably, civic duty is a source of motivation to turn out.

Habit   Voting is a habitual behavior, meaning that voting once increases the likelihood of voting again (Gerber, Green, & Shachar, 2003; Plutzer, 2002), for several possible reasons. First, the social and psychological forces that inspired voting the first time may have enhanced impact directing future voting decisions (Gerber, Green, & Shachar, 2003; Verba & Nie, 1972). After being successfully mobilized to vote once, a citizen may attract repeated mobilization efforts at the times of subsequent elections (Goldstein & Ridout, 2002). Voting may be self-reinforcing, meaning that the social and psychic rewards one enjoys after voting once may be memorable and motivating at the times of subsequent elections (Gerber, Green, & Shachar, 2003; Plutzer, 2002). And the act could change a person's self-perception into one of an active, civically engaged individual. Finally, by voting once, a voter might realize the ease of doing it and may therefore be less inhibited from doing it again.

Patience   The costs of voting are entailed before Election Day (e.g., learning about the candidates, registering), whereas the benefits of voting are not reaped until after the act is performed (e.g., feeling virtuous, seeing one's preferred candidate win). Not surprisingly, then, turnout is greater among people who are patient and willing to wait for bigger rewards later instead of preferring smaller rewards sooner (Fowler & Kam, 2006).

Altruism   Voting may sometimes be done selflessly, to help other people. That is, people could reasonably believe that the election of their preferred candidate will help many other people by increasing the chances of the passage of legislation that will yield good outcomes for those individuals. Consistent with this reasoning, people who are highly altruistic are especially likely to turn out on Election Day (Fowler, 2006; Knack, 1992; Jankowski, 2004).

Religiosity   People who attend church regularly are especially likely to vote (Gerber, Green, & Latimer, 2008).

Personality   Extraverts are especially likely to vote, as are people high in emotional stability (Gerber, Green, & Latimer, 2008). One might imagine that people with authoritarian personalities might be especially likely to vote, because voting is a behavior commanded (or at least requested) and organized by government authorities. However, Lane (1955) found that the degree to which people scored high in authoritarian personality did not predict whether or not they voted.

Genetics   A large proportion of the variance in turnout might be explained by individual genes (Fowler, Baker,

& Dawes, 2008). Identical twins manifest turnout that is much more similar than is manifested by nonidentical twins (see also Fowler & Dawes, 2008). Genes may influence turnout by shaping any of the psychological factors discussed previously.

Characteristics of a Particular Election

Strength of Candidate Preference   The bigger the gap between a person's attitude toward one candidate and the person's attitude toward a competing candidate, the more likely the person is to vote (Holbrook, Krosnick, Visser, Gardner, & Cacioppo, 2001; Rosenstone & Hansen, 1993). However, this gap is much less consequential if the citizen likes both candidates than if the citizen dislikes one or both candidates (Holbrook, Krosnick, Visser, Gardner, & Cacioppo, 2001).

Candidate Similarity in Policy Preferences   The more similar to one another the competing candidates appear to be in terms of their policy preferences, the less likely citizens are to vote in a race, because the outcomes would not differ much in utility (Abramowitz & Stone, 2006; Plane & Gershtenson, 2004). Further, the more dissimilar a citizen is from the most similar candidate running in a race in terms of policy preferences, the less likely the citizen is to vote (Plane & Gershtenson, 2004; Zipp, 1985). Distance from the closest candidate appears to be a more powerful determinant of turnout than similarity between the candidates (Zipp, 1985).

Closeness of the Race   Many observers have speculated that the closer a race appears to be prior to Election Day, the more likely voters are to believe that their votes might determine the election outcome. And the belief that one's vote matters enhances turnout (Acevedo & Krueger, 2004). So when preelection polls suggest a race is likely to be a blowout, turnout may be depressed as a result. This notion has received some empirical support (Matsusaka, 1993; Patterson & Caldeira, 1983). Campaign efforts are usually greatest in areas in which a race is close (Cox & Munger, 1989), and such campaign expenditures increase turnout (Caldeira & Patterson, 1982; Patterson & Caldeira, 1983). Even after controlling for expenditures, however, the apparent closeness of the race can influence turnout (Cox & Munger, 1989; c.f., Foster, 1984; Knack & Kropf, 1998).

Negative Advertising   Negative ads criticize one candidate while sometimes praising a competitor. One theory asserts that negative campaigns encourage cynicism about candidates and apathy among citizens, which demobilizes them (Ansolabehere & Iyengar, 1995; Min, 2004). Another perspective argues instead that negative ads strengthen attitudes toward candidates (either positive or negative) and create more interest in a campaign (Freedman & Goldstein, 1999; Goldstein & Freedman, 2002; Wattenberg & Brians, 1999). A third line of theoretical reasoning has asserted that negative ads exert no overall effect on turnout, because they depress turnout among some individuals and stimulate it among others (Clinton & Lapinski, 2004; Lau & Pomper, 2001; Martin, 2004).

Different methods investigating the effects of negative ads on turnout have yielded different results. Support for the demobilization hypothesis has mostly been produced by experimental work that showed participants sets of television news stories with positive and negative ads in the commercial breaks (Ansolabehere & Iyengar, 1995; Ansolabehere, Iyengar, Simon, & Valentino, 1994). Furthermore, archival analysis of 34 U.S. Senate Races indicated that in races with lots of negative advertising, turnout was about two percentage points less than in races with neither positive nor negative advertising, and turnout in those latter races was about two percentage points less than in races dominated by positive advertising (Ansolabehere & Iyengar, 1995).

In contrast, experiments embedded in surveys of nationally representative samples of adults and more detailed correlational studies of real elections failed to turn up any evidence that negative ads discourage turnout (Clinton & Lapinski, 2004; Freedman & Goldstein, 1999; see also Lau, Sigelman, Heldman, & Babbitt, 1999).

The inconsistency of these findings may be due in part to differences across types of negative advertisements. People may distinguish between negative information presented in a reasonable manner and negative information presented as mudslinging—the former may increase turnout, whereas the latter may not (Kahn & Kenney, 1999).

Other Campaigns   Turnout in a particular race can be affected by events that occur in other, simultaneous campaigns. For example, the appearance of an unconventional and surprisingly popular candidate, such as Ross Perot when he ran for president in 1992, can inspire disaffected citizens to vote when they otherwise would not have done so (Lacy & Burden, 1999). Furthermore, presidential, gubernatorial, and senate elections and ballot propositions can sometimes increase the rate at which people cast votes in other races by attracting particular people to the polls (Abramowitz & Stone, 2006; Campbell, 1960; Cover, 1985; Jackson, 2002).

Effects of Canvassing, Polling, and Election Outcome Projects

Canvassing   Canvassing efforts involve asking or encouraging people to vote and can have substantial

effects on turnout. Knocking on doors and reminding people to vote seems to be the most effective (Green, 2004a; Green, Gerber, & Nickerson, 2003; Gerber & Green, 2000a, 2005; Michelson, 2003). Mailing or delivering a written encouragement to people seems to be less effective (Gerber & Green, 2000a, 2005; Gerber, Green, & Green, 2003). Canvassing may enhance turnout because it helps citizens determine where to go to vote, reminds them about the election date to permit advance planning, enables citizens by giving them information about the candidates and issues, or induces citizens to make oral commitments to participating in the election, which can be self-fulfilling.

Despite enormous amounts of money paid for telephone calls to potential voters by campaigns and other organizations, such calls seem to have no effects on turnout at all (Cardy, 2005; Gerber & Green, 2000a, b, 2001, 2005; Green, 2004b; McNulty, 2005).

Preelection Polls   Prior to elections, survey researchers often conduct polls to gauge the popularity of the competing candidates. These "horse race" polls are often heavily covered by the news media and might influence turnout, especially if the polls show that a race is not as close as citizens thought. Surprisingly, however, one experimental test of this hypothesis found no evidence that such polls influence turnout (Ansolabehere & Iyengar, 1994).

Predictions of Election Outcomes on Election Day   Some observers have posited that if the new media project the outcome of an election before the polls have closed all across the country, some citizens may be discouraged from casting votes. Some studies suggest that Election Day forecasting of election results has no effect on turnout (Epstein & Strom, 1981). But other studies suggest that Election Day forecasting of election results does slightly depress turnout (Crespin & Vander Wielen, 2002; Delli Carpini, 1984; Jackson, 1983).

Being Interviewed for a Political Survey   A number of studies have explored the possibility that interviewing citizens about politics prior to an election may inspire them to vote at a higher rate. Such an interview may enhance feelings of efficacy and civic duty and might activate a desire to avoid the guilt of not voting. An extensive interview might also remind people of reasons why they might want to vote. Consistent with this reasoning, participating in a preelection survey does increase turnout, sometimes dramatically (Granberg & Holmberg, 1992; Yalch, 1976). Even participating in an extremely short survey simply asking people whether they plan to vote on Election Day has the capacity to increase turnout (Greenwald, Carnot, Beach, & Young, 1987; c.f., Smith, Gerber, & Orlich, 2003).

Conclusions

Some of the findings reviewed earlier are consistent with the general notion that a person will vote if the information and time costs of doing so are outweighed by the benefits of potentially casting the deciding vote and the rewards (or avoided costs) from voting. And the literature is also consistent with the general claim that citizens' decisions about whether to vote are a function of their motivation to vote, ability to vote, and the difficulty of the task. Many of the factors discussed so far might affect more than one of these general classes of mediators. For instance, a high level of education could motivate an individual to vote and might enable the person to vote or might decrease the costs of voting. Moving frequently could reduce people's ability to vote (because they may not have had time to acquire the needed information about local candidates and issues) and could make it harder for a person to figure out where to vote, thus increasing costs.

Why do Some People Decide to Pressure Government?

Citizen activism in democratic societies can guide government policy making in numerous ways. People can do work to help elect candidates with whom they agree on policy issues (Verba, Schlozman, & Brady, 1995). They can support interest groups that lobby legislators on particular issues (Cigler & Loomis, 1995; Hansen, 1991). And in the extreme, citizens can join together and catalyze social movements to demand more radical social change (Smelser, 1962).

A great deal of research has explored why particular citizens choose to join particular groups to direct government in particular ways (see Baumgartner & Leech, 1998). Underlying all of this work is the notion that people who share a common interest have an incentive to work with one another to pursue and protect that interest. But many people share common interests with one another and yet do not collaborate as activists. Therefore, driven importantly by Olson's (1965) landmark work, scholars have sought to identify the costs and benefits of participating, presuming that action only occurs when the latter outweigh the former (e.g., Salisbury, 1969). Past work has focused especially on the impact of selective incentives, solidary and purposive rewards, beliefs about a group's ability to succeed, the individual's access to necessary resources, and many more factors (e.g., Dahl, 1961; Finkel, Muller, & Opp, 1989; Olson, 1965).

One way to analyze issue-focused activism begins by decomposing the set of citizens within a society who share the common desire to see a particular public policy enacted. Among these people, the most effort would presumably come from staff members employed by interest group organizations devoted to lobbying elected representatives. Somewhat less effort would be expected from members of what might be called the "active public," people who voluntarily give their time and money to groups, attend rallies, and write letters. And other citizens could be called "passive sympathizers," people supportive of groups' efforts but who do nothing to help.

Who Acts?

The existing literature on activism points to a number of important determinants of whether a person will be among the active public or among the passive sympathizers at any given moment in time. Some factors are attributes of the individual. For example, people with more necessary resources available (e.g., free time and disposable income) are less taxed by participation (Verba, Schlozman, & Brady, 1995). Highly educated people are better equipped with civic skills, which presumably confer a sense of confidence that one's efforts can be successful and make a difference (Verba & Nie, 1972; Verba, Schlozman, & Brady, 1995). And people who care deeply about a particular policy issue or who link their own identities to a group affected by the issue are most likely to participate (Hinkle, Fox-Cardamone, Haseleu, Brown, & Irwin, 1996; Krosnick & Telhami, 1995; Miller, Gurin, Gurin, & Malanchuk, 1981; Morris & Mueller, 1992; Verba, Schlozman, & Brady, 1995).

The Coordination of Collective Action

The behavior of interest group coordinators also helps determine when people will be politically active. For example, recruitment efforts are terrifically consequential; people are much more likely to participate when invited to do so than when they must invest the effort to locate a group to join and a strategy for doing so (Gamson, 1975; Verba, Schlozman, & Brady, 1995; Walker, 1991). Groups can offer selective incentives, tangible rewards (e.g., discounted goods or services) that only active members can receive (Gamson, 1975; Olson, 1965). Groups can also take steps to demonstrate that they are effective in influencing policy (Moe, 1980; Opp, 1986) and to convince people that their participation will make a real difference in enhancing the group's chances of success (Muller, Dietz, & Finkel, 1991).

Real-World Conditions

Changes in real-world conditions can inspire activism as well. Societies may evolve into comfortable states of equilibrium, which are punctuated by occasional disturbances (Truman, 1951). When a disturbance causes a decline in people's quality of life, they are motivated to rectify the situation, at times through political activism. Thus, an important motivator is the sense of dissatisfaction with undesirable current life circumstances and the concomitant desire to change them (Barnes & Kaase, 1979; Chubb, 1983; Dalton, 1988; Gamson, 1975; Loomis & Cigler, 1995; Rosenstone & Hansen, 1993).

This theme is especially prominent in the social movements' literature. The French Revolution, the Civil Rights movement, and other such movements all emerged in response to dissatisfaction with governmental policies or social structures that appeared to treat people unfairly (e.g., Smelser, 1962). Likewise, interest groups have often formed to oppose newly created government programs that disadvantaged the group or to oppose other citizen groups that took actions with which the group disagreed (Baumgartner & Leech, 1998; Loomis & Cigler, 1995; Walker, 1991). And Hansen (1985) demonstrated that when people suffered serious economic hardships, they were especially likely to join activist groups that could help alleviate the hardships.

Less prominent in this literature is a somewhat different notion: that *satisfaction* with current circumstances and the desire to defend them can also motivate activism. Various scholars have argued that when people face threats of undesirable economic, social, or political changes in the future, they are especially likely to join others to protect the status quo (Hansen, 1985; Loomis & Cigler, 1995; Moen, 1992). In other words, it may not be necessary for life circumstances to take a turn for the worse before people will become active. The appearance that things may become worse in the future may be effectively motivating as well.

When it comes to democratic politics, citizens can experience various types of threats. One is "policy change threat"—the perception that a politically powerful individual or individuals are mobilizing to change a public policy that one supports. Perceptions of policy change threat should come about when a citizen, upon surveying the political landscape, becomes aware that a single individual or group of people are taking action to change a policy that the citizen does not want to see changed. For example, a newly elected president may express a commitment to changing a law. An election can shift the leadership of the Congress from one political party to the other, thereby giving special legislative power to a group that places priority on changing a law. Or powerful social groups outside of government, such as commercial firms or professional associations, can initiate public efforts to change a law that governs their operation. By their actions, these agents threaten losses to citizens who disagree with the proposed change, and these threats may inspire activism (see, e.g., Diamond, 1995; Loomis & Ciglar, 1995; MacKuen, 2000; Marcus, Neuman, & Moen, 1992). Indeed, interest group fundraisers routinely send direct mail solicitations pointing out threats of undesirable policy changes to motivate people to join their organizations (Godwin, 1988).

Many studies suggest that threat inspires activism. Gusfield (1963) documented how the temperance movement emerged because the Protestant middle class perceived lower-class urban immigrants to have compromised the moral character of society and threatened to do so further. The threat of nuclear war inspired political activism among people who perceived that threat most powerfully (Fiske, Pratto, & Pavelchak, 1983; Tyler & McGraw, 1983). The perception that the quality of the environment was threatened and was likely to decline in the future has inspired activism as well (McKenzie-Mohr et al., 1995).

Other evidence consistent with the notion that threat inspires activism involves trends over time in public support for environmental lobbying groups. Controlling for many factors (including aspects of interest group behavior) and correcting for inflation, financial contributions to such groups were higher during the Reagan and Bush administrations than during the Carter administration or during the first two years of the Clinton administration (Lowry, 1997; Richer, 1995). And membership in the Sierra Club and the Audubon Society grew much less rapidly during the Kennedy and Johnson administrations than during the Nixon and Ford administrations (Mitchell, 1979). These higher levels of activism during Republican administrations may have reflected environmentalists' perceptions of greater threat of undesirable policy change at those times.

Support for the threat hypothesis also comes from correlational evidence from surveys, experiments embedded within surveys, and field experiments (Miller & Krosnick, 2004; Miller, Tahk, Krosnick, Holbrook, & Lowe, 2009). Survey respondents who perceived a higher level of threat of undesirable policy change in the future were especially likely to have been active in expressing their policy preferences on an issue, especially if they attached a great deal of personal importance to the issue. Respondents who were given information suggesting that considerable undesirable policy change threat existed were inspired to perform such behavior in the future, again more so if they attached considerably personal importance to the issue. And participants in a field experiment who received letters describing efforts by legislators to bring about undesirable policy changes were more effective at inspiring real attitude expressive activism than were letters without this information.

Why do Some People Participate in Political Opinion Surveys?

Another way to express one's preferences on government policy issues is to participate in surveys, the results of which may be conveyed by the news media to government, thereby exerting pressure on political actors. Consistent with this logic, people who participate in surveys are more likely to vote in elections and to express interest in politics than people who do not participate in surveys (Knack & Kropf, 1998; Voogt & Saris, 2003).

CAUSES OF POLITICAL ATTITUDES AND BELIEFS

How do People Decide Which Candidate to Vote For?

A huge literature has accumulated during the past 80 years at least on the factors that influence citizens' decisions about which candidate to vote for (for a partial review, see, e.g., Kinder & Sears, 1985). Books such as *Voting* (Berelson, Lazarsefld, & McPhee, 1954), *The American Voter* (Campbell, Converse, Miller, & Stokes, 1960), *The Changing American Voter* (Nie, Verba, & Petrocik, 1979), *The New American Voter* (Miller & Shanks, 1996), *The American Voter Revisited* (Lewis-Beck, Jacoby, Norpoth, & Weisberg, 2008), and many more line the shelves of countless scholars. And countless articles have filled many journals exploring the considerations that influence citizens' candidate choices. Our selective review of some of this work emphasizes perhaps the consideration of most interest to political theorists: policy preferences. Responsible citizens, say the theorists, base votes on attitudes about what those citizens want government to do. This section of the chapter therefore reviews psychological work plumbing the depths of this issue, with special attention to moderators, and then reviews other recent work on bandwagon effects, the influence of voters' personalities, ballot layout, and the processes of information integration when making vote choices.

Policy Preferences

One mechanism by which citizens could elect representatives who implement government policies that they favor is if citizens' candidate preferences are determined in part by the match between their attitudes toward government policies (i.e., their *policy attitudes*) and their perceptions of candidates' attitudes toward those policies. This notion, referred to as *policy voting*, is consistent with the many social-psychological theories that assert that social attraction is based in part on attitudinal similarity (Byrne, 1971; Festinger, 1954; Heider, 1958).

Perceptions of Candidates' Attitudes Toward Government Policies

For a citizen to cast a vote to express an attitude on an issue of government policy, the citizen must presumably know the positions of the competing candidates on that issue. Two different theoretical accounts attempt to explain how these perceptions might be translated into candidate choices. So-called "spatial models" propose that citizen attitudes toward a policy fall along a continuum from very favorable to very unfavorable, and perceptions of candidates can be placed on the same continuum. The candidate who is perceived to be closer to the citizen is thought to gain in appeal from this proximity (Downs, 1957). The second account is the "directional theory" of voting, which proposes that citizens like candidates who are on the same side of the neutral point as they are more than they like candidates on the opposite side of the neutral point. And the more extremely the candidate is on the citizen's side of the neutral point, the more the candidate will appeal to the citizen (Rabinowitz & Macdonald, 1989).

Adjudicating between these two models appeared for quite a while to be impossible to accomplish, because which model wins depends completely on what assumptions the researcher makes (see Lewis & King, 1999; Tomz & Van Houweling, 2008). But recently, a series of experimental studies have presented participants with descriptions of hypothetical candidates and assessed how the participants used that information when evaluating the candidates. Lacy & Paolino (2004) found evidence in favor of proximity model. Although Claassen (2009) found support for the directional model for some issues and for the proximity model for others, Claassen (2007) reported another experiment yielding evidence of proximity voting but not of directional voting. And Tomz and Van Houweling (2008) found that proximity voting was much more common than directional voting, which did occur among a small proportion of participants. Thus, these studies suggest proximity voting may be the more prevalent approach employed by citizens.

Needless to say, central components of these accounts of policy-driven votes are citizens' perceptions of the positions that candidates take on policy issues. To cast a vote based on an issue, a voter must perceive the competing candidates as taking clear and different positions on the issue. And a number of studies have yielded support for this notion (e.g., Brody & Page, 1972; Krosnick, 1988a).

Personal Importance of Policy Issues

Psychological theories suggest that the impact of any given policy issue is likely to hinge on how strong a voter's attitude is on the issue. Strong attitudes are defined as those that possess four key features: They are tenaciously resistant to change, are highly stable over time during the course of daily life, exert powerful influences on information processing and decision making, and are potent determinants of social behaviors (Krosnick & Petty, 1995). Thus, by definition, strong policy preferences should have powerful impact on evaluations of candidates and vote choices.

A great deal of research in social psychology has explored various ways of identifying strong attitudes. For example, some investigators have examined the intensity of an individual's feelings about an attitude object (e.g., Krosnick & Schuman, 1988). Others have focused on the certainty with which people hold their attitudes (e.g., Budd, 1986). And still others have concentrated on the accessibility of attitudes, the ease with which they come to mind spontaneously during social information processing (e.g., Fazio, 1986). All of these attitude attributes, as well as a variety of others, can successfully identify attitudes that possess the four hallmarks of strength.

Although most of these attitude attributes have not yet been employed in studies of policy voting, many studies have explored the role of attitude importance, partly because many national surveys have included measures of the amount of personal importance that citizens attach to specific policy issues, thus equipping analysts to explore this matter. Attitude importance is defined as a person's subjective self-perception of the degree of personal importance attached to a particular attitude (e.g., Boninger, Krosnick, Berent, & Fabrigar, 1995; Krosnick, 1988b). To attach great personal importance to an attitude is to care passionately about it and to be deeply concerned about it. Attitude importance is thought to be consequential precisely because of its status as a subjective perception: Perceiving an attitude to be personally important presumably leads individuals to use it deliberately in processing information and making decisions.

Americans vary a great deal in the amount of personal importance they attach to their attitudes on policy issues, and small groups of citizens (rarely more than 15%) attach the highest importance to any one issue (see Anand & Krosnick, 2003; Krosnick, 1990). Importance ratings are very stable over time, as would be expected if they represent meaningful cognitive and emotional commitments to an issue (Krosnick, 1986). Importance appears to be issue specific—it is difficult to predict the importance a person attaches to one issue knowing how much importance that person attaches to another (Anand & Krosnick, 2003; Krosnick, 1990). Citizens who attach the highest level of personal importance to an issue are referred to as that issue's "issue public" (Converse, 1964; Krosnick, 1990).

As would be expected based on social-psychological theories of attitude strength, more important attitudes on policy issues are themselves more stable over time (Krosnick, 1988b) and more resistant to change (Fine, 1957; Gorn, 1975). The more importance people attach to a policy preference, the better their position on that issue predicts their vote choices (e.g., Anand & Krosnick,

2003; Bélanger & Meguid, 2008; Fournier, Blais, Nadeau, Gidengil, & Nevitte, 2003; Krosnick, 1988a; Miller, Krosnick, & Fabrigar, 2009; Visser, Krosnick, & Simmons, 2003). The more important people consider a policy issue to be, the more likely they are to mention the issue as a reason to vote for or against a candidate when asked for such reasons (Krosnick, 1988a). And the more important people consider a policy issue to be, the more impact they say it had on vote choices (Krosnick & Telhami, 1995; Miller et al., 2009). This may occur because more important policy preferences are more accessible in long-term memory (Bizer & Krosnick, 2001; Krosnick, 1989; Miller, Krosnick, & Fabrigar, 2009).

People who are passionate about a policy issue are also very emotional when processing relevant information. For example, when watching a television news story on a policy issue, people who attach more personal importance to the issue have more intense emotional reactions (Miller, Krosnick, & Fabrigar, 2009). This tendency toward emotion might raise concerns about whether issue public members can be trusted to make judgments in wise ways.

Reassuring in this regard is evidence that attaching personal importance to an issue inspires people to gather information on the issue voraciously, to think carefully and often about that information, and to become highly knowledgeable on the issue as a result (Holbrook, Berent, Krosnick, Visser, & Boninger, 2005). Issue public members manifest no evidence of bias toward remembering information with which they agree and toward forgetting disagreeable information (Holbrook, Berent, Krosnick, Visser, & Boninger, 2005). In fact, issue public members are especially likely to have accurate perceptions of where candidates stand on their issue (Krosnick, 1988a; 1990) and to accurately remember relevant information (Holbrook, Berent, Krosnick, Visser, & Boninger, 2005). The large store of accurate information that issue public members accumulate in long-term memory is highly organized in a way that facilitates information use (Berent & Krosnick, 1995).

The Projection Hypothesis

If issue-based voting depends on citizens' perceptions of candidates' issue positions, then the value of votes cast presumably depends on the accuracy of those candidate perceptions. If voters misperceive candidates, then vote choices will not clearly communicate wishes about directions for future policy making. Many researchers have explored a prediction of considerable inaccuracy in perceptions: the projection hypothesis.

Cognitive consistency theories (Festinger, 1957; Heider, 1958; Osgood & Tannenbaum, 1955) suggest that candidate perceptions may be systematically distorted to maintain cognitive harmony. Cognitive consistency exists when a voter's attitude toward the policy agrees with the perceived policy attitude of a liked candidate. Cognitive consistency also exists when a voter's own policy attitude disagrees with the perceived policy attitude of a disliked candidate. If voters believe they disagree with a liked candidate or agree with a disliked candidate, inconsistency exists. Such an inconsistency can be resolved by changing one's candidate evaluations (called *policy-based evaluation*), by changing one's policy preference (called *persuasion*), or by changing one's perception of the candidates' positions (called *projection*).

Projection is not only likely to be regulated by sentiment toward candidates but, according to balance theory, is also likely to be regulated by *unit relations* with candidates. A unit relation specifies the degree to which a voter is linked to or associated with a candidate, regardless of liking. One possible unit relation between a candidate and a voter would be determined by the voter's belief about the likelihood that the candidate will be elected (Kinder, 1978). Voters who see a candidate as likely to be elected will have a unit relation and will be disposed toward positive projection of that candidate's policy attitudes. Voters who see a candidate as unlikely to be elected will not have a unit relation and may be likely to displace that candidate's attitude away from their own (see Heider, 1958, p. 202). Alternatively, a unit relation might be established by shared political party affiliation, shared race or ethnic identity, or some other shared characteristic.

Projection may occur via a number of possible mechanisms (see Kinder, 1978). First, it may occur by *selective attention* during encoding when individuals are exposed to new information about a candidate. Voters may pay close attention to and devote extensive thought to statements that reinforce their preferred view of a candidate's attitude. Second, projection may occur as the result of *selective retention*. Citizens may strategically forget pieces of information that challenge their preferred perceptions of a candidate's attitude. Third, projection may occur through *selective rationalization*. When voters acquire a piece of information that is inconsistent with their beliefs regarding the position of a candidate on an issue, the voters may spend an unusually large amount of cognitive effort reinterpreting the information so that it is consistent with their preference (Hastie & Kumar, 1979).

Early research on social perception found evidence of a possible asymmetry in the effects of sentiment toward others. Although people clearly seemed to prefer to agree with others they like, people seemed not to be so concerned about disagreeing with disliked others (for a review, see Kinder, 1978). This may occur because people disengage from others they dislike and are therefore less aware of

and bothered by cognitive inconsistencies involving their attitudes (Newcomb, 1953, 1968). This is the theoretical justification for the *asymmetry* hypothesis in candidate perception, which states that positive projection onto liked candidates will be stronger than negative projection onto disliked candidates.

Some tests of the projection hypothesis examined cross-sectional relations between sentiment toward a candidate and agreement between a respondent's issue position and the respondent's perception of the candidate's position (e.g., Brent & Granberg, 1982; Conover & Feldman, 1982; Kinder, 1978; Shaffer, 1981). However, the cross-sectional correlations taken to be evidence of positive projection could instead be attributable to at least five other processes: (1) perspective effects (e.g., Ostrom & Upshaw, 1968); (2) policy-based candidate evaluation; (3) persuasion by liked candidates; (4) systematic variation in how candidates describe their positions to different audiences (e.g., Miller & Sigelman, 1978); and (5) the false consensus effect (Marks & Miller, 1987). Although many studies sought to overcome these confounds with cross-sectional data (Bartels, 1988; Conover & Feldman, 1986; Judd, Kenny, & Krosnick, 1983; Martinez, 1988; Otatti, Fishbein, & Middlestadt, 1988), those analyses universally rested on assumptions that are not likely to be plausible (see Krosnick, 2002). Only three studies have used testing methods not subject to these problems, and none of them yielded compelling evidence of projection (Anderson & Avery, 1978; Krosnick, 1991; Shaffer, 1981).

Thus, this literature has yielded no evidence of systematic, motivated misperception of the positions that political candidates take on policy issues. This is reassuring from a normative point of view—citizens do not appear to be distorting their images of political actors simply to satisfy a need for cognitive harmony.

Candidate Ambiguity

Election analysts have long recognized that candidates may be better off making it difficult for citizens to discern their issue positions. Candidates may win more votes through vagueness than they do by taking clear stands on policy issues (Bartels, 1988; Downs, 1957; Page, 1976, 1978; Shepsle, 1972). And indeed, ambiguity is more the norm than the exception, because candidates rarely state their positions on issues (Page, 1978; Tomz & Van Houweling, 2009). Candidates frequently endorse the "end states" they find desirable, such as peace and prosperity, but they rarely describe the policy *means* by which they would achieve those end states (McGinniss, 1969).

Is ambiguity in fact advantageous for candidates? Some studies have suggested that uncertainty about candidates' issue positions is counted against them by citizens when they decide for whom to vote (Alvarez, 1998; Bartels, 1986; Brady & Ansolabehere, 1989), but other studies have shown no price paid by candidates for ambiguity (Berinsky & Lewis, 2007; Campbell, 1983). A recent survey-embedded experiment with hypothetical candidates suggested that ambiguity did not discourage voters from supporting a candidate and that ambiguity can help candidates gain votes from members of their own party (Tomz & Van Houweling, 2009).

However, an important wrinkle in that experiment's findings suggests caution before presuming that its finding generalizes to real elections. In such elections, voters have much, much more information about the candidates than the experimental participants did (on only one policy issue and political party affiliations). So in real elections, voters can choose to place weight on any of a wide array of policy issues. Decisions about which issues to focus on are likely to be governed by the strength of people's attitudes on specific issues: People who hold strong favorable or unfavorable attitudes toward a policy are especially likely to use that issue as a basis for their vote choice. Among people with such strong attitudes, candidate ambiguity did reduce the chances of gaining support from a voter (Tomz & Van Houweling, 2009). So among the people who count in the situations that count, ambiguity may indeed affect a candidate's chances of victory.

Bandwagon Effects: The Influence of Social Norms

For decades, the news media have saturated the American public with the results of surveys done to measure the status of the horserace via straw polls (Broh, 1983). Scholars have long speculated that such reports might create bandwagon effects (whereby people gravitate toward popular candidates) or underdog effects (whereby people gravitate toward candidates who are not doing well). Bandwagon effects can be thought of as ordinary conformity effects, resulting either from informational social influence or normative social influence (Noelle-Neuman, 1984; Scheufele & Moy, 2000). And underdog effects might occur as the result of feelings of sympathy or empathy (Fey, 1997; Kirchgässner & Wolters, 1987; McKelvey & Ordeshook, 1985; Simon, 1954). Many laboratory experiments have found evidence of bandwagon effects (Ansolabehere & Iyengar, 1994; Atkin, 1969; Cook & Welch, 1940; Forsythe, Myerson, Rietz, & Weber, 1993; Mehrabian, 1998), as have correlational studies (Schmitt-Beck, 1996; Skalaban, 1988). And two experimental studies found evidence of underdog effects (Ceci & Kain, 1982; Laponce, 1966).

The Voter's Personality

Recent work has explored how voters' personalities might shape their candidate choices. People who score high in openness to experience are especially likely to have voted for Democratic candidates (Rentfrow, Jost, Gosling, & Potter, 2009). Agreeableness and openness to experience are also associated with voting for Democrats, whereas emotional stability and conscientiousness are associated with voting for Republicans (Barbaranelli, Caprara, Vecchione, & Fraley, 2006). These initial findings are likely to inspire future work illuminating their meanings.

Design of the Ballot

Ballot Layout

The 2000 U.S. presidential election called attention to many aspects of the procedure by which Americans have cast votes, one of which was the design of ballots. One especially interesting instance involved ballots in Palm Beach County, Florida, that listed two columns of candidate names on either side of a column of holes to punch. The layout of the names and holes was sufficiently confusing to induce some people who meant to vote for Al Gore to vote for Pat Buchanan instead (Agresti & Presnell, 2002; Wand et al., 2001). Thus, poor ballot design can induce unintended votes.

Candidate Name Order

At least since the beginning of the last century, seasoned political observers have believed that the ordering of candidates' names on ballots has some influence on the outcomes of elections (e.g., Harris, 1934; Wilson, 1910). These observers speculated that being listed first helps a candidate to win an election, especially when many candidates are competing, when voters are not well informed about a race for a little-known office, or when party affiliations cannot facilitate voters' selections.

Name order effects are easy to imagine. American voters are often asked to vote on many candidate races and referenda, and learning information to make informed choices would be tremendously burdensome, so it seems plausible that some voters might find themselves in voting booths without much information to yield informed choices in some races. And people might sometimes find themselves feeling torn between two competing candidates, unable to choose between them on substantive grounds.

If people feel obligated to vote under such circumstances, they may be inclined to select the first name they see in a list of candidates, creating what is called a "primacy effect" (Krosnick, 1991). People tend to evaluate objects with a confirmatory bias: People usually begin a search of memory for information about a choice option by looking for reasons to select it, rather than reasons not to select it (Klayman & Ha, 1987; Koriat, Lichtenstein, & Fischhoff, 1980). So when considering a list of candidates, voters may search memory primarily for reasons to vote for each contender rather than reasons to vote against him or her. And when working through a list of options, people may think less and less about each subsequent alternative, because they become increasingly fatigued, and short-term memory becomes increasingly clogged with thoughts. Therefore, people may be more likely to generate supportive thoughts about candidates listed initially, biasing them toward voting for these individuals.

According to many studies, primacy effects occur often (for a review, see Miller & Krosnick, 1998; see also Brockington, 2003; Koppell & Steen, 2004; Krosnick, Miller, & Tichy, 2004). These effects appear to be less common when voters have substantive information with which to choose between the competitors: when candidates' party affiliations are listed on the ballot, when a race has been well publicized, and when an incumbent is running for reelection. Name order effects are also especially likely to occur among voters who are less educated, presumably because they are less knowledgeable about political affairs. Experimental simulations of elections have also yielded evidence of primacy effects (Coombs, Peters, & Strom, 1974; Kamin, 1958; Taebel, 1975), and these effects were weakened when participants were given other information with which to choose between candidates (Coombs, Peters, & Strom, 1974).

Through What Cognitive Processes do People Form Candidate Preference?

Memory-Based Evaluations

For decades, the process of candidate preference formation was presumed to involve the retrieval and integration of information available in memory on Election Day. Citizens were presumed to canvass their memories for positive and negative information about each candidate, use that information to derive overall attitudes toward the candidates, and support the candidate with the higher overall favorability (e.g., Kelley & Mirer, 1974). When asked what they liked and disliked about presidential candidates during the weeks before elections, many national survey respondents have generated few reasons or none at all (e.g., Gant & Davis, 1984), fueling perennial concerns among social scientists about citizen competence and the democratic process.

Consistent with the work of Norman Anderson (1981), one account of the process suggests that it is quite simple:

> The voter canvasses his likes and dislikes of the leading candidates and major parties involved in an election. Weighing

each like and dislike equally, he votes for the candidate toward whom he has the greatest net number of favorable attitudes, if there is such a candidate. If no candidate has such an advantage, the voter votes consistently with his party affiliation, if he has one. (Kelley & Mirer, 1974, p.. 574)

Online Evaluations

An alternative account proposes that citizens may instead form and continually update candidate preferences through an online process (Lodge, McGraw, & Stroh, 1989). Over the course of a campaign, citizens have many opportunities to learn new things about the candidates for office. From the news media, political advertisements, conversations with friends and associates, and even late night comedians, citizens learn a vast array of information about each candidate. As each new piece of information is received, its evaluative implications may be integrated into citizens' existing summary attitudes toward the candidate. Consequently, candidate evaluations may be continually updated over the course of a campaign.

A good deal of evidence suggests that citizens do indeed form their candidate preferences in this way (e.g., Lodge, McGraw, & Stroh, 1989; Lodge, Steenbergen, & Brau, 1995; McGraw, Lodge, & Stroh, 1990). This online process is especially likely when people know they will eventually need to make a judgment (Hastie & Park, 1986), which is certainly the case for citizens who anticipate participating in an election. Online candidate evaluation is also more prevalent among political experts than political novices (McGraw, Lodge, & Stroh, 1990).

This evidence puts a different spin on the finding that citizens are often hard pressed to articulate clear reasons for their candidate preferences. If citizens form such preferences online, they need not retain the specific pieces of information on which preferences are based. Therefore, it is not troubling that citizens cannot list all the considerations underlying their preferences.

Other evidence suggests that the online updating process is much more nuanced than Kelley and Mirer's (1974) simpler proposal (see Holbrook, Krosnick, Visser, Gardner, & Cacioppo, 2001). First, citizens bring an optimistic perspective with them whenever evaluating a new political candidate: They expect the best of him or her, and this expectation gives all candidates a slight edge on the positive side of neutral before citizens know anything about them. Second, first impressions are self-sustaining—the first few pieces of information that a citizen gets about a candidate have more impact on final evaluations than do pieces of information acquired later. And people place greater weight on unfavorable information than on favorable information when evaluating candidates.

Consistent with this account are experimental findings as well (Moskowitz & Stroh, 1996). In one such study, participants read a newspaper editorial that created either favorable or unfavorable impressions of a hypothetical candidate, and then participants read about the policy positions of the candidates. When unfavorable impressions had been created initially, participants placed more weight on issues on which they disagreed with the candidate when evaluating him. When favorable impressions had been created initially, participants placed less weight on issues on which they disagreed with the candidate when evaluating him. However, creating an initial positive impression did not change the weight placed on evaluation criteria, perhaps because participants would have had positive expectations regarding the candidate even in the absence of an editorial creating such expectations. Thus, it appeared that unfavorable initial impressions were self-sustaining and especially powerful.

Interestingly, the relation of candidate preferences with the information that drives them is not unidirectional. Citizens certainly derive their candidate preferences from attributes held by the candidates that they like and dislike. But once a candidate preference begins to form, citizens adjust what they like and dislike about the candidates to rationalize their candidate preferences. Liking a candidate initially leads people to grow the number of the candidate's attributes that they like. And disliking a candidate initially leads people to grow the number of the candidate's attributes that they dislike. The longer before Election Day a citizen forms a candidate preference, the more apparent these rationalization processes are on election day (Rahn, Krosnick, & Breuning, 1994). Thus, citizens' beliefs about candidates and their candidate preferences end up more consistent on Election Day than they were at the time the candidate preferences were formed (see also Krosnick, Pfent, & Courser, 2003).

"Thin Slice" Judgments

The online and memory-based models specify different cognitive processes by which candidate evaluations can be formed, but they share the assumption that such evaluations are deliberately derived from substantive information about the candidates. Recent research suggests that candidate evaluations may also arise spontaneously and quite effortlessly on the basis of minimal information, called "thin slices" (Ambady & Rosenthal, 1992). One especially provocative set of findings suggests that automatic inferences about a candidate's traits based on the candidate's facial appearance may play a role in electoral outcomes (Todorov, Mandisodza, Goren, & Hall, 2005; see Ambady & Weisbuch, Macrae & Quadflieg, volume 1).

For example, some experiment participants looked at headshot photographs of unfamiliar candidates for various Congressional seats and were asked to guess the candidates' traits (Todorov, Mandisodza, Goren, & Hall, 2005). Candidates who were thought to appear more competent had in fact been more successful in winning past elections. Judgments of candidate competence based on facial appearance also predict subsequent election outcomes (Ballew & Todorov, 2007; Todorov, Mandisodza, Goren, & Hall, 2005). A wide array of other judgments that participants made based on candidate appearance (e.g., honesty, trustworthiness, likeability, charisma, attractiveness, age) did not predict election outcomes. These findings suggest that the automatic inferences of competence may play a role in candidate preference formation.

Other Determinants of Candidate Choices

Past studies have examined many other factors that might shape people's candidate selections, including:

- Identification with a political party (Campbell, Converse, Miller, & Stokes, 1960)
- Performance of the incumbent administration in running the country (Fiorina, 1981)
- Pursuit of the interests of particular social groups (Lazarsfeld, Berelson, & Gaudet, 1948)
- Perceptions of the candidates' personalities (Kinder, 1986)
- The emotions that the candidates evoke in voters (Abelson, Kinder, Peters, & Fiske, 1982).

Countless regressions have predicted candidate preferences with large arrays of such variables, and they always explained a large amount of variance—in fact, a huge amount of variance. So much that the results can often be unstable and inconsistent across different investigators' attempts to explain voters' decisions in the same election. Because the vast majority of work in this literature simply reports correlations and partial correlations of purported predictors with vote choices, evidence of the causal impact of considerations on candidate selections is not yet strong. Some attempts at discerning causal influence more directly have occurred but have led different investigators to contradictory conclusions (see, e.g., Niemi & Weisberg, 2001) The most exciting innovations in the voting literature will no doubt occur when political psychologists finally discern how and when various considerations shape candidate choices using more convincing analytic methods.

How do People Decide Which Government Policies to Favor and Oppose?

Public opinion has become a ubiquitous element of the political landscape. More than ever before, American citizens have the opportunity to voice their views on the issues of the day. And these views are consequential: When public opinion shifts, policy shifts often follow (e.g., Page & Shapiro, 1983). This would seem to provide prima facie evidence that the U.S. political system is living up to the ideals of democracy. Before reaching that conclusion, though, one must consider how citizens form their policy preferences. As it turns out, many factors that influence these preferences, and their normative implications for democracy vary greatly.

Ideology

Given the frequency with which political elites couch policy debates in broad ideological terms, it seems quite reasonable to assume that many, if not most, citizens derive their policy preferences from a set of general ideological principles to which they subscribe. These foundational assumptions (e.g., about how society should be structured, about the proper aims of government) might be expected to provide structure to attitudes on a wide range of issues, all of which are logically related through their shared bases in the underlying ideology. Try as they might, however, social scientists have largely failed to find evidence that citizens' attitudes toward specific policies are derived from broader ideological principles (for more extensive reviews of these efforts, see Kinder, 1983, 2006; Kinder & Sears, 1985).

The quest for evidence of ideology was inspired by Philip Converse (1964). In a densely packed and enormously influential chapter, he spelled out several criteria that might indicate the degree to which citizens' policy preferences are organized into ideologically constrained belief systems. Using data from national surveys, Converse demonstrated that by every one of these criteria, the vast majority of Americans failed to exhibit anything even remotely resembling ideologically constrained belief systems.

For example, Converse demonstrated that knowing whether citizens held liberal or conservative attitudes in one policy domain offered virtually no guidance in predicting their attitudes in other domains. In fact, knowing citizens' policy positions offered only the most modest indication of what their position on the very same issue would be a couple of years later. And when asked to explain their attitudes toward the major political parties and presidential candidates, virtually none drew on ideological principles or language. From all of this, Converse concluded that very few citizens held clear political preferences that were derived in any meaningful way from broad ideological principles. And in fact, Converse said, most citizens do not even have attitudes at all toward any given policy. When pressed to offer policy opinions in surveys, people usually report what Converse called "nonattitudes," top of the head responses to questions that reflect little deliberation or understanding.

Converse's bold claims inspired a tidal wave of research, much of which sought to rehabilitate the tattered image of the American citizen. Some scholars suggested that Converse's findings were unique to the politically quiescent Eisenhower years, and that a more ideologically charged political atmosphere would lead citizens to exhibit more ideologically constrained policy preferences (e.g., Nie, Verba, & Petrocik, 1979). Others offered methodological critiques, suggesting that the apparent incoherence and instability of citizens' issues positions were a function of poorly designed survey questions (e.g., Achen, 1975; Erikson, 1979; Judd & Milburn, 1980). Still others criticized Converse's strategy of aggregating across individual citizens in search of a universal organizing structure and overlooking the possibility of idiosyncratic organizing principles (e.g., Lane, 1962, 1969, 1973; Marcus, Tabb, & Sullivan, 1974).

Thorough investigation of these critiques has, for the most part, vindicated Converse's (1964) original claims. Citizens are often quite willing to place themselves on a liberal–conservative ideological continuum, but these self-placements often reflect affective reactions to the groups and symbols associated with the terms liberal and conservative rather than endorsement of abstract ideological principles (e.g., Conover & Feldman, 1981; Valentino, Traugott, & Hutchings, 2002). Even when ideological self-placement does predict specific issue positions, it seems unwise to attribute these issue positions to derivation from broad ideological principles.

Self-Interest

If citizens usually do not derive their policy preferences from abstract ideologies, on what are these preferences based? One intuitively appealing answer is self-interest: the pursuit of immediate material benefits for oneself. Perhaps citizens develop positive attitudes toward policies from which they personally stand to benefit and develop negative attitudes toward policies that are likely to have a negative impact on their own material interests.

In fact, however, self-interest defined in this way explains astonishing little of the variance in policy preferences (for reviews, see Citrin & Green, 1990; Sears & Funk, 1991). For example, having children enrolled in public schools does not increase support for government spending on education (Jennings, 1979); being unemployed does not increase support for government interventions to ensure that everyone who wants to work has a job (Sears, Lau, Tyler, & Allen, 1980); having a potential personal stake in affirmative action policies has no impact on attitudes toward such policies (Kinder & Sanders, 1996); living in a high-crime neighborhood renders people no less supportive of laws that protect the rights of the accused

(Sears, Lau, Tyler, & Allen, 1980); and being personally affected by the Vietnam War (e.g., because one's son or daughter is currently serving in the war) had no impact on attitudes toward that war (Lau, Brown, & Sears, 1978). In these and countless other policy arenas, having a personal stake in a policy debate has virtually no impact on attitudes toward the policy.

Exceptions to this general rule do exist, and they help to clarify the conditions under which considerations of personal interests do and do not influence policy preferences. For example, smokers are much more opposed to policies that restrict smoking and policies that increase cigarette taxes than are nonsmokers (Dixon, Lowery, Levy, & Ferraro, 1991; Green & Gerken, 1989). Likewise, homeowners who stood to benefit directly from a highly publicized and concrete tax cut were more supportive of the referendum than were people who did not own homes and would not receive the tax cut (Sears & Citrin, 1982).

These are unusual cases in which the impact of a policy on individuals' immediate material interests was unusually large, salient, and certain (e.g., Mansbridge, 1990; Sears & Funk, 1991). Consistent with this interpretation, experimental manipulations that enhance the magnitude of personal costs or benefits (e.g., Green, 1988) or the salience of people's own material interests (e.g., Sears & Lau, 1983) immediately before attitudes are expressed strengthen the relation between self-interest and policy attitudes. Similarly, self-interest plays a more limited role in shaping attitudes toward policies with less clear-cut implications for the evaluators (e.g., Lowery & Sigelman, 1981). Most of the time, then, self-interest plays virtually no role in determining which policies citizens favor and which policies they oppose.

Groups, Group Identification, and Intergroup Competition

Although citizens' policy preferences rarely hinge on perceptions of their own material interests, they do often appear to depend on loyalties to social groups (for more on social groups, see Dovidio & Gaertner, this volume; Yzerbyt & Demoulin, this volume). In Converse's (1964) fruitless quest for evidence of ideological constraint, for example, he found that when citizens were asked to explain their evaluations of political candidates and parties, the most common explanations involved social groups. Some citizens may support the Democratic Party, for example, because it is "the party of the working class," whereas other citizens may favor the Republican Party because it "looks out for small business owners."

In this way, social groups sometimes provide a framework for organizing the political landscape (Brady &

Sniderman, 1985). Preferences are sometimes driven by citizens' affective reactions to the groups who are helped or hurt by a policy. For example, people favor policies that benefit groups they like and oppose policies that will benefit groups they dislike (e.g., Sniderman, Hagen, Tetlock, & Brady, 1986). In one instance, attitudes toward affirmative action were shown to be shaped by attitudes toward the social groups that would be advantaged by the policy (e.g., Kinder & Sanders, 1996; Sears, Hensler, & Speer, 1979), and this is true for an array of other policies as well, including welfare (e.g., Gilens, 1995, 1996), international relations (e.g., Hurwitz & Pefley, 1987), spending to fight AIDS (e.g., Price & Hsu, 1992; Sniderman et al., 1991), and immigration reform (e.g., Citrin, Reingold, & Green, 1990).

Policy preferences are influenced not only by attitudes toward particular groups but also by membership in such groups. For example, even among citizens who are sympathetic to the plight of working women, women who belong to and identify with this group express more consistently prowomen policies than people who do not belong to this group (Conover, 1988).

Not surprisingly, group cleavages are sometimes especially pronounced when groups are competing for scarce resources. Regardless of reality, it is understandable that citizens might think that government spending on programs to aid one group comes at the expense of spending on programs to aid other groups. Similarly, hiring policies or university admissions criteria that give preferential treatment to members of some social groups might be seen as limiting the opportunities of members of other groups. Consequently, realistic group conflict can account for important political attitudes in some contexts (e.g., Glaser, 1994; Key, 1949; Quillian, 1995).

Actual competition between groups for limited material resources is not necessary to produce intergroup conflict (Tajfel, 1978; Tajfel & Turner, 1979). Simply perceiving group boundaries can set into motion efforts to positively distinguish one's ingroup from one's outgroup. It would be unwise, therefore, to attribute all group-centric policy preferences to actual competition for scarce resources.

Some scholars have suggested that many policy preferences are affected by a particular form of intergroup antipathy: *symbolic racism* (e.g., Sears, 1988, 1993; Sears, Van Laar, Carrillo, & Kosterman, 1997). When directed at African Americans, this form of racism is thought to be a subtler successor to the blatant, "old fashioned" prejudice of the Jim Crow era. Symbolic racism is thought to be a blend of the antiBlack affect (the residue of having been socialized in a culture that devalues African Americans) and the perception that African Americans violate traditional American values such as the Protestant work ethic, traditional morality, and respect for traditional authority (Sears, Van Laar, Carrillo, & Kosterman, 1997). Symbolic racists are thought to hold four core beliefs: that racial discrimination is a thing of the past, that contemporary disadvantages are attributable to poor work ethic, that continuing demands for assistance are without merit, and that special advantages are illegitimate (e.g., Henry & Sears, 2002; Sears & Henry 2003).

Endorsement of this belief system does predict citizens' attitudes toward a range of race-related policies (e.g., Gilens, 1996; Kinder & Sanders, 1996; McConahay, 1986; McConahay, Hardee, & Batts, 1981; Sears, 1988, 1993; Sears, Van Laar, Carrillo, & Kosterman, 1997). For example, symbolic racism is a strong predictor of attitudes toward policies to guarantee equal opportunities for African Americans, federal assistance to African Americans, and affirmative action policies (Sears, Van Laar, Carrillo, & Kosterman, 1997). In fact, symbolic racism is often the strongest predictor of these policy preferences, overshadowing the impact of political ideology, party identification, and social welfare policy attitudes.

Work on symbolic racism and other subtle forms of prejudice has not been without controversy. Some have criticized inconsistencies in conceptualization and measurement of symbolic racism (e.g., Bobo, 1988; Schuman, Steeh, & Bobo, 1997; Sniderman & Tetlock, 1986; Stoker, 1998). Others have questioned the unidimensionality of symbolic racism (e.g., Kluegel & Bobo, 1993; Kluegel & Smith, 1986; Stoker, 1998). Still others have suggested that associations between symbolic racism and policy preferences stem from content overlap in the two sets of measures and not from the causal impact of the former on the latter (e.g., Chong, 2000; Hurwitz & Peffley, 1998; Schuman, 2000; Sidanius et al., 1999; Sniderman, Crosby, & Howell, 2000). Finally, critics have suggested that measures of symbolic racism actually reflect other factors (e.g., political conservatism, endorsement of individualistic values, anti-egalitarianism, authoritarianism) that drive the observed association (e.g., Kluegel & Bobo, 1993; Sidanius, Levin, Rabinowitz, & Federico, 1999; Sniderman & Carmines, 1997; Sniderman & Piazza, 1993; Sniderman & Tetlock, 1986). Sears and his colleagues have directly addressed each of these critiques and have presented evidence they say is consistent with the original formulation of symbolic racism (Tarman & Sears, 2005).

Values

Other scholars have nominated *core values* as the bedrock principles that give rise to particular policy preferences (e.g., Feldman, 1988; Feldman & Steenbergen, 2001; Feldman & Zaller, 1992; Peffley & Hurwitz, 1987;

Rokeach, 1973; Rokeach & Ball-Rokeach, 1988; Tetlock, 1986, 2000). These scholars have assumed that "underlying all political belief systems are ultimate or terminal values that specify the end-states of public policy. These values—which may take such diverse forms as economic efficiency, social equality, individual freedom, crime control, national security, and racial purity—function as the back stops of belief systems" (Tetlock, 2000, p. 247). From this perspective, then, particular policies are supported or opposed to the extent that they uphold or challenge fundamental beliefs about desirable end states or modes of conduct.

Ample evidence is consistent with the notion that core values give rise to and constrain policy preferences (e.g., Feldman, 1988; Feldman & Zaller, 1992; Peffley & Hurwitz, 1987). When asked to justify their attitudes toward specific welfare policies, for example, citizens often spontaneously invoke core values (Feldman & Zaller, 1992; Hochschild, 1981). Indeed, according to citizens' own rationales for their policy preferences, values play a considerably larger role in the development of political attitudes than do abstract political ideologies (Feldman & Zaller, 1992). Citizens' core values predict a broad range of policy preferences (e.g., Feldman, 1988; Peffley & Hurwitz, 1987). Commitment to equality, for example, predicts attitudes toward many social policies, including welfare programs, government provision of jobs and an acceptable standard of living, and others (Feldman, 1988).

Competition between values can also shape policy preferences. Many debates about government policy pit competing values against one another, requiring difficult trade-offs (Rokeach, 1973; Tetlock, 1986). In the wake of the terrorist attacks of September 11, for example, new sweeping national security measures sought to enhance the safety of Americans but came at a heavy cost to personal freedom. According to the value pluralism model (Tetlock, 1986), policy preferences often hinge on the relative priority placed on competing values. Consistent with this notion, value hierarchies predict policy preferences. For example, shifts over time in the priority that Americans assigned to equality directly mirrored changes over time in support for policies designed to enhance equality (Rokeach & Ball-Rokeach, 1988).

And at the individual level, the priority placed on particular values strongly predicts attitudes toward specific policies. In one investigation, for example, participants rank ordered a set of core values according to their personal importance, and they expressed their views on a broad range of policies (Tetlock, 1986). As expected, value hierarchies strongly predicted policy preferences. The more participants prioritized freedom over national security, for example, the more strongly they opposed domestic

C.I.A. surveillance. And the more participants prioritized a world of beauty over personal prosperity, the more strongly they opposed opening public park lands for drilling and mining to promote economic growth. Across six diverse public policies, value rankings proved to be robust predictors of individuals' policy preferences.

News Media Influence

Policy preferences are also influenced by the ways in which the media cover those issues and, in particular, by the way those issues are *framed* (for more on framing, see Gilovich & Griffin, volume 1). Framing has two relatively distinct meanings, both of which concern the way an issue or problem is presented. In the first meaning, frames refer to the narrative packaging of an issue, which highlights some elements as central to the issue and relegates other elements to the periphery (e.g., Gamson, 1992; Iyengar, 1991; Nelson & Kinder, 1996). In this way, a frame communicates the essence of an issue (Gamson & Modigliani, 1987). And indeed, framing manipulations of this sort can alter reports of public opinion (e.g., Bobo & Kluegel, 1997; Iyengar, 1991; Nelson, Clawson, & Oxley, 1997). A second, related form of framing comes from the decision-making literature and refers to "the decision maker's conception of the acts, outcomes, and contingencies associated with a particular choice" (Tversky & Kahneman, 1981, p. 453). Even when the expected value of the two courses of action is equivalent, these frames powerfully shape decisions (e.g., Kahneman & Tversky, 1981, 1986; Tversky & Kahneman, 1980, 1981, 1986).

Presidential Rhetoric

Few if any political actors have the capacity to capture the attention of the American public more reliably than sitting U.S. presidents, putting them in a prime position to shape citizens' policy preferences. And indeed, studies have documented striking examples of presidential rhetoric influencing public opinion (e.g., Barton, 1974–1975; Kernell, 1976).

The impact of presidential rhetoric on public opinion is thought to be especially strong during international crises and periods of war because (1) the president occupies a unique position of legitimacy on issues of foreign policy; (2) presidents and their administrations are typically the primary source of information regarding the country's involvement in international affairs; and (3) presidents can often make their case at the start of such crises, affording the opportunity to control the framing of the situation (e.g., Bennett, 1990; Cook, 2005; Fuchs & Lorek, 2005; Mermin, 1999; Thrall, 2000). Consistent with this notion, experimental evidence suggests that presidential rhetoric is more consequential on issues of foreign policy than on domestic issues (Hurwitz, 1989).

Of course, the president is not always successful in swaying public opinion, even on foreign policy issues. Despite President George W. Bush's vigorous efforts to rally public support for the war in Iraq, for example, citizens rapidly turned against the administration as the initial rationale for the war was called into question, progress appeared to be stalling, and casualties mounted (Patrick & Thrall, 2007).

Not surprisingly, well-liked presidents are more effective in swaying public opinion than are less popular presidents (e.g., Kernell, 1993; Mondak, 1993; Page & Shapiro, 1984; Page, Shapiro, & Dempsey, 1987). In fact, unpopular presidents sometimes produce movement in the opposite direction of their advocacy (Sigelman & Sigelman, 1981).

Presumably in part because of this popularity effect, the impact of presidential rhetoric on citizens' attitudes sometimes depends on the political party with which citizens identify. In 1997, for example, President Clinton and his administration launched an aggressive campaign to build public support for the Kyoto treaty, an international agreement to limit levels of greenhouse gasses in an effort to curb global warming. Central to this effort was the White House Conference on Global Climate Change, a gathering of government, industry, and scientific experts who delivered presentations on the issue of global warming. These presentations, which were nationally televised, kicked off an unprecedented wave of attention to global warming.

Were the Clinton administration's efforts effective? Among fellow Democrats, they were indeed quite effective, but Republicans were not moved by Clinton's efforts (Krosnick, Holbrook, & Visser, 2000). For example, in the months preceding the White House Conference on Global Climate Change, 73% of strong Democrats believed that global warming was happening, whereas 68% of strong Republicans thought so, a gap of 5%. In the wake of the conference, those figures were 87% and 69%, a gap of 18% (Krosnick, Holbrook, & Visser, 2000). Thus, a president's effectiveness in moving public opinion appears sometimes to be limited to those members of the public who share the president's political party.

Separate from their ability to shape citizens' policy preferences, presidents can sometimes draw attention to a particular issue, increasing its apparent national importance. For example, the more attention the president pays to a particular policy domain in the State of the Union address (e.g., the economy, civil rights, foreign policy), the more concern citizens express about that domain in subsequent public opinion surveys (e.g., Cohen, 1995). Other speeches also appear to influence the perceived national importance of policy domains (e.g., Behr & Iyengar, 1985).

It is difficult to fully disentangle the effect of presidential rhetoric from the impact of the media, though. Presidential speeches set the agenda for the news media to some degree (e.g., Behr & Iyengar, 1985; Edwards & Wood, 1999; Gonzenbach, 1996; Wanta & Foote, 1994), and presidential focus on an issue is inspired partly by heightened media attention to it (Edwards & Wood, 1999; Flemming, Wood, & Bohte, 1999; Gonzenbach, 1996; Wood & Peake, 1998). But the existing evidence suggests that presidential rhetoric can contribute to judgments of national seriousness.

Personality

A number of scholars have raised the possibility that some policy preferences may be influenced by core dispositions that vary across individuals. The most widely investigated of these dispositions is authoritarianism. After a number of false starts (for a review, see Altemeyer, 1981), scholars have established a conceptually coherent and empirically validated model of authoritarianism, which is defined as an interrelated set of predispositions toward submissiveness to authority, aggression toward deviants, and strict adherence to conventional traditions and norms (e.g., Altemeyer, 1981, 1988a,b, 1996).

And indeed, a number of investigations have demonstrated that individual differences in authoritarianism predict a broad range of policy preferences. For example, relative to individuals who are lower in authoritarianism, high authoritarians are more likely to support extreme and punitive policies to deal with drugs and the spread of AIDS, more likely to minimize the importance of environmental conservation and to express hostility toward environmentalists, and more like to blame the homeless for their circumstances (Peterson, Doty, & Winter, 1993). Authoritarians are also less tolerant of homosexuals (e.g., Altemeyer, 1998), more prejudiced against racial and ethnic minorities (e.g., Altemeyer, 1998), more likely to support restrictions on human rights (e.g., Moghaddam & Vuksanovic, 1990), and more supportive of war as a means of settling international disputes (e.g., Doty, Winter, Peterson, & Kemmelmeier, 1997).

Recent work suggests that the strength of these associations between authoritarianism and policy preferences varies depending on the immediate context. When the social order is perceived to be jeopardized—by leaders who falter, institutions that betray the trust of citizens, a polarized and divisive political atmosphere, or by other threatening circumstances—authoritarian predispositions become relevant and the policy gap between low and high authoritarians widens substantially (e.g., Feldman, 2003; Feldman & Stenner, 1997; Stenner, 2005).

A second dispositional factor related to policy preferences is social dominance orientation, or individual differences in the preference for hierarchical social systems over systems that are more egalitarian (e.g., Pratto, Sidanius, Stallworth, & Malle, 1994; Sidanius, Mitchell, Haley, & Navarrete, 2006). Like authoritarianism, social dominance orientation does predict policy preferences. For example, those high in social dominance orientation are less supportive of gay and lesbian rights, less supportive of women's rights, more supportive of military programs, more supportive of law and order policies, and less supportive of environmental conservation (e.g., Pratto, Sidanius, Stallworth, & Malle, 1994).

The conceptual and empirical similarities between authoritarianism and social dominance orientation have not escaped the notice of scholars. And indeed, the two constructs are related, though the correlations are typically relatively weak (e.g., Duckitt, 2001; Heaven & Connors, 2001; Heaven & St. Quintin, 2003). Further, multivariate analyses indicate that the two constructs each account for unique variance in policy preferences (e.g., Altemeyer, 1998; Van Hiel & Mervielde, 2002). And in some cases, the two constructs predict endorsement of different types of policies. For example, authoritarianism predicts punitive reactions to those who deviate from traditional norms, whereas social dominance orientation predicts punitive reactions to those from low status groups (e.g., Duckitt, 2001, 2006; Duckitt, Wagner, du Plessis, & Birum, 2002). And authoritarianism tends to predict socially conservative policy preferences whereas social dominance orientation tends to predict economically conservative policy preferences (Van Hiel, Pandelaere, & Duriez, 2004).

HOW DO PEOPLE DECIDE WITH WHICH POLITICAL PARTY TO AFFILIATE?

The nature and origins of party affiliation have been debated for decades. Simplifying only a little, the debate boils down to two different conceptualizations of party affiliation. Some have characterized party affiliation as a psychological attachment to a particular political party with roots in early socialization processes, whereas others have conceived of party affiliation in more rational terms, as a calculated decision based on policy positions, evaluations of party performance, and other criteria. Each of these perspectives is reviewed next.

Childhood Socialization

Partisanship took center stage in the study of political behavior with the publication of *The American Voter*

(Campbell, Converse, Miller, & Stokes, 1960). This conceptualization of party affiliation, which was central to what became known as the "Michigan model" of voting, was heavily influenced by social psychology. At its core was the acknowledgment that most individuals identify with particular reference groups, and that these identifications are often deeply psychologically meaningful and of great consequence. Campbell and colleagues suggested that political parties are one such reference group with which many individuals identify, and that this identification powerfully shapes political thoughts and behavior.

Campbell and his colleagues suggested that these party identifications develop through socialization processes during childhood. Much like religious affiliation, children learn from their parents to identify with a particular political party. And in part because they color the way new information is perceived, these early partisan attachments were proposed to be quite enduring (e.g., Campbell, Converse, Miller, & Stokes, 1960; Easton & Dennis, 1969; Greenstein, 1965; Hess & Torney, 1967).

For the most part the literature on political socialization supports these claims—children do tend to adopt the party identification of their parents, and these identifications do tend to be quite persistent. One of the most elaborate investigations of this issue, for example, involved a longitudinal survey of adolescents and their parents. Interviews were conducted when the children were in their late teens, and again when the children were in their mid-20s (Jennings & Niemi, 1978). The correspondence between the party identification of parents and their children was striking. Only 7% of family units involved parents who identified as Democrats or Republicans and children who identified with the other party. And for the most part this parent–child correspondence tended to persist as the children progressed from adolescence into early adulthood.

In addition to parent–child correspondence, this conceptualization of party identification also implies that partisanship should be quite stable over time. And indeed, a number of longitudinal investigations have revealed high levels of stability in party identification over several decades (e.g., Alwin, Cohen, & Newcomb, 1991; Green & Palmquist, 1994; Jennings & Markus, 1984; Sears & Funk, 1990). Although perturbations in response to extreme political circumstances have occurred, partisan orientations have tended to remain highly stable over time (for a review, see Bartels, 2000).

Partisan correspondence between parents and children is not inevitable, of course, and its occurrence is especially likely under some circumstances. For example, children are particularly likely to adopt the party identification of their parents in more politicized households, and in households in which parents have stable political attitudes themselves

(Beck & Jennings, 1991; Jennings, Stoker, & Bowers, 1999), at least in part because parents' partisan orientations are communicated more clearly and effectively in such households (Tedin, 1980). The political times also matter. Political socialization accelerates during national elections (Sears & Valentino, 1997), primarily because these salient political events serve as catalysts for political conversations between parents and children (Valentino & Sears, 1998).

Policy Preference Correspondence

As our discussion up to this point implies, party identification has often been conceived of as "an unmoved mover" (e.g., Johnston, 2006), a bedrock predisposition that determines the way political issues and events are perceived, but it is almost never determined by perceptions of those issues and events. A very different perspective suggests that party identification is indeed determined by individuals' assessments of salient issues, events, and individuals of the day.

This perspective is rooted in Downs' (1957) conceptualization of party identification as a heuristic that efficiently captures the correspondence between the party platforms and an individual's own policy preferences. Building on this foundation, some have characterized party identification as a "running tally" that summarizes the various political attitudes that citizens form over time (e.g., Fiorina, 1981). As people acquire additional information and form new attitudes, party identification presumably shifts in a Bayesian updating process (Achen, 1992). From this perspective, then, party identification is a direct function of political attitudes: Citizens identify with the party that best represents their own current political preferences.

And like a glass seen as half full or half empty, the stability of party identification (or lack thereof) has sometimes been offered as evidence for this view. That is, although stability may be the rule, scholars have provided evidence that party identification sometimes fluctuates in response to policy preferences, attitudes toward particular political candidates, and past voting behavior (e.g., Brody & Rothenberg, 1988; Fiorina, 1981; Franklin & Jackson 1983; Markus & Converse, 1979), suggesting that it is at least in part a consequence of these factors.

Reconciling these Divergent Perspectives

Is party identification an "unmoved mover," an early-formed and enduring predisposition that shapes other political attitudes, or is it instead the product of these other political attitudes? A growing body of work suggests that the causal relation between party identification and policy attitudes can run both ways, but the former tends to have a considerably stronger impact than the latter.

Setting to rest an earlier debate, for example, it has become clear that when measurement error is taken into account, party identification is tremendously stable over long spans of time and a wide array of changing political circumstances (e.g., Carsey & Layman, 2006; Green, Palmquist, & Schickler, 2002). These findings pose a strong challenge to the notion that party identification is updated in response to currently salient policy debates, political candidates, and performance evaluations.

When party identification responds to current policy preferences, the impact is small and more than offset by the reciprocal influence of party identification on current policy preferences: Even on hot-button issues like abortion, government services, and government assistance for African Americans, citizens bring their attitudes into line with their party identification (Carsey & Layman, 2006; see also Cohen, 2003). Furthermore, the effect of immediate political events on party identification is often short-lived: Citizens usually "snap back" to their earlier party identification (Green, Palmquist, & Schickler, 2002).

All of this suggests that, just as *The American Voter* proposed, party identification appears to reflect an enduring and psychologically meaningful attachment to a group. Like other important social identities, party identification appears to be deeply entrenched. And as subsequent sections of this chapter explore more fully, party identification often has far reaching consequences for thought and behavior.

Genetics?

Scholars have recently questioned whether the transmission of party identification from parent to child may occur more directly than Campbell and his colleagues ever imagined. Specifically, recent findings of a genetic component to basic political attitudes (e.g., Martin et al., 1986; Tesser, 1993) and voting behavior (e.g., Fowler, Baker, & Dawes, 2008) raise the possibility that party identification might also be at least partially transmitted through genes. In fact, however, evidence from monozygotic and dizygotic twins suggests that correspondence between parents and children in party identification is due to socialization processes and not heredity (Alford, Funk, & Hibbing, 2005).

CAUSES OF OTHER POLITICAL JUDGMENTS

National Issue Priorities

At any moment in history, large nations face complex multiplicities of problems, and no government can make significant headway in addressing all of them simultaneously. Consequently, choices must be made about which direction to devote legislative attention at any given time, and democratic policy makers make these decisions guided partly by the polity's concerns and desires (e.g., Cobb & Elder, 1972; Kingdon, 1995; Walker, 1977). These decisions are shaped by many forces, including statistical indicators of national conditions, dramatic "focusing events" that call attention to those conditions, lobbying efforts by interest groups, the development of innovative technological solutions to long-standing social problems, and more.

One of these forces is "national mood" (Kingdon, 1995). Letters and telephone calls from constituents provide an impetus for a Representative to focus legislative efforts on particular issues. And news media opinion polls identifying problems that the public considers most important for the country call legislators' attention to them and deflect their attention away from others (Cohen, 1973; Kingdon, 1981, 1995; Peters & Hogwood, 1985). Therefore, understanding the ups and downs of an issue on the legislative agenda requires understanding the issue's ups and downs on the public's agenda.

The most frequently used survey measure of the public's agenda is the so-called "most important problem" (MIP) question, developed by George Gallup in the 1930s, and variants of it. Answers to the MIP question have always been remarkably diverse, including everything from the domestic economy to crime and drugs to education to moral breakdown. Only very rarely has a single problem been mentioned by even as many as one quarter of Americans over the years, and answers are very volatile, meaning that any given problem is likely to be widely cited for only a short period, after which some other problem emerges at the top of Americans' priorities.

A look through the public opinion literature in political science, sociology, communication, and related disciplines surprisingly turns up only one widely researched explanation for the volatility in the public's national priorities. According to the media agenda-setting hypothesis, the more attention the news media accord to a problem, the more likely Americans are to consider it nationally important (McCombs & Shaw, 1972). This section describes this hypothesis, in two principal forms, outlines other related theoretical claims about the origins of citizens' national priorities, and reviews the available evidence evaluating each one.

News Media Agenda-Setting

Hypothesis One version of the notion of the media agenda-setting hypothesis begins with the presumption that political affairs are far off on the periphery of most people's thinking throughout the course of their daily lives. So when a survey researcher asks people what the most important problem facing the country is, they must work hard to generate even a single answer to this question and cite whatever comes to mind first.

According to this version of media agenda-setting, what happens to come to mind for people is at least partly and perhaps principally a function of the behavior of the news media. The more attention the media have paid to a particular problem recently, the more people have presumably thought about it. Because recent thought about a topic makes knowledge about it especially accessible in memory (Higgins & King, 1981), people seem especially likely to retrieve problems on which media attention has focused. Thus, media attention is thought to render a problem particularly accessible, leading people to cite it as the nation's most important (Iyengar, 1991, 1993; Price & Tewksbury, 1995). According to this line of thinking, agenda setting occurs because people answer the MIP question based upon relatively superficial thinking.

A second version of the media agenda-setting hypothesis does not posit it to be the result of such a passive process, mediated by the mere activation of knowledge bits in memory. This version proposes that the news media tell people what to think about (Cohen, 1963). The key word here is "telling;" the idea is that the media, by its decisions about which issues to focus upon, communicate implicit but nonetheless very clear messages about what the members of the press feel are the most significant issues facing the nation and therefore deserving of people's cognitive focus (see also McCombs & Shaw, 1972). Thus, to the extent that the staffs of the news media are perceived to be credible and authoritative observers of the national and international scenes, their views about problem importance may be adopted by their readers and viewers as well. According to this vision of the process, agenda-setting results from inferences people make about which problems they should consider important.

In either of these two versions, the agenda-setting hypothesis suggests a relatively simple relation between the volume of news media coverage of an issue and the proportion of Americans citing it as the nation's most important. The more such coverage, the more such citing should occur. At one level, this assertion might seem hopelessly naïve, because it ignores the content of news media coverage altogether. That is, the same positive relation between volume of coverage and frequency of citing is predicted, regardless of whether the news stories say that an issue is a serious problem or that it is becoming less serious.

However, this prediction is not as implausible as it may first appear, because news media stories almost never announce that a particular problem has been completely solved. Certainly, news stories sometimes report that inflation or unemployment rates have dropped, but it is very rare indeed to hear the pronouncement that issues like crime or drug abuse or pollution or honesty in government or even rising prices or joblessness are no longer problems at all for the nation. Therefore, it seems quite reasonable that even a "good news" story about an issue might enhance the accessibility of that issue in people's memories while not simultaneously convincing people that the issue is not a problem and is therefore an inappropriate answer to the MIP question. Likewise, a "good news" story may suggest an improvement in social conditions, but may simultaneously suggest that the purveyors of news think the problem is serious enough to merit attention.

Evidence   Evidence in support of the media agenda-setting hypothesis has come from a wide range of different sorts of studies. For example, the initial demonstration was a simple cross-sectional study of North Carolina undecided voters during the 1968 U.S. presidential election campaign (McCombs & Shaw, 1972). A ranking of issues from those addressed the most often to those addressed the least often corresponded almost perfectly to the frequency with which issues were cited as the ones about which respondents were "most concerned" and believed that "government should concentrate on doing something about." Various other studies have confirmed this sort of cross-sectional relation between amount of media coverage and frequency of citing problems as the nation's most important (see also Bowers, 1973; Palmgreen & Clarke, 1977; Wanta & Hu, 1994).

Other cross-sectional studies have gained empirical leverage by focusing on differences in opinions between individuals who are exposed to different media sources that themselves differ in content (e.g., Erbring, Goldenberg, & Miller, 1980). For example, McLeod (1965) studied readers of two different newspapers, one of which emphasized the control of nuclear weapons during the 1964 presidential election campaign, while the other emphasized federal spending policies. Readers of the former reported nuclear weapons to be the more important issue, whereas readers of the latter described federal spending policies as the more important issue (see also Miller & Wanta, 1996; Wanta, 1997).

Laboratory experiments have also been conducted to test this hypothesis. In many such studies, exposure to particular news stories was experimentally manipulated (e.g., Iyengar & Kinder, 1987; Iyengar, Peters, & Kinder, 1982). Consistent with the agenda-setting notion, people exposed to news coverage of a given issue subsequently rate the issue to be more important (see also Wanta, 1988). Field experiments involving exposure to actual news broadcasts in people's own homes have yielded similar findings (e.g., Cook et al., 1983; Leff, Protess, & Brooks, 1986). However, experiments to date have only documented very short-term effects on public concern (lasting up to a week), leaving open the question of whether agenda-setting has the power to yield meaningful political consequences in the course of ordinary daily life over the longer term.

In this light, the most important body of evidence regarding agenda-setting involves analysis of time series data on changes in media coverage and public concerns over time. Many such studies have yielded evidence that increases in media coverage of problems preceded increases in selections of a problem as the most important issue (e.g., Behr & Iyengar, 1985; Iyengar & Simon, 1993; MacKuen & Coombs, 1981; Watt, Mazza, & Snyder, 1993).

The Real-World Cues Hypothesis

To date, researchers have explored only one strong challenge to this last set of evidence: the real-world cues hypothesis. According to this perspective, the time–series evidence apparently consistent with agenda-setting is attributable to the fact that the news media and ordinary Americans respond similarly to changes in the objective seriousness of problems. When a problem truly becomes more serious, the media may be the first to recognize this and to convey this information to the public. A bit more slowly, the public may come to learn of this change in real circumstances, and the more news media attention is devoted to it, the more quickly the public learns. So the surge in public concern about a problem following increased media coverage of it may be due not merely to enhanced accessibility of the problem in people's memories or to acceptance of the implicit message that news media personnel believe a problem is important. Rather, it may be due to people coming to recognize what the media have already seen: that the problem has in fact become more significant. Consistent with this argument, the frequency with which people cite a problem as the nation's most important is a function of real-world cues about the seriousness of the problem (e.g., Behr & Iyengar, 1985; Hill, 1998; Iyengar & Kinder, 1987; Schuman, Ludwig, & Krosnick, 1986).

The Issue-Attention Cycle

The issue-attention cycle offers another conceptualization of the origins of MIP question responses (Downs, 1972). According to this vision, the processes at work are quite a bit more thoughtful and responsible than those described by the agenda-setting hypothesis. A foundation of this view is the assumption that contemporary society is complex and multifaceted; millions of Americans are attempting to manage a wide range of different problems challenging the country from many different directions. At any given moment, most people may be occupied by a series of problems that are consensually recognized as serious. But in the background, unnoticed by most people, other problems are emerging as significant.

Public consciousness may progress through a series of stages (Downs,1972). Stage 1 is what Downs called the "preproblem" stage, during which an objectively serious problem exists, but without the awareness of the vast majority of the public. Movement to Stage 2 occurs when a dramatic event suddenly calls people's attention to the highly undesirable situation, to which they had been oblivious (see also Cobb & Elder, 1972; Hilgartner & Bosk, 1988; Kingdon, 1995). The sharp surge in public concern that occurs at this time is partly the result of this new awareness, but also the result of optimistic and enthusiastic rhetoric from political leaders, asserting that the problem is important and can be solved with minimal disruption to the social order, as long as enough resources are devoted to ameliorative efforts.

Stage 3 begins when people begin to realize that the initially optimistic rhetoric regarding the problem's tractability was most likely unrealistic. People come to see that the actual financial costs of solving the problem will be substantial, and that many people will experience major lifestyle inconveniences in the course of implementing effective solutions. Stage 4 begins when the realizations of Stage 3 provoke some people to become discouraged about the prospects of solving the problem, others to feel threatened by the proposed solutions (and therefore to defensively downplay the problem's significance), and still others to become bored with the public discussion that has no promise of a happy outcome (see also Hilgartner & Bosk, 1988). At this time, some other issue moves into Stage 2, taking center stage in public debate, and people running the news media recognize that the public is becoming bored. The media therefore shift their focus elsewhere, pushing the target issue into Stage 5, the postproblem stage, during which people are no longer explicitly concerned about it.

This account of shifts in public concern certainly implicates the news media, because they are the conduits through which public discussions take place and information is shared throughout a society. So the media are essential for the process to unfold. But the impact of the media's actions is thought to be due to the content of the messages they deliver about the state of social reality, not to the media's ability to alter the mere accessibility of knowledge or to communicate the views of their staffs about what issues are significant. Thus, this account is fundamentally quite different from the agenda-setting notion.

Presidential Approval

Presidents have more success in achieving their legislative agendas when they enjoy high levels of approval from the American public (Bond, Fleisher, & Wood, 2003;

Canes-Wrone & de Marchi, 2002; Ostrom & Simon, 1985; Rivers & Rose, 1985). Furthermore, high levels of presidential approval significantly enhance the chances that the president's political party will gain seats in midterm Congressional elections, affecting the reelection prospects most of representatives who supported the president the most (Abramowitz, 1984, 1985; Abramowitz & Segal, 1992; Gronke, Koch, & Wilson, 2003). And popular approval of the president is an important determinant of whether the president's political party retains the White House in the next election (e.g., Sigelman, 1979). Not surprisingly, then, presidents routinely take steps to try to increase their approval ratings (see Brody, 1991; Brody & Sigelman, 1983). And job approval ratings of the president seem likely to be an important determinant of the degree of confidence that citizens have in their government. Thus, the forces that drive presidential approval up and down are terrifically consequential, and a great deal of research has explored these forces.

Honeymoon Period

For most presidents, a honeymoon period of high ratings occurs at the beginning of their terms; approval declines thereafter (Brace & Hinckley, 1991; Norpoth, 1996; Stimson, 1976). One possible explanation for this pattern is that every major policy decision angers or disappoints some citizens, and the more time passes, the more such decisions are made, and the more dissatisfied citizens accumulate (Mueller, 1970, 1973). An alternative account proposes that people who are generally uninterested in politics pay attention during campaigns when presidents promise to solve problems, and these people then become disappointed as time passes and these goals are not achieved quickly (Stimson, 1976). Citizens who are more attentive to politics may attend instead to campaign promises about specific policies to be implemented, and when presidents fail to pass those policies, they may suffer disapproval.

In fact, the decline is mostly among people who identify with the major party that is not the president's (Presser & Converse, 1976–77). These are just the people who are likely to be most dissatisfied with the policies pursued by the president, suggesting that the disappointment is due not to failure to implement promised policies but instead is due to efforts to pursue undesirable policies.

When a new president is elected, public optimism about what that person will accomplish is high (see Sigelman & Knight, 1983, 1985). But as time passes after the election, the public gradually lowers its beliefs about what the president can accomplish during the term, and these expectations about likely accomplishments are important determinants of approval levels (see also Ostrom & Simon, 1985).

Impact of Events and Beliefs

Many investigations have identified specific beliefs that shape overall approval and the process by which this shaping occurs. Most generally, a president's approval is driven by approval of the president's handling of specific issues (Druckman & Holmes, 2004; Iyengar, Peters, Kinder, & Krosnick, 1984; Malhotra & Krosnick, 2007; Newman, 2003). That is, presidents are seen as doing a better job overall if they are perceived to be doing a better job at handling the economy, international relations, and an array of other challenges facing the country.

An especially large amount of research has drilled down beneath this seemly simple surface to identify what aspects of the economy are especially consequential in citizens' thinking about the president.

Macroeconomic Indicators To do so, some researchers have predicted changes over time in aggregate approval levels using various different indicators of the health of the national economy, such as the national unemployment and inflation rates. And in general, these indicators have usually been found to predict approval as expected, though not always. For example, some studies have shown that as inflation rises, presidential approval declines (e.g., Burden & Mughan, 2003; Gronke & Brehm, 2002; Nicholson, Segura, & Woods, 2002; c.f., Clarke, Rapkin, & Stewart, 1994; MacKuen, Erikson, & Stimson, 1992), and some studies have found that as unemployment rises, presidential approval falls (e.g., Burden & Mughan, 2003; Gronke & Brehm, 2002; Kriner, 2006; c.f., Geys & Vermeir, 2008; Nicholson, Segura, & Woods, 2002).

Studies of other macroeconomic indicators have also generally yielded expected findings, though not always. Presidential approval appears to increase when GDP increases (Nicholson, Segura, & Woods, 2002), when the tax burden of Americans declines (Clarke, Rapkin, & Stewart, 1994; Geys & Vermeir, 2008), when the federal deficit declines (Geys & Vermeir, 2008), and when people's incomes increase (Clarke, Rapkin, & Stewart, 1994; Kriner, 2006; Monroe & Laughlin, 1983). Whereas one study found that presidential approval rises when success of U.S. trade with other nations increases (Burden & Mughan, 2003), another study found no such relation (Monroe, 1979). And presidential approval appeared to be unrelated to interest rates (Monroe, 1978, 1979) or to improvements in the stock market (Monroe, 1978; Monroe & Laughlin, 1983).

So it appears that conclusions about the relations of macroeconomic indicators hinge on exactly which survey data are used, which time period is studied, and what control variables are included in an analysis. Although it seems that presidents enjoy benefits when the nation's economy improves and suffer when the economy declines, more work is needed to illuminate the conditions under which these effects appear.

Perceptions of the Economy Two contrasting hypotheses attempt to account for the relations of approval with macroeconomic indicators. The "pocketbook" hypothesis was long taken for granted by observers: The better the economy is doing, the more individual citizens are enjoying good or improving economic circumstances. And these people translate their personal pleasure into approval for the president. The "sociotropic" hypothesis suggests instead that people are not focused only on their own fortunes and misfortunes. Instead, people are thought to evaluate the nation's economy and to credit the president for its improvements and blame the president for its declines. Of course, both of these hypotheses could be true—some people might make pocketbook-based judgments whereas others make sociotropic judgments. Or the same individuals might take both sorts of considerations into account when evaluating the president.

Two contrasting hypotheses have also been offered about temporal orientation. The retrospective hypothesis proposes that people look at recent changes in the economy in the past. When their own or the nation's conditions are improving, citizens are thought to reward the president. The prospective hypothesis suggests that people look into the future and make predictions about the likely trajectory of their own or the nation's financial conditions. When things are looking up, presidents are thought to be rewarded.

Studies have sometimes looked at the relation of presidential approval to objective indicators of people's own personal economic conditions and have generally found no such relations. For example, Lau and Sears (1981) found no lower approval ratings among people who were unemployed or underemployed or experienced recent declines in personal income.

Most studies in this area have compared the impact of subjective retrospective and prospective judgments of personal and national economic conditions. And these studies have yielded nearly unanimous support for the retrospective and prospective sociotropic hypotheses (Clarke & Stewart, 1994; Clarke, Rapkin, & Stewart, 1994; Clarke, Stewart, Ault, & Elliott, 2004; Druckman & Holmes, 2004; Greene, 2001). Studies that focused on perceptions of improvements and declines in "business conditions" have also yielded mostly supportive evidence (MacKuen, Erikson, & Stimson, 1992; Norpoth, 1996).

Fewer studies have gauged the impact of judgments of personal economic conditions on approval ratings, but the

majority of them have also yielded confirmatory evidence. People who say that their personal financial situations have improved (Clarke, Stewart, Ault, & Elliott, 2004; Druckman & Holmes, 2004; Nicholson, Segura, & Woods, 2002) or will improve in the future (Clarke, Stewart, Ault, & Elliott, 2004; Nicholson, Segura, & Woods, 2002) are more likely to approve of the president's performance.

Some scholars have argued that these latter findings involving judgments of personal economic conditions are artifactual (Lau, Sears, & Jessor, 1990; Sears & Lau, 1983). When survey questions measuring perceptions of personal economic experiences are asked immediately before or immediately after questions assessing presidential approval, these measures are strongly associated with one another, whereas when the questions are asked during different interviews, they are no longer associated with one another.

However, the apparent impact of personal economic experiences may be underestimated in analyses like these (Kinder & Mebane, 1983). People's perceptions of the nation's economic circumstances are partly shaped by their own personal economic circumstances. That is, people sometimes generalize from their own lives to the nation as a whole. People who are suffering economically are especially inclined to believe that the nation is doing badly economically. And people who are enjoying economic successes are especially likely to think that the country is doing well economically. So, personal grievances can impact incumbent evaluations indirectly by shaping perceptions of the nation as a whole.

If personal economic conditions are not in fact determinants of presidential approval, one possible explanation may involve attributions (Brody & Sniderman, 1977; Sniderman & Brody, 1977). Personal economic suffering may only impact presidential approval among citizens who believe that government should be doing more to help solve their economic problems. Although most Americans hold their government responsible for solving national problems, citizens rarely hold government responsible for solving their own personal problems (Kinder & Mebane, 1983). This is because people rarely hold government responsible for causing their own personal traumas.

Consistent with this reasoning, people who blame government for national economic problems place more weight on their perceptions of those problems when evaluating the president (Kinder & Mebane, 1983). Similarly, the impact of perceptions of the economy on presidential approval is most pronounced among people who hold the president responsible for economic events (Rudolph, 2003).

International Conflict Presidential approval is also influenced by international events and perceptions of them.

When the United States becomes engaged in an international conflict, presidential approval typically increases. This can be in the form of an attack on the United States or its interests by another nation, or it can be in the form of aggressive action by the United States toward another nation, presumably signaling that the nation is perceived to pose a threat. For example, approval spiked at the time of the start of the first and second Gulf wars, the Iraq invasion of Kuwait, the U.S. bombing of Libya in 1986, the U.S. invasion of Granada, the September 11 attacks on the World Trade Center and the Pentagon, and the U.S. invasion of Panama (Geys & Vermeir, 2008; Gronke & Brehm, 2002; Nadeau, Niemi, Fan, & Amato, 1999; Ostrom & Job, 1986; Peffley, Langley, & Goidel, 1995).

These are examples of what Mueller (1970, 1973) called "rally round the flag" events, and many studies have documented short-lived increases in approval following rally events (e.g., Brody & Shapiro, 1989a; Lian & Oneal, 1993; Mueller, 1970, 1973; Oneal, Lian, & Joyner, 1996). Some people think this is due to the temporary disappearance of criticism of the president by other political elites (Brody & Shapiro, 1989b) and the coming together of diverse partisans in support of the president's response (Oneal et al., 1996).

Nonmilitary events that signal conflicts between the United States and another nation can also instigate surges in public approval of the president, such as the Tiananmen Square incident in China, the taking of the Iranian hostages, the Cuban Missile Crisis, and the Soviet invasion of Afghanistan (e.g., Clarke, Stewart, Ault, & Elliott, 2004; Nadeau, Niemi, Fan, & Amato 1999). When a nonmilitary international conflict between nations occurs, presidents increase their approval most by responding vigorously *without* using military force (James & Rioux, 1998). Use of military force actually decreases approval initially, in contrast to the more sizable increase in approval that can follow a vigorous nonmilitary response by the president.

Following an international attack on the United States, public approval increases most after the president makes a nationwide speech about the attack, thus presumably taking responsibility for action and articulating a plan (Peffley, Langley, & Goidel, 1995). Consistent with this logic, the post–September 11 increase in presidential approval was more pronounced among people who saw President Bush's speech reassuring the nation than among people who did not (Schubert, Stewart, & Curran, 2002).

The outcomes of short-term international conflicts have interesting and perhaps surprising effects on presidential approval. When an international conflict leads to a compromise between the United States and its opponent(s), presidential approval increases as a result of the compromise. But if the conflict leads to a stalemate, to the defeat of the United States, or, most surprisingly, a victory for the United States, presidential approval does not change as a result (James & Rioux, 1998).

When international military conflicts last a long time, presidential approval declines gradually and predictably. This may occur because Americans are willing to support a war with enthusiasm if no U.S. casualties are incurred, but people become increasingly unhappy with the president as the number of fatalities accumulates (Mueller, 1973). Consistent with this logic, many investigators have found that the more American troops die in combat during a president's term, the lower the president's approval ratings fall (Hibbs, 1982; Kriner, 2006; Mueller, 1973).

Even the increased threat of international conflict can translate into increased presidential approval. Presidential approval increases after government-issued warnings about the possibility of an impending terrorist attack (Willer, 2004).

Policy Successes Not surprisingly, presidential approval increases after visible successes of government efforts. For example, President George W. Bush's approval increased after Sadam Hussein was finally captured, following a prolonged hunt for him (Willer, 2004). Likewise, the signing of the Camp David Peace Accords increased President Carter's approval rating (Nadeau, Niemi, Fan, & Amato, 1999).

Scandals Also not surprisingly, presidential approval drops follow the public revelation of scandalous behavior by the president or members of the administration. This occurred following the revelation of the Iran–Contra scandal involving President Reagan (Clarke, Stewart, Ault, & Elliott, 2004; Geys & Vermeir, 2008) and Watergate (Geys & Vermeir, 2008; Gronke & Brehm, 2002; Newman, 2002).

Personal Trauma Presidential approval increases following personal traumas experienced by the president, such as the assassination attempt on President Reagan (Clarke, Stewart, Ault, & Elliott, 2004; Nadeau, Niemi, Fan, & Amato, 1999).

Presidential Travel Abroad Although some people have speculated that simply taking a trip abroad is sufficient to increase a president's approval rating, this appears not to be the case (Simon & Ostrom, 1989).

Presidential Speeches Presidential approval has sometimes surged following presidential speeches addressing the nation (Kriner, 2006; Ragsdale, 1984). However, a presidential speech alone does not increase or decrease approval (Simon & Ostrom, 1989). A presidential speech occurring during the time of an approval-enhancing event increases approval more than the event alone would, and a presidential speech occurring during the time of an approval-diminishing event decreases approval more than would have occurred without the speech.

Political Party Conventions   A president's approval rating increases when the president's political party holds its national convention prior to an upcoming election (Clarke, Rapkin, & Stewart, 1994), perhaps because such conventions involve many visible endorsements of the president.

Tone of News Coverage   When news coverage of the president turns negative, approval ratings tend to decline as a result. And when news coverage praises presidential successes, approval ratings increase as a result (Brody, 1991; West, 1991).

Perceptions of the President's Personality   Not surprisingly, presidential approval is generally higher among citizens who believe the president is more competent (Gilens, 1988; Greene, 2001; Newman, 2003), has more integrity (Druckman & Holmes, 2004; Greene, 2001; Newman, 2003), and is a stronger leader (Druckman & Holmes, 2004; West, 1991). Interestingly, approval seems not to be driven by the extent to which the president is perceived to be empathetic to the needs and experiences of the nation's citizens (Druckman & Holmes, 2004).

Emotions Evoked by the President   When presidents evoke more positive emotions and fewer negative emotions from citizens, they tend to enjoy higher approval ratings (Gilens, 1988).

Divided Government   When things go badly in the country, the president runs the risk of being blamed (Nicholson, Segura, & Woods, 2002). But when the Congress is not controlled by the president's political party, responsibility for national conditions can be partly blamed on Congressional representatives. Therefore, in times of divided government, presidents tend to enjoy higher approval ratings (Nicholson, Segura, & Woods, 2002; Baum, 2002; Burden & Mughan, 2003).

Sharing the President's Party Identification and Ideology
Citizens who share the president's party affiliation tend to approve at higher rates than citizens who do not share that affiliation (e.g., Greene, 2001; Newman, 2003; Nicholson, Segura, & Woods, 2002; Rudolph, 2003). Likewise, citizens who share the president's liberal or conservative ideology tend to approve at higher rates than citizens who do

not share that ideology (Rudolph, 2003; Newman, 2003; Nicholson, Segura, & Woods, 2002).

Agreement on Policy Issues   Presidential approval is enhanced among people who shared more of the president's positions on key policy issues, such as military spending, government assistance programs for the poor, women's rights, and the environment (Gilens, 1988; Thomas, Sigelman, & Baas, 1984).

Citizen Personality   Approval of Republican presidents is most likely by citizens who are high in consciousness and stability and low in openness to new experiences but is unrelated to extraversion, and agreeableness (Gerber, Green, & Latimer, 2008).

News Media Priming

A large amount of literature has posed that the criteria used to make presidential approval judgments shift over time as the result of changes in the volume of news media attention to issues. According to the original formulation of the "news media priming" hypothesis, people base their overall presidential evaluations most heavily on the issues that are most accessible in long-term memory. That is, when asked to evaluate the present, people use whatever issues happen to come to mind, which are those made most accessible by recent, frequent activation. A large number of news stories about an issue were thought to increase the accessibility of related knowledge in people's memories, thereby enhancing the issue's impact on approval ratings (Iyengar & Kinder, 1987; Iyengar, Peters, Kinder, & Krosnick, 1984; Price & Tewksbury, 1997).

Two forms of evidence support this hypothesis: (1) laboratory experiments contrasting people who saw or read no news stories or programs about an issue with people who saw or read many such stories (e.g. Holbrook & Hill, 2005; Iyengar, Peters, Kinder, & Krosnick, 1984; Iyengar & Kinder, 1987; Miller & Krosnick, 2000; Valentino, Traugott, & Hutchings, 2002); and (2) surveys comparing the correlations among attitudes of Americans when an issue got little or no media attention with those correlations during a later period when the issue received a huge amount of national news coverage (e.g., Kiousis, 2003; Krosnick & Kinder, 1990; Stoker, 1993; van der Brug, Semetko, & Valkenburg, 2007). Thus, the independent variable (amount of media coverage) was varied between essentially zero and a large amount across samples of people. Both of these methods are valid approaches to assessing whether consumption of a large amount of news media coverage of a domain causes citizens to use that domain in judging the president to a greater extent than people who consumed no coverage.

A close examination of the language in those papers and wider discussions of their findings in print reveals an interesting leap made by analysts: that as news media attention to an issue increases, so does the weight that people attach to the domain when evaluating the president. That is, this language posits a *dosage-response hypothesis*. It is not merely that the presence of news media coverage causes priming, but the *amount* of priming is presumed to increase monotonically with the *amount* of coverage (Krosnick & Brannon, 1993; Krosnick & Kinder, 1990; Stoker, 1993).

Direct tests of the dosage hypothesis are rare. Some studies have not supported it (Iyengar & Kinder, 1987; Malhotra & Krosnick, 2007). However, other studies have provided more supportive evidence (Althaus & Kim, 2006; McAvoy, 2006; Togeby, 2007). Thus, it appears that volume of media coverage does not regulate issue impact on presidential approval in a simple way. Clearly, substantial coverage of an issue focuses public attention on that issue, but smaller shifts in the volume of coverage may not be especially consequential. And perhaps the effect of coverage does not happen quickly—rather, perhaps coverage needs to focus on an issue for an extended period of time for it to have enhanced impact. Further work on the dosage hypothesis is merited.

Another challenge to the original version of the priming hypothesis involves its purported cognitive mechanism: accessibility. News stories about an issue were thought to increase the accessibility of relevant information in long-term memory, which in turn was thought to enhance the issue's impact on presidential approval judgments. But laboratory experimental evidence showed that although news stories on an issue do increase the accessibility of relevant knowledge, this increase in accessibility is not responsible for the issue's increased impact on presidential evaluations. That is, the people who manifest the strongest increases in accessibility are not the people who manifested the strongest priming effects (Althaus & Kim, 2006; Miller & Krosnick, 2000).

Other evidence suggests that quite a different mechanism is at work (Miller & Krosnick, 2000). Priming occurs exclusively among people who trust the news media to provide accurate and balanced information on appropriate issues. This suggests that people who manifest news media priming choose to be influenced by the news media. That is, these citizens believe that the media focus their attention on issues that are especially nationally important and deserve special weight when evaluating political actors. So these citizens accept that recommendation from this trusted source and construct their presidential approval ratings accordingly. Interestingly, priming is especially pronounced among people who are highly knowledgeable about politics, perhaps suggesting that keeping a running tally of news media attention to particular issues is especially likely among political experts and less likely among people who know little about politics, perhaps pay less attention to political news stories, and do not keep conscious track of what issues have received extensive coverage.

Impact of Presidential Rhetoric

The news media are not the only source of priming effects. Presidents themselves can change the criteria that the public uses to evaluate them. By focusing their public statements on particular issues, presidents can lead citizens to place extra weight on those issues when constructing overall performance evaluations (Druckman & Holmes, 2004).

Personal Importance Attached to Policy Issues

As was discussed earlier, the amount of personal importance that citizens attach to their attitudes toward policies is an especially significant factor facilitating responsible electoral behavior. The more importance people attach to an issue, the more informed they become about it, the more thoughtful they are about it, the more the issue shapes their vote choices, and the more likely they are to express relevant policy preferences to government officials. As reassuring as all this sounds in terms of the functioning of democracy, that assessment cannot be made without an understanding of who attaches importance to which policy issues and why.

Two primary and quite different hypotheses address this issue. The first has its roots clearly in the writings of Gabriel Almond (1950), who proposed that political engagement is concentrated among a relatively small proportion of a democratic electorate. He referred to these individuals as "the attentive public," who might make up 15% of a polity. These are people who are highly educated about political and civic affairs, attend closely to all aspects of politics, stay up to the minute on national and international developments, are widely informed about and engaged in a wide array of policy issues, know a great deal about political actors and current debates, and therefore manifest all the hallmarks of issue public membership for the full array of issues facing a nation at any one time. In contrast, the vast majority of citizens were thought to be uninformed, disengaged, and uninvolved. Thus, according to this vision, a small fraction of the population speaks on behalf of many, many others (see also Price & Zaller, 1993).

The contrasting hypothesis envisions issue public memberships as widely dispersed across a nation. Rather than concentrating the effort and responsibility among a small group of citizens, this hypothesis proposes that effort and responsibility are shared broadly—different people choose to engage in different issues. Thus, the work entailed in directing government activities is widely distributed across the population. And the assignment of issues to individuals is thought to be driven by three psychological forces.

First, an issue may become important to individuals who perceive the attitude object to be linked to their material self-interests (e.g., Apsler & Sears, 1968; Petty, Cacioppo, & Haugtvedt, 1991). Self-interest-based importance develops when people perceive an issue to be linked to their tangible rights, privileges, or lifestyle. Perceived self-interest is likely to be high among people who feel their own personal well-being may be directly affected by an issue in some immediate and concrete manner (Modigliani & Gamson, 1979; Popkin, Gorman, Phillips, & Smith, 1976). Thus, for example, a gun owner in a high-crime neighborhood who learns that local gun control laws are being considered will be more likely to consider his attitude toward gun control to be personally important than someone who does not own a gun and lives in a low-crime neighborhood.

An issue may also become personally important to someone as a result of social identification with reference groups or reference individuals. Strong identification with a social group may lead an issue to become important to a person if the group's rights or privileges are perceived to be at stake (Key, 1961; Modigliani & Gamson, 1979). Thus, a Black Wall Street executive who identifies closely with Blacks as a group may care deeply about social welfare programs for the urban poor, even though she is unlikely to be affected directly by such programs. Strong identification with a group that consensually considers an issue to be important can serve as an impetus for importance, independent of whether rewards for the group are in question (Sherif & Hovland, 1961). For example, people who strongly identify with Catholics are likely to care deeply about abortion, because the Catholic Church has publicly declared that issue's importance and has taken a strong stand on it. Similarly, importance may develop as a result of identification with reference individuals whose interests are perceived to be at stake or who are perceived to care deeply about a particular issue.

Finally, an issue may become personally important to people if they come to view it as relevant to their basic social and personal values. Values are abstract beliefs (not specific to any attitude object) about proper modes of behavior, about how the world ought to be, or about the worthiness of various long-term goals (Rokeach, 1968). Values may also tell people which policy issues to consider personally important. Therefore, the closer the perceived linkage between an issue and an individual's values, and the more important the values, the more important the issue

is likely to be to him or her (Campbell, Converse, Miller, & Stokes, 1960; Katz, 1960; Rosenberg, 1956).

A good deal of evidence is consistent with this latter account. For example, when people are asked to explain why they do or do not attach personal importance to a particular policy issue, most of the explanations cite either self-interest, social identification, or value relevance, with self-interest dominating (Boninger, Krosnick, & Berent, 1995). Likewise, statistical analyses of survey data show that issue importance ratings are best predicted by self-interest ratings and that ratings of social identification and value relevance explain additional variance as well (Boninger, Krosnick, & Berent, 1995; Holbrook, Berent, Krosnick, Visser, & Boninger, 2005). In an experiment, inducing participants to imagine themselves getting into a car accident led them to see their self-interest as more at stake in the issue of traffic safety laws, which in turn induced these people to attach personal importance to the issue. Likewise, when other experimental participants were told that an impending policy change would affect them personally, this led them to perceive greater self-interest at stake in the issue, which in turn induced more personal importance being attached to it (Bizer & Krosnick, 2001).

Taken together, these studies suggest that self-interest is consistently a primary determinant of the degree of personal importance people attach to their attitudes. Values were also fairly consistent causes of personal importance, but much weaker ones. Social identification's effects appeared sometimes and not others, apparently depending on the prominence of major social cleavages over the issue involved.

These findings suggest that issue public membership is likely to be idiosyncratic, such that each individual attaches personal importance to just a few issues that touch him or her directly somehow. And indeed, other evidence supports this conclusion by showing that issue public membership is not concentrated among a small portion of the population. Knowing the amount of personal importance that a person attaches to one policy issue affords very little ability to predict the amount of importance that person attaches to another issue (Krosnick, 1986). The amount of personal importance an individual attaches to any one issue is also essentially uncorrelated with indicators of general political engagement, such as the degree to which people say they are interested in politics and the amount of formal education people have (Krosnick, 1986). Furthermore, the impact of personal importance in regulating issue impact on vote choices remains robust even when controlling for the role of general political involvement in regulating this impact (Anand & Krosnick, 2003). All this sustains the portrait of issue public membership as being distributed broadly across the American populace, which reinforces the claim that sharing responsibility in this fashion allows people to be thoughtful and responsible in their limited issue domains.

CAUSES OF POLITICAL KNOWLEDGE

We began this chapter by contemplating the demands that democracy places on its citizens for the system to function effectively. Chief among these requirements is the possession of relevant information, which enables citizens to formulate preferences and effectively advocate for their desired outcomes. But how do citizens acquire the information that they need to meet these demands? To understand this question, it is useful to consider the general processes by which people become knowledgeable about topics.

For the most part, people gain knowledge about an object through two processes: (1) through direct experience with the object (Fazio & Zanna, 1981; Wood, Rhodes, & Biek, 1995); and (2) through exposure and attention to information about the object from other people, received during informal conversations (Robinson & Levy, 1986), formal schooling (Nie, Junn, & Stehlik-Barry, 1996), or through the mass media (McGuire, 1986; Roberts & Maccoby, 1985). Knowledge about social and political issues is especially likely to be acquired through the latter route: through exposure and attention to information provided by other people, especially by the news media (Clarke & Fredin, 1978; Clarke & Kline, 1974; Perse, 1990).

But exposure to information is just the first of several steps that must unfold for knowledge acquisition to occur. Having been exposed to a new piece of information, an individual must then devote perceptual attention to the information, bringing it into short-term or working memory (Baddeley & Hitch, 1974). The world is altogether too complex for people to attend to all of the stimuli that bombard their senses at any given moment, so people selectively attend to some things and filter out the vast majority of others. Some of the information that is brought into short-term or working memory undergoes elaboration, during which an individual actively thinks about the new information and relates it to information already stored in memory. Through this, process-associative links are built, connecting new information to previously acquired information (Craik & Lockhart, 1972). The more extensively an individual processes new information, the stronger the neural trace and the more likely it is that the new information will be available for later retrieval (e.g., Craik, 1977; Tyler, Hertel, MacCallum, & Ellis, 1979). Thus, the process of acquiring knowledge about the political world is costly, imposing tremendous cognitive demands (Downs, 1957).

These demands are especially high for people who have little political knowledge to begin with. Prior knowledge on a particular topic improves people's ability to comprehend new information, enabling them to efficiently extract the central elements of a message and draw appropriate inferences (Eckhardt, Wood, & Jacobvitz, 1991; Recht & Leslie, 1988). Prior knowledge also enhances people's ability to store new information on that topic and retrieve the information later (e.g., Cooke, Atlas, Lane, & Berger, 1993; Fiske, Lau, & Smith, 1990; McGraw & Pinney, 1990; Recht & Leslie, 1988; Schneider, Gruber, Gold, & Opwis, 1993). So the less political information a person has stored in memory, the more difficult it is for him or her to acquire new information.

In addition to the substantial cognitive burdens it imposes, the acquisition of political knowledge also involves other costs. In particular, it reduces the resources available for acquiring information about other topics. The more people are exposed to information about political issues and objects, and the more resources they devote to attending to and elaborating this information, the less likely it is that other available information will be stored in long-term memory and available for later retrieval (e.g., Kahneman, 1973). Thus, becoming more knowledgeable about political matters often comes at the cost of gaining knowledge about other topics.

Determinants of Political Knowledge

Under what circumstances are people willing to bear the cognitive burdens and opportunity costs of becoming politically knowledgeable? And how do people select among the myriad political issues and objects that vie for their attention?

Incidental Media Exposure   People sometimes learn about the political world through incidental exposure to news media coverage of politics (Krugman & Hartley, 1970; Zukin & Snyder, 1984). For example, people with no particular interest in politics may nonetheless become politically knowledgeable because they routinely watch the evening news, either out of habit or because another household member regularly tunes in. This type of passive learning may be especially likely for televised news broadcasts, which often contain vivid graphics and visual images that require fewer cognitive resources to decode and retain in memory (Graber, 1990).

Nonselective Media Exposure   People also intentionally expose themselves to information about the political world. Many people tune into general television or radio news programs that cover a range of political topics, for example, and doing so leads to increases in political knowledge (e.g., Delli Carpini & Keeter, 1996; Roberts & Maccoby, 1985). The flowing nature of television and radio news programs does not easily afford news media consumers opportunities to selectively expose themselves to some stories and not others. Therefore, choosing to watch or hear such programs typically brings with it non-selective exposure to information on many topics.

The decision to tune in to television or radio news broadcasts is of course influenced by interest in politics: Those who find politics intrinsically interesting are much more likely to intentionally expose themselves to news programming than those who are disinterested in politics (e.g., Delli Carpini & Keeter, 1996; Luskin, 1990). News media consumption is also influenced by more general surveillance motives: Those who are more intrinsically motivated to monitor their environment pay more attention and give more thought to news broadcasts than those who are lower in this motivation (e.g., Eveland, Shah, & Kwak, 2003).

Issue-Specific Selective Attention   People are selective not only in terms of the overall amount of attention they pay to the news media, but also regarding the amount of attention they pay to media coverage of specific issues. Indeed, people sometimes actively seek out information about some issue but make no special effort to gain information about other issues, rendering them deeply knowledgeable about the former and less informed about the latter.

How do people decide which issues to attend to? One answer is suggested by the positive correlation between the volume of knowledge a person has stored in memory about an object and the personal importance people attach to their attitudes toward the object. People consider themselves more knowledgeable about an object when their attitudes toward it are important to them (e.g., Bassili, 1996; Krosnick, Boninger, Chuang, Berent, & Carnot, 1993; Prislin, 1996; Visser, 1998), and they are in fact able to retrieve more information about the attitude object from memory (Berent & Krosnick, 1995; Krosnick, Boninger, Chuang, Berent, & Carnot, 1993; Wood, 1982). The knowledge accompanying more important attitudes is also more likely to be accurate (Krosnick, 1990). These associations suggest that attitude importance may provide the impetus for knowledge acquisition, motivating people to gather and retain information about some attitude objects at the expense of learning about others.

This occurs because attitude importance guides people's choices when they are deciding to which information they will attend (Holbrook, Berent, Krosnick, Visser, & Boninger, 2005). They selectively attend to information relevant to their more important attitudes, particularly when available information is abundant and time or cognitive resources are limited. After people are exposed to

information, they process it more deeply if it is relevant to important attitudes, because such processing is likely to serve strategic purposes later. As a result, this new information is more likely to be stored in long-term memory and available for later retrieval.

SUMMARY

Clearly, a great deal of research has explored the forces that drive political thinking and action. And our review covers only a subset of this literature—much more fascinating work has explored many other aspects of the cognition and behavior of ordinary citizens, of political leaders, and of nations. And much of this work illuminates fundamentals of human perception, judgment, decision making, choice, social influence, and action.

As is presumably apparent, this literature is quite a bit more flattering to citizens than many past accounts have suggested. Most of the determinants of political outcomes seem quite reasonable normatively. To be sure, evidence that votes are influenced by the order of candidate names on the ballot, for example, is at least a bit troubling. But relative to the magnitude of other influences on vote choices, name order effects are quite small, which itself is reassuring. And the conditions under which these effects occur point the finger of blame more to the tremendous demands placed on voters to express preferences in many races without easy access to information with which to make substantive judgments, rather than to laziness or incompetence of voters themselves. The literature on the causes of vote choices, presidential approval, turnout, and other such phenomena point, for the most part, to factors that seem reasonable rather than dooming contemporary democracies to destruction.

Consider, for example, the work on presidential approval: These judgments appear to be based on many sensible considerations. Rewarding the president for domestic and international successes seems quite reasonable, as does punishing the president for national failures. Of course, a more refined view of events might lead an observer to say that some such rewarding and punishing is not deserved, either because the president was neither responsible for causing nor creating a problem, nor are there obvious government-based mechanisms for solving it. But issues of causal responsibility and solvability are no doubt debatable, so it seems difficult to justify a claim that tying the president's approval ratings to the health of the nation is obviously a mistake or clearly unfair. In this light, evidence that citizens' linkages of national conditions to presidential approval sometimes hinges on causal attributions is also flattering for the polity.

Evidence that the country initially rallies around its president in times of international crisis also seems normatively desirable, as does the evidence that public support for presidents ultimately hinges on what they say and what they do, not the mere existence of crisis. And the evidence that presidential approval responds to news of personal traumas that the president endures, speeches the president makes, political party conventions, the tone of news coverage, the existence of divided government, agreement with the president on policy issues all suggest that the public is paying attention to the flow of news between elections and using that news to update their evaluations. Finally, the fact that news media priming seems to occur only among people who trust the media and choose to follow its suggestions about how to evaluate the president also seems more normatively admirable than the counterclaim that priming happens automatically and outside of the awareness of the citizens who manifest it, due to shifts in mere accessibility.

We look forward to future research in political psychology, continuing to illuminate and clarify the processes and variables discussed previously, and taking a balanced approach to considering the normative implications of the discoveries that are uncovered. Such work will no doubt help to advance psychology's understanding of the human mind and of social interaction but may also equip governments to interpret the actions of their citizens more accurately and to conduct their activities in ways that maximize the longevity and prosperity of societies.

REFERENCES

Abelson, R. P., Kinder, D. R., Peters, M. D., & Fiske, S. T. (1982). Affective and semantic components in political person perception. *Journal of Personality and Social Psychology, 42,* 619–630.

Abramowitz, A. I. (1984). National issues, strategic politicians, and voting behavior in the 1980 and 1982 Congressional elections. *American Journal of Political Science, 28*(4), 710–721.

Abramowitz, A. I. (1985). Economic conditions, presidential popularity, and voting behavior in midterm Congressional elections. *The Journal of Politics, 47*(1), 31–43.

Abramowitz, A. I., & Segal, J. A. (1992). *Senate elections.* Ann Arbor: University of Michigan Press.

Abramowitz, A. I., & Stone, W. J. (2006). The Bush effect: Polarization, turnout, and activism in the 2004 presidential election. *Presidential Studies Quarterly, 36*(2), 141–154.

Achen, C. H. (1975). Mass political attitudes and the survey response. *American Political Science Review, 69*(4), 1218–1231.

Achen, C. H. (1992). Social psychology, demographic variables, and linear regression: Breaking the iron triangle in voting research. *Political Behavior, 14*(3), 195–211.

Acevedo, M., & Krueger, J. I. (2004). Two egocentric sources of the decision to vote: The voter's illusion and the belief in personal relevance. *Political Psychology, 25*(1), 115–134.

Acock, A., Clarke, H. D., & Stewart, M. C. (1985). A new model for old measures: A covariance structure analysis of political efficacy. *The Journal of Politics, 47*(4), 1062–1084.

Agresti, A., & Presnell, B. (2002). Misvotes, undervotes and overvotes: The 2000 presidential election in Florida. *Statistical Science, 17*(4), 436–440.

Aldrich, J. H., & McKelvey, R. D. (1977). A method of scaling with applications to the 1968 and 1972 presidential elections. *American Political Science Review, 71*(1), 111–130.

Alex-Assensoh, Y., & Assensoh, A. B. (2001). Inner-city contexts, church attendance, and African American political participation. *The Journal of Politics, 63*(3), 886–901.

Alford, J. R., Funk, C. L., & Hibbing, J. R. (2005). Are political orientations genetically transmitted? *American Political Science Review, 99*(2), 153–167.

Allport, G. W. (1954). *The nature of prejudice.* Reading, MA: Addison-Wesley.

Allport, G. W. (1985). The historical background of social psychology. In G. Lindzey & E. Aronson (Eds.), *Handbook of social psychology* (Vol. 1, pp. 1–46). Hillsdale, NJ: Lawrence Erlbaum Associates, Inc.

Almond, G. A. (1950). *The American people and foreign policy.* New York: Harcourt Brace.

Alt, J. E., & Chrystal, K. A. (1983). *Political economies.* Berkeley: University of California Press.

Altemeyer, B. (1981). *Right-wing authoritarianism.* Winnipeg: University of Manitoba Press.

Altemeyer, B. (1988a). *Enemies of freedom: Understanding right-wing authoritarianism.* San Francisco: Jossey-Bass.

Altemeyer, B. (1988b). *The authoritarian specter.* Cambridge, MA: Harvard University Press.

Altemeyer, B. (1996). *The authoritarian specter.* Cambridge, MA: Harvard University Press.

Altemeyer, B. (1998). The other " authoritarian personality ." *Advances in Experimental Social Psychology, 30,* 47–91.

Althaus, S. L., & Kim, Y. M. (2006). Priming effects in complex information environments: Reassessing the impact of news discourse on presidential approval. *Journal of Politics, 68*(4), 960–976.

Alvarez, R. M. (1998). *Information and elections.* Ann Arbor: University of Michigan Press.

Alwin, D. F., Cohen, R. C., & Newcomb, T. M. (1991). *Political attitudes over the life span.* Madison: University of Wisconsin Press.

Ambady, N., & Rosenthal, R. (1992). Thin slices of expressive behavior as predictors of interpersonal consequences: A meta-analysis. *Psychological Bulletin, 111,* 256–274.

Anand, S., & Krosnick, J. A. (2003). The impact of attitudes toward foreign policy goals on public preferences among presidential candidates: A study of issue publics and the attentive public in the 2000 U.S. presidential election. *Presidential Studies Quarterly, 33,* 31–71.

Anderson, B., Silver, B., & Abramson, P. (1988a). The effects of race of the interviewer on measures of electoral participation by blacks in SRC national election studies. *Public Opinion Quarterly, 52*(1), 53–83.

Anderson, B., Silver, B., & Abramson, P. (1988b). The effects of the race of interviewer on race-related attitudes of Black respondents in SCR/CPS National Election Studies. *Public Opinion Quarterly, 52*(3), 289–324.

Anderson, J. A., & Avery, R. K. (1978). An analysis of changes in voter perceptions of candidates' positions. *Communication Monographs, 45,* 354–361.

Anderson, N. (1981). *Foundations of information integration theory.* Boston: Academic Press.

Ansolabehere, S., & Iyengar, S. (1994). Horseshoes and horse races: Experimental evidence of the effect of polls on campaigns. *Political Communication, 11*(4), 413–429.

Ansolabehere, S., & Iyengar, S. (1995). *Going negative: How attack ads shrink and polarize the electorate*. New York: Free Press.

Ansolabehere, S., Iyengar, S., Simon, A., & Valentino, N. (1994). Does attack advertising demobilize the electorate? *American Political Science Review, 88*(4), 829–838.

Aoki, A. L., & Nakanishi, D. T. (2001). Asian Pacific Americans and the new minority politics. *PS: Political Science and Politics, 34*(3), 605–610.

Apsler, R., & Sears, D. O. (1968). Warning, personal involvement, and attitude change. *Journal of Personality and Social Psychology, 9*(2), 162–166.

Armstrong, J. S., Denniston, W. B., & Gordon, M. M. (1975). The use of the decomposition principle in making judgments. *Organizational Behavior and Human Performance, 14*, 257–263.

Arneson, B. A. (1925). Nonvoting in a typical Ohio community. *American Political Science Review, 19*(4), 816–825.

Arneson, B. A., & Eels, W. H. (1950). Voting behavior in 1948 as compared with 1924 in a typical Ohio community. *American Political Science Review, 44*(2), 432–434.

Ashenfelter, O., & Kelley, S. (1975). Determinants of participation in presidential elections. *Journal of Law and Economics, 18(3)*, 695–733.

Atkin, S. (1969). Psychoanalytic considerations of language and thought. *Psychoanalysis Quarterly, 38*, 549–582.

Baddeley, A. D., & Hitch, G. J. (1974). Working memory. In G. A. Bower (Ed.), *The psychology of learning and motivation: Advances in research and theory* (pp. 47–89). New York: Academic Press.

Ballew, C. C., & Todorov, A. (2007). Predicting political elections from rapid and unreflective face judgments. *Proceedings of the National Academy of Sciences of the USA, 104*(46), 17948–17953.

Barabas, J. (2002). Another look at the measurement of political knowledge. *Political Analysis, 10*(2), 1–14.

Barbaranelli, C., Caprara, G. V., Vecchione, M., & Fraley, R. C. (2006). Voters' personality traits in presidential elections. *Personality and Individual Differences, 42*(7), 1199–1208.

Barnes, S. H., & Kaase, M. (1979). *Political action: Mass participation in five western democracies*. Beverly Hills, CA: Sage.

Barreto, M. A. (2005). Latino immigrants at the polls: Foreign-born voter turnout in the 2002 election. *Political Research Quarterly, 58*(1), 79–86.

Bartels, L. M. (1986). Issue voting under uncertainty: An empirical test. *American Journal of Political Science, 30*, 709–728.

Bartels, L. M. (1988). *Presidential primaries and the dynamics of public choice*. Princeton, NJ: Princeton University Press.

Bartels, L. M. (2000). Partisanship and voting behavior, 1952–1996. *American Journal of Political Science, 44*, 35–50.

Barton, A.H. (1974-75). Conflict and consensus among American leaders. *Public Opinion Quarterly, 38*, 507–30.

Bassili, J. N. (1996). Meta-judgmental versus operative indexes of psychological attributes: The case of measures of attitude strength. *Journal of Personality and Social Psychology, 71*(4), 637–653.

Baum, M. A. (2002). The constituent foundations of the rally-round-the-flag phenomenon. *International Studies Quarterly, 46*(2), 263–298.

Baumgartner, F.R., & Leech, B. L. (1998). *Basic interests: The importance of groups in politics and in political science*. Princeton, NJ: Princeton University Press.

Beck, P.A., Dalton, R. J., Greene, S., & Huckfeldt, R. (2002). The social calculus of voting: Interpersonal, media, and organizational influences on presidential choices. *American Political Science Review, 96*(1), 57–73.

Beck, P.A., & Jennings, M. K. (1979). Political periods and political participation. *American Political Science Review, 73*(3), 737–750.

Beck, P.A., & Jennings, M. K. (1991). Family traditions, political periods, and the development of partisan orientations. *Journal of Politics, 53*, 742–763.

Behr, R.L., & Iyengar, S. (1985). Television news, real-world cues, and changes in the public agenda. *Public Opinion Quarterly, 49*, 1–38.

Bélanger, E., & Meguid, B. M. (2008). Issue salience, issue ownership, and issue-based vote choice. *Electoral Studies, 27*(3), 477–491.

Bem, D. J. (1967). Self-perception: An alternative interpretation of cognitive dissonance phenomena. *Psychological Review, 74*(3), 183–200.

Benjamin, L. T., Jr. (2007). *A brief history of modern psychology*. Malden, MA: Blackwell Publishing.

Bennett, J. T., & Orzechowski, W. P. (1983). The voting behavior of bureaucrats—some empirical evidence. *Public Choice, 41*(2), 271–283.

Bennett, S. E. (1990). The uses and abuses of registration and turnout data: An analysis of Piven and Cloward's studies of nonvoting in America. *PS: Political Science and Politics, 23*(2), 166–171.

Bennett, W. L. (1990). Toward a theory of press–state relations in the United States. *Journal of Communication, 40*(2), 103–125.

Berelson, B. R., Lazarsfeld, P. F., & McPhee, W. N. (1954). *Voting: A study of opinion formation in a presidential campaign*. Chicago: University of Chicago Press.

Berent, M. K., & Krosnick, J. A. (1995). The relation between political attitude importance and knowledge structure. In M. Lodge & K.M. McGraw (Eds.), *Political judgment: Structure and process* (pp. 91–109). Ann Arbor: University of Michigan Press.

Berinsky, A., & Lewis, J. (2007). An estimate of risk aversion in the U.S. electorate. *Quarterly Journal of Political Science, 2*(2), 139–154.

Berinsky, A. J., Burns, N., & Traugott, M. W. (2001). Who votes by mail? *Public Opinion Quarterly, 65*(2), 178–197.

Bizer, G. Y., & Krosnick, J. A. (2001). Exploring the structure of strength-related attitude features: The relation between attitude importance and attitude accessibility. *Journal of Personality and Social Psychology, 81*(4), 566–596.

Blair, I. V., Judd, C. M., & Chapleau, K. M. (2004). The influence of Afrocentric facial features in criminal sentencing. *Psychological Science, 15*, 674–679.

Bobo, L. (1988). Group conflict, prejudice and the paradox of contemporary racial attitudes. In P. Katz & D. Taylor (Eds.), *Eliminating racism: Profiles in controversy* (pp. 85–116). New York: Plenum.

Bobo, L., & Gilliam, F. D., Jr. (1990). Race, sociopolitical participation, and black empowerment. *The American Political Science Review, 84*(2), 377–393.

Bobo, L., & Kluegel, J. R. (1997). Status, ideology, and dimensions of whites' racial beliefs and attitudes: Progress and stagnation. In S. A. Tuch & J. K. Martin (Eds.), *Racial attitudes in the 1990s: Continuity and change* (pp. 93–120). Greenwood, CT: Praeger.

Bond, J. R., Fleisher, R., & Wood, B. D. (2003). The marginal and time varying effect of public approval on presidential success in Congress. *Journal of Politics, 65*, 92–110.

Boninger, D. S., Krosnick, J. A., & Berent, M. K. (1995). The origins of attitude importance: Self-interest, social identification, and value relevance. *Journal of Personality and Social Psychology, 68*(1), 61–80.

Boninger, D. S., Krosnick, J. A., Berent, M. K., & Fabrigar, L. R. (1995). The causes and consequences of attitude importance. In R. E. Petty & J. A. Krosnick (Eds.), *Attitude strength: Antecedents and consequences*. Hillsdale, NJ: Lawrence Erlbaum Associates.

Borgida, E., Frederico, C. M., & Sullivan, J. L. (Eds.). (2009). *The political psychology of democratic citizenship*. New York: Oxford University Press.

Bosso, C. J. (1997). Seizing back the day: The challenge to environmental activism in the 1990s. In N. J. Vig & M. E. Kraft (Eds.), *Environmental Policy in the 1990s*. Washington, DC: CQ Press.

Bowers, K. S. (1973). Situationism in psychology: An analysis and a critique. *Psychological Review, 80*(5), 307–336.

Boyd, R. W. (1989). The effects of primaries and statewide races on voter turnout. *Journal of Politics, 51*(3), 730–739.

Brace, P., & Hinckley, B. (1991). The structure of presidential approval: Constraints within and across presidencies. *Journal of Politics, 53,* 993–1017.

Brace, K., Handley, L., Niemi, R. G., & Stanley, H. W. (1995). Minority turnout and the creation of majority–minority districts. *American Politics Quarterly, 23*(2), 90(14).

Bradburn, N., & Caplovitz, D. (1964). *Reports on happiness.* Chicago: Aldine.

Brady, H. E. (2000). Contributions of survey research to political science. *PS: Political Science and Politics, 33,* 47–57.

Brady, H. E., & Ansolabehere, S. (1989). The nature of utility functions in mass publics. *American Political Science Review, 83,* 143–163.

Brady, H. E, & McNulty, J. E. (2004). The costs of voting: Evidence from a natural experiment. Paper presented at the annual meeting of the Midwest Political Science Association.

Brady, H., & Sniderman, P. M. (1985). Attitude attribution: A group basis for political reasoning. *American Political Science Review, 79,* 1061–1078.

Brady, H. E., Herron, M. C., Mebane, W. R., Jr., Sekhon, J.S.S., Shotts, K. W., & Wand, J. (2001). Law and data: The butterfly ballot episode. *PS: Political Science & Politics, 34,* 59–69.

Brent, E. E., & Granberg, D. (1982). Subjective agreement with the presidential candidates of 1976 and 1980. *Journal of Personality and Social Psychology, 42*(3), 393–403.

Brehm, J. (1993). *The Phantom respondents: Opinion surveys and political representation.* Ann Arbor: University of Michigan Press.

Brians, C. L., & Grofman, B. (2001). Election Day registration's effect on U.S. voter turnout (statistical data included). *Social Science Quarterly, 82*(1), 170–184.

Brockington, D. (2003). Injustice and conservation: Is local support necessary for sustainable protected areas? *Policy Matters, 12,* 22–30.

Brody, R. A. (1991). *Assessing the president.* Stanford, CA: Stanford University Press.

Brody, R. A., & Page, B. I. (1972). Comment: The assessment of issue voting. *American Political Science Review, 66,* 450–458.

Brody, R. A., & Rothenberg, L. S. (1988). The instability of partisanship: An analysis of the 1980 presidential election. *British Journal of Political Science, 18*(4), 445–465.

Brody, R. A., & Shapiro, C. R. (1989a). A reconsideration of the rally phenomenon in public opinion. In S. Long (Ed.), *Political behavior annual* (Vol. 2, pp. 77–102). Denver: Westview Press.

Brody, R. A., & Shapiro, C. R. (1989b). Policy failure and public support: The Iran-Contra affair and public assessment of President Reagan. *Political Behavior, 11*(4), 353–369.

Brody, R. A., & Sigelman, L. (1983). Presidential popularity and presidential elections: An update and an extension. *Public Opinion Quarterly, 47,* 325–328.

Brody, R. A., & Sniderman, P. M. (1977). From life space to polling place: The relevance of personal concerns for voting behavior. *British Journal of Political Science, 7*(3), 337–360.

Broh, C. A. (1983). Polls, pols, and parties. *Journal of Politics, 45,* 732–744.

Brown, R. D., Jackson, R. A., & Wright, G. C. (1999). Registration, turnout, and state party systems. *Political Research Quarterly, 52*(3), 463–479.

Budd, R. J. (1986). Predicting cigarette use: The need to incorporate measures of salience in the theory of reasoned action. *Journal of Applied Social Psychology, 16,* 663–685.

Burden, B. C., & Mughan, A. (2003). The international economy and presidential approval. *Public Opinion Quarterly, 67*(4), 555–578.

Burnham, W. D. (1980). The appearance and disappearance of the American voter. In R. Rose (Ed.), *Electoral participation: A comparative perspective* (pp. 112–139). Beverly Hills, CA: Sage.

Burnham, W. D. (1982). *The current crisis in American politics.* New York: Oxford University Press.

Burnham, W. D. (1987). Elections as democratic institutions. In K. L. Schlozman (Ed.), *Elections in America* (pp. 27–60). Boston: Allen & Unwin.

Burnham, W. D. (1987). The turnout problem. In A. J. Reichley (Ed.), *Elections American style* (pp. 97–133). Washington, DC: Brookings.

Byrne, D. (1971). *The attraction paradigm.* New York: Academic Press.

Cain, B. E., & McCue, K. (1985). The efficacy of registration drives. *Journal of Politics, 47*(4), 1221–1230.

Caldeira, G. A., & Patterson, S. C. (1982). Contextual influences on participation in U. S. state legislative elections. *Legislative Studies Quarterly, 7*(3), 359–381.

Caldeira, G. A., Patterson, S. C., & Markko, G. A. (1985). The mobilization of voters in Congressional elections. *Journal of Politics, 47*(2), 490–509.

Campbell, A. (1960). Surge and decline: A study of electoral change. *Public Opinion Quarterly, 24*(3), 397–418.

Campbell, A., Converse, P. E., Miller, W. E., & Stokes, D. E. (1960). *The American voter.* New York: Wiley.

Campbell, J. E. (1983). Ambiguity in the issue positions of presidential candidates: A causal analysis. *American Journal of Political Science, 27*(2), 284–293.

Canes-Wrone, B., & de Marchi, S. (2002). Presidential approval and legislative success. *Journal of Politics, 64,* 491–509.

Cantril, A. H. (1980). *Polling on the issues.* Cabin John, MD: Seven Locks Press.

Cardy, E. A. (2005). An experimental field study of the GOTV and persuasion effects of partisan direct mail and phone calls. *The Annals of the American Academy of Political and Social Science, 601,* 28–40.

Carmines, E. G., & Merriman, W. R., Jr. (1993). The changing American dilemma: Liberal values and racial policies. In P. Sniderman, P. E. Tetlock, & E.G. Carmines (Eds.), *Prejudice, politics, and the American dilemma.* Stanford, CA: Stanford University Press.

Carsey, T. M., & Layman, G. C. (2006). Changing sides or changing minds? Party identification and policy preferences in the American electorate. *American Journal of Political Science, 50,* 464–477.

Cavanagh, T. E. (1981). Changes in American voter turnout, 1964–1976. *Political Science Quarterly, 96*(1), 53.

Ceci, S. J., & Kain, E. L. (1982). Jumping on the bandwagon with the underdog: The impact of attitude polls on poll behavior. *Public Opinion Quarterly, 46,* 228–242.

Chamberlain, G., & Rothschild, M. (1981). A note on the probability of casting a decisive vote. *Journal of Economic Theory, 25*(1), 152–162.

Cho, W.K.T. (1999). Naturalization, socialization, participation: Immigrants and (non)voting. *Journal of Politics, 61*(4), 1140–1155.

Chong, D. (2000). *Rational lives: Norms and values in politics and society.* Chicago: University of Chicago Press.

Chubb, J. E. (1983). *Interest groups and the bureaucracy: The politics of energy.* Stanford, CA: Stanford University Press.

Cigler, A. J., & Loomis, B. A. (1995). *Interest group politics.* Washington, DC: CQ Press.

Citrin, J. (1974). Comment: The political relevance of trust in government. *American Political Science Review, 68*(3), 973–988.

Citrin, J., & Green, D. (1990). The self-interest motive in American public opinion. In S. Long (Ed.), *Research in micropolitics* (pp 1–28). Boulder, CO: Westview Press.

Citrin, J., Reingold, B., & Green, D. P. (1990). American identity and the politics of ethnic change. *Journal of Politics, 52*, 1124–1154.

Citrin, J., Schickler, E., & Sides, J. (2003). What if everyone voted? Simulating the impact of increased turnout in Senate elections. *American Journal of Political Science, 47*(1), 75–90.

Citrin, J. E. (1977). Political alienation as a social indicator: Attitudes and action. *Social Indicators Research, 4*(1), 381–419.

Civics Quiz. (2009). Retrieved February 25, 2009, from Intercollegiate Studies Institute American Civil Liberties Program Web site: http://www.americancivicliteracy.org/resources/quiz.aspx.

Claassen, R.L. (2007). Ideology and evaluation in an experimental setting: Comparing the proximity and the directional models. *Political Research Quarterly, 60*(2), 263–273.

Claassen, R. L. (2009). Direction versus proximity: Amassing experimental evidence. *American Politics Research, 37*, 227–253.

Clarke, H. D., Rapkin, J., & Stewart, M. C. (1994). A president out of work: A note on the political economy of presidential approval in the Bush years. *British Journal of Political Science, 24*(4), 535–548.

Clarke, H. D., & Stewart, M. C. (1994). Prospections, retrospections, and rationality: The "bankers" model of presidential approval reconsidered. *American Journal of Political Science, 38*(4), 1104–1123.

Clarke, H. D., Stewart, M. C., Ault, M., & Elliott, E. (2004). Men, women, and the dynamics of presidential approval. *British Journal of Political Science, 35*(1), 31–51.

Clarke, P., & Fredin, E. (1978). Newspapers, television and political reasoning. *Public Opinion Quarterly, 42*(2), 143–160.

Clarke, P., & Kline, F. (1974). Media effects reconsidered. *Communication Research, 1*(2), 224–240.

Clausen, A. R. (1968). Response validity: Vote report. *Public Opinion Quarterly, 32*, 588–606.

Clinton, J. D., & Lapinski, J. S. (2004). "Targeted" advertising and voter turnout: An experimental study of the 2000 presidential election. *Journal of Politics, 66*(1), 69–96.

Coate, S., & Conlin, M. (2004). A group rule–utilitarian approach to voter turnout: Theory and evidence. *The American Economic Review, 94*(5), 1476–1504.

Cobb R., & Elder, C. (1972). *Participation in American politics.* Baltimore, MD: John Hopkins University Press.

Cohen, B. (1963). *The press and foreign policy.* Princeton, NJ: Princeton University Press.

Cohen, B. (1973). *The public's impact on foreign policy.* Boston: Little, Brown

Cohen, G. L. (2003). Party over policy: The dominating impact of group influence on political beliefs. *Journal of Personality and Social Psychology, 85*(5), 808–822.

Cohen, J. (1983). The cost of dichotomization. *Applied Psychological Measurement, 7*, 249–253.

Cohen, J. (1995). Presidential rhetoric and the public agenda. *American Journal of Political Science, 39*, 87–107.

Cohen, J. (1997). Deliberation and democratic legitimacy. In J. F. Bohman & W. Rehg (Eds.), *Deliberative democracy: Essays on reason and politics.* Cambridge, MA: MIT Press.

Coleman, S. (2004). The effect of social conformity on collective voting behavior. *Political Analysis, 12*(1), 76–96.

Cook, C. E. (2005). Did 2004 transform U.S. politics? *The Washington Quarterly, 28*(2), 173–186.

Cook, F. L., Tyler, T. R., Goetz, E. G., Gordon, M. T., Protess, D., Leff, D. R., & Molotch, H. L. (1983). Media and agenda setting: Effects on the public, interest group leaders, policy makers, and policy. *Public Opinion Quarterly, 47,* 16–35.

Cook, S. W., & Welch, A. E. (1940). Methods of measuring the practical effect of polls on public opinion. *Journal of Applied Psychology, 24,* 441–454.

Cooke, N. J., Atlas, R. S., Lane, D. M., & Berger, R. C. (1993). Role of high-level knowledge in memory for chess positions. *American Journal of Psychology, 106*(3), 321–351.

Coombs, F. S., Peters, J. G., & Strom, G. S. (1974). Bandwagon, ballot position and party effects: An experiment in voting choice. *Experimental Study of Politics, 3,* 31–57.

Conover, P. J. (1988). Feminists and the gender gap. *Journal of Politics, 50,* 985–1010.

Conover, P. J., & Feldman, S. (1981). The origins and meaning of liberal–conservative self-identifications. *American Journal of Political Science, 25,* 617–645.

Conover, P. J., & Feldman, S. (1982). Projection and the perception of candidates' issue positions. *Political Research Quarterly, 35,* 228–244.

Conover, P. J., & Feldman, S. (1986). Emotional reactions to the economy: I'm mad as hell and I'm not going to take it anymore. *American Journal of Political Science, 30,* 50–78.

Converse, P. E. (1964). The nature of belief systems in mass publics. In D. E. Apter (Ed.), *Ideology and discontent.* New York: Free Press.

Corey, E. C., & Garand, J. C. (2002). Are government employees more likely to vote? An analysis of turnout in the 1996 U.S. national election. *Public Choice, 111*(3–4), 259–283.

Corr, P. I., Pickering, A. D., & Gray, J. A. (1997). Personality, punishment, and procedural learning: A test of J. A. Gray's anxiety theory. *Journal of Personality and Social Psychology, 73*(2), 337–344.

Costa, D. L., & Kahn, M. E. (2004). Civic engagement and community heterogeneity: An economist's perspective. *Perspectives on Politics, 1*(1), 103–111.

Cover, A. D. (1985). Surge and decline in Congressional elections. *Western Political Quarterly, 38*(4), 606–619.

Cox, G. W., & Munger, M. C. (1989). Closeness, expenditures, and turnout in the 1982 U.S. House elections. *American Political Science Review, 83*(1), 217–231.

Cox, M. (2003). When trust matters: Explaining differences in voter turnout. *Journal of Common Market Studies, 41*(4), 757–770.

Craig, S. C., & Maggiotto, M. A. (1982). Measuring political efficacy. *Political Methodology, 8,* 85–109.

Craik, F.I.M., & Lockhart, R. S. (1972). Levels of processing: A framework for memory research. *Journal of Verbal Learning and Verbal Behavior, 11,* 671–684.

Craik, F.I.M. (1977). *Handbook of the psychology of aging.* New York: Van Nostrand Reinhold.

Crespin, M. H., & Vander Wielen, D. J. (2002). The influence of media projections on voter turnout in presidential elections from 1980–2000. Paper presented at the 2002 Annual Meeting of the Midwest Political Science Association, Chicago, Illinois, April 25–28.

Dahl, R. A. (1961). *Who governs?* New Haven, CT: Yale University Press.

Dalton, R. (1988). *Citizen politics: Public opinion and political parties in advanced western democracies.* Chatham, NJ: Chatham House Publishers.

Darcy, R., & McAllister, I. (1990). Ballot position effects. *Electoral Studies, 9*(1), 5–17.

Davis, D. W. (1997). The direction of race of interviewer effects among African Americans: Donning the Black Mask. *American Journal of Political Science, 41*(1), 309–322.

Davis, D. W., & Silver, B. D. (2003). Stereotype threat and race of interviewer effects in a survey on political knowledge. *American Journal of Political Science, 47*(1), 33–45.

Delli Carpini, M. X. (1984). Scooping the voters? The consequences of the networks' early call of the 1980 presidential race. *Journal of Politics, 46*(3), 866–885.

Delli Carpini, M. X., & Keeter, S. (1993). Measuring political knowledge: Putting first things first. *American Journal of Political Science, 37*(4), 1179–1206.

Delli Carpini, M. X., & Keeter, S. (1996). *What Americans know about politics and why it matters.* New Haven, CT: Yale University Press.

Delli Carpini, M. X., Keeter, S., & Webb, S. (1997). The impact of presidential debates. In P. Norris (Ed.), *Politics and the press* (pp. 145–164). Boulder, CO: Rienner.

DeRouen, K., Jr. (1977). Presidents and the diversionary use of force: A research note. *International Studies Quarterly, 44*, 317–339.

Diamond, S. (1995). *Roads to dominion: Right-wing movements and political power in the United States.* New York: Guilford Press.

Dixon, R. D., Lowery, R. C., Levy, D. E., & Ferraro, K. F. (1991). Self-interest and public opinion toward smoking policies: A replication and extension. *Public Opinion Quarterly, 55*, 241–254.

Dizney, H. F., & Roskens, R. W. (1962). An investigation of the bandwagon effect in a college straw election. *Journal of Educational Sociology, 36*, 108–114.

Domke, D. (2001). Racial cues and political ideology: An examination of associative priming. *Communication Research, 28*(6), 772–801.

Domke, D., Shah, D. V., & Wackman, D. B. (1998). Media priming effects: Accessibility, association, and activation. *International Journal of Public Opinion Research, 10*, 51–74.

Doty, R. M., Peterson, B. E., & Winter, D. G. (1991). Threat and authoritarianism in the United States, 1978–1987. *Journal of Personality and Social Psychology, 61*(4), 629–640.

Doty, R. M., Winter, D. G., Peterson, B. E., & Kemmelmeier, M. (1997). Authoritarianism and American students' attitudes about the Gulf War, 1990–1996. *Personality and Social Psychology Bulletin, 23*, 1133–1143.

Downs, A. (1957). *An economic theory of democracy.* New York: Harper & Row.

Downs, A. (1972). Up and down with ecology: The "issue-attention cycle." *Public Interest, 28*, 38–50.

Druckman, J. M., & Holmes, J. W. (2004). Does presidential rhetoric matter? Priming and presidential approval. *Presidential Studies Quarterly, 34*(4), 755–778.

Duckitt, J. (2001). A dual process cognitive–motivational theory of ideology and prejudice. *Advances in Experimental Social Psychology, 33*, 41–113.

Duckitt, J. (2006). Differential effects of right wing authoritarianism and social dominance orientation on outgroup attitudes and their mediation by threat from and competitiveness to outgroups. *Personality and Social Psychology Bulletin, 32*, 1–13.

Duckitt, J., Wagner, C., du Plessis, I., & Birum, I. (2002). The psychological basis of ideology and prejudice: Testing a dual process model. *Journal of Personality and Social Psychology, 82*, 75–93.

Easton, D., & Dennis, J. (1969). *Children in the political system: Origins of political legitimacy.* New York: McGraw-Hill.

Eberhardt, J. L., Davies, P. G., Purdie-Vaughns, V. J., & Johnson, S. L. (2006). Looking deathworthy: Perceived stereotypicality of black defendants predicts capital-sentencing outcomes. *Psychological Science, 17*, 383–386.

Eckhardt, B. B., Wood, M. R., & Jacobvitz, R. S. (1991). Verbal ability and prior knowledge: Contributions to adults' comprehension of television. *Communication Research, 18*, 636–649.

Edwards, G. C., Mitchell, W., & Welch, R. (1995). Explaining presidential approval: The significance of issue salience. *American Journal of Political Science, 39*, 108–134.

Edwards, G., & Wood, B. D. (1999). Who influences whom? The president and the public agenda. *American Political Science Review, 93*(2), 327–344.

Elden, J. M. (1981). Political efficacy at work: The connection between more autonomous forms of workplace organization and a more participatory politics. *American Political Science Review, 75*(1), 43–58.

Ellison, C. G., & London, B. (1992). The social and political participation of Black Americans: Compensatory and ethnic community perspectives revisited. *Social Forces, 70*(3), 681–701.

Enelow, J., & Hinich, M. (1984a). *The spatial theory of voting: An introduction.* New York: Cambridge University Press.

Enelow, J., & Hinich, M. (1984b). Probabilistic voting and the importance of centrist ideologies in democratic elections. *Journal of Politics, 46*, 459–478.

Enelow, J. M. (1986). The linkage between predictive dimensions and candidate issue positions in American presidential campaigns: An examination of group differences. *Political Behavior, 8*(3), 245–261.

Entman, R. M. (2004). *Projections of power: Framing news, public opinion, and U.S. foreign policy.* Chicago: University of Chicago Press.

Epstein, L. K., & Strom, G. S. (1981). Election night projections and west coast turnout. *American Politics Quarterly, 9*(4), 479–491.

Erbring, L., Goldenberg, E. N., & Miller, A. H. (1980). Front-page news and real-world cues: A new look at agenda-setting by the media. *American Journal of Political Science, 24*(1), 16–49.

Erikson, R. S. (1979). The SRC panel data and mass political attitudes. *British Journal of Political Science, 9*, 89–114.

Eveland, W. P., Jr., Shah, D. V., & Kwak, N. (2003). Assessing causality in the cognitive mediation model: A panel study of motivations, information processing and learning during Campaign 2000. *Communication Research, 30*, 359–386.

Fazio, R. H. (1986). How do attitudes guide behavior? In R. M. Sorrentino & E. T. Higgins (Eds.), *Handbook of motivation and cognition: Foundations of social behavior* (pp. 204–243). New York: Guilford Press.

Fazio, R. H. & Zanna, M. P. (1981). Direct experience and attitude–behavior consistency. In L. Berkowitz (Ed.), *Advances in experimental social psychology* (Vol. 14, pp. 161–202). New York: Academic Press.

Feldman, S. (1988). Structure and consistency in public opinion: The role of core beliefs and values. *American Journal of Political Science 32*(2), 416–440.

Feldman, S. (2003). Enforcing social conformity: A theory of authoritarianism. *Political Psychology, 24,* 41–74.

Feldman, S., & Conover, P. J. (1983). Candidates, issues, and voters: The role of inference in political perception. *Journal of Politics, 45*, 810–839.

Feldman, S., & Steenbergen, M. R. (2001). The humanitarian foundation of public support for social welfare. *American Journal of Political Science, 45*(3), 658–677.

Feldman, S., & Stenner, K. (1997). Perceived threat and authoritarianism. *Political Psychology, 18*, 741–770.

Feldman, S., & Zaller, J. (1992). Political culture of ambivalence: Ideological responses to the welfare state. *American Journal of Political Science, 36*, 268–307.

Fenster, M. J. (1994). The impact of allowing day of registration voting on turnout in U.S. elections from 1960 to 1992. *American Politics Quarterly, 22*(1), 74–87.

Ferejohn, J. A., & Fiorina, M. P. (1974). The paradox of not voting: A decision theoretic analysis. *American Political Science Review, 68*(2), 525–536.

Festinger, L. (1954). A theory of social comparison processes. *Human Relations, 7*(2), 117–140.

Festinger, L. (1957). *A theory of cognitive dissonance*. Stanford, CA: Stanford University Press.

Fey, M. (1997). Stability and coordination in Duverger's Law: A formal model of preelection polls and strategic voting. *American Political Science Review, 91*, 135–147.

Filer, J. E., Kenny, L. W., & Morton, R. B. (1993). Redistribution, income, and voting. *American Journal of Political Science, 37*(1), 63–87.

Fine, B. J. (1957). Conclusion-drawing, communicator credibility, and anxiety as factors in opinion change. *Journal of Abnormal and Social Psychology, 54*, 369–374.

Finkel, S. E., & Opp, K.D. (1991). Party Identification and Participation in Collective Political Action. *Journal of Politics 53*, 339–371.

Finkel, S. E., Muller, E. N., & Opp, K. D. (1989). Personal influence, collective rationality and mass political action. *American Political Science Review, 83*(3), 885–904.

Fiorina, M. P. (1981). *Retrospective voting in American national elections*. New Haven, CT: Yale University Press.

Fiske, S. T., Lau, R. R., & Smith, R. A. (1990). On the varieties and utilities of political expertise. *Social Cognition, 8*(1), 31–48.

Fiske, S. T., Pratto, F., & Pavelchak, M. A. (1983). Citizen's images of nuclear war: Contents and consequences. *Journal of Social Issues, 39*, 41–66.

Fleitas, D. W. (1971). Bandwagon and underdog effects in minimal information elections. *American Political Science Review, 65*, 434–438.

Flemming, R. B., Wood, B. D., & Bohte, J. (1999). Attention to issues in a system of separate powers: The macrodynamics of American policy agendas. *Journal of Politics, 61*(1), 76–108.

Forsythe, R., Myerson, R. B., Rietz, T. A., & Weber, R. J. (1993). An experiment on coordination in multicandidate elections: The importance of polls and election histories. *Social Choice and Welfare, 10*(3), 223–247.

Foster, C. B. (1984). The performance of rational voter models in recent presidential elections. *American Political Science Review, 78*(3), 678–690.

Fournier, P., Blais, A., Nadeau, R., Gidengil, E., & Nevitte, N. (2003). Issue importance and performance voting. *Political Behavior 25*(1), 51–67.

Fowler, J. H. (2005). Turnout in a small world. In A. Zuckerman (Ed.), *Social Logic of Politics* (pp. 269–287). Philadelphia: Temple University Press.

Fowler, J. H. (2006). Altruism and turnout. *Journal of Politics, 68*(3), 674–683.

Fowler, J. H., & Dawes, C. T. (2008). Two genes predict voter turnout. *Journal of Politics, 70*, 579–594.

Fowler, J. H., & Kam, C. D. (2006). Patience as a political virtue: Delayed gratification and turnout. *Political Behavior, 28*, 113–128.

Fowler, J. H., Baker, L. A., & Dawes, C. T. (2008). Genetic variation in political participation. *American Political Science Review, 102*, 233–248.

Fox, J. (1984). *Linear statistical models and related methods*. New York: Wiley.

Fox, M. (2008, December 7). Robert Zajonc, who looked at mind's ties to actions, is dead at 85. *New York Times*. p. A42.

Franklin, C. H. (1984). Isues preferences, socialization, and the evolution of party identification. *American Journal of Political Science, 28*, 459–478.

Franklin, D. P., & Grier, E. E. (1997). Effects of motor voter legislation: Voter turnout, registration, and partisan advantage in the 1992 presidential election. *American Politics Quarterly, 25*(1), 104–117.

Franklin, C. H., & Jackson, J. E. (1983). The dynamics of party identification. *American Political Science Review, 77*, 957–973.

Freedman, P., & Goldstein, K. (1999). Measuring media exposure and the effects of negative campaign ads. *American Journal of Political Science, 43*(4), 1189–1208.

Frenkel, O. J., & Doob, A. N. (1976). Post-decision dissonance at the polling booth. *Canadian Journal of Behavioural Science, 8*(4), 347–350.

Frey, B. S. (1971). Why do high income people participate more in politics? *Public Choice, 11*, 101.

Fuchs, D. A. (1966). Election-day radio–television and western voting. *The Public Opinion Quarterly, 30*(2), 226–236.

Fuchs, D., & Lorek, S. (2005). Sustainable consumption governance: A history of promises and failures. *Journal of Consumer Policy, 28*, 361–370.

Gamson, W. (1992). *Talking politics*. New York: Cambridge University Press.

Gamson, W. A. (1975). *The strategy of social protest*. Homewood, IL: The Dorsey Press.

Gamson, W. A., & Modigliani, A. (1987). The changing culture of affirmative action. *Research in Political Sociology, 3*, 137–177.

Gant, M. M. (1983). Citizen uncertainty and turnout in the 1980 presidential campaign. *Political Behavior, 5*(3), 257–275.

Gant, M., & Davis, D. (1984). Mental economy and voter rationality: The informed citizen problem in voting research. *Journal of Politics, 46*, 132–153.

Gerber, A. S., & Green, D. P. (2000a). The effect of a nonpartisan get-out-the-vote drive: An experimental study of leafleting. *Journal of Politics, 62*(3), 846–857.

Gerber, A. S., & Green, D. P. (2000b). The effects of canvassing, telephone calls, and direct mail on voter turnout: A field experiment. *American Political Science Review, 94*(3), 653–663.

Gerber, A. S., & Green, D. P. (2001). Do phone calls increase voter turnout? *Public Opinion Quarterly, 65*(1), 75–85.

Gerber, A. S., & Green, D. P. (2005). Correction to Gerber and Green (2000), replication of disputed findings, and reply to Imai (2005). *American Political Science Review, 99*(2), 301(13).

Gerber, A. S., Green, D. P., & Green, M. (2003). Partisan mail and voter turnout: Results from randomized field experiments. *Electoral Studies, 22*(4), 563–579.

Gerber, A. S., Green, D. P., & Shachar, R. (2003). Voting may be habit-forming: Evidence from a randomized field experiment. *American Journal of Political Science, 47*(3), 540–550.

Gerber, A. S., Green, D.P., & Larimer, C. W. (2008). Social pressure and voter turnout: Evidence from a large-scale field experiment. *American Political Science Review, 102*(1), 33–48.

Gershtenson, J. (2003). Mobilization strategies of the Democrats and Republicans, 1956–2000. *Political Research Quarterly, 56*(3), 293–308.

Geys, B., & Vermeir, J. (2008). Taxation and presidential approval: Separate effects from tax burden and tax structure turbulence? *Public Choice, 135*(3–4), 301–317.

Gibson, J. L., & Caldeira, G. A. (2009). Confirmation politics and the legitimacy of the U.S. Supreme Court: Institutional loyalty, positivity bias, and the Alito nomination. *American Journal of Political Science, 53*(1), 139–155.

Gilbert, R. K. (1988). The dynamics of inaction: Psychological factors inhibiting arms control activism. *American Psychologist, 43*, 755–764.

Gilens, M. (1988). Gender and support for Reagan: A comprehensive model of presidential approval. *American Journal of Political Science, 32*(1), 19–49.

Gilens, M. (1995). Racial attitudes and opposition to welfare. *Journal of Politics, 57*, 994–1014.

Gilens, M. (1996). "Race coding" and white opposition to welfare. *America Political Science Review, 90*, 593–604.

Gimpel, J. G., & Schuknecht, J. E. (2003). Political participation and the accessibility of the ballot box. *Political Geography, 22*(5), 471–488.

Gimpel, J., Dyck, J., & Shaw, D. (2004). Registrants, voters, and turnout variability across neighborhoods. *Political Behavior, 26*(4), 343–375.

Glaser, J. (1994). Back to the black belt: Racial environment and white racial attitudes in the South. *Journal of Politics, 56*(1), 21–41.

Glaser, W. A. (1959). The family and voting turnout. *Public Opinion Quarterly, 23*(4), 563–570.

Godwin, K. R. (1988). *One billion dollars of influence: The direct marketing of politics.* Chatham, NJ: Chatham House Publishers.

Goidel, R. K., Shields, T. G., & Peffley, M. (1997). Priming theory and RAS models: Toward an integrated perspective of media influence. *American Politics Quarterly, 25*(3), 287–318.

Goldstein, K., & Freedman, P. (2002). Campaign advertising and voter turnout: New evidence for a stimulation effect. *Journal of Politics, 64*(3), 721–740.

Goldstein, K. M., & Ridout, T. N. (2002). The politics of participation: Mobilization and turnout over time. *Political Behavior, 24*(1), 3–29.

Gonzenbach, W. J. (1996). *The media, the president, and public opinion: A longitudinal analysis of the drug issue, 1984–1991.* Mahwah, NJ: Lawrence Erlbaum.

Gore, P. M., & Rotter, J. B. (1963). A personality correlate of social action. *Journal of Personality, 31*(1), 58–64.

Gorn, G. J. (1975). The effects of personal involvement, communication discrepancy, and source prestige on reactions to communications on separatism. *Canadian Journal of Behavioral Science, 7*, 369–386.

Graber, D. (1991). The mass media and election campaigns in the United States of America. In F. J. Fletcher (Ed.), *Media, elections and democracy* (pp. 139–177). Toronto: Dundurn Press.

Graber, D. A. (1990). Seeing is remembering: How visuals contribute to learning from television news. *Journal of Communication, 40*(3), 134–156.

Granberg, D. (1985). An anomaly in political perception. *Political Opinion Quarterly, 49*, 504–516.

Granberg, D. (1987). Candidate preference, membership group, and estimates of voting behavior. *Social Cognition, 5*, 323–335.

Granberg, D., & Brent, E. E. (1974). Dove–hawk placements in the 1968 election: Application of social judgment and balance theories. *Journal of Personality and Social Psychology, 29*(5), 687–695.

Granberg, D., & Brent, E. E. (1980). Perceptions of issue positions in presidential candidates. *American Scientist, 68*(6), 617–625.

Granberg, D., & Holmberg, S. (1986a). Political perception in Sweden and the United States: Analyses of issues with explicit alternatives. *Western Political Quarterly, 39*, 7–28.

Granberg, D., & Holmberg, S. (1986b). Preference, expectations, and voting behavior in Sweden's referendum on nuclear power. *Social Science Quarterly, 66*, 379–392.

Granberg, D., & Holmberg, S. (1988). *The political system matters: Social psychology and voting behavior in Sweden and the United States.* Cambridge, England: Cambridge University Press.

Granberg, D., & Holmberg, S. (1991). Self-reported turnout and voter validation. *American Journal of Political Science, 35*(2), 448–460.

Granberg, D., & Holmberg, S. (1992). The Hawthorne effect in election studies: The impact of survey participation on voting. *British Journal of Political Science, 22*(2), 240–247.

Granberg, D., & Jencks, R. (1977). Assimilation and contrast effects in the 1972 election. *Human Relations, 30*, 623–640.

Granberg, D., & King, M. (1980). Cross-lagged panel analysis of the relation between attraction and perceived similarity. *Journal of Experimental Social Psychology, 16*(6), 573–581.

Granberg, D., & Seidel, J. (1976). Social judgments of the urban and Vietnam issues in 1968 and 1972. *Social Forces, 55*, 1–15.

Granberg, D., Harris, W., & King, M. (1981). Assimilation but little contrast in the 1976 U.S. presidential election. *Journal of Psychology, 108*, 241–247.

Granberg, D., Kasmer, J., & Nanneman, T. (1988). An empirical examination of two theories of political perception. *Political Research Quarterly, 41*, 29–46.

Gray, J. A. (1987). *The psychology of fear and stress.* New York: Cambridge University Press.

Gray, J. A. (1990). Brain systems that mediate both emotion and cognition. *Cognition and Emotion, 4*(3), 269–288.

Green, D. (1988). On the dimensionality of public sentiment toward partisan and ideological groups. *American Journal of Political Science, 32*, 758–780.

Green, D. (2004a). Get out the vote: What works? *Social Policy, 34*(2/3), 60(3).

Green, D. (2004b). Mobilizing African American voters using direct mail and commercial phone banks: A field experiment. *Political Research Quarterly, 57*(2), 245(11).

Green, D., & Gerkin, A. E. (1989). Self-interest and public opinion toward smoking restrictions and cigarette taxes. *Public Opinion Quarterly, 53*, 1–16.

Green, D., & Palmquist, B. (1990). Of artifacts and partisan instability. *American Journal of Political Science, 34*, 872–902.

Green, D., & Palmquist, B. (1994). How stable is party identification? *Political Behavior, 43*, 437–466.

Green, D., & Shachar, R. (2000). Habit formation and political behaviour: Evidence of consuetude in voter turnout. *British Journal of Political Science, 30*(4), 561.

Green, D., Gerber, A. S., & Nickerson, D. W. (2003). Getting out the vote in local elections: Results from six door-to-door canvassing experiments. *Journal of Politics, 65*(4), 1083–1096.

Green, D., Palmquist, B., & Schickler, E. (2002). *Partisan hearts and minds.* New Haven, CT: Yale Univeristy Press.

Greenberg, E. S. (1981). Industrial self-management and political attitudes. *The American Political Science Review, 75*(1), 29–42.

Greene, S. (2001). The role of character assessments in presidential approval. *American Politics Research, 29*(2), 196–210.

Greenstein, F. I. (1965). *Children and politics.* New Haven, CT: Yale University Press.

Greenwald, A. G., Carnot, C. G., Beach, R., & Young, B. (1987). Increasing voting behavior by asking people if they expect to vote. *Journal of Applied Psychology, 72*, 315–318.

Gronke, P., & Brehm, J. (2002). History, heterogeneity, and presidential approval: A modified ARCH approach. *Electoral Studies, 21*(3), 425–452.

Gronke, P., & Toffey, D. K. (2008b). The psychological and institutional determinants of early voting. *Journal of Social Issues, 64*(3), 503–524.

Gronke, P., Koch, J., & Wilson, J. M. (2003). Presidential approval, presidential support, and representatives' electoral fortunes. *Journal of Politics, 65*, 785–808.

Gurr, T. R. (1970). *Why men rebel.* Princeton, NJ: Princeton University Press.

Gusfield, J. E. (1963). *Symbolic crusade: Status politics and the American temperance movement.* Urbana: University of Illinois Press.

Guterbock, T. M., & London, B. (1983). Race, political orientation, and participation: An empirical test of four competing theories. *American Sociological Review, 48*(4), 439–453.

Hackley, S., Bazerman, M., Ross, L., & Shapiro, D. (2005). Psychological dimensions of the Israeli settlements issue: Endowments and identities. *Negotiation Journal, 21*, 209–219.

Hallin, D. C. (1986). *The "uncensored war:" The media and Vietnam.* New York: Oxford University Press.

Hambrick, D. Z. (2003). Why are some people more knowledgeable than others? A longitudinal study of knowledge acquisition. *Memory & Cognition, 31*(6), 902–917.

Hamermesh, D., & Biddle, J. (1994). Beauty and the labor market. *The American Economic Review, 84,* 1174–1194.

Hamilton, C. V. (1977). Voter registration drives and turnout: A report on the Harlem electorate. *Political Science Quarterly, 92*(1), 43–46.

Haney, C., Banks, W., & Zimbardo, P. (1973). Interpersonal dynamics in a simulated prison. *International Journal of Criminology and Penology, 1,* 69–97.

Hansen, J. M. (1985). The political economy of group membership. *American Political Science Review, 79,* 79–96.

Hansen, J. M. (1991). *Gaining access: Congress and the farm lobby, 1919–1981.* Chicago: University of Chicago Press.

Harris, J. P. (1934). *Election administration in the United States.* Washington, DC: Brookings Institute Press.

Hassin, R., & Trope, Y. (2000). Facing faces: Studies on the cognitive aspects of physiognomy. *Journal of Personality and Social Psychology, 78,* 837–852.

Hastie, R., & Kumar, P. A. (1979). Person memory: Personality traits as organizing principles in memory for behaviors. *Journal of Personality and Social Psychology, 37*(1), 25–38.

Hastie, R., & Park, B. (1986). The relationship between memory and judgment depends on whether the judgment task is memory-based or online. *Psychological Review, 93,* 258–268.

Heaven, P.C.L., & Connors, J. R. (2001). A note on the value correlates of social dominance orientation and right-wing authoritarianism. *Personality and Individual Differences, 31,* 925–930.

Heaven, P. C., & St. Quintin, D. S. (2003). Personality factors predict racial prejudice. *Personality and Individual Differences, 34,* 625–634.

Heider, F. (1958). *The psychology of interpersonal relations.* Hillsdale, NJ: Lawrence Erlbaum Associates.

Helliwell, J. F., & Putnam, R. D. (1999). *Education and social capital. NBER Working Paper 7121.* Cambridge, MA: National Bureau of Economic Research.

Henshel, R. L., & Johnston, W. (1987). The emergence of bandwagon effects: A theory. *Sociological Quarterly, 28,* 493–511.

Henry, P. J., & Sears, D. O. (2002). The symbolic racism 2000 scale. *Political Psychology, 23*(2), 253–283.

Hermann, M. (Ed.). (1986). *Handbook of political psychology.* San Francisco: Jossey-Bass.

Herring, C. (1989). Acquiescence or activism? Political behavior among the politically alienated. *Political Psychology, 10*(1), 135–153.

Hess, R. D., & Torney, J. V. (1967). *The development of political attitudes in children.* Chicago: Aldine.

Hester, J. B., & Gibson, R. (2003). The economy and second-level agenda setting: A time-series analysis of economic news and public opinion about the economy. *Journalism and Mass Communication Quarterly, 80*(1), 73–90.

Hetherington, M. J. (1999). The effect of political trust on the presidential vote, 1968–1996. *American Political Science Review, 93*(2), 311–326.

Hibbs, D. A. (1982). Public concern about inflation and unemployment in the United States: Trends, correlates and political implications. In R. E. Hall (Ed.), *Inflation: Causes and effects* (pp. 211–231). Chicago: University of Chicago Press.

Higgins, E. T., & King, G. (1981). Accessibility of social constructs: Information-processing consequences of individual and contextual variability. In N. Cantor & J. Kihlstrom (Eds.), *Personality, cognition, and social interaction* (pp. 69–121). Hillsdale, NJ: Erlbaum.

Highton, B. (1997). Easy registration and voter turnout. *Journal of Politics, 59*(2), 565–575.

Highton, B. (2000). Residential mobility, community mobility, and electoral participation. *Political Behavior, 22*(2), 109–120.

Highton, B., & Wolfinger, R. E. (1998). Estimating the effects of the National Voter Registration Act of 1993. *Political Behavior, 20*(2), 79–104.

Hilgartner, S., & Bosk, C. L. (1988). The rise and fall of social problems: A public arenas model. *The American Journal of Sociology, 94*(1), 53–78.

Hill, D. (2003). A two-step approach to assessing composition effects of the National Voter Registration Act. *Electoral Studies, 22*(4), 703–720.

Hill, K. Q. (1998). The policy agendas of the president and the mass public: A research validation and extension. *American Journal of Political Science, 42,* 1328–1334.

Hill, K. Q., & Leighley, J. E. (1992). The policy consequences of class bias in state electorates. *American Journal of Political Science, 36*(2), 351–365.

Hillygus, S.D. (2005). The missing link: Exploring the relationship between higher education and political engagement. *Political Behavior, 27*(1), 25–47.

Hinkel, S., Fox-Cardamone, L., Haseleu, J. A., Brown, R., & Irwin, L. M. (1996). Grassroots political action as an intergroup phenomenon. *Journal of Social Issues, 52*(Spring), 39–52.

Ho, D., & Imai, K. (2008). Estimating causal effects of ballot order from a randomized natural experiment: The California alphabet lottery, 1978–2002. *Public Opinion Quarterly. 72*(2), 216–240.

Hochschild, J. L. (1981). *What's fair: American beliefs about distributive justice.* Cambridge, MA: Harvard University Press.

Holbrook, R. A., & Hill, T. G. (2005). Agenda-setting and priming in prime time television: Crime dramas as political cue. *Political Communication, 22*(3), 277–295.

Holbrook, A. L., Berent, M. K., Krosnick, J. A., Visser, P. S., & Boninger, D. S. (2005). Attitude importance and the accumulation of attitude-relevant information in memory. *Journal of Personality and Social Psychology, 88,* 749–769.

Holbrook, A. L., Krosnick, J. A., Visser, P. S., Gardner, W. L., & Cacioppo, J. T. (2001). Attitudes toward presidential candidates and political parties: Initial optimism, inertial first impressions, and a focus on flaws. *American Journal of Political Science, 45*(4), 930–950.

Huckfeldt, R. R. (1979). Political participation and the neighborhood social context. *American Journal of Political Science, 23*(3), 579–592.

Hurwitz, J. (1989). Presidential leadership and public fellowship. In M. Margolis & G. A. Mauser (Eds.), *Manipulating public opinion: Essays on public opinion as a dependent variable* (pp. 222–249). Pacific Grove, CA: Brooks Cole Publishing Company.

Hurwitz, J., & Peffley, M. (1987). How are foreign policy attitudes structured? A hierarchical model. *American Political Science Review, 81,* 1099–1120.

Hurwitz, J., & Peffley, M. (1998). Introduction. In J. Hurwitz & M. Peffley (Eds.), *Perception and prejudice: Race and politics in the United States* (pp. 1–16). New Haven, CT: Yale University Press.

Hutchings, K. (2001). The nature of critique in critical international relations theory. In R. W. Jones (Ed.), *Critical Theory and World Politics* (pp. 79–90). London: Lynne Rienner.

Hutchings, V. L. (2003). *Public opinion and democratic accountability: How citizens learn about politics.* Princeton, NJ: Princeton University Press.

Hyman, H. (1959). *Political socialization.* Glencoe, IL: Free Press.

Hyman, H. H., & Sheatsley, P. B. (1947). Some reasons why information campaigns fail. *Public Opinion Quarterly, 11,* 412–423.

Imai, K. (2005). Do get-out-the-vote calls reduce turnout? The importance of statistical methods for field experiments. *American Political Science Review, 99*(2), 283–301.

Ingham, A. G., Levinger, G., Graves, J., & Peckman, V. (1974). The Ringelmann effect: Studies of group size and group performance. *Journal of Experimental Social Psychology, 10*(July), 371–384.

Iyengar, S. (1991). *Is anyone responsible? How television frames political issues.* Chicago: University of Chicago Press.

Iyengar, S. (1993). Agenda-setting and beyond: television news and the strength of political issues. In W. Riker (Ed.), *Agenda formation* (pp. 1–27). Ann Arbor: University of Michigan Press.

Iyengar, S., & Kinder, D. R. (1987). *News that matters: Television and American opinion.* Chicago: The University of Chicago Press.

Iyengar, S., & McGuire, W. (Eds.). (1993). *Handbook of political psychology.* Durham, NC: Duke University Press.

Iyengar, S., & Simon, A. (1993). News coverage of the Gulf crisis and public opinion. *Communication Research, 20*(3), 365–383.

Iyengar, S., Hahn, K., Krosnick, J., & Walker J. (2008). Selective exposure to campaign communication: The role of anticipated agreement and issue public membership. *Journal of Politics, 70,* 186–200.

Iyengar, S., Peters, M. D., & Kinder, D. R. (1982). Experimental demonstrations of the "not-so-minimal" consequences of television news programs. *The American Political Science Review, 76*(4), 848–858.

Iyengar, S., Peters, M. D., Kinder, D. R., & Krosnick, J. A. (1984). The evening news and presidential evaluations. *Journal of Personality and Social Psychology, 46*(4), 778–787.

Jackman, R. W., & Miller, R. A. (1996). A renaissance of political culture? *American Journal of Political Science, 40*(3), 632–659.

Jackson, J. E. (1975). Issues, party choices, and presidential votes. *American Journal of Political Science, 19,* 161–185.

Jackson, J. E. (1979). Statistical estimation of possible response bias in close-ended issue questions. *Political Methodology,* 393–423.

Jackson, J. E. (1983). The systematic beliefs of the mass public: Estimating policy preferences with survey data. *Journal of Politics, 45,* 840–865.

Jackson, J. E., & Franklin, C. H. (1983). The dynamics of party identification. *American Political Science Review, 77*(4), 957–973.

Jackson, R. A. (2002). Gubernatorial and senatorial campaign mobilization of voters. *Political Research Quarterly, 55*(4), 825–844.

James, P., & Rioux, J. S. (1998). International crises and linkage politics: The experiences of the United States, 1953–1994. *Political Research Quarterly, 51*(3), 781–812.

Jankowski, R. (2004). Altruism and the decision to vote: Explaining and testing high voter turnout. Paper presented at the Annual Meeting of the American Political Science Association.

Jankowski, T. B., & Strate, J. M. (1995). Modes of participation over the adult life span. *Political Behavior, 17*(1), 89–106.

Jenkins, J. C. (1983). Resource mobilization theory and the study of social movements. *Annual Review of Sociology, 9,* 527–553.

Jennings, M. K. (1979). Another look at the life cycle and political participation. *American Journal of Political Science, 23,* 755–771.

Jennings, M. K., & Markus, G. B. (1984). Partisan orientations over the long haul: Results from the three-wave political socialization panel study. *American Political Science Review, 78,* 1000–1018.

Jennings, M. K., & Markus, G. B. (1988). Political involvement in the later years: A longitudinal survey. *American Journal of Political Science, 32*(2), 302–316.

Jennings, M. K., & Niemi, R. G. (1978). The persistence of political orientations: An overtime analysis of two generations. *British Journal of Political Science, 8,* 333–363.

Jennings, M. K., Stoker, L., & Bowers, J. (1999). Politics across generations: Family transmission reexamined. Paper presented to the American Political Science Association, Atlanta, Georgia.

Jerit, J. (2007). How predictive appeals shape policy opinions. Paper presented at the annual meeting of the Midwest Political Science Association, Chicago, IL.

Johnson, M., Shively, W. P., & Stein, R. M. (2002). Contextual data and the study of elections and voting behavior: Connecting individuals to environments. *Electoral Studies, 21*(2), 219–233.

Johnston, R. (2006). Party identification: Unmoved mover or sum of preferences? *Annual Review of Political Science, 9,* 329–351.

Jordan, D. L., & Page, B. I. (1992). Shaping foreign policy opinions. *Journal of Conflict Resolution, 36*(2), 227–241.

Jost, J., & Sidanius, J. (Eds.). (2004). *Political psychology: Key readings.* Philadelphia: Psychology Press.

Judd, C. M., & DePaulo, B. M. (1979). The effect of perspective differences on the measurement of involving attitudes. *Social Psychology Quarterly 42,* 185–189.

Judd, C. M., & Johnson, J. T. (1981). Attitudes, polarization, and diagnosticity: Exploring the effects of affect. *Journal of Personality and Social Psychology, 41,* 26–36.

Judd, C. M., & McClelland, G. H. (1989). *Data analysis: A model–comparison approach.* San Diego, CA: Harcourt Brace Jovanovich.

Judd, C. M., & Milburn, M. A. (1980). The structure of attitude systems in the general public: Comparisons of a structural equation model. *American Sociological Review, 45,* 627–643.

Judd, C. M., Kenny, D. A., & Krosnick, J. A. (1983). Judging the positions of political candidates: Models of assimilation and contrast. *Journal of Personality and Social Psychology, 44*(5), 952–963.

Kahn, K. F., & Kenney, P. J. (1999). Do negative campaigns mobilize or suppress turnout? Clarifying the relationship between negativity and participation. *American Political Science Review, 93*(4), 877–889.

Kahneman, D. (1973). *Attention and effort.* Englewood Cliffs, NJ: Prentice Hall.

Kahneman, D., & Tversky, A. (1979). Prospect theory: An analysis of decision under risk. *Econometrica, 47* (March), 263–291.

Kahneman, D., & Tversky A. (1981). The framing of decisions and the psychology of choice. *Science, 211,* 453–458.

Kahneman, D., & Tversky A. (1986). Rational choice and the framing of decisions. *Journal of Business, 59,* S251–S278.

Kamin, L. J. (1958). Ethnic and party affiliations of candidates as determinants of voting. *Canadian Journal of Psychology, 12,* 205–212.

Karp, J. A., & Banducci, S. A. (2000). Going postal: How all-mail elections influence turnout. *Political Behavior, 22*(3), 223–239.

Kaufman, C. (2004). Threat inflation and the failure of the marketplace of ideas: The selling of the Iraq war. *International Security, 29,* 5–48.

Katosh, J. P., & Traugott, M. W. (1982). Costs and values in the calculus of voting. *American Journal of Political Science, 26*(2), 361–376.

Katz, D. (1960). The functional approach to the study of attitudes. *Public Opinion Quarterly, 24,* 163–204.

Kelley, S., Jr., & Mirer, T. (1974). The simple act of voting. *American Political Science Review, 61,* 572–591.

Kelley, S., Jr., Ayres, R. E., & Bowen, W. G. (1967). Registration and voting: Putting first things first. *American Political Science Review, 61*(2), 359–379.

Kelman, H. C. (1982). Creating the conditions for Israeli-Palestinian negotiations. *Journal of Conflict Resolution, 26,* 39–75.

Kelman, H. C. (1983). Conversations with Arafat: A social–psychological assessment of the prospects for Israeli–Palestinian peace. *American Psychologist, 38,* 203–216.

Kernell, S. (1976). The Truman Doctrine speech: A case study of the dynamics of presidential opinion leadership. *Social Science History, 1,* 20–45.

Kernell, S. (1993). *Going public: New strategies of presidential leadership* (2nd ed.). Washington, DC: Congressional Quarterly, Inc.

Key, V.O. (1949). *Southern politics.* New York: Alfred A. Knopf, Inc.

Key, V. O. (1961). *Public opinion and American democracy.* New York: Alfred A. Knopf, Inc.

Kim, J., Petrocik, J. R., & Enokson, S. N. (1975). Voter turnout among the American states: Systemic and individual components. *American Political Science Review, 69*(1), 107–123.

Kinder, D. R. (1978). Political person perception: The asymmetrical influence of sentiment and choice on perceptions of presidential candidates. *Journal of Personality and Social Psychology, 36,* 859–871.

Kinder, D. R. (1983). Diversity and complexity in American public opinion. In A. Finifter (Ed.), *Political science: The state of the discipline* (pp. 391–401). Washington, DC: American Political Science Association.

Kinder, D. R. (1986). Presidential character revisited. In R.R. Lau & D. O. Sears (Eds.), *Political cognition* (pp. 233–255). Hillsdale, NJ: Erlbaum.

Kinder D. R. (1998). Opinion and action in the realm of politics. In D. Gilbert, S. Fiske, & G. Lindsey (Eds.), *Handbook of social psychology* (4th ed., pp. 778–867). Boston: McGraw- Hill.

Kinder, D. R. (2006). Politics and the life cycle. *Science, 312*(5782), 1905–1908.

Kinder, D. R., & Mebane, W. (1983). Politics and economics in everyday life. In K. R. Monroe (Ed.), *The political process and economic change* (pp. 141–180). New York: Agathon Press.

Kinder, D. R., & Sanders, L. M. (1990). Mimicking political debate with survey questions: The case of White opinion on affirmative action for Blacks. *Social Cognition, 8*(1), 73–103.

Kinder, D. R., & Sanders, L. M. (1996). *Divided by color: Racial politics and democratic ideals.* Chicago: University of Chicago Press.

Kinder, D. R., & Sears, D. O. (1985). Public opinion and political action. In G. Lindzey & E. Aronson (Eds.), *Handbook of social psychology* (3rd ed., pp. 659–741). New York: Random House.

King, D.C., & Walker J.L., (1991). An ecology of interest groups in America. In J. L. Walker (Ed.), *Mobilizing interest groups in America.* Ann Arbor: University of Michigan Press.

King, G. (1988). Statistical models for political science event counts: Bias in conventional procedures and evidence for the exponential poisson regression model. *American Journal of Political Science* 30 (August), 838–863.

King, G. (1989a). Variance specification in event count models: From restrictive assumptions to a generalized estimator. *American Journal of Political Science, 33* (August), 767–784.

King, G. (1989b). *Unifying political methodology: The likelihood theory of statistical inference.* Cambridge, MA: Cambridge University Press.

King, P. (1978). Affective response of the analyst to the patient's communications. *International Journal of Psychoanalysis, 59,* 329–334.

Kingdon, J. W. (1995). *Agenda, alternatives, and public policies* (2nd ed.). New York: Harper Collins.

Kingdon, J. W. (1981). *Congressmen's voting decisions.* New York: Harper and Row.

Kingdon, J. W. (1995). *Agendas, alternatives and public policies.* New York: Harper Collins.

Kingston, P. W., & Finkel, S. E. (1987). Is there a marriage gap in politics? *Journal of Marriage and the Family, 49*(1), 57–64.

Kiousis, S. (2003). Job approval and favorability: The impact of media attention to the Monica Lewinsky scandal on public opinion of President Bill Clinton. *Mass Communication & Society, 6*(4), 435–451.

Kirchgässner, G., & Wolters, J. (1987). U.S.–European interest rate linkage: A time series analysis for West Germany, Switzerland, and the United States. *Review of Economics and Statistics, 69,* 675–684

Klandermans, B. (1983). Rotter's I. E. scale and sociopolitical action-taking: The balance of 20 years of research. *European Journal of Social Psychology,* 13(4), 399–415.

Klayman, J., & Ha, Y. (1987). Confirmation, disconfirmation, and information in hypothesis testing. *Psychological Review, 94,* 211–228.

Kluegel, J. R., & Bobo, L. (1993). Opposition to race-targeting: Self-interest, stratification ideology, or racial attitudes? *American Sociological Review, 58,* 443–464.

Kluegel, J. R., & Smith, E. R. (1986). *Beliefs about inequality: Americans' views of what is and what ought to be.* New York: Aldine de Gruyter.

Kline, P. (1986). *A handbook of test construction: Introduction to psychometric design.* London, UK: Methuen & Co.

Knack, S. (1992). Civic norms, social sanctions, and voter turnout. *Rationality and Society, 4*(2), 133–156.

Knack, S. (1994). Does rain help the Republicans? Theory and evidence on turnout and the vote. *Public Choice, 79,* 187–209.

Knack, S. (1995). Does "motor voter" work? Evidence from state-level data. *Journal of Politics, 57*(3), 796–811.

Knack, S., & Kropf, M.E. (1998). For shame! The effect of community cooperative context on the probability of voting. *Political Psychology, 19*(3), 585–599.

Knack, S., & White, J. (2000). Election-day registration and turnout inequality. *Political Behavior, 22*(1), 29–44.

Knutson, J. (Ed.). (1973). *Handbook of political psychology.* San Francisco, CA: Jossey-Bass.

Koriat, A., Lichtenstein, S., & Fischhoff, B. (1980). Reasons for overconfidence. *Journal of Experimental Psychology: Human Learning and Memory, 6,* 107–118.

Kornhauser, W. (1959). *The politics of mass society.* Glencoe, IL: The Free Press.

Koppell, J.G.S., & Steen, J. S. (2004). The effects of ballot position on election outcomes. *Journal of Politics, 66,* 267–281.

Kressel, N. (Ed.). (1993). *Political psychology: Classic and contemporary readings.* New York: Paragon House.

Kriner, D. L. (2006). Examining variance in presidential approval: The case of FDR in World War II. *Public Opinion Quarterly, 70*(1), 23–47.

Krosnick, J. A. (1986). Policy voting in American presidential elections: An application of psychological theory to American politics. Unpublished doctoral dissertation, University of Michigan.

Krosnick, J. A. (1988a). The role of attitude importance in social evaluation: A study of policy preferences, presidential candidate evaluations, and voting behavior. *Journal of Personality and Social Psychology, 55,* 196–210.

Krosnick, J. A. (1988b). Attitude importance and attitude change. *Journal of Experimental Social Psychology Bulletin, 24,* 240–255.

Krosnick, J. A. (1989). Attitude importance and attitude accessibility. *Personality and Social Psychology Bulletin, 15,* 297–308.

Krosnick, J. A. (1990). Government policy and citizen passion: A study of issue publics in contemporary America. *Political Behavior, 12*(1): 59–92.

Krosnick, J. A. (1991). Response strategies for coping with the cognitive demands of attitude measures in surveys. *Applied Cognitive Psychology, 5*(3), 213–236.

Krosnick, J. A. (2002). The challenges of political psychology: Lessons to be learned from research on attitude perception. In J. Kuklinski (Ed.), *Thinking about political psychology* (pp. 115–152). New York: Cambridge University Press.

Krosnick, J. A., & Brannon, L. A. (1993). The impact of the Gulf War on the ingredients of presidential evaluations: Multidimensional effects of political involvement. *American Political Science Review, 87,* 963–975.

Krosnick, J. A., & Kinder, D. R. (1990). Altering the foundations of support for the president through priming. *American Political Science Review, 84*, 497–512.

Krosnick, J. A., & Lupia, A. (2008). *Problems with ANES questions measuring political knowledge.* Ann Arbor, MI: American National Election Studies Report.

Krosnick, J. A., & Petty, R. E. (1995). Attitude strength: An overview. In R. E. Petty & J. A. Krosnick (Eds.), *Attitude strength: Antecedents and consequences* (pp. 1–24) Hillsdale, NJ: Erlbaum.

Krosnick J. A., & Schuman, H. (1988). Attitude intensity, importance, and certainty and susceptibility to response effects. *Journal of Personality Social Psychology, 54*, 940–952.

Krosnick, J. A., & Telhami, S. (1995). Public attitudes toward Israel: A study of the attentive and issue publics. *International Studies Quarterly, 59* (December), 535–554.

Krosnick, J. A., Boninger, D. S., Chuang, Y. C., Berent, M. K., & Carnot, C. G. (1993). Attitude strength: One construct or many related constructs? *Journal of Personality and Social Psychology, 65*, 1132–1151.

Krosnick, J. A., Holbrook, A. L., & Visser, P. S. (2000). The impact of the fall 1997 debate about global warming on American public opinion. *Public Understanding of Science, 9*(3), 239–260.

Krosnick, J. A., Miller, J. M., & Tichy, M. P. (2004). An unrecognized need for ballot reform: The effects of candidate name order on election outcomes. In A. N. Crigler, M. R. Just, & E. J. McCaffery (Eds.), *Rethinking the vote: The politics and prospects of American election reform* (pp. 51–73). New York: Oxford University Press.

Krosnick, J. A., Pfent, A., & Courser, M. (2003). Rationalization and derivation processes in the 2000 presidential election: New evidence about the determinants of citizens' vote choices. Paper presented at the annual meeting of the American Association for Public Opinion Research,Nashville, TN, August 16.

Krugman, H. E., & Hartley, E. L. (1970). Passive learning from television. *Public Opinion Quarterly, 34*, 184–190.

La Due Lake, R., & Huckfeldt, R. (1998). Social capital, social networks, and political participation. *Political Psychology, 19*(3), 567–584.

Lacy, D., & Burden, B. C. (1999). The vote-stealing and turnout effects of Ross Perot in the 1992 U.S. presidential election. *American Journal of Political Science, 43*(1), 233–255.

Lacy, D., & Paolino, P. (2004). An experimental test of proximity and directional voting. Paper presented at the annual meeting of the Midwest Political Science Association, Chicago, IL.

Lane, R. E. (1955). Political personality and electoral choice. *American Political Science Review, 49*, 173–190.

Lane, R. E. (1962). *Political ideology: Why the American common man believes what he does.* New York: Free Press.

Lane, R. E. (1969). *Political thinking and consciousness.* Chicago: Markham.

Lane, R. E. (1973). Patterns of political belief. In J. Knuston (Ed.), *Handbook of political psychology* (pp. 83–116). San Francisco: Jossey Bass.

Laponce, J. A. (1966). An experimental method to measure the tendency to equibalance in a political system. *American Political Science Review, 60*, 982–993.

Latane, B. (1981). The psychology of social impact. *American Psychologist, 36*(April), 343–356.

Lau, R. R., & Pomper, G. M. (2001). Effects of negative campaigning on turnout in U.S. Senate elections, 1988–1998. *Journal of Politics, 63*(3), 804–819.

Lau, R. R., Brown, T. A., & Sears, D. O. (1978). Self-interest and civilians' attitudes toward the Vietnam War. *Public Opinion Quarterly, 42*, 464–483.

Lau, R. R., & Sears, D. O. (1981). Cognitive links between economic grievances and political responses. *Political Behavior, 3*(4), 1981.

Lau, R. R., Sears, D. O., & Jessor, T. (1990). Fact or artifact revisited: Survey instrument effects and pocketbook politics. *Political Behavior, 12*, 217–242.

Lau, R. R., Sigelman, L., Heldman, C., & Babbitt, P. (1999). The effects of negative political advertisements: A meta-analytic assessment. *American Political Science Review, 93*(4), 851–875.

Lavrakas, P. J., & Holley, J. K. (1991). *Polling and presidential election coverage.* Newbury Park, CA: Sage Publications.

Lavrakas, P. J., Holley, J. K., & Miller, P. V. (1991). Public reactions to polling news during the 1988 presidential election campaign. In P. J. Lavrakas & J. K. Holley (Eds.), *Polling and presidential election coverage.* Newbury Park, CA: Sage.

Lazarsfeld, P. M., Berelson, B. R., & Gaudet, H. (1948). *The people's choice: How the voter makes up his mind in a presidential campaign.* New York: Duell, Sloan & Pearce.

LeDoux, J. E. (1996). *The emotional brain: The mysterious underpinnings of emotional life.* New York: Simon & Shuster.

Leff, D. R., Protess, D. L., & Brooks, S. C. (1986). Crusading journalism: Changing public attitudes and policy-making agendas. *Public Opinion Quarterly, 50*, 300–315.

Leighley, J. E., & Nagler, J. (1992). Individual and systemic influences on turnout: Who votes? 1984. *Journal of Politics, 54*(3), 718–740.

Leighley, J. E., & Nagler, J. (1992). Socioeconomic class bias in turnout, 1964–1988: The voters remain the same. *American Political Science Review, 86*(3), 725–736.

Leighley, J. E., & Vedlitz, A. (1999). Race, ethnicity, and political participation: Competing models and contrasting explanations. *Journal of Politics, 61*(4), 1092–1114.

Levi, M., & Stoker, L. (2000). Political trust and trustworthiness. *Annual Review of Political Science, 3*(1), 475–507.

Lewis, J. B., & King, G. (1999). No evidence on directional versus proximity voting. *Political Analysis, 8*(1), 21–33.

Lewis-Beck, M. S., Jacoby, W. G., Norpoth, H., & Weisberg, H. (2008). *The American voter revisited.* Ann Arbor: University of Michigan Press.

Lian, B., & Oneal, J. R. (1993). Presidents, the use of military force, and public opinion. *Journal of Conflict Resolution, 37*(2), 277–300.

Lien, P., Collet, C., Wong, J., & Ramakrishnan, S. K. (2001). Asian Pacific–American public opinion and political participation. *PS: Political Science and Politics, 34*(3), 625–630.

Lodge, M., McGraw, K., & Stroh, P. (1989). An impression-driven model of candidate evaluation. *American Political Science Review. 83*, 399–420.

Lodge, M., Steenbergen, M. R., & Brau, S. (1995). The responsive voter: Campaign information and the dynamics of candidate evaluation. *American Political Science Review, 89*, 309–326.

Loomis, B. A., & Cigler, A. J. (1995). Introduction: The changing nature of interest group politics. In A. J. Cigler & B. A. Loomis (Eds.), *Interest group politics* (pp. 1–30). Washington, DC: CQ Press.

Lowery, D., & Sigelman, L. (1981). Understanding the tax revolt: Eight explanations. *American Political Science Review, 75*, 963–974.

Lowry, R. C. (1997). The private production of public goods: Organizational maintenance, managers' objectives, and collective goals. *American Political Science Review, 91*(2) (June), 308–323.

Lupia, A. (2006). How elitism undermines the study of voter competence. *Critical Review, 18*, 217–232.

Lupia, A., & McCubbins, M. D. (1998). *The Democratic dilemma: Can citizens learn what they need to know?* New York: Cambridge University Press.

Luskin, R. C. (1990). Explaining political sophistication. *Political Behavior, 12*(4), 331–361.

Lyons, W., & Alexander, R. (2000). A tale of two electorates: Generational replacement and the decline of voting in presidential elections. *Journal of Politics, 62*(4), 1014–1034.

MacKuen, M., & Coombs, S. L. (1981). More than news: Media power in public affairs. Beverly Hills, CA: Sage.

MacKuen, M. B., Erikson R. S., & Stimson, J. A. (1992). Peasant or bakers? The American electorate and the U.S. economy. *The American Political Science Review, 86*(3), 597-611.

Malhotra, N. & Krosnick, J. A. (2007). The effect of survey mode and sampling on inferences about political attitudes and behavior: Comparing the 2000 and 2004 ANES to internet surveys with nonprobablility samples. *Political Analysis, 15*, 286–323.

Malhotra, Y. (2000). Role of organizational controls in knowledge management: Is knowledge management really an oxymoron? In Y. Malhotra (Ed.), *Knowledge management and virtual organizations* (pp. 245–257). Hershey, PA: Idea Group Publishing.

Mangum, M. (2003). Psychological involvement and Black voter turnout. *Political Research Quarterly, 56*(1), 41(8).

Manis, M., Cornell, S. D., & Moore, J. C. (1974). Transmission of attitude-relevant information through a communication chain. *Journal of Personality and Social Psychology, 30*, 81–94.

Mansbridge, J. (Ed.). (1990). *Beyond self-interest*. Chicago: University of Chicago Press.

Marcus, G., Tabb, D., & Sullivan, J. (1974). The application of individual differences scaling to the measurement of political ideologies. *American Journal of Political Science, 18*, 405–420.

Marcus, G. E., Neuman, W. R., & MacKuen. M. B. (2000). *Affective intelligence and political judgment*. Chicago: University of Chicago Press.

Marcus, G.E., Sullivan, J.L., Theiss-Morse, E., & Wood, S.L. (1995). *With malice toward some: How people make civil liberties judgments*. New York: Cambridge University Press.

Marks, G., & Miller, N. (1987). Ten years of research on the false-consensus effect: An empirical and theoretical review. *Psychological Bulletin, 102*, 72–90.

Markus, G. B., & Converse, P. E. (1979). A dynamic simultaneous equation model of electoral choice. *American Political Science Review, 73*, 1055–1070.

Marrow, A.J. (1984). *The practical theorist: The life and work of Kurt Lewin*. New York: B.D.R. Learning Products.

Martin, N.G., Eaves, L.J., Heath, A.C., Jardine, R., Feingold, L.M., & Eysenck, H.J. (1986). Transmission of social attitudes. *Proceedings of the National Academy of Sciences, USA, 83*, 4364–4368.

Martin, P. S. (2004). Inside the black box of negative campaign effects: Three reasons why negative campaigns mobilize. *Political Psychology, 25*, 545–562.

Martinez, M. D. (1988). Political involvement and the projection process. *Political Behavior, 10*, 151–167.

Matsusaka, J.G.E. (1993). Election closeness and voter turnout: Evidence from California ballot propositions. *Public Choice, 76*(4), 313–334.

Matthews, D. R., & Prothro, J. W. (1966). *Negroes and the new Southern politics*. New York: Harcourt, Brace & World.

Mazur, A., & Mueller, U. (1996). Channel modeling: From West Point cadet to general. *Public Administration Review. 56*, 191–198.

McAdam, D. (1985). *Political process and the development of Black insurgency, 1930–1970*. Chicago: University of Chicago Press.

McAvoy, G. E. (2006). Stability and change: The time varying impact of economic and foreign policy evaluations on presidential approval. *Political Research Quarterly, 59*(1), 71–83.

McCann, S.J.H. (1997). Threatening times, "strong" presidential popular vote winners, and the victory margin, 1824–1964. *Journal of Personality and Social Psychology, 73*(1), 160–170.

McCarthy, J. D., & Zald, M. D. (1978). Resource mobilization and social movements: A partial theory. *American Journal of Sociology, 82* (May), 1212–1241.

McClurg, S. (2006). Political disagreement in context: The conditional effect of neighborhood context, disagreement, and political talk on electoral participation. *Political Behavior, 28,* 349–366.

McCombs, M. E., & Shaw, D. L. (1972). The agenda-setting function of mass media. *Public Opinion Quarterly, 36,* 176–187.

McConahay, J. B. (1986). Modern racism, ambivalence, and the modern racism scale. In J. F. Dovidio & S. L. Gaertner (Eds.), *Prejudice, discrimination and racism: Theory and research,* (pp. 91–125). New York: Academic Press.

McConahay, J. B., Hardee, B. B., & Batts, V. (1981). Has racism declined in America? It depends on who is asking and what is asked. *Journal of Conflict Resolution, 25*(4), 563–579.

McGinniss, J. (1969). *The selling of the president, 1968*. New York: Trident.

McGraw, K. M., & Pinney, N. (1990). The effects of general and domain-specific expertise on political memory and judgment. *Social Cognition, 8,* 9–30.

McGraw, K., Lodge, M., & Stroh, P. (1990). Online processing in candidate evaluation: The effects of issue order, issue importance, and sophistication. *Political Behavior, 12,* 41–58.

McGuire, W. J. (1986). The myth of massive media impact: Savagings and salvagings. *Public Communication and Behavior, 1,* 173–257.

McKelvey, R. D., & Ordeshook, P. C. (1985). Sequential elections with limited information. *American Journal of Political Science, 29,* 480–512.

McKenzie-Mohr, D., Nemiroff, L. S., Beers, S., & Desmarais, S. (1995). Determinants of responsible environmental behavior. *Journal of Social Issues, 51,* 139–156.

McLeod, J. M. (1965). Political conflict and information seeking. Paper presented at the annual meeting of the American Psychological Association, Chicago, Illinois.

McNulty, J. E. (2005). Phone-based GOTV—what's on the line? Field experiments with varied partisan components, 2002–2003. *Annals of the American Academy of Political and Social Science, 601,* 41.

Mehrabian, A. (1998). The effects of poll reports on voter preferences. *Journal of Applied Social Psychology, 28,* 2119–2130.

Mendelsohn, G. A. (1966). Effects of client personality and client–counselor similarity on the duration of counseling: A replication and extension. *Journal of Counseling Psychology, 13,* 228–234.

Mermin, J. (1999). *Debating war and peace: Media coverage of U.S. intervention in the post–Vietnam era*. Princeton, NJ: Princeton University Press.

Michelson, M. R. (2003). Getting out the Latino vote: How door-to-door canvassing influences voter turnout in rural central California. *Political Behavior, 25*(3), 247–263.

Milbrath, L. W., & Goel, M. L. (1977). *Political participation: How and why do people get involved in politics*? Chicago: Rand McNally.

Miller, A. H., Gurin, P., Gurin, G., & Malanchuk, O. (1981). Group consciousness and political participation. *American Journal of Political Science, 25*(3), 494–511.

Miller, J. M. 2000. Threats and opportunities as motivators of political activism. Ph.D. dissertation. Ohio State University.

Miller, J. M., & Krosnick, J. A. (1998). The impact of candidate name order on election outcomes. *Public Opinion Quarterly, 62*(3), 291–330.

Miller, J. M., & Krosnick, J. A. (2000). News media impact on the ingredients of presidential evaluations: Politically knowledgeable citizens are guided by a trusted source. *American Journal of Political Science, 44,* 295–309.

Miller, J.M., & Krosnick, J.A. (2004). Threat as a motivator of political activism: A field experiment. *Political Psychology, 25*(4), 507–523.

Miller, J. M., Krosnick, J. A., & Fabrigar, L. R. (2009). The origins of policy issue salience: Personal and national importance impact on behavioral, cognitive, and emotional issue engagement. Unpublished manuscript, University of Minnesota.

Miller, J. M., Tahk, A., Krosnick, J. A., Holbrook, A. L., & Lowe, L. (2009). *The impact of policy change threat on financial contributions to interest groups.* Unpublished manuscript. University of Minnesota, Minneapolis, MN.

Miller, L. W., & Sigelman, L. (1978) Is the audience the message? A note on LBJ's Vietnam statements. *Public Opinion Quarterly, 42,* 71–80.

Miller, R. E., & Wanta, W. (1996). Sources of the public agenda: The president-press-public relationship. *International Journal of Public Opinion Research, 8,* 390–402.

Miller, W. E. (1980). Disinterest, disaffection, and participation in presidential politics. *Political Behavior,* 2(1), 7–32.

Miller, W. E. (1992). Generational changes and party identification. *Political Behavior,* 14(3), 333–352.

Miller, W. E. (1992). The puzzle transformed: Explaining declining turnout. *Political Behavior,* 14(1), 1–43.

Miller, W. E., & Shanks, J. M. (1996). *The new American voter.* Cambridge, MA: Harvard University Press.

Min, Y. (2004). News coverage of negative political campaigns: An experiment of negative campaign effects on turnout and candidate preference. *Harvard International Journal of Press/Politics,* 9(4), 95–111.

Mitchell, G. E., & Wlezien, C. (1995). The impact of legal constraints on voter registration, turnout, and the composition of the American electorate. *Political Behavior,* 17(2), 179–202.

Mitchell, R. C. (1979). National environmental lobbies and the apparent illogic of collective action. In C.S. Russell (Ed.), *Collective decision making: Applications from public choice theory* (pp. 87–123). Baltimore, MD: Johns Hopkins University Press.

Mitchell, R. C. (1990). Public opinion and the green lobby: Poised for the 1990s? In N.J. Vig & M.E, Kraft (Eds.), *Environmental policy in the 1990s* (pp. 81–99). Washington, DC: Congressional Quarterly Press.

Modigliani, A., & Gamson, W. A. (1979). Thinking about politics. *Political Behavior,* 1(1), 5–30.

Moe, T. M. (1980). *The organization of interests: Incentives and the internal dynamics of political interest groups.* Chicago: The University of Chicago Press.

Moen, M. C. 1992. *The transformation of the Christian right.* Tuscaloosa: The University of Alabama Press.

Moghaddam, F. M., & Vuksanovic, V. (1990). Attitudes and behavior toward human rights across different contexts: The role of right-wing authoritarianism, political ideology, and religiosity. *International Journal of Psychology, 25,* 455–474.

Mondak, J. J. (1993). Public opinion and heuristic processing of source cues. *Political Behavior, 15,* 167–192.

Mondak, J. J., & Davis, B. C. (2001). Asked and answered: Knowledge levels when we will not take "don't know" for an answer. *Political Behavior,* 23(3), 199–224.

Monroe, K. (Ed.). (2002). *Handbook of political psychology.* Hillsdale, NJ: Erlbaum.

Monroe, K. R. (1978). Economic influences on presidential popularity. *Public Opinion Quarterly,* 42(3), 360–369.

Monroe, K. R. (1979). Inflation and presidential popularity. *Presidential Studies Quarterly, 9,* 334–340.

Monroe, K. R., & Laughlin, D. M. (1983). Economic influences on presidential popularity among key political and socioeconomic groups: A review of the evidence and some new findings. *Political Behavior,* 5(3), 309–345.

Morris, A.D., & McClurg Mueller, C. (1992). *Frontiers in social movement theory.* New Haven, CT: Yale University Press.

Morwitz, V. G., & Pluzinski, C. (1996). Do polls reflect opinions or do opinions reflect polls? The impact of political polling on voters'

expectations, preferences, and behavior. *Journal of Consumer Research,* 23(1), 53–67.

Moskowitz, D., & Stroh, P. (1996). Expectation-driven assessments of political candidates. *Political Psychology.* 17(4), 695–712.

Mueller, J. E. (1970). Presidential popularity from Truman to Johnson. *American Political Science Review, 64,* 18–34.

Mueller, J. (1973). *War, presidents, and public opinion.* New York: Wiley.

Mueller, J. (1994). *Policy and opinion in the Gulf war.* Chicago: University of Chicago Press.

Mueller, U., & Mazur, A. (1996). Facial dominance in West Point cadets predicts military rank 20+ years later. *Social Forces.* 74, 823–850.

Muller, E. N., Dietz, H. A., & Finkel, S. E. (1991). Discontent and the expected utility of rebellion: The case of Peru. *American Political Science Review, 85,* 1261–1282.

Mutz, D. C. (2002a). Cross-cutting social networks: Testing democratic theory in practice. *American Political Science Review,* 96(1), 111–126.

Mutz, D. C. (2002b). The consequences of cross-cutting networks for political participation. *American Journal of Political Science,* 46(4), 838–855.

Nadeau, R., Niemi, R. G., & Amato, T. (1995). Emotions, issue importance, and political learning. *American Journal of Political Science* 39 (August), 558–574.

Nadeau, R., Niemi, R. G., Fan, D. P., & Amato, T. (1999). Elite economic forecasts economic news, mass economic judgments, and presidential approval. *Journal of Politics,* 61(1), 109–135.

Nagel, J. H., & McNulty, J. E. (1996). Partisan effects of voter turnout in senatorial and gubernatorial elections. *American Political Science Review,* 90(4), 780–793.

Nagler, J. (1991). The effect of registration laws and education on U.S. voter turnout. *American Political Science Review,* 85(4), 1393–1405.

Nelson, T. E., Kinder, D. R. (1996). Issue framing and group-centrism in American public opinion. *Journal of Politics, 58,* 1055–1078.

Nelson, T. E., Clawson, R. A., & Oxley, Z. M. (1997). Media framing of a civil liberties conflict and its effect on tolerance. *American Political Science Review,* 91(3), 567–583.

Newcomb, T. M. (1953). An approach to the study of communicative acts. *Psychological Review,* 60(6), 393–404.

Newcomb, T. M. (1968). Interpersonal balance. In R. Abelson, E. Aronson, W. McGuire, T. Newcomb, M. Rosenberg & P. Tannenbaum (Eds.), *Theories of cognitive consistency: A sourcebook* (pp. 28–51). Chicago: Rand McNally.

Newman, B. (2002). Bill Clinton's approval ratings: The more things change, the more they stay the same. *Presidential Research Quarterly,* 55, 781–804.

Newman, B. (2003). *Standards of judgment: The foundations of presidents' popular support.* Ph.D. dissertation Duke University.

Nicholson, S.P., Segura, G.M., & Woods, N.D. (2002). Presidential approval and the mixed blessing of divided government. *The Journal of Politics, 64(3),* 701–720.

Nie, N. H., & Hillygus, S. D. (2001). Education and democratic citizenship: Explorations into the effects of what happens in pursuit of the baccalaureate. In D. Ravitch, & J. Viteritti (Eds.), *Education and civil society* (pp. 30–57). New Haven, CT: Yale University Press.

Nie, N. H., Junn, J., & Stehlik-Barry, K. (1996). *Education and democratic citizenship in America.* Chicago: University of Chicago Press.

Nie, N., Verba, S., & Petrocik, J. (1979). *The changing American voter.* Cambridge, MA: Harvard University Press.

Niemi, R., & Weisberg, H. F. (1981). *Controversies in voting behavior.* Washington, DC: CQ Press.

Noelle-Neuman, E. (1984). *The spiral of silence.* Chicago: The University of Chicago Press.

Norpoth, H. (1996). Presidents and the prospective voter. *Journal of Politics, 58(3)*, 776–792.

Olson, M. (1965). *The logic of collective action*. Cambridge, MA: Harvard University Press.

Oneal, J. R., Lian, B., & Joyner, J.H., Jr. (1996). Are the American people "pretty prudent?" Public responses to U.S. uses of force, 1950–1988. *International Studies Quarterly, 40*, 261–276.

Oneal, J. R., Oneal, F. H., Maoz, Z., & Russett, B. (1996). The liberal peace: Interdependence, democracy, and international conflict, 1950–1985. *Journal of Peace Research, 33*, 11–28.

Opp, K.D. (1986). Soft incentives and collective action: Participation in the anti-nuclear movement. *British Journal of Political Science, 16* (January), 87–112.

Ornstein, N. J., & Elder, S. (1978). *Interest groups, lobbying, and policy-making*. Washington, DC: CQ Press.

Orum, A. M. (1966). A reappraisal of the social and political participation of Negroes. *American Journal of Sociology, 72*(1), 32–46.

Osgood, C. E., & Tannenbaum, P. H. (1955). The principle of congruity in the prediction of attitude change. *Psychological Review, 62*(1), 42–55.

Ostrom, C., & Job, B. (1986). The president and the political use of force. *American Political Science Review, 80*, 541–566.

Ostrom, C., & Simon, D. (1985). Promise and performance: A dynamic model of presidential popularity. *American Political Science Review, 79*(2), 334–358.

Ostrom, T. M., & Upshaw, H. S. (1968). Psychological perspective and attitude change. In A. G. Greenwald, T. C. Brock, & T. M. Ostrom (Eds.), *Psychological foundations of attitudes* (pp. 217–242). New York: Academic Press.

Ottati, V., Fishbein, M., & Middlestadt, S. (1988). Determinants of voters' beliefs about the candidates' stands on the issues: The role of evaluative bias heuristics and the candidates' expressed message. *Journal of Personality and Social Psychology, 55*, 1–13.

Pacheco, J., & Plutzer, E. (2008) Political participation and cumulative disadvantage: The impact of economic and social hardship on young citizens. *The Journal of Social Issues, 64*, 571–593.

Page, B. I. (1976). The theory of political ambiguity. *American Political Science Review, 70*, 742–752.

Page, B. I. (1978). *Choices and echoes in presidential elections: Rational man and electoral democracy*. Chicago: University of Chicago Press.

Page, B. I., & Brody, R. A. (1972). Policy voting and the electoral process: The Vietnam War issue. *American Political Science Review, 66*, 979–995.

Page, B. I., & Jones, C. (1979). Reciprocal effects of policy preferences, party loyalties and the vote. *American Political Science Review, 73*, 1071–1089.

Page, B., & Shapiro, R. (1983). Effects of public opinion on policy. *American Political Science Review, 77*(1), 175–190.

Page, B. I., & Shapiro, R.Y. (1984). Presidents as opinion leaders: Some new evidence. *Policy Studies Journal, 12*, 649–661.

Page, B. I., Shapiro, R. Y., & Dempsey, G. R. (1987). What moves public opinion? *American Political Science Review, 81*(1), 23–43.

Palmgreen, P., & Clarke, P. (1977). Agenda-setting with local and national issues. *Communication Research, 4*(4), 435–452.

Pan, Z., & Kosicki, G.M. (1997). Priming and media impact on the evaluations of the president's performance. *Communication Research, 24(1)*, 3–30.

Panning, W. H. (1982). Uncertainty and political participation. *Political Behavior, 4*(1), 69–81.

Parker, S. L. (1995). Toward an understanding of "rally effects": Public opinion in the Persian Gulf War. *Public Opinion Quarterly, 59*, 526–546.

Parry, H. J., & Crossley, H. M. (1950). Validity of responses to survey questions. *Public Opinion Quarterly, 14* (Spring), 61–80.

Patrick, B., & Thrall, A.T. (2007). Beyond hegemony: Classical propaganda theory and presidential communication strategy after the invasion of Iraq. *Mass Communication & Society, 10*(1), 95–118.

Patterson, S. C., & Caldeira, G. A. (1983). Getting out the vote: Participation in gubernatorial elections. *American Political Science Review, 77*(3), 675–689.

Patton, G. W., & Smith, B. (1980). The effect of taking issue positions on ratings of political candidates. *Political Psychology, 2*, 20–34.

Peake, D., & Jeffrey, S. (1998). The dynamics of foreign policy agenda setting. *American Political Science Review, 92*(1), 173–185.

Peffley, M., & Hurwitz, J. (1987). Foreign policy attitudes and political behavior. *Report prepared for the National Election Service 1987 Pilot Study*.

Peffley, M., & Hurwitz, J. (2002). The racial component of "race-neutral" crime policy attitudes. *Political Psychology, 23*, 59–74.

Peffley, M., Langley, R. E., & Goidel, R. K. (1995). Public responses to the presidential use of military force: A panel analysis. *Political Behavior, 17*(3), 307–337.

Perse, E. M. (1990). Media involvement and local news effects. *Journal of Broadcasting & Electronic Media, 34(1)*, 17–36.

Peters, B. G., & Hogwood, B. W. (1985). In search of the issue-attention cycle. *Journal of Politics, 47*, 239–253.

Peterson, B., Doty, R., & Winter, D. (1993). Authoritarianism and attitudes toward contemporary social issues. *Personality and Social Psychology Bulletin, 19*, 174–184.

Petrocik, J. R. (1991). An algorithm for estimating turnout as a guide to predicting elections. *Public Opinion Quarterly, 55*(4), 643–647.

Petrocik, J. R., & Shaw, D. (1991). Non-voting in America: Attitudes in context. In W. Crotty (Ed.), *Political participation and American democracy* (pp. 67–88). New York: Greenwood.

Petty, R. E., Cacioppo, J. T., & Haugtvedt, C. (1991). Ego involvement and persuasion: An appreciative look at the Sherif's contribution to the study of self-relevance and attitude change. In. D. Granberg & G. Sarup (Eds.), *Social judgment and intergroup relations: A Festschrift for Muzifer Sherif* (pp. 147–174). New York: Springer-Verlag.

Piven, F. F., & Cloward, R. A. (1988). National voter registration reform: How it might be won. *PS: Political Science and Politics, 21*(4), 868–875.

Piven, F. F., & Cloward, R. A. (2000). *Why Americans still don't vote: And why politicians want it that way* (Rev.). Boston: Beacon Press.

Plane, D. L., & Gershtenson, J. (2004). Candidates' ideological locations, abstention, and turnout in U.S. midterm Senate elections. *Political Behavior, 26*(1), 69–93.

Plutzer, E. (2002). Becoming a habitual voter: Inertia, resources, and growth in young adulthood. *American Political Science Review, 96*(1), 41(16).

Pomper, M, G., & Sernekos, A, L. (1991). Bake sales and voting. *Society, 28*(5), 10.

Popkin, S. L., Gorman, J., Smith, J., & Phillips, C. (1976). Comment: Toward an investment theory of voting behavior—what have you done for me lately? *American Political Science Review, 70, 3* (September), 779–805.

Pratto, F., Sidanius, J., Stallworth, L.M., & Malle, B.F. (1994). Social dominance orientation: A personality variable predicting social and political attitudes. *Journal of Personality and Social Psychology, 67*, pp. 741–763.

Presser, S., & Converse, J. (1976–1977). On Stimson's interpretation of declines in presidential popularity. *Public Opinion Quarterly, 40*, 538–541.

Presser, S., Traugott, M., & Traugott, S. (1990). *Vote "over" reporting in surveys: The records or the respondents.* Ann Arbor, MI: American National Election Studies Technical Report Series, No. nes010157.

Price, V., & Hsu, M. (1992). Public opinion about AIDS policies: The role of misinformation and attitudes toward homosexuals. *The Public Opinion Quarterly, 56*(1), 29–52.

Price, V., & Tewksbury, D. (1995). News values and public opinion—A process: How political advertising and TV news prime viewers to think about issues and candidates. In F. Biocca (Ed.), *Television and Political Advertising* (pp. 265–309). Hillsdale, NJ: Lawrence Erlbaum Associates.

Price, V., & Tewksbury, D. (1997). News values and public opinion: A theoretical account of media priming and framing. *Progress in Communication Sciences, 13*, 173–212.

Price, V., & Zaller, J. (1993). Who gets the news? Alternative measures of news reception and their implications for research. *Public Opinion Quarterly, 57*, 133–164.

Prior, M. (2009a). Improving media effects research through better measurement of news exposure. *Journal of Politics, 71*, 893–908.

Prior, M. (2009b). The immensely inflated News audience: Assessing bias in self-reported news exposure. *Public Opinion Quarterly, 73*, 130–143

Prior, M., & Lupia, A. (2008). Money, time, and political knowledge: Distinguishing quick recall and political learning skills. *American Journal of Political Science, 52*(1), 169–183.

Prislin, R. (1996). Attitude stability and attitude strength: One is enough to make it stable. *European Journal of Social Psychology, 26*, 447–477.

Putnam, R. D. (2000). *Bowling alone: The collapse and revival of American community.* New York: Simon & Schuster.

Quattrone, G. A. & Tversky, A. (1984). Causal versus diagnostic contingencies: On self-deception and on the voter's illusion. *Journal of Personality and Social Psychology, 46*(2), 237–248.

Quillian, L. (1995). Prejudice as a response to perceived group threat: Population composition and anti-immigrant and racial prejudice in Europe. *American Sociological Review, 60*, 586–611.

Rabinowitz, G., & Macdonald, S. E. (1989). A Directional Theory of Issue Voting. *The American Political Science Association, 83*(1), 93–121.

Rabinowitz, G., Prothro, J. W., & Jacoby, W. (1982). Salience as a factor in the impact of issues on candidate evaluation. *Journal of Politics, 44*, 41–63.

Radcliff, B. (1992). The welfare state, turnout, and the economy: A comparative analysis. *American Political Science Review, 86*(2), 444–454.

Ragsdale, L., (1984). The politics of presidential speechmaking, 1949–1980. *American Political Science Review, 78*, 971–984.

Rahn, W., Krosnick, J., & Breuning, M. (1994). Rationalization and derivation processes in survey studies of political candidate evaluation. *American Journal of Political Science, 38*, 582–600.

Recht, D.R., & Leslie, L. (1988). Effect of prior knowledge on good and poor readers' memory of text. *Journal of Educational Psychology, 80*(1), 16–20.

Regan, D.T., & Kilduff, M. (1988). Optimism about elections: Dissonance reduction at the ballot box. *Political Psychology, 9*(1), 101–107.

Reiter, H. L. (1979). Why is turnout down? *Public Opinion Quarterly, 43*(3), 297–311.

Rentfrow, P. J., Jost, J. T., Gosling, S. D., & Potter, J. (2009). Statewide differences in personality predict voting patterns in 1996–2004 U.S. presidential elections. In J. T. Jost, A. C. Kay, and H. Thorisdottir (Eds.), *Social and Psychological Bases of Ideology and System Justification* (pp. 314–349). Oxford University Press.

Rhine, S. L. (1996). An analysis of the impact of registration factors on turnout in 1992. *Political Behavior, 18*(2), 171–185.

Richer, J. (1995). *Green giving: An analysis of contributions to major U.S. environmental groups. Discussion Paper 95–39.* Washington, DC: Resources for the Future.

Riker, W. H., & Ordeshook, P. C. (1968). A theory of the calculus of voting. *American Political Science Review, 62*(1), 25–42.

Rivers, D., & Rose, N. L. (1985). Passing the president's program: Public opinion and presidential influence in Congress. *American Journal of Political Science, 29*, 183–196.

Roberts, D. F., & Maccoby, N. (1985). Effects of mass communication. In G. Lindzey & E. Aronson (Eds.), *The Handbook of Social Psychology* (3rd ed., Vol. 2, pp. 539–598). New York: Random House.

Robinson, J., & Levy, M. (1986). *The main source: Learning from television news.* Beverly Hills, CA: Sage.

Rokeach, M. (1960). *The open and closed mind.* New York: Basic Books.

Rokeach, M. (1968). *Beliefs, attitudes, and values: A theory of organization and change.* San Francisco, CA: Jossey-Bass.

Rokeach, M. (1973). *The nature of human values.* New York: Free Press.

Rokeach, M., & Ball-Rokeach, S. J. (1988). Stability and change in American values priorities, 1968–1981. Presented at the Meeting of the American Association for Public Opinion Research, Toronto, Canada.

Roseneau, J. N. (1974). *Citizenship between elections: An inquiry into the mobilizable American.* New York: The Free Press.

Rosenberg, M.J. (1956). Cognitive structure and attitudinal affect. *Journal of Abnormal Social Psychology, 53*, 367–372.

Rosenstone, S. J. (1982). Economic adversity and voter turnout. *American Journal of Political Science, 26*(1), 25–46.

Rosenstone, S. J., & Hansen, J. M. (1993). *Mobilization, participation, and democracy in America.* New York: Macmillan.

Rothman, A. J., & Salovey, P. (1997). Shaping perceptions to motivate healthy behavior: The role of message framing. *Psychological Bulletin, 121*(1), 3–19.

Rudolph, T.J. (2003). Who's responsible for the economy? The formation and consequences of responsibility attributions. *American Journal of Political Science, 47*(4), 698–713.

Salisbury, R. H. (1969). An exchange theory of interest groups. *Midwest Journal of Political Science, 13*, 1–32.

Salmon, C. T., & Nichols, J. S. (1983). The next-birthday method of respondent selection. *Public Opinion Quarterly, 47*, 270–276.

Sandell, J., & Plutzer, E. (2005). Families, divorce and voter turnout in the United States. *Political Behavior, 27*(2), 133–162.

Schaffer, S. D. (1981). A multivariate explanation of decreasing turnout in presidential elections, 1960–1976. *American Journal of Political Science, 25*(1), 68–95.

Scheufele, D. A., & Moy, P. (2000). Twenty-five years of the spiral of silence: A conceptual review and empirical outlook. *International Journal of Public Opinion Research, 12*, 3–28.

Schlichting, K., Tuckel, P., & Maisel, R. (1998). Racial segregation and voter turnout in urban America. *American Politics Quarterly, 26*(2), 218–219.

Schlozman, K. L., Burns, N., & Verba, S. (1999). What happened at work today? A multistage model of gender, employment, and political participation. *Journal of Politics, 61*(1), 29–53.

Schlozman, K. L., Burns, N., Verba, S., & Donahue, J. (1995). Gender and citizen participation: Is there a different voice? *American Journal of Political Science, 39*(2), 267–293.

Schmitt-Beck, R. (1996). Mass media, the electorate, and the bandwagon: A study of communication effects on vote choice. *International Journal of Public Opinion Research, 8*(3), 266–291.

Schneider, W., Gruber, H., Gold, A., & Opwis, K. (1993). Chess expertise and memory for chess positions in children and adults. *Journal of Experimental Child Psychology, 56*, 328–349.

Schubert, J. N., Stewart, P. A., & Curran, M. A. (2002). A defining presidential moment: 9/11 and the rally effect. *Political Psychology, 23*, 559–583.

Schuman, H. (2000). The perils of correlation, the lure of labels, and the beauty of negative results. In D. O. Sears, J. Sidanius, & L. Bobo (Eds.), *Racialized politics: The debate about racism in America* (pp. 302–323). Chicago: University of Chicago Press.

Schuman, H., & Converse, J. M. (1971). The effects of black and white interviewers on black responses in 1968. *Public Opinion Quarterly, 35*(1), 44–68.

Schuman, H., & Presser, S. (1981). *Questions and answers in attitude surveys*. New York: Academic Press.

Schuman, H., Ludwig, J., & Krosnick, J. A. (1986). The perceived threat of nuclear war, salience, and open questions. *Public Opinion Quarterly, 50*, 519–536.

Schuman, H., Steeh, C., & Bobo, L. (1997). *Racial attitudes in America: Trends and interpretations*. Cambridge, MA: Harvard University Press.

Schur, L. A., & Kruse, D. L. (2000). What determines voter turnout? Lessons from citizens with disabilities. *Social Science Quarterly, 81*(2), 571.

Schur, L., Shields, T., Kruse, D., & Schriner, K. (2002). Enabling democracy: Disability and voter turnout. *Political Research Quarterly, 55*(1), 167–190.

Sears, D. O. (1975). Political socialization. In F. I. Greenstein & N. W. Polsby (Eds.), *Handbook of political science* (Vol. 2, pp. 93–153). Reading, MA: Addison-Wesley.

Sears, D. O. (1988). Symbolic racism. In P. A. Katz & D. A. Taylor (Eds.), *Eliminating racism: Profiles in controversy* (pp. 53–84). New York: Plenum Press.

Sears, D. O. (1993). Symbolic politics: A socio-psychological theory. In S. Iyengar & W. J. McGuire (Eds.), *Explorations in political psychology* (pp. 113–149). Durham, NC: Duke University Press.

Sears, D.O., & Citrin, J. (1982). *Tax revolt: Something for nothing in California*. Cambridge, MA: Harvard University Press.

Sears, D. O., & Funk, C. (1990). Self-interest in Americans' political opinions. In J. Mansbridge (Ed.), *Beyond self-interest* (pp. 97–110). Chicago: University of Chicago Press.

Sears, D. O., & Funk, C. (1991). The role of self-interest in social and political attitudes. *Advances in Experimental Social Psychology, 24*, 1–92.

Sears, D. O., & Henry, P. J. (2003). The origins of symbolic racism. *Journal of Personality and Social Psychology, 85*, 259–275.

Sears, D. O., & Lau, R. R. (1983). Inducing apparently self-interested political preferences. *American Journal of Political Science, 27*, 223–252.

Sears, D. O., & Valentino, N.A. (1997). Politics matters: Political events as catalysts for preadult socialization. *American Political Science Review, 91*, 45–65.

Sears, D. O., Hensler, C. P., & Speer, L. K. (1979). Whites' opposition to "busing": Self-interest or symbolic politics? *The American Political Science Review, 73*(2), 369–384.

Sears, D. O., Huddy, L., & Jervis, R. (Eds.). (2003). *Handbook of political psychology*. New York: Oxford University Press.

Sears, D. O., Lau, R. R., Tyler, T. R., & Allen, H. M. (1980). Self-interest versus symbolic politics in policy attitudes and presidential voting. *American Political Science Review, 74*(3), 670–684.

Sears, D. O., Van Laar, C., Carrillo, M., & Kosterman, R. (1997). Is it really racism? The origins of White Americans' opposition to race-targeted policies. *Public Opinion Quarterly, 61*(1), 16–53.

Sears, D. O., & Valentino, N. A. (1997). Politics matters: Political events as catalysts for preadult socialization. *American Political Science Review, 91*(1), 45–65.

Shachar, R., & Nalebuff, B. (1999). Follow the leader: Theory and evidence on political participation. *American Economic Review, 89*(3), 525–547.

Shaffer, M. L. (1981). Minimum population sizes for species conservation. *Bioscience, 31*, 131–134.

Shapiro, M. J. (1969). Rational political man: A synthesis of economic and social-psychological perspectives. *American Political Science Review, 63*, 1106–1119.

Shaw, D., de la Garza, R. O., & Lee, J. (2000). Examining Latino turnout in 1996: A three-state, validated survey approach. *American Journal of Political Science, 44*(2), 338–346.

Shepsle, K. A. (1972). The strategy of ambiguity: Uncertainty and electoral competition. *American Political Science Review, 66*, 555–568.

Sherif, M., & Hovland, C.I. (1961). *Social judgment: Assimilation and contrast effects in communication and attitude change*. New Haven, CT: Yale University Press.

Sherrod, D. R. (1974). Crowding, perceived control, and behavioral aftereffects. *Journal of Applied Social Psychology, 4*(2), 171–186.

Shields, T. G., & Goidel, R. K. (1997). Participation rates, socioeconomic class biases, and Congressional elections: A cross-validation. *American Journal of Political Science, 41*(2), 683–691.

Shinn, A. M. (1971). A note on voter registration and turnout in Texas, 1960–1970. *Journal of Politics, 33*(4), 1120–1129.

Sidanius, J., Levin, S., Rabinowitz, J. L., & Federico, C. M. (1999). Peering into the jaws of the beast: The integrative dynamics of social identity, symbolic racism, and social dominance. In D. A. Prentice & D. T. Miller (Eds.), *Cultural divides: Understanding and overcoming group conflict* (pp. 80–132). New York: Russell Sage Foundation.

Sidanius, J., Mitchell, M., Haley, H., & Navarrete, C. D. (2006). Support for harsh criminal sanctions and criminal justice beliefs: A social dominance perspective. *Social Justice Research, 19*, 433–449.

Sigelman, L. (1979). Presidential popularity and presidential elections. *The Public Opinion Quarterly, 43*(4), 532–534.

Sigelman, L., & Knight, K. (1983). Why does presidential popularity decline? A test of the expectation–disillusion theory. *Public Opinion Quarterly, 47*, 310–324.

Sigelman, L., & Knight, K. (1985). Public opinion and presidential responsibility for the economy: Understanding personalization. *Political Behavior, 7*, 167–191.

Sigelman, L., & Sigelman, C. K. (1981). Presidential leadership of public opinion: From "benevolent leader" to "kiss of death?" *Experimental Study of Politics, 7*, 1–22.

Simon, D.M., & Ostrom, C.W. (1989). The impact of televised speeches and foreign travel on presidential approval. *Public Opinion Quarterly, 53*, 58–82.

Simon, H. A. (1954). Spurious correlation: A causal interpretation. *Journal of the American Statistical Association, 49*, 467–479.

Sinclair, R. C., Moore, M, S. E., Lavis, C. A., & Soldat, A. S. (2000). An electoral butterfly effect. *Nature, 408*, 665–666.

Skalaban, A. (1988). Do the polls affect elections? Some 1980 evidence. *Political Behaviour, 10*, 136–150.

Smelser, N. J. (1962). *Theory of collective behavior*. New York: Free Press.

Smelser, N. J. (1995). *Sociology*. Englewood Cliffs, NJ: Prentice-Hall.

Smith, J. K., Gerber, A. S., & Orlich, A. (2003). Self-prophecy effects and voter turnout: An experimental replication. *Political Psychology, 24*(3), 593–604.

Sniderman, P. M., & Brody, R. A. (1977). Coping: The ethic of self-reliance. *American Journal of Political Science, 21*(3), 501–521.

Sniderman, P. M., & Carmines, E. G. (1997). *Reading beyond race*. Cambridge, MA: Harvard University Press.

Sniderman, P. M., & Douglas, B. G. (1996). Innovations in experimental design in attitude surveys. *Annual Review of Sociology, 22,* 377–399.

Sniderman, P. M., & Piazza, T. (1993). *The scare of race.* Boston: Harvard University Press.

Sniderman, P. M., & Tetlock, P. E. (1986). Symbolic racism: Problems of motive attribution in political analysis. *Journal of Social Issues, 42*(2), 129–150.

Sniderman, P. M., Crosby, G., & Howell, W. (2000). The politics of race. In D. O. Sears, J. Sidanius, & L. Bobo (Eds.), *Racialized politics: The debate about racism in America* (pp. 236–279). Chicago: University of Chicago Press.

Sniderman, P. M., Hagen, M. G., Tetlock, P. E., & Brady, H. E. (1986). Reasoning chains: Causal models of policy reasoning in mass publics. *British Journal of Political Science, 16,* 405–430.

Sniderman, P. M., Piazza, T., Tetlock, P. E., & Kendrick, A. (1991). The new racisim. *American Journal of Political Science, 35*(2), 423–447.

Sobel, R. (1993). From occupational involvement to political participation: An exploratory analysis. *Political Behavior, 15*(4), 339–353.

Spencer, S. J., Steele, C. M., & Quinn, D. M. (1999). Stereotype threat and women's math performance. *Journal of Experimental Social Psychology, 35*(1), 4–28.

Squire, P., Wolfinger, R. E., & Glass, D. P. (1987). Residential mobility and voter turnout. *American Political Science Review, 81*(1), 45–66.

Stenner, K. (2005). *The authoritarian dynamic.* New York: Cambridge University Press.

Sterling, C. W. (1983). Time-off laws & voter turnout. *Polity, 16*(1), 143–149.

Stimson, J. A. (1976). Public support for American presidents: A cyclical model. *Public Opinion Quarterly, 40,* 1–21.

Stoker, L. (1998). Understanding whites' resistance to affirmative action: The role of principled commitments and racial prejudice. In J. Hurwitz & M. Peffley (Eds.), *Perception and prejudice: Race and politics in the United States.* New Haven, CT: Yale University Press.

Stoker, L., & Jennings, M. K. (1995). Life-cycle transitions and political participation: The case of marriage. *American Political Science Review, 89*(2), 421–433.

Stoker, T.M. (1993). Empirical approaches to the problem of aggregation over individuals. *Journal of Economic Literature, 33,* 1827–1874.

Straits, B. C. (1990). The social context of voter turnout. *Public Opinion Quarterly, 54*(1), 64–73.

Strate, J. M., Parrish, C. J., Elder, C. D., & Ford, C. (1989). Life span civic development and voting participation. *American Political Science Review, 83*(2), 443–464.

Sudman, S. (1986). Do exit polls influence voting behavior? *Public Opinion Quarterly, 50*(3), 331–339.

Sweeney, J. W. (1973). An experimental investigation of the free rider problem. *Social Science Research, 2,* 277–292.

Taebel, D. (1975).The effect of ballot position and electoral success. *American Journal of Political Science, 19*(3), 519–526.

Tajfel, H. (Ed). (1978). *Differentiation between social groups: Studies in the social psychology of intergroup relations.* London: Academic Press.

Tajfel, H., & Turner, J. C. (1979). *The social psychology of intergroup relations.* Monterey, CA: Brooks/Cole Publishing Co.

Tarman, C., & Sears, D. O. (2005). The conceptualization and measurement of symbolic racism. *The Journal of Politics, 67,* 731–761.

Tarrow, S. (1998). *Power in movement.* New York: Cambridge University Press.

Tate, K. (1991). Black political participation in the 1984 and 1988 presidential elections. *American Political Science Review, 85*(4), 1159–1176.

Tedin, K. L. (1980). Assessing peer and parent influence on adolescent political attitudes. *American Journal of Political Science, 24*(1), 136–154.

Teixeira, R. A. (1987). *Why Americans don't vote: Turnout decline in the United States, 1960–1984.* New York: Greenwood Press.

Teixeira, R. A. (1992). *The disappearing American voter.* Washington, DC: Brookings Institution.

Tenn, S. (2005). An alternative measure of relative education to explain voter turnout. *Journal of Politics, 67*(3), 271–282.

Tenn, S. (2007). The effect of education on voter turnout. *Political Analysis, 15*(4), 446–464.

Tesser, A. (1993). On the importance of heritability in psychological research: The case of attitudes. *Psychological Review, 100,* 129–142.

Tetlock, P. E. (1986). A value pluralism model of ideological reasoning. *Journal of Personality and Social Psychology, 50,* 819–827.

Tetlock, P. E. (1994). Political psychology or politicized psychology: Is the road to hell paved with good moral intentions? *Political Psychology 15,* 509–530.

Tetlock, P. E. (1998). Social psychology and world politics. In S. Fiske, D. Gilbert, & G. Lindzey (Eds.), *Handbook of social psychology* (4th ed., pp. 868–912). New York: McGraw-Hill.

Tetlock, P. E. (2000). Cognitive biases and organizational correctives: Do both disease and cure depend on the ideological beholder? *Administrative Science Quarterly, 42*(5), 293–326.

Thomas, D.B., Sigelman, L., & Baas, L.R. (1984). Public evaluations of the president: Policy, partisan, and "personal" determinants. *Political Psychology, 5,* 531–542.

Thorpe, J. (2005). Champions of psychology. *APS Observer, 18*(1), Retrieved February 19, 2009, from http://www.psychologicalscience.org/observer/getArticle.cfm?id=1711.

Thrall, A. T. (2000). *War in the media age.* Cresskill, NJ: Hampton Press Inc.

Timpone, R. J. (1998a). Structure, behavior, and voter turnout in the United States. *American Political Science Review, 92*(1), 145–158.

Timpone, R. J. (1998b). Ties that bind: Measurement, demographics, and social connectedness. *Political Behavior, 20*(1), 53–77.

Toch, H. (1965). *The social psychology of social movements.* Indianapolis, IN: Bobbs-Merrill.

Todorov, A., & Uleman, J. S. (2002). Spontaneous trait inferences are bound to actors' faces: Evidence from a false recognition paradigm. *Journal of Personality and Social Psychology, 83,* 1051–1065.

Todorov, A., & Uleman, J. S. (2003). The efficiency of binding spontaneous trait inferences to actors' faces. *Journal of Experimental Social Psychology, 39,* 549–562.

Todorov, A., Mandisodza, A. N., Goren, A., & Hall, C. C. (2005). Inferences of competence from faces predict election outcomes. *Science, 308,* 1623–1626.

Togeby, L. (2007). The context of priming. *Scandinavian Political Studies, 30*(3), 345–376.

Tolleson-Rinehart, S. (1992). *Gender consciousness and politics.* New York: Routledge.

Tomz, M., & Van Houweling, R. P. (2008). Candidate positioning and voter choice. *American Political Science Review, 102*(3), 303–318.

Tomz, M., & Van Houweling, R. P. (2009). Government calling: Public service motivation as an element in selecting government as an employer of choice. *Journal of the American Society for Information Science and Technology, 59*(14), 2210–2231.

Traugott, M. W., & Katosh, J. P. (1979). Response validity in surveys. *Public Opinion Quarterly, 43,* 359–377.

Truman, D. B. (1951). *The governmental process: Political interests and public opinion.* New York: Alfred A Knopf.

Tucker, H. J., Vedlitz, A., & DeNardo, J. (1986). Does heavy turnout help Democrats in presidential elections? *American Political Science Review, 80*(4), 1291–1304.

Turner, M. J., Shields, T. G., & Sharp, D. (2001). Changes and continuities in the determinants of older adults' voter turnout, 1952–1996. *The Gerontologist, 41*(6), 805–818.

Tversky, A., & Kahneman, D. (1980). Causal schemas in judgments under uncertainty. In M. Fishbein (Ed.), *Progress in social psychology* (pp. 49–72). Hillsdalc, N.J.: Erlbaum.

Tversky, A., & Kahneman, D. (1981). The framing of decisions and the psychology of choice. *Science, 211*(4481), 453–458.

Tversky, A., & Kahneman, D. (1986). Rational choice and the framing of decisions. *Journal of Business, 59*(4), Part 2, 251–278.

Tyler, S. W., Hertel, P. T., McCallum, M. C., & Ellis, H. C. (1979). Cognitive effort and memory. *Journal of Experimental Psychology: Human Learning and Memory, 9,* 607–661.

Tyler, T. R., & McGraw, K. M. (1983). The threat of nuclear war: Risk interpretation and behavioral response. *Journal of Social Issues, 39,* 25–40.

Uhlaner, C. J., Cain, B. E., & Kiewiet, D. R. (1989). Political participation of ethnic minorities in the 1980s. *Political Behavior, 11*(3), 195–231.

Ulbig, S. G., & Funk, C. L. (1999). Conflict avoidance and political participation. *Political Behavior, 21*(3), 265–282.

Uleman, J. S., Blader, S., & Todorov, A. (2005). Implicit impressions. In R. Hassin, J. S. Uleman, & J. A. Bargh (Eds.), *The new unconscious* (pp. 362–392). New York: Oxford University Press.

Van der Brug, W., Semetko, H. A., & Valkenburg, P. (2007). Priming in a multi-party context: The impact of European summit news on evaluations of political leaders. *Political Behavior, 29*(1), 115–141.

Van Hiel, A., & Mervielde, I. (2002). Explaining conservative beliefs and political preferences: A comparison of social dominance orientation and authoritarianism. *Journal of Applied Social Psychology, 32,* 965–976.

Van Hiel, A., Pandelaere, M., & Duriez, B. (2004). The impact of need for closure on conservative beliefs and racism: Differential mediation by authoritarian submission and authoritarian dominance. *Personality and Social Psychology Bulletin, 30,* 824–837.

Valentino N. A., Hutchings V. L., & White, I. K. (2002). Cues that matter: How political ads prime racial attitudes during campaigns. *American Political Science Review, 96,* 75–90.

Valentino, N. A., & Sears, D. O. (1998). Event-driven political communication and the preadult socialization of partisanship. *Political Behavior, 20*(2), 127–154.

Valentino, N. A., Traugott, M. W., Hutchings, V.L. (2002). Group cues and ideological constraint: A replication of political advertising effects studies in the lab and the field. *Political Communication, 19,* 29–48.

Vallone, R. P., Ross, L., & Lepper, M. R. (1985). The hostile media phenomenon: Biased perception of perceptions of media bias in coverage of the Beirut massacre. *Journal of Personality and Social Psychology, 49,* 577–585.

Vedlitz, A. (1985). Voter registration drives and black voting in the South. *Journal of Politics, 47*(2), 643–651.

Verba, S., & Nie, N. H. (1972). *Participation in America: Political democracy and social equality.* New York: Harper & Row.

Verba, S., Burns, N., & Schlozman, K. L. (1997). Knowing and caring about politics: Gender and political engagement. *Journal of Politics, 59*(4), 1051–1072.

Verba, S., Schlozman, K. L., & Brady, H. E. (1995). *Voice and equality: Civic voluntarism in American politics.* Cambridge, MA: Harvard University Press.

Visser, P. (1998). Assessing the structure and function of attitude strength: Insights from a new approach. Unpublished doctoral dissertation, The Ohio State University.

Visser, P. S., Krosnick, J. A., & Simmons, J. P. (2003). Distinguishing the cognitive and behavioral consequences of attitude importance and certainty: A test of the common-factor model of attitude strength. *Journal of Experimental Social Psychology, 39,* 118–141.

Voogt, R.J.J., & Saris, W. E. (2003). To participate or not to participate: The link between survey participation, electoral participation, and political interest. *Political Analysis, 11,* 164–179.

Walker, J. L. (1977). *Evolution of the atmosphere.* New York: Macmillan.

Walker, J. L. (1991). *Mobilizing interest groups in America: Patrons, professions, and social movements.* Ann Arbor: The University of Michigan Press.

Wand, J. N., Shotts, K. W., Sekhon, J. S., Mebane, W. R., Herron, M. C., & Brady, H. E. (2001). The butterfly did it: The aberrant vote for Buchanan in Palm Beach County, Florida. *American Political Science Review, 95,* 793–810.

Wanta, W. (1988). The effects of dominant photographs: An agenda-setting experiment. *Journalism Quarterly, 65,* 107–111.

Wanta, W. (1997). *The public and the national agenda: How people learn about important issues.* Mahwah, NJ: Lawrence Erlbaum.

Wanta, W., & Foote, J. (1994). The president–news media relationship: Time series analysis of agenda-setting. *Journal of Broadcasting & Electronic Media, 38,* 437.

Wanta, W., & Hu, Y.W. (1994). Time-lag differences in the agenda-setting process: An examination of five news media. *International Journal of Public Opinion Research, 6*(3), 225–240.

Watt, J. H., Mazza, M., & Snyder, L. (1993). Agenda-setting effects of television news coverage and the effect decay curve. *Communication Research, 20,* 408–435.

Wattenberg, M. P., & Brians, C. L. (1999). Negative campaign advertising: Demobilizer or mobilizer? *American Political Science Review, 93*(4), 891–899.

West, D. M. (1991). Polling effects in election campaigns. *Political Behavior, 13*(2), 151–163.

Willer, R. (2004). The effects of government-issued terror warnings on presidential approval ratings. *Current Research in Social Psychology, 10,* 1–12.

Willis, J., & Todorov, A. (2006). First impressions: Making up your mind after 100-ms exposure to a face. *Psychological Science, 17,* 592–598.

Wilson, W. (1910). Hide-and-seek politics. *North American Review, 191,* 585–601.

Wolfinger, R. E., & Linquitti, P. (1981). Network Election Day predictions and western voters. *Public Opinion* (February–March), 56–60.

Wolfinger, R. E., & Rosenstone, S. J. (1980). *Who votes?* New Haven, CT: Yale University Press.

Wolfinger, R.E., & Rosenstone, S. J. (1993). *Mobilization, participation, and democracy in America.* New York: Macmillan Press.

Wolfinger, R. E., Glass, D.P., & Squire, P. (1990). Predictors of electoral turnout: An international comparison. *Policy Studies Review, 9,* 551–574.

Wood, D. B., & Peake, J. S. (1998). The dynamics of foreign policy agenda setting. *American Political Science Review, 92,* 173–184.

Wood, W. (1982). Retrieval of attitude-relevant information from memory: Effects on susceptibility to persuasion and on intrinsic motivation. *Journal of Personality and Social Psychology, 42*(5), 798–910.

Wood, W., Rhodes, N., & Biek, M. (1995). Working knowledge and attitude strength: An information processing analysis. In R. E. Petty & J. A. Krosnick (Eds.), *Attitude strength: Antecedents and consequences* (pp. 283–313). Mahwah, NJ: Lawrence Erlbaum Associates, Inc.

Wright, G. C., Jr. (1976). Community structure and voting in the South. *Public Opinion Quarterly, 40*(2), 201–215.

Yalch, R. F. (1976). Preelection interview effects on voter turnout. *Public Opinion Quarterly, 40*(3), 331–336.

Zipp, J. F. (1985). Perceived representativess and voting: An assessment of the impact of "choices" versus "echoes." *American Political Science Review, 79*(1), 50–61.

Zuckerman, A. S. (2005). *The social logic of politics: Personal networks as contexts for political behavior*. Philadelphia: Temple University Press.

Zukin, C., & Snyder, R. (1984). Passive learning: When the media environment is the message. *Public Opinion Quarterly, 48,* 629–638.

Chapter 35

Social Psychology and Law

MARGARET BULL KOVERA AND EUGENE BORGIDA

One significant value of much social science research is that it makes clearer what we only dimly perceive, if we perceive it at all. It is not surprising to hear people say about many psychological findings that, "of course, we knew this all along." Yet, very often, what we thought we knew all along is not quite correct or, more importantly, not quite correct in substantial detail.

(Faigman, Kaye, Saks, & Sanders, 2005, p. 568).

Common sense and intuitive beliefs about human behavior are fundamental to why people claim, "Of course, we knew this all along." Social science now impressively documents the human tendency to rely on common sense and intuition when engaged in social cognition (Fiske & Borgida, 2008). At the same time, many insights from psychological science, including theory and research in social psychology, challenge the intuitive understandings that people hold about a wide range of behavioral domains. Many of these behavioral domains intersect with legal processes (e.g., eyewitness identification, jury selection and pretrial publicity, false confessions, polygraphs and lie detection, stereotyping, prejudice, and discrimination) and reveal a substantive "disconnect" between intuitive conceptions of human behavior (i.e., what people assume to be true about eyewitness behavior or the effects of pretrial publicity or why people confess to crimes they did not commit) and the pertinent scientific database (Borgida & Fiske, 2008).

This chapter highlights various applications of social psychology (both theory and methods) to the legal system, with a focus on examining the ways in which the U.S. criminal justice system implicates common sense and intuitive assumptions about human behavior that are empirically testable and have legal or theoretical significance, or both. There are many topical candidates for such an exercise, but the selected examples—the reliability of eyewitness identification, interrogations and confessions, jury selection, pretrial publicity effects on juror decision making, and legal decision makers' evaluations of expert evidence—exemplify this tradition and also reflect an accumulation of quality science that provides the foundation for generating insights about the disconnect between legal standards and their assumptions and science-based understandings. In so doing, several other central topics at the intersection of psychology and law (e.g., risk assessment, competency issues, offender treatment) that are studied primarily by clinical and developmental psychologists are purposely sidestepped. A few other topics (e.g., history of the field, attribution of responsibility, media violence, juror competence, and jury deliberation) were expertly reviewed in the fourth edition of the *Handbook of Social Psychology* (Ellsworth & Mauro, 1998). Similarly, a discussion of theory and research on social justice (Tyler, 2001; Tyler & Smith, 1997) and moral actions and judgments (e.g., Carlsmith, Darley, & Robinson, 2002), topics that occupy territory at the intersection of social psychology and law, also are not included because these topics are covered extensively in other chapters in this volume.

ROLE OF SOCIAL AND BEHAVIORAL SCIENCE IN THE LAW

Quality science provides the foundation for applications of social and psychological science to the law. To be admissible in court, for example, expert testimony must be legally relevant to the case at hand and scientifically valid (Faigman, 2008). The scientific validity of many social scientists' conclusions is impressive. Contemporary social scientists generally base their understanding of phenomena not on single studies but on large groups of studies that have been submitted to rigorous statistical analysis to examine the magnitude and consistency of their findings across samples and methods.

After a relatively large number of such studies accumulate, scientists may not be able to summarize them reliably merely by reading the studies and giving their impression of the most common findings. Such qualitative, informal summaries are likely to be flawed. Therefore, scientists increasingly use quantitative methods to summarize findings across studies. These techniques, known as meta-analysis, involve statistically combining a group of studies to produce a general answer to a question (Lipsey & Wilson, 2001; Schmidt & Hunter, 2004). Because this method clarifies similarities and differences in the findings of related studies, it facilitates the orderly accumulation of scientific facts.

Meta-analyses evaluating the robustness of findings across related studies occasionally establish that findings have not proven to be stable across studies and therefore should be dismissed as having insufficient scientific validity. Alternatively, a finding could prove to be reliable only under certain conditions. Another possible outcome of meta-analyses is that findings prove to be equally strong across a wide range of conditions. A comparison of the generalizability of well-known meta-analytic findings in physics and psychology demonstrated the stability of many findings in psychology (Hedges, 1987). This comparison involved 13 reviews from the Particle Data Group in physics and 13 reviews from psychology (e.g., the effects of teacher expectancy on IQ; the effects of desegregation on educational achievement; sex differences in spatial ability). The psychological reviews proved to be slightly more consistent across studies than the physics reviews, despite evidence of some inconsistencies in both fields. All in all, multiple replications have confirmed many findings in social psychology in particular and the social sciences in general, and quantitative, meta-analytic reviewing has established their robustness. Depending on the specifics of this evidence, such findings can be applied in a wide range of contexts or within a context where they are maximally applicable.

Take the specific case of social psychological research on gender prejudice and stereotyping. Research on explicit and implicit gender prejudice represents an example of scientific research that has been presented to legal fact finders (Eagly & Koenig, 2008; Faigman, Dasgupta, & Ridgeway, 2008; Hunt, Borgida, Burgess, & Kelly, 2002). Research on gender stereotyping shows that the content of stereotypes of men and women differs reliably: Women are seen as communal, and men are seen as agentic (Diekman & Eagly, 2000). Although people do not attribute more positive qualities to men than they do to women (Eagly & Mladinic, 1989), the qualities they ascribe have implications for evaluations of women in the workplace. Specifically, women are evaluated positively when they are thought of in traditional ways (i.e., homemakers, mothers) but not when they work in masculine-typed occupations, such as management (Heilman, 1995). In a situation in which women's presumed qualities do not "fit" the tasks judged necessary for the job, evaluations of their performance are likely to suffer, and their chances for success are likely to be compromised (Heilman, 1983, 2001). Extensive research has established a reliable scientific relationship between gender stereotypes and a range of work-related outcomes (Eagly & Carli, 2007).

Individuals also may hold implicit gender stereotypes that influence attitudes and behavior. Implicit bias occurs outside an individual's awareness and exists even among individuals who report explicit positive attitudes toward a group (Hofmann, Gawronski, Gschwendner, Le, & Schmitt, 2005). For many years, social psychological researchers have documented implicit bias using experimental designs that conceal the fact that gender is a factor in an individual's decision (e.g., Correll, Benard, & Paik, 2007; Dovidio & Gaertner, 1983). More recently, implicit bias has been measured with reaction-time methods borrowed from cognitive psychology, such as priming tasks and the Implicit Association Test (Fazio & Olson, 2003). Although some claim that reaction-time measures capture stereotypes generally present in the culture rather than individual prejudice, measures such as the Implicit Association Test reliably predict meaningful behavioral outcomes (Greenwald, Poehlman, Uhlmann, & Banaji, 2009).

In addition, scientists have worked toward a more nuanced understanding of gender prejudice and discrimination by identifying moderator variables. Research has identified various circumstances that foster discrimination. Studies have shown, for example, that prejudice and discrimination against women are typically stronger when fewer women occupy a particular type of position (e.g., Davison & Burke, 2000; Eagly, Makhijani, & Klonsky, 1992) or when the cultural stereotype of occupants of the position is more masculine (Eagly & Karau, 2002). Similarly, personnel evaluations consisting of subjective appraisals of workplace performance produce greater discrimination than more objective appraisals (Heilman & Haynes, 2008). In addition, male evaluators generally judge women more harshly than female evaluators do (Eagly, Karau, & Makhijani, 1995; Eagly et al., 1992).

To the extent that such conditions characterize the case in question, discrimination is rendered more understandable from the perspective of the scientific literature. A substantial body of quality science illuminating the moderating conditions that affect the likelihood that discrimination is more or less likely to occur provides the scientific foundation for experts testifying in court to more confidently "rule in" or "rule out" explanatory accounts of the discriminatory behavior in issue. In this way, then, gender prejudice research provides insights into the potential cause(s) of a workplace outcome that would be informative and useful in the legal context. The next few sections of the chapter present additional topics for which the legal system has developed commonsense assumptions about how people behave: eyewitness behavior, interrogations and confessions, jury selection, pretrial publicity, and expert scientific evidence. Sometimes these assumptions have proven correct; more often, the assumptions have proven flawed.

(UN)RELIABILITY OF EYEWITNESS IDENTIFICATIONS

People are convicted for crimes every day based solely on the testimony of a single eyewitness who identifies them as the perpetrator of a crime. Yet the evidence continues to mount that eyewitness memory, like other forms of memory, is fallible. For many years, studies of the underlying causes of wrongful convictions have identified mistaken eyewitness identifications as a primary source of error in these cases, with eyewitness errors appearing in 50% to 90% of the cases studied (Borchard & Lutz, 1932; Garrett, 2008; Huff, Rattner, & Sagarin, 1986; Rattner, 1988; Scheck, Neufeld, & Dwyer, 2000; Wells et al., 1998). In most cases, the exonerated men and women have spent many years in prison, with 80% spending more than 5 years in prison and the majority spending more than 10 years (Gross, Jacoby, Matheson, Montgomery, & Patel, 2005). Thus, eyewitness misidentification has significant societal costs.

It would be an error to think that multiple identifications of a suspect would protect against mistaken identifications. In several of the cases in which people have been exonerated by DNA evidence that excludes them as the perpetrator, multiple witnesses—sometimes as many as five witnesses—had identified the exoneree as the perpetrator (e.g., Wells et al., 1998). There are variables, however, that provide information about the relative likelihood that a witness has made an accurate identification. Two types of variables have been proposed: estimator and system variables (Wells, 1978). Estimator variables are characteristics of the crime, the witness, and the perpetrator that are present in the witnessing context and can be used to postdict witness accuracy. System variables, in contrast, are characteristics of the identification procedure that are under the control of the actors in the criminal justice system and are related to eyewitness accuracy.

Much of the research on the effects of estimator and system variables on eyewitness identification accuracy uses a mock witness simulation paradigm in which mock witnesses—generally college undergraduates—watch a simulated crime video in which a perpetrator appears.

Subsequently, witnesses participate in one of several types of identification procedures. A showup consists of the presentation of a single suspect, either in person or via a photograph. This is the most common procedure used in actual crime investigations (Flowe, Ebbesen, Burke, & Chivabunditt, 2001; Gonzalez, Ellsworth, & Pembroke, 1993), but there are limits to its use because the presentation of a single suspect does not allow for an assessment of witness guessing, because any witness guess would result in the identification of the suspect. Showups do not allow for estimating witness guessing and may be more inherently suggestive because they are often conducted with the suspect handcuffed or in the back of a police car. Because of concerns about the suggestiveness of showups, police officers may only conduct showups soon after the crime was committed when their use will shorten the time between the witnessed event and the identification procedure and consequently prevent time from decaying the witness's memory of the perpetrator.

Both live lineup and photo array identification tasks involve the presentation of a suspect and some number of known innocents (referred to as "fillers") to the witness. This procedure is thought to be fairer than a showup because the fillers provide some safeguard against witness guessing, because unbiased arrays should evenly distribute witness guesses across the suspect and multiple fillers. However, actual police lineups and photo arrays are biased against the suspect in that the suspect draws more guesses than do other known innocent members in the lineup (Brigham, Meissner, & Wasserman, 1999; Py, DeMarchi, Ginet, & Wasiak, 2003; Valentine & Heaton, 1999; Wells & Bradfield, 1999).

Although some scholars have advocated for increased study of identifications conducted in the field (Mecklenburg, Bailey, & Larson, 2008), others have noted that laboratory experiments provide information that cannot be gained through the archival study of actual identifications or through field experimentations (Wells, 2008). In laboratory experiments, researchers can manipulate whether the perpetrator is present or absent in the lineup, photo array, or showup. This manipulation allows researchers to assess correct identifications and incorrect rejections of the lineup when the perpetrator is present and mistaken identifications and correct rejections of the lineup when the perpetrator is absent; it also allows researchers to estimate the extent of witness guessing by examining the rates at which witnesses identify fillers. Use of this method can help researchers identify factors that increase the rate of correct identifications and decrease the rate of mistaken identifications.

Estimator Variables

Researchers have identified a number of variables that affect rates of correct identifications, mistaken identifications, or both. These factors include whether the perpetrator and the witness are of the same race; whether the perpetrator wore something that obscured his face, hair, or hairline; whether the witness had seen the suspect in a context other than as the perpetrator of the crime; whether the witness experienced stress during the witnessed event; whether the perpetrator carried a weapon; and whether the duration of the witness's exposure to the perpetrator and the interval between the witnessed event and the identification task were short or long.

Own-Race Bias

Although witness race does not influence witness accuracy independently nor are perpetrators of particular races more easily identified, witness and perpetrator race interact to affect witness reliability. People are more accurate in their identifications of perpetrators with whom they share racial group membership than of perpetrators who are members of a different racial group. This phenomenon has been termed the own-race identification bias or the cross-race identification effect (Meissner & Brigham, 2001) and it appears across racial and ethnic groups (Ng & Lindsay, 1994; Platz & Hosch, 1988). A meta-analysis of more than 30 studies of the own-race bias suggests that it is robust across a variety of settings and materials (Meissner & Brigham, 2001). The analysis confirms that the effect of the own-race bias on the rate of correct identifications is similar for both Black and White participants but suggests that White participants exhibited a larger own-race bias on the rate of mistaken identifications than did Black participants, although the effect size was significant for both groups. The size of the cross-race effect was moderated by exposure duration and retention interval such that the identifications of witnesses who viewed the perpetrator's face for shorter periods of time and who waited longer to complete the identification task were more prone to exhibit the bias.

Several hypotheses have been offered to explain the own-race bias. Although some have suggested that the effect represents a form of prejudice against outgroup members, the meta-analysis failed to find a relationship between prejudicial attitudes and the size of the own-race bias (Meissner & Brigham, 2001). Another explanation rests on the assumption that people who have greater contact with those of other races will be better able to differentiate among members of those other races. The findings from studies examining group differences in the own-race bias of people who live in integrated neighborhoods versus those who live in racially segregated neighborhoods are

mixed, with some studies supporting the contact hypothesis and others failing to find these group differences (for a review, see Meissner & Brigham, 2001). It may be that one must be practiced in differentiating among members of other-race groups. A study of own-race bias among White basketball fans and those who are not fans found that those who follow professional basketball—and therefore must regularly differentiate among the players who are primarily Black—are less prone to the own-race bias than are those who are not professional basketball fans (Li, Dunning, & Malpass, 1998). In summary, substantial evidence of an own-race bias in the accuracy of eyewitness identifications exists but the psychological mechanisms underlying this bias remain uncertain.

Disguises

It may be common sense that when a perpetrator wears a disguise such as a ski mask, witnesses have more difficulty making accurate identifications. However, even more subtle obscuring of facial cues, such as covering the hairline with a baseball cap or bandana, may lower witness identification accuracy. In one eyewitness simulation, half of the witnesses viewed a perpetrator who wore a hat that covered his hair and hairline; the remaining witnesses viewed a perpetrator without a hat. Almost twice as many witnesses could correctly identify the perpetrator without a hat from a subsequent lineup than could identify the perpetrator whose hair and hairline were covered (Cutler, Penrod, & Martens, 1987a). A review of six studies ($N > 1,300$ witnesses) examining the effects of a head covering on witness accuracy further supports the finding that perpetrators who cover their hair and hairlines are more difficult to identify than the same perpetrators with bare heads (Cutler, 2006). Alterations in appearance due to glasses, hairstyle, facial hair, and age also make it more difficult for witnesses to make accurate identifications (Read, 1995; Read, Tollestrup, Hammersley, McFadzen, & Christensen, 1990).

Unconscious Transference

Sometimes witnesses are shown a lineup or a photo array that contains a suspect whom they have seen previously but who is not a perpetrator. Perhaps the innocent suspect and the witness both live in the neighborhood in which the crime took place. Perhaps they went to the same school, attended the same party, or frequented the same bar. Because of this previous contact, the innocent suspect appears familiar to the witness, who mistakenly believes that familiarity is due to the fact that the suspect was the person who committed the witnessed crime. Because the witness is not aware that the suspect is familiar because of exposure in a context other than that of the crime perpetrator, this phenomenon is known as *unconscious transference*.

One paradigm that has been used to study unconscious transference has participants witness an event, with some participants viewing only a target/perpetrator and other participants viewing both the target and a bystander to the event (e.g., Read et al., 1990, Exp. 5). All witnesses attempt an identification from a photo array that contains a picture of the bystander and four previously unseen foils (i.e., all arrays are perpetrator-absent). Witnesses who previously saw the bystander are more likely mistakenly to identify the bystander as the perpetrator. In another paradigm, witnesses view a series of mug shots between witnessing an event and making an identification attempt from a photo array or lineup (e.g., Gorenstein & Ellsworth, 1980). Mere exposure to mug shots between witnessing an event and attempting to identify a target face increases the likelihood that a person depicted in a mug shot will be mistakenly identified as the perpetrator of the witnessed event (Brown, Deffenbacher, & Sturgill, 1977).

A recent meta-analytic review provides support for transference effects on eyewitness identification accuracy (Deffenbacher, Bornstein, & Penrod, 2006). A meta-analysis of 32 tests of the mug shot exposure effect confirmed that when witnesses were exposed to mug shots, they were less likely to identify perpetrators correctly when they were present and more likely to identify innocent lineup members than were those not exposed to mug shots. These effects were larger if the witness had chosen the person from a mug-shot array and then saw that person in a subsequent identification procedure than if the witness had not committed to choosing the person in the mug shot previously. Moreover, merely viewing mug shots that did not contain depictions of any of the people who appeared in the subsequent identification procedure did not affect witness accuracy. Thus, for mug-shot exposure to produce a negative effect on witness accuracy, it had to allow for transference errors by including an innocent person among the lineup members who also appeared in the mug shots. An additional meta-analysis of 19 tests of studies testing for transference effects using either mug-shot exposure or bystander paradigms also found significant transference effects on the accuracy of eyewitness identifications, but those effects were smaller when using the bystander paradigm.

Stress

Witnesses frequently view crimes under extremely stressful conditions, including circumstances in which their lives are threatened by a weapon-wielding perpetrator. Witnessing crimes is not always stressful; perhaps a witness sees a perpetrator fleeing from a crime scene but does not yet realize that a crime has been committed and therefore has no reason to be scared. Scholars have tried to examine the effects of stress on accuracy by categorizing witnesses on the basis of the likely stress that they experienced and then examining the rates at which these categories of witnesses identified the suspect in actual lineups (Behrman & Davey, 2001; Tollestrup, Turtle, & Yuille, 1994; Valentine, Pickering, & Darling, 2003). These field studies of the stress–accuracy relationship have provided no clear picture of the relationship between these two variables, perhaps because the categorizations did not accurately reflect differences in experienced stress.

Laboratory studies that manipulate experienced stress are less likely to suffer from this criticism, but they are often criticized because the levels of stress that one can induce in the lab are ethically constrained and likely do not reach the high levels of stress experienced by witnesses whose lives are threatened by actual weapon-brandishing perpetrators. One exception is a study conducted with more than 500 military personnel enrolled in a survival-training program in which participants learn to withstand high-stress interrogations involving physical confrontation (Morgan et al., 2004). Personnel experienced a high-stress interrogation, a low-stress interrogation that lacked physical confrontation, or both types of interrogation and then attempted to identify their interrogators from photo arrays. Irrespective of how the identification procedure was administered (e.g., live vs. photographic, simultaneous vs. sequential), participants who experienced low-stress interrogations were more likely to make a correct identification of their interrogator when the interrogator was present than were participants who experienced high-stress interrogations. However, the stressfulness of the interrogation did not influence the rate of mistaken identifications that the participants made when the interrogator was not present in the lineup.

How does a witness's level of stress influence identification accuracy? For years, the relationship between stress and memory accuracy was hypothesized to be an inverted U-shaped curve. Low levels of stress would not cause the witness to orient toward the relevant features of the crime, including the perpetrator. Moderate levels of stress would improve accuracy by increasing orienting responses and witnesses' attention to important event details. High levels of stress were hypothesized to interfere with witnesses' cognitive processing, lowering witness identification accuracy (Deffenbacher, 1983). More recent theorizing about the relationship between stress and memory has moved away from a discussion of an inverted-U relationship and instead posited that levels of cognitive and somatic anxiety are important for predicting the stress-accuracy relationship. When levels of cognitive anxiety are high—as would be the case if witnesses are aware that they are witnessing a crime, increasing levels of somatic anxiety would at first result in steadily improving performance accuracy. At some critical point, however, the increasing somatic anxiety would cause a precipitous drop in performance (Deffenbacher, 1994).

A meta-analysis of 27 tests of the effects of stress on identification accuracy was recently conducted (Deffenbacher, Bornstein, Penrod, & McGorty, 2004) that included only those studies that contained an experimental manipulation of stress that produced a change in experienced stress as measured by changes either in the physiological state of witnesses or in witnesses' self-reported arousal. This analysis confirmed that stress negatively influences the accuracy of witness identifications. Consistent with the findings from Morgan and colleagues' (2004) study of military personnel in survival training camp, the meta-analysis found that high stress reduced the rate of correct identifications but did not increase mistaken identifications. Stress had a greater negative influence in studies using an ecologically valid eyewitness paradigm compared with studies using more traditional facial recognition paradigms in which participants are shown a number of faces during the study phase and then asked to differentiate between faces they had seen previously and new faces at the recognition phase.

In summary, despite the lack of an effect of stress on target-absent lineups, the decrease in correct identifications means that when considering results from both target-present and target-absent lineups together, lower stress witnessing conditions will produce a higher percentage of accurate identifications than will higher stress conditions. This effect of stress on the mix of accurate and inaccurate identifications will be even greater when the choice of foils biases the witness toward choosing the suspect, as appears to be the case for a significant proportion of lineups and photo arrays used in real cases (Brigham et al., 1999; Py et al., 2003; Valentine & Heaton, 1999; Wells & Bradfield, 1999).

Weapon Focus

Many factors may cause a witness to experience high stress while witnessing an event, including the presence of a weapon. In contrast to other factors that contribute to the stress a witness may experience, weapons have a unique influence on witness accuracy because they tend to draw the attention of the witness, leaving fewer attentional resources to be allocated to the perpetrator's facial and physical characteristics. Thus, when witnesses see a weapon during the commission of a crime, they are less likely to encode the characteristics of the perpetrator's face, negatively influencing their ability to make accurate identification decisions, than when there is no weapon present.

This effect of weapon presence on eyewitness accuracy is known as *weapon focus* (Steblay, 1992).

Laboratory studies of weapon focus have taken one of two forms: Witnesses watch a videotaped crime reenactment that manipulates the presence of a weapon—often a gun (O'Rourke, Penrod, Cutler, & Stuve, 1989)—or witnesses experience a live situation that manipulates the presence of an object which could be construed as a weapon (e.g., a syringe; Maass & Kohnken, 1989). The two paradigms complement each other as the videotaped reenactment paradigm allows a presentation of weapons that cannot be ethically presented to participants in live crime simulations. Questions arise, however, about whether the effects obtained in these situations in which the witnesses are not physically confronted with a weapon may differ from the results obtained when witnesses view the weapon in vivo. Indeed a meta-analysis of 19 tests of weapon focus found that the effect of weapon presence was significant but was larger in studies that were more ecologically valid (e.g., brief exposure to the perpetrator and long delays between viewing the perpetrator and the memory test) and for studies in which the weapon was a gun (Steblay, 1992), stressing the importance of the use of both paradigms when studying the phenomenon. Studies conducted since this meta-analysis suggest that children are also susceptible to the weapon focus effect (Davies, Smith, & Blincoe, 2008; Pickel, Narter, Jameson, & Lenhardt, 2008).

There are two leading hypotheses regarding the underlying psychological mechanism for the weapon focus effect. From some studies, it appears that the effects of weapon presence may be due to increased attentional focus to the weapon. In one study in which witnesses watched a customer at a fast-food restaurant either point a gun at or hand a check to a cashier, eye-tracking data revealed that witnesses made more frequent fixations on the gun than on the check (Loftus, Loftus, & Messo, 1987). Yet other studies suggest that the unusualness of an object rather than its status as a weapon causes attention to be diverted from the perpetrator to the weapon. In one such study (Pickel, 1998), a simulated crime was filmed in a hair salon; the perpetrator carried an item that varied in how threatening and how unusual it was for the setting. High-threat items were a gun (unusual) and scissors (usual), whereas the low-threat items were a wallet (usual) and a raw chicken (unusual). Threat did not affect participants' memory for the perpetrator, but participants remembered fewer details about the perpetrator when he held an unusual object than a common one. Moreover, carrying a weapon may not always negatively influence participants' reports of information about a target person if the weapon is consistent with the context in which the weapon is viewed (e.g., carried by a police officer rather than a priest or at a shooting range rather than a baseball game; Pickel, 1999). A recent study suggests that both unusualness and threat contribute to decreased attention to target appearance (Hope & Wright, 2007), reinforcing the conclusion that weapon presence reduces eyewitness accuracy.

Exposure Duration and Retention Interval

Not surprisingly, the amount of time a witness has to view the perpetrator's face (exposure duration) and the length of time between viewing the perpetrator and the subsequent identification task (retention interval) both influence the accuracy of witness identifications. With lengthened exposure to perpetrators, witnesses are better able to encode their physical characteristics and consequently make more accurate identification decisions. Some studies of exposure duration have been conducted using traditional facial recognition paradigms in which participants are shown a large number of faces for varying amounts of time and then view a new set of faces, some of which they have seen before and some of which they have not. In these studies, participants were more accurate making judgments when they had seen the faces for the longer duration (e.g., Laughery, Alexander, & Lane, 1971). Studies using more ecologically valid eyewitness paradigms also find that witnesses are more likely to make correct identifications and less likely to make false identifications when the exposure duration is longer rather than shorter (e.g., 45 vs. 12 seconds; Memon, Hope, & Bull, 2003). Archival studies of actual crimes generally produce similar results with witnesses identifying suspects more frequently when exposure times were longer as opposed to shorter (Klobuchar, Steblay, & Caligiuri, 2006; Valentine et al., 2003).

Another temporal variable that affects eyewitness accuracy is the retention interval, the amount of time that passes between viewing a crime and the eyewitness identification. Sometimes identification procedures can take place a relatively short time after the crime occurred, as happens when a suspect is apprehended in the neighborhood relatively soon after the crime takes place and is brought to the witness for a showup identification. Sometimes it takes the police days, weeks, months, or even years to produce a suspect to place in an identification array. In laboratory and field experiments, shorter retention intervals are related to more accurate identifications (Cutler, Penrod, O'Rourke, & Martens, 1986; Krafka & Penrod, 1985). Archival studies of actual crimes confirm that witnesses identified fewer suspects as the length of time between the crime and the identification procedure increased (Behrman & Davey, 2001; Tollestrup et al., 1994).

A quantitative meta-analysis of facial recognition research—including eyewitness identification research—supports the robustness of the effects of both exposure time and retention interval on eyewitness accuracy (Shapiro & Penrod, 1986). Across eight tests of the effects of exposure time on rates of correct identifications, exposure time had a moderate to large effect ($d = .61$). As expected, longer exposure times produced more correct identifications. The effect of exposure time was smaller for mistaken identifications ($d = .22$), but again shorter exposure times produced more false identifications. Similarly, the meta-analysis supported the proposition that retention intervals are related to increased identification accuracy. Across 18 tests of the effects of retention interval on the rate of correct identifications, retention interval was negatively related to correct identifications ($d = .43$). Their analysis of 14 tests of the effects of retention interval on rates of mistaken identifications demonstrated a small to moderate effect of retention interval ($d = .33$) with longer intervals resulting in more mistakes.

Thus, overall, a variety of characteristics associated with the conditions present when someone witnesses a crime—disguises, stress, weapon presence, exposure to other faces in temporal contiguity to the crime, and whether the witness and perpetrator belong to the same racial and ethnic group—influence the accuracy of the witness identifications of perpetrators. When estimating the likely accuracy of a witness, it is helpful to know whether any of the features that decrease witness accuracy were present. However, studying these estimator variables provides no information about how to increase the accuracy of eyewitnesses because actors in the criminal justice system cannot control whether they are present when someone witnesses a crime. To help improve the quality of eyewitness identifications that may subsequently be entered into evidence against a defendant, it is important to identify variables associated with the collection of eyewitness identification evidence that investigators can control.

System Variables

System variables are those features of a lineup administration that are under the control of actors in the criminal justice system. An identification task can be thought of as an experiment in which the hypothesis being tested is that the suspect and the perpetrator are the same person (Wells & Luus, 1990). The same types of experimental features that can lead to problems in drawing inferences from experiments also make it problematic to infer that a suspect is the perpetrator even when a witness positively identifies the suspect. For example, the instructions given by the lineup administrator might bias the witness toward supporting the hypothesis that the suspect is the perpetrator. Administrators may unintentionally leak their hypothesis to witnesses, or they may interpret the witnesses' responses in a manner that is consistent with their hypothesis. The materials (e.g., the lineup members) may contain demand characteristics that communicate the hypothesis (Wells & Luus, 1990). These observations have led researchers to focus their efforts on studying the effects of lineup composition, lineup instructions, the method of presenting lineup members to witnesses, and administrator behavior on witness accuracy.

Lineup Composition

The method of selecting fillers for photo arrays and lineups can influence the accuracy of witnesses. There are two primary methods for selecting fillers to pair with a suspect. Using the first approach, known as "match-to-suspect," an administrator would select fillers that resemble the suspect. In the second approach, known as "match-to-description," the administrator selects fillers that match the description that the witness gave of the perpetrator. The fillers must possess any characteristic that is mentioned in the witness's description but may vary on characteristics that were omitted from the description. Thus, if the witness reports that the perpetrator had brown hair, all lineup members must have brown hair, but their hair may be straight or curly because this is not a characteristic mentioned by the witness.

Researchers have promoted the match-to-description method because it reduces the likelihood that witness guessing or deduction would result in the false identification of an innocent suspect. Imagine a lineup in which the suspect is the only lineup member who matches the description of the perpetrator given by the witness. In that situation, a witness may deduce who the suspect is and choose that person on the basis of their deduction paired with an assumption that the police have placed the suspect in the lineup for a reason (e.g., other evidence implicates the suspect in the crime). Match-to-description lineups are thought to guard against this type of deduction because all of the lineup members will match the witness's description. In match-to-suspect lineups, lineup members may match the suspect on features that were omitted from the description but fail to match the description on included features, leaving open the possibility that the witness could deduce the suspect's identity on the basis of his or her match to the description.

Match-to-description photo arrays appear to increase correct identifications and decrease mistaken identifications in comparison to match-to-suspect arrays. In one study (S. Clark & Tunnicliff, 2001), 30 minutes after watching a staged crime, undergraduates viewed one of three types of photo arrays: a culprit-present array in which the fillers were matched to the culprit, a culprit-absent array in which the fillers were matched to the innocent suspect, or a culprit-absent array in which fillers were matched to the

culprit. When the photo array did not contain the perpetrator, witnesses were more likely to identify the innocent suspect from the photo array in which the fillers were matched to the suspect than from the array in which the fillers were matched to the culprit. Thus, matching the fillers to the suspect seems to increase the likelihood of mistaken identifications of innocent suspects.

In a more direct test of the benefits of the match-to-description method of selecting foils, researchers constructed individual photo arrays for each witness to a staged theft (Wells, Rydell, & Seelau, 1993). Depending on the condition, they either matched fillers to the suspect or to the witness's description of the perpetrator or they selected fillers that did not match the witness's description of the culprit. The researchers also varied whether the culprit was present in the lineup. When the perpetrator was present, witnesses were more likely to make correct identifications when they viewed an array in which the fillers were chosen on the basis of whether they matched the witness's description of the perpetrator than when the fillers were matched to the suspect. Although there was no difference between the proportion of witnesses who made correct identifications from arrays that were chosen to match or mismatch the witnesses' description of the culprit, deduction may have played a role in identifications from the lineups chosen to mismatch the description. In contrast, when the culprit was absent from the photo spread, witnesses were more likely to make false identifications when they viewed the arrays in which the fillers did not match the description than when they viewed either the suspect-matched or the match-to-description arrays. Overall, it was the arrays in which filler selection was based on a match-to-description strategy that produced the best ratio of correct identifications to false identifications.

Lineup Instructions

The instructions that lineup administrators give to witnesses who are about to view a lineup or photo spread have the potential to influence the likelihood that a witness will make a choice from the lineup (i.e., make a positive identification). When lineup administrators deliver instructions suggesting that the perpetrator is one of the lineup members or that the witness is expected to make a positive identification, witnesses are more likely to make a choice from the lineup. In contrast, when a lineup administrator instructs the witness that the perpetrator may not appear in the lineup, witnesses are less likely to make a positive identification (Steblay, 1997). In an early laboratory study of the effects of lineup instruction, witnesses who heard biased instructions ("We believe that the [perpetrator] is present in the lineup. Look carefully at each of the five individuals in the lineup. Which of these is the person you saw?") were more likely to choose a lineup member than were witnesses who heard unbiased instructions ("The [perpetrator] may be one of the five individuals in the lineup. It is also possible that he is not in the lineup."; Malpass & Devine, 1981). Similar results have been obtained in other laboratory studies (e.g., Cutler, Penrod, & Martens, 1987b).

In the first quantitative meta-analysis of the literature, 19 tests of the effect were examined (Steblay, 1997). The meta-analysis found that biased instructions produce more false identifications than unbiased instructions when the perpetrator is absent from the lineup but that instruction suggestiveness does not affect correct identification rates. A qualitative reanalysis of the studies in this meta-analysis reached a somewhat different conclusion: Unbiased instructions produce a small decrease in correct identifications from culprit-present photo spreads (S. E. Clark, 2005). Despite this different conclusion about whether instruction suggestiveness significantly influence correct identification rates, both authors agreed that the size of any decrease in correct identifications from culprit-present arrays due to the use of unbiased instructions is far smaller than the decrease in mistaken identifications from culprit-absent arrays.

Lineup Administration

Typically, the lead investigator will be the person who administers the lineup or photo spread to the witness. Thus, administrators of lineups generally know which member of the lineup is the suspect, and this knowledge has the potential to influence their behavior in a way that might steer the witnesses toward the suspect and away from fillers. This change in behavior need not be intentional to exert influence on the witness (Greathouse & Kovera, 2009). When lineup administrators know the identity of the suspect in a lineup, this is called a single-blind administration, because the witness is blind to the suspect's identity but the lineup administrator is not. In contrast, double-blind administration refers to the situation in which an investigator who is not involved in the case and does not know the identity of the suspect administers the lineup or photo spread because both the witness and the administrator are blind to the suspect's identity. Of course, the idea that investigators can communicate—intentionally or unintentionally—their expectations to participants and that these expectations influence participants' behavior is a well-established principle of research methods in psychology (Rosenthal, 2002). Several laboratory studies have confirmed that when lineup administrators know the suspect's identity and therefore have a hypothesis that the witness will choose the suspect, the witness will indeed choose the suspect more frequently when there is contact between the administrator and the witness (Greathouse & Kovera, 2009; Haw & Fisher,

2004; Phillips, McAuliff, Kovera, & Cutler, 1999; Russano, Dickinson, Greathouse, & Kovera, 2006).

Most recently, researchers have begun to examine whether other features of the lineup administration moderate the effects of investigator knowledge of the suspect's identity on witness accuracy (Greathouse & Kovera, 2009). Specifically, do other variables—such as biased instructions and simultaneous presentation—that increase the likelihood a witness will make a positive identification (i.e., choose) from a lineup also increase the effect of investigator knowledge? If an administrator fails to warn a witness that the culprit may not be in the lineup, might a witness who is prone to guessing because of lineup features that promote choosing search the administrator's behavior for cues to the suspect's identity?

Research suggests that the answer is yes. When witnesses received biased instructions and viewed simultaneous lineups, they were more likely to identify suspects in single-blind than in double-blind lineups (Greathouse & Kovera, 2009). This effect obtained irrespective of whether the target was in the lineup or not. The pattern of witnesses' identifications of fillers and suspects suggests that the increase in mistaken identifications due to administrator knowledge of the suspect's identity was the result of a shift in filler identifications to suspect identifications. That is, witnesses rejected the lineups (i.e., made no identifications) equally often in single- and double-blind lineups; however, filler identifications that were made under double-blind conditions were redistributed to suspect identifications under single-blind conditions. Essentially, administrator knowledge did not sway those who believed the perpetrator was not present but shifted those who had made filler identifications to suspect identifications, especially under conditions that would promote guessing (and a higher rate of filler identifications under double-blind conditions). Moreover, the diagnosticity of identifications made when the administrator was blind to the suspect's identity was twice that of identifications made when the administrator knew who the suspect was. These findings provide support for the recommendations that all lineups be conducted with blind administrators (e.g., Wells et al., 1998).

Lineup Presentation

Most lineup administrators present lineup members or photos from a photo spread to witnesses simultaneously and ask the witness whether the perpetrator is among the people presented (Wogalter, Malpass, & McQuiston, 2004). In contrast, some scholars have suggested that a preferable method of presentation is to show the photos or lineup members to witnesses one at a time, asking witnesses to make a judgment as to whether the person is the perpetrator after each presentation (Wells et al., 1998). This second method of presentation is known as a sequential lineup.

In the first study of the relative merits of simultaneous and sequential lineups, witnesses to staged thefts attempted eyewitness identifications from culprit-absent or culprit-present photo spreads (Lindsay & Wells, 1985). Half of these arrays were presented simultaneously, and the other half were presented sequentially. When the culprit was present in the lineup, the rate of correct identifications was similar for simultaneous and sequential lineups. However, when the culprit was absent from the lineup, witnesses were more likely to make false identifications from simultaneously than from sequentially presented lineups. In part, the increase in false identifications is due to the fact that witnesses are more likely to make positive identifications (i.e., choices) from simultaneous lineups (Meissner, Tredoux, Parker, & MacLin, 2005).

This basic sequential superiority effect has been replicated by others (e.g., Cutler & Penrod, 1988) and confirmed in a meta-analysis of the studies testing the effects of presentation style on witness accuracy (Steblay, Dysart, Fulero, & Lindsay, 2001). This meta-analysis revealed that witnesses were more likely to make correct identifications from simultaneous lineups than from sequential lineups when the culprit was present in the lineup. When the culprit was not present in the identification procedure, witnesses who viewed sequential lineups were more likely to decide that the perpetrator was not there and less likely to make mistaken identifications than witnesses who viewed simultaneous lineups and photo spreads. Although the sequential procedure does reduce correct identifications, the reduction is small and much smaller than the reduction in false identifications produced by sequential presentation.

Despite these demonstrated benefits of sequential presentation, some have begun to question whether the push to make sequential presentation standard operating procedure is wise. Some scholars have argued that the push to change public policy is premature given that the psychological mechanisms underlying the sequential superiority effect are not well understood (McQuiston-Surrett, Malpass, & Tredoux, 2006). These authors are especially concerned about understanding whether certain features such as backloading of pictures (i.e., not letting the witness know how many people are in the photo spread), the stopping rule (i.e., whether photo presentation stops when a witness makes an identification or does the presentation continue until the witness sees all the photos), and the treatment of multiple identification decisions are necessary for the benefits of sequential presentation to obtain.

Practitioners have also questioned the benefits of sequential presentation based on the results of the Illinois Pilot Program on Sequential Double-Blind Identification Procedures (Mecklenburg, 2006), a field experiment in which researchers randomly assigned the identification procedures that police would use when conducting a lineup. The study compared double-blind sequential lineup administration with single-blind simultaneous administration and found that witnesses were more likely to identify suspects and less likely to identify fillers from single-blind simultaneous lineups. Although conducting a field test of these methods is admirable, this pilot study is seriously flawed for several reasons. First, equating identifications of the suspect with correct identifications is unwise because in the field, the accuracy of an identification is unknown unless DNA evidence confirms the identification. Second, the researchers confounded the manipulation of lineup presentation with the manipulation of blind presentation, rendering it difficult to make valid inferences about the effects of either variable (Schacter et al., 2008). Finally, although filler identifications are mistakes, it is possible that officers record the same witness behaviors toward fillers differently depending on whether they are blind to who are the fillers (Wells, 2008). For example, a witness who says, "I think it may have been Number Three, but I am not sure" may be recorded as a filler identification by a police officer who is blind to the suspect's identity and therefore does not know whether the uncertain identification is of the suspect or a filler but as a nonidentification by a nonblind police officer because of the witness's uncertainty. Because of these concerns about the methods of the pilot study, many commentators have cautioned against the use of these data to support public policy (Diamond, 2008; S. J. Ross & Malpass, 2008; Schacter et al., 2008; Steblay, 2008; Wells, 2008), especially in light of the controlled laboratory studies that routinely find that sequential presentation reduces mistaken identifications.

Showups Versus Lineups

When planning to collect identification evidence from witnesses, investigators must make a choice between conducting a showup, in which a witness views a single suspect and makes an identification decision, or a procedure in which the witness views the suspect along with a group of known innocent fillers (i.e., a lineup or photo array). Generally, an investigator will choose to conduct a showup when a suspect is found quickly near the area where the crime was committed. Under those circumstances, the suspect is brought to the witness, or the witness is brought to the location where the suspect is being held. On occasion, investigators will present a single photo to a witness. The potential suggestiveness of showup is a concern because, unlike a lineup, any positive identification results in the identification of the suspect, so there is no method of assessing the extent to which a witness is guessing as is the case when the lineup contains fillers. Courts have upheld the use of showups when they are conducted within 30 minutes of the crime, arguing that the short retention interval contributes to greater witness accuracy and that waiting for the construction of a lineup would eliminate this advantage (*People v. Brnja*, 1980; *Singletary v. United States*, 1978). Moreover, because a showup can be thought of as the first photo in a sequential photo spread, with no other photos to follow, some might argue that the data suggesting that witnesses are less likely to make false identifications from sequential lineups would support a hypothesis that showups are less likely to produce false identifications than simultaneous lineup procedures.

Do accuracy rates differ between showups and lineups? One study found that witnesses made more correct identifications from showups than from lineups when the culprit was present in the identification task but they also made more than twice the number of false identifications (Yarmey, Yarmey, & Yarmey, 1996). Longer retention intervals and clothing bias (when the innocent suspect wears clothing similar to the perpetrator's) exacerbated problems associated with showups (Yarmey et al., 1996). A meta-analysis of field and laboratory research testing the effects of showups versus lineups on witness accuracy confirmed these findings (Steblay, Dysart, Fulero, & Lindsay, 2003). Witnesses made fewer choices (i.e., positive identifications) from showups than from lineups and photo spreads. Because witnesses made fewer choices from showups, they were also more likely to reject correctly a culprit-absent showup than a culprit-absent lineup or photospread. Although overall, showups produced the same rate of correct and false identifications as lineups and photospreads, showups were most likely to produce false identifications when the innocent suspect more closely resembled the perpetrator. Thus, it appears that showups are more dangerous under some conditions (e.g., longer delays, the suspect looks like the perpetrator or is wearing similar clothes) than others. Because in real cases it is unknown whether some of these conditions are present, it would be safer to conduct lineups to avoid any chance of increasing false identifications.

Postdictors of Witness Accuracy

Those in a position to postdict witness accuracy (e.g., police officers, prosecutors, judges, jurors) may use another class of variables in addition to estimator and system variables. These variables include witness confidence, the accuracy of a witness's description of a perpetrator, witness consistency, and identification speed. Of these variables, identification speed is the most promising.

Witness Confidence

U.S. case law specifies that judges should consider the confidence with which witnesses make their identification of a lineup member when evaluating whether the identification resulting from suggestive lineup procedures is reliable despite the circumstances under which it was obtained (*Manson v. Braithwaite*, 1977). Judges may instruct jurors to consider witness confidence when evaluating the weight to give eyewitness identification evidence when arriving at a verdict (*United States v. Telfaire*, 1978). But does witness confidence deserve the status given to it by these legal decisions? Is witness confidence an accurate predictor of witness accuracy?

There are numerous studies that measure both witness confidence and witness accuracy. The most comprehensive of the meta-analyses that examine the relationship between witness confidence and accuracy (Sporer, Penrod, Read, & Cutler, 1995) found a relatively weak relationship between these variables; however, the relationship was much stronger for choosers (e.g., witnesses who made a positive identification from the lineup) than for nonchoosers (e.g., witnesses who rejected the lineup). Viewing conditions also moderated the confidence–accuracy correlation. Better, more optimal viewing conditions produced higher confidence–accuracy correlations than did less optimal viewing conditions, according to the *optimality hypothesis* (Deffenbacher, 1980).

One reason that confidence may be only weakly related to witness accuracy is that witness confidence appears mutable. The confidence–accuracy relationship is stronger when confidence data are collected immediately after the identification than when witnesses have the opportunity to receive information that confirms or disconfirms their identification. In the first investigation of confidence malleability, pairs of witnesses viewed a staged theft (Luus and Wells, 1994). If witnesses heard that their cowitness identified the same person whom they identified, their confidence in the accuracy of their identification increased. In contrast, if witnesses heard that their cowitness had identified a different lineup member or had failed to choose anyone from the lineup, their confidence in the accuracy of their identification decreased.

Additional studies have demonstrated that feedback not only alters witnesses' confidence in the accuracy of their identification but also alters their reports of the conditions under which they viewed the crime. In one study (Bradfield, Wells, & Olson, 2002), confirming feedback not only reduced the accuracy–confidence correlation, it also caused witnesses to report that they had a better view of the perpetrator, paid more attention to the video, had a better basis for their identification, made their identification more easily, were more willing to testify, and had a better image of the perpetrator's face in their mind than did witnesses who did not receive feedback. An archival study of actual crimes shows a similar effect of feedback on reported viewing conditions (Wright & Skagerberg, 2007).

A meta-analysis of 20 studies of the effects of post-identification feedback on confidence malleability reveals that this effect is robust and quite large ($d = .79$), with confirming feedback increasing confidence and disconfirming feedback decreasing confidence. The effects of postidentification feedback on witnesses' reports of how good a view they had and how much attention they paid to the perpetrator were somewhat smaller but still moderate effects according to conventions of evaluating effect sizes. These effects are problematic given that case law in *Manson v. Braithwaite* (1977) requires that judges who are ruling on the admissibility of an identification obtained using suggestive procedures may rule in favor of admissibility if they find the identification to be reliable despite the suggestiveness of the procedures. Three of the criteria that find are to use when evaluating the reliability of the identification are the very variables that are altered by postidentification feedback: how good of a view the witness had, how much attention the witness paid to the perpetrator, and witness confidence (Wells & Quinlivan, 2009).

Witness Description Accuracy

When defense attorneys consult with experts on eyewitness identifications, they will often argue that their client must be innocent because the witness gave a description of the perpetrator that does not match their client. To what extent are witness descriptions related to identification accuracy? Are the identifications of witnesses who provide complete descriptions of the perpetrator, a large number of accurate details, a small number of inaccurate details, or descriptions that are congruent with the identified suspect any more accurate than the identifications provided by witnesses who provide poorer descriptions?

In one field study, an experimenter visited banks and approached tellers to deposit blatantly altered money orders (Pigott, Brigham, & Bothwell, 1990). When the tellers refused to cash the money orders, the experimenter became quite angry and departed. Later that same day, a different experimenter posed as an investigator and collected descriptions and identifications from the clerks. After coding the descriptions for accuracy, completeness, and congruence, the experimenters tested whether these features of the descriptions correlated with identification accuracy. All of the correlations were positive, but none were significant. Subsequent studies have replicated the weak to nonexistent relationship between witness descriptions and witness accuracy (Susa & Meissner, 2008).

Witness Consistency

Litigation manuals suggest that trial attorneys attempt to extract inconsistencies from witnesses when they testify and to impeach the witness with these testimonial inconsistencies. This strategy is not particularly difficult to practice given that witnesses are normally interviewed multiple times over the course of an investigation, and these multiple accounts of the witnessed event are likely to contain different details about the event and the perpetrator. But to what extent do these inconsistencies in eyewitness reports relate to identification accuracy?

In four studies that examined the relationship between identification accuracy and the consistency of eyewitness reports, witnesses viewed staged thefts and then provided descriptions of the perpetrators—sometimes multiple perpetrators for each theft—and the events at two times (Fisher & Cutler, 1996). At the end of each interview, the witnesses attempted identifications of the culprits from photo spreads, videotaped lineups, or live lineups. The researchers coded these descriptions for consistency across the two interviews and then correlated witness consistency with witness identification accuracy. The correlations were small, and all but one was nonsignificant, suggesting that witness consistency is not a particularly good postdictor of witness accuracy.

Identification Speed

Sometimes when witnesses view a photo spread or a lineup, they immediately identify one of the lineup members as the perpetrator. At other times, witnesses may deliberate on the lineup members and take a relatively long time to make a positive identification. Does response latency prove to be a significant postdictor of identification accuracy? Four crime-simulation studies suggest that those witnesses who make their identifications within 10 to 12 seconds of viewing a photo spread are more accurate than those witnesses who take more time before making a choice (Dunning & Perretta, 2002). In one of these studies, undergraduates viewed a videotape of a purse snatching. The witnesses wrote their descriptions of the events and attempted to make identifications from culprit-absent and culprit-present photo spreads. Witnesses who made correct identifications did so more quickly than did those witnesses who made false identifications. Subsequent research has not supported the 10- to 12-second decision rule but did support the inverse relationship of response latency and identification accuracy (Weber, Brewer, Wells, Semmler, & Keast, 2004). There was no relationship between the time witnesses took to reject a lineup and the accuracy of that decision.

Identification speed and accuracy may also be related in real crimes (Valentine et al., 2003). In their study of 600 identification attempts by 600 witnesses to real crimes, Valentine and colleagues found that witnesses whom police officers dubbed "fast" choosers were more than twice as likely to choose the suspect from the lineup than were witnesses labeled "average" or "slow" choosers. Identification speed was unrelated to witnesses' known mistakes (i.e., choices of fillers from the lineups). Although investigators' knowledge of the suspect's identity could have influenced their judgments of identification speed—artificially creating a relationship between speed and accuracy—the consistency of these findings with those from laboratory simulations suggests that faster identifications may be more accurate.

In conclusion, the commonsense notion that eyewitnesses to crime will reliably identify perpetrators is untenable. Eyewitnesses are not as reliable as jurors believe them to be (Cutler, Penrod, & Dexter, 1990; Schmechel, O'Toole, Easterly, & Loftus, 2006). Characteristics of events that interfere with witness memory for faces—targets and perceivers from different racial or ethnic groups, weapon presence, stress, disguised target faces—are often present in witnessed crimes. Although research supports the adoption of several procedural changes (e.g., instructions warning the witness that the perpetrator may not be in the lineup, sequential presentation, double-blind administrators), many in the position to implement these changes have resisted doing so (e.g., Mecklenburg, Bailey, & Larson, 2008). Without the implementation of these evidence-based procedures, juries likely will continue to wrongfully convict at least some defendants because of mistaken eyewitness identification evidence.

INTERROGATIONS AND CONFESSIONS

Just as there are many crimes for which no DNA evidence links a perpetrator to a crime, there are also crimes for which the only witness—or at least the only surviving witness—is the perpetrator. In cases in which there are no eyewitnesses and no physical evidence to identify the perpetrator, a confession from the suspect may be the only evidence linking a suspect to the crime (Kassin, 2005). Confessions, like eyewitness identifications, represent a powerful form of evidence; jurors rarely question the validity of an obtained confession (Kassin & Sukel, 1997).

But are confessions always reliable? Are there circumstances under which an innocent suspect will confess to committing a crime that was perpetrated by someone else?

Reviews of DNA exonerations of the wrongfully convicted suggest that 15% to 20% of the exonerated had falsely confessed to the crimes (Garrett, 2008; Scheck et al., 2001). People have even falsely confessed to committing extremely horrific crimes, including five boys who falsely confessed to raping and brutally beating a jogger in Central Park (Kassin & Gudjonsson, 2004). These confessions were not elicited with brutal beatings or threats of harm; instead, more subtle psychological factors seem to be at work in most false confession cases. A number of variables increase the likelihood of false confessions, including the tendency for innocent suspects to waive the legal protections to which they are entitled (e.g., *Miranda* rights), interrogators' presumption of the suspect's guilt, and problematic interrogation tactics (Kassin & Gudjonsson, 2004). Moreover, after a defendant's confession is entered into evidence, jurors are swayed by the defendant's admission of guilt even when evidence exists that the confession may have been obtained under dubious circumstances (Kassin & Sukel, 1997).

Innocence and Waiver of Legal Rights

Suspects in criminal investigations have a variety of constitutional rights intended to protect them. Among these rights is the Fifth Amendment right to freedom from coercion intended to elicit self-incriminating statements. In *Miranda v. Arizona* (1966), the Supreme Court held that investigators must warn suspects of these rights (e.g., the right to remain silent, the right to an attorney). Suspects must voluntarily waive these rights before issuing a self-incriminating statement if the state wishes to use this statement in the prosecution of that suspect. *Miranda* has its critics, with some arguing that it ties the hands of investigators and prosecutors, reducing the number of confessions they obtain, with the consequence that sometimes potentially dangerous offenders are returned into society (Cassell, 1996a, b; Cassell & Hayman, 1996). Others have argued that *Miranda* has important benefits to society because it encourages more humane police practices and has informed citizens of their constitutional rights (Leo, 1996a).

Relatively little research informs these debates about *Miranda*, but a small body of research speaks to whether these warnings protect innocent suspects from bad outcomes in criminal prosecutions. For *Miranda* warnings to be effective, people must understand these warnings and when they waive their rights, suspects must do so "voluntarily, knowingly, and intelligently" (*Miranda v. Arizona*, 1996). Three competencies are required for this test to be met (Grisso, 1981). First, suspects must understand the words in the *Miranda* warnings. Second, suspects must understand the intended protections provided by *Miranda*, including that the assistance of counsel will protect them from the adversarial nature of an interrogation. Third, suspects must have the ability to think reasonably about the consequences that will arise from waiving or preserving their constitutional rights.

A variety of factors influence suspects' competencies to waive their *Miranda* rights, including age (Feld, 2006; Grisso, 1998; Oberlander & Goldstein, 2001; Viljoen & Roesch, 2005; Viljoen, Zapf, & Roesch, 2007), psychiatric status (Cooper & Zapf, 2008), and intelligence (Fulero & Everington, 1995; O'Connell, Garmoe, & Goldstein, 2005), with children under age 14, those experiencing psychiatric symptoms, and suspects who are mentally retarded being less likely to show competence in these areas than older children, adults, and those of normal intelligence and with no psychiatric symptoms. Indeed, children who are 15 or younger are more likely than older children to waive their rights and to confess, and their decisions to do so appear unrelated to the strength of the evidence against them (Viljoen, Klaver, & Roesch, 2005). Although some have criticized the assessment tools used to establish the deficiencies in these populations' abilities to competently waive their *Miranda* rights (Rogers, Jordan, & Harrison, 2004), the content of *Miranda* warnings may be responsible for some of the difficulties these groups experience, with warnings used ranging in reading level from Grade 2.2 to postgraduate (Rogers, Harrison, Shuman, Sewell, & Hazelwood, 2007; Rogers, Hazelwood, Sewell, Shuman, & Blackwood, 2008).

Although *Miranda* comprehension is important, an examination of live and videotaped interrogations suggests that approximately 80% of suspects waive their rights (Leo, 1996c). The police appear to achieve these high rates of waiver by establishing rapport, presenting themselves as sympathetic to the suspect's plight, and minimizing the importance of the rights to be waived (Leo, 1996c). Who waives their rights? Those who have no previous history with the criminal justice system (i.e., no police record) are more likely to waive their rights than are suspects who have criminal justice histories (Leo, 1996b). This disparity suggests the possibility that innocent suspects, who are less likely to have previous records than suspects who actually committed crimes, may be especially likely to waive their rights (Kassin, 2005). However, it is difficult to draw any strong causal conclusions from these data.

Kassin and Norwick (2004) developed a mock-crime paradigm to provide an experimental test of the hypothesis that innocent suspects may be more likely to waive their *Miranda* rights. The "guilty" participants were to enter a nearby room, open a drawer, and take $100 from the drawer. The "innocent" participants entered the room, opened and shut the drawer, but did not take any money. After leaving the room, all participants were taken to another room where they met a "detective" who was blind to whether the participant had taken the money. The detective informed the participant that he was there to question the participant about some stolen money, but first he needed the participant to sign a *Miranda* rights waiver form. It did not matter whether the detective acted kindly or aggressively; the demeanor of the detective did not influence participants' willingness to waive their *Miranda* rights. In contrast, innocence significantly predicted whether participants signed away their constitutional rights, with innocent suspects waiving their rights at a 2:1 ratio to guilty suspects.

What reasons did participants provide for relinquishing these protections? Guilty participants were afraid they would appear guilty if they did not cooperate. Although innocent participants mentioned this concern as well, they were more likely to report that they waived their rights precisely because they were innocent and had nothing to hide (Kassin & Norwick, 2004). Mock suspects in another study believed that others who watched their denials of guilt would accurately judge whether they are guilty or innocent (Kassin & Fong, 1999). Thus, it appears that the very people who need protection—the innocent—are more likely to surrender those protections voluntarily (Kassin, 2005).

After suspects have waived their *Miranda* rights, the interrogation may commence; yet interrogators seem to conclude that suspects are guilty before the interrogation even starts. Joseph Buckley (2004), one of the authors of the leading manuals of interrogation techniques (Inbau, Reid, Buckley, & Jayne, 2001), is reported to have said that he was unconcerned about whether his techniques might promote false confessions from innocent people because "we don't interrogate innocent people" (Kassin & Gudjonsson, 2004, p. 36). How can interrogators be so certain that everyone they interrogate is guilty? The popular Reid technique encourages detectives first to conduct a preinterrogation interview with the suspect to allow the investigator to determine whether the suspect is guilty and trains interrogators to examine verbal and nonverbal behaviors for cues to deception. The interrogator may make this determination of suspect guilt on the basis of whether the suspect fits a particular profile (e.g., an unfaithful husband to a murdered wife; Davis & Follette, 2002; Wells, 2003), whether the suspect displays behavioral cues that the Reid technique manual claims indicate deception (Inbau et al., 2001), or merely a suspicion developed by the investigator (Kassin & Gudjonsson, 2004). This technique raises two questions. First, how accurate are people, including interrogators, at judging whether someone is being deceptive? Second, after an investigator determines that a suspect is being deceptive in his or her denials of guilt, how does the interrogator's presumption of guilt influence the remainder of the interrogation process?

Deception Detection

If the first task of an interrogator is to judge whether the denials proffered by a suspect in a preinterrogation interview are true or false, then understanding how well people—including investigators—detect deception is important. Both laypeople and scholars expect that liars will experience guilt while lying and that truth-tellers will not experience guilt, that guilt will engender nervousness and discomfort in the liar, and that this nervousness and discomfort will manifest itself in behavior (DePaulo & Morris, 2004). Similarly, people who are lying may not be able to create a story that is as compelling and free of contradictions as someone who is telling the truth (DePaulo & Morris, 2004). A meta-analysis of studies testing behavioral cues—both verbal and nonverbal—to deception suggests that there are behaviors that help distinguish liars from truth-tellers, including pupil dilation, tension, and voice pitch; however, other behaviors that are thought to be related to lying (e.g., fidgeting, blinking) were not reliably related to deception (DePaulo et al., 2003). Despite the existence of behavioral cues to deception, people perform at chance levels when asked to evaluate whether someone is lying or telling the truth (Ambady & Weisbuch, volume 1; Bond & DePaulo, 2006; Leach et al., 2009; Memon, Vrij, & Bull, 2003; Vrij, 2000; Zuckerman, DePaulo, & Rosenthal, 1981).

Perhaps experience with lie detection improves one's ability to differentiate truth from lies. Yet people who have jobs that require deception detection ability do not appear to have special abilities to detect lies, with customs inspectors, judges, mental health professionals, police investigators, and polygraph examiners detecting deception at rates only slightly better than chance (Bull, 1989; DePaulo, 1994; DePaulo & Pfeifer, 1986; Ekman & O'Sullivan, 1991; Elaad, 2003; Garrido & Masip, 1999; Garrido, Masip, & Herrero, 2004; Koehnken, 1987; Leach, Talwar, Lee, Bala, & Lindsay, 2004; Porter, Woodwirth, & Birt, 2000). Although some scholars have claimed that they have identified a small number of lie-detection "wizards" (O'Sullivan, 2005, 2007), some have questioned whether these people with special lie-detecting abilities exist (Bond & Uysal, 2007), whereas others have failed to find a reliable individual difference in deception-detection ability (Leach et al., 2009).

Experience may not be the best measure of ability. After all, someone can practice a skill, but without any feedback about how one is performing, practice may have no positive effect on one's abilities. Perhaps those who are in professions that practice lie detection have been attempting lie detection without receiving any special training for how best to do it. Although one might suspect that people who are trained to detect deception may prove to be more adept at differentiating liars from truth-tellers, evaluations of training programs suggest that they improve lie detection performance very little (Bull, 1989; Kassin & Fong, 1999; Porter et al., 2000; Vrij, 1994; Zuckerman, Koestner, & Alton, 1984). For example, undergraduates trained in the Reid technique for deception detection before they watched videotapes of the interrogations of fellow students, half of whom had committed one of four mock crimes (breaking and entering, vandalism, shoplifting, computer break-in) and the other half who had committed similar but noncriminal acts (Kassin & Fong, 1999). Consistent with the general literature on deception detection, these observers were not able to differentiate reliably between guilty and innocent suspects, performing at levels that did not significantly differ from chance. What is surprising is that trained observers did no better than untrained observers at discriminating between truth-tellers and liars; they were actually worse at detecting deception but more confident in their deception judgments. Rather than providing observers with skills that would aid deception detection, the training caused observers to see deception more frequently.

In a follow-up study using the same materials, police officers' deception detection performance was no different from chance, but they were more confident in the accuracy of their judgments than were the untrained college students, suggesting that interrogators may have a bias toward presuming deceptiveness in suspects (Meissner & Kassin, 2002). These results were confirmed with a meta-analysis of the literature examining the effects of training—with training assumed by testing different groups who varied on whether lie detection was a skill needed in their profession or manipulated—on deception detection and bias (Meissner & Kassin, 2002). Again, training produced a bias toward viewing others as deceptive.

Presumption of Guilt

What effects does this presumption of guilt have on the interrogation process and outcome? Social psychologists have been studying the effects of interpersonal expectancies on social interactions (e.g., Rosenthal, 2002; Snyder & Swann, 1978; Snyder, Tanke, & Berscheid, 1977). Specifically, behavioral confirmation processes are thought to have three stages, in which (1) perceivers develop an expectation about a target, (2) the perceivers' expectancies alter their behavior toward the target in expectancy-congruent ways, and (3) the perceivers' behavioral changes produce target responses that confirm the perceivers' expectancies (Klein & Snyder, 2003; Snyder, 1992; Snyder & Klein, 2005; Snyder & Stukas, 1999).

Does the investigator's presumption of guilt initiate behavioral confirmation processes that cause suspects to behave in a manner that makes them look guilty? In another mock-crime simulation, some participants stole $100 from a specified location, whereas others did not (Kassin, Goldstein, & Savitsky, 2003). Student investigators interviewed all participants—innocent and guilty—via headphones from a separate location. The researchers instructed half of the investigators that 80% of the suspects in the study were guilty and the other half of the investigators that 20% of the suspects were innocent. Interrogators who were led to expect a guilty suspect asked more questions that presumed the guilt of the suspect than did those who were led to expect an innocent suspect. Innocence also worked against suspects in this experiment in that interrogators reported trying harder to get a confession from and exerting more pressure on suspects who were innocent, even though the interrogators did not know the guilt status of the suspects. The suspects' ratings of how hard the interrogator worked to get a confession and how much pressure the interrogator applied during the interview mirrored those from the interrogators, with the innocent suspects reporting that they were subjected to more high-pressured interviews. The interrogators' expectation about the suspect's guilt predicted their ultimate judgments about whether the suspect was guilty, with guilt-presumptive interrogators judging more suspects guilty, but the actual guilt of the suspect was unrelated to interrogators' judgments of suspect guilt. Observers, blind to the experimental condition, also rated suspects interviewed by guilt-expecting interrogators to be more anxious and defensive than those interviewed by interrogators led to expect innocence and were more likely to judge suspects interviewed by guilt-presumptive interrogators to be guilty (Kassin et al., 2003). These results have been replicated in a study conducted in the United Kingdom using a similar paradigm (Hill, Memon, & McGeorge, 2008). Thus, it appears as if the presumption of guilt prevalent among interrogators has the potential to put innocent suspects at risk because it results in the use of more pressure and guilt-presumptive questions during interrogations, which in turn causes suspects to confirm the guilt presumption by behaving anxiously and defensively.

Police Interrogation Tactics

What types of interrogation tactics do the police use, and which of those tactics, if any, are related to confessions and—more important—to false confessions? The Reid technique of interrogations contains nine steps that investigators

can take when questioning a suspect to a crime (Inbau et al., 2001), which others have reduced to three primary processes (Kassin & Gudjonsson, 2004; see also Hogg, this volume, on social influence tactics). The first process is custody and isolation, which involves removing suspects from their typical surroundings, holding them at the police station, and preventing contact from familiar others who may provide comfort. The second process involves confrontation, including accusations of guilt, expressed certainty of the suspect's guilt, the presentation of fabricated evidence to support the suspect's guilt, and the prohibition of denials of guilt from the suspect. The third process involves minimization, in which the interrogator provides suspects with justifications for why they may have committed the crime, implies that suspects will be treated more leniently if they confess, and that confession is the only behavior that will result in the suspect being released from custody.

How often do interrogators use these high-pressure techniques? A survey of police investigators about their interrogation practices suggested that the use of high-pressure techniques may be relatively uncommon (Kassin et al., 2007). Given the problematic nature of some of these techniques, investigators may have been motivated to underreport their use of these tactics. Findings from an observational study of close to 200 live and videotaped confessions demonstrating that the use of Reid techniques was relatively frequent (Leo, 1996b) lend support to this self-presentational explanation for the low frequency of reported high-pressure tactic use in the Kassin survey. Even if high-pressure techniques are relatively infrequent, at least some police officers use two of these tactics—fabricating independent evidence of the suspect's guilt and minimization strategies—in some interrogations. Laboratory studies suggest that both of these techniques increase the rate of false confessions (Horselenberg, Merckelbach, & Josephs, 2003; Kassin & Kiechel, 1996; Redlich & Goodman, 2003; Russano, Meissner, Narchet, & Kassin, 2005), although admittedly the confessions are not to crimes but to other types of transgressions.

In the first experimental study to examine the effects of presenting false evidence on rates of false confessions, researchers instructed participants to type letters into a computer while avoiding a particular key that if struck purportedly would cause the computer to crash (Kassin & Kiechel, 1996). To manipulate whether participants would be vulnerable to the influence of false evidence, participants were instructed to strike the keys quickly or slowly. While the participants were entering their keystrokes, the computer did crash even though they did not strike the key they were to avoid. The researcher then accused the participants of causing the computer crash and causing all data to be lost by pressing the prohibited key. For half of the participants, a confederate presented false evidence, claiming that she had witnessed the participant striking the key.

Three forms of influence have been measured: compliance, internalization, and confabulation (Kassin & Kiechel, 1996). If participants signed a confession written by the experimenter, they were deemed compliant. Participants were judged to have internalized the confession if, when describing their experience to a confederate whom they encountered after the experiment, they accepted responsibility for crashing the computer (e.g., they admitted that they hit the prohibited key, causing the computer to crash). To measure confabulation, the experimenter questioned the participants about how the computer crash could have happened; participants confabulated if they provided details describing how they hit the offending key. Across all conditions, participants were more likely to sign the confession (e.g., comply; 69%) than they were to internalize the confession (29%) or confabulate (9%), but vulnerability and false evidence moderated these effects. When participant vulnerability was low (e.g., the typing pace was slow) and there was no false evidence, not a single participant internalized a confession or confabulated details—although a third of the participants did sign the confession written by the experimenter. When vulnerability was high (e.g., the typing pace was fast) and there was false evidence presented of the participant's guilt, all of the participants signed the confession, two-thirds internalized the confession, and one-third confabulated details. Thus, susceptibility to making a false confession increased with the presentation of false evidence. Using the same paradigm, these effects have been replicated in other labs (Forrest, Wadkins, & Larson, 2006), other countries (e.g., the Netherlands; Horselenberg et al., 2003, 2006), with children (Candel, Merckelbach, Loyen, & Reyskens, 2005; Redlich & Goodman, 2003), and when a cost is associated with confessing (Redlich & Goodman, 2003). Participants are less likely to confess falsely using this paradigm when the prohibited key would be harder to hit accidentally (e.g., the "esc" key as opposed to the "alt" key; Klaver, Lee, & Rose, 2008).

Experimental simulations also suggest that minimization tactics increase the likelihood that an innocent suspect will falsely confess. With minimization tactics, investigators provide suspects with a variety of justifications or excuses for their involvement in the criminal act of which they are accused (Kassin & Gudjonsson, 2004). Even without explicit promises of leniency, the use of minimization tactics in interrogations leads people to believe that leniency in sentencing is forthcoming if a confession is proffered. Participants who read a transcript of an interrogation containing minimization tactics, explicit promises of leniency, or neither tactic provided an estimate of the expected sentence that the suspect would receive (Kassin & McNall, 1991). Participants who read an interrogation containing minimization or promises of leniency predicted that the suspect would receive a shorter sentence than participants who read the interrogation using neither of these tactics; the estimates of those reading interrogations using minimization tactics and promises of leniency did not differ.

Do these expectations of leniency translate into an increased likelihood of false confessions when interrogators use minimization tactics? Using a new problem-solving paradigm for producing confessions, researchers tested whether minimization tactics affected the diagnosticity of confessions obtained (e.g., the ratio of true to false confessions; Russano et al., 2005). In the first phase of the study, participants worked on solving a set of problems with a confederate who induces the participants to cheat or not, depending on the condition. At the conclusion of the first phase, the experimenter accused all participants of cheating. During the interrogation of the participants, the experimenter orthogonally varied whether the interrogation contained promises of leniency and minimization of the offense.

Although participants were more likely to confess to cheating when they were guilty than when they were innocent, they were also more likely to confess when the interrogator promised leniency or used minimization. The diagnosticity of a confession—which is calculated by dividing the rate of true confessions by the rate of false confessions—was greatest when neither tactic was used (Russano et al., 2005). Thus, it appears that the police can skirt the law prohibiting them from directly promising leniency by using minimization techniques, which are legal, cause suspects to infer promises of leniency, and exert similar pressures to confess as do the illegal promises (Kassin & Gudjonsson, 2004).

Confessions and the Jury

False confessions are most problematic if they lead to the wrongful conviction of innocent people. Like other forms of evidence that may be unreliable—such as eyewitness evidence—jurors have the role of evaluating the evidence and determining what weight they should give it when weighing which verdict is appropriate. When confession evidence has been presented at trial, jurors are to evaluate the circumstances under which a confession was obtained and use that information to determine whether the confession was voluntary or whether the suspect was coerced into providing it. Thus, even if police practices produce some false confessions, injustice may be averted if jurors can appropriately judge the coerciveness of an interrogation and make accurate predictions about whether a confession is true or false.

For justice to be served, jurors viewing confessions obtained under coercive circumstances must infer that the suspects' confessions were the product of coercive interrogations, rather than the product of something internal to the suspects (e.g., their guilt). Research on correspondent inference (also known as the fundamental attribution error) suggests that people may find it quite difficult to estimate the extent to which situational constraints might overcome dispositional tendencies to influence behavior (E. E. Jones, 1990; L. Ross, 1977). Even if people do assign some weight to the situational influences in producing a behavior, they may insufficiently adjust their initial dispositional inferences to account for the situation (Gilbert & Malone, 1995).

Research examining the effects of confession evidence on jurors' decisions is consistent with the research on correspondence bias: Jurors underestimate the influence of some types of situational pressures on suspects to confess (Kassin & Sukel, 1997; Kassin & Wrightsman, 1980). In general, confession evidence is persuasive, even more persuasive than eyewitness or character testimony (Kassin & Neumann, 1997). Mock jurors do discount confessions obtained through threats of physical harm (Kassin & Wrightsman, 1980). In contrast, jurors are just as likely to vote guilty when a confession was elicited through promises of leniency than when no promises were made, even though they do acknowledge that the voluntariness of the confession is questionable (Kassin & Wrightsman, 1980). This effect persists in the face of jury deliberation (Kassin & Wrightsman, 1985) and judicial instructions to disregard involuntary confessions (Kassin & Wrightsman, 1981). Thus, even when jurors acknowledge that a confession is involuntary (e.g., a police officer waved a gun in a threatening way during an aggressive interrogation) and claim that the confession did not influence their decisions, they are more likely to render guilty verdicts than are jurors who are not exposed to the involuntary confession (Kassin & Sukel, 1997).

Jurors' failure to consider the role of the interrogator in eliciting a confession is exacerbated if they view a videotape of the confession that focuses solely on the suspect (Lassiter & Irvine, 1986; Lassiter, Slaw, Briggs, & Scanlan, 1992). Jurors are more likely to consider situational factors in their inferences of voluntariness and their verdicts when they watch a videotaped confession that contains both the interrogator and the suspect in the scene (Lassiter & Geers, 2004; Lassiter, Geers, Handley, Weiland, & Munhall, 2002; Lassiter, Geers, Munhall, Handley, & Beers, 2001). Even experienced legal professionals and law enforcement offers fall prey to the camera-perspective bias (Lassiter,

Diamond, Schmidt, & Elek, 2007). The bias appears to be perceptually based (Ratcliff, Lassiter, Schmidt, & Snyder, 2006), with new eye-tracking data confirming that this effect of camera view is in part due to increased visual attention to the interrogator (Ware, Lassiter, Patterson, & Ransom, 2008).

These studies suggest that jurors do not appropriately adjust the weight they give to a confession based on the conditions under which it was obtained but none of these studies allowed jurors to view an actual confession to determine whether it was true or false. People viewing confessions elicited from innocent and guilty mock suspects who had participated in a replication of the alt-key computer-crash paradigm (Kassin & Kiechel, 1996) were unable to detect which suspects were guilty and which were innocent at better than chance rates (Lassiter, Clark, Daniels, & Soinski, 2004). Neither college students nor police officers were able to predict accurately whether confessions offered by prison inmates—who confessed to the crime of which they had been convicted or to another inmate's crime—were true or false, although students were less likely to judge false confessions to be true than were police officers who were biased toward inferring guilt (Kassin, Meissner, & Norwick, 2005). In archival studies of proven false confessions cases in which defendants proceeded to trial, 73% (Leo & Ofshe, 1998) to 81% (Drizin & Leo, 2004) of the juries returned guilty verdicts.

JURY SELECTION

Once sufficient evidence exists against a suspect, either from a positive identification by an eyewitness, a confession from the suspect, or some other form of evidence, the suspect will be charged with the crime, brought before a grand jury, and potentially indicted and brought to trial. When suspects become defendants and are tried for the crimes with which they have been charged, they have constitutional rights to be tried by an impartial jury of their peers. Similarly, in civil cases in which jurors must make decisions about whether defendants engaged in behaviors that violated their duties to prevent harm of others, juries are assembled to determine defendant liability for a plaintiff's harm and, if so, what compensation that plaintiff should receive for the harm suffered. To assemble that jury, members of the community are assembled at the courthouse to form a pool from which jurors will be drawn. This pool of community members is called a *venire*. After the venire is assembled, a judge and attorneys representing the two sides question the venirepersons to determine whether they hold any biases that would prevent them from hearing the evidence fairly or following the relevant laws when making their decisions. This pretrial proceeding in which jurors are questioned to uncover bias and the attorneys challenge jurors whom they perceive to be biased is known as *voir dire*.

During *voir dire*, attorneys attempt to identify jurors who will be biased against their case so that they might be removed from service. So in reality, juries are not selected; rather, jurors are chosen for exclusion from the jury in one of two ways. With a challenge for cause, if an attorney can demonstrate to a judge that a venireperson is unfit for jury service, perhaps because of relationships with the parties in the case, preconceptions about the defendant's guilt, or attitudinal bias that would prevent them from following the law, then the judge will excuse the venireperson from serving on the jury. A judge may grant an unlimited number of challenges for cause; all that is required is for the attorney to convince the judge that the venireperson is unfit for service. Sometimes rather than granting the challenge for cause, judges may attempt to rehabilitate venirepersons, extracting promises from them that they will put aside any biases they possess and will follow the law. With these promises, venirepersons are deemed unbiased and fit for service. Research on the effectiveness of this process is in nascent stages, but early findings suggest that this rehabilitation process may induce biased jurors to adopt less biased attitudes (Crocker & Kovera, 2009). The second method of removing a venireperson is a peremptory challenge; attorneys are given a limited number of these challenges, which they may use to eliminate a potential juror without stating their reasons for doing so unless the opposing side accuses them of removing jurors because of their race (*Batson v. Kentucky*, 1986) or gender (*J. E. B. v. Alabama*, 1994), which is impermissible.

Jury selection, as attorneys traditionally practice it, generally involves attorneys relying on stereotypes, implicit theories of attitudes and personality, and folklore based on other attorneys' trial experience (Fulero & Penrod, 1990a, 1990b). Some of the different beliefs about defendant wealth include the following: wealthy jurors are bad defense jurors unless they are trying a white-collar criminal; poor jurors are good defense jurors in civil cases because they are uncomfortable with large sums of money; and poor jurors are bad jurors for civil defendants because their dissatisfaction with their own financial status would lead them to play "Robin Hood" by delivering large awards to plaintiffs who are harmed by wealthy corporations (Fulero & Penrod, 1990b; Page, 2005). Some attorneys hypothesize that jurors who are similar to their client will have more empathy for them and will therefore be desirable (Blue, 1991; Kerr, Hymes, Anderson, & Weathers, 1995). In contrast to this defendant-similarity hypothesis, some attorneys fear that similar jurors may

want to distance themselves from in-group members who have committed very bad acts, viewing them as black sheep and not worthy of their support (Marques, Abrams, Paz, & Martinez-Taboada, 1998). These examples clearly illustrate that attorneys' commonsense notions of what makes a desirable juror are often contradictory and raise questions about whether traditional jury selection is likely to be effective.

Effectiveness of Traditional Jury Selection

There have been a few attempts to empirically evaluate the efficacy of attorneys' jury selection efforts. In one of the earliest of these evaluations (Zeisel & Diamond, 1978), venirepersons who were excluded from serving on 12 federal juries through peremptory challenges observed the cases from which they were excluded and then rendered a verdict at the conclusion of the trial. Researchers compared the verdicts obtained by the seated juries with the verdicts that would have been rendered by the juries that would have been seated if no peremptory challenges were allowed. Although peremptory challenges influenced the outcomes in a small number of cases, overall there was no influence on verdicts. In a similar study, researchers compared the verdicts decided by 10 actual juries, 10 juries composed of randomly selected venirepersons, and 10 juries consisting of challenged venirepersons (Diamond & Zeisel, 1974). Actual juries were less likely to convict than the two constructed juries. Although there are obvious limitations to these studies that make strong causal inferences difficult (e.g., only the actual juries deliberated or made decisions with real consequences), they remain classic investigations into the effectiveness of traditional jury selection.

Using a different methodology, researchers evaluated attorneys' jury selection performance in a series of studies assessing their strategies for judging juries (Olczak, Kaplan, & Penrod, 1991). Attorneys read a series of venireperson profiles and indicated what types of information they would seek from the prospective jurors during *voir dire*. The participants then read one of two felony trial transcripts and rated the venirepersons on their bias toward the defendant and a variety of personality traits, including leniency, intelligence, and attractiveness. Attorneys relied on a very small number of characteristics when making inferences about prospective jurors, and their strategies for selecting jurors did not differ from those used by college students. In another study, law students and attorneys read a summary of a manslaughter case, reviewed characteristics of a series of prospective jurors, and then rated their desirability as jurors. The prospective jurors had actually served as mock jurors in a different study and had rendered verdicts in the manslaughter case in question. Both the law students and the attorneys accepted more jurors who had previously voted to convict the defendant as opposed to acquit, despite being tasked with finding desirable defense jurors.

A study of attorney-conducted *voir dire* in four felony trials also demonstrates its ineffectiveness (Johnson & Haney, 1994). Both prosecutors and defense attorneys effectively used their peremptory challenges to eliminate the most extremely biased jurors at both ends of the prosecution–defense continuum. However, the attitudes of the seated jurors were no different from the attitudes of the juries composed of the first 12 venirepersons or of 12 randomly chosen venirepersons. Thus, it appears that traditional attorney-conducted *voir dire* may identify extremely biased jurors but that more subtle biases are unlikely to be detected.

Scientific Jury Selection

In the early 1970s, a team of social scientists (Schulman, Shaver, Coltman, Emrich, & Christie, 1973) first attempted what is now known as scientific jury selection when they used empirical methods to assist a team of attorneys defend the "Harrisburg Seven," a group of antiwar activists charged with conspiracy to kidnap then–Secretary of State Henry Kissinger. Through community surveys, they identified demographic and attitudinal characteristics that correlated with potential jurors' biases for and against the defendants. The scientists used the results of these surveys to develop profiles of favorable jurors, and the defense team relied on these profiles to guide their use of peremptory challenges. The use of scientists to assist in jury selection in this case represents the birth of what is now a multimillion–dollar industry in litigation consulting (Seltzer, 2006). In addition to conducting case-specific surveys to determine correlates of verdicts in a specific case, litigation consultants may rely on the research that has identified demographic, personality, and attitudinal correlates of verdicts when developing juror profiles.

Demographic Predictors of Verdict

The identification of demographic predictors of verdict is desirable given that some states (e.g., California) and jurisdictions (e.g., federal court) severely limit the time and scope of *voir dire*. Under these circumstances, attorneys are often left with little information other than demographic characteristics on which to base their decisions about which jurors to challenge. Unfortunately for attorneys, demographic variables are only weakly and inconsistently related to verdict. In one study, juror age, gender, marital status, and occupation did not predict damage awards in a civil case (Goodman, Loftus, &

Greene, 1990). Other studies found relationships among income, occupation, education, and verdicts, with jurors having higher incomes, prestigious occupations, and more advanced education being more likely to convict than jurors with lower incomes, menial occupations, and less education (Adler, 1973; Simon, 1967).

Juror race does not reliably predict verdict either. Some early research suggested that Black mock jurors were more likely to find a defendant not guilty by reason of insanity than were White mock jurors (Simon, 1967). More recently, race was related to community members' perceptions of O. J. Simpson's culpability in his ex-wife's death (Brigham & Wasserman, 1999). At every stage of the trial—before it began, after the evidence was presented, and after the verdict was rendered—Blacks were less likely to believe that Simpson murdered his ex-wife than were Whites. However, other evidence suggests that upper-middle-class Black jurors may be more punitive toward Black defendants, especially those who are charged with committing violent crimes (Nietzel & Dillehay, 1986), providing some evidence for the blacksheep effect discussed earlier (Marques et al., 1998).

In contrast to race, gender appears to be a reliable predictor of verdict, at least in certain types of trials. Women are more punitive toward child sexual abuse defendants than are men (Bottoms, Davis, & Epstein, 2004; Bottoms & Goodman, 1994; Kovera, Gresham, Borgida, Gray, & Regan, 1997; Kovera, Levy, Borgida, & Penrod, 1994; McCoy & Gray, 2007; Quas, Bottoms, Haegerich, & Nysse-Carris, 2002). This gender bias generalizes to other types of cases in which women are more likely to be the complainants than are men, such as rape (Brekke & Borgida, 1988; Wenger & Bornstein, 2006), intimate partner violence (Feather, 1996; Kern, Libkuman, & Temple, 2007), and sexual harassment (Blumenthal, 1998; Gutek et al., 1999; Huntley & Costanzo. 2003; Kovera, McAuliff, & Hebert, 1999; O'Connor, Gutek, Stodale, Geer, & Melançon, 2004; Wayne, Riordan, & Thomas, 2001). The effect is not limited to cases in which women are disproportionately likely to be the victims; women are also more likely to acquit women with a history of domestic violence victimization who are charged with murdering their allegedly abusive partners (Schuller, 1992; Schuller & Hastings, 1996). Overall, these findings suggest that gender differences arise when one gender may be better able to take the perspective of the complainant or the defendant (O'Connor et al., 2004; Wiener, Watts, Goldkamp, & Gasper, 1995). Little evidence exists to suggest that gender reliably predicts verdicts in cases in which gender differences in perspective taking are irrelevant.

Although gender does not appear to predict verdicts reliably across different types of cases, it may predict whether a particular juror will be influential during jury deliberations.

Studies have found that men may exercise greater influence in deliberations than women; men spoke more frequently (James, 1959), were more likely to be selected to be the jury foreperson (Dillehay & Nietzel, 1985; Strodbeck, James, & Hawkins, 1957), and changed their votes less frequently (Golding, Bradshaw, Dunlap, & Hodell, 2007) than women. Thus, it may not be possible to predict verdict with gender, but it may be possible to ensure that a particular viewpoint is expressed during jury deliberations if a significant proportion of the men seated hold that view.

Personality Predictors of Verdict

Although demographic information is the most easily collected information about venirepersons, if given the opportunity to question jurors, it may be possible for attorneys to collect some information about venirepersons' personality traits during *voir dire*. Like demographic predictors, the relationship between personality traits and verdict is weak and inconsistent, which may account for why attorneys fail to pick jurors based on their Big Five personality traits (J. Clark, Boccaccini, Caillouet, & Chaplin, 2007). For example, a belief in a just world—the belief that bad outcomes happen to bad people—sometimes is associated with holding victims responsible for what happened to them and sometimes is associated with punitiveness toward defendants (Gerbasi, Zuckerman, & Reis, 1977; Moran & Comfort, 1982).

Individual differences in jurors' beliefs about personal responsibility predict verdicts at least some of the time. Some research shows that jurors who have an internal locus of control are more likely to convict a defendant than those with an external locus of control, especially when the evidence against the defendant is weak (Phares & Wilson, 1972). Similarly, jurors who hold strong beliefs in personal responsibility are more likely to hold plaintiffs responsible for experienced harm if they contributed even partially to that harm (Hans, 1992). Extraversion also appears to influence juror verdicts, with extraverts being more likely than introverts to acquit criminal defendants (J. Clark et al., 2007).

The personality trait that best predicts verdict across a variety of cases is authoritarianism. People with an authoritarian personality are more likely to respect authority, adhere to conventional views, and to punish those who fail to conform to authority or convention (Adorno, Frenkel-Brunswik, Levinson, & Sanford, 1950). An early measure of authoritarianism was developed in the context of research on prejudice (Adorno et al., 1950), but others have constructed measures of authoritarianism that are specific to the legal system, including the Legal Attitudes Questionnaire (LAQ; Boehm, 1968) and the

revised LAQ (Kravitz, Cutler, & Brock, 1993). A meta-analysis of the studies that tested the relationship between authoritarianism and verdict confirmed that jurors who are high in authoritarianism are more likely to convict defendants than jurors who are low in authoritarianism (Narby, Cutler, & Moran, 1993). This relationship is even stronger when authoritarianism was measured using a scale specifically created to measure legal authoritarianism (Narby et al., 1993). Authoritarianism also predicts sentencing, with authoritarian jurors recommending longer sentences (Bray & Noble, 1978) and recommending death sentences at higher rates (Butler & Moran, 2007) than nonauthoritarian jurors. If an authority figure (e.g., a police officer) is the person accused of wrongdoing, then authoritarians may be less punitive than nonauthoritarians (Nietzel & Dillehay, 1986). Thus, an authoritarian personality is related to verdicts that are consistent with upholding conventional norms and the legitimacy of authority figures.

Attitudinal Predictors of Verdict

Several attempts have been made to develop attitudinal measures of general juror bias for or against the prosecution. The Juror Bias Scale (JBS), which consists of two subscales, one measuring respondents' beliefs that people charged with crimes probably committed those crimes (probability of commission) and the other measuring respondents' beliefs about reasonable doubt, represents one of these attempts (Kassin & Wrightsman, 1983). More recent investigations have used confirmatory factor analysis to refine the scale and improve its predictive validity (Myers & Lecci, 1998). The scale has proved useful in predicting verdicts in studies conducted in other countries, such as Spain (De La Fuente, De La Fuente, & Garcia, 2003) and in reactions to real trials such as the O. J. Simpson case (Chapdelaine & Griffin, 1997). The items tapping beliefs about reasonable doubt are better predictors of verdict than are the items tapping beliefs about the probability of commission (Lecci & Myers, 2002).

Because the original item pool for the JBS is limited to items tapping beliefs about probability of commission and reasonable doubt, the items may underrepresent the construct of juror bias, leading to poor prediction of juror verdicts (Lecci & Myers, 2008). To correct this perceived problem, Lecci and Myers generated additional items designed to tap beliefs about conviction proneness, system confidence, cynicism toward the defense, racial bias, social justice, and innate criminality. Not only did this new scale, which they named the Pretrial Juror Attitude Questionnaire (PJAQ), significantly predict verdicts in five of the six trial summaries that mock jurors read, it also showed incremental validity in that it predicted verdicts even after controlling for mock jurors' JBS and RLAQ scores.

Demographic characteristics and personality traits serve as proxies for jurors' beliefs and attitudes; at best, they can suggest a general tendency for a juror to evaluate evidence in a particular way. Similarly, most measures of juror bias assess general tendencies toward supporting crime control versus due process issues. Perhaps one of the reasons that there are few identified demographic variables, personality traits, or general attitudinal measures that predict verdict is that they provide insight into general evaluative tendencies rather than more case-specific attitudes or beliefs. Social-psychological research on the attitude–behavior relationship suggests that specific attitudes are stronger predictors of behavior than are more general attitudes (Kraus, 1995). Perhaps more specific case-relevant attitudes would serve as better predictors of verdicts.

Evidence that case-specific attitudes are good predictors of juror verdict inclinations before trial has grown over the years. Attitudes toward tort reform predict verdict inclinations, with jurors favoring reform more likely to favor the defense in civil trials (Moran, Cutler, & DeLisa, 1994). Similarly, attitudes toward psychiatrists predict verdict inclinations in insanity cases, with favorable attitudes related to a greater likelihood of voting not guilty by reason of insanity (Cutler, Moran, & Narby, 1992), and attitudes toward drugs predict ratings of defendant guilt in drug cases (Moran, Cutler, & Loftus, 1990). However, all of these studies used a survey methodology, and the researchers assessed the predictive validity of the attitudinal measures without the presentation of any evidence.

For those studies that have tested the predictive validity of specific attitudes after the presentation of evidence, results are more mixed. Despite a psychometrically strong measure of jurors' attitudes toward eyewitnesses, these attitudes were unrelated to mock juror verdicts in a robbery case containing eyewitness evidence (Narby & Cutler, 1994). Belief in a litigation crisis significantly predicted verdict in a tobacco and a pharmaceutical case, but not in an insurance case (Vinson, Costanzo, & Berger, 2008). Other researchers, however, have found attitudes that predict verdicts. Attitudes toward the insanity defense predict mock juror verdicts in insanity cases (Skeem, Louden, & Evans, 2004), and attitudes toward the death penalty predict verdicts in capital cases (O'Neil, Patry, & Penrod, 2004). Similarly, the attitudes of formerly impaneled jurors toward the death penalty predicted whether they had voted guilty in the trial in which they had served, irrespective of whether it had been a capital trial in which the death penalty was an option (Moran & Comfort, 1986).

Effectiveness of Scientific Jury Selection

How effective is scientific jury selection? This question is best answered in relation to the effectiveness of traditional attorney-conducted jury selection because it is the default method of jury selection. Even concluding that there are juror characteristics that allow the prediction of jurors' verdict choices, attorneys may be just as good at predicting jurors' verdict inclinations without the additional expense of scientific methods. Only one published study has compared the efficacy of traditional and scientific jury selections (Horowitz, 1980). In this study, researchers trained law students to use either traditional or scientific selection methods and collected their predictions of mock jurors' verdicts in four simulated trials. The results from this study were mixed, with two cases showing a superiority of scientific jury selection, one case showing the superiority of traditional jury selection, and one case showing no preference for jury selection type. Scientific jury selection performed better only when there was a strong relationship between the predictors—personality, demographic, and attitudinal characteristics—and verdict.

Bias in and From Jury Selection

Jury selection has several purposes. It provides judges and attorneys an opportunity to introduce jurors to the general issues that they expect will arise in the case and to educate jurors on the relevant law. When judges provide attorneys with latitude in *voir dire*, attorneys may use the opportunity to ingratiate themselves with jurors. The most important purpose of *voir dire*, however, is to identify jurors who are unfit for jury service because of bias and to eliminate them from the jury pool. The research reviewed so far suggests that traditional attorney-conducted *voir dire* allows attorneys to perform at about chance levels when identifying biased jurors (Olczak et al., 1991), that traditional jury selection produces juries that have the same attitudinal composition as juries produced through random selection from the venire (Johnson & Haney, 1994), and that scientific jury selection only sometimes produces better attorney decisions than does traditional jury selection (Horowitz, 1980). Given the spotty record of jury selection for the identification of juror bias, it is troubling that racial bias is evident in jury selection decisions and that *voir dire* may actually produce bias in jurors.

Race and Peremptory Challenges

Attorneys are prohibited from using peremptory challenges to eliminate jurors because of their race (*Batson v. Kentucky*, 1986) or gender (*J. E. B. v. Alabama*, 1994). Yet each year, a number of appellants question verdicts because they allege that race played a role in attorneys' decisions to eliminate jurors from a venire. Several studies of jury selection in actual cases have found that Black venirepersons are more likely to be excused by the prosecution than by the defense (J. Clark et al., 2007; Rose, 1999). The Supreme Court recently ruled that racial bias in the use of peremptory challenges could be established by demonstrating either (a) that attorneys asked different *voir dire* questions of jurors belonging to different racial groups or (b) that the justifications used to provide a non-race-based explanation for peremptory challenges used to dismiss member of one race were equally applicable to members of a different racial group who were not dismissed (*Miller-El v. Dretke*, 2005; *Snyder v. Louisiana*, 2008). Despite these rulings, appeals of verdicts based on the improper exclusion of jurors usually fail (Gabbidon, Kowal, Jordan, Roberts, & Vincenzi, 2008), in part because attorneys are skilled at providing reasons other than race for excluding jurors, even when race has likely played a role in their decision making (Sommers & Norton, 2008).

To test whether venireperson race influences attorneys' use of peremptory challenges, prosecuting attorneys read profiles of two venirepersons for a case in which a Black defendant was charged with robbery and aggravated assault (Sommers & Norton, 2007). Irrespective of the other characteristics in the profile, attorneys were more likely to exclude a Black venireperson than a White venireperson. When asked why they chose to exclude the juror, the attorneys provided race-neutral explanations for their decision. Thus, racial bias in jury selection may go undetected because attorneys provide compelling race-neutral justifications for their racially biased decisions (Page, 2005). In fact, in his dissenting opinion in *State v. Snyder* (2006), Justice Johnson observed that "Verbalized facially neutral reasons can be a pretext for conscious or unconscious racism" (p. 506).

Conviction-Proneness and Voir Dire in Capital Cases

When prosecutors seek the death penalty for a defendant (i.e., in capital cases), special jury selection procedures are required to determine whether jurors' attitudes toward the death penalty would interfere with their ability to consider the evidence impartially and to follow the law (*Wainwright v. Witt*, 1985; *Witherspoon v. Illinois*, 1968). A capital case has two phases: a guilt phase in which evidence of the defendant's guilt—and sometimes innocence—is presented and the jury determines whether the defendant is guilty of the crimes as charged, and a penalty phase that occurs only if the defendant is convicted in the guilt phase. In this penalty phase, evidence is presented about aggravating and mitigating factors that would argue for or against sanctioning defendants by taking their lives. Jurors may

not serve in either phase of a capital trial if their attitudes toward the death penalty would render them incapable of following the law, either because they would be unwilling to impose the death penalty or because they could not fairly evaluate the evidence supporting the defendant's guilt knowing that a conviction could result in the death of the defendant. The special *voir dire* process by which jurors are evaluated for their fitness to serve in a capital case is called death qualification.

Death qualification produces a jury that has different demographic and attitudinal characteristics than a jury seated in noncapital cases (Fitzgerald & Ellsworth, 1984; Moran & Comfort, 1986). In a sample of impaneled felony jurors (Moran & Comfort, 1986) and two random samples of community members (Fitzgerald & Ellsworth, 1984; Haney, Hurtado, & Vega, 1994), African Americans, women, Democrats, and the poor were significantly more likely to oppose the death penalty than were European Americans, men, Republicans, and the wealthy. Meta-analysis confirms that women and minorities are more likely to hold attitudes that would systematically exclude them from capital juries (Filkins, Smith, & Tindale, 1998). Thus, the death qualification process reduces the likelihood that specific groups of people will serve on a jury. This reduction in the diversity of jurors minimizes the chances that alternative points of view will be expressed during deliberation (e.g., Sommers, 2006).

In addition to the possibility that jurors—both those from underrepresented groups and those of European descent—will be less likely to exchange pertinent information on the less diverse juries created through death qualification, the jurors who remain after death qualification are more likely to convict a defendant than are those who oppose the death penalty (e.g., Cowan, Thompson, & Ellsworth, 1984; Moran & Comfort, 1986; Thompson, Cowan, Ellsworth, & Harrington, 1984). Three meta-analyses of the studies testing the relationship between death penalty attitudes and verdicts confirm that those who favor the death penalty are more conviction prone (Allen, Mabry, & McKelton, 1998; Filkins et al., 1998; Nietzel, McCarthy, & Kern, 1999), with death-qualified jurors approximately 25% to 44% more likely to render a guilty verdict than are jurors who oppose the death penalty. Juries composed of death-qualified jurors are more critical of defense evidence and generally remember less evidence than do juries that contain jurors with a mix of death penalty attitudes (Cowan et al., 1984). Merely watching a death-qualifying *voir dire* makes jurors more conviction-prone; death-qualified mock jurors who watched a death-qualification *voir dire* provided pretrial ratings indicating that they thought it was more likely that the defendant was guilty than did mock jurors who watched a standard voir dire (Haney, 1984). Thus, death-qualifying *voir dire* appears to bias jurors toward conviction.

Behavioral Confirmation and the Voir Dire Process

Researchers are just beginning to study the *voir dire* process and how it might lead to the creation of bias rather than its identification and elimination. There are several points during the *voir dire* process at which attorneys may be led astray when trying to predict the bias of individual venirepersons. In the information-seeking stage, attorneys' stereotypes or expectations about venirepersons may influence the types of questions that attorneys ask of jurors, including questions that are biased toward confirming the attorney's hypothesis or that lack diagnosticity. In the information-generation stage, attorneys' questions may influence the information gathered from venirepersons, especially if venirepersons are motivated to provide socially appropriate responses. In the inferential stage, the questions asked by attorneys, the hypotheses they hold, and the answers they receive from venirepersons may bias the conclusions that attorneys draw from venirepersons' responses to *voir dire* questions. Finally, the very act of endorsing a trial-relevant attitude, even an endorsement that is evoked through behavioral confirmation processes (Snyder & Klein, 2005), may increase the likelihood that jurors will vote to convict or acquit a defendant.

Early research on how attorneys gather information during *voir dire* and how venirepersons react to their questions suggests that *voir dire* may bias jurors because attorneys engage in biased hypothesis testing and their expectations influence jurors to change their expectation-relevant attitudes. In one study, attorneys were told to test a particular hypothesis about a venireperson. Specifically, attorneys generated two *voir dire* questions that they would use to test whether a juror held legal authoritarian attitudes or civil libertarian attitudes, or to determine which of these attitudes a venireperson held (Crocker, Kennard, Greathouse, & Kovera, 2009). Attorneys used a positive test strategy (e.g., asked hypothesis-confirming questions) in that they were most likely to ask a question that legal authoritarians would answer "yes" when they were testing the legal authoritarian hypothesis and least likely to ask this type of question when they were testing the civil libertarian hypothesis.

In another study, researchers manipulated the expectation that a mock attorney held about a venireperson by providing the attorney with data from a "juror questionnaire" (Greathouse, Crocker, Kennard, Austin, & Kovera, 2009). The data accurately reported demographic information, but researchers randomly manipulated whether attitudinal information portrayed the venireperson as pro-prosecution or pro-defense. After receiving this expectation, attorneys

conducted a capital *voir dire* with a community member, subsequently providing ratings of the mock venireperson's defense and prosecution bias. The mock attorneys' expectations about the mock venirepersons predicted their ratings of the venirepersons bias even after controlling for the venirepersons' post–*voir dire* death penalty attitudes and blind coders' ratings of the pro-defense and pro-prosecution bias exhibited in the venirepersons' behavior. Moreover, venirepersons questioned by attorneys holding pro-prosecution expectancies held more positive attitudes toward the death penalty after *voir dire* than did venirepersons questioned by attorneys with pro-defense expectations, despite the attitudinal similarity of these groups prior to *voir dire*. These studies, taken together with the research on the ability of attorneys to identify favorable jurors, suggest that biased hypothesis testing and behavioral confirmation processes may be at work in *voir dire* and question whether the process serves the purpose for which it is intended: seating a fair and impartial jury.

PRETRIAL PUBLICITY

Juror bias can also be created through extralegal means. Certain types of information, if it is released before trial in the press, can prejudice the jury pool against a defendant, endangering the impartiality of the jury pool. Because of concerns about the prejudicial impact of this information on jury decisions, the American Bar Association (2000) recommended that attorneys avoid discussing or releasing entire categories of information before the start of a trial, including but not limited to (a) the defendant's prior criminal record; (b) information about the defendant's character or reputation; (c) any confession or admission against interest produced by the defendant (or the refusal to provide information); (d) whether the defendant has or has not submitted to any examination or test; and (e) any opinion about the defendant's guilt or about the sufficiency of the evidence against the defendant. Any information of this nature could lead a juror to infer that a defendant is guilty. This inference of guilt is problematic for two reasons: (a) This prejudicial information is often not admissible at trial because it tends to be unreliable and therefore should have no influence on jurors' decisions and (b) even if it is admissible, jurors are required to presume defendants' innocence unless the trial evidence proves their guilt.

Despite the prejudicial nature of some types of trial-relevant information, the First Amendment guarantees freedom of the press to publicize newsworthy information. But can pretrial exposure to these types of information about a defendant abrogate a defendant's Sixth Amendment right to a fair and impartial jury, negatively affecting the way jurors evaluate defendants and the evidence against them? Pretrial publicity (PTP) exposure negatively affects not only pretrial judgments of defendant guilt but also posttrial judgments (Studebaker & Penrod, 1997, 2005), meaning that the effect of PTP on jurors' decisions survives the presentation of trial evidence (Chrzanowski, 2005; Otto, Penrod, & Dexter, 1994; Ruva, McEvoy, & Bryant, 2007). Negative effects of media exposure are seen even when jurors are exposed to media that is not specific to the case they are trying. General PTP—media that is topically related to a case but does not include prejudicial information about the defendant in the specific case—can increase the likelihood that jurors will convict the defendant (Greene & Loftus, 1984; Greene & Wade, 1988; Imrich, Mullin, & Linz, 2005; Kovera, 2002).

The prejudicial effects of PTP on jurors' guilt judgments are generally robust. Although most of the studies of PTP have been conducted in the context of criminal cases, PTP also affects judgments in civil trials, with PTP exposure increasing the probability that jurors found the defendant liable in a personal injury case (Bornstein, Whisenhunt, & Nemeth, 2002). A meta-analysis of 23 studies and 44 tests of the effects of PTP exposure demonstrated that there was a small to moderate effect of PTP on jurors' judgments of defendant guilt across a variety of participants, settings, trial stimuli, PTP types, and research methods (Steblay, Besirevic, Fulero, & Jimenez-Lorente, 1999). As the number of types of prejudicial information to which jurors are exposed increases, so does the size of the PTP effect. When jurors read or hear about multiple categories of prejudicial information, they are more likely to find a defendant guilty than when they read or hear only one type of prejudicial information (Steblay et al., 1999).

Methods Used in Pretrial Publicity Studies

Researchers of PTP effects have generally used one of two types of methods (Studebaker & Penrod, 2005). The more ecologically valid research method tests the effects of naturally occurring PTP exposure on community members' pretrial judgments about defendants in real cases. In these studies, researchers survey community members in the venue in which the real case is to be tried, asking the respondents questions designed to measure the extent of their exposure to PTP, the content of what they recall or recognize about the case, and their pretrial judgments about the defendant's guilt. Although it is possible to test the effects of PTP surveying only members of the potential venire by correlating self-reported extent of exposure with judgments of defendant guilt, researchers often survey a comparison group of community members from another venue that has not been saturated with publicity

about the case, allowing for the comparison of guilt judgments across the two venues that naturally differ in PTP exposure. The strength of the method lies in its use of real potential jurors and exposure to PTP in natural settings that allow people to pay as much or as little attention to the PTP as they would in real cases. However, this approach has several limitations, including an inability to draw strong causal conclusions about PTP effects because certain types of people may seek PTP exposure, which creates selection confounds. In addition, these studies assess PTP effects on juror judgments without allowing for the potential curative effects of trial evidence, judicial instruction to ignore the PTP, or deliberation.

The second method involves the experimental manipulation of PTP exposure followed by a trial simulation, allowing for random assignment of participants to level of PTP exposure, removing the potential for selection confounds present in the field studies of PTP. Within this general paradigm, researchers may also test the effects of other variables (e.g., type of prejudicial information, time between PTP exposure and trial, judicial instructions) by manipulating them. Although some criticize these methods because they usually lack the features of real trials (e.g., prolonged PTP exposure, sworn jurors, consequential decisions, deliberation), the trial simulation method has strong internal validity and allows for causal conclusions about the effects of PTP. Moreover, a comparison of the effects of naturally occurring and experimentally manipulated PTP found that exposure to prejudicial PTP led to increased perceptions of the defendant's guilt, irrespective of whether the exposure came from naturally occurring or experimental sources (Chrzanowski, 2005).

Although this study suggests that researchers should not be concerned about the external validity of findings obtained using experimentally manipulated PTP exposure, other study characteristics may moderate the effect of PTP on jurors' trial judgments. A meta-analysis of the PTP literature (Steblay et al., 1999) found that survey studies, which typically test the effects of PTP on pretrial judgments rather than on judgments made after considering trial evidence, produced larger PTP effects than did experimental studies, which almost always include the presentation of trial evidence (for an example of an experimental study that did not contain the presentation of trial evidence, see Ogloff & Vidmar, 1994). In the PTP literature, survey and experimental studies typically differ not only in terms of the research design but also in terms of the participant sample, with survey studies generally sampling from community members and experimental studies using a college student sample. However, exposure to prejudicial information about the defendant causes jurors to adopt a pro-prosecution bias when evaluating the trial evidence that they subsequently hear (Hope, Memon, & McGeorge, 2004). This predecisional distortion serves to reinforce rather than mitigate the effects of PTP even in the face of trial evidence.

Remedies for Pretrial Publicity Effects

Certain procedural remedies are presumed to eliminate or at least mitigate the harms associated with prejudicial PTP, including *voir dire*—which is often extended in cases involving PTP to identify jurors who may have been prejudiced by exposure to PTP and to educate jurors on the need to ignore the PTP. Other remedies include judicial instructions to ignore PTP, delays of the trial (i.e., continuances) to allow the PTP to subside, jury sequestration, and changes of venue to a location where there was no PTP or at least where the nature and extent of the PTP was less prejudicial (American Bar Association, 2000). Holdings in several Supreme Court cases task judges with taking steps to ensure that extensive prejudicial pretrial media does not abrogate a defendant's Sixth Amendment rights to a fair trial (*Irvin v. Dowd*, 1961; *Rideau v. Louisiana*, 1963; *Sheppard v. Maxwell*, 1966). Although these cases primarily focused on changes of venue as a remedy for the prejudicial effects of PTP, the court did also suggest that other remedies for PTP could be effective, including extended *voir dire* and the rehabilitation of biased jurors, sequestration of juries, and judicial admonitions to disregard the PTP. Despite the court's faith in these remedies, the empirical evidence suggests that this faith may be misplaced.

Deliberation

Before considering these procedures specifically designed to combat PTP effects, it is important to consider whether deliberation—a process that occurs in every jury trial—provides an opportunity to correct the negative effects of PTP exposure. Some legal practitioners and scholars have criticized research showing PTP effects by arguing that all of the survey studies and most of the experimental studies fail to contain opportunities for jurors to deliberate, during which—they presume—fellow jurors will admonish other jurors who mention prejudicial information obtained from PTP, thereby minimizing any effects it could have. The few studies that have included deliberation report that jurors rarely referred to prejudicial news reports during deliberation (Kline & Jess, 1966; Kramer, Kerr, & Carroll, 1990). When jurors do mention PTP in deliberations, other jury members did remind the group that the pretrial information was prohibited from consideration (Kramer et al., 1990). Yet these admonitions to disregard PTP did not correct the PTP effects because juries exposed to prejudicial PTP were still more punitive than were juries that

were not exposed, even after participating in deliberation. Deliberations exacerbated the negative effects of emotional PTP. Deliberations did not eliminate PTP effects when the evidence against the defendant was strong; when the evidence against the defendant was more ambiguous, deliberation increases the effects of PTP (Kerr, Niedermeier, & Kaplan, 1999). Overall, this research suggests that the justice system cannot count on deliberation to correct for prejudicial effects of PTP exposure.

Voir Dire

Extended *voir dire*—in which attorneys receive increased latitude to question jurors—is the remedy on which judges rely most often in their attempts to correct the prejudicial effects of PTP. In cases in which extensive pretrial media attention has presented potentially prejudicial information, judges may use their discretion to allow attorneys to explore the extent to which the venire has been tainted by PTP exposure. In addition to allowing more extensive questioning, the judge may provide the attorneys with the opportunity to use *voir dire* as an educational tool, providing jurors with information about the dangers of relying on PTP when making decisions, encouraging potential jurors to disregard any information about the case that is not in evidence at trial, and seeking commitments from venirepersons that they will ignore information learned pretrial if they sit on the jury.

For *voir dire* to serve as an effective remedy for PTP, several conditions must be met. First, attorneys must be able to identify jurors who have been prejudiced by PTP and then have them removed from the jury pool either by challenging them for cause or by using a peremptory challenge if they fail to convince a judge that the venireperson has been tainted. There are no studies that directly test attorneys' abilities to identify tainted jurors, but the research reviewed in the earlier section on jury selection suggests that attorneys may have difficulty identifying biased jurors.

Second, the success of *voir dire* rests on the supposition that venirepersons' self-reports will accurately reflect the extent to which they have been biased by PTP exposure. Both social desirability concerns and lack of self-awareness can limit the validity of data obtained through self-report, but courts routinely rely on venirepersons' self-reports to determine bias (Posey & Dahl, 2002). Although a positive relationship between venirepersons' exposure to PTP and their perceptions of defendant guilt exists (Costantini & King, 1980/81; Moran & Cutler, 1991), jurors' self-reported ability to remain impartial is uncorrelated with their pretrial judgments of a defendant's culpability (Costantini & King, 1980/81; Kerr, 1989; Kerr, Kramer, Carroll, & Alfini, 1991; Moran & Cutler, 1991;

Simon & Eimermann, 1971; Sue, Smith, & Pedroza, 1975). For example, in one community survey, people residing in a venue with extensive media attention to a case were more likely to have prejudged the defendant to be guilty than those residing in the alternate venue where there was little media attention, but the members of each venue reported the same ability to remain impartial if they were to serve as a juror in the case (Moran & Cutler, 1991).

A lack of relationship between venirepersons' reports of impartiality and their judgments of defendant culpability should not be surprising given social psychological research suggesting that people lack the ability to access and report the cognitive processes driving their decisions (Nisbett & Wilson, 1977). Even if people were able to appreciate the causal factors in their decisions, they believe that they are able to disregard information accurately if they choose to do so, whereas others are less capable and more biased (Pronin, Gilovich, & Ross, 2004). Yet evidence suggests that in social and legal contexts, prohibited information still influences people's judgments even when they are instructed to disregard it (Steblay, Hosch, Culhane, & McWethy, 2006; Wyer & Budesheim, 1987; Wyer & Unverzagt, 1985). So any venirepersons who lack awareness that they have been biased by PTP are likely to be seated on a jury because they report being impartial and once seated are unlikely to follow instructions to disregard the PTP when forming their decisions of defendant guilt.

Social desirability concerns demonstrably influence jurors' responses during *voir dire*. Venirepersons may pick up on verbal or nonverbal cues from judges and attorneys that certain answers to questions about PTP are more satisfactory than others and could encourage socially desirable responding (LeVan, 1984). Ex-jurors have reported that when they felt anxious about being evaluated during *voir dire*, they were less likely to provide honest answers (Marshall & Smith, 1986). Prospective jurors are less likely to succumb to social desirability concerns when questioned by attorneys than by a judge (S. E. Jones, 1987). In a mock *voir dire*, community members completed a pretrial legal attitudes questionnaire and then participated in a *voir dire* conducted by a judge or attorneys. After *voir dire*, participants again completed the attitudinal questionnaire, with participants questioned by the judge changing their posttrial attitudes from their pretrial attitudes nearly twice as often as those questioned by attorneys.

One study of PTP effects on juror judgments specifically tested whether social desirability affected jurors' self-reports of bias by analyzing the responses of venirepersons to a questionnaire that they completed before *voir dire* (Chrzanowski, 2005). The questionnaire assessed their knowledge of the case and their self-reported ability to remain impartial and hear the case fairly. Chrzanowski compared these data from the actual venirepersons with the responses to the same questions provided by community members residing in the trial venue during a telephone survey. Seventy percent of the telephone survey respondents reported an inability to hear the case fairly in contrast to 10% of the venirepersons in the case. These data suggest that the social pressures inherent in the courtroom may prevent venirepersons from accurately reporting their abilities to put aside information gleaned from PTP when deciding a case.

Even if the identification of jurors who are biased by PTP may prove difficult, perhaps *voir dire* serves as a mechanism to encourage jurors to set aside their biases. Only one study has provided a proper test of whether *voir dire* might correct juror bias from PTP exposure, and its findings are not particularly promising (Dexter, Cutler, & Moran, 1992). In this study, researchers manipulated participants' exposure to PTP and whether they participated in a standard or an extended *voir dire*. For *voir dire* to correct PTP bias, one must observe an interaction between *voir dire* type and PTP exposure, such that the extended *voir dire* eliminates the difference between the punitiveness of those who are exposed to PTP and those who are not. No such interaction was observed (Dexter et al., 1992). Despite this empirical evidence suggesting that the *voir dire* remedy is ineffective, it continues to be a popular remedy among judges, perhaps because it is relatively inexpensive to implement and judges believe that it works (Kovera & Greathouse, 2008).

Judicial Instruction

The courts have also suggested that if a judge instructs jurors to ignore information about a case that was obtained before trial, the effects of PTP will be eliminated. In these instructions, judges tell jurors of their duty to avoid the influence of PTP and to base their verdict only on the evidence that is presented at trial. It seems unlikely that judicial instruction to disregard PTP will be effective; a recent meta-analysis shows that jurors generally do not follow instructions to disregard inadmissible evidence that is mistakenly presented at trial (Steblay et al., 2006). However, the meta-analysis does suggest that people are better able to follow instructions when they understand the justification for disregarding the inadmissible evidence; so perhaps if judicial instructions help jurors understand why they must ignore PTP, the instructions will reduce or eliminate PTP effects.

Early research on PTP instructions suggested that judicial admonitions would reduce PTP effects (Kline & Jess, 1996; Simon, 1966); however, these early studies contained design features—missing control groups and demand characteristics—that make it difficult to draw strong inferences from their findings. A less promising picture is painted by methodologically sound studies, which generally fail to find a curative effect of judicial instructions on PTP (Fein, McCloskey, & Tomlinson, 1977; Sue, Smith, & Gilbert, 1974). The failure of PTP instructions to remedy the negative effects of prejudicial PTP on jurors' judgments of defendant culpability applies to PTP that presents facts and PTP that arouses emotion (Kramer, Kerr, & Carroll, 1990) and to PTP effects in civil cases (Bornstein et al., 2002). Thus, one cannot rely on judicial instruction to eliminate the negative effects of PTP exposure.

Continuances

Another possible remedy for PTP is a continuance—a delay of the start of a trial. If pretrial media coverage of a case is extensive, the defense can move to delay the start of the trial with the hope that media coverage will dissipate during the delay. Although media coverage of a case may decrease if a trial date is moved to a future date, it will probably rebound as the new trial date approaches. However, if a continuance does decrease trial coverage immediately before the trial, what effects, if any, does PTP exposure have on juror judgments when there is a delay between exposure and judgment?

Few studies have specifically tested the effects of delaying a trial for a period of time after PTP exposure. In the best of these studies (Kramer et al., 1990), researchers manipulated exposure to factual PTP (e.g., publicity that presents inculpatory information suggesting the defendant's guilt) and emotional PTP (e.g., publicity that does not speak to the defendant's guilt but is designed to arouse emotions of those exposed). They also manipulated whether participants were exposed to the PTP several days or immediately before they began the experimental session in which they watched the videotaped trial simulation. Delay reduced the effects of factual PTP but did not reduce the effects of emotional PTP (Kramer et al., 1990).

The delay in the Kramer et al. study was relatively short—only several days. Continuances are often longer than this, so delays could counteract even emotional PTP if they were relatively longer. A meta-analysis examined whether the length of delay between PTP exposure and trial judgments moderated the strength of PTP effects (Steblay et al., 1999). The results suggest that PTP effects are greater when the delay between PTP exposure and trial judgments exceeds 7 days, although their results must be viewed with caution given that there were few tests that manipulated delay within a single study; therefore, other characteristics may systematically vary with delay to produce these results, although no such characteristics were easily identifiable. Although there are few studies that manipulate delay that allow us to confirm this meta-analytic

finding, delay might exacerbate PTP effects because it increases source-monitoring errors such that people find it harder to remember whether information that they know about a case was learned pretrial or gleaned from trial evidence when the delay between PTP exposure and trial increases (Ruva & McEvoy, 2008). If one is going to ignore PTP, one needs to be able to discriminate remembered information that was obtained from PTP from information that was obtained during the trial. If continuances decrease people's ability to make this discrimination, then it is not surprising that delays might increase the influence of pretrial publicity.

Change of Venue

A final method to remedy a venire that is tainted by PTP exposure is to move the trial to a different community that has not been exposed to publicity surrounding the case or at least has been less biased by it. Assuming that the venire in the new venue has less exposure to prejudicial PTP than did the venire in the original venue, a change of venue should be a highly effective method to combat the negative effects of PTP. This condition should usually be met because research has repeatedly demonstrated that community members in counties where a highly publicized trial is to be tried are more likely to hold negative attitudes toward the defendant than are community members in other nearby counties (Costantini & King, 1980/81; Moran & Cutler, 1991; Nietzel & Dillehay, 1983; Simon & Eimmerman, 1971; Vidmar & Judson, 1981). Despite its efficacy, judges are often reluctant to grant changes of venue because it is costly to move a trial to a new location.

Judges may grant a change of venue motion if they are convinced that the community is so prejudiced against the defendant that he or she would not be able to have a fair trial anywhere within that jurisdiction. Results from a survey about the case from the current venue and at least one alternative venue often are submitted to support motions for changes of venue (Nietzel & Dillehay, 1983). Another method to establish whether venues have been saturated with prejudicial PTP is content analysis of local media coverage (Studebaker, Robbennolt, Pathak-Sharma, & Penrod, 2000). With content analysis, one can establish the amount of PTP in a venue, its prominence (e.g., lead stories, front page, above the fold of the newspaper), as well as the type (e.g., emotional vs. factual, pro-prosecution vs. pro-defense). If coverage is more extensive, prominent, and negative in the current venue than in an identified alternative venue, the content analysis could provide evidence of prejudice that would enable a judge to grant a change of venue motion. Even in extremely high-profile cases, such as Timothy McVeigh's prosecution in the Oklahoma City bombing case, it has been possible to demonstrate that media coverage was more extensive and more prominent than it was in at least one alternate venue (Studebaker et al., 2000).

In sum, exposure to pretrial media coverage that casts doubt on the defendant's innocence or otherwise portrays the defendant in a negative light results in juries rendering guilty verdicts more often than they would without exposure to prejudicial PTP. Although the courts have developed safeguards intended to remedy the prejudicial effects of PTP, many of them (*voir dire*, judicial instruction, continuances, deliberation) do not fully protect defendants' rights to an impartial jury. Of the remedies available, a change of venue has the most empirical support.

EXPERT EVIDENCE

Although jurors' reactions to different types of evidence have been extensively studied over the past 50 years (Devine, Clayton, Dunford, Seying, & Pryce, 2001), one type of evidence that has received considerable research attention recently is scientific evidence presented by experts. In the latter half of the 1990s, the focus of research on expert testimony shifted from whether expert testimony on particular topics influenced jurors to whether jurors—and other legal decision makers—had the ability to evaluate the quality of scientific and other expert evidence. The primary impetus for this shift was the Supreme Court ruling in *Daubert v. Merrell Dow Pharmaceuticals* (1993), which addressed the legal debate over the rules governing the admissibility of scientific evidence—including psychological evidence—in federal court. In the *Daubert* decision, the Court established a two-prong test for the admissibility of scientific evidence. First, evidence has to be relevant to an issue to be decided in the case. Second, the evidence must be reliable; specifically, the methodology used to produce the science must be scientifically valid. The Court specified a nonexhaustive list of criteria for determining the reliability of scientific evidence, including whether the theory on which the expert relied and the hypotheses being tested were falsifiable, whether a known error rate is associated with the topic of the expert testimony, whether the research had been subjected to peer review, and whether the research findings were generally accepted by the relevant scientific community. Judges in federal courts and the many state courts that have adopted the *Daubert* standard are tasked with serving as the gatekeepers, determining whether scientific evidence proffered in a case meets these standards of admissibility. Those states that have not adopted *Daubert*-like standards likely follow the *Frye* standard, which holds that judges should admit novel scientific evidence if it is generally accepted by the

relevant scientific community. A subsequent Supreme Court decision clarified that the *Daubert* standard should be applied to the evaluation of nonscientific expert evidence as well (*Kumho Tire Co. v. Carmichael*, 1999).

Several psychological assumptions underlie the *Daubert* decision. First, the Court assumed that judges are capable of identifying flawed evidence and barring its admission from evidence. Although the Court presumed that judges were up to the task of identifying flawed science, the justices acknowledged that there might be circumstances under which invalid science is admitted into evidence. The second assumption made by the court is that procedural safeguards already in place—cross-examination, opposing experts, and judicial instruction on the standard of proof—were sufficient to educate the jury, allowing them to evaluate the validity of science and weight it appropriately. These assumptions clearly rest on the ability of judges and jurors to recognize invalid science but also on the abilities of attorneys because it is attorneys who will file motions to exclude expert testimony—in which they must be able to highlight the inadequacies of the science for the judge, cross-examine expert witnesses, and make decisions about when it is appropriate to call their own expert to discredit the other side (Kovera, Russano, & McAuliff, 2002). Do judges, attorneys, and jurors have the capabilities to evaluate the quality of the scientific evidence that the courts presume that they have?

Because most judges, attorneys, and jurors have not received any formal training in the scientific method (Kovera & McAuliff, 2000; Lehman, Lempert, & Nisbett, 1988; McAuliff & Kovera, 2008), it is likely that their scientific reasoning abilities are similar to the abilities of other laypeople. Laypeople often fail to recognize flaws in research (Nisbett, 1993). People do not understand the importance of a control group when testing the effect of a variable, and they do not apply statistical concepts when reasoning about common social behaviors (Jepson, Krantz, & Nisbett, 1983; Nisbett, Fong, Lehman, & Cheng, 1987; Tversky & Kahneman, 1974). Jurors are laypeople and therefore should perform no better than other laypeople on these tasks unless something about trial procedure (e.g., cross-examination) or evidence (e.g., opposing experts) helps to educate them. Law school education does not improve people's ability to reason about methodology or statistics (Lehman et al., 1988). Thus, social psychological evidence suggests that the legal decision makers may not have the abilities that the *Daubert* decision presumes; however, there may be factors present in the legal environment that improve the abilities of these decision makers. To test this possibility, researchers have been actively investigating the ability of legal decision makers to evaluate scientific evidence.

Judges' Evaluations of Scientific Evidence

Law school curricula rarely include scientific training (Lehman et al., 1988), but through their experience on the bench evaluating expert evidence or through continuing legal or judicial education, judges may have been exposed to scientific principles often enough that they have developed an ability to differentiate between flawed and valid expert evidence. Surveys and archival studies suggest that judges are not engaging in high-level scientific reasoning when making admissibility decisions about scientific evidence. Judges' self-reports suggest that they rely on experts' credentials and experience and not the content of their testimony when evaluating expert testimony (Shuman, Whitaker, & Champagne, 1994). Another survey of judges revealed that only a small percentage (4%–6%) of them accurately understand the *Daubert* criteria of falsifiability and error rates (Gatowski et al., 2001). Despite mentioning *Daubert* in their appellate decisions about the admissibility of expert evidence, judges do not write about specific features of reliability in those decisions (Groscup, Penrod, Studebaker, Huss, & O'Neil, 2002).

There has been only one experimental test of whether judges are sensitive to variations in the methodological quality of scientific evidence (Kovera & McAuliff, 2000). Embedded in a survey sent to Florida circuit court judges was a description of the fact pattern in a hostile work environment sexual harassment case and the expert testimony that the plaintiff intended to proffer at trial. Some judges received a description of a valid study about which the expert would testify, whereas others received an altered version of the study that introduced one of three internal validity flaws: a missing control group, a confound, or a confederate who was not blind to experimental conditions. The study's internal validity did not affect judges' ratings of the study quality or their willingness to admit the testimony (Kovera & McAuliff, 2000). Judges with some self-reported training in the scientific method did rate the internally valid study more positively than did untrained judges. Untrained judges rated the study with the confound more positively than did trained judges, and their responses to open-ended questions indicated that their appreciation of this particular version of the study stemmed from their misunderstanding of appropriate scientific method (Kovera et al., 2002). Training did not increase judges' sensitivity to missing control groups or the potential for experimenter expectancy effects from a confederate who was not blind to condition.

Taken together, these studies suggest that methodological quality exerts little to no influence on judges' ratings of scientific quality or their admissibility decisions. What

variables do influence these judgments? Whether a study had been peer-reviewed did not influence judges' decisions in one study (Kovera & McAuliff, 2000). Other research suggests that judges' sociopolitical attitudes influence their decisions to admit expert evidence, with judges more likely to admit findings that support their political orientation toward a particular issue (Redding & Reppucci, 1999).

Attorneys' Evaluations of Expert Evidence

Attorneys need to be able to identify flawed research if they are to argue effectively to judges that they should exclude invalid research from evidence or to cross-examine expert witnesses in a manner that highlights its flaws for jurors. Motions *in limine* to oppose the admission of a particular topic of expert testimony into evidence is one method through which judges could receive information that would help them evaluate the methodological quality of proffered science. A motion *in limine* is a pretrial motion submitted by an attorney, and in the context of expert evidence, it would contain arguments for or against the admission of a particular expert or topic of expert testimony. If the motion *in limine* is unsuccessful and invalid research is admitted into evidence, attorneys need to be able to understand scientific methodology to be able to demonstrate problems with invalid science during cross-examination or to know that it would be helpful to hire an expert to present evidence on why the science presented by the other side has methodological problems. Whether motions *in limine* can serve to educate judges about the characteristics of valid and invalid science, whether attorneys can craft a cross-examination that highlights scientific flaws, or whether attorneys hire opposing experts to help combat flawed science entered into evidence by the other side is predicated on attorneys' ability to recognize when and why science is invalid.

At the end of law school, law students still lack the ability to reason about methodology in everyday situations (Lehman et al., 1988). A national sample of attorneys specializing in employment law responded to the same expert evidence used in the survey of judges described earlier, including the manipulation of whether the study described in the expert testimony was valid, missing a control group, confounded, or had a confederate who was not blind to condition (Kovera & McAuliff, 2009). The study also manipulated the general acceptance of the research; in one set of conditions, the relevant scientific community had generally accepted the expert's findings, and in another set, the research had just been completed, which did not allow time for the findings to become generally accepted. The manipulations of internal validity did not influence attorneys' ratings of the quality of the expert's study, but the manipulation of general acceptance did, with attorneys responding more positively to the generally accepted research. The study characteristics also had no effect on attorneys' reports of whether they would file a motion to exclude the expert evidence—close to 95% reported that they would—and their reports of the grounds on which they would base their objection to the testimony rarely mentioned the three methodological flaws contained in the study. Half of the attorneys who did cite one of these flaws did so when the flaw was not present, suggesting that attorneys might well provide incorrect information to judges who are already struggling to evaluate the scientific evidence without the proper skills and abilities that would allow them to do so.

Juror Decisions About Expert Evidence

Jurors also have difficulty evaluating expert scientific evidence. Mock jurors who watched a trial simulation containing an expert who testified about research she had conducted on the influence of exposure to sexually suggestive material in the workplace noticed a manipulation of construct validity, but the manipulation did not affect their ratings of the quality of the study, the expert, or their verdicts (Kovera et al., 1999). In contrast, manipulations of the representativeness of the expert's sample and general acceptance did influence jurors' trial judgments. Another study found that whether the expert's study contained a control group did not affect the reactions of community members who had reported for jury duty to a trial summary containing expert testimony unless the community member was high in Need for Cognition (McAuliff & Kovera, 2008) In a follow-up study, the presence of a control group, but not the presence of a confound or a nonblind confederate, affected jury-eligible community members' judgments of study quality and the expert's credibility (McAuliff, Kovera, & Nunez, 2009).

These studies raise concerns about jurors' abilities to recognize methodological flaws in scientific evidence. These findings are consistent with other research showing that jurors have difficulty reasoning about statistical evidence (Schklar & Diamond, 1999; Smith, Penrod, Otto, & Park, 1996; Thompson & Schumann, 1987). Of course, jurors do not make these decisions in a vacuum, and procedural safeguards such as cross-examination, opposing expert testimony, and judicial instruction may sensitize jurors to flaws that could exist in scientific evidence entered into evidence.

Instruction on the Standard of Proof

In the majority opinion of *Daubert*, the Court held that careful instruction on the standard of proof could assist jurors in assigning appropriate weight to unreliable expert evidence. There are currently no published studies that directly tested this assumption. However, the logic underlying the argument seems faulty given that the instructions provide no guidance on how to determine which evidence is reliable and which is not; the instruction on the standard of proof should only serve to make jurors more or less skeptical of expert testimony rather than sensitive to variations in validity. Moreover, a survey of previously impaneled jurors suggests that most jurors do not understand the standards of proof even after receiving instruction on them (Reifman, Gusick, & Ellsworth, 1992). Other research testing people's understanding of proof instructions similarly finds they have poor comprehension (Strawn & Buchanan, 1976). Given the available data, increased skepticism of scientific expert evidence may be the most reasonable expectation to hold for judicial instructions on the standard of proof.

Cross-Examination

For cross-examination to be an effective procedural safeguard, two conditions must be met. First, attorneys must be able to identify methodological flaws in scientific research and then pose the expert questions about those flaws during cross-examination. Second, cross-examination must make jurors sensitive to those methodological flaws rather than merely make them skeptical of all expert evidence, irrespective of whether it is valid or invalid. The currently available evidence does not support either of these conditions.

Regarding the first condition, as noted previously, variations in internal validity did not affect attorneys' ratings of a study's methodological quality (Kovera & McAuliff, 2009). In their study of attorneys' reactions to variations in the internal validity of a study, attorneys generated cross-examination questions that they would use to cross-examine the hypothetical expert described in the scenario they read (Kovera & McAuliff, 2009). Attorneys rarely mentioned internal validity issues in the questions they crafted, and when they did, they were equally likely to mention internal validity characteristics when cross-examining the expert presenting the valid study than when cross-examining the expert presenting one of the studies with a serious flaw. Rather than focusing their cross-examination questions on issues of methodology, the attorneys tended to focus on the expert's qualifications or potential sources of bias, such as the expert's fees or history of testifying on behalf of plaintiffs.

So it is unlikely that attorneys will highlight methodological flaws in their cross-examinations of experts presenting flawed science, but what would happen if jurors heard an attorney attack the methodological foundation of an expert's research? Would a scientifically informed cross-examination educate jurors so that they could identify flawed science and weight it appropriately? Two studies have examined the effects of cross-examination on jurors' evaluations of clinical versus actuarial testimony on future dangerousness. The first manipulated the basis of the expert's testimony—clinical opinion versus actuarial prediction—on the risk that the defendant would be dangerous in the future (Krauss & Sales, 2001). Despite the stronger scientific basis for the actuarial expert's prediction, jurors preferred the clinical expert. Although cross-examination did produce less positive ratings of the expert and reduced the perceived future risk of dangerousness, even after exposure to cross-examination, the jurors responded more favorably to clinical than to the more scientifically based actuarial testimony. The addition of jury deliberations to the design did not improve cross-examination's efficacy in countering clinical testimony (Krauss & Lee, 2003).

In a different study, mock jurors heard evidence from an expert that varied in its construct validity; an attorney questioned that expert using a scientifically naïve cross-examination that only addressed the expert's qualifications and credibility or a scientifically informed cross-examination that also addressed the construct validity of the expert's study (Kovera et al., 1999). Although manipulation checks indicated that participants noticed the differences in the expert's study, the differences did not affect their trial judgments, even after exposure to the scientifically informed cross-examination. On the basis of the research to date, cross-examination does not sensitize jurors to the methodological quality of expert scientific evidence, at least not as it is currently practiced.

Opposing Experts

Perhaps one of the reasons that cross-examination does not influence jurors' evaluations of scientific evidence is because the methodological criticisms come from a partisan advocate who is not a trained scientist. Would criticism conveyed by another expert more effectively sensitize jurors to methodological flaws in scientific evidence? For the opposing expert safeguard to be effective, attorneys would need to consult their own expert when the testimony proffered by the other side contains methodological flaws. Yet manipulations of internal validity had no effect on attorneys' self-reported intentions to hire their own expert. Attorneys' perceptions of the quality of the expert evidence—which were unrelated to the manipulations of internal validity—were correlated with their willingness to hire an expert but in an unexpected way (Kovera & McAuliff, 2009). Attorneys reported being more likely to hire their own expert when they believed that the other side's expert was providing higher quality testimony, perhaps believing themselves up to the task of discrediting an expert providing lower quality testimony.

Can an opposing expert help jurors better evaluate the validity of the other expert's testimony? One jury simulation study manipulated (a) the internal validity of research on child suggestibility presented by a defense expert and (b) whether an opposing expert testified for the prosecution and, if so, whether the opposing expert attacked the defense expert's willingness to generalize from laboratory studies to real-world contexts only or also testified about the internal validity of the defense expert's study. In this research, the opposing expert did little to sensitize jurors to the quality of the defense expert's study, even when directly addressing its internal validity (Levett & Kovera, 2008). Instead, the opposing expert served to make the jurors skeptical of the defense expert, irrespective of the quality of that expert's testimony and whether the opposing expert addressed that quality. The skepticism effect created by the opposing expert appears to be mediated by juror judgments about the general acceptance of the original expert's testimony (Levett & Kovera, 2009). Specifically, when an opposing expert was present, jurors inferred that scientists did not generally accept the original expert's findings, and this inference led to more guilty verdicts (i.e., verdicts more in line with the opposing expert's position).

In sum, research conducted since the late 1990s suggests that legal decision makers do not have the abilities to evaluate scientific evidence that courts presume they have. Moreover, the legal safeguards designed to assist jurors in their evaluations of unreliable scientific evidence—especially cross-examination and opposing expert testimony—appear ineffective. This lack of efficacy appears due in part to attorneys' inability to deploy them effectively and in part because even if the safeguards are deployed, they do not seem to sensitize jurors effectively to methodological flaws.

SUMMARY

The lawyer and the judge and the juryman are sure that they do not need the experimental psychologist. They do not wish to see that in this field preeminently applied experimental psychology has made strong strides . . . . They go on thinking that their legal instinct and their common sense supplies them with all that is needed and somewhat more; and if the time is ever to come when the jurist is to show some concession to the spirit of modern psychology, public opinion will have to exert some pressure.

(Munsterberg, 1908, pp. 10–11)

At the beginning of and late into the 20th century, Hugo Munsterberg's analysis of the law's skepticism about psychological science was widely shared. Yet as the applications of social psychology to the legal context covered in this chapter suggest, this skepticism has begrudgingly yielded to a greater openness to the "spirit" and reality of "modern psychology." Not only has theory and research from social psychology been applied to a variety of legal questions and problems, but theory and research in the field has been stimulated by the legal context. This type of reciprocal influence is surely a hallmark of interdisciplinary research more generally. However, as the research discussed in this chapter suggests, substantive applications of social psychology to various legal contexts, more so than theory development per se, characterize the relationship between law and social psychology even now in the 21st century.

Several critical and complex questions face social psychology and law researchers at this juncture. How should existing social science research, including but not limited to theory and research from social psychology, be used in litigation and policy formulations? Under what circumstances will general social science findings help courts and juries? What sorts of use-specific opinions should courts allow experts to give, and how should experts proffer these opinions? These questions have spawned a lively and wide-ranging debate among researchers and legal scholars at the intersection of social psychology and antidiscrimination law (e.g., Krieger & Fiske, 2006; Lane, Kang, & Banaji, 2007; Mitchell & Tetlock, 2006; Tetlock & Mitchell, in press; Wax, 2008). Crucial to addressing all of these questions is the basic tenet that quality, peer-reviewed science should be the foundation for any expert testimony. Quality science provides the best scientific context for understanding how people make sense of each other (Fiske & Borgida, 2008). For social scientists, the adversarial context also has the potential to raise vital scientific issues and to enrich theory development by posing empirically testable research questions (e.g., see special issue of *Industrial and Organizational Psychology: Perspectives on Science and Practice*, December 2008).

Quality research presented at the aggregate level (general causation) can inform fact finders without any testimony necessarily making specific causal claims (specific causation) in a given case (Faigman, 2008; Faigman & Monahan, 2005). This distinction between general and specific causation arises from medical causation and toxic tort cases (Faigman, Saks, Sanders, & Cheng, 2007). *General causation* concerns whether causality between two factors exists at all (e.g., is there a relationship between exposure to media violence and interpersonal aggression?), and *specific causation* refers to whether the phenomenon of interest occurred in a particular context (e.g., did exposure to media violence cause a specific homicide?). State and federal courts are increasingly accepting of research presented in the form of a *social framework* that uses science to provide context and to educate fact finders (Monahan, Walker, & Mitchell, 2008); however, some scholars have called for social framework testimony to be limited to testimony that educates fact finders about general causation but not specific causation issues (Monahan et al., 2008). There also has to be appropriate "fit" between the scientific evidence that is presented and the specific legal issues(s) to which it is directed, with some scholars arguing that there is a lack of fit between extant aggregate-level research findings and specific employer decisions in employment discrimination disputes (Faigman et al., 2008).

But this question of social frameworks and their "linkage" to the specific facts of a case has emerged as perhaps the key question for understanding the application and use of research in criminal and civil law contexts. Some have argued that using science to provide a context for the fact finder is appropriate, but making specific applications to the facts of the case is inappropriate and should be precluded in all instances (Monahan et al., 2008). Others do not agree about the categorical exclusion of "linkage" between general causation and specific causation and *how* social framework testimony should be offered, arguing that Federal Rule of Evidence 702 (on expert testimony) is flexible and not subject to categorical exclusions and that expert testimony may properly include opinions on facts at issue in a case (Hart & Secunda, in press). "What the Supreme Court decisions, as well as numerous opinions from the lower courts, demonstrate is that the admissibility of expert opinion testimony linking a field of knowledge with the case facts is an open domain, sensitive to the circumstances" (Hart & Secunda, in press). On the other hand, social framework testimony may not always be permitted. If judicial determinations about linkage will be at the district court level, then decisions about "linkage" testimony will and should continue to be individualized (Hart & Secunda, in press).

Another approach to this question of general versus specific causation from a scientific perspective relies on an analogy from medical science (Borgida, Eagly, & Deason, 2009). Typical physician diagnosis behavior, for example, does not follow this "general causation" model. Instead, physicians offer diagnoses as if they were applied scientists. Because symptoms can arise from several diseases, physicians begin by *ruling out* some diseases that can produce the symptoms (Borgida et al., 2009). Based on experience and scientific expertise, the physician then would evaluate the plausibility of each of the most likely causes.

Although physicians are certainly not perfect (see Groopman, 2007), they generally have the superior knowledge of the science that is relevant to diagnosing a patient's condition. This expertise is a valuable resource in a complicated world where casual ad hoc explanations are more plentiful than correct conclusions. After the physician offers a diagnosis, the patient has many options. They may accept or refuse the recommended treatment, seek the opinion of other physicians, consult a faith healer, adopt a strategy of watchful waiting, engage in psychological denial, or adopt a wide variety of other strategies. The physician's judgment informs the patient without usurping his or her role as the ultimate judge of which disease most plausibly explains the symptom.

The social science expert serves a similar purpose when, for example, attempting a "diagnosis" of the causes of a negative workplace outcome or the factors that could contribute to a mistaken identification or false confession (Borgida et al., 2009). Although the social scientist's judgment is not perfect, it is likely to be superior to uninformed judgment and can assist the trier of fact without usurping the decision-making role (Borgida & Fiske, 2008). Social scientists may be able to rule out some possible causes of the focal event (e.g., job termination, eyewitness identification, confession) and rule *in* one or more other causes, much like a physician applying his or her knowledge to a particular patient and set of symptoms. Analogous to physicians' ability to correctly diagnose a patient's physical symptoms, scientists' ability to correctly discern the linkage between general and specific causation for the individual case depends on the quality of the scientific evidence and the scientist's expertise and ability to reason based on this evidence.

The adversarial nature of the court system seldom gives social scientists the opportunity to freely invoke the power of the available science. Scientific experts are retained either by those who wish to rule in a cause or by those who wish to rule it out; a full scientific analysis is rarely welcomed by either side of the typical courtroom exchange. The often proposed idea that the courts should retain neutral science advisors to achieve some sort of scientific consensus remains appealing though without any practical momentum (Saks & Faigman, 2005). In the end, it is the responsibility of the scientists who bring their insights into court to resist these adversarial pressures to present the science in a selective and partisan manner and to present fact finders with quality science.

REFERENCES

Adler, F. (1973). Socioeconomic factors influencing jury verdicts. *New York University Review of Law and Social Change, 3*, 1–10.

Adorno, T., Frenkel-Brunswik, E., Levinson, D., & Sanford, N. (1950). *The authoritarian personality*. New York: Harper.

Allen, M., Mabry, E., & McKelton, D. (1998). Impact of juror attitudes about the death penalty on juror evaluations of guilt and punishment: A meta-analysis. *Law and Human Behavior, 22*, 715–731.

American Bar Association. (2000). *Model rules of professional conduct*, 2003 Edition. Chicago: Author.

Batson v. Kentucky, 476 U.S. 79 (1986).

Behrman, B. W., & Davey, S. L. (2001). Eyewitness identification in actual criminal cases: An archival analysis. *Law and Human Behavior, 25*, 475–491.

Blue, L. A. (1991). Jury selection in a civil case. *Trial Lawyers Quarterly, 21*, 11–25.

Blumenthal, J. A. (1998). The reasonable woman standard: A meta-analytic review of gender differences in perceptions of sexual harassment. *Law and Human Behavior, 22*, 33–57.

Boehm, V. (1968). Mr. Prejudice, Miss Sympathy, and the authoritarian personality: An application of psychological measuring techniques to the problem of jury bias. *Wisconsin Law Review, 1968*, 734–750.

Bond, C. F., Jr., & DePaulo, B. M. (2006). Accuracy of deception judgments. *Personality and Social Psychology Review, 10*, 214–234.

Bond, C. F., Jr., & Uysal, A. (2007). On lie detection "wizards." *Law and Human Behavior, 31*, 109–115.

Borchard, E. M., & Lutz, E. R. (1932). *Convicting the innocent: Errors of criminal justice*. New Haven, CT: Yale University Press.

Borgida, E., Eagly, A., & Deason, G. (2009). What does expert testimony on stereotyping research have to offer lawyers in discrimination cases? Issues of general vs. specific causation vs. scientists' continuum framework. Unpublished manuscript, University of Minnesota and Northwestern University.

Borgida, E., & Fiske, S. T. (Eds.). (2008). *Beyond common sense: Psychological science in the courtroom*. Malden, MA: Blackwell.

Bornstein, B. H., Whisenhunt, B. L., & Nemeth, R. J. (2002). Pretrial publicity and civil cases: A two-way street? *Law & Human Behavior, 21*, 3–17.

Bottoms, B. L., Davis, S. L., & Epstein, M. A. (2004). Effects of victim and defendant race on jurors' decisions in child sexual abuse cases. *Journal of Applied Social Psychology, 34*, 1–33.

Bottoms, B. L., & Goodman, G. S. (1994). Perceptions of children's credibility in sexual assault cases. *Journal of Applied Social Psychology, 24*, 702–732.

Bradfield, A. L., Wells, G. L., & Olson, E. A. (2002). The damaging effect of confirming feedback on the relation between eyewitness certainty and identification accuracy. *Journal of Applied Psychology, 87*, 112–120.

Bray, R. M., & Noble, A. M. (1978). Authoritarianism and decisions of mock juries: Evidence of jury bias and group polarization. *Journal of Personality and Social Psychology, 36*, 1424–1430.

Brekke, N., & Borgida, E. (1988). Expert psychological testimony in rape trials: A social-cognitive analysis. *Journal of Personality and Social Psychology, 55*, 372–386.

Brigham, J. C., Meissner, C. A., & Wasserman, A. W. (1999). Applied issues in the construction and expert assessment of photo lineups. *Applied Cognitive Psychology, 13*, S73–S92.

Brigham, J. C., & Wasserman, A. W. (1999). The impact of race, racial attitude, and gender on reactions to the criminal trial of O. J. Simpson. *Journal of Applied Social Psychology, 29*, 1333–1370.

Brown, E. L., Deffenbacher, K. A., & Sturgill, W. (1977). Memory for faces and the circumstances of encounter. *Journal of Applied Psychology, 62*, 311–318.

Buckley, J. P. (2004, February). *The Reid technique: Challenges and opportunities*. Paper presented at the International Symposium on Police Interviewing. Nicolet, Quebec, Canada.

Bull, R. (1989). Can training enhance the detection of deception? In J. C. Yuille (Ed.), *Credibility assessment* (pp. 83–99). London: Kluwer Academic.

Butler, B., & Moran, G. (2007). The impact of death qualification, belief in a just world, legal authoritarianism, and locus of control on venirepersons' evaluations of aggravating and mitigating circumstances in capital trials. *Behavioral Sciences and the Law, 25*, 57–68.

Candel, I., Merckelbach, H., Loyen, S., & Reyskens, H. (2005). "I hit the shift-key and then the computer crashed": Children and false admissions. *Personality and Individual Differences, 38*, 1381–1387.

Carlsmith, K. M., Darley J. M., & Robinson, P. H. (2002). Why do we punish? Deterrence and just deserts as motives for punishment. *Journal of Personality and Social Psychology, 83*, 1–16.

Cassell, P. G. (1996a). All benefits, no costs: The grand illusion of *Miranda*'s defenders. *Northwestern University Law Review, 90*, 1084–1124.

Cassell, P. G. (1996b). *Miranda*'s social costs: An empirical reassessment. *Northwestern University Law Review, 90*, 387–499.

Cassell, P. G., & Hayman, B. S. (1996). Police interrogation in the 1990s: An empirical study of the effects of *Miranda*. *UCLA Law Review, 43*, 839–931.

Chapdelaine, A., & Griffin, S. F. (1997). Beliefs of guilt and recommended sentence as a function of juror bias in the O. J. Simpson trial. *Journal of Social Issues, 53*, 477–485.

Chrzanowski, L. M. (2005). *Rape? Truth? And the media: Laboratory and field assessments of pretrial publicity in a real case.* Unpublished doctoral dissertation, City University of New York.

Clark, J., Boccaccini, M. T., Caillouet, B., & Chaplin, W. F. (2007). Five factor model personality traits, jury selection, and case outcomes in criminal and civil cases. *Criminal Justice and Behavior, 34*, 641–660.

Clark, S., & Tunnicliff, J. L. (2001). Selecting lineup foils in eyewitness identification experiments: Experimental control and real-world simulation. *Law and Human Behavior, 25*, 199–216.

Clark, S. E. (2005). A re-examination of the effects of biased lineup instructions in eyewitness identification. *Law and Human Behavior, 29*, 395–42.

Costantini, E., & King, J. (1980/81). The partial juror: Correlates and causes of prejudgment. *Law and Society Review, 15*, 9–40.

Cooper, V. G., & Zapf, P. A. (2008). Psychiatric patients' comprehension of *Miranda* rights. *Law and Human Behavior, 32*, 390–405.

Correll, S. J., Benard, S. & Paik, I. (2007). Getting a job: Is there a motherhood penalty? *American Journal of Sociology, 112*, 1297–1338.

Cowan, C. L., Thompson, W. C., & Ellsworth, P. C. (1984). The effects of death qualification on jurors: Predisposition to convict and on the quality of deliberation. *Law and Human Behavior, 8*, 53–79.

Crocker, C. B., Kennard, J. B., Greathouse, S. M., & Kovera, M. B. (2009, March). *An investigation of attorneys' questioning strategies during voir dire.* Paper presented at the meeting of the American Psychology-Law Society, San Antonio, TX.

Crocker, C. B., & Kovera, M. B. (2009). The effects of rehabilitative voir dire on juror bias and decision making. *Law and Human Behavior.* DOI 10.1007/s10979-009-9193-9.

Cutler, B. L. (2006). A sample of witness, crime, and perpetrator characteristics affecting eyewitness identification accuracy. *Cardozo Public Law, Policy, and Ethics Journal, 4*, 327–340.

Cutler, B. L., Moran, G. P., & Narby, D. J. (1992). Jury selection in insanity defense cases. *Journal of Research in Personality, 26*, 165–182.

Cutler, B. L., & Penrod, S. D. (1988). Improving the reliability of eyewitness identification: Lineup construction and presentation. *Journal of Applied Psychology, 73*, 281–290.

Cutler, B. L., Penrod, S. D., & Dexter, H. R. (1990). Juror sensitivity to eyewitness identification evidence. *Law and Human Behavior, 14*, 185–191.

Cutler, B. L., Penrod, S. D., & Martens, T. K. (1987a). The reliability of eyewitness identification: The role of system and estimator variables. *Law and Human Behavior, 11*, 223–238.

Cutler, B. L., Penrod, S. D., & Martens, T. K. (1987b). Improving the reliability of eyewitness identification: Putting context into context. *Journal of Applied Psychology, 72*, 629–637.

Cutler, B. L., Penrod, S. D., O'Rourke, T. E., & Martens, T. K. (1986). Unconfounding the effects of contextual cues on eyewitness identification accuracy. *Social Behaviour, 1*, 113–134.

Davies, G. M., Smith, S., & Blincoe, C. (2008). A "weapon focus" effect in children. *Psychology, Crime, & Law, 14*, 19–28.

Davis, D., & Follette, W. C. (2002). Rethinking probative value of evidence: Base rates, intuitive profiling and the postdiction of behavior. *Law and Human Behavior, 26*, 133–158.

Davison, H. K., & Burke, M. J. (2000). Sex discrimination in simulated employment contexts: A meta-analytic investigation. *Journal of Vocational Behavior, 56*, 225–248.

Daubert v. Merrell Dow Pharmaceuticals, Inc., 113 S.Ct. 2786 (1993).

Deffenbacher, K. A. (1980). Eyewitnesses accuracy and confidence: Can we infer anything about their relationship? *Law and Human Behavior, 4*, 243–260.

Deffenbacher, K. A. (1983). The influence of arousal on reliability of testimony. In S. M. A. Lloyd- Bostock & B. R. Clifford (Eds.), *Evaluating witness evidence* (pp. 235–251). Chichester, England: Wiley.

Deffenbacher, K. A. (1994). Effects of arousal on everyday memory. *Human Performance, 7*, 141–161.

Deffenbacher, K. A., Bornstein, B. H., & Penrod, S. L. (2006). Mug shot exposure effects: Retroactive interference, mug shot commitment, source confusion, and unconscious transference. *Law and Human Behavior, 30*, 287–307.

Deffenbacher, K. A., Bornstein, B. H., Penrod, S. D., & McGorty, E. K. (2004). A meta-analytic review of the effects of high stress on eyewitness memory. *Law and Human Behavior, 28*, 687–706.

De La Fuente, L., De La Fuente, E. I., & Garcia, J. (2003). Effects of pretrial juror bias, strength of evidence and deliberation process on juror decisions: New validity evidence of the Juror Bias Scale scores. *Psychology, Crime, & Law, 9*, 197–209.

DePaulo, B. M. (1994). Spotting lies: Can humans learn to do better? *Current Directions in Psychological Science, 3*, 83–86.

DePaulo, B. M., Lindsay, J. J., Malone, B. E., Muhlenbruck, L., Charlton, K., & Cooper, H. (2003). Cues to deception. *Psychological Bulletin, 129*, 74–118.

DePaulo, B. M., & Morris, W. L. (2004). Discerning lies from truth: Behavioural cues to deception and the indirect pathway of intuition. In P. A. Granhag & L. A. Stromwell (Eds.), *The detection of deception in forensic contexts* (pp. 15–40). Cambridge, England: Cambridge University Press.

DePaulo, B. M., & Pfeifer, R. L. (1986). On-the-job experience and skill at detecting deception. *Journal of Applied Social Psychology, 16*, 249–267.

Devine, D. J., Clayton, L. D., Dunford, B. B., Seying, R., & Pryce, J. (2001). Jury decision making: 45 years of empirical research on deliberating groups. *Psychology, Public Policy, and Law, 7*, 622–727.

Dexter, H. R., Cutler, B. L., & Moran, G. (1992). A test of *voir dire* as a remedy for the prejudicial effects of pretrial publicity. *Journal of Applied Social Psychology, 22*, 819–832.

Diamond, S. S. (2008). Psychological contributions to evaluating witness testimony. In E. Borgida & S. T. Fiske (Eds.), *Beyond common sense: Psychological science in the courtroom* (pp. 353–365). Malden: Blackwell.

Diamond, S. S., & Zeisel, H. (1974). A courtroom experiment on juror selection and decision-making. *Personality and Social Psychology Bulletin, 1*, 276–277.

Diekman, A. B., & Eagly, A. H. (2000). Stereotypes as dynamic constructs: Women and men of the past, present, and future. *Personality and Social Psychology Bulletin, 26*, 1171–1188.

Dillehay, R. C., & Nietzel, M. T. (1985). Juror experience and jury verdicts. *Law and Human Behavior, 9*, 179–191.

Douglass, A. B., & Steblay, N. (2006). Memory distortion in eyewitnesses: A meta-analysis of the post-identification feedback effect. *Applied Cognitive Psychology, 20*, 859–869.

Dovidio, J. F., & Gaertner, S. L. (1983). The effects of sex, status, and ability on helping behavior. *Journal of Applied Social Psychology, 13*, 191–205.

Drizin, S. A., & Leo, R. A. (2004). The problem of false confessions in the post-DNA world. *North Carolina Law Review, 82*, 891–1007.

Dunning, D., & Perretta, S. (2002). Automaticity and eyewitness accuracy: A 10- to 12-second rule for distinguishing accurate from inaccurate positive identifications. *Journal of Applied Psychology, 87*, 951–962.

Eagly, A. H., & Carli, L. L. (2007). *Through the labyrinth: The truth about how women become leaders.* Boston: Harvard Business School Press.

Eagly, A. H., & Karau, S. J. (2002). Role congruity theory of prejudice toward female leaders. *Psychological Review, 109*, 573–598.

Eagly, A. H., Karau, S. J., & Makhijani, M. G. (1995). Gender and the effectiveness of leaders: A meta-analysis. *Psychological Bulletin, 117*, 125–145.

Eagly, A. H., & Koenig, A. M. (2008). Gender prejudice: On the risks of occupying incongruent roles. In E. Borgida & S. T. Fiske (Eds.), *Beyond common sense: Psychological science in the courtroom* (pp. 63–82). Malden, MA: Blackwell.

Eagly, A. H., Makhijani, M. G., & Klonsky, B. G. (1992). Gender and the evaluation of leaders: A meta-analysis. *Psychological Bulletin, 111*, 3–22.

Eagly, A. H., & Mladinic, A. (1989). Gender stereotypes and attitudes toward women and men. *Personality and Social Psychology Bulletin, 15*, 543–558.

Ekman, P., & O'Sullivan, M. (1991). Who can catch a liar? *American Psychologist, 46*, 913–920.

Elaad, R. (2003). Effects of feedback on the overestimated capacity to detect lies and the underestimated ability to tell lies. *Applied Cognitive Psychology, 17*, 349–363.

Ellsworth, P. C., & Mauro, R. (1998). Psychology and law. In D. T. Gilbert, S. T. Fiske, & G. Lindzey (Eds.), *Handbook of social psychology* (4th ed., pp. 684–732). New York: McGraw-Hill.

Faigman, D. L. (2008). The limits of science in the courtroom. In E. Borgida & S. T. Fiske (Eds.), *Beyond common sense: Psychological science in the courtroom* (pp. 303–314). Malden, MA: Blackwell.

Faigman, D. L., Dasgupta, N., & Ridgeway, C. L. (2008). A matter of fit: The law of discrimination and the science of implicit bias. *University of California Hastings Law Journal, 60*, 1389–1434.

Faigman, D. L., Kaye, D. H., Saks, M. J., & Sanders, J. (Eds.). (2005). *Modern scientific evidence: The law and science of expert testimony.* (2005–2006 ed., Vol. 2, pp. 567–620). Eagan, MN: Thomson West.

Faigman, D. L., & Monahan, J. (2005). Psychological evidence at the dawn of the law's scientific age. *Annual Review of Psychology, 56*, 631–659.

Faigman, D. L., Saks, M. J., Sanders, J., & Cheng, E. K. (2007). Gender stereotyping: Legal issues. In D. Faigman, D. H. Kaye, M. J. Saks, & J. Sanders & E. K. Cheung (Eds.), *Modern scientific evidence: The law and science of expert testimony,* (Vol. 2, pp. 625–643). St. Paul, MN: Thomson West.

Fazio, R. H., & Olson, M. A. (2003). Implicit measures in social cognition: Their meaning and use. *Annual Review of Psychology, 54*, 297–327.

Feather, N. T. (1996). Domestic violence, gender, and perceptions of justice. *Sex Roles, 35*, 507–519.

Fein, S., McCloskey, A. L., & Tomlinson, T. M. (1997). Can the jury disregard that information? The use of suspicion to reduce the prejudicial effects of pretrial publicity and inadmissible testimony. *Personality and Social Psychology Bulletin, 23*, 1215–1226.

Feld, B. C. (2006). Juveniles' competence to exercise Miranda rights: An empirical study of policy and practice. *Minnesota Law Review, 91*, 26.

Filkins, J. W., Smith, C. M., & Tindale, R. S. (1998). An evaluation of the biasing effects of death qualification: A meta-analytic/computer simulation approach. In R. S. Tindale & L. Heath (Eds.), *Theory and research on small groups.* New York: Plenum Press.

Fisher, R. P., & Cutler, B. L. (1996). The relation between consistency and accuracy of eyewitness testimony. In G. M. Davies, S. Lloyd-Bostock, M. McMurran, & C. Wilson (Eds.), *Psychology and law: Advances in research.* Berlin: De Gruyter (pp. 21–28).

Fiske, S. T., & Borgida, E. (2008). Providing expert knowledge in an adversarial context: Social cognitive science in employment discrimination cases. *Annual Review of Law and Social Science, 4*, 11.1–11.26.

Fitzgerald, R., & Ellsworth, P. C. (1984). Due process vs. crime control: Death qualification and jury attitudes. *Law and Human Behavior, 8*, 31–51.

Flowe, H., Ebbesen, E. B., Burke, C., & Chivabunditt, P. (2001). *At the scene of the crime: An examination of the external validity of published studies on line-up identification accuracy.* Paper presented at the meetings of the American Psychological Society, Toronto, Canada.

Forrest, K. D., Wadkins, T. A., & Larson, B. A. (2006). Suspect personality, police interrogations, and false confessions: Maybe it is not just the situation. *Personality and Individual Differences, 40*, 621–628.

Fulero, S. M., & Everington, C. (1995). Assessing competency to waive *Miranda* rights in defendants with mental retardation. *Law and Human Behavior, 19*, 533–543.

Fulero, S. M., & Penrod, S. D. (1990a). Attorney jury selection folklore: What do they think and how can psychologists help? *Forensic Reports, 3*, 233–259.

Fulero, S. M., & Penrod, S. D. (1990b). The myths and realities of attorney jury selection folklore and scientific jury selection: What works? *Ohio Northern University Law Review, 17*, 229–253.

Gabbidon, S. L., Kowal, L. K., Jordan, K. L., Roberts, J. L., & Vincenzi, N. (2008). Race-based peremptory challenges: An empirical analysis of litigation from the U. S. Courts of Appeals, 2002–2006. *American Journal of Criminal Justice, 33*, 59–68.

Garrett, B. (2008). Judging innocence. *Columbia Law Review, 108*, 55–142.

Garrido, E., & Masip, J. (1999). How good are police officers at spotting lies? *Forensic Update, 58*, 14–21.

Garrido, E., Masip, J., & Herrero, C. (2004). Police officers' credibility judgments: Accuracy and estimated ability. *International Journal of Psychology, 39*, 254–275.

Gatowski, S. I., Dobbin, S. A., Richardson, J. T., Ginsburg, G. P., Merlino, M. L., & Dahir, V. (2001). Asking the gatekeepers: A national survey of judges on judging expert evidence in a post-*Daubert* World. *Law and Human Behavior, 25*, 433–458.

Gerbasi, K. C., Zuckerman, M., & Reis, H. T. (1977). Justice needs a new blindfold: A review of mock jury research. *Psychological Bulletin, 84*, 323–345.

Gilbert, D. T., & Malone, P. S. (1995). The correspondence bias. *Psychological Bulletin, 117*, 21–38.

Golding, J. M., Bradshaw, G. S., Dunlap, E. E., & Hodell, E. C. (2007). The impact of mock jury gender composition on deliberations and conviction rates in a child sexual assault trial. *Child Maltreatment, 12*, 182–190.

Gonzalez, R., Ellsworth, P. C., & Pembroke, M. (1993). Response biases in lineups and showups. *Journal of Personality and Social Psychology, 64*, 525–537.

Goodman, J., Loftus, E. F., & Greene, E. (1990). Matters of money: *Voir dire* in civil cases. *Forensic Reports, 3,* 303–329.

Gorenstein, G. W., & Ellsworth, P. C. (1980). Effect of choosing an incorrect photograph on a later identification by an eyewitness. *Journal of Applied Psychology, 65,* 616–622.

Greathouse, S. M., Crocker, C. B., Kennard, J. B., Austin, J., & Kovera, M. B. (2009). *Do attorney expectations influence the* voir dire *process?* Unpublished manuscript, John Jay College, City University of New York.

Greathouse, S. M., & Kovera, M. B. (2009). Instruction bias and lineup presentation moderate the effects of administrator knowledge on eyewitness identification. *Law and Human Behavior, 33,* 70–82.

Greene, E., & Loftus, E. F. (1984). What's new in the news? The influence of well-publicized news events on psychological research and courtroom trials. *Basic and Applied Social Psychology, 5,* 211–221.

Greene, E., & Wade, R. (1988). Of private talk and public print: General pre-trial publicity and juror decision-making. *Applied Cognitive Psychology, 2,* 123–135.

Greenwald, A. G., Poehlman, T. A., Uhlmann, E. L., & Banaji, M. R. (2009). Understanding and using the Implicit Association Test: III. Meta-analysis of predictive validity. *Journal of Personality and Social Psychology, 97,* 17–41.

Grisso, T. (1981). *Juveniles' waiver of rights: Legal and psychological competence.* New York: Plenum Press.

Grisso, T. (1998). *Forensic evaluation of juveniles.* Sarasota, FL: Professional Resource Press.

Groopman, J. (2007). *How doctors think.* Boston: Houghton Mifflin.

Groscup, J. L., Penrod, S. D., Studebaker, C. A., Huss, M. T., & O'Neil, K. M. (2002). The effects of *Daubert* on the admissibility of expert testimony in state and federal criminal cases. *Psychology, Public Policy, and Law, 8,* 339–372.

Gross, S. R., Jacoby, K., Matheson, D. J., Montgomery, N., & Patel, S. (2004). Exonerations in the United States from 1989 through 2003. *Journal of Criminal Law and Criminology, 95,* 523–560.

Gutek, B. A., O'Connor, M. A, Melançon, R., Stockdale, M. S., Geer, T. M., & Done, R. S. (1999). The utility of the reasonable woman legal standard in hostile environment sexual harassment cases: A multimethod, multistudy examination. *Psychology, Public Policy, and Law, 5,* 596–629.

Haney, C. (1984). On the selection of capital juries: The biasing effects of the death-qualification process. *Law and Human Behavior, 8,* 121–132.

Haney, C., Hurtado, A., & Vega, L. (1994). Modern death qualification: New data on its biasing effects. *Law and Human Behavior, 18,* 619–633.

Hans, V. P. (1992). Judgments of justice. *Psychological Science, 3,* 218–220.

Hart, M., & Secunda, P. (in press). A matter of context: Social framework evidence in employment discrimination class actions. *Fordham Law Review.*

Haw, R. M., & Fisher, R. P. (2004). Effects of administrator-witness contact on eyewitness identification accuracy. *Journal of Applied Psychology, 89,* 1106–1112.

Hedges, L. V. (1987). How hard is hard science, how soft is soft science? The empirical cumulativeness of research. *American Psychologist, 42,* 443–455.

Heilman, M. E. (1983). Sex bias in work settings: The lack of fit model. *Research and Organizational Behavior, 5,* 269–298.

Heilman, M. E. (1995). Sex stereotypes: Do they influence perceptions of managers? *Journal of Social Behavior and Personality, 10,* 237–252.

Heilman, M. E. (2001). Description and prescription: How gender stereotypes prevent women's ascent up the organizational ladder. *Journal of Social Issues, 57,* 657–674.

Heilman, M. E., & Haynes, M. C. (2008). Subjectivity in the appraisal process: A facilitator of gender bias in work settings. In E. Borgida & S. T. Fiske (Eds.), *Beyond common sense: Psychological science in the courtroom* (pp. 127–155). Malden, MA: Blackwell.

Hill, C., Memon, A., & McGeorge, P. (2008). The role of confirmation bias in suspect interviews: A systematic evaluation. *Legal and Criminological Psychology, 13,* 357–371.

Hofmann, W., Gawronski, B., Gschwendner, T., Le, H., & Schmitt, M. (2005). A meta-analysis on the correlation between the implicit association test and explicit self-report measures. *Personality and Social Psychology Bulletin, 31,* 1369–1385.

Hope, L., Memon, A., & McGeorge, P. (2004). Understanding pretrial publicity: Predecisional distortion of evidence by mock jurors. *Journal of Experimental Psychology: Applied, 10,* 111–119.

Hope, L., & Wright, D. (2007). Beyond unusual? Examining the role of attention in the weapon focus effect. *Applied Cognitive Psychology, 21,* 951–961.

Horowitz, I. A. (1980). Juror selection: A comparison of two methods in several criminal trials. *Journal of Applied Social Psychology, 10,* 86–99.

Horselenberg, R., Merckelbach, H., & Josephs, S. (2003). Individual differences and false confessions: A conceptual replication of Kassin and Kiechel (1996). *Psychology, Crime, and Law, 9,* 1–18.

Horselenberg, R., Merckelbach, H., Smeets, T., Franssens, D., Peters, G. Y., & Zeles, G. (2006). False confessions in the lab: Do plausibility and consequences matter? *Psychology, Crime, & Law, 12,* 61–75.

Huff, R., Rattner, A., & Sagarin, E. (1986). Guilty until proven innocent. *Crime and Delinquency, 32,* 518–544.

Hunt, J. S., Borgida, E., Kelly, K. A., & Burgess, D. (2002). Gender stereotyping: Scientific status. In D. Faigman, D. H. Kaye, M. J. Saks, & J. Sanders (Eds.), *Modern scientific evidence: The law and science of expert testimony* (pp. 374–426). St. Paul, MN: West Publishing Co.

Huntley, J. E., & Costanzo, M. (2003). Sexual harassment stories: Testing a story-mediate model of juror decision-making in civil litigation. *Law and Human Behavior, 27,* 29–51.

Imrich, D., Mullin, C., & Linz, D. (1995). Measuring the extent of pretrial publicity in major American newspapers: A content analysis. *Journal of Communication, 45,* 94–117.

Inbau, F. E., Reid, J. E., Buckley, J. P., & Jayne, B. C. (2001). *Criminal interrogation and confessions* (4th ed.). Gaithersburg, MD: Aspen.

Irvin v. Dowd, 366 U.S. 717 (1961).

J. E. B. v. Alabama ex rel. T. B., 114 S.Ct. 1419 (1994).

James, R. (1959). Status and competence of juries. *American Journal of Sociology, 64,* 563–570.

Jepson, C., Krantz, D. H., & Nisbett, R. E. (1983). Inductive reasoning: Competence or skill? *Behavioral and Brain Sciences, 6,* 494–501.

Johnson, C., & Haney, C. (1994). Felony *voir dire:* An exploratory study of its content and effect. *Law and Human Behavior, 18,* 487–506.

Jones, E. E. (1990). *Interpersonal perception.* New York: Freeman.

Jones, S. E. (1987). Judge- versus attorney-conducted *voir dire:* An empirical investigation or juror candor. *Law and Behavior: 11,* 131–146.

Kassin, S. M. (2005). On the psychology of confessions: Does innocence put innocents at risk? *American Psychologist, 60,* 215–228.

Kassin, S. M., & Fong, C. T. (1999). "I'm innocent!" Effects of training on judgments of truth and deception in the interrogation room. *Law and Human Behavior, 23,* 499–516.

Kassin, S. M., Goldstein, C. J., & Savitsky, K. (2003). Behavioral confirmation in the interrogation room: On the dangers of presuming guilt. *Law and Human Behavior, 27,* 187–203.

Kassin, S. M., & Gudjonsson, G. H. (2004). The psychology of confessions: A review of the literature and issues. *Psychological Science in the Public Interest, 5,* 35–69.

Kassin, S. M., & Kiechel, K. L. (1996). The social psychology of false confessions. Compliance, internalization, and confabulation. *Psychological Science, 7,* 125–128.

Kassin, S. M., Leo, R. A., Meissner, C. A., Richman, K. D., Colwell, L. H., Leach, A. M., & La Fon, D. (2007). Police interviewing and interrogation: A self-report survey of police practices and beliefs. *Law and Human Behavior, 31,* 381–400.

Kassin, S. M., & McNall, K. (1991). Police interrogations and confessions: Communicating promises and threats by pragmatic implication. *Law and Human Behavior, 15,* 233–251.

Kassin, S. M., Meissner, C. A., & Norwick, R. I. (2005). "I'd know a false confession if I saw one": A comparative study of college students and police investigators. *Law and Human Behavior, 29,* 211–227.

Kassin, S. M., & Neumann, K. (1997). On the power of confession evidence: An experimental test of the "fundamental difference" hypothesis. *Law and Human Behavior, 21,* 469–484.

Kassin, S. M., & Norwick, R. J. (2004). Why suspects waive their *Miranda* rights: The power of innocence. *Law and Human Behavior, 28,* 211–221.

Kassin, S. M., & Sukel, H. (1997). Coerced confessions and the jury: An experimental test of the "harmless error" rule. *Law and Human Behavior, 21,* 27–46.

Kassin, S. M., & Wrightsman, L. S. (1980). Prior confessions and mock juror verdicts. *Journal of Applied Social Psychology, 10,* 133–146.

Kassin, S. M., & Wrightsman, L. S. (1981). Coerced confessions, judicial instruction, and mock juror verdicts. *Journal of Applied Social Psychology, 11,* 489–506.

Kassin, S. M., & Wrightsman, L. S. (1983). The construction and validation of a juror bias scale. *Journal of Research in Personality, 17,* 423–442.

Kassin, S. M., & Wrightsman, L. S. (1985). Confession evidence. In S. M. Kassin & L. S. Wrightsman (Eds.), *The psychology of evidence and trial procedure* (pp. 67–94). Beverly Hills, CA: Sage.

Kern, R., Libkuman, T. M., & Temple, S. L. (2007). Perceptions of domestic violence and mock jurors' sentencing decisions. *Journal of Interpersonal Violence, 22,* 1515–1535.

Kerr, N. L. (1989). The effects of pretrial publicity on jurors' values. *American Courts,* 190.

Kerr, N. L., Hymes, R. W., Anderson, A. B., & Weathers, J. E. (1995). Defendant–juror similarity and mock juror judgments. *Law and Human Behavior, 19,* 545–567.

Kerr, N. L., Kramer, G. P., Carroll, J. S., & Alfini, J. J. (1991). On the effectiveness of voir dire in criminal cases with prejudicial pretrial publicity: An empirical study. *American University Law Review, 40,* 665–701.

Kerr, N. L., Niedermeier, K. E., & Kaplan, M. F. (1999). Bias in jurors vs. bias in juries: New evidence from the SDS perspective. *Organizational Behavior and Human Decision Processes, 80,* 70–86.

Klaver, J. R., Lee, Z., & Rose, V. G. (2008). Effects of personality, interrogation techniques and plausibility in an experimental false confession paradigm. *Legal and Criminological Psychology, 13,* 71–88.

Klein, O., & Snyder, M. (2003). Stereotypes and behavioral confirmation: From interpersonal to intergroup perspectives. In M. P. Zanna (Ed.), *Advances in experimental social psychology* (Vol. 35, pp. 153–234). San Diego: Academic Press.

Kline, F. G., & Jess, P. H. (1966). Prejudicial publicity: Its effects on law school mock juries. *Journalism Quarterly, 43,* 113–116.

Klobuchar, A., Steblay, N., & Caligiuri, H. (2006). Improving eyewitness identifications: Hennepin County's blind sequential lineup project. *Cardozo Public Law, Policy, and Ethics Journal, 4,* 381–413.

Koehnken, G. (1987). Training police officers to detect deceptive eyewitness statements: Does it work? *Social Behavior, 2,* 1–17.

Kovera, M. B. (2002). The effects of general pretrial publicity on juror decisions: An examination of moderators and mediating mechanisms. *Law and Human Behavior, 26,* 43–72.

Kovera, M. B., & Greathouse, S. M. (2008). Pretrial publicity: Effects, remedies and judicial knowledge. In E. Borgida and S. T. Fiske (Eds.), *Beyond common sense: Psychological science in the courtroom* (pp. 261–280). Oxford: Wiley-Blackwell.

Kovera, M. B., Gresham, A. W., Borgida, E., Gray, E., & Regan, P. C. (1997). Does expert testimony inform or influence juror decision-making? A social cognitive analysis. *Journal of Applied Psychology, 82,* 178–191.

Kovera, M. B., Levy, R. J., Borgida, E., & Penrod, S. D. (1994). Expert witnesses in child sexual abuse cases: Effects of expert testimony and cross-examination. *Law and Human Behavior, 18,* 653–674.

Kovera, M. B., & McAuliff. B. D. (2000). The effects of peer review and evidence quality on judge evaluations of psychological science: Are judges effective gatekeepers? *Journal of Applied Psychology, 85,* 574–586.

Kovera, M. B., & McAuliff, B. D. (2009). *Attorneys' evaluations of psychological science: Does evidence quality matter?* Manuscript submitted for publication.

Kovera, M. B., McAuliff, B. D., & Hebert, K. S. (1999). Reasoning about scientific evidence: Effects of juror gender and evidence quality on juror decisions in a hostile work environment case. *Journal of Applied Psychology, 84,* 362–375.

Kovera, M. B., Russano, M. B., & McAuliff, B. D. (2002). Assessment of the commonsense psychology underlying *Daubert*: Legal decision makers' abilities to evaluate expert evidence in hostile work environment cases. *Psychology, Public Policy, and Law, 8,* 180–200.

Krafka, C., & Penrod, S. (1985). Reinstatement of context in a field experiment on eyewitness identification. *Journal of Personality and Social Psychology, 49,* 58–69.

Kramer, G. P., Kerr, N. L., & Carroll, J. S. (1990). Pretrial publicity, judicial remedies, and jury bias. *Law and Human Behavior, 14,* 409–438.

Kraus, S. J. (1995). Attitudes and the prediction of behavior: A meta-analysis of the empirical literature. *Personality and Social Psychology Bulletin, 21,* 58–75.

Krauss, D. A., & Lee, D. H. (2003). Deliberating on dangerousness and death: Jurors' ability to differentiate between expert actuarial and clinical predictions of dangerousness. *International Journal of Law and Psychiatry, 26,* 113–137.

Krauss, D. A., & Sales, B. D. (2001). The effects of clinical and scientific expert testimony on juror decision making in capital sentencing. *Psychology, Public Policy, and Law, 7,* 267–310.

Kravitz, D. A., Cutler, B. L., & Brock., P. (1993). Reliability and validity of the original and revised Legal Attitudes Questionnaire. *Law and Human Behavior, 17,* 661–667.

Krieger, L., & Fiske, S. T. (2006). Behavioral realism in employment discrimination law: Implicit bias and disparate treatment. *California Law Review, 94,* 997–1062.

Kumho Tire Co. v. Carmichael, 526 U.S. 137 (1999).

Lane, K. A., Kang, J., & Banaji, M. R. (2007). Implicit social cognition and law. *Annual Review of Law and Social Science, 3,* 427–451.

Lassiter, G. D., Clark, J. K., Daniels, L. E., & Soinski, M. (2004, March). *Can we recognize false confessions and does the presentation format make a difference?* Paper presented at the annual meeting of the American Psychology-Law Society, Scottsdale, AZ.

Lassiter, G. D., Diamond, S. S., Schmidt, H. C., & Elek, J. K. (2007). Evaluating videotaped confessions: Expertise provides no defense against the camera-perspective effect. *Psychological Science, 18,* 224–226.

Lassiter, G. D., & Geers, A. L. (2004). Evaluation of confession evidence: Effects of presentation format. In G. D. Lassiter (Ed.), *Interrogations, confessions, and entrapment* (pp. 197–214). New York: Kluwer Academic.

Lassiter, G. D., Geers, A. L., Handley, I. M., Weiland, P. E., & Munhall, P. J. (2002). Videotaped confessions and interrogations: A simple change in camera perspective alters verdicts in simulated trials. *Journal of Applied Psychology, 87*, 867–874.

Lassiter, G. D., Geers, A. L., Munhall, P. J., Handley, I. M., & Beers, M. J. (2001). Videotaped confessions: Is guilt in the eye of the camera? *Advances in Experimental Social Psychology, 33*, 189–254.

Lassiter, G. D., & Irvine, A. A. (1986). Videotaped confessions: The impact of camera point of view on judgments of coercion. *Journal of Applied Social Psychology, 16*, 268–276.

Lassiter, G. D., Slaw, R. D., Briggs, M. A., & Scanlan, C. R. (1992). The potential for bias in videotaped confessions. *Journal of Applied Social Psychology, 22*, 1838–1851.

Laughery, K. R., Alexander, J. F., & Lane, A. B. (1971). Recognition of human faces: Effects of target exposure time, target position, and type of photograph. *Journal of Applied Psychology, 59*, 490–496.

Leach, A.-M., Lindsay, R. C. L., Koehler, R., Beaudry, J. L., Bala, J. C., Lee, K., & Talwar, V. (2009). The reliability of lie detection performance. *Law and Human Behavior, 33*, 96–109.

Leach, A.-M., Talwar, V., Lee, K., Bala, N., & Lindsay, R. C. L. (2004). "Intuitive" lie detection and children's deception by law enforcement officials and university students. *Law and Human Behavior, 28*, 661–685.

Lecci, L., & Myers, B. (2002). Examining the construct validity of the original and revised JBS: A cross-validation of sample and method. *Law and Human Behavior, 26*, 455–463.

Lecci, L., & Myers, B. (2008). Individual differences in attitudes relevant to juror decision making: Development and validation of the Pretrial Juror Attitude Questionnaire (PJAQ). *Journal of Applied Social Psychology, 38*, 2010–2038.

Lehman, D. R., Lempert, R. O., & Nisbett, R. E. (1988). The effects of graduate training on reasoning: Formal discipline and thinking about everyday life events. *American Psychologist, 43*, 431–443.

Leo, R. A. (1996a). The impact of *Miranda* revisited. *The Journal of Criminal Law and Criminology, 86*, 621–692.

Leo, R. A. (1996b). Inside the interrogation room. *The Journal of Criminal Law and Criminology, 86*, 266–303.

Leo, R. A. (1996c). *Miranda*'s revenge: Police interrogation as a confidence game. *Law and Society Review, 30*, 259–288.

Leo, R. A., & Ofshe, R. J. (1998). The consequences of false confessions: Deprivations of liberty and miscarriages of justice in the age of psychological interrogation. *Journal of Criminal Law and Criminology, 88*, 429–496.

LeVan, E. A. (1984). Nonverbal communication in the courtroom: Attorney beware. *Law and Psychology Review, 8*, 83–104.

Levett, L. M., & Kovera, M. B. (2008). The effectiveness of educating jurors about unreliable expert evidence using an opposing witness. *Law and Human Behavior, 32*, 363–374.

Levett, L. M., & Kovera, M. B. (2009). Psychological mediators of the effects of opposing expert testimony on juror decisions. *Psychology, Public Policy, and Law, 15*, 124–148.

Li, J. C., Dunning, D. & Malpass, R. S. (1998, March). *Cross-racial identification among European-Americans: Basketball fandom and the contact hypothesis.* Paper presented at the biennial meeting of the American Psychology-Law Society, Redondo Beach, CA.

Lindsay, R. C. L., & Wells, G. L. (1985). Improving eyewitness identification from lineups: Simultaneous versus sequential lineup presentations. *Journal of Applied Psychology, 70*, 556–564.

Lipsey, M. W., & Wilson, D. B. (2001). *Practical meta-analysis.* Thousand Oaks, CA: Sage.

Loftus, E. F., Loftus, G. R., & Messo, J. (1987). Some facts about "weapon focus." *Law and Human Behavior, 11*, 55–62.

Luus, C. A. E., & Wells, G. L. (1994). The malleability of eyewitness confidence: Co-witness and perseverance effects. *Journal of Applied Psychology, 79*, 714–723.

Maass, A., & Kohnken, G. (1989). Eyewitness identification: Simulating the "weapon effect." *Law and Human Behavior, 13*, 397–408.

Malpass, R. S., & Devine, P.G. (1981). Eyewitness identification: Lineup instructions and the absence of the offender. *Journal of Applied Psychology, 66*, 482–489.

Manson v. Braithwaite, 432 U.S. 98, 1977.

Marques, J. M., Abrams, D., Paez, D., & Martinez-Taboada, C. (1998). The role of categorization and in-group norms in judgments of groups and their members. *Journal of Personality and Social Psychology, 75*, 976–988.

Marshall, L. L., & Smith, A. (1986). The effects of demand characteristics, evaluation anxiety, and expectancy effects on juror honesty during *voir dire*. *Journal of Psychology, 120*, 205–217.

McAuliff, B. D., & Kovera, M. B. (2008). Juror need for cognition and sensitivity to methodological flaws in expert evidence. *Journal of Applied Social Psychology, 38*, 385–408.

McAuliff, B. D., Kovera, M. B., & Nunez, G. (2009). Can jurors recognize missing control groups, confounds, and experimenter bias in psychological science? *Law and Human Behavior, 33*, 247–257.

McCoy, M. L., & Gray, J. M. (2007). The impact of defendant gender and relationship to victim on juror decisions in a child sexual abuse case. *Journal of Applied Social Psychology, 37*, 1578–1593.

McQuiston-Surrett, D. E., Malpass, R. S., & Tredoux, C. G. (2006). Sequential vs. simultaneous lineups: A review of methods, data, and theory. *Psychology, Public Policy and Law, 12*, 137–169.

Mecklenburg, S. H. (2006). *Report to the legislature of the state of Illinois: The Illinois pilot program on double-blind, sequential lineup procedures.* Retrieved on June 10, 2008, from http://www.chicagopolice.org/IL%20Pilot%20on%20Eyewitness%20ID.pdf.

Mecklenburg, S. H., Bailey, P., & Larson, M. (2008). The Illinois Field Study: A significant contribution to understanding real world eyewitness identification issues. *Law and Human Behavior, 32*, 22–27.

Meissner, C. A., & Brigham, J. C. (2001). Thirty years of investigating the own race bias in memory for faces: A meta-analytic review. *Psychology, Public Policy, and Law, 7*, 3–35.

Meissner, C. A., & Kassin, S. M. (2002). "He's guilty!": Investigator bias in judgments of truth and deception. *Law and Human Behavior, 26*, 469–480.

Meissner, C. A., Tredoux, C. G., Parker, J. F., & MacLin, O. H. (2005). Eyewitness decisions in simultaneous and sequential lineups: A dual-process signal detection theory analysis. *Memory and Cognition, 33*, 783–792.

Memon, A., Hope, L., & Bull, R. (2003) Exposure duration: Effects on eyewitness accuracy and confidence, *British Journal of Psychology, 94*, 339–354.

Memon, A., Vrij, A., & Bull, R. (2003). *Psychology and law: Truthfulness, accuracy and credibility.* London: Jossey-Bass.

Miller-El v. Dretke, 545 U.S. 231 (2005).

Miranda v. Arizona, 384 U.S. 336 (1966).

Mitchell, G., & Tetlock, P. E. (2006). Antidiscrimination law and the perils of mindreading. *The Ohio State University Law Review, 67*, 1023–1122.

Monahan, J., Walker, L., & Mitchell, G. (2008). Contextual evidence of gender discrimination: The ascendance of "social frameworks." *Virginia Law Review, 94*, 1715–1749.

Moran, G., & Comfort, J. C. (1982). Scientific juror selection: Sex as a moderator of demographic and personality predictors of impaneled felony juror behavior. *Journal of Personality and Social Psychology, 43*, 1052–1063.

Moran, G., & Comfort, J. C. (1986). Neither "tentative" nor "fragmentary": Verdict preference of impaneled felony jurors as a function of attitude toward capital punishment. *Journal of Applied Psychology, 71*, 146–155.

Moran, G., & Cutler, B. L. (1991). The prejudicial impact of pretrial publicity. *Journal of Applied Social Psychology, 21*, 345–367.

Moran, G., Cutler, B. L., & De Lisa, A. (1994). Attitudes toward tort reform, scientific jury selection, and juror bias: Verdict inclination in criminal and civil trials. *Law and Psychology Review, 18*, 309–328.

Moran, G., Cutler, B. L., & Loftus, E. F. (1990). Jury selection in major controlled substance trials: The need for extended voir dire. *Forensic Reports, 3*, 331–348.

Morgan, C. A., III, Hazlett, G., Doran, A., Garrett, S., Hoyt, G., Thomas, P., Baranoski, M., & Southwick, S. M. (2004). Accuracy of eyewitness memory for persons encountered during exposure to highly intense stress. *International Journal of the Law and Psychiatry, 27*, 265–279.

Munsterberg, H. (1908). *On the witness stand.* New York: Doubleday, Page & Co.

Myers, B., & Lecci, L. (1998). Revising the factor structure of the Juror Bias Scale: A method for the empirical evaluation of theoretical constructs. *Law and Human Behavior, 22*, 239–256.

Narby, D. J., & Cutler, B. L. (1994). Effectiveness of *voir dire* as a safeguard in eyewitness cases. *Journal of Applied Psychology, 79*, 724–729.

Narby, D. J., Cutler, B. L., & Moran, G. (1993). A meta-analysis of the association between authoritarianism and jurors' perceptions of defendant culpability. *Journal of Applied Psychology, 78*, 34–42.

Ng, W., & Lindsay, R. C. L. (1994). Cross-race facial recognition. *Journal of Cross-Cultural Psychology, 2*, 217–232.

Nietzel, M. T., & Dillehay, R. C. (1983). Psychologists as consultants for changes in venue. *Law and Human Behavior, 7*, 309–355.

Nietzel, M. T., & Dillehay, R. C. (1986). *Psychological consultation in the courtroom.* New York: Pergamon Press.

Nietzel, M. T., McCarthy, D. M., & Kern, M. J. (1999). Juries: The current state of the empirical literature. In R. Roesch, S. D. Hart, & J. R. P. Ogloff (Eds.), *Psychology and law: The state of the discipline* (pp. 23–52). Dordrecht, Netherlands: Kluwer Academic.

Nisbett, R. E. (1993). *Rules for reasoning.* Hillsdale, NJ: Erlbaum.

Nisbett, R. E., Fong, G. T., Lehman, D. R., & Cheng, P. W. (1987). Teaching reasoning. *Science, 238*, 625–631.

Nisbett, R. E., & Wilson, T. D. (1977). Telling more than we can know: Verbal reports on mental processes. *Psychology Review, 84*, 231–259.

Oberlander, L. B., & Goldstein, N. E. A review and update on the practice of evaluating *Miranda* comprehension. *Behavioral Sciences and the Law, 19*, 453–471.

O'Connell, M. J., Garmoe, W., & Goldstein, N. E. S. (2005). *Miranda* comprehension in adults with mental retardation and the effects of feedback style on suggestibility. *Law and Human Behavior, 29*, 359–369.

O'Connor, M., Gutek, B. A., Stockdale, M., Geer, T. M., & Melançon, R. (2004). Explaining sexual harassment judgments: Looking beyond gender of the rater. *Law and Human Behavior, 28*, 69–95.

Ogloff, J. R. P., & Vidmar, N. (1994). The impact of pretrial publicity on jurors. A study to compare the relative effects of television and print media in a child sex abuse case. *Law and Human Behavior, 18*, 507–525.

Olczak, P. V., Kaplan, M. F., & Penrod, S. (1991). Attorney's lay psychology and its effectiveness in selecting jurors: Three empirical studies. *Journal of Social Behavior and Personality, 6*, 431–452.

O'Neil, K. M., Patry, M. W., & Penrod, S. D. (2004). Exploring the effects of attitudes toward the death penalty on capital sentencing verdicts. *Psychology, Public Policy, and Law, 10*, 443–470.

O'Rourke, T. E., Penrod, S. D., Cutler, B. L., & Stuve, T. E. (1989). The external validity of eyewitness identification research: Generalizing across subject populations. *Law and Human Behavior, 13*, 385–395.

O'Sullivan, M. (2005). Emotional intelligence and deception detection: Why most people can't "read" others, but a few can. In R. E. Riggio & R. S. Feldman (Eds.), *Applications of nonverbal communication* (pp. 215–253). Mahwah, NJ: Erlbaum.

O'Sullivan, M. (2007). Unicorns or Tiger Woods: Are lie detection experts myths or rarities? A response to "On lie detection 'Wizards'" by Bond and Uysal. *Law and Human Behavior, 31*, 117–123.

Otto, A. L., Penrod, S., & Dexter, H. R. (1994). The biasing effects of pretrial publicity on juror judgments. *Law and Human Behavior, 18*, 453–469.

Page, A. (2005). Batson's blind-spot: Unconscious stereotyping and the peremptory challenge. *Boston University Law Review, 85*, 155.

People v. Brnja, 70 A.D.2d 17, 419 N.Y.S.2d 591 (1979), aff'd, 50 N.Y.2d 366, 406 N.E.2d 1066, 429 N.Y.S.2d 173 (1980).

Phares, E. J., & Wilson, K. G. (1972). Responsibility attribution: Role of outcome severity, situational ambiguity, and internal-external control. *Journal of Personality, 40*, 392–406.

Phillips, M. R., McAuliff, B. D., Kovera, M. B., & Cutler, B. L. (1999). Double-blind photoarray administration as a safeguard against investigator bias. *Journal of Applied Psychology, 84*, 940–951.

Pickel, K. L. (1998). Unusualness and threat as possible causes of the "weapon focus." *Memory, 6*, 277–295.

Pickel, K. L. (1999). The influence of context on the "weapon focus" effect. *Law and Human Behavior, 23*, 299–311.

Pickel, K. L., Narter, D. B., Jameson, M. M., & Lenhardt, T. T. (2008). The weapon focus effect in child eyewitnesses. *Psychology, Crime, & Law, 14*, 61–72.

Pigott, M. A., Brigham, J. C., & Bothwell, R. K. (1990). A field study of the relationship between quality of eyewitnesses' descriptions and identification accuracy. *Journal of Police Science and Administration, 17*, 84–88.

Platz, S. J., & Hosch, H. M. (1988). Cross-racial/ethnic eyewitness identification: A field study. *Journal of Applied Social Psychology, 18*, 972–984.

Porter, S., Woodworth, M., & Birt, A. R. (2000). Truth, lies, and videotape: An investigation of the ability of federal parole officers to detect deception. *Law and Human Behavior, 24*, 643–658.

Posey, A. J., & Dahl, L. M. (2002). Beyond pretrial publicity: Legal and ethical issues associated with change of venue surveys. *Law and Human Behavior, 26*. 107–125.

Pronin, E., Gilovich, T., Ross, L. (2004). Objectivity in the eye of the beholder: Divergent perceptions of bias in self versus others. *Psychological Review, 111*, 781–799.

Py, J., DeMarchi, S, Ginet, M., & Wasiak, L. (2003). *"Who is the suspect?" A complementary instruction to the standard mock witness paradigm.* Paper presented at the American Psychology-Law Society and European Association of Psychology and Law 2003 Conference, Edinburgh.

Quas, J. A., Bottoms, B. L., Haegerich, T. M., & Nysse-Carris, K L. (2002). Effects of victim, defendant, and juror gender on decisions in child sexual assault cases. *Journal of Applied Social Psychology, 32*, 1993–2021.

Ratcliff, J. J., Lassiter, G. D., Schmidt, H. C., & Snyder, C. J. (2006). Camera perspective bias in videotaped confessions: Experimental evidence of its perceptual basis. *Journal of Experimental Psychology, 12*, 197–206.

Rattner, A. (1988). Convicted but innocent. *Law and Human Behavior, 12*, 283–294.

Read, J. D. (1995). The availability heuristic in person identification: The sometimes misleading consequences of enhanced contextual information. *Applied Cognitive Psychology, 9*, 91–122.

Read, J. D., Tollestrup, P., Hammersley, R., McFadzen, E., & Christensen, A. (1990). The unconscious transference effect: Are innocent bystanders ever misidentified? *Applied Cognitive Psychology, 4*, 3–31.

Redding, R. E., & Reppucci, N. D. (1999). Effects of lawyers' socio-political attitudes on their judgments of social science in legal decision making. *Law and Human Behavior, 23*, 31–54.

Redlich, A. D., & Goodman, G. S. (2003). Taking responsibility for an act not committed: The influence of age and suggestibility. *Law and Human Behavior, 27*,141–156.

Reifman, A., Gusick, S. M., & Ellsworth, P. C. (1992). Real jurors' understanding of the law in real cases. *Law and Human Behavior, 16*, 539–554.

Rideau v. Louisiana, 373 U.S. 723 (1963).

Rogers, R., Harrison, K. S., Shuman, D. W., Sewell, K. W., & Hazelwood, L. L. (2007). An analysis of *Miranda* warnings and waivers: Comprehension and coverage. *Law and Human Behavior, 31*, 177–192.

Rogers, R., Hazelwood, L. L., Sewell, K. W., Shuman, D. W., & Blackwood, H. L. (2008). The comprehensibility and content of juvenile *Miranda* warnings. *Psychology, Public Policy, and Law, 14*, 63–87.

Rogers, R., Jordan, M. J., & Harrison, K. S. (2004). A critical review of published competency-to-confess measures. *Law and Human Behavior, 28*, 707–718.

Rose, M. R. (1999). The peremptory challenge accused of race or gender discrimination? Some data from one county. *Law and Human Behavior, 23*, 695–702.

Rosenthal, R. (2002). Covert communication in classrooms, clinics, courtrooms, and cubicles. *American Psychologist, 57*, 839–849.

Ross, L. (1977). The intuitive psychologist and his shortcomings: Distortions in the attribution process. *Advances in Experimental Social Psychology, 10*, 174–221.

Ross, S. J., & Malpass, R. M. (2008). Moving forward: Responses to "Studying eyewitness investigations in the field." *Law and Human Behavior, 32*, 16–21.

Russano, M. B., Dickinson, J. J., Greathouse, S. M., & Kovera, M. B. (2006). "Why don't you take another look at number three?" Investigator knowledge and its effects on eyewitness confidence and identification decisions. *Cardozo Public Law, Policy, and Ethics Journal, 4*, 355–379,

Russano, M. B., Meissner, C. A., Narchet, F. M., & Kassin, S. M. (2005). Investigating true and false confessions within a novel experimental paradigm. *Psychological Science, 16*, 481–486.

Ruva, C. L., & McEvoy, C. (2008). Negative and positive pretrial publicity affect juror memory and decision making. *Journal of Experimental Psychology: Applied, 14*, 226–235.

Ruva, C. L., McEvoy, C., & Bryant, J. B. (2007). Effects of pre-trial publicity and jury deliberation on juror bias and source memory errors. *Applied Cognitive Psychology, 21*, 45–67.

Saks, M. J., & Faigman, D.L. (2005). Expert evidence after *Daubert*. *Annual Review of Law and Social Science, 1*, 105–30.

Schacter, D., Dawes, R., Jacoby, L. L., Kahneman, D., Lempert, R., Roediger, H. L., & Rosenthal, R. (2008). Policy forum: Studying eyewitness investigations in the field. *Law and Human Behavior, 32*, 3–5.

Scheck, B., Neufeld, P., & Dwyer, W. (2000). *Actual innocence*. New York: Harper.

Schklar, J., & Diamond, S. S. (1999). Juror reactions to DNA evidence: Errors and expectancies. *Law and Human Behavior, 23*, 159–184.

Schmechel, R. S., O'Toole, T. P., Easterly, C. & Loftus, E. F. (2006) Beyond the ken: Testing jurors' understanding of eyewitness reliability evidence. *Jurimetrics Journal, 46*, 177–214.

Schmidt, F. L., & Hunter, J. (2004). *Methods of meta-analysis: Correcting error and bias in research findings*. Thousand Oaks, CA: Sage.

Schuller, R. A. (1992). The impact of battered woman syndrome evidence on jury decision processes. *Law and Human Behavior, 16*, 597–620.

Schuller, R. A. & Hastings, P. A. (1996). Trials of battered women who kill: The impact of alternative forms of expert testimony. *Law and Human Behavior, 2*, 167–188.

Schulman, J., Shaver, P., Colman, R., Emrich, B., & Christie, R. (1973, May). Recipe for a jury. *Psychology Today*, 37–84.

Seltzer, R. O. (2006). Scientific jury selection: Does it work? *Journal of Applied Social Psychology, 36*, 2417–2435.

Shapiro, P., & Penrod, S.D. (1986). A meta-analysis of the facial identification literature. *Psychological Bulletin, 100*, 139, 156.

Sheppard v. Maxwell, 384 U.S. 333, 362 (1966).

Shuman, D. W., Whitaker, E., & Champagne, A. (1994). An empirical examination of the use of expert witnesses in the courts—Part two: A three city study. *Jurimetrics Journal of Law, Science and Technology, 34*, 193–208.

Simon, R. J. (1966). Murder, juries, and the press. *Transaction, 3*, 40–42.

Simon, R. J. (1967). *The jury and the defense of insanity*. Boston: Little, Brown.

Simon, R. J., & Eimermann, R. (1971). The jury finds not guilty: Another look at media influence on the jury. *Journalism Quarterly, 66*, 427–434.

Singletary v. United States, 383 A.2d 1064 (D.C. 1978).

Skeem, J. L., Louden, J. E., & Evans, J. (2004). Venirepersons' attitudes toward the insanity defense: Developing, refining, and validating a scale. *Law and Human Behavior, 28*, 623–648.

Smith, B. C., Penrod, S. D., Otto, A. L., & Park, R. C. (1996). Jurors' use of probabilistic evidence. *Law and Human Behavior, 20*, 49–82.

Snyder, M. (1992). Motivational foundations of behavioral confirmation. *Advances in Experimental Social Psychology, 25*, 67–114.

Snyder, M., & Klein, O. (2005). Construing and constructing others: On the reality and the generality of the behavioral confirmation scenario. *Interaction Studies, 6*, 53–67.

Snyder, M., & Stukas, A. (1999). Interpersonal processes: The interplay of cognitive, motivational, and behavioral activities in social interaction. *Annual Review of Psychology, 50*, 273–303.

Snyder, M., & Swann, W. B., Jr. (1978). Hypothesis-testing processes in social interaction. *Journal of Personality and Social Psychology, 36*, 1202–1212.

Snyder, M., Tanke, E. D., & Berscheid, E. (1977). Social perception and interpersonal behavior: On the self-fulfilling nature of social stereotypes. *Journal of Experimental Social Psychology, 35*, 656–666.

Snyder v. Louisiana, 128 S. Ct. 1203 (2008).

Sommers, S. R. (2006). On racial diversity and group decision making: Identifying multiple effects of racial composition on jury deliberations. *Journal of Personality and Social Psychology, 90*, 597–612.

Sommers, S. R., & Norton, M. I. (2007). Race-based judgments, race-neutral justifications: Experimental examination of peremptory use and the Batson challenge procedure. *Law and Human Behavior, 31*, 261–273.

Sommers, S. R., & Norton, M. I. (2008). Race and jury selection: Psychological perspectives on the peremptory challenge debate. *American Psychologist, 63*, 527–539.

Sporer, S. L., Penrod, S., Read, D., & Cutler, B. (1995). Choosing, confidence, and accuracy: A meta-analysis of the confidence-accuracy relation in eyewitness identification studies. *Psychological Bulletin, 118*, 315–327.

State v. Snyder, 942 So. 2d 484, 500 (La. 2006).

Steblay, N. M. (1992). A meta-analytic review of the weapon focus effect. *Law and Human Behavior, 16*, 413–424.

Steblay, N. M. (1997). Social influences in eyewitness recall: A meta-analytic review of lineup instruction effects. *Law & Human Behavior, 21*, 283–297.

Steblay, N. M. (2008). Commentary on "Studying eyewitness investigations in the field": A look forward. *Law and Human Behavior, 32,* 11–15.

Steblay, N., Besirevic, J., Fulero, S., & Jimenez-Lorente, B. (1999). The effects of pretrial publicity on jury verdicts: A meta-analytic review. *Law and Human Behavior, 23,* 219–235.

Steblay, N. M., Dysart, J., Fulero, S., & Lindsay, R. C. L. (2001). Eyewitness accuracy rates in sequential and simultaneous line-up presentations: A meta-analytic comparison. *Law and Human Behavior, 25,* 459–474.

Steblay, N. M., Dysart, J., Fulero, S., & Lindsay, R. C. L. (2003). Eyewitness accuracy rates in police showup and lineup presentations: A meta-analytic comparison. *Law and Human Behavior, 27,* 523–540.

Steblay, N., Hosch, H. M., Culhane, S. E., & McWethy, A. (2006). The impact on juror verdicts of judicial instruction to disregard inadmissible evidence: A meta-analysis. *Law and Human Behavior, 30,* 469–492.

Strawn, D. J., & Buchanan, R. W. (1976). Jury confusion: A threat to justice. *Judicature, 59,* 478–483.

Studebaker, C. A., & Penrod, S. D. (1997). Pretrial publicity: The media, the law, and common sense. *Psychology, Public Policy, and Law, 3,* 428–460.

Studebaker, C. A., & Penrod, S. D. (2005). Pretrial publicity and its influence on juror decision making. In N. Brewer & K. D. Williams, *Psychology and law: An empirical perspective* (pp. 254–275). New York: Guilford Press.

Studebaker, C. A., Robbennolt, J. L., Pathak-Sharma, M. K., & Penrod, S. D. (2000). Assessing pretrial publicity effects: Integrating content analytic results. *Law and Human Behavior, 24,* 317–336.

Sue, S., Smith, R., & Gilbert, R. (1974). Biasing effects of pretrial publicity on judicial decisions. *Journal of Criminal Justice, 2,* 163–171.

Sue, S., Smith, R. E., & Pedroza, G. (1975). Authoritarianism, pretrial publicity and awareness of bias in simulated jurors. *Psychological Reports, 37,* 1299–1302.

Susa, K. J., & Meissner, C. A. (2008). Eyewitness descriptions, accuracy of. In B. L. Cutler (Ed.), *Encyclopedia of Psychology and Law.* Thousand Oaks, CA: Sage.

Tetlock, P. E., & Mitchell, P. G. (in press). Implicit bias and accountability systems: What must organizations do to prevent discrimination? *Research in Organizational Behavior.*

Thompson, W. C., Cowan, C. L., Ellsworth, P. C., & Harrington, J. C. (1984). Death penalty attitudes and conviction proneness. *Law and Human Behavior, 8,* 95–113.

Thompson, W. C., & Schumann, E. L. (1987). Interpretation of evidence in criminal trials: The prosecutor's fallacy and the defense attorney's fallacy. *Law and Human Behavior, 11,* 167–187.

Tollestrup, P., Turtle, J., & Yuille, J. (1994). Actual victims and witnesses to robbery and fraud: An archival analysis. In D. F. Ross, J. D. Read, & M. P. Toglia (Eds.), *Adult eyewitness testimony: Current trends and developments* (pp. 144–160). New York: Cambridge University Press.

Tversky, A., & Kahneman, D. (1974, September). Judgment under uncertainty: Heuristics and biases. *Science, 185,* 1124–1131.

Tyler, T. R. (2001). *Social justice.* In R. Brown & S. Gaertner (Eds.), *Blackwell handbook of social psychology. Volume 4: Intergroup processes* (pp. 344–366). London: Blackwell.

Tyler, T. R., & Smith, H. (1997). *Social justice and social movements.* In D. Gilbert, S. Fiske, & G. Lindzey (Eds.), *Handbook of social psychology* (4th ed., Vol. 2, pp. 595–629). New York: McGraw-Hill.

United States v. Telfaire, 1978 469 F.2d 552, 558–59.

Valentine, T., & Heaton, P. (1999). An evaluation of the fairness of police line-ups and video identifications. *Applied Cognitive Psychology, 13,* S59–S72.

Valentine, T., Pickering, A., & Darling, S. (2003). Characteristics of eyewitness identifications that predict the outcome of real lineups. *Applied Cognitive Psychology, 17,* 969–993.

Vidmar, N., & Judson, J. (1981). The use of social sciences in a change of venue application. *Canadian Bar Review, 59,* 76–102.

Viljoen, J. L., Klaver, J., & Roesch, R. (2005). Legal decisions of pre-adolescent and adolescent defendants: Predictors of confessions, pleas, communication with attorneys, and appeals. *Law and Human Behavior, 29,* 253–277.

Viljoen, J. L., & Roesch, R. (2005). Competence to waive interrogation rights and adjudicative competence in adolescent defendants: Cognitive development, attorney contact, and psychological symptoms. *Law and Human Behavior, 29,* 723–742.

Viljoen, J. L., Zapf, P. A., & Roesch, R. (2007). Adjudicative competence and comprehension of *Miranda* rights in adolescent defendants: A comparison of legal standards. *Behavioral Sciences & the Law, 25,* 1–19.

Vinson, K. V., Costanzo, M. A., & Berger, D. E. (2008). Predictors of verdict and punitive damages in high-stakes civil litigation. *Behavioral Sciences and the Law, 26,* 167–186.

Vrij, A. (1994). The impact of information and setting on detection of deception by police detectives. *Journal of Nonverbal Behavior, 18,* 117–132.

Vrij, A. (2000). *Detecting lies and deceit: The psychology of lying and the implications for professional practice.* London: Wiley.

Wainwright v. Witt, 469 U.S. 412 d 841 (1985).

Ware, L. J., Lassiter, G. D., Patterson, S. M., & Ransom, M. R. (2008). Camera perspective bias in videotaped confessions: Evidence that visual attention is a mediator. *Journal of Experimental Psychology: Applied, 14,* 192–200.

Wax, A. L. (2008). The discriminating mind: Define it, prove it. *Connecticut Law Review, 40,* 979–1020.

Wayne, J. H., Riordan, C. M., & Thomas, K. M. (2001). Is all sexual harassment viewed the same? Mock juror decisions in same- and cross-gender cases. *Journal of Applied Psychology, 86,* 179–187.

Weber, N., Brewer, N., Wells, G. L., Semmler, C., & Keast, A. (2004). Eyewitness identification accuracy and response latency: The unruly 10–12 second rule. *Journal of Experimental Psychology: Applied, 10,* 139–147.

Wells, G. L. (1978). Applied eyewitness-testimony research: System variables and estimator variables. *Journal of Personality and Social Psychology, 36,* 1546–1557.

Wells, G. L. (2003). Murder, extramarital affairs, and the issue of probative value. *Law and Human Behavior, 27,* 623–627.

Wells, G. L. (2008). Field experiments on eyewitness identification: Towards a better understanding of pitfalls and prospects. *Law and Human Behavior, 32,* 6–10.

Wells, G. L., & Bradfield, A. L. (1999). Measuring the goodness of lineups: Parameter estimation, question effects, and limits to the mock witness paradigm. *Applied Cognitive Psychology, 13,* S27–S39.

Wells, G. L., & Luus, E. (1990). Police lineups as experiments: Social methodology as a framework for properly-conducted lineups. *Personality and Social Psychology Bulletin, 16,* 106–117.

Wells, G. L., & Quinlivan, D. S. (2009). Suggestive eyewitness identification procedures and the Supreme Court's reliability test in light of eyewitness science: 30 years later. *Law and Human Behavior, 33,* 1–24.

Wells, G. L., Rydell, S. M., & Seelau, E. P. (1993). On the selection of distracters for eyewitness lineups. *Journal of Applied Psychology, 78,* 835–844.

Wells, G. L., Small, M., Penrod, S., Malpass, R. S., Fulero, S. M., & Brimacombe, C. A. E. (1998). Eyewitness identification procedures: Recommendations for lineups and photospreads. *Law and Human Behavior, 22,* 1–39.

Wenger, A. A., & Bornstein, B. H. (2006). The effects of victim's substance use and relationship closeness on mock jurors' judgments in an acquaintance rape case. *Sex Roles, 54,* 547–555.

Wiener, R. L., Watts, B. A., Goldkamp, K. H., & Gasper, C. (1995). Social analytic investigation of hostile work environments: A test of the reasonable woman standard. *Law and Human Behavior, 19*, 263–281.

Witherspoon v. Illinois, 391 U.S. 510 (1968).

Wright, D. B., & Skagerberg, E. M. (2007). Post-identification feedback affects real eyewitnesses. *Psychological Science, 18*, 172–178.

Wogalter, M. S., Malpass, R. S., & McQuiston, D. E. (2004). A national survey of police on preparation and conduct of identification lineups. *Psychology, Crime and Law, 10*, 69–82.

Wyer, R. S., & Budesheim, T. L. (1987). Person memory and judgments: The impact of information that one is told to disregard. *Journal of Personality and Social Psychology, 53*, 14–29.

Wyer, R. S., & Unverzagt, W. H. (1985). Effects of instructions to disregard information on its subsequent recall and use in making judgments. *Journal of Personality and Social Psychology, 48*, 533–549.

Yarmey, A. D., Yarmey, M. J., & Yarmey, A. L. (2006). Accuracy of eyewitness identifications in showups and lineups. *Law and Human Behavior, 20*, 459–477.

Zeisel, H., & Diamond, S. S. (1978). The effect of peremptory challenges on jury and verdict: An experiment in a federal district court. *Stanford Law Review, 30*, 491–531.

Zuckerman, M., DePaulo, B. M., & Rosenthal, R. (1981). Verbal and nonverbal communication of deception. *Advances in Experimental Social Psychology, 14*, 1–59.

Zuckerman, M., Koestner, R., & Alton, A.O. (1984). Learning to detect deception. *Journal of Personality and Social Psychology, 46*, 519–528.

Chapter 36

Social Psychology and Language

Words, Utterances, and Conversations

THOMAS HOLTGRAVES

Words matter. So much so that politicians constantly battle to secure the linguistic high ground, to control the language of a debate, and hence to frame the manner in which issues are considered. The importance of language is not limited to politics, of course. In fact, language pervades so many social activities that it is easy to overlook its importance. Historically, the field of social psychology has recognized this. Early theorists such as G. H. Mead made language central to their theories, and every version of the *Handbook of Social Psychology* has had a chapter devoted to the topic. Yet this interest has generally not resulted in a comparable empirical payoff. There are important exceptions, of course, and social psychological interest in language has waxed and waned over the years; currently it seems to be waxing.

Language is an extremely complex phenomenon that can be viewed at multiple levels. At its heart, however, it is social, and it is social in multiple ways. The acquisition of a first language, for example, requires other people (no one has yet acquired an initial language on their own), and it is with other people that language is typically used. Hence, the development and use of language are embedded within social and cultural systems, and because of this, the social psychological antecedents and consequences of language are extensive. The structure I use for this chapter is an old one, a traditional means of discussing language in terms of its constituent parts, in this case, words, sentences/utterances, and conversations. This is arbitrary, of course; word meaning is dependent on the sentence of which it is a part, just as sentence meaning often cannot be determined apart from the conversation within which it occurs. Hence this structure should be viewed largely as an analytic convenience.

WORDS

Words are the smallest meaningful unit of language and the building blocks of sentences, utterances, conversations, novels, and so on. Children begin acquiring words early and quickly. Although estimates vary, on average a 2-year-old actively produces and comprehends 500 words and a 5-year-old up to 3,000 words (Aitchison, 2003). Although humans may have a natural capacity to acquire words (e.g., Pinker, 1994), they are acquired in context and for specific, communicative purposes (Clark & Clark, 1977; Vygotsky, 1962). From the beginning, words are tools that are designed to alter the world in some way.

Words can function as tools because there is some consensus among language users regarding their meaning. This type of word meaning is explicit and is essentially the intended sense and reference of a word. In addition, words can have important social–cognitive consequences beyond their explicit meaning and "can trigger extralinguistic behaviors independently of the language symbols' referential meaning" (Fiedler, 2008, p. 41). Such automatic reactions have been demonstrated many times with various priming procedures. Hence, the presentation of a word can activate associate representations that influence how quickly a subsequent word is recognized (Neely, 1977), an effect that can occur even when participants are not able to recognize consciously the presented word (Marcel, 1983). Particularly relevant for social psychology is the manner in which words can prime person categories and hence influence subsequent judgments about people (Srull & Wyer, 1979) or directly activate particular social behaviors (Bargh, Chen, & Burrows, 1996; Dijksterhuis & van Knippenberg, 1998).

The writing of this chapter was supported by a sabbatical leave from Ball State University.

The social–cognitive consequences of words are not limited to simple associations. There is, in fact, a relatively rich history of social psychological interest in the implicit social information that can be encoded in words. For example, Heider's (1958) classic *The Psychology of Interpersonal Relations* involved a detailed conceptual analysis of the properties of common verbs such as "can," "try," and "want," an attempt to discover and elucidate the social concepts underlying these words and the relationships existing between them. Similarly, Allport's (1954) *The Nature of Prejudice* placed considerable weight on language as a primary mode for the expression and transmission of prejudice. Allport outlined a variety of ways in which prejudice is linguistically manifested, and his analysis of stereotypes pointed to the directive function of language in "building fences for our mental categories and our emotional responses" (p. 289).

Implicit Causality

More sustained, systematic investigations of implicit lexical information began in the 1960s when Robert Abelson and others (Abelson & Kanouse, 1966; Gilson & Abelson, 1965; Kanouse, 1972) reported on some of the inferential properties of verbs. Most notable was their discovery that certain verbs functioned as implicit quantifiers, thereby implicitly specifying the object class to which they applied. They made a basic contrast between manifest verbs such as "like," verbs that implicitly apply to a relatively large number of objects, and subjective verbs such as "buy" that implicitly apply to a much smaller number. So, the sentence "Helen likes movies" implies that Helen likes most movies, but the sentence "Helen buys movies" implies that she buys only a subset (a few) of all available movies.

One of the features of verbs noted by Abelson and colleagues was their implicit causality, and it is this feature of verbs that prompted a fair amount of sustained empirical attention. Early research on implicit causality was provided by Garvey and Caramazza (1974), but it was R. Brown and Fish (1983) who were responsible for initiating much of the interest in this phenomena. In general, implicit causality refers to a tendency for interpersonal verbs to imply a particular causal focus (see Table 36.1). For action verbs such as "help," people are more likely to assign greater causal weight to the agent (the person performing the action) than to the patient (the person who is the recipient of the action). For state verbs such as "like," people tend to assign greater causal weight to the person who brings about the state (the stimulus) rather than the person who experiences the state (the experiencer). So, on hearing that "Bob helped Tom," people are more likely to believe that Bob is the cause of the helping rather than Tom, whereas on hearing that "Bob likes Tom," people are likely to judge Tom as more responsible for the liking than Bob.

It is important to note that implicit causality represents a bias because definitions of interpersonal verbs are neutral with respect to their causal focus. For example, there is nothing inherent in the meaning of the verb "help" specifying the agent as causally responsible. It could be, for example, that Tom (the patient) is a particularly needy person, and it is this neediness that causes Bob to help rather than anything about Bob per se. It is also important to note that this is not a grammatical effect; the agent is assigned greater causal weight regardless of whether it is the grammatical subject or object (although see Rudolph & Forsterling, 1997).

The most common method for investigating implicit causality has been to present participants with minimal sentences (e.g., Ted helped Joe) and ask them to indicate whether this occurred because of something about the subject (Ted) or something about the object (Joe). With these and related tasks, the research has generally supported the implicit causality predictions for state verbs (stimulus attributions are far more likely than experiencer attributions; e.g., Au, 1986; R. Brown & Fish, 1983; Corrigan, 1988; Hoffman & Tchir, 1990). The results for action verbs have generally been in line with predictions, although some contradictory findings have been reported by

Table 36.1   Categories and Examples From the Linguistic Category (Semin & Fiedler, 1988) and Implicit Causality (Brown & Fish, 1983) Models

Implicit Causality Model	Linguistic Category Model	Example
Action Verb	Descriptive action verb	Hit
	Interpretation action verb	Hurt
(State) stimulus–experiencer	State action verb	Anger
(State) experiencer–stimulus	State verb	Hate
	Adjective	Aggressive
	Noun	Assassin

Note: Categories are ordered in terms of increasing abstractness.

Au (1986); Van Kleek, Hillger, and Brown (1988); and others. These contradictory results appear to be explained if action verbs are subdivided according to whether the action was initiated by the agent or was a response to something in the environment (primarily the other person). A distinction along these lines was made by Heider (1958) and has been adopted by many researchers working in this area (e.g., Au, 1986; Corrigan, 1993; Rudolph & Fosterling, 1997). For action verbs that are evoked, the tendency is to assign greater causal weight to the patient; for action verbs that are not reactions, it is usually the agent that is the perceived causal locus.

There has been some debate about the mechanisms underlying implicit causality, a debate that mirrors some of the issues surrounding the Whorfian hypothesis (to be discussed later in the chapter). One possibility (termed the *lexical hypothesis* by R. Brown and Fish, 1983) is that interpersonal verbs have associated dispositional terms that parallel the causal reasoning tendencies for these verbs. For example, most of the associated dispositional terms for action verbs reference the agent rather than the patient (e.g., help → helpful), thereby mirroring the tendency to perceive the agent rather than patient as the causal locus. In an extensive analysis of approximately 900 English interpersonal verbs, Hoffman and Tchir (1990) found that more than 90% of action verbs had dispositional terms referencing the agent, and only 25% of the terms referenced the patient. For state verbs, more than 75% had terms referencing the stimulus and fewer than 50% referencing the experiencer. Moreover, there is experimental evidence suggesting that implicit causality effects are larger for verbs that possess associated dispositional terms (Hoffman & Tchir, 1990; Holtgraves & Raymond, 1995; but see Rudolph & Fosterling, 1997). This view, then, suggests that a particular feature of language (the asymmetrical distribution of dispositional terms for interpersonal verbs) plays a role in our perceptions of causality.

An alternative view (termed the *covariation hypothesis*) is that people have primitive schemas for thinking about interpersonal causality, and it is these schemas (e.g., agents are causally responsible) that have resulted in the development of an asymmetrical distribution of dispositional terms (R. Brown & Fish, 1983). These schemas are presumed to reflect reality. Specifically, emotional states (e.g., like, hate, etc.) are assumed to be experienced by all humans; it is part of the biological makeup of the species. Hence, if a stimulus elicits an emotional state in one person, the same state should tend to be elicited in others (high consensus). Because the state covaries with the entity and not the experiencer, it is the former rather than the latter that is presumed to be causally responsible. There is support for this view in so far as ratings of consensus and distinctiveness

vary systematically over verb type, and when judgments of consensus and distinctiveness are treated as covariates, the effect of verb type on judgments of causality are no longer significant (R. Brown & Fish, 1983; Hoffman & Tchir, 1990; Rudolph & Fosterling, 1997; see also McArthur, 1972).

To a certain extent, these two explanations are not mutually exclusive. A tendency to perceive agents as responsible (the covariation hypothesis) may influence the development of the lexicon such that there are more dispositional terms referencing agents rather than patients. However, the existence of this linguistic asymmetry may also influence the thought processes of language users when they use language on a particular occasion (the lexical hypothesis). In addition, which of these two mechanisms operates may depend on the specific judgments that participants are asked to make. For example, Semin and Marsman (1994) demonstrated that if participants are asked to make dispositional inferences, then the lexical hypothesis receives support; participants are more likely to make dispositional inferences as a function of whether there is an associated dispositional term for the verb. In contrast, if participants are asked to make judgments of causality, then the existence of the dispositional term has relatively little effect on these judgments.

Linguistic Abstractness

A conceptually similar approach—termed the Linguistic Category Model—was advanced by Gun Semin and Klaus Fiedler in the late 1980s (Semin & Fiedler, 1988, 1991). This model has been particularly popular and today remains a vibrant area of research (e.g., see special issue of *Journal of Language and Social Psychology*, Sutton & Douglas, 2008). Their approach extended work in this area by documenting additional implicit dimensions of words and doing so with syntactic categories in addition to verbs. They proposed that verbs and adjectives (and later, nouns) are linguistic categories that can be ordered on a continuum of linguistic abstractness (see Table 36.1). At one end of this continuum are descriptive action verbs (e.g., "talk"), verbs that are concrete and relatively easy to verify. Somewhat more abstract are interpretive action verbs such as "help," words that are subject to greater observer disagreement; it is less easy to identify a behavior as constituting help than a behavior as constituting talk. The continuum then continues with state action verbs (e.g., "surprise"), followed by state verbs (e.g., "like"), and finally adjectives (e.g., "honest"). Because they represent internal states, state verbs are less observable—and hence less verifiable and agreed on—than action verbs. State verbs are also more enduring than state action verbs and hence more abstract and revealing about the person (an internal reaction that persists reveals more of an actor than one that is a momentary reaction to an event). Relative to verbs, adjectives (e.g., "honest") are more abstract (they are not tied to a specific behavior) and reveal more about the person being described. Relatedly, they are less objective and verifiable than verbs. Recently, it has been argued that the model should be expanded to include nouns, a category that is more abstract than adjectives (Carnaghi et al., 2008).

The same interpersonal event or person can be described at varying levels of abstraction, and the level of linguistic abstractness can have important psychological antecedents and consequences. Foremost in this regard has been the Linguistic Intergroup Bias (LIB), a phenomenon that captures the role of linguistic abstractness in stereotyping. The LIB, first documented by Maass, Salvi, Arcuri, and Semin (1989), refers to a tendency to use differing levels of abstraction when describing the positive and negative actions of ingroup and outgroup members. In experiments conducted by Maass et al. (1989), participants were asked to describe people who belonged to different riding clubs, including each participant's own club (and hence one's ingroup) as well as other clubs (outgroups). When the ingroup members were engaged in positive behaviors, participants were more likely to use adjectives to describe them, words that reflect relatively enduring and stable qualities. When ingroup members were depicted as engaging in negative behaviors, participants described the behavior more concretely (with descriptive action verbs), thereby implying that the behaviors were unique and unstable and not revealing of the personal qualities of the actor. This tendency was reversed for outgroup members; their positive behaviors were described concretely (descriptive action verbs) and their negative behaviors more abstractly (although the results were stronger for the positive than for the negative behaviors). This general effect is relatively robust and has been replicated many times (Fiedler, Semin, & Finkenauer, 1993; Maass, 1999; Maass & Arcuri, 1996; Maass, Milesi, Zabbini, & Stahlberg, 1995; Maass, Salvi, Arcuri, & Semin, 1989; Wigboldus & Douglas, 2007).

The LIB appears to be driven, in part, by a motivational tendency to protect one's social identity; the effect increases when one's ingroup is threatened (Maass, Ceccarelli, & Rudin, 1996), and it is larger for people scoring high on the need for cognitive closure (a desire to possess a definitive answer on some topic; Webster, Kruglanski, & Pattison, 1997; also see Maass, Cadinu, Boni, & Borini, 2005). However, the bias is not entirely motivated and may sometimes reflect the violation of expectations (e.g., Miller & Ross, 1975). That is, speakers may use more abstract language for behaviors that conform to expectations, a phenomenon referred to as the Linguistic Expectancy Effect

(LEB; Maass et al., 1995; Wigboldus, Semin, & Spears, 2000). Because positive behaviors are generally expected for ingroup members, there is a tendency to use more abstract language when referring to them. Evidence for this cognitive explanation has been provided by studies demonstrating the use of more abstract language for expected behaviors regardless of behavioral valence (Maass et al., 1995), and by Semin and Smith's (1999) finding of a relationship between linguistic abstractness and memory; the more temporally distant an event, the more likely it will be represented with an abstract term. In this regard, linguistic abstractness overlaps with construal-level theory, or the tendency to construe more abstractly things that are relatively more distant (temporally, spatially, etc.; Trope & Liberman, 2003; see also Vallacher & Wegner, 1989). More recently, researchers have documented the existence of other psychological antecedents of linguistic abstractness, including positive mood (Beukeboom & Semin, 2005, 2006), proprioceptive cues of approach such as arm flexion (Beukenboom & deJong, 2008) and culture (to be described in detail subsequently).

Linguistic abstractness is an indicator of stereotyping, but it can also play a role in the transmission and maintenance of stereotypes (see also Ruscher, 1998, and van Dijk, 1984, for additional discussions of the role of language in prejudice and stereotyping). Specifically, recipients who receive more abstract descriptions of the negative behaviors of an outgroup are likely to form more stereotypical views of the outgroup; the abstract language serves to induce dispositional attributions regarding the negative evaluations (e.g., Wigboldus, Semin, & Spears, 2000). There is also some research suggesting that the LIB can help to maintain a speaker's beliefs as well. In a study conducted by Karpinsky and von Hippel (1996), participants displayed the LIB when describing a fictional target for others, and their subsequent attitudes were then influenced by the descriptions they had provided.

Some research suggests the LIB is an automatic encoding effect. Evidence for this comes from the fact that the LIB correlates with implicit but not explicit measures of prejudice (Gorham, 2006; von Hippel, Sekaquaptewa, & Vargas, 1997; see also Wigboldus, Dijksterhuis, & van Knippenberg, 2003). In terms of encoding, Wenneker, Wigboldus, and Spears (2005) showed that the LIB occurred when the group membership of a target was known at the time of encoding; it did not occur when group membership was not known (see also Stewart, Weeks, & Lupfer, 2003; Wigboldus et al., 2003). On the other hand, there are clear boundary conditions for the LIB (Douglas, Sutton, & Wilkin, 2008). Douglas and Sutton (2003), for example, showed that the LIB can be overridden when participants are asked to provide descriptions designed to accomplish a particular goal (e.g., derogate a target). Similarly, Fiedler, Bluemke, Friese, and Hofmann (2003) demonstrated that a speaker's level of linguistic abstraction can vary as a function of the recipient's identity and presumed knowledge. These findings suggest that linguistic abstraction can be used strategically, as a means of influencing others in various ways. For example, prosecution lawyers tend to describe a defendant's actions with abstract language (to imply dispositionality); defense lawyers tend to use more concrete language (as a means to imply situationality; Schmid & Fiedler, 1996, 1998; Schmid, Fiedler, Englich, Ehrenberger, & Semin, 1996). Other research has demonstrated that the verb forms used in questions can systematically influence respondents' answers (Semin & DePoot, 1996; Semin, Rubini, & Fiedler, 1995). Consistent with research on implicit causality, questions containing action verbs (e.g., "Why do you eat at Joe's?") tend to elicit responses with the subject as the causal origin ("Because I…"); questions with state verbs (e.g., "Why do you like Joe's?") tend to elicit responses with the object as the causal origin (e.g., "Because Joe's is…"). Other applied settings for which linguistic abstractness has proven useful include health communication (Watson & Gallois, 2002), politics (Maass, Corvino, & Arcuri, 1994), and personnel selection (Rubini & Menegatti, 2008).

Language, Gender, and Syntax

One pervasive and specific type of implicit word meaning concerns gender. Although the fundamental social category of gender is represented in some way in all languages, there are differences between languages in the nature and extent of this representation (Stahlberg, Braun, Irmen, & Sczesny, 2007). For some languages (e.g., German), gender is coded as a grammatical category (e.g., nouns must be either feminine or masculine); for others (e.g., English), there is only a subset of forms that code for gender (e.g., personal pronouns); and for other languages (e.g., Finnish), gender has no grammatical relevance. An interesting yet unexamined question is whether these between-language differences are related in any way to between-language differences in gender attitudes. What is clear, however, is that the distribution of terms for expressing gender in most (and probably all) languages is not symmetrical. In most languages, for example, female reference is usually the marked form (i.e., not the default form) thereby indicating that the male form is the norm. This asymmetry is also revealed in lexical gaps such as the lack of a term for one of the two sexes (e.g., "miss" in English) and word pairs whereby the feminine version expresses reduced status (e.g., governor–governess).

The most well-known and potentially far-reaching asymmetry is for masculine generics, forms that function both generically and sex-specifically. Although manifested differently, masculine generics appear to occur in all languages and have been the target of feminist critiques of language (Henley, 1989). Almost all of the empirical research on the social–cognitive consequences of these forms demonstrates a masculine bias (i.e., the referent is assumed to be male). For example, participants in a story completion task were more likely to generate male (rather than female) targets following the occurrence of a generic pronoun (Moulton, Robinson, & Elias, 1978). Using a priming procedure, Banaji and Hardin (1996) demonstrated that terms frequently assumed to be generic (e.g., chairman) prime masculine rather than neutral pronouns. This suggests that the masculine bias for generic terms is automatic, an interpretation that is consistent with much other research in this area (e.g., Boroditsky, Schmidt, & Phillips, 2003; Ng, 1990).

Language and Social Thought: Between-Language Effects

The unintended and implicit consequences of words is reminiscent of the well-known Whorf–Sapir hypothesis (or more commonly, the Whorfian hypothesis), a cluster of ideas based on the writings of Benjamin Whorf (1956) and Edward Sapir (1921).[1] The Whorfian hypothesis—or the idea that the language one speaks affects how one thinks—has had a checkered history. Although largely discredited by the 1970s (at least among psychologists), there has been a clear resurgence of interest in these ideas (e.g., see volumes edited by Gentner & Goldin-Meadow, 2003, and Gumperz & Levinson, 1996). The Whorfian hypothesis was never a clearly specified theory or hypothesis, and interpretations have ranged from the trivial (that language plays some role in thought) to the impossible (that language determines our perceptions). Until recently, this has had the unfortunate effect of hindering research on the role of language in social thought. Fortunately, more recent work in this domain has formulated hypotheses regarding the language-thought relationship in more specific (and hence testable) ways.

Early tests of Whorf's hypothesis examined perceptions of, and memory for, color. Because linguistic communities differ in the manner in which the color spectrum is lexicalized, there was an expectation of corresponding differences in perceptions of, and memory for, color. There was some early research consistent with this idea, but other studies,

---

[1]Although Whorf and Sapir are frequently cited as originators, the basic ideas actually have a relatively long history (see Gumperz & Levinson, 1996).

in particular those of Rosch (1973; Heider, 1972; Heider & Olivier, 1972) and Berlin and Kay (1969), provided what many regarded as evidence that strongly disconfirmed the hypothesis. Particularly influential was Rosch's (1973) study of color memory in the Dani, an aboriginal people in Papua, New Guinea. The Dani language has only two color terms, black and white. However, in a color-naming task, Dani participants performed better for focal colors, despite the fact that their language had no words for those colors. Rosch and others argued that the physiology of color perception undercuts any effects that language might have in this domain (but see Roberson, Davies, & Davidoff, 2000).

More recently, however, research examining the categorical perception of color (people perceive color categorically—as blues, reds, etc.—even though the color spectrum is a continuum reflecting wavelength variation) has demonstrated that language can affect certain aspects of color perception. For example, the Turkish language has two color terms for the English term "blue." Compared with English speakers, Turkish participants exaggerate the differences between colors straddling the boundary of the two Turkish color terms. Similarly, in a free grouping task, Turkish speakers tend to separate colors on the basis of this boundary; English speakers do not (Ozgen, 2004; Ozgen & Davies, 1998; see Winawer et al., 2007, for Russian–English differences in color categorization speed).

Additional, recent work in this vein has explored between-language differences in the perception of time (Boroditsky, 2001), space (Levinson, 1997; Levinson, Kita, Haun, & Rasch, 2002; but see Li & Gleitman, 2002), and the acquisition of categories (Lupyan, Rakison, & McClelland, 2007). This research demonstrates that certain lexical and syntactic differences between languages can be associated with differences in the nature and speed of related cognitive processes.

One between-language difference with social-psychological relevance is person perception, or the assignment of people to categories, including dispositional categories. Languages differ in the lexical items that are available for categorizing others, and this creates the possibility that speakers of different languages may vary in their impressions of others. A classic study conducted by Hoffman, Lau, and Johnson (1986) demonstrated this quite clearly. They presented Chinese–English bilinguals with personality descriptors that were either consistent with a label in English (but not Chinese; e.g., artistic type), or with a label in Chinese (but not in English; e.g., *shi gu*; a person who is worldly, experienced, reserved, socially skilled, and devoted to his or her family). Participants (who were randomly assigned to read the descriptions either in Chinese

or in English) demonstrated schematic processing of the descriptions when the language they used provided a label for the description; their impressions were more congruent with the label, and they were more likely to endorse non-presented traits consistent with the label.

Perhaps the most well-known (and controversial) demonstration of a Whorfian effect in the social domain is Bloom's (1981) research on counterfactual thinking. Bloom argued that Chinese differs from English by its absence of linguistic devices (e.g., the subjunctive) for expressing counterfactual thoughts, and the existence of counterfactual devices in English (but not in Chinese) allows speakers of the former language to engage more easily and accurately in counterfactual reasoning than speakers of the latter language. The results of Bloom's research were consistent with this idea, but his methodology was open to serious criticism (e.g., Au, 1983, 1984; Cheng, 1985; Liu, 1985), with the most frequent objection being that the Chinese translations he used were less idiomatic than the English versions.

Within-Language Effects: Language Use

There are inherent difficulties in investigating the thought–language relationship using between-language comparisons. Perhaps the most fundamental difficulty (as in Bloom's research) is achieving between-language equivalence independent of the cognitive processes that are being investigated. An alternative research strategy is to undertake within-language tests. This can involve examining the effects of using one linguistic construction versus another on some unrelated cognitive or perceptual process or by examining the effects of using versus not using language on subsequent cognitive processes (Chiu, Krauss, & Lau, 1998; Holtgraves, 2002). An example of the former is a series of studies conducted by Stapel and Semin (2007) examining the effects of linguistic abstractness (adjectives vs. verbs) on basic perceptual processes. Participants in these experiments were primed with concrete (action verbs) or abstract (adjectives) categories and then asked to perform an ostensibly unrelated perceptual task. In all experiments, the activation of abstract categories (via adjectives) resulted in a more global perceptual focus than did the activation of concrete categories (via verbs). Importantly, this research demonstrates the impact of language use not on the content of cognition but rather on content-free, low-level, perceptual processes.

There is a variety of research demonstrating the subsequent cognitive effects of using versus not using language. The verbal overshadowing effect (Schooler & Engstler-Schooler, 1990), for example, suggests that verbally describing a nonverbal stimulus (such as a face) can impair subsequent attempts at identifying the stimulus. In terms of decision making, T. D. Wilson and colleagues have conducted a number of studies demonstrating that using language to verbalize reasons for a decision can influence various aspects of the decision-making process, including the quality of the decision itself (Wilson & Schooler, 1991; Wilson et al., 1993). In general, participants who are asked to verbalize their reasons for a decision make less optimal decisions than participants who are not asked to verbalize their reasons, largely because doing so causes them to attend to nonoptimal criteria, an effect that is similar to research demonstrating differences in the quality of decisions as a function of whether the decision making is done consciously (language-based) or not (Dijksterhuis, 2004).

Another relevant area of research involves using language to identify emotional states, an activity that can alter the representation of those states. For example, talking about another's emotion can bias memory for the expression of that emotion (Halberstadt, 2003). In terms of labeling one's own emotional state, Lieberman (2009) has argued that affective labeling has the consequence of activating the reflective neural system (C-system) and dampening the reflexive neural system (X-system). Hence, when one uses language to label an emotional state, the underlying physiology of that state is altered. More specifically, at least for negatively valenced images, linguistic processing of the image lessens activation of the amygdala (Hariri, Bookheimer, & Mazziotta, 2000; Lieberman et al., 2007). This may be one of the reasons the linguistic expression (e.g., journal writing) of traumatic events can have a beneficial effect on one's well-being (Pennebaker & Graybeal, 2001); talking and writing about one's experiences allows one to organize and structure those experiences, thereby allowing one to complete and hence bring those negative experiences to an end.

Words, Identity, and Impressions of Others

The words that people use—and how they use them—are a rich source of information about one's identity, including, especially, one's group identification(s). Linguistic (word) variation both reflects a person's personality and social background and simultaneously is a mechanism useful in the presentation and maintenance of one's identity (Bell, 1984). Hence, linguistic variation can be both strategic (Goffman's [1959] impressions given) and nonstrategic (Goffman's impressions given off), thereby playing a role in both person perception and impression management.

The relationship between identity and linguistic variation has been a focal concern for the field of sociolinguistics. Specifically, sociolinguists have attempted to map the relationship between linguistic variables (e.g., phonological variability) and social variables (e.g., ethnicity, social class, group membership, etc.). Classic and highly influential research in this vein was conducted by William Labov who investigated the stratification of linguistic variables in New York City (Labov, 1966; Labov, 1972a; see also Milroy & Milroy, 1978; Trudgill, 1974). In a field study now regarded as a classic, Labov (1972a) asked department store employees for the location of a particular item known to be on the fourth floor, thereby requiring speakers to pronounce two words (fourth, floor) containing "r." The stores he examined varied in status (Saks, Macy's, Klein's), as did the age of the respondents. As predicted, Labov found that the pronunciation of "r" increased with social class and decreased with age (but only for the high- and low-, and not the middle-class, respondents), thereby demonstrating the linguistic marking of social class and age. Respondents were also more likely to pronounce "r" when they had to repeat these words and hence were paying greater attention to their speech, leading Labov (1972a) to postulate a general link between class marking and attention to speech: People tend to use upper-class pronunciations when they attend carefully to how they talk.

Other sociolinguistic research has demonstrated the existence of social class differences in a variety of linguistic variables including syntax (Lavandera, 1978), lexical choice (Sankoff, Thibault, & Berube, 1978), intonation (Guy & Vonwiller, 1984), and others. The manner in which identity, especially group identity, is related to linguistic variation has been studied extensively and includes, for example, studies of the verbal interactions of people with differing sexual orientation (Hajek & Giles, 2005), police–civilian contact (Giles, Willemyns, Gallois, & Anderson, 2007), and gender differences (Boggs & Giles, 1999). Intergenerational interaction has been a topic of particular interest (Harwood, 2007; A. Williams & Nussbaum, 2001), as has research on African American vernacular English (Labov, 1972b; Rickford, 1999).

What is probably most important for social psychologists is that there is a psychological reality for the meaning of some linguistic variability. New Yorkers, but not necessarily others (see Labov, 2001), are aware of the social class stratification of "r," as demonstrated by the attention–accent link (Labov, 1972a), and by the fact that perceptions of speakers are influenced by this linguistic variability (Labov, 1966). One important innovation in this area was the development of the matched-guise technique, a procedure created by Wallace Lambert and his colleagues (Lambert, Frankle, & Tucker, 1960; Lambert, Hodgson, Gardner, & Fillenbaum, 1966) that allowed for the controlled, covert examination of the effects of languages and language varieties on perceptions of a speaker. Researchers use recordings created by the same person (to control for idiosyncratic aspects of speech) speaking in different ways (e.g., different languages, accents, etc.) to examine perceptions of people who speak in those ways. This technique has been popular and used for examining the effects of language choices in many countries (e.g., Canada: W. E. Lambert et al., 1966; Spain: Woolard & Gahng, 1990) as well as regional varieties within countries (e.g., Appalachian English: Luhman, 1990; Chicano English: Bradac & Wisegarver, 1984; Japanese- and Chinese-accented English: Cargile, 1997).

The results of this research demonstrate that language varieties in a speech community can be ordered on a continuum of prestige and that evaluations of speakers of these varieties parallel this ordering (see Bradac, 1990; Giles & Coupland, 1991). In Great Britain, for example, received pronunciation (RP) is the prestigious standard, and speakers of that dialect are evaluated more favorably than are speakers of urban varieties such as Cockney and Birmingham (Giles, 1970). With the advent of sophisticated and easy-to-use digital manipulation techniques, it has become possible to manipulate and examine a wide range of specific language markers. For example, Campbell-Kibler (2007) used the matched-guise technique to examine the impact of the English "ing" variable (e.g., *reading* vs. *readin*; or dropping one's "gs," in lay terms). The occurrence of "ing" forms was associated with greater perceived education, articulateness, and urbanity relative to the "in" form.

Consistent with other research on person perception (S. T. Fiske, Cuddy, & Glick, 2007), language-based perceptions tend to coalesce around the two basic dimensions of status and solidarity. The pattern that usually emerges is that speakers of the standard language variety receive higher ratings on status dimensions such as competence, intelligence, confidence, and so on, but speakers of the nonstandard variety frequently receive higher ratings on solidarity dimensions such as friendliness and generosity (e.g., Marlow & Giles, 2008; Ryan, Giles, & Sebastian, 1982; but see B. L. Brown, Giles, & Thackerar, 1985). Hence, for language varieties, there appears to be both overt prestige—the standard variety associated with status—and covert prestige—the nonstandard varieties associated with solidarity (Labov, 1972a).

Linguistic variation also has behavioral consequences (e.g., Bourhis & Giles, 1976), particularly in educational settings where several studies have demonstrated that it is an important cue in teacher evaluations of pupils (e.g., Choy & Dodd, 1976; Seligman, Tucker, & Lambert, 1972). Linguistic variation has also been shown to play an important role in medical encounters (Fielding & Evered, 1980), legal settings (Dixon, Mahoney, & Cocks; 2002; Seggie, 1983), employment contexts (Kalin & Rayko,

1980), helping behavior (Gaertner & Bickman, 1971), and housing discrimination (Purnell, Idsardi, & Baugh, 1999).

Linguistic variation can influence speaker perceptions through several possible paths, both direct and indirect (e.g., see Cargile & Bradac, 2001; Cargile, Giles, Ryan, & Bradac, 1994). Accents, for example, can function much like any other visible feature (e.g., appearance) that activates a particular stereotype, with the activated stereotype then influencing evaluations. Hence, nonstandard language varieties may lead to an inference that the speaker is from a lower social class, and this categorization may result in negative evaluations of the speaker on the status–competence dimension (Ryan & Sebastian, 1980, but see Giles & Sassoon, 1983). Top-down effects are possible as well, and social categories can influence speech perception. Thakerar and Giles (1981) found that when participants believed a speaker to be high status, they perceived his speech rate to be more standard than when they believed he was lower in status (see also F. Williams, Whitehead, & Miller, 1972). It is also possible for linguistic variation to influence evaluations without activation of a specific social category. Affective reactions to a speaker's language can occur even though an accent cannot be identified and associated with a particular group. Such affective reactions could arise simply because a speaker is not perceived to be a member of one's ingroup. It also is possible for certain sounds to elicit evaluative reactions automatically. Garcia and Bargh (2003), for example, used a priming procedure to demonstrate that superficial phonetic qualities of nonsense stimuli are capable of automatically activating evaluative responses.

Paralinguistic Variation

People are able to infer certain physical characteristics of a speaker on the basis of noncontent voice samples (Krauss, Freyberg, & Morsella, 2002). In addition, communication researchers have examined the effects of a variety of noncontent speech variables (e.g., speech rate, lexical diversity, utterance length, response latency, etc.) on perceptions of a speaker. Many of these noncontent variables appear to load on the dimension of speaker competence (similar to prestige language varieties). Specifically, lexical diversity has been shown to be associated with perceived competence and control (Bradac & Wisegarver, 1984), higher status (Bradac, Bowers, & Courtright, 1979) and low anxiety (Howeler, 1972), utterance length with perceived dominance (Scherer, 1979), and formality with perceptions of greater competence (Levin, Giles, & Garrett, 1994). In addition, research indicates that high speech rate is associated with perceptions of speaker competence (B. L. Brown, 1980), but only up to a point (Street, Brady, & Putnam, 1983). Similarly, shorter pauses and response latencies are associated with perceptions of competence (Scherer, 1979). Further, the effect of speech rate extends to perceptions of credibility, with a corresponding effect on a speaker's persuasiveness (S. M. Smith & Schaffer, 1995). In terms of personality, people who are high in either state or trait anxiety tend to speak more rapidly (Siegman & Pope, 1972), and shorter response latencies appear to be more typical of extroverts than of introverts (Ramsey, 1966).

Content Variables

There has been a resurgence of interest in the psychological analysis of the content of words, due in part to the Linguistic Inquiry and Word Count (LIWC) program, a computerized text analysis program developed by James Pennebaker and colleagues (Pennebaker, Booth, & Francis, 2007; Pennebaker, Francis, & Booth, 2001). Although computerized text analysis programs have existed for some time (dating back at least to the 1960s with the development of the General Inquirer program by Stone, Dunphy, Smith, & Ogilvie, 1966), many of these programs were developed for use in clinical contexts (see Pennebaker, Mehl, & Niederhoffer, 2003, for a review) and generally were ignored by social and personality psychologists.

The LIWC was originally developed as a means to examine efficiently the content of participants' emotional writing, and to relate those features to their subsequent health (Pennebaker & Francis, 1996). The program consists of a dictionary of words (approximately 4,500 in the current version) that tap a number of hierarchically ordered dimensions. Samples of talk are analyzed on a word-by-word basis, each word being compared against the dictionary file. In the current version (Pennebaker et al., 2007), there are 22 standard linguistic categories (e.g., percentage of verbs, articles, etc.), 32 psychological construct categories (e.g., affect, cognition, etc.), seven personal concern categories (work, home, etc.), and several additional categories (e.g., punctuation, paralinguistic). The LIWC has been shown to have good internal consistency and temporal reliability (Pennebaker, Chung, Ireland, Gonzales, & Booth, 2007).

Research demonstrates that people are relatively consistent over time in their linguistic style, suggesting that this feature of talk represents an important, stable aspect of personality (Berry, Pennebaker, Mueller, & Hiller, 1997; Fast & Funder, 2008; Mehl, Gosling, & Pennebaker, 2006; Mehl & Pennebaker, 2003; Oberlander & Gill, 2006; Pennebaker & King, 1999). Neuroticism has been found to correlate positively with the occurrence of negative emotion words and negatively with positive emotion words, extraversion to correlate positively with the occurrence of positive emotion words and words associated with

social processes, and agreeableness to correlate positively with the occurrence of positive emotion words and negatively with negative emotion words (Berry et al., 1997; Pennebaker & King, 1999). Correlations between more molecular personality traits (e.g., certainty) and word categories were reported by Fast and Funder (2008), and Mehl et al. (2006) reported the existence of some gender differences in personality trait–word category correlations.

In addition, the LIWC program has been used to examine linguistic differences as a function of age (e.g., age is associated with more positive emotion and future tense words and fewer negative emotion words, self-references, and past tense verbs; Pennebaker & Stone, 2003), gender (e.g., women tend to use more filler words, more discrepancy words, and more positive emotions, whereas men use higher rates of swear words and anger words; Mehl & Pennebaker, 2003), and deception (Bond & Lee, 2005).

The LIWC program is clearly an efficient means for assessing linguistic content. Its primary weakness is that it does not take into account linguistic structure or context (Evans, Walters & Hatch-Woodruff, 1999), although some linguistic context can be incorporated by taking multiple word combinations rather than single words (see Oberlander & Gill, 2006). For the most part the LIWC program has been used in an inductive manner, although there is no reason why it cannot be used for testing theories.

UTTERANCES

Words do not exist in isolation. They are combined with other words and actions to create sentences and utterances. Traditionally, sentences have been the fundamental unit for most psycholinguistic research, but it is utterances (or a speaker's conversational turn), that in many respects are most relevant for social psychology. Sentences can be produced and read in isolation, but utterances cannot. Utterances must be produced and interpreted in the context of others and hence a variety of interpersonal considerations come into play (P. Brown & Levinson, 1987; Goffman 1967; Holtgraves, 1998). Moreover, unlike sentences, the meaning of a person's conversational turn must be recognized immediately if the exchange is to have any chance of success. These two features—interpersonal considerations and an immediate search for meaning—serve as the organizing principles for material in this section.

Utterances and Meaning

Humans appear to have both the need and the ability to perceive others as intentional agents, to see others' actions as a result of their intentional states (Carston, 2002; Gibbs,

1999; Malle, 2001; Sperber & Wilson, 2002). This is certainly true for language, and a fundamental assumption on the part of language users is that speakers are saying something meaningful—that there is something to be extracted from their words.[2] This assumption is fundamental to many psychological theories of comprehension (e.g., Gibbs, 1999), including relevance theory (Sperber & Wilson, 1986/1995, 2002) and speech act theory (Austin, 1962; Searle, 1969, 1979), as well as certain computational models (Cohen & Perrault, 1979; Stone, 2005) and models of text processing (Graesser, Singer, and Trabasso, 1994). If language users are primed to search for meaning, then for what type of meaning do they search? What exactly is meaning, and can it be captured in a systematic way? There are several, relevant frameworks in this regard.

Meaning as Action

One way to approach conversational meaning is to focus on language use as a type of action. There are two different approaches, one originating in philosophy and the other in cognitive science, that are relevant.

Speech Act Theory

Speech act theory was developed by the philosophers John Austin (1962) and John Searle (1969; see also Wittgenstein, 1953). This action view of language emerged, in part, in opposition to truth-conditional views of language (i.e., the view that language is to be evaluated in terms of its correspondence with external reality). Austin argued that for many utterances truth or falsity is simply irrelevant; instead, speakers are using language to perform specific actions. For example, when Marty says, "I promise to do it tomorrow," he is performing the act of promising, and whether the utterance is true or false is simply irrelevant. What is relevant, of course, is whether the promise is sincere, and linguistic actions (termed *speech acts*) can be judged on a variety of criteria such as sincerity (termed *felicity conditions*) but not in terms of their truth.[3] More specifically, speech act theorists argue that speakers are simultaneously performing multiple acts when they use language. They are producing an utterance with a certain propositional content (termed the *locutionary act*), and (given that certain conditions are met) simultaneously performing a specific speech

act such as promising, apologizing, criticizing, and so on (termed the *illocutionary act*). By performing this action, the speaker is ultimately altering the world (principally the recipient) in some way (termed the *perlocutionary act*). The recipient of Marty's promise, for example, may come to believe that Marty will indeed do it tomorrow.

Speech act theorists have been concerned with clarifying the nature of speech acts, developing speech act classification schemes, and specifying the relationship between speech acts, speakers (e.g., their beliefs and desires), and the external world (Bach & Harnish, 1979; Searle, 1979; Searle & Vanderveken, 1985; Yabuuchi, 1996). The fundamental insight of speech act theory—that language involves an action dimension—provides one perspective on the nature of conversational meaning. Illocutionary force captures the intended action a speaker performs with a particular conversation turn, and it is the recipient's recognition of that action (e.g., that Marty is performing a promise) that constitutes understanding of that conversational turn (Amrhein, 1992; Holtgraves, 2008; Holtgraves & Ashley, 2001).

An important feature of speech acts is that there is no one-to-one mapping between illocutionary force and a specific utterance, and when people use language, they are not always explicit regarding the actions that they are performing. When Marty says, "I'll definitely do it tomorrow" (rather than "I promise to do it tomorrow"), he does not explicitly state that he is performing a promise. Yet recipients will frequently recognize the act as a promise. To accomplish this, recipients must go beyond the literal dictionary meaning of the words. People search for meaning in the remarks of others, and this meaning must, to a certain extent, be constructed by the recipient, an issue that is dealt with by inferential theories as discussed later.

Speech act theory has continued to develop in philosophy and pragmatics (Levinson, 1983; Vanderveken & Kubo, 2002) but surprisingly has had relatively little impact in psycholinguistics and social psychology (but see Wish, D'Andrade, & Goodenough, 1980). This is unfortunate because speech act theory can provide a useful conceptual framework for examining many social psychological features of language use.

Embodied Cognition

Embodied approaches to cognition also view language as action but in a way that is different from speech act theory. In this view, cognition is for doing and is functional and adaptive rather than abstract and disembodied (Barsalou, 1999; Gibbs, 2006; G. Lakoff & Johnson, 1980; E. R. Smith & Semin, 2004; M. Wilson, 2002). Like other aspects of cognition, linguistic meaning must be grounded. The meaning of single words, for example, cannot be

---

[2]The concern here is with utterance meaning and speaker meaning rather than word meaning (Clark, 1985).

[3]Obviously, truthfulness is a relevant dimension of conversational utterances (e.g., see Grice, 1975), but only in terms of propositional content and not in terms of action.

captured solely by other words (cf. Landauer, Foltz, & Laham, 1998) but must be grounded outside of the linguistic system itself. Linguistic symbols become meaningful only when they are mapped onto nonlinguistic actions and perceptions.

There are now numerous demonstrations, much of it provided by Glenberg and colleagues (Glenberg et al., 2008; Glenberg, Havas, Becker, & Rinck, 2005; Glenberg & Kaschak, 2002), that the physical instantiations of words can facilitate or hinder comprehension. This suggests that understanding linguistic meaning involves the activation of some type of perceptual experience rather than just the activation of abstract, arbitrary nodes. For example, Glenberg and Kaschak (2002) asked participants to judge the sensibility of sentences by making a response that required movement either away from or toward their bodies. Responses were faster when this hand movement was consistent with the action implied by the sentence. The sentence "Close the door," for example, implies movement away from the body, and this sentence was verified more quickly when a "yes" response required movement away from rather than toward the participant; the reverse occurred for the sentence "Open the door."

Related research has demonstrated the role of perceptual experience in the comprehension of metaphor. Following G. Lakoff and Johnson (1980), these theorists argue that meaning is largely metaphorical and involves the mapping of abstract entities onto concrete ones (Gibbs, 2006). Consider vertical metaphors such as "I'm feeling down" or "Things are looking up." Meier and Robinson (2004) asked participants to evaluate negative and positive words that appeared either in the top half or the bottom half of a computer screen. Reaction times were significantly faster for positive words presented on the top half and negative words presented on the bottom half (for individual differences in this regard, see Meier, Sellbom, & Wygant, 2007). Similar results have been found regarding the spatial representation of power (Schubert, 2005) and abstract concepts such as the divine (Meier et al., 2007). These studies demonstrate that real-world experience with objects can influence the comprehension of sentences referencing those objects (see also Estes, Verges, & Barsalou, 2008; Stanfield & Zwaan, 2001; Zwaan & Yaxley, 2003).

Meaning as Inference

Inferential models assume that recipients must go beyond the simple decoding of an utterance (see Krauss & Fussell, 1996, for a discussion of code vs. inferential models of communication). Instead, recipients must construct an interpretation based on the utterance in conjunction with relevant background information, the context, and so on. In certain respects, a linguistic code is not even necessary; only a speaker's intention is required. Hence, these approaches overlap somewhat with theory of mind research and theorizing (Sperber & Wilson, 2002).[4] There are two, related, high-level models—Grice's model of conversational implicative and Relevance Theory—that have dominated work in this area.

Grice's Model

A major focus of the work of the philosopher H. Paul Grice has been the nature of language-based communication and meaning. His most influential contribution has been his theory of conversational implicature (1975, 1989). Grice argued that people frequently mean more than they say because they mutually abide by what he termed the cooperative principle (CP), a simple and straightforward rule stating that one should: "Make your conversational contribution such as is required, at the stage at which it occurs, by the accepted purpose or direction of the talk exchange in which you are engaged" (1975, p. 45). This general requirement was further specified in terms of the following four conversational maxims:

1. Quantity—make your contribution as informative as required (i.e., do not be either overinformative or underinformative).
2. Quality—try to make your contribution true; one for which you have evidence.
3. Manner—be clear. That is, avoid ambiguity, obscurity, and so on.
4. Relation—make your contribution relevant for the exchange.

Of course people often violate these rules; sometimes subtly and sometimes not so subtly (i.e., they flout the maxim). The critical point, however, is that people mutually assume adherence to the CP and maxims, and this assumption serves as a frame for the interpretation of a speaker's utterances. Hence, a speaker's utterance will be interpreted *as if* it were clear, relevant, truthful, and informative. These interpretations (or conversational implicatures) serve to preserve adherence to the CP and maxims, and they cannot be derived from a speaker's words alone (i.e., they are pragmatic rather than semantic). For example, during the 2008 U.S. presidential campaign, an ABC television interviewer asked former U.S.

---

[4]There also are extreme versions of this view (e.g., Fish, 1980) that deny any role for the speaker's original intention; in this view, meaning is entirely constructed by the recipient.

President Clinton if he thought Barack Obama was qualified to be president:

> Snow: You think he's completely qualified to be president?
>
> Clinton: The Constitution sets qualifications for the president, and then the people decide who they think would be the better president.

Clinton's reply was quite narrow and underinformative (it violated the quantity maxim) and as a result was interpreted by most commentators as a less than ringing endorsement of candidate Obama.

Conversational implicatures can vary in many ways, and Grice (1975) made an important distinction between generalized and particularized implicatures. Generalized implicatures are context-independent and have preferred interpretations that occur without reference to the context. Examples of generalized implicatures include figurative expressions (e.g., "He spilled the beans" usually implicates that he revealed a secret), scalar implicatures as described by Levinson (2000; e.g., "Some of the students attended class" implies that not all of the students attended class), "What is X doing Y?" (WXDY) constructions as described by Kay and Fillmore (1999; e.g., "What are you doing in my chair?" implies that one shouldn't be in the chair), and the illocutionary force of an utterance (see Table 36.2). In contrast, particularized implicatures are context-dependent and require a consideration of the utterance in terms of a context, most notably the prior discourse context. A common particularized implicature is to violate the relation maxim (e.g., subtly change the topic) when asked a sensitive question (Holtgraves, 1998). For example, when Celia asks Deidre what she thought of her class presentation, and Deidre replies, "It's hard to give a good presentation," Celia is likely to interpret Deidre's reply as conveying a negative opinion of her presentation. In contrast to generalized implicatures, this interpretation can be derived only by considering the utterance in terms of its relation to the preceding discourse context.

An utterance can result in both generalized and particularized implicatures as in the following example (from Levinson, 2000):

A: Did the children's summer camp go well?
B: Some of them got stomach "flu."

Generalized Implicature: Not all the children got stomach "flu."

Particularized Implicature: The summer camp didn't go as well as hoped.

Grice's theory of conversational implicative has had a dramatic influence on several research areas, including social psychology (discussed later). It has not, however, been without criticism. One major concern has been the cross-cultural validity of the maxims. It has been suggested that Grice's view, with its emphasis on individual autonomy, has relevance only in Western cultures (Fitch & Sanders, 1994). In a well-known paper, Keenan (1976) argued that people in Malagasy routinely withhold information from one another (information is a culturally prized commodity), an action that is in clear violation of the quantity maxim. As a result, violations of this maxim do not usually result in conversational implicatures (as presumably would be the case in most other cultures). It is likely that any maxims that people follow in communicating cooperatively will vary over cultures, reflecting, perhaps, differences in what is regarded as rational interaction. However, it is equally likely that conversational maxims, whatever they look like, will serve as an interpretive frame in the comprehension of conversational meaning.

Relevance Theory

Relevance theory provides an expansion and extensive reworking of Grice's theory of conversational implicature (for reviews, see Carston, 2002; D. Wilson & Sperber, 2004). The theory was originally published by Dan Sperber and Deidre Wilson in 1986 with important updates by these authors appearing in 1995 and 2002. Relevance theory retains the fundamental insight of Grice's model—language users have conversational expectancies that guide them in the recognition of a speaker's meaning—but expands it in various ways. First, the cooperative principle and four maxims are no longer viewed as necessary and are replaced with the overarching principle

Table 36.2 Examples of Generalized Implicatures

Type	Example	Implicature
Figurative expression (idiom)	"He spilled the beans."	He revealed a secret.
Scalar	"I tried to play the stock market."	I lost money playing the stock market.
WXDY	"What are you doing with my book?"	You shouldn't have my book.
Speech act	"I'll definitely do it tomorrow."	I promise to do it tomorrow.

of relevance; all utterances come with a presumption of relevance. Second, relevance is defined explicitly in terms of processing considerations. Specifically, an utterance is relevant to an individual "to the extent that the contextual effects achieved when it is optimally processed are large" and "to the extent that the efforts required to process it are small" (1986, p. 145). In general, then, the presumption of relevance combined with these processing effects suggests that comprehenders search for the first interpretation (least effort) consistent with the principle of relevance (maximum contextual effects). Third, in contrast to the standard Gricean model in which inferential processing occurs only after what has been said (i.e., literal meaning) has been decoded, in relevance theory inferential processing is required for what is said (explicatures) as well as what is meant (implicatures; see also Gibbs 1999; Terkourafi, 2009; for a counterview, see Levinson, 2000).

Evidence for Inferential Processing

Empirical research on inferential processing models has focused on several issues, with the major issue being the role of literal meaning, or "what is said" in the comprehension of a speaker's intended meaning. In Grice's (1975) model (but not in relevance theory), hearers are assumed first to recognize and then reject the "literal" meaning of a remark and then generate an alternative meaning (an implicature). For example, when Marsha tells Frank that "Sam spilled the beans," Frank would presumably first need to decode Marsha's literal meaning (Sam spilled some beans), recognize the inappropriateness of that meaning (i.e., it violates the relation maxim), and then recognize the intended meaning (Sam revealed a secret). However, research has demonstrated that this type of time-consuming inference process is not required for the comprehension of many indirect forms. People simply do not take more time to understand the meaning of figurative expressions than they do equivalent literal expressions (Gibbs, 1980; Ortony, Schallert, Reynolds, & Antos, 1978). Other research has demonstrated that the nonliteral meaning of a figure of speech is activated even when the literal meaning is acceptable in context (Gildea & Glucksberg, 1983; Glucksberg, Gildea, & Bookin, 1982; Keysar, 1989), and sometimes people recognize the literal meaning only after first considering and then rejecting the nonliteral meaning, the reverse of the predicted ordering (Keysar, 1994). A related issue concerns the necessity of inferences in the recognition of literal meaning (what is said). Consistent with relevance theory, Gibbs and Moise (1997; see also Nicolle & Clark, 1999) demonstrated that presumably literal interpretations of utterances involve some nonsemantic fleshing out (they are explicatures; but see Terkourafi, 2009).

For the most part, psycholinguistic research on nonliteral meaning has focused on a narrow range of utterance types, primarily figures of speech and conventional indirect requests, both of which represent generalized implicatures. Research on particularized implicatures, in contrast, has been rare but generally supportive of Grice's model. Holtgraves (1998, 1999) examined some of the processing consequences of violations of the relation maxim, specifically, instances in which a speaker failed to directly answer a personal question. The results demonstrated that a time-consuming inference process was required for these utterances and involved a recognition and then rejection of the literal meaning of the utterance (consistent with Grice's model).

Conversational Inferencing and Self-Report Measures

Inferential processing models have had an important impact in one area of social psychology—namely, how participants in psychology experiments provide self-reports. Psychology experiments, and social psychology experiments in particular, involve communication between an experimenter and study participants, and participants' responses sometimes reflect the operation of conversational maxims and inferential processing rather than the presumed intrapersonal processes that are the object of the study. Specifically, an experimenter may provide participants with a piece of information to see whether they use it. However, participants will use it simply because of its assumed relevance (for reviews, see Hilton & Slugoski, 2001; Hilton, 1995; Schwarz, 1996).

The classic Kahneman and Tversky (1973) studies have been interpreted in just this way. Participants in these studies made judgments about the likely occupation of a target person based on personality descriptions and occupational base-rate information. The resulting judgments were far more influenced by occupation stereotypes than by occupation base-rate information, thereby demonstrating the presumed operation of the representativeness heuristic. Conversational inferencing accounts provide an alternative interpretation, however. Specifically, participants were told that the target description was based on personality tests administered by a panel of psychologists. Because the experimenter gave this information to participants as part of the experimental procedure, it seems reasonable that participants will assume this information is relevant (as suggested by relevance theory) and should be used. Several studies have demonstrated that if the presumed relevance of the individuating information is undermined in various ways (e.g., by telling participants the descriptions were randomly generated), people are far less likely to use it (Igou & Bless, 2003; Krosnick, Li, & Lehman, 1990; Schwarz, Strack, Hilton, & Naderer, 1991).

Other judgmental "biases" can be interpreted in this way as well. For example, in the classic Jones and Harris (1967) study, participants read an essay presumably written by another student and inferred the author's position to be in line with the position advocated in the essay, even when that position had been assigned and hence was not diagnostic of the writer's true opinion. Wright and Wells (1988) replicated the Jones and Harris (1967) study but told some participants that the information given to them had been randomly selected and hence might not be relevant for the judgment task they were to perform. In this condition, the fundamental attribution error was dramatically reduced (although not completely eliminated).

Because research participants may sometimes generate inferences to maximize the relevance of the experimenter's communications, pragmatic processes may play a role in how people respond to virtually any self-report measure. For example, Strack, Schwarz, and Wanke (1991) asked respondents to rate their happiness and their satisfaction with life, two questions that are obviously highly related. For some participants the two items were presented together at the end of a questionnaire; for others, the life satisfaction item was presented as the first item in an ostensibly unrelated questionnaire. In the first situation, the second question would appear to be redundant (it violates the quantity maxim) and so participants might reason that it must mean something different from the first question. Responses to the two questions differed significantly when they were part of the same questionnaire but not when they were part of two separate questionnaires. There are similar implications for the construction of response scales (Schwarz, 1996; Schwarz et al., 1991; Schwarz, Hippler, Deutsch, & Strack, 1985). Other judgmental biases that have been interpreted in this way include order effects in persuasion (Igou & Bless, 2003), the dilution effect (Igou & Bless, 2005), and the conjunction fallacy (Dulany & Hilton, 1991). For the latter two areas, there has been some dispute regarding the extent and nature of these effects (see Kemmelmeier, 2007, and Igou, 2007, for dilution; see Donnovan & Epstein, 1997, for the conjunction fallacy).

The importance of assumed conversational cooperativeness and relevance extends beyond self-report measures. It is relevant any time people discuss their thoughts, attitudes, beliefs, and so on with others. For example, denying a proposition presumes (via the relation maxim) that there is some factual basis for the denied proposition (why else would it be denied?). Hence, denying a proposition (e.g., Nixon's assertion that "I am not a crook") can actually increase belief in the denied proposition (Gilbert, Tafarodi, & Malone, 1993; Gruenfeld & Wyer, 1992; Holtgraves & Grayer, 1994; Wegner, Coulton, & Wenzlaff, 1985). Similarly, claiming that one is not arrogant can boomerang and

increase one's perceived arrogance (El-Alayli, Myers, Peterson, & Lystad, 2008). This is why it is recommended that politicians should not deny a claim made by an opponent unless they can be reasonably sure the audience has heard the claim that is to be denied. Hearing a claim denied when one is not aware of the claim itself can serve to increase belief in that claim.

Interpersonal Underpinnings of Utterance Production and Comprehension

Language users have goals that exist at varying levels of abstraction. There are the relatively clear, lower-level goals (to request, compliment, threaten, and so on) that are captured by speech act theory. There are also higher-level interpersonal goals such as being liked, impressing others, establishing closeness and rapport, and so on (e.g., Nezlek, Schütz, & Sellin, 2007). These interpersonal goals play an important role in language and can be viewed through the lens of face-work (Goffman, 1967) and politeness theory (P. Brown & Levinson, 1978, 1987).

Face Management and Politeness Theory

Penelope Brown and Stephen Levinson's politeness theory is an attempt to explain how people phrase their utterances as a function of various social concerns. The concepts of face and face-work as articulated by Ervin Goffman (1967) are central to this approach, and in fact, their theory can be viewed as a merging of Gricean pragmatics with Goffman's microsociology. Originally published as a chapter in 1978 and then later reissued as a book in 1987, its influence has been and continues to be substantial in pragmatics and sociolinguistics. In social psychology, Roger Brown's (1988) endorsement resulted in a brief flurry of social psychological activity (Ambady, Koo, Lee, & Rosenthal, 1996; Brown & Gilman, 1989; Holtgraves & Yang, 1990; 1992).

According to Goffman (1967), one's face, or public identity, is always at stake when interacting with others, and because of this, people are strongly motivated to protect and manage their face. Moreover, because face can only be given by others (one might claim a particular identity, but it must be ratified by others), it is in everyone's best interest to maintain each other's face. Politeness theory is an attempt to specify precisely how this happens linguistically, to specify the linguistic means by which face-work is accomplished. Based on Durkheim's (1915) concepts of negative and positive rites, Brown and Levinson divided face into two basic and universal desires: negative face, or the desire for autonomy of action, and positive face, or the desire for closeness with others. Importantly, negative and positive face match up well with the basic interpersonal dimensions that have been suggested by other researchers such as Bakan's (1966) agency and communion, McAdam's (1985) power and intimacy, and A. Fiske's (1992) authority and communal sharing.

Both negative face and positive face are subject to continued threat during social interaction. Requests, for example, are the prototypical negative face-threatening act because they clearly impose on the recipient. People are aware of this; in fact, they tend to overestimate the extent to which a request is threatening (Flynn & Lake, 2008). Criticisms and disagreements are examples of acts that threaten the recipient's positive face. The speaker's own face may be threatened as well. Promises, for example, threaten the speaker's negative face (by restricting subsequent freedom), and apologies threaten the speaker's positive face (via an admission of harming the other). Social interaction thus presents a dilemma for interactants. On the one hand, they are motivated to maintain each other's positive and negative face. On the other hand, they are motivated to perform acts that threaten those very desires. This conflict is solved (to varying degrees) by engaging in face-work or, more precisely, by being polite.

The essence of politeness is to acknowledge (symbolically) that a threat is being made. This is accomplished by deviating from maximally efficient communication (i.e., communication adhering to Grice's [1975] maxims). Consider how requests are typically made. The imperative (e.g., "Get me a beer") reflects the complete absence of politeness and is used infrequently. Instead, speakers will use politeness strategies that minimize the imposition of the act (e.g., "Would you mind getting me a beer?") or that emphasize the closeness of the relationship (e.g., "How about getting us a beer?"). The latter strategy is termed positive politeness and the former negative politeness. Another (even more polite) strategy is to be ambiguous and use an off-record form (e.g., "I sure am thirsty"). Although P. Brown and Levinson (1987) focus on linguistic politeness, it is clear that politeness can be conveyed nonverbally as well (e.g., Ambady, Koo, Lee, & Rosenthal, 1996; LaPlante & Ambady, 2004; Trees & Manusov, 1998).

In general, research has demonstrated that the perceived politeness of the strategies proposed by Brown and Levinson vary as predicted (Blum-Kulka, 1987; Clark & Schunk, 1980; Fraser & Nolan, 1981; Hill, Sachiko, Shoko, Kawasaki, & Ogino, 1986; Holtgraves & Yang, 1990). Moreover, people appear to attend spontaneously to politeness; memory for wording that conveys politeness is better than chance (Holtgraves, 1997a). However, one relatively consistent and interesting deviation from the model has been the finding that ambiguous (i.e., off-record) forms are usually not perceived as the most polite

form (Blum-Kulka, 1987; Holtgraves & Yang, 1990), either because they carry a cost by violating an efficiency maxim (Blum-Kulka, 1987; Leech, 1983), or because they have the appearance of manipulativeness (Lakoff, 1973). This would suggest that greater deviation from efficient communication does not necessarily result in greater conveyed politeness. Instead, maximum face support may be conveyed by tailoring the form of one's utterance to the specific face threat (Holtgraves, 1992). Another weakness of the politeness continuum is that it does not capture aggressive face-work, or impoliteness, well (Bousfield & Locher, 2008).

Interpersonal Underpinnings

Although politeness is driven by face concerns, these concerns can vary over time, settings, individuals, cultures, and so on. The original Brown and Levinson model cut a wide swath by assuming that three broad variables—the culturally determined imposition of the act, the psychological distance between the interactants, and the hearer's power over the speaker, would affect these concerns (see also Leech, 1983, for a consideration of the effects of similar social variables). More specifically, as hearer power, distance, and act imposition increase, so, too, does the overall weightiness of the act, and increased politeness is assumed to reflect increased weightiness.

Imposition

Fairly consistent support has been found for the imposition variable, with increasing imposition associated with increasing politeness. This effect has been found for requests (R. Brown & Gilman, 1989; Holtgraves & Yang, 1992; Leichty & Applegate, 1991), expressions of gratitude (Okamoto & Robinson, 1997), recommendations versus reports (B. L. Lambert, 1996), accounts (Gonzales, Pederson, Manning, & Wetter, 1990; McLaughlin, Cody, & O'Hair, 1983), as well as other speech acts (R. Brown & Gilman, 1989; Leitchy & Applegate, 1991). Some null findings have been reported (Baxter, 1984), but they are in the minority.

Power

The relationship between power and language has been investigated across a number of domains (Ng & Bradac, 1993). In terms of politeness, the basic prediction is that higher speaker power (relative to the recipient) will be associated with lower levels of politeness. In general, research has demonstrated this to be the case. This effect has been found with experimental studies of requests (Holtgraves & Yang, 1990, 1992; Leichty & Applegate, 1991; Lim & Bowers, 1991) as well as with observational studies of actual requests (Blum-Kulka, Danet, &

Gherson, 1985). In addition, power has been found to have the predicted effects on the politeness of messages conveying bad news (Ambady, Koo, Lee, & Rosenthal, 1996), teasing (Keltner et al., 1998), reminders and complaints (Leitchy & Applegate, 1991), criticisms (Lim & Bowers, 1991), accounts (Gonzales et al., 1990), and questions (Holtgraves, 1986). Some of these effects have been replicated cross-culturally (Ambady, Koo, Lee, & Rosenthal, 1996; Holtgraves & Yang, 1992). Because the relationship between politeness and power is reciprocal, variations in politeness should result in differing perceptions of a speaker's power. Holtgraves and Yang (1990) found perceived speaker power to be a linear function of the directness of a speaker's request. Relatedly, other research using speech act coding schemes has demonstrated that perceptions of dominance are positively correlated with the relative frequency of a speaker's forceful requests and negatively correlated with the use of forceless assertions (Wish et al., 1980), and more presumptuous speech acts (e.g., advisements, interpretations, etc.) are more common for speakers relatively high in status (Cansler & Stiles, 1981; Stiles, Putnam, & Jacob, 1982).

The relationship between power and language has been investigated by researchers in many different domains (e.g., Bourdieu, 1991), and some of this research can be interpreted within politeness theory. Early on, for example, Roger Brown and colleagues (R. Brown & Ford, 1961; see also Ervin-Tripp, 1968; Wood & Kroger, 1991) drew attention to, and provided some initial analyses of, the manner in which terms of address both reflect power differentials and serve as a means of negotiating power, findings that are completely consistent with Brown and Levinson's politeness theory. Similarly, language variation (as discussed earlier) can and has been interpreted in terms of power; some language varieties are assumed to be more prestigious and hence a marker of speaker power (Giles & Powesland, 1975). Similarly, variation in speech rate, lexical diversity, and language intensity are related to perceived speaker competence and hence to power.

One particularly important subarea within this domain is research on powerful versus powerless language. The concept of powerless language comes from Robin Lakoff's (1975) writings regarding the "female" register.[5] Research has demonstrated that this register is not unique to women but instead reflects power differences (Crosby &

Nyquist, 1977; Erickson, Lind, Johnson, & O'Barr, 1978). In general, a powerless linguistic style refers to the presence of linguistic features such as tag questions, hesitations, disclaimers, hedges, polite forms, and so on. Powerful language refers to the absence of these features. Hence, consistent with politeness theory, greater indirectness is associated with decreased power. Researchers have examined the impact of a powerless linguistic style in a variety of contexts and found that the use of a powerful style (relative to a powerless style) results in perceptions of greater credibility regardless of gender (Burrell & Koper, 1998; Erickson et al., 1978), as well as higher scores on other dimensions associated with overall competence (Bradac & Mulac, 1984; Gibbons, Busch, & Bradac, 1991; Hosman & Wright, 1987). Depending on the context, messages phrased in a powerful style can be more persuasive than the same message phrased in a powerless style (Blankenship & Holtgraves, 2005; Holtgraves & Lasky, 1999), although Carli (1990) provided evidence that this effect depends on the gender of the speaker and the recipient.

Distance

The relationship between distance and politeness has also been investigated across several domains. Unlike power, however, the results have been mixed. Consistent with politeness theory, some researchers have reported greater politeness as a function of increasing distance between interlocutors (Holtgraves & Yang, 1992; Wood & Kroger, 1991); others have reported the exact opposite (Baxter, 1984; R. Brown & Gilman, 1989). And some (e.g., B. L. Lambert, 1996) have reported no relationship between distance and politeness. Distance is a multifaceted variable that has been measured and manipulated in a variety of ways. As noted by Slugoski and Turnbull (1988; see also R. Brown & Gilman, 1989), researchers have sometimes confounded distance (i.e., familiarity) and affect (i.e., liking). Higher levels of politeness have been found to be associated with greater interpersonal distance (i.e., interactants are more polite with people with whom they are less familiar) but also with greater liking (people are more polite with those whom they like).

The relationship between distance and language also has been investigated independent of politeness theory. Communication variables that are correlated with relationship distance include verbal immediacy (Mehrabian, 1971), responsiveness (Davis, 1982; Reis, Clark, & Holmes, 2004), construal level (Trope & Liberman, 2003), speech accommodation (Giles, 1973), and others. Analyses of language in marital communication have been undertaken as well (Gottman, 1979; Noller & Feeney, 2002). Recently, researchers have investigated referents as markers of perceptions of a relationship. In English, speakers have options when referring to people with whom they may

---

[5]There is a fairly extensive literature on gender differences in language use. Although there is support for some gender differences (see Leaper & Ayres, 2007, for a review), early claims of broad, cross-situational gender differences seem to be somewhat overdone.

be associated. One basic contrast is between a plural pronoun (e.g., "We went to the movies") versus separate referents (e.g., "Mark and I went to the movies"). Fitzsimons and Kay (2004; see also Agnew, Van Lange, Rusbult, & Langston, 1998) found that the use of first-person plurals results in perceptions of a closer relationship than the use of separate referents.

Politeness Theory Summary

One of the strengths of Brown and Levinson's theory is the inclusion of power and distance, two of the major dimensions underlying social interaction, at least in Western cultures (Bakan, 1966; McAdams, 1985). There have been calls, however, to broaden the model so as to incorporate other interpersonal dimensions (e.g., Tracy, 1990). It is important to note, however, that power, distance, and imposition are high-level, abstract variables that should subsume more specific variables. For example, gender, ethnicity, occupational differences, and so on are variables that feed into power and distance, and ultimately, politeness. Even mood states may be incorporated in the model in this way. For example, Forgas (1999a, 1999b) demonstrated that people in sad moods prefer greater politeness than people in happy moods. Sad moods generally result in reduced confidence and hence less perceived power. As politeness theory predicts, lower perceived power should increase the speaker's level of politeness.

There are, of course, many reasons for speaking indirectly. Recently Pinker (2007; Pinker, Nowak, & Lee, 2008) has used game theory to argue that there is an evolutionary basis for linguistic indirectness. Rather than emphasizing the role of indirectness in facilitating cooperative exchanges, Pinker argues that indirectness can play an important role in competitive exchanges. For example, indirect utterances (i.e., off-record forms) can provide a speaker with plausible deniability. This is advantageous in certain situations (e.g., offering a bribe) because it maximizes the sum of the potential outcomes (i.e., the negative outcomes of offering the bribe if caught are lessened because the bribe intent can be denied). Research is needed to test predictions derived from this model.

Face-Work and Language Comprehension

The role of face-work in language comprehension has received much less attention than its role in language production. However, given the coordination required for language use (Clark, 1996) it seems likely that face-work—and the variables that affect it—will play a parallel role in language comprehension. Because face-work is a motive for being indirect, it should serve as a frame for the interpretation of indirect remarks. Consistent with this

logic, Holtgraves (1998, 1999) demonstrated that indirect replies that involve violating the relation maxim (Grice, 1975) will be comprehended more quickly when face management processes are operative than when they are absent.

Other speaker variables such as occupation (Katz & Pexman, 1997), personality (Demeure, Bonnefon, & Raufaste, 2008, experiment 2), and status (Holtgraves, 1994; Holtgraves, Srull, & Socall, 1989) can influence remark interpretation via the operation of face management. In addition, Bonnefon and Villejoubert (2006) recently demonstrated that an expectation that speakers will tend to be polite when conveying face-threatening information can influence the interpretation of probability terms. Specifically, with statements that describe the probability of a medical problem, people tend to overestimate the conveyed probability of more severe conditions (relative to less severe conditions) because they interpret "possibility" as a politeness marker rather than as a marker of uncertainty.

Language, Culture, and Meaning

Language and culture are closely intertwined, with language reflecting aspects of culture and simultaneously playing a crucial role in the creation, maintenance, and transmission of culture (Conway & Schaller, 2007; E. Kashima & Kashima, 1998).

Cross-Cultural Misunderstandings

There is a sizable literature on cross-cultural miscommunication (House, Kasper, & Ross, 2003; Ting-Toomey, 1999), and some of these misunderstandings can be explained in terms of the interpersonal underpinnings of politeness and indirectness. For example, the meaning and distribution of power and distance can vary cross-culturally, resulting in different interaction systems with the corresponding potential for communicative misunderstandings. More specifically, cultures may differ in terms of the default values for power and distance and in terms of the weighting given to these variables. As an example of the former, Scollon and Scollon (1981) report that Athabaskans tend to assume greater distance when interacting with unacquainted individuals than do English-speaking Americans. As a result, the former display a preference for negative (i.e., deferential) politeness strategies and the latter a preference for positive (i.e., approach-based) politeness strategies, preferences that can result in misunderstanding when members of these groups interact. In terms of the weighting of the variables, Holtgraves and Yang (1992) and Ambady et al. (1996) have demonstrated that South Koreans weight power and distance more heavily than do U.S. Americans. Hence, South Koreans tend to vary the politeness of their remarks as a function of power and distance to a greater extent than do U.S. Americans.

Culture and Linguistic Contextualization

Languages differ in terms of the role played by the context in communication. Hall (1976, 1983) categorized cultures as being high context (background context plays a relatively large role in language use) and low context (communicated information is contained in the language rather than inferred based on context). Almost all high-context cultures would be classified as collectivist cultures and almost all low-context cultures as individualistic cultures. Demonstrations that South Koreans (a collectivist culture) vary their levels of politeness as a function of the social context more so than North Americans (an individualistic culture) is consistent with this difference (Ambady et al., 1996; Holtgraves & Yang, 1992), as is the demonstration that the former tend to speak more indirectly (and hence rely more on the context) than the latter (Holtgraves, 1997b).

More recently, Kashima and Kashima (E. Kashima & Kashima, 1998, Y. Kashima & Kashima, 2003) distinguished between languages in terms of whether or not pronouns are optional. Speakers of English usually reference themselves and others with pronouns when reporting on their actions (e.g., "I went to the show last night"); speakers of other languages (e.g., Japanese) often do not do this (e.g., "Went to the show last night"). The explicit mentioning of a pronoun highlights the person to whom the pronoun refers, and hence the target is decontextualized. In contrast, dropping a pronoun contextualizes the target in the context of speech. The former is a linguistic practice consistent with individualism's emphasis on the person; the latter is a linguistic practice consistent with collectivism. Countries in which people speak a language in which pronouns are required score significantly higher on Hofstede's (1980) individualism scale (and related cultural variables) than countries in which people speak a language in which pronouns are optional (E. Kashima & Kashima, 1998; Y. Kashima & Kashima, 2003).

A related cross-cultural difference is the linguistic abstractness (as described earlier in the section on words) with which social objects are described. Y. Kashima, Kashima, Kim, and Gelfand (2006) report that South Korean speakers tend to use verbs, but English speakers tend to use adjectives, to describe a variety of social objects. Likewise, Maass, Karasawa, Politi, and Suga (2006) showed that Italians were more likely to use adjectives when describing other individuals and groups, and Japanese speakers were more likely to use verbs. Adjectives are more abstract and devoid of contextual referents and hence represent a decontextualizing linguistic

practice. Relatedly, Y. Kashima et al. (2006) reported that South Koreans were more likely to provide contextual qualifiers to a description of a social object (e.g., sociable when I am with friends) than were Australian English speakers. Again, people in collectivist cultures tend to be less abstract and emphasize the context more than people in individualistic cultures.

These cross-cultural differences in linguistic contextualization have important social psychological implications. For example, Maass et al. (2006) showed that there are memory effects paralleling the practice of lexical choice (adjective vs. verb) in person and group perceptions. Just as Italians tended to use adjectives and Japanese, verbs, Italians were more likely to transform behavioral information (verbs) into traits (adjectives), whereas Japanese participants tended to falsely recall verbs when they had seen traits. In this case, cultural differences in cognitive styles and linguistic preferences showed clear parallel trends, a result that is consistent with the finding that different linguistic practices may encourage different attentional processes (Stapel & Semin, 2007).

More generally, differences in language and linguistic contextualization may play a mediating role in cross-cultural differences in certain basic social psychological processes. For example, the correspondence bias in attribution appears to be somewhat more pronounced in English-speaking cultures than in Asia (Choi, Nisbett, & Norenzayan, 1999; Y. Kashima, 2001; Miller, 1984). Similarly, person descriptions produced by Westerners are more trait-based than those produced by Asians (e.g., Trafimow, Triandis, & Goto, 1991). These cross-cultural attributional differences may reflect linguistic differences. One possibility is that English includes a relatively greater number of trait words, thereby facilitating a tendency to think about and explain behavior in terms of their trait-like properties (but see Maass et al., 2006). Another possibility is that cultural differences in linguistic contextualization underlie these attributional differences as demonstrated by Y. Kashima et al. (2006; see also Miyamoto & Kitayama, 2002). For discussions of the reciprocal relationship between language, culture, and social behavior, see Holtgraves and Kashima (2008) and Ji, Zhang, and Nisbett (2004).

CONVERSATIONS

Utterances usually occur with other utterances, that is, they are usually embedded in a conversational context. Interactive language use—and conversation in particular—complicates considerably our understanding of language. One way to appreciate conversational complexity is to examine the complete transcript of a conversation, a transcript that captures all of the false starts, incomplete sentences, repetition, backtracking, noncontent words or phrases (Oh, well, etc.), and so on. Real conversations look far different from the idealized conversations seen in novels and plays, and this reflects their collaborative and emergent nature. At the same time, conversations are typically structured in some way, even though the specifics of that structure cannot be specified in advance. Interactants are not playing individual roles in a conversation drama. Rather, participants are together jointly creating a conversation.

Conversational Structure

Much of the early work on the structure of conversations was conducted by researchers working within a framework termed *conversation analysis* (CA). CA was developed in the 1960s by the sociologist Harvey Sacks and his colleagues Emanuel Schegloff and Gail Jefferson. Conversation analysis has its roots in ethnomethodology, a branch of sociology developed by Harold Garfinkel (1967) that takes as its central argument the idea that the social order is continuously created by people as they use language to make sense of their behavior and that of others. Conversational analysis, like ethnomethodology, focuses on these common linguistic practices. The general strategy is to examine actual (not contrived) verbal interactions in great detail (e.g., telephone conversations). These recordings are then transcribed, keeping as much detail (e.g., overlap talking, pauses, breathiness, word and syllable stress, etc.) as possible. A fairly standardized transcript system, developed primarily by Gail Jefferson (2004), exists for this purpose.

The goal of the analyst is to identify regularities or patterns in the sequential organization of talk. This is an empirical, inductive approach and no a priori concepts or theories are applied at the outset. In contrast to other approaches to language covered in this chapter, no reference is ever made to internal states and events (e.g., conversational implicatures, positive face wants, etc.). It is an approach that takes talk, and only talk, as the object of study (Heritage, 1984).

Adjacency Pairs

In this approach, the most fundamental unit is termed an *adjacency pair* (Schegloff, 1968, 2007; Schegloff & Sacks, 1973). Goffman (1976) used the term *couplet* for a similar unit, and Clark (2004) referred to them as *projective* pairs. Adjacency pairs consist of two utterances, spoken by two people, with the utterances paired such that given the occurrence of the first pair part, the second pair part becomes conditionally relevant. Examples of adjacency

pairs include question–answer, apology–minimization, offer–acceptance, greeting–greeting, summons–answer, request–promise, and so on (see Table 36.3).

Adjacency pairs have a number of important features (Schegloff, 2007). First, they are useful for coordinating interactants' understanding. For example, the occurrence of an answer in response to a question displays the second interactant's understanding of what was accomplished with the first speaker's utterance, that the first speaker has asked a question. Second, adjacency pairs represent a template for the production of talk. Given the occurrence of a first pair part, the second pair part becomes *conditionally relevant* (Schegloff, 1968); it is expected, and if not forthcoming, its absence is noticeable, a feature that is similar to the effects of violating a conversation maxim (Grice, 1975).[6] Third, the second pair part of an adjacency pair need not immediately follow the first pair part because embedded sequences of talk, termed *insertion sequences* (Schegloff, 1972) or *side sequences* (Jefferson, 1972), can occur between the first and second pair part. Insertion sequences can become quite lengthy, with adjacency pairs becoming embedded within other adjacency pairs.

Fourth, not all second pair parts are of equal status; some (e.g., agreements) are preferred over others (e.g., disagreements; Levinson, 1983).[7] The former are referred to as preferred turns or seconds, and the latter as dispreferred turns or seconds. Dispreferred seconds are marked in a variety of ways. Quite often they are delayed, indirect, longer, less clear, and prefaced in various ways, relative to their direct counterparts. Interestingly, the manner in which dispreferred seconds are marked is constant over all adjacency pairs; these markings have been documented for disagreements (Holtgraves, 1997c; Pomerantz, 1984), blamings (Atkinson & Drew, 1979), rejections (Davidson, 1984), and many other actions as well (e.g., Heritage, 1984; Sacks, 1987).

Fifth, adjacency pairs figure prominently in the manner in which conversations are opened and terminated. To begin a conversation, potential interactants must indicate to one another their availability and willingness to enter into a conversation, the parties must recognize each other, and a topic must be brought up and sustained. These problems are handled economically with a particular type of adjacency pair termed a *summons–answer* pair (Schegloff, 1968). A summons (hey, hi, yo, telephone ring, etc.) obligates a response from the person to whom it is directed.

---

[6]Although CA researchers would eschew any reference to internal constructions such as implicatures.

[7]When the first-pair part is a self-deprecation, however, the preferred response is a disagreement (Pomerantz, 1984).

The answer to the summons (hello, hi, yeah?) often serves as both a second pair part (an answer) and a first pair part (question) that further serves to align potential interactants into a conversation. In a similar fashion, adjacency pairs aid in closing conversations (via preclosings; e.g., Well …), making requests (through prerequests; e.g., Are you busy?), issuing invitations (through preinvitations; Doing anything Friday?), and situating stories (through preannouncements; e.g., Did I tell you about …?). Adjacency pairs play a clear and fundamental role in the structuring of verbal interactions; they are the primordial conversational unit (see Table 36.3).

Turn-Taking and Repair

Conversations are normally quite orderly: One speaker speaks at a time and speaker transitions occur with relatively little overlap. Moreover, this orderliness occurs regardless of the number of speakers, the size of the turns, the topic of the conversation, and so on. In a seminal article, Sacks, Schegloff, and Jefferson (1974) proposed a model to account for this turn-taking regularity. This model has two components, a turn-construction component and a turn-allocation component. The first component refers to the syntactical and intonational features of a turn that result in its projectability; after a conversational turn has begun, interactants can quickly identify the type of turn that is underway and the point at which the turn will be complete (termed a *transition-relevance place*). The necessity of such a component comes from the fact that conversationalists are capable of quickly processing conversation turns; transitions are brief and overlap rare (and when overlap occurs, its repair is quite orderly (Jefferson, 1986).

The second component refers to an ordered set of rules for allocating turns within a conversation. The first rule, for example, is that the current speaker has the right (at the first transition relevance place) to either continue speaking or to select the next speaker (who is then obligated to speak). These rules have received some criticism (e.g., Schegloff, 1992; Searle, 1992), especially from those who argue for a greater role for nonverbal signaling in maintaining turn-taking orderliness (e.g., Argyle, 1973; S. Duncan & Fiske, 1977).

Conversation analysis remains a relatively small but thriving research orientation. Its impact on other areas of research on language use, with the exception of Clark's (1996) work (discussed subsequently), has been relatively small. However, there have been some non-CA studies examining the processing consequences of dispreferred markers (also referred to as *discourse* markers), with the general finding that such markers are communicative and facilitate recipients' comprehension of a speaker's meaning (Fox Tree, 2002; Fox Tree & Schrock, 1999; Holtgraves, 2000).

Perspective Taking

To converse successfully requires perspective taking, and some theorists have argued that perspective taking is one of the most fundamental tasks in successful language use (R. Brown, 1965; Clark, 1985, 1996; Fussell & Krauss, 1992; Krauss & Fussell, 1991; Mead, 1934; Rommetveit, 1974). Perspective taking is critical because linguistic meaning is not entirely fixed. Words can have multiple meanings, and these meanings are activated simultaneously, at least initially (Swinney, 1979). By definition, deictic

Table 36.3 Examples of Adjacency Pair Functions

Adjacency Pair Function	Example
Prerequest (with insertion sequence)	A: Will you be in your office?
	B: Tuesday or Wednesday?
	A: Tuesday.
	B: No.
	A does not make request
Preinvitation	A: Are you busy tomorrow night?
	B: No
	A issues an invitation
Preannouncement	A: Did I tell you about Sam's adventure?
	B: No
	A tells story about Sam
Preoffer	A: Do you need any help?
	B: I do.
	A makes offer to help
Opening a conversation	A: Hello …
	B: Hi …
Closing a conversation	A: So …, guess I better get going …
	B: Yeah, … me too ….

expressions (e.g., It's over *there*) have a meaning that can only be determined in context. Further, words can be used in new and innovative ways (Clark & Gerrig, 1983; Lakoff, 1987), such as when a waitress refers to a customer as the "ham sandwich." Ambiguity is not limited to word meaning. The meaning of a speaker's utterance, as described earlier, is frequently ambiguous and hence may require perspective taking for successful disambiguation. Moreover, it is not just the recipient who must engage in perspective taking; speakers, too, must attempt to estimate the perspective of their addressee to construct conversation contributions that will be successfully understood.

Perspective taking is necessary but not sufficient for successful communication. Rather, *mutual* perspective taking of some sort is required. The concept of mutual perspective taking has been captured most clearly with the concept of common ground (Clark, 1996; Clark & Marshal, 1981).[8] In general, "X" is in common ground when two interactants each know "X," and each knows that the other knows "X." Mutual perspective taking, then, is the attempt to establish what is in common ground.

Although the concepts of mutual perspective taking and common ground are intuitively reasonable, the nature, extent, and success of perspective taking remain a matter of considerable debate and continue to be an active area of research (for reviews see Barr & Keysar, 2007; Schober & Brennan, 2003). A major impetus for research in this area was the development of a laboratory referential communication task by Robert Krauss and colleagues (Krauss & Weinheimer, 1964, 1966). In the referential communication task (variations of which continue to be used today), participants are asked to describe figures (often nonsense figures) so that they can be identified by someone else.

One of the major findings with this task is that the descriptions that people provide typically vary as a function of what the intended audience can be presumed to know (Fussell & Krauss, 1989a, 1989b; Krauss & Weinheimer, 1964, 1966), a phenomenon referred to as audience design (Clark & Murphy, 1983). For example, messages designed for another person tend to be longer and more literal than messages designed for oneself (Fussell & Krauss, 1989a). Similarly, Isaacs and Clark (1987; see also Clark & Wilkes-Gibbs, 1986) demonstrated that New Yorkers produce longer descriptions of New York City landmarks for non–New Yorkers (of whom they can assume less New York knowledge) than they do for New Yorkers. Further, messages designed for friends tend to be shorter than messages designed for unknown others (Fussell & Krauss, 1989b). With friends, much can be left unsaid because of the relatively large amount of shared knowledge (Kent, Davis, & Shapiro, 1981). Interestingly, audience design occurs not just with humans but with robots as well; people make assumptions about what a robot "knows" and adjust their message based on this assessment (Torrey, Fussell, & Kiesler, in press).

A potential problem with these studies is that they do not demonstrate directly that perspective taking is the factor influencing message formulation (see Barr & Keysar, 2007; Keysar, 1997). Fussell and Krauss (1992), however, used a procedure in which participants' assumptions about what their addressee knew were explicitly measured, and these estimates were significantly related to the amount of descriptive information in a message. Hence, speakers' messages were based, in part, on their estimates of what their adressees knew.

At the same time, however, perspective taking is far from perfect. Numerous studies, for example, have demonstrated that speakers often fail to use linguistic expressions that would allow recipients to disambiguate a syntactically ambiguous sentence (Arnold, Wasow, Asudeh, & Alrenga, 2004; Ferreira & Dell, 2000), thereby suggesting a lack of attention to a recipient's perspective. One potential obstacle in perspective taking is that speakers may wrongly assume that their audience will know what they know—that is, they demonstrate the false consensus effect (Ross, Greene, & House, 1977). For example, when Fussell and Krauss (1991, 1992) asked participants both to identify various objects and to estimate the percentage of others who could correctly identify the objects, participants were far more likely to estimate that others could identify an object if they themselves could identify the object. Consistent with this, several studies using a referential task procedure have demonstrated that participants are frequently egocentric and use information that they know is not available to their interaction partners (Keysar, Barr, Balin, & Paek, 1998; Keysar, Lin, & Barr, 2003).

Egocentricity is not limited to referent identification. Keysar and Bly (1995), for example, demonstrated a transparency of meaning effect: When people come to believe that an idiomatic expression has a particular meaning, they tend to assume others will arrive at the same meaning, and in this way they fail to consider the possibility of alternative interpretations of the expression. Similarly, egocentricity has been found for the interpretation of potentially sarcastic expressions (Keysar, 1994), and more recently, Holtgraves (2005) demonstrated a speaker–addressee discrepancy in utterance interpretation that may be associated with their respective perspectives. An interesting variation on this problem occurs for people who are familiar with

---

[8]The concepts of common ground, and especially the related concept of mutual knowledge, have been somewhat controversial (see Clark & Marshall, 1981; Sperber & Wilson, 1982).

each other. When common ground is large because of a high level of familiarity, there is the risk of assuming that more is shared than is actually the case, thereby leading to perspective-taking errors and miscommunication (Wu & Keysar, 2007a). This failure to consider alternative perspectives may be one reason people overestimate the extent to which a message they generate will be understood by another person (Keysar & Henley, 2002).

Clearly, perspective taking is not perfect. But it is also not static (see Eply, volume 1). One model that attempts to chart the time course of perspective taking is the perspective adjustment model developed by Keysar and colleagues (Epley, Keysar, Van Boven, & Gilovich, 2004; Horton & Keysar, 1996; Keysar, 1998; Keysar, Barr, Balin, & Brauner, 2000; Keysar et al., 1998). This model assumes that the initial, default interpretation for both speakers and addressees is egocentric. Interactants do not consider common ground; instead, any available information is used regardless of whether it might be mutually known. Hence, participants in a referential communication task will look initially at objects that cannot be seen by their interaction partner and therefore are not in common ground (Keysar et al., 1998; Keysar, Lin, & Barr, 2003). People are not completely unaware of the importance of common ground, however, and they sometimes do take it into account. This occurs during an adjustment process, a process that attempts to correct the initial egocentric interpretation. Unlike the initial egocentric interpretation, the adjustment process is slow and effortful. It also constitutes a major difference between children and adults; the latter are more likely than the former to adjust an initial egocentric perspective (Epley, Morewedge, & Keysar, 2004).

There has been some question about the nature of the initial egocentricity implied by the perspective adjustment model. Some researchers, for example, have suggested that although people do use privileged information (thereby reflecting some egocentricity), the extent to which they do so is constrained (at the beginning of the process) by an awareness of what is in common ground (Hanna, Tanenhaus, & Trueswell, 2003; see also Nadig & Sedivy, 2002). Recently, Barr (2008) has provided evidence that people have an expectation that common ground will be used, but they are still unable to control their egocentricity. Overall, current evidence favors—at least for low-level processing of referents—an initial (and probably automatic and uncontrollable) egocentricity. Although biases have been demonstrated for higher-level language processes, the exact nature of these biases remains unknown and largely underresearched.

Finally, research has demonstrated individual, social, and cultural differences in the extent to which people engage in perspective taking. In terms of the former, Kruglanski and colleagues (e.g., Richter & Kruglanski, 1999; Webster & Kruglanski, 1994) have shown, using a referential communication task, that people high in need for closure tend to produce messages for others that are shorter and more nonliteral than those produced by participants low in need for closure, thereby reflecting a tendency not to take into account the perspective of the recipient. In terms of social variables, Galinsky, Magee, Inesi, and Gruenfeld (2006) have demonstrated higher power to be associated with a reduced tendency to take the perspective of another person. In terms of culture, Wu and Keysar (2007b) found that native Chinese participants were less egocentric in a referential communication task than were non-Asian Americans, an effect they interpret as reflecting the broad cultural differences of interdependence (Chinese) and independence (North American). Future research on individual and cultural variability in perspective taking is clearly warranted given its importance for communication success.

Grounding and Collaboration

The interactive nature of perspective taking, coupled with the structural regularities found in conversation analytic research, has been incorporated into models of conversation proposed and investigated by Herb Clark and colleagues (Clark, 1996, 2004; Clark & Brennan, 1991; Clark & Krych, 2004; Clark & Schaeffer, 1989; Clark & Wilkes-Gibbs, 1986; Schrober & Clark, 1989). Conversations are viewed as collaborative and emergent (this is the dialogic perspective described by Krauss & Fussell, 1996), and emphasis is placed on the linguistic and non-linguistic mechanisms that facilitate this accomplishment. Clark (2004) referred to these mechanisms as collateral signals.

A key assumption with this approach is that interlocutors must *ground* their contributions to an exchange (Clark, 1996; Clark & Schaefer, 1989; Clark & Wilkes-Gibbs, 1986), that is, make sure that their contribution is mutually understood. This is a two-step process involving a presentation phase and an acceptance phase. The presentation phase refers to a conversational contribution (an utterance, phrase, etc.) that must be evaluated in terms of its mutual understandability. Because grounding is collaborative, the presentation phase is often tentative (Clark, 1996; Clark & Brennan, 1991; Clark & Wilkes-Gibbs, 1986). Sometimes this tentativeness is underscored with a try marker (rising intonation following the referent; Sacks & Schegloff, 1979), followed by a pause. If this initial identification is not accepted, the speaker can provide additional detail (e.g., "The door" . . . pause . . . "The one that's open" . . .). Sometimes, a recipient will provide an alternative description of a proposed referent, which the first speaker can then accept or reject (Clark & Brennan, 1991; Clark & Krych, 2004).

The acceptance phase of the grounding process refers to the evidence provided by the other interlocutors regarding their understanding of the contribution, a step that is required for the conversation to stay on track. Clark argued that the absence of negative evidence (huh? what?) is not sufficient; people ultimately seek positive evidence of understanding, and this can be accomplished in several ways. First, there is *direct acknowledgment* of understanding, or back-channel responses (Yngve, 1970). These include continuers (uh, huh, yeah, etc.; Schegloff, 1982), assessments of a contribution (wow, really?, no kidding?, etc.; Goodwin, 1986), and many gestures such as head nods and so on (Clark & Kyrch, 2004). Usually direct acknowledgments do not occupy a separate turn at talk but instead overlap with the contribution of the other interactant.[9]

A second form of positive evidence is a subsequent turn that displays, through its orientation to the prior utterance, an understanding of that utterance. For example, an acceptance, answer, and refusal following an offer, question, and request, all indicate the second person's understanding of the first pair part of the adjacency pair (Sacks, Schegloff, & Jefferson, 1974). Note that the occurrence of a relevant response is both an acceptance (of the prior turn) and a presentation for the other interactant; the other interactant must now provide evidence regarding the acceptance of this contribution. The third and most basic form of positive evidence is continued attention to the current speaker. There are numerous devices that addressees can use to verify that they are attending to the speaker, and many of these are nonverbal (e.g., gaze; Argyle & Cook, 1976).[10] Speakers monitor addressees for understanding and will seek evidence of the addressees' attention (Clark & Krych, 2004). Speakers may, for example, begin a turn and then wait until the addressee

indicates attention before attempting to complete the turn; they can then either finish the turn or repeat the part that had been presented (Goodwin, 1986).

An additional feature of conversation that illustrates its collaborative nature is what Clark (1996; Clark & Brennan, 1991) termed the *principle of least collective effort,* a principle stating that conversation participants try to minimize their collective effort, the work that the two of them do. This principle is similar to proposals regarding a tendency for people to minimize their individual communicative effort, such as Grice's (1975) maxim of quantity (say no more than is required) and the tendency for people to "overassume" what their interlocutors know and "undertell" (i.e., assume the recipient can assess the relevant information; Sacks & Schegloff, 1979). The difference is in the emphasis on collective rather than individual effort. This principle is consistent with a number of findings, such as the tendency in object-naming tasks to provide only brief descriptions at the outset and then wait for confirmation of understanding (Fussell & Krauss, 1992). It is more efficient, collectively, to wait for information allowing one to then construct a tailor-made message (if necessary). Conversational repair also illustrates least collective effort. Interactants have a strong preference for repairing their own utterances (self-repair) rather than allowing another to do so (other-repair; Schegloff, Jefferson, & Sacks, 1977); fewer turns are required for the former relative to the latter. A preference for other-recognition rather than self-identification in telephone openings can be interpreted in the same way; other-recognition eliminates the turns required for mutual recognition of the involved parties (Schegloff, 1979).[11]

The approach of Clark and colleagues illustrates the collaborative nature of conversational understanding and the manner in which people work together to establish mutually what is in common ground. This is probably why both interactants are blamed when pragmatic errors occur (Kreuz & Roberts, 1993). This approach has particular relevance for the investigation of human–computer interaction because it focuses on the moment-by-moment coordination required to successfully use language (e.g., Brennan, 1998; Clark & Brennan, 1991; Kiesler, Powers, Fussell, & Torrey, 2008).

---

[9]There can be ambiguities with some of these devices (see Holtgraves, 2002). For example, direct acknowledgments (back channel responses) can be mistaken as indicating agreement when it is only understanding (grounding) of the prior contribution that is intended. Although the conversation system contains mechanisms that allow such misunderstandings to be corrected and repaired, it is possible for people to misunderstand one another and yet not be aware of that misunderstanding (and hence a repair sequence is not initiated).

[10]There is a fairly extensive literature on the role of gestures in communication, and especially how they work together with language (see S. D. Duncan, Cassell, & Levy, 2007; Krauss, Morrels-Samuels, & Colasante, 1991; McNeil, 2005).

---

[11]Note that there are also good interpersonal reasons for these effects. To initiate repair of another's utterance imposes on that person. Hence, self-repair avoids the imposition created by other-repair and lessens the threat to the other person's negative face. Other-identification in telephone openings displays closeness with the other (I know you well enough to recognize you), in effect, a positive politeness strategy.

Interactive Alignment and Synchrony

A different approach to conversation coordination and perspective taking is the interactive alignment model developed by Pickering and Garrod (2004; Garrod & Pickering, 2004). This model is based on the well-known finding in the psycholinguistics literature that a sentence can prime a syntactic structure (termed *syntactic* or *structural priming*), which then influences subsequent sentence production (Bock, 1986; see Pickering & Ferreira, 2008, for a review). For example, the probability of a speaker using a passive construction (e.g., "The sandwich was eaten by Mark") is increased if the prior speaker used a passive construction. This effect appears to be automatic and effortless and represents implicit learning rather than an intentional matching process (Pickering & Ferreira, 2008). Importantly, structural priming occurs across all dimensions of language (e.g., lexical, syntactic, conceptual, etc.) and greatly facilitates conversation participation. More specifically, these alignment mechanisms promote the activation of syntactical, lexical, and other representations that are shared by interactants, and these momentarily shared representations allow interactants to coordinate their conversational contributions more easily. In certain respects, these processes bear a resemblance to the direct and automatic perception–behavior link proposed by Bargh and colleagues (Bargh & Chartrand, 1999; Dijksterhuis & Bargh, 2001), except that in this case, it is representations rather than overt behaviors that are activated. Evidence for interactive alignment has been provided by experiments demonstrating that interactants spontaneously (without explicit negotiation) match one another across a variety of levels including syntax (Bock, 1986), conceptualization (Garrod & Doherty, 1994), lexical choice (Garrod & Anderson, 1987), and others.

The interactive alignment model can be viewed as an instance of the broader phenomenon of synchrony. According to Semin (2007), synchrony is a fundamental, jointly recruited process through which correspondence between organisms is established across a variety of levels (perceptual, neural, etc.). Synchrony is fundamental in the sense that it precedes language both evolutionarily and ontogenetically, is emphatically social, and occurs without explicit communicative intent. Evidence taken as support for synchrony comes from a variety of research areas including demonstrations of the existence of common neurons for observation and action (i.e., mirror neurons; Rizzolatti & Craighero, 2004), syntactic priming (Bock, 1986), matching of speech rate (Street, 1984) and other behaviors (Chartrand & Bargh, 1999), motor mimicry (Bavelas, Black, Chovil, Lemery, & Mullett, 1986; Bavelas, Black, Lemery, & Mullett, 1988), and so on. Synchrony is important for communication in several ways. It is part of the process through which potential interactants recognize a sense of sameness (i.e., mutual recognition and intelligibility) and develop rapport and liking. Most important, it is an essential building block for communication through its automatic alignment of behavioral and perceptual processes (as in the interactive alignment model). Note that synchrony is prelinguistic; it underlies communication between nonhumans as well as humans.

Speech Accommodation

An approach that focuses on the interpersonal underpinnings of alignment is speech accomodation theory (SAT; now referred to as *communication accomodation* theory), originally formulated by Howard Giles (1973; for reviews, see Gallois, Ogay, & Giles, 2005; Giles et al., 2007). The theory assumes, based on the similarity-attraction effect (Byrne, 1971), that people tend to like those whose speech characteristics are similar to their own and dislike those who are different. Moreover, people are capable of modulating their speech so as to be similar (termed *convergence*) or dissimilar (termed *divergence*) to that of their conversation partner. People can converge or diverge on many dimensions such as word frequency (Levin & Lim, 1988) and phonology (Coupland, 1984), and they may converge on some dimensions but simultaneously diverge on other dimensions (Bilous & Krauss, 1988). Convergence may be symmetrical (both interactants converging) or nonsymmetrical (one interactant converges toward the other). Accommodation is thus strategic and dynamic, and its existence has been documented in several languages (Gallois et al., 2005; Giles, Coupland, & Coupland, 1991).

The primary motives for convergence are to establish closeness and affiliation with the other person (Giles, Mulac, Bradac, & Johnson, 1987; Natale, 1975) and to demonstrate mutual membership in a group (Bourhis, 1983). Speech divergence, in contrast, is viewed as a desire to emphasize one's identity with a reference group that is external to the current situation. Such a motive is most likely to be salient when communicating with outgroup members, and especially when one's social identity has been threatened (Bourhis & Giles, 1976).

Conversational Activities and Their Cognitive Implications

One common conversation activity is storytelling, and the telling of stories figures prominently in narrative approaches that have been developed in personality (McAdams, 1993, 2006) and social psychology (Schank & Abelson, 1995).[12]

Conversational stories (like conversation in general) are largely joint constructions, collaboratively constructed during the course of a conversation (Clark, 1996), and Pasupathi and colleagues (2001; Pasupathi, Alderman, & Shaw, 2007) have investigated some of the effects of collaborative storytelling on subsequent representations. For example, Pasupathi et al. (2007) examined the influence of self-conceptions regarding a computer game on narratives about a game-playing session and the subsequent effects of those narratives on self-conceptions. A bidirectional relationship was found such that self-conceptions influenced narrative contributions, and narrative contributions influenced subsequent self-conceptions. The research of Pasupathi and others has demonstrated several basic principles regarding storytelling and its cognitive consequences.

First, storytelling requires some selectivity because not everything can be included in a story. Details must be glossed over and a sequence of events forced into a narrative structure (regardless of the nature of the original representation). In other words, the construction of a story is influenced by a storytelling schema (Rummlehart, 1975). Second, stories need to be constructed on the basis of what a speaker assumes an audience knows (perspective taking). For example, speakers are unlikely to include information that they believe the audience already knows (e.g., Slugoski, Lalljee, Lamb, & Ginsburg, 1993). Third, speakers may alter the nature of their story based on assumptions regarding the recipients' attitude toward the story topic. In a classic early demonstration, Higgins and Rholes (1978) showed that participants would alter the valence of their message to be consistent with the attitude of the message recipient. Finally, people tell stories for different reasons, and these different motivations can produce different stories (Dudukovic, Marsh, & Tversky, 2004; Marsh & Tversky, 2004; McGregor & Holmes, 1999).

These interactional constraints on storytelling ultimately influence the storyteller's (and recipient's) representation of the story topic. In the Higgins and Rholes (1978) study, for example, subsequent memory and impressions of the target described in the story were biased in the direction of the message (termed "saying is believing" [SIB]); those who provided more positive descriptions had more positive impressions and memory of the target (see McCann & Higgins, 1990, for a review). There have now been several additional studies demonstrating how the act of telling a story influences what people remember about the story topic (Dudukovic et al., 2004; Marsh, 2007; Pasupathi, 2001; Pasupathi et al., 2007; Schank & Ableson, 1995). More recent research, however, suggests that motivation can moderate this effect. For example, Echterhoff and colleagues (Echterhoff, Higgins, & Groll, 2005; Echterhoff, Higgins, Kopietz, & Groll, 2008) demonstrated the occurrence of an audience-congruence memory bias only when the message-production goal served the function of creating a shared reality, an effect that disappeared when other motives (e.g., to be polite or because of an incentive) were in play.

SUMMARY

At some point, most reviews of language and social psychology typically lament the lack of attention that social psychologists have paid to the topic of language. This regret is duly noted here. Social psychologists *have* tended to ignore the role of language in social psychological processes. Still, there is reason for optimism. There have been important developments across a fairly wide swath of social psychology, as well as related disciplines, that focus on language and its role in social psychological processes, as well as the social psychological underpinnings of language use. A brief summary of those developments follows.

Language, Prejudice, and Discrimination

The important role played by language in prejudice and discrimination has long been noted (e.g., Allport, 1954), but it is only more recently that sustained empirical attention has been brought to bear on these topics. This research has shown, in a variety of ways, how the use of language serves as a tool for the creation, maintenance, and dissemination of prejudices, and how language as an abstract system can serve as the repository for the prejudices of its users. Both theoretical and empirical contributions to this literature are expected and warranted.

Language Use and Social Cognition

There has been increasing recognition of the important role played by language in various aspects of social cognition.

---

[12]The idea that talking about events is central to how those events are represented is also fundamental to social constructionism (e.g., Gergen, 1985) and discursive psychology (Edwards & Potter; 1992; Potter & Wetherall, 1987), approaches that attempt to illuminate the role played by language in the creation of social reality. At this point, however, the methodological gulf between discursive psychology and other language research has hindered any cross-fertilization.

The shift from between-language comparisons to within-language comparisons (i.e., language use) has been important in this regard and should continue to be the primary avenue for this research. Particularly important here is the collaboration required to use language with others, and the manner in which that collaboration can influence subsequent representations.

Pragmatics and Social Psychology

Pragmatics may be the language discipline with the most to offer social psychology (e.g., Wyer & Gruenfeld, 1995). The most obvious example of this is the application of conversational principles to understanding participants' responses in psychology experiments. The fundamental insight of this work, that social psychological products emerge in the context of interactive language use, could easily be applied outside the lab. At the same time, social psychology has much to offer the field of pragmatics, especially in terms of the development and testing of models that specify the role of social psychological variables in language use. In short, there is a pragmatic component to many social psychological processes and products, and social psychological processes underlie a wide variety of pragmatic phenomena.

Language and Culture

Research on the cultural underpinnings of psychological processes has increased exponentially in recent years. Yet the possible role played by language in mediating this variability has not received a corresponding degree of attention. It is obviously difficult to disentangle the reciprocal relationships between language, culture, and social psychological processes. Still, understanding the cultural underpinnings of social psychological processes necessitates a consideration of the role played by language in those processes.

Language, Person Perception, and Impression Management

Verbal interactions are often the stage for our attempts at impression management as well as the site for our perceptions of others. Speakers' accents; the content of their words; the way those words are spoken; when, where, and why those words are spoken; and so on are all pieces of the impression management–formation puzzle. Hence, rather than being abstract, disembodied processes, both impression management and person perception are grounded in verbal interactions, and there is much to be gained by examining the role of language use in these processes.

Emerging Communication Technologies

Social interaction in general, and language use in particular, are changing in fundamental ways because of the development and adoption of new electronic communication technologies. Mediated communication represents both a challenge and an opportunity for social psychologists because these changes raise questions regarding the generalizability of earlier findings (e.g., Is face management just as relevant in virtual interaction as it is in face-to-face interaction?) as well as questions regarding new social psychological processes that may be engaged in virtual interactions.

To study language is to study how people produce and comprehend meaning. Every topic covered in this chapter is in some way concerned with meaning, from communicative intentions and speech acts, to the social meaning associated with accents or politeness levels (both intentionally and unintentionally conveyed), to the implicit causality of different verb forms. To study language, then, is to study the social construction of meaning, one of the earliest and most fundamental concerns of social psychology.

REFERENCES

Abelson, R. P., & Kanouse, D. E. (1966). Subjective acceptance of verbal generalizations. In S. Feldman (Ed.), *Cognitive consistency: Motivation antecedents and behavioral consequents* (pp. 171–197). New York: Academic Press.

Agnew, C. R., Van Lange, P. A., Rusbult, C. E., & Langston, C. A. (1998). Cognitive interdependence: Commitment and the mental representation of close relationships. *Journal of Personality and Social Psychology, 74*, 939–954.

Aitchison, J. (2003). *Words in the mind: An introduction to the mental lexicon* (3rd ed.). Oxford: Blackwell.

Allport, G. W. (1954). *The nature of prejudice.* New York: Addison-Wesley.

Ambady N., Koo, J., Lee, F., & Rosenthal, R. (1996). More than words: Linguistic and nonlinguistic politeness in two cultures. *Journal of Personality and Social Psychology, 70*, 996–1011.

Amrhein, P. C. (1992). The comprehension of quasi-performative verbs in verbal commitments: New evidence for componential theories of lexical meaning. *Journal of Memory and Language, 31*, 756–784.

Argyle, M. (1973). *Social interaction.* London: Tavistock.

Argyle, M., & Cook, M. (1976). *Gaze and mutual gaze.* Cambridge, England: Cambridge University Press.

Arnold, J. E., Wasow, T., Asudeh, A., & Alrenga, P. (2004). Avoiding attachment ambiguities: The role of constituent ordering. *Journal of Memory and Language, 51*, 55–70.

Atkinson, J. M., & Drew, P. (1979). *Order in the court: The organization of verbal interaction in judicial settings.* London: Macmillan.

Au, T. (1983). Chinese and English counterfactuals: The Sapir–Whorf hypothesis revisited. *Cognition, 15*, 155–187.

Au, T. (1984). Counterfactuals: In reply to Alfred Bloom. *Cognition, 17*, 289–302.

Au, T. (1986). A verb is worth a thousand words: The causes and consequences of interpersonal events implicit in language. *Journal of Memory and Language, 25,* 104–122.

Austin, J. L. (1962). *How to do things with words.* Oxford: Clarendon Press.

Bach, K., & Harnish, R. M. (1979). *Linguistic communication and speech acts.* Cambridge, MA: MIT press.

Bakan, D. (1966). *The duality of human existence.* Chicago: Rand McNally.

Banaji, M. R., & Hardin, C. D. (1996). Automatic stereotyping. *Psychological Science, 7,* 136–141.

Bargh, J. A., & Chartrand, T. L. (1999). The unbearable automaticity of being. *American Psychologist, 54,* 462–479.

Bargh, J. A., Chen, M., & Burrows, L. (1996). The automaticity of social behaviour: Direct effects of trait concept and stereotype activation on action. *Journal of Personality and Social Psychology, 71,* 230–244.

Barr, D. J. (2008). Pragmatic expectations and linguistic evidence: Listeners anticipate but do not integrate common ground. *Cognition, 109,* 18–40.

Barr, D. J., & Keysar, B. (2007). Perspective taking and the coordination of meaning in language use. In M. Traxler & M. A. Gernsbacher (Eds.), *Handbook of psycholinguistics* (2nd ed., pp. 901–938). London: Elsevier.

Barsalou, L. (1999). Perceptual symbol systems. *Behavioral and Brain Sciences, 22,* 577–660.

Bavelas, J. B., Black, A., Chovil, N., Lemery, C. R., & Mullett, L. (1988). Form and function in motor mimicry: Topographic evidence that the primary function is communicative. *Human Communication Research, 14,* 275–299.

Bavelas, J. B., Black, A., Lemery, C. R., & Mullett, L. (1986). I show how you feel: Motor mimicry as a communicative act. *Journal of Personality and Social Psychology, 50,* 322–329.

Baxter, L. A. (1984). An investigation of compliance gaining as politeness. *Human Communication Research, 10,* 427–456.

Bell, A. (1984). Language style as audience design. *Language in Society, 13,* 145–204.

Berlin, B., & Kay, P. (1969). *Basic color terms: Their universality and evolution.* Berkeley: University of California Press.

Berry, D. S., Pennebaker, J. W., Mueller, J. S., & Hiller, W. S. (1997). Linguistic bases of social perception. *Personality and Social Psychology Bulletin, 23,* 526–537.

Beukeboom, C. J., & de Jong, E. M. (2008). When feelings speak: How affective and proprioceptive cues change language abstraction. *Journal of Language and Social Psychology, 27,* 110–122.

Beukeboom, C. J., & Semin, G. R. (2005). Mood and representations of behavior: The how and why. *Cognition and Emotion, 19,* 1242–1251.

Beukeboom, C. J., & Semin, G. R. (2006). How mood turns on language. *Journal of Experimental Social Psychology, 42,* 553–566.

Bilous, F. R., & Krauss, R. M. (1988). Dominance and accommodation in the conversational behaviors of same and mixed gender dyads. *Language and Communication, 8,* 183–194.

Blankenship, K., & Holtgraves, T. (2005). The role of different markers of linguistic powerlessness in persuasion. *Journal of Language and Social Psychology, 24,* 3–24.

Bloom, A. H. (1981). *The linguistic shaping of thought: A study in the impact of language on thinking in China and the West.* Hillsdale, NJ: Erlbaum.

Blum-Kulka, S. (1987). Indirectness and politeness in requests: Same or different? *Journal of Pragmatics, 11,* 131–146.

Blum-Kulka, S., Danet, B., & Gherson, R. (1985). The language of requesting in Israeli society. In J. Forgas (Ed.), *Language in social situations* (pp. 113–139). New York: Springer-Verlag.

Bock, J. K. (1986). Syntactic priming in language production. *Cognitive Psychology, 18,* 355–387.

Boggs, C., & Giles, H. (1999). The canary in the coal mine: The nonaccommodation cycle in the gendered workplace. *International Journal of Applied Linguistics, 9,* 223–245.

Bond, G. D., & Lee, A. Y. (2005). Language of lies in prison: Linguistic classification of prisoners' truthful and deceptive natural language. *Applied Cognitive Psychology, 19,* 313–329.

Bonnefon, J. F., & Villejoubert, G. (2006). Tactful, or doubtful? Expectations of politeness explain the severity bias in the interpretation of probability phrases. *Psychological Science, 17,* 747–751.

Boroditsky, L. (2001). Does language shape thought?: Mandarin and English speakers' conceptions of time. *Cognitive Psychology, 43,* 1–22.

Boroditsky, L., Schmidt, L., & Phillips, W. (2003). Sex, syntax, and semantics. In D. Gentner & S. Goldin-Meadow (Eds.), *Language in mind: Advances in the study of language and thought* (pp. 61–79). Cambridge, MA: MIT Press.

Bourdieu, P. (1991). *Language and symbolic power.* Cambridge, MA: Polity Press.

Bourhis, R. Y. (1983). Language attitudes and self-reports of French-English usage in Quebec. *Journal of Multilingual and Multicultural Development, 4,* 163–179.

Bourhis, R. Y., & Giles, H. (1976). The language of co-operation in Wales: A field study. *Language Sciences, 42,* 13–16.

Bousfield, D., & Locher, M. A. (2008). *Impoliteness in language: Studies on its interplay with power in theory and practice.* Berlin: Mouton De Gruyter.

Bradac, J. J. (1990). Language attitudes and impression formation. In H. Giles & W. P. Robinson (Eds.), *Handbook of language and social psychology* (pp. 287–421). Chichester, England: Wiley.

Bradac, J. J., Bowers, J. W., & Courtright, J. A. (1979). Three language variables in communication research: Intensity, immediacy, and diversity. *Human Communication Research, 5,* 257–269.

Bradac, J. J., & Mulac, A. (1984). A molecular view of powerful and powerless speech styles: Attributional consequences of specific language features and communicator intentions. *Communication Monographs, 51,* 307–319.

Bradac, J. J., & Wisegarver, R. (1984). Ascribed status, lexical diversity, and accent: Determinants of perceived status, solidarity, and control of speech style. *Journal of Language and Social Psychology, 3,* 239–256.

Brennan, S. E. (1998). The grounding problem in conversations with and through computers. In S. Fussell & R. Kreuz (Eds.), *Social and cognitive approaches to interpersonal communication* (pp. 201–225). Mahwah, NJ: Erlbaum.

Brown, B. L. (1980). Effects of speech rate on personality attributions and competency evaluations. In H. Giles, W. P. Robinson, & P. Smith (Eds.), *Language: Social psychological perspectives* (pp. 294–300). Oxford: Pergamon.

Brown, B. L., Giles, H., & Thackerar, J. N. (1985). Speaker evaluations as a function of speech rate, accent and context. *Language and Communication, 5,* 107–220.

Brown, P., & Levinson, S. (1978). Universals in language usage: Politeness phenomena. In E. Goody (Ed.), *Questions and politeness* (pp. 56–289). Cambridge, England: Cambridge University Press.

Brown, P., & Levinson, S. (1987). *Politeness: Some universals in language usage.* Cambridge, England: Cambridge University Press.

Brown, R. (1965). *Social psychology.* New York: The Free Press.

Brown, R. (1988). More than Ps and Qs. *Contemporary Psychology, 33,* 749–750.

Brown, R., & Fish, D. (1983). The psychological causality implicit in language. *Cognition, 14,* 237–273.

Brown, R., & Ford, M. (1961). Address in American English. *Journal of Abnormal and Social Psychology, 62*, 375–385.

Brown, R., & Gilman, A. (1989). Politeness theory and Shakespeare's four major tragedies. *Language in Society, 18*, 159–212.

Byrne, D. (1971). *The attraction paradigm.* New York: Academic Press.

Burrell, N. A., & Koper, R. J. (1998). The efficacy of powerful/powerless language on attitudes and source credibility. In M. Allen & R. W. Preiss (Eds.), *Persuasion: Advances through meta-analysis* (pp. 203–215). Cresskill, NJ: Hampton Press.

Campbell-Kibler, K. (2007). Accent, (ing), and the social logic of listener's perceptions. *American Speech, 82*, 32–64.

Cansler, D. C., & Stiles, W. B. (1981). Relative status and interpersonal presumptuousness. *Journal of Experimental Social Psychology, 17*, 459–471.

Cargile, A. C. (1997) Attitudes toward Chinese-accented speech: An investigation in two contexts. *Journal of Language and Social Psychology 16*, 434–443.

Cargile, A. C., & Bradac, J. J. (2001) Attitudes toward language: A review of speaker-evaluation research and a general process model. In W. B. Gudykunst (Ed.), *Communication yearbook 25* (pp. 347–382). Mahwah, NJ: Erlbaum.

Cargile, A. C., Giles, H., Ryan, E. B., & Bradac, J. J. (1994). Language attitudes as a social process: A conceptual model and new directions. *Language and Communication, 14*, 211–236.

Carli, L. (1990). Gender, language and influence. *Journal of Personality and Social Psychology, 59*, 941–951.

Carnaghi, A., Maass, A., Gresta, S., Bianchi, M., Cadinu, M., & Arcuri, L. (2008). Nomina sunt omina: On the inductive potential of nouns and adjectives in person perception. *Journal of Personality and Social Psychology, 94*, 839–859.

Carston, R. (2002). *Thoughts and utterances: The pragmatics of explicit communication.* Malden, MA: Blackwell.

Chartrand, T. L., & Bargh, J. A. (1999). The chameleon effect: The perception-behavior link and social interaction. *Journal of Personality and Social Psychology, 76*, 893–910.

Cheng, P. W. (1985). Pictures of ghosts: A critique of Alfred Bloom's *The Linguistic Shaping of Thought. American Anthropologist, 87*, 917–922.

Chiu, C.-Y., Krauss, R. M., & Lau, I. Y-M. (1998). Some cognitive consequences of communication. In S. R. Fussell & R. J. Kreuz (Eds.), *Social and cognitive approaches to interpersonal communication* (pp. 259–278). Mahwah, NJ: Erlbaum.

Choi, I., Nisbett, R. E., & Norenzayan, A. (1999). Causal attribution across cultures: Variation and universality. *Psychological Bulletin, 125*, 47–63.

Choy, S., & Dodd, D. (1976). Standard-English speaking and non-standard Hawaiian-English speaking children: Comprehension of both dialects and teachers' evaluations. *Journal of Educational Psychology, 68*, 184–193.

Clark, H. H. (1985). Language use and language users. In G. Lindzey & E. Aronson (Eds.), *The handbook of social psychology* (3rd ed., Vol. 2, pp. 179–232) Reading, MA: Addison-Wesley.

Clark, H. H. (1996). *Using language.* Cambridge, England: Cambridge University Press.

Clark, H. H. (2004). Pragmatics of language performance. In L. R. Horn & G. Ward (Eds.), *The handbook of pragmatics* (pp. 365–382). Malden, MA: Blackwell.

Clark, H. H., & Brennan, S. E. (1991). Grounding in communication. In L. B. Resnick, J. M. Levine, & S. D. Teasley (Eds.), *Perspectives on socially shared cognition* (pp. 127–149). Washington, DC: American Psychological Association.

Clark, H. H., & Clark, E. V. (1977). *Psychology and language: An introduction to psycholinguistics.* San Diego: Harcourt Brace Jovanovich.

Clark, H. H., & Gerrig, R. J. (1983). Understanding old words with new meanings. *Journal of Verbal Learning and Verbal Behavior, 22*, 591–608.

Clark, H. H., & Krych, M. A. (2004). Speaking while monitoring addressees for understanding. *Journal of Memory and Language, 50*, 62–81.

Clark, H. H., & Marshall, C. R. (1981). Definite reference and mutual knowledge. In A. K. Joshi, B. L. Webber, & I. A. Sag (Eds.), *Elements of discourse understanding* (pp. 10–63). Cambridge, England: Cambridge University Press.

Clark, H. H., & Murphy, G. L. (1983). Audience design in meaning and reference. In J. F. Le Ny & W. Kintsch (Eds.), *Language and comprehension* (pp. 287–299). New York: North Holland.

Clark, H. H., & Schaefer, E. F. (1989). Contributing to discourse. *Cognitive Science, 13*, 259–204.

Clark, H. H., & Schunk, D. (1980). Polite responses to polite requests. *Cognition, 8*, 111–143.

Clark, H. H., & Wilkes-Gibbs, D. (1986). Referring as a collaborative process. *Cognition, 22*, 1–39.

Cohen, P. R., & Perrault, C. R. (1979). Elements of a plan based theory of speech acts. *Cognitive Science, 3*, 177–212.

Conway, L. G., & Schaller, M. (2007). How communication shapes culture. In K. Fiedler (Ed.), *Social communication* (pp. 107–128). New York: Psychology Press.

Corrigan, R. (1988). Who dun it? The influence of actor-patient animacy and type of verb in the making of causal attributions. *Journal of Memory and Language, 27*, 447–465.

Corrigan, R. (1993). Causal attributions to states and events described by different classes of verbs. *British Journal of Social Psychology, 32*, 335–348.

Coupland, N. (1984). Accommodation at work: Some phonological data and their implications. *International Journal of the Sociology of Language, 46*, 49–70.

Crosby, F., & Nyquist, L. (1977). The female register: An empirical study of Lakoff's hypothesis. *Language in Society, 6*, 313–322.

Davidson, J. (1984). Subsequent versions of invitations, offers, requests and proposals dealing with potential or actual rejection. In J. M. Atkinson & J. C. Heritage (Eds.), *Structures of social action: Studies in conversation analysis* (pp. 102–128). Cambridge, England: Cambridge University Press.

Davis, D. (1982). Determinants of responsiveness in dyadic interaction. In W. Ickes & E. Knowles (Eds.), *Personality, roles, and social behavior* (pp. 85–139). New York: Springer-Verlag.

Demeure, V., Bonnefon, J. F., & Raufaste, E. (2008). Utilitarian relevance and face-management in the interpretation of ambiguous question/request statements. *Memory & Cognition, 36*, 873–881.

Dijksterhuis, A. (2004). Think different: the merits of unconscious thought in preference development and decision making. *Journal of Personality and Social Psychology, 87*, 586–598.

Dijksterhuis, A., & Bargh, J. A. (2001). The perception-behavior expressway: Automatic effects of social perception on social behavior. In M. Zanna (Ed.), *Advances in Experimental Social Psychology* (Vol. 33, pp. 1–40). San Diego: Academic Press.

Dijksterhuis, A., & van Knippenberg, A. (1998). The relation between perception and behavior or how to win a game of Trivial Pursuit. *Journal of Personality and Social Psychology, 74*, 865–877.

Dixon, J. A., Mahoney, B., & Cocks, R. (2002). Accents of guilt: Effects of regional accent, race, and crime type on attributions of guilt. *Journal of Language and Social Psychology, 21*, 162–168.

Donovan, S., & Epstein, S. (1997). The difficulty in the Linda conjunction problem can be attributed to its simultaneous concrete and unnatural representation, and not to conversational implicature. *Journal of Experimental Social Psychology, 33*, 1–20.

Douglas, K. M., & Sutton, R. M. (2003). Effects of communication goals and expectancies on language abstraction. *Journal of Personality and Social Psychology, 84*, 682–696.

Douglas, K. M., Sutton, R. M., & Wilkin, K. (2008). Could you mind your language? An investigation of communicators' ability to inhibit linguistic bias. *Journal of Language and Social Psychology, 27*, 123–139.

Dudukovic, N. M., Marsh, E. J., & Tversky, B. (2004). Telling a story or telling it straight: The effects of entertaining versus accurate retellings on memory. *Applied Cognitive Psychology, 18*, 125–143.

Dulany, D. E., & Hilton, D. J. (1991). Conversational implicature, conscious representation, and the conjunction fallacy. *Social Cognition, 9*, 85–110.

Duncan, S., & Fiske, D. W. (1977). *Face to face interaction: Research, methods and theory*. Hillsdale, NJ: Erlbaum.

Duncan, S. D., Cassell, J., & Levy, E. (Eds.). (2007). *Gesture and the dynamic dimension of language*. Amsterdam: John Benjamins.

Durkheim, E. (1915). *The elementary forms of religious life*. London: Allen & Unwin.

Echterhoff, G., Higgins, E. T., & Groll, S. (2005). Audience-tuning effects on memory: The role of shared reality. *Journal of Personality and Social Psychology, 89*, 257–276.

Echterhoff, G., Higgins, E. T., Kopietz, R., & Groll, S. (2008). How communication goals determine when audience tuning biases memory. *Journal of Experimental Psychology: General, 137*, 133–144.

Edwards, D., & Potter, J. (1992). *Discursive psychology*. London: Sage.

El-Alayli, A., Myers, C. J., Peterson, T. L., & Lystad, A. L. (2008). "I don't mean to sound arrogant, but...." The effects of using disclaimers on person perception. *Personality and Social Psychology Bulletin, 34*, 130–143.

Epley, N., Keysar, B., Van Boven, L., & Gilovich, T. (2004). Perspective taking as egocentric anchoring and adjustment. *Journal of Personality and Social Psychology, 87*, 327–339.

Epley, N., Morewedge, C., & Keysar, B. (2004). Perspective taking in children and adults: Equivalent egocentrism but differential correction. *Journal of Experimental Social Psychology, 40*, 760–768.

Erickson, B., Lind, A. E., Johnson, B. C., & O'Barr, W. M. (1978). Speech style and impression formation in a court setting: The effects of "powerful" and "powerless" speech. *Journal of Experimental Social Psychology, 14*, 266–279.

Ervin-Tripp, S. M. (1968). Sociolinguistics. In L. Berkowitz (Ed.), *Advances in experimental social psychology* (Vol. 4, pp. 91–165). New York: Academic Press.

Estes, Z., Verges, M., & Barsalou, L. W. (2008). Head up, foot down: Object words orient attention to the object's typical location. *Psychological Science, 19*, 93–97.

Evans J. W.; Walters A. S.; Hatch-Woodruff M. L. (1999). Deathbed scene narratives: A construct and linguistic analysis. *Death Studies, 23*, 715–733.

Fast, L. A., & Funder, D. C. (2008). Personality as manifest in word use: Correlations with self-report, acquaintance report, and behavior. *Journal of Personality and Social Psychology, 94*, 334–346.

Ferreira, V. S., & Dell, G. S. (2000). Effect of ambiguity and lexical availability on syntactic and lexical production. *Cognitive Psychology, 40*, 296–340.

Fiedler, K. (2008). Language: A toolbox for sharing and influencing social reality. *Perspectives on Psychological Science, 3*, 38–47.

Fiedler, K., Bluemke, M., Friese, M., & Hofmann, W. (2003). On the different uses of linguistic abstractness: From LIB to LEB and beyond. *European Journal of Social Psychology, 33*, 441–453.

Fiedler, K., Semin, G. R., & Finkenauer, C. (1993). The battle of words between gender groups: A language-based approach to intergroup processes. *Human Communication Research, 19*, 409–441.

Fielding, G., & Evered, C. (1980). The influence of patients' speech upon doctors. In R. N. St. Clair & H. Giles (Eds.), *The social and psychological contexts of language* (pp. 51–72). Hillsdale, NJ: Erlbaum.

Fish, S. (1980). *Is there a text in this class? The authority of interpretive communities*. Cambridge, MA: Harvard University Press.

Fiske, A. (1992). The four elementary forms of sociality: Framework for a unified theory of social relations. *Psychological Review, 99*, 689–723.

Fiske, S. T., Cuddy, A. J. C., & Glick, P. (2007). Universal dimensions of social perception: Warmth and competence. *Trends in Cognitive Science, 11*, 77–83.

Fitch, K. L., & Sanders, R. E. (1994). Culture, communication, and preferences for directness in expression of directives. *Communication Theory, 4*, 219–245.

Fitzsimons, G. M., & Kay, A. C. (2004). Language and interpersonal cognition: Causal effects of variations in pronoun usage on perceptions of closeness. *Personality and Social Psychology Bulletin, 30*, 547–557.

Flynn, F. J., & Lake, V. K. B. (2008). If you need help, just ask: Understanding compliance with direct requests for help. *Journal of Personality and Social Psychology, 95*, 128–143.

Forgas, J. P. (1999a). Feeling and speaking: Mood effects on verbal communication strategies. *Personality and Social Psychology Bulletin, 25*, 850–863.

Forgas, J. P. (1999b). On feeling good and being rude: Affective influences on language use and request formulations. *Journal of Personality and Social Psychology, 76*, 928–939.

Fox Tree, J. E. (2002). Interpretations of pauses and ums at turn exchanges. *Discourse Processes, 34*, 37–55.

Fox Tree, J. E., & Schrock, J. C. (1999). Discourse markers in spontaneous speech: Oh what a difference an "oh" makes. *Journal of Memory and Language, 40*, 280–295.

Fraser, B., & Nolan, W. (1981). The association of deference with linguistic form. *International Journal of the Sociology of Language, 26*, 93–109.

Fussell, S. R., & Krauss, R. (1989a). The effects of intended audience on message production and comprehension: Reference in a common ground framework. *Journal of Experimental Social Psychology, 25*, 203–219.

Fussell, S. R., & Krauss, R. (1989b). Understanding friends and strangers: The effects of audience design on message comprehension. *European Journal of Social Psychology, 19*, 509–526.

Fussell, S. R., & Krauss, R. (1991). Accuracy and bias in estimates of others' knowledge. *European Journal of Social Psychology, 21*, 445–454.

Fussell, S. R., & Krauss, R. (1992). Coordination of knowledge in communication: Effects of speakers' assumptions about what others know. *Journal of Personality and Social Psychology, 62*, 378–391.

Gaertner, S., & Bickman, L. (1971). Effects of race on the elicitation of helping behavior. *Journal of Personality and Social Psychology, 20*, 218–222.

Galinsky, A., Magee, J. C., Inesi, M. E., & Gruenfeld, D. (2006). Power and perspectives not taken. *Psychological Science, 17*, 1068–1074.

Gallois, C., Ogay, T., & Giles, H. (2005). Communication accommodation theory: A look back and a look ahead. In W. Gudykunst (Ed.), *Theorizing about intercultural communication* (pp. 121–148). Thousand Oaks, CA: Sage.

Garcia, M. T., & Bargh, J. A. (2003). Automatic evaluation of novel words: The role of superficial phonetics. *Journal of Language and Social Psychology, 22*, 414–433.

Garfinkel, H. (1967). *Studies in ethnomethodology*. Englewood Cliffs, NJ: Prentice-Hall.

Garrod, S., & Anderson, A. (1987). Saying what you mean in dialogue: A study in conceptual and semantic co-ordination. *Cognition, 27*, 181–218.

Garrod, S., & Doherty, G. (1994). Conversation, co-ordination and convention: An empirical investigation of how groups establish linguistic conventions. *Cognition, 53*, 181–215.

Garrod, S., & Pickering, M. J. (2005). Why is conversation so easy? *Trends in Cognitive Sciences, 8*, 8–11.

Garvey, C., & Caramazza, A. (1974). Implicit causality in verbs. *Linguistic Inquiry, 5*, 459–464.

Gentner, D., & Goldin-Meadow, S. (Eds.). (2003). *Language in mind.* Cambridge, MA: MIT Press.

Gergen, K. J. (1985). The social constructionist movement in modern psychology. *The American Psychologist, 40*, 266–275.

Gibbons. P., Busch, J., & Bradac, J. J. (1991). Powerful versus powerless language: Consequences for persuasion, impression formation, and cognitive response. *Journal of Language and Social Psychology, 10*, 115–113.

Gibbs, R. W., Jr. (1980). Spilling the beans on understanding and memory for idioms. *Memory & Cognition, 8*, 449–456.

Gibbs, R. W., Jr. (1999). *Intentions in the experience of meaning.* Cambridge, England: Cambridge University Press.

Gibbs, R. W., Jr. (2006). *Embodiment and cognitive science.* New York: Cambridge University Press.

Gibbs, R. W., Jr., & Moise, J. F. (1997). Pragmatics in understanding what is said, *Cognition, 62*, 51–74.

Gilbert, D. T., Tafarodi, R. W., & Malone, P. S. (1993). You can't not believe everything you read. *Journal of Personality and Social Psychology, 65*, 221–233.

Gildea, P., & Glucksberg, S. (1983). On understanding metaphor: The role of context. *Journal of Verbal Learning and Verbal Behavior, 22*, 577–590.

Giles, H. (1970). Evaluative reactions to accents. *Educational Review, 22*, 211–227.

Giles, H. (1973). Accent mobility: A model and some data. *Anthropological Linguistics, 15*, 87–105.

Giles, H., & Coupland, N. (1991). *Language: Contexts and consequences.* Pacific Grove, CA: Brooks/Cole.

Giles, H., Coupland, J., & Coupland, N. (1991). *Contexts of accommodation: Developments in applied sociolinguistics.* Cambridge, England: Cambridge University Press.

Giles, H., Mulac, A., Bradac, J. J., & Johnson, P. (1987). Speech accommodation theory: The first decade and beyond. In M. L. McLaughlin (Ed.), *Communication Yearbook* (Vol. 10, pp. 13–48). Beverly Hills, CA: Sage.

Giles, H., & Sassoon, C. (1983). The effects of speakers' accent, social class, background and message style on British listeners' social judgments. *Language and Communication, 3*, 305–313.

Giles, H., & Powesland, P. F. (1975). *Speech style and social evaluation.* London, Academic Press.

Giles, H., Willemyns, M., Gallois, C., & Anderson, M. C. (2007). Accommodating a new frontier: The context of law enforcement. In K. Fiedler (Ed.), *Social communication* (pp. 129–162). New York: Psychology Press.

Gilson, C, & Abelson, R. P. (1965). The subjective use of inductive evidence. *Journal of Personality and Social Psychology, 2*, 301–310.

Glenberg, A. M. Havas, D., Becker, R., & Rinck, M. (2005). Grounding language in bodily states: The case for emotion. In R. Zwaan & D. Pecher (Eds.), *The grounding of cognition: The role of perception and action in memory, language, and thinking.* Cambridge, England: Cambridge University Press.

Glenberg, A. M., & Kaschak, M. P. (2002). Grounding language in action. *Psychonomic Bulletin & Review, 9*, 558–565.

Glenberg, A. M., Sato, M., Cattaneo, L., Riggio, L., Palumbo, D., & Buccino, G. (2008). Processing abstract language modulates motor system activity, *The Quarterly Journal of Experimental Psychology, 61*, 905–919.

Glucksberg, S., Gildea, P., & Bookin, H. (1982). On understanding nonliteral speech: Can people ignore metaphors? *Journal of Verbal Learning and Verbal Behavior, 21*, 85–98.

Goffman, E. (1959). *The presentation of self in everyday life.* Garden City, NY: Doubleday Anchor.

Goffman, E. (1967). *Interaction ritual: Essays on face to face behavior.* Garden City, NY: Doubleday.

Goffman, E. (1976). Replies and responses. *Language in Society, 5*, 257–13.

Gonzales, M. H., Pederson, J., Manning, D., & Wetter, D. W. (1990). Pardon my gaffe: Effects of sex, status, and consequence severity on accounts. *Journal of Personality and Social Psychology, 58*, 610–621.

Goodwin, C. (1986). *Conversational organization: Interaction between speakers and hearers.* New York: Academic Press.

Gorham, B. W. (2006). News media's relationship with stereotyping: The linguistic intergroup bias in response to crime news. *Journal of Communication, 56*, 289–308.

Gottman, J. M. (1979). *Marital interaction: Experimental investigations.* New York: Academic Press.

Graesser, A. C., Singer, M., & Trabasso, T. (1994). Constructing inferences during narrative text comprehension. *Psychological Review, 101*, 371–395.

Grice, H. P. (1975). Logic and conversation. In P. Cole & J. Morgan (Eds.), *Syntax and semantics, Volume 3. Speech acts* (pp. 41–58). New York: Academic Press.

Grice, H. P. (1989). *Studies in the way of words.* Cambridge, MA: Harvard University Press.

Gruenfeld, D. H., & Wyer, R. S., Jr. (1992). Semantics and pragmatics of social influence: How affirmations and denials affect beliefs in referent propositions. *Journal of Personality and Social Psychology, 62*, 38–49.

Gumperz, J. J., & Levinson, S. C. (Eds.). (1996). *Rethinking linguistic relativity.* Cambridge, England: Cambridge University Press.

Guy, G. R., & Vonwiller, J. (1984). The meaning of intonation in Australian English. *Australian Journal of Linguistics, 4.1*, 1–17.

Hajek, C., & Giles, H. (2005). Intergroup communication schemas: Cognitive representations of talk with gay men. *Language and Communication, 25*, 1161–1182.

Halberstadt, J. (2003). The paradox of emotion attribution: Explanation biases perceptual memory for emotional expressions. *Current Directions in Psychological Science, 12*, 197–201.

Hall, E. T. (1976). *Beyond culture.* New York: Doubleday.

Hall, E. T. (1983). *The dance of life.* New York: Doubleday.

Hanna, J. E., Tanenhaus, M. K., & Trueswell, J. C. (2003). The effects of common ground and perspective on domains of referential interpretation. *Journal of Memory and Language, 49*, 43–61.

Hariri, A. R., Bookheimer, S. Y., & Mazziotta, J. C. (2000). Modulating emotional response: Effects of neocortical network on the limbic system. *NeuroReport, 11*, 43–48.

Harwood, J. (2007). *Understanding communication and aging: Developing knowledge and awareness.* Thousand Oaks, CA: Sage.

Heider, E. R. (1972). Universals in color naming and memory. *Journal of Experimental Psychology, 93*, 10–20.

Heider, E. R., & Olivier, D. C. (1972). The structure of the color space in naming and memory for two languages. *Cognitive Psychology, 3*, 337–354.

Heider, F. (1958). *The psychology of interpersonal relations.* New York: Wiley.

Henley, N. M. (1989). Molehill or mountain? What we know and don't know about sex bias in language. In M. Crawford & M. Gentry (Eds.),

Gender and thought: Psychological perspectives (pp. 57–78). New York: Springer.

Heritage, J. C. (1984). *Garfinkel and ethnomethodology.* Cambridge: Polity Press.

Higgins, E. T., & Rholes, W. S. (1978). "Saying is believing": Effects of message modification on memory and liking for the person described. *Journal of Experimental Social Psychology, 14,* 363–378.

Hill, B., Sachiko, I., Shoko, I., Kawasaki, A., & Ogino, T. (1986). Universals of linguistic politeness. *Journal of Pragmatics, 10,* 347–371.

Hilton, D. J. (1995). The social context of reasoning: Conversational inference and rational judgment. *Psychological Bulletin, 118,* 248–271.

Hilton, D. J., & Slugoski, B. R. (2001). Conversational processes in reasoning and explanation. In A. Tesser & N. Schwarz (Eds.), *Blackwell handbook of social psychology, Volume 1. Intraindividual processes* (pp. 181–206). Oxford: Basil Blackwell.

Hoffman, C., Lau, I., & Johnson, D. R. (1986). The linguistic relativity of person cognition: An English-Chinese comparison. *Journal of Personality and Social Psychology, 51,* 1097–1105.

Hoffman, C., & Tchir, M. A. (1990). Interpersonal verbs and dispositional adjectives: The psychology of causality embodied in language. *Journal of Personality and Social Psychology, 58,* 767–778.

Hofstede, G. (1980). *Culture's consequences: International differences in work related values.* Thousand Oaks, CA: Sage Publications, Inc.

Holtgraves, T. (1986). Language structure in social interaction: Perceptions of direct and indirect speech acts and interactants who use them. *Journal of Personality and Social Psychology, 51,* 305–314.

Holtgraves, T. (1992). The linguistic realization of face management: Implications for language production and comprehension, person perception, and cross-cultural communication. *Social Psychology Quarterly, 55,* 141–159.

Holtgraves, T. (1994). Communication in context: The effects of speaker status on the comprehension of indirect requests. *Journal of Experimental Psychology: Learning, Memory, and Cognition. 20,* 1205–1218.

Holtgraves, T. M. (1997a). Politeness and memory for the wording of remarks. *Memory and Cognition, 25,* 106–116.

Holtgraves, T. M. (1997b). Styles of language use: Individual and cultural variability in conversational indirectness. *Journal of Personality and Social Psychology, 73,* 624–637.

Holtgraves, T. M. (1997c). Yes, but. . . . Positive politeness in conversation arguments. *Journal of Language and Social Psychology, 16,* 222–239.

Holtgraves T. M. (1998). Interpreting indirect replies. *Cognitive Psychology, 37,* 1–27.

Holtgraves, T. M. (1999). Comprehending indirect replies: When and how are their conveyed meanings activated? *Journal of Memory and Language, 41,* 519–540.

Holtgraves, T. M. (2000). Preference organization and reply comprehension. *Discourse Processes, 30,* 87–106.

Holtgraves, T. M. (2002). *Language as social action: Social psychology and language use.* Mahwah, NJ: Erlbaum.

Holtgraves, T. (2005). Diverging interpretations associated with the perspectives of the speaker and recipient in conversations. *Journal of Memory and Language, 53,* 551–566.

Holtgraves, T. (2008). Automatic intention recognition in conversation processing. *Journal of Memory and Language, 58,* 627–645.

Holtgraves, T. M., & Ashley, A. (2001). Comprehending illocutionary force. *Memory & Cognition, 29,* 83–90.

Holtgraves, T., & Grayer, A. (1994). I am not a crook: Effects of denials on perceptions of a defendant's guilt, personality, and motives. *Journal of Applied Social Psychology, 24,* 2132–2150.

Holtgraves, T. M., & Kashima, Y. (2008). Language, meaning, and social cognition. *Personality and Social Psychology Review, 12,* 73–94.

Holtgraves, T. M., & Lasky, B. (1999). Linguistic power and persuasion. *Journal of Language and Social Psychology, 18,* 196–204.

Holtgraves, T., & Raymond, S. (1995). Implicit causality and memory: Evidence for a priming model. *Personality and Social Psychology Bulletin, 21,* 5–12.

Holtgraves, T., Srull, T., & Socall, D. (1989). Conversation memory: The effects of speaker status on memory for the assertiveness of conversation remarks. *Journal of Personality and Social Psychology, 56,* 149–160.

Holtgraves, T., & Yang, J. N. (1990). Politeness as universal: Cross-cultural perceptions of request strategies and inferences based on their use. *Journal of Personality and Social Psychology, 59,* 719–729.

Holtgraves, T., & Yang, J. (1992). The interpersonal underpinnings of request strategies: General principles and differences due to culture and gender. *Journal of Personality and Social Psychology, 62,* 246–256.

Horton, W. S., & Keysar, B. (1996). When do speakers take into account common ground? *Cognition, 59,* 91–117.

Hosman, L. A., & Wright, J. W., II. (1987). The effects of hedges and hesitations on impression formation in a simulated courtroom context. *Western Journal of Speech Communication, 51,* 173–188.

House, J., Kasper, K., & Ross, S. (Eds.). (2003). *Misunderstanding in social life.* London: Longman.

Howeler, M. (1972). Diversity of word usage as a stress indicator in an interview situation. *Journal of Psycholinguistic Research, 1,* 243–248.

Igou, E. R. (2007). Additional thoughts on conversational and motivational sources of the dilution effect. *Journal of Language and Social Psychology, 26,* 61–68.

Igou, E. R., & Bless, H. (2003). Inferring the importance of arguments: Order effects and conversation rules. *Journal of Experimental Social Psychology, 39,* 91–99.

Igou, E. R., & Bless, H. (2005). The conversational basis for the dilution effect. *The Journal of Language and Social Psychology, 24,* 25–35.

Isaacs, E. A., & Clark, H. H. (1987). References in conversations between experts and novices. *Journal of Experimental Psychology: General, 116,* 26–37.

Jefferson, G. (1972). Side sequences. In D. Sudnow (Ed.), *Studies in social interaction* (pp. 294–338). New York: Free Press.

Jefferson, G. (1986). Notes on latency in overlap onset. *Human Studies, 9,* 153–183.

Jefferson, G. (2004). Glossary of transcript symbols with an introduction. In G. H. Lerner (Ed.), *Conversation analysis: Studies from the first generation* (pp. 13–31). Amsterdam/Philadelphia: John Benjamins.

Ji, L-J., Zhang, Z., & Nisbett, R. E. (2004). Is it culture or is it language? Examination of language effects in cross-cultural research on categorization. *Journal of Personality and Social Psychology, 87,* 57–65.

Jones, E. E., & Harris, V. A. (1967). The attribution of attitudes. *Journal of Experimental Social Psychology, 3,* 1–24.

Kahneman, D., & Tversky, A. (1973). On the psychology of prediction. *Psychological Review, 80,* 237–251.

Kalin, R., & Rayko, D. (1980). The social significance of speech in the job interview. In R. N. St. Clair and H. Giles (Eds.), *The social and psychological contexts of language* (pp. 39–50). Hillsdale, NJ: Erlbaum.

Kanouse, D. E. (1972). Verbs as implicit quantifiers. *Journal of Verbal Learning and Verbal Behavior, 11,* 141–147.

Karpinsky, A., & von Hippel, W. (1996). The role of the linguistic intergroup bias in expectancy-maintenance. *Social Cognition, 14,* 141–163.

Kashima, E., & Kashima, Y. (1998). Culture and language: The case of cultural dimensions and personal pronoun use. *Journal of Cross-Cultural Psychology, 29,* 461–486.

Kashima, Y. (2001). Culture and social cognition: Toward a social psychology of cultural dynamics. In D. Matsumoto (Ed.), *The handbook of culture and psychology* (pp. 325–360). New York: Oxford University Press.

Kashima, Y., & Kashima, E. (2003). Individualism, GNP, climate, and pronoun drop: Is individualism determined by affluence and climate, or does language use play a role? *Journal of Cross-Cultural Psychology, 34*, 125–134.

Kashima, Y., Kashima, E., Kim, U., & Gelfand, G. (2006). Describing the social world: How is a person, a group, and a relationship described in the East and the West. *Journal of Experimental Social Psychology, 42*, 388–396.

Katz, A. M., & Pexman, P. M. (1997). Interpreting figurative statements: Speaker occupation can change metaphor to irony. *Metaphor and Symbol, 12*, 19–41.

Kay, P., & Fillmore, C. J. (1999). Grammatical constructions and linguistic generalizations: The what's X doing Y? construction. *Language, 75*, 1–33.

Keenan, E. O. (1976). The universality of conversational implicature. *Language in Society, 5*, 67–80.

Keltner, D., Young, R. C., Heerey, E. A., Oemig, C., & Monarch, N. D. (1998). Teasing in hierarchical and intimate relations. *Journal of Personality, and Social Psychology, 75*, 1231–1247.

Kemmelmeier, M. (2007). Does the dilution effect have a conversational basis? *Journal of Language and Social Psychology, 26*, 48–60.

Kent, G. G., Davis, J. D., & Shapiro, D. A. (1978). Resources required in the construction and reconstruction of conversation. *Journal of Personality and Social Psychology, 36*, 13–22.

Keysar, B. (1989). On the functional equivalence of literal and metaphorical interpretation in discourse. *Journal of Memory and Language, 28*, 375–385.

Keysar, B. (1994). The illusory transparency of intention: Linguistic perspective taking in text. *Cognitive Psychology, 26*, 165–208.

Keysar, B. (1997). Unconfounding common ground. *Discourse Processes, 24*, 253–270.

Keysar, B. (1998). Language users as problem solvers: Just what ambiguity problem do they solve? In S. Fussell & R. Kreuz (Eds.), *Social and cognitive approaches to interpersonal communication* (pp. 175–200). Mahwah, NJ: Erlbaum.

Keysar, B., Barr, D. J., Balin, J. A., & Brauner, J. S. (2000). Taking perspective in conversation: The role of mutual knowledge in comprehension. *Psychological Science, 11*, 32–38.

Keysar, B., Barr, D. J., Balin, J. A., & Paek, T. (1998). Definite reference and mutual knowledge: A processing model of common ground in comprehension. *Journal of Memory and Language, 39*, 1–20.

Keysar, B., & Bly, B. (1995). Intuitions of the transparency of idioms: Can one keep a secret by spilling the beans? *Journal of Memory and Language, 34*, 89–109.

Keysar, B., & Henley, A. S. (2002). Speaker's overestimation of their effectiveness. *Psychological Science, 13*, 207–212.

Keysar, B., Lin, S., & Barr, D. J. (2003). Limits on theory of mind use in adults. *Cognition, 89*, 25–41.

Kiesler, S., Powers, A., Fussell, S. R., & Torrey, C. (2008). Anthropomorphic interactions with a robot and robot-like agent. *Social Cognition, 26*, 189–191.

Krauss, R. M., & Chiu, C. (1998). Language and social behavior. In D. Gilbert, S. Fiske, & G. Lindsey (Eds.), *Handbook of social psychology* (Vol. 2, pp. 41–88). Boston: McGraw-Hill.

Krauss, R. M., Freyberg, R., & Morsella, E. (2002). Inferring speaker's physical attributes from their voices. *Journal of Experimental Social Psychology, 38*, 618–625.

Krauss, R. M., & Fussell, S. R. (1991). Perspective taking in communication: Representations of others' knowledge in reference. *Social Cognition, 9*, 2–24.

Krauss, R. M., & Fussell, S. R. (1996). Social psychological models of interpersonal communication. In E. T. Higgins & A. W. Kruglanski (Eds.), *Social psychology: Handbook of basic principles* (pp. 655–701). New York: Guilford Press.

Krauss, R. M., Morrels-Samuels, P., & Colasante, C. (1991). Do conversational gestures communicate? *Journal of Personality and Social Psychology, 61*, 743–754.

Krauss, R. M., & Weinheimer, S. (1964). Changes in length of reference phrases as a function of social interaction: A preliminary study. *Psychonomic Science, 1*, 113–114.

Krauss, R. M., & Weinheimer, S. (1966). Concurrent feedback, confirmation and the encoding of referents in verbal communication. *Journal of Personality and Social Psychology, 4*, 343–346.

Kreuz, R. J., & Roberts, R. M. (1993). When collaboration fails: Consequences of pragmatic errors in conversation. *Journal of Pragmatics, 19*, 239–252.

Krosnick, J., Li, F., & Lehman, D. R. (1990). Conversational conventions, order of information acquisition, and the effect of base rates and individuating information on social judgment. *Journal of Personality and Social Psychology, 59*, 1140–1152.

Labov, W. (1966). *The social stratification of English in New York City.* Washington, DC: Center for Applied Linguistics.

Labov, W. (1972a). *Sociolinguistic patterns.* Philadelphia: University of Pennsylvania Press.

Labov, W. (1972b). *Language in the inner city.* Philadelphia: University of Pennsylvania Press.

Labov, W. (2001). *Principles of linguistic change: Social factors.* Oxford: Blackwell.

Lakoff, G. (1987). *Women, fire, and dangerous things.* Chicago: University of Chicago Press.

Lakoff, G., & Johnson, M. (1980). *Metaphors we live by.* Chicago: The University of Chicago Press.

Lakoff, R. (1973). The logic of politeness: Or, minding your p's and q's. *Papers from the Ninth Regional Meeting of the Chicago Linguistic Society* (pp. 292–305). Chicago: Chicago Linguistics Society.

Lakoff, R. (1975). *Language and woman's place.* New York: Harper & Row.

Lambert, B. L. (1996). Face and politeness in pharmacist–physician interaction. *Social Science and Medicine, 43*, 1189–1199.

Lambert, W. E., Frankle, H., & Tucker, G. R. (1966). Judging personality through speech: A French-Canadian example. *The Journal of Communication, 16*, 305–321.

Lambert, W. E., Hodgson, R., Gardner, R. C., & Fillenbaum S. (1960). Evaluative reactions to spoken languages. *Journal of Abnormal and Social Psychology, 60*, 44–51.

Landauer, T. K., Foltz, P. W., & Laham, D. (1998). An introduction to latent semantic analysis. *Discourse Processes, 25*, 259–284.

LaPlante, D., & Ambady, N. (2004). On how things are said: Voice tone, voice intensity, verbal content, and perceptions of politeness. *Journal of Language and Social Psychology, 22*, 434–441.

Lavandera, B. (1978). Where does the sociolinguistic variable stop? *Language in Society, 7*, 171–182.

Leaper, C., & Ayres, M. M. (2007). A meta-analytic review of gender variations in adult's language use: Talkativeness, affiliative speech, and assertive speech. *Personality and Social Psychology Review, 11*, 328–363.

Leech, G. (1983). *Principles of pragmatics.* London: Longman.

Leichty, G., & Applegate, J. L. (1991). Social-cognitive and situational influences on the use of face-saving persuasive strategies. *Human Communication Research, 7*, 451–484.

Levin, H., Giles, H., & Garrett, P. (1994). The effects of lexical formality and accent on trait attributions. *Language and Communication. 14*, 265–274.

Levin, H., & Lim, T. (1988). An accommodating witness. *Language and Communication, 8*, 195–198.

Levinson, S. (1983). *Pragmatics*. Cambridge, England: Cambridge University Press.

Levinson, S. (1997). Language and cognition: The cognitive consequences of spatial description in Guugu Yimithirr. *Journal of Linguistic Anthropology, 7*, 98–131.

Levinson, S. (2000). *Presumptive meanings: The theory of generalized conversational implicative*. Cambridge, MA: MIT Press.

Levinson, S., Kita, S., Haun, D., & Rasch, B. (2002). Re-turning the tables: Language affects spatial reasoning. *Cognition, 84*, 155–188.

Li, P., & Gleitman, L. (2002). Turning the tables: Language and spatial reasoning. *Cognition, 83*, 265–294.

Lieberman, M. (2007). The X- and C- systems: The neural basis of automatic and controlled social cognition. In E. Harmon-Jones & P. Winkelman (Eds.), *Fundamentals of social neuroscience* (pp. 290–315). New York: Guilford Press.

Lieberman, M., Eisenberger, N. I., Crockett, M. J., Tom, S. M., Pfeifer, J. H., & Way, B. W. (2007). Putting feelings into words. *Psychological Science, 18*, 421–428.

Lim, T., & Bowers, J. W. (1991). Face-work, solidarity, approbation, and tact. *Human Communication Research, 17*, 415–450.

Liu, L. G. (1985). Reasoning counterfactually in Chinese: Are there any obstacles? *Cognition, 21*, 239–270.

Luhman, R. (1990). Appalachian English stereotypes: Language attitudes in Kentucky. *Language in Society, 19*, 331–48.

Lupyan, G., Rakison, D. H., & McClelland, J. L. (2007). Language is not just for talking: Redundant labels facilitate learning of novel categories. *Psychological Science, 18*, 1077–1083.

Maass, A. (1999). Linguistic intergroup bias: Stereotype perpetuation through language. *Advances in Experimental Social Psychology, 31*, 79–121.

Maass, A., & Arcuri, S. (1996). Language and stereotyping. In C. N. Macrae, C. Stangor, & M. Hewstone (Eds.), *Stereotypes and stereotyping* (pp. 193–226). New York: Guilford Press.

Maass, A., Cadinu, M., Boni, M., & Borini, C. (2005). Converting verbs into adjectives: Asymmetrical memory distortions for stereotypic and counterstereotypic information. *Group Processes and Intergroup Relations, 8*, 271–290.

Maass, A., Ceccarelli, R., & Rudin, S. (1996). Linguistic intergroup bias: Evidence for ingroup protective motivation. *Journal of Personality and Social Psychology, 71*, 512–526.

Maass, A., Corvino, P., & Arcuri, L., (1994). Linguistic intergroup bias and the mass media. *Revue de Psychologie Sociale 1*, 31–43.

Maass, A., Karasawa, M., Politi, F., & Suga, S. (2006). Do verbs and adjectives play different roles in different cultures? A cross-linguistic analysis of person representation. *Journal of Personality and Social Psychology, 90*, 734–750.

Maass, A., Milesi, A., Zabbini, S., & Stahlberg, D. (1995). The linguistic intergroup bias: Differential expectancies or ingroup protection? *Journal of Personality and Social Psychology, 68*, 116–126.

Maass, A., Salvi, D., Arcuri, L., & Semin, G. (1989). Language use in intergroup contexts: The linguistic intergroup bias. *Journal of Personality and Social Psychology, 57*, 981–993.

Malle, B. F. (2001). Folk explanations of intentional action. In B. F. Malle, L. J. Moses, & D. A. Baldwin (Eds.), *Intentions and intentionality: Foundations of social cognition* (pp. 265–286). Cambridge, MA: MIT Press.

Marlow, M. L., & Giles, H. (2008). Who you tink you, talkin propah? Hawaiian pidgin demarginalized. *Journal of Multicultural Discourse, 3*, 53–68.

Marcel, A. J. (1983). Conscious and unconscious perception: Experiments on visual masking and word recognition. *Cognitive Psychology, 15*, 197–237.

Marsh, E. J. (2007). Retelling is not the same as recalling: Implications for memory. *Current Directions in Psychological Science, 16*, 16–20.

Marsh, E. J., & Tversky, B. (2004). Spinning the stories of our lives. *Applied Cognitive psychology, 18*, 491–503.

McAdams, D. P. (1985). *Power, intimacy, and the life story*. Homewood, IL: Dempsey.

McAdams, D. P. (1993). *The stories we live by: Personal myths and the making of the self*. New York: William Morrow.

McAdams, D. P. (2006). *The redemptive self: Stories Americans live by*. New York: Oxford University Press.

McArthur, L. Z. (1972). The how and what of why: Some determinants and consequences of causal attributions. *Journal of Personality and Social Psychology, 22*, 171–188.

McCann, C. D. & Higgins, E. T. (1990). Social cognition and communication. In H. Giles & W. P. Robinson (Eds.), *Handbook of language and social psychology* (pp. 13–32). Oxford, UK: Wiley.

McGregor, I., & Holmes, J. G. (1999). How storytelling shapes memory and impressions of relationship events over time. *Journal of Personality and Social Psychology, 76*, 403–419.

McLaughlin, M. L., Cody, M., & O'Hair, H. D. (1983). The management of failure events: Some contextual determinants of accounting behavior. *Human Communication Research, 9*, 208–224.

McNeil, D. (2005). *Gesture and thought*. Chicago: University of Chicago Press.

Mead, G. H. (1934). *Mind, self, and society*. Chicago: University of Chicago Press.

Mehl, M. R., Gosling, S. D., & Pennebaker, J. W. (2006). Personality in its natural habitat: Manifestations and implicit folk theories of personality in daily life. *Journal of Personality and Social Psychology, 90*, 862–877.

Mehl, M. R., & Pennebaker, J. W. (2003). The sounds of social life: A psychometric analysis of students' daily social environments and conversations. *Journal of Personality and Social Psychology, 84*, 857–870.

Mehrabian, A. (1971). *Silent messages*. Belmont, CA: Wadsworth.

Meier, B. P., Hauser, D. J., Robinson, M. D., Friesen, C. K., & Schjeldah, K. (2007). What's "up" with God?: Vertical space as a representation of the divine. *Journal of Personality and Social Psychology, 93*, 699–710.

Meier, B. P., & Robinson, M. D. (2004). Why the sunny side is up: Associations between affect and vertical position. *Psychological Science, 15*, 243–247.

Meier, B. P., Sellbom, M., & Wygant, D. B. (2007). Failing to take the moral high ground: Psychopathy and the vertical representation of morality. *Personality and Individual Differences, 43*, 757–767.

Miller, D. T., & Ross, M. (1975). Self-serving biases in attribution of causality: Fact or fiction? *Psychological Bulletin, 82*, 213–225.

Miller, J. (1984). Culture and the development of everyday social explanation. *Journal of Personality and Social Psychology, 46*, 961–978.

Miyamoto, Y., & Kitayama, S. (2002). Cultural variation in correspondence bias: The critical role of attitude diagnosticity of socially constrained behavior. *Journal of Personality and Social Psychology, 83*, 1239–1248.

Milroy, L., & Milroy, J. (1978). Speech and context in an urban setting. *Belfast Working Papers in Language and Linguistics, 2*, 1–85.

Moulton, J., Robinson, G. M., & Elias, C. (1978). Sex bias in language use: "Neutral" pronouns that aren't. *American Psychologist, 33*, 1032–1036.

Nadig, A. S., & Sedivy, J. C. (2002). Evidence of perspective taking constraints in children's on-line reference resolution. *Psychological Science, 13*, 329–336.

Natale, M. (1975). Convergence of mean vocal intensity in dyadic communications as a function of social desirability. *Journal of Personality and Social Psychology, 32*, 790–804.

Neely, J. H. (1977). Semantic priming and retrieval from lexical memory: Roles of inhibitionless spreading activation and limited-capacity attention. *Journal of Experimental Psychology: General, 106, 3*, 226–54.

Nezlek, J. B., Schütz, A., & Sellin, I. (2007). Self-presentational success in daily social interaction. *Self and Identity, 6*, 361–379.

Ng, S. H. (1990). Androcentric coding of man and his in memory by language users. *Journal of Experimental Social Psychology, 26*, 455–464.

Ng, S. H., & Bradac, J. J. (1993). *Power in language.* Newbury Park, CA: Sage.

Nicolle, S., & Clark B. (1999) Experimental pragmatics and what is said: A response to Gibbs and Moise, *Cognition, 69*, 337–354.

Noller, P., & Feeney, J. A. (Eds.). (2002). *Understanding marriage: Developments in the study of marital interaction.* New York: Cambridge University Press.

Oberlander, J., & Gill, A. J. (2006). Language with character: A corpus-based study of individual differences in e-mail communication. *Discourse Processes, 42*, 239–270.

Okamoto, S., & Robinson, W. P. (1997). Determinants of gratitude expression in England. *Journal of Language and Social Psychology, 16*, 411–433.

Ortony, A., Reynolds, R., Schallert, D., & Antos, S. (1978). Interpreting metaphors and idioms: Some effects of context on comprehension. *Journal of Verbal Learning and Verbal Behavior, 16*, 465–477.

Ozgen, E. (2004). Language, learning, and color perception. *Current Directions in Psychological Science, 13*, 95–98.

Ozgen, E., & Davies, I. R. I. (1998). Turkish color terms: Tests of Berlin and Kay's theory of color universals and linguistic relativity. *Linguistics, 36*, 919–956.

Pasupathi, M. (2001). The social construction of the personal past and its implication for adult development. *Psychological Bulletin, 127*, 651–672.

Pasupathi, M., Alderman, K., & Shaw, D. (2007). Talking the talk: Collaborative remembering and self-perceived expertise. *Discourse Processes, 43*, 55–77.

Pennebaker, J. W., Booth, R. J., & Francis, M. E. (2007). *Linguistic inquiry and word count (LIWC) 2007.* Retrieved September 5, 2009, from http://www.liwc.net.

Pennebaker, J. W., Chung, C. K., Ireland, M., Gonzales, A., & Booth, R. J. (2007). *The development and psychometric properties of LIWC2007* [software manual]. Austin, TX: LIWC.net.

Pennebaker, J. W., & Francis, M. E. (1996). Cognitive, emotional, and language processes in disclosure. *Cognition and Emotion, 10*, 601–626.

Pennebaker, J. W., Francis, M. E., & Booth, R. J. (2001). *Linguistic inquiry and word count (LIWC).* Retrieved September 5, 2009, from http://www.liwc.net.

Pennebaker, J. W., & Graybeal, A. (2001). Patterns of natural language use: Disclosure, personality, and social integration. *Current Directions in Psychological Science, 10*, 90–93.

Pennebaker, J. W., & King, L. (1999). Linguistic styles: Language use as an individual difference. *Journal of Personality and Social Psychology, 77*, 1296–1312.

Pennebaker, J. W., Mehl, M. R., & Niederhoffer, K. (2003). Psychological aspects of natural language use: Our words, our selves. *Annual Review of Psychology, 54*, 547–577.

Pennebaker, J. W., & Stone, L. D. (2003). Words of wisdom: Language use over the lifespan. *Journal of Personality and Social Psychology, 85*, 291–301.

Pickering, M. J, & Ferreira, V. S. (2008). Structural priming: A critical review. *Psychological Bulletin, 134*, 427–459.

Pickering, M. J., & Garrod, S. (2004). Toward a mechanistic psychology of dialogue. *Behavioral and Brain Sciences, 27*, 169–190.

Pinker, S. (1994). *The language instinct.* New York: William Morrow.

Pinker, S. (2007). *The stuff of thought: Language as a window into human nature.* New York: Viking.

Pinker, S., Nowak, M. A., & Lee, J. J. (2008) The logic of indirect speech. *Proceedings of the National Academy of Sciences, 105*, 833–838.

Pomerantz, A. (1984). Agreeing and disagreeing with assessments: some features of preferred/dispreferred turn-shapes. In J. Atkinson & J. Heritage (Eds.), *Structures of social action: Studies in conversation analysis* (pp. 79–112). Cambridge, England: Cambridge University Press.

Potter, J., & Wetherall, M. (1987). *Discourse and social psychology: Beyond attitudes and behavior.* London: Sage.

Purnell, T., Idsardi, W., & Baugh, J. (1999). Perceptual and phonetic experiments on American English dialect identification. *Journal of Language and Social Psychology, 18*, 10–30.

Ramsey, R. (1966). Personality and speech. *Journal of Personality and Social Psychology, 4*, 116–118.

Reis, H. T., Clark, M. S., & Holmes, J. G. (2004). Perceived partner responsiveness as an organizing construct in the study of intimacy and closeness. In D. Mashek & A. Aron (Eds.), *The handbook of closeness and intimacy* (pp. 201–225). Mahwah, NJ: Erlbaum.

Richter, L., & Kruglanski, A. W. (1999). Motivated search for common ground: Need for closure effects on audience design in interpersonal communication. *Personality and Social Psychology Bulletin, 25*, 1101–1114.

Rickford, J. (1999). *African American vernacular English.* Oxford: Blackwell.

Rizzolatti, G., & Craighero, L. (2004). The mirror-neuron system. *Annual Review of Neuroscience, 27*, 169–192.

Roberson, D., Davies, I., & Davidoff, J. (2000). Color categories are not universal: Replications and new evidence from a stone-age culture. *Journal of Experimental Psychology: General, 129*, 369–398.

Rommetveit, R. (1974). *On message structure: A framework for the study of language and communication.* New York: Wiley.

Rosch, E. (1973). Natural categories. *Cognitive Psychology, 4*, 328–350.

Ross, L., Greene, D., & House, P. (1977). The "false consensus" effect: An egocentric bias in the perception and attribution process. *Journal of Experimental Social Psychology, 13*, 279–301.

Rubini, M., & Menegatti, M. (2008). Linguistic bias in personnel selection. *Journal of Language and Social Psychology, 27*, 168–181.

Rudolph, U., & Fosterling, F. (1997). The psychological causality implicit in verbs: A review. *Psychological Bulletin, 121*, 192–218.

Rumelhart, D. E. (1975). Notes on a schema for stories. In D. G. Bobrow & A. Collins (Eds.), *Representation and understanding* (pp. 185–210). New York: Academic Press.

Ruscher, J. B. (1998). Prejudice and stereotyping in everyday conversation. In M. Zanna (Ed.), *Advances in experimental social psychology* (Vol. 30, pp. 241–307). San Diego: Academic Press.

Ryan, E. B., Giles, H., & Sebastian, R. (1982). An integrative perspective for the study of attitudes toward language variation. In E. B. Ryan & H. Giles (Eds.), *Attitudes toward language variation* (pp. 1–19). London: Edward Arnold.

Ryan, E. B., & Sebastian, R. (1980). The effects of speech style and social class background on social judgments of speakers. *British Journal of Social and Clinical Psychology, 19*, 229–233.

Sacks, H. (1987). On the preference for agreement and contiguity in sequences in conversation. In G. Button & J. R. E. Lee (Eds.), *Talk and social organization* (pp. 54–69). Clevedon, England: Multilingual Matters.

Sacks, H., & Schegloff, E. A. (1979). Two preferences in the organization of reference to persons in conversation and their interaction.

In G. Psathas (Ed.), *Everyday language: Studies in ethnomethodology* (pp. 15–21). Hillsdale, NJ: Erlbaum.

Sacks, H., Schegloff, E. A., & Jefferson, G. (1974). A simplist systematics for the organization of turn-taking in conversation. *Language, 4,* 696–735.

Sankoff, D., Thibault, P., & Berube, H. (1978). Semantic field variability. In D. Sankoff (Ed.), *Linguistic variation: models and methods* (pp. 23–44). New York: Academic Press.

Sapir, E. (1921). *Language: An introduction to the study of speech.* New York: Harcourt, Brace.

Schank, R. C., & Abelson, R. P. (1995). Knowledge and memory: The real story. In R. J. Wyer, Jr. (Ed.), *Advances in social cognition* (Vol. 8, pp. 1–86). Hillsdale, NJ: Erlbaum Press.

Schegloff, E. A. (1968). Sequencing in conversational openings. *American Anthropologist, 70,* 1075–1095.

Schegloff, E. A. (1972). Notes on a conversational practice: Formulating place. In D. Sudnow (Ed.), *Studies in social interaction* (pp. 75–119). New York: Free Press.

Schegloff, E. A. (1979). Identification and recognition in telephone conversation openings. In G. Psathas (Ed.), *Everyday language: Studies in ethnomethodology* (pp. 23–78). New York: Irvington.

Schegloff, E. A. (1982). Discourse as an interactional achievement: Some uses of "uh huh" and other things that come between sentences. In D. Tannen (Ed.), *Analyzing discourse: Text and talk. Georgetown University Roundtable on Languages and Linguistics* (pp. 71–93). Washington, DC: Georgetown University Press.

Schegloff, E. A. (1992). To Searle on conversation: A note in return. In H. Parret & J. Verschueren (Eds.), *(On) Searle on conversation* (pp. 113–128). Philadelphia: John Benjamins.

Schegloff, E. A. (2007). *Sequence organization in interaction: A primer in conversation analysis, Volume 1.* Cambridge, England: Cambridge University Press.

Schegloff, E. A., Jefferson, G., & Sacks, H. (1977). The preference for self-correction in the organization of repair in conversation. *Language, 53,* 361–382.

Schegloff, E., & Sacks, H. (1973). Opening up closings. *Semiotica, 8,* 289–327.

Scherer, K. (1979). Personality markers in speech. In K. Scherer & H. Giles (Eds.), *Social markers in speech* (pp. 147–209). Cambridge, England: Cambridge University Press.

Schmid, J., & Fiedler, K. (1996). Language and implicit attributions in the Nuremberg trials. *Human Communication Research, 22,* 371–398.

Schmid, J., & Fiedler, K. (1998). The backbone of closing speeches: The impact of prosecution versus defense language on judicial attributions. *Journal of Applied Social Psychology, 28,* 1140–1172.

Schmid, J., Fiedler, K., Englich, B., Ehrenberger, T., & Semin, G. R. (1996). Taking sides with the defendant: Grammatical choice and the influence of implicit attributions in prosecution and defense speeches, *International Journal of Psycholinguistics, 12,* 127–148.

Schober, M. F., & Brennan, S. E. (2003). Processes of interactive spoken discourse: The role of the partner. In A. C. Graesser, M. A. Gernsbacher, & S. R. Goldman (Eds.), *Handbook of discourse processes* (pp. 123–164). Hillsdale, NJ: Lawrence Erlbaum.

Schober, M. R., & Clark, H. H. (1989). Understanding by addressees and overhearers. *Cognitive Psychology, 21,* 211–232. University of Chicago Press.

Schooler, J. W., & Engstler-Schooler, T. Y. (1990). Verbal overshadowing of visual memories: Some things are better left unsaid. *Cognitive Psychology, 22,* 36–71.

Schubert, T. W. (2005). Your highness: Vertical positions as perceptual symbols of power. *Journal of Personality and Social Psychology, 89,* 1–21.

Schwarz, N. (1996). *Cognition and communication: Judgmental biases, research methods, and the logic of conversation.* Mahwah, NJ: Erlbaum.

Schwarz, N., Hippler, H. J., Deutsch, B., & Strack, F. (1985). Response scales: Effects of category range on reported behavior and subsequent judgments. *Public Opinion Quarterly, 49,* 388–395.

Schwarz, N., Strack, F., Hilton, D. J., & Naderer, G. (1991). Judgmental biases and the logic of conversation: The contextual relevance of irrelevant information. *Social Cognition, 9,* 67–84.

Scollon, R., & Scollon, S. (1981). *Narrative, literacy, and face in interethnic communication.* Norwood, NJ: Ablex.

Searle, J. R. (1969). *Speech acts.* Cambridge, England: Cambridge University Press.

Searle, J. R. (1979). *Expression and meaning.* Cambridge, England: Cambridge University Press.

Searle, J. R. (1992). Conversation. In H. Parret & J. Verschueren (Eds.), *(On) Searle on conversation* (pp. 7–30). Philadelphia: John Benjamins.

Searle, J. R, & Vanderveken, D. (1985). *Foundations of illocutionary logic.* Cambridge, England: Cambridge University Press.

Seggie, I. (1983). Attribution of guilt as a function of ethnic accent and type of crime. *Journal of Multilingual and Multicultural Development, 4,* 197–206.

Seligman, C., Tucker, G. R., & Lambert, W. E. (1972). The effects of speech style and other attributes on teachers' attitudes toward pupils. *Language in Society, 1,* 131–142.

Semin G. R. (2007). Grounding communication: Synchrony. In A. Kruglanski & E. T. Higgins (Eds.), *Social psychology: Handbook of basic principles* (2nd ed., pp. 630–649). New York: Guilford Press.

Semin, G. R., & DePoot, C. J. (1997). The question-answer paradigm: You might regret not noticing how a question is worded. *Journal of Personality and Social Psychology, 73,* 472–480.

Semin, G. R., & Fiedler, K. (1988). The cognitive functions of linguistic categories in describing persons: Social cognition and language. *Journal of Personality and Social Psychology, 54,* 558–568.

Semin, G. R., & Fiedler, K. (1991). The linguistic category model, its bases, applications and range. In W. Stroebe & M. Hewstone (Eds.), *European review of social psychology* (Vol. 2, pp. 1–30). Chichester, England: Wiley.

Semin, G. R., & Marsman, (1994). "Multiple inference-inviting properties" of interpersonal verbs: Event instigation, dispositional inference, and implicit causality. *Journal of Personality and Social Psychology, 67,* 836–849.

Semin, G. R., Rubini, M., & Fiedler, K. (1995). The answer is in the question: The effect of verb causality on locus of explanation. *Personality and Social Psychology, 21,* 834–841.

Semin, G. R., & Smith, E. R. (1999). Revisiting the past and back to the future: Memory systems and the linguistic representation of social events. *Journal of Personality and Social Psychology, 76,* 877–892.

Siegman, A. W., & Pope, B. (1972). *Studies in dyadic communication.* New York: Pergamon.

Slugoski, B., Lalljee, M., Lamb, R., & Ginsburg, G. P. (1993). Attributions in conversational context: Effects of mutual knowledge on explanation giving. *European Journal of Social Psychology, 23,* 219–238.

Slugoski, B., & Turnbull, W. (1988). Cruel to be kind and kind to be cruel: Sarcasm, banter and social relations. *Journal of Language and Social Psychology, 7,* 101–121.

Smith, E. R., & Semin, G. R. (2004). Socially situated cognition: Cognition in its social context. In M. P. Zanna (Ed.), *Advances in Experimental Social Psychology* (Vol. 36, pp. 57–121). Academic Press.

Smith, S. M., & Schaffer, D. R. (1995) Speed of speech and persuasion: Evidence for multiple effects. *Personality and Social Psychology Bulletin, 21,* 1051–1060.

Sperber, D., & Wilson, D. (1982). Mutual knowledge and relevance in theories of comprehension. In N. Smith (Ed.), *Mutual knowledge* (pp. 61–85). London, Academic Press.

Sperber, D., & Wilson, D. (1986/1995). *Relevance* (1st and 2nd eds.). Cambridge, MA: Cambridge University Press.

Sperber, D., & Wilson, D. (2002). Pragmatics, modularity, and mind reading. *Mind and Language, 17*, 3–23.

Sridhara, A. (1984). A study of language stereotype in children. *Journal of Psychological Researches, 28*, 45–51.

Srull, T. K., & Wyer, R. S. (1979). The role of category accessibility in the interpretation of information about persons: Some determinants and implications. *Journal of Personality and Social Psychology, 37*, 1660–1672.

Stahlberg, D., Braun, F., Irmen, L., & Sczesny, S. (2007). Representation of the sexes in language. In K. Fiedler (Ed.), *Social communication* (pp. 163–188). New York: Psychology Press.

Stanfield, R. A., & Zwaan, R. A. (2001). The effect of implied orientation derived from verbal context on picture recognition. *Psychological Science, 12*, 153–156.

Stapel, D. A., & Semin, G. R. (2007). The magic spell of language: Linguistic categories and their perceptual consequences. *Journal of Personality and Social Psychology, 93*, 23–33.

Stewart, T. L., Weeks, M., & Lupfer, M. B. (2003). Spontaneous stereotyping: A matter of prejudice? *Social Cognition, 21*, 263–298.

Stiles, W., Putnam, S. M., & Jacob, M. C. (1982). Verbal exchange structure of initial medical interviews. *Health Psychology, 1*, 315–336.

Stone, M. (2005). Communicative intentions and conversational processes in human-human and human-computer dialogue. In J. C. Trueswell & M. K. Tanenhaus (Eds.), *Approaches to studying world-situated language use* (pp. 39–69). Cambridge, MA: MIT Press.

Stone, P. J., Dunphy, D. C., Smith, M. S., & Ogilvie, D. M. (1966). *The general inquirer: A computer approach to content analysis.* Cambridge, MA: MIT Press.

Strack, F., Schwarz, N., & Wanke, M. (1991). Semantic and pragmatic aspects of context effects in social and psychological research. *Social cognition, 9*, 111–125.

Street, R. L., Jr. (1984). Speech convergence and speech evaluation in fact-finding interviews. *Human Communication Research, 11*, 139–169.

Street, R. L., Jr., Brady, R. M., & Putnam, W. B. (1983). The influence of speech rate stereotypes and rate similarity on listeners' evaluations of speakers. *Journal of Language and Social Psychology, 2*, 37–356.

Sutton, R. M., & Douglas, K. (2008). Celebrating two decades of linguistic bias research [Special issue]. *Journal of Language and Social Psychology, 27.*

Swinney, D. (1979). Lexical access during sentence comprehension: (Re)consideration of context effects. *Journal of Verbal Learning and Verbal Behavior, 18*, 645–660.

Terkourafi, M. (2009). What use is what is said? In M. Kissine & P. de Brabanter (Eds.), *Utterance interpretation and cognitive models. Current research in the semantics/pragmatics interface series* (pp. 27–58). Amsterdam: Emerald.

Thakerar, J. N., & Giles, H. (1981). They are—so they speak: Noncontent speech stereotypes. *Language and Communication, 1*, 251–256.

Ting-Toomey, S. (1999). *Communicating across cultures.* New York: Guilford Press.

Torrey, C. T., Fussell, S. R., & Kiesler, S. (in press). What robots could teach us about perspective-taking. In E. Morsella (Ed.), *Expressing oneself/Expressing one's self: A Festschrift in honor of Robert M. Krauss.* London: Taylor and Francis.

Tracy, K. (1990). The many faces of face-work. In H. Giles & P. Robinson (Eds.), *Handbook of language and social psychology* (pp. 209–226). London: Wiley.

Trafimow, D., Triandis, H., & Goto, S. G. (1991). Some tests of the distinction between the private self and the collective self. *Journal of Personality and Social Psychology, 60*, 649–655.

Trees, A. R., & Manusov, V. (1998). Managing face concerns in criticism: Integrating nonverbal behaviors as a dimension of politeness in female friendship dyads. *Human Communication Research, 24*, 564–583.

Trope, Y., & Liberman, N. (2003). Temporal construal. *Psychological Review, 110*, 403–421.

Trudgill, P. (1974). *The social differentiation of English in Norwich.* Cambridge, England: Cambridge University Press.

Vallacher, R. R., & Wegner, D. M. (1989). Levels of personal agency: Individual variation in action identification. *Journal of Personality and Social Psychology, 57*, 660–671.

van Dijk T. (1984). *Prejudice in discourse.* Amsterdam: Benjamins.

Van Kleek, M. H., Hillger, L. A., & Brown, R. (1988). Pitting verbal schemas against information variables in attribution. *Social Cognition, 6*, 89–106.

Vanderveken, D., & Kubo, S. (Eds.). (2002). *Essays in speech act theory.* Philadelphia: J. Benjamins.

von Hippel, W., Sekaquaptewa, D., & Vargas, P. (1997). The linguistic intergroup bias as an implicit indicator of prejudice. *Journal of Experimental Social Psychology, 33*, 490–509.

Vygotsky, L. S. (1962). *Thought and language.* Cambridge, MA: MIT Press.

Watson, B., & Gallois, C. (2002) Patients' interactions with health providers: A linguistic category model approach. *Journal of Language and Social Psychology, 21*, 32–52.

Webster, D. M., & Kruglanski, A. (1994). Individual differences in need for cognitive closure. *Journal of Personality and Social Psychology, 67*, 1049–1062.

Webster, D. M., Kruglanski, A. W., & Pattison, D. W. (1997). Motivated language use in intergroup contexts: Need for closure effects on the linguistic intergroup bias. *Journal of Personality and Social Psychology, 72*, 1122–1131.

Wegner, D. M., Coulton, G. F., & Wenzlaff, R. (1985). The transparency of denial: Briefing in the debriefing paradigm. *Journal of Personality and Social Psychology, 49*, 338–346.

Wenneker, C. P. J., Wigboldus, D. H. J., & Spears, R. (2005). Biased language use in stereotype maintenance: The role of encoding and goals. *Journal of Personality and Social Psychology, 89*, 504–516.

Whorf, B. L. (1956). *Language, thought, and reality* (J. B. Carroll, Ed.). Cambridge, MA: MIT Press.

Wigboldus, D. H. J., Dijksterhuis, A., & Van Knippenberg, A. (2003). When stereotypes get in the way: Stereotypes obstruct stereotype-inconsistent trait inferences. *Journal of Personality and Social Psychology, 84*, 470–484.

Wigboldus, D. H. J., & Douglas, K. M. (2007). Language, expectancies, and intergroup relations. In K. Fiedler (Ed.), *Social communication* (pp. 79–106). New York: Psychology Press.

Wigboldus, D. H. J., Semin, G. R., & Spears, R. (2000). How do we communicate stereotypes? Linguistic biases and inferential consequences. *Journal of Personality and Social Psychology, 78*, 5–18.

Williams, A., & Nussbaum, J. F. (2001). *Intergenerational communication across the lifespan.* Mahwah, NJ: Erlbaum.

Williams, F., Whitehead, J. L., & Miller, L. (1972). Relations between attitudes and teacher expectancy. *American Educational Research Journal, 9*, 263–277.

Wilson, D., & Sperber, D. (2004). Relevance theory. In L. R. Horn & G. Ward (Eds.), *The handbook of pragmatics* (pp. 607–632). Malden, MA: Blackwell.

Wilson, M. (2002). Six views of embodied cognition. *Psychonomic Bulletin and Review, 9*, 625–636.

Wilson, T. D., Lisle, D. J., Schooler, J. W., Hodges, S. D., Klaaren, K. J., & LaFleur, S. J. (1993). Introspecting about reasons can reduce post-choice satisfaction. *Personality and Social Psychology Bulletin, 19*, 331–339.

Wilson, T. D., & Schooler, J. W. (1991). Thinking too much: Introspection can reduce the quality of preferences and decisions. *Journal of Personality and Social Psychology, 60*, 181–192.

Winawer, J., Witthoft, N., Frank, M. C., Wu, L., Wade, A., & Boroditsky, L. (2007). The Russian blues: Effects of language on color discrimination. *Proceedings of the National Academy of Sciences, 108*, 7780–7785.

Wish, M., D'Andrade, R. G., & Goodenough, J. E. (1980). Dimensions of interpersonal communication: Correspondences between structures for speech acts and bipolar scales. *Journal of Personality and Social Psychology, 39*, 848–860.

Wittgenstein, L. (1953). *Philosophical investigations.* Oxford: Blackwell.

Wood, L. A., & Kroger, R. O. (1991). Politeness and forms of address. *Journal of Language and Social Psychology, 10*, 145–168.

Woolard, K. A., & Gahng, T.-J.(1990). Changing language policies and attitudes in autonomous Catalonia. *Language in Society, 19*, 311–330.

Wright, E. F., & Wells, G. L. (1988). Is the attitude-attribution paradigm suitable for investigating the dispositional bias? *Personality and Social Psychology Bulletin, 14*, 183–190.

Wu, S., & Keysar, B. (2007a). The effect of communication overlap on communication effectiveness. *Cognitive Science, 31*, 169–181.

Wu, S., & Keysar, B. (2007b). Cultural effects on perspective taking. *Psychological Science, 18*, 600–606.

Wyer, R. S., & Gruenfeld, D. H. (1995). Information processing in social contexts: Implications for social memory and judgment. In M. P. Zanna (Ed.), *Advances in experimental social psychology* (Vol. 27, pp. 52–93). New York: Academic Press.

Yabuuchi, A. (1996). Diagraming discourse structures: Illocution, interaction, or text? *Semiotica, 110*, 197–229.

Yngve, V. H. (1970). On getting a word in edgewise. In *Papers from the sixth regional meeting of the Chicago Linguistics Society*. Chicago: Chicago Linguistics Society.

Zwaan, R. A., & Yaxley, R. H. (2003). Spatial iconicity affects semantic relatedness judgments. *Psychonomic Bulletin & Review, 10*, 954–958.

Chapter 37

Cultural Psychology

STEVEN J. HEINE

We are members of a cultural species. That is, we depend critically on cultural learning in virtually all aspects of our lives. Whether we are trying to manage our resources, woo a mate, protect our family, enhance our status, or form a political alliance—goals that are pursued by people in all cultures—we do so in culturally grounded ways. That is, in all our actions we rely on ideas, values, feelings, strategies, and goals that have been shaped by our cultural experiences. Human activity is inextricably wrapped up in cultural meanings; on no occasions do we cast aside our cultural dressings to reveal the naked universal human mind. To be sure, much regularity exists across humans from all cultures with respect to many psychological phenomena; at the same time, there remain many pronounced differences (for a review, see Norenzayan & Heine, 2005). Yet the point is that all psychological phenomena, whether largely similar or different across cultures, remain entangled in cultural meanings. The challenge for comprehending the mind of a cultural species is that it requires a rich understanding of how the mind is constrained and afforded by cultural learning. The field of cultural psychology has emerged in response to this challenge.

Cultural psychologists share the key assumption that not all psychological processes are so inflexibly hardwired into the brain that they appear in identical ways across cultural contexts. Rather, psychological processes are seen to arise from evolutionarily shaped biological potentials becoming attuned to the particular cultural meaning system within which the individual develops. At the same time, cultures can be understood to emerge through the processes by which humans interact with and seize meanings and resources from their cultures. In this way, culture and the mind can be said to be mutually constituted (Shweder, 1990). An effort to understand either one without considering the other is bound to reveal an incomplete picture.

Although psychologists have been studying culture at least since Wilhelm Wundt published his 10-volume tome *Elements of Folk Psychology* in 1921, the study of cultural psychology has had its most impactful influence on mainstream psychology over the past 20 years. Around 1990, several seminal papers and books emerged that articulated how cultural experiences were central to and inextricably linked with psychological processing (Bruner, 1990; Markus & Kitayama, 1991; Stigler, Shweder, & Herdt, 1990; Triandis, 1989). Since then, much empirical research has demonstrated the cultural foundation of many psychological phenomena that had hitherto been viewed largely as invariant across the species.

This chapter reviews various ways in which culture shapes people's thoughts and behaviors. The term "culture" is used in two contexts. First, culture refers to any kind of *information* that is acquired from members of one's species through social learning that is capable of affecting an individual's behaviors (Richerson & Boyd, 2005). Second, culture refers to *groups of people* who exist within a shared context, where they are exposed to similar institutions, engage in similar practices, and communicate with one another regularly. This chapter explores how culture is uniquely implicated in human nature; how researchers can study cultural effects on psychology; how people are enculturated as they develop; and how culture shapes people's self-concepts, personalities, relationships, motivation, cognition and perception, language use, emotions, and moral reasoning.

This chapter was funded by a grant from the Social Science and Humanities Research Council of Canada (410-2008-0155). I am especially grateful to the extremely helpful feedback that I received from Emma Buchtel, Adam Cohen, Carl Falk, Takeshi Hamamura, Sheena Iyengar, Will Maddux, Yuri Miyamoto, Beth Morling, Dick Nisbett, Ara Norenzayan, Shige Oishi, Jeffrey Sanchez-Burks, Rick Shweder, and Jeanne Tsai.

HUMANS AS A CULTURAL SPECIES

Humans are unique in the extent of their dependence on culture. In this section, human cultural learning is contrasted with that of other species. Further, some implications of the cultural nature of humans are discussed in terms of generalizing findings from particular cultural contexts to the species at large.

One defining characteristic of humans is that they engage in cultural learning—that is, they acquire information from conspecifics through social transmission (Richerson & Boyd, 2005). Engaging in cultural learning, by itself, is not a uniquely human characteristic, as many diverse species show evidence for cultural learning; for example, rats (Galef, 1988), pigeons (Lefebvre & Giraldeau, 1994), and guppies (Lachlan, Crooks, & Laland, 1998) engage in some kinds of learning from conspecifics. In some species, such as chimpanzees (Whiten et al., 1999) and orcas (Whitehead, 1998), the degree of cultural learning is quite substantial. Humans are thus not unique in the animal kingdom for engaging in cultural learning, although they are unique in the fidelity of their cultural learning. No other species have shown the capacity to learn from conspecifics as well as humans do (Hermann, Call, Hernandez-Lloreda, Hare, & Tomasello, 2007).

The high-fidelity cultural learning of humans is fostered by two unique human capabilities. First, humans have unrivalled linguistic abilities (e.g., Pinker, 1994), which allow for precise communication and transmission of cultural ideas. Second, humans have a well-developed theory of mind (e.g., Tomasello, 1999), which allows them to consider the intentions of their compatriots and thus engage in true imitative learning. In imitative learning the learner internalizes the model's goals and behavioral strategies and works to reproduce them. Other species, such as chimpanzees, can also engage in social learning from conspecifics. However, because chimpanzees are less able to attend to other's perspectives or intentions, and in particular, have difficulties engaging in joint-shared attention, their learning is not fully imitative (Tomasello, Carpenter, Call, Behne, & Moll, 2005). Rather, the social learning of chimpanzees is better characterized as emulative, in which they attend to the affordances of the objects in the environment (e.g., they learn that termites will stick to twigs inserted in termite mounds) but do not attend to the goals of the model, and this significantly limits the fidelity of the information that can be learned (Tomasello, Kruger, & Ratner, 1993).

Humans' sophisticated cultural learning skills are surely the result of their large brains relative to other species—the encephalization quotient of humans is 4.6, which is almost double the value (2.5) for chimpanzees (the largest for nonhuman primates), and the values for other species of primates are considerably larger than those for other mammals (Aiello & Wheeler, 1995). The unusually large brains of primates appear to be an adaptation to the complex social environments in which many species of primates live (Dunbar, 1993). In contrast to the social nature of many other primate species, humans appear to be "ultrasocial" (Boyd & Richerson, 1996). This is evident in experiments contrasting the cognitive capacities of human children with those of other great apes. Whereas chimpanzees, orangutans, and 2.5-year-old human children perform similarly on various cognitive tasks, the children significantly outperform both species of apes on social tasks involving communication, theory of mind, and in particular, social learning (Hermann et al., 2007).

Hence, although many species have cultural learning, no other species is able to learn as well from conspecifics as do humans. With the possible exception of various species of matrilineal whales (in which the extent of their cultural learning is not yet well understood; Whitehead, 1998), humans are the only species with evidence for substantial cultural evolution (Boyd & Richerson, 1996; Tomasello, 1999). Cultural learning in humans is of high enough fidelity that cultural information tends to accumulate over time (a process known as the ratchet effect; Tomasello et al., 1993), whereby cultural ideas are learned by an individual, they are subsequently modified, and the modified ideas are then learned by others, ad infinitum. This cultural evolution tends to accelerate over time, as there are a growing number of ideas that can be modified or connected, provided there is open communication among individuals (Henrich, 2004; Nolan & Lenski, 2004). Consequently, humans live in vastly more complex cultural worlds than any other species, and their experiences vary widely from culture to culture.

The point that humans are unique in having significant cultural evolution is important for understanding their psychology. Unlike other species, humans do not just inhabit physical and social worlds; they also exist within cultural worlds constructed on a foundation of cultural information that has accumulated over time (Luria, 1928). For example, contemporary American undergraduates (the sample on which most of the empirical database of social psychology is based; Arnett, 2008) live in a world that includes culturally evolved products such as technologies that they use (e.g., cars, fast food, and printed paper), institutions in which they participate (e.g., democratic governments, higher education, and medical care), and ideas that are championed (e.g., being unique, justice and individual rights, and freely entering and exiting casual relationships). Many shared ideas that constitute the cultural contexts of contemporary American undergraduates are relatively unique in the context of world history, and these are paralleled by unique psychological tendencies (Henrich, Heine, & Norenzayan, in press). People are born into particular cultural worlds, and they are continually learning, and being influenced by, the shared ideas that constitute those worlds. Coming to understand why people behave and think in the ways in which they do means we need to also consider the kinds of cultural information that people encounter in their daily lives.

Cross-Cultural Generalizability of Psychological Findings

The cultural nature of humans makes it challenging to draw conclusions about psychological universals. What aspects of human psychology are common to all, and what aspects are specific to particular cultural contexts? This question is of great significance for many social psychological theories, although in many cases data to evaluate it are insufficient (Heine & Norenzayan, 2006).

Many social psychological phenomena do indeed vary significantly across cultural contexts and emerge at different levels of universality (see Norenzayan & Heine, 2005, for a framework to interpret cultural universals and variability). On the one hand, pronounced cultural variance has been identified in such fundamental psychological phenomena as perceptions of fairness (e.g., Henrich et al., 2005), approach–avoidance motivations (e.g., Lee, Aaker, & Gardner, 2000), the nature of unspoken thoughts (Kim, 2002), attention (Chua, Boland, & Nisbett, 2005), preferences for formal reasoning (e.g., Norenzayan, Smith, Kim, & Nisbett, 2002), the need for high self-esteem (e.g., Heine, Lehman, Markus, & Kitayama, 1999), and moral reasoning (e.g., Miller & Bersoff, 1992). At the same time, for many key psychological phenomena varying degrees of universality have been compellingly established, such as facial expressions of emotions (Ekman, Sorenson, & Friesen, 1969), some mating preferences (Buss, 1989), sex differences in violence (Daly & Wilson, 1988), and the structure of personality (McCrae et al., 2005). Some psychological phenomena manifest in more culturally variable ways than others, and it is typically not clear *a priori* which phenomena should be the most similar across cultures. Hence, data from an array of samples are needed to assess the universality of a particular phenomenon.

A major obstacle for assessing universality is the limited nature of the psychological database. For example, a recent review of all papers in the *Journal of Personality and Social Psychology* from 2003 to 2007 (Arnett, 2008) found that 94% of the samples were from Western countries, with 62% coming from the United States alone (also see Quinones-Vidal, Lopez-Garcia, Penaranda-Ortega,

& Tortosa-Gil, 2004). Moreover, 67% of the American samples (and 80% of the non-American samples) were composed solely of undergraduates in psychology courses at research universities. Similar proportions were found for other disciplines in psychology. Curiously, this American dominance of psychology is unparalleled by other disciplines—a larger proportion of citations come from American researchers in psychology than they do for any of the other 19 sciences that were compared in one extensive international survey (May, 1997). For the most part, psychologists simply do not know whether a given phenomenon is universal because the database rarely covers a sufficient range of cultural contexts (although several important exceptions exist).

What makes identifying the universality of psychological processes so problematic is that the results of studies conducted on American undergraduates are often outliers within the context of an international database for many key domains in the behavioral sciences. That is, the available cross-cultural data find that, for several fundamental psychological phenomena (e.g., some visual illusions, decisions in behavioral economic games, moral reasoning, self-concept, social motivations, analytic reasoning, and spatial perception), (1) people from industrialized societies respond differently than those from small-scale societies; (2) people from Western societies demonstrate more pronounced responses than those from non-Western societies; (3) Americans show yet more extreme responses than other Westerners; and (4) the responses of contemporary American college students are even further different from those of non-college-educated American adults (Henrich et al., in press). That is, discerning human universals is not just a challenge because psychologists tend to have focused on such a narrow sample; it is greatly compounded because psychologists have focused on such an *unrepresentative* sample (see Henrich et al., in press, for detailed discussion of this point). Gaining an understanding of the universal and culturally specific ways in which human minds operate requires that we collect meaningful data regarding how people compare across cultures in their thinking and behavior. However, collecting such data requires several important methodological considerations.

CONSIDERATIONS FOR CONDUCTING RESEARCH ACROSS CULTURES

Cultural psychology uses methods from virtually all areas of psychology; thus, it inherits the methodological shortcomings of each of those particular methods. However, many additional and unique methodological challenges are involved when comparing psychological phenomena across cultures.

First, researchers studying participants who share their own cultural background are at a distinct advantage in being able to be relatively confident that the measures that they create will be interpreted by the participants in the ways in which the researcher intends. When participants' cultural backgrounds differ from that of the researcher, however, such confidence can be greatly weakened. For example, Patricia Greenfield (1997) reported on her experience of interviewing Zincantecan participants with a standard psychological instrument in which she asked her participants a set series of related questions. Although the instrument was well validated in Western contexts, her series of questions only annoyed and offended her Zincantecan participants, as the interview violated conversational norms of relevance. After offering a thoughtful answer to a question, the participants were surprised and offended that the researcher then asked them what seemed to be pretty much the same question, worded slightly differently, with apparently no regard to the answer that they had just provided. In sum, to be able to gather meaningful data from people of different cultural backgrounds, it is essential that some members of the research team have much knowledge and familiarity with those cultural backgrounds so that appropriate methods can be developed and responses can be meaningfully interpreted. Such cultural knowledge can be gained by reading rich and descriptive texts and ethnographies about the cultures under study. Better still, collaborators with much familiarity with the relevant cultures could be included in the project. Ideally, these collaborators should be intimately involved with the development of the study from the onset, thereby ensuring that the methods are culturally appropriate, rather than only distributing previously developed surveys. Even more cultural knowledge can be gained if primary investigators learn about the relevant cultures as anthropologists have done for more than a century—by immersing themselves in the culture for lengthy periods—such that the researcher is able to develop intuitions about the participants under study in ways similar to those achieved by people who study participants from their own culture. Some combination of these efforts would seem most likely to ensure that the research is culturally informed (see Shweder, 1997, for more discussion).

A second challenge faced in cross-cultural research is that often the cultures being compared differ in the languages they speak. One strategy for dealing with this is to only study people who have sufficient familiarity with the same language, for example, studying immigrants to the United States with English materials. A key downside of such a strategy is one of power. It is likely that immigrants who learn English well enough to understand the materials as well as a native speaker have also learned associated psychological phenomena. Furthermore, much research on language priming finds that bilinguals show evidence for different psychological phenomena depending on the language that they are speaking (e.g., Ross, Xun, & Wilson, 2002). This means that when all participants are speaking the same language they are also being primed with similar cultural meanings, which would further reduce the magnitude of any existing cultural differences. Hence, it is quite possible that one would find no cultural differences between two divergent cultural groups assessed in the same language, whereas one could find pronounced cultural differences between the same cultural groups if they were assessed in their respective native languages.

The second strategy for resolving language differences is to translate the materials into the respective languages of the cultures being studied. Translations are challenging at the best of times, and the nuances inherent in many measures of psychological phenomena can be difficult to capture veridically in translation. If no member of the research team has sufficient familiarity with the languages of the cultures under study, then one should employ the backtranslation method (Brislin, 1970), where the original materials are translated into the other language by a translator, and then an independent translator translates the translation back into the first language, enabling the researchers to compare the similarities between the original and the backtranslated materials. Backtranslations are not ideal, however, as they can result in unnatural or difficult-to-understand translations, without that necessarily being evident to the researchers. Ideally, some of the investigators will have expertise in the respective languages and can go over the translations themselves to ensure that the materials are not awkward and capture all subtle nuances—this is the most commonly used translation method in professional translations (Wilss, 1982).

A third challenge in cross-cultural research emerges in that people from different cultures can maintain different response styles. For example, African Americans and Hispanic Americans are more likely to use the extreme points of Likert scales than are European Americans (Bachman & O'Malley, 1984; Hui & Triandis, 1989), who, in turn, are less likely to use the middle points of Likert scales than are East Asians (Chen, Lee, & Stevenson, 1995)—the former relative tendency is known as an extremity bias and the latter as a moderacy bias. Another example is that East Asians are more likely to show a relative acquiescence bias, and agree with a greater percentage of items, than are European Americans (e.g., Choi & Choi, 2002; Grimm & Church, 1999; Spencer-Rodgers, Peng, Wang, & Hou, 2004). A challenge with dealing with these different response styles is that it is not always clear whether these represent stylistic differences in expressing one's thoughts that should be statistically controlled or whether they reflect "real" differences in ways of thinking across cultures that should be preserved (Hamamura, Heine, & Paulhus, 2008; Paulhus, 1986).

Another problem that is inherent in cross-cultural comparisons of subjective responses arises from people's tendencies to evaluate themselves by comparing themselves with similar others (Festinger, 1954). Because people from different cultures are surrounded by different people, with different norms and standards, such comparisons with others may be confounded, and the results reduce the size of any obtained cultural differences. This is termed the reference-group effect (Heine, Lehman, Peng, & Greenholtz, 2002; Peng, Nisbett, & Wong, 1997). For example, a man who is 5 feet 10 inches in height would be more likely to describe himself as tall if he lived in a culture where the average height for men was 5 feet 8 inches than in a culture where the average male height was 6 feet. The same height, attitude, or behavior can come to mean something quite different depending on how it compares with the norms and standards that surround a person (cf. Biernat & Manis, 1994). Some evidence for problems that emerge from the reference-group effect can be seen, for example, in that cross-cultural comparisons of self-report means of individualism and collectivism scales yield effects that are considerably smaller than those observed in cross-cultural comparisons of cultural products (e.g., television and magazine advertisements, newspaper articles, and public behaviors; see the meta-analysis by Morling & Lamoreaux, 2008). Likewise, whereas most cross-cultural comparisons looking at means of self-report measures related to lay theories of self yield null effects (e.g., Heine et al., 2001; Hong et al., 1999), studies with experimental manipulations, or items with more objective response options, yield more pronounced effects (Heine et al., 2001). Furthermore, studies employing people's concrete responses to behavioral scenarios, and studies that explicitly specify the referent group, yield better convergence with validity criteria than those that compare subjective means (Heine et al., 2002; Peng et al., 1997). The reference-group effect remains a pernicious challenge for interpreting the means of subjective responses across cultures.

In sum, various challenges are inherent in cross-cultural comparisons of subjective questionnaire responses. Many cross-cultural researchers aspire to ensure measurement equivalence of their constructs before they compare them across cultures (e.g., ensuring that the constructs have similar factor structures and item functioning; e.g., Poortinga, 1989; van de Vijver & Tanzer, 2004); however, such efforts hinge on the assumption that the construct under study is cross-culturally universal—a question that is often the focus of the investigation. Given the various challenges inherent in comparisons of questionnaire responses across cultures, I recommend viewing any cross-cultural comparison of subjective Likert scale means with a grain of salt until convergent findings are demonstrated with other methods.

Experiments provide a powerful means to avoid many complications that plague cross-cultural comparisons of questionnaire responses. When an independent variable is manipulated within cultures, comparisons across conditions are often not affected by the issues discussed earlier because the conditions within each culture share similar response styles and reference groups. The experimental method thus allows meaningful comparisons to be made across cultures. In general, cross-cultural differences that are obtained with experimental measures appear to yield a more consistent pattern of results across studies than those obtained with cross-cultural comparisons of self-report measures (for discussion, see Heine et al., 2002). The success of the experiment in cultural psychological research may derive from the study of culture being in many ways similar to the study of the social environment. If culture is the social situation writ large, then it perhaps follows that the experimental methods applied by social psychologists would be most appropriate for studying many questions regarding how culture affects people's thoughts and behaviors.

HUMANS ARE ENCULTURATED AS THEY DEVELOP

This section reviews how humans accumulate cultural learning as they develop. It discusses some differences in cultural experiences that are evident among infants and young children, and it considers how cultural differences in various psychological processes often become more pronounced with age.

The central focus of inquiry for cultural psychology is the process by which biological entities become meaningful ones (Markus & Kitayama, 1998). That is, the field grapples with how mental capacities that are largely similar around the world (indeed, humans have far less genetic variability than do chimpanzees, underscoring how recently human populations diverged from a common ancestor; Boyd & Silk, 2006) become interpenetrated by diverse cultural meanings and thereby manifest themselves in different ways across cultures. The *universal mind* that is present at birth is expressed in *multiple mentalities* across cultural contexts (Shweder et al., 1998). In the words of Clifford Geertz (1973, p. 45), "we all begin with the natural equipment to live a thousand kinds of life but end in the end having lived only one." People acquire particular cultural characteristics as the result of their enculturation experiences in the course of development.

People come to think in different ways across cultures, because their experiences differ, and they do so in many ways from a very young age. For example, whereas the most common sleeping arrangement for American infants is in a crib in a separate room from their mothers, this arrangement was not observed in any other society studied in a large-scale survey of 100 societies around the world (Burton & Whiting, 1961). Rather, in approximately two thirds of societies, infants sleep in the same bed as their mothers; in most other cases, infants sleep in the same room as their mothers but in a different bed (Whiting, 1964; also see Shweder, Jensen, & Goldstein, 1995). Likewise, American mothers chat with their babies in a different way than do Japanese mothers, with American mothers being more likely to elicit "happy vocals" and Japanese mothers being more likely to soothe "unhappy vocals" (Caudill & Weinstein, 1969). Similarly, Canadian mothers were shown to communicate nouns more effectively to infants, whereas Chinese mothers were more effective at communicating verbs (as evidenced by college students being able to guess what was being communicated in a silent video; Lavin, Hall, & Waxman, 2006). In sum, even the cultural experiences of prelinguistic children differ in various ways across cultures.

Cultural variation in the experiences of infants and children is paralleled by cultural variation in many psychological processes. One domain in which this is clearly evident is in attachment styles. The distribution of the three attachment styles varies significantly across cultures. For example, whereas the most common attachment style among Americans is the secure attachment (approximately 62% of mother–child relationships; Campos, Barrett, Lamb, Goldsmith, & Stenberg, 1983), in northern Germany the most commonly found attachment style is the avoidant attachment (approximately 48% of relationships; Grossman, Grossman, Spangler, Suess, & Unzner, 1985). Among children reared in Israeli kibbutzim, the anxious–ambivalent style is most commonly found (approximately 50% of relationships; Sagi et al., 1985). Furthermore, in some cultural contexts, researchers have not been able to identify all three attachment styles; for example, some researchers could not identify any avoidant attachments among Japanese (Miyake, 1993) or Dogon mother–child pairs (True, Pisani, & Oumar, 2001). It has even been questioned whether the assumptions underlying attachment theory (e.g., particularly the notions of dependence and autonomy) make sense in some non-Western cultural contexts (Rothbaum, Weisz, Pott, Miyake, & Morelli, 2000).

Another domain in which young children differ across cultures is language learning. Much research with English learners has revealed pronounced evidence for a "noun bias," where most new words that toddlers learn are nouns (e.g., Huttenlocher & Smiley, 1987). Early theories focused on the salience and concreteness of nouns, which were believed to make them more easily learned (Gentner, 1982; Gleitman, 1990). However, these accounts are challenged by findings that noun biases are not readily found in all cultures. For example, in one study Chinese toddlers were found to use more verbs than nouns (Tardif, 1996), and another showed no evidence of a noun bias among Korean toddlers (Choi & Gopnik, 1995). The kinds of words learned first by young children vary across cultural and linguistic contexts.

Because cultural information is acquired as children are socialized, it follows that cultural differences in psychological processes should become more pronounced with age and socializing experiences. Aside from phenomena that are delimited by an early sensitive window for their acquisition (Johnson & Newport, 1989; McCauley & Henrich, 2006; Minoura, 1992), adults should differ more in their ways of thinking across cultures than should children. Evidence for such trends has emerged in several domains. For example, (1) cultural differences in the tendency to make nonlinear predictions of the future become more pronounced in magnitude with age (Ji, 2008); (2) tendencies to make situation attributions increase with age among Indians, whereas tendencies to make dispositional attributions increase with age among Americans (Miller, 1984); and (3) cultural differences in social loafing become more pronounced with age (Gabrenya, Wang, & Latané, 1985).

SELF-CONCEPT

Research on culture and the self-concept has been central to the field of cultural psychology. This research has focused much on distinctions between independent and interdependent self-concepts and how these different self-views manifest with respect to self-consistency versus flexibility, insider versus outsider phenomenologies, and incremental versus entity theories of self. This section also discusses the psychological experiences of those with multicultural selves.

Independent Versus Interdependent Self-Concepts

Cultural psychology maintains that the process of becoming a self is contingent on people interacting with and seizing meanings from their cultural environments. Thus, the resultant self-concepts that emerge from participating in distinct cultural contexts may vary considerably. For example, cultural variation in self-concept can be seen in studies that ask people to freely describe aspects of themselves using the Twenty Statements Test (Kuhn & McPartland, 1954). Such studies reveal that people from various individualistic cultural contexts, such as Australia, Britain, Canada, and Sweden, tend to describe themselves most commonly with statements that reflect their inner psychological characteristics, such as their attitudes, personality traits, and abilities. In contrast, people from various collectivistic cultural contexts, such as Cook Islanders, Native Americans, Malaysians, Puerto Ricans, Indians, and various East Asian populations, show a greater tendency, relative to Westerners, to describe themselves by indicating relational roles and memberships that they possess (see Heine, 2008, for a review). Such cultural differences are already evident among kindergarten-aged children (Wang, 2004). As one stark example of this cultural difference, a study that contrasted American college students and various samples in Kenya found that 48% of American self-descriptions consisted of statements regarding their psychological characteristics whereas only 2% of the statements of indigenous Kenyan tribes (the Masai and the Samburu) referred to such characteristics (Ma & Schoeneman, 1997). On the other hand, statements regarding roles and memberships constituted more than 60% of the statements by the Masai and the Samburu in contrast to only 7% of American self-descriptions. In sum, the ways in which people describe themselves vary considerably across cultures.

These different patterns of responses in self-descriptions suggest that people might conceptualize their selves in at least two different ways. One way, as evident in many statements made by the American students in Ma and Schoeneman's study, is that the self can largely derive its identity from its inner attributes—a self-contained model of self that Markus and Kitayama (1991) labeled an independent self-concept. These attributes are assumed to reflect the essence of an individual in that they are viewed as stable across situations and across the life span, they are perceived to be unique (in that no one else is expected to have the same configuration of attributes), they are viewed as significant for regulating behavior, and individuals feel obligated to publicly advertise themselves in ways consistent with these attributes. A second way that people can conceptualize themselves, evident in many statements of the Masai and Samburu, is to view the self as largely deriving its identity from its relations with significant others—this model is termed an interdependent self-concept (Markus & Kitayama, 1991). With this view of self, people recognize that their behavior is contingent upon their perceptions of other's thoughts, feelings, and actions; they attend to how their behaviors affect others; and they consider their relevant roles within each social context. The interdependent self is not so much a separate and distinct entity as it is embedded in a larger social group.

This distinction in self-concepts (which relates to individualism–collectivism; Triandis, 1989) has been related to widely varying psychological processes, such as motivations for uniqueness (e.g., Kim & Markus, 1999), self-enhancement (e.g., Heine et al., 1999), feelings of agency (e.g., Morling, Kitayama, & Miyamoto, 2002), kinds of emotional experiences (e.g., Mesquita, 2001), perspectives on relationships (e.g., Adams, 2005), and analytic versus holistic reasoning styles (e.g., Nisbett, Peng, Choi, & Norenzayan, 2001). This distinction presently stands as the most fruitful way of making sense of many cultural differences in psychological processes (Oyserman, Coon, & Kemmelmeier, 2002). Numerous other dimensions of cultural variation have been offered in the literature, such as power distance, uncertainty avoidance (Hofstede, 1980), vertical–horizontal social structure (Triandis, 1996), relationship structure (Fiske, 1992), intellectual autonomy (Schwartz, 1994), context dependence (Hall, 1976), social cynicism, social complexity (Leung & Bond, 2004), and societal tightness (Triandis, 1989). These are all interesting and important dimensions; however, thus far, none of these have had anything like the success of the individualism–collectivism construct in being linked to other kinds of psychological processes. The field will certainly benefit when researchers can demonstrate the unique predictive validity of other dimensions of cultural variability. At present, there appears to be something about individualism and collectivism that is more fundamental to human psychology than these other dimensions. Perhaps this centrality derives from the universal tension that arises from every human ultimately being a distinct individual, unique from everyone else, yet at the same time being a member of an ultrasocial species. The conflict between the pursuit of individual and social goals may prove to be the most fundamental aspect in which cultures differ in their psychology.

Self-Consistency Versus Flexibility

Several differences appear in the ways in which the self emerges across cultures that relate to the construct of independent and interdependent self-concepts. First, consider how the self is experienced across different contexts. The notion that people strive to maintain a consistent self-concept has been central to many seminal theories regarding the self (e.g., Festinger, 1957; Heider, 1958; Ross, 1989; Swann, Wenzlaff, Krull, & Pelham, 1992). However, much of this research has targeted cultural samples in which independent self-concepts predominate. This fact is of much relevance because the independent self tends to be viewed as a relatively bounded and autonomous entity, complete in and of itself, that exists separately from others and the surrounding social context (Geertz, 1975; Markus & Kitayama, 1991). Because independent selves are perceived of as similar to objects in that they are viewed as whole, unified, integrated, stable, and inviolate entities (Shweder et al., 1998), core representations of the self tend to remain largely uninfluenced by the presence of others (although situations may activate different aspects of the working self-concept; Markus & Kunda, 1986). The independent self is experienced as relatively unchanging and constant across situations, and people are often willing to make rather costly sacrifices to preserve a semblance of self-consistency (Swann & Bosson, this volume). The premium placed on a consistent self is further evident in that several key theories have maintained that psychological health is associated with a consistent and integrated knowledge of oneself (Deci & Ryan, 2000; Jourard, 1965; Maslow, 1954).

In contrast, for people with interdependent views of self, an individual's relationships and roles take precedence over abstracted and internalized attributes, such as attitudes, traits, and abilities. Hence, changing situations find the interdependent self in new roles bearing different obligations, and these should lead to different experiences of the self. Indeed, much research with participants from cultures where interdependent selves are common reveals less evidence for a self-concept that is consistent across contexts compared with cultures where independent selves predominate. For example, Bond and Cheung (1983) found that Japanese respondents tended not to describe themselves by abstracting features across situations as much as did Americans. Other research has found that East Asians are more likely than Americans to describe themselves with reference to social roles or memberships, aspects of identity that are fluid with respect to the situation that one is in (Cousins, 1989; Rhee, Uleman, Lee, & Roman, 1995).

The cross-situational fluidity of the interdependent self has been demonstrated in various paradigms. Kanagawa, Cross, and Markus (2001) found that Japanese (but not American) self-descriptions varied significantly depending on who was in the room with them when they completed their questionnaires. For example, Japanese participants became significantly more self-critical in front of a professor than when they were alone. Similarly, Suh (2002) asked Koreans and Americans to evaluate themselves on numerous traits in several hypothetical situations. The Americans showed relatively little change in their self-descriptions across situations, whereas Koreans viewed themselves in highly variable terms. These cultural differences in consistency have also been observed in people's

affective experiences: European Americans show less variability in their emotions across situations than do Japanese, Hispanic Americans, and Indians (the latter difference only emerged for negative emotions; Oishi, Diener, Scollon, & Biswas-Diener, 2004).

East Asians also endorse more contradictory self-views than Westerners. For example, Chinese self-evaluations are more ambivalent (they contain both positive and negative statements) than are those of Americans (Spencer-Rodgers et al., 2004). Likewise, whereas measures of positive and negative affect tend to be orthogonal, or slightly negatively correlated, in North American samples, among Chinese these two measures show a slight positive correlation (Bagozzi, Wong, & Yi, 1999). Similarly, East Asians tend to endorse contradictory items about their personalities; for example, Koreans are more likely than Americans to state that they are both introverted *and* extraverted (Choi & Choi, 2002), and Japanese were more likely than Canadians to endorse both positively worded and reverse-scored items regarding the Big Five personality traits (Hamamura et al., 2008). Such contradictory self-knowledge is more readily available, and is simultaneously accessible, among East Asian participants than among Americans (Spencer-Rodgers, Boucher, Mori, Wang, & Peng, 2009). More generally, this tolerance for apparent contradiction (termed naïve dialecticism; Peng & Nisbett, 1999) extends to reasoning styles more generally. For example, when presented with two contradictory arguments, Americans tend to reject the weak argument in favor of the stronger one (and become even more convinced in the validity of the stronger one when the weaker argument is presented alongside it; also see Lord, Ross, & Lepper, 1979); in contrast, Chinese tend to accept both arguments and even come to view a weak argument as more convincing when it is paired with a contradictory stronger argument (Peng & Nisbett, 1999).

Whereas psychological consistency has been linked with well-being among Westerners, the benefits of being consistent across situations are less apparent for East Asians. Suh (2002) found that whereas consistency across situations was associated with greater degrees of well-being, social skills, and being liked by others for Americans, these relations were far weaker for Koreans. Similarly, Campbell et al. (1996) found a weaker correlation between Japanese participants' self-concept clarity (a construct that captures the consistency of the self across situations and time) and self-esteem than was found for Canadians. Well-being and positive feelings about the self do not seem to be as tethered to a consistent identity for East Asians as they do for North Americans.

The preceding studies converge in demonstrating that people from cultures characterized by interdependent views of self have weaker tendencies for self-consistency than do those from cultures characterized by independent views of self (although this conclusion is weakened in that most data from interdependent cultural contexts have been limited to people from East Asian cultures; cf. Oishi et al., 2004). However, one alternative perspective is that people with interdependent selves have *different* kinds of consistency needs. For example, although little evidence indicates that East Asians strive to keep their attitudes and behaviors consistent (Kashima, Siegal, Tanaka, & Kashima, 1992) or to reduce dissonance to the extent Westerners do (Heine & Lehman, 1997b; Hiniker, 1969), East Asians do show some consistency motivations when others are involved. For example, Asian Canadians rationalize decisions that they make for others even though they do not rationalize the decisions that they make for themselves (Hoshino-Browne et al., 2005). Moreover, Kitayama, Snibbe, Markus, and Suzuki (2004) found that although Japanese would not rationalize their decisions in a standard dissonance condition, they showed pronounced dissonance when placed in a subtly activated interpersonal context. Similarly, Cialdini, Wosinska, and Barrett (1999) found that while the intentions of American participants were more consistent with their own past behaviors, Polish participants were more likely to be consistent with the behavior of others (also see Petrova, Cialdini, & Sills, 2007). In sum, these studies reveal that people from more interdependent cultures aspire for consistency when they consider themselves in relation to others.

There is another way in which the self-views of people from interdependent cultural contexts appear to be quite consistent. The studies with East Asians described earlier tended to find less self-consistency than did those with Westerners; however, this does not mean that the interdependent self is random or unstable across contexts. Rather, East Asians appear to develop several stable but context-specific self-views depending on the relationships and roles that are activated in a given context. English and Chen (2007) demonstrated that although East Asians describe themselves in less consistent terms than European Americans across relationship contexts (e.g., self with roommate vs. self with parents), they described themselves as roughly equal in consistency when they considered themselves across situations (e.g., at the gym vs. at the cafeteria). Moreover, the self-descriptions of East Asians in particular situations or relationship contexts remained as stable across time (i.e., 25 weeks apart) as did those of European Americans. These findings suggest that the self-concept of those with interdependent selves can best be understood as a series of "if–then" rules, where particular aspects of the self become accessible when particular roles are activated, and that these if–then rules

remain quite stable across time (e.g., Mischel, Shoda, & Mendoza-Denton, 2002).

Insider Versus Outsider Phenomenologies

Self-concepts also vary across cultures in terms of the perspective that people habitually adopt. People may prioritize their own perspective, thereby making sense of the world in terms of how it unfolds in front of their eyes. Alternatively, people may prioritize the perspective of an audience and attend to the world and themselves in terms of how they imagine it appears to others. Cohen, Hoshino-Browne, and Leung (2007) refer to these two perspectives as insider and outsider phenomenologies, respectively. In interdependent cultural contexts, where individuals need to adjust themselves to fit in better with the ingroup, it becomes crucial to know how one is being evaluated by others. In independent cultural contexts, in contrast, where people's identity rests largely on the inner attributes that they possess, the cultural imperative is to "know oneself" and to elaborate on one's unique perspective.

Much recent evidence supports this cultural difference in phenomenologies. For example, Cohen and Gunz (2002) demonstrated that East Asians were more likely to recall memories of themselves when they were at the center of attention from a third-person perspective than were Westerners. Apparently, East Asians' attention to an audience leaked into and distorted their memories of themselves. Similarly, Leung and Cohen (2007) demonstrated that East Asians were slower than Westerners to process social stories in which the story was told from their own perspective, whereas Westerners were slower than East Asians to process the stories when they were told from the perspective of someone else. Furthermore, East Asians outperformed Westerners on a visual task in which they needed to take the perspective of their partner, making fewer visual fixations on objects that were not visible to their partner (Wu & Keysar, 2007).

Cross-cultural research on self-awareness also identifies similar divergences in phenomenologies. When individuals are aware of how they appear to others, they are said to be in the state of objective self-awareness (Duval & Wicklund, 1972), and this leads to several predictable responses (e.g., people become more self-critical and are less likely to engage in counternormative behaviors; Diener & Wallbom, 1976; Fejfar & Hoyle, 2000). In a state of objective self-awareness, people are aware of how they appear to others (a "me") in contrast to the experience of being a subject (an "I"). It follows that to the extent that East Asians are aware of an audience, and are adjusting their behaviors to that audience, they should more likely be in a habitual state of objective self-awareness than North Americans. This suggests that stimuli that enhance objective self-awareness (e.g., seeing oneself in front of a mirror) should have little effect on East Asians. Even without a mirror present, East Asians should be considering themselves in terms of how they appear to others. Some recent cross-cultural research corroborates this hypothesis: Whereas North Americans were more self-critical and were less likely to cheat on a test when a mirror was present compared with when it was absent, the presence of a mirror had no effect on Japanese for either dependent variable (Heine, Takemoto, Moskalenko, Lasaleta, & Henrich, 2008).

Incremental Versus Entity Theories of Self

Another difference in the nature of the self-concept that relates to independent and interdependent self-views is with regard to the perceived fluidity of people's traits and abilities. One way to conceive of the self is to view it as arising from a set of relatively fixed and innate attributes. This kind of "entity theory" (Dweck & Leggett, 1988) of the self reflects beliefs that the self is founded on an underlying stable essence (also see Chiu, Hong, & Dweck, 1997). As people with entity theories become older, their collection of attributes is viewed as staying largely the same. These theories are particularly likely among people with independent views of self, who perceive their identity to be largely grounded in a set of relatively context-independent inner attributes.

A second way of conceiving of the self is to view it as being malleable and ultimately improvable with efforts. This kind of "incremental theory" of self reflects a belief in the key role of effort underlying one's abilities and traits. The attributes that one possesses (e.g., one's soccer-playing skill, one's extraversion, or one's intelligence) are not seen to remain constant across one's life but are perceived as reflecting how hard one has worked on them. Incremental theories are more common among people from interdependent cultural contexts, which place greater emphasis on individuals adjusting themselves to meet group expectations (Heine et al., 2001).

The theory of self that one embraces is predictive of the amount of effort that one will make on a related task. For example, people with more incremental theories have been shown to respond to failures by focusing on their efforts and the strategies that they used (Henderson & Dweck, 1990) and taking remedial courses (Hong, Chiu, Dweck, Lin, & Wan, 1999). To the extent that abilities are a function of efforts, it follows that one should increase one's efforts when performance is lacking.

In contrast, people with entity theories of intelligence view their intelligence as a reflection of an underlying essence that remains largely removed from the efforts that they make. Rather than increasing effort on the same

task, people with entity theories tend to respond to failures by searching for an alternative task—one that better fits with their innate talents (Heyman & Dweck, 1998). Furthermore, to the extent that one's self is perceived to be founded on a set of relatively fixed, unchangeable, and consistent inner attributes, a motivation to see the self and its component features in the most positive light takes on increased importance. Discovering weaknesses in the self is especially debilitating if those are viewed as relatively permanent inadequacies.

People from different cultures do appear to differ in the extent to which they embrace incremental views of self. Indeed, it appears that North Americans are less likely to view their selves as incremental compared with people from some interdependent cultural contexts. For example, Japanese children are more likely than American children to believe that negative traits can become more positive with age, and they are more likely to attribute individual differences in traits to efforts (Lockhart, Nakashima, Inagai, & Keil, 2008). Mexicans and Filipinos are also less likely than Americans to view traits as stable across the life span (Church et al., 2005). Several studies have identified greater tendencies for East Asians compared with North Americans to attribute school achievement to efforts, not to abilities (e.g., Holloway, 1988; Stevenson & Stigler, 1992; Tobin, Wu, & Davidson, 1989). In one study, European Americans estimated that 36% of intelligence comes from one's efforts, whereas Asian Americans estimated 45% and Japanese 55% (Heine et al., 2001). Furthermore, experimental manipulations of incremental theories of abilities corroborate the cultural differences. Leading Japanese to believe that performance on an experimental task is enhanced by effort has no impact on their persistence after failure relative to a Japanese control group; they apparently endorse this belief in the absence of the manipulation. In contrast, leading Americans to believe that performance on a task is enhanced by effort leads to significantly greater persistence after failure than the results of a control group. Apparently, this manipulation provides novel information for Americans. The opposite pattern holds across cultures when participants are led to believe that the experimental task measures innate, stable abilities (Heine et al., 2001). In sum, much evidence indicates that people from interdependent cultural contexts are more likely to embrace incremental theories of the self (but see mixed evidence on cultural comparisons of Likert scale measures of malleability; e.g., Heine et al., 2001; Hong et al., 1999; Norenzayan, Choi, & Nisbett, 2002).

Multicultural Selves

Much cross-cultural research has also explored the self-concepts of those with multiple cultural experiences. If culture shapes the self, how do people from multiple cultural backgrounds represent the self? There are two complementary perspectives on this. One perspective is that multicultural people have multiple self-concepts that are simultaneously accessible, and their typical thoughts and responses reflect a blending of these. Evidence for this can be seen in that Asian Americans, for example, tend to perform intermediately on many psychological tasks compared with European Americans and Asians in Asia (Heine & Hamamura, 2007; Iyengar, Lepper, & Ross, 1999; Tsai, Simeonova, & Watanabe, 2004).

A second perspective is that multicultural people sequentially activate their different self-concepts, depending on situation or primes; this perspective is known as frame switching (Hong, Morris, Chiu, & Benet-Martínez, 2000). For example, Anderson (1999) describes how inner-city African American children quickly learn how to discriminate between the norms and unwritten rules that govern their schools and mainstream society and those that govern the streets. Much recent evidence shows that multiculturals engage in frame switching for various psychological processes. For example, in one study, researchers primed Hong Kong Chinese with Chinese, American, or neutral thoughts by showing them cultural icons (or neutral images) and asking them to write about them; they were subsequently asked to make attributions for the behaviors of computerized images of fish (Hong et al., 2000). Those who were primed with American icons made fewer external attributions for the fish's behavior than those who were primed with Chinese icons, with the attributions of those in the neutral prime condition falling between those results. Likewise, another study found that these same kinds of primes affected the cooperation of Chinese Americans in a prisoner's dilemma game. Those who saw Chinese primes came to cooperate more with a friend than those primed with American primes (again, the control condition was intermediate). In contrast, the primes did not affect people's cooperation toward strangers (Wong & Hong, 2005; for another recent priming example, see Wang & Ross, 2005). This kind of frame switching is not equally likely for all biculturals; people are more likely to frame-switch if they see their dual cultural identities as integrated than if they see them in opposition (Benet-Martínez, Leu, Lee, & Morris, 2002) and if they were second-generation as opposed to first-generation immigrants (Tsai, Ying, & Lee, 2000).

Although the preceding findings demonstrate that multiculturals often frame-switch, a question arises whether such frame switching is limited to those with multicultural experiences. The kinds of ideas that have been primed in frame-switching studies (e.g., thoughts regarding interdependence, external attributions, and cooperation with ingroup members) are thoughts that are likely accessible to people from all cultures (they are existential universals; Norenzayan & Heine, 2005). To the extent that monocultural people have different knowledge structures associated with ideas such as interdependence from those with ideas such as independence, then people should not require experiences in more than one culture to frame-switch when different knowledge networks are activated. Indeed, in numerous demonstrations people with largely monocultural experiences also frame-switch in similar ways (Heine et al., 2001; Kühnen, Hannover, & Schubert, 2001; Mandel, 2003; Trafimow, Triandis, & Goto, 1991; for a meta-analysis, see Oyserman & Lee, 2008). For example, whereas much research finds that East Asians display more pronounced avoidance motivations than Westerners (e.g., Elliot, Chirkov, Kim, & Sheldon, 2001; Hamamura, Meijer, Heine, Kamaya, & Hori, 2009), priming European Americans with interdependent thoughts (i.e., asking them to think of a team's tennis performance in contrast to an individual's) led them to become more avoidant oriented as well (Lee et al., 2000). That is, interdependent-primed European Americans demonstrated similar motivations as nonprimed East Asians. This suggests that the relations between interdependence and avoidance motivations exist across cultural groups so that anyone, multicultural or not, who thinks interdependent thoughts also becomes more avoidant oriented. Frame switching thus does not appear to be limited to multiculturals. Nonetheless, multiculturals apparently do show more extreme degrees of frame switching than do monoculturals (Gardner, Gabriel, & Dean, 2004), suggesting that the knowledge structures of multiculturals regarding ideas such as independence and interdependence are more clearly demarcated than they are for monoculturals.

Another tendency for people with multicultural selves is that they appear to be more creative. People with experience adapting to different cultural environments need to adopt a flexible style in the way they approach problems, and this has been shown to be associated with enhanced creativity on several creative tasks (Leung, Maddux, Galinsky, & Chiu, 2008; Maddux & Galinsky, 2009). This is particularly true among those with higher levels of identity integration (i.e., those who perceive compatibility between their two cultural identities; Cheng, Sanchez-Burks, & Lee, 2008).

PERSONALITY

Culture is quite clearly implicated in people's self-concepts. What is the role of culture in their personalities? Several large-scale research programs have investigated questions regarding the similarities and differences in personality structure and trait levels across cultures. These investigations have largely contrasted cultures on measures of the five-factor model of personality (McCrae & Costa, 1987). This research raises some interesting and important questions regarding personality across cultures: Is the five-factor structure something basic about human nature, something that we should find in the personalities of people in all cultures that we look at? Or, alternatively, does the five-factor model reflect ideas about personhood that are limited to the West, where most of this research has been conducted?

Apparent Universality of Personality Structure

Various measures of the Big Five (the NEO Personality Inventory; NEO-PI-R; Costa & McCrae, 1992) have been translated into several languages and have been distributed to thousands of people in dozens of cultures around the world. Early cross-cultural comparisons of the factor structure of the Big Five were promising: Four out of five factors (all except openness) emerged in Hong Kong (Bond, 1979), Japan (Bond, Nakazato, & Shiraishi, 1975), and the Philippines (Guthrie & Bennett, 1971), revealing considerable similarity in the structure of personality across these diverse cultures. More recent studies with some other cultures have fared even better: All five factors emerged in cultures as diverse as Israel (Montag & Levin, 1994), Korea (Piedmont & Chae, 1997), and Turkey (Somer & Goldberg, 1999). One large-scale study investigated people from 50 different cultures from all continents except Antarctica and had participants evaluate someone they knew well on trait adjectives that assessed the Big Five (McCrae et al., 2005). In most of the 50 cultures, the factor structure of the Big Five was replicated. In several developing cultures (e.g., Botswana, Ethiopia, Lebanon, Malaysia, Puerto Rico, and Uganda), the factor structure was not so evident. However, in these latter cultures the data quality was rather poor, suggesting that people may not have fully understood the questions or were unfamiliar with answering questions in that format (McCrae et al., 2005). To the extent that unfamiliarity with Western measures can account for the cultures where the data fit was poor, this is good evidence that the Big Five reflect the universal structure of personality (also see Allik & McCrae, 2004; Yik, Russell, Ahn, Fernandez-Dols, & Suzuki, 2002). Still, stronger support for universality would be found if convergent evidence emerged from studies of developing and small-scale societies (cf. Henrich et al., 2005).

It is important to note that the measures of the Big Five were initially developed through the exploration of English personality terms. The challenge with factor analyses is that they only speak to the structure that emerges from the universe of items that were considered. It is possible that a different set of items, particularly those that were more meaningful in other cultural contexts, might reveal a different underlying personality structure. Indeed, explorations for personality dimensions among Chinese indigenous personality terms conducted by Cheung and colleagues (Cheung et al., 1996; Cheung, Cheung, Leung, Ward, & Leong, 2003) revealed an additional factor of "interpersonal relatedness" that was not correlated with any of the Big Five factors. Likewise, Church, Reyes, Katigbak, and Grimm (1997; also see Church, Katigbak, & Reyes, 1998) explored indigenous Filipino personality traits and found two additional factors to the Big Five: temperamentalness and a negative valence dimension. Similarly, Benet-Martínez and Waller (1995, 1997) found that an investigation of Spanish personality constructs revealed seven underlying personality factors, although these did not map well onto the Big Five. Similarly, Saucier, Georgiades, Tsaousis, and Goldberg (2005) found a six-factor solution emerged from indigenous Greek terms that was somewhat at odds with the Big Five. In general, investigations with indigenous traits reveal that although the Big Five personality traits appear to be reasonably robust across cultures, they may not be an exhaustive list of the ways in which personality can emerge in other cultures. When exploring personality structures from indigenous personality terms, some alternative dimensions have emerged, and future research is necessary to determine the robustness and universality of these other factors.

Cross-Cultural Variability in Levels of Personality Traits

Given the evidence that the Big Five model of personality appears to adequately capture the structure of personality traits in many cultures, researchers have recently begun to compare mean levels of personality traits across large samples of cultures (e.g., McCrae, 2002; McCrae et al., 2005; Schmitt et al., 2007). As of this writing, aggregate personality means from the NEO-PI-R (Costa & McCrae, 1992) have been reported for self-ratings from 36 cultures (McCrae, 2002) and for peer ratings from 51 cultures (McCrae et al., 2005), and a modified Big Five measure was used to collect people's perceptions of their national character in 49 cultures (Terracciano et al., 2005). Another popular measure, the Big Five Inventory (BFI; Benet-Martínez & John, 1998), has been used to collect self-ratings in 56 nations (Schmitt et al., 2007). Direct comparisons of self-report means in this hard-won wealth of data have found, for example, that according to the self-report means (McCrae, 2002), the world champions of neuroticism are the Spaniards, the most extraverted people in the world are from Denmark, the nationality that is most open to new experiences is Austrian, the most agreeable people in the world are Malaysian, and the world's least conscientious nation of people is Japan.

However, considerable debate has occurred regarding the validity of cross-cultural comparisons of means on self-report scales (Hamamura et al., 2008; Heine et al., 2002; Kitayama, 2002) and for personality traits in particular (Ashton, 2007; McGrath & Goldberg, 2006; Perugini & Richetin, 2007). Some noted challenges have been made to the validity of these aggregate national personality profiles. First, the emergent rank orderings of countries are not very similar when compared across different assessment techniques. No significant correlations were found for any of the Big Five between measures of self-report and perceptions of national character (Terracciano et al., 2005). Likewise, correlations between the country scores for the self-report measures of the Big Five as assessed by the NEO-PI-R and as assessed by the BFI ranged from .22 to .45 (Schmitt et al., 2007), which are quite modest given that these are measures of the same constructs. Perhaps more disturbing, the country scores from BFI and those from NEO-PI-R measures correlate *more weakly* for the corresponding traits than they do for their noncorresponding traits in four of the Big Five traits (e.g., the BFI measure of *openness* correlates .73 with the NEO-PI-R measure of *extraversion* but only .27 with the NEO-PI-R measure of openness; Schmitt et al., 2007), which is in direct violation of the multitrait–multimethod matrix approach to validating personality traits (Campbell & Fiske, 1959). Furthermore, at least for the measure of conscientiousness, behavioral and demographic validity criteria show negative or null correlations with the self-report and peer-report measures of the Big Five (average rs ranged from $-.43$ to .06), although these same validity criteria demonstrated strong positive correlations with perceptions of national character (average $r = .61$; Heine, Buchtel, & Norenzayan, 2008). In sum, more evidence of validity would seem to be needed before we can identify which rank orderings of countries' personality profiles are the most accurate. However, comparisons of self-reported traits between regions within a single country, where people likely share similar reference groups, appear to have stronger correlations with behavioral and demographic criteria (e.g., Rentfrow, Gosling, & Potter, 2009).

RELATIONSHIPS

Central to the distinction between independent and interdependent self-concepts is the notion that culture shapes the ways in which people relate with others. This section reviews how the self-concept is related to the way in which people distinguish between ingroups and outgroups, how people with more independent self-concepts tend to have more opportunities for forming new relationships and dissolving older relationships than do those with more interdependent self-concepts, and how this difference in relational mobility is associated with various aspects of people's relationships.

The interdependent self, as discussed earlier, is importantly sustained and defined by its significant relationships within the ingroup (Markus & Kitayama, 1991). This suggests that an interdependent individual's ingroup relationships represent a unique class of relationships within the universe of potential relationships that the individual might have. To put it succinctly, an interdependent self cannot be interdependent with everyone, and the self-defining nature of ingroup relationships suggests that these relationships should hold a particularly privileged position. In contrast, the independent self is a self-contained entity that remains relatively the same regardless of its interaction partners, and fewer consequences are associated with distinguishing between ingroup and outgroup members in many situations. As such, the demarcation of ingroups from outgroups should be more salient and stable in interdependent cultural contexts.

Much evidence supports this reasoning. For example, Iyengar et al. (1999) report the results of several studies contrasting ingroups and outgroups between East Asians and Americans. They found that whereas European Americans made a clear distinction between themselves and others in an actor–observer bias task (i.e., they viewed more traits to be descriptive of others than themselves), they did not differ in their evaluations of ingroup versus outgroup members. In contrast, East Asians did not show any difference between their evaluations for themselves and their friends but showed a more pronounced actor–observer bias for an outgroup member than they did for an ingroup member (i.e., they viewed more traits to be descriptive of an outgroup member than for an ingroup member). Iyengar and Lepper (1999) also found that whereas European Americans reacted negatively when choices were made for them by someone else, regardless of whether the choice-maker was their mother or a stranger, Asian American children only reacted negatively when the choice-maker was a stranger. When their mother had made the choice for them, they were just as willing to work on the task as when they had chosen it for themselves. As another example, whereas Americans showed evidence for social loafing regardless of whether they were working with ingroup or outgroup members, both Israeli and Chinese only loafed with outgroup members. In contrast, they showed evidence for social striving (i.e., working harder than they did as individuals) when working with ingroup members (Earley, 1993).

Furthermore, an extensive review of studies using Solomon Asch's (1956) conformity paradigm reveals that the conformity of people from interdependent cultures appears to be more contingent on the nature of the majority group than it is for people from independent cultures (Bond & Smith, 1996). When in a situation with strangers, people from interdependent cultures conform to a comparable degree as those from independent ones or even show some evidence of anticonformity (e.g., Frager, 1970). However, when in a situation with their peers, people from interdependent cultures show evidence of heightened conformity; indeed, the largest amount of conformity in Bond and Smith's meta-analysis involved Fijian Indians and Japanese participants conforming to groups that included their peers (Chandra, 1973; Williams & Sogon, 1984; but see Takano & Sogon, 2008, for a critical review). In contrast, the degree of conformity for people from independent cultures does not appear to be contingent on the relationships between the subjects and those of the majority group. Likewise, Wong and Hong (2005) found that priming thoughts of interdependence increases the likelihood that one would cooperate more with a friend than a stranger, compared with neutral or independent primes. In a similar vein, Yamagishi and Yamagishi (1994) find that Americans have higher levels of general trust toward strangers than do Japanese (but see Yuki, Maddux, Brewer, & Takemura, 2005, for further complexities regarding ingroup and outgroup distinctions among Japanese). In sum, the distinction between ingroup and outgroup members varies in salience across cultures, and this raises the possibility that minimal group designs might be less effective at eliciting a sense of shared belongingness among people with interdependent self-concepts.

Relationships also vary across cultures in terms of the ease with which people can form them. Relationships among those in independent cultures are entered into, and are maintained, on a somewhat mutually voluntary basis. In such contexts, people have relatively high relational mobility (Yuki et al., 2009; also see Oishi, Lun, & Sherman, 2007), and individuals can seek new relationships or dissolve unsatisfying older relationships. Importantly, a relationship must in some way benefit the independent individual; otherwise, individuals would not devote the efforts necessary to cultivating it. Hence, people in such contexts actively seek positive and rewarding relationships and often will not devote much effort or resources to any relationship that does not appear to be beneficial or may allow those relationships to wither (Adams, 2005; Anderson, Adams, & Plaut, 2008; Heine, Foster, & Spina, in press; Schug, Yuki, Horikawa, & Takemura, 2009). The

Western social psychological literature on relationships tends to be focused largely on relationship formation and dissolution, suggesting that conditional relationships have thus far been the primary focus of inquiry—indeed, relatively few references have been made to less contingent relationships, such as those with kin (e.g., Lieberman, Tooby, & Cosmides, 2007).

In contrast, relationships among those from interdependent cultures are often viewed in less conditional terms. One is born into a relatively fixed interpersonal network, and over the course of a lifetime an individual subsequently joins a select few interpersonal networks that remain somewhat stable over the years. Relatively few opportunities appear to form new relationships or to dissolve any existing ones at any given point in time, and this holds true whether one's relationships are rewarding or not. As a consequence, people with more interdependent selves (particularly in West African contexts) tend to have more ambivalent feelings toward friendship (Adams & Plaut, 2003), are more likely to say that they have enemies (often from within their own ingroups) than those with more independent selves (Adams, 2005), and have a weaker relationship between physical attractiveness and positive life outcomes (Anderson et al., 2008). The lower relational mobility of people from interdependent cultures also is associated with people showing a weaker similarity-attraction effect (Schug et al., 2009), and weaker self-enhancing motivations (Falk, Heine, Yuki, & Takemura, 2009; Yuki et al., 2009; also see Oishi et al., 2007, for further implications of relational mobility).

Such cultural differences in the voluntary and conditional nature of relationships are also relevant to how people seek social support. Much research has documented the many health benefits that people receive from social support in times of distress (e.g., Cohen & Wills, 1985; Seeman, 1996); however, most of this research has been conducted in the United States. Indeed, much research conducted with East Asians and Asian Americans finds that these samples seek *less* social support than do European Americans, and the nature of their social support also appears to be different (for a review, see Kim, Sherman, & Taylor, 2008). The tendency for people from Asian cultural backgrounds to seek less social support than those from European American backgrounds appears to be primarily due to concerns that seeking social support would cause them to lose face and disrupt group harmony (Kim, Sherman, Ko, & Taylor, 2006; Taylor et al., 2004). However, people from Asian backgrounds appear to use more implicit social support strategies, where they turn to close relations for comfort, but do not explicitly disclose their stressful life events (Taylor, Welch, Kim, & Sherman, 2007). This observed cultural difference in social support seeking has much relevance both for understanding how people cope with stress and for mental health professionals dealing with clients from varied cultural backgrounds.

MOTIVATION

Cultural experiences also importantly influence motivations. Much research has explored how some key motivations appear differently across cultures, including motivations for self-enhancement, approach–avoidance motivations, agency and control, motivations to fit in or to stick out, achievement motivations, and motivations for honor. Each of these is reviewed in the sections that follow.

Motivations for Self-Enhancement and Self-Esteem

The motivation that has been researched the most across cultures is the motivation to *self-enhance*, that is, a desire to view oneself positively. A great deal of research, from a diverse array of methodologies, reveals that Westerners apparently have a strong need to view themselves in positive terms. For example, most North Americans score much above the theoretical midpoint of self-esteem scales (Baumeister, Tice, & Hutton, 1989), show much evidence for unrealistically positive views of themselves (e.g., Greenwald, 1980; Taylor & Brown, 1988), and engage in various compensatory self-protective responses when they encounter threats to their self-esteem (e.g., Steele, 1988; Tesser, Crepaz, Beach, Cornell, & Collins, 2000; Wills, 1981).

This research reveals quite clearly that motivations for positive self-views are powerful and pervasive among Westerners. However, given that Westerners tend to endorse more independent views of self, and that much research has identified a pronounced positive relationship between independent self-construals and positive self-views within various cultures (correlations range between .33 and .51; e.g., Heine, 2003a; Oyserman et al., 2002; Singelis, Bond, Lai, & Sharkey, 1999), this research raises the possibility that such positive self-views will be more elusive in cultural contexts that are less characterized by independence.

Much research has investigated motivations for positive self-views in interdependent cultures, and overall, the evidence suggests that these motivations are less pronounced in such contexts. For example, Mexicans (Tropp & Wright, 2003), Native Americans (Fryberg & Markus, 2003), Chileans (Heine & Raineri, 2009), and Fijians (Rennie & Dunne, 1994) score lower on various measures of positive self-views than do Westerners. Indeed, in some

cultural contexts, most notably East Asian ones, evidence for self-serving biases is particularly weak (e.g., Mezulis, Abramson, Hyde, & Hankin, 2004). A recent meta-analysis on self-enhancing motivations among Westerners and East Asians found significant cultural differences in every study for 30 of the 31 methodologies that were used (the one exception being comparisons of self-esteem using the Implicit Association Test; Greenwald & Farnham, 2000; see also Falk et al., 2009; Kitayama & Uchida, 2003; Yamaguchi et al., 2007; cf. Szeto et al., 2009). The average effect size for the cultural differences across all studies was $d = .84$. Furthermore, whereas the average effect size for self-enhancing motivations was large ($d = .86$) within the Western samples, these motivations were largely absent among the East Asian samples ($d = -.02$), with Asian Americans falling between the two results ($d = .33$). Apparently, East Asians possess little motivation to self-enhance, and in many situations they instead appear especially attentive to negative information about themselves that allows for self-improvement (Heine et al., 1999).

Numerous alternative explanations have been offered to account for this cultural difference. One possibility is that East Asians are more motivated to enhance their group selves rather than their individual selves, and comparisons of people's individual self-enhancing tendencies thus obscure their group self-enhancing motivations. Despite the intuitive appeal of this account, the evidence in support of it is lacking. Studies have found that East Asians enhance their group selves more than their individual selves (e.g., Muramoto & Yamaguchi, 1997), but similar findings have emerged with Westerners (Heine & Lehman, 1997a). As of yet, no published studies find that East Asians enhance their group selves more than Westerners, whereas several studies find that Westerners show more group enhancement than East Asians (Heine, 2003b; Snibbe, Markus, Kitayama, & Suzuki, 2003).

A second possibility is that East Asians value a different set of traits than those explored in research thus far; if they were asked to evaluate themselves on traits that they viewed to be especially important, the cultural differences would likely be reduced. Although some evidence is in support of this alternative account, using the "better-than-average effect" paradigm (e.g., Sedikides, Gaertner, & Vevea, 2005, 2007), studies with other methodologies reveal that East Asians are *more* self-critical for especially important traits than they are for less important ones (e.g., Heine & Renshaw, 2002; Kitayama, Markus, Matsumoto, & Norasakkunkit, 1997). The most extensive meta-analysis on this topic finds no correlation between self-enhancement and importance for East Asians ($r = -.01$) in contrast to a positive correlation for Westerners ($r = .18$; Heine, Kitayama, & Hamamura, 2007a), but discussion has taken place regarding whether studies should be excluded from this meta-analysis (Heine, Kitayama, & Hamamura, 2007b; Sedikides et al., 2007). The better-than-average effect appears to yield different results from other self-enhancement methodologies because of the difficulties that people have in considering distributed targets (e.g., the average person) in contrast to specific targets (e.g., the self or one's best friend; Chambers & Windschitl, 2004; Hamamura, Heine, & Takemoto, 2007; Klar & Giladi, 1997; Krizan & Suls, 2008).

A third alternative account to consider is that East Asians are presenting themselves self-critically but are privately evaluating themselves in a self-enhancing manner (or Westerners are privately more self-critical than they present themselves; Kurman, 2003; Yamaguchi et al., 2007). Evidence with implicit measures of self-esteem is largely consistent with this account in that there are few cultural differences with these measures (see Heine & Hamamura, 2007, for a review), although studies that employ hidden behavioral measures in anonymous situations reveal similar cultural differences to those that employ questionnaires (e.g., Heine et al., 2001; Heine, Takata, & Lehman, 2000). That the Implicit Association Test measure of self-esteem has thus far failed to show reliable correlations with other implicit or explicit measures of self-esteem, or external criteria (Bosson, Swann, & Pennebaker, 2000; Falk et al., 2009; Hofmann, Gawronski, Gschwendner, Le, & Schmitt, 2005), makes it difficult to evaluate the conflicting results from these studies (but see Banaji & Heiphetz, volume 1).

Variation in self-esteem has also been identified across historical periods. A meta-analysis from 1965 to 1995 of studies using the Rosenberg (1965) self-esteem scale with American college students found that self-esteem scores had increased substantially over that time ($d = .6$; Twenge & Campbell, 2001). These increases in self-esteem parallel increases in independence over the same period (as measured in terms of people's changing habits of interacting with others and belonging to groups; Putnam, 2000). However, another paper found no increase in narcissism (which correlates strongly with the Rosenberg scale) over that time among students at the University of California's Berkeley and Davis campuses (Trzesniewski, Donnellan, & Robins, 2008). One account for this null effect may be the increasing percentage of Asian-descent students on these campuses over that period (Twenge, Konrath, Foster, Campbell, & Bushman, 2008).

Approach and Avoidance Motivations

Similar to cultural differences in self-enhancement motivations between East Asians and Westerners, parallel cultural differences are found in approach and avoidance motivations. Given that both self-enhancement and approach motivations reflect concerns about obtaining positive benefits for the self, and that both self-improvement and avoidance motivations entail attending to potential costs to the self, it is possible that these motivations might share a common basis (Heine, 2005; Higgins, 2008). Much research finds that, in general, East Asians show relatively more evidence for avoidance motivation, and relatively less evidence for approach motivation, compared with Westerners. For example, compared with North Americans, East Asians embrace more personal avoidance goals (Elliot et al., 2001), rate opportunities to lose as more important than opportunities to win (Lee et al., 2000), persist more on a task after failure and less after success (Heine et al., 2001; Oishi & Diener, 2003), perform better while attending to weaknesses or losses (Hamamura & Heine, 2009; Peters & Williams, 2006), are motivated more by negative role models (Lockwood, Marshall, & Sadler, 2005), recall events better if they contain prevention information, and view book reviews to be more helpful if those reviews contain prevention information (Hamamura et al., 2009). One account for these cultural differences is that "face" is a critical resource in East Asian cultural contexts, and because face is more easily lost than it is gained, people come to habitually attend to avoidance information (Heine, 2005).

Agency and Control

The ways in which individuals attend to their needs and desires are shaped by the theories that they embrace regarding where they can exert control. As discussed earlier, Dweck and colleagues (Dweck, Hong, & Chiu, 1993; Dweck & Leggett, 1988) discuss implicit theories that people have regarding the malleability of their selves: namely, incremental and entity theories of self. In addition, people have implicit theories about the malleability of the world. For example, people can see the world as something that is fixed and beyond their control to change (an entity theory of the world), or they can think of the world as flexible and responsive to their efforts to change (an incremental theory of the world). To the extent that people have implicit theories that the world is malleable but selves are stable, they have different experiences of control than people who view the world as largely impervious to change yet their selves to be quite malleable (Su et al., 1999). Those who tend to see the world as malleable and their selves stable are more likely to maintain a sense of primary control (Rothbaum, Weisz, & Snyder, 1982) in which they strive to shape existing realities to fit their perceptions, goals, or wishes. In contrast, those who are more likely to see the world as stable and their selves as malleable are more likely to engage in secondary control strategies. People strive to achieve secondary control by aligning themselves with existing realities, leaving the realities unchanged, but exerting control over their psychological impact.

In hierarchical collectivistic cultures, such as in East Asia, the social world remains somewhat impervious to efforts by a lone individual to change things (e.g., Chiu, Dweck, Tong, & Fu, 1997). Power and agency tend to be concentrated in groups or are mandated by the role that an individual occupies; thus, many domains exist in which people are unable to exert much direct influence. Likewise, East Asians are more likely to have a flexible and incremental view of themselves (Heine et al., 2001; Norenzayan, Choi, et al., 2002). When the self is perceived to be more mutable than the social world, it follows that people would be quite willing to adjust themselves to better fit in with the demands of their social worlds.

In contrast, people from Western cultures tend to stress the malleability of the world relative to the self (Su et al., 1999). When people view individuals to be the center of experience and action, they accordingly look to individuals as a source of control. Moreover, the independent self is experienced as relatively immutable and consistent (Heine et al., 2001; Suh, 2002). This view that the self is an immutable entity, working within the context of a mutable world, sustains a perception of primary control.

Much research finds that people from different cultures differ in their tendencies to pursue primary and secondary control strategies (Morling & Evered, 2006; Weisz, Rothbaum, & Blackburn, 1984). For example, in one study, participants were asked to list occasions when either they had tried to influence people or objects that surrounded them (i.e., primary control experiences) or they had tried to adjust themselves to these people or objects (i.e., secondary control experiences; Morling et al., 2002). Americans were better able to recall influencing situations than adjusting ones, whereas Japanese remembered more adjusting situations than influencing ones. Furthermore, although both Japanese and Americans evaluated influencing situations as making them feel more powerful than did adjusting ones, suggesting that primary control might universally be experienced as powerful, Japanese reported feeling more powerful about their adjusting situations than the Americans did. Various other studies have found comparable cultural differences in experiences of control (e.g., Bond & Tornatzky, 1973; Chang, Chua, & Toh, 1997; Morling & Fiske, 1999; Seginer, Trommsdorff, & Essau, 1993).

In addition, East Asians appear to view groups as more agentic than do Westerners. For example, in their reporting of rogue traders in various stock scandals, Japanese newspapers are more likely than American newspapers to describe the scandal in terms of the organizations that were involved as opposed to the individual traders. Likewise, Chinese are more likely than Americans to explain deviant animal behaviors as being due to the actions of a group (an unruly herd) than to the actions of an individual (a rogue cow; Menon, Morris, Chiu, & Hong, 1999).

Cultural differences in agency are also evident in the ways in which people make choices. In independent cultural contexts, people are less dependent on the actions of others than they are in interdependent ones. People in interdependent contexts should, on average, be more concerned with the goals of their groups, and, as such, be more willing to adjust their behaviors (and reduce their choices) so that they can coordinate the actions of the group toward those goals. One stark example of this cultural difference is that in many interdependent cultural contexts today (and perhaps in a majority of cultures several centuries ago) critical life decisions such as whom one would marry or what job one would pursue have been made by families rather than the individuals (e.g., Lee & Stone, 1980).

Examples of how perceptions of choice differ across cultures can be seen in several studies. As discussed earlier, Iyengar and Lepper (1999) found that Asian American children prefer tasks that are chosen for them by ingroup members, whereas European American children prefer tasks that they choose for themselves (children from both cultural groups do not prefer tasks that are chosen for them by outgroup members). Similarly, several studies have found that East Indians differ in their choice making from Americans, in that the Indians are slower to make choices, are less likely to choose according to their preferences, and are less motivated to express their preferences in their choices (Savani, Markus, & Conner, 2008). Cultural variation in choice making does not just differ between those from Eastern and Western cultural contexts—middle-class Americans, specifically, seem quite unusual in their high desire for choice (Schwartz, 2004). For example, in a survey of people from six Western countries, only Americans preferred making a choice from 50 ice cream flavors compared with 10 flavors. Likewise, Americans (and Britons) prefer to have more choices on menus from upscale restaurants than do those from other European countries (Rozin, Fischler, Shields, & Masson, 2006). Further, people from American working-class cultures are less protective of their choices (i.e., they do not seem particularly bothered when an experimenter denies them their original choice) compared with middle-class Americans (Snibbe & Markus, 2005). In sum, the ways in which people make choices, and express agency more generally, differ in several important aspects across cultures.

Motivations to Fit In or to Stick Out

People have competing motivations to fit in with others or to stick out from a crowd. Asch (1956) most famously documented the motivation of Americans to conform with a unanimous majority in line-comparison studies. This conformity paradigm has been immensely influential, and it has been replicated well more than 100 times in 17 countries. A meta-analysis of these studies revealed one clear trend: Although Americans show a great deal of conformity in this paradigm, people from more interdependent cultures conform even more (Bond & Smith, 1996). Motivations to fit in appear to be stronger in cultural contexts that encourage people to maintain strong relationships with others (at least in studies like Asch's that target a normative influence for conformity—weaker cultural differences for informational influences for conformity are possible).

In contrast to a motivation to conform, we can consider people's motivations to stick out and to be unique. In general, it appears that people from independent cultural contexts evince a stronger motivation to be unique. For example, Kim and Markus (1999) found that, when considering an array of shapes, European Americans rated the unusual shapes as more desirable than the more common ones, in contrast to the ratings of East Asians. Moreover, when given a choice of pens, European Americans were more likely to choose a minority-colored pen whereas East Asians were more likely to choose a majority-colored pen. Parallel differences in pen preferences have also been observed in contrasts of middle- and working-class Americans (Stephens, Markus, & Townsend, 2007). Likewise, advertisements targeting East Asians and working-class Americans are more likely to emphasize themes of connection with others than are advertisements that target middle-class Americans, which are more likely to emphasize uniqueness (Kim & Markus, 1999; Stephens et al., 2007).

Religion and Achievement Motivation

Psychological research on achievement motivation has an interesting past, as much of it was inspired by a rather outlandish idea of a sociologist. In 1904–05, Max Weber published a highly influential and controversial series of essays titled *The Protestant Ethic and the Spirit of Capitalism,* in which he proposed the intriguing thesis that some key motivations for achievement, and the psychological foundation for capitalism more generally, were rooted in the Protestant Reformation. Weber maintained that some key features of Enlightenment-era Protestant thought, including ideas regarding individualism, a calling, and predestination, led to a moralized work ethic, where working on tasks related to one's unique calling acquired spiritual significance. Although some of these Protestant beliefs (particularly predestination) only lasted for a few generations, Weber argued that they were

around long enough to be converted into a more enduring secular code of behavior that included honesty, diligence, seriousness and focus at work, and thrifty use of money and time.

Evidence consistent with Weber's thesis comes from various disciplines. For example, some economists and historians note that power and wealth in Europe moved from places like Spain and northern Italy before the Protestant Reformation began in 1517 to Northern European Protestant centers in Germany, the Netherlands, and England, followed by its most colossal bloom in the 20th-century United States (e.g., Landes, 1999). Likewise, comparisons of per capita income worldwide have found that nations that were largely Protestant earned more than those that were mixed Protestant and Catholic and that these earned more still than those nations that were predominantly Catholic (e.g., Furnham, 1990), although gross domestic product (GDP) rankings have fluctuated since then. Jackson, Fox, and Crockett (1970) demonstrated that Protestants in the United States were more likely to enter high-status nonmanual occupations than Catholics of the same occupational origin, controlling for various other societal variables. McClelland (1961) also found that Protestant nations were far more industrialized than their Catholic counterparts.

Much psychological evidence also supports Weber's thesis. McClelland (1961) demonstrated that Protestant parents expected their children to become self-reliant at an earlier age compared with Catholic parents and that stories written by German Protestant boys had higher need for achievement scores than those written by German Catholic boys. Giorgi and Marsh (1990) found pronounced differences in the embracing of an intrinsic work ethic between Western European Catholics and mainstream Protestants (interestingly, the relation was clear both by contrasting individuals of different religions *within* countries and by comparing countries), as evident in a measure of work values. Furthermore, this relation was identifiable regardless of individuals' level of religiosity, suggesting that the work ethic has become secularized. The Protestant ethic has also been associated with negative attitudes toward laziness and being overweight (Quinn & Crocker, 1999) and a concern with self-esteem and self-deception (Baumeister, 1987; Crocker & Park, 2004).

Recently, Sanchez-Burks and colleagues (Sanchez-Burks, 2002; Sanchez-Burks et al., 2003; Sanchez-Burks, Nisbett, & Ybarra, 2000) investigated Weber's thesis in the laboratory. Sanchez-Burks (2002) was interested in exploring whether Protestants become entirely focused on their morally sanctioned work and thus maintain a rather impassive attitude toward potential distractions, such as other people (Bendix, 1977; Hampden-Turner & Trompenaars,

1993; Weber, 1947). In one study, Protestant Americans engaged in a work task were found to be less attentive to their relationships with others (i.e., they were less likely to show unconscious mimicry of others[1]) than they were when engaged in a casual task. In contrast, Catholic Americans were just as attentive to their relationships, regardless of the nature of the tasks. In addition, Americans (who are predominantly Protestant) maintain more separate personal and professional networks than do people from non-Protestant countries (i.e., Poland and India; Kacperczyk, Sanchez-Burks, & Baker, 2009).

However, fuelling the controversy in Weber's thesis are some cross-cultural studies that compare Likert scale means on various self-report measures of the Protestant work ethic that are not consistent with Weber's thesis. Indeed, studies that have compared the means on these scales reveal either no cultural difference in the Protestant work ethic or a weaker work ethic among nations of a largely Protestant background (e.g., the United States, Australia, and Britain) than among people from countries with little exposure to Protestant ideology (e.g., India, Malaysia, Mexico, Sri Lanka, Uganda, and Zimbabwe; Baguma & Furnham, 1993; Furnham, Bond, & Heaven, 1993; Furnham & Muhiudeen, 1984; Isonio & Garza, 1987; Niles, 1994)—findings that would seem to challenge the face validity of the measure. That is, the evidence for an association between Protestantism and achievement motivation is far more consistent in laboratory studies (e.g., Sanchez-Burks, 2002), and in studies that measure various cultural products (e.g., children's stories; McClelland, 1961), than it is in studies that use cross-cultural comparisons of means from self-report measures. Again, this is consistent with a growing body of evidence that comparisons of means of subjective Likert scale measures across cultures are often compromised by various response artifacts and yield results of dubious validity (Heine et al., 2002; Peng et al., 1997).

Motivations for Honor

Much cross-cultural research has investigated motivations for honor, particularly between the South and the North in the United States (Cohen, Nisbett, Bowdle, & Schwarz, 1996; Cohen, Vandello, Puente, & Rantilla, 1999; Nisbett, 1993; Nisbett & Cohen, 1996). Since the 18th century, the U.S. South has had a greater number of

lynchings, sniper attacks, feuds, homicides, duels, and violent pastimes than the North (Fischer, 1989; Gastil, 1989). Several explanations have been proposed for this, including the more uncomfortable hot temperatures, the greater poverty, and the longer history of slavery in the South. In contrast, Nisbett and Cohen (1996) proposed that the South's relatively greater penchant for violence is due to its maintenance of a culture of honor. A culture of honor is a culture where people (especially men) strive to protect their reputation through aggression. Nisbett and Cohen argue that cultures of honor are common in contexts in which people's wealth is vulnerable and those that have little institutionalized protection (e.g., in inner cities, various Middle Eastern herding cultures, and some small-scale African societies; Anderson, 1999; Galaty & Bonte, 1991). In the case of the U.S. South, this state of affairs emerged because herding was a key component of the South's early economy, herders have vulnerable wealth (livestock can easily be stolen), and the sparse population of herding lands made it difficult to police. The establishment of a personal reputation for aggressive revenge for insults, therefore, emerged as a method for preventing herd rustling. Although herding is no longer the primary economic activity of most Southerners, Nisbett and Cohen argue that these cultural norms have persisted as a culture of honor represents a stable equilibrium point (see Cohen, 2001).

Various kinds of data converge to support this thesis. For example, archival data reflect that the relatively greater amount of violence in the South is largely limited to argument-related violence (in which the defense of one's honor is often implicated), and this is especially common in the rural herding regions of the South (Nisbett & Cohen, 1996). Similarly, survey data reveal that Southerners are more likely than Northerners to offer violent solutions to problems, but only if those involve a threat to an individual's or family's honor (Cohen & Nisbett, 1994). Experimental evidence further reveals that when Southerners are insulted they are more likely than Northerners to be angry, show heightened cortisol and testosterone responses (these hormone levels tend to increase with aggression), and act more physically aggressive (Cohen et al., 1996). Likewise, field studies reveal that Southerners, compared with Northerners, are warmer toward someone who committed violence in defense of their honor (but not for other kinds of violent acts; Cohen & Nisbett, 1997). Further, compared with Northerners, Southerners have maintained more institutional practices consistent with honor motivations, such as having more laws that allow for (1) more freedom in defending one's home, (2) corporal punishment in the schools, and (3) capital punishment by the state; at the same time, Southerners have fewer laws mandating punishment for domestic violence incidents (Cohen, 1996).

---

[1]The effects for Protestants were limited to Protestant men. Protestant women remained relationally attuned in both work and casual settings, perhaps reflecting a heightened relational sensitivity among women than among men (see Sanchez-Burks, 2002, for discussion).

Much evidence thus converges on the notion that the U.S. South maintains more of a culture of honor than the U.S. North (also see Vandello & Cohen, 2003, for further explorations of behavioral correlates of a culture of honor).

COGNITION AND PERCEPTION

Many psychologists assume that research from the area of cognition and perception targets the most basic and fundamental psychological processes. Given this perspective, it is interesting that cross-cultural research on cognition and perception reveals some of the clearest evidence for cultural variation. Research contrasting analytic and holistic ways of thinking reveals much cultural variation in how people attend to objects and fields, in how they reason, and in how they explain the behavior of others.

Analytic Versus Holistic Thinking

Richard Nisbett and colleagues (Nisbett, 2003; Nisbett et al., 2001) have investigated whether various cognitive and perceptual tasks explained under the labels of analytic and holistic thinking varied across cultural contexts, particularly between North American and East Asian cultures. By analytic thinking they mean a focus on objects, which are perceived as existing independently from their contexts and are understood in terms of their underlying attributes. These attributes are further used as a basis to categorize objects, and a set of fixed abstract rules are used for predicting and explaining the behavior of them. In contrast, by holistic thinking Nisbett and colleagues are referring to an orientation to the context as a whole. This is an associative way of thinking, where people attend to the relations among objects and among the objects and the surrounding context. These relations are used to explain and predict the behavior of objects. Further, holistic thinking has an emphasis on knowledge that is gained through experience rather than the application of fixed abstract rules. Dozens of studies have been conducted that demonstrate how cultures vary in these two ways of thinking (for a review, see Norenzayan, Choi, & Peng, 2007). In general, analytic thinking is especially common in Western cultures, whereas holistic thinking is more normative in the rest of the world, particularly in East Asia, where most of the cross-cultural research has been conducted. This distinction between analytic and holistic thinking has been studied in several ways.

Attention to Objects and Fields

Various experimental paradigms have revealed that Americans and other Westerners attend less to the background (i.e., are

more field independent) than are people from other non-Western societies, with the likely exception of migratory foragers. The first evidence for this cultural difference came from cross-cultural comparisons of Rorschach ink blots, where it was found that European Americans were more likely than Chinese Americans to focus their responses on a fraction of the card rather than attending to the entire image (Abel & Hsu, 1949). Dozens of years later, using evidence derived mostly from the Rod and Frame Test and the Embedded Figures Test, Witkin and Berry (1975) summarized a range of evidence from work with migratory and sedentary foraging populations (Arctic, Australia, and Africa), sedentary agriculturalists, and industrialized Westerners and found that only Westerners and migratory foragers appeared at the field-independent end of the spectrum. Recent work among East Asians in industrialized societies using the Rod and Frame Test (Ji, Peng, & Nisbett, 2000) show Westerners as more field independent than East Asians (also see Kitayama, Duffy, Kawamura, & Larsen, 2003). Research using the Embedded Figure Test comparing Americans, Germans, Malaysians, and Russians (Kühnen, Hannover, & Schubert, 2001) shows Americans and Germans to both be more field independent than Malays and Russians. Norenzayan (2009) found that Canadians showed less field-dependent processing on the Group Embedded Figures Test than Chinese, who in turn were less field dependent than Arabs. Integrative cognitive styles, which is similar to field dependence, are more pronounced among Middle Easterners than European Canadians (and exposure to a Western-style university education was found to lead to less integrative thinking among the Middle Easterners; Zebian & Denny, 2001). More recently, studies find that Americans show significantly more focused attention in the Framed Line Test than do people from other European countries (Britain and Germany) or from Japan (Kitayama, Park, Sevincer, Karasawa, & Uskul, 2009), and middle-class Americans show more evidence for object-focused attention than do working-class Americans (Na, Grossmann, Varnum, Kitayama, & Nisbett, 2009). These studies raise the possibility that Americans, particularly the college-educated Americans that make up the bulk of the psychological database, are unusual with respect to their analytic perceptual styles.

Further evidence for a greater attention to objects can be seen in studies where people were asked whether they have seen a focal object before in scenes in which the background has been switched. East Asians' recall for the objects is worse than it is for Americans if the background has been replaced with a new one (Masuda & Nisbett, 2001), indicating that they are attending to the field. This difference in attention toward the field has also been found in the eye movements of people as measured with eye trackers in both social and nonsocial scenes (Chua et al., 2005; Masuda, Akase, Radford, & Wang, 2008; Masuda, Ellsworth, et al., 2008). In these studies, the attention of Americans rarely leaves the focal object, whereas, after an initial 1,000 ms or so of attending to the focal object, East Asians are more likely to shift their gaze to the background.

Moreover, distinct neural activation appears to be associated with these different attentional styles across cultures. In the Framed Line Test (Kitayama et al., 2003), Westerners tend to do better on absolute judgments, whereas East Asians are superior on relative judgments. When asked to make absolute judgments (the more difficult task for East Asians), Asian Americans showed greater activation in regions of the left inferior parietal lobule and the right precentral gyrus—regions that are associated with attentional control. In contrast, European American participants showed greater activation in these same regions when they were asked to make relative judgments (the more difficult task for Westerners; Hedden, Ketay, Aron, Markus, & Gabrieli, 2008). That is, people from both cultural groups showed increased attentional control when engaged in tasks that were not preferred in their respective cultures. These differences were further associated with the degree to which individuals embraced independent values or had acculturated to the United States. In addition, when looking at pictorial scenes, Americans show more activation of brain regions that are implicated in object processing (e.g., the bilateral middle temporal gyrus, left superior parietal or angular gyrus, and right superior temporal or supramarginal gyrus) than do East Asians. In contrast, few cultural differences were found in regions associated with background processing (Gutchess, Welsh, Boduroglu, & Park, 2006; also see Goh et al., 2007).

This cultural difference in attention to the field is further evident in different artistic traditions between the West and East Asia, where Western paintings tend to have a horizon that is approximately 15% higher than it is in East Asian paintings (the higher horizon calls attention to the depth of the setting and allows for the different objects and places in a scene to be seen in relation to one another). Western portraits also include focal figures that are approximately three times as large as those in East Asian portraits. Further, when American college students draw a scene, or take a photograph of someone, they are more likely to draw a lower horizon, include fewer objects in their drawings, and zoom in to photograph a larger focal figure than are Japanese students (Masuda, Gonzalez, Kwan, & Nisbett, 2008). In sum, these findings converge to show that Westerners perceive the world in some importantly different ways than do those from other cultural contexts.

Reasoning Styles

Westerners are more likely to group objects on the basis of categories and rules, whereas people from many other cultural groups are more likely to group objects based on similarity or functional relationships. For example, Ji, Zhang, and Nisbett (2004) found that Chinese were more likely to group objects that shared a functional (e.g., pencil–notebook) or contextual (e.g., sky–sunshine) relationship. Americans were more likely to group objects if they belonged to the same category defined by a simple rule (e.g., notebook–magazine). Similar cultural differences were found between Northern and Southern Italy (Southern Italians gave more holistic responses; Knight & Nisbett, 2007). In a similar vein, Norenzayan and colleagues found that Chinese were more likely to group objects if they shared a strong family resemblance, whereas Americans were more likely to group the same objects if they could be assigned to that group on the basis of a deterministic rule (Norenzayan, Smith, et al., 2002). Norenzayan, Henrich, and McElreath (2009) examined classification among the Mapuche and Sangu subsistence farmers in Chile and Tanzania, respectively, and found that their classification resembled the Chinese pattern, although it was more exaggerated toward holistic reasoning. These cultural differences in reasoning appear to be a product of social interdependence; even within the same linguistic and geographical regions of Turkey, farmers and fishermen, who have more socially connected lifestyles, showed more evidence for holistic reasoning on this same task (and on other related tasks) than did herders, who are more isolated (Uskul, Kitayama, & Nisbett, 2008).

Other cultural variation in reasoning has been demonstrated in experiments exploring a "belief bias" in deductive reasoning. A belief bias exists where more plausible conclusions are judged as more logically valid than less plausible ones (Revlin, Leirer, Yop, & Yop, 1980). This bias was found to be greater for Koreans than for Americans, but only for valid arguments (Norenzayan, Smith, et al., 2002)—although, importantly, this difference was not due to any difference in abstract logical reasoning ability between the two cultural groups. This belief bias was also compared among student samples of Canadians, Chinese, and Arabs, and the bias was most pronounced among Arabs, followed by the Chinese and then Canadians (Norenzayan, 2009).

Further, as discussed earlier, pronounced cultural differences occur in reasoning with respect to how people reason about contradiction. A holistic orientation suggests that everything is perceived to be fundamentally connected and in flux, which suggests that real contradiction might not be possible. The Aristotelian law of contradiction, in which *A* cannot equal *not A,* is not as compelling if *A* is connected with *not A* and if *A* and *not A* are always changing. This naïve dialecticism is more common among East Asians and is associated with a greater tolerance for contradiction compared with Westerners across various tasks (Peng & Nisbett, 1999). The fluid and contradictory nature of East Asian beliefs is also reflected in their predictions of future changes. Whereas Westerners tend to make rather linear future predictions for change (e.g., if the stock market has been dropping over the past year it will probably continue to drop next year as well), East Asian future predictions are considerably more nonlinear (Ji, Nisbett, & Su, 2001). Moreover, this cultural difference in predictions about change is already evident in childhood and becomes more pronounced with age (Ji, 2008). This less linear view of the future may be due to East Asians perceiving events as having a broader net of consequences compared with Westerners (Maddux & Yuki, 2006). It remains to be seen whether people from other cultures view contradiction in ways more similar to East Asians or to Westerners.

Explaining the Behavior of Others

Given the previously described cultural differences in attention and reasoning, we might therefore expect that Westerners would be inclined to explain events by reference to properties of the object, whereas non-Westerners would be inclined to explain the same events with reference to interactions between the object and the field. Several classic studies, which were initially conducted exclusively with Western participants, found that when asked to explain the behavior of others, people tend to largely attend to the person's disposition as a means for explaining the behavior, even when compelling situational constraints are available (Jones & Harris, 1967; Ross, Amabile, & Steinmetz, 1977)—a tendency robust enough that it has been termed the "fundamental attribution error" (Ross et al., 1977). However, research in non-Western cultures often reveals a somewhat different pattern. Geertz (1975) described how Balinese do not tend to conceive of people's behaviors in terms of underlying dispositions but instead see it as emerging out of the roles that they have. Shweder and Bourne (1982) found that Indians tended to eschew trait descriptions of others' behaviors but rather would explain their behaviors in descriptive terms. Building on this idea, Miller (1984) found that Indian adults tended to favor situational information over dispositional accounts. More recently, several studies conducted with East Asians and Americans reveal that whereas Americans attend to dispositions first, regardless of how compelling the situational

information may be (Gilbert & Malone, 1995), East Asians are more likely than Americans to infer that behaviors are controlled by the situation (Norenzayan, Choi, et al., 2002) and to attend to situational information (Miyamoto & Kitayama, 2002; Morris & Peng, 1994; Van Boven, Kamada, & Gilovich, 1999), particularly when that information is especially salient (Choi & Nisbett, 1998). Similarly, East Asians are less likely than Americans to use trait adjectives when describing someone's behaviors (Maass, Karasawa, Politi, & Suga, 2006). Furthermore, in an investigation of people's lay beliefs about personality across eight cultures, Church et al. (2006) found that people from Western cultural backgrounds (i.e., American and European Australian) strongly endorsed implicit-trait beliefs, such as the notions that traits remain stable over time and predict behavior over many situations. In contrast, they found that those from non-Western cultural backgrounds (i.e., Asian Australian, Chinese Malaysian, Filipino, Japanese, Mexican, and Malay) more strongly endorsed contextual beliefs about personality, such as ideas that traits do not fully describe a person as well as roles or duties and that trait-related behavior will change from situation to situation. In sum, while stronger tendencies to consider dispositional information over situational information tend to be found cross-culturally, the fundamental attribution error appears to be attenuated in non-Western cultures (Choi, Nisbett, & Norenzayan, 1999; also see conflicting evidence regarding whether East Asians automatically consider situational information before dispositional information; Knowles, Morris, Chiu, & Hong, 2001; Lieberman, Jarcho, & Obayashi, 2005).

LANGUAGE

One of the most salient markers of cultural groups is language. It permeates all activities and thoughts, is learned early in life, and in addition to the obvious linguistic differences among languages (e.g., variations in lexicon and grammar), different cultural groups vary in many ways with regard to how they use language. This section reviews research regarding how language and psychology are related, including studies that assess the relation between thinking and talking, implicit and explicit communication, language priming, and studies that test the linguistic relativity hypothesis.

Relationship Between Thinking and Talking

One way that language use can vary across cultures is in terms of its relation to unspoken thoughts. When people think to themselves, are they talking silently to themselves, or are they thinking in nonverbal terms? One instance of the latter can be seen in facial perception. People do not recognize faces by verbally describing them. Research on verbal overshadowing, for example, demonstrates that verbalizing one's thoughts about faces interferes with facial recognition (Schooler & Engstler-Schooler, 1990).

Cultures also appear to differ in the degree that people verbalize their thoughts. Kim (2002) explored this question by having Asian Americans and European Americans solve two sets of IQ items. Participants first attempted to solve the initial set of items while remaining silent. Then, participants were assigned to one of two conditions: In one condition, people were asked to talk aloud as they solved the next set of items. In another condition, people recited the alphabet as they solved the next set of items. The results indicated that the European Americans performed about as well on the items that they completed in silence as those that they completed while talking aloud. In contrast, the Asian Americans performed significantly worse when talking aloud than when solving them silently. Apparently, saying one's thoughts aloud disrupted the thinking of the Asian Americans. On the other hand, the performance of the European Americans was significantly worse when they recited the alphabet than when they were silent. In contrast, reciting the alphabet did not significantly affect the performance of Asian Americans. These results suggest that the unspoken thoughts about the IQ items vary across these two cultural groups. Apparently, the Asian Americans are processing the IQ items in a holistic manner, but when they are asked to say their thoughts aloud this forces them to arrange their thoughts sequentially, which is a more analytic way of thinking. It is difficult to easily describe holistic thoughts, as they entail multiple interrelated parts. Hence, the problem solving of Asian Americans is disrupted when they verbalize their thoughts; however, they are relatively unaffected by the alphabet recitation task, as this easy verbal task did not interfere with their holistic thoughts about the IQ items. In contrast, European Americans appear to be verbalizing their thoughts so that thinking aloud is a straightforward task, whereas reciting the alphabet interferes with their verbal thoughts about the IQ items. In sum, the two cultural groups appear to be thinking about the same task in quite different ways. Other research has demonstrated that verbalizing one's thoughts is more effortful among East Asians than among Americans, as assessed through a heightened cortisol response (which indicates increased stress; Kim, 2008). Furthermore, verbalized thoughts are associated with more commitment among European Americans than among Asian Americans, demonstrating the relatively greater power of the spoken word among Westerners (Kim & Sherman, 2007).

Implicit Versus Explicit Communication

Another way in which cultures vary in their language use is in terms of the degree to which people attend to the explicit meaning of what is said. Edward Hall (1976) made a distinction between "high context" cultures, in which much shared information guides behaviors, and "low context" cultures, which have less shared information so that people have to communicate more explicitly. Japan and the United States, respectively, are exemplars of this distinction. One test of this hypothesized cultural difference in explicit communication provided Japanese and Americans with a Stroop task in which the literal meaning and the vocal tone of words were in conflict. For example, people would hear the word "failure" spoken in a happy, upbeat tone. Participants were either asked to attend to the literal meaning of the words or to the tone that they were spoken in. The findings indicated that Americans had a more difficult time ignoring the literal meaning of the words whereas Japanese had more difficulty ignoring the tone in which the words were expressed (Kitayama & Ishii, 2002), although the American effects may be limited to when they are in work contexts (Sanchez-Burks et al., 2003). Bilingual English–Tagalog-speaking Filipinos also showed the same pattern as the Japanese, even when speaking English, indicating that the results were not specific to features in the languages themselves (Ishii, Reyes, & Kitayama, 2003). Other evidence for cultural differences in explicit communication can be seen in how people use answering machines. Miyamoto and Schwarz (2006) find that Japanese are less likely to use answering machines than Americans because it is more difficult for them to communicate without receiving the nonverbal feedback that is present in a regular telephone conversation. In one study, Japanese participants performed worse on a cognitive task than Americans while trying to leave a message on an answering machine (but not in other conditions), apparently because leaving a message, in the absence of feedback, was more cognitively demanding for them. These studies converge to show that Americans do not need to attend as much to various implicit aspects of communication as do those from some other cultures (also see Ambady, Koo, Lee, & Rosenthal, 1996).

Language Priming

As reviewed earlier, various kinds of primes have been used to activate different aspects of the self-concept, both among biculturals and among monoculturals (e.g., Hong et al., 2000). The centrality of language to thought is evident in research that compares the responses of bilinguals depending on the language in which they are tested. For example, Chinese Canadians were found to describe themselves in far more positive terms when they completed an open-ended questionnaire in English than when they completed it in Chinese (Ross et al., 2002). Other research has shown that bilinguals respond differently in their two languages when they make decisions (Briley, Morris, & Simonson, 2005), describe their self-concepts (Kemmelmeier & Cheng, 2004), make categorizations (Ji et al., 2004), or report on their personality (Ramirez-Esparza, Gosling, Benet-Martínez, Potter, & Pennebaker, 2006). These studies demonstrate that speaking a particular language involves activating a broad network of thoughts that are less accessible in other languages.

Linguistic Relativity

The hypothesis that people's thoughts are bounded by the language in which they speak has been one of the more controversial research questions in psycholinguistics (e.g., Pinker, 1994; Roberson, Davies, & Davidoff, 2000; Whorf, 1956). The stronger version of this linguistic relativity hypothesis, that language determines thought, has been almost universally rejected. The weaker version of this hypothesis, that language influences thought, has sparked much research interest and controversy.

One domain that has been especially suitable for testing linguistic relativity has been color perception, as color varies on a continuum yet different languages parse up the color space in divergent ways (although a small set of solutions are relied on in every language for labeling colors; Berlin & Kay, 1969). A seminal series of studies was conducted by Rosch Heider (Rosch Heider, 1972; Rosch Heider & Olivier, 1972) to see whether the Dani of Irian Java, who had only two color terms, would perform differently on various color-perception tasks compared with English-speaking Americans. The evidence from these studies was interpreted as showing that the color perception of the Dani was identical to that of Americans. However, other researchers have called into question both the interpretation of these findings and the methodology that was used (e.g., Lucy & Shweder, 1979; Ratner, 1989; Saunders & Van Brakel, 1997). More recently, research by Roberson and colleagues (Roberson, Davidoff, Davies, & Shapiro, 2005; Roberson et al., 2000) has attempted to address some criticisms of Rosch Heider's earlier studies. Roberson's studies have investigated Berinmo speakers from Papua New Guinea and Himba speakers from Namibia. Both of these languages contain five basic colors, although their boundaries and focal colors vary. The results of these studies show that people perceive two colors that fall within the same color category as more

similar to each other than to a color from another color category, even if the colors are equidistant in terms of hue. Importantly, the categories that affect people's color-similarity judgments are those from their own language— their judgments are unaffected by the color categories from other languages. In sum, category labels do appear to affect people's perception of colors (also see Winawer et al., 2007, for parallel evidence between Russian and English speakers, but see Kay & Regier, 2007, for contrary views).

Spatial perception also appears to be influenced by language. Several languages lack words for relativistic directions (e.g., right of and in front of); instead, people communicate directions solely in absolute terms, using the cardinal points of a compass. When asked to arrange objects as they had seen them before, Guugu Ymithirr speakers from Australia, Tzeltal speakers from Mexico, and Hai//om speakers from Namibia (all of whom lack relativistic direction terms) arranged them in a geocentric pattern, meaning that they arranged them in a different order when they went to a room in which they faced a new cardinal direction, whereas Dutch speakers arrange them in an egocentric manner, preserving the order relative to themselves (Boroditsky & Gaby, 2006; Haun, Rapold, Call, Janzen, & Levinson, 2006; Levinson, 1997, 2003). The availability of language terms to express egocentric spatial arrangements appears to be associated with people's perceptions (but for a contrary view, see Papafragou, Hulbert, & Trueswell, 2008).

Numerical cognition also appears to be influenced by language. Members of the Piraha tribe of the Amazon do not have any numerical markers above the number two. In a series of studies, they appeared unable to represent numerical quantities for numbers much larger than two, although they estimated general quantities with reasonable accuracy (Gordon, 2004; for similar findings with another culture, the Mundrukuku of the Amazon, see Pica, Lerner, Izard, & Dehaene, 2004). These findings suggest that the lack of a counting system in the language affects numerical cognition (but for alternative accounts, see Everett, 2005; Gelman & Gallistel, 2004).

EMOTION

The relation between culture and emotional experience has attracted much research interest. Two aspects of emotions have received the greatest amount of study across cultures: facial expressions of emotion and people's subjective reports of their emotions, including people's reports of the intensity of their emotional experiences, emotion terms, and kinds of emotional experiences. Further, much study has focused on the nature of positive emotional experiences, such as subjective well-being and happiness, across cultures.

Emotions and Facial Expressions

Charles Darwin (1872/1965) was one of the first scientists to consider seriously whether emotional facial expressions were universal features of the human species or were the products of cultural learning. He noted several similarities in the facial expressions of various primates and humans and proposed that these expressions should be shared by all humans. Paul Ekman and colleagues have done the most on following up on Darwin's hypothesis and have conducted several studies to investigate whether emotional expressions are universally shared. For example, Ekman and Friesen (1971) posed a series of photos corresponding to what they referred to as a set of "basic emotions" (viz., anger, disgust, fear, happiness, sadness, and surprise) to participants from Argentina, Brazil, Chile, Japan, and the United States, asking them to match the expressions with emotion terms. Whereas chance performance would have been 16.7% correct, participants tended to get between 80% and 90% of the questions correct, regardless of cultural background, indicating much universality in recognition of the expressions. In efforts to rule out the possibility that cultural learning had occurred across these different countries, the researchers posed the same kinds of expressions to the Fore of New Guinea, who had little exposure to Western culture; in general, the Fore also made similar judgments to the expressions (Ekman, Sorenson, & Freisen, 1969; but see Russell's 1994 critique of the inconsistency of the findings). This evidence, combined with findings that the same facial expressions made by adults are made by very young infants (Izard, 1994), including those who are congenitally blind (reviewed in Ekman, 1973), demonstrates that facial expressions for the basic emotions are innate. Proposals have been made that some other emotions, in particular, contempt, shame, embarrassment, pride, and interest, are universally recognized enough to justify being added to this set (e.g., Keltner, 1995). For example, a bodily posture associated with feelings of pride appears to be universally recognized and spontaneously produced across cultures (Tracy & Robins, 2008), including among those who are congenitally blind (Tracy & Matsumoto, 2008).

Although this research reveals that, regardless of culture, people are able to recognize the facial expressions of many emotions, some intriguing cultural differences have been found. For example, the success rates for identifying American-posed faces were better among English speakers than they were for other Indo-European language speakers (e.g., Swedish, Greek, and Spanish); these samples

performed better than those who spoke non-Indo-European languages (e.g., Japanese, Turkish, and Malaysian); and all of these groups performed better than those from preliterate societies (e.g., the Fore and Dani from New Guinea; Russell, 1994). All groups performed significantly better than chance, but Americans performed the best at identifying the emotions posed by American actors.

Building on this observation, a meta-analysis of all past research on cross-cultural recognition of facial expressions noted that, on average, people were about 9% more accurate in judging the facial expressions of people from their own culture than in judging those of another culture (with, on average, people showing about 58% accuracy overall; Elfenbein & Ambady, 2002). Moreover, the more people had been exposed to another culture, the more accurate they were at decoding facial expressions from that culture. Likewise, urban dwellers have been found to be more accurate at identifying facial expressions than people from rural communities, apparently because they have had contact with a more diverse array of people (e.g., Ducci, Arcuri, Georgis, & Sineshaw, 1982). Further, people are able to reliably distinguish among the nationalities of targets when they are making emotional expressions but not when they make neutral expressions. For example, American participants could reliably distinguish between Australian and American faces (Marsh, Elfenbein, & Ambady, 2007) and between Japanese and Japanese American faces (Marsh, Elfenbein, & Ambady, 2003), but only when they were expressing emotions. These findings suggest that the recognition of facial expressions for emotions are best categorized as functional universals (i.e., they serve the same function everywhere) and do not meet the criteria for accessibility universals (i.e., cultural variability appears in the extent to which people recognize particular expressions; Norenzayan & Heine, 2005).

Moreover, across cultures people appear to attend to different parts of the face when deciphering facial expressions. Yuki, Maddux, and Masuda (2007) proposed that in cultures with stronger cultural norms to regulate emotional expressions, such as Japan, people would be more likely to attend to those aspects of the face that were more difficult to regulate (i.e., the eyes). In contrast, in cultures with weaker norms for emotional regulation, such as the United States, people would attend to the largest visual cues (i.e., the mouth). Indeed, studies found that independent manipulations of the mouth and eyes in facial expressions affected Japanese and Americans differently—Japanese attended more to the eyes than Americans, whereas Americans attended more to the mouth than Japanese (Yuki et al., 2007).

While Ekman and colleagues have argued that the capacity to produce and recognize particular facial expressions is identical across cultures, cultural variation is anticipated in the form of "display rules" (Ekman & Friesen, 1969). Display rules are the culturally specific rules that govern when, how intensely, and what facial expressions are appropriate in a given situation. For example, Darwin noted that his English compatriots were less emotionally expressive than were people from various other European countries (Darwin, 1872/1965). Several studies and ethnographical accounts provide evidence that cultures differ in the degree to which emotions are expressed. For example, in response to recalled situations in which participants report feeling the same amount of happiness, Hmong Americans are less likely to smile than are European Americans (Tsai, Chentsova-Dutton, Freire-Bebeau, & Przymus, 2002; also see Abu-Lughod, 1986; Briggs, 1970). Furthermore, in many countries around the world, particularly Old World countries in the Northern Hemisphere, people from southern regions of the countries are perceived by their compatriots to be more emotionally expressive than those from northern regions of the same countries (Pennebaker, Rimé, & Blankenship, 1996). The ways in which emotions are expressed can thus vary across cultures. This notion of display rules assumes that even though people in different cultures vary considerably in how strongly they express certain emotions, they may be experiencing the same underlying feelings.

In addition to governing the intensity with which emotions are expressed, display rules are also seen to shape the kinds of facial expressions that people might display. For example, often Indians express their embarrassment by biting their tongues, which is distinct from a prototypical embarrassment expression (Keltner, 1995), and the tongue bite is not reliably produced or recognized in many other cultures. This suggests that the tongue bite represents an expression that is voluntarily produced, rather than reflexively generated (Haidt & Keltner, 1999), and is termed an example of a ritualized display. The notion of display rules adds considerable complexity to the task of interpreting emotional expressions across cultures. It is not always obvious whether one is making a universal facial expression or enacting a cultural display rule. Furthermore, as people's facial expressions can affect their emotional experience (e.g., Strack, Martin, & Stepper, 1988), it is possible that cultures differ not just in their display rules but also in their emotional experiences.

Intensity of Emotional Experience

The preceding findings that Japanese appear to regulate their emotional expressions more than Americans raise the question of whether people differ in their emotional experiences across cultures. One study found that Americans reported feeling their emotions longer and more intensely than the Japanese did (Matsumoto, Kudoh, Scherer, & Wallbott, 1988). Similarly, in a diary study Japanese participants were about three times as likely as Americans to report that they had *not* been feeling any emotions when prompted (Mesquita & Karasawa, 2002; for similar findings, also see Kitayama et al., 2000; Wang, 2004). These studies suggest that the cultural display rules governing the relative deamplifying and masking of emotions in Japan might be leading them to experience fewer and less intense emotions compared with Americans.

Suppressing some emotions (particularly anger) has been found to lead to less cardiac regulation of heart rate and thus a slower recovery of the heart rate following an initial angering event (e.g., Brosschot & Thayer, 1998). However, in East Asian cultural contexts, where inhibition of emotional expressions is more common, people appear to show quicker recovery of their heart rate following an angering event. This appears to be due to East Asian participants being more likely to reappraise events in a less anger-provoking way (Anderson & Linden, 2006; also see Butler, Lee, & Gross, 2007).

Emotion and Language

Although a set of basic emotions are recognized comparably around the world, considerable cultural variability exists in the terms that people use to describe their emotions (see Russell, 1991, for a review). On one extreme is the English language, which has more than 2,000 different emotion words. On the other extreme is the Chewong of Malaysia, who have only 8 emotion words (only 3 of which, anger, fear, and shame, map onto Ekman's basic emotions). Further, across cultures people categorize their emotions in very different ways. For example, the Buganda of Uganda do not make a distinction between sorrow and anger. Among the Gidjingali aborigines of Australia, they use one word (*gurakadj*) to express both shame and fear. Samoans use one word, *alofa,* to express both love and pity. The Utku Eskimos do not distinguish between feelings of kindness and gratitude. And the Ifaluk in Micronesia do not even have a specific word for "emotion" but instead lump all internal states together (Lutz, 1988). It largely remains an open question whether these cultural differences in emotion terms are mirrored by cultural differences in emotional experiences (for conflicting views on this point, see Pinker, 1994; Russell, 1991).

Kinds of Emotional Experiences

Independent and interdependent self-concepts provide a useful framework to make sense of cultural variation in emotional experiences. The self-concept should shape how one appraises an emotionally relevant situation. Those with interdependent selves are more concerned with maintaining a sense of interpersonal harmony and thus should consider more about how events in the world affect close others, as well as themselves. Those with independent selves, in contrast, should focus more intently on how events affect themselves or how events might distinguish themselves from others. Mesquita (2001) contrasted those from a more interdependent culture (Surinamese and Turkish immigrants to Holland) with those from a more independent culture (mainstream Dutch citizens of Holland) and found that the Surinamese and Turks expressed having more relational concerns and attended more closely about how situations affected others compared with the Dutch. Moreover, the Surinamese and Turks were more likely than Dutch to ensure that others attended to the same events, thereby sharing the experience with the participants.

Along a similar line, Kitayama, Markus, and Kurokawa (2000) compared descriptions of daily emotional experiences among Japanese and Americans. People reported how often they experienced emotions that varied both in terms of their valence and in terms of the extent to which they were interpersonally engaged. The findings revealed that general positive feelings were especially correlated with the frequency that the person felt positive interpersonally *engaged* emotions (e.g., respect and friendly feelings) among Japanese, whereas general positive feelings for Americans were especially correlated with the frequency that the person felt positive interpersonally *disengaged* emotions (e.g., pride and feeling on top of the world). In sum, what makes people feel good varies across cultures (see Kitayama, Mesquita, & Karasawa, 2006, for similar findings).

Cultural Variation in Subjective Well-Being and Happiness

Is there variability in people's happiness and subjective well-being across cultures? One piece of evidence comes from the study reviewed earlier that compared Japanese and American daily emotional experiences (Kitayama et al., 2000). When comparing the frequency with how often participants reported feeling the different kinds of emotions, the two cultures showed an intriguing pattern: Japanese participants reported that they felt about the same amount of positive and negative emotions. In contrast, American participants reported that they experienced far more positive emotions than they did negative emotions. Similar kinds of cultural differences in subjective well-being are commonly found (also see Diener, Oishi, & Lucas, 2003; Plaut, Markus, & Lachman, 2002).

In general, the nations that score highest on this measure are Scandinavian and Nordic countries, much of Latin America, various English-speaking countries, and Western Europe. On the low end are the former Soviet republics, and some impoverished countries in Africa and South Asia (Diener & Diener, 1995; Diener, Diener, & Diener, 1995; Inglehart & Klingemann, 2000).

Many factors contribute to influence the overall satisfaction that people have with their lives. Wealth as assessed by GDP positively correlates with the overall well-being of a country. However, this relation is not linear; money and happiness are most closely connected at very low levels of wealth, where a little extra money can make the difference between surviving or not. For example, income and life satisfaction are correlated at .45 among respondents in the slums of Calcutta (Biswas-Diener & Diener, 2002). In contrast, above an average GDP of 40% of that of the United States, no pronounced relation remains between money and subjective well-being (Diener et al., 1995). In addition, human rights and overall equality of a country are associated with greater subjective well-being (Diener et al., 1995).

In addition, some factors predict life satisfaction differently across cultures. Suh, Diener, Oishi, and Triandis (1998) found that life satisfaction is more highly correlated with overall positive affect in individualistic cultures than in collectivist ones. On the other hand, people in collectivistic cultures showed a higher correlation between their life-satisfaction scores and being respected by others for living up to cultural norms compared with people from individualistic cultures.

Furthermore, the *kinds* of positive emotions that people desire also vary across cultures. Some work by Tsai and colleagues (e.g., Tsai, Knutson, & Fung, 2006) reveals that Americans seek out positive emotions that are high in arousal more than East Asians do, whereas East Asians prefer low-arousal positive emotions more than do Americans. Evidence for this cultural difference comes from various sources. For example, a comparison of facial expressions that were shown in characters in American and Taiwanese children's storybooks revealed that the American faces more often showed feelings of excitement and had significantly bigger smiles than the Taiwanese faces. Moreover, European American preschool children preferred the pictures of excited faces more than the Taiwanese preschoolers did; they also felt more similar to the characters who were engaged in high-arousal activities than did Taiwanese children (Tsai, Louie, Chen, & Uchida, 2006). Furthermore, a content analysis of classic Christian and Buddhist texts (the Gospels of the Bible and the Lotus Sutra, respectively), as well as contemporary Christian and Buddhist self-help books, revealed that high-arousal states were encouraged more in the Christian texts than in Buddhist texts, whereas the low-arousal states were more encouraged in the Buddhist texts than in the Christian texts (Tsai, Miao, & Seppala, 2007). In sum, cultures vary in their happiness, in part, because they appear to have quite different ideas about what happiness is and what it is derived from (also see Falk, Dunn, & Norenzayan, 2009).

To summarize the cross-cultural research on emotions, much similarity exists across cultures with respect to facial expressions of emotions (although some important variability is found here, too). In the domain of emotional experience, in contrast, the evidence for cultural variation is more pronounced.

MORALITY

Much cross-cultural work has explored the way in which people's moral reasoning compares across cultures. This section reviews cross-cultural research targeting the moral ethics associated with justice (autonomy), community, and divinity; whether thoughts are judged to be moral concerns; and perceptions of fairness.

The most influential model of moral reasoning in psychology has been a framework proposed by Lawrence Kohlberg (1971). Kohlberg argued that people's abilities to reason morally hinge on cognitive abilities that develop as individuals matured and were educated. Kohlberg proposed that people everywhere progressed through the same three levels: (1) Young children started out at a preconventional level and view what is right or wrong based on the physical or hedonistic consequences of their actions; (2) children then progressed to a conventional level, where moral behavior is perceived to be that which maintains the social order of their group; and (3) some people would finally progress further to a postconventional level and view what is right and wrong on the basis of abstract ethical principles that emphasized justice and individual rights—the moral code inherent in the U.S. Constitution.

Much cross-cultural research has explored the cultural generalizability of Kohlberg's model. One review explored the 45 studies that had been conducted up until that point, which had investigated the levels of moral reasoning in 27 cultural areas from around the world (Snarey, 1985). The results indicated some universality in moral reasoning. All cultural groups had adults who reasoned at conventional levels, and in no cultural groups did the average adult reason at the preconventional level, although many samples of children revealed evidence of preconventional reasoning. This review suggests that Kohlberg's model might be universally applicable in explaining preconventional and conventional moral reasoning around the world. However,

evidence of postconventional reasoning—reasoning based on justice and individual rights—was not universally found. Although every urban Western sample contained at least some individuals who showed reasoning based on justice and individual rights, not one person from the traditional tribal and village folk populations that were studied showed such reasoning.

Furthermore, it is not just that formal education is necessary to achieve Kohlberg's postconventional level. Some highly educated non-Western populations do not show Kohlberg's postconventional reasoning. At Kuwait University, for example, faculty members score lower on Kohlberg's schemes than the typical norms for Western adults, and the elder faculty at the university scored no higher than the younger ones, contrary to Western patterns (Al-Shehab, 2002; also see Miller, Bersoff, & Harwood, 1990).

Research in moral psychology also indicates that non-Western adults rely on a wider range of moral principles than a morality of justice (e.g., Baek, 2002; Haidt, Koller, & Dias, 1993; Miller & Bersoff, 1992). Shweder, Much, Mahapatra, and Park (1997) proposed that in addition to a dominant justice-based morality, which they termed an ethic of autonomy, two other ethics are commonly found outside the West: an ethic of community, which viewed morality as deriving from the fulfillment of interpersonal obligations, and an ethic of divinity, in which moral decisions were based on the fit with a perceived natural order. These three moral codes appear to be associated with specific emotional states—anger signals violations of the ethic of autonomy, contempt signals community violations, and disgust is particularly salient in divinity violations (Rozin, Lowery, Imada, & Haidt, 1999). Moreover, Haidt and Graham (2007) further parsed the moral spectrum into five moral foundations: harm–care, fairness–reciprocity, ingroup–loyalty, authority–respect, and purity–sanctity. Initial evidence shows that Americans with liberal political values make their moral decisions largely on the basis of harm and fairness judgments, and do not give much heed to the other three foundations. In contrast, American conservatives (and, ostensibly, people from other non-Western contexts who attend to ethics of community and divinity), base their moral decisions on all five moral foundations.

People also vary in the domains that they view to be morally relevant. Christians and Jews differ in their beliefs about the moral standing of thoughts. Judaism tends to emphasize practice over belief, in that various traditional practices are to be observed (e.g., keeping kosher) and scant emphasis is placed on a person's feelings about these practices (e.g., one is still a good Jew if one craves a cheeseburger, as long as one does not eat it). Further, membership in Judaism is defined by descent and not belief.

In contrast, several passages in the New Testament emphasize that beliefs themselves have moral grounds. Spiritual purity in Christianity is attained by keeping pure thoughts, and membership into the church, particularly with some Protestant sects, hinges on one's personal beliefs (for a review, see Cohen, Siegel, & Rozin, 2003). Supporting this distinction, research by Cohen and Rozin (2001) found that whereas Protestants and Jews do not differ in their condemnation of immoral behaviors, Protestants hold more critical attitudes toward a target who engages in immoral thoughts. Moreover, they found that Protestants believe that thoughts are more under one's control, and believe that thoughts are more likely to ultimately lead to behaviors, than do Jews.

People from different cultures also vary in their perceptions of fairness, such as in the ways they distribute resources. Several studies find that Westerners are more likely to favor distributing resources on the basis of an equity norm (i.e., the ratio between inputs and outputs is held constant) than are people from some non-Western cultures. In contrast, Indians have been shown to prefer norms based on need more than Westerners do (Berman, Murphy-Berman, & Singh, 1985; Murphy-Berman, Berman, Singh, Pachauri, & Kuman, 1984), and Japanese tend to prefer equality norms in comparison with Westerners (Kashima, Siegal, Tanaka, & Isaka, 1988). These cultural differences also emerge in negotiation strategies. Whereas people from various non-Western cultures are more likely to prefer seeking compromises in negotiations, where both sides stand to gain or lose similarly (akin to an equality rule), people from several Western cultures tend to pursue adversarial strategies, in which they push for one side (their own side) to gain maximally over their opponents (e.g., Leung, Au, Fernandez-Dols, & Iwawaki, 1992; Leung, Bond, Carment, Krishnan, & Liebrand, 1990).

Perceptions of fairness also differ across cultures in other ways. For example, the Ultimatum Game is often used to study people's capacity for fair and punishing behavior, where one person is given the opportunity to distribute money between himself or herself and a partner and the partner has the choice of either accepting the money that is given or rejecting the offer, thereby ensuring that both players receive nothing. In this game, partners (who are typically from Western industrialized societies; Camerer, 2003; Fehr & Gächter, 1998) often reject offers to them that seem unfair—even though the rules of the game make it such that they would earn more money by accepting an unfair offer than by rejecting it. Nowak, Page, and Sigmund (2000) made sense of the seemingly nonrational behavior of people by proposing that they were concerned about maintaining their reputation and that this concern had seeped into the experiment, even though the one-shot anonymous circumstances of the Ultimatum Game preclude any reputational information from being shared. A formal mathematical evolutionary model that included the variable of reputational information predicted people's behaviors as they typically unfolded and provided an argument for how fairness motivations evolved. However, results from many other cultures do not fit the model of Nowak and colleagues. Two unified cross-cultural projects have deployed the Ultimatum Game across 15 small-scale human societies, including foragers, horticulturalists, pastoralists, and subsistence farmers, drawn from Africa, Amazonia, Oceania, Siberia, and New Guinea (Henrich et al., 2004, 2005, 2006). Multiple experiments show that the experimentally measured behaviors of people in industrialized societies remain outliers in the distribution of all cultures studied using the Ultimatum Game. Notably, some populations from small-scale societies with only daily face-to-face interaction behaved in a manner reminiscent of the model of Nowak et al. (2000) *before* they added the reputational information. That is, these people made low offers and did not reject even the most unfair offers. Further, regression analyses of these behavioral data show that the degree of market integration (i.e., the proportion of calories exchanged in a market economy) and the population size of the settlements both independently predict higher offers and more punishment. Norms and institutions for dealing with and trusting anonymous others appear to have culturally coevolved with markets and expanding sedentary populations. In some cases, at least in their most efficient forms, neither markets nor large populations are feasible before such norms and institutions emerge (Henrich et al., 2006).

In addition, cooperation has been argued to have emerged because people evolved to engage in altruistic punishment—that is, people are willing to spend resources to punish free-riders and thus create a context where people have incentives to cooperate (Fehr & Gächter, 2002). However, again, this model of the evolution of cooperation was initially derived from people from Western industrialized societies. Recently, efforts to replicate people's willingness to punish free-riders have been conducted in various cultural contexts, including Australia, Belarus, China, Denmark, Germany, Greece, Korea, Oman, Russia, Saudi Arabia, Switzerland, Turkey, and the United States (Gächter, Herrmann, & Thoni, 2005; Herrmann, Thoni, & Gächter, 2007). These efforts have revealed that the initial patterns that emerged for Westerners (and most strongly with American samples) do not all generalize well to those from non-Western cultural contexts. In the non-Western cultures, the tendency was often for people to punish cooperators in addition to the free-riders. These non-Western findings call into question the arguments that motives for cooperation depended on altruistic punishment.

SUMMARY

Humans are a cultural species, and a rich understanding of how humans' minds operate would be facilitated by a psychological science that is attentive to people's cultural experiences. Research in cultural psychology has grown substantially, particularly in the past two decades. This growing database has revealed that many key psychological processes, some of which were hitherto viewed as psychological universals, manifest in distinct ways across cultures. Further, although some psychological phenomena appear in more invariant forms across cultures than others, it is often not clear which phenomena should be expected to vary the most. Pronounced cultural variation has been identified in many fundamental psychological phenomena; thus, it is crucial to seek cross-cultural data before one can confidently make inferences about the cultural generalizability of a phenomenon (Henrich et al., in press).

Such evidence for cultural variability in basic processes underscores how many psychological phenomena do not unfold reflexively, regardless of context, but are importantly shaped by engagement in the particular scripts, practices, and situations that each culture provides. In this way, psychological processes can be seen as entangled with "meaning"—and because particular meanings can vary substantially across cultural contexts, so must the psychological process (Bruner, 1990; Heine, Proulx, & Vohs, 2006).

The recent growth in cultural psychology over the past two decades has been built on a foundation of theoretical advances (particularly, ideas of the mutual constitution of culture and psyche and the distinction between independent and interdependent selves) and has benefited from the application of rigorous experimental methods. The study of culture and psychology appears to be more firmly established as a discipline than at any previous time in history. In what direction will the field go from here? With the humility to recognize that such prognostications are always wrong, here are a few thoughts regarding where the field may be heading.

A serious shortcoming of the cultural psychological database thus far is that a large portion of it is constituted by comparisons of North Americans and East Asians. While there have been good theoretical and methodological reasons to build on the differences that have been identified between these groups, much of the world remains largely unexplored territory. In particular, the role of culture in psychological functioning should become especially evident when small-scale societies are studied, which differ from the industrialized West in many profound ways. Already, much excellent and influential work has been conducted with such groups (e.g., Atran, Medin, & Ross,

2005; Bailenson, Shum, Atran, Medin, & Coley, 2002; Cole, Gay, & Glick, 1968; Gordon, 2004; Henrich et al., 2005; Levinson, 1997; Segall, Campbell, & Herskiovits, 1963), much of it done to make arguments for psychological universals (e.g., Barrett & Behne, 2005; Ekman et al., 1969; Levenson, Ekman, Heider, & Friesen, 1992).

Attention to other cultural samples will likely uncover some psychological phenomena that are less familiar to Western psychologists. For example, the notion of "face" is far more elaborated and takes on different meanings within East Asia than in the West, and this leads to specific psychological predictions that can be tested (e.g., Chang & Holt, 1994; Heine, 2005; Ting-Toomey, 1994). Likewise, a type of dialectical thinking that emphasizes constant change and is tolerant of apparent contradiction (distinct from the Hegelian dialectic) likely would not have been investigated among Westerners if it had not been first identified among Chinese (e.g., Peng & Nisbett, 1999). It is likely that many more such examples will be found in other cultural contexts (e.g., *simpatia* in Hispanic contexts; Sanchez-Burks et al., 2000; Triandis, Marin, Lisansky, & Betancourt, 1984), and these phenomena would stand to greatly advance our understanding of cultural variation and the universality of psychological processes.

There will likely continue to be much interest in using cultural variation in psychological processes as a means to identify the underlying mechanisms. Such research has already increased our understanding of mechanisms in ways that it could not have done had the research been restricted to monocultural samples. This search for mechanisms has adopted various methods, such as employing trait measures to mediate the cultural differences (e.g., Diener & Diener, 1995; Singelis et al., 1999; but see Heine & Norenzayan, 2006, for discussion regarding limitations in the use of trait measures for understanding cultural differences), priming cultural constructs (e.g., Adams, 2005; Kühnen et al., 2001; Spencer-Rodgers et al., 2004), varying degrees of exposure to certain cultural experiences (e.g., Koo & Choi, 2005), situation-sampling (e.g., Kitayama et al., 1997; Morling et al., 2002), applying experimental methods that assess people's default thoughts across cultures (e.g., Heine et al., 2001), and using triangulation strategies that contrast multiple groups in different sets of cultural variables (e.g., Bailenson et al., 2002; Medin & Atran, 2004). These and other methods will surely continue to be used to identify the mechanisms underlying cultural differences.

Last, with the growing research in genetic differences among populations (e.g., Beja-Pereira et al., 2003; Jablonski & Chaplin, 2000), cultural psychology is likely to find itself in the position of helping to identify the degree to which population differences in psychological functioning are due to inherited or acquired tendencies.

We can anticipate that future research will find evidence that genes associated with particular psychological tendencies are not distributed with identical frequencies around the world (e.g., Taylor et al., 2007). Such findings would raise the question of whether any observed group variation in those same psychological tendencies could be seen as due to differences in gene frequencies, differences in the expression of genes, differences in cultural learning, or some combination of all of these. Addressing such questions will require targeting particular samples, such as immigrants and children adopted from other cultures, to control for variations in cultural experiences and genomes. Such research will be important and likely controversial.

REFERENCES

Abel, T. M., & Hsu, F. I. (1949). Some aspects of personality of Chinese as revealed by the Rorschach Test. *Journal of Projective Techniques, 13,* 285–301.

Abu-Lughod, L. (1986). *Veiled sentiments.* Berkeley: University of California Press.

Adams, G. (2005). The cultural grounding of personal relationship: Enemyship in West African worlds. *Journal of Personality and Social Psychology, 88,* 948–968.

Adams, G. & Plaut, V. C. (2003). The cultural grounding of personal relationship: Friendship in North American and West African worlds. *Personal Relationships, 10,* 333–348.

Aiello, L. C., & Wheeler, P. (1995). The expensive-tissue hypothesis: The brain and the digestive system in human and primate evolution. *Current Anthropology, 36,* 199–221.

Allik, J., & McCrae, R. R. (2004). Toward a geography of personality traits: Patterns of profiles across 36 cultures. *Journal of Cross-Cultural Psychology, 35,* 13–28.

Ambady, N., Koo, J., Lee, F., & Rosenthal, R. (1996). More than words: Linguistic and nonlinguistic politeness in two cultures. *Journal of Personality and Social Psychology, 70,* 996–1011.

Anderson, E. (1999). *Code of the street: Decency, violence, and the moral life of the inner city.* New York: Norton.

Anderson, J. C., & Linden, W. (2006, April). *The influence of culture on cardiovascular response to anger.* Citation poster session presented at the annual meeting of the American Psychosomatic Society, Denver, CO.

Anderson, S. L., Adams, G., & Plaut, V. C. (2008). The cultural grounding of personal relationship: The importance of attractiveness in everyday life. *Journal of Personality and Social Psychology, 95,* 352–368.

Arnett, J. (2008). The neglected 95%: Why American psychology needs to become less American. *American Psychologist, 63,* 602–614.

Asch, S. (1956). Studies of independence and conformity: A minority of one against a unanimous majority. *Psychological Monographs, 70*(9, Whole No. 416).

Ashton, M. C. (2007). Self-reports and stereotypes: A comment on McCrae et al. *European Journal of Personality, 21,* 983–986.

Atran, S., Medin, D. L., & Ross, N. O. (2005). The cultural mind: Environmental decision making and cultural modeling within and across populations. *Psychological Review, 112,* 744–776.

Bachman, J. G., & O'Malley, P. M. (1984). Yea-saying, nay-saying, and going to extremes: Black–white differences in response styles. *Public Opinion Quarterly, 48,* 491–509.

Baguma, P., & Furnham, A. (1993). The Protestant work ethic in Great Britain and Uganda. *Journal of Cross-Cultural Psychology, 24,* 495–507.

Bagozzi, R., Wong, N., & Yi, Y. (1999). The role of culture and gender in the relationship between positive and negative affect. *Cognition and Emotion, 13,* 641–672.

Bailenson, J. N., Shum, M., Atran, S., Medin, D. L., & Coley, J. (2002). A bird's eye view: Biological categorization and reasoning within and across cultures. *Cognition, 84,* 1–53.

Barrett, H. C., & Behne, T. (2005). Children's understanding of death as the cessation of agency: A test using sleep versus death. *Cognition, 96,* 93–108.

Baumeister, R. F. (1987). How the self became a problem: A psychological review of historical research. *Journal of Personality and Social Psychology, 52,* 163–176.

Baumeister, R. F., Tice, D. M., & Hutton, D. G. (1989). Self-presentational motivations and personality differences in self-esteem. *Journal of Personality, 57,* 547–579.

Beja-Pereira, A., Luikart, G., England, P. R., Bradley, D. G., Jann, O. C., Bertorelle, G., Chamberlain, A. T., Nunes, T. P., Metodlev, S., Ferrand, N., & Erhadt, G. (2003). Gene–culture coevolution between cattle milk protein genes and human lactase genes. *Nature Genetics, 35,* 311–313.

Bendix, R. (1977). *Max Weber: An intellectual portrait.* Berkeley: University of California Press.

Benet-Martínez, V., & John, O. P. (1998). *Los cinco grandes* across cultures and ethnic groups: Multitrait multimethod analysis of the Big Five in Spanish and English. *Journal of Personality and Social Psychology, 75,* 729–750.

Benet-Martínez, V., Leu, J., Lee, F., & Morris, M. W. (2002). Negotiating biculturalism: Cultural frame switching in biculturals with oppositional versus compatible cultural identities. *Journal of Cross-Cultural Psychology, 33,* 492–516.

Benet-Martínez, V., & Waller, N. G. (1995). The Big Seven factor model of personality description: Evidence for its cross-cultural generality in a Spanish sample. *Journal of Personality and Social Psychology, 69,* 701–718.

Benet-Martínez, V., & Waller, N. G. (1997). Further evidence for the cross-cultural generality of the Big Seven factor model: Indigenous and imported Spanish personality constructs. *Journal of Personality, 65,* 567–598.

Berlin, B., & Kay, P. (1969). *Basic color terms: Their universality and evolution.* Berkeley and Los Angeles: University of California Press.

Berman, J. J., Murphy-Berman, V., & Singh, P. (1985). Cross-cultural similarities and differences in perceptions of fairness. *Journal of Cross-Cultural Psychology, 16,* 55–67.

Biernat, M., & Manis, M. (1994). Shifting standards and stereotype-based judgments. *Journal of Personality and Social Psychology, 66,* 5–20.

Biswas-Diener, R., & Diener, E. (2002). Making the best of a bad situation: Satisfaction in the slums of Calcutta. *Social Indicators Research, 55,* 329–352.

Bond, M. H. (1979). Dimensions of personality used in perceiving peers: Cross-cultural comparisons of Hong Kong, Japanese, American, and Filipino university students. *International Journal of Psychology, 14,* 47–56.

Bond, M. H., & Cheung, T. (1983). College students' spontaneous self-concept. *Journal of Cross-Cultural Psychology, 14,* 153–171.

Bond, M. H., Nakazato, H., & Shiraishi, D. (1975). Universality and distinctiveness in dimensions of Japanese person perception. *Journal of Cross-Cultural Psychology, 6,* 346–357.

Bond, R., & Smith, P. B. (1996). Culture and conformity: A meta-analysis of studies using Asch's (1952b, 1956) line judgment task. *Psychological Bulletin, 119,* 111–137.

Bond, M. H., & Tornatzky, L. G. (1973). Locus of control in students from Japan and the United States: Dimensions and levels of response. *Psychologia, 16,* 209–213.

Boroditsky, L., & Gaby, A. (2006). East of Tuesday: Consequences of spatial orientation for thinking about time. In R. Sun (Ed.), *Proceedings of the 28th Annual Meeting of the Cognitive Science Society* (p. 2657). Hillsdale, NJ: Lawrence Erlbaum.

Bosson, J. K., Swann, W. B., & Pennebaker, J. W. (2000). Stalking the perfect measure of implicit self-esteem: The blind men and the elephant revisited? *Journal of Personality and Social Psychology, 79,* 631–643.

Boyd, R., & Richerson, P. J. (1996). Why culture is common, but cultural evolution is rare. *Proceedings of the British Academy, 88,* 77–93.

Boyd, R., & Silk, J. B. (2006). *How humans evolved* (4th ed.). New York: Norton.

Briggs, J. L. (1970). *Never in anger: Portrait of an Eskimo family.* Cambridge, MA: Harvard University Press.

Briley, D. A., Morris, M. W., & Simonson, I. (2005). Cultural chameleons: Biculturals, conformity motives, and decision making. *Journal of Consumer Psychology, 15,* 351–362.

Brislin, R. W. (1970). Back-translation for cross-cultural research. *Journal of Cross-Cultural Psychology, 1,* 185–216.

Brosschot, J. F., & Thayer, J. F. (1998). Anger inhibition, cardiovascular recovery, and vagal function: A model of the link between hostility and cardiovascular disease. *Annals of Behavior Medicine, 20,* 326–332.

Bruner, J. (1990). *Acts of meaning.* Cambridge, MA: Harvard University Press.

Burton, R., & Whiting, J. (1961). The absent father and cross-sex identity. *Merrill-Palmer Quarterly, 7,* 85–95.

Buss, D. M. (1989). Sex differences in human mate preferences: Evolutionary hypotheses tested in 37 cultures. *Behavioral and Brain Sciences, 12,* 1–49.

Butler, E. A., Lee, T. L., & Gross, J. J. (2007). Emotion regulation and culture: Are the social consequences of emotion suppression culture-specific? *Emotion, 7,* 30–48.

Camerer, C. (2003). *Behavior game theory: Experiments in strategic interaction.* Princeton, NJ: Princeton University Press.

Campbell, D. T., & Fiske, D. W. (1959). Convergent and discrimination validation by the multi-trait multimethod matrix. *Psychological Bulletin, 56,* 81–105.

Campbell, J. D., Trapnell, P., Heine, S. J., Katz, I. M., Lavallee, L. F., & Lehman, D. R. (1996). Self-concept clarity: Measurement, personality correlates, and cultural boundaries. *Journal of Personality and Social Psychology, 70,* 141–156.

Campos, J. J., Barrett, K. C., Lamb, M. E., Goldsmith, H. H., & Stenberg, C. (1983). Socioemotional development. In M. M. Haith & J. J. Campos (Eds.), *Handbook of child psychology: Infancy and psychobiology* (Vol. 2, pp. 783–915). New York: Wiley.

Caudill, W., & Weinstein, H. (1969). Maternal care and infant behavior in Japan and America. *Psychiatry, 32,* 12–43.

Chambers, J. R., & Windschitl, P. D. (2004). Biases in social comparative judgments: The role of nonmotivated factors in above-average and comparative-optimism effects. *Psychological Bulletin, 130,* 813–838.

Chandra, S. (1973). The effects of group pressure in perception: A cross-cultural conformity study. *International Journal of Psychology, 8,* 37–39.

Chang, H.-C., & Holt, G. R. (1994). A Chinese perspective on face as interrelational concern. In S. Ting-Toomey (Ed.), *The challenge of facework:* *Cross-cultural and interpersonal issues* (pp. 95–132). Albany, NY: State University of New York Press.

Chang, W. C., Chua, W. L., & Toh, Y. (1997). The concept of psychological control in the Asian context. In K. Leung, U. Kim, S. Yamaguchi, & Y. Kashima (Eds.), *Progress in Asian social psychology* (pp. 95–117). Singapore: Wiley.

Chen, C., Lee, S.-Y., & Stevenson, H. W. (1995). Response style and cross-cultural comparisons of rating scales among East Asian and North American students. *Psychological Science, 6,* 170–175.

Cheng, C., Sanchez-Burks, J., & Lee, F. (2008). Connecting the dots within: Creative performance and identity integration. *Psychological Science, 19,* 1178–1184.

Cheung, F. M., Cheung, S. F., Leung, K., Ward, C., & Leong, F. (2003). The English version of the Chinese Personality Assessment Inventory. *Journal of Cross-Cultural Psychology, 34,* 433–452.

Cheung, F. M., Leung, K., Fan, R. M., Song, W., Zhang, J., & Zhang, J. (1996). Development of the Chinese Personality Assessment Inventory. *Journal of Cross-Cultural Psychology, 27,* 181–199.

Chiu, C., Dweck, C. S., Tong, J. U., & Fu, J. H. (1997). Implicit theories and conceptions of morality. *Journal of Personality and Social Psychology, 73,* 923–940.

Chiu, C., Hong, Y., & Dweck, C. S. (1997). Lay dispositionism and implicit theories of personality. *Journal of Personality and Social Psychology, 73,* 19–30.

Choi, I., & Choi, Y. (2002). Culture and self-concept flexibility. *Personality and Social Psychology Bulletin, 28,* 1508–1517.

Choi, I., & Nisbett, R. E. (1998). Situational salience and cultural differences in the correspondence bias and in the actor–observer bias. *Personality and Social Psychology Bulletin, 24,* 949–960.

Choi, I., Nisbett, R. E., & Norenzayan, A. (1999). Causal attribution across cultures: Variation and universality. *Psychological Bulletin, 125,* 47–63.

Choi, S., & Gopnik, A. (1995). Early acquisition of verbs in Korean: A cross-linguistic study. *Journal of Child Language, 22,* 497–529.

Chua, H. F., Boland, J. E., & Nisbett, R. E. (2005). Cultural variation in eye movements during scene perception. *Proceedings of the National Academy of Sciences, 102,* 12629–12633.

Church, A. T., Katigbak, M. S., Del Prado, A. M., Ortiz, F. A., Mastor, K. A., Harumi, Y., et al. (2006). Implicit theories and self-perceptions of traitedness across cultures: Toward integration of cultural and trait psychology perspectives. *Journal of Cross-Cultural Psychology, 37*(6), 694–716.

Church, A. T., Katigbak, M. S., Ortiz, F. A., Del Prado, A. M., Vargas-Flores, J. J., Ibanez-Reyes, J., Reyes, J. A. S., Pe-Pua, R., & Cabrera, H. F. (2005). Investigating implicit trait theories across cultures. *Journal of Cross-Cultural Psychology, 36,* 476–496.

Church, A. T., Katigbak, M. S., & Reyes, J. A. S. (1998). Further exploration of Filipino personality structure using the lexical approach: Do the Big-Five or Big-Seven dimensions emerge? *European Journal of Personality, 12,* 249–269.

Church, A. T., Reyes, J. A. S., Katigbak, M. S., & Grimm, S. D. (1997). Filipino personality structure and the Big Five model: A lexical approach. *Journal of Personality, 65,* 477–528.

Cialdini, R. B., Wosinska, W., & Barrett, D. W. (1999). Compliance with a request in two cultures: The differential influence of social proof and commitment/consistency on collectivists and individualists. *Personality and Social Psychology Bulletin, 25,* 1242–1253.

Cohen, A. B., & Rozin, P. (2001). Religion and the morality of mentality. *Journal of Personality and Social Psychology, 81,* 697–710.

Cohen, A. B., Siegel, J. I., & Rozin, P. (2003). Faith versus practice: Different bases for religiosity judgments by Jews and Protestants. *European Journal of Social Psychology, 33,* 287–295.

Cohen, D. (1996). Law, social policy, and violence: The impact of regional cultures. *Journal of Personality and Social Psychology, 70,* 961–978.

Cohen, D. (2001). Cultural variation: Considerations and implications. *Psychological Bulletin, 127,* 451–471.

Cohen, D., & Gunz, A. (2002). As seen by the other…: Perspectives on the self in the memories and emotional perceptions of Easterners and Westerners. *Psychological Science, 13,* 55–59.

Cohen, D., Hoshino-Browne, E., & Leung, A. (2007). Culture and the structure of personal experience: Insider and outsider phenomenologies of the self and social world. In M. P. Zanna (Ed.), *Advances in experimental social psychology* (Vol. 39). San Diego: Academic Press.

Cohen, D., & Nisbett, R. E. (1994). Self-protection and the culture of honor: Explaining southern homicide. *Personality and Social Psychology Bulletin, 20,* 551–567.

Cohen, D., & Nisbett, R. E. (1997). Field experiments examining the culture of honor: The role of institutions in perpetuating norms about violence. *Personality and Social Psychology Bulletin, 23,* 1188–1199.

Cohen, D., Nisbett, R. E., Bowdle, B. F., & Schwarz, N. (1996). Insult, aggression, and the southern culture of honor: An "experimental ethnography." *Journal of Personality and Social Psychology, 70,* 945–960.

Cohen, D., Vandello, J., Puente, S., & Rantilla, A. (1999). "When you call me that, smile!": How norms for politeness, interaction styles, and aggression work together in southern culture. *Social Psychology Quarterly, 62,* 257–275.

Cohen, S., & Wills, T. A. (1985). Stress, social support, and the buffering hypothesis. *Psychological Bulletin, 98,* 310–357.

Cole, M., Gay, J., & Glick, J. (1968). Some experimental studies of Kpelle quantitative behavior. *Psychonomic Monograph Supplements, 2,* 173–190.

Costa, P. T., Jr., & McCrae, R. R. (1992). *Revised NEO Personality Inventory (NEO-PI-R) and NEO Five-Factor Inventory (NEO-FFI) professional manual.* Odessa, FL: Psychological Assessment Resources.

Cousins, S. D. (1989). Culture and selfhood in Japan and the U.S. *Journal of Personality and Social Psychology, 56,* 124–131.

Crocker, J., & Park, L. E. (2004). The costly pursuit of self-esteem. *Psychological Bulletin, 130,* 392–414.

Daly, M., & Wilson, M. (1988). *Homicide.* New York: Aldine de Gruyter.

Darwin, C. (1872/1965). *The expression of emotions in man and animals.* Chicago: University of Chicago Press.

Deci, E. L., & Ryan, R. M. (2000). The "what" and "why" of goal pursuits: Human needs and the self-determination of behavior. *Psychological Inquiry, 11,* 227–268.

Diener, E., & Diener, M. (1995). Cross-cultural correlates of life satisfaction and self-esteem. *Journal of Personality and Social Psychology, 68,* 653–663.

Diener, E., Diener, M., & Diener, C. (1995). Factors predicting the subjective well-being of nations. *Journal of Personality and Social Psychology, 69,* 851–864.

Diener, E., Oishi, S., & Lucas, R. E. (2003). Personality, culture, and subjective-well-being: Emotional and cognitive evaluations of life. *Annual Review of Psychology, 54,* 403–425.

Diener, E., & Wallbom, M. (1976). Effects of self-awareness on antinormative behavior. *Journal of Research in Personality, 10,* 107–111.

Ducci, L., Arcuri, L. W., Georgis, T., & Sineshaw, T. (1982). Emotion recognition in Ethiopia. *Journal of Cross-Cultural Psychology, 13,* 340–351.

Dunbar, R. I. M. (1993). The co-evolution of neocortical size, group size and language in humans. *Behavioural and Brain Sciences, 16,* 681–735.

Duval, S., & Wicklund, R. (1972). *A theory of objective self-awareness.* New York: Academic Press.

Dweck, C. S., Hong, Y., & Chiu, C. (1993). Implicit theories: Individual differences in the likelihood and meaning of dispositional inference. *Personality and Social Psychology Bulletin, 19,* 644–656.

Dweck, C. S., & Leggett, E. L. (1988). A social-cognitive approach to motivation and personality. *Psychological Review, 95,* 256–273.

Earley, P. C. (1993). East meets West meets Mideast: Further explorations of collectivistic and individualistic work groups. *Academy of Management Journal, 36,* 319–348.

Ekman, P. (1973). Universal facial expressions in emotion. *Studia Psychologica, 15,* 140–147.

Ekman, P., & Friesen, W. V. (1969). The repertoire of nonverbal behavior: Categories, origins, usage, and coding. *Semiotica, 1,* 49–98.

Ekman, P., & Friesen, W. V. (1971). Constants across cultures in the face and emotion. *Journal of Personality and Social Psychology, 17,* 124–129.

Ekman, P., Sorenson, E. R., & Friesen, W. (1969). Pancultural elements in facial displays of emotion. *Science, 164,* 86–88.

Elfenbein, H. A., & Ambady, N. (2002). On the universality and cultural specificity of emotion recognition: A meta-analysis. *Psychological Bulletin, 128,* 203–235.

Elliot, A. J., Chirkov, V. I., Kim, Y., & Sheldon, K. M. (2001). A cross-cultural analysis of avoidance (relative to approach) personal goals. *Psychological Science, 12,* 505–510.

English, T., & Chen, S. (2007). Culture and self-concept stability: Consistency across and within contexts among Asian-American and European-Americans. *Journal of Personality and Social Psychology, 93,* 478–490.

Everett, D. L. (2005). Cultural constraints on grammar and cognition in Piraha. *Current Anthropology, 46,* 621–646.

Falk, C. F., Dunn, E. W., & Norenzayan, A. (2009). *Cultural variation in the importance of expected emotions for decision-making.* Unpublished manuscript. University of British Columbia.

Falk, C. F., Heine, S. J., Yuki, M., & Takemura, K. (2009). Why do Westerners self-enhance more than East Asians? *European Journal of Personality, 23,* 183–209.

Fehr, E., & Gächter, S. (1998). Reciprocity and economics: The economic implications of *Homo reciprocans. European Economic Review, 42,* 845–859.

Fehr, E., & Gächter, S. (2002). Altruistic punishment in humans. *Nature, 415,* 137–140.

Fejfar, M. C., & Hoyle, R. H. (2000). Effect of private self-awareness on negative affect and self-referent attribution: A quantitative review. *Personality and Social Psychology Review, 4,* 132–142.

Festinger, L. (1954). A theory of social comparison processes. *Human Relations, 7,* 117–140.

Festinger, L. (1957). *A theory of cognitive dissonance.* Stanford, CA: Stanford University Press.

Fischer, D. H. (1989). *Albion's seed: Four British folkways in America.* New York: Oxford University Press.

Fiske, A. P. (1992). The four elementary forms of sociality: Framework for a unified theory of social relations. *Psychological Review, 99,* 689–723.

Frager, R. (1970). Conformity and anti-conformity in Japan. *Journal of Personality and Social Psychology, 15,* 203–210.

Fryberg, S. A., & Markus, H. R. (2003). On being American Indian: Current and possible selves. *Self and Identity, 2,* 325–344.

Furnham, A. (1990). *The Protestant work ethic: The psychology of work-related beliefs and behaviors.* London: Routledge.

Furnham, A., Bond, M. H., & Heaven, P. (1993). A comparison of Protestant work ethic beliefs in thirteen nations. *Journal of Social Psychology, 133,* 185–197.

Furnham, A., & Muhiudeen, C. (1984). The Protestant work ethic in Britain and Malaysia. *Journal of Social Psychology, 122,* 157–161.

Gabrenya, W. K., Wang, Y., & Latané, B. (1985). Social loafing on an optimizing task: Cross-cultural differences among Chinese and Americans. *Journal of Cross-Cultural Psychology, 16,* 223–242.

Gächter, S., Herrmann, B., & Thoni, C. (2005). Cross-cultural differences in norm enforcement. *Behavioral and Brain Sciences, 28,* 822–823.

Galaty, J. G., & Bonte, P. (Eds.). (1991). *Herders, warriors, and traders: Pastoralism in Africa.* Boulder, CO: Westview.

Galef, B. G., Jr. (1988). Imitation in animals: History, definition, and interpretation of data from the psychological laboratory. In T. R. Zentall & B. G. Galef Jr. (Eds.), *Social learning: Psychological and biological perspectives* (pp. 3–29). Hillsdale, NJ: Lawrence Erlbaum.

Gardner, W. L., Gabriel, S., & Dean, K. K. (2004). The individual as "melting pot": The flexibility of bicultural self-construals. *Cahiers de Psychologie Cognitive, 22,* 181–201.

Gastil, R. D. (1989). Violence, crime, and punishment. In C. R. Wilson & W. Ferris (Eds.) *Encyclopedia of southern culture.* Chapel Hill: University of North Carolina Press.

Geertz, C. (1973). *The interpretation of cultures.* New York: Basic Books.

Geertz, C. (1975). On the nature of anthropological understanding. *American Scientist, 63,* 4–53.

Gelman, R., & Gallistel, C. R. (2004). Language and the origin of number concepts. *Science, 306,* 441–443.

Gentner, D. (1982). Why nouns are learned before verbs: Linguistic relativity versus natural partitioning. In S. Kuczaj (Ed.), *Language development: Language, cognition and culture.* Hillsdale, NJ: Erlbaum.

Gilbert, D. T., & Malone, P. S. (1995). The correspondence bias. *Psychological Bulletin, 117,* 21–38.

Giorgi, L., & Marsh, C. (1990). The Protestant work ethic as a cultural phenomenon. *European Journal of Social Psychology, 20,* 499–517.

Gleitman, L. (1990). The structural sources of verb meaning. *Language Acquisition: A Journal of Developmental Linguistics, 1,* 3–55.

Goh, J. H. O., Chee, M. W., Tan, J. C., Venkatraman, V., Hebrank, A., Leshikar, E. D., et al. (2007). Age and culture modulate object processing and object–scene binding in the ventral visual area. *Cognitive, Affective, & Behavioral Neuroscience, 7,* 44–52.

Gordon, P. (2004). Numerical cognition without words: Evidence from Amazonia. *Science, 306,* 496–499.

Greenfield, P. M. (1997). Culture as process: Empirical methods for cultural psychology. In J. W. Berry, Y. H. Poortinga, & J. Pandey (Eds.), *Handbook of cross-cultural psychology* (Vol. 1, pp. 301–346). Boston: Allyn & Bacon.

Greenwald, A. G. (1980). The totalitarian ego: Fabrication and revision of personal history. *American Psychologist, 35,* 603–618.

Greenwald, A. G., & Farnham, S. D. (2000). Using the Implicit Association Test to measure self-esteem and self-concept, *Journal of Personality and Social Psychology, 79,* 1022–1038.

Grimm, S. D., & Church, A. T. (1999). A cross-cultural study of response biases in personality measures. *Journal of Research in Personality, 33,* 415–441.

Grossmann, K., Grossmann, K. E., Spangler, S., Suess, G., & Unzner, L. (1985). Maternal sensitivity and newborn attachment orientation responses as related to quality of attachment in northern Germany. In I. Bretherton & E. Waters (Eds.), *Growing points of attachment theory. Monographs of the Society of Research in Child Development, 50*(1–2, Serial No. 209), 233–256.

Gutchess, A. H., Welsh, R. C., Boduroglu, A., & Park, D. C. (2006). Cultural differences in neural function associated with object processing. *Cognitive, Affective, & Behavioral Neuroscience, 6,* 102–109.

Guthrie, G. M., & Bennett, A. B. (1971). Cultural differences in implicit personality theory. *International Journal of Psychology, 6,* 305–312.

Haidt, J., & Graham, J. (2007). When morality opposes justice: Conservatives have moral intuitions that liberals may not recognize. *Social Justice Research, 20,* 98–116.

Haidt, J., & Keltner, D. (1999). Culture and facial expression: Open-ended methods find more expressions and a gradient of recognition. *Cognition and Emotion, 13,* 225–266.

Haidt, J., Koller, S. H., & Dias, M. G. (1993). Affect, culture, and morality, or is it wrong to eat your dog? *Journal of Personality and Social Psychology, 65,* 613–628.

Hall, E. T. (1976). *Beyond culture.* New York: Anchor Books.

Hamamura, T., & Heine, S. J. (2009). *Enhanced motivation under regulatory fit: A cross-cultural analysis.* Unpublished manuscript. Chinese University of Hong Kong.

Hamamura, T., Heine, S. J., & Paulhus, D. L. (2008). Cultural differences in response styles: The role of dialectical thinking. *Personality and Individual Differences, 44,* 932–942.

Hamamura, T., Heine, S. J., & Takemoto, T. (2007). Why the better-than-average effect is a worse-than-average measure of self-enhancement: An investigation of conflicting findings from studies of East Asian self-evaluations. *Motivation and Emotion, 31,* 247–259.

Hamamura, T., Meijer, Z., Heine, S. J., Kamaya, K., & Hori, I. (2009). Approach-avoidance motivations and information processing: A cross-cultural analysis. *Personality and Social Psychology Bulletin, 35,* 454–462.

Hampden-Turner, C., & Trompenaars, A. (1993). *The seven cultures of capitalism: Value systems for creating wealth in the United States, Japan, Germany, France, Britain, Sweden, and the Netherlands.* New York: Doubleday.

Haun, D. B. M., Rapold, C. J., Call, J., Janzen, G., & Levinson, S. C. (2006). Cognitive cladistics and cultural override in hominid spatial cognition. *Proceedings of the National Academy of Sciences, 103,* 17568–17573.

Hedden, T., Ketay, S., Aron, A., Markus, H. R., & Gabrieli, J. D. E. (2008). Cultural influences on neural substrates of attentional control. *Psychological Science, 19,* 12–17.

Heider, F. (1958). *The psychology of interpersonal relations.* New York: John Wiley & Sons.

Heine, S. J. (2003a). An exploration of cultural variation in self-enhancing and self-improving motivations. In V. Murphy-Berman & J. J. Berman (Eds.), *Nebraska Symposium on Motivation: Cross-cultural differences in perspectives on the self* (Vol. 49, pp. 101–128). Lincoln: University of Nebraska Press.

Heine, S. J. (2003b). Self-enhancement in Japan? A reply to Brown and Kobayashi. *Asian Journal of Social Psychology, 6,* 75–84.

Heine, S. J. (2005). Constructing good selves in Japan and North America. In R. M. Sorrentino, D. Cohen, J. M. Olson, & M. P. Zanna (Eds.), *Culture and social behavior: The Tenth Ontario Symposium* (pp. 95–116). Hillsdale, NJ: Lawrence Erlbaum.

Heine, S. J. (2008). *Cultural psychology.* New York: W. W. Norton.

Heine, S. J., Buchtel, E. E., & Norenzayan, A. (2008). What do cross-national comparisons of personality traits tell us? The case of conscientiousness. *Psychological Science, 19,* 309–313.

Heine, S. J., Foster, J. A., & Spina, R. (in press). Do birds of a feather universally flock together? Cultural variation in the similarity-attraction effect. *Asian Journal of Social Psychology.*

Heine, S. J., & Hamamura, T. (2007). In search of East Asian self-enhancement. *Personality and Social Psychology Review, 11,* 4–27.

Heine, S. J., Kitayama, S., & Hamamura, T. (2007a). The inclusion of additional studies yields different conclusions: A reply to Sedikides, Gaertner, & Vevea (2005), *JPSP. Asian Journal of Social Psychology, 10,* 49–58.

Heine, S. J., Kitayama, S., & Hamamura, T. (2007b). Which studies test the question of pancultural self-enhancement? A reply to Sedikides,

Gaertner, & Vevea, 2007. *Asian Journal of Social Psychology, 10,* 198–200.

Heine, S. J., Kitayama, S., Lehman, D. R., Takata, T., Ide, E., Leung, C., & Matsumoto, H. (2001). Divergent consequences of success and failure in Japan and North America: An investigation of self-improving motivations and malleable selves. *Journal of Personality and Social Psychology, 81,* 599–615.

Heine, S. J., & Lehman, D. R. (1997a). The cultural construction of self-enhancement: An examination of group-serving biases. *Journal of Personality and Social Psychology, 72,* 1268–1283.

Heine, S. J., & Lehman, D. R. (1997b). Culture, dissonance, and self-affirmation. *Personality and Social Psychology Bulletin, 23,* 389–400.

Heine, S. J., Lehman, D. R., Markus, H. R., & Kitayama, S. (1999). Is there a universal need for positive self-regard? *Psychological Review, 106,* 766–794.

Heine, S. J., Lehman, D. R., Peng, K., & Greenholtz, J. (2002). What's wrong with cross-cultural comparisons of subjective Likert scales? The reference-group problem. *Journal of Personality and Social Psychology, 82,* 903–918.

Heine, S. J., & Norenzayan, A. (2006). Towards a psychological science for a cultural species. *Perspectives on Psychological Science, 1,* 251–269.

Heine, S. J., Proulx, T., & Vohs, K. D. (2006). Meaning maintenance model: On the coherence of social motivations. *Personality and Social Psychology Review, 10,* 88–110.

Heine, S. J., & Raineri, A. (2009). Self-improving motivations and culture: The case of Chileans. *Journal of Cross-Cultural Psychology, 40,* 158–163.

Heine, S. J., & Renshaw, K. (2002). Interjudge agreement, self-enhancement, and liking: Cross-cultural divergences. *Personality and Social Psychology Bulletin, 28,* 578–587.

Heine, S. J., Takata, T., & Lehman, D. R. (2000). Beyond self-presentation: Evidence for self-criticism among Japanese. *Personality and Social Psychology Bulletin, 26,* 71–78.

Heine, S. J., Takemoto, T., Moskalenko, S., Lasaleta, J., & Henrich, J. (2008). Mirrors in the head: Cultural variation in objective self-awareness. *Personality and Social Psychology Bulletin, 34,* 879–887.

Henderson, V., & Dweck, C. S. (1990). Motivation and achievement. In S. S. Feldman & G. R. Elliott (Eds.), *At the threshold: The developing adolescent* (pp. 308–329). Cambridge, MA: Harvard University Press.

Henrich, J. (2004). Demography and cultural evolution: Why adaptive cultural processes produced maladaptive losses in Tasmania. *American Antiquity, 69,* 197–214.

Henrich, J., Boyd, R., Bowles, S., Camerer, C., Fehr, E., & Gintis, H. (Eds.). (2004). *Foundations of human sociality: Economic experiments and ethnographic evidence from fifteen small-scale societies.* Oxford: Oxford University Press.

Henrich, J., Boyd, R., Bowles, S., Camerer, C., Fehr, E., Gintis, H., et al. (2005). "Economic man" in cross-cultural perspective: Behavioral experiments in 15 small-scale societies. *Behavioral & Brain Sciences, 28,* 795–855.

Henrich, J., Heine, S. J., & Norenzayan, A. (in press). The weirdest people in the world? *Behavioral and Brain Sciences.*

Henrich, J., McElreath, R., Barr, A., Ensminger, J., Barrett, C., Bolyanatz, A., et al. (2006). Costly punishment across human societies. *Science, 312,* 1767–1770.

Herrmann, B., Thoni, C., & Gächter, S. (2007). Anti-social punishment across societies. *Science, 319,* 1362–1367.

Herrmann, E., Call, J., Hernandez-Lloreda, M. V., Hare, B., & Tomasello, M. (2007). Humans have evolved specialized skills of social cognition: The cultural intelligence hypothesis. *Science, 317,* 1360–1366.

Heyman, G. D., & Dweck, C. S. (1998). Children's thinking about traits: Implications for judgments of the self and others. *Child Development, 69,* 391–403.

Higgins, E. T. (2008). Culture and personality: Variability across universal motives as the missing link. *Social and Personality Psychology Compass, 2,* 608–634.

Hiniker, P. J. (1969). Chinese reactions to forced compliance: Dissonance reduction or national character. *Journal of Social Psychology, 77,* 157–176.

Hofmann, W., Gawronski, B., Gschwendner, T., Le, H., & Schmitt, M. (2005). A meta-analysis on the correlation between the implicit association test and explicit self-report measures. *Personality and Social Psychology Bulletin, 31,* 1369–1385.

Hofstede, G. (1980). *Culture's consequences: International differences in work-related values.* Beverly Hills, CA: Sage.

Holloway, S. D. (1988). Concepts of ability and effort in Japan and the United States. *Review of Educational Research, 58,* 327–345.

Hong, Y., Chiu, C., Dweck, C. S., Lin, D. M., & Wan, W. (1999). Implicit theories, attributions, and coping: A meaning system approach. *Journal of Personality and Social Psychology, 77,* 588–599.

Hong, Y., Morris, M. W., Chiu, C., & Benet-Martínez, V. (2000). Multicultural minds: A dynamic constructivist approach to culture and cognition. *American Psychologist, 55,* 705–720.

Hoshino-Browne, E., Zanna, A. S., Spencer, S. J., Zanna, M. P., Kitayama, S., & Lackenbauer, S. (2005). On the cultural guises of cognitive dissonance: The case of Easterners and Westerners. *Journal of Personality and Social Psychology, 89,* 294–310.

Hui, C. H., & Triandis, H. C. (1989). Effects of culture and response format on extreme response style. *Journal of Cross-Cultural Psychology, 20,* 296–309.

Huttenlocher, J., & Smiley, P. (1987). Early word meaning: The case of object names. *Cognitive Psychology, 19,* 63–89.

Inglehart, R., & Klingemann, H. (2000). Genes, culture, democracy, and happiness. In E. Diener & E. Suh (Eds.), *Culture and subjective well-being* (pp. 165–184). Cambridge, MA: MIT Press.

Ishii, K., Reyes, J. A., & Kitayama, S. (2003). Spontaneous attention to word content versus emotional tone: Differences among three cultures. *Psychological Science, 14,* 39–46.

Isonio, S. A., & Garza, R. T. (1987). Protestant work ethic endorsement among Anglo Americans, Chicanos, and Mexicans: A comparison of factor structures. *Hispanic Journal of Behavioral Sciences, 9,* 413–425.

Iyengar, S. S., & Lepper, M. R. (1999). Rethinking the value of choice: A cultural perspective on intrinsic motivation. *Journal of Personality and Social Psychology, 76,* 349–366.

Iyengar, S. S., Lepper, M. R., & Ross, L. (1999). Independence from whom? Interdependence with whom? Cultural perspectives on ingroups versus outgroups. In D. Miller & D. Prentice (Eds.), *Cultural divides: Understanding and overcoming group conflict* (pp. 273–301). New York: Sage.

Izard, C. E. (1994). Innate and universal facial expressions: Evidence from developmental and cross-cultural research. *Psychological Bulletin, 115,* 288–299.

Jablonski, N. G., & Chaplin, G. (2000). The evolution of human skin coloration. *Journal of Human Evolution, 39,* 57–106.

Jackson, E. F., Fox, W. S., & Crockett, H. J. (1970). Religion and occupational achievement. *American Sociological Review, 35,* 48–63.

Ji, L. J. (2008). The leopard cannot change his spots, or can he? Culture and the development of lay theories of change. *Personality and Social Psychology Bulletin, 34,* 613–622.

Ji, L. J., Nisbett, R. E., & Su, Y. (2001). Culture, change, and prediction. *Psychological Science, 12,* 450–456.

Ji, L. J., Peng, K., & Nisbett, R. E. (2000). Culture, control, and perception of relationships in the environment. *Journal of Personality and Social Psychology, 78,* 943–955.

Ji, L. J., Zhang, Z., & Nisbett, R. E. (2004). Is it culture or is it language? Examination of language effects in cross-cultural research on categorization. *Journal of Personality and Social Psychology, 87,* 57–65.

Johnson, J., & Newport, E. L. (1989). Critical period effects in second language learning: The influence of maturational state on the acquisition of English as a second language. *Cognitive Psychology, 21,* 60–99.

Jones, E. E., & Harris, V. A. (1967). The attribution of attitudes. *Journal of Experimental Social Psychology, 3,* 1–24.

Jourard, S. M. (1965). *Personal adjustment: An approach through the study of healthy personality.* New York: Macmillan.

Kacperczyk, A., & Sanchez-Burks, J., & Baker, W. (2009). Social isolation in the workplace: A cross-cultural and longitudinal analysis. Manuscript submitted for publication.

Kanagawa, C., Cross, S. E., & Markus, H. R. (2001). "Who am I?": The cultural psychology of the conceptual self. *Personality and Social Psychology Bulletin, 27,* 90–103.

Kashima, Y., Siegal, M., Tanaka, K., & Isaka, H. (1988). Universalism in lay conceptions of distributive justice: A cross-cultural examination. *International Journal of Psychology, 23,* 51–64.

Kashima, Y., Siegal, M., Tanaka, K., & Kashima, E. S. (1992). Do people believe behaviors are consistent with attitudes? Towards a cultural psychology of attribution processes. *British Journal of Social Psychology, 31,* 111–124.

Kay, P., & Regier, T. (2007). Color naming universals: The case of Berinmo. *Cognition, 102,* 289–298.

Keltner, D. (1995). Signs of appeasement. Evidence for the distinct displays of embarrassment, amusement, and shame. *Journal of Personality and Social Psychology, 68,* 441–454.

Kemmelmeier, M., & Cheng, B. Y. (2004). Language and self-construal priming: A replication and extension in a Hong Kong sample. *Journal of Cross-Cultural Psychology, 3,* 705–712.

Kim, H. S. (2002). We talk, therefore we think? A cultural analysis of the effect of talking on thinking. *Journal of Personality and Social Psychology, 83,* 828–842.

Kim, H. S. (2008). Culture and the cognitive and neuroendocrine responses to speech. *Journal of Personality and Social Psychology, 94,* 32–47.

Kim, H. S., & Markus, H. R. (1999). Deviance or uniqueness, harmony or conformity? A cultural analysis. *Journal of Personality and Social Psychology, 77,* 785–800.

Kim, H. S., & Sherman, D. K. (2007). "Express yourself": Culture and the effect of self-expression on choice. *Journal of Personality and Social Psychology, 92,* 1–11.

Kim, H. S., Sherman, D. K., Ko, D., & Taylor, S. E. (2006). Pursuit of happiness and pursuit of harmony: Culture, relationships, and social support seeking. *Personality and Social Psychology Bulletin, 32,* 1595–1607.

Kim, H. S., Sherman, D. K., & Taylor, S. E. (2008). Culture and social support. *American Psychologist, 63,* 518–526.

Kitayama, S. (2002). Culture and basic psychological processes—Toward a system view of culture: Comment on Oyserman et al. (2002). *Psychological Bulletin, 128,* 89–96.

Kitayama, S., Duffy, S., Kawamura, T., & Larsen, J. T. (2003). Perceiving an object and its context in different cultures: A cultural look at New Look. *Psychological Science, 14,* 201–206.

Kitayama, S., & Ishii, K. (2002). Word and voice: Spontaneous attention to emotional utterances in two languages. *Cognition and Emotion, 16,* 29–59.

Kitayama, S., Markus, H. R., & Kurokawa, M. (2000). Culture, emotion, and well-being: Good feelings in Japan and the United States. *Cognition and Emotion, 14,* 93–124.

Kitayama, S., Markus, H. R., Matsumoto, H., & Norasakkunkit, V. (1997). Individual and collective processes in the construction of the self: Self-enhancement in the United States and self-criticism in Japan. *Journal of Personality and Social Psychology, 72,* 1245–1267.

Kitayama, S., Mesquita, B., & Karasawa, M. (2006). Cultural affordances and emotional experience: Socially engaging and disengaging emotions in Japan and the United States. *Journal of Personality and Social Psychology, 91,* 890–903.

Kitayama, S., Park, H., Sevincer, A. T., Karasawa, M., & Uskul, A. K. (2009). A cultural task analysis of implicit independence: Comparing North America, Western Europe, and East Asia. *Journal of Personality and Social Psychology, 97,* 236–255.

Kitayama, S., Snibbe, A. C., Markus, H. R., & Suzuki, T. (2004). Is there any "free" choice? Self and dissonance in two cultures. *Psychological Science, 15,* 527–533.

Kitayama, S., & Uchida, Y. (2003). Explicit self-criticism and implicit self-regard: Evaluating self and friend in two cultures. *Journal of Experimental Social Psychology, 39,* 476–482.

Klar, Y., & Giladi, E. E. (1997). No one in my group can be below the group's average: A robust positivity bias in favor of anonymous peers. *Journal of Personality and Social Psychology, 73,* 885–901.

Knight, N., & Nisbett, R. E. (2007). Culture, class and cognition: Evidence from Italy. *Journal of Cognition and Culture, 7,* 283–291.

Knowles, E. D., Morris, M. W., Chiu, C., & Hong, Y. (2001). Culture and the process of person perception: Evidence for automaticity among East Asians in correcting for situational influences on behavior. *Personality and Social Psychology Bulletin, 27,* 1344–1356.

Kohlberg, L. (1971). From is to ought: How to commit the naturalistic fallacy and get away with it in the study of moral development. In L. Mischel (Ed.), *Cognitive development and epistemology* (pp. 151–284). New York: Academic Press.

Koo, M., & Choi, I. (2005). Becoming a holistic thinker: Training effect of oriental medicine on reasoning. *Personality and Social Psychology Bulletin, 31,* 1264–1272.

Krizan, X., & Suls, J. (2008). Losing sight of oneself in the above-average effect: When egocentrism, focalism, and group diffuseness collide. *Journal of Experimental Social Psychology, 44,* 929–942.

Kuhn, M. H., & McPartland, T. (1954). An empirical investigation of self-attitudes. *American Sociological Review, 19,* 68–76.

Kühnen, U., Hannover, B., & Schubert, B. (2001). The semantic–procedural interface model of the self: The role of self-knowledge for context-dependent versus context-independent modes of thinking. *Journal of Personality and Social Psychology, 80,* 397–409.

Kurman, J. (2003). Why is self-enhancement low in certain collectivist cultures? An investigation of two competing explanations. *Journal of Cross-Cultural Psychology, 34,* 496–510.

Lachlan, R. F., Crooks, L., & Laland, K. N. (1998). Who follows whom? Shoaling preferences and social learning of foraging information in guppies. *Animal Behavior, 56,* 181–190.

Landes, D. S. (1999). *The wealth and poverty of nations.* New York: Norton.

Lavin, T. A., Hall, D. G., & Waxman, S. R. (2006). East and West: A role for culture in the acquisition of nouns and verbs. In K. Hirsh-Pasek & R. M. Golinkoff (Eds.), *Action meets word: How children learn verbs* (pp. 525–543). New York: Oxford University Press.

Lee, A. Y., Aaker, J. L., & Gardner, W. L. (2000). The pleasures and pains of distinct self-construals: The role of interdependence in regulatory focus. *Journal of Personality and Social Psychology, 78,* 1122–1134.

Lee, G. R., & Stone, L. H. (1980). Mate-selection systems and criteria: Variation according to family structure. *Journal of Marriage and the Family, 42,* 319–326.

Lefebvre, L., & Giraldeau, L. A. (1994). Cultural transmission in pigeons is affected by the number of tutors and bystanders present. *Animal Behaviour, 47,* 331–337.

Leung, A. K., & Cohen, D. (2007). The soft embodiment of culture: Camera angles and motion through time and space. *Psychological Science, 18,* 824–830.

Leung, A. K., Maddux, W. W., Galinsky, A. D., & Chiu, C. (2008). Multicultural experience enhances creativity: The when and how. *American Psychologist, 63,* 169–181.

Leung, K., Au, Y., Fernandez-Dols, J. M., & Iwawaki, S. (1992). Preference for methods of conflict processing in two collectivist cultures. *International Journal of Psychology, 27,* 195–209.

Leung, K., & Bond, M. H. (2004). Social axioms: A model for social beliefs in multicultural perspective. In M. Zanna (Ed.), *Advances in Experimental Social Psychology, 36,* 119–197.

Leung, K., Bond, M. H., Carment, D. W., Krishnan, L., & Liebrand, W. B. G. (1990). Effects of cultural femininity on preference for methods of conflict processing: A cross-cultural study. *Journal of Experimental Social Psychology, 26,* 373–388.

Levenson, R. W., Ekman, P., Heider, K., & Friesen, W. V. (1992). Emotion and autonomic nervous system activity in the Minangkabau of West Sumatra. *Journal of Personality and Social Psychology, 62,* 972–988.

Levinson, S. C. (1997). Language and cognition: The cognitive consequences of spatial description in Guugu Yimithirr. *Journal of Linguistic Anthropology, 7,* 98–131.

Levinson, S. C. (2003). *Space in language and cognition.* Cambridge, England: Cambridge University Press.

Lieberman, D., Tooby, J., & Cosmides, L. (2007). The architecture of human kin detection. *Nature, 445,* 727–731.

Lieberman, M. D., Jarcho, J. M., & Obayashi, J. (2005). Attributional inference across cultures: Similar automatic attributions and different controlled corrections. *Personality and Social Psychology Bulletin, 31,* 889–901.

Lockhart, K. L., Nakashima, N., Inagaki, K., & Keil, F. C. (2008). From ugly duckling to swan? Japanese and American beliefs about the stability and origins of traits. *Cognitive Development, 23,* 155–179.

Lockwood, P., Marshall, T. C., & Sadler, P. (2005). Promoting success or preventing failure: Cultural differences in motivation by positive and negative role models. *Personality and Social Psychology Bulletin, 31,* 379–392.

Lord, C., Ross, L., & Lepper, M. (1979). Biased assimilation and attitude polarization: The effects of prior theories on subsequently considered evidence. *Journal of Personality and Social Psychology, 37,* 2098–2109.

Lucy, J. A., & Shweder, R. A. (1979). Whorf and his critics: Linguistic and nonlinguistic influences on color memory. *American Anthropologist, 81,* 581–605.

Luria, A. R. (1928). The problem of the cultural development of the child. *Journal of Genetic Psychology, 35,* 493–506.

Lutz, C. (1988). *Unnatural emotions.* Chicago: University of Chicago Press.

Ma, V., & Schoeneman, T. J. (1997). Individualism versus collectivism: A comparison of Kenyan and American self-concepts. *Basic and Applied Social Psychology, 19,* 261–273.

Maass, A., Karasawa, M., Politi, F., & Suga, S. (2005). Do verbs and adjectives play different roles in different cultures? A cross-linguistic analysis of person representation. *Journal of Personality and Social Psychology, 90,* 734–750.

Maddux, W. W., & Galinsky, A. D. (2009). Cultural barriers and mental borders: Living in and adapting to foreign cultures facilitates creativity. *Journal of Personality and Social Psychology, 96,* 1047–1061.

Maddux, W. W., & Yuki, M. (2006). The "ripple effect": Cultural differences in perceptions of the consequences of events. *Personality and Social Psychology Bulletin, 32,* 669–683.

Mandel, N. (2003). Shifting selves and decision making: The effects of self construal priming on consumer risk taking. *Journal of Consumer Research, 30,* 30–40.

Markus, H. R., & Kitayama, S. (1991). Culture and the self: Implications for cognition, emotion, and motivation. *Psychological Review, 98,* 224–253.

Markus, H. R., & Kitayama, S. (1998). The cultural psychology of personality. *Journal of Cross-Cultural Psychology, 29,* 63–87.

Markus, H. R., & Kunda, Z. (1986). Stability and malleability of the self-concept. *Journal of Personality and Social Psychology, 51,* 858–866.

Marsh, A. A., Elfenbein, H. A., & Ambady, N. (2003). Nonverbal "accents": Cultural differences in facial expressions of emotion. *Psychological Science, 14,* 373–376.

Marsh, A. A., Elfenbein, H. A., & Ambady, N. (2007). Separated by a common language: Nonverbal accents and cultural stereotypes about Americans and Australians. *Journal of Cross-Cultural Psychology, 38,* 284–301.

Maslow, A. H. (1954). *Motivation and personality.* New York: Harper & Brothers.

Masuda, T., Akase, M., Radford, M. H. B., & Wang, H. (2008). Effect of contextual factors on patterns of eye-movement: Comparing sensitivity to background information between Japanese and Westerners. *Japanese Journal of Psychology, 79,* 35–43.

Masuda, T., Ellsworth, P. C., Mesquita, B., Leu, J., Tanida, S., & van de Veerdonk, E. (2008). Placing the face in context: Cultural differences in the perception of facial emotion. *Journal of Personality and Social Psychology, 94,* 365–381.

Masuda, T., Gonzalez, R., Kwan, L., & Nisbett, R. E. (2008). Culture and aesthetic preference: Comparing the attention to context of East Asians and European Americans. *Personality and Social Psychology Bulletin, 34,* 1260–1275.

Masuda, T., & Nisbett, R. E. (2001). Attending holistically vs. analytically: Comparing the context sensitivity of Japanese and Americans. *Journal of Personality and Social Psychology, 81,* 922–934.

Matsumoto, D., Kudoh, T., Scherer, K., & Wallbott, H. (1988). Antecedents of and reactions to emotions in the United States and Japan. *Journal of Cross-Cultural Psychology, 19,* 267–286.

May, R. M. (1997). The scientific wealth of nations. *Science, 275,* 793–796.

McCauley, R. N., & Henrich, J. (2006). Susceptibility to the Muller-Lyer Illusion, theory-neutral observation, and the diachronic penetrability of the visual input system. *Philosophical Psychology, 19,* 1–23.

McClelland, D. (1961). *The achieving society.* Princeton, NJ: Van Nostrand.

McCrae, R. R. (2002). NEO-PI-R data from 36 cultures: Further intercultural comparisons. In R. R. McCrae & J. Allik (Eds.), *The five-factor model of personality across cultures* (pp. 105–126). New York: Kluwer.

McCrae. R. R., & Costa, P. T., Jr. (1987). Validation of the five-factor model of personality across instruments and observers. *Journal of Personality and Social Psychology, 52,* 82–90.

McCrae, R. R., Terracciano, A., and 78 members of the Personality Profiles of Cultures Project. (2005). Universal features of personality traits from the observer's perspective: Data from 50 cultures. *Journal of Personality and Social Psychology, 88,* 547–561.

McGrath, R. E., & Goldberg, L. R. (2006). How to measure national stereotypes? *Science, 311,* 776–777.

Medin, D. L., & Atran. S. (2004). The native mind: Biological categorization, reasoning and decision making in development and across cultures. *Psychological Review, 111,* 960–983.

Menon, T., Morris, M. W., Chiu, C., & Hong, Y. (1999). Culture and the construal of agency: Attribution to individual versus group dispositions. *Journal of Personality and Social Psychology, 76,* 701–717.

Mesquita, B. (2001). Emotions in collectivist and individualist contexts. *Journal of Personality and Social Psychology, 80,* 68–74.

Mesquita, B., & Karasawa, M. (2002). Different emotional lives. *Cognition and Emotion, 17,* 127–141.

Mezulis, A. H., Abramson, L. Y., Hyde, J. S., & Hankin, B. L. (2004). Is there a universal positive bias in attributions? A meta-analytic review of individual, developmental, and cultural differences in the self-serving attributional bias. *Psychological Bulletin, 130,* 711–747.

Miller, J. G. (1984). Culture and the development of everyday social explanation. *Journal of Personality and Social Psychology, 46,* 961–978.

Miller, J. G., & Bersoff, D. M. (1992). Culture and moral judgment: How are conflicts between justice and interpersonal responsibilities resolved? *Journal of Personality and Social Psychology, 62,* 541–554.

Miller, J. G., Bersoff, D. M., & Harwood, R. L. (1990). Perceptions of social responsibilities in India and the United States: Moral imperatives or personal decisions? *Journal of Personality and Social Psychology, 58,* 33–47.

Minoura, Y. (1992). A sensitive period for the incorporation of a cultural meaning system: A study of Japanese children growing up in the United States. *Ethos, 20,* 304–339.

Mischel, W., Shoda, Y., & Mendoza-Denton, R. (2002). Situation-behavior profiles as a locus of consistency in personality. *Current Directions in Psychological Science, 11,* 50–54.

Miyake, K. (1993). Temperament, mother-infant interaction, and early development. *The Japanese Journal of Research on Emotions, 1,* 48–55.

Miyamoto, Y., & Kitayama, S. (2002). Cultural variation in correspondence bias: The critical role of attitude diagnosticity of socially constrained behavior. *Journal of Personality and Social Psychology, 83,* 1239–1248.

Miyamoto, Y., & Schwarz, N. (2006). When conveying a message may hurt the relationship: Cultural differences in the difficulty of using an answering machine. *Journal of Experimental Social Psychology, 42,* 540–547.

Montag, L., & Levin, J. (1994). The five-factor personality model in applied settings. *European Journal of Personality, 8,* 1–11.

Morling, B., & Evered, S. (2006). Secondary control reviewed and defined. *Psychological Bulletin, 132,* 269–296.

Morling, B., & Fiske, S. T. (1999). Defining and measuring harmony control. *Journal of Research in Personality, 33,* 379–414.

Morling, B., Kitayama, S., & Miyamoto, Y. (2002). Cultural practices emphasize influence in the United States and adjustment in Japan. *Personality and Social Psychology Bulletin, 28,* 311–323.

Morling, B., & Lamoreaux, M. (2008). Measuring culture outside the head: A meta-analysis of individualism–collectivism in cultural products. *Personality and Social Psychology Review, 12,* 199–221.

Morris, M., & Peng, K. (1994). Culture and cause: American and Chinese attributions for social and physical events. *Journal of Personality and Social Psychology, 67,* 949–971.

Muramoto, Y., & Yamaguchi, S. (1997). Another type of self-serving bias: Coexistence of self-effacing and group-serving tendencies in attribution in the Japanese culture. *Japanese Journal of Experimental Social Psychology, 37,* 65–75.

Murphy-Berman, V., Berman, J. J., Singh, P., Pachauri, A., Kuman, P. (1984). Factors affecting allocation to needy and meritorious recipients: A cross-cultural comparison. *Journal of Personality and Social Psychology, 46,* 1267–1272.

Na, J., Grossmann, I., Varnum, M., Kitayama, S., & Nisbett, R. E. (2009). Unpublished raw data. Ann Arbor: University of Michigan.

Niles, F. S. (1994). The work ethic in Australia and Sri Lanka. *Journal of Social Psychology, 134,* 55–59.

Nisbett, R. E. (1993). Violence and U.S. regional culture. *American Psychologist, 48,* 441–449.

Nisbett, R. E. (2003). *The geography of thought.* New York: Free Press.

Nisbett, R. E., & Cohen, D. (1996). *Culture of honor: The psychology of violence in the South.* Boulder, CO: Westview.

Nisbett, R. E., Peng, K., Choi, I., & Norenzayan, A. (2001). Culture and systems of thought: Holistic vs. analytic cognition. *Psychological Review, 108,* 291–310.

Nolan, P., & Lenski, G. (2004). *Human societies: An introduction to macrosociology.* Boulder, CO: Paradigm.

Norenzayan, A. (2009). *Middle Eastern cognition in cross-cultural context.* Unpublished manuscript, University of British Columbia.

Norenzayan, A., Choi, I., & Nisbett, R. E. (2002). Cultural similarities and differences in social inference: Evidence from behavioral predictions and lay theories of behavior. *Personality and Social Psychology Bulletin, 28,* 109–120.

Norenzayan, A., Choi, I., & Peng, K. (2007). Perception and cognition. In S. Kitayama & D. Cohen (Eds.), *Handbook of cultural psychology* (pp. 569–594). New York: Guilford.

Norenzayan, A., & Heine, S. J. (2005). Psychological universals: What are they and how can we know? *Psychological Bulletin, 131,* 763–784.

Norenzayan, A., Henrich, J., & McElreath, R. (2009). More Chinese than the Chinese. Unpublished manuscript. University of British Columbia.

Norenzayan, A., Smith, E. E., Kim, B., & Nisbett, R. E. (2002). Cultural preferences for formal versus intuitive reasoning. *Cognitive Science, 26,* 653–684.

Nowak, M. A., Page, K. M., & Sigmund, K. (2000). Fairness versus reason in the Ultimatum Game. *Science, 289,* 1773–1775.

Oishi, S., & Diener, E. (2003). Culture and well-being: The cycle of action, evaluation, and decision. *Personality and Social Psychology Bulletin, 29,* 939–949.

Oishi, S., Diener, E., Scollon, C. N., & Biswas-Diener, R. (2004). Cross-situational consistency of affective experiences across cultures. *Journal of Personality and Social Psychology, 86,* 460–472.

Oishi, S., Lun, J., & Sherman, G. D. (2007). Residential mobility, self-concept, and positive affect in social interactions. *Journal of Personality and Social Psychology, 93,* 131–141.

Oyserman, D., Coon, H. M., & Kemmelmeier, M. (2002). Rethinking individualism and collectivism: Evaluation of theoretical assumptions and meta-analyses *Psychological Bulletin, 128,* 3–72.

Oyserman, D., & Lee, S. W. S. (2008). Does culture influence what and how we think: Effects of priming individualism and collectivism. *Psychological Bulletin, 134,* 311–342.

Papafragou, A., Hulbert, J., & Trueswell, J. (2008). Does language guide event perception? Evidence from eye movements. *Cognition, 108,* 155–184.

Paulhus, D. L. (1986). Self-deception and impression management in test responses. In A. Angleiter & J. S. Wiggins (Eds.), *Personality assessment via questionnaire: Current issues in theory and measurement.* Berlin: Springer-Verlag.

Peng, K., & Nisbett, R. E. (1999). Culture, dialectics, and reasoning about contradiction. *American Psychologist, 54,* 741–754.

Peng, K., Nisbett, R. E., & Wong, N. Y. C. (1997). Validity problems comparing values across cultures and possible solutions. *Psychological Methods, 2,* 329–344.

Pennebaker, J. W., Rimé, B., & Blankenship, V. E. (1996). Stereotypes of emotional expressiveness of Northerners and Southerners: A cross-cultural test of Montesquieu's hypotheses. *Journal of Personality and Social Psychology, 70,* 372–380.

Perugini, M., & Richetin, J. (2007). In the land of the blind, the one-eyed man is king. *European Journal of Personality, 21,* 977–981.

Peters, H. J., & Williams, J. M. (2006). Moving cultural background to the foreground: An investigation of self-talk, performance, and persistence following feedback. *Journal of Applied Sport Psychology, 18,* 240–253.

Petrova, P. K., Cialdini, R. B., & Sills, S. J. (2007). Consistency-based compliance across cultures. *Journal of Experimental Social Psychology, 43,* 104–111.

Pica, P., Lerner, C., Izard, V., & Dehaene, S. (2004). Exact and approximate arithmetic in an Amazonian indigenous group. *Science, 306,* 499–501.

Piedmont, R. L., & Chae, J. H. (1997). Cross-cultural generalizability of the five-factor model of personality. *Journal of Cross-Cultural Psychology, 28,* 131–155.

Pinker, S. (1994). *The language instinct.* New York: HarperCollins.

Plaut, V. C., Markus, H. R., & Lachman, M. E. (2002). Place matters: Consensual features and regional variation in American well-being and self. *Journal of Personality and Social Psychology, 83,* 160–184.

Poortinga, Y. H. (1989). Equivalence of cross-cultural data: An overview of basic issues. *International Journal of Psychology, 24,* 737–756.

Putnam, R. D. (2000). *Bowling alone: The collapse and revival of American community.* New York: Simon & Schuster.

Quinn, D. M., & Crocker, J. (1999). When ideology hurts: Effects of belief in the Protestant ethic and feeling overweight on the psychological well-being of women. *Journal of Personality and Social Psychology, 77,* 402–414.

Quinones-Vidal, E., Lopez-Garcia, J. J., Penaranda-Ortega, M., & Tortosa-Gil, F. (2004). The nature of social and personality psychology as reflected in JPSP, 1965–2000. *Journal of Personality and Social Psychology, 86,* 435–452.

Ramirez-Esparza, N., Gosling, S. D., Benet-Martínez, V., Potter, J. P., & Pennebaker, J. W. (2006). Do bilinguals have two personalities: A special case of cultural frame switching. *Journal of Research in Personality, 40,* 99–120.

Ratner, C. (1989). A sociohistorical critique of naturalistic theories of color perception. *Journal of Mind and Behavior, 10,* 361–373.

Rennie, L. J., & Dunne, M. N. (1994). Gender, ethnicity, and student's perceptions about science and science-related careers in Fiji. *Science Education, 78,* 285–300.

Rentfrow, P. J., Gosling, S. D., & Potter, J. (2009). A theory of the emergence, persistence, and expression of geographic variation in psychological characteristics. *Perspectives on Psychological Science, 3,* 339–369.

Revlin, R., Leirer, V., Yop, H., & Yop, R. (1980). The belief-bias effect in formal reasoning: The influence of knowledge on logic. *Memory and Cognition, 8,* 584–592.

Rhee, E., Uleman, J. S., Lee, H. K., & Roman, R. J. (1995). Spontaneous self-descriptions and ethnic identities in individualistic and collectivistic cultures. *Journal of Personality & Social Psychology, 69,* 142–152.

Richerson, P. J., & Boyd, R. (2005). *Not by genes alone.* Chicago: University of Chicago Press.

Roberson, D., Davidoff, J., Davies, I., & Shapiro, L. (2005). Colour categories in Himba: Evidence for the cultural relativity hypothesis. *Cognitive Psychology, 50,* 378–411.

Roberson, D., Davies, I., & Davidoff, J. (2000). Color categories are not universal: Replications and new evidence from a stone-age culture. *Journal of Experimental Psychology: General, 129,* 369–398.

Rosch Heider, E. (1972). Universals in color naming and memory. *Journal of Experimental Psychology, 93,* 10–20.

Rosch Heider, E., & Olivier, D. C. (1972). The structure of the color space in naming and memory for two languages. *Cognitive Psychology, 3,* 337–354.

Rosenberg, M. (1965). *Society and the adolescent self-image.* Princeton, NJ: Princeton University Press.

Ross, L. D., Amabile, T. M., & Steinmetz, J. L. (1977). Social roles, social control, and biases in social-perception processes. *Journal of Personality and Social Psychology, 35,* 485–494.

Ross, M. (1989). Relation of implicit theories to the construction of personal histories. *Psychological Review, 96,* 341–357.

Ross, M., Xun, W. Q. E., & Wilson, A. E. (2002). Language and the bicultural self. *Personality and Social Psychology Bulletin, 28,* 1040–1050.

Rothbaum, F., Weisz, J., Pott, M., Miyake, K., & Morelli, G. (2000). Attachment and culture: Security in the United States and Japan. *American Psychologist, 55,* 1093–1104.

Rothbaum, F., Weisz, J. R., & Snyder, S. S. (1982). Changing the world and changing the self: A two-process model of perceived control. *Journal of Personality and Social Psychology, 42,* 5–37.

Rozin, P., Fischler, C., Shields, C., & Masson, E. (2006). Attitudes towards large numbers of choices in the food domain: A cross-cultural study of five countries in Europe and the USA. *Appetite, 46,* 304–308.

Rozin, P., Lowery, L., Imada, S., & Haidt, J. (1999). The CAD triad hypothesis: A mapping between three moral emotions (contempt, anger, disgust) and three moral codes (community, autonomy, divinity). *Journal of Personality and Social Psychology, 76,* 574–586.

Russell, J. A. (1991). Culture and the categorization of emotions. *Psychological Bulletin, 110,* 426–450.

Russell, J. A. (1994). Is there universal recognition of emotion from facial expression? A review of the cross-cultural studies. *Psychological Bulletin, 115,* 102–141.

Sagi, A., Lamb, M. E., Lewkowicz, K. S., Shoham, R., Dvir, R., & Estes, D. (1985). Security of infant–mother, –father, and metapelet attachments among kibbutz reared Israeli children. In I. Bretherton & E. Waters (Eds.), *Growing point in attachment theory. Monographs of the Society for Research in Child Development, 50*(1–2, Serial No. 209), 257–275.

Sanchez-Burks, J. (2002). Protestant relational ideology and (in)attention to relational work settings. *Journal of Personality and Social Psychology, 83,* 919–929.

Sanchez-Burks, J., Lee, F., Choi, I., Nisbett, R., Zhao, S., & Koo, J. (2003). Conversing across cultures: East-West communication styles in work and nonwork contexts. *Journal of Personality and Social Psychology, 85,* 363–372.

Sanchez-Burks, J., Nisbett, R. E., & Ybarra, O. (2000). Cultural styles, relational schemas and prejudice against outgroups. *Journal of Personality and Social Psychology, 79,* 174–189.

Saucier, G., Georgiades, S., Tsaousis, I., & Goldberg, L. R. (2005). The factor structure of Greek personality adjectives. *Journal of Personality and Social Psychology, 88,* 856–875.

Saunders, B. A. C., & Van Brakel, J. (1997). Are there non-trivial constraints on colour categorization? *Behavioral and Brain Sciences, 20,* 167–178.

Savani, K., Markus, H. R., & Conner, A. L. (2008). Let your preference be your guide? Preferences and choices are more tightly linked for North Americans than for Indians. *Journal of Personality and Social Psychology, 95,* 861–876.

Schmitt, D. P., Allik, J., McCrae, R. R., & Benet-Martínez, V. (2007). The geographic distribution of Big Five personality traits: Patterns and profiles of human self-description across 56 nations. *Journal of Cross-Cultural Psychology, 38,* 173–212.

Schooler, J. W., & Engstler-Schooler, T. Y. (1990). Verbal overshadowing of visual memories: Some things are better left unsaid. *Cognitive Psychology, 22,* 36–71.

Schug, J., Yuki, M., Horikawa, H., & Takemura, K. (2009). Similarity attraction and actually selecting similar others: How cross-societal differences in relational mobility affect interpersonal similarity in Japan and the United States. *Asian Journal of Social Psychology, 12,* 95–103.

Schwartz, B. (2004). *The paradox of choice: Why more is less.* New York: HarperCollins.

Schwartz, S. H. (1994). Beyond individualism/collectivism: New cultural dimensions of values. In U. Kim, H. C. Triandis, C. Kagitcibasi, S.-C. Choi, & G. Yoon (Eds.), *Individualism and collectivism: Theory, method, and applications* (pp. 85–119). Thousand Oaks, CA: Sage.

Sedikides, C., Gaertner, L., & Vevea, J. (2005). Pancultural self-enhancement reloaded: A meta-analytic reply to Heine (2005). *Journal of Personality and Social Psychology, 89,* 539–551.

Sedikides, C., Gaertner, L., & Vevea, J. (2007). Inclusion of theory-relevant moderators yield the same conclusions as Sedikides, Gaertner, and Vevea (2005): A meta-analytical reply to Heine, Kitayama, and Hamamura (2007). *Asian Journal of Social Psychology, 10,* 59–67.

Seeman, T. E. (1996). Social ties and health: The benefits of social integration. *Annals of Epidemiology, 6,* 442–451.

Segall, M. H., Campbell, D. T., & Herskiovits, M. J. (1963). Cultural differences in the perception of geometric illusions. *Science, 193,* 769–771.

Seginer, R., Trommsdorff, G., & Essau, C. (1993). Adolescent control beliefs: Cross-cultural variations of primary and secondary orientations. *International Journal of Behavioral Development, 16,* 243–260.

Shweder, R. A. (1990). Cultural psychology: What is it? In J. W. Stigler, R. A. Shweder, & G. Herdt (Eds.), *Cultural psychology: Essays on comparative human development* (pp. 1–43). Cambridge, England: Cambridge University Press.

Shweder, R. A. (1997). The surprise of ethnography. *Ethos, 25,* 152–163.

Shweder, R. A., & Bourne, E. J. (1982). Does the concept of the person vary cross-culturally? In A. J. Marsella & G. M. White (Eds.), *Cultural conceptions of mental health and therapy.* New York: Kluwer.

Shweder, R. A., Goodnow, J., Hatano, G., LeVine, R. A., Markus, H., & Miller, P. (1998). The cultural psychology of development: One mind, many mentalities. In W. Damon & R. M. Lerner (Eds.), *Handbook of child psychology* (Vol. 1, pp. 865–937). New York: John Wiley & Sons.

Shweder, R. A., Jensen, L. A., & Goldstein, W. M. (1995). Who sleeps by whom revisited: A method for extracting the moral goods implicit in practice. In J. J. Goodnow et al. (Eds.), *Cultural practices as contexts for development: New directions in child development* (Vol. 67, pp. 21–39). San Francisco: Jossey Bass.

Shweder, R. A., Much, N. C., Mahapatra, M., & Park, L. (1997). The "big three" of morality (autonomy, community, divinity) and the "big three" explanations of suffering. In A. M. Brandt & P. Rozin (Eds.), *Morality and health* (pp. 119–169). New York: Routledge.

Singelis, T. M., Bond, M. H., Lai, S. Y., & Sharkey, W. F. (1999). Unpackaging culture's influence on self-esteem and embarrassability: The role of self-construals. *Journal of Cross-Cultural Psychology, 30,* 315–331.

Snarey, J. R. (1985). The cross-cultural universality of social-moral development: A critical review of Kohlbergian research. *Psychological Bulletin, 97*(2), 202–232.

Snibbe, A. C., & Markus, H. R. (2005). You can't always get what you want: Social class, agency, and choice. *Journal of Personality and Social Psychology, 88,* 703–720.

Snibbe, A. C., Markus, H. R., Kitayama, S., & Suzuki, T. (2003). "They saw a game": Self and group enhancement in Japan and the U.S. *Journal of Cross-Cultural Psychology, 34,* 581–595.

Somer, O., & Goldberg, L. R. (1999). The structure of Turkish trait-descriptive adjectives. *Journal of Personality and Social Psychology, 76,* 431–450.

Spencer-Rodgers, J., Boucher, H. C., Mori, S. C., Wang, L., & Peng, K. (2009). The dialectical self-concept: Contradiction, change, and holism in East Asian cultures. *Personality and Social Psychology Bulletin, 35,* 29–44.

Spencer-Rodgers, J., Peng, K., Wang, L., & Hou, Y. (2004). Dialectical self-esteem and East–West differences in psychological well-being. *Personality and Social Psychology Bulletin, 30,* 1416–1432.

Steele, C. M. (1988). The psychology of self-affirmation: Sustaining the integrity of the self. In L. Berkowitz (Ed.), *Advances in experimental social psychology* (Vol. 21, pp. 261–302). San Diego: Academic Press.

Stephens, N. M., Markus, H. R., & Townsend, S. S. M. (2007). Choice as an act of meaning: The case of social class. *Journal of Personality and Social Psychology, 93,* 814–830.

Stevenson, H. W., & Stigler, J. W. (1992). *The learning gap: Why our schools are failing and what we can learn from Japanese and Chinese education.* New York: Summit Books.

Stigler, J. W., Shweder, R. A., & Herdt, G. (1990). *Cultural psychology: Essays on comparative human development.* Cambridge, England: Cambridge University Press.

Strack, F., Martin, L. L., & Stepper, S. (1988). Inhibiting and facilitating conditions of the human smile: A nonobtrusive test of the facial feedback hypothesis. *Journal of Personality and Social Psychology, 54,* 768–777.

Su, S. K., Chiu, C.-Y., Hong, Y.-Y., Leung, K., Peng, K., & Morris, M. W. (1999). Self organization and social organization: American and Chinese constructions. In T. R. Tyler, R. Kramer, & O. John (Eds.), *The psychology of the social self* (pp. 193–222). Mahwah, NJ: Lawrence Erlbaum.

Suh, E. M. (2002). Culture, identity consistency, and subjective well-being. *Journal of Personality and Social Psychology, 83,* 1378–1391.

Suh, E., Diener, E., Oishi, S., & Triandis, H. C. (1998). The shifting basis of life satisfaction judgments across cultures: Emotions versus norms. *Journal of Personality and Social Psychology, 74,* 482–493.

Swann, W. B., Wenzlaff, R. M., Krull, D. S., & Pelham, B. W. (1992). Allure of negative feedback: Self-verification strivings among depressed persons. *Journal of Abnormal Psychology, 101,* 293–306.

Szeto, A., Sorrentino, R. M., Yasunaga, S., Otsubo, Y., Kouhara, S., & Sasayama, I. (2009). Using the IAT across cultures: A case of implicit self-esteem in Japan and Canada. *Asian Journal of Social Psychology, 12,* 211–220.

Takano, Y., & Sogon, S. (2008). Are Japanese more collectivistic than Americans? Examining conformity in in-groups and the reference-group effect. *Journal of Cross-Cultural Psychology, 39,* 237–250.

Tardif, T. (1996). Nouns are not always learned before verbs: Evidence from Mandarin speakers' early vocabularies. *Developmental Psychology, 32,* 492–504.

Taylor, S. E., & Brown, J. D. (1988). Illusion and well-being: A social psychological perspective on mental health. *Psychological Bulletin, 103,* 193–210.

Taylor, S. E., Sherman, D. K., Kim, H. S., Jarcho, J., Takagi, K., & Dunagan, M. S. (2004). Culture and social support: Who seeks it and why? *Journal of Personality and Social Psychology, 87,* 354–362.

Taylor, S. E., Welch, W., Kim, H. S., & Sherman, D. K. (2007). Cultural differences in the impact of social support on psychological and biological stress responses. *Psychological Science, 18,* 831–837.

Terracciano, A., Abdel-Khalek, A. M., Ádám, N., Adamovová, L., Ahn, C.-K., Ahn, H.-N., et al. (2005). National character does not reflect mean personality trait levels in 49 cultures. *Science, 310*(5745), 96–100.

Tesser, A., Crepaz, N., Beach, S. R. H., Cornell, D., & Collins, J. C. (2000). Confluence of self-esteem regulation mechanisms: On integrating the self-zoo. *Personality and Social Psychology Bulletin, 26,* 1476–1489.

Ting-Toomey, S. (Ed.). (1994). *The challenge of facework: Cross-cultural and interpersonal issues.* Albany, NY: State University of New York Press.

Tobin, J. J., Wu, D. Y. H., & Davidson, D. (1989). *Preschool in three cultures.* New Haven, CT: Yale University Press.

Tomasello, M. (1999). *The cultural origins of human cognition.* Cambridge, MA: Harvard University Press.

Tomasello, M., Carpenter, M., Call, J., Behne, T., & Moll, H. (2005). Understanding and sharing intentions: The origins of cultural cognition. *Behavioral and Brain Sciences, 28,* 675–735.

Tomasello, M., Kruger, A. C., & Ratner, H. H. (1993). Cultural learning. *Behavioral and Brain Sciences, 16,* 495–552.

Tracy, J. L., & Matsumoto, D. (2008). The spontaneous display of pride and shame: Evidence for biologically innate nonverbal displays. *Proceedings of the National Academy of Science, 105,* 11655–11660.

Tracy, J. L., & Robins, R. W. (2008). The nonverbal expression of pride: Evidence for cross-cultural recognition. *Journal of Personality and Social Psychology, 94,* 516–530.

Trafimow, D., Triandis, H. C., & Goto, S. G. (1991). Some tests of the distinction between the private self and the collective self. *Journal of Personality and Social Psychology, 60,* 649–655.

Triandis, H. C. (1989). The self and social behavior in differing cultural contexts. *Psychological Review, 96,* 506–520.

Triandis, H. C. (1996). The psychological measurement of cultural syndromes. *American Psychologist, 51,* 407–415.

Triandis, H. C., Marin, G., Lisansky, J., & Betancourt, H. (1984). Simpatia as a cultural script of Hispanics. *Journal of Personality and Social Psychology, 47,* 1363–1375.

Tropp, L. R., & Wright, S. C. (2003). Evaluations and perceptions of self, ingroup, and outgroup: Comparisons between Mexican-American and European-American children. *Self and Identity, 2,* 203–221.

True, M. M., Pisani, L., & Oumar, F. (2001). Infant–mother attachment among the Dogon of Mali. *Child Development, 72,* 1451–1466.

Trzesniewski, K. H., Donnellan, M. B., & Robins, R. W. (2008). Do today's young people really think they are so extraordinary? An examination of secular changes in narcissism and self-enhancement. *Psychological Science, 19,* 181–188.

Tsai, J. L., Chentsova-Dutton, Y., Freire-Bebeau, L., & Przymus, D. E. (2002). Emotional expression and physiology in European-Americans and Hmong Americans. *Emotion, 2,* 380–397.

Tsai, J. L., Knutson, B. K., & Fung, H. H. (2006). Cultural variation in affect valuation. *Journal of Personality and Social Psychology, 90,* 288–307.

Tsai, J. L., Louie, J. Y., Chen, E. E., & Uchida, Y. (2006). Learning what feelings to desire: Socialization of ideal affect through children's storybooks. *Personality and Social Psychology Bulletin, 32,* 1–14.

Tsai, J. L., Miao, F. F., & Seppala, E. (2007). Good feelings in Christianity and Buddhism: Religious differences in ideal affect. *Personality and Social Psychology Bulletin, 33,* 409–421.

Tsai, J. L., Simeonova, D. I., & Watanabe, J. T. (2004). Somatic and social: Chinese Americans talk about emotion. *Personality and Social Psychology Bulletin, 30,* 1226–1238.

Tsai, J. L., Ying, Y., & Lee, P. A. (2000). The meaning of "being Chinese" and "being American": Variation among Chinese American young adults. *Journal of Cross-Cultural Psychology, 31,* 302–332.

Twenge, J. M., & Campbell, W. K. (2001). Age and birth cohort differences in self-esteem: A cross-temporal meta-analysis. *Personality and Social Psychology Review, 5,* 321–344.

Twenge, J. M., Konrath, S., Foster, J. D., Campbell, W. K., & Bushman, B. J. (2008). Further evidence of an increase in narcissism among college students. *Journal of Personality, 76,* 919–927.

Uskul, A. K., Kitayama, S., & Nisbett, R. E. (2008). Ecocultural basis of cognition: Farmers and fishermen are more holistic than herders. *Proceedings of the National Academy of Sciences, 105,* 8552–8556.

Van Boven, L., Kamada, A., & Gilovich, T. (1999). The perceiver as perceived: Everyday intuitions about the correspondence bias. *Journal of Personality and Social Psychology, 77,* 1188–1199.

van de Vijver, F., & Tanzer, N. K. (2004). Bias and equivalence in cross-cultural assessment: An overview. *European Review of Applied Psychology, 54,* 119–135.

Vandello, J. A., & Cohen, D. (2003). Male honor and female fidelity: Implicit cultural scripts that perpetuate domestic violence. *Journal of Personality and Social Psychology, 84,* 997–1010.

Wang, Q. (2004). The emergence of cultural self-constructs: Autobiographical memory and self-description in European American and Chinese children. *Developmental Psychology, 40,* 3–15.

Wang, Q., & Ross, M. (2005). What we remember and what we tell: The effects of culture and self-priming on memory representations and narratives. *Memory, 13,* 594–606.

Weber, M. (1947). *The theory of social and economic organization* (T. Parsons, Trans.). New York: Free Press.

Weisz, J. R., Rothbaum, F. M., & Blackburn, T. C. (1984). Standing out and standing in: The psychology of control in America and Japan. *American Psychologist, 39,* 955–969.

Whitehead, H. (1998). Cultural selection and genetic diversity in matrilineal whales. *Science, 282,* 1708–1711.

Whiten, A., Goodall, J., McGrew, W. C., Nishida, T., Reynolds, V., Sugiyama, Y., Tutin, C. E. G., Wrangham, R. W., & Boesch, C. (1999). Cultures in chimpanzees. *Nature, 399,* 682–685.

Whiting, J. W. M. (1964). The effects of climate on certain cultural practices. In W. H. Goodenough (Ed.), *Explorations in cultural anthropology: Essays in honor of George Peter Murdock* (pp. 511–544). New York: McGraw-Hill.

Whorf, B. L. (1956). *Language, thought, and reality.* Cambridge, MA: MIT Press.

Williams, T. P., & Sogon, S. (1984). Group composition and conforming behavior in Japanese students. *Japanese Psychological Research, 26,* 231–234.

Wills, T. A. (1981). Downward comparison principles in social psychology. *Psychological Bulletin, 90,* 245–271.

Wilss, W. (1982). *The science of translation: Problems and methods.* Tübingen, Germany: Narr.

Winawer, J., Witthoft, N., Frank, M. C., Wu, L., Wade, A. R., & Boroditsky, L. (2007). Russian blues reveal effects of language on color discrimination. *Proceedings of the National Academy of Sciences, 104,* 7780–7785.

Witkin, H. A., & Berry, J. W. (1975). Psychological differentiation in cross-cultural perspective. *Journal of Cross-Cultural Psychology, 6,* 4–87.

Wong, R. Y. M., & Hong, Y. (2005). Dynamic influences of culture on cooperation in the prisoner's dilemma. *Psychological Science, 16,* 429–434.

Wu, S., & Keysar, B. (2007). Cultural effects on perspective taking. *Psychological Science, 18,* 600–606.

Wundt, W. (1921). *Elements of folk psychology.* London: Allen & Unwin.

Yamagishi, T., & Yamagishi, M. (1994). Trust and commitment in the United States and Japan. *Motivation and Emotion, 18,* 9–66.

Yamaguchi, S., Greenwald, A. G., Banaji, M. R., Murakami, F., Chen, D., Shiomura, K., et al. (2007). Apparent universality of positive implicit self-esteem. *Psychological Science, 18,* 498–500.

Yik, M. S. M., Russell, J. A., Ahn, C., Fernandez-Dols, J. M., & Suzuki, N. (2002). Relating the five-factor model of personality to a circumplex model of affect: A five language study. In R. R. McCrae & J. Allik (Eds.), *The five-factor model of personality across cultures* (pp. 79–104). New York: Kluwer.

Yuki, M., Maddux, W. W., Brewer, M. B., & Takemura, K. (2005). Cross-cultural differences in relationship- and group-based trust. *Personality and Social Psychology Bulletin, 31,* 48–62.

Yuki, M., Maddux, W. W., & Masuda, T. (2007). Are the windows to the soul the same in the East and West? Cultural differences in using the eyes and mouth as cues to recognize emotions in Japan and the United States. *Journal of Experimental Social Psychology, 43,* 303–311.

Yuki, M., Schug, J. R., Horikawa, H., Takemura, K., Sato, K., Yokota, K., & Kamaya, K. (2009). *Development of a scale to measure perceptions of relational mobility in society.* Unpublished manuscript. Hokkaido University.

Zebian, S., & Denny, J. P. (2001). Integrative cognitive style in Middle Eastern and Western groups: Multidimensional classification and major and minor classification sorting. *Journal of Cross-Cultural Psychology, 32,* 58–75.

Author Index

Gibbard, A., 801

Gibbons, F. X., 600, 602, 700, 701, 702, 703

Gibbons, P. A., 367

Gibbons. P., 1401

Gibbs, J. C., 799

Gibbs, R. W., Jr., 1394, 1395, 1395, 1396, 1398

Gibson, A., 374

Gibson, C. B., 1215, 1229, 1271

Gibson, J. J., 479, 766

Gibson, J. L., 1064, 1141, 1146, 1150

Gibson, K. S., 886

Gidengil, E., 1302

Giebels, E., 1004

Giesbrecht, B., 153

Giese, M. A., 443, 445, 446

Giesler, R. B., 600, 608, 614, 903

Gifford, R. K., 479, 556, 683

Gigerenzer, G., 252 253, 253, 255, 552, 554, 571, 672, 802, 1237

Gigone, D., 1260

Gijselaers, W. H., 1230

Gil-Rivas, V., 708

Gil-White, F. J., 779

Gil, K. M., 130

Giladi, E. E., 604, 1438

Gilbert, D. T., 4, 12, 22, 25, 37, 38, 52, 53, 57, 58, 62, 63, 67, 72, 73, 74, 144, 152, 171, 177, 236, 240, 241, 242, 301, 327, 328, 353, 354, 355, 412, 415, 428 435, 429, 438, 450, 470, 477, 498, 501, 503, 512, 514, 515, 516, 518, 522, 524, 527, 528, 542, 549, 554, 556, 566, 568, 569, 577, 578, 593, 600, 603, 608, 633, 681, 682, 688, 689, 690, 691, 771, 778, 949, 959, 1032, 1033, 1034, 1105, 1190, 1196, 1360, 1399, 1444

Gilbert, D., 252, 802

Gilbert, G. M., 954, 1032

Gilbert, R., 1370

Gilbert, S. J., 153, 163, 169, 284

Gilboa, A., 163

Gildea, P., 1398

Gilens, M., 1308, 1309, 1319

Giles, H., 478, 946, 951, 953, 1391, 1392, 1393, 1401, 1409

Giles, L., 905

Gilin, D., 502, 504

Gill, A. J., 1394

Gill, M. J., 512, 514, 516, 616, 917

Gill, M., 396, 400

Gill, S., 482

Gillath, O., 170, 728, 910, 920, 921, 922, 923, 925

Gillberg, C., 153

Gillette, J. C., 410, 411, 413, 945, 1219

Gilliam, F. D., Jr., 1295

Gilligan, C., 656, 799

Gillihan, S. J., 152

Gillis, L., 502

Gillis, M. M., 165

Gilman, A., 1399, 1400, 1401

Gilmore, G. C., 430

Gilmour, R., 469, 474

Gilovich, T., 8, 10, 18, 23, 26, 27, 33, 164, 471, 500, 507, 512, 515, 516, 518, 519, 520, 526, 528, 546, 550, 551, 553, 554, 559, 563, 564, 571, 574, 578, 604, 672, 797, 917, 1369, 1407, 1444

Gilson, C., 1387

Gilson, L. L., 1209, 1239

Gilson, M., 702

Gimpel, J., 1296

Giner-Sorolla, R., 358, 363, 525, 805, 1039

Ginet, M., 1345

Gingras, I., 602

Ginnett, R. C., 1236, 1238

Ginsburg, G. P., 1372, 1410

Ginter, H., 172

Gintis, H., 565, 773, 801, 824, 1425, 1451

Giorgi, L., 1440

Giovanazzi, A., 611, 1039

Giraldeau, L. A., 1424

Girotto, V., 547

Gist, M. E., 1237

Gitelman, D. R., 151

Gittell, J. H., 1223

Gittleman, J. H., 481

Giuliano, T., 241

Gladstein, D. L., 1236

Gladue, B. A., 846

Gladwell, M., 25, 30, 1235

Glanz, K., 96

Glaser, D. E., 157, 447

Glaser, J., 91, 337, 358, 363, 367, 381, 382, 610, 678, 823, 955, 1110, 1130, 1133, 1138, 1147, 1149

Glaser, R., 143, 218, 715

Glaser, W. A., 1295

Glasman, L. R., 408, 409, 410, 411, 413

Glass, B., 634

Glass, D. C., 1000

Glass, D. P., 1295, 1296

Glassman, N. S., 909

Gleason, C. A., 161, 258

Gleason, M. E. J., 713, 923, 927, 1131

Gleeson, K., 874

Gleicher, F., 559

Gleitman, L., 1391, 1428

Glenberg, A. M., 198, 1398

Glenn, A. L., 167, 172, 804

Glenn, S., 160

Gleser, G. C., 134

Glick, J., 1452

Glick, P., 301, 337, 358, 467, 594, 606, 632, 634, 643, 648, 651, 654, 657, 771, 772, 946, 947, 948, 949, 951, 952, 953, 957, 963, 964, 965, 1025, 1034, 1039, 1041, 1044, 1045, 1047, 1053, 1058, 1059, 1085, 1393

Gliga, T., 449

Glinder, J. G., 709

Glomb, T. M., 1266

Glover, G., 163

Glover, J., 812

Gluck, M. A., 451

Glucksberg, S., 1398

Glueck, E., 672

Glueck, S., 672

Gobbini, M. A., 428, 429, 438, 442, 443, 445, 450, 451, 452

Gobbini, M. I., 150, 153, 169, 170, 438, 439, 441, 445

Godbey, G., 96

Godfrey, D. K., 472

Godwin, K. R., 1300

Goebel, R., 445

Goeke-Morey, M., 100

Goel, V., 165

Goethals, G. R., 512, 812, 1037, 1166, 1255

Goetz, A. T., 777

Goetz, J., 334, 339, 504, 968

Goff, P. A., 31, 520, 525, 956, 963, 964, 1039, 1111

Goffin, R. D., 360

Goffman, E., 29, 215, 220, 573, 590, 877, 942, 966, 1057, 1399, 1404

Goh, J. H. O., 1443

Goidel, R. K., 1294, 1318

Golan, O., 484

Golan, Y., 484

Golby, A. J., 171, 442, 956

Gold, A. L., 445

Gold, A., 1322

Gold, J. A., 868

Goldband, S., 197

Goldberg, I. I., 163

Goldberg, J. H., 329, 330

Goldberg, L. R., 433, 594, 675, 678, 679, 708, 865, 1434, 1435

Goldenberg, E. N., 1314

Goldenberg, J. L., 610, 728, 748

Goldenberg, J., 728

Goldhagen, D. J., 10

Goldin-Meadow, S., 471, 473, 476, 1390

Goldin, C., 1056, 1256

Goldin, P. R., 165

Golding, J. M., 1363

Golding, S. L., 523

Goldkamp, K. H., 1362

Goldman, A. I., 158, 509, 511

Goldman, A., 478, 513, 1151

Goldman, B. M., 740, 741, 994, 1144

Goldman, B. N., 596

Goldman, M., 1171

Goldman, R., 72, 945

Goldsher, D., 159

Goldsmith, D. R., 167, 172, 804

Goldsmith, H. H., 149, 317, 952, 1428

Subject Index